COLLINS

PAPERBACK

ENCYCLOPEDIA

HarperCollins*Publishers*

HarperCollins*Publishers*
P.O.Box, Glasgow G4 0NB

© Helicon Publishing Ltd 1995

Maps and diagrams © Helicon Publishing Ltd 1995

Reprint 10 9 8 7 6 5 4 3 2 1 0

ISBN 0 00 470856-3

British Library Cataloguing in Publication Data

A catalogue record for this book is available from the
British Library

Printed and bound in Great Britain by
The Bath Press, Avon

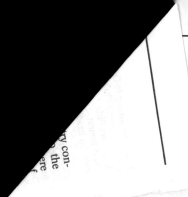

PREFACE

The *Collins Paperback Encyclopedia* is an illustrated single-volume companion to world events, history, arts, and sciences, for home, school, or library use. The aim throughout has been to provide up-to-date, readable entries, using clear and non-technical language.

Arrangement of entries

Entries are ordered alphabetically, as if there were no spaces between words. Thus, entries for words beginning 'national' follow the order:

    national insurance
    nationalism
    National Party

However, we have avoided a purely mechanical alphabetization in cases where a different order corresponds more with human logic. For example, sovereigns with the same name are grouped according to country before number, so that King George II of England is placed before King George III of England, and not next to George II of Greece. Words beginning 'Mc' and 'Mac' are treated as if they begin 'Mac'; and 'St' and 'Saint' are both treated as if they were spelt 'Saint'.

Foreign names and titles

Names of foreign sovereigns and places are usually shown in their English form, except where the foreign name is more familiar; thus, there are entries for Charles V of Spain, but Juan Carlos (not John Charles), and for Florence, not Firenze. Entries for titled people are under the name by which they are best known to the general reader: thus, Anthony Eden, not Lord Avon. Cross-references have been provided in cases where confusion is possible.

Cross-references

These are shown by a *symbol immediately preceding the reference. Cross-referencing is selective; a cross-reference is shown when another entry contains material directly relevant to the subject matter of an entry, and which the reader may not otherwise think of looking. To assist the reader, we have avoided as far as possible entries which consist only of a cross-reference; even the shortest cross-reference gives some indication of the subject involved. Common alternative spellings, where there is no agreed consistent form, are also shown.

Units

SI (metric) units are used throughout for scientific entries. Measurements of distances, temperatures, sizes, and so on, usually include an approximate imperial equivalent.

Science and technology

Entries are generally placed under the better-known name (thus, acetylene is placed under A and not under its technically correct name ethyne), but the technical term is also given. To aid comprehension, particularly for the non-specialist, technical terms are frequently explained when used within the text of an entry, even though they may have their own entry elsewhere.

Chinese names

Pinyin, the preferred system for transcribing Chinese names of people and places, is generally used: thus, there is an entry at Mao Zedong, not Mao Tse-tung; an exception is made for a few names which are more familiar in their former (Wade–Giles) form, such as Sun Yat-sen and Chiang Kai-Shek. Where confusion is likely, Wade–Giles forms are given as a cross-reference.

Comments and suggestions

We welcome comments from readers on suggested improvements or alterations to the Encyclopedia.

Aachen (French *Aix-la-Chapelle*) German cathedral city and spa in the *Land* of North Rhine–Westphalia, 72 km/45 mi SW of Cologne; population (1988) 239,000. It has thriving electronic, glass, and rubber industries, and is one of Germany's principal railway junctions.

Aalborg (Danish *Ålborg*) port in Denmark 32 km/20 mi inland from the Kattegat, on the south shore of the Limfjord; population (1990) 155,000. One of Denmark's oldest towns, it has a castle and the fine Budolfi church. It is the capital of Nordjylland county in Jylland (Jutland); the port is linked to Nørresundby on the north side of the fjord by a tunnel built 1969.

Aalto Alvar 1898–1976. Finnish architect and designer. One of Finland's first Modernists, he had a unique architectural style, characterized by asymmetry, curved walls, and contrast of natural materials. He invented a new form of laminated bent-plywood furniture 1932 and won many design awards for household and industrial items.

aardvark (Afrikaans 'earth pig') nocturnal mammal *Orycteropus afer*, order Tubulidentata, found in central and southern Africa. A timid, defenceless animal about the size of a pig, it has a long head, piglike snout, and large asinine ears. It feeds on termites, which it licks up with its long sticky tongue.

aardwolf nocturnal mammal *Proteles cristatus* of the *hyena family, Hyaenidae. It is found in eastern and southern Africa, usually in the burrows of the aardvark, and feeds on termites.

Aarhus (Danish *Århus*) second-largest city of Denmark, on the east coast overlooking the Kattegat; population (1990) 261,400. It is the capital of Aarhus county in Jylland (Jutland) and a shipping and commercial centre.

Aaron c. 13th century BC. In the Old Testament, the elder brother of Moses and co-leader of the Hebrews in their march from Egypt to the Promised Land of Canaan. He made the Golden Calf for the Hebrews to worship when they despaired of Moses' return from Mount Sinai, but he was allowed to continue as high priest. All his descendants are hereditary high priests, called the *cohanim*, or cohens, and maintain a special place in worship and ceremony in the synagogue.

abacus method of calculating with a handful of stones on 'a flat surface' (Latin *abacus*), familiar to the Greeks and Romans, and used by earlier peoples, possibly even in ancient Babylon; it still survives in the more sophisticated bead-frame form of the Russian *schoty* and the Japanese *soroban*. The abacus has been superseded by the electronic calculator.

Abadan Iranian oil port on the E side of the Shatt-al-Arab waterway; population (1986) 294,000. Abadan is the chief refinery and shipping centre for Iran's oil industry, nationalized 1951. This measure was the beginning of the worldwide movement by oil-producing countries to assume control of profits from their own resources.

abalone edible marine snail of the worldwide genus *Haliotis*, family Haliotidae. Abalones have flattened, oval, spiralled shells, which have holes around the outer edge and a bluish mother-of-pearl lining. This lining is used in ornamental work.

Abbadid dynasty 11th century. Muslim dynasty based in Seville, Spain, which lasted from 1023 until 1091. The dynasty was founded by Abu-el-Kasim Muhammad Ibn Abbad, who led the townspeople against the Berbers when the Spanish caliphate fell. The dynasty continued under Motadid (1042–1069) and Motamid (1069–1091) when the city was taken by the *Almoravids.

Abbado Claudio 1933– . Italian conductor, long associated with the La Scala opera house, Milan. Principal conductor of London Symphony Orchestra from 1979, he also worked with the European Community Youth Orchestra from 1977.

Abbas I the Great c. 1557–1629. Shah of Persia from 1588. He expanded Persian territory by conquest, defeating the Uzbeks near Herat 1597 and also the Turks. The port of Bandar-Abbas is named after him. At his death his empire reached from the river Tigris to the Indus. He was a patron of the arts.

Abbas II Hilmi 1874–1944. Last *khedive (viceroy) of Egypt, 1892–1914. On the outbreak of war between Britain and Turkey in 1914, he sided with Turkey and was deposed following the establishment of a British protectorate over Egypt.

Abbasid dynasty family of rulers of the Islamic empire, whose *caliphs reigned in Baghdad 750–1258. They were descended from Abbas, the prophet Muhammad's uncle, and some of them, such as Harun al-Rashid and Mamun (reigned 813–33), were outstanding patrons of cultural development. Later their power dwindled, and in 1258 Baghdad was burned by the Tatars.

Abbey Theatre playhouse in Dublin associated with the Irish literary revival of the early 1900s. The theatre, opened in 1904, staged the works of a number of Irish dramatists, including Lady Gregory, W B Yeats, J M Synge, and Sean O'Casey. Burned down in 1951, the Abbey Theatre was rebuilt 1966.

Abbott and Costello stage names of William Abbott (1895–1974) and Louis Cristillo (1906–1959) US comedy duo. They moved to films from vaudeville, and most, including *Buck Privates* 1941 and *Lost in a Harem* 1944, were showcases for their routines. They also appeared on radio and televison.

Abd Allah Sudanese dervish leader *Abdullah el Taaisha* 1846–1899. Successor to the Mahdi as Sudanese ruler from 1885, he was defeated by British forces under General *Kitchener at Omdurman 1898 and later killed in Kordofan.

Abd al-Malik Ibn Marwan AD 647– . Caliph who reigned 685–705. Based in Damascus, he waged military campaigns to unite Muslim groups and battled against the Greeks. He instituted a purely Arab coinage and replaced Syriac, Coptic, and Greek with Arabic as the language for his lands. His reign was turbulent but succeeded in extending and strengthening the power of the Omayyad dynasty. He was also a patron of the arts.

Abd el-Krim el-Khettabi 1881–1963. Moroccan chief known as the 'Wolf of the *Riff'. With his brother Muhammad, he led the **Riff revolt** against the French and Spanish invaders, inflicting disastrous defeat on the Spanish at Anual in 1921, but surrendered to a large French army under Pétain in 1926. Banished to the island of Réunion, he was released in 1947 and died in voluntary exile in Cairo.

abdication crisis in British history, the constitutional upheaval of the period 16 Nov 1936 to 10 Dec 1936, brought about by the English king Edward VIII's decision to marry Wallis Simpson, an American divorcee. The marriage of the 'Supreme Governor' of the Church of England to a divorced person was considered unsuitable and the king was finally forced to abdicate on 10 Dec and left for voluntary exile in France. He was created Duke of Windsor and married Mrs Simpson on 3 June 1937.

abdomen in invertebrates, the part of the body below the *thorax, containing the digestive organs; in insects and other arthropods, it is the hind part of the body. In mammals, the abdomen is separated from the thorax by the diaphragm, a sheet of muscular tissue; in arthropods, commonly by a narrow constriction. In insects and spiders, the abdomen is characterized by the absence of limbs.

Abdul-Hamid II 1842–1918. Last sultan of Turkey 1876–1909. In 1908 the *Young Turks under Enver Pasha forced Abdul-Hamid to restore the constitution of 1876 and in 1909 insisted on his deposition. He died in confinement. For his part in the *Armenian massacres suppressing the revolt of 1894–96 he was known as 'the Great Assassin'.

Abdullah ibn Hussein 1882–1951. King of Jordan from 1946. He worked with the British guerrilla leader T E *Lawrence in the Arab revolt of World War I. Abdullah became king of Trans-Jordan 1946; on the incorporation of Arab Palestine (after the 1948–49 Arab–Israeli War) he renamed the country the Hashemite Kingdom of Jordan. He was assassinated.

Abdullah Sheik Muhammad 1905–1982. Indian politician, known as the 'Lion of Kashmir'. He headed the struggle for constitutional government against the Maharajah of Kashmir, and in 1948, following a coup, became prime minister. He agreed to the accession of the state to India, but was dismissed and imprisoned from 1953 (with brief intervals) until 1966, when he called for Kashmiri self-determination. He became chief minister of Jammu and Kashmir 1975, accepting the sovereignty of India.

Abel in the Old Testament, the second son of Adam and Eve; as a shepherd, he made burnt offerings of meat to God which were more acceptable than the fruits offered by his brother Cain; he was killed by the jealous Cain.

Abel Frederick Augustus 1827–1902. British scientist and inventor who developed explosives. As a chemist to the War Department, he introduced a method of making gun-cotton and was joint inventor with James *Dewar of cordite. He also invented the Abel close-test instrument for determining the *flash point (ignition temperature) of petroleum.

Abel John Jacob 1857–1938. US biochemist, discoverer of *adrenaline. He studied the chemical composition of body tissues, and this led, in 1898, to the discovery of adrenaline, the first hormone to be identified, which Abel called epinephrine. He later became the first to isolate *amino acids from blood.

Abel Niels Henrik 1802–1829. Norwegian mathematician. He demonstrated that the general quintic equation

$$ax^5 + bx^4 + cx^3 + dx^2 + ex + f = 0$$

could not be solved algebraically. Subsequent work covered elliptic functions, integral equations, infinite series, and the binomial theorem.

Abelard Peter 1079–1142. French scholastic philosopher who worked on logic and theology. His romantic liaison with his pupil *Héloïse caused a medieval scandal. Details of his controversial life are contained in the autobiographical *Historia Calamitatum Mearum/The History of My Misfortunes*.

Abercrombie Leslie Patrick 1879–1957. Pioneer of British town planning. He is known for his work replanning British cities after damage in World War II (such as the Greater London Plan, 1944) and for the policy of creating new towns and *garden cities.

Aberdeen city and seaport on the E coast of Scotland, administrative headquarters of Grampian region; population (1991) 201,100. Industries include agricultural machinery, paper, and textiles; fishing; ship-building; granite-quarrying; and engineering. There are shore-based maintenance and service depots for the North Sea oil rigs. Aberdeen is Scotland's third largest city.

Aberdeen George Hamilton Gordon, 4th Earl of Aberdeen 1784–1860. British Tory politician, prime minister 1852–55 when he resigned because of the criticism aroused by the miseries and mismanagement of the Crimean War.

Aberfan mining village in Mid Glamorgan, Wales. Coal waste overwhelmed a school and houses in 1966; of 144 dead, 116 were children.

aberration of starlight apparent displacement of a star from its true position, due to the combined effects of the speed of light and the speed of the Earth in orbit around the Sun (about 30 km per second/18.5 mi per second).

Abidja'n port and former capital (to 1983) of the Republic of Ivory Coast, W Africa; population (1982) 1,850,000. Products include coffee, palm oil, cocoa, and timber (mahogany). It was replaced as capital by Yamoussoukro.

abiotic factor a nonorganic variable within the ecosystem, affecting the life of organisms. Examples include temperature, light, and soil structure. Abiotic factors can be harmful to the environment, as when sulphur dioxide emissions from power stations produce acid rain.

Abkhazia autonomous republic in Georgia, situated on the Black Sea
capital Sukhumi
area 8,600 sq km/3,320 sq mi
products tin, fruit, and tobacco
population (1989) 526,000
history The region has been the scene of secessionist activity on the part of the minority Muslim Abkhazi community since 1989, culminating in the republic's declaration of independence 1992. Georgian troops invaded and took control Aug 1992, but secessionist guerrillas subsequently gained control of the northern half of the republic.

ablative in the grammar of certain inflected languages, such as Latin, the ablative case is the form of a noun, pronoun, or adjective used to indicate the agent in passive sentences or the instrument, manner, or place of the action described by the verb.

ablution washing for a religious purpose, to purify the soul. Hindus, for example, believe that bathing in the river Ganges will purify them. Similar beliefs are found in Christianity and Shinto (for example, the mythical Izanagi purifies himself by diving to the bottom of the sea and washing himself).

Åbo Swedish name for *Turku, a port in Finland.

abolitionism in UK and US history, a movement culminating in the late 18th and early 19th centuries that aimed first to end the slave trade, and then to abolish the institution of *slavery and emancipate slaves.

abominable snowman or *yeti* legendary creature, said to resemble a human, with long arms and a thickset body covered with reddish-grey hair. Reports of its existence in the Himalayas have been made since 1832, and they gained substance from a published photograph of a huge footprint in the snow in 1951. No further 'evidence' has been found.

aborigine (Latin *ab origine* 'from the beginning') any indigenous inhabitant of a region or country. The word often refers to the original peoples of areas colonized by Europeans, and especially to *Australian Aborigines.

abortion ending of a pregnancy before the fetus is developed sufficiently to survive outside the uterus. Loss of a fetus at a later gestational age is termed premature stillbirth. Abortion may be accidental (miscarriage) or deliberate (termination of pregnancy).

Aboukir Bay, Battle of also known as the *Battle of the Nile*; naval battle between Great Britain and France, in which Admiral Nelson defeated Napoleon's fleet at the Egyptian seaport of Aboukir on 1 Aug 1798.

Abraham *c.* 2300 BC. In the Old Testament, founder of the Jewish nation. In his early life he was called Abram. God promised him heirs and land for his people in Canaan (Israel), renamed him Abraham ('father of many nations'), and tested his faith by a command (later retracted) to sacrifice his son Isaac.

Abraham, Plains of plateau near Québec, Canada, where the British commander *Wolfe defeated the French under *Montcalm, 13 Sept 1759, during the French and Indian War (1754–63). The outcome of the battle established British supremacy in Canada.

abrasive substance used for cutting and polishing or for removing small amounts of the surface of hard materials. There are two types: natural and artificial abrasives, and their hardness is measured using the *Mohs' scale. Natural abrasives include quartz, sandstone, pumice, diamond, and corundum; artificial abrasives include rouge, whiting, and carborundum.

Abruzzi mountainous region of S central Italy, comprising the provinces of L'Aquila, Chieti, Pescara, and Teramo; area 10,800 sq km/4,169 sq mi; population (1990) 1,272,000; capital L'Aquila. Gran Sasso d'Italia, 2,914 m/9,564 ft, is the highest point of the *Apennines.

Absalom in the Old Testament, the favourite son of King David; when defeated in a revolt against his father he fled on a mule, but caught his hair in a tree branch and was killed by Joab, one of David's officers.

abscissa in *coordinate geometry, the x-coordinate of a point – that is, the horizontal distance of that point from the vertical or y-axis. For example, a point with the coordinates (4, 3) has an abscissa of 3. The y-coordinate of a point is known as the *ordinate.

abscissin or *abscissic acid* plant hormone found in all higher plants. It is involved in the process of abscission and also inhibits stem elongation, germination of seeds, and the sprouting of buds.

abscission in botany, the controlled separation of part of a plant from the main plant body – most commonly, the falling of leaves or the dropping of fruit. In *deciduous plants the leaves are shed before the winter or dry season, whereas *evergreen plants drop their leaves continually throughout the year. Fruit drop, the abscission of fruit while still immature, is a naturally occurring process.

absolute value or *modulus* in mathematics, the value, or magnitude, of a number irrespective of its sign. The absolute value of a number n is written $|n|$ (or sometimes as mod n), and is defined as the positive square root of n^2. For example, the numbers –5 and 5 have the same absolute value: $|5| = |-5| = 5$.

absolute zero lowest temperature theoretically possible, zero degrees kelvin, equivalent to –273.16°C/–459.67°F, at which molecules are motionless. Although the third law of *thermodynamics indicates the impossibility of reaching absolute zero exactly, a temperature within 3 × 10^{-8} kelvin of it was produced 1984 by Finnish scientists. Near absolute zero, the physical properties of some materials change substantially (see *cryogenics); for example, some metals lose their electrical resistance and become superconductive.

absolutism or *absolute monarchy* system of government in which the ruler or rulers have unlimited power. The principle of an absolute monarch, given a right to rule by God (see *divine right of kings), was extensively used in Europe during the 17th and 18th centuries.

Absolute monarchy is contrasted with limited or constitutional monarchy, in which the sovereign's powers are defined or limited.

absorption in science, the taking up of one substance by another, such as a liquid by a solid (ink by blotting paper) or a gas by a liquid (ammonia by water). In biology, absorption describes the passing of nutrients or medication into and through tissues such as intestinal walls and blood vessels. In physics, absorption is the phenomenon by which a substance retains radiation of particular wavelengths; for example, a piece of blue glass absorbs all visible light except the wavelengths in the blue part of the spectrum; it also refers to the partial loss of energy resulting from light and other electromagnetic waves passing through a medium. In nuclear physics, absorption is the capture by elements, such as boron, of neutrons produced by fission in a reactor.

abstract art nonrepresentational art. Ornamental art without figurative representation occurs in most cultures. The modern abstract movement in sculpture and painting emerged in Europe and North America between 1910 and 1920. Two approaches produce different abstract styles: images that have been 'abstracted' from nature to the point where they no longer reflect a conventional reality and nonobjective, or 'pure', art forms, supposedly without reference to reality.

Abstract Expressionism US movement in abstract art that emphasized the act of painting, the expression inherent in paint itself, and the interaction of artist, paint, and canvas. Abstract Expressionism emerged in New York in the early 1940s. Arshile Gorky, Franz Kline, Jackson Pollock, and Mark Rothko are associated with the movement.

Absurd, Theatre of the avant-garde drama originating with a group of playwrights in the 1950s, including Beckett, Ionesco, Genet, and Pinter. Their work expressed the belief that in a godless universe human existence has no meaning or purpose and therefore all communication breaks down. Logical construction and argument gives way to irrational and illogical speech and to its ultimate conclusion, silence, as in Beckett's play *Breath* 1970.

Abu Bakr or *Abu-Bekr* 573–634. 'Father of the virgin', name used by Abd-el-Ka'aba from about 618 when the prophet Muhammad married his daughter Ayesha. He was a close adviser to Muhammad in the period 622–32. On the prophet's death, he became the first *caliph, adding Mesopotamia to the Muslim world and instigating expansion into Iraq and Syria.

Abu Dhabi sheikdom in SW Asia, on the Arabian Gulf, capital of the *United Arab Emirates. Formerly under British protection, it has been ruled since 1971 by Sheik Sultan Zayed bin al-Nahayan, who is also president of the Supreme Council of Rulers of the United Arab Emirates.

Abuja city in Nigeria that began construction 1976 as a replacement for Lagos. Shaped like a crescent, it was designed by the Japanese architect Kenzo Tange.

Abu Musa small island in the Persian Gulf. Formerly owned by the ruler of Sharjah, it was forcibly occupied by Iran 1971.

Abu Simbel former site of two ancient temples cut into the rock on the banks of the Nile in S Egypt during the reign of Ramses II, commemorating him and his wife Nefertari. The temples were moved, in sections, 1966–67 before the site was flooded by the Aswan High Dam.

abyssal plain broad expanse of sea floor lying 3–6 km/2–4 mi below sea level. Abyssal plains are found in all the major oceans, and they extend from bordering continental rises to mid-oceanic ridges.

abyssal zone dark ocean area 2,000–6,000 m/ 6,500–19,500 ft deep; temperature 4°C/39°F. Three-quarters of the area of the deep ocean floor lies in the abyssal zone, which is too far from the surface for photosynthesis to take place. Some fish and crustaceans living there are blind or have their own light sources. The region above is the bathyal zone; the region below, the hadal zone.

Abyssinia former name of *Ethiopia.

AC in physics, abbreviation for *alternating current*.

acacia any of a large group of shrubs and trees of the genus *Acacia* of the legume family Leguminosae. Acacias include the thorn trees of the African savanna and the gum arabic tree *A. senegal* of N Africa, and several North American species of the SW USA and Mexico. Acacias are found in warm regions of the world, particularly Australia.

Academy Award annual award in many categories, given since 1927 by the American Academy of Motion Picture Arts and Sciences (founded by Louis B Mayer of Metro-Goldwyn-Mayer 1927). Arguably the film community's most prestigious accolade, the award is a gold-plated statuette, which has been nicknamed 'Oscar' since 1931.

Academy, French or *Académie Française* literary society concerned with maintaining the purity of the French language, founded by *Richelieu 1635. Membership is limited to 40 'Immortals' at a time.

acanthus any herbaceous plant of the genus *Acanthus* with handsome lobed leaves. Twenty species are found in the Mediterranean region and Old World tropics, including bear's breech *A. mollis*, whose leaves were used as a motif in classical architecture, especially on Corinthian columns.

a cappella (Italian 'in the style of the chapel') choral music sung without instrumental accompaniment. It is characteristic of *gospel music, *doo-wop, and the evangelical Christian church movement.

Acapulco or *Acapulco de Juarez* port and holiday resort in S Mexico; population (1990) 592,200. There is deep-sea fishing, and tropical products are exported. Acapulco was founded 1550 and was Mexico's major Pacific coast port until about 1815.

ACAS acronym for *Advisory, Conciliation, and Arbitration Service*.

acceleration rate of change of the velocity of a moving body. It is usually measured in metres per second per second ($m\ s^{-2}$) or feet per second per second ($ft\ s^{-2}$). Because velocity is a *vector quantity (possessing both magnitude and direction) a body travelling at constant speed

ACADEMY AWARDS: RECENT WINNERS

1978 Best Picture: *The Deer Hunter*; Best Director: Michael Cimino *The Deer Hunter*; Best Actor: Jon Voight *Coming Home*; Best Actress: Jane Fonda *Coming Home*

1979 Best Picture: *Kramer vs Kramer*; Best Director: Robert Benton *Kramer vs Kramer*; Best Actor: Dustin Hoffman *Kramer vs Kramer*; Best Actress: Sally Field *Norma Rae*

1980 Best Picture: *Ordinary People*; Best Director: Robert Redford *Ordinary People*; Best Actor: Robert De Niro *Raging Bull*; Best Actress: Sissy Spacek *Coal Miner's Daughter*

1981 Best Picture: *Chariots of Fire*; Best Director: Warren Beatty *Reds*; Best Actor: Henry Fonda *On Golden Pond*; Best Actress: Katharine *On Golden Pond*

1982 Best Picture: *Gandhi*; Best Director: Richard Attenborough *Gandhi*; Best Actor: Ben Kingsley *Gandhi*; Best Actress: Meryl Streep *Sophie's Choice*

1983 Best Picture: *Terms of Endearment*; Best Director: James L Brooks *Terms of Endearment*; Best Actor: Robert Duvall *Tender Mercies*; Best Actress: Shirley MacLaine *Terms of Endearment*

1984 Best Picture: *Amadeus*; Best Director: Milos Forman *Amadeus*; Best Actor: F Murray Abraham *Amadeus*; Best Actress: Sally Field *Places in the Heart*

1985 Best Picture: *Out of Africa*; Best Director: Sidney Pollack *Out of Africa*; Best Actor: William Hurt *Kiss of the Spiderwoman*; Best Actress: Geraldine Page *The Trip to Bountiful*

1986 Best Picture: *Platoon*; Best Director: Oliver Stone *Platoon*; Best Actor: Paul Newman *The Color of Money*; Best Actress: Marlee Matlin *Children of a Lesser God*

1987 Best Picture: *The Last Emperor*; Best Director: Bernardo Bertolucci *The Last Emperor*; Best Actor: Michael Douglas *Wall Street*; Best Actress: Cher *Moonstruck*

1988 Best Picture: *Rain Man*; Best Director: Barry Levinson *Rain Man*; Best Actor: Dustin Hoffman *Rain Man*; Best Actress: Jodie Foster *The Accused*

1989 Best Picture: *Driving Miss Daisy*; Best Director: Oliver Stone *Born on the 4th of July*; Best Actor: Daniel Day-Lewis *My Left Foot*; Best Actress: Jessica Tandy *Driving Miss Daisy*

1990 Best Picture: *Dances with Wolves*; Best Director: Kevin Costner *Dances with Wolves*; Best Actor: Jeremy Irons *Reversal of Fortune*; Best Actress: Kathy Bates *Misery*

1991 Best Picture: *The Silence of the Lambs*; Best Director: Jonathan Demme *The Silence of the Lambs*; Best Actor: Anthony Hopkins *The Silence of the Lambs*; Best Actress: Jodie Foster *The Silence of the Lambs*

1992 Best Picture: *Unforgiven*; Best Director: Clint Eastwood *Unforgiven*; Best Actor: Al Pacino *Scent of a Woman*; Best Actress: Emma Thompson *Howards End*

1993 Best Picture: *Schindler's List*; Best Director: Steven Spielberg *Schindler's List*; Best Actor: Tom Hanks *Philadelphia*; Best Actress: Holly Hunter *The Piano*

1994 Best Picture: *Forrest Gump*; Best Director: Robert Zemeckis *Forrest Gump*; Best Actor: Tom Hanks *Forrest Gump*; Best Actress: Jessica Lange *Blue Sky*

---

may be said to be accelerating if its direction of motion changes. According to Newton's second law of motion, a body will only accelerate if it is acted upon by an unbalanced, or resultant, *force.

accelerator in physics, a device to bring charged particles (such as protons and electrons) up to high speeds and energies, at which they can be of use in industry, medicine, and pure physics. At low energies, accelerated particles can be used to produce the image on a television screen and generate X-rays (by means of a *cathode-ray tube), destroy tumour cells, or kill bacteria. When high-energy particles collide with other particles, the fragments formed reveal the nature of the fundamental forces of nature. For particles to achieve the energies required, successive applications of a high voltage are given to electrodes placed in the path of the particles. During acceleration, the particles are confined within a circular or linear track using a magnetic field.

accent way of speaking that identifies a person with a particular country, region, language, social class, linguistic style, or some mixture of these.

accessory in law, an accessory is a criminal accomplice who aids in commission of a crime that is actually committed by someone else. An accomplice may be either 'before the fact' (assisting, ordering, or procuring another to commit a crime) or 'after the fact' (giving assistance after the crime). An accomplice present when the crime is committed is an 'abettor'.

access time or *reaction time* in computing, the time taken by a computer, after an instruction has been given, to read from or write to *memory.

acclimation or *acclimatization* the physiological changes induced in an organism by exposure to new environmental conditions. When humans move to higher altitudes, for example, the number of red blood cells rises to increase the oxygen-carrying capacity of the blood in order to compensate for the lower levels of oxygen in the air.

accommodation in biology, the ability of the *eye to focus on near or far objects by changing the shape of the lens.

accomplice in law, a person who acts with another in the commission or attempted commission of a crime, either as a principal or as an *accessory.

accordion musical instrument of the free-reed organ type comprising left and right wind chests connected by flexible bellows. The right hand plays melody on a piano-style keyboard of 26 to 34 keys while the left hand has a system of push buttons for selecting single notes or chord harmonies.

accounting the principles and practice of systematically recording, presenting, and interpreting financial *accounts; financial record keeping and management of businesses and other organizations, from balance sheets to policy decisions, for tax or operating purposes. Forms of inflation accounting, such as CCA (current cost accounting) and CPP (current purchasing power)

distant object

house far away
from the eye

large pupil

lens long
and thin

tight
ligaments

close object

pencil near
the eye

small pupil

lens short
and fat

slack
ligaments

accommodation *The process by which the shape of the lens in the eye is changed so that clear images of objects, whether distant or near, can be focused on the retina.*

are aimed at providing valid financial comparisons over a period in which money values change.

Accra capital and port of Ghana; population (1984) 964,800. The port trades in cacao, gold, and timber. Industries include engineering, brewing, and food processing. Osu (Christiansborg) Castle is the presidential residence.

accumulator in electricity, a storage *battery – that is, a group of rechargeable secondary cells. A familiar example is the lead–acid car battery.

accumulator collective bet, usually on horse races (normally four or more), such that the winnings from one race are carried forward as the stake on the next, resulting in a potentially enormous return for a small initial outlay.

accumulator in computing, a special register, or memory location, in the *arithmetic and logic unit of the computer processor. It is used to hold the result of a calculation temporarily or to store data that is being transferred.

accusative in the grammar of some inflected languages, such as Latin, Greek, and Russian, the accusative case is the form of a noun, pronoun, or adjective used when it is the direct object of a verb. The accusative is also used for the object of certain prepositions.

Acer genus of trees and shrubs of the temperate regions of the northern hemisphere with over 115 species, many of them popular garden specimens in Australia. *Acer* includes *sycamore and *maple.

acesulfame-K non-carbohydrate sweetener that is up to 300 times as sweet as sugar. It is used in soft drinks and desserts.

acetate common name for *ethanoate.

acetic acid common name for *ethanoic acid.

acetone common name for *propanone.

acetylene common name for *ethyne.

Achaea in ancient Greece, and also today, an area of the N Peloponnese. The *Achaeans* were the predominant society during the Mycenaean period and are said by Homer to have taken part in the siege of Troy.

Achaean League union in 275 BC of most of the cities of the N Peloponnese, which managed to defeat *Sparta, but was itself defeated by the Romans 146 BC.

Achaemenid dynasty family ruling the Persian Empire 550–330 BC, and named after Achaemenes, ancestor of Cyrus the Great, founder of the empire. His successors included Cambyses, Darius I, Xerxes, and Darius III, who, as the last Achaemenid ruler, was killed after defeat in battle against Alexander the Great 330 BC.

Achard Franz Karl 1753–1821. German chemist who was largely responsible for developing the industrial process by which table sugar (sucrose) is extracted from beet. He improved the quality of available beet and erected the first factory for the extraction of sugar in Silesia (now in Poland) 1802.

Achebe Chinua 1930– . Nigerian novelist whose themes include the social and political impact of European colonialism on African people, and the problems of newly independent African nations. His novels include the widely acclaimed *Things Fall Apart* 1958 and *Anthills of the Savannah* 1987.

achene dry, one-seeded *fruit that develops from a single *ovary and does not split open to disperse the seed. Achenes commonly occur in groups, for example, the fruiting heads of buttercup *Ranunculus* and clematis. The outer surface may be smooth, spiny, ribbed, or tuberculate, depending on the species.

Achilles Greek hero of Homer's *Iliad*. He was the son of Peleus, king of the Myrmidons in Thessaly, and the sea nymph Thetis, who rendered him invulnerable, except for the heel by which she held him, by dipping him in the river Styx. Achilles killed Hector in the Trojan War and was himself killed by Paris who shot a poisoned arrow into Achilles' heel.

Achilles tendon tendon pinning the calf muscle to the heel bone. It is one of the largest in the human body.

achromatic lens combination of lenses made from materials of different refractive indexes, constructed in such a way as to minimize chromatic aberration (which in a single lens causes coloured fringes around images because the lens diffracts the different wavelengths in white light to slightly different extents).

acid compound that, in solution in an ionizing solvent (usually water), gives rise to hydrogen ions (H^+ or protons). In modern chemistry, acids are defined as substances that are proton donors and accept electrons to form *ionic bonds. Acids react with *bases to form salts, and they act as solvents. Strong acids are corrosive; dilute acids have a sour or sharp taste, although in some organic acids this may be partially masked by other flavour characteristics.

acid house type of *house music. The derivation of the term is disputed but may be from 'acid burning', Chicago slang for 'sampling', a recording technique much featured in acid house (see *digital sampling).

acid rain acidic rainfall, thought to be caused principally by the release into the atmosphere of sulphur dioxide (SO_2) and oxides of nitrogen. Sulphur dioxide is formed from the burning of fossil fuels, such as coal, that contain high quantities of sulphur; nitrogen oxides are contributed from various industrial activities and from car exhaust fumes.

acid salt chemical compound formed by the partial neutralization of a dibasic or tribasic *acid (one that contains two or three hydrogen atoms). Although a salt, it contains replaceable hydrogen, so it may undergo the typical reactions of an acid. Examples are sodium hydrogen sulphate ($NaHSO_4$) and acid phosphates.

aclinic line the magnetic equator, an imaginary line near the equator, where the compass needle balances horizontally, the attraction of the north and south magnetic poles being equal.

acne skin eruption, mainly occurring among adolescents and young adults, caused by inflammation of the sebaceous glands which secrete an oily substance (sebum), the natural lubricant of the skin. Sometimes the openings of the glands become blocked and they swell; the contents decompose and pimples form on the face, back, and chest.

Aconcagua extinct volcano in the Argentine Andes, the highest peak in the Americas; 6,960 m/22,834 ft. It was first climbed by Vines and Zeebruggen 1897.

aconite or **monkshood** herbaceous Eurasian plant *Aconitum napellus* of the buttercup family Ranunculaceae, with hooded blue-mauve flowers. It produces aconitine, a powerful alkaloid with narcotic and analgesic properties.

acorn fruit of the oak tree, a *nut growing in a shallow cup.

acoustic coupler device that enables computer data to be transmitted and received through a normal telephone handset; the handset rests on the coupler to make the connection. A small speaker within the device is used to convert the computer's digital output data into sound signals, which are then picked up by the handset and transmitted through the telephone system. At the receiving telephone, a second acoustic coupler converts the sound signals back into digital data for input into a computer.

acoustic ohm unit of acoustic impedance (the ratio of the sound pressure on a surface to the sound flux through the surface). It is analogous to the ohm as the unit of electrical *impedance.

acoustics in general, the experimental and theoretical science of sound and its transmission; in particular, that branch of the science that has to do with the phenomena of sound in a particular space such as a room or theatre.

acquired character feature of the body that develops during the lifetime of an individual, usually as a result of repeated use or disuse, such as the enlarged muscles of a weightlifter.

acquired immune deficiency syndrome full name for the disease *AIDS.

acquittal in law, the setting free of someone charged with a crime after a trial.

acre traditional English land measure equal to 4,840 square yards (4,047 sq m/0.405 ha). Originally meaning a field, it was the size that a yoke of oxen could plough in a day. It may be subdivided into 160 square rods (one square rod equalling 25.29 sq m/30.25 sq yd).

Acre or **'Akko** seaport in Israel; population (1983) 37,000. Taken by the Crusaders 1104, it was captured by Saladin 1187 and retaken by Richard I (the Lionheart) 1191. Napoleon failed in a siege 1799. British field marshal Allenby captured the port 1918. From being part of British mandated Palestine, it became part of Israel 1948.

acridine $C_{13}H_9N$ organic compound that occurs in coal tar. It is extracted by dilute acids but can also be obtained synthetically. It is used to make dyes and drugs.

acronym word formed from the initial letters and/or syllables of other words, intended as a pronounceable abbreviation, for example NATO (**N**orth **A**tlantic **T**reaty **O**rganization), radar (**ra**dio **d**etecting **a**nd **r**anging), and sitrep (**sit**uation **rep**ort).

acropolis (Greek 'high city') citadel of an ancient Greek town. The Acropolis of Athens contains the ruins of the Parthenon and surrounding complexes, built there during the days of the Athenian empire. The term is also used for analogous structures, as in the massive granite-built ruins of Great *Zimbabwe.

acrostic (Greek 'at the extremity of a line or row') a number of lines of writing, usually verse, whose initial letters (read downwards) form a word, phrase, or sentence. A **single acrostic** is formed by the initial letters of lines only, while a **double acrostic** is formed by both initial and final letters.

acrylic fibre synthetic fibre often used as a substitute for wool. It was first developed 1947 but not produced in great volumes until the 1950s. Strong and warm, acrylic fibre is often used for sweaters and tracksuits, and as linings for boots and gloves.

actinide any of a series of 15 radioactive metallic chemical elements with atomic numbers 89 (actinium) to 103 (lawrencium). Elements 89 to 95 occur in nature; the rest of the series are synthesized elements only. Actinides are grouped together because of their chemical similarities (for example, they are all bivalent), the properties differing only slightly with atomic number. The series is set out in a band in the *periodic table of the elements, as are the *lanthanides.

actinium (Greek *aktis* 'ray') white, radioactive, metallic element, the first of the actinide series, symbol Ac, atomic number 89, relative atomic mass 227; it is a weak emitter of high-energy alpha particles. Actinium occurs with uranium and radium in *pitchblende and other ores, and can be synthesized by bombarding radium with neutrons. The longest-lived isotope, Ac-227, has a half-life of 21.8 years (all the other isotopes have very short half-lives). Actinium was discovered in 1899 by the French chemist André Debierne.

action in law, one of the proceedings whereby a person or agency seeks to enforce rights in a civil court.

ActionAid UK charity founded 1972 to help people in the Third World to secure lasting improvements in the quality of their lives. It has sister organizations in other industrialized countries and by 1990 had projects in 18 countries in Africa, Asia, and Latin America, concentrating on long-term integrated rural development in the areas of water, health, agriculture, education, and income generation.

action and reaction in physical mechanics, equal and opposite effects produced by a force acting on an object. For example, the pressure of expanding gases from the burning of fuel in a rocket engine (a force) produces an equal and opposite reaction, which causes the rocket to move.

action painting or *gesture painting* in US art, a dynamic school of Abstract Expressionism. It emphasized the importance of the physical act of painting, sometimes expressed with both inventiveness and aggression, and on occasion performed for the camera. Jackson *Pollock was the leading exponent.

action potential in biology, a change in the potential difference (voltage) across the membrane of a nerve cell when an impulse passes along it. A change in potential (from about –60 to +45 millivolts) accompanies the passage of sodium and potassium ions across the membrane.

Actium, Battle of naval battle in which Octavian defeated the combined fleets of *Mark Antony and *Cleopatra 31 BC to become the undisputed ruler of the Roman world (as the emperor *Augustus). The site is at Akri, a promontory in W Greece.

activation energy in chemistry, the energy required in order to start a chemical reaction. Some elements and compounds will react together merely by bringing them into contact (spontaneous reaction). For others it is necessary to supply energy in order to start the reaction, even if there is ultimately a net output of energy. This initial energy is the activation energy.

act of Congress in the USA, a bill or resolution passed by both houses of Congress, the Senate and the House of Representatives, which becomes law with the signature of the president. If vetoed by the president, it may still become law if it returns to Congress again and is passed by a majority of two-thirds in each house.

act of God legal term meaning some sudden

and irresistible act of nature that could not reasonably have been foreseen or prevented, such as floods, storms, earthquakes, or sudden death.

act of Parliament in Britain, a change in the law originating in Parliament and called a statute. Before an act receives the royal assent and becomes law it is a *bill*. The US equivalent is an *act of Congress.

Actors Studio theatre workshop in New York City, established 1947 by Cheryl Crawford and Elia Kazan. Under Lee Strasberg, who became artistic director 1948, it became known for the study of Konstantin Stanislavsky's *Method acting.

actuary mathematician who makes statistical calculations concerning human life expectancy and other risks, on which insurance premiums are based.

acupuncture system of inserting long, thin metal needles into the body at predetermined points to relieve pain, as an anaesthetic in surgery, and to assist healing. The needles are rotated manually or electrically. The method, developed in ancient China and increasingly popular in the West, is thought to work by somehow stimulating the brain's own painkillers, the *endorphins.

acute in medicine, pertaining to a condition that develops and resolves quickly; for example, the common cold and meningitis. In contrast, a *chronic* condition develops and remains over a long period.

acute angle an angle between 0° and 90°.

AD in the Christian calendar, abbreviation for *Anno Domini* (Latin 'in the year of the Lord'); used with dates.

ADA high-level computer-programming language, developed and owned by the US Department of Defense, designed for use in situations in which a computer directly controls a process or machine, such as a military aircraft. The language took more than five years to specify, and became commercially available only in the late 1980s. It is named after English mathematician Ada Augusta *Byron.

Adam family of Scottish architects and designers. *William Adam* (1689–1748) was the leading Scottish architect of his day, and his son *Robert Adam* (1728–1792) is considered one of the greatest British architects of the late 18th century, who transformed the prevailing Palladian fashion in architecture to a Neo-Classical style. He designed interiors for many great country houses and earned a considerable reputation as a furniture designer. With his brother *James Adam* (1732–1794), also an architect, he speculatively developed the Adelphi near Charing Cross, London, largely rebuilt 1936.

Adam (Hebrew *adham* 'man') in the Old Testament, founder of the human race. Formed by God from dust and given the breath of life, Adam was placed in the Garden of Eden, where *Eve was created from his rib and given to him as a companion. Because she tempted him, he tasted the forbidden fruit of the Tree of Knowledge of Good and Evil, for which trespass they were expelled from the Garden.

Adams Ansel 1902–1984. US photographer

known for his printed images of dramatic land-scapes and organic forms of the American West.

Adams Gerry (Gerard) 1948– . Northern Ireland politician, president of Provisional Sinn Féin (the political wing of the Irish Republican Army) from 1978. He declined to take up his Westminster 1983 seat, stating that he did not believe in the British government. In Aug 1994 he announced a 'complete cessation of military operations'. The British government sub-sequently removed all restrictions on his public appearances and freedom to travel to the UK (in force since 1988).

Adams John 1735–1826. 2nd president of the USA 1797–1801, and vice president 1789–97. He was a member of the Continental Congress 1774–78 and signed the Declaration of Indepen-dence. In 1779 he went to France and negotiated the treaties that ended the American Revolution. Although suspicious of the French Revolution, he resisted calls for war with France. He became the first US ambassador in London 1785.

Adams John Coolidge 1947– . US composer and conductor. He was director of the New Music Ensemble 1972–81, and artistic adviser to the San Francisco Symphony Orchestra from 1978. His minimalist techniques are displayed in *Electric Wake* 1968, *Heavy Metal* 1971, *Bridge of Dreams* 1982, and the operas *Nixon in China* 1988 and *The Death of Klinghoffer* 1990.

Adams John Couch 1819–1892. English astron-omer who mathematically deduced the existence of the planet Neptune 1845 from the effects of its gravitational pull on the motion of Uranus, although it was not found until 1846 by German astronomer J G Galle (1812–1910). Adams also studied the Moon's motion, the Leonid meteors, and terrestrial magnetism.

Adams John Quincy 1767–1848. 6th president of the USA 1825–29. Eldest son of President John Adams, he was born in Quincy, Massachusetts, and became US minister in The Hague, Berlin, St Petersburg, and London. He negotiated the Treaty of Ghent to end the *War of 1812 (fought between Britain and the USA) on generous terms for the USA. In 1817 he became *Monroe's sec-retary of state, formulated the *Monroe Doctrine 1823, and was elected president by the House of Representatives, despite receiving fewer votes than his main rival, Andrew *Jackson. As presi-dent, Adams was an advocate of strong federal government.

Adams Richard 1920– . English novelist. A civil servant 1948–72, he wrote *Watership Down* 1972, a tale of a rabbit community, which is read by adults and children. Later novels include *Shardik* 1974, *The Plague Dogs* 1977, and *Girl on a Swing* 1980.

Adams Samuel 1722–1803. US politician, second cousin of President John Adams. He was the chief instigator of the Boston Tea Party (see *American Revolution). He was also a signatory to the Declaration of Independence, served in the *Continental Congress, and anticipated the French emperor Napoleon in calling the British a 'nation of shopkeepers'.

Adamson Robert R 1821–1848. Scottish photographer who, with David Octavius Hill, produced 2,500 *calotypes (mostly portraits) in five years from 1843.

Adana capital of Adana (Seyhan) province, S Turkey; population (1990) 916,150. It is a major cotton-growing centre and Turkey's fourth largest city.

adaptation in biology, any change in the struc-ture or function of an organism that allows it to survive and reproduce more effectively in its environment. In *evolution, adaptation is thought to occur as a result of random variation in the genetic make-up of organisms (produced by *mutation and *recombination) coupled with *natural selection.

adaptive radiation in evolution, the forma-tion of several species, with *adaptations to dif-ferent ways of life, from a single ancestral type. Adaptive radiation is likely to occur whenever members of a species migrate to a new habitat with unoccupied ecological niches. It is thought that the lack of competition in such niches allows sections of the migrant population to develop new adaptations, and eventually to become new species.

The colonization of newly formed volcanic islands has led to the development of many unique species. The 13 species of Darwin's finch on the Galápagos Islands, for example, are prob-ably descended from a single species from the South American mainland. The parent stock evolved into different species that now occupy a range of diverse niches.

Addams Charles 1912–1988. US cartoonist, creator of the ghoulish family featured in the *New Yorker* magazine. A successful television comedy series was based on the cartoon in the 1960s.

Addams Jane 1860–1935. US sociologist and campaigner for women's rights. In 1889 she founded and led the social settlement of Hull House, Chicago, one of the earliest community centres. She was vice president of the National American Women Suffrage Alliance 1911–14, and in 1915 led the Women's Peace Party and the first Women's Peace Congress. She shared the Nobel Peace Prize 1931.

addax light-coloured *antelope *Addax nasom-aculatus* of the family Bovidae. It lives in the Sahara desert where it exists on scanty vegetation without drinking. It is about 1.1 m/3.5 ft at the shoulder, and both sexes have spirally twisted horns.

added value in economics, the difference between the cost of producing something and the price at which it is sold. Added value is the basis of VAT or *value-added tax, a tax on the value added at each stage of the production process of a commodity.

adder European venomous snake, the common *viper *Vipera berus*. Growing to about 60 cm/24 in in length, it has a thick body, triangular head, a characteristic V-shaped mark on its head and, often, zigzag markings along the back. It feeds on small mammals and lizards. The puff adder *Bitis arietans* is a large, yellowish, thick-bodied viper up to 1.6 m/5 ft long, living in Africa and Arabia.

addiction state of dependence on drugs, alco-hol, or other substances. Symptoms include uncontrolled craving, tolerance, and symptoms of withdrawal when access is denied. Habitual use produces changes in chemical processes in

adder *The puff adder, from Africa and western Arabia, grows up to 1.6 m/5 ft long.*

the brain; when the substance is withheld, severe neurological manifestations, even death, may follow. These are reversed by the administration of the addictive substance, and mitigated by a gradual reduction in dosage.

Addis Ababa or **Adis Abeba** capital of Ethiopia; population (1984) 1,413,000. It was founded 1887 by Menelik, chief of Shoa, who ascended the throne of Ethiopia 1889. His former residence, Menelik Palace, is now occupied by the government. The city is the headquarters of the *Organization of African Unity.

Addison Joseph 1672–1719. English writer. In 1704 he celebrated *Marlborough's victory at Blenheim in a poem, 'The Campaign', and subsequently held political appointments, including undersecretary of state and secretary to the Lord-Lieutenant of Ireland 1708. In 1709 he contributed to the *Tatler* magazine, begun by Richard *Steele, with whom he was cofounder 1711 of the *Spectator*.

Addison's disease rare deficiency or failure of the *adrenal glands to produce corticosteroid hormones; it is treated with hormones. The condition, formerly fatal, is characterized by anaemia, weakness, low blood pressure, and brownish pigmentation of the skin.

addition reaction chemical reaction in which the atoms of an element or compound react with a double bond or triple bond in an organic compound by opening up one of the bonds and becoming attached to it, for example

$$CH_2=CH_2 + HCl \rightarrow CH_3CH_2Cl.$$

An example is the addition of hydrogen atoms to *unsaturated compounds in vegetable oils to produce margarine.

additive in food, any natural or artificial chemical added to prolong the shelf life of processed foods (salt or nitrates), alter the colour or flavour of food, or improve its food value (vitamins or minerals). Many chemical additives are used and they are subject to regulation, since individuals may be affected by constant exposure even to traces of certain additives and may suffer side effects ranging from headaches and hyperactivity to cancer.

address in a computer memory, a number indicating a specific location. At each address, a single piece of data can be stored. For microcomputers, this normally amounts to one *byte (enough to represent a single character, such as a letter or number).

Adelaide capital and industrial city of South Australia; population (1990) 1,049,100. Indus-

tries include oil refining, shipbuilding, and the manufacture of electrical goods and cars. Grain, wool, fruit, and wine are exported. Founded 1836, Adelaide was named after William IV's queen.

Aden (Arabic *'Adan*) main port and commercial centre of Yemen, on a rocky peninsula at the SW corner of Arabia, commanding the entrance to the Red Sea; population (1984) 318,000. The city's economy is based on oil refining, fishing, and shipping. A British territory from 1839, Aden became part of independent South Yemen 1967; it was the capital of South Yemen until 1990.

Adenauer Konrad 1876–1967. German Christian Democrat politician, chancellor of West Germany 1949–63. With the French president de Gaulle he achieved the postwar reconciliation of France and Germany and strongly supported all measures designed to strengthen the Western bloc in Europe.

adenoids masses of lymphoid tissue, similar to *tonsils, located in the upper part of the throat, behind the nose. They are part of a child's natural defences against the entry of germs but usually shrink and disappear by the age of ten.

Ader Clément 1841–1925. French aviation pioneer and inventor. He demonstrated stereophonic sound transmission by telephone at the 1881 Paris Exhibition of Electricity. His steam-driven aeroplane, the *Eole*, made the first powered takeoff in history 1890, but it could not fly. In 1897, with his *Avion III*, he failed completely, despite false claims made later.

adhesion in medicine, the abnormal binding of two tissues as a result of inflammation. The moving surfaces of joints or internal organs may merge together if they have been inflamed.

adhesive substance that sticks two surfaces together. Natural adhesives (glues) include gelatin in its crude industrial form (made from bones, hide fragments, and fish offal) and vegetable gums. Synthetic adhesives include thermoplastic and thermosetting resins, which are often stronger than the substances they join; mixtures of *epoxy resin and hardener that set by chemical reaction; and elastomeric (stretching) adhesives for flexible joints. Superglues are fast-setting adhesives used in very small quantities.

adiabatic in physics, a process that occurs without loss or gain of heat, especially the expansion or contraction of a gas in which a change takes place in the pressure or volume, although no heat is allowed to enter or leave.

Adi Granth or **Guru Granth Sahib** the holy book of Sikhism.

adipose tissue type of *connective tissue of vertebrates that serves as an energy reserve, and also pads some organs. It is commonly called fat tissue, and consists of large spherical cells filled with fat. In mammals, major layers are in the inner layer of skin and around the kidneys and heart.

Adjani Isabelle 1955– . French actress of Algerian-German descent. She played the title role in Truffaut's *L'Histoire d'Adèle H/The Story of Adèle H* 1975 and has since appeared in international productions including *Le Locataire/ The Tenant, Nosferatu Phantom der Nacht* 1979, and *Ishtar* 1987.

adjective grammatical *part of speech for words that describe nouns (for example, *new* and *beautiful*, as in 'a new hat' and 'a beautiful day'). Adjectives generally have three degrees (grades or levels for the description of relationships): the positive degree (*new, beautiful*), the comparative degree (*newer, more beautiful*), and the superlative degree (*newest, most beautiful*).

Adler Alfred 1870–1937. Austrian psychologist. Adler saw the 'will to power' as more influential in accounting for human behaviour than the sexual drive theory. A dispute over this theory led to the dissolution of his ten-year collaboration with *Freud.

administrative law law concerning the powers and control of government agencies or those agencies granted statutory powers of administration.

admiral highest-ranking naval officer.

admiral any of several species of butterfly in the same family (Nymphalidae) as the tortoiseshells. The red admiral *Vanessa atalanta*, wingspan 6 cm/2.5 in, is found worldwide in the northern hemisphere. It migrates south each year from northern areas to subtropical zones.

Admiral's Cup sailing series first held in 1957 and held biennially. National teams consisting of three boats compete over three inshore courses (in the Solent) and two offshore courses (378 km/235 mi across the Channel from Cherbourg to the Isle of Wight and 1,045 km/650 mi from Plymouth to Fastnet lighthouse off Ireland, and back). The highlight is the Fastnet race.

Admiralty, Board of the in Britain, the controlling department of state for the Royal Navy from the reign of Henry VIII until 1964, when most of its functions – apart from that of management – passed to the Ministry of Defence. The 600-year-old office of Lord High Admiral reverted to the sovereign.

adobe in architecture, building with earth bricks. The formation of earth bricks ('adobe') and the construction of walls by enclosing earth within moulds (*pisé de terre*) are the two principal methods of earth building. The techniques are commonly found in Spain, Latin America, and the southwestern USA.

adolescence in the human life cycle, the period between the beginning of puberty and adulthood.

Adonis in Greek mythology, a beautiful youth beloved by the goddess *Aphrodite. He was killed while boar-hunting but was allowed to return from the lower world for six months every year to rejoin her. The anemone sprang from his blood.

adoption permanent legal transfer of parental rights and duties in respect of a child from one person to another.

adrenal gland or *suprarenal gland* gland situated on top of the kidney. The adrenals are soft and yellow, and consist of two parts: the cortex and medulla. The **cortex** (outer part) secretes various steroid hormones, controls salt and water metabolism, and regulates the use of carbohydrates, proteins, and fats. The **medulla** (inner part) secretes the hormones adrenaline and noradrenaline which, during times of stress, cause the heart to beat faster and harder, increase blood flow to the heart and muscle cells, and

dilate airways in the lungs, thereby delivering more oxygen to cells throughout the body and in general preparing the body for 'fight or flight'.

adrenaline or *epinephrine* hormone secreted by the medulla of the *adrenal glands.

Adrian IV (Nicholas Breakspear) *c.* 1100–1159. Pope 1154–59, the only British pope. He secured the execution of *Arnold of Brescia; crowned Frederick I Barbarossa as German emperor; refused Henry II's request that Ireland should be granted to the English crown in absolute ownership; and was at the height of a quarrel with the emperor when he died.

Adriatic Sea large arm of the Mediterranean Sea, lying NW to SE between the Italian and the Balkan peninsulas. The W shore is Italian; the E is Croatian, Yugoslav, and Albanian. The sea is about 805 km/500 mi long, and its area is 135,250 sq km/52,220 sq mi.

adsorption taking up of a gas or liquid at the surface of another substance, usually a solid (for example, activated charcoal adsorbs gases). It involves molecular attraction at the surface, and should be distinguished from *absorption (in which a uniform solution results from a gas or liquid being incorporated into the bulk structure of a liquid or solid).

adult education in the UK, voluntary classes and courses for adults provided mainly in further-education colleges, adult-education institutes, and school premises. Adult education covers a range of subjects from flower arranging to electronics and can lead to examinations and qualifications. Small fees are usually charged. The *Open College, *Open University, and Workers' Educational Association are adult-education bodies.

adultery voluntary sexual intercourse between a married person and someone other than his or her legal partner.

advanced gas-cooled reactor (AGR) type of *nuclear reactor widely used in W Europe. The AGR uses a fuel of enriched uranium dioxide in stainless-steel cladding and a moderator of graphite. Carbon dioxide gas is pumped through the reactor core to extract the heat produced by the *fission of the uranium. The heat is transferred to water in a steam generator, and the steam drives a turbogenerator to produce electricity.

Adventist person who believes that Jesus will return to make a second appearance on Earth. Expectation of the Second Coming of Christ is found in New Testament writings generally. Adventist views are held by the Seventh-Day Adventists, Christadelphians, Jehovah's Witnesses, and the Four Square Gospel Alliance.

adventitious root in plants, a root developing in an unusual position, as in ivy, where roots grow sideways out of the stem and cling to trees or walls.

adverb grammatical *part of speech for words that modify or describe verbs ('She ran *quickly*'), adjectives ('a *beautifully* clear day'), and adverbs ('They did it *really* well'). Most adverbs are formed from adjectives or past participles by adding -*ly* (*quick: quickly*) or -*ally* (*automatic: automatically*).

advertising any of various methods used by a

company to increase the sales of its products or to promote a brand name. Advertising can be seen by economists as either beneficial (since it conveys information about a product and so brings the market closer to a state of *perfect competition) or as a hindrance to perfect competition, since it attempts to make illusory distinctions (such as greater sex appeal) between essentially similar products.

Advertising Standards Authority (ASA) organization founded by the UK advertising industry 1962 to promote higher standards of advertising in the media (excluding television and radio, which have their own authority). It is financed by the advertisers, who pay 0.1% supplement on the cost of advertisements. It recommends to the media that advertisements which might breach the British Code of Advertising Practice are not published, but has no statutory power.

Advisory, Conciliation, and Arbitration Service (ACAS) UK independent body set up under the Employment Protection Act 1975 to improve industrial relations. Specifically, ACAS aims to encourage the extension of collective bargaining and, wherever possible, the reform of collective-bargaining machinery.

advocate (Latin *advocatus*, one summoned to one's aid, especially in a lawcourt) professional pleader in a court of justice.

Advocates, Faculty of professional organization for Scottish advocates, the equivalent of English *barristers. It was incorporated 1532 under James V.

Aegean civilization the cultures of Bronze Age Greece, including the *Minoan civilization* of Crete and the *Mycenaean civilization* of the E Peloponnese.

Aegean Islands islands of the Aegean Sea, but more specifically a region of Greece comprising the Dodecanese islands, the Cyclades islands, Lesvos, Samos, and Chios; population (1991) 460,800; area 9,122 sq km/3,523 sq mi.

Aegean Sea branch of the Mediterranean between Greece and Turkey; the Dardanelles connect it with the Sea of Marmara. The numerous islands in the Aegean Sea include Crete, the Cyclades, the Sporades, and the Dodecanese. There is political tension between Greece and Turkey over sea limits claimed by Greece around such islands as Lesvos, Chios, Samos, and Kos.

Aelfric c. 955–1020. Anglo-Saxon writer and abbot, author of two collections of *Catholic Homilies* 990–92, sermons, and the *Lives of the Saints* 996–97, written in vernacular Old English prose.

Aeneas in Classical legend, a Trojan prince who became the ancestral hero of the Romans. According to Homer, he was the son of Anchises and the goddess Aphrodite. During the Trojan War he owed his life to the frequent intervention of the gods. The legend on which Virgil's epic poem the *Aeneid* is based describes his escape from Troy and his eventual settlement in Latium, on the Italian peninsula.

Aeneid epic poem by Virgil, written in Latin in 12 books of hexameters and composed during the last 11 years of his life (30–19 BC). It celebrates the founding of Rome through the legend of Aeneas. After the fall of Troy, Aeneas wanders the Mediterranean for seven years and is shipwrecked off North Africa. He is received by Dido, Queen of Carthage, and they fall in love. Aeneas, however, renounces their love and sails on to Italy where he settles as the founder of Latium and the Roman state.

Aeolian harp wind-blown instrument consisting of a shallow soundbox supporting gut strings at low tension and tuned to the same pitch. It produces an eerie harmony that rises and falls with the changing pressure of the wind. It was common in parts of central Europe during the 19th century.

aerial or *antenna* in radio and television broadcasting, a conducting device that radiates or receives electromagnetic waves. The design of an aerial depends principally on the wavelength of the signal. Long waves (hundreds of metres in wavelength) may employ long wire aerials; short waves (several centimetres in wavelength) may employ rods and dipoles; microwaves may also use dipoles – often with reflectors arranged like a toast rack – or highly directional parabolic dish aerials. Because microwaves travel in straight lines, giving line-of-sight communication, microwave aerials are usually located at the tops of tall masts or towers.

aerial bombardment another name for *Blitzkrieg.

aerobic in biology, a description of those living organisms that require oxygen (usually dissolved in water) for the efficient release of energy contained in food molecules, such as glucose. They include almost all living organisms (plants as well as animals) with the exception of certain bacteria.

aerodynamics branch of fluid physics that studies the forces exerted by air or other gases in motion – for example, the airflow around bodies (such as land vehicles, bullets, rockets, and aircraft) moving at speed through the atmosphere. For maximum efficiency, the aim is usually to design the shape of an object to produce a streamlined flow, with a minimum of turbulence in the moving air.

aerogenerator wind-powered electricity generator. These range from wind farms (see *wind turbine) to battery chargers used on yachts.

aeronautics science of travel through the Earth's atmosphere, including aerodynamics, aircraft structures, jet and rocket propulsion, and aerial navigation.

aeroplane (North American *airplane*) powered heavier-than-air craft supported in flight by fixed wings. Aeroplanes are propelled by the thrust of a jet engine or airscrew (propeller). They must be designed aerodynamically, since streamlining ensures maximum flight efficiency. The Wright brothers flew the first powered plane (a biplane) in Kitty Hawk, North Carolina, USA, 1903. (See also *flight.)

aerosol particles of liquid or solid suspended in a gas. Fog is a common natural example. Aerosol cans, which contain pressurized gas mixed with a propellant, are used to spray liquid in the form of tiny drops of such products as scents and cleaners. Most aerosols used chlorofluorocarbons (CFCs) as propellants until these were found to cause destruction of the *ozone layer in the stratosphere.

Aeschines lived 4th century BC. Orator of ancient Athens, a rival of *Demosthenes.

Aeschylus c. 525–c. 456 BC. Greek dramatist, widely regarded as the founder of Greek tragedy (with *Euripides and *Sophocles). By the introduction of a second actor he made true dialogue and dramatic action possible. Aeschylus wrote some 90 plays between 499 and 458 BC, of which seven survive. These are *The Suppliant Women* performed about 490 BC, *The Persians* 472 BC, *Seven against Thebes* 467 BC, *Prometheus Bound* c. 460 BC, and the *Oresteia* trilogy 458 BC.

Aesir principal gods of Norse mythology – Odin, Thor, Balder, Loki, Freya, and Tyr – whose dwelling place was Asgard.

Aesop traditional writer of Greek fables. According to the historian Herodotus, he lived in the reign of Amasis of Egypt (mid-6th century BC) and was a slave of Iadmon, a Thracian. The fables, for which no evidence of his authorship exists, are anecdotal stories using animal characters to illustrate moral or satirical points.

Aesthetic movement English artistic movement of the late 19th century, dedicated to the doctrine of 'art for art's sake' – that is, art as selfsufficient, not needing to justify its existence by serving any particular use. Artists associated with the movement include Aubrey *Beardsley and James *Whistler. The writer Oscar *Wilde was, in his twenties, an exemplary aesthete.

aesthetics branch of philosophy that deals with the nature of beauty, especially in art. It emerged as a distinct branch of enquiry in the mid-18th century.

aestivation in zoology, a state of inactivity and reduced metabolic activity, similar to *hibernation, that occurs during the dry season in species such as lungfish and snails. In botany, the term is used to describe the way in which flower petals and sepals are folded in the buds. It is an important feature in plant classification.

Aetolia district of ancient Greece on the NW of the gulf of Corinth. The **Aetolian League** was a confederation of the cities of Aetolia which, following the death of Alexander the Great, became the chief rival of Macedonian power and the Achaean League.

affidavit legal document, used in court applications and proceedings, in which a person swears that certain facts are true.

affiliation order in English law, formerly a court order for maintenance against the alleged father of an illegitimate child. Under the Family Law Reform Act 1987, either parent can apply for a court order for maintenance of children, no distinction being made between legitimate and illegitimate children.

affinity in law, relationship by marriage not blood (for example, between a husband and his wife's blood relatives, between a wife and her husband's blood relatives, or step-parent and stepchild), which may legally preclude their marriage. It is distinguished from consanguinity or blood relationship. In Britain, the right to marry was extended to many relationships formerly prohibited by the Marriage (Prohibited Degrees of Relationship) Act 1986.

affinity in chemistry, the force of attraction (see *bond) between atoms that helps to keep them in combination in a molecule. The term is also applied to attraction between molecules, such as those of biochemical significance (for example, between *enzymes and substrate molecules). This is the basis for affinity *chromatography, by which biologically important compounds are separated.

affirmative action government policy of positive discrimination that favours members of minority ethnic groups and women in such areas as employment and education, designed to counter the effects of long-term discrimination against them. In Europe, Sweden, Belgium, the Netherlands, and Italy actively promote affirmative action through legal and financial incentives.

affluent society society in which most people have money left over after satisfying their basic needs such as food and shelter. They are then able to decide how to spend their excess ('disposable') income, and become 'consumers'. The term was popularized by the US economist John Kenneth *Galbraith.

afforestation planting of trees in areas that have not previously held forests. (**Reafforestation** is the planting of trees in deforested areas.) Trees may be planted (1) to provide timber and wood pulp; (2) to provide firewood in countries where this is an energy source; (3) to bind soil together and prevent soil erosion; and (4) to act as windbreaks.

Afghan hound breed of fast hunting dog resembling the *saluki in build, though slightly smaller and more thickly coated. It was first introduced to the West by British army officers serving on India's North-West Frontier along the Afghanistan border in the late 19th century. The Afghan hound is about 70 cm/28 in tall and has a long, silky coat.

Afghanistan Republic of (*Jamhuria Afghanistan*)

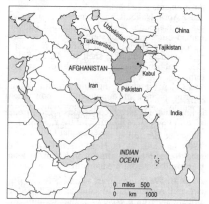

area 652,090 sq km/251,707 sq mi
capital Kabul
towns Kandahar, Herat, Mazar-i-Sharif
physical mountainous in centre and NE, plains in N and SW
environment an estimated 95% of the urban population is without access to sanitation services

head of state Burhanuddin Rabbani from 1992
head of government vacant
political system emergent democracy
exports dried fruit, natural gas, fresh fruits,
carpets; small amounts of rare minerals, karakul
lamb skins, and Afghan coats
currency afgháni
population (1993 est) 17,400,000 (more than 5
million became refugees after 1979); growth rate
0.6% p.a.
languages Pushtu, Dari (Persian)
religion Muslim (80% Sunni, 20% Shi'ite)
GNP $250 per head
chronology
1747 Afghanistan became an independent
emirate.
1839–42 and 1878–80 Afghan Wars instigated
by Britain to counter the threat to British India
from expanding Russian influence in
Afghanistan.
1919 Afghanistan recovered full independence
following Third Afghan War.
1953 Lt-Gen Daud Khan became prime minister
and introduced reform programme.
1963 Daud Khan forced to resign and constitutional monarchy established.
1973 Monarchy overthrown in coup by Daud
Khan.
1978 Daud Khan ousted by Taraki and the
PDPA.
1979 Taraki replaced by Hafizullah Amin; USSR
entered country to prop up government; it
installed Babrak Karmal in power. Amin
executed.
1986 Replacement of Karmal as leader by Dr
Najibullah Ahmadzai. Partial Soviet troop withdrawal.
1988 New non-Marxist constitution adopted.
1989 Complete withdrawal of Soviet troops;
state of emergency imposed in response to intensification of civil war.
1991 US and Soviet military aid withdrawn.
Mujaheddin began talks with Russians and Kabul
government.
1992 April: Najibullah government overthrown.
June: mujaheddin leader Burhanuddin Rabbani
named interim head of state; Islamic law introduced. Sept: Hezb-i-Islami barred from government participation after shell attacks on Kabul.
Dec: Rabbani elected president for two-year
term.
1993 Jan: intensive fighting around Kabul;
interim parliament appointed by constituent
assembly. March: peace agreement signed
between Rabbani and dissident Hezb-i-Islami
leader Gulbuddin Hekmatyar, under which Hekmatyar became prime minister.
1994 Jan: alliance of Hezb-i-Islami and other
rebel forces renewed attacks on Kabul; Hekmatyar dismissed from premiership.

Afghan Wars three wars waged between Britain and Afghanistan to counter the threat to
British India from expanding Russian influence
in Afghanistan.
First Afghan War 1838–42, when the British
garrison at Kabul was wiped out.
Second Afghan War 1878–80, when General
*Roberts captured Kabul and relieved Kandahar.
Third Afghan War 1919, when peace followed
the dispatch by the UK of the first aeroplane ever
seen in Kabul.

AFL–CIO abbreviation for **American Federation of Labor and Congress of Industrial
Organizations**.

Africa second largest of the continents, three
times the area of Europe
area 30,097,000 sq km/11,620,451 sq mi
largest cities (population over 1 million) Cairo,
Algiers, Lagos, Kinshasa, Abidjan, Cape Town,
Nairobi, Casablanca, El Gîza, Addis Ababa,
Luanda, Dar es Salaam, Ibadan, Douala,
Mogadishu
physical dominated by a uniform central plateau
comprising a southern tableland with a mean
altitude of 1,070 m/3,000 ft that falls northwards
to a lower elevated plain with a mean altitude of
400 m/1,300 ft. Although there are no great
alpine regions or extensive coastal plains, Africa
has a mean altitude of 610 m/2,000 ft, two times
greater than Europe. The highest points are
Mount Kilimanjaro 5,900 m/19,364 ft, and
Mount Kenya 5,200 m/17,058 ft; the lowest point
is Lac Assal in Djibouti −144 m/−471 ft. Compared with other continents, Africa has few broad
estuaries or inlets and therefore has proportionately the shortest coastline (24,000 km/
15,000 mi). The geographical extremities of the
continental mainland are Cape Hafun in the E,
Cape Almadies in the W, Ras Ben Sekka in the
N, and Cape Agulhas in the S. The Sahel is a
narrow belt of savanna and scrub forest which
covers 700 million hectares/1.7 billion acres of
W and central Africa; 75% of the continent lies
within the tropics
products has 30% of the world's minerals
including diamonds (51%) and gold (47%); produces 11% of the world's crude petroleum, 58%
of the world's cocoa (Ivory Coast, Ghana,
Cameroon, Nigeria), 23% of the world's coffee
(Uganda, Ivory Coast, Zaire, Ethiopia,
Cameroon, Kenya); 20% of the world's groundnuts (Senegal, Nigeria, Sudan, Zaire), and 21%
of the world's hardwood timber (Nigeria, Zaire,
Tanzania, Kenya)
population (1988) 610 million; more than
double the 1960 population of 278 million, and
rising to an estimated 900 million by 2000;
annual growth rate 3%
languages over 1,000 languages spoken in
Africa; Niger-Kordofanian languages including
Mandinke, Kwa, Lingala, Bemba, and Bantu
(Zulu, Swahili, Kikuyu), spoken over half of
Africa from Mauritania in the W to South Africa;
Nilo-Saharan languages, including Dinka, Shil-
luk, Nuer, and Masai, spoken in Central Africa
from the bend of the Niger river to the foothills
of Ethiopia; Afro-Asiatic (Hamito-Semitic) languages, including Arabic, Berber, Ethiopian, and
Amharic, N of equator; Khoisan languages with
'click' consonants spoken in SW by Kung,
Khoikhoi, and Nama people of Namibia
religions Islam in the N and on the E coast
as far S as N Mozambique; animism below the
Sahara, which survives alongside Christianity
(both Catholic and Protestant) in many central
and S areas.

African National Congress (ANC) South
African political party, founded 1912 as a multiracial nationalist organization with the aim of
extending the franchise to the whole population
and ending all racial discrimination. Its president
from 1991 is Nelson *Mandela.

The ANC was banned by the government from 1960 to Jan 1990. During the early 1990s fighting between supporters of the ANC and the Zulu-based *Inkatha movement racked the townships, leaving thousands dead. Talks between the ANC and the South African government began Dec 1991, culminating in the adoption of a nonracial constitution 1993 and the ANC's agreement to participate in a power-sharing administration, as a prelude to full majority rule. In the country's first multiracial elections April 1994, the ANC won a sweeping victory, capturing 62% of the vote, and Mandela was elected president.

African nationalism political movement for the unification of Africa. African nationalism has its roots among the educated elite (mainly 'returned' Americans of African descent and freed slaves or their descendants in W Africa in the 19th century. Christian mission-educated, many challenged overseas mission control and founded independent churches. These were often involved in anticolonial rebellions, for example, in Natal 1906 and Nyasaland 1915. The Kitwala (Watchtower Movement) and Kimbanguist churches provided strong support for the nationalist cause in the 1950s. Early African political organizations included the Aborigines Rights Protection Society in the Gold Coast 1897, the African National Congress in South Africa 1912, and the National Congress of West Africa 1920.

After World War I nationalists fostered moves for self-determination. The *Fourteen Points encouraged such demands in Tunisia, and delegates to London 1919 from the Native National Congress in South Africa stressed the contribution to the war effort by the South African Native Labour Corps. Most nationalist groups functioned within the territorial boundaries of single colonies, for example, the Tanganyika African Association and the Rhodesian Bantu Voters Association. One or two groups, including the National Congress of British West Africa, had wider pan-African visions. The first pan-African Congress was held in London 1900 and others followed after 1919. By 1939 African nationalist groups existed in nearly every territory of the continent. Africa's direct involvement in World War II, the weakening of the principal colonial powers, increasing anticolonialism from America (the Atlantic Charter 1941 encouraged self-government), the Soviet criticism of imperialism inspired African nationalists. Since 1958 pan-Africanism has become partially absorbed into wider Third World movements. In May 1963 it was decided to establish the *Organization of African Unity (OAU).

African violet herbaceous plant *Saintpaulia ionantha* from tropical central and E Africa, with velvety green leaves and scentless purple flowers. Different colours and double varieties have been bred.

Afrikaans language an official language (with English) of the Republic of South Africa and Namibia. Spoken mainly by the Afrikaners – descendants of Dutch and other 17th-century colonists – it is a variety of the Dutch language, modified by circumstance and the influence of German, French, and other immigrant as well as local languages. It became a standardized written language about 1875.

African violet The deep-blue African violet *Saintpaulia ionantha is a popular houseplant.*

Afrika Korps German army in the western desert of N Africa 1941–43 during World War II, commanded by Field Marshall Erwin Rommel. They were driven out of N Africa by May 1943.

Afrikaner (formerly known as *Boer*) inhabitant of South Africa descended from the original Dutch, Flemish, and *Huguenot settlers of the 17th century. Comprising approximately 60% of the white population in South Africa, they were originally farmers but have now become mainly urbanized. Their language is Afrikaans.

Afro-Caribbean West Indian person of African descent. Afro-Caribbeans are the descendants of W Africans captured or obtained in trade from African procurers. European slave traders then shipped them to the West Indies to English, French, Dutch, Spanish, and Portuguese colonies founded from the 16th century. Since World War II many Afro-Caribbeans have migrated to North America and to Europe, especially to the USA, the UK, and the Netherlands.

afterbirth in mammals, the placenta, umbilical cord and ruptured membranes, which become detached from the uterus and expelled soon after birth. In the natural world it is often eaten.

afterburning method of increasing the thrust of a gas turbine (jet) aeroplane engine by spraying additional fuel into the hot exhaust duct between the turbojet and the tailpipe where it ignites. Used for short-term increase of power during take-off, or during combat in military aircraft.

afterimage persistence of an image on the retina of the eye after the object producing it has been removed. This leads to persistence of vision, a necessary phenomenon for the illusion of continuous movement in films and television. The term is also used for the persistence of sensations other than vision.

after-ripening process undergone by the seeds of some plants before germination can occur. The length of the after-ripening period in different species may vary from a few weeks to many months. It helps seeds to germinate at a time when conditions are most favourable for growth. In some cases the embryo is not fully mature at the time of dispersal and must develop further before germination can take place. Other seeds do not germinate even when the embryo is mature, probably owing to growth inhibitors within the seed that must be leached out or broken down before germination can begin.

Aga Khan IV 1936– . Spiritual head (*imam*) of the **Ismaili** Muslim sect (see *Islam). He succeeded his grandfather 1957.

agama lizard of the Old World family Agamidae, especially the genus *Agama*. There are about 280 species, found throughout the warmer regions of the Old World. Many are brilliantly coloured and all are capable of changing the colour of their skin.

Agamemnon in Greek mythology, a Greek hero, son of Atreus, king of Mycenae. He married Clytemnestra, and their children included Electra, Iphigenia, and *Orestes. He led the capture of Troy, received Priam's daughter Cassandra as a prize, and was murdered by Clytemnestra and her lover, Aegisthus, on his return home. His children Orestes and Electra later killed the guilty couple.

agar jellylike carbohydrate, obtained from seaweeds. It is used mainly in microbiological experiments as a culture medium for growing bacteria and other microorganisms. The agar is resistant to breakdown by microorganisms, remaining a solid jelly throughout the course of the experiment.

agaric fungus of typical mushroom shape. Agarics include the field mushroom *Agaricus campestris* and the cultivated edible mushroom *A. brunnesiens*. Closely related is the often poisonous *Amanita* genus, including the fly agaric *Amanita muscaria*.

Agassiz Jean Louis Rodolphe 1807–1873. Swiss-born US palaeontologist and geologist, one of the foremost scientists of the 19th century. He established his name through his work on the classification of the fossil fishes. Unlike Darwin, he did not believe that individual species themselves changed, but that new species were created from time to time.

agate banded or cloudy type of *chalcedony, a silica, SiO_2, that forms in rock cavities. Agates are used as ornamental stones and for art objects.

agave any of several related plants with stiff sword-shaped spiny leaves arranged in a rosette. All species of the genus *Agave* come from the warmer parts of the New World. They include *A. sisalina*, whose fibres are used for rope making, and the Mexican century plant *A. americana*. Alcoholic drinks such as *tequila and pulque are made from the sap of agave plants.

ageing in common usage, the period of deterioration of the physical condition of a living organism that leads to death; in biological terms, the entire life process.

ageism discrimination against older people in employment, pensions, housing, and health care.

Agent Orange selective *weedkiller, notorious for its use in the 1960s during the Vietnam War by US forces to eliminate ground cover which could protect enemy forces. It was subsequently discovered to contain highly poisonous *dioxin. Thousands of US troops who had handled it later developed cancer or fathered deformed babies.

agglutination in biology, the clumping together of *antigens, such as blood cells or bacteria, to form larger, visible masses, under the influence of *antibodies. As each antigen clumps only in response to its particular antibody, agglutination provides a way of determining *blood groups and the identity of unknown bacteria.

aggression in biology, behaviour used to intimidate or injure another organism (of the same or of a different species), usually for the purposes of gaining territory, a mate, or food. Aggression often involves an escalating series of threats aimed at intimidating an opponent without having to engage in potentially dangerous physical contact. Aggressive signals include roaring by red deer, snarling by dogs, the fluffing up of feathers by birds, and the raising of fins by some species of fish.

Agincourt, Battle of battle of the Hundred Years' War in which Henry V of England defeated the French on 25 Oct 1415, mainly through the overwhelming superiority of the English longbow. The French lost more than 6,000 men to about 1,600 English casualties. As a result of the battle, Henry gained France and the French princess, Catherine of Valois, as his wife. The village of Agincourt (modern **Azincourt**) is south of Calais, in N France.

agnosticism belief that the existence of God cannot be proven; that in the nature of things the individual cannot know anything of what lies behind or beyond the world of natural phenomena. The term was coined 1869 by T H *Huxley.

agoraphobia *phobia involving fear of open spaces and crowded places.
The anxiety produced can be so severe that some sufferers are confined to their homes for many years.

agouti small rodent of the genus *Dasyprocta*, family Dasyproctidae. It is found in the forests of Central and South America. The agouti is herbivorous, swift-running, and about the size of a rabbit.

Agra city of Uttar Pradesh, India, on the river Jumna, 160 km/100 mi SE of Delhi; population (1981) 747,318. A commercial and university centre, it was the capital of the Mogul empire 1527–1628, from which period the Taj Mahal dates.

agribusiness commercial farming on an industrial scale, often financed by companies whose main interests lie outside agriculture; for example, multinational corporations. Agribusiness farms are mechanized, large in size, highly structured, and reliant on chemicals.

Agricola Gnaeus Julius AD 37–93. Roman general and politician. Born in Provence, he became Consul of the Roman Republic AD 77, and then governor of Britain AD 78–85. He extended Roman rule to the Firth of Forth in Scotland and won the battle of Mons Graupius. His fleet sailed round the north of Scotland and proved Britain an island.

agricultural revolution sweeping changes that took place in British agriculture over the period 1750–1850 in response to the increased demand for food from a rapidly expanding population. Recent research has shown these changes to be only part of a much larger, ongoing process of development.

agriculture the practice of farming, including the cultivation of the soil (for raising crops) and the raising of domesticated animals. Crops are for human nourishment, animal fodder, or commodities such as cotton and sisal. Animals are raised for wool, milk, leather, dung (as fuel), or meat. The units for managing agricultural production vary from small holdings and individually owned farms to corporate-run farms and collective farms run by entire communities.

Agriculture developed in the Middle East and Egypt at least 10,000 years ago. Farming communities soon became the base for society in China, India, Europe, Mexico, and Peru, then spread throughout the world. Reorganization along more scientific and productive lines took place in Europe in the 18th century in response to dramatic population growth. Mechanization made considerable progress in the USA and Europe during the 19th century. After World War II, there was an explosive growth in the use of agricultural chemicals: herbicides, insecticides, fungicides, and fertilizers. In the 1960s there was development of high-yielding species, especially in the *green revolution* of the Third World, and the industrialized countries began intensive farming of cattle, poultry, and pigs. In the 1980s, hybridization by genetic engineering methods and pest control by the use of chemicals plus *pheromones were developed. However, there was also a reaction against some forms of intensive agriculture because of the pollution and habitat destruction caused. One result of this was a growth of alternative methods, including organic agriculture.

agrimony herbaceous plant *Agrimonia eupatoria* of the rose family Rosaceae, with small yellow flowers on a slender spike.
It grows along hedges and in fields.

Agrippa Marcus Vipsanius 63–12 BC. Roman general. He commanded the victorious fleet at the battle of Actium and married Julia, daughter of the emperor *Augustus.

agrochemical artificially produced chemical used in modern, intensive agricultural systems. Agrochemicals include nitrate and phosphate fertilizers, pesticides, some animal-feed additives, and pharmaceuticals. Many are responsible for pollution and almost all are avoided by organic farmers.

agronomy study of crops and soils, a branch of agricultural science. Agronomy includes such topics as selective breeding (of plants and animals), irrigation, pest control, and soil analysis and modification.

AH with reference to the Muslim calendar, abbreviation for *anno hegirae* (Latin 'year of the flight' – of *Muhammad, from Mecca to Medina).

Ahab c. 875–854 BC. King of Israel. His empire included the suzerainty of Moab, and Judah was his subordinate ally, but his kingdom was weakened by constant wars with Syria. By his marriage with Jezebel, princess of Sidon, Ahab introduced into Israel the worship of the Phoenician god Baal, thus provoking the hostility of Elijah and other prophets. Ahab died in battle against the Syrians at Ramoth Gilead.

Ahasuerus (Latinized Hebrew form of the Persian *Khshayarsha*, Greek *Xerxes*) name of several Persian kings in the Bible, notably the husband of *Esther. Traditionally it was also the name of the *Wandering Jew.

ahimsa in Hinduism, Buddhism, and Jainism, the doctrine of respect for all life (including the lowest forms and even the elements themselves) and consequently an extreme form of nonvio-

lence. It arises in part from the concept of *karma*, which holds that a person's actions (and thus any injury caused to any form of life) are carried forward from one life to the next, determining each stage of reincarnation.

Ahmadiyya Islamic religious movement founded by Mirza Ghulam Ahmad (1839–1908). His followers reject the doctrine that Muhammad was the last of the prophets and accept Ahmad's claim to be the Mahdi and Promised Messiah. In 1974 the Ahmadis were denounced as non-Muslims by other Muslims.

Ahmad Shah Durrani 1724–1773. Founder and first ruler of Afghanistan. Elected shah in 1747, he had conquered the Punjab by 1751.

Ahmedabad or *Ahmadabad* capital of Gujarat, India; population (1981) 2,515,195. It is a cotton-manufacturing centre, and has many sacred buildings of the Hindu, Muslim, and Jain faiths.

Ahriman in Zoroastrianism, the supreme evil spirit, lord of the darkness and death, waging war with his counterpart Ahura Mazda (Ormuzd) until a time when human beings choose to lead good lives and Ahriman is finally destroyed.

Ahura Mazda or *Ormuzd* in Zoroastrianism, the spirit of supreme good. As god of life and light he will finally prevail over his enemy, Ahriman.

Ahváz industrial capital of the province of Khuzestan, on the river Karun, W Iran; population (1986) 590,000. The ancient city was rebuilt in the 3rd century AD; it became a prosperous city in the 20th century after the discovery of oil.

AI abbreviation for *artificial intelligence*.

AI(D) abbreviation for *artificial insemination (by donor)*. AIH is *artificial insemination by husband*.

Aidan, St c. 600–651. Irish monk who converted Northumbria to Christianity and founded Lindisfarne monastery on Holy Island off the NE coast of England. His feast day is 31 Aug.

aid, development money given or lent on concessional terms to developing countries or spent on maintaining agencies for this purpose. In the late 1980s official aid from governments of richer nations amounted to $45–60 billion annually whereas voluntary organizations in the West received about $2.4 billion a year for the Third World. The *World Bank is the largest dispenser of aid. In 1990 it transferred $467 billion to developing countries. All industrialized United Nations (UN) member countries devote a proportion of their gross national product to aid, ranging from 0.20% of GNP (Ireland) to 1.10% (Norway) (1988 figures). Each country spends more than half this contribution on direct bilateral assistance to countries with which they have historical or military links or hope to encourage trade. The rest goes to international organizations such as UN and World Bank agencies, which distribute aid multilaterally.

aid, foreign another name for *development aid* (see *aid, development).

AIDS (acronym for *acquired immune deficiency syndrome*) the gravest of the *sexually transmitted diseases, or STDs. It is caused by the human immunodeficiency virus (HIV), now known to be a *retrovirus, an organism first identified 1983. HIV is transmitted in body fluids, mainly blood and sexual secretions.

Aiken Howard 1900– . US mathematician and computer pioneer. In 1939, in conjunction with engineers from *IBM, he started work on the design of an automatic calculator using standard business-machine components. In 1944 the team completed one of the first computers, the Automatic Sequence Controlled Calculator (known as the Mark 1), a programmable computer controlled by punched paper tape and using punched cards.

aikido Japanese art of self-defence; one of the *martial arts. Two main systems of aikido are tomiki and uyeshiba.

ailanthus any tree or shrub of the genus *Ailanthus* of the quassia family. All have compound leaves made up of pointed leaflets and clusters of small greenish flowers with an unpleasant smell. The tree of heaven *Ailanthus altissima*, native to E Asia, is grown worldwide as an ornamental. It can grow to 100 ft/30 m in height and 3 ft/1 m in diameter.

Ailey Alvin 1931–1989. US dancer, choreographer, and director whose Alvin Ailey City Center Dance Theater, formed 1958, was the first truly interracial dance company and opened dance to a wider audience. Ailey studied modern, ethnic, jazz, and academic dance, and his highly individual work celebrates rural and urban black America in pieces like *Blues Suite* 1958 and the company signature piece *Revelations* 1960.

Ainu aboriginal people of Japan, driven north in the 4th century AD by ancestors of the Japanese. They now number about 25,000, inhabiting Japanese and Russian territory on Sakhalin, Hokkaido, and the Kuril Islands. Their language has no written form, and is unrelated to any other.

air see *atmosphere.

air conditioning system that controls the state of the air inside a building or vehicle. A complete air-conditioning unit controls the temperature and humidity of the air, removes dust and odours from it, and circulates it by means of a fan. US inventor W H Carrier developed the first effective air-conditioning unit 1902 for a New York printing plant.

aircraft any aeronautical vehicle, which may be lighter than air (supported by buoyancy) or heavier than air (supported by the dynamic action of air on its surfaces). *Balloons and *airships are lighter-than-air craft. Heavier-than-air craft include the *aeroplane, glider, autogyro, and helicopter.

aircraft carrier ocean-going naval vessel with a broad, flat-topped deck for launching and landing military aircraft; an effort to provide a floating military base for warplanes too far from home for refuelling, repairing, reconnaissance, escorting, and various attack and defence operations.

air-cushion vehicle (ACV) craft that is supported by a layer, or cushion, of high-pressure air. The *hovercraft is one form of ACV.

Airedale terrier breed of large *terrier dog, about 60 cm/2 ft tall, with a rough red-brown coat. It originated about 1850 in England, as a cross of the otter hound and Irish and Welsh terriers.

air force a nation's fighting aircraft and the organization that maintains them.

air lock airtight chamber that allows people to pass between areas of different pressure; also an air bubble in a pipe that impedes fluid flow. An airlock may connect an environment at ordinary pressure and an environment that has high air pressure (such as a submerged caisson used for tunnelling or building dams or bridge foundations). An airlock may also permit someone wearing breathing apparatus to pass into an airless environment (into water from a submerged submarine or into the vacuum of space from a spacecraft).

air pollution contamination of the atmosphere caused by the discharge, accidental or deliberate, of a wide range of toxic airborne substances. Often the amount of the released substance is relatively high in a certain locality, so the harmful effects become more noticeable. The cost of preventing any discharge of pollutants into the air is prohibitive, so attempts are more usually made to reduce gradually the amount of discharge and to disperse this as quickly as possible by using a very tall chimney, or by intermittent release.

air sac in birds, a thin-walled extension of the lungs. There are nine of these and they extend into the abdomen and bones, effectively increasing lung capacity. In mammals, it is another name for the alveoli in the lungs, and in some insects, for widenings of the trachea.

airship or *dirigible* any aircraft that is lighter than air and power-driven, consisting of an elliptical balloon that forms the streamlined envelope or hull and has below it the propulsion system (propellers), steering mechanism, and space for crew, passengers and/or cargo. The balloon section is filled with lighter-than-air gas, either the nonflammable helium or, before helium was industrially available in large enough quantities, the easily ignited and flammable hydrogen. The envelope's form is maintained by internal pressure in the nonrigid (blimp) and semirigid types (in which the nose and tail sections have a metal framework connected by a rigid keel). The rigid type (zeppelin) maintains its form using an internal metal framework. Airships have been used for luxury travel, polar exploration, warfare, and advertising.

air transport means of conveying goods or passengers by air from one place to another. See *flight.

Airy George Biddell 1801–1892. English astronomer. He installed a transit telescope at the Royal Observatory at Greenwich, England, and accurately measured *Greenwich Mean Time by the stars as they crossed the meridian.

Ajaccio capital and second-largest port of Corsica; population (1982) 55,279. Founded by the Genoese 1492, it was the birthplace of Napoleon; it has been French since 1768.

Ajax Greek hero in Homer's *Iliad*. Son of Telamon, king of Salamis, he was second only to Achilles among the Greek heroes in the Trojan War. When *Agamemnon awarded the armour of the dead Achilles to *Odysseus, Ajax is said to have gone mad with jealousy, and then committed suicide in shame.

Ajman smallest of the seven states that make up the *United Arab Emirates; area 250 sq km/96 sq mi; population (1985) 64,318.

ajolote Mexican reptile of the genus *Bipes*. It and several other tropical burrowing species are placed in the Amphisbaenia, a group separate from lizards and snakes among the Squamata. Unlike the others, however, which have no legs, it has a pair of short but well-developed front legs. In line with its burrowing habits, the skull is very solid, the eyes small, and external ears absent. The scales are arranged in rings, giving the body a wormlike appearance.

Akbar Jalal ud-Din Muhammad 1542–1605. Mogul emperor of N India from 1556, when he succeeded his father. He gradually established his rule throughout N India. He is considered the greatest of the Mogul emperors, and the firmness and wisdom of his rule won him the title 'Guardian of Mankind'; he was a patron of the arts.

à Kempis Thomas see *Thomas à Kempis, religious writer.

Akhenaton another name for *Ikhnaton, pharaoh of Egypt.

Akhetaton capital of ancient Egypt established by the monotheistic pharaoh *Ikhnaton as the centre for his cult of the Aton, the sun's disc; it is the modern Tell el Amarna 300 km/190 mi S of Cairo. Ikhnaton's palace had formal enclosed gardens. After his death it was abandoned, and the *Amarna tablets*, found in the ruins, were probably discarded by his officials.

Akihito 1933– . Emperor of Japan from 1989, succeeding his father Hirohito (Showa). His reign is called the Heisei ('achievement of universal peace') era.

Akkad northern Semitic people who conquered the Sumerians in 2350 BC and ruled Mesopotamia. The ancient city of Akkad in central Mesopotamia, founded by *Sargon I, was an imperial centre in the 3rd millennium BC; the site is unidentified, but it was on the Euphrates.

Akkaia alternative form of *Achaea.

Akron (Greek 'summit') city in Ohio, USA, on the Cuyahoga River, 56 km/35 mi SE of Cleveland; population (1990) 660,000. Known as the 'Rubber Capital of the World,' it is home to the headquarters of several major tyre and rubber companies, although production there ended by 1982.

Aksai Chin part of Himalayan Kashmir lying to the east of the Karakoram range. It is occupied by China but claimed by India.

Aksum ancient Greek-influenced Semitic kingdom that flourished 1st–6th centuries AD and covered a large part of modern Ethiopia as well as the Sudan. The ruins of its capital, also called Aksum, lie NW of Aduwa, but the site has been developed as a modern city.

al- for Arabic names beginning *al-*, see rest of name; for example, for 'al-Fatah', see *Fatah, al-.

Alabama state in southern USA; nickname Heart of Dixie/Cotton State
area 134,700 sq km/51,994 sq mi
capital Montgomery
towns Birmingham, Mobile, Huntsville, Tuscaloosa
physical the state comprises the Cumberland Plateau in the north; the Black Belt, or Canebrake, which is excellent cotton-growing country, in the centre; and south of this, the coastal plain of Piny Woods. The Alabama river is the largest in the state
products cotton still important though no longer prime crop; soya beans, peanuts, wood products, coal, iron, chemicals, textiles, paper
population (1990) 4,040,600
famous people Nat King Cole, Helen Keller, Joe Louis, Jesse Owens, Booker T Washington
history first settled by the French in the early 18th century, it was ceded to Britain 1763, passed to the USA 1783, and became a state 1819. It was one of the states in the *Confederacy in the American Civil War.

alabaster naturally occurring fine-grained white or light-coloured translucent form of *gypsum, often streaked or mottled. It is a soft material, used for carvings, and ranks second on the *Mohs' scale of hardness.

Alain-Fournier pen name of Henri-Alban Fournier 1886–1914. French novelist. His haunting semi-autobiographical fantasy *Le Grand Meaulnes/The Lost Domain* 1913 was a cult novel of the 1920s and 1930s. His life is intimately recorded in his correspondence with his brother-in-law Jacques Rivière. He was killed in action on the Meuse in World War I.

Alamein, El, Battles of in World War II, two decisive battles in the western desert, N Egypt. In the *First Battle of El Alamein* 1–27 July 1942 the British 8th Army under Auchinleck held the German and Italian forces under Rommel. In the *Second Battle of El Alamein* 23 Oct–4 Nov 1942 *Montgomery defeated Rommel.

Alamo, the mission fortress in San Antonio, Texas, USA. It was besieged 23 Feb–6 March 1836 by *Santa Anna and 4,000 Mexicans; they killed the garrison of about 180, including Davy *Crockett and Jim *Bowie.

Alamogordo town in New Mexico, USA, associated with nuclear testing. The first atom bomb was exploded nearby at Trinity Site 16 July 1945. It is now a test site for guided missiles.

Alanbrooke Alan Francis Brooke, 1st Viscount Alanbrooke 1883–1963. British army officer, Chief of Staff in World War II and largely responsible for the strategy that led to the German defeat.

Alaric c. 370–410. King of the Visigoths. In 396 he invaded Greece and retired with much booty to Illyria. In 400 and 408 he invaded Italy, and in 410 captured and sacked Rome, but died the same year on his way to invade Sicily. The river Busento was diverted by his soldiers so that he could be buried in its course with his treasures; the labourers were killed to keep the secret.

Alaska largest state of the USA, on the NW extremity of North America, separated from the lower 48 states by British Columbia; nickname Last Frontier
total area 1,530,700 sq km/591,004 sq mi
land area 1,478,457 sq km/570,833 sq mi
capital Juneau
towns Anchorage, Fairbanks, Fort Yukon, Holy Cross, Nome
physical much of Alaska is mountainous and includes Mount McKinley (Denali), 6,194 m/20,322 ft, the highest peak in North America,

surrounded by Denali National Park. Caribou thrive in the Arctic tundra, and elsewhere there are extensive forests

products oil, natural gas, coal, copper, iron, gold, tin, fur, salmon fisheries and canneries, lumber

population (1990) 550,000; including 9% American Indians, Aleuts, and Inuits

history various groups of Indians crossed the Bering land bridge 60,000–15,000 years ago; the Eskimo began to settle the Arctic coast from Siberia about 2000 BC; the Aleuts settled the Aleutian archipelago about 1000 BC. The first European to visit Alaska was Vitus Bering 1741. Alaska was a Russian colony from 1744 until purchased by the USA 1867 for $7,200,000; gold was discovered five years later. It became a state 1959. A Congressional act 1980 gave environmental protection to 42 million ha/104 million acres. Valuable mineral resources have been exploited from 1968, especially in the Prudhoe Bay area to the SE of Point Barrow. An oil pipeline (1977) runs from Prudhoe Bay to the port of Valdez. Oilspill from a tanker in Prince William Sound caused great environmental damage 1989. Under construction is an underground natural-gas pipeline to Chicago and San Francisco.

Albania Republic of (*Republika e Shqipërisë*)

area 28,748 sq km/11,097 sq mi
capital Tiranë
towns Shkodër, Elbasan, Vlorë, chief port Durrës
physical mainly mountainous, with rivers flowing E–W, and a narrow coastal plain
head of state Sali Berisha from 1992
head of government Alexandr Meksi from 1992
political system emergent democracy
exports crude oil, bitumen, chrome, iron ore, nickel, coal, copper wire, tobacco, fruit, vegetables
currency lek
population (1993) 3,400,000; growth rate 1.9% p.a.
languages Albanian, Greek
religion Muslim 70%, although all religion banned 1967–90
GNP $930 per head

GDP $1.3 bn; $543 per head
chronology
c. 1468 Albania made part of the Ottoman Empire.
1912 Independence achieved from Turkey.
1925 Republic proclaimed.
1928–39 Monarchy of King Zog.
1939–44 Under Italian and then German rule.
1946 Communist republic proclaimed under the leadership of Enver Hoxha.
1949 Admitted into Comecon.
1961 Break with Khrushchev's USSR.
1967 Albania declared itself the 'first atheist state in the world'.
1978 Break with 'revisionist' China.
1985 Death of Hoxha.
1987 Normal diplomatic relations restored with Canada, Greece, and West Germany.
1988 Attendance of conference of Balkan states for the first time since the 1930s.
1990 One-party system abandoned; first opposition party formed.
1991 Party of Labour of Albania (PLA) won first multiparty elections; Ramiz Alia re-elected president; three successive governments formed. PLA renamed PSS.
1992 Presidential elections won by PSDS; Sali Berisha elected president. Alia and other former communist officials charged with corruption and abuse of power; totalitarian and communist parties banned.
1993 Jan: Nexhmije Hoxha, widow of Enver Hoxha, sentenced to nine years' imprisonment for misuse of government funds 1985–90.

Albanian person of Albanian culture from Albania and the surrounding area. The Albanian language belongs to a separate group within the Indo-European family and has an estimated 3–4 million speakers. There are both Christian and Muslim Albanians, the latter having been converted by the Ottoman Turks. Albanians comprise the majority of Kosovo in Yugoslavia and are in conflict with the Serbs, for whom the province is historically and culturally significant.

Alban, St died AD 303. First Christian martyr in England. In 793 King Offa founded a monastery on the site of Alban's martyrdom, around which the city of St Albans grew up.

albatross large seabird, genus *Diomedea*, with long narrow wings adapted for gliding and a wingspan of up to 3 m/10 ft, mainly found in the southern hemisphere. It belongs to the order Procellariiformes, the same group as petrels and shearwaters.

albedo the fraction of the incoming light reflected by a body such as a planet. A body with a high albedo, near 1, is very bright, while a body with a low albedo, near 0, is dark. The Moon has an average albedo of 0.12, Venus 0.65, Earth 0.37.

Albee Edward 1928– . US dramatist. His internationally performed plays are associated with the Theatre of the *Absurd and include *The Zoo Story* 1960, *The American Dream* 1961, *Who's Afraid of Virginia Woolf?* 1962 (his most successful play; also filmed 1966), and *Tiny Alice* 1965. *A Delicate Balance* 1966 and *Seascape* 1975 both won Pulitzer Prizes.

Albéniz Isaac 1860–1909. Spanish nationalist composer and pianist. His works include the orchestral suites *Española* 1886 and *Catalonia* 1908, and some 250 piano works including the *Iberia* suite 1909.

Albert Prince Consort 1819–1861. Husband of British Queen *Victoria from 1840; a patron of the arts, science, and industry. Albert was the second son of the Duke of Saxe Coburg-Gotha and first cousin to Queen Victoria, whose chief adviser he became. He planned the Great Exhibition of 1851; the profit was used to buy the sites in London of all the South Kensington museums and colleges and the Royal Albert Hall, built 1871. He died of typhoid.

Alberta province of W Canada
area 661,200 sq km/255,223 sq mi
capital Edmonton
towns Calgary, Lethbridge, Medicine Hat, Red Deer
physical Rocky Mountains; dry, treeless prairie in the centre and south; towards the north this merges into a zone of poplar, then mixed forest. The valley of the Peace River is the most northerly farming land in Canada (except for Inuit pastures), and there are good grazing lands in the foothills of the Rockies
products coal; wheat, barley, oats, sugar beet in the south; more than a million head of cattle; oil and natural gas
population (1991) 2,501,400
history in the 17th century much of its area was part of a grant to the *Hudson's Bay Company for the fur trade. It became a province 1905.

Alberti Leon Battista 1404–1472. Italian *Renaissance architect and theorist who recognized the principles of Classical architecture and their modification for Renaissance practice in *On Architecture* 1452.

Albigenses heretical sect of Christians (associated with the *Cathars) who flourished in S France near Albi and Toulouse during the 11th–13th centuries. They adopted the Manichean belief in the duality of good and evil and pictured Jesus as being a rebel against the cruelty of an omnipotent God.

albinism rare hereditary condition in which the body has no tyrosinase, one of the enzymes that form the pigment melanin, normally found in the skin, hair, and eyes. As a result, the hair is white and the skin and eyes are pink. The skin and eyes are abnormally sensitive to light, and vision is often impaired. The condition occurs among all human and animal groups.

Albinoni Tomaso 1671–1751. Italian Baroque composer and violinist, whose work was studied and adapted by Johann Sebastian *Bach. He composed over 40 operas.

Albion ancient name for Britain used by the Greeks and Romans. It was mentioned by Pytheas of Massilia (4th century BC), and is probably of Celtic origin, but the Romans, having in mind the white cliffs of Dover, assumed it to be derived from *albus* (white).

Alboin 6th century. King of the *Lombards about 561–573. At that time the Lombards were settled north of the Alps. Early in his reign he attacked the Gepidae, a Germanic tribe occupying present-day Romania, killing their king and taking his daughter Rosamund to be his wife. About 568 he crossed the Alps to invade Italy, conquering the country as far S as Rome. He was

murdered at the instigation of his wife, after he forced her to drink wine from a cup made from her father's skull.

Ålborg alternative form of *Aalborg, a port in Denmark.

albumin or *albumen* any of a group of sulphur-containing *proteins. The best known is in the form of egg white; others occur in milk, and as a major component of serum. They are soluble in water and dilute salt solutions, and are coagulated by heat.

Albuquerque Afonso de 1453–1515. Viceroy and founder of the Portuguese East Indies with strongholds in Ceylon, Goa, and Malacca 1508–15, when the king of Portugal replaced him by his worst enemy. He died at sea on the way home when his ship *Flor del Mar* was lost between Malaysia and India.

Alcaeus c. 611–c. 580 BC. Greek lyric poet. Born at Mytilene in Lesvos, he was a member of the aristocratic party and went into exile when the popular party triumphed. He wrote odes, and the Alcaic stanza is named after him.

alcázar (Arabic 'fortress') Moorish palace in Spain; one of five in Toledo defended by the Nationalists against the Republicans for 71 days in 1936 during the Spanish *Civil War.

alchemy (Arabic *al-Kimya*) supposed technique of transmuting base metals, such as lead and mercury, into silver and gold by the philosopher's stone, a hypothetical substance, to which was also attributed the power to give eternal life.

Alcibiades 450–404 BC. Athenian general. Handsome and dissolute, he became the archetype of capricious treachery for his military intrigues against his native state with Sparta and Persia; the Persians eventually had him assassinated. He was brought up by *Pericles and was a friend of *Socrates, whose reputation as a teacher suffered from the association.

Alcock John William 1892–1919. British aviator. On 14 June 1919, he and Arthur Whitten Brown (1886–1948) made the first nonstop transatlantic flight, from Newfoundland to Ireland.

alcohol any member of a group of organic chemical compounds characterized by the presence of one or more aliphatic OH (hydroxyl) groups in the molecule, and which form *esters with acids. The main uses of alcohols are as solvents for gums, resins, lacquers, and varnishes; in the making of dyes; for essential oils in perfumery; and for medical substances in pharmacy. Alcohol (ethanol) is produced naturally in the *fermentation process and is consumed as part of alcoholic beverages.

alcoholic liquor intoxicating drink. *Ethanol (ethyl alcohol), a colourless liquid C_2H_5OH, is the basis of all common intoxicants: *wines, ciders, and sherry* contain alcohol produced by direct fermentation with yeasts of the sugar in the fruit forming the basis of the drink; *malt liquors* are beers and stouts, in which the starch of a grain is converted to sugar by malting, and the sugar then fermented into alcohol by yeasts (fermented drinks contain less than 20% alcohol); *spirits* are distilled from malted liquors or wines, and can contain up to 55% alcohol.

Alcoholics Anonymous (AA) voluntary self-help organization established 1934 in the USA to combat alcoholism; branches now exist in many other countries.

alcohol strength measure of the amount of alcohol in a drink. Wine is measured as the percentage volume of alcohol at 20°C; spirits in litres of alcohol at 20°C, although the percentage volume measure is also commonly used. A 75 cl bottle at 40% volume is equivalent to 0.3 litres of alcohol. See also *proof spirit.

Alcott Louisa May 1832–1888. US author. Her children's classic *Little Women* 1869 drew on her own home circumstances, the heroine Jo being a partial self-portrait.

Alcuin (Flaccus Albinus Alcuinus) 735–804. English scholar. Born in York, he went to Rome 780, and in 782 took up residence at Charlemagne's court in Aachen. From 796 he was abbot of Tours. He disseminated Anglo-Saxon scholarship, organized education and learning in the Frankish empire, gave a strong impulse to the Carolingian Renaissance, and was a prominent member of Charlemagne's academy.

Aldebaran or *Alpha Tauri* brightest star in the constellation Taurus and the 14th brightest star in the sky; it marks the eye of the 'bull'. Aldebaran is a red giant 60 light years away, shining with a true luminosity of about 100 times that of the Sun.

aldehyde any of a group of organic chemical compounds prepared by oxidation of primary alcohols, so that the OH (hydroxyl) group loses its hydrogen to give an oxygen joined by a double bond to a carbon atom (the aldehyde group, with the formula CHO).

alder any tree or shrub of the genus *Alnus*, in the birch family Betulaceae, found mainly in cooler parts of the northern hemisphere and characterized by toothed leaves and catkins.

alderman (Old English *ealdor mann* 'older man') Anglo-Saxon term for the noble governor of a shire; after the Norman Conquest the office was replaced with that of sheriff. From the 19th century aldermen were the senior members of the borough or county councils in England and Wales, elected by the other councillors, until the abolition of the office 1974; the title is still used in the City of London, and for members of a municipal corporation in certain towns in the USA.

Aldermaston village in Berkshire, England; site of an atomic and biological weapons research establishment, which employs some 7,000 people to work on the production of nuclear warheads. During 1958–63 the Campaign for Nuclear Disarmament (CND) made it the focus of an annual Easter protest march.

Aldiss Brian 1925– . English science-fiction writer, anthologist, and critic. His novels include *Non-Stop* 1958, *The Malacia Tapestry* 1976, and the 'Helliconia' trilogy. *Trillion Year Spree* 1986 is a history of science fiction.

Aldrin Edwin (Eugene 'Buzz') 1930– . US astronaut who landed on the Moon with Neil *Armstrong during the *Apollo 11* mission in July 1969, becoming the second person to set foot on the Moon.

aleatory music (Latin *alea* 'dice') method of composition (pioneered by John *Cage) dating from about 1945 in which the elements are assembled by chance by using, for example, dice or computer.

Alentejo region of E central Portugal divided into the districts of Alto Alentejo and Baixo Alentejo. The chief towns are Evora, Neja, and Portalegre.

Aleppo (Syrian *Halab*) ancient city in NW Syria; population (1981) 977,000. There has been a settlement on the site for at least 4,000 years.

Aletsch most extensive glacier in Europe, 23.6 km/14.7 mi long, beginning on the southern slopes of the Jungfrau in the Bernese Alps, Switzerland.

Aleut member of a people indigenous to the Aleutian Islands; a few thousand remain worldwide, most in the Aleutian Islands and mainland Alaska. They were exploited by Russian fur traders in the 18th and 19th centuries, and their forced evacuation 1942–45 earned the USA a United Nations reprimand 1959; compensation was paid 1990. From the 1980s concern for wildlife and diminishing demand for furs threatened their traditional livelihood of seal trapping.

Aleutian Islands volcanic island chain in the N Pacific, stretching 1,200 mi/1,900 km SW of Alaska, of which it forms part; population 6,000 Aleuts (most of whom belong to the Orthodox Church, plus a large US defence establishment). There are 14 large and more than 100 small islands running along the Aleutian Trench. The islands are mountainous, barren, and treeless; they are ice-free all year but are often foggy, with only about 25 days of sunshine recorded annually.

A level or *Advanced level* in the UK, examinations taken by some students in no more than four subjects at one time, usually at the age of 18 after two years' study. Two A-level passes are normally required for entry to a university degree course.

Alexander eight popes, including:

Alexander III (Orlando Barninelli) Pope 1159–81. His authority was opposed by Frederick I Barbarossa, but Alexander eventually compelled him to render homage 1178. He supported Henry II of England in his invasion of Ireland, but imposed penance on him after the murder of Thomas à *Becket.

Alexander VI (Rodrigo Borgia) 1431–1503. Pope 1492–1503. Of Spanish origin, he bribed his way to the papacy, where he furthered the advancement of his illegitimate children, who included Cesare and Lucrezia *Borgia. When *Savonarola preached against his corrupt practices Alexander had him executed.

Alexander three tsars of Russia:

Alexander I 1777–1825. Tsar from 1801. Defeated by Napoleon at Austerlitz 1805, he made peace at Tilsit 1807, but economic crisis led to a break with Napoleon's *continental system and the opening of Russian ports to British trade; this led to Napoleon's ill-fated invasion of Russia 1812. After the Congress of Vienna 1815, Alexander hoped through the Holy Alliance with Austria and Prussia to establish a new Christian order in Europe.

Alexander II 1818–1881. Tsar from 1855. He embarked on reforms of the army, the government, and education, and is remembered as 'the Liberator' for his emancipation of the serfs 1861, but he lacked the personnel to implement his reforms. However, the revolutionary element remained unsatisfied, and Alexander became increasingly autocratic and reactionary. He was assassinated by an anarchistic terrorist group, the *Nihilists.

Alexander III 1845–1894. Tsar from 1881, when he succeeded his father, Alexander II. He pursued a reactionary policy, promoting Russification and persecuting the Jews. He married Dagmar (1847–1928), daughter of Christian IX of Denmark and sister of Queen Alexandra of Britain, 1866.

Alexander three kings of Scotland:

Alexander I *c.* 1078–1124. King of Scotland from 1107, known as **the Fierce**. He ruled to the north of the rivers Forth and Clyde while his brother and successor David ruled to the south. He assisted Henry I of England in his campaign against Wales 1114, but defended the independence of the church in Scotland. Several monasteries, including the abbeys of Inchcolm and Scone, were established by him.

Alexander II 1198–1249. King of Scotland from 1214, when he succeeded his father William the Lion. Alexander supported the English barons in their struggle with King John after *Magna Carta.

Alexander III 1241–1285. King of Scotland from 1249, son of Alexander II. In 1263, by military defeat of Norwegian forces, he extended his authority over the Western Isles, which had been dependent on Norway. He strengthened the power of the central Scottish government.

Alexander Karageorgevich 1888–1934. Regent of Serbia 191–21 and king of Yugoslavia 1921–34, as dictator from 1929. Second son of *Peter I, king of Serbia, he was declared regent for his father 1912 and on his father's death became king of the state of South Slavs – Yugoslavia – that had come into being 1918.

Alexander Nevski, St 1220–1263. Russian military leader, son of the grand duke of Novgorod. In 1240 he defeated the Swedes on the banks of the Neva (hence Nevski), and 1242 defeated the Teutonic Knights on the frozen Lake Peipus.

alexanders strong-smelling tall herbaceous plant *Smyrnium olusatrum* of the carrot family Umbelliferae. It is found along hedgerows and on cliffs. Its yellow flowers appear in spring and early summer.

Alexander Severus AD 208–235. Roman emperor from 222, when he succeeded his cousin Heliogabalus. He was born in Palestine. His campaign against the Persians 232 achieved some success, but in 235, on his way to defend Gaul against German invaders, he was killed in a mutiny.

Alexander technique method of correcting established bad habits of posture, breathing, and muscular tension which Australian therapist F M Alexander maintained cause many ailments. Back troubles, migraine, asthma, hypertension, and some gastric and gynaecological disorders are among the conditions said to be alleviated by the technique, which is also effective in the prevention of disorders, particularly those of later life. The technique also acts as a general health promoter, promoting relaxation and enhancing vitality.

Alexander the Great 356–323 BC. King of Macedonia and conqueror of the large Persian empire. As commander of the vast Macedonian army he conquered Greece 336. He defeated the Persian king Darius in Asia Minor 333, then moved on to Egypt, where he founded Alexandria. He defeated the Persians again in Assyria 331, then advanced further east to reach the Indus. He conquered the Punjab before diminished troops forced his retreat.

Alexandra 1936– . Princess of the UK. Daughter of the Duke of Kent and Princess Marina, she married Angus Ogilvy (1928–), younger son of the earl of Airlie. They have two children, James (1964–) and Marina (1966–).

Alexandra 1872–1918. Last tsarina of Russia 1894–1917. She was the former Princess Alix of Hessen and granddaughter of Britain's Queen Victoria. She married *Nicholas II and, from 1907, fell under the spell of *Rasputin, a 'holy man' brought to the palace to try to cure her son of haemophilia. She was shot with the rest of her family by the Bolsheviks in the Russian Revolution.

Alexandria or *El Iskandariya* city, chief port, and second largest city of Egypt, situated between the Mediterranean and Lake Maryut; population (1986) 5,000,000. It is linked by canal with the Nile and is an industrial city (oil refining, gas processing, and cotton and grain trading). Founded 331 BC by Alexander the Great, Alexandria was the capital of Egypt for over 1,000 years.

Alexandria, Library of library in Alexandria, Egypt, founded 330 BC by *Ptolemy I Soter. It was the world's first state-funded scientific institution, and comprised a museum, teaching facilities, and a library that contained 700,000 scrolls, including much ancient Greek literature. It was used by *Euclid and *Eratosthenes, and after initial depradations was burned down AD 640 at the time of the Arab conquest.

Alexandria, school of group of writers and scholars of Alexandria who made the city the chief centre of culture in the Western world from about 331 BC to AD 642. They include the poets Callimachus, Apollonius Rhodius, and Theocritus; Euclid, pioneer of geometry; Eratosthenes, the geographer; Hipparchus, who developed a system of trigonometry; the astronomer Ptolemy, who gave his name to the Ptolemaic system of astronomy that endured for over 1,000 years; and the Jewish philosopher Philo. The Gnostics and Neo-Platonists also flourished in Alexandria.

Alexeev Vasiliy 1942– . Soviet weightlifter who broke 80 world records 1970–77, a record for any sport.

Alexius five emperors of Byzantium, including:

Alexius I (Comnenus) 1048–1118. Byzantine emperor 1081–1118. The Latin (W European) Crusaders helped him repel Norman and Turkish invasions, and he devoted great skill to buttressing the threatened empire. His daughter *Anna Comnena chronicled his reign.

Alexius III (Angelos) died *c.* 1210. Byzantine emperor 1195–1203. He gained power by deposing and blinding his brother Isaac II, but Isaac's Venetian allies enabled him and his son Alexius IV to regain power as coemperors.

Alexius IV (Angelos) 1182–1204. Byzantine emperor from 1203, when, with the aid of the army of the Fourth Crusade, he deposed his uncle Alexius III. He soon lost the support of the Crusaders (by that time occupying Constantinople), and was overthrown and murdered by another Alexius, Alexius Mourtzouphlus (son-in-law of Alexius III) 1204, an act which the Crusaders used as a pretext to sack the city the same year.

alfalfa or **lucerne** perennial tall herbaceous plant *Medicago sativa* of the pea family Leguminosae. It is native to Eurasia and bears spikes of small purple flowers in late summer. It is now a major fodder crop, generally processed into hay, meal, or silage. Alfalfa sprouts, the sprouted seeds, have become a popular salad ingredient.

Alfieri Vittorio, Count Alfieri 1749–1803. Italian dramatist. The best of his 28 plays, most of them tragedies, are *Saul* 1782 and *Mirra* 1786.

Alfonsín Foulkes Raúl Ricardo 1927– . Argentine politician, president 1983–89, leader of the moderate Radical Union Party (UCR). As president from the country's return to civilian government, he set up an investigation of the army's human-rights violations. Economic problems caused him to seek help from the International Monetary Fund and introduce austerity measures.

Alfonso kings of Portugal; see *Afonso.

Alfonso thirteen kings of León, Castile, and Spain, including:

Alfonso VII c. 1107–1157. King of León and Castile from 1126 who attempted to unite Spain. Although he protected the Moors, he was killed trying to check a Moorish rising.

Alfonso (X) el Sabio ('the Wise') 1221–1284. King of Castile from 1252. His reign was politically unsuccessful but he contributed to learning: he made Castilian the official language of the country and commissioned a history of Spain and an encyclopedia, as well as several translations from Arabic concerning, among other subjects, astronomy and games.

Alfonso (XI) the Avenger 1311–1350. King of Castile and León from 1312. He ruled cruelly, repressed a rebellion by his nobles, and defeated the last Moorish invasion 1340.

Alfonso XII 1857–1885. King of Spain from 1875, son of *Isabella II. He assumed the throne after a period of republican government following his mother's flight and effective abdication 1868. His rule was peaceful. He ended the civil war started by the Carlists and drafted a constitution, both 1876.

Alfonso XIII 1886–1941. King of Spain 1886–1931. He assumed power 1906 and married Princess Ena, granddaughter of Queen Victoria of the United Kingdom, in the same year. He abdicated 1931 soon after the fall of the Primo de Rivera dictatorship 1923–30 (which he supported), and Spain became a republic. His assassination was attempted several times.

Alfred the Great c. 848–c. 900. King of Wessex from 871. He defended England against Danish invasion, founded the first English navy, and put into operation a legal code. He encouraged the translation of works from Latin (some he translated himself), and promoted the development of the *Anglo-Saxon Chronicle.

algae (singular **alga**) diverse group of plants (including those commonly called seaweeds) that shows great variety of form, ranging from single-celled forms to multicellular seaweeds of considerable size and complexity. Marine algae help combat global warming by removing carbon dioxide from the atmosphere during photosynthesis.

Algarve ancient kingdom in S Portugal, the modern district of Faro, a popular holiday resort; population (1981) 323,500. Industries include agriculture, fishing, wine, mining, and tourism. The Algarve began to be wrested from the *Moors in the 12th century and was united with Portugal as a kingdom 1253.

algebra system of arithmetic applying to any set of non-numerical symbols (usually letters), and the axioms and rules by which they are combined or operated upon; sometimes known as **generalized arithmetic**.

Algeria Democratic and Popular Republic of (*al-Jumhuriya al-Jazairiya ad-Dimuqratiya ash-Shabiya*)

area 2,381,741 sq km/919,352 sq mi
capital Algiers (al-Jazair)
towns Constantine (Qacentina); ports are Oran (Ouahran), Annaba
physical coastal plains backed by mountains in N; Sahara desert in S
head of state Liamine Zeroual from 1994
head of government Mokdad Sifi from 1994
political system military rule
exports oil, natural gas, iron, wine, olive oil
currency dinar
population (1993) 26,600,000 (83% Arab, 17% Berber); growth rate 3.0% p.a.
languages Arabic (official); Berber, French
religion Sunni Muslim (state religion)
GNP $2,090 per head (1991)
chronology
1954 War for independence from France led by the FLN.
1962 Independence achieved from France. Republic declared. Ahmed Ben Bella elected prime minister.
1963 Ben Bella elected Algeria's first president.

1965 Ben Bella deposed by military, led by Colonel Houari Boumédienne.
1976 New constitution approved.
1978 Death of Boumédienne.
1979 Benjedid Chadli elected president. Ben Bella released from house arrest. FLN adopted new party structure.
1981 Algeria helped secure release of US prisoners in Iran.
1983 Chadli re-elected.
1988 Riots in protest at government policies; 170 killed. Reform programme introduced. Diplomatic relations with Egypt restored.
1989 Constitutional changes proposed, leading to limited political pluralism.
1990 Fundamentalist Islamic Salvation Front (FIS) won Algerian municipal and provincial elections.
1991 Dec: FIS won first round of multiparty elections.
1992 Jan: Chadli resigned; military took control of government; Mohamed Boudiaf became president; FIS leaders detained. Feb: State of emergency declared. March: FIS ordered to disband. June: Boudiaf assassinated; Ali Kafi chosen as new head of state.
1993 Worsening civil strife; assassinations of politicians and other public figures. Government human-rights abuses reported. Nov: killings of foreign workers began following expiry of FIS deadline for foreigners to leave the country.
1994 National conference of political parties boycotted by FLN and FIS. Military leader and former minister of defence, Gen Liamine Zeroual, replaced Kafi as president. Fundamentalists stepped up campaign of violence.

Algiers (Arabic *al-Jazair*; French *Alger*) capital of Algeria, situated on the narrow coastal plain between the Atlas Mountains and the Mediterranean; population (1984) 2,442,300.

Algiers, Battle of bitter conflict in Algiers 1954–62 between the Algerian nationalist population and the French colonial army and French settlers. The conflict ended with Algerian independence 1962.

alginate salt of alginic acid, $(C_6H_8O_6)_{dn}$, obtained from brown seaweeds and used in textiles, paper, food products, and pharmaceuticals.

ALGOL (acronym for *algorithmic language*) in computing, an early high-level programming language, developed in the 1950s and 1960s for scientific applications. A general-purpose language, ALGOL is best suited to mathematical work and has an algebraic style. Although no longer in common use, it has greatly influenced more recent languages, such as ADA and PASCAL.

Algol or *Beta Persei* *eclipsing binary, a pair of rotating stars in the constellation Perseus, one of which eclipses the other every 69 hours, causing its brightness to drop by two-thirds.

Algonquin member of the Algonquian-speaking hunting and fishing people formerly living around the Ottawa River in E Canada. Many now live on reservations in NE USA, E Ontario, and W Québec; others have chosen to live among the general populations of Canada and the USA.

algorithm procedure or series of steps that can be used to solve a problem. In computer science, it describes the logical sequence of operations to be performed by a program. A *flow chart is a visual representation of an algorithm.

Alhambra fortified palace in Granada, Spain, built by Moorish kings mainly between 1248 and 1354. It stands on a rocky hill and is the finest example of Moorish architecture.

Ali c. 598–660. 4th caliph of Islam. He was born in Mecca, the son of Abu Talib, uncle to the prophet Muhammad, who gave him his daughter Fatima in marriage. On Muhammad's death 632, Ali had a claim to succeed him, but this was not conceded until 656. After a stormy reign, he was assassinated. Around Ali's name the controversy has raged between the Sunni and the Shi'ites (see *Islam), the former denying his right to the caliphate and the latter supporting it.

Ali (Ali Pasha) 1741–1822. Turkish politician, known as *Arslan* ('the Lion'). An Albanian, he was appointed pasha (governor) of the Janina region 1788 (now Ioánnina, Greece). His court was visited by the British poet Byron. He was assassinated.

Ali Muhammad. Adopted name of Cassius Marcellus Clay, Jr, 1942– . US boxer. Olympic light-heavyweight champion 1960, he went on to become world professional heavyweight champion 1964, and was the only man to regain the title twice. He was known for his fast footwork and extrovert nature.

Alia Ramiz 1925– . Albanian communist politician, head of state 1982–92. He relaxed the isolationist policies of Enver Hoxha and introduced political and economic reforms, including free elections 1991, when he was elected executive president. In 1994 Alia was convicted of abuse of power while in office and sentenced to nine years' imprisonment.

alibi (Latin 'elsewhere') in law, a provable assertion that the accused was at some other place when a crime was committed.

alien in law, a person who is not a citizen of a particular nation.

alienation sense of isolation, powerlessness, and therefore frustration; a feeling of loss of control over one's life; a sense of estrangement from society or even from oneself. As a concept it was developed by the German philosophers Hegel and Marx; the latter used it as a description and criticism of the condition that developed among workers in capitalist society.

Aligarh city in Uttar Pradesh, north central India; population (1981) 320,000. Industries include agricultural manufacturing and processing, engineering, and textiles. The city is also named Koil; Aligarh is the name of a nearby fort.

alimentary canal in animals, the tube through which food passes; it extends from the mouth to the anus. It is a complex organ, adapted for *digestion. In human adults, it is about 9 m/30 ft long, consisting of the mouth cavity, pharynx, oesophagus, stomach, and the small and large intestines.

alimony in the USA, money allowance given by court order to a former spouse after separation or *divorce. The right has been extended to relationships outside marriage and is colloquially termed *palimony. Alimony is separate and distinct from court orders for child support.

Ali Pasha Mehmed Emin 1815–1871. Grand

vizier (chief minister) of the Ottoman empire 1855–56, 1858–59, 1861, and 1867–71, noted for his attempts to westernize the Ottoman Empire.

aliphatic compound any organic chemical compound in which the carbon atoms are joined in straight chains, as in hexane (C_6H_{14}), or in branched chains, as in 2-methylpentane ($CH_3CH(CH_3)CH_2CH_2CH_3$).

alkali (Arabic *al-qualty* 'ashes') in chemistry, a compound classed as a *base that is soluble in water. Alkalis neutralize acids and are soapy to the touch. The hydroxides of metals are alkalis; those of sodium (sodium hydroxide, NaOH) and of potassium (potassium hydroxide, KOH) being chemically powerful; both were derived from the ashes of plants.

alkali metal any of a group of six metallic elements with similar chemical bonding properties: lithium, sodium, potassium, rubidium, caesium, and francium. They form a linked group in the *periodic table of the elements. They are univalent (have a valency of one) and of very low density (lithium, sodium, and potassium float on water); in general they are reactive, soft, low-melting-point metals.

alkaline-earth metal any of a group of six metallic elements with similar bonding properties: beryllium, magnesium, calcium, strontium, barium, and radium. They form a linked group in the *periodic table of the elements. They are strongly basic, bivalent (have a valency of two), and occur in nature only in compounds.

alkaloid any of a number of physiologically active and frequently poisonous substances contained in some plants. They are usually organic bases and contain nitrogen. They form salts with acids and, when soluble, give alkaline solutions.

alkane member of a group of *hydrocarbons having the general formula C_nH_{2n+2}, commonly known as *paraffins*. Lighter alkanes, such as methane, ethane, propane, and butane, are colourless gases; heavier ones are liquids or solids. In nature they are found in natural gas and petroleum. As alkanes contain only single *covalent bonds, they are said to be saturated.

alkene member of the group of *hydrocarbons having the general formula C_nH_{2n}, formerly known as *olefins*. Lighter alkenes, such as ethene and propene, are gases, obtained from the *cracking of oil fractions. Alkenes are unsaturated compounds, characterized by one or more double bonds between adjacent carbon atoms. They react by addition, and many useful compounds, such as poly(ethene) and bromoethane, are made from them.

alkyne member of the group of *hydrocarbons with the general formula C_nH_{2n-2}, formerly known as the *acetylenes*. They are unsaturated compounds, characterized by one or more triple bonds between adjacent carbon atoms. Lighter alkynes, such as ethyne, are gases; heavier ones are liquids or solids.

Allah (Arabic *al-Ilah* 'the God') Islamic name for God.

Allahabad ('city of god') historic city in Uttar Pradesh state, NE India, 580 km/360 mi SE of Delhi, on the Yamuna River where it meets the Ganges and the mythical Seraswati River; population (1981) 642,000. A Hindu religious festival is held here every 12 years with the participants washing away sin and sickness by bathing in the rivers.

allegory in literature, the description or illustration of one thing in terms of another; a work of poetry or prose in the form of an extended metaphor or parable that makes use of symbolic fictional characters.

allegro (Italian 'merry, lively') in music, a lively or quick passage, movement, or composition.

allele one of two or more alternative forms of a *gene at a given position (locus) on a chromosome, caused by a difference in the *DNA. Blue and brown eyes in humans are determined by different alleles of the gene for eye colour.

Allen Woody. Adopted name of Allen Stewart Konigsberg 1935– . US film writer, director, and actor, known for his cynical, witty, often self-deprecating parody and offbeat humour. His film *Annie Hall* 1975 won him three Academy Awards.

Allende (Gossens) Salvador 1908–1973. Chilean left-wing politician. Elected president 1970 as the candidate of the Popular Front alliance, Allende never succeeded in keeping the electoral alliance together in government. His failure to solve the country's economic problems or to deal with political subversion allowed the army, backed by the CIA, to stage the 1973 coup which brought about the death of Allende and many of his supporters.

allergy special sensitivity of the body that makes it react, with an exaggerated response of the natural immune defence mechanism, especially with *histamines, to the introduction of an otherwise harmless foreign substance (*allergen*).

alliance agreement between two or more states to come to each other's assistance in the event of war. Alliances were criticized after World War I as having contributed to the outbreak of war but NATO has been a major part of the post-1945 structure of international relations (as was the Warsaw Pact until its dissolution 1991).

Alliance, the in UK politics, a loose union 1981–87 formed by the *Liberal Party and *Social Democratic Party (SDP) for electoral purposes.

Allied Coordination Committee or *Operation Stay Behind* or *Gladio* secret right-wing paramilitary network in W Europe set up in the 1950s to arm guerrillas chosen from the civilian population in the event of Soviet invasion or communist takeover. Initiated and partly funded by the CIA, it is linked to NATO. Its past or present existence was officially acknowledged 1990 by Belgium, France, (West) Germany, Greece, Italy, the Netherlands, Norway, and Portugal; in the UK the matter is covered by the Official Secrets Act. In 1990 those governments that confirmed their countries' participation said that the branches had been or would be closed down; the European Parliament set up a commission of inquiry.

Allied Mobile Force (AMF) permanent multinational military force established 1960 to move immediately to any NATO country under threat of attack. Its headquarters are in Heidelberg, Germany.

Allies, the in World War I, the 23 countries allied against the Central Powers (Germany, Austria–Hungary, Turkey, and Bulgaria), including France, Italy, Russia, the UK, Australia and other Commonwealth nations, and, in the latter part of the war, the USA; and in World War II, the 49 countries allied against the *Axis powers (Germany, Italy, and Japan), including France, the UK, Australia and other Commonwealth nations, the USA, and the USSR.

alligator reptile of the genus *Alligator*, related to the crocodile. There are two species: *A. mississipiensis*, the Mississippi alligator of the southern states of the USA, and *A. sinensis* from the swamps of the lower Chang Jiang River in China. The former grows to about 4 m/12 ft, but the latter only to 1.5 m/5 ft. Alligators lay their eggs in sand; they swim well with lashing movements of the tail; they feed on fish and mammals but seldom attack people.

alliteration in poetry and prose, the use, within a line or phrase, of words beginning with the same sound, as in 'Two tired toads trotting to Tewkesbury'. It was a common device in Old English poetry, and its use survives in many traditional English phrases, such as *kith and kin*, *hearth and home*.

Allium genus of plants belonging to the lily family Liliaceae. Members of the genus are usually strong-smelling with a sharp taste, but form bulbs in which sugar is stored. Cultivated species include onion, garlic, chive, and leek.

allometry in biology, a regular relationship between a given feature (for example, the size of an organ) and the size of the body as a whole, when this relationship is not a simple proportion of body size. Thus, an organ may increase in size proportionately faster, or slower, than body size does. For example, a human baby's head is much larger in relation to its body than is an adult's.

allopathy the usual contemporary method of treating disease, using therapies designed to counteract the manifestations of the disease. In strict usage, allopathy is the opposite of *homeopathy.

allotment small plot of rented land used for growing vegetables and flowers. Allotments originated in the UK during the 18th and 19th centuries, when much of the common land was enclosed (see *enclosure) and efforts were made to provide plots for poor people to cultivate.

allotropy property whereby an element can exist in two or more forms (allotropes), each possessing different physical properties but the same state of matter (gas, liquid, or solid). The allotropes of carbon are diamond and graphite. Sulphur has several different forms (flowers of sulphur, plastic, rhombic, and monoclinic). These solids have different crystal structures, as do the the white and grey forms of tin and the black, red, and white forms of phosphorus.

alloy metal blended with some other metallic or nonmetallic substance to give it special qualities, such as resistance to corrosion, greater hardness, or tensile strength. Useful alloys include bronze, brass, cupronickel, duralumin, German silver, gunmetal, pewter, solder, steel, and stainless steel.

All Saints' Day or *All-Hallows* or *Hallowmas* festival on 1 Nov for all Christian saints and martyrs who have no special day of their own.

All Souls' Day festival in the Roman Catholic church, held on 2 Nov (following All Saints' Day) in the conviction that through prayer and self-denial the faithful can hasten the deliverance of souls expiating their sins in purgatory.

allspice spice prepared from the dried berries of the evergreen pimento tree or West Indian pepper tree *Pimenta dioica* of the myrtle family, cultivated chiefly in Jamaica. It has an aroma similar to that of a mixture of cinnamon, cloves, and nutmeg.

alluvial deposit layer of broken rocky matter, or sediment, formed from material that has been carried in suspension by a river or stream and dropped as the velocity of the current changes. River plains and deltas are made entirely of alluvial deposits, but smaller pockets can be found in the beds of upland torrents.

alluvial fan a roughly triangular sedimentary formation found at the base of slopes. An alluvial fan results when a sediment-laden stream or river rapidly deposits its load of gravel and silt as its speed is reduced on entering a plain.

Alma-Ata formerly (to 1921) *Vernyi* capital of *Kazakhstan; population (1991) 1,151,300. Industries include engineering, printing, tobacco processing, textile manufacturing, and leather products.

Almagest (Arabic *al* 'the' and Greek *majisti* 'greatest') book compiled by the Greek astronomer *Ptolemy during the 2nd century AD, which included the idea of an Earth-centred universe. It survived in an Arabic translation. Some medieval books on astronomy, astrology, and alchemy were given the same title.

alma mater (Latin 'bounteous mother') term applied to universities and schools, as though they are the foster mothers of their students. Also, the official school song. It was the title given by the Romans to Ceres, the goddess of agriculture.

Almansa, Battle of in the War of the Spanish Succession, battle 25 April 1707 in which British, Portuguese and Spanish forces were defeated by the French under the Duke of Berwick at a Spanish town in Albacete, about 80 km/50 mi NW of Alicante.

Alma-Tadema Laurence 1836–1912. Dutch painter who settled in the UK 1870. He painted romantic, idealized scenes from Greek, Roman, and Egyptian life in a distinctive, detailed style.

Almohad Berber dynasty 1130–1269 founded by the Berber prophet Muhammad ibn Tumart (*c.* 1080–1130). The Almohads ruled much of Morocco and Spain, which they took by defeating the *Almoravids; they later took the area that today forms Algeria and Tunis. Their policy of religious 'purity' involved the forced conversion and massacre of the Jewish population of Spain. The Almohads were themselves defeated by the Christian kings of Spain 1212, and in Morocco 1269.

almond tree *Prunus amygdalus*, family Rosaceae, related to the peach and apricot. Dessert almonds are the kernels of the fruit of the sweet variety *P. amygdalus dulcis*, which is also the source of a low-cholesterol culinary oil. Oil of bitter almonds, from the variety *P. amygdalus amara*, is used in flavouring. Almond oil is also used for cosmetics, perfumes, and fine lubricants.

Almoravid Berber dynasty 1056–1147 founded by the prophet Abdullah ibn Tashfin, ruling much of Morocco and Spain in the 11th-12th centuries. The Almoravids came from the Sahara and in the 11th century began laying the foundations of an empire covering the whole of Morocco and parts of Algeria; their capital was the newly founded Marrakesh. In 1086 they defeated Alfonso VI of Castile to gain much of Spain. They were later overthrown by the *Almohads.

aloe plant of the genus *Aloe* of African plants, family Liliaceae, distinguished by their long, fleshy, spiny-edged leaves. The drug usually referred to as 'bitter aloes' is a powerful cathartic prepared from the juice of the leaves of several of the species.

alpaca *The alpaca is related to the llama, and has been known since 200 BC.*

alpaca domesticated South American hoofed mammal *Lama pacos* of the camel family, found in Chile, Peru, and Bolivia, and herded at high elevations in the Andes. It is bred mainly for its long, fine, silky wool, and stands about 1 m/3 ft tall at the shoulder with neck and head another 60 cm/2 ft.

alpha and omega first (α) and last (ω) letters of the Greek alphabet, a phrase hence meaning the beginning and end, or sum total, of anything.

alphabet set of conventional symbols used for writing, based on a correlation between individual symbols and spoken sounds, so called from *alpha* (α) and *beta* (β), the names of the first two letters of the classical Greek alphabet. The earliest known alphabet is from Palestine, about 1700 BC. Alphabetic writing now takes many forms, for example the Hebrew *aleph-beth* and the Arabic script, both written from right to left; the Devanagari script of the Hindus, in which the symbols 'hang' from a line common to all the symbols; and the Greek alphabet, with the first clearly delineated vowel symbols.

Alpha Centauri or *Rigil Kent* brightest star in the constellation Centaurus and the third brightest star in the sky. It is actually a triple star (see *binary star); the two brighter stars orbit each other every 80 years, and the third, Proxima Centauri, is the closest star to the Sun, 4.2 light years away, 0.1 light years closer than the other two.

alpha decay disintegration of the nucleus of an atom to produce an *alpha particle. See also *radioactivity.

alphanumeric data data made up of any of the letters of the alphabet and any digit from 0 to 9. The classification of data according to the type or types of character contained enables computer *validation systems to check the accuracy of data: a computer can be programmed to reject entries that contain the wrong type of character. For example, a person's name would be rejected if it contained any numeric data, and a bank-account number would be rejected if it contained any alphabetic data. A car's registration number, by comparison, would be expected to contain alphanumeric data but no punctuation marks.

alpha particle positively charged, high-energy particle emitted from the nucleus of a radioactive *atom. It is one of the products of the spontaneous disintegration of radioactive elements (see *radioactivity) such as radium and thorium, and is identical with the nucleus of a helium atom – that is, it consists of two protons and two neutrons. The process of emission, *alpha decay*, transforms one element into another, decreasing the atomic (or proton) number by two and the atomic mass (or nucleon number) by four.

Alps mountain chain, the barrier between N Italy and France, Germany and Austria.

Famous peaks include *Mont Blanc*, the highest at 4,809 m/15,777 ft, first climbed by Jacques Balmat and Michel Paccard 1786; *Matterhorn* in the Pennine Alps, 4,479 m/14,694 ft, first climbed by Edward Whymper 1865 (four of the party of seven were killed when a rope broke during their descent); *Eiger* in the Bernese Alps/Oberland, 3,970 m/13,030 ft, with a near-vertical rock wall on the N face, first climbed 1858; *Jungfrau*, 4,166 m/13,673 ft; and *Finsteraarhorn* 4,275 m/14,027 ft.

Famous passes include *Brenner*, the lowest, Austria/Italy; *Great St Bernard*, one of the highest, 2,472 m/8,113 ft, Italy/Switzerland (by which Napoleon marched into Italy 1800); *Little St Bernard*, Italy/France (which Hannibal is thought to have used); and *St Gotthard*, S Switzerland, which Suvorov used when ordered by the tsar to withdraw his troops from Italy. All have been superseded by all-weather road/rail tunnels. The Alps extend into Yugoslavia and N Albania with the Julian and Dinaric Alps.

Alps, Lunar mountain range on the Moon, NE of the Sea of Showers, cut by a valley 150 km/93 mi long.

Alsace region of France; area 8,300 sq km/3,204 sq mi; population (1986) 1,600,000. It consists of the *départements* of Bas-Rhin and Haut-Rhin, and its capital is Strasbourg.

Alsace-Lorraine area of NE France, lying west of the river Rhine. It forms the French regions of *Alsace and *Lorraine. The former iron and steel industries are being replaced by electronics, chemicals, and precision engineering. The German dialect spoken does not have equal rights with French, and there is autonomist sentiment.

Alsatia old name for *Alsace, formerly part of Germany.

Alsatian breed of dog known officially from 1977 as the **German shepherd**. It is about 63 cm/26 in tall and has a wolflike appearance, a thick coat with many varieties of colouring, and a distinctive gait. Alsatians are used as police dogs because of their high intelligence.

Altai territory of the Russian Federation, in SW Siberia; area 261,700 sq km/101,043 sq mi; capital Barnaul; population (1985) 2,744,000. Industries include mining, light engineering, chemicals, and timber. Altai was colonized by the Russians from the 18th century.

Altair or **Alpha Aquilae** brightest star in the constellation Aquila and the 12th brightest star in the sky. It is a white star 16 light years away and forms the so-called Summer Triangle with the stars Deneb (in the constellation Cygnus) and Vega (in Lyra).

Altamira caves decorated with Palaeolithic wall paintings, the first such to be discovered, 1879. The paintings are realistic depictions of bison, deer, and horses in polychrome (several colours). The caves are near the village of Santillana del Mar in Santander province, N Spain; other well-known Palaeolithic cave paintings are in *Lascaux, SW France.

Altdorfer Albrecht c. 1480–1538. German painter and printmaker, active in Regensburg, Bavaria. Altdorfer's work, inspired by the linear, Classical style of the Italian Renaissance, often depicts dramatic landscapes that are out of scale with the figures in the paintings. His use of light creates tension and effects of movement. Many of his works are of religious subjects.

alternate angles a pair of angles that lie on opposite sides and at opposite ends of a transversal (a line that cuts two or more lines in the same plane). The alternate angles formed by a transversal of two parallel lines are equal.

alternating current (AC) electric current that flows for an interval of time in one direction and then in the opposite direction, that is, a current that flows in alternately reversed directions through or around a circuit. Electric energy is usually generated as alternating current in a power station, and alternating currents may be used for both power and lighting.

alternation of generations typical life cycle of terrestrial plants and some seaweeds, in which there are two distinct forms occurring alternately: **diploid** (having two sets of chromosomes) and **haploid** (one set of chromosomes). The diploid generation produces haploid spores by *meiosis, and is called the sporophyte, while the haploid generation produces gametes (sex cells), and is called the gametophyte. The gametes fuse to form a diploid *zygote which develops into a new sporophyte; thus the sporophyte and gametophyte alternate.

alternative energy see *energy, alternative

alternative medicine see *medicine, alternative.

alternator electricity *generator that produces an alternating current.

Althing parliament of Iceland, established about 930, the oldest in the world. It was dissolved 1800, revived 1843 as an advisory body,

and became a legislative body again 1874. It has an upper and a lower house comprising one-third and two-thirds of its members respectively.

altimeter instrument used in aircraft that measures altitude, or height above sea level. The common type is a form of aneroid *barometer, which works by sensing the differences in air pressure at different altitudes. This must continually be recalibrated because of the change in air pressure with changing weather conditions. The *radar altimeter measures the height of the aircraft above the ground, measuring the time it takes for radio pulses emitted by the aircraft to be reflected. Radar altimeters are essential features of automatic and blind-landing systems.

Altiplano densely populated upland plateau of the Andes of South America, stretching from S Peru to NW Argentina. The height of the Altiplano is 3,000–4,000 m/10,000–13,000 ft.

altitude in geometry, the perpendicular distance from a *vertex (corner) of a figure, such as a triangle, to the base (the side opposite the vertex).

altitude measurement of height, usually given in metres above sea level.

Altman Robert 1925– . US maverick film director. His antiwar comedy *M.A.S.H.* 1970 was a critical and commercial success; subsequent films include *McCabe and Mrs Miller* 1971, *The Long Goodbye* 1973, *Nashville* 1975, *Popeye* 1980, and *The Player* 1992.

alto (Italian 'high') voice or instrument between *tenor and *soprano. The sound of the traditional high male alto voice (also known as counter tenor) is trumpetlike and penetrating; the low-register female contralto is rich and mellow in tone. The alto range is centred on the octave above middle C on the piano. Alto is also another name for the French viola.

altruism in biology, helping another individual of the same species to reproduce more effectively, as a direct result of which the altruist may leave fewer offspring itself. Female honey bees (workers) behave altruistically by rearing sisters in order to help their mother, the queen bee, reproduce, and forego any possibility of reproducing themselves.

alum any double sulphate of a monovalent metal or radical (such as sodium, potassium, or ammonium) and a trivalent metal (such as aluminium or iron). The commonest alum is the double sulphate of potassium and aluminium, $K_2Al_2(SO_4)_4.24H_2O$, a white crystalline powder that is readily soluble in water. It is used in curing animal skins. Other alums are used in papermaking and to fix dye in the textile industry.

alumina or **corundum** Al_2O_3 oxide of aluminium, widely distributed in clays, slates, and shales. It is formed by the decomposition of the feldspars in granite and used as an abrasive. Typically it is a white powder, soluble in most strong acids or caustic alkalis but not in water. Impure alumina is called 'emery'. Rubies and sapphires are corundum gemstones.

aluminium lightweight, silver-white, ductile and malleable, metallic element, symbol Al, atomic number 13, relative atomic mass 26.9815. It is the third most abundant element (and the most abundant metal) in the Earth's crust, of which it makes up about 8.1% by mass. It is an excellent conductor of electricity and oxidizes easily, the layer of oxide on its surface making it highly resistant to tarnish.

aluminium ore raw material from which aluminium is extracted. The main ore is bauxite, a mixture of minerals, found in economic quantities in Australia, Guinea, West Indies, and several other countries.

Alva or **Alba** Ferdinand Alvarez de Toledo, duke of 1508–1582. Spanish politician and general. He successfully commanded the Spanish armies of the Holy Roman emperor Charles V and his son Philip II of Spain. In 1567 he was appointed governor of the Netherlands, where he set up a reign of terror to suppress Protestantism and the revolt of the Netherlands. In 1573 he was recalled at his own request. He later led a successful expedition against Portugal 1580–81.

alveolus (plural *alveoli*) one of the many thousands of tiny air sacs in the *lungs in which exchange of oxygen and carbon dioxide takes place between air and the bloodstream.

Alzheimer's disease common manifestation of *dementia, thought to afflict one in 20 people over 65. Attacking the brain's 'grey matter', it is a disease of mental processes rather than physical function, characterized by memory loss and progressive intellectual impairment.

AM abbreviation for *amplitude modulation*.

a.m. or **A.M.** abbreviation for *ante meridiem* (Latin 'before noon').

Amal radical Lebanese *Shi'ite military force, established by Musa Sadr in the 1970s; its headquarters are in Borj al-Barajneh. The movement split into extremist and moderate groups 1982, but both sides agreed on the aim of increasing Shi'ite political representation in Lebanon.

Amalekite in the Old Testament, a member of an ancient Semitic people of SW Palestine and the Sinai peninsula. According to Exodus 17 they harried the rear of the Israelites after their crossing of the Red Sea, were defeated by Saul and David, and were destroyed in the reign of Hezekiah.

amalgam any alloy of mercury with other metals. Most metals will form amalgams, except iron and platinum. Amalgam is used in dentistry for filling teeth, and usually contains copper, silver, and zinc as the main alloying ingredients. This amalgam is pliable when first mixed and then sets hard, but the mercury leaches out and may cause a type of heavy-metal poisoning.

Amanita genus of fungi (see *fungus), distinguished by a ring, or *volva*, round the stem, warty patches on the cap, and the clear white colour of the gills. Many of the species are brightly coloured and highly poisonous.

Amarna tablets collection of Egyptian clay tablets with cuneiform inscriptions, found in the ruins of the ancient city of *Akhetaton on the east bank of the Nile. The majority of the tablets, which comprise royal archives and letters of 1411–1375 BC, are in the British Museum.

Amaterasu in Japanese mythology, the sun-goddess, grandmother of Jimmu Tenno, first ruler of Japan, from whom the emperors claimed to be descended.

Amati Italian family of violin-makers, who worked in Cremona, about 1550–1700. *Nicolo*

Amati (1596–1684) taught Andrea *Guarneri and Antonio *Stradivari.

Amazon (Indian *Amossona* 'destroyer of boats') South American river, the world's second longest, 6,570 km/4,080 mi, and the largest in volume of water. Its main headstreams, the Marañón and the Ucayali, rise in central Peru and unite to flow E across Brazil for about 4,000 km/2,500 mi. It has 48,280 km/30,000 mi of navigable waterways, draining 7,000,000 sq km/2,750,000 sq mi, nearly half the South American land mass. It reaches the Atlantic on the equator, its estuary 80 km/50 mi wide, discharging a volume of water so immense that 64 km/40 mi out to sea, fresh water remains at the surface. The Amazon basin covers 7.5 million sq km/3 million sq mi, of which 5 million sq km/2 million sq mi is tropical forest containing 30% of all known plant and animal species (80,000 known species of trees, 3,000 known species of land vertebrates, 2,000 freshwater fish). It is the wettest region on Earth; average rainfall 2.54 m/8.3 ft a year. Independent estimates and Landsat surveys indicated a deforestation of 12% by 1985 (up from 0.6% in 1975).

Amazon in Greek mythology, a member of a group of legendary female warriors living near the Black Sea, who cut off their right breasts to use the bow more easily. Their queen, Penthesilea, was killed by Achilles at the siege of Troy. The term Amazon has come to mean a large, strong woman.

Amazonia those regions of Brazil, Colombia, Ecuador, Peru, and Bolivia lying within the basin of the Amazon River.

Amazonian Indian indigenous inhabitant of the Amazon River Basin in South America. The majority of the societies are kin-based; traditional livelihood includes hunting and gathering, fishing, and shifting cultivation. A wide range of indigenous languages are spoken. Numbering perhaps 2.5 million in the 16th century, they had been reduced to perhaps one-tenth of that number by the 1820s. Their rainforests are being destroyed for mining and ranching, and Indians are being killed, transported, or assimilated.

Amazon Pact treaty signed 1978 by Bolivia, Brazil, Colombia, Ecuador, Guyana, Peru, Surinam, and Venezuela to protect and control the industrial or commercial development of the Amazon River.

ambassador officer of the highest rank in the diplomatic service, who represents the head of one sovereign state at the court or capital of another.

amber fossilized resin from coniferous trees of the Middle Tertiary period. It is often washed ashore on the Baltic coast with plant and animal specimens preserved in it; many extinct species have been found preserved in this way. It ranges in colour from red to yellow, and is used to make jewellery.

ambergris fatty substance, resembling wax, found in the stomach and intestines of the sperm *whale. It is found floating in warm seas, and is used in perfumery as a fixative.

amblyopia reduced vision without apparent eye disorder.

Ambrose, St *c.* 340–397. One of the early Christian leaders and theologians known as the Fathers of the Church. Feast day 7 Dec.

ambrosia (Greek 'immortal') food of the gods, which was supposed to confer eternal life upon all who ate it.

amen Hebrew word signifying affirmation ('so be it'), commonly used at the close of a Jewish or Christian prayer or hymn. As used by Jesus in the New Testament it was traditionally translated 'verily'.

Amenhotep four Egyptian pharaohs, including:

Amenhotep III King of Egypt (c. 1400 BC) who built great monuments at Thebes, including the temples at Luxor. Two portrait statues at his tomb were known to the Greeks as the colossi of Memnon; one was cracked, and when the temperature changed at dawn it gave out an eerie sound, then thought supernatural. His son **Amenhotep IV** changed his name to *Ikhnaton.

America western hemisphere of the Earth, containing the continents of *North America and *South America, with *Central America in between. This great land mass extends from the Arctic to the Antarctic, from beyond 75° N to past 55° S. The area is about 42,000,000 sq km/16,000,000 sq mi, and the estimated population is over 500 million.

American Civil War 1861–65; see *Civil War, American.

American Federation of Labor and Congress of Industrial Organizations (AFL–CIO) federation of North American trade unions, currently representing about 20% of the workforce in North America.

American football see *football, American

American Independence, War of alternative name of the *American Revolution, the revolt 1775–83 of the British North American colonies that resulted in the establishment of the United States of America.

American Indian one of the aboriginal peoples of the Americas. Columbus named them Indians 1492 because he believed he had found not the New World, but a new route to India. The Asian ancestors of the Indians are thought to have entered North America on the land bridge, Beringia, exposed by the lowered sea level between Siberia and Alaska during the last ice age, 60,000–35,000 BC.

AMERICAN INDIANS: MAJOR CULTURAL GROUPS

area	people
North America	
Arctic	Inuit, Aleut
subarctic	Algonquin, Cree, Ottawa
NE woodlands	Huron, Iroquois, Mohican, Shawnee (Tecumseh)
SE woodlands	Cherokee, Choctaw, Creek, Hopewell, Natchez, Seminole
Great Plains	Blackfoot, Cheyenne, Comanche, Pawnee, Sioux
NW coast	Chinook, Tlingit, Tsimshian
desert west	Apache, Navajo, Pueblo, Hopi, Mojave, Shoshone
Central America	Maya, Toltec, Aztec, Mexican
South America	
eastern	Carib, Xingu
central	Guaraní, Miskito
western	Araucanian, Aymara, Chimú, Inca, Jivaro, Quechua

American Revolution revolt 1775–83 of the British North American colonies that resulted in the establishment of the United States of America. It was caused by colonial resentment at the contemporary attitude that commercial or industrial interests of any colony should be subordinate to those of the mother country; and by the unwillingness of the colonists to pay for a standing army. It was also fuelled by the colonists' antimonarchist sentiment and a desire to participate in the policies affecting them.

American Samoa see *Samoa, American.

America's Cup international yacht-racing trophy named after the US schooner *America*, owned by J L Stevens, who won a race around the Isle of Wight 1851.

americium radioactive metallic element of the *actinide series, symbol Am, atomic number 95, relative atomic mass 243.13; it was first synthesized 1944. It occurs in nature in minute quantities in *pitchblende and other uranium ores, where it is produced from the decay of neutron-bombarded plutonium, and is the element with the highest atomic number that occurs in nature. It is synthesized in quantity only in nuclear reactors by the bombardment of plutonium with neutrons. Its longest-lived isotope is Am-243, with a half-life of 7,650 years.

amethyst variety of *quartz, SiO_2, coloured violet by the presence of small quantities of manganese; used as a semiprecious stone. Amethysts are found chiefly in the Ural Mountains, India, the USA, Uruguay, and Brazil.

Amhara member of an ethnic group comprising approximately 25% of the population of Ethiopia; 13 million (1987). The Amhara are traditionally farmers. They speak Amharic, a language of the Semitic branch of the Afro-Asiatic family. Most are members of the Ethiopian Christian Church.

Amida Buddha the 'Buddha of immeasurable light'. Japanese name for *Amitābha*, the Buddha venerated in Pure Land Buddhism. He presides over the Western Paradise (the Buddha-land of his own creation), and through his unlimited compassion and power to save, true believers can achieve enlightenment and be reborn.

amide any organic chemical derived from a fatty acid by the replacement of the hydroxyl group (–OH) by an amino group (–NH_2). One of the simplest amides is acetamide (CH_3CONH_2), which has a strong mousy odour.

Amies (Edwin) Hardy 1909– . English couturier, one of Queen Elizabeth II's dressmakers. Noted from 1934 for his tailored clothes for women, he also designed for men from 1959.

Amin (Dada) Idi 1926– . Ugandan politician, president 1971–79. He led the coup that deposed Milton Obote 1971, expelled the Asian community 1972, and exercised a reign of terror over his people. He fled to Libya when insurgent Ugandan and Tanzanian troops invaded the country 1979.

amine any of a class of organic chemical compounds in which one or more of the hydrogen atoms of ammonia (NH_3) have been replaced by other groups of atoms.

amino acid water-soluble organic *molecule,

mainly composed of carbon, oxygen, hydrogen, and nitrogen, containing both a basic amine group (NH_2) and an acidic carboxyl (COOH) group. When two or more amino acids are joined together, they are known as *peptides; *proteins are made up of interacting polypeptides (peptide chains consisting of more than three amino acids) and are folded or twisted in characteristic shapes.

Amis Kingsley 1922– . English novelist and poet. His works include *Lucky Jim* 1954, a comic portrayal of life in a provincial university, and *Take a Girl Like You* 1960. He won the UK's Booker Prize 1986 for *The Old Devils*. He is the father of Martin Amis.

Amis Martin 1949– . English novelist. His works are characterized by their savage wit and include *The Rachel Papers* 1974, *Money* 1984, *London Fields* 1989, and *Time's Arrow* 1991.

Amman capital and chief industrial centre of Jordan; population (1986) 1,160,000. It is a major communications centre, linking historic trade routes across the Middle East.

ammeter instrument that measures electric current, usually in *amperes.

Ammon in Egyptian mythology, the king of the gods, the equivalent of *Zeus or *Jupiter. The name is also spelled Amen/Amun, as in the name of the pharaoh Tutankh*amen*. In art, he is represented as a ram, as a man with a ram's head, or as a man crowned with feathers. He had temples at Siwa oasis, Libya, and Thebes, Egypt.

ammonia NH_3 colourless pungent-smelling gas, lighter than air and very soluble in water. It is made on an industrial scale by the *Haber process, and used mainly to produce nitrogenous fertilizers, some explosives, and nitric acid.

ammonite extinct marine *cephalopod mollusc of the order Ammonoidea, related to the modern nautilus. The shell was curled in a plane spiral and made up of numerous gas-filled chambers, the outermost containing the body of the animal. Many species flourished between 200 million and 65 million years ago, ranging in size from that of a small coin to 2 m/6 ft across.

ammonium chloride or *sal ammoniac* NH_4Cl a volatile salt that forms white crystals around volcanic craters. It is prepared synthetically for use in 'dry-cell' batteries, fertilizers, and dyes.

amnesia loss or impairment of memory. As a clinical condition it may be caused by disease or injury to the brain, or by shock; in some cases it may be a symptom of an emotional disorder.

amnesty release of political prisoners under a general pardon, or a person or group of people from criminal liability for a particular action; for example, the occasional amnesties in the UK for those who surrender firearms that they hold illegally.

Amnesty International human-rights organization established in the UK 1961 to campaign for the release of political prisoners worldwide; it is politically unaligned. Amnesty International has 700,000 members, and section offices in 43 countries. The organization was awarded the Nobel Peace Prize 1977.

amniocentesis sampling the amniotic fluid surrounding a fetus in the womb for diagnostic purposes. It is used to detect Down's syndrome and other genetic abnormalities.

amnion innermost of three membranes that enclose the embryo within the egg (reptiles and birds) or within the uterus (mammals). It contains the amniotic fluid that helps to cushion the embryo.

amoeba (plural *amoebae*) one of the simplest living animals, consisting of a single cell and belonging to the *protozoa group. The body consists of colourless protoplasm. Its activities are controlled by the nucleus, and it feeds by flowing round and engulfing organic debris. It reproduces by *binary fission. Some species of amoeba are harmful parasites.

Amos book of the Old Testament written c. 750 BC. One of the *prophets, Amos was a shepherd who foretold the destruction of Israel because of the people's abandonment of their faith.

amp in physics, abbreviation for ampere, a unit of electrical current.

ampere SI unit (abbreviation amp, symbol A) of electrical current. Electrical current is measured in a similar way to water current, in terms of an amount per unit time; one ampere represents a flow of about 6.28×10^{18} *electrons per second, or a rate of flow of charge of one coulomb per second.

Ampère's rule rule developed by André Ampère connecting the direction of an electric current and its associated magnetic currents. It states that if a person were travelling along a current-carrying wire in the direction of conventional current flow (from the positive to the negative terminal), and carrying a magnetic compass, then the north pole of the compass needle would be deflected to the left-hand side.

amphetamine or *speed* powerful synthetic *stimulant. Benzedrine was the earliest amphetamine marketed, used as a pep pill in World War II to help soldiers overcome fatigue, and until the 1970s amphetamines were prescribed by doctors as an appetite suppressant for weight loss; as an antidepressant, to induce euphoria; and as a stimulant, to increase alertness. Indications for its use today are very restricted because of severe side effects, including addiction and distorted behaviour. It is a sulphate or phosphate form of $C_9H_{13}N$.

amphibian (Greek 'double life') member of the vertebrate class Amphibia, which generally spend their larval (tadpole) stage in fresh water, transferring to land at maturity (after *metamorphosis) and generally returning to water to breed. Like fish and reptiles, they continue to grow throughout life, and cannot maintain a temperature greatly differing from that of their environment. The class includes caecilians (wormlike in appearance), salamanders, frogs, and toads.

amphibole any one of a large group of rock-forming silicate minerals with an internal structure based on double chains of silicon and oxygen, and with a general formula $X_2Y_5Si_8O_{22}(OH)_2$; closely related to *pyroxene. Amphiboles form orthorhombic, monoclinic, and triclinic *crystals.

amphitheatre large oval or circular building used by the Romans for gladiatorial contests, fights of wild animals, and other similar events; it is a structure with an open space surrounded by rising rows of seats; the arena of an amphitheatre is completely surrounded by the seats of the spectators, hence the name (Greek *amphi* 'around'). The *Colosseum in Rome, completed AD 80, held 50,000 spectators.

amphoteric term used to describe the ability of some chemical compounds to behave either as an *acid or as a *base depending on their environment. For example, the metals aluminium and zinc, and their oxides and hydroxides, act as bases in acidic solutions and as acids in alkaline solutions.

amplifier electronic device that magnifies the strength of a signal, such as a radio signal. The ratio of output signal strength to input signal strength is called the *gain* of the amplifier. As well as achieving high gain, an amplifier should be free from distortion and able to operate over a range of frequencies. Practical amplifiers are usually complex circuits, although simple amplifiers can be built from single transistors or valves.

amplitude maximum displacement of an oscillation from the equilibrium position. For a wave motion, it is the height of a crest (or the depth of a trough). With a sound wave, for example, amplitude corresponds to the intensity (loudness) of the sound. In AM (amplitude modulation) radio broadcasting, the required audio-frequency signal is made to modulate (vary slightly) the amplitude of a continuously transmitted radio carrier wave.

amplitude or *argument* in mathematics, the angle θ (theta) between the position vector of a *complex number and the real axis. For the complex number z, the amplitude of $z = r(\cos \theta + i \sin \theta)$, in which r is the radius and $i = \sqrt{-1}$.

amplitude modulation (AM) method by which radio waves are altered for the transmission of broadcasting signals. AM is constant in frequency, and varies the amplitude of the transmitting wave in accordance with the signal being broadcast.

ampulla in the inner *ear, a slight swelling at the end of each semicircular canal, able to sense the motion of the head. The sense of balance largely depends on sensitive hairs within the ampulla responding to movements of fluid within the canal.

Amritsar industrial city in the Punjab, India; population (1981) 595,000. It is the holy city of *Sikhism, with the Guru Nanak University (named after the first Sikh guru) and the Golden Temple from which armed demonstrators were evicted by the Indian army under General Dayal 1984, 325 being killed. Subsequently, Indian prime minister Indira Gandhi was assassinated in reprisal. In 1919 it was the scene of the Amritsar Massacre.

Amritsar Massacre also called *Jallianwallah Bagh massacre* the killing of 379 Indians (and wounding of 1,200) in Amritsar, at the site of a Sikh religious shrine in the Punjab 1919. British troops under General Edward Dyer (1864–1927) opened fire without warning on a crowd of some 10,000, assembled to protest against the arrest of two Indian National Congress leaders (see *Congress Party).

Amsterdam capital of the Netherlands; population (1991) 1,02,400. Canals cut through the city link it with the North Sea and the Rhine, and as a Dutch port it is second only to Rotterdam. There is shipbuilding, printing, food processing, banking, and insurance.

Amundsen Roald 1872–1928. Norwegian explorer who in 1903–06 became the first person to navigate the *Northwest Passage. Beaten to the North Pole by US explorer Robert Peary 1910, he reached the South Pole ahead of Captain Scott 1911.

Amur river in E Asia. Formed by the Argun and Shilka rivers, the Amur enters the Sea of Okhotsk. At its mouth at Nikolaevsk it is 16 km/10 mi wide. For much of its course of over 4,400 km/2,730 mi it forms, together with its tributary, the Ussuri, the boundary between Russia and China.

amyl alcohol former name for *pentanol.

amylase one of a group of *enzymes that break down starches into their component molecules (sugars) for use in the body. It occurs widely in both plants and animals. In humans, it is found in saliva and in pancreatic juices.

Anabaptist (Greek 'baptize again') member of any of various 16th-century radical Protestant sects. They believed in adult rather than child baptism, and sought to establish utopian communities. Anabaptist groups spread rapidly in N Europe, particularly in Germany, and were widely persecuted.

anabolic steroid any *hormone of the *steroid group that stimulates tissue growth. Its use in medicine is limited to the treatment of some anaemias and breast cancers; it may help to break up blood clots. Side effects include aggressive behaviour, masculinization in women, and, in children, reduced height.

anabolism process of building up body tissue, promoted by the influence of certain hormones. It is the constructive side of *metabolism, as opposed to catabolism.

anabranch (Greek *ana* 'again') stream that branches from a main river, then reunites with it. For example, the Great Anabranch in New South Wales, Australia, leaves the Darling near Menindee, and joins the Murray below the Darling–Murray confluence.

anaconda South American snake *Eunectes murinus*, a member of the python and boa family, the Boidae. One of the largest snakes, growing to 9 m/30 ft or more, it is found in and near water, where it lies in wait for the birds and animals on which it feeds. The anaconda is not venomous, but kills its prey by coiling round it and squeezing until the creature suffocates.

anaemia condition caused by a shortage of haemoglobin, the oxygen-carrying component of red blood cells. The main symptoms are fatigue, pallor, breathlessness, palpitations, and poor resistance to infection. Treatment depends on the cause.

anaerobic (of living organisms) not requiring oxygen for the release of energy from food molecules such as glucose. Anaerobic organisms include many bacteria, yeasts, and internal parasites.

anaesthetic drug that produces loss of sensation or consciousness; the resulting state is **anaesthesia**, in which the patient is insensitive to stimuli. Anaesthesia may also happen as a result of nerve disorder.

Analects the most important of the four books that contain the teachings and ideas of *Confucianism.

analgesic agent for relieving *pain. *Opiates alter the perception or appreciation of pain and are effective in controlling 'deep' visceral (internal) pain. Non-opiates, such as *aspirin, *paracetamol, and NSAIDs (nonsteroidal anti-inflammatory drugs), relieve musculoskeletal pain and reduce inflammation in soft tissues.

analogous in biology, term describing a structure that has a similar function to a structure in another organism, but not a similar evolutionary path. For example, the wings of bees and of birds have the same purpose – to give powered flight – but have different origins. Compare *homologous.

analogue (of a quantity or device) changing continuously; by contrast a *digital quantity or device varies in series of distinct steps. For example, an analogue clock measures time by means of a continuous movement of hands around a dial, whereas a digital clock measures time with a numerical display that changes in a series of discrete steps.

analogue computer computing device that performs calculations through the interaction of continuously varying physical quantities, such as voltages (as distinct from the more common *digital computer, which works with discrete quantities). An analogue computer is said to operate in real time (corresponding to time in the real world), and can therefore be used to monitor and control other events as they happen.

analysis branch of mathematics concerned with limiting processes on axiomatic number systems; *calculus of variations and infinitesimal calculus is now called analysis.

analysis in chemistry, the determination of the composition of substances; see *analytical chemistry.

analytic in philosophy, a term derived from *Kant: the converse of *synthetic. In an analytic judgement, the judgement provides no new knowledge; for example: 'All bachelors are unmarried.'

analytical chemistry branch of chemistry that deals with the determination of the chemical composition of substances. *Qualitative analysis* determines the identities of the substances in a given sample; *quantitative analysis* determines how much of a particular substance is present.

analytical geometry another name for *coordinate geometry.

anarchism (Greek *anarkhos* 'without ruler') political belief that society should have no government, laws, police, or other authority, but should be a free association of all its members. It does not mean 'without order'; most theories of anarchism imply an order of a very strict and symmetrical kind, but they maintain that such order can be achieved by cooperation. Anarchism must not be confused with nihilism (a purely negative and destructive activity directed against

society); anarchism is essentially a pacifist movement.

Anastasia 1901–1918. Russian Grand Duchess, youngest daughter of *Nicholas II. During the Russian Revolution she was presumed shot with her parents by the Bolsheviks after the Revolution of 1917, but it has been alleged that Anastasia escaped.

anatomy study of the structure of the body and its component parts, especially the *human body, as distinguished from physiology, which is the study of bodily functions.

Anaximander c. 610–c. 546 BC. Greek astronomer and philosopher. He claimed that the Earth was a cylinder three times wider than it is deep, motionless at the centre of the universe, and he is credited with drawing the first geographical map. He said that the celestial bodies were fire seen through holes in the hollow rims of wheels encircling the Earth. According to Anaximander, the first animals came into being from moisture and the first humans grew inside fish, emerging once fully developed.

ANC abbreviation for ***African National Congress***, a South African nationalist organization.

ancestor worship religious rituals and beliefs oriented towards deceased members of a family or group, as a symbolic expression of values or in the belief that the souls of the dead remain involved in this world and are capable of influencing current events.

Anchorage port and largest city of Alaska, USA, at the head of Cook Inlet; population (1990) 226,340. Established 1918, Anchorage is an important centre of administration, communication, and commerce. Oil and gas extraction and fish canning are also important to the local economy.

anchovy small fish *Engraulis encrasicholus* of the *herring family. It is fished extensively, being abundant in the Mediterranean, and is also found on the Atlantic coast of Europe and in the Black Sea. It grows to 20 cm/8 in.

ancien régime the old order; the feudal, absolute monarchy in France before the French Revolution 1789.

ancient art art of prehistoric cultures and the ancient civilizations around the Mediterranean that predate the classical world of Greece and Rome: for example, Sumerian and Aegean art. Artefacts range from simple relics of the Palaeolithic period, such as pebbles carved with symbolic figures, to the sophisticated art forms of anicent Egypt and Assyria; for example, mural paintings, sculpture, and jewellery.

Andalusia (Spanish *Andalucía*) fertile autonomous region of S Spain, including the provinces of Almería, Cádiz, Córdoba, Granada, Huelva, Jaén, Málaga, and Seville; area 87,300 sq km/33,698 sq mi; population (1986) 6,876,000. Málaga, Cádiz, and Algeciras are the chief ports and industrial centres. The *Costa del Sol* on the south coast has many tourist resorts, including Marbella and Torremolinos.

andalusite aluminium silicate Al_xSiO_5, a white to pinkish mineral crystallizing as square- or rhomb-based prisms. It is common in metamorphic rocks formed from clay sediments under low pressure conditions. Andalusite, kyanite, and sillimanite are all polymorphs of Al_2SiO_5.

Andaman and Nicobar Islands two groups of islands in the Bay of Bengal, between India and Myanmar, forming a Union Territory of the Republic of India; capital Port Blair; area 8,300 sq km/3,204 sq mi; population (1991) 278,000. The economy is based on fishing, timber, rubber, fruit, and rice.

andante in music, a passage or movement to be performed at a walking pace; that is, at a moderately slow tempo.

Andean Indian any indigenous inhabitant of the Andes range in South America, stretching from Ecuador to Peru to Chile, and including both the coast and the highlands. Many Andean civilizations developed in this region from local fishing-hunting-farming societies, all of which predated the *Inca, who consolidated the entire region and ruled from about 1200 to the 1530s, when the Spanish arrived and conquered. The earliest pan-Andean civilization was the Chavin, about 1200–800 BC, which was followed by large and important coastal city-states, such as the Mochica, the Chimú, the Nazca, and the Paracas. The region was dominated by the Tiahuanaco when the Inca started to expand, took them and outlying peoples into their empire, and imposed the Quechua language on all. It is now spoken by over 10 million people and is a member of the Andean-Equatorial family.

Andersen Hans Christian 1805–1875. Danish writer of fairy tales. Well-known examples include 'The Ugly Duckling', 'The Snow Queen', 'The Little Mermaid', and 'The Emperor's New Clothes'. Their inventiveness, sensitivity, and strong sense of wonder have given these stories perennial and universal appeal; they have been translated into many languages. He also wrote adult novels and travel books.

Anderson Carl David 1905–1991. US physicist who discovered the positive electron (positron) in 1932; he shared the Nobel Prize for Physics in 1936.

Anderson Elizabeth Garrett 1836–1917. The first English woman to qualify in medicine. Refused entry into medical school, Anderson studied privately and was licensed by the Society of Apothecaries in London 1865. She was physician to the Marylebone Dispensary for Women and Children (later renamed the Elizabeth Garrett Anderson Hospital), a London hospital now staffed by women and serving women patients.

Anderson Marian 1902–1993. US contralto whose voice was remarkable for its range and richness. She toured Europe 1930, but in 1939 she was barred from singing at Constitution Hall, Washington, DC, because she was black. In 1955 she sang at the Metropolitan Opera, the first black singer to appear there. In 1958 she was appointed an alternate (deputizing) delegate to the United Nations.

Andes great mountain system or *cordillera* that forms the western fringe of South America, extending through some 67° of latitude and the republics of Colombia, Venezuela, Ecuador, Peru, Bolivia, Chile, and Argentina. The mountains exceed 3,600 m/12,000 ft for half their length of 6,500 km/4,000 mi.

andesite volcanic igneous rock, intermediate in silica content between rhyolite and basalt. It is characterized by a large quantity of feldspar *minerals, giving it a light colour. Andesite erupts from volcanoes at destructive plate margins (where one plate of the Earth's surface moves beneath another; see *plate tectonics), including the Andes, from which it gets its name.

Andhra Pradesh state in E central India
area 276,700 sq km/106,845 sq mi
capital Hyderabad
towns Secunderabad
products rice, sugar cane, tobacco, groundnuts, cotton
population (1991) 66,304,900
languages Telugu, Urdu, Tamil
history formed 1953 from the Telegu-speaking areas of Madras, and enlarged 1956 from the former Hyderabad state.

Andorra Principality of (*Principat d'Andorra*)

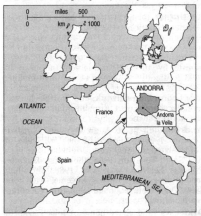

area 468 sq km/181 sq mi
capital Andorra la Vella
towns Les Escaldes
physical mountainous, with narrow valleys
heads of state Joan Marti i Alanis (bishop of Urgel, Spain) and François Mitterrand (president of France)
head of government Oscar Riba Reig from 1989
political system co-principality
political party Democratic Party of Andorra
exports main industries tourism and tobacco
currency French franc and Spanish peseta
population (1993) 59,000 (30% Andorrans, 61% Spanish, 6% French)
languages Catalan (official); Spanish, French
religion Roman Catholic
GDP $300 million (1985)
chronology
1278 Treaty signed making Spanish bishop and French count joint rulers of Andorra (through marriage the king of France later inherited the count's right).
1970 Extension of franchise to third-generation female and second-generation male Andorrans.
1976 First political organization (Democratic Party of Andorra) formed.
1977 Franchise extended to first-generation Andorrans.

1981 First prime minister appointed by General Council.

1982 With the appointment of an Executive Council, executive and legislative powers were separated.

1993 Andorra's first constitution approved in referendum.

Andrea del Sarto (Andrea d'Agnola) 1486–1531. Italian Renaissance painter active in Florence, one of the finest portraitists and religious painters of his time. His style is serene and noble, characteristic of High Renaissance art.

Andreas Capellanus Latin name for André le Chapelain.

André le Chapelain 12th century. French priest and author. He wrote *De Arte Honest Amandi/The Art of Virtuous Love*, a seminal work in courtly love literature, at the request of *Marie de France, while he was chaplain at her court in Troyes, E France.

Andreotti Giulio 1919– . Italian Christian Democrat politician. He headed seven post-war governments: 1972–73, 1976–79 (four successive terms), and 1989–92 (two terms). In addition he was defence minister eight times, and foreign minister five times. He is a fervent European. In 1993 Andreotti was among several high-ranking politicians accused of possible involvement in Italy's corruption network, and in 1995 he was formally charged with using his influence to protect Mafia leaders.

Andrew (full name Andrew Albert Christian Edward) 1960– . Prince of the UK, Duke of York, second son of Queen Elizabeth II. He married Sarah Ferguson 1986; their first daughter, Princess Beatrice, was born 1988, and their second daughter, Princess Eugenie, was born 1990. The couple separated 1992. Prince Andrew is a naval helicopter pilot.

Andrews Julie. Stage name of Julia Elizabeth Wells 1935– . British-born US singer and actress. A child performer with her mother and stepfather in British music halls, she first appeared in the USA in the Broadway production *The Boy Friend* 1954. She was the original Eliza Doolittle in *My Fair Lady* 1956. In 1960 she appeared in Lerner and Loewe's *Camelot* on Broadway. Her films include *Mary Poppins* 1964, *The Americanization of Emily* 1963, *The Sound of Music* 1965, '*10*' 1980, and *Victor/Victoria* 1982.

Andrew, St New Testament apostle. According to tradition, he went with John to Ephesus, preached in Scythia, and was martyred at Patras on an X-shaped cross (*St Andrew's cross*). He is the patron saint of Scotland. Feast day 30 Nov.

Androcles traditionally, a Roman slave who fled from a cruel master into the African desert, where he encountered and withdrew a thorn from the paw of a crippled lion. Recaptured and sentenced to combat a lion in the arena, he found his adversary was his old friend. The emperor Tiberius was said to have freed them both.

androecium male part of a flower, comprising a number of *stamens.

androgen general name for any male sex hormone, of which *testosterone is the most important. They are all *steroids and are principally involved in the production of male *secondary sexual characters (such as facial hair in humans).

Andromache in Greek mythology, the faithful wife of Hector and mother of Astyanax. After the fall of Troy she was awarded to Neoptolemus, Achilles' son; she later married a Trojan seer called Helenus. Andromache is the heroine of Homer's *Iliad* and the subject of a play by Euripides.

Andromeda major constellation of the northern hemisphere, visible in autumn. Its main feature is the Andromeda galaxy. The star Alpha Andromedae forms one corner of the Square of Pegasus. It is named after the princess of Greek mythology.

Andromeda galaxy galaxy 2.2 million light years away from Earth in the constellation Andromeda, and the most distant object visible to the naked eye. It is the largest member of the *Local Group of galaxies. Like the Milky Way, it is a spiral orbited by several companion galaxies but contains about twice as many stars. It is about 200,000 light years across.

Andropov Yuri 1914–1984. Soviet communist politician, president of the USSR 1983–84. As chief of the KGB 1967–82, he established a reputation for efficiently suppressing dissent.

anechoic chamber room designed to be of high sound absorbency. All surfaces inside the chamber are covered by sound-absorbent materials such as rubber. The walls are often covered with inward-facing pyramids of rubber, to minimize reflections. It is used for experiments in *acoustics and for testing audio equipment.

anemometer device for measuring wind speed and liquid flow. The most basic form, the **cup-type anemometer**, consists of cups at the ends of arms, which rotate when the wind blows. The speed of rotation indicates the wind speed.

anemone any plant of the genus *Anemone* of the buttercup family Ranunculaceae. The function of petals is performed by its sepals. The garden anemone *A. coronaria* is white, blue, red, or purple.

anemophily type of *pollination in which the pollen is carried on the wind. Anemophilous flowers are usually unscented, have either very reduced petals and sepals or lack them altogether, and do not produce nectar. In some species they are borne in catkins. Male and female reproductive structures are commonly found in separate flowers. The male flowers have numerous exposed stamens, often on long filaments; the female flowers have long, often branched, feathery stigmas.

aneroid barometer kind of *barometer.

aneurysm weakening in the wall of an artery, causing it to balloon outwards, with the risk of rupture and serious, often fatal, blood loss. If detected in time and accessible, some aneurysms can be excised.

Angad 1504–1552. Indian religious leader, second guru (teacher) of Sikhism 1539–52, succeeding Nanak. He popularized the alphabet known as **Gurmukhi**, in which the Sikh scriptures are written.

angel (Greek *angelos* 'messenger') in Jewish, Christian, and Muslim belief, a supernatural being intermediate between God and humans.

The Christian hierarchy has nine orders: *Seraphim*, *Cherubim*, *Thrones* (who contemplate God and reflect his glory), *Dominations*, *Virtues*, *Powers* (who regulate the stars and the universe), *Principalities*, *Archangels*, and *Angels* (who minister to humanity). In traditional Catholic belief every human being has a guardian angel. The existence of angels was reasserted by Pope John Paul II 1986.

angel dust popular name for the anaesthetic *phencyclidine*, a depressant drug.

Angel Falls highest waterfalls in the world, on the river Caroní in the tropical rainforest of Bolívar Region, Venezuela; total height 978 m/3,210 ft. They were named after the aviator and prospector James Angel who flew over the falls and crash-landed nearby 1935.

angelfish any of a number of unrelated fishes. The freshwater *angelfish*, genus *Pterophyllum*, of South America, is a tall, side-to-side flattened fish with a striped body, up to 26 cm/10 in long, but usually smaller in captivity. The *angelfish* or *monkfish* of the genus *Squatina* is a bottom-living shark up to 1.8 m/6 ft long with a body flattened from top to bottom. The *marine angelfishes*, *Pomacanthus* and others, are long narrow-bodied fish with spiny fins, often brilliantly coloured, up to 60 cm/2 ft long, living around coral reefs in the tropics.

angelica any plant of the genus *Angelica* of the carrot family Umbelliferae. Mostly Eurasian in distribution, they are tall, perennial herbs with divided leaves and clusters of white or greenish flowers. The roots and fruits have long been used in cooking and for medicinal purposes.

Angelico Fra (Guido di Pietro) *c.* 1400–1455. Italian painter of religious scenes, active in Florence. He was a monk and painted a series of frescoes at the monastery of San Marco, Florence, begun after 1436. He also produced several altarpieces in a simple style.

Angelou Maya (born Marguerite Johnson) 1928– . US novelist, poet, playwright, and short-story writer. Her powerful autobiographical works, *I Know Why the Caged Bird Sings* 1970 and its three sequels, tell of the struggles towards physical and spiritual liberation of a black woman growing up in the South.

Anger Kenneth 1929– . US avant-garde filmmaker, brought up in Hollywood. His films, which dispense with conventional narrative, often use homosexual iconography and a personal form of mysticism. They include *Fireworks* 1947, *Scorpio Rising* 1964, and *Lucifer Rising* 1973.

Angevin relating to the reigns of the English kings Henry II and Richard I (also known, with the later English kings up to Richard III, as the *Plantagenets*). Angevin derives from Anjou, the region in France controlled by English kings at this time. The *Angevin Empire* comprised the territories (including England) that belonged to the Anjou dynasty.

angina or *angina pectoris* severe pain in the chest due to impaired blood supply to the heart muscle because a coronary artery is narrowed. Faintness and difficulty in breathing accompany the pain. Treatment is by drugs, such as nitroglycerin and amyl nitrite; rest is important.

angiosperm flowering plant in which the seeds are enclosed within an ovary, which ripens to a fruit. Angiosperms are divided into *monocotyledons (single seed leaf in the embryo) and *dicotyledons (two seed leaves in the embryo). They include the majority of flowers, herbs, grasses, and trees except conifers.

Angle member of the Germanic tribe that invaded Britain in the 5th century; see *Anglo-Saxon.

angle pair of rays (half-lines) that share a common endpoint but do not lie on the same line. Angles are measured in *degrees (°) or *radians, and are classified generally by their degree measures. *Acute angles* are less than 90°; *right angles* are exactly 90°; *obtuse angles* are greater than 90° but less than 180°; *reflex angles* are greater than 180° but less than 360°. Angles can be measured by using a protractor. No angle is classified as having a measure of 180°, as by definition such an 'angle' is actually a straight line.

angler any of an order of fishes Lophiiformes, with flattened body and broad head and jaws. Many species have small, plantlike tufts on their skin. These act as camouflage for the fish as it waits, either floating among seaweed or lying on the sea bottom, twitching the enlarged tip of the threadlike first ray of its dorsal fin to entice prey.

Anglican Communion family of Christian churches including the Church of England, the US Episcopal Church, and those holding the same essential doctrines, that is the Lambeth Quadrilateral 1888 Holy Scripture as the basis of all doctrine, the Nicene and Apostles' Creeds, Holy Baptism and Holy Communion, and the historic episcopate.

angling fishing with rod and line. It is the largest participant sport in the UK. Competition angling exists and world championships take place for most branches of the sport. The oldest is the World Freshwater Championship, inaugurated 1957.

Anglo-Irish Agreement or *Hillsborough Agreement* concord reached 1985 between the UK premier Margaret Thatcher and Irish premier Garret FitzGerald. One sign of the improved relations between the two countries was increased cooperation between police and security forces across the border with Northern Ireland. The pact also gave the Irish Republic a greater voice in the conduct of Northern Ireland's affairs. However, the agreement was rejected by Northern Ireland Unionists as a step towards renunciation of British sovereignty. In March 1988 talks led to further strengthening of the agreement.

Anglo-Saxon one of the several Germanic invaders (Angles, Saxons, and Jutes) who conquered much of Britain between the 5th and 7th centuries. After the conquest a number of kingdoms were set up, commonly referred to as the *Heptarchy*; these were united in the early 9th century under the overlordship of Wessex. The Norman invasion 1066 brought Anglo-Saxon rule to an end.

Anglo-Saxon art painting and sculpture of England from the 7th century to 1066. Sculpted crosses and ivories, manuscript painting, and gold and enamel jewellery survive. The relics of the Sutton Hoo ship burial, 7th century, and the *Lindisfarne Gospels*, about 690 (both British Museum, London), have typical Celtic ornamental patterns, but in manuscripts of southern England a different style emerged in the 9th century, with delicate, lively pen-and-ink figures and heavily decorative foliage borders.

Anglo-Saxon Chronicle history of England from the Roman invasion to the 11th century, in the form of a series of chronicles written in Old English by monks, begun in the 9th century (during the reign of King Alfred), and continuing to the 12th century.

Anglo-Saxon language group of dialects spoken by the *Anglo-Saxon peoples who, in the 5th to 7th centuries, invaded and settled in Britain (in what became England and Lowland Scotland). Anglo-Saxon is traditionally known as Old English. See *English language.

Angola People's Republic of (*República Popular de Angola*)

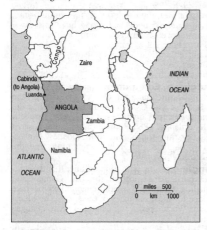

area 1,246,700 sq km/481,226 sq mi
capital and chief port Luanda
towns Lobito and Benguela, also ports; Huambo, Lubango
physical narrow coastal plain rises to vast interior plateau with rainforest in NW; desert in S
head of state José Eduardo dos Santos from 1979
head of government Marcolino José Carlos Moco from 1992
political system socialist republic
exports oil, coffee, diamonds, palm oil, sisal, iron ore, fish
currency kwanza
population (1993) 10,770,000 (largest ethnic group Ovimbundu); growth rate 2.5% p.a.
languages Portuguese (official); Bantu dialects
religions Roman Catholic 68%, Protestant 20%, animist 12%
GNP $620 per head
chronology
1951 Angola became an overseas territory of Portugal.
1956 First independence movement formed, the People's Movement for the Liberation of Angola (MPLA).
1961 Unsuccessful independence rebellion.

1962 Second nationalist movement formed, FNLA.
1966 Third nationalist movement formed, UNITA.
1975 Independence achieved from Portugal. MPLA proclaimed People's Republic of Angola under the presidency of Dr Agostinho Neto. FNLA and UNITA proclaimed People's Democratic Republic of Angola.
1976 MPLA gained control of most of the country. South African troops withdrawn, but Cuban units remained.
1977 MPLA restructured to become MPLA–PT.
1979 Death of Neto, succeeded by José Eduardo dos Santos.
1980 UNITA guerrillas, aided by South Africa, continued raids against the Luanda government and bases of the South West Africa People's Organization (SWAPO) in Angola.
1984 The Lusaka Agreement.
1985 South African forces officially withdrawn.
1986 Further South African raids into Angola. UNITA continued to receive South African support.
1988 Peace treaty, providing for the withdrawal of all foreign troops, signed with South Africa and Cuba.
1989 Cease-fire agreed with UNITA broke down and guerrilla activity restarted.
1990 Peace offer by rebels. Return to multiparty politics promised.
1991 Peace agreement signed, civil war between MPLA–PT and UNITA officially ended. Amnesty for all political prisoners.
1992 MPLA–PT's general-election victory fiercely disputed by UNITA, plunging the country into renewed civil war.
1993 Fighting escalated. Dos Santos government recognized by USA. United Nations sanctions imposed against UNITA.
1994 Agreement between government and UNITA to ensure fair presidential elections.

angostura flavouring prepared from oil distilled from the bitter, aromatic bark of either of two South American trees *Galipea officinalis* or *Cusparia trifoliata* of the rue family. It is blended with herbs and other flavourings to give **angostura bitters**, which was first used as a stomach remedy and is now used to season food, fruit, and alcoholic drinks.

Angry Young Men group of British writers who emerged about 1950 after the creative hiatus that followed World War II. They included Kingsley Amis, John Wain, John Osborne, and Colin Wilson. Also linked to the group were Iris Murdoch and Kenneth Tynan.

angst (German 'anxiety') an emotional state of anxiety without a specific cause. In *existentialism, the term refers to a general condition of anxiety at having free will, that is, of being responsible for one's actions.

angstrom unit (symbol Aå) of length equal to 10^{-10} metre or one-ten-millionth of a millimetre, used for atomic measurements and the wavelengths of electromagnetic radiation. It is named after the Swedish scientist A J Aångström.

Aångström Anders Jonas 1814–1874. Swedish astrophysicist whose main achievements were in spectroscopy and solar physics. In 1861 Aångström identified the presence of hydrogen in the Sun. His major work *Recherches sur le spectre solaire* 1868, an atlas of solar spectra, presented the measurements of 1,000 spectral lines expressed in units of one-ten-millionth of a millimetre, the unit which later became the angstrom.

Anguilla island in the E Caribbean

area 160 sq km/62 sq mi

capital The Valley

exports lobster, salt

currency Eastern Caribbean dollar

population (1988) 7,000

language English, Creole

government from 1982, governor, executive council, and legislative house of assembly (chief minister Emile Gumbs from 1984)

history a British colony from 1650, Anguilla was long associated with St Christopher-Nevis but revolted against alleged domination by the larger island and in 1969 declared itself a republic. A small British force restored order, and Anguilla retained a special position at its own request, since 1980 a separate dependency of the UK.

angular momentum see *momentum.

Anhui or *Anhwei* province of E China, watered by the Chang Jiang (Yangtze River)

area 139,900 sq km/54,000 sq mi

capital Hefei

products cereals in the north; cotton, rice, tea in the south

population (1990) 56,181,000.

anhydride chemical compound obtained by the removal of water from another compound; usually a dehydrated acid. For example, sulphur(VI) oxide (sulphur trioxide, SO_3) is the anhydride of sulphuric acid (H_2SO_4).

anhydrous of a chemical compound, containing no water. If the water of crystallization is removed from blue crystals of copper(II) sulphate, a white powder (anhydrous copper sulphate) results. Liquids from which all traces of water have been removed are also described as being anhydrous.

aniline (Portuguese *anil* 'indigo') $C_6H_5NH_2$ or *phenylamine* one of the simplest aromatic chemicals (a substance related to benzene, with its carbon atoms joined in a ring). When pure, it is a colourless oily liquid; it has a characteristic odour, and turns brown on contact with air. It occurs in coal tar, and is used in the rubber industry and to make drugs and dyes. It is highly poisonous.

animal or *metazoan* member of the kingdom Animalia, one of the major categories of living things, the science of which is *zoology*. Animals are all *heterotrophs (they obtain their energy from organic substances produced by other organisms); they have eukaryotic cells (the genetic material is contained within a distinct nucleus) bounded by a thin cell membrane rather than the thick cell wall of plants. Most animals are capable of moving around for at least part of their life cycle.

animal liberation loose international movement against the infliction of suffering on animals, whether for scientific, military, or commercial research, or in being raised for food. The movement was sparked by the book *Animal Liberation* 1975 by Peter Singer and encompasses many different organizations.

animism in psychology and physiology, the view of human personality that attributes human life and behaviour to a force distinct from matter. In religious theory, the conception of a spiritual reality behind the material one: for example, beliefs in the soul as a shadowy duplicate of the body capable of independent activity, both in life and death. In anthropology, the concept of spirits residing in all natural phenomena and objects.

anion ion carrying a negative charge. An electrolyte, such as the salt zinc chloride ($ZnCl_2$), is dissociated in aqueous solution or in the molten state into doubly-charged Zn^{2+} zinc *cations and singly-charged Cl^- anions. During electrolysis, the zinc cations flow to the cathode (to become discharged and liberate zinc metal) and the chloride anions flow to the anode.

anise plant *Pimpinella anisum*, of the carrot family Umbelliferae, whose fragrant seeds are used to flavour foods. Aniseed oil is used in cough medicines.

Ankara (formerly *Angora*) capital of Turkey; population (1990) 2,559,500. Industries include cement, textiles, and leather products. It replaced Istanbul as capital 1923.

Anna Comnena 1083–after 1148. Byzantine historian, daughter of the emperor *Alexius I, who was the historian of her father's reign. After a number of abortive attempts to alter the imperial succession in favour of her husband, Nicephorus Bryennius (*c.* 1062–1137), she retired to a convent to write her major work, the *Alexiad*. It describes the Byzantine view of public office, as well as the religious and intellectual life of the period.

Annamese member of the majority ethnic group in Vietnam, comprising 90% of the population. The Annamese language is distinct from Vietnamese, though it has been influenced by Chinese and has loan words from Khmer. Their religion combines elements of Buddhism, Confucianism, and Taoism, as well as ancestor worship.

Annapurna mountain 8,075 m/26,502 ft in the Himalayas, Nepal. The north face was first climbed by a French expedition (Maurice Herzog) 1950 and the south by a British team 1970.

Anne 1665–1714. Queen of Great Britain and Ireland 1702–14. She was the second daughter of James, Duke of York, who became James II, and Anne Hyde. She succeeded William III 1702. Events of her reign include the War of the Spanish Succession, Marlborough's victories at Blenheim, Ramillies, Oudenarde, and Malplaquet, and the union of the English and Scottish parliaments 1707. Anne was succeeded by George I.

Anne (full name Anne Elizabeth Alice Louise) 1950– . Princess of the UK, second child of Queen Elizabeth II, declared Princess Royal 1987. She is an excellent horsewoman, winning a gold medal at the 1976 Olympics, and is actively involved in global charity work, especially for children. In 1973 she married Capt Mark Phillips (1949–); they separated 1989 and were divorced 1992. She married Commander Timothy Lawrence Dec 1992.

annealing process of heating a material (usually glass or metal) for a given time at a given temperature, followed by slow cooling, to increase ductility and strength. It is a common form of *heat treatment.

annelid any segmented worm of the phylum Annelida. Annelids include earthworms, leeches, and marine worms such as lugworms.

Anne of Austria 1601–1666. Queen of France from 1615 and regent 1643–61. Daughter of Philip III of Spain, she married Louis XIII of France (whose chief minister, Cardinal Richelieu, worked against her). On her husband's death she became regent for their son, Louis XIV, until his majority.

Anne of Cleves 1515–1557. Fourth wife of *Henry VIII of England 1540. She was the daughter of the Duke of Cleves, and was recommended to Henry as a wife by Thomas *Cromwell, who wanted an alliance with German Protestantism against the Holy Roman Empire. Henry did not like her looks, had the marriage declared void after six months, pensioned her, and had Cromwell beheaded.

Anne of Denmark 1574–1619. Queen consort of James VI of Scotland (later James I of Great Britain 1603). She was the daughter of Frederick II of Denmark and Norway, and married James 1589. Anne was suspected of Catholic leanings and was notably extravagant.

annihilation in nuclear physics, a process in which a particle and its 'mirror image' particle or *antiparticle collide and disappear, with the creation of a burst of energy. The energy created is equivalent to the mass of the colliding particles in accordance with the *mass-energy equation. For example, an electron and a positron annihilate to produce a burst of high-energy X-rays. Not all particle-antiparticle interactions result in annihilation; the exception concerns the group called mesons, which are composed of *quarks and their antiquarks.

anno Domini (Latin 'in the year of our Lord') in the Christian chronological system, refers to dates since the birth of Jesus, denoted by the letters AD. There is no year 0, so AD 1 follows immediately after the year 1 BC (before Christ). The system became the standard reckoning in the Western world after being adopted by the English historian Bede in the 8th century. The abbreviations CE (Common Era) and BCE (before Common Era) are often used instead by scholars and writers as objective, rather than religious, terms.

annual general meeting (AGM) yearly meeting of the shareholders of a company or the members of an organization, at which business including consideration of the annual report and accounts, the election of officers, and the appointment of auditors is normally carried out.

annual percentage rate (APR) charge (including *interest) for granting consumer credit, expressed as an equivalent once-a-year percentage figure of the amount of the credit granted. It is usually approximately double the flat rate of interest, or simple interest. In the UK, lenders are legally required to state the APR when advertising loans.

annual plant plant that completes its life cycle within one year, during which time it germinates, grows to maturity, bears flowers, produces seed, and then dies.

annual rings or **growth rings** concentric rings visible on the wood of a cut tree trunk or other woody stem. Each ring represents a period of growth when new *xylem is laid down to replace tissue being converted into wood (secondary xylem). The wood formed from xylem produced in the spring and early summer has larger and more numerous vessels than the wood formed from xylem produced in autumn when growth is slowing down. The result is a clear boundary between the pale spring wood and the denser, darker autumn wood. Annual rings may be used to estimate the age of the plant (see *dendrochronology), although occasionally more than one growth ring is produced in a given year.

annulus (Latin 'ring') in geometry, the plane area between two concentric circles, making a flat ring.

Annunciation in the New Testament, the announcement to Mary by the archangel Gabriel that she was to be the mother of Christ; the feast of the Annunciation is 25 March (also known as Lady Day).

anode in chemistry, the positive electrode of an electrolytic *cell, towards which negative particles (anions), usually in solution, are attracted. See *electrolysis.

anodizing process that increases the resistance to *corrosion of a metal, such as aluminium, by building up a protective oxide layer on the surface. The natural corrosion resistance of aluminium is provided by a thin film of aluminium oxide; anodizing increases the thickness of this film and thus the corrosion protection.

anomalous expansion of water expansion of water as it is cooled from 4°C to 0°C. This behaviour is unusual because most substances contract when they are cooled. It means that water has a greater density at 4°C than at 0°C. Hence ice floats on water, and the water at the bottom of a pool in winter is warmer than at the surface. As a result large lakes freeze slowly in winter and aquatic life is more likely to survive.

anomie in the social sciences, a state of 'normlessness' created by the breakdown of commonly agreed standards of behaviour and morality; the term often refers to situations where the social order appears to have collapsed. The concept was developed by the French sociologist Émile Durkheim.

anorexia lack of desire to eat, especially the pathological condition of **anorexia nervosa**, usually found in adolescent girls and young women, who may be obsessed with the desire to lose weight. Compulsive eating, or *bulimia, often accompanies anorexia.

Anouilh Jean 1910–1987. French dramatist. His plays, influenced by the Neo-Classical tradition, include *Antigone* 1942, *L'Invitation au château/Ring Round the Moon* 1947, *Colombe* 1950, and *Becket* 1959, about St Thomas à Becket and Henry II.

anoxaemia shortage of oxygen in the blood; insufficient supply of oxygen to the tissues. It may be due to breathing air deficient in oxygen (for instance, at high altitude or where there are noxious fumes), a disease of the lungs, or some disorder where the oxygen-carrying capacity of the blood is impaired.

Anschluss (German 'union') the annexation of Austria with Germany, accomplished by the German chancellor Adolf Hitler 12 March 1938.

Anselm, St c. 1033–1109. Medieval priest and philosopher. As abbot from 1078, he made the abbey of Bec in Normandy, France, a centre of scholarship in Europe. He was appointed arch-bishop of Canterbury by William II of England 1093, but was later forced into exile. He holds an important place in the development of *Schol-asticism.

Anson George, 1st Baron Anson 1697–1762. English admiral who sailed around the world 1740–44. In 1740 he commanded the squadron attacking the Spanish colonies and shipping in South America; he returned home by circumnavi-gating the world, with £500,000 of Spanish treas-ure. He carried out reforms at the Admiralty, which increased the efficiency of the British fleet and contributed to its success in the Seven Years' War (1756–63) against France.

ant insect belonging to the family Formicidae, and to the same order (Hymenoptera) as bees and wasps. Ants are characterized by a conspicuous 'waist' and elbowed antennae. About 10,000 dif-ferent species are known; all are social in habit, and all construct nests of various kinds. Ants are found in all parts of the world, except the polar regions. It is estimated that there are about 10 million billion ants.

Antabuse proprietary name for disulfiram, a synthetic chemical used in the treatment of alcoholism. It produces unpleasant side effects if combined with alcohol, such as nausea, head-aches, palpitations, and collapse. The 'Antabuse effect' is produced coincidentally by certain anti-biotics.

antacid any substance that neutralizes stomach acid, such as sodium bicarbonate or magnesium hydroxide ('milk of magnesia'). Antacids are weak *bases, swallowed as solids or emulsions. They may be taken between meals to relieve symptoms of hyperacidity, such as pain, bloating, nausea, and 'heartburn'. Excessive or prolonged need for antacids should be investigated medically.

antagonistic muscles in the body, a pair of muscles allowing coordinated movement of the skeletal joints. The extension of the arm, for example, requires one set of muscles to relax, while another set contracts. The individual com-ponents of antagonistic pairs can be classified into extensors (muscles that straighten a limb) and flexors (muscles that bend a limb).

Antananarivo (formerly *Tananarive*) capital of Madagascar, on the interior plateau, with a rail link to Tamatave; population (1986) 703,000. Industries include tobacco, food processing, leather goods, and clothing.

Antarctica continent surrounding the South Pole, arbitrarily defined as the region lying S of the Antarctic Circle. Occupying 10% of the world's surface, Antarctica contains 90% of the world's ice and 70% of its fresh water
area 13,900,000 sq km/5,400,000 sq mi (the size of Europe and the USA combined)

physical formed of two blocs of rock with an area of about 8 million sq km/3 million sq mi, Antarctica is covered by a cap of ice that flows slowly towards its 22,400 km/14,000 mi coast-line, reaching the sea in high ice cliffs. The most southerly shores are near the 78th parallel in the Ross and Weddell seas. E Antarctica is a massive bloc of ancient rocks that surface in the Transant-arctic Mountains of Victoria Land. Separated by a deep channel, W Antarctica is characterized by the mountainous regions of Graham Land, the Antarctic Peninsula, Palmer Land, and Ellsworth Land; the highest peak is Vinson Massif (5,139 m/16,866 ft). Little more than 1% of the land is ice-free. With an estimated volume of 24 million cu m/5.9 million cu mi, the ice-cap has a mean thickness of 1,880 m/6,170 ft and in places reaches depths of 5,000 m/16,000 ft or more. Each annual layer of snow preserves a record of global conditions, and where no melting at the surface of the bedrock has occurred the ice can be a million years old
climate winds are strong and temperatures are cold, particularly in the interior where tempera-tures can drop to –70°C/–100°F and below. Pre-cipitation is largely in the form of snow or hoar-frost rather than rain which rarely exceeds 50 mm/2 in per year (less than the Sahara Desert)
flora and fauna the Antarctic ecosystem is characterized by large numbers of relatively few species of higher plants and animals, and a short food chain from iny marine plants to whales, seals, penguins, and other sea birds. Only two species of vascular plant are known, but there are about 60 species of moss, 100 species of lichen, and 400 species of algae
products cod, Antarctic icefish, and krill are fished in Antarctic waters. Whaling, which began in the early 20th century, ceased during the 1960s as a result of overfishing. Petroleum, coal, and minerals, such as palladium and platinum exist, but their exploitation is prevented by a 50-year ban on commercial mining agreed by 39 nations 1991
population no permanent residents; settlement limited to scientific research stations with maximum population of 2,000 to 3,000 during the summer months. Sectors of Antarctica are claimed by Argentina, Australia, Chile, France, the UK, Norway, and New Zealand.

Antarctic Circle imaginary line that encircles the South Pole at latitude 66° 32' S. The line encompasses the continent of Antarctica and the Antarctic Ocean.

Antarctic Peninsula mountainous peninsula of W Antarctica extending 1,930 km/1,200 mi N towards South America; originally named *Palmer Land* after a US navigator, Captain Nathaniel Palmer, who was the first to explore the region 1820. It was claimed by Britain 1832, Argentina 1940, and Chile 1942. Its name was changed to the Antarctic Peninsula 1964.

Antarctic Treaty international agreement aiming to promote scientific research and keep Antarctica free from conflict. It dates from 1961 and in 1991 a 50-year ban on mining activity was secured.

Antares or *Alpha Scorpii* brightest star in the constellation Scorpius and the 15th brightest star in the sky. It is a red supergiant several hundred times larger than the Sun and perhaps 10,000 times as luminous, lies about 300 light years away, and fluctuates slightly in brightness.

anteater mammal of the family Myrmecophagidae, order Edentata, native to Mexico, Central America, and tropical South America. An anteater lives almost entirely on ants and termites. It has toothless jaws, an extensile tongue, and claws for breaking into the nests of its prey.

antelope any of numerous kinds of even-toed, hoofed mammals belonging to the cow family, Bovidae. Most antelopes are lightly built and good runners. They are grazers or browsers, and chew the cud. They range in size from the dik-diks and duikers, only 30 cm/1 ft high, to the eland, which can be 1.8 m/6 ft at the shoulder.

antenna in zoology, an appendage ('feeler') on the head. Insects, centipedes, and millipedes each have one pair of antennae but there are two pairs in crustaceans, such as shrimps. In insects, the antennae are usually involved with the senses of smell and touch; they are frequently complex structures with large surface areas that increase the ability to detect scents.

antenna in radio and television, another name for *aerial.

anthem in music, a short, usually elaborate, religious choral composition, sometimes accompanied by the organ; also a song of loyalty and devotion.

anther in a flower, the terminal part of a stamen in which the *pollen grains are produced. It is usually borne on a slender stalk or filament, and has two lobes, each containing two chambers, or pollen sacs, within which the pollen is formed.

antheridium organ producing the male gametes, *antherozoids, in algae, bryophytes (mosses and liverworts), and pteridophytes (ferns, club mosses, and horsetails). It may be either single-celled, as in most algae, or multicellular, as in bryophytes and pteridophytes.

antherozoid motile (or independently moving) male gamete produced by algae, bryophytes (mosses and liverworts), pteridophytes (ferns, club mosses, and horsetails), and some gymnosperms (notably the cycads). Antherozoids are formed in an antheridium and, after being released, swim, by means of one *flagellum or more, to the female gametes. Higher plants have nonmotile male gametes contained within *pollen grains.

Anthony Susan B(rownell) 1820–1906. US pioneering campaigner for women's rights who also worked for the antislavery and temperance movements. Her causes included equality of pay for women teachers, married women's property rights, and women's suffrage. In 1869, with Elizabeth Cady *Stanton, she founded the National Woman Suffrage Association.

Anthony, St *c.* 251–356. Also known as Anthony of Thebes. He was the founder of Christian monasticism. At the age of 20, he renounced all his possessions and began a hermetic life of study and prayer, later seeking further solitude in a cave in the desert.

anthracite (from Greek *anthrax*, 'coal') hard, dense, shiny variety of *coal, containing over 90% carbon and a low percentage of ash and impurities, which causes it to burn without flame, smoke, or smell.

anthrax cattle and sheep disease occasionally transmitted to humans, usually via infected hides and fleeces. It may develop as black skin pustules or severe pneumonia. Treatment is with antibiotics.

anthropology (Greek *anthropos* 'man' and *logos* 'discourse') study of humankind, which developed following 19th-century evolutionary theory to investigate the human species, past and present, physically, socially, and culturally.

anthropomorphism the attribution of human characteristics to animals, inanimate objects, or deities. It appears in the mythologies of many cultures and as a literary device in fables and allegories.

antibiotic drug that kills or inhibits the growth of bacteria and fungi. It is derived from living organisms such as fungi or bacteria, which distinguishes it from synthetic antimicrobials.

antibody protein molecule produced in the blood by *lymphocytes in response to the presence of invading substances, or *antigens, including the proteins carried on the surface of microorganisms. Antibody production is only one aspect of *immunity in vertebrates.

anticholinergic any drug that blocks the passage of certain nerve impulses in the *central nervous system by inhibiting the production of acetylcholine, a neurotransmitter.

Antichrist in Christian theology, the opponent of Christ. The appearance of the Antichrist was believed to signal the Second Coming, at which Christ would conquer his opponent. The concept may stem from the idea of conflict between Light and Darkness, which is present in Persian, Babylonian, and Jewish literature and which influenced early Christian thought.

anticline in geology, a fold in the rocks of the Earth's crust in which the layers or beds bulge upwards to form an arch (seldom preserved intact).

anticoagulant substance that suppresses the formation of blood clots. Common anticoagulants are heparin, produced by the liver and lungs, and derivatives of coumarin. Anticoagulants are used medically in treating heart attacks, for example. They are also produced by blood-feeding animals, such as mosquitoes, leeches, and vampire bats, to keep the victim's blood flowing.

anticonvulsant any drug used to prevent epileptic seizures (convulsions or fits); see *epilepsy.

Anti-Corn Law League in UK history, an extra-parliamentary pressure group formed 1838, led by the Liberals *Cobden and *Bright, which argued for free trade and campaigned successfully against duties on the import of foreign corn to Britain imposed by the *Corn Laws, which were repealed 1846.

anticyclone area of high atmospheric pressure caused by descending air, which becomes warm and dry. Winds radiate from a calm centre, taking a clockwise direction in the northern hemisphere and an anticlockwise direction in the southern hemisphere. Anticyclones are characterized by clear weather and the absence of rain and violent winds. In summer they bring hot, sunny days and in winter they bring fine, frosty spells, although fog and low cloud are not uncommon in the UK. *Blocking anticyclones*, which prevent the normal air circulation of an area, can cause summer droughts and severe winters.

antidepressant any drug used to relieve symptoms in depressive illness. The two main groups are the tricyclic antidepressants (TCADs) and the monoamine oxidase inhibitors (MAOIs), which act by altering chemicals available to the central nervous system. Both may produce serious side effects and are restricted.

anti-emetic any substance that counteracts nausea or vomiting.

antifreeze substance added to a water-cooling system (for example, that of a car) to prevent it freezing in cold weather.

antifungal any drug that acts against fungal infection, such as ringworm and athlete's foot.

antigen any substance that causes the production of *antibodies by the body's immune system. Common antigens include the proteins carried on the surface of bacteria, viruses, and pollen grains. The proteins of incompatible blood groups or tissues also act as antigens, which has to be taken into account in medical procedures such as blood transfusions and organ transplants.

Antigone in Greek legend, a daughter of Jocasta, by her son *Oedipus. She is the subject of a tragedy by Sophocles.

Antigonus 382–301 BC. A general of Alexander the Great, after whose death 323 Antigonus made himself master of Asia Minor. He was defeated and slain by *Seleucus I at the battle of Ipsus.

Antigua and Barbuda State of
area Antigua 280 sq km/108 sq mi, Barbuda 161 sq km/62 sq mi, plus Redonda 1 sq km/0.4 sq mi
capital and chief port St John's
towns Codrington (on Barbuda)
physical low-lying tropical islands of limestone and coral with some higher volcanic outcrops; no rivers and low rainfall result in frequent droughts and deforestation
head of state Elizabeth II from 1981, represented by governor general James B Carlisle from 1993
head of government Lester Bird from 1993
political system liberal democracy
exports sea-island cotton, rum, lobsters
currency Eastern Caribbean dollar
population (1993 est) 77,000; growth rate 1.3% p.a.
language English
religion Christian (mostly Anglican)
GNP $4,770 per head (1991)
chronology
1493 Antigua visited by Christopher Columbus.
1632 Antigua colonized by English settlers.
1667 Treaty of Breda formally ceded Antigua to Britain.
1871–1956 Antigua and Barbuda administered as part of the Leeward Islands federation.
1967 Antigua and Barbuda became an associated state within the Commonwealth, with full internal independence.
1971 PLM won the general election by defeating the ALP.
1976 PLM called for early independence, but ALP urged caution. ALP won the general election.

1981 Independence from Britain achieved.
1983 Assisted US invasion of Grenada.
1984 ALP won a decisive victory in the general election and were re-elected 1985.
1989 ALP re-elected under Vere Bird.
1991 Bird resisted calls for his resignation.
1993 and 1994 Lester Bird and ALP re-elected.

antihistamine any substance that counteracts the effects of *histamine. Antihistamines may be naturally produced (such as vitamin C and epinephrin) or synthesized (pseudepinephrin).

anti-inflammatory any substance that reduces swelling in soft tissues. Antihistamines relieve allergic reactions; aspirin and nonsteroidal anti-inflammatory drugs are effective in joint and musculoskeletal conditions; rubefacients (counterirritant liniments) ease painful joints, tendons, and muscles.

antiknock substance added to petrol to reduce knocking in car engines. It is a mixture of dibromoethane and tetraethyl lead.

Antilles whole group of West Indian islands, divided N–S into the *Greater Antilles* (Cuba, Jamaica, Haiti–Dominican Republic, Puerto Rico) and *Lesser Antilles*, subdivided into the Leeward Islands (Virgin Islands, St Kitts–Nevis, Antigua and Barbuda, Anguilla, Montserrat, and Guadeloupe) and the Windward Islands (Dominica, Martinique, St Lucia, St Vincent and the Grenadines, Barbados, and Grenada).

antimatter in physics, a form of matter in which most of the attributes (such as electrical charge, magnetic moment, and spin) of *elementary particles are reversed. Such particles (antiparticles) can be created in particle accelerators, such as those at *CERN in Geneva, Switzerland, and at Fermilab in Illinois, USA.

antimony silver-white, brittle, semimetallic element (a metalloid), symbol Sb (from Latin *stibium*), atomic number 51, relative atomic mass 121.75. It occurs chiefly as the ore stibnite, and is used to make alloys harder; it is also used in photosensitive substances in colour photography, optical electronics, fireproofing, pigment, and medicine. It was employed by the ancient Egyptians in a mixture to protect the eyes from flies.

antinode in physics, the position in a *standing wave pattern at which the amplitude of vibration is greatest (compare *node). The standing wave of a stretched string vibrating in the fundamental mode has one antinode at its midpoint. A vibrating air column in a pipe has an antinode at the pipe's open end and at the place where the vibration is produced.

Antioch ancient capital of the Greek kingdom of Syria, founded 300 BC by Seleucus Nicator in memory of his father Antiochus, and famed for its splendour and luxury. Under the Roman and Byzantine empires it was an early centre of Christianity. It was captured by the Arabs 637. After a five-month siege 1098 Antioch was taken by the crusaders, who held it until 1268. The site is now occupied by the Turkish town of Antakya.

Antiochus thirteen kings of Syria of the Seleucid dynasty, including:

Antiochus I *c.* 324–*c.* 261 BC. King of Syria from 281 BC, son of Seleucus I, one of the generals of Alexander the Great. He earned the title of Antiochus Soter, or Saviour, by his defeat of the Gauls in Galatia 278.

Antiochus II c. 286–c. 246 BC. King of Syria 261–246 BC, son of Antiochus I. He was known as Antiochus Theos, the Divine. During his reign the eastern provinces broke away from the Graeco-Macedonian rule and set up native princes. He made peace with Egypt by marrying the daughter of Ptolemy Philadelphus, but was a tyrant among his own people.

Antiochus III the Great c. 241–187 BC. King of Syria from 223 BC, nephew of Antiochus II. He secured a loose suzerainty over Armenia and Parthia 209, overcame Bactria, received the homage of the Indian king of the Kabul valley, and returned by way of the Persian Gulf 204. He took possession of Palestine, entering Jerusalem 198. He crossed into NW Greece, but was decisively defeated by the Romans at Thermopylae 191 and at Magnesia 190. He had to abandon his domains in Anatolia, and was killed by the people of Elymais.

Antiochus IV c. 215–164 BC. King of Syria from 175 BC, known as Antiochus Epiphanes, the Illustrious; second son of Antiochus III. He occupied Jerusalem about 170, seizing much of the Temple treasure, and instituted worship of the Greek type in the Temple in an attempt to eradicate Judaism. This produced the revolt of the Hebrews under the Maccabees; Antiochus died before he could suppress it.

Antiochus VII Sidetes c. 159–129 BC. King of Syria from 138 BC. The last strong ruler of the Seleucid dynasty, he took Jerusalem 134, reducing the Maccabees to subjection, and fought successfully against the Parthians.

Antiochus XIII Asiaticus 1st century BC. King of Syria 69–65 BC, the last of the Seleucid dynasty. During his reign Syria was made a Roman province by Pompey the Great.

antioxidant any substance that prevents deterioration by oxidation in fats, oils, paints, plastics, and rubbers. When used as *food additives, antioxidants prevent fats and oils from becoming rancid when exposed to air, and thus extend their shelf life.

antiparticle in nuclear physics, a particle corresponding in mass and properties to a given *elementary particle but with the opposite electrical charge, magnetic properties, or coupling to other fundamental forces. For example, an electron carries a negative charge whereas its antiparticle, the positron, carries a positive one. When a particle and its antiparticle collide, they destroy each other, in the process called 'annihilation', their total energy being converted to lighter particles and/or photons. A substance consisting entirely of antiparticles is known as *antimatter.

antiphony in music, a form of composition using widely spaced choirs or groups of instruments to create perspectives in sound. It was developed in 17th-century Venice by organist Giovanni Gabrieli (c. 1555–1612) and his German pupil Heinrich Schütz (1585–1672).

antipodes (Greek 'opposite feet') places at opposite points on the globe.

antipope rival claimant to the elected pope for the leadership of the Roman Catholic Church, for instance in the Great Schism 1378–1417 when there were rival popes in Rome and Avignon.

antipruritic any skin preparation or drug administered to relieve itching.

antipyretic any drug, such as aspirin, used to reduce fever.

anti-Semitism literally, prejudice against Semitic people (see *Semite), but in practice it has meant prejudice or discrimination against, and persecution of, the Jews as an ethnic group. Historically this was practised for almost 2,000 years by European Christians. Anti-Semitism was a tenet of Hitler's Germany, and in the Holocaust 1933–45 about 6 million Jews died in concentration camps and in local extermination *pogroms, such as the siege of the Warsaw ghetto. In eastern Europe, as well as in Islamic nations, anti-Semitism exists and is promulgated by neofascist groups. It is a form of *racism.

antiseptic any substance that kills or inhibits the growth of microorganisms. The use of antiseptics was pioneered by Joseph *Lister. He used carbolic acid (*phenol), which is a weak antiseptic; substances such as TCP are derived from this.

antispasmodic any drug that reduces motility, the spontaneous action of the muscle walls. *Anticholinergics are a type of antispasmodic that act indirectly by way of the autonomic nervous system, which controls involuntary movement. Other drugs act directly on the smooth muscle to relieve spasm (contraction).

antitrust laws in economics, regulations preventing or restraining trusts, monopolies, or any business practice considered to be unfair or uncompetitive. In the US, antitrust laws prevent mergers and acquisitions that might create a monopoly situation or ones in which restrictive practices might be stimulated.

antitussive any substance administered to suppress a cough. Coughing, however, is an important reflex in clearing secretions from the airways; its suppression is usually unnecessary and possibly harmful, unless damage is being done to tissue during excessive cough spasms.

antiviral any drug that acts against viruses, usually preventing them from multiplying. Most viral infections are not susceptible to antibiotics. Antivirals have been difficult drugs to develop, and do not necessarily cure viral diseases.

antivivisection opposition to vivisection, that is, experiments on living animals, which is practised in the pharmaceutical and cosmetics industries on the grounds that it may result in discoveries of importance to medical science. Antivivisectionists argue that it is immoral to inflict pain on helpless creatures, and that it is unscientific because results achieved with animals may not be paralleled with human beings.

antler 'horn' of a deer, often branched, and made of bone rather than horn. Antlers, unlike true horns, are shed and regrown each year. Reindeer of both sexes grow them, but in all other types of deer, only the males have antlers.

ant lion larva of one of the insects of the family Myrmeleontidae, order Neuroptera, which traps ants by waiting at the bottom of a pit dug in loose, sandy soil. Ant lions are mainly tropical, but also occur in parts of Europe and in the USA, where they are called doodlebugs.

Antofagasta port of N Chile, capital of the region of Antofagasta; population (1990) 218,800. The area of the region is 125,300 sq km/ 48,366 sq mi; its population (1982) 341,000. Nitrates from the Atacama Desert are exported.

Antonello da Messina c. 1430–1479. Italian painter, born in Messina, Sicily, a pioneer of the technique of oil painting, which he is said to have introduced to Italy from N Europe. Flemish influence is reflected in his technique, his use of light, and sometimes in his imagery. Surviving works include bust-length portraits and sombre religious paintings.

Antonine Wall Roman line of fortification built AD 142–200. It was the Roman Empire's northwest frontier, between the Clyde and Forth rivers, Scotland.

Antoninus Pius AD 86–161. Roman emperor who had been adopted 138 as Hadrian's heir, and succeeded him later that year. He enjoyed a prosperous reign, during which he built the Antonine Wall. His daughter married *Marcus Aurelius Antoninus.

Antonioni Michelangelo 1912– . Italian film director, famous for his subtle presentations of neuroses and personal relationships among the leisured classes. His work includes *L'Avventura* 1960, *Blow Up* 1966, and *The Passenger* 1975.

antonymy near or precise oppositeness between or among words. *Good* and *evil* are antonyms, and therefore *evil* and *bad* are synonyms in this context.

Antrim county of Northern Ireland
area 2,830 sq km/1,092 sq mi
towns Belfast (county town), Larne (port)
products potatoes, oats, linen, synthetic textiles
population (1981) 642,000.

Antwerp (Flemish **Antwerpen**, French **Anvers**) port in Belgium on the river Scheldt, capital of the province of Antwerp; population (1991) 467,500. One of the world's busiest ports, it has shipbuilding, oil-refining, petrochemical, textile, and diamond-cutting industries. The home of the artist Rubens is preserved, and many of his works are in the Gothic cathedral. The province of Antwerp has an area of 2,900 sq km/ 1,119 sq mi; population (1987) 1,588,000.

Anubis in Egyptian mythology, the jackal-headed god of the dead, son of Osiris. Anubis presided over the funeral cult, including embalming, and led the dead to judgement.

anus opening at the end of the alimentary canal that allows undigested food and associated materials to pass out of an animal. It is found in all types of multicellular animal except the coelenterates (sponges) and the platyhelminthes (flat worms), which have a mouth only.

anxiety emotional state of fear or apprehension. Anxiety is a normal response to potentially dangerous situations. Abnormal anxiety can either be free-floating, experienced in a wide range of situations, or it may be phobic, when the sufferer is excessively afraid of an object or situation.

anxiolytic any drug that reduces an anxiety state.

ANZAC (acronym for **Australian and New Zealand Army Corps**) general term for all troops of both countries serving in World War I and to some extent those in World War II.

Anzio, Battle of in World War II, the beachhead invasion of Italy 22 Jan–23 May 1944 by Allied troops; failure to use information gained by deciphering German codes (see *Ultra) led to Allied troops being stranded temporarily after German attacks. Anzio is a seaport and resort on the W coast of Italy, 53 km/33 mi SE of Rome; population (1984) 25,000. It is the site of the Roman town of Antium and the birthplace of Emperor Nero.

aorta the chief *artery, the dorsal blood vessel carrying oxygenated blood from the left ventricle of the heart in birds and mammals. It branches to form smaller arteries, which in turn supply all body organs except the lungs. Loss of elasticity in the aorta provides evidence of *atherosclerosis, which may lead to heart disease.

Aotearoa (Maori 'land of the long white cloud') Maori name for *New Zealand.

Aouita Said 1960– . Moroccan runner. Outstanding at middle and long distances, he won the 1984 Olympic and 1987 World Championship 5,000-metres title, and has set many world records.

Aoun Michel 1935– . Lebanese soldier and Maronite Christian politician, president 1988–90. As commander of the Lebanese army, he was made president without Muslim support, his appointment precipitating a civil war between Christians and Muslims. His unwillingness to accept a 1989 Arab League-sponsored peace agreement increased his isolation until the following year when he surrendered to military pressure. He left the country 1991 and was pardoned by the new government the same year.

Apache member of a group of North *American Indian peoples who lived as hunters in the Southwest. They are related to the Navajo, and now number about 10,000, living in reservations in Arizona, SW Oklahoma, and New Mexico. They were known as fierce raiders and horse warriors in the 18th and 19th centuries. Apache also refers to any of several southern Athabaskan languages and dialects spoken by these people.

apartheid racial-segregation policy of the government of South Africa, legislated 1948, when the Afrikaner National Party gained power. Nonwhites – classified as Bantu (black), coloured (mixed), or Indian – did not share full rights of citizenship with the 4.5 million whites (for example, the 23 million black people could not vote in parliamentary elections), and many public facilities and institutions were until 1990 restricted to one race only; the establishment of *Black National States was another manifestation of apartheid. In 1991 President de Klerk repealed the key elements of apartheid legislation and by 1994 apartheid had ceased to exist.

apatite common calcium phosphate mineral, $Ca_5(PO_4CO_3)_3(F,OH,Cl)$. Apatite has a hexagonal structure and occurs widely in igneous rocks, such as pegmatite, and in contact metamorphic rocks, such as marbles. It is used in the manufacture of fertilizer and as a source of phosphorus. Apatite is the chief constituent of tooth enamel while hydroxyapatite, $Ca_{10}(PO_4)_6(OH)_2$, is the chief inorganic constituent of bone marrow. Apatite ranks 5 on the *Mohs' scale of hardness.

apatosaurus large plant-eating dinosaur, formerly called **brontosaurus**, which flourished about 145 million years ago. Up to 21 m/69 ft long and 30 tonnes in weight, it stood on four elephantlike legs and had a long tail, long neck, and small head. It probably snipped off low-growing vegetation with peglike front teeth, and swallowed it whole to be ground by pebbles in the stomach.

ape *primate of the family Pongidae, closely related to humans, including gibbon, orang-utan, chimpanzee, and gorilla.

Apennines chain of mountains stretching the length of the Italian peninsula. A continuation of the Maritime Alps, from Genoa it swings across the peninsula to Ancona on the E coast, and then back to the W coast and into the 'toe' of Italy. The system is continued over the Strait of Messina along the N Sicilian coast, then across the Mediterranean Sea in a series of islands to the Atlas Mountains of N Africa. The highest peak is Gran Sasso d'Italia at 2,914 m/9,560 ft.

aperture in photography, an opening in the camera that allows light to pass through the lens to strike the film. Controlled by shutter speed and the iris diaphragm, it can be set mechanically or electronically at various diameters.

aphasia difficulty in speaking, writing, and reading, usually caused by damage to the brain.

aphelion the point at which an object, travelling in an elliptical orbit around the Sun, is at its furthest from the Sun.

aphid any of the family of small insects, Aphididae, in the order Homoptera, that live by sucking sap from plants. There are many species, often adapted to particular plants.

Aphrodite in Greek mythology, the goddess of love (Roman Venus, Phoenician Astarte, Babylonian Ishtar); said to be either a daughter of Zeus (in Homer) or sprung from the foam of the sea (in Hesiod). She was the unfaithful wife of Hephaestus, the god of fire, and the mother of Eros.

Apia capital and port of Western *Samoa, on the N coast of Upolu Island, in the W Pacific; population (1981) 33,000. It was the final home of the writer Robert Louis Stevenson from 1888–94.

Apis ancient Egyptian god with a human body and a bull's head, linked with Osiris (and later merged with him into the Ptolemaic god Serapis); his cult centres were Memphis and Heliopolis, where sacred bulls were mummified.

Apocrypha appendix to the Old Testament of the Bible, not included in the final Hebrew canon but recognized by Roman Catholics. There are also disputed New Testament texts known as Apocrypha.

apogee the point at which an object, travelling in an elliptical orbit around the Earth, is at its furthest from the Earth.

Apollinaire Guillaume. Pen name of Guillaume Apollinaire de Kostrowitsky 1880–1918. French poet of aristocratic Polish descent. He was a leader of the avant-garde in Parisian literary and artistic circles. His novel *Le Poète assassiné/The Poet Assassinated* 1916, followed by the experimental poems *Alcools/Alcohols* 1913 and *Calligrammes/Word Pictures* 1918, show

him as a representative of the Cubist and Futurist movements.

Apollo in Greek and Roman mythology, the god of sun, music, poetry, prophecy, agriculture, and pastoral life, and leader of the Muses. He was the twin child (with Artemis) of Zeus and Leto. Ancient statues show Apollo as the embodiment of the Greek ideal of male beauty.

Apollo asteroid member of a group of *asteroids whose orbits cross that of the Earth. They are named after the first of their kind, Apollo, discovered 1932 and then lost until 1973. Apollo asteroids are so small and faint that they are difficult to see except when close to Earth (Apollo is about 2 km/1.2 mi across).

Apollonius of Perga c. 260–c. 190 BC. Greek mathematician, called 'the Great Geometer'. In his work *Conic Sections* he showed that a plane intersecting a cone will generate an ellipse, a parabola, or a hyperbola, depending on the angle of intersection. In astronomy, he used a system of circles called epicycles and deferents to explain the motion of the planets; this system, as refined by Ptolemy, was used until the Renaissance.

Apollonius of Rhodes c. 220–180 BC. Greek poet, author of the epic *Argonautica*, which tells the story of Jason and the Argonauts and their quest for the Golden Fleece.

Apollo project US space project to land a person on the Moon, achieved 20 July 1969, when Neil Armstrong was the first to set foot there. He was accompanied on the Moon surface by Col Edwin E Aldrin Jr; Michael Collins remained in the orbiting command module.

Apo, Mount active volcano and highest peak in the Philippines, rising to 2,954 m/9,692 ft on the island of Mindanao.

aposematic coloration in biology, the technical name for *warning coloration markings that make a dangerous, poisonous, or foul-tasting animal particularly conspicuous and recognizable to a predator. Examples include the yellow and black stripes of bees and wasps, and the bright red or yellow colours of many poisonous frogs. See also *mimicry.

a posteriori (Latin 'from the latter') in logic, an argument that deduces causes from their effects; inductive reasoning; the converse of *a priori.

apostle (Greek 'messenger') in the New Testament, any of the chosen 12 *disciples sent out by Jesus after his resurrection to preach the Gospel. In the earliest days of Christianity the term was extended to include some who had never known Jesus in the flesh, notably St Paul.

Apostles' Creed one of the three ancient *creeds of the Christian church.

apostolic succession doctrine in the Christian church that certain spiritual powers were received by the first apostles directly from Jesus, and have been handed down in the ceremony of 'laying on of hands' from generation to generation of bishops.

apostrophe mark (') used in written English and some other languages. In English it serves primarily to indicate either a missing letter (*mustn't* for *must not*) or number ('*47* for *1947*), or grammatical possession ('*John's* camera', '*women's* dresses'). It is often omitted in proper names (Publishers Association, Actors Studio,

Collins Dictionary). Many people otherwise competent in writing have great difficulty with the apostrophe, which has never been stable at any point in its history.

apothecaries' weights obsolete units of mass, formerly used in pharmacy: 20 grains made one scruple; three scruples made one drachm; eight drachms made an apothecary's ounce (oz apoth.), and 12 such ounces made an apothecary's pound (lb apoth.). There are 7,000 grains in one pound avoirdupois (0.454 kg).

apothecary person who prepares and dispenses medicines; a pharmacist.

Appalachians mountain system of E North America, stretching about 2,400 km/1,500 mi from Alabama to Québec, composed of very ancient eroded rocks. The chain includes the Allegheny, Catskill, and Blue Ridge mountains, the last-named having the highest peak, Mount Mitchell, 2,045 m/6,712 ft. The eastern edge has a fall line to the coastal plain where Philadelphia, Baltimore, and Washington stand.

appeal in law, an application for a rehearing of all or part of an issue that has already been dealt with by a lower court or tribunal. The outcome can be a new decision on all or part of the points raised, or the previous decision may be upheld. In criminal cases, an appeal may be against conviction and either the prosecution or the defence may appeal against sentence.

appeasement historically, the conciliatory policy adopted by the British government, in particular under Neville Chamberlain, towards the Nazi and Fascist dictators in Europe in the 1930s in an effort to maintain peace. It was strongly opposed by Winston Churchill, but the *Munich Agreement 1938 was almost universally hailed as its justification. Appeasement ended when Germany occupied Bohemia–Moravia March 1939.

appendicitis inflammation of the appendix, a small, blind extension of the bowel in the lower right abdomen. In an acute attack, the pus-filled appendix may burst, causing a potentially lethal spread of infection (peritonitis). Treatment is by removal (appendectomy).

appendix area of the mammalian gut, associated with the digestion of cellulose. In herbivores it may be large, containing millions of bacteria that secrete enzymes to digest grass. No vertebrate can produce the type of digestive enzyme that will digest cellulose, the main constituent of plant cell walls. Those herbivores that rely on cellulose for their energy have all evolved specialist mechanisms to make use of the correct type of bacteria.

apple fruit of *Malus pumila*, a tree of the family Rosaceae. There are several hundred varieties of cultivated apples, grown all over the world, which may be divided into eating, cooking, and cider apples. All are derived from the wild crab apple.

Appleton layer band containing ionized gases in the Earth's upper atmosphere, above the *E layer (formerly the Kennelly–Heaviside layer). It can act as a reflector of radio signals, although its ionic composition varies with the sunspot cycle. It is named after the English physicist Edward Appleton.

application in computing, a program or job designed for the benefit of the end user, such as a payroll system or a *word processor. The term is used to distinguish such programs from those that control the computer or assist the programmer, such as a *compiler.

applications package in computing, the set of programs and related documentation (such as instruction manuals) used in a particular application. For example, a typical payroll applications package would consist of separate programs for the entry of data, updating the master files, and printing the pay slips, plus documentation in the form of program details and instructions for use.

appliqué embroidery used to create pictures or patterns by 'applying' pieces of material onto a background fabric. The pieces are cut into the appropriate shapes and sewn on, providing decoration for wall hangings, furnishing textiles, and clothes.

Appomattox village in Virginia, USA, scene of the surrender 9 April 1865 of the Confederate army under Robert E Lee to the Union army under Ulysses S Grant, which ended the American Civil War.

APR abbreviation for *annual percentage rate*.

apricot fruit of *Prunus armeniaca*, a tree of the rose family Rosaceae, closely related to the almond, peach, plum, and cherry. It has yellow-fleshed fruit. Although native to the Far East, it has long been cultivated in Armenia, from where it was introduced into Europe and the USA.

April Fools' Day the first day of April, when it is customary in W Europe and the USA to expose people to ridicule by a practical joke, causing them to believe some falsehood or to go on a fruitless errand.

a priori (Latin 'from what comes before') in logic, an argument that is known to be true, or false, without reference to experience; the converse of *a posteriori.

Apuleius Lucius lived c. AD 160. Roman lawyer, philosopher, and author of *Metamorphoses*, or *The *Golden Ass*.

Apulia English form of *Puglia, region of Italy.

Aqaba, Gulf of gulf extending for 160 km/100 mi between the Negev and the Red Sea; its coastline is uninhabited except at its head, where the frontiers of Israel, Egypt, Jordan, and Saudi Arabia converge. The two ports of Eilat (Israeli 'Elath') and Aqaba, Jordan's only port, are situated here.

aquaculture or *fish farming* raising fish and shellfish (molluscs and crustaceans) under controlled conditions in tanks and ponds, sometimes in offshore pens. It has been practised for centuries in the Far East, where Japan alone produces some 100,000 tonnes of fish a year. In the 1980s one-tenth of the world's consumption of fish was farmed, notably carp, catfish, trout, salmon, turbot, eel, mussels, clams, oysters, and shrimp.

aqualung or *scuba* underwater breathing apparatus worn by divers, developed in the early 1940s by French diver Jacques Cousteau. Compressed-air cylinders strapped to the diver's back are regulated by a valve system and by a mouth tube to provide air to the diver at the same pressure as that of the surrounding water (which increases with the depth).

aquamarine blue variety of the mineral *beryl. A semiprecious gemstone, it is used in jewellery.

aquaplaning phenomenon in which the tyres of a road vehicle cease to make direct contact with the road surface, owing to the presence of a thin film of water. As a result, the vehicle can go out of control (particularly if the steered wheels are involved).

Aquarius zodiacal constellation a little south of the celestial equator near Pegasus. Aquarius is represented as a man pouring water from a jar. The Sun passes through Aquarius from late Feb to early March. In astrology, the dates for Aquarius are between about 20 Jan and 18 Feb (see *precession).

aquatint printmaking technique, usually combined with *etching to produce areas of subtle tone as well as more precisely etched lines. Aquatint became common in the late 18th century.

aqueduct any artificial channel or conduit for water, often an elevated structure of stone, wood, or iron built for conducting water across a valley. The Greeks built a tunnel 1,280 m/4,200 ft long near Athens, 2,500 years ago. Many Roman aqueducts are still standing, for example the one at Nîmes in S France, built about AD 18 (which is 48 m/160 ft high).

aqueous humour watery fluid found in the space between the cornea and lens of the vertebrate eye. Similar to blood serum in composition, it is renewed every four hours.

aqueous solution solution in which the solvent is water.

aquifer any rock formation containing water. The rock of an aquifer must be porous and permeable (full of interconnected holes) so that it can absorb water. Aquifers supply *artesian wells, and are actively sought in arid areas as sources of drinking and irrigation water.

Aquila constellation on the celestial equator (see *celestial sphere). Its brightest star is first-magnitude *Altair, flanked by the stars Beta and Gamma Aquilae. It is represented by an eagle.

Aquinas St Thomas c. 1226–1274. Neapolitan philosopher and theologian, the greatest figure of the school of *Scholasticism. He was a Dominican monk, known as the 'Angelic Doctor'. In 1879 his works were recognized as the basis of Catholic theology. His *Summa contra Gentiles/Against the Errors of the Infidels* 1259–64 argues that reason and faith are compatible. He assimilated the philosophy of Aristotle into Christian doctrine.

Aquino (Maria) Corazon (born Cojuangco) 1933– . President of the Philippines 1986–92. She was instrumental in the nonviolent overthrow of President Ferdinand Marcos 1986. As president, she sought to rule in a conciliatory manner, but encountered opposition from left (communist guerrillas) and right (army coup attempts), and her land reforms were seen as inadequate.

Aquitaine region of SW France; capital Bordeaux; area 41,300 sq km/15,942 sq mi; population (1986) 2,718,000. It comprises the *départements* of Dordogne, Gironde, Landes, Lot-et-Garonne, and Pyrénées-Atlantiques. Red wines (Margaux, St Julien) are produced in the Médoc district, bordering the Gironde. Aquitaine was an English possession 1152–1452.

Arab any of a Semitic (see *Semite) people native to the Arabian peninsula, but now settled throughout North Africa and the nations of the Middle East.

Arab Common Market organization providing for the abolition of customs duties on agricultural products, and reductions on other items, between the member states: Egypt, Iraq, Jordan, and Syria. It was founded 1965.

Arab Emirates see *United Arab Emirates.

arabesque in ballet, a pose in which the dancer stands on one leg, straight or bent, with the other leg raised behind, fully extended. The arms are held in a harmonious position to give the longest possible line from fingertips to toes. It is one of the fundamental positions in ballet.

Arabia peninsula between the Persian Gulf and the Red Sea, in SW Asia; area 2,600,000 sq km/1,000,000 sq mi. The peninsula contains the world's richest oil and gas deposits. It comprises the states of Bahrain, Kuwait, Oman, Qatar, Saudi Arabia, the United Arab Emirates, and Yemen.

Arabian Nights tales in oral circulation among Arab storytellers from the 10th century, probably of Indian origin. They are also known as *The Thousand and One Nights* and include 'Ali Baba', 'Aladdin', 'Sinbad the Sailor', and 'The Old Man of the Sea'.

Arabian Sea NW branch of the *Indian Ocean.

Arabic language major Semitic language of the Hamito-Semitic family of W Asia and North Africa, originating among the Arabs of the Arabian peninsula. It is spoken today by about 120 million people in the Middle East and N Africa. Arabic script is written from right to left.

Arabic numerals or **Hindu-Arabic numerals** the symbols 0, 1, 2, 3, 4, 5, 6, 7, 8, 9, early forms of which were in use among the Arabs before being adopted by the peoples of Europe during the Middle Ages in place of *Roman numerals. The symbols appear to have originated in India and probably reached Europe by way of Spain.

Arab-Israeli Wars series of wars between Israel and various Arab states in the Middle East since the founding of the state of Israel 1948.
First Arab-Israeli War 15 May 1948–13 Jan/24 March 1949. When the independent state of Israel was proclaimed by the Jews, it was invaded by combined Arab forces. The Israelis defeated them and went on to annex territory until they controlled 75% of what had been Palestine under British mandate.
Second Arab-Israeli War 29 Oct–4 Nov 1956. After Egypt had taken control of the Suez Canal and blockaded the Straits of Tiran, Israel, with British and French support, invaded and captured Sinai and the Gaza Strip, from which it withdrew under heavy US pressure after the entry of a United Nations force.
Third Arab-Israeli War 5–10 June 1967, the **Six-Day War**. It resulted in the Israeli capture of the Golan Heights from Syria; the eastern half of Jerusalem and the West Bank from Jordan; and, in the south, the Gaza Strip and Sinai peninsula as far as the Suez Canal.

Fourth Arab-Israeli War 6–24 Oct 1973, the 'October War' or **Yom Kippur War**, so called because the Israeli forces were taken by surprise on the Day of *Atonement. It started with the recrossing of the Suez Canal by Egyptian forces who made initial gains, though there was some later loss of ground by the Syrians in the north.

Fifth Arab-Israeli War From 1978 the presence of Palestinian guerrillas in Lebanon led to Arab raids on Israel and Israeli retaliatory incursions, but on 6 June 1982 Israel launched a full-scale invasion. By 14 June Beirut was encircled, and *Palestine Liberation Organization (PLO) and Syrian forces were evacuated (mainly to Syria) 21–31 Aug, but in Feb 1985 there was a unilateral Israeli withdrawal from the country without any gain or losses incurred. Israel maintains a 'security zone' in S Lebanon and supports the South Lebanese Army militia as a buffer against Palestinian guerrilla incursions.

Arab League organization of Arab states established in Cairo 1945 to promote Arab unity, primarily in opposition to Israel. The original members were Egypt, Syria, Iraq, Lebanon, Transjordan (Jordan 1949), Saudi Arabia, and Yemen. They were later joined by Algeria, Bahrain, Djibouti, Kuwait, Libya, Mauritania, Morocco, Oman, Palestine, Qatar, Somalia, Sudan, Tunisia, and the United Arab Emirates.

arable farming cultivation of crops, as opposed to the keeping of animals. Crops may be *cereals, vegetables, or plants for producing oils or cloth. Arable farming generally requires less attention than livestock farming. In a *mixed farming system, crops may therefore be found farther from the farm centre than animals.

Arachne (Greek 'spider') in Greek mythology, a Lydian woman who was so skilful a weaver that she challenged the goddess Athena to a contest. Athena tore Arachne's beautiful tapestries to pieces and Arachne hanged herself. She was transformed into a spider, and her weaving became a cobweb.

arachnid or **arachnoid** type of arthropod, including spiders, scorpions, and mites. They differ from insects in possessing only two main body regions, the cephalothorax and the abdomen, and in having eight legs.

Arafat Yassir 1929– . Palestinian nationalist politician, cofounder of al-*Fatah 1957 and president of the *Palestine Liberation Organization (PLO) from 1969. His support for Saddam Hussein after Iraq's invasion of Kuwait 1990 weakened his international standing, but he was subsequently influential in the Middle East peace talks and in Sept 1993 reached a historic peace accord of mutual recognition with Israel, under which the Gaza Strip and Jericho were transferred to PLO control. In July 1994 he returned to the former occupied territories as head of an embryonic Palestinian state. He was awarded the 1994 Nobel Prize for Peace jointly with Yitzhak Rabin and Shimon Peres.

Aragon autonomous region of NE Spain including the provinces of Huesca, Teruel, and Zaragoza; area 47,700 sq km/18,412 sq mi; population (1986) 1,215,000. Its capital is Zaragoza, and products include almonds, figs, grapes, and olives. Aragón was an independent kingdom 1035–1479.

Aragon Louis 1897–1982. French poet and novelist. Beginning as a Dadaist, he became one of the leaders of Surrealism, published volumes of verse, and in 1930 joined the Communist Party. Taken prisoner in World War II, he escaped to join the Resistance; his experiences are reflected in the poetry of Le Crève-coeur 1942 and Les Yeux d'Elsa 1944.

Aral Sea inland sea divided between Kazakhstan and Uzbekistan, the world's fourth largest lake; former area 62,000 sq km/24,000 sq mi, but decreasing. Water from its tributaries, the Amu Darya and Syr Darya, has been diverted for irrigation and city use, and the sea is disappearing, with long-term consequences for the climate.

Aramaic language Semitic language of the Hamito-Semitic family of W Asia, the everyday language of Palestine 2,000 years ago, during the Roman occupation and the time of Jesus.

Aran Islands three rocky islands (Inishmore, Inishmaan, Inisheer) in the mouth of Galway Bay, Republic of Ireland; population approximately 4,600. The capital is Kilronan. J M *Synge used the language of the islands in his plays.

Ararat double-peaked mountain on the Turkish-Iranian border; the higher, Great Ararat, 5,137 m/16,854 ft, was the reputed resting place of Noah's Ark after the Flood.

araucaria coniferous tree of the genus Araucaria, allied to the firs, with flat, scalelike needles. Once widespread, it is now native only to the southern hemisphere. Some grow to gigantic size. Araucarias include the monkey-puzzle tree A. araucana, the Australian bunya bunya pine A. bidwillii, and the Norfolk Island pine A. heterophylla.

Arawak member of an indigenous American people of the Caribbean and NE Amazon Basin. Arawaks lived mainly by shifting cultivation in tropical forests. They were driven out of many West Indian islands by another American Indian people, the Caribs, shortly before the arrival of the Spanish in the 16th century. Subsequently, their numbers on *Hispaniola declined from some 4 million in 1492 to a few thousand after their exploitation by the Spanish in their search for gold; the remaining few were eradicated by disease (smallpox was introduced 1518). Arawakan languages belong to the Andean-Equatorial group.

Arbil Kurdish town in a province of the same name in N Iraq; population (1985) 334,000. Occupied since Assyrian times, it was the site of a battle 331 BC at which Alexander the Great defeated the Persians under Darius III. In 1974 Arbil became the capital of a Kurdish autonomous region set up by the Iraqi government.

arbitrageur in finance, a person who buys securities (such as currency or commodities) in one country or market for immediate resale in another market, to take advantage of different prices.

arbitration submission of a dispute to a third, unbiased party for settlement. It may be personal litigation, a trade-union issue, or an international dispute.

arboretum collection of trees. An arboretum

may contain a wide variety of species or just closely related species or varieties – for example, different types of pine tree.

arbor vitae any of several coniferous trees or shrubs of the genus *Thuja* of the cypress family, having flattened branchlets covered in overlapping aromatic green scales. In North America, the northern white cedar *Thuja occidentalis* and the western red cedar *T. plicata* are representatives. The Chinese or Oriental species *T. orientalis*, reaching 60 ft/18 m in height, is grown widely as an ornamental.

Arbuthnot John 1667–1735. Scottish writer and physician, attendant on Queen Anne 1705–14. He was a friend of Alexander Pope, Thomas Gray, and Jonathan Swift and was the chief author of the satiric *Memoirs of Martinus Scriblerus*. He created the English national character of John Bull, a prosperous farmer, in his *History of John Bull* 1712, pamphlets advocating peace with France.

arc in geometry, a section of a curved line or circle. A circle has three types of arc: a *semicircle*, which is exactly half of the circle; *minor arcs*, which are less than the semicircle; and *major arcs*, which are greater than the semicircle.

Arc de Triomphe arch at the head of the Champs Elysées in the Place de l'Etoile, Paris, France, begun by Napoleon 1806 and completed 1836. It was intended to commemorate Napoleon's victories of 1805–06 and commissioned from Jean Chalgrin (1739–1811). Beneath it rests France's 'Unknown Soldier'.

arch curved structure of masonry that supports the weight of material over an open space, as in a bridge or doorway. The first arches consisted of several wedge-shaped stones supported by their mutual pressure. The term is also applied to any curved structure that is an arch in form only.

Archaean or *Archaeozoic* the earliest period of geological time; the first part of the Precambrian era, from the formation of Earth up to about 2,500 million years ago. It was a time when no life existed, and with every new discovery of ancient life its upper boundary is being pushed further back.

archaebacteria three groups of bacteria whose DNA differs significantly from that of other bacteria (called the 'eubacteria'). All are strict anaerobes, that is, they are killed by oxygen. This is thought to be a primitive condition and to indicate that the archaebacteria are related to the earliest life forms, which appeared about 4 billion years ago, when there was little oxygen in the Earth's atmosphere.

archaeology study of history (primarily but not exclusively the prehistoric and ancient periods), based on the examination of physical remains. Principal activities include preliminary field (or site) surveys, excavation (where necessary), and the classification, dating, and interpretation of finds. Since 1958 radiocarbon dating has been used to establish the age of archaeological strata and associated materials.

archaeopteryx extinct primitive bird, known from fossilized remains, about 160 million years old, found in limestone deposits in Bavaria, Germany. It is popularly known as 'the first bird', although some earlier bird ancestors are now known. It was about the size of a crow and had feathers and wings, but in many respects its skeleton is reptilian (teeth and a long, bony tail) and very like some small meat-eating dinosaurs of the time.

archbishop in the Christian church, a bishop of superior rank who has authority over other bishops in his jurisdiction and often over an ecclesiastical province. The office exists in the Roman Catholic, Eastern Orthodox, and Anglican churches.

archdeacon originally an ordained dignitary of the Christian church charged with the supervision of the deacons attached to a cathedral. Today in the Roman Catholic church the office is purely titular; in the Church of England an archdeacon still has many business duties, such as the periodic inspection of churches. It is not found in other Protestant churches.

archegonium female sex organ found in bryophytes (mosses and liverworts), pteridophytes (ferns, club mosses, and horsetails), and some gymnosperms. It is a multicellular, flask-shaped structure consisting of two parts: the swollen base or venter containing the egg cell, and the long, narrow neck. When the egg cell is mature, the cells of the neck dissolve, allowing the passage of the male gametes, or *antherozoids.

archerfish surface-living fish of the family Toxotidae, such as the genus *Toxotes*, native to SE Asia and Australia. The archerfish grows to about 25 cm/10 in and is able to shoot down insects up to 1.5 m/5 ft above the water by spitting a jet of water from its mouth.

archery use of the bow and arrow, originally in hunting and warfare, now as a competitive sport. The world governing body is the Fédération Internationale de Tir à l'Arc (FITA) founded 1931. In competitions, results are based on double FITA rounds; that is, 72 arrows at each of four targets at 90, 70, 50, and 30 metres (70, 60, 50, and 30 for women). The best possible score is 2,880.

Archimedes *c.* 287–212 BC. Greek mathematician who made major discoveries in geometry, hydrostatics, and mechanics. He formulated a law of fluid displacement (Archimedes' principle), and is credited with the invention of the Archimedes screw, a cylindrical device for raising water.

Archimedes' principle in physics, law stating that an object totally or partly submerged in a fluid displaces a volume of fluid that weighs the same as the apparent loss in weight of the object (which, in turn, equals the upwards force, or upthrust, experienced by that object).

Archimedes screw one of the earliest kinds of pump, thought to have been invented by Archimedes. It consists of a spiral screw revolving inside a close-fitting cylinder. It is used, for example, to raise water for irrigation.

archipelago group of islands, or an area of sea containing a group of islands. The islands of an archipelago are usually volcanic in origin, and they sometimes represent the tops of peaks in areas around continental margins flooded by the sea.

Archipenko Alexander 1887–1964. Ukrainian-

ARCHAEOLOGY: CHRONOLOGY

14th–16th centuries	The Renaissance revived interest in Classical Greek and Roman art and architecture, including ruins and buried art and artefacts.
1748	The buried Roman city of Pompeii was discovered under lava from Vesuvius.
1784	Thomas Jefferson excavated an Indian burial mound on the Rivanna River in Virginia and wrote a report on his finds.
1790	John Frere identified Old Stone Age (Palaeolithic) tools and large extinct animals.
1822	Jean François Champollion deciphered Egyptian hieroglyphics.
1836	Christian Thomsen devised the Stone, Bronze, and Iron Age classification.
1840s	Austen Layard excavated the Assyrian capital of Nineveh.
1868	The Great Zimbabwe ruins in E Africa were first seen by Europeans.
1871	Heinrich Schliemann began excavations at Troy.
1879	Stone Age paintings were first discovered at Altamira, Spain.
1880s	Augustus Pitt-Rivers developed the concept of stratigraphy (identification of successive layers of soil within a site with successive archaeological stages; the most recent at the top).
1891	Flinders Petrie began excavating Akhetaton in Egypt.
1899–1935	Arthur Evans excavated Minoan Knossos in Crete.
1900–44	Max Uhle began the systematic study of the civilizations of Peru.
1911	The Inca city of Machu Picchu was discovered by Hiram Bingham in the Andes.
1911–12	The Piltdown skull was 'discovered'; it was proved to be a fake 1949.
1914–18	Osbert Crawford developed the technique of aerial survey of sites.
1917–27	John Eric Thompson (1898–1975) discovered the great Mayan sites in Yucatán, Mexico.
1922	Tutankhamen's tomb in Egypt was opened by Howard Carter.
1926	A kill site in Folsom, New Mexico, was found with human-made spearpoints in association with ancient bison.
1935	Dendrochronology (dating events in the distant past by counting tree rings) was developed by A E Douglas.
1939	An Anglo-Saxon ship-burial treasure was found at Sutton Hoo, England.
1947	The first of the Dead Sea Scrolls was discovered.
1948	The *Proconsul* prehistoric ape was discovered by Mary Leakey in Kenya.
1950s–1970s	Several early hominid fossils were found by Louis Leakey in Olduvai Gorge.
1953	Michael Ventris deciphered Minoan Linear B.
1960s	Radiocarbon and thermoluminescence measurement techniques were developed as aids for dating remains.
1961	The Swedish warship *Wasa* was raised at Stockholm.
1963	Walter Emery pioneered rescue archaeology at Abu Simbel before the site was flooded by the Aswan Dam.
1969	Human remains found at Lake Mungo, Australia, were dated at 26,000 years; earliest evidence of ritual cremation.
1974	The Tomb of Shi Huangdi was discovered in China. The footprints of a hominid called 'Lucy', 3 to 3.7 million years old, were found at Laetoli in Ethiopia.
1978	The tomb of Philip II of Macedon (Alexander the Great's father) was discovered in Greece.
1979	The Aztec capital Tenochtitlán was excavated beneath a zone of Mexico City.
1982	The English king Henry VIII's warship *Mary Rose* of 1545 was raised and studied with new techniques in underwater archaeology.
1985	The tomb of Maya, Tutankhamen's treasurer, was discovered at Saqqara, Egypt.
1989	The remains of the Globe and Rose theatres, where many of Shakespeare's plays were originally performed, were discovered in London.
1991	Body of man from 5300 years ago, with clothing, bow, arrows, a copper axe, and other implements, found preserved in Italian Alps.
1993	Charcoal drawings at Cosquer Cave, France, were dated by radiocarbon to 27,110 and c. 19,000 years ago, making this the oldest directly dated cave art in the world.

born abstract sculptor who lived in France from 1908 and in the USA from 1923. He pioneered Cubist works composed of angular forms and spaces and later experimented with clear plastic and sculptures incorporating lights.

architecture art of designing structures. The term covers the design of the visual appearance of structures; their internal arrangements of space; selection of external and internal building materials; design or selection of natural and artificial lighting systems, as well as mechanical, electrical, and plumbing systems; and design or selection of decorations and furnishings. Architectural style may emerge from evolution of techniques and styles particular to a culture in a given time period with or without identifiable individuals as architects, or may be attributed to specific individuals or groups of architects working together on a project.

archon (Greek 'ruler') in ancient Greece, title of the chief magistrate in many cities.

arc lamp or *arc light* electric light that uses the illumination of an electric arc maintained between two electrodes. The British scientist Humphry Davy developed an arc lamp 1808, and its main use in recent years has been in cinema projectors. The lamp consists of two carbon electrodes, between which a very high voltage is maintained. Electric current arcs (jumps) between the two, creating a brilliant light.

arc minute, arc second units for measuring small angles, used in geometry, surveying, map-making, and astronomy. An arc minute (symbol ') is one-sixtieth of a degree, and an arc second (symbol ″) is one-sixtieth of an arc minute. Small distances in the sky, as between two close stars or the apparent width of a planet's disc, are expressed in minutes and seconds of arc.

arco (Italian 'with the bow') in music, a direction that cancels a previous instruction to a bowed string player to play pizzicato (plucked string.)

Arctic, the that part of the northern hemisphere surrounding the North Pole; arbitrarily defined as the region lying N of the Arctic Circle (66° 32″N) or N of the tree line. There is no Arctic continent; the greater part of the region comprises the Arctic Ocean, which is the world's smallest ocean. Arctic climate, fauna, and flora extend over the islands and northern edges of continental land masses that surround the Arctic Ocean (Svalbard, Iceland, Greenland, Siberia, Scandinavia, Alaska, and Canada)
area 36,000,000 sq km/14,000,000 sq mi
physical pack-ice floating on the Arctic Ocean occupies almost the entire region between the North Pole and the coasts of North America and Eurasia, covering an area that ranges in diameter from 3,000 km/1,900 mi to 4,000 km/2,500 mi. The pack-ice reaches a maximum extent in Feb when its outer limit (influenced by the cold Labrador Current and the warm Gulf Stream) varies from 50°N along the coast of Labrador to 75°N in the Barents Sea N of Scandinavia. In spring the pack-ice begins to break up into ice floes which are carried by the south-flowing Greenland Current to the Atlantic Ocean. Arctic ice is at its minimum area in Aug. The greatest concentration of icebergs in Arctic regions is found in Baffin Bay. They are derived from the glaciers of W Greenland, then carried along Baffin Bay and down into the N Atlantic where they melt off Labrador and Newfoundland. The Bering Straits are icebound for more than six months each year, but the Barents Sea between Scandinavia and Svalbard is free of ice and is navigable throughout the year. Arctic coastlines, which have emerged from the sea since the last Ice Age, are characterized by deposits of gravel and disintegrated rock. The area covered by the Arctic icecap shrank 2% 1978–87
climate permanent ice sheets and year-round snow cover are found in regions where average monthly temperatures remain below 0°C/32°F, but on land areas where one or more summer months have average temperatures between freezing point and 10°C/50°F, a stunted, treeless tundra vegetation is found. Mean annual temperatures range from –23°C at the North Pole to –12°C on the coast of Alaska. In winter the Sun disappears below the horizon for a time, but the cold is less severe than in parts of inland Siberia or Antarctica. During the short summer season there is a maximum of 24 hours of daylight at the summer solstice on the Arctic Circle and six months' constant light at the North Pole. Countries with Arctic coastlines established the International Arctic Sciences Committee in 1987 to study ozone depletion and climatic change
flora and fauna the plants of the relatively infertile Arctic tundra (lichens, mosses, grasses, cushion plants, and low shrubs) spring to life during the short summer season and remain dormant for the remaining ten months of the year. There are no annual plants, only perennials. Animal species include reindeer, caribou, musk ox, fox, hare, lemming, wolf, polar bear, seal, and walrus. There are few birds except in summer when insects, such as mosquitoes, are plentiful
natural resources the Arctic is rich in coal (Svalbard, Russia), oil and natural gas (Alaska, Canadian Arctic, Russia), and mineral resources including gold, silver, copper, uranium, lead, zinc, nickel, and bauxite. Because of climatic conditions, the Arctic is not suited to navigation and the exploitation of these resources. Murmansk naval base on the Kola Peninsula is the largest in the world
population there are about 1 million aboriginal people including the Aleuts of Alaska, North American Indians, the Lapps of Scandinavia and Russia, the Yakuts, Samoyeds, Komi, Chukchi, Tungus, and Dolgany of Russia, and the Inuit of Siberian Russia, the Canadian Arctic and Greenland.

Arctic Circle imaginary line that encircles the North Pole at latitude 66° 32′ N. Within this line there is at least one day in the summer during which the Sun never sets, and at least one day in the winter during which the Sun never rises.

Arctic Ocean ocean surrounding the North Pole; area 14,000,000 sq km/5,400,000 sq mi. Because of the Siberian and North American rivers flowing into it, it has comparatively low salinity and freezes readily.

Arcturus or **Alpha Boötis** brightest star in the constellation Boötes and the fourth brightest star in the sky. Arcturus is a red giant about 28 times larger than the Sun and 70 times more luminous, 34 light years away from Earth.

Ardennes wooded plateau in NE France, SE Belgium, and N Luxembourg, cut through by the river Meuse; also a *département* of *Champagne-Ardenne. There was heavy fighting here in World Wars I and II (see *Bulge, Battle of the).

are metric unit of area, equal to 100 square metres (119.6 sq yd); 100 ares make one *hectare.

area the size of a surface. It is measured in square units, usually square centimetres (cm^2), square metres (m^2), or square kilometres (km^2). Surface area is the area of the outer surface of a solid.

areca any palm tree of the genus *Areca*, native to Asia and Australia. The *betel nut comes from the species *A. catechu*.

Arecibo site in Puerto Rico of the world's largest single-dish *radio telescope, 305 m/1,000 ft in diameter. It is built in a natural hollow and uses the rotation of the Earth to scan the sky. It has been used both for radar work on the planets and for conventional radio astronomy, and is operated by Cornell University, USA.

Ares in Greek mythology, the god of war (Roman *Mars). The son of Zeus and Hera, he was worshipped chiefly in Thrace.

arête (German **grat**; North American **combe-ridge**) sharp narrow ridge separating two *glacial troughs, or valleys. The typical U-shaped cross sections of glacial troughs give arêtes very steep sides. Arêtes are common in glaciated mountain regions such as the Rockies, the Himalayas, and the Alps.

Aretino Pietro 1492–1556. Italian writer. He earned his living, both in Rome and Venice, by publishing satirical pamphlets while under the protection of a highly placed family. His *Letters 1537–57* are a unique record of the cultural and political events of his time, and illustrate his vivacious, exuberant character. He also wrote poems and comedies.

argali wild sheep *Ovis ammon* of Central Asia. The male can grow to 1.2 m/4 ft at the shoulder, and has massive spiral horns.

Argand diagram in mathematics, a method for representing complex numbers by Cartesian coordinates (x, y). Along the x-axis (horizontal axis) are plotted the real numbers, and along the y-axis (vertical axis) the nonreal, or *imaginary, numbers.

Argentina Republic of (*República Argentina*)

area 2,780,092 sq km/1,073,116 sq mi
capital Buenos Aires (to move to Viedma)
towns Rosario, Córdoba, Tucumán, Mendoza, Santa Fe; ports are La Plata and Bahía Blanca
physical mountains in W, forest and savanna in N, pampas (treeless plains) in E central area, Patagonian plateau in S; rivers Colorado, Salado, Paraná, Uruguay, Río de la Plata estuary
territories part of Tierra del Fuego; disputed claims to S Atlantic islands and part of Antarctica
environment an estimated 20,000 sq km/7,700 sq mi of land has been swamped with salt water
head of state and government Carlos Menem from 1989
political system emergent democratic federal republic
exports livestock products, cereals, wool, tannin, peanuts, linseed oil, minerals (coal, copper, molybdenum, gold, silver, lead, zinc, barium, uranium); the country has huge resources of oil, natural gas, hydroelectric power
currency peso = 10,000 australs (which it replaced 1992)
population (1993 est) 33,500,000 (mainly of Spanish or Italian origin, only about 30,000 American Indians surviving); growth rate 1.5% p.a.
languages Spanish (official); English, Italian, German, French
religion Roman Catholic (state-supported)
GNP $2,780 per head (1991)

chronology
1816 Independence achieved from Spain, followed by civil wars.
1946 Juan Perón elected president, supported by his wife 'Evita'.
1952 'Evita' Perón died.
1955 Perón overthrown and civilian administration restored.
1966 Coup brought back military rule.
1973 A Peronist party won the presidential and congressional elections. Perón returned from exile in Spain as president, with his third wife, Isabel, as vice president.
1974 Perón died, succeeded by Isabel.
1976 Coup resulted in rule by a military junta led by Lt-Gen Jorge Videla. Congress dissolved, and hundreds of people, including Isabel Perón, detained.
1976–83 Ferocious campaign against left-wing elements, the 'dirty war'.
1978 Videla retired. Succeeded by General Roberto Viola, who promised a return to democracy.
1981 Viola died suddenly. Replaced by General Leopoldo Galtieri.
1982 With a deteriorating economy, Galtieri sought popular support by ordering an invasion of the British-held Falkland Islands. After losing the short war, Galtieri was removed and replaced by General Reynaldo Bignone.
1983 Amnesty law passed and 1853 democratic constitution revived. General elections won by Raúl Alfonsín and his party. Armed forces under scrutiny.
1984 National Commission on the Disappearance of Persons (CONADEP) reported on over 8,000 people who had disappeared during the 'dirty war' of 1976–83.
1985 A deteriorating economy forced Alfonsín to seek help from the International Monetary Fund and introduce an austerity programme.
1986 Unsuccessful attempt on Alfonsín's life.
1988 Unsuccessful army coup attempt.
1989 Carlos Menem, of the Justicialist Party, elected president.
1990 Full diplomatic relations with the UK restored. Menem elected Justicialist Party leader. Revolt by army officers thwarted.

argon (Greek *argos* 'idle') colourless, odourless, nonmetallic, gaseous element, symbol Ar, atomic number 18, relative atomic mass 39.948. It is grouped with the *inert gases, since it was long believed not to react with other substances, but observations now indicate that it can be made to combine with boron fluoride to form compounds. It constitutes almost 1% of the Earth's atmosphere, and was discovered 1894 by British chemists John Rayleigh (1842–1919) and William Ramsay after all oxygen and nitrogen had been removed chemically from a sample of air. It is used in electric discharge tubes and argon lasers.

argonaut or *paper nautilus* octopus living in the open sea, genus *Argonauta*. The female of the common paper nautilus, *A. argo*, is 20 cm/8 in across, and secretes a spiralled papery shell for her eggs from the web of the first pair of arms. The male is a shell-less dwarf, 1 cm/0.4 in across.

Argonauts in Greek legend, the band of heroes who accompanied *Jason when he set sail in the *Argo* to find the *Golden Fleece.

Argos city in ancient Greece, at the head of the Gulf of Nauplia, which was once a cult centre of the goddess Hera. In the Homeric age the name 'Argives' was sometimes used instead of 'Greeks'.

Argus in Greek mythology, a giant with 100 eyes. When he was killed by Hermes, Hera transplanted his eyes into the tail of her favourite bird, the peacock.

Aårhus alternative form of *Aarhus, a port in Denmark.

aria (Italian 'air') solo vocal piece in an opera or oratorio, often in three sections, the third repeating the first after a contrasting central section.

Ariadne in Greek mythology, the daughter of Minos, King of Crete. When Theseus came from Athens as one of the sacrificial victims offered to the Minotaur, she fell in love with him and gave him a ball of thread, which enabled him to find his way out of the labyrinth.

Ariane launch vehicle built in a series by the European Space Agency (first flight 1979). The launch site is at Kourou in French Guiana. Ariane is a three-stage rocket using liquid fuels. Small solid-fuel and liquid-fuel boosters can be attached to its first stage to increase carrying power.

Arianism system of Christian theology that denied the complete divinity of Jesus. It was founded about 310 by *Arius, and condemned as heretical at the Council of Nicaea 325.

arid zone infertile area with a small, infrequent rainfall that rapidly evaporates because of high temperatures. The aridity of a region is defined by its *aridity index* – a function of the rainfall and also of the temperature, and hence the rate of evaporation. There are arid zones in Morocco, Pakistan, Australia, the USA, and elsewhere.

Aries zodiacal constellation in the northern hemisphere between Pisces and Taurus, near Auriga, represented as the legendary ram whose golden fleece was sought by Jason and the Argonauts.

aril accessory seed cover other than a *fruit; it may be fleshy and sometimes brightly coloured, woody, or hairy. Examples of arils include the bright-red, fleshy layer surrounding the yew seed and the network of hard filaments that partially covers the nutmeg seed and yields the spice known as mace.

Ariosto Ludovico 1474–1533. Italian poet who wrote Latin poems and comedies on Classical lines, including the poem *Orlando Furioso* 1516, published 1532, an epic treatment of the *Roland* story, the perfect poetic expression of the Italian Renaissance.

Aristarchus of Samos *c.* 280–264 BC. Greek astronomer. The first to argue that the Earth moves around the Sun, he was ridiculed for his beliefs. He was also the first astronomer to estimate the sizes of the Sun and Moon and their distances from the Earth.

Aristide Jean-Bertrand 1953– . President of Haiti 1990–1991 and from Oct 1994. A left-wing Catholic priest opposed to the right-wing regime of the Duvalier family, he campaigned for the National Front for Change and Democracy, and won 70% of the vote. He was deposed by the military 1991 and took refuge in the USA, returning 1994.

Aristides *c.* 530–468 BC. Athenian politician.

He was one of the ten Athenian generals at the battle of *Marathon 490 BC and was elected chief archon, or magistrate.

Aristophanes *c.* 448–380 BC. Greek comedic dramatist. Of his 11 extant plays (of a total of over 40), the early comedies are remarkable for the violent satire with which he ridiculed the democratic war leaders. He also satirized contemporary issues such as the new learning of Socrates in *The Clouds* 423 BC and the power of women in *Lysistrata* 411 BC. The chorus plays a prominent role, frequently giving the play its title, as in *The Wasps* 422 BC, *The Birds* 414 BC, and *The Frogs* 405 BC.

Aristotle 384–322 BC. Greek philosopher who advocated reason and moderation. He maintained that sense experience is our only source of knowledge, and that by reasoning we can discover the essences of things, that is, their distinguishing qualities. In his works on ethics and politics, he suggested that human happiness consists in living in conformity with nature. He derived his political theory from the recognition that mutual aid is natural to humankind, and refused to set up any one constitution as universally ideal. Of Aristotle's works some 22 treatises survive, dealing with logic, metaphysics, physics, astronomy, meteorology, biology, psychology, ethics, politics, and literary criticism.

arithmetic branch of mathematics concerned with the study of numbers and their properties. The fundamental operations of arithmetic are addition, subtraction, multiplication, and division. Raising to powers (for example, squaring or cubing a number), the extraction of roots (for example, square roots), percentages, fractions, and ratios are developed from these operations.

arithmetic and logic unit (ALU) in a computer, the part of the *central processing unit (CPU) that performs the basic arithmetic and logic operations on data.

arithmetic mean the average of a set of n numbers, obtained by adding the numbers and dividing by n. For example, the arithmetic mean of the set of 5 numbers 1, 3, 6, 8, and 12 is $(1 + 3 + 6 + 8 + 12)/5 = 30/5 = 6$.

arithmetic progression or *arithmetic sequence* sequence of numbers or terms that have a common difference between any one term and the next in the sequence. For example, 2, 7, 12, 17, 22, 27, . . . is an arithmetic sequence with a common difference of 5.

Arizona state in southwestern USA; nickname Grand Canyon State
area 294,100 sq km/113,500 sq mi
capital Phoenix
cities Tucson, Scottsdale, Tempe, Mesa, Glendale, Flagstaff
physical Colorado Plateau in the N and E, desert basins and mountains in the S and W, Colorado River, Grand Canyon
products cotton under irrigation, livestock, copper, molybdenum, silver, electronics, aircraft
population (1990) 3,665,000; including 4.5% American Indians (Navajo, Hopi, Apache), who by treaty own 25% of the state
famous people Cochise, Wyatt Earp, Geronimo, Barry Goldwater, Zane Grey, Frank Lloyd Wright
history part of New Spain 1715; part of Mexico

armadillo *The horny bands and plates of the armadillo serve as armour.*

1824; passed to the USA after Mexican War 1848; territory 1863; statehood achieved 1912.

Arjan Indian religious leader, fifth guru (teacher) of Sikhism from 1581. He built the Golden Temple in *Amritsar and compiled the *Adi Granth*, the first volume of Sikh scriptures. He died in Muslim custody.

Arkansas state in S central USA; nickname Wonder State/Land of Opportunity
area 137,800 sq km/53,191 sq mi
capital Little Rock
cities Fort Smith, Pine Bluff, Fayetteville
physical Ozark Mountains and plateau in the W, lowlands in the E; Arkansas River; many lakes
products cotton, soya beans, rice, oil, natural gas, bauxite, timber, processed foods
population (1990) 2,350,700
famous people Johnny Cash, Bill Clinton, J William Fulbright, Douglas MacArthur, Winthrop Rockefeller
history explored by Hernando de Soto 1541; European settlers 1648, who traded with local Indians; part of Louisiana Purchase 1803; statehood achieved 1836.

Arkwright Richard 1732–1792. English inventor and manufacturing pioneer who developed a machine for spinning cotton (he called it a 'spinning frame') 1768. He set up a water-powered spinning factory 1771 and installed steam power in another factory 1790.

Armada fleet sent by Philip II of Spain against England 1588. See *Spanish Armada.

armadillo mammal of the family Dasypodidae, with an armour of bony plates on its back. Some 20 species live between Texas and Patagonia and range in size from the fairy armadillo at 13 cm/5 in to the giant armadillo, 1.5 m/4.5 ft long. Armadillos feed on insects, snakes, fruit, and carrion. Some can roll into an armoured ball if attacked; others rely on burrowing for protection.

Armageddon in the New Testament (Revelation 16), the site of the final battle between the nations that will end the world; it has been identified with *Megiddo in Israel.

Armagh county of Northern Ireland
area 1,250 sq km/483 sq mi
towns Armagh (county town), Lurgan, Portadown, Keady
physical flat in the N, with many bogs; low hills in the S; Lough Neagh
products chiefly agricultural: apples, potatoes, flax
population (1981) 119,000.

Armani Giorgio 1935– . Italian fashion designer. He launched his first menswear collection 1974 and the following year started designing women's clothing. His work is known for understated styles, precise tailoring, and fine fabrics. He designs for young men and women under the Emporio label.

armature in a motor or generator, the wire-wound coil that carries the current and rotates in a magnetic field. (In alternating-current machines, the armature is sometimes stationary.) The pole piece of a permanent magnet or electromagnet and the moving, iron part of a *solenoid, especially if the latter acts as a switch, may also be referred to as armatures.

armed forces state military organizations; see *services, armed.

Armenia Republic of

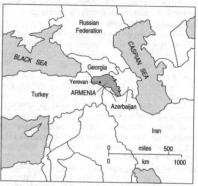

area 29,800 sq km/11,500 sq mi
capital Yerevan
towns Kumayri (formerly Leninakan)
physical mainly mountainous (including Mount Ararat), wooded
head of state Levon Ter-Petrossian from 1990
head of government Gagik Arutyunyan from 1991
political system emergent democracy
products copper, molybdenum, cereals, cotton, silk
population (1992) 3,426,000 (90% Armenian, 5% Azeri, 2% Russian, 2% Kurd)
language Armenian
religion traditionally Armenian Christian
chronology
1918 Became an independent republic.
1920 Occupied by the Red Army.
1936 Became a constituent republic of the USSR.
1988 Feb: demonstrations in Yerevan called for transfer of Nagorno-Karabakh from Azerbaijan to Armenian control. Dec: earthquake claimed around 25,000 lives and caused extensive damage.
1989 Jan–Nov: strife-torn Nagorno-Karabakh placed under direct rule from Moscow. Pro-autonomy Armenian National Movement founded. Nov: civil war erupted with Azerbaijan over Nagorno-Karabakh.
1990 March: Armenia boycotted USSR constitutional referendum. Aug: nationalists secured control of Armenian supreme soviet; former dissident Levon Ter-Petrossian indirectly elected

president; independence declared. Nakhichevan republic affected by Nagorno-Karabakh dispute. **1991** March: overwhelming support for independence in referendum. Dec: Armenia joined new Commonwealth of Independent States; Nagorno-Karabakh declared its independence; Armenia granted diplomatic recognition by USA. **1992** Admitted into United Nations and the Conference on Security and Cooperation in Europe. Conflict over Nagorno-Karabakh worsened. **1993** Russo-Turkish peace plan for Nagorno-Karabakh proved ineffectual.

Armenian member of the largest ethnic group inhabiting Armenia. There are Armenian minorities in Azerbaijan, as well as in Turkey and Iran. Christianity was introduced to the ancient Armenian kingdom in the 3rd century. There are 4–5 million speakers of Armenian, which belongs to the Indo-European family of languages.

Armenian church form of Christianity adopted in Armenia in the 3rd century. The Catholicos, or exarch, is the supreme head, and Echmiadzin (near Yerevan) is his traditional seat. Believers number about 2 million.

Armenian language one of the main divisions of the Indo-European language family. Old Armenian, the classic literary language, is still used in the liturgy of the Armenian Church. Armenian was not written down until the 5th century AD, when an alphabet of 36 (now 38) letters was evolved. Literature flourished in the 4th to 14th centuries, revived in the 18th, and continued throughout the 20th.

Armenian massacres series of massacres of Armenians by Turkish soldiers between 1895 and 1915. Reforms promised to Armenian Christians by Turkish rulers never materialized; unrest broke out and there were massacres by Turkish troops 1895. Again in 1909 and 1915, the Turks massacred altogether more than a million Armenians and deported others into the N Syrian desert, where they died of starvation; those who could fled to Russia or Persia. Only some 100,000 were left.

Arminius 17 BC–19 AD. German chieftain. An ex-soldier of the Roman army, he annihilated a Roman force led by Varus in the Teutoburger Forest area AD 9, and saved Germany from becoming a Roman province. He was later treacherously killed by some of his kinsmen.

Arminius Jacobus. Latinized name of Jakob Harmensen 1560–1609. Dutch Protestant priest who founded Arminianism, a school of Christian theology opposed to Calvin's doctrine of predestination. His views were developed by Simon Episcopius (1583–1643). Arminianism is the basis of Wesleyan *Methodism.

armistice cessation of hostilities while awaiting a peace settlement. 'The Armistice' refers specifically to the end of World War I between Germany and the Allies 11 Nov 1918. On 22 June 1940 French representatives signed an armistice with Germany in the same railway carriage at Compiègne as in 1918. No armistice was signed with either Germany or Japan 1945; both nations surrendered and there was no provision for the suspension of fighting. The Korean armistice, signed at Panmunjom 27 July 1953, terminated the Korean War 1950–53.

Armistice Day anniversary of the armistice signed 11 Nov 1918, ending World War I.

armour body protection worn in battle. Body armour is depicted in Greek and Roman art. Chain mail was developed in the Middle Ages but the craft of the armourer in Europe reached its height in design in the 15th century, when knights were completely encased in plate armour that still allowed freedom of movement. Medieval Japanese armour was articulated, made of iron, gilded metal, leather, and silk. Contemporary bulletproof vests and riot gear are forms of armour. The term is used in a modern context to refer to a mechanized armoured vehicle, such as a tank.

arms control attempts to limit the arms race between the superpowers by reaching agreements to restrict the production of certain weapons; see *disarmament.

arms trade sale of weapons from a manufacturing country to another nation. Nearly 56% of the world's arms exports end up in Third World countries. Iraq, for instance, was armed in the years leading up to the 1991 Gulf War mainly by the USSR but also by France, Brazil, and South Africa.

Armstrong Louis ('Satchmo') 1901–1971. US jazz cornet and trumpet player and singer. His Chicago recordings in the 1920s with the Hot Five and Hot Seven brought him recognition for his warm and pure trumpet tone, his skill at improvisation, and his quirky, gravelly voice. From the 1930s he also appeared in films.

Armstrong Neil Alden 1930– . US astronaut. In 1969, he became the first person to set foot on the Moon, and said, 'That's one small step for a man, one giant leap for mankind.' The Moon landing was part of the *Apollo project.

Armstrong William George 1810–1900. English engineer who developed a revolutionary method of making gun barrels 1855, by building a breech-loading artillery piece with a steel and wrought-iron barrel (previous guns were muzzle-loaded and had cast-bronze barrels). By 1880 the 150 mm/16 in Armstrong gun was the standard for all British ordnance.

army organized military force for fighting on the ground. A national army is used to further a political policy by force either within the state or on the territory of another state. Most countries have a national army, maintained by taxation, and raised either by conscription (compulsory military service) or voluntarily (paid professionals). Private armies may be employed by individuals and groups.

Arnhem, Battle of in World War II, airborne operation by the Allies, 17–26 Sept 1944, to secure a bridgehead over the Rhine, thereby opening the way for a thrust towards the Ruhr and a possible early end to the war. It was only partially successful, with 7,600 casualties. Arnhem is a city in the Netherlands, on the Rhine SE of Utrecht; population (1991) 131,700. It produces salt, chemicals, and pharmaceuticals.

Arnim Ludwig Achim von 1781–1831. German Romantic poet and novelist. Born in Berlin, he wrote short stories, a romance (*Gräfin Dolores/Countess Dolores* 1810), and plays, but left the historical novel *Die Kronenwächter* 1817 unfinished. With Clemens Brentano he collected the German folk songs in *Des Knaben Wunderhorn/ The Boy's Magic Horn* 1805–08.

Arnold Benedict 1741–1801. US soldier and military strategist who, during the American Revolution, won the turning point battle at Saratoga 1777 for the Americans. He is chiefly remembered as a traitor to the American side. A merchant in New Haven, Connecticut, he joined the colonial forces but in 1780 plotted to betray the strategic post at West Point to the British.

Arnold Matthew 1822–1888. English poet and critic. His poems, characterized by their elegiac mood and pastoral themes, include *The Forsaken Merman* 1849, *Thyrsis* 1867 (commemorating his friend Arthur Hugh Clough), *Dover Beach* 1867, and *The Scholar Gypsy* 1853. Arnold's critical works include *Essays in Criticism* 1865 and 1888, and *Culture and Anarchy* 1869, which attacks 19th-century philistinism.

aromatherapy use of aromatic essential oils to relieve tension or to induce a feeling of well-being, usually in combination with massage. It is also used to relieve minor skin complaints. Common in the Middle East for centuries, the practice was reintroduced to the West in France during the 1960s.

aromatic compound organic chemical compound in which some of the bonding electrons are delocalized (shared among several atoms within the molecule and not localized in the vicinity of the atoms involved in bonding). The commonest aromatic compounds have ring structures, the atoms comprising the ring being either all carbon or containing one or more different atoms (usually nitrogen, sulphur, or oxygen). Typical examples are benzene (C_6H_6) and pyridine (C_5H_5N).

Arp Hans or Jean 1887–1966. French abstract painter and sculptor. He was one of the founders of the *Dada movement about 1917, and later was associated with the Surrealists. His innovative wood sculptures use organic shapes in bright colours.

arpeggio (Italian 'like a harp') in music, a chord played as a cascade of notes played in succession.

arrest apprehension and detention of a person suspected of a crime. In Britain, an arrest may be made on a magistrate's warrant, but a police constable is empowered to arrest without warrant in all cases where he or she has reasonable ground for thinking a serious offence has been committed.

Arrhenius Svante August 1859–1927. Swedish scientist, the founder of physical chemistry. Born near Uppsala, he became a professor at Stockholm in 1895, and made a special study of electrolysis. He wrote *Worlds in the Making* and *Destinies of the Stars*, and in 1903 received the Nobel Prize for Chemistry. In 1905 he predicted global warming as a result of carbon dioxide emission from burning fossil fuels.

arrhythmia disturbance of the natural rhythm of the heart. There are various kinds of arrhythmia, some innocent, some indicative of heart disease.

arrowroot starchy substance derived from the roots and tubers of various tropical plants with thick, clumpy roots. The true arrowroot *Maranta arundinacea* was used by the Indians of South America as an antidote against the effects of poisoned arrows.

arsenic brittle, greyish-white, semimetallic element (a metalloid), symbol As, atomic number 33, relative atomic mass 74.92. It occurs in many ores and occasionally in its elemental state, and is widely distributed, being present in minute quantities in the soil, the sea, and the human body. In larger quantities, it is poisonous. The chief source of arsenic compounds is as a by-product from metallurgical processes. It is used in making semiconductors, alloys, and solders.

arson malicious and wilful setting fire to property.

art in the broadest sense, all the processes and products of human skill, imagination, and invention; the opposite of nature. In contemporary usage, definitions of art usually reflect aesthetic criteria, and the term may encompass literature, music, drama, painting, and sculpture. Popularly, the term is most commonly used to refer to the visual arts. In Western culture, aesthetic criteria introduced by the ancient Greeks still influence our perceptions and judgements of art.

Artaud Antonin 1896–1948. French theatre director. Although his play, *Les Cenci/The Cenci* 1935, was a failure, his concept of the Theatre of *Cruelty, intended to release feelings usually repressed in the unconscious, has been an important influence on modern dramatists such as Albert Camus and Jean Genet and on directors and producers. Declared insane 1936, Artaud was confined in an asylum.

Art Deco style in art and architecture that emerged in Europe in the 1920s and continued through the 1930s, using rather heavy, geometric simplification of form: for example, Radio City Music Hall, New York. It was a self-consciously modern style, with sharp lines, and dominated the decorative arts. The graphic artist Erté (1893–1989) was a fashionable exponent.

Artemis in Greek mythology, the goddess (Roman Diana) of chastity, the Moon, and the hunt. She is the twin sister of *Apollo. Her cult centre was at Ephesus.

arteriosclerosis nontechnical term for *atherosclerosis.

artery vessel that carries blood from the heart to the rest of the body. It is built to withstand considerable pressure, having thick walls that are impregnated with muscle and elastic fibres. During contraction of the heart muscles, arteries expand in diameter to allow for the sudden increase in pressure that occurs; the resulting *pulse or pressure wave can be felt at the wrist. Not all arteries carry oxygenated (oxygen-rich) blood; the pulmonary arteries convey deoxygenated (oxygen-poor) blood from the heart to the lungs.

artesian well well that is supplied with water rising from an underground water-saturated rock layer (*aquifer). The water rises from the aquifer under its own pressure. Such a well may be drilled into an aquifer that is confined by impermeable rocks both above and below. If the water table (the top of the region of water saturation) in that aquifer is above the level of the well head, hydrostatic pressure will force the water to the surface.

arthritis inflammation of the joints, with pain, swelling, and restricted motion. Many conditions may cause arthritis, including gout and trauma to the joint.

arthropod member of the phylum Arthropoda; an invertebrate animal with jointed legs and a segmented body with a horny or chitinous casing (exoskeleton), which is shed periodically and replaced as the animal grows. Included are arachnids such as spiders and mites, as well as crustaceans, millipedes, centipedes, and insects.

Arthur 6th century AD. Legendary British king and hero in stories of *Camelot and the quest for the *Holy Grail. Arthur is said to have been born in Tintagel, Cornwall, and buried in Glastonbury, Somerset. He may have been a Romano-Celtic leader against pagan Saxon invaders.

Arthur Chester Alan 1830–1886. 21st president of the USA 1881–85, a Republican. In 1880 he was chosen as James *Garfield's vice president, and was his successor when Garfield was assassinated the following year.

artichoke either of two plants of the composite or sunflower family Compositae. The common or globe artichoke *Cynara scolymus* is native to the Mediterranean, and is a form of thistle. It is tall, with purplish blue flowers; the bracts of the unopened flower are eaten. The Jerusalem artichoke *Helianthus tuberosus* is a sunflower, native to North America. It has edible tubers, and its common name is a corruption of the Italian for sunflower, *girasole*.

article grammatical *part of speech. There are two articles in English: the *definite article the*, which serves to specify or identify a noun (as in 'This is *the* book I need'), and the *indefinite article a* or (before vowels) *an*, which indicates a single unidentified noun (as in 'They gave me *a* piece of paper and *an* envelope').

articles of association in the UK, the rules governing the relationship between a registered company, its members (shareholders), and its directors. The articles of association are deposited with the registrar of companies. In the USA they are called *by-laws*.

artificial insemination (AI) introduction by instrument of semen from a sperm bank or donor into the female reproductive tract to bring about fertilization. Originally used by animal breeders to improve stock with sperm from high-quality males, in the 20th century it has been developed for use in humans, to help the infertile. In *in vitro fertilization, the egg is fertilized in a test tube and then implanted in the womb. In zygote intrafallopian transfer (ZIFT) the mixed egg and sperm are reintroduced into the fallopian tube.

artificial intelligence (AI) branch of science concerned with creating computer programs that can perform actions comparable with those of an intelligent human. Current AI research covers such areas as planning (for robot behaviour), language understanding, pattern recognition, and knowledge representation.

artificial limb device to replace a limb that has been removed by surgery or one that is mal-

formed because of genetic defects. It is one form of *prosthesis.

artificial radioactivity natural and spontaneous radioactivity arising from radioactive isotopes or elements that are formed when elements are bombarded with subatomic particles – protons, neutrons, or electrons – or small nuclei.

artificial respiration maintenance of breathing when the natural process is suspended. If breathing is permanently suspended, as in paralysis, an *iron lung* is used; in cases of electric shock or apparent drowning, for example, the first choice is the expired-air method, the *kiss of life* by mouth-to-mouth breathing until natural breathing is resumed.

artificial selection in biology, selective breeding of individuals that exhibit the particular characteristics that a plant or animal breeder wishes to develop. In plants, desirable features might include resistance to disease, high yield (in crop plants), or attractive appearance. In animal breeding, selection has led to the development of particular breeds of cattle for improved meat production (such as the Aberdeen Angus) or milk production (such as Jerseys).

artillery collective term for military *firearms too heavy to be carried. Artillery can be mounted on ships or aeroplanes and includes cannons and missile launchers.

Art Nouveau art style of about 1890–1910 in Europe, named after a shop in Paris that opened 1895, which makes marked use of sinuous lines, stylized flowers and foliage, and flame shapes. In England, it appears in the illustrations of Aubrey Beardsley; in Spain, in the architecture of Antonio Gaudí; in France, in the architecture of Hector Guimard and the art glass of René Lalique; in Belgium, in the houses and shops of Victor Horta; in the USA, in the lamps and metal work of Louis Comfort Tiffany; and in Scotland, in the interior and exterior designs of Charles Rennie Mackintosh. Art Nouveau was also known as *Jugendstil* in Germany and *Stile Liberty* in Italy, after the fashionable London department store.

Arts and Crafts movement English social movement, largely antimachine in spirit, based in design and architecture and founded by William Morris in the latter half of the 19th century. It was supported by the architect A W Pugin and by John *Ruskin and stressed the importance of handcrafting. The *Art Nouveau style succeeded it.

Arts Council of Great Britain UK organization, incorporated 1946, which aids music, drama, and visual arts with government funds. It began 1940 as the Council for the Encouragement of Music and the Arts (CEMA) with a grant from the Pilgrim Trust.

Aruba island in the Caribbean, the westernmost of the Lesser Antilles; an overseas part of the Netherlands
area 193 sq km/75 sq mi
population (1989) 62,400
history Aruba obtained separate status from the other Netherlands Antilles 1986 and has full internal autonomy.

arum any plant of the genus *Arum*, family Araceae, especially the Old World genus *Arum*. The arum called the trumpet lily *Zantedeschia aethiopica*, an ornamental plant, is a native of South Africa.

Arunachal Pradesh state of India, in the Himalayas on the borders of Tibet and Myanmar
area 83,600 sq km/32,270 sq mi
capital Itanagar
products rubber, coffee, spices, fruit, timber
population (1991) 858,400.
languages 50 different dialects
history formerly nominally part of Assam, known as the renamed Arunachal Pradesh ('Hills of the Rising Sun'). It became a state 1986.

Aryan Indo-European family of languages; also the hypothetical parent language of an ancient people who are believed to have lived between central Asia and E Europe and to have reached Persia and India in one direction and Europe in another, sometime in the 2nd century BC, diversifying into the various Indo-European language speakers of later times. In Nazi Germany Hitler and other theorists erroneously propagated the idea of the Aryans as a white-skinned, blue-eyed, fair-haired master race.

Aryan languages 19th-century name for the *Indo-European languages; the languages of the Aryan peoples of India. The name Aryan is no longer used by language scholars because of its association with the Nazi concept of white supremacy.

Arya Samaj Hindu religious sect founded by Dayanand Saraswati (1825–1888) about 1875. He renounced idol worship and urged a return to the purer principles of the Vedas (Hindu scriptures). For its time the movement was quite revolutionary in its social teachings, which included forbidding *caste practices, prohibiting child-marriage, and allowing widows to remarry.

asbestos any of several related minerals of fibrous structure that offer great heat resistance because of their nonflammability and poor conductivity. Commercial asbestos is generally made from olivine, a *serpentine mineral, tremolite (a white *amphibole), and riebeckite (a blue amphibole, also known as crocidolite when in its fibrous form). Asbestos usage is now strictly controlled because exposure to its dust can cause cancer.

Ascension British island of volcanic origin in the S Atlantic, a dependency of *St Helena since 1922; population (1982) 1,625. The chief settlement is Georgetown.

Ascension Day or *Holy Thursday* in the Christian calendar, the feast day commemorating Jesus' ascension into heaven. It is the 40th day after Easter.

Ascham Roger c. 1515–1568. English scholar and royal tutor, author of *The Scholemaster* 1570 on the art of education.

ASCII (acronym for *American standard code for information interchange*) in computing, a coding system in which numbers are assigned to letters, digits, and punctuation symbols. Although computers work in *binary number code, ASCII numbers are usually quoted as decimal or *hexadecimal numbers. For example, the decimal number 45 (binary 0101101) represents a hyphen, and 65 (binary 1000001) a capital A.

The first 32 codes are used for control functions, such as carriage return and backspace.

ascorbic acid $C_6H_8O_6$ or *vitamin C* a relatively simple organic acid found in fresh fruits and vegetables. It is soluble in water and destroyed by prolonged boiling, so soaking or overcooking of vegetables reduces their vitamin C content. Lack of ascorbic acid results in scurvy.

ASEAN acronym for *Association of South East Asian Nations*.

asepsis practice of ensuring that bacteria are excluded from open sites during surgery, wound dressing, blood sampling, and other medical procedures. Aseptic technique is a first line of defence against infection.

asexual reproduction in biology, reproduction that does not involve the manufacture and fusion of sex cells, nor the necessity for two parents. The process carries a clear advantage in that there is no need to search for a mate nor to develop complex pollinating mechanisms; every asexual organism can reproduce on its own. Asexual reproduction can therefore lead to a rapid population build-up.

Asgard in Scandinavian mythology, the place where the gods lived. It was reached by a bridge called Bifrost, the rainbow.

ash *Ash is the name given to a few northern European trees and shrubs of the* Fraxinus *genus.*

ash any tree of the worldwide genus *Fraxinus*, belonging to the olive family Oleaceae, with winged fruits. *F. excelsior* is the European species; its timber is of importance. The *mountain ash* or *rowan* belongs to the family Rosaceae.

Ashbee Charles Robert 1863–1942. British designer, architect, and writer, one of the major figures of the *Arts and Crafts movement. He founded a Guild and School of Handicraft in the East End of London in 1888, but later modified his views, accepting the importance of machinery and design for industry.

Ashcan school group of US painters active about 1908–14, also known as *the Eight*. Members included Robert Henri (1865–1929), George Luks (1867–1933), William Glackens (1870–1938), Everett Shinn (1876–1953), and John Sloan (1871–1951). Their style is realist; their subjects centered on city life, the poor, and the outcast. They organized the Armory Show in New York 1913, an exhibition that introduced modern European art to the USA.

Ashcroft Peggy 1907–1991. English actress. Her Shakespearean roles included Desdemona in *Othello* (with Paul Robeson) and Juliet in *Romeo and Juliet* 1935 (with Laurence Olivier and John Gielgud), and she appeared in the British TV play *Caught on a Train* 1980 (BAFTA award), the series *The Jewel in the Crown* 1984, and the film *A Passage to India* 1985.

Ashdown Paddy (Jeremy John Durham) 1941– . English politician, leader of the merged Social and Liberal Democrats from 1988. He served in the Royal Marines as a commando, leading a Special Boat Section in Borneo, and was a member of the Diplomatic Service 1971–76. He became a Liberal member of Parliament 1983. His constituency is Yeovil, Somerset.

Ashe Arthur Robert, Jr 1943–1993. US tennis player and coach. He won the US national men's singles title at Forest Hills and the first US Open 1968, the Australian men's title 1970 and Wimbledon 1975.

Ashes, the cricket trophy theoretically held by the winning team in the England-Australia test series.

Ashikaga in Japanese history, the family who held the office of shogun 1338–1573, a period of civil wars. Nō drama evolved under the patronage of Ashikaga shoguns. Relations with China improved intermittently and there was trade with Korea. The last (15th) Ashikaga shogun was ousted by Oda Nobunaga at the start of the Momoyama period. The Ashikaga belonged to the *Minamoto clan.

Ashkenazi (plural **Ashkenazim**) a Jew of German or E European descent, as opposed to a Sephardi, of Spanish, Portuguese, or N African descent.

Ashkenazy Vladimir 1937– . Russian-born pianist and conductor. His keyboard technique differs slightly from standard Western technique. In 1962 he was joint winner of the Tchaikovsky Competition with John Ogdon. He excels in Rachmaninov, Prokofiev, and Liszt.

Ashkhabad capital of Turkmenistan; population (1989) 402,000. Industries include glass, carpets ('Bukhara' carpets are made here), cotton; the spectacular natural setting has been used by the film-making industry.

Ashmole Elias 1617–1692. English antiquary, whose collection forms the basis of the Ashmolean Museum, Oxford, England.

ashram Indian community whose members lead a simple life of discipline and self-denial and devote themselves to social service. Noted ashrams are those founded by Mahatma Gandhi at Wardha and the poet Rabindranath Tagore at Santiniketan.

Ashton Frederick 1904–1988. British choreographer, director of the Royal Ballet, London, 1963–70. He studied with Marie Rambert before joining the Vic-Wells (now Royal) Ballet 1935 as chief choreographer. His long association with Ninette de Valois and Margot Fonteyn, for whom he created many roles, gave the Royal Ballet a worldwide reputation.

Ash Wednesday first day of Lent, the period in the Christian calendar leading up to Easter; in the Roman Catholic church the foreheads of the congregation are marked with a cross in ash, as a sign of penitence.

Asia largest of the continents, occupying one-third of the total land surface of the world
area 44,000,000 sq km/17,000,000 sq mi
largest cities (population over 5 million) Tokyo, Shanghai, Osaka, Beijing, Seoul, Calcutta, Bombay, Jakarta, Bangkok, Tehran, Hong Kong, Delhi, Tianjin, Karachi
physical lying in the eastern hemisphere, Asia extends from the Arctic Circle to just over 10° S of the equator. The Asian mainland, which forms the greater part of the Eurasian continent, lies entirely in the northern hemisphere and stretches from Cape Chelyubinsk at its N extremity to Cape Piai at the S tip of the Malay Peninsula. From Dezhneva Cape in the E, the mainland extends W over more than 165° longitude to Cape Baba in Turkey. Containing the world's highest mountains and largest inland seas, Asia can be divided into five physical units: 1) at the heart of the continent, a central triangle of plateaus at varying altitudes (Tibetan Plateau, Tarim Basin, Gobi Desert), surrounded by huge mountain chains which spread in all directions (Himalayas, Karakoram, Hindu Kush, Pamirs, Kunlun, Tien Shan, Altai); 2) the W plateaus and ranges (Elburz, Zagros, Taurus, Great Caucasus mountains) of Afghanistan, Iran, N Iraq, Armenia, and Turkey; 3) the lowlands of Turkestan and Siberia which stretch N of the central mountains to the Arctic Ocean and include large areas in which the subsoil is permanently frozen; 4) the fertile and densely populated E lowlands and river plains of Korea, China, and Indochina, and the islands of the East Indies and Japan; 5) the southern plateaus of Arabia, and the Deccan, with the fertile alluvial plains of the Euphrates, Tigris, Indus, Ganges, Brahmaputra, and Irrawaddy rivers. In Asiatic Russia are the largest areas of coniferous forest (taiga) in the world. The climate shows great extremes and contrasts, the heart of the continent becoming bitterly cold in winter and extremely hot in summer. When the heated air over land rises, moisture-laden air from the surrounding seas flows in, bringing heavy monsoon rains to all SE Asia, China, and Japan between May and Oct.
level; rivers (over 3,200 km/2,000 mi) include Chiang Jiang (Yangtze), Huang He (Yellow River), Ob-Irtysh, Amur, Lena, Mekong, Yeni sei; lakes (over 18,000 sq km/7,000 sq mi) include Caspian Sea (the largest lake in the world), Aral Sea, Baikal (largest freshwater lake in Eurasia), Balkhash; deserts include the Gobi, Takla Makan, Syrian Desert, Arabian Desert, Negev
products 62% of the population are employed in agriculture; Asia produces 46% of the world's cereal crops (91% of the world's rice); other crops include mangoes (India), groundnuts (India, China), 84% of the world's copra (Philippines, Indonesia), 93% of the world's rubber (Indonesia, Malaysia, Thailand), tobacco (China), flax (China, Russia), 95% of the world's jute (India, Bangladesh, China), cotton (China, India, Pakistan), silk (China, India), fish (Japan, China, Korea, Thailand); China produces 55% of the world's tungsten; 45% of the world's tin

is produced by Malaysia, China, and Indonesia; Saudi Arabia is the world's largest producer of oil **population** (1988) 2,996,000; the world's largest, though not the fastest growing population, amounting to more than half the total number of people in the world; between 1950 and 1990 the death rate and infant mortality were reduced by more than 60%; annual growth rate 1.7%; projected to increase to 3,550,000 by the year 2000 **languages** predominantly tonal languages (Chinese, Japanese) in the E, Indo-Iranian languages (Hindi, Urdu, Persian) in S Asia, Altaic languages (Mongolian, Turkish) in W and Central Asia, Semitic languages (Arabic, Hebrew) in SW **religions** the major religions of the world had their origins in Asia – Judaism and Christianity in the Middle East, Islam in Arabia, Buddhism, Hinduism, and Sikhism in India, Confucianism in China, and Shintoism in Japan.

Asia Minor historical name for **Anatolia**, the Asian part of Turkey.

Asian Development Bank (ADB) bank founded 1966 to stimulate growth in Asia and the Far East by administering direct loans and technical assistance. Members include 30 countries within the region and 14 countries of W Europe and North America. The headquarters are in Manila, Philippines.

Asia-Pacific Economic Cooperation Conference (APEC) trade group comprising 12 Pacific Asian countries, formed Nov 1989 to promote multilateral trade and economic cooperation between member states. Its members are the USA, Canada, Japan, Australia, New Zealand, South Korea, Brunei, Indonesia, Malaysia, the Philippines, Singapore, and Thailand.

Asimov Isaac 1920–1992. Russian-born US author and editor of science fiction and nonfiction. He published more than 400 books including his science fiction *I, Robot* 1950 and the *Foundation* trilogy 1951–53, continued in *Foundation's Edge* 1983.

AS level General Certificate of Education **A**dvanced **S**upplementary examinations introduced in the UK 1988 as the equivalent to 'half an *A level' as a means of broadening the sixth-form (age 16–18) curriculum and including more students in the examination system.

Asmara or **Asmera** capital of Eritrea; 64 km/40 mi SW of Massawa on the Red Sea; population (1984) 275,385. Products include beer, clothes, and textiles. It has a naval school. In 1974 unrest here precipitated the end of the Ethiopian Empire.

Asoka *c.* 273–232 BC. Emperor of India *c.* 268–232 BC, the greatest of the *Mauryan rulers. He inherited an empire covering most of north and south-central India which, at its height, had a population of at least 30 million, with its capital at *Pataliputra. A devout Buddhist, he renounced militarism and concentrated on establishing an efficient administration with a large standing army and a secret police.

asp any of several venomous snakes, including *Vipera aspis* of S Europe, allied to the adder, and the Egyptian cobra *Naja haje*, reputed to have been used by the Egyptian queen Cleopatra for her suicide.

asparagus any plant of the genus *Asparagus*, family Liliaceae, with small scalelike leaves and many needlelike branches. Native to Eurasia, *A. officinalis* is cultivated, and the young shoots are eaten as a vegetable.

aspartame noncarbohydrate sweetener used in foods under the trade-name Nutrasweet. It is about 200 times as sweet as sugar and, unlike saccharine, has no aftertaste.

aspen any of several species of *poplar tree, genus *Populus*. The European quaking aspen *P. tremula* has flattened leafstalks that cause the leaves to flutter with every breeze. The soft, light-coloured wood is used for matches and paper pulp.

asphalt mineral mixture containing semisolid brown or black *bitumen, used in the construction industry. Asphalt is mixed with rock chips to form paving material, and the purer varieties are used for insulating material and for water-proofing masonry. It can be produced artificially by the distillation of *petroleum.

asphodel either of two related Old World genera (*Asphodeline* and *Asphodelus*) of plants of the lily family Liliaceae. *Asphodelus albus*, the white asphodel or king's spear, is found in Italy and Greece, sometimes covering large areas, and providing grazing for sheep. *Asphodeline lutea* is the yellow asphodel.

asphyxia suffocation; a lack of oxygen that produces a build-up of carbon dioxide waste in the tissues.

aspidistra Asiatic plant of the genus *Aspidistra* of the lily family Liliaceae. The Chinese *A. elatior* has broad, lanceolate leaves and, like all members of the genus, grows well in warm indoor conditions.

aspirin acetylsalicylic acid, a popular pain-relieving drug (*analgesic) developed in the late 19th century as a household remedy for aches and pains. It relieves pain and reduces inflammation and fever. It is derived from the white willow tree *Salix alba*.

Asquith Herbert Henry, 1st Earl of Oxford and Asquith 1852–1928. British Liberal politician, prime minister 1908–16. As chancellor of the Exchequer he introduced old-age pensions 1908. He limited the powers of the House of Lords and attempted to give Ireland Home Rule.

ass any of several horselike, odd-toed, hoofed mammals of the genus *Equus*, family Equidae. Species include the African wild ass *E. asinus*, and the Asian wild ass *E. hemionus*. They differ from horses in their smaller size, larger ears, tufted tail, and characteristic bray. Donkeys and burros are domesticated asses.

Assad Hafez al 1930– . Syrian Ba'athist politician, president from 1971. He became prime minister after a bloodless military coup 1970, and the following year was the first president to be elected by popular vote. Having suppressed dissent, he was re-elected 1978 and 1985. He is a Shia (Alawite) Muslim.

Assam state of NE India
area 78,400 sq km/30,262 sq mi
capital Dispur
towns Guwahati
products half India's tea is grown and half its oil produced here; rice, jute, sugar, cotton, coal
population (1991) 24,294,600, including 12

million Assamese (Hindus), 5 million Bengalis (chiefly Muslim immigrants from Bangladesh), Nepalis, and 2 million indigenous people (Christian and traditional religions)

language Assamese

history a thriving region from 1000 BC; Assam migrants came from China and Myanmar (Burma). After Burmese invasion 1826, Britain took control and made Assam a separate province 1874; it was included in the Dominion of India, except for most of the Muslim district of Silhet, which went to Pakistan 1947. Ethnic unrest started in the 1960s when Assamese was declared the official language. After protests, the Gara, Khasi, and Jainitia tribal hill districts became the state of Meghalaya 1971; the Mizo hill district became the Union Territory of Mizoram 1972. There were massacres of Muslim Bengalis by Hindus 1983. In 1987 members of the Bodo ethnic group began fighting for a separate homeland. Direct rule was imposed by the Indian government Nov 1990 following separatist violence from the Marxist-militant United Liberation Front of Assam (ULFA), which had extorted payments from tea-exporting companies. In March 1991 it was reported that the ULFA, operating from the jungles of Myanmar, had been involved in 97 killings, mainly of Congress I politicians, since 27 Nov 1990.

assassination murder, usually of a political, royal, or public person. The term derives from the order of the Assassins, a Muslim sect that, in the 11th and 12th centuries, murdered officials to further its political ends.

assault intentional act or threat of physical violence against a person. In English law it is both a crime and a *tort (a civil wrong). The kinds of criminal assault are common (ordinary); aggravated (more serious, such as causing actual bodily harm); or indecent (of a sexual nature).

assay in chemistry, the determination of the quantity of a given substance present in a sample. Usually it refers to determining the purity of precious metals.

assembler in computing, a program that translates a program written in an assembly language into a complete *machine-code program that can be obeyed by a computer. Each instruction in the assembly language is translated into only one machine-code instruction.

assembly code computer-programming language closely related to a computer's internal codes. It consists chiefly of a set of short sequences of letters (mnemonics), which are translated, by a program called an assembler, into *machine code for the computer's *central processing unit (CPU) to follow directly. In assembly language, for example, 'JMP' means 'jump' and 'LDA' means 'load accumulator'. Assembly code is used by programmers who need to write very fast or efficient programs.

assembly line method of mass production in which a product is built up step-by-step by successive workers adding one part at a time.

asset in business accounting, a term that covers the land or property of a company or individual, payments due from bills, investments, and anything else owned that can be turned into cash. On a company's balance sheet, total assets must be equal to liabilities (money and services owed).

asset stripping sale or exploitation by other means of the assets of a business, often one that has been taken over for that very purpose. The parts of the business may be potentially more valuable separately than together. Asset stripping is a major force for the more efficient use of assets.

assimilation in animals, the process by which absorbed food molecules, circulating in the blood, pass into the cells and are used for growth, tissue repair, and other metabolic activities. The actual destiny of each food molecule depends not only on its type, but also on the body requirements at that time.

Assisted Places Scheme in UK education, a scheme established 1980 by which the government assists parents with the cost of fees at *independent schools on a means-tested basis.

assize in medieval Europe, the passing of laws, either by the king with the consent of nobles, as in the Constitutions of *Clarendon 1164 by Henry II of England, or as a complete system, such as the *Assizes of Jerusalem*, a compilation of the law of the feudal kingdom of Jerusalem in the 13th century.

Association of South East Asian Nations (ASEAN) regional alliance formed in Bangkok 1967; it took over the nonmilitary role of the Southeast Asia Treaty Organization 1975. Its members are Indonesia, Malaysia, the Philippines, Singapore, Thailand, and (from 1984) Brunei; its headquarters are in Jakarta, Indonesia.

associative operation in mathematics, an operation in which the outcome is independent of the grouping of the numbers or symbols concerned. For example, multiplication is associative, as $4 \times (3 \times 2) = (4 \times 3) \times 2 = 24$; however, division is not, as $12 \div (4 \div 2) = 6$, but $(12 \div 4) \div 2 = 1.5$. Compare *commutative operation and *distributive operation.

assortative mating in population genetics, selective mating in a population between individuals that are genetically related or have similar characteristics. If sufficiently consistent, assortative mating can theoretically result in the evolution of new species without geographical isolation (see *speciation).

Assyria empire in the Middle East c. 2500–612 BC, in N Mesopotamia (now Iraq); early capital Ashur, later Nineveh. It was initially subject to Sumer and intermittently to Babylon. The Assyrians adopted in the main the Sumerian religion and structure of society. At its greatest extent the empire included Egypt and stretched from the E Mediterranean coast to the head of the Persian Gulf.

Astaire Fred. Adopted name of Frederick Austerlitz 1899–1987. US dancer, actor, singer, and choreographer who starred in numerous films, including *Top Hat* 1935, *Easter Parade* 1948, and *Funny Face* 1957, many containing inventive sequences he designed and choreographed himself. He made ten classic films with the most popular of his dancing partners, Ginger Rogers. He later played straight dramatic roles in such films as *On the Beach* 1959.

Astarte alternative name for the Babylonian and Assyrian goddess *Ishtar.

astatine (Greek *astatos* 'unstable') nonmetallic, radioactive element, symbol At, atomic number 85, relative atomic mass 210. It is a member of the *halogen group, and is very rare in nature. Astatine is highly unstable, with many isotopes; the longest lived has a half-life of about eight hours.

aster any plant of the large genus *Aster*, family Compositae, belonging to the same subfamily as the daisy. All asters have starlike flowers with yellow centres and outer rays (not petals) varying from blue and purple to white and the genus comprises a great variety of size. Many are cultivated as garden flowers, including the Michaelmas daisy *A. nova-belgii*.

asterisk starlike punctuation mark (*) used to link the asterisked word with a note at the bottom of a page, and to indicate that certain letters are missing from a word (usually a taboo word such as 'f**k').

asteroid or *minor planet* any of many thousands of small bodies, composed of rock and iron, that orbit the Sun. Most lie in a belt between the orbits of Mars and Jupiter, and are thought to be fragments left over from the formation of the *Solar System. About 100,000 may exist, but their total mass is only a few hundredths the mass of the Moon.

asthenosphere division of the Earth's structure lying beneath the *lithosphere, at a depth of approximately 70 km/45 mi to 260 km/160 mi. It is thought to be the soft, partially molten layer of the *mantle on which the rigid plates of the Earth's surface move to produce the motions of *plate tectonics.

asthma difficulty in breathing due to spasm of the bronchi (air passages) in the lungs. Attacks may be provoked by allergy, infection, stress, or emotional upset. It may also be increasing as a result of air pollution and occupational hazards. Treatment is with *bronchodilators to relax the bronchial muscles and thereby ease the breathing, and in severe cases by inhaled *steroids that reduce inflammation of the bronchi.

astigmatism aberration occurring in lenses, including that in the eye. It results when the curvature of the lens differs in two perpendicular planes, so that rays in one plane may be in focus while rays in the other are not. With astigmatic eyesight, the vertical and horizontal cannot be in focus at the same time; correction is by the use of a cylindrical lens that reduces the overall focal length of one plane so that both planes are seen in sharp focus.

Aston Francis William 1877–1945. English physicist who developed the mass spectrometer, which separates *isotopes by projecting their ions (charged atoms) through a magnetic field. He received the Nobel Prize for Chemistry 1922.

Astor prominent US and British family. *John Jacob Astor* (1763–1848) was a US millionaire. His great-grandson *Waldorf Astor*, 2nd Viscount Astor (1879–1952), was Conservative member of Parliament for Plymouth 1910–19, when he succeeded to the peerage. He was chief proprietor of the British *Observer* newspaper. His US-born wife Nancy Witcher Langhorne (1879–1964), *Lady Astor*, was the first woman member of Parliament to take a seat in the House of Commons 1919, when she succeeded her husband for the constituency of Plymouth. Government policy was said to be decided at Cliveden, their country home.

astrolabe ancient navigational instrument, forerunner of the sextant. Astrolabes usually consisted of a flat disc with a sighting rod that could be pivoted to point at the Sun or bright stars. From the altitude of the Sun or star above the horizon, the local time could be estimated.

astrology (Greek *astron* 'star', *legein* 'speak') study of the relative position of the planets and stars in the belief that they influence events on Earth. The astrologer casts a *horoscope based on the time and place of the subject's birth. Astrology has no proven scientific basis, but has been widespread since ancient times. Western astrology is based on the 12 signs of the zodiac; Chinese astrology is based on a 60-year cycle and lunar calendar.

astrometry measurement of the precise positions of stars, planets, and other bodies in space. Such information is needed for practical purposes including accurate timekeeping, surveying and navigation, and calculating orbits and measuring distances in space. Astrometry is not concerned with the surface features or the physical nature of the body under study.

astronaut person making flights into space; the term *cosmonaut* is used in the West for any astronaut from the former Soviet Union.

astronomical unit unit (symbol AU) equal to the mean distance of the Earth from the Sun: 149,597,870 km/92,955,800 mi. It is used to describe planetary distances. Light travels this distance in approximately 8.3 minutes.

astronomy science of the celestial bodies: the Sun, the Moon, and the planets; the stars and galaxies; and all other objects in the universe. It is concerned with their positions, motions, distances, and physical conditions; and with their origins and evolution. Astronomy thus divides into fields such as astrophysics, celestial mechanics, and cosmology. See also *gamma-ray astronomy, *infrared astronomy, *radio astronomy, *ultraviolet astronomy, and *X-ray astronomy.

astrophotography use of photography in astronomical research. The first successful photograph of a celestial object was the daguerreotype plate of the Moon taken by John W Draper (1811–1882) of the USA in March 1840. The first photograph of a star, Vega, was taken by US astronomer William C Bond (1789–1859) in 1850. Modern-day astrophotography uses techniques such as *charge-coupled devices (CCDs).

astrophysics study of the physical nature of stars, galaxies, and the universe. It began with the development of spectroscopy in the 19th century, which allowed astronomers to analyse the composition of stars from their light. Astrophysicists view the universe as a vast natural laboratory in which they can study matter under conditions of temperature, pressure, and density that are unattainable on Earth.

Asturias autonomous region of N Spain; area 10,600 sq km/4,092 sq mi; population (1986) 1,114,000. Half of Spain's coal comes from the mines of Asturias. Agricultural produce includes maize, fruit, and livestock. Oviedo and Gijón are the main industrial towns.

Asturias Miguel Ángel 1899–1974. Guatemalan author and diplomat. He published poetry, Guatemalan legends, and novels, such as *El señor presidente/The President* 1946, *Men of Corn* 1949, and *Strong Wind* 1950, attacking Latin-American dictatorships and 'Yankee imperialism'. Nobel prize 1967.

Asunción capital and port of Paraguay, on the Paraguay River; population (1984) 729,000. It produces textiles, footwear, and food products. Founded 1537, it was the first Spanish settlement in the La Plata region.

Aswan winter resort town in Upper Egypt; population (1985) 183,000. It is near the High Dam, built 1960–70, which keeps the level of the Nile constant throughout the year without flooding. It produces steel and textiles.

asylum, political in international law, refuge granted in another country to a person who, for political reasons, cannot return to his or her own country without putting himself or herself in danger. A person seeking asylum is a type of *refugee.

asymptote in *coordinate geometry, a straight line that a curve approaches more and more closely but never reaches. The x and y axes are asymptotes to the graph of xy = constant (a rectangular *hyperbola).

Atacama Desert desert in N Chile; area about 80,000 sq km/31,000 sq mi. There are mountains inland, and the coastal area is rainless and barren. The Atacama has silver and copper mines, and extensive nitrate deposits.

Atahualpa *c.* 1502–1533. Last emperor of the Incas of Peru. He was taken prisoner 1532 when the Spaniards arrived, and agreed to pay a substantial ransom, but was accused of plotting against the conquistador Pizarro and sentenced to be burned. On his consenting to Christian baptism, the sentence was commuted to strangulation.

Atatürk Kemal. Name assumed 1934 by Mustafa Kemal Pasha 1881–1938. (Atatürk 'Father of the Turks') Turkish politician and general, first president of Turkey from 1923. After World War I he established a provisional rebel government and in 1921–22 the Turkish armies under his leadership expelled the Greeks who were occupying Turkey. He was the founder of the modern republic, which he ruled as virtual dictator, with a policy of consistent and radical westernization.

Atatürk Dam dam on the river Euphrates, in the province of Gaziantep, S Turkey, completed Jan 1990. The lake, 550 km/340 mi SE of Ankara, covers 815 sq km/315 sq mi, and submerged 25 villages, whose 55,000 inhabitants were relocated.

atavism (Latin *atavus* 'ancestor') in *genetics, the reappearance of a characteristic not apparent in the immediately preceding generations; in psychology, the manifestation of primitive forms of behaviour.

ataxia loss of muscular coordination due to neurological damage or disease.

Athanasian creed one of the three ancient *creeds of the Christian church. Mainly a definition of the Trinity and Incarnation, it was written many years after the death of Athanasius, but was attributed to him as the chief upholder of Trinitarian doctrine.

Athanasius, St 298–373. Bishop of Alexandria, supporter of the doctrines of the Trinity and Incarnation. He was a disciple of St Anthony the hermit, and an opponent of *Arianism in the great Arian controversy. Following the official condemnation of Arianism at the Council of Nicaea 325, Athanasius was appointed bishop of Alexandria 328. The Athanasian creed was not actually written by him, although it reflects his views.

atheism nonbelief in, or the positive denial of, the existence of a God or gods. A related concept is *agnosticism.

Athelney, Isle of area of firm ground in marshland near Taunton in Somerset, England, in 878 the headquarters of King *Alfred the Great when he was in hiding from the Danes. The legend of his burning the cakes is set here.

Athelstan *c.* 895–939. King of the Mercians and West Saxons. Son of Edward the Elder and grandson of Alfred the Great, he was crowned king 925 at Kingston upon Thames. He subdued parts of Cornwall and Wales, and defeated the Welsh, Scots, and Danes at Brunanburh 937.

Athena in Greek mythology, the goddess (Roman Minerva) of war, wisdom, and the arts and crafts, who was supposed to have sprung fully grown from the head of Zeus. Her chief cult centre was Athens, where the *Parthenon was dedicated to her.

Athens (Greek *Athinai*) capital city of Greece and of ancient Attica; population (1981) 885,000, metropolitan area (1991) 3,096,800. Situated 8 km/5 mi NE of its port of Piraeus on the Gulf of Aegina, it is built around the rocky hills of the Acropolis 169 m/555 ft and the Areopagus 112 m/368 ft, and is overlooked from the northeast by the hill of Lycabettus, 277 m/909 ft high. It lies in the south of the central plain of Attica, watered by the mountain streams of Cephissus and Ilissus. It has less green space than any other European capital (4%) and severe air and noise pollution.

features The Acropolis dominates the city. Remains of ancient Greece include the Parthenon, the Erechtheum, and the temple of Athena Nike. Near the site of the ancient Agora (marketplace) stands the Theseum, and south of the Acropolis is the theatre of Dionysus. To the southeast stand the gate of Hadrian and the columns of the temple of Olympian Zeus. Nearby is the marble stadium built about 330 BC and restored 1896.

history The site was first inhabited about 3000 BC, and Athens became the capital of a united Attica before 700 BC. Captured and sacked by the Persians 480 BC, subsequently under Pericles it was the first city of Greece in power and culture. After the death of Alexander the Great the city fell into comparative decline, but it flourished as an intellectual centre until AD 529, when the philosophical schools were closed by Justinian. In 1458 it was captured by the Turks who held it until 1833; it was chosen as the capital of Greece 1834. Among present-day buildings are the royal palace and several museums.

atheroma furring-up of the interior of an artery

by deposits, mainly of cholesterol, within its walls.

atherosclerosis thickening and hardening of the walls of the arteries, associated with atheroma.

athletics competitive track and field events consisting of running, throwing, and jumping disciplines. *Running events* range from sprint races (100 metres) and hurdles to the marathon (26 miles 385 yards). *Jumping events* are the high jump, long jump, and – for men only – the triple jump and pole vault (the latter two for men only). *Throwing events* are javelin, discus, shot put, and – for men only – hammer throw.

Atlanta capital and largest city of Georgia, USA; population (1990) 394,000, metropolitan area 2,010,000. It was founded 1837 and was partly destroyed by General *Sherman 1864. There are Ford and Lockheed assembly plants, and it is the headquarters of Coca-Cola. In 1990 it was chosen as the host city for the 1996 summer Olympic Games.

Atlantic, Battle of the continuous battle fought in the Atlantic Ocean during World War II by the sea and air forces of the Allies and Germany, to control the supply routes to the UK. The number of U-boats destroyed by the Allies during the war was nearly 800. At least 2,200 convoys of 75,000 merchant ships crossed the Atlantic, protected by US naval forces. Before the US entry into the war 1941, destroyers were supplied to the British under the Lend-Lease Act 1941.

Atlantic, Battle of the German campaign during World War I to prevent merchant shipping from delivering food supplies from the USA to the Allies, chiefly the UK. By 1917, some 875,000 tons of shipping had been lost. The odds were only turned by the belated use of naval *convoys* and *depth charges* to deter submarine attack.

Atlantic Ocean ocean lying between Europe and Africa to the E and the Americas to the W, probably named after the legendary island of Atlantis; area of basin 81,500,000 sq km/ 31,500,000 sq mi; including the Arctic Ocean and Antarctic seas, 106,200,000 sq km/41,000,000 sq mi. The average depth is 3 km/2 mi; greatest depth the Milwaukee Depth in the Puerto Rico Trench 8,648 m/28,374 ft. The Mid-Atlantic Ridge, of which the Azores, Ascension, St Helena, and Tristan da Cunha form part, divides it from N to S. Lava welling up from this central area annually increases the distance between South America and Africa. The N Atlantic is the saltiest of the main oceans, and has the largest tidal range. In the 1960s–80s average wave heights increased by 25%, the largest from 12 m/ 39 ft to 18 m/59 ft.

Atlas in Greek mythology, one of the *Titans who revolted against the gods; as a punishment, Atlas was compelled to support the heavens on his head and shoulders. Growing weary, he asked *Perseus to turn him into stone, and he was transformed into Mount Atlas.

Atlas Mountains mountain system of NW Africa, stretching 2,400 km/1,500 mi from the Atlantic coast of Morocco to the Gulf of Gabes, Tunisia, and lying between the Mediterranean on the N and the Sahara on the S. The highest peak is Mount Toubkal 4,167 m/13,670 ft.

atman in Hinduism, the individual soul or the eternal essential self.

atmosphere mixture of gases that surrounds the Earth, prevented from escaping by the pull of the Earth's gravity. Atmospheric pressure decreases with height in the atmosphere. In its lowest layer, the atmosphere consists of nitrogen (78%) and oxygen (21%), both in molecular form (two atoms bounded together). The other 1% is largely argon, with very small quantities of other gases, including water vapour and carbon dioxide. The atmosphere plays a major part in the various cycles of nature (the *water cycle, *carbon cycle, and *nitrogen cycle). It is the principal industrial source of nitrogen, oxygen, and argon, which are obtained by fractional distillation of liquid air.

atmosphere or *standard atmosphere* in physics, a unit (symbol atm) of pressure equal to 760 torr, 1013.25 millibars, or 1.01325×10^5 newtons per square metre. The actual pressure exerted by the atmosphere fluctuates around this value, which is assumed to be standard at sea level and 0°C, and is used when dealing with very high pressures.

atom smallest unit of matter that can take part in a chemical reaction, and which cannot be broken down chemically into anything simpler. An atom is made up of protons and neutrons in a central nucleus surrounded by electrons (see *atomic structure). The atoms of the various elements differ in atomic number, relative atomic mass, and chemical behaviour. There are 109 different types of atom, corresponding with the 109 known elements as listed in the *periodic table of the elements.

atom bomb bomb deriving its explosive force from nuclear fission (see *nuclear energy) as a result of a neutron chain reaction, developed in the 1940s in the USA into a usable weapon.

atomic clock timekeeping device regulated by various periodic processes occurring in atoms and molecules, such as atomic vibration or the frequency of absorbed or emitted radiation.

atomic energy another name for *nuclear energy.

atomicity number of atoms of an *element that combine together to form a molecule. A molecule of oxygen (O_2) has atomicity 2; sulphur (S_8) has atomicity 8.

atomic mass unit or *dalton unit* (symbol amu or u) unit of mass that is used to measure the relative mass of atoms and molecules. It is equal to one-twelfth of the mass of a carbon-12 atom, which is equivalent to the mass of a proton or 1.66×10^{-27} kg. The *relative atomic mass of an atom has no units; thus oxygen-16 has an atomic mass of 16 daltons, but a relative atomic mass of 16.

atomic number or *proton number* the number (symbol Z) of protons in the nucleus of an atom. It is equal to the positive charge on the nucleus. In a neutral atom, it is also equal to the number of electrons surrounding the nucleus. The 109 elements are arranged in the *periodic table of the elements according to their atomic number. The atomic number is also an element in nuclear notation.

atomic radiation energy given out by disintegrating atoms during *radioactive decay, whether natural or synthesized. The energy may be in the form of fast-moving particles, known as *alpha particles and *beta particles, or in the form of high-energy electromagnetic waves known as *gamma radiation. Overlong exposure to atomic radiation can lead to *radiation sickness. Radiation biology studies the effect of radiation on living organisms.

atomic structure internal structure of an *atom. The core of the atom is the **nucleus**, a dense body only one ten-thousandth the diameter of the atom itself. The simplest nucleus, that of hydrogen, comprises a single stable positively charged particle, the **proton**. Nuclei of other elements contain more protons and additional particles, called **neutrons**, of about the same mass as the proton but with no electrical charge. Each element has its own characteristic nucleus with a unique number of protons, the atomic number. The number of neutrons may vary. Where atoms of a single element have different numbers of neutrons, they are called *isotopes. Although some isotopes tend to be unstable and exhibit *radioactivity, they all have identical chemical properties. The nucleus is surrounded by a number of moving **electrons**, each of which has a negative charge equal to the positive charge on a proton, but which weighs only $1/_{1,839}$ times as much. In a neutral atom, the nucleus is surrounded by the same number of electrons as it contains protons. According to *quantum theory, the position of an electron is uncertain; it may be found at any point. However, it is more likely to be found in some places than others. The region of space in which an electron is most likely to be found is called an orbital (see *orbital, atomic). The chemical properties of an element are determined by the ease with which its atoms can gain or lose electrons from its outer orbitals. High-energy physics research has discovered the existence of subatomic particles (see *particle physics) other than the proton, neutron, and electron. More than 300 kinds of particle are now known, and these are classified into several classes according to their mass, electric charge, spin, magnetic moment, and interaction. The **elementary particles**, which include the electron, are indivisible and may be regarded as the fundamental units of matter; the **hadrons**, such as the proton and neutron, are composite particles made up of either two or three elementary particles called quarks. Atoms are held together by the electrical forces of attraction between each negative electron and the positive protons within the nucleus. The latter repel one another with enormous forces; a nucleus holds together only because an even stronger force, called the strong nuclear force, attracts the protons and neutrons to one another. The strong force acts over a very short range -the protons and neutrons must be in virtual contact with one another. If, therefore, a fragment of a complex nucleus, containing some protons, becomes only slightly loosened from the main group of neutrons and protons, the natural repulsion between the protons will cause this fragment to fly apart from the rest of the nucleus at high speed. It is by such fragmentation of atomic nuclei (nuclear *fission) that nuclear energy is released.

atomic weight another name for *relative atomic mass.

atomizer device that produces a spray of fine droplets of liquid. A vertical tube connected with a horizontal tube dips into a bottle of liquid, and at one end of the horizontal tube is a nozzle, at the other a rubber bulb. When the bulb is squeezed, air rushes over the top of the vertical tube and out through the nozzle. Following *Bernoulli's principle, the pressure at the top of the vertical tube is reduced, allowing the liquid to rise. The air stream picks up the liquid, breaks it up into tiny drops, and carries it out of the nozzle as a spray.

Aton in ancient Egypt, the Sun's disc as an emblem of the single deity whose worship was promoted by *Ikhnaton in an attempt to replace the many gods traditionally worshipped.

atonality music in which there is an apparent absence of *key; often associated with an expressionist style.

atonement in Christian theology, the doctrine that Jesus suffered on the cross to bring about reconciliation and forgiveness between God and humanity.

Atonement, Day of Jewish holy day (**Yom Kippur**) held on the tenth day of Tishri (Sept–Oct), the first month of the Jewish year. It is a day of fasting, penitence, and cleansing from sin, ending the Ten Days of Penitence that follow **Rosh Hashanah**, the Jewish New Year.

ATP abbreviation for **adenosine triphosphate**, a nucleotide molecule found in all cells. It can yield large amounts of energy, and is used to drive the thousands of biological processes needed to sustain life, growth, movement, and reproduction. Green plants use light energy to manufacture ATP as part of the process of *photosynthesis. In animals, ATP is formed by the breakdown of glucose molecules, usually obtained from the carbohydrate component of a diet, in a series of reactions termed *respiration. It is the driving force behind muscle contraction and the synthesis of complex molecules needed by individual cells.

atrium in architecture, an open inner courtyard. Originally the central court or main room of an ancient Roman house, open to the sky, often with a shallow pool to catch water.

atrophy in medicine, a diminution in size and function, or output, of a body tissue or organ. It is usually due to nutritional impairment, disease, or disuse (muscle).

atropine alkaloid derived from belladonna, a plant with toxic properties. It acts as an *anticholinergic, inhibiting the passage of certain nerve impulses. As atropine sulphate, it is administered as a mild antispasmodic drug.

attainder, bill of legislative device that allowed the English Parliament to declare guilt and impose a punishment on an individual without bringing the matter before the courts. Such bills were used intermittently from the Wars of the Roses until 1798. Some acts of attainder were also passed by US colonial legislators during the American Revolution to deal with 'loyalists' who continued to support the English crown.

attempt in law, a partial or unsuccessful commission of a crime. An attempt must be more than preparation for a crime; it must involve actual efforts to commit a crime.

Attenborough David 1926– . English traveller and zoologist, brother of the actor and director Richard Attenborough. He was director of programmes for BBC Television 1969–72, and writer and presenter of the television series *Life on Earth* 1979, *The Living Planet* 1983, and *The Trials of Life* 1990.

Attenborough Richard 1923– . English actor, director, and producer. He began his acting career in war films and comedies. His later films include *Brighton Rock* 1947 and *10 Rillington Place* 1970 (as actor), and *Oh! What a Lovely War* 1969, *Gandhi* (which won eight Academy Awards) 1982, and *Cry Freedom* 1987 (as director).

Attica (Greek *Attiki*) region of Greece comprising Athens and the district around it; area 3,381 sq km/1,305 sq mi. It is renowned for its language, art, and philosophical thought in Classical times. It is a prefecture of modern Greece with Athens as its capital.

Attila *c.* 406–453. King of the Huns in an area from the Alps to the Caspian Sea from 434, known to later Christian history as the 'Scourge of God'. He twice attacked the Eastern Roman Empire to increase the quantity of tribute paid to him, 441–443 and 447–449, and then attacked the Western Roman Empire 450–52.

Attila Line line dividing Greek and Turkish Cyprus, so called because of a fanciful identification of the Turks with the Huns.

Attis in Classical mythology, a Phrygian god whose death and resurrection symbolized the end of winter and the arrival of spring. Beloved by the goddess Cybele, who drove him mad as a punishment for his infidelity, he castrated himself and bled to death.

Attlee Clement (Richard), 1st Earl 1883–1967. British Labour politician. In the coalition government during World War II he was Lord Privy Seal 1940–42, dominions secretary 1942–43, and Lord President of the Council 1943–45, as well as deputy prime minister from 1942. As prime minister 1945–51 he introduced a sweeping programme of nationalization and a whole new system of social services.

attorney person who represents another in legal matters. In the USA, attorney is the formal title for a lawyer.

Attorney General in the UK, principal law officer of the crown and head of the English Bar; the post is one of great political importance. In the USA, it is the chief law officer of the government and head of the Department of Justice.

Atwood Margaret (Eleanor) 1939– . Canadian novelist, short-story writer, and poet. Her novels, which often treat feminist themes with wit and irony, include *The Edible Woman* 1969, *Life Before Man* 1979, *Bodily Harm* 1981, *The Handmaid's Tale* 1986, and *Cat's Eye* 1989.

Auber Daniel François Esprit 1782–1871. French operatic composer who studied under the Italian composer and teacher Cherubini. He wrote about 50 operas, including *La Muette de Portici/The Mute Girl of Portici* 1828 and the comic opera *Fra Diavolo* 1830.

aubergine or *eggplant* plant *Solanum melongena*, a member of the nightshade family Solanaceae. The aubergine is native to tropical Asia. Its purple-skinned, sometimes white, fruits are eaten as a vegetable.

Aubrey John 1626–1697. English biographer and antiquary. His *Lives*, begun in 1667, contains gossip, anecdotes, and valuable insights into the celebrities of his time. Unpublished during his lifetime, a standard edition of the work appeared as *Brief Lives* 1898 in two volumes (edited by A Clark). Aubrey was the first to claim Stonehenge as a Druid temple.

Auckland largest city in New Zealand, situated in N North Island; population (1989) 850,900. It fills the isthmus that separates its two harbours (Waitemata and Manukau), and its suburbs spread north across the Harbour Bridge. It is the country's chief port and leading industrial centre, having iron and steel plants, engineering, car assembly, textiles, food processing, sugar refining, and brewing.

auction bridge card game played by two pairs of players using all 52 cards in a standard deck. The chief characteristic is the selection of trumps by a preliminary bid or auction. It has been succeeded by *contract bridge.

Auden W(ystan) H(ugh) 1907–1973. English-born US poet. He wrote some of his most original poetry, such as *Look, Stranger!* 1936, in the 1930s when he led the influential left-wing literary group that included Louis MacNeice, Stephen Spender, and Cecil Day Lewis. He moved to the USA 1939, became a US citizen 1946, and adopted a more conservative and Christian viewpoint, for example in *The Age of Anxiety* 1947.

audiometer electrical instrument used to test hearing.

audit official inspection of a company's accounts by a qualified accountant as required by law each year to ensure that the company balance sheet reflects the true state of its affairs.

Audit Commission independent body in the UK established by the Local Government Finance Act 1982. It administers the District Audit Service (established 1844) and appoints auditors for the accounts of all UK local authorities. The Audit Commission consists of 15 members: its aims include finding ways of saving costs, and controlling illegal local-authority spending.

auditory canal tube leading from the outer *ear opening to the eardrum. It is found only in animals whose eardrums are located inside the skull, principally mammals and birds.

Audubon John James 1785–1851. US naturalist and artist. In 1827, after extensive travels and observations of birds, he published the first part of his *Birds of North America*, with a remarkable series of colour plates. Later he produced a similar work on North American quadrupeds.

Augean stables in Greek mythology, the stables of Augeas, king of Elis in Greece. One of the labours of *Heracles was to clean out the stables, which contained 3,000 cattle and had never been cleaned before. He was given only one day to do the labour and so diverted the river Alpheus through their yard.

Augsburg, Confession of statement of the Protestant faith as held by the German

Reformers, composed by Philip *Melanchthon. Presented to the holy Roman emperor Charles V, at the conference known as the Diet of Augsburg 1530, it is the creed of the modern Lutheran church.

augur member of a college of Roman priests who interpreted the will of the gods from signs or 'auspices' such as the flight of birds, the condition of entrails of sacrificed animals, and the direction of thunder and lightning. Their advice was sought before battle and on other important occasions. Consuls and other high officials had the right to consult the auspices themselves, and a campaign was said to be conducted 'under the auspices' of the general who had consulted the gods.

Augustan Age golden age of the Roman emperor *Augustus, during which art and literature flourished. The name is also given to later periods which used Classical ideals, such as that of Queen Anne in England.

Augustine of Hippo, St 354–430. One of the early Christian leaders and writers known as the Fathers of the Church. He was converted to Christianity by Ambrose in Milan and became bishop of Hippo (modern Annaba, Algeria) 396. Among Augustine's many writings are his *Confessions*, a spiritual autobiography, and *De Civitate Dei/The City of God*, vindicating the Christian church and divine providence in 22 books.

Augustine, St first archbishop of Canterbury, England. He was sent from Rome to convert England to Christianity by Pope Gregory I. He landed at Ebbsfleet in Kent 597, and soon after baptized Ethelbert, King of Kent, along with many of his subjects. He was consecrated bishop of the English at Arles in the same year, and appointed archbishop 601, establishing his see at Canterbury. Feast day 26 May.

Augustinian member of a religious community that follows the Rule of St *Augustine of Hippo. It includes the Canons of St Augustine, Augustinian Friars and Hermits, Premonstratensians, Gilbertines, and Trinitarians.

Augustus 63 BC–AD 14. Title of Octavian (Gaius Julius Caesar Octavianus), first of the Roman emperors. He joined forces with Mark Antony and Lepidus in the Second Triumvirate. Following Mark Antony's liaison with the Egyptian queen Cleopatra, Augustus defeated her troops at Actium 31 BC. As emperor (from 27 BC) he reformed the government of the empire, the army, and Rome's public services, and was a patron of the arts. The period of his rule is known as the *Augustan Age.

auk any member of the family Alcidae, consisting of marine diving birds including razorbills, puffins, murres, and guillemots. Confined to the northern hemisphere, they feed on fish and use their wings to 'fly' underwater in pursuit.

Aung San 1916–1947. Burmese politician. He was a founder and leader of the Anti-Fascist People's Freedom League, which led Burma's fight for independence from Great Britain. During World War II he collaborated first with Japan and then with the UK. In 1947 he became head of Burma's provisional government but was assassinated the same year by political opponents; Burma (now Myanmar) became independent 1948.

Aurangzeb or **Aurungzebe** 1618–1707. Mogul emperor of N India from 1658. Third son of Shah Jahan, he made himself master of the court by a palace revolution. His reign was the most brilliant period of the Mogul dynasty, but his despotic tendencies and Muslim fanaticism aroused much opposition. His latter years were spent in war with the princes of Rajputana and Maratha.

Aurelian (Lucius Domitius Aurelianus) *c.* AD 214–275. Roman emperor from 270. A successful soldier, he was chosen emperor by his troops on the death of Claudius II. He defeated the Goths and Vandals, defeated and captured *Zenobia of Palmyra, and was planning a campaign against Parthia when he was murdered. The **Aurelian Wall**, a fortification surrounding Rome, was built by Aurelian 271. It was made of concrete, and substantial ruins exist. The **Aurelian Way** ran from Rome through Pisa and Genoa to Antipolis (Antibes) in Gaul.

Aurelius Antoninus Marcus Roman emperor; see *Marcus Aurelius Antoninus.

Auric Georges 1899–1983. French composer. He was one of the musical group called *Les Six. Auric composed a comic opera, several ballets, and incidental music to films of Jean Cocteau.

Auriga constellation of the northern hemisphere, represented as a man driving a chariot. Its brightest star is the first-magnitude *Capella, about 45 light-years from Earth; Epsilon Aurigae is an *eclipsing binary star with a period of 27 years, the longest of its kind (last eclipse 1983).

Aurignacian in archaeology, an Old Stone Age culture that came between the Mousterian and the Solutrian in the Upper Palaeolithic. The name is derived from a cave at Aurignac in the Pyrenees of France. The earliest cave paintings are attributed to the Aurignacian peoples of W Europe about 16,000 BC.

aurochs (plural **aurochs**) extinct species of long-horned wild cattle *Bos primigenius* that formerly roamed Europe, SW Asia, and N Africa. It survived in Poland until 1627. Black to reddish or grey, it was up to 1.8 m/6 ft at the shoulder. It is depicted in many cave paintings, and is considered the ancestor of domestic cattle.

aurora coloured light in the night sky near the Earth's magnetic poles, called **aurora borealis**, 'northern lights', in the northern hemisphere and **aurora australis** in the southern hemisphere. An aurora is usually in the form of a luminous arch with its apex towards the magnetic pole followed by arcs, bands, rays, curtains, and coronas, usually green but often showing shades of blue and red, and sometimes yellow or white. Auroras are caused at heights of over 100 km/60 mi by a fast stream of charged particles from solar flares and low-density 'holes' in the Sun's corona. These are guided by the Earth's magnetic field towards the north and south magnetic poles, where they enter the upper atmosphere and bombard the gases in the atmosphere, causing them to emit visible light.

Aurora Roman goddess of the dawn. The Greek equivalent is **Eos**.

Auschwitz (Polish **Oswiecim**) town near

Kraków in Poland, the site of a notorious *concentration camp used by the Nazis in World War II to exterminate Jews and other political and social minorities, as part of the 'final solution'. Each of the four gas chambers could hold 6,000 people.

auscultation evaluation of internal organs by listening, usually with the aid of a stethoscope.

Austen Jane 1775–1817. English novelist who described her raw material as 'three or four families in a Country Village'. *Sense and Sensibility* was published 1811, *Pride and Prejudice* 1813, *Mansfield Park* 1814, *Emma* 1816, *Northanger Abbey* and *Persuasion* 1818, all anonymously. She observed speech and manners with wit and precision, revealing her characters' absurdities in relation to high standards of integrity and appropriateness.

Austerlitz, Battle of battle on 2 Dec 1805 in which the French forces of Emperor Napoleon defeated those of Alexander I of Russia and Francis II of Austria at a small town in Czechoslovakia (formerly in Austria), 19 km/12 mi E of Brno.

Australasia loosely applied geographical term, usually meaning Australia, New Zealand, and neighbouring islands.

Australia Commonwealth of

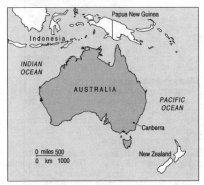

area 7,682,300 sq km/2,966,136 sq mi
capital Canberra
towns Adelaide, Alice Springs, Brisbane, Darwin, Melbourne, Perth, Sydney, Hobart, Geelong, Newcastle, Townsville, Wollongong
physical the world's smallest, flattest, and driest continent (40% lies in the tropics, one-third is desert, and one-third is marginal grazing); Great Sandy Desert; Gibson Desert; Great Victoria Desert; Simpson Desert; the Great Barrier Reef (largest coral reef in the world, stretching 2,000 km/1,250 mi off E coast of Queensland); Great Dividing Range and Australian Alps in the E (Mount Kosciusko, 2,229 m/7,136 ft, Australia's highest peak). The fertile SE region is watered by the Darling, Lachlan, Murrumbidgee, and Murray rivers; rivers in the interior are seasonal. Lake Eyre basin and Nullarbor Plain in the S
territories Norfolk Island, Christmas Island, Cocos (Keeling) Islands, Ashmore and Cartier Islands, Coral Sea Islands, Heard Island and McDonald Islands, Australian Antarctic Territory
environment an estimated 75% of Australia's northern tropical rain forest has been cleared for

agriculture or urban development since Europeans first settled there in the early 19th century
head of state Elizabeth II from 1952, represented by governor general
head of government Paul Keating from 1991
political system federal constitutional monarchy
exports world's largest exporter of sheep, wool, diamonds, alumina, coal, lead and refined zinc ores, and mineral sands; other exports include cereals, beef, veal, mutton, lamb, sugar, nickel (world's second largest producer), iron ore; principal trade partners are Japan, the USA, and EC member states
currency Australian dollar
population (1993) 17,800,000; growth rate 1.5% p.a.
languages English, Aboriginal languages
religions Anglican 26%, other Protestant 17%, Roman Catholic 26%
literacy 98.5.% (1988)
GNP $16,590 per head (1991)
chronology
1901 Creation of Commonwealth of Australia.
1927 Seat of government moved to Canberra.
1942 Statute of Westminster Adoption Act gave Australia autonomy from UK in internal and external affairs.
1944 Liberal Party founded by Robert Menzies.
1951 Australia joined New Zealand and the USA as a signatory to the ANZUS Pacific security treaty.
1966 Menzies resigned after being Liberal prime minister for 17 years, and was succeeded by Harold Holt.
1967 A referendum was passed giving Aborigines full citizenship rights.
1968 John Gorton became prime minister after Holt's death.
1971 Gorton succeeded by William McMahon, heading a Liberal–Country Party coalition.
1972 Gough Whitlam became prime minister, leading a Labor government.
1975 Senate blocked the government's financial legislation; Whitlam dismissed by the governor general, who invited Malcolm Fraser to form a Liberal–Country Party caretaker government. This action of the governor general, John Kerr, was widely criticized. 1992
1978 Northern Territory attained self-government.
1983 Labor Party returned to power under Bob Hawke, convened meeting of employers and unions to seek consensus on economic policy to deal with growing unemployment.
1986 Australia Act passed by UK government, eliminating last vestiges of British legal authority in Australia.
1988 Labor foreign minister Bill Hayden appointed governor general designate. Free-trade agreement with New Zealand signed.
1990 Hawke won record fourth election victory, defeating Liberal Party by small majority.
1991 Paul Keating became new Labor Party leader and prime minister.
1992 Keating's popularity declined as economic problems continued. Oath of allegiance to British crown abandoned.
1993 Labor Party won general election, entering fifth term of office.

Australia Day Australian national day and

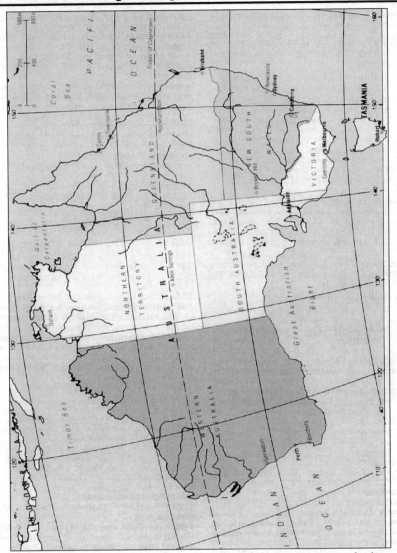

public holiday, the anniversary of Captain Phillip's arrival on 26 Jan 1788 at Sydney Cove in Port Jackson and the founding of the colony of New South Wales.

Australian Aboriginal religions beliefs associated with the creation legends recorded in the *Dreamtime stories.

Australian Aborigine any of the 500 groups of indigenous inhabitants of the continent of Australia, who migrated to this region from S Asia about 40,000 years ago. They were hunters and gatherers, living throughout the continent in small kin-based groups before European settlement. Several hundred different languages developed, the most important being Aranda (Arunta), spoken in central Australia, and Murngin, spoken in Arnhem Land. In recent years there has been a movement for the recognition of Aborigine rights and campaigning against racial discrimination in housing, education, wages, and medical facilities.

Australian Antarctic Territory islands and territories south of 60° S, between 160° E and 45° E longitude, excluding Adélie Land; area 6,044,000 sq km/2,332,984 sq mi of land and 75,800 sq km/29,259 sq mi of ice shelf. The population on the Antarctic continent is limited to research personnel.

Australian Capital Territory territory ceded to Australia by New South Wales 1911 to provide the site of *Canberra, with its port at Jervis Bay, ceded 1915; area 2,400 sq km/926 sq mi; population (1987) 261,000.

Austral Islands alternative name for *Tubuai Islands, part of *French Polynesia.

Austria Republic of (*Republik Österreich*)

area 83,500 sq km/32,374 sq mi
capital Vienna
towns Graz, Linz, Salzburg, Innsbruck
physical landlocked mountainous state, with Alps in W and S and low relief in E where most of the population is concentrated
environment Hainburg, the largest primeval forest left in Europe, under threat from a dam project (suspended 1990)
head of state Thomas Klestil from 1992
head of government Franz Vranitzky from 1986
political system democratic federal republic
exports lumber, textiles, clothing, iron and steel, paper, machinery and transport equipment, foodstuffs
currency schilling
population (1993 est) 7,900,000; growth rate 0.1% p.a.
language German
religions Roman Catholic 85%, Protestant 6%
GNP $23,256 per head (1992)
chronology
1867 Emperor Franz Josef established dual monarchy of Austria-Hungary.
1914 Archduke Franz Ferdinand assassinated by a Serbian nationalist; Austria-Hungary invaded Serbia, precipitating World War I.
1918 Habsburg empire ended, republic proclaimed.
1938 Austria incorporated into German Third Reich by Hitler (the *Anschluss*).
1945 Under Allied occupation, 1920 constitution reinstated and coalition government formed by the SPÖ and the ÖVP.
1955 Allied occupation ended, and the independence of Austria formally recognized.
1966 ÖVP in power with Josef Klaus as chancellor.
1970 SPÖ formed a minority government, with Dr Bruno Kreisky as chancellor.
1983 Kreisky resigned, was replaced by Dr Fred Sinowatz, leading a coalition.
1986 Dr Kurt Waldheim elected president. Sinowatz resigned, succeeded by Franz Vranitzky. No party won an overall majority;

Vranitzky formed a coalition of the SPÖ and the ÖVP, with ÖVP leader, Dr Alois Mock, as vice chancellor.
1989 Austria sought European Community membership.
1990 Vranitzky re-elected.
1991 Bid for EC membership endorsed by the Community.
1992 Thomas Klestil elected president, replacing Waldheim.

Austrian Succession, War of the war 1740–48 between Austria (supported by England and Holland) and Prussia (supported by France and Spain).
1740 The Holy Roman emperor Charles VI died and the succession of his daughter Maria Theresa was disputed by a number of European powers. Frederick the Great of Prussia seized *Silesia* from Austria.
1743 At *Dettingen* an army of British, Austrians, and Hanoverians under the command of George II was victorious over the French.
1745 An Austro-English army was defeated at *Fontenoy* but British naval superiority was confirmed, and there were gains in the Americas and India.
1748 The war was ended by the Treaty of Aix-la-Chapelle.

Austro-Hungarian Empire the Dual Monarchy established by the Habsburg Franz Joseph 1867 between his empire of Austria and his kingdom of Hungary (including territory that became Czechoslovakia as well as parts of Poland, the Ukraine, Romania, Yugoslavia, and Italy). It collapsed autumn 1918 with the end of World War I. Only two king-emperors ruled: Franz Joseph 1867–1916 and Charles 1916–18.

Austronesian languages (also known as *Malayo-Polynesian*) family of languages spoken in Malaysia, the Indonesian archipelago, parts of the region that was formerly Indochina, Taiwan, Madagascar, Melanesia, and Polynesia (excluding Australia and most of New Guinea). The group contains some 500 distinct languages, including Malay in Malaysia, Bahasa in Indonesia, Fijian, Hawaiian, and Maori.

autarchy national economic policy that aims at achieving self-sufficiency and eliminating the need for imports (by imposing tariffs, for example). Such a goal may be difficult, if not impossible, for a small country. Countries that take protectionist measures and try to prevent free trade are sometimes described as autarchical.

authoritarianism rule of a country by a dominant elite who repress opponents and the press to maintain their own wealth and power. They are frequently indifferent to activities not affecting their security, and rival power centres, such as trade unions and political parties, are often allowed to exist, although under tight control. An extreme form is *totalitarianism.

autism, infantile rare syndrome, generally present from birth, characterized by a withdrawn state and a failure to develop normally in language or social behaviour, although the autistic child may, rarely, show signs of high intelligence in other areas, such as music. Many have impaired intellect, however. The cause is unknown, but is thought to involve a number of interacting factors, possibly including an inherent abnormality of the child's brain.

autobiography a person's own biography, or written account of his or her life, distinguished from the journal or diary by being a connected narrative, and from memoirs by dealing less with contemporary events and personalities. *The Boke of Margery Kempe* about 1432–36 is the oldest extant autobiography in English.

autochrome in photography, a single-plate additive colour process devised by the *Lumière brothers 1903. It was the first commercially available process, in use 1907–35.

autoclave pressurized vessel that uses superheated steam to sterilize materials and equipment such as surgical instruments. It is similar in principle to a pressure cooker.

autocracy form of government in which one person holds absolute power. The autocrat has uncontrolled and undisputed authority. Russian government under the tsars was an autocracy extending from the mid-16th century to the early 20th century. The title *Autocratix* (a female autocrat) was assumed by Catherine II of Russia in the 18th century.

auto-da-fé (Portuguese 'act of faith') religious ceremony, including a procession, solemn mass, and sermon, which accompanied the sentencing of heretics by the Spanish *Inquisition before they were handed over to the secular authorities for punishment, usually burning.

autogiro or *autogyro* heavier-than-air craft that supports itself in the air with a rotary wing, or rotor. The Spanish aviator Juan de la *Cierva designed the first successful autogiro 1923. The autogiro's rotor provides only lift and not propulsion; it has been superseded by the helicopter, in which the rotor provides both. The autogiro is propelled by an orthodox propeller.

autoimmunity in medicine, condition where the body's immune responses are mobilized not against 'foreign' matter, such as invading germs, but against the body itself. Diseases considered to be of autoimmune origin include *myasthenia gravis, rheumatoid *arthritis, and *lupus erythematosus.

autolysis in biology, the destruction of a *cell after its death by the action of its own *enzymes, which break down its structural molecules.

automatic pilot control device that keeps an aeroplane flying automatically on a given course at a given height and speed. Devised by US business executive Lawrence Sperry 1912, the automatic pilot contains a set of *gyroscopes that provide references for the plane's course. Sensors detect when the plane deviates from this course and send signals to the control surfaces – the ailerons, elevators, and rudder – to take the appropriate action. Autopilot is also used in missiles.

automation widespread use of self-regulating machines in industry. Automation involves the addition of control devices, using electronic sensing and computing techniques, which often follow the pattern of human nervous and brain functions, to already mechanized physical processes of production and distribution; for example, steel processing, mining, chemical production, and road, rail, and air control.

automatism performance of actions without awareness or conscious intent. It is seen in sleepwalking and in some (relatively rare) psychotic states.

automaton mechanical figure imitating human or animal performance. Automatons are usually designed for aesthetic appeal as opposed to purely functional robots. The earliest recorded automaton is an Egyptian wooden pigeon of 400 BC.

autonomic nervous system in mammals, the part of the nervous system that controls the involuntary activities of the smooth muscles (of the digestive tract, blood vessels), the heart, and the glands. The *sympathetic* system responds to stress, when it speeds the heart rate, increases blood pressure and generally prepares the body for action. The *parasympathetic* system is more important when the body is at rest, since it slows the heart rate, decreases blood pressure, and stimulates the digestive system.

autonomy in politics, term used to describe political self-government of a state or, more commonly, a subdivision of a state. Autonomy may be based upon cultural or ethnic differences and often leads eventually to independence.

autopsy or *post-mortem* examination of the internal organs and tissues of a dead body, performed to try to establish the cause of death.

autoradiography in biology, a technique for following the movement of molecules within an organism, especially a plant, by labelling with a radioactive isotope that can be traced on photographs. It is used to study *photosynthesis, where the pathway of radioactive carbon dioxide can be traced as it moves through the various chemical stages.

autosome any *chromosome in the cell other than a sex chromosome. Autosomes are of the same number and kind in both males and females of a given species.

autosuggestion conscious or unconscious acceptance of an idea as true, without demanding rational proof, but with potential subsequent effect for good or ill. Pioneered by the French psychotherapist Emile Coué (1857–1926) in healing, it is used in modern psychotherapy to conquer nervous habits and dependence on tobacco, alcohol, and so on.

autotroph any living organism that synthesizes organic substances from inorganic molecules by using light or chemical energy. Autotrophs are the *primary producers* in all food chains since the materials they synthesize and store are the energy sources of all other organisms. All green plants and many planktonic organisms are autotrophs, using sunlight to convert carbon dioxide and water into sugars by *photosynthesis.

autumnal equinox see *equinox.

autumn crocus any member of the genus *Colchicum*, family Liliaceae. One species, the mauve *meadow saffron* *C. autumnale*, yields *colchicine*, which is used in treating gout and in plant breeding (it causes plants to double the numbers of their chromosomes, forming *polyploids).

Auvergne ancient province of central France and a modern region comprising the *départe-*

ments Allier, Cantal, Haute-Loire, and Puy-de-Dôme

area 26,000 sq km/10,036 sq mi

population (1986) 1,334,000

capital Clermont-Ferrand

physical mountainous, composed chiefly of volcanic rocks in several masses

products cattle, wheat, wine, and cheese

history named after the ancient Gallic Avenni tribe whose leader, Vercingetorix, led a revolt against the Romans 52 BC. In the 14th century the Auvergne was divided into a duchy, dauphiny, and countship. The duchy and dauphiny were united by the dukes of Bourbon before being confiscated by Francis I 1527. The countship united with France 1615.

auxin plant *hormone that promotes stem and root growth in plants. Auxins influence many aspects of plant growth and development, including cell enlargement, inhibition of development of axillary buds, *tropisms, and the initiation of roots. **Synthetic auxins** are used in rooting powders for cuttings, and in some weedkillers, where high auxin concentrations cause such rapid growth that the plants die. They are also used to prevent premature fruitdrop in orchards. The most common naturally occurring auxin is known as indoleacetic acid, or IAA. It is produced in the shoot apex and transported to other parts of the plant.

avalanche (from French *avaler* 'to swallow') fall of a mass of snow and ice down a steep slope. Avalanches occur because of the unstable nature of snow masses in mountain areas.

Avalokiteśvara in Mahāyāna Buddhism, one of the most important *bodhisattvas, seen as embodying compassion. Known as **Guanyin** in China and **Kannon** in Japan, he is one of the attendants of Amida Buddha.

avant-garde (French 'advanced guard') in the arts, those artists or works that are in the forefront of new developments in their media. The term was introduced (as was 'reactionary') after the French Revolution, when it was used to describe any socialist political movement.

avatar in Hindu mythology, the descent of a deity to Earth in a visible form, for example the ten avatars of *Vishnu.

Avebury Europe's largest stone circle (diameter 412 m/1,352 ft), in Wiltshire, England. It was probably constructed in the Neolithic period 3,500 years ago, and is linked with nearby *Silbury Hill. The village of Avebury was built within the circle, and many of the stones were used for building material.

Avedon Richard 1923– . US photographer. A fashion photographer with *Harper's Bazaar* magazine in New York from the mid-1940s, he moved to *Vogue* 1965. He later became the highest-paid fashion and advertising photographer in the world. Using large-format cameras, his work consists of intensely realistic images, chiefly portraits.

Ave Maria (Latin 'Hail, Mary') Christian prayer to the Virgin Mary, which takes its name from the archangel Gabriel's salutation to the Virgin Mary when announcing that she would be the mother of the Messiah (Luke 11:28).

avens any of several low-growing plants of the genus *Geum*, family Rosaceae. Species are distributed throughout Eurasia and N Africa.

average the typical member of a set of data, technically the *arithmetic mean. The term is also used to refer to the middle member of the set when it is sorted in ascending or descending order (the *median), and the most commonly occurring item of data (the *mode), as in 'the average family'.

Averroës (Arabic ***Ibn Rushd***) 1126–1198. Arabian philosopher who argued for the eternity of matter and against the immortality of the individual soul. His philosophical writings, including commentaries on Aristotle and on Plato's *Republic*, became known to the West through Latin translations. He influenced Christian and Jewish writers into the Renaissance, and reconciled Islamic and Greek thought in that philosophic truth comes through reason. St Thomas Aquinas opposed this position.

Avicenna (Arabic ***Ibn Sina***) 979–1037. Arabian philosopher and physician. He was the most renowned philosopher of medieval Islam. His *Canon Medicinae* was a standard work for many centuries. His philosophical writings were influenced by al-Farabi, Aristotle, and the neo-Platonists, and in turn influenced the scholastics of the 13th century.

Avignon city in Provence, France, capital of Vaucluse *département*, on the river Rhône NW of Marseilles; population (1982) 174,000. An important Gallic and Roman city, it has a 12th-century bridge (only half still standing), a 13th-century cathedral, 14th-century walls, and two palaces built during the residence here of the popes, Le Palais Vieux (1334–42) and Le Palais Nouveau (1342–52). Avignon was papal property 1348–1791.

avocado tree *Persea americana* of the laurel family, native to Central America. Its dark-green, thick-skinned, pear-shaped fruit has buttery-textured flesh and is used in salads.

avocet wading bird, genus *Recurvirostra*, family Recurvirostridae, with a characteristic long, narrow, upturned bill used in sifting water as it feeds in the shallows. It is about 45 cm/18 in long, and has long legs, partly webbed feet, and black and white plumage. There are four species. Stilts belong to the same family.

Avogadro's hypothesis in chemistry, the law stating that equal volumes of all gases, when at the same temperature and pressure, have the same numbers of molecules. It was first propounded by Amadeo Avogadro.

Avogadro's number or **Avogadro's constant** the number of carbon atoms in 12 g of the carbon-12 isotope (6.022045×10^{23}). The relative atomic mass of any element, expressed in grams, contains this number of atoms. It is named after Amadeo Avogadro.

avoirdupois system of units of mass based on the pound (0.45 kg), which consists of 16 ounces (each of 16 drams) or 7,000 grains (each equal to 65 mg).

Avon county in SW England

area 1,340 sq km/517 sq mi

towns Bristol (administrative headquarters), Bath, Weston-super-Mare

products aircraft and other engineering, tobacco, chemicals, printing, dairy products
population (1987) 919,800
famous people John Cabot, Thomas Chatterton, W G Grace
history formed 1974 from the city and county of Bristol, part of S Gloucestershire, and part of N Somerset.

Avon any of several rivers in England and Scotland. The Avon in Warwickshire is associated with Shakespeare.

AWACS (acronym for ***Airborne Warning And Control System***) surveillance system that incorporates a long-range surveillance and detection radar mounted on a Boeing E-3 sentry aircraft. It was used with great success in the 1991 Gulf War.

Awe, Loch longest (37 km/23 mi) of the Scottish freshwater lochs, in Strathclyde, SE of Oban. It is drained by the river Awe into Loch Etive.

Axelrod Julius 1912– . US neuropharmacologist who shared the 1970 Nobel Prize for Medicine with the biophysicists Bernard Katz and Ulf von Euler (1905–1983) for his work on neurotransmitters (the chemical messengers of the brain).

axil upper angle between a leaf (or bract) and the stem from which it grows. Organs developing in the axil, such as shoots and buds, are termed axillary, or lateral.

axiom in mathematics, a statement that is assumed to be true and upon which theorems are proved by using logical deduction; for example, two straight lines cannot enclose a space. The Greek mathematician Euclid used a series of axioms that he considered could not be demonstrated in terms of simpler concepts to prove his geometrical theorems.

axis (plural ***axes***) in geometry, one of the reference lines by which a point on a graph may be located. The horizontal axis is usually referred to as the *x*-axis, and the vertical axis as the *y*-axis. The term is also used to refer to the imaginary line about which an object may said to be symmetrical (***axis of symmetry***) – for example, the diagonal of a square – or the line about which an object may revolve (***axis of rotation***).

Axis alliance of Nazi Germany and Fascist Italy before and during World War II. The ***Rome–Berlin Axis*** was formed 1936, when Italy was being threatened with sanctions because of its invasion of Ethiopia (Abyssinia). It became a full military and political alliance May 1939. A ten-year alliance between Germany, Italy, and Japan (***Rome–Berlin–Tokyo Axis***) was signed Sept 1940 and was subsequently joined by Hungary, Bulgaria, Romania, and the puppet states of Slovakia and Croatia. The Axis collapsed with the fall of Mussolini and the surrender of Italy 1943 and Germany and Japan 1945.

axolotl (Aztec 'water monster' aquatic larval form ('tadpole') of any of several North American species of salamander, belonging to the family Ambystomatidae. Axolotls are remarkable because they can breed without changing to the adult form and will only metamorphose into adult salamanders in response to the drying-up of their ponds. The adults then migrate to another pond.

axon long threadlike extension of a *nerve cell that conducts electrochemical impulses away from the cell body towards other nerve cells, or towards an effector organ such as a muscle. Axons terminate in *synapses, junctions with other nerve cells, muscles, or glands.

axonometric projection three-dimensional drawing of an object, such as a building, in which the floor plan provides the basis for the visible elevations, thus creating a diagram that is true to scale but incorrect in terms of perspective. Vertical lines are projected up from the plan at the same scale; the usual angle of projection is 45°. An ***isometric projection*** is a slightly flattened variation.

ayatollah honorific title awarded to Shi'ite Muslims in Iran by popular consent, as, for example, to Ayatollah Ruhollah *Khomeini.

Ayckbourn Alan 1939– . English dramatist. His prolific output, characterized by comic dialogue and experiments in dramatic structure, includes *The Norman Conquests* (a trilogy) 1974, *A Woman in Mind* 1986, *Henceforward* 1987, and *Man of the Moment* 1988.

aye-aye *The aye-aye is a nocturnal animal that lives in the dense forests of Madagascar.*

aye-aye nocturnal tree-climbing prosimian *Daubentonia madagascariensis* of Madagascar, related to the lemurs. It is just over 1 m/3 ft long, including a tail 50 cm/20 in long.

Ayer A(lfred) J(ules) 1910–1989. English philosopher. He wrote *Language, Truth and Logic* 1936, an exposition of the theory of 'logical positivism', presenting a criterion by which meaningful statements (essentially truths of logic, as well as statements derived from experience) could be distinguished from meaningless metaphysical utterances (for example, claims that there is a God or that the world external to our own minds is illusory).

Ayers Rock (Aboriginal *Uluru*) vast ovate mass of pinkish rock in Northern Territory, Australia; 335 m/1,110 ft high and 9 km/6 mi around. For the Aboriginals, whose paintings decorate its caves, it has magical significance.

Aymara member of an American Indian people of Bolivia and Peru, builders of a great culture, who were conquered first by the Incas and then by the Spaniards. Today 1.4 million Aymara farm and herd llamas and alpacas in the highlands; their language, belonging to the Andean-Equatorial language family, survives, and their

Roman Catholicism incorporates elements of their old beliefs.

Ayurveda basically naturopathic system of medicine widely practised in India and based on principles derived from the ancient Hindu scriptures, the *Vedas. Hospital treatments and remedial prescriptions tend to be nonspecific and to coordinate holistic therapies for body, mind, and spirit.

azalea any of various deciduous flowering shrubs, genus *Rhododendron*, of the heath family Ericaceae. There are several species native to Asia and North America, and from these many cultivated varieties have been derived. Azaleas are closely related to the evergreen *rhododendrons of the same genus.

Azerbaijan Republic of

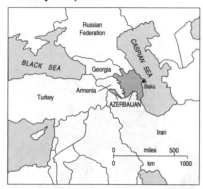

area 86,600 sq km/33,400 sq mi
capital Baku
towns Gyandzha (formerly Kirovabad), Sumgait
physical Caspian Sea; the country ranges from semidesert to the Caucasus Mountains
head of state Geidar Aliyev from 1993
head of government vacant
political system emergent democracy
products oil, iron, copper, fruit, vines, cotton, silk, carpets
currency manat
population (1993 est) 7,200,000 (83% Azeri, 6% Russian, 6% Armenian)
language Turkic
religion traditionally Shi'ite Muslim
GNP $1,670 per head (1991)
chronology
1917–18 A member of the anti-Bolshevik Transcaucasian Federation.
1918 Became an independent republic.
1920 Occupied by the Red Army.
1922–36 Formed part of the Transcaucasian Federal Republic with Georgia and Armenia.
1936 Became a constituent republic of the USSR.
1988 Riots followed Nagorno-Karabakh's request for transfer to Armenia.
1989 Jan–Nov: Nagorno-Karabakh placed under direct rule from Moscow. Azerbaijan Popular Front established. Nov: civil war with Armenia.
1990 Jan: Soviet troops dispatched to Baku to restore order. Aug: communists won parliamentary elections.
1991 Aug: Azeri leadership supported attempted anti-Gorbachev coup; independence declared.

Sept: former communist Ayaz Mutalibov elected president. Dec: joined new Commonwealth of Independent States; Nagorno-Karabakh declared independence.
1992 March: admitted into United Nations; accorded diplomatic recognition by the USA; Mutalibov resigned. June: Albulfaz Elchibey, leader of the Popular Front, elected president; renewed campaign to capture Nagorno-Karabakh.
1993 June: President Elchibey fled military revolt, replaced by former Communist Party leader Geidar Aliyev. Rebel military leader Surat Huseynov appointed prime minister. July: Nagorno-Karabakh overtaken by Armenian forces. Oct: Aliyev elected president.
1994 Huseynov dismissed from premiership.

Azerbaijani or *Azeri* native of the Azerbaijan region of Iran (population 5,500,000) or of Azerbaijan (formerly a Soviet republic) (population 7,145,600). Azerbaijani is a Turkic language belonging to the Altaic family. Of the total population of Azerbaijanis, 70% are Shi'ite Muslims and 30% Sunni Muslims.

Azerbaijan, Iranian two provinces of NW Iran, *Eastern Azerbaijan* (capital Tabriz), population (1986) 4,114,000, and *Western Azerbaijan* (capital Orúmiyeh), population (1986) 1,972,000. Azerbaijanis in Iran, as in the Republic of Azerbaijan, are mainly Shi'ite Muslim ethnic Turks, descendants of followers of the Khans from the Mongol Empire.

Azhar, El Muslim university and mosque in Cairo, Egypt. Founded 970, it is claimed to be the oldest university in the world. It is now primarily a school of Koranic teaching.

Azilian archaeological period following the close of the Old Stone (Palaeolithic) Age and one of the cultures of the Mesolithic Age. It was first recognized at Mas d'Azil, a village in Ariège, France.

azimuth in astronomy, the angular distance of an object eastwards along the horizon, measured from due north, between the astronomical *meridian (the vertical circle passing through the centre of the sky and the north and south points on the horizon) and the vertical circle containing the celestial body whose position is to be measured.

azo dye synthetic dye containing the azo group of two nitrogen atoms (N=N) connecting aromatic ring compounds. Azo dyes are usually red, brown, or yellow, and make up about half the dyes produced. They are manufactured from aromatic *amines.

Azores group of nine islands in the N Atlantic, belonging to Portugal; area 2,247 sq km/ 867 sq mi; population (1987) 254,000. They are outlying peaks of the Mid-Atlantic Ridge and are volcanic in origin. The capital is Ponta Delgada on the main island, San Miguel.

Azov (Russian *Azovskoye More*) inland sea of Europe forming a gulf in the NE of the Black Sea, between Ukraine and Russia; area 37,555 sq km/ 14,500 sq mi. Principal ports include Rostov-on-Don, Kerch, and Taganrog. Azov is a good source of freshwater fish.

AZT drug used in the treatment of AIDS; see *zidovudine.

Aztec member of a Mexican American Indian people that migrated south into the valley of Mexico in the 12th century, and in 1325 began reclaiming lake marshland to build their capital, Tenochtitlán, on the site of present-day Mexico City. Under Montezuma I (reigned from 1440), the Aztecs created a tribute empire in central Mexico. After the conquistador Cortés landed 1519, Montezuma II (reigned from 1502) was killed and Tenochtitlán subsequently destroyed. Nahuatl is the Aztec language; it belongs to the Uto-Aztecan family of languages.

B

Baader-Meinhof gang popular name for the West German left-wing guerrilla group the *Rote Armee Fraktion/Red Army Faction*, active from 1968 against what it perceived as US imperialism. The three main founding members were Andreas Baader (1943–1977), Gudrun Ensslin, and Ulrike Meinhof (1934–1976).

Baal divine title given to their chief male gods by the Phoenicians, or Canaanites. Their worship as fertility gods, often orgiastic and of a phallic character, was strongly denounced by the Hebrew prophets.

Baalbek city of ancient Syria, now in Lebanon, 60 km/36 mi NE of Beirut. It was originally a centre of Baal worship. The Greeks identified Baal with Helios, the Sun, and renamed Baalbek *Heliopolis*. Its ruins, including Roman temples, survive; the Temple of Bacchus, built in the 2nd century AD, is still almost intact.

Ba'ath Party ruling political party in Iraq and Syria. Despite public support of pan-Arab unity and its foundations 1943 as a party of Arab nationalism, its ideology has been so vague that it has fostered widely differing (and often opposing) parties in Syria and Iraq.

Bab, the name assumed by Mirza Ali Mohammad 1819–1850. Persian religious leader, born in Shiraz, founder of *Babism, an offshoot of Islam. In 1844 he proclaimed that he was a gateway to the Hidden Imam, a new messenger of Allah who was to come. He gained a large following whose activities caused the Persian authorities to fear a rebellion, and who were therefore persecuted. The Bab was executed for heresy.

Babangida Ibrahim 1941– . Nigerian politician and soldier, president 1985–93. He became head of the Nigerian army in 1983 and in 1985 led a coup against President Buhari, assuming the presidency himself. From 1992 he promised a return to civilian rule but resigned Aug 1993, his commitment to democracy increasingly in doubt.

Babbage Charles 1792–1871. English mathematician who devised a precursor of the computer. He designed an analytical engine, a general-purpose mechanical computing device for performing different calculations according to a program input on punched cards (an idea borrowed from the Jacquard loom). This device was never built, but it embodied many of the principles on which present digital computers are based.

Babbit metal soft, white metal, an *alloy of tin, lead, copper, and antimony, used to reduce friction in bearings, developed by the US inventor Isaac Babbit 1839.

Babbitt Milton 1916– . US composer and theorist. He pioneered the application of information theory to music in the 1950s, developing a personal style of *serialism. His works include four string quartets, works for orchestra, *Philomel* for soprano and electronic tape 1964, and *Ensembles for Synthesizer* 1967, both composed using the 1960 RCA Princeton-Columbia Mark II Synthesizer, which he helped to design.

babbler bird of the thrush family Muscicapidae with a loud babbling cry. Babblers, subfamily Timaliinae, are found in the Old World, and there are some 250 species in the group.

Babel Hebrew name for the city of *Babylon, chiefly associated with the **Tower of Babel** which, in the Genesis story in the Old Testament, was erected in the plain of Shinar by the descendants of Noah. It was a ziggurat, or staged temple, seven storeys high (100 m/300 ft) with a shrine of Marduk on the summit. It was built by Nabopolassar, father of Nebuchadnezzar, and was destroyed when Sennacherib sacked the city 689BC.

Babel Isaak Emmanuilovich 1894–1939/40. Russian writer. Born in Odessa, he was an ardent supporter of the Revolution and fought with Budyenny's cavalry in the Polish campaign of 1921–22, an experience which inspired *Red Cavalry* 1926. His other works include *Stories from Odessa* 1924, which portrays the life of the Odessa Jews.

Babi faith alternative name for *Baha'i faith.

Babington Anthony 1561–1586. English traitor who hatched a plot to assassinate Elizabeth I and replace her with *Mary Queen of Scots; its discovery led to Mary's execution and his own.

babirusa wild pig *Babirousa babyrussa*, becoming increasingly rare, found in the moist forests and by the water of Sulawesi, Buru, and nearby Indonesian islands. The male has large upper tusks which grow upwards through the skin of the snout and curve back towards the forehead. The babirusa is up to 80 cm/2.5 ft at the shoulder. It is nocturnal, and swims well.

Babism religious movement founded during the 1840s by Mirza Ali Mohammad ('the *Bab'). An offshoot of Islam, its main difference lies in the belief that Muhammad was not the last of the prophets. The movement split into two groups after the death of the Bab; Baha'ullah, the leader of one of these groups, founded the *Baha'i faith.

Babi Yar ravine near Kiev, Ukraine, where more than 100,000 people (80,000 Jews; the others were Poles, Russians, and Ukrainians) were killed by the Nazis 1941. The site was ignored until the Soviet poet Yevtushenko wrote a poem called 'Babi Yar' 1961 in protest at plans for a sports centre on the site.

baboon large monkey of the genus *Papio*, with a long doglike muzzle and large canine teeth, spending much of its time on the ground in open country. Males, with head and body up to 1.1 m/3.5 ft long, are larger than females, and dominant males rule the 'troops' in which baboons live. They inhabit Africa and SW Arabia.

Babur (Arabic 'lion') (Zahir ud-Din Muham-

baboon *Hamadryas baboon of Ethiopia, Somalia, and southern Saudi Arabia.*

mad) 1483–1530. First Great Mogul of India from 1526. He was the great-grandson of the Mogul conqueror Tamerlane. In 1526 he captured Delhi and *Agra and established a dynasty that lasted until 1858.

Babylon capital of ancient Babylonia, on the bank of the lower Euphrates River. The site is now in Iraq, 88 km/55 mi S of Baghdad and 8 km/5 mi N of Hilla, which is built chiefly of bricks from the ruins of Babylon. The Hanging Gardens of Babylon, one of the *Seven Wonders of the World, were probably erected on a vaulted stone base, the only stone construction in the mud-brick city. They formed a series of terraces, irrigated by a hydraulic system.

Babylonian captivity exile of Jewish deportees to Babylon after Nebuchadnezzar II's capture of Jerusalem 586 BC. According to tradition, the captivity lasted 70 years, but Cyrus of Persia, who conquered Babylon, actually allowed them to go home in 536 BC. By analogy, the name has also been applied to the papal exile to Avignon, France, 1309–77.

Bacall Lauren. Stage name of Betty Joan Perske 1924– . US actress. She became an overnight star when cast by Howard Hawks opposite Humphrey Bogart in *To Have and Have Not* 1944. She and Bogart married 1945 and starred together in *The Big Sleep* 1946. She also appeared in *Murder on the Orient Express* 1974 and *The Shootist* 1976.

Bacchus in Greek and Roman mythology, the god of fertility (see *Dionysus) and of wine; his rites (the ***Bacchanalia***) were orgiastic.

Bach Carl Philip Emmanuel 1714–1788. German composer. He was the third son of J S Bach. He introduced a new 'homophonic' style, light and easy to follow, which influenced Mozart, Haydn, and Beethoven.

Bach Johann Christian 1735–1782. German composer. The 11th son of J S Bach, he became celebrated in Italy as a composer of operas. In 1762 he was invited to London, where he became music master to the royal family. He remained in England until his death, enjoying great popularity both as a composer and a performer.

Bach Johann Sebastian 1685–1750. German composer. He was a master of *counterpoint, and his music epitomizes the Baroque polyphonic style. His orchestral music includes the six *Bran-denburg Concertos* 1721, other concertos for keyboard instrument and violin, and four orchestral suites. Bach's keyboard music, for clavier and organ, his fugues, and his choral music are of equal importance. He also wrote chamber music and songs.

Bach Wilhelm Friedemann 1710–1784. German composer. He was also an organist, improviser, and master of *counterpoint. He was the eldest son of J S Bach.

bacille Calmette-Guérin tuberculosis vaccine *BCG.

bacillus member of a group of rodlike *bacteria that occur everywhere in the soil and air. Some are responsible for diseases such as anthrax or for causing food spoilage.

backgammon board game for two players, often used in gambling. It was known in Mesopotamia, Greece, and Rome and in medieval England.

background radiation radiation that is always present in the environment. By far the greater proportion (87%) of it is emitted from natural sources. Alpha and beta particles, and gamma radiation are radiated by the traces of radioactive minerals that occur naturally in the environment and even in the human body, and by radioactive gases such as radon and thoron, which are found in soil and may seep upwards into buildings. Radiation from space (*cosmic radiation) also contributes to the background level.

back pain aches in the region of the spine. Low back pain can be caused by a very wide range of medical conditions. About half of all episodes of back pain will resolve within a week, but severe back pain can be chronic and disabling. The causes include muscle sprain, a prolapsed intervertebral disc, and vertebral collapse due to *osteoporosis or cancer. Treatment methods include rest, analgesics, physiotherapy, osteopathy, and exercises.

'back to basics' phrase used by British prime minister John Major at the Conservative Party conference in Oct 1993, in which he argued for a return to 'traditional British values'. It was subsequently adopted as a slogan by the Conservative Party, some members of which emphasized the morality aspect.

backup system in computing, a duplicate computer system that can take over the operation of a main computer system in the event of equipment failure.

Bacon Francis 1561–1626. English politician, philosopher, and essayist. He became Lord Chancellor 1618, and the same year confessed to bribe-taking, was fined £40,000 (which was later remitted by the king), and spent four days in the Tower of London. His works include *Essays* 1597, characterized by pith and brevity; *The Advancement of Learning* 1605, a seminal work discussing scientific method; the *Novum Organum* 1620, in which he redefined the task of natural science, seeing it as a means of empirical discovery and a method of increasing human power over nature; and *The New Atlantis* 1626, describing a utopian state in which scientific knowledge is systematically sought and exploited.

Bacon Francis 1909–1992. Irish painter. Self-taught, he practised abstract art, then developed a stark Expressionist style characterized by distorted, blurred figures enclosed in loosely defined space. One of his best-known works is *Study after Velázquez's Portrait of Pope Innocent X* 1953 (Museum of Modern Art, New York).

Bacon Roger 1214–1292. English philosopher, scientist, and a teacher at Oxford University. He was interested in alchemy, the biological and physical sciences, and magic. Many discoveries have been credited to him, including the magnifying lens. He foresaw the extensive use of gunpowder and mechanical cars, boats, and planes.

bacteria (singular **bacterium**) microscopic unicellular organisms with prokaryotic cells (see *prokaryote). They usually reproduce by *binary fission (dividing into two equal parts), and since this may occur approximately every 20 minutes, a single bacterium is potentially capable of producing 16 million copies of itself in a day. It is thought that 1–10% of the world's bacteria have been identified.

bacteriophage virus that attacks *bacteria. Such viruses are now of use in genetic engineering.

Bactria former region of central Asia (now divided between Afghanistan, Pakistan, and Tajikistan) which was partly conquered by *Alexander the Great. During the 3rd–6th centuries BC it was a centre of East-West trade and cultural exchange.

Bactrian species of *camel *Camelus bactrianus* found in the Gobi Desert in Central Asia. Body fat is stored in two humps on the back. It has very long winter fur which is shed in ragged lumps. The head and body length is about 3 m/10 ft, and the camel is up to 2.1 m/6.8 ft tall at the shoulder. Most Bactrian camels are domesticated and are used as beasts of burden in W Asia.

Baden former state of SW Germany, which had Karlsruhe as its capital. Baden was captured from the Romans in 282 by the Alemanni; later it became a margravate and in 1806, a grand duchy. A state of the German empire 1871–1918, then a republic, and under Hitler a *Gau* (province), it was divided between the *Länder* of Württemberg-Baden and Baden in 1945 and in 1952 made part of *Baden-Württemberg.

Baden-Powell Robert Stephenson Smyth, 1st Baron Baden-Powell 1857–1941. British general, founder of the Scout Association. He fought in defence of Mafeking (now Mafikeng) during the Second South African War. After 1907 he devoted his time to developing the Scout movement, which rapidly spread throughout the world. He was created a peer in 1929.

Baden-Württemberg administrative region (German *Land*) of Germany;
area 35,800 sq km/13,819 sq mi
capital Stuttgart
towns Mannheim, Karlsruhe, Freiburg, Heidelberg, Heilbronn, Pforzheim, Ulm
physical Black Forest; Rhine boundary S and W; source of the Danube; see also *Swabia
products wine, jewellery, watches, clocks, musical instruments, textiles, chemicals, iron, steel, electrical equipment, surgical instruments
population (1988) 9,390,000
history formed 1952 (following a plebiscite) by the merger of the *Länder* Baden, Württemberg-Baden, and Württemberg-Hohenzollern.

Bader Douglas 1910–1982. British fighter pilot. He lost both legs in a flying accident 1931, but had a distinguished flying career in World War II. He was knighted 1976 for his work with disabled people.

badger large mammal of the weasel family with molar teeth of a crushing type adapted to a partly vegetable diet, and short strong legs with long claws suitable for digging. The Eurasian *common badger Meles meles* is about 1 m/3 ft long, with long, coarse, greyish hair on the back, and a white face with a broad black stripe along each side. Mainly a woodland animal, it is harmless and nocturnal, and spends the day in a system of burrows called a 'sett'. It feeds on roots, a variety of fruits and nuts, insects, worms, mice, and young rabbits.

badlands barren landscape cut by erosion into a maze of ravines, pinnacles, gullies and sharp-edged ridges. Areas in South Dakota and Nebraska, USA, are examples.

badminton racket game similar to lawn *tennis but played on a smaller court and with a shuttlecock (a half sphere of cork or plastic with a feather or nylon skirt) instead of a ball. The object of the game is to prevent the opponent from being able to return the shuttlecock.

Badoglio Pietro 1871–1956. Italian soldier and Fascist politician. A veteran of campaigns against the peoples of Tripoli and Cyrenaica, in 1935 he became commander in chief in Ethiopia, adopting ruthless measures to break patriot resistance. He was created viceroy of Ethiopia and duke of Addis Ababa in 1936. He resigned during the disastrous campaign into Greece 1940 and succeeded Mussolini as prime minister of Italy from July 1943 to June 1944, negotiating the armistice with the Allies.

Baekeland Leo Hendrik 1863–1944. Belgian-born US chemist. He invented *Bakelite, the first commercial plastic, made from formaldehyde and *phenol. He later made a photographic paper, Velox, which could be developed in artificial light.

Baffin William 1584–1622. English explorer and navigator. In 1616, he and Robert Bylot explored Baffin Bay, NE Canada, and reached latitude 77° 45′ N, which for 236 years remained the 'furthest north'.

Bagehot Walter 1826–1877. British writer and economist, author of *The English Constitution* 1867, a classic analysis of the British political system. He was editor of *The Economist* magazine 1860–77.

Baghdad historic city and capital of Iraq, on the river Tigris; population (1985) 4,649,000. Industries include oil refining, distilling, tanning, tobacco processing, and the manufacture of textiles and cement. Founded 762, it became Iraq's capital 1921.

bagpipe ancient wind instrument used outdoors and incorporating a number of reed pipes powered from a single inflated bag. Known in Roman times, it is found in various forms throughout Europe including Ireland and Greece. The most famous, that of the Highlands, is the Scottish national instrument.

Bahadur Shah II 1775–1862. Last of the Mogul emperors of India. He reigned, though in name only, as king of Delhi 1837–57, when he was hailed by the mutineers of the *Indian Mutiny as an independent emperor at Delhi. After the rebellion he was exiled to Burma (now Myanmar) with his family.

Baha'i Faith religion founded in the 19th century from a Muslim splinter group, *Babism, by the Persian *Baha'ullah. His message in essence was that all great religious leaders are manifestations of the unknowable God and all scriptures are sacred. There is no priesthood: all Baha'is are expected to teach, and to work towards world unification. There are about 4.5 million Baha'is worldwide.

Bahamas Commonwealth of the

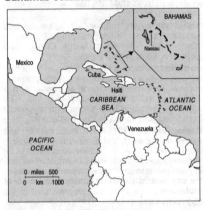

area 13,864 sq km/5,352 sq mi
capital Nassau on New Providence
towns Alice Town, Andros Town, Hope Town, Spanish Wells, Freeport, Moss Town, George Town
physical comprises 700 tropical coral islands and about 1,000 cays
principal islands Andros, Grand Bahama, Great Abaco, Eleuthera, New Providence, Berry Islands, Biminis, Great Inagua, Acklins, Exumas, Mayaguana, Crooked Island, Long Island, Cat Island, Rum Cay, Watling (San Salvador) Island
head of state Elizabeth II from 1973 represented by governor general
head of government Hubert Ingraham from 1992
political system constitutional monarchy
exports cement, pharmaceuticals, petroleum products, crawfish, salt, aragonite, rum, pulpwood; over half the islands' employment comes from tourism
currency Bahamian dollar
population (1993 est) 270,000; growth rate 1.8% p.a.
languages English and some Creole
religions 29% Baptist, 23% Anglican, 22% Roman Catholic
GNP $11,720 per head (1991)
chronology
1964 Independence achieved from Britain.
1967 First national assembly elections.
1972 Constitutional conference to discuss full independence.

1973 Full independence achieved.
1983 Allegations of drug trafficking by government ministers.
1984 Deputy prime minister and two cabinet ministers resigned. Pindling denied any personal involvement and was endorsed as party leader.
1987 Pindling re-elected despite claims of frauds.
1992 FNM led by Hubert Ingraham won absolute majority in assembly elections.

Baha'ullah title of Mirza Hosein Ali 1817–1892. Persian founder of the *Baha'i religion. Baha'ullah, 'God's Glory', proclaimed himself as the prophet the *Bab had foretold.

Bahrain State of (*Dawlat al Bahrayn*)

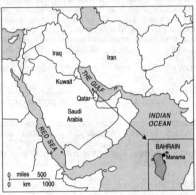

area 688 sq km/266 sq mi
capital Manama on the largest island (also called Bahrain)
towns Muharraq, Jidd Hafs, Isa Town; oil port Mina Sulman
physical 35 islands, composed largely of sand-covered limestone; generally poor and infertile soil; flat and hot
environment a wildlife park features the oryx on Bahrain; most of the south of the island is preserved for the ruling family's falconry
head of state and government Sheik Isa bin Sulman al-Khalifa (1933–) from 1961
political system absolute emirate
exports oil, natural gas, aluminium, fish
currency Bahrain dinar
population (1993 est) 538,000 (two-thirds are nationals); growth rate 4.4% p.a.
languages Arabic (official); Farsi, English, Urdu
religion 85% Muslim (Shi'ite 60%, Sunni 40%)
GNP $6,910 per head (1991)
chronology
1861 Became British protectorate.
1968 Britain announced its intention to withdraw its forces. Bahrain formed, with Qatar and the Trucial States, the Federation of Arab Emirates.
1971 Qatar and the Trucial States withdrew from the federation and Bahrain became an independent state.
1973 New constitution adopted, with an elected national assembly.
1975 Prime minister resigned and national assembly dissolved. Emir and his family assumed virtually absolute power.
1986 Gulf University established in Bahrain. A

causeway was opened linking the island with Saudi Arabia.

1988 Bahrain recognized Afghan rebel government.

1991 Bahrain joined United Nations coalition that ousted Iraq from its occupation of Kuwait.

Baikal (Russian *Baykal Ozero*) largest freshwater lake in Asia, and the eighth largest in the world (area 31,500 sq km/12,150 sq mi); also the deepest in the world (up to 1,640 m/5,700 ft), in S Siberia, Russia. Fed by more than 300 rivers, it is drained only by the Lower Angara. It has sturgeon fisheries and rich fauna.

Baikonur launch site for spacecraft, located at Tyuratam, Kazakhstan, near the Aral Sea: the first satellites and all Soviet space probes and crewed Soyuz missions were launched from here. It covers an area of 12,200 sq km/4,675 sq mi, much larger than its US equivalent, the *Kennedy Space Center in Florida.

bail the setting at liberty of a person in legal custody on an undertaking (usually backed by some security, given either by that person or by someone else) to attend at a court at a stated time and place. If the person does not attend, the bail may be forfeited.

Bailey David 1938– . British fashion photographer, chiefly associated with *Vogue* magazine from the 1960s. He has published several books of his work, exhibited widely, and also made films.

Bainbridge Beryl 1934– . English novelist, originally an actress, whose works have the drama and economy of a stage play. They include *The Dressmaker* 1973, *The Bottle Factory Outing* 1974, *Injury Time* 1977, *Young Adolf* 1978, *The Winter Garden* 1980, the collected short stories in *Mum and Mr Armitage* 1985, and *The Birthday Boys* 1991.

Baird John Logie 1888–1946. Scottish electrical engineer who pioneered television. In 1925 he gave the first public demonstration of television and in 1926 pioneered fibre optics, radar (in advance of Robert *Watson-Watt), and 'noctovision', a system for seeing at night by using infrared rays.

Bakelite first synthetic *plastic, created by Leo *Baekeland in 1909. Bakelite is hard, tough, and heatproof, and is used as an electrical insulator. It is made by the reaction of phenol with formaldehyde, producing a powdery resin that sets solid when heated. Objects are made by subjecting the resin to compression moulding (simultaneous heat and pressure in a mould).

Baker Benjamin 1840–1907. English engineer who designed (with English engineer John Fowler (1817–1898)) London's first underground railway (the Metropolitan and District) in 1869, the Forth Bridge, Scotland, 1890, and the original Aswan Dam on the river Nile, Egypt.

Baker James (Addison), III 1930– . US Republican politician. Under President Reagan, he was White House Chief of Staff 1981–85 and Treasury secretary 1985–88. After managing George Bush's successful presidential campaign 1988, Baker was appointed secretary of state 1989 and played a prominent role in the 1990–91 Gulf crisis and the subsequent search for a lasting Middle East peace settlement. In 1992 he left the State Department to head Bush's re-election campaign. After Democrat Bill Clinton's victory, Baker took over as White House Chief of Staff until the new president's inauguration Jan 1993.

Baker Janet 1933– . English mezzo-soprano noted for the emotional strength and richness of her interpretations of lieder (musical settings for poems), oratorio, and opera from Purcell to Britten, including a notable Dido in Purcell's *Dido and Aeneas*. She retired from the stage 1981.

Baker Kenneth (Wilfrid) 1934– . British Conservative politician, home secretary 1990–92. He was environment secretary 1985–86, education secretary 1986–89, and chair of the Conservative Party 1989–90, retaining his cabinet seat, before becoming home secretary in John Major's government.

baking powder mixture of bicarbonate of soda (*sodium hydrogencarbonate), an acidic compound, and a nonreactive filler (usually starch or calcium sulphate), used in baking as a raising agent. It gives a light open texture to cakes and scones, and is used as a substitute for yeast in making soda bread.

Baku capital city of the Republic of Azerbaijan, industrial port (oil refining) on the Caspian Sea; population (1987) 1,741,000. It is a major oil centre and is linked by pipelines with Batumi on the Black Sea. In Jan 1990 there were violent clashes between the Azeri majority and the Armenian minority, and Soviet troops were sent to the region; over 13,000 Armenians subsequently fled from the city. In early March 1992, opposition political forces sponsored protests in the city that led to the resignation of President Mutalibov.

Bakunin Mikhail 1814–1876. Russian anarchist, active in Europe. In 1848 he was expelled from France as a revolutionary agitator. In Switzerland in the 1860s he became recognized as the leader of the anarchist movement. In 1869 he joined the First International (a coordinating socialist body) but, after stormy conflicts with Karl Marx, was expelled 1872.

Balaclava, Battle of in the Crimean War, an engagement on 25 Oct 1854 near a town in Ukraine, 10 km/6 mi SE of Sevastopol. It was the scene of the ill-timed *Charge of the Light Brigade* of British cavalry against the Russian entrenched artillery. Of the 673 soldiers who took part, there were 272 casualties. *Balaclava helmets* were knitted hoods worn here by soldiers in the bitter weather.

Balakirev Mily Alexeyevich 1837–1910. Russian composer. He wrote orchestral works including the fantasy *Islamey* 1869/1902, piano music, songs, and a symphonic poem *Tamara*, all imbued with the Russian national character and spirit. He was leader of the group known as the Five and taught its members, Mussorgsky, Cui, Rimsky-Korsakov, and Borodin.

balalaika Russian musical instrument, resembling a guitar. It has a triangular sound box, frets, and two, three, or four strings played by strumming with the fingers.

balance apparatus for weighing or measuring mass. The various types include the *beam balance* consisting of a centrally pivoted lever with pans hanging from each end, and the *spring* *balance*, in which the object to be weighed stretches (or compresses) a vertical coil spring fitted with a pointer that indicates the weight on a scale. Kitchen and bathroom scales are balances.

balance of nature in ecology, the idea that there is an inherent equilibrium in most *ecosystems, with plants and animals interacting so as to produce a stable, continuing system of life on earth. Organisms in the ecosystem are adapted to each other – for example, waste products produced by one species are used by another and resources used by some are replenished by others; the oxygen needed by animals is produced by plants while the waste product of animal respiration, carbon dioxide, is used by plants as a raw material in photosynthesis. The nitrogen cycle, the water cycle, and the control of animal populations by natural predators are other examples. The activities of human beings can, and frequently do, disrupt the balance of nature.

balance of payments in economics, a tabular account of a country's debit and credit transactions with other countries. Items are divided into the *current account*, which includes both visible trade (imports and exports) and invisible trade (such as transport, tourism, interest, and dividends), and the *capital account*, which includes investment in and out of the country, international grants, and loans. Deficits or surpluses on these accounts are brought into balance by buying and selling reserves of foreign currencies.

balance of power in politics, the theory that the best way of ensuring international order is to have power so distributed among states that no single state is able to achieve a dominant position. The term, which may also refer more simply to the actual distribution of power, is one of the most enduring concepts in international relations. Since the development of nuclear weapons, it has been asserted that the balance of power has been replaced by a *balance of terror*.

balance sheet statement of the financial position of a company or individual on a specific date, showing both *assets and *liabilities.

Balanchine George 1904–1983. Russian-born US choreographer. After leaving the USSR in 1924, he worked with *Diaghilev in France. Moving to the USA in 1933, he became a major influence on dance, starting the New York City Ballet in 1948. He was the most influential 20th-century choreographer of ballet in the USA. He developed an 'American Neo-Classic' dance style and made the New York City Ballet one of the world's great companies. He also pioneered choreography in Hollywood films.

Balboa Vasco Núñez de 1475–1519. Spanish *conquistador. He founded a settlement at Darien (now Panama) 1511 and crossed the Isthmus in search of gold, reaching the Pacific Ocean (which he called the South Sea) on 25 Sept 1513, after a 25-day expedition. He was made admiral of the Pacific and governor of Panama but was removed by Spanish court intrigue, imprisoned, and executed.

Balcon Michael 1896–1977. British film producer, responsible for the influential 'Ealing comedies' of the 1940s and early 1950s, such as *Kind Hearts and Coronets* 1949, *Whisky Galore!* 1949, and *The Lavender Hill Mob* 1951.

Balder in Norse mythology, the son of *Odin and *Freya and husband of Nanna, and the best, wisest, and most loved of all the gods. He was killed, at *Loki's instigation, by a twig of mistletoe shot by the blind god Hodur.

Baldwin James 1924–1987. US writer, born in New York City, who portrayed the condition of black Americans in contemporary society. His works include the novels *Go Tell It on the Mountain* 1953, *Another Country* 1962, and *Just Above My Head* 1979; the play *The Amen Corner* 1955; and the autobiographical essays *Notes of a Native Son* 1955 and *The Fire Next Time* 1963. He was active in the civil-rights movement.

Baldwin Stanley, 1st Earl Baldwin of Bewdley 1867–1947. British Conservative politician, prime minister 1923–24, 1924–29, and 1935–37; he weathered the general strike 1926, secured complete adult suffrage 1928, and handled the *abdication crisis of Edward VIII 1936, but failed to prepare Britain for World War II.

Baldwin I 1058–1118. King of Jerusalem from 1100. A French nobleman, he joined his brother Godfrey de Bouillon (*c.* 1060–1100) on the First Crusade in 1096 and established the kingdom of Jerusalem in 1100. It was destroyed by Islamic conquest in 1187.

Balearic Islands (Spanish *Baleares*) group of Mediterranean islands forming an autonomous region of Spain; including *Majorca, *Minorca, *Ibiza, Cabrera, and Formentera
area 5,000 sq km/1,930 sq mi
capital Palma de Mallorca
products figs, olives, oranges, wine, brandy, coal, iron, slate; tourism is crucial
population (1986) 755,000
history a Roman colony from 123 BC, the Balearic Islands were an independent Moorish kingdom 1009–1232; they were conquered by Aragón 1343.

Balfour Arthur James, 1st Earl of Balfour 1848–1930. British Conservative politician, prime minister 1902–05 and foreign secretary 1916–19, when he issued the Balfour Declaration 1917 and was involved in peace negotiations after World War I, signing the Treaty of Versailles.

Balfour Declaration letter, dated 2 Nov 1917, from the British foreign secretary A J Balfour to Lord Rothschild (chair, British Zionist Federation) stating: 'HM government view with favour the establishment in Palestine of a national home for the Jewish people.' It led to the foundation of Israel 1948.

Bali island of Indonesia, E of Java, one of the Sunda Islands
area 5,800 sq km/2,240 sq mi
capital Denpasar
physical volcanic mountains
products gold and silver work, woodcarving, weaving, copra, salt, coffee
population (1989) 2,787,000
history Bali's Hindu culture goes back to the 7th century; the Dutch gained control of the island by 1908.

Baliol John de *c.* 1250–1314. King of Scotland 1292–96. As an heir to the Scottish throne on the death of Margaret, the Maid of Norway, his cause was supported by the English king, Edward I, against 12 other claimants. Having paid homage to Edward, Baliol was proclaimed king but soon rebelled and gave up the kingdom when English forces attacked Scotland.

Balkans (Turkish 'mountains') peninsula of SE Europe, stretching into the Mediterranean Sea between the Adriatic and Aegean seas, comprising Albania, Bosnia-Herzegovina, Bulgaria, Croatia, Greece, Romania, Slovenia, Turkey-in-Europe, and Yugoslavia. It is joined to the rest of Europe by an isthmus 1,200 km/750 mi wide between Rijeka on the west and the mouth of the Danube on the Black Sea to the east.

Balkan Wars two wars 1912–13 and 1913 (preceding World War I) which resulted in the expulsion by the Balkan states of Ottoman Turkey from Europe, except for a small area around Istanbul.

Ball John died 1381. English priest, one of the leaders of the *Peasants' Revolt 1381, known as 'the mad priest of Kent'. A follower of John Wycliffe and a believer in social equality, he was imprisoned for disagreeing with the archbishop of Canterbury. During the revolt he was released from prison, and when in Blackheath, London, incited people against the ruling classes by preaching from the text 'When Adam delved and Eve span, who was then the gentleman?' When the revolt collapsed he escaped but was captured near Coventry and executed.

Ball Lucille 1911–1989. US comedy actress, famed as TV's Lucy. From 1951 to 1957 she starred with her husband, Cuban bandleader Desi Arnaz, in *I Love Lucy*, the first US television show filmed before an audience. It was followed by *The Lucy Show* 1962–68 and *Here's Lucy* 1968–74.

ballad (Latin *ballare* 'to dance') popular poem that tells a story. Of simple metrical form and dealing with some strongly emotional event, the ballad is halfway between the lyric and the epic. Most English ballads date from the 15th century but may describe earlier events. Poets of the Romantic movement both in England and in Germany were greatly influenced by the ballad revival, as seen in, for example, the *Lyrical Ballads* 1798 of *Wordsworth and *Coleridge.

ballade in literature, a poetic form developed in France in the later Middle Ages from the ballad, generally consisting of one or more groups of three stanzas of seven or eight lines each, followed by a shorter stanza or envoy, the last line being repeated as a chorus. In music, a ballade is an instrumental piece based on a story.

Balladur Edouard 1929– . French Conservative politician, prime minister 1993–95. His first year of 'co-habitation' with socialist president François Mitterrand demonstrated the sureness of his political touch. By skilful manoeuvre and a readiness to compromise he retained popular support despite active opposition to his policies from various sectors of French society. He was a protégé of the former president Georges Pompidou, and economy and finance minister under Jacques *Chirac's prime ministership 1986–88.

ball-and-socket joint a joint allowing considerable movement in three dimensions, for instance the joint between the pelvis and the

femur. To facilitate movement, such joints are rimmed with cartilage and lubricated by synovial fluid. The bones are kept in place by ligaments and moved by muscles.

Ballard J(ames) G(raham) 1930– . English novelist. His works include science fiction on the theme of catastrophe and collapse of the urban landscape, such as *The Drowned World* 1962, *Crash!* 1973, and *High-Rise* 1975; the partly autobiographical *Empire of the Sun* 1984, dealing with his internment in China during World War II; and the autobiographical novel *The Kindness of Women* 1991. His fundamentally moral vision is expressed with an untrammelled imagination and pessimistic irony.

Ballesteros Seve(riano) 1957– . Spanish golfer who came to prominence 1976 and has won several leading tournaments in the USA, including the Masters Tournament 1980 and 1983. He has also won the British Open three times: in 1979, 1984, and 1988.

ballet theatrical representation in dance form in which music also plays a major part in telling a story or conveying a mood. Western ballet as we know it today first appeared in Italy. From there it was brought by Catherine de' Medici to France in the form of a spectacle combining singing, dancing, and declamation. In the 20th century, Russian ballet has had a vital influence on the classical tradition in the West, and ballet developed further in the USA through the work of George Balanchine and the American Ballet Theater, and in the UK through the influence of Marie Rambert. *Modern dance is a separate development.

ballistics study of the motion and impact of projectiles such as bullets, bombs, and missiles. For projectiles from a gun, relevant exterior factors include temperature, barometric pressure, and wind strength; and for nuclear missiles these extend to such factors as the speed at which the Earth turns.

balloon lighter-than-air craft that consists of a gasbag filled with gas lighter than the surrounding air and an attached basket, or gondola, for carrying passengers and/or instruments. In 1783, the first successful human ascent was in Paris, in a hot-air balloon designed by the *Montgolfier brothers. In 1785, a hydrogen-filled balloon designed by French physicist Jacques Charles travelled across the English Channel.

ballot the process of voting in an election. In political elections in democracies ballots are usually secret: voters indicate their choice of candidate on a voting slip that is placed in a sealed ballot box. ***Ballot rigging*** is a term used to describe elections that are fraudulent because of interference with the voting process or the counting of *votes.

Balmoral Castle residence of the British royal family in Scotland on the river Dee, 10.5 km/ 6½ mi NE of Braemar, Grampian region. The castle, built of granite in the Scottish baronial style, is dominated by a square tower and circular turret rising 30 m/100 ft. It was rebuilt 1853–55 by Prince Albert, who bought the estate in 1852.

balsam any of various garden plants of the genus *Impatiens* of the balsam family. They are usually annuals with spurred red or white flowers and pods that burst and scatter their seeds when ripe. In medicine and perfumery, balsam refers to various oily or gummy aromatic plant resins, such as balsam of Peru from the Central American tree *Myroxylon pereirae*.

Baltic Sea large shallow arm of the North Sea, extending NE from the narrow Skagerrak and Kattegat, between Sweden and Denmark, to the Gulf of Bothnia between Sweden and Finland. Its coastline is 8,000 km/5,000 mi long, and its area, including the gulfs of Riga, Finland, and Bothnia, is 422,300 sq km/163,000 sq mi. Its shoreline is shared by Denmark, Germany, Poland, the Baltic States, Russia, Finland, and Sweden.

Baltic States collective name for the states of *Estonia, *Latvia, and *Lithuania, former constituent republics of the USSR (from 1940). They regained independence Sept 1991.

Baltimore industrial port and largest city in Maryland, USA, on the western shore of Chesapeake Bay, NE of Washington DC; population (1990) 736,000. Industries include shipbuilding, oil refining, food processing, and the manufacture of steel, chemicals, and aerospace equipment.

Baltistan region in the Karakoram range of NE Kashmir, held by Pakistan since 1949. It is the home of Balti Muslims of Tibetan origin. The chief town is Skardu, but Ghyari is of greater significance to Muslims as the site of a mosque built by Sayyid Ali Hamadani, a Persian who brought the Shia Muslim religion to Baltistan in the 14th century.

Baluchistan mountainous desert area, comprising a province of Pakistan, part of the Iranian province of Sistán and Balúchestan, and a small area of Afghanistan. The Pakistani province has an area of 347,200 sq km/134,019 sq mi and a population (1985) of 4,908,000; its capital is Quetta. Sistán and Balúchestan has an area of 181,600 sq km/70,098 sq mi and a population (1986) of 1,197,000; its capital is Zahedan. The port of Gwadar in Pakistan is strategically important, situated on the Indian Ocean and the Strait of Hormuz. The common religion of the Baluch (or Baluchi) people is Islam, and they speak Baluchi, a member of the Iranian branch of the Indo-European language family. In the drier areas they make use of tents, moving when it becomes too arid. Although they practise nomadic pastoralism, many are settled agriculturalists.

history Originally a loose tribal confederation, Baluchistan was later divided into four principalities that were sometimes under Persian, sometimes under Afghan suzerainty. In the 19th century British troops tried to subdue the inhabitants until a treaty 1876 gave them autonomy in exchange for British army outposts along the Afghan border and strategic roads. On the partition of India 1947 the khan of Khalat declared Baluchistan independent; the insurrection was crushed by the new Pakistani army after eight months. Three rebellions followed, the last being from 1973 to 1977, when 3,300 Pakistani soldiers and some 6,000 Baluch were killed.

Balzac Honoré de 1799–1850. French novelist. His first success was *Les Chouans/The Chouans* and *La Physiologie du mariage/The Physiology of Marriage* 1829, inspired by Walter Scott. This was the beginning of the long series of novels *La Comédie humaine/The Human Comedy*. He also wrote the Rabelaisian *Contes drolatiques/Ribald Tales* 1833.

Bamako capital and port of Mali on the river Niger; population (1976) 400,000. It produces pharmaceuticals, chemicals, textiles, tobacco, and metal products.

bamboo any of numerous plants of the subgroup Bambuseae within the grass family Gramineae, mainly found in tropical and subtropical regions. Some species grow as tall as 36 m/120 ft. The stems are hollow and jointed and can be used in furniture, house, and boat construction. The young shoots are edible; paper is made from the stem.

banana any of several treelike tropical plants of the genus *Musa*, family Musaceae, which grow up to 8 m/25 ft high. The edible banana is the fruit of a sterile hybrid form.

band music group, usually falling into a special category: for example, *military*, comprising woodwind, brass, and percussion; *brass*, solely of brass and percussion; *marching*, a variant of brass; *dance* and *swing*, often like a small orchestra; *jazz*, with no fixed instrumentation; *rock and pop*, generally electric guitar, bass, and drums, variously augmented; and *steel*, from the West Indies, in which percussion instruments made from oildrums sound like marimbas.

Banda Hastings Kamuzu 1902– . Malawi politician, president 1966–94. He led his country's independence movement and was prime minister of Nyasaland (former name of Malawi) from 1963. He became Malawi's first president 1966 and president for life 1971; his rule was authoritarian. In the first free presidential elections for 30 years 1994, he was defeated by Bakili Muluzi.

Bandaranaike Sirimavo (born Ratwatte) 1916–. Sri Lankan politician, who succeeded her husband Solomon Bandaranaike to become the world's first female prime minister 1960–65 and 1970–77, but was expelled from parliament 1980 for abuse of her powers while in office. She was largely responsible for the new constitution 1972.

Bandaranaike Solomon West Ridgeway Dias 1899–1959. Sri Lankan nationalist politician. In 1952 he founded the Sri Lanka Freedom party and in 1956 became prime minister, pledged to a socialist programme and a neutral foreign policy. He failed to satisfy extremists and was assassinated by a Buddhist monk.

Bandar Seri Begawan formerly *Brunei Town* capital of Brunei; population (1983) 57,600.

bandicoot small marsupial mammal inhabiting Australia and New Guinea. There are about 11 species, family Peramelidae, rat-or rabbit-sized and living in burrows. They have long snouts, eat insects, and are nocturnal. A related group, the rabbit bandicoots or bilbys, is reduced to a single species that is now endangered and protected by law.

banding in UK education, the division of school pupils into broad streams by ability. Banding is used by some local authorities to ensure that comprehensive schools receive an intake of children spread right across the ability range. It is used internally by some schools as a means of avoiding groups of widely mixed ability.

Bandung commercial city and capital of Jawa Barat province on the island of Java, Indonesia; population (1980) 1,463,000. Bandung is the third largest city in Indonesia and was the administrative centre when the country was the Netherlands East Indies.

Bandung Conference first conference 1955 of the Afro-Asian nations, proclaiming anticolonialism and neutrality between East and West.

Bangalore capital of Karnataka state, S India; population (1981) 2,600,000. Industries include electronics, aircraft and machine-tools construction, and coffee.

Bangkok capital and port of Thailand, on the river Chao Phraya; population (1990) 6,019,000. Products include paper, ceramics, cement, textiles, and aircraft. It is the headquarters of the Southeast Asia Treaty Organization (SEATO).

Bangladesh People's Republic of (*Gana Prajatantri Bangladesh*) (formerly **East Pakistan**)

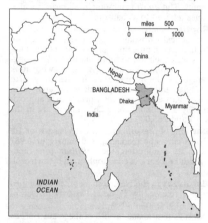

area 144,000 sq km/55,585 sq mi
capital Dhaka (formerly Dacca)
towns ports Chittagong, Khulna
physical flat delta of rivers Ganges (Padma) and Brahmaputra (Jamuna), the largest estuarine delta in the world; annual rainfall of 2,540 mm/100 in; some 75% of the land is less than 3 m/10 ft above sea level and vulnerable to flooding and cyclones; hilly in extreme SE and NE
environment deforestation on the slopes of the Himalayas increases the threat of flooding in the coastal lowlands of Bangladesh, which are also subject to devastating monsoon storms. The building of India's Farakka Barrage has reduced the flow of the Ganges in Bangladesh and permitted salt water to intrude further inland. Increased salinity has destroyed fisheries, contaminated drinking water, and damaged forests
head of state Abdur Rahman Biswas from 1991
head of government Begum Khaleda Zia from 1991
political system emergent democratic republic
exports jute, tea, garments, fish products
currency taka
population (1993 est) 118,700,000; growth rate 2.17% p.a.; just over 1 million people live in small ethnic groups in the tropical Chittagong Hill Tracts, Mymensingh, and Sylhet districts

language Bangla (Bengali)
religions Sunni Muslim 85%, Hindu 14%
GNP $220 per head (1991)
chronology
1947 Formed into eastern province of Pakistan on partition of British India.
1970 Half a million killed in flood.
1971 Bangladesh emerged as independent nation, under leadership of Sheik Mujibur Rahman, after civil war.
1975 Mujibur Rahman assassinated. Martial law imposed.
1976–77 Maj-Gen Zia ur-Rahman assumed power.
1978–79 Elections held and civilian rule restored.
1981 Assassination of Maj-Gen Zia.
1982 Lt-Gen Ershad assumed power in army coup. Martial law reimposed.
1986 Elections held but disputed. Martial law ended.
1987 State of emergency declared in response to opposition demonstrations.
1988 Assembly elections boycotted by main opposition parties. State of emergency lifted. Islam made state religion. Monsoon floods left 30 million homeless and thousands dead.
1989 Power devolved to Chittagong Hill Tracts to end 14-year conflict between local people and army-protected settlers.
1990 Following mass antigovernment protests, President Ershad resigned; Shahabuddin Ahmad became interim president.
1991 Feb: elections resulted in coalition government with BNP dominant. April: cyclone killed around 139,000 and left up to 10 million homeless. Sept: parliamentary government restored; Abdur Rahman Biswas elected president.

Bangui capital and port of the Central African Republic, on the River Ubangi; population (1988) 597,000. Industries include beer, cigarettes, office machinery, and timber and metal products.

banjo resonant stringed musical instrument, with a long fretted neck and circular drum-type sound box covered on the topside only by stretched skin (now usually plastic). It is played with a plectrum.

Banjul capital and chief port of Gambia, on an island at the mouth of the river Gambia; population (1983) 44,536. Established 1816 as a settlement for freed slaves, it was known as Bathurst until 1973.

bank financial institution that uses funds deposited with it to lend money to companies or individuals, and also provides financial services to its customers. In terms of assets, seven of the world's top ten banks were Japanese in 1988.

bank holiday in the UK, a public holiday, when banks are closed by law. Bank holidays were instituted by the Bank Holiday Acts 1871 and 1875.

Bank of Commerce and Credit International (BCCI) international bank, founded 1972. By 1990 BCCI had offices in 69 countries, $15 billion in deposits, and $20 billion in assets. In July 1991 evidence of widespread systematic fraud at BCCI led regulators in seven countries to seize the bank's assets, and its operations in most of the remaining 62 countries were then also shut down. A subsequent investigation resulted in a New York criminal indictment of the institution and four of its units, and the arrest of some 20 BCCI officials in Abu Dhabi for alleged fraud.

Bank of England UK central bank founded by act of Parliament 1694. It was entrusted with the note issue 1844 and nationalized 1946. It is banker to the clearing banks and the UK government. As the government's bank, it manages and arranges the financing of the *public-sector borrowing requirement and the national debt, implements monetary policy and exchange-rate policy through intervention in foreign-exchange markets, and supervises the UK banking system.

bank rate interest rate fixed by the Bank of England as a guide to mortgage, hire purchase rates, and so on, which was replaced 1972 by the **minimum lending rate** (lowest rate at which the Bank acts as lender of last resort to the money market), which from 1978 was again a 'bank rate' set by the Bank.

bankruptcy process by which the property of a person (in legal terms, an individual or corporation) unable to pay debts is taken away under a court order and divided fairly among the person's creditors, after preferential payments such as taxes and wages. Proceedings may be instituted either by the debtor (voluntary bankruptcy) or by any creditor for a substantial sum (involuntary bankruptcy). Until 'discharged', a bankrupt is severely restricted in financial activities.

banksia any shrub or tree of the genus *Banksia*, family Proteaceae, native to Australia and including the honeysuckle tree. The genus is named after Joseph Banks.

Bannister Roger Gilbert 1929–. English track and field athlete, the first person to run a mile in under four minutes. He achieved this feat at Oxford, England, on 6 May 1954 in a time of 3 min 59.4 sec.

Bannockburn, Battle of battle on 24 June 1314 in which *Robert I of Scotland (known as Robert the Bruce) defeated the English under Edward II, who had come to relieve the besieged Stirling Castle. Named after the town of Bannockburn, S of Stirling.

bantam small variety of domestic chicken. Bantams can either be a small version of one of the large breeds, or a separate type. Some are prolific layers. Bantam cocks have a reputation as spirited fighters.

Banting Frederick Grant 1891–1941. Canadian physician who discovered a technique for isolating the hormone insulin 1921 when, experimentally, he and his colleague Charles *Best tied off the ducts of the *pancreas to determine the function of the cells known as the islets of Langerhans. This allowed for the treatment of diabetes. Banting and John J R Macleod (1876–1935), his mentor, shared the 1923 Nobel Prize for Medicine, and Banting divided his prize with Best.

Bantu languages group of related languages belonging to the Niger-Congo family, spoken widely over the greater part of Africa south of the Sahara, including Swahili, Xhosa, and Zulu. Meaning 'people' in Zulu, the word Bantu itself illustrates a characteristic use of prefixes: *mu-ntu* 'man', *ba-ntu* 'people'.

Bantustan or **homeland** name until 1978 for a *Black National State in the Republic of South Africa.

banyan tropical Asian fig tree *Ficus benghalensis*, family Moraceae. It produces aerial roots that grow down from its spreading branches, forming supporting pillars that have the appearance of separate trunks.

baobab tree of the genus *Adansonia*, family Bombacaceae. It has rootlike branches, hence its nickname 'upside-down tree', and a disproportionately thick girth, up to 9 m/30 ft in diameter. The pulp of its fruit is edible and is known as monkey bread.

baptism (Greek 'to dip') immersion in or sprinkling with water as a religious rite of initiation. It was practised long before the beginning of Christianity. In the Christian baptism ceremony, sponsors or godparents make vows on behalf of the child, which are renewed by the child at confirmation. It is one of the seven sacraments. The *amrit* ceremony in Sikhism is sometimes referred to as baptism.

Baptist member of any of several Protestant and evangelical Christian sects that practise baptism by immersion only upon profession of faith. Baptists seek their authority in the Bible. They originated among English Dissenters who took refuge in the Netherlands in the early 17th century, and spread by emigration and, later, missionary activity. Of the world total of approximately 31 million, some 26.5 million are in the USA and 265,000 in the UK.

bar unit of pressure equal to 10^5 pascals or 10^6 dynes/cm^2, approximately 750 mmHg or 0.987 atm. Its diminutive, the **millibar** (one-thousandth of a bar), is commonly used by meteorologists.

Barabbas in the New Testament, a condemned robber released by Pilate at Passover instead of Jesus to appease a mob.

barb general name for fish of the genus *Barbus* and some related genera of the family Cyprinidae. As well as the *barbel, barbs include many small tropical Old World species, some of which are familiar aquarium species. They are active egg-laying species, usually of 'typical' fish shape and with barbels at the corner of the mouth.

Barbados
area 430 sq km/166 sq mi
capital Bridgetown
towns Speightstown, Holetown, Oistins
physical most easterly island of the West Indies; surrounded by coral reefs; subject to hurricanes June–Nov
head of state Elizabeth II from 1966, represented by governor general Dame Nita Barrow from 1990
head of government Owen Arthur from 1994
political system constitutional monarchy
exports sugar, rum, electronic components, clothing, cement
currency Barbados dollar
population (1993 est) 265,000; growth rate 0.5% p.a.
languages English and Bajan (Barbadian English dialect)
religions 70% Anglican, 9% Methodist, 4% Roman Catholic
GNP $6,630 per head (1991)

chronology
1627 Became British colony; developed as a sugar-plantation economy, initially on basis of slavery.
1834 Slaves freed.
1951 Universal adult suffrage introduced. BLP won general election.
1954 Ministerial government established.
1961 Independence achieved from Britain. DLP, led by Errol Barrow, in power.
1966 Barbados achieved full independence within Commonwealth. Barrow became the new nation's first prime minister.
1972 Diplomatic relations with Cuba established.
1976 BLP, led by Tom Adams, returned to power.
1985 Adams died; Bernard St John became prime minister.
1986 DLP, led by Barrow, returned to power.
1987 Barrow died; Erskine Lloyd Sandiford became prime minister.
1989 New NDP opposition formed.
1991 DLP, under Erskine Sandiford, won general election.
1994 BLP, led by Owen Arthur, returned to power.

Barbarossa nickname 'red beard' given to the Holy Roman emperor *Frederick I, and also to two brothers, Horuk and Khair-ed-Din, who were Barbary pirates. Horuk was killed by the Spaniards 1518; Khair-ed-Din took Tunis 1534 and died in Constantinople 1546.

Barbary ape tailless, yellowish-brown macaque monkey *Macaca sylvanus*, found in the mountains and wilds of Algeria and Morocco. It was introduced to Gibraltar, where legend has it that the British will leave if the ape colony dies out.

barbastelle insect-eating bat *Barbastella barbastellus* with 'frosted' black fur and a wingspan of about 25 cm/10 in, occasionally found in the UK but more common in Europe.

barbed wire cheap fencing material made of strands of galvanized wire (see *galvanizing), twisted together with sharp barbs at close intervals. In 1873 an American, Joseph Glidden, devised a machine to mass-produce barbed wire. Its use on the open grasslands of 19th-century America led to range warfare between farmers and cattle ranchers; the latter used to drive their herds cross-country.

barbel freshwater fish *Barbus barbus* found in fast-flowing rivers with sand or gravel bottoms in Britain and Europe. Long-bodied, and up to 1 m/3 ft long, the barbel has four *barbels* ('little beards' – sensory fleshy filaments) near the mouth.

Barber Samuel 1910–1981. US composer of a Neo-Classical, later somewhat dissonant style, whose works include *Adagio for Strings* 1936 and the opera *Vanessa* 1958, which won him one of his two Pulitzer prizes. Another Barber opera, *Antony and Cleopatra* 1966, was commissioned for the opening of the new Metropolitan Opera House at Lincoln Center, New York City. Barber's music is lyrical and fastidiously worked. His later works include *The Lovers* 1971.

barbershop in music, a style of unaccompanied close-harmony singing of sentimental ballads, revived in the USA during the 19th century. Traditionally sung by four male voices, since the 1970s it has developed as a style of *a cappella choral singing for both male and female voices.

Barbie Klaus 1913–1991. German Nazi, a member of the *SS from 1936. During World War II he was involved in the deportation of Jews from the occupied Netherlands 1940–42 and in tracking down Jews and Resistance workers in France 1942–45. He was arrested 1983 and convicted of crimes against humanity in France 1987.

Barbirolli John 1899–1970. English conductor. He made his name as a cellist, and in 1937 succeeded Toscanini as conductor of the New York Philharmonic Orchestra. He returned to England 1943, where he remained conductor of the Hallé Orchestra, Manchester, until his death.

barbiturate hypnosedative drug, commonly known as a 'sleeping pill', consisting of any salt or ester of barbituric acid $C_4H_4O_3N_2$. They work by depressing brain activity. Most barbiturates, being highly addictive, are no longer prescribed and are listed as controlled substances.

Barbizon school French school of landscape painters of the mid-19th century, based at Barbizon in the forest of Fontainebleau. Members included Jean-François Millet, Diaz de la Peña (1807–1876), and Théodore Rousseau (1812–1867). They aimed to paint fresh, realistic scenes, sketching and painting their subjects in the open air.

Barbour John c. 1316–1395. Scottish poet whose chronicle poem *The Brus* is among the earliest Scottish poetry.

Barbuda one of the islands that form the state of *Antigua and Barbuda.

Barcelona capital, industrial city (textiles, engineering, chemicals), and port of Catalonia, NE Spain; population (1991) 1,653,200. As the chief centre of anarchism and Catalonian nationalism, it was prominent in the overthrow of the monarchy 1931 and was the last city of the republic to surrender to Franco 1939. In 1992 the city hosted the Summer Olympics.

bar code pattern of bars and spaces that can be read by a computer. Bar codes are widely used in retailing, industrial distribution, and public libraries. The code is read by a scanning device; the computer determines the code from the widths of the bars and spaces.

Bardeen John 1908–1991. US physicist who won a Nobel prize 1956, with Walter Brattain and William Shockley, for the development of the transistor 1948. In 1972 he became the first double winner of a Nobel prize in the same subject (with Leon Cooper and John Schrieffer) for his work on superconductivity.

Bardot Brigitte 1934– . French film actress whose sensual appeal did much to popularize French cinema internationally. Her films include *Et Dieu créa la femme/And God Created Woman* 1950, *Viva Maria* 1965, and *Shalako* 1968.

Barebones Parliament English assembly called by Oliver *Cromwell to replace the 'Rump Parliament' July 1653. It consisted of 140 members nominated by the army and derived its name from one of its members, Praise-God Barbon. Although they attempted to pass sensible legislation (civil marriage; registration of births, deaths, and marriages; custody of lunatics), its members' attempts to abolish tithes, patronage, and the court of chancery, and to codify the law, led to the resignation of the moderates and its dissolution Dec 1653.

Barenboim Daniel 1942– . Israeli pianist and conductor, born in Argentina. Pianist/conductor with the English Chamber Orchestra from 1964, he became conductor of the New York Philharmonic Orchestra 1970 and musical director of the Orchestre de Paris 1975. Appointed artistic and musical director of the Opéra de la Bastille, Paris, July 1987, he was dismissed from his post July 1989, a few months before its opening, for reasons which he claimed were more political than artistic. His dismissal was the subject of a highly publicized and controversial dispute. He is a celebrated interpreter of Mozart and Beethoven.

Barents Willem c. 1550–1597. Dutch explorer and navigator. He made three expeditions to seek the *Northeast Passage; he died on the last voyage. The Barents Sea, part of the Arctic Ocean N of Norway, is named after him.

Bari capital of Puglia region, S Italy, and industrial port on the Adriatic; population (1988) 359,000. It is the site of Italy's first nuclear power station; the part of the town known as Tecnopolis is the Italian equivalent of *Silicon Valley.

Barikot garrison town in Konar province, E Afghanistan, near the Pakistan frontier. Besieged by Mujaheddin rebels 1985, the relief of Barikot by Soviet and Afghan troops was one of the largest military engagements of the Afghan war during Soviet occupation.

baritone male voice pitched between bass and tenor centred in the octave below middle C and rising to the F or G above. The range is well suited to *lieder.

barium (Greek *barytes* 'heavy') soft, silver-white, metallic element, symbol Ba, atomic number 56, relative atomic mass 137.33. It is one of the alkaline-earth metals, found in nature as barium carbonate and barium sulphate. As the sulphate it is used in medicine: taken as a suspension (a 'barium meal'), its progress is followed by using X-rays to reveal abnormalities of the alimentary canal. Barium is also used in alloys, pigments, and safety matches and, with strontium, forms the emissive surface in cathode-ray tubes. It was first discovered in barytes or heavy spar.

bark protective outer layer on the stems and roots of woody plants, composed mainly of dead cells. To allow for expansion of the stem, the bark is continually added to from within, and the outer surface often becomes fissured or is shed as scales. The bark from the cork oak *Quercus suber* is economically important and harvested commercially. The spice *cinnamon and the drugs cascara (used as a laxative and stimulant) and *quinine all come from bark.

barley cereal belonging to the grass family (Gramineae). Cultivated barley *Hordeum vulgare* comprises three main varieties – six-rowed, four-rowed, and two-rowed. Barley was one of the earliest cereals to be cultivated, about 5000 BC in Egypt, and no other cereal can thrive in so wide a range of climatic conditions; polar barley is sown and reaped well within the Arctic Circle in Europe. Barley is no longer much used in bread-making, but it is used in soups and stews and as a starch. Its high-protein form finds a wide use for animal feeding, and its low-protein form is used in brewing and distilling alcoholic beverages.

bar mitzvah (Hebrew 'son of the commandment') in Judaism, initiation of a boy, which takes place at the age of 13, into the adult Jewish community; less common is the *bat* or *bas mitzvah* for girls aged 12. The child reads a passage from the Torah in the synagogue on the Sabbath, and is subsequently regarded as a full member of the congregation.

Barnabas, St in the New Testament, a 'fellow labourer' with St Paul; he went with St Mark on a missionary journey to Cyprus, his birthplace. Feast day 11 June.

barnacle marine crustacean of the subclass Cirripedia. The larval form is free-swimming, but when mature, it fixes itself by the head to rock or floating wood. The animal then remains attached, enclosed in a shell through which the cirri (modified legs) protrude to sweep food into the mouth. Barnacles include the stalked *goose barnacle Lepas anatifera* found on ships' bottoms, and the *acorn barnacles*, such as *Balanus balanoides*, common on rocks.

Barnard Christiaan (Neethling) 1922– . South African surgeon who performed the first human heart transplant 1967 in Cape Town. The patient, 54-year-old Louis Washkansky, lived for 18 days.

Barnardo Thomas John 1845–1905. British philanthropist, who was known as Dr Barnardo, although not medically qualified. He opened the first of a series of homes for destitute children 1867 in Stepney, E London.

Barnard's star second closest star to the Sun, six light years away in the constellation Ophiuchus. It is a faint red dwarf of 10th magnitude, visible only through a telescope. It is named after the US astronomer Edward E Barnard (1857–1923), who discovered 1916 that it has the fastest proper motion of any star, crossing 1 degree of sky every 350 years.

Barnet, Battle of in the English Wars of the *Roses, the defeat of Lancaster by York on 14 April 1471 in Barnet (now in NW London).

Barnum Phineas T(aylor) 1810–1891. US showman. In 1871, after an adventurous career, he established the 'Greatest Show on Earth', which included the midget 'Tom Thumb', a circus, a menagerie, and an exhibition of 'freaks', conveyed in 100 railway carriages. He coined the phrase 'there's a sucker born every minute'.

barograph device for recording variations in atmospheric pressure. A pen, governed by the movements of an aneroid *barometer, makes a continuous line on a paper strip on a cylinder that rotates over a day or week to create a *barogram*, or permanent record of variations in atmospheric pressure.

barometer instrument that measures atmospheric pressure as an indication of weather. Most often used are the *mercury barometer* and the *aneroid barometer*.

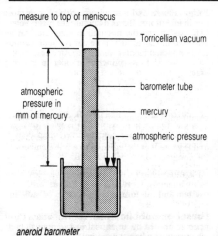

measure to top of meniscus

Torricellian vacuum

barometer tube

atmospheric pressure in mm of mercury

mercury

atmospheric pressure

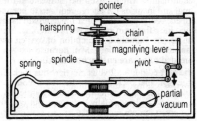

aneroid barometer

pointer

hairspring

chain

magnifying lever

spring   spindle

pivot

partial vacuum

barometer *(top) The mercury barometer and (bottom) the aneroid barometer.*

baron rank in the *peerage of the UK, above a baronet and below a viscount.

baronet British order of chivalry below the rank of baron, but above that of knight, created 1611 by James I to finance the settlement of Ulster. It is a hereditary honour, although women cannot succeed to a baronetcy. A baronet does not have a seat in the House of Lords, but is entitled to the style *Sir* before his name. The sale of baronetcies was made illegal 1937.

Barons' Wars civil wars in England:
1215–17 between King *John and his barons, over his failure to honour *Magna Carta
1264–67 between *Henry III (and the future *Edward I) and his barons (led by Simon de *Montfort)
1264 14 May **Battle of Lewes** at which Henry III was defeated and captured
1265 4 Aug Simon de Montfort was defeated by the future Edward I at Evesham and killed.

Baroque style of art and architecture characterized by extravagance in ornament, asymmetry of design, and great expressiveness. It dominated European **art** for most of the 17th century, with artists such as the painter Rubens and the sculptor Bernini. In **architecture**, it often involved large-scale designs, such as Bernini's piazza in Rome and the palace of Versailles in France. In **music**, the Baroque period lasted from about 1600 to 1750, and its composers included Monteverdi, Vivaldi, J S Bach, and Handel.

barracuda large predatory fish *Sphyraena bar-*

racuda found in the warmer seas of the world. It can grow over 2 m/6 ft long, and has a superficial resemblance to a pike. Young fish shoal but the older ones are solitary. The barracuda has very sharp shearing teeth, and may attack people.

Barranquilla seaport in N Colombia, on the river Magdalena; population (1985) 1,120,900. Products include chemicals, tobacco, textiles, furniture, and footwear.

Barras Paul François Jean Nicolas, Count 1755–1829. French revolutionary. He was elected to the National Convention 1792 and helped to overthrow Robespierre 1794. In 1795 he became a member of the ruling Directory (see *French Revolution). In 1796 he brought about the marriage of his former mistress, Joséphine de Beauharnais, with Napoleon and assumed dictatorial powers. After Napoleon's coup d'état 19 Nov 1799, Barras fell into disgrace.

Barrault Jean-Louis 1910–1994. French actor and director. His films include *La Symphonie fantastique* 1942, *Les Enfants du paradis* 1945, and *La Ronde* 1950.

Barre Raymond 1924– . French politician, member of the centre-right Union pour la Démocratie Française; prime minister 1976–81, when he also held the Finance Ministry portfolio and gained a reputation as a tough and determined budget-cutter.

barrel unit of liquid capacity, the value of which depends on the liquid being measured. It is used for petroleum, a barrel of which contains 159 litres/35 imperial gallons; a barrel of alcohol contains 189 litres/41.5 imperial gallons.

barrel organ portable pipe organ, played by turning a handle. The handle works a pump and drives a replaceable cylinder upon which a pattern of ridges controls the passage of air to certain pipes, producing a variety of tunes.

Barrett Browning Elizabeth 1806–1861. English poet. In 1844 she published *Poems* (including 'The Cry of the Children'), which led to her friendship with and secret marriage to Robert Browning 1846. The *Sonnets from the Portuguese* 1847 were written during their courtship. Later works include *Casa Guidi Windows* 1851 and the poetic novel *Aurora Leigh* 1857.

Barrie J(ames) M(atthew) 1860–1937. Scottish playwright and novelist, author of *The Admirable Crichton* 1902 and the children's fantasy *Peter Pan* 1904.

barrier island long island of sand, lying offshore and parallel to the coast. Some are over 100 km/60 mi in length. Most barrier islands are derived from marine sands piled up by shallow longshore currents that sweep sand parallel to the seashore. Others are derived from former spits, connected to land and built up by drifted sand, that were later severed from the mainland.

barrier reef *coral reef that lies offshore, separated from the mainland by a shallow lagoon.

barrister in the UK, a lawyer qualified by study at the *Inns of Court to plead for a client in court. In Scotland such lawyers are called *advocates. Barristers also undertake the writing of opinions on the prospects of a case before trial. They act for clients through the intermediary of *solicitors.

Barrois de Chamorro Violeta. President of Nicaragua from 1990; see *Chamorro.

barrow burial mound, usually composed of earth but sometimes of stones, examples of which are found in many parts of the world. The two main types are **long**, dating from the New Stone Age, or Neolithic, and **round**, dating from the later Mesolithic peoples of the early Bronze Age.

Barry Charles 1795–1860. English architect of the Neo-Gothic Houses of Parliament at Westminster, London, 1840–60, in collaboration with Augustus *Pugin.

Barry Comtesse du. See *Du Barry, mistress of Louis XV of France.

Barstow Stan 1928– . English novelist born in W Yorkshire. His novels describe northern working-class life and include *A Kind of Loving* 1960.

Barth John 1930– . US novelist and short-story writer who was influential in the 'academic' experimental movement of the 1960s. His works are usually interwoven fictions based on language games, since he is concerned with the relationship of language and reality. They include the novels *The Sot-Weed Factor* 1960, *Giles Goat-Boy* 1966, *Letters* 1979, *Sabbatical: A Romance* 1982, and *The Tidewater Tales* 1987. He also wrote the novella *Chimera* 1972 and *Lost in the Funhouse* 1968, a collection of short stories.

Barthes Roland 1915–1980. French critic and theorist of *semiology, the science of signs and symbols. One of the French 'new critics' and an exponent of *structuralism, he attacked traditional literary criticism in his early works, including *Le Degré zéro de l'ecriture/Writing Degree Zero* 1953 and *Sur Racine/On Racine* 1963.

Bartholomew, Massacre of St see *St Bartholomew, Massacre of.

Bartholomew, St in the New Testament, one of the apostles. Some legends relate that after the Crucifixion he took Christianity to India; others that he was a missionary in Anatolia and Armenia, where he suffered martyrdom by being flayed alive. Feast day 24 Aug.

Bartók Béla 1881–1945. Hungarian composer who developed a personal musical language, combining folk elements with mathematical concepts of tone and rhythmic proportion. His large output includes six string quartets, concertos, an opera, and graded teaching pieces for piano.

Bartolommeo Fra, also called **Baccio della Porta** c. 1472–c. 1517. Italian religious painter of the High Renaissance, active in Florence. His painting of *The Last Judgment* 1499 (Museo di San Marco, Florence) influenced Raphael.

Barton Edmund 1849–1920. Australian politician. He was leader of the federation movement from 1896 and first prime minister of Australia 1901–03.

baryon in nuclear physics, a heavy subatomic particle made up of three indivisible elementary particles called quarks. The baryons form a subclass of the *hadrons, and comprise the nucleons (protons and neutrons) and hyperons.

Baryshnikov Mikhail 1948– . Latvian-born dancer, now based in the USA. He joined the Kirov Ballet 1967 and became one of their most brilliant soloists. After defecting from the Soviet Union 'on artistic, not political grounds' while on tour in Canada 1974, he danced with various companies, and later joined the American Ballet Theater (ABT) as principal dancer, partnering Gelsey Kirkland. He left to join the New York City Ballet 1978–80, but rejoined ABT as director 1980–90. From 1990 he has danced for various companies.

baryte barium sulphate, $BaSO_4$, the most common mineral of barium. It is white or light-coloured, and has a comparatively high density (specific gravity 4.6); the latter property makes it useful in the production of high-density drilling muds. Baryte occurs mainly in ore veins, where it is often found with calcite and with lead and zinc minerals. It crystallizes in the orthorhombic system and can form tabular crystals or radiating fibrous masses.

basal metabolic rate (BMR) amount of energy needed by an animal just to stay alive. It is measured when the animal is awake but resting, and includes the energy required to keep the heart beating, sustain breathing, repair tissues, and keep the brain and nerves functioning. Measuring the animal's consumption of oxygen gives an accurate value for BMR, because oxygen is needed to release energy from food.

basalt commonest volcanic *igneous rock, and the principal rock type on the ocean floor; it is basic, that is, it contains relatively little silica: under 50%. It is usually dark grey, but can also be green, brown, or black.

bascule bridge type of drawbridge in which one or two counterweighted deck members pivot upwards to allow shipping to pass underneath. One example is the double bascule Tower Bridge, London.

base in mathematics, the number of different single-digit symbols used in a particular number system. In our usual (decimal) counting system of numbers (with symbols 0, 1, 2, 3, 4, 5, 6, 7, 8, 9) the base is 10. In the *binary number system, which has only the symbols 1 and 0, the base is two. A base is also a number that, when raised to a particular power (that is, when multiplied by itself a particular number of times as in $10^2 = 10 \times 10 = 100$), has a *logarithm equal to the power. For example, the logarithm of 100 to the base ten is 2. In geometry, the term is used to denote the line or area on which a polygon or solid stands.

base in chemistry, a substance that accepts protons, such as the hydroxide ion (OH^-) and ammonia (NH_3). Bases react with acids to give a salt. Those that dissolve in water are called *alkalis.

baseball national summer game of the USA, derived in the 19th century from the English game of *rounders. Baseball is a bat-and-ball game played between two teams, each of nine players, on a pitch ('field') marked out in the form of a diamond, with a base at each corner. The ball is struck with a cylindrical bat, and the players try to score ('make a run') by circuiting the bases. A 'home run' is a circuit on one hit.

Basel or **Basle** (French **Bâle**) financial, commercial, and industrial (dyes, vitamins, agrochemicals, dietary products, genetic products) city in Switzerland; population (1990) 171,000. Basel was a strong military station under the Romans. In 1501 it joined the Swiss confederation and later developed as a centre for the Reformation.

basenji breed of dog originating in Central Africa, where it is used as a hunter. About 41 cm/ 1.3 ft tall, it has a wrinkled forehead, curled tail, and short glossy coat. It is remarkable because it has no true bark.

base pair in biochemistry, the linkage of two base (purine or pyrimidine) molecules in *DNA. They are found in nucleotides, and form the basis of the genetic code.

base rate in economics, the rate of interest to which most bank lending is linked, the actual rate depending on the status of the borrower. A prestigious company might command a rate only 1% above base rate, while an individual would be charged several points above.

Bashkir autonomous republic of Russia, with the Ural Mountains on the east
area 143,600 sq km/55,430 sq mi
capital Ufa
products minerals, oil, natural gas
population (1982) 3,876,000
languages Russian, Bashkir (about 25%)
history annexed by Russia 1557; became the first Soviet autonomous republic 1919. Since 1989 Bashkirs have demanded greater independence.

Bashō Pen name of Matsuo Munefusa 1644–1694. Japanese poet who was a master of the *haiku*, a 17-syllable poetic form with lines of 5, 7, and 5 syllables, which he infused with subtle allusiveness. His *Oku-no-hosomichi/The Narrow Road to the Deep North* 1694, an account of a visit to northern and western Honshu, consists of haiku interspersed with prose passages.

BASIC (acronym for *beginner's all-purpose symbolic instruction code*) high-level computer-programming language, developed 1964, originally designed to take advantage of *multiuser systems (which can be used by many people at the same time). The language is relatively easy to learn and is popular among microcomputer users.

basicity number of replaceable hydrogen atoms in an acid. Nitric acid (HNO_3) is monobasic, sulphuric acid (H_2SO_4) is dibasic, and phosphoric acid (H_3PO_4) is tribasic.

basic-oxygen process most widely used method of steelmaking, involving the blasting of oxygen at supersonic speed into molten pig iron.

basidiocarp spore-bearing body, or 'fruiting body', of all basidiomycete fungi (see *fungus), except the rusts and smuts. A well known example is the edible mushroom *Agaricus brunnescens*. Other types include globular basidiocarps (puffballs) or flat ones that project from tree trunks (brackets). They are made up of a mass of tightly packed, intermeshed *hyphae.

Basie Count (William) 1904–1984. US jazz band leader, pianist, and organist who developed the big-band sound and a simplified, swinging style of music. He led impressive groups of musicians in a career spanning more than 50 years. Basie's compositions include 'One O'Clock Jump' and 'Jumpin at the Woodside'.

basil or *sweet basil* plant *Ocimum basilicum* of the mint family Labiatae. A native of the tropics, it is cultivated in Europe as a culinary herb.

Basil II *c.* 958–1025. Byzantine emperor from 976. His achievement as emperor was to contain, and later decisively defeat, the Bulgarians, earning for himself the title 'Bulgar-Slayer' after a victory 1014. After the battle he blinded almost all 15,000 of the defeated, leaving only a few men with one eye to lead their fellows home. The Byzantine empire had reached its largest extent at the time of his death.

basilica Roman public building; a large roofed hall flanked by columns, generally with an aisle on each side, used for judicial or other public business. The earliest known basilica, at Pompeii, dates from the 2nd century BC. This architectural form was adopted by the early Christians for their churches.

Basilicata mountainous region of S Italy, comprising the provinces of Potenza and Matera; area 10,000 sq km/3,860 sq mi; population (1990) 624, 500. Its capital is Potenza. It was the Roman province of Lucania.

basilisk South American lizard, genus *Basiliscus*. It is able to run on its hind legs when travelling fast (about 11 kph/7 mph) and may dash a short distance across the surface of water. The male has a well-developed crest on the head, body, and tail.

Basil, St *c.* 330–379. Cappadocian monk, known as 'the Great', founder of the Basilian monks. Elected bishop of Caesarea 370, Basil opposed the heresy of *Arianism. He wrote many theological works and composed the 'Liturgy of St Basil', in use in the Eastern Orthodox Church. His feast day is 2 Jan.

basketball ball game between two teams of five players on an indoor enclosed court. The object is, via a series of passing moves, to throw the large inflated ball through a circular hoop and net positioned at each end of the court, 3.05 m/ 10 ft above the ground. The first world championship for men was held in 1950, and in 1953 for women. They are now held every four years.

basketry ancient craft (Mesolithic–Neolithic) used to make a wide range of objects (from baskets to furniture) by interweaving or braiding, rushes, cane, or other equally strong, natural fibres. Wickerwork is a more rigid type of basketry worked onto a sturdy frame, usually made from strips of willow.

Basle alternative form of *Basel, city in Switzerland.

Basov Nikolai Gennadievich 1912– . Soviet physicist who in 1953, with his compatriot Aleksandr Prokhorov, developed the microwave amplifier called a *maser. They were both awarded the Nobel Prize for Physics 1964, which they shared with Charles Townes of the USA.

Basque member of a people inhabiting the *Basque Country of central N Spain and the extreme SW of France. The Basques are a pre-Indo-European people who largely maintained their independence until the 19th century. During the Spanish Civil War 1936–39, they were on the republican side defeated by Franco. Their language (*Euskara*) is unrelated to any other language. The Basque separatist movement ETA

(*Euskadi ta Askatasuna*, 'Basque Nation and Liberty') and the French organization Iparretarrak ('ETA fighters from the North Side') have engaged in guerrilla activity from 1968 in an attempt to secure a united Basque state.

Basque Country (Basque *Euskal Herria*) homeland of the Basque people in the W Pyrenees, divided by the Franco-Spanish border. The Spanish Basque Country (Spanish *País Vasco*) is an autonomous region (created 1979) of central N Spain, comprising the provinces of Vizcaya, Alava, and Guipúzcoa (Basque *Bizkaia*, *Araba*, and *Gipuzkoa*); area 7,300 sq km/2,818 sq mi; population (1988) 2,176,790. The French Basque Country (French *Pays Basque*) comprises the *département* of Pyrénées-Atlantiques, including the arrondissements of Labourd, Basse-Navarre, and Soule (Basque *Lapurdi*, *Nafarroa Beherea*, and *Zuberoa*); area 7,633 sq km/4770 sq mi; population (1981) 555,700. To Basque nationalists *Euskal Herria* also includes the autonomous Spanish province of Navarre.

Basra (Arabic *al-Basrah*) principal port in Iraq, in the Shatt-al-Arab delta, 97 km/60 mi from the Persian Gulf, founded in the 7th century; population (1977) 1.5 million (1991) 850,000. Exports include wool, oil, cereal, and dates. Aerial bombing during the 1991 Gulf War destroyed bridges, factories, power stations, water-treatment plants, sewage-treatment plants, and the port. A Shi'ite rebellion March 1991 was crushed by the Iraqi army, causing further death and destruction.

bass long-bodied scaly sea fish *Morone labrax* found in the N Atlantic and Mediterranean. They grow to 1 m/3 ft, and are often seen in shoals.

Bassein port in Myanmar (Burma), in the Irrawaddy delta, 125 km/78 mi from the sea; population (1983) 355,588. Bassein was founded in the 13th century.

Basse-Normandie or *Lower Normandy* coastal region of NW France lying between Haute-Normandie and Brittany (Bretagne). It includes the *départements* of Calvados, Manche, and Orne; area 17,600 sq km/6,794 sq mi; population (1986) 1,373,000. Its capital is Caen. Apart from stock farming, dairy farming, and textiles, the area produces Calvados (apple brandy).

basset type of dog with a long low body, wrinkled forehead, and long pendulous ears, originally bred in France for hunting hares.

Basseterre capital and port of St Kitts-Nevis, in the Leeward Islands; population (1980) 14,000. Industries include data processing, rum, clothes, and electrical components.

basset horn musical *woodwind instrument resembling a clarinet, pitched in F and ending in a brass bell. Its range lies between the clarinet and the bass clarinet.

bassoon double-reed *woodwind instrument, the bass of the oboe family. It doubles back on itself in a tube about 2.5 m/7.5 ft long. Its tone is rich and deep.

Bass Strait channel between Australia and Tasmania, named after British explorer George Bass; oil was discovered there in the 1960s.

Bastille castle of St Antoine, built about 1370 as part of the fortifications of Paris. It was made a state prison by Cardinal *Richelieu and was

stormed by the mob that set the French Revolution in motion 14 July 1789. Only seven prisoners were found in the castle when it was stormed; the governor and most of the garrison were killed, and the Bastille was razed.

Basutoland former name for *Lesotho, a kingdom in southern Africa.

bat flying mammal in which the forelimbs are developed as wings capable of rapid and sustained flight. There are two main groups of bats: *megabats*, or *flying foxes*, which eat fruit, and *microbats*, which mainly eat insects. Although by no means blind, many microbats rely largely on echolocation for navigation and finding prey, sending out pulses of high-pitched sound and listening for the echo. Bats are nocturnal, and those native to temperate countries hibernate in winter. There are about 1,000 species of bats forming the order Chiroptera, making this the second-largest mammalian order; bats make up nearly one-quarter of the world's mammals. Although bats are widely distributed, bat populations have declined alarmingly and many species are now endangered.

Bataan peninsula in Luzon, the Philippines, which was defended against the Japanese in World War II by US and Filipino troops under General MacArthur 1 Jan–9 April 1942. MacArthur was evacuated, but some 67,000 Allied prisoners died on the *Bataan Death March* to camps in the interior.

Batak member of the several distinct but related peoples of N Sumatra in Indonesia. Numbering approximately 2.5 million, the Batak speak languages belonging to the Austronesian family.

batch processing in computing, a system for processed during regular 'runs' (for example, each night). This allows efficient use of the computer and is well suited to applications of a repetitive nature, such as a company payroll.

Bates H(enry) W(alter) 1825–1892. English naturalist and explorer, who spent 11 years collecting animals and plants in South America and identified 8,000 new species of insects. He made a special study of *camouflage in animals, and his observation of insect imitation of species that are unpleasant to predators is known as 'Batesian mimicry'.

Bates H(erbert) E(rnest) 1906–1974. English author. Of his many novels and short stories, *The Jacaranda Tree* 1949 and *The Darling Buds of May* 1958 demonstrate the fineness of his natural observation and compassionate portrayal of character. *Fair Stood the Wind for France* 1959 was based on his experience as a squadron leader in World War II.

Bath historic city in Avon, England; population (1991) 79,900

features Hot springs; the ruins of the baths after which it is named, as well as a great temple, are the finest Roman remains in Britain. Excavations 1979 revealed thousands of coins and 'curses', offered at a place which was thought to be the link between the upper and lower worlds. The Gothic Bath Abbey has an unusually decorated west front and fan vaulting. There is much 18th-century architecture, notably the Royal Crescent by John Wood. The Assembly Rooms 1771 were destroyed in an air raid 1942 but reconstructed 1963. The University of Technology was established 1966. The Bath Festival Orchestra is based here.

history The Roman city of Aquae Sulis ('waters of Sul' – the British goddess of wisdom) was built in the first 20 years after the Roman invasion. In medieval times the hot springs were crown property, administered by the church, but the city was transformed in the 18th century to a fashionable spa, presided over by 'Beau' *Nash. At his home here the astronomer William Herschel discovered Uranus 1781. Visitors included the novelists Tobias Smollett, Henry Fielding, and Jane Austen.

batholith large, irregular, deep-seated mass of *igneous rock, usually granite, with an exposed surface of more than 100 sq km/40 sq mi. The mass forms by the intrusion or upswelling of magma (molten rock) through the surrounding rock. Batholiths form the core of all major mountain ranges.

Bath, Order of the British order of knighthood, believed to have been founded in the reign of Henry IV (1399–1413). Formally instituted 1815, it included civilians from 1847 and women from 1970.

Báthory Stephen 1533–1586. King of Poland, elected by a diet convened 1575 and crowned 1576. Báthory succeeded in driving the Russian troops of Ivan the Terrible out of his country. His military successes brought potential conflicts with Sweden, but he died before these developed.

bathyal zone upper part of the ocean, which lies on the continental shelf at a depth of between 200 m/650 ft and 2,000 m/6,500 ft.

bathyscaph or *bathyscaphe* or *bathyscape* deep-sea diving apparatus used for exploration at great depths in the ocean. In 1960, Jacques Piccard and Don Walsh took the bathyscaph *Trieste* to a depth of 10,917 m/35,820 ft in the Challenger Deep in the *Mariana Trench off the island of Guam in the Pacific Ocean.

batik Javanese technique of dyeing fabrics in which areas to be left undyed are sealed with wax. Practised throughout Indonesia, the craft was introduced to the West by Dutch traders.

Batista Fulgencio 1901–1973. Cuban dictator 1933–44, when he stood down, and again 1952–59, after seizing power in a coup. His authoritarian methods enabled him to jail his opponents and amass a large personal fortune. He was overthrown by rebel forces led by Fidel *Castro 1959.

Batten Jean 1909–1982. New Zealand aviator who made the first return solo flight by a woman Australia–Britain 1935, and established speed records.

battery any energy-storage device allowing release of electricity on demand. It is made up of one or more electrical *cells. Primary-cell batteries are disposable; secondary-cell batteries, or *accumulators, are rechargeable. Primary-cell batteries are an extremely uneconomical form of energy, since they produce only 2% of the power used in their manufacture.

baud in engineering, a unit of electrical signalling speed equal to one pulse per second, measuring the rate at which signals are sent between electronic devices such as telegraphs and computers; 300 baud is about 300 words a minute.

Baudelaire Charles Pierre 1821–1867. French poet. His immensely influential work combined rhythmical and musical perfection with a morbid romanticism and eroticism, finding beauty in decadence and evil. His first book of verse was *Les Fleurs du mal/Flowers of Evil* 1857. He was one of the major figures in the development of *Symbolism.

Baudouin 1930–1993. King of the Belgians 1951–93. In 1950 his father, *Leopold III, abdicated and Baudouin was known until his succession July 1951 as *Le Prince Royal*. In 1960 he married Fabiola de Mora y Aragón (1928–), member of a Spanish noble family. He was succeeded by his brother, Albert.

Bauhaus German school of architecture and design founded 1919 at Weimar in Germany by the architect Walter *Gropius in an attempt to fuse art, design, architecture, and crafts into a unified whole. Moved to Dessau under political pressure 1925 (where it was housed in a building designed by Gropius), the school was closed by the Nazis 1933. Among the artists associated with the Bauhaus were the painters Klee and Kandinsky and the architect Mies van der Rohe.

Baum L(yman) Frank 1856–1919. US writer, author of the children's fantasy *The Wonderful Wizard of Oz* 1900 and its 13 sequels. The series was continued by another author after his death. The film *The Wizard of Oz* 1939 with Judy Garland became a US classic.

bauxite principal ore of *aluminium, consisting of a mixture of hydrated aluminium oxides and hydroxides, generally contaminated with compounds of iron, which give it a red colour. To produce aluminium the ore is processed into a white powder (alumina), which is then smelted by passing a large electric current through it. Chief producers of bauxite are Australia, Guinea, Jamaica, Russia, Kazakhstan, Surinam, and Brazil.

Bavaria (German *Bayern*) administrative region (German *Land*) of Germany
area 70,600 sq km/27,252 sq mi
capital Munich

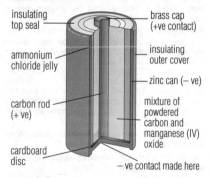

insulating top seal

brass cap (+ve contact)

ammonium chloride jelly

insulating outer cover

zinc can (– ve)

carbon rod (+ ve)

mixture of powdered carbon and manganese (IV) oxide

cardboard disc

– ve contact made here

battery *The common dry cell relies on chemical changes occurring between the electrodes – the central carbon rod and the outer zinc casing – and the ammonium chloride electrolyte to produce electricity.*

towns Nuremberg, Augsburg, Würzburg, Regensburg

products beer, electronics, electrical engineering, optics, cars, aerospace, chemicals, plastics, oil refining, textiles, glass, toys

population (1988) 11,000,000

famous people Lucas Cranach, Adolf Hitler, Franz Josef Strauss, Richard Strauss

religion 70% Roman Catholic, 26% Protestant

history the last king, Ludwig III, abdicated 1918, and Bavaria declared itself a republic.

Bax Arnold Edward Trevor 1883–1953. English composer. His works, often based on Celtic legends, include seven symphonies and *The Garden of Fand* 1913–16 and *Tintagel* 1917–19 (both tone poems). He was Master of the King's Musick 1942–53.

bay various species of *laurel, genus *Laurus*. The aromatic evergreen leaves are used for flavouring in cookery. There is also a golden-leaved variety.

Bayern German name for *Bavaria, region of Germany.

Bayeux Tapestry linen hanging made about 1067–70, which gives a vivid pictorial record of the invasion of England by William I (the Conqueror) 1066. It is an embroidery rather than a true tapestry, sewn with woollen threads in blue, green, red, and yellow, 70 m/231 ft long and 50 cm/20 in wide, and containing 72 separate scenes with descriptive wording in Latin. It is exhibited at the museum of Bayeaux in Normandy, France.

Bay of Pigs inlet on the S coast of Cuba about 145 km/90 mi SW of Havana. It was the site of an unsuccessful invasion attempt by 1,500 US-sponsored Cuban exiles 17–20 April 1961; 1,173 were taken prisoner.

bayonet short sword attached to the muzzle of a firearm. The bayonet was placed inside the barrel of the muzzle-loading muskets of the late 17th century. The **sock** or ring bayonet, invented 1700, allowed a weapon to be fired without interruption, leading to the demise of the pike.

Bayreuth town in Bavaria, S Germany, where opera festivals are held every summer; population (1983) 71,000. It was the home of composer Richard *Wagner, and the Wagner theatre was established 1876.

Bazalgette Joseph 1819–1890. British civil engineer who, as chief engineer to the London Board of Works, designed London's sewer system, a total of 155 km/83 mi of sewers, covering an area of 256 sq km/100 sq mi. It was completed 1865. He also designed the Victoria Embankment 1864–70, which was built over the river Thames and combined a main sewer, a water frontage, an underground railway, and a road.

BBC abbreviation for ***British Broadcasting Corporation**.

BC in the Christian calendar, abbreviation for **before Christ**; used with dates.

B cell or **B** *lymphocyte immune cell that produces *antibodies. Each B cell produces just one type of antibody, specific to a single *antigen. Lymphocytes are related to *T cells.

BCG (abbreviation for *bacillus of Calmette*

and Guérin) bacillus used as a vaccine to confer active immunity to *tuberculosis (TB).

Beach Boys, the US pop group formed 1961. They began as exponents of vocal-harmony surf music with Chuck Berry guitar riffs (their hits include 'Surfin' USA' 1963 and 'Help Me, Rhonda' 1965) but the compositions, arrangements, and production by Brian Wilson (1942–) became highly complex under the influence of psychedelic rock, peaking with 'Good Vibrations' 1966. Wilson spent most of the next 20 years in retirement but returned with a solo album 1988.

beagle short-haired hound with pendant ears, sickle tail, and a bell-like voice for hunting hares on foot ('beagling').

beak horn-covered projecting jaws of a bird, or other horny jaws such as those of the tortoise or octopus. The beaks of birds are adapted by shape and size to specific diets.

Beaker people people thought to be of Iberian origin who spread out over Europe from the 3rd millennium BC. They were skilled in metalworking, and are identified by their use of distinctive earthenware beakers with stamped designs, of which the bell-beaker type was widely distributed throughout Europe. They favoured inhumation (burial of the intact body), in a trench or under a round *barrow, or secondary burials in some form of chamber tomb. A beaker accompanied each burial, to hold a drink for the deceased on their final journey.

beam balance instrument for measuring mass (or weight). A simple form consists of a beam pivoted at its midpoint with a pan hanging at each end. The mass to be measured, in one pan, is compared with a variety of standard masses placed in the other. When the beam is balanced, the masses' turning effects or moments under gravity, and hence the masses themselves, are equal.

bean any seed of numerous leguminous plants. Beans are rich in nitrogenous or protein matter and are grown both for human consumption and as food for cattle and horses. Varieties of bean are grown throughout Europe, the USA, South America, China, Japan, SE Asia, and Australia.

bear *The polar bear ranges over the coasts and ice floes of the Arctic Ocean, to the southern limit of the ice.*

bear large mammal with a heavily built body, short powerful limbs, and a very short tail. Bears breed once a year, producing one to four cubs. In northern regions they hibernate, and the young are born in the winter den. They are found mainly in North America and N Asia. The skin of the polar bear is black to conserve 80–90% of the solar energy trapped and channelled down the hollow hairs of its fur.

bear in business, a speculator who sells stocks or shares on the stock exchange expecting a fall in the price in order to buy them back at a profit, the opposite of a *bull. In a bear market, prices fall, and bears prosper.

bearberry any of several species of evergreen trailing shrub, genus *Arctostaphylos*, of the heath family, found on uplands and rocky places. Most bearberries are North American but *A. uva-ursi* is also found in Asia and Europe in northern mountainous regions. It bears small pink flowers in spring, followed by red berries that are edible but dry.

Beardsley Aubrey (Vincent) 1872–1898. British illustrator. His meticulously executed black-and-white work displays the sinuous line and decorative mannerisms of Art Nouveau and was often charged with being grotesque and decadent.

bearing device used in a machine to allow free movement between two parts, typically the rotation of a shaft in a housing. *Ball bearings* consist of two rings, one fixed to a housing, one to the rotating shaft. Between them is a set, or race, of steel balls. They are widely used to support shafts, as in the spindle in the hub of a bicycle wheel.

bearing the direction of a fixed point, or the path of a moving object, from a point of observation on the Earth's surface, expressed as an angle from the north. Bearings are taken by *compass and are measured in degrees (°), given as three-digit numbers increasing clockwise. For instance, north is 000°, northeast is 045°, south is 180°, and southwest is 225°.

beat regular variation in the loudness of the sound when two notes of nearly equal pitch or *frequency are heard together. Beats result from the *interference between the sound waves of the notes. The frequency of the beats equals the difference in frequency of the notes.

Beat Generation or *Beat movement* beatniks of the 1950s and 1960s, usually in their teens and early twenties, who rejected conventional lifestyles and opted for life on the road, drug experimentation, and antimaterialist values; and the associated literary movement whose members included William S Burroughs, Lawrence Ferlinghetti, Allen *Ginsberg, and Jack *Kerouac (who is credited with coining the term).

beatification in the Catholic church, the first step towards *canonization. Persons who have been beatified can be prayed to, and the title 'Blessed' can be put before their names.

Beatitudes in the New Testament, the sayings of Jesus reported in Matthew 6: 1–12 and Luke 6: 20–38, depicting the spiritual qualities that characterize members of the Kingdom of God.

Beatles, the English pop group 1960–70. The members, all born in Liverpool, were John Lennon (1940–80, rhythm guitar, vocals), Paul McCartney (1942– , bass, vocals), George Harrison (1943– , lead guitar, vocals), and Ringo

Starr (formerly Richard Starkey, 1940– , drums). Using songs written largely by Lennon and McCartney, the Beatles dominated rock music and pop culture in the 1960s.

beat music pop music that evolved in the UK in the early 1960s, known in its purest form as *Mersey beat, and as British Invasion in the USA. The beat groups characteristically had a simple, guitar-dominated line-up, vocal harmonies, and catchy tunes. They included the Beatles (1960–70), the Hollies (1962–), and the Zombies (1962–67).

Beaton Cecil 1904–1980. English portrait and fashion photographer, designer, illustrator, diarist, and conversationalist. He produced portrait studies and also designed scenery and costumes for ballets, and sets for plays and films.

Beatrix 1936– . Queen of the Netherlands. The eldest daughter of Queen *Juliana, she succeeded to the throne on her mother's abdication 1980. In 1966 she married West German diplomat Claus von Amsberg (1926–), who was created Prince of the Netherlands. Her heir is Prince Willem Alexander (1967–).

Beatty Warren. Stage name of Warren Beaty 1937– . US actor and director, popular for such films as *Splendour in the Grass* 1961, *Bonnie and Clyde* 1967, and *Heaven Can Wait* 1978. His more recent productions include *Reds* 1981 (Academy Award for Best Producer), *Ishtar* 1987, and *Dick Tracy* 1990.

Beaufort Henry 1375–1447. English priest, bishop of Lincoln from 1398, of Winchester from 1405. As chancellor of England, he supported his half-brother Henry IV, and made enormous personal loans to Henry V to finance war against France. As a guardian of Henry VI from 1421, he was in effective control of the country until 1426. In the same year he was created a cardinal. In 1431 he crowned Henry VI as king of France in Paris.

Beaufort scale system of recording wind velocity, devised by Francis Beaufort 1806. It is a numerical scale ranging from 0 to 17, calm being indicated by 0 and a hurricane by 12; 13–17 indicate degrees of hurricane force.

Beaumarchais Pierre Augustin Caron de 1732–1799. French dramatist. His great comedies *Le Barbier de Seville/The Barber of Seville* 1775 and *Le Mariage de Figaro/The Marriage of Figaro* (1778, but prohibited until 1784) form the basis of operas by *Rossini and *Mozart.

Beaumont Francis 1584–1616. English dramatist and poet. From about 1608 he collaborated with John *Fletcher. Their joint plays include *Philaster* 1610, *The Maid's Tragedy* about 1611, and *A King and No King* about 1611. *The Woman Hater* about 1606 and *The Knight of the Burning Pestle* about 1607 are ascribed to Beaumont alone.

Beauvoir Simone de 1908–1986. French socialist, feminist, and writer who taught philosophy at the Sorbonne university in Paris 1931–43. Her book *Le Deuxième sexe/The Second Sex* 1949 became a seminal work for many feminists.

beaver aquatic rodent *Castor fiber* with webbed hind feet, a broad flat scaly tail, and thick waterproof fur. It has very large incisor teeth and fells trees to feed on the bark and to use the logs to construct the 'lodge', in which the young are reared, food is stored, and where much of the winter is spent.

Beaverbrook (William) Max(well) Aitken, 1st Baron Beaverbrook 1879–1964. British financier, newspaper proprietor, and politician, born in Canada. He bought a majority interest in the *Daily Express* 1919, founded the *Sunday Express* 1921, and bought the London *Evening Standard* 1929. He served in Lloyd George's World War I cabinet and Churchill's World War II cabinet.

bebop or *bop* hot jazz style, rhythmically complex, virtuosic, and highly improvisational, developed in New York 1940–55 by Charlie Parker, Dizzy Gillespie, Thelonius Monk, and other black musicians disaffected with dance bands.

Bechuanaland former name until 1966 of *Botswana.

Beckenbauer Franz 1945– . German footballer who made a record 103 appearances for his country. He captained West Germany to the 1972 European Championship and the 1974 World Cup, and was twice European Footballer of the Year. He is the only person both to captain and manage a winning World Cup team.

Becker Boris 1967– . German tennis player. In 1985, at the age of 17, he became the youngest winner of a singles title at Wimbledon. He has won the title three times and helped West Germany to win the Davis Cup 1988 and 1989. He also won the US Open 1989.

Becket St Thomas à 1118–1170. English priest and politician. He was chancellor to *Henry II 1155–62, when he was appointed archbishop of Canterbury. The interests of the church soon conflicted with those of the crown and Becket was assassinated; he was canonized 1172.

Beckett Samuel 1906–1989. Irish novelist and dramatist who wrote in French and English. His *En attendant Godot/Waiting for Godot* 1952 is possibly the most universally known example of Theatre of the *Absurd, in which life is taken to be meaningless. This genre is taken to further extremes in *Fin de Partie/Endgame* 1957 and *Happy Days* 1961. Nobel Prize for Literature 1969.

becquerel SI unit (symbol Bq) of *radioactivity, equal to one radioactive disintegration (change in the nucleus of an atom when a particle or ray is given off) per second.

Becquerel Antoine Henri 1852–1908. French physicist who discovered penetrating radiation coming from uranium salts, the first indication of *radioactivity, and shared a Nobel prize with Marie and Pierre *Curie 1903.

bed in geology, a single *sedimentary rock unit with a distinct set of physical characteristics or contained fossils, readily distinguishable from those of beds above and below. Well-defined partings called *bedding planes* separate successive beds or strata.

bedbug flattened wingless red-brown insect *Cimex lectularius* with piercing mouthparts. It hides by day in crevices or bedclothes, and emerges at night to suck human blood.

Bede c. 673–735. English theologian and historian, known as *the Venerable Bede*, active

in Durham and Northumbria. He wrote many scientific, theological, and historical works. His *Historia Ecclesiastica Gentis Anglorum/Ecclesiastical History of the English People* 731 is a seminal source for early English history.

Bedfordshire county in S central England; *area* 1,240 sq km/479 sq mi; *towns* Bedford (administrative headquarters), Luton, Dunstable *products* cereals, vegetables, agricultural machinery, electrical goods *population* (1991) 514,200 *famous people* John Bunyan, John Howard, Joseph Paxton.

Bedlam (abbreviation of *Bethlehem*) the earliest mental hospital in Europe. The hospital was opened in the 14th century in London and is now sited in Surrey. It is now used as a slang word meaning chaos.

Bedouin (Arabic 'desert-dweller') Arab of any of the nomadic peoples occupying the desert regions of Arabia and N Africa, now becoming increasingly settled. Their traditional trade was the rearing of horses and camels.

bee four-winged insect of the superfamily Apoidea in the order Hymenoptera, usually with a sting. There are over 12,000 species, of which fewer than 1 in 20 are social in habit. The *hive* or *honey bee Apis mellifera* establishes perennial colonies of about 80,000, the majority being infertile females (workers), with a few larger fertile males (drones), and a single very large fertile female (the queen). Worker bees live for no more than a few weeks, while a drone may live a few months, and a queen several years. Queen honey bees lay two kinds of eggs: fertilized, female eggs, which have two sets of chromosomes and develop into workers or queens, and unfertilized, male eggs, which have only one set of chromosomes and develop into drones.

beech any tree of the genera *Fagus* and *Nothofagus*, family Fagaceae. The common beech *F. sylvaticus*, found in European forests, has a smooth grey trunk and edible nuts, or 'mast', which are used as animal feed or processed for oil. The timber is used in furniture.

Beecham Thomas 1879–1961. British conductor and impresario. He established the Royal Philharmonic Orchestra 1946 and fostered the works of composers such as Delius, Sibelius, and Richard Strauss.

Beecher Harriet Unmarried name of Harriet Beecher *Stowe, author of *Uncle Tom's Cabin*.

Beecher Lyman 1775–1863. US Congregational and Presbyterian minister, one of the most popular pulpit orators of his time. He was the father of Harriet Beecher *Stowe and Henry Ward Beecher.

Beeching Richard, Baron Beeching 1913–1985. British scientist and administrator. He was chair of the British Railways Board 1963–65, producing the controversial *Beeching Report* 1963, which advocated concentrating resources on intercity passenger traffic and freight, at the cost of closing many rural and branch lines.

Beeching Report 1963 official report on the railway network of Britain, which recommended the closure of loss-making lines and the improvement of money-making routes. Hundreds of lines and several thousand stations were closed as a result.

bee-eater bird *Merops apiaster* found in Africa, S Europe, and Asia. It feeds on a variety of insects, including bees, which it catches in its long narrow bill. Chestnut, yellow, and blue-green, it is gregarious, and generally nests in river banks and sandpits.

Beelzebub (Hebrew 'lord of the flies') in the New Testament, the leader of the devils, sometimes identified with Satan and sometimes with his chief assistant (see *devil). In the Old Testament Beelzebub was a fertility god worshipped by the Philistines and other Semitic groups (Baal).

beer alcoholic drink made from water and malt (fermented barley or other grain), flavoured with hops. Beer contains between 1% and 6% alcohol. One of the oldest alcoholic drinks, it was brewed in ancient China, Egypt, and Babylon.

Beersheba industrial town in Israel; population (1987) 115,000. It is the chief centre of the Negev desert and has been a settlement from the Stone Age.

beet plant of the genus *Beta* of the goosefoot family Chenapodiaceae. The common beet *B. vulgaris* is used in one variety to produce sugar, and another, the mangelwurzel, is grown as cattle fodder. The beetroot, or red beet, *B. rubra* is a salad plant.

Beethoven Ludwig van 1770–1827. German composer and pianist whose mastery of musical expression in every genre made him the dominant influence on 19th-century music. Beethoven's repertoire includes concert overtures; the opera *Fidelio*; five piano concertos and two for violin (one unfinished); 32 piano sonatas, including the *Moonlight* and *Appassionata*; 17 string quartets; the *Mass in D* (*Missa solemnis*); and nine symphonies, as well as many youthful works. He usually played his own piano pieces and conducted his orchestral works until he was hampered by deafness 1801; nevertheless he continued to compose.

beetle common name of insects in the order Coleoptera (Greek 'sheath-winged') with leathery forewings folding down in a protective sheath over the membranous hindwings, which are those used for flight. They pass through a complete metamorphosis. They include some of the largest and smallest of all insects: the largest is the *Hercules beetle Dynastes hercules* of the South American rainforests, 15 cm/6 in long; the smallest is only 0.05 cm/0.02 in long. Comprising more than 50% of the animal kingdom, beetles number some 370,000 named species, with many not yet described.

Beeton, Mrs (Isabella Mary Mayson) 1836–1865. British writer on cookery and domestic management. She produced *Beeton's Household Management* 1859, the first comprehensive work on domestic science.

Begin Menachem 1913–1992. Israeli politician. He was leader of the extremist Irgun Zvai Leumi organization in Palestine from 1942, and prime minister of Israel 1977–83, as head of the right-wing Likud party. In 1978 Begin shared a Nobel Peace Prize with President Sadat of Egypt for work on the *Camp David Agreements for a Middle East peace settlement.

begonia any plant of the genus *Begonia* of the tropical and subtropical family Begoniaceae. Begonias have fleshy and succulent leaves, and some have large, brilliant flowers. There are numerous species native to the tropics, in particular South America and India.

Behan Brendan 1923–1964. Irish dramatist. His early experience of prison and knowledge of the workings of the *IRA (recounted in his autobiography *Borstal Boy* 1958) provided him with two recurrent themes in his plays. *The Quare Fellow* 1954 was followed by the tragicomedy *The Hostage* 1958, first written in Gaelic.

behaviourism school of psychology originating in the USA, of which the leading exponent was John B *Watson. Behaviourists maintain that all human activity can ultimately be explained in terms of conditioned reactions or reflexes and habits formed in consequence. Leading behaviourists include Ivan *Pavlov and B F *Skinner.

behaviour therapy in psychology, the application of behavioural principles, derived from learning theories, to the treatment of clinical conditions such as *phobias, *obsessions, sexual and interpersonal problems. For example, in treating a phobia the person is taken into the feared situation in gradual steps. Over time, the fear typically reduces, and the problem becomes less acute.

behemoth (Hebrew 'beasts') in the Old Testament (Job 40), an animal cited by God as evidence of his power; usually thought to refer to the hippopotamus. It is used proverbially to mean any giant and powerful creature.

Behn Aphra 1640–1689. English novelist and playwright, the first woman in England to earn her living as a writer. Her writings were criticized for their explicitness; they frequently present events from a woman's point of view. Her novel *Oronooko* 1688 is an attack on slavery.

Behrens Peter 1868–1940. German architect. He pioneered the adaptation of architecture to industry, and designed the AEG turbine factory in Berlin 1909, a landmark in industrial design. He taught *Le Corbusier and Walter *Gropius.

Behring Emil von 1854–1917. German physician who discovered that the body produces antitoxins, substances able to counteract poisons released by bacteria. Using this knowledge, he developed new treatments for diseases such as *diphtheria.

Beiderbecke Bix (Leon Bismarck) 1903–1931. US jazz cornetist, composer, and pianist. A romantic soloist with King Oliver, Louis Armstrong, and Paul Whiteman's orchestra, Beiderbecke was the first acknowledged white jazz innovator. He was inspired by the classical composers Debussy, Ravel, and Stravinsky.

Beijing or *Peking* capital of China; part of its NE border is formed by the Great Wall of China; population (1989) 6,800,000. The municipality of Beijing has an area of 17,800 sq km/6,871 sq mi and a population (1990) of 10,819,000. Industries include textiles, petrochemicals, steel, and engineering.

Beirut or *Beyrouth* capital and port of *Lebanon, devastated by civil war in the 1970s and 1980s, when it was occupied by armies of neighbouring countries; population (1988 est)

1,500,000. The city is divided into a Christian eastern and a Muslim western sector by the Green Line.

Bekka, the or *El Beqa'a* governorate of E Lebanon separated from Syria by the Anti-Lebanon mountains. The Bekaa Valley was of strategic importance in the Syrian struggle for control of N Lebanon. In the early 1980s the valley was penetrated by Shia Muslims who established an extremist Hezbollah stronghold.

Belarus Republic of

area 207,600 sq km/80,100 sq mi
capital Minsk (Mensk)
towns Gomel, Vitebsk, Mogilev, Bobruisk, Grodno, Brest
physical more than 25% forested; rivers W Dvina, Dnieper and its tributaries; the Pripet Marshes in the E; mild and damp climate
head of state Alexandr Lukashenko from 1994
head of government Mikhail Chigir from 1994
political system emergent democracy
products peat, agricultural machinery, fertilizers, glass, textiles, leather, salt, electrical goods, meat, dairy produce
currency rouble and dukat
population (1993 est) 10,400,000 (77% Byelorussian 'Eastern Slavs', 13% Russian, 4% Polish, 1% Jewish)
languages Byelorussian, Russian
religions Roman Catholic, Russian Orthodox, with Baptist and Muslim minorities
chronology
1918–19 Briefly independent from Russia.
1937–41 More than 100,000 people were shot in mass executions ordered by Stalin.
1941–44 Occupied by Nazi Germany.
1945 Became a founding member of the United Nations.
1986 April: fallout from the Chernobyl nuclear reactor in Ukraine contaminated a large area.
1989 The nationalist Byelorussian Popular Front established.
1990 Sept: Byelorussian established as state language and republican sovereignty declared.
1991 Aug: declared independence; Communist Party suspended. Sept: reformist Shushkevich elected president. Dec: accorded diplomatic recognition by USA; Commonwealth of Independent States formed in Minsk.
1993 Ratified START I; agreement to adhere to

Nuclear Nonproliferation Treaty. Communist party reestablished.
1994 Merger of Russian and Belarusian economies agreed. President Shushkevich ousted. New constitution adopted. Alexandr Lukashenko elected president.

Belau, Republic of (formerly *Palau*)
area 508 sq km/196 sq mi
capital Koror (on Koror Island)
physical more than 350 islands and atolls; humid climate, susceptible to typhoons
head of state and government Kuniwo Nakamura from 1992
political system democratic republic
currency US dollar
population (1990) 15,100
languages Palauan and English
religion Christianity, principally Roman Catholicism
chronology
1899 Held by Germany, then known as Palau.
1921 Administered by Japan under League of Nations mandate.
1944 Occupied by US forces as base for attack on the Philippines.
1947 Administered by USA as part of the United Nations (UN) Trust Territory of the Pacific Islands.
1981 Acquired autonomy as the Republic of Belau.
1985 President Haruo Remelik assassinated; succeeded by Lazarus Salii.
1988 President Salii found dead; succeeded by Ngiratkel Etpison.
1992 Kuniwo Nakamura elected president. Referendum approved constitutional amendment allowing implementation of Compact of Free Association with USA.
1994 Independence achieved. UN membership agreed.

bel canto (Italian 'beautiful song') 18th-century Italian style of singing with emphasis on perfect technique and beautiful tone. It reached its peak in the operas of Rossini, Donizetti, and Bellini.

Belfast industrial port (shipbuilding, engineering, electronics, textiles, tobacco) and capital of Northern Ireland since 1920; population (1985) 300,000 (Protestants form the majority in E Belfast, Catholics in the W). Since 1968 the city has been heavily damaged by civil disturbances.

Belgian Congo former name (1908–60) of *Zaire.

Belgium Kingdom of (French *Royaume de Belgique*, Flemish *Koninkrijk België*)
area 30,510 sq km/11,784 sq mi
capital Brussels
towns Ghent, Liège, Charleroi, Bruges, Mons, Namur, Leuven; ports are Antwerp, Ostend, Zeebrugge
physical fertile coastal plain in NW, central rolling hills rise eastwards, hills and forest in SE
head of state King Albert from 1993
head of government Jean-Luc Dehaene from 1992
political system liberal democracy
exports iron, steel, textiles, manufactured goods, petrochemicals, plastics, vehicles, diamonds

currency Belgian franc

population (1993) 10,050,000 (comprising Flemings and Walloons); growth rate 0.1% p.a.

languages in the N (Flanders) Flemish (a Dutch dialect, known as *Vlaams*) 55%; in the S (Wallonia) Walloon (a French dialect) 32%; bilingual 11%; German (E border) 0.6%; all are official

religion Roman Catholic 75%

GNP $19,300 per head (1991)

chronology

1830 Belgium became an independent kingdom.

1914 Invaded by Germany.

1940 Again invaded by Germany.

1948 Belgium became founding member of Benelux Customs Union.

1949 Belgium became founding member of Council of Europe and NATO.

1951 Leopold III abdicated in favour of his son Baudouin.

1957 Belgium became founding member of the European Economic Community.

1971 Steps towards regional autonomy taken.

1972 German-speaking members included in the cabinet for the first time.

1973 Linguistic parity achieved in government appointments.

1974 Leo Tindemans became prime minister.

1978 Wilfried Martens succeeded Tindemans as prime minister.

1980 Open violence over language divisions. Regional assemblies for Flanders and Wallonia and a three-member executive for Brussels created.

1981 Short-lived coalition led by Mark Eyskens was followed by the return of Martens.

1987 Martens head of caretaker government after break-up of coalition.

1988 Following a general election, Martens formed a new five-party coalition.

1992 Martens-led coalition collapsed; Jean-Luc Dehaene formed a new centre-left-led coalition.

1993 Federal system adopted, based on Flanders, Wallonia, and Brussels. King Baudouin died; succeeded by his brother, Prince Albert of Liege.

Belgrade (Serbo-Croatian *Beograd*) capital of Yugoslavia and Serbia, and Danube river port; population (1981) 1,470,000. Industries include light engineering, food processing, textiles, pharmaceuticals, and electrical goods.

Belize (formerly *British Honduras*)

area 22,963 sq km/8,864 sq mi

capital Belmopan

towns ports Belize City, Dangriga, Punta Gorda; Orange Walk, Corozal

physical tropical swampy coastal plain, Maya Mountains in S; over 90% forested

head of state Elizabeth II from 1981, represented by governor general

head of government Manuel Esquivel from 1993

political system constitutional monarchy

exports sugar, citrus fruits, rice, fish products, bananas

currency Belize dollar

population (1993) 230,000 (including Mayan minority in the interior); growth rate 2.5% p.a.

languages English (official); Spanish (widely spoken), native Creole dialects

religions Roman Catholic 60%, Protestant 35%

GDP $247 million (1988); $1,220 per head

chronology

1862 Belize became a British colony.

1954 Constitution adopted, providing for limited internal self-government. General election won by George Price.

1964 Self-government achieved from the UK (universal adult suffrage introduced).

1965 Two-chamber national assembly introduced, with Price as prime minister.

1970 Capital moved from Belize City to Belmopan.

1973 British Honduras became Belize.

1975 British troops sent to defend the disputed frontier with Guatemala.

1981 Full independence achieved. Price became prime minister.

1984 Price defeated in general election. Manuel Esquivel formed the government. The UK reaffirmed its undertaking to defend the frontier.

1989 Price and the centre-left People's United Party won the general election.

1993 The moderate-conservative United Democratic Party won general election. Manuel Esquivel returned as prime minister. British government relinquished responsibility for external defence of the country.

bell musical instrument, made in many sizes, comprising a suspended resonating vessel swung by a handle or from a pivoted frame to make contact with a beater which hangs inside the bell. Church bells are among the most massive structures to be cast in bronze in one piece; their shape, a flared bowl with a thickened rim, is engineered to produce a clangorous mixture of tones. Miniature **handbells** are tuned to resonate harmoniously. Orchestral **tubular bells** are tuned to a chromatic scale of pitches and are played by striking with a wooden mallet.

Bell Alexander Graham 1847–1922. Scottish-born US scientist and inventor of the telephone. He patented his invention 1876, and later experimented with a type of phonograph and, in aeronautics, invented the tricycle undercarriage.

Bell John 1928–1990. British physicist who in 1964 devised a test to verify a point in *quantum theory: whether two particles that were once connected are always afterwards interconnected even if they become widely separated. He also contributed to the design of particle accelerators.

belladonna or *deadly nightshade* poisonous plant *Atropa belladonna*, found in Europe and Asia. The dried powdered leaves contain *alkaloids from which the drugs *atropine and *hyoscine are extracted. Belladonna extract acts medicinally as an *anticholinergic (blocking the passage of certain nerve impulses), and is highly toxic in large doses.

belles lettres (French 'fine letters') literature that is appreciated more for its aesthetic qualities than for its content.

bellflower general name for many plants of the family Campanulaceae, notably those of the genus *Campanula*. The Canterbury bell *C. medium* is the garden variety, originally from S Europe. The *harebell is also a *Campanula*.

Bellini family of Italian Renaissance painters. Jacopo and his sons Gentile and Giovanni were founders of the Venetian school in the fifteenth and early sixteenth centuries.

Bellini Vincenzo 1801–1835. Italian opera composer whose lyrical, melodic treatments of classic themes include *La Sonnambula* 1831, *Norma* 1831, and *I Puritani* 1835.

Bellow Saul 1915– . Canadian-born US novelist. Novels such as *Herzog* 1964, *Humboldt's Gift* 1975, and *The Dean's December* 1982 show his method of inhabiting the consciousness of a central character, frequently a Jewish-American intellectual, to portray an individual's frustration with the ongoing events of an indifferent society. His finely styled works and skilled characterizations won him the Nobel Prize for Literature 1976.

bell ringing or *campanology* art of ringing church bells by hand, by means of a rope fastened to a wheel rotating the entire bell mechanism. *Change ringing* is an English art of ringing all the possible sequences of a number of bells in strict order, using one player to each bell. Fixed permutations of 5–12 bells are rung. In Europe and the USA, the *carillon* performs arrangements of well-known music for up to 70 static bells. It is played by a single operator using a keyboard system of levers and pulleys acting on the striking mechanisms only. *Handbell* ringing is played solo or by a team of ringers selecting from a range of lightweight bells of pure tone resting on a table.

Belmopan capital of *Belize from 1970; population (1991) 4,000. It replaced Belize City as administrative centre of the country.

Belo Horizonte industrial city (steel, engineering, textiles) in SE Brazil, capital of the fast-developing state of Minas Gerais; population (1991) 2,103,300. Built in the 1890s, it was Brazil's first planned modern city.

Belorussia or *Byelorussia* former name 1919–91 of the Republic of *Belarus.

Belsen site of a Nazi *concentration camp in Lower Saxony, Germany.

Belshazzar in the Old Testament, the last king of Babylon, son of Nebuchadnezzar. During a feast (known as *Belshazzar's Feast*) he saw a message, interpreted by *Daniel as prophesying the fall of Babylon and death of Belshazzar.

Bemba member of a people native to NE Zambia and neighbouring areas of Zaire and Zimbabwe, although many reside in urban areas such as Lusaka and Copperbelt. They number about three million. The Bemba language belongs to the Bantu branch of the Niger–Congo family.

Ben Ali Zine el Abidine 1936– . Tunisian politician, president from 1987. After training in France and the USA, he became director-general of national security. He was made minister of the interior and then prime minister under president for life, Habib *Bourguiba, whom he deposed 1987 in a bloodless coup with the aid of ministerial colleagues. He ended the personality cult established by Bourguiba and moved toward a pluralist political system. He was re-elected 1994, with 99% of the popular vote.

Benares alternative transliteration of *Varanasi, holy city in India.

Ben Bella Ahmed 1916– . Algerian politician. He was leader of the National Liberation Front (FLN) from 1952, the first prime minister of independent Algeria 1962–63, and its first president 1963–65. In 1965 Ben Bella was overthrown by Col Houari *Boumédienne and detained until 1979. In 1985 he founded a new party, Mouvement pour la Démocratie en Algérie, and returned to Algeria 1990 after nine years in exile.

Benbow John 1653–1702. English admiral, hero of several battles with France. He ran away to sea as a boy, and from 1689 served in the navy. He fought at the battles of Beachy Head 1690 and La Hogue 1692, and died of wounds received in a fight with the French off Jamaica.

bends popular name for a paralytic affliction of deep-sea divers, arising from too rapid a release of nitrogen from solution in their blood. If a diver surfaces too quickly, nitrogen that had dissolved in the blood under increasing water pressure is suddenly released, forming bubbles in the bloodstream and causing paralysis. Immediate treatment is compression and slow decompression in a special chamber.

Benedictine order religious order of monks and nuns in the Roman Catholic church, founded by St *Benedict at Subiaco, Italy, in the 6th century. It had a strong influence on medieval learning and reached the height of its prosperity early in the 14th century.

Benedict, St *c.* 480–*c.* 547. Founder of Christian monasticism in the West and of the *Benedictine order. He founded the monastery of Monte Cassino, Italy. Here he wrote out his rule for monastic life, and was visited shortly before his death by the Ostrogothic king Totila, whom he converted to the Christian faith. His feast day is 11 July.

benefice in the early Middle Ages, a donation of land or money to the Christian church as an act of devotion; from the 12th century, the term came to mean the income enjoyed by clergy.

Benelux (acronym from *Belgium, the Netherlands, and Luxembourg*) customs union agreed by Belgium, the Netherlands, and Luxembourg 1948, fully effective 1960. It was the precursor of the European Community.

Beneš Eduard 1884–1948. Czechoslovak politician. He worked with Tomáš *Masaryk towards Czechoslovak nationalism from 1918 and was foreign minister and representative at the League of Nations. He was president of the republic from 1935 until forced to resign by the Germans; he headed a government in exile in London during World War II. He returned home as president 1945 but resigned again after the Communist coup 1948.

Bengal former province of British India, divided 1947 into *West Bengal, a state of India, and East Bengal, from 1972 *Bangladesh. A famine in 1943, caused by a slump in demand for jute and a bad harvest, resulted in over 3 million deaths.

Bengal, Bay of part of the Indian Ocean lying between the east coast of India and the west coast of Myanmar (Burma) and the Malay Peninsula. The Irrawaddy, Ganges, and Brahmaputra rivers flow into the bay. The principal islands are to be found in the Andaman and Nicobar groups.

Bengali person of Bengali culture from Bangladesh and India (W Bengal, Tripura). There are 80–150 million speakers of Bengali, an Indo-Iranian language belonging to the Indo-European family. It is the official language of Bangladesh and of the state of Bengal, and is also used by emigrant Bangladeshi and Bengali communities in such countries as the UK and the USA. Bengalis in Bangladesh are predominantly Muslim, whereas those in India are mainly Hindu.

Benghazi or **Banghazi** historic city and industrial port in N Libya on the Gulf of Sirte; population (1982) 650,000. It was controlled by Turkey between the 16th century and 1911, and by Italy 1911–42; a major naval supply base during World War II.

Ben-Gurion David. Adopted name of David Gruen 1886–1973. Israeli statesman and socialist politician, one of the founders of the state of Israel, the country's first prime minister 1948–53, and again 1955–63.

Benin People's Republic of (*République Populaire du Bénin*)

area 112,622 sq km/43,472 sq mi
capital Porto Novo (official), Cotonou (de facto)
towns Abomey, Natitingou, Parakou; chief port Cotonou
physical flat to undulating terrain; hot and humid in S; semiarid in N
head of state and government Nicéphore Soglo from 1991
political system socialist pluralist republic
exports cocoa, peanuts, cotton, palm oil, petroleum, cement, sea products
currency CFA franc

population (1993 est) 5,010,000; growth rate 3% p.a.
languages French (official); Fon 47% and Yoruba 9% in south; six major tribal languages in north
religions animist 65%, Christian 17%, Muslim 13%
GNP $380 per head (1991)
chronology
1851 Under French control.
1958 Became self-governing dominion within the French Community.
1960 Independence achieved from France.
1960–72 Acute political instability, with switches from civilian to military rule.
1972 Military regime established by General Mathieu Kerekou.
1974 Kerekou announced that the country would follow a path of 'scientific socialism'.
1975 Name of country changed from Dahomey to Benin.
1977 Return to civilian rule under a new constitution.
1980 Kerekou formally elected president by the national revolutionary assembly.
1989 Marxist-Leninism dropped as official ideology. Strikes and protests against Kerekou's rule mounted; demonstrations banned and army deployed against protesters.
1990 Referendum support for multiparty politics.
1991 Multiparty elections held. Kerekou defeated in presidential elections by Nicéphore Soglo.

Benin former African kingdom 1200–1897, now part of Nigeria. It reached the height of its power in the 14th–17th centuries when it ruled the area between the Niger Delta and Lagos.

Benn Tony (Anthony Wedgwood) 1925– . British Labour politician, formerly the leading figure on the party's left wing. He was minister of technology 1966–70 and of industry 1974–75, but his campaign against entry to the European Community led to his transfer to the Department of Energy 1975–79. A skilled parliamentary orator, he unsuccessfully contested the Labour Party leadership 1988.

Bennett Alan 1934– . English playwright. His works (set in his native north of England) treat subjects such as class, senility, illness, and death with macabre comedy. They include TV films, for example *An Englishman Abroad* 1982; the cinema film *A Private Function* 1984; and plays such as *Forty Years On* 1968, *Getting On* 1971, *Kafka's Dick* 1986, and *The Madness of George III* 1991.

Bennett (Enoch) Arnold 1867–1931. English novelist. He became a London journalist 1893 and editor of *Woman* 1896. His many novels include *Anna of the Five Towns* 1904, *The Old Wives' Tale* 1908, and the trilogy *Clayhanger*, *Hilda Lessways*, and *These Twain* 1910–16.

Bennett Richard Rodney 1936– . English composer of jazz, film music, symphonies, and operas. His film scores for *Far from the Madding Crowd* 1967, *Nicholas and Alexandra* 1971, and *Murder on the Orient Express* 1974 all received Oscar nominations. His operas include *The Mines of Sulphur* 1963 and *Victory* 1970.

Ben Nevis highest mountain in the British Isles (1,343 m/4,406 ft), in the Grampians, Scotland.

bent or **bent grass** any grasses of the genus *Agrostris*. Creeping bent grass *A. stolonifera*, also known as fiorin, is common in N North America and Eurasia, including lowland Britain. It spreads by *stolons and bears large attractive panicles of yellow or purple flowers on thin stalks. It is often used on lawns and golf courses.

Bentham Jeremy 1748–1832. English philosopher, legal and social reformer, and founder of *utilitarianism. The essence of his moral philosophy is found in the pronouncement of his *Principles of Morals and Legislation* (written 1780, published 1789): that the object of all legislation should be 'the greatest happiness for the greatest number'.

Bentley John Francis 1839–1902. English architect, a convert to Catholicism, who designed Westminster Cathedral, London (1895–1903). It is outwardly Byzantine but inwardly shaped by shadowy vaults of bare brickwork. The campanile is the tallest church tower in London.

Benz Karl Friedrich 1844–1929. German automobile engineer who produced the world's first petrol-driven motor vehicle. He built his first model engine 1878 and the petrol-driven car 1885.

benzaldehyde C_6H_5CHO colourless liquid with the characteristic odour of almonds. It is used as a solvent and in the making of perfumes and dyes. It occurs in certain leaves, such as the cherry, laurel, and peach, and in a combined form in certain nuts and kernels. It can be extracted from such natural sources, but is usually made from *toluene.

benzene C_6H_6 clear liquid hydrocarbon of characteristic odour, occurring in coal tar. It is used as a solvent and in the synthesis of many chemicals.

benzoic acid C_6H_5COOH white crystalline solid, sparingly soluble in water, that is used as a preservative for certain foods and as an antiseptic. It is obtained chemically by the direct oxidation of benzaldehyde and occurs in certain natural resins, some essential oils, and as hippuric acid.

Beograd Serbo-Croatian form of *Belgrade, capital of Yugoslavia.

Beowulf Anglo-Saxon poem (composed *c.* 700), the only complete surviving example of Germanic folk epic. It exists in a single manuscript copied about 1000 in the Cottonian collection of the British Museum.

Berber member of a non-Semitic Caucasoid people of North Africa who since prehistoric times inhabited Barbary, the Mediterranean coastlands from Egypt to the Atlantic. Their language, present-day Berber (a member of the Afro-Asiatic language family), is spoken by about one-third of Algerians and nearly two-thirds of Moroccans, 10 million people. Berbers are mainly agricultural, but some are still nomadic.

Bérégovoy Pierre 1925–1993. French socialist politician, prime minister 1992–93. A close ally of François *Mitterrand, he was named chief of staff 1981 after managing the successful presidential campaign. He was social affairs minister 1982–84 and finance minister 1984–86 and 1988–92. Shortly after the Socialist defeat in 1993's general election he committed suicide.

Berengaria of Navarre 1165–1230. Queen of England. The only English queen never to set foot in England, she was the daughter of King Sancho VI of Navarre. She married Richard I of England in Cyprus 1191, and accompanied him on his crusade to the Holy Land.

Berg Alban 1885–1935. Austrian composer. He studied under Arnold *Schoenberg and was associated with him as one of the leaders of the serial, or 12-tone, school of composition. His output includes orchestral, chamber, and vocal music as well as two operas, *Wozzeck* 1925, a grim story of working-class life, and the unfinished *Lulu* 1929–35.

Berg Paul 1926– . US molecular biologist. In 1972, using gene-splicing techniques developed by others, Berg spliced and combined into a single hybrid *DNA from an animal tumour virus (SV40) and DNA from a bacterial virus. Berg's work aroused fears in other workers and excited continuing controversy. For his work on recombinant DNA, he shared the 1980 Nobel Prize for Chemistry with Walter *Gilbert and Frederick *Sanger.

bergamot small, evergreen tree *Citrus bergamia* of the rue family Rutaceae. From the rind of its fruit a fragrant orange-scented essence used as a perfume is obtained. The sole source of supply is S Calabria, Italy, but the name comes from the town of Bergamo, in Lombardy.

Bergen industrial port (shipbuilding, engineering, fishing) in SW Norway; population (1991) 213,300. Founded 1070, Bergen was a member of the *Hanseatic League.

Bergius Friedrich Karl Rudolph 1884–1949. German research chemist who invented processes for converting coal into oil and wood into sugar. He shared a Nobel prize 1931 with Carl Bosch for his part in inventing and developing high-pressure industrial methods.

Bergman Ingmar 1918– . Swedish stage producer (from the 1930s) and film director (from the 1950s). His work deals with complex moral, psychological, and metaphysical problems and is tinged with pessimism. His films include *Wild Strawberries* 1957, *The Seventh Seal* 1957, *Persona* 1966, and *Fanny and Alexander* 1982.

Bergman Ingrid 1917–1982. Swedish actress whose films include *Intermezzo* 1939, *Casablanca, For Whom the Bell Tolls* both 1943, and *Gaslight* 1944, for which she won an Academy Award.

Bergson Henri 1859–1941. French philosopher who believed that time, change, and development were the essence of reality. He thought that time was not a succession of distinct and separate instants but a continuous process in which one period merged imperceptibly into the next. Nobel Prize for Literature 1928.

Beria Lavrenti 1899–1953. Soviet politician who in 1938 became minister of the interior and head of the Soviet police force that imprisoned, liquidated, and transported millions of Soviet citizens. On Stalin's death 1953, he attempted to seize power but was foiled and shot after a secret trial. Apologists for Stalin have blamed Beria for the atrocities committed by Soviet police during Stalin's dictatorship.

Bering Vitus 1681–1741. Danish explorer, the

first European to sight Alaska. He died on Bering Island in the Bering Sea, both named after him, as is the Bering Strait, which separates Asia (Russia) from North America (Alaska).

Bering Sea section of the N Pacific between Alaska and Siberia, from the Aleutian Islands north to the Bering Strait.

Bering Strait strait between Alaska and Siberia, linking the N Pacific and Arctic oceans.

Berio Luciano 1925– . Italian composer. His style has been described as graceful *serialism, and he has frequently experimented with electronic music and taped sound. His works include nine *Sequenzas/Sequences* 1957–75 for various solo instruments or voice, *Sinfonia* 1969 for voices and orchestra, *Points on the curve to find ... 1974*, and a number of dramatic works, including the opera *Un re in ascolto/A King Listens* 1984.

Berkeley Busby. Stage name of William Berkeley Enos 1895–1976. US choreographer and film director who used ingenious and extravagant sets and teams of female dancers to create large-scale kaleidoscopic patterns through movement and costume when filmed from above, as in *Footlight Parade* 1933.

Berkeley Lennox (Randal Francis) 1903–1989. English composer. His works for the voice include *The Hill of the Graces* 1975, verses from Spenser's *Fairie Queene* set for eight-part unaccompanied chorus; and his operas *Nelson* 1953 and *Ruth* 1956.

berkelium synthesized, radioactive, metallic element of the actinide series, symbol Bk, atomic number 97, relative atomic mass 247. It was first produced 1949 by Glenn Seaborg and his team, at the University of California at Berkeley, USA, after which it is named.

Berkshire or *Royal Berkshire* county in S central England
area 1,260 sq km/486 sq mi
towns Reading (administrative headquarters), Eton, Slough, Maidenhead, Ascot, Bracknell, Newbury, Windsor
products general agricultural and horticultural goods, electronics, plastics, pharmaceuticals
population (1991) 716,500
famous people Jethro Tull, William Laud, Stanley Spencer.

Berlin industrial city (machine tools, electrical goods, paper, printing) and capital of the Federal Republic of Germany; population (1990) 3,102,500. The Berlin Wall divided the city from 1961 to 1989, but in Oct 1990 Berlin became the capital of a unified Germany, once more the 16th *Land* (state) of the Federal Republic.

Berlin Irving. Adopted name of Israel Baline 1888–1989. Russian-born US songwriter. His songs include such hits as 'Alexander's Ragtime Band' 1911, 'Always' 1925, 'God Bless America' 1939, and 'White Christmas' 1942, and the musicals *Top Hat* 1935, *Annie Get Your Gun* 1946, and *Call Me Madam* 1950. He also provided songs for films like *Blue Skies* 1946 and *Easter Parade* 1948.

Berlin blockade the closing of entry to Berlin from the west by Soviet forces June 1948–May 1949. It was an attempt to prevent the other Allies (the USA, France, and the UK) unifying the western part of Germany. The British and US forces responded by sending supplies to the city by air for over a year (the *Berlin airlift*). In May 1949 the blockade was lifted; the airlift continued until Sept. The blockade marked the division of the city into Eastern and Western sectors.

Berlin Wall dividing barrier between East and West Berlin 1961–89, erected by East Germany to prevent East Germans from leaving for West Germany. Escapers were shot on sight.

Berlioz (Louis) Hector 1803–1869. French Romantic composer. He is noted as the founder of modern orchestration. Much of his music was inspired by drama and literature and has a theatrical quality. He wrote symphonic works, such as *Symphonie fantastique* 1830–31 and *Roméo et Juliette* 1839; dramatic cantatas including *La Damnation de Faust* 1846 and *L'Enfance du Christ* 1854; sacred music; and three operas.

Berlusconi Silvio 1936– . Italian businessman and right-of-centre politician. After building a multi-million business empire, Fininvest, he turned his Milan-based pressure group, Forza Italia, into a political party to fight the 1994 general election. He capitalized on popular disillusionment with the established political parties and, with the federalist Northern League and right-wing National Alliance, won a clear parliamentary majority. His administration soon ran into difficulties over an alleged conflict of interest between his business concerns and political responsibilities, and in Dec 1994 he resigned.

Bermuda British colony in the NW Atlantic Ocean
area 54 sq km/21 sq mi
capital and chief port Hamilton
products Easter lilies, pharmaceuticals; tourism and banking are important
currency Bermuda dollar
population (1988) 58,100
language English
religion Christian
government under the constitution of 1968, Bermuda is a fully self-governing British colony, with a governor (Lord Waddington from 1992), senate, and elected House of Assembly (premier from 1982 John Swan, United Bermuda Party)
history the islands were named after Juan de Bermudez, who visited them 1515, and were settled by British colonists 1609. Indian and African slaves were transported from 1616 and soon outnumbered the white settlers. Racial violence 1977 led to intervention, at the request of the government, by British troops.

Bern (French *Berne*) capital of Switzerland and of Bern canton, in W Switzerland on the Aare River; population (1990) 134,600; canton 945,600. It joined the Swiss confederation 1353 and became the capital 1848. Industries include textiles, chocolate, pharmaceuticals, light metal and electrical goods.

Bernadette, St 1844–1879. French saint, born in Lourdes in the French Pyrenees. In Feb 1858 she had a vision of the Virgin Mary in a grotto, and it became a centre of pilgrimage. Many sick people who were dipped in the water of a spring there were said to have been cured. Her feast day is 16 April.

Bernadotte Count Folke 1895–1948. Swedish

diplomat and president of the Swedish Red Cross. In 1945 he conveyed Nazi commander Himmler's offer of capitulation to the British and US governments, and in 1948 was United Nations mediator in Palestine, where he was assassinated by Israeli Stern Gang guerrillas. He was a nephew of Gustaf VI of Sweden.

Bernard Claude 1813–1878. French physiologist and founder of experimental medicine. Bernard first demonstrated that digestion is not restricted to the stomach, but takes place throughout the small intestine. He discovered the digestive input of the pancreas, several functions of the liver, and the vasomotor nerves which dilate and contract the blood vessels and thus regulate body temperature. This led him to the concept of the *milieu intérieur* ('internal environment') whose stability is essential to good health.

Bernard of Menthon, St or **Bernard of Montjoux** 923–1008. Christian priest, founder of the hospices for travellers on the Alpine passes that bear his name. The large, heavily built **St Bernard** dogs, formerly employed to find travellers lost in the snow, were also named after him. He is the patron saint of mountaineers. His feast day is 28 May.

Bernhard Prince of the Netherlands 1911– . Formerly Prince Bernhard of Lippe-Biesterfeld, he married Princess *Juliana in 1937. When Germany invaded the Netherlands in 1940, he escaped to England and became liaison officer for the Dutch and British forces, playing a part in the organization of the Dutch Resistance.

Bernhardt Sarah. Stage name of Rosine Bernard 1845–1923. French actress who dominated the stage of her day, frequently performing at the Comédie-Française in Paris. She excelled particularly in tragic roles, including Cordelia in Shakespeare's *King Lear*, the title role in Racine's *Phèdre*, and the male roles of Hamlet and of Napoleon's son in Edmond *Rostand's *L'Aiglon*.

Bernini Giovanni Lorenzo 1598–1680. Italian sculptor, architect, and painter, a leading figure in the development of the Baroque style. His work in Rome includes the colonnaded piazza in front of St Peter's Basilica (1656), fountains (as in the Piazza Navona), and papal monuments. His sculpture includes *The Ecstasy of St Theresa* 1645–52 (Sta Maria della Vittoria, Rome) and numerous portrait busts.

Bernoulli Swiss family that produced many mathematicians and scientists in the 17th, 18th, and 19th centuries, in particular the brothers *Jakob* (1654–1705) and *Johann* (1667–1748).

Bernoulli's principle law stating that the speed of a fluid varies inversely with pressure, an increase in speed producing a decrease in pressure (such as a drop in hydraulic pressure as the fluid speeds up flowing through a constriction in a pipe) and vice versa. The principle also explains the pressure differences on each surface of an aerofoil, which gives lift to the wing of an aircraft. The principle is named after Swiss mathematician and physicist Daniel Bernoulli.

Bernstein Leonard 1918–1990. US composer, conductor, and pianist, one of the most energetic and versatile of US musicians in the 20th century. His works, which established a vogue for realistic, contemporary themes, include symphonies such as *The Age of Anxiety* 1949, ballets such as *Fancy Free* 1944, and scores for musicals, including *Wonderful Town* 1953, *West Side Story* 1957, and *Mass* 1971 in memory of President J F Kennedy.

berry fleshy, many-seeded *fruit that does not split open to release the seeds. The outer layer of tissue, the exocarp, forms an outer skin that is often brightly coloured to attract birds to eat the fruit and thus disperse the seeds. Examples of berries are the tomato and the grape.

Berry Chuck (Charles Edward) 1926– . US rock-and-roll singer, prolific songwriter, and guitarist. His characteristic guitar riffs became staples of rock music, and his humorous storytelling lyrics were also emulated. He had a string of hits in the 1950s and 1960s beginning with 'Maybellene' 1955.

Bertolucci Bernardo 1940– . Italian film director whose work combines political and historical perspectives with an elegant and lyrical visual appeal. His films include *The Spider's Stratagem* 1970, *Last Tango in Paris* 1972, *1900* 1976, *The Last Emperor* 1987, for which he received an Academy Award, and *The Sheltering Sky* 1990.

beryl mineral, beryllium aluminium silicate, $Be_3Al_2Si_6O_{18}$, which forms crystals chiefly in granite. It is the chief ore of beryllium. Two of its gem forms are aquamarine (light-blue crystals) and emerald (dark-green crystals).

beryllium hard, light-weight, silver-white, metallic element, symbol Be, atomic number 4, relative atomic mass 9.012. It is one of the *alkaline-earth metals, with chemical properties similar to those of magnesium; in nature it is found only in combination with other elements. It is used to make sturdy, light alloys and to control the speed of neutrons in nuclear reactors. Beryllium oxide was discovered in 1798 by French chemist Louis-Nicolas Vauquelin (1763–1829), but the element was not isolated until 1828, by Friedrich Wöhler and Antoine-Alexandre-Brutus Bussy independently.

Berzelius Jöns Jakob 1779–1848. Swedish chemist who accurately determined more than 2,000 relative atomic and molecular masses. He devised (1813–14) the system of chemical symbols and formulae now in use and proposed oxygen as a reference standard for atomic masses. His discoveries include the elements cerium (1804), selenium (1817), and thorium (1828); he was the first to prepare silicon in its amorphous form and to isolate zirconium. The words *isomerism*, *allotropy*, and *protein* were coined by him.

Bessarabia region in SE Europe, divided between Moldova and Ukraine. Bessarabia was annexed by Russia 1812, but broke away at the Russian Revolution to join Romania. The cession was confirmed by the Allies, but not by Russia, in a Paris treaty of 1920; the USSR reoccupied it 1940 and divided it between the Moldavian and Ukrainian republics (now independent Moldova and Ukraine). Romania recognized the position in the 1947 peace treaty.

Bessel Friedrich Wilhelm 1784–1846. German astronomer and mathematician, the first person to find the approximate distance to a star by direct methods when he measured the *parallax (annual displacement) of the star 61 Cygni in

1838. In mathematics, he introduced the series of functions now known as *Bessel functions*.

Bessemer Henry 1813–1898. British engineer and inventor who developed a method of converting molten pig iron into steel (the *Bessemer process*).

Bessemer process the first cheap method of making *steel, invented by Henry Bessemer in England 1856. It has since been superseded by more efficient steelmaking processes, such as the *basic-oxygen process. In the Bessemer process compressed air is blown into the bottom of a converter, a furnace shaped like a cement mixer, containing molten pig iron. The excess carbon in the iron burns out, other impurities form a slag, and the furnace is emptied by tilting.

Best Charles Herbert 1899–1978. Canadian physiologist, one of the team of Canadian scientists including Frederick *Banting whose research resulted in 1922 in the discovery of insulin as a treatment for diabetes.

bestiary in medieval times, a book with stories and illustrations which depicted real and mythical animals or plants to illustrate a (usually Christian) moral. The stories were initially derived from the Greek *Physiologus*, a collection of 48 such stories, written in Alexandria around the 2nd century AD.

beta-blocker any of a class of drugs that block impulses that stimulate certain nerve endings (beta receptors) serving the heart muscles. This reduces the heart rate and the force of contraction, which in turn reduces the amount of oxygen (and therefore the blood supply) required by the heart. Beta-blockers are banned from use in competitive sports. They may be useful in the treatment of angina, arrhythmia, and raised blood pressure, and following myocardial infarctions. They must be withdrawn from use gradually.

beta particle electron or positron ejected with great velocity from a radioactive atom that is undergoing spontaneous disintegration. Beta particles do not exist in the nucleus but are created on disintegration, beta decay, when a neutron converts to a proton to emit an electron.

Betelgeuse or *Alpha Orionis* red supergiant star in the constellation of Orion and the tenth brightest star in the sky, although its brightness varies. It is over 300 times the diameter of the Sun, about the same size as the orbit of Mars, is over 10,000 times as luminous as the Sun, and lies 650 light years from Earth.

betel nut fruit of the areca palm *Areca catechu*, used together with lime and betel pepper as a masticatory stimulant by peoples of the East and Papua New Guinea. Chewing it results in blackened teeth and a mouth stained deep red.

Bethe Hans Albrecht 1906– . German-born US physicist who worked on the first atom bomb. He was awarded a Nobel prize 1967 for his discoveries concerning energy production in stars.

Bethlehem (Hebrew *Beit-Lahm*) town on the W bank of the river Jordan, S of Jerusalem. Occupied by Israel in 1967; population (1980) 14,000. In the Bible it is mentioned as the birthplace of King David and Jesus.

Betjeman John 1906–1984. English poet and essayist, originator of a peculiarly English light verse, nostalgic, and delighting in Victorian and Edwardian architecture. His *Collected Poems* appeared in 1968 and a verse autobiography, *Summoned by Bells*, in 1960. He became poet laureate 1972.

betony plant, *Stachys* (formerly *Betonica*) *officinalis*, of the mint family, formerly used in medicine and dyeing. It has a hairy stem and leaves, and reddish-purple flowers.

Bettelheim Bruno 1903–1990. Austrian-born US child psychologist. At the University of Chicago he founded a treatment centre for emotionally disturbed children based on the principle of a supportive home environment. Among his most influential books are *Love is Not Enough* 1950, *Truants from Life* 1954, and *Children of the Dream* 1962.

Beuys Joseph 1921–1986. German sculptor and performance artist, one of the leaders of avant-garde art in Europe during the 1970s and 1980s. His sculpture makes use of unusual materials such as felt and fat.

He was strongly influenced by his wartime experiences.

Bevan Aneurin (Nye) 1897–1960. British Labour politician. Son of a Welsh miner, and himself a miner at 13, he became member of Parliament for Ebbw Vale 1929–60. As minister of health 1945–51, he inaugurated the National Health Service (NHS); he was minister of labour Jan– April 1951, when he resigned (with Harold Wilson) on the introduction of NHS charges and led a Bevanite faction against the government. In 1956 he became chief Labour spokesperson on foreign affairs, and deputy leader of the Labour party 1959. He was an outstanding speaker.

Beveridge William Henry, 1st Baron Beveridge 1879–1963. British economist. A civil servant, he acted as Lloyd George's lieutenant in the social legislation of the Liberal government before World War I. The *Beveridge Report* 1942 formed the basis of the welfare state in Britain.

Bevin Ernest 1881–1951. British Labour politician. Chief creator of the Transport and General Workers' Union, he was its general secretary from 1921 to 1940, when he entered the war cabinet as minister of labour and national service. He organized the 'Bevin boys', chosen by ballot to work in the coal mines as war service, and was foreign secretary in the Labour government 1945–51.

Bewick Thomas 1753–1828. English wood engraver, excelling in animal subjects. His illustrated *A General History of Quadrupeds* 1790 and *A History of British Birds* 1797–1804 display his skill.

Beza Théodore (properly *De Bèsze*) 1519–1605. French church reformer. He settled in Geneva, Switzerland, where he worked with the Protestant leader John Calvin and succeeded him as head of the reformed church there 1564. He wrote in defence of the burning of *Servetus (1554) and translated the New Testament into Latin.

Bezier curve curved line that connects a series of points (or 'nodes') in the smoothest possible way. The shape of the curve is governed by a series of complex mathematical formulae. They are used in *computer graphics and *CAD.

BFI abbreviation for the *British Film Institute*.

Founded in 1933, the organization was created to promote the cinema as a 'means of entertainment and instruction'. It includes the National Film Archive (1935) and the National Film Theatre (1951).

Bhagavad-Gītā (Hindu 'the Song of the Blessed') religious and philosophical Sanskrit poem, dating from around 300 BC, forming an episode in the sixth book of the *Mahābhārata*, one of the two great Hindu epics. It is the supreme religious work of Hinduism.

bhakti (Sanskrit 'devotion') in Hinduism, a tradition of worship that emphasizes love and devotion rather than ritual, sacrifice, or study.

bhangra pop music evolved in the UK in the late 1970s from traditional Punjabi music, combining electronic instruments and ethnic drums.

Bhindranwale Sant Jarnail Singh 1947–1984. Indian Sikh fundamentalist leader who campaigned for the creation of a separate state of Khalistan during the early 1980s, precipitating a bloody Hindu–Sikh conflict in the Punjab. Having taken refuge in the Golden Temple complex in Amritsar and built up an arms cache for guerrilla activities, Bhindranwale, along with around 500 followers, died at the hands of Indian security forces who stormed the temple in 'Operation Blue Star' June 1984.

Bhopal industrial city (textiles, chemicals, electrical goods, jewellery); capital of Madhya Pradesh, central India; population (1981) 672,000. Nearby Bhimbetka Caves, discovered 1973, have the world's largest collection of prehistoric paintings, about 10,000 years old. In 1984 some 2,600 people died from an escape of the poisonous gas methyl isocyanate from a factory owned by US company Union Carbide; another 300,000 suffer from long-term health problems.

Bhumibol Adulyadej 1927– . King of Thailand from 1946. Born in the USA and educated in Bangkok and Switzerland, he succeeded to the throne on the assassination of his brother. In 1973 he was active, with popular support, in overthrowing the military government of Marshal Thanom Kittikachorn and thus ended a sequence of army-dominated regimes in power from 1932.

Bhutan Kingdom of (*Druk-yul*)
area 46,500 sq km/17,954 sq mi
capital Thimbu (Thimphu)
towns Paro, Punakha, Mongar
physical occupies southern slopes of the Himalayas; cut by valleys formed by tributaries of the Brahmaputra; thick forests in S
head of state and government Jigme Singye Wangchuk from 1972
political system absolute monarchy
exports timber, talc, fruit and vegetables, cement, distilled spirits, calcium carbide
currency ngultrum; also Indian currency
population (1993) 1,700,000; growth rate 2% p.a. (75% Ngalops and Sharchops, 25% Nepalese)
languages Dzongkha (official, a Tibetan dialect), Sharchop, Bumthap, Nepali, and English
religions 75% Lamaistic Buddhist (state religion), 25% Hindu
GNP $468 per head (1990)
chronology
1907 First hereditary monarch installed.

1910 Anglo-Bhutanese Treaty signed.
1949 Indo-Bhutan Treaty of Friendship signed.
1952 King Jigme Dorji Wangchuk installed.
1953 National assembly established.
1959 4,000 Tibetan refugees given asylum.
1968 King established first cabinet.
1972 King died and was succeeded by his son Jigme Singye Wangchuk.
1979 Tibetan refugees told to take Bhutanese citizenship or leave; most stayed.
1983 Bhutan became a founding member of the South Asian Regional Association for Cooperation.
1988 King imposed 'code of conduct' suppressing Nepalese customs.
1990 Hundreds of people allegedly killed during prodemocracy demonstrations.

Bhutto Benazir 1953– . Pakistani politician, leader of the Pakistan People's Party (PPP) from 1984 (in exile until 1986), and prime minister of Pakistan 1988–90 when the opposition manoeuvred her from office and charged her with corruption. She was the first female leader of a Muslim state. She was re-elected as prime minister 1993.

Bhutto Zulfikar Ali 1928–1979. Pakistani politician, president 1971–73; prime minister from 1973 until the 1977 military coup led by General *Zia ul-Haq. In 1978 Bhutto was sentenced to death for conspiring to murder a political opponent and was hanged the following year. He was the father of Benazir Bhutto.

Biafra, Republic of African state proclaimed in 1967 when fears that Nigerian central government was increasingly in the hands of the rival Hausa tribe led the predominantly Ibo Eastern Region of Nigeria to secede under Lt Col Odumegwu Ojukwu. On the proclamation of Biafra, civil war ensued with the rest of the federation. In a bitterly fought campaign federal forces confined the Biafrans to a shrinking area of the interior by 1968, and by 1970 Biafra ceased to exist.

Bible the sacred book of the Jewish and Christian religions. The Hebrew Bible, recognized by both Jews and Christians, is called the *Old Testament* by Christians. The *New Testament* comprises books recognized by the Christian church from the 4th century as canonical. The Roman Catholic Bible also includes the *Apocrypha.

bicarbonate of soda or *baking soda* (technical name *sodium hydrogencarbonate*) $NaHCO_3$ white crystalline solid that neutralizes acids and is used in medicine to treat acid indigestion. It is also used in baking powders and effervescent drinks.

bicycle pedal-driven two-wheeled vehicle used in *cycling. It consists of a metal frame mounted on two large wire-spoked wheels, with handlebars in front and a seat between the front and back wheels. The bicycle is an energy-efficient, nonpolluting form of transport, and it is estimated that 800 million bicycles are in use throughout the world – outnumbering cars three to one.

Bidault Georges 1899–1983. French politician, prime minister 1946, 1949–50. He was a leader of the French Resistance during World War II and foreign minister and president in de Gaulle's provisional government. He left the Gaullists over Algerian independence, and in 1962 he became head of the *Organisation de l'Armée Secrète (OAS), formed 1961 by French settlers devoted to perpetuating their own rule in Algeria. He was charged with treason 1963 and left the country, but was allowed to return 1968.

Biedermeier early- to mid-19th-century Germanic style of art and furniture design, derogatorily named after Gottlieb Biedermeier, a humorous pseudonym used by several German poets, embodying bourgeois taste.

biennial plant plant that completes its life cycle in two years. During the first year it grows vegetatively and the surplus food produced is stored in its *perennating organ, usually the root. In the following year these food reserves are used for the production of leaves, flowers, and seeds, after which the plant dies. Many root vegetables are biennials, including the carrot *Daucus carota* and parsnip *Pastinaca sativa*. Some garden plants that are grown as biennials are actually perennials, for example, the wallflower *Cheiranthus cheiri*.

Bierce Ambrose (Gwinett) 1842–*c.* 1914. US author. After service in the American Civil War, he established his reputation as a master of the short story, his themes being war and the supernatural, as in *Tales of Soldiers and Civilians* 1891 and *Can Such Things Be?* 1893. He also wrote *The Devil's Dictionary* 1911 (first published as *The Cynic's Word Book* 1906), a collection of ironic definitions showing his sardonic humour. He disappeared in Mexico 1913.

bigamy in law, the offence of marrying a person while already lawfully married to another. In some countries marriage to more than one wife or husband is lawful; see also *polygamy.

big-band jazz *swing music created in the late 1930s and 1940s by bands of 13 or more players, such as those of Duke *Ellington and Benny *Goodman. Big-band jazz relied on fixed arrangements, where there is more than one instrument to some of the parts, rather than improvisation. Big bands were mainly dance bands, and they ceased to be economically viable in the 1950s.

Big Bang in astronomy, the hypothetical 'explosive' event that marked the origin of the universe as we know it. At the time of the Big Bang, the entire universe was squeezed into a hot, superdense state. The Big Bang explosion threw this compacted material outwards, producing the expanding universe (see *red shift). The cause of the Big Bang is unknown; observations of the current rate of expansion of the universe suggest that it took place about 10 to 20 billion years ago. The Big Bang theory began modern *cosmology.

Big Bang in economics, popular term for the changes instituted in late 1986 to the organization and practices of the City of London as Britain's financial centre, including the liberalization of the London *Stock Exchange. This involved merging the functions of jobber (dealer in stocks and shares) and broker (who mediates between the jobber and the public), introducing negotiated commission rates, and allowing foreign banks and financial companies to own British brokers/jobbers, or themselves to join the London Stock Exchange.

Big Ben popular name for the bell in the clock tower of the Houses of Parliament in London, cast at the Whitechapel Bell Foundry in 1858, and known as 'Big Ben' after Benjamin Hall, First Commissioner of Works at the time. It weighs 13.7 tonnes.

Bihar or *Behar* state of NE India
area 173,900 sq km/67,125 sq mi
capital Patna
products copper, iron, coal, rice, jute, sugar cane, grain, oilseed
population (1991) 86,338,900
language Hindi, Bihari
famous people Chandragupta, Asoka
history the ancient kingdom of Magadha roughly corresponded to central and S Bihar. Many Bihari people were massacred as a result of their protest at the establishment of Bangladesh 1971.

Bihari member of a N Indian people, also living in Bangladesh, Nepal, and Pakistan, and numbering over 40 million. The Bihari are mainly Muslim. The Bihari language is related to Hindi and has several widely varying dialects. It belongs to the Indic branch of the Indo-European family. Many Bihari were massacred during the formation of Bangladesh, which they opposed.

Bikini atoll in the *Marshall Islands, W Pacific, where the USA carried out 23 atomic-and hydrogen-bomb tests (some underwater) 1946–58.

Biko Steve (Stephen) 1946–1977. South African civil-rights leader. An active opponent of *apartheid, he was arrested in Sept 1977; he died in detention six days later. Since his death in the custody of South African police, he has been a symbol of the anti-apartheid movement.

bilateralism in economics, a trade agreement between two countries or groups of countries in which they give each other preferential treatment. Usually the terms agreed result in balanced trade and are favoured by countries with limited foreign exchange reserves. Bilateralism is incompatible with free trade.

Bilbao industrial port (iron and steel, chemicals, cement, food) in N Spain, capital of Biscay province; population (1991) 372,200.

bilberry several species of shrubs of the genus *Vaccinium* of the heath family Ericaceae, closely related to North American blueberries.

Bildungsroman (German 'education novel') novel that deals with the psychological and emotional development of its protagonist, tracing his or her life from inexperienced youth to maturity. The first example of the type is generally considered to be C M Wieland's *Agathon* 1765–66, but it was *Goethe's *Wilhelm Meisters Lehrjahr/Wilhelm Meister's Apprenticeship* 1795–96 that established the genre. Although taken up by writers in other languages, it remained chiefly a German form; later examples include Thomas *Mann's *Der Zauberberg/The Magic Mountain* 1924.

bile brownish fluid produced by the liver. In most vertebrates, it is stored in the gall bladder and emptied into the small intestine as food passes through. Bile consists of bile salts, bile pigments, cholesterol, and lecithin. *Bile salts* assist in the breakdown and absorption of fats; *bile pigments* are the breakdown products of old red blood cells that are passed into the gut to be eliminated with the faeces.

bilharzia or *schistosomiasis* disease that causes anaemia, inflammation, formation of scar tissue, dysentery, enlargement of the spleen and liver, cancer of the bladder, and cirrhosis of the liver. It is contracted by bathing in water contaminated with human sewage. Some 300 million people are thought to suffer from this disease in the tropics.

billabong (Australian *billa bung* 'dead river') a stagnant pond.

billiards indoor game played, normally by two players, with tapered poles (cues) and composition balls (one red, two white) on a rectangular table covered with a green, feltlike cloth (baize). The table has six pockets, one at each corner and in each of the long sides at the middle. Scoring strokes are made by potting the red ball, potting the opponent's ball, or potting another ball off one of these two. The cannon (when the cue ball hits the two other balls on the table) is another scoring stroke.

billion the cardinal number represented by a 1 followed by nine zeros (1,000,000,000), equivalent to a thousand million.

bill of exchange form of commercial credit instrument, or IOU, used in international trade. In Britain, a bill of exchange is defined by the Bills of Exchange Act 1882 as an unconditional order in writing addressed by one person to another, signed by the person giving it, requiring the person to whom it is addressed to pay on demand or at a fixed or determinable future time a certain sum in money to or to the order of a specified person, or to the bearer. US practice is governed by the Uniform Negotiable Instruments Law, drafted on the same lines as the British, and accepted by all states by 1927.

bill of lading document giving proof of particular goods having been loaded on a ship. The person to whom the goods are being sent normally needs to show the bill of lading in order to obtain the release of the goods. For air freight, there is an *air waybill*.

Bill of Rights in the USA, the first ten amendments to the US *Constitution:
1 guarantees freedom of worship, of speech, of the press, of assembly, and to petition the government;
2 grants the right to keep and bear arms;
3 prohibits billeting of soldiers in private homes in peacetime;
4 forbids unreasonable search and seizure;
5 guarantees none be 'deprived of life, liberty or property without due process of law' or compelled in any criminal case to be a witness against him- or herself;
6 grants the right to speedy trial, to call witnesses, and to have defence counsel;
7 grants the right to trial by jury of one's peers;
8 prevents the infliction of excessive bail or fines, or 'cruel and unusual punishment;'
9, *10* provide a safeguard to the states and people for all rights not specifically delegated to the central government.

Bill of Rights in Britain, an act of Parliament 1689 which established it as the primary governing body of the country. The Bill of Rights embodied the Declarations of Rights which contained the conditions on which William and Mary were offered the throne. It made provisions limiting *royal prerogative with respect to legislation, executive power, money levies, courts, and the army and stipulated Parliament's consent to many government functions.

Billy the Kid nickname of William H Bonney 1859–1881. US outlaw, a leader in the 1878 Lincoln County cattle war in New Mexico, who allegedly killed his first victim at 12 and was reputed to have killed 21 men by age 22, when he died.

bimetallic strip strip made from two metals each having a different coefficient of thermal expansion; it therefore bends when subjected to a change in temperature. Such strips are used widely for temperature measurement and control.

binary fission in biology, a form of *asexual reproduction, whereby a single-celled organism, such as the amoeba, divides into two smaller 'daughter' cells. It can also occur in a few simple multicellular organisms, such as sea anemones, producing two smaller sea anemones of equal size.

binary number system or *binary number code* system of numbers to *base two, using combinations of the digits 1 and 0. Binary numbers play a key role in digital computers, in which they form the basis of the internal coding of information, the values of *bits (short for 'binary digits') being represented as on/off (1 and 0) states of switches and high/low voltages in circuits.

binary search in computing, a rapid technique used to find any particular record in a list of records held in sequential order. The computer is programmed to compare the record sought with the record in the middle of the ordered list. This being done, the computer discards the half of the list in which the record does not appear, thereby reducing the number of records left to search by half. This process of selecting the middle record and discarding the unwanted half of the list is repeated until the required record is found.

binary star pair of stars moving in orbit around their common centre of mass. Observations show that most stars are binary, or even multiple -for example, the nearest star system to the Sun, *Alpha Centauri.

binary weapon in chemical warfare, weapon consisting of two substances that in isolation are harmless but when mixed together form a poisonous nerve gas. They are loaded into the delivery system separately and combine after launch.

binding energy in physics, the amount of energy needed to break the nucleus of an atom into the neutrons and protons of which it is made.

bind over in law, a UK court order that requires a person to carry out some act, usually by an order given in a magistrates' court. A person may be bound over to appear in court at a particular time if bail has been granted or, most commonly, be bound over not to commit some offence; for example, causing a breach of the peace.

Binet Alfred 1857–1911. French psychologist who introduced the first *intelligence tests 1905.

They were standardized so that the last of a set of graded tests the child could successfully complete gave the level described as 'mental age'. If the test was passed by most children over 12, for instance, but failed by those younger, it was said to show a mental age of 12. Binet published these in collaboration with Theodore Simon.

binoculars optical instrument for viewing an object in magnification with both eyes; for example, field glasses and opera glasses. Binoculars consist of two telescopes containing lenses and prisms, which produce a stereoscopic effect as well as magnifying the image. Use of prisms has the effect of 'folding' the light path, allowing for a compact design.

binomial in mathematics, an expression consisting of two terms, such as $a + b$ or $a - b$.

binomial system of nomenclature in biology, the system in which all organisms are identified by a two-part Latinized name. Devised by the biologist *Linnaeus, it is also known as the Linnaean system. The first name is capitalized and identifies the *genus; the second identifies the *species within that genus.

binturong shaggy-coated mammal *Arctitis binturong*, the largest member of the mongoose family, nearly 1 m/3 ft long excluding a long muscular tail with a prehensile tip. Mainly nocturnal and tree-dwelling, the binturong is found in the forests of SE Asia, feeding on fruit, eggs, and small animals.

biochemistry science concerned with the chemistry of living organisms: the structure and reactions of proteins (such as enzymes), nucleic acids, carbohydrates, and lipids. See page 103.

biodegradable capable of being broken down by living organisms, principally bacteria and fungi. In biodegradable substances, such as food and sewage, the natural processes of decay lead to compaction and liquefaction, and to the release of nutrients that are then recycled by the ecosystem. Nonbiodegradable substances, such as glass, heavy metals, and most types of plastic, present serious problems of disposal.

biodynamic farming agricultural practice based on the principle of *homeopathy: tiny quantities of a substance are applied to transmit vital qualities to the soil. It is a form of *organic farming, and was developed by the Austrian holistic mystic Rudolf *Steiner and Ehrenfried Pfiffer.

bioengineering the application of engineering to biology and medicine. Common applications include the design and use of artificial limbs, joints, and organs, including hip joints and heart valves.

biofeedback modification or control of a biological system by its results or effects. For example, a change in the position or *trophic level of one species affects all levels above it.

biofeedback in medicine, the use of electrophysiological monitoring devices to 'feed back' information about internal processes and thus facilitate conscious control. Developed in the USA in the 1960s, independently by neurophysiologist Barbara Brown and neuropsychiatrist Joseph Kamiya, the technique is effective in alleviating hypertension and preventing associated organic and physiological dysfunctions.

biofuel any solid, liquid, or gaseous fuel produced from organic (once living) matter, either directly from plants or indirectly from industrial, commercial, domestic, or agricultural wastes. There are three main ways for the development of biofuels: the burning of dry organic wastes (such as household refuse, industrial and agricultural wastes, straw, wood, and peat); the fermentation of wet wastes (such as animal dung) in the absence of oxygen to produce biogas (containing up to 60% methane), or the fermentation of sugar cane or corn to produce alcohol; and energy forestry (producing fast-growing wood for fuel).

biogenesis biological term coined 1870 by T H Huxley to express the hypothesis that living matter always arises out of other similar forms of living matter. It superseded the opposite idea of *spontaneous generation or abiogenesis (that is, that living things may arise out of nonliving matter).

biogeography study of how and why plants and animals are distributed around the world, in the past as well as in the present; more specifically, a theory describing the geographical distribution of *species developed by Robert MacArthur and E O *Wilson. The theory argues that for many species, ecological specializations mean that suitable habitats are patchy in their occurrence. Thus for a dragonfly, ponds in which to breed are separated by large tracts of land, and for edelweiss adapted to alpine peaks the deep valleys between cannot be colonized.

biography account of a person's life. When it is written by that person, it is an *autobiography. Biography can be simply a factual narrative, but it was also established as a literary form in the 18th and 19th centuries. Among ancient biographers are Xenophon, Plutarch, Tacitus, Suetonius, and the authors of the Gospels of the New Testament. In the English language Lytton Strachey's *Eminent Victorians* opened the new era of frankness; 20th-century biographers include Richard Ellmann (James Joyce and Oscar Wilde), Michael Holroyd (1935–) (Lytton Strachey and George Bernard Shaw) and Elizabeth Longford (Queen Victoria and Wellington).

Bioko island in the Bight of Bonny, W Africa, part of Equatorial Guinea; area 2,017 sq km/786 sq mi; products include coffee, cacao, and copra; population (1983) 57,190. Formerly a Spanish possession, as *Fernando Po*, it was known 1973–79 as *Macías Nguema Bijogo*.

biological clock regular internal rhythm of activity, produced by unknown mechanisms, and not dependent on external time signals. Such clocks are known to exist in almost all animals, and also in many plants, fungi, and unicellular organisms. In higher organisms, there appears to be a series of clocks of graded importance. For example, although body temperature and activity cycles in human beings are normally 'set' to 24 hours, the two cycles may vary independently, showing that two clock mechanisms are involved.

biological control control of pests such as insects and fungi through biological means, rather than the use of chemicals. This can include breeding resistant crop strains; inducing sterility in the pest; infecting the pest species with disease organisms; or introducing the pest's natural pred-

BIOCHEMISTRY: CHRONOLOGY

c. 1830 Johannes Müller discovered proteins.
1833 Anselme Payen and J F Persoz first isolated an enzyme.
1862 Haemoglobin was first crystallized.
1869 The genetic material DNA (deoxyribonucleic acid) was discovered by Friedrich Mieschler
1899 Emil Fischer postulated the lock-and-key hypothesis to explain the specificity of enzyme action.
1913 Leonor Michaelis and M L Menten developed a mathematical equation describing the rate of enzyme-catalysed reactions.
1915 The hormone thyroxine was first isolated from thyroid-gland tissue.
1920 The chromosome theory of heredity was postulated by Thomas H Morgan; growth hormone was discovered by Herbert McLean Evans and J A Long.
1921 Insulin was first isolated from the pancreas by Frederick Banting and Charles Best.
1927 Thyroxine was first synthesized.
1928 Alexander Fleming discovered penicillin.
1931 Paul Karrer deduced the structure of retinol (vitamin A); vitamin D compounds were obtained in crystalline form by Adolf Windaus and Askew, independently of each other.
1932 Charles Glen King isolated ascorbic acid (vitamin C).
1933 Tadeus Reichstein synthesized ascorbic acid.
1935 Richard Kuhn and Karrer established the structure of riboflavin (vitamin B$_2$).
1936 Robert Williams established the structure of thiamine (vitamin B$_1$); biotin was isolated by Kogl and Tonnis.
1937 Niacin was isolated and identified by Conrad Arnold Elvehjem.
1938 Pyridoxine (vitamin B$_6$) was isolated in pure crystalline form.
1939 The structure of pyridoxine was determined by Kuhn.
1940 Hans Krebs proposed the citric acid (Krebs) cycle; Hickman isolated retinol in pure crystalline form; Williams established the structure of pantothenic acid; biotin was identified by Albert Szent-Györgyi, Vincent Du Vigneaud, and co-workers.
1941 Penicillin was isolated and characterized by by Howard Florey and Ernst Chain.
1943 The role of DNA in genetic inheritance was first demonstrated by Oswald Avery, Colin MacLeod, and Maclyn McCarty.
1950 The basic components of DNA were established by Erwin Chargaff; the alpha-helical structure of proteins was established by Linus Pauling and R B Corey.
1953 James Watson and Francis Crick determined the molecular structure of DNA.
1956 Mahlon Hoagland and Paul Zamecnick discovered transfer RNA; mechanisms for the biosynthesis of RNA and DNA were discovered by Arthur Kornberg and Severo Ochoa.
1957 Interferon was discovered by Alick Isaacs and Jean Lindemann.
1958 The structure of RNA was determined.
1960 Messenger RNA was discovered by Sydney Brenner and François Jacob.
1961 Marshall Nirenberg and Ochoa determined the chemical nature of the genetic code.
1965 Insulin was first synthesized.
1966 The immobilization of enzymes was achieved by Chibata.
1968 Brain hormones were discovered by Roger Guillemin and Andrew Schally.
1975 J Hughes and Hans Kosterlitz discovered encephalins.
1976 Guillemin discovered endorphins.
1977 J Baxter determined the genetic code for human growth hormone.
1978 Human insulin was first produced by genetic engineering.
1979 The biosynthetic production of human growth hormone was announced by Howard Goodman and Baxter of the University of California, and by D V Goeddel and Seeburg of Genentech.
1982 Louis Chedid and Michael Sela developed the first synthesized vaccine.
1983 The first commercially available product of genetic engineering (Humulin) was launched.
1985 Alec Jeffreys devised genetic fingerprinting.
1990 Jean-Marie Lehn, Ulrich Koert, and Margaret Harding reported the synthesis of a new class of compounds, called nucleohelicates, that mimic the double helical structure of DNA, turned inside out.
1993 UK researchers introduced a healthy version of the gene for cystic fibrosis into the lungs of mice with induced cystic fibrosis, restoring normal function.

ator. Biological control tends to be naturally self-regulating, but as ecosystems are so complex, it is difficult to predict all the consequences of introducing a biological controlling agent.

biological oxygen demand (BOD) the amount of dissolved oxygen taken up by microorganisms in a sample of water. Since these microorganisms live by decomposing organic matter, and the amount of oxygen used is proportional to their number and metabolic rate, BOD can be used as a measure of the extent to which the water is polluted with organic compounds.

biological shield shield around a nuclear reactor that is intended to protect personnel from the effects of *radiation. It usually consists of a thick wall of steel and concrete.

biological warfare the use of living organisms, or of infectious material derived from them, to bring about death or disease in humans, animals, or plants. At least ten countries have this capability.

biology science of life. Strictly speaking, biology includes all the life sciences – for example, anatomy and physiology, cytology, zoology and botany, ecology, genetics, biochemistry and biophysics, animal behaviour, embryology, and plant breeding. During the 1990s an important focus of biological research will be the

BIOLOGY: CHRONOLOGY

c. 500 BC	First studies of the structure and behaviour of animals, by the Greek Alcmaeon of Creton.
c. 450	Hippocrates of Cos undertook the first detailed studies of human anatomy.
c. 350	Aristotle laid down the basic philosophy of the biological sciences and outlined a theory of evolution.
c. 300	Theophrastus carried out the first detailed studies of plants.
c. AD 175	Galen established the basic principles of anatomy and physiology.
c. 1500	Leonardo da Vinci studied human anatomy to improve his drawing ability and produced detailed anatomical drawings.
1628	William Harvey described the circulation of the blood and the function of the heart as a pump.
1665	Robert Hooke used a microscope to describe the cellular structure of plants.
1672	Marcelle Malphigi undertook the first studies in embryology by describing the development of a chicken egg.
1736	Carolus (Carl) Linnaeus published his systematic classification of plants, so establishing taxonomy.
1768–79	James Cook's voyages of discovery in the Pacific revealed an undreamed-of diversity of living species, prompting the development of theories to explain their origin.
1796	Edward Jenner established the practice of vaccination against smallpox, laying the foundations for theories of antibodies and immune reactions.
1809	Jean-Baptiste Lamarck advocated a theory of evolution through inheritance of acquired characteristics.
1839	Theodor Schwann proposed that all living matter is made up of cells.
1857	Louis Pasteur established that microorganisms are responsible for fermentation, creating the discipline of microbiology.
1859	Charles Darwin published On the Origin of Species, expounding his theory of the evolution of species by natural selection.
1866	Gregor Mendel pioneered the study of inheritance with his experiments on peas.
1883	August Weismann proposed his theory of the continuity of the germ plasm.
1900	Mendel's work was rediscovered and the science of genetics founded.
1935	Konrad Lorenz published the first of many major studies of animal behaviour, which founded the discipline of ethology.
1953	James Watson and Francis Crick described the molecular structure of DNA.
1964	William Hamilton recognized the importance of inclusive fitness, so paving the way for the development of sociobiology.
1975	Discovery of endogenous opiates (the brain's own painkillers) opened up a new phase in the study of brain chemistry.
1976	Har Gobind Khorana and his colleagues constructed the first artificial gene to function naturally when inserted into a bacterial cell, a major step in genetic engineering.
1982	Gene databases were established at Heidelberg, Germany, for the European Molecular Biology Laboratory, and at Los Alamos, USA, for the US National Laboratories.
1985	The first human cancer gene, retinoblastoma, was isolated by researchers at the Massachusetts Eye and Ear Infirmary and the Whitehead Institute, Massachusetts.
1988	The Human Genome Organization (HUGO) was established in Washington, DC with the aim of mapping the complete sequence of DNA.
1992	Researchers at the University of California, USA, stimulated the multiplication of isolated brain cells of mice, overturning the axiom that mammalian brains cannot produce replacement cells once birth has taken place.
1994	Scientists from Pakistan and the USA unearthed a 50–million-year-old fossil whale with hind legs that would have enabled it to walk on land.

international Human Genome Project, which will attempt to map the entire genetic code contained in the 23 pairs of human chromosomes.

bioluminescence production of light by living organisms. It is a feature of many deep-sea fishes, crustaceans, and other marine animals. On land, bioluminescence is seen in some nocturnal insects such as glow-worms and fireflies, and in certain bacteria and fungi. Light is usually produced by the oxidation of luciferin, a reaction catalysed by the *enzyme luciferase. This reaction is unique, being the only known biological oxidation that does not produce heat. Animal luminescence is involved in communication, camouflage, or the luring of prey, but its function in other organisms is unclear.

biomass the total mass of living organisms present in a given area. It may be specified for a particular species (such as earthworm biomass) or for a general category (such as herbivore biomass). Estimates also exist for the entire global plant biomass. Measurements of biomass

can be used to study interactions between organisms, the stability of those interactions, and variations in population numbers.

biome broad natural assemblage of plants and animals shaped by common patterns of vegetation and climate. Examples include the tundra biome and the desert biome.

biomechanics study of natural structures to improve those produced by humans. For example, mother-of-pearl is structurally superior to glass fibre, and deer antlers have outstanding durability because they are composed of microscopic fibres. Such natural structures may form the basis of high-tech composites.

bionics (from 'biological electronics') design and development of electronic or mechanical artificial systems that imitate those of living things. The bionic arm, for example, is an artificial limb (*prosthesis) that uses electronics to amplify minute electrical signals generated in body muscles to work electric motors, which operate the joints of the fingers and wrist.

biophysics application of physical laws to the properties of living organisms. Examples include using the principles of *mechanics to calculate the strength of bones and muscles, and *thermodynamics to study plant and animal energetics.

biopsy removal of a living tissue sample from the body for diagnostic examination.

biorhythm rhythmic change, mediated by *hormones, in the physical state and activity patterns of certain plants and animals that have seasonal activities. Examples include winter hibernation, spring flowering or breeding, and periodic migration. The hormonal changes themselves are often a response to changes in day length (*photoperiodism); they signal the time of year to the animal or plant. Other biorhythms are innate and continue even if external stimuli such as day length are removed. These include a 24-hour or *circadian rhythm, a 28-day or circalunar rhythm (corresponding to the phases of the Moon), and even a year-long rhythm in some organisms.

biosphere the narrow zone that supports life on our planet. It is limited to the waters of the Earth, a fraction of its crust, and the lower regions of the atmosphere.

BioSphere 2 (BS2) ecological test project, a 'planet in a bottle', in Arizona, USA from summer 1991–93. Under a sealed glass dome, several different habitats are recreated, with representatives of nearly 4,000 species, including eight humans, to see how well air, water, and waste can be recycled and whether a stable ecosystem can be created.

biosynthesis synthesis of organic chemicals from simple inorganic ones by living cells -for example, the conversion of carbon dioxide and water to glucose by plants during *photosynthesis. Other biosynthetic reactions produce cell constituents including proteins and fats.

biotechnology industrial use of living organisms to manufacture food, drugs, or other products. The brewing and baking industries have long relied on the yeast microorganism for *fermentation purposes, while the dairy industry employs a range of bacteria and fungi to convert milk into cheeses and yoghurts. *Enzymes, whether extracted from cells or produced artificially, are central to most biotechnological applications.

biotic factor organic variable affecting an ecosystem - for example, the changing population of elephants and its effect on the African savanna.

biotin or *vitamin H* vitamin of the B complex, found in many different kinds of food; egg yolk, liver, legumes, and yeast contain large amounts.

biotite dark mica, $K(Mg, Fe)_3Al Si_3O_{10}(OH, F)_2$, a common silicate mineral It is colourless to silvery white with shiny surfaces, and like all micas, it splits into very thin flakes along its one perfect cleavage. Biotite is a mineral of igneous rocks such as granites, and metamorphic rocks such as schists and gneisses.

birch any tree of the genus *Betula*, including about 40 species found in cool temperate parts of the northern hemisphere. Birches grow rapidly, and their hard, beautiful wood is used for veneers and cabinet work.

bird backboned animal of the class Aves, the biggest group of land vertebrates, characterized by warm blood, feathers, wings, breathing through lungs, and egg-laying by the female. There are nearly 8,500 species of birds.

Bird Isabella 1832–1904. British traveller and writer who wrote extensively of her journeys in the USA, Persia, Tibet, Kurdistan, China, Japan, and Korea.

bird of paradise one of 40 species of crowlike birds, family Paradiseidae, native to New Guinea and neighbouring islands. Females are drably coloured, but the males have bright and elaborate plumage used in courtship display. Hunted almost to extinction for their plumage, they are now subject to conservation.

Birdseye Clarence 1886–1956. US inventor who pioneered food refrigeration processes. While working as a fur trader in Labrador 1912–16 he was struck by the ease with which food could be preserved in an Arctic climate. Back in the USA he found that the same effect could be obtained by rapidly freezing prepared food between two refrigerated metal plates. To market his products he founded the General Sea Foods Co. 1924, which he sold to General Foods 1929.

Birendra Bir Bikram Shah Dev 1945– . King of Nepal from 1972, when he succeeded his father Mahendra; he was formally crowned 1975. King Birendra has overseen Nepal's return to multiparty politics and introduced a new constitution 1990.

Birmingham industrial city in the West Midlands, second largest city of the UK; population (1991 est) 934,900, metropolitan area 2,632,000. Industries include motor vehicles, machine tools, aerospace control systems, plastics, chemicals, and food.

Birmingham commercial and industrial city (iron, steel, chemicals, building materials, computers, cotton textiles) and largest city in Alabama, USA; population (1990) 266,000.

Birmingham Six Irish victims of a miscarriage of justice who spent nearly 17 years in British prisons convicted of an IRA terrorist bombing in Birmingham 1974. They were released 1991 when the Court of Appeal quashed their convictions. The methods of the police and prosecution were called into question.

Biro Lazlo 1900–1985. Hungarian-born Argentine who invented a ballpoint pen 1944. His name became generic for ballpoint pens in the UK.

birth control another name for *family planning; see also *contraceptive.

birth rate the number of live births per year per thousand of the population. Birth rate is a factor in *demographic transition. It is sometimes called *crude birth rate* because it takes in the whole population, including men and women who are too old to bear children.

Birtwistle Harrison 1934– . English avant-garde composer. He has specialized in chamber music, for example, his chamber opera *Punch and Judy* 1967 and *Down by the Greenwood Side* 1969.

Biscay, Bay of bay of the Atlantic Ocean between N Spain and W France, known for rough seas and exceptionally high tides.

bise cold dry northerly wind experienced in southern France and Switzerland.

bishop (Greek 'overseer') priest next in rank to an archbishop in the Roman Catholic, Eastern Orthodox, Anglican or episcopal churches. A bishop has charge of a district called a *diocese*.

Bishop Isabella. Married name of the travel writer Isabella *Bird.

Bismarck Otto Eduard Leopold, Prince von 1815–1898. German politician, prime minister of Prussia 1862–90 and chancellor of the German Empire 1871–90. He pursued an aggressively expansionist policy, waging wars against Denmark 1863–64, Austria 1866, and France 1870–71, which brought about the unification of Germany.

Bismarck in World War II, a small German battleship sunk 1942 in the Atlantic by the British Royal Navy.

Bismarck Archipelago group of over 200 islands in SW Pacific Ocean, part of *Papua New Guinea; area 49,660 sq km/19,200 sq mi. The largest island is New Britain.

bismuth hard, brittle, pinkish-white, metallic element, symbol Bi, atomic number 83, relative atomic mass 208.98. It has the highest atomic number of all the stable elements (the elements from atomic number 84 up are radioactive). Bismuth occurs in ores and occasionally as a free metal (*native metal). It is a poor conductor of heat and electricity, and is used in alloys of low melting point and in medical compounds to soothe gastric ulcers.

bison large, hoofed mammal of the bovine family. There are two species, both brown. The *European bison* or *wisent Bison bonasus*, of which only a few protected herds survive, is about 2 m/7 ft high and weighs up to 1,100 kg/2,500 lb. The *North American bison* (often known as 'buffalo') *Bison bison* is slightly smaller, with a heavier mane and more sloping hindquarters. Formerly roaming the prairies in vast numbers, it was almost exterminated in the 19th century, but survives in protected areas.

Bissau capital and chief port of Guinea-Bissau, on an island at the mouth of the Geba river; population (1988) 125,000. Originally a fortified slave-trading centre, Bissau became a free port 1869.

bit in computing, the smallest unit of information; a binary digit or place in a binary number. A *byte contains eight bits (four bits is sometimes called a nybble).

Bithynia district of NW Asia that became a Roman province 74 BC.

bittern any of several small herons, in particular the common bittern *Botaurus stellaris* of Europe and Asia. It is shy, stoutly built, has a streaked camouflage pattern and a loud, booming call. An inhabitant of marshy country, it is now quite rare in Britain.

bittersweet alternative name for the woody *nightshade plant.

bitumen impure mixture of hydrocarbons, including such deposits as petroleum, asphalt, and natural gas, although sometimes the term is restricted to a soft kind of pitch resembling asphalt.

bivalent in biology, a name given to the pair of homologous chromosomes during reduction division (*meiosis). In chemistry, the term is sometimes used to describe an element or group with a *valency of two, although the term 'divalent' is more common.

bivalve marine or freshwater mollusc whose body is enclosed between two shells hinged together by a ligament on the dorsal side of the body.

Bizet Georges (Alexandre César Léopold) 1838–1875. French composer of operas, among them *Les Pêcheurs de perles/The Pearl Fishers* 1863, and *La jolie Fille de Perth/The Fair Maid of Perth* 1866. He also wrote the concert overture *Patrie* and incidental music to Daudet's *L'Arlésienne*. His operatic masterpiece *Carmen* was produced a few months before his death 1875.

Bjelke-Petersen Joh(annes) 1911– . Australian right-wing politician, leader of the Queensland National Party (QNP) and premier of Queensland 1968–87.

black English term first used 1625 to describe West Africans, now used to refer to Africans south of the Sahara and to people of African descent living outside Africa. In some countries such as the UK (but not in North America) the term is sometimes also used for people originally from the Indian subcontinent, for Australian Aborigines, and peoples of Melanesia.

Black Conrad (Moffat) 1940– . Canadian newspaper publisher. Between 1985 and 1990 he gained control of the right-wing *Daily Telegraph*, *Sunday Telegraph*, and *Spectator* weekly magazine in the UK, and he owns a number of Canadian newspapers.

Black Joseph 1728–1799. Scottish physicist and chemist who in 1754 discovered carbon dioxide (which he called 'fixed air'). By his investigations in 1761 of latent heat and specific heat, he laid the foundation for the work of his pupil James Watt.

Black and Tans nickname of a special auxiliary force of the Royal Irish Constabulary employed by the British 1920–21 to combat the Sinn Féiners (Irish nationalists) in Ireland; the name derives from the colours of the uniforms, khaki with black hats and belts.

blackberry prickly shrub *Rubus fruticosus* of the rose family, closely allied to raspberries and dewberries, that is native to northern parts of Europe. It produces pink or white blossoms and edible, black, compound fruits.

blackbird bird *Turdus merula* of the thrush family. The male is black with a yellow bill and eyelids, the female dark brown with a dark beak. About 25 cm/10 in long, it lays three to five bluegreen eggs with brown spots. Its song is rich and flutelike.

black body in physics, a hypothetical object that completely absorbs all thermal (heat) radiation striking it. It is also a perfect emitter of thermal radiation.

black box popular name for the unit containing an aeroplane's flight and voice recorders. These monitor the plane's behaviour and the crew's conversation, thus providing valuable clues to the cause of a disaster. The box is nearly indestructible and usually painted orange for easy recovery. The name also refers to any compact electronic device that can be quickly connected or disconnected as a unit.

blackbuck antelope *Antilope cervicapra* found in central and NW India. It is related to the gazelle, from which it differs in having spirally-twisted horns. The male is black above and white beneath, whereas the female and young are fawn-coloured above. It is about 76 cm/2.5 ft in height.

blackcap *warbler *Sylvia atricapilla*. The male has a black cap, the female a reddish-brown one. About 14 cm/5.5 in long, the blackcap likes wooded areas, and is a summer visitor to N Europe.

blackcock large grouse *Lyrurus tetrix* found on moors and in open woods in N Europe and Asia. The male is mainly black with a lyre-shaped tail, and grows up to 54 cm/1.7 ft in height. The female is speckled brown and only 40 cm/1.3 ft tall.

Black Country central area of England, around and to the N of Birmingham. Heavily industrialized, it gained its name in the 19th century from its belching chimneys, but antipollution laws have changed its aspect.

Black Death great epidemic of bubonic *plague that ravaged Europe in the 14th century, killing between one-third and half of the population. The cause of the plague was the bacterium *Pasteurella pestis*, transmitted by fleas borne by migrating Asian black rats. The name Black Death was first used in England in the early 19th century.

black economy unofficial economy of a country, which includes undeclared earnings from a second job ('moonlighting'), and enjoyment of undervalued goods and services (such as company 'perks'), designed for tax evasion purposes. In industrialized countries, it has been estimated to equal about 10% of *gross domestic product.

blackfly plant-sucking insect, a type of *aphid.

Blackfoot member of a Plains *American Indian people, some 10,000 in number and consisting of three subtribes: the Blackfoot proper, the Blood, and the Piegan, who live in Montana, USA, and Saskatchewan and Alberta, Canada. They were skilled, horse-riding buffalo hunters until their territories were settled by Europeans. Their name derives from their black moccasins. Their language belongs to the Algonquian family.

Black Forest (German *Schwarzwald*) mountainous region of coniferous forest in Baden-Württemberg, W Germany. Bounded W and S by the Rhine, which separates it from the Vosges, it has an area of 4,660 sq km/1,800 sq mi and rises to 1,493 m/4,905 ft in the Feldberg. Parts of the forest have recently been affected by *acid rain.

black hole object in space whose gravity is so great that nothing can escape from it, not even light. Thought to form when massive stars shrink at the ends of their lives, a black hole sucks in more matter, including other stars, from the space around it. Matter that falls into a black hole is squeezed to infinite density at the centre of the hole. Black holes can be detected because gas falling towards them becomes so hot that it emits X-rays.

Black Hole of Calcutta incident in Anglo-Indian history: according to tradition, the nawab (ruler) of Bengal confined 146 British prisoners on the night of 20 June 1756 in one small room, of whom only 23 allegedly survived. Later research reduced the death count to 43, assigning negligence rather than intention.

blacking in an industrial dispute, the refusal of workers to handle particular goods or equipment, or to work with particular people.

blackmail criminal offence of extorting money with menaces or threats of detrimental action, such as exposure of some misconduct on the part of the victim.

Black Monday worldwide stockmarket crash that began 19 Oct 1987, prompted by the announcement of worse-than-expected US trade figures. Between 19 and 23 Oct, the New York Stock Exchange fell by 33%, the London Stock Exchange Financial Times 100 Index by 25%, the European index by 17%, and Tokyo by 12%. The expected world recession did not occur; by the end of 1988 it was clear that the main effect had been a steadying in stock market activity and only a slight slowdown in world economic growth.

Blackmore R(ichard) D(oddridge) 1825–1900. English novelist, author of *Lorna Doone* 1869, a romance set on Exmoor, SW England, in the late 17th century.

Black Muslim member of a religious group founded 1929 in the USA and led, from 1934, by Elijah Muhammad (then Elijah Poole) (1897–1975) after he had a vision of *Allah. Its growth from 1946 as a black separatist organization was due to Malcolm X (1926–1965), the son of a Baptist minister who, in 1964, broke away and founded his own Organization for Afro-American Unity, preaching 'active self-defence'. Under the leadership of Louis Farrakhan, the movement underwent a recent revival.

black nationalism movement towards black separatism in the USA during the 1960s; see *Black Power.

Black National State area in the Republic of South Africa set aside, from 1971, for development in self-government by black Africans, in accordance with *apartheid. Before 1980 these areas were known as *black homelands* or *bantustans*. Those that achieved nominal independence were Transkei 1976, Bophuthatswana 1977, Venda 1979, and Ciskei 1981. They were not recognized outside South Africa because of their racial basis. Under the interim nonracial constitution, which came into effect April 1994, they became part of the republic's provincial structure, with guaranteed legislative and executive power.

Blackpool seaside resort in Lancashire, England, 45 km/28 mi N of Liverpool; population (1981) 148,000. The largest holiday resort in N England, the amusement facilities include 11 km/7 mi of promenades, known for their 'illuminations' of coloured lights. Political party conferences are often held here.

Black Power movement towards black separatism in the USA during the 1960s, embodied in the **Black Panther Party** founded 1966 by Huey Newton and Bobby Seale. Its declared aim was the establishment of a separate black state in the USA established by a black plebiscite under the aegis of the United Nations. Following a National Black Political Convention 1972, a National Black Assembly was established to exercise pressure on the Democratic and Republican parties.

Black Prince nickname of *Edward, Prince of Wales, eldest son of Edward III of England.

Black Sea (Russian **Chernoye More**) inland sea in SE Europe, linked with the seas of Azov and Marmara, and via the Dardanelles with the Mediterranean. Uranium deposits beneath it are among the world's largest. It is heavily polluted by agricultural fertilizers.

Black September guerrilla splinter group of the *Palestine Liberation Organization formed 1970. Operating from bases in Syria and Lebanon, it was responsible for the kidnappings at the Munich Olympics 1972 that led to the deaths of 11 Israelis, and more recent hijack and bomb attempts. The group is named after the month in which Palestinian guerrillas were expelled from Jordan by King Hussein.

Blackshirts term widely used to describe fascist paramilitary organizations. Originating with Mussolini's fascist Squadristi in the 1920s, it was also applied to the Nazi SS (*Schutzstaffel*) and to the followers of Oswald Mosley's British Union of Fascists.

blacksnake any of several species of snake. The blacksnake *Pseudechis porphyriacus* is a venomous snake of the cobra family found in damp forests and swamps in E Australia. The blacksnake *Coluber constrictor* from E USA, is a relative of the European grass snake, growing up to 1.2 m/4 ft long, and without venom.

Black Stone in Islam, the sacred stone built into the east corner of the *Kaaba which is a focal point of the *hajj*, or pilgrimage, to Mecca. There are a number of stories concerning its origin, one of which states that it was sent to Earth at the time of the first man, Adam; Muhammad declared that it was given to Abraham by Gabriel. It has been suggested that it is of meteoric origin.

blackthorn densely branched spiny European bush *Prunus spinosa*, family Rosaceae. It produces white blossom on black and leafless branches in early spring. Its sour, plumlike, blue-black fruit, the sloe, is used to make sloe gin.

Black Thursday day of the Wall Street stock market crash 29 Oct 1929, which precipitated the *Depression in the USA and throughout the world.

black widow North American spider *Latrodectus mactans*. The male is small and harmless, but the female is 1.3 cm/0.5 in long with a red patch below the abdomen and a powerful venomous bite.

bladder hollow elastic-walled organ in the *urinary systems of some fishes, most amphibians, some reptiles, and all mammals. Urine enters the bladder through two ureters, one leading from each kidney, and leaves it through the urethra.

bladderwort any of a large genus *Utricularia* of carnivorous aquatic plants of the family Lenti-bulariaceae. They have leaves with bladders that entrap small aquatic animals.

Blair Tony (Anthony Charles Lynton) 1953– . British politician, leader of the Labour Party from 1994. A centrist in the manner of his predecessor John *Smith, he became Labour's youngest leader by a large majority in the first fully democratic elections to the post July 1994.

Blake George 1922– . British double agent who worked for MI6 (see *intelligence) and also for the USSR. Blake was unmasked by a Polish defector 1960 and imprisoned, but escaped to the Eastern bloc 1966. He is said to have betrayed at least 42 British agents to the Soviet side.

Blake Quentin 1932– . English book illustrator whose animated pen-and-ink drawings for children's books are instantly recognizable. His own picture books include *The Marzipan Pig* 1986; he has illustrated more than 200 books.

Blake William 1757–1827. English poet, artist, engraver, and visionary. His lyrics, as in *Songs of Innocence* 1789 and *Songs of Experience* 1794 express spiritual wisdom in radiant imagery and symbolism. Prophetic books like *The Marriage of Heaven and Hell* 1790, *America* 1793, and *Milton* 1804 yield their meaning to careful study. He created a new composite art form in engraving and hand-colouring his own works.

Blanco Serge 1958– . French rugby union player. Blanco played a world-record 93 internationals before his retirement in 1991, scoring 38 tries of which 34 were from full back – another world record.

blank verse in literature, the unrhymed iambic pentameter or ten-syllable line of five stresses. First used by the Italian Gian Giorgio Trissino in his tragedy *Sofonisba* 1514–15, it was introduced to England about 1540 by the Earl of Surrey, and developed by Christopher Marlowe. More recent exponents of blank verse in English include Thomas Hardy, T S Eliot, and Robert Frost.

Blanqui Louis Auguste 1805–1881. French revolutionary politician. He formulated the theory of the 'dictatorship of the proletariat', used by Karl Marx, and spent a total of 33 years in prison for insurrection. Although in prison, he was elected president of the Commune of Paris 1871. His followers, the Blanquists, joined with the Marxists 1881.

Blantyre-Limbe chief industrial and commercial centre of Malawi, in the Shire highlands; population (1987) 331,600. It produces tea, coffee, rubber, tobacco, and textiles.

Blarney small town in County Cork, Republic of Ireland, possessing, inset in the wall of the 15th-century castle, the **Blarney Stone**, reputed to give persuasive speech to those kissing it.

Blashford-Snell John 1936– . British explorer and soldier. His expeditions have included the first descent and exploration of the Blue Nile 1968; the journey N to S from Alaska to Cape Horn, crossing the Darien Gap between Panama and Colombia for the first time 1971–72; and the first complete navigation of the Zaïre River, Africa 1974–75.

blasphemy (Greek 'evil-speaking') written or spoken insult directed against religious belief or sacred things with deliberate intent to outrage believers.

blast furnace smelting furnace in which temperature is raised by the injection of an air blast. It is used to extract metals from their ores, chiefly pig iron from iron ore.

blastocyst in mammals, a stage in the development of the *embryo that is roughly equivalent to the *blastula of other animal groups.

blastomere in biology, a cell formed in the first stages of embryonic development, after the splitting of the fertilized ovum, but before the formation of the *blastula or blastocyst.

blastula early stage in the development of a fertilized egg, when the egg changes from a solid mass of cells (the morula) to a hollow ball of cells (the blastula), containing a fluid-filled cavity (the blastocoel). See also *embryology.

Blaue Reiter, der ('the Blue Rider') group of German Expressionist painters based in Munich, some of whom had left *die *Brücke*. They were interested in the value of colours, in folk art, and in the necessity of painting 'the inner, spiritual side of nature', but styles were highly varied. Wassily Kandinsky and Franz Marc published a book of their views 1912, and there were two exhibitions 1911, 1912.

bleaching decolorization of coloured materials. The two main types of bleaching agent are the *oxidizing bleaches*, which bring about the *oxidation of pigments, and include the ultraviolet rays in sunshine, hydrogen peroxide, and chlorine in household bleaches; and the *reducing bleaches*, which bring about *reduction, and include sulphur dioxide.

bleak freshwater fish *Alburnus alburnus* of the carp family. It is up to to 20 cm/8 in long, and lives in still or slow-running clear water in Britain and Europe.

blenny any fish of the family Blenniidae, mostly small fishes found near rocky shores, with elongated slimy bodies tapering from head to tail, no scales, and long pelvic fins set far forward.

Blériot Louis 1872–1936. French aviator who, in a 24-horsepower monoplane of his own construction, made the first flight across the English Channel on 25 July 1909.

blesbok African antelope *Damaliscus albifrons*, about 1 m/3 ft high, with curved horns, brownish body, and a white blaze on the face. It was seriously depleted in the wild at the end of the 19th century. A few protected herds survive in South Africa. It is farmed for meat.

Bligh William 1754–1817. English sailor who accompanied Captain James *Cook on his second voyage around the world 1772–74, and in 1787 commanded HMS *Bounty* on an expedition to the Pacific. On the return voyage the crew mutinied 1789, and Bligh was cast adrift in a boat with 18 men. He was appointed governor of New South Wales 1805, where his discipline again provoked a mutiny 1808 (the Rum Rebellion). He returned to Britain, and was made an admiral 1811.

blimp airship: any self-propelled, lighter-than-air craft that can be steered. A blimp with a soft frame is also called a *dirigible*; a *zeppelin is rigid-framed.

blind spot area where the optic nerve and blood vessels pass through the retina of the *eye.

No visual image can be formed as there are no light-sensitive cells in this part of the retina.

Bliss Arthur (Drummond) 1891–1975. English composer and conductor who became Master of the Queen's Musick 1953. Among his works are *A Colour Symphony* 1922, music for ballets *Checkmate* 1937, *Miracle in the Gorbals* 1944, and *Adam Zero* 1946; an opera *The Olympians* 1949; and dramatic film music, including *Things to Come* 1935. He conducted the first performance of Stravinsky's *Ragtime* for eleven instruments 1918.

Blitzkrieg (German 'lightning war') swift military campaign, as used by Germany at the beginning of World War II 1939–41. The abbreviated *Blitz* was applied to the attempted saturation bombing of London by the German air force between Sept 1940 and May 1941.

Blixen Karen, born Karen Dinesen 1885–1962. Danish writer. Her autobiography *Out of Africa* 1937 is based on her experience of running a coffee plantation in Kenya. She wrote fiction, mainly in English, under the pen name Isak Dinesen.

Bloch Konrad 1912– . German-born US chemist whose research concerned cholesterol. Making use of the *radioisotope carbon-14 (the radioactive form of carbon), Bloch was able to follow the complex steps by which the body chemically transforms acetic acid into cholesterol. For his work in this field Bloch shared the 1964 Nobel Prize for Medicine with Feodor Lynen (1911–1979).

Bloemfontein capital of the Orange Free State and judicial capital of the Republic of South Africa; population (1985) 204,000. Founded 1846, the city produces canned fruit, glassware, furniture, and plastics.

Blomberg Werner von 1878–1946. German general and Nazi politician, minister of defence 1933–35, minister of war, and head of the *Wehrmacht* (army) 1935–38 under Hitler's chancellorship. He was discredited by his marriage to a prostitute and dismissed in Jan 1938, enabling Hitler to exercise more direct control over the armed forces. In spite of his removal from office, Blomberg was interrogated about war crimes by the Nuremberg tribunal. He died during the trial and was never in the dock.

blood liquid circulating in the arteries, veins, and capillaries of vertebrate animals; the term also refers to the corresponding fluid in those invertebrates that possess a closed *circulatory system. Blood carries nutrients and oxygen to individual cells and removes waste products, such as carbon dioxide. It is also important in the immune response and, in many animals, in the distribution of heat throughout the body.

Blood Thomas 1618–1680. Irish adventurer, known as Colonel Blood, who attempted to steal the crown jewels from the Tower of London, England, 1671.

blood clotting complex series of events that prevents excessive bleeding after injury. The result is the formation of a meshwork of protein fibres (fibrin) and trapped blood cells over the cut blood vessels.

blood group any of the blood groups into which blood is classified according to antigenic activity. Red blood cells of one individual may carry molecules on their surface that act as *antigens in another individual whose red blood cells lack these molecules. The two main antigens are designated A and B. These give rise to four blood groups: having A only (A), having B only (B), having both (AB), and having neither (O). Each of these groups may or may not contain the *rhesus factor. Correct typing of blood groups is vital in transfusion, since incompatible types of donor and recipient blood will result in blood clotting, with possible death of the recipient.

bloodhound ancient breed of dog. Black and tan in colour, it has long, pendulous ears and distinctive wrinkled head and face. It grows to a height of about 65 cm/26 in at the shoulder. The breed originated as a hunting dog in Belgium in the Middle Ages, and its excellent powers of scent have been employed in tracking and criminal detection from very early times.

blood poisoning condition in which poisons are spread throughout the body by *pathogens in the bloodstream.

blood pressure pressure, or tension, of the blood against the inner walls of blood vessels, especially the arteries, due to the muscular pumping activity of the heart. Abnormally high blood pressure (see *hypertension) may be associated with various conditions or arise with no obvious cause; abnormally low blood pressure (hypotension) occurs in *shock and after excessive fluid or blood loss from any cause.

blood test laboratory evaluation of a blood sample. There are numerous blood tests, from simple typing to establish the *blood group to sophisticated biochemical assays of substances, such as hormones, present in the blood only in minute quantities.

blood transfusion see *transfusion.

blood vessel specialized tube that carries blood around the body of multicellular animals. Blood vessels are highly evolved in vertebrates, where the three main types–the arteries, veins, and capillaries–are all adapted for their particular role within the body.

Bloom Claire 1931– . British film actress, who first made her reputation on the stage in Shakespearean roles. Her films include *Richard III* 1956 and *The Brothers Karamazov* 1958; television appearances include *Brideshead Revisited* 1980.

Bloomer Amelia Jenks 1818–1894. US campaigner for women's rights. In 1849, when unwieldy crinolines were the fashion, she introduced a knee-length skirt combined with loose trousers gathered at the ankles, which became known as *bloomers* (also called 'rational dress'). She published the magazine *The Lily* 1849–54, which campaigned for women's rights and dress reform, and lectured with Susan B *Anthony in New York, USA.

Bloomsbury Group group of writers and artists based in *Bloomsbury, London. The group included the artists Duncan *Grant and Vanessa Bell, and the writers Lytton *Strachey and Leonard (1880–1969) and Virginia *Woolf.

Blow John 1648–1708. British composer. He taught *Purcell, and wrote church music, for example the anthem 'I Was Glad when They Said

unto Me' 1697. His masque *Venus and Adonis* 1685 is sometimes called the first English opera.

blowfly any fly of the genus *Calliphora*, also known as bluebottle, or of the related genus *Lucilia*, when it is greenbottle. It lays its eggs in dead flesh, on which the maggots feed.

blubber thick layer of *fat under the skin of marine mammals, which provides an energy store and an effective insulating layer, preventing the loss of body heat to the surrounding water. Blubber has been used (when boiled down) in engineering, food processing, cosmetics, and printing, but all of these products can now be produced synthetically, thus saving the lives of animals.

Blücher Gebhard Leberecht von 1742–1819. Prussian general and field marshal, popularly known as 'Marshal Forward'. He took an active part in the patriotic movement, and in the War of German Liberation defeated the French as commander in chief at Leipzig 1813, crossed the Rhine to Paris 1814, and was made prince of Wahlstadt (Silesia).

Bluebeard folktale character, popularized by the writer Charles Perrault in France about 1697, and historically identified with French marshal Gilles de Rais (1404–1440). Bluebeard murdered six wives for disobeying his command not to enter a locked room, but was himself killed before he could murder the seventh. Bluebeard inspired operas by Dukas and *Bartók.

bluebell The bluebell is a bulbous plant abundant in woods, hedgerows, and meadows adjoining woods.

bluebell name given in Scotland to the harebell *Campanula rotundifolia*, and in England to the wild hyacinth *Endymion nonscriptus*, belonging to the family Liliaceae.

blueberry any of various North American acid-soil shrubs of the genus *Vaccinium* of the heath family. The genus also includes huckleberries, bilberries, deerberries, and cranberries, many of which resemble each other and are difficult to distinguish from blueberries. All have small, elliptical short-stalked leaves, slender green or reddish twigs, and whitish bell-like blossoms. Only true blueberries, however, have tiny granular speckles on their twigs. Blueberries have black or blue edible fruits, often covered with a white powder.

bluebird three species of a North American bird, genus *Sialia*, belonging to the thrush subfamily, Turdinae. The eastern bluebird *Sialia sialis* is regarded as the herald of spring. About 18 cm/ 7 in long, it has a reddish breast, the upper plumage being sky-blue, and a distinctive song.

blue chip in business and finance, a stock that is considered strong and reliable in terms of the dividend yield and capital value. Blue-chip companies are favoured by stock-market investors more interested in security than risk taking.

bluegrass dense, spreading grass of the genus *Poa*, which is bluetinted and grows in clumps. Various species are known from the northern hemisphere. Kentucky bluegrass *P. pratensis*, introduced to the USA from Europe, provides pasture for horses.

blue-green algae or *cyanobacteria* single-celled, primitive organisms that resemble bacteria in their internal cell organization, sometimes joined together in colonies or filaments. Blue-green algae are among the oldest known living organisms and, with bacteria, belong to the kingdom Monera; remains have been found in rocks up to 3.5 billion years old. They are widely distributed in aquatic habitats, on the damp surfaces of rocks and trees, and in the soil.

blue gum either of two Australian trees: Tasmanian blue gum *Eucalyptus globulus* of the myrtle family, with bluish bark, a chief source of eucalyptus oil; or Sydney blue gum *E. saligna*, a tall, straight tree. The former is cultivated extensively in California and has also been planted in South America, India, parts of Africa, and S Europe.

Blue Mountains part of the *Great Dividing Range, New South Wales, Australia, ranging 600–1,100 m/2,000–3,600 ft and blocking Sydney from the interior until the crossing 1813 by surveyor William Lawson, Gregory Blaxland, and William Wentworth.

Blue Nile (Arabic *Bahr el Azraq*) river rising in the mountains of Ethiopia. Flowing W then N for 2,000 km/1,250 mi, it eventually meets the White Nile at Khartoum. The river is dammed at Roseires where a hydroelectric scheme produces 70% of Sudan's electricity.

blueprint photographic process used for copying engineering drawings and architectural plans, so called because it produces a white copy of the original against a blue background.

blue riband or *blue ribbon* the highest distinction in any sphere; for example, the blue riband of horse racing in the UK is held by the winner of the Derby.

Blue Ridge Mountains range extending from West Virginia to Georgia, USA, and including Mount Mitchell 2,045 m/6,712 ft; part of the *Appalachians.

blues African-American music that originated in the rural American South in the late 19th century, characterized by a 12-bar construction and frequently melancholy lyrics. Blues guitar and vocal styles have played a vital part in the development of jazz and pop music in general.

blue shift in astronomy, a manifestation of the *Doppler effect in which an object appears bluer when it is moving towards the observer or the observer is moving towards it (blue light is of a higher frequency than other colours in the spectrum). The blue shift is the opposite of the *red shift.

Blum Léon 1872–1950. French politician. He was converted to socialism by the *Dreyfus affair 1899 and in 1936 became the first socialist prime minister of France. He was again premier for a few weeks 1938. Imprisoned under the *Vichy

government 1942 as a danger to French security, he was released by the Allies 1945. He again became premier for a few weeks 1946.

Blunt Anthony 1907–1983. British art historian and double agent. As a Cambridge lecturer, he recruited for the Soviet secret service and, as a member of the British Secret Service 1940–45, passed information to the USSR. In 1951 he assisted the defection to the USSR of the British agents Guy *Burgess and Donald Maclean (1913–1983). He was the author of many respected works on French and Italian art. Unmasked 1964, he was given immunity after his confession.

Blyton Enid 1897–1968. British writer of children's books. She created the character Noddy and the adventures of the 'Famous Five' and 'Secret Seven', but has been criticized by educationalists for social, racial, and sexual stereotyping.

boa any of various nonvenomous snakes of the family Boidae, found mainly in tropical and subtropical parts of the New World. Boas feed mainly on small mammals and birds. They catch these in their teeth or kill them by constriction (crushing the creature within their coils until it suffocates). The boa constrictor *Constrictor constrictor* can grow up to 5.5 m/18.5 ft long, but rarely reaches more than 4 m/12 ft. Other boas include the anaconda and the emerald tree boa *Boa canina*, about 2 m/6 ft long and bright green.

Boadicea alternative spelling of British queen *Boudicca.

boar wild member of the pig family, such as the Eurasian wild boar *Sus scrofa*, from which domestic pig breeds derive. The wild boar is sturdily built, being 1.5 m/4.5 ft long and 1 m/3 ft high, and possesses formidable tusks. Of gregarious nature and mainly woodland-dwelling, it feeds on roots, nuts, insects, and some carrion.

boardsailing another name for *windsurfing, a watersport combining elements of surfing and sailing, also called sailboarding.

boat people illegal emigrants travelling by sea, especially those Vietnamese who left their country after the takeover of South Vietnam 1975 by North Vietnam. Some 160,000 Vietnamese fled to Hong Kong, many being attacked at sea by Thai pirates, and in 1989 50,000 remained there in cramped, squalid refugee camps. The UK government began forced repatriation 1990.

Boat Race annual UK *rowing race between the crews of Oxford and Cambridge universities. It is held during the Easter vacation over a 6.8 km/4.25 mi course on the river Thames between Putney and Mortlake, SW London.

bobcat cat *Felis rufa* living in a variety of habitats from S Canada through to S Mexico. It is similar to the lynx, but only 75 cm/2.5 ft long, with reddish fur and less well-developed ear tufts.

bobsleighing or *bobsledding* sport of racing steel-bodied, steerable toboggans, crewed by two or four people, down mountain ice chutes at speeds of up to 130 kph/80 mph. It was introduced as an Olympic event 1924 and world championships have been held every year since 1931. Included among the major bobsleighing events are the Olympic Championships (the four-crew event was introduced at the 1924 Winter Olympics and the two-crew 1932) and the World Championships, the four-crew championship introduced in 1924 and the two-crew in 1931. In Olympic years winners automatically become world champions.

Boccaccio Giovanni 1313–1375. Italian poet, chiefly known for the collection of tales called the *Decameron* 1348–53.

Boccherini (Ridolfo) Luigi 1743–1805. Italian composer and cellist. He studied in Rome, made his mark in Paris 1768, and was court composer in Prussia and Spain. Boccherini composed some 350 instrumental works, an opera, and oratorios.

Boccioni Umberto 1882–1916. Italian painter and sculptor. One of the founders of the Futurist movement, he was a pioneer of abstract art.

Bode's law numerical sequence that gives the approximate distances, in astronomical units (distance between Earth and Sun = one astronomical unit), of the planets from the Sun by adding 4 to each term of the series 0, 3, 6, 12, 24, ... and then dividing by 10. Bode's law predicted the existence of a planet between *Mars and *Jupiter, which led to the discovery of the asteroids.

Bodhidharma 6th century AD. Indian Buddhist and teacher. He entered China from S India about 520, and was the founder of the Ch'an school (*Zen is the Japanese derivation). Ch'an focuses on contemplation leading to intuitive meditation, a direct pointing to and stilling of the human mind. In the 20th century, the Japanese variation, Zen, has attracted many followers in the west.

bodhisattva in Mahāyāna Buddhism, someone who seeks *enlightenment in order to help other living beings. A bodhisattva is free to enter *nirvana but voluntarily chooses to be reborn until all other beings have attained that state. Bodhisattvas are seen as intercessors to whom believers may pray for redemption.

Bodin Jean 1530–1596. French political philosopher whose six-volume *De la République* 1576 is considered the first work on political economy.

Bodley Thomas 1545–1613. English scholar and diplomat, after whom the Bodleian Library in Oxford is named. After retiring from Queen Elizabeth I's service 1597, he restored the university's library, which was opened as the Bodleian Library 1602.

Boeing US military and commercial aircraft manufacturer. Among the models Boeing has produced are the B-17 Flying Fortress, 1935; the B-52 Stratofortress, 1952; the Chinook helicopter, 1961; the first jetliner, the Boeing 707, 1957; the jumbo jet or Boeing 747, 1970; and the *jetfoil, 1975.

Boeotia ancient district of central Greece, of which *Thebes was the chief city. The *Boeotian League* (formed by 10 city states in the 6th century BC) superseded *Sparta in the leadership of Greece in the 4th century BC.

Boer Dutch settler or descendant of Dutch and Huguenot settlers in South Africa; see also *Afrikaner.

Boer War the second of the *South African Wars 1899–1902, waged between the Dutch settlers in South Africa and the British.

Boethius Anicius Manilus Severinus AD 480–524. Roman philosopher. While imprisoned on suspicion of treason by the emperor *Theodoric the Great, he wrote treatises on music and mathematics and *De Consolatione Philosophiae/The Consolation of Philosophy*, a dialogue in prose. It was translated into European languages during the Middle Ages; English translations by Alfred the Great, Geoffrey Chaucer, and Queen Elizabeth I.

bog type of wetland where decomposition is slowed down and dead plant matter accumulates as *peat. Bogs develop under conditions of low temperature, high acidity, low nutrient supply, stagnant water, and oxygen deficiency. Typical bog plants are sphagnum moss, rushes and cotton grass; insectivorous plants such as sundews and bladderworts are common in bogs (insect prey make up for the lack of nutrients).

Bogarde Dirk. Stage name of Derek van den Bogaerde 1921– . English actor who appeared in comedies and adventure films such as *Doctor in the House* 1954 and *Campbell's Kingdom* 1957, before acquiring international recognition for complex roles in Joseph Losey's *The Servant* 1963 and *Accident* 1967, and Luchino Visconti's *Death in Venice* 1971.

Bogart Humphrey 1899–1957. US film actor who achieved fame as the gangster in *The Petrified Forest* 1936. He became an international cult figure as the tough, romantic 'loner' in such films as *The Maltese Falcon* 1941 and *Casablanca* 1943, a status resurrected in the 1960s and still celebrated today. He won an Academy Award for his role in *The African Queen* 1952.

bogbean or **buckbean** aquatic or bog plant *Menyanthes trifoliata* of the gentian family, with a creeping rhizome and leaves and pink flower spikes held above water. It is found over much of the northern hemisphere.

Bogomils Christian heretics who originated in 10th-century Bulgaria and spread throughout the Byzantine empire. Their name derives from Bogomilus, or Theophilus, who taught in Bulgaria 927–950. Despite persecution, they were expunged by the Ottomans only after the fall of Constantinople 1453.

Bogotá capital of Colombia, South America; 2,640 m/8,660 ft above sea level on the edge of the plateau of the E Cordillera; population (1985) 4,185,000. It was founded 1538.

Bohemia area of the Czech Republic, a kingdom of central Europe from the 9th century. It was under Habsburg rule 1526–1918, when it was included in Czechoslovakia. The name Bohemia derives from the Celtic Boii, its earliest known inhabitants.

Bohr Aage 1922– . Danish physicist who produced a new model of the nucleus 1952, known as the collective model. For this work, he shared the 1975 Nobel Prize for Physics. He was the son of Niels Bohr.

Bohr Niels Henrik David 1885–1962. Danish physicist. His theoretic work produced a new model of atomic structure, now called the Bohr model, and helped establish the validity of *quantum theory.

Boileau Nicolas 1636–1711. French poet and critic. After a series of contemporary satires, his *Epîtres/Epistles* 1669–77 led to his joint appointment with Racine as royal historiographer 1677. Later works include *L'Art poétique/The Art of Poetry* 1674 and the mock-heroic *Le Lutrin/The Lectern* 1674–83.

boiler any vessel that converts water into steam. Boilers are used in conventional power stations to generate steam to feed steam *turbines, which drive the electricity generators. They are also used in steamships, which are propelled by steam turbines, and in steam locomotives. Every boiler has a furnace in which fuel (coal, oil, or gas) is burned to produce hot gases, and a system of tubes in which heat is transferred from the gases to the water.

boiling point for any given liquid, the temperature at which the application of heat raises the temperature of the liquid no further, but converts it into vapour.

Bokassa Jean-Bédel 1921– . President of the Central African Republic 1966–79 and later self-proclaimed emperor 1977–79. Commander in chief from 1963, in Dec 1965 he led the military coup that gave him the presidency. On 4 Dec 1976 he proclaimed the Central African Empire and one year later crowned himself as emperor for life. His regime was characterized by arbitrary state violence and cruelty. Overthrown in 1979, Bokassa was in exile until 1986. Upon his return he was sentenced to death, but this was commuted to life imprisonment 1988.

bolero Spanish dance in triple time for a solo dancer or a couple, usually with castanet accompaniment. It was used as the title of a one-act ballet score by Ravel, choreographed by Nijinsky for Ida Rubinstein 1928.

boletus genus of fleshy fungi belonging to the class Basidiomycetes, with thick stems and caps of various colours. The European *Boletus edulis* is edible, but some species are poisonous.

Boleyn Anne 1507–1536. Queen of England 1533–36. Henry VIII broke with the pope (see *Reformation) in order to divorce his first wife and marry Anne. She was married to him 1533 and gave birth to the future Queen Elizabeth I in the same year. Accused of adultery and incest with her half-brother (a charge invented by Thomas *Cromwell), she was beheaded.

Bolger Jim (James) Brendan 1935– . New Zealand politician and prime minister from 1990. A successful sheep and cattle farmer, Bolger was elected to Parliament 1972. He held a variety of cabinet posts under Robert Muldoon's leadership 1977–84 and was an effective, if uncharismatic, leader of the opposition from March 1986, taking the National Party to electoral victory Oct 1990. His subsequent failure to honour election pledges, leading to cuts in welfare provision, led to a sharp fall in his popularity.

Bolingbroke title of Henry of Bolingbroke, *Henry IV of England.

Bolingbroke Henry St John, Viscount Bolingbroke 1678–1751. British Tory politician and political philosopher. He was foreign secretary 1710–14 and a Jacobite conspirator. His books, such as *Idea of a Patriot King* 1738 and *The Dissertation upon Parties* 1735, laid the foundations for 19th-century Toryism.

Bolívar Simón 1783–1830. South American nationalist, leader of revolutionary armies, known as *the Liberator*. He fought the Spanish colonial forces in several uprisings and eventually liberated his native Venezuela 1821, Colombia and Ecuador 1822, Peru 1824, and Bolivia (a new state named after him, formerly Upper Peru) 1825.

Bolivia Republic of (*República de Bolivia*)

area 1,098,581 sq km/424,052 sq mi
capital La Paz (seat of government), Sucre (legal capital and seat of judiciary)
towns Santa Cruz, Cochabamba, Oruro, Potosí
physical high plateau (Altiplano) between mountain ridges (cordilleras); forest and lowlands (llano) in the E
head of state and government Gonzalo Sanchez de Lozado from 1993
political system emergent democratic republic
exports tin, antimony (second largest world producer), other nonferrous metals, oil, gas (piped to Argentina), agricultural products, coffee, sugar, cotton
currency boliviano
population (1993) 8,010,000; (Quechua 25%, Aymara 17%, mestizo (mixed) 30%, European 14%); growth rate 2.7% p.a.
languages Spanish, Aymara, Quechua (all official)
religion Roman Catholic 95% (state-recognized)
GNP $650 per head (1991)
chronology
1825 Liberated from Spanish rule by Simón Bolívar; independence achieved (formerly known as Upper Peru).
1952 Dr Víctor Paz Estenssoro elected president.
1956 Dr Hernán Siles Zuazo became president.
1960 Estenssoro returned to power.
1964 Army coup led by the vice president, General René Barrientos.
1966 Barrientos became president.
1967 Uprising, led by 'Che' Guevara, put down with US help.
1969 Barrientos killed in plane crash, replaced

by Vice President Siles Salinas. Army coup deposed him.

1970 Army coup put General Juan Torres González in power.

1971 Torres replaced by Col Hugo Banzer Suárez.

1973 Banzer promised a return to democratic government.

1974 Attempted coup prompted Banzer to postpone elections and ban political and trade-union activity.

1978 Elections declared invalid after allegations of fraud.

1980 More inconclusive elections followed by another coup, led by General Luis García. Allegations of corruption and drug trafficking led to cancellation of US and EC aid.

1981 García forced to resign. Replaced by General Celso Torrelio Villa.

1982 Torrelio resigned. Replaced by military junta led by General Guido Vildoso. Because of worsening economy, Vildoso asked congress to install a civilian administration. Dr Siles Zuazo chosen as president.

1983 Economic aid from USA and Europe resumed.

1984 New coalition government formed by Siles. Abduction of president by right-wing officers. The president undertook a five-day hunger strike as an example to the nation.

1985 President Siles resigned. Election result inconclusive; Dr Paz Estenssoro chosen by congress as president.

1989 Jaime Paz Zamora elected president in power-sharing arrangement with Hugo Banzer Suárez, pledged to maintain fiscal and monetary discipline and preserve free-market policies.

1993 Centre-right National Revolutionary Movement party, under leadership of Gonzalo Sanchez de Lozado, won congressional and presidential elections.

Bolkiah Hassanal 1946– . Sultan of Brunei from 1967, following the abdication of his father, Omar Ali Saifuddin (1916–1986). As absolute ruler, Bolkiah also assumed the posts of prime minister and defence minister on independence 1984.

Böll Heinrich 1917–1985. German novelist. A radical Catholic and anti-Nazi, he attacked Germany's political past and the materialism of its contemporary society. His many publications include poems, short stories, and novels which satirized West German society, for example *Billard um Halbzehn/Billiards at Half-Past Nine* 1959 and *Gruppenbild mit Dame/Group Portrait with Lady* 1971. Nobel Prize for Literature 1972.

boll weevil small American beetle *Anthonomus grandis* of the weevil group. The female lays her eggs in the unripe pods or 'bolls' of the cotton plant, and on these the larvae feed, causing great destruction.

Bologna industrial city and capital of Emilia-Romagna, Italy, 80 km/50 mi N of Florence; population (1988) 427,000. It was the site of an Etruscan town, later of a Roman colony, and became a republic in the 12th century. It came under papal rule 1506 and was united with Italy 1860.

Bolshevik member of the majority of the Rus-

sian Social Democratic Party who split from the *Mensheviks 1903. The Bolsheviks, under *Lenin, advocated the destruction of capitalist political and economic institutions, and the setting-up of a socialist state with power in the hands of the workers. The Bolsheviks set the *Russian Revolution 1917 in motion. They changed their name to the Russian Communist Party 1918.

Bolshoi Ballet (Russian 'great') Russian ballet company founded 1776 and based at the Bolshoi Theatre in Moscow. With their mixed repertory of classics and new works, the Bolshoi is noted for its grand scale productions and the dancers' dramatic and eloquent technique. From 1964 its artistic director has been the choreographer Yuri Grigorovich (1927–   ).

Boltzmann constant in physics, the constant (symbol k) that relates the kinetic energy (energy of motion) of a gas atom or molecule to temperature. Its value is 1.380662×10^{-23} joules per Kelvin. It is equal to the gas constant R, divided by *Avogadro's number.

bomb container filled with explosive or chemical material and generally used in warfare. There are also *incendiary bombs and nuclear bombs and missiles (see *nuclear warfare). Any object designed to cause damage by explosion can be called a bomb (car bombs, letter bombs). Initially dropped from aeroplanes (from World War I), bombs were also launched by rocket (*V1, V2) in World War II. The 1960s saw the development of missiles that could be launched from aircraft, land sites, or submarines. In the 1970s laser guidance systems were developed to hit small targets with accuracy.

Bombay industrial port (textiles, engineering, pharmaceuticals, diamonds), commercial centre, and capital of Maharashtra, W India; population (1981) 8,227,000. It is the centre of the Hindi film industry.

Bombay duck or *bummalow* small fish *Harpodon nehereus* found in the Indian Ocean. It has a thin body, up to 40 cm/16 in long, and sharp, pointed teeth. It feeds on shellfish and other small fish. It is valuable as a food fish, and is eaten, salted and dried, with dishes such as curry.

Bomberg David 1890–1957. English painter. He applied forms inspired by Cubism and Vorticism to figurative subjects in such early works as *The Mud Bath* 1914 (Tate Gallery, London). Moving away from semi-abstraction in the mid-1920s, his work became more representational.

bona fide legal phrase used to signify that a contract is undertaken without intentional misrepresentation.

Bonaparte Corsican family of Italian origin that gave rise to the Napoleonic dynasty: see *Napoleon I, *Napoleon II, and *Napoleon III. Others were the brothers and sister of Napoleon I:

Joseph (1768–1844) whom Napoleon made king of Naples 1806 and Spain 1808

Lucien (1775–1840) whose handling of the Council of Five Hundred on 10 Nov 1799 ensured Napoleon's future;

Louis (1778–1846) the father of Napoleon III, who was made king of Holland 1806–10;

Caroline (1782–1839) who married Joachim *Murat 1800;
Jerome (1784–1860) made king of Westphalia 1807.

Bonar Law British Conservative politician; see *Law, Andrew Bonar.

bond in chemistry, the result of the forces of attraction that hold together atoms of an element or elements to form a molecule. The principal types of bonding are *ionic, *covalent, *metallic, and *intermolecular (such as hydrogen bonding).

bond in commerce, a security issued by a government, local authority, company, bank, or other institution on fixed interest. Usually a long-term security, a bond may be irredeemable (with no date of redemption), secured (giving the investor a claim on the company's property or on a part of its assets), or unsecured (not protected by a lien). Property bonds are nonfixed securities with the yield fixed to property investment. See also *Eurobond.

Bond Alan 1938– . English-born Australian entrepreneur. He was chair of the Bond Corporation 1969–90. The collapse of the Bond empire 1990 left thousands of investors impoverished and shook both Australian and international business confidence. Declared bankrupt April 1992 with debts of at least £110 million, Bond was jailed on criminal charges relating to the collapse of an Australian merchant bank.

Bond Edward 1935– . English dramatist. His early work aroused controversy because of the savagery of some of his imagery, for example, the brutal stoning of a baby by bored youths in *Saved* 1965. Other works include *Early Morning* 1968, the last play to be banned in the UK by the Lord Chamberlain; *Lear* 1972, a reworking of Shakespeare's play; *Bingo* 1973, an account of Shakespeare's last days; and *The War Plays* 1985.

Bondfield Margaret Grace 1873–1953. British socialist who became a trade-union organizer to improve working conditions for women. She was a Labour member of Parliament 1923–24 and 1926–31, and was the first woman to enter the cabinet – as minister of labour 1929–31.

bondservant another term for a slave or serf used in the Caribbean in the 18th and 19th centuries; a person who was offered a few acres of land in return for some years of compulsory service. The system was a means of obtaining labour from Europe.

bone hard connective tissue comprising the *skeleton of most vertebrate animals. It consists of a network of collagen fibres impregnated with inorganic salts, especially calcium phosphate. Enclosed within this solid matrix are bone cells, blood vessels, and nerves.

bone china or *softpaste* semiporcelain made of 5% bone ash added to 95% kaolin; first made in the West in imitation of Chinese porcelain, whose formula was kept secret by the Chinese.

bone marrow substance found inside the cavity of bones. In early life it produces red blood cells but later on lipids (fat) accumulate and its colour changes from red to yellow.

bongo Central African antelope *Boocercus eurycerus*, living in dense humid forests. Up to 1.4 m/4.5 ft at the shoulder, it has spiral horns which may be 80 cm/2.6 ft or more in length. The body is rich chestnut, with narrow white stripes running vertically down the sides, and a black belly.

Bonhoeffer Dietrich 1906–1945. German Lutheran theologian and opponent of Nazism. Involved in a plot against Hitler, he was executed by the Nazis in Flossenburg concentration camp. His *Letters and Papers from Prison* 1953 became the textbook of modern radical theology, advocating the idea of a 'religionless' Christianity.

Boniface name of nine popes, including:

Boniface VIII Benedict Caetani *c.* 1228–1303. Pope from 1294. He clashed unsuccessfully with Philip IV of France over his taxation of the clergy, and also with Henry III of England.

Boniface, St 680–754. English Benedictine monk, known as the 'Apostle of Germany'; originally named Wynfrith. After a missionary journey to Frisia 716, he was given the task of bringing Christianity to Germany 718 by Pope Gregory II, and was appointed archbishop of Mainz 746. He returned to Frisia 754 and was martyred near Dockum. His feast day is 5 June.

bonito any of various species of medium-sized tuna, predatory fish of the genus *Sarda*, in the mackerel family. The ocean bonito *Katsuwonus pelamis* grows to 1 m/3 ft and is common in tropical seas. The Atlantic bonito *Sarda sarda* is found in the Mediterranean and tropical Atlantic and grows to the same length but has a narrower body.

Bonn industrial city (chemicals, textiles, plastics, aluminium) and seat of government of the Federal Republic of Germany, 18 km/15 mi SSE of Cologne, on the left bank of the Rhine; population (1988) 292,000.

Bonnard Pierre 1867–1947. French Post-Impressionist painter. With other members of *les* *Nabis, he explored the decorative arts (posters, stained glass, furniture). He painted domestic interiors and nudes.

Bonneville Salt Flats bed of a prehistoric lake in Utah, USA, of which the Great Salt Lake is the surviving remnant. The flats, near the Nevada border, have been used to set many land speed records.

Bonnie and Clyde Bonnie Parker (1911–1934) and Clyde Barrow (1900–1934). Infamous US criminals who carried out a series of small-scale robberies in Texas, Oklahoma, New Mexico, and Missouri between Aug 1932 and May 1934. They were eventually betrayed and then killed in a police ambush.

Bonnie Prince Charlie Scottish name for *Charles Edward Stuart, pretender to the throne.

bonsai (Japanese 'bowl cultivation') art of producing miniature trees by selective pruning. It originated in China many centuries ago and later spread to Japan. Some specimens in China are about 1,000 years old and some in the imperial Japanese collection are more than 300 years old.

bonus issue another term for *scrip issue, or the issue of free shares to existing shareholders.

booby tropical seabird of the genus *Sula*, in the same family, Sulidae, as the northern *gannet. There are six species, including the circumtropical brown booby *S. leucogaster*. They inhabit

booby *Abbott's booby.*

coastal waters, and dive to catch fish. The name was given by sailors who saw the bird's tameness as stupidity.

boogie-woogie jazz played on the piano, using a repeated motif for the left hand. It was common in the USA from around 1900 to the 1950s. Boogie-woogie players included Pinetop Smith (1904–1929), Meade 'Lux' Lewis (1905–1964), and Jimmy Yancey (1898–1951). Rock-and-roll pianist Jerry Lee Lewis adapted the style.

bookbinding securing of the pages of a book between protective covers by sewing and/or gluing. Cloth binding was first introduced 1822, but from the mid-20th century synthetic bindings were increasingly employed, and most hardback books are bound by machine.

Booker Prize for Fiction British literary prize of £20,000 awarded annually (from 1969) to a Commonwealth writer by the Booker company (formerly Booker McConnell) for a novel published in the UK during the previous year.

BOOKER PRIZE: RECENT WINNERS

1985	Keri Hulme *The Bone People*
1986	Kingsley Amis *The Old Devils*
1987	Penelope Lively *Moon Tiger*
1988	Peter Carey *Oscar and Lucinda*
1989	Kazuo Ishiguro *The Remains of the Day*
1990	A S Byatt *Possession*
1991	Ben Okri *The Famished Road*
1992	Barry Unsworth *Sacred Hunger*; Michael Ondaatje *The English Patient*
1993	Roddy Doyle *Paddy Clarke Ha Ha Ha*
1994	James Kelman *How Late It Was, How Late*

Boole George 1815–1864. English mathematician whose work *The Mathematical Analysis of Logic* 1847 established the basis of modern mathematical logic, and whose ***Boolean algebra*** can be used in designing computers.

boomerang hand-thrown, flat wooden hunting missile shaped in a curved angle, formerly used throughout the world but developed by the Australian Aborigines to a great degree of diversity and elaboration. It is used to kill game and as a weapon or, in the case of the returning boomerang, as recreation.

boomslang rear-fanged venomous African snake *Dispholidus typus*, often green but sometimes brown or blackish, and growing to a length of 2 m/6 ft. It lives in trees, and feeds on tree-dwelling lizards such as chameleons. Its venom can be fatal to humans; however, boomslangs rarely attack people.

Boone Daniel 1734–1820. US pioneer who explored the Wilderness Road (East Virginia–Kentucky) 1775 and paved the way for the first westward migration of settlers.

boot or ***bootstrap*** in computing, the process of starting up a computer. Most computers have a small, built-in boot program that starts automatically when the computer is switched on – its only task is to load a slightly larger program, usually from a disc, which in turn loads the main *operating system. In microcomputers the operating system is often held in the permanent *ROM memory and the boot program simply triggers its operation.

Boötes constellation of the northern hemisphere represented by a herdsman driving a bear (Ursa Major) around the pole. Its brightest star is *Arcturus (or Alpha Bootis) about 36 light-years from Earth.

Booth John Wilkes 1839–1865. US actor and fanatical Confederate sympathizer who assassinated President Abraham *Lincoln 14 April 1865; he escaped with a broken leg and was later shot in a barn in Virginia when he refused to surrender.

Booth William 1829–1912. British founder of the *Salvation Army 1878, and its first 'general'.

Boothroyd Betty 1929–   . British Labour politician, Speaker of the House of Commons from 1992. The first woman in this office, she has controlled Parliamentary proceedings with a mixture of firmness and good humour. Born in Yorkshire, she has been MP for West Bromwich in the West Midlands since 1973 and was a member of the European Parliament 1975–77.

bootlegging illegal manufacture, distribution, or sale of a product. The term originated in the USA, when the sale of alcohol to American Indians was illegal and bottles were hidden for sale in the legs of the jackboots of unscrupulous traders. The term was later used for all illegal liquor sales during the period of *Prohibition in the USA 1920–33, and is often applied to unauthorized commercial tape recordings and the copying of computer software.

bop short for *bebop, a style of jazz.

Bophuthatswana Republic of; self-governing black homeland within South Africa until annexed by the South African government 1994; under a new nonracial constitution, adopted Dec 1993, homelands were to progressively disappear
area 40,330 sq km/15,571 sq mi
capital Mmbatho or Sun City, a casino resort frequented by many white South Africans
exports platinum, chromium, vanadium, asbestos, manganese
currency South African rand
population (1985) 1,627,000
languages Setswana, English
religion Christian
recent history first 'independent' Black National State from 1977, but not recognized by any country other than South Africa. It was annexed by South Africa 1994 after rioting broke out in the run-up to the first multiracial elections and white extremists attempted to seize power.

Bora-Bora one of the 14 Society Islands of French Polynesia; situated 225 km/140 mi NW of Tahiti; area 39 sq km/15 sq mi. Exports include mother-of-pearl, fruit, and tobacco.

borage salad plant *Borago officinalis* native to S Europe and used in salads and medicinally. It has small blue flowers and hairy leaves.

borax hydrous sodium borate, $Na_2B_4O_7.10H_2O$, found as soft, whitish crystals or encrustations on the shores of hot springs and in the dry beds of salt lakes in arid regions, where it occurs with other borates, halite, and *gypsum. It is used in bleaches and washing powders.

Bordeaux port on the Garonne, capital of Aquitaine, SW France, a centre for the wine trade, oil refining, and aeronautics and space industries; population (1982) 640,000. Bordeaux was under the English crown for three centuries until 1453. In 1870, 1914, and 1940 the French government was moved here because of German invasion.

Border Allan 1955– . Australian cricketer, left-handed batsman, and captain of Australia 1985–94. He retired from international cricket in 1994 with several world records, including most test runs (11,174), most test matches as captain (93), and most appearances in test matches (156).

Borders region of Scotland;
area 4,700 sq km/1,815 sq mi
towns Newtown St Boswells (administrative headquarters), Hawick, Jedburgh
products knitted goods, tweed, electronics, timber
population (1991) 102,600
famous people Duns Scotus, James Murray, Mungo Park.

Bordet Jules 1870–1961. Belgian bacteriologist and immunologist who researched the role of blood serum in the human immune response. He was the first to isolate 1906 the whooping cough bacillus.

bore surge of tidal water up an estuary or a river, caused by the funnelling of the rising tide by a narrowing river mouth. A very high tide, possibly fanned by wind, may build up when it is held back by a river current in the river mouth. The result is a broken wave, a metre or a few feet high, that rushes upstream.

Borelli Giovanni Alfonso 1608–1679. Italian scientist who explored the links between physics and medicine and showed how mechanical principles could be applied to animal *physiology. This approach, known as iatrophysics, has proved basic to understanding how the mammalian body works.

Borg Björn 1956– . Swedish tennis player who won the men's singles title at Wimbledon five times 1976–80, a record since the abolition of the challenge system 1922. He also won six French Open singles titles 1974–75 and 1978–81 inclusive.

Borges Jorge Luis 1899–1986. Argentine poet and short-story writer, an exponent of *magic realism. In 1961 he became director of the National Library, Buenos Aires, and was professor of English literature at the university there. He is known for his fantastic and paradoxical work *Ficciones/Fictions* 1944.

Borgia Cesare 1476–1507. Italian general, illegitimate son of Pope *Alexander VI. Made a cardinal at 17 by his father, he resigned to become captain-general of the papacy, campaigning successfully against the city republics of Italy. Ruthless and treacherous in war, he was an able ruler (the model for Machiavelli's *The Prince*), but his power crumbled on the death of his father. He was a patron of artists, including Leonardo da Vinci.

Borgia Lucrezia 1480–1519. Duchess of Ferrara from 1501. She was the illegitimate daughter of Pope *Alexander VI and sister of Cesare Borgia. She was married at 12 and again at 13 to further her father's ambitions, both marriages being annulled by him. At 18 she was married again, but her husband was murdered 1500 on the order of her brother, with whom (as well as with her father) she was said to have committed incest. Her final marriage was to the duke of Este, the son and heir of the duke of Ferrara. She made the court a centre of culture and was a patron of authors and artists such as Ariosto and Titian.

boric acid or ***boracic acid*** H_3BO_3, acid formed by the combination of hydrogen and oxygen with nonmetallic boron. It is a weak antiseptic and is used in the manufacture of glass and enamels. It is also an efficient insecticide against ants and cockroaches.

Boris Godunov 1552–1605. See Boris *Godunov, tsar of Russia from 1598.

Bormann Martin 1900–1945. German Nazi leader. He took part in the abortive Munich putsch (uprising) 1923 and rose to high positions in the Nazi (National Socialist) Party, becoming party chancellor May 1941.

Born Max 1882–1970. German physicist who received a Nobel prize 1954 for fundamental work on the *quantum theory. He left Germany for the UK during the Nazi era.

Borna disease virus disease-causing virus. It affects a wide range of animals, causing behavioural changes such as increased aggression and excitability. It is fatal in horses.

Borneo third largest island in the world, one of the Sunda Islands in the W Pacific; area 754,000 sq km/290,000 sq mi. It comprises the Malaysian territories of *Sabah and *Sarawak; *Brunei; and, occupying by far the largest part, the Indonesian territory of *Kalimantan. It is mountainous and densely forested. In coastal areas the people of Borneo are mainly of Malaysian origin, with a few Chinese, and the interior is inhabited by the indigenous Dyaks. It was formerly under both Dutch and British colonial influence until Sarawak was formed 1841.

Bornu kingdom of the 9th–19th centuries to the west and south of Lake Chad, W central Africa. Converted to Islam in the 11th century, Bornu reached its greatest strength in the 15th–18th centuries. From 1901 it was absorbed in the British, French, and German colonies in this area, which became the states of Niger, Cameroon, and Nigeria. The largest section of ancient Bornu is now the *state of Bornu* in Nigeria.

Borodin Alexander Porfir'yevich 1833–1887. Russian composer. Born in St Petersburg, the illegitimate son of a Russian prince, he became by profession an expert in medical chemistry, but in his spare time devoted himself to music. His principal work is the opera *Prince Igor*, left unfinished; it was completed by Rimsky-Korsakov and Glazunov and includes the Polovtsian Dances.

Borodino, Battle of battle 7 Sept 1812 where French troops under Napoleon defeated the Russians under Kutusov. Named after the village of Borodino, 110 km/70 mi NW of Moscow.

boron nonmetallic element, symbol B, atomic number 5, relative atomic mass 10.811. In nature it is found only in compounds, as with sodium and oxygen in borax. It exists in two allotropic forms (see *allotropy): brown amorphous powder and very hard, brilliant crystals. Its compounds are used in the preparation of boric acid, water softeners, soaps, enamels, glass, and pottery glazes.

Boross Peter 1928– . Hungarian politician, prime minister 1993–94. Brought into Joszef *Antall's government as a nonpolitical technocrat, he succeeded him upon his death 1993.

borough unit of local government in the UK from the 8th century until 1974, when it continued as an honorary status granted by royal charter to a district council, entitling its leader to the title of mayor.

Borromini Francesco 1599–1667. Italian Baroque architect. He was one of the two most important architects (with *Bernini, his main rival) in 17th-century Rome. Whereas Bernini designed in a florid, expansive style, his pupil Borromini developed a highly idiosyncratic and austere use of the Classical language of architecture. His genius may be seen in the cathedrals of San Carlo alle Quatro Fontane 1637–41, San Ivo della Sapienza 1643–60, and the Oratory of St Philip Neri 1638–50.

borstal in the UK, formerly a place of detention for offenders aged 15–21. The name was taken from Borstal prison near Rochester, Kent, where the system was first introduced 1908. They have now been replaced by ***young offender institutions**.

borzoi breed of large dog originating in Russia. It is of the greyhound type, white with darker markings, with a thick, silky coat, and stands 75 cm/30 in or more at the shoulder.

Bosch Carl 1874–1940. German metallurgist and chemist. He developed Fritz Haber's small-scale technique for the production of ammonia into an industrial high-pressure process that made use of water gas as a source of hydrogen; see *Haber process. He shared the Nobel Prize for Chemistry 1931 with Friedrich Bergius.

Bosch Hieronymus (Jerome) *c.* 1450–1516. Early Dutch painter. His fantastic visions of weird and hellish creatures, as shown in *The Garden of Earthly Delights* about 1505–10 (Prado, Madrid), show astonishing imagination. His religious subjects focused on the mass of ordinary witnesses, placing the religious event in a contemporary Dutch context and creating cruel caricatures of human sinfulness.

Bosnia-Herzegovina Republic of
area 51,129 sq km/19,745 sq mi
capital Sarajevo
towns Banja Luka, Mostar, Prijedor, Tuzla, Zenica

physical barren, mountainous country
head of state Alija Izetbegović from 1990
head of government Haris Silajdzic from 1993
political system emergent democracy
products citrus fruits and vegetables; iron, steel, and leather goods; textiles
population (1993 est) 4,400,000 including 44% Muslims, 33% Serbs, 17% Croats
language Serbian variant of Serbo-Croatian
religions Sunni Muslim, Serbian Orthodox, Roman Catholic
chronology
1918 Incorporated in the future Yugoslavia.
1941 Occupied by Nazi Germany.
1945 Became republic within Yugoslav Socialist Federation.
1980 Upsurge in Islamic nationalism.
1990 Ethnic violence erupted between Muslims and Serbs. Communists defeated in multiparty elections; coalition formed by Serb, Muslim, and Croatian parties.
1991 Aug: Serbia revealed plans to annex the SE part of the republic. Sept: Bosnian Serb enclaves established by force. Oct: 'sovereignty' declared. Nov: plebiscite by Bosnian Serbs favoured remaining within Yugoslavia; Bosnian Serbs and Croats established autonomous communities.
1992 Feb–March: Bosnian Muslims and Croats voted in favour of Bosnia-Herzegovina's independence; referendum boycotted by Bosnian Serbs. April: USA and EC recognized Bosnian independence. Ethnic hostilities escalated, with Bosnian Serb forces occupying E and Bosnian Croat forces much of W; all-out civil war ensued. May: admitted into UN. June: UN forces drafted into Sarajevo to break three-month siege of city by Bosnian Serbs. Accusations of 'ethnic cleansing' being practised, particularly by Bosnian Serbs. Oct: UN ban on military flights over Bosnia-Herzegovina. First British troops deployed, under UN control.
1993 UN–EC peace plan failed. USA began air-drops of food and medical supplies. Six UN 'safe areas' created, intended as havens for Muslim civilians. Bosnian Croat-Serb partition plan rejected by Muslims.
1994 Feb: Bosnian Serb siege of Sarajevo lifted after UN–NATO ultimatum; Russian intervention accelerated Serb withdrawal. Bosnian Croat--Muslim federation formed after cease-fire in

north. April: NATO bombed Bosnian Serb control positions around Gorazde (a UN-declared 'safe area'). Bosnian Serbs later withdrew in response to UN ultimatum. Aug: Serbia imposed blockade against Bosnian Serbs. Hostilities renewed around Sarajevo and 'safe area' of Bihac. Nov: USA unilaterally lifted arms embargo against Bosnian Muslims.

boson in physics, an elementary particle whose spin can only take values that are whole numbers or zero. Bosons may be classified as *gauge bosons (carriers of the four fundamental forces) or *mesons. All elementary particles are either bosons or *fermions.

Bosporus (Turkish **Karadeniz Boğazi**) strait 27 km/17 mi long, joining the Black Sea with the Sea of Marmara and forming part of the water division between Europe and Asia; its name may be derived from the Greek legend of *Io. Istanbul stands on its west side. The **Bosporus Bridge** 1973, measuring 1,621 m/5,320 ft, links Istanbul and Anatolia (the Asian part of Turkey). In 1988 a second bridge across the straits was opened, linking Asia and Europe.

Boston industrial and commercial centre, capital of Massachusetts, USA; population (1990) 574,300; metropolitan area 4,171,600. It is a publishing centre and industrial port on Massachusetts Bay, but the economy is dominated by financial and health services and government. Boston and Northeastern universities are here; Harvard University and the Massachusetts Institute of Technology are in neighbouring Cambridge, across the Charles River.

Boston Tea Party protest 1773 by colonists against the tea tax imposed on them by the British in Massachusetts, America, before the *American Revolution.

Boswell James 1740–1795. Scottish biographer and diarist. He was a member of Samuel *Johnson's London Literary Club and the two men travelled to Scotland together 1773, as recorded in Boswell's *Journal of the Tour to the Hebrides* 1785. His classic English biography *Life of Samuel Johnson* was published 1791.

Bosworth, Battle of last battle of the Wars of the *Roses, fought on 22 Aug 1485. Richard III, the Yorkist king, was defeated and slain by Henry of Richmond, who became Henry VII. The battlefield is near the village of Market Bosworth, 19 km/12 mi W of Leicester, England.

botanical garden place where a wide range of plants is grown, providing the opportunity to see a botanical diversity not likely to be encountered naturally. Among the earliest forms of botanical garden was the **physic garden**, devoted to the study and growth of medicinal plants; an example is the Chelsea Physic Garden in London, established 1673 and still in existence. Following increased botanical exploration, botanical gardens were used to test the commercial potential of new plants being sent back from all parts of the world.

botany the study of plants. It is subdivided into a number of specialized studies, such as the identification and classification of plants (taxonomy), their external formation (plant morphology), their internal arrangement (plant anatomy), their microscopic examination (plant histology), their functioning and life history (plant physiology), and their distribution over the Earth's surface in relation to their surroundings (plant ecology). Palaeobotany concerns the study of fossil plants, while economic botany deals with the utility of plants. Horticulture, agriculture, and forestry are branches of botany.

Botany Bay inlet on the E coast of Australia, 8 km/5 mi S of Sydney, New South Wales. Chosen 1787 as the site for a penal colony, it proved unsuitable. Sydney now stands on the site of the former settlement. The name Botany Bay continued to be popularly used for any convict settlement in Australia.

botfly any fly of the family Oestridae. The larvae are parasites that feed on the skin (warblefly of cattle) or in the nasal cavity (nostrilflies of sheep and deer). The horse botfly belongs to another family, the Gasterophilidae. It has a parasitic larva that feeds in the horse's stomach.

Botha Louis 1862–1919. South African soldier and politician, a commander in the Second South African War (Boer War). In 1907 Botha became premier of the Transvaal and in 1910 of the first Union South African government. On the outbreak of World War I 1914 he rallied South Africa to the Commonwealth, suppressed a Boer revolt, and conquered German South West Africa.

Botha P(ieter) W(illem) 1916– . South African politician, prime minister from 1978. Botha initiated a modification of *apartheid, which later slowed in the face of Afrikaner (Boer) opposition. In 1984 he became the first executive state president. In 1989 he unwillingly resigned both party leadership and presidency after suffering a stroke, and was succeeded by F W de Klerk.

Botham Ian (Terrence) 1955– . English cricketer whose test record places him among the world's greatest all-rounders. He has played county cricket for Somerset, Worcestershire, and Durham, as well as playing in Australia. He played for England 1977–89 and returned to the England side 1991.

Bothwell James Hepburn, 4th Earl of Bothwell c. 1536–1578. Scottish nobleman, third husband of *Mary Queen of Scots, 1567–70, alleged to have arranged the explosion that killed Darnley, her previous husband, 1567.

bo tree or **peepul** Indian *fig tree *Ficus religiosa*, said to be the tree under which the Buddha became enlightened.

Botswana Republic of
area 582,000 sq km/225,000 sq mi
capital Gaborone
towns Mahalpye, Serowe, Tutume, Francistown
physical desert in SW, plains in E, fertile lands and swamp in N
environment the Okavango Swamp is threatened by plans to develop the area for mining and agriculture
head of state and government Quett Ketamile Joni Masire from 1980
political system democratic republic
exports diamonds (third largest producer in world), copper, nickel, meat products, textiles
currency pula
population (1993 est) 1,400,000 (80% Bamangwato, 20% Bangwaketse); growth rate 3.5% p.a.

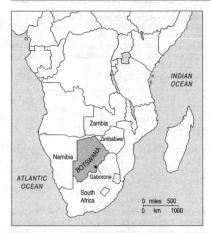

languages English (official), Setswana (national)
religions Christian 50%, animist 50%
GNP $2,590 per head (1991)
chronology
1885 Became a British protectorate.
1960 New constitution created a legislative council.
1963 End of rule by High Commission.
1965 Capital transferred from Mafeking to Gaborone. Internal self-government achieved. Sir Seretse Khama elected head of government.
1966 Independence achieved from Britain. New constitution came into effect; name changed from Bechuanaland to Botswana; Seretse Khama elected president.
1980 Seretse Khama died; succeeded by Vice President Quett Masire.
1984 Masire re-elected.
1985 South African raid on Gaborone.
1987 Joint permanent commission with Mozambique established, to improve relations.
1989 and 1994 The BDP and Masire re-elected.

Botticelli Sandro 1445–1510. Florentine painter of religious and mythological subjects. He was patronized by the ruling *Medici family, for whom he painted *Primavera* 1478 and *The Birth of Venus* about 1482–84 (both in the Uffizi, Florence). From the 1490s he was influenced by the religious fanatic *Savonarola and developed a harshly expressive and emotional style.

bottlebrush any of several trees or shrubs common in Australia, belonging to the genus *Callistemon* of the myrtle family, with characteristic cylindrical, composite flower heads in green, yellow, white, various shades of red, and violet.

Bottomley Virginia 1948– . British Conservative politician, health secretary from April 1992, member of Parliament for Surrey Southwest from 1984. Before entering Parliament she was a magistrate and psychiatric social worker. As an MP she became parliamentary private secretary to Chris Patten, then to Geoffrey Howe, and was made a junior environment minister 1988. Her husband, Peter Bottomley (1944–), is Conservative MP for Eltham.

botulism rare, often fatal type of *food poisoning. Symptoms include muscular paralysis and disturbed breathing and vision. It is caused by a toxin produced by the bacterium *Clostridium botulinum*, sometimes found in improperly canned food.

Boucher François 1703–1770. French Rococo painter, court painter from 1765. He was much patronized for his light-hearted, decorative scenes: for example *Diana Bathing* 1742 (Louvre, Paris).

Boudicca Queen of the Iceni (native Britons), often referred to by the Latin form **Boadicea**. Her husband, King Prasutagus, had been a tributary of the Romans, but on his death AD 60 the territory of the Iceni was violently annexed. Boudicca was scourged and her daughters raped. Boudicca raised the whole of SE England in revolt, and before the main Roman armies could return from campaigning in Wales she burned Londinium (London), Verulamium (St Albans), and Camolodunum (Colchester). Later the Romans under governor Suetonius Paulinus defeated the British between London and Chester; they were virtually annihilated and Boudicca poisoned herself.

Boudin Eugène 1824–1898. French artist, a forerunner of the Impressionists, known for his fresh seaside scenes painted in the open air.

Bougainville Louis Antoine de 1729–1811. French navigator. After service with the French in Canada during the Seven Years' War, he made the first French circumnavigation of the world 1766–69 and the first systematic observations of longitude.

bougainvillea any plant of the genus of South American tropical vines *Bougainvillea*, of the four o'clock family Nyctaginaceae, now cultivated in warm countries throughout the world for the red and purple bracts that cover the flowers. They are named after the French navigator Louis Bougainville.

Boulanger Nadia (Juliette) 1887–1979. French music teacher and conductor. A pupil of Fauré, and admirer of Stravinsky, she included among her composition pupils at the American Conservatory in Fontainebleau (from 1921) Aaron Copland, Roy Harris, Walter Piston, and Philip Glass.

boulder clay another name for *till, a type of glacial deposit.

boules (French 'balls') French game (also called *boccie* and *pétanque*) between two players or teams; it is similar to bowls.

Boulez Pierre 1925– . French composer and conductor. He studied with *Messiaen and promoted contemporary music with a series of innovative *Domaine Musical* concerts and recordings in the 1950s, as conductor of the BBC Symphony and New York Philharmonic orchestras during the 1970s, and as founder and director of IRCAM, a music research studio in Paris opened 1977.

boulle or **buhl** type of *marquetry in brass and tortoiseshell. Originally Italian, it has acquired the name of its most skilful exponent, the French artisan André-Charles Boulle (1642–1732).

Boulting John 1913–1985 and Roy 1913– . British director–producer team that was successful in the years following World War II. Their films include *Brighton Rock* 1947, *Lucky Jim* 1957, and *I'm All Right Jack* 1959. They were twins.

Boulton Matthew 1728–1809. British factory owner who helped to finance James *Watt's development of the steam engine.

Boumédienne Houari. Adopted name of Mohammed Boukharouba 1925–1978. Algerian politician who brought the nationalist leader Ben Bella to power by a revolt 1962, and superseded him as president in 1965 by a further coup.

***Bounty*, Mutiny on the** Naval mutiny in the Pacific 1789 against British captain William *Bligh.

Bourbon Charles, Duke of 1490–1527. Constable of France, honoured for his courage at the Battle of Marignano 1515. Later he served the Holy Roman Emperor Charles V, and helped to drive the French from Italy. In 1526 he was made duke of Milan, and in 1527 allowed his troops to sack Rome. He was killed by a shot the artist Cellini claimed to have fired.

Bourbon, duchy of originally a seigneury (feudal domain) created in the 10th century in the county of Bourges, central France, held by the Bourbon family. It became a duchy 1327.

Bourbon dynasty French royal house (succeeding that of *Valois) beginning with Henry IV, and ending with Louis XVI, with a brief revival under Louis XVIII, Charles X, and Louis Philippe. The Bourbons also ruled Spain almost uninterruptedly from Philip V to Alfonso XIII and were restored in 1975 (*Juan Carlos); at one point they also ruled Naples and several Italian duchies. The Grand Duke of Luxembourg is also a Bourbon by male descent.

Bourdon gauge instrument for measuring pressure, invented by Eugène Bourdon 1849. The gauge contains a C-shaped tube, closed at one end. When the pressure inside the tube increases, the tube uncurls slightly causing a small movement at its closed end. A system of levers and gears magnifies this movement and turns a pointer, which indicates the pressure on a circular scale. Bourdon gauges are often fitted to cylinders of compressed gas used in industry and hospitals.

Bourgeois Léon Victor Auguste 1851–1925. French politician. Entering politics as a Radical, he was prime minister in 1895, and later served in many cabinets. He was one of the pioneer advocates of the League of Nations. He was awarded the Nobel Peace Prize 1920.

bourgeoisie (French) the middle classes. The French word originally meant 'the freemen of a borough'. It came to mean the whole class above the workers and peasants, and below the nobility. Bourgeoisie (and *bourgeois*) has also acquired a contemptuous sense, implying commonplace, philistine respectability. By socialists it is applied to the whole propertied class, as distinct from the proletariat.

Bourgogne region of France that includes the *départements* of Côte-d'Or, Nièvre, Sâone-et-Loire, and Yonne; area 31,600 sq km/ 12,198 sq mi; population (1986) 1,607,000. Its capital is Dijon.

Bourguiba Habib ben Ali 1903– . Tunisian politician, first president of Tunisia 1957–87. Educated at the University of Paris, he became a journalist and was frequently imprisoned by the French for his nationalist aims as leader of the Néo-Destour party. He became prime minister 1956, president (for life from 1974) and prime minister of the Tunisian republic 1957; he was overthrown in a bloodless coup 1987.

Bournonville August 1805–1879. Danish dancer and choreographer. He worked with the Royal Danish Ballet for most of his life, giving Danish ballet a worldwide importance. His ballets, many of which have been revived in the last 50 years, include *La Sylphide* 1836 (music by Lövenskjöld) and *Napoli* 1842.

Boutros-Ghali Boutros 1922– . Egyptian diplomat and politician, secretary general of the United Nations from Jan 1992. He worked towards peace in the Middle East in the foreign-ministry posts he held 1977–91, and was deputy prime minister 1991–92.

Bouvines, Battle of victory for Philip II (Philip Augustus) of France in 1214, near the village of Bouvines in Flanders, over the Holy Roman emperor Otto IV and his allies. The battle, one of the most decisive in medieval Europe, ensured the succession of Frederick II as emperor and confirmed Philip as ruler of the whole of N France and Flanders; it led to the renunciation of all English claims to the region.

bovine somatotropin (BST) hormone that increases an injected cow's milk yield by 10–40%. It is a protein naturally occurring in milk and breaks down within the human digestive tract into harmless amino acids. However, doubts have arisen recently as to whether such a degree of protein addition could in the long term be guaranteed harmless either to cattle or to humans.

bovine spongiform encephalopathy (BSE) disease of cattle, allied to *scrapie, that renders the brain spongy and may drive an animal mad. First identified in 1986, it is almost entirely confined to the UK. By early 1994 it had claimed 115,000 British cattle. The organism causing it is unknown; it is not a conventional virus because it is more resistant to chemicals and heat, cannot be seen even under an electron microscope, cannot be grown in tissue culture, and does not appear to provoke an immune response in the body.

Bow Clara 1905–1965. US film actress known as a Jazz Baby and the 'It Girl' after her portrayal of a glamorous flapper in the silent film *It* 1927.

Bowdler Thomas 1754–1825. British editor whose prudishly expurgated versions of Shakespeare and other authors gave rise to the verb *bowdlerize*.

bower bird New Guinean and N Australian bird of the family Ptilonorhynchidae, related to the *birds of paradise. The males are dull-coloured, and build elaborate bowers of sticks and grass, decorated with shells, feathers, or flowers, and even painted with the juice of berries, to attract the females. There are 17 species.

bowfin North American fish *Amia calva* with a swim bladder highly developed as an air sac, enabling it to breathe air. It is the only surviving member of a primitive group of bony fishes.

bowhead Arctic whale *Balaena mysticetus* with strongly curving upper jawbones supporting the plates of baleen with which it sifts planktonic crustaceans from the water. Averaging 15 m/50 ft long and 90 tonnes/100 tons in weight, these slow-moving, placid whales were once extremely common, but by the 17th century were already becoming scarce through hunting. Only an estimated 3,000 remain, and continued hunting by the Inuit may result in extinction.

Bowie David. Stage name of David Jones 1947– . English pop singer, songwriter, and actor. He became a rock star with the release of the album *The Rise and Fall of Ziggy Stardust and the Spiders from Mars* 1972, and collaborated in the mid-1970s with the electronic virtuoso Brian Eno (1948–) and Iggy Pop. He has also acted in plays and films, including Nicolas Roeg's *The Man Who Fell to Earth* 1976.

Bowie James 'Jim' 1796–1836. US frontiersman and folk hero. A colonel in the Texan forces during the Mexican War, he is said to have invented the single-edge, guarded hunting and throwing knife known as a *Bowie knife*. He was killed in the battle of the *Alamo.

bowls outdoor and indoor game popular in Commonwealth countries. It has been played in Britain since the 13th century and was popularized by Francis Drake, who is reputed to have played bowls on Plymouth Hoe as the Spanish Armada approached 1588.

Bowman's capsule in the vertebrate kidney, a microscopic filtering device used in the initial stages of waste-removal and urine formation.

box any of several small evergreen trees and shrubs, genus *Buxus*, of the family Buxaceae, with small, leathery leaves. Some species are used as hedge plants and for shaping into garden ornaments.

boxer breed of dog, about 60 cm/2 ft tall, with a smooth coat and a set-back nose. The tail is usually docked. Boxers are usually brown but may be brindled or white.

Boxer member of the *I ho ch'üan* ('Righteous Harmonious Fists'), a society of Chinese nationalists dedicated to fighting European influence. The *Boxer Rebellion* or *Uprising* 1900 was instigated by the Dowager Empress Tzu Hsi (1834–1908). European and US legations in Beijing were besieged and thousands of Chinese Christian converts and missionaries murdered. An international punitive force was dispatched, Beijing was captured 14 Aug 1900, and China agreed to pay a large indemnity.

boxfish or *trunkfish* any fish of the family Ostraciodontidae, with scales that are hexagonal bony plates fused to form a box covering the body, only the mouth and fins being free of the armour. Boxfishes swim slowly. The cowfish, genus *Lactophrys*, with two 'horns' above the eyes, is a member of this group.

boxing fighting with gloved fists, almost entirely a male sport. The sport dates from the 18th century, when fights were fought with bare knuckles and untimed rounds. Each round ended with a knockdown. Fighting with gloves became the accepted form in the latter part of the 19th century after the formulation of the Queensberry Rules 1867.

boyar landowner in the Russian aristocracy. During the 16th century boyars formed a power-ful interest group threatening the tsar's power, until their influence was decisively broken in 1565 when Ivan the Terrible confiscated much of their land.

Boycott Geoffrey 1940– . English cricketer born in Yorkshire, England's most prolific run-maker with 8,114 runs in test cricket until overtaken by David Gower in 1992. He was banned as a test player in 1982 for taking part in matches against South Africa.

Boyd-Orr John 1880–1971. British nutritionist and health campaigner. He was awarded the Nobel Prize for Peace in 1949 in recognition of his work towards alleviating world hunger.

Boyle's law law stating that the volume of a given mass of gas at a constant temperature is inversely proportional to its pressure. For example, if the pressure of a gas doubles, its volume will be reduced by a half, and vice versa. The law was discovered in 1662 by Robert Boyle and is one of the chief gas laws.

Boyne river in the Irish Republic. Rising in the Bog of Allen in County Kildare, it flows 110 km/69 mi NE to the Irish Sea near Drogheda. The Battle of the Boyne was fought at Oldbridge near the mouth of the river in 1690.

Boyne, Battle of the battle fought 1 July 1690 in E Ireland, in which James II was defeated by William III and fled to France. It was the decisive battle of the War of English Succession, confirming a Protestant monarch. It took its name from the river Boyne which rises in County Kildare and flows 110 km/69 mi NE to the Irish Sea.

Boy Scout member of the *Scout organization.

Brabant (Flemish *Braband*) former duchy of W Europe, comprising the Dutch province of *North Brabant and the Belgian provinces of Brabant and Antwerp. They were divided when Belgium became independent 1830. The present-day Belgian province of Brabant has an area of 3,400 sq km/1,312 sq mi and a population (1987) of 2,245,900.

Brabham Grand Prix racing team started 1962 by the top Australian driver Jack Brabham (1926–). Their first car, designed by Ron Tauranac, had its first win 1964, and in 1966 Brabham won the world title in his own Repco engine-powered car.

Brachiopod any member of the phylum Brachiopoda, marine invertebrates with two shells, resembling but totally unrelated to bivalves. There are about 300 living species; they were much more numerous in past geological ages. They are suspension feeders, ingesting minute food particles from water. A single internal organ, the iophophore, handles feeding, aspiration, and excretion.

bracken large fern, especially *Pteridium aquilinum*, abundant in the northern hemisphere. A perennial rootstock throws up coarse fronds.

bracket fungus any *fungus of the class Basidiomycetes, with fruiting bodies that grow like shelves from trees.

bract leaflike structure in whose *axil a flower or inflorescence develops. Bracts are generally green and smaller than the true leaves. However, in some plants they may be brightly coloured and conspicuous, taking over the role of attracting pollinating insects to the flowers, whose own petals are small; examples include poinsettia *Euphorbia pulcherrima* and bougainvillea.

Bradbury Malcolm 1932– . British novelist and critic, whose writings include comic and satiric portrayals of academic life. He became professor of American studies at the University of East Anglia 1970, and his major work is *The History Man* 1975, set in a provincial English university. Other works include *Rates of Exchange* 1983.

Bradford industrial city (engineering, machine tools, electronics, printing) in West Yorkshire, England, 14 km/9 mi W of Leeds; population (1981) 281,000.

Bradlaugh Charles 1833–1891. British freethinker and radical politician. In 1880 he was elected Liberal member of Parliament for Northampton, but was not allowed to take his seat until 1886 because, as an atheist, he (unsuccessfully) claimed the right to affirm instead of taking the oath. He was associated with the feminist Annie Besant.

Bradley Omar Nelson 1893–1981. US general in World War II. In 1943 he commanded the 2nd US Corps in their victories in Tunisia and Sicily, leading to the surrender of 250,000 Axis troops, and in 1944 led the US troops in the invasion of France. His command, as the 12th Army Group, grew to 1.3 million troops, the largest US force ever assembled.

Bradman Don(ald George) 1908– . Australian test cricketer with the highest average in test history. From 52 test matches he averaged 99.94 runs per innings. He only needed four runs from his final test innings to average 100 but was dismissed second ball.

Bragança capital of a province of the same name in NE Portugal, 176 km/110 mi NE of Oporto. Population (1981) 13,900. It was the original family seat of the House of Braganza which ruled Portugal 1640–1910.

Braganza the royal house of Portugal whose members reigned 1640–1910; another branch were emperors of Brazil 1822–89.

Brahe Tycho 1546–1601. Danish astronomer who made accurate observations of the planets from which the German astronomer and mathematician Johann *Kepler proved that planets orbit the Sun in ellipses. His discovery and report of the 1572 supernova brought him recognition, and his observations of the comet of 1577 proved that it moved on an orbit among the planets, thus disproving the Greek view that comets were in the Earth's atmosphere.

Brahma in Hinduism, the creator of the cosmos, who forms with Vishnu and Siva the Trimurti, or three aspects of the absolute spirit.

Brahman in Hinduism, the supreme being, an abstract, impersonal world-soul into whom the *atman*, or individual soul, will eventually be absorbed when its cycle of rebirth is ended.

Brahmanism earliest stage in the development of *Hinduism. Its sacred scriptures are the *Vedas, with their accompanying literature of comment and explanation known as Brahmanas, Aranyakas, and Upanishads.

Brahmaputra river in Asia 2,900 km/1,800 mi long, a tributary of the Ganges.

Brahms Johannes 1833–1897. German composer, pianist, and conductor. Considered one of the greatest composers of symphonic music and of songs, his works include four symphonies; *lieder (songs); concertos for piano and for violin; chamber music; sonatas; and the choral *A German Requiem* 1868. He performed and conducted his own works.

Braille system of writing for the blind. Letters are represented by a combination of raised dots on paper or other materials, which are then read by touch. It was invented in 1829 by *Louis Braille* (1809–1852), who became blind at the age of three.

brain in higher animals, a mass of interconnected *nerve cells, forming the anterior part of the *central nervous system, whose activities it coordinates and controls. In *vertebrates the brain is contained by the skull. An enlarged portion of the upper spinal cord, the *medulla oblongata*, contains centres for the control of respiration, heartbeat rate and strength, and blood pressure. Overlying this is the *cerebellum*, which is concerned with coordinating complex muscular processes such as maintaining posture and moving limbs. The cerebral hemispheres (*cerebrum*) are paired outgrowths of the front end of the forebrain, in early vertebrates mainly concerned with the senses, but in higher vertebrates greatly developed and involved in the integration of all sensory input and motor output, and in intelligent behaviour.

Braine John 1922–1986. English novelist. His novel *Room at the Top* 1957 created the character of Joe Lampton, one of the first of the northern working-class antiheroes.

brake device used to slow down or stop the movement of a moving body or vehicle. The mechanically applied caliper brake used on bicycles uses a scissor action to press hard rubber blocks against the wheel rim. The main braking system of a car works hydraulically: when the driver depresses the brake pedal, liquid pressure forces pistons to apply brakes on each wheel.

Bramah Joseph 1748–1814. British inventor of a flushing water closet 1778, an 'unpickable' lock 1784, and the hydraulic press 1795. The press made use of *Pascal's principle (that pressure in fluid contained in a vessel is evenly distributed) and employed water as the hydraulic fluid; it enabled the 19th-century bridge-builders to lift massive girders.

Bramante Donato *c.* 1444–1514. Italian Renaissance architect and artist. Inspired by Classical designs, he was employed by Pope Julius II in rebuilding part of the Vatican and St Peter's in Rome.

bramble any prickly bush of a genus *Rubus* belonging to the rose family Rosaceae. Examples are *blackberry, raspberry, and dewberry.

Branagh Kenneth 1960– . British actor and director. He cofounded, with David Parfitt, the Renaissance Theatre Company 1987, was a notable Hamlet and Touchstone in 1988, and in 1989 directed and starred in a film of Shakespeare's *Henry V*.

Brancusi Constantin 1876–1957. Romanian sculptor, active in Paris from 1904, a pioneer of abstract forms and conceptual art. He developed

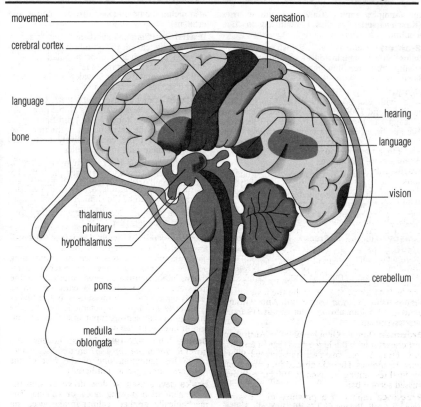

movement
cerebral cortex
language
bone
thalamus
pituitary
hypothalamus
pons
medulla
oblongata

sensation
hearing
language
vision
cerebellum

brain *The structure of the human brain.*

increasingly simplified natural or organic forms, such as the sculpted head that gradually came to resemble an egg (*Sleeping Muse* 1910, Musée National d'Art Moderne, Paris).

Brandeis Louis Dembitz 1856–1941. US jurist. As a crusader for progressive causes, he helped draft social-welfare and labour legislation. In 1916, with his appointment to the US Supreme Court by President Wilson, he became the first Jewish justice and maintained his support of individual rights in his opposition to the 1917 Espionage Act and in his dissenting opinion in the first wiretap case, *Olmstead* v *US* 1928.

Brandenburg administrative *Land* (state) of Germany;
area 25,000 sq km/10,000 sq mi
capital Potsdam
towns Cottbus, Brandenburg, Frankfurt-on-Oder
products iron and steel, paper, pulp, metal products, semiconductors
population (1990) 2,700,000
history the Hohenzollern rulers who took control of Brandenburg in 1415 later acquired the powerful duchy of Prussia and became emperors of Germany. At the end of World War II, Brandenburg lost over 12,950 sq km/5,000 sq mi of territory when Poland advanced its frontier to the line of the Oder and Neisse rivers. The remainder,

which became a region of East Germany, was divided 1952 into the districts of Frankfurt-on-Oder, Potsdam, and Cottbus. When Germany was reunited 1990, Brandenburg reappeared as a state of the Federal Republic.

Brando Marlon 1924– . US actor whose casual style, mumbling speech, and use of *Method acting earned him a place as a distinctive actor. He won best-actor Academy Awards for *On the Waterfront* 1954 and *The Godfather* 1972.

Brandt Bill 1905–1983. British photographer who produced a large body of richly printed and romantic black-and-white studies of people, London life, and social behaviour.

Brandt Willy. Adopted name of Karl Herbert Frahm 1913–1992. German socialist politician, federal chancellor (premier) of West Germany 1969–74. He played a key role in the remoulding of the Social Democratic Party (SPD) as a moderate socialist force (leader 1964–87). As mayor of West Berlin 1957–66, Brandt became internationally known during the Berlin Wall crisis 1961. Nobel Peace Prize 1971.

brandy (Dutch *brandewijn* 'burnt wine') alcoholic drink distilled from fermented grape juice (wine). The best-known examples are produced in France, notably Armagnac and Cognac. Brandy can also be prepared from other fruits, for example, apples (Calvados) and cherries (Kirschwasser). Brandies contain up to 55% alcohol.

Branson Richard 1950– . British entrepreneur whose Virgin company developed quickly, diversifying from retailing records to the airline business.

Braque Georges 1882–1963. French painter who, with Picasso, founded the Cubist movement around 1907–10. They worked together at L'Estaque in the south of France and in Paris. Braque began to experiment in collages and invented a technique of gluing paper, wood, and other materials to canvas. His later work became more decorative.

Brasília capital of Brazil from 1960, 1,000 m/3,000 ft above sea level; population (1991) 1,841,000. It was designed by Lucio Costa (1902–1963), with Oscar Niemeyer as chief architect, as a completely new city to bring life to the interior.

Braşov (Hungarian *Brassó*, German *Kronstadt*) industrial city (machine tools, industrial equipment, chemicals, cement, woollens) in central Romania at the foot of the Transylvanian Alps; population (1985) 347,000. It belonged to Hungary until 1920.

brass metal *alloy of copper and zinc, with not more than 5% or 6% of other metals. The zinc content ranges from 20% to 45%, and the colour of brass varies accordingly from coppery to whitish yellow. Brasses are characterized by the ease with which they may be shaped and machined; they are strong and ductile, resist many forms of corrosion, and are used for electrical fittings, ammunition cases, screws, household fittings, and ornaments.

Brassäi adopted name of Gyula Halesz 1899–1986. French photographer of Hungarian origin. From the early 1930s on he documented, mainly by flash, the nightlife of Paris, before turning to more abstract work.

Brassica genus of plants of the family Cruciferae. The most familiar species is the common cabbage *Brassica oleracea*, with its varieties broccoli, cauliflower, kale, and brussels sprouts.

brass instrument in music, any instrument made of brass or other metal, which is directly blown through a 'cup' or 'funnel' mouthpiece. In the symphony orchestra they comprise: the *French horn*, a descendant of the natural hunting horn, valved, and curved into a circular loop, with a wide bell; the *trumpet*, a cylindrical tube curved into an oblong, with a narrow bell and three valves (the state *fanfare trumpet* has no valves); the *trombone*, an instrument with a 'slide' to vary the effective length of the tube (the *sackbut*, common from the 14th century, was its forerunner; the *tuba*, normally the lowest toned instrument of the orchestra, which is valved and with a very wide bore to give sonority, and a bell that points upward. In the brass band (in descending order of pitch) they comprise: the *cornet*, three-valved instrument, looking like a shorter, broader trumpet, and with a wider bore; the *flugelhorn*, valved instrument, rather similar in range to the cornet; the *tenor horn*; *B-flat baritone*; *euphonium*; *trombone*; and *bombardon* (bass tuba). A brass band normally

also includes bass and side drums, triangle, and cymbals.

Bratislava (German *Pressburg*) industrial port (engineering, chemicals, oil refining) in Czechoslovakia, on the river Danube; population (1991) 441,500. It was the capital of Hungary 1526–1784 and is now capital of the Slovak Socialist Republic and second largest city in Czechoslovakia.

Brattain Walter Houser 1902–1987. US physicist. In 1956 he was awarded a Nobel prize jointly with William Shockley and John Bardeen for their work on the development of the transistor, which replaced the comparatively costly and clumsy vacuum tube in electronics.

Braun Eva 1910–1945. German mistress of Adolf Hitler. Secretary to Hitler's photographer and personal friend, Heinrich Hoffmann, she became Hitler's mistress in the 1930s and married him in the air-raid shelter of the Chancellery in Berlin on 29 April 1945. The next day they committed suicide together.

Brazil Federative Republic of (*República Federativa do Brasil*)

area 8,511,965 sq km/3,285,618 sq mi
capital Brasília
towns São Paulo, Belo Horizonte, Curitiba, Manaus, Fortaleza; ports are Rio de Janeiro, Belém, Recife, Pôrto Alegre, Salvador
physical the densely forested Amazon basin covers the northern half of the country with a network of rivers; the south is fertile; enormous energy resources, both hydroelectric (Itaipú dam on the Paraná, and Tucuruí on the Tocantins) and nuclear (uranium ores)
environment Brazil has one-third of the world's tropical rainforest. It contains 55,000 species of flowering plants (the greatest variety in the world) and 20% of all the world's bird species. During the 1980s at least 7% of the Amazon rainforest was destroyed by settlers who cleared the land for cultivation and grazing
head of state and government Fernando Henrique Cardoso from 1994
political system democratic federal republic
exports coffee, sugar, soya beans, cotton, textiles, timber, motor vehicles, iron, chrome,

manganese, tungsten, and other ores, as well as quartz crystals, industrial diamonds, gemstones; the world's sixth largest arms exporter
currency real
population (1993 est) 159,100,000 (including 200,000 Indians, survivors of 5 million, especially in Rondônia and Mato Grosso, mostly living on reservations); growth rate 2.2% p.a.
languages Portuguese (official); 120 Indian languages
religions Roman Catholic 89%; Indian faiths
GNP $2,680 per head (1987)
chronology
1822 Independence achieved from Portugal; ruled by Dom Pedro, son of the refugee King John VI of Portugal.
1889 Monarchy abolished and republic established.
1891 Constitution for a federal state adopted.
1930 Dr Getúlio Vargas became president.
1945 Vargas deposed by the military.
1946 New constitution adopted.
1951 Vargas returned to office.
1954 Vargas committed suicide.
1956 Juscelino Kubitschek became president.
1960 Capital moved to Brasília.
1961 João Goulart became president.
1964 Bloodless coup made General Castelo Branco president; he assumed dictatorial powers, abolishing free political parties.
1967 New constitution adopted. Branco succeeded by Marshal da Costa e Silva.
1969 Da Costa e Silva resigned and a military junta took over.
1974 General Ernesto Geisel became president.
1978 General Baptista de Figueiredo became president.
1979 Political parties legalized again.
1984 Mass calls for a return to fully democratic government.
1985 Tancredo Neves became first civilian president in 21 years. Neves died and was succeeded by the vice president, José Sarney.
1988 New constitution approved, transferring power from the president to the congress. Measures announced to halt large-scale burning of Amazonian rainforest for cattle grazing.
1989 Fernando Collor (PRN) elected president, pledging free-market economic policies.
1990 Government won the general election offset by mass abstentions.
1992 Collor charged with corruption and replaced by Vice President Itamar Franco. Hosted Earth Summit.
1993 April: referendum rejected replacement of presidential system with parliamentary system or monarchy. Collor accused of 'passive corruption'.
1994 New currency introduced. Fernando Henrique Cardoso, of the PSDB, elected president.

Brazil nut seed, rich in oil and highly nutritious, of the gigantic South American tree *Bertholletia excelsa*. The seeds are enclosed in a hard outer casing, each fruit containing 10–20 seeds arranged like the segments of an orange. The timber of the tree is also valuable.

brazing method of joining two metals by melting an *alloy into the joint. It is similar to soldering but takes place at a much higher temperature. Copper and silver alloys are widely used for brazing, at temperatures up to about 900°C/1,650°F.

Brazzaville capital of the Congo, industrial port (foundries, railway repairs, shipbuilding, shoes, soap, furniture, bricks) on the river Zaïre, opposite Kinshasa; population (1984) 595,000. There is a cathedral 1892 and the Pasteur Institute 1908. It stands on Pool Malebo (Stanley Pool).

bread food baked from a kneaded dough or batter made with ground cereals, usually wheat, and water; many other ingredients may be added. The dough may be unleavened or raised (usually with yeast). Bread has been a staple of human diet in many civilizations as long as agriculture has been practised, and some hunter-gatherer peoples made it from crushed acorns or beech nuts. Potato, banana, and cassava bread are among some local varieties, but most breads are made from fermented cereals which form glutens when mixed with water.

breadfruit fruit of the tropical trees *Artocarpus communis* and *A. altilis* of the mulberry family Moraceae. It is highly nutritious and when baked is said to taste like bread. It is native to many South Pacific islands.

Breakspear Nicholas. Original name of *Adrian IV, the only English pope.

bream deep-bodied, flattened fish *Abramis brama* of the carp family, growing to about 50 cm/1.6 ft, typically found in lowland rivers across Europe.

breast one of a pair of organs on the upper front of the human female, also known as a *mammary gland. Each of the two breasts contains milk-producing cells, and a network of tubes or ducts that lead to an opening in the nipple.

Breathalyzer trademark for an instrument for on-the-spot checking by police of the amount of alcohol consumed by a suspect driver. The driver breathes into a plastic bag connected to a tube containing a chemical (such as a diluted solution of potassium dichromate in 50% sulphuric acid) that changes colour in the presence of alcohol. Another method is to use a gas chromatograph, again from a breath sample.

breathing in terrestrial animals, the muscular movements whereby air is taken into the lungs and then expelled, a form of *gas exchange. Breathing is sometimes referred to as external respiration, for true respiration is a cellular (internal) process.

breccia coarse clastic *sedimentary rock, made up of broken fragments (clasts) of pre-existing rocks. It is similar to *conglomerate but the fragments in breccia are large and jagged.

Brecht Bertolt 1898–1956. German dramatist and poet who aimed to destroy the 'suspension of disbelief' usual in the theatre and to express Marxist ideas. He adapted John Gay's *Beggar's Opera* as *Die Dreigroschenoper/The Threepenny Opera* 1928, set to music by Kurt Weill. Later plays include *Mutter Courage/Mother Courage* 1941, set during the Thirty Years' War, and *Der kaukasische Kreidekreis/The Caucasian Chalk Circle* 1949.

Breda, Treaty of 1667 treaty that ended the Second Anglo-Dutch War (1664–67). By the terms of the treaty, England gained New Amsterdam, which was renamed New York.

breeder reactor or *fast breeder* alternative names for *fast reactor, a type of nuclear reactor.

breeding in biology, the crossing and selection of animals and plants to change the characteristics of an existing breed or cultivar (variety), or to produce a new one.

breeding in nuclear physics, a process in a reactor in which more fissionable material is produced than is consumed in running the reactor.

Bremen industrial port (iron, steel, oil refining, chemicals, aircraft, shipbuilding, cars) in Germany, on the Weser 69 km/43 mi from the open sea; population (1988) 522,000.

Bremen administrative region (German *Land*) of Germany, consisting of the cities of Bremen and Bremerhaven; area 400 sq km/154 sq mi; population (1988) 652,000.

Brendel Alfred 1931– . Austrian pianist, known for his fastidious and searching interpretations of Beethoven, Schubert, and Liszt. He is the author of *Musical Thoughts and Afterthoughts* 1976 and *Music Sounded Out* 1990.

Brennan William Joseph, Jr 1906– . US jurist and associate justice of the US Supreme Court 1956–90. He wrote many important Supreme Court majority decisions that assured the freedoms set forth in the First Amendment and established the rights of minority groups. He is especially noted for writing the majority opinion in *Baker* v *Carr* 1962, in which state voting reapportionment ensured 'one person, one vote', and in *US* v *Eichman* 1990, which ruled that the law banning desecration of the flag was a violation of the right to free speech as provided for in the First Amendment.

Brenner Sidney 1927– . South African scientist, one of the pioneers of genetic engineering. Brenner discovered messenger *RNA (a link between *DNA and the *ribosomes in which proteins are synthesized) 1960.

Brenner Pass lowest of the Alpine passes, 1,370 m/4,495 ft; it leads from Trentino–Alto Adige, Italy, to the Austrian Tirol, and is 19 km/12 mi long.

Brenton Howard 1942– . British dramatist, whose works include *The Romans in Britain* 1980, and a translation of Brecht's *The Life of Galileo*.

Brescia (ancient *Brixia*) historic and industrial city (textiles, engineering, firearms, metal products) in N Italy, 84 km/52 mi E of Milan; population (1988) 199,000. It has medieval walls and two cathedrals (12th and 17th century).

Breslau German name of *Wrocław, town in Poland.

Brest naval base and industrial port (electronics, engineering, chemicals) on *Rade de Brest* (Brest Roads), a great bay at the western extremity of Bretagne, France; population (1983) 201,000. Occupied as a U-boat base by the Germans 1940–44, the town was destroyed by Allied bombing and rebuilt.

Brest-Litovsk, Treaty of bilateral treaty signed 3 March 1918 between Russia and Germany, Austria–Hungary, and their allies. Under its terms, Russia agreed to recognize the independence of Georgia, Ukraine, Poland and the Baltic States, and pay heavy compensation. Under the

Nov 1918 Armistice that ended World War I, it was annulled, since Russia was one of the winning allies.

Bretagne region of NW France, see *Brittany.

Brétigny, Treaty of treaty made between Edward III of England and John II of France in 1360 at the end of the first phase of the Hundred Years' War, under which Edward received Aquitaine and its dependencies in exchange for renunciation of his claim to the French throne.

Breton André 1896–1966. French author, among the leaders of the *Dada art movement. *Les Champs magnétiques/Magnetic Fields* 1921, an experiment in automatic writing, was one of the products of the movement. He was also a founder of Surrealism, publishing *Le Manifeste de surréalisme/Surrealist Manifesto* 1924. Other works include *Najda* 1928, the story of his love affair with a medium.

Breton language member of the Celtic branch of the Indo-European language family; the language of Brittany in France, related to Welsh and Cornish, and descended from the speech of Celts who left Britain as a consequence of the Anglo-Saxon invasions of the 5th and 6th centuries. Officially neglected for centuries, Breton is now a recognized language of France.

Bretton Woods township in New Hampshire, USA, where the United Nations Monetary and Financial Conference was held in 1944 to discuss postwar international payments problems. The agreements reached on financial assistance and measures to stabilize exchange rates led to the creation of the International Bank for Reconstruction and Development in 1945 and the International Monetary Fund (IMF).

Breuer Josef 1842–1925. Viennese physician, one of the pioneers of psychoanalysis. He applied it successfully to cases of hysteria, and collaborated with Freud in *Studien über Hysterie/Studies in Hysteria* 1895.

Breuer Marcel 1902–1981. Hungarian-born architect and designer who studied and taught at the *Bauhaus school in Germany. His tubular steel chair 1925 was the first of its kind. He moved to England, then to the USA, where he was in partnership with Walter Gropius 1937–40. His buildings show an affinity with natural materials; the best known is the Bijenkorf, Rotterdam, the Netherlands (with Elzas) 1953.

brewing making of beer, ale, or other alcoholic beverage from *malt and *barley by steeping (mashing), boiling, and fermenting. Mashing the barley releases its sugars. Yeast is then added, which contains the enzymes needed to convert the sugars into ethanol (alcohol) and carbon dioxide. Hops are added to give a bitter taste.

Brezhnev Leonid Ilyich 1906–1982. Soviet leader. A protégé of Stalin and Khrushchev, he came to power (after he and *Kosygin forced Khrushchev to resign) as general secretary of the Soviet Communist Party (CPSU) 1964–82 and was president 1977–82. Domestically he was conservative; abroad the USSR was established as a military and political superpower during the Brezhnev era, extending its influence in Africa and Asia.

Brian Havergal 1876–1972. English composer of 32 symphonies in visionary Romantic style, including the *Gothic* 1919–27 for large choral and orchestral forces.

Brian known as *Brian Boru* ('Brian of the Tribute') 926–1014. High king of Ireland from 976, who took Munster, Leinster, and Connacht to become ruler of all Ireland. He defeated the Norse at Clontarf, thus ending Norse control of Dublin, although he was himself killed. He was the last high king with jurisdiction over most of Scotland. His exploits were celebrated in several chronicles.

Briand Aristide 1862–1932. French radical socialist politician. He was prime minister 1909–11, 1913, 1915–17, 1921–22, 1925–26 and 1929, and foreign minister 1925–32. In 1925 he concluded the *Locarno pact (settling Germany's western frontier) and in 1928 the *Kellogg–Briand Pact renouncing war; in 1930 he outlined a scheme for a United States of Europe.

bribery corruptly receiving or agreeing to receive, giving or promising to give, any gift, loan, fee, reward, or advantage as an inducement or reward to persons in certain positions of trust. For example, it is an offence to improperly influence in this way judges or other judicial officers, members and officers of public bodies, or voters at public elections.

brick common building material, rectangular in shape, made of clay that has been fired in a kiln. Bricks are made by kneading a mixture of crushed clay and other materials into a stiff mud and extruding it into a ribbon. The ribbon is cut into individual bricks, which are fired at a temperature of up to about 1,000°C/1,800°F. Bricks may alternatively be pressed into shape in moulds.

bridewealth or *brideprice* goods or property presented by a man's family to his prospective wife's as part of the marriage agreement. It was the usual practice among many societies in Africa, Asia, and the Pacific, and among many American Indian groups. In most European and S Asian countries the alternative custom was *dowry.

bridewell jail or house of correction. The word comes from the royal palace of Bridewell, built 1522 by Henry VIII. In 1555 it was converted to a type of prison where the 'sturdy and idle' as well as certain petty criminals were made to labour. Various other towns set up their own institutions following the same regime.

bridge structure that provides a continuous path or road over water, valleys, ravines, or above other roads. The basic designs and composites of these are based on the way they bear the weight of the structure and its load. *Beam*, or *girder*, bridges are supported at each end by the ground with the weight thrusting downwards. *Cantilever* bridges are a complex form of girder. *Arch* bridges thrust outwards but downwards at their ends; they are in compression. *Suspension* bridges use cables under tension to pull inwards against anchorages on either side of the span, so that the roadway hangs from the main cables by the network of vertical cables. Some bridges are too low to allow traffic to pass beneath easily, so they are designed with movable parts, like swing and draw bridges.

bridge card game derived from whist. First played among members of the Indian Civil Service about 1900, bridge was brought to England in 1903 and played at the Portland Club in 1908. It is played in two forms: *auction bridge and *contract bridge.

Bridge Frank 1879–1941. English composer, the teacher of Benjamin Britten. His works include the orchestral suite *The Sea* 1912, and *Oration* 1930 for cello and orchestra.

Bridgetown port and capital of Barbados, founded 1628; population (1987) 8,000. Sugar is exported through the nearby deep-water port.

Bridgewater Francis Egerton, 3rd Duke of 1736–1803. Pioneer of British inland navigation. With James *Brindley as his engineer, he constructed 1762–72 the *Bridgewater canal* from Worsley to Manchester and on to the Mersey, a distance of 67.5 km/42 mi. Initially built to carry coal, the canal crosses the Irwell valley on an aqueduct.

brigade military formation consisting of a minimum of two battalions, but more usually three or more, as well as supporting arms. There are typically about 5,000 soldiers in a brigade, which is commanded by a brigadier. Two or more brigades form a *division.

Bright John 1811–1889. British Liberal politician, a campaigner for free trade, peace, and social reform. A Quaker millowner, he was among the founders of the Anti-Corn Law League in 1839, and was largely instrumental in securing the passage of the Reform Bill of 1867.

brill flatfish *Scophthalmus laevis*, living in shallow water over sandy bottoms in the NE Atlantic and Mediterranean. It is a freckled sandy brown, and grows to 60 cm/2 ft.

Brindley James 1716–1772. British canal builder, the first to employ tunnels and aqueducts extensively, in order to reduce the number of locks on a direct-route canal. He built 580 km/360 mi of canals, including the Bridgewater (Manchester–Liverpool) and Grand Union (Manchester–Potteries) canals.

brine common name for a solution of sodium chloride (NaCl) in water. Brines are used extensively in the food-manufacturing industry for canning vegetables, pickling vegetables (sauerkraut manufacture), and curing meat. Industrially, brine is the source from which chlorine, caustic soda (sodium hydroxide), and sodium carbonate are made.

Brinell hardness test test of the hardness of a substance according to the area of indentation made by a 10 mm/0.4 in hardened steel or sintered tungsten carbide ball under standard loading conditions in a test machine. The resulting Brinell number is equal to the load (kg) divided by the surface area (mm^2) and is named after its inventor Johann Brinell.

Brisbane industrial port (brewing, engineering, tanning, tobacco, shoes; oil pipeline from Moonie), capital of Queensland, E Australia, near the mouth of Brisbane River, dredged to carry ocean-going ships; population (1990) 1,301,700.

Brisbane Thomas Makdougall 1773–1860. Scottish soldier, colonial administrator, and astronomer. After serving in the Napoleonic Wars under Wellington, he was governor of New South

Wales 1821–25. Brisbane in Queensland is named after him. He catalogued over 7,000 stars.

Brissot Jacques Pierre 1754–1793. French revolutionary leader, born in Chartres. He became a member of the legislative assembly and the National Convention, but his party of moderate republicans, the *Girondins, or Brissotins, fell foul of Robespierre, and Brissot was guillotined.

bristlecone pine The oldest living species of *pine.

bristletail primitive wingless insect of the order Thysanura. Up to 2 cm/0.8 in long, bristletails have a body tapering from front to back, two long antennae, and three 'tails' at the rear end. They include the *silverfish* Lepisma saccharina and the *firebrat* Thermobia domestica. Two-tailed bristletails constitute another insect order, the Diplura. They live under stones and fallen branches, feeding on decaying material.

Bristol industrial port (aircraft engines, engineering, microelectronics, tobacco, chemicals, paper, printing), administrative headquarters of Avon, SW England; population (1991 est) 370,300. The old docks have been redeveloped for housing, industry, yachting facilities, and the National Lifeboat Museum. Further developments include a new city centre, with Brunel's Temple Meads railway station at its focus, and a weir across the Avon nearby to improve the waterside environment.

Bristow Eric 1957– . English darts player nicknamed 'the Crafty Cockney'. He has won all the game's major titles, including the world professional title a record five times between 1980 and 1986.

Britain or **Great Britain** island off the NW coast of Europe, one of the British Isles. It consists of *England, *Scotland, and *Wales, and is part of the *United Kingdom. The name is derived from the Roman name Britannia, which in turn is derived from ancient Celtic name of the inhabitants, *Bryttas*.

Britain, ancient period in the history of the British Isles (excluding Ireland) from prehistory to the Roman occupation. After the last glacial retreat of the Ice Age about 15,000 BC, Britain was inhabited by hunters who became neolithic farming villagers. They built stone circles and buried their chiefs in *barrow mounds. Around 400 BC Britain was conquered by the *Celts and 54 BC by the Romans under Julius Caesar; *Boudicca led an uprising against their occupation.

Britain, Battle of World War II air battle between German and British air forces over Britain lasting 10 July–31 Oct 1940.

Britannicus Tiberius Claudius *c.* AD 41–55. Roman prince, son of the Emperor Claudius and Messalina; so-called from his father's expedition to Britain. He was poisoned by Nero.

British Antarctic Territory colony created in 1962 and comprising all British territories S of latitude 60° S: the South Orkney Islands, the South Shetland Islands, the Antarctic Peninsula and all adjacent lands, and Coats Land, extending to the South Pole; total land area 660,000 sq km/170,874 sq mi. Population (exclusively scientific personnel): about 300.

British Broadcasting Corporation (BBC) the UK state-owned broadcasting network. It operates television and national and local radio stations, and is financed solely by the sale of television viewing licences; it is not allowed to carry advertisements. Overseas radio broadcasts (World Service) have a government subsidy.

British Columbia province of Canada on the Pacific
area 947,800 sq km/365,851 sq mi
capital Victoria
towns Vancouver, Prince George, Kamloops, Kelowna
physical Rocky Mountains and Coast Range; deeply indented coast; rivers include the Fraser and Columbia; over 80 lakes; more than half the land is forested
products fruit and vegetables; timber and wood products; fish; coal, copper, iron, lead; oil and natural gas; hydroelectricity
population (1991) 3,185,900
history Captain Cook explored the coast in 1778; a British colony was founded on Vancouver Island in 1849, and the gold rush of 1858 extended settlement to the mainland; it became a province in 1871. In 1885 the Canadian Pacific Railroad linking British Columbia to the E coast was completed.

British Council semiofficial organization set up 1935 (royal charter 1940) to promote a wider knowledge of the UK, excluding politics and commerce, and to develop cultural relations with other countries.

British Empire various territories all over the world conquered or colonized by Britain from about 1600, most now independent or ruled by other powers; the British Empire was at its largest at the end of World War I, with over 25% of the world's population and area. The *Commonwealth is composed of former and remaining territories of the British Empire.

British Empire, Order of the British order of chivalry, instituted by George V in 1917. There are military and civil divisions, and the ranks are GBE, Knight Grand Cross or Dame Grand Cross; KBE, Knight Commander; DBE, Dame Commander; CBE, Commander; OBE, Officer; MBE, Member.

British Expeditionary Force (BEF) British army serving in France in World War I 1914–18. Also the 1939–40 army in Europe in World War II, which was evacuated from Dunkirk, France.

British Honduras former name (until 1973) of *Belize.

British Indian Ocean Territory British colony in the Indian Ocean directly administered by the Foreign and Commonwealth Office. It consists of the Chagos Archipelago some 1,900 km/1,200 mi NE of Mauritius
area 60 sq km/23 sq mi
products copra, salt fish, tortoiseshell
population (1982) 3,000
history purchased in 1965 for $3 million by Britain from Mauritius to provide a joint US/UK base. The islands of Aldabra, Farquhar, and Desroches, some 485 km/300 mi N of Madagascar, originally formed part of the British Indian Ocean Territory but were returned to the administration of the Seychelles in 1976.

British Isles group of islands off the NW coast of Europe, consisting of Great Britain (England,

Wales, and Scotland), Ireland, the Channel Islands, the Orkney and Shetland islands, the Isle of Man, and many other islands that are included in various counties, such as the Isle of Wight, Scilly Isles, Lundy Island, and the Inner and Outer Hebrides. The islands are divided from Europe by the North Sea, Strait of Dover, and the English Channel, and face the Atlantic to the west.

British Legion organization to promote the welfare of British veterans of war service and their dependants. Established under the leadership of Douglas Haig in 1921 (royal charter 1925) it became the *Royal British Legion* 1971; it is nonpolitical. The sale on Remembrance Sunday of Flanders poppies made by disabled members raises much of its funds.

British Library national library of the UK. Created 1973, it comprises the *reference division* (the former library departments of the British Museum, being rehoused in Euston Road, London); *lending division* at Boston Spa, Yorkshire, from which full text documents and graphics can be sent by satellite link to other countries; *bibliographic services division* (incorporating the British National Bibliography); and the *National Sound Archive* in South Kensington, London.

British Museum largest museum of the UK. Founded in 1753, it opened in London in 1759. Rapid additions led to the constuction of the present buildings (1823–47). In 1881 the Natural History Museum was transferred to South Kensington.

British Petroleum (BP) one of the world's largest oil concerns and Britain's largest company, with more than 128,000 employees in 70 countries. It was formed as the Anglo-Persian Oil Company 1909 and acquired the chemical interests of the Distillers Company 1967.

British Somaliland British protectorate comprising over 176,000 sq km/67,980 sq mi of territory on the Somali coast of E Africa from 1884 until the independence of Somalia in 1960. British authorities were harassed by Somali nationalists under the leadership of Muhammad bin Abdullah Hassan.

British Standards Institute (BSI) UK national standards body. Although government funded, the institute is independent. The BSI interprets international technical standards for the UK, and also sets its own.

British Telecom (BT) British company that formed part of the Post Office until 1980, and was privatized in 1984. It is responsible for *telecommunications, including the telephone network, and radio and television broadcasting. Previously a monopoly, it now faces commercial competition for some of its services. It operates Britain's *viewdata network called *Prestel.

British Virgin Islands part of the *Virgin Islands group in the West Indies.

Brittany (French *Bretagne*, Breton *Breiz*) region of NW France in the Breton peninsula between the Bay of Biscay and the English Channel; area 27,200 sq km/10,499 sq mi; population (1987) 2,767,000. Its capital is Rennes and includes the *départements* of Côtes-du-Nord,

Finistère, Ille-et-Vilaine, and Morbihan. It is a farming region.

history Brittany was the Gallo-Roman province of Armorica after being conquered by Julius Caesar 56 BC. It was devastated by Norsemen after the Roman withdrawal. It was established under the name of Brittany in the 5th century AD by Celts fleeing the Anglo-Saxon invasion of Britain. It became a strong, expansionist state that maintained its cultural and political independence, despite pressure from the Carolingians, Normans, and Capetians. In 1171, the duchy of Brittany was inherited by Geoffrey, son of Henry II of England, and remained in the Angevin dynasty's possession until 1203, when Geoffrey's son Arthur was murdered by King *John, and the title passed to the Capetian Peter of Dreux. Under the Angevins, feudalism was introduced, and French influence increased under the Capetians. By 1547 it had been formally annexed by France, and the *Breton language was banned in education. A separatist movement developed after World War II, and there has been guerrilla activity.

Britten (Edward) Benjamin 1913–1976. English composer. He often wrote for the individual voice; for example, the role in the opera *Peter Grimes* 1945, based on verses by George Crabbe, was created for Peter *Pears. Among his many works are the *Young Person's Guide to the Orchestra* 1946; the chamber opera *The Rape of Lucretia* 1946; *Billy Budd* 1951; *A Midsummer Night's Dream* 1960; and *Death in Venice* 1973.

brittle-star any member of the echinoderm class Ophiuroidea. A brittle-star resembles a starfish, and has a small, central, rounded body and long, flexible, spiny arms used for walking. The small brittle-star *Amphipholis squamata* is greyish, about 4.5 cm/2 in across, and found on sea bottoms worldwide. It broods its young, and its arms can be luminous.

BRM abbreviation for *British Racing Motors* racing-car manufacturer founded 1949 by Raymond Mays (1899–1980). Their first Grand Prix win was 1959, and in the next 30 years they won 17 Grands Prix. Their world champions include Graham Hill.

Brno industrial city in central Czechoslovakia (chemicals, arms, textiles, machinery); population (1991) 388,000. Now the third largest city in Czechoslovakia, Brno was formerly the capital of the Austrian crown land of Moravia.

broadcasting the transmission of sound and vision programmes by *radio and *television. Broadcasting may be organized under private enterprise, as in the USA, or may operate under a compromise system, as in Britain, where there is a television and radio service controlled by the state-regulated *British Broadcasting Corporation (BBC) and also the commercial *Independent Television Commission (known as the Independent Broadcasting Authority before 1991).

Broadcasting Complaints Commission UK body responsible for dealing with complaints of invasion of privacy or unjust treatment on television or radio. It is a statutory body, formed 1981.

broad-leaved tree another name for a tree belonging to the *angiosperms, such as ash, beech, oak, maple, or birch. The leaves are generally broad and flat, in contrast to the needlelike leaves of most *conifers. See also *deciduous tree.

Broadmoor special hospital (established 1863) in Crowthorne, Berkshire, England, for those formerly described as 'criminally insane'. Patients are admitted if considered by a psychiatrist to be both mentally disordered and potentially dangerous. The average length of stay is eight years; in 1991 patients numbered 515.

Broads, Norfolk area of navigable lakes and rivers in England, see *Norfolk Broads.

Broadway major avenue in New York running from the tip of Manhattan NW and crossing Times Square at 42nd Street, at the heart of the theatre district, where Broadway is known as 'the Great White Way'. New York theatres situated outside this area are described as *off-Broadway*; those even smaller and farther away are *off-off-Broadway*.

broccoli variety of *cabbage.

Brodsky Joseph 1940– . Russian poet who emigrated to the USA in 1972. His work, often dealing with themes of exile, is admired for its wit and economy of language, particularly in its use of understatement. Many of his poems, written in Russian, have been translated into English (*A Part of Speech* 1980). More recently he has also written in English. He was awarded the Nobel Prize for Literature in 1987 and became US poet laureate 1991.

Broglie Louis de, 7th Duc de Broglie 1892–1987. French theoretical physicist. He established that all subatomic particles can be described either by particle equations or by wave equations, thus laying the foundations of wave mechanics. He was awarded the 1929 Nobel Prize for Physics.

Broglie Maurice de, 6th Duc de Broglie 1875–1960. French physicist. He worked on X-rays and gamma rays, and helped to establish the Einsteinian description of light in terms of photons. He was the brother of Louis de Broglie.

brome grass any annual grasses of the genus *Bromus* of the temperate zone; some are used for forage, but many are weeds.

bromeliad any tropical or subtropical plant of the pineapple family Bromeliaceae, usually with stiff leathery leaves and bright flower spikes.

bromide salt of the halide series containing the Br⁻ ion, which is formed when a bromine atom gains an electron.

bromine (Greek *bromos* 'stench') dark, reddish-brown, nonmetallic element, a volatile liquid at room temperature, symbol Br, atomic number 35, relative atomic mass 79.904. It is a member of the *halogen group, has an unpleasant odour, and is very irritating to mucous membranes. Its salts are known as bromides.

bromocriptine drug that mimics the actions of the naturally occurring biochemical substance dopamine, a neurotransmitter. Bromocriptine acts on the pituitary gland to inhibit the release of prolactin, the hormone that regulates lactation, and thus reduces or suppresses milk production. It is also used in the treatment of *Parkinson's disease.

bronchiole small-bore air tube found in the vertebrate lung responsible for delivering air to the main respiratory surfaces. Bronchioles lead off from the larger bronchus and branch extensively before terminating in the many thousand alveoli that form the bulk of lung tissue.

bronchitis inflammation of the bronchi (air passages) of the lungs, usually caused initially by a viral infection, such as a cold or flu. It is aggravated by environmental pollutants, especially smoking, and results in a persistent cough, irritated mucus-secreting glands, and large amounts of sputum.

bronchodilator drug that relieves obstruction of the airways by causing the bronchi and bronchioles to relax and widen. It is most useful in the treatment of *asthma.

bronchus one of a pair of large tubes (bronchii) branching off from the windpipe and passing into the vertebrate lung. Apart from their size, bronchii differ from the bronchioles in possessing cartilaginous rings, which give rigidity and prevent collapse during breathing movements.

Bronson Charles. Stage name of Charles Bunchinsky 1921– . US film actor. His films are mainly violent thrillers such as *Death Wish* 1974. He was one of *The Magnificent Seven* 1960.

Brontë three English novelists, daughters of a Yorkshire parson. *Charlotte* (1816–1855), notably with *Jane Eyre* 1847 and *Villette* 1853, reshaped autobiographical material into vivid narrative. *Emily* (1818–1848) in *Wuthering Heights* 1847 expressed the intensity and nature mysticism which also pervades her poetry (*Poems* 1846). The more modest talent of *Anne* (1820–1849) produced *Agnes Grey* 1847 and *The Tenant of Wildfell Hall* 1848.

brontosaurus former name of a type of large, plant-eating dinosaur, now better known as *apatosaurus.

bronze alloy of copper and tin, yellow or brown in colour. It is harder than pure copper, more suitable for *casting, and also resists *corrosion. Bronze may contain as much as 25% tin, together with small amounts of other metals, mainly lead.

Bronze Age stage of prehistory and early history when bronze became the first metal worked extensively and used for tools and weapons. It developed out of the Stone Age, preceded the Iron Age and may be dated 5000–1200 BC in the Middle East and about 2000–500 BC in Europe. Recent discoveries in Thailand suggest that the Far East, rather than the Middle East, was the cradle of the Bronze Age.

Bronzino Agnolo 1503–1572. Italian painter active in Florence, court painter to Cosimo I, Duke of Tuscany. He painted in an elegant, Mannerist style and is best known for portraits and the allegory *Venus, Cupid, Folly and Time* about 1545 (National Gallery, London).

Brook Peter 1925– . English director renowned for his experimental productions. His work with the Royal Shakespeare Company included a production of Shakespeare's *A Midsummer Night's Dream* 1970, set in a white gymnasium and combining elements of circus and commedia dell'arte. In the same year he established Le Centre International de Créations Théâtrales/The International Centre for Theatre

Research in Paris. Brook's later productions transcend Western theatre conventions and include *The Conference of the Birds* 1973, based on a Persian story, and *The Mahabarata* 1985/8, a cycle of three plays based on the Hindu epic. His films include *Lord of the Flies* 1962 and *Meetings with Remarkable Men* 1979.

Brooke Rupert (Chawner) 1887–1915. English poet, symbol of the World War I 'lost generation'. His five war sonnets, the best known of which is 'The Patriot', were published posthumously. Other notable works include 'Grantchester' and 'The Great Lover'.

Brookeborough Basil Brooke, Viscount Brookeborough 1888–1973. Unionist politician of Northern Ireland. He entered Parliament in 1929, held ministerial posts 1933–45, and was prime minister of Northern Ireland 1943–63. He was a staunch advocate of strong links with Britain.

Brooklands former UK motor racing track near Weybridge, Surrey. One of the world's first purpose-built circuits, it was opened 1907 as a testing ground for early motorcars. It was the venue for the first British Grand Prix (then known as the RAC Grand Prix) 1926. It was sold to aircraft builders Vickers 1946.

Brookner Anita 1928– . British novelist and art historian, whose novels include *Hotel du Lac* 1984, winner of the Booker prize, *A Misalliance* 1986, and *Latecomers* 1988.

Brooks Louise 1906–1985. US actress, known for her roles in silent films such as *A Girl in Every Port* 1928, *Die Büchse der Pandora/Pandora's Box*, and *Das Tagebuch einer Verlorenen/Diary of a Lost Girl* both 1929 and both directed by G W Pabst (1885–1967). At 25 she had appeared in 17 films. She retired from the screen 1938.

Brooks Mel. Stage name of Melvin Kaminsky 1926– . US film director and comedian, known for madcap and slapstick verbal humour. He became well known with his record album *The 2,000-Year-Old Man* 1960. His films include *The Producers* 1968, *Blazing Saddles* 1974, *Young Frankenstein* 1975, *History of the World Part I* 1981, and *To Be or Not to Be* 1983.

broom any shrub of the family Leguminosae, especially species of the *Cytisus* and *Spartium*, often cultivated for their bright yellow flowers.

Brouwer Adriaen 1605–1638. Flemish painter who studied with Frans Hals. He excelled in scenes of peasant revelry.

Brown Capability (Lancelot) 1715–1783. English landscape gardener. He acquired his nickname because of his continual enthusiasm for the 'capabilities' of natural landscapes.

Brown Charles Brockden 1771–1810. US novelist and magazine editor. He introduced the American Indian into fiction and is called the 'father of the American novel' for his *Wieland* 1798, *Ormond* 1799, *Edgar Huntly* 1799, and *Arthur Mervyn* 1800. His works also pioneered the Gothic and fantastic traditions in US fiction.

Brown Earle 1926– . US composer who pioneered *graphic notation and mobile form during the 1950s, as in *Available Forms II* 1958 for ensemble and two conductors. He was an associate of John *Cage.

Brown Ford Madox 1821–1893. British painter associated with the *Pre-Raphaelite Brotherhood. His pictures include *The Last of England* 1855 (Birmingham Art Gallery) and *Work* 1852–65 (City Art Gallery, Manchester), packed with realistic detail and symbolic incident.

Brown George, Baron George-Brown 1914–1985. British Labour politician. He entered Parliament in 1945, was briefly minister of works 1951, and contested the leadership of the party on the death of Gaitskell, but was defeated by Harold Wilson. He was secretary for economic affairs 1964–66 and foreign secretary 1966–68. He was created a life peer 1970.

Brown James 1928– . US rhythm-and-blues singer, a pioneer of funk. Staccato horn arrangements and shouted vocals characterize his hits, which include 'Please, Please, Please' 1956, 'Papa's Got a Brand New Bag' 1965, and 'Say It Loud, I'm Black and I'm Proud' 1968.

Brown John 1800–1859. US slavery abolitionist. With 18 men, on the night of 16 Oct 1859, he seized the government arsenal at Harper's Ferry in W Virginia, apparently intending to distribute weapons to runaway slaves who would then defend the mountain stronghold, which Brown hoped would become a republic of former slaves. On 18 Oct the arsenal was stormed by US Marines under Col Robert E *Lee. Brown was tried and hanged on 2 Dec, becoming a martyr and the hero of the popular song 'John Brown's Body' about 1860.

Brown John 1825–1883. Scottish servant and confidant of Queen Victoria from 1858.

Brown Robert 1773–1858. Scottish botanist, a pioneer of plant classification and the first to describe and name the cell nucleus.

brown dwarf hypothetical object less massive than a star, but heavier than a planet. Brown dwarfs would not have enough mass to ignite nuclear reactions at their centres, but would shine by heat released during their contraction from a gas cloud. Because of the difficulty of detection, no brown dwarfs have been spotted with certainty, but some astronomers believe that vast numbers of them may exist throughout the Galaxy.

Browne Thomas 1605–1682. English author and physician. Born in London, he travelled widely in Europe before settling in Norwich in 1637. His works display a richness of style as in *Religio Medici/The Religion of a Doctor* 1643, a justification of his profession; *Vulgar Errors* 1646, an examination of popular legend and superstition; *Urn Burial* and *The Garden of Cyrus* 1658; and *Christian Morals*, published posthumously in 1717.

Brownian movement the continuous random motion of particles in a fluid medium (gas or liquid) as they are subjected to impact from the molecules of the medium. The phenomenon was explained by Albert Einstein in 1905 but was observed as long ago as 1827 by the Scottish botanist Robert Brown.

Browning Robert 1812–1889. English poet, married to Elizabeth Barrett Browning. His work is characterized by the use of dramatic monologue and an interest in obscure literary and historical figures. It includes the play *Pippa Passes*

1841 and the poems 'The Pied Piper of Hamelin' 1842, 'My Last Duchess' 1842, 'Home Thoughts from Abroad' 1845, and 'Rabbi Ben Ezra' 1864.

Browns Ferry site of a nuclear power station on the Alabama River, central Alabama, USA. A nuclear accident in 1975 resulted in the closure of the plant for 18 months. This incident marked the beginning of widespread disenchantment with nuclear power in the USA.

Brownshirts the SA (*Sturmabteilung*), or Storm Troops, the private army of the German Nazi party, who derived their name from the colour of their uniform.

Bruce one of the chief Scottish noble houses. *Robert I (Robert the Bruce) and his son, David II, were both kings of Scotland descended from Robert de Bruis (died 1094), a Norman knight who arrived in England with William the Conqueror 1066.

Bruce James 1730–1794. Scottish explorer, the first European to reach the source of the Blue Nile 1770, and to follow the river downstream to Cairo 1773.

Bruce Robert. King of Scotland; see *Robert I.

Brücke, die (German 'the bridge') German Expressionist art movement 1905–13, formed in Dresden. Ernst Ludwig Kirchner was one of its founders, and Emil Nolde was a member 1906–07. Influenced by African art, they strove for spiritual significance, using raw colours to express different emotions. In 1911 the *Blaue Reiter took over as the leading group in German art.

Bruckner (Joseph) Anton 1824–1896. Austrian Romantic composer. He was cathedral organist at Linz 1856–68, and from 1868 he was professor at the Vienna Conservatoire. His works include many choral pieces and 11 symphonies, the last unfinished. His compositions were influenced by Richard *Wagner and Beethoven.

Brüderhof (German 'Society of Brothers') Christian Protestant sect with beliefs similar to the *Mennonites. They live in groups of families (single persons are assigned to a family), marry only within the sect (divorce is not allowed), and retain a 'modest' dress for women (cap or headscarf, and long skirts). In the USA they are known as Hutterites.

Brueghel family of Flemish painters. *Pieter Brueghel the Elder* (c. 1525–69) was one of the greatest artists of his time. He painted satirical and humorous pictures of peasant life, many of which include symbolic details illustrating folly and inhumanity, and a series of Months (five survive), including *Hunters in the Snow* (Kunsthistorisches Museum, Vienna).

Bruges (Flemish **Brugge**) historic city in NW Belgium; capital of W Flanders province, 16 km/ 10 mi from the North Sea, with which it is connected by canal; population (1991) 117,100. Bruges was the capital of medieval *Flanders and was the chief European wool manufacturing town as well as its chief market.

Brummell Beau (George Bryan) 1778–1840. British dandy and leader of fashion. He introduced long trousers as conventional day and evening wear for men. A friend of the Prince of Wales, the future George IV, he later quarrelled

with him. Gambling losses drove him in 1816 to exile in France, where he died in an asylum.

Brundtland Gro Harlem 1939– . Norwegian Labour politician. Environment minister 1974–76, she briefly took over as prime minister 1981, and was elected prime minister 1986 and again 1990. She chaired the World Commission on Environment and Development which produced the Brundtland Report, published as *Our Common Future* 1987.

Brundtland Report the findings of the World Commission on Environment and Development, published 1987 as *Our Common Future*. It stressed the necessity of environmental protection and popularized the phrase 'sustainable development'. The commission was chaired by the Norwegian prime minister Gro Harlem Brundtland.

Brunei Islamic Sultanate of (*Negara Brunei Darussalam*)
area 5,765 sq km/2,225 sq mi
capital Bandar Seri Begawan
towns Tutong, Seria, Kuala Belait
physical flat coastal plain with hilly lowland in W and mountains in E; 75% of the area is forested; the Limbang valley splits Brunei in two, and its cession to Sarawak 1890 is disputed by Brunei
head of state and of government HM Muda Hassanal Bolkiah Mu'izzaddin Waddaulah, Sultan of Brunei, from 1968
political system absolute monarchy
exports liquefied natural gas (world's largest producer) and oil, both expected to be exhausted by the year 2000
currency Brunei dollar
population (1993 est) 280,000 (65% Malay, 20% Chinese – few Chinese granted citizenship); growth rate 12% p.a.
languages Malay (official), Chinese (Hokkien), English
religion 60% Muslim (official)
GNP $14,120 per head (1987)
chronology
1888 Brunei became a British protectorate.
1941–45 Occupied by Japan.
1959 Written constitution made Britain responsible for defence and external affairs.
1962 Sultan began rule by decree.
1963 Proposal to join Malaysia abandoned.
1967 Sultan abdicated in favour of his son, Hassanal Bolkiah.
1971 Brunei given internal self-government.
1975 United Nations resolution called for independence for Brunei.
1984 Independence achieved from Britain, with Britain maintaining a small force to protect the oil-and gasfields.
1985 A 'loyal and reliable' political party, the Brunei National Democratic Party (BNDP), legalized.
1986 Death of former sultan, Sir Omar. Formation of multiethnic BNUP.
1988 BNDP banned.

Brunei Town former name (until 1970) of *Bandar Seri Begawan, Brunei.

Brunel Isambard Kingdom 1806–1859. British engineer and inventor. In 1833 he became engineer to the Great Western Railway, which adopted the 2.1 m/7 ft gauge on his advice. He built the

Clifton Suspension Bridge over the river Avon at Bristol and the Saltash Bridge over the river Tamar near Plymouth. His shipbuilding designs include the *Great Western* 1838, the first steamship to cross the Atlantic regularly; the *Great Britain* 1845, the first large iron ship to have a screw propeller; and the *Great Eastern* 1858, which laid the first transatlantic telegraph cable.

Brunel Marc Isambard 1769–1849. French-born British engineer and inventor, father of Isambard Kingdom Brunel. He constructed the Rotherhithe tunnel under the river Thames in London from Wapping to Rotherhithe 1825–43.

Brunelleschi Filippo 1377–1446. Italian Renaissance architect. One of the earliest and greatest Renaissance architects, he pioneered the scientific use of perspective. He was responsible for the construction of the dome of Florence Cathedral (completed 1438), a feat deemed impossible by many of his contemporaries.

Bruno Frank 1961– . English heavyweight boxer who challenged for the World Boxing Association (WBA) World Title against Tim Witherspoon in 1986 and for the Undisputed World Title against Mike Tyson in 1989. He retired 1989 but made a successful comeback 1992.

Bruno Giordano 1548–1600. Italian philosopher. He entered the Dominican order of monks 1563, but his sceptical attitude to Catholic doctrines forced him to flee Italy 1577. After visiting Geneva and Paris, he lived in England 1583–85, where he wrote some of his finest works. He was arrested by the *Inquisition 1593 in Venice and burned at the stake for his adoption of Copernican astronomy and his heretical religious views.

Bruno, St 1030–1101. German founder of the monastic Catholic *Carthusian order. He was born in Cologne, became a priest, and controlled the cathedral school of Rheims 1057–76. Withdrawing to the mountains near Grenoble after an ecclesiastical controversy, he founded the monastery at Chartreuse in 1084. Feast day 6 Oct.

Brunswick (German *Braunschweig*) industrial city (chemical engineering, precision engineering, food processing) in Lower Saxony, Germany; population (1988) 248,000. It was one of the chief cities of N Germany in the Middle Ages and a member of the *Hanseatic League. It was capital of the duchy of Brunswick from 1671.

Brussels (Flemish *Brussel*; French *Bruxelles*) capital of Belgium, industrial city (lace, textiles, machinery, chemicals); population (1987) 974,000 (80% French-speaking, the suburbs Flemish-speaking). It is the headquarters of the European Economic Community and since 1967 of the international secretariat of *NATO. First settled in the 6th century, and a city from 1312, Brussels became the capital of the Spanish Netherlands 1530 and of Belgium 1830.

Brussels sprout one of the small edible buds along the stem of a variety (*Brassica oleracea* var. *gemmifera*) of *cabbage.

Brussels, Treaty of pact of economic, political, cultural, and military alliance established 17 March 1948, for 50 years, by the UK, France, and the Benelux countries, joined by West Germany and Italy 1955. It was the forerunner of the North Atlantic Treaty Organization and the European Community.

Brutalism architectural style of the 1950s and 1960s that evolved from the work of Le Corbusier and Mies van der Rohe. It stresses fuctionalism and honesty to materials; steel and concrete are favoured. In the UK the style was developed by Alison and Peter Smithson (1928–).

Bruton John 1947– . Irish politician, leader of Fine Gael (United Ireland Party) from 1990 and prime minister from 1994. The collapse of the Fianna Fáil–Labour government Nov 1994 thrust Bruton, as leader of a new coalition with Labour, into the prime ministerial vacancy. He pledged himself to the continuation of the Anglo-Irish peace process as pursued by his predecessor Albert *Reynolds.

A trained lawyer and working farmer, Bruton made steady progress as party spokesman on agriculture, education, and industry and commerce before serving in the government of Garret FitzGerald 1982–87 and succeeding him as leader of Fine Gael 1990.

Brutus Marcus Junius *c.* 78–42 BC. Roman soldier, a supporter of *Pompey (against *Caesar) in the civil war. Pardoned by Caesar and raised to high office by him, he nevertheless plotted Caesar's assassination to restore the purity of the Republic. Brutus committed suicide when he was defeated (with *Cassius) by *Mark Antony, Caesar's lieutenant, at Philippi 42 BC.

Bruxelles French form of *Brussels, capital of Belgium.

Brynner Yul 1915–1985. Actor, in the USA from 1940, who made a shaven head his trademark. He played the king in *The King and I* both on stage 1951 and on film 1956, and was the leader of *The Magnificent Seven* 1960.

bryony either of two hedgerow climbing plants found in Britain: *white bryony* Bryonia dioca belonging to the gourd family Cucurbitaceae, and *black bryony* Tamus communis of the yam family Dioscoreaceae.

bryophyte member of the Bryophyta, a division of the plant kingdom containing three classes: the Hepaticae (*liverwort), Musci (*moss), and Anthocerotae (*hornwort). Bryophytes are generally small, low-growing, terrestrial plants with no vascular (water-conducting) system as in higher plants. Their life cycle shows a marked *alternation of generations. Bryophytes chiefly occur in damp habitats and require water for the dispersal of the male gametes (*antherozoids).

BSE abbreviation for *bovine spongiform encephalopathy*.

BST abbreviation for *British Summer Time*; *bovine somatotropin*.

BT abbreviation for *British Telecom*.

bubble chamber in physics, a device for observing the nature and movement of atomic particles, and their interaction with radiations. It is a vessel filled with a superheated liquid through which ionizing particles move and collide. The paths of these particles are shown by strings of bubbles, which can be photographed and studied. By using a pressurized liquid medium instead of a gas, it overcomes drawbacks inherent in the earlier *cloud chamber. It was invented by Donald *Glaser 1952.

bubble memory in computing, a memory device based on the creation of small 'bubbles' on a magnetic surface. Bubble memories typically store up to 4 megabits (4 million *bits) of information. They are not sensitive to shock and vibration, unlike other memory devices such as disc drives, yet, like magnetic discs, they are non-volatile and do not lose their information when the computer is switched off.

Bubiyan island off Kuwait, occupied by Iraq 1990. On 28 Feb 1991, following Allied success in the *Gulf War, Iraqi troops were withdrawn.

Bubka Sergey 1963– . Russian pole vaulter who achieved the world's first six-metre vault in 1985. World champion in 1983, he was unbeaten in a major event from 1981 to 1990. From 1984 he has broken the world record on 28 occasions.

bubonic plague epidemic disease of the Middle Ages; see *plague and *Black Death.

Bucaramanga industrial (coffee, tobacco, cacao, cotton) and commercial city in N central Colombia; population (1985) 493,929. It was founded by the Spanish 1622.

buccaneer member of any of various groups of seafarers who plundered Spanish ships and colonies on the Spanish American coast in the 17th century. Unlike true pirates, they were acting on (sometimes spurious) commission.

Bucer Martin 1491–1551. German Protestant reformer, Regius professor of divinity at Cambridge University from 1549, who tried to reconcile the views of his fellow Protestants Luther and Zwingli with the significance of the eucharist.

Buchan John, Baron Tweedsmuir 1875–1940. Scottish politician and author. Called to the Bar 1901, he was Conservative member of Parliament for the Scottish universities 1927–35, and governor general of Canada 1934–40. His adventure stories, today criticized for their anti-semitism, include *The Thirty-Nine Steps* 1915, *Greenmantle* 1916, and *The Three Hostages* 1924.

Bucharest (Romanian **Bucureşti**) capital and largest city of Romania; population (1985) 1,976,000, the conurbation of Bucharest district having an area of 1,520 sq km/587 sq mi and a population of 2,273,000. It was originally a citadel built by Vlad the Impaler (see *Dracula) to stop the advance of the Ottoman invasion in the 14th century. Bucharest became the capital of the princes of Wallachia 1698 and of Romania 1861. Savage fighting took place in the city during Romania's 1989 revolution.

Buchenwald site of a Nazi *concentration camp 1937–45 at a village NE of Weimar, E Germany.

Buchner Eduard 1860–1917. German chemist who researched the process of fermentation. In 1897 he observed that fermentation could be produced mechanically, by cell-free extracts. Buchner argued that it was not the whole yeast cell that produced fermentation, but only the presence of the enzyme he named zymase. Nobel prize 1907.

Buck Pearl S(ydenstricker) 1892–1973. US novelist. Daughter of missionaries to China, she spent much of her life there and wrote novels about Chinese life, such as *East Wind–West Wind* 1930 and *The Good Earth* 1931, for which she received a Pulitzer prize 1932. She received the Nobel Prize for Literature 1938.

Buckingham George Villiers, 1st Duke of Buckingham 1592–1628. English courtier, adviser to James I and later Charles I. After Charles's accession, Buckingham attempted to form a Protestant coalition in Europe, which led to war with France, but he failed to relieve the Protestants (*Huguenots) besieged in La Rochelle 1627. This added to his unpopularity with Parliament, and he was assassinated.

Buckingham George Villiers, 2nd Duke of Buckingham 1628–1687. English politician, a member of the *Cabal under Charles II. A dissolute son of the first duke, he was brought up with the royal children. His play *The Rehearsal* satirized the style of the poet Dryden, who portrayed him as Zimri in *Absalom and Achitophel*.

Buckingham Palace London home of the British sovereign, built 1703 for the duke of Buckingham, but bought by George III 1762 and reconstructed by John *Nash 1821–36; a new front was added 1913.

Buckinghamshire county in SE central England
area 1,880 sq km/726 sq mi
towns Aylesbury (administrative headquarters), Buckingham, High Wycombe, Beaconsfield, Olney, Milton Keynes
products furniture, chiefly beech; agricultural goods
population (1991) 619,500
famous people William Herschel, George Gilbert Scott, Edmund Waller, John Hampden, Ben Nicholson.

buckminsterfullerene form of carbon, made up of molecules (buckyballs) consisting of 60 carbon atoms arranged in 12 pentagons and 20 hexagons to form a perfect sphere. It was named after the US architect and engineer Buckminster *Fuller because of its structural similarity to the geodesic dome that he designed. See *fullerene.

Bucks abbreviation for ***Buckinghamshire**.

buckthorn any of several thorny shrubs of the family Rhamnaceae. The buckthorn *Rhamnus catharticus* is native to Britain and has berries formerly used in medicine as a purgative.

buckwheat any of several plants of the genus *Fagopyrum*, family Polygonaceae. The name usually refers to *F. esculentum*, which grows to about 1 m/3 ft and can grow on poor soil in a short summer. The highly nutritious black, triangular seeds (groats) are consumed by both animals and humans. They can be eaten either cooked whole or or as a cracked meal (kasha) or ground into flour, often made into pancakes.

bud undeveloped shoot usually enclosed by protective scales; inside is a very short stem and numerous undeveloped leaves, or flower parts, or both. Terminal buds are found at the tips of shoots, while axillary buds develop in the *axils of the leaves, often remaining dormant unless the terminal bud is removed or damaged. Adventitious buds may be produced anywhere on the plant, their formation sometimes stimulated by an injury, such as that caused by pruning.

Budapest capital of Hungary, industrial city

(chemicals, textiles) on the river Danube; population (1989) 2,115,000. Buda, on the right bank of the Danube, became the Hungarian capital 1867 and was joined with Pest, on the left bank, 1872.

Buddha 'enlightened one', title of Prince **Gautama Siddhārtha** c. 563–483 BC. Religious leader, founder of Buddhism, born at Lumbini in Nepal. At the age of 29 he left his wife and son and a life of luxury, to escape from the material burdens of existence. After six years of austerity he realized that asceticism, like overindulgence, was futile, and chose the middle way of meditation. He became enlightened under a bo, or bodhi, tree near Buddh Gaya in Bihar, India. He began teaching at Varanasi, and founded the Sangha, or order of monks. He spent the rest of his life travelling around N India, and died at Kusinagara in Uttar Pradesh.

Buddhism one of the great world religions, which originated in India about 500 BC. It derives from the teaching of the Buddha, who is regarded as one of a series of such enlightened beings; there are no gods. The chief doctrine is that of **karma**, good or evil deeds meeting an appropriate reward or punishment either in this life or (through reincarnation) a long succession of lives. The main divisions in Buddhism are **Theravāda** (or **Hīnayāna**) in SE Asia and **Mahāyāna** in N Asia; **Lamaism** in Tibet and **Zen** in Japan are among the many Mahāyāna sects. Its symbol is the lotus. There are over 247.5 million Buddhists worldwide.

budding type of *asexual reproduction in which an outgrowth develops from a cell to form a new individual. Most yeasts reproduce in this way.

buddleia any shrub or tree of the tropical genus *Buddleia*, family Buddleiaceae. The purple or white flower heads of the butterfly bush *B. davidii* attract large numbers of butterflies.

Budge Donald 1915– . US tennis player. He was the first to perform the Grand Slam when he won the Wimbledon, French, US, and Australian championships all in 1938.

budgerigar small Australian parakeet *Melopsittacus undulatus* that feeds mainly on grass seeds. Normally it is bright green, but yellow, white, blue, and mauve varieties have been bred for the pet market.

budget estimate of income and expenditure for some future period, used in financial planning. National budgets set out estimates of government income and expenditure and generally include projected changes in taxation and growth. Interim budgets are not uncommon, in particular, when dramatic changes in economic conditions occur. Governments will sometimes construct a budget deficit or surplus as part of macroeconomic policy.

Buenos Aires capital and industrial city of Argentina, on the S bank of the Río de la Plata; population (1991) 2,961,000, metropolitan area 7,950,400. It was founded 1536, and became the capital 1853.

buffalo either of two species of wild cattle. The Asiatic water buffalo *Bubalis bubalis* is found domesticated throughout S Asia and wild in parts of India and Nepal. It likes moist conditions.

Usually grey or black, up to 1.8 m/6 ft high, both sexes carry large horns. The African buffalo *Syncerus caffer* is found in Africa, south of the Sahara, where there is grass, water, and cover in which to retreat. There are a number of subspecies, the biggest up to 1.6 m/5 ft high, and black, with massive horns set close together over the head. The name is also commonly applied to the American *bison.

buffer in computing, a part of the *memory used to store data temporarily while it is waiting to be used. For example, a program might store data in a printer buffer until the printer is ready to print it.

buffer mixture of chemical compounds chosen to maintain a steady *pH. The commonest buffers consist of a mixture of a weak organic acid and one of its salts or a mixture of acid salts of phosphoric acid. The addition of either an acid or a base causes a shift in the *chemical equilibrium, thus keeping the pH constant.

bug in computing, an error in a program. It can be an error in the logical structure of a program or a syntax error, such as a spelling mistake. Some bugs cause a program to fail immediately; others remain dormant, causing problems only when a particular combination of events occurs. The process of finding and removing errors from a program is called **debugging**.

bug in entomology, an insect belonging to the order Hemiptera. All these have two pairs of wings with forewings partly thickened. They also have piercing mouthparts adapted for sucking the juices of plants or animals, the 'beak' being tucked under the body when not in use.

Bugatti racing and sports-car company, founded by the Italian Ettore Bugatti (1881–1947). The first car was produced 1908, but it was not until 1924 that one of the great Bugattis, Type 35, was produced. Bugatti cars are credited with more race wins than any others. The company was taken over by Hispano Suiza after Bugatti's death 1947.

buggery or *sodomy* anal intercourse by a man with another man or a woman, or sexual intercourse by a man or woman with an animal (bestiality). In English law, buggery may be committed by a man with his wife, or with another man in private if both parties consent and are over 21 years old. In all other circumstances it is an offence.

bugle in music, a valveless brass instrument with a shorter tube and less flared bell than the trumpet. Constructed of copper plated with brass, it has long been used as a military instrument for giving a range of signals based on the tones of a harmonic series. The bugle is conical whereas the trumpet is cylindrical.

bugle any of a genus *Ajuga* of low-growing plants of the mint family Labiatae, with spikes of white, pink, or blue flowers. They are often grown as ground cover.

bugloss any of several genera of plants of the family Boraginaceae, distinguished by their rough, bristly leaves and small blue flowers.

buhl alternative spelling for *boulle, a type of marquetry.

building society in the UK, a financial institution that attracts investment in order to lend money, repayable at interest, for the purchase or building of a house on security of a *mortgage. Since the 1970s building societies have considerably expanded their services and in many ways now compete with clearing banks.

Bujones Fernando 1955– . US ballet dancer who joined American Ballet Theater 1972. A virtuoso performer, he has danced leading roles both in the major classics and in contemporary ballets, including *Swan Lake*, *Bayadere*, and *Fancy Free*.

Bukharest alternative form of *Bucharest, capital of Romania.

Bukharin Nikolai Ivanovich 1888–1938. Soviet politician and theorist. A moderate, he was the chief Bolshevik thinker after Lenin. Executed on Stalin's orders for treason 1938, he was posthumously rehabilitated 1988.

Bulawayo industrial city and railway junction in Zimbabwe; population (1982) 415,000. It lies at an altitude of 1,355 m/4,450 ft on the river Matsheumlope, a tributary of the Zambezi, and was founded on the site of the kraal (enclosed village), burned down 1893, of the Matabele chief, Lobenguela. It produces agricultural and electrical equipment. The former capital of Matabeleland, Bulawayo developed with the exploitation of gold mines in the neighbourhood.

bulb underground bud with fleshy leaves containing a reserve food supply and with roots growing from its base. Bulbs function in vegetative reproduction and are characteristic of many monocotyledonous plants such as the daffodil, snowdrop, and onion. Bulbs are grown on a commercial scale in temperate countries, such as England and the Netherlands.

bulbul small fruit-eating passerine bird of the family Pycnonotidae. There are about 120 species, mainly in the forests of the Old World tropics.

Bulgakov Mikhail Afanasyevich 1891–1940. Russian novelist and dramatist. His novel *The White Guard* 1924, dramatized as *The Days of the Turbins* 1926, deals with the Revolution and the civil war.

Bulganin Nikolai 1895–1975. Soviet politician and military leader. His career began in 1918 when he joined the Cheka, the Soviet secret police. He helped to organize Moscow's defence in World War II, became a marshal of the USSR 1947, and was minister of defence 1947–49 and 1953–55. On the fall of Malenkov he became prime minister (chair of Council of Ministers) 1955–58 until ousted by Khrushchev.

Bulgaria Republic of (*Republika Bulgaria*)
area 110,912 sq km/42,812 sq mi
capital Sofia
towns Plovdiv, Ruse; Black Sea ports Burgas and Varna
physical lowland plains in N and SE separated by mountains that cover three-quarters of the country
head of state Zhelyu Zhelev from 1990
head of government (interim) Reneta Indjova from 1994
political system emergent democratic republic
exports textiles, leather, chemicals, nonferrous metals, timber, machinery, tobacco, cigarettes (world's largest exporter)

currency lev
population (1993 est) 9,020,000 (including 900,000–1,500,000 ethnic Turks, concentrated in S and NE); growth rate 0.1% p.a.
languages Bulgarian, Turkish
religions Eastern Orthodox Christian 90%, Sunni Muslim 10%
GNP $1,840 per head (1991)
chronology
1908 Bulgaria became a kingdom independent of Turkish rule.
1944 Soviet invasion of German-occupied Bulgaria.
1946 Monarchy abolished and communist-dominated people's republic proclaimed.
1947 Soviet-style constitution adopted.
1949 Death of Georgi Dimitrov, the communist government leader.
1954 Election of Todor Zhivkov as Communist Party general secretary; made nation a loyal satellite of USSR.
1971 Constitution modified; Zhivkov elected president.
1985–89 Large administrative and personnel changes made haphazardly under Soviet stimulus.
1987 New electoral law introduced multicandidate elections.
1989 Programme of 'Bulgarianization' resulted in mass exodus of Turks to Turkey. Nov: Zhivkov ousted by Petar Mladenov. Dec: opposition parties allowed to form.
1990 April: BCP renamed Bulgarian Socialist Party (BSP). Aug: Dr Zhelyu Zhelev elected president. Nov: government headed by Andrei Lukanov resigned, replaced Dec by coalition led by Dimitur Popov.
1991 July: new constitution adopted. Oct: UDF beat BSP in general election by narrow margin; formation of first noncommunist, UDF-minority government under Filip Dimitrov.
1992 Zhelev became Bulgaria's first directly elected president. Dimitrov replaced by Lyuben Berov and nonparty government.
1993 Formal invitation to apply for European Community (now European Union) membership.
1994 Berov resigned due to ill-health. Parliament

dissolved; Reneta Indjova appointed interim premier pending general election.

Bulgarian member of an ethnic group living mainly in Bulgaria. There are 8–8.5 million speakers of Bulgarian, a Slavic language belonging to the Indo-European family. The Bulgarians use the Cyrillic alphabet.

Bulge, Battle of the or *Ardennes offensive* in World War II, Hitler's plan, code-named 'Watch on the Rhine', for a breakthrough by his field marshal *Rundstedt aimed at the US line in the Ardennes 16 Dec 1944–28 Jan 1945. There were 77,000 Allied casualties and 130,000 German, including Hitler's last powerful reserve, his Panzer elite. Although US troops were encircled for some weeks at Bastogne, the German counteroffensive failed.

bulgur wheat cracked whole wheat, made by cooking the grains, then drying and cracking them. It is widely eaten in the Middle East. Coarse bulgur may be cooked in the same way as rice; more finely ground bulgur is mixed with minced meat to make a paste that may be eaten as a dip with salad, or shaped and stuffed before being grilled or fried.

bulimia (Greek 'ox hunger') condition of continuous, uncontrolled hunger. Considered a counteraction to stress or depression, this eating disorder is found chiefly in young women. When compensated for by forced vomiting or overdoses of laxatives, the condition is called *bulimia nervosa*. It is sometimes associated with *anorexia.

bull speculator who buys stocks or shares on the stock exchange expecting a rise in the price in order to sell them later at a profit, the opposite of a *bear. In a bull market, prices rise and bulls profit.

bull or *papal bull* document or edict issued by the pope; so called from the circular seals (medieval Latin *bulla*) attached to them. Some of the most celebrated bulls include Leo X's condemnation of Luther 1520 and Pius IX's proclamation of papal infallibility 1870.

Bull John. Imaginary figure personifying England; see *John Bull.

Bull John c. 1562–1628. British composer, organist, and virginalist. Most of his output is for keyboard, and includes *'God Save the King'. He also wrote sacred vocal music.

bulldog British dog of ancient but uncertain origin. The head is broad and square, with deeply wrinkled cheeks, small folded ears, and the nose laid back between the eyes. The bulldog grows to about 45 cm/18 in at the shoulder.

bullfighting the national sport of Spain (where there are more than 400 bullrings), which is also popular in Mexico, Portugal, and much of Latin America. It involves the ritualized taunting of a bull in a circular ring, until its eventual death at the hands of the matador. Originally popular in Greece and Rome, it was introduced into Spain by the Moors in the 11th century.

bullfinch Eurasian finch *Pyrrhula pyrrhula*, with a thick head and neck, and short heavy bill. It is small and blue-grey or black, the males being reddish and the females brown on the breast. Bullfinches are 15 cm/6 in long, and usually seen in pairs. They feed on tree buds as well as seeds and berries, and are usually seen in woodland.

They also live in the Aleutians and on the Alaska mainland.

bullhead or *miller's thumb* small fish *Cottus gobio* found in fresh water in the northern hemisphere, often under stones. It has a large head, a spine on the gill cover, and grows to 10 cm/4 in.

bullroarer musical instrument used by Australian Aborigines during religious rites. It consists of a piece of wood or stone, fastened to a cord, and is twirled around the head to make a whirring noise. It is a highly sacred object carved with mythical designs.

Bull Run, Battles of in the American Civil War, two victories for the Confederate army under General Robert E Lee at *Manassas* Junction, NE Virginia: *First Battle of Bull Run* 21 July 1861; *Second Battle of Bull Run* 29–30 Aug 1862.

bull terrier heavily built, smooth-coated breed of dog, usually white, originating as a cross between a terrier and a bulldog. It grows to about 40 cm/16 in tall, and was formerly used in *bull-baiting. Pit bull terriers are used in illegal dog fights.

Bülow Bernhard, Prince von 1849–1929. German diplomat and politician. He was chancellor of the German Empire 1900–09 under Kaiser Wilhelm II and, holding that self-interest was the only rule for any state, adopted attitudes to France and Russia that unintentionally reinforced the trend towards opposing European power groups: the *Triple Entente (Britain, France, Russia) and *Triple Alliance (Germany, Austria–Hungary, Italy).

bulrush either of two plants: the great reed mace or cat's tail *Typha latifolia* with chocolate-brown tight-packed flower spikes reaching up to 15 cm/6 in long; and a type of sedge *Scirpus lacustris* with tufts of reddish-brown flowers at the top of a rounded, rushlike stem.

bumblebee any large *bee, 2–5 cm/1–2 in, usually dark-coloured but banded with yellow, orange, or white, belonging to the genus *Bombus*.

Bunker Hill, Battle of the first significant engagement in the *American Revolution, 17 June 1775, near a small hill in Charlestown (now part of Boston), Massachusetts, USA; the battle actually took place on Breed's Hill. Although the colonists were defeated they were able to retreat to Boston and suffered fewer casualties than the British.

Bunsen Robert Wilhelm von 1811–1899. German chemist credited with the invention of the *Bunsen burner*. His name is also given to the carbon–zinc electric cell, which he invented 1841 for use in arc lamps. In 1859 he discovered two new elements, caesium and rubidium.

bunsen burner gas burner used in laboratories, consisting of a vertical metal tube through which a fine jet of fuel gas is directed. Air is drawn in through airholes near the base of the tube and the mixture is ignited and burns at the tube's upper opening.

Bunshaft Gordon 1909–1990. US architect whose Modernist buildings include the first to be completely enclosed in curtain walling (walls which hang from a rigid steel frame), the Lever Building 1952 in New York. He also designed the Heinz Company's UK headquarters 1965 at Hayes Park, London.

bunting any of a number of sturdy, finchlike, passerine birds with short, thick bills, of the family Emberizidae, especially the genera *Passerim* and *Emberiza*. Most of these brightly coloured birds are native to the New World.

Buñuel Luis 1900–1983. Spanish Surrealist film director. He collaborated with Salvador Dali on *Un Chien andalou* 1928 and *L'Age d'or/The Golden Age* 1930, and established his solo career with *Los olvidados/The Young and the Damned* 1950. His works are often anticlerical, with black humour and erotic imagery.

Bunyan John 1628–1688. English author. A Baptist, he was imprisoned in Bedford 1660–72 for unlicensed preaching. During a second jail sentence 1675 he started to write *The Pilgrim's Progress*, the first part of which was published 1678. Other works include *Grace Abounding* 1666, *The Life and Death of Mr Badman* 1680, and *The Holy War* 1682.

buoy floating object used to mark channels for shipping or warn of hazards to navigation. Buoys come in different shapes, such as a pole (spar buoy), cylinder (car buoy), and cone (nun buoy). Light buoys carry a small tower surmounted by a flashing lantern, and bell buoys house a bell, which rings as the buoy moves up and down with the waves. Mooring buoys are heavy and have a ring on top to which a ship can be tied.

buoyancy lifting effect of a fluid on a body wholly or partly immersed in it. This was studied by *Archimedes in the 3rd century BC.

bur or *burr* in botany, a type of 'false fruit' or *pseudocarp, surrounded by numerous hooks; for instance, that of burdock *Arctium*, where the hooks are formed from bracts surrounding the flowerhead. Burs catch in the feathers or fur of passing animals, and thus may be dispersed over considerable distances.

Burbage Richard *c.* 1567–1619. English actor. He is thought to have been Shakespeare's original Hamlet, Othello, and Lear. He also appeared in first productions of works by Ben Jonson, Thomas Kyd, and John Webster. His father *James Burbage* (*c.* 1530–1597) built the first English playhouse, known as 'the Theatre'; his brother *Cuthbert Burbage* (*c.* 1566–1636) built the original *Globe Theatre 1599 in London.

burbot long, rounded fish *Lota lota* of the cod family, the only one living entirely in fresh water. Up to 1 m/3 ft long, it lives on the bottom of clear lakes and rivers, often in holes or under rocks, throughout Europe, Asia, and North America.

burdock any of the bushy herbs belonging to the genus *Arctium* of the family Compositae, characterized by hairy leaves and ripe fruit enclosed in *burs with strong hooks.

bureaucracy organization whose structure and operations are governed to a high degree by written rules and a hierarchy of offices; in its broadest sense, all forms of administration, and in its narrowest, rule by officials.

Burgenland federal state of SE Austria, extending S from the Danube along the western border of the Hungarian plain; area 4,000 sq km/ 1,544 sq mi; population (1989) 267,200. It is a largely agricultural region adjoining the Neusiedler See, and produces timber, fruit, sugar, wine, lignite, antimony, and limestone. Its capital is Eisenstadt.

Burges William 1827–1881. English Gothic Revival architect and designer. His style is characterized by sumptuous interiors with carving, painting, and gilding. His chief works are Cork Cathedral 1862–76, and additions to and the remodelling of Cardiff Castle 1868–85 and Castle Coch near Cardiff 1875–91.

Burgess Anthony. Pen name of Anthony John Burgess Wilson 1917–1993. English novelist, critic, and composer. His prolific work includes *A Clockwork Orange* 1962, set in a future London terrorized by teenage gangs, and the panoramic *Earthly Powers* 1980. His vision has been described as bleak and pessimistic, but his work is also comic and satiric, as in his novels featuring the poet Enderby.

Burgess Shale Site site of unique fossil-bearing rock formations created 530 million years ago by a mud slide, in Yoho National Park, British Columbia, Canada. The shales in this corner of the Rocky Mountains contain more than 120 species of marine invertebrate fossils. Although discovered 1909 by US geologist Charles Walcott, the Burgess Shales have only recently been used as evidence in the debate concerning the evolution of life. In *Wonderful Life* 1990 Stephen Jay Gould drew attention to a body of scientific opinion interpreting the fossil finds as evidence of parallel early evolutionary trends extinguished by chance rather than natural selection. However, recently both Gould's theories and the site's supposed uniqueness have been called into question by Richard Fortey and Derek Briggs after they re-examined the Burgess Shale fauna.

burgh former unit of Scottish local government, referring to town enjoying degree of self-government, abolished 1975; the terms **burgh** and *royal burgh* once gave mercantile privilege but are now only an honorary distinction.

burgh (burh or borough) archaic form of *borough.

Burgh Hubert de died 1243. English *justiciar and regent of England. He began his career in the administration of Richard I, and was promoted to the justiciarship by King John; he remained in that position under Henry III from 1216 until his dismissal. He was a supporter of King John against the barons, and ended French intervention in England by his defeat of the French fleet in the Strait of Dover 1217. He reorganized royal administration and the Common Law.

Burghley William Cecil, Baron Burghley 1520–1598. English politician, chief adviser to Elizabeth I as secretary of state from 1558 and Lord High Treasurer from 1572. He was largely responsible for the religious settlement of 1559, and took a leading role in the events preceding the execution of Mary Queen of Scots 1587.

burgher term used from the 11th century to describe citizens of *burghs who were freemen of a burgh, and had the right to participate in its government. They usually had to possess a house within the burgh.

burglary offence committed when a trespasser

enters a building intending to steal, do damage to property, grievously harm any person, or rape a woman. Entry needs only be effective so, for example, a person who puts their hand through a broken shop window to steal something may be guilty of burglary.

Burgoyne John 1722–1792. British general and dramatist. He served in the American War of Independence and surrendered 1777 to the colonists at Saratoga, New York State, in one of the pivotal battles of the war. He wrote comedies, among them *The Maid of the Oaks* 1775 and *The Heiress* 1786. He figures in George Bernard Shaw's play *The Devil's Disciple* 1896.

Burgundy ancient kingdom in the valleys of the rivers Rhône and Saône in E France and SW Germany, partly corresponding with modern-day Burgundy. Settled by the Teutonic Burgundi around AD 443, and brought under Frankish control 534, Burgundy played a central role in the medieval history of NW Europe.

Burgundy (French *Bourgogne*) modern region and former duchy of France that includes the *départements* of Côte-d'Or, Nièvre, Sâone-et-Loire, and Yonne; area 31,600 sq km/12,198 sq mi; population (1986) 1,607,000. Its capital is Dijon.

Burke Edmund 1729–1797. British Whig politician and political theorist, born in Dublin, Ireland. In Parliament from 1765, he opposed the government's attempts to coerce the American colonists, for example in *Thoughts on the Present Discontents* 1770, and supported the emancipation of Ireland, but denounced the French Revolution, for example in *Reflections on the Revolution in France* 1790.

Burke Martha Jane *c.* 1852–1903. Real name of US heroine *Calamity Jane.

Burke Robert O'Hara 1820–1861. Australian explorer who made the first south-north crossing of Australia (from Victoria to the Gulf of Carpentaria), with William Wills (1834–1861). Both died on the return journey, and only one of their party survived. He was born in Galway, Ireland, and became a police inspector in the goldfields of Victoria.

Burke William 1792–1829. Irish murderer. He and his partner William Hare, living in Edinburgh, sold the body of an old man who had died from natural causes in their lodging house. After that, they increased their supplies by murdering at least 15 people. Burke was hanged on the evidence of Hare. Hare is said to have died a beggar in London in the 1860s.

Burke's Peerage popular name of the *Genealogical and Heraldic History of the Peerage, Baronetage, and Knightage of the United Kingdom*, first issued by John Burke 1826. The most recent edition was 1970.

Burkina Faso The People's Democratic Republic of (formerly *Upper Volta*)
area 274,122 sq km/105,811 sq mi
capital Ouagadougou
towns Bobo-Dioulasso, Koudougou
physical landlocked plateau with hills in W and SE; headwaters of the river Volta; semiarid in N, forest and farmland in S
environment tropical savanna subject to overgrazing and deforestation

head of state Blaise Compaoré from 1987
head of government Roch Christian Kabore from 1994
political system transitional
exports cotton, groundnuts, livestock, hides, skins, sesame, cereals
currency CFA franc
population (1993 est) 9,810,000; growth rate 2.4% p.a.
languages French (official); about 50 native Sudanic languages spoken by 90% of population
religions animist 53%, Sunni Muslim 36%, Roman Catholic 11%
GNP $350 per head (1991)
chronology
1958 Became a self-governing republic within the French Community.
1960 Independence from France, with Maurice Yaméogo as the first president.
1966 Military coup led by Col Lamizana. Constitution suspended, political activities banned, and a supreme council of the armed forces established.
1969 Ban on political activities lifted.
1970 Referendum approved a new constitution leading to a return to civilian rule.
1974 After experimenting with a mixture of military and civilian rule, Lamizana reassumed full power.
1977 Ban on political activities removed. Referendum approved a new constitution based on civilian rule.
1978 Lamizana elected president.
1980 Lamizana overthrown in bloodless coup led by Col Zerbo.
1982 Zerbo ousted in a coup by junior officers. Major Ouédraogo became president and Thomas Sankara prime minister.
1983 Sankara seized complete power.
1984 Upper Volta renamed Burkina Faso, 'land of upright men'.
1987 Sankara killed in coup led by Blaise Compaoré.
1989 New government party ODP–MT formed by merger of other pro-government parties. Coup against Compaoré foiled.
1991 New constitution approved. Compaoré re-elected president.
1992 Multiparty elections won by FP–Popular Front, renamed the CNPP–PSD. New government formed.

burlesque in the 17th and 18th centuries, a form of satirical comedy parodying a particular play or dramatic genre. For example, John *Gay's *The Beggar's Opera* 1728 is a burlesque of 18th-century opera, and Richard Brinsley *Sheridan's *The Critic* 1777 satirizes the sentimentality in contemporary drama. In the USA from the mid-19th century, burlesque referred to a sex and comedy show invented by Michael Bennett Leavitt 1866 with acts including acrobats, singers, and comedians. During the 1920s striptease was introduced in order to counteract the growing popularity of the movies; Gypsy Rose Lee was the most famous stripper. Burlesque was frequently banned in the USA.

Burlington Richard Boyle, 3rd Earl of Burlington 1694–1753. British architectural patron and architect; one of the premier exponents of the Palladian style in Britain. His buildings, such as Chiswick House, London, 1725–29, are characterized by absolute adherence to the Classical rules. His major protégé was William *Kent.

Burman member of the largest ethnic group in Myanmar (formerly Burma). The Burmans, speakers of a Sino-Tibetan language, migrated from the hills of Tibet, settling in the areas around Mandalay by the 11th century AD.

burn in medecine, destruction of body tissue by extremes of temperature, corrosive chemicals, electricity, or radiation. *First-degree burns* may cause reddening; *second-degree burns* cause blistering and irritation but usually heal spontaneously; *third-degree burns* are disfiguring and may be life-threatening.

Burne-Jones Edward Coley 1833–1898. English painter. In 1856 he was apprenticed to the Pre-Raphaelite painter Dante Gabriel *Rossetti, who remained a dominant influence. His paintings, inspired by legend and myth, were characterized by elongated forms as in *King Cophetua and the Beggar Maid* 1880–84 (Tate Gallery, London). He later moved towards Symbolism. He also designed tapestries and stained glass in association with William *Morris.

burnet herb *Sanguisorba minor* of the rose family, also known as *salad burnet*. It smells of cucumber and can be used in salads. The term is also used for other members of the genus *Sanguisorba*.

Burnett Frances (Eliza) Hodgson 1849–1924. English writer who emigrated with her family to the USA 1865. Her novels for children include the rags-to-riches tale *Little Lord Fauntleroy* 1886 and the sentimental *The Secret Garden* 1909.

Burney Frances (Fanny) 1752–1840. English novelist and diarist, daughter of musician Dr Charles Burney (1726–1814). She achieved success with *Evelina*, published anonymously 1778, became a member of Dr *Johnson's circle, received a post at court from Queen Charlotte, and in 1793 married the French émigré General d'Arblay. She published three further novels, *Cecilia* 1782, *Camilla* 1796, and *The Wanderer* 1814; her diaries and letters appeared 1842.

Burnham Forbes 1923–1985. Guyanese Marxist-Leninist politician. He was prime minister 1964–80, leading the country to independence 1966 and declaring it the world's first cooperative republic 1970. He was executive president 1980–85. Resistance to the US landing in Grenada 1983 was said to be due to his forewarning the Grenadans of the attack.

Burns Robert 1759–1796. Scottish poet. He used the Scots dialect at a time when it was not considered suitably 'elevated' for literature. Burns's first volume, *Poems, Chiefly in the Scottish Dialect*, appeared 1786. In addition to his poetry, Burns wrote or adapted many songs, including 'Auld Lang Syne'.

Burr Aaron 1756–1836. US politician, Republican vice president 1800–04, in which year he killed his political rival Alexander *Hamilton in a duel.

Burroughs Edgar Rice 1875–1950. US novelist. He wrote *Tarzan of the Apes* 1914, the story of an aristocratic child lost in the jungle and reared by apes, and followed it with over 20 more books about the Tarzan character. He also wrote a series of novels about life on Mars.

Burroughs William S(eward) 1914– . US writer. One of the most culturally influential postwar writers, his work is noted for its experimental methods, black humour, explicit homo-eroticism, and apocalyptic vision. In 1944 he met Allen Ginsberg and Jack Kerouac, all three becoming leading members of the *Beat Generation. His first novel, *Junkie* 1953, documented his heroin addiction and expatriation to Mexico, where in 1951, he accidentally killed his common-law wife. He settled in Tangier 1954 and wrote his celebrated anti-novel *Naked Lunch* 1959. In Paris, he developed collage-based techniques of writing, resulting in his 'cut-up' science-fiction trilogy, *The Soft Machine* 1961, *The Ticket That Exploded* 1962, and *Nova Express* 1964.

Burton Richard Francis 1821–1890. British explorer and translator (he knew 35 oriental languages). He travelled mainly in the Middle East and NE Africa, often disguised as a Muslim; made two attempts to find the source of the Nile, 1855 and 1857–58 (on the second, with John *Speke, he reached Lake Tanganyika); and wrote many travel books. He translated oriental erotica and the *Arabian Nights* 1885–88.

Burton Richard. Stage name of Richard Jenkins 1925–1984. Welsh stage and screen actor. He had a rich, dramatic voice but his career was dogged by an often poor choice of roles. Films in which he appeared with his wife, Elizabeth *Taylor, include *Cleopatra* 1962 and *Who's Afraid of Virginia Woolf?* 1966. Among his later films are *Equus* 1977 and *Nineteen Eighty-Four* 1984.

Burundi Republic of (*Republika y'Uburundi*)
area 27,834 sq km/10,744 sq mi
capital Bujumbura
towns Gitega, Bururi, Ngozi, Muyinga
physical landlocked grassy highland straddling watershed of Nile and Congo
head of state (interim) Sylvestre Ntibantunganya from 1994
head of government Anatole Kanyenkino from 1994
political system emergent democratic republic
exports coffee, cotton, tea, nickel, hides, livestock, cigarettes, beer, soft drinks
currency Burundi franc
population (1993 est) 5,970,000 (of whom 15% are the Nilotic Tutsi, still holding most of the land and political power; 1% are Pygmy Twa, the remainder Bantu Hutu); growth rate 2.8%p.a.
languages Kirundi (a Bantu language) and French (both official), Kiswahili
religions Roman Catholic 62%, Protestant 5%, Muslim 1%, animist 32%
GNP $210 per head (1991)
chronology
1962 Separated from Ruanda-Urundi, as Burundi, and given independence as a monarchy under King Mwambutsa IV.
1966 King deposed by his son Charles, who became Ntare V; he was in turn deposed by his prime minister, Capt Michel Micombero, who declared Burundi a republic.
1972 Ntare V killed, allegedly by the Hutu ethnic group. Massacres of 150,000 Hutus by the rival Tutsi ethnic group, of which Micombero was a member.

1973 Micombero made president and prime minister.

1974 UPRONA declared the only legal political party, with the president as its secretary general.

1976 Army coup deposed Micombero. Col Jean-Baptiste Bagaza appointed president by the Supreme Revolutionary Council.

1981 New constitution adopted.

1984 Bagaza elected president as sole candidate.

1987 Bagaza deposed in coup Sept. Maj Pierre Buyoya headed new Military Council for National Redemption.

1988 Some 24,000 majority Hutus killed by Tutsis.

1993 June: Melchior Ndadaye, a Hutu, elected president. Oct: Ndadye killed in military coup. Intertribal massacres followed.

1994 Jan: Cyprien Ntaryamira, a Hutu, elected president. Ntaryamira killed in air crash. Sylvestre Ntibantunganya became interim head of state. Power-sharing agreement between main political factions.

bus in computing, the electrical pathway through which a computer processor communicates with some of its parts and/or peripherals. Physically, a bus is a set of parallel tracks that can carry digital signals; it may take the form of copper tracks laid down on the computer's *printed circuit boards (PCBs), or of an external cable or connection.

Bush George 1924– . 41st president of the USA 1989–93, a Republican. He was director of the Central Intelligence Agency (CIA) 1976–81 and US vice president 1981–89. As president, his response to the Soviet leader Gorbachev's diplomatic initiatives were initially criticized as inadequate, but his sending of US troops to depose his former ally, General *Noriega of Panama, proved a popular move at home. Success in the 1991 Gulf War against Iraq further raised his standing. Domestic economic problems 1991–92 were followed by his defeat in the 1992 presidential elections by Democrat Bill Clinton.

bushbuck antelope *Tragelaphus scriptus* found over most of Africa S of the Sahara. Up to 1 m/3 ft high, the males have keeled horns twisted into spirals, and are brown to blackish. The females are generally hornless, lighter, and redder. All have white markings, including stripes or vertical rows of dots down the sides. Rarely far from water, bushbuck live in woods and thick brush.

bushel dry or liquid measure equal to eight gallons or four pecks (2,219.36 cu in/36.37 litres) in the UK; some US states have different standards according to the goods measured.

bushido chivalric code of honour of the Japanese military caste, the *samurai. Bushido means 'the way of the warrior'; the code stresses simple living, self-discipline, and bravery.

Bushman former name for the *Kung, *San, and other hunter-gatherer groups (for example, the Gikwe, Heikom, and Sekhoin) living in and around the Kalahari Desert in southern Africa. They number approximately 50,000 and speak San and other languages of the *Khoisan family. They are characteristically small-statured and brown-skinned.

bushman's rabbit or *riverine rabbit* a wild rodent *Bunolagus monticularis* found in dense riverine bush in South Africa. It lives in small populations, and individuals are only seen very occasionally; it is now at extreme risk of extinction owing to loss of habitat to agriculture. Very little is known about its life or habits.

bushmaster large snake *Lachesis muta*. It is a type of pit viper, and is related to the rattlesnakes. Up to 4 m/12 ft long, it is found in wooded areas of South and Central America, and is the largest venomous snake in the New World. When alarmed, it produces a noise by vibrating its tail among dry leaves.

bushranger Australian armed robber of the 19th century. The first bushrangers were escaped convicts. The last gang was led by Ned *Kelly and his brother Dan in 1878–80. They form the subject of many Australian ballads.

business plan key management tool that focuses on business objectives, the products or services involved, estimated market potential, expertise in the firm, projected financial results, the money required from investors, and the likely investment return.

Busoni Ferruccio (Dante Benvenuto) 1866–1924. Italian pianist, composer, and music critic. Much of his music was for the piano, but he also composed several operas including *Doktor Faust*, completed by Philipp Jarnach after his death. An apostle of Futurism, he encouraged the French composer Edgard Varèse.

Bustamante (William) Alexander (born Clarke) 1884–1977. Jamaican socialist politician. As leader of the Labour Party, he was the first prime minister of independent Jamaica 1962–67.

bustard bird of the family Otididae, related to cranes but with a rounder body, a thicker neck, and a relatively short beak. Bustards are found on the ground on open plains and fields.

butane C_4H_{10} one of two gaseous alkanes (paraffin hydrocarbons) having the same formula but differing in structure. Normal butane is derived from natural gas; isobutane is a by-product of petroleum manufacture. Liquefied under pressure, it is used as a fuel for industrial and domestic purposes (for example, in portable cookers).

Bute John Stuart, 3rd Earl of Bute 1713–1792. British Tory politician, prime minister 1762–63. On the accession of George III in 1760, he became the chief instrument in the king's policy for breaking the power of the Whigs and establishing the personal rule of the monarch through Parliament.

Buthelezi Chief Gatsha 1928– . South African Zulu leader and politician. He is the president of the Zulu-based *Inkatha Freedom Party, which he founded 1975 as a paramilitary organization for attaining a nonracial democratic political system. His threatened boycott of South Africa's first multiracial elections led to a dramatic escalation in pre-election violence, but he was eventually persuaded to participate and in May 1994 was appointed home affairs minister in the first post-apartheid government.

Butler Richard Austen ('Rab'), Baron Butler 1902–1982. British Conservative politician. As minister of education 1941–45, he was responsible for the 1944 Education Act; he was chancellor of the Exchequer 1951–55, Lord Privy Seal

1955–59, and foreign minister 1963–64. As a candidate for the prime ministership, he was defeated by Harold Macmillan in 1957 (under whom he was home secretary 1957–62), and by Alec Douglas-Home in 1963.

Butler Samuel 1835–1902. English author. He made his name 1872 with a satiric attack on contemporary utopianism, *Erewhon* (*nowhere* reversed), but is now remembered for his autobiographical *The Way of All Flesh* written 1872–85 and published 1903.

Butlin Billy (William) 1899–1980. British holiday-camp entrepreneur. Born in South Africa, he went in early life to Canada, but later entered the fairground business in the UK. He originated a chain of camps (the first was at Skegness 1936) that provided accommodation, meals, and amusements at an inclusive price.

buttercup plant of the genus *Ranunculus* of the buttercup family with divided leaves and yellow flowers.

Butterfield William 1814–1900. English Gothic Revival architect. His work is characterized by vigorous, aggressive forms and multicoloured striped and patterned brickwork, as in the church of All Saints, London, 1850–59, and Keble College, Oxford 1867–83.

butterfly insect belonging, like moths, to the order Lepidoptera, in which the wings are covered with tiny scales, often brightly coloured. There are some 15,000 species of butterfly, many of which are under threat throughout the world because of the destruction of habitat.

butterfly fish any of several fishes, not all related. The freshwater butterfly fish *Pantodon buchholzi* of W Africa can leap from the water and glide for a short distance on its large winglike pectoral fins. Up to 10 cm/4 in long, it lives in stagnant water. The tropical marine butterfly fishes, family Chaetodontidae, are brightly coloured with laterally flattened bodies, often with long snouts which they poke into crevices in rocks and coral when feeding.

butterwort insectivorous plant, genus *Pinguicula*, of the bladderwort family, with purplish flowers and a rosette of flat leaves covered with a sticky secretion that traps insects.

button (French *bouton* 'bud', 'knob') fastener for clothing, originating with Bronze Age fasteners. In medieval Europe buttons were replaced by pins but were reintroduced in the 13th century as a decorative trim and in the 16th century as a functional fastener.

buttress reinforcement in brick or masonry, built against a wall to give it strength. A *flying buttress* is an arc transmitting the force of the wall to be supported to an outer buttress, common in Gothic architecture.

Buxtehude Diderik 1637–1707. Danish composer and organist at Lübeck, Germany, who influenced *Bach and *Handel. He is remembered for his organ works and cantatas, written for his evening concerts or *Abendmusiken*.

buyer's market market having an excess of goods and services on offer and where prices are likely to be declining. The buyer benefits from the wide choice and competition available.

buzzard any of a number of species of medium-sized hawks with broad wings, often seen soaring. The **common buzzard** *Buteo buteo* of Europe and Asia is about 55 cm/1.8 ft long with a wingspan of over 1.2 m/4 ft. It preys on a variety of small animals up to the size of a rabbit.

Byatt A(ntonia) S(usan) 1936– . English novelist and critic. Her fifth novel, *Possession*, won the 1990 Booker Prize. *The Virgin in the Garden* 1978 is a confident, zestfully handled account of a varied group of characters putting on a school play during Coronation year, 1953. It has a sequel, *Still Life* 1985.

Byblos ancient Phoenician city (modern Jebeil), 32 km/20 mi N of Beirut, Lebanon. Known to the Assyrians and Babylonians as *Gubla*, it had a thriving export of cedar and pinewood to Egypt as early as 1500 BC. In Roman times it boasted an amphitheatre, baths, and a temple dedicated to an unknown male god, and was known for its celebration of the resurrection of Adonis, worshipped as a god of vegetation.

Byelorussian or *Belorussian* 'White Russian' native of Belarus. Byelorussian, a Balto-Slavic language belonging to the Indo-European family, is spoken by about 10 million people, including some in Poland. It is written in the Cyrillic script. Byelorussian literature dates to the 11th century AD.

Byrd Richard Evelyn 1888–1957. US aviator and explorer. The first to fly over the North Pole (1926), he also flew over the South Pole (1929), and led five overland expeditions in Antarctica.

Byrd William 1543–1623. English composer. His church choral music (set to Latin words, as he was a firm Catholic), notably masses for three, four, and five voices, is among the greatest Renaissance music. He also composed secular vocal and instrumental music.

Byron Augusta Ada 1815–1851. English mathematician, a pioneer in writing programs for Charles *Babbage's analytical engine. In 1983 a new, high-level computer language, ADA, was named after her. She was the daughter of the poet Lord Byron.

Byron George Gordon, 6th Baron Byron 1788–1824. English poet who became the symbol of Romanticism and political liberalism throughout Europe in the 19th century. His reputation was established with the first two cantos of *Childe Harold* 1812. Later works include *The Prisoner of Chillon* 1816, *Beppo* 1818, *Mazeppa* 1819, and, most notably, the satirical *Don Juan* 1819–24. He left England in 1816, spending most of his later life in Italy.

byte in computing, a basic unit of storage of information. A byte contains 8 *bits and can specify 256 values, such as the numbers from 0 to 255, or 256 colours at one byte per pixel (picture element). Three bytes (24 bits) can specify 16,777,216 values. Twenty-four-bit colour graphics with 16.8 million colours can provide a photo-realistic colour display.

Byzantine Empire the *Eastern Roman Empire* 395–1453, with its capital at Constantinople (formerly Byzantium, modern Istanbul).

Byzantine style style in the visual arts and architecture that originated in the 4th–5th centuries in Byzantium (the capital of the Eastern Roman Empire), and spread to Italy, throughout the Balkans, and to Russia, where it survived for many centuries. It is characterized by heavy stylization, strong linear emphasis, the use of rigid artistic stereotypes and rich colours such as gold. Byzantine artists excelled in mosaic work and manuscript painting. In architecture, the dome supported on pendentives was in widespread use.

Byzantium (modern Istanbul) ancient Greek city on the Bosporus, founded as a colony of the Greek city of Megara, near Corinth, about 660 BC. In AD 330 the capital of the Roman Empire was transferred there by Constantine the Great, who renamed it *Constantinople.

C high-level general-purpose computer-programming language popular on minicomputers and microcomputers. Developed in the early 1970s from an earlier language called BCPL, C was first used as the language of the operating system *Unix, though it has since become widespread beyond Unix. It is useful for writing fast and efficient systems programs, such as operating systems (which control the operations of the computer).

c. abbreviation for *circa* (Latin 'about'); used with dates that are uncertain.

C abbreviation for *centum* (Latin 'hundred'); *century*; *centigrade*; *Celsius*.

°C symbol for degrees *Celsius*, commonly called centigrade.

CAB acronym for *Citizens' Advice Bureau*.

Cabal, the (from *kabbala*) group of politicians, the English king Charles II's counsellors 1667–73, whose initials made up the word by coincidence – **C**lifford (Thomas Clifford 1630–1673), **A**shley (Anthony Ashley Cooper, 1st Earl of *Shaftesbury), *B**uckingham (George Villiers, 2nd Duke of Buckingham), **A**rlington (Henry Bennett, 1st Earl of Arlington 1618–1685), and *L**auderdale (John Maitland, Duke of Lauderdale).

cabbage plant *Brassica oleracea* of the cress family Cruciferae, allied to the turnip and wild mustard, or charlock. It is a table vegetable, known to be cultivated as early as 2000 BC, and the numerous commercial varieties include kale, Brussels sprouts, common cabbage, savoy, cauliflower, sprouting broccoli, and kohlrabi.

cabbala alternative spelling of *kabbala.

caber, tossing the (Gaelic *cabar* 'pole') Scottish athletic sport, a *Highland Games event. The caber (a tapered tree trunk about 6 m/20 ft long, weighing about 100 kg/220 lb) is held in the palms of the cupped hands and rests on the shoulder. The thrower runs forward and tosses the caber, rotating it through 180 degrees so that it lands on its opposite end and falls forward. The best competitors toss the caber about 12 m/40 ft.

Cabinda or *Kabinda* African coastal enclave, a province of *Angola; area 7,770 sq km/3,000 sq mi; population (1980) 81,300. The capital is Cabinda. There are oil reserves. Cabinda, which was attached to Angola in 1886, has made claims to independence.

cabinet (a small room, implying secrecy) in politics, the group of ministers holding a country's highest executive offices who decide government policy. In Britain the cabinet system originated under the Stuarts. Under William III it became customary for the king to select his ministers from the party with a parliamentary majority. The US cabinet, unlike the British, does not initiate legislation, and its members, appointed by the president, must not be members of Congress.

cable unit of length, used on ships, originally the length of a ship's anchor cable or 120 fathoms (219 m/720 ft), but now taken as one-tenth of a *nautical mile (185.3 m/608 ft).

cable car method of transporting passengers up steep slopes by cable. In the **cable railway**, passenger cars are hauled along rails by a cable wound by a powerful winch. A pair of cars usually operates together on the funicular principle, one going up as the other goes down. The other main type is the **aerial cable car**, where the passenger car is suspended from a trolley that runs along an aerial cableway.

Cable News Network (CNN) international television news channel; the 24-hour service was founded 1980 by US entrepreneur Ted Turner and has its headquarters in Atlanta, Georgia. It established its global reputation 1991 with eyewitness accounts from Baghdad of the beginning of the Gulf War.

cable television distribution of broadcast signals through cable relay systems. Narrow-band systems were originally used to deliver services to areas with poor regular reception; systems with wider bands, using coaxial and fibreoptic cable, are increasingly used for distribution and development of home-based interactive services.

Cabot Sebastian 1474–1557. Italian navigator and cartographer, the second son of Giovanni *Caboto. He explored the Brazilian coast and the Río de la Plata for the Holy Roman Emperor Charles V 1526–30.

Caboto Giovanni or *John Cabot* 1450–1498. Italian navigator. Commissioned, with his three sons, by Henry VII of England to discover unknown lands, he arrived at Cape Breton Island on 24 June 1497, thus becoming the first European to reach the North American mainland (he thought he was in NE Asia). In 1498 he sailed again, touching Greenland, and probably died on the voyage.

cacao tropical American evergreen tree *Theobroma cacao* of the Sterculia family, now also cultivated in W Africa and Sri Lanka. Its seeds are cocoa beans, from which *cocoa and chocolate are prepared. The trees mature at five to eight years and produce two crops a year.

cache memory in computing, a reserved area of the *immediate-access memory used to increase the running speed of a computer program.

cactus (plural *cacti*) plant of the family Cactaceae, although the term is commonly applied to many different succulent and prickly plants. True cacti have a woody axis (central core) overlaid with an enlarged fleshy stem, which assumes various forms and is usually covered with spines (actually reduced leaves). They all have special adaptations to growing in dry areas.

cactus *The cactus has no leaves, an adaptation for conserving water; photosynthesis occurs in green stems.*

CAD (acronym for *computer-aided design*) the use of computers in creating and editing design drawings. CAD also allows such things as automatic testing of designs and multiple or animated three-dimensional views of designs. CAD systems are widely used in architecture, electronics, and engineering, for example in the motor-vehicle industry, where cars designed with the assistance of computers are now commonplace. A related development is *CAM (computer-assisted manufacture).

caddis fly insect of the order Trichoptera. Adults are generally dull brown, mothlike, with wings covered in tiny hairs. Mouthparts are poorly developed, and many caddis flies do not feed as adults. They are usually found near water.

Cadiz Spanish city and naval base, capital and seaport of the province of Cadiz, standing on Cadiz Bay, an inlet of the Atlantic, 103 km/64 mi S of Seville; population (1991) 156,600. After the discovery of the Americas 1492, Cadiz became one of Europe's most vital trade ports. The English adventurer Francis *Drake burned a Spanish fleet here 1587 to prevent the sailing of the *Armada.

cadmium soft, silver-white, ductile, and malleable metallic element, symbol Cd, atomic number 48, relative atomic mass 112.40. Cadmium occurs in nature as a sulphide or carbonate in zinc ores. It is a toxic metal that, because of industrial dumping, has become an environmental pollutant. It is used in batteries, electroplating, and as a constituent of alloys used for bearings with low coefficients of friction; it is also a constituent of an alloy with a very low melting point.

Cadmus in Greek mythology, a Phoenician from Tyre, brother of *Europa. He founded the city of Thebes in Greece. Obeying the oracle of Athena, Cadmus killed the sacred dragon that guarded the spring of Ares. He sowed the teeth of the dragon, from which sprang a multitude of fierce warriors who fought among themselves; the sur-

vivors were considered to be the ancestors of the Theban aristocracy.

Cadwalader 7th century. Welsh hero. The son of Cadwallon, king of Gwynedd, N Wales, he defeated and killed Eadwine of Northumbria in 633. About a year later he was killed in battle.

caecilian tropical amphibian of wormlike appearance. There are about 170 species known, forming the amphibian order Apoda (also known as Caecilia or Gymnophiona). Caecilians have a grooved skin that gives a 'segmented' appearance; they have no trace of limbs, and mostly live below ground. Some species bear live young, others lay eggs.

caecum in the *digestive system of animals, a blind-ending tube branching off from the first part of the large intestine, terminating in the appendix. It has no function in humans but is used for the digestion of cellulose by some grass-eating mammals.

Caedmon 7th century. Earliest known English poet. According to the Northumbrian historian Bede, when Caedmon was a cowherd at the Christian monastery of Whitby, he was commanded to sing by a stranger in a dream, and on waking produced a hymn on the Creation. The poem is preserved in some manuscripts.

Caernarvon or *Caernarfon* administrative headquarters of Gwynedd, N Wales, situated on the SW shore of the Menai Strait. Formerly a Roman station, it is now a market town and port. The first Prince of Wales (later Edward II) was born in Caernarvon Castle; Edward VIII was invested here 1911 and Prince Charles 1969.

Caesar powerful family of ancient Rome, which included Gaius Julius Caesar, whose grand-nephew and adopted son *Augustus assumed the name of Caesar and passed it on to his adopted son *Tiberius. From then on, it was used by the successive emperors, becoming a title of the Roman rulers. The titles 'tsar' in Russia and 'kaiser' in Germany were both derived from the name Caesar.

Caesar Gaius Julius *c.* 100–44 BC. Roman statesman and general. He formed with Pompey and Crassus the First Triumvirate 60 BC. He conquered Gaul 58–50 and invaded Britain 55 and 54. He fought against Pompey 49–48, defeating him at Pharsalus. After a period in Egypt Caesar returned to Rome as dictator from 46. He was assassinated by conspirators on the *Ides of March 44.

Caesarea ancient city in Palestine (now Qisarya). It was built by Herod the Great 22–12 BC, who also constructed a port (*portus Augusti*). Caesarea was the administrative capital of the province of Judaea.

Caesarean section surgical operation to deliver a baby by cutting through the mother's abdominal and intrauterine walls. It may be recommended for obstetric complications implying a threat to mother or baby.

caesium (Latin *caesius* 'bluish-grey') soft, silvery-white, ductile metallic element, symbol Cs, atomic number 55, relative atomic mass 132.905. It is one of the *alkali metals, and is the most electropositive of all the elements. In air it ignites spontaneously, and it reacts vigorously with water. It is used in the manufacture of photoelectric cells. The name comes from the blueness of its spectral line.

caffeine *alkaloid organic substance found in tea, coffee, and kola nuts; it stimulates the heart and central nervous system. When isolated, it is a bitter crystalline compound, $C_8H_{10}N_4O_2$. Too much caffeine (more than six average cups of tea or coffee a day) can be detrimental to health.

Cage John 1912–1992. US composer. A pupil of Arnold *Schoenberg, he maintained that all sounds should be available for musical purposes; for example, he used 24 radios, tuned to random stations, in *Imaginary Landscape No 4* 1951. He also worked to reduce the control of the composer over the music, introducing randomness (*aleatory music) and inexactitude and allowing sounds to 'be themselves'. Cage's unconventional ideas have had a profound impact on 20th-century music.

Cagliari capital and port of Sardinia, Italy, on the Gulf of Cagliari; population (1988) 222,000.

Cagney James 1899–1986. US actor who moved to films from Broadway. Usually associated with gangster roles (*The Public Enemy* 1931), he was an actor of great versatility, playing Bottom in *A Midsummer Night's Dream* 1935 and singing and dancing in *Yankee Doodle Dandy* 1942.

Cahora Bassa largest hydroelectric project in Africa, created as a result of the damming of the Zambezi River to form a reservoir 230 km/144 mi long in W Mozambique.

Cain in the Old Testament, the first-born son of Adam and Eve. Motivated by jealousy, he murdered his brother Abel because the latter's sacrifice was more acceptable to God than his own.

Cain James M(allahan) 1892–1977. US novelist. He was the author of *The Postman Always Rings Twice* 1934, *Mildred Pierce* 1941, and *Double Indemnity* 1943, which epitomized the 'hard-boiled' fiction of the 1930s and 1940s.

Caine Michael. Stage name of Maurice Micklewhite 1933– . English actor, an accomplished performer with an enduring Cockney streak. His films include *Alfie* 1966, *The Man Who Would Be King* 1975, *Educating Rita* 1983, and *Hannah and Her Sisters* 1986.

cairn Scottish breed of *terrier. Shaggy, short-legged, and compact, it can be sandy, greyish brindle, or red. It was formerly used for flushing out foxes and badgers.

Cairo ((Arabic *El Qahira*)) capital of Egypt, on the E bank of the Nile 13 km/8 mi above the apex of the delta and 160 km/100 mi from the Mediterranean; the largest city in Africa and in the Middle East; population (1985) 6,205,000; metropolitan area (1987) 13,300,000. An earthquake in a suburb of the city Oct 1992 left over 500 dead.

history El Fustat (Old Cairo) was founded by Arabs about AD 642, Al Qahira about 1000 by the *Fatimid ruler Gowhar. Cairo was the capital of the Ayyubid dynasty, one of whose sultans, Saladin, built the Citadel in the late 1100s.

Cajun member of a French-speaking community of Louisiana, USA, descended from French-Canadians who, in the 18th century, were driven there from Nova Scotia (then known as Acadia, from which the name Cajun comes). *Cajun*

music has a lively rhythm and features steel guitar, fiddle, and accordion.

CAL (acronym for *computer-assisted learning*) the use of computers in education and training: the computer displays instructional material to a student and asks questions about the information given; the student's answers determine the sequence of the lessons.

calabash tropical South American evergreen tree *Crescentia cujete*, family Bignoniaceae, with gourds 50 cm/20 in across, which are used as water containers. The Old World tropical vine bottle gourd *Lagenaria siceraria* of the gourd family Cucurbitaceae is sometimes called calabash, and it produces equally large true gourds.

Calabria mountainous earthquake region occupying the 'toe' of Italy, comprising the provinces of Catanzaro, Cosenza, and Reggio; capital Catanzaro; area 15,100 sq km/5,829 sq mi; population (1990) 2,153,700. Reggio is the industrial centre.

calamine $ZnCO_3$ zinc carbonate, an ore of zinc. The term also refers to a pink powder made of a mixture of zinc oxide and iron(II) oxide used in lotions and ointments as an astringent for treating, for example, sunburn, eczema, measles rash, and insect bites and stings.

Calamity Jane nickname of Martha Jane Burke *c.* 1852–1903. US heroine of Deadwood, South Dakota. She worked as a teamster, transporting supplies to the mining camps, adopted male dress and, as an excellent shot, promised 'calamity' to any aggressor. Many fictional accounts of the Wild West featured her exploits.

calceolaria plant of the *Calceolaria* figwort genus, family Scrophulariaceae, with brilliantly coloured slipper-shaped flowers. Native to South America, calceolarias were introduced to Europe and the USA in the 1830s.

calcite colourless, white, or light-coloured common rock-forming mineral, calcium carbonate, $CaCO_3$. It is the main constituent of *limestone and marble, and forms many types of invertebrate shell.

calcium (Latin *calcis* 'lime') soft, silvery-white metallic element, symbol Ca, atomic number 20, relative atomic mass 40.08. It is one of the *alkaline-earth metals. It is the fifth most abundant element (the third most abundant metal) in the Earth's crust. It is found mainly as its carbonate $CaCO_3$, which occurs in a fairly pure condition as chalk and limestone (see *calcite). Calcium is an essential component of bones, teeth, shells, milk, and leaves, and it forms 1.5% of the human body by mass.

calcium carbonate $CaCO_3$ white solid, found in nature as limestone, marble, and chalk. It is a valuable resource, used in the making of iron, steel, cement, glass, slaked lime, bleaching powder, sodium carbonate and bicarbonate, and many other industrially useful substances.

calculus (Latin 'pebble') branch of mathematics that permits the manipulation of continuously varying quantities, used in practical problems involving such matters as changing speeds, problems of flight, varying stresses in the framework of a bridge, and alternating current theory. *Integral calculus* deals with the method of summation or adding together the effects of continuously varying quantities. **Differential calculus** deals in a similar way with rates of change. Many of its applications arose from the study of the gradients of the tangents to curves.

Calcutta largest city of India, on the river Hooghly, the westernmost mouth of the river Ganges, some 130 km/80 mi N of the Bay of Bengal. It is the capital of West Bengal; population (1981) 9,166,000. It is chiefly a commercial and industrial centre (engineering, shipbuilding, jute, and other textiles). Calcutta was the seat of government of British India 1773–1912. There is severe air pollution.

caldera in geology, a very large basin-shaped *crater. Calderas are found at the tops of volcanoes, where the original peak has collapsed into an empty chamber beneath. The basin, many times larger than the original volcanic vent, may be flooded, producing a crater lake, or the flat floor may contain a number of small volcanic cones, produced by volcanic activity after the collapse.

Calderón de la Barca Pedro 1600–1681. Spanish dramatist and poet. After the death of Lope de Vega 1635, he was considered to be the leading Spanish dramatist. Most celebrated of the 118 plays is the philosophical *La vida es sueño/Life is a Dream* 1635.

calendar division of the *year into months, weeks, and days and the method of ordering the years. From year one, an assumed date of the birth of Jesus, dates are calculated backwards (BC 'before Christ' or BCE 'before common era') and forwards (AD, Latin *anno Domini* 'in the year of the Lord', or CE 'common era'). The *lunar month* (period between one new moon and the next) naturally averages 29.5 days, but the Western calendar uses for convenience a *calendar month* with a complete number of days, 30 or 31 (Feb has 28). For adjustments, since there are slightly fewer than six extra hours a year left over, they are added to Feb as a 29th day every fourth year (*leap year*), century years being excepted unless they are divisible by 400. For example, 1896 was a leap year; 1900 was not. 1996 is the next leap year.

Calgary city in Alberta, Canada, on the Bow River, in the foothills of the Rockies; at 1,048 m/3,440 ft it is one of the highest Canadian towns; population (1986) 671,000. It is the centre of a large agricultural region and is the oil and financial centre of Alberta and W Canada. The 1988 Winter Olympic Games were held here.

Cali city in SW Colombia, in the Cauca Valley 975 m/3,200 ft above sea level; population (1985) 1,398,276. Cali was founded 1536. It has textile, sugar, and engineering industries.

California Pacific-coast state of the USA; nicknamed the Golden State (originally because of its gold mines, more recently because of its orange groves and sunshine)
area 411,100 sq km/158,685 sq mi
capital Sacramento
cities Los Angeles, San Diego, San Francisco, San José, Fresno
physical Sierra Nevada, including Yosemite and Sequoia national parks, Lake Tahoe, Mount Whitney (4,418 m/14,500 ft, the highest mountain in the lower 48 states); the Coast Range; Death Valley (282 ft/86 m below sea level, the

lowest point in the western hemisphere); Colorado and Mojave deserts; Monterey Peninsula; Salton Sea; the San Andreas fault; huge, offshore underwater volcanoes with tops 5 mi/8 km across
products leading agricultural state with fruit (peaches, citrus, grapes in the valley of the San Joaquin and Sacramento rivers), nuts, wheat, vegetables, cotton, and rice, all mostly grown by irrigation, the water being carried by immense concrete-lined canals to the Central and Imperial valleys; beef cattle; timber; fish; oil; natural gas; aerospace technology; electronics (Silicon Valley); food processing; films and television programmes; great reserves of energy (geothermal) in the hot water that lies beneath much of the state
population (1990) 29,760,000, the most populous state of the USA (white 69.9%, Hispanic 25.8%, Asian and Pacific islander including many Vietnamese 9.6%, black 7.4%, American Indian 0.8%)
famous people Luther Burbank, Walt Disney, William Randolph Hearst, Jack London, Marilyn Monroe, Richard Nixon, Ronald Reagan, John Steinbeck
history colonized by Spain 1769; ceded to the USA after the Mexican War 1848; became a state 1850. The discovery of gold in the Sierra Nevada Jan 1848 was followed by the gold rush 1849–56.

California current cold ocean *current in the E Pacific Ocean flowing southwards down the west coast of North America. It is part of the North Pacific gyre (a vast, circular movement of ocean water).

californium synthesized, radioactive, metallic element of the actinide series, symbol Cf, atomic number 98, relative atomic mass 251. It is produced in very small quantities and used in nuclear reactors as a neutron source. The longest-lived isotope, Cf-251, has a half-life of 800 years.

Caligula Gaius Caesar AD 12–41. Roman emperor, son of Germanicus and successor to Tiberius AD 37. Caligula was a cruel tyrant and was assassinated by an officer of his guard. Believed to have been mentally unstable, he is remembered for giving a consulship to his horse Incitatus.

caliph title of civic and religious heads of the world of Islam. The first caliph was *Abu Bakr. Nominally elective, the office became hereditary, held by the Ummayyad dynasty 661–750 and then by the *Abbasid dynasty. After the death of the last Abbasid (1258), the title was claimed by a number of Muslim chieftains in Egypt, Turkey, and India. The most powerful of these were the Turkish sultans of the Ottoman Empire.

Callaghan (Leonard) James, Baron Callaghan 1912– . British Labour politician. As chancellor of the Exchequer 1964–67, he introduced corporation and capital-gains taxes, and resigned following devaluation. He was home secretary 1967–70 and prime minister 1976–79 in a period of increasing economic stress.

Callao chief commercial and fishing port of Peru, 12 km/7 mi SW of Lima; population (1988) 318,000. Founded 1537, it was destroyed by an earthquake 1746. It is Peru's main naval base, and produces fertilizers.

Callas Maria. Adopted name of Maria Kalogeropoulos 1923–1977. US lyric soprano, born in New York of Greek parents. With a voice of fine range and a gift for dramatic expression, she excelled in operas including *Norma*, *La Sonnambula*, *Madame Butterfly*, *Aïda*, *Lucia di Lammermoor*, and *Medea*.

calligraphy art of handwriting, regarded in China and Japan as the greatest of the visual arts, and playing a large part in Islamic art because the depiction of the human and animal form is forbidden.

callipers measuring instrument used, for example, to measure the internal and external diameters of pipes. Some callipers are made like a pair of compasses, having two legs, often curved, pivoting about a screw at one end. The ends of the legs are placed in contact with the object to be measured, and the gap between the ends is then measured against a rule. The slide calliper looks like an adjustable spanner, and carries a scale for direct measuring, usually with a vernier scale for accuracy.

Callisto second largest moon of Jupiter, 4,800 km/3,000 mi in diameter, orbiting every 16.7 days at a distance of 1.9 million km/1.2 million mi from the planet. Its surface is covered with large craters.

callus in botany, a tissue that forms at a damaged plant surface. Composed of large, thin-walled *parenchyma cells, it grows over and around the wound, eventually covering the exposed area.

Calmette Albert 1863–1933. French bacteriologist. A student of Pasteur, he developed (with Camille Guérin, 1872–1961) the *BCG vaccine against tuberculosis in 1921.

calomel Hg_2Cl_2 (technical name **mercury(I) chloride**) white, heavy powder formerly used as a laxative, now used as a pesticide and fungicide.

calorie cgs unit of heat, now replaced by the *joule (one calorie is approximately 4.2 joules). It is the heat required to raise the temperature of one gram of water by 1°C. In dietetics, the calorie or kilocalorie is equal to 1,000 calories.

calorific value the amount of heat generated by a given mass of fuel when it is completely burned. It is measured in joules per kilogram. Calorific values are measured experimentally with a bomb calorimeter.

calorimeter instrument used in physics to measure heat. A simple calorimeter consists of a heavy copper vessel that is polished (to reduce heat losses by radiation) and covered with insulating material (to reduce losses by convection and conduction).

calotype paper-based photograph using a wax paper negative, the first example of the *negative/positive process invented by the English photographer Fox Talbot around 1834.

Calvary (Aramaic *Golgotha* 'skull') in the New Testament, the site of Jesus' crucifixion at Jerusalem. Two chief locations are suggested: the site where the Church of the Sepulchre now stands, and the hill beyond the Damascus gate.

Calvin John (also known as **Cauvin** or **Chauvin**) 1509–1564. French-born Swiss Protestant church reformer and theologian. He was a leader of the Reformation in Geneva and set up a strict religious community there. His theo-logical system is known as Calvinism, and his church government as *Presbyterianism. Calvin wrote (in Latin) *Institutes of the Christian Religion* 1536 and commentaries on the New Testament and much of the Old Testament.

Calvin Melvin 1911– . US chemist who, using radioactive carbon-14 as a tracer, determined the biochemical processes of *photosynthesis, in which green plants use *chlorophyll to convert carbon dioxide and water into sugar and oxygen. Nobel prize 1961.

Calvinism Christian doctrine as interpreted by John Calvin and adopted in Scotland, parts of Switzerland, and the Netherlands; by the *Puritans in England and New England, USA; and by the subsequent Congregational and Presbyterian churches in the USA. Its central doctrine is predestination, under which certain souls (the elect) are predestined by God through the sacrifice of Jesus to salvation, and the rest to damnation. Although Calvinism is rarely accepted today in its strictest interpretation, the 20th century has seen a Neo-Calvinist revival through the work of Karl *Barth.

Calypso in Greek mythology, a sea *nymph who waylaid the homeward-bound Odysseus for seven years.

calypso West Indian satirical ballad with a syncopated beat. Calypso is a traditional song form of Trinidad, a feature of its annual carnival, with roots in W African praise singing. It was first popularized in the USA by Harry Belafonte (1927–) in 1956. Mighty Sparrow (1935–) is Trinidad's best-known calypso singer.

calyx collective term for the *sepals of a flower, forming the outermost whorl of the *perianth. It surrounds the other flower parts and protects them while in bud. In some flowers, for example, the campions *Silene*, the sepals are fused along their sides, forming a tubular calyx.

cam part of a machine that converts circular motion to linear motion or vice versa. The **edge cam** in a car engine is in the form of a rounded projection on a shaft, the camshaft. When the camshaft turns, the cams press against linkages (plungers or followers) that open the valves in the cylinders.

CAM (acronym for **computer-aided manufacture**) the use of computers to control production processes; in particular, the control of machine tools and *robots in factories. In some factories, the whole design and production system has been automated by linking *CAD (computer-aided design) to CAM.

Camargue marshy area of the *Rhône delta, S of Arles, France; about 780 sq km/300 sq mi. Bulls and horses are bred here, and the nature reserve, which is known for its bird life, forms the southern part.

cambium in botany, a layer of actively dividing cells (lateral *meristem), found within stems and roots, that gives rise to *secondary growth in perennial plants, causing an increase in girth. There are two main types of cambium: **vascular cambium**, which gives rise to secondary *xylem and *phloem tissues, and **cork cambium** (or phellogen), which gives rise to secondary cortex and cork tissues (see *bark).

Cambodia State of (formerly *Khmer Republic* 1970–76, *Democratic Kampuchea* 1976–79, *People's Republic of Kampuchea* 1979–89)

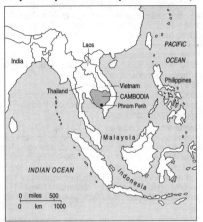

area 181,035 sq km/69,880 sq mi
capital Phnom Penh
towns Battambang, the seaport Kompong Som
physical mostly flat forested plains with mountains in SW and N; Mekong River runs N–S
head of state Prince Norodom Sihanouk from 1991
head of government Prince Norodom Ranariddh from 1993
political system transitional
exports rubber, rice, pepper, wood, cattle
currency Cambodian riel
population (1993) 12,000,000; growth rate 2.2% p.a.
languages Khmer (official), French
religion Theravāda Buddhist 95%
GNP $200 per head (1991)
chronology
1863–1941 French protectorate.
1941–45 Occupied by Japan.
1946 Recaptured by France.
1953 Independence achieved from France.
1970 Prince Sihanouk overthrown by US-backed Lon Nol.
1975 Lon Nol overthrown by Khmer Rouge.
1976–78 Khmer Rouge introduced an extreme communist programme, forcing urban groups into rural areas and bringing over 2.5 million deaths from famine, disease, and maltreatment.
1978–79 Vietnamese invasion and installation of Heng Samrin government.
1982 The three main anti-Vietnamese resistance groups formed an alliance under Prince Sihanouk.
1987 Vietnamese troop withdrawal began.
1989 Sept: completion of Vietnamese withdrawal. Nov: United Nations peace proposal rejected by Phnom Penh government.
1991 Oct: Peace agreement signed in Paris, providing for a UN Transitional Authority in Cambodia (UNTAC) to administer country in transition period in conjunction with all-party Supreme National Council; communism abandoned. Nov: Sihanouk returned as head of state.
1992 Political prisoners released; freedom of speech and party formation restored. Oct: Khmer

Rouge refused to disarm in accordance with peace process. Dec: UN Security Council voted to impose limited trade embargo on area of country controlled by Khmer Rouge guerrillas.
1993 Free general elections (boycotted by Khmer Rouge) resulted in surprise win by United Front for an Independent, Neutral, Peaceful, and Cooperative Cambodia (FUNCINPEC) over the Cambodian People's Party (CPP). Sihanouk reinstated as constitutional monarch. Prince Norodom Ranariddh, FUNCINPEC leader, appointed prime minister. Khmer Rouge continued fighting.

Cambrai, Battles of two battles in World War I at Cambrai in NE France: *First Battle* Nov–Dec 1917, the city was almost captured by the British when large numbers of tanks were used for the first time. *Second Battle* 26 Aug–5 Oct 1918, the town was taken during the final British offensive.

Cambrian period of geological time 570–510 million years ago; the first period of the Palaeozoic era. All invertebrate animal life appeared, and marine algae were widespread. The earliest fossils with hard shells, such as trilobites, date from this period.

Cambridge city in England, on the river Cam (a river sometimes called by its earlier name, Granta), 80 km/50 mi N of London; population (1989) 101,000. It is the administrative headquarters of Cambridgeshire. The city is centred on Cambridge University (founded 12th century), whose outstanding buildings, including Kings College Chapel, back onto the river.

Cambridgeshire county in E England
area 3,410 sq km/1,316 sq mi
towns Cambridge (administrative headquarters), Ely, Huntingdon, Peterborough
products mainly agricultural
population (1991) 640,700
famous people Oliver Cromwell, Octavia Hill, John Maynard Keynes.

camcorder another name for a *video camera.

camel large cud-chewing mammal of the even-toed hoofed order Artiodactyla. Unlike typical ruminants, it has a three-chambered stomach. It has two toes which have broad soft soles for walking on sand, and hooves resembling nails. There are two species, the single-humped **Arabian camel** *Camelus dromedarius* and the twin-humped **Bactrian camel** *C. bactrianus* from Asia. They carry a food reserve of fatty tissue in the hump; go without drinking for long periods; feed on salty vegetation; and withstand extremes of heat and cold, thus being well adapted to desert conditions.

camellia any oriental evergreen shrub with roselike flowers of the genus *Camellia*, tea family Theaceae. Numerous species, including *C. japonica* and *C. reticulata*, have been introduced into Europe, the USA, and Australia.

cameo small relief carving of semiprecious stone, shell, or glass, in which a pale-coloured surface layer is carved to reveal a darker ground. Fine cameos were produced in ancient Greece and Rome, during the Renaissance, and in the Victorian era. They were used for decorating goblets and vases, and as jewellery.

camera apparatus used in *photography, consisting of a lens system set in a light-proof box inside of which a sensitized film or plate can be placed. The lens collects rays of light reflected from the subject and brings them together as a sharp image on the film; it has marked numbers known as *apertures, or f-stops, that reduce or increase the amount of light. Apertures also control depth of field. A shutter controls the amount of time light has to affect the film. There are small-, medium-, and large-format cameras; the format refers to the size of recorded image and the dimensions of the print obtained.

camera obscura darkened box with a tiny hole for projecting the inverted image of the scene outside on to a screen inside. For its development as a device for producing photographs, see *photography.

Cameron Julia Margaret 1815–1879. British photographer. She made lively and dramatic portraits of the Victorian intelligentsia, using a large camera, five-minute exposures, and wet plates. Her sitters included Alfred Lord Tennyson and Charles Darwin.

Cameroon Republic of (*République du Cameroun*)
area 475,440 sq km/183,638 sq mi
capital Yaoundé
towns chief port Douala; Nkongsamba, Garova
physical desert in far north in the Lake Chad basin, mountains in W, dry savanna plateau in the intermediate area, and dense tropical rainforest in S
environment the Korup National Park preserves 1,300 sq km/500 sq mi of Africa's fast-disappearing tropical rainforest. Scientists have identified nearly 100 potentially useful chemical substances produced naturally by the plants of this forest
head of state and of government Paul Biya from 1982
political system emergent democratic republic
exports cocoa, coffee, bananas, cotton, timber, rubber, groundnuts, gold, aluminium, crude oil
currency CFA franc
population (1993 est) 12,800,000; growth rate 2.7% p.a.
languages French and English in pidgin variations (official); there has been some discontent with the emphasis on French – there are 163 indigenous peoples with their own African languages
religions Roman Catholic 35%, animist 25%, Muslim 22%, Protestant 18%
GNP $940 per head (1991)
chronology
1884 Treaty signed establishing German rule.
1916 Captured by Allied forces in World War I.
1922 Divided between Britain and France.
1946 French Cameroon and British Cameroons made UN trust territories.
1960 French Cameroon became the independent Republic of Cameroon. Ahmadou Ahidjo elected president.
1961 Northern part of British Cameroon merged with Nigeria and southern part joined the Republic of Cameroon to become the Federal Republic of Cameroon.
1966 One-party regime introduced.
1972 New constitution made Cameroon a unitary state, the United Republic of Cameroon.
1973 New national assembly elected.

1982 Ahidjo resigned and was succeeded by Paul Biya.
1983 Biya began to remove his predecessor's supporters; accused by Ahidjo of trying to create a police state. Ahidjo went into exile in France.
1984 Biya re-elected; defeated a plot to overthrow him. Country's name changed to Republic of Cameroon.
1988 Biya re-elected.
1990 Widespread public disorder. Biya granted amnesty to political prisoners.
1991 Constitutional changes made.
1992 Ruling RDPC won in first multiparty elections for 28 years. Biya's presidential victory challenged by opposition.

Camoëns or **Camões** Luís Vaz de 1524–1580. Portuguese poet and soldier. He went on various military expeditions, and was shipwrecked in 1558. His poem *Os Lusiades/The Lusiads* 1572 tells the story of the explorer Vasco da Gama and incorporates much Portuguese history; it has become the country's national epic. His posthumously published lyric poetry is also now valued.

Camorra Italian secret society formed about 1820 by criminals in the dungeons of Naples and continued once they were freed. It dominated politics from 1848, was suppressed 1911, but many members eventually surfaced in the US *Mafia. The Camorra still operates in the Naples area.

camouflage colours or structures that allow an animal to blend with its surroundings to avoid detection by other animals. Camouflage can take the form of matching the background colour, of countershading (darker on top, lighter below, to counteract natural shadows), or of irregular patterns that break up the outline of the animal's body. More elaborate camouflage involves closely resembling a feature of the natural environment, as with the stick insect; this is closely akin to *mimicry.

Campaign for Nuclear Disarmament (CND) nonparty-political British organization advocating the abolition of nuclear weapons worldwide. CND seeks unilateral British initiatives to help start the multilateral process and end the arms race. It was founded 1958.

Campania agricultural region (wheat, citrus, wine, vegetables, tobacco) of S Italy, including the volcano *Vesuvius; capital Naples; industrial centres Benevento, Caserta, and Salerno; area 13,600 sq km/5,250 sq mi; population (1990) 5,853,900. There are ancient sites at Pompeii, Herculaneum, and Paestum.

Campbell Colin, 1st Baron Clyde 1792–1863. British field marshal. He commanded the Highland Brigade at *Balaclava in the Crimean War and, as commander in chief during the Indian Mutiny, raised the siege of Lucknow and captured Cawnpore.

Campbell Donald Malcolm 1921–1967. British car and speedboat enthusiast, son of Malcolm Campbell, who simultaneously held the land-speed and water-speed records. In 1964 he set the world water-speed record of 444.57 kph/276.3 mph on Lake Dumbleyung, Australia, with the turbojet hydroplane *Bluebird*, and achieved the land-speed record of 648.7 kph/403.1 mph at Lake Eyre salt flats, Australia. He was killed in an attempt to raise his water-speed record on Coniston Water, England.

Campbell Malcolm 1885–1948. British racing driver who once held both land- and water-speed records. He set the land-speed record nine times, pushing it up to 484.8 kph/301.1 mph at Bonneville Flats, Utah, USA, in 1935, and broke the water-speed record three times, the best being 228.2 kph/141.74 mph on Coniston Water, England, in 1939. His car and boat were both called *Bluebird*.

Campbell Mrs Patrick (born Beatrice Stella Tanner) 1865–1940. British actress whose roles included Paula in Pinero's *The Second Mrs Tanqueray* 1893 and Eliza in *Pygmalion*, written for her by G B Shaw, with whom she had an amusing correspondence.

Campbell-Bannerman Henry 1836–1908. British Liberal politician, prime minister 1905–08. It was during his term of office that the South African colonies achieved self-government, and the Trades Disputes Act 1906 was passed.

Camp David official country home of US presidents, situated in the Appalachian mountains, Maryland; it was originally named Shangri-la by F D Roosevelt, but was renamed Camp David by Eisenhower (after his grandson).

Camp David Agreements two framework agreements signed 1978 by Israeli prime minister Begin and Egyptian president Sadat at Camp David, Maryland, USA, under the guidance of US president Carter, covering an Egypt–Israel peace treaty and phased withdrawal of Israel from Sinai, which was completed 1982, and an overall Middle East settlement including the election by the West Bank and Gaza Strip Palestinians of a 'self-governing authority'. The latter issue has stalled repeatedly over questions of who should represent the Palestinians and what form the self-governing body should take.

Camperdown (Dutch *Kamperduin*) village on the NW Netherlands coast, off which a British fleet defeated the Dutch 11 Oct 1797 in the Revolutionary Wars.

Campese David 1962– . Australian rugby union player, one of the outstanding entertainers of the game. He holds the world record for the most tries scored in international rugby (60).

camphor $C_{10}H_{16}O$ volatile, aromatic *ketone substance obtained from the camphor tree *Cinnamomum camphora*. It is distilled from chips of the wood, and is used in insect repellents and medicinal inhalants and liniments, and in the manufacture of celluloid.

campion any of several plants of the genera *Lychnis* and *Silene*, belonging to the pink family Caryophyllaceae and including the garden campion *L. coronaria*, the wild white and red campions *S. alba* and *S. dioica*, and the bladder campion *S. vulgaris*.

Campion Jane 1954– . New Zealand film director and screenwriter. One of the few women directors to win international acclaim, she made her feature debut with *Sweetie* 1989. She went on to make *An Angel at My Table* 1990, based on the autobiography of writer Janet Frame. Her international status was confirmed by the success of *The Piano* 1993, for which she won an Academy Award for the screenplay.

Campo-Formio, Treaty of peace settlement 1797 during the Revolutionary Wars between Napoleon and Austria, by which France gained the region that is now Belgium and Austria was compensated with Venice and part of an area that now reaches into Slovenia and Croatia.

Campylobacter genus of bacteria that cause serious outbreaks of gastroenteritis. They grow best at 43°C, and so are well suited to the digestive tract of birds. Poultry is therefore the most likely source of a *Campylobacter* outbreak, although the bacteria can also be transmitted via beef or milk. *Campylobacter* can survive in water for up to 15 days, so may be present in drinking water if supplies are contaminated by sewage or reservoirs are polluted by seagulls.

Camus Albert 1913–1960. Algerian-born French writer. A journalist in France, he was active in the Resistance during World War II. His novels, which owe much to *existentialism, include *L'Etranger/The Outsider* 1942, *La Peste/The Plague* 1948, and *L'Homme révolté/The Rebel* 1952. Nobel Prize for Literature 1957.

Canaan ancient region between the Mediterranean and the Dead Sea, called in the Bible the 'Promised Land' of the Israelites. It was occupied as early as the 3rd millennium BC by the Canaanites, a Semitic-speaking people who were known to the Greeks of the 1st millennium BC as Phoenicians. The capital was Ebla (now Tell Mardikh, Syria).

Canada

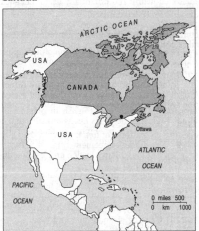

area 9,970,610 sq km/3,849,674 sq mi
capital Ottawa
cities Toronto, Montréal, Vancouver, Edmonton, Calgary, Winnipeg, Quebec, Hamilton, Saskatoon, Halifax
physical mountains in W, with low-lying plains in interior and rolling hills in E. Climate varies from temperate in S to arctic in N
head of state Elizabeth II from 1952, represented by governor general
head of government Jean Chretien from 1993

political system federal constitutional monarchy

exports wheat, timber, pulp, newsprint, fish, furs, oil, natural gas, aluminium, asbestos (world's second largest producer), coal, copper, iron, zinc, nickel (world's largest producer), uranium (world's largest producer), motor vehicles and parts, industrial and agricultural machinery, fertilizers, chemicals

currency Canadian dollar

population (1993) 28,100,000 – including 300,000 North American Indians, of whom 75% live on more than 2,000 reservations in Ontario and the four Western provinces; some 300,000 Métis (people of mixed race) and 19,000 Inuit of whom 75% live in the Northwest Territories. Over half Canada's population lives in Ontario and Québec. Growth rate 1.1% p.a.

languages English, French (both official; about 70% speak English, 20% French, and the rest are bilingual); there are also North American Indian languages and the Inuit Inuktitut

religion Roman Catholic 46%, Protestant 35%

GNP $21,260 per head (1991)

chronology

1867 Dominion of Canada founded.

1949 Newfoundland joined Canada.

1957 Progressive Conservatives returned to power after 22 years in opposition.

1961 NDP formed.

1963 Liberals elected under Lester Pearson.

1968 Pearson succeeded by Pierre Trudeau.

1979 Joe Clark, leader of the Progressive Conservatives, formed a minority government; defeated on budget proposals.

1980 Liberals under Trudeau returned with a large majority. Québec referendum rejected demand for independence.

1982 Canada Act removed Britain's last legal control over Canadian affairs; 'patriation' of Canada's constitution.

1983 Clark replaced as leader of the Progressive Conservatives by Brian Mulroney.

1984 Trudeau retired and was succeeded as Liberal leader and prime minister by John Turner. Progressive Conservatives won the federal election with a large majority, and Mulroney became prime minister.

1988 Conservatives re-elected with reduced majority on platform of free trade with the USA.

1989 Free-trade agreement signed. Turner resigned as Liberal Party leader, and Ed Broadbent as NDP leader.

1992 Gradual withdrawal of Canadian forces in Europe announced. Self-governing homeland for Inuit approved. Constitutional reform package, the Charlottetown Accord, rejected in national referendum.

1993 Mulroney resigned leadership of Conservative Party. Kim Campbell became prime minister. North American Free Trade Agreement (NAFTA) with USA and Mexico ratified. Oct: Conservatives defeated in general election. Liberal leader Jean Chretien became prime minister.

canal artificial waterway constructed for drainage, irrigation, or navigation. **Irrigation canals** carry water for irrigation from rivers, reservoirs, or wells, and are designed to maintain an even flow of water over the whole length. **Navigation and ship canals** are constructed at one level between *locks, and frequently link with rivers or sea inlets to form a waterway system. The Suez Canal 1869 and the Panama Canal 1914 eliminated long trips around continents and dramatically shortened shipping routes.

Canaletto Antonio (Giovanni Antonio Canale) 1697–1768. Italian painter. He is celebrated for his paintings of views (*vedute*) of Venice (his native city) and of London and the river Thames 1746–56.

Canaries current cold ocean current in the North Atlantic Ocean flowing SW from Spain along the NW coast of Africa. It meets the northern equatorial current at a latitude of 20° N.

canary bird *Serinus canaria* of the finch family, found wild in the Canary Islands and Madeira. It is greenish with a yellow underside. Canaries have been bred as cage birds in Europe since the 15th century, and many domestic varieties are yellow or orange.

Canary Islands (Spanish **Canarias**) group of volcanic islands 100 km/60 mi off the NW coast of Africa, forming the Spanish provinces of Las Palmas and Santa Cruz de Tenerife; area 7,300 sq km/2,818 sq mi; population (1986) 1,615,000.

features The chief centres are Santa Cruz on Tenerife (which also has the highest peak in extracontinental Spain, Pico de Teide, 3,713 m/ 12,186 ft), and Las Palmas on Gran Canaria. The province of Santa Cruz comprises Tenerife, Palma, Gomera, and Hierro; the province of Las Palmas comprises Gran Canaria, Lanzarote, and Fuerteventura. There are also six uninhabited islets. The Northern Hemisphere Observatory (1981) is on the island of La Palma. Observation conditions are exceptionally good because there is no moisture, no artificial light pollution, and little natural airglow. The Organization of African Unity (OAU) supports an independent Guanch Republic and revival of the Guanch language.

Canary Wharf large-scale office development on the Isle of Dogs in London's *Docklands, the first phase of which was completed 1992. The complex of offices, surrounding landscaped squares, is best known for its central skyscraper, the second tallest in Europe at 244 m/800 ft. Designed by US architect Cesar Pelli (1926–), it sports a pyramid-shaped crown in stainless steel.

Canberra capital of Australia (since 1908), situated in the Australian Capital Territory, enclosed within New South Wales, on a tributary of the Murrumbidgee River; area (Australian Capital Territory including the port at Jervis Bay) 2,432 sq km/939 sq mi; population (1988) 297,300.

cancer group of diseases characterized by abnormal proliferation of cells. Cancer (malignant) cells are usually degenerate, capable only of reproducing themselves (tumour formation). Malignant cells tend to spread from their site of origin by travelling through the bloodstream or lymphatic system.

Cancer faintest of the zodiacal constellations (its brightest stars are fourth magnitude). It lies in the Northern hemisphere, between Leo and Gemini, and is represented as a crab. Cancer's most distinctive feature is the star cluster Praesepe, popularly known as the Beehive. The Sun passes through the constellation during late July and early Aug. In astrology, the dates for Cancer are between about 22 June and 22 July (see *precession).

Cancún resort in Yucatan, Mexico, created on a barrier island 1974 by the Mexican government to boost tourism; population around 30,000 (almost all involved in the tourist industry). It is Mexico's most popular tourist destination, with beaches, a coral reef, and lagoon. In 1981, a North-South summit was held here to discuss the widening gap between the industrialized countries and the Third World.

candela SI unit (symbol cd) of luminous intensity, which replaced the old units of candle and standard candle. It measures the brightness of a light itself rather than the amount of light falling on an object, which is called *illuminance* and measured in *lux.

Candida albicans yeastlike fungus present in the human digestive tract and in the vagina, which causes no harm in most healthy people. However, it can cause problems if it multiplies excessively, as in vaginal candidiasis or *thrush, the main symptom of which is intense itching. The most common form of thrush is oral, which often occurs in those taking steroids or prolonged courses of antibiotics.

cane reedlike stem of various plants such as the sugar cane, bamboo, and, in particular, the group of palms called rattans, consisting of the genus *Calamus* and its allies. Their slender stems are dried and used for making walking sticks, baskets, and furniture.

Canes Venatici constellation of the northern hemisphere near Ursa Major, identified with the hunting dogs of *Boötes, the herder. Its stars are faint, and it contains the Whirlpool galaxy (M51), the first spiral galaxy to be recognized.

Canetti Elias 1905–1994. Bulgarian-born writer. He was exiled from Austria as a Jew 1938 and settled in England 1939. His books, written in German, include *Die Blendung/Auto da Fé* 1935. Nobel Prize for Literature 1981.

canine in mammalian carnivores, any of the long, often pointed teeth found at the front of the mouth between the incisors and premolars. Canine teeth are used for catching prey, for killing, and for tearing flesh. They are absent in herbivores such as rabbits and sheep, and are much reduced in humans.

Canis Major brilliant constellation of the southern hemisphere, identified with one of the two dogs following at the heel of Orion. Its main star, *Sirius, is the brightest star in the sky.

Canis Minor small constellation along the celestial equator, identified with the second of the two dogs of Orion (the other dog is Canis Major). Its brightest star is Procyon.

cannabis dried leaves and female flowers (marijuana) and resin (hashish) of certain varieties of *hemp *Cannabis sativa*, which are smoked or eaten and have an intoxicating effect.

Cannes Film Festival international film festival held every year in Cannes, France. A number of important prizes are awarded, including the Palme d'Or (Golden Palm) for the best film.

canning food preservation in hermetically sealed containers by the application of heat. Originated by Nicolas Appert in France 1809 with glass containers, it was developed by Peter Durand in England 1810 with cans made of sheet steel thinly coated with tin to delay corrosion. Cans for beer and soft drinks are now generally made of aluminium.

Canning Charles John, 1st Earl 1812–1862. British administrator, first viceroy of India from 1858. As governor general of India from 1856, he suppressed the Indian Mutiny with a fair but firm hand which earned him the nickname 'Clemency Canning'. He was the son of George Canning.

Canning George 1770–1827. British Tory politician, foreign secretary 1807–10 and 1822–27, and prime minister 1827 in coalition with the Whigs. He was largely responsible, during the Napoleonic Wars, for the seizure of the Danish fleet and British intervention in the Spanish peninsula.

Cannizzaro Stanislao 1826–1910. Italian chemist who revived interest in the work of Avogadro that had, in 1811, revealed the difference between *atoms and *molecules, and so established atomic and molecular weights as the basis of chemical calculations.

Cannon Annie Jump 1863–1941. US astronomer who, from 1896, worked at Harvard College Observatory and carried out revolutionary work on the classification of stars by examining their spectra. Her system, still used today, has spectra arranged according to temperature and runs from O through B, A, F, G, K, and M. O-type stars are the hottest, with surface temperatures of over 25,000 K.

Cano Juan Sebastian del *c.* 1476–1526. Spanish voyager. It is claimed that he was the first sea captain to sail around the world. He sailed with Magellan 1519 and, after the latter's death in the Philippines, brought the *Victoria* safely home to Spain.

canoeing sport of propelling a lightweight, shallow boat, pointed at both ends, by paddles or sails. Currently, canoes are made from fibreglass, but original boats were of wooden construction covered in bark or skin. Canoeing was popularized as a sport in the 19th century.

canon in theology, the collection of writings that is accepted as authoritative in a given religion, such as the *Tripitaka* in Theravāda Buddhism. In the Christian church, it comprises the books of the *Bible.

canon in music, an echo form for two or more parts repeating and following a leading melody at regular time intervals to achieve a harmonious effect. It is often found in classical music, for example *Vivaldi and J S *Bach.

canonical hours in the Catholic church, seven set periods of devotion: *matins* and *lauds*, *prime*, *terce*, *sext*, *nones*, *evensong* or *vespers*, and *compline*.

canonization in the Catholic church, the admission of one of its members to the Calendar of *Saints. The evidence of the candidate's exceptional piety is contested before the Congregation for the Causes of Saints by the Promotor Fidei, popularly known as the *devil's advocate*. Papal ratification of a favourable verdict results in *beatification, and full sainthood (conferred in St

Peter's basilica, the Vatican) follows after further proof.

canon law rules and regulations of the Christian church, especially the Greek Orthodox, Roman Catholic, and Anglican churches. Its origin is sought in the declarations of Jesus and the apostles. In 1983 Pope John Paul II issued a new canon law code reducing offences carrying automatic excommunication, extending the grounds for annulment of marriage, removing the ban on marriage with non-Catholics, and banning trade union and political activity by priests.

Canopus or *Alpha Carinae* second brightest star in the sky (after Sirius), lying in the constellation Carina. It is a yellow-white supergiant about 120 light years from Earth, and thousands of times more luminous than the Sun.

Canova Antonio 1757–1822. Italian Neo-Classical sculptor, based in Rome from 1781. He received commissions from popes, kings, and emperors for his highly finished marble portrait busts and groups. He made several portraits of Napoleon.

Cantab abbreviation for *Cantabrigiensis* (Latin 'of Cambridge').

Cantabria autonomous region of N Spain; area 5,300 sq km/2,046 sq mi; population (1986) 525,000; capital Santander.

cantaloupe any of several small varieties of muskmelon *Cucumis melo*, distinguished by their round, ribbed fruits with orange-coloured flesh.

cantata in music, an extended work for voices, from the Italian, meaning 'sung', as opposed to *sonata* ('sounded') for instruments. A cantata can be sacred or secular, sometimes uses solo voices, and usually has orchestral accompaniment. The first printed collection of sacred cantata texts dates from 1670.

Canterbury historic cathedral city in Kent, England, on the river Stour, 100 km/62 mi SE of London; population (1984) 39,000. In 597 King Ethelbert welcomed *Augustine's mission to England here, and the city has since been the metropolis of the Anglican Communion and seat of the archbishop of Canterbury.

Canterbury, archbishop of primate of all England, archbishop of the Church of England (Anglican), and first peer of the realm, ranking next to royalty. He crowns the sovereign, has a seat in the House of Lords, and is a member of the Privy Council. He is appointed by the prime minister.

cantilever beam or structure that is fixed at one end only, though it may be supported at some point along its length; for example, a diving board. The cantilever principle, widely used in construction engineering, eliminates the need for a second main support at the free end of the beam, allowing for more elegant structures and reducing the amount of materials required. Many large-span bridges have been built on the cantilever principle.

canton in France, an administrative district, a subdivision of the *arrondissement*; in Switzerland, one of the 23 subdivisions forming the Confederation.

Canton alternative spelling of Kwangchow or *Guangzhou in China.

cantor (Latin *cantare* 'to sing') in Judaism, the prayer leader and choir master in a synagogue; the cantor is not a rabbi, and the position can be held by any lay person.

Canute c. 995–1035. King of England from 1016, Denmark from 1018, and Norway from 1028. Having invaded England 1013 with his father, Sweyn, king of Denmark, he was acclaimed king on his father's death 1014 by his *Viking army. Canute defeated *Edmund II Ironside at Assandun, Essex, 1016, and became king of all England on Edmund's death. He succeeded his brother Harold as king of Denmark 1018, compelled King Malcolm to pay homage by invading Scotland about 1027, and conquered Norway 1028. He was succeeded by his illegitimate son Harold I.

Canute VI (*Cnut VI*) 1163–1202. King of Denmark from 1182, son and successor of Waldemar Knudsson. With his brother and successor, Waldemar II, he resisted Frederick I's northward expansion, and established Denmark as the dominant power in the Baltic.

canyon (Spanish *cañon* 'tube') deep, narrow valley or gorge running through mountains. Canyons are formed by stream down-cutting, usually in arid areas, where the stream or river receives water from outside the area.

cap another name for a *diaphragm contraceptive.

CAP abbreviation for *Common Agricultural Policy*.

capacitance, electrical property of a capacitor that determines how much charge can be stored in it for a given potential difference between its terminals. It is equal to the ratio of the electrical charge stored to the potential difference. It is measured in *farads.

capacitor or *condenser* device for storing electric charge, used in electronic circuits; it consists of two or more metal plates separated by an insulating layer called a dielectric.

capacity in economics, the maximum amount that can be produced when all the resources in an economy, industry, or firm are employed as fully as possible. Capacity constraints can be caused by lack of investment and skills shortages, and spare capacity can be caused by lack of demand.

Cape Canaveral promontory on the Atlantic coast of Florida, USA, 367 km/228 mi N of Miami, used as a rocket launch site by *NASA.

Cape Cod hook-shaped peninsula in SE Massachusetts, USA, 100 km/60 mi long and 1.6–32 km/1–20 mi wide. Its beaches and woods make it a popular tourist area. It is separated from the rest of the state by the Cape Cod Canal. The islands of Martha's Vineyard and Nantucket are just south of the cape.

cape gooseberry plant *Physalis peruviana* of the potato family. Originating in South America, it is grown in South Africa, from where it takes its name. It is cultivated for its fruit, a yellow berry surrounded by a papery *calyx.

Cape Horn southernmost point of South America, in the Chilean part of the archipelago of *Tierra del Fuego; notorious for gales and heavy seas. It was named 1616 by Dutch explorer Willem Schouten (1580–1625) after his birthplace (Hoorn).

Čapek Karel 1890–1938. Czech writer whose works often deal with social injustice in an imaginative, satirical way. *R.U.R.* 1921 is a play in which robots (a term he coined) rebel against their controllers; the novel *Válka s Mloky/War with the Newts* 1936 is a science-fiction classic.

Capella or *Alpha Aurigae* brightest star in the constellation Auriga and the sixth brightest star in the sky. It consists of a pair of yellow giant stars 41 light years from Earth, orbiting each other every 104 days.

Cape of Good Hope South African headland forming a peninsula between Table Bay and False Bay, Cape Town. The first European to sail around it was Bartholomew Diaz 1488. Formerly named Cape of Storms, it was given its present name by King John II of Portugal.

Cape Province (Afrikaans *Kaapprovinsie*) largest province of the Republic of South Africa, named after the Cape of Good Hope
area 641,379 sq km/247,638 sq mi, excluding Walvis Bay
capital Cape Town
towns Port Elizabeth, East London, Kimberley, Grahamstown, Stellenbosch
physical Orange River, Drakensberg, Table Mountain (highest point Maclear's Beacon, 1,087 m/3,567 ft); Great Karoo Plateau, Walvis Bay
products fruit, vegetables, wine; meat, ostrich feathers; diamonds, copper, asbestos, manganese
population (1985) 5,041,000; officially including 44% coloured; 31% black; 25% white; 0.6% Asian
history Dutch traders established the first European settlement on the Cape 1652, but it was taken by the British 1795, after the French Revolutionary armies had occupied the Netherlands, and was sold to Britain for £6 million 1814. The Cape achieved self-government 1872. It was an original province of the Union 1910.

caper trailing shrub *Capparis spinosa*, native to the Mediterranean and belonging to the family Capparidaceae. Its flower buds are preserved in vinegar as a condiment.

Capet Hugh 938–996. King of France from 987, when he claimed the throne on the death of Louis V. He founded the *Capetian dynasty*, of which various branches continued to reign until the French Revolution, for example, *Valois and *Bourbon.

Cape Town (Afrikaans *Kaapstad*) port and oldest town in South Africa, situated in the SW on Table Bay; population (1985) 776,617. Industries include horticulture and trade in wool, wine, fruit, grain, and oil. It is the legislative capital of the Republic of South Africa and capital of Cape Province; it was founded 1652.

Cape Verde Republic of (*República de Cabo Verde*)
area 4,033 sq km/1,557 sq mi
capital Praia
towns Mindelo, Sal-Rei, Porto Novo
physical archipelago of ten volcanic islands 565 km/350 mi W of Senegal; the windward (Barlavento) group includes Santo Antão, São Vicente, Santa Luzia, São Nicolau, Sal, and Boa Vista; the leeward (Sotovento) group comprises Maio, São Tiago, Fogo, and Brava; all but Santa Luzia are inhabited
head of state Mascarenhas Monteiro from 1991
head of government Carlos Viega from 1991
political system socialist pluralist state
exports bananas, salt, fish
currency Cape Verde escudo
population (1993 est) 350,000 (including 100,000 Angolan refugees); growth rate 1.9% p.a.
language Creole dialect of Portuguese
religion Roman Catholic 80%
GNP $750 per head (1991)
chronology
15th century First settled by Portuguese.
1951–74 Ruled as an overseas territory by Portugal.
1974 Moved towards independence through a transitional Portuguese–Cape Verde government.
1975 Independence achieved from Portugal. National people's assembly elected. Aristides Pereira became the first president.
1980 Constitution adopted providing for eventual union with Guinea-Bissau.
1981 Union with Guinea-Bissau abandoned and the constitution amended; became one-party state.
1991 First multiparty elections held. New party, MPD, won majority in assembly. Pereira replaced by Mascarenhas Monteiro.

capillarity spontaneous movement of liquids up or down narrow tubes, or capillaries. The movement is due to unbalanced molecular attraction at the boundary between the liquid and the tube. If liquid molecules near the boundary are more strongly attracted to molecules in the material of the tube than to other nearby liquid molecules, the liquid will rise in the tube. If liquid molecules are less attracted to the material of the tube than to other liquid molecules, the liquid will fall.

capillary narrowest blood vessel in vertebrates, 0.008–0.02 mm in diameter, barely wider than a red blood cell. Capillaries are distributed as *beds*, complex networks connecting arteries and veins. Capillary walls are extremely thin, consisting of a single layer of cells, and so nutrients, dissolved gases, and waste products can easily pass through them. This makes the capillaries the main area of exchange between the fluid (*lymph) bathing body tissues and the blood.

capillary in physics, a very narrow, thick-walled tube, usually made of glass, such as in a thermometer. Properties of fluids, such as surface tension and viscosity, can be studied using capillary tubes.

capital in architecture, a stone placed on the top of a column, pier, or pilaster, and usually wider on the upper surface than the diameter of the supporting shaft. A capital consists of three parts: the top member, called the *abacus*, a block that acts as the supporting surface to the superstructure; the middle portion, known as the bell or *echinus*; and the lower part, called the necking or *astragal*.

capital in economics, accumulated or inherited wealth held in the form of assets (such as stocks and shares, property, and bank deposits). In stricter terms, capital is defined as the stock of goods used in the production of other goods, and may be *fixed capital* (such as buildings, plant, and machinery) that is durable, or *circulating capital* (raw materials and components) that is used up quickly.

capital bond in economics, an investment bond that is purchased by a single payment, set up for a fixed period, and offered for sale by a life insurance company. The emphasis is on capital growth of the lump sum invested rather than on income.

capitalism economic system in which the principal means of production, distribution, and exchange are in private (individual or corporate) hands and competitively operated for profit. A *mixed economy* combines the private enterprise of capitalism and a degree of state monopoly, as in nationalized industries.

capital punishment punishment by death. Capital punishment is retained in 92 countries and territories (1990), including the USA (37 states), China, and Islamic countries. It was abolished in the UK 1965 for all crimes except treason. Methods of execution include electrocution, lethal gas, hanging, shooting, lethal injection, garrotting, and decapitation.

Capone Al(phonse 'Scarface') 1898–1947. US gangster. During the *Prohibition period, he built a formidable criminal organization in Chicago. He was brutal in his pursuit of dominance, killing seven members of a rival gang in the St Valentine's Day massacre. He was imprisoned 1931–39 for income-tax evasion, the only charge that could be sustained against him.

Capote Truman. Pen name of Truman Streckfus Persons 1924–1984. US novelist, journalist, and playwright. He wrote *Breakfast at Tiffany's* 1958; set a trend with the first 'nonfiction novel', *In Cold Blood* 1966, reconstructing a Kansas killing; and mingled recollection and fiction in *Music for Chameleons* 1980.

Cappadocia ancient region of Asia Minor, in E central Turkey. It was conquered by the Persians 584 BC but in the 3rd century BC became an independent kingdom. The region was annexed as a province of the Roman Empire AD 17.

Capra Frank 1897–1991. Italian-born US film director. His films, satirical social comedies that often have idealistic heroes, include *It Happened One Night* 1934, *Mr Deeds Goes to Town* 1936, and *You Can't Take It With You* 1938, for each of which he received an Academy Award.

Capricornus zodiacal constellation in the southern hemisphere next to Sagittarius. It is represented as a fish-tailed goat, and its brightest stars are third magnitude. The Sun passes through it late Jan to mid-Feb. In astrology, the dates for Capricornus (popularly known as Capricorn) are between about 22 Dec and 19 Jan (see *precession).

Caprivi Georg Leo, Graf von 1831–1899. German soldier and politician. While chief of the admiralty (1883–88) he reorganized the German navy. He became imperial chancellor 1890–94 succeeding Bismarck and renewed the Triple Alliance but wavered between European allies and Russia. Although he strengthened the army, he alienated the conservatives.

Caprivi Strip NE part of Namibia, a narrow strip between Angola and Botswana, giving the country access to the Zambezi River.

capsicum any pepper plant of the genus *Capsicum* of the nightshade family Solanaceae, native to Central and South America. The differing species produce green to red fruits that vary in size. The small ones are used whole to give the hot flavour of chilli, or ground to produce cayenne pepper; the large pointed or squarish pods, known as sweet peppers, are mild-flavoured and used as a vegetable.

capsule in botany, a dry, usually many-seeded fruit formed from an ovary composed of two or more fused *carpels, which splits open to release the seeds. The same term is used for the spore-containing structure of mosses and liverworts; this is borne at the top of a long stalk or seta.

capuchin monkey of the genus *Cebus* found in Central and South America, so called because the hairs on the head resemble the cowl of a Capuchin monk. Capuchins live in small groups, feed on fruit and insects, and have a long tail that is semiprehensile and can give support when climbing through the trees.

Capuchin member of the Franciscan order of monks in the Roman Catholic church, instituted by the Italian monk Matteo di Bassi (died 1552), who wished to return to the literal observance of the rule of St Francis. The Capuchin rule was drawn up 1529 and the order recognized by the pope 1619. The name was derived from the French term for the brown habit and pointed hood (*capuche*) that they wore. The order has been involved in missionary activity.

capybara world's largest rodent *Hydrochoerus hydrochaeris*, up to 1.3 m/4 ft long and 50 kg/110 lb in weight. It is found in South America, and belongs to the guinea-pig family. The capybara inhabits marshes and dense vegetation around water. It has thin, yellowish hair, swims well, and can rest underwater with just eyes, ears, and nose above the surface.

car small, driver-guided, passenger-carrying motor vehicle; originally the automated version of the horse-drawn carriage, meant to convey people and their goods over streets and roads. Over 300 million motor vehicles are produced each year worldwide. Most are four-wheeled and have water-cooled, piston-type internal-combustion engines fuelled by petrol or diesel. Variations have existed for decades that use ingenious and often nonpolluting power plants, but the motor industry long ago settled on this general formula for the consumer market. Experimental and sports models are streamlined, energy-efficient, and hand-built.

Caracalla Marcus Aurelius Antoninus AD 186–217. Roman emperor. He succeeded his father Septimus Severus AD 211, ruled with cruelty and extravagance, and was assassinated. He was nicknamed after the Celtic cloak (*caracalla*) that he wore.

Caracas chief city and capital of Venezuela, situated on the Andean slopes, 13 km/8 mi S of its port La Guaira on the Caribbean coast; population of metropolitan area (1989) 3,373,100. Founded 1567, it is now a large industrial and commercial centre, notably for oil companies.

Caractacus died c. AD 54. British chieftain who headed resistance to the Romans in SE England AD 43–51, but was defeated on the Welsh border. Shown in Claudius's triumphal procession, he was released in tribute to his courage and died in Rome.

carambola small evergreen tree *Averrhoa carambola* of SE Asia. The fruits, called **star fruit**, are yellowish, about 12 cm/4 in long, with a five-pointed star-shaped cross-section. They may be eaten raw, cooked, or pickled, and are juicily acidic. The juice is also used to remove stains from hands and clothes.

caramel complex mixture of substances produced by heating sugars, without charring, until they turn brown. Caramel is used as colouring and flavouring in foods. Its production in the manufacture of sugar confection gives rise to a toffeelike sweet of the same name.

carat (Arabic *quirrat* 'seed') unit for measuring the mass of precious stones; it is equal to 0.2 g/ 0.00705 oz, and is part of the troy system of weights. It is also the unit of purity in gold (US karat). Pure gold is 24-carat; 22-carat (the purest used in jewellery) is 22 parts gold and two parts alloy (to give greater strength).

Caravaggio Michelangelo Merisi da 1573–1610. Italian early Baroque painter, active in Rome 1592–1606, then in Naples, and finally in Malta. His life was as dramatic as his art (he had to leave Rome after killing a man). He created a forceful style, using contrasts of light and shade and focusing closely on the subject figures, sometimes using dramatic foreshortening.

caraway herb *Carum carvi* of the carrot family Umbelliferae. Native to northern temperate Eurasian regions, it is grown for its spicy, aromatic seeds, which are used in cookery, medicine, and perfumery.

carbide compound of carbon and one other chemical element, usually a metal, silicon, or boron.

carbohydrate chemical compound composed of carbon, hydrogen, and oxygen, with the basic formula $C_m(H_2O)_n$, and related compounds with the same basic structure but modified *functional groups. As sugar and starch, carbohydrates form a major energy-providing part of the human diet.

carbolic acid common name for the aromatic compound *phenol.

carbon (Latin *carbo* (*carbonaris*) 'coal') nonmetallic element, symbol C, atomic number 6, relative atomic mass 12.011. It is one of the most widely distributed elements, both inorganically and organically, and occurs in combination with other elements in all plants and animals. The atoms of carbon can link with one another in rings or chains, giving rise to innumerable complex compounds. It occurs in nature (1) in the pure state in three crystalline forms of graphite, diamond and various fullerenes; (2) as calcium carbonate ($CaCO_3$) in carbonaceous rocks such as chalk and limestone; (3) as carbon dioxide (CO_2) in the atmosphere; and (4) as hydrocarbons in the fossil fuels petroleum, coal, and natural gas. Noncrystalline forms of pure carbon include charcoal and coal.

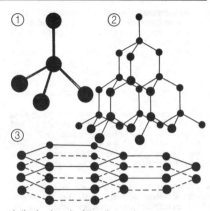

1. the basic unit of the diamond structure
2. *diamond*, a giant three-dimensional structure
3. *graphite*, a two-dimensional structure

carbon *Molecular structure of diamond and graphite.*

Carbonari secret revolutionary society in S Italy in the first half of the 19th century that advocated constitutional government. The movement spread to N Italy but support dwindled after the formation of *Mazzini's nationalist Young Italy movement, although it helped prove the way for the unification of Italy (see *Risorgimento).

carbonate CO_3^{2-} ion formed when carbon dioxide dissolves in water; any salt formed by this ion and another chemical element, usually a metal.

carbonated water water in which carbon dioxide is dissolved under pressure. It forms the basis of many fizzy soft drinks such as soda water and lemonade.

carbon cycle sequence by which *carbon circulates and is recycled through the natural world. The carbon element from carbon dioxide, released into the atmosphere by living things as a result of *respiration, is taken up by plants during *photosynthesis and converted into carbohydrates; the oxygen component is released back into the atmosphere. The simplest link in the carbon cycle occurs when an animal eats a plant and carbon is transferred from, say, a leaf cell to the animal body. Today, the carbon cycle is in danger of being disrupted by the increased consumption and burning of fossil fuels, and the burning of large tracts of tropical forests, as a result of which levels of carbon dioxide are building up in the atmosphere and probably contributing to the *greenhouse effect.

carbon dating alternative name for *radiocarbon dating.

carbon dioxide CO_2 colourless, odourless gas, slightly soluble in water and denser than air. It is formed by the complete oxidation of carbon.

carbon fibre fine, black, silky filament of pure carbon produced by heat treatment from a special grade of Courtelle acrylic fibre, used for reinforcing plastics. The resulting composite is very stiff and, weight for weight, has four times the strength of high-tensile steel. It is used in the aerospace industry, cars, and electrical and sports equipment.

Carboniferous period of geological time 360–286 million years ago, the fifth period of the Palaeozoic era. In the USA it is divided into two periods: the Mississippian (lower) and the Pennsylvanian (upper). Typical of the lower-Carboniferous rocks are shallow-water *limestone, while upper-Carboniferous rocks have *delta deposits with *coal (hence the name). Amphibians were abundant, and reptiles evolved during this period.

carbon monoxide CO colourless, odourless gas formed when carbon is oxidized in a limited supply of air. It is a poisonous constituent of car exhaust fumes, forming a stable compound with haemoglobin in the blood, thus preventing the haemoglobin from transporting oxygen to the body tissues.

Carborundum trademark for a very hard, black abrasive, consisting of silicon carbide (SiC), an artificial compound of carbon and silicon. It is harder than *corundum but not as hard as *diamond.

carboxyl group –COOH in organic chemistry, the acidic functional group that determines the properties of fatty acids (carboxylic acids) and amino acids.

carboxylic acid alternative name for *fatty acid.

carbuncle in medicine, a bacterial infection of the skin, similar to a boil but deeper and more widespread. It is treated with drawing salves, lancing, or antibiotics.

carburation mixing of a gas, such as air, with a volatile hydrocarbon fuel, such as petrol, kerosene, or fuel oil, in order to form an explosive mixture. The process, which increases the amount of potential heat energy released during combustion, is used in internal-combustion engines. In most petrol engines the liquid fuel is atomized and mixed with air by means of a device called a **carburettor**.

Carchemish (now **Karkamis**, Turkey) centre of the *Hittite New Empire (c. 1400–1200 BC) on the river Euphrates, 80 km/50 mi NE of Aleppo, and taken by Sargon II of Assyria 717 BC. Nebuchadnezzar II of Babylon defeated the Egyptians here 605 BC.

carcinogen any agent that increases the chance of a cell becoming cancerous (see *cancer), including various chemical compounds, some viruses, X-rays, and other forms of ionizing radiation. The term is often used more narrowly to mean chemical carcinogens only.

carcinoma malignant *tumour arising from the skin, the glandular tissues, or the mucous membranes that line the gut and lungs.

Cárdenas Lázaro 1895–1970. Mexican centre-left politician and general, president 1934–40. A civil servant in early life, Cárdenas took part in the revolutionary campaigns 1915–29 that followed the fall of President Díaz (1830–1915). As president of the republic, he attempted to achieve the goals of the revolution by building schools, distributing land to the peasants, and developing transport and industry. He was minister of defence 1943–45.

cardiac pertaining to the *heart.

Cardiff (Welsh **Caerdydd**) capital of Wales (from 1955) and administrative headquarters of

South and Mid Glamorgan, at the mouth of the Taff, Rhymney, and Ely rivers; population (1991) 272,600. Besides steelworks, there are car-component, flour-milling, paper, cigar, and other industries.

Cardin Pierre 1922– . French pioneering fashion designer whose clothes are bold and fantastic. He was the first to launch menswear (1960) and ready-to-wear collections (1963) and has given his name to a perfume.

cardinal in the Roman Catholic church, the highest rank next to the pope. Cardinals act as an advisory body to the pope and elect him. Their red hat is the badge of office. The number of cardinals has varied; there were 151 in 1989.

cardinal number in mathematics, one of the series of numbers 0, 1, 2, 3, 4, ... Cardinal numbers relate to quantity, whereas ordinal numbers (first, second, third, fourth, ...) relate to order.

cardioid heart-shaped curve traced out by a point on the circumference of a circle, resulting from the circle rolling around the edge of another circle of the same diameter.

Cardwell Edward, Viscount Cardwell 1813–1886. British Liberal politician. He entered Parliament as a supporter of the Conservative prime minister *Peel 1842, and was secretary for war under Gladstone 1868–74, when he carried out many reforms, including the abolition of the purchase of military commissions and promotions.

care order in Britain, a court order that places a child in the care of a local authority.

Carew Thomas c. 1595–c. 1640. English poet. He was a gentleman of the privy chamber to Charles I in 1628, and a lyricist as well as member of the school of *Cavalier poets.

Carey George Leonard 1935– . 103rd archbishop of Canterbury from 1991. A product of a liberal evangelical background, he was appointed bishop of Bath and Wells 1987.

Carey Peter 1943– . Australian novelist. His works include Bliss 1981, Illywhacker (Australian slang for 'con man') 1985, and Oscar and Lucinda 1988, which won the Booker Prize. The Tax Inspector 1991 is set in modern-day Sydney, and depicts an eccentric Greek family under investigation for tax fraud.

cargo cult Melanesian religious movement, dating from the 19th century. Adherents believe the arrival of cargo is through the agency of a messianic spirit figure, heralding a new paradise free of white dominance. The movement became active during and after World War II with the apparently miraculous dropping of supplies from aeroplanes.

Carib member of a group of *American Indian people of the northern coast of South America and the islands of the southern West Indies in the Caribbean. Those who moved north to take the islands from the Arawak Indians were alleged by the conquering Spaniards to be fierce cannibals. In 1796, the English in the West Indies deported most of them to Roatan Island, off Honduras. Carib languages belong to the Ge-Pano-Carib family.

Caribbean Community and Common Market (CARICOM) organization for economic and foreign policy coordination in the

Caribbean region, established by the Treaty of Chaguaramas 1973 to replace the former Caribbean Free Trade Association. Its members are Antigua and Barbuda, Bahamas, Barbados, Belize, Dominica, Grenada, Guyana, Jamaica, Montserrat, St Christopher–Nevis, St Lucia, St Vincent and the Grenadines, and Trinidad and Tobago. The British Virgin Islands and the Turks and Caicos Islands are associate members, and the Dominican Republic, Haiti, Mexico, Puerto Rico, Surinam, and Venezuela are observers. CARICOM headquarters are in Kingston, Jamaica.

Caribbean Sea western part of the Atlantic Ocean between the south coast of North America and the north coasts of South America. Central America is to the west and the West Indies are the islands within the sea, which is about 2,740 km/1,700 mi long and 650–1,500 km/400–900 mi wide. It is from here that the *Gulf Stream turns towards Europe.

caribou the *reindeer of North America.

caricature exaggerated portrayal of individuals or types, aiming to ridicule or otherwise expose the subject. Classical and medieval examples survive. Artists of the 18th, 19th, and 20th centuries have often used caricature as a way of satirizing society and politics. Notable exponents include the French artist Honore1 Daumier and the German George Grosz.

CARICOM abbreviation for ***Caribbean Community and Common Market**.

caries decay and disintegration, usually of the substance of teeth (cavity) or bone. It is caused by acids produced when the bacteria that live in the mouth break down sugars in the food. Fluoride, a low sugar intake, and regular brushing are all protective. Caries form mainly in the 45 minutes following an intake of sugary food, so the most dangerous diet for the teeth is one in which frequent sugary snacks and drinks are consumed.

Carina constellation of the southern hemisphere, represented as a ship's keel. Its brightest star is Canopus; it also contains Eta Carinae, a massive and highly luminous star embedded in a gas cloud, perhaps 8,000 light years away. It has varied unpredictably in the past; some astronomers think it is likely to explode as a supernova within 10,000 years.

Carinthia (German *Kärnten*) federal province of Alpine SE Austria, bordering Italy and Slovenia in the south; capital Klagenfurt; area 9,500 sq km/3,667 sq mi; population (1987) 542,000. It was an independent duchy from 976 and a possession of the Habsburg dynasty 1276–1918.

Carl XVI Gustaf 1946– . King of Sweden from 1973. He succeeded his grandfather Gustaf VI, his father having been killed in an air crash 1947. Under the new Swedish constitution, which became effective on his grandfather's death, the monarchy was stripped of all power at his accession.

Carlist supporter of the claims of the Spanish pretender Don Carlos de Bourbon (1788–1855), and his descendants, to the Spanish crown. The Carlist revolt continued, primarily in the Basque provinces, until 1839. In 1977 the Carlist political party was legalized and Carlos Hugo de Bourbon Parma (1930–) renounced his claim as pretender and became reconciled with King Juan Carlos. See also *Bourbon.

Carlos I 1863–1908. King of Portugal, of the Braganza-Coburg line, from 1889 until he was assassinated in Lisbon with his elder son Luis. He was succeeded by his younger son Manuel.

Carlos Don 1545–1568. Spanish prince. Son of Philip II, he was recognized as heir to the thrones of Castile and Aragon but became mentally unstable and had to be placed under restraint following a plot to assassinate his father. His story was the subject of plays by Friedrich von Schiller, Vittorio Alfieri, Thomas Otway, and others.

Carlos four kings of Spain; see *Charles.

Carlow county in the Republic of Ireland, in the province of Leinster; county town Carlow; area 900 sq km/347 sq mi; population (1991) 40,900. Mostly flat except for mountains in the south, the land is fertile, and well suited to dairy farming.

Carlson Chester 1906–1968. US scientist who invented *xerography. A research worker with Bell Telephone, he lost his job 1930 during the Depression and set to work on his own to develop an efficient copying machine. By 1938 he had invented the Xerox photocopier.

Carlsson Ingvar (Gösta) 1934– . Swedish socialist politician, leader of the Social Democratic Party, deputy prime minister 1982–86 and prime minister 1986–91.

Carlucci Frank (Charles) 1930– . US politician. A former diplomat and deputy director of the CIA, he was national security adviser 1986–87 and defence secretary 1987–89 under Reagan, supporting Soviet–US arms reduction.

Carlyle Thomas 1795–1881. Scottish essayist and social historian. His works include *Sartor Resartus* 1833–34, describing his loss of Christian belief, *French Revolution* 1837, *Chartism* 1839, and *Past and Present* 1843. His prose style was idiosyncratic, encompassing grand, thunderous rhetoric and deliberate obscurity.

Carmelite order mendicant order of friars in the Roman Catholic church. The order was founded on Mount Carmel in Palestine by Berthold, a crusader from Calabria, about 1155, and spread to Europe in the 13th century. The Carmelites have devoted themselves largely to missionary work and mystical theology. They are known as **White Friars** because of the white overmantle they wear (over a brown habit).

Carmichael Hoagy (Hoagland Howard) 1899–1981. US composer, pianist, singer, and actor. His songs include 'Stardust' 1927, 'Rockin' Chair' 1930, 'Lazy River' 1931, and 'In the Cool, Cool, Cool of the Evening' 1951 (Academy Award).

Carnarvon alternative spelling of *Caernarvon, a town in Gwynedd, NW Wales.

carnassial tooth powerful scissorlike pair of molars, found in all mammalian carnivores except seals. Carnassials are formed from an upper premolar and lower molar, and are shaped to produce a sharp cutting surface. Carnivores such as dogs transfer meat to the back of the mouth, where the carnassials slice up the food ready for swallowing.

carnation any of numerous double-flowered cultivated varieties of a plant *Dianthus caryophyllus* of the pink family. The flowers smell like cloves; they are divided into flake, bizarre, and picotees, according to whether the petals exhibit one or more colours on their white ground, have the colour dispersed in strips, or have a coloured border to the petals.

carnauba palm *Copernicia cerifera*, native to South America. It produces fine timber and a hard wax, used for polishes and lipsticks.

Carné Marcel 1909– . French director known for the romantic fatalism of such films as *Drôle de Drame* 1936, *Hôtel du Nord* 1938, *Le Quai des brumes/Port of Shadows* 1938, and *Le Jour se lève/Daybreak* 1939. His masterpiece, *Les Enfants du paradis/The Children of Paradise* 1943–45, was made with his longtime collaborator, the poet and screenwriter Jacques Prévert (1900–1977).

Carnegie Andrew 1835–1919. US industrialist and philanthropist, born in Scotland, who developed the Pittsburgh iron and steel industries, making the USA the world's leading producer. He endowed public libraries, education, and various research trusts.

Carnegie Dale 1888–1955. US author and teacher who wrote the best-selling self-help book *How to Win Friends and Influence People* 1937.

carnelian semiprecious gemstone variety of *chalcedony consisting of quartz (silica) with iron impurities, which give it a translucent red colour. It is found mainly in Brazil, India, and Japan.

carnivore animal that eats other animals. Although the term is sometimes confined to those that eat the flesh of *vertebrate prey, it is often used more broadly to include any animal that eats other animals, even microscopic ones. Carrion-eaters may or may not be included.

Carnot (Nicolas Leonard) Sadi 1796–1832. French scientist and military engineer who founded the science of *thermodynamics. His pioneering work was *Réflexions sur la puissance motrice du feu/On the Motive Power of Fire*.

Carnot Lazare Nicolas Marguerite 1753–1823. French general and politician. A member of the National Convention in the French Revolution, he organized the armies of the republic. He was war minister 1800–01 and minister of the interior 1815 under Napoleon. His work on fortification, *De la Défense de places fortes* 1810, became a military textbook. Minister of the interior during the *Hundred Days, he was proscribed at the restoration of the monarchy and retired to Germany.

Carnot cycle series of changes in the physical condition of a gas in a reversible heat engine, necessarily in the following order: (1) isothermal expansion (without change of temperature), (2) adiabatic expansion (without change of heat content), (3) isothermal compression, and (4) adiabatic compression.

carnotite potassium uranium vanadate, $K_2(UO_2)_2(VO_4)_2.3H_2O$, a radioactive ore of vanadium and uranium with traces of radium. A yellow powdery mineral, it is mined chiefly in the Colorado Plateau, USA; Radium Hill, Australia; and Shaba, Zaire.

carob small Mediterranean tree *Ceratonia siliqua* of the legume family Leguminosae. Its pods, 20 cm/8 in long, are used as animal fodder; they are also the source of a chocolate substitute.

carol song that in medieval times was associated with a round dance; now those that are sung at annual festivals, such as Easter and Christmas.

Carol two kings of Romania:

Carol I 1839–1914. First king of Romania 1881–1914. A prince of the house of Hohenzollern-Sigmaringen, he was invited to become prince of Romania, then part of the Ottoman Empire, 1866. In 1877, in alliance with Russia, he declared war on Turkey, and the Congress of Berlin 1878 recognized Romanian independence.

Carol II 1893–1953. King of Romania 1930–40. Son of King Ferdinand, he married Princess Helen of Greece and they had a son, Michael. In 1925 he renounced the succession because of his affair with Elena Lupescu and went into exile in Paris. Michael succeeded to the throne 1927, but in 1930 Carol returned to Romania and was proclaimed king. In 1938 he introduced a new constitution under which he practically became an absolute ruler. He was forced to abdicate by the pro-Nazi *Iron Guard Sept 1940, went to Mexico, and married his mistress 1947.

Carolina two separate states of the USA; see *North Carolina and *South Carolina.

Caroline of Anspach 1683–1737. Queen of George II of Great Britain and Ireland. The daughter of the Margrave of Brandenburg-Anspach, she married George, Electoral Prince of Hanover, 1705, and followed him to England 1714 when his father became King George I. She was the patron of many leading writers and politicians such as Alexander Pope, John Gay, and the Earl of Chesterfield. She supported Sir Robert Walpole and kept him in power and acted as regent during her husband's four absences.

Caroline of Brunswick 1768–1821. Queen of George IV of Great Britain, who unsuccessfully attempted to divorce her on his accession to the throne 1820.

Carolines scattered archipelago in Micronesia, Pacific Ocean, consisting of over 500 coral islets; area 1,200 sq km/463 sq mi. The chief islands are Ponape, Kusai, and Truk in the eastern group, and Yap and Belau in the western group.

Carolingian dynasty Frankish dynasty descending from *Pepin the Short (died 768) and named after his son Charlemagne; its last ruler was Louis V of France (reigned 966–87), who was followed by Hugh *Capet, first ruler of the Capetian dynasty.

carotene naturally occurring pigment of the *carotenoid group. Carotenes produce the orange, yellow, and red colours of carrots, tomatoes, oranges, and crustaceans.

carotenoid any of a group of yellow, orange, red, or brown pigments found in many living organisms, particularly in the *chloroplasts of plants. There are two main types, the **carotenes** and the **xanthophylls**. Both types are long-chain lipids (*fats).

Carothers Wallace 1896–1937. US chemist who carried out research into polymerization. By 1930 he had discovered that some polymers were fibreforming, and in 1937 he produced *nylon.

carp fish *Cyprinus carpio* found all over the world. It commonly grows to 50 cm/1.8 ft and 3 kg/7 lb, but may be even larger. It lives in lakes, ponds, and slow rivers. The wild form is drab, but cultivated forms may be golden, or may have few large scales (mirror carp) or be scaleless (leather carp). *Koi* carp are highly prized and can grow up to 1 m/3 ft long with a distinctive pink, red, white, or black colouring.

Carpaccio Vittorio 1450/60–1525/26. Italian painter known for scenes of his native Venice. His series *The Legend of St Ursula* 1490–98 (Accademia, Venice) is full of detail of contemporary Venetian life. His other great series is the lives of saints George and Jerome 1502–07 (S Giorgio degli Schiavoni, Venice).

Carpathian Mountains Central European mountain system, forming a semicircle through Czechoslovakia, Poland, Ukraine and Romania, 1,450 km/900 mi long. The central *Tatra mountains* on the Czechoslovakia–Poland frontier include the highest peak, Gerlachovka, 2,663 m/ 8,737 ft.

carpel female reproductive unit in flowering plants (*angiosperms). It usually comprises an *ovary containing one or more ovules, the stalk or style, and a *stigma at its top which receives the pollen. A flower may have one or more carpels, and they may be separate or fused together. Collectively the carpels of a flower are known as the *gynoecium.

carpet thick textile fabric, generally made of wool, used for covering floors and stairs. There is a long tradition of fine handmade carpets in the Middle East, India, Pakistan, and China. Western carpets are machine-made. Carpets and rugs have also often been made in the home as a pastime, cross and tent stitch on canvas being widely used in the 18th and 19th centuries.

carpetbagger in US history, derogatory name for any of the entrepreneurs and politicians from the North who moved to the Southern states during *Reconstruction 1861–65 after the Civil War.

Carracci Italian family of painters in Bologna, whose forte was murals and ceilings. The foremost of them, *Annibale Carracci* (1560–1609), decorated the Farnese Palace, Rome, with a series of mythological paintings united by simulated architectural ornamental surrounds (completed 1604).

carragheen species of deep-reddish, branched seaweed *Chondrus crispus.* Named after Carragheen in Ireland, it is found on rocky shores on both sides of the Atlantic. It is exploited commercially in food and medicinal preparations and as cattle feed.

Carrel Alexis 1873–1944. US surgeon born in France, whose experiments paved the way for organ transplantation. Working at the Rockefeller Institute, New York City, he devised a way of joining blood vessels end to end (anastomosing). This was a key move in the development of transplant surgery, as was his work on keeping organs

viable outside the body, for which he was awarded the Nobel Prize for Medicine 1912.

Carreras José 1947– . Spanish tenor whose roles include Handel's Samson and whose recordings include *West Side Story* 1984. In 1987, he became seriously ill with leukaemia, but resumed his career in 1988.

Carrhae, Battle of battle 53 BC in which the invading Roman general Crassus was defeated and killed by the Parthians. The ancient town of Carrhae is near Haran, Turkey.

carrier in medicine, anyone who harbours an infectious organism without ill effects but can pass the infection to others. The term is also applied to those who carry a recessive gene for a disease or defect without manifesting the condition.

Carroll Lewis. Pen name of Charles Lutwidge Dodgson 1832–1898. English author of children's classics *Alice's Adventures in Wonderland* 1865 and its sequel *Through the Looking-Glass* 1872. Among later works was the mock-heroic nonsense poem *The Hunting of the Snark* 1876. An Oxford don, he also published mathematical works.

carrot hardy European biennial *Daucus carota* of the family Umbelliferae. Cultivated since the 16th century for its edible root, it has a high sugar content and also contains *carotene, which is converted by the human liver to vitamin A.

carrying capacity in ecology, the maximum number of animals of a given species that a particular area can support. When the carrying capacity is exceeded, there is insufficient food (or other resources) for the members of the population. The population may then be reduced by emigration, reproductive failure, or death through starvation.

Carson Edward Henry, Baron Carson 1854–1935. Irish politician and lawyer who played a decisive part in the trial of the writer Oscar Wilde. In the years before World War I he led the movement in Ulster to resist Irish *Home Rule by force of arms if need be.

Carson Kit (Christopher) 1809–68. US frontier settler, guide, and Indian agent, who later fought for the Federal side in the Civil War. Carson City, Nevada, was named after him.

Carson Willie (William) 1942– . Scottish jockey who has ridden four Epsom Derby winners as well as the winners of most major races worldwide.

Carson City capital of Nevada, USA; population (1990) 40,400. Settled as a trading post 1851, it was named after the frontier guide Kit Carson 1858. It flourished as a boom town after the discovery of the nearby Comstock silver-ore lode 1859.

Cartagena or *Cartagena de los Indes* port, industrial centre, and capital of the department of Bolívar, NW Colombia; population (1985) 531,000. Plastics and chemicals are produced here.

carte blanche (French 'white paper') no instructions, complete freedom to do as one wishes.

cartel (German *Kartell* 'a group') agreement among national or international firms to set mutually acceptable prices for their products. A cartel may restrict supply, or output, or raise prices to prevent entrants to the market and increase member profits. It therefore represents a form of *oligopoly. *OPEC, for example, is an oil cartel.

Carter Angela 1940–1992. English writer of the *magic realist school. Her novels include *The Magic Toyshop* 1967 (filmed by David Wheatley 1987) and *Nights at the Circus* 1984. She co-wrote the script for the film *The Company of Wolves* 1984, based on one of her stories. Her last novel was *Wise Children* 1991.

Carter Elliott (Cook) 1908– . US composer. His early work shows the influence of Igor *Stravinsky, but after 1950 his music became increasingly intricate and densely written in a manner resembling Charles *Ives. He invented 'metrical modulation', which allows different instruments or groups to stay in touch while playing at different speeds. He wrote four string quartets, the *Symphony for Three Orchestras* 1967, and the song cycle *A Mirror on Which to Dwell* 1975.

Carter Jimmy (James Earl) 1924– . 39th president of the USA 1977–81, a Democrat. In 1976 he narrowly wrested the presidency from Gerald Ford. Features of his presidency were the return of the Panama Canal Zone to Panama, the Camp David Agreements for peace in the Middle East, and the Iranian seizure of US embassy hostages. He was defeated by Ronald Reagan 1980.

Cartesian coordinates in *coordinate geometry, the components of a system used to show the position of a point on a plane (two dimensions) or in space (three dimensions) with reference to a set of two or more axes. For a plane defined by two axes at right angles (a horizontal x-axis and a vertical y-axis), the coordinates of a point are given by its perpendicular distances from the y-axis and x-axis, written in the form (x,y). For example, a point P that lies three units from the y-axis and four units from the x-axis has Cartesian coordinates (3,4) (see *abscissa). In three-dimensional coordinate geometry, points are located with reference to a third, z-axis.

Carthage ancient Phoenician port in N Africa; it lay 16 km/10 mi N of Tunis, Tunisia. A leading trading centre, it was in conflict with Greece from the 6th century BC, and then with Rome, and was destroyed by Roman forces 146 BC at the end of the *Punic Wars*. About 45 BC, Roman colonists settled in Carthage, and it became the wealthy capital of the province of Africa. After its capture by the Vandals AD 439 it was little more than a pirate stronghold. From 533 it formed part of the Byzantine Empire until its final destruction by Arabs 698, during their conquest in the name of Islam.

Carthusian order Roman Catholic order of monks and, later, nuns, founded by St Bruno 1084 at Chartreuse, near Grenoble, France. Living chiefly in unbroken silence, they ate one vegetarian meal a day and supported themselves by their own labours; the rule is still one of severe austerity.

Cartier Georges Étienne 1814–1873. French-Canadian politician. He fought against the British in the rebellion 1837, was elected to the Canadian parliament 1848, and was joint prime minister with John A Macdonald 1858–62. He brought Québec into the Canadian federation 1867.

Cartier Jacques 1491–1557. French navigator who was the first European to sail up the St Lawrence River 1534. He named the site of Montréal.

Cartier-Bresson Henri 1908– . French photographer, considered one of the greatest photographic artists. His documentary work was shot in black and white, using a small-format camera. His work is remarkable for its tightly structured composition and his ability to capture the decisive moment.

cartilage flexible bluish-white connective *tissue made up of the protein collagen. In cartilaginous fish it forms the skeleton; in other vertebrates it forms the greater part of the embryonic skeleton, and is replaced by *bone in the course of development, except in areas of wear such as bone endings, and the discs between the back-bones. It also forms structural tissue in the larynx, nose, and external ear of mammals.

Cartland Barbara 1904– . English romantic novelist. She published her first book, *Jigsaw* 1921 and since then has produced a prolific stream of stories of chastely romantic love, usually in idealized or exotic settings, for a mainly female audience (such as *Love Climbs In* 1978 and *Moments of Love* 1981).

cartography art and practice of drawing *maps.

cartoon humorous or satirical drawing or *caricature; a strip cartoon or *comic strip; traditionally, the base design for a large fresco, mosaic, or tapestry, transferred to wall or canvas by tracing or picking out (pouncing). Surviving examples include Leonardo da Vinci's *Virgin and St Anne* (National Gallery, London).

Cartwright Edmund 1743–1823. British inventor. He patented the power loom 1785, built a weaving mill 1787, and patented a wool-combing machine 1789.

Caruso Enrico 1873–1921. Italian operatic tenor. In 1902 he starred, with Nellie Melba, in Puccini's *La Bohème*. He was one of the first opera singers to profit from gramophone recordings.

Carver George Washington 1864–1943. US agricultural chemist. Born a slave in Missouri, he was kidnapped and raised by his former owner, Moses Carver. He devoted his life to improving the economy of the US South and the condition of blacks. He advocated the diversification of crops, promoted peanut production, and was a pioneer in the field of plastics.

Cary (Arthur) Joyce (Lunel) 1888–1957. British novelist. He used his experiences gained in Nigeria in the Colonial Service (which he entered 1918) as a backdrop to such novels as *Mister Johnson* 1939. Other books include *The Horse's Mouth* 1944.

caryatid building support or pillar in the shape of a woman, the name deriving from the Karyatides, who were priestesses at the temple of Artemis at Karyai; the male equivalent is a *telamon* or *atlas*.

caryopsis dry, one-seeded *fruit in which the wall of the seed becomes fused to the carpel wall during its development. It is a type of *achene, and therefore develops from one ovary and does not split open to release the seed. Caryopses are typical of members of the grass family (Gramineae), including the cereals.

Casablanca (Arabic *Dar el-Beida*) port, commercial and industrial centre on the Atlantic coast of Morocco; population (1982) 2,139,000. It trades in fish, phosphates, and manganese. The Great Hassan II Mosque, completed 1989, is the world's largest; it is built on a platform (40,000 sq m/430,000 sq ft) jutting out over the Atlantic, with walls 60 m/200 ft high, topped by a hydraulic sliding roof, and a minaret 175 m/574 ft high.

Casals Pablo 1876–1973. Catalan cellist, composer, and conductor. As a cellist, he was celebrated for his interpretations of J S Bach's unaccompanied suites. He left Spain 1939 to live in Prades, in the French Pyrenees, where he founded an annual music festival. In 1956 he moved to Puerto Rico, where he launched the Casals Festival 1957, and toured extensively in the USA. He wrote instrumental and choral works, including the Christmas oratorio *The Manger*.

Casanova de Seingalt Giovanni Jacopo 1725–1798. Italian adventurer, spy, violinist, librarian, and, according to his *Memoirs*, one of the world's great lovers. From 1774 he was a spy in the Venetian police service. In 1782 a libel got him into trouble, and after more wanderings he was appointed 1785 librarian to Count Waldstein at his castle of Dûx in Bohemia. Here Casanova wrote his *Memoirs* (published 1826–38, although the complete text did not appear until 1960–61).

casein main protein of milk, from which it can be separated by the action of acid, the enzyme rennin, or bacteria (souring); it is also the main component of cheese. Casein is used commercially in cosmetics, glues, and as a sizing for coating paper.

Casement Roger David 1864–1916. Irish nationalist. While in the British consular service, he exposed the ruthless exploitation of the people of the Belgian Congo and Peru, for which he was knighted 1911 (degraded 1916). He was hanged for treason by the British for his involvement in the Irish nationalist cause.

Cash Johnny 1932– . US country singer, songwriter, and guitarist. His early hits, recorded for Sun Records in Memphis, Tennessee, include the million-selling 'I Walk the Line' 1956. Many of his songs have become classics.

cash crop crop grown solely for sale rather than for the farmer's own use, for example, coffee, cotton, or sugar beet. Many Third World countries grow cash crops to meet their debt repayments rather than grow food for their own people. The price for these crops depends on financial interests, such as those of the multinational companies and the International Monetary Fund.

cashew tropical American tree *Anacardium occidentale*, family Anacardiaceae. Extensively cultivated in India and Africa, it produces poisonous kidney-shaped nuts that become edible after being roasted.

cash flow input of cash required to cover all expenses of a business, whether revenue or capital. Alternatively, the actual or prospective balance between the various outgoing and incoming movements which are designated in total, positive or negative according to which is greater.

cashmere natural fibre originating from the wool of the goats of Kashmir, India, used for shawls, scarves, sweaters, and coats.
It can also be made artificially.

Caslavska Vera 1943– . Czechoslovak gymnast, the first of the great present-day stylists. She won a record 21 world, Olympic, and European gold medals 1959–68; she also won eight silver and three bronze medals.

Caspian Sea world's largest inland sea, divided between Iran, Azerbaijan, Russia, Kazakhstan, and Turkmenistan; area about 400,000 sq km/155,000 sq mi, with a maximum depth of 1,000 m/3,250 ft. The chief ports are Astrakhan and Baku. Drainage in the north and damming of the Volga and Ural rivers for hydroelectric power left the sea approximately 28 m/90 ft below sea level. In June 1991 opening of sluices in the dams caused the water level to rise dramatically, threatening towns and industrial areas.

Cassandra in Greek mythology, the daughter of *Priam, king of Troy. Her prophecies (for example, of the fall of Troy) were never believed, because she had rejected the love of Apollo. She was murdered with Agamemnon by his wife Clytemnestra.

Cassatt Mary 1845–1926. US Impressionist painter and printmaker. In 1868 she settled in Paris. Her popular, colourful pictures of mothers and children show the then-new influence of Japanese prints, for example *The Bath* 1892 (Art Institute, Chicago).

cassava or *manioc* plant *Manihot utilissima*, belonging to the spurge family Euphorbiaceae. Native to South America, it is now widely grown throughout the tropics for its starch-containing roots, from which tapioca and bread are made.

cassia bark of a SE Asian plant *Cinnamomum cassia* of the laurel family Lauraceae. It is aromatic and closely resembles true cinnamon, for which it is a widely used substitute. *Cassia* is also a genus of pod-bearing tropical plants of the family Caesalpiniaceae, many of which have strong purgative properties; *Cassia senna* is the source of the laxative drug senna.

Cassini joint space probe of the US agency NASA and the European Space Agency to the planet Saturn. *Cassini* is scheduled to be launched Nov 1995 and to go into orbit around Saturn Dec 2003, dropping off a sub-probe, *Huygens*, to land on Saturn's largest moon, Titan.

Cassiopeia prominent constellation of the northern hemisphere, named after the mother of Andromeda. It has a distinctive W-shape, and contains one of the most powerful radio sources in the sky, Cassiopeia A, the remains of a *supernova (star explosion).

cassiterite or *tinstone* chief ore of tin, consisting of reddish-brown to black stannic oxide (SnO_2), usually found in granite rocks. When fresh it has a bright ('adamantine') lustre. It was formerly extensively mined in Cornwall, England; today Malaysia is the world's main supplier. Other sources of cassiterite are Africa, Indonesia, and South America.

Cassius Gaius died 42 BC. Roman soldier, one of the conspirators who killed Julius *Caesar 44 BC. He fought at Carrhae 53, and with the republicans against Caesar at Pharsalus 48, was pardoned and appointed praetor, but became a leader in the conspiracy of 44, and after Caesar's death joined Brutus. He committed suicide after his defeat at *Philippi 42.

Cassivelaunus chieftain of the British tribe, the Catuvellauni, who led the British resistance to the Romans under Caesar 54 BC.

cassowary large flightless bird, genus *Casuarius*, found in New Guinea and N Australia, usually in forests. Related to the emu, the cassowary has a bare head with a horny casque, or helmet, on top, and brightly coloured skin on the neck. Its loose plumage is black and its wings tiny, but it can run and leap well and defends itself by kicking. Cassowaries stand up to 1.5 m/ 5 ft tall.

Castagno Andrea del *c.* 1421–1457. Italian Renaissance painter, active in Florence. In his frescoes in Sta Apollonia, Florence, he adapted the pictorial space to the architectural framework and followed *Masaccio's lead in perspective.

castanets Spanish percussion instrument made of two hollowed wooden shells, clapped in the hand to produce a rhythmic accompaniment to dance.

caste (Portuguese *casta* 'race') stratification of Hindu society into four main groups: **Brahmans** (priests), **Kshatriyas** (nobles and warriors), **Vaisyas** (traders and farmers), and **Sudras** (servants); plus a fifth group, **Harijan** (untouchables). No upward or downward mobility exists, as in classed societies. The system dates from ancient times, and there are more than 3,000 subdivisions.

Castiglione Baldassare, Count Castiglione 1478–1529. Italian author and diplomat who described the perfect Renaissance gentleman in *Il Cortegiano/The Courtier* 1528.

Castile kingdom founded in the 10th century, occupying the central plateau of Spain. Its union with *Aragon 1479, based on the marriage of *Ferdinand V and *Isabella, effected the foundation of the Spanish state, which at the time was occupied and ruled by the *Moors. Castile comprised the two great basins separated by the Sierra de Gredos and the Sierra de Guadarrama, known traditionally as Old and New Castile. The area now forms the regions of *Castilla–León and *Castilla–La Mancha.

Castilian language member of the Romance branch of the Indo-European language family, originating in NW Spain, in the provinces of Old and New Castile. It is the basis of present-day standard Spanish (see *Spanish language) and is often seen as the same language, the terms *castellano* and *español* being used interchangeably in both Spain and the Spanish-speaking countries of the Americas.

Castilla–La Mancha autonomous region of central Spain; area 79,200 sq km/30,571 sq mi; population (1986) 1,665,000. It includes the provinces of Albacete, Ciudad Real, Cuenca, Guadalajara, and Toledo. Irrigated land produces

grain and chickpeas, and merino sheep graze here.

Castilla–León autonomous region of central Spain; area 94,100 sq km/36,323 sq mi; population (1986) 2,600,000. It includes the provinces of Ávila, Burgos, León, Palencia, Salamanca, Segovia, Soria, Valladolid, and Zamora. Irrigated land produces wheat and rye. Cattle, sheep, and fighting bulls are bred in the uplands.

casting process of producing solid objects by pouring molten material into a shaped mould and allowing it to cool. Casting is used to shape such materials as glass and plastics, as well as metals and alloys.

cast iron cheap but invaluable constructional material, most commonly used for car engine blocks. Cast iron is partly refined pig (crude) *iron, which is very fluid when molten and highly suitable for shaping by casting; it contains too many impurities (for example, carbon) to be readily shaped in any other way. Solid cast iron is heavy and can absorb great shock but is very brittle.

castle private fortress of a king or noble. The earliest castles in Britain were built following the Norman Conquest, and the art of castle building reached a peak in the 13th century. By the 15th century, the need for castles for domestic defence had largely disappeared, and the advent of gunpowder made them largely useless against attack. See also *château.

Castle Barbara, Baroness Castle (born Betts) 1911– . British Labour politician, a cabinet minister in the Labour governments of the 1960s and 1970s. She led the Labour group in the European Parliament 1979–89.

Castle Hill rising Irish convict revolt in New South Wales, Australia, 4 March 1804; a number were killed while parleying with the military under a flag of truce.

Castlereagh Robert Stewart, Viscount Castlereagh 1769–1822. British Tory politician. As chief secretary for Ireland 1797–1801, he suppressed the rebellion of 1798 and helped the younger Pitt secure the union of England, Scotland, and Ireland 1801. As foreign secretary 1812–22, he coordinated European opposition to Napoleon and represented Britain at the Congress of Vienna 1814–15.

Castor and Pollux/Polydeuces in Greek mythology, twin sons of Leda (by *Zeus), brothers of *Helen and *Clytemnestra. Protectors of mariners, they were transformed at death into the constellation Gemini.

castor-oil plant tall, tropical and subtropical shrub *Ricinus communis* of the spurge family Euphorbiaceae. The seeds, in North America called castor beans, yield the purgative castor oil and also ricin, one of the most powerful poisons known, which can be targeted to destroy cancer cells, while leaving normal cells untouched.

castration removal of the testicles. Male domestic animals may be castrated to prevent reproduction, to make them larger or more docile, or to remove a disease site.

Castries port and capital of St Lucia, on the NW coast of the island in the Caribbean; population (1988) 53,000. It produces textiles, chemicals, tobacco, and wood and rubber products.

Castro (Ruz) Fidel 1927– . Cuban communist politician, prime minister 1959–76 and president from 1976. He led two unsuccessful coups against the right-wing Batista regime and led the revolution that overthrew the dictator 1959. He raised the standard of living for most Cubans but dealt harshly with dissenters.

cat small, domesticated, carnivorous mammal *Felis catus*, often kept as a pet or for catching small pests such as rodents. Found in many colour variants, it may have short, long, or no hair, but the general shape and size is constant. All cats walk on the pads of their toes, and have retractile claws. They have strong limbs, large eyes, and acute hearing. The canine teeth are long and well-developed, as are the shearing teeth in the side of the mouth.

catabolism in biology, the destructive part of *metabolism where living tissue is changed into energy and waste products. It is the opposite of *anabolism. It occurs continuously in the body, but is accelerated during many disease processes, such as fever, and in starvation.

catacomb underground cemetery, such as the catacombs of the early Christians. Examples include those beneath the basilica of St Sebastian in Rome, where bodies were buried in niches in the walls of the tunnels.

Catalan language member of the Romance branch of the Indo-European language family, an Iberian language closely related to Provençal in France. It is spoken in Catalonia in NE Spain, the Balearic Islands, Andorra, and a corner of SW France.

Catalonia (Spanish **Cataluña**, Catalan **Catalunya**) autonomous region of NE Spain; area 31,900 sq km/12,313 sq mi; population (1986) 5,977,000. It includes Barcelona (the capital), Gerona, Lérida, and Tarragona. Industries include wool and cotton textiles; hydroelectric power is produced.

catalpa any tree of the genus *Catalpa* belonging to the trumpet creeper Bignoniaceae family, found in North America, China, and the West Indies. The northern catalpa *C. speciosa* of North America grows to 30 m/100 ft and has heart-shaped, deciduous leaves and tubular white flowers with purple borders.

Cataluña Spanish name for *Catalonia.

catalyst substance that alters the speed of, or makes possible, a chemical or biochemical reaction but remains unchanged at the end of the reaction. *Enzymes are natural biochemical catalysts. In practice most catalysts are used to speed up reactions.

catalytic converter device for reducing toxic emissions from the *internal-combustion engine. It converts harmful exhaust products to relatively harmless ones by passing exhaust gases over a mixture of catalysts. *Oxidation catalysts* convert hydrocarbons into carbon dioxide and water; *three-way catalysts* convert oxides of nitrogen back into nitrogen.

catamaran (Tamil 'tied log') twin-hulled sailing vessel, based on the aboriginal craft of South America and the Indies, made of logs lashed together, with an outrigger. A similar vessel with three hulls is known as a trimaran. Car ferries with a wave-piercing catamaran design are also in use in parts of Europe and North America. They have a pointed main hull and two outriggers and travel at a speed of 35 knots (84.5 kph/52.5 mph).

Catania industrial port in Sicily; population (1988) 372,000. It exports local sulphur.

cataract eye disease in which the crystalline lens or its capsule becomes opaque, causing blindness. Fluid accumulates between the fibres of the lens and gives place to deposits of *albumin. These coalesce into rounded bodies, the lens fibres break down, and areas of the lens or the lens capsule become filled with opaque products of degeneration.

catastrophe theory mathematical theory developed by René Thom in 1972, in which he showed that the growth of an organism proceeds by a series of gradual changes that are triggered by, and in turn trigger, large-scale changes or 'catastrophic' jumps. It also has applications in engineering – for example, the gradual strain on the structure of a bridge that can eventually result in a sudden collapse – and has been extended to economic and psychological events.

catastrophism theory that the geological features of the Earth were formed by a series of sudden, violent 'catastrophes' beyond the ordinary workings of nature. The theory was largely the work of Georges *Cuvier. It was later replaced by the concepts of *uniformitarianism and *evolution.

catch crop crop such as turnip that is inserted between two principal crops in a rotation in order to provide some quick livestock feed or soil improvement at a time when the land would otherwise be lying idle.

catchment area area from which water is collected by a river and its tributaries. In the social sciences the term may be used to denote the area from which people travel to obtain a particular service or product, such as the area from which a school draws its pupils.

catechism teaching by question and answer on the Socratic method, but chiefly as a means of instructing children in the basics of the Christian creed. A person being instructed in this way in preparation for baptism or confirmation is called a *catechumen*.

category in philosophy, a fundamental concept applied to being that cannot be reduced to anything more elementary. Aristotle listed ten categories: substance, quantity, quality, relation, place, time, position, state, action, and passion.

caterpillar larval stage of a *butterfly or *moth. Wormlike in form, the body is segmented, may be hairy, and often has scent glands. The head has strong biting mandibles, silk glands, and a spinneret.

caterpillar track endless flexible belt of metal plates on which certain vehicles such as tanks and bulldozers run, which takes the place of ordinary tyred wheels and improves performance on wet or uneven surfaces.

catfish fish belonging to the order Siluriformes, in which barbels (feelers) on the head are well-developed, so giving a resemblance to the whiskers of a cat. Catfishes are found worldwide, mainly but not exclusively in fresh water, and are plentiful in South America.

Cathar (medieval Latin 'the pure') member of a sect in medieval Europe usually numbered among the Christian heretics. Influenced by *Manichaeism, they started about the 10th century in the Balkans where they were called 'Bogomils', spread to SW Europe where they were often identified with the *Albigenses, and by the middle of the 14th century had been destroyed or driven underground by the Inquisition.

cathedral (Latin *cathedra*, 'seat' or 'throne') Christian church containing the throne of a bishop or archbishop, which is usually situated on the south side of the choir. A cathedral is governed by a dean and chapter.

Catherine I 1684–1727. Empress of Russia from 1725. A Lithuanian peasant, born Martha Skavronsky, she married a Swedish dragoon and eventually became the mistress of Peter the Great. In 1703 she was rechristened Katarina Alexeievna. The tsar divorced his wife 1711 and married Catherine 1712. She accompanied him on his campaigns, and showed tact and shrewdness. In 1724 she was proclaimed empress, and after Peter's death 1725 she ruled capably with the help of her ministers. She allied Russia with Austria and Spain in an anti-English bloc.

Catherine II *the Great* 1729–1796. Empress of Russia from 1762, and daughter of the German prince of Anhalt-Zerbst. In 1745, she married the Russian grand duke Peter. Catherine was able to dominate him; six months after he became Tsar Peter III 1762, he was murdered in a coup and Catherine ruled alone. During her reign Russia extended its boundaries to include territory from wars with the Turks 1768–74, 1787–92, and from the partitions of Poland 1772, 1793, and 1795, as well as establishing hegemony over the Black Sea.

Catherine de' Medici 1519–1589. French queen consort of Henry II, whom she married 1533; daughter of Lorenzo de' Medici, Duke of Urbino; and mother of Francis II, Charles IX, and Henry III. At first outshone by Henry's mistress Diane de Poitiers (1490–1566), she became regent 1560–63 for Charles IX and remained in power until her death 1574.

Catherine of Alexandria, St Christian martyr. According to legend she disputed with 50 scholars, refusing to give up her faith and marry Emperor Maxentius. Her emblem is a wheel, on which her persecutors tried to kill her (the wheel broke and she was beheaded). Feast day 25 Nov.

Catherine of Aragon 1485–1536. First queen of Henry VIII of England, 1509–33, and mother of Mary I. Catherine had married Henry's elder brother Prince Arthur 1501 and on his death 1502 was betrothed to Henry, marrying him on his accession. She failed to produce a male heir and Henry divorced her without papal approval, thus beginning the English *Reformation.

Catherine of Siena 1347–1380. Italian mystic, born in Siena. She persuaded Pope Gregory XI to return to Rome from Avignon 1376. In 1375 she is said to have received on her body the stigmata, the impression of Jesus' wounds. Her *Dialogue* is a classic mystical work. Feast day 29 April.

Catherine of Valois 1401–1437. Queen of Henry V of England, whom she married 1420; the mother of Henry VI. After the death of Henry V, she secretly married Owen Tudor (c. 1400–1461) about 1425, and their son Edmund Tudor became the father of Henry VII.

catheter fine tube inserted into the body to introduce or remove fluids. The original catheter was the urinary one, passed by way of the urethra (the duct that leads urine away from the bladder). In today's practice, catheters can be inserted into blood vessels, either in the limbs or trunk, to provide blood samples and local pressure measurements, and to deliver drugs and/or nutrients directly into the bloodstream.

cathode in chemistry, the negative electrode of an electrolytic *cell, towards which positive particles (cations), usually in solution, are attracted. See *electrolysis.

cathode in electronics, the part of an electronic device in which electrons are generated. In a thermionic valve, electrons are produced by the heating effect of an applied current; in a photoelectric cell, they are produced by the interaction of light and a semiconducting material. The cathode is kept at a negative potential relative to the device's other electrodes (anodes) in order to ensure that the liberated electrons stream away from the cathode and towards the anodes.

cathode-ray tube vacuum tube in which a beam of electrons is produced and focused onto a fluorescent screen. It is an essential component of television receivers, computer visual display units, and oscilloscopes.

Catholic church whole body of the Christian church, though usually referring to the Roman Catholic Church (see *Roman Catholicism).

Catholic Emancipation in British history, acts of Parliament passed 1780–1829 to relieve Roman Catholics of civil and political restrictions imposed from the time of Henry VIII and the Reformation.

Catiline (Lucius Sergius Catilina) c. 108–62 BC. Roman politician. Twice failing to be elected to the consulship in 64/63 BC, he planned a military coup, but *Cicero exposed his conspiracy. He died at the head of the insurgents.

cation *ion carrying a positive charge. During electrolysis, cations in the electrolyte move to the cathode (negative electrode).

Cato Marcus Porcius 234–149 BC. Roman politician. Appointed censor (senior magistrate) in 184 BC, he excluded from the Senate those who did not meet his high standards. He was so impressed by the power of *Carthage, on a visit 157, that he ended every speech by saying: 'Carthage must be destroyed.' His farming manual is the earliest surviving work in Latin prose.

CAT scan or *CT scan* (acronym for *computerized axial tomography*) sophisticated method of X-ray imaging. Quick and noninvasive, CAT scanning is used in medicine as an aid to diagnosis, helping to pinpoint problem areas without the need for exploratory surgery. It is also used in archaeology to examine mummies.

cat's eyes reflective studs used to mark the limits of traffic lanes, invented by Percy Shaw (1890–1976) in England, as a road safety device in 1934.

cattle any large, ruminant, even-toed, hoofed

mammal of the genus *Bos*, family Bovidae, including wild species such as the yak, gaur, gayal, banteng, and kouprey, as well as domestic breeds. Asiatic water buffaloes *Bubalus*, African buffaloes *Syncerus*, and American bison *Bison* are not considered true cattle. Cattle are bred for meat (beef cattle) or milk (dairy cattle).

Catullus Gaius Valerius *c*. 84–54 BC. Roman lyric poet, born in Verona of a well-to-do family. He moved in the literary and political society of Rome and wrote lyrics describing his unhappy love affair with Clodia, probably the wife of the consul Metellus, calling her Lesbia. His longer poems include two wedding songs. Many of his poems are short verses to his friends.

Caucasoid or *Caucasian* former racial classification used for any of the light-skinned peoples; so named because the German anthropologist J F Blumenbach (1752–1840) theorized that they originated in the Caucasus.

Caucasus series of mountain ranges between the Caspian and Black seas, in the republics of Russia, Georgia, Armenia, and Azerbaijan; 1,200 km/750 mi long. The highest peak is Elbruz, 5,633 m/18,480 ft.

caucus in the USA, a closed meeting of regular party members; for example, to choose a candidate for office. The term was originally used in the 18th century in Boston, Massachusetts.

cauliflower variety of *cabbage *Brassica oleracea*, distinguished by its large, flattened head of fleshy, aborted flowers. It is similar to broccoli but less hardy.

causality in philosophy, a consideration of the connection between cause and effect, usually referred to as the 'causal relationship'. If an event is assumed to have a cause, two important questions arise: what is the relationship between cause and effect, and must it follow that every event is caused? The Scottish philosopher David Hume considered these questions to be, in principle, unanswerable.

cauterization in medicine, the use of special instruments to burn or fuse small areas of body tissue to destroy dead cells, prevent the spread of infection, or seal tiny blood vessels to minimize blood loss during surgery.

Cauthen Steve 1960– . US jockey. He rode Affirmed to the US Triple Crown 1978 at the age of 18 and won 487 races 1977. He twice won the Derby, on Slip Anchor 1985 and on Reference Point 1987, and was UK champion jockey 1984, 1985, and 1987.

caution legal term for a warning given by police questioning a suspect, which in the UK must be couched in the following terms: 'You do not have to say anything unless you wish to do so, but what you say may be given in evidence.' Persons not under arrest must also be told that they do not have to remain at the police station or with the police officer but that if they do, they may obtain legal advice if they wish. A suspect should be cautioned again after a break in questioning and upon arrest.

Cauvery or *Kaveri* river of S India, rising in the W Ghats and flowing 765 km/475 mi SE to meet the Bay of Bengal in a wide delta. It has been a major source of hydroelectric power since 1902 when India's first hydropower plant was built on the river.

Cavaco Silva Anibal 1939– . Portuguese politician, finance minister 1980–81, and prime minister and Social Democratic Party (PSD) leader from 1985. Under his leadership Portugal joined the European Community 1985 and the Western European Union 1988.

cavalier horseman of noble birth, but mainly used to describe a male supporter of Charles I in the English Civil War (Cavalier), typically with courtly dress and long hair (as distinct from a Roundhead); also a supporter of Charles II after the Restoration.

Cavalier poets poets of Charles I's court, including Thomas Carew, Robert Herrick, Richard Lovelace, and John Suckling. They wrote witty, light-hearted love lyrics.

Cavalli (Pietro) Francesco 1602–1676. Italian composer, organist at St Mark's, Venice, and the first to make opera a popular entertainment with such works as *Xerxes* 1654, later performed in honour of Louis XIV's wedding in Paris. 27 of his operas survive.

Cavan agricultural county of the Republic of Ireland, in the province of Ulster; area 1,890 sq km/730 sq mi; population (1991) 52,800.

cave roofed-over cavity in the Earth's crust usually produced by the action of underground water or by waves on a seacoast. Caves of the former type commonly occur in areas underlain by limestone, such as Kentucky and many Balkan regions, where the rocks are soluble in water. A *pothole* is a vertical hole in rock caused by water descending a crack; it is thus open to the sky.

caveat emptor (Latin 'let the buyer beware') dictum that professes the buyer is responsible for checking that the goods or services they purchase are satisfactory.

Cavell Edith Louisa 1865–1915. British matron of a Red Cross hospital in Brussels, Belgium, in World War I, who helped Allied soldiers escape to the Dutch frontier. She was court-martialled by the Germans and condemned to death.

Cavendish Frederick Charles, Lord Cavendish 1836–1882. British administrator, second son of the 7th Duke of Devonshire. He was appointed chief secretary to the lord lieutenant of Ireland in 1882. On the evening of his arrival in Dublin he was murdered in Phoenix Park with Thomas Burke, the permanent Irish undersecretary, by members of the Irish Invincibles, a group of Irish Fenian extremists founded 1881.

Cavendish Henry 1731–1810. English physicist. He discovered hydrogen (which he called 'inflammable air') 1766, and determined the compositions of water and of nitric acid.

caviar salted roe (eggs) of sturgeon, salmon, and other fishes. Caviar is prepared by beating and straining the egg sacs until the eggs are free from fats and then adding salt. Russia and Iran are the main exporters of the most prized variety of caviar, derived from Caspian Sea sturgeon. Iceland produces various high-quality, lower-priced caviars.

Cavour Camillo Benso di, Count 1810–1861. Italian nationalist politician. He was the editor of *Il *Risorgimento* from 1847. As prime minister of Piedmont 1852–59 and 1860–61, he enlisted the support of Britain and France for the concept of a united Italy achieved 1861; after expelling the Austrians 1859, he assisted Garibaldi in liberating southern Italy 1860.

cavy short-tailed South American rodent, family Caviidae, of which the guinea-pig *Cavia porcellus* is an example. Wild cavies are greyish or brownish with rather coarse hair. They live in small groups in burrows, and have been kept for food since ancient times.

Cawnpore former spelling of *Kanpur, Indian city.

Caxton William *c.* 1422–1491. The first English printer. He learned the art of printing in Cologne, Germany, 1471 and set up a press in Belgium where he produced the first book printed in English, his own version of a French romance, *Recuyell of the Historyes of Troye* 1474. Returning to England 1476, he established himself in London, where he produced the first book printed in England, *Dictes or Sayengis of the Philosophres* 1477.

Cayenne capital and chief port of French Guiana, on Cayenne island at the mouth of the river Cayenne; population (1982) 38,135.

cayenne pepper condiment derived from the dried fruits of various species of *capsicum (especially *Capsicum frutescens*), a tropical American genus of plants of the family Solanaceae. It is wholly distinct in its origin from black or white pepper, which is derived from an East Indian plant (*Piper nigrum*).

cayman or *caiman* large reptile, resembling the *crocodile.

Cayman Islands British island group in the West Indies
area 260 sq km/100 sq mi
features comprises three low-lying islands: Grand Cayman, Cayman Brac, and Little Cayman
government governor, executive council, and legislative assembly
exports seawhip coral, a source of *prostaglandins; shrimps; honey; jewellery
currency CI dollar
population (1988) 22,000
language English
history discovered by Christopher Columbus 1503; acquired by Britain following the Treaty of Madrid 1670; a dependency of Jamaica 1863, In 1962 the islands became a separate colony, although the inhabitants chose to remain British. From that date, changes in legislation attracted foreign banks and the Caymans are now an international financial centre and tax haven as well as a tourist resort.

CBI abbreviation for ***Confederation of British Industry**.

cc symbol for *cubic centimetre*; abbreviation for *carbon copy/copies*.

CD abbreviation for *compact disc; *certificate of deposit*.

CD-i abbreviation for *compact disc-interactive*, a format, developed by Philips, of *CD-ROM used with a computerized reader, which responds intelligently to the user's instructions. The disc stores a combination of video, audio,

text, and pictures, and can be used for both the consumer market and for training purposes.

CD-ROM (abbreviation for *compact-disc read-only memory*) computer storage device developed from the technology of the audio *compact disc. It consists of a plastic-coated metal disc, on which binary digital information is etched in the form of microscopic pits. This can then be read optically by passing a light beam over the disc. CD-ROMs typically hold about 550 *megabytes of data, and are used in distributing large amounts of text and graphics, such as encyclopedias, catalogues, and technical manuals.

Ceauşescu Nicolae 1918–1989. Romanian politician, leader of the Romanian Communist Party (RCP), in power 1965–89. He pursued a policy line independent and critical of the USSR. He appointed family members, including his wife *Elena Ceauşescu*, to senior state and party posts, and governed in an increasingly repressive manner, zealously implementing schemes that impoverished the nation. The Ceauşescus were overthrown in a bloody revolutionary coup Dec 1989 and executed.

Cebu chief city and port of the island of Cebu in the Philippines; population (1990) 610,400; area of the island 5,086 sq km/1,964 sq mi. The oldest city of the Philippines, Cebu was founded as San Miguel 1565 and became the capital of the Spanish Philippines.

Cecil Robert, 1st Earl of Salisbury 1563–1612. Secretary of state to Elizabeth I of England, succeeding his father, Lord Burghley; he was afterwards chief minister to James I (James VI of Scotland) whose accession to the English throne he secured. He discovered the *Gunpowder Plot, the conspiracy to blow up the King and Parliament 1605. James I created him Earl of Salisbury 1605.

cedar any of an Old World genus *Cedrus* of coniferous trees of the pine family Pinaceae. The *cedar of Lebanon C. libani* grows to great heights and age in the mountains of Syria and Asia Minor. Of the historic forests on Mount Lebanon itself, only a few stands of trees remain.

Ceefax one of Britain's two *teletext systems (the other is Teletext), or 'magazines of the air', developed by the BBC and first broadcast 1973.

celandine either of two plants belonging to different families, and resembling each other only in their bright yellow flowers. The *greater celandine Chelidonium majus* belongs to the poppy family, and is common in hedgerows. The *lesser celandine Ranunculus ficaria* is a member of the buttercup family, and is a familiar wayside and meadow plant in Europe.

Celebes English name for *Sulawesi, an island of Indonesia.

celeriac variety of garden celery *Apium graveolens* var. *rapaceum* of the carrot family Umbelliferae, with an edible, turniplike root and small, bitter stems.

celery Old World plant *Apium graveolens* of the carrot family Umbelliferae. It grows wild in ditches and salt marshes and has a coarse texture and acrid taste. Cultivated varieties of celery are grown under cover to make them less bitter.

celesta keyboard glockenspiel producing high-pitched sounds of glistening purity. It was invented by Auguste Mustel 1886 and first used to effect by Tchaikovsky in the *Nutcracker* ballet 1890.

celestial mechanics the branch of astronomy that deals with the calculation of the orbits of celestial bodies, their gravitational attractions (such as those that produce the Earth's tides), and also the orbits of artificial satellites and space probes. It is based on the laws of motion and gravity laid down by Isaac *Newton.

celestial sphere imaginary sphere surrounding the Earth, on which the celestial bodies seem to lie. The positions of bodies such as stars, planets, and galaxies are specified by their coordinates on the celestial sphere. The equivalents of latitude and longitude on the celestial sphere are called *declination and *right ascension (which is measured in hours from 0 to 24). The *celestial poles* lie directly above the Earth's poles, and the *celestial equator* lies over the Earth's equator. The celestial sphere appears to rotate once around the Earth each day, actually a result of the rotation of the Earth on its axis.

cell in biology, a discrete, membrane-bound portion of living matter, the smallest unit capable of an independent existence. All living organisms consist of one or more cells, with the exception of *viruses. Bacteria, protozoa, and many other microorganisms consist of single cells, whereas a human is made up of billions of cells. Essential features of a cell are the membrane, which encloses it and restricts the flow of substances in and out; the jellylike material within, the *cytoplasm; the *ribosomes, which carry out protein synthesis; and the *DNA, which forms the hereditary material.

cell, electrical or *voltaic cell* or *galvanic cell* device in which chemical energy is converted into electrical energy; the popular name for this device is *'battery', but this name actually refers to a collection of cells in one unit. The reactive chemicals of a *primary cell* cannot be replenished, whereas *secondary cells* – such as storage batteries – are rechargeable: their chemical reactions can be reversed and the original condition restored by applying an electric current. It is dangerous to attempt to recharge a primary cell.

cell, electrolytic device to which electrical energy is applied in order to bring about a chemical reaction; see *electrolysis.

Cellini Benvenuto 1500–1571. Italian sculptor and goldsmith working in the Mannerist style; author of an arrogant autobiography (begun 1558). Among his works are a graceful bronze *Perseus* 1545–54 (Loggia dei Lanzi, Florence) and a gold salt cellar made for Francis I of France 1540–43 (Kunsthistorisches Museum, Vienna), topped by nude reclining figures.

cell membrane or *plasma membrane* thin layer of protein and fat surrounding cells that controls substances passing between the cytoplasm and the intercellular space. The cell membrane is semipermeable, allowing some substances to pass through and some not.

cello abbreviation for *violoncello*, a member of the violin family and fourth member of a string quartet. The cello has been much in demand as a solo instrument because of its exceptional range

and brilliance of tone, and its repertoire extends from Bach to Beethoven, Dvořák, and Elgar.

cellophane transparent wrapping film made from wood *cellulose, widely used for packaging, first produced by Swiss chemist Jacques Edwin Brandenberger 1908.

cell sap dilute fluid found in the large central vacuole of many plant cells. It is made up of water, amino acids, glucose, and salts. The sap has many functions, including storage of useful materials, and provides mechanical support for non-woody plants.

cellular phone or *cellphone* mobile radio telephone, one of a network connected to the telephone system by a computer-controlled communication system. Service areas are divided into small 'cells', about 5 km/3 mi across, each with a separate low-power transmitter.

cellulite fatty compound alleged by some dietitians to be produced in the body by liver disorder and to cause lumpy deposits on the hips and thighs. Medical opinion generally denies its existence, attributing the lumpy appearance to a type of subcutaneous fat deposit.

celluloid transparent or translucent, highly flammable, plastic material (a thermoplastic) made from cellulose nitrate and camphor. It was once used for toilet articles, novelties, and photographic film, but has now been replaced by the nonflammable substance cellulose acetate.

cellulose complex *carbohydrate composed of long chains of glucose units. It is the principal constituent of the cell wall of higher plants, and a vital ingredient in the diet of many *herbivores. Molecules of cellulose are organized into long, unbranched microfibrils that give support to the cell wall. No mammal produces the enzyme (cellulase) necessary for digesting cellulose; mammals such as rabbits and cows are only able to digest grass because the bacteria present in their gut manufacture the appropriate enzyme.

cellulose nitrate or *nitrocellulose* series of esters of cellulose with up to three nitrate (NO_3) groups per monosaccharide unit. It is made by the action of concentrated nitric acid on cellulose (for example, cotton waste) in the presence of concentrated sulphuric acid. Fully nitrated cellulose (gun cotton) is explosive, but esters with fewer nitrate groups were once used in making lacquers, rayon, and plastics, such as coloured and photographic film, until replaced by the nonflammable cellulose acetate. *Celluloid is a form of cellulose nitrate.

cell wall in plants, the tough outer surface of the cell. It is constructed from a mesh of *cellulose and is very strong and relatively inelastic. Most living cells are turgid (swollen with water) and develop an internal hydrostatic pressure (wall pressure) that acts against the cellulose wall. The result of this turgor pressure is to give the cell, and therefore the plant, rigidity. Plants that are not woody are particularly reliant on this form of support.

Celsius scale of temperature, previously called Centigrade, in which the range from freezing to boiling of water is divided into 100 degrees, freezing point being 0 degrees and boiling point 100 degrees.

Celt (Greek *Keltoi*) member of an Indo-European people that originated in Alpine Europe and spread to the Iberian peninsula and beyond. They were ironworkers and farmers. In the 1st century BC they were defeated by the Roman Empire and by Germanic tribes and confined largely to Britain, Ireland, and N France.

Celtic art style of art that originated about 500 BC, probably on the Rhine, and spread as the Celts moved westwards to Gaul and the British Isles and southwards to Italy and Turkey. Celtic manuscript illumination and sculpture from Ireland and Anglo-Saxon Britain of the 6th–8th centuries has intricate spiral and geometric ornament, as in *The Book of Kells* (Trinity College, Dublin) and the *Lindisfarne Gospels* (British Museum, London).

Celtic languages branch of the Indo-European family, divided into two groups: the *Brythonic* or *P-Celtic* (Welsh, Cornish, Breton, and Gaulish) and the *Goidelic* or *Q-Celtic* (Irish, Scottish, and Manx Gaelic). Celtic languages once stretched from the Black Sea to Britain, but have been in decline for centuries, limited to the so-called 'Celtic fringe' of western Europe.

Celtic League nationalist organization based in Ireland, aiming at an independent Celtic federation. It was founded 1975 with representatives from Alba (Scotland), Breizh (Brittany), Eire, Kernow (Cornwall), Cymru (Wales), and Ellan Vannin (Isle of Man).

cement any bonding agent used to unite particles in a single mass or to cause one surface to adhere to another. *Portland cement* is a powder obtained from burning together a mixture of lime (or chalk) and clay, and when mixed with water and sand or gravel, turns into mortar or concrete. In geology, a chemically precipitated material such as carbonate that occupies the interstices of clastic rocks is called cement.

cenotaph (Greek 'empty tomb') monument to commemorate a person or persons not actually buried at the site, as in the Whitehall Cenotaph, London, designed by Edwin Lutyens to commemorate the dead of both world wars.

Cenozoic or *Caenozoic* era of geological time that began 65 million years ago and is still in process. It is divided into the Tertiary and Quaternary periods. The Cenozoic marks the emergence of mammals as a dominant group, including humans, and the formation of the mountain chains of the Himalayas and the Alps.

censor in ancient Rome, either of two senior magistrates, high officials elected every five years to hold office for 18 months. Their responsibilities included public morality, a census of the citizens, and a revision of the senatorial list.

censorship suppression by authority of material considered immoral, heretical, subversive, libellous, damaging to state security, or otherwise offensive. It is generally more stringent under totalitarian or strongly religious regimes and in wartime.

censorship, film control of the content and presentation of films. Film censorship dates back almost as far as the cinema. In Britain, censorship was established in 1912, in the USA 1922. In some countries, self-regulation of the industry has not been regarded as sufficient; in the USSR,

for example, state censorship forbade the treatment of certain issues.

census official count of the population of a country, originally for military call-up and taxation, later for assessment of social trends as other information regarding age, sex, and occupation of each individual was included. They may become unnecessary as computerized databanks are developed.

centaur in Greek mythology, a creature half-human and half-horse. Centaurs were supposed to live in Thessaly, and be wild and lawless; the mentor of Heracles, Chiron, was an exception.

Centaurus large bright constellation of the southern hemisphere, represented as a centaur. It contains the closest star to the Sun, Proxima Centauri. Omega Centauri, the largest and brightest globular cluster of stars in the sky, is 16,000 light years away. Centaurus A, a peculiar galaxy 15 million light years away, is a strong source of radio waves and X-rays.

centigrade common name for the *Celsius temperature scale.

centipede jointed-legged animal of the group Chilopoda, members of which have a distinct head and a single pair of long antennae. Their bodies are composed of segments (which may number nearly 200), each of similar form and bearing a single pair of legs. Most are small, but the tropical *Scolopendra gigantea* may reach 30 cm/1 ft in length. *Millipedes*, class Diplopoda, have fewer segments (up to 100), but have two pairs of legs on each.

Central African Republic (*République Centrafricaine*)

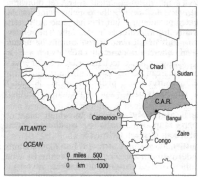

area 622,436 sq km/240,260 sq mi
capital Bangui
towns and cities Berbérati, Bouar, Bossangoa
physical landlocked flat plateau, with rivers flowing N and S, and hills in NE and SW; dry in N, rainforest in SW
environment an estimated 87% of the urban population is without access to safe drinking water
head of state Ange-Felix Patasse from 1993
head of government Jean-Luc Mandaba from 1993
political system emergent democratic republic

exports diamonds, uranium, coffee, cotton, timber, tobacco
currency CFA franc
population (1993 est) 3,200,000 (more than 80 ethnic groups); growth rate 2.3% p.a.
languages Sangho (national), French (official), Arabic, Hunsa, and Swahili
religions Protestant 25%, Roman Catholic 25%, Muslim 10%, animist 10%
GNP $390 per head (1991)
chronology
1960 Central African Republic achieved independence from France; David Dacko elected president.
1962 The republic made a one-party state.
1965 Dacko ousted in military coup led by Col Bokassa.
1966 Constitution rescinded and national assembly dissolved.
1972 Bokassa declared himself president for life.
1977 Bokassa made himself emperor of the Central African Empire.
1979 Bokassa deposed by Dacko.
1981 Dacko deposed by General André Kolingba, and an all-military government established.
1983 Clandestine opposition movement formed.
1984 Political amnesty.
1985 New constitution promised, with some civilians in the government.
1986 Bokassa returned. He was imprisoned and sent to trial. General Kolingba re-elected. New constitution approved by referendum.
1988 Bokassa found guilty and received death sentence, later commuted to life imprisonment.
1991 Opposition parties allowed to form.
1992 Abortive debate held on political reform; multiparty elections promised but then postponed.
1993 Sept: Kolingba released several thousand prisoners, including Bokassa. Ange-Felix Patasse elected president, ending twelve years of military dictatorship. Jean-Luc Mandaba appointed prime minister at head of coalition government. Nov: Bokassa stripped of his military rank.

Central America the part of the Americas that links Mexico with the Isthmus of Panama, comprising Belize, Costa Rica, El Salvador, Guatemala, Honduras, Nicaragua, and Panama. It is also an isthmus, crossed by mountains that form part of the Cordilleras, rising to a maximum height of 4,220 m/13,845 ft. There are numerous active volcanoes. Central America is about 523,000 sq km/200,000 sq mi in area and has a population (1980) estimated at 22,700,000, mostly Indians or mestizos (of mixed white-Indian ancestry). Tropical agricultural products and other basic commodities and raw materials are exported.

Central American Common Market CACM (***Mercado Común Centroamericana*** MCCA) economic alliance established 1960 by El Salvador, Guatemala, Honduras (seceded 1970), and Nicaragua; Costa Rica joined 1962. Formed to encourage economic development and cooperation between the smaller Central American nations and to attract industrial capital, CACM failed to live up to early expectations: nationalist interests remained strong and by the mid-1980s political instability in the region and border conflicts between members were hindering its activities.

Central Asian Republics group of five republics: *Kazakhstan, *Kyrgyzstan, *Tajikistan, *Turkmenistan, and *Uzbekistan. Formerly part of the Soviet Union, their independence was recognized 1991. All five republics belong to the Commonwealth of Independent States (CIS). They comprise a large part of the geographical region of *Turkestan and are the home of large numbers of Muslims.

central business district (CBD) area of a town or city where most of the commercial activity is found. This area is dominated by shops, offices, entertainment venues, and local-government buildings. Usually the CBD is characterized by high rents and rates, tall buildings, and chain stores, and is readily accessible to pedestrians. It may also occupy the historic centre of the city and is often located where transport links meet.

Central Command military strike force consisting of units from the US army, navy, and air force, which operates in the Middle East and North Africa. Its headquarters are in Fort McDill, Florida. It was established 1979, following the Iranian hostage crisis and the Soviet invasion of Afghanistan, and was known as the Rapid Deployment Force until 1983. It commanded coalition forces in the Gulf War 1991.

Central Criminal Court in the UK, crown court in the City of London, able to try all treasons and serious offences committed in the City or Greater London. First established 1834, it is popularly known as the ***Old Bailey*** after part of the medieval defences of London; the present building is on the site of Newgate Prison.

central dogma in genetics and evolution, the fundamental belief that *genes can affect the nature of the physical body, but that changes in the body (for example, through use or accident) cannot be translated into changes in the genes.

Central Intelligence Agency (CIA) US intelligence organization established 1947. It has actively intervened overseas, generally to undermine left-wing regimes or to protect US financial interests; for example, in the Congo (now Zaire) and Nicaragua. From 1980 all covert activity by the CIA has by law to be reported to Congress, preferably beforehand, and must be authorized by the president. Robert James Woolsey became CIA director 1993. In 1994 the CIA's estimated budget was around $28 billion.

Central Lowlands one of the three geographical divisions of Scotland, occupying the fertile and densely populated plain that lies between two geological fault lines, which run nearly parallel NE–SW across Scotland from Stonehaven to Dumbarton and from Dunbar to Girvan.

central nervous system the part of the nervous system with a concentration of *nerve cells which coordinates various body functions. In *vertebrates, the central nervous system consists of a brain and a dorsal nerve cord (the spinal cord) within the spinal column. In worms, insects, and crustaceans, it consists of a paired ventral nerve cord with concentrations of nerve cells, known as ***ganglia*** (see *ganglion), in each segment, and a small brain in the head.

Central Powers originally the signatories of the *Triple Alliance 1882: Germany, Austria-Hungary, and Italy. During the World War I, Italy remained neutral before joining the *Allies.

central processing unit (CPU) main component of a computer, the part that executes individual program instructions and controls the operation of other parts. It is sometimes called the central processor or, when contained on a single integrated circuit, a microprocessor.

Central Scotland region of Scotland, formed 1975 from the counties of Stirling, S Perthshire, and West Lothian
area 2,600 sq km/1,004 sq mi
towns Stirling (administrative headquarters), Falkirk, Alloa, Grangemouth
products agriculture; industries including brewing and distilling, engineering, electronics
population (1991) 268,000
famous people William Alexander (founder of Nova Scotia), Rob Roy Macgregor.

Centre region of N central France; area 39,200 sq km/15,131 sq mi; population (1986) 2,324,000. It includes the *départements* of Cher, Eure-et-Loire, Indre, Indre-et-Loire, Loire-et-Cher, and Loiret. Its capital is Orléans.

centre of mass or *centre of gravity* point in or near an object from which its total weight appears to originate and can be assumed to act. A symmetrical homogeneous object such as a sphere or cube has its centre of mass at its physical centre; a hollow shape (such as a cup) may have its centre of mass in space inside the hollow.

Centre Party (German *Zentrumspartei*) German political party established 1871 to protect Catholic interests. Although alienated by Chancellor Bismarck's *Kulturkampf* 1873–78, in the following years the *Zentrum* became an essential component in the government of imperial Germany. The party continued to play a part in the politics of Weimar Germany before being barred by Hitler in the summer of 1933.

centrifugal force useful concept in physics, based on an apparent (but not real) force. It may be regarded as a force that acts radially outwards from a spinning or orbiting object, thus balancing the *centripetal force (which is real). For an object of mass m moving with a velocity v in a circle of radius r, the centrifugal force F equals mv^2/r (outwards).

centrifuge apparatus that rotates at high speeds, causing substances inside it to be thrown outwards. One use is for separating mixtures of substances of different densities.

centriole structure found in the *cells of animals that plays a role in the processes of *meiosis and *mitosis (cell division).

centripetal force force that acts radially inwards on an object moving in a curved path. For example, with a weight whirled in a circle at the end of a length of string, the centripetal force is the tension in the string. For an object of mass m moving with a velocity v in a circle of radius r, the centripetal force F equals mv^2/r (inwards). The reaction to this force is the *centrifugal force.

centromere part of the *chromosome where there are no *genes. Under the microscope, it usually appears as a constriction in the strand of the chromosome, and is the point at which the spindle fibres are attached during *meiosis and *mitosis (cell division).

cephalopod any predatory marine mollusc of the class Cephalopoda, with the mouth and head surrounded by tentacles. Cephalopods are the most intelligent, the fastest-moving, and the largest of all animals without backbones, and there are remarkable luminescent forms which swim or drift at great depths. They have the most highly developed nervous and sensory systems of all invertebrates, the eye in some closely paralleling that found in vertebrates. Examples include octopus, squid, and cuttlefish. Shells are rudimentary or absent in most cephalopods.

Cepheid variable yellow supergiant star that varies regularly in brightness every few days or weeks as a result of pulsations. The time that a Cepheid variable takes to pulsate is directly related to its average brightness; the longer the pulsation period, the brighter the star.

Cepheus constellation of the north polar region, named after King Cepheus of Greek mythology, husband of Cassiopeia and father of Andromeda. It contains the Garnet Star (Mu Cephei), a red supergiant of variable brightness that is one of the reddest-coloured stars known, and Delta Cephei, prototype of the *Cepheid variables.

ceramic nonmetallic mineral (clay) used to form articles that are then fired at high temperatures. Ceramics are divided into heavy clay products (bricks, roof tiles, drainpipes, sanitary ware), refractories or high-temperature materials (linings for furnaces used to manufacture steel, fuel elements in nuclear reactors), and pottery, which uses china clay, ball clay, china stone, and flint. Superceramics, such as silicon carbide, are lighter, stronger, and more heat-resistant than steel for use in motor and aircraft engines and have to be cast to shape since they are too hard to machine.

Cerberus in Greek mythology, the three-headed dog guarding the entrance to *Hades, the underworld.

cereal grass grown for its edible, nutrient-rich, starchy seeds. The term refers primarily to wheat, oats, rye, and barley, but may also refer to maize, millet, and rice. Cereals contain about 75% complex carbohydrates and 10% protein, plus fats and fibre (roughage). They store well. If all the world's cereal crop were consumed as wholegrain products directly by humans, everyone could obtain adequate protein and carbohydrate; however, a large proportion of cereal production in affluent nations is used as animal feed to boost the production of meat, dairy products, and eggs.

cerebellum part of the brain of *vertebrate animals which controls muscular movements, balance, and coordination. It is relatively small in lower animals such as newts and lizards, but large in birds since flight demands precise coordination. The human cerebellum is also well developed, because of the need for balance when walking or running, and for coordinated hand movements.

cerebral haemorrhage or *apoplectic fit* in medicine, a *stroke in which a blood vessel bursts in the brain, caused by factors such as high blood pressure combined with hardening of the arteries, or chronic poisoning with lead or alcohol. It may cause death or damage parts of the brain, leading to paralysis or mental impairment. The effects are usually long-term and the condition may recur.

cerebral palsy any nonprogressive abnormality of the brain caused by oxygen deprivation before birth, injury during birth, haemorrhage, meningitis, viral infection, or faulty development. It is characterized by muscle spasm, weakness, lack of coordination, and impaired movement. Intelligence is not always affected.

cerebrum part of the vertebrate *brain, formed from the two paired cerebral hemispheres. In birds and mammals it is the largest part of the brain. It is covered with an infolded layer of grey matter, the cerebral cortex, which integrates brain functions. The cerebrum coordinates the senses, and is responsible for learning and other higher mental faculties.

Ceres the largest asteroid, 940 km/584 mi in diameter, and the first to be discovered (by Giuseppe Piazzi 1801). Ceres orbits the Sun every 4.6 years at an average distance of 414 million km/257 million mi. Its mass is about one-seventieth of that of the Moon.

Ceres in Roman mythology, the goddess of agriculture; see *Demeter.

cerium malleable and ductile, grey, metallic element, symbol Ce, atomic number 58, relative atomic mass 140.12. It is the most abundant member of the lanthanide series, and is used in alloys, electronic components, nuclear fuels, and lighter flints. It was discovered 1804 by the Swedish chemists Jöns Berzelius and Wilhelm Hisinger (1766–1852), and, independently, by Martin Klaproth. The element was named after the then recently discovered asteroid Ceres.

cermet bonded material containing ceramics and metal, widely used in jet engines and nuclear reactors. Cermets behave much like metals but have the great heat resistance of ceramics. Tungsten carbide, molybdenum boride, and aluminium oxide are among the ceramics used; iron, cobalt, nickel, and chromium are among the metals.

CERN nuclear research organization founded 1954 as a cooperative enterprise between European governments. It has laboratories at Meyrin, near Geneva, Switzerland. It was originally known as the *Conseil Européen pour la Recherche Nucléaire* but subsequently renamed *Organisation Européenne pour la Recherche Nucléaire*, although still familiarly known as CERN. It houses the world's largest particle *accelerator, the Large Electron–Positron Collider (LEP), with which notable advances have been made in *particle physics.

certiorari in UK *administrative law, a remedy available by *judicial review whereby a superior court may quash an order or decision made by an inferior body. It has become less important in recent years following the extension of alternative remedies by judicial review. It originally took the form of a prerogative *writ.

Cervantes Saavedra, Miguel de 1547–1616. Spanish novelist, playwright, and poet whose masterpiece *Don Quixote* (in full *El ingenioso hidalgo Don Quixote de la Mancha*) was published 1605. In 1613, his *Novelas ejemplares/ Exemplary Novels* appeared, followed by *Viaje del Parnaso/The Voyage to Parnassus* 1614. A spurious second part of *Don Quixote* prompted Cervantes to bring out his own second part 1615,

often considered superior to the first in construction and characterization.

cervical cancer *cancer of the cervix (the neck of the womb).

cervical smear removal of a small sample of tissue from the cervix (neck of the womb) to screen for changes implying a likelihood of cancer. The procedure is also known as the *Pap test* after its originator, George Papanicolau.

cervix (Latin 'neck') abbreviation for *cervix uteri*, the neck of the womb.

Cetewayo (Cetshwayo) c. 1826–1884. King of Zululand, South Africa, 1873–83, whose rule was threatened by British annexation of the Transvaal 1877. Although he defeated the British at Isandhlwana 1879, he was later that year defeated by them at Ulundi. Restored to his throne 1883, he was then expelled by his subjects.

Cetus (Latin 'whale') constellation straddling the celestial equator (see *celestial sphere), represented as a sea monster. Cetus contains the long-period variable star *Mira, and *Tau Ceti, one of the nearest stars visible with the naked eye.

Ceylon former name (until 1972) of *Sri Lanka.

Cézanne Paul 1839–1906. French Post-Impressionist painter, a leading figure in the development of modern art. He broke away from the Impressionists' spontaneous vision to develop a style that captured not only light and life, but the structure of natural forms in landscapes, still lifes, portraits, and his series of bathers.

cf. abbreviation for *confer* (Latin 'compare').

CFC abbreviation for *chlorofluorocarbon*.

c.g.s. system or *C.G.s system* system of units based on the centimetre, gram, and second, as units of length, mass, and time respectively. It has been replaced for scientific work by the *SI units to avoid inconsistencies in definition of the thermal calorie and electrical quantities.

Chabrol Claude 1930– . French film director. Originally a critic, he was one of the New Wave directors. His works of murder and suspense, which owe much to Hitchcock, include *Les Cousins/The Cousins* 1959, *Les Biches/The Girlfriends* 1968, *Le Boucher/The Butcher* 1970, and *Cop au Vin* 1984.

Chaco province of Argentina; area 99,633 sq km/38,458 sq mi; population (1991) 838,300. Its capital is Resistencia, in the SE. The chief crop is cotton, and there is forestry.

Chad Republic of (*République du Tchad*)
area 1,284,000 sq km/495,624 sq mi
capital Ndjamena (formerly Fort Lamy)
towns Sarh, Moundou, Abéché
physical landlocked state with mountains and part of Sahara Desert in N; moist savanna in S; rivers in S flow NW to Lake Chad
head of state and government Idriss Deby from 1990
political system emergent democratic republic
exports cotton, meat, livestock, hides, skins
currency CFA franc
population (1993 est) 6,290,000; growth rate 2.3% p.a. Nomadic tribes move N–S seasonally in search of water
languages French, Arabic (both official), over 100 African languages spoken

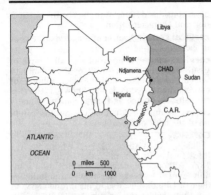

religions Muslim 44% (N), Christian 33%, animist 23% (S)

GNP $267 per head (1992)

chronology

1960 Independence achieved from France, with François Tombalbaye as president.

1963 Violent opposition in the Muslim north, led by the Chadian National Liberation Front (Frolinat), backed by Libya.

1968 Revolt quelled with France's help.

1975 Tombalbaye killed in military coup led by Félix Malloum. Frolinat continued its resistance.

1978 Malloum tried to find a political solution by bringing the former Frolinat leader Hissène Habré into his government but they were unable to work together.

1979 Malloum forced to leave the country; an interim government was set up under General Goukouni. Habré continued his opposition with his Army of the North (FAN).

1981 Habré now in control of half the country. Goukouni fled and set up a 'government in exile'.

1983 Habré's regime recognized by the Organization for African Unity (OAU), but in the north Goukouni's supporters, with Libya's help, fought on. Eventually a cease-fire was agreed, with latitude 16°N dividing the country.

1984 Libya and France agreed to a withdrawal of forces.

1985 Fighting between Libyan-backed and French-backed forces intensified.

1987 Chad, France, and Libya agreed on cease-fire proposed by OAU.

1988 Full diplomatic relations with Libya restored.

1989 Libyan troop movements reported on border; Habré re-elected, amended constitution.

1990 President Habré ousted in coup led by Idriss Deby. New constitution adopted.

1991 Several anti-government coups foiled.

1992 Anti-government coup foiled. Two new opposition parties approved.

Chad, Lake lake on the NE boundary of Nigeria. It once varied in extent between rainy and dry seasons from 50,000 sq km/20,000 sq mi to 20,000 sq km/7,000 sq mi, but a series of droughts 1979–89 reduced its area by 80%. The S Chad irrigation project used the lake waters to irrigate the surrounding desert, but the 4,000 km/2,500 mi of canals dug for the project are now permanently dry because of the shrinking size of the lake. The Lake Chad basin is being jointly developed for oil and natron by Cameroon, Chad, Niger, and Nigeria.

Chadli Benjedid 1929– . Algerian socialist politician, president 1979–92. An army colonel, he supported Boumédienne in the overthrow of Ben Bella 1965, and succeeded Boumédienne 1979, pursuing more moderate policies. Chadli resigned Jan 1992 following a victory for Islamic fundamentalists in the first round of assembly elections.

Chadwick James 1891–1974. British physicist. In 1932 he discovered the particle in the nucleus of an atom that became known as the neutron because it has no electric charge. He received the Nobel Prize for Physics 1935.

chafer beetle of the family Scarabeidae. The adults eat foliage or flowers, and the underground larvae feed on roots, chiefly those of grasses and cereals, and can be very destructive. Examples are the *cockchafer* and the **rose chafer** *Cetonia aurata*, about 2 cm/0.8 in long and bright green.

chaffinch bird *Fringilla coelebs* of the finch family, common throughout much of Europe and W Asia. About 15 cm/6 in long, the male is olive-brown above, with a bright chestnut breast, a bluish-grey cap, and two white bands on the upper part of the wing; the female is duller.

Chagall Marc 1887–1985. Russian-born French painter and designer; much of his highly coloured, fantastic imagery was inspired by the village life of his boyhood and by Jewish and Russian folk tradition. He also designed stained glass, mosaics (for Israel's Knesset in the 1960s), the ceiling of the Paris Opera House 1964, tapestries, and stage sets. He was an original figure, often seen as a precursor of Surrealism, as in *The Dream* (Metropolitan Museum of Art, New York).

Chain Ernst Boris 1906–1979. German-born British biochemist who worked on the development of *penicillin. Chain fled to Britain from the Nazis 1933. After the discovery of penicillin by Alexander Fleming, Chain worked to isolate and purify it. For this work, he shared the 1945 Nobel Prize for Medicine with Fleming and Howard Florey. Chain also discovered penicillinase, an enzyme that destroys penicillin.

chain reaction in chemistry, a succession of reactions, usually involving free radicals, where the products of one stage are the reactants of the next. A chain reaction is characterized by the continual generation of reactive substances.

chain reaction in nuclear physics, a fission reaction that is maintained because neutrons released by the splitting of some atomic nuclei themselves go on to split others, releasing even more neutrons. Such a reaction can be controlled (as in a nuclear reactor) by using moderators to absorb excess neutrons. Uncontrolled, a chain reaction produces a nuclear explosion (as in an atom bomb).

Chaka alternative spelling of *Shaka, Zulu chief.

Chalatenango department on the N frontier of El Salvador; area 2,507 sq km/968 sq mi; population (1981) 235,700; capital Chalatenango.

chalaza glutinous mass of transparent albumen

supporting the yolk inside birds' eggs. The chalaza is formed as the egg slowly passes down the oviduct, when it also acquires its coiled structure.

Chalcedon, Council of ecumenical council of the early Christian church, convoked 451 by the Roman emperor Marcian, and held at Chalcedon (now Kadiköy, Turkey). The council, attended by over 500 bishops, resulted in the *Definition of Chalcedon*, an agreed doctrine for both the eastern and western churches.

chalcedony form of quartz, SiO_2, in which the crystals are so fine-grained that they are impossible to distinguish with a microscope (cryptocrystalline). Agate, onyx, tiger's eye, and carnelian are *gem varieties of chalcedony.

chalcopyrite copper iron sulphide, $CuFeS_2$, the most common ore of copper. It is brassy yellow in colour and may have an iridescent surface tarnish. It occurs in many different types of mineral vein, in rocks ranging from basalt to limestone.

Chaliapin Fyodor Ivanovich 1873–1938. Russian bass singer, born in Kazan. His greatest role was that of Boris Godunov in Mussorgsky's opera of the same name. Chaliapin left the USSR 1921 to live and sing in the world's capitals.

chalice cup, usually of precious metal, used in celebrating the *Eucharist in the Christian church.

chalk soft, fine-grained, whitish rock composed of calcium carbonate, $CaCO_3$, extensively quarried for use in cement, lime, and mortar, and in the manufacture of cosmetics and toothpaste. *Blackboard chalk* in fact consists of *gypsum (calcium sulphate, $CaSO_4$).

Chalmers Thomas 1780–1847. Scottish theologian. At the Disruption of the *Church of Scotland 1843, Chalmers withdrew from the church along with a large number of other priests, and became principal of the Free Church college, thus founding the *Free Church of Scotland.

Chamberlain (Arthur) Neville 1869–1940. British Conservative politician, son of Joseph Chamberlain. He was prime minister 1937–40; his policy of appeasement towards the fascist dictators Mussolini and Hitler (with whom he concluded the *Munich Agreement 1938) failed to prevent the outbreak of World War II. He resigned 1940 following the defeat of the British forces in Norway.

Chamberlain (Joseph) Austen 1863–1937. British Conservative politician, elder son of Joseph Chamberlain; as foreign secretary 1924–29 he negotiated the Pact of *Locarno, for which he won the Nobel Peace Prize 1925, and signed the *Kellogg–Briand pact to outlaw war 1928.

Chamberlain Joseph 1836–1914. British politician, reformist mayor of and member of Parliament for Birmingham; in 1886, he resigned from the cabinet over Gladstone's policy of home rule for Ireland, and led the revolt of the Liberal-Unionists.

Chamberlain Owen 1920– . US physicist whose graduate studies were interrupted by wartime work on the Manhattan Project at Los Alamos. After World War II, working with Italian physicist Emilio Segrè, he discovered the existence of the antiproton. Both men were awarded the Nobel Prize for Physics 1959.

Chamberlain, Lord in the UK, chief officer of the royal household who engages staff and appoints retail suppliers. Until 1968 the Lord Chamberlain licensed and censored plays before their public performance. The office is temporary, and appointments are made by the government.

Chamberlain, Lord Great in the UK, the only officer of state whose position survives from Norman times; responsibilities include the arrangements for the opening of Parliament, assisting with the regalia at coronations, and organizing the ceremony when bishops and peers are created.

chamber music music suitable for performance in a small room or chamber, rather than in the concert hall, and usually written for instrumental combinations, played with one instrument to a part, as in the string quartet.

chameleon *Meller's chameleon of the savanna of Tanzania and Malawi is the largest chameleon found outside Madagascar, about 55 cm/1.7ft long.*

chameleon any of some 80 or so species of lizard of the family Chameleontidae. Some species have highly developed colour-changing abilities, which are caused by changes in the intensity of light, of temperature, and of emotion altering the dispersal of pigment granules in the layers of cells beneath the outer skin.

chamois goatlike mammal *Rupicapra rupicapra* found in mountain ranges of S Europe and Asia Minor. It is brown, with dark patches running through the eyes, and can be up to 80 cm/2.6 ft high. Chamois are very sure-footed, and live in herds of up to 30 members.

Chamorro Violeta Barrios de *c.* 1939– . President of Nicaragua from 1990. With strong US support, she was elected to be the candidate for the National Opposition Union (UNO) 1989, winning the presidency from David Ortega Saavedra Feb 1990 and thus ending the period of Sandinista rule.

champagne sparkling white wine invented by Dom Pérignon, a Benedictine monk, 1668. It is made from a blend of grapes (*pinot noir* and *pinot chardonnay*) grown in the Marne River region around Reims and Epernay, in Champagne, NE France. After a first fermentation, sugar and yeast are added to the still wine, which, when bottled, undergoes a second fermentation to produce the sparkle. Sugar syrup may be added to make the wine sweet (*sec*) or dry (*brut*).

Champagne-Ardenne region of NE France; area   25,600 sq km/9,882 sq mi;   population

(1986) 1,353,000. Its capital is Reims, and it comprises the *départements* of Ardennes, Aube, Marne, and Haute-Marne. It has sheep and dairy farming and vineyards.

Champaigne Philippe de 1602–1674. French artist, the leading portrait painter of the court of Louis XIII. Of Flemish origin, he went to Paris 1621 and gained the patronage of Cardinal Richelieu. His style is elegant, cool, and restrained.

champignon any of a number of edible fungi of the family Agaricaceae. The *fairy ring champignon Marasmius oreades* is so called because its fruiting bodies (mushrooms) occur in rings around the outer edge of the underground mycelium (threadlike tubes) of the fungus.

Champlain Samuel de 1567–1635. French pioneer, soldier, and explorer in Canada. Having served in the army of Henry IV and on an expedition to the West Indies, he began his exploration of Canada 1603. In a third expedition 1608 he founded and named Québec, and was appointed lieutenant governor of French Canada 1612.

Champlain, Lake lake in NE USA (extending some 10 km/6 mi into Canada) on the New York–Vermont border; length 201 km/125 mi; area 692 sq km/430 sq mi. It is linked by canal to the St Lawrence and Hudson rivers.

Champollion Jean François, le Jeune 1790–1832. French Egyptologist who in 1822 deciphered Egyptian hieroglyphics with the aid of the *Rosetta Stone.

chance likelihood, or *probability, of an event taking place, expressed as a fraction or percentage. For example, the chance that a tossed coin will land heads up is 50%.

Chancellor, Lord UK state official, originally the royal secretary, today a member of the cabinet, whose office ends with a change of government. The Lord Chancellor acts as Speaker of the House of Lords, may preside over the Court of Appeal, and is head of the judiciary.

chancellor of the Duchy of Lancaster in the UK, honorary post held by a cabinet minister who has other nondepartmental responsibilities. The chancellor of the Duchy of Lancaster was originally the monarch's representative controlling the royal lands and courts within the duchy.

chancellor of the Exchequer in the UK, senior cabinet minister responsible for the national economy. The office, established under Henry III, originally entailed keeping the Exchequer seal.

Chancery in the UK, a division of the High Court that deals with such matters as the administration of the estates of deceased persons, the execution of trusts, the enforcement of sales of land, and *foreclosure of mortgages. Before reorganization of the court system 1875, it administered the rules of *equity as distinct from *common law.

chancroid acute localized, sexually transmitted ulcer on or about the genitals caused by the bacterium *Hemophilus ducreyi*. The ulcer forms at the point of inoculation from a sexual partner and leads to painful enlargement and suppuration of lymph nodes in the groin area.

Chandelā or *Candella* Rajput dynasty that ruled the Bundelkhand region of central India from the 9th to the 11th century. The Chandelās fought against Muslim invaders, until they were replaced by the Bundelās.

Chandigarh city of N India, in the foothills of the Himalayas; population (1981) 421,000. It is also a Union Territory; area 114 sq km/44 sq mi; population (1991) 640,725.

Chandler Raymond 1888–1959. US novelist. He turned the pulp detective mystery form into a successful genre of literature and created the quintessential private eye in the tough but chivalric loner, Philip Marlowe. Marlowe is the narrator of such books as *The Big Sleep* 1939 (filmed 1946), *Farewell My Lovely* 1940 (filmed 1944), *The Lady in the Lake* 1943 (filmed 1947), and *The Long Goodbye* 1954 (filmed 1975). He also wrote numerous screenplays, notably *Double Indemnity* 1944, *Blue Dahlia* 1946, and *Strangers on a Train* 1951.

Chandragupta Maurya ruler of N India *c.* 325–*c.* 297 BC, founder of the Mauryan dynasty. He overthrew the Nanda dynasty 325 and then conquered the Punjab 322 after the death of *Alexander the Great, expanding his empire west to Persia. He is credited with having united most of India.

Chandrasekhar Subrahmanyan 1910– . Indian-born US astrophysicist who made pioneering studies of the structure and evolution of stars. The *Chandrasekhar limit* of 1.4 Suns is the maximum mass of a *white dwarf before it turns into a *neutron star. Nobel Prize for Physics 1983.

Chanel Coco (Gabrielle) 1883–1971. French fashion designer. She was renowned as a trendsetter and her designs have been copied worldwide. She created the 'little black dress', the informal cardigan suit, costume jewellery, and perfumes.

Changchun industrial city and capital of Jilin province, China; population (1989) 2,020,000. Machinery and motor vehicles are manufactured. It is also the centre of an agricultural district.

change of state in science, a change in the physical state (solid, liquid, or gas) of a material. For instance, melting, boiling, evaporation, and their opposites, solidification and condensation, are changes of state. The former set of changes are brought about by heating or decreased pressure; the latter by cooling or increased pressure.

Chang Jiang or *Yangtze Kiang* longest river of China, flowing about 6,300 km/3,900 mi from Tibet to the Yellow Sea. It is a main commercial waterway.

Changsha port on the river Chang Jiang, capital of Hunan province, China; population (1989) 1,300,000. It trades in rice, tea, timber, and nonferrous metals; works antimony, lead, and silver; and produces chemicals, electronics, porcelain, and embroideries.

Channel Islands group of islands in the English Channel, off the northwest coast of France; they are a possession of the British crown. They comprise the islands of Jersey, Guernsey, Alderney, Great and Little Sark, with the lesser Herm, Brechou, Jethou, and Lihou.

Channel Tunnel tunnel built beneath the English Channel, linking Britain with mainland Europe. It comprises twin rail tunnels, 50 km/31 mi long and 7.3 m/24 ft in diameter, located 40 m/130 ft beneath the seabed. It was begun 1986, and the French and English sections were linked Dec 1990. It was officially opened 6 May 1994. The shuttle train service for cars and lorries, Le Shuttle, opened to commercial freight June 1994 and to fare-paying passengers Dec 1994. The tunnels high-speed train service, Eurostar, opened Nov 1994.

chanson song type common in France and Italy, often based on a folk tune that originated with the *troubadours. Josquin *Desprez was a chanson composer.

chanson de geste epic poetry of the High Middle Ages in Europe. It probably developed from oral poetry recited in royal or princely courts, and takes as its subject the exploits of heroes, such as those associated with Charlemagne and the crusades. The best-known example is the *Chanson de Roland*.

Chanson de Roland 11th-century epic poem which tells of the real and imaginary deeds of Roland and other knights of Charlemagne, and their last stand against the Basques at Roncesvalles. It is an example of the *chanson de geste*.

chant ritual incantation by an individual or group, for confidence or mutual support. Chants can be secular (football supporters' chants) or religious. Ambrosian and *Gregorian chants are forms of *plainsong.

chanterelle edible fungus *Cantharellus cibarius* that is bright yellow and funnel-shaped. It grows in deciduous woodland.

chantry in medieval Europe, a religious foundation in which, in return for an endowment of land, the souls of the donor and the donor's family and friends would be prayed for. A chantry could be held at an existing altar, or in a specially constructed *chantry chapel*, in which the donor's body was usually buried.

chaos theory or *chaology* branch of mathematics used to deal with chaotic systems – for example, an engineered structure, such as an oil platform, that is subjected to irregular, unpredictable wave stress.

chapel place of worship used by some Christian denominations; also, a part of a building used for Christian worship. A large church or cathedral may have several chapels.

Chapel Royal in the UK, the royal retinue of priests, singers, and musicians (including Tallis, Byrd, and Purcell) of the English court from 1135.

Chaplin Charlie (Charles Spencer) 1889–1977. English film actor and director. He made his reputation as a tramp with a smudge moustache, bowler hat, and twirling cane in silent comedies from the mid-1910s, including *The Rink* 1916, *The Kid* 1920, and *The Gold Rush* 1925. His work often contrasts buffoonery with pathos, and his later films combine dialogue with mime and music, as in *The Great Dictator* 1940 and *Limelight* 1952. He was one of cinema's most popular and greatest stars.

Chapman George 1559–1634. English poet and dramatist. His translations of the Greek epics of Homer (completed 1616) were celebrated; his

plays include the comedy *Eastward Ho!* (with Jonson and Marston) 1605 and the tragedy *Bussy d'Amboise* 1607.

char or *charr* fish *Salvelinus alpinus* related to the trout, living in the Arctic coastal waters, and also in Europe and North America in some upland lakes. It is one of Britain's rarest fish, and is at risk from growing acidification.

characin freshwater fish belonging to the family Characidae. There are over 1,300 species, mostly in South and Central America, but also in Africa. Most are carnivores. In typical characins, unlike the somewhat similar carp family, the mouth is toothed, and there is a small dorsal adipose fin in front of the tail.

character set in computing, the complete set of symbols that can be used in a program or recognized by a computer. It may include letters, digits, spaces, punctuation marks, and special symbols.

charcoal black, porous form of *carbon, produced by heating wood or other organic materials in the absence of air. It is used as a fuel in the smelting of metals such as copper and zinc, and by artists for making black line drawings. *Activated charcoal* has been powdered and dried so that it presents a much increased surface area for adsorption; it is used for filtering and purifying liquids and gases – for example, in drinking-water filters and gas masks.

Charcot Jean-Martin 1825–1893. French neurologist who studied hysteria, sclerosis, locomotor ataxia, and senile diseases. Among his pupils was Sigmund *Freud.

Chardin Jean-Baptiste-Siméon 1699–1779. French painter of naturalistic still lifes and quiet domestic scenes that recall the Dutch tradition. His work is a complete contrast to that of his contemporaries, the Rococo painters. He developed his own technique using successive layers of paint to achieve depth of tone and is generally considered one of the finest exponents of the genre.

Chardonnet Hilaire Bernigaud 1839–1924. French chemist who developed artificial silk 1883, the first artificial fibre.

charge see *electric charge.

charge-coupled device (CCD) device for forming images electronically, using a layer of silicon that releases electrons when struck by incoming light. The electrons are stored in *pixels and read off into a computer at the end of the exposure. CCDs have now almost entirely replaced photographic film for applications such as astrophotography where extreme sensitivity to light is paramount.

charged particle beam high-energy beam of electrons or protons that does not burn through the surface of its target like a *laser, but cuts through it. Such beams are being developed as weapons.

Charge of the Light Brigade disastrous attack by the British Light Brigade of cavalry against the Russian entrenched artillery on 25 Oct 1854 during the Crimean War at the Battle of *Balaclava.

chariot horse-drawn carriage with two wheels, used in ancient Egypt, Greece, and Rome, for fighting, processions, and races; it is thought to have originated in Asia. Typically, the fighting chariot contained a driver and a warrior, who would fight on foot, with the chariot providing rapid mobility.

charismatic movement late 20th-century movement within the Christian church that emphasizes the role of the Holy Spirit in the life of the individual believer and in the life of the church. See *Pentecostal movement.

Charlemagne Charles I *the Great* 742–814. King of the Franks from 768 and Holy Roman emperor from 800. By inheritance (his father was *Pepin the Short) and extensive campaigns of conquest, he united most of W Europe by 804, when after 30 years of war the Saxons came under his control. He reformed the legal, judicial, and military systems; established schools; and promoted Christianity, commerce, agriculture, arts, and literature. In his capital, Aachen, scholars gathered from all over Europe.

Charles (Mary) Eugenia 1919– . Dominican politician, prime minister from 1980; cofounder and first leader of the centrist Dominica Freedom Party (DFP). Two years after Dominica's independence the DFP won the 1980 general election and she became the Caribbean's first female prime minister.

Charles Jacques Alexandre César 1746–1823. French physicist who studied gases and made the first ascent in a hydrogen-filled balloon 1783. His work on the expansion of gases led to the formulation of *Charles's law.

Charles Ray 1930– . US singer, songwriter, and pianist whose first hits were 'I've Got A Woman' 1955, 'What'd I Say' 1959, and 'Georgia on My Mind' 1960. He has recorded gospel, blues, rock, soul, country, and rhythm and blues.

Charles two kings of Britain:

Charles I 1600–1649. King of Great Britain and Ireland from 1625, son of James I of England (James VI of Scotland). He accepted the *petition of right 1628 but then dissolved Parliament and ruled without a parliament 1629–40. His advisers were *Strafford and *Laud, who persecuted the Puritans and provoked the Scots to revolt. The *Short Parliament, summoned 1640, refused funds, and the *Long Parliament later that year rebelled. Charles declared war on Parliament 1642 but surrendered 1646 and was beheaded 1649. He was the father of Charles II.

Charles II 1630–1685. King of Great Britain and Ireland from 1660, when Parliament accepted the restoration of the monarchy after the collapse of Cromwell's Commonwealth; son of Charles I. His chief minister Clarendon, who arranged his marriage 1662 with Catherine of Braganza, was replaced 1667 with the *Cabal of advisers. His plans to restore Catholicism in Britain led to war with the Netherlands 1672–74 in support of Louis XIV of France and a break with Parliament, which he dissolved 1681. He was succeeded by James II.

Charles (full name Charles Philip Arthur George) 1948– . Prince of the UK, heir to the British throne, and Prince of Wales since 1958 (invested 1969). He is the first-born child of Queen Elizabeth II and the Duke of Edinburgh. He studied at Trinity College, Cambridge, 1967–70, before serving in the Royal Air Force

and Royal Navy. He is the first royal heir since 1659 to have an English wife, Lady Diana Spencer, daughter of the 8th Earl Spencer. They have two sons and heirs, William (1982–) and Henry (1984–). Charles and Diana separated 1992.

Charles ten kings of France, including:

Charles I king of France, better known as the Holy Roman emperor *Charlemagne.

Charles II *the Bald* king of France, see *Charles II, Holy Roman emperor.

Charles III *the Simple* 879–929. King of France 893–922, son of Louis the Stammerer. He was crowned at Reims. In 911 he ceded what later became the duchy of Normandy to he Norman chief Rollo.

Charles IV *the Fair* 1294–1328. King of France from 1322, when he succeeded Philip V as the last of the direct Capetian line.

Charles V *the Wise* 1337–1380. King of France from 1364. He was regent during the captivity of his father, John II, in England 1356–60, and became king on John's death. He reconquered nearly all France from England 1369–80.

Charles VI *the Mad* or *the Well-Beloved* 1368–1422. King of France from 1380, succeeding his father Charles V; he was under the regency of his uncles until 1388. He became mentally unstable 1392, and civil war broke out between the dukes of Orléans and Burgundy. Henry V of England invaded France 1415, conquering Normandy, and in 1420 forced Charles to sign the Treaty of Troyes, recognizing Henry as his successor.

Charles VII 1403–1461. King of France from 1429. Son of Charles VI, he was excluded from the succession by the Treaty of Troyes, but recognized by the south of France. In 1429 Joan of Arc raised the siege of Orléans and had him crowned at Reims. He organized France's first standing army and by 1453 had expelled the English from all of France except Calais.

Charles VIII 1470–1498. King of France from 1483, when he succeeded his father, Louis XI. In 1494 he unsuccessfully tried to claim the Neapolitan crown, and when he entered Naples 1495 was forced to withdraw by a coalition of Milan, Venice, Spain, and the Holy Roman Empire. He defeated them at Fornovo, but lost Naples. He died while preparing a second expedition.

Charles IX 1550–1574. King of France from 1560. Second son of Henry II and Catherine de' Medici, he succeeded his brother Francis II at the age of ten but remained under the domination of his mother's regency for ten years while France was torn by religious wars. In 1570 he fell under the influence of the *Huguenot leader Gaspard de Coligny (1517–1572); alarmed by this, Catherine instigated his order for the Massacre of *St Bartholomew, which led to a new religious war.

Charles X 1757–1836. King of France from 1824. Grandson of Louis XV and brother of Louis XVI and Louis XVIII, he was known as the comte d'Artois before his accession. He fled to England at the beginning of the French Revolution, and when he came to the throne on the death of Louis XVIII, he attempted to reverse the achievements of the Revolution. A revolt ensued 1830, and he again fled to England.

Charles seven rulers of the Holy Roman Empire, including:

Charles I Holy Roman emperor, better known as *Charlemagne.

Charles II the Bald 823–877. Holy Roman emperor from 875 and (as Charles II) king of France from 843. Younger son of Louis I (the Pious), he warred against his eldest brother, Emperor Lothair I. The Treaty of Verdun 843 made him king of the West Frankish Kingdom (now France and the Spanish Marches).

Charles III the Fat 839–888. Holy Roman emperor 881–87; he became king of the West Franks 885, thus uniting for the last time the whole of Charlemagne's dominions, but was deposed.

Charles IV 1316–1378. Holy Roman emperor from 1355 and king of Bohemia from 1346. Son of John of Luxembourg, king of Bohemia, he was elected king of Germany 1346 and ruled all Germany from 1347. He was the founder of the first German university in Prague 1348.

Charles V 1500–1558. Holy Roman emperor 1519–56. Son of Philip of Burgundy and Joanna of Castile, he inherited vast possessions, which led to rivalry from Francis I of France, whose alliance with the Ottoman Empire brought Vienna under siege 1529 and 1532. Charles was also in conflict with the Protestants in Germany until the Treaty of Passau 1552, which allowed the Lutherans religious liberty.

Charles VI 1685–1740. Holy Roman emperor from 1711, father of *Maria Theresa, whose succession to his Austrian dominions he tried to ensure, and himself claimant to the Spanish throne 1700, thus causing the War of the *Spanish Succession.

Charles VII 1697–1745. Holy Roman emperor from 1742, opponent of *Maria Theresa's claim to the Austrian dominions of Charles VI.

Charles (Karl Franz Josef) 1887–1922. Emperor of Austria and king of Hungary from 1916, the last of the Habsburg emperors. He succeeded his great-uncle Franz Josef 1916 but was forced to withdraw to Switzerland 1918, although he refused to abdicate. In 1921 he attempted unsuccessfully to regain the crown of Hungary and was deported to Madeira, where he died.

Charles (Spanish **Carlos**) four kings of Spain, including:

Charles I 1500–1558. See *Charles V, Holy Roman emperor.

Charles II 1661–1700. King of Spain from 1665. The second son of Philip IV, he was the last of the Spanish Habsburg kings. Mentally handicapped from birth, he bequeathed his dominions to Philip of Anjou, grandson of Louis XIV, which led to the War of the *Spanish Succession.

Charles III 1716–1788. King of Spain from 1759. Son of Philip V, he became duke of Parma 1732 and conquered Naples and Sicily 1734. On the death of his half-brother Ferdinand VI (1713–1759), he became king of Spain, handing over Naples and Sicily to his son Ferdinand (1751–1825). During his reign, Spain was twice at war with Britain: during the Seven Years' War, when he sided with France and lost Florida; and when he backed the colonists in the American Revolution and regained it. At home he car-

ried out a programme of reforms and expelled the Jesuits.

Charles IV 1748–1819. King of Spain from 1788, when he succeeded his father, Charles III; he left the government in the hands of his wife and her lover, the minister Manuel de Godoy (1767–1851). In 1808 Charles was induced to abdicate by Napoleon's machinations in favour of his son Ferdinand VII (1784–1833), who was subsequently deposed by Napoleon's brother Joseph. Charles was awarded a pension by Napoleon and died in Rome.

Charles (Swedish **Carl**) fifteen kings of Sweden (the first six were local chieftains), including:

Charles VIII 1408–1470. King of Sweden from 1448. He was elected regent of Sweden 1438, when Sweden broke away from Denmark and Norway. He stepped down 1441 when Christopher III of Bavaria (1418–1448) was elected king, but after his death became king. He was twice expelled by the Danes and twice restored.

Charles IX 1550–1611. King of Sweden from 1604, the youngest son of Gustavus Vasa. In 1568 he and his brother John led the rebellion against Eric XIV (1533–1577); John became king as John III and attempted to Catholicize Sweden, and Charles led the opposition. John's son Sigismund, king of Poland and a Catholic, succeeded to the Swedish throne 1592, and Charles led the Protestants. He was made regent 1595 and deposed Sigismund 1599. Charles was elected king of Sweden 1604 and was involved in unsuccessful wars with Russia, Poland, and Denmark. He was the father of Gustavus Adolphus.

Charles X 1622–1660. King of Sweden from 1654, when he succeeded his cousin Christina. He waged war with Poland and Denmark and in 1657 invaded Denmark by leading his army over the frozen sea.

Charles XI 1655–1697. King of Sweden from 1660, when he succeeded his father Charles X. His mother acted as regent until 1672 when Charles took over the government. He was a remarkable general and reformed the administration.

Charles XII 1682–1718. King of Sweden from 1697, when he succeeded his father, Charles XI. From 1700 he was involved in wars with Denmark, Poland, and Russia. He won a succession of victories until, in 1709 while invading Russia, he was defeated at Poltava in the Ukraine, and forced to take refuge in Turkey until 1714. He was killed while besieging Fredrikshall, Norway, although it was not known whether he was murdered by his own side or by the enemy.

Charles XIII 1748–1818. King of Sweden from 1809, when he was elected; he became the first king of Sweden and Norway 1814.

Charles XIV (Jean Baptiste Jules *Bernadotte) 1763–1844. King of Sweden and Norway from 1818. A former marshal in the French army, in 1810 he was elected crown prince of Sweden under the name of Charles John (Carl Johan). Loyal to his adopted country, he brought Sweden into the alliance against Napoleon 1813, as a reward for which Sweden received Norway. He was the founder of the present dynasty.

Charles XV 1826–1872. King of Sweden and Norway from 1859, when he succeeded his father

Oscar I. A popular and liberal monarch, his main achievement was the reform of the constitution.

Charles Albert 1798–1849. King of Sardinia from 1831. He showed liberal sympathies in early life, and after his accession introduced some reforms. On the outbreak of the 1848 revolution he granted a constitution and declared war on Austria. His troops were defeated at Custozza and Novara. In 1849 he abdicated in favour of his son Victor.

Charles Augustus 1757–1828. Grand Duke of Saxe-Weimar in Germany. He succeeded his father in infancy, fought against the French in 1792–94 and 1806, and was the patron and friend of the writer Goethe.

Charles Edward Stuart the *Young Pretender* or *Bonnie Prince Charlie* 1720–1788. British prince, grandson of James II and son of James, the Old Pretender. In the Jacobite rebellion 1745 Charles won the support of the Scottish Highlanders; his army invaded England to claim the throne but was beaten back by the duke of *Cumberland and routed at *Culloden 1746. Charles went into exile.

Charles Martel *c.* 688–741. Frankish ruler (Mayor of the Palace) of the E Frankish kingdom from 717 and the whole kingdom from 731. His victory against the Moors at Moussais-la-Bataille near Tours 732 earned him his nickname of Martel, 'the Hammer', because he halted the Islamic advance by the *Moors into Europe.

Charles's law law stating that the volume of a given mass of gas at constant pressure is directly proportional to its absolute temperature (temperature in kelvin). It was discovered by Jacques Charles 1787, and independently by Joseph Gay-Lussac 1802.

Charles the Bold Duke of Burgundy 1433–1477. Son of Philip the Good, he inherited Burgundy and the Low Countries from him 1465. He waged wars attempting to free the duchy from dependence on France and restore it as a kingdom. He was killed in battle.

Charleston capital and chief city of West Virginia, USA, on the Kanawha River; population (1990) 57,300. It is the centre of a region that produces coal, natural gas, salt, clay, timber, oil, and chemicals. Charleston developed from a fort built 1788.

Charleston back-kicking dance of the 1920s that originated in Charleston, South Carolina, and became an American craze.

charlock or *wild mustard* annual plant *Sinapis arvensis* of the family Cruciferae.

Charlotte Amalie capital, tourist resort, and free port of the US Virgin Islands; population (1980) 11,756.

Charlotte Augusta Princess 1796–1817. Only child of George IV and Caroline of Brunswick, and heir to the British throne. In 1816 she married Prince Leopold of Saxe-Coburg (later Leopold I of the Belgians), but died in childbirth 18 months later.

Charlotte Sophia 1744–1818. British queen consort. The daughter of the German duke of Mecklenburg-Strelitz, she married George III of Great Britain and Ireland 1761, and they had nine sons and six daughters.

Charlottetown capital of Prince Edward Island, Canada; population (1986) 16,000. The city trades in textiles, fish, timber, vegetables, and dairy produce. It was founded by French settlers in the 1720s.

Charlton Bobby (Robert) 1937– . English footballer, younger brother of Jack Charlton, who scored a record 49 goals in 106 appearances. An elegant midfield player who specialized in fierce long-range shots, he spent most of his playing career with Manchester United and played in the England team that won the World Cup 1966.

Charlton Jack 1935– . English footballer, older brother of Robert (Bobby) Charlton. He spent all his playing career with Leeds United and played more than 750 games for them. He was appointed manager of the Republic of Ireland national squad 1986.

charm in physics, a property possessed by one type of *quark (very small particles found inside protons and neutrons), called the charm quark. The effects of charm are only seen in experiments with particle *accelerators. See *elementary particles.

Charon in Greek mythology, the boatman who ferried the dead over the rivers Acheron and Styx to Hades, the underworld. A coin placed on the tongue of the dead paid for their passage.

Charter 88 British political campaign begun 1988, calling for a written constitution to prevent what it termed the development of 'an elective dictatorship'. Those who signed the charter, including many figures from the arts, objected to what they saw as the autocratic premiership of Margaret Thatcher.

Chartism radical British democratic movement, mainly of the working classes, which flourished around 1838–50. It derived its name from the People's Charter, a six-point programme comprising universal male suffrage, equal electoral districts, secret ballot, annual parliaments, and abolition of the property qualification for, and payment of, members of Parliament. Greater prosperity, lack of organization, and rivalry in the leadership led to its demise.

Chartreuse, La Grande the original home of the Carthusian order of Roman Catholic monks, established by St Bruno around 1084, in a valley near Grenoble, France.

Charybdis in Greek mythology, a whirlpool formed by a monster of the same name on one side of the narrow straits of Messina, Sicily, opposite the monster Scylla.

chasing indentation of a design on metal by small chisels and hammers. This method of decoration was familiar in ancient Egypt, Assyria, and Greece; it is used today on fine silverware.

chasuble the outer garment worn by the priest in the celebration of the Christian Mass. The colour of the chasuble depends on which feast is being celebrated.

château country house or important residence in France. The term originally applied to a French medieval castle, and the château was first used as a domestic building in the late 15th century; by the reign of Louis XIII (1610–43) fortifications such as moats and keeps were no longer used for defensive purposes, but merely as decorative features. The Loire valley contains some fine examples of châteaux.

Chateaubriand François René, vicomte de 1768–1848. French author. In exile from the French Revolution 1794–99, he wrote *Atala* 1801 (after his encounters with North American Indians) and the autobiographical *René*, which formed part of *Le Génie du Christianisme* 1802. He later wrote *Mémoires d'outre tombe/Memoirs from Beyond the Tomb* 1849–50.

Chatterton Thomas 1752–1770. English poet whose medieval-style poems and brief life inspired English Romanticism. Born in Bristol, he studied ancient documents from the Church of St Mary Redcliffe and composed poems he ascribed to a 15th-century monk, 'Thomas Rowley', which were accepted as genuine.

Chatwin Bruce 1940–1989. English writer. His works include *The Songlines* 1987, written after living with Aborigines; the novel *Utz* 1988, a novel about a manic porcelain collector in Prague; and travel pieces and journalism collected in *What Am I Doing Here* 1989.

Chaucer Geoffrey *c.* 1340–1400. English poet. *The Canterbury Tales*, a collection of stories told by a group of pilgrims on their way to Canterbury, reveals his knowledge of human nature and his stylistic variety, from urbane and ironic to simple and bawdy. Early allegorical poems, including *The Book of the Duchess*, were influenced by French poems like the *Roman de la Rose*.

chauvinism warlike, often unthinking patriotism, as exhibited by Nicholas Chauvin, one of Napoleon I's veterans and his fanatical admirer. In the mid-20th century the expression *male chauvinism* was coined to mean an assumed superiority of the male sex over the female.

Chávez Carlos 1899–1978. Mexican composer. A student of the piano and of the complex rhythms of his country's folk music, he founded the Mexico Symphony Orchestra. He composed a number of ballets, seven symphonies, and concertos for both violin and piano.

Chechnya or **Chechenya** breakaway part of the former Russian autonomous republic of Checheno-Ingush on the northern slopes of the Caucasus Mountains; official name **Noxcijn Republika Ickery** from 1994
area 17,300 sq km/6,680 sq mi
capital Grozny
population (1989) 1,070,000 (Chechen 90%)
religion Muslim
industries oil extraction (at one of the largest Russian oilfields); engineering, chemicals, building materials; timber
history After decades of resistance, the region was conquered by Russia 1859. It was an autonomous region of the USSR 1922–36 when it was joined to Ingushetia as the Autonomous Republic of Checheno-Ingush.
   In Nov 1991, following the seizure of power by General Dzhokhar Dudayev, the region declared its independence. After a brief, unsuccessful attempt to quell the rebellion, Moscow entered into negotiations over the republic's future, and in 1992 Chechnya became an autonomous republic in its own right. Later the same year fighting broke out between forces loyal to Dudayev and anti-separatist opposition forces, backed by Russia. Civil war developed Aug 1994 and in Dec 1994 Russian forces entered Chechnya and bombed the capital. By March 1995 an estimated 40,000 civilians had been killed and 250,000 were refugees. Chechnya's independence has not received international recognition.

check digit in computing, a digit attached to an important code number as a *validation check.

Checkpoint Charlie Western-controlled crossing point for non-Germans between West Berlin and East Berlin, opened 1961 as the only crossing point between the Allied and Soviet sectors. Its dismantling in June 1990 was seen as a symbol of the ending of the *Cold War.

cheese food made from the *curds* (solids) of soured milk from cows, sheep, or goats, separated from the *whey* (liquid), then salted, put into moulds, and pressed into firm blocks. Cheese is ripened with bacteria or surface fungi, and kept for a time to mature before eating.

cheetah large wild cat *Acinonyx jubatus* native to Africa, Arabia, and SW Asia, but now rare in some areas. Yellowish with black spots, it has a slim lithe build. It is up to 1 m/3 ft tall at the shoulder, and up to 1.5 m/5 ft long. It can reach 110 kph/70 mph, but tires after about 400 metres. Cheetahs live in open country where they hunt small antelopes, hares, and birds.

Cheka secret police operating in the USSR 1917–23. It originated from the tsarist Okhrana (the security police under the tsar 1881–1917), and became successively the OGPU (GPU) 1923–34, NKVD 1934–46, MVD 1946–53, and the *KGB from 1954.

Chekhov Anton (Pavlovich) 1860–1904. Russian dramatist and writer of short stories. His plays concentrate on the creation of atmosphere and delineation of internal development, rather than external action. His first play, *Ivanov* 1887, was a failure, as was *The Seagull* 1896 until revived by Stanislavsky 1898 at the Moscow Art Theatre, for which Chekhov went on to write his finest plays: *Uncle Vanya* 1899, *The Three Sisters* 1901, and *The Cherry Orchard* 1904.

chelate chemical compound whose molecules consist of one or more metal atoms or charged ions joined to chains of organic residues by coordinate (or dative covalent) chemical *bonds.

Chelyabinsk industrial town and capital of Chelyabinsk region, W Siberia, Russia; population (1987) 1,119,000. It has iron and engineering works and makes chemicals, motor vehicles, and aircraft.

chemical change change that occurs when two or more substances (reactants) interact with each other, resulting in the production of different substances (products) with different chemical compositions. A simple example of chemical change is the burning of carbon in oxygen to produce carbon dioxide.

chemical equation method of indicating the reactants and products of a chemical reaction by using chemical symbols and formulae. A chemical equation gives two basic pieces of information: (1) the reactants (on the left-hand side) and products (right-hand side); and (2) the reacting proportions (stoichiometry) – that is, how many units of each reactant and product are involved. The equation must balance; that is, the total number of atoms of a particular element on the left-hand side must be the same as the number of atoms of that element on the right-hand side.

chemical equilibrium condition in which the products of a reversible chemical reaction are formed at the same rate at which they decompose back into the reactants, so that the concentration of each reactant and product remains constant.

chemical warfare use in war of gaseous, liquid, or solid substances intended to have a toxic effect on humans, animals, or plants. Together with *biological warfare, it was banned by the Geneva Protocol 1925 and the United Nations in 1989 also voted for a ban. The total US stockpile 1989 was estimated at 30,000 tonnes and the Soviet stockpile at 50,000 metric tons. In June 1990, the USA and USSR agreed bilaterally to reduce their stockpile to 5,000 tonnes each by 2002. The USA began replacing its stocks with new nerve-gas *binary weapons.

chemical weathering form of *weathering brought about by a chemical change in the rocks affected. Chemical weathering involves the 'rotting', or breakdown, of the minerals within a rock, and usually produces a claylike residue (such as china clay and bauxite). Some chemicals are dissolved and carried away from the weathering source.

chemisorption the attachment, by chemical means, of a single layer of molecules, atoms, or ions of gas to the surface of a solid or, less frequently, a liquid. It is the basis of catalysis (see *catalyst) and is of great industrial importance.

chemistry science concerned with the composition of matter (gas, liquid, or solid) and of the changes that take place in it under certain conditions.

chemosynthesis method of making *protoplasm (contents of a cell) using the energy from chemical reactions, in contrast to the use of light energy employed for the same purpose in *photosynthesis. The process is used by certain bacteria, which can synthesize organic compounds from carbon dioxide and water using the energy from special methods of *respiration.

chemotherapy any medical treatment with chemicals. It usually refers to treatment of cancer with cytotoxic and other drugs. The term was coined by the German bacteriologist Paul Ehrlich for the use of synthetic chemicals against infectious diseases.

chemotropism movement by part of a plant in response to a chemical stimulus. The response by the plant is termed 'positive' if the growth is towards the stimulus or 'negative' if the growth is away from the stimulus.

Chen Kaige 1952– . Chinese film director and screenwriter. A member of the 'Fifth Generation' of filmmakers that graduated from the Beijing Film Academy in the early 1980s, Chen's films often explore Chinese social and political history from a highly personal viewpoint. They include *Huang Tudi/Yellow Earth* 1984, *Da Yuebing/The Big Parade* 1986, *Haizi Wang/King of Children* 1988, and *Ba Wang Bie Ji/Farewell My Concubine* 1993.

Cherenkov Pavel 1904–1990. Soviet physicist. In 1934 he discovered **Cherenkov radiation**; this occurs as a bluish light when charged atomic particles pass through water or other media at a speed in excess of that of light. He shared a Nobel prize 1958 with his colleagues Ilya *Frank and Igor Tamm for work resulting in a cosmic-ray counter.

Chernobyl town in central Ukraine; site of a nuclear power station. In April 1986 a leak, caused by overheating, occurred in a nonpressurized boiling-water nuclear reactor. The resulting clouds of radioactive isotopes were traced as far away as Sweden; over 250 people were killed, and thousands of square miles contaminated.

Cherokee member of a North *American Indian people, formerly living in the S Allegheny Mountains of what is now Alabama, the Carolinas, Georgia, and Tennessee. Their scholarly leader Sequoyah (c. 1770–1843) devised the syllabary used for writing their language. Their language belongs to the Macro-Siouan family.

cherry any of various trees of the genus *Prunus*, belonging to the rose family. Cherry trees are distinguished from plums and apricots by their fruits, which are spherical and smooth and not covered with a bloom. They grow best in deep fertile soil.

chervil any of several plants of the carrot family Umbelliferae. The garden chervil *Anthriscus cerefolium* has leaves with a sweetish odour, resembling parsley. It is used as a garnish and in soups. Chervil originated on the borders of Europe and Asia and was introduced to W Europe by the Romans.

NOBEL PRIZE FOR CHEMISTRY

recent prizewinners

1986	Dudley Herschbach (USA), Yuan Lee (USA), and John Polanyi (Canada): dynamics of chemical elementary processes
1987	Donald Cram (USA), Jean-Marie Lehn (France), and Charles Pedersen (USA): molecules with highly selective structure-specific interactions
1988	Johann Deisenhofer (West Germany), Robert Huber (West Germany), and Hartmut Michel (West Germany): three-dimensional structure of the reaction centre of photosynthesis
1989	Sydney Altman (USA) and Thomas Cech (USA): discovery of catalytic function of RNA
1990	Elias James Corey (USA): new methods of synthesizing chemical compounds
1991	Richard R Ernst (Switzerland): improvements in the technology of nuclear magnetic resonance (NMR) imaging
1992	Rudolph A Marcus (USA): theoretical discoveries relating to reduction and oxidation reactions
1993	Kary Mullis (USA): invention of the polymerase chain reaction technique for amplifying DNA. Michael Smith (Canada): development of techniques for splicing foreign genetic segments into an organism's DNA in order to modify the proteins produced
1994	George A Olah (USA): development of technique for examining hydrocarbon molecules

Chesapeake Bay largest of the inlets on the Atlantic coast of the USA, bordered by Maryland and Virginia. It is about 320 km/200 mi in length and 6–64 km/4–40 mi in width.

Cheshire county in NW England
area 2,320 sq km/896 sq mi
towns Chester (administrative headquarters), Warrington, Crewe, Widnes, Macclesfield, Congleton
physical chiefly a fertile plain; rivers: Mersey, Dee, Weaver Britain; Quarry Bank Mill at Styal is a cotton-industry museum
products textiles, chemicals, dairy products
population (1991) 937,300
famous people Charles Dodgson (Lewis Carroll); the novelist Mrs Gaskell lived at Knutsford (the locale of *Cranford*).

chess board game originating as early as the 2nd century AD. Two players use 16 pieces each, on a board of 64 squares of alternating colour, to try to force the opponent into a position where the main piece (the king) is threatened and cannot move to another position without remaining threatened.

Chesterton G(ilbert) K(eith) 1874–1936. English novelist, essayist, and satirical poet, author of a series of novels featuring as detective a naive priest, Father Brown. Other novels include *The Napoleon of Notting Hill* 1904 and *The Man Who Knew Too Much* 1922.

chestnut tree of the genus *Castanea*, belonging to the beech family Fagaceae. The Spanish or sweet chestnut *C. sativa* produces edible nuts inside husks; its timber is also valuable. *Horse chestnuts are quite distinct, belonging to the genus *Aesculus*, family Hippocastanaceae.

Chetnik member of a Serbian nationalist group that operated underground during the German occupation of Yugoslavia during World War II. Led by Col Draza *Mihailovič, the Chetniks initially received aid from the Allies, but this was later transferred to the communist partisans led by Tito. The term has also popularly been applied to Serb militia forces in the 1991–92 Yugoslav civil war.

Chevalier Maurice 1888–1972. French singer and actor. He began as dancing partner to the revue artiste Mistinguett at the Folies-Bergère cabaret theatre, and made numerous films, including *Innocents of Paris* 1929, which revived his song 'Louise', *The Merry Widow* 1934, and *Gigi* 1958.

chewing gum gummy confectionery to be chewed not swallowed. It is composed mainly of chicle (milky juice of the tropical sapodilla tree *Achras zapota* of Central America), usually flavoured with mint, sweetened, and pressed flat. The first patent was taken out in the USA in 1871. *Bubble gum* is a variety that allows chewers to blow bubbles.

Chiang Ching alternative transliteration of *Jiang Qing, Chinese actress, third wife of *Mao Zedong.

Chiang Kai-shek (Pinyin *Jiang Jie Shi*) 1887–1975. Chinese nationalist *Guomindang (Kuomintang) general and politician, president of China 1928–31 and 1943–49, and of Taiwan from 1949, where he set up a US-supported rightwing government on his expulsion from the mainland by the Communist forces. He was a commander in the civil war that lasted from the end of imperial rule 1911 to the Second *Sino-Japanese War and beyond, having split with the Communist leader Mao Zedong 1927.

Chiba industrial city (paper, steel, textiles) in Kanton region, E Honshu island, Japan, 40 km/25 mi W of Tokyo; population (1989) 815,500.

Chicago financial and industrial city in Illinois, on Lake Michigan. It is the third largest US city; population (1990) 2,783,700, metropolitan area 8,065,000. Industries include iron, steel, chemicals, electrical goods, machinery, meatpacking and food processing, publishing, and fabricated metals. The once famous stockyards are now closed.

Chicano citizen or resident of the USA of Mexican descent. The term was originally used for those who became US citizens after the *Mexican War.

Chichen Itzá Toltec city situated among the Mayan city-states of Yucatán, Mexico. It flourished AD 900–1200 and displays Classic and Post-Classic architecture of the Toltec style. The site has temples with sculptures and colour reliefs, an observatory, and a sacred well into which sacrifices, including human beings, were cast.

Chichester Francis 1901–1972. English sailor and navigator. In 1931 he made the first east-west crossing of the Tasman Sea in *Gipsy Moth*, and in 1966–67 circumnavigated the world in his yacht *Gipsy Moth IV*.

chickenpox or *varicella* common acute disease, caused by a virus of the *herpes group and transmitted by airborne droplets. Chickenpox chiefly attacks children under the age of ten. The incubation period is two to three weeks. One attack normally gives immunity for life.

chickpea annual plant *Cicer arietinum*, family Leguminosae, which is grown for food in India and the Middle East. Its short, hairy pods contain edible pealike seeds.

Chiclayo capital of Lambayeque department, NW Peru; population (1988) 395,000.

chicory plant *Cichorium intybus*, family Compositae. Native to Europe and W Asia, it has large, usually blue, flowers. Its long taproot is used dried and roasted as a coffee substitute. As a garden vegetable, grown under cover, its blanched leaves are used in salads. It is related to *endive.

chiffchaff bird *Phylloscopus collybita* of the warbler family, found in woodlands and thickets in Europe and N Asia during the summer, migrating south for winter. About 11 cm/4.3 in long, olive above, greyish below, with an eyestripe and usually dark legs, it looks similar to a willow warbler but has a distinctive song.

chigger or *harvest mite* scarlet or rusty brown *mite of the family Trombiculidae, common in summer and autumn. Their tiny red larvae cause intensely irritating bites.

chihuahua smallest breed of dog, 15 cm/10 in high, developed in the USA from Mexican origins. It may weigh only 1 kg/2.2 lb. The domed head and wide-set ears are characteristic, and the skull is large compared to the body. It can be almost any colour, and occurs in both smooth (or even hairless) and long-coated varieties.

Chihuahua capital of Chihuahua state, Mexico, 1,285 km/800 mi NW of Mexico City; population (1984) 375,000. Founded 1707, it is the centre of a mining district and has textile mills.

chilblain painful inflammation of the skin of the feet, hands, or ears, due to cold. The parts turn red, swell, itch violently, and are very tender. In bad cases, the skin cracks, blisters, or ulcerates.

child abuse the molesting of children by parents and other adults. It can give rise to various criminal charges and has become a growing concern since the early 1980s.

Child, Convention on the Rights of the United Nations document designed to make the wellbeing of children an international obligation. It was adopted 1989 and covers children from birth up to 18.

Childers (Robert) Erskine 1870–1922. Irish Sinn Féin politician, author of the spy novel *The Riddle of the Sands* 1903. He was executed as a Republican terrorist.

Children's Crusade *crusade by some 10,000 children from France, the Low Countries, and Germany, in 1212, to recapture Jerusalem for Christianity. Motivated by religious piety, many of them were sold into slavery or died of disease.

children's literature works specifically written for children. The earliest known illustrated children's book in English is *Goody Two Shoes* 1765, possibly written by Oliver Goldsmith. *Fairy tales* were originally part of a vast range of oral literature, credited only to the writer who first recorded them, such as Charles Perrault. During the 19th century several writers, including Hans Christian Andersen, wrote original stories in the fairy tale genre; others, such as the Grimm brothers, collected (and sometimes adapted) existing stories.

Chile Republic of (*República de Chile*)

```
                        :
                     PACIFIC
                     OCEAN
          Peru
                  Bolivia
PACIFIC
OCEAN                        ATLANTIC
          CHILE                 OCEAN
       Santiago   Argentina

 0    500  miles
 0    1000 km
```

area 756,950 sq km/292,257 sq mi
capital Santiago
towns Concepción, Viña del Mar, Temuco; ports Valparaíso, Antofagasta, Arica, Iquique, Punta Arenas
physical Andes mountains along E border, Ata-

cama Desert in N, fertile central valley, grazing land and forest in S
territories Easter Island, Juan Fernández Islands, part of Tierra del Fuego, claim to part of Antarctica
head of state and government Eduardo Frei from 1994
political system emergent democratic republic
exports copper (world's leading producer), iron, molybdenum (world's second largest producer), nitrate, pulp and paper, steel products, fishmeal, fruit
currency peso
population (1993) 13,440,000 (mainly of European origin or mestizos, of mixed American Indian and Spanish descent); growth rate 1.6% p.a.
language Spanish
religion Roman Catholic 89%
GNP $2,800 per head (1992)
chronology
1818 Achieved independence from Spain.
1964 PDC formed government under Eduardo Frei.
1970 Dr Salvador Allende became the first democratically elected Marxist president; he embarked on an extensive programme of nationalization and social reform.
1973 Government overthrown by the CIA-backed military, led by General Augusto Pinochet. Allende killed. Policy of repression began during which all opposition was put down and political activity banned.
1983 Growing opposition to the regime from all sides, with outbreaks of violence.
1988 Referendum on whether Pinochet should serve a further term resulted in a clear 'No' vote.
1989 President Pinochet agreed to constitutional changes to allow pluralist politics. Patricio Aylwin (PDC) elected president; Pinochet remained as army commander in chief.
1990 Aylwin reached accord on end to military junta government. Pinochet censured by president.
1993 Ruling coalition successful in general election.
1994 PDC leader Eduardo Frei sworn in as president.

Chilean Revolution in Chile, the presidency of Salvador *Allende 1970–73, the Western hemisphere's first democratically elected Marxist-oriented president of an independent state.

chilli (North American *chili*) pod, or powder made from the pod, of a variety of *capsicum, *Capsicum frutescens*, a hot, red pepper. It is widely used in cooking.

Chiltern Hundreds, stewardship of in the UK, a nominal office of profit under the crown. British members of Parliament must not resign; therefore, if they wish to leave office during a Parliament, they may apply for this office, a formality that disqualifies them from being an MP.

chimaera fish of the group Holocephali. Chimaeras have thick bodies that taper to a long thin tail, large fins, smooth skin, and a cartilaginous skeleton. They can grow to 1.5 m/4.5 ft. Most chimaeras are deep-water fish, and even *Chimaera monstrosa*, a relatively shallow-living form caught around European coasts, lives at a depth of 300–500 m/1,000–1,600 ft.

Chimbote largest fishing port in Peru; population (1981) 216,000.

chimera in biology, an organism composed of tissues that are genetically different. Chimeras can develop naturally if a *mutation occurs in a cell of a developing embryo, but are more commonly produced artificially by implanting cells from one organism into the embryo of another.

chimera or *chimaera* in Greek mythology, a fire-breathing animal with a lion's head, a goat's body, and tail in the form of a snake; hence any apparent hybrid of two or more creatures. The chimera was killed by the hero Bellerophon on the winged horse Pegasus.

chimpanzee highly intelligent African ape *Pan troglodytes* that lives mainly in rainforests but sometimes in wooded savanna. Chimpanzees are covered in thin but long black body hair, except for the face, hands, and feet, which may have pink or black skin. They normally walk on all fours, supporting the front of the body on the knuckles of the fingers, but can stand or walk upright for a short distance. They can grow to 1.4 m/4.5 ft tall, and weigh up to 50 kg/110 lb. They are strong and climb well, but spend time on the ground, living in loose social groups. The bulk of the diet is fruit, with some leaves, insects, and occasional meat. Chimpanzees can use 'tools', fashioning twigs to extract termites from their nests.

Chimu South American civilization that flourished on the coast of Peru from about 1250 to about 1470, when it was conquered by the Incas. The Chimu people produced fine work in gold, realistic portrait pottery, savage fanged feline images in clay, and possibly a system of writing or recording by painting patterns on beans. They built aqueducts carrying water many miles, and the huge, mazelike city of Chan Chan, 36 sq km/14 sq mi, on the coast near Trujillo.

China People's Republic of (*Zhonghua Renmin Gonghe Guo*)

area 9,596,960 sq km/3,599,975 sq mi
capital Beijing (Peking)
towns Chongqing (Chungking), Shenyang (Mukden), Wuhan, Nanjing (Nanking), Harbin; ports Tianjin (Tientsin), Shanghai, Qingdao (Tsingtao), Lüda (Lü-ta), Guangzhou (Canton)
physical two-thirds of China is mountains or desert (N and W); the low-lying E is irrigated by rivers Huang He (Yellow River), Chang Jiang (Yangtze-Kiang), Xi Jiang (Si Kiang)
head of state Jiang Zemin from 1993
head of government Li Peng from 1987
political system communist republic
political party Chinese Communist Party (CCP), Marxist-Leninist-Maoist
exports tea, livestock and animal products, silk, cotton, oil, minerals (China is the world's largest producer of tungsten and antimony), chemicals, light industrial goods
currency yuan
population (1993 est) 1,185,000,000 (the majority are Han or ethnic Chinese; the 67 million of other ethnic groups, including Tibetan, Uigur, and Zhuang, live in border areas). The number of people of Chinese origin outside China, Taiwan, and Hong Kong is estimated at 15–24 million. Growth rate 1.2% p.a.
languages Chinese, including Mandarin (official), Cantonese, and other dialects
religions officially atheist, but traditionally Taoist, Confucianist, and Buddhist; Muslim 13 million; Catholic 3–6 million (divided between the 'patriotic' church established 1958 and the 'loyal' church subject to Rome); Protestant 3 million
GNP $370 per head (1991)
chronology
1949 People's Republic of China proclaimed by Mao Zedong.
1954 Soviet-style constitution adopted.
1956–57 Hundred Flowers Movement encouraged criticism of the government.
1958–60 Great Leap Forward commune experiment to achieve 'true communism'.
1960 Withdrawal of Soviet technical advisers.
1962 Sino-Indian border war.
1962–65 Economic recovery programme under Liu Shaoqi; Maoist 'socialist education movement' rectification campaign.
1966–69 Great Proletarian Cultural Revolution; Liu Shaoqi overthrown.
1969 Ussuri River border clashes with USSR.
1970–76 Reconstruction under Mao and Zhou Enlai.
1971 Entry into United Nations.
1972 US president Nixon visited Beijing.
1975 New state constitution. Unveiling of Zhou's 'Four Modernizations' programme.
1976 Deaths of Zhou Enlai and Mao Zedong; appointment of Hua Guofeng as prime minister and Communist Party chair. Vice Premier Deng Xiaoping in hiding. Gang of Four arrested.
1977 Rehabilitation of Deng Xiaoping.
1979 Economic reforms introduced. Diplomatic relations opened with USA. Punitive invasion of Vietnam.
1980 Zhao Ziyang appointed prime minister.
1981 Hu Yaobang succeeded Hua Guofeng as party chair. Imprisonment of Gang of Four.
1982 New state constitution adopted.
1984 'Enterprise management' reforms for industrial sector.
1986 Student prodemocracy demonstrations.
1987 Hu was replaced as party leader by Zhao, with Li Peng as prime minister. Deng left Politburo but remained influential.
1988 Yang Shangkun replaced Li Xiannian as state president. Economic reforms encountered increasing problems; inflation rocketed.

1989 Over 2,000 killed in prodemocracy student demonstrations in Tiananmen Square; international sanctions imposed.

1991 March: European Community and Japanese sanctions lifted. May: normal relations with USSR resumed. Sept: UK prime minister John Major visited Beijing. Nov: relations with Vietnam normalized.

1992 China promised to sign 1968 Nuclear Non-Proliferation Treaty. Full diplomatic relations with Israel established.

1993 Jiang Zemin, Chinese Communist Party general secretary replaced Yang Shangkun as President.

china clay clay mineral formed by the decomposition of *feldspars. The alteration of aluminium silicates results in the formation of **kaolinite**, $Al_2Si_2O_5(OH)_2$, from which **kaolin**, or white china clay, is derived.

China Sea area of the Pacific Ocean bordered by China, Vietnam, Borneo, the Philippines, and Japan. Various groups of small islands and shoals, including the Paracels, 500 km/300 mi E of Vietnam, have been disputed by China and other powers because they lie in oil-rich areas.

chincherinchee poisonous plant *Ornithogalum thyrsoides* of the lily family Liliaceae. It is native to South Africa, and has spikes of long-lasting, white or yellow, waxlike flowers.

chinchilla South American rodent *Chinchilla laniger* found in high, rather barren areas of the Andes in Bolivia and Chile. About the size of a small rabbit, it has long ears and a long bushy tail, and shelters in rock crevices. These gregarious animals have thick, soft, silver-grey fur, and were hunted almost to extinction for it. They are now farmed and protected in the wild.

Chinese native to or an inhabitant of China and Taiwan, or a person of Chinese descent. The Chinese comprise more than 25% of the world's population, and the Chinese language (Mandarin) is the largest member of the Sino-Tibetan family.

Chinese art the painting and sculpture of China. From the Bronze Age to the Cultural Revolution, Chinese art shows a stylistic unity unparalleled in any other culture. From about the 1st century AD Buddhism inspired much sculpture and painting. The **Han dynasty** (206 BC–AD 220) produced outstanding metalwork, ceramics, and sculpture. The **Song dynasty** (960–1278) established standards of idyllic landscape and nature painting in a delicate calligraphic style.

Chinese language language or group of languages of the Sino-Tibetan family, spoken in China, Taiwan, Hong Kong, Singapore, and Chinese communities throughout the world. Varieties of spoken Chinese differ greatly, but all share a written form using thousands of ideographic symbols – characters – which have changed little in 2,000 years. Nowadays, *putonghua* ('common speech'), based on the educated Beijing dialect known as Mandarin Chinese, is promoted throughout China as the national spoken and written language.

Chinese Revolution series of great political upheavals in China 1911–49 that eventually led to Communist party rule and the establishment of the People's Republic of China. In 1912, a Nationalist revolt overthrew the imperial Manchu (or Ching) dynasty. Led by Sun Yat-sen 1923–25, and by Chiang Kai-shek 1925–49, the Nationalists, or Guomindang, were increasing challenged by the growing Communist movement. The 10,000 km/6,000 mi **Long March** to the NW by the Communists 1934–35 to escape from attacks by the Nationalist forces resulted in Mao Zedong's emergence as Communist leader. During World War II 1939–45, the various Chinese political groups pooled military resources against the Japanese invaders. After World War II, the conflict reignited into open civil war 1946–49, until the Nationalists were defeated at Nanking and forced to flee to Taiwan. Communist rule was established in the People's Republic of China under the leadership of Mao.

chinook (American Indian 'snow-eater') warm dry wind that blows downhill on the eastern side of the Rocky Mountains of North America. It often occurs in winter and spring when it produces a rapid thaw, and so is important to the agriculture of the area.

chintz printed fabric, usually glazed, popular for furnishings. In England in the late 16th and 17th centuries the term was used for Indian painted and printed cotton fabrics (calicos) and later for European printed fabrics.

chip or **silicon chip** another name for an *integrated circuit*, a complete electronic circuit on a slice of silicon (or other semiconductor) crystal only a few millimetres square.

chipmunk any of several species of small ground squirrel with characteristic stripes along its side. Chipmunks live in North America and E Asia, in a variety of habitats, usually wooded, and take shelter in burrows. They have pouches in their cheeks for carrying food. They climb well but spend most of their time on or near the ground.

Chippendale Thomas *c.* 1718–1779. English furniture designer. He set up his workshop in St Martin's Lane, London 1753. His book *The Gentleman and Cabinet Maker's Director* 1754, was a significant contribution to furniture design. He favoured Louis XVI, Chinese, Gothic, and Neo-Classical styles, and worked mainly in mahogany.

Chirac Jacques 1932– . French conservative politician, prime minister 1974–76 and 1986–88 and president from 1995. He established the neo-Gaullist Rassemblement pour la République (RPR) 1976, and became mayor of Paris 1977.

Chirico Giorgio de 1888–1978. Italian painter born in Greece, whose style presaged Surrealism in its use of enigmatic imagery and dreamlike settings, for example, *Nostalgia of the Infinite* 1911, Museum of Modern Art, New York.

Chiron unusual Solar-System object orbiting between Saturn and Uranus, discovered 1977 by US astronomer Charles T Kowal (1940–). Initially classified as an asteroid, it is now believed to be a giant cometary nucleus about 200 km/120 mi across, composed of ice with a dark crust of carbon dust.

chiropractic technique of manipulation of the spine and other parts of the body, based on the principle that disorders are attributable to aberrations in the functioning of the nervous system, which manipulation can correct.

Chissano Joaquim 1939– . Mozambique nationalist politician, president from 1986; foreign minister 1975–86. In Oct 1992 Chissano signed a peace accord with the leader of the rebel Mozambique National Resistance (MNR) party, bringing to an end 16 years of civil war, and in 1994 won the first free presidential elections.

chitin complex long-chain compound, or *polymer; a nitrogenous derivative of glucose. Chitin is found principally in the *exoskeleton of insects and other arthropods. It combines with protein to form a covering that can be hard and tough, as in beetles, or soft and flexible, as in caterpillars and other insect larvae.

Chittagong city and port in Bangladesh, 16 km/10 mi from the mouth of the Karnaphuli River, on the Bay of Bengal; population (1981) 1,388,476. Industries include steel, engineering, chemicals, and textiles.

chive or **chives** bulbous perennial European plant *Allium schoenoprasum* of the lily family Liliaceae. It has long, tubular leaves and dense, round flower heads in blue or lilac, and is used as a garnish for salads.

chlamydia single-celled bacterium that can live only parasitically in animal cells. Chlamydiae are thought to be descendants of bacteria that have lost certain metabolic processes. In humans, they cause *trachoma, a disease found mainly in the tropics (a leading cause of blindness), and psittacosis, a disease that may be contracted from birds; venereally transmitted chlamydiae cause genital and urinary infections.

chloral or **trichloroethanal** CCl_3CHO oily, colourless liquid with a characteristic pungent smell, produced by the action of chlorine on ethanol. It is soluble in water and its compound chloral hydrate is a powerful sleep-inducing agent.

chloramphenicol the first broad-spectrum antibiotic to be used commercially. It was discovered 1947 in a Venezuelan soil sample containing the bacillus *Streptomyces venezuelae*, which produces the antibiotic substance $C_{11}H_{12}Cl_2N_2O_5$, now synthesized. Because of its toxicity, its use is limited to treatment of life-threatening infections, such as meningitis and typhoid fever.

chlorate any salt derived from an acid containing both chlorine and oxygen and possessing the negative ion ClO^-, ClO_2^-, ClO_3^-, or ClO_4^-. Common chlorates are those of sodium, potassium, and barium. Certain chlorates are used in weedkillers.

chloride Cl^- negative ion formed when hydrogen chloride dissolves in water, and any salt containing this ion, commonly formed by the action of hydrochloric acid (HCl) on various metals or by direct combination of a metal and chlorine. Sodium chloride (NaCl) is common table salt.

chlorinated solvent any liquid organic compound that contains chlorine atoms, often two or more. These compounds are very effective solvents for fats and greases, but many have toxic properties. They include trichloromethane (chloroform, $CHCl_3$), tetrachloromethane

(carbon tetrachloride, CCl_4), and trichloroethene ($CH_2ClCHCl_2$).

chlorine (Greek *chloros* 'green') greenish-yellow, gaseous, nonmetallic element with a pungent odour, symbol Cl, atomic number 17, relative atomic mass 35.453. It is a member of the *halogen group and is widely distributed, in combination with the *alkali metals, as chlorates or chlorides.

chlorofluorocarbon (CFC) synthetic chemical that is odourless, nontoxic, nonflammable, and chemically inert. CFCs have been used as propellants in *aerosol cans, as refrigerants in refrigerators and air conditioners, and in the manufacture of foam packaging. They are partly responsible for the destruction of the *ozone layer. In June 1990 representatives of 93 nations, including the UK and the USA, agreed to phase out production of CFCs and various other ozone-depleting chemicals by the end of the 20th century.

chloroform (technical name **trichloromethane**) $CHCl_3$ clear, colourless, toxic, carcinogenic liquid with a characteristic pungent, sickly sweet smell and taste, formerly used as an anaesthetic.

chlorophyll green pigment present in most plants; it is responsible for the absorption of light energy during *photosynthesis. The pigment absorbs the red and blue-violet parts of sunlight but reflects the green, thus giving plants their characteristic colour.

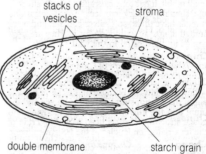

chloroplast Green chlorophyll within the chloroplast captures light energy to produce food by photosynthesis.

chloroplast structure (*organelle) within a plant cell containing the green pigment chlorophyll. Chloroplasts occur in most cells of the green plant that are exposed to light, often in large numbers. Typically, they are flattened and disclike, with a double membrane enclosing the stroma, a gel-like matrix. Within the stroma are stacks of fluid-containing cavities, or vesicles, where *photosynthesis occurs.

chlorosis abnormal condition of green plants in which the stems and leaves turn pale green or yellow. The yellowing is due to a reduction in the levels of the green chlorophyll pigments. It may be caused by a deficiency in essential elements (such as magnesium, iron, or manganese), a lack of light, genetic factors, or viral infection.

chocolate powder, syrup, confectionery, or beverage derived from cacao seeds. See *cocoa and chocolate.

Choiseul Étienne François, duc de Choiseul 1719–1785. French politician. Originally a protégé of Madame de Pompadour, the mistress of Louis XV, he became minister for foreign affairs 1758, and held this and other offices until 1770. He banished the Jesuits, and was a supporter of the Enlightenment philosophers Diderot and Voltaire.

choke coil in physics, a coil employed to limit or suppress alternating current without stopping direct current, particularly the type used as a 'starter' in the circuit of fluorescent lighting.

cholecalciferol or **vitamin D** fat-soluble chemical important in the uptake of calcium and phosphorous for bones. It is found in liver, fish oils and margarine. It can be produced in the skin, provided that the skin is adequately exposed to sunlight. Lack of vitamin D leads to rickets and other bone diseases.

cholecystectomy surgical removal of the *gall bladder. It is carried out when gallstones or infection lead to inflammation of the gall bladder, which may then be removed either by conventional surgery or by 'keyhole' procedure (see *endoscopy).

cholera disease caused by infection with various strains of the bacillus *Vibrio cholerae*, transmitted in contaminated water and characterized by violent diarrhoea and vomiting. It is prevalent in many tropical areas.

cholesterol white, crystalline *sterol found throughout the body, especially in fats, blood, nerve tissue, and bile; it is also provided in the diet by foods such as eggs, meat, and butter. A high level of cholesterol in the blood is thought to contribute to atherosclerosis (hardening of the arteries).

Chomsky Noam 1928– . US professor of linguistics. He proposed a theory of transformational generative grammar, which attracted widespread interest because of the claims it made about the relationship between language and the mind and the universality of an underlying language structure. He has been a leading critic of the imperialist tendencies of the US government.

Chongqing or **Chungking**, also known as **Pahsien** city in Sichuan province, China, that stands at the confluence of the *Chang Jiang and Jialing Jiang rivers; population (1984) 2,733,700. Industries include iron, steel, chemicals, synthetic rubber, and textiles.

Chopin Frédéric (François) 1810–1849. Polish composer and pianist. He made his debut as a pianist at the age of eight. As a performer, Chopin revolutionized the technique of pianoforte-playing, turning the hands outward and favouring a light, responsive touch. His compositions for piano, which include two concertos and other works with orchestra, are characterized by great volatility of mood, and rhythmic fluidity.

chord in geometry, a straight line joining any two points on a curve. The chord that passes through the centre of a circle (its longest chord) is the diameter. The longest and shortest chords of an ellipse (a regular oval) are called the major and minor axes respectively.

chord in music, a group of three or more notes sounded together. The resulting combination of tones may be either harmonious or dissonant.

chordate animal belonging to the phylum Chordata, which includes vertebrates, sea squirts, amphioxi, and others. All these animals, at some stage of their lives, have a supporting rod of tissue (notochord or backbone) running down their bodies.

chorea condition featuring involuntary movements of the face muscles and limbs. It is seen in a number of neurological diseases, including *Huntington's chorea. See also *St Vitus's dance.

choreography art of creating and arranging ballet and dance for performance; originally, in the 18th century, the art of dance notation.

chorion outermost of the three membranes enclosing the embryo of reptiles, birds, and mammals; the *amnion is the innermost membrane.

chorionic villus sampling (CVS) *biopsy of a small sample of placental tissue, carried out in early pregnancy at 10–12 weeks' gestation. Since the placenta forms from embryonic cells, the tissue obtained can be tested to reveal genetic abnormality in the fetus. The advantage of CVS over *amniocentesis is that it provides an earlier diagnosis, so that if any abnormality is discovered, and the parents opt for an abortion, it can be carried out more safely.

chorus in classical Greek drama, the group of actors who jointly comment on the main action or advise the main characters. The action in Greek plays took place offstage; the chorus provided a link in the drama when the principals were offstage. The chorus did not always speak in unison; it was common for members of the chorus to show some individuality. The device of a chorus has also been used by later dramatists.

Chou En-lai alternative transliteration of *Zhou Enlai.

chough bird *Pyrrhocorax pyrrhocorax* of the crow family, about 38 cm/15 in long, black-feathered, and with red bill and legs. It lives on sea cliffs and mountains from Europe to E Asia, but is now rare.

chow chow breed of dog originating in China in ancient times. About 45 cm/1.5 ft tall, it has a broad neck and head, round catlike feet, a soft woolly undercoat with a coarse outer coat, and a mane. Its coat should be of one colour, and it has an unusual blue-black tongue.

Chretien Jean 1934– . Canadian politician, prime minister from 1993. He won the leadership of the Liberal Party 1990 and defeated Kim Campbell in the Oct 1993 election. He has been a vigorous advocate of national unity and, although himself Quebeçois, has consistently opposed the province's separatist ambitions.

Chrétien de Troyes Lived second half of the 12th century. French poet. His epics, which introduced the concept of the *Holy Grail, include *Lancelot, ou le chevalier de la charrette*; *Perceval, ou le conte du Graal*, written for Philip, Count of Flanders; *Erec*; *Yvain, ou le chevalier au Lion*; and other Arthurian romances.

Christ the *Messiah as prophesied in the Hebrew Bible, or Old Testament.

christening Christian ceremony of *baptism of infants, including giving a name.

Christian ten kings of Denmark and Norway, including:

Christian I 1426–1481. King of Denmark from 1448, and founder of the Oldenburg dynasty. In 1450 he established the union of Denmark and Norway that lasted until 1814.

Christian IV 1577–1648. King of Denmark and Norway from 1588. He sided with the Protestants in the Thirty Years' War (1618–48), and founded Christiania (now Oslo, capital of Norway). He was succeeded by Frederick II 1648.

Christian IX 1818–1906. King of Denmark from 1863. His daughter Alexandra married Edward VII of the UK and another, Dagmar, married Tsar Alexander III of Russia; his second son, George, became king of Greece. In 1864 he lost the duchies of Schleswig and Holstein after a war with Austria and Prussia.

Christian X 1870–1947. King of Denmark and Iceland from 1912, when he succeeded his father Frederick VIII. He married Alexandrine, Duchess of Mecklenburg-Schwerin, and was popular for his democratic attitude. During World War II he was held prisoner by the Germans in Copenhagen. He was succeeded by Frederick IX.

Christianity world religion derived from the teaching of Jesus in the first third of the 1st century, with a present-day membership of about 1 billion. It is divided into groups or denominations that differ in some areas of belief and practice. Its main divisions are the *Roman Catholic, *Eastern Orthodox, and *Protestant churches.

beliefs Christians believe in one God with three aspects: God the Father, God the Son (Jesus), and God the Holy Spirit, who is the power of God working in the world. God created everything that exists and showed his love for the world by coming to Earth as Jesus, and suffering and dying in order to be reconciled with humanity. Christians believe that three days after his death by crucifixion Jesus was raised to life by God's power, appearing many times in bodily form to his followers, and that he is now alive in the world through the Holy Spirit. Christians speak of the sufferings they may have to endure because of their faith, and the reward of everlasting life in God's presence which is promised to those who have faith in Jesus Christ and who live according to his teaching.

Christian Science or *the Church of Christ, Scientist* sect established in the USA by Mary Baker Eddy 1879. Christian Scientists believe that since God is good and is a spirit, matter and evil are not ultimately real. Consequently they refuse all medical treatment. The church has its own daily newspaper, the *Christian Science Monitor.*

Christie Agatha (born Miller) 1890–1976. English detective novelist who created the characters Hercule Poirot and Miss Jane Marple. She wrote more than 70 novels, including *The Murder of Roger Ackroyd* 1926 and *Ten Little Indians* 1939. Her play *The Mousetrap*, which opened in London 1952, is the longest continuous running show in the world.

Christie Linford 1960– . Jamaican-born English sprinter who, at the 1992 Barcelona Olympics, won a gold medal in the 100 metres race. At the 1988 Seoul Olympics, he won silver medals in the 100 metres and 4 × 100 metres relay. In 1990 he won gold medals in the Commonwealth

Games for the 100 metres and 4 × 100 metres relay.

Christina 1626–1689. Queen of Sweden 1632–54. Succeeding her father Gustavus Adolphus at the age of six, she assumed power 1644, but disagreed with the former regent Axel Oxenstjerna (1583–1654). Refusing to marry, she eventually nominated her cousin Charles Gustavus (Charles X) as her successor. As a secret convert to Roman Catholicism, which was then illegal in Sweden, she had to abdicate 1654, and went to live in Rome, twice returning to Sweden unsuccessfully to claim the throne.

Christine de Pisan 1364–1430. French poet and historian. Her works include love lyrics, philosophical poems, a poem in praise of Joan of Arc, a history of Charles V, and various defences of women, including *La Cité des dames/The City of Ladies* 1405.

Christmas Christian religious holiday, observed throughout the Western world on Dec 25 and traditionally marked by feasting and gift-giving. In the Christian church, it is the day on which the birth of Jesus is celebrated, although the actual birth date is unknown. Many of its customs have a non-Christian origin and were adapted from celebrations of the winter *solstice.

Christmas rose see *hellebore.

Christmas tree any evergreen tree brought indoors and decorated for Christmas. The custom was a medieval German tradition and is now practised in many Western countries.

Christophe Henri 1767–1820. West Indian slave, one of the leaders of the revolt against the French 1791, who was proclaimed king of Haiti 1811. His government distributed plantations to military leaders. He shot himself when his troops deserted him because of his alleged cruelty.

Christopher, St patron saint of travellers. His feast day, 25 July, was dropped from the Roman Catholic liturgical calendar 1969.

chromatic scale musical scale proceeding by semitones. All 12 notes in the octave are used rather than the 7 notes of the diatonic scale.

chromatography (Greek *chromos* 'colour') technique used for separating the components of a mixture. This is brought about by means of two immiscible substances, one of which (*the mobile phase*) transports the sample mixture through the other (*the stationary phase*). The mobile phase may be a gas or a liquid; the stationary phase may be a liquid or a solid, and may be in a column, on paper, or in a thin layer on a glass or plastic support. The components of the mixture are absorbed or impeded by the stationary phase to different extents and therefore become separated.

chromite $FeCr_2O_4$, iron chromium oxide, the main chromium ore. It is one of the spinel group of minerals, and crystallizes in dark-coloured octahedra of the cubic system. Chromite is usually found in association with ultrabasic and basic rocks; in Cyprus, for example, it occurs with *serpentine, and in South Africa it forms continuous layers in a layered *intrusion.

chromium (Greek *chromos* 'colour') hard, brittle, grey-white, metallic element, symbol Cr, atomic number 24, relative atomic mass 51.996. It takes a high polish, has a high melting point, and is very resistant to corrosion. It is used in chromium electroplating, in the manufacture of stainless steel and other alloys, and as a catalyst. Its compounds are used for tanning leather and for *alums. In human nutrition it is a vital trace element. In nature, it occurs chiefly as chrome iron ore or chromite ($FeCr_2O_4$). Kazakhstan, Zimbabwe, and Brazil are sources.

chromium ore essentially chromite, $FeCr_2O_4$, from which chromium is extracted. South Africa and Zimbabwe are major producers.

chromosome structure in a cell nucleus that carries the *genes. Each chromosome consists of one very long strand of DNA, coiled and folded to produce a compact body. The point on a chromosome where a particular gene occurs is known as its locus. Most higher organisms have two copies of each chromosome (they are *diploid) but some have only one (they are *haploid). There are 46 chromosomes in a normal human cell. See also *mitosis and *meiosis.

chromosphere (Greek 'colour' and 'sphere') layer of mostly hydrogen gas about 10,000 km/6,000 mi deep above the visible surface of the Sun (the photosphere). It appears pinkish red during *eclipses of the Sun.

chronic in medicine, term used to describe a condition that is of slow onset and then runs a prolonged course, such as rheumatoid arthritis or chronic bronchitis. In contrast, an *acute* condition develops quickly and may be of relatively short duration.

Chronicles two books of the Old Testament.

chronometer instrument for measuring time precisely, originally used at sea. It is designed to remain accurate through all conditions of temperature and pressure. The first accurate marine chronometer, capable of an accuracy of half a minute a year, was made 1761 by John Harrison in England.

chrysanthemum any plant of the genus *Chrysanthemum* of the family Compositae, with about 200 species. There are hundreds of cultivated varieties, whose exact wild ancestry is uncertain. In the Far East the common chrysanthemum has been cultivated for more than 2,000 years and is the imperial emblem of Japan. Chrysanthemums may be grown from seed, but are more usually propagated by cutting or division.

chrysolite alternative name for the mineral *olivine.

Chuang member of the largest minority group in China, numbering about 15 million. They live in S China, where they cultivate rice fields. Their religion includes elements of ancestor worship. The Chuang language belongs to the Tai family.

chub freshwater fish *Leuciscus cephalus* of the carp family. Thickset and cylindrical, it grows up to 60 cm/2 ft, is dark greenish or grey on the back, silvery yellow below, with metallic flashes on the flanks. It lives generally in clean rivers throughout Europe.

Chubu mountainous coastal region of central Honshu island, Japan; area 66,774 sq km/25,791 sq mi; population (1986) 20,694,000. The chief city is Nagoya.

Chugoku SW region of Honshu island, Japan; area 31,881 sq km/12,314 sq mi; population (1986) 7,764,000. The chief city is Hiroshima.

Chun Doo-hwan 1931– . South Korean military ruler who seized power 1979, president 1981–88 as head of the newly formed Democratic Justice Party.

church building designed as a Christian place of worship. Churches were first built in the 3rd century, when persecution ceased under the Holy Roman emperor Constantine. The original church design was based on the Roman *basilica, with a central nave, aisles either side, and an apse at one end.

Church Army religious organization within the Church of England founded 1882 by Wilson Carlile (1847–1942), an industrialist converted after the failure of his textile firm, who took orders 1880. Originally intended for evangelical and social work in the London slums, it developed along Salvation Army lines, and has done much work among ex-prisoners and for the soldiers of both world wars.

Churchill Caryl 1938– . English playwright. Her predominantly radical and feminist works include *Top Girls* 1982, a study of the hazards encountered by 'career' women throughout history; *Serious Money* 1987, which satirized the world of London's brash young financial brokers; and *Mad Forest* 1990, set in Romania during the overthrow of the Ceauşescu regime. *The Skriker* 1994 is a fairytale-inspired piece with much alliteration and wordplay.

Churchill Randolph (Henry Spencer) 1849–1895. British Conservative politician, chancellor of the Exchequer and leader of the House of Commons 1886; father of Winston Churchill.

Churchill Winston (Leonard Spencer) 1874–1965. British Conservative politician, prime minister 1940–45 and 1951–55. In Parliament from 1900, as a Liberal until 1923, he held a number of ministerial offices, including First Lord of the Admiralty 1911–15 and chancellor of the Exchequer 1924–29. Absent from the cabinet in the 1930s, he returned Sept 1939 to lead a coalition government 1940–45, negotiating with Allied leaders in World War II to achieve the unconditional surrender of Germany 1945; he led a Conservative government 1951–55. He received the Nobel Prize for Literature 1953.

Church in Wales the Welsh Anglican church, independent from the Church of England since 1920. It comprises six dioceses with an archbishop.

Church of England established form of Christianity in England, a member of the Anglican Communion. It was dissociated from the Roman Catholic Church 1534. There were approximately 1,100,000 regular worshippers in 1988.

Church of Scotland established form of Christianity in Scotland, first recognized by the state 1560. It is based on the Protestant doctrines of the reformer Calvin and governed on Presbyterian lines. The Church went through several periods of episcopacy in the 17th century, and those who adhered to episcopacy after 1690 formed the Episcopal Church of Scotland, an autonomous church in communion with the Church of England. In 1843, there was a split in the Church of Scotland (the Disruption), in which almost a third of its ministers and members left and formed the Free Church of Scotland. Its membership 1988 was about 850,000.

chyme general term for the stomach contents. Chyme resembles a thick creamy fluid and is made up of partly digested food, hydrochloric acid, and a range of enzymes.

CIA abbreviation for the US *Central Intelligence Agency*.

Ciano Galeazzo 1903–1944. Italian Fascist politician. Son-in-law of the dictator Mussolini, he was foreign minister and member of the Fascist Supreme Council 1936–43. He voted against Mussolini at the meeting of the Grand Council July 1943 that overthrew the dictator, but was later tried for treason and shot by the Fascists.

Cibachrome in photography, a process of printing directly from transparencies. It can be home-processed and the rich, saturated colours are highly resistant to fading. It was introduced 1963.

cicada any of several insects of the family Cicadidae. Most species are tropical, but a few occur in Europe and North America. Young cicadas live underground, for up to 17 years in some species. The adults live on trees, whose juices they suck. The males produce a loud, almost continuous, chirping by vibrating membranes in resonating cavities in the abdomen.

Cicero Marcus Tullius 106–43 BC. Roman orator, writer, and politician. His speeches and philosophical and rhetorical works are models of Latin prose, and his letters provide a picture of contemporary Roman life. As consul 63 BC he exposed the Roman politician Catiline's conspiracy in four major orations.

cichlid any freshwater fish of the family Cichlidae. Cichlids are somewhat perchlike, but have a single nostril on each side instead of two. They are mostly predatory, and have deep, colourful bodies, flattened from side to side so that some are almost disc-shaped. Many are territorial in the breeding season and may show care of the young. There are more than 1,000 species found in South and Central America, Africa, and India.

CID abbreviation for *Criminal Investigation Department*.

Cid, El Rodrigo Díaz de Bivar 1040–1099. Spanish soldier, nicknamed **El Cid** ('the lord') by the *Moors. Born in Castile of a noble family, he fought against the king of Navarre and won his nickname *el Campeador* ('the Champion') by killing the Navarrese champion in single combat. Essentially a mercenary, fighting both with and against the Moors, he died while defending Valencia against them, and in subsequent romances became Spain's national hero.

cider in the UK, a fermented drink made from the juice of the apple; in the USA, the term cider usually refers to unfermented (nonalcoholic) apple juice. Cider has been made for more than 2,000 years, and for many centuries has been a popular drink in France and England, which are now its main centres of production.

Cierva Juan de la 1895–1936. Spanish engineer. In trying to produce an aircraft that would not stall and could fly slowly, he invented the *autogiro, the forerunner of the helicopter but differing from it in having unpowered rotors that revolve freely.

cif in economics, abbreviation for *cost, insurance, and freight* or *charged in full*. Many countries value their imports on this basis, whereas exports are usually valued *fob*. For balance of payments purposes, figures are usually adjusted to include the freight and insurance costs.

cigar compact roll of cured tobacco leaves, contained in a binder leaf, which in turn is surrounded by a wrapper leaf. The cigar was originally a sheath of palm leaves filled with tobacco, smoked by the Indians of Central America. Cigar smoking was introduced into Spain soon after 1492 and spread all over Europe in the next few centuries. From about 1890 cigar smoking was gradually supplanted in popularity by cigarette smoking.

cigarette (French 'little cigar') thin paper tube stuffed with shredded tobacco for smoking, now usually plugged with a filter. The first cigarettes were the *papelitos* smoked in South America about 1750. The habit spread to Spain and then throughout the world; today it is the most general form of tobacco smoking, although it is dangerous to the health of both smokers and nonsmokers who breathe in the smoke.

cilia (singular *cilium*) small threadlike organs on the surface of some cells, composed of contractile fibres that produce rhythmic waving movements. Some single-celled organisms move by means of cilia. In multicellular animals, they keep lubricated surfaces clear of debris. They also move food in the digestive tracts of some invertebrates.

ciliary muscle ring of muscle surrounding and controlling the lens inside the vertebrate eye, used in *accommodation (focusing). Suspensory ligaments, resembling spokes of a wheel, connect the lens to the ciliary muscle and pull the lens into a flatter shape when the muscle relaxes. On contraction, the lens returns to its normal spherical state.

Cilicia ancient region of Asia Minor, now forming part of Turkey, situated between the Taurus Mountains and the Mediterranean.

Cimabue Giovanni (Cenni de Peppi) c. 1240–1302. Italian painter, active in Florence, traditionally styled the 'father of Italian painting'. His paintings retain the golden background of Byzantine art but the figures have a new naturalism. Among the works attributed to him are *Madonna and Child* (Uffizi, Florence), a huge Gothic image of the Virgin that nevertheless has a novel softness and solidity that points forwards to Giotto.

cimbalom in music, a type of *dulcimer.

Cimino Michael 1943– . US film director whose reputation was made by *The Deer Hunter* 1978, a moral epic set against the Vietnam War (five Academy Awards). A later film, the Western *Heaven's Gate* 1980, lost its backers, United Artists, some $30 million, and subsequently became a byword for commercial disaster in the industry.

cinchona any shrub or tree of the tropical American genus *Chinchona* of the madder family Rubiaceae. *Quinine is produced from the bark of some species, and these are now cultivated in India, Sri Lanka, the Philippines, and Indonesia.

Cincinnatus Lucius Quintus 5th century BC. Roman general. Appointed dictator 458 BC, he defeated the Aequi (an Italian people) in a brief campaign, then resumed life as a yeoman farmer.

cine camera camera that takes a rapid sequence of still photographs – 24 frames (pictures) each second. When the pictures are projected one after the other at the same speed on to a screen, they appear to show movement, because our eyes hold on to the image of one picture before the next one appears.

cinema 20th-century form of art and entertainment consisting of 'moving pictures' in either black and white or colour, projected onto a screen. Cinema borrows from the other arts, such as music, drama, and literature, but is entirely dependent for its origins on technological developments, including the technology of action photography, projection, sound reproduction, and film processing and printing (see *photography).

CinemaScope trade name for a wide-screen process using anamorphic lenses, in which images are compressed during filming and then extended during projection over a wide curved screen. The first film to be made in CinemaScope was *The Robe* 1953.

cinéma vérité (French 'cinema truth') filmmaking that aims to capture truth on film by observing, recording, and presenting real events and situations as they occur without major directorial, editorial, or technical control.

Cinerama wide-screen process devised 1937 by Fred Waller of Paramount's special-effects department. Originally three 35-mm cameras and three projectors were used to record and project a single image. Three aspects of the image were recorded and then projected on a large curved screen with the result that the images blended together to produce an illusion of vastness. The first Cinerama film was *How the West Was Won* 1962. It was eventually abandoned in favour of a single-lens 70-mm process.

cinnabar mercuric sulphide, HgS, the only commercially useful ore of mercury. It is deposited in veins and impregnations near recent volcanic rocks and hot springs. The mineral itself is used as a red pigment, commonly known as **vermilion**. Cinnabar is found in the USA (California), Spain (Almadén), Peru, Italy, and Slovenia.

cinnamon dried inner bark of a tree *Cinnamomum zeylanicum* of the laurel family, grown in India and Sri Lanka. The bark is ground to make the spice used in curries and confectionery. Oil of cinnamon is obtained from waste bark and is used as flavouring in food and medicine.

cinquefoil any plant of the genus *Potentilla* of the rose family, usually with five-lobed leaves and brightly coloured flowers. It is widespread in northern temperate regions.

Cinque Ports group of ports in S England, originally five, Sandwich, Dover, Hythe, Romney, and Hastings, later including Rye, Winchelsea, and others. Probably founded in Roman times, they rose to importance after the Norman conquest and until the end of the 15th century were bound to supply the ships and men necessary against invasion.

CIO abbreviation for *Congress of Industrial Organizations*.

circadian rhythm metabolic rhythm found in most organisms, which generally coincides with the 24-hour day. Its most obvious manifestation is the regular cycle of sleeping and waking, but body temperature and the concentration of *hormones that influence mood and behaviour also vary over the day. In humans, alteration of habits (such as rapid air travel round the world) may result in the circadian rhythm being out of phase with actual activity patterns, causing malaise until it has had time to adjust.

Circe in Greek mythology, an enchantress living on the island of Aeaea. In Homer's *Odyssey*, she turned the followers of Odysseus into pigs. Odysseus, bearing the herb moly provided by Hermes to protect him from the same fate, forced her to release his men.

circle perfectly round shape. Each circle comprises a **centre**, a **radius** (distance from centre to boundary), a **circumference** (the boundary), **diameters** (lines crossing the circle through the centre), **chords** (lines joining two points on the circumference), **tangents** (lines that touch the circumference at one point only), **sectors** (regions inside the circle between two radii), and **segments** (regions between a chord and the circumference).

circuit in physics or electrical engineering, an arrangement of electrical components through which a current can flow. There are two basic circuits, series and parallel. In a **series circuit**, the components are connected end to end so that the current flows through all components one after the other. In a **parallel circuit**, components are connected side by side so that part of the current passes through each component. A circuit diagram shows in graphical form how components are connected together, using standard symbols for the components.

circuit breaker switching device designed to protect an electric circuit from excessive current. It has the same action as a *fuse, and many houses now have a circuit breaker between the incoming mains supply and the domestic circuits. Circuit breakers usually work by means of *solenoids. Those at electricity-generating stations have to be specially designed to prevent dangerous arcing (the release of luminous discharge) when the high-voltage supply is switched off. They may use an air blast or oil immersion to quench the arc.

circulatory system system of vessels in an animal's body that transports essential substances (blood or other circulatory fluid) to and from the different parts of the body. Except for simple animals such as sponges and coelenterates (jellyfishes, sea anemones, corals), all animals have a circulatory system.

circumcision surgical removal of all or part of the foreskin (prepuce) of the penis, usually performed on the newborn; it is practised among Jews and Muslims. In some societies in Africa and the Middle East, female circumcision or clitoridectomy (removal of the labia minora and/or clitoris) is practised on adolescents as well as babies; it is illegal in the West.

CINEMA: CHRONOLOGY

1826–34	Various machines invented to show moving images: the stroboscope, zoetrope, and thaumatrope.
1872	Eadweard Muybridge demonstrated movement of horses' legs by using 24 cameras.
1877	Invention of Praxinoscope; developed as a projector of successive images on screen 1879 in France.
1878–95	Marey, a French physiologist, developed various types of camera for recording human and animal movements.
1887	Augustin le Prince produced the first series of images on a perforated film; Thomas A Edison, having developed the phonograph, took the first steps in developing a motion-picture recording and reproducing device to accompany recorded sound.
1888	William Friese-Greene (1855–1921) showed the first celluloid film and patented a movie camera.
1889	Edison invented 35-mm film.
1890–94	Edison, using perforated film, developed his Kinetograph camera and Kinetoscope individual viewer; developed commercially in New York, London, and Paris.
1895	The Lumière brothers projected, to a paying audience, a film of an oncoming train arriving at a station. Some of the audience fled in terror.
1896	Charles Pathé introduced the Berliner gramophone, using discs in synchronization with film. Lack of amplification, however, made the performances ineffective.
1899	Edison tried to improve amplification by using banks of phonographs.
1900	Attempts to synchronize film and disc were made by Leon Gaumont (1863–1946) in France and Goldschmidt in Germany, leading later to the Vitaphone system of the USA.
1902	Georges Méliès made *Le Voyage dans la Lune/A Trip to the Moon*.
1903	The first Western was made in the USA: *The Great Train Robbery* by Edwin Porter.
1906	The earliest colour film (Kinemacolor) was patented in Britain by George Albert Smith (1864–1959).
1907–11	The first films shot in the Los Angeles area called Hollywood. In France, Emile Cohl (1857–1938) experimented with film animation.
1910	With the influence of US studios and fan magazines, film actors and actresses began to be recognized as international stars.
1911	The first Hollywood studio, Horsley's Centaur Film Company, was established, followed in 1915 by Carl Laemmle's Universal City and Thomas Ince's studio.
1912	In Britain, Eugene Lauste designed experimental 'sound on film' systems.
1914–18	Full newsreel coverage of World War I.
1915	*The Birth of a Nation*, D W Griffith's epic on the American Civil War, was released in the USA.
1917	35 mm was officially adopted as the standard format for motion picture film by the Society of Motion Picture Engineers of America.
1918–19	A sound system called Tri-Ergon was developed in Germany, which led to sound being recorded on film photographically. Photography with sound was also developed in the USA by Lee De Forest in his Phonofilm system.
1923	First sound film (as Phonofilm) demonstrated.
1926	*Don Juan*, a silent film with a synchronized music score, was released.
1927	Release of the first major sound film, *The Jazz Singer*, consisting of some songs and a few moments of dialogue, by Warner Brothers, New York City. The first Academy Awards (Oscars) were presented.
1928	Walt Disney released his first Mickey Mouse cartoon, *Steamboat Willie*. The first all-talking film, *Lights of New York*, was released.
1930	*The Big Trail*, a Western filmed and shown in 70-mm rather than the standard 35-mm format, was released. 70 mm is still used, mainly for big-budget epics such as *Lawrence of Arabia*.
1932	Technicolor (three-colour) process introduced and used for a Walt Disney cartoon film.
1935	*Becky Sharp*, the first film in three-colour Technicolor was released.
1937	Walt Disney released the first feature-length (82 minutes) cartoon, *Snow White and the Seven Dwarfs*.
1939	*Gone With the Wind*, regarded as one of Hollywood's greatest achievements, was released.
1952	Cinerama, a wide-screen presentation using three cameras and three projectors, was introduced in New York.
1953	Commercial 3-D (three-dimensional) cinema and wide-screen CinemaScope were launched in the USA. CinemaScope used a single camera and projector to produce a wide-screen effect with an anamorphic lens. The new wide-screen cinema was accompanied by the introduction of Stereographic sound, which eventually became standard.
1959	The first film in Smell-O-Vision, *The Scent of Mystery*, was released. The process did not catch on.
1970	Most major films were released in Dolby stereo.
1982	One of the first and most effective attempts at feature-length, computer-generated animation was *Tron*, Walt Disney's $20-million bid to break into the booming fantasy market.
1987	US House Judiciary Committee petitioned by leading Hollywood filmmakers to protect their work from electronic 'colorization', the new process by which black-and-white films were tinted for television transmission.
1988	Robert Zemeckis' (1952–) *Who Framed Roger Rabbit* set new technical standards in combining live action with cartoon animation.

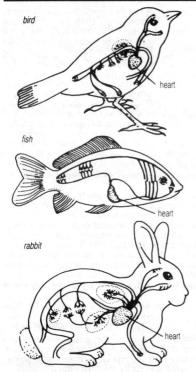

circulatory system *The circulatory systems of the fish, the bird, and the rabbit.*

circumference in geometry, the curved line that encloses a plane figure, for example a *circle or an ellipse. Its length varies according to the nature of the curve, and may be ascertained by the appropriate formula. The circumference of a circle is $2\pi r$, where r is the radius and π is the constant pi, approximately equal to 3.1416.

circumnavigation sailing around the world. The first ship to sail around the world was the *Victoria*, one of a Spanish squadron of five vessels that sailed from Seville Aug 1519 under the Portuguese navigator Ferdinand Magellan.

circus (Latin 'circle') entertainment, often held in a large tent ('big top'), involving performing animals, acrobats, and clowns. In 1871 Phineas T *Barnum created the 'Greatest Show on Earth' in the USA. The popularity of animal acts decreased in the 1980s. Originally, in Roman times, a circus was an arena for chariot races and gladiatorial combats.

cire perdue or **lost-wax technique** bronze-casting method. A model is made of wax and enclosed in an envelope of clay and plaster, with a small hole in the bottom. The whole is baked, the wax melts and runs away through the hole, and the clay and plaster becomes a hard mould. Molten bronze is poured in and allowed to cool; then the clay envelope is cut away.

cirrhosis any degenerative disease in an organ of the body, especially the liver, characterized by excessive development of connective tissue, causing scarring and painful swelling. Cirrhosis of the liver may be caused by an infection such as viral hepatitis, by chronic alcoholism or drug use, blood disorder, or malnutrition. If cirrhosis is diagnosed early, it can be arrested by treating the cause; otherwise it will progress to jaundice, oedema, vomiting of blood, coma, and death.

CIS abbreviation for *Commonwealth of Independent States*, established 1992 by 11 former Soviet republics.

Cisalpine Gaul region of the Roman province of Gallia (N Italy) south of the Alps; *Transalpine Gaul*, the region north of the Alps, comprised what is now Belgium, France, the Netherlands, and Switzerland.

CISC (acronym for *complex instruction set computer*) in computing, a microprocessor (processor on a single chip) that can carry out a large number of *machine-code instructions – for example, the Intel 80386. The term was introduced to distinguish them from the more rapid *RISC (reduced instruction set computer) processors, which handle only a smaller set of instructions.

Ciskei, Republic of Bantu homeland in South Africa, which became independent 1981, although this is not recognized by any other country
area 7,700 sq km/2,974 sq mi
capital Bisho
products wheat, sorghum, sunflower, vegetables, timber, metal products, leather, textiles
population (1985) 925,000
language Xhosa
government president (Brig Oupa Gqozo from 1990), with legislative and executive councils
recent history In Sept 1992 Ciskei troops fired on African National Congress (ANC) demonstrators demanding the ousting of the territory's military leader, Brig Gqozo; 28 people were slain and about 200 injured. Brig Gqozo had assumed power in a military takeover 1990. Initially sympathetic to the aims of the ANC, he had pledged to restore civilian rule and called for the reincorporation of Ciskei into South Africa. Subsequently, he turned against the organization and had been accused of repressing its supporters.

Cistercian order Roman Catholic monastic order established at Cîteaux 1098 by St Robert de Champagne, abbot of Molesme, as a stricter form of the Benedictine order. Living mainly by agricultural labour, the Cistercians made many advances in farming methods in the Middle Ages. The *Trappists*, so called from the original house at La Trappe in Normandy (founded by Dominique de Rancé 1664), followed a particularly strict version of the rule.

cistron in genetics, the segment of *DNA that is required to synthesize a complete polypeptide chain. It is the molecular equivalent of a *gene.

CITES (abbreviation for *Convention on International Trade in Endangered Species*) international agreement regulating trade in *endangered species of animals and plants. The agreement came into force 1975 and by 1991 had been signed by 110 states, but is not closely observed. It prohibits any trade in a category of 8,000 highly endangered species and controls trade in a further 30,000 species.

cithara ancient musical instrument, resembling

a lyre but with a flat back. It was strung with wire and plucked with a plectrum or (after the 16th century) with the fingers. The bandurria and laud, still popular in Spain, are instruments of the same type.

Citizens' Advice Bureau (CAB) UK organization established 1939 to provide information and advice to the public on any subject, such as personal problems, financial, house purchase, or consumer rights.

citizens' band (CB) short-range radio communication facility (around 27 MHz) used by members of the public in the USA and many European countries to talk to one another or call for emergency assistance.

Citizen's Charter series of proposals aimed at improving public services in the UK, unveiled by Prime Minister John Major 1991. Major's 'programme for a decade' covered the activities of a range of public-sector bodies, including the police, the health service, schools, local authorities, and public and private utility companies.

citizenship status as a member of a state. In most countries citizenship may be acquired either by birth or by naturalization. The status confers rights such as voting and the protection of the law and also imposes responsibilities such as military service, in some countries.

citric acid $HOOCCH_2C(OH)(COOH)CH_2$-$COOH$ organic acid widely distributed in the plant kingdom; it is found in high concentrations in citrus fruits and has a sharp, sour taste. At one time it was commercially prepared from concentrated lemon juice, but now the main source is the fermentation of sugar with certain moulds.

citronella lemon-scented oil used in cosmetics and insect repellents, obtained from the S Asian grass *Cymbopogon nardus*.

citrus any tree or shrub of the genus *Citrus*, family Rutaceae. Citruses are found in Asia and other warm parts of the world. They are evergreen and aromatic, and several species – the orange, lemon, lime, citron, and grapefruit – are cultivated for fruit.

City, the the financial centre of London, England.

city technology college in the UK, one of a planned network of some 20 schools, financed jointly by government and industry, designed to teach technological subjects in inner-city areas to students aged 11 to 18. By 1991 only seven schools had opened, industry having proved reluctant to fund the scheme.

Ciudad Juárez city on the Rio Grande, in Chihuahua, N Mexico, on the US border; population (1990) 797,650. It is a centre for cotton.

civet small to medium-sized carnivorous mammal found in Africa and Asia, belonging to the family Viverridae, which also includes *mongooses* and *genets*. Distant relations of cats, they generally have longer jaws and more teeth. All have a scent gland in the inguinal (groin) region. Extracts from this gland are taken from the *African civet* Civettictis civetta and used in perfumery.

Civic Forum (Czech *Občanske Forum*) Czech democratic movement, formed Nov 1989, led by Václav *Havel. In Dec 1989 it participated in forming a coalition government after the collapse of communist rule in Czechoslovakia. The party began to splinter during 1991: from it emerged the right-of-centre Civic Democratic Party, led by Václav Klaus, and the social-democratic Civic Movement, led by Jiri Dienstbier.

civil aviation operation of passenger and freight transport by air. With increasing traffic, control of air space is a major problem, and in 1963 Eurocontrol was established by Belgium, France, West Germany, Luxembourg, the Netherlands, and the UK to supervise both military and civil movement in the air space over member countries. There is also a tendency to coordinate services and other facilities between national airlines; for example, the establishment of Air Union 1963 by France (Air France), West Germany (Lufthansa), Italy (Alitalia), and Belgium (Sabena).

civil disobedience deliberate breaking of laws considered unjust, a form of nonviolent direct action; the term was coined by the US writer Henry Thoreau in an essay of that name 1849. It was advocated by Mahatma *Gandhi to prompt peaceful withdrawal of British power from India. Civil disobedience has since been employed by, for instance, the US civil-rights movement in the 1960s and the peace movement in the 1980s.

civil law legal system based on *Roman law. It is one of the two main European legal systems, *English (common) law being the other. Civil law may also mean the law relating to matters other than criminal law, such as *contract and *tort.

civil list in the UK, the annual sum provided from public funds to meet the official expenses of the sovereign and immediate dependents; private expenses are met by the *privy purse.

civil-list pension in the UK, a pension paid to persons in need who have just claims on the royal beneficence, who have rendered personal service to the crown, or who have rendered service to the public by their discoveries in science and attainments in literature, art, or the like. The recipients are nominated by the prime minister, and the list is approved by Parliament. The pensions were originally paid out of the sovereign's civil list, but have been granted separately since the accession of Queen Victoria.

civil rights rights of the individual citizen. In many countries they are specified (as in the Bill of Rights of the US constitution) and guaranteed by law to ensure equal treatment for all citizens. In the USA, the struggle to obtain civil rights for former slaves and their descendants, both through legislation and in practice, has been a major theme since the Civil War. The *civil-rights movement* is a general term for this aspect of US history; see *history* under *black.

civil service body of administrative staff appointed to carry out the policy of a government. Members of the UK civil service may not take an active part in politics, and do not change with the government.

civil society part of a society or culture outside the government and state-run institutions. For Karl Marx and G W F Hegel, civil society was that part of society where self-interest and materialism were rampant, although Adam *Smith believed that enlightened self-interest would promote the general good. Classical writers and earlier political theorists such as John *Locke used the term to describe the whole of a civilized society.

civil war war between rival groups within the same country.

Civil War, American also called **War Between the States** war 1861–65 between the Southern or Confederate States of America and the Northern or Union States. The former wished to maintain certain 'states' rights', in particular the right to determine state law on the institution of slavery, and claimed the right to secede from the Union; the latter fought primarily to maintain the Union, with slave emancipation (proclaimed 1863) a secondary issue.

Civil War, English in British history, the conflict between King Charles I and the Royalists (Cavaliers) on one side and the Parliamentarians (also called Roundheads) under Oliver *Cromwell on the other. Hostilities began 1642 and a series of Royalist defeats (Marston Moor 1644, Naseby 1645) culminated in Charles's capture 1647 and execution 1649. The war continued until the final defeat of Royalist forces at Worcester 1651. Cromwell became Protector (ruler) 1651 until his death 1658.

Civil War, Spanish war 1936–39 precipitated by a military revolt led by General Franco against the Republican government. Inferior military capability led to the gradual defeat of the Republicans by 1939, and the establishment of Franc's dictatorship.

cladistics method of biological *classification (taxonomy) that uses a formal step-by-step procedure for objectively assessing the extent to which organisms share particular characters, and for assigning them to taxonomic groups. Taxonomic groups (for example, *species, *genus, family) are termed *clades*.

cladode in botany, a flattened stem that is leaflike in appearance and function. It is an adaptation to dry conditions because a stem contains fewer *stomata than a leaf, and water loss is thus minimized. The true leaves in such plants are usually reduced to spines or small scales. Examples of plants with cladodes are butcher's-broom *Ruscus aculeatus*, asparagus, and certain cacti. Cladodes may bear flowers or fruit on their surface, and this distinguishes them from leaves.

Clair René. Adopted name of René-Lucien Chomette 1898–1981. French filmmaker, originally a poet, novelist, and journalist. His *Sous les toits de Paris/Under the Roofs of Paris* 1930 was one of the first sound films. His other films include *Entr'acte* 1924, *Le Million*, and *A nous la Liberté* both 1931.

clam common name for a *bivalve mollusc. The giant clam *Tridacna gigas* of the Indopacific can grow to 1 m/3 ft across in 50 years and weigh, with the shell, 500 kg/1,000 lb.

Clapton Eric 1945– . English blues and rock guitarist, singer, and composer, member of the Yardbirds 1963–65 and Cream 1966–68. Originally a blues purist, then one of the pioneers of heavy rock with Cream and on the album *Layla* 1970 (released under the name of Derek and the Dominos), he later adopted a more laid-back style in his solo career, as on *Journeyman* 1989.

Clare county on the W coast of the Republic of Ireland, in the province of Munster; area 3,190 sq km/1,231 sq mi; population (1991) 90,800.

Clare John 1793–1864. English poet. His work includes *Poems Descriptive of Rural Life and Scenery* 1820, *The Village Minstrel* 1821, and *The Shepherd's Calendar* 1827. Clare's work was largely rediscovered in the 20th century.

Clarendon Edward Hyde, 1st Earl of Clarendon 1609–1674. English politician and historian, chief adviser to Charles II 1651–67. A member of Parliament 1640, he joined the Royalist side 1641. The **Clarendon Code** 1661–65, a series of acts passed by the government, was directed at Nonconformists (or Dissenters) and were designed to secure the supremacy of the Church of England.

Clarendon, Constitutions of in English history, a series of resolutions agreed by a council summoned by Henry II at Clarendon in Wiltshire 1164. The Constitutions aimed at limiting the secular power of the clergy, and were abandoned after the murder of Thomas à Becket. They form an early English legal document of great historical value.

Clare, St c. 1194–1253. Christian saint. Born in Assisi, Italy, at 18 she became a follower of St Francis, who founded for her the convent of San Damiano. Here she gathered the first members of the **Order of Poor Clares**. In 1958 she was proclaimed the patron saint of television by Pius XII, since in 1252 she saw from her convent sickbed the Christmas services being held in the Basilica of St Francis in Assisi. Feast day 12 Aug.

clarinet musical *woodwind instrument, developed in Germany in the 18th century, with a single reed and a cylindrical tube, broadening at the end. At the lower end of its range it has a rich 'woody' tone, which becomes increasingly brilliant towards the upper register. Its ability both to blend and to contrast with other instruments make it popular for chamber music and as a solo instrument. It is also heard in military and concert bands and as a jazz instrument.

Clark Jim (James) 1936–1968. Scottish-born motor-racing driver who was twice world champion 1963 and 1965. He spent all his Formula One career with Lotus.

Clark Kenneth, Lord Clark 1903–1983. British art historian, director of the National Gallery, London, 1934–45. His books include *Leonardo da Vinci* 1939 and *The Nude* 1956.

Clark Michael 1962– . Scottish avant-garde dancer whose bare-bottomed costumes and zany stage props have earned him as much celebrity as his innovative dance technique. A graduate of the Royal Ballet school, he formed his own company, the Michael Clark Dance Company, in the mid-1980s and became a leading figure in the British *avant-garde dance scene. He premiered his *Mmm... Modern Masterpiece* 1992.

Clarke Arthur C(harles) 1917– . English science-fiction and nonfiction writer, who originated the plan for a system of communications satellites in geostationary orbit 1945. His works include *Childhood's End* 1953 and *2001: A Space Odyssey* 1968 (which was made into a film by Stanley Kubrick), and *2010: Odyssey Two* 1982.

Clarke Jeremiah 1659–1707. English composer.

Organist at St Paul's, he composed 'The Prince of Denmark's March', a harpsichord piece that was arranged by Henry *Wood as a 'Trumpet Voluntary' and wrongly attributed to Purcell.

Clarke Kenneth (Harry) 1940– . British Conservative politician, member of Parliament from 1970, a cabinet minister from 1985, education secretary 1990–92, and home secretary from 1992–93. He succeeded Norman Lamont as Chancellor of the Exchequer May 1993.

Clarke Marcus Andrew Hislop 1846–1881. Australian writer. Born in London, he went to Australia when he was 18 and worked as a journalist in Victoria. He wrote *For the Term of his Natural Life* 1874, a novel dealing with life in the early Australian prison settlements.

Clarke orbit alternative name for *geostationary orbit*, an orbit 35,900 km/22,300 mi high, in which satellites circle at the same speed as the Earth turns. This orbit was first suggested by space writer Arthur C Clarke 1945.

Clarkson Thomas 1760–1846. British philanthropist. From 1785 he devoted himself to a campaign against slavery. He was one of the founders of the Anti-Slavery Society 1823 and was largely responsible for the abolition of slavery in British colonies 1833.

class in biological classification, a group of related *orders. For example, all mammals belong to the class Mammalia and all birds to the class Aves. Among plants, all class names end in 'idae' (such as Asteridae) and among fungi in 'mycetes'; there are no equivalent conventions among animals. Related classes are grouped together in a *phylum.

class action in law, a court procedure where one or more claimants represent a larger group of people who are all making the same kind of claim against the same defendant. The court's decision is binding on all the members of the group.

classical economics school of economic thought that dominated 19th-century thinking. It originated with Adam *Smith's *The Wealth of Nations* 1776, which embodied many of the basic concepts and principles of the classical school. Smith's theories were further developed in the writings of John Stuart Mill and David Ricardo. Central to the theory were economic freedom, competition, and laissez faire government. The idea that economic growth could best be promoted by free trade, unassisted by government, was in conflict with *mercantilism.

Classicism in art, music, and literature, a style that emphasizes the qualities traditionally considered characteristic of ancient Greek and Roman art, that is, reason, balance, objectivity, restraint, and strict adherence to form. The term Classicism (also *Neo-Classicism) is often used to characterize the culture of 18th-century Europe, and contrasted with 19th-century Romanticism.

classification in biology, the arrangement of organisms into a hierarchy of groups on the basis of their similarities in biochemical, anatomical, or physiological characters. The basic grouping is a *species, several of which may constitute a *genus, which in turn are grouped into families,

and so on up through orders, classes, phyla (in plants, sometimes called divisions), to kingdoms.

class interval in statistics, the range of each class of data, used when dealing with large amounts of data. To obtain an idea of the distribution, the data are broken down into convenient classes, which must be mutually exclusive and are usually equal. The class interval defines the range of each class; for example if the class interval is five and the data begin at zero, the classes are 0–4, 5–9, 10–14, and so on.

clathrate compound formed when the small molecules of one substance fill in the holes in the structural lattice of another, solid, substance – for example, sulphur dioxide molecules in ice crystals. Clathrates are therefore intermediate between mixtures and true compounds (which are held together by *ionic or covalent chemical bonds).

Claudel Paul 1868–1955. French poet and dramatist. A fervent Catholic, he was influenced by the Symbolists and achieved an effect of mystic allegory in such plays as *L'Annonce faite à Marie/Tidings Brought to Mary* 1912 and *Le Soulier de satin/The Satin Slipper* 1929, set in 16th-century Spain. His verse includes *Cinq grandes odes/Five Great Odes* 1910.

Claude Lorrain (Claude Gelée) 1600–1682. French landscape painter, active in Rome from 1627. His distinctive, luminous, Classical style had great impact on late 17th-and 18th-century taste. His subjects are mostly mythological and historical, with insignificant figures lost in great expanses of poetic scenery, as in *The Enchanted Castle* 1664 (National Gallery, London).

Claudian (Claudius Claudianus) *c.* 370–404. Last of the great Latin poets of the Roman Empire, probably born in Alexandria, Egypt. He wrote official panegyrics, epigrams, and the epic *The Rape of Proserpine.*

Claudius Tiberius Claudius Nero 10 BC–AD 54. Nephew of *Tiberius, made Roman emperor by his troops AD 41, after the murder of his nephew Caligula. Claudius was a scholar, historian, and able administrator. During his reign the Roman Empire was considerably extended, and in 43 he took part in the invasion of Britain.

Clause 28 in British law, section 28 of the Local Government Act 1988 that prohibits local authorities promoting homosexuality by publishing material, or by promoting the teaching in state schools of the acceptability of homosexuality as a 'pretended family relationship'. There was widespread opposition to the introduction of the provision.

clausius in engineering, a unit of *entropy (the loss of energy as heat in any physical process). It is defined as the ratio of energy to temperature above absolute zero.

Clausius Rudolf Julius Emanuel 1822–1888. German physicist, one of the founders of the science of thermodynamics. In 1850 he enunciated its second law: heat cannot pass from a colder to a hotter body.

claustrophobia *phobia involving fear of enclosed spaces.

Claverhouse John Graham, Viscount Dundee 1649–1689. Scottish soldier. Appointed by Charles II to suppress the *Covenanters from

1677, he was routed at Drumclog 1679, but three weeks later won the battle of Bothwell Bridge, by which the rebellion was crushed. Until 1688 he was engaged in continued persecution and became known as 'Bloody Clavers', regarded by the Scottish people as a figure of evil. His army then joined the first Jacobite rebellion and defeated the loyalist forces in the pass of Killiecrankie, where he was mortally wounded.

clavichord stringed keyboard instrument, common in Renaissance Europe and in 18th-century Germany. Notes are sounded by a metal blade striking the string. The clavichord was a forerunner of the pianoforte.

clavicle the collar bone of many vertebrates. In humans it is vulnerable to fracture; falls involving a sudden force on the arm may result in excessive stress passing into the chest region by way of the clavicle and other bones.

claw hard, hooked, pointed outgrowth of the digits of mammals, birds, and most reptiles. Claws are composed of the protein keratin, and grow continuously from a bundle of cells in the lower skin layer. Hooves and nails are modified structures with the same origin as claws.

clay very fine-grained *sedimentary deposit that has undergone a greater or lesser degree of consolidation. When moistened it is plastic, and it hardens on heating, which renders it impermeable. It may be white, grey, red, yellow, blue, or black, depending on its composition. Clay minerals consist largely of hydrous silicates of aluminium and magnesium together with iron, potassium, sodium, and organic substances. The crystals of clay minerals have a layered structure, capable of holding water, and are responsible for its plastic properties. According to international classification, in mechanical analysis of soil, clay has a grain size of less than 0.002 mm/0.00008 in.

Clay Cassius Marcellus, Jr, original name of boxer Muhammad *Ali.

Clay Henry 1777–1852. US politician. He stood unsuccessfully three times for the presidency: as a Democratic-Republican 1824, as a National Republican 1832, and as a Whig 1844. He supported the war of 1812 against Britain, and tried to hold the Union together on the slavery issue by the Missouri Compromise of 1820, and again in the compromise of 1850. He was secretary of state 1825–29, and is also remembered for his 'American system', which favoured the national bank, internal improvements to facilitate commercial and industrial development, and the raising of protective tariffs.

clay mineral one of a group of hydrous silicate minerals that form most of the fine-grained particles in clays. Clay minerals are normally formed by weathering or alteration of other silicates. Virtually all have sheet silicate structures similar to the *micas. They exhibit the following useful properties: loss of water on heating, swelling and shrinking in different conditions, cation exchange with other media, and plasticity when wet. Examples are kaolinite, illite, and montmorillonite.

cleavage in mineralogy, the tendency of a mineral to split along defined, parallel planes related to its internal structure. It is a useful distinguishing feature in mineral identification. Cleavage occurs where bonding between atoms is weakest, and cleavages may be perfect, good, or poor, depending on the bond strengths; a given mineral may possess one, two, three, or more orientations along which it will cleave.

cleavage in geology, the tendency of a rock, especially slate, to split along parallel or sub-parallel planes that result from realignment of component minerals during deformation or metamorphism.

Cleese John 1939– . English actor and comedian who has written for and appeared in both television programmes and films. On British television, he is particularly associated with the comedy series *Monty Python's Flying Circus* and *Fawlty Towers*. His films include *Monty Python and the Holy Grail* 1974, *The Life of Brian* 1979, and *A Fish Called Wanda* 1988.

clef in music, the symbol used to indicate the pitch of the lines of the staff in musical notation.

Cleisthenes lived 6th century BC. Ruler of Athens. Inspired by the statesman Solon, he is credited with the establishment of democracy in Athens 507 BC.

cleistogamy production of flowers that never fully open and that are automatically self-fertilized. Cleistogamous flowers are often formed late in the year, after the production of normal flowers, or during a period of cold weather, as seen in several species of violet *Viola*.

clematis any temperate woody climbing plant of the genus *Clematis* with showy flowers. Clematis is a member of the buttercup family, Ranunculaceae.

Clemenceau Georges 1841–1929. French politician and journalist (prominent in the defence of Alfred *Dreyfus). He was prime minister 1906–09 and 1917–20. After World War I he presided over the peace conference in Paris that drew up the Treaty of *Versailles, but failed to secure for France the Rhine as a frontier.

Clemens Samuel Langhorne. Real name of the US writer Mark *Twain.

Clement VII 1478–1534. Pope 1523–34. He refused to allow the divorce of Henry VIII of England and Catherine of Aragon. Illegitimate son of a brother of Lorenzo de' Medici, the ruler of Florence, he commissioned monuments for the Medici chapel in Florence from the Renaissance artist Michelangelo.

clementine small orange, thought to be a hybrid between a tangerine and an orange or a variety of tangerine. It has a flowery taste and scent and is in season in winter. It is commonly grown in N Africa and Spain.

Clement of Rome, St lived late 1st century AD. One of the early Christian leaders and writers known as the Fathers of the Church. According to tradition he was the third or fourth bishop of Rome, and a disciple of St Peter. He wrote a letter addressed to the church at Corinth (First Epistle of Clement), and many other writings have been attributed to him.

Cleon Athenian demagogue and military leader in the *Peloponnesian War 431–404 BC. After the death of Pericles, to whom he was opposed, he won power as representative of the commercial classes and was for some years the foremost man in Athens. He advocated a vigorous war policy in opposition to the moderates who favoured an early peace. He was killed fighting the Spartans at Amphipolis.

Cleopatra c. 68–30 BC. Queen of Egypt 51–48 and 47–30 BC. When the Roman general Julius Caesar arrived in Egypt, he restored her to the throne from which she had been ousted. Cleopatra and Caesar became lovers and she went with him to Rome. After Caesar's assassination 44 BC she returned to Alexandria and resumed her position as queen of Egypt. In 41 BC she was joined there by Mark Antony, one of Rome's rulers. In 31 BC Rome declared war on Egypt and scored a decisive victory in the naval Battle of Actium off the W coast of Greece. Cleopatra fled with her 60 ships to Egypt; Antony abandoned the struggle and followed her. Both he and Cleopatra committed suicide.

Cleopatra's Needle either of two ancient Egyptian granite obelisks erected at Heliopolis in the 15th century BC by Thothmes III, and removed to Alexandria by the Roman emperor Augustus about 14 BC. They have no connection with Cleopatra's reign. One of the pair was taken to England 1878 and erected on the Victoria Embankment in London. The other was given by the khedive of Egypt to the USA and erected in Central Park, New York, in 1881.

Clermont-Ferrand city, capital of Puy-de-Dôme *département*, in the Auvergne region of France; population (1983) 256,000. It is a centre for agriculture, and its rubber industry is the largest in France.

Cleveland county in NE England
area 580 sq km/224 sq mi
towns Middlesbrough (administrative headquarters), Stockton on Tees, Billingham, Hartlepool
products steel, chemicals
population (1987) 555,000
famous people Capt James Cook, Thomas Sheraton, Compton Mackenzie

Cleveland largest city of Ohio, USA, on Lake Erie at the mouth of the river Cuyahoga; population (1990) 505,600, metropolitan area 2,759,800. Its chief industries are iron and steel and petroleum refining.

Cleveland (Stephen) Grover 1837–1908. 22nd and 24th president of the USA, 1885–89 and 1893–97; the first Democratic president elected after the Civil War, and the only president to hold office for two nonconsecutive terms. He attempted to check corruption in public life, and in 1895 initiated arbitration proceedings that eventually settled a territorial dispute with Britain concerning the Venezuelan boundary.

client-server architecture in computing, a system in which the mechanics of storing data are separated from the programs that use the data. For example, the 'server' might be a central database, typically located on a large computer that is reserved for this purpose. The 'client' would be an ordinary program that requests data from the server as needed.

Cliff Clarice 1899–1972. English pottery designer. Her Bizarre ware, characterized by brightly coloured floral and geometric decoration on often geometrically shaped china, became increasingly popular in the 1930s.

Clift (Edward) Montgomery 1920–1966. US film

and theatre actor. A star of the late 1940s and 1950s in films such as *Red River* 1948, *A Place in the Sun* 1951, and *From Here to Eternity* 1953, he was disfigured in a car accident in 1957 but continued to make films. He played the title role in *Freud* 1962.

climate weather conditions at a particular place over a period of time. Climate encompasses all the meteorological elements and the factors that influence them. The primary factors that determine the variations of climate over the surface of the Earth are: (a) the effect of latitude and the tilt of the Earth's axis to the plane of the orbit about the Sun (66.5°); (b) the large-scale movements of different wind belts over the Earth's surface; (c) the temperature difference between land and sea; (d) contours of the ground; and (e) location of the area in relation to ocean currents. Catastrophic variations to climate may be caused by the impact of another planetary body, or by clouds resulting from volcanic activity. The most important local or global meteorological changes brought about by human activity are those linked with *ozone depleters and the *greenhouse effect.

climate model computer simulation, based on physical and mathematical data, of the entire climatic system of the Earth. It is used by researchers to study such topics as the possible long-term disruptive effects of the greenhouse gases, or of variations in the amount of radiation given off by the Sun.

clinical psychology discipline dealing with the understanding and treatment of health problems, particularly mental disorders. The main problems dealt with include anxiety, phobias, depression, obsessions, sexual and marital problems, drug and alcohol dependence, childhood behavioural problems, psychoses (such as schizophrenia), mental disability, and brain disease (such as dementia) and damage. Other areas of work include forensic psychology (concerned with criminal behaviour) and health psychology.

Clinton Bill (William Jefferson) 1946– . 42nd president of the USA from 1993, a Democrat. He served as governor of Arkansas 1979–81 and 1983–93, establishing a liberal and progressive reputation. As president, he focused on domestic issues and sought to implement a **New Democrat** programme, combining social reform with economic conservatism as a means of bringing the country out of recession. By early 1994, the economy showed signs of recovery and Clinton secured approval of Congress for the *North American Free Trade Agreement (NAFTA), and wide-ranging anticrime measures.

Clive Robert, Baron Clive of Plassey 1725–1774. British soldier and administrator who established British rule in India by victories over French troops at Arcot 1751 and over the nawab of Bengal at Plassey 1757. He was governor of Bengal 1757–60 and 1765–66. On his return to Britain in 1766, his wealth led to allegations that he had abused his power. Although acquitted, he committed suicide.

cloaca the common posterior chamber of most vertebrates into which the digestive, urinary, and reproductive tracts all enter; a cloaca is found in most reptiles, birds, and amphibians; many fishes; and, to a reduced degree, marsupial mammals. Placental mammals, however, have a separate digestive opening (the anus) and urinogenital opening. The cloaca forms a chamber in which products can be stored before being voided from the body via a muscular opening, the cloacal aperture.

clock rate the frequency of a computer's internal electronic clock. Every computer contains an electronic clock, which produces a sequence of regular electrical pulses used by the control unit to synchronize the components of the computer and regulate the *fetch-execute cycle by which program instructions are processed. A fixed number of time pulses is required in order to execute each particular instruction. The speed at which a computer can process instructions therefore depends on the clock rate: increasing the clock rate will decrease the time required to complete each particular instruction.

cloisonné ornamental craft technique in which thin metal strips are soldered in a pattern onto a metal surface, and the resulting compartments (*cloisons*) filled with coloured *enamels and fired. The technique was probably developed in the Byzantine Middle East and traded to Asia and Europe. Cloisonné vases and brooches were made in medieval Europe, but the technique was perfected in Japan and China during the 17th, 18th, and 19th centuries.

clone an exact replica. In genetics, any one of a group of genetically identical cells or organisms. An identical *twin is a clone; so, too, are bacteria living in the same colony. The term clone has also been adopted by computer technology to describe a (nonexistent) device that mimics an actual one to enable certain software programs to run correctly.

Close Glenn 1948– . US actress. She received Academy Award nominations for her roles as the embittered 'other woman' in *Fatal Attraction* 1987 and as the scheming antiheroine of *Dangerous Liaisons* 1988.

closed in mathematics, descriptive of a set of data for which an operation (such as addition or multiplication) done on any members of the set gives a result that is also a member of the set.

closed shop a place of work, such as a factory or an office, where all workers within a section must belong to a single officially recognized trade union. Closed-shop agreements are negotiated between trade unions and management. Trade unions favour closed shops because 100% union membership gives them greater industrial power. Management can find it convenient because they can deal with workers as a group (*collective bargaining) rather than having to negotiate with individual workers. The closed shop was condemned by the European Court of Human Rights 1981. In the USA the closed shop was made illegal by the Taft-Hartley Act 1947.

clothes moth or *Tineola bisselliella* moth whose larvae feed on clothes, upholstery, and carpets. The adults are small golden or silvery moths. The natural habitat of the larvae is in the nests of animals, feeding on remains of hair and feathers, but they have adapted to human households and can cause considerable damage.

cloud water vapour condensed into minute water particles that float in masses in the atmosphere. Clouds, like fogs or mists, which occur at lower levels, are formed by the cooling of air containing water vapour, which generally condenses around tiny dust particles.

cloud chamber apparatus for tracking ionized particles. It consists of a vessel fitted with a piston and filled with air or other gas, saturated with water vapour. When the volume of the vessel is suddenly expanded by moving the piston outwards, the vapour cools and a cloud of tiny droplets forms on any nuclei, dust, or ions present. As fast-moving ionizing particles collide with the air or gas molecules, they show as visible tracks.

Clouet François c. 1515–1572. French portrait painter who succeeded his father Jean Clouet as court painter. He worked in the Italian style of Mannerism. His half-nude portrait of Diane de Poitiers, *The Lady in Her Bath* (National Gallery, Washington), is also thought to be a likeness of Marie Touchet, mistress of Charles IX.

Clouet Jean (known as **Janet**) 1486–1541. French artist, court painter to Francis I. His portraits and drawings, often compared to Holbein's, show an outstanding naturalism.

clove dried, unopened flower bud of the clove tree *Eugenia caryophyllus*. A member of the myrtle family Myrtaceae, the clove tree is a native of the Moluccas. Cloves are used for flavouring in cookery and confectionery. Oil of cloves, which has tonic and carminative qualities, is employed in medicine. The aromatic quality of cloves is shared to a large degree by the leaves, bark, and fruit of the tree.

clover any of an Old World genus *Trifolium* of low-growing leguminous plants, usually with compound leaves of three leaflets and small flowers in dense heads. Sweet clover refers to various species belonging to the related genus *Melilotus*.

Clovis 465–511. Merovingian king of the Franks from 481. He succeeded his father Childeric as king of the Salian (northern) Franks; defeated the Gallo-Romans (Romanized Gauls) near Soissons 486, ending their rule in France; and defeated the Alemanni, a confederation of Germanic tribes, near Cologne 496. He embraced Christianity and subsequently proved a powerful defender of orthodoxy against the Arian Visigoths, whom he defeated at Poitiers 507. He made Paris his capital.

Club of Rome informal international organization, set up after a meeting at the Accademia dei Lincei, Rome, in 1968, which aims to promote greater understanding of the interdependence of global economic, political, natural, and social systems.

clubroot disease affecting cabbages, turnips, and allied plants of the Cruciferae family. It is caused by a *slime mould, *Plasmodiophora brassicae*. This attacks the roots of the plant, which send out knotty outgrowths. Eventually the whole plant decays.

Cluj (German **Klausenberg**) city in Transylvania, Romania, located on the river Somes; population (1985) 310,000. It is a communications centre for Romania and the Hungarian plain. Industries include machine tools, furniture, and knitwear.

cluster in music, the effect of playing simultaneously and without emphasis all the notes within a chosen interval. Invented by US composer Henry Cowell (1897–1965) for the piano, it was adopted by Krzystof *Penderecki for string orchestra; in radio and film, an organ cluster is the traditional sound of reverie.

clutch any device for disconnecting rotating shafts, used especially in a car's transmission system. In a car with a manual gearbox, the driver depresses the clutch when changing gear, thus disconnecting the engine from the gearbox.

Clwyd county in N Wales
area 2,420 sq km/934 sq mi
towns Mold (administrative headquarters), Flint, Denbigh, Wrexham; seaside resorts: Colwyn Bay, Rhyl, Prestatyn
physical rivers: Dee, Clwyd; Clwydian Range of mountains with Offa's Dyke along the main ridge
products dairy and meat products, optical glass, chemicals, limestone, microprocessors, plastics
population (1991) 400,500
language 19% Welsh, English
famous people George Jeffreys, Henry Morton Stanley.

Clyde river in Strathclyde, Scotland; 170 km/103 mi long. The Firth of Clyde and Firth of Forth are linked by the Forth and Clyde canal, 56 km/35 mi long. The shipbuilding yards have declined in recent years.

Clytemnestra in Greek mythology, the wife of *Agamemnon. With her lover Aegisthus, she murdered her husband on his return from the Trojan War and was in turn killed by her son Orestes.

cm symbol for *centimetre*.

CMOS abbreviation for *complementary metal-oxide semiconductor* family of integrated circuits (chips) widely used in building electronic systems.

CND abbreviation for *Campaign for Nuclear Disarmament*.

Cnossus alternative form of *Knossos, city of ancient Crete.

Cnut alternative spelling of *Canute.

c/o abbreviation for *care of*.

co. abbreviation for *company*.

CO abbreviation for *commanding officer*.

CO abbreviation for *Colorado*.

coal black or blackish mineral substance of fossil origin, the result of the transformation of ancient plant matter under progressive compression. It is used as a fuel and in the chemical industry. Coal is classified according to the proportion of carbon and volatiles it contains. The main types are *anthracite* (shiny, with more than 90% carbon), *bituminous coal* (shiny and dull patches, more than 80% carbon), and *lignite* (woody, grading into *peat, 70% carbon).

coal gas gas produced when coal is destructively distilled or heated out of contact with the air. Its main constituents are methane, hydrogen, and carbon monoxide. Coal gas has been superseded by *natural gas for domestic purposes.

coastal erosion the erosion of the land by the constant battering of the sea's waves. This produces two effects. The first is a hydraulic effect, in which the force of the wave compresses air pockets in coastal rocks and cliffs, and the air then expands explosively. The second is the effect of abrasion, in which rocks and pebbles are flung against the cliffs, wearing them away.

coati or *coatimundi* any of several species of carnivores of the genus *Nasua*, in the same family, Procyonidae, as the raccoons. A coati is a good climber and has long claws, a long tail, a good sense of smell, and a long, flexible piglike snout used for digging. Coatis live in packs in the forests of South and Central America.

coaxial cable electric cable that consists of a solid or stranded central conductor insulated from and surrounded by a solid or braided conducting tube or sheath. It can transmit the high-frequency signals used in television, telephone, and other telecommunications transmissions.

cobalt (German *Kobalt* 'goblin') hard, lustrous, grey, metallic element, symbol Co, atomic number 27, relative atomic mass 58.933. It is found in various ores and occasionally as a free metal, sometimes in metallic meteorite fragments. It is used in the preparation of magnetic, wear-resistant, and high-strength alloys; its compounds are used in inks, paints, and varnishes.

cobalt ore cobalt is extracted from a number of minerals, the main ones being *smaltite*, $(CoNi)As_3$; *linnaeite*, Co_3S_4; *cobaltite*, CoAsS; and *glaucodot*, (CoFe)AsS.

Cobb Ty(rus Raymond), nicknamed 'the Georgia Peach' 1886–1961. US baseball player, one of the greatest batters and base runners of all time. He played for Detroit and Philadelphia 1905–28, and won the American League batting average championship 12 times. He holds the record for runs scored (2,254) and batting average (.367). He had 4,191 hits in his career – a record that stood for almost 60 years.

Cobbett William 1763–1835. British Radical politician and journalist, who published the weekly *Political Register* 1802–35. He spent much time in North America. His crusading essays on the conditions of the rural poor were collected as *Rural Rides* 1830.

Cobden Richard 1804–1865. British Liberal politician and economist, co-founder with John Bright of the Anti-Corn Law League 1839. A member of Parliament from 1841, he opposed class and religious privileges and believed in disarmament and free trade.

COBOL (acronym for *common business-oriented language*) high-level computer-programming language, designed in the late 1950s for commercial data-processing problems; it has become one of the major languages in this field. COBOL features powerful facilities for file handling and business arithmetic. Program instructions written in this language make extensive use of words and look very much like English sentences. This makes COBOL one of the easiest languages to learn and understand.

cobra any of several poisonous snakes, especially the genus *Naja*, of the family Elapidae, found in Africa and S Asia, species of which can grow from 1 m/3 ft to over 4.3 m/14 ft. The neck stretches into a hood when the snake is alarmed. Cobra venom contains nerve toxins powerful enough to kill humans.

Coburn James 1928– . US film actor, popular

cobra *The Indian cobra feeds on rodents, lizards, and frogs.*

in the 1960s and 1970s. His films include *The Magnificent Seven* 1960, *Pat Garrett and Billy the Kid* 1973, and *Cross of Iron* 1977.

coca South American shrub *Erythroxylon coca* of the coca family Erythroxylaceae, whose dried leaves are the source of cocaine. It was used as a holy drug by the Andean Indians.

Coca-Cola trade name of a sweetened, carbonated drink, originally made with coca leaves and flavoured with cola nuts, and containing caramel and caffeine. Invented in 1886, Coca-Cola was sold in every state of the USA by 1895 and in 155 countries by 1987.

cocaine alkaloid $C_{17}H_{21}NO_4$ extracted from the leaves of the coca tree. It has limited medical application, mainly as a local anaesthetic agent that is readily absorbed by mucous membranes (lining tissues) of the nose and throat. It is both toxic and addictive. Its use as a stimulant is illegal. *Crack is a derivative of cocaine.

coccolithophore microscopic marine alga of a type that grows within a calcite shell. They were particularly abundant during the late *Cretaceous period and their calcite remains form the chalk deposits characteristic of S England, N France, and Kansas, USA.

coccus (plural **cocci**) member of a group of globular bacteria, some of which are harmful to humans. The cocci contain the subgroups **streptococci**, where the bacteria associate in straight chains, and **staphylococci**, where the bacteria associate in branched chains.

Cochabamba city in central Bolivia, SE of La Paz; population (1988) 377,200. Its altitude is 2,550 m/8,370 ft; it is a centre of agricultural trading and oil refining.

cochlea part of the inner *ear. It is equipped with approximately 10,000 hair cells, which move in response to sound waves and thus stimulate nerve cells to send messages to the brain. In this way they turn vibrations of the air into electrical signals.

Cochran C(harles) B(lake) 1872–1951. British impresario who promoted entertainment ranging from wrestling and roller-skating to Diaghilev's *Ballets Russes*.

cockatiel Australian parrot *Nymphicus hollandicus*, about 20 cm/8 in long, with greyish plumage, yellow cheeks, a long tail, and a crest like a cockatoo. Cockatiels are popular as pets and aviary birds.

cockatoo any of several crested parrots, especially of the genus *Cacatua*. They usually have light-coloured plumage with tinges of red, yellow, or orange on the face, and an erectile crest on the head. They are native to Australia, New Guinea, and nearby islands.

cockchafer or **maybug** European beetle *Melolontha melolontha*, of the scarab family, up to 3 cm/1.2 in long, with clumsy, buzzing flight, seen on early summer evenings. Cockchafers damage trees by feeding on the foliage and flowers.

Cockcroft John Douglas 1897–1967. British physicist. In 1932 he and the Irish physicist Ernest Walton succeeded in splitting the nucleus of an atom for the first time. In 1951 they were jointly awarded a Nobel prize.

Cockerell Charles 1788–1863. English architect who built mainly in a Neo-Classical style derived from antiquity and from the work of Christopher Wren. His buildings include the Ashmolean Museum and Taylorian Institute in Oxford 1841–45.

Cockerell Christopher 1910– . British engineer who invented the *hovercraft 1959.

cockle any of over 200 species of bivalve mollusc with ribbed, heart-shaped shells. Some are edible and are sold in W European markets.

cock-of-the-rock South American bird *Rupicola peruviana* of the family Cotingidae, which also includes the cotingas and umbrella birds. The male cock-of-the-rock has brilliant orange plumage including the head crest, the female is a duller brown. Males clear an area of ground and use it as a communal display ground, spreading wings, tail, and crest to attract mates.

cockroach any of numerous insects of the family Blattidae, distantly related to mantises and grasshoppers. There are 3,500 species, mainly in the tropics. They have long antennae and biting mouthparts. They can fly, but rarely do so.

cocktail effect the effect of two toxic, or potentially toxic, chemicals when taken together rather than separately. Such effects are known to occur with some mixtures of chemicals, with one ingredient making the body more sensitive to another ingredient. This sometimes occurs because both chemicals require the same *enzyme to break them down. Chemicals such as pesticides and food additives are only ever tested singly, not in combination with other chemicals that may be consumed at the same time, so no allowance is made for cocktail effects.

cocoa and chocolate (Aztec *xocolatl*) food products made from the *cacao (or cocoa) bean, fruit of a tropical tree *Theobroma cacao*, now cultivated mainly in Africa. Chocolate as a drink was introduced to Europe from the New World by the Spanish in the 16th century; eating chocolate was first produced in the late 18th century. Cocoa and chocolate are widely used in confectionery and drinks.

coconut fruit of the coconut palm *Cocos nucifera* of the family Arecaceae, which grows throughout the lowland tropics. The fruit has a large outer husk of fibres, which is split off and used for coconut matting and ropes. Inside this is the nut exported to temperate countries. Its hard shell contains white flesh and coconut milk, both of which are nourishing and palatable.

Cocos Islands or **Keeling Islands** group of 27

small coral islands in the Indian Ocean, about 2,770 km/1,720 mi NW of Perth, Australia; area 14 sq km/5.5 sq mi; population (1986) 616. They are owned by Australia.

Cocteau Jean 1889–1963. French poet, dramatist, and film director. A leading figure in European Modernism, he worked with Picasso, Diaghilev, and Stravinsky. He produced many volumes of poetry, ballets such as *Le Boeuf sur le toit/The Ox on the Roof* 1920, plays, for example, *Orphée/Orpheus* 1926, and a mature novel of bourgeois French life, *Les Enfants terribles/Children of the Game* 1929, which he made into a film 1950.

cod any fish of the family Gadoidea, especially the Atlantic cod, *Gadus morhua* found in the N Atlantic and Baltic. It is brown to grey with spots, white below, and can grow to 1.5 m/5 ft.

COD abbreviation for *cash on delivery*.

codeine opium derivative that provides *analgesia in mild to moderate pain. It also suppresses the cough centre of the brain. It is an alkaloid, derived from morphine but less toxic and addictive.

cod-liver oil oil obtained by subjecting the fresh livers of cod to pressure at a temperature of about 85°C/185°F. It is highly nutritious, being a valuable source of the vitamins A and D; overdose can be harmful.

codon in genetics, a triplet of bases (see *base pair) in a molecule of DNA or RNA that directs the placement of a particular amino acid during the process of protein (polypeptide) synthesis. There are 64 codons in the *genetic code.

Cody (William Frederick) 'Buffalo Bill' 1846–1917. US scout and performer. From 1883 he toured the USA and Europe with a Wild West show which featured the re-creation of Indian attacks and, for a time, the cast included Chief *Sitting Bull as well as Annie *Oakley. His nickname derives from a time when he had a contract to supply buffalo carcasses to railway labourers (over 4,000 in 18 months).

Cody Samuel Franklin 1862–1913. US aviation pioneer. He made his first powered flight on 16 Oct 1908 at Farnborough, England, in a machine of his own design. He was killed in a flying accident.

Coe Sebastian 1956– . English middle-distance runner, Olympic 1,500-metre champion 1980 and 1984. After his retirement from running in 1990 he pursued a political career with the Conservative party, and in 1992 was elected member of Parliament for Falmouth and Cambourne in Cornwall.

coefficient the number part in front of an algebraic term, signifying multiplication. For example, in the expression $4x^2 + 2xy - x$, the coefficient of x^2 is 4 (because $4x^2$ means $4 \times x^2$), that of xy is 2, and that of x is –1 (because $-1 \times x = -x$).

coefficient of relationship the probability that any two individuals share a given gene by virtue of being descended from a common ancestor. In sexual reproduction of diploid species, an individual shares half its genes with each parent, with its offspring, and (on average) with each sibling; but only a quarter (on average) with its grandchildren or its siblings' offspring; an eighth with its great-grandchildren, and so on.

coelacanth lobe-finned fish *Latimeria chalumnae* up to 2 m/6 ft long. It has bone and muscle at the base of the fins, and is distantly related to the freshwater lobefins, which were the ancestors of all land animals with backbones. Coelacanths live in deep water (200 m/650 ft) around the Comoros Islands, off the coast of Madagascar. They were believed to be extinct until one was caught in 1938.

coelenterate any freshwater or marine organism of the phylum Coelenterata, having a body wall composed of two layers of cells. They also possess stinging cells. Examples are jellyfish, hydra, and coral.

coeliac disease deficiency disease, usually in young children, due to disorder of the absorptive surface of the small intestine. It is caused by an intolerance to gluten (a constituent of wheat) and characterized by diarrhoea and malnutrition.

coelom in all but the simplest animals, the fluid-filled cavity that separates the body wall from the gut and associated organs, and allows the gut muscles to contract independently of the rest of the body.

Coetzee J(ohn) M 1940– . South African author whose novel *In the Heart of the Country* 1975 dealt with the rape of a white woman by a black man. In 1983 he won Britain's prestigious *Booker Prize for *The Life and Times of Michael K*.

coevolution evolution of those structures and behaviours within a species that can best be understood in relation to another species. For example, insects and flowering plants have evolved together: insects have produced mouthparts suitable for collecting pollen or drinking nectar, and plants have developed chemicals and flowers that will attract insects to them.

coffee drink made from the roasted and ground beanlike seeds found inside the red berries of any of several species of shrubs of the genus *Coffea*, originally native to Ethiopia and now cultivated throughout the tropics. It contains a stimulant, *caffeine.

cultivation The shrub is naturally about 5 m/17 ft high, is pruned to about 2 m/7 ft, is fully fruit-bearing in 5 or 6 years, and lasts for 30 years. Coffee grows best on frost-free hillsides with moderate rainfall. The world's largest producers are Brazil, Colombia, and the Ivory Coast; others include Indonesia (Java), Ethiopia, India, Hawaii, and Jamaica.

history Coffee drinking began in Arab regions in the 14th century but did not become common in Europe until 300 years later, when the first coffee houses were opened in Vienna, and soon after in Paris and London. In the American colonies, coffee became the substitute for tea when tea was taxed by the British.

cogito, ergo sum (Latin) 'I think, therefore I am'; quotation from French philosopher René Descartes. The concept formed the basis of the philosophical doctrine of *dualism.

cognition in psychology, a general term covering the functions involved in synthesizing information – for example, perception (seeing, hearing, and so on), attention, memory, and reasoning.

cognitive therapy treatment for emotional

disorders such as *depression and *anxiety, developed by Professor Aaron T Beck in the USA. This approach encourages the patient to challenge the distorted and unhelpful thinking that is characteristic of these problems. The treatment includes *behaviour therapy and has been most helpful for people suffering from depression.

Cohan Robert Paul 1925– . US choreographer and founder of the London Contemporary Dance Theatre 1969–87; now artistic director of the Contemporary Dance Theatre. He was a student of Martha *Graham and co-director of her company 1966–69. His works include *Waterless Method of Swimming Instruction* 1974 and *Mass for Man* 1985.

coherence in physics, property of two or more waves of a beam of light or other electromagnetic radiation having the same frequency and the same *phase, or a constant phase difference.

cohesion in physics, a phenomenon in which interaction between two surfaces of the same material in contact makes them cling together (with two different materials the similar phenomenon is called adhesion). According to kinetic theory, cohesion is caused by attraction between particles at the atomic or molecular level. *Surface tension, which causes liquids to form spherical droplets, is caused by cohesion.

coil in medicine, another name for an *intrauterine device.

coin form of money. The right to make and issue coins is a state monopoly, and the great majority are tokens in that their face value is greater than that of the metal of which they consist.

COIN acronym for *counter insurgency*, the suppression by a state's armed forces of uprisings against the state. Also called internal security (IS) operations of counter-revolutionary warfare (CRW).

coke clean, light fuel produced by the carbonization of certain types of coal. When this coal is strongly heated in airtight ovens (in order to release all volatile constituents), the brittle, silver-grey remains are coke. Coke comprises 90% carbon together with very small quantities of water, hydrogen, and oxygen, and makes a useful industrial and domestic fuel. The process was patented in England 1622, but it was only in 1709 that Abraham Darby devised a commercial method of production.

Coke Edward 1552–1634. Lord Chief Justice of England 1613–17. He was a defender of common law against royal prerogative; against Charles I he drew up the *Petition of Right 1628, which defines and protects Parliament's liberties.

Coke Thomas William 1754–1842. English pioneer and promoter of the improvements associated with the Agricultural Revolution. His innovations included regular manuring of the soil, the cultivation of fodder crops in association with corn, and the drilling of wheat and turnips.

cola or *kola* any tropical tree of the genus *Cola*, especially *C. acuminata*, family Sterculiaceae. The nuts are chewed in W Africa for their high caffeine content, and in the West are used to flavour soft drinks.

Colbert Claudette. Stage name of Claudette Lily Cauchoin 1905– . French-born film actress who lived in Hollywood from childhood. She was ideally cast in sophisticated, romantic roles, but had a natural instinct for comedy and appeared in several of Hollywood's finest, including *It Happened One Night* 1934 and *The Palm Beach Story* 1942.

Colbert Jean-Baptiste 1619–1683. French politician, chief minister to Louis XIV, and controller-general (finance minister) from 1665. He reformed the Treasury, promoted French industry and commerce by protectionist measures, and tried to make France a naval power equal to England or the Netherlands, while favouring a peaceful foreign policy.

cold, common minor disease of the upper respiratory tract, caused by a variety of viruses. Symptoms are headache, chill, nasal discharge, sore throat, and occasionally cough. Research indicates that the virulence of a cold depends on psychological factors and either a reduction or an increase of social or work activity, as a result of stress, in the previous six months.

cold-blooded of animals, dependent on the surrounding temperature; see *poikilothermy*.

cold fusion in nuclear physics, the fusion of atomic nuclei at room temperature. Were cold fusion to become possible it would provide a limitless, cheap, and pollution-free source of energy, and it has therefore been the subject of research around the world. In 1989, Martin Fleischmann (1927–) and Stanley Pons (1943–) of the University of Utah, USA, claimed that they had achieved cold fusion in the laboratory, but their results could not be substantiated.

Cold Harbor, Battle of in the American Civil War, engagement near Richmond, Virginia, 1–12 June 1864, in which the Confederate Army under Robert E Lee repulsed Union attacks under Ulysses S Grant.

Colditz town in E Germany, near Leipzig, site of a castle used as a high-security prisoner-of-war camp (Oflag IVC) in World War II. Among daring escapes was that of British Captain Patrick Reid (1910–1990) and others Oct 1942. It became a museum 1989. In 1990 the castle was converted into a hotel.

Cold War ideological, political, and economic tensions 1945–90 between the USSR and Eastern Europe on the one hand and the USA and Western Europe on the other. The Cold War was exacerbated by propaganda, covert activity by intelligence agencies, and economic sanctions; it intensified at times of conflict anywhere in the world. Arms-reduction agreements between the USA and USSR in the late 1980s, and a diminution of Soviet influence in Eastern Europe, symbolized by the opening of the Berlin Wall 1989, led to a reassessment of positions, and the 'war' officially ended 1990.

coleoptile the protective sheath that surrounds the young shoot tip of a grass during its passage through the soil to the surface. Although of relatively simple structure, most coleoptiles are very sensitive to light, ensuring that seedlings grow upwards.

Coleridge Samuel Taylor 1772–1834. English poet, one of the founders of the Romantic movement. A friend of Southey and Wordsworth, he collaborated with the latter on *Lyrical Ballads* 1798. His poems include 'The Rime of the Ancient Mariner', 'Christabel', and 'Kubla Khan'; critical works include *Biographia Literaria* 1817.

Colette Sidonie-Gabrielle 1873–1954. French writer. At 20 she married Henri Gauthier-Villars, a journalist known as 'Willy', under whose name and direction her four 'Claudine' novels, based on her own early life, were written. Divorced 1906, she worked as a striptease and mime artist for a while, but continued to write. Works from this later period include *Chéri* 1920, *La Fin de Chéri/The End of Chéri* 1926, and *Gigi* 1944.

colitis inflammation of the colon (large intestine) with diarrhoea (often bloody). It may be caused by food poisoning or some types of bacterial dysentery.

collage (French 'gluing' or 'pasting') technique of pasting paper and other materials to create a picture. Several artists in the early 20th century used collage: Jean (or Hans) Arp, Georges Braque, Max Ernst, and Kurt Schwitters, among others.

collagen strong, rubbery *protein that plays a major structural role in the bodies of *vertebrates. Collagen supports the ear flaps and the tip of the nose in humans, as well as being the main constituent of tendons and ligaments. Bones are made up of collagen, with the mineral calcium phosphate providing increased rigidity.

collective bargaining the process whereby management, representing an employer, and a trade union, representing employees, agree to negotiate jointly terms and conditions of employment. Agreements can be company-based or industry-wide.

collective farm (Russian *kolkhoz*) farm in which a group of farmers pool their land, domestic animals, and agricultural implements, retaining as private property enough only for the members' own requirements. The profits of the farm are divided among its members. In cooperative farming, farmers retain private ownership of the land.

collective responsibility doctrine found in governments modelled on the British system of cabinet government. It is based on convention, or usage, rather than law, and requires that once a decision has been taken by the cabinet, all members of the government are bound by it and must support it or resign their posts.

collective security system for achieving international stability by an agreement among all states to unite against any aggressor. Such a commitment was embodied in the post-World War I League of Nations and also in the United Nations, although the League was not, and the UN has not yet been, able to live up to the ideals of its founders.

collective unconscious in psychology, the shared pool of memories inherited from ancestors that Carl Jung suggested coexists with individual *unconscious recollections. He thought it could affect individuals both for ill, in precipitating mental disturbance, and for good, in prompting achievements (for example, in the arts).

collectivism in politics, a position in which the collective (such as the state) has priority over its individual members. It is the opposite of *individualism, which is itself a variant of anarchy.

collectivization policy pursued by the Soviet leader Stalin in the USSR after 1928 to reorganize agriculture by taking land into state ownership or creating *collective farms. Much of this was achieved during the first two five-year plans for the economy, but only with much coercion and loss of life among the peasantry.

College of Arms or *Heralds' College* English heraldic body formed 1484 by Richard III incorporating the heralds attached to the royal household; reincorporated by royal charter of Philip and Mary 1555. There are three kings of arms, six heralds, and four pursuivants, who specialize in genealogical and heraldic work. The college establishes the right to a coat of arms, and the kings of arms grant arms by letters patent. In Ireland the office of Ulster king of arms was transferred 1943 to the College of Arms in London and placed with that of Norroy king of arms, who now has jurisdiction in Northern Ireland as well as in the north of England.

collenchyma plant tissue composed of relatively elongated cells with thickened cell walls, in particular at the corners where adjacent cells meet. It is a supporting and strengthening tissue found in nonwoody plants, mainly in the stems and leaves.

collie sheepdog originally bred in Britain. The rough and smooth collies are about 60 cm/2 ft tall, and have long narrow heads and muzzles. They may be light to dark brown or silver-grey, with black and white markings. The border collie is a working dog, often black and white, about 50 cm/20 in tall, with a dense coat. The bearded collie is about the same size, and is rather like an Old English sheepdog in appearance.

Collier Lesley 1947– . British ballerina, a principal dancer of the Royal Ballet from 1972. She created roles in Kenneth MacMillan's *Anastasia* 1971 and *Four Seasons* 1975, Hans van Manen's *Four Schumann Pieces* 1975, Frederick Ashton's *Rhapsody*, and Glen Tetley's *Dance of Albiar* both 1980.

collinear in mathematics, lying on the same straight line.

Collingwood Cuthbert, Baron Collingwood 1748–1810. British admiral who served with Horatio Nelson in the West Indies against France and blockaded French ports 1803–05; after Nelson's death he took command at the Battle of Trafalgar.

Collingwood Robin George 1889–1943. English philosopher who believed that any philosophical theory or position could be properly understood only within its own historical context and not from the point of view of the present. His aesthetic theory is outlined in *Principles of Art* 1938.

Collins Michael 1890–1922. Irish nationalist. He was a Sinn Féin leader, a founder and director of intelligence of the Irish Republican Army 1919, minister for finance in the provisional government of the Irish Free State 1922 (see *Ireland, Republic of), commander of the Free State forces in the civil war, and for ten days head of state before being killed.

Collins Phil(lip David Charles) 1951– . English pop singer, drummer, and actor. A member of the group Genesis from 1970, he has also pursued a successful middle-of-the-road solo career since 1981, with hits (often new versions of old songs) including 'In the Air Tonight' 1981 and 'Groovy Kind of Love' 1988.

Collins (William) Wilkie 1824–1889. English author of mystery and suspense novels. He wrote *The Woman in White* 1860 (with its fat villain Count Fosco), often called the first English detective novel, and *The Moonstone* 1868 (with Sergeant Cuff, one of the first detectives in English literature).

collision theory theory that explains how chemical reactions take place and why rates of reaction alter. For a reaction to occur the reactant particles must collide. Only a certain fraction of the total collisions cause chemical change; these are called *fruitful collisions*. The fruitful collisions have sufficient energy (activation energy) at the moment of impact to break the existing bonds and form new bonds, resulting in the products of the reaction. Increasing the concentration of the reactants and raising the temperature bring about more collisions and therefore more fruitful collisions, increasing the rate of reaction.

Collodi Carlo. Pen name of Carlo Lorenzini 1826–1890. Italian journalist and writer who in 1881–83 wrote *Le avventure di Pinocchio/The Adventure of Pinocchio*, a children's story of a wooden puppet that became a human boy.

colloid substance composed of extremely small particles of one material (the dispersed phase) evenly and stably distributed in another material (the continuous phase). The size of the dispersed particles (1–1,000 nanometres across) is less than that of particles in suspension but greater than that of molecules in true solution. Colloids involving gases include *aerosols* (dispersions of liquid or solid particles in a gas, as in fog or smoke) and *foams* (dispersions of gases in liquids). Those involving liquids include *emulsions* (in which both the dispersed and the continuous phases are liquids) and *sols* (solid particles dispersed in a liquid). Sols in which both phases contribute to a molecular three-dimensional network have a jellylike form and are known as *gels*; gelatin, starch 'solution', and silica gel are common examples.

Collor de Mello Fernando 1949– . Brazilian politician, president 1990–92. As candidate of the centre-right National Reconstruction Party (PRN), he conducted the 1989 presidential campaign on a platform of rooting out government corruption and entrenched privileges. Rumours of his own past wrongdoings were rife by 1992, leading to his constitutional removal from office by a vote of impeachment in congress in Sept.

Cologne (German *Köln*) industrial and commercial port in North Rhine–Westphalia, Germany, on the left bank of the Rhine, 35 km/22 mi from Düsseldorf; population (1988) 914,000. To the north is the Ruhr coalfield, on which many of Cologne's industries are based. They include motor vehicles, railway wagons, chemicals, and machine tools. Cologne is an important trans-shipment centre.

Colombia Republic of (*República de Colombia*)
area 1,141,748 sq km/440,715 sq mi
capital Santa Fé de Bogotá

towns Medellín, Cali, Bucaramanga; ports Barranquilla, Cartagena, Buenaventura
physical the Andes mountains run N–S; flat coastland in W and plains (llanos) in E; Magdalena River runs N to Caribbean Sea; includes islands of Providencia, San Andrés, and Mapelo
head of state and government Ernesto Samper Pizano from 1994
political system democratic republic
exports emeralds (world's largest producer), coffee (world's second largest producer), cocaine (country's largest export), bananas, cotton, meat, sugar, oil, skins, hides, tobacco
currency peso
population (1993 est) 34,900,800 (mestizo 68%, white 20%, American Indian 1%); growth rate 2.2% p.a.
language Spanish
religion Roman Catholic 95%
GNP $1,280 per head (1991)
chronology
1886 Full independence achieved from Spain. Conservatives in power.
1948 Left-wing mayor of Bogotá assassinated; widespread outcry.
1949 Start of civil war, 'La Violencia', during which over 250,000 people died.
1957 Hoping to halt the violence, Conservatives and Liberals agreed to form a National Front, sharing the presidency.
1970 National Popular Alliance (ANAPO) formed as a left-wing opposition to the National Front.
1974 National Front accord temporarily ended.
1975 Civil unrest because of disillusionment with the government.
1978 Liberals, under Julio Turbay, revived the accord and began an intensive fight against drug dealers.
1982 Liberals maintained their control of congress but lost the presidency. The Conservative president, Belisario Betancur, granted guerrillas an amnesty and freed political prisoners.
1984 Minister of justice assassinated by drug dealers; campaign against them stepped up.
1986 Virgilio Barco Vargas, Liberal, elected president by record margin.
1989 Drug cartel assassinated leading presidential candidate; Vargas declared antidrug war; bombing campaign by drug traffickers killed

hundreds; police killed José Rodríguez Gacha, one of the most wanted cartel leaders.

1990 Cesar Gaviria Trujillo elected president. Liberals maintained control of congress.

1991 New constitution prohibited extradition of Colombians wanted for trial in other countries; several leading drug traffickers arrested. Oct: Liberal Party won general election.

1992 Drug cartel leader Pablo Escobar escaped from prison. State of emergency declared.

1993 Escobar shot while attempting to avoid arrest.

1994 Ernesto Samper Pizano, Liberal, elected president.

Colombo capital and principal seaport of Sri Lanka, on the W coast near the mouth of the Kelani River; population (1990) 615,000, Greater Colombo about 1,000,000. It trades in tea, rubber, and cacao. It has iron-and steelworks and an oil refinery.

Colombo Matteo Realdo *c.* 1516–1559. Italian anatomist who discovered pulmonary circulation, the process of blood circulating from the heart to the lungs and back.

Colombo Plan plan for cooperative economic and social development in Asia and the Pacific, established 1950. The 26 member countries are Afghanistan, Australia, Bangladesh, Bhutan, Cambodia, Canada, Fiji, India, Indonesia, Iran, Japan, South Korea, Laos, Malaysia, Maldives, Myanmar (Burma), Nepal, New Zealand, Pakistan, Papua New Guinea, Philippines, Singapore, Sri Lanka, Thailand, UK, and USA. They meet annually to discuss economic and development plans such as irrigation, hydroelectric schemes, and technical training.

Colón second-largest city in Panama, at the Caribbean end of the Panama Canal; population (1990) 140,900. It has a special economic zone created 1948 used by foreign companies to avoid taxes on completed products in their home countries; $2 billion worth of goods passed through the zone in 1987, from dozens of countries and 600 companies. Unemployment in the city of Colón, outside the zone, was over 25% in 1991.

colon in anatomy, the part of the large intestine between the caecum and rectum, where water and mineral salts are absorbed from digested food, and the residue formed into faeces or faecal pellets.

colon in punctuation, a mark (:) intended to direct the reader's attention forward, usually because what follows explains or develops what has just been written (for example, *The farmer owned the following varieties of dogs: a spaniel, a pointer, a terrier, a border collie, and three mongrels*).

colonialism another name for *imperialism*.

colophon decorative device on the title page or spine of a book, the trademark of the individual publisher. Originally a colophon was an inscription on the last page of a book giving the writer or printer's name and the place and year of publication.

Colorado state of the W central USA; nicknamed Centennial State
area 269,700 sq km/104,104 sq mi
capital Denver

towns Colorado Springs, Aurora, Lakewood, Fort Collins, Greeley, Pueblo, Boulder
physical Great Plains in the E; the main ranges of the Rocky Mountains; high plateaux of the Colorado Basin in the W
products cereals, meat and dairy products, oil, coal, molybdenum, uranium, iron, steel, machinery
population (1990) 3,294,400
famous people Jack Dempsey, Douglas Fairbanks
history first visited by Spanish explorers in the 16th century; claimed for Spain 1706; E portion passed to the USA 1803 as part of the Louisiana Purchase, the rest 1845 and 1848 as a result of the Mexican War. It attracted fur traders, and Denver was founded following the discovery of gold 1858. Colorado became a state 1876.

coloratura in music, a rapid ornamental vocal passage with runs and trills. A **coloratura soprano** is a light, high voice suited to such music.

Colosseum amphitheatre in ancient Rome, begun by the emperor Vespasian to replace the one destroyed by fire during the reign of Nero, and completed by his son Titus AD 80. It was 187 m/615 ft long and 49 m/160 ft high, and seated 50,000 people. Early Christians were martyred there by lions and gladiators. It could be flooded for mock sea battles.

Colossus of Rhodes bronze statue of Apollo erected at the entrance to the harbour at Rhodes 292–280 BC. Said to have been about 30 m/100 ft high, it was counted as one of the Seven Wonders of the World, but in 224 BC fell as a result of an earthquake.

colour quality or wavelength of light emitted or reflected from an object. Visible white light consists of electromagnetic radiation of various wavelengths, and if a beam is refracted through a prism, it can be spread out into a spectrum, in which the various colours correspond to different wavelengths. From long to short wavelengths (from about 700 to 400 nanometres) the colours are red, orange, yellow, green, blue, indigo, and violet.

colour blindness hereditary defect of vision that reduces the ability to discriminate certain colours, usually red and green. The condition is sex-linked, affecting men more than women.

colouring food *additive used to alter or improve the colour of processed foods. Colourings include artificial colours, such as tartrazine and amaranth, which are made from petrochemicals, and the 'natural' colours such as chlorophyll, caramel, and carotene. Some of the natural colours are actually synthetic copies of the naturally occurring substances, and some of these, notably the synthetically produced caramels, may be injurious to health.

colours, military flags or standards carried by military regiments, so called because of the various combinations of colours employed to distinguish one country or one regiment from another.

colour therapy application of light of appropriate wavelength to alleviate ailments or facilitate healing. Coloured light affects not only psychological but also physiological states – for instance, long exposure to red light raises blood pressure and speeds up heartbeat and respiration

Coltrane John (William) 1926–1967. US jazz saxophonist who first came to prominence 1955 with the Miles *Davis quintet, later playing with Thelonious Monk 1957. He was a powerful and individual artist, whose performances featured much experimentation. His 1960s quartet was highly regarded for its innovations in melody and harmony.

colugo SE Asian climbing mammal of the genus *Cynocephalus*, order Dermoptera, about 60 cm/ 2 ft long including the tail. It glides between forest trees using a flap of skin that extends from head to forelimb to hindlimb to tail. It may glide 130 m/425 ft or more, losing little height. It feeds largely on buds and leaves, and rests hanging upside down under branches.

Colum Padraic 1881–1972. Irish poet and playwright. He was associated with the foundation of the Abbey Theatre, Dublin, where his plays *Land* 1905 and *Thomas Muskerry* 1910 were performed. His *Collected Poems* 1932 show his gift for lyrical expression.

Columba, St 521–597. Irish Christian abbot, missionary to Scotland. He was born in County Donegal of royal descent, and founded monasteries and churches in Ireland. In 563 he sailed with 12 companions to Iona, and built a monastery there that was to play a leading part in the conversion of Britain. Feast day 9 June.

Columban, St 543–615. Irish Christian abbot. He was born in Leinster, studied at Bangor, and about 585 went to the Vosges, France, with 12 other monks and founded the monastery of Luxeuil. Later, he preached in Switzerland, then went to Italy, where he built the abbey of Bobbio in the Apennines. Feast day 23 Nov.

Columbia, District of seat of the federal government of the USA, coextensive with the city of Washington, situated on the Potomac River; area 178 sq km/69 sq mi. It was ceded by Maryland as the national capital site 1790.

Columbia Pictures US film production and distribution company founded 1924. It grew out of a smaller company founded 1920 by Harry and Jack Cohn and Joe Brandt. Under Harry Cohn's guidance, Columbia became a major studio by the 1940s, producing such commercial hits as *Gilda* 1946. After Cohn's death 1958 the studio remained successful, producing such international films as *Lawrence of Arabia* 1962.

columbine any plant of the genus *Aquilegia* of the buttercup family Ranunculaceae. All are perennial herbs with divided leaves and flowers with spurred petals.

columbium (Cb) former name for the chemical element *niobium. The name is still used occasionally in metallurgy.

Columbus Christopher (Spanish *Cristóbal Colón*) 1451–1506. Italian navigator and explorer who made four voyages to the New World: 1492 to San Salvador Island, Cuba, and Haiti; 1493–96 to Guadaloupe, Montserrat, Antigua, Puerto Rico, and Jamaica; 1498 to Trinidad and the mainland of South America; 1502–04 to Honduras and Nicaragua. Believing that Asia could be reached by sailing westwards, he eventually won the support of King Ferdinand and

Queen Isabella of Spain and set off on his first voyage from Palos 3 Aug 1492 with three small ships, the *Niña*, the *Pinta*, and his flagship the *Santa Maria*. Land was sighted 12 Oct, probably Watling Island (now San Salvador Island), and within a few weeks he reached Cuba and Haiti, returning to Spain March 1493.

column in architecture, a structure, round or polygonal in plan, erected vertically as a support for some part of a building. Cretan paintings reveal the existence of wooden columns in Aegean architecture in about 1500 BC. The Hittites, Assyrians, and Egyptians also used wooden columns, and they are a feature of the monumental architecture of China and Japan. In Classical architecture there are five principal types of column; see *order.

coma in astronomy, the hazy cloud of gas and dust that surrounds the nucleus of a *comet.

coma in medicine, a state of deep unconsciousness from which the subject cannot be roused and in which the subject does not respond to pain. Possible causes include head injury, liver failure, cerebral haemorrhage, and drug overdose.

coma in optics, one of the geometrical aberrations of a lens, whereby skew rays from a point object make a comet-shaped spot on the image plane instead of meeting at a point.

Comaneci Nadia 1961– . Romanian gymnast. She won three gold medals at the 1976 Olympics at the age of 14, and was the first gymnast to record a perfect score of 10 in international competition. Upon retirement she became a coach of the Romanian team, but defected to Canada 1989.

combination in mathematics, a selection of a number of objects from some larger number of objects when no account is taken of order within any one arrangement. For example, 123, 213, and 312 are regarded as the same combination of three digits from 1234. Combinatorial analysis is used in the study of *probability.

Combination Laws laws passed in Britain 1799 and 1800 making trade unionism illegal, introduced after the French Revolution for fear that the unions would become centres of political agitation. The unions continued to exist, but claimed to be friendly societies or went underground, until the acts were repealed 1824, largely owing to the radical Francis Place.

combine harvester or *combine* machine used for harvesting cereals and other crops, so called because it combines the actions of reaping (cutting the crop) and threshing (beating the ears so that the grain separates).

combustion burning, defined in chemical terms as the rapid combination of a substance with oxygen, accompanied by the evolution of heat and usually light. A slow-burning candle flame and the explosion of a mixture of petrol vapour and air are extreme examples of combustion.

Comecon (acronym for *Council for Mutual Economic Assistance*, or *CMEA*) economic organization 1949–91, linking the USSR with Bulgaria, Czechoslovakia, Hungary, Poland, Romania, East Germany (1950–90), Mongolia (from 1962), Cuba (from 1972), and Vietnam (from 1978), with Yugoslavia as an associate member. Albania also belonged 1949–61. Its establishment was prompted by the US *Marshall Plan.

Comédie Française French national theatre (for both comedy and tragedy) in Paris, founded 1680 by Louis XIV. Its base is the Salle Richelieu on the right bank of the river Seine, and the Théâtre de l'Odéon, on the left bank, is a testing ground for avant-garde ideas.

comedy drama that aims to make its audience laugh, usually with a happy or amusing ending, as opposed to *tragedy. The comic tradition has enjoyed many changes since its Greek roots; the earliest comic tradition developed in ancient Greece, in the farcical satires of Aristophanes. Great comic playwrights include Shakespeare, Molière, Carlo Goldoni, Pierre de Marivaux, George Bernard Shaw, and Oscar Wilde. Genres of comedy include pantomime, satire, farce, black comedy, and *commedia dell'arte*.

comet small, icy body orbiting the Sun, usually on a highly elliptical path. A comet consists of a central nucleus a few kilometres across, and has been likened to a dirty snowball because it consists mostly of ice mixed with dust. As the comet approaches the Sun the nucleus heats up, releasing gas and dust which form a tenuous coma, up to 100,000 km/60,000 mi wide, around the nucleus. Gas and dust stream away from the coma to form one or more tails, which may extend for millions of kilometres.

comfrey any plant of the genus *Symphytum*, borage family Boraginaceae, with rough, hairy leaves and small bell-shaped flowers (blue, purple-pink, or white), found in Europe and W Asia.

comic book publication in strip-cartoon form. Comic books are usually aimed at children, although in Japan, Latin America, and Europe millions of adults read them. Artistically sophisticated adult comics and **graphic novels** are produced in the USA and several European countries, notably France. Comic books developed from *comic strips in newspapers or, like those of Walt *Disney, as spinoffs from animated cartoon films.

comic strip or **strip cartoon** sequence of several frames of drawings in *cartoon style. Strips, which may work independently or form instalments of a serial, are usually humorous or satirical in content. Longer stories in comic-strip form are published separately as *comic books. Some have been made into animated films.

Comines Philippe de c. 1445–1511. French diplomat in the service of Charles the Bold, Louis XI, and Charles VIII; author of *Mémoires* 1489–98.

Cominform (acronym for **Communist Information Bureau**) organization 1947–56 established by the Soviet politician Andrei Zhdanov (1896–1948) to exchange information between European communist parties. Yugoslavia was expelled 1948.

Comintern acronym for **Communist *International**.

comma punctuation mark (,) intended to provide breaks or pauses within a sentence; commas may come at the end of a clause, to set off a phrase, or in lists (for example, *apples, pears, plums, and pineapples*).

command language in computing, a set of commands and the rules governing their use, by which users control a program. For example, an *operating system may have commands such as SAVE and DELETE, or a payroll program may have commands for adding and amending staff records.

commando member of a specially trained, highly mobile military unit. The term originated in South Africa in the 19th century, where it referred to Boer military reprisal raids against Africans and, in the South African Wars, against the British. Commando units have often carried out operations behind enemy lines.

commedia dell'arte popular form of Italian improvised comic drama in the 16th and 17th centuries, performed by trained troupes of actors and involving stock characters and situations. It exerted considerable influence on writers such as Molière and Carlo Goldoni, and on the genres of *pantomime, harlequinade, and the Punch and Judy show. It laid the foundation for a tradition of mime, strong in France, that has continued with the contemporary mime of Jean-Louis Barrault and Marcel Marceau.

comme il faut (French 'as it should be') socially correct and acceptable.

commensalism in biology, a relationship between two *species whereby one (the commensal) benefits from the association, whereas the other neither benefits nor suffers. For example, certain species of millipede and silverfish inhabit the nests of army ants and live by scavenging on the refuse of their hosts, but without affecting the ants.

commissioner for oaths in English law, a person appointed by the Lord Chancellor with power to administer oaths or take affidavits. All practising solicitors have these powers but must not use them in proceedings in which they are acting for any of the parties or in which they have an interest.

committal proceedings in the UK, a preliminary hearing in a magistrate's court to decide whether there is a case to answer before a higher court. The media may only report limited facts about committal proceedings, such as the name of the accused and the charges, unless the defendant asks for reporting restrictions to be lifted.

Committee of Imperial Defence informal group established 1902 to coordinate planning of the British Empire's defence forces. Initially meeting on a temporary basis, it was established permanently 1904. Members were usually cabinet ministers concerned with defence, military leaders, and key civil servants.

Committee on Safety of Medicine UK authority processing licence applications for new drugs. The members are appointed by the secretary of state for health and in 1988 most of them had commercial links with pharmaceutical companies. Drugs are licensed on the basis of safety alone, according to the manufacturers' own data; usefulness is not considered.

commodity something produced for sale. Commodities may be consumer goods, such as radios, or producer goods, such as copper bars. **Commodity markets** deal in raw or semi-raw materials that are amenable to grading and that can be stored for considerable periods without deterioration.

Commodus Lucius Aelius Aurelius AD 161–192. Roman emperor from 180, son of Marcus Aurelius Antoninus. He was a tyrant, spending lavishly on gladiatorial combats, confiscating the property of the wealthy, persecuting the Senate, and renaming Rome 'Colonia Commodia'. There were many attempts against his life, and he was finally strangled at the instigation of his mistress and advisers, who had discovered themselves on the emperor's death list.

Common Agricultural Policy (CAP) system that allows the member countries of the European Community (EC) jointly to organize and control agricultural production within their boundaries. The objectives of the CAP were outlined in the Treaty of Rome: to increase agricultural productivity, to provide a fair standard of living for farmers and their employees, to stabilize markets, and to assure the availability of supply at a price that was reasonable to the consumer. The CAP is increasingly criticized for its role in creating overproduction, and consequent environmental damage, and for the high price of food subsidies.

common land unenclosed wasteland, forest, and pasture used in common by the community at large. Poor people have throughout history gathered fruit, nuts, wood, reeds, roots, game, and so on from common land; in dry regions of India, for example, the landless derive 20% of their annual income in this way, together with much of their food and fuel. Codes of conduct evolved to ensure that common resources were not depleted. But in the 20th century, in the Third World as elsewhere, much common land has been privatized or appropriated by the state, and what remains is overburdened by those dependent on it.

common law that part of the English law not embodied in legislation. It consists of rules of law based on common custom and usage and on judicial decisions. English common law became the basis of law in the USA and many other English-speaking countries.

common logarithm another name for a *logarithm to the base ten.

Common Market popular name for the *European Economic Community*; see *European Community (EC).

Commons, House of the lower but more powerful of the two parts of the British and Canadian *parliaments.

commonwealth body politic founded on law for the common 'weal' or good. Political philosophers of the 17th century, such as Thomas Hobbes and John Locke, used the term to mean an organized political community. In Britain it was specifically applied to the regime (**the Commonwealth**) of Oliver *Cromwell 1649–60.

Commonwealth conference any consultation between the prime ministers (or defence, finance, foreign, or other ministers) of the sovereign independent members of the British Commonwealth. These are informal discussion meetings, and the implementation of policies is decided by individual governments.

Commonwealth Day public holiday celebrated on the second Monday in March in many parts of the Commonwealth. It was called **Empire Day** until 1958 and celebrated on 24 May (Queen Victoria's birthday) until 1966.

Commonwealth Development Corporation organization founded as the Colonial Development Corporation 1948 to aid the development of dependent Commonwealth territories; the change of name and extension of its activities to include those now independent were announced 1962.

Commonwealth Games multisport gathering of competitors from British Commonwealth countries, held every four years. The first meeting (known as the British Empire Games) was in Hamilton, Canada, Aug 1930.

Commonwealth of Independent States (CIS) successor body to the *Union of Soviet Socialist Republics, initially formed as a new commonwealth of Slav republics on 8 Dec 1991 by the presidents of the Russian Federation, Belarus, and Ukraine. On 21 Dec, eight of the nine remaining non-Slav republics – Moldova, Tajikistan, Armenia, Azerbaijan, Turkmenistan, Kazakhstan, Kyrgyzstan, and Uzbekistan – joined the CIS. The CIS formally came into existence in Jan 1992 when President Gorbachev resigned and the Soviet government voted itself out of existence. It has no real, formal political institutions and its role is uncertain. Its headquarters are in Mensk (Minsk), Belarus.

Commonwealth, the (British) voluntary association of 50 countries and their dependencies that once formed part of the *British Empire and are now independent sovereign states. They are all regarded as 'full members of the Commonwealth'. Additionally, there are some 20 territories that are not completely sovereign and remain dependencies of the UK or another of the fully sovereign members, and are regarded as 'Commonwealth countries'. Heads of government meet every two years, apart from those of Nauru and Tuvalu; however, Nauru and Tuvalu have the right to participate in all functional activities. The Commonwealth has no charter or constitution, and is founded more on tradition and sentiment than political or economic factors.

commune group of people or families living together, sharing resources and responsibilities.

Commune, Paris two separate periods in the history of Paris 1789–94 and March– May 1871; see *Paris Commune.

communication in biology, the signalling of information by one organism to another, usually with the intention of altering the recipient's behaviour. Signals used in communication may be **visual** (such as the human smile or the display of colourful plumage in birds), **auditory** (for example, the whines or barks of a dog), **olfactory** (such as the odours released by the scent glands of a deer), **electrical** (as in the pulses emitted by electric fish), or **tactile** (for example, the nuzzling of male and female elephants).

communications satellite relay station in space for sending telephone, television, telex, and other messages around the world. Messages are sent to and from the satellites via ground stations. Most communications satellites are in *geostationary orbit, appearing to hang fixed over one point on the Earth's surface.

Communion, Holy in the Christian church, another name for the *Eucharist.

communism (French *commun* 'common, general') revolutionary socialism based on the theories of the political philosophers Karl Marx and Friedrich Engels, emphasizing common ownership of the means of production and a planned economy. The principle held is that each should work according to their capacity and receive according to their needs. Politically, it seeks the overthrow of capitalism through a proletarian revolution. The first communist state was the USSR after the revolution of 1917. Revolutionary socialist parties and groups united to form communist parties in other countries (in the UK 1920). After World War II, communism was enforced in those countries that came under Soviet occupation. China emerged after 1961 as a rival to the USSR in world communist leadership, and other countries attempted to adapt communism to their own needs. The late 1980s saw a movement for more individual freedoms in many communist countries, culminating in the abolition or overthrow of communist rule in Eastern European countries and Mongolia, and further state repression in China. The failed hardline coup in the USSR against President Gorbachev 1991 resulted in the effective abandonment of communism there.

Communism Peak alternative form of Pik *Kommunizma, the highest mountain in the *Pamirs.

community in the social sciences, the sense of identity, purpose, and companionship that comes from belonging to a particular place, organization, or social group. The concept dominated sociological thinking in the first half of the 20th century, and inspired the academic discipline of *community studies*.

community in ecology, an assemblage of plants, animals, and other organisms living within a circumscribed area. Communities are usually named by reference to a dominant feature such as characteristic plant species (for example, beech-wood community), or a prominent physical feature (for example, a freshwater-pond community).

community architecture movement enabling people to work directly with architects in the design and building of their own homes and neighbourhoods.

community charge in the UK, a charge levied by local authorities (commonly known as the *poll tax); to be replaced 1993 by a council tax.

community council in Wales, name for a *parish council.

Community law law of the member states of the *European Community, as adopted by the Council of Ministers. The *European Court of Justice interprets and applies EC law. Community law forms part of the law of states and prevails over national law. In the UK, community law became effective after enactment of the European Communities Act 1972.

community school/education system based on the philosophy asserting that educational institutions are more effective if they involve all members of the surrounding community.

community service in the penal systems of the UK and the USA, unpaid work in the service of the community (aiding children, the elderly, or the handicapped), performed by a convicted person by order of the court.

commutative operation in mathematics, an operation that is independent of the order of the numbers or symbols concerned. For example, addition is commutative: the result of adding 4 + 2 is the same as that of adding 2 + 4; subtraction is not as 4 −2 = 2, but 2 − 4 = −2. Compare *associative operation and *distributive operation.

commutator device in a DC (direct-current) electric motor that reverses the current flowing in the armature coils as the armature rotates. A DC generator, or *dynamo, uses a commutator to convert the AC (alternating current) generated in the armature coils into DC. A commutator consists of opposite pairs of conductors insulated from one another, connected to an external circuit by carbon or metal brushes.

Comoros Federal Islamic Republic of (*Jumhuriyat al-Qumur al-Itthadiyah al-Islamiyah*)
area 1,862 sq km/719 sq mi
capital Moroni
towns Mutsamudu, Domoni, Fomboni
physical comprises the volcanic islands of Njazídja, Nzwani, and Mwali (formerly Grande Comore, Anjouan, Moheli); at N end of Mozambique Channel
head of state Said Muhammad Djohar from 1989
head of government Muhammad Abdou Madi from 1994
political system emergent democracy
exports copra, vanilla, cocoa, sisal, coffee, cloves, essential oils
currency CFA franc
population (1993 est) 510,000; growth rate 3.1% p.a.
languages Arabic (official), Comorian (Swahili and Arabic dialect), Makua, French
religions Muslim (official) 86%, Roman Catholic 14%
GNP $500 per head (1991)
chronology
1975 Independence achieved from France, but island of Mayotte remained part of France. Ahmed Abdallah elected president. The Comoros joined the United Nations.
1976 Abdallah overthrown by Ali Soilih.
1978 Soilih killed by mercenaries working for Abdallah. Islamic republic proclaimed and Abdallah elected president.
1979 The Comoros became a one-party state; powers of the federal government increased.
1985 Constitution amended to make Abdallah head of government as well as head of state.
1989 Abdallah killed by French mercenaries who took control of government; under French and South African pressure, mercenaries left Comoros, turning authority over to French administration and interim president Said Mohammad Djohar.
1990 and 1992 Antigovernment coups foiled.
1993 General election failed to provide any one

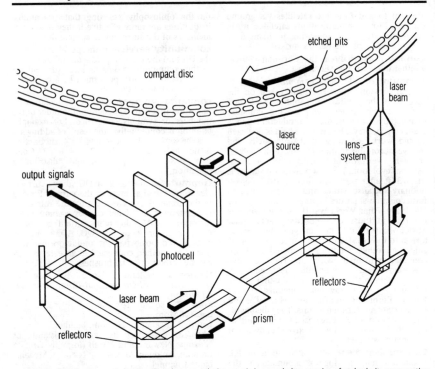

etched pits

compact disc

laser beam

laser source

lens system

output signals

photocell

laser beam

prism

reflectors

reflectors

compact disc *The compact disc is a digital storage device; music is recorded as a series of etched pits representing numbers in digital code.*

party with overall assembly majority. Post of prime minister restored.

1994 Djohar's supporters won overall majority in assembly elections.

compact disc disc for storing digital information, about 12 cm/4.5 in across, mainly used for music, when it can have over an hour's playing time. Entirely different from a conventional LP (long-playing) gramophone record, the compact disc is made of aluminium with a transparent plastic coating; the metal disc underneath is etched by a *laser beam with microscopic pits that carry a digital code representing the sounds. During playback, a laser beam reads the code and produces signals that are changed into near-exact replicas of the original sounds.

Companion of Honour British order of chivalry, founded by George V 1917. It is of one class only, and carries no title, but Companions append 'CH' to their names. The number is limited to 65 and the award is made to both men and women.

company in economics, a number of people grouped together as a business enterprise. Types of company include public limited companies, partnerships, joint ventures, sole proprietorships, and branches of foreign companies.

comparative advantage law of international trade first elaborated by David Ricardo showing that trade becomes advantageous if the cost of production of particular items differs between two countries.

compass any instrument for finding direction. The most commonly used is a magnetic compass, consisting of a thin piece of magnetic material with the north-seeking pole indicated, free to rotate on a pivot and mounted on a compass card on which the points of the compass are marked. When the compass is properly adjusted and used, the north-seeking pole will point to the magnetic north, from which true north can be found from tables of magnetic corrections.

compensation point in biology, the point at which there is just enough light for a plant to survive. At this point all the food produced by *photosynthesis is used up by *respiration. For aquatic plants, the compensation point is the depth of water at which there is just enough light to sustain life (deeper water = less light = less photosynthesis).

competition in ecology, the interaction between two or more organisms, or groups of organisms (for example, species), that use a common resource which is in short supply. Competition invariably results in a reduction in the numbers of one or both competitors, and in *evolution contributes both to the decline of certain species and to the evolution of *adaptations.

competition, perfect in economics, a market situation in which there are many potential and actual buyers and sellers, each being too small to be an individual influence on the price; the market is open to all and the products being traded are homogeneous. At the same time, the producers are seeking the maximum profit and consumers the best value for money.

compiler computer program that translates programs written in a *high-level language into machine code (the form in which they can be run by the computer). The compiler translates each high-level instruction into several machine-code instructions – in a process called *compilation* – and produces a complete independent program that can be run by the computer as often as required, without the original source program being present.

complement the set of the elements within the universal set that are not contained in the designated set. For example, if the universal set is the set of all positive whole numbers and the designated set S is the set of all even numbers, then the complement of S (denoted S') is the set of all odd numbers.

complementary angles two angles that add up to 90°.

complementary metal-oxide semiconductor (CMOS) in computing, a particular way of manufacturing integrated circuits (chips). The main advantage of CMOS chips is their low power requirement and heat dissipation, which enables them to be used in electronic watches and portable microcomputers. However, CMOS circuits are expensive to manufacture and have lower operating speeds than have circuits of the *transistor– transistor logic (TTL) family.

complementation in genetics, the interaction that can occur between two different mutant alleles of a gene in a *diploid organism, to make up for each other's deficiencies and allow the organism to function normally.

complex in psychology, a group of ideas and feelings that have become repressed because they are distasteful to the person in whose mind they arose, but are still active in the depths of the person's unconscious mind, continuing to affect his or her life and actions, even though he or she is no longer fully aware of their existence. Typical examples include the *Oedipus complex and the inferiority complex.

complex number in mathematics, a number written in the form $a + ib$, where a and b are *real numbers and i is the square root of –1 (that is, $i^2 = -1$); i used to be known as the 'imaginary' part of the complex number. Some equations in algebra, such as those of the form $x^2 + 5 = 0$, cannot be solved without recourse to complex numbers, because the real numbers do not include square roots of negative numbers.

compliance in economics in the UK, abiding by the terms of the Financial Services Act 1986. Companies undertaking any form of investment business are regulated by the act and must fulfil their obligations to investors under it, under four main headings: efficiency, competitiveness, confidence, and flexibility.

component in mathematics, one of the the vectors produced when a single vector is resolved into two or more parts. The perpendicular components add up to the original vector.

Compositae daisy family, comprising dicotyledonous flowering plants characterized by flowers borne in composite heads. It is the largest family of flowering plants, the majority being herbaceous. Birds seem to favour the family for use in nest 'decoration', possibly because many species either repel or kill insects (see *pyrethrum). Species include the daisy and dandelion; food plants such as the artichoke, lettuce, and safflower; and the garden varieties of chrysanthemum, dahlia, and zinnia.

composite in industry, any purpose-designed engineering material created by combining single materials with complementary properties into a composite form. Most composites have a structure in which one component consists of discrete elements, such as fibres, dispersed in a continuous matrix. For example, lengths of asbestos, glass, or carbon steel, or 'whiskers' (specially grown crystals a few millimetres long) of substances such as silicon carbide may be dispersed in plastics, concrete, or steel.

Composite in classical architecture, one of the five types of *column. See *order.

composite function in mathematics, a function made up of two or more other functions carried out in sequence, usually denoted by * or o, as in the relation $(f * g) x = f [g(x)]$.

compos mentis (Latin) of sound mind.

compost organic material decomposed by bacteria under controlled conditions to make a nutrient-rich natural fertilizer for use in gardening or farming. A well-made compost heap reaches a high temperature during the composting process, killing most weed seeds that might be present.

compound chemical substance made up of two or more *elements bonded together, so that they cannot be separated by physical means. Compounds are held together by ionic or covalent bonds.

compound interest interest calculated by computing the rate against the original capital plus reinvested interest each time the interest becomes due. When simple interest is calculated, only the interest on the original capital is added.

comprehensive school in the UK, a secondary school which admits pupils of all abilities, and therefore without any academic selection procedure.

Compromise of 1850 in US history, legislative proposals designed to resolve the sectional conflict between North and South over the admission of California to the Union 1850. Slavery was prohibited in California, but a new fugitive slave law was passed to pacify the slave states. The Senate debate on the compromise lasted nine months: acceptance temporarily revitalized the Union.

Compton Arthur Holly 1892–1962. US physicist known for his work on X-rays. Working at Chicago 1923 he found that X-rays scattered by such light elements as carbon increased their wavelengths. Compton concluded from this unexpected result that the X-rays were displaying both wavelike and particlelike properties, since named the *Compton effect*. He shared a Nobel prize 1927 with Scottish physicist Charles Wilson (1869–1959).

Compton-Burnett Ivy 1892–1969. English novelist. She used dialogue to show reactions of small groups of characters dominated by the

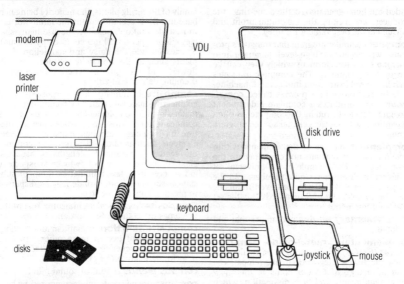

computer *A desktop computer is made of a number of connected units.*

tyranny of family relationships. Her novels, set at the turn of the century, include *Pastors and Masters* 1925, *More Women Than Men* 1933, and *Mother and Son* 1955.

computer programmable electronic device that processes data and performs calculations and other symbol-manipulation tasks. There are three types: the ***digital computer***, which manipulates information coded as binary numbers (see *binary number system); the ***analogue computer***, which works with continuously varying quantities; and the **hybrid computer**, which has characteristics of both analogue and digital computers.

computer-aided design use of computers to create and modify design drawings; see *CAD.

computer-aided manufacture use of computers to regulate production processes in industry; see *CAM.

computer-assisted learning use of computers in education and training; see *CAL.

computer generation any of the five broad groups into which computers may be classified:
first generation the earliest computers, developed in the 1940s and 1950s, made from valves and wire circuits;
second generation from the early 1960s, based on transistors and printed circuits;
third generation from the late 1960s, using integrated circuits and often sold as families of computers, such as the IBM 360 series;
fourth generation using *microprocessors, large-scale integration (LSI), and sophisticated programming languages, still in use in the 1990s; and
fifth generation based on parallel processors and very large-scale integration, currently under development.

computer graphics use of computers to display and manipulate information in pictorial form. The output may be as simple as a pie chart, or as complex as an animated sequence in a science-fiction film, or a seemingly three-dimensional engineering blueprint. Input may be achieved by drawing with a mouse or stylus on a graphics tablet, or by drawing directly on the screen with a light pen. The drawing is stored in the computer as *raster graphics or *vector graphics. Computer graphics are increasingly used in computer-aided design (*CAD), and to generate models and simulations in engineering, meteorology, medicine and surgery, and other fields of science.

computerized axial tomography medical technique, usually known as *CAT scan, for looking inside bodies without disturbing them.

computer program coded instructions for a computer; see *program.

computer simulation representation of a real-life situation in a computer program. For example, the program might simulate the flow of customers arriving at a bank. The user can alter variables, such as the number of cashiers on duty, and see the effect.

Comte Auguste 1798–1857. French philosopher regarded as the founder of sociology, a term he coined 1830. He sought to establish sociology as an intellectual discipline, using a scientific approach ('positivism') as the basis of a new science of social order and social development.

Conakry capital and chief port of the Republic of Guinea; population (1983) 705,300. It is on the island of Tumbo, linked with the mainland by a causeway and by rail with Kankan, 480 km/300 mi to the NE. Bauxite and iron ore are mined nearby.

concave of a surface, curving inwards, or away from the eye. For example, a bowl appears concave when viewed from above. In geometry, a concave polygon is one that has an interior angle

COMPUTING: CHRONOLOGY

1614	John Napier invented logarithms.
1615	William Oughtred invented the slide rule.
1623	Wilhelm Schickard (1592–1635) invented the mechanical calculating machine.
1645	Blaise Pascal produced a calculator.
1672–74	Gottfried Leibniz built his first calculator, the Stepped Reckoner.
1801	Joseph-Marie Jacquard developed an automatic loom controlled by punch cards.
1820	The first mass-produced calculator, the Arithometer, was developed by Charles Thomas de Colmar (1785–1870).
1822	Charles Babbage completed his first model for the difference engine.
1830s	Babbage created the first design for the analytical engine.
1890	Herman Hollerith developed the punched-card ruler for the US census.
1936	Alan Turing published the mathematical theory of computing.
1938	Konrad Zuse constructed the first binary calculator, using Boolean algebra.
1939	US mathematician and physicist J V Atanasoff (1903–) became the first to use electronic means for mechanizing arithmetical operations.
1943	The Colossus electronic code-breaker was developed at Bletchley Park, England. The Harvard University Mark I or Automatic Sequence Controlled Calculator (partly financed by IBM) became the first program-controlled calculator.
1946	ENIAC (acronym for electronic numerator, integrator, analyser, and computer), the first general purpose, fully electronic digital computer, was completed at the University of Pennsylvania, USA.
1948	Manchester University (England) Mark I, the first stored-program computer, was completed. William Shockley of Bell Laboratories invented the transistor.
1951	Launch of Ferranti Mark I, the first commercially produced computer. Whirlwind, the first real-time computer, was built for the US air-defence system. Grace Murray Hopper of Remington Rand invented the compiler computer program.
1952	EDVAC (acronym for electronic discrete variable computer) was completed at the Institute for Advanced Study, Princeton, USA (by John Von Neumann and others).
1953	Magnetic core memory was developed.
1958	The first integrated circuit was constructed.
1963	The first minicomputer was built by Digital Equipment (DEC). PDP-8, the first electronic calculator, was built by Bell Punch Company.
1964	Launch of IBM System/360, the first compatible family of computers. John Kemeny and Thomas Kurtz of Dartmouth College invented BASIC (Beginner's All-purpose Symbolic Instruction Code), a computer language similar to FORTRAN.
1965	The first supercomputer, the Control Data CD6600, was developed.
1971	The first microprocessor, the Intel 4004, was announced.
1974	CLIP-4, the first computer with a parallel architecture, was developed by John Backus at IBM.
1975	The first personal computer, Altair 8800, was launched.
1981	The Xerox Star system, the first WIMP system (acronym for windows, icons, menus, and pointing devices), was developed.
1985	The Inmos T414 transputer, the first 'off-the-shelf' microprocessor for building parallel computers, was announced.
1988	The first optical microchip, which uses light instead of electricity, was developed.
1989	Wafer-scale silicon memory chips, able to store 200 million characters, were launched.
1990	Microsoft released Windows 3, a windowing environment for PCs.
1991	IBM developed world's fastest high-capacity memory computer chip, SRAM (static random-access memory), able to send or receive 8 billion bits of information per second.
1992	Philips launched the CD-I (compact disc-interactive) player, based on CD audio technology.
1993	Intel launched the Pentium chip, containing 3.1 million transistors and capable of 100 MIPs (millions of instructions per second).

greater than 180°. Concave is the opposite of *convex.

concave lens converging *lens – a parallel beam of light gets wider as it passes through such a lens. A concave lens is thinner at its centre than at the edges.

concentration in chemistry, the amount of a substance (*solute) present in a specified amount of a solution. Either amount may be specified as a mass or a volume (liquids only). Common units used are *moles per cubic decimetre, grams per cubic decimetre, grams per 100 cubic centimetres, and grams per 100 grams. The term also refers to the process of increasing the concentration of a solution by removing some of the substance (*solvent) in which the solute is dissolved. In a **concentrated solution**, the solute is present in large quantities. Concentrated brine is around 30% sodium chloride in water;

concentrated caustic soda (caustic liquor) is around 40% sodium hydroxide; and concentrated sulphuric acid is 98% acid.

concentration camp prison camp for civilians in wartime or under totalitarian rule. The first concentration camps were devised by the British during the Second Boer War in South Africa 1899 for the detention of Afrikaner women and children (with the subsequent deaths of more than 20,000 people). A system of approximately 5,000 concentration camps was developed by the Nazis in Germany and occupied Europe (1933–45) to imprison political and ideological opponents after Hitler became chancellor Jan 1933. Several hundred camps were established in Germany and occupied Europe, the most infamous being the extermination camps of Auschwitz, Belsen, Dachau, Maidanek, Sobibor, and Treblinka. The total number of people who died at the camps exceeded 6 million, and some inmates were subjected to medical experimentation before being killed.

concentric-ring theory hypothetical pattern of land use within an urban area, where different activities occur at different distances from the urban centre. The result is a sequence of rings. The theory was first suggested by the US sociologist E W Burgess in 1925. He said that towns expand outwards evenly from an original core so that each zone grows by gradual colonization into the next outer ring.

concertina portable reed organ related to the *accordion but smaller in size and rounder in shape, with buttons for keys. It was invented in England in the 19th century.

concerto composition, usually in three movements, for solo instrument (or instruments) and orchestra. It developed during the 18th century from the **concerto grosso** form for string orchestra, in which a group of solo instruments is contrasted with a full orchestra.

Conchobar in Celtic mythology, king of Ulster whose intended bride, Deirdre, eloped with Noísí. She died of sorrow when Conchobar killed her husband and his brothers.

conclave ((Latin 'a room locked with a key')) secret meeting, in particular the gathering of cardinals in Rome to elect a new pope. They are locked away in the Vatican Palace until they have reached a decision. The result of each ballot is announced by a smoke signal – black for an undecided vote and white when the choice is made.

concordance book containing an alphabetical list of the important words in a major work, with reference to the places in which they occur. The first concordance was one for the Latin Vulgate Bible compiled by a Dominican monk in the 13th century.

concordat agreement regulating relations between the papacy and a secular government, for example, that for France between Pius VII and the emperor Napoleon, which lasted 1801–1905, and the concordat of 1984 in Italy in which Roman Catholicism ceased to be the Italian state religion.

Concorde the only supersonic airliner, which cruises at Mach 2, or twice the speed of sound, about 2,170 kph/1,350 mph. Concorde, the result of Anglo-French cooperation, made its first flight 1969 and entered commercial service seven years later. It is 62 m/202 ft long and has a wing span of nearly 26 m/84 ft.

concrete building material composed of cement, stone, sand, and water. It has been used since Egyptian and Roman times. During the 20th century, it has been increasingly employed as an economical alternative to materials such as brick and wood.

concrete music (French **musique concrète**) music created by reworking natural sounds recorded on disc or tape, developed in 1948 by Pierre Schaeffer and Pierre Henry in the drama studios of Paris Radio. **Concrete sound** is pre-recorded natural sound used in electronic music, as distinct from purely synthesized tones or noises.

concurrent lines two or more lines passing through a single point; for example, the diameters of a circle are all concurrent at the centre of the circle.

Condé Louis de Bourbon, Prince of Condé 1530–1569. Prominent French *Huguenot leader, founder of the house of Condé and uncle of Henry IV of France. He fought in the wars between Henry II and the Holy Roman emperor Charles V, including the defence of Metz.

Condé Louis II 1621–1686. Prince of Condé called the **Great Condé**. French commander who won brilliant victories during the Thirty Years' War at Rocroi 1643 and Lens 1648, but rebelled 1651 and entered the Spanish service. Pardoned 1660, he commanded Louis XIV's armies against the Spanish and the Dutch.

condensation in physical chemistry, conversion of a vapour to a liquid as it loses heat. This is frequently achieved by letting the vapour come into contact with a cold surface. It is an essential step in *distillation processes.

condensation in organic chemistry, a reaction in which two organic compounds combine to form a larger molecule, accompanied by the removal of a smaller molecule (usually water). This is also known as an addition–elimination reaction. Polyamides (such as nylon) and polyesters (such as Terylene) are made by condensation *polymerization.

condenser in optics, a *lens or combination of lenses with a short focal length used for concentrating a light source onto a small area, as used in a slide projector or microscope substage lighting unit. A condenser can also be made using a concave mirror. In electricity, another name for *capacitor.

conditioning in psychology, two major principles of behaviour modification. In **classical conditioning**, described by Ivan Pavlov, a new stimulus can evoke an automatic response by being repeatedly associated with a stimulus that naturally provokes a response. For example, the sound of a bell repeatedly associated with food will eventually trigger salivation, even if sounded without food being presented. In **operant conditioning**, described by Edward Lee Thorndike (1874–1949) and B F Skinner, the frequency of a voluntary response can be increased by following it with a reinforcer or reward.

condom or **sheath** or **prophylactic** barrier contraceptive, made of rubber, which fits over an erect penis and holds in the sperm produced by ejaculation. It is an effective means of preventing pregnancy if used carefully, preferably with a *spermicide. A condom with spermicide is 97% effective; one without spermicide is 85% effective. Condoms also give protection against sexually transmitted diseases, including AIDS.

condominium joint rule of a territory by two or more states, for example, Kanton and Enderbury islands in the South Pacific Phoenix group (under the joint control of Britain and the USA for 50 years from 1939).

condor large bird, a New World vulture *Vultur gryphus*, with wingspan up to 3 m/10 ft, weight up to 13 kg/28 lb, and length up to 1.2 m/3.8 ft. It is black, with some white on the wings and a white frill at the base of the neck. It lives in the

Andes and along the South American coast, and feeds on carrion. The Californian condor *Gymnogyps californianus* is a similar bird, on the verge of extinction.

Condorcet Marie Jean Antoine Nicolas Caritat, Marquis de Condorcet 1743–1794. French philosopher, mathematician, and politician, associated with the authors of the *Encyclopédie*. One of the *Girondins, he opposed the execution of Louis XVI, and was imprisoned and poisoned himself. While in prison, he wrote *Esquisse d'un tableau des progrès de l'esprit humain/Historical Survey of the Progress of Human Understanding* 1795, which envisaged inevitable future progress, though not the perfectibility of human nature.

conductance ability of a material to carry an electrical current, usually given the symbol G. For a direct current, it is the reciprocal of resistance: a conductor of resistance R has a conductance of $1/R$. For an alternating current, conductance is the resistance R divided by the impedance Z: $G = R/Z$. Conductance was formerly expressed in reciprocal ohms (or mhos); the SI unit is the siemens (S).

conduction, electrical flow of charged particles through a material that gives rise to electric current. Conduction in metals involves the flow of negatively charged free *electrons. Conduction in gases and some liquids involves the flow of *ions that carry positive charges in one direction and negative charges in the other. Conduction in a semiconductor such as silicon involves the flow of electrons and positive holes.

conduction, heat flow of heat energy through a material without the movement of any part of the material itself (compare *conduction, electrical). Heat energy is present in all materials in the form of the kinetic energy of their vibrating molecules, and may be conducted from one molecule to the next in the form of this mechanical vibration. In the case of metals, which are particularly good conductors of heat, the free electrons within the material carry heat around very quickly.

conductive education specialized method of training physically disabled children suffering from conditions such as cerebral palsy. The method was pioneered at the Peto Institute in Budapest, Hungary, and has been taken up elsewhere.

conductor any material that conducts heat or electricity (as opposed to an insulator, or nonconductor). A good conductor has a high electrical or heat conductivity, and is generally a substance rich in free electrons such as a metal. A poor conductor (such as the nonmetals glass and porcelain) has few free electrons. Carbon is exceptional in being nonmetallic and yet (in some of its forms) a relatively good conductor of heat and electricity. Substances such as silicon and germanium, with intermediate conductivities that are improved by heat, light, or voltage, are known as *semiconductors.

cone in geometry, a solid or surface consisting of the set of all straight lines passing through a fixed point (the vertex) and the points of a circle or ellipse whose plane does not contain the vertex.

cone in botany, the reproductive structure of the conifers and cycads; also known as a strobilus. It consists of a central axis surrounded by numerous, overlapping, scalelike, modified leaves (sporophylls) that bear the reproductive organs. Usually there are separate male and female cones, the former bearing pollen sacs containing pollen grains, and the larger female cones bearing the ovules that contain the ova or egg cells. The pollen is carried from male to female cones by the wind (*anemophily). The seeds develop within the female cone and are released as the scales open in dry atmospheric conditions, which favour seed dispersal.

Confederacy in US history, popular name for the **Confederate States of America**, the government established by 6 (later 11) Southern states Feb 1861 when they seceded from the Union, precipitating the *Civil War. Richmond, Virginia, was the capital, and Jefferson Davis the president. The Confederacy fell after its army was defeated 1865 and General Robert E Lee surrendered.

Confederation, Articles of in US history, the initial means by which the 13 former British colonies created a form of national government. Ratified 1781, the articles established a unicameral legislature, Congress, with limited powers of raising revenue, regulating currency, and conducting foreign affairs. But because the individual states retained significant autonomy, the confederation was unmanageable. The articles were superseded by the US Constitution 1788.

Confederation of British Industry (CBI) UK organization of employers, established 1965, combining the former Federation of British Industries (founded 1916), British Employers' Confederation, and National Association of British Manufacturers.

Conference on Security and Cooperation in Europe (CSCE) international forum attempting to reach agreement in security, economics, science, technology, and human rights. The CSCE first met at the *Helsinki Conference in Finland 1975. By the end of March 1992, having admitted the former republics of the USSR, as well as Croatia and Slovenia, its membership had risen to 51 states.

confession in religion, the confession of sins practised in Roman Catholic, Orthodox, and most Far Eastern Christian churches, and since the early 19th century revived in Anglican and Lutheran churches. The Lateran Council of 1215 made auricular confession (self-accusation by the penitent to a priest, who in Catholic doctrine is divinely invested with authority to give absolution) obligatory once a year.

confession in law, a criminal's admission of guilt. Since false confessions may be elicited by intimidation or ill treatment of the accused, the validity of confession in a court of law varies from one legal system to another. For example, in England and Wales a confession, without confirmatory evidence, is sufficient to convict; in Scotland it is not. In the USA a confession that is shown to be coerced does not void a conviction as long as it is supported by independent evidence.

confidence vote in politics, a test of support for the government in the legislature. In political systems modelled on that of the UK, the survival of a government depends on assembly support. The opposition may move a vote of 'no confidence'; if the vote is carried, it requires the government, by convention, to resign.

confirmation rite practised by a number of Christian denominations, including Roman Catholic, Anglican, and Orthodox, in which a previously baptized person is admitted to full membership of the church. In Reform Judaism there is often a confirmation service several years after the bar or bat mitzvah (initiation into the congregation).

Confucianism body of beliefs and practices based on the Chinese classics and supported by the authority of the philosopher Confucius. The origin of things is seen in the union of *yin* and *yang*, the passive and active principles. Human relationships follow the patriarchal pattern. For more than 2,000 years Chinese political government, social organization, and individual conduct was shaped by Confucian principles. In 1912, Confucian philosophy, as a basis for government, was dropped by the state.

Confucius (Latinized form of *Kong Zi*, 'Kong the master') 551–479 BC. Chinese sage whose name is given to Confucianism. He devoted his life to relieving suffering among the poor through governmental and administrative reform. His emphasis on tradition and ethics attracted a growing number of pupils during his lifetime. *The Analects of Confucius*, a compilation of his teachings, was published after his death. Within 300 years of the death of Confucius his teaching was adopted by the Chinese state.

congenital disease in medicine, a disease that is present at birth. It is not necessarily genetic in origin; for example, congenital herpes may be acquired by the baby as it passes through the mother's birth canal.

conger any large marine eel of the family Congridae, especially the genus *Conger*. Conger eels live in shallow water, hiding in crevices during the day and active by night, feeding on fish and crabs. They are valued for food and angling.

conglomerate in mineralogy, coarse clastic *sedimentary rock, composed of rounded fragments (clasts) of pre-existing rocks cemented in a finer matrix, usually sand.

Congo Republic of (*République du Congo*)
area 342,000 sq km/132,012 sq mi
capital Brazzaville

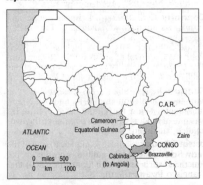

towns chief port Pointe-Noire; N'Kayi, Loubomo
physical narrow coastal plain rises to central plateau, then falls into northern basin; Zaïre (Congo) River on the border with Zaire; half the country is rainforest
environment an estimated 93% of the rural population is without access to safe drinking water
features 70% of the population lives in Brazzaville, Pointe-Noire, or in towns along the railway linking these two places
head of state Pascal Lissouba from 1992
head of government Jacques-Joachim Yhombi-Opango from 1993
political system emergent democracy
exports timber, petroleum, cocoa, sugar
currency CFA franc
population (1993) 2,700,000 (chiefly Bantu); growth rate 2.6% p.a.
languages French (official); many African languages
religions animist 50%, Christian 48%, Muslim 2%
GNP $1,120 per head (1991)
chronology
1910 Became part of French Equatorial Africa.
1960 Achieved independence from France, with Abbé Youlou as the first president.
1963 Youlou forced to resign. New constitution approved, with Alphonse Massamba-Débat as president.
1964 The Congo became a one-party state.
1968 Military coup, led by Capt Marien Ngouabi, ousted Massamba-Débat.
1970 A Marxist state, the People's Republic of the Congo, was announced, with the PCT as the only legal party.
1977 Ngouabi assassinated. Col Yhombi-Opango became president.
1979 Yhombi-Opango handed over the presidency to the PCT, who chose Col Denis Sassou-Nguessou as his successor.
1984 Sassou-Nguessou elected for another five-year term.
1990 The Congolese Labour Party (PCT) abandoned Marxist-Leninism and promised multiparty politics.
1991 1979 constitution suspended. Country renamed the Republic of Congo.
1992 New constitution approved and multiparty elections held, giving Pan-African Union for Social Democracy (UPADS) the most assembly seats. Pascal Lissouba elected president.
1993 June and Oct elections declared void; rerun scheduled.

Congregationalism form of church government adopted by those Protestant Christians known as Congregationalists, who let each congregation manage its own affairs. The first Congregationalists were the Brownists, named after Robert Browne, who defined the congregational principle 1580.

Congress national legislature of the USA, consisting of the House of Representatives (435 members, apportioned to the states of the Union on the basis of population, and elected for two-year terms) and the Senate (100 senators, two for each state, elected for six years, one-third elected every two years). Both representatives and senators are elected by direct popular vote. Congress meets in Washington DC, in the Capitol Building. An *act of Congress is a bill passed by both houses.

Congress of Industrial Organizations (CIO) branch of the *American Federation of Labor and Congress of Industrial Organizations, the federation of US trade unions.

Congress of Racial Equality (CORE) US non-violent civil-rights organization, founded in Chicago 1942.

Congress Party Indian political party, founded 1885 as the Indian National Congress. It led the movement to end British rule and was the governing party from independence 1947 until 1977, when Indira Gandhi lost the leadership she had held since 1966. Heading a splinter group, known as *Congress I*, she achieved an overwhelming victory in the elections of 1980, and reduced the main Congress Party to a minority.

Congreve William 1670–1729. English dramatist and poet. His first success was the comedy *The Old Bachelor* 1693, followed by *The Double Dealer* 1694, *Love for Love* 1695, the tragedy *The Mourning Bride* 1697, and *The Way of the World* 1700. His plays, which satirize the social affectations of the time, are characterized by elegant wit and wordplay, and complex plots.

congruent in geometry, having the same shape and size, as applied to two-dimensional or solid figures. With plane congruent figures, one figure will fit on top of the other exactly, though this may first require rotation and/or rotation of one of the figures.

conic section curve obtained when a conical surface is intersected by a plane. If the intersecting plane cuts both extensions of the cone, it yields a *hyperbola; if it is parallel to the side of the cone, it produces a *parabola. Other intersecting planes produce *circles or *ellipses.

conifer tree or shrub of the order Coniferales, in the gymnosperm or naked-seed-bearing group of plants. They are often pyramidal in form, with leaves that are either scaled or made up of needles; most are evergreen. Conifers include pines, spruces, firs, yews, junipers, monkey puzzles, and larches.

conjugation in biology, the bacterial equivalent of sexual reproduction. A fragment of the *DNA from one bacterium is passed along a thin tube, the pilus, into the cell of another bacterium.

conjunction grammatical *part of speech that serves to connect words, phrases, and clauses. Coordinating conjunctions link parts of equal grammatical value; *and*, *but*, and *or* are the most common. Subordinating conjunctions link subordinate clauses to the main clause in a sentence; among the most common are *if*, *when*, and *though*.

conjunction in astronomy, the alignment of two celestial bodies as seen from Earth. A *superior planet (or other object) is in conjunction when it lies behind the Sun. An *inferior planet (or other object) comes to *inferior conjunction* when it passes between the Earth and the Sun; it is at *superior conjunction* when it passes behind the Sun. *Planetary conjunction* takes place when a planet is closely aligned with another celestial object, such as the Moon, a star, or another planet.

conjunctivitis inflammation of the conjunctiva, the delicate membrane that lines the inside of the eyelids and covers the front of the eye. Symptoms include redness, swelling, and a watery or pus-filled discharge. It may be caused by infection, allergy, or other irritant.

Connacht province of the Republic of Ireland, comprising the counties of Galway, Leitrim, Mayo, Roscommon, and Sligo; area 17,130 sq km/6,612 sq mi; population (1991) 422,900. The chief towns are Galway, Roscommon, Castlebar, Sligo, and Carrick-on-Shannon. Mainly lowland, it is agricultural and stock-raising country, with poor land in the W.

Connecticut state in New England, USA; nicknamed Constitution State/Nutmeg State
area 13,000 sq km/5,018 sq mi
capital Hartford
towns Bridgeport, New Haven, Waterbury
physical highlands in the NW; Connecticut River restored ships)
products dairy, poultry, and market garden products; tobacco, watches, clocks, silverware, helicopters, jet engines, nuclear submarines
population (1990) 3,287,100
famous people Phineas T Barnum, George Bush, Katharine Hepburn, Harriet Beecher Stowe, Mark Twain
history settled by Puritan colonists from Massachusetts 1635, it was one of the Thirteen Colonies, and became a state 1788.

connectionist machine computing device built from a large number of interconnected simple processors, which are able both to communicate with each other and process information separately. The underlying model is that of the human brain.

connective tissue in animals, tissue made up of a noncellular substance, the *extracellular matrix, in which some cells are embedded. Skin, bones, tendons, cartilage, and adipose tissue (fat) are the main connective tissues. There are also small amounts of connective tissue in organs such as the brain and liver, where they maintain shape and structure.

Connery Sean 1930– . Scottish film actor, the first and best interpreter of James Bond in several films based on the novels of Ian Fleming. His films include *Dr No* 1962, *From Russia with Love* 1963, *Marnie* 1964, *Goldfinger* 1964, *Diamonds Are Forever* 1971, *A Bridge Too Far* 1977, *The Name of the Rose* 1986, and *The Untouchables* 1987 (Academy Award).

Connolly Cyril 1903–1974. English critic and author. As founder and editor of the literary magazine *Horizon* 1930–50, he had considerable critical influence. His works include *The Rock Pool* 1935, a novel of artists on the Riviera, and *The Unquiet Grave* 1944, a series of reflections published under the pseudonym of Palinurus.

Connors Jimmy 1952– . US tennis player who won the Wimbledon title 1974 and 1982, and subsequently won ten Grand Slam events. He was one of the first players to popularize the two-handed backhand.

conquistador (Spanish 'conqueror') any of the early Spanish explorers and adventurers in the Americas, such as Hernán Cortés (Mexico) and Francisco Pizarro (Peru).

Conrad Joseph. Pen name of Teodor Jozef Conrad Korzeniowski 1857–1924. English novelist, born in the Ukraine of Polish parents. He joined the French merchant navy at the age of 17 and first learned English at 21. His greatest works include the novels *Lord Jim* 1900, *Nostromo* 1904, *The Secret Agent* 1907, and *Under Western Eyes* 1911, and the short stories 'Heart of Darkness' 1902 and 'The Shadow Line' 1917. These combine a vivid sensuous evocation of various lands and seas with a rigorous, humane scrutiny of moral dilemmas, pitfalls, and desperation.

Conrad several kings of the Germans and Holy Roman emperors, including:

Conrad I King of the Germans from 911, when he succeeded Louis the Child, the last of the German Carolingians. During his reign the realm was harassed by *Magyar invaders.

Conrad II King of the Germans from 1024, Holy Roman emperor from 1027. He ceded the Sleswick (Schleswig) borderland, south of the Jutland peninsula, to King Canute, but extended his rule into Lombardy and Burgundy.

Conrad III 1093–1152. Holy Roman emperor from 1138, the first king of the Hohenstaufen dynasty. Throughout his reign there was a fierce struggle between his followers, the *Ghibellines*, and the *Guelphs*, the followers of Henry the Proud, duke of Saxony and Bavaria (1108–1139), and later of his son Henry the Lion (1129–1195).

Conrad IV 1228–1254. Elected king of the Germans 1237. Son of the Holy Roman emperor Frederick II, he had to defend his right of succession against Henry Raspe of Thuringia (died 1247) and William of Holland (1227–56).

Conrad V (Conradin) 1252–1268. Son of Conrad IV, recognized as king of the Germans, Sicily, and Jerusalem by German supporters of the *Hohenstaufens 1254. He led Ghibelline forces (see *Guelph and Ghibelline) against Charles of Anjou at the battle of Tagliacozzo, N Italy 1266, and was captured and executed.

conscription legislation for all able-bodied male citizens (and female in some countries, such as Israel) to serve with the armed forces. It originated in France 1792, and in the 19th and 20th centuries became the established practice in almost all European states. Modern conscription systems often permit alternative national service for conscientious objectors.

conservation in the life sciences, action taken to protect and preserve the natural world, usually from pollution, overexploitation, and other harmful features of human activity. The late 1980s saw a great increase in public concern for the environment, with membership of conservation groups, such as *Friends of the Earth, rising sharply. Globally the most important issues include the depletion of atmospheric ozone by the action of chlorofluorocarbons (CFCs), the build-up of carbon dioxide in the atmosphere (thought to contribute to an intensification of the *greenhouse effect), and the destruction of the tropical rainforests (see *deforestation).

conservation, architectural attempts to maintain the character of buildings and historical areas. In England this is subject to a growing body of legislation that has designated more

*listed buildings. There are now over 6,000 conservation areas throughout England alone.

conservation of energy in chemistry, the principle that states that in a chemical reaction, the total amount of energy in the system remains unchanged.

conservation of mass in chemistry, the principle that states that in a chemical reaction the sum of all the masses of the substances involved in the reaction (reactants) is equal to the sum of all of the masses of the substances produced by the reaction (products) – that is, no matter is gained or lost.

conservatism approach to government favouring the maintenance of existing institutions and identified with a number of Western political parties, such as the British Conservative, US Republican, German Christian Democratic, and Australian Liberal parties. It tends to be explicitly nondoctrinaire and pragmatic but generally emphasizes free-enterprise capitalism, minimal government intervention in the economy, rigid law and order, and the importance of national traditions.

Conservative Party UK political party, one of the two historic British parties; the name replaced *Tory* in general use from 1830 onwards. Traditionally the party of landed interests, it broadened its political base under Benjamin Disraeli's leadership in the 19th century. The present Conservative Party's free-market capitalism is supported by the world of finance and the management of industry.

conspiracy in law, an agreement between two or more people to do something unlawful. In the UK it is a complex offence and may be prosecuted under either the Criminal Law Act 1977 or common law. The common-law offence may include entering into an agreement to defraud, corrupt public morals, or outrage public decency. Unless others are involved, there can be no conspiracy between man and wife.

constable (Latin *comes stabuli* 'count of the stable') low-ranking police officer. In medieval Europe, a constable was an officer of the king, originally responsible for army stores and stabling, and later responsible for the army in the king's absence. In England the constable subsequently became an official at a sheriff's court of law, leading to the title's current meaning.

Constable John 1776–1837. English landscape painter. He painted scenes of his native Suffolk, including *The Haywain* 1821 (National Gallery, London), as well as castles, cathedrals, landscapes, and coastal scenes in other parts of Britain. Constable inherited the Dutch tradition of sombre realism, in particular the style of Jacob *Ruisdael, but he aimed to capture the momentary changes of nature as well as to create monumental images of British scenery, such as *The White Horse* 1819 (Frick Collection, New York) and *Flatford Mill* 1825.

Constance, Council of council held by the Roman Catholic church 1414–17 in Constance, Germany. It elected Pope Martin V, which ended the Great Schism 1378–1417 when there were rival popes in Rome and Avignon.

constant in mathematics, a fixed quantity or one that does not change its value in relation to *variables. For example, in the algebraic expression $y^2 = 5x - 3$, the numbers 3 and 5 are constants. In physics, certain quantities are regarded as universal constants, such as the speed of light in a vacuum.

Constanţa chief Romanian port on the Black Sea, capital of Constanţa region, and third-largest city of Romania; population (1985) 323,000. It has refineries, shipbuilding yards, and food factories.

constantan or **eureka** high-resistance alloy of approximately 40% nickel and 60% copper with a very low coefficient of *thermal expansion (measure of expansion on heating). It is used in electrical resistors.

constant composition, law of in chemistry, the law that states that the proportions of the amounts of the elements in a pure compound are always the same and are independent of the method by which the compound was produced.

Constant de Rebecque (Henri) Benjamin 1767–1830. French writer and politician. An advocate of the Revolution, he opposed Napoleon and in 1803 went into exile. Returning to Paris after the fall of Napoleon in 1814 he proposed a constitutional monarchy. He published the autobiographical novel *Adolphe* 1816, which reflects his affair with Madame de *Staël, and later wrote the monumental study *De la Religion* 1825–31.

Constantine II 1940– . King of the Hellenes (Greece). In 1964 he succeeded his father Paul I, went into exile 1967, and was formally deposed 1973.

Constantine the Great c. AD 280–337. First Christian emperor of Rome and founder of Constantinople. He defeated Maxentius, joint emperor of Rome AD 312, and in 313 formally recognized Christianity. As sole emperor of the west of the empire, he defeated Licinius, emperor of the east, to become ruler of the Roman world 324. He presided over the church's first council at Nicaea 325. In 330 Constantine moved his capital to Byzantium, renaming it Constantinople.

Constantinople former name (330–1453) of Istanbul, Turkey. It was named after the Roman emperor Constantine the Great when he enlarged the Greek city of Byzantium 328 and declared it the capital of the *Byzantine Empire 330. Its elaborate fortifications enabled it to resist a succession of sieges, but it was captured by crusaders 1204, and was the seat of a Latin (Western European) kingdom until recaptured by the Greeks 1261. An attack by the Turks 1422 proved unsuccessful, but it was taken by another Turkish army 29 May 1453, after nearly a year's siege, and became the capital of the Ottoman Empire.

constant prices series of prices adjusted to reflect real purchasing power. If wages were to rise by 15% from 100 per week (to 115) and the rate of inflation was 10% (requiring 110 to maintain spending power), the real wage would have risen by 5%. Also an index used to create a constant price series, unlike current prices, which express value pertaining only to a given time.

constellation one of the 88 areas into which the sky is divided for the purposes of identifying and naming celestial objects. The first constellations were simple, arbitrary patterns of stars in which early civilizations visualized gods, sacred beasts, and mythical heroes.

constitution body of fundamental laws of a state, laying down the system of government and defining the relations of the legislature, executive, and judiciary to each other and to the citizens. Since the French Revolution almost all countries (the UK is an exception) have adopted written constitutions; that of the USA (1787) is the oldest.

Constructivism revolutionary art movement founded in Moscow 1917 by the Russians Naum *Gabo, his brother Antoine Pevsner (1886–1962), and Vladimir Tatlin (1885–1953). Tatlin's abstract sculptures, using wood, metal, and clear plastic, were hung on walls or suspended from ceilings. Gabo and Pevsner soon left the USSR and joined the European avant-garde.

consul chief magistrate of ancient Rome after the expulsion of the last king 510 BC. The consuls were two annually elected magistrates, both of equal power; they jointly held full civil power in Rome and the chief military command in the field. After the establishment of the Roman Empire the office became purely honorary.

consumption in economics, the purchase of goods and services for final use, as opposed to spending by firms on capital goods, known as capital formation.

consumption (Latin *consumptio* 'wasting') in medicine, former name for the disease *tuberculosis.

contact lens lens, made of soft or hard plastic, that is worn in contact with the cornea and conjunctiva of the eye, beneath the eyelid, to correct defective vision. In special circumstances, contact lenses may be used as protective shells or for cosmetic purposes, such as changing eye colour.

contact process the main industrial method of manufacturing the chemical *sulphuric acid. Sulphur dioxide (produced by burning sulphur) and air are passed over a hot (450°C) *catalyst of vanadium(V) oxide. The sulphur trioxide produced is absorbed in concentrated sulphuric acid to make fuming sulphuric acid (oleum), which is then diluted with water to give concentrated sulphuric acid (98%). Unreacted gases are recycled.

Contadora Panamanian island of the Pearl Island group in the Gulf of Panama.

Contadora Group alliance formed between Colombia, Mexico, Panama, and Venezuela Jan 1983 to establish a general peace treaty for Central America. It was named after Contadora, the island of the Pearl Group in the Gulf of Panama where the first meeting was held.

contempt of court behaviour that shows lack of respect for the authority of a court of law, such as disobeying a court order, breach of an injunction, or improper use of legal documents. Behaviour that disrupts, prejudices, or interferes with court proceedings either inside or outside the courtroom may also be contempt. The court may punish contempt with a fine or imprisonment.

continent any one of the seven large land

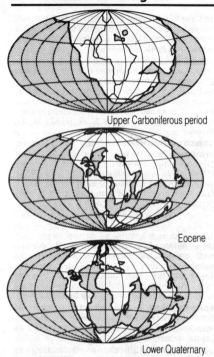

Upper Carboniferous period

Eocene

Lower Quaternary

continental drift The drifting continents.

masses of the Earth, as distinct from the oceans. They are Asia, Africa, North America, South America, Europe, Australia, and Antarctica. Continents are constantly moving and evolving (see *plate tectonics). A continent does not end at the coastline; its boundary is the edge of the shallow continental shelf, which may extend several hundred kilometres or miles out to sea.

Continental Congress in US history, the federal legislature of the original 13 states, acting as a provisional government during the *American Revolution. It was convened in Philadelphia 1774–89, when the constitution was adopted. The second Continental Congress, convened May 1775, was responsible for drawing up the Declaration of Independence.

continental drift in geology, theory proposed by the German meteorologist Alfred Wegener in 1915 that, about 200 million years ago, Earth consisted of a single large continent (*Pangaea) that subsequently broke apart to form the continents known today. Such vast continental movements could not be satisfactorily explained until the study of *plate tectonics in the 1960s.

continental rise the portion of the ocean floor rising gently from the abyssal plain toward the steeper continental slope. The continental rise is a depositional feature formed from sediments transported down the slope mainly by turbidity currents. Much of the continental rise consists of coalescing submarine alluvial fans bordering the continental slope.

continental slope sloping, submarine portion of a continent. It extends downward from the

continental margin at the edge of the continental shelf. In some places, such as south of the Aleutian Islands of Alaska, continental slopes extend directly to the ocean deeps or abyssal plain. In others, such as the E coast of North America, they grade into the gentler continental rises that in turn grade into the abyssal plains.

Continental System system of economic preference and protection within Europe created by the French emperor Napoleon in order to exclude British trade. Apart from its function as economic warfare, the system also reinforced the French economy at the expense of other European states. It lasted 1806–13 but failed owing to British naval superiority.

continuo abbreviation for *basso continuo*; in music, the bass line on which a keyboard player, often accompanied by a bass stringed instrument, built up a harmonic accompaniment in 17th-century Baroque music.

continuum in mathematics, a *set that is infinite and everywhere continuous, such as the set of points on a line.

Contra member of a Central American right-wing guerrilla force attempting to overthrow the democratically elected Nicaraguan Sandinista government 1979–90. The Contras, many of them mercenaries or former members of the deposed dictator Somoza's guard (see *Nicaraguan Revolution), operated mainly from bases outside Nicaragua, mostly in Honduras, with covert US funding, as revealed by the *Irangate hearings 1986–87.

contrabassoon larger version of the *bassoon, sounding an octave lower.

contraceptive any drug, device, or technique that prevents pregnancy. The contraceptive pill (the *Pill) contains female hormones that interfere with egg production or the first stage of pregnancy. The 'morning-after' pill can be taken up to 72 hours after unprotected intercourse. Barrier contraceptives include *condoms (sheaths) and *diaphragms, also called caps or Dutch caps; they prevent the sperm entering the cervix (neck of the womb). *Intrauterine devices, also known as IUDs or coils, cause a slight inflammation of the lining of the womb; this prevents the fertilized egg from becoming implanted. See also *family planning.

contract agreement between two or more parties that will be enforced by law according to the intention of the parties.

contract bridge card game first played 1925. From 1930 it quickly outgrew *auction bridge in popularity.

contractile root in botany, a thickened root at the base of a corm, bulb, or other organ that helps position it at an appropriate level in the ground. Contractile roots are found, for example, on the corms of plants of the genus *Crocus*. After they have become anchored in the soil, the upper portion contracts, pulling the plant deeper into the ground.

contracting out in industrial relations, an agreement between an employer and employee whereby the employee does not participate in a financial contributory scheme administered by the employer. This usually applies to pension and health insurance schemes, or payment of trade union or other subscriptions from the gross salary.

contralto in music, a low-registered female voice; also called an *alto.

contrapuntal in music, a work employing *counterpoint.

control experiment essential part of a scientifically valid experiment, designed to show that the factor being tested is actually responsible for the effect observed. In the control experiment all factors, apart from the one under test, are exactly the same as in the test experiments, and all the same measurements are carried out. In drug trials, a placebo (a harmless substance) is given alongside the substance being tested in order to compare effects.

conurbation or *metropolitan area* large continuous built-up area formed by the joining together of several urban settlements. Conurbations are often formed as a result of urban sprawl. Typically, they have populations in excess of 1 million and some are many times that size; for example, the Osaka–Kobe conurbation in Japan, which contains over 16 million people.

convection heat energy transfer that involves the movement of a fluid (gas or liquid). According to kinetic theory, molecules of fluid in contact with the source of heat expand and tend to rise within the bulk of the fluid. Less energetic, cooler molecules sink to take their place, setting up convection currents. This is the principle of natural convection in many domestic hot-water systems and space heaters.

conventional forces in Europe (CFE) treaty signed by NATO and Warsaw Pact representatives Nov 1990, reducing the number of tanks, missiles, aircraft, and other forms of military hardware held by member states. Talks between government representatives had begun in Vienna, Austria, March 1989 with the aim of reducing the 'conventional' – that is, non-nuclear – forces (US, Soviet, French, British, and German) in Europe. The dissolution of the Warsaw Pact 1991 left doubts over the verification of the treaty, but at the July 1992 Helsinki summit of the *Conference on Security and Cooperation in Europe (CSCE) a revised version of the 1990 treaty was signed by 29 states (all members of NATO or former Soviet republics). Armenia and Belarus had still to ratify the treaty.

convergence in mathematics, the property of a series of numbers in which the difference between consecutive terms gradually decreases. The sum of a converging series approaches a limit as the number of terms tends to *infinity.

convergent evolution in biology, the independent evolution of similar structures in species (or other taxonomic groups) that are not closely related, as a result of living in a similar way. Thus, birds and bats have wings, not because they are descended from a common winged ancestor, but because their respective ancestors independently evolved flight.

converse in mathematics, the reversed order of a conditional statement; the converse of the statement 'if a, then b' is 'if b, then a'. The converse does not always hold true; for example, the converse of 'if $x = 3$, then $x^2 = 9$' is 'if $x^2 = 9$, then $x = 3$', which is not true, as x could also be –3.

convertible loan stock stock or bond (paying a fixed interest) that may be converted into a stated number of shares at a specific date.

convertiplane vertical takeoff and landing craft (VTOL) with rotors on its wings that spin horizontally for takeoff, but tilt to spin in a vertical plane for forward flight.

convex of a surface, curving outwards, or towards the eye. For example, the outer surface of a ball appears convex. In geometry, the term is used to describe any polygon possessing no interior angle greater than 180°. Convex is the opposite of *concave.

convex lens converging *lens – that is, a parallel beam of light passing through it converges and is eventually brought to a focus; it can therefore produce a real image on a screen. Such a lens is wider at its centre than at the edges.

conveyor device used for transporting materials. Widely used throughout industry is the *conveyor belt*, usually a rubber or fabric belt running on rollers. Trough-shaped belts are used, for example in mines, for transporting ores and coal. *Chain conveyors* are also used in coal mines to remove coal from the cutting machines. Overhead endless chain conveyors are used to carry components and bodies in car-assembly works. Other types include *bucket conveyors* and *screw conveyors*, powered versions of the *Archimedes' screw.

convocation in the Church of England, the synods (councils) of the clergy of the provinces of Canterbury and York. The General Synod, established 1970, took over the functions and authority of the Convocation of Canterbury and York which continued to exist only in a restricted form.

convolvulus or *bindweed* any plant of the genus *Convolvulus* of the morning-glory family Convolvulaceae. They are characterized by their twining stems and by their petals, which are united into a funnel-shaped tube.

convoy system grouping of ships to sail together under naval escort in wartime. In World War I (1914–18) navy escort vessels were at first used only to accompany troopships, but the convoy system was adopted for merchant shipping when the unrestricted German submarine campaign began 1917. In World War II (1939–45) the convoy system was widely used by the Allies to keep the Atlantic sea lanes open.

convulsion series of violent contractions of the muscles over which the patient has no control. It may be associated with loss of consciousness. Convulsions may arise from any one of a number of causes, including brain disease (such as *epilepsy), injury, high fever, poisoning, and electrocution.

Cook, Mount highest point, 3,764 m/12,353 ft, of the Southern Alps, a range of mountains running through New Zealand.

Cook James 1728–1779. British naval explorer. After surveying the St Lawrence 1759, he made three voyages: 1768–71 to Tahiti, New Zealand, and Australia; 1772–75 to the South Pacific; and 1776–79 to the South and North Pacific, attempting to find the Northwest Passage and charting the Siberian coast. He was killed in Hawaii.

Cook Robin (Finlayson) 1946– . English

Labour politician. A member of the moderate-left Tribune Group, he entered Parliament 1974 and became a leading member of Labour's shadow cabinet, specializing in health matters. When John Smith assumed the party leadership in July 1992, Cook remained in the shadow cabinet as spokesperson for trade and industry. He became shadow foreign secretary under Smith's successor, Anthony Blair, Oct 1994.

Cook Thomas 1808–1892. Pioneer British travel agent and founder of Thomas Cook & Son. He introduced traveller's cheques (then called 'circular notes') in the early 1870s.

Cooke Sam 1931–1964. US soul singer and songwriter who began his career as a gospel singer and turned to pop music 1956. His hits include 'You Send Me' 1957 and 'Wonderful World' 1960 (re-released 1986).

cooking heat treatment of food to make it more palatable, digestible, and safe. It breaks down connective tissue in meat, making it tender, and softens the cellulose in plant tissue.

Cook Islands group of six large and a number of smaller Polynesian islands 2,600 km/1,600 mi NE of Auckland, New Zealand; area 290 sq km/112 sq mi; population (1991) 19,000. Their main products include fruit, copra, and crafts. They became a self-governing overseas territory of New Zealand 1965.

Cook Strait strait dividing North Island and South Island, New Zealand. A submarine cable carries electricity from South to North Island.

Coolidge (John) Calvin 1872–1933. 30th president of the USA 1923–29, a Republican. As governor of Massachusetts 1919, he was responsible for crushing a Boston police strike. As Warren *Harding's vice president 1921–23, he succeeded to the presidency on Harding's death (2 Aug 1923). He won the 1924 presidential election, and his period of office was marked by great economic prosperity.

cooling-off period in industrial relations, the practice of allowing a period of time to elapse between the start of a dispute and the taking of industrial action by a trade union. The practice may be voluntary or compulsory; in the latter case it is written into an agreement or into legislation.

Cooper Grand Prix motor racing team formed by John Cooper (1923–   ). They built Formula Two and Formula Three cars before building their revolutionary rear-engined Cooper T45 in 1958.

Cooper Gary 1901–1962. US film actor. He epitomized the lean, true-hearted Yankee, slow of speech but capable of outdoing the 'bad guys' in *Lives of a Bengal Lancer* 1935, *Mr Deeds Goes to Town* (Academy Award for best picture 1936), *Sergeant York* 1940 (Academy Award for best actor 1941), and *High Noon* (Academy Award for best actor 1952).

Cooper James Fenimore 1789–1851. US writer of 50 novels, becoming popular with *The Spy* 1821. He wrote volumes of *Leatherstocking Tales* about the frontier hero Leatherstocking and American Indians before and after the American Revolution, including *The Last of the Mohicans* 1826.

Cooper Leon 1930–   . US physicist who in 1955 began work on the puzzling phenomenon

of *superconductivity. He proposed that at low temperatures electrons would be bound in pairs (since known as **Cooper pairs**) and in this state electrical resistance to their flow through solids would disappear. He shared the 1972 Nobel Prize for Physics with John *Bardeen and John Schrieffer (1931–   ).

Cooper Susie. Married name Susan Vera Barker 1902–   . English pottery designer. Her style has varied from colourful Art Deco to softer, pastel decoration on more classical shapes. She started her own company 1929, which later became part of the Wedgwood factory, where she was senior designer from 1966.

cooperative movement banding together of groups of people for mutual assistance in trade, manufacture, the supply of credit, housing, or other services. The original principles of cooperative movement were laid down 1844 by the Rochdale Pioneers, under the influence of Robert Owen, and by Charles Fourier in France.

Cooperative Party political party founded in Britain 1917 by the cooperative movement to maintain its principles in parliamentary and local government. A written constitution was adopted 1938. The party had strong links with the Labour Party; from 1946 Cooperative Party candidates stood in elections as Cooperative and Labour Candidates and, after the 1959 general election, agreement was reached to limit the party's candidates to 30.

Cooperative Wholesale Society (CWS) British concern, the largest cooperative organization in the world, owned and controlled by the numerous cooperative retail societies, which are also its customers. Founded 1863, it acts as wholesaler, manufacturer, and banker, and owns factories, farms, and estates, in addition to offices and warehouses.

coordinate in geometry, a number that defines the position of a point relative to a point or axis. *Cartesian coordinates define a point by its perpendicular distances from two or more axes drawn through a fixed point at right angles to each other; *polar coordinates define a point in a plane by its distance from a fixed point and direction from a fixed line.

coordinate geometry or *analytical geometry* system of geometry in which points, lines, shapes, and surfaces are represented by algebraic expressions. In plane (two-dimensional) coordinate geometry, the plane is usually defined by two axes at right angles to each other, the horizontal x-axis and the vertical y-axis, meeting at O, the origin. A point on the plane can be represented by a pair of *Cartesian coordinates, which define its position in terms of its distance along the x-axis and along the y-axis from O. These distances are respectively the x and y coordinates of the point.

coot any of various freshwater birds of the genus *Fulica* in the rail family. Coots are about 38 cm/1.2 ft long, and mainly black. They have a white bill, extending up the forehead in a plate, and big feet with lobed toes.

Coote Eyre 1726–1783. Irish general in British India. His victory 1760 at Wandiwash, followed by the capture of Pondicherry, ended French hopes of supremacy. He returned to India as commander in chief 1779, and several times defeated *Hyder Ali, sultan of Mysore.

Copenhagen (Danish **København**) capital of Denmark, on the islands of Zealand and Amager; population (1990) 1,337,100 (including suburbs).

Copenhagen, Battle of naval victory 2 April 1801 by a British fleet under Sir Hyde Parker (1739–1807) and *Nelson over the Danish fleet. Nelson put his telescope to his blind eye and refused to see Parker's signal for withdrawal.

copepod *crustacean of the subclass Copepoda, mainly microscopic and found in plankton.

Copernicus Nicolaus 1473–1543. Polish astronomer who believed that the Sun, not the Earth, is at the centre of the Solar System, thus defying the Christian church doctrine of the time. For 30 years he worked on the hypothesis that the rotation and the orbital motion of the Earth were responsible for the apparent movement of the heavenly bodies. His great work *De Revolutionibus Orbium Coelestium/About the Revolutions of the Heavenly Spheres* was not published until the year of his death.

coplanar in geometry, describing lines or points that all lie in the same plane.

Copland Aaron 1900–1990. US composer. His early works, such as his piano concerto 1926, were in the jazz idiom but he gradually developed a gentler style with a regional flavour drawn from American folk music. Among his works are the ballets *Billy the Kid* 1939, *Rodeo* 1942, *Appalachian Spring* 1944 (based on a poem by Hart Crane), and *Inscape for Orchestra* 1967.

copper orange-pink, very malleable and ductile, metallic element, symbol Cu (from Latin *cuprum*), atomic number 29, relative atomic mass 63.546. It is used for its durability, pliability, high thermal and electrical conductivity, and resistance to corrosion.

copper ore any mineral from which copper is extracted, including native copper, Cu; chalcocite, Cu_2S; chalcopyrite, $CuFeS_2$; bornite, Cu_5FeS_4; azurite, $Cu_3(CO_3)_2(OH)_2$; malachite, $Cu_2CO_3(OH)_2$; and chrysocolla, $CuSiO_3.nH_2O$.

coppicing woodland management practice of severe pruning where trees are cut down to near ground level at regular intervals, typically every 3–20 years, to promote the growth of numerous shoots from the base.

Coppola Francis Ford 1939– . US film director and screenwriter. He directed *The Godfather* 1972, which became one of the biggest money-making films of all time, and its sequels *The Godfather Part II* 1974, which garnered seven Academy Awards, and *The Godfather Part III* 1990. His other films include *Apocalypse Now* 1979, *One From the Heart* 1982, *Rumblefish* 1983, *The Outsiders* 1983, and *Tucker: The Man and His Dream* 1988.

copra dried meat from the kernel of the *coconut, used to make coconut oil.

Copt descendant of those ancient Egyptians who adopted Christianity in the 1st century and refused to convert to Islam after the Arab conquest. They now form a small minority (about 5%) of Egypt's population. *Coptic* is a member of the Hamito-Semitic language family. It is descended from the language of the ancient Egyptians and is the ritual language of the Coptic

Christian church. It is written in the Greek alphabet with some additional characters derived from *demotic script.

copulation act of mating in animals with internal *fertilization. Male mammals have a *penis or other organ that is used to introduce spermatozoa into the reproductive tract of the female. Most birds transfer sperm by pressing their cloacas (the openings of their reproductive tracts) together.

copyright law applying to literary, musical, and artistic works (including plays, recordings, films, photographs, radio and television broadcasts, and, in the USA and the UK, computer programs), which prevents the reproduction of the work, in whole or in part, without the author's consent.

coral marine invertebrate of the class Anthozoa in the phylum Cnidaria, which also includes sea anemones and jellyfish. It has a skeleton of lime (calcium carbonate) extracted from the surrounding water. Corals exist in warm seas, at moderate depths with sufficient light. Some coral is valued for decoration or jewellery, for example, Mediterranean red coral *Corallum rubrum*.

Coral Sea or *Solomon Sea* part of the Pacific Ocean bounded by NE Australia, New Guinea, the Solomon Islands, Vanuatu, and New Caledonia. It contains numerous coral islands and reefs. The Coral Sea Islands are a territory of Australia; they comprise scattered reefs and islands over an area of about 1,000,000 sq km/386,000 sq mi. They are uninhabited except for a meteorological station on Willis Island. The *Great Barrier Reef lies along its western edge, just off the east coast of Australia.

cor anglais or *English horn* alto member of the *oboe family.

Corbusier, Le see *Le Corbusier, architect.

Corday Charlotte 1768–1793. French Girondin (right-wing republican during the French Revolution). After the overthrow of the Girondins by the more extreme Jacobins May 1793, she stabbed to death the Jacobin leader, Jean Paul Marat, with a bread knife as he sat in his bath in July of the same year. She was guillotined.

cordillera group of mountain ranges and their valleys, all running in a specific direction, formed by the continued convergence of two tectonic plates (see *tectonics) along a line.

Cordilleras, the mountainous western section of North America, with the Rocky mountains and the coastal ranges parallel to the contact between the North American and the Pacific plates.

core in earth science, the innermost part of the Earth. It is divided into an inner core, the upper boundary of which is 1,700 km/1,060 mi from the centre, and an outer core, 1,820 km/1,130 mi thick. Both parts are thought to consist of iron-nickel alloy, with the inner core being solid and the outer core being semisolid. The temperature may be 3,000°C/5,400°F.

CORE (acronym from *Congress of Racial Equality*) US nonviolent civil-rights organization, founded in Chicago 1942.

Corelli Arcangelo 1653–1713. Italian composer and violinist. He was one of the first virtuoso violinists and his music, marked by graceful melody, includes a set of *concerti grossi* and five sets of chamber sonatas.

Corfu (Greek *Kérkira*) northernmost and second largest of the Ionian islands of Greece, off the coast of Epirus in the Ionian Sea; area 1,072 sq km/414 sq mi; population (1981) 96,500. Its businesses include tourism, fruit, olive oil, and textiles. Its largest town is the port of Corfu (Kérkira), population (1981) 33,560. Corfu was colonized by the Corinthians about 700 BC. Venice held it 1386–1797, Britain 1815–64.

coriander Coriander is a hardy annual growing to 45–60 cm/21–24 in.

coriander pungent fresh herb, the Eurasian plant *Coriandrum sativum*, a member of the parsley family Umbelliferae, also a spice: the dried ripe fruit. The spice is used commercially as a flavouring in meat products, bakery goods, tobacco, gin, liqueurs, chilli, and curry powder. Both are much used in cooking in the Middle East, India, Mexico, and China.

Corinna lived 6th century BC. Greek lyric poet, said to have instructed Pindar. Only fragments of her poetry survive.

Corinth (Greek *Kórinthos*) port in Greece, on the isthmus connecting the Peloponnese with the mainland; population (1981) 22,650. The rocky isthmus is bisected by the 6.5 km/4 mi Corinth canal, opened 1893. The site of the ancient city-state of Corinth lies 7 km/4.5 mi SW of the port.

Corinthian in Classical architecture, one of the five types of column; see *order.

Coriolis effect the effect of the Earth's west-to-east rotation upon the atmosphere and upon all objects on the Earth's surface. In the northern hemisphere it causes winds, ocean currents, and aircraft to be deflected to the right (clockwise); in the southern hemisphere it causes deflection to the left (anticlockwise).

cork light, waterproof outer layers of the bark of the stems and roots of almost all trees and shrubs. The cork oak *Quercus suber*, a native of S Europe and N Africa, is cultivated in Spain and Portugal; the exceptionally thick outer layers of its bark provide the cork that is used commercially.

Cork largest county of the Republic of Ireland, in the province of Munster; county town Cork;

area 7,460 sq km/2,880 sq mi; population (1991) 409,800. It is agricultural, but there is also some copper and manganese mining, marble quarrying, and river and sea fishing. Natural gas and oil fields are found off the S coast at Kinsale.

corm short, swollen, underground plant stem, surrounded by protective scale leaves, as seen in the genus *Crocus*. It stores food, provides a means of *vegetative reproduction, and acts as a *perennating organ.

cormorant any of various diving seabirds, mainly of the genus *Phalacrocorax*, about 90 cm/3 ft long, with webbed feet, long neck, hooked beak, and glossy black plumage. There are some 30 species of cormorant worldwide, including a flightless form *Nannopterum harrisi* in the Galápagos Islands. Cormorants generally feed on fish and shellfish. Some species breed on inland lakes and rivers.

corn the main *cereal crop of a region – for example, wheat in the UK, oats in Scotland and Ireland, maize in the USA.

corncrake bird *Crex crex* of the rail family. About 25 cm/10 in long, it is drably coloured, shy, and has a persistent rasping call. It lives in meadows and crops in temperate regions, but has become rare where mechanical methods of cutting corn are used.

cornea transparent front section of the vertebrate *eye. The cornea is curved and behaves as a fixed lens, so that light entering the eye is partly focused before it reaches the lens.

Corneille Pierre 1606–1684. French dramatist. His many tragedies, such as *Oedipe* 1659, glorify the strength of will governed by reason, and established the French classical dramatic tradition for the next two centuries. His first play, *Mélite*, was performed 1629, followed by others that gained him a brief period of favour with Cardinal Richelieu. *Le Cid* 1636 was attacked by the Academicians, although it received public acclaim. Later plays were based on Aristotle's unities.

cornet brass band instrument. It is like a shorter, broader trumpet, with a wider bore and mellower tone, and without fixed notes. Notes of different pitch are obtained by overblowing and by means of three pistons.

cornflour in the UK, purified, fine, powdery starch made from of maize (Indian corn), used as a thickener in cooking; in the USA it is called *cornstarch*.

cornflower plant *Centaurea cyanus* of the family Compositae. It is distinguished from the knapweeds by its deep azure-blue flowers. Formerly a common weed in N European wheat fields, it is now commonly grown in gardens as a herbaceous plant.

Cornforth John Warcup 1917– . Australian chemist. Using *radioisotopes as markers, he found out how cholesterol is manufactured in the living cell and how enzymes synthesize chemicals that are mirror images of each other (optical *isomers). He shared a Nobel prize 1975 with Swiss chemist Vladimir Prelog (1906–).

Cornish language extinct member of the *Celtic languages, a branch of the Indo-European language family, spoken in Cornwall, England, until 1777. Written Cornish first appeared in 10th-century documents; some religious plays were written in Cornish in the 15th and 16th centuries, but later literature is scanty, consisting mainly of folk tales and verses. In recent years the language has been revived in a somewhat reconstructed form by members of the Cornish nationalist movement.

Corn Laws in Britain until 1846, laws used to regulate the export or import of cereals in order to maintain an adequate supply for consumers and a secure price for producers. For centuries the Corn Laws formed an integral part of the mercantile system in England; they were repealed because they became an unwarranted tax on food and a hindrance to British exports.

cornucopia (Latin 'horn of plenty') in Greek mythology, one of the horns of the goat Amaltheia, which was caused by Zeus to refill itself indefinitely with food and drink. In paintings, the cornucopia is depicted as a horn-shaped container spilling over with fruit and flowers.

Cornwall county in SW England including the *Scilly Islands (Scillies)
area (excluding Scillies) 3,550 sq km/1,370 sq mi
towns Truro (administrative headquarters), Camborne, Launceston; resorts of Bude, Falmouth, Newquay, Penzance, St Ives
physical Bodmin Moor (including Brown Willy 419 m/1,375 ft), Land's End peninsula, St Michael's Mount, rivers Tamar, Fowey, Fal, Camel
products electronics, spring flowers, tin (mined since Bronze Age, some workings renewed 1960s, though the industry has all but disappeared), kaolin (St Austell), fish
population (1991) 469,300
famous people John Betjeman, Humphry Davy, Daphne Du Maurier, William Golding
history the Stannary, established in the 11th century, ceased to meet 1752 but its powers were never rescinded at Westminster, and it was revived 1974 as a separatist movement.

Cornwallis Charles, 1st Marquess 1738–1805. British general in the *American Revolution until 1781, when his defeat at Yorktown led to final surrender and ended the war. He then served twice as governor general of India and once as viceroy of Ireland.

corolla collective name for the petals of a flower. In some plants the petal margins are partly or completely fused to form a **corolla tube**, for example in bindweed *Convolvulus arvensis*.

corona faint halo of hot (about 2,000,000°C/3,600,000°F) and tenuous gas around the Sun, which boils from the surface. It is visible at solar *eclipses or through a **coronagraph**, an instrument that blocks light from the Sun's brilliant disc. Gas flows away from the corona to form the *solar wind.

Coronado Francisco de *c.* 1500–1554. Spanish explorer who sailed to the New World 1535 in search of gold. In 1540 he set out with several hundred men from the Gulf of California on an exploration of what are today the Southern states. Although he failed to discover any gold, his expedition came across the impressive Grand Canyon of the Colorado and introduced the use of the horse to the indigenous Indians.

coronary artery disease (Latin *corona* 'crown', from the arteries' encircling of the heart) condition in which the fatty deposits of *atherosclerosis form in the coronary arteries that supply the heart muscle, making them too narrow.

coronation ceremony of investing a sovereign with the emblems of royalty, as a symbol of inauguration in office. Since the coronation of Harold 1066, English sovereigns have been crowned in Westminster Abbey, London.

Corot Jean-Baptiste-Camille 1796–1875. French painter, creator of a distinctive landscape style with cool colours and soft focus. His early work, including Italian scenes in the 1820s, influenced the Barbizon school of painters. Like them, Corot worked outdoors, but he also continued a conventional academic tradition with more romanticized paintings.

corporal punishment physical punishment of wrongdoers – for example, by whipping. It is still used as a punishment for criminals in many countries, especially under Islamic law. Corporal punishment of children by parents is illegal in some countries, including Sweden, Finland, Denmark, and Norway.

corporation organization that has its own legal identity, distinct from that of its members – for example, a *company.

corporation tax tax levied on a company's profits by public authorities. It is a form of income tax, and rates vary according to country, but there is usually a flat rate. It is a large source of revenue for governments.

corporatism belief that the state in capitalist democracies should intervene to a large extent in the economy to ensure social harmony. In Austria, for example, corporatism results in political decisions often being taken after discussions between chambers of commerce, trade unions, and the government.

corporative state state in which the members are organized and represented not on a local basis as citizens, but as producers working in a particular trade, industry, or profession. Originating with the syndicalist workers' movement, the idea was superficially adopted by the fascists during the 1920s and 1930s. Catholic social theory, as expounded in some papal encyclicals, also favours the corporative state as a means of eliminating class conflict.

Corpus Christi feast celebrated in the Roman Catholic and Orthodox churches, and to some extent in the Anglican church, on the Thursday after Trinity Sunday. It was instituted in the 13th century through the devotion of St Juliana, prioress of Mount Cornillon, near Liège, Belgium, in honour of the Real Presence of Christ in the Eucharist.

corpuscular theory hypothesis about the nature of light championed by Isaac Newton, who postulated that it consists of a stream of particles or corpuscles. The theory was superseded at the beginning of the 19th century by Thomas *Young's wave theory. *Quantum theory and wave mechanics embody both concepts.

corpus luteum temporary endocrine gland found in the mammalian *ovary. It is formed after ovulation from the Graafian follicle, a group of cells associated with bringing the egg to maturity, and secretes the hormone progesterone.

Correggio Antonio Allegri da *c.* 1494–1534. Italian painter of the High Renaissance whose style followed the Classical grandeur of Leonardo and Titian but anticipated the Baroque in its emphasis on movement, softer forms, and contrasts of light and shade.

correlation relation between two sets of information: they correlate when they vary together. If one set of data increases at the same time as the other, the relationship is said to be positive or direct. If one set of data increases as the other decreases, the relationship is negative or inverse. Correlation can be shown by plotting a best-fit line on a *scatter diagram.

correspondence in mathematics, the relation between two sets where an operation on the members of one set maps some or all of them onto one or more members of the other. For example, if *A* is the set of members of a family and *B* is the set of months in the year, *A* and *B* are in correspondence if the operation is: ' ...has a birthday in the month of... '.

corresponding society in British history, one of the first independent organizations for the working classes, advocating annual parliaments and universal male suffrage. The London Corresponding Society was founded 1792 by politicians Thomas Hardy (1752–1832) and John Horne Tooke (1736–1812). It later established branches in Scotland and the provinces. Many of its activities had to be held in secret and government fears about the spread of revolutionary doctrines led to its banning 1799.

corrie (Welsh *cwm*; French, North American *cirque*) Scottish term for a steep-walled hollow in the mountainside of a glaciated area representing the source of a melted glacier. The weight of the ice has ground out the bottom and worn back the sides.

corrosion the eating away and eventual destruction of metals and alloys by chemical attack. The rusting of ordinary iron and steel is the most common form of corrosion. Rusting takes place in moist air, when the iron combines with oxygen and water to form a brown-orange deposit of *rust (hydrated iron oxide). The rate of corrosion is increased where the atmosphere is polluted with sulphur dioxide. Salty road and air conditions accelerate the rusting of car bodies.

corsair pirate based on the N African Barbary Coast. From the 16th century onwards the corsairs plundered shipping in the Mediterranean and Atlantic, holding hostages for ransom or selling them as slaves. Although many punitive expeditions were sent against them, they were not suppressed until France occupied Algiers 1830.

Corsica (French *Corse*) island region of France, in the Mediterranean off the W coast of Italy, N of Sardinia; it comprises the *départements* of Haute Corse and Corse du Sud
area 8,700 sq km/3,358 sq mi
capital Ajaccio (port)
physical mountainous; *maquis vegetation
government its special status involves a 61-member regional parliament with the power to scrutinize French National Assembly bills applicable to the island and propose amendments
products wine, olive oil
population (1986) 249,000, including just under 50% native Corsicans. There are about 400,000 *émigrés*, mostly in Mexico and Central America, who return to retire
language French (official); the majority speak Corsican, an Italian dialect
famous people Napoleon

Cort Henry 1740–1800. British iron manufacturer. For the manufacture of *wrought iron, he invented the puddling process and developed the rolling mill, both of which were significant in the Industrial Revolution.

Cortés Hernán (Ferdinand) 1485–1547. Spanish conquistador. He conquered the Aztec empire 1519–21, and secured Mexico for Spain.

cortex in biology, the outer layer of a structure such as the brain, kidney, or adrenal gland. In botany the cortex includes non-specialized cells lying just beneath the surface cells of the root and stem.

corticosteroid any of several steroid hormones secreted by the cortex of the *adrenal glands; also synthetic forms with similar properties. Corticosteroids have anti-inflammatory and *immunosuppressive effects and may be used to treat a number of conditions including rheumatoid arthritis, severe allergies, asthma, some skin diseases, and some cancers. Side effects can be serious, and therapy must be withdrawn very gradually.

cortisone natural corticosteroid produced by the *adrenal gland, now synthesized for its anti-inflammatory qualities and used in the treatment of rheumatoid arthritis.

corundum native aluminium oxide, Al_2O_3, the hardest naturally occurring mineral known apart from diamond (corundum rates 9 on the Mohs' scale of hardness); lack of *cleavage also increases its durability. Varieties of gem-quality corundum are *ruby* (red) and *sapphire* (any colour other than red, usually blue). Poorer-quality and synthetic corundum is used in industry, for example as an *abrasive.

cosecant in trigonometry, a *function of an angle in a right-angled triangle found by dividing the length of the hypotenuse (the longest side) by the length of the side opposite the angle. Thus the cosecant of an angle *A*, usually shortened to cosec *A*, is always greater than (or equal to) 1. It is the reciprocal of the sine of the angle, that is, cosec *A* = 1/sin *A*.

Cosgrave Liam 1920– . Irish Fine Gael politician, prime minister of the Republic of Ireland 1973–77. As party leader 1965–77, he headed a Fine Gael–Labour coalition government from 1973. Relations between the Irish and UK governments improved under his premiership.

Cosgrave William Thomas 1880–1965. Irish politician. He took part in the *Easter Rising 1916 and sat in the Sinn Féin cabinet of 1919–21. Head of the Free State government 1922–33, he founded and led the Fine Gael opposition 1933–44. His eldest son is Liam Cosgrave.

cosine in trigonometry, a function of an angle in a right-angled triangle found by dividing the length of the side adjacent to the angle by the length of the hypotenuse (the longest side). It is usually shortened to cos.

cosmic background radiation or *3° radiation* electromagnetic radiation left over from the original formation of the universe in the Big Bang around 15 billion years ago. It corresponds to an overall background temperature of 3K (–270°C/–454°F), or 3°C above absolute zero.

cosmic radiation streams of high-energy particles from outer space, consisting of protons, alpha particles, and light nuclei, which collide with atomic nuclei in the Earth's atmosphere, and produce secondary nuclear particles (chiefly *mesons, such as pions and muons) that shower the Earth.

cosmid fragment of *DNA from the human genome inserted into a bacterial cell. The bacterium replicates the fragment along with its own DNA. In this way the fragments are copied for a gene library. Cosmids are characteristically 40,000 base pairs in length. The most commonly used bacterium is *Escherichia coli*. A *yeast artificial chromosome works in the same way.

cosmological principle in astronomy, a hypothesis that any observer anywhere in the *universe has the same view that we have; that is, that the universe is not expanding from any centre but all galaxies are moving away from one another.

cosmology study of the structure of the universe. Modern cosmology began in the 1920s with the discovery that the universe is expanding, which suggested that it began in an explosion, the *Big Bang. An alternative view, the *steady-state theory, claimed that the universe has no origin, but is expanding because new matter is being continually created.

Cosmos name used from the early 1960s for nearly all Soviet artificial satellites. Over 2,100 Cosmos satellites had been launched by Jan 1991.

Cossack member of any of several, formerly horse-raising groups of S and SW Russia, Ukraine, and Poland, predominantly of Russian or Ukrainian origin, who took in escaped serfs and lived in independent communal settlements (military brotherhoods) from the 15th to the 19th century. Later they held land in return for military service in the cavalry under Russian and Polish rulers. After 1917, the various Cossack communities were incorporated into the Soviet administrative and collective system.

Costa Rica Republic of (*República de Costa Rica*)

area 51,100 sq km/19,735 sq mi
capital San José
towns ports Limón, Puntarenas
physical high central plateau and tropical coasts; Costa Rica was once entirely forested, containing an estimated 5% of the Earth's flora and fauna
environment by 1983 only 17% of the forest remained; half of the arable land had been cleared for cattle ranching, leading to landlessness, unemployment, and soil erosion; the massive environmental destruction also caused incalculable loss to the gene pool. It is now one of the leading centres of conservation in Latin America, with more than 10% of the country protected by national parks, and tree replanting

proceeding at a rate of 150 sq km/60 sq mi per year
head of state and government Jose Maria Figueres Olsen from 1994
political system liberal democracy
exports coffee, bananas, cocoa, sugar, beef
currency colón
population (1993 est) 3,300,000 (including 1,200 Guaymi Indians); growth rate 2.6% p.a.
language Spanish (official)
religion Roman Catholic 95%
GNP $1,930 per head (1991)
chronology
1821 Independence achieved from Spain.
1949 New constitution adopted. National army abolished. José Figueres, cofounder of the PLN, elected president; he embarked on socialist programme.
1958–73 Mainly conservative administrations.
1974 PLN regained the presidency and returned to socialist policies.
1978 Rodrigo Carazo, conservative, elected president. Sharp deterioration in the state of the economy.
1982 Luis Alberto Monge (PLN) elected president. Harsh austerity programme introduced to rebuild the economy. Pressure from the USA to abandon neutral stance and condemn Sandinista regime in Nicaragua.
1983 Policy of neutrality reaffirmed.
1985 Following border clashes with Sandinista forces, a US-trained antiguerrilla guard formed.
1986 Oscar Arias Sánchez won the presidency on a neutralist platform.
1987 Arias won Nobel Prize for Peace for devising a Central American peace plan.
1990 Rafael Calderón (PUSC) elected president.
1994 Jose Maria Figueres Olsen (PLN) elected president.

cost–benefit analysis process whereby a project is assessed for its social and welfare benefits in addition to considering the financial return on investment. For example, this might take into account the environmental impact of an industrial plant or convenience for users of a new railway.

Costello Elvis. Stage name of Declan McManus 1954– . English rock singer, songwriter, and guitarist whose intricate yet impassioned lyrics have made him one of Britain's foremost songwriters. The great stylistic range of his work was evident from his 1977 debut *My Aim Is True*.

Coster Laurens Janszoon 1370–1440. Dutch printer. According to some sources, he invented movable type, but after his death an apprentice ran off to Mainz with the blocks and, taking Johann *Gutenberg into his confidence, began a printing business with him.

Costner Kevin 1955– . US film actor. He first achieved top-ranking success with his role as law-enforcer Elliot Ness, in the film version of the 1960s television series *The Untouchables* 1987. Increasingly identified with the embodiment of idealism and high principle, Costner went on to direct and star in *Dances With Wolves* 1990, a Western sympathetic to the native American Indian, which won several Academy Awards. Subsequent films include *Robin Hood – Prince of Thieves* 1991, *JFK* 1991, and *The Bodyguard* 1992.

cotangent in trigonometry, a *function of an angle in a right-angled triangle found by dividing the length of the side adjacent to the angle by the length of the side opposite it. It is usually written as cotan, or cot, and is the reciprocal of the tangent of the angle, so that cot A = 1/tan A, where A is the angle in question.

cot death or *sudden infant death syndrome* (SIDS) death of an apparently healthy baby, almost always during sleep. It is most common in the winter months, and strikes more boys than girls. The cause is not known but risk factors that have been identified include prematurity, respiratory infection, overheating and sleeping position.

Cotman John Sell 1782–1842. English landscape painter. With John Crome, he was a founder of the *Norwich School. His early watercolours were bold designs in simple flat washes of colour, for example *Greta Bridge, Yorkshire* about 1805 (British Museum, London).

cotoneaster any shrub or tree of the Eurasian genus *Cotoneaster*, rose family Rosaceae, closely allied to the hawthorn and medlar. The fruits, though small and unpalatable, are usually bright red and conspicuous, often persisting through the winter. Some of the shrubs are cultivated for their attractive appearance.

Cotonou chief port and largest city of Benin, on the Bight of Benin; population (1982) 487,000. Palm products and timber are exported. Although not the official capital, it is the seat of the president, and the main centre of commerce and politics.

Cotopaxi (Quechua 'shining peak') active volcano, situated to the S of Quito in Ecuador. It is 5,897 m/19,347 ft high and was first climbed 1872.

Cotswold Hills or *Cotswolds* range of hills in Avon and Gloucestershire, England, 80 km/50 mi long, between Bath and Chipping Camden. They rise to 333 m/1,086 ft at Cleeve Cloud, near Cheltenham, but average about 200 m/600 ft. The area is known for its picturesque villages, built with the local honey-coloured stone.

Cotten Joseph 1905–1994. US actor, intelligent and low-keyed, who was brought into films by Orson *Welles. Cotten gave outstanding perform-ances in *Citizen Kane* 1941, *The Magnificent Ambersons* 1942, and *The Third Man* 1949.

cotton tropical and subtropical herbaceous plant of the genus *Gossypium* of the mallow family Malvaceae. Fibres surround the seeds inside the ripened fruits, or bolls, and these are spun into yarn for cloth.

cotton gin machine that separates cotton fibres from the seed boll. Production of the gin (then called an en*gin*e) by US inventor Eli Whitney 1793 was a milestone in textile history.

cotton spinning creating thread or fine yarn from the cotton plant by spinning the raw fibre contained within the seed-pods. The fibre is separated from the pods by a machine called a *cotton gin. It is then cleaned and the fibres are separated out (carding). Finally the fibres are drawn out to the desired length and twisted together to form strong thread.

cottonwood any of several North American poplars of the genus *Populus*, with seeds topped by a thick tuft of silky hairs. The eastern cottonwood *P. deltoides*, growing to 30 m/100 ft, is native to the eastern USA. The name cottonwood is also given to the downy-leaved Australian tree *Bedfordia salaoina*.

cotyledon structure in the embryo of a seed plant that may form a 'leaf' after germination and is commonly known as a seed leaf. The number of cotyledons present in an embryo is an important character in the classification of flowering plants (*angiosperms).

couch grass European grass *Agropyron repens* of the family Gramineae. It spreads rapidly by underground stems. It is considered a troublesome weed in North America, where it has been introduced.

cougar another name for the *puma, a large North American cat.

coulomb SI unit (symbol C) of electrical charge. One coulomb is the quantity of electricity conveyed by a current of one *ampere in one second.

Coulomb Charles Auguste de 1736–1806. French scientist, inventor of the torsion balance for measuring the force of electric and magnetic attraction. The coulomb was named after him.

council in local government in England and Wales, a popularly elected local assembly charged with the government of the area within its boundaries. Under the Local Government Act 1972, they comprise three types: *county councils, *district councils, and *parish councils.

Council for the Protection of Rural England countryside conservation group founded 1926 by Patrick *Abercrombie with a brief that extends from planning controls to energy policy. A central organization campaigns on national issues and 42 local groups lobby on regional matters. The *Council for the Protection of Rural Wales* is the Welsh equivalent.

Council of Europe body constituted 1949 in Strasbourg, France (still its headquarters), to secure 'a greater measure of unity between the European countries'. The widest association of European states, it has a *Committee* of foreign ministers, a *Parliamentary Assembly* (with members from national parliaments), and a *European Commission* investigating violations of human rights.

council tax method of raising revenue for local government in Britain. It replaced the community charge, or *poll tax, from April 1993. The tax is based on property values but takes some account of the number of people occupying each property.

counterfeiting fraudulent imitation, usually of banknotes. It is countered by special papers, elaborate watermarks, skilled printing, and sometimes the insertion of a metallic strip. *Forgery is also a form of counterfeiting.

counterpoint in music, the art of combining different forms of an original melody with apparent freedom while preserving a harmonious effect. Giovanni Palestrina and J S Bach were masters of counterpoint.

Counter-Reformation movement initiated by the Catholic church at the Council of Trent 1545–63 to counter the spread of the *Reformation. Extending into the 17th century, its dominant forces included the rise of the Jesuits as an educating and missionary group and the deployment of the Spanish *Inquisition in other countries.

countertenor the highest natural male voice, also called an *alto*. It was favoured by the Elizabethans for its heroic brilliance of tone.

countervailing power in economics, the belief that too much power held by one group or company can be balanced or neutralized by another, creating a compatible relationship, such as trade unions in the case of strong management in a large company, or an opposition party facing an authoritarian government.

country and western or *country music* popular music of the white US South and West; it evolved from the folk music of the English, Irish, and Scottish settlers and has a strong blues influence. Characteristic instruments are the steel guitar, mandolin, and fiddle.

country park pleasure ground or park, often located near an urban area, providing facilities for the public enjoyment of the countryside. Country parks were introduced in the UK following the 1968 Countryside Act and are the responsibility of local authorities with assistance from the Countryside Commission. They cater for a range of recreational activities such as walking, boating, and horse-riding.

Country Party (official name *National Country Party* from 1975) Australian political party representing the interests of the farmers and people of the smaller towns; it holds the power balance between Liberals and Labor. It developed from about 1860, gained strength after the introduction of preferential voting (see *vote) 1918, and has been in coalition with the Liberals from 1949.

Countryside Commission official conservation body created for England and Wales under the Countryside Act 1968. It replaced the National Parks Commission, and had by 1980 created over 160 country parks.

county administrative unit of a country or state. In the UK it is nowadays synonymous with 'shire', although historically the two had different origins. Many of the English counties can be traced back to Saxon times. In the USA a county is a subdivision of a state; the power of counties differs widely between states. The Republic of Ireland has 26 geographical and 27 administrative counties.

county council in the UK, a unit of local government whose responsibilities include broad planning policy, highways, education, personal social services, and libraries; police, fire, and traffic control; and refuse disposal.

county court English court of law created by the County Courts Act 1846 and now governed by the Act of 1984. It exists to try civil cases, such as actions on *contract and *tort where the claim does not exceed £5,000, and disputes about land, such as between landlord and tenant. County courts are presided over by one or more circuit judges. An appeal on a point of law lies to the Court of Appeal.

county palatine in medieval England, a county whose lord held particular rights, in lieu of the king, such as pardoning treasons and murders. Under William I there were four counties palatine: Chester, Durham, Kent, and Shropshire.

coup d'état or *coup* forcible takeover of the government of a country by elements from within that country, generally carried out by violent or illegal means. It differs from a revolution in typically being carried out by a small group (for example, of army officers or opposition politicians) to install its leader as head of government, rather than being a mass uprising by the people.

Couperin François *le Grand* 1668–1733. French composer. He held various court appointments under Louis XIV and wrote vocal, chamber, and harpsichord music.

Courbet Gustave 1819–1877. French artist, a portrait, genre, and landscape painter. Reacting against academic trends, both Classicist and Romantic, he sought to establish a new realism based on contemporary life. His *Burial at Ornans* 1850 (Louvre, Paris), showing ordinary working people gathered round a village grave, shocked the public and the critics with its 'vulgarity'.

courgette small variety of marrow, *Cucurbita pepo*, of the Cucurbitaceae family. It is cultivated as a vegetable and harvested before it is fully mature, at 15–20 cm/6–8 in. In the USA and Canada it is known as a zucchini.

Courrèges André 1923– . French fashion designer who is credited with inventing the miniskirt 1964. His 'space-age' designs – square-shaped short skirts and trousers – were copied worldwide in the 1960s.

coursing chasing of hares by greyhounds, not by scent but by sight, as a sport and as a test of the greyhound's speed. It is one of the most ancient of field sports. Since the 1880s it has been practised in the UK on enclosed or park courses.

court body that hears legal actions and the building where this occurs. See *law courts and particular kinds of court, for example *county court and *Diplock court.

Court Margaret (born Smith) 1942– . Australian tennis player. The most prolific winner in the women's game, she won a record 64 Grand Slam titles, including 25 at singles.

Courtauld Samuel 1793–1881. British industrialist who developed the production of viscose rayon and other synthetic fibres from 1904. He founded the firm of Courtaulds 1816 in Bocking, Essex, and at first specialized in silk and crepe manufacture.

courtesy title in the UK, any title given to the progeny of members of the peerage. For example, the eldest son of a duke, marquess, or earl may bear one of his father's lesser titles; thus the Duke of Marlborough's son is the Marquess of Blandford. They are not peers and do not sit in the House of Lords.

Courtneidge Cicely 1893–1980. British comic actress and singer who appeared both on stage and in films. She married comedian Jack Hulbert (1892–1978), with whom she formed a successful variety partnership.

Court of Session supreme civil court in Scotland, established 1532. Cases come in the first place before one of the judges of the Outer House (corresponding to the High Court in England and Wales), and from that decision an appeal lies to the Inner House (corresponding to the Court of Appeal) which sits in two divisions called the First and the Second Division. From the decisions of the Inner House an appeal lies to the House of Lords. The court sits in Edinburgh.

Court of the Lord Lyon Scottish heraldic authority composed of one king of arms, three heralds, and three pursuivants who specialize in genealogical work. It embodies the High Sennachie of Scotland's Celtic kings.

Cousteau Jacques Yves 1910– . French oceanographer, known for his researches in command of the *Calypso* from 1951, his film and television documentaries, and his many books; he pioneered the invention of the aqualung 1943 and techniques in underwater filming.

coûte que coûte (French) whatever the cost.

covalent bond chemical *bond in which the two combining atoms share a pair of electrons. It is often represented by a single line drawn between the two atoms. Covalently bonded substances include hydrogen (H_2), water (H_2O), and most organic substances.

Covenanter in Scottish history, one of the Presbyterian Christians who swore to uphold their forms of worship in a National Covenant, signed 28 Feb 1638, when Charles I attempted to introduce a liturgy on the English model into Scotland.

Coventry industrial city in West Midlands, England; population (1981) 313,800. Manufacturing includes cars, electronic equipment, machine tools, and agricultural machinery.

Coward Noël 1899–1973. English playwright, actor, producer, director, and composer, who epitomized the witty and sophisticated man of the theatre. From his first success with *The Young Idea* 1923, he wrote and appeared in plays and comedies on both sides of the Atlantic such as *Hay Fever* 1925, *Private Lives* 1930 with Gertrude Lawrence, *Design for Living* 1933, and *Blithe Spirit* 1941.

cowfish type of *boxfish.

cow parsley or **keck** tall perennial plant, *Anthriscus sylvestris*, of the carrot family. It grows in Europe, N Asia, and N Africa.

Cowper William 1731–1800. English poet. He trained as a lawyer, but suffered a mental breakdown 1763 and entered an asylum, where he underwent an evangelical conversion. He later wrote hymns (including 'God Moves in a Mysterious Way'). His verse includes the six books of *The Task* 1785.

cowrie marine snail of the family Cypreidae, in which the interior spiral form is concealed by a double outer lip. The shells are hard, shiny, and often coloured. Most cowries are shallow-water forms, and are found in many parts of the world, particularly the tropical Indo-Pacific. Cowries have been used as ornaments and fertility charms, and also as currency, for example the Pacific money cowrie *Cypraea moneta*.

cowslip European plant *Primula veris* of the same genus as the primrose and belonging to the family Primulaceae, with yellow flowers. It is native to temperate regions of the Old World. The oxlip *P. elatior* is closely related to the cowslip.

coyote wild dog *Canis latrans*, in appearance like a small wolf, living from Alaska to Central America and east to New York. Its head and body are about 90 cm/3 ft long and brown, flecked with grey or black. Coyotes live in open country and can run at 65 kph/40 mph. Their main foods are rabbits and rodents. Although persecuted by humans for over a century, the species is very successful.

coypu South American water rodent *Myocastor coypus*, about 60 cm/2 ft long and weighing up to 9 kg/20 lb. It has a scaly, ratlike tail, webbed hind feet, a blunt-muzzled head, and large orange incisors. The fur is reddish brown. It feeds on vegetation, and lives in burrows in rivers and lake banks.

CP/M (abbreviation for *control program/monitor* or *control program for microcomputers*) one of the earliest *operating systems for microcomputers. It was produced by Digital Research Corporation, and became a standard for microcomputers based on the Intel 8080 and Zilog Z80 8-bit microprocessors. In the 1980s it was superseded by *MS-DOS, written for 16-bit microprocessors.

CPU in computing, abbreviation for *central processing unit*.

CPVE (abbreviation for *Certificate of Pre-Vocational Education*) in the UK, educational qualification introduced 1986 for students over 16 in schools and colleges who want a one-year course of preparation for work or further vocational study.

crab any decapod (ten-legged) crustacean of the division Brachyura, with a broad, rather round, upper body shell (carapace) and a small *abdomen tucked beneath the body. Crabs are related to lobsters and crayfish. Mainly marine, some crabs live in fresh water or on land. They are alert carnivores and scavengers. They have a typical sideways walk, and strong pincers on the first pair of legs, the other four pairs being used for walking. Periodically, the outer shell is cast to allow for growth. The name 'crab' is sometimes used for similar arthropods, such as the horseshoe crab, which is neither a true crab nor a crustacean.

crab apple any of 25 species of wild *apple

trees (genus *Malus*), native to temperate regions of the northern hemisphere. Numerous varieties of cultivated apples have been derived from *M. pumila*, the common native crab apple of SE Europe and central Asia. The fruit of native species is smaller and more bitter than that of cultivated varieties and used in crab-apple jelly.

Crabbe George 1754–1832. English poet. Originally a doctor, he became a cleric 1781, and wrote grimly realistic verse on the poor of his own time: *The Village* 1783, *The Parish Register* 1807, *The Borough* 1810 (which includes the story used in Benjamin Britten's opera *Peter Grimes*), and *Tales of the Hall* 1819.

Crab nebula cloud of gas 6,000 light years from Earth, in the constellation Taurus. It is the remains of a star that exploded as a *supernova (observed as a brilliant point of light on Earth 1054). At its centre is a *pulsar that flashes 30 times a second. The name comes from its crablike shape.

crack street name for a chemical derivative (bicarbonate) of *cocaine in hard, crystalline lumps; it is heated and inhaled (smoked) as a stimulant. Crack was first used in San Francisco in the early 1980s, and is highly addictive.

cracking reaction in which a large *alkane molecule is broken down by heat into a smaller alkane and a small *alkene molecule. The reaction is carried out at a high temperature (600°C or higher) and often in the presence of a catalyst. Cracking is a commonly used process in the petrochemical industry.

Cracow alternative form of *Kraków, Polish city.

Craig Edward Gordon 1872–1966. British director and stage designer. His innovations and theories on stage design and lighting effects, expounded in *On the Art of the Theatre* 1911, had a profound influence on stage production in Europe and the USA.

Craig James 1871–1940. Ulster Unionist politician, the first prime minister of Northern Ireland 1921–40. Craig became a member of Parliament 1906, and was a highly effective organizer of Unionist resistance to Home Rule. As prime minister he carried out systematic discrimination against the Catholic minority, abolishing proportional representation 1929 and redrawing constituency boundaries to ensure Protestant majorities.

crake any of several small birds related to the *corncrake.

Cranach Lucas 1472–1553. German painter, etcher, and woodcut artist, a leading light in the German Renaissance. He painted many full-length nudes and precise and polished portraits, such as *Martin Luther* 1521 (Uffizi, Florence).

cranberry any of several trailing evergreen plants of the genus *Vaccinium* in the heath family Ericaceae, allied to bilberries and blueberries. They grow in marshy places and bear small, acid, crimson berries, high in vitamin C, used for making sauce and jelly.

crane in engineering, a machine for raising, lowering, or placing in position heavy loads. The three main types are the jib crane, the overhead travelling crane, and the tower crane. Most cranes have the machinery mounted on a revolving turntable. This may be mounted on trucks or be self-propelled, often being fitted with *caterpillar tracks.

crane in zoology, a large, wading bird of the family Gruidae, with long legs and neck, and powerful wings. Cranes are marsh- and plains-dwelling birds, feeding on plants as well as insects and small animals. They fly well and are usually migratory. Their courtship includes frenzied, leaping dances. They are found in all parts of the world except South America.

Crane (Harold) Hart 1899–1932. US poet. His long mystical poem *The Bridge* 1930 uses the Brooklyn Bridge as a symbol. In his work he attempted to link humanity's present with its past, in an epic continuum. He drowned after jumping overboard from a steamer bringing him back to the USA after a visit to Mexico.

Crane Stephen 1871–1900. US writer who introduced grim realism into the US novel. His book *The Red Badge of Courage* 1895 deals vividly with the US Civil War.

crane fly or **daddy-longlegs** any fly of the family Tipulidae, with long, slender, fragile legs. They look like giant mosquitoes, but the adults are quite harmless. The larvae live in soil or water.

cranesbill any plant of the genus *Geranium*, which contains about 400 species. The plants are named after the long, beaklike protrusion attached to the seed vessels. When ripe, this splits into coiling spirals, which jerk the seeds out, assisting in their distribution.

craniotomy operation to remove or turn back a small flap of skull bone to give access to the living brain.

cranium the dome-shaped area of the vertebrate skull, consisting of several fused plates, that protects the brain. Fossil remains of the human cranium have aided the development of theories concerning human evolution.

Cranko John 1927–1973. British choreographer, born in South Africa. He joined Sadler's Wells, London, 1946, and excelled in the creation of comedy characters, as in the *Tritsch-Tratsch Polka* 1946 and *Pineapple Poll* 1951.

crankshaft essential component of piston engines that converts the up-and-down (reciprocating) motion of the pistons into useful rotary motion. The car crankshaft carries a number of cranks. The pistons are connected to the cranks by connecting rods and *bearings; when the pistons move up and down, the connecting rods force the offset crank pins to describe a circle, thereby rotating the crankshaft.

Cranmer Thomas 1489–1556. English cleric, archbishop of Canterbury from 1533. A Protestant convert, he helped to shape the doctrines of the Church of England under Edward VI. He was responsible for the issue of the Prayer Books of 1549 and 1552, and supported the succession of Lady Jane Grey 1553.

Crashaw Richard 1613–1649. English religious poet of the metaphysical school. He published a book of Latin sacred epigrams 1634, then went to Paris, where he joined the Roman Catholic Church; his collection of poems *Steps to the Temple* appeared 1646.

Crassus Marcus Licinius *c.* 108–53 BC. Roman

general who crushed the *Spartacus uprising 71 BC. In 60 BC he joined with Caesar and Pompey in the First Triumvirate and obtained command in the east 55 BC. Invading Mesopotamia, he was defeated by the Parthians at the battle of Carrhae, captured, and put to death.

crater bowl-shaped depression, usually round and with steep sides. Craters are formed by explosive events such as the eruption of a volcano or by the impact of a meteorite. A *caldera is a much larger feature.

craton or **shield** core of a continent, a vast tract of highly deformed *metamorphic rock around which the continent has been built. Intense mountain-building periods shook these shield areas in Precambrian times before stable conditions set in.

Crawford Joan. Stage name of Lucille Le Seur 1908–1977. US film actress who became a star with her performance as a flapper (liberated young woman) in *Our Dancing Daughters* 1928. Later she appeared as a sultry, often suffering, mature woman. Her films include *Mildred Pierce* 1945 (for which she won an Academy Award), *Password* 1947, and *Whatever Happened to Baby Jane?* 1962.

crawling peg or **sliding peg** or **sliding parity** or **moving parity** in economics, a method of achieving a desired adjustment in a currency exchange rate (up or down) by small percentages over a given period, rather than by major revaluation or devaluation. Some countries use a formula that triggers a change when certain conditions are met. Others change values frequently to discourage speculations.

Craxi Bettino 1934– . Italian socialist politician, leader of the Italian Socialist Party (PSI) 1976–93, prime minister 1983–87. In 1993 Craxi was included amongst politicians suspected of having links with the Mafia and was under investigation.

crayfish freshwater decapod (ten-limbed) crustacean belonging to several families structurally similar to, but smaller than, the lobster. Crayfish are brownish-green scavengers and are found in all parts of the world except Africa. They are edible, and some species are farmed.

Crazy Horse 1849–1877. Sioux Indian chief, one of the Indian leaders at the massacre of *Little Bighorn. He was killed when captured.

creationism theory concerned with the origins of matter and life, claiming, as does the Bible in Genesis, that the world and humanity were created by a supernatural Creator, not more than 6,000 years ago. It was developed in response to Darwin's theory of *evolution; it is not recognized by most scientists as having a factual basis.

creation myth legend of the origin of the world. All cultures have ancient stories of the creation of the Earth or its inhabitants. Often this involves the violent death of a primordial being from whose body everything then arises; the giant Ymir in Scandinavian mythology is an example. Marriage between heaven and earth is another common explanation, as in Greek mythology (Uranus and Gaia).

Crécy, Battle of first major battle of the Hundred Years' War 1346. Philip VI of France was defeated by Edward III of England at the village of Crécy-en-Ponthieu, now in Somme *département*, France, 18 km/11 mi NE of Abbeville.

credit in economics, means by which goods or services are obtained without immediate payment, usually by agreeing to pay interest. The three main forms are **consumer credit** (usually extended to individuals by retailers), **bank credit** (such as overdrafts or personal loans), and **trade credit** (common in the commercial world both within countries and internationally).

credit in education, a system of evaluating courses so that a partial qualification or unit from one institution is accepted by another on transfer to complete a course. At US universities and colleges, the term also refers to the number of units given upon successful completion of a course.

credit card card issued by a credit company, retail outlet, or bank, which enables the holder to obtain goods or services on credit (usually to a specified limit), payable on specified terms. The first credit card was introduced 1950 in the USA.

Cree member of a North American Indian people whose language belongs to the Algonquian family. The Cree are distributed over a vast area in Canada from Québec to Alberta. In the USA the majority of Cree live in the Rocky Boys reservation in Montana. Cree and Ojibwa languages are closely related and are spoken by around 50,000 people.

creed in general, any system of belief; in the Christian church the verbal confessions of faith expressing the accepted doctrines of the church. The different forms are the *Apostles' Creed, the *Nicene Creed, and the *Athanasian Creed. The only creed recognized by the Orthodox Church is the Nicene Creed.

Creed Frederick George 1871–1957. Canadian inventor who developed the *teleprinter. He perfected the Creed telegraphy system (teleprinter), first used in Fleet Street, the headquarters of the British press, 1912 and subsequently, usually under the name Telex, in offices throughout the world.

creep in civil and mechanical engineering, the property of a solid, typically a metal, under continuous stress that causes it to deform below its yield point (the point at which any elastic solid normally stretches without any increase in load or stress). Lead, tin, and zinc, for example, exhibit creep at ordinary temperatures, as seen in the movement of the lead sheeting on the roofs of old buildings.

creeper any small, short-legged passerine bird of the family Certhidae. They spiral with a mouselike movement up tree trunks, searching for insects and larvae with their thin, downcurved beaks.

cremation disposal of the dead by burning. The custom was universal among ancient Indo-European peoples, for example, the Greeks, Romans, and Teutons. It was discontinued among Christians until the late 19th century because of their belief in the bodily resurrection of the dead. Overcrowded urban cemeteries gave rise to its revival in the West. It has remained the usual method of disposal in the East.

crème de la crème (French 'the cream of the cream') the elite, the very best.

Creole in the West Indies and Spanish America, originally someone of European descent born in the New World; later someone of mixed European and African descent. In Louisiana and other states on the Gulf of Mexico, it applies either to someone of French or Spanish descent or (popularly) to someone of mixed French or Spanish and African descent.

creole language any *pidgin language that has ceased to be simply a trade jargon in ports and markets and has become the mother tongue of a particular community. Many creoles have developed into distinct languages with literatures of their own; for example, Jamaican Creole, Haitian Creole, Krio in Sierra Leone, and Tok Pisin, now the official language of Papua New Guinea.

creosote black, oily liquid derived from coal tar, used as a wood preservative. Medicinal creosote, which is transparent and oily, is derived from wood tar.

crescent curved shape of the Moon when it appears less than half-illuminated. It also refers to any object or symbol resembling the crescent Moon. Often associated with Islam, it was first used by the Turks on their standards after the capture of Constantinople 1453, and appears on the flags of many Muslim countries. The *Red Crescent* is the Muslim equivalent of the Red Cross.

cress any of several plants of the Cruciferae family, characterized by a pungent taste. The common European garden cress *Lepidium sativum* is cultivated worldwide.

Cresson Edith 1934– . French politician and founder member of the Socialist Party, prime minister 1991–92. Cresson held successive ministerial portfolios in François Mitterrand's government 1981–86 and 1988–90. Her government was troubled by a struggling economy, a series of strikes, and unrest in many of the country's poor suburban areas, which eventually forced her resignation.

Cretaceous (Latin *creta* 'chalk') period of geological time 144–65 million years ago. It is the last period of the Mesozoic era, during which angiosperm (seed-bearing) plants evolved, and dinosaurs and other reptiles reached a peak before almost complete extinction at the end of the period. Chalk is a typical rock type of the second half of the period.

Crete (Greek *Kríti*) largest Greek island in the E Mediterranean Sea, 100 km/62 mi SE of mainland Greece
area 8,378 sq km/3,234 sq mi
capital Khaniá (Canea)
towns Iráklion (Heraklion), Rethymnon, Aghios Nikolaos
products citrus fruit, olives, wine
population (1991) 536,900
language Cretan dialect of Greek
history it has remains of the *Minoan civilization 3000–1400 BC (see *Knossos) and was successively under Roman, Byzantine, Venetian, and Turkish rule. The island was annexed by Greece 1913.

cretonne strong unglazed cotton cloth, printed with a design and used for wall hangings and upholstery. It originally referred to a fabric with an unusual weave of hempen warp and linen weft, made in France.

Crick Francis 1916– . British molecular biologist. From 1949 he researched the molecular structure of DNA, and the means whereby characteristics are transmitted from one generation to another. For this work he was awarded a Nobel prize (with Maurice *Wilkins and James *Watson) 1962.

cricket bat-and-ball game between two teams of 11 players each. It is played with a small solid ball and long flat-sided wooden bats, on a round or oval field, at the centre of which is a finely mown pitch, 20 m/22 yd long. At each end of the pitch is a wicket made up of three upright wooden sticks (stumps), surmounted by two smaller sticks (bails). The object of the game is to score more runs than the opposing team. A run is normally scored by the batsman striking the ball and exchanging ends with his or her partner until the ball is returned by a fielder, or by hitting the ball to the boundary line for an automatic four or six runs.

cricket in zoology, an insect belonging to any of various families, especially the Grillidae, of the order Orthoptera. Crickets are related to grasshoppers. They have somewhat flattened bodies and long antennae. The males make a chirping noise by rubbing together special areas on the forewings. The females have a long needlelike egglaying organ (ovipositor). There are some 900 species known worldwide.

cri de coeur (French) cry from the heart.

Crimea northern peninsula on the Black Sea, an autonomous republic of *Ukraine; formerly a region (1954–91)
area 27,000 sq km/10,425 sq mi
capital Simferopol
towns Sevastopol, Yalta
products iron, oil
population 2.5 million (70% Russian, despite return of 150,000 Tatars since 1989)
history Since 1991 the Crimea has sought to gain independence from the Ukraine; the latter has resisted all secessionist moves. A 1994 referendum in Crimea supported demands for greater autonomy and closer links with Russia.

Crimean War war 1853–56 between Russia and the allied powers of England, France, Turkey, and Sardinia. The war arose from British and French mistrust of Russia's ambitions in the Balkans. It began with an allied Anglo-French expedition to the Crimea to attack the Russian Black Sea city of Sevastopol. The battles of the river Alma, *Balaclava (including the Charge of the Light Brigade), and Inkerman 1854 led to a siege which, owing to military mismanagement, lasted for a year until Sept 1855. The war was ended by the Treaty of Paris 1856. The scandal surrounding French and British losses through disease led to the organization of proper military nursing services by Florence Nightingale.

crime fiction variant of *detective fiction distinguished by emphasis on character and atmosphere rather than solving a mystery. Examples are the works of Dashiell Hammett and Raymond Chandler during the 1930s and, in the second half of the 20th century, Patricia Highsmith and Ruth Rendell.

crime, organized illegal operations run like a

large business. The best-known such organization is the *Mafia. In the USA, organized crime began to flourish during *Prohibition 1919–33. Japanese gangsters, also highly organized, are called *yakuza*.

Criminal Injuries Compensation Board UK board established 1964 to administer financial compensation by the state for victims of crimes of violence. Victims can claim compensation for their injuries, but not for damage to property. The compensation awarded is similar to the amount that would be obtained for a court in *damages for personal injury.

Criminal Investigation Department (CID) detective branch of the London Metropolitan Police, established 1878, comprising a force of about 4,000 men and women recruited entirely from the uniformed police and controlled by an assistant commissioner. Such branches are now also found in the regional police forces.

criminal law body of law that defines the public wrongs (crimes) that are punishable by the state and establishes methods of prosecution and punishment. It is distinct from *civil law, which deals with legal relationships between individuals (including organizations), such as contract law.

Crippen Hawley Harvey 1861–1910. US murderer of his wife, variety artist Belle Elmore. He buried her remains in the cellar of his London home and tried to escape to the USA with his mistress Ethel le Neve (dressed as a boy). He was arrested on board ship following a radio message, the first criminal captured 'by radio', and was hanged.

Cripps (Richard) Stafford 1889–1952. British Labour politician, expelled from the Labour Party 1939–45 for supporting a 'Popular Front' against Chamberlain's appeasement policy. He was ambassador to Moscow 1940–42, minister of aircraft production 1942–45, and chancellor of the Exchequer 1947–50.

crith unit of mass used for weighing gases. One crith is the mass of one litre of hydrogen gas (H_2) at standard temperature and pressure.

critical angle in optics, for a ray of light passing from a denser to a less dense medium (such as from glass to air), the smallest angle of incidence at which the emergent ray grazes the surface of the denser medium – at an angle of refraction of 90°.

critical mass in nuclear physics, the minimum mass of fissile material that can undergo a continuous *chain reaction. Below this mass, too many *neutrons escape from the surface for a chain reaction to carry on; above the critical mass, the reaction may accelerate into a nuclear explosion.

critical path analysis procedure used in the management of complex projects to minimize the amount of time taken. The analysis shows which subprojects can run in parallel with each other, and which have to be completed before other subprojects can follow on. By identifying the time required for each separate subproject and the relationship between the subprojects, it is possible to produce a planning schedule showing when each subproject should be started and finished in order to complete the whole project

most efficiently. Complex projects may involve hundreds of subprojects, and computer *applications packages for critical path analysis are widely used to help reduce the time and effort involved in their analysis.

critical temperature temperature above which a particular gas cannot be converted into a liquid by pressure alone. It is also the temperature at which a magnetic material loses its magnetism (the Curie temperature or point).

Crivelli Carlo 1435/40–1495/1500. Italian painter in the early Renaissance style, active in Venice. He painted extremely detailed, decorated religious works, sometimes festooned with garlands of fruit.

Croagh Patrick holy mountain rising to 765 m/2,510 ft in County Mayo, W Ireland, one of the three national places of pilgrimage in Ireland (with Lough Derg and Knock). An annual pilgrimage on the last Sunday of July commemorates St Patrick who fasted there for the 40 days of Lent 440 AD.

Croat member of the majority ethnic group in *Croatia. Their language is generally considered to be identical to that of the Serbs, hence *Serbo-Croatian.

Croatia Republic of

area 56,538 sq km/21,824 sq mi
capital Zagreb
towns chief port: Rijeka (Fiume); other ports: Zadar, Sibenik, Split, Dubrovnik
physical Adriatic coastline with large islands; very mountainous, with part of the Karst region and the Julian and Styrian Alps; some marshland
head of state Franjo Tudjman from 1990
head of government Nikica Valentić from 1993
political system emergent democracy
products cereals, potatoes, tobacco, fruit, livestock, metal goods, textiles
currency Croatian dinar
population (1993) 4,850,000 including 75% Croats, 12% Serbs, and 1% Slovenes
language Croatian variant of Serbo-Croatian
religions Roman Catholic (Croats); Orthodox Christian (Serbs)
GNP $1,800 per head (1992)

chronology

1918 Became part of the kingdom that united the Serbs, Croats, and Slovenes.

1929 The kingdom of Croatia, Serbia, and Slovenia became Yugoslavia. Croatia continued its campaign for autonomy.

1941 Became a Nazi puppet state following German invasion.

1945 Became constituent republic of Yugoslavia.

1970s Separatist demands resurfaced. Crackdown against anti-Serb separatist agitators.

1989 Formation of opposition parties permitted.

1990 April–May: Communists defeated by Tudjman-led Croatian Democratic Union (HDZ) in first free election since 1938. Sept: 'sovereignty' declared. Dec: new constitution adopted.

1991 Feb: assembly called for Croatia's secession. March: Serb-dominated Krajina announced secession from Croatia. June: Croatia declared independence; military conflict with Serbia; internal civil war ensued. Oct: Croatia formally seceded from Yugoslavia.

1992 Jan: United Nations peace accord reached in Sarajevo; Croatia's independence recognized by the European Community. March–April: UN peacekeeping force of 14,000 drafted into Croatia. April: independence recognized by USA. May: became a member of the United Nations. Aug: Tudjman directly elected president; HDZ won assembly elections.

1993 Jan: Croatian forces launched offensive to retake parts of Serb-held Krajina, violating 1992 UN peace accord. April: new government sworn in.

Croce Benedetto 1866–1952. Italian philosopher, historian, and literary critic; an opponent of fascism. His *Filosofia dello spirito/Philosophy of the Spirit* 1902–17 was a landmark in idealism. Like Hegel, he held that ideas do not represent reality but *are* reality; but unlike Hegel, he rejected every kind of transcendence.

crochet craft technique similar to both knitting and lacemaking, in which one hooked needle is used to produce a loosely looped network of wool or cotton.

Crockett Davy 1786–1836. US folk hero, born in Tennessee, a Democratic Congressman 1827–31 and 1833–35. A series of books, of which he may have been part-author, made him into a mythical hero of the frontier, but their Whig associations cost him his office. He died in the battle of the *Alamo during the War of Texan Independence.

crocodile large aquatic carnivorous reptile of the family Crocodiliae, related to alligators and caymans, but distinguished from them by a more pointed snout and a notch in the upper jaw into which the fourth tooth in the lower jaw fits. Crocodiles can grow up to 6 m/20 ft, and live long, powerful tails that propel them when swimming. They can live up to 100 years.

crocus any plant of the genus *Crocus* of the iris family Iridaceae, native to Northern parts of the Old World, especially S Europe and Asia Minor. It has single yellow, purple, or white flowers and narrow, pointed leaves.

Croesus 6th century BC. Last king of Lydia, famed for his wealth. His court included *Solon, who warned him that no man could be called happy until his life had ended happily. When

Croesus was overthrown by Cyrus the Great 546 BC and condemned to be burned to death, he called out Solon's name. Cyrus, having learned the reason, spared his life.

croft small farm in the Highlands of Scotland, traditionally farming common land cooperatively; the 1886 Crofters Act gave security of tenure to crofters. Today, although grazing land is still shared, arable land is typically enclosed.

Crohn's disease or **regional ileitis** chronic inflammatory bowel disease. It tends to flare up for a few days at a time, causing diarrhoea, abdominal cramps, loss of appetite, and mild fever. The cause of Crohn's disease is unknown, although stress may be a factor.

Cro-Magnon prehistoric human *Homo sapiens sapiens* believed to be ancestral to Europeans, the first skeletons of which were found 1868 in the Cro-Magnon cave near Les Eyzies, in the Dordogne region of France. They are thought to have superseded the Neanderthals in the Middle East, Africa, Europe, and Asia about 40,000 years ago. Although modern in skeletal form, they were more robust in build than some present-day humans. They hunted bison, reindeer, and horses, and are associated with Upper Palaeolithic cultures, which produced fine flint and bone tools, jewellery, and naturalistic cave paintings.

Crome John 1768–1821. British landscape painter, founder of the **Norwich school** with John Sell Cotman 1803. His works include *The Poringland Oak* 1818 (Tate Gallery, London), showing Dutch influence.

Crompton Richmal. Pen name of R C Lamburn 1890–1969. British writer. She is remembered for her stories about the mischievous schoolboy 'William'.

Crompton Samuel 1753–1827. British inventor at the time of the Industrial Revolution. He invented the 'spinning mule' 1779, combining the ideas of Richard *Arkwright and James *Hargreaves. Though widely adopted, his invention brought him little financial return.

Cromwell Oliver 1599–1658. English general and politician, Puritan leader of the Parliamentary side in the *Civil War. He raised cavalry forces (later called **Ironsides**) which aided the victories at Edgehill 1642 and *Marston Moor

crocodile The estuarine, or saltwater, crocodile of India, SE Asia, and Australasia is one of the largest and most dangerous of its family.

1644, and organized the New Model Army, which he led (with General Fairfax) to victory at Naseby 1645. He declared Britain a republic ('the Commonwealth') 1649, following the execution of Charles I. As Lord Protector (ruler) from 1653, Cromwell established religious toleration and raised Britain's prestige in Europe on the basis of an alliance with France against Spain.

Cromwell Richard 1626–1712. Son of Oliver *Cromwell, he succeeded his father as Lord Protector but resigned May 1659, having been forced to abdicate by the army. He lived in exile after the Restoration until 1680, when he returned.

Cromwell Thomas, Earl of Essex c. 1485–1540. English politician who drafted the legislation making the Church of England independent of Rome. Originally in Lord Chancellor Wolsey's service, he became secretary to Henry VIII 1534 and the real director of government policy; he was executed for treason.

Cronkite Walter 1916– . US broadcast journalist who was anchorperson of the national evening news programme for CBS, a US television network, from 1962 to 1981.

Crookes William 1832–1919. English scientist whose many chemical and physical discoveries included the metallic element thallium 1861, the radiometer 1875, and the Crookes high-vacuum tube used in X-ray techniques.

crop in birds, the thin-walled enlargement of the digestive tract between the oesophagus and stomach. It is an effective storage organ especially in seed-eating birds; a pigeon's crop can hold about 500 cereal grains. Digestion begins in the crop, by the moisturizing of food. A crop also occurs in insects and annelid worms.

crop any plant product grown or harvested for human use. Over 80 crops are grown worldwide, providing people with the majority of their food and supplying fibres, rubber, pharmaceuticals, dyes, and other materials. Crops grown for export are *cash crops. A *catch crop is one grown in the interval between two main crops.

crop circle circular area of flattened grain found in fields especially in SE England, with increasing frequency every summer since 1980. More than 1,000 such formations were reported in the UK 1991. The cause is unknown.

crop rotation system of regularly changing the crops grown on a piece of land. The crops are grown in a particular order to utilize and add to the nutrients in the soil and to prevent the build-up of insect and fungal pests. Including a legume crop, such as peas or beans, in the rotation helps build up nitrate in the soil because the roots contain bacteria capable of fixing nitrogen from the air.

croquet outdoor game played with mallets and balls on a level hooped lawn measuring 27 m/ 90 ft by 18 m/60 ft. Played in France in the 16th and 17th centuries, it gained popularity in the USA and England in the 1850s.

Crosby Bing (Harry Lillis) 1904–1977. US film actor and singer who achieved world success with his distinctive style of crooning in such songs as 'Pennies from Heaven' 1936 (featured in a film of the same name) and 'White Christmas' 1942. He won an acting Oscar for *Going My Way* 1944, and made a series of 'road' film comedies with Dorothy Lamour and Bob *Hope, the last being *Road to Hong Kong* 1962.

cross symbol of the Christian religion, in widespread use since the 3rd century. It is a symbol of the crucifixion of Jesus and the central significance of his suffering, death, and resurrection. The Latin cross is the most commonly used; other types are the Greek cross, St Anthony's cross, and St Andrew's cross. Symbolic crosses were used by pre-Christian cultures, for example the ancient Egyptian ankh (St Anthony's cross with a loop at the top), symbol of life, and the swastika, used by Hindus, Buddhists, Celts, and N American Indians before it was adopted by the Nazis.

crossbill species of bird, a *finch of the genus *Loxia*, in which the hooked tips of the upper and lower beak cross one another, an adaptation for extracting the seeds from conifer cones. The red or common crossbill *Loxia curvirostra* is found in parts of Eurasia and North America.

crossing over in biology, a process that occurs during *meiosis. While the chromosomes are lying alongside each other in pairs, each partner may twist around the other and exchange corresponding chromosomal segments. It is a form of genetic *recombination, which increases variation and thus provides the raw material of evolution.

Crossman Richard (Howard Stafford) 1907–1974. British Labour politician. He was minister of housing and local government 1964–66 and of health and social security 1968–70. His posthumous *Crossman Papers* 1975 revealed confidential cabinet discussion.

crossword puzzle in which a grid of open and blacked-out squares must be filled with interlocking words, to be read horizontally and vertically, according to numbered clues. The first crossword was devised by Arthur Wynne of Liverpool, England, in the *New York World* 1913.

croup inflammation (usually viral) of a child's larynx and trachea, with croaking breathing and hoarse coughing.

crow any of 35 species of the genus *Corvus*, family Corvidae, which also includes jays and magpies. Ravens belong to the same genus as crows. Crows are usually about 45 cm/1.5 ft long, black, with a strong bill feathered at the base, and omnivorous with a bias towards animal food. They are considered to be very intelligent.

Crowley John 1942– . US writer of science fiction and fantasy, notably *Little, Big* 1980 and *Aegypt* 1987, which contain esoteric knowledge and theoretical puzzles.

crown colony any British colony that is under the direct legislative control of the crown and does not possess its own system of representative government. Crown colonies are administered by a crown-appointed governor or by elected or nominated legislative and executive councils with an official majority. Usually the crown retains rights of veto and of direct legislation by orders in council.

crown court in England and Wales, any of several courts that hear serious criminal cases referred from *magistrates' courts after *committal proceedings. They replaced *quarter sessions and assizes, which were abolished 1971. Appeals against conviction or sentence at magistrates' courts may be heard in crown courts. Appeal from a crown court is to the Court of Appeal.

Crown Estate title (from 1956) of land in UK formerly owned by the monarch but handed to Parliament by George III in 1760 in exchange for an annual payment (called the civil list). The Crown Estate owns valuable sites in central London, and 268,400 acres in England and Scotland.

crown jewels or *regalia* symbols of royal authority. The British set (except for the Ampulla and the Anointing Spoon) were broken up at the time of Oliver Cromwell, and now date from the Restoration. In 1671 Colonel *Blood attempted to steal them, but was captured, then pardoned and pensioned by Charles II. They are kept in the Tower of London in the Crown Jewel House (1967).

crucifixion death by fastening to a cross, a form of capital punishment used by the ancient Romans, Persians, and Carthaginians, and abolished by the Roman emperor Constantine. Specifically, **the Crucifixion** refers to the execution by the Romans of *Jesus in this manner.

crude oil the unrefined form of *petroleum.

Cruelty, Theatre of theory advanced by Antonin *Artaud in his book *Le Théâtre et son double* 1938 and adopted by a number of writers and directors. It aims to shock the audience into an awareness of basic, primitive human nature through the release of visceral feelings usually repressed by conventional behaviour.

Cruft Charles 1852–1938. British dog expert. He organized his first dog show 1886, and from that year annual shows bearing his name were held in Islington, London. In 1948 the show's venue moved to Olympia and in 1979 to Earl's Court.

Cruikshank George 1792–1878. British painter and illustrator, remembered for his political cartoons and illustrations for Charles Dickens's *Oliver Twist* and Daniel Defoe's *Robinson Crusoe*.

cruise missile long-range guided missile that has a terrain-seeking radar system and flies at moderate speed and low altitude. It is descended from the German V-1 of World War II. Initial trials in the 1950s demonstrated the limitations of cruise missiles, which included high fuel consumption and relatively slow speeds (when compared to intercontinental ballistic missiles – ICBMs) as well as inaccuracy and a small warhead. Improvements to guidance systems by the use of terrain-contour matching (TERCOM) ensured pinpoint accuracy on low-level flights after launch from a mobile ground launcher (ground-launched cruise missile – GLCM), from an aircraft (air-launched cruise missile – ALCM), or from a submarine or ship (sea-launched cruise missile – SLCM).

crumple zone region at the front and rear of a motor vehicle that is designed to crumple gradually during a collision, so reducing the risk of serious injury to passengers. The progressive crumpling absorbs the kinetic energy of the vehicle more gradually than a rigid structure would, thereby diminishing the forces of deceleration acting on the vehicle and on the people inside.

crusade European war against non-Christians and heretics, sanctioned by the pope; in particular, the Crusades, a series of wars 1096–1291 undertaken by European rulers to recover Palestine from the Muslims. Motivated by religious zeal, the desire for land, and the trading ambitions of the major Italian cities, the Crusades were varied in their aims and effects.

crust the outermost part of the structure of Earth, consisting of two distinct parts, the oceanic crust and the continental crust. The **oceanic** crust is on average about 10 km/6.2 mi thick and consists mostly of basaltic types of rock. By contrast, the **continental** crust is largely made of granite and is more complex in its structure. Because of the movements of *plate tectonics, the oceanic crust is in no place older than about 200 million years. However, parts of the continental crust are over 3 billion years old.

crustacean one of the class of arthropods that includes crabs, lobsters, shrimps, woodlice, and barnacles. The external skeleton is made of protein and chitin hardened with lime. Each segment bears a pair of appendages that may be modified as sensory feelers (antennae), as mouthparts, or as swimming, walking, or grasping structures.

Cruyff Johan 1947– . Dutch footballer, an outstanding European player in the 1970s. He was capped 48 times by his country, scoring 33 goals. He was named European Footballer of the Year on three occasions.

cryogenics science of very low temperatures (approaching *absolute zero), including the production of very low temperatures and the exploitation of special properties associated with them, such as the disappearance of electrical resistance (*superconductivity).

cryolite rare granular crystalline mineral (sodium aluminium fluoride), Na_3AlF_6, used in the electrolytic reduction of *bauxite to aluminium. It is chiefly found in Greenland.

cryonics practice of freezing a body at the moment of clinical death with the aim of enabling eventual resuscitation. The body, drained of blood, is indefinitely preserved in a thermos-type container filled with liquid nitrogen at –196°C/–321°F.

cryptography science of creating and reading codes; for example, those produced by the Enigma coding machine used by the Germans in World War II and those used in commerce by banks encoding electronic fund-transfer messages, business firms sending computer-conveyed memos between headquarters, and in the growing field of electronic mail. No method of encrypting is completely unbreakable, but decoding can be made extremely complex and time consuming.

cryptosporidium waterborne parasite first discovered 1983. It infects drinking-water supplies, causing diarrhoea, abdominal cramps, vomiting, and fever, and can be fatal in people with damaged immune systems, such as AIDS sufferers or those with leukaemia.

sodium chloride

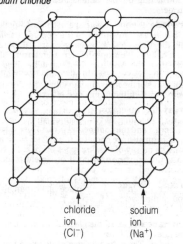

chloride   sodium
ion   ion
(Cl⁻)   (Na⁺)

crystal *The sodium chloride, or common salt, crystal is a regular cubic array of charged atoms (ions) – positive sodium atoms and negative chlorine atoms.*

crystal substance with an orderly three-dimensional arrangement of its atoms or molecules, thereby creating an external surface of clearly defined smooth faces having characteristic angles between them. Examples are table salt and quartz.

crystallography the scientific study of crystals. In 1912 it was found that the shape and size of the repeating atomic patterns (unit cells) in a crystal could be determined by passing X-rays through a sample. This method, known as *X-ray diffraction, opened up an entirely new way of 'seeing' atoms. It has been found that many substances have a unit cell that exhibits all the symmetry of the whole crystal; in table salt (sodium chloride, NaCl), for instance, the unit cell is an exact cube.

Crystal Palace glass and iron building designed by Joseph *Paxton, housing the Great Exhibition of 1851 in Hyde Park, London; later rebuilt in modified form at Sydenham Hill 1854 (burned down 1936).

CSCE abbreviation for *Conference on Security and Cooperation in Europe*.

CSE (abbreviation for *Certificate of Secondary Education*) in the UK, the examinations taken by the majority of secondary school pupils who were not regarded as academically capable of GCE *O level, until the introduction of the common secondary examination system, *GCSE, in 1988.

Ctesiphon ruined royal city of the Parthians, and later capital of the Sassanian Empire, 19 km/12 mi SE of Baghdad, Iraq. A palace of the 4th century still has its throne room standing, spanned by a single vault of unreinforced brickwork some 24 m/80 ft across.

CT scanner or *CAT scanner medical device used to obtain detailed X-ray pictures of the inside of a patient's body.

cu abbreviation for *cubic* (measure).

Cuba Republic of (*República de Cuba*)

area 110,860 sq km/42,820 sq mi
capital Havana
towns Santiago de Cuba, Camagüey
physical comprises Cuba, the largest and westernmost of the West Indies, and smaller islands including Isle of Youth; low hills; Sierra Maestra mountains in SE
head of state and government Fidel Castro Ruz from 1959
political system communist republic
political party Communist Party of Cuba (PCC), Marxist-Leninist
exports sugar, tobacco, coffee, nickel, fish
currency Cuban peso
population (1993 est) 11,000,000; 37% are white of Spanish descent, 51% mulatto, and 11% are of African origin; growth rate 0.6% p.a.
language Spanish
religions Roman Catholic 85%; also Episcopalians and Methodists
GNP $1,000 per head (1991)
chronology
1492 Christopher Columbus landed in Cuba and claimed it for Spain.
1898 USA defeated Spain in Spanish-American War; Spain gave up all claims to Cuba.
1901 Cuba achieved independence; Tomás Estrada Palma became first president of the Republic of Cuba.
1933 Fulgencia Batista seized power.
1944 Batista retired.
1952 Batista seized power again to begin an oppressive regime.
1953 Fidel Castro led an unsuccessful coup against Batista.
1956 Second unsuccessful coup by Castro.
1959 Batista overthrown by Castro. Constitution of 1940 replaced by a 'Fundamental Law', making Castro prime minister, his brother Raúl Castro his deputy, and Che Guevara his number three.
1960 All US businesses in Cuba appropriated without compensation; USA broke off diplomatic relations.
1961 USA sponsored an unsuccessful invasion at the Bay of Pigs. Castro announced that Cuba had become a communist state, with a Marxist-Leninist programme of economic development.

1962 Cuba expelled from the Organization of American States. Soviet nuclear missiles installed but subsequently removed from Cuba at US insistence.

1965 Cuba's sole political party renamed Cuban Communist Party (PCC). With Soviet help, Cuba began to make considerable economic and social progress.

1972 Cuba became a full member of the Moscow-based Council for Mutual Economic Assistance.

1976 New socialist constitution approved; Castro elected president.

1976–81 Castro became involved in extensive international commitments, sending troops as Soviet surrogates, particularly to Africa.

1984 Castro tried to improve US-Cuban relations by discussing exchange of US prisoners in Cuba for Cuban 'undesirables' in the USA.

1988 Peace accord with South Africa signed, agreeing to withdrawal of Cuban troops from Angola.

1989 Reduction in Cuba's overseas military activities.

1991 Soviet troops withdrawn.

1993 First direct parliamentary vote held. Communist seats were uncontested and all candidates won their seats.

1994 Economy deteriorated; refugee exodus.

Cuban missile crisis confrontation in international relations 1962 when Soviet rockets were installed in Cuba and US president Kennedy compelled Soviet leader Khrushchev, by an ultimatum, to remove them. The drive by the USSR to match the USA in nuclear weaponry dates from this event.

cube in geometry, a solid figure whose faces are all squares. It has six equal-area faces and 12 equal-length edges. If the length of one edge is l, the volume V of the cube is given by $V = l^3$ and its surface area $A = 6l^2$.

cubic measure measure of volume, indicated either by the word 'cubic' followed by a linear measure, as in 'cubic foot', or the word 'cubed' after a linear measure, as in 'metre cubed'.

Cubism revolutionary movement in early 20th-century painting, pioneering abstract art. Its founders, Georges Braque and Pablo Picasso, were admirers of Paul Cézanne and were inspired by his attempt to create a structure on the surface of the canvas. About 1907–10 in France the Cubists began to 'abstract' images from nature, gradually releasing themselves from the imitation of reality. Cubism announced that a work of art exists in its own right rather than as a representation of the real world, and it attracted such artists as Juan Gris, Fernand Léger, and Robert Delaunay.

cubit earliest known unit of length, which originated between 2800 and 2300 BC. It is approximately 50.5 cm/20.6 in long, which is about the length of the human forearm measured from the tip of the middle finger to the elbow.

cuboid six-sided three-dimensional prism whose faces are all rectangles. A brick is a cuboid.

Cuchulain in Celtic mythology, a legendary hero, the chief figure in a cycle of Irish legends. He is associated with his uncle Conchobar, king of Ulster; his most famous exploits are described in *Taín Bó Cuailnge/The Cattle Raid of Cuchulain*.

cuckoo species of bird, any of about 200 members of the family Cuculidae, especially the Eurasian cuckoo *Cuculus canorus*, whose name derives from its characteristic call. Somewhat hawklike, it is about 33 cm/1.1 ft long, bluish-grey and barred beneath (females sometimes reddish), and has a long, typically rounded tail. Cuckoos feed on insects, including hairy caterpillars that are distasteful to most birds. It is a 'brood parasite', laying its eggs singly, at intervals of about 48 hours, in the nests of small insectivorous birds. As soon as the young cuckoo hatches, it ejects all other young birds or eggs from the nest and is tended by its 'foster parents' until fledging. American species hatch and rear their own young.

cuckoo flower or **lady's smock** perennial plant *Cardamine pratensis*, family Cruciferae. Native to Britain, it is common in damp meadows and marshy woods. It bears pale lilac flowers, which later turn white, from April to June.

cuckoo-pint or **lords-and-ladies** perennial plant *Arum maculatum* of the Araceae family. The large arrow-shaped leaves appear in early spring, and the flower-bearing stalks are enveloped by a bract, or spathe. In late summer the bright red, berrylike fruits, which are poisonous, make their appearance.

cucumber trailing annual plant *Cucumis sativus* of the gourd family Cucurbitaceae, producing long, green-skinned fruit with crisp, translucent, edible flesh. Small cucumbers, called gherkins, usually the fruit of *C. anguria*, are often pickled.

Cugnot Nicolas-Joseph 1728–1804. French engineer who produced the first high-pressure steam engine. While serving in the French army, he was asked to design a steam-operated gun carriage. After several years, he produced a three-wheeled, high-pressure carriage capable of carrying 1,800 litres/400 gallons of water and four passengers at a speed of 5 kph/3 mph. Although he worked further on the carriage, the political upheavals of the French revolutionary era obstructed progress and his invention was ignored.

cuius regio, eius religio (Latin) those who live in a country should adopt the religion of its ruler.

Cukor George 1899–1983. US film director. He moved to the cinema from the theatre, and was praised for his skilled handling of such stars as Greta *Garbo (in *Camille* 1937) and Katharine Hepburn (in *The Philadelphia Story* 1940). He won an Academy Award for the direction of *My Fair Lady* 1964.

cul-de-sac (French 'bottom of the bag') street closed off at one end; an inescapable situation.

Culloden, Battle of defeat 1746 of the *Jacobite rebel army of the British prince *Charles Edward Stuart by the Duke of Cumberland on a stretch of moorland in Inverness-shire, Scotland. This battle effectively ended the military challenge of the Jacobite rebellion.

cultural anthropology or *social anthropology* subdiscipline of anthropology that analyses human culture and society, the nonbiological and behavioural aspects of humanity. Two principal branches are ethnography (the study at first hand of living cultures) and ethnology (the comparison of cultures using ethnographic evidence).

Cultural Revolution mass movement begun by Chinese Communist Party chair Mao Zedong 1966–69, directed against the upper middle class – bureaucrats, artists, and academics who were killed, imprisoned, humiliated, or 'resettled'. Intended to 'purify' Chinese communism, it was also an attempt by Mao to renew his political and ideological pre-eminence inside China. Half a million people are estimated to have been killed.

culture in biology, the growing of living cells and tissues in laboratory conditions.

culture in sociology and anthropology, the way of life of a particular society or group of people, including patterns of thought, beliefs, behaviour, customs, traditions, rituals, dress, and language, as well as art, music, and literature. Sociologists and anthropologists use culture as a key concept in describing and analysing human societies.

Cumae ancient city in Italy, on the coast about 16 km/10 mi W of Naples. In was the seat of the oracle of the Cumaean Sibyl.

Cuman member of a powerful alliance of Turkic-speaking peoples of the Middle Ages, which dominated the steppes in the 11th and 12th centuries and built an empire reaching from the river Volga to the Danube.

Cumberland former county of NW England, merged with Cumbria 1974.

Cumberland Ernest Augustus, Duke of Cumberland 1771–1851. King of Hanover from 1837, the fifth son of George III of Britain. A high Tory and an opponent of all reforms, he attempted to suppress the constitution but met with open resistance that had to be put down by force.

Cumberland William Augustus, Duke of Cumberland 1721–1765. British general who ended the Jacobite rising in Scotland with the Battle of Culloden 1746; his brutal repression of the Highlanders earned him the nickname of 'Butcher'.

Cumbria county in NW England
area 6,810 sq km/2,629 sq mi
towns Carlisle (administrative headquarters), Barrow, Kendal, Whitehaven, Workington, Penrith
physical Lake District National Park, including Scafell Pike 978 m/3,210 ft, highest mountain in England; Helvellyn 950 m/3,118 ft; Lake Windermere, the largest lake in England, 17 km/10.5 mi long, 1.6 km/1 mi wide; other lakes (Derwentwater, Ullswater)
products the traditional coal, iron, and steel industries of the coast towns have been replaced by newer industries including chemicals, plastics, and electronics; in the N and E there is dairying, and West Cumberland Farmers is the country's largest agricultural cooperative
population (1991) 486,900

cumin seedlike fruit of the herb *Cuminum cyminum* of the carrot family Umbelliferae, with a bitter flavour. It is used as a spice in cooking.

cummings e(dward) e(stlin) 1894–1962. US poet whose published collections of poetry

include *Tulips and Chimneys* 1923. His poems were initially notorious for their idiosyncratic punctuation and typography (he always wrote his name in lower-case letters, for example), but their lyric power has gradually been recognized.

cumulative frequency in statistics, the total frequency of a given value up to and including a certain point in a set of data. It is used to draw the cumulative frequency curve, the ogive.

cuneiform ancient writing system formed of combinations of wedge-shaped strokes, usually impressed on clay. It was probably invented by the Sumerians, and was in use in Mesopotamia as early as the middle of the 4th millennium BC.

Cunene or **Kunene** river rising near Nova Lisboa in W central Angola. It flows S to the frontier with Namibia, then W to the Atlantic; length 250 km/150 mi.

Cunningham Merce 1919– . US dancer and choreographer. Influenced by Martha *Graham, with whose company he was soloist from 1939–45, he formed his own avant-garde dance company and school in New York in 1953. His works include *The Seasons* 1947, *Antic Meet* 1958, *Squaregame* 1976, and *Arcade* 1985.

Cupid in Roman mythology, the god of love, identified with the Greek god *Eros.

cuprite Cu_2O ore (copper(I) oxide), found in crystalline form or in earthy masses. It is red to black in colour, and is often called ruby copper.

cupronickel copper alloy (75% copper and 25% nickel), used in hardware products and for coinage.

Curaçao island in the West Indies, one of the *Netherlands Antilles; area 444 sq km/171 sq mi; population (1988) 148,500. The principal industry, dating from 1918, is the refining of Venezuelan petroleum. Curaçao was colonized by Spain 1527, annexed by the Dutch West India Company 1634, and gave its name from 1924 to the group of islands renamed Netherlands Antilles in 1948. Its capital is the port of Willemstad.

curare black, resinous poison extracted from the bark and juices of various South American trees and plants. Originally used on arrowheads by Amazonian hunters to paralyse prey, it blocks nerve stimulation of the muscles. Alkaloid derivatives (called curarines) are used in medicine as muscle relaxants during surgery.

curate in the Christian church, literally, a priest who has the cure of souls in a parish, and the term is so used in mainland Europe. In the Church of England, a curate is an unbeneficed cleric who acts as assistant to a parish priest, more exactly an 'assistant curate'.

Curia Romana the judicial and administrative bodies through which the pope carries on the government of the Roman Catholic Church. It includes certain tribunals; the chancellery, which issues papal bulls; various offices including that of the cardinal secretary of state; and the Congregations, or councils of cardinals, each with a particular department of work.

Curie Marie (born Sklodovska) 1867–1934. Polish scientist. In 1898 she reported the possible existence of a new, powerfully radioactive element in pitchblende ores. Her husband, Pierre (1859–1906) abandoned his own researches to assist her, and in the same year they announced the existence of polonium and radium. They isolated the pure elements 1902. Both scientists refused to take out a patent on their discovery and were jointly awarded the Davy Medal 1903 and the Nobel Prize for Physics 1903, with Antoine *Becquerel. Marie Curie wrote a *Treatise on Radioactivity* 1910, and was awarded the Nobel Prize for Chemistry 1911.

curium synthesized, radioactive, metallic element of the *actinide* series, symbol Cm, atomic number 96, relative atomic mass 247. It is produced by bombarding plutonium or americium with neutrons. Its longest-lived isotope has a half-life of 1.7×10^7 years.

curlew wading bird of the genus Numenius of the sandpiper family, Scolopacidae. The curlew is between 36 cm/14 in and 55 cm/1.8 ft in length, and has mottled brown plumage, long legs, and a long, thin, downcurved bill. Several species live in N Europe, Asia, and North America. The name derives from its haunting flutelike call.

curling game played on ice with stones; sometimes described as 'bowls on ice'. One of the national games of Scotland, it has spread to many countries. It can also be played on artificial (cement or tarmacadam) ponds.

currant berry of a small seedless variety of cultivated grape *Vitis vinifera*. Currants are grown on a large scale in Greece and California and used dried in cooking and baking. Because of the similarity of the fruit, the name currant is also given to several species of shrubs in the genus *Ribes*, family Grossulariaceae.

current flow of a body of water or air, or of heat, moving in a definite direction. There are three basic types of *oceanic current: **drift currents** are broad and slow-moving; **stream currents** are narrow and swift-moving; and **upwelling currents** bring cold, nutrient-rich water from the ocean bottom.

current account in economics, that part of the balance of payments concerned with current transactions, as opposed to capital movements. It includes trade (visibles) and service transactions, such as investment, insurance, shipping, and tourism (invisibles). The state of the current account is regarded as a barometer of overall economic health.

current asset or *circulating* or *floating asset* any asset of a business that could be turned into cash in a limited period of time, generally less than a year. Current assets include stocks, accounts receivable or billings, short-term investments, and cash.

current liability any debt of a business that falls due within one year. Current liabilities include creditors (including employees), bank overdrafts, and interest.

current ratio in a company, the ratio of current assets to current liabilities. It is a general indication of the adequacy of an organization's working capital and its ability to meet day-to-day calls upon it.

curriculum vitae (CV) account of a person's education and previous employment, attached to a job application.

curry (Tamil *kari* 'sauce') traditional Indian mixture of spices used to flavour a dish of rice, meat, and/or vegetables. Spices include turmeric, fenugreek, cloves, chillies, cumin, cinnamon, ginger, black and cayenne pepper, coriander, and caraway.

cursor on a computer screen, the symbol that indicates the current entry position (position where the next character will appear). It usually consists of a solid rectangle or underline character, flashing on and off.

curtain wall in buildings, a lightweight wall of glass or aluminium that is not load-bearing and is hung from a metal frame rather than built up from the ground like a brick wall. Curtain walls are typically used in high-rise blocks.

Curtiz Michael. Adopted name of Mihaly Kertész 1888–1962. Hungarian-born film director who worked in Austria, Germany, and France before moving to the USA in 1926, where he made several films with Errol Flynn, directed *Mildred Pierce* 1945, which revitalized Joan Crawford's career, and *Casablanca* 1942 (Academy Award).

curve in geometry, the *locus of a point moving according to specified conditions. The circle is the locus of all points equidistant from a given point (the centre). Other common geometrical curves are the *ellipse, *parabola, and *hyperbola, which are also produced when a cone is cut by a plane at different angles.

Curzon George Nathaniel, 1st Marquess Curzon of Kedleston 1859–1925. British Conservative politician, viceroy of India 1899–1905. During World War I, he was a member of the cabinet 1916–19. As foreign secretary 1919–24, he set up a British protectorate over Persia.

Cushing Harvey Williams 1869–1939. US neurologist who pioneered neurosurgery. He developed a range of techniques for the surgical treatment of brain tumours, and also studied the link between the *pituitary gland and conditions such as dwarfism.

Cushing Peter 1913–1994. British actor who specialized in horror roles in films made at Hammer studios 1957–73, including *Dracula* 1958, *The Mummy* 1959, and *Frankenstein Must Be Destroyed* 1969. Other films include *Doctor Who and the Daleks* 1966, *Star Wars* 1977, and *Top Secret* 1984.

Cushing's syndrome condition in which the body chemistry is upset by excessive production of *steroid hormones from the adrenal cortex.

cusp point where two branches of a curve meet and the tangents to each branch coincide.

custard apple any of several tropical fruits produced by trees and shrubs of the family Annonaceae, often cultivated for their large, edible, heart-shaped fruits. *Annona reticulata*, bullock's heart, bears a large dark-brown fruit containing a sweet, reddish-yellow pulp; it is a native of the West Indies.

Custer George A(rmstrong) 1839–1876. US Civil War general, the Union's youngest brigadier general as a result of a brilliant war record. He campaigned against the Sioux from 1874, and was killed with a detachment of his troops by the forces of Sioux chief Sitting Bull in the Battle of Little Bighorn, Montana: also called *Custer's last stand*, 25 June 1876.

custody of children the legal control of a

minor by an adult. Parents often have joint custody of their children, but this may be altered by a court order, which may be made in various different circumstances. One parent may have 'care and control' over the day-to-day activities of the child while the other or both together have custody. In all cases, the court's role is to give the welfare of the child paramount consideration.

cuticle the horny noncellular surface layer of many invertebrates such as insects; in botany, the waxy surface layer on those parts of plants that are exposed to the air, continuous except for *stomata and *lenticels. All types are secreted by the cells of the *epidermis. A cuticle reduces water loss and, in arthropods, acts as an *exoskeleton.

cuttlefish any of a family, Sepiidae, of squidlike cephalopods with an internal calcareous shell (cuttlebone). The common cuttle *Sepia officinalis* of the Atlantic and Mediterranean is up to 30 cm/1 ft long. It swims actively by means of the fins into which the sides of its oval, flattened body are expanded, and jerks itself backwards by shooting a jet of water from its 'siphon'.

Cuvier Georges, Baron Cuvier 1769–1832. French comparative anatomist, the founder of palaeontology. In 1799 he showed that some species have become extinct by reconstructing extinct giant animals that he believed were destroyed in a series of giant deluges. These ideas are expressed in *Recherches sur les ossiments fossiles de quadrupèdes* 1812 and *Discours sur les révolutions de la surface du globe* 1825.

Cuyp Aelbert 1620–1691. Dutch painter. His subjects were countryside scenes, seascapes, and portraits. His idyllically peaceful landscapes are bathed in a golden light, reflecting the influence of Claude Lorrain, for example, *A Herdsman with Cows by a River* about 1650 (National Gallery, London).

Cuzco city in S Peru, capital of Cuzco department, in the Andes Mountains, over 3,350 m/ 11,000 ft above sea level and 560 km/350 mi SE of Lima; population (1988) 255,000. It was founded in the 11th century as the ancient capital of the *Inca empire and was captured by the Spanish conqueror Francisco Pizarro 1533.

CV abbreviation for *curriculum vitae*.

cwt symbol for *hundredweight*, a unit of weight equal to 112 pounds (50.802 kg); 100 lb (45.36 kg) in the USA.

cyanide CN⁻ ion derived from hydrogen cyanide (HCN), and any salt containing this ion (produced when hydrogen cyanide is neutralized by alkalis), such as potassium cyanide (KCN). The principal cyanides are potassium, sodium, calcium, mercury, gold, and copper. Certain cyanides are poisons.

cyanobacteria (singular **cyanobacterium**) alternative name for *blue-green algae.

cyanocobalamin chemical name for *vitamin B₁₂, which is normally produced by microorganisms in the gut. The richest natural source is raw liver. The deficiency disease, pernicious anaemia, is the poor development of red blood cells with possible degeneration of the spinal chord. Sufferers develop extensive bruising and recover slowly from even minor injuries.

cybernetics science concerned with how systems organize, regulate, and reproduce themselves, and also how they evolve and learn. In the laboratory, inanimate objects are created that behave like living systems. Applications range from the creation of electronic artificial limbs to the running of the fully automated factory where decision making machines operate up to managerial level.

cyberspace imaginary, interactive 'worlds' created by computers. The term refers to the electronic forum shared by millions of users of on-line computer services worldwide. Such services, which can be accessed through a home computer using a modem, include *electronic mail, electronic conferencing systems, chat lines, and electronic 'billboards', and became widely available to home users with the rapid development of on-line technology from the 1980s. Cyberspace is also used interchangeably with 'virtual world' or *virtual reality; the term was coined by the US science-fiction writer William Gibson (1948–) in his first novel *Neuromancer* 1984.

cycad plant of the order Cycadales belonging to the gymnosperms. Some have a superficial resemblance to palms, others to ferns. Their large cones contain fleshy seeds. There are ten genera and about 80–100 species, native to tropical and subtropical countries. The stems of many species yield an edible starchy substance resembling sago. Cycads were widespread during the Mesozoic era.

Cyclades (Greek *Kikládhes*) group of about 200 Greek islands in the Aegean Sea, lying between mainland Greece and Turkey; area 2,579 sq km/996 sq mi; population (1981) 88,500. They include Andros, Melos, Paros, Naxos, and Siros, on which is the capital Hermoupolis.

cyclamen any plant of the genus *Cyclamen* of perennial plants of the primrose family Primulaceae, with heart-shaped leaves and petals that are twisted at the base and bent back. The flowers are usually white or pink, and several species are cultivated.

cycle in physics, a sequence of changes that moves a system away from, and then back to, its original state. An example is a vibration that moves a particle first in one direction and then in the opposite direction, with the particle returning to its original position at the end of the vibration.

cyclic compound any of a group of organic chemicals that have rings of atoms in their molecules, giving them a closed-chain structure.

cycloid in geometry, a curve resembling a series of arches traced out by a point on the circumference of a circle that rolls along a straight line. Its applications include the study of the motion of wheeled vehicles along roads and tracks.

cyclone alternative name for a *depression, an area of low atmospheric pressure. A severe cyclone that forms in the tropics is called a tropical cyclone or *hurricane.

Cyclops in Greek mythology, one of a race of Sicilian giants, who had one eye in the middle of the forehead and lived as shepherds. *Odysseus blinded the Cyclops *Polyphemus in Homer's *Odyssey*.

Cygnus large prominent constellation of the northern hemisphere, named after its shape

(Latin 'swan'). Its brightest star is first-magnitude *Deneb.

cylinder in geometry, a tubular solid figure with a circular base. In everyday use, the term applies to a *right cylinder*, the curved surface of which is at right angles to the base.

cymbal ancient musical instrument of percussion, consisting of a shallow circular brass dish held at the centre; either used in pairs clashed together or singly, struck with a beater. Smaller finger cymbals or *crotala*, used by Debussy and Stockhausen, are more solid and pure in tone. Turkish or 'buzz' cymbals have loose rivets to extend the sound.

Cymbeline or *Cunobelin* 1st century AD. King of the Catuvellauni AD 5–40, who fought unsuccessfully against the Roman invasion of Britain. His capital was at Colchester.

Cymru Welsh name for *Wales.

Cynic school of Greek philosophy (Cynicism), founded in Athens about 400 BC by Antisthenes, a disciple of Socrates, who advocated a stern and simple morality and a complete disregard of pleasure and comfort.

cypress any coniferous tree or shrub of the genera *Cupressus* and *Chamaecyparis*, family Cupressaceae. There are about 20 species, originating from temperate regions of the northern hemisphere. They have minute, scalelike leaves and cones made up of woody, wedge-shaped scales containing an aromatic resin.

Cyprian, St *c.* 210–258. Christian martyr, one of the earliest Christian writers, and bishop of Carthage about 249. He wrote a treatise on the unity of the church. Feast day 16 Sept.

Cyprus Greek *Republic of Cyprus* (*Kypriakí Dimokratía*) in the south, and *Turkish Republic of Northern Cyprus* (*Kibris Cumhuriyeti*) in the north

Ukraine
Romania
Bulgaria
BLACK SEA
Russian Federation
Turkey
MEDITERRANEAN SEA
Syria
Iraq
Lebanon
Jordan
CYPRUS
Israel
Nicosia
Egypt
Saudi Arabia
0 miles 400
0 km 800

area 9,251 sq km/3,571 sq mi, 37% in Turkish hands

capital Nicosia (divided between Greeks and Turks)

towns ports Limassol, Larnaca, Paphos (Greek); Morphou, and ports Kyrenia and Famagusta (Turkish)

physical central plain between two E–W mountain ranges

heads of state and government Glafkos Cler-

ides (Greek) from 1993, Rauf Denktaş (Turkish) from 1976

political system democratic divided republic

exports citrus, grapes, raisins, Cyprus sherry, potatoes, clothing, footwear

currency Cyprus pound and Turkish lira

population (1994) 725,000 (Greek Cypriot 78%, Turkish Cypriot 18%); growth rate 1.2% p.a.

languages Greek and Turkish (official), English

religions Greek Orthodox 78%, Sunni Muslim 18%

GNP $8,640 per head (1991)

chronology

1878 Came under British administration.

1955 Guerrilla campaign began against the British for enosis (union with Greece), led by Archbishop Makarios and General Grivas.

1956 Makarios and enosis leaders deported.

1959 Compromise agreed and Makarios returned to be elected president of an independent Greek-Turkish Cyprus.

1960 Independence achieved from Britain, with Britain retaining its military bases.

1963 Turks set up their own government in northern Cyprus. Fighting broke out between the two communities.

1964 United Nations peacekeeping force installed.

1971 Grivas returned to start a guerrilla war against the Makarios government.

1974 Grivas died. Military coup deposed Makarios, who fled to Britain. Nicos Sampson appointed president. Turkish army sent to northern Cyprus to confirm Turkish Cypriots' control; military regime in southern Cyprus collapsed; Makarios returned. Northern Cyprus declared itself the Turkish Federated State of Cyprus (TFSC), with Rauf Denktaş as president.

1977 Makarios died; succeeded by Spyros Kyprianou.

1983 An independent Turkish Republic of Northern Cyprus proclaimed but recognized only by Turkey.

1984 United Nations (UN) peace proposals rejected.

1985 Summit meeting between Kyprianou and Denktaş failed to reach agreement.

1988 Georgios Vassiliou elected Greek president. Talks with Denktaş began under UN auspices.

1989 Peace talks abandoned.

1992 UN-sponsored peace talks collapsed.

1993 DISY leader Glafkos Clerides narrowly won presidential election to replace Vassiliou.

1994 European Court of Justice declared trade with northern Cyprus illegal.

Cyrano de Bergerac Savinien 1619–1655. French writer. He joined a corps of guards at 19 and performed heroic feats which brought him fame. He is the hero of a classic play by Edmond *Rostand, in which his excessively long nose is used as a counterpoint to his chivalrous character.

Cyrenaic member of a school of Greek *hedonistic philosophy founded about 400 BC by Aristippus of Cyrene. He regarded pleasure as the only absolutely worthwhile thing in life but taught that self-control and intelligence were necessary to choose the best pleasures.

Cyril and Methodius, Sts two brothers, both

Christian saints: Cyril 826–869 and Methodius 815–885. Born in Thessalonica, they were sent as missionaries to what is today Moravia. They invented a Slavonic alphabet, and translated the Bible and the liturgy from Greek to Slavonic. The language (known as **Old Church Slavonic**) remained in use in churches and for literature among Bulgars, Serbs, and Russians up to the 17th century. The **cyrillic alphabet** is named after Cyril and may also have been invented by him. Feast day 14 Feb.

Cyrus the Great died 529 BC. Founder of the Persian Empire. As king of Persia, he was originally subject to the *Medes, whose empire he overthrew 550 BC. He captured *Croesus 546 BC, and conquered all Asia Minor, adding Babylonia (including Syria and Palestine) to his empire 539 BC, allowing exiled Jews to return to Jerusalem. He died fighting in Afghanistan.

cystic fibrosis hereditary disease involving defects of various tissues, including the sweat glands, the mucous glands of the bronchi (air passages), and the pancreas. The sufferer experiences repeated chest infections and digestive disorders and generally fails to thrive. In 1989 the gene for cystic fibrosis was identified by teams of researchers in Michigan, USA, and Toronto, Canada. This discovery promises more reliable diagnosis of the disease in babies before birth.

cystitis inflammation of the bladder, usually caused by bacterial infection, and resulting in frequent and painful urination. Treatment is by antibiotics and copious fluids with vitamin C.

cytokine in biology, chemical messenger that carries information from one cell to another, for example the *lymphokines.

cytology the study of *cells and their functions. Major advances have been made possible in this field by the development of *electron microscopes.

cytoplasm the part of the cell outside the *nucleus. Strictly speaking, this includes all the *organelles (mitochondria, chloroplasts, and so on), but often cytoplasm refers to the jellylike matter in which the organelles are embedded (correctly termed the cytosol).

cytotoxic drug any drug used to kill the cells of a malignant tumour, or as an *immunosuppressive following organ transplantation; it may also damage healthy cells. Side effects include nausea, vomiting, hair loss, and bone-marrow damage.

czar alternative form of *tsar*, an emperor of Russia.

Czechoslovakia Former country in E central Europe that reverted to independent republics following the dissolution of the federation in 1993; see *Czech Republic and *Slovak Republic.

recent history independence was achieved from the Austro-Hungarian Empire 1918. Czechoslovakia was occupied by Germany 1938–45 and the USSR from 1968. The Communist monopoly of power ended in the bloodless revolution of 1989; complete withdrawal of Soviet troops was agreed by May 1991. Bill of rights passed 1991; new parties emerged; Czech and Slovak friction increased from 1991

until the federation was dissolved and the two became sovereign states 1 January 1993.

Czech Republic (*Česká Republika*)

area 78,864 sq km/30,461 sq mi
capital Prague
towns Brno, Ostrava, Olomouc, Liberec, Plzeň, Ustí nad Labem, Hradec Králové
physical mountainous; rivers: Morava, Labe (Elbe), Vltava (Moldau)
environment one of the most polluted areas of Europe; up to twenty times the permissible level of sulphur dioxide is released over Prague, where 75% of the drinking water fails to meet the country's health standards
head of state Václav Havel from 1993
head of government Václav Klaus from 1993
political system emergent democracy
exports machinery, vehicles, coal, iron and steel, chemicals, glass, ceramics, clothing
currency koruna (based on Czechoslovak koruna)
population (1993) 10,330,000 (with German and other minorities); growth rate 0.4% p.a.
languages Czech (official)
religions Roman Catholic (75%), Protestant, Hussite, Orthodox
GNP $2,562 per head (1990)
chronology
1526–1918 Under Habsburg domination.
1918 Independence achieved from Austro-Hungarian Empire; Czechs joined Slovaks in forming Czechoslovakia as independent nation.
1948 Communists assumed power in Czechoslovakia.
1969 Czech Socialist Republic created under new federal constitution.
1989 Nov: prodemocracy demonstrations in Prague; new political parties formed and legalized, including Czech-based Civic Forum under Václav Havel; Communist Party stripped of powers. Dec: new 'grand coalition' government formed; Havel appointed state president. Amnesty granted to 22,000 prisoners.
1990 July: Havel re-elected president in multiparty elections.
1991 Civic Forum split into Civic Democratic Party (CDP) and Civic Movement (CM); evidence of increasing Czech and Slovak separatism.

1992 June: Václav Klaus, leader of the Czech-based CDP, became prime minister; Havel resigned following Slovak gains in assembly elections. Aug: creation of separate Czech and Slovak states agreed.
1993 Jan: Czech Republic became sovereign state, with Klaus as prime minister. Havel elected president. Admitted into United Nations. Major realignment of political parties. New currency introduced. Formal invitation to apply for European Community membership.
1994 Joined NATO's 'partnership for peace' programme.

d abbreviation for *day*; *diameter*; *died*; in the UK, d was the symbol for a *penny* (Latin *denarius*) until decimalization of the currency 1971.

D abbreviation for *500* in the Roman numeral system.

DA abbreviation for *district attorney*.

dab small marine flatfish of the flounder family, especially the genus *Limanda*. Dabs live in the N Atlantic and around the coasts of Britain and Scandinavia.

Dacca alternate name for *Dhaka, the capital of Bangladesh.

dace freshwater fish *Leuciscus leuciscus* of the carp family. Common in England and mainland Europe, it is silvery and grows up to 30 cm/1 ft.

Dachau site of a Nazi *concentration camp during World War II, in Bavaria, Germany.

dachshund (German 'badger-dog') small dog of German origin, bred originally for digging out badgers. It has a long body and short legs. Several varieties are bred: standard size (up to 10 kg/22 lb), miniature (5 kg/11 lb or less), long-haired, smooth-haired, and wire-haired.

Dacia ancient region forming much of modern Romania. The various Dacian tribes were united around 60 BC, and for many years posed a threat to the Roman Empire; they were finally conquered by the Roman emperor Trajan AD 101–06, and the region became a province of the same name. It was abandoned to the invading Goths about 275.

Dada or *Dadaism* artistic and literary movement founded 1915 in Zürich, Switzerland, by the Romanian poet Tristan Tzara (1896–1963) and others in a spirit of rebellion and disillusionment during World War I. Other Dadaist groups were soon formed by the artists Marcel *Duchamp and *Man Ray in New York and Francis Picabia (1879–1953) in Barcelona. Dada had a considerable impact on early 20th-century art, questioning established artistic rules and values.

Dadd Richard 1817–1887. British painter. In 1843 he murdered his father and was committed to an asylum, but continued to paint minutely detailed pictures of fantasies and fairy tales, such as *The Fairy Feller's Master-Stroke* 1855–64 (Tate Gallery, London).

daddy-longlegs popular name for a *crane fly.

Dadra and Nagar Haveli since 1961, a Union Territory of W India; capital Silvassa; area 490 sq km/189 sq mi; population (1991) 138,500.

It was formerly part of Portuguese Daman. It produces rice, wheat, millet, and timber.

Daedalus in Greek mythology, an Athenian artisan supposed to have constructed for King Minos of Crete the labyrinth in which the *Minotaur was imprisoned. When Minos became displeased with him, Daedalus fled from Crete with his son *Icarus using wings made by them from feathers fastened with wax.

daffodil any of several Old World species of the genus *Narcissus*, family Amaryllidaceae, distinguished by their trumpet-shaped flowers. The common daffodil of N Europe *N. pseudonarcissus* has large yellow flowers and grows from a large bulb. There are numerous cultivated forms.

Dafydd ap Gwilym c. 1340–c. 1400. Welsh poet. His work is notable for its complex but graceful style, its concern with nature and love rather than with heroic martial deeds, and for its references to Classical and Italian poetry.

Dagestan autonomous republic of S Russia, situated E of the *Caucasus, bordering the Caspian Sea; capital Makhachkala; area 50,300 sq km/19,421 sq mi; population (1982) 1,700,000. It is mountainous, with deep valleys, and its numerous ethnic groups speak a variety of distinct languages. Annexed 1723 from Iran, which strongly resisted Russian conquest, it became an autonomous republic 1921.

Daguerre Louis Jacques Mande 1789–1851. French pioneer of photography. Together with Joseph Niépce, he is credited with the invention of photography (though others were reaching the same point simultaneously). In 1838 he invented the daguerreotype, a single image process superseded ten years later by *Talbot's negative/positive process.

daguerreotype in photography, a single-image process using mercury vapour and an iodine-sensitized silvered plate; it was invented by Louis Daguerre 1838.

Dahl Roald 1916–1990. British writer, celebrated for short stories with a twist, for example, *Tales of the Unexpected* 1979, and for children's books, including *Charlie and the Chocolate Factory* 1964. He also wrote the screenplay for the James Bond film *You Only Live Twice* 1967.

dahlia any perennial plant of the genus *Dahlia*, family Compositae, comprising 20 species and many cultivated forms. Dahlias are stocky plants with showy flowers that come in a wide range of colours. They are native to Mexico and Central America.

Dahomey former name (until 1975) of the People's Republic of *Benin.

Dáil Eireann lower house of the legislature of the Republic of Ireland. It consists of 148 members elected by adult suffrage on a basis of proportional representation.

Daimler Gottlieb 1834–1900. German engineer who pioneered the modern car. In 1886 he produced his first motor vehicle and a motorbicycle. He later joined forces with Karl *Benz and was one of the pioneers of the high-speed four-stroke petrol engine.

daisy any of numerous species of perennial plants in the family Compositae, especially the field daisy of Europe *Chrysanthemum leucanthemum* and the English common daisy *Bellis* *perennis*, with a single white or pink flower rising from a rosette of leaves.

daisywheel printing head in a computer printer or typewriter that consists of a small plastic or metal disc made up of many spokes (like the petals of a daisy). At the end of each spoke is a character in relief. The daisywheel is rotated until the spoke bearing the required character is facing an inked ribbon, then a hammer strikes the spoke against the ribbon, leaving the impression of the character on the paper beneath.

Dakar capital and chief port (with artificial harbour) of Senegal; population (1984) 1,000,000. It is an industrial centre, and there is a university, established 1957.

Dakhla port and capital of Western Sahara; population (1982) 17,800. First established as a Spanish trading port 1476, it was known as *Villa Cisneros*.

Daladier Edouard 1884–1970. French Radical politician. As prime minister April 1938–March 1940, he signed the *Munich Agreement 1938 (by which the Sudeten districts of Czechoslovakia were ceded to Germany) and declared war on Germany 1939. He resigned 1940 because of his unpopularity for failing to assist Finland against Russia. He was arrested on the fall of France 1940 and was a prisoner in Germany 1943–45. Following the end of World War II he was re-elected to the Chamber of Deputies 1946–58.

Dalai Lama 14th incarnation 1935– . Spiritual and temporal head of the Tibetan state until 1959, when he went into exile in protest against Chinese annexation and oppression. His people have continued to demand his return.

Dali Salvador 1904–1989. Spanish painter. In 1928 he collaborated with Luis Buñuel on the film *Un chien andalou*. In 1929 he joined the Surrealists and became notorious for his flamboyant eccentricity. Influenced by the psychoanalytic theories of Freud, he developed a repertoire of dramatic images, such as the distorted human body, limp watches, and burning giraffes in such pictures as *The Persistence of Memory* 1931 (Museum of Modern Art, New York). They are painted with a meticulous, polished clarity. He also used religious themes and painted many portraits of his wife Gala.

Dallas commercial city in Texas, USA; population (1990) 1,006,900, metropolitan area (with Fort Worth) 3,885,400. Industries include banking, insurance, oil, aviation, aerospace, and electronics. Dallas–Fort Worth Regional Airport (opened 1973) is one of the world's largest. John F *Kennedy was assassinated here 1963.

Dalmatia region divided among Croatia, Montenegro in Yugoslavia, and Bosnia-Herzegovina. The capital is Split. It lies along the eastern shore of the Adriatic Sea and includes a number of islands. The interior is mountainous. Important products are wine, olives, and fish. Notable towns in addition to the capital are Zadar, Sibenik, and Dubrovnik.

history Dalmatia became Austrian 1815 and by the treaty of Rapallo 1920 became part of the kingdom of the Serbs, Croats, and Slovenes (Yugoslavia from 1931), except for the town of Zadar (Zara) and the island of Lastovo (Lagosta), which, with neighbouring islets, were given to Italy until transferred to Yugoslavia 1947. The part of Dalmatia within Croatia was made a region 1949.

Dalmatian breed of dog, about 60 cm/2 ft tall at the shoulder, white with spots that are black or brown. Dalmatians are born white; the spots appear later. They were formerly used as coach dogs, walking beside horse-drawn carriages to fend off highwaymen.

Dalton John 1766–1844. British chemist who proposed the theory of atoms, which he considered to be the smallest parts of matter. He produced the first list of relative atomic masses in *Absorption of Gases* 1805 and put forward the law of partial pressures of gases (Dalton's law).

dam structure built to hold back water in order to prevent flooding, provide water for irrigation and storage, and to provide hydroelectric power. The biggest dams are of the earth-and rock-fill type, also called *embankment dams*. Early dams in Britain, built before about 1800, had a core made from puddled clay (clay which has been mixed with water to make it impermeable). Such dams are generally built on broad valley sites. Deep, narrow gorges dictate a *concrete dam*, where the strength of reinforced concrete can withstand the water pressures involved. The first major all-concrete dam in Britain was built at Woodhead in 1876. The first dam in which concrete was used to seal the joints in the rocks below was built at Tunstall 1879.

Dam (Henrik) Carl (Peter) 1895–1976. Danish biochemist who discovered vitamin K. For his success in this field he shared the 1943 Nobel Prize for Medicine with US biochemist Edward *Doisy (1893–1986).

damages in law, compensation for a *tort (such as personal injuries caused by negligence) or breach of contract. In the case of breach of contract the complainant can claim all the financial loss he or she has suffered. Damages for personal injuries include compensation for loss of earnings, as well as for the injury itself. The court might reduce the damages if the claimant was partly to blame. In the majority of cases, the parties involved reach an out-of-court settlement (a compromise without going to court).

Damascus (Arabic *Dimashq*) capital of Syria, on the river Barada, SE of Beirut; population (1981) 1,251,000. It produces silk, wood products, and brass and copper ware. Said to be the oldest continuously inhabited city in the world, Damascus was an ancient city even in Old Testament times; most notable of the old buildings is the Great Mosque, completed as a Christian church in the 5th century.

Dame in the UK honours system, the title of a woman who has been awarded the Order of the Bath, Order of St Michael and St George, Royal Victorian Order, or Order of the British Empire. It is also in law the legal title of the wife or widow of a knight or baronet, placed before her name.

Damocles lived 4th century BC. In Classical legend, a courtier of the elder Dionysius, ruler of Syracuse, Sicily. Having extolled the happiness of his sovereign, Damocles was invited by him to a feast, during which he saw above his head a sword suspended by a single hair. He recognized this as a symbol of the insecurity of the great.

damper any device that deadens or lessens vibrations or oscillations; for example, one used to check vibrations in the strings of a piano. The term is also used for the movable plate in the flue of a stove or furnace for controlling the draught.

Dampier William 1652–1715. English explorer and hydrographic surveyor who circumnavigated the world three times.

damselfly long, slender, colourful dragonfly of the suborder Zygoptera, with two pairs of similar wings that are generally held vertically over the body when at rest, unlike those of other dragonflies.

damson cultivated variety of plum tree *Prunus domestica* var. *institia*, distinguished by its small, oval, edible fruits, which are dark purple or blue to black.

Dana Richard Henry 1815–1882. US author and lawyer who went to sea and worked for his passage around Cape Horn to California and back, then wrote an account of the journey *Two Years before the Mast* 1840. He also published *The Seaman's Friend* 1841, a guide to maritime law.

Danby Thomas Osborne, Earl of Danby 1631–1712. British Tory politician. He entered Parliament 1665, acted as Charles II's chief minister 1673–78 and was created earl of Danby 1674, but was imprisoned in the Tower of London 1678–84. In 1688 he signed the invitation to William of Orange to take the throne. Danby was again chief minister 1690–95, and in 1694 was created Duke of Leeds.

dance rhythmic movement of the body, usually performed in time to music. Its primary purpose may be religious, magical, martial, social, or artistic – the last two being characteristic of non-traditional societies. The pre-Christian era had a strong tradition of ritual dance, and ancient Greek dance still exerts an influence on dance movement today. Although Western folk and social dances have a long history, the Eastern dance tradition long predates the Western. The European Classical tradition dates from the 15th century in Italy, the first printed dance text from 16th-century France, and the first dance school in Paris from the 17th century. The 18th century saw the development of European Classical ballet as we know it today, and the 19th century saw the rise of Romantic ballet. In the 20th century Modern dance firmly established itself as a separate dance idiom, not based on Classical ballet, and many divergent styles and ideas have grown from a willingness to explore a variety of techniques and amalgamate different traditions.

dandelion plant *Taraxacum officinale* belonging to the Compositae family. The stalk rises from a rosette of leaves that are deeply indented like a lion's teeth, hence the name (from French *dent de lion*). The flower heads are bright yellow. The fruit is surmounted by the hairs of the calyx which constitute the familiar dandelion 'clock'.

Dandie Dinmont breed of *terrier that originated in the Scottish border country. It is about 25 cm/10 in tall, short-legged and long-bodied, with drooping ears and a long tail. Its hair, about 5 cm/2 in long, can be greyish or yellowish. It is named after the character Dandie Dinmont in Walter Scott's novel *Guy Mannering* 1815.

Dane person of Danish culture from Denmark and N Germany. There are approximately 5 million speakers of Danish (including some in the USA), a Germanic language belonging to the Indo-European family. The Danes are known for their seafaring culture, which dates back to the Viking age of expansion between the 8th and 10th centuries.

danegeld in English history, a tax imposed from 991 by Anglo-Saxon kings to pay tribute to the Vikings. After the Norman Conquest the tax continued to be levied until 1162, and the Normans used it to finance military operations.

Danelaw 11th-century name for the area of N and E England settled by the Vikings in the 9th century. It occupied about half of England, from the river Tees to the river Thames. Within its bounds, Danish law, customs, and language prevailed. Its linguistic influence is still apparent.

dangling participle see *participle.

Daniel 6th century BC. Jewish folk hero and prophet at the court of Nebuchadnezzar; also the name of a book of the Old Testament, probably compiled in the 2nd century BC. It includes stories about Daniel and his companions Shadrach, Meshach, and Abednego, set during the Babylonian captivity of the Jews.

Daniell John Frederic 1790–1845. British chemist and meteorologist who invented a primary electrical cell 1836. The **Daniell cell** consists of a central zinc cathode dipping into a porous pot containing zinc sulphate solution. The porous pot is, in turn, immersed in a solution of copper sulphate contained in a copper can, which acts as the cell's anode. The use of a porous barrier prevents polarization (the covering of the anode with small bubbles of hydrogen gas) and allows the cell to generate a continuous current of electricity.

Danish language member of the North Germanic group of the Indo-European language family, spoken in Denmark and Greenland and related to Icelandic, Faroese, Norwegian, and Swedish. It has had a particularly strong influence on Norwegian. As one of the languages of the Vikings, who invaded and settled in parts of Britain during the 9th to 11th centuries, Old Danish had a strong influence on English.

Dante Alighieri 1265–1321. Italian poet. His masterpiece *La divina commedia/The Divine Comedy* 1307–21 is an epic account in three parts of his journey through Hell, Purgatory, and Paradise, during which he is guided part of the way by the poet Virgil; on a metaphorical level the journey is also one of Dante's own spiritual development. Other works include the philosophical prose treatise *Convivio/The Banquet* 1306–08, the first major work of its kind to be written in Italian rather than Latin; *Monarchia/On World Government* 1310–13, expounding his political theories; *De vulgari eloquentia/Concerning the Vulgar Tongue* 1304–06, an original Latin work on Italian, its dialects, and kindred languages; and *Canzoniere/Lyrics*, containing his scattered lyrics.

Danton Georges Jacques 1759–1794. French revolutionary. Originally a lawyer, during the early years of the Revolution he was one of the most influential people in Paris. He organized the uprising 10 Aug 1792 that overthrew

DANCE: CHRONOLOGY

1909 The first Paris season given by Diaghilev's troupe of Russian dancers, later to become known as the Ballets Russes, marked the beginning of one of the most exciting periods in Western ballet.

1913 The premiere of Stravinsky's *The Rite of Spring* provoked a scandal in Paris.

1914 The foxtrot developed from the two-step in the USA.

1926 Martha Graham, one of the most innovative figures in Modern dance, gave her first recital in New York. In England, students from the Rambert School of Ballet, opened by Marie Rambert in 1920, gave their first public performance in *A Tragedy of Fashion*, the first ballet to be choreographed by Frederick Ashton.

1928 The first performance of George Balanchine's *Apollon Musagète* in Paris, by the Ballets Russes, marked the birth of Neo-Classicism in ballet.

1931 Ninette de Valois's Vic-Wells Ballet gave its first performance in London. In 1956 the company became the Royal Ballet.

1933 The Hollywood musical achieved artistic independence through Busby Berkeley's kaleidoscopic choreography in *Forty-Second Street* and Dave Gould's airborne finale in *Flying Down to Rio*, in which Fred Astaire and Ginger Rogers appeared together for the first time.

1940 The Dance Notation Bureau was established in New York for recording ballets and dances.

1948 The New York City Ballet was founded with George Balanchine as artistic director and principal choreographer. The film *The Red Shoes* appeared, choreographed by Massine and Robert Helpmann, starring Moira Shearer.

1950 The Festival Ballet, later to become the London Festival Ballet, was created by Alicia Markova and Anton Dolin, who had first danced together with the Ballets Russes de Monte Carlo 1929.

1952 Gene Kelly starred and danced in the film *Singin' in the Rain*.

1953 The US experimental choreographer Merce Cunningham, who often worked with the composer John Cage, formed his own troupe.

1956 The Bolshoi Ballet opened its first season in the West at Covent Garden in London, with Galina Ulanova dancing in *Romeo and Juliet*.

1957 Jerome Robbins conceived and choreographed the musical *West Side Story*, demonstrating his outstanding ability to work in both popular and Classical forms.

1960 The progressive French choreographer Maurice Béjart became director of the Brussels-based *Ballet du XXième Siècle* company.

1961 Rudolf Nureyev defected from the USSR while dancing with the Kirov Ballet in Paris. He was to have a profound influence on male dancing in the West. The South African choreographer John Cranko became director and chief choreographer of the Stuttgart Ballet, transforming it into a major company.

1965 US choreographer Twyla Tharp produced her first works.

1966 The School of Contemporary Dance was founded in London, from which Robin Howard and the choreographer Robert Cohan created the London Contemporary Dance Theatre, later to become an internationally renowned company.

1968 Arthur Mitchell, the first black principal dancer to join the New York City Ballet, founded the Dance Theatre of Harlem.

1974 Mikhail Baryshnikov defected from the USSR while dancing with the Kirov Ballet in Toronto, and made his US debut with the American Ballet Theater.

1977 The release of Robert Stigwood's film *Saturday Night Fever* popularized disco dancing worldwide.

1980 Natalia Makarova, who had defected from the USSR 1979, staged the first full-length revival of Petipa's *La Bayadère* in the West with the American Ballet Theater in New York.

1981 Wayne Sleep, previously principal dancer with the Royal Ballet, starred as lead dancer in Andrew Lloyd-Webber's musical *Cats*, choreographed by Gillian Lynne.

1983 Peter Martins, principal dancer with the New York City Ballet, became choreographer and codirector with Jerome Robbins on the death of Balanchine. Break dancing became widely popular in Western inner cities.

1984 The avant-garde group Michael Clark and Company made its debut in London.

1990 *Maple Leaf Rag*, Martha Graham's final work, was premiered in New York City.

Louis XVI and the monarchy, roused the country to expel the Prussian invaders, and in April 1793 formed the revolutionary tribunal and the **Committee of Public Safety**, of which he was the leader until July of that year. Thereafter he lost power to the *Jacobins, and, when he attempted to recover it, was arrested and guillotined.

Danube (German *Donau*) second longest of European rivers, rising on the E slopes of the Black Forest, and flowing 2,858 km/1,776 mi across Europe to enter the Black Sea in Romania by a swampy delta.

Danzig German name for the Polish port of *Gdańsk.

Daphne in Greek mythology, a nymph who was changed into a laurel tree to escape from Apollo's amorous pursuit.

Darby Abraham 1677–1717. English iron manufacturer who developed a process for smelting iron ore using coke instead of the more expensive charcoal.

Dardanelles (ancient name Hellespont, Turkish name *Canakkale Boğazi*) Turkish strait connecting the Sea of Marmara with the Aegean Sea; its shores are formed by the *Gallipoli peninsula on the NW and the mainland of Turkey-in-Asia on the SE. It is 75 km/47 mi long and 5–6 km/3–4 mi wide.

Dar es Salaam (Arabic 'haven of peace') chief seaport in Tanzania, on the Indian Ocean, and capital of Tanzania until its replacement by *Dodoma 1974; population (1985) 1,394,000.

Darius I the Great c. 558–486 BC. King of Persia 521–48 BC. A member of a younger branch of the Achaemenid dynasty, he won the throne from the usurper Gaumata (died 522 BC) and reorganized the government. In 512 BC he marched against the Scythians, a people north of the Black Sea, and subjugated Thrace and Macedonia.

Darling Grace 1815–1842. British heroine. She was the daughter of a lighthouse keeper on the Farne Islands, off Northumberland. On 7 Sept 1838 the *Forfarshire* was wrecked, and Grace Darling and her father rowed through a storm to the wreck, saving nine lives. She was awarded a medal for her bravery.

Darnley Henry Stewart or Stuart, Lord Darnley 1545–1567. British aristocrat, second husband of Mary Queen of Scots from 1565, and father of James I of England (James VI of Scotland). On the advice of her secretary, David *Rizzio, Mary refused Darnley the crown matrimonial; in revenge, Darnley led a band of nobles who murdered Rizzio in Mary's presence. Darnley was assassinated 1567.

Dart Raymond 1893–1988. Australian-born South African paleontologist and anthropologist who in 1924 discovered the first fossil remains of the Australopithecenes, early hominids, near Taungs in Botswana. He named them *Australopithecus africanus*, and spent many years trying to prove to sceptics that they were early humans, since their cranial and dental characteristics were not apelike in any way. In the 1950s and 1960s, the *Leakey family found more fossils of this type and of related types in the Olduvai Gorge of E Africa, establishing that Australopithecines were hominids, walked erect, made tools, and lived as early as 5.5 million years ago. After further discoveries in the 1980s, they are today classified as *Homo sapiens australopithecus*, and Dart's assertions have been validated.

darts indoor game played on a circular board. Darts (like small arrow shafts) about 13 cm/5 in long are thrown at segmented targets and score points according to their landing place.

Darwin capital and port in Northern Territory, Australia, in NW Arnhem Land; population (1986) 69,000. It serves the uranium mining site at Rum Jungle to the south. Destroyed 1974 by a cyclone, the city was rebuilt on the same site.

Darwin Charles Robert 1809–1882. English scientist who developed the modern theory of *evolution and proposed, with Alfred Russel Wallace, the principle of *natural selection. After research in South America and the Galápagos Islands as naturalist on HMS *Beagle* 1831–36, Darwin published *On the Origin of Species by Means of Natural Selection or the Preservation of Favoured Races in the Struggle for Life* 1859. This explained the evolutionary process through the principles of natural and sexual selection. It aroused bitter controversy because it disagreed with the literal interpretation of the Book of Genesis in the Bible.

Darwinism, social in US history, an influential but misleading social theory, based upon the work of Charles Darwin and Herbert Spencer, which claimed to offer a scientific justification

for late 19th-century *laissez-faire* capitalism (the principle of unrestricted freedom in commerce).

Dasam Granth collection of the writings of the tenth Sikh guru (teacher), Gobind Singh, and of poems by a number of other writers. It is written in a script called Gurmukhi, the written form of Punjabi popularized by Guru Angad. It contains a retelling of the Krishna legends, devotional verse, and amusing anecdotes.

Das Kapital Karl Marx's exposition of his theories on economic production, published in three volumes 1867–95. It focuses on the exploitation of the worker and appeals for a classless society where the production process and its rewards are shared equally.

dasyure any *marsupial of the family Dasyuridae, also known as a 'native cat', found in Australia and New Guinea. Various species have body lengths from 25 cm/10 in to 75 cm/2.5 ft. Dasyures have long, bushy tails and dark coats with white spots. They are agile, nocturnal carnivores, able to move fast and climb.

DAT abbreviation for ***digital audio tape**.

data facts, figures, and symbols, especially as stored in computers. The term is often used to mean raw, unprocessed facts, as distinct from information, to which a meaning or interpretation has been applied.

database structured collection of data. The database makes data available to the various programs that need it, without the need for those programs to be aware of how the data are stored. There are three main types (or 'models'): hierarchical, network, and relational, of which relational is the most widely used. A *free-text database* is one that holds the unstructured text of articles or books in a form that permits rapid searching.

data communications sending and receiving data via any communications medium, such as a telephone line. The term usually implies that the data are digital (such as computer data) rather than analogue (such as voice messages). However, in the ISDN (*Integrated Services Digital Network) system, all data – including voices and video images – are transmitted digitally. See also *telecommunications.

data compression in computing, techniques for reducing the amount of storage needed for a given amount of data. They include word tokenization (in which frequently used words are stored as shorter codes), variable bit lengths (in which common characters are represented by fewer *bits than less common ones), and run-length encoding (in which a repeated value is stored once along with a count).

data preparation preparing data for computer input by transferring it to a machine-readable medium. This usually involves typing the data at a keyboard (or at a key-to-disc or key-to-tape station) so that it can be transferred directly to tapes or discs. Various methods of direct data capture, such as *bar codes, *optical mark recognition (OMR), and *optical character recognition (OCR), have been developed to reduce or eliminate lengthy data preparation before computer input.

data processing (DP) use of computers for performing clerical tasks such as stock control, payroll, and dealing with orders. DP systems are typically *batch systems, running on mainframe computers. DP is sometimes called EDP (electronic data processing).

data protection safeguarding of information about individuals stored on computers, to protect privacy. The Council of Europe adopted, in 1981, a Data Protection Convention, which led in the UK to the Data Protection Act 1984. This requires computer databases containing personal information to be registered, and users to process only accurate information and to retain the information only for a necessary period and for specified purposes. Subject to certain exemptions, individuals have a right of access to their personal data and to have any errors corrected.

date palm tree of the genus *Phoenix*. The female tree produces the fruit, dates, in bunches weighing 9–11 kg/20–25 lb. Dates are an important source of food in the Middle East, being rich in sugar; they are dried for export. The tree also supplies timber, and materials for baskets, rope, and animal feed.

dating science of determining the age of geological structures, rocks, and fossils, and placing them in the context of geological time. Dating can be carried out by identifying fossils of creatures that lived only at certain times (marker fossils), by looking at the physical relationships of rocks to other rocks of a known age, or by measuring how much of a rock's radioactive elements have changed since the rock was formed, using the process of *radiometric dating.

dative in the grammar of certain inflected languages (see *language) such as Latin, the dative case is the form of a noun, pronoun, or adjective used for the indirect object of a verb. It is also used with some prepositions.

dauphin title of the eldest son of the kings of France, derived from the personal name of a count, whose lands, known as the **Dauphiné**, traditionally passed to the heir to the throne from 1349 to 1830.

David c. 1060–970 BC. Second king of Israel. According to the Old Testament he played the harp for King Saul to banish Saul's melancholy; he later slew the Philistine giant Goliath with a sling and stone. After Saul's death David was anointed king at Hebron, took Jerusalem, and made it his capital.

David Elizabeth 1914–1992. British cookery writer. Her *Mediterranean Food* 1950 and *French Country Cooking* 1951 helped to spark an interest in foreign cuisine in Britain, and also inspired a growing school of informed, highly literate writing on food and wine.

David Jacques Louis 1748–1825. French painter in the Neo-Classical style. He was an active supporter of and unofficial painter to the republic during the French Revolution, for which he was imprisoned 1794–95. In his *Death of Marat* 1793, he turned political murder into a Classical tragedy. Later he devoted himself to the empire in paintings such as the enormous, pompous *Coronation of Napoleon* 1805–07 (Louvre, Paris).

David two kings of Scotland:

David I 1084–1153. King of Scotland from 1124. The youngest son of Malcolm III Canmore and

St *Margaret, he was brought up in the English court of Henry I, and in 1113 married *Matilda, widow of the 1st earl of Northampton. He invaded England 1138 in support of Queen Matilda, but was defeated at Northallerton in the Battle of the Standard, and again 1141.

David II 1324–1371. King of Scotland from 1329, son of *Robert I (the Bruce). David was married at the age of four to Joanna, daughter of Edward II of England. In 1346 David invaded England, was captured at the battle of Neville's Cross, and imprisoned for 11 years.

David, St or **Dewi** 5th–6th century. Patron saint of Wales, Christian abbot and bishop. According to legend he was the son of a prince of Dyfed and uncle of King Arthur; he was responsible for the adoption of the leek as the national emblem of Wales, but his own emblem is a dove. Feast day 1 March.

Davies Peter Maxwell 1934– . English composer and conductor. His music combines medieval and serial codes of practice with a heightened Expressionism as in his opera *Taverner* 1962–68.

da Vinci see *Leonardo da Vinci, Italian Renaissance artist.

Davis Angela 1944– . US left-wing activist for black rights, prominent in the student movement of the 1960s. In 1970 she went into hiding after being accused of supplying guns used in the murder of a judge who had been seized as a hostage in an attempt to secure the release of three black convicts. She was captured, tried, and acquitted. At the University of California she studied under German political philosopher Herbert Marcuse (1898–1979), and was assistant professor of philosophy at UCLA 1969–70. In 1980 she was the Communist vice-presidential candidate.

Davis Bette 1908–1989. US actress. She entered films in 1930, and established a reputation as a forceful dramatic actress with *Of Human Bondage* 1934. Later films included *Dangerous* 1935 and *Jezebel* 1938, both winning her Academy Awards, *All About Eve* which won the 1950 Academy Award for best picture, and *Whatever Happened to Baby Jane?* 1962. She continued to make films throughout the 1980s such as *How Green Was My Valley* for television, and *The Whales of August* 1987, in which she co-starred with Lillian Gish.

Davis Jefferson 1808–1889. US politician, president of the short-lived Confederate States of America 1861–65. He was a leader of the Southern Democrats in the US Senate from 1857, and a defender of 'humane' slavery; in 1860 he issued a declaration in favour of secession from the USA. During the Civil War he assumed strong political leadership, but often disagreed with military policy. He was imprisoned for two years after the war, one of the few cases of judicial retribution against Confederate leaders.

Davis Miles (Dewey, Jr) 1926–1991. US jazz trumpeter, composer, and bandleader. He recorded bebop with Charlie Parker 1945, pioneered cool jazz in the 1950s and jazz-rock fusion beginning in the late 1960s. His significant albums include *Birth of the Cool* 1957 (recorded 1949 and 1950), *Sketches of Spain* 1959, and *Bitches' Brew* 1970.

Davis Sammy, Jr 1925–1990. US actor, singer, and tap dancer. He starred in the Broadway show *Mr Wonderful* 1956, and appeared in the film version of the opera *Porgy and Bess* 1959 and in films with Frank Sinatra in the 1960s.

Davis Steve 1957– . English snooker player who has won every major honour in the game since turning professional 1978. He has been world champion six times.

Davis Cup annual lawn tennis tournament for men's international teams, first held 1900 after Dwight Filley Davis (1879–1945) donated the trophy.

Davison Emily 1872–1913. English militant suffragette who died after throwing herself under the king's horse at the Derby at Epsom (she was trampled by the horse). She joined the Women's Social and Political Union in 1906 and served several prison sentences for militant action such as stone throwing, setting fire to pillar boxes, and bombing Lloyd George's country house.

Davitt Michael 1846–1906. Irish nationalist. He joined the Fenians (forerunners of the Irish Republican Army) 1865, and was imprisoned for treason 1870–77. After his release, he and the politician Charles Parnell founded the *Land League 1879. Davitt was jailed several times for land-reform agitation. He was a member of Parliament 1895–99, advocating the reconciliation of extreme and constitutional nationalism.

Davy Humphry 1778–1829. English chemist. He discovered, by electrolysis, the metallic elements sodium and potassium in 1807, and calcium, boron, magnesium, strontium, and barium in 1808. In addition, he established that chlorine is an element and proposed that hydrogen is present in all acids. He invented the 'safety lamp' for use in mines where methane was present, enabling miners to work in previously unsafe conditions.

day time taken for the Earth to rotate once on its axis. The *solar day* is the time that the Earth takes to rotate once relative to the Sun. It is divided into 24 hours, and is the basis of our civil day. The *sidereal day* is the time that the Earth takes to rotate once relative to the stars. It is 3 minutes 56 seconds shorter than the solar day, because the Sun's position against the background of stars as seen from Earth changes as the Earth orbits it.

Day Doris. Stage name of Doris von Kappelhoff 1924– . US film actress and singing star of the 1950s and early 1960s. She appeared in musicals and, often with Rock Hudson, in coy sex comedies. Her films include *Tea for Two* 1950, *Calamity Jane* 1953, *Love Me or Leave Me* 1955, and Alfred Hitchcock's *The Man Who Knew Too Much* 1956. With *Pillow Talk* 1959, *Lover Come Back* 1962, and other 1960s light sex comedies, she played a confident but coy woman who made some of the biggest male stars capitulate.

Dayan Moshe 1915–1981. Israeli general and politician. As minister of defence 1967 and 1969–74, he was largely responsible for the victory over neighbouring Arab states in the 1967 Six-Day War, but he was criticized for Israel's alleged unpreparedness in the 1973 October War and resigned along with Prime Minister Golda Meir. Foreign minister from 1977, Dayan

resigned 1979 in protest over the refusal of the Begin government to negotiate with the Palestinians.

Day-Lewis Cecil 1904–1972. Irish poet, British poet laureate 1968–1972. With W H Auden and Stephen Spender, he was one of the influential left-wing poets of the 1930s. He also wrote detective novels under the pseudonym *Nicholas Blake*.

Day-Lewis Daniel 1958– . English actor, noted for his chameleon-like versatility. He came to prominence in *My Beautiful Laundrette* and *A Room With a View* both 1985. He won an Academy Award for his performance as Christy Brown, the painter suffering from cerebral palsy, in *My Left Foot* 1989. His other films include *The Last of the Mohicans* 1992, *The Age of Innocence*, and *In the Name of the Father* both 1993.

dBASE family of microcomputer programs used for manipulating large quantities of data; also, a related *fourth-generation language. The first version, dBASE II, appeared in 1981; it has since become the basis for a recognized standard for database applications, known as Xbase.

DCC abbreviation for *digital compact cassette*.

D-day 6 June 1944, the day of the Allied invasion of Normandy under the command of General Eisenhower, with the aim of liberating Western Europe from German occupation. The Anglo-American invasion fleet landed on the Normandy beaches on the stretch of coast between the Orne River and St Marcouf. Artificial harbours known as 'Mulberries' were constructed and towed across the Channel so that equipment and armaments could be unloaded onto the beaches. After overcoming fierce resistance the allies broke through the German defences; Paris was liberated on 25 Aug, and Brussels on 2 Sept. D-day is also military jargon for any day on which a crucial operation is planned. D+1 indicates the day after the start of the operation.

DDT abbreviation for *dichloro-diphenyl-trich-loroethane* ($ClC_6H_5)_2CHCHCl_2$) insecticide discovered 1939 by Swiss chemist Paul Müller. It is useful in the control of insects that spread malaria, but resistant strains develop. DDT is highly toxic and persists in the environment and in living tissue. Its use is now banned in most countries, but it continues to be used on food plants in Latin America.

deacon in the Roman Catholic and Anglican churches, an ordained minister who ranks immediately below a priest. In the Protestant churches, a deacon is in training to become a minister or is a lay assistant.

deadly nightshade *belladonna, a poisonous plant.

Dead Sea large lake, partly in Israel and partly in Jordan, lying 394 m/1,293 ft below sea level; area 1,020 sq km/394 sq mi. The chief river entering it is the Jordan; it has no outlet and the water is very salty.

Dead Sea Scrolls collection of ancient scrolls (rolls of writing) and fragments of scrolls found 1947–56 in caves on the W side of the Jordan, 12 km/7 mi S of Jericho and 2 km/l mi from the

N end of the Dead Sea, at *Qumran. They include copies of Old Testament books a thousand years older than those previously known to be extant. The documents date mainly from about 150 BC–AD 68, when the monastic community that owned them, the Essenes, was destroyed by the Romans because of its support for a revolt against their rule.

deafness partial or total deficit of hearing in either ear. Of assistance are hearing aids, lip-reading, a cochlear implant in the ear in combination with a special electronic processor, sign language, and 'cued speech' (manual clarification of ambiguous lip movement during speech).

dean in education, in universities and medical schools, the head of administration; in the colleges of Oxford and Cambridge, UK, the member of the teaching staff charged with the maintenance of discipline; in Roman Catholicism, senior cardinal bishop, head of the college of cardinals; in the Anglican Communion, head of the chapter of a cathedral or collegiate church (a rural dean presides over a division of an archdeaconry).

Dean James (Byron) 1931–1955. US actor. Killed in a car accident after the release of his first film, *East of Eden* 1955, he posthumously became a cult hero with *Rebel Without a Cause* 1955 and *Giant* 1956.

death permanent ending of all the functions that keep an organism alive. Death used to be pronounced when a person's breathing and heartbeat stopped. The advent of mechanical aids has made this point sometimes difficult to determine, and in controversial cases a person is now pronounced dead when the brain ceases to control the vital functions even if breath and heartbeat are maintained.

death cap fungus *Amanita phalloides*, the most poisonous mushroom known. The fruiting body has a scaly white cap and a collarlike structure near the base of the stalk.

death penalty another name for *capital punishment.

Death Valley depression 225 km/140 mi long and 6–26 km/4–16 mi wide in SE California, USA. At 85 m/280 ft below sea level, it is the lowest point in North America. Bordering mountains rise to 3,000 m/10,000 ft. It is one of the world's hottest and driest places, with temperatures sometimes exceeding 51.7°C/125°F and an annual rainfall of less than 5 cm/2 in. Borax, iron ore, tungsten, gypsum, and salts are extracted.

deathwatch beetle any wood-boring beetle of the family Anobiidae, especially *Xestobium rufovillosum*. The larvae live in oaks and willows, and sometimes cause damage by boring in old furniture or structural timbers. To attract the female, the male beetle produces a ticking sound by striking his head on a wooden surface, and this is taken by the superstitious as a warning of approaching death.

de Bono Edward 1933– . British medical doctor and psychologist whose concept of lateral thinking, first expounded in *The Use of Lateral Thinking* 1967, involves thinking round a problem rather than tackling it head-on.

Debrecen third largest city in Hungary, 193 km/120 mi E of Budapest, in the Great Plain (*Alföld*) region; population (1988) 217,000. It produces

tobacco, agricultural machinery, and pharmaceuticals. Lajos *Kossuth declared Hungary independent of the *Habsburgs here in 1849. It is a commercial centre and has a university founded 1912.

Debrett John 1753–1822. English publisher of a directory of the peerage 1802, baronetage 1808, and knightage 1866–73/4; the books are still published under his name.

de Broglie see *Broglie, de.

Debs Eugene Victor 1855–1926. US labour leader and socialist who organized the Social Democratic Party 1897. He was the founder and first president of the American Railway Union 1893, and was imprisoned for six months in 1894 for defying a federal injunction to end the Pullman strike in Chicago. He was socialist candidate for the presidency in every election from 1900 to 1920, except that of 1916.

debt something that is owed by a person or organization, usually money, goods, or services. Debt usually occurs as a result of borrowing *credit*. **Debt servicing** is the payment of interest on a debt. The **national debt** of a country is the total money owed by the national government to private individuals, banks, and so on; **international debt**, the money owed by one country to another, began on a large scale with the investment in foreign countries by newly industrialized countries in the late 19th to early 20th centuries. International debt became a global problem as a result of the oil crisis of the 1970s.

debt crisis any situation in which an individual, company, or country owes more to others than it can repay or pay interest on; more specifically, the massive indebtedness of many Third World countries that became acute in the 1980s, threatening the stability of the international banking system as many debtor countries became unable to service their debts.

debt-for-nature swap agreement under which a country's debts are written off in exchange for a commitment by the debtor country to undertake projects for environmental protection. Debt-for-nature swaps were set up by environment groups in the 1980s in an attempt to reduce the debt problem of developing countries, while simultaneously promoting conservation.

Debussy (Achille-) Claude 1862–1918. French composer. He broke with the dominant tradition of German Romanticism and introduced new qualities of melody and harmony based on the whole-tone scale, evoking oriental music. His work includes *Prélude à l'après-midi d'un faune* 1894 and the opera *Pelléas et Mélisande* 1902.

decagon in geometry, a ten-sided *polygon.

Decameron, The collection of tales by the Italian writer Giovanni Boccaccio, brought together 1348–53. Ten young people, fleeing plague-stricken Florence, amuse their fellow travellers by each telling a story on the ten days they spend together. The work had a great influence on English literature, particularly on Chaucer's *Canterbury Tales*.

decathlon two-day athletic competition for men consisting of ten events: 100 metres, long jump, shot put, high jump, 400 metres (day one); 110 metres hurdles, discus, pole vault, javelin,

1,500 metres (day two). Points are awarded for performances and the winner is the athlete with the greatest aggregate score. The decathlon is an Olympic event.

decay, radioactive see *radioactive decay.

decibel unit (symbol dB) of measure used originally to compare sound densities and subsequently electrical or electronic power outputs; now also used to compare voltages. An increase of 10 dB is equivalent to a 10-fold increase in intensity or power, and a 20-fold increase in voltage. A whisper has an intensity of 20 dB; 140 dB (a jet aircraft taking off nearby) is the threshold of pain.

deciduous of trees and shrubs, that shed their leaves at the end of the growing season or during a dry season to reduce *transpiration, the loss of water by evaporation.

decimal fraction a *fraction expressed by the use of the decimal point, that is, a fraction in which the denominator is any higher power of 10. Thus $^3/_{10}$, 51100, and 231,000 are decimal fractions and are normally expressed as 0.3, 0.51, 0.023. The use of decimals greatly simplifies addition and multiplication of fractions, though not all fractions can be expressed exactly as decimal fractions.

decimal number system or **denary number system** the most commonly used number system, to the base ten. Decimal numbers do not necessarily contain a decimal point; 563, 5.63, and –563 are all decimal numbers. Other systems are mainly used in computing and include the *binary number system, *octal number system, and *hexadecimal number system.

decision theory system of mathematical techniques for analysing decision-making problems, for example, over unpredictable factors. The system aims to minimize error. It includes game theory, risk analysis, and utility theory.

Declaration of Independence historic US document stating the theory of government on which the USA was founded, based on the right 'to life, liberty, and the pursuit of happiness'. The statement was issued by the American Continental Congress 4 July 1776, renouncing all allegiance to the British crown and ending the political connection with Britain.

Declaration of Rights in Britain, the statement issued by the Convention Parliament Feb 1689, laying down the conditions under which the crown was to be offered to *William III and Mary. Its clauses were later incorporated in the *Bill of Rights.

decoder in computing, an electronic circuit used to select one of several possible data pathways. Decoders are, for example, used to direct data to individual memory locations within a computer's immediate access memory.

decolonization gradual achievement of independence by former colonies of the European imperial powers which began after World War I. The process of decolonization accelerated after World War II and the movement affected every continent: India and Pakistan gained independence from Britain 1947; Algeria gained independence from France 1962.

decomposer in biology, any organism that breaks down dead matter. Decomposers play a vital role in the *ecosystem by freeing important chemical substances, such as nitrogen compounds, locked up in dead organisms or excrement. They feed on some of the released organic matter, but leave the rest to filter back into the soil or pass in gas form into the atmosphere. The principal decomposers are bacteria and fungi, but earthworms and many other invertebrates are often included in this group. The *nitrogen cycle relies on the actions of decomposers.

decomposition process whereby a chemical compound is reduced to its component substances. In biology, it is the destruction of dead organisms either by chemical reduction or by the action of decomposers.

decompression sickness illness brought about by a sudden and substantial change in atmospheric pressure. It is caused by a too rapid release of nitrogen that has been dissolved into the bloodstream under pressure; when the nitrogen bubbles it causes the *bends. The condition causes breathing difficulties, joint and muscle pain, and cramps, and is experienced mostly by deep-sea divers who surface too quickly.

Deconstruction in architecture, a style that fragments forms and space by taking the usual building elements of floors, walls, and ceilings and sliding them apart to create a sense of disorientation and movement. Its proponents include Zaha Hadid (1950–) in the UK, Frank Gehry (1929–) and Peter Eisenman (1932–) in the USA, and Co-op Himmelbau in Austria.

decontamination factor in radiological protection, a measure of the effectiveness of a decontamination process. It is the ratio of the original contamination to the remaining radiation after decontamination: 1,000 and above is excellent; 10 and below is poor.

Decorated in architecture, the second period of English Gothic, covering the latter part of the 13th century and the 14th century. Chief characteristics include ornate window tracery, the window being divided into several lights by vertical bars called mullions; sharp spires ornamented with crockets and pinnacles; complex church vaulting; and slender arcade piers. Exeter Cathedral is a notable example.

decretal in medieval Europe, a papal ruling on a disputed point, sent to a bishop or abbot in reply to a request or appeal. The earliest dates from Siricius 385. Later decretals were collected to form a decretum.

decretum collection of papal decrees. The best known is that collected by Gratian (died 1159) about 1140, comprising some 4,000 items. The decretum was used as an authoritative source of canon law (the rules and regulations of the church).

dedicated computer computer built into another device for the purpose of controlling or supplying information to it. Its use has increased dramatically since the advent of the *microprocessor: washing machines, digital watches, cars, and video recorders all now have their own processors.

Dee river in Grampian region, Scotland; length 139 km/87 mi. From its source in the Cairngorms, it flows east into the North Sea at

Aberdeen (by an artificial channel). It is noted for salmon fishing.

deed legal document that passes an interest in property or binds a person to perform or abstain from some action. Deeds are of two kinds: indenture and deed poll. **Indentures** bind two or more parties in mutual obligations. A **deed poll** is made by one party only, such as when a person changes his or her name.

deep-sea trench another term for *ocean trench.

deer any of various ruminant, even-toed, hoofed mammals belonging to the family Cervidae. The male typically has a pair of antlers, shed and regrown each year. Most species of deer are forest-dwellers and are distributed throughout Eurasia and North America, but are absent from Australia and Africa S of the Sahara.

deerhound large, rough-coated dog, formerly used for hunting and killing deer. Slim and long-legged, it grows to 75 cm/2.5 ft or more, usually with a bluish-grey coat.

de Falla Manuel Spanish composer. See *Falla, Manuel de.

defamation in law, an attack on a person's reputation by *libel or *slander.

Defender of the Faith one of the titles of the English sovereign, conferred on Henry VIII 1521 by Pope Leo X in recognition of the king's treatise against the Protestant Martin Luther. It appears on coins in the abbreviated form **F.D.** (Latin *Fidei Defensor*).

deferred share on the stock market, a share that typically warrants a dividend only after a specified dividend has been paid on the ordinary shares; it may, however, be entitled to a dividend on all the profits after that point.

defibrillation use of electrical stimulation to restore a chaotic heartbeat to a rhythmical pattern. In fibrillation, which may occur in most kinds of heart disease, the heart muscle contracts irregularly; the heart is no longer working as an efficient pump. Paddles are applied to the chest wall, and one or more electric shocks are delivered to normalize the beat.

deficit financing in economics, a planned excess of expenditure over income, dictated by government policy, creating a shortfall of public revenue which is met by borrowing. The decision to create a deficit is made to stimulate an economy by increasing consumer purchasing and at the same time to create more jobs.

deflation in economics, a reduction in the level of economic activity, usually caused by an increase in interest rates and reduction in the money supply, increased taxation, or a decline in government expenditure.

Defoe Daniel 1660–1731. English writer. His *Robinson Crusoe* 1719, though purporting to be a factual account of shipwreck and solitary survival, was influential in the development of the novel. The fictional *Moll Flanders* 1722 and the partly factual *A Journal of the Plague Year* 1724 are still read for their concrete realism. A prolific journalist and pamphleteer, he was imprisoned 1702–04 for the ironic *The Shortest Way with Dissenters* 1702.

deforestation destruction of forest for timber, fuel, charcoal burning, and clearing for agriculture and extractive industries, such as mining, without planting new trees to replace those lost (reafforestation) or working on a cycle that allows the natural forest to regenerate. Deforestation causes fertile soil to be blown away or washed into rivers, leading to *soil erosion, drought, flooding, and loss of wildlife. It may also increase the carbon dioxide content of the atmosphere and intensify the *greenhouse effect, because there are fewer trees absorbing carbon dioxide from the air for photosynthesis.

Degas (Hilaire Germain) Edgar 1834–1917. French Impressionist painter and sculptor. He devoted himself to lively, informal studies (often using pastels) of ballet, horse racing, and young women working. From the 1890s he turned increasingly to sculpture, modelling figures in wax in a fluent, naturalistic style.

de Gaulle Charles André Joseph Marie 1890–1970. French general and first president of the Fifth Republic 1958–69. He organized the *Free French troops fighting the Nazis 1940–44, was head of the provisional French government 1944–46, and leader of his own Gaullist party. In 1958 the national assembly asked him to form a government during France's economic recovery and to solve the crisis in Algeria. He became president at the end of 1958, having changed the constitution to provide for a presidential system, and served until 1969.

degree in mathematics, a unit (symbol °) of measurement of an angle or arc. A circle or complete rotation is divided into 360°. A degree may be subdivided into 60 minutes (symbol ′), and each minute may be subdivided in turn into 60 seconds (symbol ″). **Temperature** is also measured in degrees, which are divided on a decimal scale. See also *Celsius, and *Fahrenheit.

De Havilland Olivia 1916– . US actress. She was a star in Hollywood from the age of 19, when she appeared in *A Midsummer Night's Dream* 1935. She later successfully played challenging dramatic roles in *Gone with the Wind* 1939, *To Each His Own* (Academy Award) and *Dark Mirror* 1946, and *The Snake Pit* 1948. She won her second Academy Award for *The Heiress* 1949.

Dehaene Jean-Luc 1940– . Belgian politician, prime minister from 1992. He successfully negotiated constitutional changes to make Belgium a federal state. His proposed appointment as European Commission president was vetoed 1994 by UK prime minister John Major.

Deighton Len 1929– . English author of spy fiction. His novels include *The Ipcress File* 1963 and the trilogy *Berlin Game, Mexico Set*, and *London Match* 1983–85, featuring the spy Bernard Samson. Samson was also the main character in Deighton's trilogy *Spy Hook* 1988, *Spy Line* 1989, and *Spy Sinker* 1990.

Deimos one of the two moons of Mars. It is irregularly shaped, 15 × 12 × 11 km/9 × 7.5 × 7 mi, orbits at a height of 24,000 km/15,000 mi every 1.26 days, and is not as heavily cratered as the other moon, Phobos. Deimos was discovered 1877 by US astronomer Asaph Hall (1829–1907), and is thought to be an asteroid captured by Mars's gravity.

Deirdre in Celtic mythology, the beautiful

intended bride of *Conchobar. She eloped with Noísi, and died of sorrow when Conchobar killed him and his brothers.

deism belief in a supreme being; but the term usually refers to a movement of religious thought in the 17th and 18th centuries, characterized by the belief in a rational 'religion of nature' as opposed to the orthodox beliefs of Christianity. Deists believed that God is the source of natural law but does not intervene directly in the affairs of the world, and that the only religious duty of humanity is to be virtuous.

de Klerk F(rederik) W(illem) 1936– . South African National Party politician, president 1989–94. He served in the cabinets of B J Vorster and P W Botha 1978–89, and replaced Botha as National Party leader Feb 1989 and as state president Aug 1989. In Feb 1990 he ended the ban on the *African National Congress opposition movement and released its effective leader, Nelson Mandela. In Feb 1991 de Klerk promised the end of all apartheid legislation and a new multi-racial constitution, and by June of the same year had repealed all racially discriminating laws. In Feb 1993 he and Mandela agreed to the formation of a government of national unity after free, nonracial elections in April 1994, which were won by the ANC. He was joint winner of the Nobel Peace Prize 1993 with Mandela.

de Kooning Willem 1904– . Dutch-born US painter who emigrated to the USA 1926, initially working as a commercial artist. After World War II he became, together with Jackson Pollock, one of the leaders of the Abstract Expressionist movement., His *Women* series, exhibited 1953, was criticized for its grotesque figurative style.

Delacroix Eugène 1798–1863. French Romantic painter. His prolific output included religious and historical subjects and portraits of friends, among them the musicians Paganini and Chopin. Antagonistic to the French academic tradition, he evolved a highly coloured, fluid style, as in *The Death of Sardanapalus* 1829 (Louvre, Paris).

de la Mare Walter 1873–1956. English poet. He is known for his verse for children, such as *Songs of Childhood* 1902, and the novels *The Three Royal Monkeys* 1910 for children and, for adults, *The Memoirs of a Midget* 1921. He excelled at creating a sense of eeriness and supernatural mystery.

Delaunay Robert 1885–1941. French painter. He was a pioneer of abstract art. With his wife Sonia Delaunay-Terk, he developed a style known as *Orphism, an early variation of Cubism, focusing on the effects of pure colour contrasts.

Delaunay-Terk Sonia 1885–1979. French painter and textile designer. Born in Russia, she was active in Paris from 1905. With her husband Robert Delaunay, she was a pioneer of abstract art.

De Laurentiis Dino 1919– . Italian film producer. His early films, including Fellini's *La strada/The Street* 1954, brought more acclaim than later epics such as *Waterloo* 1970. He then produced a series of Hollywood films: *Death Wish* 1974, *King Kong* (remake) 1976, and *Dune* 1984.

Delaware state in northeastern USA; nickname First State/Diamond State
area 5,300 sq km/2,046 sq mi
capital Dover
towns Wilmington, Newark
physical divided into two physical areas, one hilly and wooded, the other gently undulating
products dairy, poultry, and market-garden produce; chemicals, motor vehicles, and textiles
population (1990) 666,200
famous people J P Marquand
history the first settlers were Dutch 1631 and Swedes 1638, but the area was captured by the British 1664. Delaware was made a separate colony 1704 and organized as a state 1776.

de Lesseps Ferdinand, Vicomte. French engineer; see de *Lesseps.

Delhi capital of India, comprising the walled city of *Old Delhi*, situated on the west bank of the river Jumna, and *New Delhi* to the S, largely designed by English architect Edwin Lutyens and chosen to replace Calcutta as the seat of government 1912 (completed 1929; officially inaugurated 1931). Delhi is the administrative centre of the Union Territory of Delhi and India's largest commercial and communications centre; population (1991) 9,370,400.

Delibes (Clément Philibert) Léo 1836–1891. French composer. His lightweight, perfectly judged works include the ballets *Coppélia* 1870 and *Sylvia* 1876, and the opera *Lakmé* 1883.

Delilah in the Old Testament, the Philistine mistress of *Samson. Following instructions from the lords of the Philistines she sought to find the source of Samson's great strength. When Samson eventually revealed that his physical power lay in the length of his hair, she shaved his head while he slept and then delivered him into the hands of the Philistines.

deliquescence phenomenon of a substance absorbing so much moisture from the air that it ultimately dissolves in it to form a solution.

delirium in medicine, a state of acute confusion in which the subject is incoherent, frenzied, and out of touch with reality. It is often accompanied by delusions or hallucinations.

Delius Frederick (Theodore Albert) 1862–1934. English composer. His haunting, richly harmonious works include the opera *A Village Romeo and Juliet* 1901; the choral pieces *Appalachia* 1903, *Sea Drift* 1904, *A Mass of Life* 1905; orchestral works such as *In a Summer Garden* 1908 and *A Song of the High Hills* 1911; chamber music; and songs.

della Robbia Italian family of artists; see *Robbia, della.

Delors Jacques 1925– . French socialist politician, finance minister 1981–84. As president of the European Commission 1984–95 he has overseen significant budgetary reform and the move towards a free European Community market in 1992, with increased powers residing in Brussels.

Delphi city of ancient Greece, situated in a rocky valley north of the gulf of Corinth, on the southern slopes of Mount Parnassus, site of a famous *oracle in the temple of Apollo. The site was supposed to be the centre of the Earth and was marked by a conical stone, the *omphelos*.

The oracle was interpreted by priests from the inspired utterances of the Pythian priestess until it was closed down by the Roman emperor Theodosius I AD 390.

delphinium any plant of the genus *Delphinium* belonging to the buttercup family Ranunculaceae. There are some 250 species, including the butterfly or Chinese delphinium *D. grandiflorum*, an Asian form and one of the ancestors of the garden delphinium. Most species have blue, purple, or white flowers on a long spike.

del Sarto Andrea Italian Renaissance painter; see *Andrea del Sarto.

delta tract of land at a river's mouth, composed of silt deposited as the water slows on entering the sea. Familiar examples of large deltas are those of the Mississippi, Ganges and Brahmaputra, Rhône, Po, Danube, and Nile; the shape of the Nile delta is like the Greek letter *delta* Δ, and thus gave rise to the name.

Delta Force US antiguerrilla force, based at Fort Bragg, North Carolina, and modelled on the British *Special Air Service.

delta wing aircraft wing shaped like the Greek letter *delta* Δ. Its design enables an aircraft to pass through the *sound barrier with little effect. The supersonic airliner *Concorde and the US *space shuttle have delta wings.

de Maiziere Lothar 1940– . German politician, leader 1989–90 of the conservative Christian Democratic Union in East Germany. He became premier after East Germany's first democratic election April 1990 and negotiated the country's reunion with West Germany. In Dec 1990 he resigned from Chancellor Kohl's cabinet and as deputy leader of the CDU, following allegations that he had been an informer to the Stasi (East German secret police). In Sept 1991, he resigned as deputy chairman of the CDU and from the legislature, effectively leaving active politics.

demand in economics, the quantity of a product or service that customers want to buy at any given price. Also, the desire for a commodity, together with ability to pay for it.

dementia mental deterioration as a result of physical changes in the brain. It may be due to degenerative change, circulatory disease, infection, injury, or chronic poisoning. *Senile dementia*, a progressive loss of mental faculties such as memory and orientation, is typically a disease process of old age, and can be accompanied by *depression.

demesne in the Middle Ages in Europe, land kept in the lord's possession, not leased out, but, under the system of *villeinage, worked by villeins to supply the lord's household.

Demeter in Greek mythology, the goddess of agriculture (Roman Ceres), daughter of Kronos and Rhea, and mother of Persephone by Zeus. Demeter and Persephone were worshipped in a sanctuary at Eleusis, where one of the foremost *mystery religions of Greece was celebrated. She was later identified with the Egyptian goddess *Isis.

DeMille Agnes 1909–1993. US dancer and choreographer. One of the most significant contributors to the American Ballet Theater with dramatic ballets like *Fall River Legend* 1948, she also led the change on Broadway to new-style musicals with her choreography of *Oklahoma!* 1943, *Carousel* 1945, and others.

DeMille Cecil B(lount) 1881–1959. US film director and producer. He entered films 1913 with Jesse L Lasky (with whom he later established Paramount Pictures), and was one of the founders of Hollywood. He specialized in biblical epics, such as *The Sign of the Cross* 1932 and *The Ten Commandments* 1923; remade 1956. He also made the 1952 Academy-Award-winning *The Greatest Show on Earth*.

Demirel Suleiman 1924– . Turkish politician. Leader from 1964 of the Justice Party, he was prime minister 1965–71, 1975–77, and 1979–80. He favoured links with the West, full membership in the European Community, and foreign investment in Turkish industry. He became head of state in 1993.

democracy (Greek *demos* 'the community', *kratos* 'sovereign power') government by the people, usually through elected representatives. In the modern world, democracy has developed from the American and French revolutions.

Democratic Party one of the two main political parties of the USA. It tends to be the party of the working person, as opposed to the Republicans, the party of big business, but the distinctions between the two are not clear cut. Its stronghold since the Civil War has traditionally been industrial urban centres and the Southern states, but conservative Southern Democrats were largely supportive of Republican positions and helped elect President Reagan.

Democritus *c.* 460–361 BC. Greek philosopher and speculative scientist who made a significant contribution to metaphysics with his atomic theory of the universe: all things originate from a vortex of atoms and differ according to the shape and arrangement of their atoms.

demography study of the size, structure, dispersement, and development of human *populations to establish reliable statistics on such factors as birth and death rates, marriages and divorces, life expectancy, and migration.

Demosthenes *c.* 384–322 BC. Athenian politician, famed for his oratory. From 351 BC he led the party that advocated resistance to the growing power of *Philip of Macedon, and in his *Philippics*, a series of speeches, incited the Athenians to war. This policy resulted in the defeat of Chaeronea 338, and the establishment of Macedonian supremacy. After the death of Alexander he organized a revolt; when it failed, he took poison to avoid capture by the Macedonians.

Demotic Greek common or vernacular variety of the modern *Greek language.

demotic script cursive (joined) writing derived from Egyptian hieratic script, itself a cursive form of *hieroglyphic. Demotic documents are known from the 6th century BC to about AD 470. It was written horizontally, from right to left.

Dempsey Jack (William Harrison) 1895–1983. US heavyweight boxing champion, nicknamed 'the Manassa Mauler'. He beat Jess Willard 1919 to win the title and held it until 1926, when he lost it to Gene Tunney. He engaged in the 'Battle of the Long Count' with Tunney 1927.

Dench Judi (Judith Olivia) 1934– . English actress. She made her professional debut as Ophelia in *Hamlet* 1957 with the Old Vic Company. Her Shakespearean roles include Viola in *Twelfth Night* 1969, Lady Macbeth 1976, and Cleopatra 1987. She is also a versatile comedy actress and has directed *Much Ado about Nothing* 1988 and John Osborne's *Look Back in Anger* 1989 for the Renaissance Theatre Company.

dendrite part of a *nerve cell or neuron. The dendrites are slender filaments projecting from the cell body. They receive incoming messages from many other nerve cells and pass them on to the cell body. If the combined effect of these messages is strong enough, the cell body will send an electrical impulse along the axon (the thread-like extension of a nerve cell). The tip of the axon passes its message to the dendrites of other nerve cells.

dendrochronology analysis of the *annual rings of trees to date past events. Samples of wood are obtained by means of a narrow metal tube that is driven into a tree to remove a core extending from the bark to the centre. Samples taken from timbers at an archaeological site can be compared with a master core on file for that region or by taking cores from old, living trees; the year when they were felled can be determined by locating the point where the rings of the two samples correspond and counting back from the present.

Deneb or *Alpha Cygni* brightest star in the constellation Cygnus, and the 19th brightest star in the sky. It is one of the greatest supergiant stars known, with a true luminosity of about 60,000 times that of the Sun. Deneb is about 1,800 light years from Earth.

Deng Xiaoping or *Teng Hsiao-ping* 1904– . Chinese political leader. A member of the Chinese Communist Party (CCP) from the 1920s, he took part in the Long March 1934–36. He was in the Politburo from 1955 until ousted in the Cultural Revolution 1966–69. Reinstated in the 1970s, he gradually took power and introduced a radical economic modernization programme. He retired from the Politburo 1987 and from his last official position (as chair of State Military Commission) March 1990, but remained influential behind the scenes.

Den Haag Dutch form of The *Hague, a town in the Netherlands.

denier unit used in measuring the fineness of yarns, equal to the mass in grams of 9,000 metres of yarn. Thus 9,000 metres of 15 denier nylon, used in nylon stockings, weighs 15 g/0.5 oz, and in this case the thickness of thread would be 0.00425 mm/0.0017 in. The term is derived from the French silk industry; the *denier* was an old French silver coin.

denim cotton twill fabric with coloured warp (lengthwise yarns) and undyed weft, originating in France (hence the name 'de Nîmes'). In its most classic form, indigo blue and heavyweight, it is used for jeans and dungarees. It became fashionable in the early 1970s, and many variations followed, including lighter-weight dress fabrics and stone-washed, overdyed, and brushed finishes in many colours.

De Niro Robert 1943– . US actor of great magnetism and physical presence. He won Academy Awards for his performances in *The Godfather Part II* 1974 and *Raging Bull* 1980, for which role he put on weight in the interests of authenticity as the boxer gone to seed, Jake La-Motta. His other films include *Mean Streets* 1973, *Taxi Driver* 1976, *The Deer Hunter* 1978, *The King of Comedy* 1982, *The Untouchables* 1987, *Midnight Run* 1988, and *Cape Fear* 1991. He made his debut as a director with *A Bronx Tale* 1993.

denitrification process occurring naturally in soil, where bacteria break down *nitrates to give nitrogen gas, which returns to the atmosphere.

Denktaş Rauf R 1924– . Turkish-Cypriot nationalist politician. In 1975 the Turkish Federated State of Cyprus (TFSC) was formed in the northern third of the island, with Denktaş as its head, and in 1983 he became president of the breakaway Turkish Republic of Northern Cyprus (TRNC).

Denmark Kingdom of (*Kongeriget Danmark*)

area 43,075 sq km/16,627 sq mi
capital Copenhagen
towns Aarhus, Odense, Aalborg, Esbjerg, all ports
physical comprises the Jutland peninsula and about 500 islands (100 inhabited) including the island of Bornholm in the Baltic Sea; the land is flat and cultivated; sand dunes and lagoons on the W coast and long inlets (fjords) on the E; the main island is Sjælland (Zealand), where most of Copenhagen is located (the rest of it is on the island of Amager)
territories the dependencies of Faeroe Islands and Greenland
head of state Queen Margrethe II from 1972
head of government Poul Nyrup Rasmussen from 1993
political system liberal democracy
exports bacon, dairy produce, eggs, fish, mink pelts, car and aircraft parts, electrical equipment, textiles, chemicals
currency kroner
population (1993 est) 5,180,000; growth rate 0% p.a.
languages Danish (official); there is a German-speaking minority
religion Lutheran 97%
GNP $23,660 per head (1991)
chronology
1940–45 Occupied by Germany.

1945 Iceland's independence recognized.
1947 Frederik IX succeeded Christian X.
1948 Home rule granted for Faeroe Islands.
1949 Became a founding member of NATO.
1960 Joined European Free Trade Association (EFTA).
1972 Margrethe II became Denmark's first queen in nearly 600 years.
1973 Left EFTA and joined European Economic Community (EEC).
1979 Home rule granted for Greenland.
1985 Strong non-nuclear movement in evidence.
1990 General election; another coalition government formed.
1992 Rejection of Maastricht Treaty in national referendum.
1993 Poul Schlüter resigned; replaced by Poul Nyrup Rassmussen at head of Social Democrat-led coalition. Country votes in favour of Maastricht Treaty in second referendum.

Denpasar capital town of Bali in the Lesser Sunda Islands of Indonesia; population (1980) 88,100.

density measure of the compactness of a substance; it is equal to its mass per unit volume and is measured in kg per cubic metre/lb per cubic foot. Density is a *scalar quantity. The density D of a mass m occupying a volume V is given by the formula: $D = m/V$. *Relative density is the ratio of the density of a substance to that of water at 4°C. In photography, density refers to the degree of opacity of a negative; in population studies, it is the quantity or number per unit area. In electricity, current density is the amount of current passing through a conductor in a given amount of time.

dentistry care and treatment of the teeth and gums. *Orthodontics* deals with the straightening of the teeth for aesthetic and clinical reasons, and *periodontics* with care of the supporting tissue (bone and gums).

dentition type and number of teeth in a species. Different kinds of teeth have different functions; a grass-eating animal will have large molars for grinding its food, whereas a meat-eater will need powerful canines for catching and killing its prey. The teeth that are less useful may be reduced in size or missing altogether.

denudation natural loss of soil and rock debris, blown away by wind or washed away by running water, that lays bare the rock below. Over millions of years, denudation causes a general lowering of the landscape.

Denver city and capital of Colorado, USA, on the South Platte River, near the foothills of the Rocky Mountains; population (1990) 467,600, Denver–Boulder metropolitan area 1,848,300. It is a processing and distribution centre for a large agricultural area and for natural resources (minerals, oil, gas).

deontology ethical theory that the rightness of an action consists in its conformity to duty, regardless of the consequences that may result from it. Deontological ethics is thus opposed to any form of utilitarianism or pragmatism.

deoxyribonucleic acid full name of *DNA.

De Palma Brian 1941– . US film director, especially of thrillers. His technical mastery and enthusiasm for spilling blood are shown in films

such as *Sisters* 1973, *Carrie* 1976, and *The Untouchables* 1987.

Depardieu Gérard 1948– . French actor renowned for his imposing physique and screen presence. His films include *Deux hommes dans la ville* 1973, *Mon oncle d'Amérique* 1980, *Jean de Florette* 1985, *Cyrano de Bergerac* 1990. His English-speaking roles include the US romantic comedy *Green Card* 1990 and *1492 – Conquest of Paradise* 1992, and *My Father the Hero* 1994.

deposit account in banking, an account in which money is left to attract interest, sometimes for a fixed term. Unlike a current account, the deposit account does not give constant access.

depreciation in economics, the decline of a currency's value in relation to other currencies. Depreciation also describes the fall in value of an asset (such as factory machinery) resulting from age, wear and tear, or other circumstances. It is an important factor in assessing company profits and tax liabilities.

depression in economics, a period of low output and investment, with high unemployment. Specifically, the term describes two periods of crisis in world economy: 1873–96 and 1929–mid-1930s.

depression or *cyclone* or *low* in meteorology, a region of low atmospheric pressure. A depression forms as warm, moist air from the tropics mixes with cold, dry polar air, producing warm and cold boundaries (*fronts) and unstable weather – low cloud and drizzle, showers, or fierce storms. The warm air, being less dense, rises above the cold air to produce the area of low pressure on the ground. Air spirals in towards the centre of the depression in an anticlockwise direction in the northern hemisphere, clockwise in the southern hemisphere, generating winds up to gale force. Depressions tend to travel eastwards and can remain active for several days.

depression emotional state characterized by sadness, unhappy thoughts, apathy, and dejection. Sadness is a normal response to major losses such as bereavement or unemployment. After childbirth, *postnatal depression is common. However, clinical depression, which is prolonged or unduly severe, often requires treatment, such as antidepressant medication, *cognitive therapy, or, in very rare cases, electro-convulsive therapy (ECT), in which an electrical current is passed through the brain.

De Quincey Thomas 1785–1859. English author whose works include *Confessions of an English Opium-Eater* 1821 and the essays 'On the Knocking at the Gate in Macbeth' 1823 and 'On Murder Considered as One of the Fine Arts' 1827. He was a friend of the poets Wordsworth and Coleridge.

Derby industrial city in Derbyshire, England; population (1991) 214,000. Products include rail locomotives, Rolls-Royce cars and aero engines, chemicals, paper, electrical, mining, and engineering equipment. The museum collections of Crown Derby china, the Rolls-Royce collection of aero engines, and the Derby Playhouse are here.

Derby *blue riband of the English horse-racing season. It is run over 2.4 km/1.5 mi at Epsom,

Surrey, every June. It was established 1780 and named after the 12th Earl of Derby. The USA has an equivalent horse race, the **Kentucky Derby**.

Derby Edward (George Geoffrey Smith) Stanley, 14th Earl of Derby 1799–1869. British politician, prime minister 1852, 1858–59, and 1866–68. Originally a Whig, he became secretary for the colonies 1830, and introduced the bill for the abolition of slavery. He joined the Tories 1834, and the split in the Tory Party over Robert Peel's free-trade policy gave Derby the leadership for 20 years.

Derbyshire county in N central England
area 2,630 sq km/1,015 sq mi
towns Matlock (administrative headquarters), Derby, Chesterfield, Ilkeston
products cereals; dairy and sheep farming; there have been pit and factory closures, but the area is being redeveloped, and there are large reserves of fluorite
population (1991) 915,000
famous people Thomas Cook, Marquess Curzon of Kedleston, Samuel Richardson.

deregulation US term for freeing markets from protection, with the aim of improving competitiveness. It often results in greater monopoly control.

Derg, Lough lake in County Donegal, NW Ireland, with an island (Station Island or St Patrick's Purgatory) that is the country's leading place of pilgrimage. Associated with St Patrick, a monastery flourished here from early times.

derivative or **differential coefficient** in mathematics, the limit of the gradient of a chord linking two points on a curve as the distance between the points tends to zero; in a function with a single variable, $y = f'(x)$, it is denoted by $f'(x)$, $Df(x)$, or dy/dx, and is equal to the gradient of the curve.

dermatitis inflammation of the skin (see *eczema), usually related to allergy. **Dermatosis** refers to any skin disorder and may be caused by contact or systemic problems.

dermatology science of the skin, its nature and diseases. It is a rapidly expanding field owing to the proliferation of industrial chemicals affecting workers, and the universal use of household cleaners, cosmetics, and sun screens.

De Roburt Hammer 1923–1992. President of Nauru 1968–76, 1978–83, and 1987–89. During the country's occupation 1942–45, he was deported to Japan. He became head chief of Nauru 1956 and was elected the country's first president 1968. He secured only a narrow majority in the 1987 elections and in 1989 was ousted on a no-confidence motion.

derrick simple lifting machine consisting of a pole carrying a block and tackle. Derricks are commonly used on ships that carry freight. In the oil industry the tower used for hoisting the drill pipes is known as a derrick.

Derry county of Northern Ireland
area 2,070 sq km/799 sq mi
towns Derry (county town, formerly Londonderry), Coleraine, Portstewart
products mainly agricultural, but farming is hindered by the very heavy rainfall; flax, cattle, sheep, food processing, textiles, light engineering
population (1981) 187,000

famous people Joyce Cary.

Derry (Gaelic **doire** 'a place of oaks') historic city and port on the river Foyle, County Derry, Northern Ireland; population (1981) 89,100. Known as Londonderry until 1984, Derry dates from the foundation of a monastery by St Columba AD 546. James I of England granted the borough and surrounding land to the citizens of London and a large colony of imported Protestants founded the present city which they named Londonderry. Textiles and chemicals are produced.

dervish in Iran and Turkey, a religious mendicant; throughout the rest of Islam a member of an Islamic religious brotherhood, not necessarily mendicant in character. The Arabic equivalent is **fakir**. There are various orders of dervishes, each with its rule and special ritual. The 'whirling dervishes' claim close communion with the deity through ecstatic dancing; the 'howling dervishes' gash themselves with knives to demonstrate the miraculous feats possible to those who trust in Allah.

Derwent river in N Yorkshire, NE England; length 112 km/70 mi. Rising in the N Yorkshire moors, it joins the river Ouse SE of Selby.

desalination removal of salt, usually from sea water, to produce fresh water for irrigation or drinking. Distillation has usually been the method adopted, but in the 1970s a cheaper process, using certain polymer materials that filter the molecules of salt from the water by reverse osmosis, was developed.

De Savary Peter 1944– . British entrepreneur. He acquired Land's End, Cornwall, England, 1987 and built a theme park there. He revived Falmouth dock and the port of Hayle in N Cornwall.

Descartes René 1596–1650. French philosopher and mathematician. He believed that commonly accepted knowledge was doubtful because of the subjective nature of the senses, and attempted to rebuild human knowledge using as his foundation *cogito ergo sum* ('I think, therefore I am'). He also believed that the entire material universe could be explained in terms of mathematical physics, and founded coordinate geometry as a way of defining and manipulating geometrical shapes by means of algebraic expressions. *Cartesian coordinates, the means by which points are represented in this system, are named after him. Descartes also established the science of optics, and helped to shape contemporary theories of astronomy and animal behaviour.

deselection in Britain, removal or withholding of a sitting member of Parliament's official status as a candidate for a forthcoming election. The term came into use in the 1980s with the efforts of many local Labour parties to revoke the candidature of MPs viewed as too right-wing.

desert arid area without sufficient rainfall and, consequently, vegetation to support human life. The term includes the ice areas of the polar regions (known as cold deserts). Almost 33% of Earth's land surface is desert, and this proportion is increasing.

desertification creation of deserts by changes in climate, or by human-aided processes. The latter include overgrazing, destruction of forest belts, and exhaustion of the soil by intensive cultivation without restoration of fertility – all of which are usually prompted by the pressures of an expanding population. Desertification can be reversed by special planting (marram grass, trees) and by the use of water-absorbent plastic grains, which, added to the soil, enable crops to be grown. About 135 million people are directly affected by desertification, mainly in Africa, the Indian subcontinent, and South America.

Desert Storm, Operation codename of the military action to eject the Iraqi army from Kuwait 1991. The build-up phase was code-named *Operation Desert Shield* and lasted from Aug 1990, when Kuwait was first invaded by Iraq, to Jan 1991 when Operation Desert Storm was unleashed, starting the *Gulf War. Desert Storm ended with the defeat of the Iraqi army in the Kuwaiti theatre of operations late Feb 1991. The cost of the operation was $53 billion.

De Sica Vittorio 1901–1974. Italian director and actor. He won his first Oscar with *Bicycle Thieves* 1948, a film of subtle realism. Later films included *Umberto D* 1952, *Two Women* 1960, and *The Garden of the Finzi-Continis* 1971. His considerable acting credits include *Madame de ...* 1953 and *The Millionaires* 1960.

desiccator airtight vessel, traditionally made of glass, in which materials may be stored either to dry them or to prevent them, once dried, from reabsorbing moisture.

desktop publishing (DTP) use of micro-computers for small-scale typesetting and page make-up. DTP systems are capable of producing camera-ready pages (pages ready for photograph-ing and printing), made up of text and graphics, with text set in different typefaces and sizes. The page can be previewed on the screen before final printing on a laser printer.

Desmoulins Camille 1760–1794. French revolutionary who summoned the mob to arms on 12 July 1789, so precipitating the revolt that culminated in the storming of the Bastille. A prominent left-wing *Jacobin, he was elected to the National Convention 1792. His *Histoire des Brissotins* was largely responsible for the overthrow of the right-wing *Girondins, but shortly after he was sent to the guillotine as too moderate.

de Soto Hernando *c.* 1496–1542. Spanish explorer who sailed with d'Avila (*c.* 1400–1531) to Darien, Central America, 1519, explored the Yucatán Peninsula 1528, and travelled with Francisco Pizarro in Peru 1530–35. In 1538 he was made governor of Cuba and Florida. In his expedition of 1539, he explored Florida, Georgia, and the Mississippi River.

Desprez Josquin Franco-Flemish composer; see *Josquin Desprez.

Dessalines Jean Jacques *c.* 1758–1806. Emperor of Haiti 1804–06. Born in Guinea, he was taken to Haiti as a slave, where in 1802 he succeeded *Toussaint L'Ouverture as leader of the black revolt against the French. After defeating the French, he proclaimed Haiti's independence and made himself emperor. He was killed when trying to suppress an uprising provoked by his cruelty.

Dessau Paul 1894–1979. German composer. His work includes incidental music to Bertolt Brecht's theatre pieces; an opera, *Der Verurtei-lung des Lukullus* 1949, also to a libretto by Brecht; and numerous choral works and songs.

destroyer small, fast warship designed for anti-submarine work. Destroyers played a critical role in the convoy system in World War II.

detective fiction novel or short story in which a mystery is solved mainly by the action of a professional or amateur detective. Where the mystery to be solved concerns a crime, the work may be called *crime fiction*. The earliest work of detective fiction as understood today was *Murders in the Rue Morgue* 1841 by Edgar Allan Poe, and his detective Dupin became the model for those who solved crimes by deduction from a series of clues. A popular deductive sleuth was Sherlock Holmes in the stories by Arthur Conan Doyle.

détente (French) reduction of political tension and the easing of strained relations between nations, for example, the ending of the Cold War 1989–90, although it was first used in the 1970s to describe the easing East–West relations, trade agreements, and cultural exchanges.

detention in law, depriving a person of liberty following arrest. In England and Wales, the Police and Criminal Evidence Act 1984 established a wide-ranging statutory framework for the regime of detention. Limitations were placed on the length of time that suspects may be held in custody by the police without being charged (to a maximum of 96 hours) and systems of record-keeping and supervision by designated 'custody officers' were introduced.

detention centre in the UK penal system, an institution where young offenders (aged 14–21) are confined for short periods. Treatment is designed to be disciplinary; for example, the 'short, sharp shock' regime introduced by the Conservative government 1982.

detergent surface-active cleansing agent. The common detergents are made from *fats (hydrocarbons) and sulphuric acid, and their long-chain molecules have a type of structure similar to that of *soap molecules: a salt group at one end attached to a long hydrocarbon 'tail'. They have the advantage over soap in that they do not produce scum by forming insoluble salts with the calcium and magnesium ions present in hard water.

determinism in philosophy, the view that denies human freedom of action. Everything is strictly governed by the principle of cause and effect, and human action is no exception. It is the opposite of free will, and rules out moral choice and responsibility.

deterrence underlying conception of the nuclear arms race: the belief that a potential aggressor will be discouraged from launching a 'first strike' nuclear attack by the knowledge that the adversary is capable of inflicting 'unaccept-able damage' in a retaliatory strike. This doctrine is widely known as that of *mutual assured destruction (MAD)*. Three essential characteristics of deterrence are: the 'capability to act', 'credibility', and the 'will to act'.

de Tocqueville Alexis French politician; see *Tocqueville, Alexis de.

detonator or *blasting cap* or *percussion cap* small explosive charge used to trigger off a main charge of high explosive. The relatively unstable compounds mercury fulminate and lead acid are often used in detonators, being set off by a lighted fuse or, more commonly, an electric current.

detritus in biology, the organic debris produced during the *decomposition of animals and plants.

Detroit city in Michigan, USA, situated on Detroit River; population (1990) 1,028,000, metropolitan area 4,665,200. It is an industrial centre with the headquarters of Ford, Chrysler, and General Motors, hence its nickname, *Motown (from 'motor town'). Other manufactured products include metal products, machine tools, chemicals, office machines, and pharmaceuticals. Detroit is a port on the St Lawrence Seaway and the home of Wayne State University and its Medical Center complex. The University of Detroit and the Detroit Institute of Arts are also here.

deus ex machina (Latin 'a god from a machine') far-fetched or unlikely event that resolves an intractable difficulty. The phrase was originally used in drama to indicate a god descending from heaven to resolve the plot.

deuterium naturally occurring heavy isotope of hydrogen, mass number 2 (one proton and one neutron), discovered by Harold Urey 1932. It is sometimes given the symbol D. In nature, about one in every 6,500 hydrogen atoms is deuterium. Combined with oxygen, it produces 'heavy water' (D₂O), used in the nuclear industry.

deuteron nucleus of an atom of deuterium (heavy hydrogen). It consists of one proton and one neutron, and is used in the bombardment of chemical elements to synthesize other elements.

Deuteronomy book of the Old Testament; fifth book of the *Torah. It contains various laws, including the Ten Commandments, and gives an account of the death of Moses.

Dev Kapil 1959– . Indian cricketer who is one of the world's outstanding all-rounders. At the age of 20 he became the youngest player to complete the 'double' of 1,000 runs and 100 wickets in test cricket. In 1992 he followed Richard Hadlee as the second bowler to reach 400 wickets.

de Valera Eámon 1882–1975. Irish nationalist politician, prime minister of the Irish Free State/Eire/Republic of Ireland 1932–48, 1951–54, and 1957–59, and president 1959–73. Repeatedly imprisoned, he participated in the Easter Rising 1916 and was leader of the nationalist *Sinn Féin party 1917–26, when he formed the republican *Fianna Fáil party; he directed negotiations with Britain 1921 but refused to accept the partition of Ireland until 1937.

de Valois Ninette. Stage name of Edris Stannus 1898– . Irish dancer, choreographer, and teacher. A pioneer of British national ballet, she worked with Sergei Diaghilev in Paris before opening a dance academy in London 1926. Collaborating with Lilian Baylis at the *Old Vic, she founded the Vic-Wells Ballet 1931, which later became the Royal Ballet and Royal Ballet School.

Among her works are *Job* 1931 and *Checkmate* 1937.

devaluation in economics, the lowering of the official value of a currency against other currencies, so that exports become cheaper and imports more expensive. Used when a country is badly in deficit in its balance of trade, it results in the goods the country produces being cheaper abroad, so that the economy is stimulated by increased foreign demand.

developed world or *First World* or *the North* the countries that have a money economy and a highly developed industrial sector. They generally also have a high degree of urbanization, a complex communications network, high *GDP (over US $2,000) per person, low birth and death rates, high energy consumption, and a large proportion of the workforce employed in manufacturing or service industries (secondary to quaternary *industrial sectors). The developed world includes the USA, Canada, Europe, Japan, Australia, and New Zealand.

development or *Third World* or *the South* countries with a largely subsistence economy where the output per person and the average income are both low. These countries typically have low life expectancy, high birth and death rates, poor communications, low literacy levels, high national debt, and low energy consumption per person. The developing world includes much of Africa and parts of Asia and South America. Terms like 'developing world' and 'less developed countries' are often criticized for implying that a highly industrialized economy (as in the *developed world) is a desirable goal.

development in the social sciences, the acquisition by a society of industrial techniques and technology; hence the common classification of the 'developed' nations of the First and Second Worlds and the poorer, 'developing' or 'underdeveloped' nations of the Third World. The assumption that development in the sense of industrialization is inherently good has been increasingly questioned since the 1960s.

development in biology, the process whereby a living thing transforms itself from a single cell into a vastly complicated multicellular organism, with structures, such as limbs, and functions, such as respiration, all able to work correctly in relation to each other. Most of the details of this process remain unknown, although some of the central features are becoming understood.

development aid see *aid, development.

deviance abnormal behaviour; that is, behaviour that deviates from the norms or the laws of a society or group, and so invokes social sanctions, controls, or stigma.

devil in Jewish, Christian, and Muslim theology, the supreme spirit of evil (*Beelzebub, Lucifer, Iblis*), or an evil spirit generally.

devil ray any of several large rays of the genera *Manta* and *Mobula*, fish in which two 'horns' project forwards from the sides of the huge mouth. These flaps of skin guide the plankton on which the fish feed into the mouth. The largest of these rays can be 7 m/23 ft across, and weigh 1,000 kg/2,200 lb. They live in warm seas.

Devil's Island (French *Ile du Diable*) smallest of the Iles du Salut, off French Guiana, 43 km/

27 mi NW of Cayenne. The group of islands was collectively and popularly known by the name Devil's Island and formed a penal colony notorious for its terrible conditions.

devolution delegation of authority and duties; in the later 20th century, the movement to decentralize governmental power, as in the UK where a bill for the creation of Scottish and Welsh assemblies was introduced 1976 (rejected by referendums in Scotland and Wales 1979).

Devolution, War of war waged unsuccessfully 1667–68 by Louis XIV of France to gain Spanish territory in the Netherlands, of which ownership had allegedly 'devolved' on his wife Maria Theresa.

Devon or **Devonshire** county in SW England
area 6,720 sq km/2,594 sq mi
towns Exeter (administrative headquarters), Plymouth; resorts: Paignton, Torquay, Teignmouth, and Ilfracombe
products mainly agricultural, with sheep and dairy farming; cider and clotted cream; kaolin in the S; Honiton lace; Dartington glass
population (1991) 1,008,300
famous people Francis Drake, John Hawkins, Charles Kingsley, Robert F Scott.

Devonian period of geological time 408–360 million years ago, the fourth period of the Palaeozoic era. Many desert sandstones from North America and Europe date from this time. The first land plants flourished in the Devonian period, corals were abundant in the seas, amphibians evolved from air-breathing fish, and insects developed on land.

Devoy Susan 1964– . New Zealand squash player who won the World Open Championship a record three times 1985,1987, and 1990. She also won seven consecutive British Open titles 1984–90.

De Vries Hugo 1848–1935. Dutch botanist who conducted important research on osmosis in plant cells and was a pioneer in the study of plant evolution. His work led to the rediscovery of *Mendel's laws and the discovery of spontaneously occurring *mutations.

dew precipitation in the form of moisture that collects on the ground. It forms after the temperature of the ground has fallen below the *dew point of the air in contact with it. As the temperature falls during the night, the air and its water vapour become chilled, and condensation takes place on the cooled surfaces.

Dewar James 1842–1923. Scottish chemist and physicist who invented the *vacuum flask (Thermos) 1872 during his research into the properties of matter at extremely low temperatures.

Dewey Melvil 1851–1931. US librarian. In 1876, he devised the Dewey decimal system of classification for accessing, storing, and retrieving books, widely used in libraries. The system uses the numbers 000 to 999 to designate the major fields of knowledge, then breaks these down into more specific subjects by the use of decimals.

dew point temperature at which the air becomes saturated with water vapour. At temperatures below the dew point, the water vapour condenses out of the air as droplets. If the drop-

lets are large they become deposited on the ground as dew; if small they remain in suspension in the air and form mist or fog.

dewpond drinking pond for farm animals on arid hilltops such as chalk downs. In the UK, dewponds were excavated in the 19th century and lined with mud and clay. It is uncertain where the water comes from but it may be partly rain, partly sea mist, and only a small part dew.

Dhaka or **Dacca** capital of Bangladesh from 1971, in Dhaka region, west of the river Meghna; population (1984) 3,600,000. It trades in jute, oilseed, sugar, and tea and produces textiles, chemicals, glass, and metal products.

dharma (Sanskrit 'justice, order') in Hinduism, the consciousness of forming part of an ordered universe, and hence the moral duty of accepting one's station in life. In Buddhism, dharma is anything that increases generosity and wisdom, and so leads towards enlightenment.

Dhaulagiri mountain in the *Himalayas of W central Nepal, rising to 8,172 m/26,811 ft.

Dhofar mountainous western province of *Oman, on the border with Yemen; population (1982) 40,000. South Yemen supported guerrilla activity here in the 1970s, while Britain and Iran supported the government's military operations. The capital is Salalah, which has a port at Rasut.

dhole wild dog *Cuon alpinus* found in Asia from Siberia to Java. With head and body up to 1 m/3 ft long, variable in colour but often reddish above and lighter below, the dhole lives in groups of from 3 to 30 individuals. The species is becoming rare and is protected in some areas.

DHSS abbreviation for **Department of Health and Social Security**, UK government department until divided 1988; see *social security.

diabetes disease *diabetes mellitus* in which a disorder of the islets of Langerhans in the *pancreas prevents the body producing the hormone *insulin, so that sugars cannot be used properly. Treatment is by strict dietary control and oral or injected insulin.

diagenesis or **lithification** in geology, the physical and chemical changes by which a sediment becomes a *sedimentary rock. The main processes involved include compaction of the grains, and the cementing of the grains together by the growth of new minerals deposited by percolating groundwater.

Diaghilev Sergei Pavlovich 1872–1929. Russian ballet impresario who in 1909 founded the Ballets Russes/Russian Ballet (headquarters in Monaco), which he directed for 20 years. Through this company he brought Russian ballet to the West, introducing and encouraging a dazzling array of dancers, choreographers, and composers, such as Anna Pavlova, Vaslav Nijinsky, Mikhail Fokine, Léonide Massine, George Balanchine, Igor Stravinsky, and Sergey Prokofiev.

dialect variation of a spoken language shared by those in a particular area or a particular social group or both. The term is used both objectively, to indicate a geographical area ('northern dialects') or social group ('black dialect'), and subjectively, in a judgemental and sometimes dismissive way.

dialectic Greek term, originally associated with the philosopher Socrates' method of argument through dialogue and conversation. **Hegelian dialectic**, named after the German philosopher *Hegel, refers to an interpretive method in which the contradiction between a thesis and its antithesis is resolved through synthesis.

dialectical materialism political, philosophical, and economic theory of the 19th-century German thinkers Karl Marx and Friedrich Engels, also known as *Marxism.

dialysis in medicine, the process used to mimic the effects of the kidneys. It may be life-saving in some types of poisoning. Dialysis is usually performed to compensate for failing kidneys; there are two main methods, haemodialysis and peritoneal dialysis.

diamond generally colourless, transparent mineral, the hard crystalline form of carbon. It is regarded as a precious gemstone, and is the hardest natural substance known (10 on the *Mohs' scale). Industrial diamonds are used for cutting, grinding, and polishing.

Diana in Roman mythology, the goddess of chastity, hunting, and the Moon (Greek *Artemis), daughter of Jupiter and twin of Apollo.

Diana Princess of Wales 1961– . The daughter of the 8th Earl Spencer, she married Prince Charles in St Paul's Cathedral, London 1981, the first English bride of a royal heir since 1659. She is descended from the only sovereigns from whom Prince Charles is not descended, Charles II and James II. Diana and Charles separated 1992.

DIANE (acronym from *direct information access network for Europe*) collection of information suppliers, or 'hosts', for the European computer network.

diaphragm muscular sheet separating the thorax from the abdomen in mammals. Its rhythmical movements affect the size of the thorax and cause the pressure changes within the lungs that result in breathing.

diaphragm or *cap* or *Dutch cap* barrier *contraceptive that is pushed into the vagina and fits over the cervix (neck of the uterus), preventing sperm from entering the uterus. For a cap to be effective, a *spermicide must be used and the diaphragm left in place for 6–8 hours after intercourse. This method is 97% effective if practised correctly.

diarrhoea excessive action of the bowels so that the faeces are fluid or semifluid. It is caused by intestinal irritants (including some drugs and poisons), infection with harmful organisms (as in dysentery, salmonella, or cholera), or allergies.

diary informal record of day-to-day events, observations, or reflections, usually not intended for a general readership. One of the earliest diaries extant is that of a Japanese noblewoman, the *Kagerō Nikki* 954–974, and the earliest diary extant in English is that of Edward VI (ruled 1547–53). Notable diaries include those of Samuel Pepys, the writer John Evelyn, the Quaker George Fox, and in the 20th century those of Anne Frank and the writers André Gide and Katherine Mansfield.

Diaspora dispersal of the Jews, initially from Palestine after the Babylonian conquest 586 BC, and then following the Roman sack of Jerusalem

AD 70 and their crushing of the Jewish revolt of 135. The term has come to refer to all the Jews living outside Israel.

diatom microscopic alga of the division Bacillariophyta found in all parts of the world. Diatoms consist of single cells, sometimes grouped in colonies.

diatomic molecule molecule composed of two atoms joined together. In the case of an element such as oxygen (O_2), the atoms are identical.

diatonic in music, a scale consisting of the seven notes of any major or minor key.

Diaz Bartolomeu *c.* 1450–1500. Portuguese explorer, the first European to reach the Cape of Good Hope 1488, and to establish a route around Africa. He drowned during an expedition with Pedro Cabral (1460–1526).

Díaz Porfirio 1830–1915. Dictator of Mexico 1877–80 and 1884–1911. After losing the 1876 election, he overthrew the government and seized power. He was supported by conservative landowners and foreign capitalists, who invested in railways and mines. He centralized the state at the expense of the peasants and Indians, and dismantled all local and regional leadership. He faced mounting and revolutionary opposition in his final years and was forced into exile 1911.

Diaz de Solís Juan 1471–*c.* 1516. Spanish explorer in South America who reached the estuary of the Río de la Plata, and was killed and reputedly eaten by cannibals.

Dickens Charles 1812–1870. English novelist, popular for his memorable characters and his portrayal of the social evils of Victorian England. In 1836 he published the first number of the *Pickwick Papers*, followed by *Oliver Twist* 1838, the first of his 'reforming' novels; *Nicholas Nickleby* 1839; *Barnaby Rudge* 1840; *The Old Curiosity Shop* 1841; and *David Copperfield* 1849. Among his later books are *A Tale of Two Cities* 1859 and *Great Expectations* 1861.

Dickinson Emily 1830–1886. US poet. Born in Amherst, Massachusetts, she lived in near seclusion there from 1862. Very few of her many short, mystical poems were published during her lifetime, and her work became well known only in the 20th century.

dicotyledon major subdivision of the *angiosperms, containing the great majority of flowering plants. Dicotyledons are characterized by the presence of two seed leaves, or *cotyledons, in the embryo, which is usually surrounded by an *endosperm. They generally have broad leaves with netlike veins.

dictatorship term or office of an absolute ruler, overriding the constitution. (In ancient Rome a dictator was a magistrate invested with emergency powers for six months.) Although dictatorships were common in Latin America during the 19th century, the only European example during this period was the rule of Napoleon III. The crises following World War I produced many dictatorships, including the regimes of Atatürk and Piłsudski (nationalist); Mussolini, Hitler, Primo de Rivera, Franco, and Salazar (all right-wing); and Stalin (Communist).

dictatorship of the proletariat Marxist term for a revolutionary dictatorship established during the transition from capitalism to *communism after a socialist revolution.

Diderot Denis 1713–1784. French philosopher. He is closely associated with the Enlightenment, the European intellectual movement for social and scientific progress, and was editor of the enormously influential *Encyclopédie* 1751–80.

didjeridu musical wind instrument, made from a hollow bamboo section 1.5 m/4 ft long and blown to produce rhythmic, booming notes. It was first developed and played by Australian Aborigines.

Dido Phoenician princess, legendary founder of Carthage, N Africa, who committed suicide to avoid marrying a local prince. In the Latin epic *Aeneid*, Virgil claims that it was because *Aeneas deserted her.

diecasting form of *casting in which molten metal is injected into permanent metal moulds or dies.

Dien Bien Phu, Battle of decisive battle in the *Indochina War at a French fortress in North Vietnam, near the Laotian border. French troops were besieged 13 March–7 May 1954 by the communist Vietminh. The fall of Dien Bien Phu resulted in the end of French control of Indochina.

Diesel Rudolf 1858–1913. German engineer who patented the diesel engine. He began his career as a refrigerator engineer and, like many engineers of the period, sought to develop a more efficient power source than the conventional steam engine. Able to operate with greater efficiency and economy, the diesel engine soon found a ready market.

diesel engine *internal-combustion engine that burns a lightweight fuel oil. The diesel engine operates by compressing air until it becomes sufficiently hot to ignite the fuel. It is a piston-in-cylinder engine, like the *petrol engine, but only air (rather than an air-and-fuel mixture) is taken into the cylinder on the first piston stroke (down). The piston moves up and compresses the air until it is at a very high temperature. The fuel oil is then injected into the hot air, where it burns, driving the piston down on its power stroke. For this reason the engine is called a compression-ignition engine.

diesel oil lightweight fuel oil used in diesel engines. Like petrol, it is a petroleum product. When used in vehicle engines, it is also known as **derv** – *d*iesel-*e*ngine *r*oad *v*ehicle.

diet a particular selection of food, or the overall intake and selection of food for a particular person or people. A special diet may be recommended for medical reasons, to balance, limit, or increase certain nutrients; undertaken to lose weight, by a reduction in calorie intake or selection of specific foods; or observed on religious, moral, or emotional grounds. An adequate diet is one that fulfils the body's nutritional requirements and gives an energy intake proportional to the person's activity level (the average daily requirement is 2,400 calories for men, less for women, more for active children). In the Third World and in famine or poverty areas some 450 million people in the world subsist on fewer than 1,500 calories per day, whereas in the developed countries the average daily intake is 3,300 calories.

diet meeting or convention of the princes and other dignitaries of the Holy Roman (German) Empire, for example, the Diet of Worms 1521 which met to consider the question of Luther's doctrines and the governance of the empire under Charles V.

dietetics specialized branch of human nutrition, dealing with the promotion of health through the proper kinds and quantities of food.

Dietrich Marlene (Maria Magdalene) 1904–1992. German-born US actress and singer who appeared with Emil Jannings in both the German and American versions of the film *The Blue Angel* 1930, directed by Josef von Sternberg. She stayed in Hollywood, becoming a US citizen 1937. Her husky, sultry singing voice added to her appeal. Her other films include *Blonde Venus* 1932, *Destry Rides Again* 1939, and *Just a Gigolo* 1978.

difference in mathematics, the result obtained when subtracting one number from another. Also, those elements of one *set that are not elements of another.

difference engine mechanical calculating machine designed (and partly built 1822) by British mathematician Charles *Babbage to produce reliable tables of life expectancy. A precursor of the *analytical engine, it was to calculate mathematical functions by solving the differences between values given to *variables within equations. Babbage designed the calculator so that once the initial values for the variables were set it would produce the next few thousand values without error.

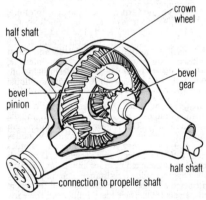

differential The differential lies midway between the driving wheels of a motorcar.

differential arrangement of gears in the final drive of a vehicle's transmission system that allows the driving wheels to turn at different speeds when cornering. The differential consists of sets of bevel gears and pinions within a cage attached to the crown wheel. When cornering, the bevel pinions rotate to allow the outer wheel to turn faster than the inner.

differential calculus branch of *calculus involving applications such as the determination of maximum and minimum points and rates of change.

differentiation in mathematics, a procedure for determining the gradient of the tangent to a curve $f(x)$ at any point x.

differentiation in embryology, the process whereby cells become increasingly different and specialized, giving rise to more complex structures that have particular functions in the adult organism. For instance, embryonic cells may develop into nerve, muscle, or bone cells.

diffraction spreading of a wave motion (such as light or sound) as it passes an obstacle and expands into a region not exposed directly to incoming waves behind the obstacle. This accounts for interference phenomena observed at the edges of opaque objects, or discontinuities between different media in the path of a wave train. The phenomena give rise to slight spreading of light into coloured bands at the shadow of a straight edge.

diffusion spontaneous and random movement of molecules or particles in a fluid (gas or liquid) from a region in which they are at a high concentration to a region in which they are at a low concentration, until a uniform concentration is achieved throughout. No mechanical mixing or stirring is involved. For instance, if a drop of ink is added to water, its molecules will diffuse until their colour becomes evenly distributed throughout.

digestion process whereby food eaten by an animal is broken down physically, and chemically by *enzymes, usually in the *stomach and *intestines, to make the nutrients available for absorption and cell metabolism.

digestive system mouth, stomach, intestine, and associated glands of animals, which are responsible for digesting food. The food is broken down by physical and chemical means in the *stomach; digestion is completed, and most nutrients are absorbed in the small intestine; what remains is stored and concentrated into faeces in the large intestine. In birds, additional digestive organs are the *crop and *gizzard.

Diggers or *true* *Levellers English 17th-century radical sect that attempted to dig common land. The Diggers became prominent April 1649 when, headed by Gerrard Winstanley (c. 1609–1660), they set up communal colonies near Cobham, Surrey, and elsewhere. These colonies were attacked by mobs and, being pacifists, the Diggers made no resistance. The support they attracted alarmed the government and they were dispersed 1650. Their ideas influenced the early *Quakers.

digit in mathematics, any of the numbers from 0 to 9 in the decimal system. Different bases have different ranges of digits. For example, the *hexadecimal system has digits 0 to 9 and A to F, whereas the binary system has two digits (or *bits), 0 and 1.

digital in electronics and computing, a term meaning 'coded as numbers'. A digital system uses two-state, either on/off or high/low voltage pulses, to encode, receive, and transmit information. A *digital display* shows discrete values as numbers (as opposed to an analogue signal,

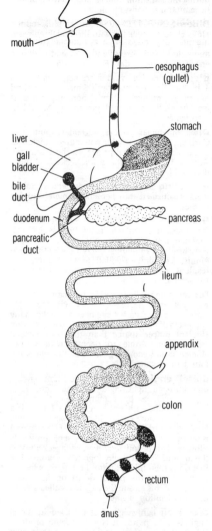

digestive system The human digestive system.

such as the continuous sweep of a pointer on a dial).

digital audio tape (DAT) digitally recorded audio tape produced in cassettes that can carry two hours of sound on each side and are about half the size of standard cassettes. DAT players/recorders were developed 1987 but not marketed in the UK until 1989. Prerecorded cassettes are copy-protected. The first DAT for computer data was introduced 1988.

digital compact cassette (DCC) digitally recorded audio cassette that is roughly the same size as a standard cassette. It cannot be played on a normal tape recorder, though standard tapes can be played on a DCC machine; this is known as 'backwards compatibility'. The playing time is 90 minutes.

digital computer computing device that operates on a two-state system, using symbols that are internally coded as binary numbers (numbers made up of combinations of the digits 0 and 1); see *computer.

digital data transmission in computing, a way of sending data by converting all signals (whether pictures, sounds, or words) into numeric (normally binary) codes before transmission, then reconverting them on receipt. This virtually eliminates any distortion or degradation of the signal during transmission, storage, or processing.

digitalis plant of the genus *Digitalis* of the figwort family Scrophulariaceae, which includes the *foxgloves. The leaves of the common foxglove *Digitalis purpurea* are the source of the drug *digitalis* used in the treatment of heart disease.

digitalis drug that increases the efficiency of the heart by strengthening its muscle contractions and slowing its rate. It is derived from the leaves of the common European woodland plant *Digitalis purpurea* (foxglove).

digital recording technique whereby the pressure of sound waves is sampled more than 30,000 times a second and the values converted by computer into precise numerical values. These are recorded and, during playback, are reconverted to sound waves.

digital sampling electronic process used in *telecommunications for transforming a constantly varying (analogue) signal into one composed of discrete units, a digital signal. In the creation of recorded music, sampling enables the composer, producer, or remix engineer to borrow discrete vocal or instrumental parts from other recorded work (it is also possible to sample live sound).

digitizer in computing, a device that converts an analogue video signal into a digital format so that video images can be input, stored, displayed, and manipulated by a computer. The term is sometimes used to refer to a *graphics tablet.

dik-dik Dik-diks are shy, secretive animals.

dik-dik any of several species of tiny antelope, genus *Madoqua*, found in Africa south of the Sahara in dry areas with scattered brush. Dik-diks are about 60 cm/2 ft long and 35 cm/1.1 ft tall, and are often seen in pairs. Males have short, pointed horns. The dik-dik is so named because of its alarm call.

dilatation and curettage (D and C) common gynaecological procedure in which the cervix (neck of the womb) is widened, or dilated, giving access so that the lining of the womb can be scraped away (curettage). It may be carried out to terminate a pregnancy, treat an incomplete miscarriage, discover the cause of heavy menstrual bleeding, or for biopsy.

dill herb *Anethum graveolens* of the carrot family Umbelliferae, whose bitter seeds and aromatic leaves are used for culinary and medicinal purposes.

dilution process of reducing the concentration of a solution by the addition of a solvent.

DiMaggio Joe 1914– . US baseball player with the New York Yankees 1936–51. In 1941 he set a record by getting hits in 56 consecutive games. He was an outstanding fielder, played centre field, hit 361 home runs, and had a career average of .325. DiMaggio was married to the actress Marilyn Monroe. He was elected to the Baseball Hall of Fame.

dimension in science, any directly measurable physical quantity such as mass (M), length (L), and time (T), and the derived units obtainable by multiplication or division from such quantities. For example, acceleration (the rate of change of velocity) has dimensions (LT^{-2}), and is expressed in such units as km s^{-2}. A quantity that is a ratio, such as relative density or humidity, is dimensionless.

diminishing returns, law of in economics, the principle that additional application of one factor of production, such as an extra machine or employee, at first results in rapidly increasing output but eventually yields declining returns, unless other factors are modified to sustain the increase.

Dine Jim 1935– . US Pop artist. He experimented with combinations of paintings and objects, such as a sink attached to a canvas.

Dinesen Isak 1885–1962. Pen name of Danish writer Karen *Blixen, born Karen Christentze Dinesen.

Dingaan Zulu chief who obtained the throne in 1828 by murdering his predecessor, Shaka, and became notorious for his cruelty. In warfare with the Boer immigrants into Natal he was defeated on 16 Dec 1838 – 'Dingaan's Day'. He escaped to Swaziland, where he was deposed by his brother Mpande and subsequently assassinated.

dingo wild dog of Australia. Descended from domestic dogs brought from Asia by Aborigines thousands of years ago, it belongs to the same species *Canis familiaris* as other domestic dogs. It is reddish brown with a bushy tail, and often hunts at night. It cannot bark.

dinitrogen oxide alternative name for nitrous oxide or 'laughing gas', one of the *nitrogen oxides.

Dinkins David 1927– . Mayor of New York City from Jan 1990, a Democrat. He won a reputation as a moderate and consensual community politician and was Manhattan borough president before succeeding Edward I Koch to become New York's first black mayor.

dinosaur (Greek *deinos* 'terrible', *sauros* 'lizard') any of a group (sometimes considered as two separate orders) of extinct reptiles living between 230 million and 65 million years ago. Their closest living relations are crocodiles and birds, the latter perhaps descended from the dinosaurs. Many species of dinosaur evolved during the millions of years they were the dominant large land animals. Most were large (up to 27 m/90 ft), but some were as small as chickens. They disappeared 65 million years ago for reasons not fully understood, although many theories exist.

Diocletian Gaius Valerius Diocletianus AD 245–313. Roman emperor 284–305, when he abdicated in favour of Galerius. He reorganized and subdivided the empire, with two joint and two subordinate emperors, and in 303 initiated severe persecution of Christians.

diode combination of a cold anode and a heated cathode (or the semiconductor equivalent, which incorporates a $p-n$ junction). Either device allows the passage of direct current in one direction only, and so is commonly used in a *rectifier to convert alternating current (AC) to direct current (DC).

Diogenes c. 412–323 BC. Ascetic Greek philosopher of the *Cynic school. He believed in freedom and self-sufficiency for the individual, and that the virtuous life was the simple life; he did not believe in social mores. His writings do not survive.

Dion Cassius AD 150–235. Roman historian. He wrote, in Greek, a Roman history in 80 books (of which 26 survive), covering the period from the founding of the city to AD 229, including the only surviving account of the invasion of Britain by Claudius 43 BC.

Dionysius two tyrants of the ancient Greek city of Syracuse in Sicily. *Dionysius the Elder* (432–367 BC) seized power 405 BC. His first two wars with Carthage further extended the power of Syracuse, but in a third (383–378 BC) he was defeated. He was a patron of *Plato. He was succeeded by his son, *Dionysius the Younger* (c. 390–344 BC), who was driven out of Syracuse by Dion 356; he was tyrant again 353, but in 343 returned to Corinth.

Dionysus in Greek mythology, the god of wine (son of Semele and Zeus), and also of orgiastic excess, who was attended by women called maenads, who were believed to be capable of tearing animals to pieces with their bare hands when under his influence. He was identified with the Roman *Bacchus, whose rites were less savage.

dioptre optical unit in which the power of a *lens is expressed as the reciprocal of its focal length in metres. The usual convention is that convergent lenses are positive and divergent lenses negative. Short-sighted people need lenses of power about –0.66 dioptre; a typical value for long sight is about +1.5 dioptre.

Dior Christian 1905–1957. French couturier. He established his own Paris salon 1947 and made an impact with the 'New Look' – long, cinch-waisted, and full-skirted – after wartime austerity.

diorite igneous rock intermediate in composition; the coarse-grained plutonic equivalent of *andesite.

Diouf Abdou 1935– . Senegalese left-wing politician, president from 1980. He became prime minister 1970 under President Leopold Senghor and, on his retirement, succeeded him, being re-elected in 1983 and 1988. His presidency has been characterized by authoritarianism.

dioxin any of a family of over 200 organic chemicals, all of which are heterocyclic hydrocarbons (see *cyclic compounds). The term is commonly applied, however, to only one member of the family, 2,3,7,8-tetrachlorodibenzodioxin (2,3,7,8-TCDD), a highly toxic chemical that occurs as an impurity in the defoliant Agent Orange, used in the Vietnam War, and in the weedkiller 2,4,5-T. It has been associated with a disfiguring skin complaint (chloracne), birth defects, miscarriages, and cancer.

diphtheria acute infectious disease in which a membrane forms in the throat (threatening death by *asphyxia), along with the production of a powerful neurotoxin that poisons the system. The organism responsible is a bacterium (*Corynebacterium diphtheriae*). Its incidence has been reduced greatly by immunization.

Diplock court in Northern Ireland, a type of court established 1972 by the British government under Lord Diplock (1907–1985) to try offences linked with guerrilla violence. The right to jury trial was suspended and the court consisted of a single judge, because potential jurors were allegedly being intimidated and were unwilling to serve. Despite widespread criticism, the Diplock courts have remained in operation.

diplodocus plant-eating sauropod dinosaur that lived about 145 million years ago, the fossils of which have been found in the W USA. Up to 27 m/88 ft long, most of which was neck and tail, it weighed about 11 tonnes. It walked on four elephantine legs, had nostrils on top of the skull, and peglike teeth at the front of the mouth.

diploid having two sets of *chromosomes in each cell. In sexually reproducing species, one set is derived from each parent, the *gametes, or sex cells, of each parent being *haploid (having only one set of chromosomes) due to *meiosis (reduction cell division).

diplomacy process by which states attempt to settle their differences through peaceful means such as negotiation or *arbitration. See *foreign relations.

dip, magnetic angle at a particular point on the Earth's surface between the direction of the Earth's magnetic field and the horizontal. It is measured using a *dip circle*, which has a magnetized needle suspended so that it can turn freely in the vertical plane of the magnetic field. In the northern hemisphere the needle dips below the horizontal, pointing along the line of the magnetic field towards its north pole. At the magnetic north and south poles, the needle dips vertically and the angle of dip is 90°.

dipole uneven distribution of magnetic or electrical characteristics within a molecule or substance so that it behaves as though it possesses two equal but opposite poles or charges, a finite distance apart. The uneven distribution of electrons within a molecule composed of atoms of different *electronegativities may result in an apparent concentration of electrons towards one end of the molecule and a deficiency towards the other, so that it forms a dipole consisting of apparently separated positive and negative charges. A bar magnet behaves as though its magnetism were concentrated in separate north and south magnetic poles because of the uneven distribution of its magnetic field.

dipper any of various passerine birds of the family Cinclidae, found in hilly and mountainous regions across Eurasia and North America, where there are clear, fast-flowing streams. It can swim, dive, or walk along the bottom, using the pressure of water on its wings and tail to keep it down, while it searches for insect larvae and other small animals.

Dirac Paul Adrien Maurice 1902–1984. British physicist who worked out a version of quantum mechanics consistent with special *relativity. The existence of the positron (positive electron) was one of its predictions. He shared the Nobel Prize for Physics 1933 with Austrian physicist Erwin Schrödinger (1887–1961).

Dire Straits UK rock group formed 1977 by the guitarist, singer, and songwriter Mark Knopfler (1949–). Their tasteful musicianship was tailor-made for the new compact-disc audience, and their 1985 LP *Brothers in Arms* went on to sell 20 million copies.

direct current (DC) electric current that flows in one direction, and does not reverse its flow as *alternating current does. The electricity produced by a battery is direct current.

direct debit in banking, an instruction by a depositor with the bank to pay a certain sum of money at regular intervals.

directed number an *integer with a positive (+) or negative (–) sign attached, for example +5 or –5. On a graph, a positive sign shows a movement to the right or upwards; a negative sign indicates movement downwards or to the left.

Director of Public Prosecutions (DPP) in the UK, the head of the Crown Prosecution Service (established 1985), responsible for the conduct of all criminal prosecutions in England and Wales. The DPP was formerly responsible only for the prosecution of certain serious crimes, such as murder.

directory in computing, a list of file names, together with information that enables a computer to retrieve those files from *backing storage. The computer operating system will usually store and update a directory on the backing storage to which it refers. So, for example, on each *disc used by a computer a directory file will be created listing the disc's contents.

dirigible another name for *airship.

disaccharide *sugar made up of two monosaccharides or simple sugars, such as glucose or fructose. Sucrose, $C_{12}H_{22}O_{11}$, or table sugar, is a disaccharide.

disarmament reduction of a country's weapons of war. Most disarmament talks since World War II have been concerned with nuclear-arms verification and reduction, but biological, chemical, and conventional weapons have also come under discussion at the United Nations and in other forums. Attempts to limit the arms race between the USA and (until its demise) the USSR

included the *Strategic Arms Limitation Talks (SALT) of the 1970s and the *Strategic Arms Reduction Talks (START) of the 1980s–90s. Russia's president, Boris Yeltsin, continued the process of strategic arms reductions into 1992.

disc in computing, a common medium for storing large volumes of data (an alternative is magnetic tape.) A magnetic disc is rotated at high speed in a disc-drive unit as a read/write (playback or record) head passes over its surfaces to record or 'read' the magnetic variations that encode the data. There are several types, including *floppy discs, *hard discs, and *CD-ROM.

disc drive mechanical device that reads data from and writes data to a magnetic *disc.

disc formatting in computing, preparing a blank magnetic disc so that data can be stored on it. Data are recorded on a disc's surface on circular tracks, each of which is divided into a number of sectors. In formatting a disc, the computer's operating system adds control information such as track and sector numbers, which enables the data stored to be accessed correctly by the disc-drive unit.

discharge tube device in which a gas conducting an electric current emits visible light. It is usually a glass tube from which virtually all the air has been removed (so that it 'contains' a near vacuum), with electrodes at each end. When a high-voltage current is passed between the electrodes, the few remaining gas atoms in the tube (or some deliberately introduced ones) ionize and emit coloured light as they conduct the current along the tube. The light originates as electrons change energy levels in the ionized atoms.

disciple follower, especially of a religious leader. The word is used in the Bible for the early followers of Jesus. The 12 disciples closest to him are known as the *apostles.

discrimination distinction made (social, economic, political, legal) between individuals or groups such that one has the power to treat the other unfavourably. **Negative discrimination**, often based on *stereotype, includes anti-Semitism, apartheid, caste, racism, sexism, and slavery. **Positive discrimination**, or 'affirmative action', is sometimes practised in an attempt to counter-act the effects of previous long-term discrimination. Minorities and, in some cases, majorities have been targets for discrimination.

discus circular disc thrown by athletes who rotate the body to gain momentum from within a circle 2.5 m/8 ft in diameter. The men's discus weighs 2 kg/4.4 lb and the women's 1 kg/2.2 lb. Discus throwing was a competition in ancient Greece at gymnastic contests, such as those of the Olympic Games. It is an event in the modern Olympics and athletics meetings.

disease any condition that impairs the normal state of an organism, and usually alters the functioning of one or more of its organs or systems. A disease is usually characterized by a set of specific symptoms and signs, although these may not always be apparent to the sufferer. Diseases may be inborn (see *congenital disease) or acquired through infection, injury, or other cause. Many diseases have unknown causes.

disinvestment withdrawal of investments in a country for political reasons. The term is also used in economics to describe non-replacement of stock as it wears out.

Disney Walt(er Elias) 1901–1966. US filmmaker and animator, a pioneer of family entertainment. He established his own studio in Hollywood 1923, and his first Mickey Mouse cartoons (*Plane Crazy*, which was silent, and *Steamboat Willie*, which had sound) appeared 1928. In addition to short cartoons, the studio made feature-length animated films, including *Snow White and the Seven Dwarfs* 1938, *Pinocchio* 1940, and *Dumbo* 1941. Disney's cartoon figures, for example Donald Duck, also appeared in comic books worldwide. In 1955, Disney opened the first theme park, Disneyland, in California.

dispersion in optics, the splitting of white light into a spectrum; for example, when it passes through a prism or a diffraction grating. It occurs because the prism (or grating) bends each component wavelength to a slightly different extent. The natural dispersion of light through raindrops creates a rainbow.

Disraeli Benjamin, Earl of Beaconsfield 1804–1881. British Conservative politician and novelist. Elected to Parliament 1837, he was chancellor of the Exchequer under Lord *Derby 1852, 1858–59, and 1866–68, and prime minister 1868 and 1874–80. His imperialist policies brought India directly under the crown, and he was personally responsible for purchasing control of the Suez Canal. The central Conservative Party organization is his creation. His popular, political novels reflect an interest in social reform and include *Coningsby* 1844 and *Sybil* 1845.

dissection cutting apart of bodies to study their organization. This was considered a crime in parts of the world in the Middle Ages. In the UK before 1832, hanged murderers were the only legal source of bodies, supplemented by grave-robbing (*Burke and Hare were the most notorious grave robbers). The Anatomy Act 1832 authorized the use of deceased institutionalized people unclaimed by next of kin, and by the 1940s bequests of bodies had been introduced.

Dissenter former name for a Protestant refusing to conform to the established Christian church. For example, Baptists, Presbyterians, and Independents (now known as Congregationalists) were Dissenters.

dissident in one-party states, a person intellectually dissenting from the official line. Dissidents have been sent into exile, prison, labour camps, and mental institutions, or deprived of their jobs. In the USSR the number of imprisoned dissidents declined from more than 600 in 1986 to fewer than 100 in 1990, of whom the majority were ethnic nationalists. In China the number of prisoners of conscience increased after the 1989 Tiananmen Square massacre, and in South Africa, despite the release of Nelson Mandela in 1990, numerous political dissidents remained in jail.

dissociation in chemistry, the process whereby a single compound splits into two or more smaller products, which may be capable of recombining to form the reactant.

distance ratio in a machine, the distance moved by the input force, or effort, divided by the distance moved by the output force, or load. The ratio indicates the movement magnification

achieved, and is equivalent to the machine's *velocity ratio.

distemper any of several infectious diseases of animals characterized by catarrh, cough, and general weakness. Specifically, it refers to a virus disease in young dogs, also found in wild animals, which can now be prevented by vaccination. In 1988 an allied virus killed over 10,000 common seals in the Baltic and North seas.

distillation technique used to purify liquids or to separate mixtures of liquids possessing different boiling points. **Simple distillation** is used in the purification of liquids (or the separation of substances in solution from their solvents) – for example, in the production of pure water from a salt solution.

distributive operation in mathematics, an operation, such as multiplication, that bears a relationship to another operation, such as addition, such that $a \times (b + c) = (a \times b) + (a \times c)$. For example, $3 \times (2 + 4) = (3 \times 2) + (3 \times 4) = 18$. Multiplication may be said to be distributive over addition. Addition is not, however, distributive over multiplication because $3 + (2 \times 4) = (3 + 2) \times (3 + 4)$.

distributor device in the ignition system of a piston engine that distributes pulses of high-voltage electricity to the *spark plugs in the cylinders. The electricity is passed to the plug leads by the tip of a rotor arm, driven by the engine camshaft, and current is fed to the rotor arm from the ignition coil. The distributor also houses the contact point or breaker, which opens and closes to interrupt the battery current to the coil, thus triggering the high-voltage pulses. With electronic ignition it is absent.

district council unit of local government in England and Wales. District-council responsibilities cover housing, local planning and development, roads (excluding trunk and classified), bus services, environmental health (refuse collection, clean air, food safety and hygiene, and enforcement of the Offices, Shops and Railway Premises Act), poll tax, museums and art galleries, parks and playing fields, swimming baths, cemeteries, and so on. In metropolitan district councils education, personal social services, and libraries are also included.

District of Columbia federal district of the USA, see *Washington DC.

diuretic any drug that rids the body of fluid accumulated in the tissues by increasing the output of urine by the kidneys. It may be used in the treatment of heart disease, high blood pressure, kidney or liver disease, and some endocrine disorders. A potassium supplement is prescribed where potassium loss would be dangerous.

diver also called **loon** any of four species of bird specialized for swimming and diving, found in northern regions of the northern hemisphere. The legs are set so far back that walking is almost impossible, and divers come to land only to nest, but they are powerful swimmers and good flyers. They have straight bills and long bodies, and feed on fish, crustaceans, and some water plants. Of the four species, the largest is the white-billed diver *Gavia adamsii*, an Arctic species 75 cm/2.5 ft long.

diversification in business, a corporate strategy of entering distinctly new products or markets as opposed to simply adding to an existing product range. A company may diversify in order to spread its risks or because its original area of operation is becoming less profitable.

diverticulitis inflammation of diverticula (pockets of herniation) in the large intestine. It is usually controlled by diet and antibiotics.

divertissement (French 'entertainment') dance, or group of dances, within a ballet or opera that has no connection with the plot, such as the character dances in the last act of *Coppélia* by Delibes.

dividend in business, the amount of money that company directors decide should be taken out of profits for distribution to shareholders. It is usually declared as a percentage or fixed amount per share.

divination art of ascertaining future events or eliciting other hidden knowledge by supernatural or nonrational means. Divination played a large part in the ancient civilizations of the Egyptians, Greeks (see *oracle), Romans, and Chinese (see *I Ching*), and is still practised throughout the world.

Divine Comedy, The epic poem by Dante Alighieri 1307–21, describing a journey through Hell, Purgatory, and Paradise. The poet Virgil is Dante's guide through Hell and Purgatory; to each of the three realms, or circles, Dante assigns historical and contemporary personages according to their moral (and also political) worth. In Paradise Dante finds his lifelong love Beatrice. The poem makes great use of symbolism and allegory, and influenced many English writers including Milton, Byron, Shelley, and T S Eliot.

Divine Light Mission religious movement founded in India in 1960, which gained a prominent following in the USA in the 1970s. It proclaims *Guru Maharaj Ji* as the present age's successor to the gods or religious leaders Krishna, Buddha, Jesus, and Muhammad. He is believed to be able to provide his followers with the knowledge required to attain salvation.

divine right of kings Christian political doctrine that hereditary monarchy is the system approved by God, hereditary right cannot be forfeited, monarchs are accountable to God alone for their actions, and rebellion against the lawful sovereign is therefore blasphemous.

diving sport of entering water either from a springboard 1 m/3 ft or 3 m/10 ft above the water, or from a platform, or highboard, 10 m/33 ft above the water. Various differing starts are adopted, facing forwards or backwards, and somersaults, twists, and combinations thereof are performed in midair before entering the water. A minimum pool depth of 5 m/16.5 ft is needed for high or platform diving. Points are awarded and the level of difficulty of each dive is used as a multiplying factor.

diving apparatus any equipment used to enable a person to spend time underwater. Diving bells were in use in the 18th century, the diver breathing air trapped in a bell-shaped chamber. This was followed by cumbersome diving suits in the early 19th century. Complete freedom of movement came with the *aqualung, invented by Jacques *Cousteau in the early

1940s. For work at greater depths the technique of saturation diving was developed in the 1970s by which divers live for a week or more breathing a mixture of helium and oxygen at the pressure existing on the seabed where they work (as in tunnel building).

division military formation consisting of two or more brigades. A major general at divisional headquarters commands the brigades and also additional artillery, engineers, attack helicopters, and other logistic support. There are 10,000 or more soldiers in a division. Two or more divisions form a corps.

divorce legal dissolution of a lawful marriage. It is distinct from an annulment, which is a legal declaration that the marriage was invalid. The ease with which a divorce can be obtained in different countries varies considerably and is also affected by different religious practices.

Diwali ('garland of lamps') Hindu festival in Oct/Nov celebrating Lakshmi, goddess of light and wealth. It is marked by the lighting of lamps and candles, feasting, and the exchange of gifts.

Dixie southern states of the USA. The word probably derives from the *Mason–Dixon line.

Dixieland jazz jazz style that originated in New Orleans, USA, in the early 20th century, dominated by cornet, trombone, and clarinet. The trumpeter Louis Armstrong emerged from this style. The *trad jazz* movement in the UK in the 1940s–50s was a Dixieland revival.

Djakarta variant spelling of *Jakarta, capital of Indonesia.

Djibouti Republic of (*Jumhouriyya Djibouti*)
area 23,200 sq km/8,955 sq mi
capital (and chief port) Djibouti
towns Tadjoura, Obock, Dikhil
physical mountains divide an inland plateau from a coastal plain; hot and arid
head of state Hassan Gouled Aptidon from 1977
head of government Barkat Gourad Hamadou from 1988
political system authoritarian nationalism
exports acts mainly as a transit port for Ethiopia
currency Djibouti franc
population (1992) 557,000 (Issa 47%, Afar 37%, European 8%, Arab 6%); growth rate 3.4% p.a.
languages French (official), Somali, Afar, Arabic
religion Sunni Muslim
GNP $475 per head (1986)
chronology
1884 Annexed by France as part of French Somaliland.
1967 French Somaliland became the French Territory of the Afars and the Issas.
1977 Independence achieved from France; Hassan Gouled was elected president.
1979 All political parties combined to form the People's Progress Assembly (RPP).
1981 New constitution made RPP the only legal party. Gouled re-elected. Treaties of friendship signed with Ethiopia, Somalia, Kenya, and Sudan.
1984 Policy of neutrality reaffirmed.
1987 Gouled re-elected.

1992 Constitution amended to provide for a multiparty system.
1993 Gouled re-elected.
1994 Peace agreement reached with Afar militants, ending civil war.

Djilas Milovan 1911– . Yugoslav political writer and dissident. A former close wartime colleague of Marshal Tito, in 1953 he was dismissed from high office and subsequently imprisoned because of his advocacy of greater political pluralism. He was released 1966 and formally rehabilitated 1989.

DM abbreviation for **Deutschmark**, the unit of currency in Germany.

DNA (**deoxyribonucleic acid**) complex two-stranded molecule that contains, in chemically coded form, all the information needed to build, control, and maintain a living organism. DNA is a ladderlike double-stranded *nucleic acid that forms the basis of genetic inheritance in all organisms, except for a few viruses that have only *RNA. In eukaryotes (all organisms except bacteria and blue-green algae), it is organized into *chromosomes and contained in the cell nucleus.

Dnepropetrovsk city in Ukraine, on the right bank of the river Dnieper; population (1987) 1,182,000. It is the centre of an major industrial region, with iron, steel, chemical, and engineering industries. It is linked with the Dnieper Dam, 60 km/37 mi downstream.

Dnieper or **Dnepr** river rising in the Smolensk region of Russia and flowing south through Belarus, Ukraine to enter the Black Sea east of Odessa; total length 2,250 km/1,400 mi.

D-notice in the UK, a censorship notice issued by the Department of Defence to the media to prohibit the publication of information on matters alleged to be of national security. The system dates from 1922.

Dobermann or **Dobermann pinscher** smooth-coated dog with a docked tail, much used as a guard dog. It stands up to 70 cm/2.2 ft tall, has a long head with a flat, smooth skull, and is often black with brown markings. It takes its name from the man who bred it in 19th-century Germany.

Dobzhansky Theodosius 1900–1975. US geneticist of Ukrainian origin. A pioneer of modern genetics and evolutionary theory, he showed that genetic variability between individuals of the same species is very high and that this diversity is vital to the process of evolution. His book *Genetics and the Origin of Species* was published in 1937.

dock or **sorrel** in botany, any of a number of plants of the genus *Rumex* of the buckwheat family Polygonaceae. They are tall, annual to perennial herbs, often with lance-shaped leaves and small, greenish flowers. Native to temperate regions, there are 30 North American and several British species.

Doc Pomus (Jerome Solon Felder) 1925–1991. US pop-music songwriter who worked primarily in partnership with Mort Shuman (1936–). The team had its greatest successes in the early 1960s with hits for the Drifters ('Save the Last Dance for Me' 1960) and Elvis Presley ('Little Sister' and 'His Latest Flame' 1961). Fluent in a number of styles, they were innovators in none.

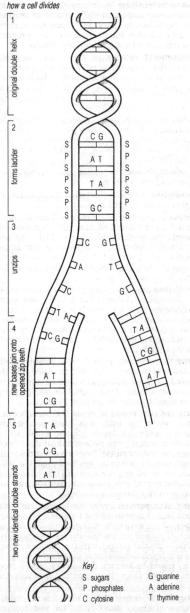

how a cell divides

1 — original double helix
2 — forms ladder
3 — unzips
4 — new bases join onto opened zip teeth
5 — two new identical double strands

Key
S sugars	G guanine
P phosphates	A adenine
C cytosine	T thymine

DNA How the DNA molecule divides.

document in computing, data associated with a particular application. For example, a **text document** might be produced by a *word processor and a **graphics document** might be produced with a *CAD package. An *OMR or *OCR document is a paper document containing data that can be directly input to the computer using a *document reader.

documentation in computing, the written information associated with a computer program or *applications package. Documentation is usually divided into two categories: program documentation and user documentation.

document reader in computing, an input device that reads marks or characters, usually on preprepared forms and documents. Such devices are used to capture data by *optical mark recognition (OMR), *optical character recognition (OCR), and *mark sensing.

dodder parasitic plant, genus *Cuscuta*, of the morning-glory family Convolvulaceae, without leaves or roots. The thin stem twines around the host, and penetrating suckers withdraw nourishment.

dodecaphonic in music, the *twelve-tone system of composition.

Dodgson Charles Lutwidge. Real name of writer Lewis *Carroll.

dodo extinct bird *Raphus cucullatus* formerly found on the island of Mauritius, but exterminated before the end of the 17th century. Although related to the pigeons, it was larger than a turkey, with a bulky body and very short wings and tail. Flightless and trusting, it was easy prey to humans.

Dodoma capital (replacing Dar es Salaam 1974) of Tanzania; 1,132 m/3,713 ft above sea level; population (1985) 85,000. It is a centre of communications, linked by rail with Dar es Salaam and Kigoma on Lake Tanganyika, and by road with Kenya to the north and Zambia and Malawi to the south.

Doe Samuel Kenyon 1950–1990. Liberian politician and soldier, head of state 1980–90. He seized power in a coup. Having successfully put down an uprising April 1990, Doe was deposed and killed by rebel forces Sept 1990.

dog any carnivorous mammal of the family Canidae, including wild dogs, wolves, jackals, coyotes, and foxes. Specifically, the domestic dog *Canis familiaris*, the earliest animal descended from the wolf or jackal. Dogs were first domesticated over 10,000 years ago, and migrated with humans to all the continents. They have been selectively bred into many different varieties for use as working animals and pets.

dog, dangerous any of the breeds listed in a 1991 amendment to the UK Dangerous Dogs Act 1989, which have to be muzzled in public. These include pit-bull terriers (which must also be registered with the police) and the Japanese *tosa*. Earlier legislation includes the Dogs Act 1871, with regard to keeping dogs under proper control, and the Dogs (Protection of Livestock) Act 1953.

doge chief magistrate in the ancient constitutions of Venice and Genoa. The first doge of Venice was appointed 697 with absolute power (modified 1297), and from his accession dates Venice's prominence in history. The last Venetian doge, Lodovico Manin, retired 1797 and the last Genoese doge 1804.

Dōgen 1200–1253. Japanese Buddhist monk, pupil of Eisai; founder of the Sōtō school of Zen. He did not reject study, but stressed the importance of *zazen*, seated meditation, for its own sake.

dogfish any of several small sharks found in the NE Atlantic, Pacific, and Mediterranean.

dogwood any of a genus *Cornus* of trees and shrubs of the dogwood family (Cornaceae), native to temperate regions of North America and Eurasia. The flowering dogwood *Cornus florida* of the E USA is often cultivated as an ornamental for its beautiful blooms consisting of clusters of small greenish flowers surrounded by four large white or pink petal-like *bracts.

Doha (Arabic *Ad Dawḥah*) capital and chief port of Qatar; population (1986) 217,000. Industries include oil refining, refrigeration plants, engineering, and food processing. It is the centre of vocational training for all the Persian Gulf states.

Dohnányi Ernst von (Ernö) 1877–1960. Hungarian pianist, conductor, and composer, whose influence is maintained through the examinations repertoire. His compositions include *Variations on a Nursery Song* 1914 and *Second Symphony for Orchestra* 1948.

Doisy Edward 1893–1986. US biochemist. In 1939 he succeeded in synthesizing vitamin K, a compound discovered earlier by Carl *Dam, with whom he shared the 1943 Nobel Prize for Medicine.

doldrums area of low atmospheric pressure along the equator, in the intertropical convergence zone where the NE and SE trade winds converge. The doldrums are characterized by calm or very light westerly winds, during which there may be sudden squalls and stormy weather. For this reason the areas are avoided as far as possible by sailing ships.

Dolin Anton. Stage name of Patrick Healey-Kay 1904–1983. British dancer and choreographer, a pioneer of UK ballet. After studying under Vaslav Nijinsky, he was a leading member of Sergei Diaghilev's company 1924–29. He formed the Markova–Dolin Ballet with Alicia Markova 1935–38, and was a guest soloist with the American Ballet Theater 1940–46.

Doll William Richard 1912– . British physician who, working with Professor Bradford Hill (1897–) provided the first statistical proof of the link between smoking and lung cancer in 1950. In a later study of the smoking habits of doctors, they were able to show that stopping smoking immediately reduces the risk of cancer.

dollar monetary unit containing 100 cents, adopted as the standard unit in the USA in 1785; also by Australia, Canada, Hong Kong, and a number of other countries.

Dollfuss Engelbert 1892–1934. Austrian Christian Socialist politician. He was appointed chancellor in 1932, and in 1933 suppressed parliament and ruled by decree. In Feb 1934 he crushed a protest by the socialist workers by force, and in May Austria was declared a 'corporative' state. The Nazis attempted a coup d'état on 25 July; the Chancellery was seized and Dollfuss murdered.

dolmen prehistoric monument in the form of a chamber built of large stone slabs, roofed over by a flat stone which they support. Dolmens are grave chambers of the Neolithic period, found in Europe and Africa, and occasionally in Asia as far east as Japan.

dolomite white mineral with a hexagonal structure, calcium magnesium carbonate (CaMg $(CO_3)_2$). The term also applies to a type of limestone rock where the calcite content is replaced by the mineral dolomite. Dolomite rock may be white, grey, brown, or reddish in colour, commonly crystalline. It is used as a building material. The region of the Alps known as the Dolomites is a fine example of dolomite formation.

dolomite in geology, a sedimentary rock containing a high proportion of the mineral dolomite; a variety of limestone, or marble (if metamorphosed). The magnesian limestone of N England is a dolomite.

dolomite in mineralogy, calcium magnesium carbonate, CaMg(Co$_{32}$). It is similar to calcite but often forms rhombohedral crystals with curved faces. Dolomite occurs with ore minerals in veins; it can form by replacement of other carbonates in rocks, and can also precipitate from seawater.

dolphin The bottlenosed dolphin lives in groups of up to 15 individuals.

dolphin any of various highly intelligent aquatic mammals of the family Delphinidae, which also includes porpoises. There are about 60 species. The name 'dolphin' is generally applied to species having a beaklike snout and slender body, whereas the name 'porpoise' is reserved for the smaller species with a blunt snout and stocky body. Dolphins use sound (echolocation) to navigate, to find prey, and for communication.

Domagk Gerhard 1895–1964. German pathologist, discoverer of antibacterial sulphonamide drugs. He found in 1932 that a coal-tar dye called Prontosil red contains chemicals with powerful antibacterial properties. Sulphanilamide became the first of the sulphonamide drugs, used before *antibiotics were discovered to treat a wide range of conditions, including pneumonia and septic wounds. Domagk was awarded the 1939 Nobel Prize for Physiology and Medicine.

domain small area in a magnetic material that behaves like a tiny magnet. The magnetism of the material is due to the movement of electrons in the atoms of the domain. In an unmagnetized sample of material, the domains point in random directions, or form closed loops, so that there is no overall magnetization of the sample. In a magnetized sample, the domains are aligned so that their magnetic effects combine to produce a strong overall magnetism.

Domenichino real name Domenico Zampieri 1582–1641. Italian Baroque painter and architect, active in Bologna, Naples, and Rome. He began as an assistant to the *Carracci family of painters and continued the early Baroque style in, for example, frescoes 1624–28 in the choir of S Andrea della Valle, Rome.

Dome of the Rock building in Jerusalem dating from the 7th century AD that enshrines the rock from which, in Muslim tradition, Muhammad ascended to heaven on his *Night Journey. It stands on the site of the Jewish national Temple and is visited by pilgrims.

Domesday Book record of the survey of England carried out 1086 by officials of William the Conqueror in order to assess land tax and other dues, ascertain the value of the crown lands, and enable the king to estimate the power of his vassal barons. The name is derived from the belief that its judgement was as final as that of Doomsday.

dominance in genetics, the masking of one allele (an alternative form of a gene) by another allele. For example, if a *heterozygous person has one allele for blue eyes and one for brown eyes, his or her eye colour will be brown. The allele for blue eyes is described as *recessive and the allele for brown eyes as dominant.

dominant in music, the fifth degree of the scale, for example, G in the C major scale.

Domingo Placido 1937– . Spanish tenor who excels in romantic operatic roles. He made his debut 1960 as Alfredo in Verdi's *La Traviata*, then spent four years with the Israel National Opera. He sang at the New York City Opera 1965 and has since performed diverse roles in opera houses worldwide. In 1986 he starred in the film version of *Otello*.

Dominica Commonwealth of
area 751 sq km/290 sq mi
capital Roseau, with a deepwater port
towns Portsmouth, Marigot
physical second largest of the Windward Islands, mountainous central ridge with tropical rainforest
head of state Clarence Seignoret from 1983
head of government Eugenia Charles from 1980
political system liberal democracy
exports bananas, coconuts, citrus, lime, bay oil
currency E Caribbean dollar, pound sterling, French franc
population (1993 est) 88,000 (mainly black African in origin, but with a small Carib reserve of some 500); growth rate 1.3% p.a.
language English (official), but the Dominican patois reflects earlier periods of French rule
religion Roman Catholic 80%
GNP $2,440 per head (1991)
chronology
1763 Became British possession.
1978 Independence achieved from Britain. Patrick John, leader of Dominica Labour Party (DLP), elected prime minister.
1980 Dominica Freedom Party (DFP), led by Eugenia Charles, won convincing victory in general election.
1981 Patrick John implicated in plot to overthrow government.
1982 John tried and acquitted.
1985 John retried and found guilty. Regrouping

of left-of-centre parties resulted in new Labour Party of Dominica (LPD). DFP, led by Eugenia Charles, re-elected.
1990 Charles elected to a third term.
1991 Integration into Windward Islands confederation proposed.

Dominican order Roman Catholic order of friars founded 1215 by St Dominic. The Dominicans are also known as Friars Preachers, Black Friars, or Jacobins. The order is worldwide and there is also an order of contemplative nuns; the habit is black and white.

Dominican Republic (*República Dominicana*)

area 48,442 sq km/18,700 sq mi
capital Santo Domingo
towns Santiago de los Caballeros, San Pedro de Macoris
physical comprises eastern two-thirds of island of Hispaniola; central mountain range with fertile valleys
head of state and government Joaquín Balaguer Ricardo from 1986
political system democratic republic
exports sugar, gold, silver, tobacco, coffee, nickel
currency peso
population (1993 est) 7,600,000; growth rate 2.3% p.a.
language Spanish (official)
religion Roman Catholic 95%
GNP $950 per head (1991)
chronology
1492 Visited by Christopher Columbus.
1844 Dominican Republic established.
1930 Dictatorship of Rafael Trujillo.
1961 Trujillo assassinated.
1962 First elections. Juan Bosch as president.
1963 Bosch overthrown in military coup.
1965 US Marines intervened to restore order and protect foreign nationals.
1966 New constitution adopted. Joaquín Balaguer, leader of PRSC, became president.
1978 PRD returned to power, with Silvestre Antonio Guzmán as president.
1982 PRD re-elected, with Jorge Blanco as president.
1985 Blanco forced by International Monetary Fund to adopt austerity measures to save the economy.

1986 PRSC returned to power, with Balaguer re-elected president.
1990 Balaguer re-elected by a small majority.
1994 Balaguer re-elected; election results disputed by opposition but eventually declared valid.

Dominic, St 1170–1221. Founder of the Roman Catholic Dominican order of preaching friars. Feast day 7 Aug.

Dominions the name formerly applied to the self-governing divisions of the *British Empire – for example Australia, New Zealand, Canada, and South Africa.

Domino 'Fats' (Antoine) 1928– . US rock-and-roll pianist, singer, and songwriter, exponent of the New Orleans style. His hits include 'Ain't That a Shame' 1955 and 'Blueberry Hill' 1956.

domino theory idea popularized by US president Eisenhower in 1954 that if one country came under communist rule, adjacent countries were likely to become communist as well.

Domitian Titus Flavius Domitianus AD 51–96. Roman emperor from AD 81. He finalized the conquest of Britain (see *Agricola), strengthened the Rhine–Danube frontier, and suppressed immorality as well as freedom of thought in philosophy (see *Epictetus) and religion (Christians were persecuted). His reign of terror led to his assassination.

Don river in Russia, rising to the S of Moscow and entering the NE extremity of the Sea of Azov; length 1,900 km/1,180 mi. In its lower reaches the Don is 1.5 km/1 mi wide, and for about four months of the year it is closed by ice. Its upper course is linked with the river Volga by a canal.

Donatello (Donato di Niccolo) 1386–1466. Italian sculptor of the early Renaissance, born in Florence. He was instrumental in reviving the Classical style, as in his graceful bronze statue of the youthful *David* (Bargello, Florence) and his equestrian statue of the general *Gattamelata* 1443 (Padua). The course of Florentine art in the 15th century was strongly influenced by his style.

Donau German name for the river *Danube.

Donegal mountainous county in Ulster province in the NW of the Republic of Ireland, surrounded on three sides by the Atlantic; area 4,830 sq km/1,864 sq mi; population (1991) 127,900. The county town is Lifford; the market town and port of Donegal is at the head of Donegal Bay in the SW. Commercial activities include sheep and cattle raising, tweed and linen manufacture, and some deep-sea fishing. The river Erne hydroelectric project (1952) involved the building of large power stations at Ballyshannon.

Donen Stanley 1924– . US film director, formerly a dancer, who co-directed two of Gene Kelly's best musicals, *On the Town* 1949 and *Singin' in the Rain* 1952. His other films include *Charade* 1963 and *Two for the Road* 1968.

Donetsk city in Ukraine; capital of Donetsk region, situated in the Donets Basin, a major coal-mining area, 600 km/372 mi SE of Kiev; population (1987) 1,090,000. It has blast furnaces, rolling mills, and other heavy industries.

Dönitz Karl 1891–1980. German admiral, originator of the wolf-pack submarine technique, which sank 15 million tonnes of Allied shipping in World War II. He succeeded Hitler in 1945, capitulated, and was imprisoned 1946–56.

Donizetti Gaetano 1797–1848. Italian composer who created more than 60 operas, including *Lucrezia Borgia* 1833, *Lucia di Lammermoor* 1835, *La Fille du régiment* 1840, *La Favorite* 1840, and *Don Pasquale* 1843. They show the influence of Rossini and Bellini, and are characterized by a flow of expressive melodies.

Don Juan character of Spanish legend, Don Juan Tenorio, supposed to have lived in the 14th century and notorious for his debauchery. Tirso de Molina, Molière, Mozart, Byron, and George Bernard Shaw have featured the legend in their works.

donkey another name for *ass.

Donne John 1571–1631. English metaphysical poet. His work consists of love poems, religious poems, verse satires, and sermons, most of which were first published after his death. His religious poems show the same passion and ingenuity as his love poetry. A Roman Catholic in his youth, he converted to the Church of England and finally became dean of St Paul's Cathedral, where he is buried.

Doolittle Hilda. Pen name *HD* 1886–1961. US poet who went to Europe 1911, and was associated with Ezra Pound and the British writer Richard *Aldington (to whom she was married 1913–37) in founding the Imagist school of poetry, advocating simplicity, precision, and brevity. Her work includes the *Sea Garden* 1916 and *Helen in Egypt* 1916.

Doomsday Book variant spelling of *Domesday Book, the English survey of 1086.

Doors, the US psychedelic rock group formed 1965 in Los Angeles by Jim Morrison (1943–1971, vocals), Ray Manzarek (1935– , keyboards), Robby Krieger (1946– , guitar), and John Densmore (1944– , drums). Their first hit was 'Light My Fire' from their debut album *The Doors* 1967. They were noted for Morrison's poetic lyrics and flamboyant performance.

doo-wop US pop-music form of the 1950s, a style of harmony singing without instrumental accompaniment or nearly so, almost exclusively by male groups. The name derives from the practice of having the lead vocalist singing the lyrics against a backing of nonsense syllables from the other members of the group. Many of the doo-wop groups were named after birds; for example, the Ravens and the Orioles.

dopamine neurotransmitter, hydroxytyramine $C_8H_{11}NO_2$, an intermediate in the formation of adrenaline. There are special nerve cells (neurones) in the brain that use dopamine for the transmission of nervous impulses. One such area of dopamine neurones lies in the basal ganglia, a region that controls movement. Patients suffering from the tremors of Parkinson's disease show nerve degeneration in this region. Another dopamine brain area lies in the limbic system, a region closely involved with emotional responses. It has been found that schizophrenic patients respond well to drugs that act on limbic dopamine receptors in the brain.

doppelgänger (German 'double-goer') apparition of a living person, a person's double, or a guardian spirit. The German composer and writer E T A Hoffman wrote a short story called *Die Doppelgänger* in 1821. English novelist Charles Williams used the idea to great effect in his novel *Descent into Hell* 1937.

Doppler effect change in the observed frequency (or wavelength) of waves due to relative motion between the wave source and the observer. The Doppler effect is responsible for the perceived change in pitch of a siren as it approaches and then recedes, and for the *red shift of light from distant stars. It is named after the Austrian physicist Christian Doppler (1803–1853).

Dordogne river in SW France, rising in Puy-de-Dôme *département* and flowing 490 km/300 mi to join the river Garonne, 23 km/14 mi N of Bordeaux. It gives its name to a *département* and is a major source of hydroelectric power.

Doré Gustave 1832–1883. French artist, chiefly known as a prolific illustrator, and also active as a painter, etcher, and sculptor. He produced closely worked engravings of scenes from, for example, Rabelais, Dante, Cervantes, the Bible, Milton, and Edgar Allan Poe.

Dorian people of ancient Greece. They entered Greece from the north and took most of the Peloponnese from the Achaeans, destroying the *Mycenaean civilization; this invasion appears to have been completed before 1000 BC. Their chief cities were Sparta, Argos, and Corinth.

Doric in Classical architecture, one of the five types of column; see *order.

dormancy in botany, a phase of reduced physiological activity exhibited by certain buds, seeds, and spores. Dormancy can help a plant to survive unfavourable conditions, as in annual plants that pass the cold winter season as dormant seeds, and plants that form dormant buds.

dormancy in the UK, state of a peerage or baronetcy when it is believed that heirs to the title exist, but their whereabouts are unknown. This sometimes occurs when a senior line dies out and a cadet line has long since gone off to foreign parts.

dormitory town rural settlement that has a high proportion of *commuters in its population. The original population may have been displaced by these commuters and the settlements enlarged by housing estates. Dormitory towns have increased in the UK since 1960 as a result of *counterurbanization.

dormouse small rodent, of the family Gliridae, with a hairy tail. There are about ten species, living in Europe, Asia, and Africa. They are arboreal (live in trees) and nocturnal, and they hibernate during winter in cold regions.

Dorset county in SW England
area 2,650 sq km/1,023 sq mi
towns Dorchester (administrative headquarters), Poole, Shaftesbury, Sherborne; resorts: Bournemouth, Lyme Regis, Weymouth
population (1987) 649,000
famous people Anthony Ashley Cooper, Thomas Hardy, Thomas Love Peacock.

Dorsey Jimmy 1904–1957. Tommy 1905–1956. US bandleaders, musicians, and composers during the *swing era. They worked together in the Dorsey Brothers Orchestra 1934–35 and 1953–56, but led separate bands in the intervening period. The Tommy Dorsey band featured the singer Frank Sinatra 1940–42. Both Dorsey bands featured in a number of films in the 1940s, and the brothers appeared together in *The Fabulous Dorseys* 1947.

Dortmund industrial centre in the *Ruhr, Germany, 58 km/36 mi NE of Düsseldorf; population (1988) 568,000. It is the largest mining town of the Westphalian coalfield and the southern terminus of the Dortmund–Ems canal. Industries include iron, steel, construction machinery, engineering, and brewing.

dory marine fish *Zeus faber* found in the Mediterranean and Atlantic. It grows up to 60 cm/2 ft, and has nine or ten long spines at the front of the dorsal fin, and four at the front of the anal fin. It is considered to be an excellent food fish and is also known as *John Dory*.

DOS (acronym for *disc operating system*) computer *operating system specifically designed for use with disc storage; also used as an alternative name for a particular operating system, *MS-DOS.

Dos Santos José Eduardo 1942– . Angolan left-wing politician, president from 1979, a member of the People's Movement for the Liberation of Angola (MPLA). By 1989, he had negotiated the withdrawal of South African and Cuban forces, and in 1991 a peace agreement to end the civil war. In Sept 1992 his victory in multiparty elections was disputed by UNITA rebel leader Jonas Savimbi, and fighting resumed, escalating into full-scale civil war 1993. Representatives of the two leaders signed a peace agreement 1994.

Dostoevsky Fyodor Mihailovich 1821–1881. Russian novelist. Remarkable for their profound psychological insight, Dostoevsky's novels have greatly influenced Russian writers, and since the beginning of the 20th century have been increasingly influential abroad. In 1849 he was sentenced to four years' hard labour in Siberia, followed by army service, for printing socialist propaganda. *The House of the Dead* 1861 recalls his prison experiences, followed by his major works *Crime and Punishment* 1866, *The Idiot* 1868–69, and *The Brothers Karamazov* 1880.

dot matrix printer computer printer that produces each character individually by printing a pattern, or matrix, of very small dots. The printing head consists of a vertical line or block of either 9 or 24 printing pins. As the printing head is moved from side to side across the paper, the pins are pushed forwards selectively to strike an inked ribbon and build up the dot pattern for each character on the paper beneath.

dotterel bird *Eudromias morinellus* of the plover family, nesting on high moors and tundra in Europe and Asia, and migrating south for the winter. About 23 cm/9 in long, it is clad in a pattern of black, brown, and white in summer, duller in winter, but always with white eyebrows and breastband. Females are larger than males, and the male incubates and rears the brood.

Douala or *Duala* chief port and industrial centre (aluminium, chemicals, textiles, pulp) of Cameroon, on the Wouri River estuary; population (1981) 637,000. Known as Kamerunstadt until 1907, it was capital of German Cameroon 1885–1901.

double bass large bowed four-stringed musical instrument, the bass of the *violin family, tuned in fourths, and descended from the violone of the *viol family.

double decomposition reaction between two chemical substances (usually *salts in solution) that results in the exchange of a constituent from each compound to create two different compounds.

double entendre (French 'double meaning') an ambiguous word or phrase, usually one that is coarse or indelicate.

double star two stars that appear close together. Most double stars attract each other due to gravity, and orbit each other, forming a genuine *binary star, but other double stars are at different distances from Earth, and lie in the same line of sight only by chance. Through a telescope both types of double star look the same.

dough mixture consisting primarily of flour, water, and yeast, which is used in the manufacture of bread.

Douglas capital of the Isle of Man in the Irish Sea; population (1981) 20,000. A holiday resort and terminus of shipping routes to and from Fleetwood and Liverpool.

Douglas Gavin (or Gawain) 1475–1522. Scottish poet whose translation into Scots of Virgil's *Aeneid* 1515 was the first translation from the classics into a vernacular of the British Isles.

Douglas Kirk. Stage name of Issur Danielovitch Demsky 1916– . US film actor. Usually cast as a dynamic and intelligent hero, as in *Spartacus* 1960, he was a major star of the 1950s and 1960s in such films as *Ace in the Hole* 1951, *The Bad and the Beautiful* 1953, *Lust for Life* 1956, *The Vikings* 1958, *Seven Days in May* 1964, and *The War Wagon* 1967. He continues to act and produce, along with his son Michael Douglas.

Douglas Michael 1944– . US film actor and producer. One of the biggest box-office draws of the late 1980s and 1990s, Douglas won an Academy Award for his portrayal of a ruthless corporate raider in *Wall Street* 1987. His acting range includes both romantic and heroic leads in films such as *Romancing the Stone* 1984 and *Jewel of the Nile* 1985, both of which he produced. Among his other films are *Fatal Attraction* 1987 and *Basic Instinct* 1991.

Douglas fir any of some six species of coniferous evergreen tree of the family Pinaceae. The most common is *Pseudotsuga menziesii*, native to western North America and E Asia. It grows 60–90 m/200–300 ft, has long, flat, spirally-arranged needles and hanging cones, and produces hard, strong timber. *P. glauca* has shorter, bluish needles and grows to 30 m/100 ft in mountainous areas.

Douglas-Hamilton family name of dukes of Hamilton, seated at Lennoxlove, East Lothian, Scotland.

Douglas-Home Alec British politician, see *Home.

Douglass Frederick *c.* 1817–1895. US antislavery campaigner. Born a slave in Maryland, he escaped in 1838. He wrote three autobiographies including *Narrative of the Life of Frederick Douglass* 1845, which aroused support in northern states for the abolition of slavery. After the Civil War, he held several US government posts.

Doulton Henry 1820–1897. English ceramicist. He established the world's first stoneware-drain-pipe factory 1846. From 1870 he created art pottery and domestic tablewares in Lambeth, S London, and Burslem, near Stoke-on-Trent.

Doumer Paul 1857–1932. French politician. He was elected president of the Chamber in 1905, president of the Senate in 1927, and president of the republic in 1931. He was assassinated.

Dounreay experimental nuclear reactor site on the N coast of Scotland, 12 km/7 mi W of Thurso. Development started in 1974 and continued until a decision was made in 1988 to decommission the site by 1994.

Douro (Spanish *Duero*) river rising in N central Spain and flowing through N Portugal to the Atlantic at Porto; length 800 km/500 mi.

dove another name for *pigeon.

dove person who takes a moderate, sometimes pacifist, view on political issues. The term originated in the US during the Vietnam War. Its counterpart is a *hawk. In more general usage today, a dove is equated with liberal policies, and a hawk with conservative ones.

Dover, Strait of (French *Pas-de-Calais*) stretch of water separating England from France, and connecting the English Channel with the North Sea. It is about 35 km/22 mi long and 34 km/21 mi wide at its narrowest part. It is one of the world's busiest sea lanes.

dowager the style given to the widow of a peer or baronet.

Dow Chemical US chemical manufacturing company, one of the largest in the world, founded 1897. It has large chemical plants in many countries, including the Netherlands, Germany, Brazil, and Japan.

Dowell Anthony 1943– . British ballet dancer in the Classical style. He was principal dancer with the Royal Ballet 1966–86, and director 1986–89.

Dow Jones average New York Stock Exchange index, the most widely used indicator of US stock market prices. The average (no longer simply an average but today calculated to take into account changes in the constituent companies) is based on prices of 30 major companies, such as IBM and Walt Disney. It was first compiled 1884 by Charles Henry Dow, cofounder of Dow Jones & Co., publishers of the *Wall Street Journal*.

Dow Jones Index (*Dow Jones Industrial 30 Share Index*) scale for measuring the average share price and percentage change of 30 major US industrial companies. It has been calculated and published since 1897 by the financial news publisher Dow Jones & Co.

Dowland John 1563–1626. English composer. He is remembered for his songs to lute accompaniment as well as music for lute alone, such as *Lachrymae* 1605.

Down county in SE Northern Ireland, facing the Irish Sea on the E; area 2,470 sq km/953 sq mi; population (1981) 53,000. To the S are the Mourne mountains, to the E Strangford sea lough. The county town is Downpatrick; the main industry is dairying.

Downing Street street in Westminster, London, leading from Whitehall to St James's Park, named after Sir George Downing (died 1684), a diplomat under Cromwell and Charles II. **Number 10** is the official residence of the prime minister and **number 11** is the residence of the chancellor of the Exchequer. **Number 12** is the office of the government whips.

Downing Street Declaration statement, issued jointly by UK prime minister John Major and Irish premier Albert Reynolds 15 Dec 1993, setting out general principles for holding all-party talks on securing peace in Northern Ireland. The Declaration was warmly welcomed by mainstream politicians in both the UK and the Republic of Ireland, but the reception by Northern Ireland parties was more guarded. However, after initial hesitation, Republican and Loyalist ceasefires were declared 1994 and an Ulster framework document, intended to guide the peace negotiations, issued by the UK and Irish governments Feb 1995.

Down's syndrome condition caused by a chromosomal abnormality (the presence of an extra copy of chromosome 21) which in humans produces mental retardation; a flattened face; coarse, straight hair; and a fold of skin at the inner edge of the eye (hence the former name 'mongolism').

dowry property or money given by the bride's family to the groom or his family as part of the marriage agreement; the opposite of *bride-wealth. In 1961 dowries were made illegal in India; however, in 1992 the Indian government reported more than 15,000 murders or suicides between 1988 and 1991 that were a direct result of insufficient dowries.

dowsing ascertaining the presence of water or minerals beneath the ground with a forked twig or pendulum. Unconscious muscular action by the dowser is thought to move the twig, usually held with one fork in each hand, possibly in response to a local change in the pattern of electrical forces. The ability has been known since at least the 16th century and, though not widely recognized by science, it has been used commercially and in archaeology.

Doyle Arthur Conan 1859–1930. British writer, creator of the detective Sherlock Holmes and his assistant Dr Watson, who first appeared in *A Study in Scarlet* 1887 and featured in a number of subsequent stories, including *The Hound of the Baskervilles* 1902. Conan Doyle also wrote historical romances (*Micah Clarke* 1889 and *The White Company* 1891) and the scientific romance *The Lost World* 1912.

D'Oyly Carte Richard 1844–1901. British producer of the Gilbert and Sullivan operas at the Savoy Theatre, London, which he built. The old D'Oyly Carte Opera Company founded 1876 was disbanded 1982, but a new one opened its first season 1988. Since 1991 the company has moved to the Alexandra Theatre in Birmingham.

DPhil abbreviation for *Doctor of Philosophy*.

DPP abbreviation for *Director of Public Prosecutions*.

Drabble Margaret 1939– . British writer. Her novels include *The Millstone* 1966 (filmed as *The Touch of Love*), *The Middle Ground* 1980, *The Radiant Way* 1987, and *A Natural Curiosity* 1989. She edited the 1985 edition of the *Oxford Companion to English Literature*.

Draco 7th century BC. Athenian politician, the first to codify the laws of the Athenian city-state. These were notorious for their severity; hence *draconian*, meaning particularly harsh.

Draco in astronomy, a large but faint constellation, representing a dragon coiled around the north celestial pole. The star Alpha Draconis (Thuban) was the pole star 4,800 years ago.

Dracula in the novel *Dracula* 1897 by Bram *Stoker, the caped count who, as a *vampire, drinks the blood of beautiful women. The original of Dracula is thought to have been Vlad Țepeș, or Vlad the Impaler, ruler of medieval Wallachia, who used to impale his victims and then mock them.

draft compulsory military service; also known as *conscription.

drag resistance to motion a body experiences when passing through a fluid – gas or liquid. The aerodynamic drag aircraft experience when travelling through the air represents a great waste of power, so they must be carefully shaped, or streamlined, to reduce drag to a minimum. Cars benefit from streamlining, and aerodynamic drag is used to slow down spacecraft returning from space. Boats travelling through water experience hydrodynamic drag on their hulls, and the fastest vessels are *hydrofoils, whose hulls lift out of the water while cruising.

dragon Euro-Asian mythical reptilian beast, often portrayed as breathing fire. The name is popularly given to various sorts of lizard. These include the *flying dragon *Draco volans* of SE Asia and the komodo dragon *Varanus komodoensis* of Indonesia, at over 3 m/10 ft the largest living lizard.

dragonfly any of numerous insects of the order Odonata, including the *damselfly. They all have long narrow bodies, two pairs of almost equal-sized, glassy wings with a network of veins; short, bristlelike antennae; powerful, 'toothed' mouthparts; and very large compound eyes which may have up to 30,000 facets.

dragoon mounted soldier who carried an infantry weapon such as a 'dragon', or short musket, as used by the French army in the 16th century. The name was retained by some later regiments after the original meaning became obsolete.

drag racing motor sport popular in the USA. High-powered single-seater cars with large rear and small front wheels are timed over a 402.2 m/440 yd strip. Speeds of up to 450 kph/280 mph have been attained.

Drake Francis *c.* 1545–1596. English buccaneer and explorer. Having enriched himself as a pirate against Spanish interests in the Caribbean 1567–72, he was sponsored by Elizabeth I for an expedition to the Pacific, sailing round the world 1577–80 in the *Golden Hind*, robbing Spanish ships as he went. This was the second circumnavigation of the globe (the first was by the Portuguese explorer Ferdinand Magellan). Drake also helped to defeat the Spanish Armada 1588 as a vice admiral in the *Revenge*.

DRAM (acronym for *dynamic random-access memory*) computer memory device in the form of a silicon chip commonly used to provide the immediate-access memory of microcomputers. DRAM loses its contents unless they are read and rewritten every 2 milliseconds or so. This process is called *refreshing* the memory. DRAM is slower but cheaper than *SRAM, an alternative form of silicon-chip memory.

drama in theatre, any play performed by actors for an audience. The term is also used collectively to group plays into historical or stylistic periods – for example, Greek drama, Restoration drama – as well as referring to the whole body of work written by a dramatist for performance. Drama is distinct from literature in that it is a performing art open to infinite interpretation, the product not merely of the playwright but also of the collaboration of director, designer, actors, and technical staff. See also *comedy, *tragedy, *mime, and *pantomime.

dramatis personae (Latin) the characters in a play.

draughts board game (known as *checkers* in the USA and Canada because of the chequered board of 64 squares) with elements of a simplified form of chess. Each of the two players has 12 men (disc-shaped pieces), and attempts either to capture all the opponent's men or to block their movements.

Dravidian group of non-Indo-European peoples of the Deccan region of India and in N Sri Lanka. The Dravidian language family is large, with about 20 languages spoken in S India; the main ones are Tamil; Kanarese; Telugu; Malayalam; and Tulu.

Dreadnought class of battleships built for the British navy after 1905 and far superior in speed and armaments to anything then afloat. The first modern battleship to be built, it was the basis of battleship design for more than 50 years. It was first launched 18 February 1906, with armaments consisting entirely of big guns.

dream series of events or images perceived through the mind during sleep. Their function is unknown, but Sigmund *Freud saw them as wish fulfilment (nightmares being failed dreams prompted by fears of 'repressed' impulses). Dreams occur in periods of rapid eye movement (REM) by the sleeper, when the cortex of the brain is approximately as active as in waking hours. Dreams occupy about a fifth of sleeping time.

Dreamtime or *Dreaming* mythical past of the Australian Aborigines, the basis of their religious beliefs and creation stories. In the Dreamtime spiritual beings shaped the land, the first people were brought into being and set in their proper territories, and laws and rituals were established. Belief in a creative spirit in the form of a huge snake, the Rainbow Serpent, occurs over much of Aboriginal Australia, usually associated with waterholes, rain, and thunder.

Drenthe low-lying northern province of the Netherlands
area 2,660 sq km/1,027 sq mi
population (1988) 437,000
towns capital Assen; Emmen, Hoogeveen
physical fenland and moors; well-drained clay and peat soils

products livestock, arable crops, horticulture, petroleum

history governed in the Middle Ages by provincial nobles and by bishops of Utrecht, Drenthe was eventually acquired by Charles V of Spain 1536. It developed following land drainage initiated in the mid-18th century and was established as a separate province of the Netherlands 1796.

Dresden capital of the state of Saxony, Germany; population (1990) 520,000. Industries include chemicals, machinery, glassware, and musical instruments. It was one of the most beautiful German cities until its devastation by Allied fire-bombing 1945. Dresden county has an area of 6,740 sq km/2,602 sq mi and a population of 1,772,000.

dressage (French 'preparation') method of training a horse to carry out a predetermined routine of specified movements. Points are awarded for discipline and style.

Dreyer Carl Theodor 1889–1968. Danish film director. His wide range of films include the austere silent classic *La Passion de Jeanne d'Arc/The Passion of Joan of Arc* 1928 and the Expressionist horror film *Vampyr* 1932, after the failure of which Dreyer made no full-length films until *Vredens Dag/Day of Wrath* 1943. His two late masterpieces are *Ordet/The Word* 1955 and *Gertrud* 1964.

Dreyfus Alfred 1859–1935. French army officer, victim of miscarriage of justice, anti-Semitism, and cover-up. Employed in the War Ministry, in 1894 he was accused of betraying military secrets to Germany, court-martialled, and sent to the penal colony on *Devil's Island, French Guiana. When his innocence was discovered 1896 the military establishment tried to conceal it, and the implications of the Dreyfus affair were passionately discussed in the press until he was exonerated in 1906.

drill in military usage, the repetition of certain fixed movements in response to set commands. Drill is used to get a body of soldiers from one place to another in an orderly fashion, and for parades and ceremonial purposes.

drilling common woodworking and metal machinery process that involves boring holes with a drill *bit. The commonest kind of drill bit is the fluted drill, which has spiral grooves around it to allow the cut material to escape. In the oil industry, rotary drilling is used to bore oil wells. The drill bit usually consists of a number of toothed cutting wheels, which grind their way through the rock as the drill pipe is turned, and mud is pumped through the pipe to lubricate the bit and flush the ground-up rock to the surface.

driver in computing, a program that controls a peripheral device. Every device connected to the computer needs a driver program. The driver ensures that communication between the computer and the device is successful.

dromedary variety of Arabian *camel. The dromedary or one-humped camel has been domesticated since 400 BC. During a long period without water, it can lose up to one-quarter of its bodyweight without ill effects.

drone in music, an accompanying tone or harmony that never varies. It is heard in folk music

dromedary *The dromedary is superbly adapted for life in hot, dry climates.*

and reproduced by many instruments, including the Jew's harp, bagpipe, and hurdy-gurdy.

drug any of a range of chemicals voluntarily or involuntarily introduced into the bodies of humans and animals in order to enhance or suppress a biological function. Most drugs in use are medicines (pharmaceuticals), used to prevent or treat diseases, or to relieve their symptoms; they include antibiotics, cytotoxic drugs, immunosuppressives, sedatives, and pain-relievers (analgesics).

drug, generic any drug produced without a brand name that is identical to a branded product. Usually generic drugs are produced when the patent on a branded drug has expired, and are cheaper than their branded equivalents.

drug misuse illegal use of drugs for nonmedicinal purposes. Under the UK Misuse of Drugs Acts drugs used illegally comprise: (1) **most harmful** heroin, morphine, opium, and other narcotics; hallucinogens, such as mescalin and LSD, and injectable amphetamines, such as methedrine; (2) **less harmful** narcotics such as codeine and cannabis; stimulants of the amphetamine type, such as Benzedrine and barbiturates; (3) **least harmful** milder drugs of the amphetamine type. **Designer drugs**, for example ecstasy, are usually modifications of the amphetamine molecule, altered in order to evade the law as well as for different effects, and may be many times more powerful and dangerous. Crack, a smokable form of cocaine, became available to drug users in the 1980s.

Druidism religion of the Celtic peoples of the pre-Christian British Isles and Gaul. The word is derived from Greek *drus* 'oak'. The Druids regarded this tree as sacred; one of their chief rites was the cutting of mistletoe from it with a golden sickle. They taught the immortality of the soul and a reincarnation doctrine, and were expert in astronomy. The Druids are thought to have offered human sacrifices.

drum percussion instrument, essentially a piece of skin (parchment, plastic, or nylon) stretched over a resonator and struck with a stick or the hands, one of the oldest instruments. Electronic drums, first marketed 1980, are highly touch- and force-sensitive and can also be controlled by computer.

drupe fleshy *fruit containing one or more seeds

which are surrounded by a hard, protective layer – for example cherry, almond, and plum. The wall of the fruit (*pericarp) is differentiated into the outer skin (exocarp), the fleshy layer of tissues (mesocarp), and the hard layer surrounding the seed (endocarp).

Drury Lane Theatre theatre first opened 1663 on the site of earlier London playhouses. It was twice burned; the present building dates from 1812.

Druse or **Druze** religious sect in the Middle East of some 500,000 people. They are monotheists, preaching that the Fatimid caliph al-Hakim (996–1021) is God; their scriptures are drawn from the Bible, the Koran, and Sufi allegories. Druse militia groups form one of the three main factions involved in the Lebanese civil war (the others are Amal Shi'ite Muslims and Christian Maronites). The Druse military leader (from the time of his father's assassination 1977) is Walid Jumblatt.

dryad in Greek mythology, a forest nymph or tree spirit.

Dryden John 1631–1700. English poet and dramatist, noted for his satirical verse and for his use of the heroic couplet. His poetry includes the verse satire *Absalom and Achitophel* 1681, *Annus Mirabilis* 1667, and 'St Cecilia's Day' 1687. Plays include the comedy *Marriage à la Mode* 1672 and *All for Love* 1678, a reworking of Shakespeare's *Antony and Cleopatra*.

dry ice solid carbon dioxide (CO_2), used as a refrigerant. At temperatures above −79°C/ −110.2°F, it sublimes (turns into vapour without passing through a liquid stage) to gaseous carbon dioxide.

dry point in printmaking, a technique of engraving on copper, using a hard, sharp tool. The resulting lines tend to be fine and angular, with a strong furry edge created by the metal shavings.

dry rot infection of timber in damp conditions by fungi, such as *Merulius lacrymans*, that form a threadlike surface. Whitish at first, the fungus later reddens as reproductive spores are formed. Fungoid tentacles also enter the fabric of the timber, rendering it dry-looking and brittle. Dry rot spreads rapidly through a building.

DTP abbreviation for *desktop publishing*.

Dual Entente alliance between France and Russia that lasted from 1893 until the Bolshevik Revolution of 1917.

dualism in philosophy, the belief that reality is essentially dual in nature. The French philosopher René *Descartes, for example, refers to thinking and material substance. These entities interact but are fundamentally separate and distinct. Dualism is contrasted with *monism, the theory that reality is made up of only one substance.

Duarte José Napoleon 1925–1990. El Salvadorean politician, president 1980–82 and 1984–88. He was mayor of San Salvador 1964–70, and was elected president 1972, but exiled by the army 1982. On becoming president again 1984, he sought a negotiated settlement with the left-wing guerrillas 1986, but resigned on health grounds.

dub in pop music, a *remix, usually instrumen-

tal, of a reggae recording, stripped down to the rhythm track. Dub originated in Jamaica with the disc jockeys of mobile sound systems, who would use their playback controls to drop out parts of tracks; later it became common practice to produce a studio dub version as the B-side of a single.

Dubai one of the *United Arab Emirates.

du Barry Marie Jeanne Bécu, Comtesse 1743–1793. Mistress of *Louis XV of France from 1768. At his death 1774 she was banished to a convent, and during the Revolution fled to London. Returning to Paris 1793, she was guillotined.

Dubček Alexander 1921–1992. Czechoslovak liberal socialist politician. As first secretary of the Communist Party 1967–69, he launched a liberalization campaign (called the Prague Spring). To stamp it out, the USSR invaded Czechoslovakia 1968; Dubček was arrested and, in 1970, expelled from the party. In 1989 he gave speeches at prodemocracy rallies and, after the fall of the hardline regime, was elected speaker of the national assembly.

Dublin county in Leinster province, Republic of Ireland, facing the Irish Sea; area 920 sq km/ 355 sq mi; population (1986) 1,021,000. It is mostly level and low-lying, but rises in the south to 753 m/2,471 ft in Kippure, part of the Wicklow Mountains. The river Liffey enters Dublin Bay. Dublin, the apital of the Republic of Ireland, and Dun Laoghaire are the two major towns.

Dublin (Gaelic *Baile Atha Cliath*) capital and port on the E coast of the Republic of Ireland, at the mouth of the river Liffey, facing the Irish Sea; population (1981) 526,000, Greater Dublin (including Dun Laoghaire) 921,000. It is the site of one of the world's largest breweries (Guinness); other industries include textiles, pharmaceuticals, electrical goods, and machine tools. It was the centre of English rule from 1171 (exercised from Dublin Castle 1220) until 1922.

Dubuffet Jean 1901–1985. French artist. He originated *l'art brut*, 'raw or brutal art', in the 1940s. He used a variety of materials in his paintings and sculptures (plaster, steel wool, straw, and so on) and was inspired by graffiti and children's drawings.

Duccio di Buoninsegna c. 1255–1319. Italian painter, a major figure in the Sienese school. His greatest work is his altarpiece for Siena Cathedral, the *Maestà* 1308–11; the figure of the Virgin is Byzantine in style, with much gold detail, but Duccio also created a graceful linear harmony in drapery hems, for example, and this proved a lasting characteristic of Sienese style.

Duce (Italian 'leader') title bestowed on the fascist dictator Benito *Mussolini by his followers and later adopted as his official title.

Duchamp Marcel 1887–1968. US artist, born in France. He achieved notoriety with his *Nude Descending a Staircase* 1912 (Philadelphia Museum of Art), influenced by Cubism and Futurism. An active exponent of *Dada, he invented 'ready-mades', everyday items like a bicycle wheel on a kitchen stool, which he displayed as works of art.

duck any of several short-legged waterbirds with webbed feet and flattened bills, of the family Anatidae, which also includes the larger geese and swans. Ducks were domesticated for eggs, meat, and feathers by the ancient Chinese and the ancient Maya (see *poultry). Most ducks live in fresh water, feeding on worms and insects as well as vegetable matter. They are generally divided into dabbling ducks and diving ducks.

duckweed any of a family of tiny plants of the family Lemnaceae, especially of the genus *Lemna*, found floating on the surface of still water throughout most of the world, except the polar regions and tropics. Each plant consists of a flat, circular, leaflike structure 0.4 cm/0.15 in or less across, with a single thin root up to 15 cm/ 6 in long below.

duel fight between two people armed with weapons. A duel is usually fought according to pre-arranged rules with the aim of settling a private quarrel.

due process of law legal principle, dating from the *Magna Carta, the charter of rights granted by King John of England 1215, and now enshrined in the fifth and fourteenth amendments to the US Constitution, that no person shall be deprived of life, liberty, or property without due process of law (a fair legal procedure). In the USA, the provisions have been given a wide interpretation, to include, for example, the right to representation by an attorney.

Dufay Guillaume 1400–1474. Flemish composer. He is recognized as the foremost composer of his time, of both secular songs and sacred music (including 84 songs and eight masses). His work marks a transition between the music of the Middle Ages and that of the Renaissance and is characterized by expressive melodies and rich harmonies.

Dufourspitze second highest of the alpine peaks, 4,634 m/15,203 ft high. It is the highest peak in the Monte Rosa group of the Pennine Alps on the Swiss-Italian frontier.

Du Fu another name for the Chinese poet *Tu Fu.

Dufy Raoul 1877–1953. French painter and designer. He originated a fluent, brightly coloured style in watercolour and oils, painting scenes of gaiety and leisure, such as horse racing, yachting, and life on the beach. He also designed tapestries, textiles, and ceramics.

dugong marine mammal *Dugong dugong* of the order Sirenia (sea cows), found in the Red Sea, the Indian Ocean, and W Pacific. It can grow to 3.6 m/11 ft long, and has a tapering body with a notched tail and two fore-flippers. It is herbivorous, feeding on sea grasses and seaweeds.

duiker (Afrikaans *diver*) any of several antelopes of the family Bovidae, common in Africa. Duikers are shy and nocturnal, and grow to 30–70 cm/12–28 in tall.

Duiker Johannes 1890–1935. Dutch architect of the 1920s and 1930s avant-garde period. His works demonstrate great structural vigour, and include the Zonnestraal sanatorium 1926, and the Open Air School 1932 and the Cineac News Cinema 1933, both in Amsterdam.

Duisburg river port and industrial city in North Rhine– Westphalia, Germany, at the confluence of the Rhine and Ruhr rivers; population (1987)

515,000. It is the largest inland river port in Europe. Heavy industries include oil refining and the production of steel, copper, zinc, plastics, and machinery.

Dukas Paul (Abraham) 1865–1935. French composer. His orchestral scherzo *L'Apprenti sorcier/ The Sorcerer's Apprentice* 1897 is full of the colour and energy that characterizes much of his work.

duke highest title in the English peerage. It originated in England 1337, when Edward III created his son Edward, Duke of Cornwall.

dulcimer musical instrument consisting of a shallow soundbox strung with many wires that are struck with small wooden hammers. In Hungary it is called a *cimbalom.

Dulles John Foster 1888–1959. US politician. Senior US adviser at the founding of the United Nations, he was largely responsible for drafting the Japanese peace treaty of 1951. As secretary of state 1952–59, he secured US intervention in support of South Vietnam following the expulsion of the French 1954 and was critical of Britain during the Suez Crisis 1956.

Dulong Pierre 1785–1838. French chemist and physicist. In 1819 he discovered, along with the physicist Alexis Petit, the law that, for many elements solid at room temperature, the product of *relative atomic mass and *specific heat capacity is approximately constant. He had earlier, in 1811, and at the cost of an eye, discovered the explosive nitrogen trichloride.

Duma in Russia, before 1917, an elected assembly that met four times following the short-lived 1905 revolution. With progressive demands the government could not accept, the Duma was largely powerless. After the abdication of Nicholas II, the Duma directed the formation of a provisional government.

Dumas Alexandre 1802–1870. French author, known as Dumas *père* (the father). He is remembered for his romances, the reworked output of a 'fiction-factory' of collaborators. They include *Les trois mousquetaires/The Three Musketeers* 1844 and its sequels. Dumas *fils* was his son.

Dumas Alexandre 1824–1895. French author, known as Dumas *fils* (the son of Dumas *père*) and remembered for the play *La Dame aux camélias/The Lady of the Camellias* 1852, based on his own novel and the source of Verdi's opera *La Traviata*.

Du Maurier Daphne 1907–1989. British novelist whose romantic fiction includes *Jamaica Inn* 1936, *Rebecca* 1938, and *My Cousin Rachel* 1951. *Jamaica Inn*, *Rebecca*, and her short story 'The Birds' were made into films by the English director Alfred Hitchcock.

Dumfries and Galloway region of Scotland
area 6,500 sq km/2,510 sq mi
towns Dumfries (administrative headquarters) Ruthwell Cross, a runic cross of about 800 at the village of Ruthwell; Stranraer provides the shortest sea route to Ireland
products horses and cattle (for which the Galloway area was renowned), sheep, timber
population (1987) 147,000
famous people Robert I (Robert the Bruce), Robert Burns, Thomas Carlyle.

Dumfriesshire former county of S Scotland,

merged 1975 in the region of Dumfries and Galloway.

dump in computing, the process of rapidly transferring data to external memory or to a printer. It is usually done to help with debugging (see **bug*) or as part of an error-recovery procedure designed to provide data security. A screen dump makes a printed copy of the current screen display.

dumping in international trade, the selling of goods by one country to another at below marginal cost or at a price below that in its own country. Countries dump in order to get rid of surplus produce or to improve their competitive position in the recipient country. The practice is widely condemned by protectionists (opponents of free trade) because of the unfair competition it represents.

Duna Hungarian name for the river *Danube.

Dunarea Romanian name for the river *Danube.

Dunaway Faye 1941– . US actress whose first starring role was in *Bonnie and Clyde* 1967. Her subsequent films, including *Network* 1976 (for which she won an Academy Award) and *Mommie Dearest* 1981, received a varying critical reception. She also starred in Roman Polanski's *Chinatown* 1974 and *The Handmaid's Tale* 1990.

Duncan Isadora 1878–1927. US dancer and teacher. An influential pioneer of Modern dance, she adopted an expressive free form, dancing barefoot and wearing a loose tunic, inspired by the ideal of Hellenic beauty. She toured extensively, often returning to Russia after her initial success there 1905.

Dundee city and fishing port, administrative headquarters of Tayside, Scotland, on the N side of the Firth of Tay; population (1981) 175,000. It is an important shipping and rail centre with marine engineering, watch and clock, and textile industries.

dune mound or ridge of wind-drifted sand. Loose sand is blown and bounced along by the wind, up the windward side of a dune. The sand particles then fall to rest on the lee side, while more are blown up from the windward side. In this way a dune moves gradually downwind.

Dunedin port on Otago harbour, South Island, New Zealand; population (1986) 106,864. It is a road, rail, and air centre, with engineering and textile industries. The city was founded 1848 by members of the Free Church of Scotland.

Dunfermline industrial town near the Firth of Forth in Fife region, Scotland; population (1981) 52,000. It is the site of the naval base of Rosyth; industries include engineering, shipbuilding, electronics, and textiles. Many Scottish kings, including Robert the Bruce, are buried in Dunfermline Abbey. It is the birthplace of the industrialist Andrew Carnegie.

Dunkirk (French *Dunkerque*) seaport on the N coast of France, in Nord *département*, on the Strait of Dover; population (1983) 83,760, conurbation 196,000. Its harbour is one of the foremost in France, and it has widespread canal links with the rest of France and with Belgium; there is a ferry service to Ramsgate, England. Industries include oil refining, fishing, and the

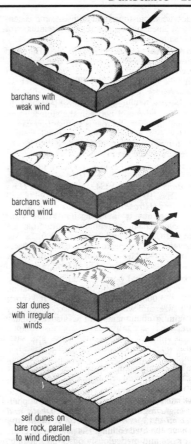

barchans with weak wind

barchans with strong wind

star dunes with irregular winds

seif dunes on bare rock, parallel to wind direction

dune *The shape of a dune indicates the prevailing wind pattern.*

manufacture of textiles, machinery, and soap. Dunkirk was close to the front line during much of World War I, and in World War II, 337,131 Allied troops (including about 110,000 French) were evacuated from the beaches as German forces approached.

Dun Laoghaire (former name *Kingstown*) port and suburb of Dublin, Republic of Ireland. It is a terminal for ferries to Britain, and there are fishing industries.

Dunlop John Boyd 1840–1921. Scottish inventor who founded the rubber company that bears his name. In 1887, to help his child win a tricycle race, he bound an inflated rubber hose to the wheels. The same year he developed commercially practical pneumatic tyres, first patented by Robert William Thomson (1822–1873) 1846 for bicycles and cars.

dunnock European bird *Prunella modularis* similar in size and colouring to the sparrow, but with a slate-grey head and breast, and more slender bill. It nests in bushes and hedges, and is often called the 'hedge sparrow'.

Dunstable John *c.* 1385–1453. English composer who wrote songs and anthems, and is generally considered one of the founders of Renaissance music.

duodecimal system system of arithmetic notation using twelve as a base, at one time considered superior to the decimal number system in that 12 has more factors (2, 3, 4, 6) than 10 (2, 5).

duodenum in vertebrates, a short length of alimentary canal found between the stomach and the small intestine. Its role is in digesting carbohydrates, fats, and proteins. The smaller molecules formed are then absorbed, either by the duodenum or the ileum.

Duras Marguerite 1914– . French author. Her work includes short stories (*Des Journées entières dans les arbres* 1954, stage adaption *Days in the Trees* 1965), plays (*La Musica* 1967), and film scripts (*Hiroshima mon amour* 1960). She also wrote novels including *Le Vice-Consul* 1966, evoking an existentialist world from the setting of Calcutta, and *Emily L.* 1989. *La Vie materielle* 1987 appeared in England as *Practicalities* 1990. Her autobiographical novel, *La Douleur* 1986, is set in Paris in 1945.

Durban principal port of Natal, South Africa, and second port of the republic; population (1985) 634,000, urban area 982,000. It exports coal, maize, and wool, imports heavy machinery and mining equipment, and is also a holiday resort.

Dürer Albrecht 1471–1528. German artist, the leading figure of the northern Renaissance. He was born in Nuremberg and travelled widely in Europe. Highly skilled in drawing and a keen student of nature, he perfected the technique of woodcut and engraving, producing woodcut series such as the *Apocalypse* 1498 and copperplate engravings such as *The Knight, Death, and the Devil* 1513, and *Melancholia* 1514; he may also have invented etching. His paintings include altarpieces and meticulously observed portraits, including many self-portraits.

Durga Hindu goddess; one of the many names for the 'great goddess' *Mahādevī*.

Durham county in NE England
area 2,440 sq km/942 sq mi
towns Durham (administrative headquarters), Darlington, Peterlee, Newton Aycliffe
products sheep and dairy produce; site of one of Britain's richest coalfields
population (1987) 599,000
famous people Elizabeth Barrett Browning, Anthony Eden.

Durkheim Emile 1858–1917. French sociologist, one of the founders of modern sociology, who also influenced social anthropology. He worked to establish sociology as a respectable and scientific discipline, capable of diagnosing social ills and recommending possible cures.

Durrell Gerald (Malcolm) 1925–1995. British naturalist, director of Jersey Zoological Park. He was the author of travel and natural history books, and the humorous memoir *My Family and Other Animals* 1956. He was the brother of Lawrence Durrell.

Durrell Lawrence (George) 1912–1990. British novelist and poet. Born in India, he joined the foreign service and lived mainly in the E Mediter-

ranean, the setting of his novels, including the Alexandria Quartet: *Justine, Balthazar, Mountolive,* and *Clea* 1957–60; he also wrote travel books. He was the brother of the naturalist Gerald Durrell.

Dürrenmatt Friedrich 1921–1991. Swiss dramatist, author of grotesquely farcical tragicomedies, for example *The Visit* 1956 and *The Physicists* 1962.

Durrës chief port of Albania; population (1983) 72,000. It is a commercial and communications centre, with flour mills, soap and cigarette factories, distilleries, and an electronics plant. It was the capital of Albania 1912–21.

Dushanbe formerly (1929–69) *Stalinabad* capital of Tajikistan, 160 km/100 mi N of the Afghan frontier; population (1987) 582,000. It is a road, rail, and air centre. Industries include cotton mills, tanneries, meat-packing factories, and printing works. It is the seat of Tajik state university. A curfew was imposed Feb 1990–Jan 1991 in response to antigovernment rioting and pogroms; a state of emergency remained in force after Jan. In March–May 1992 antigovernment protests left more than 100 dead and in Aug protestors stormed the presidential palace demanding President Nabiyev's resignation. Nabiyev was seized while trying to flee the capital and resigned.

Düsseldorf industrial city of Germany, on the right bank of the river Rhine, 26 km/16 mi NW of Cologne, capital of North Rhine–Westphalia; population (1988) 561,000. It is a river port and the commercial and financial centre of the Ruhr area, with food processing, brewing, agricultural machinery, textile, and chemical industries.

dust bowl area in the Great Plains region of North America (Texas to Kansas) that suffered extensive wind erosion as the result of drought and poor farming practice in once fertile soil. Much of the topsoil was blown away in the droughts of the 1930s and the 1980s.

Dutch cap common name for a barrier method of contraception; see *diaphragm.

Dutch East India Company trading monopoly of the 17th and 18th centuries; see *East India Company, Dutch.

Dutch East Indies former Dutch colony, which in 1945 became independent as *Indonesia.

Dutch elm disease disease of elm trees *Ulmus,* principally Dutch, English, and American elm, caused by the fungus *Certocystis ulmi.* The fungus is usually spread from tree to tree by the elm-bark beetle, which lays its eggs beneath the bark. The disease has no cure and control methods involve injecting insecticide into the trees annually to prevent infection, or the destruction of all elms in a broad band around an infected area, to keep the beetles out.

Dutch Guiana former Dutch colony, which in 1975 became independent as *Surinam.

Dutch language member of the Germanic branch of the Indo-European language family, often referred to by scholars as Netherlandic and taken to include the standard language and dialects of the Netherlands (excluding Frisian) as well as Flemish (in Belgium and N France) and, more remotely, its offshoot Afrikaans in South Africa.

Duvalier François 1907–1971. Right-wing president of Haiti 1957–71. Known as *Papa Doc*, he ruled as a dictator, organizing the Tontons Macoutes ('bogeymen') as a private security force to intimidate and assassinate opponents of his regime. He rigged the 1961 elections in order to have his term of office extended until 1967, and in 1964 declared himself president for life. He was excommunicated by the Vatican for harassing the church, and was succeeded on his death by his son Jean-Claude Duvalier.

Duvalier Jean-Claude 1951– . Right-wing president of Haiti 1971–86. Known as *Baby Doc*, he succeeded his father François Duvalier, becoming, at the age of 19, the youngest president in the world. He continued to receive support from the USA but was pressured into moderating some elements of his father's regime, yet still tolerated no opposition. In 1986, with Haiti's economy stagnating and with increasing civil disorder, Duvalier fled to France, taking much of the Haitian treasury with him.

Dvořák Antonin (Leopold) 1841–1904. Czech composer. International recognition came with his series of *Slavonic Dances* 1877–86, and he was director of the National Conservatory, New York, 1892–95. Works such as his *New World Symphony* 1893 reflect his interest in American folk themes, including black and native American. He wrote nine symphonies; tone poems; operas, including *Rusalka* 1900; large-scale choral works; the *Carnival* 1891–92 and other overtures; violin and cello concertos; chamber music; piano pieces; and songs. His Romantic music extends the Classical tradition of Beethoven and Brahms and displays the influence of Czech folk music.

Dyak or *Dayak* several indigenous peoples of Indonesian Borneo (Kalimantan) and Sarawak, including the Bahau of central and E Borneo, the Land Dyak of SW Borneo, and the Iban of Sarawak (sometimes called Sea Dyak). Their languages belong to the Austronesian family. Some anthropologists now call all Dyak peoples Iban.

dybbuk (Hebrew 'a clinging thing') in Jewish folklore, the soul of a dead sinner which has entered the body of a living person.

Dyck Anthony Van 1599–1641. Flemish painter. Born in Antwerp, Van Dyck was an assistant to Rubens 1618–20, then briefly worked in England at the court of James I, and moved to Italy 1622. In 1626 he returned to Antwerp, where he continued to paint religious works and portraits. From 1632 he lived in England and produced numerous portraits of royalty and aristocrats, such as *Charles I on Horseback* about 1638 (National Gallery, London).

dye substance that, applied in solution to fabrics, imparts a colour resistant to washing. *Direct dyes* combine with the material of the fabric, yielding a coloured compound; *indirect dyes* require the presence of another substance (a mordant), with which the fabric must first be treated; *vat dyes* are colourless soluble substances that on exposure to air yield an insoluble coloured compound.

Dyfed county in SW Wales
area 5,770 sq km/2,227 sq mi
towns Carmarthen (administrative headquarters), Llanelli, Haverfordwest, Aberystwyth, Cardigan, Lampeter
population (1987) 343,000
languages 46% Welsh, English
famous people Dafydd ap Gwilym, Giraldus Cambrensis.

Dylan Bob. Adopted name of Robert Allen Zimmerman 1941– . US singer and songwriter whose lyrics provided catchphrases for a generation and influenced innumerable songwriters. He began in the folk-music tradition. His early songs, as on his albums *Freewheelin'* 1963 and *The Times They Are A-Changin'* 1964, were associated with the US civil-rights movement and antiwar protest. From 1965 he worked in an individualistic rock style, as on the albums *Highway 61 Revisited* 1965 and *Blonde on Blonde* 1966.

dynamics or *kinetics* in mechanics, the mathematical and physical study of the behaviour of bodies under the action of forces that produce changes of motion in them.

dynamite explosive consisting of a mixture of nitroglycerine and diatomaceous earth (diatomite, an absorbent, chalklike material). It was first devised by Alfred Nobel.

dynamo simple generator, or machine for transforming mechanical energy into electrical energy. A dynamo in basic form consists of a powerful field magnet between the poles of which a suitable conductor, usually in the form of a coil (armature), is rotated. The mechanical energy of rotation is thus converted into an electric current in the armature.

dysentery infection of the large intestine causing abdominal cramps and painful *diarrhoea with blood. There are two kinds of dysentery: *amoebic* (caused by a protozoan), common in the tropics, which may lead to liver damage; and *bacterial*, the kind most often seen in the temperate zones.

dyslexia (Greek 'bad', 'pertaining to words') malfunction in the brain's synthesis and interpretation of sensory information, popularly known as 'word blindness'. It results in poor ability to read and write, though the person may otherwise excel, for example, in mathematics. A similar disability with figures is called dyscalculia.

dysprosium (Greek *dusprositos* 'difficult to get near') silver-white, metallic element of the *lanthanide series, symbol Dy, atomic number 66, relative atomic mass 162.50. It is among the most magnetic of all known substances and has a great capacity to absorb neutrons.

dystopia imaginary society whose evil qualities are meant to serve as a moral or political warning. The term was coined in the 19th century by the English philosopher John Stuart *Mill, and is the opposite of a *Utopia. George Orwell's *1984* 1949 and Aldous Huxley's *Brave New World* 1932 are examples of novels about dystopias. Dystopias are common in science fiction.

eagle any of several genera of large birds of prey of the family Accipitridae, including the golden eagle *Aquila chrysaetos* of Eurasia and North America, which has a 2 m/6 ft wingspan and is dark brown.

Ealing Studios British film-producing company headed by Michael *Balcon 1937–58. The studio is best remembered for a series of comedies, which had an understated, self-deprecating humour such as *Passport to Pimlico, Kind Hearts and Coronets, Whisky Galore!* all 1949, *The Man in the White Suit* 1951, and *The Ladykillers* 1955. In 1994 film production began again at Ealing after an interval of nearly 40 years.

Eanes António dos Santos Ramalho 1935– . Portuguese politician. He helped plan the 1974 coup that ended the Caetano regime, and as army chief of staff put down a left-wing revolt Nov 1975. He was president 1976–86.

ear organ of hearing in animals. It responds to the vibrations that constitute sound, and these are translated into nerve signals and passed to the brain. A mammal's ear consists of three parts: outer ear, middle ear, and inner ear. The **outer ear** is a funnel that collects sound, directing it down a tube to the **ear drum** (tympanic membrane), which separates the outer and **middle ear**. Sounds vibrate this membrane, the mechanical movement of which is transferred to a smaller membrane leading to the **inner ear** by three small bones, the auditory ossicles. Vibrations of the inner ear membrane move fluid contained in the snail-shaped cochlea, which vibrates hair cells that stimulate the auditory nerve connected to the brain. Three fluid-filled canals of the inner ear detect changes of position; this mechanism, with other sensory inputs, is responsible for the sense of balance.

Earhart Amelia 1898–1937. US aviation pioneer and author, who in 1928 became the first woman to fly across the Atlantic. With copilot Frederick Noonan, she attempted a round-the-world flight 1937. Somewhere over the Pacific their plane disappeared.

earl in the British peerage, the third title in order of rank, coming between marquess and viscount.

Early English in architecture, name given by Thomas Rickman (1776–1841) to the first of the three periods of the English Gothic style. It covers the period from about 1189 to 1280, and is characterized by tall, elongated windows (lancets) without mullions (horizontal bars), often grouped in threes, fives, or sevens; the

pointed arch; pillars of stone centres surrounded by shafts of black Purbeck marble; and dog-tooth (zig-zag) ornament. Salisbury Cathedral is almost entirely Early English.

Early English in language, general name for the range of dialects spoken by Germanic settlers in England between the fifth and eleventh centuries AD. The literature of the period includes *Beowulf*, an epic in West Saxon dialect, shorter poems of melancholic dignity such as *The Wanderer* and *The Seafarer*, and prose chronicles, Bible translations, spells, and charms.

earth electrical connection between an appliance and the ground. In the event of a fault in an electrical appliance, for example, involving connection between the live part of the circuit and the outer casing, the current flows to earth, causing no harm to the user.

Earth third planet from the Sun. It is almost spherical, flattened slightly at the poles, and is composed of three concentric layers: the *core, the *mantle, and the *crust. 70% of the surface (including the north and south polar icecaps) is covered with water. The Earth is surrounded by a life-supporting atmosphere and is the only planet on which life is known to exist
mean distance from the Sun 149,500,000 km/ 92,860,000 mi
equatorial diameter 12,756 km/7,923 mi
circumference 40,070 km/24,900 mi
rotation period 23 hr 56 min 4.1 sec
year (complete orbit, or sidereal period) 365 days 5 hr 48 min 46 sec. Earth's average speed around the Sun is 30 kps/18.5 mps; the plane of its orbit is inclined to its equatorial plane at an angle of 23.5°, the reason for the changing seasons
atmosphere nitrogen 78.09%; oxygen 20.95%; argon 0.93%; carbon dioxide 0.03%; and less than 0.0001% neon, helium, krypton, hydrogen, xenon, ozone, radon
surface land surface 150,000,000 sq km/ 57,500,000 sq mi (greatest height above sea level 8,872 m/29,118 ft Mount Everest); water surface 361,000,000 sq km/139,400,000 sq mi (greatest depth 11,034 m/36,201 ft *Mariana Trench in the Pacific). The interior is thought to be an inner core about 2,600 km/1,600 mi in diameter, of solid iron and nickel; an outer core about 2,250 km/1,400 mi thick, of molten iron and nickel; and a mantle of mostly solid rock about 2,900 km/1,800 mi thick, separated by the *Mohorovičić discontinuity from the Earth's crust. The crust and the topmost layer of the mantle form about 12 major moving plates, some of which carry the continents. The plates are in constant, slow motion, called tectonic drift
satellite the *Moon
age 4.6 billion years. The Earth was formed with the rest of the *solar system by consolidation of interstellar dust. Life began 3.5–4 billion years ago.

earthenware pottery made of porous clay and fired to temperatures of up to 1,150°C/2,101°F. Earthenware may be unglazed (flowerpots, winecoolers) or glazed (most tableware); the glaze and body characteristics form quite separate layers.

earthquake shaking of the Earth's surface as a result of the sudden release of stresses built up in the Earth's crust. The study of earthquakes is called *seismology. Most earthquakes occur along *faults (fractures or breaks) in the crust. *Plate tectonic movements generate the major proportion: as two plates move past each other they can become jammed and deformed, and a series of shock waves (seismic waves) occur when they spring free. Their force is measured on the *Richter scale, and the effect of an earthquake is measured on the Mercalli scale. The point at which an earthquake originates is the **sesmic focus**; the point on the Earth's surface directly above this is the **epicentre**.

earth sciences scientific study of the planet Earth as a whole, a synthesis of several traditional subjects such as *geology, *meteorology, oceanography, *geophysics, *geochemistry, and *palaeontology.

Earth Summit (official name **United Nations Conference on Environment and Development**) international meeting in Rio de Janeiro, Brazil, June 1992 which drew up measures towards world environmental protection. Treaties were made to combat global warming and protect wildlife ('biodiversity') (the latter was not signed by the USA).

earthworm *annelid worm of the class Oligochaeta. Earthworms are hermaphroditic, and deposit their eggs in cocoons. They live by burrowing in the soil, feeding on the organic matter it contains. They are vital to the formation of humus, aerating the soil and levelling it by transferring earth from the deeper levels to the surface as castings.

earwig nocturnal insect of the order Dermaptera. The fore-wings are short and leathery and serve to protect the hind-wings, which are large and are folded like a fan when at rest. Earwigs seldom fly. They have a pincerlike appendage in the rear. The male is distinguished by curved pincers, those of the female are straight. Earwigs are regarded as pests because they feed on flowers and fruit, but they also eat other insects, dead or alive. Eggs are laid beneath the soil, and the female cares for the young even after they have hatched. The male dies before the eggs have hatched.

easement in law, rights that a person may have over the land of another. A common example is a right of way; others are the right to bring water over another's land and the right to a sufficient quantity of light.

east one of the four cardinal points of the compass, indicating that part of the horizon where the Sun rises; when facing north, east is to the right.

East Anglia region of E England, formerly a Saxon kingdom, including Norfolk, Suffolk, and parts of Essex and Cambridgeshire. Norwich is the principal city of East Anglia. The University of East Anglia was founded in Norwich 1962, and includes the Sainsbury Centre for the Visual Arts, opened 1978, which has a collection of ethnographic art and sculpture. East Anglian ports such as Harwich and Felixstowe have greatly developed as trade with the rest of Europe increases.

Easter spring feast of the Christian church, commemorating the Resurrection of Jesus. It is a moveable feast, falling on the first Sunday following the full moon after the vernal equinox (21 March), that is, between 22 March and 25 April.

Easter Island or **Rapa Nui** Chilean island in the S Pacific Ocean, part of the Polynesian group, about 3,500 km/2,200 mi W of Chile; area about 166 sq km/64 sq mi; population (1985) 2,000. It was first reached by Europeans on Easter Sunday 1722. On it stand over 800 huge carved statues (moai) and the remains of boat-shaped stone houses, the work of neolithic peoples of unknown origin. The chief centre is Hanga-Roa.

Eastern Orthodox Church see *Orthodox Church.

Easter Rising or **Easter Rebellion** in Irish history, a republican insurrection that began on Easter Monday, April 1916, in Dublin. It was inspired by the Irish Republican Brotherhood (IRB) in an unsuccessful attempt to overthrow British rule in Ireland. It was led by Patrick Pearce of the IRB and James Connolly of Sinn Fé in.

East Germany see *Germany, East.

East India Company commercial company 1600–1858 chartered by Queen Elizabeth I and given a monopoly of trade between England and the Far East. In the 18th century the company became, in effect, the ruler of a large part of India, and a form of dual control by the company and a committee responsible to Parliament in London was introduced by Pitt's India Act 1784. The end of the monopoly of China trade came 1834, and after the *Indian Mutiny 1857 the crown took complete control of the government of British India; the India Act 1858 abolished the company.

East India Company, Dutch (**VOC**, or **Vereenigde Oost-Indische Compagnie**) trading company chartered by the States General (parliament) of the Netherlands, and established in the N Netherlands 1602. It was given a monopoly on Dutch trade in the Indonesian archipelago, and certain sovereign rights such as the creation of an army and a fleet.

Eastman George 1854–1932. US entrepreneur and inventor who founded the Eastman Kodak photographic company 1892. From 1888 he marketed his patented daylight-loading flexible roll films (to replace the glass plates used previously) and portable cameras. By 1900 his company was selling a pocket camera for as little as one dollar.

East Pakistan former province of *Pakistan, now Bangladesh.

East Sussex county in SE England
area 1,800 sq km/695 sq mi
towns Lewes (administrative headquarters), Newhaven (cross-Channel port), Brighton, Eastbourne, Hastings, Bexhill, Winchelsea, Rye
products electronics, gypsum, timber
population (1987) 698,000

East Timor disputed territory on the island of *Timor in the Malay Archipelago; prior to 1975, it was a Portuguese colony for almost 460 years
area 14,874 sq km/5,706 sq mi
capital Dili
products coffee
population (1980) 555,000
history Following Portugal's withdrawal 1975, the left-wing Revolutionary Front of Independent East Timor (Fretilin) occupied the capital, Dili,

calling for independence. In opposition, troops from neighbouring Indonesia invaded the territory, declaring East Timor (**Loro Sae**) the 17th province of Indonesia July 1976. This claim is not recognized by the United Nations. In Nov 1991, at least 19 people were killed and 91 injured when Indonesian troops fired on pro-independence demonstrators.

Eastwood Clint 1930– . US film actor and director. As the 'Man with No Name' in *A Fistful of Dollars* 1964 and *The Good, the Bad, and the Ugly* 1966, he started the vogue for 'spaghetti Westerns'. Later Westerns which he both starred in and directed include *High Plains Drifter* 1973, *The Outlaw Josey Wales* 1976, and *Unforgiven* 1992 (Academy Award for best director). Other films include *In The Line of Fire* 1993.

ebony any of a group of hardwood trees of the ebony family Ebenaceae, especially some tropical persimmons of the genus *Diospyros*, native to Africa and Asia.

Eboracum Roman name for the English city of *York. The archbishop of York signs himself 'Ebor'.

EC abbreviation for **European Community**, renamed 1993 *****European Union**.

eccentricity in geometry, a property of a *conic section (circle, ellipse, parabola, or hyperbola). It is the distance of any point on the curve from a fixed point (the focus) divided by the distance of that point from a fixed line (the directrix). A circle has an eccentricity of zero; for an ellipse it is less than one; for a parabola it is equal to one; and for a hyperbola it is greater than one.

ecclesiastical law church law. In England, the Church of England has special ecclesiastical courts to administer church law. Each diocese has a consistory court with a right of appeal to the Court of Arches (in the archbishop of Canterbury's jurisdiction) or the Chancery Court of York (in the archbishop of York's jurisdiction). They deal with the constitution of the Church of England, church property, the clergy, services, doctrine, and practice.

ecdysis periodic shedding of the *exoskeleton by insects and other arthropods to allow growth. Prior to shedding, a new soft and expandable layer is first laid down underneath the existing one. The old layer then splits, the animal moves free of it, and the new layer expands and hardens.

ECG abbreviation for *****electrocardiogram**.

echidna or **spiny anteater** toothless, egg-laying, spiny mammal of the order Monotremata, found in Australia and New Guinea. There are two species: *Tachyglossus aculeatus*, the short-nosed echidna, and the rarer *Zaglossus bruijni*, the long-nosed echidna. They feed entirely upon ants and termites, which they dig out with their powerful claws and lick up with their prehensile tongues. When attacked, an echidna rolls itself into a ball, or tries to hide by burrowing in the earth.

echinoderm marine invertebrate of the phylum Echinodermata ('spiny-skinned'), characterized by a five-radial symmetry. Echinoderms have a water-vascular system which transports substances around the body. They include starfishes (or sea stars), brittlestars, sea-lilies, sea-urchins, and sea-cucumbers. The skeleton is external,

made of a series of limy plates, and echinoderms generally move by using tube-feet, small water-filled sacs that can be protruded or pulled back to the body.

echo repetition of a sound wave, or of a *radar or *sonar signal, by reflection from a surface. By accurately measuring the time taken for an echo to return to the transmitter, and by knowing the speed of a radar signal (the speed of light) or a sonar signal (the speed of sound in water), it is possible to calculate the range of the object causing the echo (*echolocation).

Echo in Greek mythology, a nymph who pined away until only her voice remained, after being rejected by Narcissus.

echolocation or **biosonar** method used by certain animals, notably bats, whales and dolphins, to detect the positions of objects by using sound. The animal emits a stream of high-pitched sounds, generally at ultrasonic frequencies (beyond the range of human hearing), and listens for the returning echoes reflected off objects to determine their exact location.

echo sounder or **sonar device** device that detects objects under water by means of *sonar – by using reflected sound waves. Most boats are equipped with echo sounders to measure the water depth beneath them. An echo sounder consists of a transmitter, which emits an ultrasonic pulse (see *ultrasound), and a receiver, which detects the pulse after reflection from the seabed. The time between transmission and receipt of the reflected signal is a measure of the depth of water. Fishing boats also use echo sounders to detect shoals of fish.

eclipse passage of an astronomical body through the shadow of another. The term is usually employed for solar and lunar eclipses, which may be either partial or total, but also, for example, for eclipses by Jupiter of its satellites. An eclipse of a star by a body in the Solar System is called an occultation.

eclipsing binary binary (double) star in which the two stars periodically pass in front of each other as seen from Earth.

ecliptic path, against the background of stars, that the Sun appears to follow each year as the Earth orbits the Sun. It can be thought of as the plane of the Earth's orbit projected on to the *celestial sphere (imaginary sphere around the Earth).

Eco Umberto 1932– . Italian writer, semiologist, and literary critic. His works include *The Role of the Reader* 1979, the 'philosophical thriller' *The Name of the Rose* 1983, and *Foucault's Pendulum* 1988.

ecology (Greek *oikos* 'house') study of the relationship among organisms and the environments in which they live, including all living and nonliving components. The term was coined by the biologist Ernst Haeckel 1866.

economic community or **common market** organization of autonomous countries formed to promote trade. Examples include the European Community (EC) 1957, Caribbean Community (Caricom) 1973, Latin American Economic System 1975, and Central African Economic Community 1985.

economic growth rate of growth of output of

all goods and services in an economy, usually measured as the percentage increase in gross domestic product or gross national product from one year to the next. It is regarded as an indicator of the rate of increase or decrease (if economic growth is negative) in the standard of living.

economics (Greek 'household management') social science devoted to studying the production, distribution, and consumption of wealth. It consists of the disciplines of *microeconomics*, the study of individual producers, consumers, or markets, and *macroeconomics*, the study of whole economies or systems (in particular, areas such as taxation and public spending).

economies of scale in economics, when production capacity is increased at a financial cost that is more than compensated for by the greater volume of output. In a dress factory, for example, a reduction in the unit cost may be possible only by the addition of new machinery, which would be worthwhile only if the volume of dresses produced were increased and there were sufficient market demand for them.

ecosystem in *ecology, an integrated unit consisting of the *community of living organisms and the physical environment in a particular area. The relationships among species in an ecosystem are usually complex and finely balanced, and removal of any one species may be disastrous. The removal of a major predator, for example, can result in the destruction of the ecosystem through overgrazing by herbivores.

ECOWAS acronym for *Economic Community of West African States*.

ecstasy or *MDMA* (3,4-methylenedioxymethamphetamine) illegal drug in increasing use from the 1980s. It is a modified amphetamine with mild psychedelic effects, and works by depleting serotonin (a neurotransmitter) in the brain.

ECT abbreviation for *electroconvulsive therapy*.

ectoparasite *parasite that lives on the outer surface of its host.

ectopic in medicine, term applied to an anatomical feature that is displaced or found in an abnormal position. An ectopic pregnancy is one occurring outside the womb, usually in a Fallopian tube.

ectotherm 'cold-blooded' animal (see *poikilothermy), such as a lizard, that relies on external warmth (ultimately from the sun) to raise its body temperature so that it can become active. To cool the body, ectotherms seek out a cooler environment.

ECTU abbreviation for *European Confederation of Trade Unions*.

ECU abbreviation for *European Currency Unit*, the official monetary unit of the European Community. It is based on the value of the different currencies used in the *European Monetary System (EMS).

Ecuador Republic of (*República del Ecuador*)
area 270,670 sq km/104,479 sq mi
capital Quito
towns Cuenca; chief port Guayaquil
physical coastal plain rises sharply to Andes

Mountains, which are divided into a series of cultivated valleys; flat, low-lying rainforest in E
environment about 25,000 species became extinct 1965–90 as a result of environmental destruction
head of state and government Sixto Duran Ballen from 1992
political system emergent democracy
exports bananas, cocoa, coffee, sugar, rice, fruit, balsa wood, fish, petroleum
currency sucre
population (1993 est) 10,980,000; (mestizo 55%, Indian 25%, European 10%, black African 10%); growth rate 2.9% p.a.
languages Spanish (official), Quechua, Jivaro, and other Indian languages
religion Roman Catholic 95%
GNP $1,020 per head (1991)

chronology
1830 Independence achieved from Spain.
1925–48 Great political instability; no president completed his term of office.
1948–55 Liberals in power.
1956 First conservative president in 60 years.
1960 Liberals returned, with José Velasco as president.
1961 Velasco deposed and replaced by the vice president.
1962 Military junta installed.
1968 Velasco returned as president.
1972 A coup put the military back in power.
1978 New democratic constitution adopted.
1979 Liberals in power but opposed by right- and left-wing parties.
1982 Deteriorating economy provoked strikes, demonstrations, and a state of emergency.
1983 Austerity measures introduced.
1984–85 No party with a clear majority in the national congress; Febres Cordero narrowly won the presidency for the Conservatives.
1988 Rodrigo Borja Cevallos elected president for moderate left-wing coalition.
1989 Guerrilla left-wing group, *Alfaro Vive, Carajo* ('Alfaro lives, Dammit'), numbering about 1,000, laid down arms after nine years.
1992 PUR leader, Sixto Duran Ballen, elected president; PSC became largest party in congress.

ecumenical council (Greek *oikoumenikos* 'of the whole world') meeting of church leaders worldwide to determine Christian doctrine; their results are binding on all church members. Seven such councils are accepted as ecumenical by both Eastern and Western churches, while the Roman Catholic Church accepts a further 14 as ecumenical.

ecumenical movement movement for reunification of the various branches of the Christian church. It began in the 19th century with the extension of missionary work to Africa and Asia, where the divisions created in Europe were incomprehensible; the movement gathered momentum from the need for unity in the face of growing secularism in Christian countries and of the challenge posed by such faiths as Islam. The *World Council of Churches* was founded 1948.

eczema inflammatory skin condition, a form of dermatitis, marked by dryness, rashes, itching, the formation of blisters, and the exudation of fluid. It may be allergic in origin and is sometimes complicated by infection.

Edberg Stefan 1966– . Swedish tennis player, twice winner of Wimbledon 1988 and 1990. He won the junior Grand Slam 1983 and his first Grand Slam title, the Australian Open, 1985, repeated 1987. Other Grand Slam singles titles include the US Open 1991 and 1992. At Wimbledon in 1987 he became the first male player in 40 years to win a match without conceding a game.

Edda two collections of early Icelandic literature that together constitute our chief source for Old Norse mythology. The term strictly applies to the *Younger* or *Prose Edda*, compiled by Snorri Sturluson, a priest, about AD 1230.

Eddery Pat(rick) 1952– . Irish-born flat-racing jockey who has won the jockey's championship eight times, including four in succession.

Eddy Mary Baker 1821–1910. US founder of the Christian Science movement. She founded the Christian Science Association 1876. In 1879 the Church of Christ, Scientist, was established, and although living in retirement after 1892 she continued to direct the activities of the movement until her death.

edelweiss perennial alpine plant *Leontopodium alpinum*, family Compositae, with a white, woolly, star-shaped bloom, found in the high mountains of Eurasia.

Eden river in Cumbria, NW England; length 104 km/65 mi. From its source in the Pennines, it flows NW to enter the Solway Firth NW of Carlisle.

Eden Anthony, 1st Earl of Avon 1897–1977. British Conservative politician, foreign secretary 1935–38, 1940–45, and 1951–55; prime minister 1955–57, when he resigned after the failure of the Anglo-French military intervention in the *Suez Crisis.

Eden, Garden of in the Old Testament book of Genesis and in the Koran, the 'garden' in which Adam and Eve lived after their creation, and from which they were expelled for disobedience.

Edgar the Peaceful 944–975. King of all England from 959. He was the younger son of

Edmund I, and strove successfully to unite English and Danes as fellow subjects.

Edgehill, Battle of first battle of the English Civil War. It took place 1642, on a ridge in S Warwickshire, between Royalists under Charles I and Parliamentarians under the Earl of Essex. The result was indecisive.

Edinburgh capital of Scotland and administrative centre of the region of Lothian, near the southern shores of the Firth of Forth; population (1985) 440,000. A cultural centre, it holds an annual festival of music and the arts; the university was established 1583. Industries include printing, publishing, banking, insurance, chemical manufactures, distilling, brewing, and some shipbuilding.

Edinburgh, Duke of title of Prince *Philip of the UK.

Edison Thomas Alva 1847–1931. US scientist and inventor, with over 1,000 patents. In Menlo Park, New Jersey, 1876–87, he produced his most important inventions, including the electric light bulb 1879. He constructed a system of electric power distribution for consumers, the telephone transmitter, and the phonograph.

Edmonton capital of Alberta, Canada, on the North Saskatchewan River; population (1986) 576,200. It is the centre of an oil and mining area to the N and also an agricultural and dairying region. Petroleum pipelines link Edmonton with Superior, Wisconsin, USA, and Vancouver, British Columbia.

Edmund II Ironside c. 989–1016. King of England 1016, the son of Ethelred II the Unready. He led the resistance to *Canute's invasion 1015, and on Ethelred's death 1016 was chosen king by the citizens of London, whereas the Witan (the king's council) elected Canute. In the struggle for the throne, Edmund was defeated by Canute at Assandun (Ashington), Essex, and then divided the kingdom between them; when Edmund died the same year, Canute ruled the whole kingdom.

Edmund, St c. 840–870. King of East Anglia from 855. In 870 he was defeated and captured by the Danes at Hoxne, Suffolk, and martyred on refusing to renounce Christianity. He was canonized and his shrine at Bury St Edmunds became a place of pilgrimage.

education process, beginning at birth, of developing intellectual capacity, manual skill, and social awareness, especially by instruction. In its more restricted sense, the term refers to the process of imparting literacy, numeracy, and a generally accepted body of knowledge.

educational psychology the work of psychologists primarily in schools, including the assessment of children with achievement problems and advising on problem behaviour in the classroom.

education, conductive training for the physically disabled; see *conductive education.

education spending government budget for all schools, universities, and other educational institutions. In the UK, education spending as a proportion of gross national product reached a peak of 6.3% in 1975–76 and fell steadily thereafter to 4.9% in 1986–87. The period saw a fall in the number of schools and pupils, but an increase in the proportion staying in school or college after 16 and moving into higher education at 18. The pupil:teacher ratio in state schools fell from 23:1 in 1971 to 19:1 in 1981 and 17:1 in 1987. By 1989 it had begun to climb again and stood at 18:1. In fee-paying schools in 1989 the pupil:teacher ratio was 11:1. Over the same period the value of teachers' salaries was eroded, standing at 136% of average non-manual earnings in 1974 and falling to 99% of the average in 1991.

Edward (full name Edward Antony Richard Louis) 1964– . Prince of the UK, third son of Queen Elizabeth II. He is seventh in line to the throne after Charles, Charles's two sons, Andrew, and Andrew's two daughters.

Edward the *Black Prince* 1330–1376. Prince of Wales, eldest son of Edward III of England. The epithet (probably posthumous) may refer to his black armour. During the Hundred Years' War he fought at the Battle of Crécy 1346 and captured the French king at Poitiers 1356. He ruled Aquitaine 1360–71; during the revolt that eventually ousted him, he caused the massacre of Limoges 1370.

Edward eight kings of England or the UK:

Edward I 1239–1307. King of England from 1272, son of Henry III. Edward led the royal forces against Simon de Montfort in the *Barons' War 1264–67, and was on a crusade when he succeeded to the throne. He established English rule over all Wales 1282–84, and secured recognition of his overlordship from the Scottish king, although the Scots (under Wallace and Bruce) fiercely resisted actual conquest. In his reign Parliament took its approximate modern form with the *Model Parliament 1295. He was succeeded by his son Edward II.

Edward II 1284–1327. King of England from 1307. Son of Edward I and born at Caernarvon Castle, he was created the first Prince of Wales 1301. His invasion of Scotland 1314 to suppress revolt resulted in defeat at *Bannockburn. He was deposed 1327 by his wife Isabella (1292–1358), daughter of Philip IV of France, and her lover Roger de *Mortimer, and murdered in Berkeley Castle, Gloucestershire. He was succeeded by his son Edward III.

Edward III 1312–1377. King of England from 1327, son of Edward II. He assumed the government 1330 from his mother, through whom in 1337 he laid claim to the French throne and thus began the *Hundred Years' War. He was succeeded by Richard II.

Edward IV 1442–1483. King of England 1461–70 and from 1471. He was the son of Richard, Duke of York, and succeeded Henry VI in the Wars of the *Roses, temporarily losing the throne to Henry when Edward fell out with his adviser *Warwick, but regaining it at the Battle of Barnet 1471. He was succeeded by his son Edward V.

Edward V 1470–1483. King of England 1483. Son of Edward IV, he was deposed three months after his accession in favour of his uncle (*Richard III), and is traditionally believed to have been murdered (with his brother) in the Tower of London on Richard's orders.

Edward VI 1537–1553. King of England from 1547, son of Henry VIII and Jane Seymour. The government was entrusted to his uncle the Duke of Somerset (who fell from power 1549), and then to the Earl of Warwick, later created Duke of Northumberland. He was succeeded by his sister, Mary I.

Edward VII 1841–1910. King of Great Britain and Ireland from 1901. As Prince of Wales he was a prominent social figure, but his mother Queen Victoria considered him too frivolous to take part in political life. In 1860 he made the first tour of Canada and the USA ever undertaken by a British prince.

Edward VIII 1894–1972. King of Great Britain and Northern Ireland Jan–Dec 1936, when he renounced the throne to marry Wallis Warfield *Simpson (see *abdication crisis). He was created Duke of Windsor and was governor of the Bahamas 1940–45, subsequently settling in France.

Edward the Confessor c. 1003–1066. King of England from 1042, the son of Ethelred II. He lived in Normandy until shortly before his accession. During his reign power was held by Earl Godwin (died 1053) and his son Harold (see *Harold II), while the king devoted himself to religion, including the rebuilding of Westminster Abbey (consecrated 1065), where he is buried. His childlessness led ultimately to the Norman Conquest 1066. He was canonized 1161.

Edward the Elder c. 870–924. King of the West Saxons. He succeeded his father *Alfred the Great 899. He reconquered SE England and the Midlands from the Danes, uniting Wessex and *Mercia with the help of his sister, Athelflad. By the time Edward died, his kingdom was the most powerful in the British Isles. He was succeeded by his son *Athelstan.

Edward the Martyr c. 963–978. King of England from 975. Son of King Edgar, he was murdered at Corfe Castle, Dorset, probably at his stepmother Aelfthryth's instigation (she wished to secure the crown for her son, Ethelred). He was canonized 1001.

EEC abbreviation for *European Economic Community*; see *European Community.

EEG abbreviation for *electroencephalogram*.

eel any fish of the order Anguilliformes. They are snakelike, with elongated dorsal and anal fins. They include the freshwater eels of Europe and North America (which breed in the Atlantic), the marine conger eels, and the morays of tropical coral reefs.

EEPROM (acronym for *electrically erasable programmable read-only memory*) computer memory that can record data and retain it indefinitely. The data can be erased with an electrical charge and new data recorded.

efficiency output of a machine (work done by the machine) divided by the input (work put into the machine), usually expressed as a percentage. Because of losses caused by friction, efficiency is always less than 100%, although it can approach this for electrical machines with no moving parts (such as a transformer).

EFTA acronym for *European Free Trade Association*.

EFTPOS (acronym for *electronic funds transfer at point of sale*) transfer of funds from one bank account to another by electronic means.

For example, a customer inserts a plastic card into a point-of-sale computer terminal in a super-market, and telephone lines are used to make an automatic debit from the customer's bank account to settle the bill. See also *credit card.

egalitarianism belief that all citizens in a state should have equal rights and privileges. Interpretations of this can vary, from the notion of equality of opportunity to equality in material welfare and political decision-making. Some states clearly reject any thought of egalitarianism; most accept the concept of equal opportunities but recognize that people's abilities vary widely. Even those states which claim to be socialist find it necessary to have hierarchical structures in the political, social, and economic spheres. Egalitarianism was one of the principles of the French Revolution.

egg in animals, the ovum, or female *gamete (reproductive cell). After fertilization by a sperm cell, it begins to divide to form an embryo. Eggs may be deposited by the female (*ovipary) or they may develop within her body (*vivipary and *ovovivipary). In the oviparous reptiles and birds, the egg is protected by a shell, and well supplied with nutrients in the form of yolk.

eggplant another name for *aubergine.

ego (Latin 'I') in psychology, a general term for the processes concerned with the self and a person's conception of himself or herself, encompassing values and attitudes. In Freudian psychology, the term refers specifically to the element of the human mind that represents the conscious processes concerned with reality, in conflict with the *id (the instinctual element) and the *superego (the ethically aware element).

egret any of several herons with long feathers on the head or neck.

Egypt Arab Republic of (*Jumhuriyat Misr al-Arabiya*)

area 1,001,450 sq km/386,990 sq mi
capital Cairo
towns and cities Gīza; ports Alexandria, Port Said, Suez, Damietta
physical mostly desert; hills in E; fertile land along Nile valley and delta; cultivated and settled area is about 35,500 sq km/13,700 sq mi
environment the Aswan Dam (opened 1970) on the Nile has caused widespread salinization and an increase in waterborne diseases in the area. A dramatic fall in the annual load of silt deposited downstream has reduced the fertility of cropland and led to coastal erosion
head of state Muhammad Hosni Mubarak from 1981
head of government Atif Sidqi from 1981
political system democratic republic
exports cotton and textiles, petroleum, fruit and vegetables
currency Egyptian pound
population (1993) 56,430,000; growth rate 2.4% p.a.
languages Arabic (official); ancient Egyptian survives to some extent in Coptic
religions Sunni Muslim 95%, Coptic Christian 5%
GNP $620 per head (1991)
chronology
1914 Egypt became a British protectorate.
1936 Independence achieved from Britain. King Fuad succeeded by his son Farouk.
1946 Withdrawal of British troops except from Suez Canal Zone.
1952 Farouk overthrown by army in bloodless coup.
1953 Egypt declared a republic, with General Neguib as president.
1956 Neguib replaced by Col Gamal Nasser. Nasser announced nationalization of Suez Canal; Egypt attacked by Britain, France, and Israel. Cease-fire agreed because of US intervention.
1967 Six-Day War with Israel ended in Egypt's defeat and Israeli occupation of Sinai and Gaza Strip.
1970 Nasser died suddenly; succeeded by Anwar Sadat.
1973 Attempt to regain territory lost to Israel led to fighting; cease-fire arranged by US secretary of state Henry Kissinger.
1978–79 Camp David talks in the USA resulted in a treaty between Egypt and Israel. Egypt expelled from the Arab League.
1981 Sadat assassinated, succeeded by Hosni Mubarak.
1984 Mubarak's party victorious in the people's assembly elections.
1987 Mubarak re-elected. Egypt readmitted to Arab League.
1989 Improved relations with Libya; diplomatic relations with Syria restored. Mubarak proposed a peace plan.
1990 Gains for independents in general election.
1991 Participation in Gulf War on US-led side. Major force in convening Middle East peace conference in Spain.
1992 Outbreaks of violence between Muslims and Christians.
1993 Islamic militant campaign against government escalated. Mubarak sworn in for third term.

Egyptian religion in the civilization of ancient Egypt, totemic animals, believed to be the ancestors of the clan, were worshipped. Totems later developed into gods, represented as having animal heads. One of the main cults was that of *Osiris, the god of the underworld. Immortality, conferred by the magical rite of mummification, was originally the sole prerogative of the king, but was extended under the New Kingdom to all who could afford it; they were buried with the *Book of the Dead*.

Egyptology the study of ancient Egypt. Interest

in the subject was aroused by the Napoleonic expedition's discovery of the *Rosetta Stone 1799. Various excavations continued throughout the 19th century and gradually assumed a more scientific character, largely as a result of the work of the British archaeologist Flinders *Petrie from 1880 onwards and the formation of the Egyptian Exploration Fund 1892. In 1922 another British archaeologist, Howard Carter, discovered the tomb of Tutankhamen, the only royal tomb with all its treasures intact.

Ehrlich Paul 1854–1915. German bacteriologist and immunologist who produced the first cure for *syphilis. He developed the arsenic compounds, in particular Salvarsan, that were used in the treatment of syphilis prior to the discovery of antibiotics. He shared the 1908 Nobel Prize for Medicine with Ilya *Mechnikov for his work on immunity.

Eichmann (Karl) Adolf 1906–1962. Austrian Nazi. As an *SS official during Hitler's regime (1933–1945), he was responsible for atrocities against Jews and others, including the implementation of genocide. He managed to escape at the fall of Germany 1945, but was discovered in Argentina 1960, abducted by Israeli agents, tried in Israel 1961 for *war crimes, and executed.

eider large marine *duck, *Somateria mollissima*, highly valued for its soft down, which is used in quilts and cushions for warmth. The adult male has a black cap and belly and a green nape. The rest of the plumage is white with pink breast and throat while the female is a mottled brown. The bill is large and flattened. It is found on the northern coasts of the Atlantic and Pacific Oceans.

Eid ul-Adha Muslim festival which takes place during the *hajj*, or pilgrimage to Mecca, and commemorates Abraham's willingness to sacrifice his son *Ishmael at the command of Allah.

Eid ul-Fitr Muslim festival celebrating the end of Ramadan, the month of fasting.

Eiffel (Alexandre) Gustave 1832–1923. French engineer who constructed the *Eiffel Tower* for the 1889 Paris Exhibition. The tower, made of iron, is 320 m/1,050 ft high, and stands in the Champ de Mars, Paris.

Einstein Albert 1879–1955. German-born US physicist who formulated the theories of *relativity, and worked on radiation physics and thermodynamics. In 1905 he published the special theory of relativity, and in 1915 issued his general theory of relativity. He received the Nobel Prize for Physics 1921. His latest conception of the basic laws governing the universe was outlined in his *unified field theory, made public 1953.

einsteinium in chemistry, a synthesized, radioactive, metallic element of the actinide series, symbol Es, atomic number 99, relative atomic mass 254.

Eire Gaelic name for the Republic of *Ireland.

Eisenach industrial town (pottery, vehicles, machinery) in the state of Thuringia, Germany; population (1981) 50,700. Martin *Luther made the first translation of the Bible into German in Wartburg Castle and the composer J S Bach was born here.

Eisenhower Dwight David ('Ike') 1890–1969.

34th president of the USA 1953–60, a Republican. A general in World War II, he commanded the Allied forces in Italy 1943, then the Allied invasion of Europe, and from Oct 1944 all the Allied armies in the West. As president he promoted business interests at home and conducted the *Cold War abroad. His vice president was Richard Nixon.

Eisenstein Sergei Mikhailovich 1898–1948. Latvian film director who pioneered film theory and introduced the use of montage (the juxtaposition of shots to create a particular effect) as a means of propaganda, as in *The Battleship Potemkin* 1925.

eisteddfod (Welsh 'sitting') traditional Welsh gathering lasting up to a week and dedicated to the encouragement of the bardic arts of music, poetry, and literature; it dates from pre-Christian times.

Ekaterinburg formerly (1924–90) *Sverdlovsk, industrial town (copper, iron, platinum, engineering, and chemicals) in Russia in the eastern foothills of the Urals; population (1987) 1,331,000. Tsar Nicholas II and his family were murdered here 1918.

eland largest species of *antelope, *Taurotragus oryx*. Pale fawn in colour, it is about 2 m/6 ft high, and both sexes have spiral horns about 45 cm/18 in long. It is found in central and southern Africa.

elasticity in economics, the measure of response of one variable to changes in another. If the price of butter is reduced by 10% and the demand increases by 20%, the elasticity measure is 2. Such measures are used to test the effects of changes in prices, incomes, and supply and demand. Inelasticity may exist in the demand for necessities such as water, the demand for which will remain the same even if the price changes considerably.

elasticity in physics, the ability of a solid to recover its shape once deforming forces (stresses modifying its dimensions or shape) are removed. An elastic material obeys *Hooke's law: that is, its deformation is proportional to the applied stress up to a certain point, called the *elastic limit*, beyond which additional stress will deform it permanently. Elastic materials include metals and rubber; however, all materials have some degree of elasticity.

E layer (formerly called the Kennelly–Heaviside layer) the lower regions of the *ionosphere, which refract radio waves, allowing their reception around the surface of the Earth. The E layer approaches the Earth by day and recedes from it at night.

Elbe one of the principal rivers of Germany, 1,166 km/725 mi long, rising on the southern slopes of the Riesengebirge, Czechoslovakia, and flowing NW across the German plain to the North Sea.

Elbruz or *Elbrus* highest mountain (5,642 m/ 18,510 ft) on the continent of Europe, in the Caucasus, Georgia.

elder small tree or shrub of the genus *Sambucus*, family Caprifoliaceae. The common *S. nigra* of Europe, N Africa, and W Asia has pinnate leaves and heavy heads of small, sweet-scented, white flowers in early summer. These are succeeded by clusters of small, black berries. The scarlet-berried *S. racemosa* is found in parts of Europe, Asia, and North America.

elder in the Presbyterian church, a lay member who assists the minister (or teaching elder) in running the church.

El Dorado fabled city of gold believed by the 16th-century Spanish and other Europeans to exist somewhere in the area of the Orinoco and Amazon rivers.

Eleanor of Aquitaine *c.* 1122–1204. Queen of France 1137–51 as wife of Louis VII, and of England from 1154 as wife of Henry II. Henry imprisoned her 1174–89 for supporting their sons, the future Richard I and King John, in revolt against him.

Eleanor of Castile *c.* 1245–1290. Queen of Edward I of England, the daughter of Ferdinand III of Castile. She married Prince Edward 1254, and accompanied him on his crusade 1270. She died at Harby, Nottinghamshire, and Edward erected stone crosses in towns where her body rested on the funeral journey to London. Several *Eleanor Crosses* are still standing, for example at Northampton.

election process of appointing a person to public office or a political party to government by voting. Elections were occasionally held in ancient Greek democracies; Roman tribunes were regularly elected.

elector (German *Kurfürst*) any of originally seven (later ten) princes of the Holy Roman Empire who had the prerogative of electing the emperor (in effect, the king of Germany). The electors were the archbishops of Mainz, Trier, and Cologne, the court palatine of the Rhine, the Duke of Saxony, the Margrave of Brandenburg, and the king of Bohemia (in force to 1806). Their constitutional status was formalized 1356 in the document known as the *Golden Bull*, which granted them extensive powers within their own domains, to act as judges, issue coins, and impose tolls.

electoral college in the US government, the indirect system of voting for the president and vice president. The people of each state officially vote not for the presidential candidate, but for a list of electors nominated by each party. The whole electoral-college vote of the state then goes to the winning party (and candidate). A majority is required for election.

electoral system see *vote and *proportional representation.

electric arc a continuous electric discharge of high current between two electrodes, giving out a brilliant light and heat. The phenomenon is exploited in the carbon-arc lamp, once widely used in film projectors. In the electric-arc furnace an arc struck between very large carbon electrodes and the metal charge provides the heating. In arc *welding an electric arc provides the heat to fuse the metal. The discharges in low-pressure gases, as in neon and sodium lights, can also be broadly considered as electric arcs.

electric charge property of some bodies that causes them to exert forces on each other. Two bodies both with positive or both with negative charges repel each other, whereas bodies with opposite or 'unlike' charges attract each other,

since each is in the *electric field of the other. In atoms, *electrons possess a negative charge, and *protons an equal positive charge. The *SI unit of electric charge is the coulomb (symbol C).

electric current the flow of electrically charged particles through a conducting circuit due to the presence of a *potential difference. The current at any point in a circuit is the amount of charge flowing per second; its SI unit is the ampere (coulomb per second).

electric field in physics, a region in which a particle possessing electric charge experiences a force owing to the presence of another electric charge. It is a type of electromagnetic field.

electricity all phenomena caused by *electric charge, whether static or in motion. Electric charge is caused by an excess or deficit of electrons in the charged substance, and an electric current by the movement of electrons around a circuit. Substances may be electrical conductors, such as metals, which allow the passage of electricity through them, or insulators, such as rubber, which are extremely poor conductors. Substances with relatively poor conductivities that can be improved by the addition of heat or light are known as *semiconductors.

electric motor a machine that converts electrical energy into mechanical energy. There are various types, including direct-current and induction motors, most of which produce rotary motion. A linear induction motor produces linear (sideways) rather than rotary motion.

electric ray another name for the *torpedo.

electrocardiogram (ECG) graphic recording of the electrical changes in the heart muscle, as detected by electrodes placed on the chest. Electrocardiography is used in the diagnosis of heart disease.

electrochemistry the branch of science that studies chemical reactions involving electricity. The use of electricity to produce chemical effects, *electrolysis, is employed in many industrial processes, such as the manufacture of chlorine and the extraction of aluminium. The use of chemical reactions to produce electricity is the basis of electrical *cells, such as the dry cell and the *Leclanché cell.

electroconvulsive therapy (ECT) or *electroshock therapy* treatment for *schizophrenia and *depression, given under anaesthesia and with a muscle relaxant. An electric current is passed through the brain to induce alterations in the brain's electrical activity. The treatment can cause distress and loss of concentration and memory, and so there is much controversy about its use and effectiveness.

electrocution death caused by electric current. It is used as a method of execution in some US states. The condemned person is strapped into a special chair and a shock of 1,800–2,000 volts is administered. See *capital punishment.

electrode any terminal by which an electric current passes in or out of a conducting substance; for example, the anode or cathode in a battery or the carbons in an arc lamp. The terminals that emit and collect the flow of electrons in thermionic *valves (electron tubes) are also called electrodes: for example, cathodes, plates, and grids.

electrodynamics the branch of physics dealing with electric currents and associated magnetic forces. *Quantum electrodynamics (QED) studies the interaction between charged particles and their emission and absorption of electromagnetic radiation. This field combines quantum theory and relativity theory, making accurate predictions about subatomic processes involving charged particles such as electrons and protons.

electroencephalogram (EEG) graphic record of the electrical discharges of the brain, as detected by electrodes placed on the scalp. The pattern of electrical activity revealed by electroencephalography is helpful in the diagnosis of some brain disorders, such as epilepsy.

electrolysis in archaeological conservation, a cleaning process, especially of material from underwater archaeology, involving immersing the object in a chemical solution and passing a weak current between it and a surrounding metal grille. Corrosive salts move slowly from the object (cathode) to the grille (anode), leaving the artefact clean.

electrolysis in chemistry, the production of chemical changes by passing an electric current through a solution or molten salt (the electrolyte), resulting in the migration of ions to the electrodes: positive ions (cations) to the negative electrode (cathode) and negative ions (anions) to the positive electrode (anode).

electrolysis cosmetic hair removal using an electric current. It can be very effective in experienced hands, but is slow and therefore expensive.

electrolyte a solution or molten substance in which an electric current is made to flow by the movement and discharge of ions in accordance with Faraday's laws of *electrolysis.

electromagnet an iron bar with coils of wire around it, which acts as a magnet when an electric current flows through the wire. Electromagnets have many uses: in switches, electric bells, solenoids, and metal-lifting cranes.

electromagnetic field in physics, the agency by which a particle with an *electric charge experiences a force in a particular region of space. If it does so only when moving, it is in a pure **magnetic field**; if it does so when stationary, it is in an **electric field**. Both can be present simultaneously.

electromagnetic force one of the four fundamental *forces of nature, the other three being gravity, the strong nuclear force, and the weak nuclear force. The *elementary particle that is the carrier for the electromagnetic (em) force is the photon.

electromagnetic induction in electronics, the production of an *electromotive force (emf) in a circuit by a change of magnetic flux through the circuit or by relative motion of the circuit and the magnetic flux. In a closed circuit an *induced current will be produced. All dynamos and generators make use of this effect. When magnetic tape is driven past the playback head (a small coil) of a tape-recorder, the moving magnetic field induces an emf in the head, which is then amplified to reproduce the recorded sounds.

electromagnetic waves oscillating electric and magnetic fields travelling together through space at a speed of nearly 300,000 km/ 186,000 mi per second. The (limitless) range of possible wavelengths or *frequencies of electromagnetic waves, which can be thought of as making up the **electromagnetic spectrum**, includes radio waves, infrared radiation, visible light, ultraviolet radiation, X-rays, and gamma rays.

electron stable, negatively charged *elementary particle; it is a constituent of all atoms, and a member of the class of particles known as *leptons. The electrons in each atom surround the nucleus in groupings called shells; in a neutral atom the number of electrons is equal to the number of protons in the nucleus. This electron structure is responsible for the chemical properties of the atom (see *atomic structure).

electronegativity the ease with which an atom can attract electrons to itself. Electronegative elements attract electrons, so forming negative ions.

electronic funds transfer (EFT) method of transferring funds automatically from one account to another by electronic means, for example **electronic funds transfer at point of sale** (EFTPOS), which provides for the automatic transfer of money from buyer to seller at the time of sale. For example, a customer inserts a plastic card into a point-of-sale computer terminal in a supermarket, and telephone lines are used to make an automatic debit from the customer's bank account to settle the bill.

electronic music term first applied 1954 to edited tape music composed primarily of electronically generated and modified tones, serially organized to objective scales of differentiation, to distinguish it from the more intuitive methodology of *concrete music. The term was subsequently extended to include prerecorded vocal and instrumental sounds organized in a similar way, as in Stockhausen's *Gesang der Jünglinge/ Song of the Youths* 1955 and Berio's *Differences* 1957. Other pioneers of electronic music are Milton Babbitt and Bruno Maderna (1920–1973).

electronic point of sale (EPOS) system used in retailing in which a bar code on a product is scanned at the cash till and the information relayed to the store computer. The computer will then relay back the price of the item to the cash till.

electronic publishing the distribution of information using computer-based media such as *multimedia and *Hypertext in the creation of electronic 'books'. Critical technologies in the development of electronic publishing are *CD-ROM, with its massive yet compact storage capabilities, and the advent of computer networking with its ability to deliver information instantaneously anywhere in the world.

electronics branch of science that deals with the emission of *electrons from conductors and *semiconductors, with the subsequent manipulation of these electrons, and with the construction of electronic devices. The first electronic device was the thermionic *valve, or vacuum tube, in which electrons moved in a vacuum, and led to such inventions as *radio, *television, *radar, and the digital *computer. Replacement of valves with the comparatively tiny and reliable transistor from 1948 revolutionized electronic development. Modern electronic devices are based on minute *integrated circuits (silicon chips), wafer-thin crystal slices holding tens of thousands of electronic components.

electron microscope instrument that produces a magnified image by using a beam of *electrons instead of light rays, as in an optical *microscope. An **electron lens** is an arrangement of electromagnetic coils that control and focus the beam. Electrons are not visible to the eye, so instead of an eyepiece there is a fluorescent screen or a photographic plate on which the electrons form an image. The wavelength of the electron beam is much shorter than that of light, so much greater magnification and resolution (ability to distinguish detail) can be achieved.

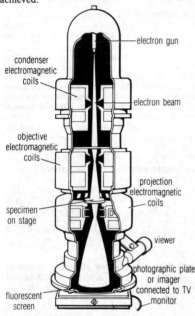

- electron gun
- condenser electromagnetic coils
- electron beam
- objective electromagnetic coils
- projection electromagnetic coils
- specimen on stage
- viewer
- photographic plate or imager connected to TV monitor
- fluorescent screen

electron microscope *The transmission electron microscope.*

electron volt unit (symbol eV) for measuring the energy of a charged particle (*ion or *electron) in terms of the energy of motion an electron would gain from a potential difference of one volt. Because it is so small, more usual units are mega- (million) and giga- (billion) electron volts (MeV and GeV).

electrophoresis the *diffusion of charged particles through a fluid under the influence of an electric field.

electroplating deposition of metals upon metallic surfaces by electrolysis for decorative and/or protective purposes. It is used in the preparation of printers' blocks, 'master' audio discs, and in many other processes.

electropositivity in chemistry, a measure of the ability of elements (mainly metals) to donate electrons to form positive ions. The greater the metallic character, the more electropositive the element.

electroscope an apparatus for detecting *electric charge. The simple gold-leaf electroscope consists of a vertical conducting (metal) rod ending in a pair of rectangular pieces of gold foil, mounted inside and insulated from an earthed metal case. An electric charge applied to the end of the metal rod makes the gold leaves diverge, because they each receive a similar charge (positive or negative) and so repel each other.

electrovalent bond another name for an *ionic bond, a chemical bond in which the combining atoms lose or gain electrons to form ions.

electrum naturally occurring alloy of gold and silver used by early civilizations to make the first coins, about the 6th century BC.

element substance that cannot be split chemically into simpler substances. The atoms of a particular element all have the same number of protons in their nuclei (their atomic number). Elements are classified in the periodic table (see *periodic table of the elements). Of the 109 known elements, 95 are known to occur in nature (those with atomic numbers 1–95). Those from 96 to 109 do not occur in nature and are synthesized only, produced in particle accelerators. Eighty-one of the elements are stable; all the others, which include atomic numbers 43, 61, and from 84 up, are radioactive.

elementary particle in physics, a subatomic particle that is not made up of smaller particles, and so can be considered one of the fundamental units of matter. There are three groups of elementary particles: quarks, leptons, and gauge bosons.

elephant mammal belonging to either of two surviving species of the order Proboscidea: the Asian elephant *Elephas maximus* and the Afri-

Asiatic Elephant

African Elephant

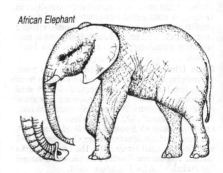

elephant *The elephant is the largest and most powerful land mammal.*

can elephant *Loxodonta africana.* Elephants can grow to 4 m/13 ft and weigh up to 8 tonnes; they have a thick, grey, wrinkled skin, a large head, a long trunk used to obtain food and water, and upper incisors or tusks, which grow to a considerable length. The African elephant has very large ears and a flattened forehead, and the Asian species has smaller ears and a convex forehead. In India, Myanmar (Burma), and Thailand, Asiatic elephants are widely used for transport and logging.

elephantiasis in the human body, a condition of local enlargement and deformity, most often of a leg, the scrotum, a labium of the vulva, or a breast, caused by the blocking of lymph channels.

Eleusinian Mysteries ceremonies in honour of the Greek deities *Demeter, *Persephone, and *Dionysus, celebrated in the remains of the temple of Demeter at Eleusis, Greece. Worshippers saw visions in the darkened temple, supposedly connected with the underworld.

Elgar Edward (William) 1857–1934. English composer. His *Enigma Variations* appeared 1899, and although his celebrated choral work, the oratorio setting of John Henry Newman's *The Dream of Gerontius*, was initially a failure, it was well received at Düsseldorf in 1902. Many of his earlier works were then performed, including the *Pomp and Circumstance* marches.

Elgin marbles collection of ancient Greek sculptures mainly from the Parthenon at Athens, assembled by the 7th Earl of Elgin. Sent to England 1812, and bought for the nation 1816 for £5,000, they are now in the British Museum. Greece has repeatedly asked for them to be returned to Athens.

Elijah *c.* mid-9th century BC. In the Old Testament, a Hebrew prophet during the reigns of the Israelite kings Ahab and Ahaziah. He came from Gilead. He defeated the prophets of *Baal, and was said to have been carried up to heaven in a fiery chariot in a whirlwind. In Jewish belief, Elijah will return to Earth to herald the coming of the Messiah.

Eliot George. Pen name of Mary Ann Evans 1819–1880. English novelist whose works include the pastoral *Adam Bede* 1859, *The Mill on the Floss* 1860, with its autobiographical elements, *Silas Marner* 1861, which contains elements of the folktale, and *Daniel Deronda* 1876. *Middlemarch*, published serially in 1871–2, is considered her greatest novel for its confident handling of numerous characters and central social and moral issues. Her work is pervaded by a penetrating and compassionate intelligence.

Eliot T(homas) S(tearns) 1888–1965. US poet, playwright, and critic who lived in London from 1915. His first volume of poetry, *Prufrock and Other Observations* 1917, introduced new verse forms and rhythms; further collections include *The Waste Land* 1922, *The Hollow Men* 1925, and *Old Possum's Book of Practical Cats* 1939. His plays include *Murder in the Cathedral* 1935 and *The Cocktail Party* 1949. His critical works include *The Sacred Wood* 1920. He was awarded the Nobel Prize for Literature 1948.

Elisabethville former name of *Lubumbashi, a town in Zaire.

Elizabeth in the New Testament, mother of John the Baptist. She was a cousin of Jesus' mother Mary, who came to see her shortly after the Annunciation; on this visit (called the Visitation), Mary sang the hymn of praise later to be known as the 'Magnificat'.

Elizabeth the *Queen Mother* 1900– . Wife of King George VI of England. She was born Lady Elizabeth Angela Marguerite Bowes-Lyon, and on 26 April 1923 she married Albert, Duke of York, who became King George VI in 1936. Their children are Queen Elizabeth II and Princess Margaret.

Elizabeth two queens of England or the UK:

Elizabeth I 1533–1603. Queen of England 1558–1603, the daughter of Henry VIII and Anne Boleyn. Through her Religious Settlement of 1559 she enforced the Protestant religion by law. She had *Mary, Queen of Scots, executed 1587. Her conflict with Roman Catholic Spain led to the defeat of the *Spanish Armada 1588. The Elizabethan age was expansionist in commerce and geographical exploration, and arts and literature flourished. The rulers of many European states made unsuccessful bids to marry Elizabeth, and she used these bids to strengthen her power. She was succeeded by James I.

Elizabeth II 1926– . Queen of Great Britain and Northern Ireland from 1952, the elder daughter of George VI. She married her third cousin, Philip, the Duke of Edinburgh, 1947. They have four children: Charles, Anne, Andrew, and Edward.

Elizabeth 1709–1762. Empress of Russia from 1741, daughter of Peter the Great. She carried through a palace revolution and supplanted her cousin, the infant Ivan VI (1730–1764), on the throne. She continued the policy of westernization begun by Peter and allied herself with Austria against Prussia.

Elizabethan literature literature produced during the reign of Elizabeth I of England (1558–1603). This period saw a remarkable florescence of the arts in England, and the literature of the time is characterized by a new energy, richness, and confidence. Renaissance humanism, Protestant zeal, and geographical discovery all contributed to this upsurge of creative power. Drama was the dominant form of the age, and *Shakespeare and *Marlowe were popular with all levels of society. Other writers of the period include Edmund Spenser, Sir Philip Sidney, Francis Bacon, Thomas Lodge, Robert Greene, and John Lyly.

elk large deer *Alces alces* inhabiting N Europe, Asia, Scandinavia, and North America, where it is known as the moose. It is brown in colour, stands about 2 m/6 ft at the shoulders, has very large palmate antlers, a fleshy muzzle, short neck, and long legs. It feeds on leaves and shoots. In North America, the *wapiti is called an elk.

Ellice Islands former name of *Tuvalu, a group of islands in the W Pacific Ocean.

Ellington Duke (Edward Kennedy) 1899–1974. US pianist who had an outstanding career as a composer and arranger of jazz. He wrote numerous pieces for his own jazz orchestra, accentuating the strengths of individual virtuoso instrumentalists, and became one of the leading figures in jazz over a 55-year period. Some of his most popular compositions include 'Mood Indigo', 'Sophisticated Lady', 'Solitude', and 'Black and Tan Fantasy'. He was one of the founders of big-band jazz.

ellipse curve joining all points (loci) around two fixed points (foci) such that the sum of the distances from those points is always constant. The diameter passing through the foci is the major axis, and the diameter bisecting this at right angles is the minor axis. An ellipse is one of a series of curves known as *conic sections. A slice across a cone that is not made parallel to, and does not pass through, the base will produce an ellipse.

Ellis Island island in New York Harbor, USA; area 11 hectares/27 acres. A former reception centre for steerage-class immigrants during the immigration waves between 1892–1943 (12 million people passed through it 1892–1924), it was later used as a detention centre for non-residents without documentation, or for those who were being deported. It was declared a National Historic Site 1964 by President Lyndon Johnson.

elm any tree of the family Ulmaceae, found in temperate regions of the northern hemisphere and in mountainous parts of the tropics. The common English elm *Ulmus procera* is widely distributed throughout Europe. It reaches 35 m/115 ft, with tufts of small, purplish-brown flowers, which appear before the leaves.

El Niño (Spanish 'the child') warm ocean surge of the *Peru Current, so called because it tends to occur at Christmas, recurring every 5–8 years or so in the E Pacific off South America. It warms the nutrient-rich waters along the coast of Ecuador and Peru, killing cold-water fishes and plants, and is an important factor in global weather.

El Paso city in Texas, USA, situated at the base of the Franklin Mountains, on the Rio Grande, opposite the Mexican city of Ciudad Juárez; population (1990) 515,000. It is the centre of an agricultural and cattle-raising area, and there are electronics, food processing, packing, and leather industries, as well as oil refineries and industries based on local iron and copper mines.

El Salvador Republic of (*República de El Salvador*)
area 21,393 sq km/8,258 sq mi

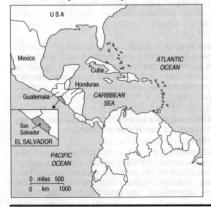

capital San Salvador
towns Santa Ana, San Miguel
physical narrow coastal plain, rising to mountains in N with central plateau
head of state and government Armando Calderón Sol from 1994
political system emergent democracy
exports coffee, cotton, sugar
currency colón
population (1993 est) 5,580,000 (mainly of mixed Spanish and Indian ancestry; 10% Indian); growth rate 2.9% p.a.
languages Spanish, Nahuatl
religion Roman Catholic 97%
GNP $1,070 per head (1991)
chronology
1821 Independence achieved from Spain.
1972 Allegations of human-rights violations; growth of left-wing guerrilla activities. General Carlos Romero elected president.
1979 A coup replaced Romero with a military-civilian junta.
1980 Archbishop Oscar Romero assassinated; country on verge of civil war. José Duarte became first civilian president since 1931.
1981 Mexico and France recognized the guerrillas as a legitimate political force, but the USA actively assisted the government in its battle against them.
1982 Assembly elections boycotted by left-wing parties and held amid considerable violence.
1986 Duarte sought a negotiated settlement with the guerrillas.
1988 Duarte resigned.
1989 Alfredo Cristiani (ARENA) became president in rigged elections; rebel attacks intensified.
1991 United Nations-sponsored peace accord signed by representatives of the government and the socialist guerrilla group, the FMLN.
1992 Peace accord validated; FMLN became political party.
1993 March: UN-sponsored commission published report on war atrocities. April: government amnesty cleared those implicated. July: top military leaders officially retired.
1994 Armando Calderón Sol (ARENA) elected president.

Elton Charles 1900–1991. British ecologist, a pioneer of the study of animal and plant forms in their natural environments, and of animal behaviour as part of the complex pattern of life. He defined the concept of *food chains and was an early conservationist, instrumental in establishing (1949) the Nature Conservancy Council of which he was a member 1949–56, and much concerned with the impact of introduced species on natural systems.

Eluard Paul. Pen name of Eugène Grindel 1895–1952. French poet, born in Paris. He expressed the suffering of poverty in his verse, and was a leader of the Surrealists. He fought in World War I, which inspired his *Poèmes pour la paix/Poems for Peace* 1918, and was a member of the Resistance in World War II. His books include *Poésie et vérité/Poetry and Truth* 1942 and *Au Rendezvous allemand/To the German Rendezvous* 1944.

Elysée Palace (*Palais de l'Elysée*) building in Paris erected 1718 for Louis d'Auvergne, Count of Evreux. It was later the home of Mme de Pompadour, Napoleon I, and Napoleon III, and became the official residence of the presidents of France 1870.

Elysium in Greek mythology, the Islands of the Blessed, situated at the western end of the Earth, near the river Oceanus, to which favoured heroes are sent by the gods to enjoy a life after death. Later a region in *Hades.

Emancipation Proclamation, The in US history, President Lincoln's Civil War announcement, 22 Sept 1862, stating that from the beginning of 1863 all black slaves in states still engaged in rebellion against the federal government would be emancipated. Slaves in border states still remaining loyal to the Union were excluded.

embargo the legal prohibition by a government of trade with another country, forbidding foreign ships to leave or enter its ports. Trade embargoes may be imposed on a country seen to be violating international laws.

embezzlement in law, theft by an employee of property entrusted to him or her by an employer.

emblem any visible symbol; a moral maxim expressed pictorially with an explanatory epigram. Books of emblems were popular in Renaissance Europe. The first emblem book was by Andrea Alciati of Milan; first printed in Augsburg 1531, it had some 175 editions in several languages. In England *Emblems* 1635, a religious work, was compiled by Francis Quarles (1592–1644).

embolism blockage of a blood vessel by an obstruction called an embolus (usually a blood clot, fat particle, or bubble of air).

embossing relief decoration on metals, which can be cast, chased, or repoussé, and executed by hand or machine. In the 16th century the term was also used for carved decorations on wood. Embossed bindings for books were developed from the early 19th century; the leather is embossed before binding.

embroidery the art of decorating cloth with a needle and thread. It includes broderie anglaise, gros point, and petit point, all of which have been used for the adornment of costumes, gloves, book covers, furnishings, and ecclesiastical vestments.

embryo early development stage of an animal or a plant following fertilization of an ovum (egg cell), or activation of an ovum by *parthenogenesis. In humans, the term embryo describes the fertilized egg during its first seven weeks of existence; from the eighth week onwards it is referred to as a fetus.

embryology study of the changes undergone by an organism from its conception as a fertilized ovum (egg) to its emergence into the world at hatching or birth. It is mainly concerned with the changes in cell organization in the embryo and the way in which these lead to the structures and organs of the adult (the process of *differentiation).

emerald a clear, green gemstone variety of the mineral *beryl. It occurs naturally in Colombia, the Ural Mountains, in Russia, Zimbabwe, and Australia.

emergent properties features of a system that are due to the way in which its components are structured in relation to each other, rather than to the individual properties of those compo-nents. Thus the distinctive characteristics of chemical *compounds are emergent properties of the way in which the constituent elements are organized, and cannot be explained by the particular properties of those elements taken in isolation. In biology, *ecosystem stability is an emergent property of the interaction between the constituent species, and not a property of the species themselves.

Emerson Ralph Waldo 1803–1882. US philosopher, essayist, and poet. He settled in Concord, Massachusetts, which he made a centre of *transcendentalism, and wrote *Nature* 1836, which states the movement's main principles emphasizing the value of self-reliance and the Godlike nature of human souls. His two volumes of *Essays* (1841, 1844) made his reputation: 'Self-Reliance' and 'Compensation' are among the best known.

emery greyish-black opaque metamorphic rock consisting of *corundum and magnetite, together with other minerals such as hematite. It is used as an *abrasive.

emetic any substance administered to induce vomiting. Emetics are used to empty the stomach in many cases of deliberate or accidental ingestion of a poison. The most frequently used is ipecacuanha.

emf in physics, abbreviation for *electro-motive force*.

Emilia-Romagna region of N central Italy including much of the Po valley; area 22,100 sq km/8,531 sq mi; population (1988) 3,924,000. The capital is Bologna; other towns include Reggio, Rimini, Parma, Ferrara, and Ravenna. Agricultural produce includes fruit, wine, sugar beet, beef, and dairy products; oil and natural-gas resources have been developed in the Po valley.

éminence grise (French 'grey eminence') a power behind a throne: that is, a manipulator of power without immediate responsibility. The nickname was originally applied (because of his grey cloak) to the French monk François Leclerc du Tremblay (1577–1638), also known as Père Joseph, who in 1612 became the close friend and behind-the-scenes adviser of Cardinal Richelieu.

eminent domain in the USA, the right of federal and state government and other authorized bodies to compulsorily purchase land that is needed for public purposes. The owner is entitled to receive a fair price for the land.

Emin Pasha Mehmed. Adopted name of Eduard Schnitzer 1849–1892. German explorer, doctor, and linguist. Appointed by General Gordon as chief medical officer and then governor of the Equatorial province of S Sudan, he carried out extensive research in anthropology, botany, zoology, and meteorology.

emotivism a philosophical position in the theory of ethics. Emotivists deny that moral judgements can be true or false, maintaining that they merely express an attitude or an emotional response.

Empedocles c. 490–430 BC. Greek philosopher and scientist. He lived at Acragas (Agrigentum) in Sicily, and proposed that the universe is composed of four elements – fire, air, earth, and water – which through the action of love and discord are eternally constructed, destroyed, and constructed anew. According to tradition, he committed suicide by throwing himself into the crater of Mount Etna.

emphysema incurable lung condition characterized by disabling breathlessness. Progressive loss of the thin walls dividing the air spaces (alveoli) in the lungs reduces the area available for the exchange of oxygen and carbon dioxide, causing the lung tissue to expand. The term 'emphysema' can also refer to any abnormal swelling of body tissues caused by the accumulation of air.

empiricism (Greek *empeiria* 'experience' or 'experiment') in philosophy, the belief that all knowledge is ultimately derived from sense experience. It is suspicious of metaphysical schemes based on *a priori* propositions, which are claimed to be true irrespective of experience. It is frequently contrasted with *rationalism.

Employment, Department of (DE) UK government department responsible for policies relating to workers, the promotion of equal employment opportunities, the payment of unemployment benefits, the collection of labour statistics, the overseeing of industrial relations, and the administration of employment legislation.

employment exchange agency for bringing together employers requiring labour and workers seeking employment. Employment exchanges may be organized by central government or a local authority (formerly known in the UK as Job Centres), or as private business ventures (employment agencies).

employment law law covering the rights and duties of employers and employees. During the 20th century, statute law rather than common law has increasingly been used to give new rights to employees. Industrial tribunals are statutory bodies that adjudicate in disputes between employers and employees or trade unions and deal with complaints concerning unfair dismissal, sex or race discrimination, and equal pay.

EMS abbreviation for *European Monetary System*.

emu flightless bird *Dromaius novaehollandiae* native to Australia. It stands about 1.8 m/6 ft high and has coarse brown plumage, small rudimentary wings, short feathers on the head and neck, and powerful legs, well adapted for running and kicking. The female has a curious bag or pouch in the windpipe that enables her to emit the characteristic loud booming note.

EMU abbreviation for *economic and monetary union*, the proposed European Community policy for a single currency and common economic policies.

emulator in computing, an item of software or firmware that allows one device to imitate the functioning of another. Emulator software is commonly used to allow one make of computer to run programs written for a different make of computer. This allows a user to select from a wider range of *applications programs, and perhaps to save money by running programs designed for an expensive computer on a cheaper model.

emulsifier food *additive used to keep oils dispersed and in suspension, in products such as mayonnaise and peanut butter. Egg yolk is a naturally occurring emulsifier, but most of the emulsifiers in commercial use today are synthetic chemicals.

emulsion a stable dispersion of a liquid in another liquid – for example, oil and water in some cosmetic lotions.

enamel vitrified (glass-like) coating of various colours used for decorative purposes on a metallic or porcelain surface. In *cloisonné* the various sections of the design are separated by thin metal wires or strips. In *champlevé* the enamel is poured into engraved cavities in the metal surface.

encaustic painting an ancient technique of painting, commonly used by the Egyptians, Greeks, and Romans, in which coloured pigments were mixed with molten wax and painted on panels.

encephalitis inflammation of the brain, nearly always due to virus infection but also to parasites, fungi, or malaria. It varies widely in severity, from short-lived, relatively slight effects of headache, drowsiness, and fever to paralysis, coma, and death. One such type of viral infection is also sometimes called 'sleeping sickness'.

Encke's comet comet with the shortest known orbital period, 3.3 years. It is named after German mathematician and astronomer Johann Franz Encke (1791–1865) who calculated the orbit in 1819 from earlier sightings.

enclosure appropriation of common land as private property, or the changing of open-field systems to enclosed fields (often used for sheep). This process began in Britain in the 14th century and became widespread in the 15th and 16th centuries. It caused poverty, homelessness, and rural depopulation, and resulted in revolts 1536, 1569, and 1607.

encumbrance in law, a right or interest in land, for example a mortgage, lease, restrictive covenant, or right of way, which benefits someone other than the owner of the land.

encyclopedia or *encyclopaedia* work of reference covering either all fields of knowledge or one specific subject. Although most encyclopedias are alphabetical, with cross-references, some are organized thematically with indexes, to keep related subjects together.

endangered species plant or animal species whose numbers are so few that it is at risk of becoming extinct. A quarter of the world's plants are in danger of becoming extinct by the year 2020. Officially designated endangered species are listed by the International Union for the Conservation of Nature.

endive cultivated annual plant *Cichorium endivia*, family Compositae, the leaves of which are used in salads and cooking. One variety has narrow, curled leaves; another has wide, smooth leaves. It is related to *chicory.

endocrine gland gland that secretes hormones into the bloodstream to regulate body processes. Endocrine glands are most highly developed in vertebrates, but are also found in other animals, notably insects. In humans the main endocrine glands are the pituitary, thyroid, parathyroid, adrenal, pancreas, ovary, and testis.

endometriosis common gynaecological complaint in which patches of endometrium (the lining of the womb) are found outside the uterus.

endoplasmic reticulum (ER) membranous system of tubes, channels, and flattened sacs that form compartments within cells in *eukaryotes (organisms other than bacteria). The ER stores and transports proteins within cells and also carries various enzymes needed for the synthesis of *fats. The *ribosomes, or the organelles that carry out protein synthesis, are attached to parts of the ER.

endorphin natural substance (a polypeptide) that modifies the action of nerve cells. Endorphins are produced by the pituitary gland and hypothalamus of vertebrates. They lower the perception of pain by reducing the transmission of signals between nerve cells.

endorsement in law, the procedure by which a court notes the particulars of a driving offence on an offender's driving licence. Endorsements are given on conviction for most traffic offences, except parking offences and causing an obstruction.

endoscopy examination of internal organs or tissues by an instrument allowing direct vision. An endoscope is equipped with an eyepiece, lenses, and its own light source to illuminate the field of vision. The endoscope that examines the alimentary canal is a flexible fibreoptic instrument swallowed by the patient.

endoskeleton the internal supporting structure of vertebrates, made up of cartilage or bone. It provides support, and acts as a system of levers to which muscles are attached to provide movement. Certain parts of the skeleton (the skull and ribs) give protection to vital body organs.

endosperm nutritive tissue in the seeds of most flowering plants. It surrounds the embryo and is produced by an unusual process that parallels the *fertilization of the ovum by a male gamete. A second male gamete from the pollen grain fuses with two female nuclei within the *embryo sac. Thus endosperm cells are triploid (having three sets of chromosomes); they contain food reserves such as starch, fat, and protein that are utilized by the developing seedling.

endotherm 'warm-blooded', or homeothermic, animal. Endotherms have internal mechanisms for regulating their body temperatures to levels different from the environmental temperature. See *homeothermy.

endothermic reaction chemical reaction that requires an input of energy in the form of heat for it to proceed; the energy is absorbed from the surroundings by the reactants.

endowment insurance a type of life insurance that may produce profits. An endowment policy will run for a fixed number of years during which it accumulates a cash value; it can provide a savings plan for a retirement fund, and may be used to help with a house purchase, linked to a building society mortgage.

Endymion in Greek mythology, a beautiful young man loved by Selene, the Moon goddess. He was granted eternal sleep in order to remain forever young. Keats's poem *Endymion* 1818 is an allegory of searching for perfection.

energy capacity for doing *work. Potential energy (PE) is energy deriving from position; thus a stretched spring has elastic PE, and an object raised to a height above the Earth's surface, or the water in an elevated reservoir, has gravitational PE. A lump of coal and a tank of petrol, together with the oxygen needed for their combustion, have chemical energy. Other sorts of energy include electrical and nuclear energy, and light and sound. Moving bodies possess kinetic energy (KE). Energy can be converted from one form to another, but the total quantity stays the same (in accordance with the *conservation of energy principle that governs many natural phenomena). For example, as an apple falls, it loses gravitational PE but gains KE.

energy, alternative energy from sources that are renewable and ecologically safe, as opposed to sources that are nonrenewable with toxic by-products, such as coal, oil, or gas (fossil fuels), and uranium (for nuclear power). The most important alternative energy source is flowing water, harnessed as *hydroelectric power. Other sources include the oceans' tides and waves (see *tidal power station and *wave power), wind (harnessed by windmills and wind turbines), the Sun (*solar energy), and the heat trapped in the Earth's crust (*geothermal energy).

energy conservation methods of reducing energy use through insulation, increasing energy efficiency, and changes in patterns of use. Profligate energy use by industrialized countries contributes greatly to air pollution and the *greenhouse effect when it draws on nonrenewable energy sources.

energy of reaction energy released or absorbed during a chemical reaction, also called *enthalpy of reaction* or *heat of reaction*. In a chemical reaction, the energy stored in the reacting molecules is rarely the same as that stored in the product molecules. Depending on which is the greater, energy is either released (an exothermic reaction) or absorbed (an endothermic reaction) from the surroundings (see *conservation of energy). The amount of energy released or absorbed by the quantities of substances represented by the chemical equation is the energy of reaction.

Engels Friedrich 1820–1895. German social and political philosopher, a friend of, and collaborator with, Karl *Marx on *The Communist Manifesto* 1848 and other key works. His later interpretations of Marxism, and his own philosophical and historical studies such as *Origins of the Family, Private Property, and the State* 1884 (which linked patriarchy with the development of private property), developed such concepts as historical materialism.

engine device for converting stored energy into useful work or movement. Most engines use a fuel as their energy store. The fuel is burnt to produce heat energy – hence the name 'heat engine' – which is then converted into movement. Heat engines can be classified according to the fuel they use (*petrol engine or *diesel engine), or according to whether the fuel is burnt inside (*internal combustion engine) or outside (*steam engine) the engine, or according to whether they produce a reciprocating or rotary motion (*turbine or *Wankel engine).

engineering the application of science to the

design, construction, and maintenance of works, machinery, roads, railways, bridges, harbour installations, engines, ships, aircraft and airports, spacecraft and space stations, and the generation, transmission, and use of electrical power. The main divisions of engineering are aerospace, chemical, civil, electrical, electronic, gas, marine, materials, mechanical, mining, production, radio, and structural.

England largest division of the *United Kingdom
area 130,357 sq km/50,318 sq mi
capital London
towns Birmingham, Cambridge, Coventry, Leeds, Leicester, Manchester, Newcastle-upon-Tyne, Nottingham, Oxford, Sheffield, York; ports Bristol, Dover, Felixstowe, Harwich, Liverpool, Portsmouth, Southampton
exports cereals, rape, sugar beet, potatoes; meat and meat products; electronic (software) and telecommunications equipment; scientific instruments; textiles and fashion goods; North Sea oil and gas, petrochemicals, pharmaceuticals, fertilizers. Tourism is important.
currency pound sterling
population (1986) 47,255,000
languages English; over 100 minority languages
religions Christian, with the Church of England as the established church, 31,500,000; and various Protestant groups, of which the largest is the Methodist 1,400,000; Roman Catholic about 5,000,000; Muslim 900,000; Jewish 410,000; Sikh 175,000; Hindu 140,000.
For **history**, see *Britain, ancient; *England: history; *United Kingdom.

England: history for earlier history, see *Britain, ancient.
AD 43 Roman invasion.
5th–7th centuries Anglo-Saxons overran all England except Cornwall and Cumberland, forming independent kingdoms including Northumbria, Mercia, Kent, and Wessex.
c. 597 England converted to Christianity by St Augustine.
829 Egbert of Wessex accepted as overlord of all England.
878 Alfred ceded N and E England to the Danish invaders but kept them out of Wessex.
1066 Norman Conquest; England passed into French hands under William the Conqueror.
1172 Henry II became king of Ireland and established a colony there.
1215 King John forced to sign Magna Carta.
1284 Conquest of Wales, begun by the Normans, completed by Edward I.
1295 Model Parliament set up.
1338–1453 Hundred Years' War with France enabled parliament to secure control of taxation and, by impeachment, of the king's choice of ministers.
1348–49 Black Death killed 30% of the population.
1381 Social upheaval led to the *Peasants' Revolt, which was brutally repressed.
1399 Richard II deposed by Parliament for absolutism.
1414 Lollard revolt repressed.
1455–85 Wars of the Roses.
1497 Henry VII ended the power of the feudal nobility with the suppression of the Yorkist revolts.

1529 Henry VIII became head of the Church of England after breaking with Rome.
1536–43 Acts of Union united England and Wales after conquest.
1547 Edward VI adopted Protestant doctrines.
1553 Return to Roman Catholicism under Mary I.
1558 Elizabeth I adopted a religious compromise.
1588 Attempted invasion of England by the Spanish Armada.
1603 James I united the English and Scottish crowns; parliamentary dissidence increased.
1642–52 Civil War between royalists and parliamentarians, resulting in victory for Parliament.
1649 Charles I executed and the Commonwealth set up.
1653 Oliver Cromwell appointed Lord Protector.
1660 Restoration of Charles II.
1685 Monmouth's rebellion.
1688 William of Orange invited to take the throne; flight of James II.
1707 Act of Union between England and Scotland under Queen Anne, after which the countries became known as Great Britain. For further history, see *United Kingdom.

English Channel stretch of water between England and France, leading in the W to the Atlantic Ocean, and in the east via the Strait of Dover to the North Sea; also known as **La Manche** (French 'the sleeve') from its shape.

English horn alternative name for *cor anglais, musical instrument of the oboe family.

English language member of the Germanic branch of the Indo-European language family. It is traditionally described as having passed through four major stages over about 1,500 years: **Old English** or **Anglo-Saxon** (c. 500–1050), rooted in the dialects of invading settlers (Jutes, Saxons, Angles, and Frisians); **Middle English** (c. 1050–1550), influenced by Norman French after the Conquest 1066 and by ecclesiastical Latin; **Early Modern English** (c. 1550–1700), including a standardization of the diverse influences of Middle English; and **Late Modern English** (c. 1700 onwards), including in particular the development and spread of current Standard English. Through extensive exploration, colonization, and trade, English spread worldwide from the 17th century onwards and remains the most important international language of trade and technology. It is used in many variations, for example, British, American, Canadian, West Indian, Indian, Singaporean, and Nigerian English, and many pidgins and creoles.

English law one of the major European legal systems, *Roman law being the other. English law has spread to many other countries, including former English colonies such as the USA, Canada, Australia, and New Zealand.

engraving art of creating a design by means of inscribing blocks of metal, wood, or some other hard material with a point. **Intaglio prints** are made mainly on metal by *dry point, and *etching.

enharmonic in music, a harmony capable of different interpretations, or of leading into different keys.

enlightenment in Buddhism, the term used to translate the Sanskrit *bodhi*, awakening: perceiving the reality of the world, or the unreality of the self, and becoming liberated from suffering (Sanskrit *duhkha*). It is the gateway to nirvana.

Enlightenment European intellectual movement that reached its high point in the 18th century. Enlightenment thinkers were believers in social progress and in the liberating possibilities of rational and scientific knowledge. They were often critical of existing society and were hostile to religion, which they saw as keeping the human mind chained down by superstition.

enosis (Greek 'union') movement, developed from 1930, for the union of *Cyprus with Greece. The campaign (led by *EOKA and supported by Archbishop Makarios) intensified from the 1950s. In 1960 independence from Britain, without union, was granted, and increased demands for union led to its proclamation 1974. As a result, Turkey invaded Cyprus, ostensibly to protect the Turkish community, and the island was effectively partitioned.

entail in law, the settlement of land or other property on a successive line of people, usually succeeding generations of the original owner's family. An entail can be either *general*, in which case it simply descends to the heirs, or *special*, when it descends according to a specific arrangement – for example, to children by a named wife.

Entebbe town in Uganda, on the NW shore of Lake Victoria, 20 km/12 mi SW of Kampala, the capital; 1,136 m/3,728 ft above sea level; population (1983) 21,000. Founded 1893, it was the administrative centre of Uganda 1894–1962.

Entente Cordiale (French 'friendly understanding') agreement reached by Britain and France 1904 recognizing British interests in Egypt and French interests in Morocco. It formed the basis for Anglo-French cooperation before the outbreak of World War I 1914.

enterprise zone special zone designated by government to encourage industrial and commercial activity, usually in economically depressed areas. Investment is attracted by means of tax reduction and other financial incentives.

enthalpy in chemistry, alternative term for *energy of reaction, the heat energy associated with a chemical change.

entomology study of *insects.

entrepreneur in business, a person who successfully manages and develops an enterprise through personal skill and initiative. Examples include John D *Rockefeller and Henry *Ford.

entropy in *thermodynamics, a parameter representing the state of disorder of a system at the atomic, ionic, or molecular level; the greater the disorder, the higher the entropy. Thus the fast-moving disordered molecules of water vapour have higher entropy than those of more ordered liquid water, which in turn have more entropy than the molecules in solid crystalline ice.

E number code number for additives that have been approved for use by the European Commission (EC). The E written before the number stands for European. E numbers do not have to be displayed on lists of ingredients, and the manufacturer may choose to list *additives by their name instead. E numbers cover all categories of additives apart from flavourings. Additives,

other than flavourings, that are not approved by the EC, but are still used in Britain, are represented by a code number without an E.

Enver Pasha 1881–1922. Turkish politician and soldier. He led the military revolt 1908 that resulted in the Young Turks' revolution (see *Turkey). He was killed fighting the Bolsheviks in Turkestan.

environment in ecology, the sum of conditions affecting a particular organism, including physical surroundings, climate, and influences of other living organisms. See also *biosphere and *habitat.

Environmentally Sensitive Area (ESA) scheme introduced by the UK Ministry of Agriculture 1984, as a result of EC legislation, to protect some of the most beautiful areas of the British countryside from the loss and damage caused by agricultural change. The first areas to be designated ESAs are in the Pennine Dales, the North Peak District, the Norfolk Broads, the Breckland, the Suffolk River Valleys, the Test Valley, the South Downs, the Somerset Levels and Moors, West Penwith, Cornwall, the Shropshire Borders, the Cambrian Mountains, and the Lleyn Peninsula.

Environmental Protection Agency (EPA) US agency set up 1970 to control water and air quality, industrial and commercial wastes, pesticides, noise, and radiation. In its own words, it aims to protect 'the country from being degraded, and its health threatened, by a multitude of human activities initiated without regard to long-ranging effects upon the life-supporting properties, the economic uses, and the recreational value of air, land, and water'.

environment–heredity controversy see *nature–nurture controversy*.

enzyme biological *catalyst produced in cells, and capable of speeding up the chemical reactions necessary for life by converting one molecule (substrate) into another. Enzymes are not themselves destroyed by this process. They are large, complex *proteins, and are highly specific, each chemical reaction requiring its own particular enzyme. The enzyme fits into a 'slot' (active site) in the substrate molecule, forming an enzyme–substrate complex that lasts until the substrate is altered or split, after which the enzyme can fall away. The substrate may therefore be compared to a lock, and the enzyme to the key required to open it.

Eocene second epoch of the Tertiary period of geological time, 55–38 million years ago. Originally considered the earliest division of the Tertiary, the name means 'early recent', referring to the early forms of mammals evolving at the time, following the extinction of the dinosaurs.

EOKA acronym for *Ethnikí Organósis Kipriakóu Agónos* (National Organization of Cypriot Struggle) an underground organization formed by General George *Grivas 1955 to fight for the independence of Cyprus from Britain and ultimately its union (*enosis*) with Greece. In 1971, 11 years after the independence of Cyprus, Grivas returned to the island to form EOKA B and to resume the fight for *enosis*, which had not been achieved by the Cypriot government.

Eos in Greek mythology, the goddess of the dawn, equivalent to the Roman Aurora.

ephedrine drug that acts like adrenaline on the sympathetic *nervous system (sympathomimetic). Once used to relieve bronchospasm in *asthma, it has been superseded by safer, more specific drugs. It is contained in some cold remedies as a decongestant. Side effects include rapid heartbeat, tremor, dry mouth, and anxiety.

ephemeral plant plant with a very short life cycle, sometimes as little as six or eight weeks. It may complete several generations in one growing season.

Ephesus ancient Greek seaport in Asia Minor, a centre of the *Ionian Greeks, with a temple of Artemis destroyed by the Goths AD 262. Now in Turkey, it is one of the world's largest archaeological sites. St Paul is said to have visited the city, and addressed a letter (*epistle) to the Christians there.

epic narrative poem or cycle of poems dealing with some great deed – often the founding of a nation or the forging of national unity – and often using religious or cosmological themes. The two major epic poems in the Western tradition are *The Iliad* and *The Odyssey*, attributed to Homer, and which were probably intended to be chanted in sections at feasts.

epicentre the point on the Earth's surface immediately above the seismic focus of an *earthquake. Most damage usually takes place at an earthquake's epicentre. The term sometimes refers to a point directly above or below a nuclear explosion ('at ground zero').

Epictetus c. AD 55–135. Greek Stoic philosopher who encouraged people to refrain from self-interest and to promote the common good of humanity. He believed that people were in the hands of an all-wise providence and that they should endeavour to do their duty in the position to which they were called.

Epicureanism system of philosophy that claims soundly based human happiness is the highest good, so that its rational pursuit should be adopted. It was named after the Greek philosopher Epicurus. The most distinguished Roman Epicurean was *Lucretius.

Epicurus 341–270 BC. Greek philosopher, founder of Epicureanism, who taught at Athens from 306 BC.

epicyclic gear or *sun-and-planet gear* gear system that consists of one or more gear wheels moving around another. Epicyclic gears are found in bicycle hub gears and in automatic gearboxes.

epicycloid in geometry, a curve resembling a series of arches traced out by a point on the circumference of a circle that rolls around another circle of a different diameter. If the two circles have the same diameter, the curve is a *cardioid.

Epidaurus or *Epidavros* ancient Greek city and port on the E coast of Argolis, in the NE Peloponnese. The site contains a well-preserved theatre of the 4th century BC; nearby are the ruins of the temple of Aesculapius, the god of healing.

epidemic outbreak of infectious disease affecting large numbers of people at the same time. A widespread epidemic that sweeps across many countries (such as the *Black Death in the late Middle Ages) is known as a *pandemic*.

epidermis outermost layer of *cells on an organism's body. In plants and many invertebrates such as insects, it consists of a single layer of cells. In vertebrates, it consists of several layers of cells.

epiglottis small flap found in the throats of mammals. It moves during swallowing to prevent food from passing into the windpipe and causing choking.

epigram short poem, originally a religious inscription but later a short, witty, and pithy saying.

epilepsy medical disorder characenized by a tendency to develop fits, which are convulsions or abnormal feelings caused by abnormal electrical discharges in the cerebral hemispheres of the *brain. Epilepsy can be controlled with a number of *anticonvulsant drugs.

Epiphany festival of the Christian church, held 6 Jan, celebrating the coming of the Magi (the three Wise Men) to Bethlehem with gifts for the infant Jesus, and symbolizing the manifestation of Jesus to the world. It is the 12th day after Christmas, and marks the end of the Christmas festivities.

epiphyte any plant that grows on another plant or object above the surface of the ground, and has no roots in the soil. An epiphyte does not parasitize the plant it grows on but merely uses it for support. Its nutrients are obtained from rainwater, organic debris such as leaf litter, or from the air.

Epirus (Greek *Ipiros*) region of NW Greece; area 9,200 sq km/3,551 sq mi; population (1981) 325,000. Its capital is Yannina, and it consists of the provinces (nomes) of Arta, Thesprotia, Yannina, and Preveza. There is livestock farming.

episcopacy in the Christian church, a system of government in which administrative and spiritual power over a district (diocese) is held by a bishop.

Episcopalianism US term for the Anglican Communion.

epistemology branch of philosophy that examines the nature of knowledge and attempts to determine the limits of human understanding. Central issues include how knowledge is derived and how it is to be validated and tested.

epistle in the New Testament, any of the 21 letters to individuals or to the members of various churches written by Christian leaders, including the 13 written by St *Paul. The term also describes a letter with a suggestion of pomposity and literary affectation, and a letter addressed to someone in the form of a poem, as in the epistles of *Horace and *Pope.

EPLF abbreviation for *Eritrean People's Liberation Front*; see *Eritrea.

EPNS abbreviation for *electroplated nickel silver*; see *electroplating.

epoch subdivision of a geological period in the geological time scale. Epochs are sometimes given their own names (such as the Palaeocene, Eocene, Oligocene, Miocene, and Pliocene epochs comprising the Tertiary period), or they are referred to as the late, early, or middle portions of a given period (as the Late Cretaceous or the Middle Triassic epoch).

epoxy resin synthetic *resin used as an *adhesive and as an ingredient in paints. Household epoxy resin adhesives come in component form as two separate tubes of chemical, one tube containing resin, the other a curing agent (hardener). The two chemicals are mixed just before application, and the mix soon sets hard.

EPROM (acronym for **erasable programmable read-only memory**) computer memory device in the form of an *integrated circuit (chip) that can record data and retain it indefinitely. The data can be erased by exposure to ultraviolet light, and new data recorded. Other kinds of computer memory chips are *ROM (read-only memory), *PROM (programmable read-only memory), and *RAM (random-access memory).

Epsom salts $MgSO_4.7H_2O$ hydrated magnesium sulphate, used as a relaxant and laxative and added to baths to soothe the skin. The name is derived from a bitter saline spring at Epsom, Surrey, England, which contains the salt in solution.

Epstein Jacob 1880–1959. British sculptor, born in New York. He experimented with abstract forms, but is chiefly known for his controversial muscular nude figures such as *Genesis* 1931 (Whitworth Art Gallery, Manchester). He was better appreciated as a portraitist (bust of Einstein, 1933), and in later years executed several monumental figures, notably the expressive bronze of *St Michael and the Devil* 1959 (Coventry Cathedral).

equal opportunities the right to be employed or considered for employment without discrimination on the grounds of race, gender, physical or mental handicap.

Equal Opportunities Commission commission established by the UK government 1975 to implement the Sex Discrimination Act 1975. Its aim is to prevent discrimination, particularly on sexual or marital grounds.

equation in mathematics, expression that represents the equality of two expressions involving constants and/or variables, and thus usually includes an equals sign (=). For example, the equation $A = \pi r^2$ equates the area A of a circle of radius r to the product πr^2. The algebraic equation $y = mx + c$ is the general one in coordinate geometry for a straight line.

equation in chemistry, representation of a chemical reaction by symbols and numbers; see *chemical equation.

equator the *terrestrial equator* is the *great circle whose plane is perpendicular to the Earth's axis (the line joining the poles). Its length is 40,092 km/24,901.8 mi, divided into 360 degrees of longitude. The *celestial equator* is the circle in which the plane of the Earth's equator intersects the *celestial sphere.

Equatorial Guinea Republic of (*República de Guinea Ecuatorial*)
area 28,051 sq km/10,828 sq mi
capital Malabo (Bioko)
towns Bata, Mbini (Río Muni)
physical comprises mainland Río Muni, plus the small islands of Corisco, Elobey Grande and

Elobey Chico, and Bioko (formerly Fernando Po) together with Annobón (formerly Pagalu)
head of state and government Teodoro Obiang Nguema Mbasogo from 1979
political system one-party military republic
political party Democratic Party of Equatorial Guinea (PDGE), militarily controlled
exports cocoa, coffee, timber
currency ekuele; CFA franc
population (1993 est) 390,000 (plus 110,000 estimated to live in exile abroad); growth rate 2.2% p.a.
languages Spanish (official); pidgin English is widely spoken, and on Annobón (whose people were formerly slaves of the Portuguese) a Portuguese dialect; Fang and other African dialects spoken on Río Muni
religions nominally Christian, mainly Catholic, but in 1978 Roman Catholicism was banned
GNP $330 per head (1991)
chronology
1778 Fernando Po (Bioko Island) ceded to Spain.
1885 Mainland territory came under Spanish rule; colony known as Spanish Guinea.
1968 Independence achieved from Spain. Francisco Macias Nguema became first president, soon assuming dictatorial powers.
1979 Macias overthrown and replaced by his nephew, Teodoro Obiang Nguema Mbasogo, who established a military regime. Macias tried and executed.
1982 Obiang elected president unopposed for another seven years. New constitution adopted.
1989 Obiang re-elected president.
1992 New constitution adopted; elections held, but president continued to nominate those for top government posts.

equestrianism skill in horse riding, as practised under International Equestrian Federation rules. An Olympic sport, there are three main branches of equestrianism: showjumping, dressage, and three-day eventing.

equilateral of a geometrical figure, having all sides of equal length.

equilibrium in physics, an unchanging condition in which the forces acting on a particle or system of particles (a body) cancel out, or in which energy is distributed among the particles of a system in the most probable way; or the state in which a body is at rest or moving at constant velocity. A body is in **thermal equilibrium** with its surroundings if no heat enters or leaves it, so that all its parts are at the same temperature as the surroundings.

equinox the points in spring and autumn at which the Sun's path, the *ecliptic, crosses the celestial equator, so that the day and night are of approximately equal length. The **vernal equinox** occurs about 21 March and the **autumnal equinox**, 23 Sept.

equity system of law supplementing the ordinary rules of law where the application of these would operate harshly in a particular case; sometimes it is regarded as an attempt to achieve 'natural justice'. So understood, equity appears as an element in most legal systems, and in a number of legal codes judges are instructed to apply both the rules of strict law and the principles of equity in reaching their decisions.

equity a company's assets, less its liabilities, which are the property of the owner or shareholders. Popularly, equities are stocks and shares which do not pay interest at fixed rates but pay dividends based on the company's performance. The value of equities tends to rise over the long term, but in the short term they are a risk investment because of fluctuating values. Equity is also used to refer to the paid value of mortgaged real property, most commonly a house.

Equity common name for the *British Actors' Equity Association*, the UK trade union for professional actors in theatre, film, and television, founded 1929. In the USA its full name is the *American Actors' Equity Association* and it deals only with performers in the theatre.

era any of the major divisions of geological time, each including several periods, but smaller than an eon. The currently recognized eras all fall within the Phanerozoic eon – or the vast span of time, starting about 590 million years ago, when fossils are found to become abundant. The eras in ascending order are the Palaeozoic, Mesozoic, and Cenozoic. We are living in the Recent epoch of the Quaternary period of the Cenozoic era.

Erasmus Desiderius *c.* 1466–1536. Dutch scholar and leading humanist of the Renaissance era, who taught and studied all over Europe and was a prolific writer. His pioneer translation of the Greek New Testament 1516 exposed the Vulgate as a second-hand document. Although opposed to dogmatism and abuse of church power, he remained impartial during Martin *Luther's conflict with the pope.

Erastianism belief that the church should be subordinated to the state. The name is derived from Thomas Erastus (1534–83), a German-Swiss theologian and opponent of Calvinism, who maintained in his writings that the church should not have the power of excluding people as a punishment for sin.

Eratosthenes *c.* 276–194 BC. Greek geographer and mathematician whose map of the ancient world was the first to contain lines of latitude and longitude, and who calculated the Earth's circumference with an error of about 10%. His mathematical achievements include a method for duplicating the cube, and for finding *prime numbers (Eratosthenes' sieve).

Eratosthenes' sieve a method for finding *prime numbers. It involves writing in sequence all numbers from 2. Then, starting with 2, cross out every second number (but not 2 itself), thus eliminating numbers that can be divided by 2. Next, starting with 3, cross out every third number (but not 3 itself), and continue the process for 5, 7, 11, 13, and so on. The numbers that remain are primes.

erbium soft, lustrous, greyish, metallic element of the *lanthanide series, symbol Er, atomic number 68, relative atomic mass 167.26. It occurs with the element yttrium or as a minute part of various minerals. It was discovered 1843 by Carl Mosander (1797–1858), and named after the town of Ytterby, Sweden, where the lanthanides (rare-earth elements) were first found.

Erebus, Mount the world's southernmost active volcano, 3,794 m/12,452 ft high, on Ross Island, Antarctica.

Erebus in Greek mythology, the god of darkness and the intermediate region between upper Earth and *Hades.

Erfurt city in Germany on the river Gera, capital of the state of Thuringia; population (1990) 217,000. It is in a rich horticultural area, and its industries include textiles, typewriters, and electrical goods.

ergonomics study of the relationship between people and the furniture, tools, and machinery they use at work. The object is to improve work performance by removing sources of muscular stress and general fatigue: for example, by presenting data and control panels in easy-to-view form, making office furniture comfortable, and creating a generally pleasant environment.

ergot certain parasitic fungi (especially of the genus *Claviceps*), whose brown or black grain-like masses replace the kernels of rye or other cereals. *C. purpurea* attacks the rye plant. Ergot poisoning is caused by eating infected bread, resulting in burning pains, gangrene, and convulsions.

ergotamine *alkaloid $C_{33}H_{35}O_5N_5$ administered to treat migraine. Isolated from ergot, a fungus that colonizes rye, it relieves symptoms by causing the cranial arteries to constrict. Its use is limited by severe side effects, including nausea and abdominal pain.

Erhard Ludwig 1897–1977. West German Christian Democrat politician, chancellor of the Federal Republic 1963–66. The 'economic miracle' of West Germany's recovery after World War II is largely attributed to Erhard's policy of social free enterprise (German *Marktwirtschaft*), which he initiated during his period as federal economics minister (1949–63).

erica in botany, any plant of the genus *Erica*, family Ericaceae, including the heathers. There are about 500 species, distributed mainly in South Africa with some in Europe.

Ericsson John 1803–1889. Swedish-born US engineer who took out a patent to produce screw-propeller powered paddle-wheel ships 1836. He built a number of such ships, including the *Monitor*, which was successfully deployed during the American Civil War.

Ericsson Leif *c.* AD 1000. Norse explorer, son of Eric the Red, who sailed west from Greenland about 1000 to find a country first sighted by Norsemen 986. Landing with 35 companions in North America, he called it Vinland, because he discovered grape vines growing there.

Eric the Red 940–1010. Allegedly the first European to find Greenland. According to a 13th-century saga, he was the son of a Norwegian chieftain, and was banished from Iceland about 982 for murder. He then sailed westward and discovered a land that he called Greenland.

Eridu ancient city of Mesopotamia about 5000 BC, according to tradition the cradle of Sumerian civilization. On its site is now the village of Tell Abu Shahrain, Iraq.

Erie, Lake fourth largest of the Great Lakes of North America, connected to Lake Ontario by the Niagara River and bypassed by the Welland Canal; area 9,930 sq mi/25,720 sq km.

Eritrea State of
area 125,000 sq km/48,250 sq mi

capital Asmara
towns Keren, Adigrat; ports: Asab, Massawa
physical coastline along the Red Sea 1,000 km/
620 mi; narrow coastal plain that rises to an
inland plateau
head of state and government Issaias
Afwerki from 1993
political system emergent democracy
products coffee, salt, citrus fruits, grains, cotton
currency birr
population (1993 est) 3,500,000
languages Amharic (official), Tigrinya (official),
Arabic, Afar, Bilen, Hidareb, Kunama, Nara,
Rashaida, Saho, and Tigre
religions Muslim, Coptic Christian
GNP $77 per head (1991)
chronology
1962 Annexed by Ethiopia; secessionist movement began.
1974 Ethiopian emperor Haile Selassie deposed
by military; Eritrean People's Liberation Front
(EPLF) continued struggle for independence.
1990 Port of Massawa captured by Eritrean
forces.
1991 Ethiopian president Mengistu Haile
Mariam overthrown. EPLF secured whole of
Eritrea.
1993 Independence approved in regional referendum and formally recognized by Ethiopia.
Transitional government established for four-year
period. Issaias Afwerki elected president; independence formally declared.
1994 EPLF renamed the PFDJ. New national
assembly and state council created.

ERM abbreviation for *Exchange Rate
Mechanism.*

ermine the *stoat during winter, when its coat
becomes white. In northern latitudes the coat
becomes completely white, except for a black tip
on the tail, but in warmer regions the back may
remain brownish. The fur is used commercially.

Ernst Max 1891–1976. German Surrealist artist.
He worked in France 1922–38 and in the USA
from 1941. He was an active Dadaist, experimenting with collage, photomontage, and surreal
images, and helped found the Surrealist movement 1924.

Eros in Greek mythology, boy-god of love, traditionally armed with bow and arrows. He was the
son of *Aphrodite, and fell in love with *Psyche.
He is identified with the Roman Cupid.

Eros in astronomy, an asteroid, discovered 1898,
that can pass 22 million km/14 million mi from
the Earth, as observed in 1975. Eros was the
first asteroid to be discovered that has an orbit
coming within that of Mars. It is elongated, measures about 36 × 12 km/22 × 7 mi, rotates around
its shortest axis every 5.3 hours, and orbits the
Sun every 1.8 years.

erosion wearing away of the Earth's surface,
caused by the breakdown and transportation of
particles of rock or soil (by contrast, *weathering
does not involve transportation). Agents of erosion include the sea, rivers, glaciers, and wind.
Water, consisting of sea waves and currents,
rivers, and rain; ice, in the form of glaciers; and
wind, hurling sand fragments against exposed
rocks and moving dunes along, are the most
potent forces of erosion. People also contribute
to erosion by bad farming practices and the cut-

ting down of forests, which can lead to the formation of dust bowls.

erratic in geology, a displaced rock that has
been transported by a glacier or some other
natural force to a site of different geological composition. For example, in East Anglia, England,
erratics have been found that have been transported from as far away as Scotland and Scandinavia.

error in computing, a fault or mistake, either in
the software or on the part of the user, that causes
a program to stop running (crash) or produce
unexpected results. Program errors, or bugs, are
largely eliminated in the course of the programmer's initial testing procedure, but some will
remain in most programs. All computer operating
systems are designed to produce an **error
message** (on the display screen, or in an error
file or printout) whenever an error is detected,
reporting that an error has taken place and,
wherever possible, diagnosing its cause.

error detection in computing, the techniques
that enable a program to detect incorrect data.
A common method is to add a check digit to
important codes, such as account numbers and
product codes. The digit is chosen so that the
code conforms to a rule that the program can
verify. Another technique involves calculating the
sum (called the hash total) of each instance of a
particular item of data, and storing it at the end
of the data.

Ershad Hussain Mohammad 1930– . Military
ruler of Bangladesh 1982–90. He became chief of
staff of the Bangladeshi army 1979 and assumed
power in a military coup 1982. As president from
1983, Ershad introduced a successful rural-
oriented economic programme. He was re-
elected 1986 and lifted martial law, but faced
continuing political opposition, which forced
him to resign Dec 1990.

Erskine Ralph 1914– . British architect who
specialized in *community architecture before it
was named as such. A deep social consciousness
and a concern to mould building form in
response to climate determine his architecture.
His Byker Estate in Newcastle-upon-Tyne
(1969–80), where a great sheltering wall of dwellings embraces the development, involved a lengthy process of consultation with the residents. A
later project is the 'Ark', an office building in
Hammersmith, London (1989–91). Its shiplike
form shelters the internal activities from an
adjoining motorway.

Erté adopted name of Romain de Tirtoff
1892–1990. Russian designer and illustrator. He
was active in France and the USA. He was an
exponent of *Art Deco and designed sets and
costumes for opera, theatre, and ballet. His drawings were highly stylized and expressive, featuring elegant, curvilinear women.

erysipelas in medicine, an acute disease of the
skin or mucous membranes due to infection by
a streptococcus bacterium. Starting at some point
where the skin is broken or injured, the infection
spreads, producing a swollen red patch with
small blisters and generalized fever. The condition is now rare.

erythrocyte another name for *red blood cell.

erythropoietin in biology, a naturally occurring hormone that increases the production of red blood cells, which carry oxygen around the body. It is released in response to a lowered percentage of oxygen in the blood reaching the kidneys, such as in anaemic subjects. Recombinant erythropoietin is used therapeutically but also illegally by athletes to enhance their performance.

Esaki Leo 1925– . Japanese physicist who in 1957 noticed that electrons could sometimes 'tunnel' through the barrier formed at the junctions of certain semiconductors. The effect is now widely used in the electronics industry. For this early discovery Esaki shared the 1973 Nobel Prize for Physics with British physicist Brian Josephson and Norwegian-born US physicist Ivar Giaever (1929–).

escalator automatic moving staircase that carries people between floors or levels. It consists of treads linked in an endless belt arranged to form strips (steps), powered by an electric motor that moves both steps and handrails at the same speed. Towards the top and bottom the steps flatten out for ease of passage. The first escalator was exhibited in Paris 1900.

escape velocity in physics, minimum velocity with which an object must be projected for it to escape from the gravitational pull of a planetary body. In the case of the Earth, the escape velocity is 11.2 kps/6.9 mps; the Moon 2.4 kps/1.5 mps; Mars 5 kps/3.1 mps; and Jupiter 59.6 kps/37 mps.

Escher M(aurits) C(ornelis) 1902–1972. Dutch graphic artist. His prints are often based on mathematical concepts and contain paradoxes and illusions. The lithograph *Ascending and Descending* 1960, with interlocking staircases creating a perspective puzzle, is a typical work.

Escorial, El monastery and palace in the Guadarrama Mountains, 42 km/26 mi NW of Madrid, Spain. El Escorial was built 1536–84 for Philip II. Designed by Juan Bautista de Toledo and Juan de Herrera, it houses a famous art collection and a fine library.

Esenin or **Yesenin**, Sergey 1895–1925. Soviet poet, born in Konstantinovo (renamed Esenino in his honour). He went to Petrograd 1915, attached himself to the Symbolists, welcomed the Russian Revolution, revived peasant traditions and folklore, and initiated the Imaginist group of poets 1919. A selection of his poetry was translated in *Confessions of a Hooligan* 1973. He was married briefly to US dancer Isadora Duncan 1922–23.

esker geologic feature of formerly glaciated areas consisting of a long, steep-walled narrow ridge, often sinuous and sometimes branching. Eskers consist of stratified glacial drift and are thought to form by the deposits of streams running through tunnels underneath melting stagnant ice. When the glacier finally disappeared, the old stream deposits were left standing as a high ridge. Eskers vary in height 3–30 m/ 10–100 ft and can run to about 160 km/100 mi in length.

Eskimo (Algonquian 'eater of raw meat') member of a group of Asian, North American, and Greenland Arctic peoples who migrated east from Siberia about 2,000 years ago, exploiting the marine coastal environment and the tundra.

Eskişehir city in Turkey, 200 km/125 mi W of Ankara; population (1985) 367,000. Products include meerschaum, chromium, magnesite, cotton goods, tiles, and aircraft.

ESP abbreviation for **extrasensory perception*.

esparto grass *Stipa tenacissima*, native to S Spain, S Portugal, and the Balearics, but now widely grown in dry, sandy locations throughout the world. The plant is just over 1 m/3 ft high, producing greyish-green leaves, which are used for making paper, ropes, baskets, mats, and cables.

Esperanto language devised 1887 by Polish philologist Ludwig L Zamenhof (1859–1917) as an international auxiliary language. For its structure and vocabulary it draws on Latin, the Romance languages, English, and German.

espionage the practice of spying; a way to gather *intelligence.

Esquipulas pilgrimage town in Chiquimula department, SE Guatemala; seat of the 'Black Christ' which is a symbol of peace throughout Central America. In May 1986 five Central American presidents met here to discuss a plan for peace in the region.

essay short piece of nonfiction, often dealing from a personal point of view with some particular subject. The essay became a recognized genre with the French writer Montaigne's *Essais* 1580. Francis Bacon's *Essays* 1597 are among the most famous in English. From the 19th century the essay was increasingly used in Europe and the USA as a vehicle for literary criticism.

Essen city in North Rhine–Westphalia, Germany; population (1988) 615,000. It is the administrative centre of the Ruhr, with textile, chemical, and electrical industries.

Essene member of an ancient Jewish religious sect located in the area near the Dead Sea *c*. 200 BC–AD 200, whose members lived a life of denial and asceticism, as they believed that the day of judgement was imminent.

Essequibo the longest river in Guyana, South America, rising in the Guiana Highlands of S Guyana; length 1,014 km/630 mi. Part of the district of Essequibo, which lies to the west of the river, is claimed by Venezuela.

Essex county in SE England
area 3,670 sq km/1,417 sq mi
towns Chelmsford (administrative headquarters), Colchester; ports: Harwich, Tilbury; resorts: Southend, Clacton
features Epping Forest; Stansted, London's third airport
products dairying, cereals, fruit
population (1987) 1,522,000.

Essex Robert Devereux, 2nd Earl of Essex 1566–1601. English soldier and politician. He became a favourite with Queen Elizabeth I from 1587, but was executed because of his policies in Ireland.

estate in law, the rights that a person has in relation to any property. *Real estate* is an interest in any land; *personal estate* is an interest in any other kind of property.

estate in European history, an order of society that enjoyed a specified share in government. In medieval theory, there were usually three estates – the **nobility**, the **clergy**, and the **commons** – with the functions of, respectively, defending society from foreign aggression and internal disorder, attending to its spiritual needs, and working to produce the base with which to support the other two orders.

ester organic compound formed by the reaction between an alcohol and an acid, with the elimination of water. Unlike *salts, esters are covalent compounds.

Esther in the Old Testament, the wife of the Persian king Ahasuerus (Xerxes I), who prevented the extermination of her people by the king's vizier Haman. Their deliverance is celebrated in the Jewish festival of Purim. Her story is told in the Old Testament Book of Esther.

Estonia Republic of

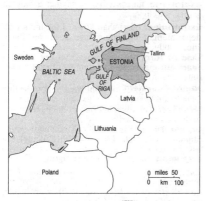

area 45,000 sq km/17,000 sq mi
capital Tallinn
towns Tartu, Narva, Kohtla-Järve, Pärnu
physical lakes and marshes in a partly forested plain; 774 km/481 mi of coastline; mild climate
head of state Lennart Meri from 1992
head of government Andres Tarand from 1994
political system emergent democracy
products oil and gas (from shale), wood products, flax, dairy and pig products
currency kroon
population (1993 est) 1,620,000 (Estonian 62%, Russian 30%, Ukrainian 3%, Byelorussian 2%)
language Estonian, allied to Finnish
religion traditionally Lutheran
GNP $3,380 per head (1991)
chronology
1918 Estonia declared its independence. March: Soviet forces, who had tried to regain control from occupying German forces during World War I, were overthrown by German troops. Nov: Soviet troops took control after German withdrawal.
1919 Soviet rule overthrown with help of British navy; Estonia declared a democratic republic.
1934 Fascist coup replaced government.
1944 USSR regained control.
1988 Adopted own constitution, with power of veto on all centralized Soviet legislation. Popular Front established to campaign for democracy. Estonia's state assembly voted to declare the

republic autonomous in all matters except military and foreign affairs; rejected by USSR as unconstitutional.
1989 Estonian replaced Russian as main language.
1990 Feb: Communist Party monopoly of power abolished; multiparty system established. March: pro-independence candidates secured majority after republic elections; coalition government formed with Popular Front leader Edgar Savisaar as prime minister; Arnold Rüütel became president. May: prewar constitution partially restored.
1991 March: independence approved by national vote. Aug: full independence declared after abortive anti-Gorbachev coup; Communist Party outlawed. Sept: independence recognized.
1992 Jan: Savisaar resigned over food and energy shortages; new government formed by Tiit Vahl. June: new constitution adopted. Sept: presidential and parliamentary elections inconclusive. Oct: Fatherland Group leader Lennart Meri chosen by parliament to replace Rüütel; Mart Laar became prime minister.
1994 Russian troops withdrawn. Sept: Laar resigned after losing vote of confidence. Oct: Andres Tarand became prime minister.

Estonian member of the largest ethnic group in Estonia. There are 1 million speakers of the Estonian language, a member of the Finno-Ugric branch of the Uralic family. Most live in Estonia.

estoppel in law, a conclusive admission that cannot be denied. For the rule of estoppel to operate in law, a denial of the truth of the statement or facts relating to it must have been made, and the person hoping to benefit from the estoppel must have acted upon the denial before the true position was known (usually to his or her detriment).

estuary river mouth widening into the sea, where fresh water mixes with salt water and tidal effects are felt.

etching printmaking technique in which a metal plate (usually copper or zinc) is covered with a waxy overlayer (ground) and then drawn on with an etching needle. The exposed areas are then 'etched', or bitten into, by a corrosive agent (acid), so that they will hold ink for printing.

Etesian wind north-northwesterly wind in the E Mediterranean and Aegean Sea, which blows June–Sept.

ethanal common name **acetaldehyde** CH_3CHO one of the chief members of the group of organic compounds known as *aldehydes. It is a colourless inflammable liquid boiling at 20.8°C/69.6°F. Ethanal is formed by the oxidation of ethanol or ethene and is used to make many other organic chemical compounds.

ethanoate common name **acetate** $CH_3CO_2^-$ negative ion derived from ethanoic (acetic) acid; any salt containing this ion. In textiles, acetate rayon is a synthetic fabric made from modified cellulose (wood pulp) treated with ethanoic acid; in photography, acetate film is a non-flammable film made of cellulose ethanoate.

ethanoic acid common name **acetic acid** CH_3CO_2H one of the simplest fatty acids (a series of organic acids). In the pure state it is a colourless liquid with an unpleasant pungent odour; it solidifies to an icelike mass of crystals at 16.7°C/62.4°F, and hence is often called glacial ethanoic acid. Vinegar contains 5% or more ethanoic acid, produced by fermentation.

ethanol common name *ethyl alcohol* C_2H_5OH alcohol found in beer, wine, cider, spirits, and other alcoholic drinks. When pure, it is a colourless liquid with a pleasant odour, miscible with water or ether; it burns in air with a pale blue flame. The vapour forms an explosive mixture with air and may be used in high-compression internal combustion engines. It is produced naturally by the fermentation of carbohydrates by yeast cells. Industrially, it can be made by absorption of ethene and subsequent reaction with water, or by the reduction of ethanal in the presence of a catalyst, and is widely used as a solvent.

Ethelbert *c.* 552–616. King of Kent 560–616. He was defeated by the West Saxons 568 but later became ruler of England S of the river Humber. Ethelbert received the Christian missionary Augustine 597 and later converted to become the first Christian ruler of Anglo-Saxon England. He issued the first written code of laws known in England.

Ethelred (II) the Unready *c.* 968–1016. King of England from 978. He tried to buy off the Danish raiders by paying Danegeld. In 1002, he ordered the massacre of the Danish settlers, provoking an invasion by Sweyn I of Denmark. War with Sweyn and Sweyn's son, Canute, occupied the rest of Ethelred's reign. He was nicknamed the 'Unready' because of his apparent lack of foresight.

ethene common name *ethylene* C_2H_4 colourless, flammable gas, the first member of the *alkene series of hydrocarbons. It is the most widely used synthetic organic chemical and is used to produce the plastics polyethene (polyethylene), polychloroethene, and polyvinyl chloride (PVC). It is obtained from natural gas or coal gas, or by the dehydration of ethanol.

ether in chemistry, any of a series of organic chemical compounds having an oxygen atom linking the carbon atoms of two hydrocarbon radical groups (general formula R-O-R'); also the common name for ethoxyethane $C_2H_5OC_2H_5$ (also called diethyl ether). This is used as an anaesthetic and as an external cleansing agent before surgical operations. It is also used as a solvent, and in the extraction of oils, fats, waxes, resins, and alkaloids.

Etherege George *c.* 1635–1691. English Restoration dramatist. His play *Love in a Tub* 1664 was the first attempt at the comedy of manners (a genre further developed by Congreve and Sheridan). Later plays include *She Would If She Could* 1668 and *The Man of Mode, or Sir Fopling Flutter* 1676.

ethics area of *philosophy concerned with human values, which studies the meanings of moral terms and theories of conduct and goodness; also called *moral philosophy*. It is one of the three main branches of contemporary philosophy.

Ethiopia People's Democratic Republic of (*Hebretesebawit Ityopia*, formerly known as *Abyssinia*)
area 1,096,900 sq km/423,403 sq mi
capital Addis Ababa
towns Jimma, Dire Dawa, Harar

physical a high plateau with central mountain range divided by Rift Valley; plains in E; source of Blue Nile River
environment more than 90% of the forests of the Ethiopian highlands have been destroyed since 1900
head of state Meles Zenawi from 1991
head of government Tamirat Layne from 1991
political system transition to democratic socialist republic
exports coffee, pulses, oilseeds, hides, skins
currency birr
population (1993) 51,980,000 (Oromo 40%, Amhara 25%, Tigré 12%, Sidamo 9%); growth rate 2.5% p.a.
languages Amharic (official), Tigrinya, Orominga, Arabic
religions Sunni Muslim 45%, Christian (Ethiopian Orthodox Church, which has had its own patriarch since 1976) 40%
GNP $120 per head (1991). The country's debt-service payments 1993–95 will be $2 billion
chronology
1889 Abyssinia reunited by Menelik II.
1930 Haile Selassie became emperor.
1962 Eritrea annexed by Haile Selassie; resistance movement began.
1974 Haile Selassie deposed and replaced by a military government led by General Teferi Benti. Ethiopia declared a socialist state.
1977 Teferi Benti killed and replaced by Col Mengistu Haile Mariam.
1977–79 'Red Terror' period in which Mengistu's regime killed thousands of innocent people.
1981–85 Ethiopia spent at least $2 billion on arms.
1984 Workers' Party of Ethiopia (WPE) declared the only legal political party.
1985 Worst famine in more than a decade; Western aid sent and forcible internal resettlement programmes undertaken.
1987 New constitution adopted, Mengistu Mariam elected president. New famine; food aid hindered by guerrillas.
1988 Mengistu agreed to adjust his economic policies in order to secure IMF assistance. Influx of refugees from Sudan.
1989 Coup attempt against Mengistu foiled. Peace talks with Eritrean rebels mediated by former US president Carter reported some progress.
1990 Rebels captured port of Massawa.

1991 Mengistu overthrown; transitional government set up by EPRDF. EPLF secured Eritrea; Eritrea's right to secede recognized. Meles Zenawi elected Ethiopia's new head of state and government.

1993 Eritrean independence recognized after referendum.

1994 Assembly elections won by ruling EPLF.

ethnic cleansing the forced expulsion or killing of one ethnic group by another. The term was applied particularly to the actions of Bosnian Serbs in *Bosnia-Herzegovina from 1992. In a policy of creating a Greater Serbia, Bosnian-Serb forces killed thousands of non-Serbs and forced many more to abandon their homes, allowing Serb families from other parts of the former Yugoslavia to occupy them. The practice, reminiscent of the Nazi purge of the Jews in Germany, created nearly 700,000 refugees and was widely condemned by the international community.

ethnicity (from Greek *ethnos* 'a people') people's own sense of cultural identity; a social term that over-laps with such concepts as race, nation, class, and religion.

ethnography study of living cultures, using anthropological techniques like participant observation (where the anthropologist lives in the society being studied) and a reliance on informants. Ethnography has provided many data of use to archaeologists as analogies.

ethnology study of contemporary peoples, concentrating on their geography and culture, as distinct from their social systems. Ethnologists make a comparative analysis of data from different cultures to understand how cultures work and why they change, with a view to deriving general principles about human society.

ethnomethodology the study of social order and routines used by people in their daily lives, to explain how everyday reality is created and perceived. Ethnomethodologists tend to use small-scale studies and experiments to examine the details of social life and structure (such as conversations) that people normally take for granted, rather than construct large-scale theories about society.

ethology comparative study of animal behaviour in its natural setting. Ethology is concerned with the causal mechanisms (both the stimuli that elicit behaviour and the physiological mechanisms controlling it), as well as the development of behaviour, its function, and its evolutionary history.

ethyl alcohol common name for *ethanol.

ethylene common name for *ethene.

ethylene glycol alternative name for *glycol.

ethyne common name **acetylene** CHCH colourless inflammable gas produced by mixing calcium carbide and water. It is the simplest member of the *alkyne series of hydrocarbons. It is used in the manufacture of the synthetic rubber neoprene, and in oxyacetylene welding and cutting.

etiolation in botany, a form of growth seen in plants receiving insufficient light. It is characterized by long, weak stems, small leaves, and a pale yellowish colour (*chlorosis) owing to a lack of chlorophyll. The rapid increase in height enables a plant that is surrounded by others to quickly reach a source of light, after which a return to normal growth usually occurs.

Etna volcano on the east coast of Sicily, 3,323 m/10,906 ft, the highest in Europe. About 90 eruptions have been recorded since 1800 BC, yet because of the rich soil, the cultivated zone on the lower slopes is densely populated, including the coastal town of Catania. The most recent eruption was in Dec 1985.

Eton College most prestigious of English *public schools (that is, private schools) for boys. It provided the UK with 19 prime ministers and more than 20% of all government ministers between 1900 and 1985.

Etruscan member of an ancient people inhabiting Etruria, Italy (modern-day Tuscany and part of Umbria) from the 8th to 4th centuries BC. The Etruscan dynasty of the Tarquins ruled Rome 616–509 BC. At the height of their civilization, in the 6th century BC, the Etruscans achieved great wealth and power from their maritime strength. They were driven out of Rome 509 BC and eventually dominated by the Romans.

etymology study of the origin and history of words within and across languages. It has two major aspects: the study of the phonetic and written forms of words, and of the semantics or meanings of those words, with relation to the changes both have undergone.

EU abbreviation for ***European Union**.

Euboea (Greek **Evvoia**) mountainous island off the east coast of Greece, in the Aegean sea; area 3,755 sq km/1,450 sq mi; about 177 km/110 mi long; population (1981) 188,410. Mount Delphi reaches 1,743 m/5,721 ft. The chief town, Chalcis, is connected by a bridge to the mainland.

eucalyptus any tree of the genus *Eucalyptus* of the myrtle family Myrtaceae, native to Australia and Tasmania, where they are commonly known as gum trees. About 90% of Australian timber belongs to the eucalyptus genus, which comprises about 500 species. The trees have dark hardwood timber which is used principally for heavy construction as in railway and bridge building. They are tall, aromatic, evergreen trees with pendant leaves and white, pink, or red flowers.

Eucharist chief Christian sacrament, in which bread is eaten and wine drunk in memory of the death of Jesus. Other names for it are the **Lord's Supper**, **Holy Communion**, and (among Roman Catholics, who believe that the bread and wine are transubstantiated, that is, converted to the body and blood of Christ) the **Mass**. The doctrine of transubstantiation was rejected by Protestant churches during the Reformation.

Euclid *c.* 330–*c.* 260 BC. Greek mathematician, who lived in Alexandria and wrote the *Stoicheia/Elements* in 13 books, of which nine deal with plane and solid geometry and four with number theory. His great achievement lay in the systematic arrangement of previous discoveries, based on axioms, definitions, and theorems.

Eudoxus of Cnidus *c.* 390–*c.* 340 BC. Greek mathematician and astronomer. He devised the first system to account for the motions of celestial bodies, believing them to be carried around the Earth on sets of spheres. Probably Eudoxus regarded these spheres as a mathematical device for ease of computation rather than as physically real, but the idea of celestial spheres was taken up by Aristotle and became entrenched in astronomical thought until the time of Tycho *Brahe. Eudoxus also described the constellations in a work called *Phaenomena*, providing the basis of the constellation system stil in use today.

Eugène Prince of Savoy 1663–1736. Austrian general who had many victories against the Turkish invaders (whom he expelled from Hungary 1697 in the Battle of Zenta) and against France in the War of the *Spanish Succession (battles of Blenheim, Oudenaarde, and Malplaquet).

eugenics (Greek 'well-born') study of ways in which the physical and mental quality of a people can be controlled and improved by selective breeding, and the belief that this should be done. The idea was abused by the Nazi Party in Germany during the 1930s to justify the attempted extermination of entire groups of people. Eugenics can try to control the spread of inherited genetic abnormalities by counselling prospective parents.

Eugénie Marie Ignace Augustine de Montijo 1826–1920. Empress of France, daughter of the Spanish count of Montijo. In 1853 she married Louis Napoleon, who had become emperor as *Napoleon III. She encouraged court extravagance, Napoleon III's intervention in Mexico, and urged him to fight the Prussians. After his surrender to the Germans at Sedan, NE France, 1870 she fled to England.

eukaryote in biology, one of the two major groupings into which all organisms are divided. Included are all organisms, except bacteria and cyanobacteria (*blue-green algae), which belong to the *prokaryote grouping.

Eumenides ('kindly ones') in Greek mythology, appeasing name for the *Furies.

eunuch (Greek *eunoukhos* 'one in charge of a bed') castrated man. Originally eunuchs were bedchamber attendants in harems in the East, but as they were usually castrated to keep them from taking too great an interest in their charges, the term became applied more generally. In China, eunuchs were employed within the imperial harem from some 4,000 years ago and by medieval times wielded considerable political power. Eunuchs often filled high offices of state in India and Persia.

euphemism a *figure of speech whose name in Greek means 'speaking well (of something)'. To speak or write euphemistically is to use a milder, more polite, less direct, or even less honest expression rather than one that is considered too blunt, vulgar, direct, or revealing.

euphonium type of *brass instrument, like a small tuba.

Euphrates (Arabic **Furat**) river, rising in E Turkey, flowing through Syria and Iraq and joining the river Tigris above Basra to form the river Shatt-al-Arab, at the head of the Persian/Arabian Gulf; 3,600 km/2,240 mi in length. The ancient cities of Babylon, Eridu, and Ur were situated along its course.

Eurasian former term in India and the East Indies for a person born of mixed European and Asian parentage or ancestry.

Eureka Stockade incident at Ballarat, Australia, when about 150 goldminers, or 'diggers', rebelled against the Victorian state police and military authorities. They took refuge behind a wooden stockade, which was taken in a few minutes by the military on 3 Dec 1854. Some 30 gold diggers were killed, and a few soldiers killed or wounded, but the majority of the rebels were taken prisoner. Among those who escaped was Peter Lalor, their leader. Of the 13 tried for treason, all were acquitted, thus marking the emergence of Australian democracy.

eurhythmics practice of coordinated bodily movement as an aid to musical development. It was founded about 1900 by Swiss musician Emil Jaques-Dalcroze (1865–1950), professor of harmony at the Geneva conservatoire. He devised a series of 'gesture' songs, to be sung simultaneously with certain bodily actions.

Euripides *c.* 484–407 BC. Greek dramatist whose plays deal with the emotions and reactions of ordinary people and social issues rather than with deities and the grandiose themes of his contemporaries. He wrote more than 80 plays, of which 18 survive, including *Alcestis* 438 BC, *Medea* 431 BC, *Andromache* 426 BC, *The Trojan Women* 415 BC, *Electra* 417 BC, *Iphigenia in Tauris* 413 BC, *Iphigenia in Aulis* 405 BC, and *Bacchae* 405 BC. His influence on later drama was probably greater than that of the other two accomplished tragedians, Aeschylus and Sophocles.

Eurobond in finance, a bond underwritten by an international syndicate and sold in countries other than the country of the currency in which the issue is denominated. It provides longer-term financing than is possible with loans in Eurodollars.

Eurocodes series of codes giving design rules for all types of engineering structures, except certain very specialized forms, such as nuclear reactors. The codes will be given the status of ENs (European standards) and will be administered by CEN (European Committee for Standardization). ENs will eventually replace national codes, in Britain currently maintained by the BSI (British Standards Institute), and will include parameters to reflect local requirements.

Eurocommunism policy followed by communist parties in Western Europe to seek power within the framework of national political initiative rather than by revolutionary means. In addition, Eurocommunism enabled these parties to free themselves from total reliance on the USSR.

Eurodollar in finance, US currency deposited outside the USA and held by individuals and institutions, not necessarily in Europe. Eurodollars originated in the 1960s when East European countries deposited their US dollars in West European banks. Banks holding Eurodollar deposits may lend in dollars, usually to finance trade, and often redeposit with other foreign banks. The practice is a means of avoiding credit controls and exploiting interest rate differentials.

Europa in astronomy, the fourth largest moon of the planet Jupiter, diameter 3,140 km/1,950 mi, orbiting 671,000 km/417,000 mi from the planet every 3.55 days. It is covered by ice and criss-crossed by thousands of thin cracks, each some 50,000 km/30,000 mi long.

Europa in Greek mythology, the daughter of the king of Tyre, carried off by Zeus (in the form of a bull); she personifies the continent of Europe.

Europe second-smallest continent, occupying 8% of the Earth's surface

area 10,400,000 sq km/4,000,000 sq mi

largest cities (population over 1.5 million) Athens, Barcelona, Berlin, Birmingham, Bucharest, Budapest, Hamburg, Istanbul, Kharkov, Kiev, Lisbon, London, Madrid, Manchester, Milan, Moscow, Paris, Rome, St Petersburg, Vienna, Warsaw

physical conventionally occupying that part of Eurasia to the west of the Ural Mountains, north of the Caucasus Mountains and north of the Sea of Marmara; Europe lies entirely in the northern hemisphere between 36° N and the Arctic Ocean. About two-thirds of the continent is a great plain which covers the whole of European Russia and spreads westwards through Poland to the Low Countries and the Bay of Biscay. To the north lie the Scandinavian highlands rising to 2,472 m/8,110 ft at Glittertind in the Jotenheim range of Norway. To the south, a series of mountain ranges stretch east to west (Caucasus, Balkans, Carpathians, Apennines, Alps, Pyrenees, and Sierra Nevada). The most westerly point of the mainland is Cape Roca in Portugal; the most southerly location is Tarifa Point in Spain; the most northerly point on the mainland is Nordkynn in Norway. A line from the Baltic to the Black Sea divides Europe between an eastern continental region and a western region characterized by a series of peninsulas that include Scandinavia (Norway, Sweden, and Finland), Jutland (Denmark and Germany), Iberia (Spain and Portugal), and Italy and the Balkans (Greece, Albania, Croatia, Slovenia, Bosnia-Herzegovina, Yugoslavia, Bulgaria, and European Turkey). Because of the large number of bays, inlets, and peninsulas, the coastline is longer in proportion to its size than that of any other continent. The largest islands adjacent to continental Europe are the British Isles, Novaya Zemlya, Sicily, Sardinia, Crete, Corsica, Gotland (in the Baltic Sea) and the Balearic Islands; other more distant islands associated with Europe include Iceland, Svalbard, Franz Josef Land, Madeira, the Azores, and the Canary Islands. The greater part of Europe falls within the northern temperate zone which is modified by the Gulf Stream in the northwest; Central Europe has warm summers and cold winters; the Mediterranean coast has comparatively mild winters and hot summers

products nearly 50% of the world's cars are produced in Europe (Germany, France, Italy, Spain, Russia, Georgia, Ukraine, Latvia, Belarus, UK); the rate of fertilizer consumption on agricultural land is four times greater than that in any other continent; Europe produces 43% of the world's barley (Germany, Spain, France, UK), 41% of its rye (Poland, Germany), 31% of its oats (Poland, Germany, Sweden, France), and 24% of its wheat (France, Germany, UK, Romania); Italy, Spain, and Greece produce more than 70% of the world's olive oil

population (1985) 496 million (excluding Turkey and the ex-Soviet republics); annual growth rate 0.3%, projected population of 512 million by 2000

languages mostly Indo-European, with a few exceptions, including Finno-Ugrian (Finnish and Hungarian), Basque and Altaic (Turkish); apart from a fringe of Celtic, the NW is Germanic; Letto-Lithuanian languages separate the Germanic from the Slavonic tongues of E Europe; Romance languages spread E–W from Romania through Italy and France to Spain and Portugal

religions Christianity (Protestant, Roman Catholic, Eastern Orthodox), Muslim (Turkey, Albania, Yugoslavia, Bulgaria), Judaism.

European any person native to or an inhabitant of the continent of Europe. The term is also sometimes applied to people of European descent living in other continents, as in the Americas and Australia.

European Atomic Energy Commission (Euratom) organization established by the second Treaty of Rome 1957, which seeks the cooperation of member states of the European Community in nuclear research and the rapid and large-scale development of nonmilitary nuclear energy.

European Community (EC) former name (until 1993) of political and economic alliance between European counties; see *European Union.

European Court of Human Rights court that hears cases referred from the European Commission of Human Rights, if the commission has failed to negotiate a friendly settlement in a case where individuals' rights have been violated by a member state. The court sits in Strasbourg and comprises one judge for every state that is a party to the 1950 convention. Court rulings have forced the Republic of Ireland to drop its constitutional ban on homosexuality, and Germany to cease to exclude political left- and right-wingers from the civil service.

European Court of Justice the court of the *European Union that is responsible for interpreting *Community law and ruling on breaches by member states and others of such law. It sits in Luxembourg with judges from the member states.

European Economic Area agreement 1991 between the European Community (now the *European Union) and the *European Free Trade Association (EFTA) to create a zone of economic cooperation, allowing their 380 million citizens to transfer money, shares, and bonds across national borders and to live, study, or work in one another's countries. The pact, which took effect Jan 1994, has been seen as a temporary arrangement since most EFTA members hope, eventually, to join the EU.

European Economic Community (EEC) popularly called the *Common Market* organization established 1957 with the aim of creating a single European market for the products of member states by the abolition of tariffs and other restrictions on trade.

European Free Trade Association (EFTA) organization established 1960 consisting of Austria, Finland, Iceland, Norway, Sweden, Switzerland, and (from 1991) Liechtenstein, previously a nonvoting associate member. There are no import duties between members. EFTA is seen as a temporary body since most members expect to join the *European Union. EU membership of Austria, Finland, Norway, and Sweden was agreed 1994. Of the original members, Britain and Denmark left (1972) to join the European Community, as did Portugal (1985). In 1991 an agreement between the EC and EFTA provided for a *European Economic Area to be set up, which took effect from Jan 1994.

European Monetary Cooperation Fund (EMCOF) institution funded by the members of the Exchange Rate Mechanism (ERM) of the *European Monetary System to stabilize the exchange rates of member countries if they fluctuate by more than the range permitted by the ERM: if the exchange rate of a currency falls too far, EMCOF will buy quantities of the currency on the foreign-exchange market, and if it rises too far, EMCOF will sell enough of the currency to bring down the exchange rate.

European Monetary System (EMS) attempt by the European Community (now the *European Union) to bring financial cooperation and monetary stability to Europe. It was established 1979 in the wake of the 1974 oil crisis, which brought growing economic disruption to European economies because of floating exchange rates. Central to the EMS is the *Exchange Rate Mechanism* (ERM), a voluntary system of semifixed exchange rates based on the European Currency Unit (ECU).

European Monetary Union (EMU) the proposed *European Union) policy for a single currency and common economic policies for EU member states. The proposal was announced by a European Community committee headed by EU Commission president Jacques Delors April 1989.

European Parliament the parliament of the European Union, which meets in Strasbourg to comment on the legislative proposals of the European Commission. Members are elected for a five-year term. The European Parliament has 567 seats, apportioned on the basis of population, of which Germany has 99; the UK, France, and Italy have 87 each; Spain 64; the Netherlands 31; Belgium, Greece, and Portugal 25 each; Denmark 16; the Republic of Ireland 15; and Luxembourg 6.

European Space Agency (ESA) an organization of European countries (Austria, Belgium, Denmark, France, Germany, Ireland, Italy, the Netherlands, Norway, Spain, Sweden, Switzerland, and the UK) that engages in space research and technology. It was founded 1975, with headquarters in Paris.

European Union (EU; formerly until 1993 *European Community*) political and economic alliance consisting of the European Coal and Steel Community (1952), European Economic Community (EEC, popularly called the Common Market, 1957), and the European Atomic Energy Commission (Euratom, 1957). The original six members – Belgium, France, West Germany, Italy, Luxembourg, and the Netherlands – were joined by the UK, Denmark, and the Republic of Ireland 1973, Greece 1981, and Spain and Portugal 1986. East Germany was incorporated on German reunification 1990. Membership terms for Austria, Finland, Sweden, and Norway were agreed March 1994 (to take effect Jan 1995), and approved in national referendums in all but Norway, which rejected membership. Association agreements – providing for free trade within ten years and the possibility of full membership – were signed with Czechoslovakia, Hungary, and Poland 1991, subject to ratification, and with Romania 1992. In 1994 there were more than 340 million people in the EU countries.

europium soft, greyish, metallic element of the *lanthanide series, symbol Eu, atomic number 63, relative atomic mass 151.96. It is used in lasers and as the red phosphor in colour televisions; its compounds are used to make control rods for nuclear reactors. It was named in 1901 by French chemist Eugène Demarçay (1852–1904) after the continent of Europe, where it was first found.

Euskal Herria Basque name for the *Basque Country.

eusociality form of social life found in insects such as honey bees and termites, in which the colony is made up of special castes (for example, workers, drones, and reproductives) whose membership is biologically determined.

Eustachian tube small air-filled canal connecting the middle *ear with the back of the throat. It is found in all land vertebrates and equalizes the pressure on both sides of the eardrum.

Euston Road School group of British artists based at an art school in Euston Road, London, 1937–39. William Coldstream (1908–1987) and Victor Pasmore were teachers there. Despite its brief existence, the school influenced many British painters with its emphasis on careful, subdued naturalism.

Eutelsat acronym for *European Telecommunications Satellite Organization*.

euthanasia in medicine, mercy killing of someone with a severe and incurable condition or illness. The Netherlands legalized voluntary euthanasia 1983, but is the only country to have done so. Approximately 2,700 patients there formally request euthanasia each year.

eutrophication excessive enrichment of rivers, lakes, and shallow sea areas, primarily by nitrate fertilizers washed from the soil by rain, by phosphates from fertilizers, and from nutrients in municipal sewage, and by sewage itself. These encourage the growth of algae and bacteria which use up the oxygen in the water, thereby making it uninhabitable for fishes and other animal life.

evangelicalism the beliefs of some Protestant Christian movements that stress biblical authority, faith, and the personal commitment of the 'born again' experience.

Evangelical Movement in Britain, a 19th-century group that stressed basic Protestant beliefs and the message of the four Gospels. The movement was associated with Rev Charles Simeon (1783–1836). It aimed to raise moral enthusiasm and ethical standards among Church of England clergy.

evangelist person travelling to spread the Christian gospel, in particular the authors of the four Gospels in the New Testament: Matthew, Mark, Luke, and John. See also *televangelist.

Evans Arthur John 1851–1941. English archaeologist. His excavation of *Knossos on Crete resulted in the discovery of pre-Phoenician Minoan script and proved the existence of the legendary Minoan civilization.

Evans Edith 1888–1976. English character actress. She performed on the London stage and on Broadway. Her many imposing performances include the Nurse in *Romeo and Juliet* (first performed 1926); her film roles include Lady Bracknell in Wilde's comedy *The Importance of Being Earnest* 1952 and Betsy in the television version of *David Copperfield* 1969. Among her other films are *Tom Jones* 1963 and *Crooks and Coronets* 1969.

Evans Walker 1903–1975. US photographer. He is best known for his documentary photographs of people in the rural American South during the Great Depression. Many of his photographs appeared in James Agee's book *Let Us Now Praise Famous Men* 1941.

evaporation process in which a liquid turns to a vapour without its temperature reaching boiling point. A liquid left to stand in a saucer eventually evaporates because, at any time, a proportion of its molecules will be fast enough (have enough kinetic energy) to escape through the attractive intermolecular forces at the liquid surface into the atmosphere. The temperature of the liquid tends to fall because the evaporating molecules remove energy from the liquid. The rate of evaporation rises with increased temperature because as the mean kinetic energy of the liquid's molecules rises, so will the number possessing enough energy to escape.

evaporite sedimentary deposit precipitated on evaporation of salt water. With a progressive evaporation of seawater, the most common salts are deposited in a definite sequence: calcite (calcium carbonate), gypsum (hydrous calcium sulphate), halite (sodium chloride), and finally salts of potassium and magnesium.

Eve in the Old Testament, the first woman, wife of *Adam. She was tempted by Satan (in the form of a snake) to eat the fruit of the Tree of Knowledge of Good and Evil, and then tempted Adam to eat of the fruit as well, thus bringing about their expulsion from the Garden of Eden.

Evelyn John 1620–1706. English diarist and author. He was a friend of Samuel Pepys, like him remained in London during the Plague and the Great Fire. He wrote some 300 books, including his diary, first published 1818, which covers the period 1640–1706.

evening primrose any plant of the genus *Oenothera*, family Onagraceae. Some 50 species are native to North America, several of which now also grow in Europe. Some are cultivated for their oil, which is used in treating eczema, premenstrual tension, and chronic fatigue syndrome.

Everest, Mount (Chinese *Qomolungma* 'goddess mother of the snows/world'; Nepalese *Sagarmatha* 'head of the earth') the world's highest mountain above sea level, in the Himalayas, on the China–Nepal frontier; height 8,872 m/29,118 ft (recently measured by satellite to this new height from the former official height of 8,848 m/29,028 ft). It was first climbed by Edmund Hillary and Tenzing Norgay 1953. More than 360 climbers have reached the summit; over 100 have died during the ascent.

Everglades area of swamps, marsh, and lakes in S *Florida; area 5,000 sq mi/12,950 sq km. A national park covers the southern tip.

evergreen in botany, a plant such as pine, spruce, or holly, that bears its leaves all year round. Most *conifers are evergreen. Plants that shed their leaves in autumn or during a dry season are described as *deciduous.

Evert Chris(tine) 1954– . US tennis player. She won her first Wimbledon title 1974, and has since won 21 Grand Slam titles. She became the first woman tennis player to win $1 million in prize money. Evert retired from competitive tennis 1989.

evidence in law, the testimony of witnesses and production of documents and other material in court proceedings, in order to prove or disprove facts at issue in the case. Witnesses must swear or affirm that their evidence is true. In English law, giving false evidence is the crime of *perjury.

evolution slow process of change from one form to another, as in the evolution of the universe from its formation in the *Big Bang to its present state, or in the evolution of life on Earth. Some Christians and Muslims deny the theory of evolution as conflicting with the belief that God created all things (see *creationism).

evolutionary stable strategy (ESS) in *sociobiology, an assemblage of behavioural or physical characters (collectively termed a 'strategy') of a population that is resistant to replacement by any forms bearing new traits, because the new traits will not be capable of successful reproduction.

Evvoia Greek name for the island of *Euboea.

exam results in the UK, the success rate in public examinations at 16 and 18. This improved steadily throughout the 1970s and early 1980s, levelled off, and then began to improve again after the replacement of O level and CSE with *GCSE in 1988. The proportion of 18-year-olds achieving at least two A-level passes increased from 14% 1970–71 to 16% 1987–88, and the proportion of 16-year-olds achieving at least five O levels (or equivalent) increased from 26% 1970–71 to 32% 1987–88. The proportion of young people leaving school with no qualifications at all dropped from 15.5% in 1980–81 to 11% in 1987–88.

excavation or *dig* in archaeology, the systematic recovery of data through the exposure of buried sites and artefacts. Excavation is destructive, and is therefore accompanied by a comprehensive recording of all material found and its three-dimensional locations (its context). As much material and information as possible must be recovered from any dig. A full record of all the techniques employed in the excavation itself must also be made, so that future archaeologists will be able to evaluate the results of the work accurately.

exchange rate the price at which one currency is bought or sold in terms of other currencies, gold, or accounting units such as the special drawing right (SDR) of the *International Monetary Fund. Exchange rates may be fixed by international agreement or by government policy; or they may be wholly or partly allowed to 'float' (that is, find their own level) in world currency markets.

Exchange Rate Mechanism (ERM) voluntary system for controlling exchange rates within the European Community's *European Monetary System. The member currencies of the ERM are fixed against each other within a narrow band of fluctuation based on a central European Currency Unit (ECU) rate, but floating against non-member countries. If a currency deviates significantly from the central ECU rate, the *European Monetary Cooperation Fund and the central banks concerned intervene to stabilize the currency.

excise duty levied on certain goods produced within a country; it is collected by the government's *Customs and Excise department.

exclamation mark or *exclamation point* punctuation mark (!) used to indicate emphasis or strong emotion ('That's terrible!'). It is appropriate after interjections ('Rats!'), emphatic greetings ('Yo!'), and orders ('Shut up!'), as well as those sentences beginning *How* or *What* that are not questions ('How embarrassing!', 'What a surprise!').

exclusion principle in physics, a principle of atomic structure originated by Wolfgang *Pauli. It states that no two electrons in a single atom may have the same set of *quantum numbers. Hence, it is impossible to pack together certain elementary particles, such as electrons, beyond a certain critical density, otherwise they would share the same location and quantum number. A white dwarf star is thus prevented from contracting further by the exclusion principle and never collapses.

excommunication in religion, exclusion of an offender from the rights and privileges of the Roman Catholic Church; King John, Henry VIII, and Elizabeth I were all excommunicated.

excretion in biology, the removal of waste products from the cells of living organisms. In plants and simple animals, waste products are removed by diffusion, but in higher animals they are removed by specialized organs. In mammals, for example, carbon dioxide and water are removed via the lungs, and nitrogenous compounds and water via the liver, the kidneys, and the rest of the urinary system.

executor in law, a person appointed in a will to carry out the instructions of the deceased. A person so named has the right to refuse to act. The executor also has a duty to bury the deceased, prove the will, and obtain a grant of probate (that is, establish that the will is genuine and obtain official approval of his or her actions).

exemplum in Western medieval and Renaissance literature, a short narrative text that contains a moral. Examples include works by the French essayist *Montaigne, the philosopher *Pascal, and the Italian political theorist *Machiavelli.

existentialism branch of philosophy based on the concept of an absurd universe where humans have free will. Existentialists argue that philosophy must begin from the concrete situation of the individual in such a world, and that humans are responsible for and the sole judge of their actions as they affect others, though no one else's existence is real to the individual. The origin of existentialism is usually traced back to the Danish philosopher *Kierkegaard; among its proponents were Martin Heidegger in Germany and Jean-Paul *Sartre in France.

exocrine gland gland that discharges secretions, usually through a tube or a duct, onto a surface. Examples include sweat glands which release sweat onto the skin, and digestive glands which release digestive juices onto the walls of the intestine. Some animals also have *endocrine glands (ductless glands) that release hormones directly into the bloodstream.

Exodus second book of the Old Testament, which relates the departure of the Israelites from slavery in Egypt, under the leadership of *Moses, for the Promised Land of Canaan. The journey included the miraculous parting of the Red Sea, with the Pharaoh's pursuing forces being drowned as the waters returned.

exorcism rite used in a number of religions for the expulsion of so-called evil spirits. In Christianity it is employed, for example, in the Roman Catholic and Pentecostal churches.

exoskeleton the hardened external skeleton of insects, spiders, crabs, and other arthropods. It provides attachment for muscles and protection for the internal organs, as well as support. To permit growth it is periodically shed in a process called ecdysis.

exothermic reaction a chemical reaction during which heat is given out (see *energy of reaction).

expansion in physics, the increase in size of a constant mass of substance caused by, for example, increasing its temperature (*thermal expansion) or its internal pressure. The *expansivity*, or coefficient of thermal expansion, of a material is its expansion (per unit volume, area, or length) per degree rise in temperature.

expansion board or *expansion card* printed circuit board that can be inserted into a computer in order to enhance its capabilities (for example, to increase its memory) or to add facilities (such as graphics).

ex parte (Latin 'on the part of one side only') in law, term indicating that an order has been made after hearing only the party that made the application; for example, an ex parte injunction. It may also be used in law reports to indicate whom the application is in behalf of.

expectorant any substance, often added to cough mixture, intended to help expel mucus from the airways. It is debatable whether expectorants have an effect on lung secretions.

experience curve observed effect of improved performance of individuals and organizations as experience of a repeated task increases.

experiment in science, a practical test designed with the intention that its results will be relevant to a particular theory or set of theories. Although some experiments may be used merely for gathering more information about a topic that is already well understood, others may be of crucial importance in confirming a new theory or in undermining long-held beliefs.

experimental psychology application of

scientific methods to the study of mental processes and behaviour.

expert system computer program for giving advice (such as diagnosing an illness or interpreting the law) that incorporates knowledge derived from human expertise. It is a kind of *knowledge-based system containing rules that can be applied to find the solution to a problem. It is a form of *artificial intelligence.

explanation in science, an attempt to make clear the cause of any natural event, by reference to physical laws and to observations.

Explorer series of US scientific satellites. *Explorer 1*, launched Jan 1958, was the first US satellite in orbit and discovered the Van Allen radiation belts around the Earth.

explosive any material capable of a sudden release of energy and the rapid formation of a large volume of gas, leading when compressed to the development of a high-pressure wave (blast).

exponent or *index* in mathematics, a number that indicates the number of times a term is multiplied by itself; for example $x^2 = x \times x$, $4^3 = 4 \times 4 \times 4$.

exponential in mathematics, descriptive of a *function in which the variable quantity is an exponent (a number indicating the power to which another number or expression is raised).

export goods or service produced in one country and sold to another. Exports may be visible (goods physically exported) or invisible (services provided in the exporting country but paid for by residents of another country).

export credit loan, finance, or guarantee provided by a government or a financial institution enabling companies to export goods and services in situations where payment for them may be delayed or subject to risk.

export file in computing, a file stored by the computer in a standard format so that it can be accessed by other programs, possibly running on different makes of computer.

exposition in music, the opening statement of a sonata form in which the principal themes are clearly outlined.

exposure meter instrument used in photography for indicating the correct exposure – the length of time the camera shutter should be open under given light conditions. Meters use substances such as cadmium sulphide and selenium as light sensors. These materials change electrically when light strikes them, the change being proportional to the intensity of the incident light. Many cameras have a built-in exposure meter that sets the camera controls automatically as the light conditions change.

Expressionism style of painting, sculpture, and literature that expresses inner emotions; in particular, a movement in early 20th-century art in northern and central Europe. Expressionists tended to distort or exaggerate natural appearance in order to create a reflection of an inner world; the Norwegian painter Edvard Munch's *Skriket/The Scream* 1893 (National Gallery, Oslo) is perhaps the most celebrated example. Expressionist writers include August Strindberg and Frank Wedekind.

extensor a muscle that straightens a limb.

extinction in biology, the complete disappearance of a species. In the past, extinctions are believed to have occurred because species were unable to adapt quickly enough to a naturally changing environment. Today, most extinctions are due to human activity. Some species, such as the *dodo of Mauritius, the *moas of New Zealand, and the passenger *pigeon of North America, were exterminated by hunting. Others became extinct when their habitat was destroyed. See also *endangered species.

extracellular matrix strong material naturally occurring in animals and plants, made up of protein and long-chain sugars (polysaccharides) in which cells are embedded. It is often called a 'biological glue', and forms part of *connective tissues such as bone and skin.

extradition surrender, by one state or country to another, of a person accused of a criminal offence in the state or country to which that person is extradited.

extrasensory perception (ESP) form of perception beyond and distinct from the known sensory processes. The main forms of ESP are clairvoyance (intuitive perception or vision of events and situations without using the senses); precognition (the ability to foresee events); and telepathy or thought transference (communication between people without using any known visible, tangible, or audible medium). Verification by scientific study has yet to be achieved.

Extremadura autonomous region of W Spain including the provinces of Badajoz and Cáceres; area   41,600 sq km/16,058 sq mi;   population (1986) 1,089,000. Irrigated land is used for growing wheat; the remainder is either forest or used for grazing.

extroversion or *extraversion* personality dimension described by *Jung and later by *Eysenck. The typical extrovert is sociable, impulsive, and carefree. The opposite of extroversion is introversion; the typical introvert is quiet and inward-looking.

extrusion common method of shaping metals, plastics, and other materials. The materials, usually hot, are forced through the hole in a metal die and take its cross-sectional shape. Rods, tubes, and sheets may be made in this way.

Exxon Corporation the USA's largest oil concern, founded 1888 as the *Standard Oil Company (New Jersey), selling petrol under the brand name Esso from 1926 and under the name Exxon in the USA from 1972. The company was responsible for *oil spills in Alaska 1989 and New York harbour 1990.

Eyck Aldo van 1918– . Dutch architect with a strong commitment to social architecture. His works include an Orphans' Home 1957–60, and a refuge for single mothers, Mothers' House 1978; both are in Amsterdam.

Eyck Jan van *c.* 1390–1441. Flemish painter of the early northern Renaissance, one of the first to work in oils. His paintings are technically brilliant and sumptuously rich in detail and colour. In his *Arnolfini Wedding* 1434 (National Gallery, London) the bride and groom appear in a domestic interior crammed with disguised symbols, as a kind of pictorial marriage certificate.

eye the organ of vision. In the human eye, the light is focused by the combined action of the curved *cornea*, the internal fluids, and the *lens*. The insect eye is compound – made up of many separate facets – known as ommatidia, each of which collects light and directs it separately to a receptor to build up an image. Invertebrates have much simpler eyes, with no lens. Among molluscs, cephalopods have complex eyes similar to those of vertebrates. The mantis shrimp's eyes contain ten colour pigments with which to perceive colour; some flies and fishes have five, while the human eye has only three.

eyebright any flower of the genus *Euphrasia*, family Scrophulariaceae. They are 2–30 cm/1–12 in high, bearing whitish flowers streaked with purple. The name indicates its traditional use as an eye-medicine.

Eyre Richard (Charles Hastings) 1943– . English stage and film director who succeeded Peter Hall as artistic director of the National Theatre, London, 1988. His stage productions include *Guys and Dolls* 1982, *Bartholomew Fair* 1988, and *Richard III* 1990, which he set in 1930s Britain. His films include *The Ploughman's Lunch* 1983 and *Laughterhouse* 1984.

Eyre, Lake Australia's largest lake, in central South Australia, which frequently runs dry, becoming a salt marsh in dry seasons; area up to 9,000 sq km/3,500 sq mi. It is the continent's lowest point, 12 m/39 ft below sea level.

Eysenck Hans Jurgen 1916– . English psychologist. His work concentrates on personality theory and testing by developing *behaviour therapy. He is an outspoken critic of psychoanalysis as a therapeutic method.

°F symbol for degrees *Fahrenheit*.

Fabergé Peter Carl 1846–1920. Russian goldsmith and jeweller. Among his masterpieces was a series of jewelled Easter eggs, the first of which was commissioned by Alexander III for the tsarina 1884.

Fabian Society UK socialist organization for research, discussion, and publication, founded in London 1884. Its name is derived from the Roman commander Fabius Maximus, and refers to the evolutionary methods by which it hopes to attain socialism by a succession of gradual reforms. Early members included the playwright George Bernard Shaw and Beatrice and Sidney Webb. The society helped to found the Labour Representation Committee in 1900, which became the Labour Party in 1906.

Fabius Laurent 1946– . French politician, leader of the Socialist Party 1992–93. As prime minister 1984–86, he introduced a liberal, free-market economic programme, but his career was damaged by the 1985 *Greenpeace sabotage scandal.

fable story, either in verse or prose, in which animals or inanimate objects are endowed with the mentality and speech of human beings to point out a moral. Fabulists include Aesop, Babrius, Phaedrus, Avianus, and La Fontaine.

Fabricius Geronimo 1537–1619. Italian anatomist and embryologist. He made a detailed study of the veins and discovered the valves that direct the blood flow towards the heart. He also studied the development of chick embryos.

facsimile transmission full name for *fax* or *telefax*.

factor a number that divides into another number exactly. For example, the factors of 64 are 1, 2, 4, 8, 16, 32, and 64. In algebra, certain kinds of polynomials (expressions consisting of several or many terms) can be factorized. For example, the factors of $x^2 + 3x + 2$ are $x + 1$ and $x + 2$, since $x^2 + 3x + 2 = (x + 1)(x + 2)$. This is called factorization. See also *prime number.

factorial of a positive number, the product of all the whole numbers (integers) inclusive between 1 and the number itself. A factorial is indicated by the symbol '!'. Thus $6! = 1 \times 2 \times 3 \times 4 \times 5 \times 6 = 720$. Factorial zero, $0!$, is defined as 1.

factoring lending money to a company on the security of money owed to that company; this is often done on the basis of collecting those debts. The lender is known as the factor. Factoring may also describe acting as a commission agent for the sale of goods.

factory farming intensive rearing of poultry or animals for food, usually on high-protein foodstuffs in confined quarters. Chickens for eggs and meat, and calves for veal are commonly factory farmed. Some countries restrict the use of antibiotics and growth hormones as aids to factory farming, because they can persist in the flesh of the animals after they are slaughtered. Many people object to factory farming for moral as well as health reasons.

factory system the basis of manufacturing in the modern world. In the factory system workers are employed at a place where they carry out specific tasks, which together result in a product. This is called the division of labour. Usually these workers will perform their tasks with the aid of machinery. Such mechanization is another feature of the factory system, which leads to *mass production.

factotum (Latin 'do everything') someone employed to do all types of work.

FA Cup abbreviation for *Football Association Cup*, the major annual soccer knockout competition in England and Wales, open to all member clubs of the British Football Association. First held 1871–72, it is the oldest football knockout competition.

Faenza city on the river Lamone in Ravenna province, Emilia-Romagna, Italy; population (1985) 54,900. It has many medieval remains, including the 15th-century walls. It gave its name to 'faience' pottery, a type of tin-glazed earthenware first produced there.

Faeroe Islands or *Faeroes* alternative spelling of the *Faroe Islands, in the N Atlantic.

Fagatogo capital of American *Samoa, situated on Pago Pago Harbour, Tutuila Island, population (1980) 30,124.

Fahd 1921– . King of Saudi Arabia from 1982, when he succeeded his half-brother Khalid. As head of government, he has been active in trying to bring about a solution to the Middle East conflicts.

Fahrenheit scale a temperature scale invented 1714 by Gabriel Fahrenheit which was commonly used in English-speaking countries up until the 1970s, after which the *Celsius scale was generally adopted, in line with the rest of the world. In the Fahrenheit scale, intervals are measured in degrees (°F); °F = (°C × ⁹/₅) + 32.

fainting sudden, temporary loss of consciousness caused by reduced blood supply to the brain. It may be due to emotional shock or physical factors, such as pooling of blood in the legs from standing still for long periods.

Fairbanks Douglas, Sr. Stage name of Douglas Elton Ulman 1883–1939. US actor. He played acrobatic swashbuckling heroes in silent films such as *The Mark of Zorro* 1920, *The Three Musketeers* 1921, *Robin Hood* 1922, *The Thief of Bagdad* 1924, and *Don Quixote* 1925. He was married to film star Mary Pickford ('America's Sweetheart') 1920–33. In 1919 founded United Artists with Charlie Chaplin and D W Griffith.

Fairbanks Douglas, Jr 1909– . US actor who appeared in the same type of swashbuckling film roles as his father, Douglas Fairbanks; for example, in *Catherine the Great* 1934 and *The Prisoner of Zenda* 1937.

Fair Deal the policy of social improvement advocated by Harry S Truman, President of the USA 1945–53. The Fair Deal proposals, first mooted in 1945 after the end of World War II, aimed to extend the *New Deal on health insurance, housing development, and the laws to maintain farming prices. Although some bills became law – for example a Housing Act, a higher minimum wage, and wider social security benefits – the main proposals were blocked by a hostile Congress.

Fairfax Thomas, 3rd Baron Fairfax of Cameron 1612–1671. English general, commander in chief of the Parliamentary army in the English Civil War. With Oliver Cromwell he formed the *New Model Army and defeated Charles I at Naseby. He opposed the king's execution, resigned in protest 1650 against the invasion of Scotland, and participated in the restoration of Charles II after Cromwell's death.

Fair Trading, Office of UK government department established 1973 to keep commercial activities under review. It covers the areas of consumer affairs and credit, monopolies and mergers, and anti-competitive and *restrictive trade practices. The USA has a Bureau of Consumer Protection with similar scope.

fairy tale magical story, usually a folk tale in origin. Typically in European fairy tales, a poor, brave, and resourceful hero or heroine goes through testing adventures to eventual good fortune. The Germanic tales collected by the *Grimm brothers have been retold in many variants. The form may also be adapted for more individual moral and literary purposes, as was done by Danish writer Hans Christian *Andersen.

Faisal Ibn Abdul Aziz 1905–1975. King of Saudi Arabia from 1964. He was the younger brother of King Saud, on whose accession 1953 he was declared crown prince. He was prime minister from 1953–60 and from 1962–75. In 1964 he emerged victorious from a lengthy conflict with his brother and adopted a policy of steady modernization of his country. He was assassinated by his nephew.

Faisal I 1885–1933. King of Iraq 1921–33. An Arab nationalist leader during World War I, he was instrumental in liberating the Near East from Ottoman control and was declared king of Syria in 1918 but deposed by the French in 1920. The British then installed him as king in Iraq, where he continued to foster pan-Arabism.

fait accompli (French 'accomplished fact') something that has been done and cannot be undone.

fakir originally a Muslim mendicant of some religious order, but in India a general term for an ascetic.

Falange Española (Spanish 'phalanx') former Spanish Fascist Party, founded 1933 by José Antonio de Rivera (1903–1936), son of military ruler Miguel *Primo de Rivera. It was closely modelled in programme and organization on the Italian fascists and on the Nazis. In 1937, when *Franco assumed leadership, it was declared the only legal party, and altered its name to Traditionalist Spanish Phalanx.

Falasha member of a small community of black Jews in Ethiopia. They suffered discrimination there, and, after being accorded Jewish status by Israel 1975, began a gradual process of resettlement in Israel. In the early 1980s only about 30,000 Falashim remained in Ethiopia.

falcon any bird of prey of the genus *Falco*, family Falconidae, order Falconiformes. Falcons are the smallest of the hawks (15–60 cm/6–24 in). They nest in high places and kill their prey by 'stooping' (swooping down at high speed). They include the peregrine and kestrel.

falconry the use of specially trained falcons and hawks to capture birds or small mammals. Practised since ancient times in the Middle East, falconry was introduced from continental Europe to Britain in Saxon times.

Faldo Nick 1957– . English golfer who was the first Briton in 54 years to win three British Open titles, and the only person after Jack *Nicklaus to win two successive US Masters titles (1989 and 1990). He is one of only six golfers to win the Masters and British Open in the same year.

Falkland Islands British crown colony in the S Atlantic
area 12,173 sq km/4,700 sq mi, made up of two main islands: East Falkland 6,760 sq km/2,610 sq mi, and West Falkland 5,413 sq km/2,090 sq mi
capital Stanley; new port facilities opened 1984, Mount Pleasant airport 1985
products wool, alginates (used as dyes and as a food additive) from seaweed beds
population (1986) 1,916

Falklands War war between Argentina and Britain over disputed sovereignty of the Falkland Islands initiated when Argentina invaded and occupied the islands 2 April 1982. On the following day, the United Nations Security Council passed a resolution calling for Argentina to withdraw. A British task force was immediately dispatched and, after a fierce conflict in which over 1,000 Argentine and British lives were lost, 12,000 Argentine troops surrendered and the islands were returned to British rule 14–15 June 1982.

Falla Manuel de 1876–1946. Spanish composer. His opera *La vida breve/Brief Life* 1905 (performed 1913) was followed by the ballets *El amor brujo/Love the Magician* 1915 and *El sombrero de tres picos/The Three-Cornered Hat* 1919, and his most ambitious concert work, *Noches en los jardines de España/Nights in the Gardens of Spain* 1916. The folk idiom of southern Spain is an integral part of his compositions. He also wrote songs and pieces for piano and guitar.

Fall of Man, the myth that explains the existence of evil as the result of some primeval wrongdoing by humanity. It occurs independently in many cultures. In the Bible it is recorded in the Old Testament in Genesis 3, which provided the inspiration for the epic poem *Paradise Lost* 1667 by John *Milton.

Fallopian tube or *oviduct* in mammals, one of two tubes that carry eggs from the ovary to the uterus. An egg is fertilized by sperm in the

Fallopian tubes, which are lined with cells whose *cilia move the egg towards the uterus.

fallout harmful radioactive material released into the atmosphere in the debris of a nuclear explosion – accidental or in nuclear warfare – and descending to the surface of the Earth. Such material can enter the food chain, cause *radiation sickness, and last for hundreds of thousands of years (see *half-life).

false-colour imagery graphic technique that displays images in false (not true-to-life) colours so as to enhance certain features. It is widely used in displaying electronic images taken by spacecraft; for example, Earth-survey satellites such as *Landsat*. Any colours can be selected by a computer processing the received data.

false memory syndrome syndrome occurring in some patients undergoing psychotherapy or hypnosis, in which the individual 'remembers' events that never happened. For example, the patient may recall having been sexually abused as a child. As it is very difficult to establish whether or not memories are genuine, the syndrome is surrounded by controversy.

falsetto in music, a male voice singing in the female (soprano or alto) register.

falsificationism in philosophy of science, the belief that a scientific theory must be under constant scrutiny and that its merit lies only in how well it stands up to rigorous testing. It was first expounded by philosopher Karl *Popper in his *Logic of Scientific Discovery* 1934.

Famagusta seaport on the E coast of Cyprus, in the Turkish Republic of Northern Cyprus; population (1985) 19,500. It was the chief port of the island until the Turkish invasion 1974.

family in biological classification, a group of related genera (see *genus). Family names are not printed in italic (unlike genus and species names), and by convention they all have the ending -idae (animals) or -aceae (plants and fungi). For example, the genera of hummingbirds are grouped in the hummingbird family, Trochilidae. Related families are grouped together in an *order.

family group of people related to each other by blood or by marriage. Families are usually described as either 'extended' (a large group of relations living together or in close contact with each other) or 'nuclear' (a family consisting of two parents and their children).

family planning spacing or preventing the birth of children. Access to family-planning services (see *contraceptive) is a significant factor in women's health as well as in limiting population growth. If all those women who wished to avoid further childbirth were able to do so, the number of births would be reduced by 27% in Africa, 33% in Asia, and 35% in Latin America; and the number of women who die during pregnancy or childbirth would be reduced by about 50%.

famine severe shortage of food affecting a large number of people. Almost 750 million people (equivalent to double the population of Europe) worldwide suffer from hunger and malnutrition. The **food availability deficit** (FAD) theory explains famines as being caused by insufficient food supplies. A more recent theory is that famines arise when one group in a society loses its opportunity to exchange its labour or possessions for food.

Fang Lizhi 1936– . Chinese political dissident and astrophysicist. He advocated human rights and encouraged his students to campaign for democracy. In 1989, after the Tiananmen Square massacre, he sought refuge in the US embassy in Beijing and, over a year later, received official permission to leave China.

fanjet another name for *turbo fan, the jet engine used by most airliners.

fantasia *fantasy* or *fancy* in music, a freeform instrumental composition of improvised character.

fantasy fiction nonrealistic fiction. Much of the world's fictional literature could be classified under this term but, as a commercial and literary genre, fantasy started to thrive after the success of J R R Tolkien's *Lord of the Rings* 1954–55.

FAO abbreviation for *__Food and Agriculture Organization__*.

farad SI unit (symbol F) of electrical capacitance (how much electricity a *capacitor can store for a given voltage). One farad is a capacitance of one *coulomb per volt. For practical purposes the microfarad (one millionth of a farad) is more commonly used.

Faraday Michael 1791–1867. English chemist and physicist. In 1821 he began experimenting with electromagnetism, and ten years later discovered the induction of electric currents and made the first dynamo. He subsequently found that a magnetic field will rotate the plane of polarization of light (see *polarized light). Faraday also investigated electrolysis.

Faraday's constant constant (symbol F) representing the electric charge carried on one mole of electrons. It is found by multiplying Avogadro's constant by the charge carried on a single electron, and is equal to 9.648×10^4 coulombs per mole. One *faraday* is this constant used as a unit. The constant is used to calculate the electric charge needed to discharge a particular quantity of ions during *electrolysis.

Faraday's laws three laws of electromagnetic induction, and two laws of electrolysis, all proposed originally by Michael Faraday: *induction* (1) a changing magnetic field induces an electromagnetic force in a conductor; (2) the electromagnetic force is proportional to the rate of change of the field; (3) the direction of the induced electromagnetic force depends on the orientation of the field; *electrolysis* (1) the amount of chemical change during electrolysis is proportional to the charge passing through the liquid; (2) the amount of chemical change produced in a substance by a given amount of electricity is proportional to the electrochemical equivalent of that substance.

Far East geographical term for all Asia E of the Indian subcontinent.

Fargo William George 1818–1881. US long-distance transport pioneer. In 1844 he established with Henry Wells (1805–1878) and Daniel Dunning the first express company to carry freight west of Buffalo. He also established **Wells, Fargo & Company** 1851, carrying goods express between New York and San Francisco via Panama.

Farnese an Italian family, originating in upper Lazio, who held the duchy of Parma 1545–1731. Among the family's most notable members were Alessandro Farnese (1468–1549), who became Pope Paul III in 1534 and granted his duchy to his illegitimate son Pier Luigi (1503–1547); Elizabeth (1692–1766), niece of the last Farnese duke, married Philip V of Spain and was a force in European politics of the time.

Faroe Islands or **Faeroe Islands** or **Faeroes** (Danish **Faerøerne**, 'Sheep Islands') island group (18 out of 22 inhabited) in the N Atlantic, between the Shetland Islands and Iceland, forming an outlying part of *Denmark

area 1,399 sq km/540 sq mi; largest islands are Strømø, Østerø, Vagø, Suderø, Sandø, and Bordø

capital Thorshavn on Strømø, population (1986) 15,287

products fish, crafted goods

currency Danish krone

population (1986) 46,000

language Faerøese, Danish

government since 1948 the islands have had full self-government; they do not belong to the EC

history first settled by Norsemen in the 9th century, the Faroes were a Norwegian province 1380–1709. Their parliament was restored 1852. They withdrew from the European Free Trade Association 1972.

Farouk 1920–1965. King of Egypt 1936–52. He succeeded his father *Fuad I. In 1952 a coup headed by General Muhammed Neguib and Colonel Gamal Nasser compelled him to abdicate, and his son Fuad II was temporarily proclaimed in his place.

Farquhar George 1677–1707. Irish dramatist. His plays *The Recruiting Officer* 1706 and *The Beaux' Stratagem* 1707 are in the tradition of the Restoration comedy of manners, although less robust.

Farrell Terry 1938– . British architect working in a Post-Modern idiom, largely for corporate clients seeking an alternative to the rigours of High Tech or Modernist office blocks. His Embankment Place scheme 1991 sits theatrically on top of Charing Cross station in Westminster, London, and has been likened to a giant jukebox.

Farrow Mia 1945– . US film and television actress. Popular since the late 1960s, she has been associated with the director Woody Allen since 1982, both on and off screen. She starred in his films *Zelig* 1983, *Hannah and Her Sisters* 1986, and *Crimes and Misdemeanors* 1990, as well as in Roman Polanski's *Rosemary's Baby* 1968.

Fars province of SW Iran, comprising fertile valleys among mountain ranges running NW–SE; population (1982) 2,035,600; area 133,300 sq km/51,487 sq mi. The capital is Shiraz, and there are imposing ruins of Cyrus the Great's city of Parargardae and of *Persepolis.

Farsi or **Persian** language belonging to the Indo-Iranian branch of the Indo-European family, and the official language of Iran (formerly Persia). It is also spoken in Afghanistan, Iraq, and Tajikistan.

farthing formerly the smallest English coin, a quarter of a penny. It was introduced as a silver coin in Edward I's reign. The copper farthing became widespread in Charles II's reign, and the bronze 1860. It was dropped from use 1961.

fasces in ancient Rome, bundles of rods carried in procession by the lictors (minor officials) in front of the chief magistrates, as a symbol of the latter's power over the lives and liberties of the people. An axe was included in the bundle. The fasces were revived in the 20th century as the symbol of *fascism.

fascism political ideology that denies all rights to individuals in their relations with the state; specifically, the totalitarian nationalist movement founded in Italy 1919 by *Mussolini and followed by Hitler's Germany 1933. Fascism was essentially a product of the economic and political crisis of the years after World War I. Units called *fasci di combattimento* (combat groups), from the Latin *fasces, were originally established to oppose communism. The fascist party, the *Partitio Nazionale Fascista*, controlled Italy 1922–43. Fascism protected the existing social order by forcible suppression of the working-class movement and by providing scapegoats for popular anger such as outsiders who lived within the state: Jews, foreigners, or blacks; it also prepared the citizenry for the economic and psychological mobilization of war.

Fassbinder Rainer Werner 1946–1982. West German film director who began as a fringe actor and founded his own 'anti-theatre' before moving into films. His works are mainly stylized indictments of contemporary German society. He made more than 40 films, including *Die bitteren Tränen der Petra von Kant/The Bitter Tears of Petra von Kant* 1972, *Angst essen Seele auf/Fear Eats the Soul* 1974, and *Die Ehe von Maria Braun/The Marriage of Maria Braun* 1979.

fast breeder or **breeder reactor** alternative names for *fast reactor, a type of nuclear reactor.

fasting the practice of voluntarily going without food. It can be undertaken as a religious observance, a sign of mourning, a political protest (hunger strike), or for slimming purposes.

fast reactor or **fast breeder reactor** *nuclear reactor that makes use of fast neutrons to bring about fission. Unlike other reactors used by the nuclear-power industry, it has little or no *moderator, to slow down neutrons. The reactor core is surrounded by a 'blanket' of uranium carbide. During operation, some of this uranium is converted into plutonium, which can be extracted and later used as fuel.

fat in the broadest sense, a mixture of *lipids – chiefly triglycerides (lipids containing three *fatty acid molecules linked to a molecule of glycerol). More specifically, the term refers to a lipid mixture that is solid at room temperature (20°C); lipid mixtures that are liquid at room temperature are called *oils. The higher the proportion of saturated fatty acids in a mixture, the harder the fat.

Fatah, al- Palestinian nationalist organization founded 1956 to bring about an independent state of Palestine. Also called the Palestine National Liberation Movement, it is the main component of the *Palestine Liberation Organization. Its leader is Yassir *Arafat.

fata morgana (Italian 'Morgan the Fairy') a mirage, often seen in the Strait of Messina and traditionally attributed to the sorcery of *Morgan le Fay. She was believed to reside in Calabria, a region of S Italy.

Fates in Greek mythology, the three female figures who determined the destiny of human lives. They were envisaged as spinners; Clotho spun the thread of life, Lachesis twisted the thread, and Atropos cut it off. They are analogous to the Roman Parcae and Norse Norns.

Father of the Church any of certain teachers and writers of the early Christian church, eminent for their learning and orthodoxy, experience, and sanctity of life. They lived between the end of the 1st and the end of the 7th century, a period divided by the Council of Nicaea 325 into the Ante-Nicene and Post-Nicene Fathers.

Father's Day a day set apart in many countries for honouring fathers, observed on the third Sunday in June in the USA, UK, and Canada. The idea for a father's day originated with Sonora Louise Smart Dodd of Spokane, Washington, USA, in 1909 (after hearing a sermon on Mother's Day), and through her efforts the first Father's Day was celebrated there in 1910.

fathom (Anglo-Saxon *faethm* 'to embrace') in mining, seafaring, and handling timber, a unit of depth measurement (1.83 m/6 ft) used prior to metrication; it approximates to the distance between an adult man's hands when the arms are outstretched.

Fatimid dynasty of Muslim Shi'ite caliphs founded 909 by Obaidallah, who claimed to be a descendant of Fatima (the prophet Muhammad's daughter) and her husband Ali, in N Africa. In 969 the Fatimids conquered Egypt, and the dynasty continued until overthrown by Saladin 1171.

fatty acid or **carboxylic acid** organic compound consisting of a hydrocarbon chain, up to 24 carbon atoms long, with a carboxyl group (–COOH) at one end. The covalent bonds between the carbon atoms may be single or double; where a double bond occurs the carbon atoms concerned carry one instead of two hydrogen atoms. Chains with only single bonds have all the hydrogen they can carry, so they are said to be **saturated** with hydrogen. Chains with one or more double bonds are said to be **unsaturated** (see *polyunsaturate).

fatwa in Islamic law, an authoritative legal opinion on a point of doctrine. In 1989 a fatwa calling for the death of English novelist Salman *Rushdie was made by the Ayatollah *Khomeini of Iran, following publication of Rushdie's controversial and allegedly blasphemous book *The Satanic Verses*.

Faulkner William 1897–1962. US novelist. He wrote in an experimental stream-of-consciousness style. His works include *The Sound and the Fury* 1929, dealing with a Southern family in decline; *As I Lay Dying* 1930; and *The Hamlet* 1940, *The Town* 1957, and *The Mansion* 1959, a trilogy covering the rise of the materialistic Snopes family. Nobel prize 1949.

fault in geology, a fracture in the Earth's crust along which the two sides have moved as a result of differing strains in the adjacent rock bodies. Displacement of rock masses horizontally or vertically along a fault may be microscopic, or it may be massive, causing major *earthquakes.

Faunus in Roman mythology, god of fertility and prophecy, with goat's ears, horns, tail and hind legs, identified with the Greek Pan.

Fauré Gabriel (Urbain) 1845–1924. French composer of songs, chamber music, and a choral *Requiem* 1888. He was a pupil of Saint-Saëns, became professor of composition at the Paris Conservatoire 1896 and was director from 1905 to 1920.

Faust legendary magician who sold his soul to the Devil. The historical Georg Faust appears to have been a wandering scholar and conjurer in Germany at the start of the 16th century. Goethe, Heine, Thomas Mann, and Paul Valéry all used the legend, and it inspired musical works by Schumann, Berlioz, Gounod, Boito, and Busoni.

Fauvism style of painting with a bold use of vivid colours inspired by van Gogh, Cézanne, and Gaugin. A short-lived but influential art movement, Fauvism originated in Paris 1905 with the founding of the Salon d'Automne by Henri *Matisse and others, when the critic Louis Vauxcelles called their gallery '*une cage aux fauves*' (a cage of wild beasts).

faux pas (French 'false step') a social blunder.

Fawkes Guy 1570–1606. English conspirator in the *Gunpowder Plot to blow up King James I and the members of both Houses of Parliament. Fawkes, a Roman Catholic convert, was arrested in the cellar underneath the House 4 Nov 1605, tortured, and executed. The event is still commemorated in Britain and elsewhere every 5 Nov with bonfires, fireworks, and the burning of the 'guy', an effigy.

fax (common name for **facsimile transmission** or **telefax**) the transmission of images over a *telecommunications link, usually the telephone network. When placed on a fax machine, the original image is scanned by a transmitting device and converted into coded signals, which travel via the telephone lines to the receiving fax machine, where an image is created that is a copy of the original. Photographs as well as printed text and drawings can be sent.

FBI abbreviation for *Federal Bureau of Investigation*, agency of the US Department of Justice.

fealty in feudalism, the loyalty and duties owed by a vassal to his lord. In the 9th century fealty obliged the vassal not to take part in any action that would endanger the lord or his property, but by the 11th century the specific duties of fealty were established and included financial obligations and military service. Following an oath of fealty, an act of allegiance and respect (homage) was made by the vassal; when a fief (estate) was granted by the lord, it was formalized in the process of investiture.

feather rigid outgrowth of the outer layer of the skin of birds, made of the protein keratin. Feathers provide insulation and facilitate flight. There are several types, including long quill feathers on the wings and tail, fluffy down feathers for retaining body heat, and contour feathers covering the body. The colouring of feathers is often important in camouflage or in courtship and other displays. Feathers are replaced at least once a year.

feather star any of an unattached, free-swimming group of sea-lilies, order Comatulida. The arms are branched into numerous projections (hence 'feather' star), and grow from a small cup-shaped body. Below the body are appendages that can hold on to a surface, but the feather star is not permanently attached.

February Revolution the first of the two political uprisings of the *Russian revolution in 1917 that led to the overthrow of the tsar and the end of the *Romanov dynasty.

fecundity the rate at which an organism reproduces, as distinct from its ability to reproduce (*fertility). In vertebrates, it is usually measured as the number of offspring produced by a female each year.

Federal Bureau of Investigation (FBI) agency of the US Department of Justice that investigates violations of federal law not specifically assigned to other agencies, being particularly concerned with internal security. The FBI was established 1908 and built up a position of powerful autonomy during the autocratic directorship of J Edgar Hoover 1924–72. Judge William Sessions has been director since 1987.

federalism system of government in which two or more separate states unite under a common central government while retaining a considerable degree of local autonomy. A federation should be distinguished from a *confederation*, a looser union of states for mutual assistance. Switzerland, the USA, Canada, Australia, and Malaysia are all examples of federal government, and many supporters of the European Community see it as the forerunner of a federal Europe.

Federalist in US history, one who advocated the ratification of the US Constitution 1787–88 in place of the Articles of *Confederation. The Federalists became in effect the ruling political party during the presidencies of George Washington and John Adams 1789–1801, legislating to strengthen the authority of the newly created federal government.

Federal Reserve System (the 'Fed') US central banking system and note-issuing authority, established 1913 to regulate the country's credit and *monetary policy. The Fed consists of the 12 federal reserve banks, their 25 branches and other facilities throughout the country; it is headed by a board of governors in Washington, DC, appointed by the president with Senate approval.

federation political entity made up from a number of smaller units or states where the central government has powers over national issues such as foreign policy and defence, while the individual states retain a high degree of regional and local autonomy. A federation should be distinguished from a *confederation*, a looser union of states for mutual assistance. Contemporary examples of federated states established since 1750 include the USA, Canada, Australia, India, and the Federal Republic of Germany.

feedback general principle whereby the results produced in an ongoing reaction become factors in modifying or changing the reaction; it is the principle used in self-regulating control systems, from a simple *thermostat and steam-engine *governor to automatic computer-controlled machine tools. A fully computerized control system, in which there is no operator intervention, is called a *closed-loop feedback* system. A system that also responds to signals from an operator is called an *open-loop feedback* system.

feedback in music, a continuous tone, usually a high-pitched squeal, caused by the overloading of circuits between electric guitar and amplifier as the sound of the speakers is fed back through the guitar pickup. Deliberate feedback is much used in rock music.

feldspar one of a group of rock-forming minerals; the chief constituents of *igneous rock. Feldspars all contain silicon, aluminium, and oxygen, linked together to form a framework; spaces within this structure are occupied by sodium, potassium, calcium, or occasionally barium, in various proportions. Feldspars form white, grey, or pink crystals and rank 6 on the *Mohs' scale of hardness.

feldspathoid any of a group of silicate minerals resembling feldspars but containing less silica. Examples are nepheline ($NaAlSiO_4$ with a little potassium) and leucite ($KAlSi_2O_6$). Feldspathoids occur in igneous rocks that have relatively high proportions of sodium and potassium. Such rocks may also contain alkali feldspar, but they do not generally contain quartz because any free silica would have combined with the feldspathoid to produce more feldspar instead.

felicific calculus or *hedonic calculus* in ethics, a technique for establishing the rightness and wrongness of an action. Using the calculus, one can attempt to work out the likely consequences of an action in terms of the pain or pleasure of those affected by the action. The calculus is attributed to English utilitarian philosopher Jeremy Bentham.

Fellini Federico 1920–1993. Italian film director and screenwriter. His work has been a major influence on modern cinema. His films combine dream and fantasy sequences with satire and autobiographical detail. They include *I vitelloni/The Young and the Passionate* 1953, *La strada/The Street* 1954 (Academy Award), *Le notti di Cabiria/Nights of Cabiria* 1956 (Academy Award), *La dolce vita* 1960, *Otto e mezzo/8½* 1963 (Academy Award), *Satyricon* 1969, *Roma/Fellini's Rome* 1972, *Amarcord* 1974 (Academy Award), *La città delle donne/City of Women* 1980, and *Ginger e Fred/Ginger and Fred* 1986. He was presented with a Special Academy Award for his life's work 1993.

female circumcision operation on women analagous to male *circumcision. There are three types: *Sunna*, which involves cutting off the hood, and sometimes the tip, of the clitoris; *clitoridectomy*, the excision of the clitoris and removal of parts of the inner and outer labia; *infibulation* (most widely practised in Sudan and Somalia), in which the labia are stitched, after excision, leaving a small hole.

feminism active belief in equal rights and opportunities for women; see *women's movement.

femur the *thighbone*; also the upper bone in the hind limb of a four-limbed vertebrate.

fencing sport of fighting with swords including the *foil*, derived from the light weapon used in practice duels; the *épée*, a heavier weapon derived from the duelling sword proper; and the *sabre*, with a curved handle and narrow V-shaped blade. In sabre fighting, cuts count as well as thrusts. Masks and protective jackets are worn, and hits are registered electronically in competitions. Men's fencing has been part of every Olympic programme since 1896; women's fencing was included from 1924 but only using the foil.

Fender (Clarence) Leo 1909–1991. US guitar-maker. He created the solid-body electric guitar, the Fender Broadcaster 1948 (renamed the Tele-caster 1950), and the first electric bass guitar, the Fender Precision, 1951. The Fender Stratocaster guitar dates from 1954. In 1965 he sold the Fender name to CBS, which continues to make the instruments.

Fenian movement Irish-American republican secret society, founded 1858 and named after the ancient Irish legendary warrior band of the Fianna. The collapse of the movement began when an attempt to establish an independent Irish republic by an uprising in Ireland 1867 failed, as did raids into Canada 1866 and 1870, and England 1867.

fennec small nocturnal desert *fox *Fennecus zerda* found in N Africa and Arabia. It is only 40 cm/1.3 ft long, and its enormous ears act as radiators to lose excess heat. It eats insects and small animals.

fennel any of several varieties of a perennial plant *Foeniculum vulgare* with feathery green leaves, of the carrot family Umbelliferae. Fennels have an aniseed flavour, and the leaves and seeds are used in seasoning.

Fens, the level, low-lying tracts of land in E England, W and S of the Wash, about 115 km/70 mi N–S and 55 km/34 mi E–W. They fall within the counties of Lincolnshire, Cambridge-shire, and Norfolk, consisting of a huge area, formerly a bay of the North Sea, but now crossed by numerous drainage canals and forming some of the most productive agricultural land in Brit-ain. The peat portion of the Fens is known as the *Bedford Level*.

Fenton Roger 1819–1869. English photog-rapher. The world's first war photographer, he went to the Crimea 1855; he also founded the Royal Photographic Society in London 1853.

Ferdinand 1861–1948. King of Bulgaria 1908–18. Son of Prince Augustus of Saxe-Coburg-Gotha, he was elected prince of Bulgaria 1887 and, in 1908, proclaimed Bulgaria's inde-pendence of Turkey and assumed the title of tsar. In 1915 he entered World War I as Germany's ally, and in 1918 abdicated.

Ferdinand five kings of Castile, including

Ferdinand I *the Great* c. 1016–1065. King of Castile from 1035. He began the reconquest of Spain from the Moors and united all NW Spain under his and his brothers' rule.

Ferdinand V 1452–1516. King of Castile from 1474, *Ferdinand II* of Aragon from 1479, and *Ferdinand III* of Naples from 1504; first king of all Spain. In 1469 he married his cousin *Isabella I, who succeeded to the throne of Castile 1474; they were known as *the Catholic Monarchs* because after 700 years of rule by the *Moors, they Catholicized Spain. When Ferdinand inherited the throne of Aragon 1479, the two great Spanish kingdoms were brought under a single government for the first time. They intro-duced the *Inquisition 1480; expelled the Jews, forced the final surrender of the Moors at Gran-ada, and financed Columbus' expedition to the Americas, 1492.

Ferdinand three Holy Roman emperors, including:

Ferdinand II 1578–1637. Holy Roman emperor from 1619, when he succeeded his uncle Mat-thias; king of Bohemia from 1617 and of Hungary from 1618. A zealous Catholic, he provoked the Bohemian revolt that led to the Thirty Years' War. He was a grandson of Ferdinand I.

Ferdinand III 1608–1657. Holy Roman emperor from 1637 when he succeeded his father Ferdinand II; king of Hungary from 1625. Although anxious to conclude the Thirty Years' War, he did not give religious liberty to Prot-estants.

Ferghana town in Uzbekistan, in the fertile *Ferghana Valley*; population (1987) 203,000. It is the capital of the major cotton-and fruit-grow-ing Ferghana region; nearby are petroleum fields. The Ferghana Valley is divided between Uzbekis-tan, Kyrgyzstan, and Tajikistan, causing inter-ethnic violence between Uzbek, Meskhetian, and Kyrgyz communities.

Fermanagh county in the southern part of Northern Ireland
area 1,680 sq km/648 sq mi
towns Enniskillen (county town), Lisnaskea, Irvinestown
physical in the centre is a broad trough of low-lying land, in which lie Upper and Lower Lough Erne
products mainly agricultural; livestock, tweeds, clothing
population (1981) 52,000.

fermentation the breakdown of sugars by bac-teria and yeasts using a method of respiration without oxygen (*anaerobic). Fermentation pro-cesses have long been utilized in baking bread, making beer and wine, and producing cheese, yoghurt, soy sauce, and many other foodstuffs.

Fermi Enrico 1901–1954. Italian-born US physi-cist who proved the existence of new radioactive elements produced by bombardment with neu-trons, and discovered nuclear reactions produced by low-energy neutrons. His theoretical work included study of the weak nuclear force, one of the fundamental forces of nature, and (with Paul Dirac) of the quantum statistics of fermion par-ticles. He was awarded a Nobel prize 1938.

fermion in physics, a subatomic particle whose spin can only take values that are half-integers, such as $\frac{1}{2}$ or $1\frac{1}{2}$. Fermions may be classified as leptons, such as the electron, and baryons, such as the proton and neutron. All elementary par-ticles are either fermions or *bosons.

fermium synthesized, radioactive, metallic element of the *actinide series, symbol Fm, atomic number 100, relative atomic mass 257.

Ten isotopes are known, the longest-lived of which, Fm-257, has a half-life of 80 days. Fermium has been produced only in minute quantities in particle accelerators.

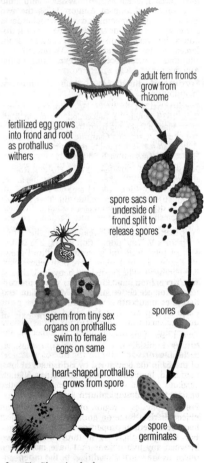

adult fern fronds grow from rhizome

fertilized egg grows into frond and root as prothallus withers

spore sacs on underside of frond split to release spores

spores

sperm from tiny sex organs on prothallus swim to female eggs on same

heart-shaped prothallus grows from spore

spore germinates

fern *The life cycle of a fern.*

fern plant of the class Filicales, related to horsetails and clubmosses. Ferns are spore-bearing, not flowering, plants, and most are perennial, spreading by low-growing roots. The leaves, known as fronds, vary widely in size and shape. Some taller types, such as tree-ferns, grow in the tropics. There are over 7,000 species.

Ferranti Sebastian de 1864–1930. British electrical engineer who established the principle of a national grid, and an electricity generating system based on alternating current (AC) (successfully arguing against *Edison's proposal). He brought electricity to much of central London. In 1881 he made and sold his first alternator.

Ferrari Enzo 1898–1988. Italian founder of the Ferrari car manufacturing company, which specializes in Grand Prix racing cars and high-quality sports cars. He was a racing driver for

Alfa Romeo in the 1920s, went on to become one of their designers and in 1929 took over their racing division. In 1947 the first 'true' Ferrari was seen. The Ferrari car has won more world championship Grands Prix than any other car.

ferret domesticated variety of the Old World *polecat. About 35 cm/1.2 ft long, it usually has yellowish-white fur and pink eyes, but may be the dark brown colour of a wild polecat. Ferrets may breed with wild polecats. They have been used since ancient times to hunt rabbits and rats.

Ferrier Kathleen (Mary) 1912–1953. English contralto who sang in oratorio and opera. In Benjamin Britten's *The Rape of Lucretia* 1946 she created the role of Lucretia, and she gave a memorable performance in Gustav Mahler's *Das Lied von der Erde* at the Edinburgh Festival 1947.

ferro-alloy alloy of iron with a high proportion of elements such as manganese, silicon, chromium, and molybdenum. Ferro-alloys are used in the manufacture of alloy steels. Each alloy is generally named after the added metal – for example, ferrochromium.

fertility an organism's ability to reproduce, as distinct from the rate at which it reproduces (see *fecundity). Individuals become infertile (unable to reproduce) when they cannot generate gametes (eggs or sperm) or when their gametes cannot yield a viable *embryo after fertilization.

fertility drug any of a range of drugs taken to increase a female's fertility, developed in Sweden in the mid-1950s. They increase the chances of a multiple birth.

fertilization in *sexual reproduction, the union of two *gametes (sex cells, often called egg and sperm) to produce a *zygote, which combines the genetic material contributed by each parent. In self-fertilization the male and female gametes come from the same plant; in cross-fertilization they come from different plants. Self-fertilization rarely occurs in animals; usually even *hermaphrodite animals cross-fertilize each other.

fertilizer substance containing some or all of a range of about 20 chemical elements necessary for healthy plant growth, used to compensate for the deficiencies of poor or depleted soil. Fertilizers may be *organic*, for example farmyard manure, composts, bonemeal, blood, and fishmeal; or *inorganic*, in the form of compounds, mainly of nitrogen, phosphate, and potash, which have been used on a very much increased scale since 1945.

Fès or *Fez* former capital of Morocco 808–1062, 1296–1548, and 1662–1912, in a valley N of the Great Atlas mountains, 160 km/100 mi E of Rabat; population (1982) 563,000. Textiles, carpets, and leather are manufactured, and the *fez*, a brimless hat worn in S and E Mediterranean countries, is traditionally said to have originated here. Kairwan Islamic University dates from 859; a second university was founded 1961.

fescue any grass of the widely distributed genus *Festuca.* Many are used in temperate regions for lawns and pasture. Many upland species are viviparous.

fetal surgery any operation on the fetus to correct a congenital condition (for example, *hydrocephalus). Fetal surgery was pioneered in the USA 1981. It leaves no scar tissue.

fetch-execute cycle or *processing cycle* in computing, the two-phase cycle used by the computer's central processing unit to process the instructions in a program. During the *fetch phase*, the next program instruction is transferred from the computer's immediate-access memory to the instruction register (memory location used to hold the instruction while it is being executed). During the *execute phase*, the instruction is decoded and obeyed. The process is repeated in a continuous loop.

fetishism in anthropology, belief in the supernormal power of some inanimate object that is known as a fetish. Fetishism in some form is common to most cultures, and often has religio-magical significance.

fetishism in psychology, the transfer of erotic interest to an object, such as an item of clothing whose real or fantasized presence is necessary for sexual gratification.

fetus or *foetus* stage in mammalian *embryo development. The human embryo is usually termed a fetus after the eighth week of development, when the limbs and external features of the head are recognizable.

feudalism (Latin *feudem* 'fief', coined 1839) main form of social organization in medieval Europe. A system based primarily on land, it involved a hierarchy of authority, rights, and power that extended from the monarch downwards. An intricate network of duties and obligations linked royalty, nobility, lesser gentry, free tenants, villeins, and serfs. Feudalism was reinforced by a complex legal system and supported by the Christian church. With the growth of commerce and industry from the 13th century, feudalism gradually gave way to the class system as the dominant form of social ranking.

Feynman Richard Phillips 1918–1988. US physicist whose work laid the foundations of quantum electrodynamics. As a member of the committee investigating the *Challenger* space-shuttle disaster 1986, he demonstrated the lethal faults in rubber seals on the shuttle's booster rocket. For his work on the theory of radiation he shared the Nobel Prize for Physics 1965 with Julian Schwinger and Sin-Itiro Tomonaga (1906–1979).

Fianna Fáil (Gaelic 'Soldiers of Destiny') Republic of Ireland political party, founded by the Irish nationalist de Valera 1926. It has been the governing party in the Republic of Ireland 1932–48, 1951–54, 1957–73, 1977–81, 1982, and 1987– . It aims at the establishment of a united and completely independent all-Ireland republic.

Fibonacci Leonardo, also known as *Leonardo of Pisa* c. 1175–c. 1250. Italian mathematician. He published *Liber abaci* in Pisa 1202, which was instrumental in the introduction of Arabic notation into Europe. From 1960, interest increased in *Fibonacci numbers*, in their simplest form a sequence in which each number is the sum of its two predecessors (1, 1, 2, 3, 5, 8, 13, ...). They have unusual characteristics with possible applications in botany, psychology, and astronomy (for example, a more exact correspondence than is given by *Bode's law to the distances between the planets and the Sun).

fibre, dietary or *roughage* plant material that cannot be digested by human digestive enzymes; it consists largely of cellulose, a carbohydrate found in plant cell walls. Fibre adds bulk to the gut contents, assisting the muscular contractions that force food along the intestine. A diet low in fibre causes constipation and is believed to increase the risk of developing diverticulitis, diabetes, gall-bladder disease, and cancer of the large bowel – conditions that are rare in non-industrialized countries, where the diet contains a high proportion of unrefined cereals.

fibreglass glass that has been formed into fine fibres, either as long continuous filaments or as a fluffy, short-fibred glass wool. Fibreglass is heat- and fire-resistant and a good electrical insulator. It has applications in the field of fibre optics and as a strengthener for plastics in *GRP (glass-reinforced plastics).

fibre optics branch of physics dealing with the transmission of light and images through glass or plastic fibres known as *optical fibres.

fibrin an insoluble blood protein used by the body to stop bleeding. When an injury occurs fibrin is deposited around the wound in the form of a mesh, which dries and hardens, so that bleeding stops. Fibrin is developed in the blood from a soluble protein, fibrinogen.

fibula the rear lower bone in the hind leg of a vertebrate. It is paired and often fused with a smaller front bone, the tibia.

fiction in literature, any work in which the content is completely or largely invented. The term describes imaginative works of narrative prose (such as the novel or the short story), and is distinguished from *nonfiction* (such as history, biography, or works on practical subjects), and *poetry*.

Fidei Defensor Latin for the title of 'Defender of the Faith' (still retained by British sovereigns) conferred by Pope Leo X on Henry VIII of England 1521 to reward his writing of a treatise against the Protestant Martin Luther.

field in physics, a region of space in which an object exerts a force on another separate object because of certain properties they both possess. For example, there is a force of attraction between any two objects that have mass when one is in the gravitational field of the other.

field enclosed area of land used for farming. Traditionally fields were measured in *acres; the current unit of measurement is the hectare (2.47 acres).

fieldfare thrush *Turdus pilaris* of the family Muscicapidae; it has a pale-grey lower back and neck and a dark tail.

Fielding Henry 1707–1754. English novelist. His greatest work, *The History of Tom Jones, a Foundling* 1749 (which he described as 'a comic epic in prose'), realized for the first time in English the novel's potential for memorable characterization, coherent plotting, and perceptive analysis. In youth a prolific playwright, he began writing novels with *An Apology for the Life of Mrs Shamela Andrews* 1741, a merciless parody of Samuel *Richardson's *Pamela*.

field marshal the highest rank in many European armies. A British field marshal is equivalent to a US *general.

Fields W C. Stage name of William Claude Dukenfield 1879–1946. US actor and screenwriter. His distinctive speech and professed attitudes such as hatred of children and dogs gained him enormous popularity in such films as *David Copperfield* 1935, *My Little Chickadee* (co-written with Mae West) and *The Bank Dick* both 1940, and *Never Give a Sucker an Even Break* 1941.

field studies study of ecology, geography, geology, history, archaeology, and allied subjects, in the natural environment as opposed to the laboratory.

Fiennes Ranulph Twisleton-Wykeham 1944– . British explorer who made the first surface journey around the world's polar circumference between 1979 and 1982. Earlier expeditions included explorations of the White Nile 1969, Jostedalsbre Glacier, Norway, 1970, and the Headless Valley, Canada, 1971. Accounts of his adventures include *A Talent for Trouble* 1970, *Hell on Ice* 1979, and the autobiographical *Living Dangerously* 1987.

fife a type of small flute. Originally from Switzerland, it was known as the Swiss pipe and has long been played by military bands.

Fife region of E Scotland (formerly the county of Fife), facing the North Sea and Firth of Forth
area 1,300 sq km/502 sq mi
towns Glenrothes (administrative headquarters); Dunfermline, St Andrews, Kirkcaldy, Cupar
physical the only high land is the Lomond Hills, in the NW; chief rivers Eden and Leven
products potatoes, cereals, electronics, petrochemicals (Mossmorran), light engineering
population (1991) 339,200.

Fifteen, the *Jacobite rebellion of 1715, led by the 'Old Pretender' *James Edward Stuart and the Earl of Mar, in order to place the former on the English throne. Mar was checked at Sheriffmuir, Scotland, and the revolt collapsed.

fifth column group within a country secretly aiding an enemy attacking from without. The term originated 1936 during the Spanish Civil War, when General Mola boasted that Franco supporters were attacking Madrid with four columns and that they had a 'fifth column' inside the city.

fifth-generation computer anticipated new type of computer based on emerging microelectronic technologies with high computing speeds and *parallel processing. The development of very large-scale integration (*VLSI) technology, which can put many more circuits on to an integrated circuit (chip) than is currently possible, and developments in computer hardware and software design may produce computers far more powerful that those in current use.

fig any tree of the genus *Ficus* of the mulberry family Moraceae, including the many cultivated varieties of *F. carica*, originally from W Asia. They produce two or three crops of fruit a year. Eaten fresh or dried, figs have a high sugar content and laxative properties.

fighting fish any of a SE Asian genus *Betta* of fishes of the gourami family, especially *B. splendens*, about 6 cm/2 in long and a popular aquarium fish. It can breathe air, using an accessory breathing organ above the gill, and can live in poorly oxygenated water. The male has large fins and various colours, including shining greens, reds, and blues. The female is yellowish brown with short fins.

figure of speech poetic, imaginative, or ornamental expression used for purposes of comparison, emphasis, or stylistic effect; usually one of a list of such forms dating from discussions of literary and rhetorical style in Greece in the 5th century BC. These figures include euphemism, hyperbole, metaphor, metonymy, onomatopoeia, oxymoron, personification, the pun, simile, and synecdoche.

figwort any Old World plant of the genus *Scrophularia* of the figwort family, which also includes foxgloves and snapdragons. Members of the genus have square stems, opposite leaves, and open two-lipped flowers in a cluster at the top of the stem.

Fiji Republic of
area 18,333 sq km/7,078 sq mi
capital Suva
towns ports Lautoka and Levuka
physical comprises 844 Melanesian and Polynesian islands and islets (about 110 inhabited), the largest being Viti Levu (10,429 sq km/ 4,028 sq mi) and Vanua Levu (5,550 sq km/2,146 sq mi); mountainous, volcanic, with tropical rainforest and grasslands
head of state Kamisese Mara from 1994
head of government Col Sitiveni Rabuka from 1992
political system democratic republic
exports sugar, coconut oil, ginger, timber, canned fish, gold; tourism is important
currency Fiji dollar
population (1993) 758,300 (46% Fijian, holding 80% of the land communally, and 49% Indian, introduced in the 19th century to work the sugar crop); growth rate 2.1% p.a.
languages English (official), Fijian, Hindi
religions Hindu 50%, Methodist 44%
GNP $1,830 per head (1991)
chronology
1874 Fiji became a British crown colony.
1970 Independence achieved from Britain; Ratu Sir Kamisese Mara elected as first prime minister.
1987 April: general election put Dr Timoci Bavadra in power. Sept: military coup by Col Sitiveni Rabuka who proclaimed Fiji a republic. Oct: Fiji ceased to be a member of the Commonwealth. Dec: civilian government restored with Rabuka retaining control of security.
1990 New constitution, favouring indigenous Fijians, introduced.
1992 General election produced coalition government; Col Rabuka (FPP) named as prime minister.
1993 President Ganilau died; Kamisese Mara became acting head of state.
1994 Mara sworn in as president. Rabuka and FPP re-elected.

file in computing, a collection of data or a program stored in a computer's external memory (for example, on *disc). It might contain anything from information on a company's employees to a program for an adventure game. **Serial files** hold information as a sequence of characters, so that, to read any particular item of data, the program must read all those that precede it. **Random-access files** allow the required data to be reached directly.

Fillmore Millard 1800–1874. 13th president of the USA 1850–53, a Whig. Born into a poor farming family in New Cayuga County, New York State, he was Zachary Taylor's vice-president from 1849, and succeeded him on Taylor's death, July 9 1850. Fillmore supported a compromise on slavery 1850 to reconcile North and South.

film, art of see *cinema.

film noir (French 'dark film') a term originally used by French critics to describe films characterized by pessimism, cynicism, and a dark, sombre tone. It has been used to describe black-and-white Hollywood films of the 1940s and 1950s that portrayed the seedy side of life.

film, photographic strip of transparent material (usually cellulose acetate) coated with a light-sensitive emulsion, used in cameras to take pictures. The emulsion contains a mixture of light-sensitive silver halide salts (for example, bromide or iodide) in gelatin. When the emulsion is exposed to light, the silver salts are invisibly altered, giving a latent image, which is then made visible by the process of *developing. Films differ in their sensitivities to light, this being indicated by their speeds. Colour film consists of several layers of emulsion, each of which records a different colour in the light falling on it.

filter in chemistry, a porous substance, such as blotting paper, through which a mixture can be passed to separate out its solid constituents. In optics, a filter is a piece of glass or transparent material that passes light of one colour only.

filter in electronics, a circuit that transmits a signal of some frequencies better than others. A low-pass filter transmits signals of low frequency and direct current; a high-pass filter transmits high-frequency signals; a band-pass filter transmits signals in a band of frequencies.

filtration technique by which suspended solid particles in a fluid are removed by passing the mixture through a porous barrier, usually paper or cloth. The particles are retained by the paper or cloth to form a residue and the fluid passes through to make up the filtrate. Soot is filtered from air while suspended solids are filtered from water.

final solution (to the Jewish question; German *Endlosung der Judenfrage*) phrase used by the Nazis to describe the extermination of Jews (and other unwanteds and opponents of the regime) before and during World War II. See *Holocaust.

Financial Times Index (FT Index) indicator measuring the daily movement of 30 major industrial share prices on the London Stock Exchange (1935 = 100), issued by the UK *Financial Times* newspaper. Other FT indices cover government securities, fixed-interest securities, gold mine shares, and Stock Exchange activity.

finch any of various songbirds of the family Fringillidae, in the order Passeriformes (perching birds).

Finch Peter 1916–1977. Australian-born English cinema actor who began his career in Australia before moving to London in 1949 to start on an international career in films such as *A Town Like Alice* 1956, *Sunday, Bloody Sunday* 1971, and *Network* 1976, for which he won an Academy Award.

Fine Gael (Gaelic 'United Ireland') Republic

of Ireland political party founded 1933 by W J *Cosgrave and led by Alan Dukes from 1987. It is socially liberal but fiscally conservative.

fingerprint ridge pattern of the skin on a person's fingertips; this is constant through life and no two are exactly alike. Fingerprinting was first used as a means of identifying crime suspects in India, and was adopted by the English police 1901; it is now widely employed in police and security work.

Finland Republic of (*Suomen Tasavalta*)

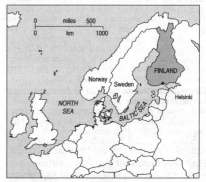

area 338,145 sq km/130,608 sq mi
capital Helsinki
towns Tampere, Rovaniemi, Lahti; ports Turku, Oulu
physical most of the country is forest, with low hills and about 60,000 lakes; one-third is within the Arctic Circle; archipelago in S; includes Aåland Islands
head of state Martti Ahtisaari from 1994
head of government Esko Aho from 1991
political system democratic republic
exports metal, chemical, and engineering products (icebreakers and oil rigs), paper, sawn wood, clothing, fine ceramics, glass, furniture
currency markka
population (1993) 5,020,000; growth rate 0.5% p.a.
languages Finnish 93%, Swedish 6% (both official), small Saami-and Russian-speaking minorities
religions Lutheran 97%, Eastern Orthodox 1.2%
GNP $21,009 per head (1992)
chronology
1809 Finland annexed by Russia.
1917 Independence declared from Russia.
1920 Soviet regime acknowledged independence.
1939 Defeated by USSR in Winter War.
1941 Allowed Germany to station troops in Finland to attack USSR; USSR bombed Finland.
1944 Concluded separate armistice with USSR.
1948 Finno-Soviet Pact of Friendship, Cooperation, and Mutual Assistance signed.
1955 Finland joined the United Nations and the Nordic Council.
1956 Urho Kekkonen elected president; re-elected 1962, 1968, 1978.
1973 Trade treaty with European Economic Community signed.
1977 Trade agreement with USSR signed.

1982 Mauno Koivisto elected president; re-elected 1988.
1989 Finland joined Council of Europe.
1991 Big swing to the centre in general election. New coalition government formed.
1992 Formal application for European Community membership.
1994 Martti Ahtisaari (Social Democratic Party) elected president. Terms of accession to European Union agreed.

Finney Albert 1936– . English actor. He created the title roles in Keith Waterhouse's stage play *Billy Liar* 1960 and John Osborne's *Luther* 1961, and was associate artistic director of the Royal Court Theatre 1972–75. Later roles for the National Theatre include Tamburlaine in Marlowe's tragedy 1976 and *Macbeth* 1978. His films include *Saturday Night and Sunday Morning* 1960, *Tom Jones* 1963, *Murder on the Orient Express* 1974, and *The Dresser* 1984.

Finnish language member of the Finno-Ugric language family, the national language of Finland and closely related to neighbouring Estonian, Livonian, Karelian, and Ingrian languages. At the beginning of the 19th century Finnish had no official status, since Swedish was the language of education, government, and literature in Finland.

Finn Mac Cumhaill legendary Irish hero, identified with a general who organized an Irish regular army in the 3rd century. James Macpherson (1736–96) featured him (as Fingal) and his followers in the verse of his popular epics 1762–63, which were supposedly written by a 3rd-century bard, *Ossian. Although challenged by the critic Dr Johnson, the poems were influential in the Romantic movement.

Finno-Ugric group or family of more than 20 languages spoken by some 22 million people in scattered communities from Norway in the west to Siberia in the east and to the Carpathian mountains in the south. Members of the family include Finnish, Lapp, and Hungarian.

finsen unit unit (symbol FU) for measuring the intensity of ultraviolet (UV) light; for instance, UV light of 2 FUs causes sunburn in 15 minutes.

fiord alternative spelling of *fjord.

fir any *conifer of the genus *Abies* in the pine family Pinaceae. The true firs include the balsam fir of N North America and the Eurasian silver fir *A. alba*. Douglas firs of the genus *Pseudotsuga* are native to W North America and the Far East.

firearm weapon from which projectiles are discharged by the combustion of an explosive. Firearms are generally divided into two main sections: *artillery* (ordnance or cannon), with a bore greater than 2.54 cm/1 in, and *small arms*, with a bore of less than 2.54 cm/1 in. Although gunpowder was known in Europe 60 years previously, the invention of guns dates from 1300 to 1325, and is attributed to Berthold Schwartz, a German monk.

firedamp gas that occurs in coal mines and is explosive when mixed with air in certain proportions. It consists chiefly of methane (CH_4, natural gas or marsh gas) but always contains small quantities of other gases, such as nitrogen, carbon dioxide, and hydrogen, and sometimes ethane and carbon monoxide.

firefly any winged nocturnal beetle of the family Lampyridae. They all emit light through the process of *bioluminescence.

fire protection methods available for fighting fires. Industrial and commercial buildings are often protected by an automatic sprinkler system: heat or smoke opens the sprinkler heads on a network of water pipes which spray the source of the fire. In circumstances where water is ineffective and may be dangerous, for example, for oil and petrol storage-tank fires, foam systems are used; for industrial plants containing flammable vapours, carbon dioxide is used; where electricity is involved, vaporizing liquids create a nonflammable barrier; for some chemicals only various dry powders can be used.

firmware computer program held permanently in a computer's *ROM (read-only memory) chips, as opposed to a program that is read in from external memory as it is needed.

First World War another name for *World War I, 1914–18.

fiscal policy that part of government policy devoted to achieving the desired level of revenue, notably through taxation, and deciding the priorities and purposes governing its expenditure.

fiscal year the financial year, which does not necessarily coincide with the calendar year.

Fischer Bobby (Robert James) 1943– . US chess champion. In 1958, after proving himself in international competition, he became the youngest grand master in history. He was the author of *Games of Chess* 1959, and was also celebrated for his unorthodox psychological tactics. He won the world title from Boris Spassky in Reykjavik, Iceland, 1972.

Fischer Emil Hermann 1852–1919. German chemist who produced synthetic sugars and from these various enzymes. His descriptions of the chemistry of the carbohydrates and peptides laid the foundations for the science of biochemistry. Nobel prize 1902.

Fischer Hans 1881–1945. German chemist awarded a Nobel prize 1930 for his discovery of haemoglobin in blood.

Fischer-Dieskau Dietrich 1925– . German baritone, renowned for his interpretation of Franz Schubert's *lieder* (songs).

fish aquatic vertebrate that uses gills for obtaining oxygen from fresh or sea water. There are three main groups, not closely related: the bony fishes or Osteichthyes (goldfish, cod, tuna); the cartilaginous fishes or Chondrichthyes (sharks, rays); and the jawless fishes or Agnatha (hagfishes, lampreys).

Fisher John, St *c.* 1469–1535. English bishop, created bishop of Rochester 1504. He was an enthusiastic supporter of the revival in the study of Greek, and a friend of the humanists Thomas More and Desiderius Erasmus. In 1535 he was tried on a charge of denying the royal supremacy of Henry VIII and beheaded.

fishing and fisheries fisheries can be classified by (1) type of water: freshwater (lake, river, pond); marine (inshore, midwater, deep sea); (2) catch: for example salmon fishing, (3) fishing method: diving, stunning or poisoning, harpooning, trawling, drifting.
marine fishing The greatest proportion of the

world's catch comes from the oceans. The primary production area is the photic zone, the relatively thin surface layer (50 m/164 ft) of water that can be penetrated by light, allowing photosynthesis by plant *plankton to take place. Plankton-eating fish tend to be small in size and include herrings and sardines. Demersal fishes, such as haddock, halibut, and cod, live primarily near the ocean floor, and feed on various invertebrate marine animals. Over 20 million tonnes of them are caught each year by trawling. Pelagic fish, such as tuna, live in the open sea, near the surface, and purse seine nets are used to catch them; the annual catch is over 30 million tonnes a year.

freshwater fishing There is large demand for salmon, trout, carp, eel, bass, pike, perch, and catfish. These inhabit ponds, lakes, rivers, or swamps, and some species have been successfully cultivated (*aquaculture).

methods Lines, seine nets, and lift nets are the common commercial methods used. Purse seine nets, which close like a purse and may be as long as 30 nautical miles, have caused a crisis in the S Pacific where Japan, Taiwan, and South Korea fish illegally in other countries' fishing zones.

history Until the introduction of refrigeration, fish was too perishable to be exported, and fishing met local needs only. Between 1950 and 1970, the global fish catch increased by an average of 7% each year. On refrigerated factory ships, filleting and processing can be done at sea. Japan evolved new techniques for locating shoals (by sonar and radar) and catching them (for example, with electrical charges and chemical baits). By the 1970s, indiscriminate overfishing had led to serious depletion of stocks, and heated confrontations between countries using the same fishing grounds. A partial solution was the extension of fishing limits to 320 km/200 mi. The North Sea countries have experimented with the artificial breeding of fish eggs and release of small fry into the sea. In 1988, overfishing of the NE Atlantic led to hundreds of thousands of starving seals on the N coast of Norway. Marine pollution is blamed for the increasing number (up to 30%) of diseased fish in the North Sea. A United Nations resolution was passed 1989 to end driftnet fishing by June 1992.

ancillary industries These include the manufacture of nets, the processing of oil and fishmeal (nearly 25% of the fish caught annually are turned into meal for animal feed), pet food, glue, manure, and drugs such as insulin and other pharmaceutical products.

fission in physics, the splitting of a heavy atomic nucleus into two or more major fragments. It is accompanied by the emission of two or three neutrons and the release of large amounts of energy (see *nuclear energy).

fistula in medicine, an abnormal pathway developing between adjoining organs or tissues, or leading to the exterior of the body. A fistula developing between the bowels and the bladder, for instance, may give rise to urinary-tract infection by intestinal organisms.

fitness in genetic theory, a measure of the success with which a genetically determined character can spread in future generations. By convention, the normal character is assigned a fitness of one, and variants (determined by other *alleles) are then assigned fitness values relative to this. Those with fitness greater than one will spread more rapidly and will ultimately replace the normal allele; those with fitness less than one will gradually die out.

Fitzgerald Edward 1809–1883. English poet and translator. In 1859 he published his poetic version of the *Rubaiyat of Omar Khayyam*, which is generally considered more an original creation than a translation.

Fitzgerald Ella 1918– . US jazz singer, recognized as one of the finest, most lyrical voices in jazz, both in solo work and with big bands. She is celebrated for her smooth interpretations of Gershwin and Cole Porter songs.

Fitzgerald F(rancis) Scott (Key) 1896–1940. US novelist and short-story writer. His early autobiographical novel *This Side of Paradise* 1920 made him known in the postwar society of the East Coast, and *The Great Gatsby* 1925, in which the narrator resembles the author, epitomizes the Jazz Age.

FitzGerald Garret 1926– . Irish politician. As Taoiseach (prime minister) 1981–82 and again 1982–86, he was noted for his attempts to solve the Northern Ireland dispute, ultimately by participating in the Anglo-Irish agreement 1985. He tried to remove some of the overtly Catholic features of the constitution to make the Republic more attractive to Northern Protestants. He retired as leader of the Fine Gael Party 1987.

Fitzherbert Maria Anne 1756–1837. Wife of the Prince of Wales, later George IV. She became Mrs Fitzherbert by her second marriage 1778 and, after her husband's death 1781, entered London society. She secretly married the Prince of Wales 1785 and finally parted from him 1803.

five pillars of Islam the five duties required of every Muslim: repeating the ***creed***, which affirms that Allah is the one God and Muhammad is his prophet; daily ***prayer*** or salat; giving ***alms***; ***fasting*** during the month of Ramadan; and, if not prevented by ill health or poverty, the hajj, or ***pilgrimage*** to Mecca, once in a lifetime.

fixed point temperature that can be accurately reproduced and used as the basis of a temperature scale. In the Celsius scale, the fixed points are the temperature of melting ice, which is 0°C (32°F), and the temperature of boiling water (at standard atmospheric pressure), which is 100°C (212°F).

fjord or ***fiord*** narrow sea inlet enclosed by high cliffs. Fjords are found in Norway, New Zealand, and western parts of Scotland. They are formed when an overdeepened glacial valley is drowned by a rise in sea-level. At the mouth of the fjord there is a characteristic lip causing a shallowing of the water. This is due to reduced glacial erosion at this point.

fl. abbreviation for ***floruit*** (Latin 'he/she flourished').

flaccidity in botany, the loss of rigidity (turgor) in plant cells, caused by loss of water from the central vacuole so that the cytoplasm no longer pushes against the cellulose cell wall. If this condition occurs throughout the plant then wilting is seen.

flag in botany, another name for *iris especially yellow flag *Iris pseudacorus*, which grows wild in damp places throughout Europe; it is a true water plant but adapts to border conditions. It has a thick rhizome, stiff, bladelike, monocotyledonous leaves, and stems up to 150 cm/5 ft high. The flowers are large and yellow.

flag in computing, an indicator that can be set or unset in order to signal whether a particular condition is true – for example, whether the end of a file has been reached, or whether an overflow error has occurred. The indicator usually takes the form of a single binary digit, or bit (either 0 or 1).

flagellant religious person who uses a whip on him- or herself as a means of penance. Flagellation was practised in many religions from ancient times; notable outbreaks of this type of extremist devotion occurred in Christian Europe in the 11th–16th centuries.

flagellum small hairlike organ on the surface of certain cells. Flagella are the motile organs of certain protozoa and single-celled algae, and of the sperm cells of higher animals. Unlike *cilia, flagella usually occur singly or in pairs; they are also longer and have a more complex whiplike action.

Flaherty Robert 1884–1951. US film director, the father of documentary filmmaking. He exerted great influence through his pioneer documentary of Inuit (Eskimo) life, *Nanook of the North* 1922, a critical and commercial success.

flamenco music and dance of the Andalusian gypsies of S Spain, evolved from Andalusian and Arabic folk music. The *cante* (song) is sometimes performed as a solo but more often accompanied by guitar music and passionate improvised dance. Hand clapping, finger clicking (castanets have been added more recently), and enthusiastic shouts are all features. Male flamenco dancers excel in powerful, rhythmic footwork while the female dancers place emphasis on the graceful and erotic movements of their hands and bodies.

flame test in chemistry, the use of a flame to identify metal *cations present in a solid.

flame tree any of various trees with brilliant red flowers, including the smooth-stemmed semideciduous tree *Brachychiton acerifolium* with scarlet bell-shaped flowers, native to Australia, but spread throughout the tropics.

flamingo long-legged and long-necked wading bird, family Phoenicopteridae, of the stork order Ciconiiformes. Largest of the family is the greater or roseate flamingo *Phoenicopterus ruber*, found in Africa, the Caribbean, and South America, with delicate pink plumage and 1.25 m/4 ft tall. They sift the mud for food with their downbent bills, and build colonies of high, conelike mud nests, with a little hollow for the eggs at the top.

Flanders region of the Low Countries that in the 8th and 9th centuries extended from Calais to the Scheldt and is now covered by the Belgian provinces of Oost Vlaanderen and West Vlaanderen (East and West Flanders), the French *département* of Nord, and part of the Dutch province of Zeeland. The language is Flemish. East Flanders, capital Ghent, has an area of 3,000 sq km/1,158 sq mi and a population (1991) of 1,335,700. West Flanders, capital Bruges, has an area of 3,100 sq km/1,197 sq mi and a population (1991) of 1,106,800.

flare, solar brilliant eruption on the Sun above a *sunspot, thought to be caused by release of magnetic energy. Flares reach maximum brightness within a few minutes, then fade away over about an hour. They eject a burst of atomic particles into space at up to 1,000 kps/600 mps. When these particles reach Earth they can cause radio blackouts, disruptions of the Earth's magnetic field, and *auroras.

flash flood flood of water in a normally arid area brought on by a sudden downpour of rain. Flash floods are rare and usually occur in mountainous areas. They may travel many kilometres from the site of the rainfall. Because of the suddenness of flash floods, little warning can be given of their occurrence. In 1972 a flash flood at Rapid City, South Dakota, USA, killed 238 people along Rapid Creek.

flash point in physics, the lowest temperature at which a liquid or volatile solid heated under standard conditions gives off sufficient vapour to ignite on the application of a small flame.

flat in music, a note or a key that is played lower in pitch than the written value, indicated by a flat sign or key signature. It can also refer to inaccurate intonation by a player.

flatfish bony fishes of the order Pleuronectiformes, having a characteristically flat, asymmetrical body with both eyes (in adults) on the upper side. Species include flounders, turbots, halibuts, plaice, and the European soles.

flatworm invertebrate of the phylum Platyhelminthes. Some are free-living, but many are parasitic (for example, tapeworms and flukes). The body is simple and bilaterally symmetrical, with one opening to the intestine. Many are hermaphroditic (with both male and female sex organs), and practise self-fertilization.

Flaubert Gustave 1821–1880. French novelist, author of *Madame Bovary* 1857, *Salammbô* 1862, *L'Education sentimentale/Sentimental Education* 1869, and *La Tentation de Saint Antoine/The Temptation of St Anthony* 1874. Flaubert also wrote the short stories *Trois contes/Three Tales* 1877. His dedication to art resulted in a meticulous prose style, realistic detail, and psychological depth, which is often revealed through interior monologue.

flax any plant of the genus *Linum*, family Linaceae. The species *L. usitatissimum* is the cultivated strain; **linen** is produced from the fibre in its stems. The seeds yield **linseed oil**, used in paints and varnishes. The plant, of almost worldwide distribution, has a stem up to 60 cm/24 in high, small leaves, and bright blue flowers.

flea wingless insect of the order Siphonaptera, with blood-sucking mouthparts. Fleas are parasitic on warm-blooded animals. Some fleas can jump 130 times their own height.

fleabane plant of the genera *Erigeron* or *Pulicaria*, family Compositae. Common fleabane *P. dysenterica* has golden-yellow flower heads and grows in wet and marshy places throughout Europe.

Fleming Alexander 1881–1955. Scottish bacteriologist who discovered the first antibiotic drug, *penicillin, in 1928. In 1922 he had discovered lysozyme, an antibacterial enzyme present in saliva, nasal secretions, and tears. While studying this, he found an unusual mould growing on a neglected culture dish, which he isolated and grew into a pure culture; this led to his discovery of penicillin. It came into use in 1941. In 1945 he won the Nobel Prize for Physiology and Medicine with Howard W Florey and Ernst B Chain, whose research had brought widespread realization of the value of penicillin.

Fleming Ian 1908–1964. English author of suspense novels featuring the ruthless, laconic James Bond, British Secret Service agent No. 007. Most of the novels were made into successful films.

Fleming John Ambrose 1849–1945. English electrical physicist and engineer who invented the thermionic valve 1904 and devised *Fleming's rules.

Fleming's rules memory aids used to recall the relative directions of the magnetic field, current, and motion in an electric generator or motor, using one's fingers. The three directions are represented by the thumb (for motion), forefinger (for field) and second finger (current), all held at right angles to each other. The right hand is used for generators and the left for motors. The rules were devised by the English physicist John Fleming.

Flemish member of the W Germanic branch of the Indo-European language family, spoken in N Belgium and the Nord *département* of France. It is closely related to Dutch.

Flemish art the style of painting developed and practised in *Flanders. A Flemish style emerged in the early 15th century. Paintings are distinguished by keen observation, minute attention to detail, bright colours, and superb technique – oil painting was a Flemish invention. Apart from portraits, they depict religious scenes, often placed in contemporary Flemish landscapes, townscapes, and interiors. Flemish sculpture shows German and French influence.

Fletcher John 1579–1625. English dramatist. He collaborated with *Beaumont, producing, most notably, *Philaster* 1609 and *The Maid's Tragedy* 1610–11. He is alleged to have collaborated with Shakespeare on *The Two Noble Kinsmen* and *Henry VIII* in 1612.

fleur-de-lis (French 'flower of the lily') heraldic device in the form of a stylized iris flower, borne on coats of arms since the 12th century and adopted by the French royal house of Bourbon.

Flevoland formerly *IJsselmeerpolders* low-lying province of the Netherlands established 1986
area 1,410 sq km/544 sq mi
population (1988) 194,000
towns capital Lelystad, Dronten, Almere
history created in 1986 out of land reclaimed from the Ijsselmeer 1950–68.

flexor any muscle that bends a limb. Flexors usually work in opposition to other muscles, the extensors, an arrangement known as antagonistic.

flight or *aviation* method of transport in which aircraft carry people and goods through the air. People first took to the air in *balloons and began powered flight 1852 in *airships, but the history of flying, both for civilian and military use, is dominated by the *aeroplane. The earliest planes were designed for *gliding; the advent of the petrol engine saw the first powered flight by the *Wright brothers 1903 in the USA. This inspired the development of aircraft throughout Europe. Biplanes were succeeded by monoplanes in the 1930s. The first jet plane (see *jet propulsion) was produced 1939, and after the end of World War II the development of jetliners brought about a continuous expansion in passenger air travel. In 1969 came the supersonic aircraft *Concorde.

flight simulator computer-controlled pilot-training device, consisting of an artificial cockpit mounted on hydraulic legs, that simulates the experience of flying a real aircraft. Inside the cockpit, the trainee pilot views a screen showing a computer-controlled projection of the view from a real aircraft, and makes appropriate adjustments to the controls.

Flinders Matthew 1774–1814. English navigator who explored the Australian coasts 1795–99 and 1801–03.

flint compact, hard, brittle mineral (a variety of chert), brown, black, or grey in colour, found in nodules in limestone or shale deposits. It consists of fine-grained silica, SiO_2, in cryptocrystalline form (usually *quartz). Flint implements were widely used in prehistory and constitute the basis of all human technology.

Flintstones, the cartoon comedy series appearing on television created by US animators William Hanna and Joseph Barbera 1960. It featured Stone Age caveman Fred Flintstone and his half-wit neighbour Barney Rubble, together with their wives Wilma and Betty living in the town of Bedrock. Fred's cry of 'Yabba dabba do!' as he tried out a new invention with Barney, became his catchphrase. It was the first cartoon series to move onto the prime time viewing slot of Friday night.

flocculation in soils, the artificially induced coupling together of particles to improve aeration and drainage. Clay soils, which have very tiny particles and are difficult to work, are often treated in this way. The method involves adding more lime to the soil.

Flodden, Battle of the defeat of the Scots by the English under the Earl of Surrey 9 Sept 1513 on a site 5 km/3 mi SE of Coldstream, Northumberland, England; many Scots, including King James IV, were killed.

Flood, the in the Old Testament, the Koran, and *The Epic of Gilgamesh* (an ancient Sumerian legend), a deluge lasting 40 days and nights, a disaster alleged to have obliterated all humanity except a chosen few (in the Old Testament, the survivors were the family of *Noah and the pairs of animals sheltered on his ark).

floppy disc in computing, a storage device consisting of a light, flexible disc enclosed in a cardboard or plastic jacket. The disc is placed in a disc drive, where it rotates at high speed. Data are recorded magnetically on one or both surfaces.

floral diagram diagram showing the arrangement and number of parts in a flower, drawn in cross section. An ovary is drawn in the centre, surrounded by representations of the other floral parts, indicating the position of each at its base. If any parts such as the petals or sepals are fused, this is also indicated. Floral diagrams allow the structure of different flowers to be compared, and are usually shown with the floral formula.

floral formula symbolic representation of the structure of a flower. Each kind of floral part is represented by a letter (K for calyx, C for corolla, P for perianth, A for androecium, G for gynoecium) and a number to indicate the quantity of the part present, for example, C5 for a flower with five petals. The number is in brackets if the parts are fused. If the parts are arranged in distinct whorls within the flower, this is shown by two separate figures, such as A5 + 5, indicating two whorls of five stamens each.

Florence (Italian **Firenze**) capital of *Tuscany, N Italy, 88 km/55 mi from the mouth of the river Arno; population (1988) 421,000. It has printing, engineering, and optical industries; many crafts, including leather, gold and silver work, and embroidery; and its art and architecture attract large numbers of tourists. Notable medieval and Renaissance citizens included the writers Dante and Boccaccio, and the artists Giotto, Leonardo da Vinci, and Michelangelo.

floret small flower, usually making up part of a larger, composite flower head. There are often two different types present on one flower head: disc florets in the central area, and ray florets around the edge which usually have a single petal known as the ligule. In the common daisy, for example, the disc florets are yellow, while the ligules are white.

Florey Howard Walter, Baron Florey 1898–1968. Australian pathologist whose research into lysozyme, an antibacterial enzyme discovered by Alexander *Fleming, led him to study penicillin (another of Fleming's discoveries), which he and Ernst *Chain isolated and prepared for widespread use. With Fleming, they were awarded the Nobel Prize for Physiology or Medicine 1945.

Florida southeasternmost state of the USA; mainly a peninsula jutting into the Atlantic, which it separates from the Gulf of Mexico; nickname Sunshine State
area 152,000 sq km/58,672 sq mi
capital Tallahassee
cities Miami, Tampa, Jacksonville
population (1990) 12,937,900, one of the fastest-growing of the states; including 15% non-white; 10% Hispanic, (especially Cuban)
physical 50% forested; lakes (including Okeechobee 1,000 sq km/695 sq mi/; Everglades National Park (5,000 sq km/1,930 sq mi), with birdlife, cypresses, alligators
products citrus fruits, melons, vegetables, fish, shellfish, phosphates, chemicals, electrical and electronic equipment, aircraft, fabricated metals
famous people Chris Evert, Henry Flagler, James Weldon Johnson, Sidney Poitier, Philip Randolph, Joseph Stilwell
history discovered by Ponce de Leon and under Spanish rule from 1513 until its cession to England 1763; was returned to Spain 1783 and purchased by the US 1819, becoming a state 1845.

flotation process common method of preparing mineral ores for subsequent processing by making use of the different wetting properties of various components. The ore is finely ground and then mixed with water and a specially selected

wetting agent. Air is bubbled through the mixture, forming a froth; the desired ore particles attach themselves to the bubbles and are skimmed off, while unwanted dirt or other ores remain behind.

flounder small flatfish *Platychthys flesus* of the NE Atlantic and Mediterranean, although it sometimes lives in estuaries. It is dully coloured and grows to 50 cm/1.6 ft.

flour foodstuff made by grinding starchy vegetable materials, usually cereal grains, into a fine powder. Flour may also be made from root vegetables such as potato and cassava, and from pulses such as soya beans and chick peas. The most commonly used cereal flour is wheat flour.

flow chart diagram, often used in computing, to show the possible paths that data can take through a system or program.

flower the reproductive unit of an *angiosperm or flowering plant, typically consisting of four whorls of modified leaves: *sepals, *petals, *stamens, and *carpels. These are borne on a central axis or *receptacle. The many variations in size, colour, number, and arrangement of parts are closely related to the method of pollination. Flowers adapted for wind pollination typically have reduced or absent petals and sepals and long, feathery *stigmas that hang outside the flower to trap airborne pollen. In contrast, the petals of insect-pollinated flowers are usually conspicuous and brightly coloured.

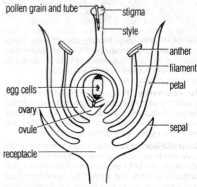

flower The parts of a flower.

flowering plant term generally used for *angiosperms, which bear flowers with various parts, including sepals, petals, stamens, and carpels. Sometimes the term is used more broadly, to include both angiosperms and *gymnosperms, in which case the *cones of conifers and cycads are referred to as 'flowers'. Usually, however, the angiosperms and gymnosperms are referred to collectively as *seed plants, or spermatophytes.

flower power youth movement of the 1960s; see *hippie.

flue-gas desulphurization process of removing harmful sulphur pollution from gases emerging from a boiler. Sulphur compounds such as sulphur dioxide are commonly produced by burning *fossil fuels, especially coal in power stations, and are the main cause of *acid rain.

flugelhorn alto brass instrument, similar in appearance to the *cornet.

fluid any substance, either liquid or gas, in which the molecules are relatively mobile and can 'flow'.

fluidization making a mass of solid particles act as a fluid by agitation or by gas passing through. Much earthquake damage is attributed to fluidization of surface soils during the earthquake shock.

fluid mechanics the study of the behaviour of fluids (liquids and gases) at rest and in motion. Fluid mechanics is important in the study of the weather, the design of aircraft and road vehicles, and in industries, such as the chemical industry, which deal with flowing liquids or gases.

fluid, supercritical fluid brought by a combination of heat and pressure to the point at which, as a near vapour, it combines the properties of a gas and a liquid. Supercritical fluids are used as solvents in chemical processes, such as the extraction of lubricating oil from refinery residues or the decaffeination of coffee, because they avoid the energy-expensive need for phase changes (from liquid to gas and back again) required in conventional distillation processes.

fluke any of various parasitic flatworms of the classes Monogenea and Digenea, that as adults live in and destroy the livers of sheep, cattle, horses, dogs, and humans. Monogenetic flukes can complete their life cycle in one host; digenetic flukes require two or more hosts, for example a snail and a human being, to complete their life cycle.

fluorescence in scientific usage, very short-lived *luminescence (a glow not caused by high temperature). Generally, the term is used for any luminescence regardless of the persistence. See *phosphorescence.

fluorescence microscopy technique for examining samples under a *microscope without slicing them into thin sections. Instead, fluorescent dyes are introduced into the tissue and used as a light source for imaging purposes.

fluoridation addition of small amounts of fluoride salts to drinking water by certain water authorities to help prevent tooth decay. Experiments in Britain, the USA, and elsewhere have indicated that a concentration of fluoride of 1 part per million in tap water retards the decay of teeth in children by more than 50%.

fluoride negative ion (Fl⁻) formed when hydrogen fluoride dissolves in water; compound formed between fluorine and another element in which the fluorine is the more electronegative element (see *electronegativity, *halide).

fluorine pale yellow, gaseous, nonmetallic element, symbol F, atomic number 9, relative atomic mass 19. It is the first member of the halogen group of elements, and is pungent, poisonous, and highly reactive, uniting directly with nearly all the elements. It occurs naturally as the minerals fluorite (CaF_2) and cryolite (Na_3AlF_6). Hydrogen fluoride is used in etching glass, and the freons, which all contain fluorine, are widely used as refrigerants.

fluorite or *fluorspar* a glassy, brittle mineral, calcium fluoride CaF_2, forming cubes and octahedra; colourless when pure, otherwise violet.

fluorocarbon compound formed by replacing the hydrogen atoms of a hydrocarbon with fluorine. Fluorocarbons are used as inert coatings, refrigerants, synthetic resins, and as propellants in aerosols.

Flushing Meadow tennis centre in New York, NY, officially the National Tennis Center and home of the US Open championships since 1978.

flute member of a group of *woodwind musical instruments (although usually made of metal), including the piccolo, the concert flute, and the bass or alto flute. Flutes are cylindrical in shape, with a narrowed end, containing a shaped aperture, across which the player blows. The air vibrations produce the note, which can be altered by placing fingers over lateral holes. Certain keys can be depressed to extend the range of the flute to three octaves.

flux in smelting, a substance that combines with the unwanted components of the ore to produce a fusible slag, which can be separated from the molten metal. For example, the mineral fluorite, CaF_2, is used as a flux in iron smelting; it has a low melting point and will form a fusible mixture with substances of higher melting point such as silicates and oxides.

flux in soldering, a substance that improves the bonding properties of solder by removing contamination from metal surfaces and preventing their oxidation, and by reducing the surface tension of the molten solder alloy. For example, with solder made of lead–tin alloys, the flux may be resin, borax, or zinc chloride.

fly any insect of the order Diptera. A fly has a single pair of wings, antennae, and compound eyes; the hind wings have become modified into knoblike projections (halteres) used to maintain equilibrium in flight. There are over 90,000 species.

flying dragon lizard *Draco volans* of the family Agamidae. It lives in SE Asia, and can glide on flaps of skin spread and supported by its ribs. This small (7.5 cm/3 in head and body) arboreal lizard can glide between trees for 6 m/20 ft or more.

flying fish any of a family, Exocoetidae, of marine bony fishes of the order Beloniformes, best represented in tropical waters. They have winglike pectoral fins that can be spread to glide over the water.

flying fox fruit-eating *bat of the suborder Megachiroptera.

flying lemur commonly used, but incorrect, name for *colugo. It cannot fly, and it is not a lemur.

flying lizard another name for *flying dragon.

flying squirrel any of numerous species of squirrel, not closely related to the true squirrels. They are characterized by a membrane along the side of the body from forelimb to hindlimb (in some species running to neck and tail) which allows them to glide through the air. Several genera of flying squirrel are found in the Old World; the New World has the genus *Glaucomys*. Most species are E Asian.

Flynn Errol. Stage name of Leslie Thompson

1909–1959. Australian-born US film actor. He is renowned for his portrayal of swashbuckling heroes in such films as *Captain Blood* 1935, *Robin Hood* 1938, *The Charge of the Light Brigade* 1938, *The Private Lives of Elizabeth and Essex* 1939, *The Sea Hawk* 1940, and *The Master of Ballantrae* 1953.

flywheel heavy wheel in an engine that helps keep it running and smooths its motion. The *crankshaft in a petrol engine has a flywheel at one end, which keeps the crankshaft turning in between the intermittent power strokes of the pistons. It also comes into contact with the *clutch, serving as the connection between the engine and the car's transmission system.

FM in physics, abbreviation for *frequency modulation*.

FNLA abbreviation for *Front National de Libération de l'Angola* (French 'National Front for the Liberation of Angola').

f-number measure of the relative aperture of a telescope or camera lens; it indicates the light-gathering power of the lens. In photography, each successive f-number represents a halving of exposure speed.

FO abbreviation for *Foreign Office*, a UK government department (see *foreign relations).

Fo Dario 1926– . Italian playwright. His plays are predominantly political satires combining black humour with slapstick. They include *Morte accidentale di un anarchico/Accidental Death of an Anarchist* 1970, and *Non si paga non si paga/Can't Pay? Won't Pay!* 1975/1981.

fob abbreviation for *free-on-board*, used in commerce to describe a valuation of goods at point of embarkation, excluding transport and insurance costs. Export values are usually expressed fob for customs and excise purposes, while imports are usually valued *cif.

focal length or *focal distance* the distance from the centre of a lens or curved mirror to the focal point. For a concave mirror or convex lens, it is the distance at which parallel rays of light are brought to a focus to form a real image (for a mirror, this is half the radius of curvature). For a convex mirror or concave lens, it is the distance from the centre to the point at which a virtual image (an image produced by diverging rays of light) is formed.

Foch Ferdinand 1851–1929. Marshal of France during World War I. He was largely responsible for the Allied victory at the first battle of the *Marne Sept 1914, and commanded on the NW front Oct 1914–Sept 1916. He was appointed commander in chief of the Allied armies in the spring of 1918, and launched the Allied counter-offensive in July that brought about the negotiation of an armistice to end the war.

fog cloud that collects at the surface of the Earth, composed of water vapour that has condensed on particles of dust in the atmosphere. Cloud and fog are both caused by the air temperature falling below *dew point. The thickness of fog depends on the number of water particles it contains. Usually, fog is formed by the meeting of two currents of air, one cooler than the other, or by warm air flowing over a cold surface. Sea fogs commonly occur where warm and cold currents meet and the air above them mixes.

Fokine Mikhail 1880–1942. Russian dancer and choreographer, born in St Petersburg. He was chief choreographer to the Ballets Russes 1909–14, and with *Diaghilev revitalized and reformed the art of ballet, promoting the idea of artistic unity among dramatic, musical, and stylistic elements. His creations for Diaghilev include *Les Sylphides* 1907, *Carnival* 1910, *The Firebird* 1910, *Le Spectre de la Rose* 1911, and *Petrushka* 1911.

fold in geology, a bend in *beds or layers of rock. If the bend is arched in the middle it is called an *anticline*; if it sags downwards in the middle it is called a *syncline*. The line along which a bed of rock folds is called its axis. The axial plane is the plane joining the axes of successive beds.

folic acid a *vitamin of the B complex. It is found in liver and green leafy vegetables, and is also synthesized by the intestinal bacteria. It is essential for growth, and plays many other roles in the body. Lack of folic acid causes anaemia because it is necessary for the synthesis of nucleic acids and the formation of red blood cells.

folk dance dance characteristic of a particular people, nation, or region. Many European folk dances are derived from the dances accompanying the customs and ceremonies of pre-Christian times. Some later became ballroom dances (for example, the minuet and waltz). Once an important part of many rituals, folk dance has tended to die out in industrialized countries. Examples of folk dance are Morris dance, farandole, and jota.

folklore the oral traditions and culture of a people, expressed in legends, riddles, songs, tales, and proverbs. The term was coined 1846 by W J Thoms (1803–85), but the founder of the systematic study of the subject was Jacob *Grimm; see also *oral literature.

folk music body of traditional music, originally transmitted orally. Many folk songs originated as a rhythmic accompaniment to manual work or to mark a specific ritual. Folk song is usually melodic, not harmonic, and the modes used are distinctive of the country of origin; see *world music.

follicle in botany, a dry, usually many-seeded fruit that splits along one side only to release the seeds within. It is derived from a single *carpel, examples include the fruits of the larkspurs *Delphinium* and columbine *Aquilegia*. It differs from a pod, which always splits open (dehisces) along both sides.

follicle in zoology, a small group of cells that surround and nourish a structure such as a hair (hair follicle) or a cell such as an egg (Graafian follicle; see *menstrual cycle).

follicle-stimulating hormone (FSH) a *hormone produced by the pituitary gland. It affects the ovaries in women, triggering off the production of an egg cell. Luteinizing hormone is needed to complete the process. In men, FSH stimulates the testes to produce sperm.

Fonda Henry 1905–1982. US actor whose engaging style made him ideal in the role of the American pioneer and honourable man. His many films include the Academy Award-winning *The Grapes of Wrath* 1940, *My Darling Clem-*

entine 1946, and *On Golden Pond* 1981, for which he won the Academy Award for best actor. He was the father of actress Jane Fonda and actor and director Peter Fonda (1939–).

Fonda Jane 1937– . US actress. Her early films include *Cat Ballou* 1965, *Barefoot in the Park* 1967, *Barbarella* 1968, *They Shoot Horses, Don't They?* 1969, *Julia*, 1977, *The China Syndrome* 1979, *On Golden Pond* 1981, in which she appeared with her father Henry Fonda, and *Agnes of God* 1985. She won Academy Awards for *Klute* 1971 and *Coming Home* 1979.

Fontainebleau school French school of Mannerist painting and sculpture. It was established at the court of Francis I, who brought Italian artists to Fontainebleau near Paris to decorate his hunting lodge: Rosso Fiorentino (1494–1540) arrived 1530, Francesco Primaticcio (1504/5–1570) came 1532. They evolved a distinctive decorative style using a combination of stucco sculpture and painting.

Fonteyn Margot. Stage name of Margaret Hookham 1919–1991. English ballet dancer. She made her debut with the Vic-Wells Ballet in *Nutcracker* 1934 and first appeared as Giselle 1937, eventually becoming prima ballerina of the Royal Ballet, London. Renowned for her perfect physique, musicality, and interpretive powers, she created many roles in Frederick *Ashton's ballets and formed a legendary partnership with Rudolf *Nureyev. She did not retire from dancing until 1979.

food anything eaten by human beings and other animals to sustain life and health. The building blocks of food are nutrients, and humans can utilize the following nutrients: *carbohydrates*, as starches found in bread, potatoes, and pasta; as simple sugars in sucrose and honey; as fibres in cereals, fruit, and vegetables; *proteins* as from nuts, fish, meat, eggs, milk, and some vegetables; *fats* as found in most animal products (meat, lard, dairy products, fish), also in margarine, nuts and seeds, olives, and edible oils; *vitamins* are found in a wide variety of foods, except for vitamin B_{12}, which is mainly found in animal foods; *minerals* are found in a wide variety of foods; good sources of calcium are milk and broccoli, for example; iodine from seafood; iron from liver and green vegetables; *water* ubiquitous in nature; *alcohol* is found in fermented distilled beverages, from 40% in spirits to 0.01% in low-alcohol lagers and beers.

Food and Agriculture Organization (FAO) United Nations agency that coordinates activities to improve food and timber production and levels of nutrition throughout the world. It is also concerned with investment in agriculture and dispersal of emergency food supplies. It has headquarters in Rome and was founded 1945.

food chain or **food web** in ecology, the sequence of organisms through which energy and other nutrients are successively transferred. Since many organisms feed at several different levels (for example, omnivores feed on both fruit and meat), the relationships often form a complex web rather than a simple chain. See also *ecosystem.

food irradiation the exposure of food to low-level *irradiation to kill microorganisms; a technique used in *food technology. Irradiation is highly effective, and does not make the food any more radioactive than it is naturally. Irradiated food is used for astronauts and immunocompromised patients in hospitals. Some vitamins are partially destroyed, such as vitamin C, and it would be unwise to eat only irradiated fruit and vegetables.

food poisoning any acute illness characterized by vomiting and diarrhoea and caused by eating food contaminated with harmful bacteria (for example, *listeriosis), poisonous food (for example, certain mushrooms, puffer fish), or poisoned food (such as lead or arsenic introduced accidentally during processing). A frequent cause of food poisoning is *salmonella bacteria. These come in many forms, and strains are found in cattle, pigs, poultry, and eggs.

Food Safety Act 1990 UK legislation that re-enacts and expands the consumer protection given in the Food Act 1984. It imposes liability on producers and importers, authorizes environmental health officers to inspect and seize any food for sale except primary agricultural produce, and empowers courts and minister to close premises and make emergency control orders in case of health risk. All hot food must be kept at or above 63°C, cold foods in controlled categories at or below 8°C, and certain foods below 5°C.

food technology the application of science to the commercial processing of foodstuffs. Food is processed to make it more palatable or digestible, for which the traditional methods include boiling, frying, flour-milling, bread-making, yoghurt- and cheese-making, brewing, or to preserve it from spoilage caused by the action of *enzymes within the food that change its chemical composition, or the growth of bacteria, moulds, yeasts, and other microorganisms. Fatty or oily foods also suffer oxidation of the fats, which makes them rancid. Traditional forms of **food preservation**, include salting, smoking, pickling, drying, bottling, and preserving in sugar. Modern food technology also uses many novel processes and *additives, which allow a wider range of foodstuffs to be preserved.

foot imperial unit of length (symbol ft), equivalent to 0.3048 m, in use in Britain since Anglo-Saxon times. It originally represented the length of a human foot. One foot contains 12 inches and equals one-third of a yard.

Foot Michael 1913– . British Labour politician and writer. A leader of the left-wing Tribune Group, he was secretary of state for employment 1974–76, Lord President of the Council and leader of the House 1976–79, and succeeded James Callaghan as Labour Party leader 1980–83.

foot-and-mouth disease contagious eruptive viral disease of cloven-hoofed mammals, characterized by blisters in the mouth and around the hooves. In cattle it causes deterioration of milk yield and abortions. It is an airborne virus which makes its eradication extremely difficult.

football, American contact sport similar to the English game of rugby, played between two teams of 11 players, with an inflated oval ball. Players are well padded for protection and wear protective helmets. The **Super Bowl**, first held in 1967, is now an annual meeting between the winners of the National and American Football Conferences.

football, association or *soccer* form of football originating in the UK, popular in Europe and Latin America. The modern game is played in the UK according to the rules laid down by the Football Association. Slight amendments to the rules take effect in certain competitions and overseas matches as laid down by the sport's world governing body, Fédération Internationale de Football Association (FIFA, 1904). FIFA organizes the competitions for the World Cup, held every four years since 1930.

football, Australian Rules game that combines aspects of Gaelic football, rugby, and association football; it is played between two teams of 18 players each, with an inflated oval ball. It is unique to Australia.

football, Gaelic kicking and catching game played mainly in Ireland. The two teams have 15 players each. The game is played on a field with an inflated spherical ball. The goalposts have a crossbar and a net across the lower half. Goals are scored by kicking the ball into the net (3 points) or over the crossbar (1 point).

foraminifera any of an order Foraminiferida of marine protozoa with shells of calcium carbonate. Their shells have pores through which filaments project. Some form part of the *plankton, others live on the sea bottom.

force in physics, any influence that tends to change the state of rest or uniform motion in a straight line of a body. It is measured by the rate of change of momentum of the body on which it acts, that is, the mass of the body multiplied by its acceleration: $F=ma$. Force is a vector quantity, possessing both magnitude and direction; its SI unit is the newton. See also *Newton's laws of motion.

force majeure (French 'superior force') in politics, the use of force rather than the seeking of a political or diplomatic solution to a problem. By this principle, a government could end a strike by sending in troops, instead of attempting to conciliate the strikers.

force ratio the magnification of a force by a machine; see *mechanical advantage.

forces, fundamental in physics, the four fundamental interactions believed to be at work in the physical universe. There are two long-range forces: *gravity*, which keeps the planets in orbit around the Sun, and acts between all particles that have mass; and the *electromagnetic force*, which stops solids from falling apart, and acts between all particles with *electric charge. There are two very short-range forces: the **weak nuclear force**, responsible for the reactions that fuel the Sun and for the emission of *beta particles from certain nuclei; and the **strong nuclear force**, which binds together the protons and neutrons in the nuclei of atoms.

Ford Gerald R(udolph) 1913– . 38th president of the USA 1974–77, a Republican. He was elected to the House of Representatives 1949, was nominated to the vice-presidency by Richard Nixon 1973 on the resignation of Spiro Agnew (1918–), and became president 1974, when Nixon was forced to resign following the *Watergate scandal. Ford pardoned Nixon and gave amnesty to those who had resisted the draft for the Vietnam War.

Ford Henry 1863–1947. US automobile manufacturer, who built his first car 1896 and founded the Ford Motor Company 1903. His Model T (1908–27) was the first car to be constructed solely by assembly-line methods and to be mass marketed; 15 million of these cars were made and sold.

Ford John 1586–*c*. 1640. English poet and dramatist. His play '*Tis Pity She's a Whore* (performed about 1626, printed 1633) is a study of incest between brother and sister.

Ford John. Adopted name of Sean O'Feeney 1895–1973. US film director. Active from the silent film era, he was one of the original creators of the 'Western', directing *The Iron Horse* 1924; *Stagecoach* 1939 became his masterpiece. He won Academy Awards for *The Informer* 1935, *The Grapes of Wrath* 1940, *How Green Was My Valley* 1941, and *The Quiet Man* 1952.

foreclosure in law, the transfer of title of a mortgaged property from the mortgagor (borrower, usually a home owner) to the mortgagee (loaner, for example a bank) if the mortgagor is in breach of the mortgage agreement, usually by failing to make a number of payments on the mortgage (loan).

Foreign Legion volunteer corps of foreigners within a country's army. The French *Légion Etrangère*, 1831, is one of a number of such forces. Enlisted volunteers are of any nationality (about half are now French), but the officers are usually French. Headquarters until 1962 was in Sidi Bel Abbés, Algeria; the main base is now Corsica, with reception headquarters at Aubagne, near Marseille, France.

foreign relations a country's dealings with other countries. Specialized diplomatic bodies first appeared in Europe during the 18th century. After 1818 diplomatic agents were divided into: *ambassadors*, papal legates, and nuncios; *envoys* extraordinary, *ministers* plenipotentiary, and other ministers accredited to the head of state; ministers resident; and *chargés d'affaires*, who may deputize for an ambassador or minister, or be themselves the representative accredited to a minor country. Other diplomatic staff may include counsellors and attachés (military, labour, cultural, press). *Consuls* are state agents with commercial and political responsibilities in foreign towns.

forensic science the use of scientific techniques to solve criminal cases. A multidisciplinary field embracing chemistry, physics, botany, zoology, and medicine, forensic science includes the identification of human bodies or traces. Traditional methods such as *fingerprinting are still used, assisted by computers; in addition, blood analysis, forensic dentistry, voice and speech spectograms, and *genetic fingerprinting are increasingly applied. Chemicals, such as poisons and drugs, are analysed by *chromatography. Ballistics (the study of projectiles, such as bullets), another traditional forensic field, makes use of tools such as the comparison microscope and the *electron microscope.

Forester C(ecil) S(cott) 1899–1966. English novelist, born in Egypt. He wrote a series of historical novels set in the Napoleonic era that, beginning with *The Happy Return* 1937, cover the career – from midshipman to admiral – of Horatio Hornblower.

forestry the science of forest management. Recommended forestry practice aims at multipurpose crops, allowing the preservation of varied plant and animal species as well as human uses (lumbering, recreation). Forestry has often been confined to the planting of a single species, such as a rapid-growing conifer providing softwood for paper pulp and construction timber, for which world demand is greatest. In tropical countries, logging contributes to the destruction of *rainforests, causing global environmental problems. Small unplanned forests are *woodland.

forget-me-not any plant of the genus *Myosotis*, family Boraginaceae, including *M. sylvatica* and *M. scorpioides*, with bright blue flowers.

forging one of the main methods of shaping metals, which involves hammering or a more gradual application of pressure. A blacksmith hammers red-hot metal into shape on an anvil, and the traditional place of work is called a forge. The blacksmith's mechanical equivalent is the drop forge. The metal is shaped by the blows from a falling hammer or ram, which is usually accelerated by steam or air pressure. Hydraulic presses forge by applying pressure gradually in a squeezing action.

formaldehyde common name for *methanal.

formalin aqueous solution of formaldehyde (methanal) used to preserve animal specimens.

Formentera smallest inhabited island in the Spanish Balearic Islands, lying south of Ibiza; area 93 sq km/36 sq mi; population (1981) 3,500. The chief town is San Francisco Javier and the main port is La Sabina. The main industry is tourism.

Formica trademark of the Formica Corporation for a heat-proof plastic laminate, widely used as a veneer on wipe-down kitchen surfaces and children's furniture. It is made from formaldehyde resins similar to *Bakelite. It was first put on the market 1913.

formic acid common name for *methanoic acid.

formula in chemistry, a representation of a molecule, radical, or ion, in which the component chemical elements are represented by their symbols. An *empirical formula* indicates the simplest ratio of the elements in a compound, without indicating how many of them there are or how they are combined. A *molecular formula* gives the number of each type of element present in one molecule. A *structural formula* shows the relative positions of the atoms and the bonds between them. For example, for ethanoic acid, the empirical formula is CH_2O, the molecular formula is $C_2H_4O_2$, and the structural formula is CH_3COOH.

Forster E(dward) M(organ) 1879–1970. English novelist, concerned with the interplay of personality and the conflict between convention and instinct. His novels include *A Room with a View* 1908, *Howard's End* 1910, and *A Passage to India* 1924. He also wrote short stories, for example 'The Eternal Omnibus' 1914; criticism, including *Aspects of the Novel* 1927; and essays, including *Abinger Harvest* 1936.

Forsyth Frederick 1938– . English thriller writer. His books include *The Day of the Jackal* 1970, *The Dogs of War* 1974, and *The Fourth Protocol* 1984.

forsythia any temperate E Asian shrub of the genus *Forsythia* of the olive family Oleaceae, which bear yellow bell-shaped flowers in early spring before the leaves appear.

Forth river in SE Scotland, with its headstreams rising on the NE slopes of Ben Lomond. It flows approximately 72 km/45 mi to Kincardine where the *Firth of Forth* begins. The Firth is approximately 80 km/50 mi long, and is 26 km/16 mi wide where it joins the North Sea.

Fort Knox US army post and gold depository in Kentucky, established 1917 as a training camp. The US Treasury gold-bullion vaults were built 1937.

FORTRAN (acronym for *formula translation*) high-level computer-programming language suited to mathematical and scientific computations. Developed in the mid-1950s, it is one of the earliest languages still in use. *BASIC was strongly influenced by FORTRAN and is similar in many ways.

Fort Sumter fort in Charleston Harbor, South Carolina, USA, 6.5 km/4 mi SE of Charleston. The first shots of the US Civil War were fired here 12 April 1861, after its commander had refused the call to surrender made by the Confederate General Beauregard.

Fort Ticonderoga fort in New York State, USA, near Lake Champlain. It was the site of battles between the British and the French 1758–59, and was captured from the British 10 May 1775 by Benedict *Arnold and Ethan Allen (leading the *Green Mountain Boys).

Fortune 500 the 500 largest publicly-owned US industrial corporations, a list compiled by the US business magazine *Fortune*. An industrial corporation is defined as one that derives at least 50% of its revenue from manufacturing or mining. General Motors topped the list in 1990 with sales of $126.017 billion.

Fort Worth city in NE Texas, USA; population (1990) 447,600. Formerly an important cattle area, it is now a grain, petroleum, aerospace, and railway centre serving the S USA.

Fossey Dian 1938–1985. US zoologist. From 1975, Fossey studied mountain gorillas in Rwanda. Living in close proximity to them, she discovered that they led peaceful family lives. She was murdered by poachers whose snares she had cut.

fossil (Latin *fossilis* 'dug up') remains of an animal or plant preserved in rocks. Fossils may be formed by refrigeration (for example, Arctic *mammoths in ice); carbonization (leaves in coal); formation of a cast (dinosaur or human footprints in mud); or mineralization of bones, more generally teeth or shells. The study of fossils is called *palaeontology.

fossil fuel fuel, such as coal, oil, and natural gas, formed from the fossilized remains of plants that lived hundreds of millions of years ago. Fossil fuels are a *nonrenewable resource and will eventually run out. Extraction of coal (mining) causes considerable environmental pollution, and burning coal contributes to problems of *acid rain and the *greenhouse effect.

Foster Greg 1958– . US hurdler. He has won three consecutive World Championship gold medals, the only athlete to achieve this feat.

Foster Jodie. Stage name of Alicia Christian Foster 1962– . US film actress and director who began as a child in a great variety of roles. She starred in *Taxi Driver* and *Bugsy Malone* both 1976, when only 14. Subsequent films include *The Accused* 1988 and *The Silence of the Lambs* 1991, for both of which she won the Academy Award for best actress.

Foster Norman 1935– . English architect of the high-tech school. His buildings include the Willis Faber office, Ipswich, 1978, the Sainsbury Centre for Visual Arts at the University of East Anglia 1974 (opened 1978), the headquarters of the Hong Kong and Shanghai Bank, Hong Kong, 1986, and Stansted Airport, Essex, 1991.

Foster Stephen Collins 1826–1864. US songwriter. He wrote sentimental popular songs including 'My Old Kentucky Home' 1853 and 'Beautiful Dreamer' 1864, and rhythmic minstrel songs such as 'Oh! Susannna' 1848 and 'Camptown Races' 1850.

Foucault Jean Bernard Léon 1819–1868. French physicist who used a pendulum to demonstrate the rotation of the Earth on its axis, and invented the gyroscope.

Foucault Michel 1926–1984. French philosopher who rejected phenomenology and existentialism. He was concerned with how forms of knowledge and forms of human subjectivity are constructed by specific institutions and practices.

fouetté (French 'whipped') in ballet, a type of *pirouette in which one leg is extended to the side and then into the knee in a whiplike action, while the dancer spins on the supporting leg. Odile performs 32 fouettés in Act III of *Swan Lake*.

fount complete set of printed or display characters of the same typeface, size, and style (bold, italic, underlined, and so on). In the UK, fount sizes are measured in points, a point being approximately 0.3 mm.

Fountains Abbey Cistercian abbey in North Yorkshire, England. It was founded about 1132, and closed 1539 at the Dissolution of the Monasteries. The ruins were incorporated into a Romantic landscape garden 1720–40 with lake, formal water garden, temples, and a deer park.

four-colour process colour *printing using four printing plates, based on the principle that any colour is made up of differing proportions of the primary colours blue, red, and green. The first stage in preparing a colour picture for printing is to produce separate films, one each for the blue, red, and green respectively in the picture (colour separations). From these separations three printing plates are made, with a fourth plate for black (for shading or outlines). Ink colours complementary to those represented on the plates are used for printing – yellow for the blue plate, cyan for the red, and magenta for the green.

Fourdrinier machine papermaking machine patented by the Fourdrinier brothers Henry and Sealy in England 1803. On the machine, liquid pulp flows onto a moving wire-mesh belt, and

water drains and is sucked away, leaving a damp paper web. This is passed first through a series of steam-heated rollers, which dry it, and then between heavy calendar rollers, which give it a smooth finish. Such machines can measure up to 90 m/300 ft in length, and are still in use.

Fourier Jean Baptiste Joseph 1768–1830. French applied mathematician whose formulation of heat flow 1807 contains the proposal that, with certain constraints, any mathematical function can be represented by trigonometrical series. This principle forms the basis of *Fourier analysis*, used today in many different fields of physics. His idea, not immediately well received, gained currency and is embodied in his *Théorie analytique de la chaleur/The Analytical Theory of Heat* 1822.

Four Noble Truths in Buddhism, a summary of the basic concepts: life is suffering (Sanskrit *duhkha*); suffering has its roots in desire (*tanha*, clinging or grasping); the cessation of desire is the end of suffering, *nirvana*; and this can be reached by the Noble Eightfold Path of *dharma* (truth).

four-stroke cycle the engine-operating cycle of most petrol and *diesel engines. The 'stroke' is an upward or downward movement of a piston in a cylinder. In a petrol engine the cycle begins with the induction of a fuel mixture as the piston goes down on its first stroke. On the second stroke (up) the piston compresses the mixture in the top of the cylinder. An electric spark then ignites the mixture, and the gases produced force the piston down on its third, power, stroke. On the fourth stroke (up) the piston expels the burned gases from the cylinder into the exhaust.

Fourteen Points the terms proposed by President Wilson of the USA in his address to Congress 8 Jan 1918, as a basis for the settlement of World War I. The creation of the League of Nations was one of the points.

fourth estate another name for the press. The term was coined by the British politician Edmund Burke in analogy with the traditional three *estates.

fourth-generation language in computing, a type of programming language designed for the rapid programming of *applications but often lacking the ability to control the individual parts of the computer. Such a language typically provides easy ways of designing screens and reports, and of using databases. Other 'generations' (the term implies a class of language rather than a chronological sequence) are *machine code (first generation); *assembly code, or low-level languages (second); and conventional high-level languages such as *BASIC and *PASCAL (third).

Fourth of July in the USA, the anniversary of the day in 1776 when the *Declaration of Independence was adopted by the Continental Congress. It is a public holiday, officially called *Independence Day*, commemorating independence from Britain.

Fourth Republic the French constitutional regime that was established between 1944 and 1946 and lasted until 4 Oct 1958: from liberation after Nazi occupation during World War II to the introduction of a new constitution by General de Gaulle.

fowl chicken or chickenlike bird. Sometimes the term is also used for ducks and geese. The red jungle fowl *Gallus gallus* is the ancestor of all domestic chickens. It is a forest bird of Asia, without the size or egg-laying ability of many domestic strains. *Guinea fowl are of African origin.

Fowler Henry Watson 1858–1933 and his brother Francis George 1870–1918. English scholars and authors of a number of English dictionaries. *Modern English Usage* 1926, the work of Henry Fowler, has become a classic reference work for matters of style and disputed usage.

fox member of the smaller species of wild dog of the family Canidae, which live in Africa, Asia, Europe, North America, and South America. Foxes feed on a wide range of animals from worms to rabbits, scavenge for food, and also eat berries. They are very adaptable, maintaining high populations close to urban areas.

Fox Charles James 1749–1806. English Whig politician, son of the 1st Baron Holland. He entered Parliament 1769 as a supporter of the court, but went over to the opposition 1774. As secretary of state 1782, leader of the opposition to Pitt, and foreign secretary 1806, he welcomed the French Revolution and brought about the abolition of the slave trade.

Fox George 1624–1691. English founder of the Society of *Friends. After developing his belief in a mystical 'inner light', he became a travelling preacher 1647, and in 1650 was imprisoned for blasphemy at Derby, where the name Quakers was first applied derogatorily to him and his followers, supposedly because he enjoined Judge Bennet to 'quake at the word of the Lord'.

foxglove Foxgloves with their erect spikes of purple, golden, or white flowers are natives of Europe, Asia, and N Africa.

foxglove any flowering plant of the genus *Digitalis*, family Scrophulariaceae, found in Europe and the Mediterranean region. It bears showy spikes of bell-like flowers, and grows up to 1.5 m/ 5 ft high.

foxhound small, keen-nosed hound, up to 60 cm/2 ft tall and black, tan, and white in colour. There are two recognized breeds: the English foxhound, bred for some 300 years to hunt foxes, and the American foxhound, not quite as stocky, used for foxes and other game.

foxtrot ballroom dance originating in the US

about 1914. It has alternating long and short steps, supposedly like the movements of the fox.

f.p.s. system system of units based on the foot, pound, and second as units of length, mass, and time, respectively. It has now been replaced for scientific work by the *SI system.

fractal (from Latin *fractus* 'broken') an irregular shape or surface produced by a procedure of repeated subdivision. Generated on a computer screen, fractals are used in creating models for geographical or biological processes (for example, the creation of a coastline by erosion or accretion, or the growth of plants).

fraction (from Latin *fractus* 'broken') in mathematics, a number that indicates one or more equal parts of a whole. Usually, the number of equal parts into which the unit is divided (denominator) is written below a horizontal line, and the number of parts comprising the fraction (numerator) is written above; thus $^2/_3$ or $^3/_4$. Such fractions are called *vulgar* or *simple* fractions. The denominator can never be zero.

fraction in chemistry, a group of similar compounds, the boiling points of which fall within a particular range and which are separated during fractional *distillation (fractionation).

fractionating column device in which many separate *distillations can occur so that a liquid mixture can be separated into its components.

fractionation or *fractional distillation* process used to split complex mixtures (such as crude oil) into their components, usually by repeated heating, boiling, and condensation; see *distillation.

Fragonard Jean Honoré 1732–1806. French painter, the leading exponent of the Rococo style (along with his master Boucher). His lighthearted subjects include *The Swing* about 1766 (Wallace Collection, London).

Frame Janet 1924– . New Zealand novelist. After being wrongly diagnosed as schizophrenic, she reflected her experiences 1945–54 in the novel *Faces in the Water* 1961 and the autobiographical *An Angel at My Table* 1984.

France French Republic (*République Française*)
area (including Corsica) 543,965 sq km/ 209,970 sq mi

capital Paris

towns Lyons, Lille, Bordeaux, Toulouse, Nantes, Strasbourg; ports Marseille, Nice, Le Havre

physical rivers Seine, Loire, Garonne, Rhône, Rhine; mountain ranges Alps, Massif Central, Pyrenees, Jura, Vosges, Cévennes; the island of Corsica

territories Guadeloupe, French Guiana, Martinique, Réunion, St Pierre and Miquelon, Southern and Antarctic Territories, New Caledonia, French Polynesia, Wallis and Futuna

head of state Jacques Chirac from 1995

head of government Alain Juppé from 1995

political system liberal democracy

exports fruit (especially apples), wine, cheese, wheat, cars, aircraft, iron and steel, petroleum products, chemicals, jewellery, silk, lace; tourism is very important

currency franc

population (1994 est) 57,800,000 (including 4,500,000 immigrants, chiefly from Portugal, Algeria, Morocco, and Tunisia); growth rate 0.3% p.a.

language French (regional languages include Basque, Breton, Catalan, and the Provençal dialect)

religions Roman Catholic 90%, Protestant 2%, Muslim 1%

GNP $20,600 per head (1991)

chronology

1944–46 De Gaulle provisional government; start of Fourth Republic.

1954 Indochina achieved independence.

1956 Morocco and Tunisia achieved independence.

1957 Entry into EEC.

1958 Recall of de Gaulle after Algerian crisis; start of Fifth Republic.

1959 De Gaulle became president.

1962 Algeria achieved independence.

1966 France withdrew from military wing of NATO.

1968 'May events' crisis.

1969 De Gaulle resigned after referendum defeat; Pompidou became president.

1974 Giscard d'Estaing elected president.

1981 Mitterrand elected Fifth Republic's first socialist president.

1986 'Cohabitation' experiment, with the conservative Jacques Chirac as prime minister.

1988 Mitterrand re-elected. Moderate socialist Michel Rocard became prime minister. Matignon Accord on future of New Caledonia approved by referendum.

1989 Greens gained 11% of vote in elections to European Parliament.

1991 French forces were part of the US-led coalition in the Gulf War. Edith Cresson became France's first woman prime minister. Mitterrand's popularity rating fell rapidly.

1992 March: Socialist Party humiliated in regional and local elections; Greens and National Front polled strongly. April: Cresson replaced by Pierre Bérégovoy. Sept: referendum narrowly endorsed Maastricht Treaty.

1993 March: Socialist Party suffered heavy defeat in National Assembly elections. Edouard Balladur appointed prime minister.

1994 Balladur's administration tainted by corruption scandals; several ministers quit.

1995 Jacques Chirac elected president.

France Anatole. Pen name of Jacques Anatole Thibault 1844–1924. French writer renowned for the wit, urbanity, and style of his works. His earliest novel was *Le Crime de Sylvestre Bonnard/The Crime of Sylvester Bonnard* 1881; later books include *Les Dieux ont soif/The Gods Are Athirst* 1912. He was awarded the Nobel Prize for Literature 1921.

Francesca Piero della See *Piero della Francesca, Italian painter.

Franche-Comté region of E France; area 16,200 sq km/6,253 sq mi; population (1987) 1,086,000. Its capital is Besançon, and it includes the *départements* of Doubs, Jura, Haute Saône, and Territoire de Belfort. In the mountainous Jura, there is farming and forestry, and elsewhere there are engineering and plastics industries.

franchise in politics, the eligibility, right or privilege to vote at public elections, especially for the members of a legislative body. In the UK adult citizens are eligible to vote from the age of 18, with the exclusion of peers, the insane, and criminals.

Francis or **François** two kings of France:

Francis I 1494–1547. King of France from 1515. He succeeded his cousin Louis XII, and from 1519 European politics turned on the rivalry between him and the Holy Roman emperor Charles V, which led to war 1521–29, 1536–38, and 1542–44. In 1525 Francis was defeated and captured at Pavia and released only after signing a humiliating treaty. At home, he developed absolute monarchy.

Francis II 1544–1560. King of France from 1559 when he succeeded his father, Henry II. He married Mary Queen of Scots 1558. He was completely under the influence of his mother, *Catherine de' Medici.

Francis II 1768–1835. Holy Roman emperor 1792–1806. He became Francis I, Emperor of Austria 1804, and abandoned the title of Holy Roman emperor 1806. During his reign Austria was five times involved in war with France, 1792–97, 1798–1801, 1805, 1809, and 1813–14. He succeeded his father Leopold II.

Franciscan order Catholic order of friars, **Friars Minor** or **Grey Friars**, founded 1209 by Francis of Assisi. Subdivisions were the strict Observants; the Conventuals, who were allowed to own property corporately; and the *Capuchins, founded 1529.

Francis Ferdinand English form of *Franz Ferdinand, archduke of Austria.

Francis of Assisi, St 1182–1226. Italian founder of the Roman Catholic Franciscan order of friars 1209 and, with St Clare, of the Poor Clares 1212. In 1224 he is said to have undergone a mystical experience during which he received the *stigmata* (five wounds of Jesus). Many stories are told of his ability to charm wild animals, and he is the patron saint of ecologists. His feast day is 4 Oct.

francium radioactive metallic element, symbol Fr, atomic number 87, relative atomic mass 223. It is one of the *alkali metals and occurs in nature in small amounts as a decay product of actinium. Its longest-lived isotope has a half-life of only 21 minutes. Francium was discovered and named in 1939 by Marguérite Perey to honour her country.

Franck James 1882–1964. US physicist. He was awarded a Nobel prize 1925 for his experiments of 1914 on the energy transferred by colliding electrons to mercury atoms, showing that the transfer was governed by the rules of *quantum theory.

Franco Francisco (Paulino Hermenegildo Teódulo Bahamonde) 1892–1975. Spanish dictator from 1939. As a general, he led the insurgent Nationalists to victory in the Spanish *Civil War 1936–39, supported by Fascist Italy and Nazi Germany, and established a dictatorship. In 1942 Franco reinstated the Cortes (Spanish parliament), which in 1947 passed an act by which he became head of state for life.

François French form of *Francis, two kings of France.

Franco-Prussian War 1870–71. The Prussian chancellor Bismarck put forward a German candidate for the vacant Spanish throne with the deliberate, and successful, intention of provoking the French emperor Napoleon III into declaring war. The Prussians defeated the French at Sedan, then besieged Paris. The Treaty of Frankfurt May 1871 gave Alsace, Lorraine, and a large French indemnity to Prussia. The war established Prussia, at the head of a newly established German Empire, as Europe's leading power.

frangipani any tropical American tree of the genus *Plumeria*, especially *P. rubra*, of the dogbane family Apocynaceae. Perfume is made from the strongly scented flowers.

Franglais French language mixed with (usually unwelcome) elements of modern, usually American, English. *Le weekend, le drugstore*, and other such mixtures have prompted moves within France to limit the growth of Franglais and protect the integrity of Standard French.

Frank member of a group of Germanic peoples prominent in Europe in the 3rd to 9th centuries. Believed to have originated in Pomerania on the Black Sea, they had settled on the Rhine by the 3rd century, spread into the Roman Empire by the 4th century, and gradually conquered most of Gaul, Italy, and Germany under the *Merovingian and *Carolingian dynasties. The kingdom of the W Franks became France, the kingdom of the E Franks became Germany.

Frank Anne 1929–1945. German diarist who fled to the Netherlands with her family 1933 to escape Nazi anti-Semitism (the *Holocaust). During the German occupation of Amsterdam, they and two other families remained in a sealed-off room, protected by Dutch sympathizers 1942–44, when betrayal resulted in their deportation and Anne's death in Belsen concentration camp. Her diary of her time in hiding was published 1947.

Frankenstein or *The Modern Prometheus* Gothic horror story by Mary Shelley, published in England 1818. Frankenstein, a scientist, discovers how to bring inanimate matter to life, and creates a man-monster. When Frankenstein fails to provide a mate to satisfy the creature's human emotions, it seeks revenge by killing Frankenstein's brother and bride. Frankenstein dies in an attempt to destroy his creation.

Frankenstein law popular name for the 1980 ruling by the US Supreme Court (Diamond v Chakrabarty) that new forms of life created in the laboratory may be patented.

Frankenthaler Helen 1928– . US Abstract Expressionist painter, inventor of the colour-staining technique whereby the unprimed, absorbent canvas is stained or soaked with thinned-out paint, creating deep, soft veils of translucent colour.

Frankfurt-am-Main city in Hessen, Germany, 72 km/45 mi NE of Mannheim; population (1988) 592,000. It is a commercial and banking centre, with electrical and machine industries, and an inland port on the river Main. An international book fair is held here annually.

frankincense resin of various African and Asian trees of the genus *Boswellia*, family Burseraceae, burned as incense. Costly in ancient times, it is traditionally believed to be one of the three gifts brought by the Magi to the infant Jesus.

Franklin Benjamin 1706–1790. US printer, publisher, author, scientist, and statesman. He proved that lightning is a form of electricity, distinguished between positive and negative electricity, and invented the lightning conductor. He was the first US ambassador to France 1776–85, and negotiated peace with Britain 1783. As a delegate to the Continental Congress from Pennsylvania 1785–88, he helped to draft the *Declaration of Independence and the US *Constitution.

Franz Ferdinand or Francis Ferdinand 1863–1914. Archduke of Austria. He became heir to his uncle, Emperor Franz Joseph, in 1884 but while visiting Sarajevo 28 June 1914, he and his wife were assassinated by a Serbian nationalist. Austria used the episode to make unreasonable demands on Serbia that ultimately precipitated World War I.

Franz Joseph or Francis Joseph 1830–1916. Emperor of Austria-Hungary from 1848, when his uncle, Ferdinand I, abdicated. After the suppression of the 1848 revolution, Franz Joseph tried to establish an absolute monarchy but had to grant Austria a parliamentary constitution 1861 and Hungary equality with Austria 1867. He was defeated in the Italian War 1859 and the Prussian War 1866. In 1914 he made the assassination of his heir and nephew Franz Ferdinand the excuse for attacking Serbia, thus precipitating World War I.

Frasch process process used to extract underground deposits of sulphur. Superheated steam is piped into the sulphur deposit and melts it. Compressed air is then pumped down to force the molten sulphur to the surface. The process was developed in the USA 1891 by German-born Herman Frasch (1851–1914).

Fraser (John) Malcolm 1930– . Australian Liberal politician, prime minister 1975–83; nicknamed 'the Prefect' because of a supposed disregard of subordinates.

Fraser Antonia 1932– . English author of biographies, including *Mary Queen of Scots* 1969; historical works, such as *The Weaker Vessel* 1984; and a series of detective novels featuring investigator Jemima Shore.

fraternity and sorority student societies

(fraternity for men; sorority for women) in some US and Canadian universities and colleges. Although mainly social and residential, some are purely honorary, membership being on the basis of scholastic distinction; Phi Beta Kappa, the earliest of the fraternities, was founded at the College of William and Mary, Virginia in 1776.

fraud in law, an act of deception resulting in injury to another. To establish fraud it has to be demonstrated that (1) a false representation (for example, a factually untrue statement) has been made, with the intention that it should be acted upon; (2) the person making the representation knows it is false or does not attempt to find out whether it is true or not; and (3) the person to whom the representation is made acts upon it to his or her detriment.

Frazer James George 1854–1941. Scottish anthropologist, author of *The Golden Bough* 1890, a pioneer study of the origins of religion and sociology on a comparative basis. It exerted considerable influence on writers such as T S Eliot and D H Lawrence, but by the standards of modern anthropology, many of its methods and findings are unsound.

Frederick V known as *the Winter King* 1596–1632. Elector palatine of the Rhine 1610–23 and king of Bohemia 1619–20 (for one winter, hence the name), having been chosen by the Protestant Bohemians as ruler after the deposition of Catholic emperor *Ferdinand II. His selection was the cause of the Thirty Years' War. Frederick was defeated at the Battle of the White Mountain, near Prague, in Nov 1620, by the army of the Catholic League and fled to Holland.

Frederick IX 1899–1972. King of Denmark from 1947. He was succeeded by his daughter who became Queen *Margrethe II.

Frederick two Holy Roman emperors:

Frederick I *Barbarossa* ('red-beard') *c.* 1123–1190. Holy Roman emperor from 1152. Originally duke of Swabia, he was elected emperor 1152, and was engaged in a struggle with Pope Alexander III 1159–77, which ended in his submission; the Lombard cities, headed by Milan, took advantage of this to establish their independence of imperial control. Frederick joined the Third Crusade, and was drowned while crossing a river in Anatolia.

Frederick II 1194–1250. Holy Roman emperor from 1212, called 'the Wonder of the World'. He led a crusade 1228–29 that recovered Jerusalem by treaty, without fighting. He quarrelled with the pope, who excommunicated him three times, and a feud began that lasted with intervals until the end of his reign. Frederick, who was a religious sceptic, is often considered the most cultured man of his age. He was the son of Henry VI.

Frederick three kings of Prussia, including:

Frederick II *the Great* 1712–1786. King of Prussia from 1740, when he succeeded his father Frederick William I. In that year he started the War of the *Austrian Succession by his attack on Austria. In the peace of 1745 he secured Silesia. The struggle was renewed in the *Seven Years' War 1756–63. He acquired West Prussia in the first partition of Poland 1772 and left Prussia as Germany's foremost state. He was an efficient and just ruler in the spirit of the Enlightenment and a patron of the arts.

Frederick III 1831–1888. King of Prussia and emperor of Germany 1888. The son of Wilhelm I, he married the eldest daughter (Victoria) of Queen Victoria of the UK 1858 and, as a liberal, frequently opposed Chancellor Bismarck. He died three months after his accession.

Frederick William 1620–1688. Elector of Brandenburg from 1640, 'the Great Elector'. By successful wars against Sweden and Poland, he prepared the way for Prussian power in the 18th century.

Frederick William four kings of Prussia:

Frederick William I 1688–1740. King of Prussia from 1713, who developed Prussia's military might and commerce.

Frederick William II 1744–1797. King of Prussia from 1786. He was a nephew of Frederick II but had little of his relative's military skill. He was unsuccessful in waging war on the French 1792–95 and lost all Prussia west of the Rhine.

Frederick William III 1770–1840. King of Prussia from 1797. He was defeated by Napoleon 1806, but contributed to his final overthrow 1813–15 and profited by being allotted territory at the Congress of Vienna.

Frederick William IV 1795–1861. King of Prussia from 1840. He upheld the principle of the *divine right of kings, but was forced to grant a constitution 1850 after the Prussian revolution 1848. He suffered two strokes 1857 and became mentally debilitated. His brother William (later emperor) took over his duties.

Free Church the Protestant denominations in England and Wales that are not part of the Church of England; for example, the Methodist Church, Baptist Union, and United Reformed Church (Congregational and Presbyterian). These churches joined for common action in the Free Church Federal Council 1940.

Free Church of Scotland the body of Scottish Presbyterians who seceded from the Established Church of Scotland in the Disruption of 1843. In 1900 all but a small section that retains the old name, and is known as the *Wee Frees*, combined with the United Presbyterian Church to form the United Free Church, which reunited with the Church of Scotland 1929.

freedom of the press absence of censorship in the press or other media; see *press, freedom of.

Freedom, Presidential Medal of the highest peacetime civilian honour in the USA. Instituted by President Kennedy 1963, it is awarded to those 'who contribute significantly to the quality of American life'. A list of recipients is published each Independence Day and often includes unknown individuals as well as artists, performers, and politicians.

free enterprise or *free market* economic system where private capital is used in business with profits going to private companies and individuals. The term has much the same meaning as *capitalism.

free fall the state in which a body is falling freely under the influence of *gravity, as in free-fall parachuting. The term *weightless* is normally used to describe a body in free fall in space.

free falling another name for *skydiving.

Free French in World War II, movement formed by General Charles *de Gaulle in the UK June 1940, consisting of French soldiers who continued to fight against the Axis after the Franco-German armistice. They took the name *Fighting France* 1942 and served in many campaigns, among them General Leclerc's advance from Chad to Tripolitania 1942, the Syrian campaigns 1941, the campaigns in the Western Desert, the Italian campaign, the liberation of France, and the invasion of Germany. Their emblem was the Cross of Lorraine, a cross with two bars.

freehold in England and Wales, ownership of land for an indefinite period. It is contrasted with a leasehold, which is always for a fixed period. In practical effect, a freehold is absolute ownership.

Freemasonry the beliefs and practices of a group of linked national organizations open to men over the age of 21, united by a common code of morals and certain traditional 'secrets'. Modern Freemasonry began in 18th-century Europe. Freemasons do much charitable work, but have been criticized in recent years for their secrecy, their male exclusivity, and their alleged use of influence within and between organizations (for example, the police or local government) to further each other's interests. There are approximately 6 million members.

free port port or sometimes a zone within a port, where cargo may be accepted for handling, processing, and reshipment without the imposition of tariffs or taxes. Duties and tax become payable only if the products are for consumption in the country to which the free port belongs.

free radical in chemistry, an atom or molecule that has an unpaired electron and is therefore highly reactive. Most free radicals are very short-lived. If free radicals are produced in living organisms they can be very damaging.

freesia any plant of the South African genus *Freesia* of the iris family Iridaceae, commercially grown for their scented, funnel-shaped flowers.

free thought post-Reformation movement opposed to Christian dogma.

Freetown capital of Sierra Leone, W Africa; population (1988) 470,000. It has a naval station and a harbour. Industries include cement, plastics, footwear, and oil refining. Platinum, chromite, diamonds, and gold are traded. It was founded as a settlement for freed slaves in the 1790s.

free trade economic system where governments do not interfere in the movement of goods between countries; there are thus no taxes on imports. In the modern economy, free trade tends to hold within economic groups such as the European Community (EC), but not generally, despite such treaties as *GATT 1948 and subsequent agreements to reduce tariffs. The opposite of free trade is *protectionism.

free verse poetry without metrical form. At the beginning of the 20th century, under the very different influences of Whitman and Mallarmé, many poets believed that the 19th century had accomplished most of what could be done with regular metre, and rejected it, in much the same spirit as Milton had rejected rhyme, preferring irregular metres that made it possible to express thought clearly and without distortion.

free will the doctrine that human beings are free to control their own actions, and that these actions are not fixed in advance by God or fate. Some Jewish and Christian theologians assert that God gave humanity free will to choose between good and evil; others that God has decided in advance the outcome of all human choices (*predestination), as in Calvinism.

freeze-drying method of preserving food; see *food technology. The product to be dried is frozen and then put in a vacuum chamber that forces out the ice as water vapour, a process known as sublimation.

freezing change from liquid to solid state, as when water becomes ice. For a given substance, freezing occurs at a definite temperature, known as the *freezing point*, that is invariable under similar conditions of pressure, and the temperature remains at this point until all the liquid is frozen. The amount of heat per unit mass that has to be removed to freeze a substance is a constant for any given substance, and is known as the latent heat of fusion.

freezing point, depression of lowering of a solution's freezing point below that of the pure solvent; it depends on the number of molecules of solute dissolved in it. For a single solvent, such as pure water, all solute substances in the same molar concentration produce the same lowering of freezing point. The depression d produced by the presence of a solute of molar concentration C is given by the equation $d = KC$, where K is a constant (called the cryoscopic constant) for the solvent concerned. Measurement of freezing-point depression is a useful method of determining the molecular weights of solutes. It is also used to detect the illicit addition of water to milk.

Frege Friedrich Ludwig Gottlob 1848–1925. German philosopher, the founder of modern mathematical logic. He created symbols for concepts like 'or' and 'if . . . then', which are now in standard use in mathematics. His *Die Grundlagen der Arithmetik/The Foundations of Arithmetic* 1884 influenced Bertrand *Russell and *Wittgenstein. His major work is *Berggriftsschrift/Conceptual Notation* 1879.

Frelimo (acronym for *Front for the Liberation of Mozambique*) nationalist group aimed at gaining independence for Mozambique from the occupying Portuguese. It began operating from S Tanzania 1963 and continued until victory 1975.

French Community former association consisting of France and those overseas territories joined with it by the constitution of the Fifth Republic, following the 1958 referendum. Many of the constituent states withdrew during the 1960s, and it no longer formally exists, but in practice all former French colonies have close economic and cultural as well as linguistic links with France.

French Fourth Republic see *Fourth Republic.

French Guiana (French *Guyane Française*) French overseas *département* from 1946, and administrative region from 1974, on the N coast of South America, bounded to the W by Suriname and to the E and S by Brazil.

area 83,500 sq km/32,230 sq mi
capital Cayenne
towns St Laurent
products timber, shrimps, gold
currency franc
population (1987) 89,000
language 90% Creole, French, Amerindian
famous people Alfred *Dreyfus
history first settled by France 1604, the territory
became a French possession 1817; penal colonies, including Devil's Island, were established
from 1852; by 1945 the shipments of convicts
from France ceased.

French horn musical *brass instrument.

French India former French possessions in
India: Pondicherry, Chandernagore, Karaikal,
Mahé, and Yanam (Yanaon). They were all transferred to India by 1954.

French language member of the Romance
branch of the Indo-European language family,
spoken in France, Belgium, Luxembourg,
Monaco, and Switzerland in Europe; also in
Canada (principally in the province of Québec),
various Caribbean and Pacific Islands (including
overseas territories such as Martinique and
French Guiana), and certain N and W African
countries (for example, Mali and Senegal).

French Polynesia French Overseas Territory
in the S Pacific, consisting of five archipelagos:
Windward Islands, Leeward Islands (the two
island groups comprising the *Society Islands),
*Tuamotu Archipelago (including *Gambier
Islands), *Tubuai Islands, and *Marquesas
Islands
total area 3,940 sq km/1,521 sq mi
capital Papeete on Tahiti
products cultivated pearls, coconut oil, vanilla;
tourism is important
population (1990) 199,100
language Tahitian (official), French
government a high commissioner (Alain Ohrel)
and Council of Government; two deputies are
returned to the National Assembly in France
history first visited by Europeans 1595; French
Protectorate 1843; annexed to France 1880–82;
became an Overseas Territory, changing its name
from French Oceania 1958; self-governing 1977.
Following demands for independence in *New
Caledonia 1984–85, agitation increased also in
Polynesia.

French Revolution the period 1789–1799 that
saw the end of the French monarchy. Although
the revolution began as an attempt to create a
constitutional monarchy, by late 1792 demands
for long-overdue reforms resulted in the proclamation of the First Republic. The violence of the
revolution, attacks by other nations, and bitter
factional struggles, riots, and counterrevolutionary uprisings consumed the republic. This helped
bring the extremists to power, and the bloody
Reign of Terror followed. French armies then succeeded in holding off their foreign enemies and
one of the generals, *Napoleon, seized power
1799.

French Sudan former name (1898–1959) of
*Mali.

French West Africa group of French colonies
administered from Dakar 1895–1958. They are
now Senegal, Mauritania, Sudan, Burkina Faso,
Guinea, Niger, Ivory Coast, and Benin.

frequency in physics, the number of periodic
oscillations, vibrations, or waves occurring per
unit of time. The unit of frequency is the hertz
(Hz), one hertz being equivalent to one cycle
per second. Human beings can hear sounds from
objects vibrating in the range 20–15,000 Hz.
Ultrasonic frequencies well above 15,000 Hz can
be detected by mammals such as bats.

frequency modulation (FM) method by
which radio waves are altered for the transmission of broadcasting signals. FM is constant
in amplitude and varies the frequency of the carrier wave in accordance with the signal being
transmitted. Its advantage over AM (*amplitude
modulation) is its better signal-to-noise ratio.

fresco mural painting technique using waterbased paint on wet plaster. Some of the earliest
frescoes (about 1750–1400 BC) were found in
Knossos, Crete (now preserved in the Heraklion
Museum). Fresco reached its finest expression in
Italy from the 13th to the 17th centuries. Giotto,
Masaccio, Michelangelo, and many other artists
worked in the medium.

Frescobaldi Girolamo 1583–1643. Italian composer of virtuoso pieces for the organ and harpsichord.

Fresnel Augustin 1788–1827. French physicist
who refined the theory of *polarized light. Fresnel realized in 1821 that light waves do not
vibrate like sound waves longitudinally, in the
direction of their motion, but transversely, at
right angles to the direction of the propagated
wave.

Freud Anna 1895–1982. Austrian-born founder
of child psychoanalysis in the UK. Her work was
influenced by the theories of her father, Sigmund
Freud. She held that understanding of the stages
of psychological development was essential to
the treatment of children, and that this knowledge could only be obtained through observation
of the child.

Freud Lucian 1922– . German-born British
painter, whose realistic portraits with the subject
staring intently from an almost masklike face
include *Francis Bacon* 1952 (Tate Gallery,
London). He is a grandson of Sigmund Freud.

Freud Sigmund 1865–1939. Austrian physician
who pioneered the study of the unconscious
mind. He developed the methods of free association and interpretation of dreams that are basic
techniques of *psychoanalysis, and formulated
the concepts of the *id, *ego, and *superego. His
books include *Die Traumdeutung/The Interpretation of Dreams* 1900, *Totem and Taboo* 1913,
and *Das Unbehagen in der Kultur/Civilization and its Discontents* 1930.

Freya or *Frigga* in Scandinavian mythology,
wife of Odin and mother of Thor, goddess of
married love and the hearth. Friday is named
after her.

friar a monk of any order, but originally the title
of members of the mendicant (begging) orders,
the chief of which were the Franciscans or
Minors (Grey Friars), the Dominicans or
Preachers (Black Friars), the Carmelites (White
Friars), and Augustinians (Austin Friars).

friction in physics, the force that opposes the
relative motion of two bodies in contact. The
coefficient of friction is the ratio of the force

required to achieve this relative motion to the force pressing the two bodies together.

Friedan Betty 1921– . US liberal feminist. Her book *The Feminine Mystique* 1963 started the contemporary women's movement, both in the US and the UK. She was a founder of the National Organization for Women (NOW) 1966 (and its president 1966–70), the National Women's Political Caucus 1971, and the First Women's Bank 1973. Friedan also helped to organize the Women's Strike for Equality 1970 and called the First International Feminist Congress 1973.

Friedman Milton 1912– . US economist. The foremost exponent of *monetarism, he argued that a country's economy, and hence inflation, can be controlled through its money supply, although most governments lack the 'political will' to control inflation by cutting government spending and thereby increasing unemployment. He was awarded the Nobel Prize for Economics 1976.

Friendly Islands another name for *Tonga.

friendly society an association that makes provisions for the needs of sickness and old age by money payments. There are some 6,500 registered societies in the UK. Among the largest are the National Deposit, Odd Fellows, Foresters, and Hearts of Oak. In the USA similar 'fraternal insurance' bodies are known as *benefit societies*; they include the Modern Woodmen of America 1883 and the Fraternal Order of Eagles 1898.

Friends of the Earth (FoE or FOE) environmental pressure group, established in the UK 1971, that aims to protect the environment and to promote rational and sustainable use of the Earth's resources. It campaigns on issues such as acid rain; air, sea, river, and land pollution; recycling; disposal of toxic wastes; nuclear power and renewable energy; the destruction of rainforests; pesticides; and agriculture. FoE has branches in 30 countries.

Friends, Society of or *Quakers* Christian Protestant sect founded by George *Fox in England in the 17th century. They were persecuted for their nonviolent activism, and many emigrated to form communities elsewhere, for example in Pennsylvania and New England, USA. They now form a worldwide movement of about 200,000. Their worship stresses meditation and the freedom of all to take an active part in the service (called a meeting, held in a meeting house). They have no priests or ministers.

Friesland maritime province of the N Netherlands, which includes the Frisian Islands and land that is still being reclaimed from the former Zuyder Zee; the inhabitants of the province are called *Frisians
area 3,400 sq km/1,312 sq mi
population (1990) 600,000
capital Leeuwarden
towns Drachten, Harlingen, Sneek, Heerenveen
products livestock (Friesian cattle originated here), dairy products, small boats
history ruled as a county of the Holy Roman Empire during the Middle Ages, Friesland passed to Saxony in 1498 and, after a revolt, to Charles V of Spain. In 1579 it subscribed to the Treaty of Utrecht, opposing Spanish rule. In 1748 its

stadholder, Prince William IV of Orange, became stadholder of all the United Provinces of the Netherlands.

frigate escort warship smaller than a destroyer. Before 1975 the term referred to a warship larger than a destroyer but smaller than a light cruiser. In the 18th and 19th centuries a frigate was a small, fast sailing warship.

fringe theatre plays that are anti-establishment or experimental, and performed in informal venues, in contrast to mainstream commercial theatre. In the UK, the term originated in the 1960s from the activities held on the 'fringe' of the Edinburgh Festival. The US equivalent is off-off-Broadway (off-Broadway is mainstream theatre that is not on Broadway).

Frisch Karl von 1886–1982. Austrian zoologist, founder with Konrad *Lorenz of *ethology, the study of animal behaviour. He specialized in bees, discovering how they communicate the location of sources of nectar by movements called 'dances'. He was awarded the Nobel Prize for Medicine 1973 together with Lorenz and Nikolaas *Tinbergen.

fritillary in zoology, any of a large grouping of butterflies of the family Nymphalidae. Mostly medium-sized, fritillaries are usually orange and reddish with a black criss-cross pattern or spots above and with silvery spots on the underside of the hindwings.

Friuli-Venezia Giulia autonomous agricultural and wine-growing region of NE Italy, bordered to the E by Slovenia; area 7,800 sq km/3,011 sq mi; population (1990) 1,201,000. Cities include Udine (the capital), Gorizia, Pordenone, and Trieste.

Frobisher Martin 1535–1594. English navigator. He made his first voyage to Guinea, West Africa, 1554. In 1576 he set out in search of the Northwest Passage, and visited Labrador, and Frobisher Bay, Baffin Island. Second and third expeditions sailed 1577 and 1578.

frog any amphibian of the order Anura (Greek 'tailless'). There are no clear rules for distinguishing between frogs and toads. Frogs usually have squat bodies, hind legs specialized for jumping, and webbed feet for swimming. Many frogs use their long, extensible tongues to capture insects. Frogs vary in size from the tiny North American little grass frog *Limnaoedus ocularis*, 12 mm/0.5 in long, to the giant aquatic frog *Telmatobius culeus*, 50 cm/20 in long, of Lake Titicaca, South America.

froghopper or *spittlebug* leaping plant-bug, of the family Cercopidae, in the same order (Homoptera) as leafhoppers and aphids. Froghoppers live by sucking the juice from plants. The pale green larvae protect themselves (from drying out and from predators) by secreting froth ('cuckoo spit') from their anuses.

Fromm Erich 1900–1980. German psychoanalyst who moved to the USA 1933 to escape the Nazis. His *The Fear of Freedom* 1941 and *The Sane Society* 1955 were source books for alternative lifestyles.

frond large leaf or leaflike structure; in ferns it is often pinnately divided. The term is also applied to the leaves of palms and less commonly to the plant bodies of certain seaweeds, liverworts, and lichens.

Fronde French revolts 1648–53 against the administration of the chief minister *Mazarin during Louis XIV's minority. In 1648–49 the Paris *parlement* attempted to limit the royal power, its leaders were arrested, Paris revolted, and the rising was suppressed by the royal army under Louis II Condé. In 1650 Condé led a new revolt of the nobility, but this was suppressed by 1653. The defeat of the Fronde enabled Louis to establish an absolutist monarchy in the later 17th century.

front in meteorology, the boundary between two air masses of different temperature or humidity. A *cold front* marks the line of advance of a cold air mass from below, as it displaces a warm air mass; a *warm front* marks the advance of a warm air mass as it rises up over a cold one.

frontal lobotomy an operation on the brain. See *lobotomy.

front-end processor small computer used to coordinate and control the communications between a large mainframe computer and its input and output devices.

frost condition of the weather that occurs when the air temperature is below freezing, 0°C/32°F. Water in the atmosphere is deposited as ice crystals on the ground or exposed objects. As cold air is heavier than warm, ground frost is more common than hoar frost, which is formed by the condensation of water particles in the same way that *dew collects.

Frost Robert (Lee) 1874–1963. US poet whose verse, in traditional form, is written with an individual voice and penetrating vision. His poems include 'Mending Wall' ('Something there is that does not love a wall'), 'The Road Not Taken', and 'Stopping by Woods on a Snowy Evening' and are collected in *A Boy's Will* 1913, *North of Boston* 1914, *New Hampshire* 1924, *Collected Poems* 1930, *A Further Range* 1936, and *A Witness Tree* 1942.

frostbite the freezing of skin or flesh, with formation of ice crystals leading to tissue damage. The treatment is slow warming of the affected area; for example, by skin-to-skin contact or with lukewarm water. Frostbitten parts are extremely vulnerable to infection, with the risk of gangrene.

FRS abbreviation for *Fellow of the *Royal Society*.

fructose $C_6H_{12}O_6$ a sugar that occurs naturally in honey, the nectar of flowers, and many sweet fruits; it is commercially prepared from glucose.

fruit (from Latin *frui* 'to enjoy') in botany, the ripened ovary in flowering plants that develops from one or more seeds or carpels and encloses one or more seeds. Its function is to protect the seeds during their development and to aid in their dispersal. Fruits are often edible, sweet, juicy, and colourful. When eaten they provide vitamins, minerals, and enzymes, but little protein. Most fruits are borne by perennial plants. When fruits are eaten by animals the seeds pass through the alimentary canal unharmed, and are passed out with the faeces.

fruit juice juice extracted from fruits, either by pressing (citrus fruits) or by spinning at high speed in a centrifuge (other fruits). Although fruit

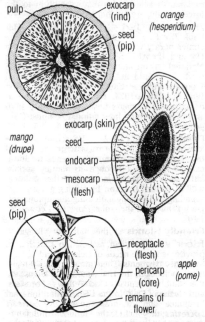

fruit A fruit contains the seeds of a plant.

juice provides no fibre, its nutritional value is close to that of the whole fruit. Most fruit juices are transported in concentrated form, and are diluted and pasteurized before being packaged.

frustum (from Latin for 'a piece cut off') in geometry, a 'slice' taken out of a solid figure by a pair of parallel planes. A conical frustum, for example, resembles a cone with the top cut off. The volume and area of a frustum are calculated by subtracting the volume or area of the 'missing' piece from those of the whole figure.

Fry Elizabeth (born Gurney) 1780–1845. English Quaker philanthropist. She formed an association for the improvement of conditions for female prisoners 1817, and worked with her brother, *Joseph Gurney* (1788–1847), on an 1819 report on prison reform.

FSH abbreviation for *follicle-stimulating hormone*.

f-stop in photography, another name for *f number.

FT Index abbreviation for *Financial Times Index*, a list of leading share prices.

Fuad two kings of Egypt, including:

Fuad I 1868–1936. King of Egypt from 1922. Son of the Khedive Ismail, he succeeded his elder brother Hussein Kiamil as sultan of Egypt 1917; when Egypt was declared independent 1922 he assumed the title of king.

Fuchs Klaus (Emil Julius) 1911–1988. German spy who worked on atom-bomb research in the USA in World War II, and subsequently in the UK. He was imprisoned 1950–59 for passing information to the USSR and resettled in eastern Germany.

Fuchs Vivian 1908– . British explorer and geologist. Before World War II, he accompanied several Cambridge University expeditions to East Africa. From 1947 he worked in the Falkland Islands as director of the Scientific Bureau. In 1957–58, he led the overland Commonwealth Trans-Antarctic Expedition and published his autobiography *A Time to Speak* in 1991.

fuchsia any shrub or herbaceous plant of the genus *Fuchsia* of the evening-primrose family Onagraceae. Species are native to South and Central America and New Zealand, and bear red, purple, or pink bell-shaped flowers that hang downward.

fuel any source of heat or energy, embracing the entire range of materials that burn (combustibles). A **nuclear fuel** is any material that produces energy by nuclear fission in a nuclear reactor.

fuel cell cell converting chemical energy directly to electrical energy. It works on the same principle as a battery but is continually fed with fuel, usually hydrogen. Fuel cells are silent and reliable (no moving parts) but expensive to produce.

fuel injection injecting fuel directly into the cylinders of an internal combustion engine, instead of by way of a carburettor. It is the standard method used in *diesel engines, and is now becoming standard for petrol engines. In the diesel engine oil is injected into the hot compressed air at the top of the second piston stroke and explodes to drive the piston down on its power stroke. In the petrol engine, fuel is injected into the cylinder at the start of the first induction stroke of the *four-stroke cycle.

Fuentes Carlos 1928– . Mexican novelist, lawyer, and diplomat whose first novel *La región más transparente/Where the Air Is Clear* 1958 encompasses the history of the country from the Aztecs to the present day.

fugue (Latin 'flight') in music, a contrapuntal form (with two or more melodies) for a number of parts or 'voices', which enter successively in imitation of each other. It was raised to a high art by J S *Bach.

Führer or *Fuehrer* title adopted by Adolf *Hitler as leader of the Nazi Party.

Fujairah or *Fujayrah* one of the seven constituent member states of the *United Arab Emirates; area 1,150 sq km/450 sq mi; population (1985) 54,000.

Fujian or *Fukien* province of SE China, bordering Taiwan Strait, opposite Taiwan
area 123,100 sq km/47,517 sq mi
capital Fuzhou
physical dramatic mountainous coastline
products sugar, rice, special aromatic teas, tobacco, timber, fruit
population (1990) 30,048,000

Fujimori Alberto 1939– . President of Peru from July 1990. As leader of the newly formed Cambio 90 (Change 90), he campaigned on a reformist ticket and defeated his more experienced Democratic Front opponent. With no assembly majority, and and increasing opposition to his policies, he imposed military rule in April 1992; elections Nov 1992 gave his coalition a majority.

Fujisankei Japanese communications group, the world's fourth largest media conglomerate, with nearly 100 companies. It owns Japan's (and the world's) largest radio network, a national newspaper and the country's most successful television chain, plus record and video concerns.

Fujiwara in Japanese history, the ruling clan 858–1185. During that period, the office of emperor became merely ceremonial, with power exercised by chancellors and regents, who were all Fujiwara and whose daughters in every generation married into the imperial family. There was a Fujiwara in Japanese government as recently as during World War II.

Fujiyama or *Mount Fuji* Japanese volcano and highest peak, on Honshu Island, near Tokyo; height 3,778 m/12,400 ft. Extinct since 1707, it has a *Shinto shrine and a weather station on its summit. Fuji has long been revered for its picturesque cone-shaped crater peak, and figures prominently in Japanese art, literature, and religion.

Fula W African empire founded by people of predominantly Fulani extraction. The Fula conquered the Hausa states in the 19th century.

Fulani member of a W African culture from the southern Sahara and Sahel. Traditionally nomadic pastoralists and traders, Fulani groups are found in Senegal, Guinea, Mali, Burkina Faso, Niger, Nigeria, Chad, and Cameroon. The Fulani language is divided into four dialects and belongs to the W Atlantic branch of the Niger—Congo family; it has more than 10 million speakers.

Fulbright (James) William 1905– . US Democratic politician. A US senator 1945–75, he was responsible for the *Fulbright Act* 1946, which provided grants for thousands of Americans to study abroad and for overseas students to study in the USA. Fulbright chaired the Senate Foreign Relations Committee 1959–74, and was a strong internationalist and supporter of the United Nations.

full employment in economics, a state in which the only unemployment is frictional (that share of the labour force which is in the process of looking for, or changing to, a new job), and when everyone wishing to work is able to find employment.

Fuller (Richard) Buckminster 1895–1983. US architect, engineer, and futurist social philosopher who embarked on an unorthodox career in an attempt to maximize energy resources through improved technology. In 1947 he invented the lightweight geodesic dome, a half-sphere of triangular components independent of buttress or vault.

fullerene form of carbon, discovered 1985, based on closed cages of carbon atoms. The molecules of the most symmetrical of the fullerenes are called buckminsterfullerenes. They are perfect spheres made up of 60 carbon atoms linked together in 12 pentagons and 20 hexagons fitted together like those of a spherical football. Other fullerenes are C_{28}, C_{32}, C_{50}, and C_{70}.

fuller's earth a soft, greenish-grey rock resembling clay, but without clay's plasticity. It is formed largely of clay minerals, rich in montmorillonite, but a great deal of silica is also present.

Its absorbent properties make it suitable for removing oil and grease, and it was formerly used for cleaning fleeces ('fulling'). It is still used in the textile industry, but its chief application is in the purification of oils. Beds of fuller's earth are found in the southern USA, Germany, Japan, and the UK.

full score in music, a complete transcript of a composition showing all parts individually, as opposed to a *short score* or *piano score* that is condensed into fewer lines of music.

full stop or *period* punctuation mark (.). It has two functions: to mark the end of a sentence and to indicate that a word has been abbreviated. It is also used in mathematics to indicate decimals and is then called a *point*.

fulmar any of several species of petrels of the family Procellariidae, which are similar in size and colour to herring gulls. The northern fulmar *Fulmarus glacialis* is found in the N Atlantic and visits land only to nest, laying a single egg.

Fulton Robert 1765–1815. US engineer and inventor who designed the first successful steamships. He produced a submarine, the *Nautilus*, for Napoleon's government in France 1801, and experimented with steam navigation on the Seine, then returned to the USA. The first steam vessel of note, known as the *Clermont*, appeared on the Hudson 1807, sailing between New York and Albany. The first steam warship was the USS *Fulton*, of 38 tonnes, built 1814–15.

fumitory any plant of the genus *Fumeria*, family Fumariaceae, native to Europe and Asia. The common fumitory *F. officinalis* grows to 50 cm/20 in tall, and produces pink flowers tipped with blackish red; it has been used in medicine for stomach and liver complaints.

Funchal capital and chief port of the Portuguese island of Madeira, on the south coast; population (1980) 100,000. Tourism and wine are the main industries.

function in computing, a small part of a program that supplies a specific value – for example, the square root of a specified number, or the current date. Most programming languages incorporate a number of built-in functions; some allow programmers to write their own. A function may have one or more arguments (the values on which the function operates). A *function key* on a keyboard is one that, when pressed, performs a designated task, such as ending a program.

function in mathematics, a function f is a nonempty set of ordered pairs $(x,f(x))$ of which no two can have the same first element. Hence, if $f(x) = x^2$, two ordered pairs are $(-2,4)$ and $(2,4)$. The set of all first elements in a function's ordered pairs is called the *domain*; the set of all second elements is the *range*. In the algebraic expression $y = 4x^3 + 2$, the dependent variable y is a function of the independent variable x, generally written as $f(x)$.

functional group in chemistry, a small number of atoms in an arrangement that determines the chemical properties of the group and of the molecule to which it is attached (for example, the carboxyl group COOH, or the amine group NH_2). Organic compounds can be considered as structural skeletons, with a high carbon content, with functional groups attached.

Functionalism in architecture and design, a 20th-century school, also called Modernism or International Style, characterized by the ideal of excluding everything that serves no practical purpose. It developed as a reaction against the 19th-century practice of imitating and combining earlier styles, and its finest achievements are in the realm of industrial architecture and office furnishings.

fundamental in musical acoustics, the lowest *harmonic of a musical tone, corresponding to the audible pitch.

fundamental constant physical quantity that is constant in all circumstances throughout the whole universe. Examples are the electric charge of an electron, the speed of light, Planck's constant, and the gravitational constant.

fundamental forces see *forces, fundamental.

fundamentalism in religion, an emphasis on basic principles or articles of faith. *Christian fundamentalism* emerged in the USA just after World War I (as a reaction to theological modernism and the historical criticism of the Bible) and insisted on belief in the literal truth of everything in the Bible. *Islamic fundamentalism* insists on strict observance of Muslim Shari'a law.

fundamental particle another term for *elementary particle.

fungicide any chemical *pesticide used to prevent fungus diseases in plants and animals. Inorganic and organic compounds containing sulphur are widely used.

fungus (plural *fungi*) any of a group of organisms in the kingdom Fungi. Fungi are not considered plants. They lack leaves and roots; they contain no chlorophyll and reproduce by spores. Moulds, yeasts, rusts, smuts, mildews, and mushrooms are all types of fungi.

funk dance music of black US origin, relying on heavy percussion in polyrhythmic patterns. Leading exponents include James Brown (1928–) and George Clinton (1940–).

fur pelts of certain animals. Fur is used as clothing, although this is vociferously criticized by environmental groups on humane grounds, because the methods of breeding or trapping animals are often cruel. Mink, chinchilla, and sable are among the most valuable, the wild furs being finer than the farmed. Fur such as mink is made up of a soft, thick, insulating layer called underfur and a top layer of longer, lustrous guard hairs.

Furies in Greek mythology, the Erinyes, appeasingly called the Eumenides ('kindly ones'). They were the daughters of Earth or of Night, represented as winged maidens with serpents twisted in their hair. They punished such crimes as filial disobedience, murder, and inhospitality.

furlong unit of measurement, originating in Anglo-Saxon England, equivalent to 220 yd (201.168 m).

furnace structure in which fuel such as coal, coke, gas, or oil is burned to produce heat for various purposes. Furnaces are used in conjunction with *boilers for heating, to produce hot water, or steam for driving turbines – in ships for propulsion and in power stations for generating electricity. The largest furnaces are those used for smelting and refining metals, such as the *blast furnace, electric furnace, and *open-hearth furnace.

furze another name for *gorse, a shrub.

fuse in electricity, a wire or strip of metal designed to melt when excessive current passes through. It is a safety device to stop at that point in the circuit when surges of current would otherwise damage equipment and cause fires. In explosives, a fuse is a cord impregnated with chemicals so that it burns slowly at a predetermined rate. It is used to set off a main explosive charge, sufficient length of fuse being left to allow the person lighting it to get away to safety.

fusel oil liquid with a characteristic unpleasant smell, obtained as a by-product of the distillation of the product of any alcoholic fermentation, and used in paints, varnishes, essential oils, and plastics. It is a mixture of fatty acids, alcohols, and esters.

fusion in physics, the fusing of the nuclei of light elements, such as hydrogen, into those of a heavier element, such as helium. The resultant loss in their combined mass is converted into energy. Stars and thermonuclear weapons work on the principle of *nuclear fusion.

future in business, a contract to buy or sell a specific quantity of a particular commodity or currency (or even a purely notional sum, such as the value of a particular stock index) at a particular date in the future. There is usually no physical exchange between buyer and seller. It is only the difference between the ground value and the market value that changes hands. Such transactions are a function of the *futures market*.

futures trading buying and selling commodities (usually cereals and metals) at an agreed price for delivery several months ahead.

Futurism literary and artistic movement 1909–14, originating in Paris. The Italian poet *Marinetti published the *Futurist Manifesto* 1909 urging Italian artists to join him in Futurism. In their works the Futurists eulogized the modern world and the 'beauty of speed and energy', trying to capture the dynamism of a speeding car or train by combining the shifting geometric planes of *Cubism with vibrant colours. As a movement Futurism died out during World War I, but the Futurists' exultation in war and violence was seen as an early manifestation of *fascism.

Fuzhou or **Foochow** industrial port and capital of Fujian province, SE China; population (1989) 1,270,000. It is a centre for shipbuilding and steel production; rice, sugar, tea, and fruit pass through the port. There are joint foreign and Chinese factories.

fuzzy logic in mathematics and computing, a form of knowledge representation suitable for notions (such as 'hot' or 'loud') that cannot be defined precisely but which depend on their context. For example, a jug of water may be described as hot or cold, depending on whether it is to be used to wash one's face or to make tea. The central idea of fuzzy logic is **probability of set membership**. For instance, referring to someone 5 ft 9 in tall, the statement 'this person is tall' (or 'this person is a member of the set of tall people') might be about 70% true if that person is a man, and about 85% true if that person is a woman. Fuzzy logic enables computerized devices to reason more like humans, responding effectively to complex messages from their control panels and sensors.

g symbol for **gram*.

G7 or **Group of Seven** the seven wealthiest nations in the world: the USA, Japan, Germany, France, the UK, Italy, and Canada. Since 1975 their heads of government have met once a year to discuss economic and, increasingly, political matters.

gabbro basic (low-silica) igneous rock formed deep in the Earth's crust. It contains pyroxene and calcium-rich feldspar, and may contain small amounts of olivine and amphibole. Its coarse crystals of dull minerals give it a speckled appearance.

Gable (William) Clark 1901–1960. US actor. A star for more than 30 years in 90 films, he played romantic roles such as Rhett Butler in *Gone With the Wind* 1939. His other films include *The Painted Desert* 1931 (his first), *It Happened One Night* 1934 (Academy Award), *Mutiny on the Bounty* 1935, and *The Misfits* 1960. He was nicknamed the 'King' of Hollywood.

Gabo Naum. Adopted name of Naum Neemia Pevsner 1890–1977. US abstract sculptor, born in Russia. One of the leading exponents of *Constructivism, he left the USSR in 1922 for Germany and taught at the Bauhaus in Berlin (a key centre of modern design). He lived in Paris and England in the 1930s, then settled in the USA in 1946. He was one of the first artists to make kinetic (moving) sculpture and often used transparent coloured plastics.

Gabon Gabonese Republic (*République Gabonaise*)
area 267,667 sq km/103,319 sq mi
capital Libreville
towns Port-Gentil and Owendo (ports); Masuku (Franceville)
physical virtually the whole country is tropical rainforest; narrow coastal plain rising to hilly interior with savanna in E and S; Ogooué River flows N–W
head of state Omar Bongo from 1967
head of government Casimir Oye-Mba from 1990
political system authoritarian nationalism
exports petroleum, manganese, uranium, timber
currency CFA franc
population (1993) 1,010,000 including 40 Bantu groups; growth rate 1.6% p.a.
languages French (official), Bantu
religions 96% Christian (Roman Catholic 65%), small Muslim minority (1%), animist 3%
GNP $3,780 per head (1991)

chronology
1889 Gabon became part of the French Congo.
1960 Independence from France achieved; Léon M'ba became the first president.
1964 Attempted coup by rival party foiled with French help. M'ba died; he was succeeded by his protégé Albert-Bernard Bongo.
1968 One-party state established.
1973 Bongo re-elected; converted to Islam, he changed his first name to Omar.
1986 Bongo re-elected.
1989 Coup attempt against Bongo defeated.
1990 Constitution amended to allow for multiparty system; widespread fraud alleged in first multiparty elections since 1964.

Gaborone capital of Botswana from 1965, mainly an administrative centre; population (1989) 120,200. Light industry includes textiles.

Gabriel in the New Testament, the archangel who foretold the birth of John the Baptist to Zacharias and of Jesus to the Virgin Mary. He is also mentioned in the Old Testament in the book of Daniel. In Muslim belief, Gabriel revealed the Koran to Muhammad and escorted him on his *Night Journey.

Gaddafi alternative form of *Khaddafi, Libyan leader.

Gaddi family of Italian painters in Florence: *Gaddo Gaddi* (*c.* 1250–1330); his son *Taddeo Gaddi* (*c.* 1300–1366), who was inspired by Giotto and painted the fresco cycle *Life of the Virgin* in Santa Croce, Florence; and grandson *Agnolo Gaddi* (active 1369–96), who also painted frescoes in Santa Croce, *The Story of the Cross* 1380s, and produced panel paintings in characteristic pale pastel colours.

gadolinium silvery-white metallic element of the lanthanide series, symbol Gd, atomic number 64, relative atomic mass 157.25. It is found in the products of nuclear fission and used in electronic components, alloys, and products needing to withstand high temperatures.

Gadsden Purchase, the in US history, the purchase of approximately 77,700 sq km/30,000 sq mi in what is now New Mexico and Arizona by the USA 1853. The land was bought from Mexico for $10 million in a treaty negotiated by James Gadsden (1788–1858) of South Carolina, to construct a transcontinental railroad route, the Southern Pacific, completed in the 1880s.

Gaelic language member of the Celtic branch of the Indo-European language family, spoken in Ireland, Scotland, and (until 1974) the Isle of Man. Gaelic has been in decline for several centuries, discouraged until recently within the British state. There is a small Gaelic-speaking community in Nova Scotia, Canada.

Gagarin Yuri (Alexeyevich) 1934–1968. Soviet cosmonaut who in 1961 became the first human in space aboard the spacecraft *Vostok 1*.

Gaia or **Ge** in Greek mythology, the goddess of the Earth. She sprang from primordial Chaos and herself produced Uranus, by whom she was the mother of the Cyclopes and Titans.

Gaia hypothesis theory that the Earth's living and nonliving systems form an inseparable whole that is regulated and kept adapted for life by living organisms themselves. The planet therefore functions as a single organism, or a giant cell. Since life and environment are so closely linked, there is a need for humans to understand and maintain the physical environment and living things around them. The Gaia hypothesis was elaborated by British scientist James (Ephraim) Lovelock (1919–) in the 1970s.

Gainsborough Thomas 1727–1788. English landscape and portrait painter. In 1760 he settled in Bath and painted society portraits. In 1774 he went to London and became one of the original members of the Royal Academy. He was one of the first British artists to follow the Dutch in painting realistic landscapes rather than imaginative Italianate scenery.

Gaitskell Hugh (Todd Naylor) 1906–1963. British Labour politician. In 1950 he became minister of economic affairs, and then chancellor of the Exchequer until Oct 1951. In 1955 he defeated Aneurin Bevan for the succession to Attlee as party leader, and tried to reconcile internal differences on nationalization and disarmament. He was re-elected leader in 1960.

Galahad in Arthurian legend, one of the knights of the Round Table. Galahad succeeded in the quest for the *Holy Grail because of his virtue. He was the son of Lancelot of the Lake.

Galápagos Islands (official name *Archipiélago de Colón*) group of 15 islands in the Pacific, belonging to Ecuador; area 7,800 sq km/3,000 sq mi; population (1982) 6,120. The capital is San Cristóbal on the island of the same name. The islands are a nature reserve. Their unique fauna (including giant tortoises, iguanas, penguins, flightless cormorants, and Darwin's finches), which inspired Charles *Darwin to formulate the principle of evolution by natural selection, is under threat from introduced species.

galaxy congregation of millions or billions of stars, held together by gravity. *Spiral galaxies*, such as the *Milky Way, are flattened in shape, with a central bulge of old stars surrounded by a disc of younger stars, arranged in spiral arms like a Catherine wheel. *Barred spirals* are spiral galaxies that have a straight bar of stars across their centre, from the ends of which the spiral arms emerge. The arms of spiral galaxies contain gas and dust from which new stars are still forming. *Elliptical galaxies* contain old stars and very little gas. They include the most massive galaxies known, containing a trillion stars. At least some elliptical galaxies are thought to be formed by mergers between spiral galaxies. There are also irregular galaxies. Most galaxies occur in clusters, containing anything from a few to thousands of members.

Galbraith John Kenneth 1908– . Canadian-born US economist; he became a US citizen 1937. His major works include the *Affluent Society* 1958, in which he documents the tendency of the 'invisible hand' of free-market capitalism to create private splendour and public squalor, *Economics and the Public Purpose* 1974, and *The Culture of Containment* 1992.

Galen c. 130–c. 200. Greek physician whose ideas dominated Western medicine for almost 1,500 years. Central to his thinking were the theories of *humours and the threefold circulation of the blood. He remained the highest medical authority until Andreas Vesalius and William Harvey exposed the fundamental errors of his system.

galena chief ore of lead, consisting of lead sulphide, PbS. It is lead-grey in colour, has a high metallic lustre and breaks into cubes because of its perfect cubic cleavage. It may contain up to 1% silver, and so the ore is sometimes mined for both metals. Galena occurs mainly among limestone deposits in Australia, Mexico, Russia, Kazakhstan, the UK, and the USA.

Galicia mountainous but fertile autonomous region of NW Spain, formerly an independent kingdom; area 29,400 sq km/11,348 sq mi; population (1986) 2,785,000. It includes La Coruña, Lugo, Orense, and Pontevedra. Industries include fishing and the mining of tungsten and tin. The language is similar to Portuguese.

Galilee, Sea of or *Lake Tiberias* lake in N Israel, 210 m/689 ft below sea level, into which the river Jordan flows; area 170 sq km/66 sq mi.

Galileo properly Galileo Galilei 1564–1642. Italian mathematician, astronomer, and physicist. He developed the astronomical telescope and was the first to see sunspots, the four main satellites of Jupiter, mountains and craters on the Moon, and the appearance of Venus going through 'phases', thus proving it was orbiting the Sun. In mechanics, Galileo discovered that freely falling bodies, heavy or light, had the same, constant acceleration (although the story of his dropping cannonballs from the Leaning Tower of Pisa is questionable) and that a body moving on a perfectly smooth horizontal surface would neither speed up nor slow down.

Galileo spacecraft launched from the space shuttle *Atlantis* Oct 1989, on a six-year journey to Jupiter. It flew past Venus Feb 1990 and passed within 970 km/600 mi of Earth Dec 1990, using the gravitational fields of these two planets to increase its velocity. The craft is scheduled to fly past Earth Dec 1992 to receive its final boost towards Jupiter.

gall abnormal outgrowth on a plant that develops as a result of attack by insects or, less commonly, by bacteria, fungi, mites, or nematodes. The attack causes an increase in the number of cells or an enlargement of existing cells in the plant. Gall-forming insects generally pass the early stages of their life inside the gall. Gall wasps are responsible for the conspicuous bud galls forming on oak trees, 2.5 to 4 cm/1 to 1.5 in across, known as 'oak apples'.

Galla or *Oromo* nomadic pastoralists inhabiting S Ethiopia and NW Kenya. Galla is an Afro-Asiatic language, and is spoken by about 12 million people.

gall bladder small muscular sac, part of the digestive system of most, but not all, vertebrates. In humans, it is situated on the underside of the liver and connected to the small intestine by the bile duct. It stores bile from the liver.

galley ship powered by oars, and usually also equipped with sails. Galleys typically had a crew of hundreds of oarsmen arranged in rows; they were used in warfare in the Mediterranean from antiquity until the 18th century.

Gallipoli port in European Turkey, giving its name to the peninsula (ancient name

Chersonesus) on which it stands. In World War I, at the instigation of Winston Churchill, an unsuccessful attempt was made Feb 1915–Jan 1916 by Allied troops to force their way through the Dardanelles and link up with Russia. The campaign was fought mainly by Australian and New Zealand (*ANZAC) forces, who suffered heavy losses. An estimated 36,000 Commonwealth troops died during the nine-month campaign.

gallium grey metallic element, symbol Ga, atomic number 31, relative atomic mass 69.75. It is liquid at room temperature. Gallium arsenide crystals are used in microelectronics, since electrons travel a thousand times faster through them than through silicon. The element was discovered in 1875 by Lecoq de Boisbaudran (1838–1912).

Gallo Robert Charles 1937– . US scientist credited with identifying the virus responsible for *AIDS. Gallo discovered the virus, now known as human immunodeficiency virus (HIV), in 1984; the French scientist Luc Montagnier (1932–) of the Pasteur Institute, Paris, discovered the virus, independently, in 1983. The sample in which Gallo discovered the virus was supplied by Montagnier, and it has been alleged that this may have been contaminated by specimens of the virus isolated by Montagnier a few months earlier.

gallon imperial liquid or dry measure, equal to 4.546 litres, and subdivided into four quarts or eight pints. The US gallon is equivalent to 3.785 litres.

gallstone pebblelike, insoluble accretion formed in the human gall bladder or bile ducts from cholesterol or calcium salts present in bile. Gallstones may be symptomless or they may cause pain, indigestion, or jaundice. They can be dissolved with medication or removed, along with the gall bladder, in an operation known as cholecystectomy.

Gallup George Horace 1901–1984. US journalist and statistician, who founded in 1935 the American Institute of Public Opinion and devised the Gallup Poll, in which public opinion is sampled by questioning a number of representative individuals.

Galsworthy John 1867–1933. English novelist and dramatist whose work examines the social issues of the Victorian period. He wrote *The Forsyte Saga* 1922 and its sequel *A Modern Comedy* 1929. His other novels include *The Country House* 1907 and *Fraternity* 1909; plays include *The Silver Box* 1906.

Galtieri Leopoldo 1926– . Argentine general, president 1981–82. Under his leadership the junta ordered the seizure 1982 of the Falkland Islands (Malvinas), a British colony in the SW Atlantic claimed by Argentina. He and his fellow junta members were tried for abuse of human rights and court-martialled for their conduct of the war; he was sentenced to 12 years in prison in 1986.

Galton Francis 1822–1911. English scientist who studied the inheritance of physical and mental attributes in humans, with the aim of improving the human species. He discovered that no two sets of human fingerprints are the same, and is considered the founder of *eugenics.

galvanizing process for rendering iron rustproof, by plunging it into molten zinc (the dipping method), or by electroplating it with zinc.

galvanometer instrument for detecting small electric currents by their magnetic effect.

Galway county on the W coast of the Republic of Ireland, in the province of Connacht; area 5,940 sq km/2,293 sq mi; population (1991) 180,300. Towns include Galway (county town), Ballinasloe, Tuam, Clifden, and Loughrea (near which deposits of lead, zinc, and copper were found 1959).

Gama Vasco da *c.* 1469–1524. Portuguese navigator who commanded an expedition in 1497 to discover the route to India around the Cape of Good Hope in modern South Africa. On Christmas Day 1497 he reached land, which he named Natal. He then crossed the Indian Ocean, arriving at Calicut May 1498, and returning to Portugal Sept 1499.

Gambia Republic of The

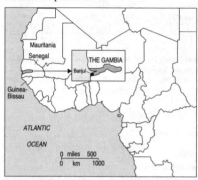

area 10,402 sq km/4,018 sq mi
capital Banjul
towns Serekunda, Bakau, Georgetown
physical banks of the river Gambia flanked by low hills
head of state and government (interim) Yahya Jammeh from 1994
political system interim military republic
exports groundnuts, palm oil, fish
currency dalasi
population (1993 est) 920,000; growth rate 1.9% p.a.
languages English (official), Mandinka, Fula and other native tongues
religions Muslim 90%, with animist and Christian minorities
GNP $360 per head (1991)
chronology
1843 The Gambia became a crown colony.
1965 Independence achieved from Britain as a constitutional monarchy within the Commonwealth, with Dawda K Jawara as prime minister.
1970 Declared itself a republic, with Jawara as president.
1981 Attempted coup foiled with the help of Senegal.
1982 Formed with Senegal the Confederation of Senegambia; Jawara re-elected.
1989 Confederation of Senegambia dissolved.
1994 Jawara ousted in military coup; Yahya Jammeh named as acting head of state.

Gambier Islands island group, part of *French Polynesia, administered with the *Tuamotu Archipelago; area 36 sq km/14 sq mi; population (1983) 582. It includes four coral islands and many small islets. The main island is Mangareva, with its town Rikitea.

gamete cell that functions in sexual reproduction by merging with another gamete to form a *zygote. Examples of gametes include sperm and egg cells. In most organisms, the gametes are haploid (they contain half the number of chromosomes of the parent), owing to reduction division or *meiosis.

game theory branch of mathematics that deals with strategic problems (such as those that arise in business, commerce, and warfare) by assuming that the people involved invariably try to employ winning strategies. The theory was developed by Oscar Morgenstern (1902–1977) and John *Von Neumann during World War II.

gametophyte the *haploid generation in the life cycle of a plant that produces gametes; see *alternation of generations.

gamma radiation very high-frequency electromagnetic radiation, similar in nature to X-rays but of shorter wavelength, emitted by the nuclei of radioactive substances during decay or by the interactions of high-energy electrons with matter. Cosmic gamma rays have been identified as coming from pulsars, radio galaxies, and quasars, although they cannot penetrate the Earth's atmosphere.

gamma-ray astronomy the study of gamma rays from space. Some sources have been identified, including the Crab nebula and the Vela pulsar (the most powerful gamma-ray source detected).

Gamsakhurdia Zviad 1939–1994. Georgian politician, president 1990–92. He was an active anti-communist and, after nationalist success in parliamentary elections, he was directly elected head of state by a huge margin in May 1991. Gamsakhurdia's increasingly dictatorial style led to his forced removal and he fled to Armenia.

Gance Abel 1889–1981. French film director. His films were grandiose melodramas. *Napoléon* 1927 was one of the most ambitious silent epic films. It features colour tinting and triple-screen sequences, as well as multiple-exposure shots, and purported to suggest that Napoleon was the fulfilment of the French Revolution.

Ganda member of the Baganda people, the majority ethnic group in Uganda; the Baganda also live in Kenya. Until the 19th century they formed an independent kingdom, the largest in E Africa. It was a British protectorate 1894–1962, and the monarchy was officially overthrown in 1966. Their language, Luganda, belongs to the Niger–Congo language family and has about 3 million speakers.

Gandhi Indira (born Nehru) 1917–1984. Indian politician, prime minister of India 1966–77 and 1980–84, and leader of the *Congress Party 1966–77 and subsequently of the Congress (I) party. She was assassinated 1984 by members of her Sikh bodyguard, resentful of her use of troops to clear malcontents from the Sikh temple at *Amritsar.

Gandhi (Mohandas Karamchand Gandhi, given the honorific name of **Mahatma** [Sanskrit 'Great Soul']) 1869–1948. Indian nationalist leader. A pacifist, he led the struggle for Indian independence from the UK by advocating nonviolent noncooperation (*satyagraha*, defence of and by truth) from 1915. He was imprisoned several times by the British authorities and was influential in the nationalist *Congress Party and in the independence negotiations 1947. He was assassinated by a Hindu nationalist in the violence that followed the partition of British India into India and Pakistan.

Gandhi Rajiv 1944–1991. Indian politician, prime minister from 1984 (following his mother Indira Gandhi's assassination) to Nov 1989. As prime minister, he faced growing discontent with his party's elitism and lack of concern for social issues. He was assassinated by a bomb at an election rally.

Ganges (Hindi **Ganga**) major river of India and Bangladesh; length 2,510 km/1,560 mi. It is the most sacred river for Hindus.

ganglion (plural **ganglia**) solid cluster of nervous tissue containing many cell bodies and *synapses, usually enclosed in a tissue sheath; found in invertebrates and vertebrates.

Gang of Four in Chinese history, the chief members of the radical faction that played a key role in directing the *Cultural Revolution and tried to seize power after the death of the communist leader Mao Zedong 1976. It included his widow, *Jiang Qing; the other members were three young Shanghai politicians: Zhang Chunqiao, Wang Hongwen, and Yao Wenyuan. The coup failed and the Gang of Four were arrested. Publicly tried in 1980, they were found guilty of treason.

gangrene death and decay of body tissue (often of a limb) due to bacterial action; the affected part gradually turns black and causes blood poisoning.

gannet N Atlantic seabird *Sula bassana* in the same family (Sulidae) as the boobies. When fully grown, it is white with black-tipped wings having a span of 1.7 m/5.6 ft. The young are speckled. It breeds on cliffs in nests made of grass and seaweed. Only one (white) egg is laid.

Gansu or **Kansu** province of NW China
area 530,000 sq km/204,580 sq mi
capital Lanzhou
products coal, oil, hydroelectric power from the Huang He (Yellow) River
population (1990) 22,371,000, including many Muslims.

Ganymede in astronomy, the largest moon of the planet Jupiter, and the largest moon in the solar system, 5,260 km/3,270 mi in diameter (larger than the planet Mercury). It orbits Jupiter every 7.2 days at a distance of 1.1 million km/700,000 mi. Its surface is a mixture of cratered and grooved terrain.

gar primitive bony fish of the order Semionotiformes, which also includes *sturgeons. Gar have long, beaklike snouts and elongated bodies covered in heavy, bony scales. All four species of gar inhabit freshwater rivers and lakes of the Mississippi drainage. See also *needlefish.

Garbo Greta. Stage name of Greta Lovisa Gustafsson 1905–1990. Swedish-born US film actress. She went to the USA 1925, where her captivating beauty and leading role in *Flesh and the Devil* 1927 made her one of Hollywood's greatest stars. Her later films include *Mata Hari* 1931, *Grand Hotel* 1932, *Queen Christina* 1933, *Anna Karenina* 1935, *Camille* 1936, and *Ninotchka* 1939. Her ethereal qualities and romantic mystery on the screen intermingled with her seclusion in private life. She retired 1941.

García Márquez Gabriel 1928–   . Colombian novelist. His sweeping novel *Cien años de soledad/One Hundred Years of Solitude* 1967 (which tells the story of a family over a period of six generations) is an example of magic realism, a technique used to heighten the intensity of realistic portrayal of social and political issues by introducing grotesque or fanciful material. Nobel Prize for Literature 1982.

García Perez Alan 1949–   . Peruvian politician, leader of the moderate, left-wing APRA party; president 1985–90. He inherited an ailing economy and had to trim his socialist programme.

garden city in the UK, a town built in a rural area and designed to combine town and country advantages, with its own industries, controlled developments, private and public gardens, and cultural centre. The idea was proposed by Sir Ebenezer Howard (1850–1928), who in 1899 founded the Garden City Association, which established the first garden city, Letchworth (in Hertfordshire).

gardenia subtropical and tropical trees and shrubs of Africa and Asia, genus *Gardenia*, of the madder family Rubiaceae, with evergreen foliage and flattened rosettes of fragrant waxen-looking blooms, often white in colour.

Garfield James A(bram) 1831–1881. 20th president of the USA 1881, a Republican. A compromise candidate for the presidency, he held office for only four months before being assassinated in Washington, DC railway station by a disappointed office-seeker. His short tenure was marked primarily by struggles within the Republican party over influence and cabinet posts.

Garibaldi Giuseppe 1807–1882. Italian soldier who played a central role in the unification of Italy by conquering Sicily and Naples 1860. From 1834 a member of the nationalist Mazzini's *Young Italy society, he was forced into exile until 1848 and again 1849–54. He fought against Austria 1848–49, 1859, and 1866, and led two unsuccessful expeditions to liberate Rome from papal rule in 1862 and 1867.

Garland Judy. Stage name of Frances Gumm 1922–1969. US singer and actress whose performances are marked by a compelling intensity. Her films include *The Wizard of Oz* (which featured the tune that was to become her theme song, 'Over the Rainbow'), *Babes in Arms* 1939, *Strike Up the Band* 1940, *Meet Me in St Louis* 1944, *Easter Parade* 1948, *A Star is Born* 1954, and *Judgment at Nuremberg* 1961.

garlic perennial plant *Allium sativum* of the lily family Liliaceae, with white flowers. The bulb, made of small segments, or cloves, is used in cookery, and its pungent essence has an active medical ingredient, allyl methyl trisulphide, which prevents blood clotting.

garnet group of silicate minerals with the formula $X_3Y_2(SiO_4)_3$, when X is calcium, magnesium, iron, or manganese, and Y is iron, aluminium, or chromium. Garnets are used as semiprecious gems (usually pink to deep red) and as abrasives. They occur in metamorphic rocks such as gneiss and schist.

Garrick David 1717–1779. British actor and theatre manager. He was a pupil of Samuel *Johnson. From 1747 he became joint licensee of the Drury Lane theatre with his own company, and instituted a number of significant theatrical conventions including concealed stage lighting and banishing spectators from the stage. He played Shakespearean characters such as Richard III, King Lear, Hamlet, and Benedick, and collaborated with George Colman (1732–1794) in writing the play *The Clandestine Marriage* 1766. He retired from the stage 1766, but continued as a manager.

Garter, Order of the senior British order of knighthood, founded by Edward III in about 1347. Its distinctive badge is a garter of dark blue velvet, with the motto of the order, *Honi soit qui mal y pense* ('Shame be to him who thinks evil of it') in gold letters.

Garvey Marcus (Moziah) 1887–1940. Jamaican political thinker and activist, an early advocate of black nationalism. He founded the UNIA (Universal Negro Improvement Association) in 1914, and moved to the USA in 1916, where he established branches in New York and other northern cities. Aiming to achieve human rights and dignity for black people through black pride and economic self-sufficiency, he was considered one of the first militant black nationalists. He led a Back to Africa movement for black Americans to establish a black-governed country in Africa. The Jamaican cult of *Rastafarianism is based largely on his ideas.

gas in physics, a form of matter, such as air, in which the molecules move randomly in otherwise empty space, filling any size or shape of container into which the gas is put.

Gascoigne Paul ('Gazza') 1967–   . English footballer who played for Tottenham Hotspur from 1988 and for Lazio, Italy, from 1992. He signed for Glasgow Rangers June 1995.

Gascony ancient province of SW France. With Guienne it formed the duchy of Aquitaine in the 12th century; Henry II of England gained possession of it through his marriage to Eleanor of Aquitaine in 1152, and it was often in English hands until 1451. It was then ruled by the king of France until it was united with the French royal domain 1607 under Henry IV.

gas-cooled reactor type of nuclear reactor; see *advanced gas-cooled reactor.

gas engine internal-combustion engine in which a gas (coal gas, producer gas, natural gas, or gas from a blast furnace) is used as the fuel. The first practical gas engine was built 1860 by Jean Etienne Lenoir, and the type was subsequently developed by Nikolaus August Otto, who introduced the *four-stroke cycle.

gas exchange in biology, the movement of gases between an organism and the atmosphere, principally oxygen and carbon dioxide. All aerobic organisms (most animals and plants) take in oxygen in order to burn food and manufacture

*ATP. The resultant oxidation reactions release carbon dioxide as a waste product to be passed out into the environment. Green plants also absorb carbon dioxide during *photosynthesis, and release oxygen as a waste product.

Gaskell 'Mrs' (Elizabeth Cleghorn, born Stevenson) 1810–1865. British novelist. Her books include *Mary Barton* 1848, *Cranford* (set in the town in which she was brought up, Knutsford, Cheshire) 1853, *North and South* 1855, *Sylvia's Lovers* 1863–64, the unfinished *Wives and Daughters* 1866, and a life of her friend Charlotte *Brontë.

gasohol motor fuel that is 90% petrol and 10% ethanol (alcohol). The ethanol is usually obtained by fermentation, followed by distillation, using maize, wheat, potatoes, or sugar cane. It was used in early cars before petrol became economical, and its use was revived during the 1940s war shortage and the energy shortage of the 1970s, for example in Brazil.

gasoline mixture of hydrocarbons derived from petroleum, whose main use is as a fuel for internal combustion engines. It is colourless and highly volatile.

gastroenteritis inflammation of the stomach and intestines, giving rise to abdominal pain, vomiting, and diarrhoea. It may be caused by food or other poisoning, allergy, or infection, and is dangerous in babies.

gastrolith stone that was once part of the digestive system of a dinosaur or other extinct animal. Rock fragments were swallowed to assist in the grinding process in the dinosaur digestive tract, much as some birds now swallow grit and pebbles to grind food in their crop. Once the animal has decayed, smooth round stones remain – often the only clue to their past use is the fact that they are geologically different from their surrounding strata.

gastropod any member of a very large class (Gastropoda) of *molluscs. Gastropods are single-shelled (in a spiral or modified spiral form), have eyes on stalks, and move on a flattened, muscular foot. They have well-developed heads and rough, scraping tongues called radulae. Some are marine, some freshwater, and others land creatures, but all tend to inhabit damp places.

gas turbine engine in which burning fuel supplies hot gas to spin a *turbine. The most widespread application of gas turbines has been in aviation. All jet engines (see under *jet propulsion) are modified gas turbines, and some locomotives and ships also use gas turbines as a power source. They are also used in industry for generating and pumping purposes.

gate in electronics, short for *logic gate.

Gatling Richard Jordan 1818–1903. US inventor of a rapid-fire gun. Patented in 1862, the Gatling gun had ten barrels arranged as a cylinder rotated by a hand crank. Cartridges from an overhead hopper or drum dropped into the breech mechanism, which loaded, fired, and extracted them at a rate of 320 rounds per minute.

GATT acronym for *General Agreement on Tariffs and Trade.

Gaudí Antonio 1852–1926. Spanish architect distinguished for his flamboyant Art Nouveau style. Gaudí worked mainly in Barcelona, designing both domestic and industrial buildings. He introduced colour, unusual materials, and audacious technical innovations. His spectacular Church of the Holy Family, Barcelona, begun 1883, is still under construction.

Gaudier-Brzeska Henri (Henri Gaudier) 1891–1915. French artist, active in London from 1911; he is regarded as one of the outstanding sculptors of his generation. He studied art in Bristol, Nuremberg, and Munich, and became a member of the English Vorticist movement, which sought to reflect the industrial age by a sense of motion and angularity. From 1913 his sculptures showed the influence of Constantin Brancusi and Jacob Epstein. He was killed in action during World War I.

gauge any scientific measuring instrument – for example, a wire gauge or a pressure gauge. The term is also applied to the width of a railway or tramway track.

gauge boson or *field particle* any of the particles that carry the four fundamental forces of nature (see *forces, fundamental). Gauge bosons are *elementary particles that cannot be subdivided, and include the photon, the graviton, the gluons, and the weakons.

Gauguin Paul 1848–1903. French Post-Impressionist painter. Going beyond the Impressionists' notion of reality, he sought a more direct experience of life in the magical rites of the people and rich colours of the South Sea islands. He disliked theories and rules of painting, and his pictures are *Expressionist compositions characterized by his use of pure, unmixed colours. Among his paintings is *Le Christe Jaune* 1889 (Albright-Knox Art Gallery, Buffalo, USA).

Gaul member of the Celtic-speaking peoples who inhabited France and Belgium in Roman times; also their territory. The Romans conquered S Gaul between the Mediterranean and the Cevennes in about 125 BC and the remaining Gauls up to the Rhine were conquered by Julius *Caesar 58–51 BC.

Gaulle Charles de. French politician, see Charles *de Gaulle.

Gaultier Jean-Paul 1952– . French fashion designer who, after working for Pierre Cardin, launched his first collection in 1978, designing clothes that went against fashion trends, inspired by London's street style. Humorous and showy, his clothes are among the most influential in the French ready-to-wear market.

gaur Asiatic wild cattle *Bos gaurus*, dark grey-brown with white 'socks', and 2 m/6 ft tall at the shoulders. The original range was from India to SE Asia and Malaysia, but numbers and range are now diminished.

gauss cgs unit (symbol Gs) of magnetic flux density, replaced by the SI unit, the *tesla, but still commonly used. The Earth's magnetic field is about 0.5 Gs, and changes to it over time are measured in gammas (one gamma equals 10^{-5} gauss).

Gautier Théophile 1811–1872. French Romantic poet whose later works emphasized the perfection of form and the polished beauty of language and imagery (for example, *Emaux et camées/Enamels and Cameos* 1852). He was also a novelist (*Mlle de Maupin* 1835) and later turned to journalism.

Gavaskar Sunil Manohar 1949– . Indian cricketer. Between 1971 and 1987 he scored a record 10,122 test runs in a record 125 matches (including 106 consecutive tests).

gavial large reptile *Gavialis gangeticus* related to the crocodile. It grows to about 7 m/23 ft long, and has a very long snout with about 100 teeth in its jaws. Gavials live in rivers in N India, where they feed on fish and frogs. They have been extensively hunted for their skins, and are now extremely rare.

Gaviria (Trujillo) Cesar 1947– . Colombian Liberal Party politician, president from 1990; he was finance minister 1986–87 and minister of government 1987–89. He has supported the extradition of drug traffickers wanted in the USA and has sought more US aid in return for stepping up the drug war.

Gawain in Arthurian legend, one of the knights of the Round Table who participated in the quest for the *Holy Grail. He is the hero of the 14th-century epic poem *Sir Gawayne and the Greene Knight*.

Gay John 1685–1732. British poet and dramatist. He wrote *Trivia* 1716, a verse picture of 18th-century London. His *The Beggar's Opera* 1728, a 'Newgate pastoral' using traditional songs and telling of the love of Polly for highwayman Captain Macheath, was an extraordinarily popular success. Its satiric political touches led to the banning of *Polly*, a sequel.

Gaye Marvin 1939–1984. US soul singer and songwriter whose hits, including 'Stubborn Kinda Fellow' 1962, 'I Heard It Through the Grapevine' 1968, and 'What's Goin' On' 1971, exemplified the Detroit *Motown sound.

Gazankulu *Black National State in Transvaal province, South Africa, with self-governing status from 1971; population (1985) 497,200.

Gaza Strip strip of Palestine under Israeli administration; capital Gaza; area 363 sq km/140 sq mi; population (1989) 645,000 of which 446,000 are refugees.

gazelle any of a number of species of lightly built, fast-running antelopes found on the open plains of Africa and S Asia, especially those of the genus *Gazella*.

GCE (abbreviation for *General Certificate of Education*) in the UK, the public examination formerly taken at the age of 16 at Ordinary level (O level) and at still taken at 18 at Advanced level (A level). The GCE O-level examination, aimed at the top 20% of the ability range, was superseded 1988 by the General Certificate of Secondary Education (*GCSE).

GCSE (*General Certificate of Secondary Education*) in the UK, from 1988, examination for 16-year-old pupils, superseding both GCE O level and CSE, and offering qualifications for up to 60% of school leavers in any particular subject.

Gdańsk (German *Danzig*) Polish port; population (1990) 465,100. Oil is refined, and textiles, televisions, and fertilizers are produced. In the 1980s there were repeated anti-government strikes at the Lenin shipyards.

GDP abbreviation for *gross domestic product*.

gear a toothed wheel that transmits the turning movement of one shaft to another shaft. Gear wheels may be used in pairs, or in threes if both shafts are to turn in the same direction. The gear ratio – the ratio of the number of teeth on the two wheels – determines the torque ratio, the turning force on the output shaft compared with the turning force on the input shaft. The ratio of the angular velocities of the shafts is the inverse of the gear ratio.

gearing, financial see *financial gearing.

Geber Latinized form of *Jabir* ibn Hayyan *c.* 721– *c.* 776. Arabian alchemist. His influence lasted for more than 600 years, and in the late 1300s his name was adopted by a Spanish alchemist whose writings spread the knowledge and practice of alchemy throughout Europe.

gecko *The tokay gecko is one of the largest and most common geckos – 28 cm/11 in long.*

gecko any lizard of the family Gekkonidae. Geckos are common worldwide in warm climates, and have large heads and short, stout bodies. Many have no eyelids. Their adhesive toe pads enable them to climb vertically and walk upside down on smooth surfaces in their search for flies, spiders, and other prey.

Geddes Patrick 1854–1932. Scottish town planner who established the importance of surveys, research work, and properly planned 'diagnoses before treatment'. His major work is *City Development* 1904. His protégé was US social critic Lewis Mumford (1895–1990).

gazelle *Thomson's gazelle from the open plains of Sudan, Kenya, and N Tanzania has a distinctive dark stripe along its sides.*

Gehenna another name for *hell; in the Old Testament, a valley S of Jerusalem where children were sacrificed to the Phoenician god Moloch and fires burned constantly.

Geiger Hans 1882–1945. German physicist who produced the Geiger counter. After studying in Germany, he spent the period 1907–12 in Manchester, England, working with Ernest Rutherford on radioactivity. In 1908 they designed an instrument to detect and count *alpha particles, positively charged ionizing particles produced by radioactive decay.

Geiger counter any of a number of devices used for detecting nuclear radiation and/or measuring its intensity by counting the number of ionizing particles produced (see *radioactivity). It detects the momentary current that passes between *electrodes in a suitable gas when a nuclear particle or a radiation pulse causes the ionization of that gas. The electrodes are connected to electronic devices that enable the number of particles passing to be measured. The increased frequency of measured particles indicates the intensity of radiation. It is named after Hans Geiger.

Geingob Hage Gottfried 1941– . Namibian politician, prime minister from 1990. Geingob was appointed the first director of the United Nations Institute for Namibia in Lusaka, 1975. He became the first prime minister of independent Namibia in March 1990.

geisha female entertainer (music, singing, dancing, and conversation) in Japanese teahouses and at private parties. Geishas survive mainly as a tourist attraction. They are apprenticed from childhood and highly skilled in traditional Japanese arts and graces. There are now only approximately 20,000 geishas in Japan compared to 100,000 before World War II.

Geissler tube high-voltage *discharge tube in which traces of gas ionize and conduct electricity. Since the electrified gas takes on a luminous colour characteristic of the gas, the instrument is also used in *spectroscopy. It was developed 1858 by the German physicist Heinrich Geissler (1814–1879).

gel solid produced by the formation of a three-dimensional cage structure, commonly of linked large-molecular-mass polymers, in which a liquid is trapped. It is a form of *colloid. A gel may be a jellylike mass (pectin, gelatin) or have a more rigid structure (silica gel).

gelatin water-soluble protein prepared from boiled hide and bone, used in cookery to set jellies, and in glues and photographic emulsions.

Gelderland (English **Guelders**) province of the E Netherlands
area 5,020 sq km/1,938 sq mi
population (1991) 1,817,000
capital Arnhem
towns Apeldoorn, Nijmegen, Ede
products livestock, textiles, electrical goods
history in the Middle Ages Gelderland was divided into Upper Gelderland (Roermond in N Limburg) and Lower Gelderland (Nijmegen, Arnhem, Zutphen). These territories were inherited by Charles V of Spain, but when the revolt against Spanish rule reached a climax 1579, Lower Gelderland joined the United Provinces of the Netherlands.

gelignite type of *dynamite.

Gell-Mann Murray 1929– . US physicist. In 1964 he formulated the theory of the *quark as one of the fundamental constituents of matter. In 1969 he was awarded a Nobel prize for his work on elementary particles and their interaction.

gem mineral valuable by virtue of its durability (hardness), rarity, and beauty, cut and polished for ornamental use, or engraved. Of 120 minerals known to have been used as gemstones, only about 25 are in common use in jewellery today; of these, the diamond, emerald, ruby, and sapphire are classified as precious, and all the others semiprecious, for example the topaz, amethyst, opal, and aquamarine.

Gemayel Amin 1942– . Lebanese politician, a Maronite Christian; president 1982–88. He succeeded his brother, president-elect **Bechir Gemayel** (1947–1982), on his assassination on 14 Sept 1982. The Lebanese parliament was unable to agree on a successor when his term expired, so separate governments were formed under rival Christian and Muslim leaders.

Gemeinschaft and **Gesellschaft** German terms (roughly, 'community' and 'association') coined 1887 by German social theorist Ferdinand Tönnies (1855–1936) to contrast social relationships in traditional rural societies with those in modern industrial societies. He saw *Gemeinschaft* (traditional) as intimate and positive, and *Gesellschaft* (modern) as impersonal and negative.

Gemini prominent zodiacal constellation in the northern hemisphere represented as the twins Castor and Pollux. Its brightest star is *Pollux; *Castor is a system of six stars. The Sun passes through Gemini from late June to late July. Each Dec, the Geminid meteors radiate from Gemini. In astrology, the dates for Gemini are between about 21 May and 21 June (see *precession).

gemma (plural **gemmae**) unit of *vegetative reproduction, consisting of a small group of undifferentiated green cells. Gemmae are found in certain mosses and liverworts, forming on the surface of the plant, often in cup-shaped structures, or gemmae cups. Gemmae are dispersed by splashes of rain and can then develop into new plants. In many species, gemmation is more common than reproduction by *spores.

gender in grammar, one of the categories into which nouns are divided in many languages, such as masculine, feminine, and neuter (as in Latin, German, and Russian), masculine and feminine (as in French, Italian, and Spanish), or animate and inanimate (as in some North American Indian languages).

gene unit of inherited material, encoded by a strand of *DNA, and transcribed by *RNA. In higher organisms, genes are located on the *chromosomes. The term 'gene', coined 1909 by the Danish geneticist Wilhelm Johannsen (1857–1927), refers to the inherited factor that consistently affects a particular character in an individual – for example, the gene for eye colour. Also termed a Mendelian gene, after Gregor *Mendel, it occurs at a particular point or *locus on a particular chromosome and may have several variants or *alleles, each specifying a particular form of that character – for example, the alleles for blue or brown eyes. Some alleles show *dominance. These mask the effect of other alleles known as *recessive.

gene amplification technique by which selected DNA from a single cell can be repeatedly duplicated until there is a sufficient amount to analyse by conventional genetic techniques.

gene bank collection of seeds or other forms of genetic material, such as tubers, spores, bacterial or yeast cultures, live animals and plants, frozen sperm and eggs, or frozen embryos. These are stored for possible future use in agriculture, plant and animal breeding, or in medicine, genetic engineering, or the restocking of wild habitats where species have become extinct. Gene banks will be increasingly used as the rate of extinction increases, depleting the Earth's genetic variety (biodiversity).

gene pool total sum of *alleles (variants of *genes) possessed by all the members of a given population or species alive at a particular time.

general senior military rank, the ascending grades being major general, lieutenant general, and general. The US rank of general of the army is equivalent to the British *field marshal.

General Agreement on Tariffs and Trade (GATT) organization within the United Nations founded 1948 with the aim of encouraging *free trade between nations through low tariffs, abolitions of quotas, and curbs on subsidies.

General Motors the USA's largest company, a vehicle manufacturer founded 1908 in Flint, Michigan, from a number of small car makers; it went on to acquire many more companies, including those that produced the Oldsmobile, Pontiac, Cadillac, and Chevrolet. It has headquarters in Detroit, Michigan, and New York.

general strike refusal to work by employees in several key industries, with the intention of paralysing the economic life of a country. In British history, the General Strike was a nationwide strike called by the Trade Union Congress on 3 May 1926 in support of the miners' union.

generator machine that produces electrical energy from mechanical energy, as opposed to an *electric motor, which does the opposite. A simple generator (dynamo) consists of a wire-wound coil (*armature) that is rotated between the poles of a permanent magnet. The movement of the wire in the magnetic field induces a current in the coil by *electromagnetic induction, which can be fed by means of a *commutator as a continuous direct current into an external circuit. Slip rings instead of a commutator produce an alternating current, when the generator is called an alternator.

gene replacement therapy (GRT) hypothetical treatment for hereditary diseases in which affected cells from a sufferer would be removed from the body, the *DNA repaired in the laboratory (*genetic engineering), and the functioning cells reintroduced. Successful experiments have been carried out on animals.

Genesis first book of the Old Testament, which includes the stories of the creation of the world, Adam and Eve, the Flood, and the history of the Jewish patriarchs Abraham, Isaac, Jacob, and Joseph (who brought his people to Egypt).

gene-splicing technique for inserting a foreign gene into laboratory cultures of bacteria to generate commercial biological products, such as synthetic insulin, hepatitis-B vaccine, and interferon. It was invented 1973 by the US scientists Stanley Cohen and Herbert Boyer, and patented in the USA 1984. See *genetic engineering.

genet small, nocturnal, meat-eating mammal, genus *Genetta*, in the mongoose and civet family (Viverridae). Most species live in Africa, but *G. genetta* is also found in Europe and the Middle East. It is about 50 cm/1.6 ft long with a 45 cm/1.5 ft tail, and greyish yellow with rows of black spots. It climbs well.

Genet Jean 1910–1986. French dramatist, novelist, and poet, an exponent of the Theatre of *Cruelty. His turbulent life and early years spent in prison are reflected in his drama, characterized by ritual, role-play, and illusion, in which his characters come to act out their bizarre and violent fantasies. His plays include *Les Bonnes/The Maids* 1947, *Le Balcon/The Balcony* 1957, and two plays dealing with the Algerian situation: *Les Nègres/The Blacks* 1959 and *Les Paravents/The Screens* 1961.

genetic code the way in which instructions for building proteins, the basic structural molecules of living matter, are 'written' in the genetic material *DNA. This relationship between the sequence of bases (the subunits in a DNA molecule) and the sequence of *amino acids (the subunits of a protein molecule) is the basis of heredity. The code employs *codons of three bases each; it is the same in almost all organisms, except for a few minor differences recently discovered in some protozoa.

genetic disease any disorder caused at least partly by defective genes or chromosomes. In humans there are some 3,000 genetic diseases, including cleft palate, cystic fibrosis, Down's syndrome, haemophilia, Huntington's chorea, some forms of anaemia, spina bifida, and Tay-Sachs disease.

genetic engineering deliberate manipulation of genetic material by biochemical techniques. It is often achieved by the introduction of new *DNA, usually by means of a virus or *plasmid. This can be for pure research or to breed functionally specific plants, animals, or bacteria. These organisms with a foreign gene added are said to be transgenic (see *transgenic organism).

genetic fingerprinting technique used for determining the pattern of certain parts of the genetic material *DNA that is unique to each individual. Like skin fingerprinting, it can accurately distinguish humans from one another, with the exception of identical siblings from multiple births.

genetics study of inheritance and of the units of inheritance (*genes). The founder of genetics was Gregor *Mendel, whose experiments with plants, such as peas, showed that inheritance takes place by means of discrete 'particles', which later came to be called genes.

Geneva (French *Genève*) Swiss city, capital of Geneva canton, on the shore of Lake Geneva; population (1990) city 167,200; canton 376,000. It is a point of convergence of natural routes and is a cultural and commercial centre. Industries include the manufacture of watches, scientific and optical instruments, foodstuffs, jewellery, and musical boxes.

Geneva Convention international agreement 1864 regulating the treatment of those wounded in war, and later extended to cover the types of weapons allowed, the treatment of prisoners and the sick, and the protection of civilians in wartime. The rules were revised at conventions held 1906, 1929, and 1949, and by the 1977 Additional Protocols.

Geneva, Lake (French *Lac Léman*) largest of the central European lakes, between Switzerland and France; area 580 sq km/225 sq mi.

Geneva Protocol international agreement 1925 designed to prohibit the use of poisonous gases, chemical weapons, and bacteriological methods of warfare. It came into force 1928 but was not ratified by the USA until 1974.

Genghis Khan *c.* 1167–1227. Mongol conqueror, ruler of all Mongol peoples from 1206. He began the conquest of N China 1213, overran the empire of the shah of Khiva 1219–25, and invaded N India, while his lieutenants advanced as far as the Crimea. When he died, his empire ranged from the Yellow Sea to the Black Sea; it continued to expand after his death to extend from Hungary to Korea. Genghis Khan controlled probably a larger area than any other individual in history. He was not only a great military leader, but the creator of a stable political system.

Genoa (Italian *Genova*) historic city in NW Italy, capital of Liguria; population (1989) 706,700. It is Italy's largest port; industries include oil-refining, chemicals, engineering, and textiles.

genocide deliberate and systematic destruction of a national, racial, religious, or ethnic group defined by the exterminators as undesirable. The term is commonly applied to the policies of the Nazis during World War II (what they called the 'final solution' – the extermination of all 'undesirables' in occupied Europe).

genome the full complement of *genes carried by a single (haploid) set of *chromosomes. The term may be applied to the genetic information carried by an individual or to the range of genes found in a given species.

genotype the particular set of *alleles (variants of genes) possessed by a given organism. The term is usually used in conjunction with *phenotype, which is the product of the genotype and all environmental effects. See also *environment–heredity controversy.

Genova Italian form of *Genoa, city in Italy.

genre painting (French *genre* 'kind', 'type') painting scenes from everyday life. Genre paintings were enormously popular in the Netherlands and Flanders in the 17th century (Vermeer, de Hooch, and Brouwer were great exponents). The term 'genre' is also used more broadly to mean a category in the arts, such as landscape painting, or literary forms, such as the detective novel.

Genscher Hans-Dietrich 1927– . German politician, chair of the West German Free Democratic Party (FDP) 1974–85, foreign minister 1974–92. A skilled and pragmatic tactician, Genscher became the reunified Germany's most popular politician.

Gentile da Fabriano *c.* 1370–1427. Italian painter of frescoes and altarpieces in the International Gothic style. Gentile was active in

Venice, Florence, Siena, Orvieto, and Rome and collaborated with the artists Pisanello and Jacopo Bellini. *The Adoration of the Magi* 1423 (Uffizi, Florence) is typically rich in detail and crammed with courtly figures.

Gentili Alberico 1552–1608. Italian jurist. He practised law in Italy but having adopted Protestantism was compelled to flee to England, where he lectured on Roman law in Oxford. His publications, such as *De Jure Belli libri tres/On the Law of War, Book Three* 1598, made him the first true international law writer and scholar.

gentry the lesser nobility, particularly in England and Wales, not entitled to sit in the House of Lords. By the later Middle Ages, it included knights, esquires, and gentlemen, and after the 17th century, baronets.

genus (plural *genera*) group of *species with many characteristics in common. Thus all dog-like species (including dogs, wolves, and jackals) belong to the genus *Canis* (Latin 'dog'). Species of the same genus are thought to be descended from a common ancestor species. Related genera are grouped into *families.

geochemistry science of chemistry as it applies to geology. It deals with the relative and absolute abundances of the chemical elements and their *isotopes in the Earth, and also with the chemical changes that accompany geologic processes.

geode in geology, a subspherical cavity into which crystals have grown from the outer wall into the centre. Geodes often contain very well-formed crystals of quartz (including amethyst), calcite, or other minerals.

geodesy methods of surveying the Earth for making maps and correlating geological, gravitational, and magnetic measurements. Geodesic surveys, formerly carried out by means of various measuring techniques on the surface, are now commonly made by using radio signals and laser beams from orbiting satellites.

Geoffrey of Monmouth *c.* 1100–1154. Welsh writer and chronicler. While a canon at Oxford, he wrote *Historia Regum Britanniae/History of the Kings of Britain c.* 1139, which included accounts of the semi-legendary kings Lear, Cymbeline, and Arthur, and *Vita Merlini*, a life of the legendary wizard. He was bishop-elect of St Asaph, N Wales, 1151 and ordained a priest 1152.

geography science of the Earth's surface; its topography, climate, and physical conditions, and how these factors affect people and society. It is usually divided into *physical geography*, dealing with landforms and climates; *biogeography*, dealing with the conditions that affect the distribution of animals and plants; and *human geography*, dealing with the distribution and activities of peoples on Earth.

geological time time scale embracing the history of the Earth from its physical origin to the present day. Geological time is divided into eras (Precambrian, Palaeozoic, Mesozoic, Cenozoic), which in turn are divided into periods, epochs, ages, and finally chrons.

geology science of the Earth, its origin, composition, structure, and history. It is divided into several branches: *mineralogy* (the minerals of

Earth), *petrology* (rocks), *stratigraphy* (the deposition of successive beds of sedimentary rocks), *palaeontology* (fossils), and *tectonics* (the deformation and movement of the Earth's crust).

geomagnetic reversal another term for *polar reversal.

geometric mean in mathematics, the *n*th root of the product of *n* positive numbers. The geometric mean *m* of two numbers *p* and *q* is such that $m = \sqrt{(p \times q)}$. For example, the mean of 2 and 8 is $\sqrt{(2 \times 8)} = \sqrt{16} = \pm 4$

geometric progression or *geometric sequence* in mathematics, a sequence of terms (progression) in which each term is a constant multiple (called the common ratio) of the one preceding it. For example, 3, 12, 48, 192, 768, ... is a geometric progression with a common ratio 4, since each term is equal to the previous term multiplied by 4.

geometry branch of mathematics concerned with the properties of space, usually in terms of plane (two-dimensional) and solid (three-dimensional) figures. The subject is usually divided into *pure geometry*, which embraces roughly the plane and solid geometry dealt with in Euclid's *Elements*, and *analytical* or *coordinate geometry*, in which problems are solved using algebraic methods. A third, quite distinct, type includes the non-Euclidean geometries.

geomorphology branch of geology that deals with the nature and origin of surface landforms such as mountains, valleys, plains, and plateaus.

geophysics branch of geology using physics to study the Earth's surface, interior, and atmosphere. Studies also include winds, weather, tides, earthquakes, volcanoes, and their effects.

George six kings of Great Britain:

George I 1660–1727. King of Great Britain and Ireland from 1714. He was the son of the first elector of Hanover, Ernest Augustus (1629–1698), and his wife *Sophia, and a great-grandson of James I. He succeeded to the electorate 1698, and became king on the death of Queen Anne. He attached himself to the Whigs, and spent most of his reign in Hanover, never having learned English.

George II 1683–1760. King of Great Britain and Ireland from 1727, when he succeeded his father, George I. His victory at Dettingen 1743, in the War of the Austrian Succession, was the last battle commanded by a British king. He married Caroline of Anspach 1705. He was succeeded by his grandson George III.

George III 1738–1820. King of Great Britain and Ireland from 1760, when he succeeded his grandfather George II. His rule was marked by intransigence resulting in the loss of the American colonies, for which he shared the blame with his chief minister Lord North, and the emancipation of Catholics in England. Possibly suffering from *porphyria, he had repeated attacks of insanity, permanent from 1811. He was succeeded by his son George IV.

George IV 1762–1830. King of Great Britain and Ireland from 1820, when he succeeded his father George III, for whom he had been regent during the king's period of insanity 1811–20. In 1785 he secretly married a Catholic widow, Maria

*Fitzherbert, but in 1795 also married Princess *Caroline of Brunswick, in return for payment of his debts. His prestige was undermined by his treatment of Caroline (they separated 1796), his dissipation, and his extravagance. He was succeeded by his brother, the duke of Clarence, who became William IV.

George V 1865–1936. King of Great Britain from 1910, when he succeeded his father Edward VII. He was the second son, and became heir 1892 on the death of his elder brother Albert, Duke of Clarence. In 1893, he married Princess Victoria Mary of Teck (Queen Mary), formerly engaged to his brother. During World War I he made several visits to the front. In 1917, he abandoned all German titles for himself and his family. The name of the royal house was changed from Saxe-Coburg-Gotha (popularly known as Brunswick or Hanover) to Windsor.

George VI 1895–1952. King of Great Britain from 1936, when he succeeded after the abdication of his brother Edward VIII, who had succeeded their father George V. Created Duke of York 1920, he married in 1923 Lady Elizabeth Bowes-Lyon (1900–   ), and their children are Elizabeth II and Princess Margaret. During World War II, he visited the Normandy and Italian battlefields.

George two kings of Greece:

George I 1845–1913. King of Greece 1863–1913. The son of Christian IX of Denmark, he was nominated to the Greek throne and, in spite of early unpopularity, became a highly successful constitutional monarch. He was assassinated by a Greek, Schinas, at Salonika.

George II 1890–1947. King of Greece 1922–23 and 1935–47. He became king on the expulsion of his father Constantine I 1922 but was himself overthrown 1923. Restored by the military 1935, he set up a dictatorship under Joannis *Metaxas, and went into exile during the German occupation 1941–45.

George Cross/Medal UK awards to civilians for acts of courage.

George, St patron saint of England. The story of St George rescuing a woman by slaying a dragon, evidently derived from the *Perseus legend, first appears in the 6th century. The cult of St George was introduced into W Europe by the Crusaders. His feast day is 23 April.

Georgetown capital and port of Guyana; population (1983) 188,000.

Georgetown or *Penang* chief port of the Federation of Malaysia, and capital of Penang, on the island of Penang; population (1980) 250,600. It produces textiles and toys.

Georgia, Republic of
area 69,700 sq km/26,911 sq mi
capital Tbilisi
towns Kutaisi, Rustavi, Batumi, Sukhumi
physical largely mountainous with a variety of landscape from the subtropical Black Sea shores to the ice and snow of the crest line of the Caucasus; chief rivers are Kura and Rioni
head of state Eduard Shevardnadze from 1992
head of government Otar Patsatsia from 1993
political system emergent democracy
products tea, citrus and orchard fruits, tung oil, tobacco, vines, silk, hydroelectricity

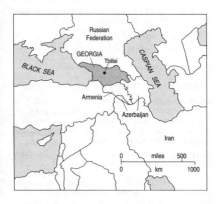

currency lari
population (1993 est) 5,600,000 (Georgian 70%, Armenian 8%, Russian 8%, Azeri 6%, Ossetian 3%, Abkhazian 2%)
language Georgian
religion Georgian Church, independent of the Russian Orthodox Church since 1917
GNP $1,640 per head (1991)
chronology
1918–21 Independent republic.
1921 Uprising quelled by Red Army and Soviet republic established.
1922–36 Linked with Armenia and Azerbaijan as the Transcaucasian Republic.
1936 Became separate republic within USSR.
1972 Drive against corruption by Georgian Communist Party (GCP) leader Eduard Shevardnadze.
1978 Outbreaks of violence by nationalists.
1981–88 Increasing demands for autonomy, spearheaded from 1988 by the Georgian Popular Front.
1989 March–April: Abkhazians demanded secession from Georgia, provoking interethnic clashes. April: GCP leadership purged. July: state of emergency imposed on Abkhazia; interethnic clashes in South Ossetia. Nov: sovereignty declared.
1990 Oct: nationalist coalition triumphed in supreme-soviet elections. Nov: Zviad Gamsakhurdia became president. Dec: GCP seceded from Communist Party of USSR; calls for Georgian independence.
1991 April: declared independence. May: Gamsakhurdia popularly elected president. Aug: GCP outlawed and all relations with USSR severed. Sept: anti-Gamsakhurdia demonstrations; state of emergency declared. Dec: Georgia failed to join new Commonwealth of Independent States (CIS).
1992 Jan: Gamsakhurdia fled to Armenia; Tengiz Sigua appointed prime minister. Eduard Shevardnadze appointed interim president. July: admitted into United Nations (UN). Aug: fighting between Georgian troops and separatists in Abkhazia. Oct: Shevardnadze elected chair of new parliament. Clashes in South Ossetia and Abkhazia continued.
1993 Conflict with Abkhazi separatists intensified; Shevardnadze forced to seek Russian military help. Georgia joined CIS. Nov: pro-

Gamsakhurdia revolt put down by government forces. Gamsakhurdia found dead.
1994 Feb: Abkhazi separatists agreed to UN peacekeeping force. Military cooperation pact signed with Russia.

Georgia state in SE USA; nicknames Empire State of the South/Peach State
area 58,904 sq mi/152,600 sq km
capital Atlanta
cities Columbus, Savannah, Macon
products poultry, livestock, tobacco, maize, peanuts, cotton, soya beans, china clay, crushed granite, textiles, carpets, aircraft, paper products
population (1990) 6,480,000
famous people Jim Bowie; Erskine Caldwell; Jimmy Carter; Ray Charles; Ty Cobb; Bobby Jones; Martin Luther King, Jr; Margaret Mitchell; James Oglethorpe; Jackie Robinson
history explored 1540 by Hernando de Soto; claimed by the British and named after George II of England; founded 1733 as a colony for the industrious poor by James Oglethorpe, a philanthropist, and was one of the original 13 states of the USA. In 1864, during the Civil War, General W T Sherman's Union troops cut a wide swath of destruction as they marched from Atlanta to the sea. The state benefited after World War II from the growth of Atlanta as the financial and transportation centre of the SE USA.

Georgian period of English architecture, furniture making, and decorative art between 1714 and 1830. The architecture is mainly Classical in style, although external details and interiors were often rich in Rococo carving. Furniture was frequently made of mahogany and satinwood, and mass production became increasingly common; designers included Thomas Chippendale, George Hepplewhite, and Thomas Sheraton. The silver of this period is particularly fine, and ranges from the earlier, simple forms to the ornate, and from the Neo-Classical style of Robert Adam to the later, more decorated pre-Victorian taste.

Georgian or *Grazinian* member of any of a number of related groups which make up the largest ethnic group in Georgia and the surrounding area. There are 3–4 million speakers of Georgian, a member of the Caucasian language family.

geostationary orbit circular path 35,900 km/ 22,300 mi above the Earth's equator on which a *satellite takes 24 hours, moving from west to east, to complete an orbit, thus appearing to hang stationary over one place on the Earth's surface. Geostationary orbits are particularly used for communications satellites and weather satellites. They were first thought of by the author Arthur C Clarke. A *geosynchronous orbit* lies at the same distance from Earth but is inclined to the equator.

geothermal energy energy extracted for heating and electricity generation from natural steam, hot water, or hot dry rocks in the Earth's crust. Water is pumped down through an injection well where it passes through joints in the hot rocks. It rises to the surface through a recovery well and may be converted to steam or run through a heat exchanger. Dry steam may be directed through turbines to produce electricity.

geranium any plant either of the family Geraniaceae, having divided leaves and pink or purple flowers, or of the family Pelargonium, having a hairy stem, and red, pink, or white flowers. Some geraniums are also called *cranesbill.

gerbil any of numerous rodents of the family Cricetidae with elongated back legs and good hopping or jumping ability. Gerbils range from mouse-to rat-size, and have hairy tails. Many of the 13 genera live in dry, sandy, or sparsely vegetated areas of Africa and Asia.

gerenuk antelope *Litocranius walleri* about 1 m/3 ft at the shoulder, with a greatly elongated neck. It browses on leaves, often balancing on its hind legs to do so. Sandy brown in colour, it is well camouflaged in its E African habitat of dry scrub.

Géricault Théodore (Jean Louis André) 1791–1824. French Romantic painter. *The Raft of the Medusa* 1819 (Louvre, Paris) was notorious for exposing a relatively recent scandal in which shipwrecked sailors had been cut adrift and left to drown. He painted *The Derby at Epsom* 1821 (Louvre, Paris) and pictures of cavalry. He also painted portraits.

germ colloquial term for a microorganism that causes disease, such as certain *bacteria and *viruses. Formerly, it was also used to mean something capable of developing into a complete organism (such as a fertilized egg, or the *embryo of a seed).

Germanic languages branch of the Indo-European language family, divided into *East Germanic* (Gothic, now extinct), *North Germanic* (Danish, Faroese, Icelandic, Norwegian, Swedish), and *West Germanic* (Afrikaans, Dutch, English, Flemish, Frisian, German, Yiddish).

Germanicus Caesar 15 BC–AD 19. roman general. He was the adopted son of the emperor *Tiberius and married the emperor *Augustus' granddaughter Agrippina. Although he refused the suggestion of his troops that he claim the throne on the death of Augustus, his military victories in Germany made Tiberius jealous. Sent to the Middle East, he died near Antioch, possibly murdered at the instigation of Tiberius. He was the father of *Caligula and Agrippina, mother of *Nero.

germanium brittle, grey-white, weakly metallic (*metalloid) element, symbol Ge, atomic number 32, relative atomic mass 72.6. It belongs to the silicon group, and has chemical and physical properties between those of silicon and tin. Germanium is a semiconductor material and is used in the manufacture of transistors and integrated circuits. The oxide is transparent to infrared radiation, and is used in military applications. It was discovered 1886 by German chemist Clemens Winkler (1838–1904).

German language member of the Germanic group of the Indo-European language family, the national language of Germany and Austria, and an official language of Switzerland. There are many spoken varieties of German, including High German (*Hochdeutsch*) and Low German (*Plattdeutsch*).

German measles or *rubella* mild, communicable virus disease, usually caught by children. It is marked by a sore throat, pinkish rash, and slight fever, and has an incubation period of two to three weeks. If a woman contracts it in the first three months of pregnancy, it may cause serious damage to the unborn child.

German shepherd breed of dog also known as the Alsatian. It is about 63 cm/25 in tall and has a wolflike appearance, a thick coat with many varieties of colouring, and a distinctive gait. German Shepherds are used as police dogs because of their courage and high intelligence.

German silver or *nickel silver* silvery alloy of nickel, copper, and zinc. It is widely used for cheap jewellery and the base metal for silver plating. The letters EPNS on silverware stand for *electroplated nickel silver.*

Germany Federal Republic of (*Bundesrepublik Deutschland*)

area 357,041 sq km/137,853 sq mi
capital Berlin
towns Cologne, Munich, Essen, Frankfurt-am-Main, Dortmund, Stuttgart, Düsseldorf, Leipzig, Dresden, Chemnitz, Magdeburg; ports Hamburg, Kiel, Cuxhaven, Bremerhaven, Rostock
physical flat in N, mountainous in S with Alps; rivers Rhine, Weser, Elbe flow N, Danube flows SE, Oder, Neisse flow N along Polish frontier; many lakes, including Müritz
environment acid rain causing *Waldsterben* (tree death) affects more than half the country's forests; industrial E Germany has the highest sulphur-dioxide emissions in the world per head of population
head of state Roman Herzog from 1994
head of government Helmut Kohl from 1982
political system liberal democratic federal republic
exports machine tools (world's leading exporter), cars, commercial vehicles, electronics, industrial goods, textiles, chemicals, iron, steel, wine, lignite (world's largest producer), uranium, coal, fertilizers, plastics
currency Deutschmark
population (1993 est) 80,800,000 (including nearly 5,000,000 'guest workers', *Gastarbeiter*, of whom 1,600,000 are Turks; the rest are Yugoslav, Italian, Greek, Spanish, and Portuguese); growth rate –0.7% p.a.
languages German, Sorbian
religions Protestant 42%, Roman Catholic 35%
GNP $23,650 per head (1991)

chronology
1945 Germany surrendered; country divided into four occupation zones (US, French, British, Soviet).
1948 Blockade of West Berlin.
1949 Establishment of Federal Republic under the 'Basic Law' Constitution with Konrad Adenauer as chancellor; establishment of the German Democratic Republic as an independent state.
1953 Uprising in East Berlin suppressed by Soviet troops.
1954 Grant of full sovereignty to both West Germany and East Germany.
1957 West Germany was a founder-member of the European Economic Community; recovery of Saarland from France.
1961 Construction of Berlin Wall.
1963 Retirement of Chancellor Adenauer.
1964 Treaty of Friendship and Mutual Assistance signed between East Germany and USSR.
1969 Willy Brandt became chancellor of West Germany.
1971 Erich Honecker elected SED leader in East Germany.
1972 Basic Treaty between West Germany and East Germany; treaty ratified 1973, normalizing relations between the two.
1974 Resignation of Brandt; Helmut Schmidt became chancellor.
1982 Helmut Kohl became West German chancellor.
1989 West Germany: rising support for far right in local and European elections, declining support for Kohl. East Germany: mass exodus to West Germany began. Honecker replaced by Egon Krenz. National borders opened in Nov, including Berlin Wall. Reformist Hans Modrow appointed prime minister. Krenz replaced.
1990 March: East German multiparty elections won by coalition led by right-wing CDU. 3 Oct: official reunification of East and West Germany. 2 Dec: first all-German elections since 1932, resulting in a victory for Kohl.
1991 Kohl's popularity declined after tax increase. The CDU lost its Bundesrat majority to the SPD. Violent attacks on foreigners.
1992 Neo-Nazi riots against immigrants continued.
1993 Severe recession. Racist violence continued. Restrictions on refugee admission introduced.
1994 Kohl's nominee, Roman Herzog, elected president. CDU returned to power in general election, but with wafer-thin majority.

Germany, East (German Democratic Republic, GDR) country 1949–90, formed from the Soviet zone of occupation in the partition of Germany following World War II. East Germany became a sovereign state 1954, and was reunified with West Germany Oct 1990. For history before 1949, see *Germany, history; for history after 1949, see *Germany, Federal Republic of.

Germany, West (Federal Republic of Germany) country 1949–90, formed from the British, US, and French occupation zones in the partition of Germany following World War II; reunified with East Germany Oct 1990. For history after 1949, see *Germany, Federal Republic of.

germination in botany, the initial stages of growth in a seed, spore, or pollen grain. Seeds germinate when they are exposed to favourable external conditions of moisture, light, and temperature, and when any factors causing dormancy have been removed.

Geronimo 1829–1909. Chief of the Chiricahua Apache Indians and war leader. From 1875 to 1885, he fought US federal troops, as well as settlers encroaching on tribal reservations in the Southwest, especially in SE Arizona and New Mexico.

Gershwin George 1898–1937. US composer who wrote both 'serious' music, such as the tone poem *Rhapsody in Blue* 1924 and *An American in Paris* 1928, and popular musicals and songs, many with lyrics by his brother **Ira Gershwin** (1896–1983), including 'I Got Rhythm', ''S Wonderful', and 'Embraceable You'. His opera *Porgy and Bess* 1935 was an ambitious work that incorporated jazz rhythms and popular song styles in an operatic format.

gerund in the grammar of certain languages, such as Latin, a noun formed from a verb and functioning as a noun to express an action or state. In English, gerunds end in *-ing*.

gestalt concept of a unified whole that is greater than, or different from, the sum of its parts; that is, a complete structure whose nature is not explained simply by analysing its constituent elements. A chair, for example, will generally be recognized as a chair despite great variations between individual chairs in such attributes as size, shape, and colour. The term was first used in psychology in Germany about 1910. It has been adopted from German because there is no exact equivalent in English.

Gestapo (contraction of **Geheime Staatspolizei**) Nazi Germany's secret police, formed 1933, and under the direction of Heinrich Himmler from 1936.

gestation in all mammals except the monotremes (duck-billed platypus and spiny anteaters), the period from the time of implantation of the embryo in the uterus to birth. This period varies among species; in humans it is about 266 days, in elephants 18–22 months, in cats about 60 days, and in some species of marsupial (such as opossum) as short as 12 days.

Gethsemane site of the garden where Judas Iscariot, according to the New Testament, betrayed Jesus. It is on the Mount of Olives, E of Jerusalem. When Jerusalem was divided between Israel and Jordan 1948, Gethsemane fell within Jordanian territory.

Getty J(ean) Paul 1892–1976. US oil billionaire, president of the Getty Oil Company from 1947, and founder of the Getty Museum (housing the world's highest-funded art gallery) in Malibu, California.

Gettysburg site in Pennsylvania of a decisive battle of the American *Civil War 1863, won by the North. The site is now a national cemetery, at the dedication of which President Lincoln delivered the **Gettysburg Address** 19 Nov 1863, a speech in which he reiterated the principles of freedom, equality, and democracy embodied in the US Constitution.

Getz Stan(ley) 1927–1991. US tenor saxophonist of the 1950s cool jazz school, closely identified with the Latin American bossa nova sound, which gave him a hit single, 'The Girl from Ipanema' 1964. He is regarded as one of the foremost tenor-sax players of his generation.

geyser natural spring that intermittently discharges an explosive column of steam and hot water into the air. One of the most remarkable geysers is Old Faithful, in Yellowstone National Park, Wyoming, USA. Geysers also occur in New Zealand and Iceland.

G-force force that pilots and astronauts experience when their craft accelerate or decelerate rapidly. One G is the ordinary pull of gravity. Early astronauts were subjected to launch and re-entry forces of up to six G or more; in the Space Shuttle, more than three G is experienced on liftoff. Pilots and astronauts wear G-suits that prevent their blood 'pooling' too much under severe G-forces, which can lead to unconsciousness.

Ghana Republic of

ATLANTIC OCEAN

0 miles 500
0 km 1000

Burkina Faso
Togo
Ivory Coast
Accra
GHANA

area 238,305 sq km/91,986 sq mi
capital Accra
towns Kumasi, and ports Sekondi-Takoradi, Tema
physical mostly tropical lowland plains; bisected by river Volta
environment forested areas have shrunk from 8.2 million sq km/3.17 million sq mi at the beginning of the 20th century to 1.9 million sq km/730,000 sq mi by 1990
head of state and government Jerry Rawlings from 1981
political system military republic
exports cocoa, coffee, timber, gold, diamonds, manganese, bauxite
currency cedi
population (1993 est) 16,700,000; growth rate 3.2% p.a.
languages English (official) and African languages
religions animist 38%, Muslim 30%, Christian 24%
GNP $400 per head (1992)
chronology
1957 Independence achieved from Britain, within the Commonwealth, with Kwame Nkrumah as president.
1960 Ghana became a republic.
1964 Ghana became a one-party state.
1966 Nkrumah deposed and replaced by General Joseph Ankrah.
1969 Ankrah replaced by General Akwasi Afrifa, who initiated a return to civilian government.
1970 Edward Akufo-Addo elected president.

1972 Another coup placed Col Acheampong at the head of a military government.
1978 Acheampong deposed in a bloodless coup led by Frederick Akuffo; another coup put Flight-Lt Jerry Rawlings in power.
1979 Return to civilian rule under Hilla Limann.
1981 Rawlings seized power again, citing the incompetence of previous governments. All political parties banned.
1989 Coup attempt against Rawlings foiled.
1992 New multiparty constitution approved. Partial lifting of ban on political parties.

Ghana, ancient trading empire that flourished in NW Africa between the 5th and 13th centuries. Founded by the Soninke people, the Ghana Empire was based, like the Mali Empire that superseded it, on the Saharan gold trade. Trade consisted mainly of the exchange of gold from inland deposits for salt from the coast. At its peak in the 11th century, it occupied an area that includes parts of present-day Mali, Senegal, and Mauritania. Wars with the Berber tribes of the Sahara led to its fragmentation and collapse in the 13th century, when much of its territory was absorbed into Mali.

Ghats, Eastern and Western twin mountain ranges in S India, E and W of the central plateau; a few peaks reach about 3,000 m/9,800 ft. The name is a European misnomer, the Indian word *ghat* meaning 'pass', not 'mountain'.

Ghazzali, al- 1058–1111. Muslim philosopher and Sufi (Muslim mystic). He was responsible for easing the conflict between the Sufi and the Ulema, a body of Muslim religious and legal scholars.

Ghent (Flemish **Gent**, French **Gand**) city and port in East Flanders, NW Belgium; population (1991) 230,200. Industries include textiles, chemicals, electronics, and metallurgy. The cathedral of St Bavon (12th–14th centuries) has paintings by van Eyck and Rubens.

ghetto (Old Venetian *gèto* 'foundry') any deprived area occupied by a minority group, whether voluntarily or not. Originally a ghetto was the area of a town where Jews were compelled to live, decreed by a law enforced by papal bull 1555. The term came into use 1516 when the Jews of Venice were expelled to an island within the city which contained an iron foundry. Ghettos were abolished, except in E Europe, in the 19th century, but the concept and practice were revived by the Germans and Italians 1940–45.

Ghiberti Lorenzo 1378–1455. Italian sculptor and goldsmith. In 1401 he won the commission for a pair of gilded bronze doors for Florence's baptistry. He produced a second pair (1425–52), the *Gates of Paradise*, one of the masterpieces of the early Italian Renaissance. They show sophisticated composition and use of perspective.

Ghirlandaio Domenico *c.* 1449–1494. Italian fresco painter, head of a large and prosperous workshop in Florence. His fresco cycle 1486–90 in Sta Maria Novella, Florence, includes portraits of many Florentines and much contemporary domestic detail. He also worked in Pisa, Rome, and San Gimignano, and painted portraits.

GI abbreviation for *government issue*; hence (in the USA) a common soldier.

Giacometti Alberto 1901–1966. Swiss sculptor and painter who trained in Italy and Paris. In the 1930s, in his Surrealist period, he began to develop his characteristic spindly constructions. His mature style of emaciated single figures, based on wire frames, emerged in the 1940s.

Giambologna (Giovanni da Bologna or Jean de Boulogne) 1529–1608. Flemish-born sculptor active mainly in Florence and Bologna. In 1583 he completed his public commission for the Loggia dei Lanzi in Florence, *The Rape of the Sabine Women*, a dynamic group of muscular figures and a prime example of Mannerist sculpture.

Giant's Causeway stretch of basalt columns forming a headland on the N coast of Antrim, Northern Ireland. It was formed by an outflow of lava in Tertiary times that has solidified in polygonal columns.

gibberellin plant growth substance (see also *auxin) that promotes stem growth and may also affect the breaking of dormancy in certain buds and seeds, and the induction of flowering. Application of gibberellin can stimulate the stems of dwarf plants to additional growth, delay the ageing process in leaves, and promote the production of seedless fruit (*parthenocarpy).

gibbon any of several small S Asian apes of the genus *Hylobates*, including the subgenus *Symphalangus*. The common or lar gibbon *H. lar* is about 60 cm/2 ft tall, with a body that is hairy except for the buttocks, which distinguishes it from other types of apes. Gibbons have long arms and no tail. They are arboreal in habit, being very agile when swinging from branch to branch. On the ground they walk upright, and are more easily caught by predators.

Gibbon Edward 1737–1794. British historian, author of *The History of the Decline and Fall of the Roman Empire* 1776–88.

Gibbons Grinling 1648–1721. British woodcarver, born in Rotterdam. He produced carved wooden panels (largely of birds, flowers, and fruit) for St Paul's Cathedral, London, and for many large houses including Petworth House, Sussex, and Hampton Court, Surrey. He became master carver to George I in 1741.

Gibbs James 1682–1754. Scottish Neo-Classical architect whose works include St Martin-in-the-Fields, London, 1722–26, Radcliffe Camera, Oxford, 1737–49, and Bank Hall, Warrington, Cheshire, 1750.

Gibbs Josiah Willard 1839–1903. US theoretical physicist and chemist who developed a mathematical approach to thermodynamics. His book *Vector Analysis* 1881 established vector methods in physics.

Gibraltar British dependency, situated on a narrow rocky promontory in S Spain
area 6.5 sq km/2.5 sq mi
exports mainly a trading centre for the import and re-export of goods
population (1988) 30,000
history captured from Spain 1704 by English admiral George Rooke (1650–1709), it was ceded to Britain under the Treaty of Utrecht 1713. A referendum 1967 confirmed the wish of the people to remain in association with the UK, but Spain continues to claim sovereignty and closed the border 1969–85. In 1989, the UK government announced it would reduce the military garrison by half.

Gibraltar, Strait of strait between N Africa and Spain, with the Rock of Gibraltar on the north side and Jebel Musa on the south, the so-called Pillars of Hercules.

Gide André 1869–1951. French novelist, born in Paris. His work is largely autobiographical and concerned with the dual themes of self-fulfilment and renunciation. It includes *L'Immoraliste/The Immoralist* 1902, *La Porte étroite/Strait Is the Gate* 1909, *Les Caves du Vatican/The Vatican Cellars* 1914, and *Les Faux-monnayeurs/The Counterfeiters* 1926; and an almost lifelong *Journal*. Nobel Prize for Literature 1947.

Gielgud John 1904– . English actor and director, renowned as one of the greatest Shakespearean actors of his time. He made his debut at the Old Vic 1921, and his numerous stage appearances ranged from roles in works by Chekhov and Sheridan to those of Alan Bennett, Harold Pinter, and David Storey. Gielgud's films include *Becket* 1964, *Oh! What a Lovely War* 1969, *Providence* 1977, and *Prospero's Books* 1991. He won an Academy Award for his role as a butler in *Arthur* 1981.

Giffard Henri 1825–1882. French inventor of the first passenger-carrying powered and steerable airship, called a dirigible, built 1852. The hydrogen-filled airship was 43 m/144 ft long, had a 3-hp steam engine that drove a three-bladed propeller, and was steered using a saillike rudder. It flew at an average speed of 5 kph/3 mph.

giga- prefix signifying multiplication by 10^9 (1,000,000,000 or 1 billion), as in *gigahertz*, a unit of frequency equivalent to 1 billion hertz.

gigabyte in computing, a measure of *memory capacity, equal to 1,024 *megabytes. It is also used, less precisely, to mean 1,000 million *bytes.

gila monster lizard *Heloderma suspectum* of SW USA and Mexico. It is one of the only two existing venomous lizards, the other being the Mexican beaded lizard of the same genus. It has poison glands in its lower jaw, but its bite is not usually fatal to humans.

Gilbert Cass 1859–1934. US architect, major developer of the *skyscraper. He designed the Woolworth Building, New York, 1913, the highest building in America (868 ft/265 m) when built and famous for its use of Gothic decorative detail.

Gilbert Humphrey *c.* 1539–1583. English soldier and navigator who claimed Newfoundland (landing at St John's) for Elizabeth I in 1583. He died when his ship sank on the return voyage.

Gilbert W(illiam) S(chwenk) 1836–1911. British humorist and dramatist who collaborated with composer Arthur *Sullivan, providing the libretti for their series of light comic operas from 1871; they include *HMS Pinafore* 1878, *The Pirates of Penzance* 1879, and *The Mikado* 1885.

Gilbert Walter 1932– . US molecular biologist who studied genetic control, seeking the mechanisms that switch genes on and off. By 1966 he had established the existence of the *lac* repressor, the molecule that suppresses lactose production. Further work on the sequencing of *DNA nucleotides won him a share of the 1980 Nobel Prize for Chemistry, with Frederick Sanger and Paul Berg.

Gilbert William 1544–1603. English scientist and physician to Elizabeth I and (briefly) James I. He studied magnetism and static electricity, deducing that the Earth's magnetic field behaves as if a bar magnet joined the North and South poles. His book on magnets, published 1600, is the first printed scientific book based wholly on experimentation and observation.

Gilbert and Ellice Islands former British colony in the Pacific, known since independence 1978 as the countries of *Tuvalu and *Kiribati.

Gilbert and George Gilbert Proesch 1943– and George Passmore 1942– . English painters and performance artists. They became known in the 1960s for their presentation of themselves as works of art – living sculpture.

gilding application of gilt (gold or a substance that looks like it) to a surface. From the 19th century, gilt was often applied to ceramics and to the relief surfaces of woodwork or plasterwork to highlight a design.

Gilgamesh hero of Sumerian, Hittite, Akkadian, and Assyrian legend. The 12 verse 'books' of the *Epic of Gilgamesh* were recorded in a standard version on 12 cuneiform tablets by the Assyrian king Ashurbanipal's scholars in the 7th century BC, and the epic itself is older than Homer's *Iliad* by at least 1,500 years.

gill in biology, the main respiratory organ of most fishes and immature amphibians, and of many aquatic invertebrates. In all types, water passes over the gills, and oxygen diffuses across the gill membranes into the circulatory system, while carbon dioxide passes from the system out into the water.

gill imperial unit of volume for liquid measure, equal to one-quarter of a pint or 4 fluid ounces (0.142 litre). It is used in selling alcoholic drinks.

Gill Eric 1882–1940. English sculptor and engraver. He designed the typefaces Perpetua 1925 and Gill Sans (without serifs) 1927, and created monumental stone sculptures with clean, simplified outlines, such as *Prospero and Ariel* 1929–31 (on Broadcasting House, London).

Gillespie Dizzy (John Birks) 1917–1993. US jazz trumpeter who, with Charlie *Parker, was the chief creator and exponent of the *bebop style. He influenced many modern jazz trumpeters, including Miles Davis.

gilt-edged securities stocks and shares issued and guaranteed by the British government to raise funds and traded on the Stock Exchange.

gin (Dutch *jenever* 'juniper') alcoholic drink made by distilling a mash of maize, malt, or rye, with juniper flavouring. It was first produced in the Netherlands.

ginger SE Asian reedlike perennial *Zingiber officinale*, family Zingiberaceae; the hot-tasting underground root is used as a condiment and in preserves.

Gingrich Newt (Newton Leyroy) 1943– . US Republican politician, speaker (leader) of the House of Representatives from 1995. A radical-right 'Reaganite', he was the driving force behind his party's sensational victory in the congressional elections Nov 1994, when it gained a House majority for the first time since 1954. On taking office, he sought to implement a conservative, populist manifesto designed to reduce federal powers, balance the budget, tackle crime and limit congressional terms.

ginkgo or ***maidenhair tree*** tree *Ginkgo biloba* of the gymnosperm (or naked-seed-bearing) division of plants. It may reach a height of 30 m/100 ft by the time it is 200 years old.

Ginsberg Allen 1926– . US poet. His 'Howl' 1956, an influential poem of the *Beat Generation, criticizes the materialism of contemporary US society. In the 1960s Ginsberg travelled widely in Asia and was a key figure in introducing Eastern thought to students of that decade.

ginseng plant *Panax ginseng*, family Araliaceae, with a thick, forked aromatic root used in medicine as a tonic.

Giolitti Giovanni 1842–1928. Italian liberal politician, born in Mondovi. He was prime minister 1892–93, 1903–05, 1906–09, 1911–14, and 1920–21. He opposed Italian intervention in World War I and pursued a policy of broad coalitions, which proved ineffective in controlling Fascism after 1921.

Giorgione del Castelfranco *c.* 1475–1510. Italian Renaissance painter, active in Venice, probably trained by Giovanni Bellini. His work influenced Titian and other Venetian painters. His subjects are imbued with a sense of mystery and treated with a soft technique, reminiscent of Leonardo da Vinci's later works, as in *The Tempest* 1504 (Accademia, Venice).

Giotto di Bondone 1267–1337. Italian painter and architect. He broke away from the conventional Gothic style of the time, and introduced a naturalistic style, painting saints as real people. He painted cycles of frescoes in churches at Assisi, Florence, and Padua.

Giotto space probe built by the European Space Agency to study *Halley's comet. Launched by an Ariane rocket in July 1985, *Giotto* passed within 600 km/375 mi of the comet's nucleus on 13 March 1986.

giraffe world's tallest mammal, *Giraffa camelopardalis*, belonging to the ruminant family Giraffidae. It stands over 5.5 m/18 ft tall, the neck accounting for nearly half this amount. The giraffe has two to four small, skin-covered, hornlike structures on its head and a long, tufted tail. The skin has a mottled appearance and is reddish brown and cream. Giraffes are found only in Africa, south of the Sahara Desert.

Giraudoux (Hippolyte) Jean 1882–1944. French playwright and novelist who wrote the plays *Amphitryon 38* 1929 and *La Folle de Chaillot/The Madwoman of Chaillot* 1945, and the novel *Suzanne et la Pacifique/Suzanne and the Pacific* 1921.

Girl Guide female member of the *Scout organization founded 1910 in the UK by Robert Baden-Powell and his sister Agnes. There are three branches: Brownie Guides (age 7–11); Guides (10–16); Ranger Guides (14–20); and Guiders (adult leaders). The World Association of Girl Guides and Girl Scouts (as they are known in the USA) has over 6.5 million members.

Girondin member of the right-wing republican party in the French Revolution, so called because a number of their leaders came from the Gironde region. They were driven from power by the *Jacobins 1793.

Giscard d'Estaing Valéry 1926– . French conservative politician, president 1974–81. He was finance minister to de Gaulle 1962–66 and Pompidou 1969–74. As leader of the Union pour la Démocratie Française, which he formed in 1978, Giscard sought to project himself as leader of a 'new centre'.

Giulini Carlo Maria 1914– . Italian conductor. Principal conductor at La Scala in Milan 1953–55, and musical director of the Los Angeles Philharmonic 1978–84, he is renowned as an interpreter of Verdi.

Giulio Romano c. 1499–1546. Italian painter and architect. An assistant to Raphael, he developed a Mannerist style, creating effects of exaggerated movement and using rich colours, for example the frescoes in the Palazzo del Tè (1526, Mantua).

Gîza, El or **al-Jizah** site of the Great Pyramids and Sphinx; a suburb of *Cairo, Egypt; population (1983) 1,500,000. It has textile and film industries.

gizzard muscular grinding organ of the digestive tract, below the *crop of birds, earthworms, and some insects, and forming part of the *stomach. The gizzard of birds is lined with a hardened horny layer of the protein keratin, preventing damage to the muscle layer during the grinding process. Most birds swallow sharp grit which aids maceration of food in the gizzard.

glacial trough or **U-shaped valley** steepsided, flat-bottomed valley formed by a glacier. The erosive action of the glacier and of the debris carried by it results in the formation not only of the trough itself but also of a number of associated features, such as truncated spurs (projections of rock that have been sheared off by the ice) and hanging valleys (smaller glacial valleys that enter the trough at a higher level than the trough floor). Features characteristic of glacial deposition, such as drumlins and eskers, are commonly found on the floor of the trough, together with linear lakes called ribbon lakes.

glacier tongue of ice, originating in mountains in snowfields above the snowline, which moves slowly downhill and is constantly replenished from its source. The scenery produced by the erosive action of glaciers is characteristic and includes *glacial troughs (U-shaped valleys), *corries, and *arêtes. In lowlands, the laying down of *moraine (rocky debris once carried by glaciers) produces a variety of landscape features.

gladiator in ancient Rome, a trained fighter, recruited mainly from slaves, criminals, and prisoners of war, who fought to the death in arenas for the entertainment of spectators. The custom, which originated in the practice of slaughtering slaves on a chieftain's grave, was introduced into Rome from Etruria in 264 BC and continued until the 5th century AD.

gladiolus any plant of the genus *Gladiolus* of S European and African cultivated perennials of the iris family Iridaceae, with brightly coloured, funnel-shaped flowers, borne in a spike; the swordlike leaves spring from a corm.

Gladstone William Ewart 1809–1898. British Liberal politician, repeatedly prime minister. He

entered Parliament as a Tory in 1833 and held ministerial office, but left the party 1846 and after 1859 identified himself with the Liberals. He was chancellor of the Exchequer 1852–55 and 1859–66, and prime minister 1868–74, 1880–85, 1886, and 1892–94. He introduced elementary education 1870 and vote by secret ballot 1872 and many reforms in Ireland, although he failed in his efforts to get a Home Rule Bill passed.

Glamorgan (Welsh **Morgannwg**) three counties of S Wales – *Mid Glamorgan, *South Glamorgan, and *West Glamorgan – created in 1974 from the former county of Glamorganshire.

gland specialized organ of the body that manufactures and secretes enzymes, hormones, or other chemicals. In animals, glands vary in size from small (for example, tear glands) to large (for example, the pancreas), but in plants they are always small, and may consist of a single cell. Some glands discharge their products internally, *endocrine glands, and others, *exocrine glands, externally. Lymph nodes are sometimes wrongly called glands.

glandular fever or **infectious mononucleosis** viral disease characterized at onset by fever and painfully swollen lymph nodes (in the neck); there may also be digestive upset, sore throat, and skin rashes. Lassitude persists for months and even years, and recovery can be slow. It is caused by the Epstein-Barr virus.

Glaser Donald Arthur 1926– . US physicist who invented the *bubble chamber in 1952, for which he received the Nobel Prize for Physics in 1960.

Glasgow city and administrative headquarters of Strathclyde, Scotland; population (1991) 654,500. Industries include engineering, chemicals, printing, and distilling.

glasnost (Russian 'openness') former Soviet leader Mikhail *Gorbachev's policy of liberalizing various aspects of Soviet life, such as introducing greater freedom of expression and information and opening up relations with Western countries. *Glasnost* was introduced and adopted by the Soviet government 1986.

glass transparent or translucent substance that is physically neither a solid nor a liquid. Although glass is easily shattered, it is one of the strongest substances known. It is made by fusing certain types of sand (silica); this fusion occurs naturally in volcanic glass (see *obsidian).

Glass Philip 1937– . US composer. As a student of Nadia *Boulanger, he was strongly influenced by Indian music; his work is characterized by repeated rhythmic figures that are continually expanded and modified. His compositions include the operas *Einstein on the Beach* 1975, *Akhnaten* 1984, and *The Making of the Representative for Planet 8* 1988.

glass snake or **glass lizard** any of a worldwide genus *Ophisaurus* of legless lizards of the family Anguidae. Their tails are up to three times the head–body length and are easily broken off.

Glauber Johann 1604–1668. German chemist who discovered the salt known variously as 'Glauber's salt' and '*sal mirabile*'. He made his living selling patent medicines.

Glauber's salt in chemistry, crystalline sodium sulphate decahydrate $Na_2SO_4.10H_2O$, which melts at 87.8°F/31°C; the latent heat stored as it solidifies makes it a convenient thermal energy store. It is used in medicine.

glaucoma condition in which pressure inside the eye (intraocular pressure) is raised abnormally as excess fluid accumulates. It occurs when the normal flow of intraocular fluid out of the eye is interrupted. As pressure rises, the optic nerve suffers irreversible damage, leading to a reduction in the field of vision and, ultimately, loss of eyesight.

Glendower Owen *c.* 1359–*c.* 1416. (Welsh *Owain Glyndwr*) Welsh nationalist leader of a successful revolt against the English in N Wales, who defeated Henry IV in three campaigns 1400–02, although Wales was reconquered 1405–13. Glendower disappeared 1416 after some years of guerrilla warfare.

Glenn John (Herschel), Jr 1921– . US astronaut and politician. On 20 Feb 1962, he became the first American to orbit the Earth, doing so three times in the Mercury spacecraft *Friendship 7*, in a flight lasting 4 hr 55 min. After retiring from *NASA, he was elected to the US Senate as a Democrat from Ohio 1974; re-elected 1980 and 1986. He unsuccessfully sought the Democratic presidential nomination 1984.

gliding the art of using air currents to fly unpowered aircraft. Technically, gliding involves the gradual loss of altitude; gliders designed for soaring flight (utilizing air rising up a cliff face or hill, warm air rising as a 'thermal' above sunheated ground, and so on) are known as sailplanes. The sport of *hang gliding was developed in the 1970s.

Glinka Mikhail Ivanovich 1804–1857. Russian composer. He broke away from the prevailing Italian influence and turned to Russian folk music as the inspiration for his opera *A Life for the Tsar* (originally *Ivan Susanin*) 1836. His later works include another opera, *Ruslan and Lyudmila* 1842, and the orchestral *Kamarinskaya* 1848.

global warming projected imminent climate change attributed to the *greenhouse effect.

globefish another name for *puffer fish.

Globe Theatre 17th-century London theatre, octagonal and open to the sky, near Bankside, Southwark, where many of Shakespeare's plays were performed by Richard Burbage and his company. Built 1599 by Cuthbert Burbage, it was burned down 1613 after a cannon, fired during a performance of *Henry VIII*, set light to the thatch. It was rebuilt in 1614 but pulled down in 1644. The site was rediscovered Oct 1989 near the remains of the contemporaneous Rose Theatre.

globular cluster spherical or near-spherical *star cluster from approximately 10,000 to millions of stars. More than a hundred globular clusters are distributed in a spherical halo around our Galaxy. They consist of old stars, formed early in the Galaxy's history. Globular clusters are also found around other galaxies.

glockenspiel percussion instrument of light metal keys mounted on a carrying frame for use in military bands or on a standing frame for use in an orchestra (in which form it resembles a small xylophone or celesta).

glomerulus in the kidney, the blood capillaries responsible for forming the fluid that passes down the tubules and ultimately becomes urine. In the human kidney there are approximately one million tubules, each possessing its own glomerulus.

Glorious Revolution in British history, the events surrounding the removal of James II from the throne and his replacement by Mary (daughter of Charles I) and William of Orange as joint sovereigns in 1689. James had become increasingly unpopular on account of his unconstitutional behaviour and Catholicism. Various elements in England, including seven prominent politicians, plotted to invite the Protestant William to invade. Arriving at Torbay on 5 Nov 1688, William rapidly gained support and James was allowed to flee to France after the army deserted him. William and Mary then accepted a new constitutional settlement, the Bill of Rights 1689, which assured the ascendency of parliamentary power over sovereign rule.

Gloucestershire county in SW England
area 2,640 sq km/1,019 sq mi
towns Gloucester (administrative headquarters), Stroud, Cheltenham, Tewkesbury, Cirencester
products cereals, fruit, dairy products; engineering, coal in the Forest of Dean
population (1991) 520,600

glow-worm wingless female of some luminous beetles (fireflies) in the family Lampyridae. The luminous organs situated under the abdomen serve to attract winged males for mating. There are about 2,000 species, distributed worldwide.

Gluck Christoph Willibald von 1714–1787. German composer who settled in Vienna as kapellmeister to Maria Theresa in 1754. In 1762 his *Orfeo ed Euridice/Orpheus and Eurydice* revolutionized the 18th-century conception of opera by giving free scope to dramatic effect. *Orfeo* was followed by *Alceste/Alcestis* 1767 and *Paride ed Elena/Paris and Helen* 1770.

glucose or *dextrose* or *grape-sugar* $C_6H_{12}O_6$ sugar present in the blood, and found also in honey and fruit juices. It is a source of energy for the body, being produced from other sugars and starches to form the 'energy currency' of many biochemical reactions also involving *ATP.

glue ear or *serous otitis media* condition commonly affecting small children, in which the Eustachian tube, which normally drains and ventilates the middle *ear, becomes blocked with mucus. The resulting accumulation of mucus in the middle ear causes muffled hearing.

glue-sniffing or *solvent misuse* inhalation of the fumes from organic solvents of the type found in paints, lighter fuel, and glue, for their hallucinatory effects. As well as being addictive, solvents are dangerous for their effects on the user's liver, heart, and lungs. It is believed that solvents produce hallucinations by dissolving the cell membrane of brain cells, thus altering the way the cells conduct electrical impulses.

gluon in physics, a *gauge boson that carries the strong nuclear force, responsible for binding quarks together to form the strongly interacting subatomic particles known as *hadrons. There are eight kinds of gluon.

gluten protein found in cereal grains, especially wheat. Gluten enables dough to stretch during rising. It has to be avoided by sufferers from coeliac disease.

glyceride *ester formed between one or more acids and glycerol (propan-1,2,3-triol). A glyceride is termed a mono-, di-, or triglyceride, depending on the number of hydroxyl groups from the glycerol that have reacted with the acids.

glycerine another name for *glycerol.

glycerol or *glycerine* or *propan-1,2,3-triol* HOCH$_2$CH(OH)CH$_2$OH thick, colourless, odourless, sweetish liquid. It is obtained from vegetable and animal oils and fats (by treatment with acid, alkali, superheated steam, or an enzyme), or by fermentation of glucose, and is used in the manufacture of high explosives, in antifreeze solutions, to maintain moist conditions in fruits and tobacco, and in cosmetics.

glycine CH$_2$(NH$_2$)COOH the simplest amino acid, and one of the main components of proteins. When purified, it is a sweet, colourless crystalline compound.

glycogen polymer (a polysaccharide) of the sugar *glucose made and retained in the liver as a carbohydrate store, for which reason it is sometimes called animal starch. It is a source of energy when needed by muscles, where it is converted back into glucose by the hormone *insulin and metabolized.

glycol or *ethylene glycol* or *ethane-1,2-diol* (CH$_2$OH)$_2$ thick, colourless, odourless, sweetish liquid. It is used in antifreeze solutions, in the preparation of ethers and esters (used for explosives), as a solvent, and as a substitute for glycerol.

Glyndebourne site of an opera house in East Sussex, England, established in 1934 by John Christie (1882–1962). Operas are staged at an annual summer festival and a touring company is also based there. A newly-built opera house opened 1994.

GmbH abbreviation for *Gesellshaft mit beschrankter Haftung* (German 'limited liability company').

GMT abbreviation for *Greenwich Mean Time*.

gnat small fly of the family Culicidae, the mosquitoes. The eggs are laid in water, where they hatch into wormlike larvae, which pass through a pupal stage to emerge as adult insects.

gneiss coarse-grained *metamorphic rock, formed under conditions of increasing temperature and pressure, and often occurring in association with schists and granites. It has a foliated, laminated structure, consisting of thin bands of micas and amphiboles alternating with granular bands of quartz and feldspar. Gneisses are formed during regional metamorphism; *paragneisses* are derived from sedimentary rocks and *orthogneisses* from igneous rocks. Garnets are often found in gneiss.

Gnosticism esoteric cult of divine knowledge (a synthesis of Christianity, Greek philosophy, Hinduism, Buddhism, and the mystery cults of the Mediterranean), which flourished during the 2nd and 3rd centuries and was a rival to, and influence on, early Christianity. The medieval French *Cathar heresy and the modern *Mandean* sect (in S Iraq) descend from Gnosticism.

GNP abbreviation for *gross national product*.

gnu or *wildebeest* either of two species of African *antelope, genus *Connochaetes*, with a cowlike face, a beard and mane, and heavy curved horns in both sexes. The body is up to 1.3 m/ 4.2 ft at the shoulder and slopes away to the hindquarters.

Goa state of India
area 3,700 sq km/1,428 sq mi
capital Panaji
population (1991) 1,168,600
history captured by the Portuguese 1510; the inland area added in the 18th century. Goa was incorporated into India as a union territory with Daman and Diu 1961 and became a state 1987.

goat ruminant mammal of the genus *Capra* in the family Bovidae, closely related to the sheep. Both males and females have horns and beards. They are sure-footed animals, and feed on shoots and leaves more than on grass.

Gobbi Tito 1913–1984. Italian baritone singer renowned for his opera characterizations of Figaro in *The Marriage of Figaro*, Scarpia in *Tosca*, and Iago in *Otello*.

Gobelins French tapestry factory, originally founded as a dyeworks in Paris by Gilles and Jean Gobelin about 1450. The firm began to produce tapestries in the 16th century, and in 1662 the establishment was bought for Louis XIV by his minister Colbert. With the support of the French government, it continues to make tapestries.

Gobi Asian desert divided between the Mongolian People's Republic and Inner Mongolia, China; 800 km/500 mi N–S, and 1,600 km/ 1,000 mi E–W. It is rich in fossil remains of extinct species.

Gobind Singh 1666–1708. Indian religious leader, the tenth and last guru (teacher) of Sikhism, 1675–1708, and founder of the Sikh brotherhood known as the *Khalsa. On his death, the Sikh holy book, the *Guru Granth Sahib*, replaced the line of human gurus as the teacher and guide of the Sikh community.

God the concept of a supreme being, a unique creative entity, basic to several monotheistic religions (for example Judaism, Christianity, Islam); in many polytheistic cultures (for example Norse, Roman, Greek), the term 'god' refers to a supernatural being who personifies the force behind an aspect of life (for example Neptune, Roman god of the sea).

Godard Jean-Luc 1930– . French film director, one of the leaders of *New Wave cinema. His works are often characterized by experimental editing techniques and an unconventional dramatic form. His films include *A bout de souffle* 1959, *Vivre sa Vie* 1962, *Weekend* 1968, and *Je vous salue, Marie* 1985.

Goddard Robert Hutchings 1882–1945. US rocket pioneer. His first liquid-fuelled rocket was launched at Auburn, Massachusetts in 1926. By 1935 his rockets had gyroscopic control and carried cameras to record instrument readings. Two years later a Goddard rocket gained the world altitude record with an ascent of 3 km/1.9 mi.

Goddard Space Flight Center NASA installation at Greenbelt, Maryland, USA, responsible for the operation of NASA's uncrewed scientific satellites, including the *Hubble Space Telescope. It is also home of the National Space Science Data centre, a repository of data collected by satellites.

Godiva Lady c. 1040–1080. Wife of Leofric, earl of Mercia (died 1057). Legend has it that her husband promised to reduce the heavy taxes on the people of Coventry if she rode naked through the streets at noon. The grateful citizens remained indoors as she did so, but 'Peeping Tom' bored a hole in his shutters and was struck blind.

'God Save the King/Queen' British national anthem. The melody resembles a composition by John Bull (1563–1628) and similar words are found from the 16th century. In its present form it dates from the 1745 Rebellion, when it was used as an anti-Jacobite Party song.

Godthaab (Greenlandic **Nuuk**) capital and largest town of Greenland; population (1982) 9,700. It is a storage centre for oil and gas, and the chief industry is fish processing.

Godunov Boris 1552–1605. Tsar of Russia from 1598, elected after the death of Fyodor I, son of Ivan the Terrible. He was assassinated by a pretender to the throne who professed to be Dmitri, a brother of Fyodor and the rightful heir. The legend that has grown up around this forms the basis of Pushkin's play *Boris Godunov* 1831 and Mussorgsky's opera of the same name 1874.

Goebbels Paul Josef 1897–1945. German Nazi leader. As minister of propaganda from 1933, he brought all cultural and educational activities under Nazi control and built up sympathetic movements abroad to carry on the 'war of nerves' against Hitler's intended victims. On the capture of Berlin by the Allies, he poisoned himself.

Goering (German **Göring**) Hermann Wilhelm 1893–1946. Nazi leader, German field marshal from 1938. He was part of Hitler's inner circle, and with Hitler's rise to power in 1933, he established the Gestapo and concentration camps. Appointed successor to Hitler in 1939, he built a vast economic empire in occupied Europe, but later lost favour and was expelled from the party in 1945. Tried at Nuremberg for war crimes, he poisoned himself before he could be executed.

Goes Hugo van der, died 1482. Flemish painter, chiefly active in Ghent. His *Portinari altarpiece* about 1475 (Uffizi, Florence) is a huge oil painting of the Nativity, full of symbolism and naturalistic detail, and the *Death of the Virgin* about 1480 (Musée Communale des Beaux Arts, Bruges) is remarkable for the varied expressions on the faces of the apostles.

Goethe Johann Wolfgang von 1749–1832. German poet, novelist, and dramatist, generally considered the founder of modern German literature, and leader of the Romantic *Sturm und Drang* movement. His works include the autobiographical *Die Leiden des Jungen Werthers/ The Sorrows of the Young Werther* 1774 and *Faust* 1808, his masterpiece. A visit to Italy 1786–88 inspired the classical dramas *Iphigenie auf Tauris/Iphigenia in Tauris* 1787 and *Torquato Tasso* 1790.

Gogh Vincent van 1853–1890. Dutch Post-Impressionist painter. He tried various careers, including preaching, and began painting in the 1880s. He met Paul *Gauguin in Paris, and when he settled in Arles, Provence, 1888, Gauguin joined him there. After a quarrel van Gogh cut off part of his own earlobe, and in 1889 he entered an asylum; the following year he committed suicide. The Arles paintings vividly testify to his intense emotional involvement in his art; among them are *The Yellow Chair* and several *Sunflowers* 1888 (National Gallery, London).

Gogol Nicolai Vasilyevich 1809–1852. Russian writer. His first success was a collection of stories, *Evenings on a Farm near Dikanka* 1831–32, followed by *Mirgorod* 1835. Later works include *Arabesques* 1835, the comedy play *The Inspector General* 1836, and the picaresque novel *Dead Souls* 1842, which satirizes Russian provincial society.

Goh Chok Tong 1941– . Singapore politician, prime minister from 1990. A trained economist, Goh became a member of Parliament for the ruling People's Action Party 1976. Rising steadily through the party ranks, he was appointed deputy prime minister 1985, and subsequently chosen by the cabinet as Lee Kuan Yew's successor.

goitre enlargement of the thyroid gland seen as a swelling on the neck. It is most pronounced in simple goitre, which is caused by iodine deficiency. More common is toxic goitre or *thyrotoxicosis, caused by overactivity of the thyroid gland.

Golan Heights (Arabic **Jawlan**) plateau on the Syrian border with Israel, bitterly contested in the *Arab-Israeli Wars and annexed by Israel on 14 Dec 1981.

gold heavy, precious, yellow, metallic element; symbol Au, atomic number 79, relative atomic mass 197.0. It is unaffected by temperature changes and is highly resistant to acids. For manufacture, gold is alloyed with another strengthening metal (such as copper or silver), its purity being measured in *carats on a scale of 24.

goldcrest smallest British bird, *Regulus regulus*, about 9 cm/3.5 in long. It is olive green, with a bright yellow streak across the crown. This warbler builds its nest in conifers.

Golden Fleece in Greek mythology, fleece of the winged ram Chrysomallus, which hung on an oak tree at Colchis and was guarded by a dragon. It was stolen by Jason and the Argonauts.

Golden Horde the invading Mongol-Tatar army that first terrorized Europe from 1237 under the leadership of Batu Khan, a grandson of Genghis Khan. *Tamerlane broke their power 1395, and *Ivan III ended Russia's payment of tribute to them 1480.

goldenrod one of several tall, leafy perennials of the North American genus *Solidago*, in the daisy family Compositae. Flower heads are mostly composed of yellow florets.

golden section visually satisfying ratio, first constructed by the Greek mathematician *Euclid and used in art and architecture. It is found by dividing a line AB at a point O such that the rectangle produced by the whole line and one of the segments is equal to the square drawn on the other segment. The ratio of the two segments is about 8:13 or 1:1.618, and a rectangle whose sides are in this ratio is called a **golden rectangle**.

goldfinch songbird of the genus *Carduelis*, found in Eurasia, N Africa, and North America.

goldfish fish *Carassius auratus* of the *carp family, found in E Asia. Greenish-brown in its natural state, it has for centuries been bred by the Chinese, taking on highly coloured and sometimes freakishly shaped forms. Goldfish can see a greater range of colours than any other animal tested.

Golding William 1911–1993. English novelist. His work is often principally concerned with the fundamental corruption and evil inherent in human nature. His first book, *Lord of the Flies* 1954, concerns the degeneration into savagery of a group of English schoolboys marooned on a Pacific island. *Pincher Martin* 1956 is a study of greed and self-delusion. Later novels include *The Spire* 1964 and *Darkness Visible* 1979. He was awarded the Nobel Prize for Literature 1983.

gold rush large influx of gold prospectors to an area where gold deposits have recently been discovered. The result is a dramatic increase in population. Cities such as Johannesburg, Melbourne, and San Francisco either originated or were considerably enlarged by gold rushes. Melbourne's population trebled from 77,000 to some 200,000 between 1851–53.

Goldsmith James 1933– . Franco-British entrepreneur, one of the UK's wealthiest people. Early in his career he built up a grocery empire, Cavenham Foods; he went on to become the owner of several industrial, commercial (he was cofounder of Mothercare), and financial enterprises. He became a director of the *Daily Telegraph* 1990.

Goldsmith Oliver 1728–1774. Irish writer. His works include the novel *The Vicar of Wakefield* 1766; the poem 'The Deserted Village' 1770; and the play *She Stoops to Conquer* 1773. In 1761 Goldsmith met Samuel Johnson, and became a member of his 'club'. *The Vicar of Wakefield* was sold (according to Johnson's account) to save him from imprisonment for debt.

gold standard system under which a country's currency is exchangeable for a fixed weight of gold on demand at the central bank. It was almost universally applied 1870–1914, but by 1937 no single country was on the full gold standard. Britain abandoned the gold standard 1931; the USA abandoned it 1971. Holdings of gold are still retained because it is an internationally recognized commodity, which cannot be legislated upon or manipulated by interested countries.

Goldwyn Samuel. Adopted name of Samuel Goldfish 1882–1974. US film producer. Born in Poland, he emigrated to the USA 1896. He founded the Goldwyn Pictures Corporation 1917, which eventually merged into Metro-Goldwyn-Mayer (MGM) 1924, although he was not part of the deal. He remained an independent producer for many years, making classics such as *Wuthering Heights* 1939, *The Little Foxes* 1941, *The Best Years of Our Lives* 1946, and *Guys and Dolls* 1955.

golf outdoor game in which a small rubber-cored ball is hit with a wooden- or iron-faced club into a series of holes using the least number of shots. On the first shot for each hole, the ball is hit from a tee, which elevates the ball slightly off the ground; subsequent strokes are played off the ground. Most courses have 18 holes and are approximately 5,500 m/6,000 yd in length.

Golgi Camillo 1844–1926. Italian cell biologist who with Santiago Ramón y Cajal produced the first detailed knowledge of the fine structure of the nervous system.

Golgi apparatus or **Golgi body** stack of flattened membranous sacs found in the cells of *eukaryotes. Many molecules travel through the Golgi apparatus on their way to other organelles or to the endoplasmic reticulum. Some are modified or asssembled inside the sacs. The Golgi apparatus is named after the Italian physician Camillo Golgi.

Goliath in the Old Testament, champion of the *Philistines, who was said to have been slain by a stone from a sling by the young *David in single combat in front of their opposing armies.

Gómez Juan Vicente 1864–1935. Venezuelan dictator 1908–35. The discovery of oil during his rule attracted US, British, and Dutch oil interests and made Venezuela one of the wealthiest countries in Latin America. Gómez amassed a considerable personal fortune and used his well-equipped army to dominate the civilian population.

Gompers Samuel 1850–1924. US labour leader. His early career in the Cigarmakers' Union led him to found and lead the *American Federation of Labor 1882.

Gomułka Władysław 1905–1982. Polish communist politician, party leader 1943–48 and 1956–70. He introduced moderate reforms, including private farming and tolerance for Roman Catholicism.

gonad the part of an animal's body that produces the sperm or egg cells (ova) required for sexual reproduction. The sperm-producing gonad is called a *testis, and the egg- producing gonad is called an *ovary.

gonadotrophin any hormone that supports and stimulates the function of the gonads (sex glands); some gonadotrophins are used as *fertility drugs.

Goncharov Ivan Alexandrovitch 1812–1891. Russian novelist. His first novel, *A Common Story* 1847, was followed 1858 by his humorous masterpiece *Oblomov*, which satirized the indolent Russian landed gentry.

Goncourt, de the brothers Edmond 1822–1896 and Jules 1830–1870. French writers. They collaborated in producing a compendium, *L'Art du XVIIIème siècle/18th-Century Art* 1859–75, historical studies, and a *Journal* published 1887–96 that depicts French literary life of their day. Edmond de Goncourt founded the Académie Goncourt, opened 1903, which awards an annual prize, the Prix Goncourt, to the author of the best French novel of the year.

Gond member of a heterogenous people of central India, about half of whom speak unwritten languages belonging to the Dravidian family. The rest speak Indo-European languages. There are over 4 million Gonds, most of whom live in Madhya Pradesh, E Maharashtra, and N Andra

Pradesh, although some live in Orissa. Traditionally, many Gonds practised shifting cultivation; agriculture and livestock remain the basis of the economy.

Gondwanaland or *Gondwana* land mass, including the continents of South America, Africa, Australia, and Antarctica, that formed the southern half of *Pangaea, the 'supercontinent' or world continent that existed between 250 and 200 million years ago. The northern half was *Laurasia. The baobab tree of Africa and Australia is a relic of Gondwanaland.

gonorrhoea common sexually transmitted disease arising from infection with the bacterium *Neisseria gonorrhoeae*, which causes inflammation of the genito-urinary tract. After an incubation period of two to ten days, infected men experience pain while urinating and a discharge from the penis; infected women often have no external symptoms.

González Márquez Felipe 1942– . Spanish socialist politician, leader of the Socialist Workers' Party (PSOE), prime minister from 1982. Although he was re-elected in 1989, his popularity suffered from economic upheaval and allegations of corruption.

Gooch Graham Alan 1953– . English cricketer who plays for Essex, England's leading run-scorer in test cricket since he overtook David Gower's record in 1993. He made his first-class cricket debut in 1973, and was first capped for England two years later.

Good Friday in the Christian church, the Friday before Easter, which is observed in memory of the Crucifixion (the death of Jesus on the cross).

Good King Henry perennial plant *Chenopodium bonus-henricus* growing to 50 cm/1.6 ft, with triangular leaves which are mealy when young. Spikes of tiny greenish-yellow flowers appear above the leaves in midsummer.

Goodman Benny (Benjamin David) 1909–1986. US clarinetist, nicknamed the 'King of Swing' for the new jazz idiom he introduced with arranger Fletcher Henderson (1897–1952). In 1934 he founded his own 12-piece band, which combined the expressive improvisatory style of black jazz with disciplined precision ensemble playing. He is associated with such numbers as 'Blue Skies' and 'Lets Dance'. He also recorded with a sextet 1939–41 that included the guitarist Charlie Christian (1916–1942).

goose aquatic bird of several genera (especially *Anser*) in the family Anatidae, which also includes ducks and swans. Both genders are similar in appearance: they have short, webbed feet, placed nearer the front of the body than in other members of the order Anatidae, and the beak is slightly hooked. They feed entirely on grass and plants.

gooseberry edible fruit of *Ribes uva-crispa*, a low-growing bush related to the currant. It is straggling in its growth, bearing straight sharp spines in groups of three, and rounded, lobed leaves. The flowers are green, and hang on short stalks. The fruits are generally globular, green, and hairy, but there are reddish and white varieties.

gopher burrowing rodent of the genus *Citellus*,

family Sciuridae. It is a kind of ground squirrel represented by some 20 species distributed across W North America and Eurasia. Length ranges from 15 cm/6 in to 90 cm/16 in, excluding the furry tail; colouring ranges from plain yellowish to striped and spotted species. The name *pocket gopher* is applied to the eight genera of the North American family Geomyidae.

Gorbachev Mikhail Sergeyevich 1931– . Soviet president, in power 1985–91. He was a member of the Politburo from 1980. As general secretary of the Communist Party (CPSU) 1985–91, and president of the Supreme Soviet 1988–91, he introduced liberal reforms at home (*perestroika and *glasnost), proposed the introduction of multiparty democracy, and attempted to halt the arms race abroad. He became head of state 1989. He was awarded the Nobel Peace Prize 1990 but his international reputation suffered in the light of harsh state repression of nationalist demonstrations in Baltic states. Following an abortive coup attempt by hardliners Aug 1991, international acceptance of independence for the Baltic states, and accelerated moves towards independence in other republics, Gorbachev's power base as Soviet president was greatly weakened and in Dec 1991 he resigned.

Gordian knot in Greek mythology, the knot tied by King Gordius of Phrygia that – so an oracle revealed – could be unravelled only by the future conqueror of Asia. According to tradition, Alexander the Great, unable to untie it, cut it with his sword in 334 BC.

Gordimer Nadine 1923– . South African novelist, an opponent of apartheid. Her first novel, *The Lying Days*, appeared in 1953, her other works include *The Conservationist* 1974, the volume of short stories *A Soldier's Embrace* 1980, and *July's People* 1981. She was awarded the Nobel Prize for Literature in 1991.

Gordon Charles (George) 1833–1885. British general sent to Khartoum in the Sudan 1884 to rescue English garrisons that were under attack by the *Mahdi, Muhammad Ahmed; he was himself besieged for ten months by the Mahdi's army. A relief expedition arrived 28 Jan 1885 to find that Khartoum had been captured and Gordon killed two days before.

Gordon George 1751–1793. British organizer of the so-called *Gordon Riots* of 1778, a protest against removal of penalties imposed on Roman Catholics in the Catholic Relief Act of 1778; he was acquitted on a treason charge. Gordon and the 'No Popery' riots figure in Charles Dickens's novel *Barnaby Rudge*.

Gore Albert 1948– . US Democratic politician, vice president from 1993. He served as congressman 1977–79, and as senator of Tennessee 1985–92. Like his running mate, Bill *Clinton, he is on the conservative wing of the party, but holds liberal views on such matters as women's rights and abortion.

Gorgon in Greek mythology, any of three sisters, Stheno, Euryale, and Medusa, who had wings, claws, enormous teeth, and snakes for hair. Medusa, the only one who was mortal, was killed by *Perseus, but even in death her head was still so frightful that it turned the onlooker to stone.

Goria Giovanni 1943–1994. Italian Christian Democrat (DC) politician, prime minister 1987–88. He entered the Chamber of Deputies 1976 and held a number of posts, including treasury minister, until he was asked to form a coalition government in 1987.

gorilla largest of the apes, *Gorilla gorilla*, found in the dense forests of West Africa and mountains of central Africa. The male stands about 1.8 m/6 ft, and weighs about 200 kg/450 lbs. Females are about half the size. The body is covered with blackish hair, silvered on the back in older males. Gorillas live in family groups; they are vegetarian, highly intelligent, and will attack only in self-defence. They are dwindling in numbers, being shot for food by some local people, or by poachers taking young for zoos, but protective measures are having some effect.

Göring Hermann. German spelling of *Goering, Nazi leader.

Gorky Maxim. Pen name of Alexei Peshkov 1868–1936. Russian writer. Born in Nizhni Novgorod (named Gorky 1932–90 in his honour), he was exiled 1906–13 for his revolutionary principles. His works, which include the play *The Lower Depths* 1902 and the memoir *My Childhood* 1913–14, combine realism with optimistic faith in the potential of the industrial proletariat.

Gorky Russian *Gor'kiy* name 1932–90 of *Nizhni Novgorod, city in central Russia.

gorse or *furze* or *whin* Eurasian genus of plants *Ulex*, family Leguminosae, consisting of thorny shrubs with spine-shaped leaves densely clustered along the stems, and bright yellow flowers.

goshawk or *northern goshawk* woodland hawk *Accipiter gentilis* that is similar in appearance to the peregrine falcon, but with shorter wings and legs. It is used in falconry.

Gospel (Middle English 'good news') in the New Testament generally, the message of Christian salvation; in particular the four written accounts of the life of Jesus by Matthew, Mark, Luke, and John. Although the first three give approximately the same account or synopsis (thus giving rise to the name 'Synoptic Gospels'), their differences from John have raised problems for theologians.

gospel music vocal music developed in the 1920s in the black Baptist churches of the US South from spirituals, which were 18th- and 19th-century hymns joined to the old African pentatonic (five-note) scale. Outstanding among the early gospel singers was Mahalia Jackson (1911–1972), but from the 1930s to the mid-1950s male harmony groups predominated, among them the Dixie Hummingbirds, the Swan Silvertones, and the Five Blind Boys of Mississippi.

Gossaert Jan, Flemish painter, known as *Mabuse.

Göteborg (German *Gothenburg*) port and industrial (ships, vehicles, chemicals) city (Sweden's second largest) on the W coast of Sweden, on the Göta Canal (built 1832), which links it with Stockholm; population (1990) 433,000.

Goth E Germanic people who settled near the Black Sea around AD 2nd century. There are two branches, the eastern Ostrogoths and the western Visigoths. The *Ostrogoths* were conquered by the Huns 372. They regained their independence 454 and under *Theodoric the Great conquered Italy 488–93; they disappeared as a nation after the Byzantine emperor *Justinian I reconquered Italy 535–55. The *Visigoths* migrated to Thrace. Under *Alaric they raided Greece and Italy 395–410, sacked Rome, and established a kingdom in S France. Expelled from there by the Franks, they established a Spanish kingdom which lasted until the Moorish conquest of 711.

Gothic architecture style of architecture that flourished in Europe from the mid-12th century to the end of the 15th century. It is characterized by vertical lines of tall pillars, spires, greater height in interior spaces, the pointed arch, rib vaulting, and the flying buttress.

Gothic art style of painting and sculpture that dominated European art from the late 12th century until the early Renaissance. The great Gothic church façades held hundreds of sculpted figures and profuse ornamentation, and manuscripts were lavishly decorated. Stained glass replaced mural painting to some extent in N European churches. The *International Gothic* style in painting emerged in the 14th century, characterized by delicate and complex ornamentation and increasing realism.

Gothic novel literary genre established by Horace Walpole's *The Castle of Otranto* 1765 and marked by mystery, violence, and horror; other exponents were the English writers Anne Radcliffe, Matthew 'Monk' Lewis, Mary Shelley, the Irish writer Bram Stoker, and Edgar Allan Poe in the USA.

Gothic revival the resurgence of interest in Gothic architecture, as displayed in 19th-century Britain and the USA. Gothic revival buildings include the Houses of Parliament and St Pancras Station, London; the Town Hall, Vienna; and Princeton University, USA.

Götterdämmerung (German 'twilight of the gods') in Scandinavian mythology, the end of the world.

Gould Stephen Jay 1941– . US palaeontologist and author. In 1972 he proposed the theory of punctuated equilibrium, suggesting that the evolution of species did not occur at a steady rate but could suddenly accelerate, with rapid change occurring over a few hundred thousand years. His books include *Ever Since Darwin* 1977, *The Panda's Thumb* 1980, *The Flamingo's Smile* 1985, and *Wonderful Life* 1990.

Gounod Charles François 1818–1893. French composer. His operas include *Sappho* 1851, *Faust* 1859, *Philémon et Baucis* 1860, and *Roméo et Juliette* 1867. He also wrote sacred songs, masses, and an oratorio, *The Redemption* 1882. His music inspired many French composers of the late 19th century.

gourd any of various members of the family Cucurbitaceae, including melons and pumpkins. In a narrower sense, the name applies only to the genus *Lagenaria*, of which the bottle gourd or *calabash *Lagenaria siceraria* is best known.

gout disease, a hereditary form of *arthritis, marked by an excess of uric acid crystals in the tissues, causing pain and inflammation in one or more joints (usually of the feet or hands). Acute attacks are treated with *anti-inflammatories.

government any system whereby political authority is exercised. Modern systems of government distinguish between liberal democracies, totalitarian (one-party) states, and autocracies (authoritarian, relying on force rather than ideology). The Greek philosopher Aristotle was the first to attempt a systematic classification of governments. His main distinctions were between government by one person, by few, and by many (monarchy, oligarchy, and democracy), although the characteristics of each may vary between states and each may degenerate into tyranny (rule by an oppressive elite in the case of oligarchy or by the mob in the case of democracy).

Government Communications Headquarters centre of the British government's electronic surveillance operations, popularly known as GCHQ.

governor in engineering, any device that controls the speed of a machine or engine, usually by regulating the intake of fuel or steam.

Gower David 1957– . English left-handed cricketer who played for Leicestershire 1975–89 and for Hampshire from 1990. He was England's record run scorer in test cricket from 1992, when he surpassed Geoffrey Boycott's record, until 1993, when his total was overtaken by Graham Gooch. He retired 1993.

Gowon Yakubu 1934– . Nigerian politician, head of state 1966–75. Educated at Sandhurst military college in the UK, he became chief of staff, and in the military coup of 1966 seized power. After the Biafran civil war 1967–70, he reunited the country with his policy of 'no victor, no vanquished'. In 1975 he was overthrown by a military coup.

Goya Francisco José de Goya y Lucientes 1746–1828. Spanish painter and engraver. He painted portraits of four kings of Spain, and his etchings include *The Disasters of War*, depicting the French invasion of Spain 1810–14. Among his later works are the 'black paintings' (Prado, Madrid), with horrific images such as *Saturn Devouring One of His Sons c.* 1822.

Graaf Regnier de 1641–1673. Dutch physician and anatomist who discovered the ovarian follicles, which were later named *Graafian follicles*. He named the ovaries and gave exact descriptions of the testicles. He was also the first to isolate and collect the secretions of the pancreas and gall bladder.

Graafian follicle fluid-filled capsule that surrounds and protects the developing egg cell inside the ovary during the *menstrual cycle. After the egg cell has been released, the follicle remains and is known as a corpus luteum.

Grable Betty (Elizabeth Ruth) 1916–1973. US actress, singer, and dancer, who starred in *Moon over Miami* 1941, *I Wake Up Screaming* 1941, and *How to Marry a Millionaire* 1953. As a publicity stunt, her legs were insured for a million dollars. Her popularity peaked during World War II when US soldiers voted her their number-one pin-up girl.

Gracchus the brothers *Tiberius Sempronius*

163–133 BC and *Gaius Sempronius* 153–121 BC. Roman agrarian reformers. As *tribune (magistrate) 133 BC, Tiberius tried to prevent the ruin of small farmers by making large slave-labour farms illegal but was murdered. Gaius, tribune 123–122 BC, revived his brother's legislation, and introduced other reforms, but was outlawed by the Senate and committed suicide.

Grace W(illiam) G(ilbert) 1848–1915. English cricketer. By profession a doctor, he became the best batsman in England. He began playing first-class cricket at the age of 16, scored 152 runs in his first test match, and scored the first triple century 1876. Throughout his career, which lasted nearly 45 years, he scored more than 54,000 runs.

Graces in Greek mythology, three goddesses (Aglaia, Euphrosyne, Thalia), daughters of Zeus and Hera, personifications of pleasure, charm, and beauty; the inspirers of the arts and the sciences.

Graf Steffi 1969– . German lawn-tennis player who brought Martina *Navratilova's long reign as the world's number-one female player to an end. Graf reached the semi-final of the US Open 1985 at the age of 16, and won five consecutive Grand Slam singles titles 1988–89.

graffiti (Italian 'scratched drawings') inscriptions or drawings carved, scratched, or drawn on public surfaces, such as walls, fences, or public-transport vehicles. *Tagging* is the act of writing an individual logo on surfaces with spray paint or large felt-tip pens.

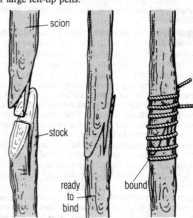

grafting Grafting, a method of artificial propagation in plants, is used particularly on roses and fruit trees.

grafting in medicine, the operation by which a piece of living tissue is removed from one organism and transplanted into the same or a different organism where it continues growing. In horticulture, it is a technique widely used for propagating plants, especially woody species. A bud or shoot on one plant, termed the *scion*, is inserted into another, the *stock*, so that they continue growing together, the tissues combining at the point of union.

Graham Billy (William Franklin) 1918– . US Protestant evangelist, known for the dramatic staging and charismatic eloquence of his preaching. Graham has preached to millions during worldwide crusades and on television, bringing many thousands to a 'decision for Christ'.

Graham Martha 1893–1991. US dancer, choreographer, teacher, and director. A leading exponent of modern dance in the USA, she developed a distinctive vocabulary of movement, the *Graham Technique*, now taught worldwide. Her pioneering technique, designed to express inner emotion and intention through dance forms, represented the first real alternative to classical ballet.

Graham Thomas 1805–1869. Scottish chemist who laid the foundations of physical chemistry (the branch of chemistry concerned with changes in energy during a chemical transformation) by his work on the diffusion of gases and liquids. *Graham's Law* 1829 states that the diffusion rate of a gas is inversely proportional to the square root of its density.

Grahame Kenneth 1859–1932. Scottish author. The early volumes of sketches of childhood, *The Golden Age* 1895 and *Dream Days* 1898, were followed by his masterpiece *The Wind in the Willows* 1908, an animal fantasy created for his young son, which was dramatized by A A Milne as *Toad of Toad Hall* 1929.

grain the smallest unit of mass in the three English systems (avoirdupois, troy, and apothecaries' weights) used in the UK and USA, equal to 0.0648 g. It was reputedly the weight of a grain of wheat. One pound avoirdupois equals 7,000 grains; one pound troy or apothecaries' weight equals 5,760 grains.

gram metric unit of mass; one-thousandth of a kilogram.

grammar (Greek *grammatike tekhne* 'art of letters') the rules for combining words into phrases, clauses, sentences, and paragraphs. Emphasis on the standardizing impact of print has meant that spoken or colloquial language is often perceived as less grammatical than written language, but all forms of a language, standard or otherwise, have their own grammatical systems of differing complexity. People often acquire several overlapping grammatical systems within one language; for example, one formal system for writing and standard communication and one less formal system for everyday and peer-group communication.

grammar school in the UK, a secondary school catering for children of high academic ability, about 20% of the total, usually measured by the Eleven Plus examination. Most grammar schools have now been replaced by *comprehensive schools. By 1991 the proportion of English children in grammar schools was less than 3%.

Grampian Region region of Scotland
area 8,600 sq km/3,320 sq mi
towns Aberdeen (administrative headquarters)
products beef cattle (Aberdeen Angus and Beef Shorthorn), fishing, North Sea oil service industries, tourism (winter skiing)
population (1991) 493,200
famous people John Barbour, James Ramsay MacDonald, Alexander Cruden.

Gramsci Antonio 1891–1937. Italian Marxist who attempted to unify social theory and political practice. He helped to found the Italian Communist Party 1921 and was elected to parliament 1924, but imprisoned by the Fascist leader Mussolini from 1926; his *Quaderni di carcere/Prison Notebooks* were published posthumously 1947.

Granada city in the Sierra Nevada in Andalusia, S Spain; population (1986) 281,000. It produces textiles, soap, and paper. *history* Founded by the Moors in the 8th century, it became the capital of an independent kingdom 1236–1492, when it was the last Moorish stronghold to surrender to the Spaniards. The *Alhambra*, a fortified hilltop palace, was built in the 13th and 14th centuries by the Moorish kings.

Gran Carajas industrial and mining project in the Brazilian Amazon region, covering an area the size of Britain and France combined. Mining and dam building are destroying huge areas of rainforest and some of the factories are being powered by charcoal from firewood, further adding to the deforestation.

Gran Chaco large lowland plain in N Argentina, W Paraguay, and SE Bolivia; area 650,000 sq km/251,000 sq mi. It consists of swamps, forests (a source of quebracho timber), and grasslands, and there is cattle-raising.

Grand Banks continental shelf in the N Atlantic off SE Newfoundland, where the shallow waters are rich fisheries, especially for cod.

Grand Canal (Chinese *Da Yune*) the world's longest canal. It is 1,600 km/1,000 mi long and runs from Hangzhou to Tianjin, China; it is 30–61 m/100–200 ft wide, and reaches depths of over 1.5 km/1 mi. The earliest section was completed 486 BC, and the northern section was built AD 1282–92, during the reign of Kublai Khan.

Grand Canyon gorge of multicoloured rock strata cut by and containing the Colorado River, N Arizona, USA. It is 350 km/217 mi long, 6–29 km/4–18 mi wide, and reaches depths of over 1.7 km/1.1 mi.

Grand Design in the early 17th century, a plan attributed by the French minister Sully to Henry IV of France (who was assassinated before he could carry it out) for a great Protestant union against the Holy Roman Empire; the term was also applied to President de Gaulle's vision of France's place in a united Europe.

Grande Dixence dam the world's highest dam, located in Switzerland, which measures 285 m/935 ft from base to crest. Completed in 1961, it contains 6 million cu m/8 million cu yd of concrete.

Grand Guignol genre of short horror play originally produced at the Grand Guignol theatre in Montmartre, Paris (named after the bloodthirsty character Guignol in late 18th-century marionette plays).

Grand National in horse-racing, any of several steeplechases, such as the one run at Aintree, England, during the Liverpool meeting in March or April over 7,242 m/4.5 mi, with 30 formidable jumps. The highest jump is the Chair at 156 cm/5 ft 2 in. It was first run 1839.

grand opera type of opera without any spoken dialogue (unlike the *opéra-comique*) as performed at the Paris Opéra 1820s–80s. Using the enormous resources of the state-subsidized opera house, grand operas were extremely long (five acts), and included incidental music and a ballet.

Grand Remonstrance petition passed by the English Parliament in Nov 1641 that listed all the alleged misdeeds of Charles I and demanded Parliamentary approval for the king's ministers and the reform of the church. Charles refused to accept the Grand Remonstrance and countered by trying to arrest five leading members of the House of Commons (Pym, Hampden, Holles, Hesilrige, and Strode). The worsening of relations between king and Parliament led to the outbreak of the English Civil War in 1642.

grand slam in tennis, the four major tournaments: the Australian Open, the French Open, Wimbledon, and the US Open. In golf, it is also the four major tournaments: the US Open, the British Open, the Masters, and the PGA (Professional Golfers Association). In baseball, a grand slam is a home run with runners on all the bases. A grand slam in bridge is when all 13 tricks are won by one team.

grand unified theory (GUT) in physics, a sought-for theory that would combine the theory of the strong nuclear force (called *quantum chromodynamics) with the theory of the weak nuclear and electromagnetic forces. The search for the grand unified theory is part of a larger programme seeking a *unified field theory, which would combine all the forces of nature (including gravity) within one framework.

Granger (James) Stewart 1913–1993. British film actor. After several leading roles in British romantic films during World War II, he moved to Hollywood in 1950 and subsequently appeared in such films as *Scaramouche* 1952, *The Prisoner of Zenda* 1952, and *The Wild Geese* 1978.

granite coarse-grained *igneous rock, typically consisting of the minerals quartz, feldspar, and mica. It may be pink or grey, depending on the composition of the feldspar. Granites are chiefly used as building materials.

Grant Cary. Stage name of Archibald Leach 1904–1986. British-born actor, a US citizen from 1942. His witty, debonair personality made him a screen favourite for more than three decades. He was directed by Alfred *Hitchcock in *Suspicion* 1941, *Notorious* 1946, *To Catch a Thief* 1955, and *North by Northwest* 1959. He received a 1970 Academy Award for general excellence.

Grant Duncan 1885–1978. Scottish painter and designer. He was a member of the *Bloomsbury Group and a pioneer of Post-Impressionism in the UK. He lived with the painter Vanessa Bell (1879–1961) from about 1914 and worked with her on decorative projects. Later works, such as *Snow Scene* 1921, show great fluency and a subtle use of colour.

Grant Ulysses S(impson) 1822–1885. US Civil War general in chief for the Union and 18th president of the USA 1869–77. As a Republican president, he carried through a liberal *Reconstruction policy in the South. He failed to suppress extensive political corruption within his own party and cabinet, which tarnished the reputation of his second term.

grant-maintained school in the UK, a state school that has voluntarily withdrawn itself from local authority support (an action called **opting out**), and instead is maintained directly by central government. The first was Skegness Grammar School in 1989. The schools are managed by their own boards of governors.

grape fruit of any vine of the genus *Vitis*, especially *V. vinifera*, of the Vitaceae family.

grapefruit round, yellow, juicy, sharp-tasting fruit of the evergreen tree *Citrus paradisi* of the Rutaceae family. The tree grows up to 10 m/30 ft and has dark shiny leaves and large white flowers. The large fruits grow in grapelike clusters (hence the name). Grapefruits were first established in the West Indies and subsequently cultivated in Florida by the 1880s; they are now also grown in Israel and South Africa. Some varieties have pink flesh.

graphical user interface (GUI) or *WIMP* in computing, a type of *user interface in which programs and files appear as icons (small pictures), user options are selected from pull-down menus, and data are displayed in windows (rectangular areas), which the operator can manipulate in various ways. The operator uses a pointing device, typically a *mouse, to make selections and initiate actions.

graphic equalizer control used in hi-fi systems that allows the distortions introduced by unequal amplification of different frequencies to be corrected.

graphics tablet or *bit pad* in computing, an input device in which a stylus or cursor is moved, by hand, over a flat surface. The computer can keep track of the position of the stylus, so enabling the operator to input drawings or diagrams into the computer.

graphite blackish-grey, laminar, crystalline form of *carbon. It is used as a lubricant and as the active component of pencil lead.

graph notation in music, an invented sign language representing unorthodox sounds objectively in pitch and time, or alternatively representing sounds of orthodox music in a visually unorthodox manner. A form of graph notation for speech patterns used in phonetics was adopted by Stockhausen in *Carré/Squared* 1959–60.

graph plotter alternative name for a *plotter.

grass plant of the large family Gramineae of monocotyledons, with about 9,000 species distributed worldwide except in the Arctic regions. The majority are perennial, with long, narrow leaves and jointed, hollow stems; hermaphroditic flowers are borne in spikelets; the fruits are grain-like. Included are bluegrass, wheat, rye, maize, sugarcane, and bamboo.

Grass Günter 1927– . German writer. The grotesque humour and socialist feeling of his novels *Die Blechtrommel/The Tin Drum* 1959 and *Der Butt/The Flounder* 1977 are also characteristic of many of his poems.

grasshopper insect of the order Orthoptera, usually with strongly developed hind legs, enabling it to leap. The femur of each hind leg in the male usually has a row of protruding joints that produce the characteristic chirping when rubbed against the hard wing veins. Members of the order include *locusts, *crickets, and katydids.

grass of Parnassus plant *Parnassia palustris*, unrelated to grasses, found growing in marshes and on wet moors in Europe and Asia. It is low-growing, with a rosette of heart-shaped, stalked leaves, and has five-petalled, white flowers with conspicuous veins growing singly on stem tips in late summer.

Grateful Dead, the US psychedelic rock group formed 1965. Their shows feature long improvisations and subtle ensemble playing, seldom fully captured in recording; albums include *Live Dead* 1969, *Workingman's Dead* 1970, and *Built to Last* 1989.

gravel coarse *sediment consisting of pebbles or small fragments of rock, originating in the beds of lakes and streams or on beaches. Gravel is quarried for use in road building, railway ballast, and for an aggregate in concrete. It is obtained from quarries known as gravel pits, where it is often found mixed with sand or clay.

Graves Robert (Ranke) 1895–1985. English poet and author. He was severely wounded on the Somme in World War I, and his frank autobiography *Goodbye to All That* 1929 is one of the outstanding war books. Other works include the poems *Over the Brazier* 1916; two historical novels of imperial Rome, *I Claudius* and *Claudius the God*, both 1934; and books on myth – for example, *The White Goddess* 1948.

gravimetry study of the Earth's gravitational field. Small variations in the gravitational field (gravimetric anomalies) can be caused by varying densities of rocks and structure beneath the surface. Such variations are measured by a device called a gravimeter, which consists of a weighted spring that is pulled further downwards where the gravity is stronger – at a positive anomaly, also known as the Bouguer anomaly – and the extension of the spring is measured. Gravimetry is used by geologists to map the subsurface features of the Earth's crust, such as underground masses of heavy rock like granite, or light rock like salt.

gravitational lensing bending of light by a gravitational field, predicted by Einstein's general theory of relativity. The effect was first detected 1917 when the light from stars was found to be bent as it passed the totally eclipsed Sun. More remarkable is the splitting of light from distant quasars into two or more images by intervening galaxies. In 1979 the first double image of a quasar produced by gravitational lensing was discovered and a quadruple image of another quasar was later found.

graviton in physics, the *gauge boson that is the postulated carrier of gravity.

gravity force of attraction that arises between objects by virtue of their masses. On Earth, gravity is the force of attraction between any object in the Earth's gravitational field and the Earth itself. It is regarded as one of the four *fundamental forces of nature, the other three being the *electromagnetic force, the *strong nuclear force, and the *weak nuclear force. The gravitational force is the weakest of the four forces, but it acts over great distances. The particle that is postulated as the carrier of the gravitational force is the *graviton.

gravure one of the three main *printing methods, in which printing is done from a plate etched with a pattern of recessed cells in which the ink is held. The greater the depth of a cell, the greater the strength of the printed ink. Gravure plates are expensive to make, but the process is economical for high-volume printing and reproduces illustrations well.

gray SI unit (symbol Gy) of absorbed radiation dose. It replaces the rad (1 Gy equals 100 rad), and is defined as the dose absorbed when one kilogram of matter absorbs one joule of ionizing radiation. Different types of radiation cause different amounts of damage for the same absorbed dose; the SI unit of ***dose equivalent*** is the *sievert.

Gray Thomas 1716–1771. English poet whose 'Elegy Written in a Country Churchyard' 1751 is one of the most quoted poems in English. Other poems include 'Ode on a Distant Prospect of Eton College', 'The Progress of Poesy', and 'The Bard'; these poems are now seen as the precursors of Romanticism.

grayling freshwater fish *Thymallus thymallus* of the family Salmonidae. It has a long multirayed dorsal fin, and a coloration shading from silver to purple. It is found in northern parts of Europe, Asia, and North America, where it was once common in the Great Lakes.

Graz capital of Styria province, and second largest city in Austria; population (1981) 243,400. Industries include engineering, chemicals, iron, and steel. It has a 15th-century cathedral and a university founded 1573. Lippizaner horses are bred near here.

Great Artesian Basin the largest area of artesian water in the world. It underlies much of Queensland, New South Wales, and South Australia, and in prehistoric times formed a sea. It has an area of 1,750,000 sq km/676,250 sq mi.

Great Australian Bight broad bay in S Australia, notorious for storms. It was discovered by a Dutch navigator, Captain Thyssen, 1627. The coast was charted by the English explorer Captain Matthew Flinders 1802.

Great Barrier Reef chain of coral reefs and islands about 2,000 km/1,250 mi long, off the E coast of Queensland, Australia, at a distance of 15–45 km/10–30 mi. It is believed to be the world's largest living organism and forms an immense natural breakwater, the coral rock forming a structure larger than all human-made structures on Earth combined. The reef is in danger from large numbers of starfish, which are reported to have infested 35% of the reef. Some scientists fear the entire reef will disappear within 50 years.

Great Bear Lake lake on the Arctic Circle, in the Northwest Territories, Canada; area 31,800 sq km/12,275 sq mi.

Great Britain official name for *England, *Scotland, and *Wales, and the adjacent islands (except the Channel Islands and the Isle of Man) from 1603, when the English and Scottish crowns were united under James I of England (James VI of Scotland). With Northern *Ireland it forms the *United Kingdom.

great circle circle drawn on a sphere such that the diameter of the circle is a diameter of the sphere. On the Earth, all meridians of longitude are half great circles; among the parallels of latitude, only the equator is a great circle.

Great Dane large, short-haired breed of dog, usually fawn in colour, standing up to 76 cm/30 in tall, and weighing up to 70 kg/154 lb. It has a long head, a large nose, and small, erect ears. It was used in Europe for hunting boar and stags.

Great Dividing Range E Australian mountain range, extending 3,700 km/2,300 mi N–S from Cape York Peninsula, Queensland, to Victoria. It includes the Carnarvon Range, Queensland, which has many Aboriginal cave paintings, the Blue Mountains in New South Wales, and the Australian Alps.

Great Exhibition world fair held in Hyde Park, London, UK, in 1851, proclaimed by its originator Prince Albert as 'the Great Exhibition of the Industries of All Nations'. In practice, it glorified British manufacture: over half the 100,000 exhibits were from Britain or the British Empire. Over 6 million people attended the exhibition. The exhibition hall, popularly known as the *Crystal Palace, was constructed of glass with a cast-iron frame, and designed by Joseph *Paxton.

Great Lakes series of five freshwater lakes along the USA-Canada border: Lakes Superior, Michigan, Huron, Erie, and Ontario; total area 245,000 sq km/94,600 sq mi.   Interconnecting canals make them navigable by large ships, and they are drained by the *St Lawrence River. The whole forms the St Lawrence Seaway. They are said to contain 20% of the world's surface fresh water.

Great Leap Forward change in the economic policy of the People's Republic of China introduced by *Mao Zedong under the second five-year plan of 1958–62. The aim was to achieve rapid and simultaneous agricultural and industrial growth through the creation of large new agro-industrial communes. The inefficient and poorly planned allocation of state resources led to the collapse of the strategy by 1960 and the launch of a 'reactionary programme', involving the use of rural markets and private subsidiary plots.

Great Patriotic War (1941–45) war between the USSR and Germany during *World War II.

Great Plains semi-arid region to the E of the Rocky Mountains, USA, stretching as far as the 100th meridian of longitude through Oklahoma, Kansas, Nebraska, and the Dakotas. The plains, which cover one-fifth of the USA, extend from Texas in the S over 2,400 km/1,500 mi N to Canada. Ranching and wheat farming have resulted in over-use of water resources to such an extent that available farmland has been reduced by erosion.

Great Power any of the major European powers of the 19th century: Russia, Austria (Austria-Hungary), France, Britain, and Prussia.

Great Red Spot prominent oval feature, 14,000 km/8,500 mi wide and some 30,000 km/ 20,000 mi long, in the atmosphere of the planet *Jupiter, S of the equator. It was first observed in the 19th century. Space probes show it to be an anticlockwise vortex of cold clouds, coloured possibly by phosphorus.

Great Rift Valley longest 'split' in the Earth's surface; see *Rift Valley, Great.

Great Schism in European history, the period 1378–1417 in which rival popes had seats in Rome and in Avignon; it was ended by the election of Martin V during the Council of Constance 1414–17.

Great Slave Lake lake in the Northwest Territories, Canada; area 28,450 sq km/10,980 sq mi. It is the deepest lake (615 m/2,020 ft) in North America.

Great Trek in South African history, the movement of 12,000–14,000 Boer (Dutch) settlers from Cape Colony 1835 and 1845 to escape British rule. They established republics in Natal and the Transvaal. It is seen by many white South Africans as the main event in the founding of the present republic and also as a justification for continuing whites-only rule.

Great Wall of China continuous defensive wall stretching from W Gansu to the Gulf of Liaodong (2,250 km/1,450 mi). It was once even longer. It was built under the Qin dynasty from 214 BC to prevent incursions by the Turkish and Mongol peoples. Some 8 m/25 ft high, it consists of a brick-faced wall of earth and stone, has a series of square watchtowers, and has been carefully restored. It is so large that it can be seen from space.

Great War another name for *World War I.

grebe any of 19 species of water birds belonging to the family Podicipedidae. The great crested grebe *Podiceps cristatus* is the largest of the Old World grebes. It lives in ponds and marshes in Eurasia, Africa, and Australia, feeding on fish. It grows to 50 cm/20 in long and has a white breast, with chestnut and black feathers on its back and head. The head and neck feathers form a crest, especially prominent during the breeding season.

Greco, El (Doménikos Theotokopoulos) 1541–1614. painter called 'the Greek' because he was born in Crete. He studied in Italy, worked in Rome from about 1570, and by 1577 had settled in Toledo, Spain. He painted elegant portraits and intensely emotional religious scenes with increasingly distorted figures and flickering light; for example, *The Burial of Count Orgaz* 1586 (church of San Tomé, Toledo).

Greece Hellenic Republic (*Elliniki Dimokratia*)

area 131,957 sq km/50,935 sq mi
capital Athens
towns Larisa; ports Piraeus, Thessaloníki, Patras, Iráklion
physical mountainous; a large number of islands, notably Crete, Corfu, and Rhodes
environment acid rain and other airborne pollutants are destroying the Classical buildings and ancient monuments of Athens
head of state Constantine Karamanlis from 1990
head of government Andreas Papandreou from 1993
political system democratic republic
exports tobacco, fruit, vegetables, olives, olive oil, textiles, aluminium, iron and steel
currency drachma
population (1993 est) 10,300,000; growth rate 0.3% p.a.
language Greek
religion Greek Orthodox 97%
GNP $6,374 per head (1992)
chronology
1829 Independence achieved from Turkish rule.
1912–13 Balkan Wars; Greece gained much land.
1941–44 German occupation of Greece.
1946 Civil war between royalists and communists; communists defeated.
1949 Monarchy re-established with Paul as king.
1964 King Paul succeeded by his son Constantine.
1967 Army coup removed the king; Col George Papadopoulos became prime minister. Martial law imposed, all political activity banned.
1973 Republic proclaimed, with Papadopoulos as president.
1974 Former premier Constantine Karamanlis recalled from exile to lead government. Martial law and ban on political parties lifted; restoration of the monarchy rejected by a referendum.
1975 New constitution adopted, making Greece a democratic republic.
1980 Karamanlis resigned as prime minister and was elected president.
1981 Greece became full member of European Economic Community. Andreas Papandreou elected Greece's first socialist prime minister.
1983 Five-year military and economic cooperation agreement signed with USA; ten-year economic cooperation agreement signed with USSR.
1985 Papandreou re-elected.
1988 Relations with Turkey improved. Mounting criticism of Papandreou.
1989 Papandreou defeated. Tzannis Tzannetakis became prime minister; his all-party government collapsed. Xenophon Zolotas formed new unity government. Papandreou charged with corruption.
1990 New Democracy Party (ND) won half of parliamentary seats in general election but no outright majority; Constantine Mitsotakis became premier; formed new all-party government. Karamanlis re-elected president.
1992 Papandreou acquitted. Greece opposed recognition of independence of the Yugoslav breakaway republic of Macedonia. Parliament ratified Maastricht Treaty.
1993 PASOK won general election and Papandreou returned as prime minister.
1994 Trade embargo imposed against Former Yugoslav Republic of Macedonia.

Greek art the sculpture, mosaic, and crafts of ancient Greece (no large-scale painting survives). It is usually divided into three periods: **Archaic** (late 8th century–480 BC), showing Egyptian influence; **Classical** (480–323 BC), characterized by dignified and eloquent realism; and **Hellenistic** (323–27 BC), more exuberant or dramatic. Sculptures of human figures dominate all periods, and vase painting was a focus for artistic development for many centuries.

Greek language member of the Indo-European language family, which has passed through at least five distinct phases since the 2nd millennium BC: **Ancient Greek** 14th–12th centuries BC; **Archaic Greek**, including Homeric epic language, until 800 BC; **Classical Greek** until 400 BC; **Hellenistic Greek**, the common language of Greece, Asia Minor, W Asia, and Egypt to the 4th century AD, and **Byzantine Greek**, used until the 15th century and still the ecclesiastical language of the Greek Orthodox Church. **Modern Greek** is principally divided into the general vernacular (**Demotic Greek**) and the language of education and literature (**Katharevousa**).

Greek Orthodox Church see *Orthodox Church.

Greeley Horace 1811–1872. US editor, publisher, and politician. He founded the *New York Tribune* 1841 and, as a strong supporter of the Whig party, advocated many reform causes in his newspaper – among them, feminism and abolitionism. He was an advocate of American westward expansion, and is remembered for his advice 'Go west, young man'. One of the founders of the Republican party 1854, Greeley was the unsuccessful presidential candidate of the breakaway Liberal Republicans 1872.

Greenaway Peter 1942– . English film director. His films are highly stylized and cerebral, richly visual, and often controversial. His feeling for perspective and lighting reveal his early training as a painter. His films, such as *A Zed & Two Noughts* 1985, are hallmarked by puzzle motifs and numerical games. Greenaway's other films include *The Draughtsman's Contract* 1982, *Belly of an Architect* 1986, *Drowning by Numbers* 1988, *The Cook, the Thief, his Wife and her Lover* 1989, *Prospero's Books* 1991, and *The Baby of Macon* 1993.

green belt area surrounding a large city, officially designated not to be built on but preserved where possible as open space (for agricultural and recreational use). In the UK the first green belts were established from 1938 around conurbations such as London in order to prevent *urban sprawl. New towns were set up to take the overspill population.

Greene (Henry) Graham 1904–1991. English writer. His novels of guilt, despair, and penitence are set in a world of urban seediness or political corruption in many parts of the world. They include *Brighton Rock* 1938, *The Power and the Glory* 1940, *The Heart of the Matter* 1948, *The Third Man* 1949, *The Honorary Consul* 1973, and *Monsignor Quixote* 1982.

greenfinch songbird *Carduelis chloris*, common in Europe and N Africa. The male is green with a yellow breast, and the female is a greenish-brown.

Greenham Common site of a continuous peace demonstration 1981–90 on common land near Newbury, Berkshire, UK, outside a US airbase. The women-only camp was established Sept 1981 in protest against the siting of US cruise missiles in the UK. The demonstrations ended with the closure of the base. Greenham Common reverted to standby status, and the last US cruise missiles were withdrawn March 1991.

greenhouse effect phenomenon of the Earth's atmosphere by which solar radiation, trapped by the Earth and re-emitted from the surface, is prevented from escaping by various gases in the air. The result is a rise in the Earth's temperature. The main greenhouse gases are carbon dioxide, methane, and *chlorofluorocarbons (CFCs). Fossil-fuel consumption and forest fires are the main causes of carbon-dioxide build-up; methane is a byproduct of agriculture (rice, cattle, sheep). Water vapour is another greenhouse gas. The United Nations Environment Programme estimates an increase in average world temperatures of 1.5°C/2.7°F with a consequent rise of 20 cm/7.7 in in sea level of 2025.

Greenland (Greenlandic *Kalaalit Nunaat*) world's largest island, lying between the North Atlantic and Arctic Oceans east of North America
area 2,175,600 sq km/840,000 sq mi
capital Godthaab (Greenlandic *Nuuk*) on the W coast
economy fishing and fish-processing
population (1990) 55,500; Inuit (Ammassalik Eskimoan), Danish, and other European
language Greenlandic (Ammassalik Eskimoan)
history Greenland was discovered about 982 by Eric the Red, who founded colonies on the W coast soon after Eskimos from the North American Arctic had made their way to Greenland. Christianity was introduced to the Vikings about 1000. In 1261 the Viking colonies accepted Norwegian sovereignty, but early in the 15th century all communication with Europe ceased, and by the 16th century the colonies had died out, but the Eskimos had moved on to the E coast. It became a Danish colony in the 18th century, and following a referendum 1979 was granted full internal self-government 1981.

greenmail payment made by a target company to avoid a takeover; for example, buying back a portion of its own shares from a potential predator (either a person or a company) at an inflated price.

Green Mountain Boys in US history, irregular troops who fought to protect the Vermont part of what was then New Hampshire colony from land claims made by neighbouring New York. In the American Revolution they captured *Fort Ticonderoga from the British. Their leader was Ethan Allen (1738–1789), who was later captured by the British. Vermont declared itself an independent republic, refusing to join the Union until 1791. It is popularly known as the Green Mountain State.

green movement collective term for the individuals and organizations involved in efforts to protect the environment. The movement encompasses political parties such as the *Green Party and organizations like *Friends of the Earth and *Greenpeace.

Green Paper publication issued by a British government department setting out various aspects of a matter on which legislation is contemplated, and inviting public discussion and suggestions. In due course it may be followed by a *White Paper, giving details of proposed legislation. The first Green Paper was published 1967.

Green Party political party aiming to 'preserve the planet and its people', based on the premise that incessant economic growth is unsustainable. The leaderless party structure reflects a general commitment to decentralization. Green parties sprang up in W Europe in the 1970s and in E Europe from 1988. Parties in different countries are linked to one another but unaffiliated with any pressure group.

Greenpeace international environmental pressure group, founded 1971, with a policy of nonviolent direct action backed by scientific research. During a protest against French atmospheric nuclear testing in the S Pacific 1985, its ship *Rainbow Warrior* was sunk by French intelligence agents, killing a crew member.

green pound exchange rate used by the European Community for the conversion of EC agricultural prices to sterling. The prices for all EC members are set in European Currency Units (ECUs) and are then converted into green currencies for each national currency.

green revolution in agriculture, a popular term for the change in methods of arable farming in Third World countries. The intent is to provide more and better food for their populations, albeit with a heavy reliance on chemicals and machinery. It was instigated in the 1940s and 1950s, but abandoned by some countries in the 1980s. Much of the food produced is exported as *cash crops, so that local diet does not always improve.

greenshank greyish shorebird *Tringa nebularia* of the sandpiper group. It has long olive-green legs and a slightly upturned bill. It breeds in N Europe and regularly migrates through the Aleutian Islands.

Greenstreet Sydney 1879–1954. British character actor. He made an impressive film debut in *The Maltese Falcon* 1941 and became one of the cinema's best-known villains. His other films include *Casablanca* 1943 and *The Mask of Dimitrios* 1944.

Greenwich inner borough of Greater London, England; population (1991) 200,800.

Greenwich Mean Time (GMT) local time on the zero line of longitude (the **Greenwich meridian**), which passes through the Old Royal Observatory at Greenwich, London. It was replaced 1986 by coordinated universal time (UTC); see *time.

Greenwich Village in New York City, a section of lower Manhattan (from 14th Street south to Houston Street and from Broadway west to the Hudson River), which from the late 19th century became the bohemian and artistic quarter of the city and, despite expensive rentals, remains so.

Greer Germaine 1939– . Australian feminist who became widely known on the publication of her book *The Female Eunuch* 1970. Later works include *The Obstacle Race* 1979, a study of contemporary women artists, and *Sex and Destiny: The Politics of Human Fertility* 1984. She is also a speaker and activist.

Gregorian chant any of a body of plainsong choral chants associated with Pope Gregory the Great (540–604), which became standard in the Roman Catholic Church.

Gregory name of 16 popes, including:

Gregory I St, the Great c. 540–604. Pope from 590 who asserted Rome's supremacy and exercised almost imperial powers. In 596 he sent St *Augustine to England. He introduced the choral *Gregorian chant* into the liturgy. Feast day 12 March.

Gregory VII or **Hildebrand** c. 1023–1085. Chief minister to several popes before his election to the papacy 1073. In 1077 he forced the Holy Roman emperor Henry IV to wait in the snow at Canossa for four days, dressed as a penitent, before receiving pardon. He was driven from Rome and died in exile. His feast day is 25 May.

Gregory XIII 1502–1585. Pope from 1572 who introduced the reformed *Gregorian calendar*, still in use, in which a century year is not a leap year unless it is divisible by 400.

Gregory of Tours, St 538–594. French Christian bishop of Tours from 573, author of a *History of the Franks*. His feast day is 17 Nov.

Grenada
area (including the Grenadines, notably Carriacou) 340 sq km/131 sq mi
capital St George's
towns Grenville, Hillsborough (Carriacou)
physical southernmost of the Windward Islands; mountainous
head of state Elizabeth II from 1974 represented by governor general
head of government Nicholas Braithwaite from 1990
political system emergent democracy
exports cocoa, nutmeg, bananas, mace
currency Eastern Caribbean dollar
population (1993 est) 95,300, 84% of black African descent; growth rate –0.2% p.a.
language English (official); some French patois spoken
religion Roman Catholic 60%
GNP $2,180 per head (1991)
chronology
1974 Independence achieved from Britain; Eric Gairy elected prime minister.
1979 Gairy removed in bloodless coup led by Maurice Bishop; constitution suspended and a People's Revolutionary Government established.
1982 Relations with the USA and Britain deteriorated as ties with Cuba and the USSR strengthened.
1983 After Bishop's attempt to improve relations with the USA, he was overthrown by left-wing opponents. A coup established the Revolutionary Military Council (RMC), and Bishop and three colleagues were executed. The USA invaded Grenada, accompanied by troops from other E Caribbean countries; RMC overthrown, 1974 constitution reinstated.
1984 The newly formed NNP won 14 of the 15 seats in the house of representatives and its leader, Herbert Blaize, became prime minister.
1989 Herbert Blaize lost leadership of NNP,

remaining as head of government; he died and was succeeded by Ben Jones.
1990 Nicholas Braithwaite of the NDC became prime minister.
1991 Integration into Windward Islands confederation proposed.

Grenadines chain of about 600 small islands in the Caribbean sea, part of the group known as the Windward Islands. They are divided between *St Vincent and *Grenada.

Grenville George 1712–1770. British Whig politician, prime minister, and chancellor of the Exchequer, whose introduction of the *Stamp Act 1765 to raise revenue from the colonies was one of the causes of the American Revolution. His government was also responsible for prosecuting the radical John *Wilkes.

Grenville Richard 1542–1591. English naval commander and adventurer who died heroically aboard his ship *The Revenge* when attacked by Spanish warships. Grenville fought in Hungary and Ireland 1566–69, and was knighted about 1577. In 1585 he commanded the expedition that founded Virginia, USA, for his cousin Walter *Raleigh. From 1586 to 1588 he organized the defence of England against the Spanish Armada.

Grenville William Wyndham, Baron 1759–1834. British Whig politician, foreign secretary from 1791; he resigned along with Prime Minister Pitt the Younger 1801 over George III's refusal to assent to Catholic emancipation. He headed the 'All the Talents' coalition of 1806–07 that abolished the slave trade.

Gretna Green village in Dumfries and Galloway region, Scotland, where runaway marriages were legal after they were banned in England 1754; all that was necessary was the couple's declaration, before witnesses, of their willingness to marry. From 1856 Scottish law required at least one of the parties to be resident in Scotland for a minimum of 21 days before the marriage, and marriage by declaration was abolished 1940.

Greville Fulke, 1st Baron Brooke 1554–1628. English poet and courtier, friend and biographer of Philip Sidney. Greville's works, none of them published during his lifetime, include *Caelica*, a sequence of poems in different metres; *The Tragedy of Mustapha* and *The Tragedy of Alaham*, tragedies modelled on the Latin Seneca; and the *Life of Sir Philip Sidney* 1652. He has been commended for his plain style and tough political thought.

grievous bodily harm (GBH) in English law, very serious physical damage suffered by the victim of a crime. The courts have said that judges should not try to define grievous bodily harm but leave it to the jury to decide.

Grey Charles, 2nd Earl Grey 1764–1845. British Whig politician. He entered Parliament 1786, and in 1806 became First Lord of the Admiralty, and foreign secretary soon afterwards. As prime minister 1830–34, he carried the Great Reform Bill that reshaped the parliamentary representative system 1832 and the act abolishing slavery throughout the British Empire 1833.

Grey Lady Jane 1537–1554. Queen of England for nine days, 10–19 July 1553, the great-granddaughter of Henry VII. She was married 1553 to Lord Guildford Dudley (died 1554), son of the

Duke of *Northumberland. Edward VI was persuaded by Northumberland to set aside the claims to the throne of his sisters Mary and Elizabeth. When Edward died on 6 July the same year, Jane reluctantly accepted the crown and was proclaimed queen four days later. Mary, although a Roman Catholic, had the support of the populace, and the Lord Mayor of London announced that she was queen 19 July. Grey was executed on Tower Green.

Grey Zane 1875–1939. US author of Westerns, such as *Riders of the Purple Sage* 1912. He wrote more than 80 books and was primarily responsible for the creation of the Western as a literary genre.

greyhound ancient breed of dog, with a long narrow muzzle, slight build, and long legs, renowned for its swiftness. It is up to 78 cm/2.6 ft tall, and can exceed 60 kph/40 mph. Greyhound racing is a popular spectator sport.

grey market dealing in shares using methods that are legal but perhaps officially frowned upon – for example, before issue and flotation.

grid network by which electricity is generated and distributed over a region or country. It contains many power stations and switching centres and allows, for example, high demand in one area to be met by surplus power generated in another. Britain has the world's largest grid system, with over 140 power stations able to supply up to 55,000 megawatts.

grid reference on a map, numbers that are used to show location. The numbers at the bottom of the map (eastings) are given before those at the side (northings). A four-figure grid reference indicates a specific square, whereas a six-figure grid reference indicates a point within a square.

Grieg Edvard Hagerup 1843–1907. Norwegian composer. Much of his music is small-scale, particularly his songs, dances, sonatas, and piano works. Among his orchestral works are the *Piano Concerto* 1869 and the incidental music for Ibsen's *Peer Gynt* 1876.

griffin mythical monster, the supposed guardian of hidden treasure, with the body, tail, and hind legs of a lion, and the head, forelegs, and wings of an eagle.

Griffith D(avid) W(ark) 1875–1948. US film director, an influential figure in the development of cinema as an art. He made hundreds of 'one-reelers' 1908–13, in which he pioneered the techniques of masking, fade-out, flashback, crosscut, close-up, and long shot. After much experimentation with photography and new techniques he directed *The Birth of a Nation* 1915, about the aftermath of the Civil War, later criticized as degrading to blacks.

griffon small breed of dog originating in Belgium; red, black, or black and tan in colour and weighing up to 5 kg/11 lb. Griffons are square-bodied and round-headed, and there are rough-and smooth-coated varieties.

Grimaldi Joseph 1779–1837. English clown. Born in London, he was the son of an Italian actor. He appeared on the stage at two years old. He gave his name 'Joey' to all later clowns, and excelled as 'Mother Goose' performed at Covent Garden 1806.

Grimm brothers Jakob Ludwig Karl (1785–1863) and Wilhelm (1786–1859), philologists and collectors of German fairy tales such as 'Hansel and Gretel' and 'Rumpelstiltskin'. Joint compilers of an exhaustive dictionary of German, they saw the study of language and the collecting of folk tales as strands in a single enterprise.

Grimm's law in linguistics, the rule (formulated 1822 by Jacob Grimm) by which certain prehistoric sound changes have occurred in the consonants of Indo-European languages: for example Latin *p* became English and German *f* sound, as in *pater – father, Vater*.

Grimond Jo(seph), Baron Grimond 1913–1993. British Liberal politician. As leader of the party 1956–67, he aimed at making it 'a new radical party to take the place of the Socialist Party as an alternative to Conservatism'.

Gris Juan 1887–1927. Spanish painter, one of the earliest Cubists. He developed a distinctive geometrical style, often strongly coloured. He experimented with paper collage and made designs for Diaghilev's *Ballets Russes* 1922–23.

Grivas George 1898–1974. Greek Cypriot general who from 1955 led the underground group EOKA's attempts to secure the union (Greek *enosis*) of Cyprus with Greece.

Gromyko Andrei 1909–1989. President of the USSR 1985–88. As ambassador to the USA from 1943, he took part in the Tehran, Yalta, and Potsdam conferences; as United Nations representative 1946–49, he exercised the Soviet veto 26 times. He was foreign minister 1957–85. It was Gromyko who formally nominated Mikhail Gorbachev as Communist Party leader 1985.

Groningen most northerly province of the Netherlands
area 2,350 sq km/907 sq mi
capital Groningen
towns Hoogezand-Sappemeer, Stadskanaal, Veendam, Delfzijl, Winschoten
physical Ems estuary, innermost W Friesian Islands
products natural gas, arable crops, dairy produce, sheep, horses
population (1991) 554,600
history under the power of the bishops of Utrecht from 1040, Groningen became a member of the Hanseatic League 1284. Taken by Spain 1580, it was recaptured by Maurice of Nassau 1594.

grooming in biology, the use by an animal of teeth, tongue, feet, or beak to clean fur or feathers. Grooming also helps to spread essential oils for waterproofing. In many social species, notably monkeys and apes, grooming of other individuals is used to reinforce social relationships.

Gropius Walter Adolf 1883–1969. German architect. He lived in the USA from 1937. He was an early exponent of the International Style defined by glass curtain walls, cubic blocks, and unsupported corners, for example, the model factory and office building at the 1914 Cologne Werkbund exhibition. A founder-director of the *Bauhaus school in Weimar 1919–28, he advocated teamwork in design and artistic standards in industrial production. He was responsible for the new Bauhaus premises at Dessau 1925–26, a hallmark of the International Style.

grosbeak any of various thick-billed finches of the family Fringillidae. The *pine grosbeak Pinicola enucleator* breeds in Arctic forests. Its plumage is similar to that of the pine *crossbill.

gross a particular figure or price, calculated before the deduction of specific items such as commission, discounts, interest, and taxes. The opposite is *net.

gross domestic product (GDP) value of the output of all goods and services produced within a nation's borders, normally given as a total for the year. It thus includes the production of foreign-owned firms within the country, but excludes the income from domestically owned firms located abroad. See also *gross national product.

Grossmith George 1847–1912. British actor and singer. Turning from journalism to the stage, in 1877 he began a long association with the Gilbert and Sullivan operas, in which he created a number of parts. He collaborated with his brother **Weedon Grossmith** (1853–1919) on the comic novel *Diary of a Nobody* 1894.

gross national product (GNP) the most commonly used measurement of the wealth of a country. GNP is defined as the total value of all goods and services produced by firms owned by the country concerned. It is measured as the *gross domestic product plus income from abroad, minus income earned during the same period by foreign investors within the country; see also *national income.

Grosz Georg 1893–1959. German Expressionist painter and graphic artist. He was a founder of the Berlin Dada movement 1918. Grosz excelled in savage satirical drawings criticizing the government and the military establishment. After numerous prosecutions he fled his native Berlin 1932 and went to the USA where he became a naturalized American 1938.

Grotefend George Frederick 1775–1853. German scholar. Although a student of the classical rather than the oriental languages, he nevertheless solved the riddle of the wedgelike *cuneiform script as used in ancient Persia: decipherment of Babylonian cuneiform followed from his work.

Grotius Hugo 1583–1645. Dutch jurist and politician, born in Delft. He became a lawyer, and later received political appointments. In 1618 he was arrested as a republican and sentenced to imprisonment for life. His wife contrived his escape 1620, and he settled in France, where he composed the *De Jure Belli et Pacis/On the Law of War and Peace* 1625, the foundation of international law. He was Swedish ambassador in Paris 1634–45.

groundnut another name for *peanut.

ground water water collected underground in porous rock strata and soils; it emerges at the surface as springs and streams. The groundwater's upper level is called the *water table*. Sandy or other kinds of beds that are filled with groundwater are called *aquifers*. Recent estimates are that usable ground water amounts to more than 90% of all the fresh water on Earth; however, keeping such supplies free of pollutants

entering the recharge areas is a critical environmental concern.

group in chemistry, a vertical column of elements in the *periodic table. Elements in a group have similar physical and chemical properties; for example, the group I elements (the alkali metals: lithium, sodium, potassium, rubidium, caesium, and francium) are all highly reactive metals that form univalent ions. There is a gradation of properties down any group: in group I, melting and boiling points decrease, and density and reactivity increase.

grouper any of several species of large sea perch (Serranidae), found in warm waters. Some species grow to 2 m/6.5 ft long, and can weigh 300 kg/660 lbs.

grouse fowl-like game bird of the subfamily Tetraonidae, in the pheasant family, Phasianidae. The subfamily also includes quail, ptarmigan, and prairie chicken. Grouse are native to North America and N Europe. They are mostly ground-living. During the mating season the males undertake elaborate courtship displays in small individual territories (*leks).

Grünewald (Mathias or Mathis Gothardt-Neithardt) *c.* 1475–1528. German painter. He was court painter, architect, and engineer to the archbishop of Mainz 1508–14. His few surviving paintings show an intense involvement with religious subjects. His *Isenheim Altarpiece* 1515 (Unterlinden Museum, Colmar, France), with its tortured figure of Jesus, recalls medieval traditions.

grunge rock-music style of the early 1990s, characterized by a thick, abrasive, distorted sound. Grunge evolved from *punk in Seattle, Washington, USA and came to prominence with the chart success of the band *Nirvana 1991.

Guadalajara industrial city (textiles, glass, soap, pottery), capital of Jalisco state, W Mexico; population (1990) 2,847,000. It is a key communications centre. It has a 16th–17th-century cathedral, the Governor's Palace, and an orphanage with murals by the Mexican painter José Orozco (1883–1949).

Guadalcanal largest of the *Solomon Islands; area 6,500 sq km/2,510 sq mi; population (1987) 71,000. Gold, copra, and rubber are produced. During World War II it was the scene of a battle that was won by US forces after six months of fighting.

Guadeloupe island group in the Leeward Islands, West Indies, an overseas *département* of France; area 1,705 sq km/658 sq mi; population (1990) 387,000. The main islands are Basse-Terre, on which is the chief town of the same name, and Grande-Terre. Sugar refining and rum distilling are the main industries.

Guam largest of the *Mariana Islands in the W Pacific, an unincorporated territory of the USA
area 540 sq km/208 sq mi
capital Agaña
towns Apra (port), Tamuning
products sweet potatoes, fish; tourism is important
currency US dollar
population (1990) 132,800
languages English, Chamorro (basically Malay-Polynesian)

religion 96% Roman Catholic
government popularly elected governor (Ricardo Bordallo from 1985) and single-chamber legislature
recent history ceded by Spain to the USA 1898; occupied by Japan 1941–44. Guam achieved full US citizenship and self-government from 1950. A referendum 1982 favoured the status of a commonwealth, in association with the USA.

guan any of several large, pheasant-like birds of the family Cracidae, living in the forests of South and Central America. They are olive-green or brown.

guanaco hoofed ruminant *Lama guanacoe* of the camel family, found in South America on pampas and mountain plateaux. It grows to 1.2 m/4 ft at the shoulder, with head and body about 1.5 m/5 ft long. It is sandy brown in colour, with a blackish face, and has fine wool. It lives in small herds and is the ancestor of the domestic *llama and *alpaca. It is also related to the other wild member of the camel family, the *vicuna.

Guangdong or **Kwantung** province of S China
area 231,400 sq km/89,320 sq mi
capital Guangzhou
features Hainan, Leizhou peninsula, and the foreign enclaves of Hong Kong and Macao in the Pearl River delta
products rice, sugar, tobacco, minerals, fish
population (1990) 62,829,000.

Guangxi or **Kwangsi Chuang** autonomous region in S China
area 220,400 sq km/85,074 sq mi
capital Nanning
products rice, sugar, fruit
population (1990) 42,246,000, including the Zhuang people, allied to the Thai, who form China's largest ethnic minority.

Guangzhou or **Kwangchow** or **Canton** capital of Guangdong province, S China; population (1989) 3,490,000. Industries include shipbuilding, engineering, chemicals, and textiles.

guano dried excrement of fish-eating birds, widely collected for use as fertilizer. Some 80% comes from the sea cliffs of Peru.

Guanyin in Chinese Buddhism, the goddess of mercy. In Japan she is **Kannon** or Kwannon, an attendant of the Amida Buddha (Amitābha). Her origins were in India as the male bodhisattva Avalokiteśvara.

guarana Brazilian woody climbing plant *Paullinia cupana*, family Sapindaceae. A drink made from its roasted seeds has a high caffeine content, and it is the source of the drug known as zoom in the USA. Starch, gum, and several oils are extracted from it for commercial use.

Guaraní member of a South American Indian people who formerly inhabited the area that is now Paraguay, S Brazil, and Bolivia. The Guaraní live mainly in reserves; few retain the traditional ways of hunting in the tropical forest, cultivation, and ritual warfare. About 1 million speak Guaraní, a member of the Tupian language group.

guard cell in plants, a specialized cell on the undersurface of leaves for controlling gas exchange and water loss. Guard cells occur in pairs and are shaped so that a pore, or *stomata, exists between them. They can change shape with the result that the pore disappears. During warm weather, when a plant is in danger of losing excessive water, the guard cells close, cutting down evaporation from the interior of the leaf.

Guardi Francesco 1712–1793. Italian painter. He produced souvenir views of his native Venice that were commercially less successful than Canaletto's but are now considered more atmospheric, with subtler use of reflected light.

Guarneri family of stringed-instrument makers of Cremona, Italy. Giuseppe 'del Gesù' Guarneri (1698–1744) produced the finest models.

Guatemala Republic of (*República de Guatemala*)

area 108,889 sq km/42,031 sq mi
capital Guatemala City
towns Quezaltenango, Puerto Barrios (naval base)
physical mountainous; narrow coastal plains; limestone tropical plateau in N; frequent earthquakes
environment between 1960 and 1980 nearly 57% of the country's forest was cleared for farming
head of state and government Ramiro de Leon Carpio from 1993
political system democratic republic
exports coffee, bananas, cotton, sugar, beef
currency quetzal
population (1993 est) 10,000,000 (Mayaquiche Indians 54%, mestizos (mixed race) 42%); growth rate 2.8% p.a. (87% of under-fives suffer from malnutrition)
languages Spanish (official); 40% speak 18 Indian languages
religion Roman Catholic 80%, Protestant 20%
GNP $930 per head (1991)
chronology
1839 Independence achieved from Spain.
1954 Col Carlos Castillo became president in US-backed coup, halting land reform.
1963 Military coup made Col Enrique Peralta president.
1981 Growth of antigovernment guerrilla movement.
1982 General Angel Anibal became president. Army coup installed General Ríos Montt as head of junta and then as president; political violence continued.

1983 Montt removed in coup led by General Mejía Victores, who declared amnesty for the guerrillas.
1985 New constitution adopted; PDCG won congressional elections; Vinicio Cerezo elected president.
1989 Coup attempt against Cerezo foiled. Over 100,000 people killed and 40,000 reported missing since 1980.
1991 Jorge Serrano Elías of the Solidarity Action Movement elected president. Diplomatic relations with Belize established.
1993 President Serrano deposed; Ramiro de Leon Carpio elected president by assembly.
1994 Referendum supported constitutional reforms aimed at combatting corruption. Peace talks held with rebels. Right-wing parties, led by FRG, won majority in congressional elections.

Guatemala City capital of Guatemala; population (1983) 1,300,000. It produces textiles, tyres, footwear, and cement. It was founded 1776 when its predecessor (Antigua) was destroyed in an earthquake. It was severely damaged by another earthquake 1976.

guava tropical American tree *Psidium guajava* of the myrtle family Myrtaceae; the astringent yellow pear-shaped fruit is used to make guava jelly, or it can be stewed or canned. It has a high vitamin C content.

Guayaquil largest city and chief port of *Ecuador; population (1986) 1,509,100. The economic centre of Ecuador, Guayaquil manufactures machinery and consumer goods, processes food, and refines petroleum. It was founded 1537 by the Spanish explorer Francisco de Orellana.

Guderian Heinz 1888–1954. German general in World War II. He created the Panzer (German 'armour') divisions that formed the ground spearhead of Hitler's *Blitzkrieg* attack strategy, achieving a significant breakthrough at Sedan in Ardennes, France 1940, and leading the advance to Moscow 1941.

gudgeon any of an Old World genus *Gobio* of freshwater fishes of the carp family, especially *G. gobio* found in Europe and N Asia on the gravel bottoms of streams. It is olive-brown, spotted with black, and up to 20 cm/8 in long, with a distinctive barbel (a sensory fleshy filament) at each side of the mouth.

guelder rose or *snowball tree* cultivated shrub or small tree *Viburnum opulus*, native to Europe and N Africa, with spherical clusters of white flowers and shiny red berries.

Guelph and Ghibelline rival parties in medieval Germany and Italy, which supported the papal party and the Holy Roman emperors respectively.

Guérin Camille 1872–1961. French bacteriologist who, with *Calmette, developed the *bacille* Calmette-Guérin (*BCG) vaccine for tuberculosis.

Guernsey second largest of the *Channel Islands; area 63 sq km/24.3 sq mi; population (1986) 55,500. The capital is St Peter Port. Products include electronics, tomatoes, flowers, and more recently butterflies; from 1975 it has been a major financial centre. Guernsey cattle, which are a distinctive pale fawn colour and give rich creamy milk, originated here.

guerrilla (Spanish 'little war') irregular soldier fighting in a small unofficial unit, typically against an established or occupying power, and engaging in sabotage, ambush, and the like, rather than pitched battles against an opposing army. Guerrilla tactics have been used both by resistance armies in wartime (for example, the Vietnam War) and in peacetime by national liberation groups and militant political extremists (for example the *PLO; Tamil Tigers).

Guevara 'Che' Ernesto 1928–1967. Latin American revolutionary. He was born in Argentina and trained there as a doctor, but left his homeland 1953 because of his opposition to the right-wing president Perón. In effecting the Cuban revolution of 1959, he was second only to Castro and Castro's brother Raúl. In 1965 he went to the Congo to fight against white mercenaries, and then to Bolivia, where he was killed in an unsuccessful attempt to lead a peasant rising. He was an orthodox Marxist, and renowned for his guerrilla techniques.

Guiana NE part of South America that includes *French Guiana, *Guyana, and *Surinam.

guild or *gild* medieval association, particularly of artisans or merchants, formed for mutual aid and protection and the pursuit of a common purpose, religious or economic. Guilds became politically powerful in Europe but after the 16th century their position was undermined by the growth of capitalism.

Guilin or *Kweilin* principal tourist city of S China, on the Li River, Guangxi province; population (1984 est) 446,900. The dramatic limestone mountains are a tourist attraction.

Guildford Four four Irish victims of miscarriage of justice who spent 18 years in prison, convicted of terrorist bombings of public houses in Guildford and Woolwich, England 1974. They were released 1992 after an investigation concluded that the arresting Surrey police had given misleading evidence and the Lord Chief Justice ruled the Four's convictions were unsafe and unsatisfactory. They were Patrick Armstrong, Gerard Conlon, Paul Hill, and Carole Richardson.

guillemot diving seabird of the auk family that breeds in large numbers on rocky N Atlantic and Pacific coasts. The common guillemot *Uria aalge* has a sharp bill and short tail, and sooty-brown and white plumage.

guillotine beheading device consisting of a metal blade that descends between two posts. It was common in the Middle Ages and was introduced 1791 in an improved design by physician Joseph Ignace Guillotin (1738–1814) in France. It was subsequently used for executions during the French Revolution. It is still in use in some countries.

guillotine in politics, a device used by UK governments in which the time allowed for debating a bill in the House of Commons is restricted so as to ensure its speedy passage to becoming law. It is also used in France.

Guinea Republic of (*République de Guinée*)
area 245,857 sq km/94,901 sq mi
capital Conakry
towns Labé, Nzérékoré, Kankan
physical flat coastal plain with mountainous

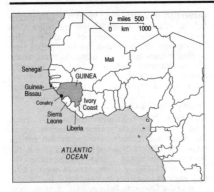

interior; sources of rivers Niger, Gambia, and Senegal; forest in SE

head of state and government Lansana Conté from 1984

political system military republic

exports coffee, rice, palm kernels, alumina, bauxite, diamonds

currency syli or franc

population (1993) 7,700,000 (chief peoples are Fulani, Malinke, Susu); growth rate 2.3% p.a.

languages French (official), African languages

religions Muslim 85%, Christian 10%, local 5%

GNP $450 per head (1991)

chronology

1958 Full independence achieved from France; Sékou Touré elected president.

1977 Strong opposition to Touré's rigid Marxist policies forced him to accept return to mixed economy.

1980 Touré returned unopposed for fourth seven-year term.

1984 Touré died. Bloodless coup established a military committee for national recovery, led by Col Lansana Conté.

1985 Attempted coup against Conté while he was out of the country was foiled by loyal troops.

1990 Sent troops to join the multinational force that attempted to stabilize Liberia.

1991 Antigovernment general strike by National Confederation of Guinea Workers (CNTG).

1993 Conté narrowly re-elected.

Guinea-Bissau Republic of (*República da Guiné-Bissau*)

area 36,125 sq km/13,944 sq mi

capital Bissau

towns Mansôa, São Domingos

physical flat coastal plain rising to savanna in E

head of state João Bernardo Vieira from 1980

head of government Carlos Correia from 1991

political system emergent democracy

exports rice, coconuts, peanuts, fish, timber

currency peso

population (1993 est) 1,050,000 (main ethnic groups are the Balanti, Fulani, Malinké, Mandjako, and Pepel); growth rate 2.4% p.a.

languages Portuguese (official), Crioulo (Cape Verdean dialect of Portuguese), African languages

religions animism 54%, Muslim 38%, Christian 8%

GNP $190 per head (1991)

chronology

1956 PAIGC formed to secure independence from Portugal.

1973 Two-thirds of the country declared independent, with Luiz Cabral as president of a state council.

1974 Independence achieved from Portugal.

1980 Cape Verde decided not to join a unified state. Cabral deposed, and João Vieira became chair of a council of revolution.

1981 PAIGC confirmed as the only legal party, with Vieira as its secretary general.

1982 Normal relations with Cape Verde restored.

1984 New constitution adopted, making Vieira head of government as well as head of state.

1989 Vieira re-elected.

1991 Other parties legalized.

1992 Multiparty electoral commission established.

1994 PAIGC and Vieira re-elected in first multiparty elections.

Guinea Coast or **Gulf of Guinea** coast of W Africa between Cape Palmas, Liberia, and Cape Lopez, Gabon. The coastline features the Bight of Benin and the Bight of Bonny, and the rivers Volta, Niger, and Ogowé reach the sea here.

guinea fowl chickenlike African bird of the family Numididae. The group includes the helmet guinea fowl *Numida meleagris*, which has a horny growth on the head, white-spotted feathers, and fleshy cheek wattles. It is the ancestor of the domestic guinea fowl.

guinea pig species of *cavy, a type of rodent.

Guinea worm parasitic, microscopic nematode worm *Dracunculus medinensis* found in India and Africa, affecting some 650,000 people in Nigeria alone. It enters the body via drinking water and migrates to break out through the skin.

Guinevere Welsh *Gwenhwyfar* in British legend, the wife of King *Arthur. Her adulterous love affair with the knight Lancelot of the Lake led ultimately to Arthur's death.

Guinness Alec 1914– . English actor of stage and screen. His films include *Kind Hearts and Coronets* 1949 (in which he played eight parts), *The Bridge on the River Kwai* 1957 (Academy Award), and *Star Wars* 1977.

Guinness affair in British law, a case of financial fraud during the takeover of Distillers by the brewing company Guinness 1986. Those accused of acting illegally to sustain Guinness share prices included Ernest Saunders, the former chief executive. The trial, lasting from Feb to Aug 1990, was widely seen as the first major test of the government's legislation aimed at increasing control of financial dealings on London's Stock Exchange.

Guise Francis, 2nd Duke of Guise 1519–1563. French soldier and politician. He led the French victory over Germany at Metz 1552 and captured Calais from the English 1558. Along with his brother **Charles** (1527–1574), he was powerful in the government of France during the reign of Francis II. He was assassinated attempting to crush the *Huguenots.

guitar six-stringed, flat-bodied musical instrument, plucked or strummed with the fingers. The **Hawaiian guitar**, laid across the lap, uses a metal bar to produce a distinctive gliding tone; the solid-bodied **electric guitar**, developed in the 1950s, mixes and amplifies vibrations from microphone contacts at different points to produce a range of tone qualities.

Guiyang or *Kweiyang* capital and industrial city of Guizhou province, S China; industries include metals and machinery; population (1989) 1,490,000.

Guizhou or *Kweichow* province of S China
area 174,000 sq km/67,164 sq mi
capital Guiyang
products rice, maize, nonferrous minerals
population (1990) 32,392,000.

Gujarat or *Gujerat* state of W India
area 196,000 sq km/75,656 sq mi
capital Ahmedabad
products cotton, petrochemicals, oil, gas, rice, textiles
language Gujarati (Gujerati), Hindi
population (1991) 41,174,000.

Gujarati inhabitant of Gujarat on the NW coast of India. The Gujaratis number approximately 30 million and speak their own Indo-European language, Gujarati, which has a long literary tradition. They are predominantly Hindu (90%), with Muslim (8%) and Jain (2%) minorities.

Gujarati language member of the Indo-Iranian branch of the Indo-European language family, spoken in and around the state of Gujarat in W India. It is written in its own script, a variant of the Devanagari script used for Sanskrit and Hindi.

Gujranwala city in Punjab province, Pakistan; population (1981) 597,000. It is a centre of grain trading. The city is a former Sikh capital and the birthplace of Sikh leader Ranjit Singh (1780–1839).

Gujrat city in Punjab province, E Pakistan, N of Lahore; products include cotton, pottery, brassware, and furniture; population (1981) 154,000. It occupies the site of a fort built 1580 by the Moghul ruler Akbar. Gujrat was the scene of the final battle between the British and the Sikhs in the Sikh Wars 1845–49.

gulag Russian term for the system of prisons and labour camps used to silence dissidents and opponents of the Soviet regime.

Gulf States oil-rich countries sharing the coastline of the *Persian Gulf (Bahrain, Iran, Iraq, Kuwait, Oman, Qatar, Saudi Arabia, and the United Arab Emirates). In the USA, the term refers to those states bordering the Gulf of Mexico (Alabama, Florida, Louisiana, Mississippi, and Texas).

Gulf Stream warm ocean *current that flows north from the warm waters of Gulf of Mexico. Part of the current is diverted east across the Atlantic, where it is known as the *North Atlantic Drift*, and warms what would otherwise be a colder climate in the British Isles and NW Europe.

Gulf War war 16 Jan–28 Feb 1991 between Iraq and a coalition of 28 nations led by the USA. (It is also another name for the *Iran–Iraq War).
The invasion and annexation of Kuwait by Iraq on 2 Aug 1990 provoked a build-up of troops in Saudi Arabia. An air offensive lasting six weeks, in which 'smart' weapons came of age, destroyed about one-third of Iraqi equipment and inflicted massive casualties. A 100-hour ground war followed, which effectively destroyed the remnants of the 500,000-strong Iraqi army in or near Kuwait.

gull seabird of the family Laridae, especially the genus *Larus*. Gulls are usually 25–75 cm/10–30 in long, white with grey or black on the back and wings, and have large beaks.

Gullit Ruud 1962– . Dutch international footballer who was captain when the Netherlands captured the European Championship 1988. After playing in the Netherlands with Haarlem, Feyenoord, and PSV Eindhoven, he moved to AC Milan 1987 for a transfer fee of £5.5 million.

gum in botany, complex polysaccharides (carbohydrates) formed by many plants and trees, particularly by those from dry regions. They form four main groups: plant exudates (gum arabic); marine plant extracts (agar); seed extracts; and fruit and vegetable extracts. Some are made synthetically.

gum arabic substance obtained from certain species of *acacia, with uses in medicine, confectionery, and adhesive manufacture.

Gummer John Selwyn 1939– . British Conservative politician, secretary of state for agriculture from 1989. He was minister of state for employment 1983–84, paymaster general 1984–85, minister for agriculture 1985–89, and chair of the party 1983–85.

gumtree common name for the *eucalyptus tree.

gun any kind of firearm or any instrument consisting of a metal tube from which a projectile is discharged; see also *artillery, *machine gun, *pistol, and *small arms.

gun metal type of *bronze, an alloy high in copper (88%), also containing tin and zinc, so-called because it was once used to cast cannons. It is tough, hard-wearing, and resists corrosion.

Gunnell Sally 1966– . British hurdler. In 1994 she became the first woman athlete to complete the athletics Grand Slam, winning gold medals over 400 m hurdles at the 1992 Olympics, 1993 World Championships (breaking the world record), 1990 and 1994 Commonwealth Games, and 1994 European Championships.

gunpowder or *black powder* the oldest known *explosive, a mixture of 75% potassium nitrate (saltpetre), 15% charcoal, and 10% sulphur. Sulphur ignites at a low temperature, charcoal burns readily, and the potassium nitrate provides oxygen for the explosion. Although progressively replaced since the late 19th century by high explosives, gunpowder is still widely used for quarry blasting, fuses, and fireworks.

Gunpowder Plot in British history, the Catholic conspiracy to blow up James I and his parliament on 5 Nov 1605. It was discovered through an anonymous letter. Guy *Fawkes was found in the cellar beneath the Palace of Westminster, ready to fire a store of explosives. Several of the conspirators were killed, and Fawkes and seven others were executed.

Guomindang Chinese National People's Party, founded 1894 by *Sun Yat-sen, which overthrew the Manchu Empire 1912. From 1927 the right wing, led by *Chiang Kai-shek, was in conflict with the left, led by Mao Zedong until the Communist victory 1949 (except for the period of the Japanese invasion 1937–45). It survives as the dominant political party of Taiwan, where it is still spelled **Kuomintang**.

gurdwara Sikh place of worship and meeting. As well as a room housing the *Guru Granth Sahib*, the holy book, the gurdwara contains a kitchen and eating area for the *langar*, or communal meal.

gurnard coastal fish of the *Trigla* genus in the family Trigilidae, which creeps along the sea bottom by means of three finger-like appendages detached from the pectoral fins. Gurnards are both tropic and temperate zone fish.

guru Hindi *gurū* Hindu or Sikh leader, or religious teacher.

Gush Emunim Israeli fundamentalist group, founded 1973, which claims divine right to settlement of the West Bank, Gaza Strip, and Golan Heights as part of Israel. The claim is sometimes extended to the Euphrates.

Gustavus Adolphus (Gustavus II) 1594–1632. King of Sweden from 1611, when he succeeded his father Charles IX. He waged successful wars with Denmark, Russia, and Poland, and in the *Thirty Years' War became a champion of the Protestant cause. Landing in Germany 1630, he defeated the German general Wallenstein at Lützen, SW of Leipzig 6 Nov 1632, but was killed in the battle. He was known as the 'Lion of the North'.

Gustavus Vasa (Gustavus) 1496–1560. King of Sweden from 1523, when he was elected after leading the Swedish revolt against Danish rule. He united and pacified the country and established Lutheranism as the state religion.

gut or **alimentary canal** in the *digestive system, the part of an animal responsible for processing food and preparing it for entry into the blood.

Gutenberg Johann *c.* 1400–1468. German printer, the inventor of printing from movable metal type, based on the Chinese wood-block-type method (although Laurens Janszoon *Coster has a rival claim).

Guthrie Woody (Woodrow Wilson) 1912–1967. US folk singer and songwriter. His left-wing protest songs, 'dustbowl ballads', and 'talking blues' influenced, among others, Bob Dylan; they include 'Deportees', 'Hard Travelin'', and 'This Land Is Your Land'.

guttation secretion of water on to the surface of leaves through specialized pores, or *hydathodes. The process occurs most frequently during conditions of high humidity when the rate of transpiration is low. Drops of water found on grass in early morning are often the result of guttation, rather than dew. Sometimes the water contains minerals in solution, such as calcium, which leaves a white crust on the leaf surface as it dries.

Guyana Cooperative Republic of
area 214,969 sq km/82,978 sq mi
capital (and port) Georgetown
towns New Amsterdam, Mabaruma
physical coastal plain rises into rolling highlands with savanna in S; mostly tropical rainforest
head of state Cheddi Jagan from 1992
head of government Sam Hinds from 1992

political system democratic republic
exports sugar, rice, rum, timber, diamonds, bauxite, shrimps, molasses
currency Guyanese dollar
population (1993) 800,000 (51% descendants of workers introduced from India to work the sugar plantations after the abolition of slavery, 30% black, 5% Amerindian); growth rate 2% p.a.
languages English (official), Hindi, Amerindian
religions Christian 57%, Hindu 33%, Sunni Muslim 9%
GNP $290 per head (1991)
chronology
1831 Became British colony under name of British Guiana.
1953 Assembly elections won by left-wing PPP; Britain suspended constitution and installed interim administration, fearing communist takeover.
1961 Internal self-government granted; Cheddi Jagan became prime minister.
1966 Independence achieved from Britain.
1970 Guyana became a republic within the Commonwealth.
1981 Forbes Burnham became first executive president under new constitution.
1985 Burnham died; succeeded by Desmond Hoyte.
1992 PPP had decisive victory in assembly elections; Cheddi Jagan became president.

Guzmán Blanco Antonio 1829–1899. Venezuelan dictator and military leader (*caudillo*), who seized power 1870 and remained absolute ruler until 1889. He modernized Caracas to become the political capital; committed resources to education, communications, and agriculture; and encouraged foreign trade.

Gwent county in S Wales
area 1,380 sq km/533 sq mi
towns Cwmbran (administrative headquarters), Abergavenny, Newport, Tredegar
products salmon and trout from the Wye and Usk rivers; iron and steel at Llanwern
population (1991) 432,300
languages 2.5% Welsh, English

Gwyn Nell (Eleanor) 1651–1687. English comedy actress from 1665, formerly an orange-seller at Drury Lane Theatre, London. The poet Dryden wrote parts for her, and from 1669 she was the mistress of Charles II.

Gwynedd county in NW Wales
area 3,870 sq km/1,494 sq mi
towns Caernarvon (administrative head-quarters), Bangor
products cattle, sheep, gold (at Dolgellau), textiles, electronics, slate
population (1991) 238,600
languages 61% Welsh, English

gymnastics physical exercises, originally for health and training (so-called from the way in which men of ancient Greece trained: *gymnos* 'naked'). The *gymnasia* were schools for training competitors for public games. **Men's gymnastics** includes high bar, parallel bars, horse vault, rings, pommel horse, and floor exercises. **Women's gymnastics** includes asymmetrical bars, side horse vault, balance beam, and floor exercises. Also popular are **sports acrobatics**, performed by gymnasts in pairs, trios, or fours to music, where the emphasis is on dance, balance, and timing, and **rhythmic gymnastics**, choreographed to music and performed by individuals or six-girl teams, with small hand apparatus such as a ribbon, ball, or hoop.

gymnosperm (Greek 'naked seed') in botany, any plant whose seeds are exposed, as opposed to the structurally more advanced *angiosperms, where they are inside an ovary.

The group includes conifers and related plants such as cycads and ginkgos, whose seeds develop in *cones. Fossil gymnosperms have been found in rocks about 350 million years old.

gynaecology in medicine, a specialist branch concerned with disorders of the female reproductive system.

gynoecium or **gynaecium** collective term for the female reproductive organs of a flower, consisting of one or more *carpels, either free or fused together.

gypsum common *mineral, composed of hydrous calcium sulphate, $CaSO_4.2H_2O$. It ranks 2 on the Mohs' scale of hardness. Gypsum is used for making casts and moulds, and for blackboard chalk.

Gypsy English name for a member of the *Romany people.

gyroscope mechanical instrument, used as a stabilizing device and consisting, in its simplest form, of a heavy wheel mounted on an axis fixed in a ring that can be rotated about another axis, which is also fixed in a ring capable of rotation about a third axis. Applications of the gyroscope principle include the gyrocompass, the gyropilot for automatic steering, and gyro-directed torpedoes.

ha symbol for *hectare*.

Haakon seven kings of Norway, including:

Haakon IV 1204–1263. King of Norway from 1217, the son of Haakon III. Under his rule, Norway flourished both militarily and culturally; he took control of the Faroe Islands, Greenland 1261, and Iceland 1262–64. His court was famed throughout N Europe.

Haakon VII 1872–1957. King of Norway from 1905. Born Prince Charles, the second son of Frederick VIII of Denmark, he was elected king of Norway on separation from Sweden, and in 1906 he took the name Haakon. In World War II he carried on the resistance from Britain during the Nazi occupation of his country. He returned 1945.

Haarlem industrial city and capital of North Holland, the Netherlands, 20 km/12 mi W of Amsterdam; population (1991) 149,500. At Velsea to the north a road-rail tunnel runs under the North Sea Canal, linking North and South Holland. Industries include chemicals, pharmaceuticals, textiles, and printing. Haarlem is renowned for flowering bulbs and has a 15th–16th-century cathedral and a Frans Hals museum.

habanera or *havanaise* slow dance in two–four time, originating in Havana, Cuba, which was introduced into Spain during the 19th century. There is a celebrated example of this dance in Bizet's opera *Carmen*.

habeas corpus (Latin 'you may have the body') in law, a writ directed to someone who has custody of a person, ordering him or her to bring the person before the court issuing the writ and to justify why the person is detained in custody.

Haber Fritz 1868–1934. German chemist whose conversion of atmospheric nitrogen to ammonia opened the way for the synthetic fertilizer industry. His study of the combustion of hydrocarbons led to the commercial 'cracking' or fractional distillation of natural oil (petroleum) into its components (for example, diesel, petrol, and paraffin). In electrochemistry, he was the first to demonstrate that oxidation and reduction take place at the electrodes; from this he developed a general electrochemical theory.

Haber process or *Haber–Bosch process* industrial process by which ammonia is manufactured by direct combination of its elements, nitrogen and hydrogen. The reaction is carried out at 400–500°C/752–932°F and at 200 atmospheres pressure. The two gases, in the proportions of 1:3 by volume, are passed over a *catalyst of finely divided iron. Around 10% of the reactants combine, and the unused gases are recycled. The ammonia is separated either by being dissolved in water or by being cooled to liquid form.

habitat localized *environment in which an organism lives, and which provides for all (or almost all) of its needs. The diversity of habitats found within the Earth's ecosystem is enormous, and they are changing all the time. Many can be considered inorganic or physical, for example the Arctic ice cap, a cave, or a cliff face. Others are more complex, for instance a woodland or a forest floor. Some habitats are so precise that they are called *microhabitats*, such as the area under a stone where a particular type of insect lives. Most habitats provide a home for many species.

Habsburg or *Hapsburg* European royal family, former imperial house of Austria–Hungary. A Hapsburg, Rudolf I, became king of Germany 1273 and began the family's control of Austria and Styria. They acquired a series of lands and titles, including that of Holy Roman emperor which they held 1273–91, 1298–1308, 1438–1740, and 1745–1806. The Hapsburgs reached the zenith of their power under the emperor Charles V (1519–1556) who divided his lands, creating an Austrian Habsburg line (which ruled until 1918) and a Spanish line (which ruled to 1700).

hacking unauthorized access to a computer, either for fun or for malicious or fraudulent purposes. Hackers generally use microcomputers and telephone lines to obtain access. In computing, the term is used in a wider sense to mean using software for enjoyment or self-education, not necessarily involving unauthorized access. See also computer *virus.

Hackman Gene 1931– . US actor. He became a star as 'Popeye' Doyle in *The French Connection* 1971 and continued to play major combative roles in such films as *The Conversation* 1974, *The French Connection II* 1975, and *Mississippi Burning* 1988.

haddock marine fish *Melanogrammus aeglefinus* of the cod family found off the N Atlantic coasts. It is brown with silvery underparts and black markings above the pectoral fins. It can grow to a length of 1 m/3 ft. Haddock are important food fish; about 45 million kg/100 million lb are taken annually off the New England fishing banks alone.

Hades in Greek mythology, the underworld where spirits went after death, usually depicted as a cavern or pit underneath the Earth, the entrance of which was guarded by the three-headed dog Cerberus. It was presided over by the god Hades or Pluto (Roman Dis). Hades was the brother of Zeus and married *Persephone, daughter of Demeter and Zeus.

Hadith collection of the teachings of *Muhammad and stories about his life, regarded by Muslims as a guide to living second only to the *Koran.

Hadlee Richard John 1951– . New Zealand cricketer. In 1987 he surpassed Ian Botham's world record of 373 wickets in test cricket and went on to set the record at 431 wickets. He played for Canterbury and Nottinghamshire in

England, and retired from international cricket 1990.

Hadrian AD 76–138. Roman emperor from 117. Born in Spain, he was adopted by his relative, the emperor Trajan, whom he succeeded. He abandoned Trajan's conquests in Mesopotamia and adopted a defensive policy, which included the building of Hadrian's Wall in Britain.

Hadrian's Wall Roman fortification built AD 122–126 to mark England's northern boundary and abandoned about 383; its ruins run 185 km/115 mi from Wallsend on the river Tyne to Maryport, W Cumbria. In some parts, the wall was covered with a glistening, white coat of mortar. The fort at South Shields, Arbeia, built to defend the eastern end, is being reconstructed.

hadron in physics, a subatomic particle that experiences the strong nuclear force. Each is made up of two or three indivisible particles called quarks. The hadrons are grouped into the *baryons (protons, neutrons, and hyperons) and the *mesons (particles with masses between those of electrons and protons). Since the 1960s, particle physicists' main interest has been the elucidation of hadron structure.

haematology branch of medicine concerned with disorders of the blood.

haemoglobin protein used by all vertebrates and some invertebrates for oxygen transport because the two substances combine reversibly. In vertebrates it occurs in red blood cells (erythrocytes), giving them their colour.

haemolymph circulatory fluid of those molluscs and insects that have an 'open' circulatory system. Haemolymph contains water, amino acids, sugars, salts, and white cells like those of blood. Circulated by a pulsating heart, its main functions are to transport digestive and excretory products around the body. In molluscs, it also transports oxygen and carbon dioxide.

haemophilia any of several inherited diseases in which normal blood clotting is impaired. The sufferer experiences prolonged bleeding from the slightest wound, as well as painful internal bleeding without apparent cause.

haemorrhage loss of blood from the circulatory system. It is 'manifest' when the blood can be seen, as when it flows from a wound, and 'occult' when the bleeding is internal, as from an ulcer or internal injury.

haemorrhoids distended blood vessels (*varicose veins) in the area of the anus, popularly called *piles*.

haemostasis natural or surgical stoppage of bleeding. In the natural mechanism, the damaged vessel contracts, restricting the flow, and blood *platelets plug the opening, releasing chemicals essential to clotting.

Hāfiz Shams al-Din Muhammad c. 1326–1390. Persian lyric poet who was born in Shiraz and taught in a Dervish college there. His *Diwan*, a collection of short odes, extols the pleasures of life and satirizes his fellow Dervishes.

hafnium (Latin *Hafnia* 'Copenhagen') silvery, metallic element, symbol Hf, atomic number 72, relative atomic mass 178.49. It occurs in nature in ores of zirconium, the properties of which it resembles. Hafnium absorbs neutrons better than most metals, so it is used in the control rods of nuclear reactors; it is also used for light-bulb filaments.

Haganah Zionist military organization in Palestine. It originated under the Turkish rule of the Ottoman Empire before World War I to protect Jewish settlements, and many of its members served in the British forces in both world wars. After World War II it condemned guerrilla activity, opposing the British authorities only passively. It formed the basis of the Israeli army after Israel was established 1948.

Haggadah in Judaism, the part of the Talmudic literature not concerned with religious law (the *Halakah*), but devoted to folklore and legends of heroes.

Haggard H(enry) Rider 1856–1925. English novelist. He used his experience in the South African colonial service in his romantic adventure tales, including *King Solomon's Mines* 1885 and *She* 1887.

haggis Scottish dish made from a sheep's or calf's heart, liver, and lungs, minced with onion, oatmeal, suet, spices, and salt, mixed with stock, and traditionally boiled in the animal's stomach for several hours.

Hagia Sophia (Greek 'holy wisdom') Byzantine building in Istanbul, Turkey, built 532–37 as an Eastern Orthodox cathedral, replacing earlier churches. From 1204 to 1261 it was a Catholic cathedral; 1453–1934 an Islamic mosque; and in 1934 it became a museum.

Hague, The (Dutch *'s-Gravenhage* or *Den Haag*) capital of South Holland and seat of the Netherlands government, linked by canal with Rotterdam and Amsterdam; population (1991) 444,200. It is also the seat of the United Nations International Court of Justice.

ha-ha in landscape gardening, a sunken boundary wall permitting an unobstructed view beyond a garden; a device much used by Capability *Brown.

Hahn Otto 1879–1968. West German physical chemist who discovered nuclear fission (see under *nuclear energy). In 1938 with Fritz Strassmann (1902–1980), he discovered that uranium nuclei split when bombarded with neutrons, which led to the development of the atom bomb. He was awarded the Nobel Prize for Chemistry 1944.

hahnium name proposed by US scientists for the element also known as *unnilpentium (atomic number 105), in honour of German nuclear physicist Otto Hahn. The symbol is Ha.

Haifa port in NE Israel; population (1988) 222,600. Industries include oil refining and chemicals.

Haig Alexander (Meigs) 1924– . US general and Republican politician. He became President Nixon's White House Chief of Staff at the height of the *Watergate scandal, was NATO commander 1974–79, and secretary of state to President Reagan 1981–82.

Haig Douglas, 1st Earl Haig 1861–1928. British army officer, commander in chief in World War I. His Somme offensive in France in the summer of 1916 made considerable advances only at enormous cost to human life, and his Passchendaele offensive in Belgium from July to Nov 1917 achieved little at a similar loss. He was created field marshal 1917 and, after retiring, became first president of the British Legion 1921.

haiku seventeen-syllable Japanese verse form, usually divided into three lines of five, seven, and five syllables. *Bashō popularized the form in the 17th century. It evolved from the 31-syllable *tanka* form dominant from the 8th century.

hail precipitation in the form of pellets of ice (hail-stones). It is caused by the circulation of moisture in strong convection currents, usually within cumulonimbus *clouds.

Haile Selassie Ras (Prince) Tafari ('the Lion of Judah') 1892–1975. Emperor of Ethiopia 1930–74. He pleaded unsuccessfully to the League of Nations against Italian conquest of his country 1935–36, and lived in the UK until his restoration 1941. He was deposed by a military coup 1974 and died in captivity the following year. Followers of the Rastafarian religion (see *Rastafarianism) believe that he was the Messiah, the incarnation of God (Jah).

Hailsham Quintin Hogg, Baron Hailsham of St Marylebone 1907– . British lawyer and Conservative politician. The 2nd Viscount Hailsham, he renounced the title in 1963 to re-enter the House of Commons, and was then able to contest the Conservative Party leadership elections, but took a life peerage 1970 on his appointment as Lord Chancellor 1970–74. He was Lord Chancellor again 1979–87.

Hainan island in the South China Sea; area 34,000 sq km/13,124 sq mi; population (1990) 6,557,000. The capital is Haikou. In 1987 Hainan was designated a Special Economic Zone; in 1988 it was separated from Guangdong and made a new province. It is China's second-largest island.

Haiphong industrial port in N Vietnam; population (1989) 456,000. Among its industries are shipbuilding and the making of cement, plastics, phosphates, and textiles.

hair fine filament growing from mammalian skin. Each hair grows from a pit-shaped follicle embedded in the second layer of the skin, the dermis. It consists of dead cells impregnated with the protein keratin.

hairstreak any of a group of butterflies, belonging to the family Lycaenidae, to which blues and coppers also belong. Hairstreaks live in both temperate and tropical regions. Most of them are brownish or greyishblue with hairlike tips at the end of their hind wings.

Haiti Republic of (*République d'Haïti*)
area 27,750 sq km/10,712 sq mi
capital Port-au-Prince
towns Cap-Haïtien, Gonaïves, Les Cayes
physical mainly mountainous and tropical; occupies W third of Hispaniola Island in Caribbean Sea; seriously deforested
head of state Jean-Bertrand Aristide from 1994
head of government Robert Malval from 1993
political system transitional
exports coffee, sugar, sisal, cotton, cocoa, bauxite
currency gourde
population (1993 est) 6,600,000; growth rate 1.7% p.a.; one of highest population densities in the world; about 1.5 million Haitians live outside Haiti (in USA and Canada); about 400,000 live

in virtual slavery in the Dominican Republic, where they went or were sent to cut sugar cane
languages French (official, spoken by literate 10% minority), Creole (spoken by 90% black majority)
religion Christian 95% of which 80% Roman Catholic, voodoo 4%
GNP $370 per head (1991)
chronology
1804 Independence achieved from France.
1915 Haiti invaded by USA; remained under US control until 1934.
1957 Dr François Duvalier (Papa Doc) elected president.
1971 Duvalier died, succeeded by his son, Jean-Claude (Baby Doc); thousands murdered during Duvalier era.
1988 Feb: Leslie Manigat became president. Namphy staged a military coup in June, but another coup in Sept led by Brig-Gen Prosper Avril replaced him with a civilian government under military control.
1991 Jean-Bertrand Aristide elected president but later overthrown in military coup led by Brig-Gen Raoul Cedras. Efforts to reinstate Aristide failed. Joseph Nerette became interim head of state. Sanctions imposed by Organization of American States (OAS) and USA.
1992 Economic sanctions eased by the USA but increased by the OAS. Marc Bazin appointed premier.
1993 June: Bazin resigned; United Nations (UN) embargo imposed. July: Aristide's return agreed under UN-brokered accord. Aug: international sanctions lifted; Robert Malval nominated premier. Oct: Aristide's return blocked by military; UN embargo reimposed. Malval resigned but remained as caretaker prime minister.
1994 Cedras appointed Emile Jonassaint, a supporter of the military regime, to replace Nerette as president. Sept: threat of US invasion led to Cedras regime recognizing Aristide as president, under agreement brokered by former US president Jimmy Carter. Oct: Cedras relinquished power and withdrew to Panama; Aristide returned.

Haitink Bernard 1929– . Dutch conductor. He has been associated with the Concertgebouw Orchestra, Amsterdam, from 1958, and the London Philharmonic Orchestra from 1967; musical director at Glyndebourne 1977–87 and at the Royal Opera House, Covent Garden, London, from 1987. He is a noted interpreter of Mahler and Shostakovitch.

hajj pilgrimage to Mecca that should be undertaken by every Muslim at least once in a lifetime, unless he or she is prevented by financial or health difficulties. A Muslim who has been on hajj may take the additional name Hajji. Many of the pilgrims on hajj also visit Medina, where the prophet Muhammad is buried.

hake any of various marine fishes of the cod family, found in N European, African, and American waters. They have silvery, elongated bodies and attain a length of 1 m/3 ft. They have two dorsal fins and one long anal fin. The silver hake *Merluccius bilinearis* is an important food fish.

Halab Arabic name of *Aleppo, a city in Syria.

halal conforming to the rules laid down by Islam. The term can be applied to all aspects of life, but usually refers to food permissible under Muslim dietary laws, including meat from animals that have been slaughtered in the correct ritual fashion.

Hale George Ellery 1868–1938. US astronomer who made pioneer studies of the Sun and founded three major observatories. In 1889 he invented the spectroheliograph, a device for photographing the Sun at particular wavelengths. In 1917 he established on Mount Wilson, California, a 2.5-m/100-in reflector, the world's largest telescope until superseded 1948 by the 5-m/200-in reflector on Mount Palomar, which Hale had planned just before he died.

Haley Bill 1927–1981. US pioneer of rock and roll who was originally a western-swing musician. His songs 'Rock Around the Clock' 1954 (recorded with his group the Comets and featured in the 1955 film *Blackboard Jungle*) and 'Shake, Rattle and Roll' 1955 became anthems of the early rock-and-roll era.

half-life in physics, the time taken for half the nuclei in a sample of a radioactive isotope to disintegrate. It may vary from millionths of a second to billions of years, even among different isotopes of the same element.

halftone process technique used in printing to reproduce the full range of tones in a photograph or other illustration. The intensity of the printed colour is varied from full strength to the lightest shades, even if one colour of ink is used. The picture to be reproduced is photographed through a screen ruled with a rectangular mesh of fine lines, which breaks up the tones of the original into areas of dots that vary in frequency according to the intensity of the tone. In the darker areas the dots run together; in the lighter areas they have more space between them.

halibut any of several large flatfishes of the genus *Hippoglossus*, in the family Pleuronectidae, found in the Atlantic and Pacific oceans. The largest of the flatfishes, they may grow to 2 m/6 ft and weigh 90–135 kg/200–300 lb. They are very dark mottled brown or green above and pure white beneath. The Atlantic halibut *H. hippoglossus* is caught offshore at depths from 180 m/600 ft to 730 m/2,400 ft.

Halicarnassus ancient city in Asia Minor (now Bodrum in Turkey), where the tomb of Mausolus, built about 350 BC by widowed Queen Artemisia, was one of the Seven Wonders of the World. The Greek historian Herodotus was born there.

halide any compound produced by the combination of a *halogen, such as chlorine or iodine, with a less electronegative element (see *electronegativity). Halides may be formed by ionic or *covalent bonds.

Halifax capital of Nova Scotia, E Canada's main port; population (1986) 296,000. Its industries include oil refining and food processing. There are six military bases in Halifax and it is a major centre of oceanography. It was founded by British settlers 1749.

halite mineral sodium chloride, NaCl, or common *salt. When pure it is colourless and transparent, but it is often pink, red, or yellow. It is soft and has a low density.

Hall (Marguerite) Radclyffe 1883–1943. English novelist. *The Well of Loneliness* 1928 brought her notoriety because of its lesbian theme. Its review in the *Sunday Express* newspaper stated: 'I had rather give a healthy boy or girl a phial of prussic acid than this novel'. Her other works include the novel *Adam's Bread* 1926 and four volumes of poetry.

Hall Peter (Reginald Frederick) 1930– . English theatre, opera, and film director. He was director of the Royal Shakespeare Theatre in Stratford-on-Avon 1960–68 and developed the Royal Shakespeare Company 1968–73 until appointed director of the National Theatre 1973–88, succeeding Laurence Olivier. He founded the Peter Hall Company 1988.

Haller Albrecht von 1708–1777. Swiss physician and scientist, founder of *neurology. He studied the muscles and nerves, and concluded that nerves provide the stimulus that triggers muscle contraction. He also showed that it is the nerves, not muscle or skin, that receive sensation.

Halley Edmond 1656–1742. English scientist. In 1682 he observed the comet named after him, predicting that it would return 1759.

Halley's comet comet that orbits the Sun about every 76 years, named after Edmond Halley who calculated its orbit. It is the brightest and most conspicuous of the periodic comets. Recorded sightings go back over 2,000 years. It travels around the Sun in the opposite direction to the planets. Its orbit is inclined at almost 20° to the main plane of the Solar System and ranges between the orbits of Venus and Neptune. It will next reappear 2061.

hallmark official mark stamped on British gold, silver, and (from 1913) platinum, instituted 1327 (royal charter of London Goldsmiths) in order to prevent fraud. After 1363, personal marks of identification were added. Now tests of metal content are carried out at authorized assay offices in London, Birmingham, Sheffield, and Edinburgh; each assay office has its distinguishing mark, to which is added a maker's mark, date letter, and mark guaranteeing standard.

Hallowe'en evening of 31 Oct, immediately preceding the Christian feast of Hallowmas or All Saints' Day. Customs associated with Hallowe'en in the USA and the UK include children wearing masks or costumes, and 'trick or treating' – going from house to house collecting sweets, fruit, or money.

Hallstatt archaeological site in Upper Austria, SW of Salzburg. The salt workings date from prehistoric times. In 1846 over 3,000 graves were discovered belonging to a 9th–5th century BC Celtic civilization transitional between the Bronze and Iron ages.

hallucinogen any substance that acts on the *central nervous system to produce changes in perception and mood and often hallucinations. Hallucinogens include *LSD, *peyote, and *mescaline. Their effects are unpredictable and they are illegal in most countries.

halogen any of a group of five nonmetallic elements with similar chemical bonding properties: fluorine, chlorine, bromine, iodine, and astatine. They form a linked group in the *periodic table of the elements, descending from fluorine, the most reactive, to astatine, the least reactive. They combine directly with most metals to form salts, such as common salt (NaCl). Each halogen has seven electrons in its valence shell, which accounts for the chemical similarities displayed by the group.

halon organic chemical compound containing one or two carbon atoms, together with *bromine and other *halogens. The most commonly used are halon 1211 (bromochlorodifluoromethane) and halon 1301 (bromotrifluoromethane). The halons are gases and are widely used in fire extinguishers. As destroyers of the *ozone layer, they are up to ten times more effective than *chlorofluorocarbons (CFCs), to which they are chemically related.

halophyte plant adapted to live where there is a high concentration of salt in the soil, for example, in salt marshes and mud flats.

halothane anaesthetic agent (a liquid, $CF_3CHBrCl$) that produces a deep level of unconsciousness when inhaled.

Hals Frans *c.* 1581–1666. Flemish-born painter of lively portraits, such as the *Laughing Cavalier* 1624 (Wallace Collection, London), and large groups of military companies, governors of charities, and others (many examples in the Frans Hals Museum, Haarlem, the Netherlands). In the 1620s he experimented with genre (domestic) scenes.

Hamburg largest inland port of Europe, in Germany, on the river Elbe; population (1988) 1,571,000. Industries include oil, chemicals, electronics, and cosmetics.

Hamilcar Barca *c.* 270–228 BC. Carthaginian general, father of *Hannibal. From 247 to 241 BC he harassed the Romans in Italy and then led an expedition to Spain, where he died in battle.

Hamilton capital (since 1815) of Bermuda, on Bermuda Island; population about (1980) 1,617. It was founded 1612.

Hamilton port in Ontario, Canada; population (1986) 557,000. Linked with Lake Ontario by the Burlington Canal, it has a hydroelectric plant and steel, heavy machinery, electrical, chemical, and textile industries.

Hamilton Alexander 1757–1804. US politician who influenced the adoption of a constitution with a strong central government and was the first secretary of the Treasury 1789–95. He led the Federalist Party, and incurred the bitter hatred of Aaron *Burr when he voted against Burr and in favour of Thomas Jefferson for the presidency 1801. Challenged to a duel by Burr, Hamilton was wounded and died the next day.

Hamilton Emma (born Amy Lyon) 1765–1815. English courtesan. In 1782 she became the mistress of Charles *Greville and in 1786 of his uncle Sir William Hamilton (1730–1803), the British envoy to the court of Naples, who married her 1791. After Admiral *Nelson's return from the Nile 1798 during the Napoleonic Wars, she became his mistress and their daughter, Horatia, was born 1801.

Hamilton James, 1st Duke of Hamilton 1606–1649. Scottish adviser to Charles I. He led an army against the *Covenanters (supporters of the National Covenant 1638 to establish Presbyterianism) 1639 and subsequently took part in the negotiations between Charles and the Scots. In the second Civil War he led the Scottish invasion of England, but was captured at Preston and executed.

Hamilton Richard 1922– . English artist, a pioneer of Pop art. His collage *Just What Is It That Makes Today's Homes So Different, So Appealing?* 1956 (Kunsthalle, Tübingen, Germany) is often cited as the first Pop art work.

Hamito-Semitic language any of a family of languages spoken throughout the world. There are two main branches, the *Hamitic* languages of N Africa and the *Semitic* languages originating in Syria, Mesopotamia, Palestine, and Arabia, but now found from Morocco in the west to the Persian Gulf in the east.

Hammarskjöld Dag 1905–1961. Swedish secretary general of the United Nations 1953–61. He opposed Britain over the *Suez Crisis 1956. His attempts to solve the problem of the Congo (now Zaire), where he was killed in a plane crash, were criticized by the USSR. He was awarded the Nobel Peace Prize 1961.

hammer in track and field athletics, a throwing event in which only men compete. The hammer is a spherical weight attached to a chain with a handle. The competitor spins the hammer over his head to gain momentum, within the confines of a circle, and throws it as far as he can. The hammer weighs 7.26 kg/16 lb, and may originally have been a blacksmith's hammer.

Hammer Armand 1898–1990. US entrepreneur, one of the most remarkable business figures of the 20th century. A pioneer in trading with the USSR from 1921, he later acted as a political mediator. He was chair of the US oil company Occidental Petroleum until his death, and was also an expert on art.

hammerhead any of several species of shark of the genus *Sphyrna*, found in tropical seas, characterized by having eyes at the ends of flattened extensions of the skull. Hammerheads can grow to 4 m/13 ft.

Hammerstein Oscar, II 1895–1960. Lyricist and librettist who collaborated with Richard *Rodgers on some of the best-known American musicals, including *Oklahoma* 1943 (Pulitzer Prize), *Carousel* 1945, *South Pacific* 1949 (Pulitzer Prize), *The King and I* 1951, and *The Sound of Music* 1959.

Hammett (Samuel) Dashiell 1894–1961. US crime novelist. His works, *The Maltese Falcon*

1930, *The Glass Key* 1931, and the *The Thin Man* 1932, introduced the 'hard-boiled' detective character into fiction.

Hammond organ electric organ invented in the USA by Laurens Hammond 1934 and widely used in gospel music. It was a precursor of the synthesizer.

Hampden John 1594–1643. English politician. His refusal in 1636 to pay *ship money, a compulsory tax levied to support the navy, made him a national figure. In the Short and Long Parliaments he proved himself a skilful debater and parliamentary strategist. King Charles's attempt to arrest him and four other leading MPs made the Civil War inevitable. He raised his own regiment on the outbreak of hostilities, and on 18 June 1643 was mortally wounded at the skirmish of Chalgrove Field in Oxfordshire.

Hampshire county of S England
area 3,770 sq km/1,455 sq mi
towns Winchester (administrative headquarters), Southampton, Portsmouth, Gosport
products agricultural including watercress growing; oil from refineries at Fawley; chemicals, pharmaceuticals, electronics
population (1991) 1,511,900
famous people Jane Austen, Charles Dickens, Gilbert White.

Hampstead district of N London, part of the borough of Camden.

Hampton Lionel 1909– . US jazz musician, a top band leader of the 1940s and 1950s. Originally a drummer, Hampton introduced the vibraphone, an electronically vibrated percussion instrument, to jazz music. With the Benny *Goodman band from 1936, he fronted his own big band 1941–65 and subsequently led small groups.

Hampton Court Palace former royal residence near Richmond, London, built 1515 by Cardinal *Wolsey and presented by him to Henry VIII 1525. Henry subsequently enlarged and improved it. In the 17th century William and Mary made it their main residence outside London, and the palace was further enlarged by Christopher Wren, although only part of his intended scheme was completed. Part of the building was extensively damaged by fire 1986.

hamster rodent of the family Cricetidae with a thickset body, short tail, and cheek pouches to carry food. Several genera are found across Asia and in SE Europe. Hamsters are often kept as pets.

Hamsun Knut 1859–1952. Norwegian novelist. His first novel *Sult/Hunger* 1890 was largely autobiographical. Other works include *Pan* 1894 and *The Growth of the Soil* 1917, which won him a Nobel prize 1920. His hatred of capitalism made him sympathize with Nazism, and he was fined in 1946 for collaboration.

Han member of the majority ethnic group in China, numbering about 990 million. The Hans speak a wide variety of dialects of the same monosyllabic language, a member of the Sino-Tibetan family. Their religion combines Buddhism, Taoism, Confucianism, and ancestor worship.

Hancock John 1737–1793. US politician and a leader of the American Revolution. As president of the Continental Congress 1775–77, he was the first to sign the Declaration of Independence 1776. Because he signed it in a large, bold hand (in popular belief, so that it would be big enough for George III to see), his name became a colloquial term for a signature in the USA. He coveted command of the Continental Army, deeply resenting the selection of George *Washington. He was governor of Massachusetts 1780–85 and 1787–93.

Hancock Tony (Anthony John) 1924–1968. English lugubrious radio and television comedian. *Hancock's Half Hour* from 1954 showed him famously at odds with everyday life. He also appeared in films, including *The Rebel* 1960 and *The Wrong Box* 1966.

hand unit used in measuring the height of a horse from front hoof to shoulder (withers). One hand equals 10.2 cm/4 in.

handball game resembling football but played with the hands instead of the feet. It was popularized in Germany in the late 19th century. The indoor game has 7 players in a team; the outer version (field handball) has 11. Indoor handball was introduced as an Olympic event in 1972 for men, and in 1976 for women.

Handel Georg Friedrich 1685–1759. German composer, a British subject from 1726. His first opera, *Almira*, was performed in Hamburg 1705. In 1710 he was appointed kapellmeister to the elector of Hanover (the future George I of England). In 1712 he settled in England, where he established his popularity with such works as the *Water Music* 1717 (written for George I). His great choral works include the *Messiah* 1742 and the later oratorios *Samson* 1743, *Belshazzar* 1745, *Judas Maccabaeus* 1747, and *Jephtha* 1752.

hang-gliding technique of unpowered flying using air currents, perfected by US engineer Francis Rogallo in the 1970s. The aeronaut is strapped into a carrier, attached to a sail wing of nylon stretched on an aluminium frame like a paper dart, and jumps into the air from a high place, where updrafts of warm air allow soaring on the 'thermals'. See *gliding.

hanging execution by suspension, usually with a drop of 0.6–2 m/2–6 ft, so that the powerful jerk of the tightened rope breaks the neck. This was once a common form of *capital punishment in Europe and is still practised in some states in the USA.

Hanging Gardens of Babylon in antiquity, gardens at Babylon, the capital of Mesopotamia, considered one of the *Seven Wonders of the World. According to legend, King Nebuchadnezzar constructed the gardens in the 6th century BC for one of his wives, who was homesick for her birthplace in the Iranian mountains. Archaeological excavations at the site of Babylon, 88 km/55 mi S of Baghdad in modern Iraq, have uncovered a huge substructure that may have supported irrigated gardens on terraces.

Hanks Tom 1956– . US actor. His amiable features and mainstream appeal, often seen to best advantage in romantic comedies such as *Sleepless in Seattle* 1993, made his casting as the AIDS-afflicted lawyer in *Philadelphia* 1993 (Academy Award) all the more controversial. His other notable films include *Big* 1988 and the title role in *Forrest Gump* 1994 (Academy Award).

Hanley Ellery 1965– . English rugby league player, a regular member of the Great Britain team since 1984 and the inspiration behind Wigan's domination of the sport in the 1980s. He joined Leeds 1991.

Hannibal 247–182 BC. Carthaginian general from 221 BC, son of Hamilcar Barca. His siege of Saguntum (now Sagunto, near Valencia) precipitated the Second *Punic War with Rome. Following a campaign in Italy (after crossing the Alps in 218), Hannibal was the victor at Trasimene in 217 and Cannae in 216, but he failed to take Rome. In 203 he returned to Carthage to meet a Roman invasion but was defeated at Zama in 202 and exiled in 196 at Rome's insistence.

Hanoi capital of Vietnam, on the Red River; population (1989) 1,088,900. Central Hanoi has one of the highest population densities in the world: 1,300 people per hectare/3,250 per acre. Industries include textiles, paper, and engineering.

Hanover industrial city, capital of Lower Saxony, Germany; population (1988) 506,000. Industries include machinery, vehicles, electrical goods, rubber, textiles, and oil refining.

Hanover German royal dynasty that ruled Great Britain and Ireland 1714–1901. Under the Act of *Settlement 1701, the succession passed to the ruling family of Hanover, Germany, on the death of Queen Anne. On the death of Queen Victoria, the crown passed to Edward VII of the house of Saxe-Coburg.

Hansard official report of the proceedings of the British Houses of Parliament, named after Luke Hansard (1752–1828), printer of the House of Commons *Journal* from 1774. It is published by Her Majesty's Stationery Office. The name *Hansard* was officially adopted 1943.

Hanseatic League confederation of N European trading cities from the 12th century to 1669. At its height in the late 14th century the Hanseatic League included over 160 cities and towns, among them Lübeck, Hamburg, Cologne, Breslau, and Kraków. The basis of the league's power was its monopoly of the Baltic trade and its relations with Flanders and England. The decline of the Hanseatic League from the 15th century was caused by the closing and moving of trade routes and the development of nation states.

Hanukkah or *Hanukah* or *Chanukkah* in Judaism, an eight-day festival of lights that takes place at the beginning of Dec. It celebrates the recapture and rededication of the Temple in Jerusalem by Judas Maccabaeus 164 BC.

Hanuman in the Sanskrit epic *Rāmāyana*, the Hindu monkey god and king of Hindustan (N India). He helped Rama (an incarnation of the god Vishnu) to retrieve his wife Sita, abducted by Ravana of Lanka (now Sri Lanka).

haploid having a single set of *chromosomes in each cell. Most higher organisms are *diploid – that is, they have two sets – but their gametes (sex cells) are haploid. Some plants, such as mosses, liverworts, and many seaweeds, are haploid, and male honey bees are haploid because they develop from eggs that have not been fertilized. See also *meiosis.

Hapsburg English form of *Habsburg, former imperial house of Austria–Hungary.

Harald III Hardrada or Harald the Ruthless (Norwegian *Harald Hardråde*) 1015–1066. King of Norway 1045–66, ruling jointly with Magnus I 1045–47. He engaged in an unsuccessful attempt to conquer Denmark 1045–62; extended Norwegian rule in Orkney, Shetland, and the Hebrides; and tried to conquer England together with Tostig, Earl of Northumbria. They were defeated by King Harold of England at Stamford Bridge and both died in battle.

Harare capital of Zimbabwe, on the Mashonaland plateau, about 1,525 m/5,000 ft above sea level; population (1982) 656,000. It is the centre of a rich farming area (tobacco and maize), with metallurgical and food processing industries.

Harbin or *Haerhpin* or *Pinkiang* port on the Songhua River, NE China, capital of Heilongjiang province; population (1989) 2,800,000. Industries include metallurgy, machinery, paper, food processing, and sugar refining, and it is a major rail junction. Harbin was developed by Russian settlers after Russia was granted trading rights there 1896, and more Russians arrived as refugees after the October Revolution 1917.

hardcore extremist rock music that evolved from punk. It entails playing (guitars and drums) as fast as possible with loud, angry shouting. *Thrash metal* and *death metal* are very similar but developed from heavy metal. *Artcore* uses noise for artistic as well as shock effect.

hard disc in computing, a storage device consisting of a rigid metal *disc coated with a magnetic material. Data are read from and written to the disc by means of a disc drive. The hard disc may be permanently fixed into the drive or in the form of a disc pack that can be removed and exchanged with a different pack. Hard discs vary from large units with capacities of over 3,000 megabytes, intended for use with mainframe computers, to small units with capacities as low as 20 megabytes, intended for use with microcomputers.

Hardicanute c. 1019–1042. King of England from 1040. Son of Canute, he was king of Denmark from 1028. In England he was considered a harsh ruler.

Hardie (James) Keir 1856–1915. Scottish socialist, member of Parliament 1892–95 and 1900–15. He worked in the mines as a boy and in 1886 became secretary of the Scottish Miners' Federation. In 1888 he was the first Labour candidate to stand for Parliament; he entered Parliament independently as a Labour member 1892 and was a chief founder of the *Independent Labour Party 1893.

Harding Warren G(amaliel) 1865–1923. 29th president of the USA 1921–23, a Republican. Harding was born in Ohio, and entered the US Senate 1914. As president he concluded the peace treaties of 1921 with Germany, Austria, and Hungary, and in the same year called the Washington Naval Conference to resolve conflicting British, Japanese, and US ambitions in the Pacific. He opposed US membership of the League of Nations. There were charges of corruption among members of his cabinet in the so-called Teapot Dome Scandal.

hardness physical property of materials that governs their use. Methods of heat treatment can increase the hardness of metals. A scale of hardness was devised by Friedrich *Mohs in the 1800s, based upon the hardness of certain minerals from soft talc (Mohs hardness 1) to diamond (10), the hardest of all materials.

Hardouin-Mansart Jules 1646–1708. French architect to Louis XIV from 1675. He designed the lavish Baroque extensions to the palace of Versailles (from 1678) and Grand Trianon. Other works include the Invalides Chapel (1680–91), the Place de Vendôme, and the Place des Victoires, all in Paris.

hardware the mechanical, electrical, and electronic components of a computer system, as opposed to the various programs, which constitute *software.

hard water water that does not lather easily with soap, and produces 'fur' or 'scale' in kettles. It is caused by the presence of certain salts of calcium and magnesium.

Hardy Oliver 1892–1957. US film comedian, member of the duo *Laurel and Hardy.

Hardy Thomas 1840–1928. English novelist and poet. His novels, set in rural 'Wessex' (his native West Country), portray intense human relationships played out in a harshly indifferent natural world. They include *Far From the Madding Crowd* 1874, *The Return of the Native* 1878, *The Mayor of Casterbridge* 1886, *The Woodlanders* 1887, *Tess of the d'Urbervilles* 1891, and *Jude the Obscure* 1895. His poetry includes the *Wessex Poems* 1898, the blank-verse epic of the Napoleonic Wars *The Dynasts* 1904–08, and several volumes of lyrics.

hare mammal of the genus *Lepus* of the family Leporidae (which also includes rabbits) in the order Lagomorpha. Hares are larger than rabbits, with very long, black-tipped ears, long hind legs, and short, upturned tails.

Hare David 1947– . British dramatist and director, whose plays include *Slag* 1970, *Teeth 'n' Smiles* 1975, *Pravda* 1985 (with Howard *Brenton), and *Wrecked Eggs* 1986.

harebell perennial plant *Campanula rotundifolia* of the *bellflower family, with bell-shaped blue flowers, found on dry grassland and heaths. It is known in Scotland as the bluebell.

Hare Krishna popular name for a member of the *International Society for Krishna Consciousness, derived from their chant.

Hargobind 1595–1644. Indian religious leader, sixth guru (teacher) of Sikhism 1606–44. He encouraged Sikhs to develop military skills in response to growing persecution. At the festival of *Diwali, Sikhs celebrate his release from prison.

Hargreaves James died 1778. English inventor who co-invented a carding machine for combing wool 1760. About 1764 he invented his 'spinning jenny', which enabled a number of threads to be spun simultaneously by one person.

Harijan (Hindi 'children of god') member of the Indian *caste of untouchables. The compassionate term was introduced by Mahatma Gandhi during the independence movement.

Harlem Globetrotters US touring basketball team that plays exhibition matches worldwide. Comedy routines as well as their great skills are features of the games. They were founded 1927 by Abraham Saperstein (1903–1966).

Harlow Jean. Stage name of Harlean Carpenter 1911–1937. US film actress, the first 'platinum blonde' and the wisecracking sex symbol of the 1930s. Her films include *Hell's Angels* 1930, *Red Dust* 1932, *Platinum Blonde* 1932, *Dinner at Eight* 1933, *China Seas* 1935, and *Saratoga* 1937, during the filming of which she died (her part was completed by a double – with rear and long shots).

harmonica or *mouth organ* pocket-sized reed organ blown directly from the mouth; it was invented by Charles Wheatstone 1829.

harmonics in music, a series of partial vibrations that combine to form a musical tone. The number and relative prominence of harmonics produced determines an instrument's tone colour (timbre). An oboe is rich in harmonics, the flute has few. Harmonics conform to successive divisions of the sounding air column or string: their pitches are harmonious.

harmonium keyboard reed organ of the 19th century, powered by foot-operated bellows.

harmony in music, any simultaneous combination of sounds, as opposed to melody, which is a succession of sounds. Although the term suggests a pleasant or agreeable sound, it is applied to any combination of notes, whether consonant or dissonant. Harmony deals with the formation of chords and their interrelation and logical progression.

Harold two kings of England:

Harold I died 1040. King of England from 1035. The illegitimate son of Canute, known as *Harefoot*, he claimed the throne 1035 when the legitimate heir Hardicanute was in Denmark. He was elected king 1037.

Harold II c. 1020–1066. King of England from Jan 1066. He succeeded his father Earl Godwin 1053 as earl of Wessex. In 1063 William of Normandy (*William I) tricked him into swearing to support his claim to the English throne, and when the Witan (a council of high-ranking religious and secular men) elected Harold to succeed Edward the Confessor, William prepared to invade. Meanwhile, Harold's treacherous brother Tostig (died 1066) joined the king of Norway, Harald III Hardrada (1015–1066), in invading Northumbria. Harold routed and killed them at Stamford Bridge 25 Sept. Three days later William landed at Pevensey, Sussex, and Harold was killed at the Battle of Hastings 14 Oct 1066.

harp plucked musical string instrument, with the strings stretched vertically within a wooden frame, normally triangular. The concert harp is now the largest musical instrument to be plucked by hand. It has up to 47 strings, and seven pedals set into the soundbox at the base to alter pitch.

Harper's Ferry village in W Virginia, USA, where the Potomac and Shenandoah rivers meet. In 1859 antislavery leader John *Brown seized the federal government's arsenal here, an action that helped precipitate the Civil War.

harpsichord keyboard musical instrument common in the 16th–18th centuries, until superseded by the piano. The strings are plucked by quills. It was revived in the 20th century for the authentic performance of early music.

Harpy (plural *Harpies*) in early Greek mythology, a wind spirit; in later legend the Harpies have horrific women's faces and the bodies of vultures.

harrier bird of prey of the genus *Circus*, family Accipitridae. Harriers have long wings and legs, short beaks and soft plumage. They are found throughout the world.

harrier breed of dog, a small hound originally used for hare-hunting.

Harrier the only truly successful vertical takeoff and landing fixed-wing aircraft, often called the *jump jet*. Built in Britain, it made its first flight 1966. It has a single jet engine and a set of swivelling nozzles. These deflect the jet exhaust vertically downwards for takeoff and landing, and to the rear for normal flight. Designed to fly from confined spaces with minimal ground support, it refuels in midair.

Harris southern part of *Lewis with Harris, in the Outer *Hebrides; area 500 sq km/193 sq mi; population (1971) 2,900. It is joined to Lewis by a narrow isthmus. Harris tweeds are produced here.

Harris Frank 1856–1931. Irish journalist, later in the USA, who wrote colourful biographies of Oscar Wilde and George Bernard Shaw, and an autobiography, *My Life and Loves* 1926, originally banned in the UK and the USA for its sexual contents.

Harris Joel Chandler 1848–1908. US author, born in Georgia. He wrote tales narrated by the former slave 'Uncle Remus', based on black folklore, and involving the characters Br'er Rabbit and the Tar Baby.

Harrison Benjamin 1833–1901. 23rd president of the USA 1889–93, a Republican. He called the first Pan-American Conference, which led to the establishment of the Pan American Union, to improve inter-American cooperation, and develop commercial ties. In 1948 this became the *Organization of American States.

Harrison Rex (Reginald Carey) 1908–1990. English film and theatre actor. He appeared in over 40 films and numerous plays, often portraying sophisticated and somewhat eccentric characters, such as the waspish Professor Higgins in *My Fair Lady* 1964, the musical version of Irish dramatist George Bernard Shaw's play *Pygmalion*. His other films include *Blithe Spirit* 1945, *The Ghost and Mrs Muir* 1947, and *Dr Doolittle* 1967.

harrow agricultural implement used to break up the furrows left by the *plough and reduce the soil to a fine consistency or tilth, and to cover the seeds after sowing. The traditional harrow consists of spikes set in a frame; modern harrows use sets of discs.

Harrow school fee-paying independent school in N London, founded 1571 and opened 1611; it became a leading public school for boys during the 18th century, and among its former pupils are the writers Byron and Sheridan and the politicians Peel, Palmerston, and Churchill.

hartebeest large African antelope *Alcelaphus buselaphus* with lyre-shaped horns set close on top of the head in both sexes. It may grow to

1.5 m/5 ft at the rather humped shoulders and up to 2 m/6 ft long. Although they are clumsy-looking runners, hartebeest can reach 65 kph/40 mph.

hart's-tongue fern *Phyllitis scolopendrium* whose straplike undivided fronds, up to 60 cm/24 in long, have prominent brown spore-bearing organs on the undersides. The plant is native to Eurasia and E North America.

Hartz Mountains range running north to south in Tasmania, Australia, with two remarkable peaks: Hartz Mountain (1,254 m/4,113 ft) and Adamsons Peak (1,224 m/4,017 ft).

Harvard University oldest educational institution in the USA, founded 1636 at New Towne (later Cambridge), Massachusetts, and named after John Harvard (1607–1638), who bequeathed half his estate and his library to it. Women were first admitted 1969; the women's college of the university is *Radcliffe College*.

harvestman arachnid of the order Opiliones, with very long, thin legs and small bodies. Harvestmen are distinguished from true spiders by the absence of a waist or constriction in the oval body. They are carnivorous and found from the Arctic to the tropics.

Harvey William 1578–1657. English physician who discovered the circulation of blood. In 1628 he published his book *De Motu Cordis/On the Motion of the Heart and the Blood in Animals*. He was court physician to James I and Charles I.

Haryana state of NW India
area 44,200 sq km/17,061 sq mi
capital Chandigarh
products sugar, cotton, oilseed, textiles, cement, iron ore
population (1991) 16,317,700
language Hindi.

Hasdrubal Barca Carthaginian general, son of Hamilcar Barca and brother of Hannibal. He remained in command in Spain when Hannibal invaded Italy and, after fighting there against Scipio until 208 BC, marched to Hannibal's relief. He was defeated and killed in the Metaurus valley, NE Italy.

hashish drug made from the resin contained in the female flowering tops of hemp (*cannabis).

Hasid or *Hassid, Chasid* (plural *Hasidim, Hassidim, Chasidim*) member of a sect of Orthodox Jews, founded in 18th-century Poland, which stressed intense emotion as a part of worship. Many of their ideas are based on the *kabbala.

Hassan II 1929– . King of Morocco from 1961. From 1976 he undertook the occupation of Western Sahara when it was ceded by Spain.

Hastings resort in East Sussex, England; population (1981) 74,803. The chief of the *Cinque Ports, it has ruins of a Norman castle.

Hastings Warren 1732–1818. British colonial administrator. A protégé of Lord Clive, who established British rule in India, Hastings carried out major reforms, and became governor of Bengal 1772 and governor general of India 1774. Impeached for corruption on his return to England 1785, he was acquitted 1795.

Hastings, Battle of battle 14 Oct 1066 at which William the Conqueror, Duke of Normandy, defeated Harold, King of England. The site is 10 km/6 mi inland from Hastings, at Senlac, Sussex; it is marked by Battle Abbey.

Hathaway Anne 1556–1623. Englishwoman, daughter of a yeoman farmer, who married William *Shakespeare 1582. She was born at Shottery, near Stratford, where her cottage can still be seen.

Hathor in ancient Egyptian mythology, the sky goddess, identified with *Isis.

Hatshepsut c. 1540–c. 1481 BC. Queen of Egypt during the 18th dynasty. She was the daughter of Thothmes I, with whom she ruled until the accession to the throne of her husband and half-brother Thothmes II. Throughout his reign real power lay with Hatshepsut, and she continued to rule after his death, as regent for her nephew Thothmes III.

Hattersley Roy 1932– . British Labour politician. On the right wing of the Labour Party, he was prices secretary 1976–79, and deputy leader of the party 1983–1992.

Hatton Derek 1948– . British left-wing politician, former deputy leader of Liverpool Council. A leading member of the *Militant Tendency, Hatton was removed from office and expelled from the Labour Party 1987.

Haughey Charles 1925– . Irish Fianna Fáil politician of Ulster descent. Dismissed 1970 from Jack Lynch's cabinet for alleged complicity in IRA gun-running, he was afterwards acquitted. He was prime minister 1979–81, March–Nov 1982, and 1986–92, when he was replaced by Albert Reynolds.

Hausa member of an agricultural Muslim people of NW Nigeria, numbering 9 million. The Hausa language belongs to the Chadic subfamily of the Afro-Asiatic language group. It is used as a trade language throughout W Africa.

haustorium (plural **haustoria**) specialized organ produced by a parasitic plant or fungus that penetrates the cells of its host to absorb nutrients. It may be either an outgrowth of hyphae (see *hypha), as in the case of parasitic fungi, or of the stems of flowering parasitic plants, as in dodders (Cuscuta). The suckerlike haustoria of a dodder penetrate the vascular tissue of the host plant without killing the cells.

Haute-Normandie or **Upper Normandy** coastal region of NW France lying between Basse-Normandie and Picardy and bisected by the river Seine; area 12,300 sq km/4,757 sq mi; population (1986) 1,693,000. It comprises the départements of Eure and Seine-Maritime; its capital is Rouen. Major ports include Dieppe and Fécamp. The area has many beech forests.

Havana capital and port of Cuba; population (1989) 2,096,100. Products include cigars and tobacco.

Havel Václav 1936– . Czech playwright and politician, president 1989–92. His plays include The Garden Party 1963 and Largo Desolato 1985, about a dissident intellectual. During the communist period, Havel became widely known as a human-rights activist. He was imprisoned 1979–83 and again 1989 for support of Charter 77 (see *Czechoslovakia). As president he sought to preserve a united Czechoslovakia, and resigned in recognition of the breakup of the fed-

eration 1992. In 1993 he became president of the newly independent Czech Republic.

Hawaii Pacific state of the USA; nickname Aloha State
area 16,800 sq km/6,485 sq mi
capital Honolulu on Oahu
towns Hilo
physical Hawaii consists of a chain of some 20 volcanic islands, of which the chief are (1) Hawaii, noted for Mauna Kea (4,201 m/ 13,788 ft), the world's highest island mountain (site of a UK infrared telescope) and Mauna Loa (4,170 m/13,686 ft), the world's largest active volcanic crater; (2) Maui, the second largest of the islands; (3) Oahu, the third largest, with the greatest concentration of population and tourist attractions – for example, Waikiki beach and the Pearl Harbor naval base; (4) Kauai; and (5) Molokai, site of a historic leper colony
products sugar, coffee, pineapples, flowers, women's clothing
population (1990) 1,108,200; 34% European, 25% Japanese, 14% Filipino, 12% Hawaiian, 6% Chinese
language English
religion Christianity; Buddhist minority
history a Polynesian kingdom from the 6th century until 1893; Hawaii became a republic 1894; ceded itself to the US 1898, and became a US territory 1900. Japan's air attack on Pearl Harbor 7 Dec 1941 crippled the US Pacific fleet and turned the territory into an armed camp, under martial law, for the remainder of the war. Hawaii became a state 1959. Tourism is the chief source of income.

hawfinch European finch Coccothraustes coccothraustes about 18 cm/7 in long. It feeds on berries and seeds, and can crack cherry stones with its large and powerful bill.

hawk any of various small to medium-sized birds of prey of the family Accipitridae, other than eagles, kites, ospreys, and vultures. The name is used especially to describe the genera Accipiter and Buteo. Hawks have short, rounded wings compared with falcons, and keen eyesight.

hawk person who believes in the use of military action rather than mediation as a means of solving a political dispute. The term first entered the political language of the USA during the 1960s, when it was applied metaphorically to those advocating continuation and escalation of the Vietnam War. Those with moderate, or even pacifist, views were known as *doves. In general usage today, a hawk is associated with conservative policies.

Hawke Bob (Robert) 1929– . Australian Labor politician, prime minister 1983–91, on the right wing of the party. He was president of the Australian Council of Trade Unions 1970–80. He announced his retirement from politics 1992.

Hawkesbury river in New South Wales, Australia; length 480 km/300 mi. It is a major source of Sydney's water.

Hawking Stephen 1942– . English physicist who has researched *black holes and gravitational field theory. His books include A Brief History of Time 1988, in which he argues that our universe is only one small part of a 'super-universe' that has existed forever and that comprises an infinite number of universes like our own.

Hawkins Coleman (Randolph) 1904–1969. US virtuoso tenor saxophonist. He was, until 1934, a soloist in the swing band led by Fletcher Henderson (1898–1952), and was an influential figure in bringing the jazz saxophone to prominence as a solo instrument.

hawk moth family of moths (Sphingidae) with more than 1,000 species distributed throughout the world, but found mainly in tropical regions.

Hawks Howard 1896–1977. US director, writer, and producer of a wide range of classic films, swift-moving and immensely accomplished, including *Scarface* 1932, *Bringing Up Baby* 1938, *The Big Sleep* 1946, and *Gentlemen Prefer Blondes* 1953.

Hawksmoor Nicholas 1661–1736. English architect, assistant to Christopher *Wren in designing London churches and St Paul's Cathedral; joint architect with John *Vanbrugh of Castle Howard and Blenheim Palace. His genius is displayed in a quirky and uncompromising style incorporating elements from both Gothic and Classical sources.

hawthorn shrub or tree of the genus *Crataegus* of the rose family Rosaceae. Species are most abundant in E North America, but there are also many in Eurasia. All have alternate, toothed leaves and bear clusters of showy white, pink, or red flowers. Small applelike fruits can be red, orange, blue, or black. Hawthorns are popular as ornamentals.

Hawthorne Nathaniel 1804–1864. US writer of *The Scarlet Letter* 1850, a powerful novel set in Puritan Boston. He wrote three other novels, including *The House of the Seven Gables* 1851, and many short stories, including *Tanglewood Tales* 1853, classic Greek legends retold for children.

Hayden William (Bill) 1933– . Australian Labor politician. He was leader of the Australian Labor Party and of the opposition 1977–83, and minister of foreign affairs 1983. He became governor general 1989.

Haydn Franz Joseph 1732–1809. Austrian composer. A teacher of Mozart and Beethoven, he was a major exponent of the classical sonata form in his numerous chamber and orchestral works (he wrote more than 100 symphonies). He also composed choral music, including the oratorios *The Creation* 1798 and *The Seasons* 1801. He was the first great master of the string quartet.

Hayes Rutherford Birchard 1822–1893. 19th president of the USA 1877–81, a Republican. Born in Ohio, he was a major general on the Union side in the Civil War. During his presidency federal troops (see *Reconstruction) were withdrawn from the Southern states and the Civil Service reformed.

hay fever allergic reaction to pollen, causing sneezing, inflammation of the eyes, and asthmatic symptoms. Sufferers experience irritation caused by powerful body chemicals related to *histamine produced at the site of entry. Treatment is by antihistamine drugs.

Hays Office film regulation body in the USA 1922–45. Officially known as the Motion Picture Producers and Distributors of America, it was created by the major film companies to improve the industry's image and provide internal regulation, including a strict moral code.

Hayworth Rita. Stage name of Margarita Carmen Cansino 1918–1987. US dancer and film actress who gave vivacious performances in 1940s musicals and steamy, erotic roles in *Gilda* 1946 and *Affair in Trinidad* 1952. She was known as Hollywood's 'Goddess' during the height of her career. She was married to Orson Welles 1943–48 and appeared in his films, including *The Lady from Shanghai* 1948. She was perfectly cast in *Pal Joey* 1957 and *Separate Tables* 1958.

hazardous substance waste substance, usually generated by industry, which represents a hazard to the environment or to people living or working nearby. Examples include radioactive wastes, acidic resins, arsenic residues, residual hardening salts, lead, mercury, nonferrous sludges, organic solvents, and pesticides. Their economic disposal or recycling is the subject of research.

hazel shrub or tree of the genus *Corylus*, family Corylaceae, including the European common hazel or cob *C. avellana*, of which the filbert is the cultivated variety. North American species include the American hazel *C. americana*.

Hazlitt William 1778–1830. English essayist and critic whose work is characterized by invective, scathing irony, and a gift for epigram. His critical essays include *Characters of Shakespeare's Plays* 1817–18, *Lectures on the English Poets* 1818–19, *English Comic Writers* 1819, and *Dramatic Literature of the Age of Elizabeth* 1820. Other works are *Table Talk* 1821–22, *The Spirit of the Age* 1825, and *Liber Amoris* 1823.

H-bomb abbreviation for *hydrogen bomb*.

HDTV abbreviation for *high-definition television*.

Healey Denis (Winston) 1917– . British Labour politician. While minister of defence 1964–70 he was in charge of the reduction of British forces east of Suez. He was chancellor of the Exchequer 1974–79. In 1976 he contested the party leadership, losing to James Callaghan, and again in 1980, losing to Michael Foot, to whom he was deputy leader 1980–83. In 1987 he resigned from the shadow cabinet.

Health and Safety Commission UK government organization responsible for securing the health, safety, and welfare of people at work, and for protecting the public against dangers to health and safety arising from work activities. It was established by the Health and Safety at Work Act 1974 and is responsible to the secretary of state for employment.

health education teaching and counselling on healthy living, including hygiene, nutrition, sex education, and advice on alcohol and drug abuse, smoking, and other threats to health. Health education in most secondary schools is also included within a course of personal and social education, or integrated into subjects such as biology, home economics, or physical education.

health screening testing large numbers of

apparently healthy people for disease; see *screening.

health service government provision of medical care on a national scale.

health, world the health of people worldwide is monitored by the *World Health Organization (WHO). Outside the industrialized world, in particular, poverty and degraded environmental conditions mean that easily preventable diseases are widespread: WHO estimated 1990 that 1 billion people, or 20% of the world's population, were diseased, in poor health, or malnourished. In North Africa and the Middle East, 25% of the population were ill.

Heaney Seamus (Justin) 1939– . Irish poet, born in County Derry, who has written powerful verse about the political situation in Northern Ireland. Collections include *North* 1975, *Field Work* 1979, and *Station Island* 1984. In 1989, he was elected professor of poetry at Oxford University.

hearing aid any device to improve the hearing of partially deaf people. Hearing aids usually consist of a battery-powered transistorized microphone/amplifier unit and earpiece. Some miniaturized aids are compact enough to fit in the ear or be concealed in the frame of eyeglasses.

Hearst William Randolph 1863–1951. US newspaper publisher, celebrated for his introduction of banner headlines, lavish illustration, and the sensationalist approach known as 'yellow journalism'. A campaigner in numerous controversies, and a strong isolationist, he was said to be the model for Citizen Kane in the 1941 film of that name by Orson Welles.

heart muscular organ that rhythmically contracts to force blood around the body of an animal with a circulatory system. Annelid worms and some other invertebrates have simple hearts consisting of thickened sections of main blood vessels that pulse regularly. An earthworm has ten such hearts. Vertebrates have one heart. A fish heart has two chambers – the thin-walled **atrium** (once called the auricle) that expands to receive blood, and the thick-walled **ventricle** that pumps it out. Amphibians and most reptiles have two atria and one ventricle; birds and mammals have two atria and two ventricles. The beating of the heart is controlled by the autonomic nervous system and an internal control centre or pacemaker, the sinoatrial node.

heart attack sudden onset of gripping central chest pain, often accompanied by sweating and vomiting, caused by death of a portion of the heart muscle following obstruction of a coronary artery by thrombosis (formation of a blood clot). Half of all heart attacks result in death within the first two hours, but in the remainder survival has improved following the widespread use of streptokinase and aspirin to treat heart-attack victims.

heart disease disorder affecting the heart; for example, *ischaemic heart disease, in which the blood supply through the coronary arteries is reduced by *atherosclerosis; *valvular heart disease, in which a heart valve is damaged; and cardiomyophathy, where the heart muscle itself is diseased.

heart-lung machine apparatus used during heart surgery to take over the functions of the heart and the lungs temporarily. It has a pump to circulate the blood around the body and is able to add oxygen to the blood and remove carbon dioxide from it. A heart-lung machine was first used for open-heart surgery in the USA 1953.

heat form of internal energy possessed by a substance by virtue of the kinetic energy in the motion of its molecules or atoms. It is measured by *temperature. Heat energy is transferred by conduction, convection, and radiation. It always flows from a region of higher temperature (heat intensity) to one of lower temperature. Its effect on a substance may be simply to raise its temperature, or to cause it to expand, melt (if a solid), vaporize (if a liquid), or increase its pressure (if a confined gas).

heat capacity in physics, the quantity of heat required to raise the temperature of a substance by one degree. The **specific heat capacity** of a substance is the heat capacity per unit of mass, measured in joules per kilogram per kelvin (J kg^{-1} K^{-1}).

Heath Edward (Richard George) 1916– . British Conservative politician, party leader 1965–75. As prime minister 1970–74 he took the UK into the European Community but was brought down by economic and industrial relations crises at home. He was replaced as party leader by Margaret Thatcher 1975, and became increasingly critical of her policies and her opposition to the UK's full participation in the EC. In 1990 he undertook a mission to Iraq in an attempt to secure the release of British hostages.

heather low-growing evergreen shrub of the heath family, common on sandy or acid soil. The common heather *Calluna vulgaris* is a carpet-forming shrub, growing up to 60 cm/24 in high and bearing pale pink-purple flowers. It is found over much of Europe and has been introduced to North America.

heat shield any heat-protecting coating or system, especially the coating (for example, tiles) used in spacecraft to protect the astronauts and equipment inside from the heat of re-entry when returning to Earth. Air friction can generate temperatures of up to 1,500°C/2,700°F on re-entry into the atmosphere.

heat storage any means of storing heat for release later. It is usually achieved by using materials that undergo phase changes, for example, Glauber's salt and sodium pyrophosphate, which melts at 70°C/158°F. The latter is used to store off-peak heat in the home: the salt is liquefied by cheap heat during the night and then freezes to give off heat during the day.

heatstroke or *sunstroke* rise in body temperature caused by excessive exposure to heat. Mild heatstroke is experienced as feverish lassitude, sometimes with simple fainting; recovery is prompt following rest and replenishment of salt lost in sweat. Severe heatstroke causes collapse akin to that seen in acute *shock, and is potentially lethal without prompt treatment of cooling the body carefully and giving fluids to relieve dehydration.

heat treatment in industry, the subjection of metals and alloys to controlled heating and cooling after fabrication to relieve internal stresses and improve their physical properties. Methods include *annealing, *quenching, and *tempering.

heaven in Christianity and some other religions, the abode of God and the destination of the virtuous after death. Theologians now usually describe it as a place or state in which the soul experiences the full reality of God.

heavy metal in music, a style of rock characterized by loudness, sex-and-violence imagery, and guitar solos. Heavy metal developed out of the hard rock of the late 1960s and early 1970s, was performed by such groups as Led Zeppelin and Deep Purple, and enjoyed a resurgence in the late 1980s. Bands include Van Halen (formed 1974), Def Leppard (formed 1977), and Guns 'n' Roses (formed 1987).

heavy metal in chemistry, a metallic element of high relative atomic mass, such as platinum, gold, and lead. Many heavy metals are poisonous and tend to accumulate and persist in living systems – for example, high levels of mercury (from industrial waste and toxic dumping) accumulate in shellfish and fish, which are in turn eaten by humans. Treatment of heavy-metal poisoning is difficult because available drugs are not able to distinguish between the heavy metals that are essential to living cells (zinc, copper) and those that are poisonous.

heavy water or **deuterium oxide** D_2O water containing the isotope deuterium instead of hydrogen (relative molecular mass 20 as opposed to 18 for ordinary water).

Hebrew member of the Semitic people who lived in Palestine at the time of the Old Testament and who traced their ancestry to *Abraham of Ur, a city of Sumer.

Hebrew Bible the sacred writings of Judaism (some dating from as early as 1200 BC), called by Christians the *Old Testament. It includes the Torah (the first five books, ascribed to Moses), historical and prophetic books, and psalms, originally written in Hebrew and later translated into Greek (*Pentateuch) and other languages.

Hebrew language member of the *Hamito-Semitic language family spoken in SW Asia by the ancient Hebrews, sustained for many centuries in the Diaspora as the liturgical language of Judaism, revived by the late-19th-century Haskala movement, and developed in the 20th century as Israeli Hebrew, the national language of the state of Israel. It is the original language of the Old Testament of the Bible.

Hebrides group of more than 500 islands (fewer than 100 inhabited) off W Scotland; total area 2,900 sq km/1,120 sq mi. The Hebrides were settled by Scandinavians during the 6th to 9th centuries and passed under Norwegian rule from about 890 to 1266.

Hebron (Arabic **El Khalil**) town on the West Bank of the Jordan. It has been a front-line position in the confrontation between Israelis and Arabs in the *Intifada. In 1994 the Hebron mosque was the scene of a massacre in which 39 Palestinians while at morning prayer were shot dead by an Israeli settler.

Hecate in Greek mythology, the goddess of witchcraft and magic, sometimes identified with *Artemis and the Moon.

Hecht Ben 1893–1964. US screenwriter and

occasional film director, who was formerly a journalist. His play *The Front Page* 1928 was adapted several times for the cinema by other writers. His own screenplays included *Gunga Din* 1939, *Spellbound* 1945, and *Actors and Sin* 1952.

hectare metric unit of area equal to 100 ares or 10,000 square metres (2.47 acres), symbol ha.

Hector in Greek mythology, a Trojan prince, son of King Priam and husband of Andromache, who, in the siege of Troy, was the foremost warrior on the Trojan side until he was killed by *Achilles.

hedge or **hedgerow** row of closely planted shrubs or low trees, generally acting as a land division and windbreak. Hedges also serve as a source of food and as a refuge for wildlife, and provide a *habitat not unlike the understorey of a natural forest.

hedgehog insectivorous mammal of the genus *Erinaceus*, native to Europe, Asia, and Africa. The body, including the tail, is 30 cm/1 ft long. It is greyish-brown in colour, has a piglike snout, and is covered with sharp spines. When alarmed it can roll itself into a ball. Hedgehogs feed on insects, slugs, and carrion.

hedge sparrow another name for *dunnock, a small bird.

hedonism ethical theory that pleasure or happiness is, or should be, the main goal in life. Hedonist sects in ancient Greece were the *Cyrenaics, who held that the pleasure of the moment is the only human good, and the *Epicureans, who advocated the pursuit of pleasure under the direction of reason. Modern hedonistic philosophies, such as those of the British philosophers Jeremy Bentham and J S Mill, regard the happiness of society, rather than that of the individual, as the aim.

Hefei or **Hofei** capital of Anhui province, China; population (1989) 980,000. Products include textiles, chemicals, and steel.

Hefner Hugh (Marston) 1926– . US publisher, founder of *Playboy* magazine 1953. With its centrefolds of nude women, and columns of opinion, fashion, and advice on sex, *Playboy* helped reshape the social attitudes of the postwar generation. Its success declined in the 1980s owing to the rise of competing men's magazines and feminist protest.

Hegel Georg Wilhelm Friedrich 1770–1831. German philosopher who conceived of consciousness and the external object as forming a unity in which neither factor can exist independently, mind and nature being two abstractions of one indivisible whole. He believed development took place through dialectic: thesis and antithesis (contradiction) and synthesis, the resolution of contradiction. For Hegel, the task of philosophy was to comprehend the rationality of what already exists; leftist followers, including Karl Marx, used Hegel's dialectic to attempt to show the inevitability of radical change and to attack both religion and the social order of the European Industrial Revolution. He wrote *The Phenomenology of Spirit* 1807, *Encyclopaedia of the Philosophical Sciences* 1817, and *Philosophy of Right* 1821.

hegemony (Greek *hegemonia* 'authority')

political dominance of one power over others in a group in which all are supposedly equal. The term was first used for the dominance of Athens over the other Greek city states, later applied to Prussia within Germany, and, in more recent times, to the USA and the USSR with regard to the rest of the world.

Hegira the flight of the prophet Muhammad; see *Hijrah.

Heian in Japanese history, the period 794–1185, from the foundation of Kyoto as the new capital to the seizure of power by the Minamoto clan. The cutoff date may also be given as 1186, 1192, or 1200. The Heian period was the golden age of Japanese literature and of a highly refined culture at court.

Heidegger Martin 1889–1976. German philosopher. In *Sein und Zeit/Being and Time* 1927 he used the methods of Edmund *Husserl's phenomenology to explore the structures of human existence. His later writings meditated on the fate of a world dominated by science and technology.

Heike alternative name for *Taira, an ancient Japanese clan.

Heike monogatari (Japanese 'tales of the Heike') Japanese chronicle, written down in the 14th century but based on oral legend describing events that took place 200 years earlier, recounting the struggle for control of the country between the rival Genji (Minamoto) and Heike (*Taira) clans. The conflict resulted in the end of the Heian period, and the introduction of the first shogunate (military dictatorship). Many subsequent Japanese dramas are based on material from the chronicle.

Heilongjiang or **Heilungkiang** province of NE China, in *Manchuria
area 463,600 sq km/178,950 sq mi
capital Harbin
products cereals, gold, coal, copper, zinc, lead, cobalt
population (1990) 35,215,000.

Heilungkiang former name of *Heilongjiang, a province of NE China.

Heine Heinrich 1797–1856. German Romantic poet and journalist who wrote *Reisebilder* 1826 and *Buch der Lieder/Book of Songs* 1827. From 1831 he lived mainly in Paris, working as a correspondent for German newspapers. Schubert and Schumann set many of his lyrics to music.

Heinkel Ernst 1888–1958. German aircraft designer who pioneered jet aircraft. He founded his firm 1922 and built the first jet aircraft 1939. During World War II his company was Germany's biggest producer of warplanes, mostly propeller-driven.

Heinlein Robert A(nson) 1907– . US science-fiction writer, associated with the pulp magazines of the 1940s, who wrote the militaristic novel *Starship Troopers* 1959 and the utopian cult novel *Stranger in a Strange Land* 1961. His work helped to increase the legitimacy of science fiction as a literary genre.

Heisenberg Werner Carl 1901–1976. German physicist who developed *quantum theory and formulated the *uncertainty principle, which concerns matter, radiation, and their reactions, and places absolute limits on the achievable accuracy of measurement. He was awarded a Nobel prize 1932.

Hejaz former independent kingdom, merged 1932 with Nejd to form *Saudi Arabia; population (1970) 2,000,000; the capital is Mecca.

Hekmatyar Gulbuddin 1949– . Afghani Islamic fundamentalist guerrilla leader, prime minister 1993–94. Strongly anticommunist, he resisted the takeover of Kabul by moderate mujaheddin forces April 1992 and refused to join the interim administration, continuing to bombard the city until being driven out. A year later he became prime minister by a peace agreement but was dismissed from the post after his forces renewed attacks on Kabul.

Hel or **Hela** in Norse mythology, the goddess of the underworld.

Helen in Greek mythology, the daughter of Zeus and Leda, and the most beautiful of women. She married Menelaus, King of Sparta, but during his absence, was abducted by Paris, Prince of Troy. This precipitated the Trojan War. Afterwards she returned to Sparta with her husband.

Helicon mountain in central Greece, on which was situated a spring and a sanctuary sacred to the *Muses.

helicopter powered aircraft that achieves both lift and propulsion by means of a rotary wing, or rotor, on top of the fuselage. It can take off and land vertically, move in any direction, or remain stationary in the air. It can be powered by piston or jet engine. The *autogiro was a precursor.

Heliopolis ancient Egyptian centre (the biblical **On**) of the worship of the sun god Ra, NE of Cairo and near the village of Matariah.

Helios in Greek mythology, the sun god and father of *Phaethon, thought to make his daily journey across the sky in a chariot.

heliotrope decorative plant of the genus *Heliotropium* of the borage family Boraginaceae, with distinctive spikes of blue, lilac, or white flowers, including the Peruvian or cherry pie heliotrope *H. peruvianum*.

helium (Greek *helios* 'Sun') colourless, odourless, gaseous, nonmetallic element, symbol He, atomic number 2, relative atomic mass 4.0026. It is grouped with the *inert gases, is nonreactive, and forms no compounds. It is the second most abundant element (after hydrogen) in the universe, and has the lowest boiling (–268.9°C/–452°F) and melting points (–272.2°C/–458°F) of all the elements. It is present in small quantities in the Earth's atmosphere from gases issuing from radioactive elements (from *alpha decay) in the Earth's crust; after hydrogen it is the second lightest element.

helix in mathematics, a three-dimensional curve resembling a spring, corkscrew, or screw thread. It is generated by a line that encircles a cylinder or cone at a constant angle.

hell in various religions, a place of posthumous punishment. In Hinduism, Buddhism, and Jainism, hell is a transitory stage in the progress of the soul, but in Christianity and Islam it is eternal (*purgatory is transitory). Judaism does not postulate such punishment.

hellebore poisonous European herbaceous plant of the genus *Helleborus* of the buttercup family Ranunculaceae. The stinking hellebore *H. foetidus* has greenish flowers early in the spring.

helleborine temperate Old World orchid of the genera *Epipactis* and *Cephalanthera*, including the marsh helleborine *E. palustris* and the hellebore orchid *E. helleborine* introduced to North America.

Hellenic period (from *Hellas*, Greek name for Greece) classical period of ancient Greek civilization, from the first Olympic Games 776 BC until the death of Alexander the Great 323 BC.

Hellenistic period period in Greek civilization from the death of Alexander 323 BC until the accession of the Roman emperor Augustus 27 BC. Alexandria in Egypt was the centre of culture and commerce during this period, and Greek culture spread throughout the Mediterranean region.

Heller Joseph 1923– . US novelist. He drew on his experiences in the US air force in World War II to write *Catch-22* 1961, satirizing war and bureaucratic methods. A film based on the book appeared 1970.

Hellespont former name of the *Dardanelles, the strait that separates Europe from Asia.

Hellman Lillian 1907–1984. US playwright whose work is concerned with contemporary political and social issues. *The Children's Hour* 1934, *The Little Foxes* 1939, and *Toys in the Attic* 1960 are all examples of the 'well-made play'.

Helmholtz Hermann Ludwig Ferdinand von 1821–1894. German physiologist, physicist, and inventor of the ophthalmoscope for examining the inside of the eye. He was the first to explain how the cochlea of the inner ear works, and the first to measure the speed of nerve impulses. In physics he formulated the law of conservation of energy, and worked in thermodynamics.

Helmont Jean Baptiste van 1577–1644. Belgian doctor who was the first to realize that there are gases other than air, and claimed to have coined the word 'gas' (from Greek *cháos*).

Héloïse 1101–1164. Abbess of Paraclete in Champagne, France, correspondent and lover of *Abelard. She became deeply interested in intellectual study in her youth and was impressed by the brilliance of Abelard, her teacher, whom she secretly married. After her affair with Abelard, and the birth of a son, Astrolabe, she became a nun 1129, and with Abelard's assistance, founded a nunnery at Paraclete. Her letters show her strong and pious character and her devotion to Abelard.

Helpmann Robert 1909–1986. Australian dancer, choreographer, and actor. The leading male dancer with the Sadler's Wells Ballet, London 1933–50, he partnered Margot *Fonteyn in the 1940s.

Helsinki (Swedish *Helsingfors*) capital and port of Finland; population (1990) 492,400, metropolitan area 978,000. Industries include shipbuilding, engineering, and textiles. The homes of the architect Eliel Saarinen and the composer Jean Sibelius outside the town are museums.

Helsinki Conference international meeting 1975 at which 35 countries, including the USSR and the USA, attempted to reach agreement on cooperation in security, economics, science, technology, and human rights. This established the *Conference on Security and Cooperation in Europe (CSCE).

Helvetius Claude Adrien 1715–1771. French philosopher. In *De l'Esprit* 1758 he argued, following David *Hume, that self-interest, however disguised, is the mainspring of all human action and that since conceptions of good and evil vary according to period and locality there is no absolute good or evil. He also believed that intellectual differences are only a matter of education.

hematite principal ore of iron, consisting mainly of iron(III) oxide, Fe_2O_3. It occurs as *specular hematite* (dark, metallic lustre), *kidney ore* (reddish radiating fibres terminating in smooth, rounded surfaces), and as a red earthy deposit.

Hemingway Ernest 1898–1961. US writer. War, bullfighting, and fishing are used symbolically in his work to represent honour, dignity, and primitivism – prominent themes in his short stories and novels, which include *A Farewell to Arms* 1929, *For Whom the Bell Tolls* 1940, and *The Old Man and the Sea* 1952. His deceptively simple writing styles attracted many imitators. He received the Nobel Prize for Literature 1954.

hemlock plant *Conium maculatum* of the carrot family Umbelliferae, native to Europe, W Asia, and N Africa. Reaching up to 2 m/6 ft high, it bears umbels of small white flowers. The whole plant, especially the root and fruit, is poisonous, causing paralysis of the nervous system. The name hemlock is also applied to members of the genus *Tsuga* of North American and Asiatic conifers of the pine family.

hemp annual plant *Cannabis sativa*, family Cannabaceae. Originally from Asia, it is cultivated in most temperate countries for its fibres, produced in the outer layer of the stem, and used in ropes, twines, and, occasionally, in a type of linen or lace. *Cannabis is obtained from certain varieties of hemp.

Henan or *Honan* province of E central China
area 167,000 sq km/64,462 sq mi
capital Zhengzhou
products cereals, cotton
population (1990) 85,510,000.

henbane poisonous plant *Hyoscyamus niger* of the nightshade family Solanaceae, found on waste ground throughout most of Europe and W Asia. A branching plant, up to 80 cm/31 in high, it has hairy leaves and a nauseous smell. The yellow flowers are bell-shaped. Henbane is used in medicine as a source of hyoscyamine and scopolamine.

Hendrix Jimi (James Marshall) 1942–1970. US rock guitarist, songwriter, and singer, legendary for his virtuoso experimental technique and flamboyance. *Are You Experienced?* 1967 was his first album. His performance at the 1969 Woodstock festival included a memorable version of 'The Star-Spangled Banner' and is recorded in the film *Woodstock*. He greatly expanded the vocabulary of the electric guitar and influenced both rock and jazz musicians.

Hendry Stephen 1970– . Scottish snooker player. He replaced Steve Davis as the top-ranking player during the 1989–90 season as well as becoming the youngest ever world champion.

Hengist 5th century AD. Legendary leader, with his brother Horsa, of the Jutes, who originated in Jutland and settled in Kent about 450, the first Anglo-Saxon settlers in Britain.

Heng Samrin 1934– . Cambodian politician, prime minister 1979–85. A former Khmer Rouge commander 1976–78, who had become disillusioned with its brutal tactics, he led an unsuccessful coup against *Pol Pot 1978 and established the Kampuchean People's Revolutionary Party in Vietnam, before returning 1979 to head the new Vietnamese-backed government. He was replaced as prime minister by the reformist Hun Sen 1985.

Henlein Konrad 1898–1945. Sudeten-German leader of the Sudeten Nazi Party in Czechoslovakia, and closely allied with Hitler's Nazis. He was partly responsible for the destabilization of the Czechoslovak state 1938, which led to the *Munich Agreement and secession of the Sudetenland to Germany.

Henley Royal Regatta UK *rowing festival on the river Thames, inaugurated 1839. It is as much a social as a sporting occasion. The principal events are the solo *Diamond Challenge Sculls* and the *Grand Challenge Cup*, the leading event for eight-oared shells. The regatta is held in July.

henna small shrub *Lawsonia inermis* of the loosestrife family Lythraceae, found in Iran, India, Egypt, and N Africa. The leaves and young twigs are ground to a powder, mixed to a paste with hot water, and applied to fingernails and hair, giving an orange-red hue. The colour may then be changed to black by applying a preparation of indigo.

Henri Robert. Adopted name of Robert Henry Cozad 1865–1929. US painter, a leading figure in the transition between 19th-century conventions and Modern art in America. He was a principal member of the *Ashcan School*.

Henrietta Maria 1609–1669. Queen of England 1625–49. The daughter of Henry IV of France, she married Charles I of England 1625. By encouraging him to aid Roman Catholics and make himself an absolute ruler, she became highly unpopular and was exiled during the period 1644–60. She returned to England at the Restoration but retired to France 1665.

henry SI unit (symbol H) of *inductance (the reaction of an electric current against the magnetic field that surrounds it). One henry is the inductance of a circuit that produces an opposing voltage of one volt when the current changes at one ampere per second.

Henry (Charles Albert David) known as *Harry* 1984– . Prince of the UK; second child of the Prince and Princess of Wales.

Henry Joseph 1797–1878. US physicist, inventor of the electromagnetic motor 1829 and of a telegraphic apparatus. He also discovered the principle of electromagnetic induction, roughly at the same time as Michael *Faraday, and the phenomenon of self-induction. A unit of inductance (henry) is named after him.

Henry Patrick 1736–1799. US politician who in 1775 supported the arming of the Virginia militia against the British by a speech ending, 'Give me

liberty or give me death!' He was governor of Virginia 1776–79 and 1784–86.

Henry William 1774–1836. British chemist. In 1803 he formulated *Henry's law*, which states that when a gas is dissolved in a liquid at a given temperature, the mass that dissolves is in direct proportion to the pressure of the gas.

Henry eight kings of England:

Henry I 1068–1135. King of England from 1100. Youngest son of William I, he succeeded his brother William II. He won the support of the Saxons by granting them a charter and marrying a Saxon princess. An able administrator, he established a professional bureaucracy and a system of travelling judges. He was succeeded by Stephen.

Henry II 1133–1189. King of England from 1154, when he succeeded *Stephen. He was the son of *Matilda and Geoffrey of Anjou (1113–1151). He curbed the power of the barons, but his attempt to bring the church courts under control had to be abandoned after the murder of Thomas à *Becket. During his reign the English conquest of Ireland began. He was succeeded by his son Richard I.

Henry III 1207–1272. King of England from 1216, when he succeeded John, but he did not rule until 1227. His financial commitments to the papacy and his foreign favourites led to de *Montfort's revolt 1264. Henry was defeated at Lewes, Sussex, and imprisoned. He was restored to the throne after the royalist victory at Evesham 1265. He was succeeded by his son Edward I.

Henry IV (Bolingbroke) 1367–1413. King of England from 1399, the son of *John of Gaunt. In 1398 he was banished by *Richard II for political activity but returned 1399 to head a revolt and be accepted as king by Parliament. He was succeeded by his son Henry V.

Henry V 1387–1422. King of England from 1413, son of Henry IV. Invading Normandy 1415 (during the Hundred Years' War), he captured Harfleur and defeated the French at *Agincourt. He invaded again 1417–19, capturing Rouen. His military victory forced the French into the Treaty of Troyes 1420, which gave Henry control of the French government. He married *Catherine of Valois 1420 and gained recognition as heir to the French throne by his father-in-law Charles VI, but died before him. He was succeeded by his son Henry VI.

Henry VI 1421–1471. King of England from 1422, son of Henry V. He assumed royal power 1442 and sided with the party opposed to the continuation of the Hundred Years' War with France. After his marriage 1445, he was dominated by his wife, *Margaret of Anjou. The unpopularity of the government, especially after the loss of the English conquests in France, encouraged Richard, Duke of *York, to claim the throne, and though York was killed 1460, his son Edward IV proclaimed himself king 1461 (see Wars of the *Roses). Henry was captured 1465, temporarily restored 1470, but again imprisoned 1471 and then murdered.

Henry VII 1457–1509. King of England from 1485, son of Edmund Tudor, Earl of Richmond (c. 1430–1456), and a descendant of *John of Gaunt. He spent his early life in Brittany until

1485, when he landed in Britain to lead the rebellion against Richard III which ended with Richard's defeat and death at *Bosworth. By his marriage to Elizabeth of York 1486 he united the houses of York and Lancaster. Yorkist revolts continued until 1497, but Henry restored order after the Wars of the *Roses by the *Star Chamber and achieved independence from Parliament by amassing a private fortune through confiscations. He was succeeded by his son Henry VIII.

Henry VIII 1491–1547. King of England from 1509, when he succeeded his father Henry VII and married Catherine of Aragon, the widow of his brother. During the period 1513–29 Henry pursued an active foreign policy, largely under the guidance of his Lord Chancellor, Cardinal Wolsey who shared Henry's desire to make England a notable nation. Wolsey was replaced by Thomas More 1529 for failing to persuade the pope to grant Henry a divorce. After 1532 Henry broke with papal authority, proclaimed himself head of the church in England, dissolved the monasteries, and divorced Catherine. His subsequent wives were Anne Boleyn, Jane Seymour, Anne of Cleves, Catherine Howard, and Catherine Parr. He was succeeded by his son Edward VI.

Henry four kings of France, including:

Henry III 1551–1589. King of France from 1574. He fought both the *Huguenots (headed by his successor, Henry of Navarre) and the Catholic League (headed by the Duke of Guise). Guise expelled Henry from Paris 1588 but was assassinated. Henry allied with the Huguenots under Henry of Navarre to besiege the city, but was assassinated by a monk.

Henry IV 1553–1610. King of France from 1589. Son of Antoine de Bourbon and Jeanne, Queen of Navarre, he was brought up as a Protestant and from 1576 led the *Huguenots. On his accession he settled the religious question by adopting Catholicism while tolerating Protestantism. He restored peace and strong government to France and brought back prosperity by measures for the promotion of industry and agriculture and the improvement of communications. He was assassinated by a Catholic extremist.

Henry seven Holy Roman emperors, including:

Henry I the Fowler c. 876–936. King of Germany from 919, and duke of Saxony from 912. He secured the frontiers of Saxony, ruled in harmony with its nobles, and extended German influence over the Danes, the Hungarians, and the Slavonic tribes. He was about to claim the imperial crown when he died.

Henry III the Black 1017–1056. King of Germany from 1028, Holy Roman emperor from 1039 (crowned 1046). He raised the empire to the height of its power, and extended its authority over Poland, Bohemia, and Hungary.

Henry IV 1050–1106. Holy Roman emperor from 1056, who was involved from 1075 in a struggle with the papacy (see *Gregory VII). Excommunicated twice (1076 and 1080), Henry deposed Gregory and set up the antipope Clement III (died 1191) by whom he was crowned Holy Roman emperor 1084.

Henry V 1081–1125. Holy Roman emperor from 1106. He continued the struggle with the church until the settlement of the *investiture contest 1122.

Henry VI 1165–1197. Holy Roman emperor from 1190. As part of his plan for making the empire universal, he captured and imprisoned Richard I of England and compelled him to do homage.

Henry, O Pen name of William Sydney Porter 1862–1910. US short-story writer whose collections include *Cabbages and Kings* 1904 and *The Four Million* 1906. His stories are written in a colloquial style and employ skilled construction with surprise endings.

Henry the Lion 1129–1195. Duke of Bavaria 1156–80, duke of Saxony 1142–80, and duke of Lüneburg 1180–85. He was granted the Duchy of Bavaria by the Emperor Frederick Barbarossa. He founded Lübeck and Munich. In 1162 he married Matilda, daughter of Henry II of England. His refusal in 1176 to accompany Frederick Barbarossa to Italy led in 1180 to his being deprived of the duchies of Bavaria and Saxony. Henry led several military expeditions to conquer territory in the East.

Henry the Navigator 1394–1460. Portuguese prince, the fourth son of John I. He set up a school for navigators 1419 and under his patronage Portuguese sailors explored and colonized Madeira, the Cape Verde Islands, and the Azores; they sailed down the African coast almost to Sierra Leone.

Henson Jim (James Maury) 1936–1990. US puppeteer who created the television Muppet characters, including Kermit the Frog, Miss Piggy, and Fozzie Bear. The Muppets became popular on the children's educational TV series *Sesame Street*, which first appeared in 1969 and soon became regular viewing in over 80 countries. In 1976 Henson created *The Muppet Show*, which ran for five years and became one of the world's most widely seen TV programmes, reaching 235 million viewers in 100 countries. Three Muppet movies followed. In 1989 the Muppets became part of the *Disney empire.

Henze Hans Werner 1926– . German composer whose large and varied output includes orchestral, vocal, and chamber music. He uses traditional symphony and concerto forms, and incorporates a wide range of styles including jazz. Operas include *Das Verratene Meer* (Berlin 1992) based on Yukio Mishima's novel *The Sailor Who Fell from Grace with the Sea*.

hepatitis any inflammatory disease of the liver, usually caused by a virus. Other causes include alcohol, drugs, gallstones, lupus erythematosus, and amoebic dysentery. Symptoms include weakness, nausea, and jaundice.

Hepburn Audrey (Audrey Hepburn-Rushton) 1929–1993. British actress of Anglo-Dutch descent who often played innocent, childlike characters. Slender and doe-eyed, she set a different style from the more ample women stars of the 1950s. After playing minor parts in British films in the early 1950s, she became a Hollywood star in such films as *Funny Face* 1957, *My Fair Lady* 1964, *Wait Until Dark* 1968, and *Robin and Marian* 1976.

Hepburn Katharine 1909– . US actress who

made feisty self-assurance her trademark. She appeared in such films as *Morning Glory* 1933 (Academy Award), *Little Women* 1933, *Bringing Up Baby* 1938, *The Philadelphia Story* 1940, *Woman of the Year* 1942, *The African Queen* 1951, *Pat and Mike* 1952 (with her frequent partner Spencer Tracy), *Guess Who's Coming to Dinner* 1967 (Academy Award), *Lion in Winter* 1968 (Academy Award), and *On Golden Pond* 1981 (Academy Award). She also had a distinguished stage career.

Hephaestus in Greek mythology, the god of fire and metalcraft (Roman Vulcan), son of Zeus and Hera, husband of Aphrodite. He was lame.

Hepplewhite George died 1786. English furniture maker. He developed a simple, elegant style, working mainly in mahogany or satinwood, adding delicately inlaid or painted decorations of feathers, shells, or ears of wheat. His book of designs, *The Cabinetmaker and Upholsterer's Guide* 1788, was published posthumously.

heptathlon multi-event athletics discipline for women consisting of seven events over two days: 100 metres hurdles, high jump, shot put, 200 metres (day one); long jump, javelin, 800 metres (day two). Points are awarded for performances in each event in the same way as the *decathlon. It replaced the pentathlon (five events) in international competition 1981.

Hepworth Barbara 1903–1975. English sculptor. She developed a distinctive abstract style, creating hollowed forms of stone or wood with spaces bridged by wires or strings; many later works are in bronze.

Hera in Greek mythology, a goddess (Roman Juno), sister-consort of Zeus, mother of Hephaestus, Hebe, and Ares; protector of women and marriage.

Heracles in Greek mythology, a hero (Roman Hercules), son of Zeus and Alcmene, famed for strength. While serving Eurystheus, King of Argos, he performed 12 labours, including the cleansing of the Augean stables.

Heraclius *c.* 575–641. Byzantine emperor from 610. His reign marked a turning point in the empire's fortunes. Of Armenian descent, he recaptured Armenia 622, and other provinces 622–28 from the Persians, but lost them to the Muslims 629–41.

Heraklion alternative name for *Iráklion*, a Greek port.

heraldry insignia and symbols representing a person, family, or dynasty. Heraldry originated with simple symbols used on banners and shields for recognition in battle. By the 14th century, it had become a complex pictorial language with its own regulatory bodies (courts of chivalry), used by noble families, corporations, cities, and realms. The world's oldest heraldic court is the English College of Arms founded by Henry V; it was incorporated 1484 by Richard III.

Herat capital of Herat province, and the largest city in W Afghanistan, on the north banks of the Hari Rud River; population (1980) 160,000. A principal road junction, it was a great city in ancient and medieval times.

herb any plant (usually a flowering plant) tasting sweet, bitter, aromatic, or pungent, used in cooking, medicine, or perfumery; technically, a herb is any plant in which the aerial parts do not remain above ground at the end of the growing season.

herbalism prescription and use of plants and their derivatives for medication. Herbal products are favoured by alternative practitioners as 'natural medicine', as opposed to modern synthesized medicines and drugs, which are regarded with suspicion because of the dangers of side-effects and dependence.

Herbert George 1593–1633. English poet. His volume of religious poems, *The Temple*, appeared in 1633, shortly before his death. His poems depict his intense religious feelings in clear, simple language.

herbicide any chemical used to destroy plants or check their growth; see *weedkiller.

herbivore animal that feeds on green plants (or photosynthetic single-celled organisms) or their products, including seeds, fruit, and nectar. The most numerous type of herbivore is thought to be the zooplankton, tiny invertebrates in the surface waters of the oceans that feed on small photosynthetic algae. Herbivores are more numerous than other animals because their food is the most abundant. They form a vital link in the food chain between plants and carnivores.

herb Robert wild *geranium *Geranium robertianum* found throughout Europe and central Asia and naturalized in North America. About 30 cm/12 in high, it bears hairy leaves and small pinkish to purplish flowers.

Herculaneum ancient city of Italy between Naples and Pompeii. Along with Pompeii, it was buried when Vesuvius erupted AD 79. It was excavated from the 18th century onwards.

Hercules Roman form of *Heracles.

Hercules in astronomy, the fifth largest constellation, lying in the northern hemisphere. Despite its size it contains no prominent stars. Its most important feature is a *globular cluster of stars 22,500 light years from Earth, one of the best examples in the sky.

Hereford and Worcester county in W central England
area 3,930 sq km/1,517 sq mi
towns Worcester (administrative headquarters), Hereford, Kidderminster, Evesham, Ross-on-Wye, Ledbury laden tea tray)
products mainly agricultural: apples, pears, cider; hops, vegetables, Hereford cattle; carpets; porcelain; some chemicals and engineering
population (1991) 667,800
famous people Edward Elgar, A E Housman, William Langland, John Masefield.

heresy (Greek *hairesis* 'parties' of believers) doctrine opposed to orthodox belief, especially in religion. Those holding ideas considered heretical by the Christian church have included Gnostics, Arians, Pelagians, Montanists, Albigenses, Waldenses, Lollards, and Anabaptists.

Hereward the Wake 11th century. English leader of a revolt against the Normans 1070. His stronghold in the Isle of Ely was captured by William the Conqueror 1071. Hereward escaped, but his fate is unknown.

Hergé Pen name of Georges Remi 1907–1983. Belgian artist, creator of the boy reporter Tintin, who first appeared in strip-cartoon form as *Tintin in the Land of the Soviets* 1929–30.

Herman Woody (Woodrow) 1913–1987. US bandleader and clarinetist. A child prodigy, he was leader of his own orchestra at 23, and after 1945 formed his famous Thundering Herd band. Soloists in this or later versions of the band included Lester *Young and Stan *Getz.

hermaphrodite organism that has both male and female sex organs. Hermaphroditism is the norm in species such as earthworms and snails, and is common in flowering plants. Cross-fertilization is the rule among hermaphrodites, with the parents functioning as male and female simultaneously, or as one or the other sex at different stages in their development.

Hermaphroditus in Greek mythology, the son of Hermes and Aphrodite. He was loved by a nymph who prayed for eternal union with him, so that they became one body with dual sexual characteristics, hence the term hermaphrodite.

hermeneutics philosophical tradition concerned with the nature of understanding and interpretation of human behaviour and social traditions. From its origins in problems of biblical interpretation, hermeneutics has expanded to cover many fields of enquiry, including aesthetics, literary theory, and science. German philosophers Wilhelm Dilthey (1833–1911) and Martin *Heidegger are influential contributors to this tradition.

Hermes in Greek mythology, a god, son of Zeus and Maia; messenger of the gods; he wore winged sandals, a wide-brimmed hat, and carried a staff around which serpents coiled. Identified with the Roman Mercury and ancient Egyptian Thoth, he protects thieves, travellers, and merchants.

hernia or *rupture* protrusion of part of an internal organ through a weakness in the surrounding muscular wall, usually in the groin or navel. The appearance is that of a rounded soft lump or swelling.

Hero and Leander in Greek mythology, a pair of lovers. Hero was a priestess of Aphrodite at Sestos on the Hellespont, in love with Leander on the opposite shore at Abydos. When he was drowned while swimming across during a storm, she threw herself into the sea.

Herod the Great 74–4 BC. King of the Roman province of Judaea, S Palestine, from 40 BC. With the aid of Mark Antony, he established his government in Jerusalem 37 BC. He rebuilt the Temple in Jerusalem, but his Hellenizing tendencies made him suspect to orthodox Jewry. His last years were a reign of terror, and in the New Testament Matthew alleges that he ordered the slaughter of all the infants in Bethlehem to ensure the death of Jesus, whom he foresaw as a rival. He was the father of Herod Antipas.

Herod Agrippa I 10 BC–AD 44. Ruler of Palestine from AD 41. His real name was Marcus Julius Agrippa, erroneously called 'Herod' in the Bible. Grandson of Herod the Great, he was made tetrarch (governor) of Palestine by the Roman emperor Caligula and king by Emperor Claudius AD 41. He put the apostle James to death and imprisoned the apostle Peter. His son was Herod Agrippa II.

Herod Agrippa II c. AD 40–93. King of Chalcis (now S Lebanon), son of Herod Agrippa I. He was appointed by the Roman emperor Claudius about AD 50, and in AD 60 tried the apostle Paul. He helped the Roman emperor Titus take Jerusalem AD 70, then went to Rome, where he died.

Herod Antipas 21 BC–AD 39. Tetrarch (governor) of the Roman province of Galilee, N Palestine, 4 BC–AD 9, son of Herod the Great. He divorced his wife to marry his niece Herodias, who persuaded her daughter Salome to ask for John the Baptist's head when he reproved Herod's action. Jesus was brought before him on Pontius Pilate's discovery that he was a Galilean and hence of Herod's jurisdiction, but Herod returned him without giving any verdict. In AD 38 Herod Antipas went to Rome to try to persuade Emperor Caligula to give him the title of king, but was instead banished.

Herodotus c. 484–424 BC. Greek historian. After four years in Athens, he travelled widely in Egypt, Asia, and eastern Europe, before settling at Thurii in S Italy 443 BC. He wrote a nine-book history of the Greek-Persian struggle that culminated in the defeat of the Persian invasion attempts 490 and 480 BC. Herodotus was the first historian to apply critical evaluation to his material.

heroin or *diamorphine* powerful *opiate analgesic, an acetyl derivative of *morphine. It is more addictive than morphine but causes less nausea. It has an important place in the control of severe pain in terminal illness, severe injuries, and heart attacks, but is widely used illegally.

heron large to medium-sized wading bird of the family Ardeidae, which also includes bitterns, egrets, night herons, and boatbills. Herons have sharp bills, broad wings, long legs, and soft plumage. They are found mostly in tropical and subtropical regions, but also in temperate zones.

Herophilus of Chalcedon c. 330–c. 260 BC. Greek physician, active in Alexandria. His handbooks on anatomy made pioneering use of dissection, which, according to several ancient sources, he carried out on live criminals condemned to death.

herpes any of several infectious diseases caused by viruses of the herpes group. *Herpes simplex I* is the causative agent of a common inflammation, the cold sore. *Herpes simplex II* is responsible for genital herpes, a highly contagious, sexually transmitted disease characterized by painful blisters in the genital area. It can be transmitted in the birth canal from mother to newborn. *Herpes zoster* causes *shingles; another herpes virus causes chickenpox.

Herrick Robert 1591–1674. English poet and cleric, born in Cheapside, London. He published *Hesperides* 1648, a collection of sacred and pastoral poetry admired for its lyric quality, including 'Gather ye rosebuds' and 'Cherry ripe'.

herring any of various marine fishes of the herring family (Clupeidae), but especially the important food fish *Clupea harengus*. A silvered greenish-blue, it swims close to the surface, and may be 25–40 cm/10–16 in long. Herring travel in schools several miles long and wide. They are found in large quantities off the E coast of North America, and the shores of NE Europe. Overfishing and pollution have reduced their numbers.

Herriot Edouard 1872–1957. French Radical socialist politician. An opponent of Poincaré, who as prime minister carried out the French occupation of the Ruhr, Germany, he was briefly prime minister 1924–25, 1926, and 1932. As president of the chamber of deputies 1940, he opposed the policies of the right-wing Vichy government and was arrested and later taken to Germany; he was released 1945 by the Soviets.

Herschel John Frederick William 1792–1871. English scientist and astronomer, son of William Herschel. He discovered thousands of close *double stars, clusters, and *nebulae, reported 1847. A friend of the photography pioneer Fox *Talbot, Herschel coined the terms 'photography', 'negative', and 'positive', discovered sodium thiosulphite as a fixer of silver halides, and invented the cyanotype process; his inventions also include astronomical instruments.

Herschel William 1738–1822. German-born English astronomer. He was a skilled telescope maker, and pioneered the study of binary stars and nebulae. He discovered the planet Uranus 1781 and infrared solar rays 1801. He catalogued over 800 double stars, and found over 2,500 nebulae, catalogued by his sister Caroline Herschel; this work was continued by his son John Herschel. By studying the distribution of stars, William established the basic form of our Galaxy, the Milky Way.

Hertfordshire county in SE England
area 1,630 sq km/629 sq mi
towns Hertford (administrative headquarters), St Albans, Watford, Hatfield, Hemel Hempstead, Bishop's Stortford, Letchworth (the first *garden city, followed by Welwyn 1919 and Stevenage 1947) station
products engineering, aircraft, electrical goods, paper and printing; general agricultural goods
population (1991) 951,500
famous people Henry Bessemer, Cecil Rhodes, Graham Greene.

hertz SI unit (symbol Hz) of frequency (the number of repetitions of a regular occurrence in one second). Radio waves are often measured in megahertz (MHz), millions of hertz, and the *clock rate of a computer is usually measured in megahertz. The unit is named after Heinrich Hertz.

Hertzog James Barry Munnik 1866–1942. South African politician, prime minister 1924–39, founder of the Nationalist Party 1913 (the United South African National Party from 1933). He opposed South Africa's entry into both world wars.

Hertzsprung–Russell diagram in astronomy, a graph on which the surface temperatures of stars are plotted against their luminosities. Most stars, including the Sun, fall into a narrow band called the *main sequence*. When a star grows old it moves from the main sequence to the upper right part of the graph, into the area of the giants and supergiants. At the end of its life, as the star shrinks to become a white dwarf, it moves again, to the bottom left area. It is named after the Dane Ejnar Hertzsprung (1873–1967) and the American Henry Norris Russell (1877–1957), who independently devised it in the years 1911–13.

Herzegovina or **Hercegovina** part of

*Bosnia-Herzegovina (which was formerly, until 1991, a republic of Yugoslavia).

Herzl Theodor 1860–1904. Austrian founder of the *Zionist* movement. He was born in Budapest and became a successful playwright and journalist, mainly in Vienna. The *Dreyfus case convinced him that the only solution to the problem of anti-Semitism was the resettlement of the Jews in a state of their own. His book *Jewish State* 1896 launched political *Zionism, and he became the first president of the World Zionist Organization 1897.

Herzog Werner 1942– . German maverick film director who often takes his camera to exotic and impractical locations. His highly original and visually splendid films include *Aguirre der Zorn Gottes/Aguirre Wrath of God* 1972, *Nosferatu Phantom der Nacht/Nosferatu Phantom of the Night* 1979, and *Fitzcarraldo* 1982.

Heseltine Michael (Ray Dibdin) 1933– . English Conservative politician, member of Parliament from 1966 (for Henley from 1974), secretary of state for trade and industry from 1992. As minister of defence from Jan 1983, he resigned Jan 1986 over the Westland affair (concerning the takeover of a British helicopter company) and was then seen as a major rival to Margaret Thatcher. However, in the 1990 leadership election he lost to John Major and became secretary of state for the environment 1990–92. In Oct 1992, adverse public reaction to his pit-closure programme forced the government to review their policy.

Hess (Walter Richard) Rudolf 1894–1987. German Nazi leader. Imprisoned with Hitler 1923–25, he became his private secretary, taking down *Mein Kampf* from his dictation. In 1932 he was appointed deputy *Führer* to Hitler. On 10 May 1941 he landed by air in the UK with compromise peace proposals and was held a prisoner of war until 1945, when he was tried at Nuremberg as a war criminal and sentenced to life imprisonment. He died in Spandau prison, Berlin.

Hess Victor 1883–1964. Austrian physicist who emigrated to the USA shortly after sharing a Nobel prize in 1936 for the discovery of cosmic radiation.

Hesse Hermann 1877–1962. German writer who became a Swiss citizen 1923. A conscientious objector in World War I and a pacifist opponent of Hitler, he published short stories, poetry, and novels, including *Peter Camenzind* 1904, *Siddhartha* 1922, and *Steppenwolf* 1927. Later works, such as *Das Glasperlenspiel/The Glass Bead Game* 1943, tend towards the mystical. He was awarded the Nobel Prize for Literature 1946.

Hessen administrative region (German *Land*) of Germany
area 21,100 sq km/8,145 sq mi
capital Wiesbaden
towns Frankfurt-am-Main, Kassel, Darmstadt, Offenbach-am-Main
products wine, timber, chemicals, cars, electrical engineering, optical instruments
population (1988) 5,550,000
religion Protestant 61%, Roman Catholic 33%
history Until 1945, Hessen was divided in two by a strip of Prussian territory, the southern

portion consisting of the valleys of the rivers Rhine and the Main, the northern being dominated by the Vogelsberg Mountains (744 m/ 2,442 ft). Its capital was Darmstadt.

Hestia in Greek mythology, the goddess (Roman Vesta) of the hearth, daughter of *Kronos (Roman Saturn) and Rhea.

Heston Charlton. Stage name of Charles Carter 1924– . US film actor who often starred in biblical and historical epics (as Moses, for example, in *The Ten Commandments* 1956, and in the title role in *Ben-Hur* 1959).

heterosexuality sexual preference for, or attraction mainly to, persons of the opposite sex.

heterostyly in botany, having *styles of different lengths. Certain flowers, such as primroses (*Primula vulgaris*), have different-sized *anthers and styles to ensure cross-fertilization (through *pollination) by visiting insects.

heterotroph any living organism that obtains its energy from organic substances produced by other organisms. All animals and fungi are heterotrophs, and they include herbivores, carnivores, and saprotrophs (those that feed on dead animal and plant material).

heterozygous in a living organism, having two different *alleles for a given trait. In *homozygous organisms, by contrast, both chromosomes carry the same allele. In an outbreeding population an individual organism will generally be heterozygous for some genes but homozygous for others.

heuristics in computing, a process by which a program attempts to improve its performance by learning from its own experience.

Hewish Antony 1924– . British radio astronomer who was awarded, with Martin *Ryle, the Nobel Prize for Physics 1974 for his work on *pulsars, rapidly rotating neutron stars that emit pulses of energy.

hexadecimal number system number system to the base 16, used in computing. In hex (as it is commonly known) the decimal numbers 0–15 are represented by the characters 0, 1, 2, 3, 4, 5, 6, 7, 8, 9, A, B, C, D, E, F. Hexadecimal numbers are easy to convert to the computer's internal *binary code and are more compact than binary numbers.

Heydrich Reinhard 1904–1942. German Nazi, head of the party's security service and Heinrich *Himmler's deputy. He was instrumental in organizing the *final solution, the policy of genocide used against Jews and others. While deputy 'protector' of Bohemia and Moravia from 1941, he was ambushed and killed by three members of the Czechoslovak forces in Britain, who had landed by parachute. Reprisals followed, including several hundred executions and the massacre of the villagers of Lidice, Czechoslovakia.

Heyerdahl Thor 1914– . Norwegian ethnologist. He sailed on the ancient-Peruvian-style raft *Kon-Tiki* from Peru to the Tuamotu Archipelago along the Humboldt Current 1947, and in 1969–70 used ancient-Egyptian-style papyrus reed boats to cross the Atlantic. His experimental approach to historical reconstruction is not regarded as having made any important scientific contribution.

Heywood Thomas *c.* 1570–*c.* 1650. English actor and dramatist. He wrote or adapted over 220 plays, including the domestic tragedy *A Woman kilde with kindnesse* 1607.

Hezbollah or *Hizbollah* (Party of God) extremist Muslim organization founded by the Iranian Revolutionary Guards who were sent to Lebanon after the 1979 Iranian revolution. Its aim is to spread the Islamic revolution of Iran among the Shi'ite population of Lebanon. Hezbollah is believed to be the umbrella movement of the groups that held many of the Western hostages taken since 1984.

HGV abbreviation for *heavy goods vehicle*.

Hiawatha 16th-century North American Indian teacher and Onondaga chieftain. He is said to have welded the Five Nations (later joined by a sixth) of the *Iroquois into the league of the **Long House**, as the confederacy was known in what is now upper New York State. Hiawatha is the hero of Longfellow's epic poem *The Song of Hiawatha*.

hibernation state of *dormancy in which certain animals spend the winter. It is associated with a dramatic reduction in all metabolic processes, including body temperature, breathing, and heart rate. It is a fallacy that animals sleep throughout the winter.

hibiscus any plant of the genus *Hibiscus* of the mallow family. Hibiscuses range from large herbaceous plants to trees. Popular as ornamental plants because of their brilliantly coloured, red to white, bell-shaped flowers, they include *H. syriacus* and *H. rosa-sinensis* of Asia and the rose mallow *H. palustris* of North America.

Hick Graeme 1966– . Rhodesian-born cricketer who became Zimbabwe's youngest professional cricketer at the age of 17. A prolific batsman, he joined Worcestershire, England, in 1984.

Hickok 'Wild Bill' (James Butler) 1837–1876. US pioneer and law enforcer, a legendary figure in the West. In the Civil War he was a sharpshooter and scout for the Union army. He then served as marshal in Kansas, killing as many as 27 men. He established his reputation as a gunfighter when he killed a fellow scout, turned traitor. He was a prodigious gambler and was fatally shot from behind while playing poker in Deadwood, South Dakota.

hickory tree of the genus *Carya* of the walnut family, native to North America and Asia. It provides a valuable timber, and all species produce nuts, although some are inedible. The pecan *C. illinoensis* is widely cultivated in the southern USA, and the shagbark *C. ovata* in the northern USA.

hieroglyphic Egyptian writing system of the mid-4th millennium BC–3rd century AD, which combines picture signs with those indicating letters. The direction of writing is normally from right to left, the signs facing the beginning of the line. It was deciphered 1822 by the French Egyptologist J F Champollion (1790–1832) with the aid of the *Rosetta Stone*, which has the same inscription carved in hieroglyphic, demotic, and Greek.

hi-fi (abbreviation of *high-fidelity*) faithful

reproduction of sound from a machine that plays recorded music or speech. A typical hi-fi system includes a turntable for playing vinyl records, a cassette tape deck to play magnetic tape recordings, a tuner to pick up radio broadcasts, an amplifier to serve all the equipment, possibly a compact-disc player, and two or more loudspeakers.

high commissioner representative of one independent Commonwealth country in the capital of another, ranking with ambassador.

high-definition television (HDTV) *television system offering a significantly greater number of scanning lines, and therefore a clearer picture, than that provided by conventional systems.

Higher in Scottish education, a public examination taken at the age of 17, one year after the Scottish O grade. Highers are usually taken in four or five subjects and qualify students for entry to *higher education. About 90% of Scottish undergraduates choose to study in Scotland.

higher education in most countries, education beyond the age of 18 leading to a university or college degree or similar qualification.

high jump field event in athletics in which competitors leap over a horizontal crossbar held between rigid uprights at least 3.66 m/12 ft apart. The bar is placed at increasingly higher levels. Elimination occurs after three consecutive failures to clear the bar.

Highland Clearances forced removal of tenants from large estates in Scotland during the early 19th century, as landowners 'improved' their estates by switching from arable to sheep farming. It led ultimately to widespread emigration to North America.

Highland Games traditional Scottish outdoor gathering that includes tossing the caber, putting the shot, running, dancing, and bagpipe playing.

Highland Region administrative region of Scotland
area 26,100 sq km/10,077 sq mi
towns Inverness (administrative headquarters), Thurso, Wick
products oil services, winter sports, timber, livestock, grouse and deer hunting, salmon fishing
population (1991) 209,400
famous people Alexander Mackenzie, William Smith.

Highlands one of the three geographical divisions of Scotland, lying to the north of a geological fault line that stretches from Stonehaven in the North Sea to Dumbarton on the Clyde. It is a mountainous region of hard rocks, shallow infertile soils, and high rainfall.

high-level language in computing, a programming language designed to suit the requirements of the programmer; it is independent of the internal machine code of any particular computer. High-level languages are used to solve problems and are often described as *problem-oriented languages* – for example, BASIC was designed to be easily learnt by first-time programmers; COBOL is used to write programs solving business problems; and FORTRAN is used for programs solving scientific and mathematical problems. In contrast, low-level languages, such as *assembly languages, closely reflect the

machine codes of specific computers, and are therefore described as *machine-oriented languages*.

Highsmith Patricia 1921–1995. US crime novelist. Her first book, *Strangers on a Train* 1950, was filmed by Alfred Hitchcock. She excelled in tension and psychological exploration of character.

high tech (abbreviation for *high technology*) in architecture, buildings that display technical innovation of a high order and celebrate structure and services to create exciting forms and spaces. The Hong Kong and Shanghai Bank, Hong Kong, is a masterpiece of this approach.

highway in Britain, any road over which there is a right of way. In the USA, any public road, especially a main road.

highwayman in English history, a thief on horseback who robbed travellers on the highway (those who did so on foot were known as *footpads*). Highwaymen continued to flourish well into the 19th century.

high-yield variety crop that has been specially bred or selected to produce more than the natural varieties of the same species. During the 1950s and 1960s, new strains of wheat and maize were developed to reduce the food shortages in poor countries (the *Green Revolution). Later, IR8, a new variety of rice that increased yields by up to six times, was developed in the Philippines. Strains of crops resistant to drought and disease were also developed. High-yield varieties require large amounts of expensive artificial fertilizers and sometimes pesticides for best results.

hijacking illegal seizure or taking control of a vehicle and/or its passengers or goods. The term dates from 1923 and originally referred to the robbing of freight lorries. In recent times it (and its derivative, 'skyjacking') has been applied to the seizure of aircraft, usually in flight, by an individual or group, often with some political aim. International treaties (Tokyo 1963, The Hague 1970, and Montreal 1971) encourage cooperation against hijackers and make severe penalties compulsory.

Hijrah or *Hegira* the trip from Mecca to Medina of the prophet Muhammad, which took place AD 622 as a result of the persecution of the prophet and his followers. The Muslim calendar dates from this event, and the day of the Hijrah is celebrated as the Muslim New Year.

Hilbert David 1862–1943. German mathematician who founded the formalist school with the publication of *Grundlagen der Geometrie/Foundations of Geometry* 1899, which was based on his idea of postulates. He attempted to put mathematics on a logical foundation through defining it in terms of a number of basic principles, which US mathematician Kurt Gödel (1906–1978) later showed to be impossible; nonetheless, his attempt greatly influenced 20th-century mathematicians.

Hill David Octavius 1802–1870. Scottish photographer who, in collaboration with Robert *Adamson, made extensive use of the *calotype process in their large collection of portraits taken in Edinburgh 1843–48.

Hill Graham 1929–1975. English motor-racing

driver. He won the Dutch Grand Prix in 1962, progressing to the world driver's title in 1962 and 1968. In 1972 he became the first world driver's champion to win the Le Mans Grand Prix d'Endurance (Le Mans 24-Hour Race). He was killed in an air crash.

Hill Rowland 1795–1879. British Post Office official who invented adhesive stamps and prompted the introduction of the penny prepaid post in 1840 (previously the addressee paid, according to distance, on receipt).

Hillary Edmund Percival 1919– . New Zealand mountaineer. In 1953, with Nepalese Sherpa mountaineer Tenzing Norgay, he reached the summit of Mount Everest, the first to climb the world's highest peak. As a member of the Commonwealth Transantarctic Expedition 1957–58, he was the first person since Scott to reach the South Pole overland, on 3 Jan 1958.

hill figure in Britain, any of a number of ancient figures, usually of animals, cut from downland turf to show the underlying chalk. Examples include the *White Horses, the Long Man of Wilmington, East Sussex, and the Cerne Abbas Giant, Dorset. Their origins are variously attributed to Celts, Romans, Saxons, Druids, or Benedictine monks.

hillfort European Iron Age site with massive banks and ditches for defence, used as both a military camp and a permanent settlement. An example is Maiden Castle, Dorset, England.

Hilliard Nicholas c. 1547–1619. English miniaturist and goldsmith, court artist to Elizabeth I from about 1579. His sitters included the explorers Francis Drake and Walter Raleigh.

Hillsborough Agreement another name for the *Anglo-Irish Agreement 1985.

Himachal Pradesh state of NW India
area 55,700 sq km/21,500 sq mi
capital Simla
products timber, grain, rice, fruit
population (1991) 5,111,000; mainly Hindu
language Pahari
history created as a Union Territory 1948, it became a full state 1971.

Himalayas vast mountain system of central Asia, extending from the Indian states of Kashmir in the west to Assam in the east, covering the southern part of Tibet, Nepal, Sikkim, and Bhutan. It is the highest mountain range in the world. The two highest peaks are Mount *Everest and *Kangchenjunga. Other major peaks include Makalu, Annapurna, and Nanga Parbat, all over 8,000 m/26,000 ft.

Himmler Heinrich 1900–1945. German Nazi leader, head of the *SS elite corps from 1929, the police and the *Gestapo secret police from 1936, and supervisor of the extermination of the Jews in E Europe. During World War II he replaced Goering as Hitler's second-in-command. He was captured May 1945 and committed suicide.

Hīnayāna (Sanskrit 'lesser vehicle') Mahāyāna Buddhist name for *Theravāda Buddhism.

Hindemith Paul 1895–1963. German composer. His Neo-Classical, contrapuntal works include chamber ensemble and orchestral pieces, such as the *Symphonic Metamorphosis on Themes of Carl Maria von Weber* 1944, and the operas *Cardillac* 1926, revised 1952, and *Mathis der Maler/Mathis the Painter* 1938.

Hindenburg Paul Ludwig Hans von Beneckendorf und Hindenburg 1847–1934. German field marshal and right-wing politician. During World War I he was supreme commander and, with Ludendorff, practically directed Germany's policy until the end of the war. He was president of Germany 1925–33.

Hindenburg Line German western line of World War I fortifications built 1916–17.

Hindi language member of the Indo-Iranian branch of the Indo-European language family, the official language of the Republic of India, although resisted as such by the Dravidian-speaking states of the south. Hindi proper is used by some 30% of Indians, in such northern states as Uttar Pradesh and Madhya Pradesh.

Hinduism (Hindu *sanatana dharma* 'eternal tradition') religion originating in N India about 4,000 years ago, which is superficially and in some of its forms polytheistic, but has a concept of the supreme spirit, *Brahman, above the many divine manifestations. These include the triad of chief gods (the Trimurti): Brahma, Vishnu, and Siva (creator, preserver, and destroyer). Central to Hinduism are the beliefs in reincarnation and *karma; the oldest scriptures are the *Vedas*. Temple worship is almost universally observed and there are many festivals. There are over 805 million Hindus worldwide. Women are not regarded as the equals of men but should be treated with kindness and respect. Muslim influence in N India led to the veiling of women and the restriction of their movements from about the end of the 12th century.

Hindu Kush mountain range in central Asia, length 800 km/500 mi, greatest height Tirich Mir, 7,690 m/25,239 ft, in Pakistan. The narrow *Khyber Pass* (53 km/33 mi long) separates Pakistan from Afghanistan and was used by *Zahir and other invaders of India. The present road was built by the British in the Afghan Wars.

Hindustan ('land of the Hindus') the whole of India, but more specifically the plain of the Ganges and Jumna rivers, or that part of India north of the Deccan.

Hindustani member of the Indo-Iranian branch of the Indo-European language family, closely related to Hindi and Urdu and originating in the bazaars of Delhi. It is a *lingua franca in many parts of the Republic of India.

hip-hop popular music originating in New York in the early 1980s. It uses scratching (a percussive effect obtained by manually rotating a vinyl record) and heavily accented electronic drums behind a *rap vocal. The term 'hip-hop' also comprises break dancing and graffiti.

Hipparchus c. 190–c. 120 BC. Greek astronomer who invented trigonometry, calculated the lengths of the solar year and the lunar month, discovered the precession of the equinoxes, made a catalogue of 800 fixed stars, and advanced Eratosthenes' method of determining the situation of places on the Earth's surface by lines of latitude and longitude.

Hipparcos (acronym for *high precision parallax collecting satellite*) satellite launched by the European Space Agency Aug 1989. Named after the Greek astronomer Hipparchus, it is the world's first *astrometry satellite designed to provide precise positions and apparent motions of stars. The accuracy of these measurements from space will be far greater than from ground-based telescopes. However, because of engine failure, *Hipparcos* is making more limited orbits than had been planned, which may restrict the data it is able to provide.

hippie member of a youth movement of the late 1960s, also known as **flower power**, which originated in San Francisco, California, and was characterized by nonviolent anarchy, concern for the environment, and rejection of Western materialism. The hippies formed a politically outspoken, antiwar, artistically prolific counterculture in North America and Europe. Their colourful psychedelic style, inspired by drugs such as *LSD, emerged in fabric design, graphic art, and music by bands such as Love (1965–71), the *Grateful Dead, Jefferson Airplane (1965–74), and *Pink Floyd.

Hippocrates *c.* 460–*c.* 370 BC. Greek physician, often called the father of medicine. Important Hippocratic ideas include cleanliness (for patients and physicians), moderation in eating and drinking, letting nature take its course, and living where the air is good. He believed that health was the result of the 'humours' of the body being in balance; imbalance caused disease. These ideas were later adopted by *Galen.

Hippolytus in Greek mythology, the son of Theseus. When he rejected the love of his stepmother, Phaedra, she falsely accused him of making advances to her and turned Theseus against him. Killed by Poseidon at Theseus' request, he was restored to life when his innocence was proven.

hippopotamus *The common hippopotamus is adapted to life in the water, where it spends most of the day.*

hippopotamus (Greek 'river horse') large herbivorous, even-toed hoofed mammal of the family Hippopotamidae. The common hippopotamus *Hippopotamus amphibius* is found in Africa. It averages over 4 m/13 ft long, 1.5 m/5 ft high, weighs about 4,500 kg/5 tons, and has a brown or slate-grey skin. It is an endangered species.

hire purchase (HP) form of credit under which the buyer pays a deposit and makes instalment payments at fixed intervals over a certain period for a particular item. The buyer has immediate possession, but does not own the item until the final instalment has been paid.

Hirohito 1901–1989. Emperor of Japan from 1926. He succeeded his father Yoshihito. After the defeat of Japan in World War II 1945, he was made constitutional monarch by the US-backed 1946 constitution. He is believed to have played a reluctant role in *Tojo's prewar expansion plans. Hirohito ruled postwar occupied Japan with dignity. His era is known as the Showa era. He was succeeded by his son *Akihito.

Hiroshige Andō 1797–1858. Japanese artist whose landscape prints, often using snow or rain to create atmosphere, include *Tōkaidō gojūsantsugi/53 Stations on the Tokaido Highway* 1833. James Whistler and Vincent van Gogh were among Western painters influenced by him.

Hiroshima industrial city and port on the S coast of Honshu, Japan, destroyed by the first wartime use of an atomic bomb 6 Aug 1945. The city has largely been rebuilt since the war; population (1989) 1,057,100.

Hispaniola (Spanish 'little Spain') West Indian island, first landing place of Columbus in the New World, 6 Dec 1492; now divided into *Haiti and the *Dominican Republic.

histamine inflammatory substance normally released in damaged tissues, which also accounts for many of the symptoms of *allergy. Substances that neutralize its activity are known as *antihistamines.

histochemistry study of plant and animal tissue by visual examination, usually with a *microscope.

histogram in statistics, a graph showing frequency of data, in which the horizontal axis details discrete units or class boundaries, and the vertical axis represents the frequency. Blocks are drawn such that their areas (rather than their height, as in a bar chart) are proportional to the frequencies within a class or across several class boundaries. There are no spaces between blocks.

histology in medicine, the laboratory study of cells and tissues.

historical novel fictional prose narrative set in the past. Literature set in the historic rather than the immediate past has always abounded, but in the West Walter Scott began the modern tradition by setting imaginative romances of love, impersonation, and betrayal in a past based on known fact; his use of historical detail, and subsequent imitations of this technique by European writers such as Manzoni, gave rise to the genre.

Hitchcock Alfred 1899–1980. British film director who became a US citizen in 1955. A master of the suspense thriller, he was noted for his meticulously drawn storyboards that determined his camera angles and for his cameo walk-ons in his own films. His *Blackmail* 1929 was the first successful British talking film; *The Thirty-Nine Steps* 1935 and *The Lady Vanishes* 1939 are British suspense classics. He went to Hollywood 1940, where he made *Rebecca* 1940, *Notorious* 1946, *Strangers on a Train* 1951, *Rear Window* 1954, *Vertigo* 1958, *Psycho* 1960, and *The Birds* 1963. He also hosted two US television mystery series, *Alfred Hitchcock Presents* 1955–62 and *The Alfred Hitchcock Hour* 1963–65.

Hitler Adolf 1889–1945. German Nazi dictator, born in Austria. He was *Führer* (leader) of the Nazi Party from 1921 and author of *Mein*

Kampf/My Struggle 1925–27. As chancellor of Germany from 1933 and head of state from 1934, he created a dictatorship by playing party and state institutions against each other and continually creating new offices and appointments. His position was not seriously challenged until the 'Bomb Plot' 20 July 1944 to assassinate him. In foreign affairs, he reoccupied the Rhineland and formed an alliance with the Italian Fascist Mussolini 1936, annexed Austria 1938, and occupied the Sudetenland under the *Munich Agreement. The rest of Czechoslovakia was annexed March 1939. The Hitler–Stalin pact was followed in Sept by the invasion of Poland and the declaration of war by Britain and France (see *World War II). He committed suicide as Berlin fell.

Hitler–Stalin pact nonaggression treaty signed by Germany and the USSR 23 Aug 1939. Under the terms of the treaty both countries agreed to remain neutral and to refrain from acts of aggression against each other if either went to war. Secret clauses allowed for the partition of Poland – Hitler was to acquire western Poland, Stalin the eastern part. On 1 Sept 1939 Hitler invaded Poland. The pact ended when Hitler invaded Russia on 22 June 1941. See also *World War II.

Hittite member of a group of people who inhabited Anatolia and N Syria from the 3rd millennium to the 1st millennium BC. The city of Hattusas (now Boğazköy in central Turkey) became the capital of a strong kingdom which overthrew the Babylonian Empire. After a period of eclipse the Hittite New Empire became a great power (about 1400–1200 BC), which successfully waged war with Egypt. The Hittite language is an Indo-European language.

HIV abbreviation for *human immunodeficiency virus*, the infectious agent that causes *AIDS.

Hmong member of a SE Asian highland people. They are predominantly hill farmers, rearing pigs and cultivating rice and grain, and many are involved in growing the opium poppy. Estimates of the size of the Hmong population vary between 1.5 million and 5 million, the greatest number being in China. Although traditional beliefs remain important, many have adopted Christianity. Their language belongs to the Sino-Tibetan family. The names *Meo* or *Miao*, sometimes used to refer to the Hmong, are considered derogatory.

Hoban James C 1762–1831. Irish-born architect who emigrated to the USA. He designed the White House, Washington, DC; he also worked on the Capitol and other public buildings.

Hobart capital and port of Tasmania, Australia; population (1986) 180,000. Products include zinc, textiles, and paper. Founded 1804 as a penal colony, it was named after Lord Hobart, then secretary of state for the colonies.

Hobbema Meindert 1638–1709. Dutch landscape painter, a pupil of Ruisdael. His early work is derivative, but later works are characteristically realistic and unsentimental.

Hobbes Thomas 1588–1679. English political philosopher and the first thinker since Aristotle to attempt to develop a comprehensive theory of nature, including human behaviour. In *The Leviathan* 1651, he advocates absolutist government as the only means of ensuring order and security; he saw this as deriving from the *social contract.

hobby small falcon *Falco subbuteo* found across Europe and N Asia. It is about 30 cm/1 ft long, with a grey back, streaked front, and chestnut thighs. It is found in open woods and heaths, and feeds on insects and small birds.

Ho Chi Minh adopted name of Nguyen That Tan 1890–1969. North Vietnamese Communist politician, premier and president 1954–69. Having trained in Moscow shortly after the *Russian Revolution, he headed the communist Vietminh from 1941 and fought against the French during the Indochina War 1946–54, becoming president and prime minister of the republic at the armistice. Aided by the Communist bloc, he did much to develop industrial potential. He relinquished the premiership 1955, but continued as president. In the years before his death, Ho successfully led his country's fight against US-aided South Vietnam in the Vietnam War 1954–75.

Ho Chi Minh City (until 1976 *Saigon*) chief port and industrial city of S Vietnam; population (1989) 3,169,100. Industries include shipbuilding, textiles, rubber, and food products. Saigon was the capital of the Republic of Vietnam (South Vietnam) from 1954 to 1976, when it was renamed.

hockey game played with hooked sticks and a ball, the object being to hit a small solid ball into the goal. It is played between two teams, each of not more than 11 players. Hockey has been an Olympic sport since 1908 for men and since 1980 for women. In North America it is known as 'field hockey', to distinguish it from *ice hockey.

Hockney David 1937– . English painter, printmaker, and designer, resident in California. He exhibited at the Young Contemporaries Show of 1961 and contributed to the Pop art movement. He developed an individual figurative style, as in his portrait *Mr and Mrs Clark and Percy* 1971, Tate Gallery, London, and has prolifically experimented with technique. His views of swimming pools reflect a preoccupation with surface pattern and effects of light. He has also produced drawings, etchings, photo collages, and sets for opera.

Hodgkin's disease rare form of cancer (also known as *lymphoadenoma*), mainly affecting the lymph nodes and spleen. It undermines the immune system, leaving the sufferer susceptible to infection. However, it responds well to radiotherapy and *cytotoxic drugs, and long-term survival is usual.

Hofei alternative transcription of *Hefei*, a city in China.

Hoffman Dustin 1937– . US actor, icon of the antiheroic 1960s. He won Academy Awards for his performances in *Kramer vs Kramer* 1979 and *Rain Man* 1988. His other films include *The Graduate* 1967, *Midnight Cowboy* 1969, *Little Big Man* 1970, *All the President's Men* 1976, *Tootsie* 1982, and *Hook* 1991. He appeared on Broadway in the 1984 revival of *Death of a Salesman* (produced for television 1985).

Hoffmann E(rnst) T(heodor) A(madeus) 1776–1822. German composer and writer. He composed the opera *Undine* 1816 and many fairy stories, including *Nussknacker/Nutcracker* 1816. His stories inspired *Offenbach's *Tales of Hoffmann*.

Hofstadter Robert 1915–1990. US high-energy physicist who revealed the structure of the atomic nucleus. He demonstrated that the nucleus is composed of a high-energy core and a surrounding area of decreasing density. He shared the 1961 Nobel Prize for Physics with Rudolf Mössbauer.

hog member of the *pig family.

Hogan Paul 1940– . Australian TV comic, film actor, and producer. The box-office hit *Crocodile Dundee* (considered the most profitable film in Australian history) 1986 and *Crocodile Dundee II* 1988 (of which he was co-writer, star, and producer) brought him international fame.

Hogarth William 1697–1764. English painter and engraver who produced portraits and moralizing genre scenes, such as the series *A Rake's Progress* 1735. His portraits are remarkably direct and full of character, for example *Heads of Six of Hogarth's Servants* c. 1750–55 (Tate Gallery, London).

Hogg Quintin. British politician; see Lord *Hailsham.

Hogmanay Scottish name for New Year's Eve.

Hohenlinden, Battle of in the French *Revolutionary Wars, a defeat of the Austrians by the French Dec 1800. Coming after the defeat at *Marengo, it led the Austrians to make peace at the Treaty of Lunéville 1801.

Hohenstaufen German family of princes, several members of which were Holy Roman emperors 1138–1208 and 1214–54. They were the first German emperors to make use of associations with Roman law and tradition to aggrandize their office, and included Conrad III; Frederick I (Barbarossa), the first to use the title Holy Roman emperor (previously the title Roman emperor was used); Henry VI; and Frederick II. The last of the line, Conradin, was executed 1268 with the approval of Pope Clement IV while attempting to gain his Sicilian inheritance.

Hohenzollern German family, originating in Württemberg, the main branch of which held the titles of *elector of Brandenburg from 1415, king of Prussia from 1701, and German emperor from 1871. The last emperor, Wilhelm II, was dethroned 1918 after the disastrous course of World War I. Another branch of the family were kings of Romania 1881–1947.

Hohhot or **Huhehot** city and capital of Inner Mongolia (Nei Mongol) autonomous region, China; population (1989) 870,000. Industries include textiles, electronics, and dairy products. There are Lamaist monasteries and temples here.

Hokkaido former name (until 1868) **Yezo** or **Ezo** or **Ezochi** northernmost of the four main islands of Japan, separated from Honshu to the south by Tsugaru Strait and from Sakhalin to the north by Soya Strait; area 83,500 sq km/ 32,231 sq mi; population (1986) 5,678,000, including 16,000 *Ainus. The capital is Sapporo. Natural resources include coal, mercury, manganese, oil and natural gas, timber, and fisheries. Coal mining and agriculture are the main industries.

Hokusai Katsushika 1760–1849. Japanese artist, the leading printmaker of his time. He published *Fugaku Sanjū-rokkei/36 Views of Mount Fuji* about 1823–29, but he produced outstanding pictures of almost every kind of subject – birds, flowers, courtesans, and scenes from legend and everyday life.

Holbein Hans, **the Elder** c. 1464–1524. German painter, active in Augsburg. His works include altarpieces, such as that of *St Sebastian* 1516 (Alte Pinakothek, Munich). He also painted portraits and designed stained glass.

Holbein Hans, **the Younger** 1497/98–1543. German painter and woodcut artist; the son and pupil of Hans Holbein the Elder. Holbein was born in Augsburg. In 1515 he went to Basel, where he became friendly with Erasmus; he painted three portraits of him in 1523, which were strongly influenced by Quentin Massys. He travelled widely in Europe and was court painter to England's Henry VIII from 1536. He also painted portraits of Thomas More and Thomas Cromwell; a notable woodcut series is *Dance of Death* about 1525. He designed title pages for Luther's New Testament and More's *Utopia*.

Holden William. Stage name of William Franklin Beedle 1918–1981. US film actor, a star in the late 1940s and 1950s. He played leading roles in *Sunset Boulevard* 1950, *Stalag 17* 1953, *The Wild Bunch* 1969, and *Network* 1976.

holding company company with a controlling shareholding in one or more subsidiaries.

Holiday Billie. Stage name of Eleanora Gough McKay 1915–1959. US jazz singer, also known as 'Lady Day'. She made her debut in Harlem clubs and became known for her emotionally charged delivery and idiosyncratic phrasing; she brought a blues feel to performances with swing bands. Songs she made her own include 'Stormy Weather', 'Strange Fruit' and 'I Cover the Waterfront'.

holiday camp site that provides an all-inclusive holiday, usually with entertainment, at an inclusive price. The first holiday camp on a permanent site was opened 1894 near Douglas, Isle of Man, by Joseph Cunningham. Billy *Butlin's first camp (accommodating 3,000 people) opened at Skegness 1935.

Holinshed Ralph c. 1520–c. 1580. English historian who published two volumes of the *Chronicles of England, Scotland and Ireland* 1578, on which Shakespeare based his history plays.

holism in philosophy, the concept that the whole is greater than the sum of its parts.

holistic medicine umbrella term for an approach that virtually all alternative therapies profess, which considers the overall health and lifestyle profile of a patient, and treats specific ailments not primarily as conditions to be alleviated but rather as symptoms of more fundamental disease.

Holland John Philip 1840–1914. Irish engineer who developed some of the first submarines. He began work in Ireland in the late 1860s and emigrated to the USA 1873. His first successful boat was launched 1881 and, after several failures, built the *Holland* 1893, which was bought by the US Navy two years later.

Hollerith Herman 1860–1929. US inventor of a

mechanical tabulating machine, the first device for data processing. Hollerith's tabulator was widely publicized after being successfully used in the 1890 census. The firm he established, the Tabulating Machine Company, was later one of the founding companies of *IBM.

holly tree or shrub of the genus *Ilex*, family Aquifoliaceae, including the English Christmas holly *I. aquifolium*, an evergreen with spiny, glossy leaves, small white flowers, and poisonous scarlet berries on the female tree. Leaves of the Brazilian holly *I. paraguayensis* are used to make the tea **yerba maté**.

Holly Buddy. Stage name of Charles Hardin Holley 1936–1959. US rock-and-roll singer, guitarist, and songwriter, born in Lubbock, Texas. Holly had a distinctive, hiccuping vocal style and was an early experimenter with recording techniques. Many of his hits with his band, the Crickets, such as 'That'll Be the Day' 1957, 'Peggy Sue' 1957, and 'Maybe Baby' 1958, have become classics. He died in a plane crash.

hollyhock plant of the genus *Althaea* of the mallow family Malvaceae. *A. rosea*, originally a native of Asia, produces spikes of large white, yellow, or red flowers, 3 m/10 ft high when cultivated as a biennial.

Hollywood district in the city of Los Angeles, California; the centre of the US film industry from 1911. It is the home of legendary film studios such as 20th Century Fox, MGM, Paramount, Columbia Pictures, United Artists, Disney, and Warner Brothers. Many film stars' homes are situated nearby in Beverly Hills and other communities adjacent to Hollywood.

Holmes, Sherlock fictitious private detective, created by the English writer Arthur Conan *Doyle in *A Study in Scarlet* 1887 and recurring in novels and stories until 1914. Holmes's ability to make inferences from slight clues always astonishes the narrator, Dr Watson.

holmium (Latin *Holmia* 'Stockholm') silvery, metallic element of the *lanthanide series, symbol Ho, atomic number 67, relative atomic mass 164.93. It occurs in combination with other rare-earth metals and in various minerals such as gadolinite. Its compounds are highly magnetic.

Holocaust, the the annihilation of more than 16 million people by the Hitler regime 1933–45 in the numerous extermination and *concentration camps, most notably Auschwitz, Sobibor, Treblinka, and Maidanek in Poland, and Belsen, Buchenwald, and Dachau in Germany. Of the victims who died during imprisonment or were exterminated, more than 6 million were Jews (over 67% of European Jewry); 10 million were Ukrainian, Polish, and Russian civilians and prisoners of war, Romanies, socialists, homosexuals, and others (labelled 'defectives'). Victims were variously starved, tortured, experimented on, and worked to death. Many thousands were executed in gas chambers, shot, or hanged. It was euphemistically termed the *final solution.

Holocene epoch of geological time that began 10,000 years ago, the second and current epoch of the Quaternary period. The glaciers retreated, the climate became warmer, and humans developed significantly.

holography method of producing three-dimensional (3-D) images by means of *laser light. Holography uses a photographic technique (involving the splitting of a laser beam into two beams) to produce a picture, or hologram, that contains 3-D information about the object photographed. Some holograms show meaningless patterns in ordinary light and produce a 3-D image only when laser light is projected through them, but reflection holograms produce images when ordinary light is reflected from them (as found on credit cards).

Holst Gustav(us Theodore von) 1874–1934. English composer. He wrote operas, including *Savitri* 1916 and *At the Boar's Head* 1925; ballets; choral works, including *Hymns from the Rig Veda* 1911 and *The Hymn of Jesus* 1920; orchestral suites, including *The Planets* 1918;

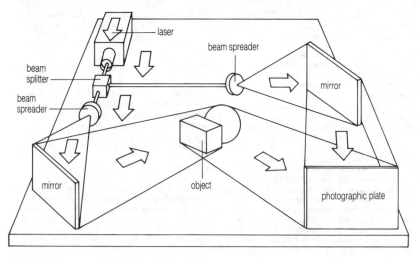

holography Recording a transmission hologram.

and songs. He was a lifelong friend of Ralph *Vaughan Williams, with whom he shared an enthusiasm for English folk music. His musical style, although tonal and drawing on folk song, tends to be severe.

Holt Harold Edward 1908–1967. Australian Liberal politician, prime minister 1966–67. His brief prime ministership was dominated by the Vietnam War, to which he committed increased Australian troops.

Holy Alliance 'Christian Union of Charity, Peace, and Love' initiated by Alexander I of Russia 1815 and signed by every crowned head in Europe. The alliance became associated with Russian attempts to preserve autocratic monarchies at any price, and served as an excuse to meddle in the internal affairs of other states.

Holy Communion another name for the *Eucharist, a Christian sacrament.

Holy Grail in medieval Christian legend, the dish or cup used by Jesus at the Last Supper, supposed to have supernatural powers. Together with the spear with which he was wounded at the Crucifixion, it was an object of quest by King Arthur's knights in certain stories incorporated in the Arthurian legend.

Holy Land Christian term for *Israel, because of its association with Jesus and the Old Testament.

Holy Office tribunal of the Roman Catholic church that deals with ecclesiastical discipline; see *Inquisition.

holy orders Christian priesthood, as conferred by the laying on of hands by a bishop. It is held by the Roman Catholic, Eastern Orthodox, and Anglican churches to have originated in Jesus' choosing of the apostles.

Holy Roman Empire empire of *Charlemagne and his successors, and the German Empire 962–1806, both being regarded as the Christian (hence 'holy') revival of the Roman Empire. At its height it comprised much of western and central Europe. See *Germany, history and *Habsburg.

Holyrood House royal residence in Edinburgh, Scotland. The palace was built 1498–1503 on the site of a 12th-century abbey by James IV. It has associations with Mary, Queen of Scots, and Charles Edward, the Young Pretender.

Holy See the diocese of the *pope.

Holy Spirit third person of the Christian *Trinity, also known as the Holy Ghost or the Paraclete, usually depicted as a white dove.

Holy Week in the Christian church, the last week of *Lent, when Christians commemorate the events that led up to the crucifixion of Jesus. Holy Week begins on Palm Sunday and includes Maundy Thursday, which commemorates the Last Supper.

Home Alec Douglas-Home, Baron Home of the Hirsel 1903– . British Conservative politician. He was foreign secretary 1960–63, and succeeded Harold Macmillan as prime minister 1963. He renounced his peerage (as 14th Earl of Home) to fight (and lose) the general election 1963, and resigned as party leader 1965. He was again foreign secretary 1970–74, when he received a life peerage. The playwright William Douglas-Home was his brother.

Home Counties the counties in close proximity to London, England: Hertfordshire, Essex, Kent, Surrey, and formerly Middlesex.

home front the organized sectors of domestic activity in wartime, mainly associated with World Wars I and II. Features of the UK home front in World War II included the organization of the black-out, evacuation, air-raid shelters, the Home Guard, rationing, and distribution of gas masks. With many men on active military service, women were called upon to carry out jobs previously undertaken only by men.

Home Guard unpaid force formed in Britain May 1940 to repel the expected German invasion, and known until July 1940 as the Local Defence Volunteers. It consisted of men aged 17–65 who had not been called up, formed part of the armed forces of the crown, and was subject to military law. Over 2 million strong in 1944, it was disbanded 31 Dec 1945, but revived 1951, then placed on a reserve basis 1955, and ceased activities 1957.

homeland or *Bantustan* before 1980, name for the *Black National States in the Republic of South Africa.

Homelands Policy South Africa's apartheid policy which set aside *Black National States for black Africans.

Home Office British government department established 1782 to deal with all the internal affairs of England except those specifically assigned to other departments. Responsibilities include the police, the prison service, immigration, race relations, and broadcasting. The home secretary, the head of the department, holds cabinet rank. There is a separate secretary of state for Scotland and another for Wales. The home secretary has certain duties in respect of the Channel Islands and the Isle of Man.

homeopathy alternative spelling of *homoeopathy*.

homeothermy maintenance of a constant body temperature in endothermic (warm-blooded) animals, by the use of chemical body processes to compensate for heat loss or gain when external temperatures change. Such processes include generation of heat by the breakdown of food and the contraction of muscles, and loss of heat by sweating, panting, and other means.

Homer lived c. 8th century BC. Legendary Greek epic poet. According to tradition, he was a blind minstrel and the author of the *Iliad* and the *Odyssey*, which are probably based on much older stories, passed on orally, concerning war with Troy in the 12th century BC.

Homer Winslow 1836–1910. US painter and lithographer, known for his seascapes, both oils and watercolours, which date from the 1880s and 1890s.

Home Rule, Irish movement to repeal the Act of *Union 1801 that joined Ireland to Britain and to establish an Irish parliament responsible for internal affairs. In 1870 Isaac Butt (1813–1879) formed the Home Rule Association and the movement was led in Parliament from 1880 by Charles *Parnell. After 1918 the demand for an independent Irish republic replaced that for home rule.

home service force (HSF) military unit established in the UK 1982, linked to the *Territorial Army (TA) and recruited from volunteers aged 18–60 with previous army (TA or regular) experience. It was introduced to guard key points and installations likely to be the target of enemy 'special forces' and saboteurs, so releasing other units for mobile defence roles.

Homestead Act in US history, an act of Congress 1862 to encourage settlement of land in the west by offering 65-hectare/160-acre plots cheaply or even free to those willing to cultivate and improve the land for a stipulated amount of time. By 1900 about 32 million hectares/80 million acres had been distributed. Homestead lands are available to this day.

homicide in law, the killing of a human being. This may be unlawful, lawful, or excusable, depending on the circumstances. Unlawful homicides include *murder, *manslaughter, *infanticide, and causing death by dangerous driving. Lawful homicide occurs where, for example, a police officer is justified in killing a criminal in the course of apprehension or when a person is killed in self-defence or defence of others.

homoeopathy or **homeopathy** system of medicine based on the principle that symptoms of disease are part of the body's self-healing processes, and on the practice of administering extremely diluted doses of natural substances found to produce in a healthy person the symptoms manifest in the illness being treated. Developed by German physician Samuel Hahnemann (1755–1843), the system is widely practised today as an alternative to allopathic medicine, and many controlled tests and achieved cures testify its efficacy.

homologous in biology, a term describing an organ or structure possessed by members of different taxonomic groups (for example, species, genera, families, orders) that originally derived from the same structure in a common ancestor. The wing of a bat, the arm of a monkey, and the flipper of a seal are homologous because they all derive from the forelimb of an ancestral mammal.

homologous series any of a number of series of organic chemicals with similar chemical properties in which members differ by a constant relative molecular mass.

homonymy aspect of language in which, through historical accident, two or more words may sound and look alike (**homonymy** proper, as in a farmer's *bull* and a papal *bull*), may sound the same but look different (**homophony**, as in *air* and *heir*; *gilt* and *guilt*), or may look the same but sound different (**homography**, as in the *wind* in the trees and roads that *wind*).

homophony in music, a melody lead and accompanying harmony, as distinct from **heterophony** and **polyphony** in which different melody lines are combined.

homosexuality sexual preference for, or attraction to, persons of one's own sex; in women it is referred to as *lesbianism. Both sexes use the term 'gay'. Men and women who are attracted to both sexes are referred to as bisexual. The extent to which homosexual behaviour is caused by biological or psychological factors is an area of disagreement among experts.

homozygous in a living organism, having two identical *alleles for a given trait. Individuals homozygous for a trait always breed true; that is, they produce offspring that resemble them in appearance when bred with a genetically similar individual; inbred varieties or species are homozygous for almost all traits. *Recessive alleles are only expressed in the homozygous condition. See also *heterozygous.

Homs or **Hums** city, capital of Homs district, W Syria, near the Orontes River; population (1981) 355,000. Silk, cereals, and fruit are produced in the area, and industries include silk textiles, oil refining, and jewellery. *Zenobia, Queen of Palmyra, was defeated at Homs by the Roman emperor *Aurelian 272.

Honan alternative name of ***Henan**, a province of China.

Honduras Republic of (*República de Honduras*)

area 112,100 sq km/43,282 sq mi
capital Tegucigalpa
towns San Pedro Sula; ports La Ceiba, Puerto Cortés
physical narrow tropical coastal plain with mountainous interior, Bay Islands
head of state and government Carlos Roberto Reina from 1993
political system democratic republic
exports coffee, bananas, meat, sugar, timber (including mahogany, rosewood)
currency lempira
population (1993 est) 5,240,000 (mestizo, or mixed, 90%; Indians and Europeans 10%); growth rate 3.1% p.a.
languages Spanish (official), English, Indian languages
religion Roman Catholic 97%
GNP $570 per head (1991)
chronology
1838 Independence achieved from Spain.
1980 After more than a century of mostly military rule, a civilian government was elected, with Dr Roberto Suazo as president; the commander in chief of the army, General Gustavo Alvarez, retained considerable power.
1983 Close involvement with the USA in providing naval and air bases and allowing Nicaraguan counter-revolutionaries ('Contras') to operate from Honduras.
1984 Alvarez ousted in coup led by junior

officers, resulting in policy review towards USA and Nicaragua.
1985 José Azcona elected president after electoral law changed, making Suazo ineligible for presidency.
1989 Peace plan to demobilize Nicaraguan Contras based in Honduras.
1990 Rafael Callejas (PN) inaugurated as president.
1992 Border dispute with El Salvador dating from 1861 finally resolved.
1993 Carlos Roberto Reina elected President.

Honecker Erich 1912–1994. German communist politician, in power 1973–89, elected chair of the council of state (head of state) 1976. He governed in an outwardly austere and efficient manner and, while favouring East–West détente, was a loyal ally of the USSR. In Oct 1989, following a wave of prodemocracy demonstrations, he was replaced as leader of the Socialist Unity Party (SED) and head of state by Egon *Krenz, and in Dec expelled from the Communist Party.

Honegger Arthur 1892–1955. Swiss composer, one of *Les Six. His work was varied in form, for example, the opera *Antigone* 1927, the ballet *Skating Rink* 1922, the oratorio *Le Roi David/King David* 1921, programme music (*Pacific 231* 1923), and the *Symphonie liturgique/Liturgical Symphony* 1946.

honey sweet syrup produced by honey *bees from the nectar of flowers. It is stored in honeycombs and made in excess of their needs as food for the winter. Honey comprises various sugars, mainly laevulose and dextrose, with enzymes, colouring matter, acids, and pollen grains. It has antibacterial properties and was widely used in ancient Egypt, Greece, and Rome as a wound salve. It is still popular for sore throats, in hot drinks or in lozenges.

honeysuckle vine or shrub of the genus *Lonicera*, family Caprifoliaceae. The common honeysuckle or woodbine *L. periclymenum* of Europe is a climbing plant with sweet-scented flowers, reddish and yellow-tinted outside and creamy-white inside; it now grows in the northeastern USA.

Hong Kong British crown colony SE of China, in the South China Sea, comprising Hong Kong Island; the Kowloon Peninsula; many other islands, of which the largest is Lantau; and the mainland New Territories. It is due to revert to Chinese control 1997.
area 1,070 sq km/413 sq mi
capital Victoria (Hong Kong City)
towns Kowloon, Tsuen Wan (in the New Territories)
exports textiles, clothing, electronic goods, clocks, watches, cameras, plastic products; a large proportion of the exports and imports of S China are transshipped here; tourism is important
currency Hong Kong dollar
population (1986) 5,431,000; 57% Hong Kong Chinese, most of the remainder refugees from the mainland
languages English, Chinese
religions Confucianist, Buddhist, Taoist, with Muslim and Christian minorities
government Hong Kong is a British depen-

dency administered by a crown-appointed governor (Chris Patten from 1992) who presides over an unelected executive council, composed of 4 ex-officio and 11 nominated members, and a legislative council composed of 3 ex-officio members, 18 appointees, and 39 elected members. In 1994 the Legislative Council, in defiance of China, passed the first stage of the constitutional reforms which lowered the voting age to 18 and provided for elected local councils.
history formerly part of China, Hong Kong Island was occupied by Britain 1841, during the first of the *Opium Wars, and ceded by China under the 1842 Treaty of Nanking. The Kowloon Peninsula was acquired under the 1860 Beijing (Peking) Convention and the New Territories secured on a 99-year lease from 1898. The colony, which developed into a major entrepôt for Sino-British trade during the late 19th and early 20th centuries, was occupied by Japan 1941–45. The restored British administration promised, after 1946, to increase self-government. These plans were shelved, however, after the 1949 Communist revolution in China. During the 1950s almost 1 million Chinese (predominantly Cantonese) refugees fled to Hong Kong. Immigration continued during the 1960s and 1970s, raising the colony's population from 1 million in 1946 to 5 million in 1980, leading to the imposition of strict border controls during the 1980s. Since 1975, 160,000 Vietnamese *boat people have fled to Hong Kong; in 1991 some 61,000 remained. The UK government began forced repatriation 1989. Hong Kong's economy expanded rapidly during the corresponding period and the colony became one of Asia's major commercial, financial, and industrial centres, boasting the world's busiest container port from 1987. As the date (1997) for the termination of the New Territories' lease approached, negotiations on Hong Kong's future were opened between Britain and China 1982. These culminated in a unique agreement, signed in Beijing 1984, in which Britain agreed to transfer full sovereignty of the islands and New Territories to China 1997 in return for Chinese assurance that Hong Kong's social and economic freedom and capitalist lifestyle would be preserved for at least 50 years.

honi soit qui mal y pense (French 'shame on him or her who thinks evil of it') the motto of England's Order of the Garter.

Honolulu (Hawaiian 'sheltered bay') capital city and port of Hawaii, on the S coast of Oahu; population (1990) 365,300. It is a holiday resort, noted for its beauty and tropical vegetation, with some industry.

honours list military and civil awards approved by the sovereign of the UK and published on New Year's Day and on her official birthday in June. Many Commonwealth countries, for example, Australia and Canada, also have their own honours list.

Honshu principal island of Japan. It lies between Hokkaido to the NE and Kyushu to the SW; area 231,100 sq km/89,205 sq mi, including 382 smaller islands; population (1986) 97,283,000. A chain of volcanic mountains runs along the island, which is subject to frequent earthquakes. The main cities are Tokyo, Yokohama, Osaka, Kobe, Nagoya, and Hiroshima.

Honthorst Gerrit van 1590–1656. Dutch painter who used extremes of light and shade, influenced by Caravaggio; with Terbrugghen he formed the **Utrecht School**.

Hooch Pieter de 1629–1684. Dutch painter, active in Delft and, later, Amsterdam. The harmonious domestic interiors and courtyards of his Delft period were influenced by Vermeer.

Hooke Robert 1635–1703. English scientist and inventor, originator of *Hooke's law, and considered the foremost mechanic of his time. His inventions included a telegraph system, the spirit level, marine barometer, and sea gauge. He coined the term 'cell' in biology.

Hooker Joseph Dalton 1817–1911. English botanist who travelled to the Antarctic and made many botanical discoveries. His works include *Flora Antarctica* 1844–47, *Genera Plantarum* 1862–83, and *Flora of British India* 1875–97.

Hooke's law in physics, law stating that the tension in a lightly stretched spring is proportional to its extension from its natural length. It was discovered by Robert Hooke 1676.

hookworm parasitic roundworm (see *worm), of the genus *Necator*, with hooks around the mouth. It lives mainly in tropic and subtropic regions, but also in humid areas in temperate climates. The eggs are hatched in damp soil, and the larvae bore into the host's skin, usually through the soles of the feet. They make their way to the small intestine, where they live by sucking blood. The eggs are expelled with faeces, and the cycle starts again. The human hookworm causes anaemia, weakness, and abdominal pain. It is common in areas where defecation occurs outdoors.

hoopoe bird *Upupa epops* in the order Coraciiformes, slightly larger than a thrush, with a long, thin bill and a bright, buff-coloured crest that expands into a fan shape. The wings are banded with black and white, and the rest of the plumage is black, white, and buff. This bird is the 'lapwing' mentioned in the Old Testament.

Hoover Herbert Clark 1874–1964. 31st president of the USA 1929–33, a Republican. He was secretary of commerce 1921–28. Hoover lost public confidence after the stock-market crash of 1929, when he opposed direct government aid for the unemployed in the Depression that followed.

Hoover J(ohn) Edgar 1895–1972. US director of the Federal Bureau of Investigation (FBI) from 1924. He built up a powerful network for the detection of organized crime. His drive against alleged communist activities after World War II, and his opposition to the Kennedy administration and others brought much criticism over abuse of power.

Hoover William Henry 1849–1932. US manufacturer who developed the *vacuum cleaner. 'Hoover' soon became a generic name for vacuum cleaner.

Hoover Dam highest concrete dam in the USA, 221 m/726 ft, on the Colorado River at the Arizona–Nevada border. It was begun built 1931–36. Known as Boulder Dam 1933–47, its name was restored by President Truman as the reputation of the former president, Herbert Hoover, was revived. It impounds Lake Meade, and has a hydroelectric power capacity of 1,300 megawatts.

Hope Bob. Stage name of Leslie Townes Hope 1903– . British-born US comedian, best remembered for seven films he made with Bing *Crosby and Dorothy Lamour between 1940 and 1953, whose titles all began *The Road to* (*Singapore, Zanzibar, Morocco, Utopia, Rio, Bali*, and *Hong Kong*).

Hopei alternative transcription of **Hebei**, a province of China.

Hope's apparatus in physics, an apparatus used to demonstrate the temperature at which water has its maximum density. It is named after Thomas Charles Hope (1766–1844).

Hopewell North American Indian agricultural culture of the central USA, dated about AD 200. The Hopewell built burial mounds up to 12 m/40 ft high and structures such as Serpent Mound in Ohio; see also *Moundbuilder.

Hopi member of a North American Indian people, numbering approximately 9,000, who live mainly in mountain villages in the SW USA, especially NE Arizona. They live in houses of stone or adobe (mud brick), forming small towns on rocky plateaus, and farm and herd sheep. Their language belongs to the Uto-Aztecan family.

Hopkins Anthony 1937– . Welsh actor. Among his stage appearances are *Equus, Macbeth, Pravda,* and the title role in *King Lear*. His films include *The Lion in Winter* 1968, *A Bridge Too Far* 1977, *The Elephant Man* 1980, *84 Charing Cross Road* 1986, and *The Silence of the Lambs* (Academy Award) 1991.

Hopkins Gerard Manley 1844–1889. English poet and Jesuit priest. His work, marked by its religious themes and use of natural imagery, includes 'The Wreck of the Deutschland' 1876 and 'The Windhover' 1877. His employment of 'sprung rhythm' greatly influenced later 20th-century poetry. His poetry was written in secret, and published 30 years after his death by his friend Robert Bridges.

Hopper Dennis 1936– . US film actor and director who caused a sensation with the antiestablishment *Easy Rider* 1969, the archetypal 'road' film, but whose *The Last Movie* 1971 was poorly received by the critics. He made a comeback in the 1980s. His work as an actor includes *Rebel Without a Cause* 1955, *The American Friend/Der amerikanische Freund* 1977, and *Blue Velvet* 1986.

Hopper Edward 1882–1967. US painter and etcher. His views of New England and New York in the 1930s and 1940s captured the loneliness and superficial glamour of city life, as in *Nighthawks* 1942 (Art Institute, Chicago).

hops female fruit-heads of the hop plant *Humulus lupulus*, family Cannabiaceae; these are dried and used as a tonic and in flavouring beer. In designated areas in Europe, no male hops may be grown, since seedless hops produced by the unpollinated female plant contain a greater proportion of the alpha acid that gives beer its bitter taste.

Horace 65–8 BC. Roman lyric poet and satirist. He became a leading poet under the patronage of Emperor Augustus. His works include *Satires

35–30 BC; the four books of *Odes* about 25–24 BC; *Epistles*, a series of verse letters; and a critical work, *Ars poetica*. They are distinguished by their style, wit, and good sense.

horehound any plant of the genus *Marrubium* of the mint family Labiatae. The white horehound *M. vulgare*, found in Europe, N Africa, and W Asia and naturalized in North America, has a thick, hairy stem and clusters of dull white flowers; it has medicinal uses.

horizon the limit to which one can see across the surface of the sea or a level plain, that is, about 5 km/3 mi at 1.5 m/5 ft above sea level, and about 65 km/40 mi at 300 m/1,000 ft.

hormone product of the *endocrine glands, concerned with control of body functions. The main glands are the thyroid, parathyroid, pituitary, adrenal, pancreas, uterus, ovary, and testis. Hormones bring about changes in the functions of various organs according to the body's requirements. The pituitary gland, at the base of the brain, is a centre for overall coordination of hormone secretion; the thyroid hormones determine the rate of general body chemistry; the adrenal hormones prepare the organism during stress for 'fight or flight'; and the sexual hormones such as oestrogen govern reproductive functions.

hormone-replacement therapy (HRT) use of oral *oestrogen and progesterone to help limit the effects of the menopause in women. The treatment was first used in the 1970s.

Hormuz or *Ormuz* small island, area 41 sq km/16 sq mi, in the Strait of Hormuz, belonging to Iran. It is strategically important because oil tankers leaving the Persian Gulf for Japan and the West have to pass through the strait to reach the Arabian Sea.

horn one of a family of wind instruments, of which the French horn is the most widely used. See *brass instrument.

Horn Philip de Montmorency, Count of Horn 1518–1568. Flemish politician. He held high offices under the Holy Roman emperor Charles V and his son Philip II. From 1563 he was one of the leaders of the opposition to the rule of Cardinal Granvella (1517–1586) and to the introduction of the Inquisition. In 1567 he was arrested, together with the Resistance leader Egmont, and both were beheaded in Brussels.

hornbeam any tree of the genus *Carpinus* of the birch family Betulaceae. They have oval, serrated leaves and bear pendant clusters of flowers, each with a nutlike seed attached to the base. The trunk is usually twisted, with smooth grey bark.

hornbill bird of the family of Bucerotidae, found in Africa, India, and Malaysia. Omnivorous, it is about 1 m/3 ft long, and has a powerful bill, usually surmounted by a bony growth or casque. During the breeding season, the female walls herself into a hole in a tree, and does not emerge until the young are hatched.

hornblende green or black rock-forming mineral, one of the *amphiboles; it is a hydrous silicate of calcium, iron, magnesium, and aluminium. Hornblende is found in both igneous and metamorphic rocks.

hornet kind of *wasp.

hornfels *metamorphic rock formed by rocks heated by contact with a hot igneous body. It is fine-grained and brittle, without foliation.

Horniman Annie Elizabeth Frederika 1860–1937. English pioneer of repertory theatre who subsidized the Abbey Theatre, Dublin, and founded the Manchester company.

hornwort underwater aquatic plant, family Ceratophyllaceae. It has whorls of finely divided leaves and is found in slow-moving water. Hornworts may be up to 2 m/7 ft long.

horoscope in Western astrology, a chart of the position of the Sun, Moon, and planets relative to the *zodiac at the moment of birth, used to assess a person's character and forecast future influences.

Horowitz Vladimir 1904–1989. Russian-born US pianist. He made his debut in the USA 1928 with the New York Philharmonic Orchestra. Noted for his commanding virtuoso style, he was a leading interpreter of Liszt, Schumann, and Rachmaninov.

horror genre of fiction and film, devoted primarily to scaring the reader or audience, but often also aiming to be cathartic through their exaggeration of the bizarre and grotesque. Dominant figures in the horror tradition are Mary Shelley (*Frankenstein* 1818), Edgar Allan Poe, Bram Stoker, H P Lovecraft and, among contemporary writers, Stephen King and Clive Barker.

horse hoofed, odd-toed, grazing mammal *Equus caballus* of the family Equidae, which also includes zebras and asses. The many breeds of domestic horse of Euro-Asian origin range in colour from white to grey, brown, and black. The yellow-brown Mongolian wild horse or Przewalski's horse *E. przewalskii*, named after its Polish 'discoverer' about 1880, is the only surviving species of wild horse.

horse chestnut any tree of the genus *Aesculus* of the family Hippocastanaceae, especially *A. hippocastanum*, originally from SE Europe but widely planted elsewhere. Horse chestnuts have large, showy spikes of bell-shaped flowers and bear large, shiny, inedible seeds in capsules (**conkers**). The horse chestnut is not related to the true chestnut. In North America it is called buckeye.

horsefly any of over 2,500 species of fly, belonging to the family Tabanidae. The females suck blood from horses, cattle, and humans; males live on plants and suck nectar. The larvae are carnivorous.

Horse Guards in the UK, the Household Cavalry, or Royal Horse Guards, formed 1661. Their headquarters, in Whitehall, London, were erected in 1753 on the site of the Tilt Yard of Whitehall Palace.

horsepower imperial unit (abbreviation hp) of power, now replaced by the *watt. It was first used by the engineer James *Watt, who employed it to compare the power of steam engines with that of horses.

horse racing sport of racing mounted or driven horses. Two forms in Britain are *flat racing*, for thoroughbred horses over a flat course, and *National Hunt racing*, in which the horses have to clear obstacles.

horseradish hardy perennial *Armoracia rusticana*, native to SE Europe but naturalized elsewhere, family Cruciferae. The thick, cream-coloured root is strong-tasting and is often made into a condiment.

horsetail plant of the genus *Equisetum*, related to ferns and club mosses; some species are also called *scouring rush*. There are about 35 living species, bearing their spores on cones at the stem tip. The upright stems are ribbed and often have spaced whorls of branches. Today they are of modest size, but hundreds of millions of years ago giant treelike forms existed.

Horthy Nicholas Horthy de Nagybánya 1868–1957. Hungarian politician and admiral. Leader of the counterrevolutionary White government, he became regent 1920 on the overthrow of the communist Bela Kun regime by Romanian and Czechoslovak intervention. He represented the conservative and military class, and retained power until World War II, trying (although allied to Hitler) to retain independence of action. In 1944 he tried to negotiate a surrender to the USSR but Hungary was taken over by the Nazis and he was deported to Germany. He was released from German captivity the same year by the Western Allies and allowed to go to Portugal, where he died.

horticulture art and science of growing flowers, fruit, and vegetables. Horticulture is practised in gardens and orchards, along with millions of acres of land devoted to vegetable farming. Some areas, like California, have specialized in horticulture because they have the mild climate and light fertile soil most suited to these crops.

Horus in ancient Egyptian mythology, the hawk-headed sun god, son of Isis and Osiris, of whom the pharaohs were declared to be the incarnation.

Hoskins Bob 1942– . English character actor. He progressed to fame from a series of supporting roles. Films include *The Long Good Friday* 1980, *The Cotton Club* 1984, *Mona Lisa* 1985, *A Prayer for the Dying* 1987, and *Who Framed Roger Rabbit?* 1988.

hospice residential facility specializing in palliative care for terminally ill patients and their relatives.

Hospitaller member of the Order of *St John.

host in biology, an organism that is parasitized by another. In *commensalism, the partner that does not benefit may also be called the host.

hostage person taken prisoner as a means of exerting pressure on a third party, usually with threats of death or injury.

HOTOL (acronym for *horizontal takeoff and landing*) reusable hypersonic spaceplane invented by British engineer Alan Bond 1983. HOTOL was to be a single-stage vehicle that could take off and land on a runway. It featured a revolutionary dual-purpose engine that enabled it to carry far less oxygen than a conventional spaceplane: it functioned as a jet engine during the initial stage of flight, taking in oxygen from the surrounding air; when the air became too thin, it was converted into a rocket, burning oxygen from an onboard supply. The project was developed by British Aerospace and Rolls-Royce but foundered for lack of capital 1988, largely because a government security order prevented

the companies from showing plans to potential overseas backers.

hot spot in geology, a hypothetical region of high thermal activity in the Earth's *mantle. Hot spots are believed to be the origin of many chains of ocean islands, such as Polynesia and the Galápagos.

Hottentot ('stammerer') South African term for a variety of different African peoples; it is non-scientific and considered derogatory by many. The name *Khoikhoi is preferred.

Houdini Harry. Stage name of Erich Weiss 1874–1926. US escapologist and conjurer. He was renowned for his escapes from ropes and handcuffs, from trunks under water, from straitjackets and prison cells.

Houphouët-Boigny Félix 1905–1993. Ivory Coast right-wing politician. He held posts in French ministries, and became president of the Republic of the Ivory Coast on independence 1960, maintaining close links with France, which helped to boost an already thriving economy and encourage political stability. Pro-Western and opposed to communist intervention in Africa, Houphouët-Boigny has been strongly criticized for maintaining diplomatic relations with South Africa. He was re-elected for a seventh term 1990 in multiparty elections, amid allegations of ballot rigging and political pressure.

hour period of time comprising 60 minutes; 24 hours make one calendar day.

Hours, Book of in medieval Europe, a collection of liturgical prayers for the use of the faithful.

housefly fly of the genus *Musca*, found in and around dwellings, especially *M. domestica*, a common worldwide species. Houseflies are grey, and have mouthparts adapted for drinking liquids and sucking moisture from food and manure.

house music dance music of the 1980s originating in the inner-city clubs of Chicago, USA, combining funk with European high-tech pop, and using dub, digital sampling, and cross-fading. *Acid house* has minimal vocals and melody, instead surrounding the mechanically emphasized 4/4 beat with stripped-down synthesizer riffs and a wandering bass line. Other variants include *hip house*, with rap elements, and *acid jazz*.

House of Representatives lower house of the US *Congress, with 435 members elected at regular two-year intervals, every even year, in Nov.

Housman A(lfred) E(dward) 1859–1936. English poet and classical scholar. His *A Shropshire Lad* 1896, a series of deceptively simple, nostalgic, ballad-like poems, was popular during World War I. This was followed by *Last Poems* 1922 and *More Poems* 1936.

Houston port in Texas, USA; population (1990) 1,630,600; linked by canal to the Gulf of Mexico. It is a major centre of the petroleum industry and of finance and commerce. It is also one of the busiest US ports.

Houston Sam 1793–1863. US general who won independence for Texas from Mexico 1836 and was president of the Republic of Texas 1836–45. Houston, Texas, is named after him.

hovercraft vehicle that rides on a cushion of

high-pressure air, free from all contact with the surface beneath, invented by British engineer Christopher Cockerell 1959. Hovercraft need a smooth terrain when operating overland and are best adapted to use on waterways. They are useful in places where harbours have not been established.

Howard Catherine *c.* 1520–1542. Queen consort of *Henry VIII of England from 1540. In 1541 the archbishop of Canterbury, Thomas Cranmer, accused her of being unchaste before marriage to Henry and she was beheaded 1542 after Cranmer made further charges of adultery.

Howard Charles, 2nd Baron Howard of Effingham and 1st Earl of Nottingham 1536–1624. English admiral, a cousin of Queen Elizabeth I. He commanded the fleet against the Spanish Armada while Lord High Admiral 1585–1618.

Howard John 1726–1790. English philanthropist whose work to improve prison conditions is continued today by the *Howard League for Penal Reform*.

Howard Michael 1947–   . British Conservative politician, home secretary from 1993. On the right of the Conservative Party, he championed the restoration of law and order as a key electoral issue, but encountered stiff opposition to his proposals for reform of the criminal justice system and for increased police powers, as embodied in the 1994 Criminal Justice and Public Order Bill.

Howard Trevor (Wallace) 1916–1989. English actor whose films include *Brief Encounter* 1945, *Sons and Lovers* 1960, *Mutiny on the Bounty* 1962, *Ryan's Daughter* 1970, and *Conduct Unbecoming* 1975.

Howe Geoffrey 1926–   . British Conservative politician, member of Parliament for Surrey East. Under Edward Heath he was solicitor general 1970–72 and minister for trade 1972–74; as chancellor of the Exchequer 1979–83 under Margaret Thatcher, he put into practice the monetarist policy which reduced inflation at the cost of a rise in unemployment. In 1983 he became foreign secretary, and in 1989 deputy prime minister and leader of the House of Commons. On 1 Nov 1990 he resigned in protest at Thatcher's continued opposition to Britain's greater integration in Europe.

Howe William, 5th Viscount Howe 1729–1814. British general. During the War of American Independence he won the Battle of Bunker Hill 1775, and as commander in chief in America 1776–78 captured New York and defeated Washington at Brandywine and Germantown. He resigned in protest at lack of home government support.

howitzer cannon, in use since the 16th century, with a particularly steep angle of fire. It was much developed in World War I for demolishing the fortresses of the trench system. The multinational NATO FH70 field howitzer is mobile and fires, under computer control, three 43 kg/95 lb shells at 32 km/20 mi range in 15 seconds.

Hoxha Enver 1908–1985. Albanian Communist politician, the country's leader from 1954. He founded the Albanian Communist Party 1941, and headed the liberation movement 1939–44. He was prime minister 1944–54, combining with foreign affairs 1946–53, and from 1954 was first secretary of the Albanian Party of Labour. In policy he was a Stalinist and independent of both Chinese and Soviet communism.

Hoyle Fred(erick) 1915–   . English astronomer and writer. In 1948 he joined with Hermann *Bondi and Thomas Gold (1920–   ) in developing the *steady-state theory. In 1957, with Geoffrey and Margaret Burbidge (1925–   and 1919–   ) and William *Fowler, he showed that chemical elements heavier than hydrogen and helium are built up by nuclear reactions inside stars. He has suggested that life originates in the gas clouds of space and is delivered to the Earth by passing comets. His science-fiction novels include *The Black Cloud* 1957.

Hsuan Tung name adopted by Henry *P'u-i on becoming emperor of China 1908.

Hua Guofeng or *Hua Kuofeng* 1920–   . Chinese politician, leader of the Chinese Communist Party (CCP) 1976–81, premier 1976–80. He dominated Chinese politics 1976–77, seeking economic modernization without major structural reform. From 1978 he was gradually eclipsed by Deng Xiaoping. Hua was ousted from the Politburo Sept 1982 but remained a member of the CCP Central Committee.

Huang He or *Hwang Ho* river in China; length 5,464 km/3,395 mi. It takes its name (meaning 'yellow river') from its muddy waters. Formerly known as 'China's sorrow' because of disastrous floods, it is now largely controlled through hydroelectric works and flood barriers.

Hubbard L(afayette) Ron(ald) 1911–1986. US science-fiction writer of the 1930s and 40s, founder in 1954 of *Scientology.

Hubble Edwin Powell 1889–1953. US astronomer who discovered the existence of other *galaxies outside our own, and classified them according to their shape. His theory that the universe is expanding is now generally accepted.

Hubble's law the law that relates a galaxy's distance from us to its speed of recession as the universe expands, announced in 1929 by Edwin Hubble. He found that galaxies are moving apart at speeds that increase in direct proportion to their distance apart. The rate of expansion is known as Hubble's constant.

Hubble Space Telescope telescope placed into orbit around the Earth, at an altitude of 610 km/380 mi, by the space shuttle *Discovery* in April 1990. The telescope's position in space means that light from distant galaxies is not obscured by the atmosphere, and it therefore performs many times better than any ground-based instrument.

Hubei or *Hupei* province of central China, through which flow the river Chang Jiang and its tributary the Han Shui
area 187,500 sq km/72,375 sq mi
capital Wuhan
features high land in the W, the river Chang breaking through from Sichuan in gorges; elsewhere low-lying, fertile land; many lakes
products beans, cereals, cotton, rice, vegetables, copper, gypsum, iron ore, phosphorous, salt
population (1990) 53,969,000.

hubris in Greek thought, an act of transgression or overweening pride. In ancient Greek tragedy, hubris was believed to offend the gods, and to lead to retribution.

Hudson river of the NE USA; length 485 km/ 300 mi. It rises in the Adirondack Mountains and flows S, emptying into a bay of the Atlantic Ocean at New York City.

Hudson Henry *c.* 1565–*c.* 1611. English explorer. Under the auspices of the Muscovy Company 1607–08, he made two unsuccessful attempts to find the Northeast Passage to China. In Sept 1609, commissioned by the Dutch East India Company, he reached New York Bay and sailed 240 km/150 mi up the river that now bears his name, establishing Dutch claims to the area. In 1610, he sailed from London in the *Discovery* and entered what is now the Hudson Strait. After an icebound winter, he was turned adrift by a mutinous crew in what is now Hudson Bay.

Hudson Rock. Stage name of Roy Scherer Jr 1925–1985. US film actor. He was a star from the mid-1950s to the mid-1960s, and appeared in several melodramas directed by Douglas Sirk and in three comedies co-starring Doris Day (including *Pillow Talk* 1959). He went on to have a successful TV career in the 1970s.

Hudson Bay inland sea of NE Canada, linked with the Atlantic Ocean by **Hudson Strait** and with the Arctic Ocean by Foxe Channel; area 1,233,000 sq km/476,000 sq mi. It is named after Henry Hudson, who reached it 1610.

Hudson River School group of US landscape painters of the early 19th century. They were inspired by the dramatic scenery of the Hudson River Valley and the Catskill Mountains in New York State, and also by the Romantic landscapes of Turner and John Martin. The first artist to depict the region was Thomas Cole. The group also included Asher B. Durand, Martin Joseph Heade, and Frederic Edwin Church.

Hudson's Bay Company chartered company founded by Prince *Rupert 1670 to trade in furs with North American Indians. In 1783 the rival North West Company was formed, but in 1851 this became amalgamated with the Hudson's Bay Company. It is still Canada's biggest fur company, but today also sells general merchandise through department stores and has oil and natural gas interests.

Hughes Howard 1905–1976. US tycoon. Inheriting wealth from his father, who had patented a successful oil-drilling bit, he created a legendary financial empire. A skilled pilot, he manufactured and designed aircraft. He formed a film company in Hollywood and made the classic film *Hell's Angels* 1930, about aviators of World War I; later successes included *Scarface* 1932 and *The Outlaw* 1944. From his middle years he was a recluse.

Hughes Ted 1930– . English poet, poet laureate from 1984. His work includes *The Hawk in the Rain* 1957, *Lupercal* 1960, *Wodwo* 1967, and *River* 1983, and is characterized by its harsh portrayal of the crueller aspects of nature. In 1956 he married the poet Sylvia Plath.

Hughes Thomas 1822–1896. English writer, author of the children's book *Tom Brown's School Days* 1857, a story of Rugby school under Thomas *Arnold. It had a sequel, *Tom Brown at Oxford* 1861.

Hugo Victor (Marie) 1802–1885. French poet, novelist, and dramatist. The *Odes et poésies diverses* appeared 1822, and his verse play *Hernani* 1830 established him as the leader of French Romanticism. More volumes of verse followed between his series of dramatic novels, which included *Notre-Dame de Paris* 1831, later filmed as *The Hunchback of Notre Dame* 1924, 1939, and *Les Misérables* 1862, adapted as a musical 1980. He died a national hero and is buried in the Panthéon, Paris.

Huguenot French Protestant in the 16th century; the term referred mainly to Calvinists. Severely persecuted under Francis I and Henry II, the Huguenots survived both an attempt to exterminate them (the *Massacre of *St Bartholomew* 24 Aug 1572) and the religious wars of the next 30 years. In 1598 Henry IV (himself formerly a Huguenot) granted them toleration under the *Edict of Nantes. Louis XIV revoked the edict 1685, attempting their forcible conversion, and 400,000 emigrated.

Huhehot former name of *Hohhot, a city in Inner Mongolia.

Hui member of one of the largest minority ethnic groups in China, numbering about 25 million. Members of the Hui live all over China, but are concentrated in the northern central region. They have been Muslims since the 10th century, for which they have suffered persecution both before and since the Communist revolution.

Hull Cordell 1871–1955. US Democratic politician. As F D Roosevelt's secretary of state 1933–44, he opposed German and Japanese aggression. He was identified with the Good Neighbour policy of nonintervention in Latin America. In his last months of office he paved the way for a system of collective security, for which he was called 'father' of the United Nations. He was awarded the Nobel Peace Prize 1945.

Hull officially **Kingston upon Hull** city and port on the north bank of the Humber estuary, England, where the river Hull flows into it, England; population (1991) 252,200. It is linked with the south bank of the estuary by the Humber Bridge. Industries include fish processing, vegetable oils, flour milling, electrical goods, textiles, paint, pharmaceuticals, chemicals, caravans, and aircraft.

human body the physical structure of the human being. It develops from the single cell of the fertilized ovum, is born at 40 weeks, and usually reaches sexual maturity between 11 and 18 years of age. The bony framework (skeleton) consists of more than 200 bones, over half of which are in the hands and feet. Bones are held together by joints, some of which allow movement. The circulatory system supplies muscles and organs with blood, which provides oxygen and food and removes carbon dioxide and other waste products. Body functions are controlled by the nervous system and hormones. In the upper part of the trunk is the thorax, which contains the lungs and heart. Below this is the abdomen, containing the digestive system (stomach and intestines); the liver, spleen, and pancreas; the urinary system (kidneys, ureters, and bladder); and, in women, the reproductive organs (ovaries, uterus, and vagina). In men, the prostate gland

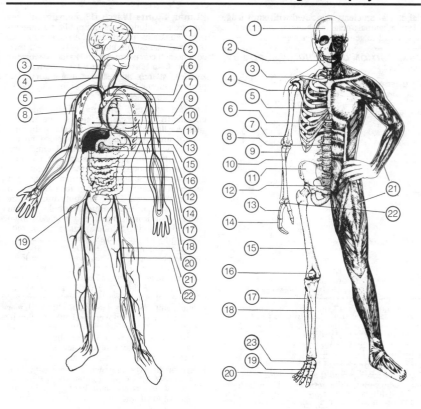

Key

1. brain	12. liver
2. eye	13. stomach
3. carotid artery	14. gall bladder
4. jugular vein	15. kidney
5. subclavian artery	16. pancreas
6. superior vena cava	17. small intestine
7. aorta	18. large intestine
8. subclavian vein	19. appendix
9. heart	20. bladder
10. lungs	21. femoral artery
11. diaphragm	22. femoral vein

Key

1. cranium (skull)	13. metacarpals
2. mandible	14. phalanges
3. clavicle	15. femur
4. scapula	16. patella
5. sternum	17. fibula
6. rib cage	18. tibia
7. humerus	19. metatarsals
8. vertebra	20. phalanges
9. ulna	21. superficial (upper)
10. radius	layer of muscles
11. pelvis	22. carpals
12. coccyx	23. tarsals

human body *The adult human body has approximately 650 muscles, 100 joints, 100,000 km/60,000 mi of blood vessels and 13,000 nerve cells.*

and seminal vesicles only of the reproductive system are situated in the abdomen, the testes being in the scrotum, which, with the penis, is suspended in front of and below the abdomen. The bladder empties through a small channel (urethra); in the female this opens in the upper end of the vulval cleft, which also contains the opening of the vagina, or birth canal; in the male, the urethra is continued into the penis. In both sexes, the lower bowel terminates in the anus, a ring of strong muscle situated between the buttocks.

human genome project research scheme, begun 1988, to map the complete nucleotide (see *nucleic acid) sequence of human *DNA. There are approximately 80,000 different *genes in the human genome, and one gene may contain more than 2 million nucleotides. The knowledge gained is expected to help prevent or treat many crippling and lethal diseases, but there are potential ethical problems associated with knowledge of an individual's genetic make-up, and fears that it will lead to genetic engineering.

COMPOSITION OF THE HUMAN BODY BY WEIGHT

class	chemical element or substance	body weight (%)
pure elements	oxygen	65
	carbon	18
	hydrogen	10
	nitrogen	3
	calcium	2
	phosphorus	1.1
	potassium	0.35
	sulphur	0.25
	sodium	0.15
	chlorine	0.15
	magnesium, iron, manganese, copper, iodine, cobalt, zinc	traces
water and solid matter	water	60–80
	total solid material	20–40
organic molecules	protein	15–20
	lipid	3–20
	carbohydrate	1–15
	small organic molecules	0–1

humanism belief in the goodness and high potential of human nature rather than in religious or transcendental values. Humanism culminated as a cultural and literary force in 16th-century Renaissance Europe in line with the period's enthusiasm for classical literature and art, growing individualism, and the ideal of the all-round male who should be statesman and poet, scholar and warrior. Sir Philip *Sidney is a great exemplar of Renaissance humanism.

human reproduction an example of *sexual reproduction, where the male produces sperm and the female eggs. These gametes contain only half the normal number of chromosomes, 23 instead of 46, so that on fertilization the resulting cell has the correct genetic complement. Fertilization is internal, which increases the chances of conception; unusually for mammals, copulation and pregnancy can occur at any time of the year. Human beings are also remarkable for the length of childhood and for the highly complex systems of parental care found in society. The use of contraception and the development of laboratory methods of insemination and fertilization are issues that make human reproduction more than a merely biological phenomenon.

Human Rights, Universal Declaration of charter of civil and political rights drawn up by the United Nations 1948. They include the right to life, liberty, education, and equality before the law; to freedom of movement, religion, association, and information; and to a nationality. Under the European Convention of Human Rights 1950, the Council of Europe established the *European Commission of Human Rights* (headquarters in Strasbourg, France), which investigates complaints by states or individuals, and its findings are examined by the *European Court of Human Rights* (established 1959), whose compulsory jurisdiction has been recognized by a number of states, including the UK.

Human Rights Watch US nonpartisan pressure group that monitors and publicizes human-rights abuses by governments, especially attacks on those who defend human rights in their own countries. It comprises *Africa Watch, Americas Watch, Asia Watch, Middle East Watch,* and *Helsinki Watch*; the last-named monitors compliance with the 1975 Helsinki accords by the 35 signatory countries.

human species, origins of evolution of humans from ancestral *primates. The African apes (gorilla and chimpanzee) are shown by anatomical and molecular comparisons to be the closest living relatives of humans. Humans are distinguished from apes by the size of their brain and jaw, their bipedalism, and their elaborate culture. Molecular studies put the date of the split between the human and African ape lines at 5–10 million years ago. There are only fragmentary remains of ape and **hominid** (of the human group) fossils from this period; the oldest known hominids, found in Ethiopia and Tanzania, date from 3.5 to 4 million years ago. These creatures are known as *Australopithecus afarensis,* and they walked upright. They were either direct ancestors or an offshoot of the line that led to modern humans. They may have been the ancestors of *Homo habilis* (considered by some to be a species of *Australopithecus*), who appeared about a million years later, had slightly larger bodies and brains, and were probably the first to use stone tools. *Australopithecus robustus* and *A. africanus* also lived in Africa at the same time, but these are not generally considered to be our ancestors.

Humber Bridge suspension bridge with twin towers 163 m/535 ft high, which spans the estuary of the river Humber in NE England. When completed 1980, it was the world's longest bridge with a span of 1,410 m/4,628 ft.

Humberside county of NE England
area 3,510 sq km/1,355 sq mi
towns Hull (administrative headquarters), Grimsby, Scunthorpe, Goole, Cleethorpes
products petrochemicals, refined oil, processed fish, cereals, root crops, cattle
population (1991) 845,200
famous people Andrew Marvell, John Wesley, Amy Johnson.

Humbert anglicized form of *Umberto, two kings of Italy.

Humboldt Friedrich Heinrich Alexander, Baron von 1769–1859. German botanist and geologist who, with the French botanist Aimé Bonpland (1773–1858), explored the regions of the Orinoco and the Amazon rivers in South America 1800–04, and gathered 60,000 plant specimens. On his return, Humboldt devoted 21 years to writing an account of his travels.

Hume David 1711–1776. Scottish philosopher. *A Treatise of Human Nature* 1739–40 is a central text of British empiricism. Hume denies the possibility of going beyond the subjective experiences of 'ideas' and 'impressions'. The effect of this position is to invalidate metaphysics.

Hume John 1937– . Northern Ireland Catholic politician, leader of the Social Democratic Labour Party (SDLP) from 1979. Hume was a founder member of the Credit Union Party, which later became the SDLP. In 1993 he held talks with Sinn Féin leader, Gerry Adams, on the possibility of securing peace in Northern Ireland, in response to which the British and Irish governments launched a joint peace initiative, which led to a general cease-fire 1994.

humidity the quantity of water vapour in a given volume of the atmosphere (absolute humidity), or the ratio of the amount of water vapour in the atmosphere to the saturation value at the same temperature (relative humidity). At *dew point the relative humidity is 100% and the air is said to be saturated. Condensation (the conversion of vapour to liquid) may then occur. Relative humidity is measured by various types of *hygrometer.

hummingbird any of various birds of the family Trochilidae, found in the Americas. The name is derived from the sound produced by the rapid vibration of their wings. Hummingbirds are brilliantly coloured, and have long, needlelike bills and tongues to obtain nectar from flowers and capture insects. They are the only birds able to fly backwards. The Cuban bee hummingbird *Mellisuga helenae*, the world's smallest bird, is 5.5 cm/2 in long, and weighs less than 2.5 g/ 0.1 oz.

humours, theory of theory prevalent in classical and medieval times that the human body was composed of four kinds of fluid: phlegm, blood, choler or yellow bile, and melancholy or black bile. Physical and mental characteristics were explained by different proportions of humours in individuals.

Humperdinck Engelbert 1854–1921. German composer. He studied music in Munich and in Italy and assisted Richard *Wagner at the Bayreuth Festival Theatre. He wrote the musical fairy operas *Hänsel und Gretel* 1893, and *Königskinder/King's Children* 1910.

Humphries (John) Barry 1934– . Australian actor and author. He is best known for his satirical one-person shows and especially for the creation of the character of Mrs (later Dame) Edna Everage. His comic strip 'The Adventures of Barry Mackenzie', published in the British weekly *Private Eye* 1963–74, was the basis for two films, *The Adventures of Barry Mackenzie* 1972 and *Barry Mackenzie Holds His Own* 1974, in which Humphries also acted.

humus component of *soil consisting of decomposed or partly decomposed organic matter, dark in colour and usually richer towards the surface. It has a higher carbon content than the original material and a lower nitrogen content, and is an important source of minerals in soil fertility.

Hun member of any of a number of nomad Mongol peoples who were first recorded historically in the 2nd century BC, raiding across the Great Wall into China. They entered Europe about AD 372, settled in the area that is now Hungary, and imposed their supremacy on the Ostrogoths and other Germanic peoples. Under the leadership of Attila they attacked the Byzantine Empire, invaded Gaul, and threatened Rome. After Attila's death in 453 their power was broken by a revolt of their subject peoples. The **White Huns**, or Ephthalites, a kindred people, raided Persia and N India in the 5th and 6th centuries.

Hunan province of S central China

area 210,500 sq km/81,253 sq mi
capital Changsha
products rice, tea, tobacco, cotton; nonferrous minerals
population (1990) 60,660,000.

hundred days in European history, the period 20 March–28 June 1815, marking the French emperor Napoleon's escape from imprisonment on Elba to his departure from Paris after losing the battle of Waterloo 18 June.

hundredweight imperial unit (abbreviation cwt) of mass, equal to 112 lb (50.8 kg). It is sometimes called the long hundredweight, to distinguish it from the short hundredweight or *cental*, equal to 100 lb (45.4 kg).

Hundred Years' War series of conflicts between England and France 1337–1453. Its origins lay with the English kings' possession of Gascony (SW France), which the French kings claimed as their *fief, and with trade rivalries over *Flanders. The two kingdoms had a long history of strife before 1337, and the Hundred Years' War has sometimes been interpreted as merely an intensification of these struggles. It was caused by fears of French intervention in Scotland, which the English were trying to subdue, and by the claim of England's *Edward III (through his mother Isabel, daughter of Charles IV) to the crown of France.

Hungarian language member of the Finno-Ugric language group, spoken principally in Hungary but also in parts of the Slovak Republic, Romania, and Yugoslavia. Hungarian is known as *Magyar* among its speakers. It is written in a form of the Roman alphabet in which *s* corresponds to English *sh*, and *sz* to *s*.

Hungary Republic of (*Magyar Köztársaság*)

area 93,032 sq km/35,910 sq mi
capital Budapest
towns Miskolc, Debrecen, Szeged, Pécs
physical Great Hungarian Plain covers E half of country; Bakony Forest, Lake Balaton, and Transdanubian Highlands in the W; rivers Danube, Tisza, and Raba
environment an estimated 35%–40% of the population live in areas with officially 'inadmissible' air and water pollution. In Budapest lead

levels have reached 30 times the maximum international standards
head of state Arpád Göncz from 1990
head of government Gyula Horn from 1994
political system emergent democratic republic
exports machinery, vehicles, iron and steel, chemicals, fruit and vegetables
currency forint
population (1993) 10,310,000 (Magyar 92%, Romany 3%, German 2.5%; Hungarian minority in Romania has caused some friction between the two countries); growth rate 0.2% p.a.
language Hungarian (or Magyar), one of the few languages of Europe with non-Indo-European origins; it is grouped with Finnish, Estonian, and others in the Finno-Ugric family
religions Roman Catholic 67%, other Christian denominations 25%
GNP $2,690 per head (1991)
chronology
1918 Independence achieved from Austro-Hungarian empire.
1919 A communist state formed for 133 days.
1920–44 Regency formed under Admiral Horthy, who joined Hitler's attack on the USSR.
1945 Liberated by USSR.
1946 Republic proclaimed; Stalinist regime imposed.
1949 Soviet-style constitution adopted.
1956 Hungarian national uprising; workers' demonstrations in Budapest; democratization reforms by Imre Nagy overturned by Soviet tanks; János Kádár installed as party leader.
1968 Economic decentralization reforms.
1983 Competition introduced into elections.
1987 VAT and income tax introduced.
1988 Kádár replaced by Károly Grosz. First free trade union recognized; rival political parties legalized.
1989 May: border with Austria opened. July: new four-person collective leadership of Hungarian Socialist Workers' Party (HSWP). Oct: new 'transitional constitution' adopted, founded on multiparty democracy and new presidentialist executive. HSWP changed name to Hungarian Socialist Party, with Nyers as new leader. Kádár 'retired'.
1990 HSP reputation damaged by 'Danubegate' bugging scandal. March–April: elections won by right-of-centre coalition, headed by Hungarian Democratic Forum (MDF). May: József Antall, leader of the MDF, appointed premier. Aug: Arpád Göncz elected president.
1991 Jan: devaluation of currency. June: legislation approved to compensate owners of land and property expropriated under communist government. Last Soviet troops departed. Dec: European Community (EC) association pact signed.
1993 June: formal invitation to apply for EC membership. Dec: József Antall died; succeeded by Peter Boross.
1994 Joined NATO 'partnership for peace' programme. HSP won clear majority in assembly elections; its leader, Gyula Horn, became prime minister. Coalition formed with centrist parties.

Hun Sen 1950– . Cambodian political leader, prime minister 1985–93, deputy prime minister from 1993. Originally a member of the Khmer Rouge army, he defected in 1977 to join Vietnam-based anti-Khmer Cambodian forces. His leadership was characterized by the promotion of economic liberalization and a thawing in relations with exiled non-Khmer opposition forces as a prelude to a compromise political settlement. After defeat of his Cambodian People's Party (CCP) in the 1993 elections, Hun Sen agreed to participate in a power-sharing arrangement as second premier.

Hunt (James Henry) Leigh 1784–1859. English poet and essayist. The appearance in his Liberal newspaper *The Examiner* of an unfavourable article that he had written about the Prince Regent caused him to be convicted for libel and imprisoned 1813.

Hunt William Holman 1827–1910. English painter. He was one of the founders of the *Pre-Raphaelite Brotherhood 1848. His works include *The Awakening Conscience* 1853 (Tate Gallery, London) and *The Light of the World* 1854 (Keble College, Oxford).

Hunter Holly 1958– . US actress. She first came to prominence with *Broadcast News* and *Raising Arizona*, both 1987; she gave a virtuoso performance as a mute woman in *The Piano* 1993 (Academy Award).

hunting dog or **painted dog** wild dog *Lycaon pictus* which once roamed over virtually the whole of sub-Saharan Africa. A pack might have a range of almost 4,000 km/2,500 mi. The species is now reduced to a fraction of its original population.

Huntington's chorea rare hereditary disease of the nervous system that mostly begins in middle age. It is characterized by involuntary movements (*chorea), emotional disturbances, and rapid mental degeneration progressing to *dementia.

Hupei alternative transcription of *Hubei, a province of China.

Hurd Douglas (Richard) 1930– . English Conservative politician, home secretary 1985–89, foreign secretary from 1989. In Nov 1990 he was an unsuccessful candidate in the Tory leadership contest following Margaret Thatcher's unexpected resignation. He retained his post as foreign secretary in Prime Minister John Major's new cabinet formed after the 1992 general election.

hurling or **hurley** stick-and-ball game played between two teams of 15 players each, popular in Ireland. Its object is to hit the ball, by means of a curved stick, into the opposing team's goal. First played over 3,000 years ago, the game was at one time outlawed. The rules were standardized 1884, and are now under the control of the Gaelic Athletic Association. The premier competition, the All-Ireland Championship, was first held 1887.

Huron second largest of the Great Lakes of North America, on the US–Canadian border; area 23,160 sq mi/60,000 sq km. It includes Georgian Bay, Saginaw Bay, and Manitoulin Island.

hurricane revolving storm in tropical regions, called **typhoon** in the N Pacific. It originates at latitudes between 5° and 20° N or S of the equator, when the surface temperature of the ocean is above 27°C/80°F. A central calm area, called the eye, is surrounded by inwardly spiralling winds (anticlockwise in the northern hemisphere) of up to 320 kph/200 mph. A hurricane is accompanied by lightning and torrential rain, and can cause extensive damage. In meteorology, a hurricane is a wind of force 12 or more on the *Beaufort scale. The most intense hurricane recorded in the Caribbean/Atlantic sector was Hurricane Gilbert in 1988, with sustained winds of 280 kph/175 mph and gusts of over 320 kph/200 mph.

Husák Gustáv 1913–1991. Leader of the Communist Party of Czechoslovakia (CCP) 1969–87 and president 1975–89. After the 1968 Prague Spring of liberalization, his task was to restore control, purge the CCP, and implement a new, federalist constitution. Deposed in the popular uprising of Nov–Dec 1989, he was expelled from the Communist Party Feb 1990.

Huscarl Anglo-Danish warrior in 10th-century Denmark and early 11th-century England. Huscarls formed the bulk of English royal armies until the Norman Conquest.

husky any of several breeds of sledge dog used in Arctic regions, growing to 70 cm/2 ft high, and weighing about 50 kg/110 lbs, with pricked ears, thick fur, and a bushy tail. The Siberian husky is the best known.

Huss John (Czech **Jan**) c. 1373–1415. Bohemian Christian church reformer, rector of Prague University from 1402, who was excommunicated for attacks on ecclesiastical abuses. He was summoned before the Council of Constance 1414, defended the English reformer John Wycliffe, rejected the pope's authority, and was burned at the stake. His followers were called Hussites.

Hussein ibn Ali c. 1854–1931. Leader of the Arab revolt 1916–18 against the Turks. He proclaimed himself king of the Hejaz 1916, accepted the caliphate 1924, but was unable to retain it due to internal fighting. He was deposed 1924 by Ibn Saud.

Hussein ibn Talal 1935– . King of Jordan from 1952. By 1967 he had lost all his kingdom west of the river Jordan in the *Arab-Israeli Wars, and in 1970 suppressed the *Palestine Liberation Organization acting as a guerrilla force against his rule on the remaining East Bank territories. Subsequently, he became a moderating force in Middle Eastern politics, and in 1994 signed a peace agreement with Israel, ending a 46-year-old 'state of war' between the two countries.

Hussein Saddam 1937– . Iraqi politician, in power from 1968, president from 1979, progressively eliminating real or imagined opposition factions as he gained dictatorial control. He fought a bitter war against Iran 1980–88, with US economic aid, and dealt harshly with Kurdish rebels seeking independence, using chemical weapons against civilian populations. In 1990 he annexed Kuwait, to universal condemnation, before being driven out by a US-dominated coalition army Feb 1991. After Iraq's defeat in the *Gulf War, the Kurds rebelled again, as did the Shi'ites in the south. Hussein used the remainder of his military force against them, causing hundreds of thousands of Kurds to flee their homes in N Iraq, and bombarding S Iraq until the UN imposed a 'no-fly zone' in the area. Infringement of the latter led to US air strikes 1993.

Husserl Edmund (Gustav Albrecht) 1859–1938.

German philosopher, regarded as the founder of *phenomenology, a philosophy concentrating on what is consciously experienced. His main works are *Logical Investigations* 1900, *Phenomenological Philosophy* 1913, and *The Crisis of the European Sciences* 1936.

Hussite follower of John *Huss. Opposed to both German and papal influence in Bohemia, the Hussites waged successful war against the Holy Roman Empire from 1419, but Roman Catholicism was finally re-established 1620.

Huston John 1906–1987. US film director, screenwriter, and actor. An impulsive and individualistic film maker, he often dealt with the themes of greed, treachery in human relationships, and the loner. His works as a director include *The Maltese Falcon* 1941 (his debut), *The Treasure of the Sierra Madre* 1948 (in which his father Walter Huston starred and for which both won Academy Awards), *The African Queen* 1951, and his last, *The Dead* 1987.

Hutton James 1726–1797. Scottish geologist, known as the 'founder of geology', who formulated the concept of *uniformitarianism. In 1785 he developed a theory of the igneous origin of many rocks.

Hutu member of the majority ethnic group of both Burundi and Rwanda, numbering around 9,500,000. The Hutu tend to live as peasant farmers, while the ruling minority, the Tutsi, are town dwellers. There is a long history of violent conflict between the two groups. The Hutu language belongs to the Bantu branch of the Niger–Congo family.

Huxley Aldous (Leonard) 1894–1963. English writer of novels, essays, and verse. From the disillusionment and satirical eloquence of *Crome Yellow* 1921, *Antic Hay* 1923, and *Point Counter Point* 1928, Huxley developed towards the Utopianism exemplified by *Island* 1962. The science fiction novel *Brave New World* 1932 shows human beings mass-produced in laboratories and rendered incapable of freedom by indoctrination and drugs. He was the grandson of Thomas Henry Huxley and brother of Julian Huxley.

Huxley Andrew 1917– . English physiologist, awarded the Nobel Prize for Physiology or Medicine 1963 with Alan Hodgkin and John Eccles, for work on nerve impulses, discovering how ionic mechanisms are used in nerves to transmit impulses.

Huxley Julian 1887–1975. English biologist, first director general of UNESCO, and a founder of the World Wildlife Fund (now the World Wide Fund for Nature).

Huxley Thomas Henry 1825–1895. English scientist and humanist. Following the publication of Charles Darwin's *On the Origin of Species* 1859, he became known as 'Darwin's bulldog', and for many years was a prominent champion of evolution. In 1869, he coined the word 'agnostic' to express his own religious attitude. His grandsons include Aldous, Andrew, and Julian Huxley.

Hu Yaobang 1915–1989. Chinese politician, Communist Party (CCP) chair 1981–87. A protégé of the communist leader Deng Xiaoping, Hu presided over a radical overhaul of the party structure and personnel 1982–86. His death ignited the prodemocracy movement, which was eventually crushed in Tiananmen Square June 1989.

Huygens Christiaan 1629–1695. Dutch mathematical physicist and astronomer who proposed the wave theory of light. He developed the pendulum clock, discovered polarization, and observed Saturn's rings.

Hwang Ho alternative transcription of *Huang He, a river in China.

hyacinth any bulb-producing plant of the genus *Hyacinthus* of the lily family Liliaceae, native to the E Mediterranean and Africa. The cultivated hyacinth *H. orientalis* has large, scented, cylindrical heads of pink, white, or blue flowers. The *water hyacinth, genus *Eichhornia*, is unrelated, a floating plant from South America.

hybrid offspring from a cross between individuals of two different species, or two inbred lines within a species. In most cases, hybrids between species are infertile and unable to reproduce sexually. In plants, however, doubling of the chromosomes (see *polyploid) can restore the fertility of such hybrids.

hydathode specialized pore, or less commonly, a hair, through which water is secreted by hydrostatic pressure from the interior of a plant leaf onto the surface. Hydathodes are found on many different plants and are usually situated around the leaf margin at vein endings. Each pore is surrounded by two crescent-shaped cells and resembles an open *stoma, but the size of the opening cannot be varied as in a stoma. The process of water secretion through hydathodes is known as *guttation.

Hyderabad capital city of the S central Indian state of Andhra Pradesh, on the river Musi; population (1981) 2,528,000. Products include carpets, silks, and metal inlay work. It was formerly the capital of the state of Hyderabad. Buildings include the Jama Masjid mosque and Golconda fort.

Hyderabad city in Sind province, SE Pakistan; population (1981) 795,000. It produces gold, pottery, glass, and furniture. The third largest city of Pakistan, it was founded 1768.

Hyder Ali c. 1722–1782. Indian general, sultan of Mysore from 1759. In command of the army in Mysore from 1749, he became the ruler of the state 1759, and rivalled British power in the area until his triple defeat by Sir Eyre Coote 1781 during the Anglo-French wars. He was the father of Tippu Sultan.

hydra in zoology, any member of the family Hydridae, or freshwater polyps, of the phylum Cnidaria (coelenterates). The body is a double-layered tube (with six to ten hollow tentacles around the mouth), 1.25 cm/0.5 in long when extended, but capable of contracting to a small knob. Usually fixed to waterweed, hydras feed on minute animals, that are caught and paralysed by stinging cells on the tentacles.

Hydra in astronomy, the largest constellation, winding across more than a quarter of the sky between Cancer and Libra in the southern hemisphere. Hydra is named after the multiheaded monster slain by Heracles. Despite its size, it is not prominent; its brightest star is second-magnitude Alphard.

Hydra in Greek mythology, a huge monster with nine heads. If one were cut off, two would grow in its place. One of the 12 labours of Heracles was to kill it.

hydrangea any flowering shrub of the genus *Hydrangea* of the saxifrage family Hydrangeaceae, native to Japan. Cultivated varieties of *H. macrophylla* normally produce round heads of pink flowers, but these may be blue if certain chemicals, such as alum or iron, are in the soil. The name is from the Greek for 'water vessel', after the cuplike seed capsules.

hydraulics field of study concerned with utilizing the properties of water and other liquids, in particular the way they flow and transmit pressure, and with the application of these properties in engineering. It applies the principles of *hydrostatics and hydrodynamics. The oldest type of hydraulic machine is the *hydraulic press*, invented by Joseph *Bramah in England 1795. The hydraulic principle of pressurized liquid increasing mechanical efficiency is commonly used on vehicle braking systems, the forging press, and the hydraulic systems of aircraft and excavators.

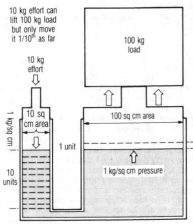

hydraulics *The hydraulic jack transmits the pressure on a small piston to a larger one.*

hydrocarbon any of a class of chemical compounds containing only hydrogen and carbon (for example, the alkanes and alkenes). Hydrocarbons are obtained industrially principally from petroleum and coal tar.

hydrocephalus potentially serious increase in the volume of cerebrospinal fluid (CSF) within the ventricles of the brain. In infants, since their skull plates have not fused, it causes enlargement of the head, and there is a risk of brain damage from CSF pressure on the developing brain.

hydrochloric acid HCl solution of hydrogen chloride (a colourless, acidic gas) in water. The concentrated acid is about 35% hydrogen chloride and is corrosive. The acid is a typical strong, monobasic acid forming only one series of salts, the chlorides. It has many industrial uses, including recovery of zinc from galvanized scrap iron and the production of chlorine. It is also produced in the stomachs of animals for the purposes of digestion.

hydrocyanic acid or **prussic acid** solution of hydrogen cyanide gas (HCN) in water. It is a colourless, highly poisonous, volatile liquid, smelling of bitter almonds.

hydrodynamics science of nonviscous fluids (such as water, alcohol, and ether) in motion.

hydroelectric power (HEP) electricity generated by moving water. In a typical HEP scheme water stored in a reservoir, often created by damming a river, is piped into water *turbines, coupled to electricity generators. In *pumped storage plants, water flowing through the turbines is recycled. A *tidal power station exploits the rise and fall of the tides. About one-fifth of the world's electricity comes from HEP.

hydrofoil wing that develops lift in the water in much the same way that an aeroplane wing develops lift in the air. A hydrofoil boat is one whose hull rises out of the water due to the lift, and the boat skims along on the hydrofoils. The first hydrofoil was fitted to a boat 1906. The first commercial hydrofoil went into operation 1956. One of the most advanced hydrofoil boats is the Boeing *jetfoil.

hydrogen (Greek *hydro* + *gen* 'water generator') colourless, odourless, gaseous, non-metallic element, symbol H, atomic number 1, relative atomic mass 1.00797. It is the lightest of all the elements and occurs on Earth chiefly in combination with oxygen as water. Hydrogen is the most abundant element in the universe, where it accounts for 93% of the total number of atoms and 76% of the total mass. It is a component of most stars, including the Sun, whose heat and light are produced through the nuclear-fusion process that converts hydrogen into helium. When subjected to a pressure 500,000 times greater than that of the Earth's atmosphere, hydrogen becomes a solid with metallic properties, as in one of the inner zones of Jupiter. Its common and industrial uses include the hardening of oils and fats by hydrogenation and the creation of high-temperature flames for welding.

hydrogen bomb bomb that works on the principle of nuclear *fusion. Large-scale explosion results from the thermonuclear release of energy when hydrogen nuclei are fused to form helium nuclei. The first hydrogen bomb was exploded at Eniwetok Atoll in the Pacific Ocean by the USA 1952.

hydrogencarbonate or **bicarbonate** compound containing the ion HCO_3^-, an acid salt of carbonic acid (solution of carbon dioxide in water). When heated or treated with dilute acids, it gives off carbon dioxide. The most important compounds are *sodium hydrogencarbonate (bicarbonate of soda), and *calcium hydrogencarbonate.

hydrogen sulphide H_2S poisonous gas with the smell of rotten eggs. It is found in certain types of crude oil where it is formed by decomposition of sulphur compounds. It is removed from the oil at the refinery and converted to elemental sulphur.

hydrology study of the location and movement of inland water, both frozen and liquid, above and below ground. It is applied to major civil engineering projects such as irrigation schemes, dams and hydroelectric power, and in planning water supply.

hydrolysis chemical reaction in which the action of water or its ions breaks down a substance into smaller molecules. Hydrolysis occurs in certain inorganic salts in solution, in nearly all nonmetallic chlorides, in esters, and in other organic substances. It is one of the mechanisms for the breakdown of food by the body, as in the conversion of starch to glucose.

hydrometer in physics, an instrument used to measure the density of liquids compared with that of water, usually expressed in grams per cubic centimetre. It consists of a thin glass tube ending in a sphere that leads into a smaller sphere, the latter being weighted so that the hydrometer floats upright, sinking deeper into less dense liquids than into denser liquids. It is used in brewing.

hydrophily *pollination in which the pollen is carried by water. Hydrophily is very rare but occurs in a few aquatic species. In Canadian pondweed *Elodea* and tape grass *Vallisneria*, the male flowers break off whole and rise to the water surface where they encounter the female flowers, which are borne on long stalks. In eel grasses *Zostera*, which are coastal plants growing totally submerged, the filamentous pollen grains are released into the water and carried by currents to the female flowers where they become wrapped around the stigmas.

hydrophobia another name for the disease *rabies.

hydrophone underwater *microphone and ancillary equipment capable of picking up waterborne sounds. It was originally developed to detect enemy submarines but is now also used, for example, for listening to the sounds made by whales.

hydrophyte plant adapted to live in water, or in waterlogged soil.

hydroponics cultivation of plants without soil, using specially prepared solutions of mineral salts. Beginning in the 1930s, large crops were grown by hydroponic methods, at first in California but since then in many other parts of the world.

hydrostatics in physics, the branch of *statics dealing with the mechanical problems of fluids in equilibrium – that is, in a static condition. Practical applications include shipbuilding and dam design.

hydrotherapy use of water, externally or internally, for health or healing.

hydroxide any inorganic chemical compound containing one or more hydroxyl (OH) groups and generally combined with a metal. Hydroxides include sodium hydroxide (caustic soda, NaOH), potassium hydroxide (caustic potash, KOH), and calcium hydroxide (slaked lime, $Ca(OH)_2$).

hydroxyl group an atom of hydrogen and an atom of oxygen bonded together and covalently bonded to an organic molecule. Common compounds containing hydroxyl groups are alcohols and phenols.

hyena any of three species of carnivorous mammals in the family Hyaenidae, living in Africa and Asia. Hyenas have extremely powerful jaws. They are scavengers, although they will also attack and kill live prey.

hygrometer in physics, any instrument for measuring the humidity, or water vapour content, of a gas (usually air). A wet and dry bulb hygrometer consists of two vertical thermometers, with one of the bulbs covered in absorbent cloth dipped into water. As the water evaporates, the bulb cools producing a temperature difference between the two thermometers. The amount of evaporation, and hence cooling of the wet bulb, depends on the relative humidity of the air.

Hymen in Greek mythology, either the son of Apollo and one of the Muses, or of Dionysus and Aphrodite. He was the god of marriage, and in painting he is represented as a youth carrying a bridal torch.

hymn song in praise of a deity. Examples include Ikhnaton's hymn to the Aton in ancient Egypt, the ancient Greek Orphic hymns, Old Testament psalms, extracts from the New Testament (such as the 'Ave Maria'), and hymns by the British writers John Bunyan ('Who would true valour see') and Charles Wesley ('Hark the herald angels sing'). *Gospel music and carols are forms of Christian hymn singing.

hyoscine or *scopolamine* drug that acts on the autonomic nervous system and is frequently included in premedication (before operations) to dry up lung secretions and as a postoperative sedative. It is an alkaloid, $C_{17}H_{21}NO_2$, obtained from various plants of the nightshade family (such as *belladonna).

hyperactivity condition of excessive activity in young children, combined with inability to concentrate and difficulty in learning. The cause is not known, although some food *additives have come under suspicion. Modification of the diet may help, and in the majority of cases there is improvement at puberty.

hyperbola in geometry, a curve formed by cutting a right circular cone with a plane so that the angle between the plane and the base is greater than the angle between the base and the side of the cone. All hyperbolae are bounded by two asymptotes (straight lines which the hyperbola moves closer and closer to but never reaches). A hyperbola is a member of the family of curves known as *conic sections.

hyperbole *figure of speech; the Greek name suggests 'going over the top'. When people use hyperbole, they exaggerate, usually to emphasize a point ('If I've told you once I've told you a thousand times not to do that').

hypercharge in physics, a property of certain *elementary particles, analogous to electric charge, that accounts for the absence of some expected behaviour (such as decay) in terms of the short-range strong nuclear force, which holds atomic nuclei together.

hyperinflation rapid and uncontrolled *inflation, or increases in prices, usually associated with political and/or social instability (as in Germany in the 1920s).

hyperon in physics, a *hadron; any of a group of highly unstable *elementary particles that includes all the *baryons with a mass greater than the *neutron. They are all composed of three quarks. The lambda, xi, sigma, and omega particles are hyperons.

hypertension abnormally high *blood pressure due to a variety of causes, leading to excessive contraction of the smooth muscle cells of the walls of the arteries. It increases the risk of kidney disease, stroke, and heart attack.

Hypertext system for viewing information (both text and pictures) on a computer screen in such a way that related items of information can easily be reached. For example, the program might display a map of a country; if the user clicks (with a *mouse) on a particular city, the program will display some information about that city.

hyperthyroidism or *thyrotoxicosis* overactivity of the thyroid gland due to enlargement or tumour. Symptoms include accelerated heart rate, sweating, anxiety, tremor, and weight loss. Treatment is by drugs or surgery.

hypha (plural *hyphae*) delicate, usually branching filament, many of which collectively form the mycelium and fruiting bodies of a *fungus. Food molecules and other substances are transported along hyphae by the movement of the cytoplasm, known as 'cytoplasmic streaming'.

hyphen punctuation mark (-) with two functions: to join words, parts of words, syllables, and so on, as an aid to sense; and to mark a word break at the end of a line. Adjectival compounds (see *adjective) are hyphenated because they modify the noun jointly rather than separately ('a small-town boy' is a boy from a small town; 'a small town boy' is a small boy from a town). The use of hyphens with adverbs is redundant unless an identical adjective exists (*well, late, long*): 'late-blooming plant' but 'brightly blooming plant'.

hypnosis artificially induced state of relaxation in which suggestibility is heightened. The subject may carry out orders after being awakened, and may be made insensitive to pain. Hypnosis is sometimes used to treat addictions to tobacco or overeating, or to assist amnesia victims.

hypnotherapy use of hypnotic trance and post-hypnotic suggestions to relieve stress-related conditions such as insomnia and hypertension, or to break health-inimical habits or addictions.

hypo in photography, a term for sodium thiosulphate, discovered 1819 by John *Herschel, and used as a fixative for photographic images since 1837.

hypocycloid in geometry, a cusped curve traced by a point on the circumference of a circle that rolls around the inside of another larger circle. (Compare *epicycloid.)

hypodermic instrument used for injecting fluids beneath the skin into either muscles or blood vessels. It consists of a small graduated tube with a close-fitting piston and a nozzle onto which a hollow needle can be fitted.

hypogeal term used to describe seed germination in which the *cotyledons remain below ground. It can refer to fruits that develop underground, such as peanuts *Arachis hypogea*.

hypoglycaemia condition of abnormally low level of sugar (glucose) in the blood, which starves the brain. It causes weakness, the shakes, and perspiration, sometimes fainting. Untreated victims have suffered paranoia and extreme anxiety. Treatment is by special diet.

hyponymy in semantics, a relationship in meaning between two words such that one (for example, *sport*) includes the other (for example, *football*), but not vice versa.

hypotenuse the longest side of a right-angled triangle, opposite the right angle. It is of particular application in Pythagoras's theorem (the square on the hypotenuse equals the sum of the squares on the other two sides), and in trigonometry where the ratios *sine and *cosine are defined as the ratios opposite/hypotenuse and adjacent/hypotenuse respectively.

hypothalamus region of the brain below the *cerebrum which regulates rhythmic activity and physiological stability within the body, including water balance and temperature. It regulates the production of the pituitary gland's hormones and controls that part of the *nervous system regulating the involuntary muscles.

hypothermia condition in which the deep (core) temperature of the body spontaneously drops. If it is not discovered, coma and death ensue. Most at risk are the aged and babies (particularly if premature).

hypothesis in science, an idea concerning an event and its possible explanation. The term is one favoured by the followers of the philosopher Karl *Popper, who argue that the merit of a scientific hypothesis lies in its ability to make testable predictions.

hyrax small mammal, forming the order Hyracoidea, that lives among rocks, in deserts, and in forests in Africa, Arabia, and Syria. It is about the size of a rabbit, with a plump body, short legs, short ears, brownish fur, and long, curved front teeth.

hyssop aromatic herb *Hyssopus officinalis* of the mint family Labiatae, found in Asia, S Europe, and around the Mediterranean. It has blue flowers, oblong leaves, and stems that are woody near the ground but herbaceous above.

hysterectomy surgical removal of all or part of the uterus (womb). The operation is performed to treat fibroids (benign tumours growing in the uterus) or cancer; also to relieve heavy menstrual bleeding. A woman who has had a hysterectomy will no longer menstruate and cannot bear children.

hysteresis phenomenon seen in the elastic and electromagnetic behaviour of materials, in which a lag occurs between the application or removal of a force or field and its effect.

hysteria according to the work of Sigmund *Freud, the conversion of a psychological conflict or anxiety feeling into a physical symptom, such as paralysis, blindness, recurrent cough, vomiting, and general malaise. The term is little used today in diagnosis.

Iaşi (German **Jassy**) city in NE Romania; population (1985) 314,000. It has chemical, machinery, electronic, and textile industries. It was the capital of the principality of Moldavia 1568–89.

Ibadan city in SW Nigeria and capital of Oyo state; population (1981) 2,100,000. Industries include chemicals, electronics, plastics, and vehicles.

Ibáñez Vicente Blasco 1867–1928. Spanish novelist and politician, born in Valencia. He was actively involved in revolutionary politics. His novels include *La barraca/The Cabin* 1898, the best of his regional works; *Sangre y arena/Blood and Sand* 1908, the story of a famous bullfighter; and *Los cuatro jinetes del Apocalipsis/The Four Horsemen of the Apocalypse* 1916, a product of the effects of World War I.

Ibarruri Dolores, known as *La Pasionaria* ('the passion flower') 1895–1989. Spanish Basque politician, journalist, and orator; she was first elected to the Cortes in 1936. She helped to establish the Popular Front government and was a Loyalist leader in the Civil War. When Franco came to power in 1939 she left Spain for the USSR, where she was active in the Communist Party. She returned to Spain in 1977 after Franco's death and was re-elected to the Cortes (at the age of 81) in the first parliamentary elections for 40 years.

ibex any of various wild goats found in mountainous areas of Europe, NE Africa, and Central Asia. They grow to 100 cm/3.5 ft, and have brown or grey coats and heavy horns. They are herbivorous and live in small groups.

ibid. abbreviation for *ibidem* (Latin 'in the same place'); used in reference citation.

ibis any of various wading birds, about 60 cm/2 ft tall, in the same family, Threskiornidae, as spoonbills. Ibises have long legs and necks, and long, curved beaks. Various species occur in the warmer regions of the world.

Ibiza one of the *Balearic Islands, a popular tourist resort; area 596 sq km/230 sq mi; population (1986) 45,000. The capital and port, also called Ibiza, has a cathedral.

IBM (abbreviation for *International Business Machines*) multinational company, the largest manufacturer of computers in the world. The company is a descendant of the Tabulating Machine Company, formed 1896 by Herman *Hollerith to exploit his punched-card machines. It adopted its present name in 1924. By 1991

it had an annual turnover of $64.8 billion and employed about 345,000 people.

Ibn Battuta 1304–1368. Arab traveller born in Tangiers. In 1325, he went on an extraordinary 120,675 km/75,000 mi journey via Mecca to Egypt, E Africa, India, and China, returning some 30 years later. During this journey he also visited Spain and crossed the Sahara to Timbuktu. The narrative of his travels, *The Adventures of Ibn Battuta*, was written with an assistant, Ibn Juzayy.

Ibn Saud 1880–1953. First king of Saudi Arabia from 1932. His father was the son of the sultan of Nejd, at whose capital, Riyadh, Ibn Saud was born. In 1891 a rival group seized Riyadh, and Ibn Saud went into exile with his father, who resigned his claim to the throne in his son's favour. In 1902 Ibn Saud recaptured Riyadh and recovered the kingdom, and by 1921 he had brought all central Arabia under his rule. In 1924 he invaded the Hejaz, of which he was proclaimed king in 1926.

Ibn Sina Arabic name of *Avicenna, scholar, and translator.

Ibo or *Igbo* member of the W African Ibo culture group occupying SE Nigeria and numbering about 18,000,000. Primarily cultivators, they inhabit the richly forested tableland, bounded by the river Niger to the west and the river Cross to the east. They are divided into five main groups, and their languages belong to the Kwa branch of the Niger-Congo family.

Ibsen Henrik (Johan) 1828–1906. Norwegian playwright and poet, whose realistic and often controversial plays revolutionized European theatre. Driven into exile 1864–91 by opposition to the satirical *Love's Comedy* 1862, he wrote the verse dramas *Brand* 1866 and *Peer Gynt* 1867, followed by realistic plays dealing with social issues, including *Pillars of Society* 1877, *A Doll's House* 1879, *Ghosts* 1881, *An Enemy of the People* 1882, and *Hedda Gabler* 1891. By the time he returned to Norway, he was recognized as the country's greatest living writer.

Icarus in Greek mythology, the son of *Daedalus, who with his father escaped from the labyrinth in Crete by making wings of feathers fastened with wax. Icarus plunged to his death when he flew too near the Sun and the wax melted.

Icarus in astronomy, an *Apollo asteroid 1.5 km/1 mi in diameter, discovered 1949. It orbits the Sun every 409 days at a distance of 28–300 million km/18–186 million mi (0.19–2.0 astronomical units). It was the first asteroid known to approach the Sun closer than does the planet Mercury. In 1968 it passed 6 million km/4 million mi from the Earth.

ice solid formed by water when it freezes. It is colourless and its crystals are hexagonal. The water molecules are held together by *hydrogen bonds.

ice form of methamphetamine that is smoked for its stimulating effect; its use has been illegal in the USA since 1989. Its effect may be followed by a period of depression and psychosis.

ice age any period of glaciation occurring in the Earth's history, but particularly that in the Pleistocene epoch, immediately preceding historic times. On the North American continent, *glaciers reached as far south as the Great Lakes, and an ice sheet spread over N Europe, leaving its remains as far south as Switzerland. There were several glacial advances separated by interglacial stages during which the ice melted and temperatures were higher than today.

iceberg floating mass of ice, about 80% of which is submerged, rising sometimes to 100 m/ 300 ft above sea level. Glaciers that reach the coast become extended into a broad foot; as this enters the sea, masses break off and drift towards temperate latitudes, becoming a danger to shipping.

ice hockey game played on ice between two teams of six, developed in Canada from hockey or bandy. A rubber disc (puck) is used in place of a ball. Players wear skates and protective clothing.

Iceland Republic of (*Lýðveldið Ísland*)

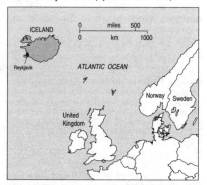

area 103,000 sq km/39,758 sq mi
capital Reykjavík
towns Akureyri, Akranes
physical warmed by the Gulf Stream; glaciers and lava fields cover 75% of the country; active volcanoes (Hekla was once thought the gateway to Hell), geysers, hot springs, and new islands created offshore (Surtsey in 1963); subterranean hot water heats 85% of Iceland's homes
head of state Vigdís Finnbogadóttir from 1980
head of government Davíð Oddsson from 1991
political system democratic republic
exports cod and other fish products, aluminium, diatomite
currency krona
population (1993 est) 270,000; growth rate 0.8% p.a.
language Icelandic, the most archaic Scandinavian language, in which some of the finest sagas were written
religion Evangelical Lutheran 95%
GNP $24,565 per head (1992)
chronology
1944 Independence achieved from Denmark.
1949 Joined NATO and Council of Europe.
1953 Joined Nordic Council.
1976 'Cod War' with UK.
1979 Iceland announced 320-km/200-mi exclusive fishing zone.
1983 Steingrímur Hermannsson appointed to lead a coalition government.

1985 Iceland declared itself a nuclear-free zone.
1987 New coalition government formed by Thorsteinn Pálsson after general election.
1988 Vigdís Finnbogadóttir re-elected president for a third term; Hermannsson led new coalition.
1991 Davíð Oddsson led new IP–SDP (Independence Party and Social Democratic Party) centre-right coalition, becoming prime minister in the general election.

Icelandic language member of the N Germanic branch of the Indo-European language family, spoken only in Iceland and the most conservative in form of the Scandinavian languages. Despite seven centuries of Danish rule, lasting until 1918, Icelandic has remained virtually unchanged since the 12th century.

iceman nickname given to the preserved body of a prehistoric man discovered in a glacier on the Austrian-Italian border in 1991. On the basis of the clothing and associated artefacts, the body was at first believed to be 4,000 years old, from the Bronze Age. Carbon dating established its age at about 5,300 years. The discovery led to a reappraisal of the boundary between the Bronze and the Stone Age.

Iceni ancient people of E England, who revolted against occupying Romans under *Boudicca.

ice-skating see *skating.

I Ching or **Book of Changes** ancient Chinese book of divination based on 64 hexagrams, or patterns of six lines. The lines may be 'broken' or 'whole' (yin or yang) and are generated by tossing yarrow stalks or coins. The enquirer formulates a question before throwing, and the book gives interpretations of the meaning of the hexagrams.

ichneumon fly any parasitic wasp of the family Ichneumonidae. There are several thousand species in Europe, North America, and other regions. They have slender bodies, and females have unusually long, curved ovipositors (egg-laying instruments) that can pierce several inches of wood. The eggs are laid in the eggs, larvae, or pupae of other insects, usually butterflies or moths.

ICI (Imperial Chemical Industries) one of the UK's largest companies, engaged in the manufacture and research of products and processes including agrochemicals, polymers, and electronics. In 1990 ICI had more than 127,000 employees, more than half of whom worked outside Britain.

icon in the Greek or Eastern Orthodox Church, a representation of Jesus, Mary, an angel, or a saint, in painting, low relief, or mosaic. The painted icons were traditionally done on wood. After the 17th century in Russia, a *riza*, or gold and silver covering which leaves only the face and hands visible (and may be adorned with jewels presented by the faithful in thanksgiving), was often added as protection.

icon in computing, a small picture on the computer screen, or *VDU, representing an object or function that the user may manipulate or otherwise use. It is a feature of *graphical user-interface (GUI) systems. Icons make computers easier to use by allowing the user to point to and click with a *mouse on pictures, rather than type commands.

iconoclast (Greek 'image-breaker') literally, a person who attacks religious images, originally in obedience to the injunction of the Second Commandment not to worship 'graven images'. Under the influence of Islam and Judaism, an iconoclastic movement calling for the destruction of religious images developed in the Byzantine empire, and was endorsed by the Emperor Leo III in 726. Fierce persecution of those who made and venerated icons followed, until iconoclasm was declared a heresy in the 9th century. The same name was applied to those opposing the use of images at the Reformation, when there was much destruction in churches. Figuratively, the term is used for a person who attacks established ideals or principles.

iconography in art history, significance attached to symbols that can help to identify subject matter (for example, a saint holding keys usually represents St Peter) and place a work of art in its historical context.

id in Freudian psychology, the instinctual element of the human mind, concerned with pleasure, which demands immediate satisfaction. It is regarded as the *unconscious element of the human psyche, and is said to be in conflict with the *ego and the *superego.

id. abbreviation for *idem* (Latin 'the same'); used in reference citation.

Idaho state of NW USA; nickname Gem State
area 216,500 sq km/83,569 sq mi
capital Boise
towns Pocatello, Idaho Falls
products potatoes, wheat, livestock, timber, silver, lead, zinc, antimony
population (1990) 1,006,700
history part of the Louisiana Purchase 1803; first permanently settled 1860 after the discovery of gold, Idaho became a state 1890.

idealism in philosophy, the theory that states that the external world is fundamentally immaterial and a dimension of the mind. Objects in the world exist but, according to this theory, they lack substance.

identikit a set of drawings of different parts of the face used to compose a likeness of a person for identification. It was evolved by Hugh C McDonald (1913–) in the USA. It has largely been replaced by *photofit, based on photographs, which produces a more realistic likeness.

Ides in the Roman calendar, the 15th day of March, May, July, and Oct, and the 13th day of all other months (the word originally indicated the full moon); Julius Caesar was assassinated on the Ides of March 44 BC.

i.e. abbreviation for *id est* (Latin 'that is').

Ignatius Loyola, St 1491–1556. Spanish noble who founded the *Jesuit order 1540, also called the Society of Jesus.

Ignatius of Antioch, St 1st–2nd century AD. Christian martyr. Traditionally a disciple of St John, he was bishop of Antioch, and was thrown to the wild beasts in Rome. He wrote seven epistles, important documents of the early Christian church. Feast day 1 Feb.

igneous rock rock formed from cooling magma or lava, and solidifying from a molten state. Igneous rocks are classified according to their crystal size, texture, chemical composition, or method of formation. They are largely composed of silica (SiO_2) and they are classified by their silica content into groups: acid (over 66% silica), intermediate (55–66%), basic (45–55%), and ultrabasic (uner 45%). Igneous rocks that crystallize below the Earth's surface are called plutonic or intrusive, depending on the depth of formation. They have large crystals produced by slow cooling; examples include dolerite and granite. Those extruded at the surface are called extrusive or volcanic. Rapid cooling results in small crystals; basalt is an example.

ignition coil *transformer that is an essential part of a petrol engine's ignition system. It consists of two wire coils wound around an iron core. The primary coil, which is connected to the car battery, has only a few turns. The secondary coil, connected via the *distributor to the *spark plugs, has many turns. The coil takes in a low voltage (usually 12 volts) from the battery and transforms it to a high voltage (about 20,000 volts) to ignite the engine.

ignition temperature or *fire point* minimum temperature to which a substance must be heated before it will spontaneously burn independently of the source of heat; for example, ethanol has an ignition temperature of 425°C and a *flash point of 12°C.

Iguaçú Falls or *Iguassú Falls* waterfall in South America, on the border between Brazil and Argentina. The falls lie 19 km/12 mi above the junction of the river Iguaçú with the Paraná. The falls are divided by forested rocky islands and form a spectacular tourist attraction. The water plunges in 275 falls, many of which have separate names. They have a height of 82 m/269 ft and a width of about 4 km/2.5 mi.

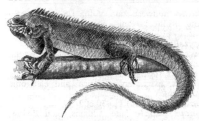

iguana The common iguana lives mainly in trees but is an excellent swimmer.

iguana any lizard, especially the genus *Iguana*, of the family Iguanidae, which includes about 700 species and is chiefly confined to the Americas. The common iguana *I. iguana* of Central and South America is a vegetarian and may reach 2 m/6 ft in length.

Ijsselmeer lake in the Netherlands, formed 1932 after the Zuider Zee was cut off by a dyke from the North Sea; freshwater since 1944. Area 1,217 sq km/470 sq mi.

ikat textile produced by resist-printing the warp or weft before *weaving. The term is Indonesian, but ikat fabrics are also produced in parts of Africa.

ikebana (Japanese 'living flower') Japanese art of flower arrangement. It dates from the 6th–7th centuries when arrangements of flowers were placed as offerings in Buddhist temples, a practice learned from China. In the 15th century, ikebana became a favourite pastime of the nobility. Oldest of the Japanese ikebana schools is Ikenobo at Kyoto (7th century).

Ikhnaton or **Akhenaton** 14th century BC. King of Egypt of the 18th dynasty (c. 1379–1362 BC), who may have ruled jointly for a time with his father Amenhotep III. He developed the cult of the Sun, *Aton, rather than the rival cult of *Ammon. Some historians believe that his attention to religious reforms rather than imperial defence led to the loss of most of Egypt's possessions in Asia.

Île-de-France region of N France; area 12,000 sq km/4,632 sq mi; population (1986) 10,251,000. It includes the French capital, Paris, and the towns of Versailles, Sèvres, and St-Cloud and comprises the *départements* of Essonne, Val-de-Marne, Val d'Oise, Ville de Paris, Seine-et-Marne, Hauts-de-Seine, Seine-Saint-Denis, and Yvelines. From here the early French kings extended their authority over the whole country.

ileum part of the small intestine of the *digestive system, between the duodenum and the colon, that absorbs digested food.

Iliescu Ion 1930– . Romanian president from 1990. A former member of the Romanian Communist Party (PCR) and of Nicolae Ceauşescu's government, Iliescu swept into power on Ceauşescu's fall as head of the National Salvation Front.

illegitimacy in law, the status of a child born to a mother who is not legally married; a child may be legitimized by subsequent marriage of the parents. The nationality of the child is usually that of the mother.

Illinois midwest state of the USA; nickname Land of Lincoln/Prairie State
area 146,100 sq km/56,395 sq mi
capital Springfield
towns Chicago, Rockford, Peoria, Decatur, Aurora
products soya beans, cereals, meat and dairy products, machinery, electrical and electronic equipment
population (1990) 11,430,600
famous people Jane Addams, Saul Bellow, Mother Cabrini, Clarence Darrow, Enrico Fermi, Ernest Hemingway, Jesse Jackson, Edgar Lee Masters, Ronald Reagan, Louis Sullivan, Frank Lloyd Wright

Illyria ancient name for the eastern coastal region on the Adriatic, N of the Gulf of Corinth, conquered by Philip of Macedon. It became a Roman province AD 9. The Albanians are the survivors of its ancient peoples.

image picture or appearance of a real object, formed by light that passes through a lens or is reflected from a mirror. If rays of light actually pass through an image, it is called a *real image*. Real images, such as those produced by a camera or projector lens, can be projected onto a screen. An image that cannot be projected onto a screen, such as that seen in a flat mirror, is known as a *virtual image*.

imaginary number term often used to describe the non-real element of a *complex number. For the complex number (a + ib), ib is

the imaginary number where i = √–1, and b any real number.

Imagism movement in Anglo-American poetry that flourished 1912–14 and affected much US and British poetry and critical thinking thereafter. A central figure was Ezra Pound, who asserted the principles of free verse, complex imagery, and poetic impersonality.

imago sexually mature stage of an *insect.

imam (Arabic 'leader') in a mosque, the leader of congregational prayer, but generally any notable Islamic leader.

IMF abbreviation for *International Monetary Fund*.

Imhotep c. 2800 BC. Egyptian physician and architect, adviser to King Zoser (3rd dynasty). He is thought to have designed the step pyramid at Sakkara, and his tomb (believed to be in the N Sakkara cemetery) became a centre of healing. He was deified as the son of Ptah and was identified with Aesculapius, the Greek god of medicine.

Immaculate Conception in the Roman Catholic Church, the belief that the Virgin Mary was, by a special act of grace, preserved free from *original sin from the moment she was conceived. This article of the Catholic faith was for centuries the subject of heated controversy, opposed by St Thomas Aquinas and other theologians, but generally accepted from about the 16th century. It became a dogma in 1854 under Pope Pius IX.

immiscible term describing liquids that will not mix with each other, such as oil and water. When two immiscible liquids are shaken together, a turbid mixture is produced. This normally forms separate layers on being left to stand.

immunity the protection that organisms have against foreign microorganisms, such as bacteria and viruses, and against cancerous cells (see *cancer). The cells that provide this protection are called white blood cells, or leucocytes, and make up the immune system. They include neutrophils and *macrophages, which can engulf invading organisms and other unwanted material, and natural killer cells that destroy cells infected by viruses and cancerous cells. Some of the most important immune cells are the *B cells and *T cells. Immune cells coordinate their activities by means of chemical messengers or *lymphokines, including the antiviral messenger *interferon. The lymph nodes play a major role in organizing the immune response.

immunization conferring immunity to infectious disease by artificial methods. The most widely used technique is *vaccination.

immunocompromised lacking a fully effective immune system. The term is most often used in connection with infections such as *AIDS where the virus interferes with the immune response (see *immunity).

immunodeficient lacking one or more elements of a working immune system. Immune deficiency is the term generally used for patients who are born with such a defect, while those who acquire such a deficiency later in life are referred to as *immunocompromised or immunosuppressed.

immunoglobulin human globulin *protein

that can be separated from blood and administered to confer immediate immunity on the recipient. It participates in the immune reaction as the antibody for a specific *antigen (disease-causing agent).

immunosuppressive any drug that suppresses the body's normal immune responses to infection or foreign tissue. It is used in the treatment of autoimmune disease (see *autoimmunity); as part of chemotherapy for leukaemias, lymphomas, and other cancers; and to help prevent rejection following organ transplantation.

impala African antelope *Aepyceros melampus* found from Kenya to South Africa in savannas and open woodland. The body is sandy brown. Males have lyre-shaped horns up to 75 cm/2.5 ft long. Impala grow up to 1.5 m/5 ft long and 90 cm/3 ft tall. They live in herds and spring high in the air when alarmed.

impeachment judicial procedure by which government officials are accused of wrongdoing and brought to trial before a legislative body. In the USA the House of Representatives may impeach offenders to be tried before the Senate, as in the case of President Andrew Johnson 1868. Richard *Nixon to resigned the US presidency 1974 when threatened by impeachment.

impedance the total opposition of a circuit to the passage of alternating electric current. It has the symbol Z. For an *alternating current (AC) it includes the reactance X (caused by *capacitance or *inductance); the impedance can then be found using the equation $Z^2 = R^2 + X^2$.

imperialism policy of extending the power and rule of a government beyond its own boundaries. A country may attempt to dominate others by direct rule or by less obvious means such as control of markets for goods or raw materials. The latter is often called *neocolonialism.

imperial system traditional system of units developed in the UK, based largely on the foot, pound, and second (f.p.s.) system.

implantation in mammals, the process by which the developing *embryo attaches itself to the wall of the mother's uterus and stimulates the development of the *placenta.

import product or service that one country purchases from another for domestic consumption, or for processing and re-exporting (Hong Kong, for example, is heavily dependent on imports for its export business). Imports may be visible (goods) or invisible (services). If an importing country does not have a counterbalancing value of exports, it may experience balance-of-payments difficulties and accordingly consider restricting imports by some form of protectionism (such as an import tariff or imposing import quotas).

Impressionism movement in painting that originated in France in the 1860s and dominated European and North American painting in the late 19th century. The Impressionists wanted to depict real life, to paint straight from nature, and to capture the changing effects of light. The term was first used abusively to describe Monet's painting *Impression, Sunrise* 1872 (stolen from the Musée Marmottan, Paris); other Impressionists were Renoir and Sisley, soon joined by Cézanne, Manet, Degas, and others.

imprinting in *ethology, the process whereby a young animal learns to recognize both specific individuals (for example, its mother) and its own species.

impromptu in music, a short instrumental piece that suggests spontaneity. Composers of piano impromptus include Schubert and Chopin.

in abbreviation for ***inch**, a measure of distance.

inbreeding in *genetics, the mating of closely related individuals. It is considered undesirable because it increases the risk that offspring will inherit copies of rare deleterious *recessive alleles (genes) from both parents and so suffer from disabilities.

Inca member of an ancient Peruvian civilization of Quechua-speaking Indians that began in the Andean highlands about 1200; by the time of the Spanish Conquest in the 1530s, the Inca ruled from Ecuador in the north to Chile in the south.

incandescence emission of light from a substance in consequence of its high temperature. The colour of the emitted light from liquids or solids depends on their temperature, and for solids generally the higher the temperature the whiter the light. Gases may become incandescent through *ionizing radiation, as in the glowing vacuum *discharge tube.

incarnation assumption of living form (plant, animal, human) by a deity, for example the gods of Greece and Rome, Hinduism, and Christianity (Jesus as the second person of the Trinity).

incendiary bomb a bomb containing inflammable matter. Usually dropped by aircraft, incendiary bombs were used in World War I, and were a major weapon in attacks on cities in World War II. To hinder firefighters, delayed-action high-explosive bombs were usually dropped with them. In the Vietnam War, US forces used *napalm in incendiary bombs.

incest sexual intercourse between persons thought to be too closely related to marry; the exact relationships which fall under the incest taboo vary widely from society to society. A biological explanation for the incest taboo is based on the necessity to avoid *inbreeding.

inch imperial unit of linear measure, a twelfth of a foot, equal to 2.54 centimetres.

Inchon formerly **Chemulpo** chief port of Seoul, South Korea; population (1990) 1,818,300. It produces steel and textiles.

incisor sharp tooth at the front of the mammalian mouth. Incisors are used for biting or nibbling, as when a rabbit or a sheep eats grass. Rodents, such as rats and squirrels, have large continually-growing incisors, adapted for gnawing. The elephant tusk is a greatly enlarged incisor.

inclination angle between the *ecliptic and the plane of the orbit of a planet, asteroid, or comet. In the case of satellites orbiting a planet, it is the angle between the plane of orbit of the satellite and the equator of the planet.

inclusive fitness in *genetics, the success with which a given variant (or allele) of a *gene is passed on to future generations by a particular individual, after copies of the allele in the individual's relatives and their offspring have been taken into account.

incomes policy government-initiated exercise to curb *inflation by restraining rises in incomes, on either a voluntary or a compulsory basis; often linked with action to control prices, in which case it becomes a prices and incomes policy.

income support in the UK, *social security benefit payable to people who are unemployed or who work for less than 24 hours per week and whose financial resources fall below a certain level. It replaced supplementary benefit 1988.

income tax direct tax levied on personal income, mainly wages and salaries, but which may include the value of receipts other than in cash. It is one of the main instruments for achieving a government's income redistribution objectives. In contrast, *indirect taxes* are duties payable whenever a specific product is purchased; examples include VAT and customs duties.

incontinence failure or inability to control evacuation of the bladder or bowel (or both in the case of double incontinence). It may arise as a result of injury, childbirth, disease, or senility.

incorporation in law, the formation of an association that has corporate personality and is therefore distinct from its individual members, who have no liability for its debts. Corporations (such as companies) can own property and have their own rights and liabilities in legal proceedings.

incubus male demon who in the popular belief of the Middle Ages had sexual intercourse with women in their sleep. Supposedly the women then gave birth to witches and demons.

indemnity in law, an undertaking to compensate another for damage, loss, trouble, or expenses, or the money paid by way of such compensation – for example, under fire insurance agreements.

indenture in law, a *deed between two or more people. Historically, an indenture was a contract between a master and apprentice. The term derives from the practice of writing the agreement twice on paper or parchment and then cutting it with a jagged edge so that both pieces fit together, proving the authenticity of each half.

indentured labour work under a restrictive contract of employment for a fixed period in a foreign country in exchange for payment of passage, accommodation, and food. Indentured labour was the means by which many British people emigrated to North America during the colonial era, and in the 19th–early 20th centuries it was used to recruit Asian workers for employment elsewhere in European colonial empires.

Independence Day public holiday in the USA, commemorating the adoption of the *Declaration of Independence 4 July 1776.

Independent Labour Party (ILP) British socialist party, founded in Bradford 1893 by the Scottish member of Parliament Keir Hardie. In 1900 it joined with trades unions and Fabians in founding the Labour Representation Committee, the nucleus of the *Labour Party. Many members left the ILP to join the Communist Party 1921, and in 1932 all connections with the Labour

Party were severed. After World War II the ILP dwindled, eventually becoming extinct. James Maxton (1885–1946) was its chair 1926–46.

independent school school run privately without direct assistance from the state. In the UK, just over 7% of children (1991) attend private fee-paying schools; the proportion rose in the 1980s. The sector includes most boarding education in the UK. Although most independent secondary schools operate a highly selective admissions policy for entrants at the age of 11 or 13, some specialize in the teaching of slow learners or difficult children and a few follow particular philosophies of progressive education. A group of old established and prestigious independent schools are known as *public schools.

Independent Television Commission (ITC) (formerly the Independent Broadcasting Authority) UK corporate body established by legislation to provide commercially funded television (ITV from 1955). During the 1980s, this role was expanded to include the setting-up of Channel 4 (launched 1982) and the provision of broadcasts directly by satellite into homes.

indeterminacy principle alternative name for *uncertainty principle.

index in economics, an indicator of a general movement in wages and prices over a specified period.

index (plural *indices*) in mathematics, another term for *exponent, the number that indicates the power to which a term should be raised.

India Republic of (Hindi *Bharat*)

area 3,166,829 sq km/1,222,396 sq mi
capital New Delhi
towns Bangalore, Hyderabad, Ahmedabad, Kanpur, Pune, Nagpur; ports Calcutta, Bombay, Madras
physical Himalaya mountains on N border; plains around rivers Ganges, Indus, Brahmaputra; Deccan peninsula S of the Narmada River forms plateau between Western and Eastern Ghats mountain ranges; desert in W; Andaman and Nicobar Islands, Lakshadweep (Laccadive Islands)
environment the controversial Narmada Valley Project is the world's largest combined hydroelectric irrigation scheme. As well as displacing

a million people, the damming of the holy Narmada River will submerge large areas of forest and farmland and create problems of waterlogging and salinization

head of state Shankar Dyal Sharma from 1992

head of government P V Narasimha Rao from 1991

political system liberal democratic federal republic

exports tea (world's largest producer), coffee, fish, iron and steel, leather, textiles, clothing, polished diamonds

currency rupee

population (1993 est) 903,000,000 (920 women to every 1,000 men); growth rate 2.0% p.a.

languages Hindi (widely spoken in N India), English, and 14 other official languages: Assamese, Bengali, Gujarati, Kannada, Kashmiri, Malayalam, Marathi, Oriya, Punjabi, Sanskrit, Sindhi, Tamil, Telugu, Urdu

religions Hindu 80%, Sunni Muslim 10%, Christian 2.5%, Sikh 2%

GNP $330 per head (1991)

chronology

1947 Independence achieved from Britain.

1950 Federal republic proclaimed.

1962 Border skirmishes with China.

1964 Death of Prime Minister Nehru. Border war with Pakistan over Kashmir.

1966 Indira Gandhi became prime minister.

1971 War with Pakistan leading to creation of Bangladesh.

1975–77 State of emergency proclaimed.

1977–79 Janata Party government in power.

1980 Indira Gandhi returned in landslide victory.

1984 Indira Gandhi assassinated; Rajiv Gandhi elected with record majority.

1987 Signing of 'Tamil' Colombo peace accord with Sri Lanka; Indian Peacekeeping Force (IPKF) sent there. Public revelation of Bofors corruption scandal.

1988 New opposition party, Janata Dal, established by former finance minister V P Singh. Voting age lowered from 21 to 18.

1989 Congress (I) lost majority in general election, after Gandhi associates implicated in financial misconduct; Janata Dal minority government formed, with V P Singh prime minister.

1990 Central rule imposed in Jammu and Kashmir. V P Singh resigned; new minority Janata Dal government formed by Chandra Shekhar. Interethnic and religious violence in Punjab and elsewhere.

1991 Central rule imposed in Tamil Nadu. Shekhar resigned; elections called for May. May: Rajiv Gandhi assassinated. June: elections resumed, resulting in a Congress (I) minority government led by P V Narasimha Rao. Separatist violence continued.

1992 Congress (I) won control of state assembly and a majority in parliament in Punjab state elections. Split in Janata Dal opposition resulted in creation of National Front coalition party (including rump of Janata Dal party). July: Shankar Dyal Sharma elected president.

Indiana state of the midwest USA; nickname Hoosier State

area 93,700 sq km/36,168 sq mi

capital Indianapolis

towns Fort Wayne, Gary, Evansville, South Bend

products maize, pigs, soya beans, limestone, machinery, electrical goods, coal, steel, iron, chemicals

population (1990) 5,544,200

famous people Hoagy Carmichael, Eugene V Debs, Theodore Dreiser, Michael Jackson, Cole Porter, Wilbur Wright

Indianapolis capital and largest city of Indiana, on the White River; population (1990) 731,300. It is an industrial centre and venue of the 'Indianapolis 500' automobile race.

Indian corn an alternative name for *maize.

Indian languages traditionally, the languages of the subcontinent of India; since 1947, the languages of the Republic of India. These number some 200, depending on whether a variety is classified as a language or a dialect. They fall into five main groups, the two most widespread of which are the Indo-European languages (mainly in the north) and the Dravidian languages (mainly in the south).

Indian music rich and diverse musical culture related to that of the Middle East. A characteristic classical ensemble consists of two to four players representing solo melody (sitar, vina), drone accompaniment (tamboura), and rhythm (tabla). Players improvise to combinations of established modes (ragas) and rhythms (talas), associated with specific emotions, ritual functions, and times of day. Sitar improvisations are intensely incantatory in style and develop continuously, often for more than an hour. A close rapport exists among players and with audiences. Popular music makes use of larger orchestras including violins and reed organ, both introduced from Europe during the 18th and 19th centuries.

Indian Mutiny or **Sepoy Rebellion** or **Mutiny** revolt 1857–58 of Indian soldiers (Sepoys) against the British in India. The uprising was confined to the north, from Bengal to the Punjab, and central India. The majority of support came from the army and recently dethroned princes, but in some areas it developed into a peasant uprising and general revolt. It included the seizure of Delhi by the rebels, its siege and recapture by the British, and the defence of Lucknow by a British garrison. The mutiny led to the end of rule by the *East India Company and its replacement by direct British crown administration.

Indian National Congress (INC) official name for the *Congress Party of India.

Indian Ocean ocean between Africa and Australia, with India to the N, and the S boundary being an arbitrary line from Cape Agulhas to S Tasmania; area 73,500,000 sq km/ 28,371,000 sq mi; average depth 3,872 m/ 12,708 ft. The greatest depth is the Java Trench 7,725 m/25,353 ft.

India of the Princes the 562 Indian states ruled by princes during the period of British control. They occupied an area of 1,854,347 sq km/ 715,964 sq mi (45% of the total area of pre-partition India) and had a population of over 93 million. At the partition of British India in 1947 the princes were given independence by the British government but were advised to adhere to either India or Pakistan. Between 1947 and 1950 all except *Kashmir were incorporated in either country.

indicator in chemistry, a compound that changes its structure and colour in response to its environment. The commonest chemical indicators detect changes in *pH (for example, *litmus), or in the oxidation state of a system (redox indicators).

indicator species plant or animal whose presence or absence in an area indicates certain environmental conditions, such as soil type, high levels of pollution, or, in rivers, low levels of dissolved oxygen. Many plants show a preference for either alkaline or acid soil conditions, while certain trees require aluminium, and are found only in soils where it is present. Some lichens are sensitive to sulphur dioxide in the air, and absence of these species indicates atmospheric pollution.

indie (short for **independent**) in music, a record label that is neither owned nor distributed by one of the large conglomerates ('majors') that dominate the industry. Without a corporate bureaucratic structure, the independent labels are often quicker to respond to new trends and more idealistic in their aims. What has become loosely known as **indie music** therefore tends to be experimental, amateurish, or at the cutting edge of street fashion.

indigo violet-blue vegetable dye obtained from plants of the genus *Indigofera*, family Leguminosae, but now replaced by a synthetic product. It was once a major export crop of India.

indium (Latin *indicum* 'indigo') soft, ductile, silver-white, metallic element, symbol In, atomic number 49, relative atomic mass 114.82. It occurs in nature in some zinc ores, is resistant to abrasion, and is used as a coating on metal parts. It was discovered 1863 by German metallurgists Ferdinand Reich (1799–1882) and Hieronymus Richter (1824–1898), who named it after the two indigo lines of its spectrum.

individualism in politics, a view in which the individual takes precedence over the collective: the opposite of *collectivism. The term **possessive individualism** has been applied to the writings of John *Locke and Jeremy *Bentham, describing society as comprising individuals interacting through market relations.

Indo-Aryan languages another name for the *Indo-European languages.

Indochina French former collective name for *Cambodia, *Laos, and *Vietnam, which became independent after World War II.

Indochina War successful war of independence 1946–54 between the nationalist forces of what was to become Vietnam and France, the occupying colonial power.

Indo-European languages family of languages that includes some of the world's major classical languages (Sanskrit and Pali in India, Zend Avestan in Iran, Greek and Latin in Europe), as well as several of the most widely spoken languages (English worldwide; Spanish in Iberia, Latin America, and elsewhere; and the Hindi group of languages in N India). Indo-European languages were once located only along a geographical band from India through Iran into

NW Asia, E Europe, the northern Mediterranean lands, N and W Europe and the British Isles.

Indo-Germanic languages former name for the *Indo-European languages.

Indonesia Republic of (*Republik Indonesia*)

area 1,919,443 sq km/740,905 sq mi
capital Jakarta
towns Bandung, Yogyakarta (Java), Medan, Banda Aceh, Palembang (Sumatra), Denpasar (Bali), Kupang (Timor); ports: Tanjung Priok, Surabaya, Semarang (Java), Ujung Pandang (Sulawesi)
physical comprises 13,677 tropical islands: the Greater Sundas (including Java, Madura, Sumatra, Sulawesi, and Kalimantan [part of Borneo]), the Lesser Sundas/Nusa Tenggara (including Bali, Lombok, Sumbawa, Flores, Sumba, Alor, Lomblen, Timor, Roti, and Savu), Maluku/Moluccas (over 1,000 islands including Ambon, Ternate, Tidore, Tanimbar, and Halmahera), and Irian Jaya (part of New Guinea)
environment comparison of primary forest and 30-year-old secondary forest has shown that logging in Kalimantan has led to a 20% decline in tree species
head of state and government T N J Suharto from 1967
political system authoritarian nationalist republic
exports timber, oil, rubber, coffee, liquid natural gas, minerals, palm oil, tea, tobacco
currency rupiah
population (1993) 187,800,000 (including 300 ethnic groups); growth rate 2% p.a. Indonesia is the world's fourth most populous country, surpassed only by China, India and USA. It has the world's largest Muslim population; Java is one of the world's most densely populated areas
languages Bahasa Indonesia (official), closely related to Malay; there are 583 regional languages and dialects; Javanese is the most widely spoken local language
religions Muslim 88%, Christian 10%, Buddhist and Hindu 2% (the continued spread of Christianity, together with an Islamic revival, have led to greater religious tensions)
GNP $620 per head (1992)
chronology
17th century Dutch rule established.
1942 Occupied by Japan; nationalist puppet government established.

1945 Japanese surrender; nationalists declared independence under Achmed Sukarno.

1965–66 Attempted communist coup; General T N J Suharto imposed emergency administration, leading to deaths of hundreds of thousands of Indonesians.

1967 Sukarno replaced as president by Suharto.

1975 Guerrillas seeking independence for S Maluku seized train and Indonesian consulate in the Netherlands; Western hostages held.

1976 Forced annexation of former Portuguese colony of East Timor.

1984 Stepping up of transmigration programme announced, to play crucial role in overall development strategy.

1989 Foreign debt reached $50 billion; Western creditors offered aid on condition that concessions were made to foreign companies and austerity measures introduced.

1991 Democracy forums launched to promote political dialogue. Massacre in East Timor.

1992 Ruling Golkar party re-elected. East Timor rebel leader arrested; more than 1,000 rebels surrendered.

1993 President Suharto re-elected for sixth consecutive five-year term; first civilian leader of Golkar installed.

1994 Sukarno's daughter, Magawati, elected head of PDI.

Indra Hindu god of the sky, shown as a four-armed man on a white elephant, carrying a thunderbolt. The intoxicating drink *soma is associated with him.

inductance in physics, a measure of the capability of an electronic circuit or circuit component to form a magnetic field or store magnetic energy when carrying a current. Its symbol is L, and its unit of measure is the *henry.

induction in obstetrics, deliberate intervention to initiate labour before it starts naturally; then it usually proceeds normally. Induction involves rupture of the fetal membranes (amniotomy) and the use of the hormone oxytocin to stimulate contractions of the womb. In biology, induction is a term used for various processes, including the production of an *enzyme in response to a particular chemical in the cell, and the *differentiation of cells in an *embryo in response to the presence of neighbouring tissues.

induction coil type of electrical transformer, similar to an *ignition coil, that produces an intermittent high-voltage alternating current from a low-voltage direct current supply.

inductor device included in an electrical circuit because of its inductance.

indulgence in the Roman Catholic church, the total or partial remission of temporal punishment for sins which remain to be expiated after penitence and confession have secured exemption from eternal punishment. The doctrine of indulgence began as the commutation of church penances in exchange for suitable works of charity or money gifts to the church, and became a great source of church revenue. This trade in indulgences roused Luther in 1517 to initiate the Reformation. The Council of Trent 1563 recommended moderate retention of indulgences, and they continue, notably in 'Holy Years'.

Indus river in Asia, rising in Tibet and flowing 3,180 km/1,975 mi to the Arabian Sea. In 1960 the use of its waters, including those of its five tributaries, was divided between India (rivers Ravi, Beas, Sutlej) and Pakistan (rivers Indus, Jhelum, Chenab).

industrial dispute disagreement between an employer and its employees, usually represented by a trade union, over some aspect of the terms or conditions of employment. A dispute is often followed by industrial action, in the form of a *strike or a *work to rule.

industrialization policy usually associated with modernization of developing countries where the process normally starts with the manufacture of simple goods that can replace imports. It is essential for economic development and largely responsible for the growth of cities.

industrial relations relationship between employers and employees, and their dealings with each other. In most industries, wages and conditions are determined by *free collective bargaining* between employers and *trade unions. Some European and American countries have *worker participation* through profit-sharing and industrial democracy. Another solution is *co-ownership*, in which a company is entirely owned by its employees. The aim of good industrial relations is to achieve a motivated, capable workforce that sees its work as creative and fulfilling.

Industrial Revolution the sudden acceleration of technical and economic development that began in Britain in the second half of the 18th century. The traditional agrarian economy was replaced by one dominated by machinery and manufacturing, made possible through technical advances such as the steam engine. This transferred the balance of political power from the landowner to the industrial capitalist and created an urban working class. From 1830 to the early 20th century, the Industrial Revolution spread throughout Europe and the USA and to Japan and the various colonial empires.

industrial sector any of the different groups into which industries may be divided: primary, secondary, tertiary, and quaternary. *Primary* industries extract or use raw materials; for example, mining and agriculture. *Secondary* industries are manufacturing industries, where raw materials are processed or components are assembled. *Tertiary* industries supply services such as retailing. The *quaternary* sector of industry is concerned with the professions and those services that require a high level of skill, expertise, and specialization. It includes education, research and development, administration, and financial services such as accountancy.

industrial tribunal court of law that hears and rules on disputes between employers and employees or trade unions relating to statutory terms and conditions of employment.

Industrial Workers of the World (IWW) labour movement founded in Chicago, USA 1905, and in Australia 1907, the members of which were popularly known as the *Wobblies*. The IWW was dedicated to the overthrow of capitalism and the creation of a single union for workers, but divided on tactics.

industry the extraction and conversion of raw materials, the manufacture of goods, and the provision of services. Industry can be either low technology, unspecialized, and labour-intensive, as in Third World countries, or highly automated, mechanized, and specialized, using advanced technology, as in the industrialized countries. Major trends in industrial activity 1960–90 were the growth of electronic, robotic, and microelectronic technologies, the expansion of the offshore oil industry, and the prominence of Japan and other Pacific-region countries in manufacturing and distributing electronics, computers, and motor vehicles.

Indus Valley civilization one of the four earliest ancient civilizations of the Old World (the other three being the *Sumerian civilization 3500 BC; *Egypt 3000 BC; and *China 2200 BC), developing in the NW of the Indian subcontinent about 2500 BC.

inert gas or **noble gas** any of a group of six elements (helium, neon, argon, krypton, xenon, and radon), so named because they were originally thought not to enter into any chemical reactions. This is now known to be incorrect: in 1962, xenon was made to combine with fluorine, and since then, compounds of argon, krypton, and radon with fluorine and/or oxygen have been described.

inertia in physics, the tendency of an object to remain in a state of rest or uniform motion until an external force is applied, as stated by Isaac Newton's first law of motion (see *Newton's laws of motion).

INF abbreviation for **intermediate nuclear forces**, as in the *Intermediate Nuclear Forces Treaty.

infante and **infanta** title given in Spain and Portugal to the sons (other than the heir apparent) and daughters, respectively, of the sovereign. The heir apparent in Spain bears the title of prince of Asturias.

infanticide in law, the killing of a child under 12 months old by its mother. More generally, any killing of a newborn child, usually as a method of population control and most frequently of girls (especially in India and China), although boys are killed in countries where bride prices are high.

infant mortality rate measure of the number of infants dying under one year of age, usually expressed as the number of deaths per 1,000 live births. Improved sanitation, nutrition, and medical care have considerably lowered figures throughout much of the world; for example in the 18th century in the USA and UK infant mortality was about 500 per thousand, compared with under 10 per thousand in 1989. In much of the Third World, however, the infant mortality rate remains high.

infection invasion of the body by disease-causing organisms (pathogens, or germs) that become established, multiply, and produce symptoms. Bacteria and viruses cause most diseases, but there are other microorganisms, protozoans, and other parasites.

inferiority complex in psychology, a *complex described by Alfred *Adler based on physical inferiority; the term has been popularly used to describe general feelings of inferiority and the overcompensation that often ensues.

infinite series in mathematics, a series of numbers consisting of a denumerably infinite sequence of terms. The sequence $n, n^2, n^3, \ldots$ gives the series $n + n^2 + n^3 + \ldots$. For example, $1 + 2 + 3 + \ldots$ is a divergent infinite arithmetic series, and $8 + 4 + 2 + 1 + \frac{1}{2} + \ldots$ is a convergent infinite geometric series that has a sum to infinity of 16.

infinity mathematical quantity that is larger than any fixed assignable quantity; symbol ∞. By convention, the result of dividing any number by zero is regarded as infinity.

inflammation defensive reaction of the body tissues to disease or damage, including redness, swelling, and heat. Denoted by the suffix -itis (as in appendicitis), it may be acute or chronic, and may be accompanied by the formation of pus. This is an essential part of the healing process.

inflation in economics, a rise in the general level of prices. The many causes include **cost-push inflation** that occurred 1974 as a result of the world price increase in oil, thus increasing production costs. **Demand-pull inflation** results when overall demand exceeds supply. Suppressed inflation occurs in controlled economies and is reflected in rationing, shortages, and black market prices. Deflation, a fall in the general level of prices, is the reverse of inflation.

inflation tax tax imposed on companies that increase wages by more than an amount fixed by law (except to take account of increased profits or because of a profit-sharing scheme).

inflection or **inflexion** in grammatical analysis, an ending or other element in a word that indicates its grammatical function (whether plural or singular, masculine or feminine, subject or object, and so on).

inflorescence flower-bearing branch, or system of branches, in plants. Inflorescences can be divided into two main types: cymose and racemose. In a cymose inflorescence, the terminal growing point produces a single flower and subsequent flowers arise on lower lateral branches, as in forget-me-not Myosotis and chickweed Stellaria; the oldest flowers are found at the apex. A racemose inflorescence consists of a main axis, bearing flowers along its length, with an active growing region at the apex, as in hyacinth and lupin; the oldest flowers are found near the base or, in cases where the inflorescence has become flattened, towards the outside.

influenza any of various virus infections primarily affecting the air passages, accompanied by *systemic effects such as fever, chills, headache, joint and muscle pains, and lassitude. Treatment is with bed rest and analgesic drugs such as aspirin and paracetamol.

information technology collective term for the various technologies involved in processing and transmitting information. They include computing, telecommunications, and microelectronics.

infrared astronomy study of infrared radiation produced by relatively cool gas and dust in space, as in the areas around forming stars. In 1983, the Infra-Red Astronomy Satellite (IRAS) surveyed the entire sky at infrared wavelengths. It found five new comets, thousands of galaxies undergoing bursts of star formation, and the possibility of planetary systems forming around several dozen stars.

infrared radiation invisible electromagnetic radiation of wavelength between about 0.75 micrometres and 1 millimetre – that is, between the limit of the red end of the visible spectrum and the shortest microwaves. All bodies above the *absolute zero of temperature absorb and radiate infrared radiation. Infrared radiation is used in medical photography and treatment, and in industry, astronomy, and criminology.

infrastructure relatively permanent facilities that service an industrial economy. Infrastructure usually includes roads, railways, other communication networks, energy and water supply, and education and training facilities. Some definitions also include socio-cultural installations such as health-care and leisure facilities.

Ingres Jean Auguste Dominique 1780–1867. French painter, a student of David and leading exponent of the Neo-Classical style. He studied and worked in Rome about 1807–20, where he began the *Odalisque* series of sensuous female nudes, then went to Florence, and returned to France 1824. His portraits painted in the 1840s–50s are meticulously detailed and highly polished.

inhibition, neural in biology, the process in which activity in one *nerve cell suppresses activity in another. Neural inhibition in networks of nerve cells leading from sensory organs, or to muscles, plays an important role in allowing an animal to make fine sensory discriminations and to exercise fine control over movements.

initiative device whereby constitutional voters may play a direct part in making laws. A proposed law is drawn up and signed by petitioners, and submitted to the legislature. A *referendum may be taken on a law that has been passed by the legislature but that will not become operative unless the voters assent to it. Switzerland was the first country to make use of the device.

injunction court order that forbids a person from doing something, or orders him or her to take certain action. Breach of an injunction is *contempt of court.

ink coloured liquid used for writing, drawing, and printing. Traditional ink (blue, but later a permanent black) was produced from gallic acid and tannic acid, but inks are now based on synthetic dyes.

Inkatha Freedom Party (IFP) South African political party, representing the nationalist aspirations of the country's largest ethnic group, the Zulus. It was founded as a paramilitary organization 1975 by its present leader, Chief Gatsha *Buthelezi, with the avowed aim of creating a nonracial democratic political situation. Fighting between Inkatha and *African National Congress (ANC) supporters during the early 1990s cost thousands of lives. In April 1994, after an initial violent boycott, Buthelezi agreed to register the IFP in the country's first multiracial elections. The party emerged with 10% of the popular vote. Buthelezi was himself appointed home affairs minister in the new power-sharing administration.

INLA abbreviation for *Irish National Liberation Army*.

inlay decorative technique used on furniture until replaced by *marquetry in the 17th century. A pattern composed of differently coloured woods or other materials such as horn or ivory is inset into the solid wood of the piece of furniture.

in loco parentis (Latin 'in place of a parent') in a parental capacity.

inner city the area that immediately borders the central business district of a town or city. In many cities this is one of the older parts and may suffer from decay and neglect, leading to social problems.

Innocent thirteen popes including:

Innocent III 1161–1216. Pope from 1198 who asserted papal power over secular princes, in particular over the succession of Holy Roman Emperors. He also made King *John of England his vassal, compelling him to accept Stephen *Langton as archbishop of Canterbury. He promoted the fourth Crusade and crusades against the non-Christian Livonians and Letts, and the Albigensian heretics of S France.

Innocents' Day or **Childermas** festival of the Roman Catholic church, celebrated 28 Dec in memory of the **Massacre of the Innocents**, the children of Bethlehem who were allegedly slaughtered by King *Herod after the birth of Jesus.

Innsbruck capital of Tirol state, W Austria; population (1981) 117,000. It is a tourist and winter sports centre and a route junction for the Brenner Pass. The 1964 and 1976 Winter Olympics were held here.

Inns of Court four private legal societies in London, England: Lincoln's Inn, Gray's Inn, Inner Temple, and Middle Temple. All barristers (advocates in the English legal system) must belong to one of the Inns of Court. The main function of each Inn is the education, government, and protection of its members. Each is under the administration of a body of Benchers (judges and senior barristers).

inoculation injection into the body of dead or weakened disease-carrying organisms or their toxins (*vaccine) to produce immunity by inducing a mild form of a disease.

inorganic chemistry branch of chemistry dealing with the chemical properties of the elements and their compounds, excluding the more complex covalent compounds of carbon, which are considered in *organic chemistry.

input device device for entering information into a computer. Input devices include keyboards, joysticks, mice, light pens, touch-sensitive screens, graphics tablets, speech-recognition devices, and vision systems. Compare *output device.

inquest inquiry held by a coroner into an unexplained death. At an inquest, a coroner is assisted by a jury of between 7 and 11 people. Evidence is on oath, and medical and other witnesses may be summoned.

Inquisition tribunal of the Roman Catholic Church established 1233 to suppress heresy (dissenting views), originally by excommunication. Sentence was pronounced during a religious ceremony, the *auto-da-fé*. The Inquisition operated in France, Italy, Spain, and the Holy Roman Empire, and was especially active following the *Reformation; it was later extended to the Americas. Its trials were conducted in secret, under torture, and penalties ranged from fines, through flogging and imprisonment, to death by burning.

insanity popular and legal term for mental disorder. In medicine the corresponding term is *psychosis.

insect any member of the class Insecta among the *arthropods or jointed-legged animals. An insect's body is divided into head, thorax, and abdomen. The head bears a pair of feelers or antennae, and attached to the thorax are three pairs of legs and usually two pairs of wings. The scientific study of insects is termed entomology. More than 1 million species are known, and several thousand new ones are discovered every year. Insects vary in size from 0.02 cm/0.007 in to 35 cm/13.5 in in length.

insecticide any chemical pesticide used to kill insects. Among the most effective insecticides are synthetic organic chemicals such as *DDT and dieldrin, which are chlorinated hydrocarbons. These chemicals, however, have proved persistent in the environment and are also poisonous to all animal life, including humans, and are consequently banned in many countries. Other synthetic insecticides include organic phosphorus compounds such as malathion. Insecticides prepared from plants, such as derris and pyrethrum, are safer to use but need to be applied frequently and carefully.

insectivore any animal whose diet is made up largely or exclusively of insects. In particular, the name is applied to mammals of the order Insectivora, which includes the shrews, hedgehogs, moles, and tenrecs.

insectivorous plant plant that can capture and digest live prey (normally insects), to obtain nitrogen compounds that are lacking in its usual marshy habitat. Some are passive traps, for example, the pitcher plants *Nepenthes* and *Sarracenia*. One pitcher-plant species has container-traps holding 1.6 l/3.5 pt of the liquid that 'digests' its food, mostly insects but occasionally even rodents. Others, for example, sundews *Drosera*, butterworts *Pinguicula* and Venus's-flytrap *Dionaea muscipula*, have an active trapping mechanism; see *leaf.

inselberg (German 'island mountain') prominent steep-sided hill of resistant solid rock, such as granite, rising out of a plain, usually in a tropical area. Its rounded appearance is caused by so-called onion-skin *weathering, in which the surface is eroded in successive layers.

insemination, artificial see *artificial insemination.

insider trading or **insider dealing** illegal use of privileged information in dealing on a stock exchange, for example when a company takeover bid is imminent. Insider trading is in theory detected by the Securities and Exchange Commission (SEC) in the USA, and by the Securities and Investment Board (SIB) in the UK. Neither agency, however, has any legal powers other than public disclosure and they do not bring prosecutions themselves.

in situ (Latin) in place, on the spot, without moving from position.

instinct in *ethology, behaviour found in all equivalent members of a given species (for example, all the males, or all the females with young) that is presumed to be genetically determined.

instrument landing system landing aid for aircraft that uses *radio beacons on the ground and instruments on the flight deck. One beacon (localizer) sends out a vertical radio beam along the centre line of the runway. Another beacon (glide slope) transmits a beam in the plane at right angles to the localizer beam at the ideal approach-path angle. The pilot can tell from the instruments how to manoeuvre to attain the correct approach path.

insulator any poor *conductor of heat, sound, or electricity. Most substances lacking free (mobile) *electrons, such as nonmetals, are electrical or thermal insulators.

insulin protein *hormone, produced by specialized cells in the islets of Langerhans in the pancreas, that regulates the metabolism (rate of activity) of glucose, fats, and proteins. Insulin was discovered by Canadian physician Frederick *Banting, who pioneered its use in treating *diabetes.

insurance contract indemnifying the payer of a premium against loss by fire, death, accident, and so on, which is known as **assurance** in the case of a fixed sum and **insurance** where the indemnity is proportionate to the loss.

intaglio gem or seal that has a pattern cut into one surface; an *engraving technique.

integer any whole number. Integers may be positive or negative; 0 is an integer, and is often considered positive. Formally, integers are members of the set $Z = 1... -3, -2, -1, 0, 1, 2, 3,....$ Fractions, such as $1/2$ and 0.35, are known as non-integral numbers ('not integers').

integral calculus branch of mathematics using the process of *integration. It is concerned with finding volumes and areas and summing infinitesimally small quantities.

integrated circuit (IC), popularly called **silicon chip**, a miniaturized electronic circuit produced on a single crystal, or chip, of a semiconducting material – usually silicon. It may contain many thousands of components and yet measure only 5 mm square and 1 mm thick. The IC is encapsulated within a plastic or ceramic case, and linked via gold wires to metal pins with which it is connected to a *printed circuit board and the other components that make up such electronic devices as computers and calculators.

Integrated Services Digital Network (ISDN) internationally developed telecommunications system for sending signals in *digital format along optical fibres and coaxial cable. It involves converting the 'local loop' – the link between the user's telephone (or private automatic branch exchange) and the digital telephone exchange – from an *analogue system into a digital system, thereby greatly increasing the amount of information that can be carried. The first large-scale use of ISDN began in Japan 1988.

integration in mathematics, a method in *calculus of evaluating definite or indefinite integrals. An example of a definite integral can be conceived of as finding the area under a curve (as represented by an algebraic expression or function) between particular values of the function's variable. In practice, integral calculus provides scientists with a powerful tool for doing calculations that involve a continually varying quantity (such as determining the position at any given instant of a space rocket that is accelerating away from Earth). Its basic principles were discovered in the late 1660s independently by the German philosopher *Leibniz and the British scientist Isaac *Newton.

intelligence in psychology, a general concept that summarizes the abilities of an individual in reasoning and problem solving, particularly in novel situations. These consist of a wide range of verbal and nonverbal skills and therefore some psychologists dispute a unitary concept of intelligence, such as the *IQ arrived at by intelligence testing.

intelligence in military and political affairs, information, often secretly or illegally obtained, about other countries. *Counter-intelligence* is information on the activities of hostile agents. Much intelligence is gained by technical means, such as satellites and the electronic interception of data.

intensity in physics, the power (or energy per second) per unit area carried by a form of radiation or wave motion. It is an indication of the concentration of energy present and, if measured at varying distances from the source, of the effect of distance on this. For example, the intensity of light is a measure of its brightness, and may be shown to diminish with distance from its source in accordance with the *inverse square law (its intensity is inversely proportional to the square of the distance).

interactive computing in computing, a system for processing data in which the operator is in direct communication with the computer, receiving immediate responses to input data. In *batch processing, by contrast, the necessary data and instructions are prepared in advance and processed by the computer with little or no intervention from the operator.

interactive video (IV) computer-mediated system that enables the user to interact with and control information (including text, recorded speech, or moving images) stored on video disc. IV is most commonly used for training purposes, using analogue video discs, but has wider applications with digital video systems such as CD-I (Compact Disc Interactive, from Philips and Sony) and DVI (Digital Video Interactive, from Intel).

inter alia (Latin) among other things.

interdict ecclesiastical punishment that excludes an individual, community, or realm from participation in spiritual activities except for communion. It was usually employed against heretics or realms whose ruler was an excommunicant.

interest in finance, a sum of money paid by a borrower to a lender in return for the loan, usually expressed as a percentage per annum. *Simple interest* is interest calculated as a straight percentage of the amount loaned or invested. In *compound interest*, the interest earned over a period of time (for example, per annum) is added to the investment, so that at the end of the next period interest is paid on that total.

interface in computing, the point of contact between two programs or pieces of equipment. The term is most often used for the physical connection between the computer and a *peripheral device, which is used to compensate for differences in such operating characteristics as speed, data coding, voltage, and power consumption. For example, a *printer interface* is the cabling and circuitry used to transfer data from a computer to a printer, and to compensate for differences in speed and coding.

interference in physics, the phenomenon of two or more wave motions interacting and combining to produce a resultant wave of larger or smaller amplitude (depending on whether the combining waves are in or out of *phase with each other).

interferometer in physics, a device that splits a beam of light into two parts, the parts being recombined after travelling different paths to form an interference pattern of light and dark bands. Interferometers are used in many branches of science and industry where accurate measurements of distances and angles are needed.

interferon naturally occurring cellular protein that makes up part of the body's defences against viral disease. Three types (alpha, beta, and gamma) are produced by infected cells and enter the bloodstream and uninfected cells, making them immune to virus attack.

Intermediate Nuclear Forces Treaty agreement signed 8 Dec 1987 between the USA and the USSR to eliminate all ground-based nuclear missiles in Europe that were capable of hitting only European targets (including European Russia). It reduced the countries' nuclear arsenals by some 2,000 (4% of the total). The treaty included provisions for each country to inspect the other's bases.

intermediate technology application of mechanics, electrical engineering, and other technologies, based on inventions and designs developed in scientifically sophisticated cultures, but utilizing materials, assembly, and maintenance methods found in technologically less advanced regions (known as the *Third World).

intermezzo in music, a one-act comic opera, such as Pergolesi's *La Serva Padrona/The Maid as Mistress* 1732; also a short orchestral interlude played between the acts of an opera to denote the passage of time. By extension, an intermezzo can also be a short piece to be played between other more substantial works.

intermolecular force or *van der Waals' force* force of attraction between molecules. Intermolecular forces are relatively weak; hence simple molecular compounds are gases, liquids, or low-melting-point solids.

internal-combustion engine heat engine in which fuel is burned inside the engine, contrasting with an external combustion engine (such as the steam engine) in which fuel is burned in a separate unit. The *diesel engine and *petrol engine are both internal-combustion engines. Gas *turbines and *jet and *rocket engines may also be considered to be internal-combustion engines because they burn their fuel inside their combustion chambers.

International, the coordinating body established by labour and socialist organizations, including:

First International or **International Working Men's Association** 1864–72, formed in London under Karl *Marx.

Second International 1889–1940, founded in Paris.

Third (Socialist) International or **Comintern** 1919–43, formed in Moscow by the Soviet leader Lenin, advocating from 1933 a popular front (communist, socialist, liberal) against the German dictator Hitler.

Fourth International or **Trotskyist International** 1938, somewhat indeterminate, anti-Stalinist.

Revived Socialist International 1951, formed in Frankfurt, Germany, a largely anti-communist association of social democrats.

International Bank for Reconstruction and Development official name of the *World Bank.

International Court of Justice main judicial organ of the *United Nations, in The Hague, the Netherlands. It hears international law disputes as well as playing an advisory role to UN organs. It was set up by the UN charter 1945 and superseded the World Court. There are 15 judges, each from a different member state.

International Date Line (IDL) imaginary line that approximately follows the 180° line of longitude. The date is put forward a day when crossing the line going west, and back a day when going east. The IDL was chosen at the International Meridian Conference 1884.

Internationale international revolutionary socialist anthem; composed 1870 and first sung 1888. The words by Eugene Pottier (1816–1887) were written shortly after Napoleon III's surrender to Prussia; the music is by Pierre Degeyter. It was the Soviet national anthem 1917–44.

International Gothic late Gothic style of painting prevalent in Europe in the 14th and 15th centuries, characterized by greater realism. Exponents include Simone *Martini and the Franco-Flemish *Limbourg brothers.

International Labour Organization (ILO) agency of the United Nations, established 1919, which formulates standards for labour and social conditions. Its headquarters are in Geneva. It was awarded the Nobel Peace Prize 1969.

international law body of rules generally accepted as governing the relations between countries, pioneered by Hugo *Grotius, especially in matters of human rights, territory, and war.

International Monetary Fund (IMF) specialized agency of the *United Nations, headquarters Washington DC, established under the 1944 *Bretton Woods agreement and operational since 1947. It seeks to promote international monetary cooperation and the growth of world trade, and to smooth multilateral payment arrangements among member states. IMF standby loans are available to members in balance-of-payments difficulties (the amount being governed by the member's quota), usually

on the basis that the country must agree to take certain corrective measures.

International Society for Krishna Consciousness (ISKCON) or **Gaudiya Vaisnavism** Hindu sect based on the demonstration of intense love for Krishna (an incarnation of the god Vishnu), especially by chanting the mantra 'Hare Krishna'. Their holy books are the Hindu scriptures and particularly the *Bhagavad-Gītā*, which they study daily.

Internet global, on-line computer network connecting governments, companies, universities, and many other networks and users. The service offers *electronic mail, conferencing and chat services, as well as the ability to access remote computers and send and retrieve files. It began in 1984 and by late 1994 was estimated to have over 40 million users on 11,000 networks in 70 countries, with an estimated one million new users joining each month.

internment detention of suspected criminals without trial. Foreign citizens are often interned during times of war or civil unrest.

interplanetary matter gas and dust thinly spread through the solar system. The gas flows outwards from the Sun as the *solar wind. Fine dust lies in the plane of the solar system, scattering sunlight to cause the *zodiacal light. Swarms of dust shed by comets enter the Earth's atmosphere to cause *meteor showers.

Interpol (acronym for **International Criminal Police Organization**) agency founded following the Second International Judicial Police Conference 1923 with its headquarters in Vienna, and reconstituted after World War II with its headquarters in Paris. It has an international criminal register, fingerprint file, and methods index.

interpreter computer program that translates and executes a program written in a high-level language. Unlike a *compiler, which produces a complete machine-code translation of the high-level program in one operation, an interpreter translates the source program, instruction by instruction, each time that program is run.

intersex individual that is intermediate between a normal male and a normal female in its appearance (for example, a genetic male that lacks external genitalia and so resembles a female).

interval in music, the pitch difference between two notes, usually measured in terms of the diatonic scale.

intestacy absence of a will at a person's death. In law, special legal rules apply on intestacy for appointing administrators to deal with the deceased person's affairs, and for disposing of the deceased person's property in accordance with statutory provisions.

intestine in vertebrates, the digestive tract from the stomach outlet to the anus. The human **small intestine** is 6 m/20 ft long, 4 cm/1.5 in in diameter, and consists of the duodenum, jejunum, and ileum; the **large intestine** is 1.5 m/5 ft long, 6 cm/2.5 in in diameter, and includes the caecum, colon, and rectum. Both are muscular tubes comprising an inner lining that secretes alkaline digestive juice, a submucous coat containing fine blood vessels and nerves, a muscular coat, and a serous coat covering all, supported by a strong peritoneum, which carries the blood and lymph vessels, and the nerves. The contents are passed along slowly by *peristalsis (waves of involuntary muscular action). The term intestine is also applied to the lower digestive tract of invertebrates.

Intifada (Arabic 'resurgence' or 'throwing off') Palestinian uprising; also the title of the involved *Liberation Army of Palestine*, a loosely organized group of adult and teenage Palestinians active since 1987 in attacks on armed Israeli troops in the occupied territories of Palestine. Their campaign for self-determination includes stone-throwing and petrol bombing.

intrauterine device IUD or coil, a contraceptive device that is inserted into the womb (uterus). It is a tiny plastic object, sometimes containing copper. By causing a mild inflammation of the lining of the uterus it prevents fertilized eggs from becoming implanted.

intrusion mass of *igneous rock that has formed by 'injection' of molten rock, or magma, into existing cracks beneath the surface of the Earth, as distinct from a volcanic rock mass which has erupted from the surface. Intrusion features include vertical cylindrical structures such as stocks and necks, sheet structures such as dykes that cut across the strata and sills that push between them, and laccoliths, which are blisters that push up the overlying rock.

intuition rapid, unconscious thought process. In philosophy, intuition is that knowledge of a concept which does not derive directly from the senses. Thus, we may be said to have an intuitive idea of God, beauty, or justice. The concept of intuition is similar to Bertrand *Russell's theory of knowledge by acquaintance. In both cases, it is contrasted with empirical knowledge (see *empiricism).

Inuit people inhabiting the Arctic coasts of North America, the E islands of the Canadian Arctic, and the ice-free coasts of Greenland. Inuktitut, their language, has about 60,000 speakers; it belongs to the Eskimo-Aleut group. The Inuit object to the name Eskimos ('eaters of raw meat') given them by the Algonquin Indians.

Invar trademark for an alloy of iron containing 36% nickel, which expands or contracts very little when the temperature changes. It is used to make precision instruments (such as pendulums and tuning forks) whose dimensions must not alter.

Invergordon Mutiny incident in the British Atlantic Fleet, Cromarty Firth, Scotland, 15 Sept 1931. Ratings refused to prepare the ships for sea following the government's cuts in their pay; the cuts were consequently modified.

Inverness town in Highland region, Scotland, lying in a sheltered site at the mouth of the river Ness; population (1985) 58,000. It is a tourist centre with tweed, tanning, engineering, and distilling industries.

inverse square law in physics, the statement that the magnitude of an effect (usually a force) at a point is inversely proportional to the square of the distance between that point and the point location of its cause.

inverse video or *reverse video* in computing, a display mode in which images on a display

screen are presented as a negative of their normal appearance. For example, if the computer screen normally displays dark images on a light background, inverse video will change all or part of the screen to a light image on a dark background.

inversion in music, the mirror-image of a melody used in counterpoint; alternatively a chord in which the natural order of notes is rearranged.

invertebrate animal without a backbone. The invertebrates comprise over 95% of the million or so existing animal species and include sponges, coelenterates, flatworms, nematodes, annelid worms, arthropods, molluscs, echinoderms, and primitive aquatic chordates, such as sea squirts and lancelets.

investment in economics, the purchase of any asset with the potential to yield future financial benefit to the purchaser (such as a house, a work of art, stocks and shares, or even a private education).

investment trust public company that makes investments in other companies on behalf of its shareholders. It may issue shares to raise capital and issue fixed interest securities.

in vitro fertilization (IVF) ('fertilization in glass') allowing eggs and sperm to unite in a laboratory to form embryos. The embryos produced may then either be implanted into the womb of the otherwise infertile mother (an extension of artificial *insemination), or used for research. The first baby to be produced by this method was born 1978 in the UK. In cases where the fallopian tubes are blocked, fertilization may be carried out by *intra-vaginal culture*, in which egg and sperm are incubated (in a plastic tube) in the mother's vagina, then transferred surgically into the uterus.

Io in astronomy, the third largest moon of the planet Jupiter, 3,630 km/2,260 mi in diameter, orbiting in 1.77 days at a distance of 422,000 km/262,000 mi. It is the most volcanically active body in the solar system, covered by hundreds of vents that erupt not lava but sulphur, giving Io an orange-coloured surface.

iodide compound formed between iodine and another element in which the iodine is the more electronegative element (see *electronegativity, *halide).

iodine (Greek *iodes* 'violet') greyish-black non-metallic element, symbol I, atomic number 53, relative atomic mass 126.9044. It is a member of the *halogen group. Its crystals give off, when heated, a violet vapour with an irritating odour resembling that of chlorine. It only occurs in combination with other elements. Its salts are known as iodides, which are found in sea water. As a mineral nutrient it is vital to the proper functioning of the thyroid gland, where it occurs in trace amounts as part of the hormone thyroxine. Absence of iodine from the diet leads to *goitre. Iodine is used in photography, in medicine as an antiseptic, and in making dyes.

iodoform (chemical name *triiodomethane*) CHI_3, an antiseptic that crystallizes into yellow hexagonal plates. It is soluble in ether, alcohol, and chloroform, but not in water.

ion atom, or group of atoms, that is either positively charged (*cation) or negatively charged (*anion), as a result of the loss or gain of electrons during chemical reactions or exposure to certain forms of radiation.

Iona island in the Inner Hebrides; area 850 hectares/2,100 acres. A centre of early Christianity, it is the site of a monastery founded 563 by St *Columba. It later became a burial ground for Irish, Scottish, and Norwegian kings. It has a 13th-century abbey.

ion engine rocket engine that uses *ions (charged particles) rather than hot gas for propulsion. Ion engines have been successfully tested in space, where they will eventually be used for gradual rather than sudden velocity changes. In an ion engine, atoms of mercury, for example, are ionized (given an electric charge by an electric field) and then accelerated at high speed by a more powerful electric field.

Ionesco Eugène 1912–1994. Romanian-born French dramatist. He was a leading exponent of the Theatre of the *Absurd. Most of his plays are in one act and concern the futility of language as a means of communication. These include *La Cantatrice chauve/The Bald Prima Donna* 1950 and *La Leçon/The Lesson* 1951. Later full-length plays include *Rhinocéros* 1958 and *Le Roi se meurt/Exit the King* 1961.

Ionia in Classical times the E coast of the Aegean Sea and the offshore islands, settled about 1000 BC by the Ionians; it included the cities of Ephesus, Miletus, and later Smyrna, and the islands of Chios and Samos.

Ionian member of a Hellenic people from beyond the Black Sea who crossed the Balkans around 1980 BC and invaded Asia Minor. Driven back by the *Hittites, they settled all over mainland Greece, later being supplanted by the Achaeans.

ionic bond or *electrovalent bond* bond produced when atoms of one element donate electrons to atoms of another element, forming positively and negatively charged *ions respectively. The electrostatic attraction between the oppositely charged ions constitutes the bond. Sodium chloride (Na^+Cl^-) is a typical ionic compound.

ionic compound substance composed of oppositely charged ions. All salts, most bases, and some acids are examples of ionic compounds. They possess the following general properties: they are crystalline solids with a high melting point; are soluble in water and insoluble in organic solvents; and always conduct electricity when molten or in aqueous solution. A typical ionic compound is sodium chloride (Na^+Cl^-).

ionization potential measure of the energy required to remove an *electron from an *atom. Elements with a low ionization potential readily lose electrons to form *cations.

ionization therapy enhancement of the atmosphere of an environment by instrumentally boosting the negative ion content of the air.

ionizing radiation radiation that knocks electrons from atoms during its passage, thereby leaving ions in its path. Alpha and beta particles are far more ionizing in their effect than are neutrons or gamma radiation.

ionosphere ionized layer of Earth's outer *atmosphere (60–1,000 km/38–620 mi) that contains sufficient free electrons to modify the way in which radio waves are propagated, for instance by reflecting them back to Earth. The ionosphere is thought to be produced by absorption of the Sun's ultraviolet radiation.

ion plating method of applying corrosion-resistant metal coatings. The article is placed in argon gas, together with some coating metal, which vaporizes on heating and becomes ionized (acquires charged atoms) as it diffuses through the gas to form the coating. It has important applications in the aerospace industry.

Iowa state of the midwest USA; nickname Hawkeye State
area 145,800 sq km/56,279 sq mi
capital Des Moines
cities Cedar Rapids, Davenport, Sioux City
products cereals, soya beans, pigs and cattle, chemicals, farm machinery, electrical goods, hardwood lumber, minerals
population (1990) 2,776,800
famous people 'Bix' Beiderbecke, Buffalo Bill Cody, Herbert Hoover, Glenn Miller, Lillian Russell, Grant Wood

ipecacuanha or *ipecac* South American plant *Psychotria ipecacuanha* of the madder family Rubiaceae, the dried roots of which are used as an emetic and in treating amoebic dysentery.

IQ (abbreviation for *intelligence quotient*) the ratio between a subject's 'mental' and chronological ages, multiplied by 100. A score of 100 × 10 in an *intelligence test is considered average.

Iqbāl Muhammad 1875–1938. Islamic poet and thinker. His literary works, in Urdu and Persian, were mostly verse in the classical style, suitable for public recitation. He sought through his writings to arouse Muslims to take their place in the modern world.

IRA abbreviation for *Irish Republican Army*.

Iráklion or *Heraklion* chief commercial port and largest city of Crete, Greece; population (1981) 102,000.

Iran Islamic Republic of (*Jomhori-e-Islami-e-Irân*; until 1935 **Persia**)

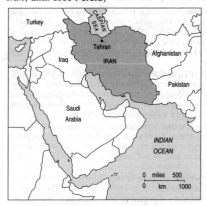

area 1,648,000 sq km/636,128 sq mi
capital Tehran
towns Isfahan, Mashhad, Tabriz, Shiraz, Ahvaz; chief port Abadan

physical plateau surrounded by mountains, including Elburz and Zagros; Lake Rezayeh; Dasht-Ekavir Desert; occupies islands of Abu Musa, Greater Tunb and Lesser Tunb in the Gulf
Leader of the Islamic Revolution Seyed Ali Khamenei from 1989
head of government Ali Akbar Hoshemi Rafsanjani from 1989
political system authoritarian Islamic republic
exports carpets, cotton textiles, metalwork, leather goods, oil, petrochemicals, fruit
currency rial
population (1993 est) 61,660,000 (including minorities in Azerbaijan, Baluchistan, Khuzestan/Arabistan, and Kurdistan); growth rate 3.2% p.a.
languages Farsi (official), Kurdish, Turkish, Arabic, English, French
religion Shi'ite Muslim (official) 92%, Sunni Muslim 5%, Zoroastrian 2%, Jewish, Baha'i, and Christian 1%
GNP $2,320 per head (1991)
chronology
1946 British, US, and Soviet forces left Iran.
1951 Oilfields nationalized by Prime Minister Muhammad Mossadeq.
1953 Mossadeq deposed and the US-backed shah took full control of the government.
1975 The shah introduced single-party system.
1978 Opposition to the shah organized from France by Ayatollah Khomeini.
1979 Shah left the country; Khomeini returned to create Islamic state. Revolutionaries seized US hostages at embassy in Tehran; US economic boycott.
1980 Start of Iran–Iraq War.
1981 US hostages released.
1984 Egyptian peace proposals rejected.
1985 Fighting intensified in Iran–Iraq War.
1988 Cease-fire; talks with Iraq began.
1989 Khomeini called for the death of British writer Salman Rushdie. June: Khomeini died; Ali Khamenei elected interim Leader of the Revolution; speaker of Iranian parliament Hoshemi Rafsanjani elected president. Secret oil deal with Israel revealed.
1990 Generous peace terms with Iraq accepted. Normal relations with UK restored.
1991 Imprisoned British business executive released. Nearly one million Kurds arrived in Iran from Iraq, fleeing persecution by Saddam Hussein after the Gulf War.
1992 Pro-Rafsanjani moderates won assembly elections.

Irangate US political scandal 1987 involving senior members of the Reagan administration (called this to echo the Nixon administration's *Watergate). Congressional hearings 1986–87 revealed that the US government had secretly sold weapons to Iran in 1985 and traded them for hostages held in Lebanon by pro-Iranian militias, and used the profits to supply right-wing Contra guerrillas in Nicaragua with arms. The attempt to get around the law (Boland amendment) specifically prohibiting military assistance to the Contras also broke other laws in the process.

Iranian language the main language of Iran, more commonly known as Persian or *Farsi.

Iran–Iraq War or *Gulf War* war between Iran and Iraq 1980–88, claimed by the former to have begun with the Iraqi offensive 21 Sept 1980, and

by the latter with the Iranian shelling of border posts 4 Sept 1980. Occasioned by a boundary dispute over the *Shatt-al-Arab waterway, it fundamentally arose because of Saddam Hussein's fear of a weakening of his absolute power base in Iraq by Iran's encouragement of the Shi'ite majority in Iraq to rise against the Sunni government. An estimated 1 million people died in the war.

Iraq Republic of (*al Jumhouriya al 'Iraqia*)

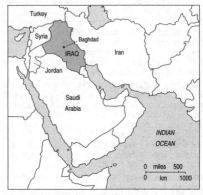

area 434,924 sq km/167,881 sq mi
capital Baghdad
towns Mosul and port of Basra
physical mountains in N, desert in W; wide valley of rivers Tigris and Euphrates NW–SE
environment a chemical-weapons plant covering an area of 65 sq km/25 sq mi, situated 80 km/50 mi NW of Baghdad, has been described by the UN as the largest toxic waste dump in the world
head of state and government Saddam Hussein al-Tikriti from 1979
political system one-party socialist republic
political party Arab Ba'ath Socialist Party, nationalist socialist
exports oil (prior to UN sanctions), wool, dates (80% of world supply)
currency Iraqi dinar
population (1993) 19,410,000 (Arabs 77%, Kurds 19%, Turks 2%); growth rate 3.6% p.a.
languages Arabic (official); Kurdish, Assyrian, Armenian
religions Shi'ite Muslim 60%, Sunni Muslim 37%, Christian 3%
GNP $3,000 per head (1987)
chronology
1920 Iraq became a British League of Nations protectorate.
1921 Hashemite dynasty established, with Faisal I installed by Britain as king.
1932 Independence achieved from British protectorate status.
1958 Monarchy overthrown; Iraq became a republic.
1963 Joint Ba'athist-military coup headed by Col Salem Aref.
1968 Military coup put Maj-Gen al-Bakr in power.
1979 Al-Bakr replaced by Saddam Hussein.
1980 War between Iraq and Iran broke out.
1985 Fighting intensified.
1988 Cease-fire; talks began with Iran. Iraq used

chemical weapons against Kurdish rebels seeking greater autonomy.

1989 Unsuccessful coup against President Hussein.

1990 Peace treaty favouring Iran agreed. Aug: Iraq invaded and annexed Kuwait, precipitating another Gulf crisis. US forces massed in Saudi Arabia at request of King Fahd. United Nations resolutions ordered Iraqi withdrawal from Kuwait and imposed total trade ban on Iraq; UN resolution sanctioning force approved. All foreign hostages released.

1991 16 Jan: US-led forces began aerial assault on Iraq; Iraq's infrastructure destroyed by bombing. 23–28 Feb: land-sea-air offensive to free Kuwait successful. Uprisings of Kurds and Shi'ites brutally suppressed by surviving Iraqi troops. Allied troops withdrew after establishing 'safe havens' for Kurds in the north, leaving a rapid-reaction force near the Turkish border. Allies threatened to bomb strategic targets in Iraq if full information about nuclear facilities denied to UN.

1992 UN imposed a 'no-fly zone' over S Iraq to protect Shi'ites.

1993 Jan: Iraqi incursions into the 'no-fly zone' prompted US-led alliance aircraft to bomb 'strategic' targets in Iraq. April: Iraq trades fire with USA in northern 'no fly zone'.

Ireland one of the British Isles, lying to the west of Great Britain, from which it is separated by the Irish Sea. It comprises the provinces of Ulster, Leinster, Munster, and Connacht, and is divided into the Republic of Ireland (which occupies the south, centre, and northwest of the island) and Northern Ireland (which occupies the northeast corner and forms part of the United Kingdom).

Ireland: history in prehistoric times Ireland underwent a number of invasions from Europe, the most important of which was that of the Gaels in the 3rd century BC. Gaelic Ireland was divided into kingdoms, nominally subject to an *Ardri* or High King; the chiefs were elected under the tribal or Brehon law, and were usually at war with one another. Christianity was introduced by St *Patrick about 432, and during the 5th and 6th centuries Ireland became the home of a civilization which sent out missionaries to Britain and Europe. From about 800 the Danes began to raid Ireland, and later founded Dublin and other coastal towns, until they were defeated by Brian Boru (king from 976) at Clontarf 1014. Anglo-Norman adventurers invaded Ireland 1167, but by the end of the medieval period English rule was still confined to the Pale, the territory round Dublin. The Tudors adopted a policy of conquest, confiscation of Irish land, and plantation by English settlers, and further imposed the *Reformation and English law on Ireland. The most important of the plantations was that of Ulster, carried out under James I 1610. In 1641 the Irish took advantage of the developing struggle in England between king and Parliament to begin a revolt which was crushed by Oliver *Cromwell 1649, the estates of all 'rebels' being confiscated. Another revolt 1689–91 was also defeated, and the Roman Catholic majority held down by penal laws. In 1739–41 a famine killed one-third of the population of 1.5 million.

The subordination of the Irish parliament to that of England, and of Irish economic interests to English, led to the rise of a Protestant patriot party, which in 1782 forced the British government to remove many commercial restrictions and grant the Irish parliament its independence. This did not satisfy the population, who in 1798, influenced by French revolutionary ideas, rose in rebellion, but were again defeated; and in 1800 William *Pitt induced the Irish parliament to vote itself out of existence by the Act of *Union, effective 1 Jan 1801, which brought Ireland under the aegis of the British crown. During another famine 1845–46, 1.5 million people emigrated, mostly to the USA. By the 1880s there was a strong movement for home rule for Ireland; Gladstone supported it but was defeated by the British Parliament. By 1914, home rule was conceded but World War I delayed implementation. The **Easter Rising** took place April 1916, when nationalists seized the Dublin general post office and proclaimed a republic. After a week of fighting, the revolt was suppressed by the British army and most of its leaders executed. From 1918 to 1921 there was guerrilla warfare against the British army, especially by the Irish Republican Army (*IRA), formed by Michael Collins 1919. This led to a split in the rebel forces, but in 1921 the Anglo-Irish Treaty resulted in partition and the creation of the Irish Free State in S Ireland. For history since that date, see *Ireland, Republic of; *Ireland, Northern.

Ireland, Northern constituent part of the UK
area 13,460 sq km/5,196 sq mi
capital Belfast
towns Londonderry, Enniskillen, Omagh, Newry, Armagh, Coleraine
exports engineering, especially shipbuilding, textile machinery, aircraft components; linen and synthetic textiles; processed foods, especially dairy and poultry products
currency pound sterling
population (1991) 1,578,000
language English
religion Protestant 54%, Roman Catholic 31%
government direct rule from the UK since 1972. Northern Ireland is entitled to send 12 members to the Westminster Parliament.
history for history pre-1921, see *Ireland, history. The creation of Northern Ireland dates from 1921 when the mainly Protestant counties of Ulster withdrew from the newly established Irish Free State. Spasmodic outbreaks of violence by the *IRA continued, but only in 1968–69 were there serious disturbances arising from Protestant political dominance and discrimination against the Roman Catholic minority in employment and housing. British troops were sent to restore peace and protect Catholics, but disturbances continued and in 1972 the parliament at Stormont was prorogued and superseded by direct rule from Westminster. Under the *Anglo-Irish Agreement 1985, the Republic of Ireland was given a consultative role (via an Anglo-Irish conference) in the government of Northern Ireland, but agreed that there should be no change in its status except by majority consent. The agreement was approved by Parliament, but all 12 Ulster members gave up their seats, so that by-elections could be fought as a form of 'referendum' on the views of the province itself. A similar boycotting of the Northern Ireland Assembly led to its dissolution 1986 by the UK government. The

question of Northern Ireland's political future was debated in talks held in Belfast April–Sept 1991 – the first direct negotiations between the political parties for 16 years. Follow-up talks between the British government and the main Northern Ireland parties Sept–Nov 1992 made little progress. In Sept 1993 it emerged that the Catholic nationalist Social Democratic Labour Party (SDLP) and Sinn Fein (political wing of the outlawed IRA) had held talks aimed at achieving a political settlement. This revelation prompted the British government to engage in bilateral talks with the main Northern Ireland parties, and in Dec 1993 London and Dublin issued a joint peace proposal, the Downing Street Declaration, for consideration by all parties.

IRA cease-fire In August 1994 the Provisional IRA announced a unilateral cease-fire in an attempt to reach a non-violent solution.

Ireland, Republic of (*Eire*)

area 70,282 sq km/27,146 sq mi
capital Dublin
towns ports Cork, Dun Laoghaire, Limerick, Waterford
physical central plateau surrounded by hills; rivers Shannon, Liffey, Boyne
head of state Mary Robinson from 1990
head of government John Bruton
political system democratic republic
exports livestock, dairy products, Irish whiskey, microelectronic components and assemblies, mining and engineering products, chemicals, clothing
currency punt
population (1993 est) 3,600,000; growth rate 0.1% p.a.
languages Irish Gaelic and English (both official)
religion Roman Catholic 94%
GNP $10,780 per head (1991)
chronology
1916 Easter Rising: nationalists against British rule seized the Dublin general post office and proclaimed a republic; the revolt was suppressed by the British army and most of the leaders were executed.
1918–21 Guerrilla warfare against British army led to split in rebel forces.

1921 Anglo-Irish Treaty resulted in creation of the Irish Free State (Southern Ireland).
1937 Independence achieved from Britain.
1949 Eire left the Commonwealth and became the Republic of Ireland.
1985 Anglo-Irish Agreement signed.
1986 Protests by Ulster Unionists against the agreement.
1987 General election won by Charles Haughey.
1988 Relations with UK at low ebb because of disagreement over extradition decisions.
1989 Haughey failed to win majority in general election. Progressive Democrats given cabinet positions in coalition government.
1990 Mary Robinson elected president; John Bruton became Fine Gael leader.
1992 Jan: Haughey resigned after losing parliamentary majority. Feb: Albert Reynolds became Fianna Fáil leader and prime minister. June: National referendum approved ratification of Maastricht Treaty. Nov: Reynolds lost confidence vote; election result inconclusive.
1993 Fianna Fáil–Labour coalition formed; Reynolds re-elected prime minister. Dec: Major and Reynolds issued joint Anglo-Irish peace proposal for Northern Ireland, the Downing Street Declaration. Six-year national development plan announced.
1994 Cease-fires announced by Catholic and Protestant paramilitaries in Northern Ireland. Nov: Reynolds resigned as premier and Fianna Fáil leader; Bertie Ahern elected new Fianna Fáil leader. Dec: new Fine Gael – Labour coalition formed under John Bruton.

Irene, St *c.* 752–*c.* 803. Byzantine emperor 797–802. The wife of Leo IV (750–80), she became regent for their son Constantine (771–805) on Leo's death. In 797 she deposed her son, had his eyes put out, and assumed the full title of *basileus* ('emperor'), ruling in her own right until exiled to Lesvos by a revolt in 802. She was made a saint by the Greek Orthodox church for her attacks on iconoclasts.

Ireton Henry 1611–1651. English Civil War general. He joined the parliamentary forces and fought at *Edgehill 1642, Gainsborough 1643, and *Naseby 1645.

Irian Jaya the western portion of the island of New Guinea, part of Indonesia
area 420,000 sq km/162,000 sq mi
capital Jayapura
population (1989) 1,555,700
history part of the Dutch East Indies 1828 as Western New Guinea; retained by the Netherlands after Indonesian independence 1949 but ceded to Indonesia 1963 by the United Nations and remained part of Indonesia by an 'Act of Free Choice' 1969. In the 1980s 283,500 hectares/700,000 acres were given over to Indonesia's controversial transmigration programme for the resettlement of farming families from overcrowded Java, causing destruction of rainforests and displacing indigenous people. In 1989 Indonesia began construction of a space launching pad on the island of Biak, near the equator where the Earth's atmosphere is least thick.

iridium (Latin *iridis* 'rainbow') hard, brittle, silver-white, metallic element, symbol Ir, atomic number 77, relative atomic mass 192.2. It is twice as heavy as lead and is resistant to tarnish and corrosion. It is one of the so-called platinum

iris The iris is a plant of northern temperate regions.

group of metals; it occurs in platinum ores and as a free metal (*native metal) with osmium in osmiridium, a natural alloy that includes platinum, ruthenium, and rhodium.

iris in anatomy, the coloured muscular diaphragm that controls the size of the pupil in the vertebrate eye. It contains radial muscle that increases the pupil diameter and circular muscle that constricts the pupil diameter. Both types of muscle respond involuntarily to light intensity.

iris in botany, perennial northern temperate flowering plants of the genus *Iris*, family Iridaceae. The leaves are usually sword-shaped; the purple, white, or yellow flowers have three upright inner petals and three outward-and-downward-curving sepals. The wild yellow iris is called *flag.

Irish person of Irish culture from Ireland or person of Irish descent. The Irish mainly speak English, though there are approximately 30,000–100,000 speakers of Irish Gaelic, a Celtic language belonging to the Indo-European family.

Irish Gaelic first official language of the Irish Republic, but much less widely used than the second official language, English. See *Gaelic language.

Irish National Liberation Army (INLA) guerrilla organization committed to the end of British rule in Northern Ireland and the incorporation of Ulster into the Irish Republic. The INLA was a 1974 offshoot of the Irish Republican Army (IRA). Among the INLA's activities was the killing of British politician Airey Neave in 1979. It declared a cease-fire 1994.

Irish Republican Army (IRA) militant Irish nationalist organization whose aim is to create a united Irish socialist republic including Ulster. The paramilitary wing of *Sinn Féin, it was founded 1919 by Michael *Collins and fought a successful war against Britain 1919–21. It came to the fore again 1939 with a bombing campaign in Britain, having been declared illegal in 1936 . Its activities intensified from 1968 onwards, as the civil-rights disorders ('the Troubles') in Northern Ireland developed. In 1970 a group in the north broke away to become the *Provisional IRA*; its objective is the expulsion of the British from Northern Ireland.

In Sept 1994 the IRA announced a cessation of its military activities, responding to a joint UK-Irish peace initiative launched Dec 1993.

Irkutsk city in S Siberian Russia; population (1987) 609,000. It produces coal, iron, steel, and machine tools. Founded 1652, it began to grow after the Trans-Siberian railway reached it 1898.

iron hard, malleable and ductile, silver-grey, metallic element, symbol Fe (from Latin *ferrum*), atomic number 26, relative atomic mass 55.847. It is the fourth most abundant element (the second most abundant metal, after aluminium) in the Earth's crust. Iron occurs in concentrated deposits as the ores hematite (Fe_2O_3), spathic ore ($FeCO_3$), and magnetite (Fe_3O_4). It sometimes occurs as a free metal, occasionally as fragments of iron or iron–nickel meteorites.

Iron Age developmental stage of human technology when weapons and tools were made from iron. Iron was produced in Thailand by about 1600 BC but was considered inferior in strength to bronze until about 1000 when metallurgical techniques improved and the alloy steel was produced by adding carbon during the smelting process.

ironclad wooden warship covered with armour plate. The first to be constructed was the French *Gloire* 1858, but the first to be launched was the British HMS *Warrior* 1859. The first battle between ironclads took place during the American Civil War, when the Union *Monitor* fought the Confederate *Virginia* (formerly the *Merrimack*) 9 March 1862. The design was replaced by battleships of all-metal construction in the 1890s.

Iron Curtain in Europe after World War II, the symbolic boundary of the *Cold War between capitalist West and communist East. The term was popularized by the UK prime minister Winston Churchill from 1945.

Iron Guard pro-fascist group controlling Romania in the 1930s. To counter its influence, King Carol II established a dictatorship 1938 but the Iron Guard forced him to abdicate 1940.

iron ore any mineral from which iron is extracted. The chief iron ores are *magnetite*, a black oxide; *hematite*, or kidney ore, a reddish oxide; *limonite, brown, impure oxyhydroxides of iron; and siderite*, a brownish carbonate.

iron pyrites or *pyrite* FeS_2 common iron ore. Brassy yellow, and occurring in cubic crystals, it is often called 'fool's gold', since only those who have never seen gold would mistake it.

irony literary technique that achieves the effect of 'saying one thing and meaning another', through the use of humour or mild sarcasm. It can be traced through all periods of literature, from classical Greek and Roman epics and dramas to the good-humoured and subtle irony of *Chaucer to the 20th-century writer's method for dealing with nihilism and despair, as in Samuel Beckett's *Waiting for Godot*.

Iroquois member of a confederation of NE North American Indians, the Six Nations (Cayuga, Mohawk, Oneida, Onondaga, and Seneca, with the Tuscarora after 1723), traditionally formed by Hiawatha (actually a priestly title) 1570.

irradiation in technology, subjecting anything to radiation, including cancer tumours. See also *food irradiation.

irrationalism feature of many philosophies

rather than a philosophical movement. Irrationalists deny that the world can be comprehended by conceptual thought, and often see the human mind as determined by unconscious forces.

irrational number a number that cannot be expressed as an exact *fraction. Irrational numbers include some square roots (for example, $\sqrt{2}$, $\sqrt{3}$ and $\sqrt{5}$ are irrational) and numbers such as π (the ratio of the circumference of a circle to its diameter, which is approximately equal to 3.14159) and e (the base of *natural logarithms, approximately 2.71828).

Irrawaddy (Myanmar **Ayeryarwady**) chief river of Myanmar (Burma), flowing roughly N to S for 2,090 km/1,300 mi across the centre of the country into the Bay of Bengal. Its sources are the Mali and N'mai rivers; its chief tributaries are the Chindwin and Shweli.

irredentist (Latin *redemptus*, bought back) person who wishes to reclaim the lost territories of a state. The term derives from an Italian political party founded about 1878 intending to incorporate Italian-speaking areas into the newly formed state.

irrigation artificial water supply for dry agricultural areas by means of dams and channels. Drawbacks are that it tends to concentrate salts, ultimately causing infertility, and that rich river silt is retained at dams, to the impoverishment of the land and fisheries below them.

Irving Henry. Stage name of John Brodribb 1838–1905. English actor. He established his reputation from 1871, chiefly at the Lyceum Theatre in London, where he became manager 1878. He staged a series of successful Shakespearean productions, including *Romeo and Juliet* 1882, with himself and Ellen Terry (1847–1928) playing the leading roles. He was the first actor to be knighted, in 1895.

Isaac in the Old Testament, Hebrew patriarch, son of *Abraham and Sarah, and father of Esau and Jacob.

Isaacs Alick 1921–1967. Scottish virologist who, with Jean Lindemann, in 1957 discovered *interferon, a naturally occurring antiviral substance produced by cells infected with viruses. The full implications of this discovery are still being investigated.

Isabella two Spanish queens:

Isabella I the Catholic 1451–1504. Queen of Castile from 1474, after the death of her brother Henry IV. By her marriage with Ferdinand of Aragon 1469, the crowns of two of the Christian states in the Moorish-held Spanish peninsula were united. In her reign, during 1492, the Moors were driven out of Spain. She introduced the *Inquisition into Castile, expelled the Jews, and gave financial encouragement to *Columbus. Her youngest daughter was Catherine of Aragon, first wife of Henry VIII of England. In 1992 the Catholic church proposes to beatify her, arousing the indignation of Jewish groups.

Isabella II 1830–1904. Queen of Spain from 1833, when she succeeded her father Ferdinand VII (1784–1833). The Salic Law banning a female sovereign had been repealed by the Cortes (parliament), but her succession was disputed by her uncle Don Carlos de Bourbon (1788–1855).

After seven years of civil war, the *Carlists were defeated. She abdicated in favour of her son Alfonso XII in 1868.

Isaiah 8th century BC. In the Old Testament, the first major Hebrew prophet. The son of Amos, he was probably of high rank, and lived largely in Jerusalem.

Isaurian 8th-century Byzantine imperial dynasty, originating in Asia Minor.

ISBN (abbreviation for **International Standard Book Number**) code number used for ordering or classifying book titles.

ischaemia reduction of blood supply to any part of the body.

ischaemic heart disease (IHD) disorder caused by reduced perfusion of the coronary arteries due to *atherosclerosis. It is the commonest cause of death in the Western world, leading to more than a million deaths each year in the USA and about 160,000 in the UK. Early symptoms of IHD include *angina or palpitations, but not infrequently a heart attack is the first indication that a person is affected.

ISDN abbreviation for *__Integrated Services Digital Network__*, a telecommunications system.

Isfahan or **Eşfahan** industrial (steel, textiles, carpets) city in central Iran; population (1986) 1,001,000. It was the ancient capital (1598–1722) of *Abbas I, and its features include the Great Square, Grand Mosque, and Hall of Forty Pillars.

Isherwood Christopher (William Bradshaw) 1904–1986. English novelist. He lived in Germany 1929–33 just before Hitler's rise to power, a period that inspired *Mr Norris Changes Trains* 1935 and *Goodbye to Berlin* 1939, creating the character of Sally Bowles (the basis of the musical *Cabaret* 1968). Returning to England, he collaborated with W H *Auden in three verse plays.

Ishiguro Kazuo 1954– . Japanese-born British novelist. His novel *An Artist of the Floating World* won the 1986 Whitbread Prize, and *The Remains of the Day* won the 1989 Booker Prize. His work is characterized by a sensitive style and subtle structure.

Ishmael in the Old Testament, son of *Abraham and his wife Sarah's Egyptian maid Hagar; traditional ancestor of Muhammad and the Arab people. He and his mother were driven away by Sarah's jealousy. Muslims believe that it was Ishmael, not Isaac, whom God commanded Abraham to sacrifice, and that Ishmael helped Abraham build the *Kaaba in Mecca.

Ishtar goddess of love and war, worshipped by the Babylonians and Assyrians, and personified as the legendary queen Semiramis.

Isidore of Seville c. 560–636. Writer and missionary. His *Ethymologiae* was the model for later medieval encyclopedias and helped to preserve classical thought during the Middle Ages; his *Chronica Maiora* remains an important source for the history of Visigothic Spain. As bishop of Seville from 600, he strengthened the church in Spain and converted many Jews and Aryan Visigoths.

isinglass pure form of gelatin obtained from the internal membranes of the swim bladder of various fishes, particularly the sturgeon. Isinglass is used in the clarification of wines and beer, and in cooking.

Isis the principal goddess of ancient Egypt. She was the daughter of Geb and Nut (Earth and Sky), and as the sister-wife of Osiris searched for his body after his death at the hands of his brother, Set. Her son Horus then defeated and captured Set but cut off his mother's head because she would not allow Set to be killed. She was later identified with *Hathor. The cult of Isis ultimately spread to Greece and Rome.

Iskandariya Arabic name for *Alexandria, Egypt.

Islam (Arabic 'submission', that is, to the will of Allah) religion founded in the Arabian peninsula in the early 7th century AD. It emphasizes the oneness of God, his omnipotence, benificence, and inscrutability. The sacred book is the **Koran** of the prophet *Muhammad, the Prophet or Messenger of Allah. There are two main Muslim sects: ***Sunni*** and ***Shi'ite***. Other schools include **Sufism**, a mystical movement originating in the 8th century.

Islamabad capital of Pakistan from 1967, in the Potwar district, at the foot of the Margala Hills and immediately NW of Rawalpindi; population (1981) 201,000. The city was designed by Constantinos Doxiadis in the 1960s. The Federal Capital Territory of Islamabad has an area of 907 sq km/350 sq mi and a population (1985) of 379,000.

Islamic architecture the architecture of the Muslim world, highly diverse but unified by climate, culture, and a love of geometric and arabesque ornament, as well as by the mobility of ideas, artisans, and architects throughout the region. The central public buildings are *mosques, often with a dome and *minaret; domestic houses face an inner courtyard and are grouped together, with vaulted streets linking the blocks.

Islamic art art and design of the Muslim world, dating from the foundation of Islam in the 7th century AD. The traditions laid down by Islam created devout craftsmen whose creative purpose was the glory of God. Elements and motifs were borrowed from *Byzantine, *Coptic, and *Persian Sassanian (AD 224–642) traditions and fused into a distinctive decorative style, based on Arabic calligraphy. Sculpture was prohibited and carvers turned instead to exquisite inlay and fretwork, notably on doors and screens, in Islamic monuments such as the Alhambra Palace, Granada, Spain, and the Taj Mahal, India.

Isle of Man see *Man, Isle of.

Isle of Wight see *Wight, Isle of.

islets of Langerhans groups of cells within the pancreas responsible for the secretion of the hormone insulin. They are sensitive to the blood sugar, producing more hormone when glucose levels rise.

Ismail 1830–1895. Khedive (governor) of Egypt 1866–79. A grandson of Mehmet Ali, he became viceroy of Egypt in 1863 and in 1866 received the title of khedive from the Ottoman sultan. He amassed huge foreign debts and in 1875 Britain, at Prime Minister Disraeli's suggestion, bought the khedive's Suez Canal shares for nearly £4 million, establishing Anglo-French control of Egypt's finances. In 1879 the UK and France persuaded the sultan to appoint Tewfik, his son, khedive in his place.

Isma'ili member of an Islamic group, the second-largest *Shi'ite community in Islam (after the *Twelver Shi'is). Isma'ilis comprise several smaller groups, the most important of which are the Nizari Isma'ilis, from 1094; the Da'udi Isma'ilis; the Musta'li Isma'ilis; and the Sulaymani Isma'ilis.

ISO in photography, a numbering system for rating the speed of films, devised by the International Standards Organization.

isobar line drawn on maps and weather charts linking all places with the same atmospheric pressure (usually measured in millibars). When used in weather forecasting, the distance between the isobars is an indication of the barometric gradient.

isolationism in politics, concentration on internal rather than foreign affairs; a foreign policy having no interest in international affairs that do not affect the country's own interests.

isomer chemical compound having the same molecular composition and mass as another, but with different physical or chemical properties owing to the different structural arrangement of its constituent atoms. For example, the organic compounds butane ($CH_3(CH_2)_2CH_3$) and methyl propane ($CH_3CH(CH_3)CH_3$) are isomers, each possessing four carbon atoms and ten hydrogen atoms but differing in the way that these are arranged with respect to each other.

isorhythm in music, a form in which a given rhythm cyclically repeats, although the corresponding melody notes may change. It was used in European medieval music, and is still practised in classical Indian music. The composers Berg, Cage, and Messiaen used isorhythmic procedures.

isotope one of two or more atoms that have the same atomic number (same number of protons), but which contain a different number of neutrons, thus differing in their atomic masses. They may be stable or radioactive, naturally occurring or synthesized. The term was coined by English chemist Frederick Soddy, pioneer researcher in atomic disintegration.

Israel State of (*Medinat Israel*)

area 20,800 sq km/8,029 sq mi (as at 1949 armistice)
capital Jerusalem (not recognized by the United Nations)
towns ports Tel Aviv/Jaffa, Haifa, Acre, Eilat; Bat-Yam, Holon, Ramat Gan, Petach Tikva, Beersheba
physical coastal plain of Sharon between Haifa and Tel Aviv noted since ancient times for fertility; central mountains of Galilee, Samariq, and Judea; Dead Sea, Lake Tiberias, and river Jordan Rift Valley along the E are below sea level; Negev Desert in the S; Israel occupies Golan Heights, West Bank, and Gaza
head of state Ezer Weizman from 1993
head of government Yitzhak Rabin from 1992
political system democratic republic
exports citrus and other fruit, avocados, chinese leaves, fertilizers, diamonds, plastics, petrochemicals, textiles, electronics (military, medical, scientific, industrial), electro-optics, precision instruments, aircraft and missiles
currency shekel
population (1993) 5,300,000 (including 750,000 Arab Israeli citizens and over 1 million Arabs in the occupied territories); under the Law of Return 1950, 'every Jew shall be entitled to come to Israel as an immigrant'; those from the East and E Europe are Ashkenazim, and those from Mediterranean Europe (Spain, Portugal, Italy, France, Greece) and Arab N Africa are Sephardim (over 50% of the population is now of Sephardic descent). Between Jan 1990 and April 1991, 250,000 Soviet Jews emigrated to Israel. An Israeli-born Jew is a Sabra. About 500,000 Israeli Jews are resident in the USA. Growth rate 1.8% p.a.
languages Hebrew and Arabic (official); Yiddish, European, and W Asian languages
religions Israel is a secular state, but the predominant faith is Judaism 83%; also Sunni Muslim, Christian, and Druse
GNP $11,330 per head (1991)
chronology
1948 Independent State of Israel proclaimed with David Ben-Gurion as prime minister; attacked by Arab nations, Israel won the War of Independence. Many displaced Arabs settled in refugee camps in the Gaza Strip and West Bank.
1952 Col Gamal Nasser of Egypt stepped up blockade of Israeli ports and support of Arab guerrillas in Gaza.
1956 Israel invaded Gaza and Sinai.
1959 Egypt renewed blockade of Israeli trade through Suez Canal.
1963 Ben-Gurion resigned, succeeded by Levi Eshkol.
1964 Palestine Liberation Organization (PLO) founded with the aim of overthrowing the state of Israel.
1967 Israel victorious in the Six-Day War. Gaza, West Bank, E Jerusalem, Sinai, and Golan Heights captured.
1968 Israel Labour Party formed, led by Golda Meir.
1969 Golda Meir became prime minister.
1973 Yom Kippur War: Israel attacked by Egypt and Syria.
1974 Golda Meir succeeded by Yitzhak Rabin.
1975 Suez Canal reopened.
1977 Menachem Begin elected prime minister. Egyptian president addressed the Knesset.

1978 Camp David talks.
1979 Egyptian-Israeli agreement signed. Israel agreed to withdraw from Sinai.
1980 Jerusalem declared capital of Israel.
1981 Golan Heights formally annexed.
1982 Israel pursued PLO fighters into Lebanon.
1983 Peace treaty between Israel and Lebanon signed but not ratified.
1985 Formation of government of national unity with Labour and Likud ministers.
1986 Yitzhak Shamir took over from Peres under power-sharing agreement.
1987 Outbreak of Palestinian uprising (Intifada) in West Bank and Gaza.
1988 Criticism of Israel's handling of Palestinian uprising in occupied territories; PLO acknowledged Israel's right to exist.
1989 New Likud–Labour coalition government formed under Shamir. Limited progress achieved on proposals for negotiations leading to elections in occupied territories.
1990 Coalition collapsed due to differences over peace process; international condemnation of Temple Mount killings. New Shamir right-wing coalition formed.
1991 Shamir gave cautious response to Middle East peace proposals. Some Palestinian prisoners released.
1992 Shamir lost majority in Knesset when ultraorthodox party withdrew from coalition. Labour Party, led by Yitzhak Rabin, won elections; coalition formed under Rabin.
1993 Ban on contacts with PLO formally lifted. Ezer Weizman elected president; Binyamin 'Bibi' Netanyahu elected leader of Likud party. Israel launched attacks against Hezbollah in S Lebanon. Sept: historic accord of mutual recognition signed by Israel and PLO, to result in partial autonomy for Palestinians and phased Israeli withdrawal from parts of occupied territories.
1994 Peace process and withdrawal threatened by extremist violence in occupied territories. May: first phase of 1993 peace accord (the Gaza–Jericho agreement) finalized and implemented; Israeli troop withdrawal begun.

Issigonis Alec 1906–1988. British engineer who designed the Morris Minor 1948 and the Mini-Minor 1959 cars, thus creating economy motoring and adding the word 'mini' to the English language.

Istanbul city and chief seaport of Turkey; population (1990) 6,620,200. It produces textiles, tobacco, cement, glass, and leather. Founded as **Byzantium** about 660 BC, it was renamed **Constantinople** AD 330 and was the capital of the *Byzantine Empire until captured by the Turks 1453. As **Istamboul** it was capital of the Ottoman Empire until 1922.

isthmus narrow strip of land joining two larger land masses. The Isthmus of Panama joins North and South America.

IT abbreviation for *information technology*.

Itagaki Taisuke 1837–1919. Japanese military and political leader, the founder of Japan's first political party, the Jiyūtō (Liberal Party) 1875–81. Involved in the overthrow of the Tokugawa shogunate and the *Meiji restoration 1866–68, Itagaki became a champion of democratic principles while continuing to serve in the government for short periods.

Itaipu world's largest hydroelectric plant, situated on the Paraná River, SW Brazil. A joint Brazilian-Paraguayan venture, it came into operation 1984; it supplies hydroelectricity to a wide area.

Italian language member of the Romance branch of the Indo-European language family, the most direct descendant of Latin. Broadcasting and films have standardized the Italian national tongue, but most Italians speak a regional dialect as well as standard Italian.

Italian Somaliland former Italian trust territory on the Somali coast of Africa extending to 502,300 sq km/194,999 sq mi. Established 1892, it was extended 1925 with the acquisition of Jubaland from Kenya; administered from Mogadishu; under British rule 1941–50. Thereafter it reverted to Italian authority before uniting with British Somaliland 1960 to form the independent state of Somalia.

italic style of printing in which the letters slope to the right *like this*, introduced by the printer Aldus Manutius of Venice in 1501. It is usually used side by side with the erect Roman type to distinguish titles of books, films, and so on, and for purposes of emphasis and (mainly in the USA) citation. The term 'italic' is also used for the handwriting style developed for popular use in 1522 by Vatican chancery scribe Ludovico degli Arrighi.

Italy Republic of (*Repubblica Italiana*)

area 301,300 sq km/116,332 sq mi
capital Rome
towns Milan, Turin; ports Naples, Genoa, Palermo, Bari, Catania, Trieste
physical mountainous (Maritime Alps, Dolomites, Apennines) with narrow coastal lowlands; rivers Po, Adige, Arno, Tiber, Rubicon; islands of Sicily, Sardinia, Elba, Capri, Ischia, Lipari, Pantelleria; lakes Como, Maggiore, Garda
head of state Oscar Luigi Scalfaro from 1992
head of government Lamberto Dini from 1995
political system democratic republic
exports wine (world's largest producer), fruit, vegetables, textiles (Europe's largest silk producer), clothing, leather goods, motor vehicles, electrical goods, chemicals, marble (Carrara), sulphur, mercury, iron, steel
currency lira

population (1993) 58,100,000; growth rate 0.1% p.a.
language Italian; German, French, Slovene, and Albanian minorities
religion Roman Catholic 100% (state religion)
GNP $18,580 per head (1991)
chronology
1946 Monarchy replaced by a republic.
1948 New constitution adopted.
1954 Trieste (claimed by Yugoslavia after World War II) was divided between Italy and Yugoslavia.
1976 Communists proposed establishment of broad-based, left–right government, the 'historic compromise'; rejected by Christian Democrats.
1978 Christian Democrat Aldo Moro, architect of the historic compromise, kidnapped and murdered by Red Brigade guerrillas infiltrated by Western intelligence agents.
1983 Bettino Craxi, a Socialist, became leader of broad coalition government.
1987 Craxi resigned; succeeding coalition fell within months.
1988 Christian Democrats' leader Ciriaco de Mita established a five-party coalition including the Socialists.
1989 De Mita resigned after disagreements within his coalition government; succeeded by Giulio Andreotti. De Mita lost leadership of Christian Democrats; Communists formed 'shadow government'.
1991 Referendum approved electoral reform.
1992 April: ruling coalition lost its majority in general election; President Cossiga resigned, replaced by Oscar Luigi Scalfaro in May. Giuliano Amato, deputy leader of PDS, accepted premiership. Sept: lira devalued and Italy withdrew from the Exchange Rate Mechanism.
1993 Investigation of corruption network exposed Mafia links with several notable politicians, including Craxi and Andreotti. Craxi resigned Socialist Party leadership; replaced by Giorgio Benvenutu and then Ottaviano del Turro. Referendum supported ending the proportional-representation electoral system. Amato resigned premiership; Carlo Ciampi, with no party allegiance, named as his successor.
1994 Jan: Ciampi resigned pending general election. March: elections won by right-wing alliance led by media tycoon and Forza Italia leader, Silvio Berlusconi. Right-wing coalition government formed with Berlusconi as premier. Dec: Berlusconi resigned.

Ithaca (Greek *Itháki*) Greek island in the Ionian Sea, area: 93 sq km/36 sq mi. Important in pre-Classical Greece, Ithaca was (in Homer's poem) the birthplace of *Odysseus, though this is sometimes identified with the island of Leukas (some archaeologists have equated ancient Ithaca with Leukas rather than modern Ithaca).

Itō Hirobumi, Prince 1841–1909. Japanese politician, prime minister 1887, 1892–96, 1898, 1900–01. He was a key figure in the modernization of Japan and was involved in the *Meiji restoration 1866–68 and in official missions to study forms of government in the USA and Europe in the 1870s and 1880s. He helped draft the Meiji constitution of 1889.

Ivan (III) the Great 1440–1505. Grand duke of Muscovy from 1462, who revolted against Tatar overlordship by refusing tribute to Grand Khan

Ahmed 1480. He claimed the title of tsar, and used the double-headed eagle as the Russian state emblem.

Ivan (IV) the Terrible 1530–1584. Grand duke of Muscovy from 1533; he assumed power 1544 and was crowned as first tsar of Russia 1547. He conquered Kazan 1552, Astrakhan 1556, and Siberia 1581. He reformed the legal code and local administration 1555 and established trade relations with England. In his last years he alternated between debauchery and religious austerities, executing thousands including his own son.

Ives Charles (Edward) 1874–1954. US composer. He experimented with *atonality, quarter tones, clashing time signatures, and quotations from popular music of the time. He wrote five symphonies, including *Holidays Symphony* 1913; chamber music, including the *Concord Sonata*; and the orchestral works *Three Places in New England* 1914.

Ives Frederic Eugene 1856–1937. US inventor who developed the *halftone process of printing photographs in 1878. The process uses a screen to break up light and dark areas into dots. By 1886 he had evolved the halftone process now generally in use. Among his many other inventions was a three-colour printing process (similar to the *four-colour process).

IVF abbreviation for **in vitro fertilization*.

ivory hard white substance of which the teeth and tusks of certain mammals are composed. Among the most valuable are elephants' tusks, which are of unusual hardness and density. Ivory is used in carving and other decorative work, and is so valuable that poachers continue to illegally destroy the remaining wild elephant herds in Africa to obtain it.

Ivory James 1928– . US film director. He established his reputation with the Indian-made *Shakespeare Wallah* 1965, which began collaborations with Ishmail *Merchant and writer Ruth Prawer Jhabvala. Ivory subsequently directed films in various genres in India, the USA and Europe, but became associated with adaptations of classic literature, including *The Bostonians* 1984, *A Room with a View* 1987, *Maurice* 1987, and *Howards End* 1992. He directed *The Remains of the Day* 1993.

Ivory Coast Republic of (*République de la Côte d'Ivoire*)
area 322,463 sq km/124,471 sq mi
capital Yamoussoukro

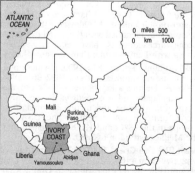

towns Bouaké, Daloa, Man; ports Abidjan, San-Pédro
physical tropical rainforest (diminishing as exploited) in S; savanna and low mountains in N
environment an estimated 85% of the country's forest has been destroyed by humans
head of state Henri Konan Bedie from 1993
head of government Daniel Kablan Duncan from 1993
political system emergent democratic republic
political party Democratic Party of the Ivory Coast (PDCI), nationalist, free-enterprise
exports coffee, cocoa, timber, petroleum products
currency franc CFA
population (1993) 13,500,000; growth rate 3.3% p.a.
languages French (official), over 60 native dialects
religions animist 65%, Muslim 24%, Christian 11%
GNP $690 per head (1991)
chronology
1904 Became part of French West Africa.
1958 Achieved internal self-government.
1960 Independence achieved from France, with Félix Houphouët-Boigny as president of a one-party state.
1985 Houphouët-Boigny re-elected, unopposed.
1986 Name changed officially from Ivory Coast to Côte d'Ivoire.
1990 Houphouët-Boigny and PDCI re-elected.
1993 Houphouët-Boigny died and was succeeded by parliamentary speaker, Henri Konan Bedie. Daniel Kablan Duncan appointed prime minister.

ivy any tree or shrub of the genus *Hedera* of the ginseng family Araliaceae. English or European ivy *H. helix* has shiny, evergreen, triangular or oval-shaped leaves, and clusters of small, yellowish-green flowers, followed by black berries. It climbs by means of rootlike suckers put out from its stem, and is injurious to trees.

Ivy League eight long-established colleges and universities in the US with prestigious academic and social reputations: Brown, Columbia, Cornell, Dartmouth, Harvard, Pennsylvania, Princeton, and Yale. The members of the Ivy League compete in intercollegiate athletics.

Iwo Jima largest of the Japanese Volcano Islands in the W Pacific Ocean, 1,222 km/760 mi S of Tokyo; area 21 sq km/8 sq mi. Annexed by Japan 1891, it was captured by the USA 1945 after fierce fighting. It was returned to Japan 1968.

Iwo Jima, Battle of intense fighting between Japanese and US forces 19 Feb–17 March 1945 during World War II. In Feb 1945, US marines landed on the island of Iwo Jima, a Japanese air base, intending to use it to prepare for a planned final assault on mainland Japan. The Japanese defences were so strong that 5,000 US marines were killed before the island was captured from the Japanese.

Izetbegović Alija 1925– . Bosnia-Herzegovinan politician, president from 1990. An opponent of communism, he founded the Party of Democratic Action (PDA) 1990, ousting the communists in the multiparty elections that year.

Adopting a moderate stance during the civil war in Bosnia-Herzegovina, he sought an honourable peace for his country in the face of ambitious demands from Serb and Croat political leaders.

Izmir (formerly **Smyrna**) port and naval base in Turkey; population (1990) 1,757,400. Products include steel, electronics, and plastics. The largest annual trade fair in the Middle East is held here. It is the headquarters of *North Atlantic Treaty Organization SE Command.

Iznik modern name of ancient *Nicaea, a town in Turkey noted for the richly decorated pottery and tiles produced there in the 15th and 16th centuries.

jabiru stork *Jabiru mycteria* found in Central and South America. It is 1.5 m/5 ft high with white plumage. The head is black and red.

jacamar insect-eating bird of the family Galbulidae, in the same order as woodpeckers. Jacamars are found in Central and South America. It has a long, sharp-pointed bill, long tail, and paired toes. The plumage is brilliantly coloured. The largest species grows up to 30 cm/12 in.

jacana one of seven species of wading birds, family Jacanidae, with very long toes and claws enabling it to walk on the flat leaves of river plants, hence the name 'lily trotter'. Jacanas are found in Mexico, Central America, South America, Africa, S Asia, and Australia. The female pheasant-tailed jacana *Hydrophasianus chirurgus* of Asia has a 'harem' of two to four males.

jacaranda any tropical American tree of the genus *Jacaranda* of the bignonia family Bignoniaceae, with fragrant wood and showy blue or violet flowers, commonly cultivated in the southern USA.

jack tool or machine for lifting, hoisting, or moving heavy weights, such as motor vehicles. A *screw jack* uses the principle of the screw to magnify an applied effort; in a car jack, for example, turning the handle many times causes the lifting screw to rise slightly, and the effort is magnified to lift heavy weights. A *hydraulic jack* uses a succession of piston strokes to increase pressure in a liquid and force up a lifting ram.

jackal any of several wild dogs of the genus *Canis*, found in S Asia, S Europe, and N Africa. Jackals can grow to 80 cm/2.7 ft long, and have greyish-brown fur and a bushy tail.

jackdaw Eurasian bird *Corvus monedula* of the crow family. It is mainly black, but greyish on sides and back of head, and about 33 cm/1.1 ft long. It nests in tree holes or on buildings.

Jackson Andrew 1767–1845. 7th president of the USA 1829–37, a Democrat. A major general in the War of 1812, he defeated a British force at New Orleans in 1815 (after the official end of the war in 1814) and was involved in the war that led to the purchase of Florida in 1819. The political organization he built as president, with Martin Van Buren, was the basis for the modern *Democratic Party.

Jackson Glenda 1936– . English actress, Labour member of Parliament from 1992. She has made many stage appearances, including

Marat/Sade 1966, and her films include the Oscar-winning *Women in Love* 1969, *Sunday Bloody Sunday* 1971, and *A Touch of Class* 1973. On television she played Queen Elizabeth I in *Elizabeth R* 1971.

Jackson Jesse 1941– . US Democrat politician, a cleric and campaigner for minority rights. He contested his party's 1984 and 1988 presidential nominations in an effort to increase voter registration and to put black issues on the national agenda. He is an eloquent public speaker.

Jackson Michael 1958– . US rock singer and songwriter whose videos and live performances are meticulously choreographed. His first solo hit was 'Got to Be There' 1971; his worldwide popularity peaked with the albums *Thriller* 1982 and *Bad* 1987. The follow-up was *Dangerous* 1991.

Jackson Stonewall (Thomas Jonathan) 1824–1863. US Confederate general in the American Civil War. He acquired his nickname and his reputation at the Battle of Bull Run, from the firmness with which his brigade resisted the Northern attack. In 1862 he organized the Shenandoah Valley campaign and assisted Robert E *Lee's invasion of Maryland. He helped to defeat General Joseph E Hooker's Union army at the battle of Chancellorsville, Virginia, but was fatally wounded by one of his own soldiers in the confusion of battle.

Jacksonville port, resort, and commercial centre in Florida, USA; population (1990) 635,200. The port has naval installations and ship-repair yards. To the north the Cross-Florida Barge Canal links the Atlantic with the Gulf of Mexico. Manufactured goods include wood and paper products, chemicals, and processed food.

Jack the Ripper popular name for the unidentified mutilator and murderer of at least five women prostitutes in the Whitechapel area of London in 1888.

Jacob in the Old Testament, Hebrew patriarch, son of Isaac and Rebecca, who obtained the rights of seniority from his twin brother Esau by trickery. He married his cousins Leah and Rachel, serving their father Laban seven years for each, and at the time of famine in Canaan joined his son Joseph in Egypt. His 12 sons were the traditional ancestors of the 12 tribes of Israel.

Jacob François 1920– . French biochemist who, with Jacques Monod, pioneered research into molecular genetics and showed how the production of proteins from *DNA is controlled. He shared the Nobel Prize for Medicine in 1965.

Jacobean style in the arts, particularly in architecture and furniture, during the reign of James I (1603–25) in England. Following the general lines of Elizabethan design, but using classical features more widely, it adopted many motifs from Italian *Renaissance design.

Jacobin member of an extremist republican club of the French Revolution founded at Versailles 1789, which later used a former Jacobin (Dominican) friary as its headquarters in Paris. Helped by *Danton's speeches, they proclaimed the French republic, had the king executed, and overthrew the moderate *Girondins 1792–93. Through the Committee of Public Safety, they began the Reign of Terror, led by *Robespierre.

After his execution 1794, the club was abandoned and the name 'Jacobin' passed into general use for any left-wing extremist.

Jacobite in Britain, a supporter of the royal house of Stuart after the deposition of James II in 1688. They include the Scottish Highlanders, who rose unsuccessfully under *Claverhouse in 1689; and those who rose in Scotland and N England under the leadership of *James Edward Stuart, the Old Pretender, in 1715, and followed his son *Charles Edward Stuart in an invasion of England that reached Derby in 1745–46. After the defeat at *Culloden, Jacobitism disappeared as a political force.

Jacquard Joseph Marie 1752–1834. French textile manufacturer who invented a punched-card system for programming designs on a carpet-making loom. In 1804 he constructed looms that used a series of punched cards to control the pattern of longitudinal warp threads depressed before each sideways passage of the shuttle. On later machines the punched cards were joined to form an endless loop that represented the 'program' for the repeating pattern of a carpet.

Jacquerie French peasant uprising 1358, caused by the ravages of the English army and French nobility during the Hundred Years' War, which reduced the rural population to destitution. The word derives from the nickname for French peasants, Jacques Bonhomme.

Jacuzzi Candido 1903–1986. Italian-born US engineer who invented the Jacuzzi, a pump that produces a whirlpool effect in a bathtub. The Jacuzzi was commercially launched as a health and recreational product in the mid-1950s.

jade semiprecious stone consisting of either jadeite, $NaAlSi_2O_6$ (a pyroxene), or nephrite, $Ca_2(Mg,Fe)_5Si_8O_{22}(OH,F)_2$ (an amphibole), ranging from colourless through shades of green to black according to the iron content. Jade ranks 5.5–6.5 on the Mohs' scale of hardness.

Jade Emperor in Chinese religion, the supreme god, Yu Huang, of pantheistic Taoism, who watches over human actions and is the ruler of life and death.

Jaffa (biblical name **Joppa**) port in W Israel, part of *Tel Aviv from 1950.

Jaffna capital of Jaffna district, Northern Province, Sri Lanka; population (1990) 129,000. It was the focal point of Hindu Tamil nationalism and the scene of recurring riots during the 1980s.

Jagan Cheddi (Berrat) 1918– . Guyanese left-wing politician, president from 1992. He led the People's Progressive Party (PPA) from 1950, and was the first prime minister of British Guyana 1961–64. As the PPA candidate for president in Aug 1992, he opposed privatization as leading to 'recolonization'; the PPA won a decisive victory, and Jagan as veteran leader replaced Desmond Hoyte.

jaguar largest species of *cat Panthera onca in the Americas, formerly ranging from the SW USA to S South America, but now extinct in most of North America. It can grow up to 2.5 m/8 ft long including the tail. The background colour of the fur varies from creamy white to brown or black, and is covered with black spots. The jaguar is usually solitary.

Jaguar British car manufacturer that has

jaguar The jaguar has been hunted for its beautiful coat.

enjoyed a long association with motor racing; owned by Ford from 1989. One of the most successful companies in the 1950s, Jaguar won the Le Mans 24-hour race five times 1951–58.

jaguarundi wild cat Felis yaguoaroundi found in forests in Central and South America. Up to 1.1 m/3.5 ft long, it is very slim with rather short legs and short rounded ears. It is uniformly coloured dark brown or chestnut. A good climber, it feeds on birds and small mammals and, unusually for a cat, has been reported to eat fruit.

Jahangir 'Conqueror of the World'. Adopted name of Salim 1569–1627. Mogul emperor of India 1605–27, succeeding his father *Akbar the Great. He designed the Shalimar Gardens in Kashmir and buildings and gardens in Lahore.

Jahweh another spelling of *Jehovah, the Lord (meaning God) in the Hebrew Bible, used by some writers instead of Adonai (Lord) or Hashem (the Name) – all names used to avoid the representation of God in any form.

jai alai another name for the ball game *pelota.

Jainism (Hindi jaina 'person who overcomes') ancient Indian religion, sometimes regarded as an offshoot of Hinduism. Jains emphasize the importance of not injuring living beings, and their code of ethics is based on sympathy and compassion for all forms of life. They also believe in *karma but not in any deity. It is a monastic, ascetic religion. There are two main sects: the Digambaras and the Swetambaras. Jainism practises the most extreme form of nonviolence (ahimsā) of all Indian sects, and influenced the philosophy of Mahatma Gandhi. Jains number approximately 6 million; there are Jain communities throughout the world but the majority live in India.

Jaipur capital of Rajasthan, India; population (1981) 1,005,000. Formerly the capital of the state of Jaipur, which was merged with Rajasthan in 1949. Products include textiles and metal products.

Jakarta or **Djakarta** (former name until 1949 **Batavia**) capital of Indonesia on the NW coast of Java; population (1980) 6,504,000. Industries include textiles, chemicals, and plastics; a canal links it with its port of Tanjung Priok where rubber, oil, tin, coffee, tea, and palm oil are among its exports; also a tourist centre. Jakarta was founded by Dutch traders in 1619.

Jakeš Miloš 1922– . Czech communist politician, a member of the Politburo from 1981 and party leader 1987–89. A conservative, he supported the Soviet invasion of Czechoslovakia in

1968. He was forced to resign in Nov 1989 following a series of pro-democracy mass rallies.

Jalalabad capital of Nangarhar province, E Afghanistan, on the road from Kabul to Peshawar in Pakistan. The city was besieged by mujaheddin rebels in 1989 after the withdrawal of Soviet troops from Afghanistan.

Jamaica

area 10,957 sq km/4,230 sq mi
capital Kingston
towns Montego Bay, Spanish Town, St Andrew
physical mountainous tropical island
head of state Elizabeth II from 1962 represented by governor general (Howard Cooke from 1991)
head of government P J Patterson from 1992
political system constitutional monarchy
exports sugar, bananas, bauxite, rum, cocoa, coconuts, liqueurs, cigars, citrus
currency Jamaican dollar
population (1993 est) 2,523,000 (African 76%, mixed 15%, Chinese, Caucasian, East Indian); growth rate 2.2% p.a.
languages English, Jamaican creole
religions Protestant 70%, Rastafarian
GNP $1,292 per head (1992)
chronology
1494 Columbus reached Jamaica.
1509–1655 Occupied by Spanish.
1655 Captured by British.
1944 Internal self-government introduced.
1962 Independence achieved from Britain, with Alexander Bustamante of the JLP as prime minister.
1967 JLP re-elected under Hugh Shearer.
1972 Michael Manley of the PNP became prime minister.
1980 JLP elected, with Edward Seaga as prime minister.
1983 JLP re-elected, winning all 60 seats.
1989 PNP won a decisive victory with Michael Manley returning as prime minister.
1992 Manley resigned, succeeded by P J Patterson.
1993 Landslide victory for PNP in general election.

James Henry 1843–1916. US novelist, who lived in Europe from 1875 and became a naturalized British subject 1915. His novels deal with the impact of sophisticated European culture on the innocent American. They include *The Portrait of a Lady* 1881, *The Bostonians* 1886, and *The Golden Bowl* 1904. He also wrote more than a hundred shorter works of fiction, notably the supernatural tale *The Turn of the Screw* 1898.

James Jesse 1847–1882. US bank and train robber, born in Missouri and a leader, with his brother Frank (1843–1915), of the Quantrill raiders, a Confederate guerrilla band in the Civil War. Frank later led his own gang. Jesse was killed by Bob Ford, an accomplice; Frank remained unconvicted and became a farmer.

James William 1842–1910. US psychologist and philosopher, brother of the novelist Henry James. He turned from medicine to psychology and taught at Harvard 1872–1907. His books include *Principles of Psychology* 1890, *The Will to Believe* 1897, and *Varieties of Religious Experience* 1902, one of the most important works on the psychology of religion.

James I the Conqueror 1208–1276. King of Aragon from 1213, when he succeeded his father. He conquered the Balearic Islands and took Valencia from the *Moors, dividing it with Alfonso X of Castile by a treaty of 1244. Both these exploits are recorded in his autobiography *Libre dels feyts/Chronicle*. He largely established Aragon as the dominant power in the Mediterranean.

James two kings of Britain:

James I 1566–1625. King of England from 1603 and Scotland (as **James VI**) from 1567. The son of Mary Queen of Scots and Lord Darnley, he succeeded on his mother's abdication from the Scottish throne, assumed power 1583, established a strong centralized authority, and in 1589 married Anne of Denmark (1574–1619). As successor to Elizabeth I in England, he alienated the Puritans by his High Church views and Parliament by his assertion of *divine right, and was generally unpopular because of his favourites, such as *Buckingham, and his schemes for an alliance with Spain. He was succeeded by his son Charles I.

James II 1633–1701. King of England and Scotland (as **James VII**) from 1685, second son of Charles I. He succeeded Charles II. James married Anne Hyde 1659 (1637–1671, mother of Mary II and Anne) and Mary of Modena 1673 (1658–1718, mother of James Edward Stuart). He became a Catholic 1671, which led first to attempts to exclude him from the succession, then to the rebellions 1685 of Lords Monmouth (1649–1685, an illegitimate son of Charles II) and Argyll (1629–1685), and finally to the Whig and Tory leaders' invitation to William of Orange to take the throne in 1688. James fled to France, then led an uprising in Ireland 1689, but after defeat at the Battle of the *Boyne 1690 remained in exile in France.

James seven kings of Scotland:

James I 1394–1437. King of Scotland 1406–37, who assumed power 1424. He was a cultured and strong monarch whose improvements in the administration of justice brought him popularity among the common people. He was assassinated by a group of conspirators led by the Earl of Atholl.

James II 1430–1460. King of Scotland from 1437, who assumed power 1449. The only surviving son of James I, he was supported by most of the nobles and parliament. He sympathized with the Lancastrians during the Wars of the *Roses, and attacked English possessions in S Scotland. He was killed while besieging Roxburgh Castle.

James III 1451–1488. King of Scotland from 1460, who assumed power 1469. His reign was marked by rebellions by the nobles, including his brother Alexander, Duke of Albany. He was murdered during a rebellion supported by his son, who then ascended the throne as James IV.

James IV 1473–1513. King of Scotland from 1488, who married Margaret (1489–1541, daughter of Henry VII) in 1503. He came to the throne after his followers murdered his father, James III, at Sauchieburn. His reign was internally peaceful, but he allied himself with France against England, invaded 1513 and was defeated and killed at the Battle of *Flodden. James IV was a patron of poets and architects as well as a military leader.

James V 1512–1542. King of Scotland from 1513, who assumed power 1528. During the long period of his minority, he was caught in a struggle between pro-French and pro-English factions. When he assumed power, he allied himself with France and upheld Catholicism against the Protestants. Following an attack on Scottish territory by Henry VIII's forces, he was defeated near the border at Solway Moss 1542.

James VI of Scotland. See *James I of England.

James VII of Scotland. See *James II of England.

James Edward Stuart 1688–1766. British prince, known as the **Old Pretender** (for the *Jacobites, he was James III). Son of James II, he was born at St James's Palace and after the revolution of 1688 was taken to France. He landed in Scotland in 1715 to head a Jacobite rebellion but withdrew through lack of support. In his later years he settled in Rome.

Jameson Leander Starr 1853–1917. British colonial administrator. In South Africa, early in 1896, he led the **Jameson Raid** from Mafeking into Transvaal to support the non-Boer colonists there, in an attempt to overthrow the government (for which he served some months in prison). Returning to South Africa, he succeeded Cecil *Rhodes as leader of the Progressive Party of Cape Colony, where he was prime minister 1904–08.

James, St the Great died 44 AD. A New Testament apostle, originally a Galilean fisher, he was the son of Zebedee and brother of the apostle John. He was put to death by *Herod Agrippa. James is the patron saint of Spain. Feast day 25 July.

James, St the Just 1st century AD. The New Testament brother of Jesus, to whom Jesus appeared after the Resurrection. Leader of the Christian church in Jerusalem, he was the author of the biblical Epistle of James.

Jammu and Kashmir state of N India
area 101,300 sq km/39,102 sq mi
capital Jammu (winter); Srinagar (summer)
towns Leh

products timber, grain, rice, fruit, silk, carpets
population (1991) 7,718,700 (Indian-occupied territory)
history part of the Mogul Empire from 1586, Jammu came under the control of Gulab Singh 1820. In 1947 Jammu was attacked by Pakistan and chose to become part of the new state of India. Dispute over the area (see *Kashmir) caused further hostilities 1971 between India and Pakistan (ended by the Simla agreement 1972). Since then, separatist agitation has developed, complicating the territorial dispute between India and Pakistan.

Janáček Leoš 1854–1928. Czech composer. He became director of the Conservatoire at Brno 1919 and professor at the Prague Conservatoire 1920. His music, highly original and influenced by Moravian folk music, includes arrangements of folk songs, operas (*Jenůfa* 1904, *The Cunning Little Vixen* 1924), and the choral *Glagolitic Mass* 1926.

Janata alliance of political parties in India formed 1971 to oppose Indira Gandhi's *Congress Party. Victory in the election brought Morarji Desai to power as prime minister but he was unable to control the various groups within the alliance and resigned 1979. His successors fared little better, and the elections of 1980 overwhelmingly returned Indira Gandhi to office.

Janata Dal (People's Party) Indian centre-left coalition, formed Oct 1988 under the leadership of V P Singh and comprising the Janata, Lok Dal (B), Congress (S), and Jan Morcha parties. In a loose alliance with the Hindu fundamentalist Bharatiya Janata Party and the Communist Party of India, the Janata Dal was victorious in the Nov 1989 general election, taking power out of the hands of the Congress (I) Party for the first time since 1947. Following internal splits, its minority government fell Nov 1990.

Janequin Clément *c.* 1472–*c.* 1560. French composer of chansons and psalms. He was choirmaster of Angers Cathedral 1534–37 and then based in Paris from 1549. His songs of the 1520s–30s are witty and richly textured in imitative effects, for example 'Le Chant des oiseaux'/ 'Birdsong', 'La Chasse'/'The Hunt', and 'Les Cris de Paris'/'Street Cries of Paris'.

janissary bodyguard of the Ottoman sultan, the Turkish standing army from the late 14th century until 1826. Until the 16th century janissaries were Christian boys forcibly converted to Islam; after this time they were allowed to marry and recruit their own children. The bodyguard ceased to exist when it revolted against the decision of the sultan in 1826 to raise a regular force.

Jansenism Christian teaching of Cornelius Jansen (1585–1638), which divided the Roman Catholic Church in France in the mid-17th century. Emphasizing the more predestinatory approach of Augustine's teaching, as opposed to that of the Jesuits, Jansenism was supported by the philosopher Pascal. Jansenists were excommunicated 1719.

jansky unit of radiation received from outer space, used in radio astronomy. It is equal to 10^{-26} watts per square metre per hertz, and is named after US engineer Karl Jansky.

Janus in Roman mythology, the god of doorways and passageways, patron of the beginning of the day, month, and year, after whom January is named; he is represented as having two faces, one looking forwards and one back. In Roman ritual, the doors of Janus in the Forum were closed when peace was established.

Japan (*Nippon*)

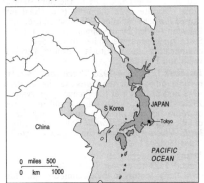

area 377,535 sq km/145,822 sq mi
capital Tokyo
towns Fukuoka, Kitakyushu, Kyoto, Sapporo; ports Osaka, Nagoya, Yokohama, Kobe, Kawasaki
physical mountainous, volcanic; comprises over 1,000 islands, the largest of which are Hokkaido, Honshu, Kyushu, and Shikoku
head of state (figurehead) Emperor Akihito (Heisei) from 1989
head of government Tomiichi Murayama from 1994
political system liberal democracy
exports televisions, cassette and video recorders, radios, cameras, computers, robots, other electronic and electrical equipment, motor vehicles, ships, iron, steel, chemicals, textiles
currency yen
population (1993 est) 124,900,000; growth rate 0.5% p.a.
language Japanese
religions Shinto, Buddhist (often combined), Christian; 30% claim a personal religious faith
GNP $29,794 per head (1992)
chronology
1867 End of shogun rule; executive power passed to emperor. Start of modernization of Japan.
1894–95 War with China; Formosa (Taiwan) and S Manchuria gained.
1902 Formed alliance with Britain.
1904–05 War with Russia; Russia ceded southern half of Sakhalin.
1910 Japan annexed Korea.
1914 Joined Allies in World War I.
1918 Received German Pacific islands as mandates.
1931–32 War with China; renewed 1937.
1941 Japan attacked US fleet at Pearl Harbor 7 Dec.
1945 World War II ended with Japanese surrender. Allied control commission took power. Formosa and Manchuria returned to China.
1946 Framing of 'peace constitution'. Emperor Hirohito became figurehead ruler.
1952 Full sovereignty regained.

1958 Joined United Nations.
1968 Bonin and Volcano Islands regained.
1972 Ryukyu Islands regained.
1974 Prime Minister Tanaka resigned over Lockheed bribes scandal.
1982 Yasuhiro Nakasone elected prime minister.
1987 Noboru Takeshita chosen to succeed Nakasone.
1988 Recruit scandal cast shadow over government and opposition parties.
1989 Emperor Hirohito (Shōwa) died; succeeded by his son Akihito. Many cabinet ministers implicated in Recruit scandal and Takeshita resigned; succeeded by Sosuke Uno. Aug: Uno resigned after sex scandal; succeeded by Toshiki Kaifu.
1990 Feb: new house of councillors' elections won by LDP. Public-works budget increased by 50% to encourage imports.
1991 Japan contributed billions of dollars to the Gulf War and its aftermath. Kaifu succeeded by Kiichi Miyazawa.
1992 Over 100 politicians implicated in new financial scandal. Emperor Akihito made first Japanese imperial visit to China. Trade surpluses reached record levels.
1993 Worst recession of postwar era but trade surpluses again reached record levels. Government lost no-confidence vote over electoral reform. LDP failed to win majority in general election, ending 38 years in power; Miyazawa resigned. New parties formed from LDP factions. Morihiro Hosokawa chosen as premier, heading non-LDP coalition.
1994 Feb: compromise political-reform package passed, after initial rejection by upper house. April: Hosokawa resigned, accused of corruption; Tsutomu Hata appointed prime minister, heading minority coalition government. June: Hata resigned; succeeded by SDJP leader, Tomiichi Murayama, leading an LDP-dominated coalition.

Japanese language language of E Asia, spoken almost exclusively in the islands of Japan. Traditionally isolated, but possibly related to Korean, Japanese was influenced by Mandarin Chinese especially in the 6th–9th centuries and is written in Chinese-derived ideograms supplemented by two syllabic systems.

Jarman Derek 1942–1994 English avant-garde film director. Jarman made several low-budget, highly innovative features, often with homoerotic associations. His films include *Sebastiane* 1976, with dialogue spoken in Latin; *Caravaggio* 1986; *Edward II* 1991, a free adaptation of Christopher Marlowe's play; *Wittgenstein* 1993; and *Blue* 1993.

Jarry Alfred 1873–1907. French satiric dramatist. His grossly farcical *Ubu Roi* 1896 foreshadowed the Theatre of the *Absurd and the French Surrealist movement in its freedom of staging and subversive humour.

Jaruzelski Wojciech 1923– . Polish general, communist leader from 1981, president 1985–90. He imposed martial law for the first year of his rule, suppressed the opposition, and banned trade-union activity, but later released many political prisoners. In 1989, elections in favour of the free trade union Solidarity forced Jaruzelski to speed up democratic reforms, overseeing a transition to a new form of 'socialist pluralist' democracy and stepping down as president 1990.

jasmine any subtropical plant of the genus *Jasminum* of the olive family Oleaceae, with white or yellow flowers. The common jasmine *J. officinale* has fragrant pure white flowers yielding jasmine oil, used in perfumes; the Chinese winter jasmine *J. nudiflorum* has bright yellow flowers that appear before the leaves.

Jason in Greek mythology, the leader of the Argonauts who sailed in the Argo to Colchis in search of the *Golden Fleece. He eloped with *Medea, daughter of the king of Colchis, who had helped him achieve his goal, but later deserted her.

Jat member of an ethnic group living in Pakistan and N India, and numbering about 11 million; they are the largest group in N India. The Jat are predominantly farmers. They speak Punjabi, a language belonging to the Iranian branch of the Indo-European family. They are thought to be related to the Romany people.

Jataka collections of Buddhist legends compiled at various dates in several countries; the oldest and most complete has 547 stories. They were collected before AD 400.

jaundice yellow discoloration of the skin and whites of the eyes caused by an excess of bile pigment in the bloodstream. Mild jaundice is common in newborns, but a serious form occurs in rhesus disease (see *rhesus factor).

Jaurès Jean Léon 1859–1914. French socialist politician and advocate of international peace. He was a lecturer in philosophy at Toulouse until his election 1885 as a deputy (member of parliament). In 1893 he joined the Socialist Party, established a united party, and in 1904 founded the newspaper *L'Humanité*, becoming its editor until his assassination.

Java or *Jawa* the most important island of Indonesia, situated between Sumatra and Bali
area (with the island of Madura) 132,000 sq km/ 51,000 sq mi
capital Jakarta (also capital of Indonesia)
towns ports include Surabaya and Semarang
physical about half the island is under cultivation, the rest being thickly forested. Mountains and sea breezes keep temperatures down, but humidity is high, with heavy rainfall from Dec to March
products rice, coffee, cocoa, tea, sugar, rubber, quinine, teak, petroleum
population (with Madura; 1989) 107,513,800, including people of Javanese, Sundanese, and Madurese origin, with differing languages
religion predominantly Muslim
history Fossilized early human remains (*Homo erectus*) were discovered 1891–92. In central Java there are ruins of magnificent Buddhist monuments and of the Sivaite temple in Prambanan. The island's last Hindu kingdom, Majapahit, was destroyed about 1520 and followed by a number of short-lived Javanese kingdoms. The Dutch East India company founded a factory in 1610. Britain took over during the Napoleonic period, 1811–16, and Java then reverted to Dutch control. Occupied by Japan 1942–45, Java then became part of the republic of *Indonesia.

Javanese member of the largest ethnic group in the Republic of Indonesia. There are more than 50 million speakers of Javanese, which belongs to the western branch of the Austronesian family. Although the Javanese have a Hindu-Buddhist heritage, they are today predominantly Muslim, practising a branch of Islam known as *Islam Jawa*, which contains many Sufi features.

javelin spear used in athletics events. The men's javelin is about 260 cm/8.5 ft long, weighing 800 g/28 oz; the women's 230 cm/7.5 ft long, weighing 600 g/21 oz. It is thrown from a scratch line at the end of a run-up. The centre of gravity on the men's javelin was altered 1986 to reduce the vast distances (90 m/100 yd) that were being thrown.

jaw one of two bony structures that form the framework of the mouth in all vertebrates except lampreys and hagfishes (the agnathous or jawless vertebrates). They consist of the upper jawbone (maxilla), which is fused to the skull, and the lower jawbone (mandible), which is hinged at each side to the bones of the temple by *ligaments.

jay any of several birds of the crow family Corvidae, generally brightly coloured and native to Eurasia and the Americas. In the Eurasian common jay *Garrulus glandarius*, the body is fawn with patches of white, blue, and black on the wings and tail.

jay The common jay ranges widely over Europe to N Africa, and Asia south to Myanmar, China, and Taiwan.

Jayawardene Junius Richard 1906– . Sri Lankan politician. Leader of the United National Party from 1973, he became prime minister 1977 and the country's first president 1978–88.

jazz polyphonic, syncopated music characterized by solo virtuosic improvisation, which developed in the USA at the turn of the 20th century. Initially music for dancing, often with a vocalist, it had its roots in black American and other popular music. As jazz grew increasingly complex and experimental, various distinct forms evolved. Seminal musicians include Louis Armstrong, Charlie Parker, and John Coltrane.

jazz dance dance based on African techniques and rhythms, developed by black Americans around 1917. It entered mainstream dance in the 1920s, mainly in show business, and from the 1960s the teachers and choreographers Matt Mattox and Luigi expanded its vocabulary. Contemporary choreographers as diverse as Jerome *Robbins and Alvin Ailey used it in their work.

Jeans James Hopwood 1877–1946. British mathematician and scientist. In physics he worked on the kinetic theory of gases, and on forms of energy radiation; in astronomy, his work focused on giant and dwarf stars, the nature of spiral nebulae, and the origin of the cosmos. He did much to popularize astronomy.

Jedda alternative spelling for the Saudi Arabian port *Jiddah.

Jefferson Thomas 1743–1826. 3rd president of the USA 1801–09, founder of the Democratic Republican Party. He published *A Summary View of the Rights of America* 1774 and as a member of the Continental Congresses of 1775–76 was largely responsible for the drafting of the *Declaration of Independence. He was governor of Virginia 1779–81, ambassador to Paris 1785–89, secretary of state 1789–93, and vice president 1797–1801.

Jeffreys Alec John 1950– . British geneticist who discovered the DNA probes necessary for accurate *genetic fingerprinting so that a murderer or rapist could be identified by, for example, traces of blood, tissue, or semen.

Jeffreys George, 1st Baron 1648–1689. Welsh judge, popularly known as the hanging judge. He became Chief Justice of the King's Bench in 1683, and presided over many political trials, notably those of Philip Sidney, Titus Oates, and Richard Baxter, becoming notorious for his brutality.

Jehosophat 4th king of Judah *c.* 873–849 BC; he allied himself with Ahab, king of Israel, in the war against Syria.

Jehovah also **Jahweh** in the Old Testament the name of God, revealed to Moses; in Hebrew texts of the Old Testament the name was represented by the letters YHVH (without the vowels 'a o a') as it was regarded as too sacred to be pronounced.

Jehovah's Witness member of a religious organization originating in the USA 1872 under Charles Taze Russell (1852–1916). Jehovah's Witnesses attach great importance to Christ's second coming, which Russell predicted would occur 1914, and which Witnesses still believe is imminent. All Witnesses are expected to take part in house-to-house preaching; there are no clergy.

Jehu king of Israel *c.* 842–815 BC. He led a successful rebellion against the family of *Ahab and was responsible for the death of Jezebel.

Jekyll Gertrude 1843–1932. English landscape gardener and writer. She created over 200 gardens, many in collaboration with the architect Edwin *Lutyens. In her books, she advocated natural gardens of the cottage type, with plentiful herbaceous borders.

jellyfish marine invertebrate of the phylum Cnidaria (coelenterates) with an umbrella-shaped body composed of a semi-transparent gelatinous substance, with a fringe of stinging tentacles. Most adult jellyfishes move freely, but during parts of their life cycle many are polyplike and attached. They feed on small animals that are paralysed by stinging cells in the jellyfishes' tentacles.

Jenkins Roy (Harris), Lord Jenkins 1920– . British politician. He became a Labour minister 1964, was home secretary 1965–67 and 1974–76, and chancellor of the Exchequer 1967–70. He was president of the European Commission 1977–81. In 1981 he became one of the founders of the Social Democratic Party and was elected 1982, but lost his seat 1987. In the same year, he was elected chancellor of Oxford University and made a life peer.

Jenner Edward 1749–1823. English physician who pioneered vaccination. In Jenner's day, smallpox was a major killer. His discovery 1796 that inoculation with cowpox gives immunity to smallpox was a great medical breakthrough. He coined the word 'vaccination' from the Latin word for cowpox, *vaccina*.

Jerablus ancient Syrian city, adjacent to Carchemish on the river Euphrates.

jerboa small, nocturnal, leaping rodent belonging to the family Dipodidae. There are about 25 species of jerboa, native to N Africa and SW Asia.

Jeremiah 7th–6th century BC. Old Testament Hebrew prophet, whose ministry continued 626–586 BC. He was imprisoned during *Nebuchadnezzar's siege of Jerusalem on suspicion of intending to desert to the enemy. On the city's fall, he retired to Egypt.

Jericho Israeli-administered town in Jordan, north of the Dead Sea. It was settled by 8000 BC, and by 6000 BC had become a walled city with 2,000 inhabitants. In the Old Testament it was the first Canaanite stronghold captured by the Israelites, and its walls, according to the Book of *Joshua, fell to the blast of Joshua's trumpets. Successive archaeological excavations since 1907 show that the walls of the city were destroyed many times.

Jeroboam 10th century BC. First king of Israel *c.* 922–901 BC after it split away from the kingdom of Judah.

Jerome Jerome K(lapka) 1859–1927. English journalist and writer. His works include the humorous essays *Idle Thoughts of an Idle Fellow* 1889, the novel *Three Men in a Boat* 1889, and the play *The Passing of the Third Floor Back* 1907.

Jerome, St *c.* 340–420. One of the early Christian leaders and scholars known as the Fathers of the Church. His Latin versions of the Old and New Testaments form the basis of the Roman Catholic Vulgate. He is usually depicted with a lion. Feast day 30 Sept.

Jersey largest of the *Channel Islands; capital St Helier; area 117 sq km/45 sq mi; population (1986) 80,000. It is governed by a lieutenant-governor representing the English crown and an assembly. Jersey cattle were originally bred here. Jersey gave its name to a woollen garment.

Jerusalem ancient city of Palestine, divided 1948 between Jordan and the new republic of Israel; area (pre-1967) 37.5 sq km/14.5 sq mi, (post-1967) 108 sq km/42 sq mi, including areas of the West Bank; population (1989) 500,000, about 350,000 Israelis and 150,000 Palestinians. In 1950 the western New City was proclaimed as the Israeli capital, and, having captured from Jordan the eastern Old City 1967, Israel affirmed 1980 that the united city was the country's capital; the United Nations does not recognize the claim.

Jerusalem artichoke a variety of *artichoke.

Jessop William 1745–1814. British canal engineer who built the first canal in England entirely dependent on reservoirs for its water supply (the Grantham Canal 1793–97), and designed (with Thomas *Telford) the 300 m/ 1,000 ft long Pontcysyllte aqueduct over the river Dee.

Jesuit member of the largest and most influential Roman Catholic religious order (also known as the **Society of Jesus**) founded by Ignatius *Loyola 1534, with the aims of protecting Catholicism against the Reformation and carrying out missionary work. During the 16th and 17th centuries Jesuits were missionaries in Japan, China, Paraguay, and among the North American Indians. The order had (1991) about 29,000 members (15,000 priests plus students and lay members), and their schools and universities are renowned.

Jesus c. 4 BC–AD 29 or 30. Hebrew preacher on whose teachings Christianity was founded. According to the accounts of his life in the four Gospels, he was born in Bethlehem, Palestine, son of God and the Virgin Mary, and brought up by Mary and her husband Joseph as a carpenter in Nazareth. After adult baptism, he gathered 12 disciples, but his preaching antagonized the Roman authorities and he was executed by crucifixion. Three days later there came reports of his resurrection and, later, his ascension to heaven.

jet hard, black variety of lignite, a type of coal. It is cut and polished for use in jewellery and ornaments. Articles made of jet have been found in Bronze Age tombs.

JET (abbreviation for **Joint European Torus**) *tokamak machine built in England to conduct experiments on nuclear fusion. It is the focus of the European effort to produce a practical fusion-power reactor.

jeté (French 'thrown') in dance, a jump from one foot to the other. A *grand jeté* is a big jump in which the dancer pushes off on one foot, holds a brief pose in midair, and lands lightly on the other foot.

jetfoil advanced type of *hydrofoil boat built by Boeing, propelled by water jets. It features horizontal, fully submerged hydrofoils fore and aft and has a sophisticated computerized control system to maintain its stability in all waters.

jet lag the effect of a sudden switch of time zones in air travel, resulting in tiredness and feeling 'out of step' with day and night. In 1989 it was suggested that use of the hormone melatonin helped to lessen the effect of jet lag by resetting the body clock. See also *circadian rhythm.

jet propulsion method of propulsion in which an object is propelled in one direction by a jet, or stream of gases, moving in the other. This follows from Isaac *Newton's third law of motion: 'To every action, there is an equal and opposite reaction.' The most widespread application of the jet principle is in the jet engine, the most common kind of aircraft engine.

Jet Propulsion Laboratory NASA installation at Pasadena, California, operated by the California Institute of Technology. It is the command centre for NASA's deep-space probes such as the *Voyager, *Magellan, and *Galileo missions, with which it communicates via the Deep Space Network of radio telescopes at Goldstone,

California; Madrid, Spain; and Canberra, Australia.

jet stream narrow band of very fast wind (velocities of over 150 kph/95 mph) found at altitudes of 10–16 km/6–10 mi in the upper troposphere or lower stratosphere. Jet streams usually occur about the latitudes of the Westerlies (35°–60°).

Jew follower of *Judaism, the Jewish religion. The term is also used to refer to those who claim descent from the ancient Hebrews, a Semitic people of the Middle East. Today, some may recognize their ethnic heritage but not practise the religious or cultural traditions. The term came into use in medieval Europe, based on the Latin name for Judeans, the people of Judah. Prejudice against Jews is termed *anti-Semitism.

Jew's harp musical instrument consisting of a two-pronged metal frame inserted between the teeth, and a springlike tongue plucked with the finger. The resulting drone excites resonances in the mouth that can be varied in pitch to produce a melody.

Jezebel in the Old Testament, daughter of the king of Sidon. She married King Ahab of Israel, and was brought into conflict with the prophet Elijah by her introduction of the worship of Baal.

Jiang Jie Shi alternative transcription of *Chiang Kai-shek.

Jiang Qing or **Chiang Ching** 1914–1991. Chinese communist politician, third wife of the party leader Mao Zedong. In 1960 she became minister for culture, and played a key role in the 1966–69 Cultural Revolution as the leading member of the Shanghai-based Gang of Four, who attempted to seize power 1976. Jiang was imprisoned 1981.

Jiangsu or **Kiangsu** province on the coast of E China
area 102,200 sq km/39,449 sq mi
capital Nanjing
products cereals, rice, tea, cotton, soya beans, fish, silk, ceramics, textiles, coal, iron, copper, cement
population (1990) 67,057,000
history Jiangsu was originally part of the Wu kingdom, and Wu is still a traditional local name for the province. Jiangsu's capture by Japan in 1937 was an important step in that country's attempt to conquer China.

Jiangxi or **Kiangsi** province of SE China
area 164,800 sq km/63,613 sq mi
capital Nanchang
products rice, tea, cotton, tobacco, porcelain, coal, tungsten, uranium
population (1990) 37,710,000
history the province was Mao Zedong's original base in the first phase of the Communist struggle against the Nationalists.

Jiang Zemin 1926– . Chinese political leader. The son-in-law of *Li Xiannian, he joined the Chinese Communist Party's politburo in 1967 after serving in the Moscow embassy and as mayor of Shanghai. He succeeded *Zhao Ziyang as party leader after the Tiananmen Square massacre of 1989. A cautious proponent of economic reform coupled with unswerving adherence to the party's 'political line', he subsequently replaced *Deng Xiaoping as head of the influential central military commission and replaced Yang Shangkun as state president 1993.

Jiddah or **Jedda** port in Hejaz, Saudi Arabia, on the E shore of the Red Sea; population (1986) 1,000,000. Industries include cement, steel, and oil refining. Pilgrims pass through here on their way to Mecca.

jihad (Arabic 'conflict') holy war undertaken by Muslims against nonbelievers. In the **Mecca Declaration** 1981, the Islamic powers pledged a jihad against Israel, though not necessarily military attack.

Jilin or **Kirin** province of NE China in central *Manchuria
area 187,000 sq km/72,182 sq mi
capital Changchun
population (1990) 24,659,000.

Jim Crow the systematic practice of segregating black Americans, which was common in the South until the 1960s. **Jim Crow laws** are laws designed to deny civil rights to blacks or to enforce the policy of segregation, which existed until Supreme Court decisions and civil-rights legislation of the 1950s and 1960s (Civil Rights Act 1964, Voting Rights Act 1965) denied their legality. See also *black.

Jinan or **Tsinan** city and capital of Shandong province, China; population (1989) 2,290,000. It has food-processing and textile industries.

jingoism blinkered, warmongering patriotism. The term originated in 1878, when the British prime minister Disraeli developed a pro-Turkish policy, which nearly involved the UK in war with Russia. His supporters' war song included the line 'We don't want to fight, but by jingo if we do ... '.

jinn in Muslim mythology, a spirit able to assume human or animal shape.

Jinnah Muhammad Ali 1876–1948. Indian politician, Pakistan's first governor general from 1947. He was president of the Muslim League (an Islamic political organization) 1916 and 1934–48, and by 1940 was advocating the need for a separate state of Pakistan; at the 1946 conferences in London he insisted on the partition of British India into Hindu and Muslim states.

Jinsha Jiang river that rises in SW China and forms the *Chang Jiang (Yangtze) at Yibin.

jive energetic American dance that evolved from the jitterbug, popular in the 1940s and 1950s.

Joan of Arc, St 1412–1431. French military leader. In 1429 at Chinon, NW France, she persuaded Charles VII that she had a divine mission to expel the occupying English from N France (see *Hundred Years' War) and secure his coronation. She raised the siege of Orléans, defeated the English at Patay, north of Orléans, and Charles was crowned in Reims. However, she failed to take Paris and was captured May 1430 by the Burgundians, who sold her to the English. She was found guilty of witchcraft and heresy by a tribunal of French ecclesiastics who supported the English. She was burned to death at the stake in Rouen 30 May 1431. In 1920 she was canonized.

Job *c.* 5th century BC. In the Old Testament, Hebrew leader who in the **Book of Job** questioned God's infliction of suffering on the righteous while enduring great sufferings himself.

job creation schemes introduced by governments at times of high or seasonal unemployment, often involving community work or training to develop marketable skills.

Jodrell Bank site in Cheshire, England, of the Nuffield Radio Astronomy Laboratories of the University of Manchester. Its largest instrument is the 76 m/250 ft radio dish (the Lovell Telescope), completed 1957 and modified 1970. A 38 × 25 m/ 125 × 82 ft elliptical radio dish was introduced 1964, capable of working at shorter wavelengths.

Joffre Joseph Jacques Césaire 1852–1931. Marshal of France during World War I. He was chief of general staff 1911. The German invasion of Belgium 1914 took him by surprise, but his stand at the Battle of the *Marne resulted in his appointment as supreme commander of all the French armies 1915. His failure to make adequate preparations at Verdun 1916 and the military disasters on the *Somme led to his replacement by Nivelle in Dec 1916.

Johannesburg largest city of South Africa, situated on the Witwatersrand River in Transvaal; population (1985) 1,609,000. It is the centre of a large gold-mining industry; other industries include engineering works, meat-chilling plants, and clothing factories.

John Augustus (Edwin) 1878–1961. British painter of landscapes and portraits, including *The Smiling Woman* 1910 (Tate Gallery, London) of his second wife, Dorelia.

John Elton. Stage name of Reginald Kenneth Dwight 1947– . English pop singer, pianist, and composer, noted for his melodies and elaborate costumes and glasses. His best-known LP, *Goodbye Yellow Brick Road* 1973, includes the hit 'Bennie and the Jets'. His output is prolific and his hits continued intermittently into the 1990s.

John Gwen 1876–1939. British painter who lived in France for most of her life. Many of her paintings depict Dominican nuns (she converted to Catholicism 1913); she also painted calm, muted interiors.

John Lackland 1167–1216. King of England from 1199 and acting king from 1189 during his brother Richard I's (the Lion-Heart) absence on the third Crusade. He lost Normandy and almost all the other English possessions in France to Philip II of France by 1205. His repressive policies and excessive taxation brought him into conflict with his barons, and he was forced to seal the *Magna Carta 1215. Later repudiation of it led to the first Barons' War 1215–17, during which he died.

John two kings of France, including:

John II 1319–1364. King of France from 1350. He was defeated and captured by the Black Prince at Poitiers 1356 and imprisoned in England. Released 1360, he failed to raise the money for his ransom and returned to England 1364, where he died.

John name of 23 popes, including:

John XXII 1249–1334. Pope 1316–34. He spent his papacy in Avignon, France, engaged in a long conflict with the Holy Roman emperor, Louis of Bavaria, and the Spiritual Franciscans, a monastic order who preached the absolute poverty of the clergy.

John XXIII Angelo Giuseppe Roncalli 1881–1963. Pope from 1958. He improved relations with the USSR in line with his encyclical *Pacem in Terris/Peace on Earth* 1963, established Roman Catholic hierarchies in newly emergent states, and summoned the Second Vatican Council, which reformed church liturgy and backed the ecumenical movement.

John three kings of Poland, including:

John III Sobieski 1624–1696. King of Poland from 1674. He became commander in chief of the army 1668 after victories over the Cossacks and Tatars. A victory over the Turks 1673 helped to get him elected to the Polish throne, and he saved Vienna from the besieging Turks 1683.

John six kings of Portugal, including:

John I 1357–1433. King of Portugal from 1385. An illegitimate son of Pedro I, he was elected by the Cortes (parliament). His claim was supported by an English army against the rival king of Castile, thus establishing the Anglo-Portuguese Alliance 1386. He married Philippa of Lancaster, daughter of *John of Gaunt.

John IV 1603–1656. King of Portugal from 1640. Originally duke of Braganza, he was elected king when the Portuguese rebelled against Spanish rule. His reign was marked by a long war against Spain, which did not end until 1668.

John Bull imaginary figure who is a personification of England, similar to the American Uncle Sam. He is represented in cartoons and caricatures as a prosperous farmer of the 18th century.

John of Gaunt 1340–1399. English politician, born in Ghent, fourth son of Edward III, Duke of Lancaster from 1362. He distinguished himself during the Hundred Years' War. During Edward's last years, and the years before Richard II attained the age of majority, he acted as head of government, and Parliament protested against his corrupt rule.

John of Salisbury c. 1115–1180. English philosopher and historian. His *Policraticus* portrayed the church as the guarantee of liberty against the unjust claims of secular authority.

John of the Cross, St 1542–1591. Spanish Roman Catholic Carmelite friar from 1564, who was imprisoned several times for attempting to impose the reforms laid down by St Teresa. His verse describes spiritual ecstasy. Feast day 24 Nov.

John Paul two popes:

John Paul I Albino Luciani 1912–1978. Pope 26 Aug–28 Sept 1978. His name was chosen as the combination of his two immediate predecessors.

John Paul II Karol Wojtyla 1920– . Pope from 1978, the first non-Italian to be elected pope since 1522. He was born near Kraków, Poland. He has upheld the tradition of papal infallibility, condemned artificial contraception, women priests, married priests, and modern dress for monks and nuns – views that have aroused criticism from liberalizing elements in the church.

Johns Jasper 1930– . US painter and printmaker who rejected the abstract in favour of such simple subjects as flags, maps, and numbers. He uses pigments mixed with wax (encaustic) to create a rich surface with unexpected delicacies of colour. He has also created collages and lithographs.

John, St 1st century AD. New Testament apostle. Traditionally, he wrote the fourth Gospel and the Johannine Epistles (when he was bishop of Ephesus), and the Book of Revelation (while exiled to the Greek island of Patmos). His emblem is an eagle; his feast day 27 Dec.

Johnson Amy 1903–1941. British aviator. She made a solo flight from England to Australia 1930, in 9½ days, and in 1932 made the fastest ever solo flight from England to Cape Town, South Africa. Her plane disappeared over the English Channel in World War II while she was serving with the Air Transport Auxiliary.

Johnson Andrew 1808–1875. 17th president of the USA 1865–69, a Democrat. He was a congressman from Tennessee 1843–53, governor of Tennessee 1853–57, senator 1857–62, and vice president 1865. He succeeded to the presidency on Lincoln's assassination (15 April 1865). His conciliatory policy to the defeated South after the Civil War involved him in a feud with the Radical Republicans, culminating in his impeachment 1868 before the Senate, which failed to convict him by one vote.

Johnson Jack 1878–1968. US heavyweight boxer. He overcame severe racial prejudice to become the first black heavyweight champion of the world 1908 when he travelled to Australia to challenge Tommy Burns. The US authorities wanted Johnson 'dethroned' because of his colour but could not find suitable challengers until 1915, when he lost the title in a dubious fight decision to the giant Jess Willard.

Johnson Lyndon Baines 1908–1973. 36th president of the USA 1963–69, a Democrat. He was elected to Congress 1937–49 and the Senate 1949–60. Born in Texas, he brought critical Southern support as J F Kennedy's vice-presidential running mate 1960, and became president on Kennedy's assassination. After the *Tonkin Gulf Incident, which escalated US involvement in the *Vietnam War, support won by Johnson's Great Society legislation (civil rights, education, alleviation of poverty) dissipated, and he declined to run for re-election 1968.

Johnson Philip (Cortelyou) 1906– . US architect who coined the term 'international style'. Originally designing in the style of *Mies van der Rohe, he later became an exponent of *Post-Modernism. He designed the giant AT&T building in New York 1978, a pink skyscraper with a Chippendale-style cabinet top.

Johnson Samuel, known as 'Dr Johnson', 1709–1784. English lexicographer, author, and critic, also a brilliant conversationalist and the dominant figure in 18th-century London literary society. His *Dictionary*, published 1755, remained authoritative for over a century, and is still remarkable for the vigour of its definitions. In 1764 he founded the Literary Club, whose members included the painter Joshua Reynolds, the political philosopher Edmund Burke, the playwright Oliver Goldsmith, the actor David Garrick, and James *Boswell, Johnson's biographer.

Johnston Atoll coral island in the mid-Pacific, lying between the *Marshall Islands and Hawaii; area 2.8 sq km. The island is only 2.4 m/8 ft above sea level and subject to hurricanes and tidal waves. It has the status of a

National Wildlife Refuge but was contaminated by fallout from nuclear-weapons testing in 1962, and has since 1971 been used as a repository for chemical weapons left over from the Korean and Vietnam wars. An unincorporated territory of the USA, it is administered by the US Defense Nuclear Agency (DNA).

John the Baptist, St *c.* 12 BC–*c.* AD 27. In the New Testament, an itinerant preacher. After preparation in the wilderness, he proclaimed the coming of the Messiah and baptized Jesus in the river Jordan. He was later executed by *Herod Antipas at the request of Salome, who demanded that his head be brought to her on a platter.

joint in any animal with a skeleton, a point of movement or articulation. In vertebrates, it is the point where two bones meet. Some joints allow no motion (the sutures of the skull), others allow a very small motion (the sacroiliac joints in the lower back), but most allow a relatively free motion. Of these, some allow a gliding motion (one vertebra of the spine on another), some have a hinge action (elbow and knee), and others allow motion in all directions (hip and shoulder joints), by means of a ball-and-socket arrangement. The ends of the bones at a moving joint are covered with cartilage for greater elasticity and smoothness, and enclosed in an envelope (capsule) of tough white fibrous tissue lined with a membrane which secretes a lubricating and cushioning *synovial fluid. The joint is further strengthened by ligaments. In invertebrates with an *exoskeleton, the joints are places where the exoskeleton is replaced by a more flexible outer covering, the arthrodial membrane, which allows the limb (or other body part) to bend at that point.

Joint European Torus experimental nuclear-fusion machine, known as *JET.

joint venture in business, an undertaking in which an individual or legal entity of one country forms a company with those of another country, with risks being shared.

Joliot-Curie Irène (born Curie) 1897–1956 and Frédéric (born Joliot) 1900–1958. French physicists who made the discovery of artificial radioactivity, for which they were jointly awarded the 1935 Nobel Prize for Chemistry.

Jonah 7th century BC. Hebrew prophet whose name is given to a book in the Old Testament. According to this, he fled by ship to evade his mission to prophesy the destruction of Nineveh. The crew threw him overboard in a storm, as a bringer of ill fortune, and he spent three days and nights in the belly of a whale before coming to land.

Jonathan Chief (Joseph) Leabua 1914–1987. Lesotho politician. A leader in the drive for independence, Jonathan became prime minister of Lesotho in 1965. His rule was ended by a coup in 1986.

Jones Inigo 1573–*c.* 1652. English classical architect. Born in London, he studied in Italy and was influenced by the works of Palladio. He was employed by James I to design scenery for Ben Jonson's masques. He designed the Queen's House, Greenwich 1616–35 and his English Renaissance masterpiece, the Banquet House in Whitehall, London, 1619–22.

Jonestown commune of the ***People's Temple Sect**, NW of Georgetown, Guyana, established 1974 by the American Jim Jones (1933–1978), who originally founded the sect among San Francisco's black community. After a visiting US congressman was shot dead, Jones enforced mass suicide on his followers by instructing them to drink cyanide; 914 died, including over 240 children.

jonquil species of small daffodil *Narcissus jonquilla*, family Amaryllidaceae, with yellow flowers. Native to Spain and Portugal, it is cultivated elsewhere.

Jonson Ben(jamin) 1572–1637. English dramatist, poet, and critic. *Every Man in his Humour* 1598 established the English 'comedy of humours', in which each character embodies a particular 'humour', or passion. This was followed by *Cynthia's Revels* 1600 and *Poetaster* 1601. His first extant tragedy is *Sejanus* 1603, with Burbage and Shakespeare as members of the original cast. The plays of his middle years include *Volpone, or The Fox* 1606, *The Alchemist* 1610, and *Bartholomew Fair* 1614.

Joplin Janis 1943–1970. US blues and rock singer, born in Texas. She was lead singer with the San Francisco group Big Brother and the Holding Company 1966–68. Her biggest hit, Kris Kristofferson's 'Me and Bobby McGee', was released on the posthumous *Pearl* LP 1971.

Joplin Scott 1868–1917. US *ragtime pianist and composer, active in Chicago. His 'Maple Leaf Rag' 1899 was the first instrumental sheet music to sell a million copies, and 'The Entertainer', as the theme tune of the film *The Sting* 1973, revived his popularity.

Jordaens Jacob 1593–1678. Flemish painter, born in Antwerp. His style follows Rubens, whom he assisted in various commissions. Much of his work is exuberant and on a large scale, including scenes of peasant life, altarpieces, portraits, and mythological subjects.

Jordan Hashemite Kingdom of (*Al Mamlaka al Urduniya al Hashemiyah*)

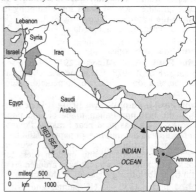

area 89,206 sq km/34,434 sq mi (West Bank 5,879 sq km/2,269 sq mi)
capital Amman
towns Zarqa, Irbid, Aqaba (the only port)

physical desert plateau in E; rift valley separates E and W banks of the river Jordan

head of state King Hussein ibn Talai from 1952

head of government Abd al-Salam al-Mujali from 1993

political system constitutional monarchy

exports potash, phosphates, citrus, vegetables

currency Jordanian dinar

population (1993 est) 4,100,000; growth rate 3.6% p.a.

languages Arabic (official), English

religions Sunni Muslim 92%, Christian 8%

GNP $1,120 per head (1991)

chronology

1946 Independence achieved from Britain as Transjordan.

1949 New state of Jordan declared.

1950 Jordan annexed West Bank.

1953 Hussein ibn Talai officially became king of Jordan.

1967 Israel captured and occupied West Bank. Martial law imposed.

1976 Lower house dissolved, political parties banned, elections postponed until further notice.

1982 Hussein tried to mediate in Arab-Israeli conflict.

1984 Women voted for the first time.

1985 Hussein and Yassir Arafat put forward framework for Middle East peace settlement. Secret meeting between Hussein and Israeli prime minister.

1988 Hussein announced decision to cease administering the West Bank as part of Jordan, passing responsibility to Palestine Liberation Organization (PLO), and the suspension of parliament.

1989 Prime Minister Zaid al-Rifai resigned; Hussein promised new parliamentary elections following criticism of economic policies. Riots over price increases of up to 50% following fall in oil revenues. First parliamentary elections for 22 years; Muslim Brotherhood won 25 of 80 seats but exiled from government; martial law lifted.

1990 Hussein unsuccessfully tried to mediate after Iraq's invasion of Kuwait. Massive refugee problems as thousands fled to Jordan from Kuwait and Iraq.

1991 24 years of martial law ended; ban on political parties lifted.

1993 King Hussein publicly distanced himself from Iraqi leader Saddam Hussein.

1994 Jan: economic cooperation pact signed with PLO. July: peace treaty signed with Israel, ending 46-year-old 'state of war'.

Joseph in the New Testament, the husband of the Virgin Mary, a descendant of King David of the Tribe of Judah, and a carpenter by trade. Although Jesus was not the son of Joseph, Joseph was his legal father. According to Roman Catholic tradition, he had a family by a previous wife, and was an elderly man when he married Mary.

Joseph in the Old Testament, the 11th and favourite son of *Jacob, sold into Egypt by his jealous half-brothers. After he had risen to power there, they and his father joined him to escape from famine in Canaan.

Joseph two Holy Roman emperors:

Joseph II 1741–1790. Holy Roman emperor from 1765, son of Francis I (1708–1765). The reforms he carried out after the death of his mother, *Maria Theresa, in 1780, provoked revolts from those who lost privileges.

Josephine Marie Josèphe Rose Tascher de la Pagerie 1763–1814. As wife of *Napoleon Bonaparte, she was empress of France 1796–1809. Born on Martinique, she married in 1779 Alexandre de Beauharnais (1760–1794), who played a part in the French Revolution, and in 1796 Napoleon, who divorced her in 1809 because she had not produced children.

Joseph of Arimathaea, St 1st century AD. In the New Testament, a wealthy Hebrew, member of the Sanhedrin (supreme court), and secret supporter of Jesus. On the evening of the Crucifixion he asked the Roman procurator Pilate for Jesus' body and buried it in his own tomb. Feast day 17 March.

Josephson Brian 1940– . British physicist, a leading authority on superconductivity. In 1973 he shared a Nobel prize for his theoretical predictions of the properties of a supercurrent through a tunnel barrier (the Josephson effect), which led to the development of the Josephson junction.

Josephson junction device used in 'superchips' (large and complex integrated circuits) to speed the passage of signals by a phenomenon called 'electron tunnelling'. Although these superchips respond a thousand times faster than the *silicon chip, they have the disadvantage that the components of the Josephson junctions operate only at temperatures close to *absolute zero. They are named after Brian Josephson.

Josephus Flavius AD 37–c. 100. Jewish historian and general, born in Jerusalem. He became a Pharisee and commanded the Jewish forces in Galilee in their revolt against Rome from AD 66 (which ended with the mass suicide at Masada). When captured, he gained the favour of the Roman emperor Vespasian and settled in Rome as a citizen. He wrote *Antiquities of the Jews*, an early history to AD 66; *The Jewish War*; and an autobiography.

Joshua 13th century BC. In the Old Testament, successor of Moses, who led the Jews in their return to and conquest of the land of Canaan. The city of Jericho was the first to fall – according to the Book of Joshua, the walls crumbled to the blast of his trumpets.

Josquin Desprez or *des Prés* 1440–1521. Franco-Flemish composer. His music combines a technical mastery with the feeling for words that became a hallmark of Renaissance vocal music. His works, which include 18 masses, over 100 motets, and secular vocal works, are characterized by their vitality and depth of feeling.

Joubert Petrus Jacobus 1831–1900. Boer general in South Africa. He opposed British annexation of the Transvaal 1877, proclaimed its independence 1880, led the Boer forces in the First *South African War against the British 1880–81, defeated *Jameson 1896, and fought in the Second South African War.

joule SI unit (symbol J) of work and energy, replacing the *calorie (one joule equals 4.2 calories).

Joule James Prescott 1818–1889. English physicist whose work on the relations between electrical, mechanical, and chemical effects led to the discovery of the first law of *thermodynamics.

Joule–Kelvin effect in physics, the fall in temperature of a gas as it expands adiabatically (without loss or gain of heat to the system) through a narrow jet. It can be felt when, for example, compressed air escapes through the valve of an inflated bicycle tyre. Only hydrogen does not exhibit the effect. It is the basic principle of most refrigerators.

journeyman in Britain, a man who served his apprenticeship in a trade and worked as a fully qualified employee. The term originated in the regulations of the medieval trade *guilds; it derives from the French *journée* ('a day') because journeymen were paid daily.

Joyce James (Augustine Aloysius) 1882–1941. Irish writer, born in Dublin, who revolutionized the form of the English novel with his 'stream of consciousness' technique. His works include *Dubliners* 1914 (short stories), *Portrait of the Artist as a Young Man* 1916, *Ulysses* 1922, and *Finnegans Wake* 1939.

joystick in computing, an input device that signals to a computer the direction and extent of displacement of a hand-held lever. It is similar to the joystick used to control the flight of an aircraft.

JP abbreviation for *justice of the peace*.

Juan Carlos 1938– . King of Spain. The son of Don Juan, pretender to the Spanish throne, he married Princess Sofia in 1962, eldest daughter of King Paul of Greece. In 1969 he was nominated by *Franco to succeed on the restoration of the monarchy intended to follow Franco's death; his father was excluded because of his known liberal views. Juan Carlos became king in 1975.

Juárez Benito 1806–1872. Mexican politician, president 1861–65 and 1867–72. In 1861 he suspended repayments of Mexico's foreign debts, which prompted a joint French, British, and Spanish expedition to exert pressure. French forces invaded and created an empire for *Maximilian, brother of the Austrian emperor. After their withdrawal in 1867, Maximilian was executed, and Juárez returned to the presidency.

Judaea or *Judea*) southern division of ancient Palestine, see *Judah.

Judah or *Judaea* or *Judea* district of S Palestine. After the death of King Solomon 937 BC, Judah adhered to his son Rehoboam and the Davidic line, whereas the rest of Israel elected Jeroboam as ruler of the northern kingdom. In New Testament times, Judah was the Roman province of Judaea, and in current Israeli usage it refers to the southern area of the West Bank.

Judaism the religion of the ancient Hebrews and their descendants the Jews, based, according to the Old Testament, on a covenant between God and Abraham about 2000 BC, and the renewal of the covenant with Moses about 1200 BC. It rests on the concept of one eternal invisible God, whose will is revealed in the *Torah* and who has a special relationship with the Jewish people. The Torah comprises the first five books of the Bible (the Pentateuch), which contains the history, laws, and guide to life for correct behaviour. Besides those living in Israel, there are large Jewish populations today in the USA, the former USSR (mostly Russia, Ukraine, Belarus, and Moldova), the UK and Commonwealth nations, and in Jewish communities throughout the world. There are approximately 18 million Jews, with about 9 million in the Americas, 5 million in Europe, and 4 million in Asia, Africa, and the Pacific.

Judas Iscariot 1st century AD. In the New Testament, the disciple who betrayed Jesus Christ. Judas was the treasurer of the group. At the last Passover supper, he arranged, for 30 pieces of silver, to point out Jesus to the chief priests so that they could arrest him. Afterwards Judas was overcome with remorse and committed suicide.

Jude, St 1st century AD. Supposed half-brother of Jesus and writer of the Epistle of Jude in the New Testament; patron saint of lost causes. Feast day 28 Oct.

judicial review in English law, action in the High Court to review the decisions of lower courts, tribunals, and administrative bodies. Various court orders can be made: *certiorari* (which quashes the decision); *mandamus* (which commands a duty to be performed); *prohibition* (which commands that an action should not be performed because it is unauthorized); a *declaration* (which sets out the legal rights or obligations); or an *injunction*.

judicial separation action in a court by either husband or wife, in which it is not necessary to prove an irreconcilable breakdown of a marriage, but in which the grounds are otherwise the same as for divorce. It does not end a marriage, but a declaration may be obtained that the complainant need no longer cohabit with the defendant. The court can make similar orders to a divorce court in relation to custody and support of children and maintenance.

judiciary in constitutional terms, the system of courts and body of judges in a country. The independence of the judiciary from other branches of the central authority is generally considered to be an essential feature of a democratic political system. This independence is often written into a nation's constitution and protected from abuse by politicians.

Judith in Biblical legend, a Jewish widow, the heroine of Bethulia, who saved her community from a Babylonian siege by killing the enemy general Holofernes. The Book of Judith is part of the Apocrypha, a section of the Old Testament.

judo (Japanese *jū do*, 'gentle way') form of wrestling of Japanese origin. The two combatants wear loose-fitting, belted jackets and trousers to facilitate holds, and falls are broken by a square mat; when one has established a painful hold that the other cannot break, the latter signifies surrender by slapping the ground with a free hand. Degrees of proficiency are indicated by the colour of the belt: for novices, white; after examination, brown (three degrees); and finally, black (nine degrees).

Juggernaut or *Jagannath* a name for Vishnu, the Hindu god, meaning 'Lord of the World'. His temple is in Puri, Orissa, India. A statue of the god, dating from about 318, is annually carried in procession on a large vehicle (hence the word 'juggernaut'). Devotees formerly threw themselves beneath its wheels.

Jugoslavia alternative spelling of *Yugoslavia.

jugular vein one of two veins in the necks of vertebrates; they return blood from the head to the superior (or anterior) vena cava and thence to the heart.

jujitsu or **jujutsu** traditional Japanese form of self-defence; the modern form is *judo.

jujube tree of the genus *Zizyphus* of the buckthorn family Thamnaceae, with berrylike fruits.

Julian the Apostate c. 331–363. Roman emperor. Born in Constantinople, the nephew of Constantine the Great, he was brought up as a Christian but early in life became a convert to paganism. Sent by Constantius to govern Gaul in 355, he was proclaimed emperor by his troops in 360, and in 361 was marching on Constantinople when Constantius' death allowed a peaceful succession. He revived pagan worship and refused to persecute heretics. He was killed in battle against the Persians.

Juliana 1909– . Queen of the Netherlands 1948–80. The daughter of Queen Wilhelmina (1880–1962), she married Prince Bernhard of Lippe-Biesterfeld in 1937. She abdicated 1980 and was succeeded by her daughter *Beatrix.

Julius II 1443–1513. Pope 1503–13. A politician who wanted to make the Papal States the leading power in Italy, he formed international alliances first against Venice and then against France. He began the building of St Peter's Church in Rome 1506 and was the patron of the artists Michelangelo and Raphael.

July Revolution revolution 27–29 July 1830 in France that overthrew the restored Bourbon monarchy of Charles X and substituted the constitutional monarchy of Louis Philippe, whose rule (1830–48) is sometimes referred to as the July Monarchy.

jumbo jet popular name for a generation of huge wide-bodied airliners including the *Boeing 747*, which is 71 m/232 ft long, has a wingspan of 60 m/196 ft, a maximum takeoff weight of nearly 380 tonnes/400 tons, and can carry more than 400 passengers.

Jung Carl Gustav 1875–1961. Swiss psychiatrist who collaborated with Sigmund *Freud until their disagreement in 1912 over the importance of sexuality in causing psychological problems. Jung studied religion and dream symbolism, saw the unconscious as a source of spiritual insight, and distinguished between introversion and extroversion. His books include *Modern Man in Search of a Soul* 1933.

jungle popular name for *rainforest.

juniper aromatic evergreen tree or shrub of the genus *Juniperus* of the cypress family Cupressaceae, found throughout temperate regions. Its berries are used to flavour gin. Some junipers are erroneously called *cedars.

junk bond derogatory term for a security officially rated as 'below investment grade'. It is issued in order to raise capital quickly, typically to finance a takeover to be paid for by the sale of assets once the company is acquired. Junk bonds have a high yield, but are a high-risk investment.

Junkers Hugo 1859–1935. German aeroplane designer. In 1919 he founded in Dessau the aircraft works named after him. Junkers planes, including dive bombers, night fighters, and troop carriers, were used by the Germans in World War II.

Juno principal goddess in Roman mythology (identified with the Greek Hera). The wife of Jupiter, the queen of heaven, she was concerned with all aspects of women's lives.

junta (Spanish 'council') the military rulers of a country after an army takeover, as in Turkey in 1980.

Jupiter or **Jove** in mythology, chief god of the Romans, identified with the Greek *Zeus. He was god of the sky, associated with lightning and thunderbolts; protector in battle; and bestower of victory. The son of Saturn, he married his sister Juno, and reigned on Mount Olympus as lord of heaven.

Jupiter the fifth planet from the Sun, and the largest in the Solar System (equatorial diameter 142,800 km/88,700 mi), with a mass more than twice that of all the other planets combined, 318 times that of the Earth's. It takes 11.86 years to orbit the Sun, at an average distance of 778 million km/484 million mi, and has at least 16 moons. It is largely composed of hydrogen and helium, liquefied by pressure in its interior, and probably with a rocky core larger than the Earth. Its main feature is the Great Red Spot, a cloud of rising gases, revolving anticlockwise, 14,000 km/8,500 mi wide and some 30,000 km/20,000 mi long.

Jura mountains series of parallel mountain ranges running SW–NE along the French-Swiss frontier between the rivers Rhône and Rhine, a distance of 250 km/156 mi. The highest peak is *Crête de la Neige*, 1,723 m/5,650 ft.

Jurassic period of geological time 213–144 million years ago; the middle period of the Mesozoic era. Climates worldwide were equable, creating forests of conifers and ferns, dinosaurs were abundant, birds evolved, and limestones and iron ores were deposited.

jurisprudence the science of law in the abstract – that is, not the study of any particular laws or legal system, but of the principles upon which legal systems are founded.

jury body of lay people (usually 12) sworn to decide the facts of a case and reach a verdict in a court of law. Juries, used mainly in English-speaking countries, are implemented primarily in criminal cases, but also sometimes in civil cases; for example, inquests and libel trials.

justice of the peace (JP) in England, an unpaid *magistrate. In the USA, where JPs receive fees and are usually elected, their courts are the lowest in the states, and deal only with minor offences, such as traffic violations; they may also conduct marriages.

justiciar the chief justice minister of Norman and early Angevin kings, second in power only to the king. By 1265, the government had been divided into various departments, such as the Exchequer and Chancery, which meant that it was no longer desirable to have one official in charge of all.

Justinian I 483–565. Byzantine emperor from 527. He recovered N Africa from the Vandals, SE Spain from the Visigoths, and Italy from the

Ostrogoths, largely owing to his great general Belisarius. He ordered the codification of Roman law, which has influenced European jurisprudence.

Justin, St c. 100–c. 163. One of the early Christian leaders and writers known as the Fathers of the Church. Born in Palestine of a Greek family, he was converted to Christianity and wrote two *Apologies* in its defence. He spent the rest of his life as an itinerant missionary, and was martyred in Rome. Feast day 1 June.

Jute member of a Germanic people who originated in Jutland but later settled in Frankish territory. They occupied Kent, SE England, about 450, according to tradition under Hengist and Horsa, and conquered the Isle of Wight and the opposite coast of Hampshire in the early 6th century.

jute fibre obtained from two plants of the genus *Corchorus* of the linden family: *C. capsularis* and *C. olitorius*. Jute is used for sacks and sacking, upholstery, webbing, twine, and stage canvas.

Jutland (Danish *Jylland*) peninsula of N Europe; area 29,500 sq km/11,400 sq mi. It is separated from Norway by the Skagerrak and from Sweden by the Kattegat, with the North Sea to the west. The larger northern part belongs to Denmark, the southern part to Germany.

Jutland, Battle of naval battle of World War I, fought between England and Germany on 31 May 1916, off the W coast of Jutland. Its outcome was indecisive, but the German fleet remained in port for the rest of the war.

Juvenal c. AD 60–140. Roman satirist and poet. His genius for satire brought him to the unfavourable notice of the emperor Domitian. Juvenal's 16 extant satires give an explicit and sometimes brutal picture of the decadent Roman society of his time.

juvenile delinquency offences against the law that are committed by young people.

K symbol for *kelvin*, a scale of temperature.

K abbreviation for *thousand*, as in a salary of £10K.

k symbol for *kilo-*, as in kg (kilogram) and km (kilometre).

K2 or *Chogori* second highest mountain above sea level, 8,611 m/28,261 ft, in the Karakoram range, Kashmir, N India. It was first climbed 1954 by an Italian expedition.

Kaaba (Arabic 'chamber') in Mecca, Saudi Arabia, the oblong building in the quadrangle of the Great Mosque, into the NE corner of which is built the Black Stone declared by the prophet Muhammad to have been given to Abraham by the archangel Gabriel, and revered by Muslims.

kabbala or *cabbala* (Hebrew 'tradition') ancient esoteric Jewish mystical tradition of philosophy containing strong elements of pantheism yet akin to neo-Platonism. Kabbalistic writing reached its peak between the 13th and 16th centuries. It is largely rejected by current Judaic thought as medieval superstition, but is basic to the *Hasid sect.

Kabinda part of Angola. See *Cabinda.

kabuki (Japanese 'music, dance, skill') drama originating in late 16th-century Japan, drawing on *Nō, puppet plays, and folk dance. Its colourful, lively spectacle became popular in the 17th and 18th centuries. Many kabuki actors specialize in particular types of character, female impersonators (*onnagata*) being the biggest stars.

Kabul capital of Afghanistan, 2,100 m/6,900 ft above sea level, on the river Kabul; population (1984) 1,179,300. Products include textiles, plastics, leather, and glass. It commands the strategic routes to Pakistan via the *Khyber Pass.

Kádár János 1912–1989. Hungarian Communist leader, in power 1956–88, after suppressing the national uprising. As Hungarian Socialist Workers' Party (HSWP) leader and prime minister 1956–58 and 1961–65, Kádár introduced a series of market-socialist economic reforms, while retaining cordial political relations with the USSR.

Kafka Franz 1883–1924. Czech novelist, born in Prague, who wrote in German. His three unfinished allegorical novels *Der Prozess/The Trial* 1925, *Der Schloss/The Castle* 1926, and *Amerika/America* 1927 were posthumously published despite his instructions that they should be destroyed. His short stories include 'Die Verwandlung/The Metamorphosis' 1915, in which a man turns into a huge insect. His vision of lonely individuals trapped in bureaucratic or legal labyrinths can be seen as a powerful metaphor for modern experience.

Kahn Louis 1901–1974. US architect, born in Estonia. A follower of Mies van der Rohe, he developed a classically romantic style, in which functional 'servant' areas, such as stairwells and air ducts, featured prominently, often as towerlike structures surrounding the main living and working, or 'served', areas. His projects are characterized by an imaginative use of concrete and brick and include the Salk Institute for Biological Studies, La Jolla, California, and the British Art Center at Yale University.

Kaiser title formerly used by the Holy Roman emperors, Austrian emperors 1806–1918, and German emperors 1871–1918. The word, like the Russian 'tsar', is derived from the Latin *Caesar*.

kakapo nocturnal, flightless parrot *Strigops habroptilus* that lives in burrows in New Zealand. It is green, yellow, and brown and weighs up to 3.5 kg/7.5 lb. When in danger, its main defence is to keep quite still. Because of the introduction of predators such as dogs, cats, rats, and ferrets, it is in danger of extinction, there being only about 40 birds left.

Kalahari Desert semi-desert area forming most of Botswana and extending into Namibia, Zimbabwe, and South Africa; area about 900,000 sq km/347,400 sq mi. The only permanent river, the Okavango, flows into a delta in the NW forming marshes rich in wildlife. Its inhabitants are the nomadic Kung.

kale type of *cabbage.

Kalevala Finnish national epic poem compiled from legends and ballads by Elias Lönnrot 1835; its hero is Väinämöinen, god of music and poetry.

Kalgan city in NE China, now known as *Zhangjiakou.

Kali in Hindu mythology, the goddess of destruction and death. She is the wife of *Siva.

Kalimantan province of the republic of Indonesia occupying part of the island of Borneo
area 543,900 sq km/210,000 sq mi
towns Banjermasin and Balikpapan
physical mostly low-lying, with mountains in the north
products petroleum, rubber, coffee, copra, pepper, timber
population (1989 est) 8,677,500.

Kali-Yuga in Hinduism, the last of the four *yugas* (ages) that make up one cycle of creation. The Kali-Yuga, in which Hindus believe we are now living, is characterized by wickedness and disaster, and leads up to the destruction of this world in preparation for a new creation and a new cycle of yugas.

Kalki in Hinduism, the last avatar (manifestation) of Vishnu, who will appear at the end of the Kali-Yuga, or final age of the world, to destroy it in readiness for a new creation.

Kaltenbrunner Ernst 1901–1946. Austrian Nazi leader. After the annexation of Austria 1938 he joined police chief Himmler's staff, and as head of the Security Police (SD) from 1943 was responsible for the murder of millions of Jews (see the *Holocaust) and Allied soldiers in World

War II. After the war, he was tried at Nuremberg for war crimes and hanged.

Kamchatka mountainous peninsula separating the Bering Sea and Sea of Okhotsk, forming (together with the Chukchi and Koryak national districts) a region of E Siberian Russia. Its capital, Petropavlovsk, is the only town; agriculture is possible only in the south. Most of the inhabitants are fishers and hunters.

Kamenev Lev Borisovich 1883–1936. Russian leader of the Bolshevik movement after 1917 who, with Stalin and Zinoviev, formed a ruling triumvirate in the USSR after Lenin's death 1924. His alignment with the Trotskyists led to his dismissal from office and from the Communist Party by Stalin 1926. Arrested 1934 after Kirov's assassination, Kamenev was secretly tried and sentenced, then retried, condemned, and shot 1936 for plotting to murder Stalin.

Kamerlingh-Onnes Heike 1853–1926. Dutch physicist who worked mainly in the field of low-temperature physics. In 1911, he discovered the phenomenon of *superconductivity (enhanced electrical conductivity at very low temperatures), for which he was awarded the 1913 Nobel Prize for Physics.

kamikaze (Japanese 'wind of the gods') pilots of the Japanese air force in World War II who deliberately crash-dived their planes, loaded with bombs, usually onto ships of the US Navy.

Kampala capital of Uganda; population (1983) 455,000. It is linked by rail with Mombasa. Products include tea, coffee, textiles, fruit, and vegetables.

Kampuchea former name (1975–89) of *Cambodia.

Kanchenjunga variant spelling of *Kangchenjunga, a Himalayan mountain.

Kandinsky Wassily 1866–1944. Russian painter, a pioneer of abstract art. Born in Moscow, he travelled widely, settling in Munich 1896. Around 1910 he produced the first known examples of purely abstract work in 20th-century art. He was an originator of the *Blaue Reiter* movement 1911–12. From 1921 he taught at the *Bauhaus school of design. He moved to Paris 1933, becoming a French citizen 1939.

Kandy city in central Sri Lanka, former capital of the kingdom of Kandy 1480–1815; population (1990) 104,000. Products include tea. One of the most sacred Buddhist shrines is situated in Kandy.

kangaroo any marsupial of the family Macropodidae found in Australia, Tasmania, and New Guinea. Kangaroos are plant-eaters and most live in groups. They are adapted to hopping, the vast majority of species having very large back legs and feet compared with the small forelimbs. The larger types can jump 9 m/30 ft at a single bound. Most are nocturnal. Species vary from small rat kangaroos, only 30 cm/1 ft long, through the medium-sized wallabies, to the large red and great grey kangaroos, which are the largest living marsupials. These may be 1.8 m/5.9 ft long with 1.1 m/3.5 ft tails.

kangaroo paw bulbous plant *Anigozanthos manglesii*, family Hameodoraceae, with a row of small white flowers emerging from velvety green

kangaroo *The giant grey kangaroo may reach a weight of 90 kg/200 lb and a height of over 1.5 m/5 ft.*

tubes with red bases. It is the floral emblem of Western Australia.

Kangchenjunga Himalayan mountain on the Nepal–Sikkim border, 8,586 m/28,170 ft high, 120 km/75 mi SE of Mount Everest. The name means 'five treasure houses of the great snows'. Kangchenjunga was first climbed by a British expedition 1955.

Ka Ngwane black homeland in Natal province, South Africa; achieved self-governing status 1971; population (1985) 392,800.

Kano capital of Kano state in N Nigeria, trade centre of an irrigated area; population (1983) 487,100. Products include bicycles, glass, furniture, textiles, and chemicals. Founded about 1000 BC, Kano is a walled city, with New Kano extending beyond the walls.

Kanpur formerly *Cawnpore* capital of Kanpur district, Uttar Pradesh, India, SW of Lucknow, on the river Ganges; a commercial and industrial centre (cotton, wool, jute, chemicals, plastics, iron, steel); population (1981) 1,688,000.

Kansas state in central USA; nickname Sunflower State
area 213,200 sq km/82,296 sq mi
capital Topeka
towns Kansas City, Wichita, Overland Park
products wheat, cattle, coal, petroleum, natural gas, aircraft, minerals
population (1990) 2,477,600
famous people Amelia Earhart; Dwight D Eisenhower; William Inge; Buster Keaton; Carry Nation; Charlie Parker
history explored by Francisco de Coronado for Spain 1541 and La Salle for France 1682; ceded to the USA 1803 as part of the Louisiana Purchase.

Kansas City twin city in the USA at the confluence of the Missouri and Kansas rivers, partly in Kansas and partly in Missouri; population (1990) of Kansas City (Kansas) 149,800, Kansas City (Missouri) 435,100. A market and agricultural distribution centre and one of the chief livestock centres of the USA. Kansas City, Missouri, has car-assembly plants and Kansas City, Kansas, has the majority of offices.

Kansu alternative spelling for the Chinese province *Gansu.

Kant Immanuel 1724–1804. German philosopher who believed that knowledge is not merely an aggregate of sense impressions but is dependent on the conceptual apparatus of the human understanding, which is itself not derived from experience. In ethics, Kant argued that right action cannot be based on feelings or inclinations but conforms to a law given by reason, the *categorical imperative*.

kaolinite white or greyish *clay mineral, hydrated aluminium silicate, $Al_2Si_2O_5(OH)_4$, formed mainly by the decomposition of feldspar in granite. China clay (kaolin) is derived from it. It is mined in France, the UK, Germany, China, and the USA.

Kapital, Das three-volume work presenting the theories of Karl *Marx on economic production, published 1867–95. It focuses on the exploitation of the worker and calls for a classless society where the production process and its rewards are shared equally.

kapok silky hairs that surround the seeds of certain trees, particularly the **kapok tree** *Bombax ceiba* of India and Malaysia, and the **silk-cotton tree** *Ceiba pentandra*, a native of tropical America. Kapok is used for stuffing cushions and mattresses and for sound insulation; oil obtained from the seeds is used in food and soap preparation.

Karachi largest city and chief seaport of Pakistan, and capital of Sind province, NW of the Indus delta; population (1981) 5,208,000. Industries include engineering, chemicals, plastics, and textiles. It was the capital of Pakistan 1947–59.

Karadzić Radovan 1945– . Montenegrin-born leader of the Bosnian Serbs from 1992. He cofounded the Serbian Democratic Party of Bosnia-Herzegovina (SDS-BH) 1990. He launched the siege of Sarajevo 1992, which escalated swiftly into a brutal civil war. Although the siege was lifted early 1994, his forces continued to shell other strategic cities in Bosnia. Distrusted in the West and viewed as an intransigent figure, for many Bosnian Serbs he is a moderate.

Karajan Herbert von 1908–1989. Austrian conductor. He dominated European classical music performance after 1947. He was principal conductor of the Berlin Philharmonic Orchestra 1955–89, artistic director of the Vienna State Opera 1957–64, and of the Salzburg Festival 1956–60. He cultivated an orchestral sound of notable smoothness and transparency.

Karakoram mountain range in central Asia, divided among China, Pakistan, and India. Peaks include K2, Masharbrum, Gasharbrum, and Mustagh Tower.

Karamanlis Constantinos 1907– . Greek politician of the New Democracy Party. A lawyer and an anticommunist, he was prime minister 1955–1958, 1958–1961, and 1961–1963 (when he went into self-imposed exile because of a military coup). He was recalled as prime minister on the fall of the regime of the 'colonels' in July 1974, and was president 1980–85.

karaoke amateur singing in public to pre-recorded backing tapes. Karaoke originated in Japan and spread to other parts of the world in the 1980s. Karaoke machines are jukeboxes of backing tracks to well-known popular songs, usually with a microphone attached and accompanying lyrics and video graphics displayed on a screen.

karate one of the *martial arts. Karate is a type of unarmed combat derived from *kempo*, a form of the Chinese Shaolin boxing. It became popular in the West in the 1930s.

Karelia autonomous republic of NW Russia
area 172,400 sq km/66,550 sq mi
capital Petrozavodsk
cities Vyborg
physical mainly forested
products fishing, timber, chemicals, coal
population (1989) 792,000
history Karelia was annexed to Russia by Peter the Great 1721 as part of the grand duchy of Finland. In 1917 part of Karelia was retained by Finland when it gained its independence from Russia. The remainder became an autonomous region 1920 and an autonomous republic 1923 of the USSR. Following the wars of 1939–40 and 1941–44, Finland ceded 46,000 sq km/18,000 sq mi of Karelia to the USSR. Part of this territory was incorporated in the Russian Soviet Republic and part in the Karelian autonomous republic. A movement for the reunification of Russian and Finnish Karelia emerged in the late 1980s.

Karen member of a group of SE Asian peoples, numbering 5.1 million. They live in E Myanmar (formerly Burma), Thailand, and the Irrawaddy delta. Their language belongs to the Thai division of the Sino-Tibetan family. In 1984 the Burmese government began a large-scale military campaign against the Karen National Liberation Army (KNLA), the armed wing of the Karen National Union (KNU).

Kariba Dam concrete dam on the Zambezi River, on the Zambia–Zimbabwe border, about 386 km/240 mi downstream from the Victoria Falls, constructed 1955–60 to supply power to both countries. The dam crosses Kariba Gorge, and the reservoir, Lake Kariba, has important fisheries.

Karloff Boris. Stage name of William Henry Pratt 1887–1969. English-born US actor. He is best known for his work in the USA. He achieved Hollywood stardom with his role as the monster in the film *Frankenstein* 1931.

karma (Sanskrit 'fate') in Hinduism, the sum of a human being's actions, carried forward from one life to the next, resulting in an improved or worsened fate. Buddhism has a similar belief, except that no permanent personality is envisaged, the karma relating only to the physical and mental elements carried on from birth to birth, until the power holding them together disperses in the attainment of nirvana.

Karmal Babrak 1929– . Afghani communist politician, president 1979–86. In 1965 he formed what became the banned People's Democratic Party of Afghanistan (PDPA) 1977. As president, with Soviet backing, he sought to broaden the appeal of the PDPA but encountered wide resistance from the *Mujaheddin Muslim guerrillas.

Karnak village of modern Egypt, on the east bank of the river Nile, that gives its name to the temple of Ammon (constructed by Seti I and Ramses I) around which the major part of the ancient city of *Thebes was built. An avenue of rams leads to *Luxor.

Karnataka formerly (until 1973) *Mysore* state in SW India
area 191,800 sq km/74,035 sq mi
capital Bangalore
products mainly agricultural; minerals include manganese, chromite, and India's only sources of gold and silver
population (1991) 44,817,400
language Kannada
famous people Hyder Ali, Tippu Sultan.

Karpov Anatoly 1951–   . Russian chess player. He succeeded Bobby Fischer of the USA as world champion 1975, and held the title until losing to Gary Kasparov 1985.

karst landscape characterized by remarkable surface and underground forms, created as a result of the action of water on permeable limestone. The feature takes its name from the Karst region on the Adriatic coast in Slovenia and Croatia, but the name is applied to landscapes throughout the world, the most dramatic of which is found near the city of Guilin in the Guangxi province of China.

karyotype in biology, the set of *chromosomes characteristic of a given species. It is described as the number, shape, and size of the chromosomes in a single cell of an organism. In humans for example, the karyotype consists of 46 chromosomes, in mice 40, crayfish 200, and in fruit flies 8.

Kashmir former part of Jammu state in the north of British India with a largely Muslim population, ruled by a Hindu maharajah, who joined it to the republic of India 1947. There was fighting between pro-India and pro-Pakistan factions, the former being the Hindu ruling class and the latter the Muslim majority, and open war between the two countries 1965–66 and 1971. It is today divided between the Pakistani area of Kashmir and the Indian state of *Jammu and Kashmir.

Kashmir Pakistan-occupied area, 30,445 sq mi/78,900 sq km, in the northwest of the former state of Kashmir, now *Jammu and Kashmir. Azad ('free') Kashmir in the west has its own legislative assembly based in Muzaffarabad while Gilgit and Baltistan regions to the north and east are governed directly by Pakistan. The *Northern Areas are claimed by India and Pakistan
population 1,500,000
towns Gilgit, Skardu

Kasparov Gary 1963–   . Russian chess player. When he beat his compatriot Anatoly Karpov to win the world title 1985, he was the youngest ever champion at 22 years 210 days.

Katmandu or *Kathmandu* capital of Nepal; population (1981) 235,000. Founded in the 8th century on an ancient pilgrim and trade route from India to Tibet and China, it has a royal palace, Buddhist temples, and monasteries.

Katowice industrial city (anthracite, iron and coal mining, iron foundries, smelting works, machine shops) in Upper Silesia, S Poland; population (1990) 366,800.

Katyn Forest forest near Smolensk, SW of Moscow, Russia, where 4,500 Polish officer prisoners of war (captured in the German-Soviet partition of Poland 1940) were shot; 10,000 others were killed elsewhere. In 1989 the USSR accepted responsibility for the massacre.

Kaunda Kenneth (David) 1924–   . Zambian politician, president 1964–91. Imprisoned in 1958–60 as founder of the Zambia African National Congress, he became in 1964 the first prime minister of Northern Rhodesia, then the first president of independent Zambia. He was elected chair of the Organization of African Unity 1987. In 1990 wide anti-government demonstrations forced him to accept a multiparty political system and, in Nov 1991, electoral defeat to Frederick Chiluba.

kauri pine New Zealand timber conifer *Agathis australis*, family Araucariaceae. Its fossilized gum deposits are valued in varnishes; the wood is used for carving and handicrafts.

Kawabata Yasunari 1899–1972. Japanese novelist, translator of Lady *Murasaki, and author of *Snow Country* 1947 and *A Thousand Cranes* 1952. His novels are characterized by melancholy and loneliness. He was the first Japanese to win the Nobel Prize for Literature, in 1968.

Kawasaki industrial city (iron, steel, shipbuilding, chemicals, textiles) on Honshu island, Japan; population (1989) 1,128,000.

Kay John 1704–*c*. 1764. British inventor who developed the flying shuttle, a machine to speed up the work of hand-loom weaving. In 1733 he patented his invention but was ruined by the litigation necessary for its defence.

Kaye Danny. Stage name of David Daniel Kaminski 1913–1987. US actor, comedian, and singer. He appeared in many films, including *Wonder Man* 1944, *The Secret Life of Walter Mitty* 1946, and *Hans Christian Andersen* 1952.

Kayseri (ancient name *Caesarea Mazaca*) capital of Kayseri province, central Turkey; population (1990) 421,400. It produces textiles, carpets, and tiles. In Roman times it was capital of the province of Cappadocia.

Kazakh or *Kazak* member of a pastoral Kyrgyz people of Kazakhstan. Kazakhs also live in China (Xinjiang, Gansu, and Qinghai), Mongolia, and Afghanistan. There are 5–7 million speakers of Kazakh, a Turkic language belonging to the Altaic family. They are predominantly Sunni Muslim, although pre-Islamic customs have survived.

Kazakhstan Republic of
area 2,717,300 sq km/1,049,150 sq mi
capital Alma-Ata
towns Karaganda, Semipalatinsk, Petropavlovsk
physical Caspian and Aral seas, Lake Balkhash; Steppe region
head of state Nursultan Nazarbayev from 1990
head of government Akezhan Kazhegeldin from 1994
political system emergent democracy
products grain, copper, lead, zinc, manganese, coal, oil
currency tenge
population (1993 est) 17,200,000 (Kazakh 40%, Russian 38%, German 6%, Ukrainian 5%)
language Russian; Kazakh, related to Turkish
religion Sunni Muslim
GNP $2,470 per head (1991)

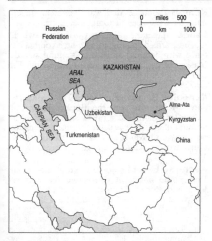

chronology

1920 Autonomous republic in USSR.

1936 Joined the USSR and became a full union republic.

1960s A large influx of Russian settlers turned the Kazakhs into a minority in their own republic.

1986 Riots in Alma-Alta after Gorbachev ousted local communist leader.

1989 Nursultan Nazarbayev became leader of the Kazakh Communist Party (KCP) and instituted economic and cultural reform programmes.

1990 Nazarbayev became head of state.

1991 Support pledged for continued union with USSR. Nazarbayev condemned attempted anti-Gorbachev coup; KCP abolished and replaced by Independent Socialist Party of Kazakhstan. Joined new Commonwealth of Independent States; independence recognized by USA.

1992 Admitted into United Nations. Trade agreement with USA.

1993 New constitution increased authority of the president and made Kazakh the state language. Offer to dismantle nuclear arsenal in exchange for US aid.

1994 Agreement to form single economic zone with Uzbekistan. First parliamentary elections won by Nazarbayev's supporters, but without working majority.

Kazan capital of Tatarstan, central Russia, on the river Volga; population (1989) 1,094,000. It is a transport, commercial, and industrial centre (engineering, oil refining, petrochemicals, textiles, large fur trade). Formerly capital of a Tatar khanate, Kazan was captured by Ivan IV 'the Terrible' 1552.

Kazan Elia 1909– . US stage and film director, a founder of the *Actors Studio 1947. Plays he directed include *The Skin of Our Teeth* 1942, *A Streetcar Named Desire* 1947, and *Cat on a Hot Tin Roof* 1955; films include *Gentlemen's Agreement* 1948, *East of Eden* 1954, and *The Visitors* 1972.

Kazantzakis Nikos 1885–1957. Greek writer whose works include the poem *I Odysseia/The Odyssey* 1938 (which continues Homer's *Odyssey*), and the novels *Zorba the Greek* 1946,

The Greek Passion, and *The Last Temptation of Christ*, both 1951.

kazoo simple wind instrument adding a buzzing quality to the singing voice on the principle of 'comb and paper' music.

KBE abbreviation for *Knight (Commander of the Order) of the British Empire*.

kcal symbol for *kilocalorie* (see *calorie).

Kean Edmund 1787–1833. British tragic actor, noted for his portrayal of villainy in the Shakespearean roles of Shylock, Richard III, and Iago.

Keating Paul 1954– . Australian politician, Labor Party (ALP) leader and prime minister from 1991. He was treasurer and deputy leader of the ALP 1983–91, and also held several posts in Labor's shadow ministry 1976–83.

Keaton Buster (Joseph Frank) 1896–1966. US comedian, actor, and film director. After being a star in vaudeville, he took up a career in 'Fatty' Arbuckle comedies, and became one of the great comedians of the silent film era, with an inimitable deadpan expression (the 'Great Stone Face') masking a sophisticated acting ability. His films include *One Week* 1920, *The Navigator* 1924, *The General* 1927, and *The Cameraman* 1928.

Keats John 1795–1821. English Romantic poet who produced work of the highest quality and promise before dying at the age of 25. *Poems* 1817, *Endymion* 1818, the great odes (particularly 'Ode to a Nightingale' and 'Ode on a Grecian Urn' 1819), and the narratives 'Lamia', 'Isabella', and 'The Eve of St Agnes' 1820, show his lyrical richness and talent for drawing on both classical mythology and medieval lore.

Keïta Salif 1949– . Malian singer and songwriter whose combination of traditional rhythms and vocals with electronic instruments made him popular in the West in the 1980s; in Mali he worked 1973–83 with the band Les Ambassadeurs and became a star throughout W Africa, moving to France 1984. His albums include *Soro* 1987 and *Amen* 1991.

Kekulé von Stradonitz Friedrich August 1829–1896. German chemist whose theory 1858 of molecular structure revolutionized organic chemistry. He proposed two resonant forms of the *benzene ring.

kelim oriental carpet or rug that is flat, pileless, and reversible. Kelims are made by a tapestry-weave technique. Weft thread of one colour is worked to and fro in one area of the pattern; the next colour continues the pattern from the adjacent warp thread, so that no weft thread runs across the full width of the carpet.

Kellogg–Briand pact agreement negotiated 1927 between the USA and France to renounce war and seek settlement of disputes by peaceful means. It took its name from the US secretary of state Frank B Kellogg (1856–1937) and the French foreign minister Aristide Briand. Most other nations subsequently signed. Some successes were achieved in settling South American disputes, but the pact made no provision for measures against aggressors and became ineffective in the 1930s, with Japan in Manchuria, Italy in Ethiopia, and Hitler in central Europe.

Kells, Book of 8th-century illuminated manuscript of the Gospels produced at the monastery of Kells in County Meath, Ireland. It is now in Trinity College library, Dublin.

Kelly Gene (Eugene Curran) 1912– . US film actor, dancer, choreographer, and director. He was a major star of the 1940s and 1950s in a series of MGM musicals, including *On the Town* 1949, *An American in Paris* 1951, and *Singin' in the Rain* 1952.

Kelly Grace (Patricia) 1928–1982. US film actress who retired from acting after marrying Prince Rainier III of Monaco 1956. She starred in *High Noon* 1952, *The Country Girl* 1954, for which she received an Academy Award, and *High Society* 1955. She also starred in three Hitchcock classics – *Dial M for Murder* 1954, *Rear Window* 1954, and *To Catch a Thief* 1955.

Kelly Ned (Edward) 1855–1880. Australian *bushranger. The son of an Irish convict, he wounded a police officer in 1878 while resisting the arrest of his brother Daniel for horse-stealing. The two brothers escaped and carried out bank robberies. Kelly wore a distinctive home-made armour. In 1880 he was captured and hanged.

Kelly Petra 1947–1992. German political activist. She was a vigourous campaigner against nuclear power and on other environmental and anti-military issues before becoming a leading member of the German Green Party. A member of Parliament 1983–1990, she then fell out with the Greens over her assertive leadership style. She also actively embraced the Tibetan nationalist cause. She was shot by her partner, the former general Gert Bastian.

keloid in medicine, overgrowth of fibrous tissue, usually produced at the site of a scar. Black skin produces more keloid than does white skin; it has a puckered appearance caused by clawlike offshoots. Surgical removal is often unsuccessful, because the keloid returns.

kelp collective name for large brown seaweeds, such as those of the Fucaceae and Laminariaceae families. Kelp is also a term for the powdery ash of burned seaweeds, a source of iodine.

Kelvin William Thomson, 1st Baron Kelvin 1824–1907. Irish physicist who introduced the *kelvin scale*, the absolute scale of temperature. His work on the conservation of energy 1851 led to the second law of *thermodynamics.

kelvin scale temperature scale used by scientists. It begins at *absolute zero (–273.16°C) and increases by the same degree intervals as the Celsius scale; that is, 0°C is the same as 273 K and 100°C is 373 K.

Kemal Atatürk Mustafa. Turkish politician; see *Atatürk.

Kemble (John) Philip 1757–1823. English actor and theatre manager. He excelled in tragedy, including the Shakespearean roles of Hamlet and Coriolanus. As manager of Drury Lane 1788–1803 and Covent Garden 1803–17 in London, he introduced many innovations in theatrical management, costume, and scenery.

Kempe Margery *c.* 1373–*c.* 1439. English Christian mystic. She converted to religious life after a period of mental derangement, and travelled widely as a pilgrim. Her *Boke of Margery Kempe* about 1420 describes her life and experiences, both religious and worldly. It has been called the first autobiography in English.

Kempis Thomas à. Medieval German monk and religious writer; see *Thomas à Kempis.

kendo (Japanese 'the way of the sword') Japanese armed *martial art in which combatants fence with bamboo replicas of samurai swords. Masks and padding are worn for protection. The earliest recorded reference to kendo is from AD 789.

Keneally Thomas (Michael) 1935– . Australian novelist who won the Booker Prize with *Schindler's Ark* 1982, a novel based on the true account of Polish Jews saved from the gas chambers in World War II by a German industrialist. Other works include *Woman of the Inner Sea* 1992.

Kennedy Edward (Moore) 'Ted' 1932– . US Democratic politician. He aided his brothers John and Robert Kennedy in the presidential campaign of 1960, and entered politics as a senator for Massachusetts 1962. He failed to gain the presidential nomination 1980, largely because of questions about his delay in reporting a car crash at Chappaquiddick Island, near Cape Cod, Massachusetts, in 1969, in which his passenger, Mary Jo Kopechne, was drowned.

Kennedy John F(itzgerald) 'Jack' 1917–1963. 35th president of the USA 1961–63, a Democrat; the first Roman Catholic and the youngest person to be elected president. In foreign policy he carried through the unsuccessful *Bay of Pigs invasion of Cuba, and in 1963 secured the withdrawal of Soviet missiles from the island. His programme for reforms at home, called the *New Frontier*, was posthumously executed by Lyndon Johnson. Kennedy was assassinated while on a state visit to Dallas, Texas, on 22 Nov 1963 by Lee Harvey Oswald (1939–1963), who was within a few days shot dead by Jack Ruby (1911–1967).

Kennedy Joseph Patrick 1888–1969. US industrialist and diplomat; ambassador to the UK 1937–40. A self-made millionaire, he ventured into the film industry, then set up the Securities and Exchange Commission (SEC) for F D Roosevelt. He groomed each of his four sons – Joseph Patrick Kennedy Jr (1915–1944), John F *Kennedy, Robert *Kennedy, and Edward *Kennedy – for a career in politics. His eldest son, Joseph, was killed in action with the naval air force in World War II.

Kennedy Nigel 1956– . British violinist, credited with expanding the audience for classical music. His 1986 recording of Vivaldi's *Four Seasons* sold more than 1 million copies.

Kennedy Robert (Francis) 1925–1968. US Democratic politician and lawyer. He was presidential campaign manager for his brother John F *Kennedy 1960, and as attorney general 1961–64 pursued a racket-busting policy and promoted the Civil Rights Act of 1964. He was also a key aide to his brother. When John Kennedy's successor, Lyndon Johnson, preferred Hubert H Humphrey for the 1964 vice-presidential nomination, Kennedy resigned and was elected senator for New York. In 1968 he campaigned for the Democratic Party's presidential nomination, but during a campaign stop in California was assassinated by Sirhan Bissara Sirhan (1944–), a Jordanian.

Kennedy Space Center *NASA launch site

on Merritt Island, near Cape Canaveral, Florida, used for Apollo and space-shuttle launches. The first flight to land on the Moon (1969) and *Skylab*, the first orbiting laboratory (1973), were launched here.

Kennelly–Heaviside layer former term for the *E layer.

Kenneth two kings of Scotland, including:

Kenneth I *MacAlpin* died 858. King of Scotland from *c.* 844. Traditionally, he is regarded as the founder of the Scottish kingdom (Alba) by virtue of his final defeat of the Picts about 844. He invaded Northumbria six times, and drove the Angles and the Britons over the river Tweed.

Kent county in SE England, nicknamed the 'garden of England'
area 3,730 sq km/1,440 sq mi
towns Maidstone (administrative headquarters), Canterbury, Chatham, Rochester, Sheerness, Tunbridge Wells; resorts: Folkestone, Margate, Ramsgate
products hops, apples, soft fruit, coal, cement, paper
population (1991) 1,485,600
famous people Charles Dickens, Edward Heath, Christopher Marlowe.

Kent Edward George Nicholas Paul Patrick, 2nd Duke of Kent 1935– . British prince, grandson of George V. His father, *George* (1902–1942), was created Duke of Kent just before his marriage in 1934 to Princess Marina of Greece and Denmark (1906–1968). The second duke succeeded when his father (George Edward Alexander Edmund) was killed in an air crash on active service with the RAF.

Kent William 1686–1748. British architect, landscape gardener, and interior designer. In architecture he was foremost in introducing the Palladian style into Britain from Italy. Later, he was a foremost exponent of the 18th-century Gothic revival, and in Romantic landscape gardening.

Kentucky state in S central USA; nickname Bluegrass State
area 104,700 sq km/40,414 sq mi
capital Frankfort
towns Louisville, Lexington, Owensboro, Covington, Bowling Green
products tobacco, cereals, textiles, coal, whiskey, horses, transport vehicles
population (1990) 3,365,300
famous people Muhammad Ali, Daniel Boone, Louis D Brandeis, Kit Carson, Henry Clay, D W Griffith, Thomas Hunt Morgan, Harland 'Colonel' Sanders, Robert Penn Warren
history the first region west of the Alleghenies settled by American pioneers. James Harrod founded Harrodsburg 1774; in 1775 Daniel Boone, who blazed his Wilderness Trail 1767, founded Boonesboro. Originally part of Virginia, Kentucky became a state 1792. Badly divided over the slavery question, the state was racked by guerrilla warfare and partisan feuds during the Civil War.

Kenya Republic of (*Jamhuri ya Kenya*)
area 582,600 sq km/224,884 sq mi
capital Nairobi
towns Kisumu, port Mombasa
physical mountains and highlands in W and centre; coastal plain in S; arid interior and tropical coast

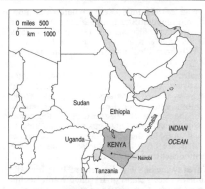

environment the elephant faces extinction as a result of poaching
head of state and government Daniel arap Moi from 1978
political system authoritarian nationalism
exports coffee, tea, pineapples, petroleum products
currency Kenya shilling
population (1993 est) 27,900,000 (Kikuyu 21%, Luo 13%, Luhya 14%, Kelenjin 11%; Asian, Arab, European); growth rate 4.2% p.a.
languages Kiswahili (official), English; there are many local dialects
religions Protestant 38%, Roman Catholic 28%, indigenous beliefs 26%, Muslim 6%
GNP $340 per head (1991)
chronology
1895 British East African protectorate established.
1920 Kenya became a British colony.
1944 African participation in politics began.
1950 Mau Mau campaign began.
1953 Nationalist leader Jomo Kenyatta imprisoned by British authorities.
1956 Mau Mau campaign defeated, Kenyatta released.
1963 Achieved internal self-government, with Kenyatta as prime minister.
1964 Independence achieved from Britain as a republic within the Commonwealth, with Kenyatta as president.
1978 Death of Kenyatta. Succeeded by Daniel arap Moi.
1982 Attempted coup against Moi foiled.
1983 Moi re-elected unopposed.
1984 Over 2,000 people massacred by government forces at Wajir.
1985–86 Thousands of forest villagers evicted and their homes destroyed to make way for cash crops.
1988 Moi re-elected. 150,000 evicted from state-owned forests.
1989 Moi announced release of all known political prisoners. Confiscated ivory burned in attempt to stop elephant poaching.
1990 Despite antigovernment riots, Moi refused multiparty politics.
1991 Moi announced that multiparty politics would be established.
1992 Constitutional amendment for presidential elections. Moi re-elected in first direct elections despite allegations of fraud.

Kenyatta Jomo. Assumed name of Kamau

Ngengi *c.* 1894–1978. Kenyan nationalist politician, prime minister from 1963, as well as the first president of Kenya from 1964 until his death. He led the Kenya African Union from 1947 (**KANU** from 1963) and was active in liberating Kenya from British rule.

Kepler Johannes 1571–1630. German mathematician and astronomer. He formulated what are now called **Kepler's laws** of planetary motion: (1) the orbit of each planet is an ellipse with the Sun at one of the foci; (2) the radius vector of each planet sweeps out equal areas in equal times; (3) the squares of the periods of the planets are proportional to the cubes of their mean distances from the Sun.

Kerala state of SW India, formed 1956 from the former princely states of Travancore and Cochin
area 38,900 sq km/15,015 sq mi
capital Trivandrum
products tea, coffee, rice, oilseed, rubber, textiles, chemicals, electrical goods
population (1991) 29,011,200
language Kannada, Malayalam, Tamil.

keratin fibrous protein found in the *skin of vertebrates and also in hair, nails, claws, hooves, feathers, and the outer coating of horns in animals such as cows and sheep.

Kerekou Mathieu (Ahmed) 1933– . Benin socialist politician and soldier, president 1980–91. In 1972, when deputy head of the Dahomey army, he led a coup to oust the ruling president and establish his own military government. He embarked on a programme of 'scientific socialism', changing his country's name to Benin to mark this change of direction. In 1987 he resigned from the army and confirmed a civilian administration. He was re-elected president 1989, but lost to Nicéphore Soglo in the 1991 presidential elections.

Kerensky Alexandr Feodorovich 1881–1970. Russian revolutionary politician, prime minister of the second provisional government before its collapse Nov 1917, during the *Russian Revolution. He was overthrown by the Bolshevik revolution and fled to France 1918 and to the USA 1940.

Kern Jerome (David) 1885–1945. US composer. Many of Kern's songs have become classics, notably 'Smoke Gets in Your Eyes' from his musical *Roberta* 1933. He wrote the operetta *Show Boat* 1927, which includes the song 'Ol' Man River'.

kernel the inner, softer part of a *nut, or of a seed within a hard shell.

kerosene thin oil obtained from the distillation of petroleum; a highly refined form is used in jet aircraft fuel. Kerosene is a mixture of hydrocarbons of the *paraffin series.

Kerouac Jack 1923–1969. US novelist. He named and epitomized the *Beat Generation of the 1950s. The first of his autobiographical, myth-making books, *The Town and the City* 1950, was followed by the rhapsodic *On the Road* 1957. Other works written with similar free-wheeling energy and inspired by his interests in jazz and Buddhism include *The Dharma Bums* 1958, *Doctor Sax* 1959, and *Desolation Angels* 1965.

Kerry county of Munster province, Republic of Ireland, E of Cork
area 4,700 sq km/1,814 sq mi
county town Tralee
physical W coastline deeply indented; N part low-lying, but in the S are the highest mountains in Ireland, including Carrantuohill 1,041 m/3,417 ft, the highest peak in Ireland; many rivers and lakes
products engineering, woollens, shoes, cutlery; tourism is important
population (1991) 121,700.

kestrel hawk *Falco tinnunculus* of the family Falconidae, which breeds in Europe, Asia, and Africa. About 30 cm/1 ft long, the male has a head and tail of bluish grey, and its back is a light chestnut brown with black spots. The female is slightly larger and reddish brown above, with bars. The kestrel hunts mainly by hovering in midair while searching for prey.

ketone member of the group of organic compounds containing the carbonyl group (C=O) bonded to two atoms of carbon (instead of one carbon and one hydrogen as in *aldehydes). Ketones are liquids or low-melting-point solids, slightly soluble in water.

Kew Gardens popular name for the Royal Botanic Gardens, Kew, Surrey, England. They were founded 1759 by the mother of King George III as a small garden and passed to the nation by Queen Victoria 1840. By then they had expanded to almost their present size of 149 hectares/368 acres and since 1841 have been open daily to the public. They contain a collection of over 25,000 living plant species and many fine buildings. The gardens are also a centre for botanical research.

key in music, the *diatonic scale around which a piece of music is written; for example, a passage in the key of C major will mainly use the notes of the C major scale. The term is also used for the lever activated by a keyboard player, such as a piano key, or the finger control on a woodwind instrument.

keyboard in computing, an input device resembling a typewriter keyboard, used to enter instructions and data. There are many variations on the layout and labelling of keys. Extra numeric keys may be added, as may special-purpose function keys, whose effects can be defined by programs in the computer.

keyhole surgery or **minimally invasive surgery** operations that do not involve cutting into the body in the traditional way. These procedures are performed either by means of *endoscopy or by passing fine instruments through catheters inserted into large blood vessels. Advocates of keyhole surgery claim it is safer and cheaper than conventional surgery, requiring a shorter hospital stay and less disruption to the patient's life. However, detractors believe that it does not yield the long-term result of open surgery.

Keynes John Maynard, 1st Baron Keynes 1883–1946. English economist, whose *The General Theory of Employment, Interest, and Money* 1936 proposed the prevention of financial crises and unemployment by adjusting demand through government control of credit and currency. He is responsible for that part of economics now known as *macroeconomics*.

Keynesian economics the economic theory

of English economist John Maynard Keynes, which argues that a fall in national income, lack of demand for goods, and rising unemployment should be countered by increased government expenditure to stimulate the economy. It is opposed by monetarists (see *monetarism).

kg symbol for *kilogram*.

KGB secret police of the USSR, the **Komitet Gosudarstvennoy Bezopasnosti**/Committee of State Security, which was in control of frontier and general security and the forced-labour system. KGB officers held key appointments in all fields of daily life, reporting to administration offices in every major town. The KGB was superseded by the Russian Federal Security Agency on the demise of the Soviet Union 1991.

Khabarovsk territory of SE Siberian Russia, bordering the Sea of Okhotsk and drained by the Amur River; area 824,600 sq km/318,501 sq mi; population (1985) 1,728,000. The capital is Khabarovsk. Mineral resources include gold, coal, and iron ore.

Khachaturian Aram Il'yich 1903–1978. Armenian composer. His use of folk themes is shown in the ballets *Gayaneh* 1942, which includes the 'Sabre Dance', and *Spartacus* 1956.

Khaddhafi or **Gaddafi** or **Qaddafi**, Moamer al 1942– . Libyan revolutionary leader. Overthrowing King Idris 1969, he became virtual president of a republic, although he nominally gave up all except an ideological role 1974. He favours territorial expansion in N Africa reaching as far as Zaire, has supported rebels in Chad, and has proposed mergers with a number of countries. His theories, based on those of the Chinese communist leader Mao Zedong, are contained in a *Green Book*.

Khalifa Sudanese leader *Abd Allah.

Khalistan projected independent Sikh state. See *Sikhism.

Khalsa the brotherhood of the Sikhs, created by Guru Gobind Singh at the festival of Baisakhi in 1699. The Khalsa was originally founded as a militant group to defend the Sikh community from persecution.

Khama Seretse 1921–1980. Botswanan politician, prime minister of Bechuanaland 1965, and first president of Botswana from 1966 until his death.

Khan Imran 1952– . Pakistani cricketer. He played county cricket for Worcestershire and Sussex in the UK, and made his test debut for Pakistan 1971, subsequently playing for his country 85 times. He captained Pakistan to victory in the World Cup in 1992.

Khan Jahangir 1963– . Pakistani squash player who won the world open championship a record six times 1981–85 and 1988. He was ten times British Open champion 1982–91, and World Amateur champion 1979, 1983, and 1985.

Khan Liaquat Ali 1895–1951. Indian politician, deputy leader of the Muslim League (an Islamic political organization) 1941–47, first prime minister of Pakistan from 1947. He was assassinated by objectors to his peace policy with India.

Khan, Aga Islamic leader, see *Aga Khan

Khardungla Pass road linking the Indian town of Leh with the high-altitude military outpost on the Siachen Glacier at an altitude of 5,662 m/ 1,744 ft in the Karakoram range, Kashmir. It is thought to be the highest road in the world.

Kharkov capital of the Kharkov region, E Ukraine, 400 km/250 mi E of Kiev; population (1987) 1,587,000. It is a railway junction and industrial city (engineering, tractors), close to the Donets Basin coalfield and Krivoy Rog iron mines. Kharkov was founded 1654 as a fortress town.

Khartoum capital and trading centre of Sudan, at the junction of the Blue and White Nile; population (1983) 476,000, and of Khartoum North, across the Blue Nile, 341,000. *Omdurman is also a suburb of Khartoum, giving the urban area a population of over 1.3 million.

Khashoggi Adnan 1935– . Saudi entrepreneur and arms dealer who built up a large property company, Triad, based in Switzerland, and through ownership of banks, hotels, and real estate became a millionaire. In 1975 he was accused by the USA of receiving bribes to secure military contracts in Arab countries, and in 1986 he was financially disadvantaged by the slump in oil prices and political problems in Sudan. In April 1989 he was arrested in connection with illegal property deals. He successfully weathered all three setbacks.

khedive title granted by the Turkish sultan to his Egyptian viceroy 1867, retained by succeeding rulers until 1914.

Khirbet Qumran archaeological site in Jordan; see *Qumran.

Khmer or **Kmer** member of the largest ethnic group in Cambodia, numbering about 7 million. Khmer minorities also live in E Thailand and S Vietnam. The Khmer language belongs to the Mon-Khmer family of Austro-Asiatic languages.

Khmer Republic former name of *Cambodia.

Khmer Rouge communist movement in Cambodia (Kampuchea) formed in the 1960s. Controlling the country 1974–78, it was responsible for mass deportations and executions under the leadership of Pol Pot. Since then it has conducted guerrilla warfare, and in 1991 gained representation in the governing body. The leader of the Khmer Rouge from 1985 is Khieu Samphan.

Khoisan the smallest group of languages in Africa. It includes fewer than 50 languages, spoken mainly by the people of the Kalahari Desert (including the Khoikhoi and Kung). Two languages from this group are spoken in Tanzania. The Khoisan languages are known for their click consonants (clicking sounds made with the tongue, which function as consonants).

Khomeini Ayatollah Ruhollah 1900–1989. Iranian Shi'ite Muslim leader, born in Khomein, central Iran. Exiled for opposition to the Shah from 1964, he returned when the Shah left the country 1979, and established a fundamentalist Islamic republic. His rule was marked by a protracted war with Iraq, and suppression of opposition within Iran, executing thousands of opponents.

Khorana Har Gobind 1922– . Indian-born US biochemist who in 1976 led the team that first synthesized a biologically active gene. In 1968 he shared the Nobel Prize for Medicine for research on the interpretation of the genetic code and its function in protein synthesis.

Khrushchev Nikita Sergeyevich 1894–1971. Soviet politician, secretary general of the Communist Party 1953–64, premier 1958–64. He emerged as leader from the power struggle following Stalin's death and was the first official to denounce Stalin, in 1956. His de-Stalinization programme gave rise to revolts in Poland and Hungary 1956. Because of problems with the economy and foreign affairs (a breach with China 1960; conflict with the USA in the *Cuban missile crisis 1962), he was ousted by Leonid Brezhnev and Alexei Kosygin.

Khufu c. 2600 BC. Egyptian king of Memphis, who built the largest of the pyramids, known to the Greeks as the pyramid of Cheops (the Greek form of Khufu).

Khulna capital of Khulna region, SW Bangladesh, situated close to the Ganges delta; population (1981) 646,000. Industry includes shipbuilding and textiles; it trades in jute, rice, salt, sugar, and oilseed.

Khwārizmī, al- Muhammad ibn-Mūsā c. 780–c. 850. Persian mathematician from Khwarizm (now Khiva, Uzbekistan), who lived and worked in Baghdad. He wrote a book on algebra, from part of whose title (al-jabr) comes the word 'algebra', and a book in which he introduced to the West the Hindu-Arabic decimal number system. The word 'algorithm' is a corruption of his name.

Khyber Pass pass 53 km/33 mi long through the mountain range that separates Pakistan from Afghanistan. The Khyber Pass was used by invaders of India. The present road was constructed by the British during the Afghan Wars.

Kiangsi alternative spelling of *Jiangxi, province of China.

Kiangsu alternative spelling of *Jiangsu, province of China.

kibbutz Israeli communal collective settlement with collective ownership of all property and earnings, collective organization of work and decision-making, and communal housing for children. A modified version, the Moshav Shitufi, is similar to the *collective farms that were typical of the former USSR. Other Israeli cooperative rural settlements include the Moshav Ovdim, which has equal opportunity, and the similar but less strict Moshav settlement.

Kidd 'Captain' (William) c. 1645–1701. Scottish pirate. He spent his youth privateering for the British against the French off the North American coast, and in 1695 was given a royal commission to suppress piracy in the Indian Ocean. Instead, he joined a group of pirates in Madagascar. On his way to Boston, Massachusetts, he was arrested 1699, taken to England, and hanged.

kidney in vertebrates, one of a pair of organs responsible for water regulation, excretion of waste products, and maintaining the ionic composition of the blood. The kidneys are situated on the rear wall of the abdomen. Each one consists of a number of long tubules; the outer parts filter the aqueous components of blood, and the inner parts selectively reabsorb vital salts, leaving waste products in the remaining fluid (urine), which is passed through the ureter to the bladder.

kidney machine medical equipment used in *dialysis.

Kierkegaard Soøren (Aabye) 1813–1855. Danish philosopher considered to be the founder of *existentialism. Disagreeing with the German dialectical philosopher *Hegel, he argued that no system of thought could explain the unique experience of the individual. He defended Christianity, suggesting that God cannot be known through reason, but only through a 'leap of faith'. He believed that God and exceptional individuals were above moral laws.

Kiev capital of Ukraine, industrial centre (chemicals, clothing, leatherwork), on the confluence of the Desna and Dnieper rivers; population (1987) 2,554,000. capital of Russia in the Middle Ages.

Kigali capital of Rwanda, central Africa; population (1981) 157,000. Products include coffee and minerals.

Kikuyu member of Kenya's dominant ethnic group, numbering about three million. The Kikuyu are primarily cultivators, although many are highly educated and have entered the professions. Their language belongs to the Bantu branch of the Niger-Congo family.

Kildare county of Leinster province, Republic of Ireland, S of Meath
area 1,690 sq km/652 sq mi
county town Naas
physical wet and boggy in the north
products oats, barley, potatoes, cattle
population (1991) 122,516.

Kilimanjaro volcano in *Tanzania, the highest mountain in Africa, 5,895 m/19,340 ft.

Kilkenny county of Leinster province, Republic of Ireland, E of Tipperary
area 2,060 sq km/795 sq mi
county town Kilkenny
products agricultural, coal
population (1991) 73,600.

killer whale or *orca* toothed whale Orcinus orca of the dolphin family, found in all seas of the world. It is black on top, white below, and grows up to 9 m/30 ft long. It is the only whale that has been observed to prey on other whales, as well as on seals and seabirds.

Killiecrankie, Battle of in British history, during the first *Jacobite uprising, defeat on 7 May 1689 of General Mackay (for William of Orange) by John Graham of *Claverhouse, a supporter of James II. Despite the victory, Claverhouse was killed and the revolt soon petered out; the remaining forces were routed on 21 Aug.

kiln high-temperature furnace used commercially for drying timber, roasting metal ores, or for making cement, bricks, and pottery. Oil- or gas-fired kilns are used to bake ceramics at up to 1,760°C/3,200°F; electric kilns do not generally reach such high temperatures.

kilo- prefix denoting multiplication by 1,000, as in kilohertz, a unit of frequency equal to 1,000 hertz.

kilobyte (K or KB) in computing, a unit of memory equal to 1,024 *bytes. It is sometimes used, less precisely, to mean 1,000 bytes.

kilogram SI unit (symbol kg) of mass equal to 1,000 grams (2.2 lb). It is defined by scientists as a mass equal to that of the international prototype, a platinum-iridium cylinder held at the International Bureau of Weights and Measures at Sèvres, France.

kilometre unit (symbol km) of length equal to 1,000 metres (3,280.89 ft or about $^5/_8$ of a mile).

kilowatt unit (symbol kW) of power equal to 1,000 watts or about 1.34 horsepower.

kilowatt-hour commercial unit of electrical energy (symbol kWh), defined as the work done by a power of 1,000 watts in one hour. It is used to calculate the cost of electrical energy taken from the domestic supply.

kimberlite an igneous rock that is ultrabasic (containing very little silica); a type of alkaline *peridotite containing mica in addition to olivine and other minerals. Kimberlite represents the world's principal source of diamonds.

Kim Dae Jung 1924– . South Korean social-democratic politician. As a committed opponent of the regime of General Park Chung Hee, he suffered imprisonment and exile.

Kim Il Sung 1912–1994. North Korean Communist politician and marshal. He became prime minister 1948 and president 1972, retaining the presidency of the Communist Workers' party. He likes to be known as the 'Great Leader' and has campaigned constantly for the reunification of Korea. His son *Kim Jong Il* (1942–), known as the 'Dear Leader', has been named as his successor.

kimono traditional Japanese costume. Worn in the Heian period (more than 1,000 years ago), it is still used by women for formal wear and informally by men.

Kim Young Sam 1927– . South Korean democratic politician, president from 1993. A member of the national assembly from 1954 and president of the New Democratic Party (NDP) from 1974, he lost his seat and was later placed under house arrest because of his opposition to President Park Chung Hee. In 1983 he led a pro-democracy hunger strike but in 1987 failed to defeat Roh Tae-Woo in the presidential election. In 1990 he merged the NDP with the ruling party to form the new Democratic Liberal Party (DLP). In the Dec 1992 presidential election he captured 42% of the national vote and assumed office Feb 1993.

Kincardineshire former county of E Scotland, merged in 1975 in Grampian Region. The county town was Stonehaven.

kindergarten (German 'children's garden') another term for *nursery school.

kinesis (plural *kineses*) in biology, a nondirectional movement in response to a stimulus; for example, woodlice move faster in drier surroundings. *Taxis* is a similar pattern of behaviour, but there the response is directional.

kinetic energy the energy of a body resulting from motion. It is contrasted with *potential energy.

kinetics branch of *dynamics dealing with the action of forces producing or changing the motion of a body; *kinematics* deals with motion without reference to force or mass.

kinetics the branch of chemistry that investigates the rates of chemical reactions.

kinetic theory theory describing the physical properties of matter in terms of the behaviour – principally movement – of its component atoms or molecules. The temperature of a substance is dependent on the velocity of movement of its constituent particles, increased temperature being accompanied by increased movement. A gas consists of rapidly moving atoms or molecules and, according to kinetic theory, it is their continual impact on the walls of the containing vessel that accounts for the pressure of the gas. The slowing of molecular motion as temperature falls, according to kinetic theory, accounts for the physical properties of liquids and solids, culminating in the concept of no molecular motion at *absolute zero (0K/–273°C). By making various assumptions about the nature of gas molecules, it is possible to derive from the kinetic theory the various gas laws (such as *Avogadro's hypothesis, *Boyle's law, and *Charles's law).

King B B (Riley) 1925– . US blues guitarist, singer, and songwriter, one of the most influential electric-guitar players, who became an international star in the 1960s. His albums include *Blues Is King* 1967, *Lucille Talks Back* 1975, and *Blues 'n' Jazz* 1983.

King Billie Jean (born Moffitt) 1943– . US tennis player. She won a record 20 Wimbledon titles 1961–79 and 39 Grand Slam titles. She won the Wimbledon singles title six times, the US Open singles title four times, the French Open once, and the Australian Open once.

King Martin Luther Jr 1929–1968. US civil-rights campaigner, black leader, and Baptist minister. He first came to national attention as leader of the *Montgomery, Alabama, bus boycott 1955, and was one of the organizers of the massive (200,000 people) march on Washington, DC 1963 to demand racial equality. An advocate of nonviolence, he was awarded the Nobel Peace Prize 1964. He was assassinated in Memphis, Tennessee, by James Earl Ray (1928–).

King Stephen 1946– . US writer of best-selling horror novels with small-town or rural settings. Many of his works have been filmed, including *Carrie* 1974, *The Shining* 1978, and *Christine* 1983.

King William Lyon Mackenzie 1874–1950. Canadian Liberal prime minister 1921–26, 1926–30, and 1935–48. He maintained the unity of the English-and French-speaking populations, and was instrumental in establishing equal status for Canada with Britain.

king crab or *horseshoe crab* marine arthropod, class Arachnida, subclass Xiphosura, which lives on the Atlantic coast of North America, and the coasts of Asia. The upper side of the body is entirely covered with a rounded shell, and it has a long spinelike tail. It is up to 60 cm/2 ft long. It is unable to swim, and lays its eggs in the sand at the high-water mark.

kingdom the primary division in biological *classification. At one time, only two kingdoms were recognized: animals and plants. Today most biologists prefer a five-kingdom system, even though it still involves grouping together organisms that are probably unrelated. One widely accepted scheme is as follows: *Kingdom Animalia* (all multicellular animals); *Kingdom Plantae* (all plants, including seaweeds and

king crab *The king crab is an ancient life form, almost identical to fossils from the Triassic period, about 225 million years ago.*

other algae); **Kingdom Fungi** (all fungi, including the unicellular yeasts, but not slime moulds); **Kingdom Protista** or **Protoctista** (protozoa, diatoms, dinoflagellates, slime moulds, and various other lower organisms with eukaryotic cells); and **Kingdom Monera** (all prokaryotes – the bacteria and cyanobacteria, or *blue-green algae). The first four of these kingdoms make up the eukaryotes.

kingfisher heavy-billed bird of the worldwide family Alcedinidae, found near streams, ponds, and coastal areas. Kingfishers plunge-dive for fish and aquatic insects. The nest is usually a burrow in a riverbank.

Kingsley Charles 1819–1875. English author. A rector, he was known as the 'Chartist clergyman' because of such social novels as *Alton Locke* 1850. His historical novels include *Westward Ho!* 1855. He also wrote *The Water-Babies* 1863.

Kingston capital and principal port of Jamaica, West Indies, the cultural and commercial centre of the island; population (1983) 101,000, metropolitan area 525,000. Founded 1693, Kingston became the capital of Jamaica 1872.

Kingston upon Hull official name of *Hull, city in Humberside in NE England.

Kingstown capital and principal port of St Vincent and the Grenadines, West Indies, in the SW of the island of St Vincent; population (1989) 29,400.

kinkajou Central and South American carnivore *Potos flavus* of the raccoon family. Yellowish-brown, with a rounded face and slim body, the kinkajou grows to 55 cm/1.8 ft with a 50 cm/ 1.6 ft tail, and has short legs with sharp claws. It spends its time in trees and has a prehensile tail. It feeds largely on fruit.

Kinki region of S Honshu island, Japan; population (1988) 22,105,000; area 33,070 sq km/ 12,773 sq mi. The chief city is Osaka.

Kinnock Neil 1942– . British Labour politician, party leader 1983–92. Born and educated in Wales, he was elected to represent a Welsh constituency in Parliament 1970 (Islwyn from 1983). As party leader (in succession to Michael Foot) he adopted a moderate position, initiating a major policy review 1988–89. He resigned as party leader after Labour's defeat in the 1992 general election. In 1994 he left parliament to become a European commissioner.

Kinsey Alfred 1894–1956. US researcher whose studies of male and female sexual behaviour 1948–53, based on questionnaires, were the first serious published research on this topic.

Kinshasa formerly **Léopoldville** capital of Zaire on the river Zaïre, 400 km/250 mi inland from Matadi; population (1984) 2,654,000. Industries include chemicals, textiles, engineering, food processing, and furniture. It was founded by the explorer Henry Stanley 1887.

kinship in anthropology, human relationship based on blood or marriage, and sanctified by law and custom. Kinship forms the basis for most human societies and for such social groupings as the family, clan, or tribe.

Kinski Klaus 1926–1991. German actor of skeletal appearance who featured in Werner Herzog's films *Aguirre Wrath of God* 1972, *Nosferatu* 1978, and *Fitzcarraldo* 1982. His other films include *For a Few Dollars More* 1965, *Dr Zhivago* 1965, and *Venom* 1982. He was the father of the actress **Nastassja Kinski** (1961–).

Kipling (Joseph) Rudyard 1865–1936. English writer, born in India. *Plain Tales from the Hills* 1888, about Anglo-Indian society, contains the earliest of his masterly short stories. His books for children, including *The Jungle Books* 1894–95, *Just So Stories* 1902, *Puck of Pook's Hill* 1906, and the novel *Kim* 1901, reveal his imaginative identification with the exotic. Poems such as 'Danny Deever', 'Gunga Din', and 'If–' express an empathy with common experience, which contributed to his great popularity, together with a vivid sense of 'Englishness' (sometimes denigrated as a kind of jingoist imperialism). His work is increasingly valued for its complex characterization and subtle moral viewpoints. Nobel prize 1907.

Kirchner Ernst Ludwig 1880–1938. German Expressionist artist, a leading member of the group *die *Brücke* in Dresden from 1905 and in Berlin from 1911. His Dresden work, which includes woodcuts, shows the influence of African art. In Berlin he turned to city scenes and portraits, using lurid colours and bold diagonal paint strokes recalling woodcut technique. He suffered a breakdown during World War I and settled in Switzerland, where he committed suicide.

Kirghiz member of a pastoral people numbering approximately 1.5 million. They inhabit the central Asian region bounded by the Hindu Kush, the Himalayas, and the Tian Shan mountains. The Kirghiz are Sunni Muslims, and their Turkic language belongs to the Altaic family.

Kiribati Republic of
area 717 sq km/277 sq mi
capital (and port) Bairiki (on Tarawa Atoll)

kingfisher *The kingfisher, with its brilliantly coloured plumage and daggerlike beak, is unmistakeable.*

physical comprises 33 Pacific coral islands: the Kiribati (Gilbert), Rawaki (Phoenix), Banaba (Ocean Island), and three of the Line Islands including Kiritimati (Christmas Island)

environment the islands are threatened by the possibility of a rise in sea level caused by global warming. A rise of approximately 30 cm/1 ft by the year 2040 will make existing fresh water brackish and undrinkable

head of state and government Teburoro Tito from 1994

political system liberal democracy

exports copra, fish

currency Australian dollar

population (1993 est) 77,000 (Micronesian); growth rate 1.7% p.a.

languages English (official), Gilbertese

religions Roman Catholic 48%, Protestant 45%

GNP $750 per head (1991)

chronology

1892 Gilbert and Ellice Islands proclaimed a British protectorate.

1937 Phoenix Islands added to colony.

1950s UK tested nuclear weapons on Kiritimati (formerly Christmas Island).

1962 USA tested nuclear weapons on Kiritimati.

1975 Ellice Islands separated to become Tuvalu.

1979 Independence achieved from Britain, within the Commonwealth, as the Republic of Kiribati, with Ieremia Tabai as president.

1985 Kiribati's first political party, the opposition Christian Democrats, formed.

1987 Tabai re-elected.

1991 Tabai re-elected but not allowed under constitution to serve further term; Teatao Teannaki won run-off presidential election.

1994 Government resigned, after losing vote of confidence. NPP defeated in general election. Teburoro Tito named head of state.

Kirin alternative name for *Jilin, Chinese province.

Kirkland Gelsey 1952– . US ballerina of effortless technique and innate musicality. She joined the New York City Ballet 1968, where George Balanchine staged a new *Firebird* for her 1970 and Jerome Robbins chose her for his *Goldberg Variations* 1971 and other ballets. In 1974 Mikhail Baryshnikov sought her out and she joined American Ballet Theater, where they danced in partnership, for example in *Giselle*.

Kirov Sergei Mironovich 1886–1934. Russian Bolshevik leader who joined the party 1904 and played a prominent part in the 1918–20 civil war. As one of *Stalin's closest associates, he became first secretary of the Leningrad Communist Party. His assassination, possibly engineered by Stalin, led to the political trials held during the next four years as part of the *purge.

Kishinev capital of the Republic of Moldova; population (1989) 565,000. Industries include cement, food processing, tobacco, and textiles.

Kissinger Henry 1923– . German-born US diplomat. After a brilliant academic career at Harvard University, he was appointed national security adviser 1969 by President Nixon, and was secretary of state 1973–77. His missions to the USSR and China improved US relations with both countries, and he took part in negotiating US withdrawal from Vietnam 1973 and in Arab-

Israeli peace negotiations 1973–75. Nobel Peace Prize 1973.

Kiswahili another name for the *Swahili language.

Kitaj Ron B 1932– . US painter and printmaker, active in Britain. His work is mainly figurative, and his distinctive decorative pale palette was in part inspired by studies of the Impressionist painter Degas.

Kitakyushu industrial port city (coal, steel, chemicals, cotton thread, plate glass, alcohol) port city in Japan, on the Hibiki Sea, N Kyushu, formed 1963 by the amalgamation of Moji, Kokura, Tobata, Yawata, and Wakamatsu; population (1989) 1,030,000. A tunnel 1942 links it with Honshu.

Kitasato Shibasaburo 1852–1931. Japanese bacteriologist who discovered the *plague bacillus while investigating an outbreak of plague in Hong Kong. Kitasato was the first to grow the tetanus bacillus in pure culture. He and the German bacteriologist Behring discovered that increasing nonlethal doses of tetanus toxin give immunity to the disease.

Kitchener Horatio Herbert, Earl Kitchener of Khartoum 1850–1916. British soldier and administrator. He defeated the Sudanese dervishes at Omdurman 1898 and reoccupied Khartoum. In South Africa, he was Chief of Staff 1900–02 during the Boer War, and commanded the forces in India 1902–09. He was appointed war minister on the outbreak of World War I, and drowned when his ship was sunk on the way to Russia.

kitchen-sink painters loose-knit group of British artists specializing in social-realistic painting, active in the late 1940s and early 1950s. They depicted drab, ordinary themes with an aggressive technique and brilliant, 'crude' colour. The best known were John Bratby (1928–), Derrick Greaves (1927–), Edward Middleditch (1923–1987), and Jack Smith (1928–). The group disbanded after a few years but interest in them revived in the 1990s.

kite one of about 20 birds of prey in the family Accipitridae, found in all parts of the world.

kiwi flightless bird *Apteryx australis* found only in New Zealand. It has long, hairlike brown plumage and a very long beak with nostrils at the tip. It is nocturnal and insectivorous. The egg is larger in relation to the bird's size (similar to a domestic chicken) than that of any other bird.

kiwi fruit or *Chinese gooseberry* fruit of a vinelike plant *Actinidithia chinensis*, family Actinidiaceae, commercially grown on a large scale in New Zealand. Kiwi fruits are egg-sized, oval, and of similar flavour to a gooseberry, with a fuzzy brown skin.

Klammer Franz 1953– . Austrian skier who won a record 35 World Cup downhill races between 1974 and 1985. Olympic gold medallist 1976. He was the combined world champion 1974, and the World Cup downhill champion 1975–78 and 1983.

Klaproth Martin Heinrich 1743–1817. German chemist who first identified the elements uranium, zirconium, cerium, and titanium.

Klee Paul 1879–1940. Swiss painter. He settled in Munich 1906, joined the *Blaue Reiter* group 1912, and worked at the Bauhaus school of art and design 1920–31, returning to Switzerland 1933. His style in the 1920s and 1930s was dominated by humorous linear fantasies.

Klein Melanie 1882–1960. Austrian child psychoanalyst. She pioneered child psychoanalysis and play studies, and was influenced by Sigmund *Freud's theories. She published *The Psychoanalysis of Children* 1960.

kleptomania (Greek *kleptēs* 'thief') behavioural disorder characterized by an overpowering desire to possess articles for which one has no need. In kleptomania, as opposed to ordinary theft, there is no obvious need or use for what is stolen and sometimes the sufferer has no memory of the theft.

Klimt Gustav 1862–1918. Austrian painter, influenced by Jugendstil ('youth style', a form of Art Nouveau); a founding member of the Vienna *Sezession* group 1897. His paintings have a jewelled effect similar to mosaics, for example *The Kiss* 1909 (Musée des Beaux-Arts, Strasbourg). His many portraits include *Judith I* 1901 (Österreichische Galerie, Vienna).

Klondike former gold-mining area in *Yukon, Canada, named after the river valley where gold was found 1896. About 30,000 people moved there during the following 15 years. Silver is still mined there.

Klopstock Friedrich Gottlieb 1724–1803. German poet whose religious epic *Der Messias/ The Messiah* 1748–73 and *Oden/Odes* 1771 anticipated Romanticism.

km symbol for *kilometre*.

knapweed any of several weedy plants of the genus *Centaurea*, family Compositae. In the common knapweed *C. nigra*, also known as *hardhead*, the hard bract-covered buds break into purple composite heads. It is native to Europe and has been introduced to North America.

Kneller Godfrey 1646–1723. German-born portrait painter who lived in England from 1674. He was court painter to Charles II, James II, William III, and George I.

Knesset the Israeli parliament, consisting of a single chamber of 120 deputies elected for a period of four years.

knighthood, order of fraternity carrying with it the rank of knight, admission to which is granted as a mark of royal favour or as a reward for public services. During the Middle Ages in Europe such fraternities fell into two classes, religious and secular. The first class, including the *Templars* and the *Knights of *St John*, consisted of knights who had taken religious vows and devoted themselves to military service against the Saracens (Arabs) or other non-Christians. The secular orders probably arose from bands of knights engaged in the service of a prince or great noble.

knitting method of making fabric by looping and knotting yarn with two needles. Knitting may have developed from *crochet*, which uses a single hooked needle, or from *netting*, using a shuttle.

Knock (also the *Basilica of Our Lady, Queen of Ireland*) church shrine in County Mayo, W of Ireland, one of three national places of pilgrimage (with Lough Derg and Croagh Patrick). On 21

Aug 1879 it was the scene of an alleged apparition of the Virgin Mary.

knocking in a spark-ignition petrol engine, a phenomenon that occurs when unburned fuel-air mixture explodes in the combustion chamber before being ignited by the spark. The resulting shock waves produce a metallic knocking sound. Loss of power occurs, which can be prevented by reducing the compression ratio, re-designing the geometry of the combustion chamber, or increasing the octane number of the petrol (usually by the use of lead tetraethyl anti-knock additives).

Knossos chief city of *Minoan Crete, near present-day Iráklion, 6 km/4 mi SE of Candia. The archaeological site excavated by Arthur *Evans 1899–1935, dates from about 2000 BC, and includes the palace throne room and a labyrinth, legendary home of the *Minotaur.

knot wading bird *Calidris canutus* of the sandpiper family. It is about 25 cm/10 in long. In the winter, it is grey above and white below, but in the breeding season, it is brick-red on the head and chest and black on the wings and back. It feeds on insects and molluscs.

knot in navigation, unit by which a ship's speed is measured, equivalent to one *nautical mile per hour (one knot equals about 1.15 miles per hour). It is also sometimes used in aviation.

knowledge-based system (KBS) computer program that uses an encoding of human knowledge to help solve problems. It was discovered during research into *artificial intelligence that adding heuristics (rules of thumb) enabled programs to tackle problems that were otherwise difficult to solve by the usual techniques of computer science.

Knox John *c.* 1505–1572. Scottish Protestant reformer, founder of the Church of Scotland. He spent several years in exile for his beliefs, including a period in Geneva where he met John *Calvin. He returned to Scotland 1559 to promote Presbyterianism. His books include *First Blast of the Trumpet Against the Monstrous Regiment of Women* 1558.

koala The koala lives in eucalyptus trees, and comes down only to pass from one tree to another.

koala marsupial *Phascolarctos cinereus* of the family Phalangeridae, found only in E Australia. It feeds almost entirely on eucalyptus shoots. It is about 60 cm/2 ft long, and resembles a bear. The popularity of its greyish fur led to its almost complete extermination by hunters. Under protection since 1936, it has rapidly increased in numbers.

kōan in Zen Buddhism, a superficially nonsensical question or riddle used by a Zen master to help a pupil achieve satori (*enlightenment). It is used in the Rinzai school of Zen.

Kobe deep-water port in S Honshu, Japan; population (1989) 1,438,200. *Port Island*, created 1960–68 from the rock of nearby mountains, area 5 sq km/2 sq mi, is one of the world's largest construction projects. An earthquake measuring 7.2 on the Richter scale hit Kobe Jan 1995, leaving more than 4,000 people dead, 25,000 injured, and over 45,000 homes destroyed.

Koøbenhavn Danish name for *Copenhagen, capital of Denmark.

Koch Robert 1843–1910. German bacteriologist. Koch and his assistants devised the techniques to culture bacteria outside the body, and formulated the rules for showing whether or not a bacterium is the cause of a disease. Nobel Prize for Medicine 1905.

Kodály Zoltán 1882–1967. Hungarian composer. With Béla *Bartók, he recorded and transcribed Magyar folk music, the scales and rhythm of which he incorporated in a deliberately nationalist style. His works include the cantata *Psalmus Hungaricus* 1923, a comic opera *Háry János* 1925–27, and orchestral dances and variations.

Koestler Arthur 1905–1983. Hungarian author. Imprisoned by the Nazis in France 1940, he escaped to England. His novel *Darkness at Noon* 1940, regarded as his masterpiece, is a fictional account of the Stalinist purges, and draws on his experiences as a prisoner under sentence of death during the Spanish Civil War. He also wrote extensively about creativity, parapsychology, politics, and culture.

Koh-i-noor (Persian 'mountain of light') diamond, originally part of the Aurangzeb treasure, seized 1739 by the shah of Iran from the Moguls in India, taken back by Sikhs, and acquired by Britain 1849 when the Punjab was annexed.

kohl (Arabic) powdered antimony sulphide, used in Asia and the Middle East to darken the area around the eyes. Commonly used eyeliners also contain carbon (bone black, lamp black, carbon black) or black iron oxide.

Kohl Helmut 1930– . German conservative politician, leader of the Christian Democratic Union (CDU) from 1976, West German chancellor (prime minister) 1982–90. He oversaw the reunification of East and West Germany 1989–90 and in 1990 won a resounding electoral victory to become the first chancellor of reunited Germany. His miscalculation of the costs of reunification and their subsequent effects on the German economy led to a dramatic fall in his popularity.

kohlrabi variety of kale *Brassica oleracea*. The leaves of kohlrabi shoot from a globular swelling on the main stem; it is used for food and resembles a turnip.

Kokoschka Oskar 1886–1980. Austrian Expressionist painter and writer who lived in England from 1938. Initially influenced by the Vienna *Sezession painters, he developed a disturbingly expressive portrait style. His writings include several plays.

kola alternative spelling of *cola, a genus of tropical tree.

Kolchak Alexander Vasilievich 1875–1920. Russian admiral, commander of the White forces in Siberia after the Russian Revolution. He proclaimed himself Supreme Ruler of Russia 1918, but was later handed over to the Bolsheviks by his own men and shot.

Kollontai Alexandra 1872–1952. Russian revolutionary, politician, and writer. In 1905 she published *On the Question of the Class Struggle*, and, as commissar for public welfare, was the only female member of the first Bolshevik government. She campaigned for domestic reforms such as acceptance of free love, simplification of divorce laws, and collective child care.

Kollwitz Käthe 1867–1945. German sculptor and printmaker. Her early series of etchings depicting workers and their environment are realistic and harshly expressive. Later themes include war, death, and maternal love.

Kommunizma, Pik or *Communism Peak* highest mountain in the *Pamirs, a mountain range in Tajikistan; 7,495 m/24,599 ft. As part of the former USSR, it was known as *Mount Garmo* until 1933 and *Mount Stalin* 1933–62.

Kongur Shan mountain peak in China, 7,719 m/25,325 ft high, part of the Pamir range (see *Pamirs). The 1981 expedition that first reached the summit was led by British climber Chris Bonington.

Kong Zi Pinyin form of *Confucius, Chinese philosopher.

Kon-Tiki legendary creator god of Peru and sun king who ruled the country later occupied by the *Incas and was supposed to have migrated out into the Pacific. The name was used by explorer Thor *Heyerdahl for his raft (made of nine balsawood logs), which he sailed from Peru to the Tuamotu Islands, near Tahiti, on the Humboldt current 1947, in an attempt to show that ancient inhabitants of South Americans might have reached Polynesia. He sailed from 28 April to 7 Aug 1947, with five companions, over about 8,000 km/5,000 mi. The Tuamotu Archipelago was in fact settled by Austronesian seafarers, and Heyerdahl's theory is largely discounted by anthropologists.

kookaburra or *laughing jackass* largest of the world's *kingfishers *Dacelo novaeguineae*, found in Australia, with an extraordinary laughing call. It feeds on insects and other small creatures. The body and tail measure 45 cm/18 in, the head is greyish with a dark eye stripe, and the back and wings are flecked brown with grey underparts. Its laugh is one of the most familiar sounds of the bush of E Australia.

kora 21-string instrument of W African origin made from gourds, with a harplike sound.

Koran (alternatively transliterated as *Quran*) sacred book of *Islam. Written in the purest Arabic, it contains 114 *suras* (chapters), and is stated to have been divinely revealed to the prophet Muhammad about 616.

Korbut Olga 1955– . Soviet gymnast who attracted world attention at the 1972 Olympic Games with her lively floor routine, winning three gold medals for the team, beam, and floor exercises.

Korda Alexander 1893–1956. Hungarian-born British film producer and director, a dominant figure during the 1930s and 1940s. His films include *The Private Life of Henry VIII* 1933, *The Third Man* 1950, and *Richard III* 1956.

Korea peninsula in E Asia, divided into *Korea, North, and *Korea, South.

Korea: history
2000 BC The foundation of the Korean state traditionally dates back to the Tangun dynasty.
1122–4th century BC The Chinese Kija dynasty.
AD 10th century After centuries of internal war and invasion, Korea was united within its present boundaries.
16th century Japan invaded Korea for the first time, later withdrawing from a country it had devastated.
1905 Japan began to treat Korea as a protectorate.
1910 It was annexed by Japan. Many Japanese colonists settled in Korea, introducing both industrial and agricultural development.
1945 At the end of World War II, the Japanese in Korea surrendered, but the occupying forces at the cease-fire – the USSR north of the 38th parallel, and the USA south of it – created a lasting division of the country as North and South Korea (see *Korea, North, and *Korea, South, for history since 1945).

Korean language language of Korea, written from the 5th century AD in Chinese characters until the invention of an alphabet by King Sejong 1443. The linguistic affiliations of Korean are unclear, but it may be distantly related to Japanese.

Korea, North Democratic People's Republic of (*Chosun Minchu-chui Inmin Konghwa-guk*)

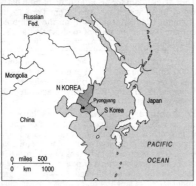

area 120,538 sq km/46,528 sq mi
capital Pyongyang
towns Chongjin, Nampo, Wonsan
physical wide coastal plain in W rising to mountains cut by deep valleys in interior
environment the building of a hydroelectric dam at Kumgangsan on a tributary of the Han River has been opposed by South Korea as a potential flooding threat to central Korea
head of state Kim Jong Il from 1994
head of government Kang Song San from 1992

political system communism
exports coal, iron, copper, textiles, chemicals
currency won
population (1993 est) 22,600,000; growth rate 2.5% p.a.
language Korean
religions traditionally Buddhist, Confucian, but religious activity curtailed by the state
GNP $1,038 per head (1991)
chronology
1910 Korea formally annexed by Japan.
1945 Russian and US troops entered Korea, forced surrender of Japanese, and divided the country in two. Soviet troops occupied North Korea.
1948 Democratic People's Republic of Korea declared.
1950 North Korea invaded South Korea to unite the nation, beginning the Korean War.
1953 Armistice agreed to end Korean War.
1961 Friendship and mutual assistance treaty signed with China.
1972 New constitution, with executive president, adopted. Talks with South Korea about possible reunification.
1980 Reunification talks broke down.
1983 Four South Korean cabinet ministers assassinated in Rangoon, Burma (Myanmar), by North Korean army officers.
1985 Improved relations with the USSR.
1989 Increasing evidence of nuclear-weapons development.
1990 Diplomatic contacts with South Korea and Japan suggested a thaw in North Korea's relations with rest of world.
1991 Became a member of the United Nations. Signed nonaggression agreement with South Korea; agreed to ban nuclear weapons.
1992 Signed Nuclear Safeguards Agreement, allowing international inspection of nuclear facilities. Also signed pact with South Korea for mutual inspection of nuclear facilities. Yon Hyong Muk replaced by Kang Song San.
1993 Threatened to withdraw from Nuclear Non-Proliferation Treaty. Resisted international inspection of nuclear-development sites; tension with USA over nuclear capability.
1994 Kim Il Sung died; succeeded by Kim Jong Il.

Korean War war 1950–53 between North Korea (supported by China) and South Korea, aided by the United Nations (the troops were mainly US). North Korean forces invaded the South 25 June 1950, and the Security Council of the United Nations, owing to a walk-out by the USSR, voted to oppose them. The North Koreans held most of the South when US reinforcements arrived Sept 1950 and forced their way through to the North Korean border with China. The Chinese retaliated, pushing them back to the original boundary Oct 1950; truce negotiations began 1951, although the war did not end until 1953.

Korea, South Republic of Korea (*Daehan Minguk*)
area 98,799 sq km/38,161 sq mi
capital Seoul
towns Taegu, ports Pusan, Inchon
physical southern end of a mountainous peninsula separating the Sea of Japan from the Yellow Sea

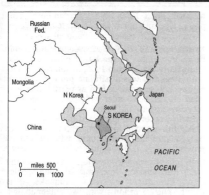

head of state Kim Young Sam from 1993
head of government Lee Young Tok from 1994
political system emergent democracy
exports steel, ships, chemicals, electronics, textiles and clothing, plywood, fish
currency won
population (1993) 44,200,000; growth rate 1.4% p.a.
language Korean
religions traditionally Buddhist, Confucian, and Chondokyo; Christian 28%
GNP $6,749 per head (1992)
chronology
1910 Korea formally annexed by Japan.
1945 Russian and US troops entered Korea, forced surrender of Japanese, and divided the country in two. US military government took control of South Korea.
1948 Republic proclaimed.
1950–53 War with North Korea.
1960 President Syngman Rhee resigned amid unrest.
1961 Military coup by General Park Chung-Hee. Industrial growth programme.
1979 Assassination of President Park.
1980 Military takeover by General Chun Doo Hwan.
1987 Adoption of more democratic constitution after student unrest. Roh Tae Woo elected president.
1988 Former president Chun, accused of corruption, publicly apologized and agreed to hand over his financial assets to the state. Seoul hosted Summer Olympic Games.
1989 Roh reshuffled cabinet, threatened crackdown on protesters.
1990 Two minor opposition parties united with Democratic Justice Party to form ruling Democratic Liberal Party (DLP). Diplomatic relations established with the USSR.
1991 Violent mass demonstrations against the government. New opposition grouping, the Democratic Party, formed. Prime Minister Ro Jai Bong replaced by Chung Won Shik. Entered United Nations. Nonaggression and nuclear pacts signed with North Korea.
1992 DLP lost absolute majority in March general election; substantial gains made by Democratic Party and newly formed UNP, led by Chung Ju Wong. Diplomatic relations with China established. Kim Young Sam, DLP candidate, won the presidential election.

1993 Feb: Hwang In Sung appointed prime minister. Dec: Lee Hoi Chang succeeded Hwang as prime minister.
1994 Mounting tension in peninsula after N Korea's refusal to allow unrestricted inspections of its nuclear-development sites.

Kościusko highest mountain in Australia (2,229 m/7,316 ft), in New South Wales.

Kościuszko Tadeusz 1746–1817. Polish general and nationalist who served with George Washington in the American Revolution (1776–83). He returned to Poland 1784, fought against the Russian invasion that ended in the partition of Poland, and withdrew to Saxony. He returned 1794 to lead the revolt against the occupation, but was defeated by combined Russian and Prussian forces and imprisoned until 1796.

kosher (Hebrew 'appropriate') conforming to religious law with regard to the preparation and consumption of food; in Judaism, conforming to the Mosaic law of the Book of Deuteronomy. For example, only animals that chew the cud and have cloven hooves (cows and sheep, but not pigs) may be eaten. There are rules governing their humane slaughter and their preparation (such as complete draining of blood) which also apply to fowl. Only fish with scales and fins may be eaten; shellfish may not. Milk products may not be cooked or eaten with meat or poultry, or until four hours after eating them. Utensils for meat must be kept separate from those for milk as well.

Kosovo autonomous region (1974–90) in S Serbia, Yugoslavia; capital Priština; area 10,900 sq km/4,207 sq mi; population (1986) 1,900,000, consisting of about 200,000 Serbs and about 1.7 million Albanians. Products include wine, nickel, lead, and zinc. Since it is largely inhabited by Albanians and bordering on Albania, there have been demands for unification with that country, while in the late 1980s Serbians agitated for Kosovo to be merged with the rest of Serbia. A state of emergency was declared Feb 1990 after fighting broke out between ethnic Albanians, police, and the Slavonic minority. The parliament and government were dissolved July 1990 and the Serbian parliament formally annexed Kosovo Sept 1990.

Kossuth Lajos 1802–1894. Hungarian nationalist and leader of the revolution of 1848. He proclaimed Hungary's independence of Habsburg rule, became governor of a Hungarian republic 1849, and, when it was defeated by Austria and Russia, fled first to Turkey and then to exile in Britain and Italy.

Kosygin Alexei Nikolaievich 1904–1980. Soviet politician, prime minister 1964–80. He was elected to the Supreme Soviet 1938, became a member of the Politburo 1946, deputy prime minister 1960, and succeeded Khrushchev as premier (while Brezhnev succeeded him as party secretary). In the late 1960s Kosygin's influence declined.

koto Japanese musical instrument; a long zither of ancient Chinese origin, having 13 silk strings supported by movable bridges. It rests on the floor and the strings are plucked with ivory plectra, producing a brittle sound.

kouprey wild cattle *Bos sauveli* native to the forests of N Cambodia. Only known to science since 1937, it is in great danger of extinction. Koupreys have cylindrical, widely separated horns and grow to 1.9 m/6 ft in height.

Kourou river and second-largest town of French Guiana, NW of Cayenne, site of the Guiana Space Centre of the European Space Agency.

Kowloon peninsula on the Chinese coast forming part of the British crown colony of Hong Kong; the town of Kowloon is a residential area.

kph or **km/h** symbol for **kilometres per hour**.

Krajina region on the frontier between Croatia and Bosnia-Herzegovina; the chief town is Knin. Dominated by Serbs, the region proclaimed itself an autonomous Serbian province after Croatia declared its independence from Yugoslavia 1991. Krajina was the scene of intense inter-ethnic fighting during the civil war in Croatia 1991–92 and, following the cease-fire Jan 1992, 10,000 UN troops were deployed here and in E and W Slavonia.

Kraków or **Cracow** city in Poland, on the river Vistula; population (1990) 750,500. It is an industrial centre producing railway wagons, paper, chemicals, and tobacco. It was capital of Poland c. 1300–1595.

Krasnodar territory of SW Russia, in the N Caucasus, adjacent to the Black Sea; area 83,600 sq km/32,290 sq mi; population (1985) 4,992,000. The capital is Krasnodar. In addition to stock rearing and the production of grain, rice, fruit, and tobacco, oil is refined.

Krasnoyarsk territory of Russia in central Siberia stretching north to the Arctic Ocean; area 2,401,600 sq km/927,617 sq mi; population (1985) 3,430,000. The capital is Krasnoyarsk. It is drained by the Yenisei River. Mineral resources include gold, graphite, coal, iron ore, and uranium.

Kravchuk Leonid 1934– . Ukrainian politician, president from July 1990. Formerly a member of the Ukrainian Communist Party (UCP), he became its ideology chief in the 1980s. After the suspension of the UCP in Aug 1991, Kravchuk became an advocate of independence and market-centred economic reform.

Krebs Hans 1900–1981. German-born British biochemist who discovered the citric acid cycle, also known as the **Krebs cycle**, the final pathway by which food molecules are converted into energy in living tissues. For this work he shared with Fritz Lipmann the 1953 Nobel Prize for Medicine.

Krebs cycle or **citric acid cycle** or **tricarbox-ylic acid cycle** final part of the chain of biochemical reactions by which organisms break down food using oxygen to release energy (respiration). It takes place within structures called *mitochondria in the body's cells, and breaks down food molecules in a series of small steps, producing energy-rich molecules of *ATP.

Kreisler Fritz 1875–1962. Austrian violinist and composer, renowned as an interpreter of Brahms and Beethoven. From 1911 he was one of the earliest recording artists of Classical music, including records of his own compositions.

kremlin citadel or fortress of Russian cities. The Moscow kremlin dates from the 12th century, and the name 'the Kremlin' was once synonymous with the Soviet government.

Krenek Ernst 1900–1991. Austrian-born composer. His jazz opera *Jonny spielt auf/Johnny plays up* 1927 received international acclaim.

Krenz Egon 1937– . German communist politician. A member of the East German Socialist Unity Party (SED) from 1955, he joined its politburo 1983 and was a hardline protégé of Erich *Honecker, succeeding him as party leader and head of state 1989 after widespread prodemocracy demonstrations. Krenz opened the country's western border and promised more open elections, but popular protest continued and he resigned Dec 1989 after only a few weeks in power.

krill any of several Antarctic crustaceans of the order Euphausiacea, the most common species being *Euphausia superba*. Shrimplike, it is about 6 cm/2.5 in long, with two antennae, five pairs of legs, seven pairs of light organs along the body, and is coloured orange above and green beneath.

Krishna incarnation of the Hindu god *Vishnu. The devotion of the *bhakti movement is usually directed towards Krishna; an example of this is the *International Society for Krishna Consciousness. Many stories are told of Krishna's mischievous youth, and he is the charioteer of Arjuna in the *Bhagavad-Gītā*.

Krishna Consciousness Movement popular name for the *International Society for Krishna Consciousness.

Kristallnacht 'night of (broken) glass' 9–10 Nov 1938 when the Nazi Sturmabteilung (SA) militia in Germany and Austria mounted a concerted attack on Jews, their synagogues, homes, and shops. It followed the assassination of a German embassy official in Paris by a Polish-Jewish youth. Subsequent measures included German legislation against Jews owning businesses or property, and restrictions on their going to school or leaving Germany. It was part of the *Holocaust.

Kristiansen Ingrid 1956– . Norwegian athlete, an outstanding long-distance runner of 5,000 metres, 10,000 metres, marathon, and cross-country races. She has won all the world's leading marathons. In 1986 she knocked 45.68 seconds off the world 10,000 metres record. She was the world cross-country champion 1988 and won the London marathon 1984–85 and 1987–88.

Kronos or **Cronus** in Greek mythology, ruler of the world and one of the *Titans. He was the father of Zeus, who overthrew him.

Kronstadt uprising revolt in March 1921 by sailors of the Russian Baltic Fleet at their headquarters in Kronstadt, outside Petrograd (now St Petersburg). On the orders of the leading Bolshevik, Leon Trotsky, Red Army troops, dressed in white camouflage, crossed the ice to the naval base and captured it on 18 March. The leaders were subsequently shot.

Kropotkin Peter Alexeivich, Prince Kropotkin 1842–1921. Russian anarchist. Imprisoned for revolutionary activities 1874, he escaped to the UK 1876 and later moved to Switzerland. Expelled from Switzerland 1881, he went to France, where he was imprisoned 1883–86. He lived in Britain until 1917, when he returned to

Moscow. Among his works are *Memoirs of a Revolutionist* 1899, *Mutual Aid* 1902, and *Modern Science and Anarchism* 1903.

Kruger Stephanus Johannes Paulus 1825–1904. President of the Transvaal 1883–1900. He refused to remedy the grievances of the uitlanders (English and other non-Boer white residents) and so precipitated the Second *South African War.

Krupp German steelmaking armaments firm, founded 1811 by *Friedrich Krupp* (1787–1826) and developed by *Alfred Krupp* (1812–1887) by pioneering the Bessemer steelmaking process. The company developed the long-distance artillery used in World War I, and supported Hitler's regime in preparation for World War II, after which the head of the firm, *Alfred Krupp* (1907–1967), was imprisoned.

krypton (Greek *kryptos* 'hidden') colourless, odourless, gaseous, nonmetallic element, symbol Kr, atomic number 36, relative atomic mass 83.80. It is grouped with the inert gases and was long believed not to enter into reactions, but it is now known to combine with fluorine under certain conditions; it remains inert to all other reagents. It is present in very small quantities in the air (about 114 parts per million). It is used chiefly in fluorescent lamps, lasers, and gas-filled electronic valves.

K-T boundary geologists' shorthand for the boundary between the rocks of the *Cretaceous and the *Tertiary periods. It marks the extinction of the dinosaurs and in many places reveals a layer of iridium, possibly deposited by a meteorite that may have caused the extinction by its impact.

Kuala Lumpur capital of the Federation of Malaysia; area 240 sq km/93 sq mi; population (1990) 1,237,900. The city developed after 1873 with the expansion of tin and rubber trading; these are now its main industries. Formerly within the state of Selangor, of which it was also the capital, it was created a federal territory 1974.

Kuanyin transliteration of *Guanyin, goddess of mercy in Chinese Buddhism.

Kublai Khan 1216–1294. Mongol emperor of China from 1259. He completed his grandfather *Genghis Khan's conquest of N China from 1240, and on his brother Mungo's death 1259 established himself as emperor of China. He moved the capital to Beijing and founded the Yuan dynasty, successfully expanding his empire into Indochina, but was defeated in an attempt to conquer Japan 1281.

Kubrick Stanley 1928– . US-born British film director, producer, and screenwriter. His films include *Paths of Glory* 1957, *Dr Strangelove* 1964, *2001: A Space Odyssey* 1968, *A Clockwork Orange* 1971, and *The Shining* 1979.

kudu either of two species of African antelope of the genus *Tragelaphus*. The greater kudu *T. strepsiceros* is fawn-coloured with thin white vertical stripes, and stands 1.3 m/4.2 ft at the shoulder, with head and body 2.4 m/8 ft long. Males have long spiral horns. The greater kudu is found in bush country from Angola to Ethiopia. The similar lesser kudu *T. imberbis* lives in E Africa and is 1 m/3 ft at the shoulder.

kudzu Japanese creeper *Pueraria lobata*, family Leguminosae, which helps fix nitrogen (see

*nitrogen cycle) and can be used as fodder, but became a pest in the southern USA when introduced to check soil erosion.

Kuhn Thomas S 1922– . US historian and philosopher of science, who showed that social and cultural conditions affect the directions of science. *The Structure of Scientific Revolutions* 1962 argued that even scientific knowledge is relative, dependent on the *paradigm* (theoretical framework) that dominates a scientific field at the time.

Ku Klux Klan US secret society dedicated to white supremacy, founded 1866 in the southern states of the USA to oppose *Reconstruction after the American *Civil War and to deny political rights to the black population. Members wore hooded white robes to hide their identity, and burned crosses at their night-time meetings. It was publicized in the 1960s for terrorizing civil-rights activists and organizing racist demonstrations.

kulak Russian term for a peasant who could afford to hire labour and often acted as village usurer. The kulaks resisted the Soviet government's policy of collectivization, and in 1930 they were 'liquidated as a class', with up to 5 million being either killed or deported to Siberia.

Kulturkampf German word for a policy introduced by Chancellor Bismarck in Germany 1873 that isolated the Catholic interest and attempted to reduce its power in order to create a political coalition of liberals and agrarian conservatives. The alienation of such a large section of the German population as the Catholics could not be sustained, and the policy was abandoned after 1876 to be replaced by an anti-socialist policy.

Kumasi second largest city in Ghana, W Africa, capital of Ashanti region, with trade in cocoa, rubber, and cattle; population (1984) 376,200.

Kumayri formerly (until 1990) *Leninakan*, town in Armenia, 40 km/25 m NW of Yerevan; population (1987) 228,000. Industries include textiles and engineering. It was founded 1837 as a fortress called Alexandropol. The city was virtually destroyed by an earthquake 1926 and again 1988.

kumquat small orange-yellow fruit of any of several evergreen trees of the genus *Fortunella*, family Rutaceae. Native to E Asia, kumquats are cultivated throughout the tropics. The tree grows 2.4–3.6 m/8–12 ft and has dark green shiny leaves and white scented flowers. The fruit is eaten fresh (the skin is edible), preserved, or candied. The oval or Nagami kumquat is the most common variety.

Kun Béla 1885–1938. Hungarian politician who created a Soviet republic in Hungary March 1919, which was overthrown Aug 1919 by a Western blockade and Romanian military actions. The succeeding regime under Admiral Horthy effectively liquidated both socialism and liberalism in Hungary.

Kundera Milan 1929– . Czech writer, born in Brno. His first novel, *The Joke* 1967, brought him into official disfavour in Prague, and unable to publish further works, he moved to France. Other novels include *The Book of Laughter and Forgetting* 1979, *The Unbearable Lightness of Being* 1984, and *Immortality* 1992.

Kung (formerly *Bushman*) member of a small group of hunter-gatherer peoples of the NE Kalahari, southern Africa, still living to some extent nomadically. Their language belongs to the *Khoisan family.

kung fu Chinese art of unarmed combat (Mandarin *ch'üan fa*), one of the *martial arts. It is practised in many forms, the most popular being *wing chun*, 'beautiful springtime'. The basic principle is to use attack as a form of defence.

Kunming formerly *Yunnan* capital of Yunnan province, China, on Lake Dian Chi, about 2,000 m/6,500 ft above sea level; population (1989) 1,500,000. Industries include chemicals, textiles, and copper smelted with nearby hydroelectric power.

Kuomintang original spelling of the Chinese nationalist party, now known (outside Taiwan) as *Guomindang.

Kurd member of the Kurdish culture, living mostly in the Taurus and Sagros mountains of W Iran and N Iraq in the region called Kurdistan. Although divided among more powerful states, the Kurds have nationalist aspirations; there are some 8 million in Turkey (where they suffer from discriminatory legislation), 5 million in Iran, 4 million in Iraq, 500,000 in Syria, and 500,000 in Azerbaijan, Armenia, and Georgia. Several million live elsewhere in Europe. Some 1 million Kurds were made homeless and 25,000 killed as a result of chemical-weapon attacks by Iraq 1984–89, and in 1991, in the wake of the Gulf War, more than 1 million were forced to flee their homes in N Iraq. The Kurdish languages (Kurmanji, Sorani Kurdish, Guraní, and Zaza) are members of the Indo-Iranian branch of the Indo-European family, and the Kurds are a non-Arab, non-Turkic ethnic group. The Kurds are predominantly Sunni Muslims, although there are some Shi'ites in Iran.

Kurdistan or *Kordestan* hilly region in SW Asia near Mount Ararat, where the borders of Iran, Iraq, Syria, Turkey, Armenia, and Azerbaijan meet; area 193,000 sq km/74,600 sq mi; total population around 18 million.

Kuril Islands or *Kuriles* chain of about 50 small islands stretching from the NE of Hokkaido, Japan, to the S of Kamchatka, Russia; area 14,765 sq km/5,700 sq mi; population (1990) 25,000. Some of them are of volcanic origin. Two of the Kurils (Etorofu and Kunashiri) are claimed by Japan and Russia.

Kuropatkin Alexei Nikolaievich 1848–1921. Russian general. He distinguished himself as chief of staff during the Russo-Turkish War 1877–78, was commander in chief in Manchuria 1903, and resigned after his defeat at Mukden 1905 in the *Russo-Japanese War. During World War I he commanded the armies on the northern front until 1916.

Kurosawa Akira 1929– . Japanese director whose film *Rashōmon* 1950 introduced Western audiences to Japanese cinema. Epics such as *Shichinin no samurai/Seven Samurai* 1954 combine spectacle with intimate human drama. The nostalgic and visionary *Yume/Dreams* 1990 has autobiographical elements.

Kuti Fela Anikulapo 1938– . Nigerian singer, songwriter, and musician, a strong proponent of African nationalism and ethnic identity. He had his first local hit 1971 and soon became a W African star. His political protest songs (in English) caused the Nigerian army to attack his commune 1974 and again 1977. His albums include *Coffin for Head of State* 1978 and *Teacher Don't Teach Me Nonsense* 1987.

Kutuzov Mikhail Larionovich, Prince of Smolensk 1745–1813. Commander of the Russian forces in the Napoleonic Wars. He commanded an army corps at *Austerlitz and the army in its reatreat 1812. After the burning of Moscow that year, he harried the French throughout their retreat and later took command of the united Prussian armies.

Kuwait State of (*Dowlat al Kuwait*)

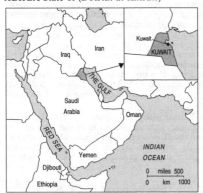

area 17,819 sq km/6,878 sq mi
capital Kuwait (also chief port)
towns Jahra, Ahmadi, Fahaheel
physical hot desert; islands of Failaka, Bubiyan, and Warba at NE corner of Arabian Peninsula
environment during the Gulf War 1990–91, 650 oil wells were set alight and about 300,000 tonnes of oil were released into the waters of the Gulf leading to pollution haze, photochemical smog, acid rain, soil contamination, and water pollution
head of state and government Jabir al-Ahmad al-Jabir al-Sabah from 1977
political system absolute monarchy
exports oil
currency Kuwaiti dinar
population (1993 est) 1,600,000 (Kuwaitis 40%, Palestinians 30%); growth rate 5.5% p.a.
languages Arabic 78%, Kurdish 10%, Farsi 4%
religion Sunni Muslim 45%, Shi'ite minority 30%
GNP $19.1 bn; $10,410 per head (1988)
chronology
1914 Britain recognized Kuwait as an independent sovereign state.
1961 Full independence achieved from Britain, with Sheik Abdullah al-Salem al-Sabah as emir.
1965 Sheik Abdullah died; succeeded by his brother, Sheik Sabah.
1977 Sheik Sabah died; succeeded by Crown Prince Jabir.
1983 Shi'ite guerrillas bombed targets in Kuwait; 17 arrested.

1987 Kuwaiti oil tankers reflagged, received US Navy protection; missile attacks by Iran.
1988 Aircraft hijacked by pro-Iranian Shi'ites demanding release of convicted guerrillas; Kuwait refused.
1989 Two of the convicted guerrillas released.
1990 Prodemocracy demonstrations suppressed. Kuwait annexed by Iraq. Emir set up government in exile in Saudi Arabia.
1991 Feb: Kuwait liberated by US-led coalition forces; extensive damage to property and environment. Emir returned to Kuwait. New government omitted any opposition representatives. Trials of alleged Iraqi collaborators criticized. Promised elections postponed.
1992 Oct: reconstituted national assembly elected on restricted franchise, with opposition party winning majority of seats.
1993 Jan: incursions by Iraq into Kuwait again created tension; US-led air strikes restored calm.

Kuwait City (Arabic *Al Kuwayt*) formerly *Qurein* chief port and capital of the state of Kuwait, on the southern shore of Kuwait Bay; population (1985) 44,300, plus the suburbs of Hawalli, population (1985) 145,100, Jahra, population (1985) 111,200, and as-Salimiya, population (1985) 153,400. Kuwait is a banking and investment centre.

Kuznetsov Anatoli 1930–1979. Russian writer. His novels *Babi Yar* 1966, describing the wartime execution of Jews at Babi Yar, near Kiev, and *The Fire* 1969, about workers in a large metallurgical factory, were seen as anti-Soviet. He lived in Britain from 1969.

kW symbol for *kilowatt*.

Kwa Ndebele black homeland in Transvaal province, South Africa; achieved self-governing status 1981; population (1985) 235,800.

Kwangchow alternative transliteration of *Guangzhou, city in China.

Kwangchu or *Kwangju* capital of South Cholla province, SW South Korea; population (1990) 1,144,700. It is at the centre of a rice-growing region. A museum in the city houses a large collection of Chinese porcelain dredged up 1976 after lying for over 600 years on the ocean floor.

Kwangsi-Chuang alternative transliteration of *Guangxi, region of China.

Kwangtung alternative transliteration of *Guangdong, province of China.

Kwannon or *Kannon* in Japanese Buddhism, a female form (known to the West as 'goddess of mercy') of the bodhisattva *Avalokiteśvara. Kwannon is sometimes depicted with many arms extending compassion.

kwashiorkor severe protein deficiency in children under five years, resulting in retarded growth and a swollen abdomen.

Kwa Zulu black homeland in Natal province, South Africa; population (1985) 3,747,000. It achieved self-governing status 1971.

Kweilin alternative transliteration of *Guilin in China.

kyanite aluminium silicate, Al_2SiO_5, a pale-blue mineral occurring as blade-shaped crystals. It is an indicator of high-pressure conditions in metamorphic rocks formed from clay sediments.

Andalusite, kyanite, and sillimanite are all polymorphs.

Kyd Thomas *c.* 1557–1595. English dramatist, author in about 1588 of a bloody revenge tragedy, *The Spanish Tragedy*, which anticipated elements present in Shakespeare's *Hamlet*.

Kyoto former capital of Japan 794–1868 (when the capital was changed to Tokyo) on Honshu island, linked by canal with Biwa Lake; population (1989) 1,407,300. Industries include electrical, chemical, and machinery plants; silk weaving; and the manufacture of porcelain, bronze, and lacquerware.

features The city's more than 2,000 temples and shrines include Tō-ji (1380), Kiyomizu-dera (1633), Ryōan-ji with its 15th-century Zen rock and sand garden, Sanjusangendo (1266), and the former Ashikaga shoguns' villas Kinkaku-ji and Ginkaku-ji (the 'gold and silver pavilions'). Other features are the Gion teahouse district with traditional geishas, the silk-weavers' district of Nishijin, 17th-century sake warehouses in Fushimi, Momoyama castle, and Japan's oldest theatre, the Minamiza kabuki theatre (early 17th century).

history Like previous Japanese capitals, Kyoto was originally laid out in a grid pattern derived from China. Civil wars, especially that between the Taira and Minamoto clans in the 12th century and the Ōnin war 1467–77, caused great destruction in the capital, and it has been periodically ravaged by fire, most recently in 1864, when almost 80% of the city was laid waste. Although the shogunate was at times based elsewhere, Kyoto remained the seat of the imperial court until the Meiji restoration 1868, and is still a cultural centre.

Kyrgyzstan Republic of

area 198,500 sq km/76,641 sq mi
capital Bishkek (formerly Frunze)
towns Osh, Przhevalsk, Kyzyl-Kiya, Tormak
physical mountainous, an extension of the Tian Shan range
head of state Askar Akayev from 1990
head of government Tursunbek Chyngyshev from 1991
political system emergent democracy
political party Democratic Kyrgyzstan,

nationalist reformist; Asaba (Banner) Party and Free Kyrgyzstan Party, both opposition groupings
products cereals, sugar, cotton, coal, oil, sheep, yaks, horses
currency som
population (1993) 4,600,000 (52% Kyrgyz, 22% Russian, 13% Uzbek, 3% Ukrainian, 2% German)
language Kyrgyz, a Turkic language
religion Sunni Muslim
chronology
GNP $1,1550 per head (1991)
1917–1924 Part of an independent Turkestan republic.
1924 Became autonomous republic within USSR.
1936 Became full union republic within USSR.
1990 June: ethnic clashes resulted in state of emergency being imposed in Bishkek. Nov: Askar Akayev chosen as state president.
1991 March: Kyrgyz voters endorsed maintenance of Union in USSR referendum. Aug: President Akayev condemned anti-Gorbachev attempted coup in Moscow; Kyrgyz Communist Party, which supported the coup, suspended. Oct: Akayev directly elected president. Dec: joined new Commonwealth of Independent States and independence recognized by USA.
1992 Admitted into Conference on Security and Cooperation in Europe (Jan) and the United Nations (March).

Kyrie eleison (Greek 'Lord have mercy') the words spoken or sung at the beginning of the mass in the Catholic, Orthodox, and Anglican churches.

Kyushu southernmost of the main islands of Japan, separated from Shikoku and Honshu by Bungo Channel and Suo Bay, but connected to Honshu by bridge and rail tunnel
area 42,150 sq km/16,270 sq mi, including about 370 small islands
capital Nagasaki
cities Fukuoka, Kumamoto, Kagoshima
physical mountainous, volcanic, with subtropical climate
products coal, gold, silver, iron, tin, rice, tea, timber
population (1986) 13,295,000.

L Roman numeral for 50.

l symbol for *litre*, a measure of liquid volume.

Labanotation comprehensive system of accurate dance notation (*Kinetographie Laban*) devised 1928 by Rudolf von Laban (1879–1958), dancer, choreographer, and dance theorist.

labelled compound or *tagged compound* chemical compound in which a radioactive isotope is substituted for a stable one. The path taken by such a compound through a system can be followed, for example by measuring the radiation emitted.

labelling in sociology, defining or describing a person in terms of his or her behaviour; for example, describing someone who has broken a law as a criminal. Labelling theory deals with human interaction, behaviour, and control, particularly in the field of deviance.

labellum lower petal of an orchid flower; it is a different shape from the two lateral petals and gives the orchid its characteristic appearance. The labellum is more elaborate and usually larger than the other petals. It often has distinctive patterning to encourage *pollination by insects; sometimes it is extended backwards to form a hollow spur containing nectar.

Labiatae family of 3,000–4,000 species of flowering plants found worldwide. The stems are often quadrangular in sections, with leaves arranged in opposite pairs at right angles to the next pair. The plants are often covered with hairs and glands that emit an aromatic fragrance. Species include basil, marjoram, oregano, peppermint, salvia, and thyme.

Labor, Knights of in US history, a national labour organization founded by Philadelphia tailor Uriah Stephens in 1869 and committed to cooperative enterprise, equal pay for both sexes, and an eight-hour day. The Knights grew rapidly in the mid-1880s under Terence V Powderly (1849–1924) but gave way to the *American Federation of Labor after 1886.

Labor Party in Australia, a political party based on socialist principles. It was founded in 1891 and first held office in 1904. It formed governments 1929–31 and 1939–49, but in the intervening periods internal discord provoked splits, and reduced its effectiveness. It returned to power under Gough Whitlam 1972–75, and again under Bob Hawke from 1983.

Labour Day legal holiday in honour of workers. In Canada and the USA, *Labor day* is celebrated on the first Monday in September. In many countries it coincides with *May Day, the first day of May.

labour market market that determines the cost and conditions of the work force, taking into consideration the demand of employers, the levels and availability of skills, and social conditions.

Labour Party UK political party based on socialist principles, originally formed to represent workers. It was founded in 1900 and first held office in 1924. The first majority Labour government 1945–51 introduced *nationalization and the National Health Service, and expanded *social security. Labour was again in power 1964–70 and 1974–79. The party leader is elected by Labour members of Parliament.

labour theory of value in classical economics, the theory that the price (value) of a product directly reflects the amount of labour it involves. According to the theory, if the price of a product falls, either the share of labour in that product has declined or that expended in the production of other goods has risen. *Marx adopted and developed the theory but it was not supported by all classical economists. The British economist, Thomas *Malthus, was a dissenter.

Labrador area of NE Canada, part of the province of Newfoundland, lying between Ungava Bay on the NW, the Atlantic Ocean on the E, and the Strait of Belle Isle on the SE; area 266,060 sq km/102,699 sq mi; population (1986) 28,741. It consists primarily of a gently sloping plateau with an irregular coastline of numerous bays, fjords, inlets, and cliffs (60 m/200 ft to 120 m/400 ft high). Industries include fisheries, timber and pulp, and many minerals. Hydroelectric resources include Churchill Falls on Churchill River, where one of the world's largest underground power houses is situated.

La Bruyère Jean de 1645–1696. French essayist. He was born in Paris, studied law, took a post in the revenue office, and in 1684 entered the service of the French commander the Prince of *Condé. His *Caractères* 1688, satirical portraits of his contemporaries, made him many enemies.

laburnum any flowering tree or shrub of the genus *Laburnum* of the pea family Leguminosae. The seeds are poisonous. *L. anagyroides*, native to the mountainous parts of central Europe, is often grown as an ornamental tree. The flowers, in long drooping clusters, are bright yellow and appear in early spring; some varieties have purple or reddish flowers.

Labyrinth in Greek mythology, the maze designed by the Athenian artisan Daedalus at Knossos in Crete for King Minos as a home for the Minotaur, a monster, half man and half bull. After killing the Minotaur, Theseus, the prince of Athens, was guided out of the Labyrinth by a thread given to him by the king's daughter, Ariadne.

labyrinthitis inflammation of the part of the inner ear responsible for the sense of balance (the labyrinth). It results in dizziness, which may then cause nausea and vomiting. It is usually caused by a viral infection of the ear (*otitis), which resolves in a few weeks. The nausea and vomiting may respond to anti-emetic drugs.

Laccadive, Minicoy, and Amindivi Islands former name of Indian island group *Lakshadweep.

laccolith intruded mass of igneous rock that forces apart two strata and forms a round lens-shaped mass many times wider than thick. The overlying layers are often pushed upward to form a dome. A classic development of laccoliths is illustrated in the Henry La Sal and Abajo mountains of SE Utah, USA, found on the Colorado plateau.

lace delicate, decorative, openwork textile fabric. Lace is a European craft with centres in Belgium, Italy, France, Germany, and England.

lacewing insect of the families Hemerobiidae (the brown lacewings) and Chrysopidae (the green lacewings) of the order Neuroptera. Found throughout the world, lacewings are so called because of the intricate veining of their two pairs of semi-transparent wings. They have narrow bodies and long thin antennae. The larvae (called aphid lions) are predators, especially on aphids.

laches in law, neglect and unreasonable delay in enforcing an equitable right. If the court is satisfied that a plaintiff has taken an unnecessarily long time in pursuing a case, the action may be struck out.

Laclos Pierre Choderlos de 1741–1803. French author. An army officer, he wrote a single novel in letter form, *Les Liaisons dangereuses/Dangerous Liaisons* 1782, an analysis of moral corruption.

lacquer waterproof resinous varnish obtained from Oriental trees *Toxicodendron verniciflua*, and used for decorating furniture and art objects. It can be applied to wood, fabric, leather, or other materials, with or without added colours. The technique of making and carving small lacquer-work objects was developed in China, probably as early as the 4th century BC, and was later adopted in Japan.

lacrosse Canadian ball game, adopted from the North American Indians, and named after a fancied resemblance of the lacrosse stick (crosse) to a bishop's crosier. Thongs across the curved end of the crosse form a pocket to carry the small rubber ball. The field is approximately 100 m/110 yd long and a minimum of 55 m/60 yd wide in the men's game, which is played with 10 players per side; the women's field is larger, and there are 12 players per side. The goals are just under 2 m/6 ft square, with loose nets. The world championship were first held in 1967 for men, and in 1969 for women.

lactation secretion of milk from the mammary glands of mammals. In late pregnancy, the cells lining the lobules inside the mammary glands begin extracting substances from the blood to produce milk. The supply of milk starts shortly after birth with the production of colostrum, a clear fluid consisting largely of water, protein, antibodies, and vitamins. The production of milk continues practically as long as the infant continues to suck.

lactic acid or **2-hydroxypropanoic acid** CH₃CHOHCOOH organic acid, a colourless, almost odourless liquid, produced by certain bacteria during fermentation and by active muscle cells when they are exercised hard and are experiencing *oxygen debt. It occurs in yoghurt, buttermilk, sour cream, poor wine, and certain plant extracts, and is used in food preservation and in the preparation of pharmaceuticals.

lactose white sugar, found in solution in milk; it forms 5% of cow's milk. It is commercially prepared from the whey obtained in cheese-making. Like table sugar (sucrose), it is a disaccharide, consisting of two basic sugar units (monosaccharides), in this case, glucose and galactose. Unlike sucrose, it is tasteless.

Ladd Alan 1913–1964. US actor whose first leading role, as the professional killer in *This Gun for Hire* 1942, made him a star. His career declined after the mid-1950s although his last role, in *The Carpetbaggers* 1964, is considered one of his best. His other films include *The Blue Dahlia* 1946 and *Shane* 1953.

Ladoga (Russian **Ladozhskoye**) largest lake on the continent of Europe, in Russia, just NE of St Petersburg; area 18,400 sq km/7,100 sq mi. It receives the waters of several rivers, including the Svir, which drains Lake Onega and runs to the Gulf of Finland by the river Neva.

Lady in the UK, the formal title of the daughter of an earl, marquis, or duke; and of any woman whose husband is above the rank of baronet or knight, as well as (by courtesy only) the wives of these latter ranks.

ladybird or **ladybug** beetle of the family Coccinellidae, generally red or yellow in colour, with black spots. There are numerous species which, as larvae and adults, feed on aphids and scale-insect pests.

Lady Day Christian festival (25 March) of the Annunciation of the Virgin Mary; until 1752 it was the beginning of the legal year in England, and it is still a quarter day (date for the payment of quarterly rates or dues).

lady's smock alternative name for the *cuckoo flower *Cardamine pratensis*.

Laënnec René Théophile Hyacinthe 1781–1826. French physician, inventor of the *stethoscope 1814. He introduced the new diagnostic technique of auscultation (evaluating internal organs by listening with a stethoscope) in his book *Traité de l'auscultation médiaté* 1819, which quickly became a medical classic.

Lafayette Marie Joseph Gilbert de Motier, Marquis de Lafayette 1757–1834. French soldier and politician. He fought against Britain in the American Revolution 1777–79 and 1780–82. During the French Revolution he sat in the National Assembly as a constitutional royalist and in 1789 presented the Declaration of the Rights of Man. After the storming of the *Bastille, he was given command of the National Guard. In 1792 he fled the country after attempting to restore the monarchy and was imprisoned by the Austrians until 1797. He supported Napoleon Bonaparte in 1815, sat in the chamber of deputies as a Liberal from 1818, and played a leading part in the revolution of 1830.

La Fontaine Jean de 1621–1695. French poet. He was born at Château-Thierry, and from 1656 lived largely in Paris, the friend of the playwrights Molière and Racine, and the poet Boileau. His works include *Fables* 1668–94 and *Contes* 1665–74, a series of witty and bawdy tales in verse.

Laforgue Jules 1860–1887. French poet who pioneered *free verse and who inspired later French and English writers.

Lagash Sumerian city N of Shatra, Iraq, under independent and semi-independent rulers from about 3000–2700 BC. Besides objects of high artistic value, it has provided about 30,000 clay tablets giving detailed information on temple administration. Lagash was discovered in 1877 and excavated by Ernest de Sarzec, then French consul in Basra.

lager type of light *beer.

Lagerkvist Pär 1891–1974. Swedish author of lyric poetry, dramas (including *The Hangman* 1935), and novels, such as *Barabbas* 1950. He was awarded the 1951 Nobel Prize for Literature.

Lagerlöf Selma 1858–1940. Swedish novelist. Her first work was the romantic historical novel *Gösta Berling's Saga* 1891. The children's fantasy *Nils Holgerssons underbara resa/The Wonderful Voyage of Nils Holgersson* 1906–07 grew from her background as a schoolteacher. She was the first woman to receive a Nobel prize, in 1909.

lagoon coastal body of shallow salt water, usually with limited access to the sea. The term is normally used to describe the shallow sea area cut off by a *coral reef or barrier islands.

Lagos chief port and former capital of Nigeria, located at the western end of an island in a lagoon and linked by bridges with the mainland via Iddo Island; population (1983) 1,097,000. Industries include chemicals, metal products, and fish. One of the most important slaving ports, Lagos was bombarded and occupied by the British 1851, becoming the colony of Lagos 1862. *Abuja was established as the new capital 1982.

Lagrange Joseph Louis 1736–1813. French mathematician. His *Mécanique analytique* 1788 applied mathematical analysis, using principles established by Newton, to such problems as the movements of planets when affected by each other's gravitational force. He presided over the commission that introduced the metric system in 1793.

Lagrangian points five locations in space where the centrifugal and gravitational forces of two bodies neutralize each other; a third, less massive body located at any one of these points will be held in equilibrium with respect to the other two. Three of the points, L1–L3, lie on a line joining the two large bodies. The other two points, L4 and L5, which are the most stable, lie on either side of this line. Their existence was predicted in 1772 by Joseph Louis Lagrange.

La Guardia Fiorello (Henrico) 1882–1947. US Republican politician; congressman 1917, 1919, 1923–33; mayor of New York 1933–45. Elected against the opposition of the powerful Tammany Hall Democratic Party organization, he improved the administration, suppressed racketeering, and organized unemployment relief, slum-clearance schemes, and social services. Although nominally a Republican, he supported the Democratic president F D Roosevelt's *New Deal. La Guardia Airport, in New York City, is named after him.

Lahore capital of the province of Punjab and second city of Pakistan; population (1981) 2,920,000. Industries include engineering, textiles, carpets, and chemicals. It is associated with the Mogul rulers Akbar, Jahangir, and Aurangzeb, whose capital it was in the 16th and 17th centuries.

Lailat ul-Barah Muslim festival, the *Night of Forgiveness*, which takes place two weeks before the beginning of the fast of Ramadan (the ninth month of the Islamic year) and is a time for asking and granting forgiveness.

Lailat ul-Isra Wal Mi'raj Muslim festival that celebrates the prophet Muhammad's *Night Journey.

Lailat ul-Qadr Muslim festival, the *Night of Power*, which celebrates the giving of the Koran to Muhammad. It usually falls at the end of Ramadan.

Laing R(onald) D(avid) 1927–1989. Scottish psychoanalyst, originator of the 'social theory' of mental illness, for example that schizophrenia is promoted by family pressure for its members to conform to standards alien to themselves. His books include *The Divided Self* 1960 and *The Politics of the Family* 1971.

laissez faire (French 'let alone') theory that the state should not intervene in economic affairs, except to break up a monopoly. The phrase originated with the Physiocrats, 18th-century French economists whose maxim was *laissez faire et laissez passer*, (literally, 'let go and let pass' – that is, leave the individual alone and let commodities circulate freely). The degree to which intervention should take place is still one of the chief problems of economics. The Scottish economist Adam *Smith justified the theory in *The Wealth of Nations*.

lake body of still water lying in depressed ground without direct communication with the sea. Lakes are common in formerly glaciated regions, along the courses of slow rivers, and in low land near the sea. The main classifications are by origin: *glacial lakes*, formed by glacial scouring; *barrier lakes*, formed by landslides and glacial moraines; *crater lakes*, found in volcanoes; and *tectonic lakes*, occurring in natural fissures.

MAJOR LAKES

name and location	sq km	sq mi
Caspian Sea (Azerbaijan/Russia/ Kazakhstan/Turkmenistan/Iran)	370,990	143,240
Superior (USA/Canada)	82,071	31,700
Victoria (Tanzania/Kenya/ Uganda)	69,463	26,820
Aral Sea (Kazakhstan/ Uzbekistan)	64,500	24,904
Huron (USA/Canada)	59,547	23,000
Michigan (USA)	57,735	22,300
Tanganyika (Malawi/Zaire/ Zambia/Burundi)	32,880	12,700
Baikal (Russia)	31,456	12,150
Great Bear (Canada)	31,316	12,096
Malawi (Tanzania/Malawi/ Mozambique)	28,867	11,150
Great Slave (Canada)	28,560	11,031
Erie (USA/Canada)	25,657	9,910
Winnipeg (Canada)	25,380	9,417
Ontario (USA/Canada)	19,547	7,550
Balkhash (Kazakhstan)	18,421	7,115
Ladoga (Russia)	17,695	6,835
Chad (Chad/Niger/Nigeria)	16,310	6,300
Maracaibo (Venezuela)	13,507	5,217

Lake District region in Cumbria, England; area 1,800 sq km/700 sq mi. It contains the principal English lakes, which are separated by wild uplands rising to many peaks, including Scafell Pike (978 m/3,210 ft).

lake dwelling prehistoric village built on piles driven into the bottom of a lake. Such villages are found throughout Europe, in W Africa, South America, Borneo, and New Guinea.

Lakshadweep group of 36 coral islands, 10 inhabited, in the Indian Ocean, 320 km/200 mi off the Malabar coast; area 32 sq km/12 sq mi; population (1991) 51,700. The administrative headquarters is on Kavaratti Island. Products include coir, copra, and fish. The religion is Muslim. The first Western visitor was Vasco da Gama in 1499. The islands were British from 1877 until Indian independence and were created a Union Territory of the Republic of India 1956. Formerly known as the Laccadive, Minicoy, and Amindivi Islands, they were renamed Lakshadweep 1973.

Lakshmi Hindu goddess of wealth and beauty, consort of Vishnu; her festival is *Diwali.

Lalique René 1860–1945. French designer and manufacturer of *Art Nouveau glass, jewellery, and house interiors. The Lalique factory continues in production at Wingen-sur-Moder, Alsace, under his son Marc and granddaughter Marie-Claude.

Lallans variant of 'lowlands' and a name for Lowland Scots, whether conceived as a language in its own right or as a northern dialect of English. Because of its rustic associations, Lallans has been known since the 18th century as 'the Doric', in contrast with the 'Attic' usage of Edinburgh ('the Athens of the North'). See *Scots language.

Lalo (Victor Antoine) Edouard 1823–1892. French composer. His Spanish ancestry and violin training are evident in the *Symphonie Espagnole* 1873 for violin and orchestra, and *Concerto for cello and orchestra* 1877. He also wrote an opera, *Le Roi d'Ys* 1887.

Lam Wilfredo 1902–1982. Cuban abstract painter. Influenced by Surrealism in the 1930s (he lived in Paris 1937–41), he created a semi-abstract style using mysterious and sometimes menacing images and symbols, mainly taken from Caribbean tradition. His *Jungle* series, for example, contains voodoo elements. He visited Haiti and Martinique in the 1940s, Paris 1952, and also made frequent visits to Italy.

Lamaism religion of Tibet and Mongolia, a form of Mahāyāna Buddhism. Buddhism was introduced into Tibet in AD 640, but the real founder of Lamaism was the Indian missionary Padma Sambhava who began his activity about 750. The head of the church is the *Dalai Lama, who is considered an incarnation of the Bodhisattva Avalokiteśvara. On the death of the Dalai Lama great care is taken in finding the infant in whom he has been reincarnated.

Lamarck Jean Baptiste de 1744–1829. French naturalist whose theory of evolution, known as **Lamarckism**, was based on the idea that acquired characteristics (changes acquired in an individual's lifetime) are inherited, and that organisms have an intrinsic urge to evolve into better-adapted forms. His works include *Philosophie Zoologique/Zoological Philosophy* 1809 and *Histoire naturelle des animaux sans vertèbres/Natural History of Invertebrate Animals* 1815–22.

Lamarckism theory of evolution, now discredited, advocated during the early 19th century by Lamarck. It differed from the Darwinian theory of evolution.

Lamartine Alphonse de 1790–1869. French poet. He wrote romantic poems, including *Méditations poétiques* 1820, followed by *Nouvelles méditations/New Meditations* 1823, and *Harmonies* 1830. His *Histoire des Girondins/History of the Girondins* 1847 helped to inspire the revolution of 1848.

Lamb Charles 1775–1834. English essayist and critic. He collaborated with his sister **Mary Lamb** (1764–1847) on *Tales from Shakespeare* 1807, and his *Specimens of English Dramatic Poets* 1808 helped to revive interest in Elizabethan plays. As 'Elia' he contributed essays to the *London Magazine* from 1820 (collected 1823 and 1833).

Lamb Willis 1913– . US physicist who revised the quantum theory of Paul *Dirac. The hydrogen atom was thought to exist in either of two distinct states carrying equal energies. More sophisticated measurements by Lamb in 1947 demonstrated that the two energy levels were not equal. This discrepancy, since known as the **Lamb shift** won him the 1955 Nobel Prize for Physics.

Lambeth Conference meeting of bishops of the Anglican Communion every ten years, presided over by the archbishop of Canterbury; its decisions on doctrinal matters are not binding.

Lamburn Richmal Crompton. Full name of British writer Richmal *Crompton.

lamina in flowering plants (*angiosperms), the blade of the *leaf on either side of the midrib. The lamina is generally thin and flattened, and is usually the primary organ of *photosynthesis. It has a network of veins through which water and nutrients are conducted. More generally, a lamina is any thin, flat plant structure, such as the *thallus of many seaweeds.

Lammas ('loaf-mass') medieval festival of harvest, celebrated 1 Aug. At one time it was an English quarter day (date for payment of quarterly rates or dues), and is still a quarter day in Scotland.

lammergeier Old World vulture *Gypaetus barbatus*, also known as the bearded vulture, with a wingspan of 2.7 m/9 ft. It ranges over S Europe, N Africa, and Asia, in wild mountainous areas. It feeds on offal and carrion and drops bones onto rocks to break them and so get at the marrow.

Lamont Norman 1942– . UK Conservative politician, chief secretary of the Treasury 1989–90, chancellor of the Exchequer 1990–93. In Sept 1992, despite earlier assurances to the contrary, he was forced to suspend Britain's membership of the *European Monetary System (EMS) and let the pound float downwards.

Lampedusa Giuseppe Tomasi di 1896–1957. Italian aristocrat, author of *The Leopard* 1958, a novel set in his native Sicily during the period following its annexation by Garibaldi in 1860. It chronicles the reactions of an aristocratic family to social and political upheavals.

lamprey any of various eel-shaped jawless fishes belonging to the family Petromyzontidae. A lamprey feeds on other fish by fixing itself by its round mouth to its host and boring into the flesh with its toothed tongue. Lampreys breed in fresh water, and the young live as larvae for about five years before migrating to the sea.

Lancashire county in NW England
area 3,040 sq km/1,173 sq mi
towns Preston (administrative headquarters), which forms part of Central Lancashire New Town (together with Fulwood, Bamber Bridge, Leyland, and Chorley); Lancaster, Accrington, Blackburn, Burnley; ports Fleetwood and Heysham; seaside resorts Blackpool, Morecambe, and Southport
products formerly a world centre of cotton manufacture, now replaced with high-technology aerospace and electronics industries
population (1991) 1,365,100.

Lancaster, Chancellor of the Duchy of public office created 1351 and attached to the crown since 1399. The office of Chancellor of the Duchy is a sinecure without any responsibilities, usually held by a member of the Cabinet with a special role outside that of the regular ministries, for example, Harold Lever as financial adviser to the Wilson–Callaghan governments from 1974.

Lancaster Burt (Burton Stephen) 1913–1994. US film actor, formerly an acrobat. A star from his first film, *The Killers* 1946, he proved himself adept both at action roles and more complex character parts as in such films as *From Here to Eternity* 1953, *The Rose Tattoo* 1955, *Elmer Gantry* 1960, and *The Leopard/Il Gattopardo* 1963.

Lancaster Osbert 1908–1986. English cartoonist and writer. In 1939 he began producing daily 'pocket cartoons' for the *Daily Express*, in which he satirized current social mores through such characters as Maudie Littlehampton. He was originally a book illustrator and muralist.

Lancaster, House of English royal house, a branch of the Plantagenets.

lancelet any one of a variety of marine animals of subphylum cephalocordates (see *chordate), genus *Amphioxus*, about 2.5 cm/1 in long. It has no skull, brain, eyes, heart, vertebral column, centralized brain, nor paired limbs, but there is a notochord (a supportive rod) which runs from end to end of the body, a tail, and a number of gill slits. Found in all seas, it burrows in the sand but when disturbed swims freely.

Lancelot of the Lake in British legend, one of King Arthur's knights, the lover of Queen Guinevere. Originally a folk hero, he first appeared in the Arthurian cycle of tales in the 12th century.

Land (plural *Länder*) federal state of Germany or Austria.

Land Edwin Herbert 1909–1991. US inventor of the Polaroid Land camera 1947, which developed the film in one minute inside the camera and produced an 'instant' photograph.

Land League Irish peasant-rights organization, formed 1879 by Michael *Davitt and Charles

*Parnell to fight against tenant evictions. Through its skilful use of the boycott against anyone who took a farm from which another had been evicted, it forced Gladstone's government to introduce a law in 1881 restricting rents and granting tenants security of tenure.

landlord and tenant in law, the relationship that exists between an owner of land or buildings (the landlord) and a person granted the right to occupy them (the tenant). The landlord grants a lease or tenancy, which may be for a year, a term of years, a week, or any other definite, limited period.

Land Registry, HM official body set up in 1925 to register legal rights to land in England and Wales. There has been a gradual introduction, since 1925, of compulsory registration of land in different areas of the country. This requires the purchaser of land to register details of his or her title and all other rights (such as mortgages and *easements) relating to the land. Once registered, the title to the land is guaranteed by the Land Registry, subject to those interests that cannot be registered; this makes the buying and selling of land easier and cheaper. The records are open to public inspection (since Dec 1990).

Landsbergis Vytautas 1932– . President of Lithuania 1990–92. He became active in nationalist politics in the 1980s, founding and eventually chairing the anticommunist Sajudis independence movement 1988. When Sajudis swept to victory in the republic's elections March 1990, Landsbergis chaired the Supreme Council of Lithuania, becoming, in effect, president. He immediately drafted the republic's declaration of independence from the USSR, which was recognized Sept 1991. In elections Nov 1992 he lost to former communist leader Algirdas Brazauskas.

Landseer Edwin Henry 1802–1873. English painter, sculptor, and engraver of animal studies. Much of his work reflects the Victorian taste for sentimental and moralistic pictures, for example *Dignity and Impudence* 1839 (Tate Gallery, London). The *Monarch of the Glen* (John Dewar and Sons Ltd) 1850, depicting a highland stag, was painted for the House of Lords. His sculptures include the lions at the base of Nelson's Column in Trafalgar Square, London, 1857–67.

Land's End promontory of W Cornwall, 15 km/9 mi WSW of Penzance, the westernmost point of England.

land set-aside scheme policy introduced by the European Community in the late 1980s, as part of the Common Agricultural Policy, to reduce overproduction of certain produce. Farmers are paid not to use land but to keep it *fallow. The policy may bring environmental benefits by limiting the amount of fertilizers and pesticides used.

landslide sudden downward movement of a mass of soil or rocks from a cliff or steep slope. Landslides happen when a slope becomes unstable, usually because the base has been undercut or because materials within the mass have become wet and slippery.

Landsteiner Karl 1868–1943. Austrian-born immunologist who discovered the ABO *blood group system 1900–02, and aided in the discovery of the Rhesus blood factors 1940. He also discovered the polio virus. He was awarded a Nobel prize in 1930.

Landtag legislature of each of the *Länder* (states) that form the federal republics of Germany and Austria.

Lang Andrew 1844–1912. Scottish historian and folklore scholar. His writings include historical works; anthropological essays, such as *Myth, Ritual and Religion* 1887 and *The Making of Religion* 1898, which involved him in controversy with the anthropologist James G *Frazer; novels; and a series of children's books, beginning with *The Blue Fairy Tale Book* 1889.

Lang Fritz 1890–1976. Austrian film director whose films are characterized by a strong sense of social realism. His German films include *Metropolis* 1927, the sensational *M* 1931, in which Peter Lorre starred as a child-killer, and the series of Dr Mabuse films, after which he fled from the Nazis to Hollywood in 1936. His US films include *Fury* 1936, *You Only Live Once* 1937, *Scarlet Street* 1945, *Rancho Notorious* 1952, and *The Big Heat* 1953. He returned to Germany and directed a third picture in the Dr Mabuse series in 1960.

lang k d 1961– . Canadian singer whose mellifluous voice and androgynous image gained her a wide following beyond the country-music field where she first established herself. Albums include *Angel With a Lariat* 1987, *Shadowland* 1988, *Absolute Torch and Twang* 1989, and the mainstream *Ingénue* 1992.

Lange David (Russell) 1942– . New Zealand Labour Party prime minister 1983–89. Lange, a barrister, was elected to the House of Representatives 1977. Labour had a decisive win in the 1984 general election on a non-nuclear military policy, which Lange immediately put into effect, despite criticism from the USA. He introduced a free-market economic policy and was re-elected 1987. He resigned Aug 1989 over a disagreement with his finance minister.

Langland William *c.* 1332–*c.* 1400. English poet. His alliterative *Vision Concerning Piers Plowman* appeared in three versions between about 1362 and 1398, but some critics believe he was only responsible for the first of these. The poem forms a series of allegorical visions, in which Piers develops from the typical poor peasant to a symbol of Jesus, and condemns the social and moral evils of 14th-century England.

Langton Stephen *c.* 1150–1228. English priest who was mainly responsible for drafting the charter of rights, the *Magna Carta.

Langtry Lillie. Stage name of Emilie Charlotte le Breton 1853–1929. English actress, mistress of the future Edward VII. She was known as the 'Jersey Lily' from her birthplace in the Channel Islands and considered to be one of the most beautiful women of her time.

language human communication through speech, writing, or both. Different nationalities or ethnic groups typically have different languages or variations on particular languages; for example, Armenians speaking the Armenian language and the British and Americans speaking distinctive varieties of the English language. One language may have various *dialects, which may be seen by those who use them as languages in their own right. The term is also used for systems of communication with language-like qualities, such as **animal language** (the way animals communicate), **body language** (gestures and expressions used to communicate ideas), **sign language** (gestures for the deaf or for use as a *lingua franca, as among American Indians), and **computer languages** (such as BASIC and COBOL).

Languedoc former province of S France, bounded by the river Rhône, the Mediterranean Sea, and the regions of Guienne and Gascony.

Languedoc-Roussillon region of S France, comprising the *départements* of Aude, Gard, Hérault, Lozère, and Pyrénées-Orientales; area 27,400 sq km/10,576 sq mi; population (1986) 2,012,000. Its capital is Montpellier, and products include fruit, vegetables, wine, and cheese.

langur any of various leaf-eating Old World monkeys of several genera, especially the genus *Presbytis*, that lives in trees in S Asia. There are about 20 species. Langurs are related to the colobus monkey of Africa.

Lansbury George 1859–1940. British Labour politician, leader in the Commons 1931–35. In 1921, while mayor of the London borough of Poplar, he went to prison with most of the council rather than modify their policy of more generous unemployment relief. He was a member of Parliament for Bow 1910–12, when he resigned to force a by-election on the issue of votes for women, which he lost. He was again member of Parliament for Bow 1922–40; he was leader of the parliamentary Labour party 1931–35, but resigned (as a pacifist) in opposition to the party's militant response to the Italian invasion of Abyssinia (present-day Ethiopia).

lanthanide any of a series of 15 metallic elements (also known as rare earths) with atomic numbers 57 (lanthanum) to 71 (lutetium). One of its members, promethium, is radioactive. All occur in nature. Lanthanides are grouped because of their chemical similarities (they are all bivalent), their properties differing only slightly with atomic number.

lanthanum (Greek *lanthanein* 'to be hidden') soft, silvery, ductile and malleable, metallic element, symbol La, atomic number 57, relative atomic mass 138.91, the first of the lanthanide series. It is used in making alloys. It was named 1839 by Swedish chemist Carl Mosander (1797–1858).

Lanzarote most easterly of the Spanish Canary Islands; area 795 sq km/307 sq mi; capital Arrecife. The desert-like volcanic landscape is dominated by the Montan6as de Fuego ('Mountains of Fire') with more than 300 volcanic cones.

Lanzhou or **Lanchow** capital of Gansu province, China, on the river Huang He, 190 km/120 mi S of the Great Wall; population (1989) 1,480,000. Industries include oil refining, chemicals, fertilizers, and synthetic rubber.

Lao people who live along the Mekong river system in Laos (2 million) and N Thailand (9 million). The Lao language is a member of the Sino-Tibetan family. The majority of Lao live in rural villages. During the wet season, May–Oct, they grow rice in irrigated fields, though some shifting or swidden cultivation is practised on hillsides. Vegetables and other crops are grown during drier weather. The Lao are predominantly Buddhist though a belief in spirits, *phi*, is included in Lao devotions. There are some Christians among the minority groups.

Laois or **Laoighis** county in Leinster province, Republic of Ireland
area 1,720 sq km/664 sq mi
county town Port Laoise
physical flat except for the Slieve Bloom Mountains in the northwest
products sugarbeets, dairy products, woollens, agricultural machinery
population (1991) 52,300.

Laos Lao People's Democratic Republic (*Saathiaranagroat Prachhathippatay Prachhachhon Lao*)

area 236,790 sq km/91,400 sq mi
capital Vientiane
towns Luang Prabang (the former royal capital), Pakse, Savannakhet
physical landlocked state with high mountains in E; Mekong River in W; jungle covers nearly 60% of land
head of state Nouhak Phoumsavan from 1992
head of government General Khamtay Siphandon from 1991
political system communism, one-party state
exports hydroelectric power from the Mekong is exported to Thailand, timber, teak, coffee, electricity
currency new kip
population (1993) 4,400,000 (Lao 48%, Thai 14%, Khmer 25%, Chinese 13%); growth rate 2.2% p.a.
languages Lao (official), French
religions Theravāda Buddhist 85%, animist beliefs among mountain dwellers
GNP $230 per head (1991)
chronology
1893–1945 Laos was a French protectorate.
1945 Temporarily occupied by Japan.
1946 Retaken by France.
1950 Granted semi-autonomy in French Union.
1954 Independence achieved from France.
1960 Right-wing government seized power.
1962 Coalition government established; civil war continued.
1973 Vientiane cease-fire agreement. Withdrawal of US, Thai, and North Vietnamese forces.

1975 Communist-dominated republic proclaimed with Prince Souphanouvong as head of state.
1986 Phoumi Vongvichit became acting president.
1988 Plans announced to withdraw 40% of Vietnamese forces stationed in the country.
1989 First assembly elections since communist takeover.
1991 Constitution approved. Kaysone Phomvihane elected president. General Khamtay Siphandon named as new premier.
1992 Phomvihane died; replaced by Nouhak Phoumsavan. New national assembly created, replacing supreme people's assembly, and general election held (effectively one-party).

Lao Zi or **Lao Tzu** *c*. 604–531 BC. Chinese philosopher, commonly regarded as the founder of *Taoism, with its emphasis on the Tao, the inevitable and harmonious way of the universe. Nothing certain is known of his life, and he is variously said to have lived in the 6th or the 4th century BC. The *Tao Tê Ching*, the Taoist scripture, is attributed to him but apparently dates from the 3rd century BC.

La Paz capital city of Bolivia, in Murillo province, 3,800 m/12,400 ft above sea level; population (1988) 1,049,800. Products include textiles and copper. Founded by the Spanish 1548 as Pueblo Nuevo de Nuestra Señora de la Paz, it has been the seat of government since 1898.

lapis lazuli rock containing the blue mineral lazurite in a matrix of white calcite with small amounts of other minerals. It occurs in silicapoor igneous rocks and metamorphic limestones found in Afghanistan, Siberia, Iran, and Chile. Lapis lazuli was a valuable pigment of the Middle Ages, also used as a gemstone and in inlaying and ornamental work.

Laplace Pierre Simon, Marquis de Laplace 1749–1827. French astronomer and mathematician. In 1796, he theorized that the solar system originated from a cloud of gas (the nebular hypothesis). He studied the motion of the Moon and planets, and published a five-volume survey of *celestial mechanics, Traité de méchanique céleste* 1799–1825. Among his mathematical achievements was the development of probability theory.

Lapland region of Europe within the Arctic Circle in Norway, Sweden, Finland, and the Kola Peninsula of NW Russia, without political definition. Its chief resources are chromium, copper, iron, timber, hydroelectric power, and tourism. The indigenous population are the *Saami (formerly known as Lapps), a seminomadic herding people. Lapland has low temperatures, with three months' continuous daylight in summer and three months' continuous darkness in winter. There is summer agriculture.

laptop computer portable microcomputer, small enough to be used on the operator's lap. It consists of a single unit, incorporating a keyboard, *floppy disc or *hard disc drives, and a screen. The screen often forms a lid that folds back in use. It uses a liquid-crystal or gas-plasma display, rather than the bulkier cathode-ray tubes found in most display terminals.

lapwing Eurasian bird *Vanellus vanellus* of the plover family, also known as the *green plover* and, from its call, as the *peewit*. Bottle-green above and white below, with a long thin crest and rounded wings, it is about 30 cm/1 ft long. It inhabits moorland in Europe and Asia, making a nest scratched out of the ground.

Lara Brian 1969– . West Indian, left-handed batsman who plays first class cricket for Trinidad and Tobago and for Warwickshire. In April 1994 he broke the world individual test batting record with an innings of 375 against England at St John's Antigua, and then went on to break the world record for an individual innings in first class cricket with an unbeaten 501 for Warwickshire against Durham at Edgbaston.

larch any tree of the genus *Larix*, of the family Pinaceae. The common larch *L. decidua* grows to 40 m/130 ft. It is one of the few *conifer trees to shed its leaves annually. The small needlelike leaves are replaced every year by new bright-green foliage, which later darkens.

Large Electron Positron Collider (LEP) the world's largest particle *accelerator, in operation from 1989 at the CERN laboratories near Geneva in Switzerland. It occupies a tunnel 3.8 m/12.5 ft wide and 27 km/16.7 mi long, which is buried 180 m/590 ft underground and forms a ring consisting of eight curved and eight straight sections. In 1989 the LEP was used to measure the mass and lifetime of the Z particle, carrier of the weak nuclear force.

lark songbird of the family Alaudidae, found mainly in the Old World, but also in North America. Larks are brownish-tan in colour and usually about 18 cm/7 in long; they nest on the ground in the open. The skylark *Alauda arvensis* sings as it rises almost vertically in the air. It breeds in Britain; it is light-brown, and 18 cm/7 in long.

Larkin Philip 1922–1985. English poet. His perfectionist, pessimistic verse includes *The North Ship* 1945, *The Whitsun Weddings* 1964, and *High Windows* 1974. He edited *The Oxford Book of 20th-Century English Verse* 1973. After his death, his letters and writings revealed an intolerance and misanthropy not found in his published material.

larkspur plant of the genus *delphinium.

La Rochefoucauld François, duc de La Rochefoucauld 1613–1680. French writer. His *Réflexions, ou sentences et maximes morales/ Reflections, or Moral Maxims* 1665 is a collection of brief, epigrammatic, and cynical observations on life and society, with the epigraph 'Our virtues are mostly our vices in disguise'. He was a lover of Mme de *Lafayette.

Lartigue Jacques-Henri 1894–1986. French photographer. He began taking photographs of his family at the age of seven, and went on to make *autochrome colour prints of women. During his lifetime he took over 40,000 photographs, documenting everyday people and situations.

larva stage between hatching and adulthood in those species in which the young have a different appearance and way of life from the adults. Examples include tadpoles (frogs) and caterpillars (butterflies and moths). Larvae are typical of the invertebrates, some of which (for example, shrimps) have two or more distinct larval stages. Among vertebrates, it is only the amphibians and some fishes that have a larval stage.

laryngitis inflammation of the larynx, causing soreness of the throat, a dry cough, and hoarseness. The acute form is due to a virus or other infection, excessive use of the voice, or inhalation of irritating smoke, and may cause the voice to be completely lost. With rest, the inflammation usually subsides in a few days.

larynx in mammals, a cavity at the upper end of the trachea (windpipe), containing the vocal cords. It is stiffened with cartilage and lined with mucous membrane. Amphibians and reptiles have much simpler larynxes, with no vocal cords. Birds have a similar cavity, called the *syrinx*, found lower down the trachea, where it branches to form the bronchi. It is very complex, with well-developed vocal cords.

la Salle René Robert Cavelier, Sieur de la Salle 1643–1687. French explorer. He made an epic voyage through North America, exploring the Mississippi River down to its mouth, and in 1682 founded Louisiana. When he returned with colonists, he failed to find the river mouth again, and was eventually murdered by his mutinous men.

Lascaux cave system in SW France with prehistoric wall paintings. It is richly decorated with realistic and symbolic paintings of buffaloes, horses, and red deer of the Upper Palaeolithic period, about 18,000 BC. The caves, near Montignac in the Dordogne, were discovered 1940. Similar paintings are found in *Altamira, Spain. The opening of the Lascaux caves to tourists led to deterioration of the paintings; the caves were closed 1963 and a facsimile opened 1983.

laser (acronym for *light amplification by stimulated emission of radiation*) a device for producing a narrow beam of light, capable of travelling over vast distances without dispersion, and of being focused to give enormous power densities (10^8 watts per cm^2 for high-energy lasers). The laser operates on a principle similar to that of the *maser (a high-frequency microwave amplifier or oscillator). The uses of lasers include communications (a laser beam can carry much more information than can radio waves), cutting, drilling, welding, satellite tracking, medical and biological research, and surgery.

laser printer computer printer in which the image to be printed is formed by the action of a laser on a light-sensitive drum, then transferred to paper by means of an electrostatic charge. Laser printers are page printers, printing a complete page at a time. The printed image, which can take the form of text or pictures, is made up of tiny dots, or ink particles. The quality of the image generated depends on the fineness of these dots – most laser printers can print up to 120 dots per cm/300 dots per in across the page.

Las Palmas or *Las Palmas de Gran Canaria* tourist resort on the NE coast of Gran Canaria, Canary Islands; population (1991) 347,700. Products include sugar and bananas.

Lassa fever acute disease caused by a virus, first detected in 1969, and spread by a species of rat found only in W Africa. It is characterized by high fever and inflammation of various organs. There is no known cure, the survival rate being less than 50%.

Las Vegas city in Nevada, USA, known for its nightclubs and gambling casinos; population (1986) 202,000. Founded 1855 in a ranching area, it is the largest city in the state.

La Tène prehistoric settlement at the east end of Lake Neuchâtel, Switzerland, which has given its name to a culture of the Iron Age. The culture lasted from the 5th century BC to the Roman conquest.

latent heat in physics, the heat absorbed or radiated by a substance as it changes state (for example, from solid to liquid) at constant temperature and pressure.

lateral line system system of sense organs in fishes and larval amphibians (tadpoles) that detects water movement. It usually consists of a row of interconnected pores on either side of the body that divide into a system of canals across the head.

Lateran Treaties series of agreements that marked the reconciliation of the Italian state with the papacy in 1929. They were hailed as a propaganda victory for the Fascist regime. The treaties involved recognition of the sovereignty of the *Vatican City State, the payment of an indemnity for papal possessions lost during unification in 1870, and agreement on the role of the Catholic church within the Italian state in the form of a concordat between Pope Pius XI and the dictator Mussolini.

latex (Latin 'liquid') fluid of some plants (such as the rubber tree and poppy), an emulsion of resins, proteins, and other organic substances. It is used as the basis for making rubber. The name is also applied to a suspension in water of natural or synthetic rubber (or plastic) particles used in rubber goods, paints, and adhesives.

latitude and longitude imaginary lines used to locate position on the globe. Lines of latitude are drawn parallel to the equator, with 0° at the equator and 90° at the north and south poles. Lines of longitude are drawn at right angles to these, with 0° (the Prime Meridian) passing through Greenwich, England. See page 488.

latifundium (Latin for 'broad' and 'farm') in ancient Rome, a large agricultural estate designed to make maximum use of cheap labour, whether free workmen or slaves.

Latimer Hugh 1490–1555. English Christian church reformer and bishop. After his conversion to Protestantism in 1524 he was imprisoned several times but was protected by Cardinal Wolsey and Henry VIII. After the accession of the Catholic Mary, he was burned for heresy.

Latin Indo-European language of ancient Italy. Latin has passed through four influential phases: as the language of (1) republican Rome, (2) the Roman Empire, (3) the Roman Catholic Church, and (4) W European culture, science, philosophy, and law during the Middle Ages and the Renaissance. During the third and fourth phases, much Latin vocabulary entered the English language. It is the parent form of the *Romance languages, noted for its highly inflected grammar and conciseness of expression.

Latin America countries of South and Central America (also including Mexico) in which Spanish, Portuguese, and French are spoken.

La Tour Georges de 1593–1652. French painter

Point X lies on longitude 60°W

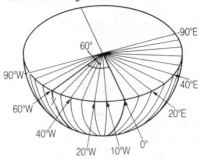

Point X lies on latitude 20°S

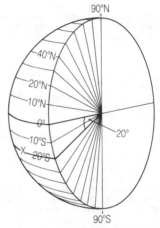

Together longitude 60°W latitude 20°S places point X on a precise position on the globe.

latitude and longitude Locating a point on a globe using latitude and longitude.

active in Lorraine. He was patronized by the duke of Lorraine and perhaps also by Louis XIII. Many of his pictures are illuminated by a single source of light, with deep contrasts of light and shade. They range from religious paintings to domestic genre scenes.

Latter-day Saint member of the Christian sect the *Mormons.

Latvia Republic of
area 63,700 sq km/24,595 sq mi
capital Riga
towns Daugavpils, Liepāja, Jurmala, Jelgava, Ventspils
physical wooded lowland (highest point 312 m/ 1,024 ft), marshes, lakes; 472 km/293 mi of coastline; mild climate
environment coast littered with wrecks of Soviet vessels; ground water around former Soviet bases contaminated; cleanup cost estimated at £10 billion (1994)
head of state Guntis Ulmanis from 1993
head of government Maris Gailis from 1994
political system emergent democratic republic

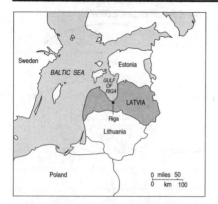

products electronic and communications equipment, electric railway carriages, motorcycles, consumer durables, timber, paper and woollen goods, meat and dairy products

currency latis

population (1993) 2,610,000 (Latvian 52%, Russian 34%, Byelorussian 5%, Ukrainian 3%)

language Latvian

religions mostly Lutheran Protestant, with a Roman Catholic minority

GNP $3,410 per head (1991)

chronology

1917 Soviets and Germans contested for control of Latvia.

1918 Feb: Soviet forces overthrown by Germany. Nov: Latvia declared independence. Dec: Soviet rule restored after German withdrawal.

1919 Soviet rule overthrown by British naval and German forces May–Dec; democracy established.

1934 Coup replaced established government.

1939 German-Soviet secret agreement placed Latvia under Russian influence.

1940 Incorporated into USSR as constituent republic.

1941–44 Occupied by Germany.

1944 USSR regained control.

1980 Nationalist dissent began to grow.

1988 Latvian Popular Front established to campaign for independence. Prewar flag readopted; official status given to Latvian language.

1989 Popular Front swept local elections.

1990 Popular Front secured majority in elections. Latvian Communist Party split into pro-independence and pro-Moscow wings.

1991 Soviet troops briefly seized key installations in Riga. Overwhelming vote for independence in referendum. Full independence declared at time of attempted anti-Gorbachev coup; CP outlawed. Independence recognized by USSR and Western nations; joined United Nations (UN).

1993 Guntis Ulmanis chosen as president, Gorbunov as parliamentary speaker, and Valdis Birkavs as premier.

1994 Birkavs and his government resigned. Russian troops departed. Maris Gailis appointed premier.

Latvian language or *Lettish* language of Latvia; with Lithuanian it is one of the two surviving members of the Balto-Slavic branch of the Indo-European language family.

Latynina Larissa Semyonovna 1935– . Soviet gymnast, winner of more Olympic medals than any person in any sport. She won 18 between 1956 and 1964, including nine gold medals. She won a total of 12 individual Olympic and world championship gold medals.

Laud William 1573–1645. English priest; archbishop of Canterbury from 1633. Laud's High Church policy, support for Charles I's unparliamentary rule, censorship of the press, and persecution of the Puritans all aroused bitter opposition, while his strict enforcement of the statutes against enclosures and of laws regulating wages and prices alienated the propertied classes. His attempt to impose the use of the Prayer Book on the Scots precipitated the English *Civil War. Impeached by Parliament 1640, he was imprisoned in the Tower of London, summarily condemned to death, and beheaded.

Lauda Niki 1949– . Austrian motor racing driver who won the world championship 1975, 1977 and 1984. He was also runner-up in 1976 just six weeks after a serious accident at Nurburgring, Germany, which left him badly burned and permanently scarred.

laudanum alcoholic solution (tincture) of the drug *opium. Used formerly as a narcotic and painkiller, it was available in the 19th century from pharmacists on demand in most of Europe and the USA.

Lauderdale John Maitland, Duke of Lauderdale 1616–1682. Scottish politician. Formerly a zealous *Covenanter, he joined the Royalists 1647, and as high commissioner for Scotland 1667–1679 persecuted the Covenanters. He was created duke of Lauderdale 1672, and was a member of the *Cabal ministry 1667–73.

laughing gas popular name for *nitrous oxide, an anaesthetic.

Laughton Charles 1899–1962. English actor who became a US citizen in 1950. Initially a classical stage actor, he joined the Old Vic 1933. His films were made in Hollywood and include such roles as the king in *The Private Life of Henry VIII* 1933 (Academy Award), Captain Bligh in *Mutiny on the Bounty* 1935, and Quasimodo in *The Hunchback of Notre Dame* 1939. In 1955 he directed *Night of the Hunter* and in 1961 appeared in *Judgment at Nuremberg*.

Laurasia former land mass or supercontinent, formed by the fusion of North America, Greenland, Europe, and Asia. It made up the northern half of *Pangaea, the 'world continent' that is thought to have existed between 250 and 200 million years ago. The southern half was *Gondwanaland. Between Laurasia and Gondwanaland was the Tethys Sea. Laurasia broke up with the separation of North America from Europe in the Upper Cretaceous period.

laurel any evergreen tree of the European genus *Laurus*, family Lauraceae, with glossy, aromatic leaves, yellowish flowers, and black berries. The leaves of sweet bay or poet's laurel *L. nobilis* are used in cooking. Several species are cultivated worldwide.

Laurel and Hardy Stan Laurel (stage name of Arthur Stanley Jefferson) (1890–1965) and Oliver Hardy (1892–1957). US film comedians who were one of the most successful comedy teams in film history (Stan was slim, Oliver rotund). Their partnership began in 1927, survived the transition from silent films to sound, and resulted in more than 200 short and feature-length films, which were revived as a worldwide cult in the 1970s. Among these are *Pack Up Your Troubles* 1932, *Our Relations* 1936, and *A Chump at Oxford* 1940.

Laurier Wilfrid 1841–1919. Canadian politician, leader of the Liberal Party 1887–1919 and prime minister 1896–1911. The first French-Canadian to hold the office, he encouraged immigration into Canada from Europe and the USA, established a separate Canadian navy, and sent troops to help Britain in the Boer War.

Lausanne resort and capital of Vaud canton, W Switzerland, above the north shore of Lake Geneva; population (1990) 123,200. Industries include chocolate, scientific instruments, and publishing.

lava molten material that erupts from a *volcano and cools to form extrusive *igneous rock. A lava high in silica is viscous and sticky and does not flow far, whereas low-silica lava can flow for long distances. Lava differs from its parent *magma in that the fluid 'fractionates' on its way to the surface of the Earth; that is, certain heavy or high-temperature minerals settle out and the constituent gases form bubbles and boil away into the atmosphere.

Laval Pierre 1883–1945. French right-wing politician. He was prime minister and foreign secretary 1931–32, and again 1935–36. In World War II he joined Pétain's *Vichy government as vice-premier in June 1940; dismissed in Dec 1940, he was reinstated by Hitler's orders as head of the government and foreign minister in 1942. After the war he was executed.

lavender sweet-smelling herb, genus *Lavandula*, of the mint family Labiatae, native to W Mediterranean countries. The bushy low-growing *L. angustifolia* has long, narrow, erect leaves of a silver-green colour. The flowers, borne on a terminal spike, vary in colour from lilac to deep purple and are covered with small fragrant oil glands. The oil is extensively used in pharmacy and the manufacture of perfumes.

Lavoisier Antoine Laurent 1743–1794. French chemist. He proved that combustion needed only a part of the air, which he called oxygen, thereby destroying the theory of phlogiston (an imaginary 'fire element' released during combustion). With Pierre de Laplace, the astronomer and mathematician, he showed that water was a compound of oxygen and hydrogen. In this way he established the basic rules of chemical combination.

law body of rules and principles under which justice is administered or order enforced in a state or nation. In western Europe there are two main systems: Roman law and English law. US law is a modified form of English law.

Law Andrew Bonar 1858–1923. British Conservative politician. Elected leader of the opposition 1911, he became colonial secretary in Asquith's coalition government 1915–16, chancellor of the Exchequer 1916–19, and Lord Privy Seal 1919–21 in Lloyd George's coalition. He formed a Conservative Cabinet 1922, but resigned on health grounds.

Law Commission in the UK, either of two statutory bodies established in 1965 (one for England and Wales and one for Scotland) which consider proposals for law reform and publish their findings. They also keep British law under constant review, systematically developing and reforming it by, for example, the repeal of obsolete and unnecessary enactments.

law courts bodies that adjudicate in legal disputes. Civil and criminal cases are usually dealt with by separate courts. In many countries there is a hierarchy of courts that provide an appeal system.

law lords in England, the ten Lords of Appeal in Ordinary who, together with the Lord Chancellor and other peers, make up the House of Lords in its judicial capacity. The House of Lords is the final court of appeal in both criminal and civil cases. Law lords rank as life peers.

Lawrence D(avid) H(erbert) 1885–1930. English writer whose work expresses his belief in emotion and the sexual impulse as creative and true to human nature. The son of a Nottinghamshire miner, Lawrence studied at University College, Nottingham, and became a teacher. His writing first received attention after the publication of the semi-autobiographical *Sons and Lovers*, which includes a portrayal of his mother (died 1911). Other novels include *Sons and Lovers* 1913, *The Rainbow* 1915, *Women in Love* 1921, and *Lady Chatterley's Lover* 1928. Lawrence also wrote short stories (for example 'The Woman Who Rode Away') and poetry.

Lawrence Ernest O(rlando) 1901–1958. US physicist. His invention of the cyclotron particle *accelerator pioneered the production of artificial *radioisotopes.

Lawrence T(homas) E(dward), known as *Lawrence of Arabia* 1888–1935. British soldier and writer. Appointed to the military intelligence department in Cairo, Egypt, during World War I, he took part in negotiations for an Arab revolt against the Ottoman Turks, and in 1916 attached himself to the emir Faisal. He became a guerrilla leader of genius, combining raids on Turkish communications with the organization of a joint Arab revolt, described in *The Seven Pillars of Wisdom* 1926.

Lawrence Thomas 1769–1830. British painter, the leading portraitist of his day. He became painter to George III 1792 and president of the Royal Academy 1820.

lawrencium synthesized, radioactive, metallic element, the last of the actinide series, symbol Lr, atomic number 103, relative atomic mass 262. Its only known isotope, Lr-257, has a half-life of 4.3 seconds and was originally synthesized at the University of California at Berkeley 1961 by bombarding californium with boron nuclei. The original symbol, Lw, was officially changed 1963.

Lawson Nigel 1932– . British Conservative politician. A former financial journalist, he was financial secretary to the Treasury 1979–81, secretary of state for energy 1981–83, and chancellor of the Exchequer from 1983. He resigned 1989 after criticism by government adviser Alan Walters over his policy of British membership of the *European Monetary System.

laxative substance used to relieve constipation

(infrequent bowel movement). Current medical opinion discourages regular or prolonged use. Regular exercise and a diet high in vegetable fibre is believed to be the best means of preventing and treating constipation.

Layamon lived about 1200. English poet, author of the *Brut*, a chronicle of about 30,000 alliterative lines on the history of Britain from the legendary Brutus onwards, which gives the earliest version of the Arthurian legend in English.

Lazio (Roman *Latium*) region of W central Italy; area 17,200 sq km/6,639 sq mi; capital Rome; population (1990) 5,191,500. Products include olives, wine, chemicals, pharmaceuticals, and textiles. Home of the Latins from the 10th century BC, it was dominated by the Romans from the 4th century BC.

LCD abbreviation for *liquid-crystal display*.

L-dopa chemical, normally produced by the body, which is converted by an enzyme to dopamine in the brain. It is essential for integrated movement of individual muscle groups.

LEA in the UK, abbreviation for *local education authority*.

Leach Bernard 1887–1979. British potter. His simple designs, inspired by a period of study in Japan, pioneered a revival of the art. He established the Leach Pottery at St Ives, Cornwall, in 1920.

leaching process by which substances are washed out of the soil. Fertilizers leached out of the soil drain into rivers, lakes, and ponds and cause water pollution. In tropical areas, leaching of the soil after the destruction of forests removes scarce nutrients and leads to a dramatic loss of soil fertility. The leaching of soluble minerals with soils can lead to the formation of distinct soil horizons as different minerals are deposited at successively lower levels.

Leacock Stephen Butler 1869–1944. Canadian humorist whose writings include *Literary Lapses* 1910, *Sunshine Sketches of a Little Town* 1912, and *Frenzied Fiction* 1918.

lead heavy, soft, malleable, grey, metallic element, symbol Pb (from Latin *plumbum*), atomic number 82, relative atomic mass 207.19. Usually found as an ore (most often in galena), it occasionally occurs as a free metal (*native metal), and is the final stable product of the decay of uranium. Lead is the softest and weakest of the commonly used metals, with a low melting point; it is a poor conductor of electricity and resists acid corrosion. As a cumulative poison, lead enters the body from lead water pipes, lead-based paints, and leaded petrol. The metal is an effective shield against radiation and is used in batteries, glass, ceramics, and alloys such as pewter and solder.

lead–acid cell type of *accumulator (storage battery).

Leadbelly stage name of Huddie Ledbetter *c.* 1889–1949. US blues and folk singer, songwriter, and guitarist who was a source of inspiration for the urban folk movement of the 1950s. He was 'discovered' in prison by folklorists John Lomax (1875–1948) and Alan Lomax (1915–), who helped him begin a professional concert and recording career 1934. His songs include 'Rock Island Line' and 'Good Night, Irene'.

leaded petrol petrol that contains *antiknock, a mixture of the chemicals tetraethyl lead and dibromoethane.

lead ore any of several minerals from which lead is extracted. The main primary ore is galena or lead sulphite PbS. This is unstable, and on prolonged exposure to the atmosphere it oxidizes into the minerals cerussite $PbCO_3$ and anglesite $PbSO_4$. Lead ores are usually associated with other metals, particularly silver – which can be mined at the same time – and zinc, which can cause problems during smelting.

leaf lateral outgrowth on the stem of a plant, and in most species the primary organ of *photosynthesis. The chief leaf types are cotyledons (seed leaves), scale leaves (on underground stems), foliage leaves, and bracts (in the axil of which a flower is produced).

leaf-hopper any of numerous species of plant-sucking insects (order Homoptera) of the family Cicadellidae. They feed on the sap of leaves. Each species feeds on a limited range of plants.

leaf insect insect of the order Phasmida, about 10 cm/4 in long, with a green, flattened body, remarkable for closely resembling the foliage on which it lives. It is most common in SE Asia.

League of Nations international organization formed after World War I to solve international disputes by arbitration. Established in Geneva, Switzerland, 1920, the league included representatives from states throughout the world, but was severely weakened by the US decision not to become a member, and had no power to enforce its decisions. It was dissolved 1946. Its subsidiaries included the *International Labour Organization* and the *Permanent Court of International Justice* in The Hague, Netherlands, both now under the auspices of the *United Nations.

Leakey Louis (Seymour Bazett) 1903–1972. British archaeologist, born in Kenya. In 1958, with his wife Mary Leakey, he discovered gigantic extinct-animal fossils in the *Olduvai Gorge in Tanzania, as well as many remains of an early human type.

Leakey Mary 1913– . British archaeologist. In 1948 she discovered, on Rusinga Island, Lake Victoria, E Africa, the prehistoric ape skull known as *Proconsul*, about 20 million years old; and human remains at Laetoli, to the south, about 3,750,000 years old.

Leakey Richard 1944– . British archaeologist. In 1972 he discovered at Lake Turkana, Kenya, an apelike skull, estimated to be about 2.9 million years old; it had some human characteristics and a brain capacity of 800 cu cm. In 1984 his team found an almost complete skeleton of *Homo erectus* some 1.6 million years old. He is the son of Louis and Mary Leakey.

Lean David 1908–1991. British film director. His films, noted for their atmospheric quality, include early work codirected with playwright Noël *Coward. *Brief Encounter* 1946 established Lean as a leading talent. Among his later films are such accomplished epics as *The Bridge on the River Kwai* 1957 (Academy Award), *Law-*

rence of Arabia 1962 (Academy Award), *Dr Zhivago* 1965, and *A Passage to India* 1984.

Lear Edward 1812–1888. English artist and humorist. His *Book of Nonsense* 1846 popularized the limerick (a five-line humorous verse). He first attracted attention by his paintings of birds, and later turned to landscapes. He travelled to Italy, Greece, Egypt, and India, publishing books on his travels with his own illustrations, and spent most of his later life in Italy.

learning theory in psychology, a theory about how an organism acquires new behaviours. Two main theories are classical and operant *conditioning.

leasehold in law, land or property held by a tenant (lessee) for a specified period, (unlike *freehold, outright ownership) usually at a rent from the landlord (lessor).

leather material prepared from the hides and skins of animals, by tanning with vegetable tannins and chromium salts. Leather is a durable and water-resistant material, and is used for bags, shoes, clothing, and upholstery. There are three main stages in the process of converting animal skin into leather: cleaning, tanning, and dressing. Tanning is often a highly polluting process.

Leavis F(rank) R(aymond) 1895–1978. English literary critic. With his wife Q D Leavis (1906–81) he cofounded and edited the review *Scrutiny* 1932–53. He championed the work of D H Lawrence and James Joyce and in 1962 attacked C P Snow's theory of 'The Two Cultures' (the natural alienation of the arts and sciences in intellectual life). His other works include *New Bearings in English Poetry* 1932 and *The Great Tradition* 1948. He was a lecturer at Cambridge University.

Lebanon Republic of (*al-Jumhouria al-Lubnaniya*)

area 10,452 sq km/4,034 sq mi
capital and port Beirut
towns ports Tripoli, Tyre, Sidon
physical narrow coastal plain; Bekka valley N–S between Lebanon and Anti-Lebanon mountain ranges
head of state Elias Hrawi from 1989
head of government Rafik al-Hariri from 1992
political system emergent democratic republic
exports citrus and other fruit, vegetables; industrial products to Arab neighbours

currency Lebanese pound
population (1993 est) 2,900 (Lebanese 82%, Palestinian 9%, Armenian 5%); growth rate –0.1% p.a.
languages Arabic, French (both official), Armenian, English
religions Muslim 57% (Shi'ite 33%, Sunni 24%), Christian (Maronite and Orthodox) 40%, Druse 3%
GNP $2,000 per head (1991)
chronology
1920–41 Administered under French mandate.
1944 Independence achieved.
1948–49 Lebanon joined first Arab war against Israel. Palestinian refugees settled in the south.
1964 Palestine Liberation Organization (PLO) founded in Beirut.
1967 More Palestinian refugees settled in Lebanon.
1971 PLO expelled from Jordan; established headquarters in Lebanon.
1975 Outbreak of civil war between Christians and Muslims.
1976 Cease-fire agreed; Syrian-dominated Arab deterrent force formed to keep the peace but considered by Christians as an occupying force.
1978 Israel invaded S Lebanon in search of PLO fighters. International peacekeeping force established. Fighting broke out again.
1979 Part of S Lebanon declared an 'independent free Lebanon'.
1982 Bachir Gemayel became president but was assassinated before he could assume office; succeeded by his brother Amin Gemayel. Israel again invaded Lebanon. Palestinians withdrew from Beirut under supervision of international peacekeeping force. PLO moved its headquarters to Tunis.
1983 Agreement reached for the withdrawal of Syrian and Israeli troops but abrogated under Syrian pressure.
1984 Most of international peacekeeping force withdrawn. Muslim militia took control of W Beirut.
1985 Lebanon in chaos; many foreigners taken hostage.
1987 Syrian troops sent into Beirut.
1988 Agreement on a Christian successor to Gemayel failed; he established a military government; Selim al-Hoss set up rival government; threat of partition hung over the country.
1989 Christian leader General Michel Aoun declared 'war of liberation' against Syrian occupation; Saudi Arabia and Arab League sponsored talks that resulted in new constitution recognizing Muslim majority; René Muhawad named president, assassinated after 17 days in office; Elias Hrawi named successor; Aoun occupied presidential palace, rejected constitution.
1990 Irish hostage Brian Keenan released. General Aoun surrendered and legitimate government restored, with Umar Karami as prime minister.
1991 Government extended control to the whole country. Treaty of cooperation with Syria signed. Western hostages Terry Anderson, Joseph Cicippio, Thomas Sutherland, and Terry Waite released. General Aoun pardoned.
1992 Karami resigned as prime minister; succeeded by Rashid al-Solh. Remaining Western hostages released. General election boycotted by

many Christians; pro-Syrian administration re-elected; Rafik al-Hariri became prime minister.

Lebensraum (German 'living space') theory developed by Hitler for the expansion of Germany into E Europe, and in the 1930s used by the Nazis to justify their annexation of neighbouring states on the grounds that Germany was overpopulated.

Lebowa black homeland in Transvaal province, South Africa; it achieved self-governing status 1972; population (1985) 1,836,000.

Le Brun Charles 1619–1690. French artist, painter to Louis XIV from 1662. In 1663 he became director of the French Academy and of the Gobelins factory, which produced art, tapestries, and furnishings for the new palace of Versailles. In the 1640s he studied under the painter Poussin in Rome. Returning to Paris in 1646, he worked on large decorative schemes including the *Galerie des glaces* (Hall of Mirrors) at Versailles. He also painted portraits.

Le Carré John. Pen name of David John Cornwell 1931– . English writer of thrillers. His low-key realistic accounts of complex espionage include *The Spy Who Came in from the Cold* 1963, *Tinker Tailor Soldier Spy* 1974, *Smiley's People* 1980, and *The Russia House* 1989. He was a member of the Foreign Service 1960–64.

Le Chatelier's principle or **Le Chatelier-Braun principle** in science, the principle that if a change in conditions is imposed on a system in equilibrium, the system will react to counteract that change and restore the equilibrium.

lecithin lipid (fat), containing nitrogen and phosphorus, that forms a vital part of the cell membranes of plant and animal cells. The name is from the Greek *lekithos* 'egg yolk', eggs being a major source of lecithin.

Leclanché Georges 1839–1882. French engineer. In 1866 he invented a primary electrical cell, the **Leclanché cell**, which is still the basis of most dry batteries. A Leclanché cell consists of a carbon rod (the *anode) inserted into a mixture of powdered carbon and manganese dioxide contained in a porous pot, which sits in a glass jar containing an *electrolyte (conducting medium) of ammonium chloride solution, into which a zinc *cathode is inserted. The cell produces a continuous current, the carbon mixture acting as a depolarizer; that is, it prevents hydrogen bubbles from forming on the anode and increasing resistance. In a dry battery, the electrolyte is made in the form of a paste with starch.

Le Corbusier assumed name of Charles-Édouard Jeanneret 1887–1965. Swiss architect. His functionalist approach to town planning in industrial society was based on the interrelationship between machine forms and the techniques of modern architecture. His concept, *La Ville radieuse*, developed in Marseille, France (1945–50) and Chandigarh, India, placed buildings and open spaces with related functions in a circular formation, with buildings based on standard-sized units mathematically calculated according to the proportions of the human figure (see *Fibonacci, *golden section).

LED abbreviation for *light-emitting diode*.

Leda in Greek mythology, the wife of Tyndareus and mother of Clytemnestra. Zeus, who came to her as a swan, was the father of her other children: Helen of Troy and the twins Castor and Pollux.

Ledoux Claude-Nicolas 1736–1806. French Neo-Classical architect, stylistically comparable to E L *Boullée in his use of austere, geometric forms, exemplified in his toll houses for Paris; for instance, the Barrière de la Villette in the Place de Stalingrad.

Le Duc Tho 1911–1990. North Vietnamese diplomat who was joint winner (with US Secretary of State Kissinger) of the 1973 Nobel Peace Prize for his part in the negotiations to end the Vietnam War. He indefinitely postponed receiving the award.

Led Zeppelin UK rock group 1969–80, founders of the heavy-metal genre. Their overblown style, with long solos, was based on rhythm and blues; songs like 'Stairway to Heaven' have become classics.

Lee Bruce. Stage name of Lee Yuen Kam 1941–1973. US 'Chinese Western' film actor, an expert in *kung fu, who popularized the oriental martial arts in the West with pictures made in Hong Kong, such as *Fists of Fury* 1972 and *Enter the Dragon* 1973, his last film.

Lee Christopher 1922– . English film actor whose gaunt figure was memorable in the title role of *Dracula* 1958 and its sequels. He has not lost his sinister image in subsequent Hollywood productions. His other films include *Hamlet* 1948, *The Mummy* 1959, *Julius Caesar* 1970, and *The Man with the Golden Gun* 1974.

Lee Laurie 1914– . English writer, born near Stroud, Gloucestershire. His works include the autobiographical novel *Cider with Rosie* 1959, a classic evocation of childhood; nature poetry such as *The Bloom of Candles* 1947; and travel writing including *A Rose for Winter* 1955.

Lee Robert E(dward) 1807–1870. US Confederate general in the *American Civil War, a military strategist. As military adviser to Jefferson *Davis, president of the Confederacy, and as commander of the army of N Virginia, he made several raids into Northern territory, but was defeated at Gettysburg and surrendered 1865 at Appomattox.

Lee Spike 1956– . US actor, writer and film director. His work presents the realities of contemporary black American life in a witty and incisive way that avoids cliché. His films, in which he usually appears, include *She's Gotta Have It* 1986, *Do The Right Thing* 1989, *Jungle Fever* 1991, and *Malcolm X* 1992.

leech annelid worm forming the class Hirudinea. Leeches inhabit fresh water, and in tropical countries infest damp forests. As bloodsucking animals they are injurious to people and animals, to whom they attach themselves by means of a strong mouth adapted to sucking.

Leeds city in W Yorkshire, England, on the river Aire; population (1991 est) 674,400. Industries include engineering, printing, chemicals, glass, and woollens. It is a centre of communications where road, rail, and canal (to Liverpool and Goole) meet.

leek onionlike plant of the genus *Allium* of the lily family Liliaceae. The cultivated leek is a variety of the wild *A. ampeloprasum* of the Mediterranean area and Atlantic islands. The lower leaf parts form the bulb, which is eaten as a vegetable.

Lee Teng-hui 1923– . Taiwanese right-wing politician, vice president 1984–88, president and Kuomintang (see *Guomindang) party leader from 1988. Lee, the country's first island-born leader, is viewed as a reforming technocrat.

Lee Tsung-Dao 1926– . Chinese physicist whose research centred on the physics of weak nuclear forces. In 1956 Lee proposed that weak nuclear forces between elementary particles might disobey certain key assumptions for instance, the conservation of parity. He shared the 1957 Nobel Prize for Physics with his colleague Yang Chen Ning (1922–).

Leeuwenhoek Anton van 1632–1723. Dutch pioneer of microscopic research. He ground his own lenses, some of which magnified up to 200 times. With these he was able to see individual red blood cells, sperm, and bacteria, achievements not repeated for more than a century.

Leeward Islands (1) group of islands, part of the *Society Islands, in *French Polynesia, S Pacific; (2) general term for the northern half of the Lesser *Antilles in the West Indies; (3) former British colony in the West Indies (1871–1956) comprising Antigua, Montserrat, St Christopher/ St Kitts–Nevis, Anguilla, and the Virgin Islands.

left-handedness in humans, using the left hand more skilfully and in preference to the right hand for most actions. It occurs in about 9% of the population, predominantly males. It is caused by dominance of the right side of the brain.

left wing in politics, the socialist parties. The term originated in the French National Assembly of 1789, where the nobles sat in the place of honour to the right of the president, and the commons sat to the left. This arrangement has become customary in European parliaments, where the progressives sit on the left and the conservatives on the right. It is also usual to speak of the right, left, and centre, when referring to the different elements composing a single party.

legacy in law, a gift of personal property made by a testator in a will and transferred on the testator's death to the legatee. *Specific legacies* are definite named objects; a *general legacy* is a sum of money or item not specially identified; a *residuary legacy* is all the remainder of the deceased's personal estate after debts have been paid and the other legacies have been distributed.

legal aid public assistance with legal costs. In Britain it is given only to those below certain thresholds of income and unable to meet the costs. There are separate provisions for civil and criminal cases. Since 1989 legal aid is administered by the Legal Aid Board.

legend (Latin *legere* 'to read') a traditional or undocumented story about famous people. The term was originally applied to the books of readings designed for use in Divine Service, and afterwards extended to the stories of saints read in monasteries. A collection of such stories was the 13th-century *Legenda Aurea* by Jacobus de Voragine.

Léger Fernand 1881–1955. French painter, associated with *Cubism. From around 1909 he evolved a characteristic style, composing abstract and semi-abstract works with cylindrical forms, reducing the human figure to constructions of pure shape. Mechanical forms are constant themes in his work, including his designs for the Swedish Ballet 1921–22, murals, and the abstract film *Ballet mécanique/Mechanical Ballet*.

legionnaire's disease pneumonia-like disease, so called because it was first identified when it broke out at a convention of the American Legion in Philadelphia in 1976. Legionnaire's disease is caused by the bacterium *Legionella pneumophila*, which breeds in warm water (for example, in the cooling towers of air-conditioning systems). It is spread in minute water droplets, which may be inhaled.

legislature law-making body or bodies in a political system. Some legislatures are unicameral (having one chamber), and some bicameral (with two).

Legitimist party in France that continued to support the claims of the house of *Bourbon after the revolution of 1830. When the direct line became extinct in 1883, the majority of the party transferred allegiance to the house of Orléans.

Legnano, Battle of defeat of Holy Roman emperor Frederick I Barbarossa by members of the Lombard League in 1176 at Legnano, northwest of Milan. It was a major setback to the emperor's plans for imperial domination over Italy and showed for the first time the power of infantry against feudal cavalry.

Le Guin Ursula K(roeber) 1929– . US writer of science fiction and fantasy. Her novels include *The Left Hand of Darkness* 1969, which questions sex roles; the *Earthsea* trilogy 1968–72; *The Dispossessed* 1974, which compares an anarchist and a capitalist society; *Orsinian Tales* 1976; and *Always Coming Home* 1985.

legume plant of the family Leguminosae, which has a pod containing dry seeds. The family includes peas, beans, lentils, clover, and alfalfa (lucerne). Legumes are important in agriculture because of their specialized roots, which have nodules containing bacteria capable of fixing nitrogen from the air and increasing the fertility of the soil. The edible seeds of legumes are called *pulses*.

Lehár Franz 1870–1948. Hungarian composer. He wrote many operettas, among them *The Merry Widow* 1905, *The Count of Luxembourg* 1909, *Gypsy Love* 1910, and *The Land of Smiles* 1929. He also composed songs, marches, and a violin concerto.

Le Havre industrial port (engineering, chemicals, oil refining) in Normandy, NW France, on the river Seine; population (1982) 255,000. It is the largest port in Europe, and has transatlantic passenger links.

Leibniz Gottfried Wilhelm 1646–1716. German mathematician and philosopher. Independently of, but concurrently with, the British scientist Isaac Newton he developed the branch of mathematics known as *calculus. In his metaphysical works, such as *The Monadology* 1714, he argued that everything consisted of innumerable units, *monads*, the individual properties of which determined each thing's past, present, and future. Monads, although independent of each other, interacted predictably; this meant that Christian faith and scientific reason need not be in conflict and that 'this is the best of all possible worlds'. His optimism is satirized in Voltaire's *Candide*.

Leicester industrial city (food processing, hosiery, footwear, engineering, electronics, printing, plastics) and administrative headquarters of Leicestershire, England, on the river Soar; population (1991) 270,600.

Leicester Robert Dudley, Earl of Leicester *c.* 1532–1588. English courtier. Son of the Duke of Northumberland, he was created Earl of Leicester 1564. Queen Elizabeth I gave him command of the army sent to the Netherlands 1585–87 and of the forces prepared to resist the threat of Spanish invasion of 1588. His lack of military success led to his recall, but he retained Elizabeth's favour until his death.

Leicestershire county in central England
area 2,550 sq km/984 sq mi
towns Leicester (administrative headquarters), Loughborough, Melton Mowbray, Market Harborough
products horses, cattle, sheep, dairy products, coal
population (1991) 860,500
famous people C P Snow, Thomas Babington Macaulay, Titus Oates.

Leics abbreviation for **Leicestershire*, county in England.

Leigh Mike 1943– . English playwright and filmmaker, noted for his sharp, carefully improvised social satires. He directs his own plays, which evolve through improvisation before they are scripted. His work for television includes *Nuts in May* 1976 and *Abigail's Party* 1977; his films include *High Hopes* 1989 and *Life Is Sweet* 1991.

Leigh Vivien. Stage name of Vivien Mary Hartley 1913–1967. English actress who appeared on the stage in London and New York, and won Academy Awards for her performances as Scarlett O'Hara in *Gone With the Wind* 1939 and as Blanche du Bois in *A Streetcar Named Desire* 1951.

Leinster SE province of the Republic of Ireland, comprising the counties of Carlow, Dublin, Kildare, Kilkenny, Laois, Longford, Louth, Meath, Offaly, Westmeath, Wexford, and Wicklow; area 19,630 sq km/7,577 sq mi; capital Dublin; population (1991) 1,860,000.

Leipzig city in W Saxony, Germany, 145 km/90 mi SW of Berlin; population (1986) 552,000. Products include furs, leather goods, cloth, glass, cars, and musical instruments.

leitmotif (German 'leading motive') in music, a recurring theme or motive used to indicate a character or idea. Wagner frequently used this technique in his operas.

Leitrim county in Connacht province, Republic of Ireland, bounded NW by Donegal Bay
area 1,530 sq km/591 sq mi
county town Carrick-on-Shannon
products potatoes, cattle, linen, woollens, pottery, coal, iron, lead
population (1991) 25,300.

lek in biology, a closely spaced set of very small *territories each occupied by a single male during the mating season. Leks are found in the mating systems of several ground-dwelling birds (such as grouse) and a few antelopes.

Lely Peter. Adopted name of Pieter van der Faes 1618–1680. Dutch painter, active in England from 1641, who painted fashionable portraits in Baroque style. His subjects included Charles I, Cromwell, and Charles II. He painted a series of admirals, *Flagmen* (National Maritime Museum, Greenwich), and one of *The Windsor Beauties* (Hampton Court, Richmond), fashionable women of Charles II's court.

Lemaître Georges Edouard 1894–1966. Belgian cosmologist who in 1927 proposed the *Big Bang theory of the origin of the universe. He predicted that the entire universe was expanding, which the US astronomer Edwin *Hubble confirmed. Lemaître suggested that the expansion had been started by an initial explosion, the Big Bang, a theory that is now generally accepted.

Le Mans industrial town in Sarthe *département*, France; population (1982) 150,000, conurbation 191,000. It has a motor-racing circuit where the annual endurance 24-hour race (established 1923) for sports cars and their prototypes is held.

lemming small rodent of the family Cricetidae, especially the genus *Lemmus*, comprising four species worldwide in northern latitudes. It is about 12 cm/5 in long, with thick brownish fur, a small head, and a short tail. Periodically, when their population exceeds the available food supply, lemmings undertake mass migrations.

Lemmon Jack (John Uhler III) 1925– . US character actor, often cast as the lead in comedy films, such as *Some Like It Hot* 1959 but equally skilled in serious roles, as in *The China Syndrome* 1979 and *Dad* 1990.

lemon sour fruit of the small, evergreen, semitropical lemon tree *Citrus limon*. It may have originated in NW India, and was introduced into Europe by the Spanish Moors in the 12th or 13th century. It is now grown in Italy, Spain, California, Florida, South Africa, and Australia.

lemon balm perennial herb *Melissa officinalis* of the mint family Labiatae, with lemon-scented leaves. It is widely used in teas, liqueurs, and medicines.

LeMond Greg 1961– . US racing cyclist, the first American to win the Tour de France 1986.

lemur prosimian *primate of the family Lemuridae, inhabiting Madagascar and the Comoro Islands. There are about 16 species, ranging from mouse-sized to dog-sized animals. Lemurs are arboreal animals, and some species are nocturnal. They have long, bushy tails, and feed on fruit, insects, and small animals. Many are threatened with extinction owing to loss of their forest habitat and, in some cases, from hunting.

Lena longest river in Asiatic Russia, 4,400 km/2,730 mi, with numerous tributaries. Its source is near Lake Baikal, and it empties into the Arctic Ocean through a delta 400 km/240 mi wide. It is ice-covered for half the year.

Lendl Ivan 1960– . Czech-born American lawn tennis player. He has won eight Grand Slam singles titles, including the US and French titles three times each. He has won more than $15 million in prize money.

lend-lease in US history, an act of Congress

passed in March 1941 that gave the president power to order 'any defense article for the government of any country whose defense the president deemed vital to the defense of the USA'. During World War II, the USA negotiated many Lend-Lease agreements, notably with Britain and the Soviet Union.

Lenglen Suzanne 1899–1938. French tennis player, Wimbledon singles and doubles champion 1919–23 and 1925, and Olympic champion 1921. She became professional in 1926. She also popularized sports clothes designed by Jean Patou (1880–1936).

Lenin Vladimir Ilyich. Adopted name of Vladimir Ilyich Ulyanov 1870–1924. Russian revolutionary, first leader of the USSR, and communist theoretician. Active in the 1905 Revolution, Lenin had to leave Russia when it failed, settling in Switzerland in 1914. He returned to Russia after the February revolution of 1917 (see *Russian Revolution). He led the Bolshevik revolution in Nov 1917 and became leader of a Soviet government, concluded peace with Germany, and organized a successful resistance to White Russian (pro-tsarist) uprisings and foreign intervention 1918–20. His modification of traditional Marxist doctrine to fit conditions prevailing in Russia became known as **Marxism-Leninism**, the basis of communist ideology.

Leningrad former name (1924–91) of the Russian city *St Petersburg.

Lennon John (Ono) 1940–1980. UK rock singer, songwriter, and guitarist, in the USA from 1971; a founder member of the *Beatles. Both before the band's break-up 1969 and in his solo career, he collaborated intermittently with his wife **Yoko Ono** (1933–). 'Give Peace a Chance', a hit 1969, became an anthem of the peace movement. His solo work alternated between the confessional and the political, as on the album *Imagine* 1971. He was shot dead by a fan.

Le Nôtre André 1613–1700. French landscape gardener, creator of the gardens at Versailles and Les Tuileries, Paris.

lens in optics, a piece of a transparent material, such as glass, with two polished surfaces – one concave or convex, and the other plane, concave, or convex – that modifies rays of light. A convex lens brings rays of light together; a concave lens makes the rays diverge. Lenses are essential to spectacles, microscopes, telescopes, cameras, and almost all optical instruments.

lens, gravitational see *gravitational lens.

Lent in the Christian church, the 40-day period of fasting that precedes Easter, beginning on Ash Wednesday, but omitting Sundays.

lentil annual Old World plant *Lens culinaris* of the pea family Leguminosae. The plant, which resembles vetch, grows 15–45 cm/6–18 in high and has white, blue, or purplish flowers. The seeds, contained in pods about 1.6 cm/0.6 in long, are widely used as food.

Lenz's law in physics, a law stating that the direction of an electromagnetically induced current (generated by moving a magnet near a wire or a wire in a magnetic field) will oppose the motion producing it. It is named after the German physicist Heinrich Friedrich Lenz (1804–1865), who announced it in 1833.

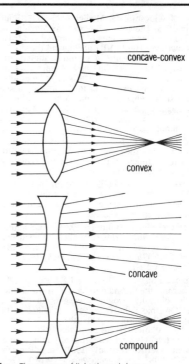

concave-convex

convex

concave

compound

lens *The passage of light through lenses.*

Leo zodiacal constellation in the northern hemisphere represented as a lion. The Sun passes through Leo from mid-Aug to mid-Sept. Its brightest star is first-magnitude Regulus at the base of a pattern of stars called the Sickle. In astrology, the dates for Leo are between about 23 July and 22 Aug (see *precession).

Leo III the Isaurian *c.* 680–740. Byzantine emperor and soldier. He seized the throne in 717, successfully defended Constantinople against the Saracens 717–18, and attempted to suppress the use of images in church worship (see *iconoclast).

Leo thirteen popes, including:

Leo I St the Great *c.* 390–461. Pope from 440 who helped to establish the Christian liturgy. Leo summoned the Chalcedon Council where his Dogmatical Letter was accepted as the voice of St Peter. Acting as ambassador for the emperor Valentinian III (425–455), Leo saved Rome from devastation by the Huns by buying off their king, Attila.

Leo III *c.* 750–816. Pope from 795. After the withdrawal of the Byzantine emperors, the popes had become the real rulers of Rome. Leo III was forced to flee because of a conspiracy in Rome and took refuge at the court of the Frankish king Charlemagne. He returned to Rome in 799 and crowned Charlemagne emperor on Christmas Day 800, establishing the secular sovereignty of the pope over Rome under the suzerainty of the emperor (who became the Holy Roman emperor).

Leo X Giovanni de' Medici 1475–1521. Pope from 1513. The son of Lorenzo the Magnificent of Florence, he was created a cardinal at 13. He bestowed on Henry VIII of England the title of Defender of the Faith. A patron of the arts, he sponsored the rebuilding of St Peter's Church, Rome. He raised funds for this by selling indulgences (remissions of punishment for sin), a sale that led the religious reformer Martin Luther to rebel against papal authority. Leo X condemned Luther in the bull *Exsurge domine* 1520 and excommunicated him in 1521.

León city in W Nicaragua; population (1985) 101,000. Industries include textiles and food processing. Founded in 1524, it was the capital of Nicaragua until 1855.

León city in Castilla-León, Spain; population (1991) 146,300. It was the capital of the kingdom of León from the 10th century until 1230, when it was merged with Castile.

Leonard Elmore (John, Jr) 1925– . US author of westerns and thrillers, marked by vivid dialogue, as in *City Primeval* 1980, *La Brava* 1983, *Stick* 1983, *Glitz* 1985, *Freaky Deaky* 1988, and *Get Shorty* 1990.

Leonard Sugar Ray 1956– . US boxer. In 1988 he became the first man to have won world titles at five officially recognized weights. In 1976 he was Olympic light-welterweight champion; he won his first professional title in 1979 when he beat Wilfred Benitez for the WBC welterweight title. He later won titles at junior middleweight (WBA version) 1981, middleweight (WBC) 1987, light-heavyweight (WBC) 1988, and super-middleweight (WBC) 1988. In 1989 he drew with Thomas Hearns.

Leonardo da Vinci 1452–1519. Italian painter, sculptor, architect, engineer, and scientist. One of the greatest figures of the Italian Renaissance, he was active in Florence, Milan, and, from 1516, France. As state engineer and court painter to the duke of Milan, he painted the *Last Supper* mural about 1495 (Sta Maria delle Grazie, Milan), and on his return to Florence painted the *Mona Lisa* (Louvre, Paris) about 1503–06. His notebooks and drawings show an immensely inventive and enquiring mind, studying aspects of the natural world from anatomy to aerodynamics.

Leoncavallo Ruggiero 1857–1919. Italian operatic composer, born in Naples. He played in restaurants, composing in his spare time, until the success of *Pagliacci* in 1892. His other operas include *La Bohème* 1897 (contemporary with Puccini's version) and *Zaza* 1900.

León de los Aldamas industrial city (leather goods, footwear) in central Mexico; population (1986) 947,000.

Leone Sergio 1928–1989. Italian film director, responsible for popularizing 'spaghetti' Westerns (Westerns made in Italy and Spain, usually with a US leading actor and a European supporting cast and crew) and making a world star of Clint Eastwood. His films include *Per un pugno di dollari/A Fistful of Dollars* 1964, *C'era una volta il West/Once Upon a Time in the West* 1968, and *C'era una volta il America/Once Upon a Time in America* 1984.

Leonidas died 480 BC. King of Sparta. He was killed while defending the pass of *Thermopylae with 300 Spartans, 700 Thespians, and 400 Thebans against a huge Persian army.

Leonov Aleksei Arkhipovich 1934– . Soviet cosmonaut. In 1965 he was the first person to walk in space, from the spacecraft *Voskhod 2*.

leopard or *panther* cat *Panthera pardus*, found in Africa and Asia. The background colour of the coat is golden, and the black spots form rosettes, that differ according to the variety; black panthers are simply a colour variation and retain the patterning as a 'watered-silk' effect. The leopard is 1.5–2.5 m/5–8 ft long, including the tail, which may measure 1 m/3 ft.

Leopold three kings of the Belgians, including:

Leopold I 1790–1865. King of the Belgians from 1831, having been elected to the throne on the creation of an independent Belgium. Through his marriage, when prince of Saxe-Coburg, to Princess Charlotte Augusta, he was the uncle of Queen Victoria of Great Britain and had considerable influence over her.

Leopold III 1901–1983. King of the Belgians 1934–51. He surrendered to the German army in World War II 1940. Postwar charges against his conduct led to a regency by his brother Charles and his eventual abdication 1951 in favour of his son Baudouin.

Léopoldville former name (until 1966) of *Kinshasa, city in Zaire.

Lepanto, Battle of sea battle 7 Oct 1571, fought in the Mediterranean Gulf of Corinth off Lepanto (Italian name of the Greek port of *Naupaktos*), then in Turkish possession, between the Ottoman Empire and forces from Spain, Venice, Genoa, and the Papal States, jointly commanded by the Spanish soldier Don John of Austria. The combined western fleets overcame Muslim sea power. The Spanish writer Cervantes was wounded in the battle.

Le Pen Jean-Marie 1928– . French extreme right-wing politician. In 1972 he formed the French National Front, supporting immigrant repatriation and capital punishment; the party gained 14% of the national vote in the 1986 election. Le Pen was elected to the European Parliament in 1984.

Lepenski Vir site of Europe's oldest urban settlement (6th millennium BC), now submerged by an artificial lake on the river Danube.

lepidoptera order of insects, including *butterflies and *moths, which have overlapping scales on their wings; the order consists of some 165,000 species.

leprosy or *Hansen's disease* chronic, progressive disease caused by a bacterium *Mycobacterium leprae* closely related to that of tuberculosis. The infection attacks the skin and nerves. Once common in many countries, leprosy is now confined almost entirely to the tropics. It is controlled with drugs.

Leptis Magna ruined city in Libya, 120 km/75 mi E of Tripoli. It was founded by the Phoenicians, then came under Carthage, and in 47 BC under Rome. Excavation in the 20th century revealed remains of fine Roman buildings.

lepton any of a class of light *elementary particles that are not affected by the strong nuclear force; they do not interact strongly with other particles or nuclei. The leptons are comprised of the *electron, muon, and tau, and their *neutrinos (the electron, muon, and tau neutrinos), plus their six *antiparticles.

Lermontov Mikhail Yurevich 1814–1841. Russian Romantic poet and novelist. In 1837 he was sent into active military service in the Caucasus for writing a revolutionary poem on the death of Pushkin, which criticized court values, and for participating in a duel. Among his works are the psychological novel *A Hero of Our Time* 1840 and a volume of poems *October* 1840.

Le Sage Alain René 1668–1747. French novelist and dramatist. Born in Brittany, he abandoned law for literature. His novels include *Le Diable boîteux/The Devil upon Two Sticks* 1707 and his picaresque masterpiece *Gil Blas* 1715–35, which is much indebted to Spanish originals.

lesbianism homosexuality (sexual attraction to one's own sex) between women, so called from the Greek island of Lesbos (now Lesvos), the home of *Sappho the poet and her followers to whom the behaviour was attributed.

Lesbos alternative spelling of *Lesvos, an island in the Aegean Sea.

lesion any change in a body tissue that is a manifestation of disease or injury.

Lesotho Kingdom of
area 30,355 sq km/11,717 sq mi
capital Maseru
towns Teyateyaneng, Mafeteng, Roma, Quthing
physical mountainous with plateaus, forming part of South Africa's chief watershed
political system military-controlled monarchy
head of state King Letsie III from 1990
head of government Ntsu Mokhehle from 1993
exports wool, mohair, diamonds, cattle, wheat, vegetables
currency maluti
population (1993 est) 1,900,000; growth rate 2.7% p.a.
life expectancy men 59, women 62 (1989)
languages Sesotho, English (official), Zulu, Xhosa
religions Protestant 42%, Roman Catholic 38%
GNP $580 per head (1991)
chronology
1868 Basutoland became a British protectorate.
1966 Independence achieved from Britain, within the Commonwealth, as the Kingdom of Lesotho, with Moshoeshoe II as king and Chief Leabua Jonathan as prime minister.
1970 State of emergency declared and constitution suspended.
1973 Pro-government interim assembly established; BNP won majority of seats.
1975 Members of the ruling party attacked by guerrillas backed by South Africa.
1985 Elections cancelled because no candidates opposed BNP.
1986 South Africa imposed border blockade, forcing deportation of 60 African National Congress members. General Lekhanya ousted Chief Jonathan in coup. National assembly abolished. Highlands Water Project agreement signed with South Africa.
1990 Moshoeshoe II dethroned by military

council; replaced by his son Mohato as King Letsie III.
1991 Lekhanya ousted in military coup led by Col Elias Tutsoane Ramaema. Political parties permitted to operate.
1992 Ex-king Moshoeshoe returned from exile.
1993 Free elections ended military rule; Ntsu Mokhehle of BCP became prime minister.

less developed country (ldc) any country late in developing an industrial base, and dependent on cash crops and unprocessed minerals. The Group of 77 was established in 1964 to pressure industrialized countries into giving greater aid to less developed countries.

Lesseps Ferdinand, Vicomte de Lesseps 1805–1894. French engineer, constructor of the *Suez Canal 1859–69; he began the *Panama Canal in 1879, but withdrew after failing to construct it without locks.

Lessing Doris (May) (née Taylor) 1919– . British novelist, born in Iran. Concerned with social and political themes, particularly the place of women in society, her work includes *The Grass is Singing* 1950, the five-novel series *Children of Violence* 1952–69, *The Good Terrorist* 1985, and *The Fifth Child* 1988. She has also written an 'inner space fiction' series *Canopus in Argus Archives* 1979–83, and under the pen name 'Jane Somers', *The Diary of a Good Neighbour* 1981.

Les Six (French 'the six') a group of French composers: Georges *Auric, Louis Durey (1888–1979), Arthur *Honegger, Darius Milhaud, Francis *Poulenc, and Germaine Tailleferre (1892–1983). Formed in 1917, the group was dedicated to producing works free from foreign influences and reflecting the contemporary world. It split up in the early 1920s.

Lesvos Greek island in the Aegean Sea, near the coast of Turkey
area 2,154 sq km/831 sq mi
capital Mytilene
products olives, wine, grain
population (1981) 104,620
history ancient name Lesbos; an Aeolian settlement, the home of the poets Alcaeus and Sappho; conquered by the Turks from Genoa 1462; annexed to Greece 1913.

Lethe in Greek mythology, a river of the underworld whose waters, when drunk, brought forgetfulness of the past.

letterpress method of printing from raised type, pioneered by Johann *Gutenberg in Europe in the 1450s.

lettre de cachet French term for an order signed by the king and closed with his seal (*cachet*); especially an order under which persons might be imprisoned or banished without trial. *Lettres de cachet* were used as a means of disposing of political opponents or criminals of high birth. The system was abolished during the French Revolution.

lettuce annual edible plant *Lactuca sativa*, family Compositae, believed to have been derived from the wild species *L. serriola*. There are many varieties, including the cabbage lettuce, with round or loose heads, and the Cos lettuce, with long, upright heads.

leucocyte another name for a *white blood cell.

leucotomy another term for frontal *lobotomy, a brain operation.

leukaemia any one of a group of cancers of the blood cells, with widespread involvement of the bone marrow and other blood-forming tissue. The central feature of leukaemia is runaway production of white blood cells that are immature or in some way abnormal. These rogue cells, which lack the defensive capacity of healthy white cells, overwhelm the normal ones, leaving the victim vulnerable to infection. Treatment is with radiotherapy and *cytotoxic drugs to suppress replication of abnormal cells, or by bone-marrow transplantation.

Le Vau Louis 1612–1670. French architect who drafted the plan of Versailles, rebuilt the Louvre, and built Les Tuileries in Paris.

levee naturally formed raised bank along the side of a river channel. When a river overflows its banks, the rate of flow in the flooded area is less than that in the channel, and silt is deposited. After the waters have withdrawn the silt is left as a bank that grows with successive floods. Eventually the river, contained by the levee, may be above the surface of the surrounding flood plain. Notable levees are found on the lower reaches of the Mississippi in the USA and the Po in Italy.

level or **spirit level** instrument for finding horizontal level, or adjusting a surface to an even level, used in surveying, building construction, and archaeology. It has a glass tube of coloured liquid, in which a bubble is trapped, mounted in an elongated frame. When the tube is horizontal, the bubble moves to the centre.

Levellers democratic party in the English Civil War. The Levellers found wide support among Cromwell's New Model Army and the yeoman farmers, artisans, and small traders, and proved a powerful political force 1647–49. Their programme included the establishment of a republic, government by a parliament of one house elected by male suffrage, religious toleration, and sweeping social reforms.

lever simple machine consisting of a rigid rod pivoted at a fixed point called the fulcrum, used for shifting or raising a heavy load or applying force in a similar way. Levers are classified into orders according to where the effort is applied, and the load-moving force developed, in relation to the position of the fulcrum.

leveraged buyout in business, the purchase of a controlling proportion of the shares of a company by its own management, financed almost exclusively by borrowing. It is so called because the ratio of a company's long-term debt to its equity (capital assets) is known as its 'leverage'.

Lévesque René 1922–1987. French-Canadian politician. In 1968 he founded the Parti Québecois, with the aim of an independent Québec, but a referendum rejected the proposal in 1980. He was premier of Québec 1976–85.

Levi Primo 1919–1987. Italian novelist. He joined the anti-Fascist resistance during World War II, was captured, and sent to the concentration camp at Auschwitz. He wrote of these experiences in *Se questo è un uomo/If This Is a Man* 1947.

Levi-Montalcini Rita 1909– . Italian neurologist who discovered nerve-growth factor, a substance that controls how many cells make up the adult nervous system. She shared the 1986 Nobel Prize for Medicine with US biochemist Stanley Cohen (1922–).

Levinson Barry 1932– . US film director and screenwriter. Working in Hollywood's mainstream, he has been responsible for some of the best adult comedy films of the 1980s and 1990s. Winning cult status for the offbeat realism of *Diner* 1982, Levinson went on to make such large-budget movies as *Good Morning Vietnam* 1987, *Tin Men* 1987, *Rain Man* 1988 (Academy Award), and *Bugsy* 1991.

Lévi-Strauss Claude 1908–1990. French anthropologist who sought to find a universal structure governing all societies, as reflected in the way their myths are constructed. His works include *Tristes Tropiques* 1955 and *Mythologiques/Mythologies* 1964–71.

levitation counteraction of gravitational forces on a body. As claimed by medieval mystics, spiritualist mediums, and practitioners of transcendental meditation, it is unproven. In the laboratory it can be produced scientifically; for example, electrostatic force and acoustical waves have been used to suspend water drops for microscopic study. It is also used in technology, for example, in magnetic levitation as in *maglev trains.

Lewes, Battle of battle in 1264 caused by the baronial opposition to the English King Henry III, led by Simon de Montfort, earl of Leicester (1208–65). The king was defeated and captured at the battle.

Lewis (William) Arthur 1915– . British economist born on St Lucia, West Indies. He specialized in the economic problems of developing countries and created a model relating the terms of trade between less developed and more developed nations to their respective levels of labor productivity in agriculture. He shared the Nobel Prize for Economics with an American, Theodore Schultz, 1979. He wrote many books, including the *Theory of Economic Growth* 1955.

Lewis Carl (Frederick Carleton) 1961– . US track and field athlete who won eight gold medals and one silver in three successive Olympic Games. At the 1984 Olympic Games he equalled the performance of Jesse *Owens, winning gold medals in the 100 and 200 metres, 400-metre relay, and long jump.

Lewis Cecil Day. Irish poet; see *Day Lewis.

Lewis C(live) S(taples) 1898–1963. British academic and writer, born in Belfast. His books include the medieval study, *The Allegory of Love* 1936, and the space fiction, *Out of the Silent Planet* 1938. He was a committed Christian and wrote essays in popular theology such as *The Screwtape Letters* 1942 and *Mere Christianity* 1952; the autobiographical *Surprised by Joy* 1955; and a series of books of Christian allegory for children, set in the magic land of Narnia, including *The Lion, the Witch, and the Wardrobe* 1950.

Lewis (Harry) Sinclair 1885–1951. US novelist. He made a reputation with satirical novels: *Main Street* 1920, depicting American small-town life; *Babbitt* 1922, the story of a real-estate dealer of the Midwest caught in the conventions of his milieu; *Arrowsmith* 1925, a study of the pettiness in medical science; and *Elmer Gantry* 1927, a satiric portrayal of evangelical religion. *Dodsworth*, a gentler novel of a US industrialist, was published 1929. He was the first American to be awarded the Nobel Prize for Literature, in 1930.

Lewis Jerry. Stage name of Joseph Levitch 1926– . US comic actor and director. Formerly in partnership with Dean Martin (1946–56), their film debut was in *My Friend Irma* 1949. He was revered as a solo performer by French critics ('Le Roi du Crazy'), but films that he directed such as *The Nutty Professor* 1963 were less well received in the USA. He appeared with Robert De Niro in *The King of Comedy* 1982.

Lewis Jerry Lee 1935– . US rock-and-roll and country singer and pianist. His trademark was the 'pumping piano' style in hits such as 'Whole Lotta Shakin' Going On' and 'Great Balls of Fire' 1957; later recordings include 'What Made Milwaukee Famous' 1968.

Lewis Meriwether 1774–1809. US explorer. He was commissioned by president Thomas Jefferson to find a land route to the Pacific with William Clark (1770–1838). They followed the Missouri River to its source, crossed the Rocky Mountains (aided by an Indian woman, Sacajawea) and followed the Columbia River to the Pacific, then returned overland to St Louis 1804–06.

Lewis (Percy) Wyndham 1886–1957. English writer and artist who pioneered *Vorticism, which with its feeling of movement sought to reflect the age of industry. He had a hard and aggressive style in both his writing and his painting. His literary works include the novels *Tarr* 1918 and *The Childermass* 1928, the essay *Time and Western Man* 1927, and autobiographies.

Lewis with Harris largest island in the Outer Hebrides; area 2,220 sq km/857 sq mi; population (1981) 23,400. Its main town is Stornoway. It is separated from NW Scotland by the Minch. There are many lakes and peat moors. Harris is famous for its tweeds.

Lewton Val. Stage name of Vladimir Ivan Leventon 1904–1951. Russian-born US film producer, responsible for a series of atmospheric B horror films made for RKO in the 1940s, including *Cat People* 1942 and *The Body Snatcher* 1946. He co-wrote several of his films under the adopted name of Carlos Keith.

Leyden Lucas van. See *Lucas van Leyden, Dutch painter.

Lhasa ('the Forbidden City') capital of the autonomous region of Tibet, China, at 5,000 m/ 16,400 ft; population (1982) 105,000. Products include handicrafts and light industry. The holy city of *Lamaism, Lhasa was closed to Westerners until 1904, when members of a British expedition led by Col Francis E Younghusband visited the city. It was annexed with the rest of Tibet 1950–51 by China, and the spiritual and temporal head of state, the Dalai Lama, fled in 1959 after a popular uprising against Chinese rule. Monasteries have been destroyed and monks killed, and an influx of Chinese settlers has generated resentment. In 1988 and 1989

nationalist demonstrators were shot by Chinese soldiers.

liability in accounting, a financial obligation. Liabilities are placed alongside assets on a balance sheet to show the wealth of the individual or company concerned at a given date.

liana woody, perennial climbing plant with very long stems, which grows around trees up to the canopy, where there is more sunlight. Lianas are common in tropical rainforests, where individual stems may grow up to 78 m/255 ft long. They have an unusual stem structure that allows them to retain some flexibility, despite being woody.

Liaoning province of NE China
area 151,000 sq km/58,300 sq mi
capital Shenyang
towns Anshan, Fushun, Liaoyang
products cereals, coal, iron, salt, oil
population (1990) 39,460,000
history developed by Japan 1905–45, including the **Liaodong Peninsula**, whose ports had been conquered from the Russians.

libel in law, defamation published in a permanent form, such as in a newspaper, book, or broadcast.

Liberal Democrats in UK politics, common name for the *Social and Liberal Democrats.

liberalism political and social theory that favours representative government, freedom of the press, speech, and worship, the abolition of class privileges, the use of state resources to protect the welfare of the individual, and international *free trade. It is historically associated with the Liberal Party in the UK and the Democratic Party in the USA.

Liberal Party British political party, the successor to the *Whig Party, with an ideology of liberalism. In the 19th century, it represented the interests of commerce and industry. Its outstanding leaders were Palmerston, Gladstone, and Lloyd George. From 1914 it declined, and the rise of the Labour Party pushed the Liberals into the middle ground. The Liberals joined forces with the Social Democratic Party (SDP) as the Alliance for the 1983 and 1987 elections. In 1988, a majority of the SDP voted to merge with the Liberals to form the *Social and Liberal Democrats.

Liberal Party, Australian political party established 1944 by Robert Menzies, after a Labor landslide, and derived from the former United Australia Party. After the voters rejected Labor's extensive nationalization plans, the Liberals were in power 1949–72 and 1975–83 and were led in succession by Harold Holt, John Gorton, William McMahon (1908–), Billy Snedden (1926–), and Malcolm Fraser.

Liberia Republic of
area 111,370 sq km/42,989 sq mi
capital and port Monrovia
towns ports Buchanan, Greenville
physical forested highlands; swampy tropical coast where six rivers enter the sea
head of state and government Amos Sawyer from 1990
political system emergent democratic republic
exports iron ore, rubber (Africa's largest

producer), timber, diamonds, coffee, cocoa, palm oil
currency Liberian dollar
population (1993 est) 2,700,000 (95% indigenous); growth rate 3% p.a.
languages English (official), over 20 Niger-Congo languages
religions animist 65%, Muslim 20%, Christian 15% **literacy** men 47%, women 23% (1985 est)
GNP $440 per head (1991)
chronology
1847 Founded as an independent republic.
1944 William Tubman elected president.
1971 Tubman died; succeeded by William Tolbert.
1980 Tolbert assassinated in coup led by Samuel Doe, who suspended the constitution and ruled through a People's Redemption Council.
1984 New constitution approved. National Democratic Party of Liberia (NDPL) founded by Doe.
1985 NDPL won decisive victory in general election. Unsuccessful coup against Doe.
1990 Rebels under former government minister Charles Taylor controlled nearly entire country by July. Doe killed during a bloody civil war between rival rebel factions. Amos Sawyer became interim head of government.
1991 Amos Sawyer re-elected president. Rebel leader Charles Taylor agreed to work with Sawyer. Peace agreement failed but later revived; peacekeeping force drafted into republic.

libido in Freudian psychology, the psychic energy, or life force, that is to be found even in a newborn child. The libido develops through a number of phases, identified by Freud as the **oral stage**, when a child tests everything by mouth, the **anal stage**, when the child gets satisfaction from control of its body, and the **genital stage**, when sexual instincts find pleasure in the outward show of love.

LIBOR acronym for **London Interbank Offered Rates**, loan rates for a specified period that are offered to first-class banks in the London interbank market. Banks link their lending to LIBOR as an alternative to the base lending rate when setting the rate for a fixed term, after which the rate may be adjusted. The LIBOR rate is the main bench mark for much of the Eurodollar loan market.

Libra faint zodiacal constellation in the southern hemisphere adjoining Scorpius, and represented as the scales of justice. The Sun passes through Libra during Nov. The constellation was once considered to be a part of Scorpius, seen as the scorpion's claws. In astrology, the dates for Libra are between about 23 Sept and 23 Oct (see *precession).

library collection of information (usually in the form of books) held for common use. The earliest was at Nineveh in Babylonian times. The first public library was opened in Athens in 330 BC. All ancient libraries were reference libraries: books could be consulted but not borrowed.

libretto (Italian 'little book') the text of an opera or other dramatic vocal work, or the scenario of a ballet.

Libreville capital of Gabon, on the estuary of the river Gabon; population (1988) 352,000. Products include timber, oil, and minerals. It was founded 1849 as a refuge for slaves freed by the French.

Libya Great Socialist People's Libyan Arab Jamahiriya (*al-Jamahiriya al-Arabiya al-Libya al-Shabiya al-Ishtirakiya al-Uzma*)

area 1,759,540 sq km/679,182 sq mi
capital Tripoli
towns ports Benghazi, Misurata, Tobruk
physical flat to undulating plains with plateaus and depressions stretch S from the Mediterranean coast to an extremely dry desert interior
environment plan to pump water from below the Sahara to the coast risks rapid exhaustion of nonrenewable supply (Great Manmade River Project)
head of state and government Moamer al-Khaddhafi from 1969
political party Arab Socialist Union (ASU), radical, left-wing
exports oil, natural gas
currency Libyan dinar
population (1993 est) 4,700,000 (including 500,000 foreign workers); growth rate 3.1% p.a.
language Arabic
religion Sunni Muslim 97%
GNP $5,410 per head (1988)
chronology
1911 Conquered by Italy.
1934 Colony named Libya.
1942 Divided into three provinces: Fezzan (under French control); Cyrenaica, Tripolitania (under British control).
1951 Achieved independence as the United Kingdom of Libya, under King Idris.
1969 King deposed in a coup led by Col Moamer al-Khaddhafi. Revolution Command Council set up and the Arab Socialist Union (ASU) proclaimed the only legal party.
1972 Proposed federation of Libya, Syria, and Egypt abandoned.
1980 Proposed merger with Syria abandoned. Libyan troops began fighting in Chad.
1981 Proposed merger with Chad abandoned.
1986 US bombing of Khaddhafi's headquarters, following allegations of his complicity in terrorist activities.
1988 Diplomatic relations with Chad restored.
1989 USA accused Libya of building a chemical-weapons factory and shot down two Libyan planes; reconciliation with Egypt.
1992 Khaddhafi under international pressure to

send suspected Lockerbie bombers for trial outside Libya.

lichen any organism of the group Lichenes, which consists of a specific fungus and a specific alga existing in a mutually beneficial relationship. Found as coloured patches or spongelike masses adhering to trees, rocks, and other substrates, lichens flourish under adverse conditions.

Lichfield Patrick Anson, 5th Earl of Lichfield 1939– . British portrait photographer.

Lichtenstein Roy 1923– . US Pop artist. He uses advertising imagery and comic-strip techniques, often focusing on popular ideals of romance and heroism, as in *Whaam!* 1963 (Tate Gallery, London). He has also produced sculptures in brass, plastic, and enamelled metal.

Liddell Hart Basil 1895–1970. British military strategist. He was an exponent of mechanized warfare, and his ideas were adopted in Germany in 1935 in creating the 1st Panzer Division, combining motorized infantry and tanks. From 1937 he advised the UK War Office on army reorganization.

Liebig Justus, Baron von 1803–1873. German chemist, a major contributor to agricultural chemistry. He introduced the theory of *radicals and discovered chloroform and chloral.

Liebknecht Karl 1871–1919. German socialist, son of Wilhelm Liebknecht. A founder of the German Communist Party, originally known as the Spartacus League (see *Spartacist) 1918, he was one of the few socialists who refused to support World War I. He and Rosa Luxemburg led an unsuccessful revolt in Berlin 1919 and were murdered by army officers.

Liebknecht Wilhelm 1826–1900. German socialist. A friend of the communist theoretician Karl Marx, with whom he took part in the *revolution of 1848, he was imprisoned for opposition to the Franco-Prussian War 1870–71. He was one of the founders of the Social Democratic Party 1875. He was the father of Karl Liebknecht.

Liechtenstein Principality of (*Fürstentum Liechtenstein*)

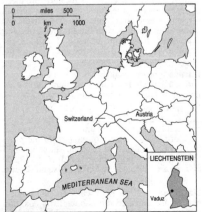

area 160 sq km/62 sq mi
capital Vaduz
towns Balzers, Schaan, Ruggell

physical landlocked Alpine; includes part of Rhine Valley in W
head of state Prince Hans Adam II from 1989
head of government Mario Frick from 1993
political system constitutional monarchy
exports microchips, dental products, small machinery, processed foods, postage stamps
currency Swiss franc
population (1993 est) 30,000 (33% foreign); growth rate 1.4% p.a.
language German (official); an Alemannic dialect is also spoken
religions Roman Catholic 87%, Protestant 8%
GNP $33,000 per head (1991)
chronology
1342 Became a sovereign state.
1434 Present boundaries established.
1719 Former counties of Schellenberg and Vaduz constituted as the Principality of Liechtenstein.
1921 Adopted Swiss currency.
1923 United with Switzerland in a customs union.
1938 Prince Franz Josef II came to power.
1984 Prince Franz Josef II handed over power to Crown Prince Hans Adam. Vote extended to women in national elections.
1989 Prince Franz Josef II died; Hans Adam II succeeded him.
1990 Became a member of the United Nations.
1991 Became seventh member of European Free Trade Association.
1993 Mario Frick (28) became Europe's youngest head of government.

lied (German 'song', plural lieder) musical setting of a poem, usually for solo voice and piano; referring to Romantic songs of Schubert, Schumann, Brahms, and Hugo Wolf.

lie detector instrument that records graphically certain body activities, such as thoracic and abdominal respiration, blood pressure, pulse rate, and galvanic skin response (changes in electrical resistance of the skin). Marked changes in these activities when a person answers a question may indicate that the person is lying.

liege in the feudal system, the allegiance owed by a vassal to his or her lord (the liege lord).

Liège (German **Luik**) industrial city (weapons, textiles, paper, chemicals), capital of Liège province in Belgium, SE of Brussels, on the river Meuse; population (1991) 194,600. The province of Liège has an area of 3,900 sq km/1,505 sq mi and a population (1991) of 999,600.

Lifar Serge 1905–1986. Ukrainian dancer and choreographer. Born in Kiev, he studied under *Nijinsky, joined the Diaghilev company in 1923, and was *maître de ballet* at the Paris Opéra 1930–44 and 1947–59.

life ability to grow, reproduce, and respond to such stimuli as light, heat, and sound. It is thought that life on Earth began about 4 billion years ago. The earliest fossil evidence of life is threadlike chains of cells discovered in 1980 in deposits in NW Australia that have been dated as 3.5 billion years old.

life cycle in biology, the sequence of developmental stages through which members of a given species pass. Most vertebrates have a simple life cycle consisting of *fertilization of sex cells or *gametes, a period of development as an *embryo, a period of juvenile growth after hatching or birth, an adulthood including *sexual reproduction, and finally death. Invertebrate life cycles are generally more complex and may involve major reconstitution of the individual's appearance (*metamorphosis) and completely different styles of life. Plants have a special type of life cycle with two distinct phases, known as *alternation of generations. Many insects such as cicadas, dragonflies, and mayflies have a long larvae or pupae phase and a short adult phase. Dragonflies live an aquatic life as larvae and an aerial life during the adult phase. In many invertebrates and protozoa there is a sequence of stages in the life cycle, and in parasites different stages often occur in different host organisms.

life expectancy average lifespan of a person at birth. It depends on nutrition, disease control, environmental contaminants, war, stress, and living standards in general.

life sciences scientific study of the living world as a whole, a new synthesis of several traditional scientific disciplines including *biology, *zoology, and *botany, and newer, more specialized areas of study such as *biophysics and *sociobiology.

LIFFE acronym for **London International Financial Futures Exchange**, one of the exchanges in London where *futures contracts are traded. It opened Sept 1982.

Liffey river in the eastern Republic of Ireland, flowing from the Wicklow Mountains to Dublin Bay; length 80 km/50 mi.

ligament strong flexible connective tissue, made of the protein collagen, which joins bone to bone at moveable joints. Ligaments prevent bone dislocation (under normal circumstances) but permit joint flexion.

Ligeti György (Sándor) 1923– . Hungarian-born Austrian composer who developed a dense, highly chromatic, polyphonic style in which melody and rhythm are sometimes lost in shifting blocks of sound. He achieved international prominence with *Atmosphères* 1961 and *Requiem* 1965, which were used for Stanley Kubrick's film epic *2001: A Space Odyssey* 1968. Other works include an opera *Le Grand Macabre* 1978, and *Poème symphonique* 1962, for 100 metronomes (clockwork time-keeping devices).

light electromagnetic waves in the visible range, having a wavelength from about 400 nanometres in the extreme violet to about 770 nanometres in the extreme red. Light is considered to exhibit particle and wave properties, and the fundamental particle, or quantum, of light is called the photon. The speed of light (and of all electromagnetic radiation) in a vacuum is approximately 300,000 km/186,000 mi per second, and is a universal constant denoted by *c*.

light bulb incandescent filament lamp, first demonstrated by Joseph Swan in the UK 1878 and Thomas Edison in the USA 1879. The present-day light bulb is a thin glass bulb filled with an inert mixture of nitrogen and argon gas. It contains a filament made of fine tungsten wire. When electricity is passed through the wire, it glows white hot, producing light.

light-dependent resistor (LDR) component of electronic circuits whose resistance varies with the level of illumination on its surface. Usually resistance decreases as illumination rises. LDRs are used in light-measuring or light-sensing instruments (for example, in the exposure-meter circuit of an automatic camera) and in switches (such as those that switch on street lights at dusk). LDRs are made from *semiconductors, such as cadmium sulphide.

light-emitting diode (LED) means of displaying symbols in electronic instruments and devices. An LED is made of *semiconductor material, such as gallium arsenide phosphide, that glows when electricity is passed through it. The first digital watches and calculators had LED displays, but many later models use *liquid-crystal displays.

lighthouse structure carrying a powerful light to warn ships or aeroplanes that they are approaching a place (usually land) dangerous or important to navigation. The light is magnified and directed out to the horizon or up to the zenith by a series of mirrors or prisms. Increasingly lighthouses are powered by electricity and automated rather than staffed; the more recent models also emit radio signals. Only a minority of the remaining staffed lighthouses still use dissolved acetylene gas as a source of power.

lightning high-voltage electrical discharge between two charged rainclouds or between a cloud and the Earth, caused by the build-up of electrical charges. Air in the path of lightning ionizes (becomes conducting), and expands; the accompanying noise is heard as thunder. Currents of 20,000 amperes and temperatures of 30,000°C/54,000°F are common.

light watt unit of radiant power (brightness of light). One light watt is the power required to produce a perceived brightness equal to that of light at a wavelength of 550 nanometres and 680 lumens.

light year in astronomy, the distance travelled by a beam of light in a vacuum in one year, approximately 9.46 trillion (million million) km/5.88 trillion miles.

lignin naturally occurring substance produced by plants to strengthen their tissues. It is difficult for *enzymes to attack lignin, so living organisms cannot digest wood, with the exception of a few specialized fungi and bacteria. Lignin is the essential ingredient of all wood and is, therefore, of great commercial importance.

lignite type of *coal that is brown and fibrous, with a relatively low carbon content. In Scandinavia it is burned to generate power.

Liguria coastal region of NW Italy, which includes the resorts of the Italian Riviera, lying between the western Alps and the Mediterranean Gulf of Genoa. The region comprises the provinces of Genova, La Spezia, Imperia, and Savona, with a population (1990) of 1,719,200 and an area of 5,418 sq km/2,093 sq mi. Genoa is the chief town and port.

Likud alliance of right-wing Israeli political parties that defeated the Labour Party coalition in the May 1977 election and brought Menachem Begin to power. In 1987 Likud became part of an uneasy national coalition with Labour, formed to solve Israel's economic crisis. In 1989 another coalition was formed under Shamir. Likud lost the 1992 general election to Labour.

lilac any flowering Old World shrub of the genus *Syringa* (such as *S. vulgaris*) of the olive family Oleaceae, bearing panicles (clusters) of small, sweetly scented, white or purplish flowers.

Lilburne John 1614–1657. English republican agitator. He was imprisoned 1638–40 for circulating Puritan pamphlets, fought in the Parliamentary army in the Civil War, and by his advocacy of a democratic republic won the leadership of the Levellers, the democratic party in the English Revolution.

Lilienthal Otto 1848–1896. German aviation pioneer who inspired the US aviators Orville and Wilbur Wright. He made and successfully flew many gliders before he was killed in a glider crash.

Lille (Flemish *Ryssel*) industrial city (textiles, chemicals, engineering, distilling), capital of Nord-Pas-de-Calais, France; population (1982) 174,000, metropolitan area 936,000. The world's first entirely automatic underground system was opened here in 1982.

Lillee Dennis 1949– . Australian cricketer regarded as the best fast bowler of his generation. He made his test debut in the 1970–71 season and subsequently played for his country 70 times. Lillee was the first to take 300 wickets in test cricket. He played Sheffield Shield cricket for Western Australia and at the end of his career made a comeback with Tasmania.

Lilongwe capital of Malawi since 1975; population (1987) 234,000. Products include tobacco and textiles.

lily plant of the genus *Lilium*, family Liliaceae, of which there are some 80 species, most with showy, trumpet-shaped flowers growing from bulbs. The lily family includes hyacinths, tulips, asparagus, and plants of the onion genus. The term 'lily' is also applied to many lilylike plants of allied genera and families.

lily of the valley plant *Convallaria majalis* of the lily family Liliaceae, growing in woods in Europe, N Asia, and North America. The small, pendant, white flowers are strongly scented. The plant is often cultivated.

Lima capital of Peru, an industrial city (textiles, chemicals, glass, cement) with its port at Callao; population (1988) 418,000, metropolitan area 4,605,000. Founded by the conquistador Pizarro 1535, it was rebuilt after destruction by an earthquake in 1746.

limbo in Christian theology, a region for the souls of those who were not admitted to the divine vision. *Limbus infantum* was a place where unbaptized infants enjoyed inferior blessedness, and *limbus patrum* was where the prophets of the Old Testament dwelt. The word was first used in this sense in the 13th century by St Thomas Aquinas.

Limbourg brothers Franco-Flemish painters, Pol, Herman, and Jan (Hennequin, Janneken), active in the late 14th and early 15th centuries, first in Paris, then at the ducal court of Burgundy. They produced richly detailed manuscript illuminations, including two Books of *Hours.

Limburg southernmost province of the Netherlands in the plain of the Maas (Meuse); area

2,170 sq km/838 sq mi; population (1991) 1,109,900. Its capital is Maastricht, the oldest city in the Netherlands. The manufacture of chemicals has now replaced coal mining but the coal industry is still remembered at Kerkrade, alleged site of the first European coal mine. The marl soils of S Limburg are used in the manufacture of cement and fertilizer. Mixed arable farming and horticulture are also important.

lime small thorny bush *Citrus aurantifolia* of the rue family Rutaceae, native to India. The white flowers are succeeded by light green or yellow fruits, limes, which resemble lemons but are more globular in shape.

lime or **linden** deciduous tree, genus *Tilia*, of the family Tiliaceae native to the northern hemisphere. The leaves are heart-shaped and coarsely toothed, and the flowers are cream-coloured and fragrant.

lime or **quicklime** CaO (technical name **calcium oxide**) white powdery substance used in making mortar and cement. It is made commercially by heating calcium carbonate ($CaCO_3$), obtained from limestone or chalk, in a lime kiln. Quicklime readily absorbs water to become calcium hydroxide ($CaOH$), known as slaked lime, which is used to reduce soil acidity.

limerick five-line humorous verse, often nonsensical, which first appeared in England about 1820 and was popularized by Edward *Lear. An example is: There was a young lady of Riga, Who rode with a smile on a tiger; They returned from the ride With the lady inside, And the smile on the face of the tiger.

Limerick county town of Limerick, Republic of Ireland, the main port of W Ireland, on the Shannon estuary; population (1991) 52,000. It was founded in the 12th century.

Limerick county in the SW Republic of Ireland, in Munster province
area 2,690 sq km/1,038 sq mi
county town Limerick
physical fertile, with hills in the south
products dairy products
population (1991) 161,900.

limestone sedimentary rock composed chiefly of calcium carbonate $CaCO_3$, either derived from the shells of marine organisms or precipitated from solution, mostly in the ocean. Various types of limestone are used as building stone.

Limitation, Statutes of in English law, acts of Parliament limiting the time within which legal action must be inaugurated. Actions for breach of contract and most other civil wrongs must be started within six years. Personal injury claims must usually be brought within three years. In actions in respect of land and of contracts under seal, the period is 12 years.

limited company company for whose debts the members are liable only to a limited extent. The capital of a limited company is divided into small units, and profits are distributed according to shareholding.

Limited Liability Acts UK acts of Parliament 1855 and 1862, which provided a legal framework for the consolidation of large companies that existed as legal entities in perpetuity; they restricted the maximum loss for individual shareholders to the purchase price of their shares.

Limits, Territorial and Fishing see *maritime law.

limnology study of lakes and other bodies of open fresh water, in terms of their plant and animal biology, and their physical properties.

Limousin former province and modern region of central France; area 16,900 sq km/6,544 sq mi; population (1986) 736,000. It consists of the *départements* of Corréze, Creuse, and Haute-Vienne. The chief town is Limoges. A thinly populated and largely unfertile region, it is crossed by the mountains of the Massif Central. Fruit and vegetables are produced in the more fertile lowlands. Kaolin is mined.

limpet any of various marine *snails belonging to several families and genera, especially *Acmaea* and *Patella*. A limpet has a conical shell and adheres firmly to rocks by its dislike foot. Limpets leave their fixed positions only to graze on seaweeds, always returning to the same spot. They are found in the Atlantic and Pacific.

Limpopo river in SE Africa, rising in the Transvaal and reaching the Indian Ocean in Mozambique; length 1,600 km/1,000 mi.

Lin Biao 1907–1971. Chinese politician and general. He joined the Communists in 1927, became a commander of *Mao Zedong's Red Army, and led the Northeast People's Liberation Army in the civil war after 1945. He became defence minister in 1959, and as vice chair of the party in 1969 he was expected to be Mao's successor. But in 1972 the government announced that Lin had been killed in an aeroplane crash in Mongolia on 17 Sept 1971 while fleeing to the USSR following an abortive coup attempt.

Lincoln Abraham 1809–1865. 16th president of the USA 1861–65, a Republican. In the American *Civil War, his chief concern was the preservation of the Union from which the Confederate (Southern) slave states had seceded on his election. In 1863 he announced the freedom of the slaves with the Emancipation Proclamation. He was re-elected in 1864 with victory for the North in sight, but was assassinated at the end of the war.

Lincolnshire county in E England
area 5,890 sq km/2,274 sq mi
towns Lincoln (administrative headquarters), Skegness
physical Lincoln Wolds; marshy coastline; the Fens in the SE; rivers: Witham, Welland
products cattle, sheep, horses, cereals, flower bulbs, oil
population (1991) 573,900
famous people Isaac Newton, Alfred Tennyson, Margaret Thatcher.

Lindbergh Charles A(ugustus) 1902–1974. US aviator who made the first solo nonstop flight in 33.5 hours across the Atlantic (Roosevelt Field, Long Island, New York, to Le Bourget airport, Paris) 1927 in the *Spirit of St Louis*, a Ryan monoplane designed by him.

linden another name for the *lime tree.

Lindow Man remains of an Iron Age man discovered in a peat bog at Lindow Marsh, Cheshire, UK, in 1984. The chemicals in the bog had kept the body in an excellent state of preservation.

linear accelerator or *linac* in physics, a device in which charged subatomic particles are accelerated to high speeds along a straight evacuated tube or waveguide by electromagnetic waves in the tube or by electric fields. Particles pass through a linear accelerator only once – unlike those in a cyclotron (a ring-shaped accelerator), which make many revolutions, gaining energy each time.

linear equation in mathematics, an equation involving two variables (x,y) of the general form $y = mx + b$, where m is the slope of the line represented by the equation and b is the y-intercept, or the value of y where the line crosses the y-axis in the *Cartesian coordinate system. Sets of linear equations can be used to describe the behaviour of buildings, bridges, trusses, and other static structures.

linear motor type of electric motor, an induction motor in which the fixed stator and moving armature are straight and parallel to each other (rather than being circular and one inside the other as in an ordinary induction motor). Linear motors are used, for example, to power sliding doors. There is a magnetic force between the stator and armature; this force has been used to support a vehicle, as in the experimental *maglev linear motor train.

Lineker Gary 1960– . English footballer who scored over 200 goals in 550 games for Leicester, Everton, Barcelona, and Tottenham. With 48 goals in 75 internationals to the end of the 1991–2 English season, he needed just two goals to beat Bobby Charlton's record of 49 goals for England. Lineker was elected Footballer of the Year in 1986 and 1992, and was leading scorer at the 1986 World Cup finals.

linen yarn spun and the textile woven from the fibres of the stem of the *flax plant. Used by the ancient Egyptians, linen was introduced by the Romans to northern Europe, where production became widespread. Religious refugees from the Low Countries in the 16th century helped to establish the linen industry in England, but here and elsewhere it began to decline in competition with cotton in the 18th century.

ling any of several deepwater long-bodied fishes of the cod family found in the N Atlantic.

ling another name for common *heather.

lingua franca (Italian 'Frankish tongue') any language that is used as a means of communication by groups who do not themselves normally speak that language; for example, English is a lingua franca used by Japanese doing business in Finland, or by Swedes in Saudi Arabia. The term comes from the mixture of French, Italian, Spanish, Greek, Turkish, and Arabic that was spoken around the Mediterranean from the time of the Crusades until the 18th century.

linguistics scientific study of language, from its origins (historical linguistics) to the changing way it is pronounced (phonetics), derivation of words through various languages (etymology), development of meanings (semantics), and the arrangement and modifications of words to convey a message (grammar).

linkage in genetics, the association between two or more genes that tend to be inherited together because they are on the same chromosome. The closer together they are on the chromosome, the less likely they are to be separated by crossing over (one of the processes of *recombination) and they are then described as being 'tightly linked'.

Linnaeus Carolus 1707–1778. Swedish naturalist and physician. His botanical work *Systema naturae* 1735 contained his system for classifying plants into groups depending on shared characteristics (such as the number of stamens in flowers), providing a much-needed framework for identification. He also devised the concise and precise system for naming plants and animals, using one Latin (or Latinized) word to represent the genus and a second to distinguish the species.

linnet Old World finch *Acanthis cannabina*. Mainly brown, the males, noted for their song, have a crimson crown and breast in summer.

linoleum (Latin *lini oleum* 'linseed oil') floor covering made from linseed oil, tall oil, rosin, cork, woodflour, chalk, clay, and pigments, pressed into sheets with a jute backing. Oxidation of the oil is accelerated by heating, so that the oil mixture solidifies into a tough, resilient material. Linoleum tiles have a backing made of polyester and glass.

Lin Piao alternative transliteration of *Lin Biao.

linseed seeds of the flax plant *Linum usitatissimum*, from which linseed oil is expressed, the residue being used as cattle feed. The oil is used in paint, wood treatments and varnishes, and in the manufacture of linoleum.

Linz industrial port (iron, steel, metalworking) on the river Danube in N Austria; population (1981) 199,900.

lion cat *Panthera leo*, now found only in Africa and NW India. The coat is tawny, the young having darker spot markings that usually disappear in the adult. The male has a heavy mane and a tuft at the end of the tail. Head and body measure about 2 m/6 ft, plus 1 m/3 ft of tail, the lioness being slightly smaller. Lions produce litters of two to six cubs, and often live in prides of several adult males and females with several young.

Li Peng 1928– . Chinese communist politician, a member of the Politburo from 1985, and head of government from 1987. During the prodemocracy demonstrations of 1989 he supported the massacre of students by Chinese troops and the subsequent execution of others. He sought improved relations with the USSR before its demise, and has favoured maintaining firm central and party control over the economy.

lipid any of a large number of esters of fatty acids, commonly formed by the reaction of a fatty acid with glycerol (see *glycerides). They are soluble in alcohol but not in water. Lipids are the chief constituents of plant and animal waxes, fats, and oils.

Li Po 705–762. Chinese poet. He used traditional literary forms, but his exuberance, the boldness of his imagination, and the intensity of his feeling have won him recognition as perhaps the greatest of all Chinese poets. Although he was mostly concerned with higher themes, he is also remembered for his celebratory verses on drinking.

Lippershey Hans *c.* 1570–1619. Dutch lens maker, credited with inventing the telescope in 1608.

Lippi Filippino 1457–1504. Italian painter of the Florentine school, trained by Botticelli. He produced altarpieces and several fresco cycles, full of detail and drama, elegant and finely drawn. He was the son of Filippo Lippi.

Lippi Fra Filippo 1406–1469. Italian painter whose works include frescoes depicting the lives of St Stephen and St John the Baptist in Prato Cathedral 1452–66. He also painted many altarpieces of Madonnas and groups of saints.

Lippmann Gabriel 1845–1921. French doctor who invented the direct colour process in photography. He was awarded the Nobel Prize for Physics in 1908.

liquefaction the process of converting a gas to a liquid, normally associated with low temperatures and high pressures (see *condensation).

liquefied petroleum gas (LPG) liquid form of butane, propane, or pentane, produced by the distillation of petroleum during oil refining. At room temperature these substances are gases, although they can be easily liquefied and stored under pressure in metal containers. They are used for heating and cooking where other fuels are not available: camping stoves and cigarette lighters, for instance, often use liquefied butane as fuel.

liquid state of matter between a *solid and a *gas. A liquid forms a level surface and assumes the shape of its container. Its atoms do not occupy fixed positions as in a crystalline solid, nor do they have freedom of movement as in a gas. Unlike a gas, a liquid is difficult to compress since pressure applied at one point is equally transmitted throughout (Pascal's principle). *Hydraulics makes use of this property.

liquid air air that has been cooled so much that it has liquefied. This happens at temperatures below about –196°C/–321°F. The various constituent gases, including nitrogen, oxygen, argon, and neon, can be separated from liquid air by the technique of *fractionation.

liquidation in economics, the termination of a company by converting all its assets into money to pay off its liabilities.

liquid-crystal display (LCD) display of numbers (for example, in a calculator) or pictures (such as on a pocket television screen) produced by molecules of a substance in a semiliquid state with some crystalline properties, so that clusters of molecules align in parallel formations. The display is a blank until the application of an electric field, which 'twists' the molecules so that they reflect or transmit light falling on them.

liquidity in economics, the state of possessing sufficient money and/or assets to be able to pay off all liabilities. *Liquid assets* are those such as shares that may be converted quickly into cash, as opposed to property.

liquorice perennial European herb *Glycyrrhiza glabra*, family Leguminosae. The long, sweet root yields an extract which is made into a hard black paste and used in confectionery and medicines.

Lisbon (Portuguese *Lisboa*) city and capital of Portugal, in the SW of the country, on the tidal lake and estuary formed by the river Tagus; population (1984) 808,000. Industries include steel,

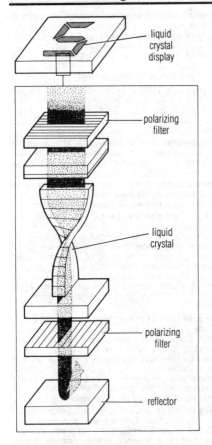

liquid crystal display

polarizing filter

liquid crystal

polarizing filter

reflector

liquid-crystal display A liquid-crystal display consists of a liquid crystal sandwiched between polarizing filters similar to polaroid sunglasses.

textiles, chemicals, pottery, shipbuilding, and fishing. It has been the capital since 1260 and reached its peak of prosperity in the period of Portugal's empire during the 16th century. In 1755 an earthquake killed 60,000 people and destroyed much of the city.

listed building in Britain, a building officially recognized as having historical or architectural interest and therefore legally protected from alteration or demolition. In England the listing is drawn up by the Secretary of State for the Environment under the advice of the English Heritage organization, which provides various resources for architectural conservation.

Lister Joseph, 1st Baron Lister 1827–1912. English surgeon and founder of antiseptic surgery, influenced by Louis *Pasteur's work on bacteria. He introduced dressings soaked in carbolic acid and strict rules of hygiene to combat wound sepsis in hospitals.

listeriosis disease of animals that may occasionally infect humans, caused by the bacterium *Listeria monocytogenes*. The bacteria multiply at temperatures close to 0°C/32°F, which means they may flourish in precooked frozen meals if the cooking has not been thorough. Listeriosis causes inflammation of the brain and its surrounding membranes, but can be treated with penicillin.

Liszt Franz 1811–1886. Hungarian pianist and composer. An outstanding virtuoso of the piano, he was an established concert artist by the age of 12. His expressive, romantic, and frequently chromatic works include piano music (*Transcendental Studies* 1851), symphonies, piano concertos, and organ music. Much of his music is programmatic; he also originated the symphonic poem. Liszt was taught by his father, then by Carl Czerny (1791–1857). He travelled widely in Europe, producing an opera *Don Sanche* in Paris at the age of 14.

Litani river rising near Baalbek in the Anti-Lebanon Mountains of E Lebanon. It flows NE–SW through the Beqa'a Valley, then E to the Mediterranean 8 km/5 mi N of Tyre. Israeli forces invaded Lebanon as far as the Litani River 1978.

litany in the Christian church, a form of prayer or supplication led by a priest with set responses by the congregation.

litchi or *lychee* evergreen tree *Litchi chinensis* of the soapberry family Sapindaceae. The delicately flavoured ovate fruit is encased in a brownish rough outer skin and has a hard seed. The litchi is native to S China, where it has been cultivated for 2,000 years.

literacy ability to read and write. The level at which functional literacy is set rises as society becomes more complex, and it becomes increasingly difficult for an illiterate person to find work and cope with the other demands of everyday life.

literary criticism establishment of principles governing literary composition, and the assessment and interpretation of literary works. Contemporary criticism offers analyses of literary works from structuralist, semiological, feminist, Marxist, and psychoanalytical perspectives, whereas earlier criticism tended to deal with moral or political ideas, or with a literary work as a formal object independent of its creator.

literature words set apart in some way from ordinary everyday communication. In the ancient oral traditions, before stories and poems were written down, literature had a mainly public function – mythic and religious. As literary works came to be preserved in writing and, eventually, printed, their role became more private, serving as a vehicle for the exploration and expression of emotion and the human situation.

lithification another term for *diagenesis.

lithium (Greek *lithos* 'stone') soft, ductile, silver-white, metallic element, symbol Li, atomic number 3, relative atomic mass 6.941. It is one of the *alkali metals, has a very low density (far less than most woods), and floats on water (specific gravity 0.57); it is the lightest of all metals. Lithium is used to harden alloys, and in batteries; its compounds are used in medicine to treat manic depression.

lithography printmaking technique originated in 1798 by Aloys Senefelder, based on the antipathy of grease and water. A drawing is made with greasy crayon on an absorbent stone, which is then wetted. The wet stone repels ink (which is greasy) applied to the surface and the crayon attracts it, so that the drawing can be printed. Lithographic printing is used in book production and has developed this basic principle into complex processes.

lithosphere topmost layer of the Earth's structure, forming the jigsaw of plates that take part in the movements of *plate tectonics. The lithosphere comprises the *crust and a portion of the upper *mantle. It is regarded as being rigid and moves about on the semi-molten *asthenosphere. The lithosphere is about 75 km/47 mi thick.

Lithuania Republic of

area 65,200 sq km/25,174 sq mi
capital Vilnius
towns Kaunas, Klaipeda, Siauliai, Panevezys
physical central lowlands with gentle hills in W and higher terrain in SE; 25% forested; some 3,000 small lakes, marshes, and complex sandy coastline
head of state Algirdas Brazauskas from 1993
head of government Adolfas Slezevicius from 1993
political system emergent democracy
exports food processing, bacon, dairy products, cereals, potatoes
currency Lithuanian rouble
population (1994) 3,740,000 (Lithuanian 80%, Russian 9%, Polish 7%, Byelorussian 2%)
language Lithuanian
religion predominantly Roman Catholic
GNP $2,710 per head (1991)
chronology
1918 Independence declared following withdrawal of German occupying troops at end of World War I; USSR attempted to regain power.
1919 Soviet forces overthrown by Germans, Poles, and nationalist Lithuanians; democratic republic established.
1920–39 Province of Vilnius occupied by Poles.
1926 Coup overthrew established government; Antanas Smetona became president.
1939 Secret German-Soviet agreement brought most of Lithuania under Soviet influence.
1940 Incorporated into USSR as constituent republic.
1941 Lithuania revolted against USSR and estab-

lished own government. During World War II Germany again occupied the country.
1944 USSR resumed rule.
1944–52 Lithuanian guerrillas fought USSR.
1972 Demonstrations against Soviet government.
1980 Growth in nationalist dissent, influenced by Polish example.
1988 Popular front formed, the Sajudis, to campaign for increased autonomy.
1989 Lithuanian declared the state language; flag of independent interwar republic readopted. Communist Party split into pro-Moscow and nationalist wings. Communist local monopoly of power abolished.
1990 Feb: nationalist Sajudis won elections. March: Vytautas Landsbergis became president; unilateral declaration of independence resulted in temporary Soviet blockade.
1991 Jan: Albertas Shiminas became prime minister. Soviet paratroopers briefly occupied key buildings in Vilnius. Sept: independence recognized by Soviet government and Western nations; Gediminas Vagnorius elected prime minister; CP outlawed; admitted into United Nations and Conference on Security and Cooperation in Europe.
1992 July: Aleksandras Abisala became prime minister. Nov: Democratic Labour Party (DLP), led by Algirdas Brazauskas, won majority vote in parliamentary elections. Dec: Bronislovas Lubys appointed prime minister.
1993 Brazauskas elected president; Adolfas Slezevicius appointed prime minister. Last Russian troops departed.
1994 Application for NATO membership.

litmus dye obtained from various lichens and used in chemistry as an indicator to test the acidic or alkaline nature of aqueous solutions; it turns red in the presence of acid, and blue in the presence of alkali.

litre metric unit of volume (symbol l), equal to one cubic decimetre (1.76 imperial pints/2.11 US pints). It was formerly defined as the volume occupied by one kilogram of pure water at 4°C at standard pressure, but this is slightly larger than one cubic decimetre.

Little Bighorn site in Montana, USA, of General George *Custer's defeat by the *Sioux Indians 25 June 1876 under their chiefs Crazy Horse and Sitting Bull, known as **Custer's last stand**.

Little Red Book book of aphorisms and quotations from the speeches and writings by *Mao Zedong, in which he adapted Marxist theory to Chinese conditions. Published 1966, the book was printed in huge numbers and read widely at the start of the *Cultural Revolution.

Little Richard stage name of Richard Penniman 1932– . US rock singer and pianist. He was one of the creators of rock and roll with his wildly uninhibited renditions of 'Tutti Frutti' 1956, 'Long Tall Sally' 1956, and 'Good Golly Miss Molly' 1957. His subsequent career in soul and rhythm and blues was interrupted by periods as a Seventh-Day Adventist cleric.

Littlewood Joan 1914– . English theatre director. She established the Theatre Workshop 1945 and was responsible for many vigorous productions at the Theatre Royal, Stratford, London, 1953–75, such as *A Taste of Honey* 1959,

Brendan Behan's *The Hostage* 1959–60, and *Oh, What a Lovely War* 1963.

liturgy in the Christian church, any service for public worship; the term was originally limited to the celebration of the *Eucharist.

Liu Shaoqi or *Liu Shao-chi* 1898–1969. Chinese communist politician, in effective control of government 1960–65. A Moscow-trained labour organizer, he was a firm proponent of the Soviet style of government based around disciplined one-party control, the use of incentive gradings, and priority for industry over agriculture. This was opposed by *Mao Zedong, but began to be implemented by Liu while he was state president 1960–65. Liu was brought down during the *Cultural Revolution.

liver large organ of vertebrates, which has many regulatory and storage functions. The human liver is situated in the upper abdomen, and weighs about 2 kg/4.5 lb. It is divided into four lobes. The liver receives the products of digestion, converts glucose to glycogen (a long-chain carbohydrate used for storage), and breaks down fats. It removes excess amino acids from the blood, converting them to urea, which is excreted by the kidneys. The liver also synthesizes vitamins, produces bile and blood-clotting factors, and removes damaged red cells and toxins such as alcohol from the blood.

Liverpool city, seaport, and administrative headquarters of Merseyside, NW England; population (1991 est) 448,300. In the 19th and early 20th centuries it exported the textiles of Lancashire and Yorkshire. Liverpool is the UK's chief Atlantic port with miles of specialized, mechanized quays on the river Mersey.

Liverpool Robert Banks Jenkinson, 2nd Earl Liverpool 1770–1825. British Tory politician. He entered Parliament 1790 and was foreign secretary 1801–03, home secretary 1804–06 and 1807–09, war minister 1809–12, and prime minister 1812–27. His government conducted the Napoleonic Wars to a successful conclusion, but its ruthless suppression of freedom of speech and of the press aroused such opposition that during 1815–20 revolution frequently seemed imminent.

Livingstone David 1813–1873. Scottish missionary explorer. In 1841 he went to Africa, reached Lake Ngami 1849, followed the Zambezi to its mouth, saw the Victoria Falls 1855, and went to East and Central Africa 1858–64, reaching Lakes Shirwa and Malawi. From 1866, he tried to find the source of the river Nile, and reached Ujiji in Tanganyika in Nov 1871. British explorer Henry Stanley joined Livingstone in Ujiji.

Livingstone Ken(neth) 1945– . British leftwing Labour politician. He was leader of the Greater London Council (GLC) 1981–86 and a member of Parliament from 1987. He stood as a candidate for the Labour Party leadership elections 1992.

living will written declaration of a person's wishes regarding medical treatment if he or she should become too ill to communicate. It is, in effect, an advance refusal of interventions to prolong a life that the patient would consider no longer tolerable. It enables patients whose condition is terminal to die with dignity. Living wills are increasingly popular in the United States.

Livonia former region in Europe on the E coast of the Baltic Sea comprising most of present-day Latvia and Estonia. Conquered and converted to Christianity in the early 13th century by the Livonian Knights, a crusading order, Livonia was independent until 1583, when it was divided between Poland and Sweden. In 1710 it was occupied by Russia, and in 1721 was ceded to Peter the Great, Tsar of Russia.

Livy (Titus Livius) 59 BC–AD 17. Roman historian. He was the author of a *History of Rome* from the city's foundation to 9 BC, based partly on legend. It was composed of 142 books, of which 35 survive, covering the periods from the arrival of Aeneas in Italy to 293 BC and from 218 to 167 BC.

Li Xiannian 1905–1992. Chinese politician, member of the Chinese Communist Party (CCP) Politburo from 1956. He fell from favour during the 1966–69 Cultural Revolution, but was rehabilitated as finance minister in 1973. He was state president 1983–88.

lizard reptile of the suborder Lacertilia, which together with snakes constitutes the order Squamata. Lizards are generally distinguishable from snakes by having four legs, moveable eyelids, eardrums, and a fleshy tongue, but some lizards are legless and snakelike in appearance. There are over 3,000 species of lizard worldwide.

Lizard Point southernmost point of England in Cornwall. The coast is broken into small bays overlooked by two cliff lighthouses.

Ljubljana (German *Laibach*) capital and industrial city (textiles, chemicals, paper, leather goods) of Slovenia; population (1981) 305,200. It has a nuclear research centre and is linked with S Austria by the Karawanken road tunnel under the Alps (1979–83).

llama South American even-toed hoofed mammal *Lama glama* of the camel family, about 1.2 m/4 ft high at the shoulder. Llamas are white, brown, or dark, sometimes with spots or patches. They are very hardy, and require little food or water. They spit profusely when annoyed.

Llewelyn two princes of Wales:

Llewelyn I 1173–1240. Prince of Wales from 1194 who extended his rule to all Wales not in Norman hands, driving the English from N Wales 1212, and taking Shrewsbury 1215. During the early part of Henry III's reign, he was several times attacked by English armies. He was married to Joanna, illegitimate daughter of King John.

Llewelyn II c. 1225–1282. Prince of Wales from 1246, grandson of Llewelyn I. In 1277 Edward I of England compelled Llewelyn to acknowledge him as overlord and to surrender S Wales. His death while leading a national uprising ended Welsh independence.

Lloyd Harold 1893–1971. US film comedian, noted for his 'trademark' of thick horn-rimmed glasses and straw hat, who invented the bumbling cliff-hanger and dangler. He appeared from 1913 in silent and talking films. His silent films include *Grandma's Boy* 1922, *Safety Last* 1923, and *The Freshman* 1925. His first talkie was *Movie Crazy* 1932. He produced films after 1938, including the reissued *Harold Lloyd's World of Comedy* 1962 and *Funny Side of Life* 1964.

Lloyd George David 1863–1945. Welsh Liberal politician, prime minister of Britain 1916–22. A pioneer of social reform, as chancellor of the Exchequer 1908–15 he introduced old-age pensions 1908 and health and unemployment insurance 1911. High unemployment, intervention in the Russian Civil War, and use of the military police force, the *Black and Tans, in Ireland eroded his support as prime minister, and the creation of the Irish Free State in 1921 and his pro-Greek policy against the Turks caused the collapse of his coalition government.

Lloyd Webber Andrew 1948– . English composer. His early musicals, with lyrics by Tim Rice, include *Joseph and the Amazing Technicolor Dreamcoat* 1968; *Jesus Christ Superstar* 1970; and *Evita* 1978, based on the life of the Argentine leader Eva Perón. He also wrote *Cats* 1981 and *The Phantom of the Opera* 1986.

Llull Ramon 1232–1316. Catalan scholar and mystic. He began his career at the court of James I of Aragon (1212–1276) in Majorca. He produced treatises on theology, mysticism, and chivalry in Catalan, Latin, and Arabic. His *Ars magna* was a mechanical device, a kind of prototype computer, by which all problems could be solved by manipulating fundamental Aristotelian categories.

loa spirit in *voodoo. Loas may be male or female, and include Maman Brigitte, the loa of death and cemeteries, and Aida-Wedo, the rainbow snake. Believers may be under the protection of one particular loa.

loach carplike freshwater fish, family Cobitidae, with a long narrow body, and no teeth in the small, downward-pointing mouth, which is surrounded by barbels. Loaches are native to Asian and European waters.

loam type of fertile soil, a mixture of sand, silt, clay, and organic material. It is porous, which allows for good air circulation and retention of moisture.

lobby individual or pressure group that sets out to influence government action. The lobby is prevalent in the USA, where the term originated in the 1830s from the practice of those wishing to influence state policy waiting for elected representatives in the lobby of the Capitol.

lobelia any temperate and tropical plant of the genus *Lobelia* of the bellflower family Lobeliaceae, with white to mauve flowers. Lobelias may grow to shrub size but are mostly small annual plants.

lobotomy in medicine, the cutting of a lobe. The term usually refers to the operation of *frontal lobotomy* (or *leucotomy*), where the frontal lobes are disconnected from the rest of the brain by cutting the white matter that joins them. This may alleviate the condition of patients with severe depression, anxiety states, or obsessive-compulsive disorders, but it is now rarely performed, and only on patients who have proved resistant to all other forms of treatment. It is irreversible and the degree of personality change is not predictable.

lobster large marine crustacean of the order Decapoda. Lobsters are grouped with freshwater *crayfish in the suborder Reptantia ('walking'), although both lobsters and crayfish can also swim, using their fanlike tails. Lobsters have eyes on stalks and long antennae, and are mainly nocturnal. They scavenge and eat dead or dying fish.

local government that part of government dealing mainly with matters concerning the inhabitants of a particular area or town, usually financed at least in part by local taxes. In the USA and UK, local government has comparatively large powers and responsibilities.

Locarno, Pact of series of diplomatic documents initialled in Locarno, Switzerland, 16 Oct 1925 and formally signed in London 1 Dec 1925. The pact settled the question of French security, and the signatories – Britain, France, Belgium, Italy, and Germany – guaranteed Germany's existing frontiers with France and Belgium. Following the signing of the pact, Germany was admitted to the League of Nations.

Lochner Stephan died 1451. German painter, active in Cologne from 1442, a master of the International Gothic style. Most of his work is still in Cologne: for example, the *Virgin in the Rose Garden* (Wallraf-Richartz Museum) and *Adoration of the Magi* (Cologne Cathedral).

Loch Ness see *Ness, Loch.

lock construction installed in waterways to allow boats or ships to travel from one level to another. The earliest form, the *flash lock*, was first seen in the East in 1st-century-AD China and in the West in 11th-century Holland. By this method barriers temporarily dammed a river and when removed allowed the flash flood to impel the waiting boat through any obstacle. This was followed in 12th-century China and 14th-century Holland by the *pound lock*. In this system the lock has gates at each end. Boats enter through one gate when the levels are the same both outside and inside. Water is then allowed in (or out of) the lock until the level rises (or falls) to the new level outside the other gate. Locks are important to shipping where canals link oceans of differing levels, such as the Panama Canal, or where falls or rapids are replaced by these adjustable water 'steps'.

lock and key devices that provide security, usually fitted to a door of some kind. In 1778 English locksmith Robert Barron made the forerunner of the *mortise lock*, which contains levers that the key must raise to an exact height before the bolt can be moved. The *Yale lock*, a pin-tumbler cylinder design, was invented by US locksmith Linus Yale, Jr, in 1865. More secure locks include *combination locks*, with a dial mechanism that must be turned certain distances backwards and forwards to open, and *time locks*, which are set to be opened only at specific times.

Locke John 1632–1704. English philosopher. His *Essay concerning Human Understanding* 1690 maintained that experience was the only source of knowledge (empiricism), and that 'we can have knowlege no farther than we have ideas' prompted by such experience. *Two Treatises on Government* 1690 helped to form contemporary ideas of liberal democracy.

Lockheed US aircraft manufacturer, the USA's largest military contractor. The company was founded in 1916 by two brothers, Allan and Malcolm Loughheed (they later changed the spelling of their name), who had built their first seaplane in 1913, with headquarters in Burbank, California. Lockheed built the Vega plane in 1926 (later used by Amelia *Earhart in her solo transatlantic flight), the first fully pressurized aircraft, the XC-35, 1937, and the TriStar passenger plane of the 1960s.

lockjaw former name for *tetanus, a type of infection.

locomotive engine for hauling railway trains. In 1804 Richard Trevithick built the first steam engine to run on rails. Locomotive design did not radically improve until George Stephenson built the *Rocket* 1829, which featured a multitube boiler and blastpipe, standard in all following **steam locomotives**. Today most locomotives are diesel or electric: **diesel locomotives** have a powerful diesel engine, and **electric locomotives** draw their power from either an overhead cable or a third rail alongside the ordinary track.

locus (Latin 'place') in mathematics, traditionally the path traced out by a moving point, but now defined as the set of all points on a curve satisfying given conditions. For example, the locus of a point that moves so that it is always at the same distance from another fixed point is a circle; the locus of a point that is always at the same distance from two fixed points is a straight line that perpendicularly bisects the line joining them.

locust swarming grasshopper, with short antennae and auditory organs on the abdomen, in the family Acrididae. As winged adults, flying in swarms, locusts may be carried by the wind hundreds of miles from their breeding grounds; on landing they devour all vegetation. Locusts occur in nearly every continent.

locust tree alternative name for the *carob, small tree of the Mediterranean region. It is also the name of several North American trees of the family Leguminosae.

lode geologic deposit rich in certain minerals, generally consisting of a large vein or set of veins containing ore minerals. A system of veins that can be mined directly forms a lode, for example the mother lode of the California gold rush.

lodestar or **loadstar** a star used in navigation or astronomy, often *Polaris, the Pole Star.

Lódź industrial town (textiles, machinery, dyes) in central Poland, 120 km/75 mi SW of Warsaw; population (1990) 848,300.

Loewe Frederick 1901–1988. US composer of musicals. In 1942 he joined forces with the lyricist Alan Jay Lerner (1918–1986), and their joint successes include *Brigadoon* 1947, *Paint Your Wagon* 1951, *My Fair Lady* 1956, *Gigi* 1958, and *Camelot* 1960.

loganberry hybrid between a *blackberry and a *raspberry with large, tart, dull-red fruit. It was developed by US judge James H Logan in 1881.

logarithm or **log** the *exponent or index of a number to a specified base – usually 10. For example, the logarithm to the base 10 of 1,000 is 3 because $10^3 = 1,000$; the logarithm of 2 is 0.3010 because $2 = 10^{0.3010}$. Before the advent of cheap electronic calculators, multiplication and division could be simplified by being replaced with the addition and subtraction of logarithms.

logic branch of philosophy that studies valid reasoning and argument. It is also the way in which one thing may be said to follow from, or be a consequence of, another (deductive logic). Logic is generally divided into the traditional formal logic of Aristotle and the symbolic logic derived from Friedrich Frege and Bertrand Russell.

logical positivism doctrine that the only meaningful propositions are those that can be verified empirically. Metaphysics, religion, and aesthetics are therefore meaningless.

logic gate or **logic circuit** in electronics, one of the basic components used in building *integrated circuits. The five basic types of gate make logical decisions based on the functions NOT, AND, OR, NAND (NOT AND), and NOR (NOT OR). With the exception of the NOT gate, each has two or more inputs.

LOGO (Greek *logos* 'word') high-level computer programming language designed to teach mathematical concepts. Developed about 1970 at the Massachusetts Institute of Technology, it became popular in schools and with home computer users because of its 'turtle graphics' feature. This allows the user to write programs that create line drawings on a computer screen, or drive a small mobile robot (a 'turtle' or 'buggy') around the floor.

Loire longest river in France, rising in the Cévennes Mountains, at 1,350 m/4,430 ft and flowing for 1,050 km/650 mi first N then W until it reaches the Bay of Biscay at St Nazaire, passing Nevers, Orléans, Tours, and Nantes. It gives its name to the *départements* of Loire, Haute-Loire, Loire-Atlantique, Indre-et-Loire, Maine-et-Loire, and Saône-et-Loire. There are many chateaux and vineyards along its banks.

Loki in Norse mythology, one of the *Aesir (the principal gods), but the cause of dissension among the gods, and the slayer of *Balder. His children are the Midgard serpent Jörmungander, which girdles the Earth, the wolf Fenris, and Hela, goddess of death.

Lollard follower of the English religious reformer John *Wycliffe in the 14th century. The Lollards condemned the doctrine of the transubstantiation of the bread and wine of the Eucharist, advocated the diversion of ecclesiastical property to charitable uses, and denounced war and capital punishment. They were active from about 1377; after the passing of the statute *De heretico comburendo* ('The Necessity of Burning Heretics') 1401 many Lollards were burned, and in 1414 they attempted an unsuccessful revolt in London.

Lombard Carole. Stage name of Jane Alice Peters 1908–1942. US comedy film actress. A warm and witty actress, she starred in some of the best comedies of the 1930s: *Twentieth Century* 1934, *My Man Godfrey* 1936, and *To Be or Not to Be* 1942.

Lombard or **Langobard** member of a Germanic people who invaded Italy in 568 and occupied Lombardy (named after them) and central Italy. Their capital was Monza. They were conquered by the Frankish ruler Charlemagne in 774.

Lombardy (Italian **Lombardia**) region of N Italy, including Lake Como; capital Milan; area

23,900 sq km/9,225 sq mi; population (1990) 8,939,400. It is the country's chief industrial area, producing chemicals, pharmaceuticals, and textiles; engineering is also a major industry.

Lomé capital and port of Togo; population (1983) 366,000. It is a centre for gold, silver, and marble crafts; industries include steel production and oil refining.

Lomé Convention convention in 1975 that established economic cooperation between the European Community and African, Caribbean, and Pacific countries. It was renewed 1979 and 1985.

Lomond, Loch largest freshwater Scottish lake, 37 km/21 mi long, area 70 sq km/27 sq mi, divided between Strathclyde and Central regions. It is overlooked by the mountain **Ben Lomond** (973 m/3,192 ft) and is linked to the Clyde estuary.

London capital of England and the UK, on the river Thames; area 1,580 sq km/610 sq mi; population (1991) 6,378,600, larger metropolitan area about 9 million. The **City of London**, known as the 'square mile', area 274 hectares/677 acres, is the financial and commercial centre of the UK. **Greater London** from 1965 comprises the City of London and 32 boroughs. Popular tourist attractions include the Tower of London, St Paul's Cathedral, Buckingham Palace, and Westminster Abbey. Roman **Londinium** was established soon after the Roman invasion AD 43; in the 2nd century London became a walled city; by the 11th century, it was the main city of England and gradually extended beyond the walls to link with the originally separate Westminster. Throughout the 19th century London was the largest city in the world (in population). Other features include the Barbican arts and conference centre; Central Criminal Court (Old Bailey) and the Inner and Middle Temples; Covent Garden, once a vegetable market, is now a tourist shopping and entertainment area.

architecture London contains buildings in all styles of English architecture since the 11th century. **Norman**: the White Tower, Tower of London; St Bartholomew's, Smithfield; the Temple Church. **Gothic**: Westminster Abbey; Westminster Hall; Lambeth Palace; Southwark Cathedral. **Tudor**: St James's Palace; Staple Inn. **17th century**: Banqueting Hall, Whitehall (Inigo Jones); St Paul's, Kensington Palace; many City churches (Wren). **18th century**: Somerset House (Chambers); St Martin-in-the-Fields; Buckingham Palace. **19th century**: British Museum (Neo-Classical); Houses of Parliament; Law Courts (Neo-Gothic); Westminster Cathedral (Byzantine style). **20th century**: Lloyd's of London.

commerce and industry From Saxon times the Port of London dominated the Thames from Tower Bridge to Tilbury; its activity is now centred outside the metropolitan area, and downstream Tilbury has been extended to cope with container traffic. The prime economic importance of modern London is as a financial centre. There are various industries, mainly on the outskirts. There are also recording, broadcasting, television, and film studios; publishing companies; and the works and offices of the national press. Tourism is important. Some of the docks in the East End of London, once the busiest in

the world, have been sold to the Docklands Development Corporation, which has built offices, houses, factories, and a railway. *Canary Wharf* is now the site of the world's largest office development project, estimated to have cost over £4 billion.

education and entertainment Museums: British, Victoria and Albert, Natural History, Science museums; galleries: National and Tate. London University is the largest in Britain, while the Inns of Court have been the training school for lawyers since the 13th century. London has been the centre of English drama since its first theatre was built by James Burbage in 1576.

government There has since 1986 been no central authority for Greater London; responsibility is divided between individual boroughs and central government. The City of London has been governed by a corporation from the 12th century. Its structure and the electoral procedures for its common councillors and aldermen are medievally complex, and it is headed by the lord mayor (who is, broadly speaking, nominated by the former and elected annually by the latter). After being sworn in at the Guildhall, he or she is presented the next day to the lord chief justice at the Royal Courts of Justice in Westminster, and the *Lord Mayor's Show* is a ceremonial procession there in November.

London Jack (John Griffith) 1876–1916. US novelist, author of the adventure stories *The Call of the Wild* 1903, *The Sea Wolf* 1904, and *White Fang* 1906. By 1906 he was the most widely read writer in the US and had been translated into 68 languages.

Londonderry former name (until 1984) of the county and city of *Derry in Northern Ireland.

London, Greater the metropolitan area of *London, England, comprising the City of London, which forms a self-governing enclave, and 32 surrounding boroughs; area 1,580 sq km/ 610 sq mi; population (1991) 6,378,600. Certain powers were exercised over this whole area by the Greater London Council (GLC) until its abolition in 1986.

London, Treaty of secret treaty signed 26 April 1915 between Britain, France, Russia, and Italy. It promised Italy territorial gains (at the expense of Austria-Hungary) on condition that it entered World War I on the side of the Triple Entente (Britain, France, and Russia). Italy's intervention did not achieve the rapid victories expected, and the terms of the treaty (revealed by Russia 1918), angered the USA. Britain and France refused to honour the treaty and, in the postwar peace treaties, Italy received far less territory than promised.

lone pair in chemistry, a pair of electrons in the outermost shell of an atom that are not used in bonding. In certain circumstances, they will allow the atom to bond with atoms, ions, or molecules (such as boron trifluoride, BF_3) that are deficient in electrons, forming coordinate covalent (dative) bonds in which they provide both of the bonding electrons.

Long Huey 1893–1935. US Democratic politician, nicknamed 'the Kingfish', governor of Louisiana 1928–31, US senator for Louisiana 1930–35, legendary as a demagogue. He was popular with poor white voters for his programme of social and economic reform, which he called the 'Share Our Wealth' programme. It represented a significant challenge to F D Roosevelt's *New Deal economic programme. Long's scheme called for massive redistribution of wealth through high inheritance taxes and confiscatory taxes on high incomes. His own extravagance, including the state capitol building at Baton Rouge built of bronze and marble, was widely criticized. He was assassinated.

Longfellow Henry Wadsworth 1807–1882. US poet, remembered for ballads ('Excelsior', 'The Village Blacksmith', 'The Wreck of the Hesperus') and the mythic narrative epics *Evangeline* 1847, *The Song of *Hiawatha* 1855, and *The Courtship of Miles Standish* 1858.

Longford county of Leinster province, Republic of Ireland
area 1,040 sq km/401 sq mi
county town Longford
population (1991) 30,300.

Longinus Dionysius lived 1st century AD. Greek critic, author of the treatise *On the Sublime*, which influenced the English poets John Dryden and Alexander Pope.

Long Island island E of Manhattan and SE of Connecticut, USA, separated from the mainland by Long Island Sound and the East River; 120 mi/193 km long by about 30 mi/48 km wide; area 1,400 sq mi/3,627 sq km; population (1984) 6,818,480.

longitude see *latitude and longitude.

long jump field event in athletics in which competitors sprint up to and leap from a take-off board into a sandpit measuring 9 metres in length. The take-off board is 1 metre from the landing area. Each competitor usually has six trials, and the winner is the one with the longest jump.

Long March in Chinese history, the 10,000 km/ 6,000 mi trek undertaken 1934–35 by *Mao Zedong and his Communist forces from SE to NW China, under harassment from the Nationalist army.

Long Parliament English Parliament 1640–53 and 1659–60, which continued through the Civil War. After the Royalists withdrew in 1642 and the Presbyterian right was excluded in 1648, the remaining *Rump ruled England until expelled by Oliver Cromwell in 1653. Reassembled 1659–60, the Long Parliament initiated the negotiations for the restoration of the monarchy.

loom any machine for weaving yarn or thread into cloth. The first looms were used to weave sheep's wool about 5000 BC. A loom is a frame on which a set of lengthwise threads (warp) is strung. A second set of threads (weft), carried in a shuttle, is inserted at right angles over and under the warp.

loop in computing, short for *program loop.

Loos Adolf 1870–1933. Austrian architect and author of the article *Ornament and Crime* 1908, in which he rejected the ornamentation and curved lines of the Viennese *Jugendstil* movement (see *Art Nouveau). His buildings include private houses on Lake Geneva 1904 and the Steiner House in Vienna 1910.

Loos Anita 1888–1981. US writer, author of the humorous fictitious diary *Gentlemen Prefer Blondes* 1925. She became a screenwriter 1912

and worked on more than 60 films, including D W *Griffith's *Intolerance* 1916.

loosestrife any of several plants of the family Primulaceae, including the yellow loosestrife *Lysimachia vulgaris*, with spikes of yellow flowers, and the low-growing creeping jenny *Lysimachia nummularia*. The striking purple loosestrife *Lythrum saclicaria* belongs to the family Lythraceae.

Lope de Vega (Carpio) Felix Spanish poet and dramatist; see *Vega, Lope de.

López Carlos Antonio 1790–1862. Paraguayan dictator (in succession to his uncle José Francia) from 1840. He achieved some economic improvement, and he was succeeded by his son Francisco López.

López Francisco Solano 1827–1870. Paraguayan dictator in succession to his father Carlos López. He involved the country in a war with Brazil, Uruguay, and Argentina, during which approximately 80% of the population died.

Lorca Federico García 1898–1936. Spanish poet and playwright, born in Granada. His plays include *Bodas de sangre/Blood Wedding* 1933 and *La casa de Bernarda Alba/The House of Bernarda Alba* 1936. His poems include *Lament*, written for the bullfighter Mejías. Lorca was shot by the Falangists during the Spanish Civil War.

Lord in the UK, prefix used informally as alternative to the full title of a marquess, earl, or viscount; normally also in speaking of a baron, and as a courtesy title before the forename and surname of younger sons of dukes and marquesses.

Lord Advocate chief law officer of the crown in Scotland who has ultimate responsibility for criminal prosecutions in Scotland. The Lord Advocate does not usually act in inferior courts, where prosecution is carried out by procurators-fiscal acting under the Lord Advocate's instructions.

Lord Chancellor UK state official; see *Chancellor, Lord.

Lord's one of England's test match grounds and the headquarters of cricket's governing body, the Marylebone Cricket Club (MCC), since 1788 when the MCC was formed following the folding of the White Conduit Club.

Lords, House of upper house of the UK *Parliament.

Lorelei in Germanic folklore, a river nymph of the Rhine who lures sailors onto the rock where she sits combing her hair. She features in several poems, including 'Die Lorelei' by the German Romantic writer Heine. The *Lurlei* rock S of Koblenz is 130 m/430 ft high.

Loren Sophia. Stage name of Sofia Scicolone 1934– . Italian film actress whose boldly sensual appeal was promoted by her husband, producer Carlo Ponti. Her work includes *Aida* 1953, *The Key* 1958, *La ciociara/Two Women* 1960, *Judith* 1965, and *Firepower* 1979.

Lorenz Konrad 1903–1989. Austrian ethologist. Director of the Max Planck Institute for the Physiology of Behaviour in Bavaria 1955–73, he wrote the studies of ethology (animal behaviour) *King Solomon's Ring* 1952 and *On Aggression* 1966. In 1973 he shared the Nobel Prize for

Medicine with Nikolaas Tinbergen and Karl von Frisch.

Lorenz Ludwig Valentine 1829–1891. Danish mathematician and physicist. He developed mathematical formulae to describe phenomena such as the relation between the refraction of light and the density of a pure transparent substance, and the relation between a metal's electrical and thermal conductivity and temperature.

Lorimer Robert Stoddart 1864–1929. Scottish architect, the most prolific architect representative of the Scottish Arts and Crafts Movement. Examples of his work include Ardkinglas House, Argyll, 1906, and Ruwallan House, Ayrshire, 1902.

loris any of various small prosimian primates of the family Lorisidae. Lorises are slow-moving, arboreal, and nocturnal. They have very large eyes; true lorises have no tails. They climb without leaping, gripping branches tightly and moving on or hanging below them.

Lorrain Claude. French painter; see *Claude Lorrain.

Lorraine region of NE France in the upper reaches of the Meuse and Moselle rivers; bounded to the N by Belgium, Luxembourg, and Germany and to the E by Alsace; area 23,600 sq km/9,095 sq mi; population (1986) 2,313,000. It comprises the *départements* of Meurthe-et-Moselle, Meuse, Moselle, and Vosges, and its capital is Nancy. There are deposits of coal, iron ore, and salt; grain, fruit, and livestock are farmed. In 1871 the region was ceded to Germany as part of Alsace-Lorraine.

Lorre Peter. Stage name of Lazlo Löwenstein 1904–1964. Hungarian character actor with bulging eyes, high voice, and melancholy mien. He made several films in Germany before moving to Hollywood in 1935. He appeared in *The Maltese Falcon* 1941, *Casablanca* 1942, *Beat the Devil* 1953, and *The Raven* 1963.

Los Alamos town in New Mexico, USA, which has had a centre for atomic and space research since 1942. In World War II the first atom (nuclear fission) bomb was designed there (under Robert *Oppenheimer), based on data from other research stations; the *hydrogen bomb was also developed there.

Los Angeles city and port in SW California, USA; population (1990) 3,485,400, the metropolitan area of Los Angeles–Long Beach 14,531,530. Industries include aerospace, electronics, motor vehicles, chemicals, clothing, printing, and food processing.

Losey Joseph 1909–1984. US film director. Blacklisted as a former communist in the *McCarthy era, he settled in England, where his films included *The Servant* 1963 and *The Go-Between* 1971.

Lost Generation, the disillusioned US literary generation of the 1920s members of which went to live in Paris. The phrase is attributed to the writer Gertrude Stein in Ernest Hemingway's early novel of 1920s Paris, *The Sun Also Rises* 1926.

lost-wax technique method of making sculptures; see *cire perdue.

Lothair 825–869. King of Lotharingia from 855, when he inherited the region from his father, the Holy Roman emperor Lothair I.

Lothair two Holy Roman emperors:

Lothair I 795–855. Holy Roman emperor from 817 in association with his father Louis I. On Louis's death in 840, the empire was divided between Lothair and his brothers; Lothair took N Italy and the valleys of the rivers Rhône and Rhine.

Lothair II c. 1070–1137. Holy Roman emperor from 1133 and German king from 1125. His election as emperor, opposed by the *Hohenstaufen family of princes, was the start of the feud between the *Guelph and Ghibelline factions, who supported the papal party and the Hohenstaufens' claim to the imperial throne respectively.

Lotharingia medieval region W of the Rhine, between the Jura mountains and the North Sea; the northern portion of the lands assigned to Lothair I when the Carolingian empire was divided. It was called after his son King Lothair, and later corrupted to Lorraine; it is now part of Alsace-Lorraine, France.

Lothian region of Scotland
area 1,800 sq km/695 sq mi
towns Edinburgh (administrative headquarters), Livingston
products bacon, vegetables, coal, whisky, engineering, electronics
population (1991) 723,700
famous people Alexander Graham Bell, Arthur Conan Doyle, R L Stevenson.

lottery game of chance in which tickets sold may win a prize. In the UK lotteries are subject to strict government regulations. A national lottery was launched by the British government Nov 1994. Its operators, the Camelot Consortium (led by Cadbury Schweppes PLC), predicted total sales of £32 billion over an initial seven-year licence period, of which £9 billion was to go towards the arts, sports, charities, national heritage, and the Millenium Fund, set up to celebrate the year 2000.

Lotto Lorenzo c. 1480–1556. Italian painter, born in Venice, active in Bergamo, Treviso, Venice, Ancona, and Rome. His early works were influenced by Giovanni Bellini; his mature style belongs to the High Renaissance. He painted dignified portraits, altarpieces, and frescoes.

lotus any of several different plants, especially the water lily *Nymphaea lotus*, frequent in Egyptian art, and *Nelumbo nucifera*, the pink Asiatic lotus, a sacred symbol in Hinduism and Buddhism, whose flower head floats erect above the water.

Lotus motorcar company founded by Colin Chapman (1928–1982), who built his first racing car in 1948, and also developed high-powered production saloon and sports cars, such as the Lotus-Cortina and Lotus Elan. Lotus has been one of the leading Grand Prix manufacturers since its first Grand Prix in 1960.

Lotus 1–2–3 *spreadsheet computer program, produced by Lotus Development Corporation. It first appeared in 1982 and its combination of spreadsheet, graphics display, and data management contributed to the rapid acceptance of the IBM Personal Computer in businesses.

Lotus Sūtra scripture of Mahāyāna Buddhism. It is Buddha Śākyamuni's final teaching, emphasizing that everyone can attain Buddhahood with the help of bodhisattvas. The original is in Sanskrit (*Saddharmapundarīka Sūtra*) and is thought to date from some time after 100 BC.

loudspeaker electromechanical device that converts electrical signals into sound waves, which are radiated into the air. The most common type of loudspeaker is the *moving-coil speaker*. Electrical signals from, for example, a radio are fed to a coil of fine wire wound around the top of a cone. The coil is surrounded by a magnet. When signals pass through it, the coil becomes an electromagnet, which by moving causes the cone to vibrate, setting up sound waves.

Louis Joe. Assumed name of Joseph Louis Barrow 1914–1981. US boxer, nicknamed 'the Brown Bomber'. He was world heavyweight champion between 1937 and 1949 and made a record 25 successful defences (a record for any weight).

Louis Morris 1912–1962. US abstract painter. From Abstract Expressionism he turned to the colour-staining technique developed by Helen *Frankenthaler, using thinned-out acrylic paints poured on rough canvas to create the illusion of vaporous layers of colour. The *Veil* paintings of the 1950s are examples.

Louis eighteen kings of France, including:

Louis I *the Pious* 788–840. Holy Roman emperor from 814, when he succeeded his father Charlemagne.

Louis III 863–882. King of N France from 879, while his brother Carloman (866–884) ruled S France. He was the son of Louis II. Louis countered a revolt of the nobility at the beginning of his reign, and his resistance to the Normans made him a hero of epic poems.

Louis IV (d'Outremer) 921–954. King of France from 936. His reign was marked by the rebellion of nobles who refused to recognize his authority. As a result of his liberality they were able to build powerful feudal lordships.

Louis VII *c.* 1120–1180. King of France from 1137, who led the Second *Crusade.

Louis X *the Stubborn* 1289–1316. King of France who succeeded his father Philip IV in 1314. His reign saw widespread discontent among the nobles, which he countered by granting charters guaranteeing seignorial rights, although some historians claim that by using evasive tactics, he gave up nothing.

Louis XI 1423–1483. King of France from 1461. He broke the power of the nobility (headed by *Charles the Bold) by intrigue and military power.

Louis XII 1462–1515. King of France from 1499. He was duke of Orléans until he succeeded his cousin Charles VIII to the throne. His reign was devoted to Italian wars.

Louis XIII 1601–1643. King of France from 1610 (in succession to his father Henry IV), he assumed royal power in 1617. He was under the political control of Cardinal *Richelieu 1624–42.

Louis XIV *the Sun King* 1638–1715. King of France from 1643, when he succeeded his father

Louis XIII; his mother was Anne of Austria. Until 1661 France was ruled by the chief minister, Jules Mazarin, but later Louis took absolute power, summed up in his saying *L'Etat c'est moi* ('I am the state'). Throughout his reign he was engaged in unsuccessful expansionist wars – 1667–68, 1672–78, 1688–97, and 1701–13 (the War of the *Spanish Succession) – against various European alliances, always including Britain and the Netherlands. He was a patron of the arts.

Louis XV 1710–1774. King of France from 1715, with the Duke of Orléans as regent until 1723. He was the great-grandson of Louis XIV. Indolent and frivolous, Louis left government in the hands of his ministers, the Duke of Bourbon and Cardinal Fleury (1653–1743). On the latter's death he attempted to rule alone but became entirely dominated by his mistresses, Madame de Pompadour and Madame Du Barry. His foreign policy led to French possessions in Canada and India being lost to England.

Louis XVI 1754–1793. King of France from 1774, grandson of Louis XV, and son of Louis the Dauphin. He was dominated by his queen, *Marie Antoinette, and French finances fell into such confusion that in 1789 the *States General (parliament) had to be summoned, and the *French Revolution began. Louis lost his personal popularity in June 1791 when he attempted to flee the country, and in Aug 1792 the Parisians stormed the Tuileries palace and took the royal family prisoner. Deposed in Sept 1792, Louis was tried in Dec, sentenced for treason in Jan 1793, and guillotined.

Louis XVII 1785–1795. Nominal king of France, the son of Louis XVI. During the French Revolution he was imprisoned with his parents in 1792 and probably died in prison.

Louis XVIII 1755–1824. King of France 1814–24, the younger brother of Louis XVI. He assumed the title of king in 1795, having fled into exile in 1791 during the French Revolution, but became king only on the fall of Napoleon I in April 1814. Expelled during Napoleon's brief return (the 'hundred days') in 1815, he resumed power after Napoleon's final defeat at the battle of Waterloo, pursuing a policy of calculated liberalism until ultra-royalist pressure became dominant after 1820.

Louisiana state in S USA; nickname Pelican State
area 135,900 sq km/52,457 sq mi
capital Baton Rouge
cities New Orleans, Shreveport, Lafayette, Lake Charles
products rice, cotton, sugar, oil, natural gas, chemicals, sulphur, fish and shellfish, salt, processed foods, petroleum products, timber, paper
population (1990) 4,219,970; including Cajuns, descendants of 18th-century religious exiles from Canada, who speak a French dialect
famous people Louis Armstrong, P G T Beauregard, Huey Long
history explored by the Spanish Piñeda 1519, Cabeza de Vaca 1528, and de Soto 1541 and by the French explorer La Salle 1862, who named it after Louis XIV and claimed it for France. It became Spanish 1762–1800, then French, then passed to the USA 1803 under the *Louisiana Purchase; admitted to the Union as a state 1812.

The Civil War destroyed the plantation economy. Recovery was slow, but in the 1930s Louisiana became one of the world's major centres of petro-chemical manufacturing, based on oil wells in the Gulf of Mexico.

Louisiana Purchase purchase by the USA from France 1803 of an area covering about 2,144,000 sq km/828,000 sq mi, including the present-day states of Louisiana, Missouri, Arkansas, Iowa, Nebraska, North Dakota, South Dakota, and Oklahoma.

Louis Philippe 1773–1850. King of France 1830–48. Son of Louis Philippe Joseph, Duke of Orléans 1747–93; both were known as *Philippe Egalité* from their support of the 1792 Revolution. Louis Philippe fled into exile 1793–1814, but became king after the 1830 revolution with the backing of the rich bourgeoisie. Corruption discredited his regime, and after his overthrow, he escaped to the UK and died there.

Lourdes town in SW France, population (1982) 18,000. Its Christian shrine to St *Bernadette has a reputation for miraculous cures.

Lourenço Marques former name of *Maputo, capital of Mozambique.

louse parasitic insect of the order Anoplura, which lives on mammals. It has a flat, segmented body without wings, and a tube attached to the head, used for sucking blood from its host.

Louth smallest county of the Republic of Ireland, in Leinster province; county town Dundalk; area 820 sq km/317 sq mi; population (1991) 90,700.

Louvre French art gallery, former palace of the French kings, in Paris. It was converted by Napoleon to an art gallery in 1793 and houses the sculpture *Venus de Milo* and Leonardo da Vinci's painting *Mona Lisa*.

Lovelace Richard 1618–1658. English poet. Imprisoned in 1642 for petitioning for the restoration of royal rule, he wrote 'To Althea from Prison', and in a second term in jail in 1648 revised his collection *Lucasta* 1649.

Low Countries region of Europe that consists of *Belgium and the *Netherlands, and usually includes *Luxembourg.

Lowe John 1947– . English darts player. He has won most of the major titles including the world championships in 1979 and 1987. In 1986 he achieved the first televised nine-dart finish at the MFI Championship at Reading.

Lowell Amy (Lawrence) 1874–1925. US poet who began her career by publishing the conventional *A Dome of Many-Colored Glass* 1912 but eventually succeeded Ezra Pound as leader of the *Imagists. Her works, in free verse, include *Sword Blades and Poppy Seed* 1916.

Lower Saxony (German *Niedersachsen*) administrative region (German *Land*) of N Germany
area 47,400 sq km/18,296 sq mi
capital Hanover
towns Brunswick, Osnabrück, Oldenburg, Göttingen, Wolfsburg, Salzgitter, Hildesheim
products cereals, cars, machinery, electrical engineering
population (1988) 7,190,000
religion 75% Protestant, 20% Roman Catholic

history formed 1946 from Hanover, Oldenburg, Brunswick, and Schaumburg-Lippe.

low-level language in computing, a programming language designed for a particular computer and reflecting its internal *machine code; low-level languages are therefore often described as *machine-oriented* languages. They cannot easily be converted to run on a computer with a different central processing unit, and they are relatively difficult to learn because a detailed knowledge of the internal working of the computer is required. Since they must be translated into machine code by an *assembler program, low-level languages are also called *assembly languages.

Lowry L(aurence) S(tephen) 1887–1976. English painter. Born in Manchester, he lived mainly in nearby Salford and painted northern industrial townscapes. His characteristic style of matchstick figures and almost monochrome palette emerged in the 1920s.

Loy Myrna. Stage name of Myrna Williams 1905– . US film actress who played Nora Charles in the *Thin Man* series (1943–47) costarring William Powell. Her other films include *The Mask of Fu Manchu* 1932 and *The Rains Came* 1939.

Loyalist member of approximately 30% of the US population remaining loyal to Britain in the *American Revolution. Many Loyalists went to E Ontario, Canada after 1783.

Loyola founder of the Jesuits. See *Ignatius Loyola.

LSD (*lysergic acid diethylamide*) psychedelic drug, a *hallucinogen. Colourless, odourless, and easily synthesized, it is nonaddictive and nontoxic, but its effects are unpredictable. Its use is illegal in most countries.

LSI (abbreviation for *large-scale integration*) the technology that enables whole electrical circuits to be etched into a piece of semiconducting material just a few millimetres square.

Ltd abbreviation for *Limited*; see *private limited company.

Luanda formerly *Loanda* capital and industrial port (cotton, sugar, tobacco, timber, paper, oil) of Angola; population (1988) 1,200,000. It was founded in 1575 and became a Portuguese colonial administrative centre as well as an outlet for slaves transported to Brazil.

Lubbers Rudolph Franz Marie (Ruud) 1939– . Dutch politician, prime minister of the Netherlands from 1982. Leader of the Christian Democratic Appeal (CDA), he is politically right of centre. He became minister for economic affairs 1973.

Lubovitch Lar 1945– . US modern-dance choreographer and director of the Lar Lubovitch Dance Company, founded 1976. He was the first to use Minimalist music, for which he created a new style of movement in works like *Marimba* 1977 and *North Star* 1978.

lubricant substance used between moving surfaces to reduce friction. Carbon-based (organic) lubricants, commonly called grease and oil, are recovered from petroleum distillation.

Lubumbashi formerly (until 1986) *Elisabethville* town in Zaire, on the Lualaba River; population (1984) 543,000. It is chief commercial centre of the Shaba copper-mining region.

Lucan (Marcus Annaeus Lucanus) AD 39–65. Latin poet, born in Córdoba, Spain, a nephew of the writer Seneca and favourite of Nero until the emperor became jealous of his verse. Lucan then joined a republican conspiracy and committed suicide on its failure. His epic *Pharsalia* deals with the civil wars of the Roman rulers Caesar and Pompey.

Lucas George 1944– . US director and producer whose imagination was fired by the comic books in his father's store. He wrote and directed (in collaboration with Steven Spielberg) *Star Wars* 1977, *The Empire Strikes Back* 1980, and *Return of the Jedi* 1983. His other films include *THX 1138* 1971, *American Graffiti* 1973, *Raiders of the Lost Ark* 1981, *Indiana Jones and the Temple of Doom* 1984, *Willow* 1988, and *Indiana Jones and the Last Crusade* 1989, most of which were box-office hits.

Lucas van Leyden 1494–1533. Dutch painter and engraver, active in Leiden and Antwerp. He was a pioneer of Netherlandish genre scenes, for example *The Chess Players* (Staatliche Museen, Berlin). His woodcuts and engravings were inspired by Albrecht *Dürer, whom he met in Antwerp in 1521.

Luce Clare Boothe 1903–1987. US journalist, playwright, and politician. She was managing editor of *Vanity Fair* magazine 1933–34, and wrote several successful plays, including *The Women* 1936 and *Margin for Error* 1940, both of which were made into films. She served as a Republican member of Congress 1943–47 and as ambassador to Italy 1953–57.

Luce Henry Robinson 1898–1967. US publisher, founder of Time Inc, which publishes the weekly news magazine *Time* 1923, the business magazine *Fortune* 1930, the pictorial magazine *Life* 1936, and the sports magazine *Sports Illustrated* 1954. He married Clare Boothe Luce in 1935.

lucerne another name for the plant *alfalfa.

Lucerne (German *Luzern*) capital and tourist centre of Lucerne canton, Switzerland, on the river Reuss where it flows out of Lake Lucerne; population (1990) city 59,440, canton 319,500. It developed around the Benedictine monastery, established about 750, and owes its prosperity to its position on the St Gotthard road and railway.

Lucian c. 125–c. 190. Greek writer of satirical dialogues, in which he pours scorn on all religions. He was born at Samosata in Syria and for a time was an advocate at Antioch, but later travelled before settling in Athens about 165. He occupied an official post in Egypt, where he died.

Lucifer (Latin 'bearer of light') in Christian theology, another name for the *devil, the leader of the angels who rebelled against God. Lucifer is also another name for the morning star (the planet *Venus).

Lucknow capital and industrial city (engineering, chemicals, textiles, many handicrafts) of the state of Uttar Pradesh, India; population (1981) 1,007,000. During the Indian Mutiny against British rule, it was besieged 2 July–16 Nov 1857.

Lucretia Roman woman, the wife of Collatinus, said to have committed suicide after being raped by Sextus, son of Tarquinius Superbus, the king of Rome. According to tradition, this incident led to the dethronement of Tarquinius and the establishment of the Roman Republic in 509 BC.

Lucretius (Titus Lucretius Carus) c. 99–55 BC. Roman poet and *Epicurean philosopher whose *De Rerum natura/On the Nature of The Universe* envisaged the whole universe as a combination of atoms, and had some concept of evolutionary theory.

Lucullus Lucius Licinius 110–56 BC. Roman general and consul. As commander against *Mithridates of Pontus 74–66 he proved to be one of Rome's ablest generals and administrators, until superseded by Pompey. He then retired from politics. His wealth enabled him to live a life of luxury, and Lucullan feasts became legendary.

Lüda or **Hüta** industrial port (engineering, chemicals, textiles, oil refining, shipbuilding, food processing) in Liaoning, China, on Liaodong Peninsula, facing the Yellow Sea; population (1986) 4,500,000. It comprises the naval base of Lüshun (known under 19th-century Russian occupation as Port Arthur) and the commercial port of Dalien (formerly Talien/Dairen).

Luddite one of a group of people involved in machine-wrecking riots in N England 1811–16. The organizer of the Luddites was referred to as General Ludd, but may not have existed. Many Luddites were hanged or transported to penal colonies, such as Australia.

Ludendorff Erich von 1865–1937. German general, chief of staff to *Hindenburg in World War I, and responsible for the eastern-front victory at the Battle of *Tannenberg in 1914. After Hindenburg's appointment as chief of general staff and Ludendorff's as quartermaster-general in 1916, he was also politically influential. He took part in the Nazi rising in Munich in 1923 and sat in the Reichstag (parliament) as a right-wing Nationalist.

Ludwig three kings of Bavaria, including:

Ludwig I 1786–1868. King of Bavaria 1825–48, succeeding his father Maximilian Joseph I. He made Munich an international cultural centre, but his association with the dancer Lola Montez, who dictated his policies for a year, led to his abdication in 1848.

Ludwig II 1845–1886. King of Bavaria from 1864, when he succeeded his father Maximilian II. He supported Austria during the Austro-Prussian War 1866, but brought Bavaria into the Franco-Prussian War as Prussia's ally and in 1871 offered the German crown to the king of Prussia. He was the composer Richard Wagner's patron and built the Bayreuth theatre for him. Declared insane 1886, he drowned himself soon after.

Ludwig III 1845–1921. King of Bavaria 1913–18, when he abdicated upon the formation of a republic.

Luening Otto 1900– . US composer. He studied in Zurich, and privately with the Italian composer Feruccio Busoni. In 1949 he joined the staff at Columbia University, and in 1951 began a series of pioneering compositions for instruments and tape, some in partnership with Vladimir Ussachevsky (1911–) (*Incantation* 1952, *Poem in Cycles and Bells* 1954). In 1959 he became co-director, with Milton *Babbitt and Ussachevsky, of the Columbia-Princeton Electronic Music Center.

Luftwaffe German air force. In World War I and, as reorganized by the Nazi leader Hermann Goering in 1933, in World War II. The Luftwaffe also covered anti-aircraft defence and the launching of the flying bombs *V1 and V2.

Lugosi Bela. Stage name of Bela Ferenc Blasko 1882–1956. Hungarian-born US film actor. Acclaimed for his performance in *Dracula* on Broadway 1927, Lugosi began acting in feature films in 1930. His appearance in the film version of *Dracula* 1931 marked the start of Lugosi's long career in horror films – among them, *Murders in the Rue Morgue* 1932, *The Raven* 1935, and *The Wolf Man* 1941.

lugworm any of a genus *Arenicola* of marine annelid worms that grow up to 25 cm/10 in long. They are common burrowers between tidemarks and are useful for their cleansing and powdering of the beach sand, of which they may annually bring to the surface about 5,000 tonnes per hectare/2,000 tons per acre.

Lu Hsün alternative transliteration of Chinese writer *Lu Xun.

Lukács Georg 1885–1971. Hungarian philosopher, one of the founders of 'Western' or 'Hegelian' Marxism, a philosophy opposed to the Marxism of the official communist movement.

Luke, St 1st century AD. Traditionally the compiler of the third Gospel and of the Acts of the Apostles in the New Testament. He is the patron saint of painters; his emblem is a winged ox, and his feast day 18 Oct.

Lully Jean-Baptiste. Adopted name of Giovanni Battista Lulli 1632–1687. French composer of Italian origin who was court composer to Louis XIV. He composed music for the ballet, for Molière's plays, and established French opera with such works as *Alceste* 1674 and *Armide et Renaud* 1686. He was also a ballet dancer.

lumbago pain in the lower region of the back, usually due to strain or faulty posture. If it occurs with *sciatica, it may be due to pressure on spinal nerves by a displaced vertebra. Treatment includes rest, application of heat, and skilled manipulation. Surgery may be needed in rare cases.

lumbar puncture or *spinal tap* insertion of a hollow needle between two lumbar (lower back) vertebrae to withdraw a sample of cerebrospinal fluid (CSF) for testing. Normally clear and colourless, the CSF acts as a fluid buffer around the brain and spinal cord. Changes in its quantity, colour, or composition may indicate neurological damage or disease.

Lumbini birthplace of *Buddha in the foothills of the Himalayas near the Nepalese-Indian frontier. A sacred garden and shrine were established here in 1970 by the Nepalese government.

lumen SI unit (symbol lm) of luminous flux (the amount of light passing through an area per second).

Lumet Sidney 1924– . US film director whose social conscience has sometimes prejudiced his invariably powerful films: *12 Angry Men* 1957, *Fail Safe* 1964, *Serpico* 1973, and *Dog Day Afternoon* 1975.

Lumière Auguste Marie 1862–1954 and Louis Jean 1864–1948. French brothers who pioneered cinematography. In 1895 they patented their cinematograph, a combined camera and projector operating at 16 frames per second, and opened the world's first cinema in Paris to show their films.

luminescence emission of light from a body when its atoms are excited by means other than raising its temperature. Short-lived luminescence is called fluorescence; longer-lived luminescence is called phosphorescence.

luminism method of painting, associated with the *Hudson River School in the 19th century, that emphasized the effects of light on water.

luminosity or *brightness* in astronomy, the amount of light emitted by a star, measured in *magnitudes. The apparent brightness of an object decreases in proportion to the square of its distance from the observer. The luminosity of a star or other body can be expressed in relation to that of the sun.

luminous paint preparation containing a mixture of pigment, oil, and a phosphorescent sulphide, usually calcium or barium. After exposure to light it appears luminous in the dark. The luminous paint used on watch faces contains radium, is radioactive and therefore does not require exposure to light.

Lumumba Patrice 1926–1961. Congolese politician, prime minister of Zaire 1960. Imprisoned by the Belgians, but released in time to attend the conference giving the Congo independence in 1960, he led the National Congolese Movement to victory in the subsequent general election. He was deposed in a coup d'état, and murdered some months later.

lung large cavity of the body, used for *gas exchange, or respiration. It is essentially a sheet of thin, moist membrane that is folded so as to occupy less space. Lungs are found in some slugs and snails, particularly those that live on land. Some fishes (lungfish) and most four-limbed vertebrates have a pair of lungs, which occupy the thorax (the upper part of the trunk). Lungs function by bringing inhaled air into close contact with the blood, so that oxygen can pass into the organism and waste carbon dioxide can be passed out; the oxygen is carried by *haemoglobin in red blood cells. The lung tissue, consisting of multitudes of air sacs and blood vessels, is very light and spongy.

lungfish three genera of fleshy-finned bony fishes of the subclass Dipnoi, found in Africa, South America, and Australia. They have elongated bodies, and grow to about 2 m/6 ft, and in addition to gills have 'lungs' with which they can breathe air during periods of drought conditions.

Luo member of the second-largest ethnic group of Kenya, living in the Lake Victoria region and in 1987 numbering some 2,650,000. The Luo traditionally live by farming livestock. The Luo language is of the Nilo-Saharan family.

Lupercalia Roman festival celebrated 15 Feb. It took place at the Lupercal, the cave where Romulus and Remus, the twin founders of Rome, were supposedly suckled by a wolf (*lupus*). Lupercalia included feasting, dancing, and sacrificing goats. Priests ran around the city carrying whips made from the hides of the sacrificed goats, a blow from which was believed to cure sterility in women.

lupin any plant of the genus *Lupinus*, which comprises about 300 species, family Leguminosae. Lupins are native to Mediterranean regions and parts of North and South America, and some species are naturalized in Britain. Their spikes of pealike flowers may be white, yellow, blue, or pink. *L. albus* is cultivated in some places for cattle fodder and for green manuring.

lupus in medicine, any of various diseases characterized by lesions of the skin. One form (lupus vulgaris) is caused by the tubercle bacillus (see *tuberculosis). The organism produces ulcers that spread and eat away the underlying tissues. Treatment is primarily with standard antituberculous drugs, but ultraviolet light may also be used.

Lusaka capital of Zambia from 1964 (of Northern Rhodesia 1935–64), 370 km/230 mi NE of Livingstone; commercial and agricultural centre (flour mills, tobacco factories, vehicle assembly, plastics, printing); population (1988) 870,000.

Lusitania ocean liner sunk by a German submarine on 7 May 1915 with the loss of 1,200 lives, including some Americans; its destruction helped to bring the USA into World War I.

lute family of stringed musical instruments of the 14th–18th century, including the mandore, theorbo, and chitarrone. Lutes are pear-shaped and are plucked with the fingers. Members of the lute family were used both as solo instruments and for vocal accompaniment, and were often played in addition to, or instead of, keyboard instruments in larger ensembles and in opera.

luteinizing hormone *hormone produced by the pituitary gland. In males, it stimulates the testes to produce androgens (male sex hormones). In females, it works together with follicle-stimulating hormone to initiate production of egg cells by the ovary. If fertilization of the egg cell occurs, it plays a part in maintaining the pregnancy by controlling the levels of the hormones oestrogen and progesterone in the body.

lutetium (Latin *Lutetia* 'Paris') silver-white, metallic element, the last of the *lanthanide series, symbol Lu, atomic number 71, relative atomic mass 174.97. It is used in the 'cracking', or breakdown, of petroleum and in other chemical processes. It was named by its discoverer, French chemist Georges Urbain, (1872–1938) after his native city.

Luther Martin 1483–1546. German Christian church reformer, a founder of Protestantism. While he was a priest at the University of Wittenberg, he wrote an attack on the sale of indulgences (remissions of punishment for sin) in 95 theses which he nailed to a church door in 1517, in defiance of papal condemnation. The Holy Roman emperor Charles V summoned him to the Diet (meeting of dignitaries of the Holy Roman Empire) of Worms in Germany, in 1521, where he refused to retract his objections. Originally intending reform, his protest led to schism, with the emergence, following the *Augsburg Confession 1530 (a statement of the Protestant faith), of a new Protestant church. Luther is regarded as the instigator of the Protestant revolution, and Lutheranism is now the major religion of many N European countries, including Germany, Sweden, and Denmark.

Lutheranism form of Protestant Christianity derived from the life and teaching of Martin Luther; it is sometimes called Evangelical to distinguish it from the other main branch of European Protestantism, the Reformed. The most generally accepted statement of Lutheranism is that of the ***Augsburg Confession*** 1530 but Luther's Shorter Catechism also carries great weight. It is the largest Protestant body, including some 80 million persons, of whom 40 million are in Germany, 19 million in Scandinavia, 8.5 million in the USA and Canada, with most of the remainder in central Europe.

Lutyens Edwin Landseer 1869–1944. English architect, one of the most important of the early 1900s. His designs ranged from picturesque to Renaissance-style country houses and ultimately evolved into a Classical style best exemplified by the Cenotaph, London, and the Viceroy's House, New Delhi.

lux SI unit (symbol lx) of illuminance or illumination (the light falling on an object). It is equivalent to one *lumen per square metre or to the illuminance of a surface one metre distant from a point source of one *candela.

Luxembourg capital of Luxembourg; population (1985) 76,000. The 16th-century Grand Ducal Palace, European Court of Justice, and European Parliament secretariat are situated here, but plenary sessions of the parliament are now held only in Strasbourg, in France. Products include steel, chemicals, textiles, and processed food.

Luxembourg Grand Duchy of (*Grand-Duché de Luxembourg*)

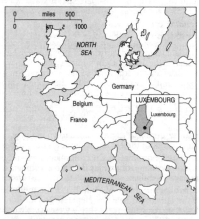

area 2,586 sq km/998 sq mi
capital Luxembourg
towns Esch-sur-Alzette, Dudelange
physical on the river Moselle; part of the Ardennes (Oesling) forest in N
head of state Grand Duke Jean from 1964
head of government Jacques Santer from 1984
political system liberal democracy
exports pharmaceuticals, synthetic textiles, steel

currency Luxembourg franc
population (1993 est) 395,200 growth rate 0% p.a.
languages French (official), local Letzeburgesch, German
religion Roman Catholic 97%
GNP $31,080 per head (1991)
chronology
1354 Became a duchy.
1482 Under Habsburg control.
1797 Ceded, with Belgium, to France.
1815 Treaty of Vienna created Luxembourg a grand duchy, ruled by the king of the Netherlands.
1830 With Belgium, revolted against Dutch rule.
1890 Link with Netherlands ended with accession of Grand Duke Adolphe of Nassau-Weilburg.
1948 With Belgium and the Netherlands, formed the Benelux customs union.
1960 Benelux became fully effective economic union.
1961 Prince Jean became acting head of state on behalf of his mother, Grand Duchess Charlotte.
1964 Grand Duchess Charlotte abdicated; Prince Jean became grand duke.
1974 Dominance of Christian Social Party challenged by Socialists.
1979 Christian Social Party regained pre-eminence.
1991 Pact agreeing European free-trade area signed in Luxembourg.
1992 Voted in favour of ratification of Maastricht Treaty.

Luxembourg Accord French-initiated agreement in 1966 that a decision of the Council of Ministers of the European Community may be vetoed by a member whose national interests are at stake.

Luxembourg, Palais du palace in Paris, France, in which the Senate sits. It was built in 1615 for the Queen Marie de' Medici by Salomon de Brosse.

Luxemburg Rosa 1870–1919. Polish-born German communist. She helped found the Polish Social Democratic Party in the 1890s (which later became the Polish Communist Party). She was a leader of the left wing of the German Social Democratic Party from 1898 and collaborator with Karl Liebknecht in founding the communist Spartacus League 1918 (see *Spartacist). She was murdered with him by army officers during the Jan 1919 Berlin workers' revolt.

Luxor (Arabic **al-Uqsur**) small town in Egypt on the E bank of the Nile near the ruins of *Thebes.

Lu Xun Pen name of Chon Shu-jêu 1881–1936. Chinese short-story writer. His three volumes of satirically realistic stories, *Call to Arms*, *Wandering*, and *Old Tales Retold*, reveal the influence of the Russian writer Nicolai Gogol.

Luzern German name of *Lucerne, town in Switzerland.

Luzon largest island of the *Philippines; area 108,130 sq km/41,750 sq mi; capital Quezon City; population (1970) 18,001,270. The chief city is Manila, capital of the Philippines. Products include rice, timber, and minerals. It has US military bases.

LW abbreviation for **long wave**, a radio wave with a wavelength of over 1,000 m/3,300 ft; one

of the main wavebands into which radio frequency transmissions are divided.

LWM abbreviation for **low water mark**.

lycanthropy in folk belief, transformation of a human being into a wolf; or, in psychology, a delusion involving this belief.

Lyceum ancient Athenian gymnasium and garden, with covered walks, where the philosopher Aristotle taught. It was SE of the city and named after the nearby temple of Apollo Lyceus.

lychee alternative spelling of *litchi, a fruit-bearing tree.

Lycurgus Spartan lawgiver. He is said to have been a member of the royal house of the ancient Greek city-state of Sparta, who, while acting as regent, gave the Spartans their constitution and system of education. Many scholars believe him to be purely mythical.

Lydgate John c. 1370–c. 1450. English poet. He was a Benedictine monk and later prior. His numerous works were often translations or adaptations, such as *Troy Book* and *Falls of Princes*.

Lydia ancient kingdom in Anatolia (7th–6th centuries BC), with its capital at Sardis. The Lydians were the first Western people to use standard coinage. Their last king, Croesus, was conquered by the Persians in 546 BC.

Lyell Charles 1797–1875. Scottish geologist. In his *Principles of Geology* 1830–33, he opposed the French anatomist Georges Cuvier's theory that the features of the Earth were formed by a series of catastrophes, and expounded the Scottish geologist James Hutton's view, known as *uniformitarianism, that past events were brought about by the same processes that occur today – a view that influenced Charles Darwin's theory of evolution.

Lyle Sandy 1958– . Scottish golfer who came to prominence in 1978 when he won the Rookie of the Year award. He won the British Open in 1985 and added the Masters and World Match-Play titles 1988. He was Europe's leading money winner in 1979, 1980, and 1985 and has played in five Ryder Cups.

Lyly John c. 1553–1606. English playwright and author of the romance *Euphues, or the Anatomy of Wit* 1578. Its elaborate stylistic devices gave rise to the word 'euphuism' to describe an affected rhetorical style.

lymph fluid found in the lymphatic system of vertebrates.

lymph nodes small masses of lymphatic tissue in the body that occur at various points along the major lymphatic vessels. Tonsils and adenoids are large lymph nodes. As the lymph passes through them it is filtered, and bacteria and other microorganisms are engulfed by cells known as macrophages.

lymphocyte type of white blood cell with a large nucleus, produced in the bone marrow. Most occur in the *lymph and blood, and around sites of infection. **B-lymphocytes** or *B cells are responsible for producing *antibodies. **T-lymphocytes** or *T-cells have several roles in the formation of *immunity.

lymphokines chemical messengers produced by lymphocytes that carry messages between the cells of the immune system (see *immunity). Examples include interferon, which initiates defensive reactions to viruses, and the interleukins, which activate specific immune cells.

Lynagh Michael 1963– . Australian rugby union player. He is Australia's most capped stand-off and, with Nicholas Farr-Jones, holds the world record of over 40 appearances as an international halfback partnership. A key member of Australia's 1991 World Cup winning team, he plays for Queensland University and Queensland.

Lynch 'Jack' (John) 1917– . Irish politician, prime minister 1966–73 and 1977–79. A Gaelic footballer and a barrister, in 1948 he entered the parliament of the republic as a Fianna Fáil member.

lynx cat *Felis lynx* found in rocky and forested regions of North America and Europe. About 1 m/3 ft in length, it has a short tail and tufted ears, and the long, silky fur is reddish brown or grey with dark spots. The North American bobcat or bay lynx *F. rufus* looks similar but is smaller. Some zoologists place the lynx, the bobcat, and the caracal *F. caracal*, which lives in deserts of Africa, Arabia and India, in a separate genus, *Lynx*.

Lyon (English **Lyons**) industrial city (textiles, chemicals, machinery, printing) and capital of Rhône *département*, Rhône-Alpes region, and third largest city of France, at the confluence of the rivers Rhône and Saône, 275 km/170 mi NNW of Marseille; population (1982) 418,476, conurbation 1,221,000. Formerly a chief fortress of France, it was the ancient **Lugdunum**, taken by the Romans in 43 BC.

Lyons Joseph 1848–1917. British entrepreneur, founder of the catering firm of J Lyons in 1894. He popularized teashops, and the 'Corner Houses' incorporating several restaurants of varying types were long a feature of London life.

lyophilization technical term for the *freeze-drying process used for foods and drugs and in the preservation of organic archaeological remains.

Lyra small but prominent constellation of the northern hemisphere, representing the lyre of Orpheus. Its brightest star is *Vega.

lyre stringed instrument of great antiquity. It consists of a soundbox with two curved arms extended upwards to a crosspiece to which four to ten strings are attached. It is played with a plectrum or the fingers. It originated in Asia, and was used in Greece and Egypt.

lyrebird any bird of the order *Passeriformes*, forming the Australian family Menuridae. There are two species, both in the genus *Menura*. The male has a large lyre-shaped tail, brilliantly coloured. Lyrebirds nest on the ground, and feed on insects, worms, and snails.

lyretail African fish *Aphyosemion australe* 6 cm/2.4 in long, whose tail has two outward-curving fin supports for a central fin area which looks like the strings of a lyre. The male is bright blue with red markings; the less brightly coloured female has plainer fins.

Lysander Spartan general. He brought the Peloponnesian War between Athens and Sparta to a successful conclusion by capturing the Athenian fleet at Aegospotami in 405 BC, and by starving Athens into surrender in the following year. He then aspired to make Sparta supreme in Greece and himself supreme in Sparta; he set up puppet governments in Athens and its former allies, and tried to secure for himself the Spartan kingship, but he was killed in battle with the Thebans.

Lysenko Trofim Denisovich 1898–1976. Soviet biologist who believed in the inheritance of *acquired characteristics (changes acquired in an individual's lifetime) and used his position under Joseph Stalin officially to exclude Gregor *Mendel's theory of inheritance. He was removed from office after the fall of Khrushchev in 1964.

Lysippus 4th century BC. Greek sculptor. He made a series of portraits of Alexander the Great (Roman copies survive, including examples in the British Museum and the Louvre) and also sculpted the *Apoxyomenos*, an athlete (copy in the Vatican), and a colossal *Hercules* (lost).

lysis in biology, any process that destroys a cell by rupturing its membrane or cell wall (see *lysosome).

lysosome membrane-enclosed structure, or organelle, inside a *cell, principally found in animal cells. Lysosomes contain enzymes that can break down proteins and other biological substances. They play a part in digestion, and in the white blood cells known as phagocytes the lysosome enzymes attack ingested bacteria.

m symbol for **metre*.

M Roman numeral for *1,000*.

MA abbreviation for *Master of Arts*, a degree of education; the state of **Massachusetts*.

Maastricht Treaty treaty on European union, signed 10 Dec 1991 by leaders of European Community (EC) nations at Maastricht in the Netherlands, at a meeting convened to agree on terms for political union. The treaty was formally endorsed by the European Parliament April 1992 but its subsequent rejection by the Danish in a June referendum placed its future in jeopardy. Survival of the treaty appeared more certain after an Edinburgh summit Dec 1992, at which EC leaders agreed to a set of compromises and it was eventually ratified by all member states 1 Nov 1993. From that date the European Community became known as the European Union (EU).

Mabuse Jan. Adopted name of Jan Gossaert *c.* 1478–*c.* 1533. Flemish painter. He was active chiefly in Antwerp. His common name derives from his birthplace, Maubeuge. His visit to Italy 1508 with Philip of Burgundy started a new vogue in Flanders for Italianate ornament and Classical detail in painting, including sculptural nude figures, as in his *Neptune and Amphitrite c.* 1516 (Staatliche Museen, Berlin).

McAdam John (Loudon) 1756–1836. Scottish engineer, inventor of the macadam road surface. It originally consisted of broken granite bound together with slag or gravel, raised for drainage. Today, it is bound with tar or asphalt.

macadamia edible nut from the tree *Macadamia ternifolia*, family Proteaceae, native to Australia and cultivated in Hawaii, South Africa, Zimbabwe, and Malawi. The nuts are slow-growing; they are harvested when they drop.

Macao Portuguese possession on the S coast of China, about 65 km/40 mi W of Hong Kong, from which it is separated by the estuary of the Canton River; it consists of a peninsula and the islands of Taipa and Colôane
area 17 sq km/7 sq mi
capital Macao, on the peninsula
currency pataca
population (1986) 426,000
languages Cantonese; Portuguese (official)
religions Buddhist, with 6% Catholic minority.

macaque Old World monkey of the genus *Macaca*. Various species of these medium-sized monkeys live in forests from the Far East to N Africa. The *rhesus and the *Barbary ape are part of this group.

MacArthur Douglas 1880–1964. US general in World War II, commander of US forces in the Far East and, from March 1942, of the Allied forces in the SW Pacific. After the surrender of Japan he commanded the Allied occupation forces there. During 1950 he commanded the UN forces in Korea, but in April 1951, after expressing views contrary to US and UN policy, he was relieved of all his commands by President Truman.

Macaulay Thomas Babington, Baron Macaulay 1800–1859. English historian, essayist, poet, and politician, secretary of war 1839–41. His *History of England* in five volumes 1849–61 celebrates the Glorious Revolution of 1688 as the crowning achievement of the Whig party.

macaw any of various large, brilliantly coloured, long-tailed tropical American *parrots, especially the genus *Ara*.

Macbeth died 1057. King of Scotland from 1040. The son of Findlaech, hereditary ruler of Moray, he was commander of the forces of Duncan I, King of Scotia, whom he killed in battle 1040. His reign was prosperous until Duncan's son Malcolm III led an invasion and killed him at Lumphanan.

Maccabee or *Hasmonaean* member of an ancient Hebrew family founded by the priest Mattathias (died 166 BC) who, with his sons, led the struggle for independence against the Syrians in the 2nd century BC. Judas (died 161) reconquered Jerusalem 164 BC, and Simon (died 135) established its independence 142 BC. The revolt of the Maccabees lasted until the capture of Jerusalem by the Romans 63 BC. The story is told in four books of the *Apocrypha.

McCarthy Joe (Joseph Raymond) 1908–1957. US right-wing Republican politician. His unsubstantiated claim 1950 that the State Department and US army had been infiltrated by communists started a wave of anticommunist hysteria, wild accusations, and blacklists, which continued until he was discredited 1954. He was censured by the US Senate for misconduct.

McCartney Paul 1942– . UK rock singer, songwriter, and bass guitarist. He was a member of the *Beatles, and leader of the pop group Wings 1971–81. His subsequent solo hits have included collaborations with Michael Jackson and Elvis Costello. Together with composer Carl Davis, McCartney wrote the *Liverpool Oratorio* 1991, his first work of classical music.

McClellan George Brinton 1826–1885. US Civil War general, commander in chief of the Union forces 1861–62. He was dismissed by President Lincoln when he delayed five weeks in following up his victory over the Confederate General Lee at Antietam (see under *Civil War, American). He was the unsuccessful Democrat presidential candidate against Lincoln 1864.

McClure Robert John le Mesurier 1807–1873. Irish-born British admiral and explorer. While on an expedition 1850–54 searching for John *Franklin, he was the first to pass through the Northwest Passage.

McColgan Elizabeth 1964– . Scottish long-distance runner who became the 1992 world 10,000 metres champion. She won consecutive gold medals at the Commonwealth games in 1986 and 1990 at the same distance.

McCullers Carson (Smith) 1917–1967. US novelist. Most of her writing, including the novels *The Heart is a Lonely Hunter* 1940 and *Reflections in a Golden Eye* 1941, is set in her native South. Her work, like that of Flannery *O'Connor, has been characterized as 'Southern Gothic' for its images of the grotesque, using physical abnormalities to project the spiritual and psychological distortions of Southern experience.

McCullin Don(ald) 1935– . English war photographer. He started out as a freelance photojournalist for the Sunday newspapers. His coverage of hostilities in the Congo 1967, Vietnam 1968, Biafra 1968 and 1970, and Cambodia 1970 are notable for their pessimistic vision. He has published several books of his work, among them *Destruction Business*.

Macdonald Flora 1722–1790. Scottish heroine who rescued Prince Charles Edward Stuart, the Young Pretender, after his defeat at Culloden 1746. Disguising him as her maid, she escorted him from her home in the Hebrides to France. She was arrested, but released 1747.

MacDonald (James) Ramsay 1866–1937. British politician, first Labour prime minister Jan–Oct 1924 and 1929–31. Failing to deal with worsening economic conditions, he left the party to form a coalition government 1931, which was increasingly dominated by Conservatives, until he was replaced by Stanley Baldwin 1935.

Macdonald John Alexander 1815–1891. Canadian Conservative politician, prime minister 1867–73 and 1878–91. In 1857 he became prime minister of Upper Canada. He took the leading part in the movement for federation, and in 1867 became the first prime minister of Canada. He was defeated 1873 but returned to office 1878 and retained it until his death.

Macedonia ancient region of the S Balkans, forming parts of modern Greece, Bulgaria, and Yugoslavia. Macedonia gained control of Greece after Philip II's victory at Chaeronea 338 BC. His son, *Alexander the Great, conquered a vast empire. Macedonia became a Roman province 146 BC.

Macedonia Former Yugoslav Republic of

area 25,700 sq km/9,920 sq mi

capital Skopje
physical mountainous; rivers: Struma, Vardar
head of state Kiro Gligorov from 1990
head of government Branko Crvenkovski from 1992
political system emergent democracy
population (1992) 2,060,000
language Macedonian, closely allied to Bulgarian and written in Cyrillic
religion Macedonian Orthodox Christian
chronology
1913 Ancient country of Macedonia divided between Serbia, Bulgaria, and Greece.
1918 Serbian part included in what was to become Yugoslavia.
1941–44 Occupied by Bulgaria.
1945 Created a republic within Yugoslav Socialist Federation.
1980 Rise of nationalism after death of Yugoslav leader Tito.
1990 Multiparty election produced inconclusive result.
1991 'Socialist' dropped from republic's name. Referendum supported independence.
1992 Independence declared, but international recognition withheld because of objections to name by Greece.
1993 Sovereignty recognized by UK and Albania; won United Nations membership under provisional name of Former Yugoslav Republic of Macedonia.
1994 Trade embargo imposed by Greece.

Macedonia (Greek *Makedhonia*) mountainous region of N Greece, part of the ancient country of Macedonia which was divided between Serbia, Bulgaria, and Greece after the Balkan Wars of 1912–13. Greek Macedonia is bounded W and N by Albania and Yugoslavia; area 34,177 sq km/13,200 sq mi; population (1991) 2,263,000. The chief city is Thessaloniki. Fertile valleys produce grain, olives, grapes, tobacco, and livestock. Mount Olympus rises to 2,918 m/9,570 ft on the border with Thessaly.

McEnroe John (Patrick) 1959– . US lawn-tennis player whose brash behaviour and fiery temper on court dominated the men's game in the early 1980s. He was three times winner of Wimbledon 1981, 1983, and 1984. He also won three successive US Open titles 1979–81 and again in 1984.

McEwan Ian 1948– . English novelist and short-story writer. His works often have sinister or macabre undertones and contain elements of violence and bizarre sexuality, as in the short stories in *First Love, Last Rites* 1975. His novels include *The Comfort of Strangers* 1981, *The Child in Time* 1987, and *Black Dogs* 1992.

Machel Samora 1933–1986. Mozambique nationalist leader, president 1975–86. Machel was active in the liberation front *Frelimo from its conception 1962, fighting for independence from Portugal. He became Frelimo leader 1966, and Mozambique's first president from independence 1975 until his death in a plane crash near the South African border.

Machiavelli Niccolò 1469–1527. Italian politician and author. His name is synonymous with cunning and cynical statecraft. In his most celebrated political writings, *Il principe/The Prince* 1513 and *Discorsi/Discourses* 1531, he discussed ways in which rulers can advance the interests of their states (and themselves) through an often amoral and opportunistic manipulation of other people.

machine device that allows a small force (the effort) to overcome a larger one (the load). There are three basic machines: the inclined plane (ramp), the lever, and the wheel and axle. All other machines are combinations of these three basic types. Simple machines derived from the inclined plane include the wedge, the gear, and the screw; the spanner is derived from the lever; the pulley from the wheel.

machine code in computing, a set of instructions that a computer's central processing unit (CPU) can understand and obey directly, without any translation. Each type of CPU has its own machine code. Because machine-code programs consist entirely of binary digits (bits), most programmers write their programs in an easy-to-use *high-level language. A high-level program must be translated into machine code – by means of a *compiler or *interpreter program – before it can be executed by a computer.

machine gun rapid-firing automatic gun. The Maxim (named after its inventor, US-born British engineer H S Maxim (1840–1916)) of 1884 was recoil-operated, but some later types have been gas-operated (Bren) or recoil assisted by gas (some versions of the Browning).

machine tool automatic or semi-automatic power-driven machine for cutting and shaping metals. Machine tools have powerful electric motors to force cutting tools into the metal: these are made from hardened steel containing heat-resistant metals such as tungsten and chromium. The use of precision machine tools in *mass-production assembly methods ensures that all duplicate parts produced are virtually identical.

Mach number ratio of the speed of a body to the speed of sound in the undisturbed medium through which the body travels. Mach 1 is reached when a body (such as an aircraft) has a velocity greater than that of sound ('passes the sound barrier'), namely 331 m/1,087 ft per second at sea level. It is named after Austrian physicist Ernst Mach (1838–1916).

Machu Picchu ruined Inca city in Peru, built about AD 1500, NW of Cuzco, discovered 1911 by Hiram Bingham. It stands at the top of cliffs 300 m/1,000 ft high and contains the well-preserved remains of houses and temples.

MacInnes Colin 1914–1976. English novelist, son of the novelist Angela Thirkell. His work is characterized by sharp depictions of London youth and subcultures of the 1950s, as in *City of Spades* 1957 and *Absolute Beginners* 1959.

Macintosh range of microcomputers produced by Apple Computers. The Apple Macintosh, introduced in 1984, was the first popular microcomputer with a *graphical user interface.

Macintosh Charles 1766–1843. Scottish manufacturing chemist who invented a waterproof fabric, lined with rubber, that was used for raincoats – hence *mackintosh*. Other waterproofing processes have now largely superseded this method.

McKellen Ian Murray 1939– . English actor acclaimed as the leading Shakespearean player of

his generation. His stage roles include Macbeth 1977, Max in Martin Sherman's *Bent* 1979, Platonov in Chekhov's *Wild Honey* 1986, Iago in *Othello* 1989, and Richard III 1990. His films include *Priest of Love* 1982 and *Plenty* 1985.

Mackendrick Alexander 1912–1993. US-born Scottish film director and teacher responsible for some of *Ealing Studios' finest comedies, including *Whisky Galore!* 1949 and *The Man in the White Suit* 1951. After *Mandy* 1952 he left for Hollywood, where he made *Sweet Smell of Success* 1957.

Mackenzie Compton 1883–1972. Scottish author. He published his first novel *The Passionate Elopement* 1911. Later works were *Carnival* 1912, *Sinister Street* 1913–14 (an autobiographical novel), and the comic *Whisky Galore* 1947. He published his autobiography in ten 'octaves' (volumes) 1963–71.

Mackenzie River river in the Northwest Territories, Canada, flowing NW from Great Slave Lake to the Arctic Ocean; about 1,800 km/1,120 mi long. It is the main channel of the Finlay-Peace-Mackenzie system, 4,241 km/2,635 mi long.

mackerel any of various fishes of the mackerel family Scombroidia, especially the common mackerel *Scomber Scombrus* found in the N Atlantic and Mediterranean. It weighs about 0.7 kg/1.5 lb, and is blue with irregular black bands down its sides, the latter and the under surface showing a metallic sheen. Like all mackerels, it has a deeply forked tail, and a sleek, streamlined body form.

McKinley William 1843–1901. 25th president of the USA 1897–1901, a republican. His term as president was marked by the USA's adoption of an imperialist policy, as exemplified by the Spanish-American war 1898 and the annexation of the Philippines. He was first elected to congress 1876. He was assassinated.

McKinley, Mount or *Denali* peak in Alaska, USA, the highest in North America, 6,194 m/20,320 ft; named after US president William McKinley.

Mackintosh Charles Rennie 1868–1928. Scottish architect, designer, and painter, whose chief work includes the Glasgow School of Art 1896, various Glasgow tea rooms 1897–about 1911, and Hill House, Helensburg, 1902–03. His early work is Art Nouveau; he subsequently developed a unique style, both rational and expressive.

MacLaine Shirley. Stage name of Shirley MacLean Beatty 1934– . Versatile US actress whose films include Alfred Hitchcock's *The Trouble with Harry* 1955 (her debut), *The Apartment* 1960, and *Terms of Endearment* 1983, for which she won an Academy Award.

McLaren racing-car company, makers of the successful Formula One Grand Prix car of the 1980s. The team was founded 1966 by New Zealand driver Bruce McLaren.

Maclean Donald 1913–1983. British spy who worked for the USSR while in the UK civil service. He defected to the USSR 1951 together with Guy *Burgess.

McLuhan (Herbert) Marshall 1911–1980. Canadian theorist of communication, famed for his views on the effects of technology on modern society. He coined the phrase 'the medium is the message', meaning that the form rather than the content of information has become crucial. His works include *The Gutenberg Galaxy* 1962 (in which he coined the phrase 'the global village' for the worldwide electronic society then emerging), *Understanding Media* 1964, and *The Medium is the Massage* (sic) 1967.

MacMahon Marie Edmé Patrice Maurice, Comte de 1808–1893. Marshal of France. Captured at Sedan 1870 during the Franco-Prussian War, he suppressed the *Paris Commune after his release, and as president of the republic 1873–79 worked for a royalist restoration until forced to resign.

Macmillan (Maurice) Harold, 1st Earl of Stockton 1894–1986. British Conservative politician, prime minister 1957–63; foreign secretary 1955 and chancellor of the Exchequer 1955–57. In 1963 he attempted to negotiate British entry into the European Economic Community, but was blocked by French president de Gaulle. Much of his career as prime minister was spent defending the retention of a UK nuclear weapon, and he was responsible for the purchase of US Polaris missiles 1962.

MacMillan Kenneth 1929–1992. Scottish choreographer. After studying at the Sadler's Wells Ballet School he was director of the Royal Ballet 1970–77 and then principal choreographer. His works included *Romeo and Juliet* for Margot Fonteyn and Rudolf Nureyev.

MacNeice Louis 1907–1963. British poet, born in Belfast. He made his debut with *Blind Fireworks* 1929 and developed a polished ease of expression, reflecting his classical training, as in *Autumn Journal* 1939. Unlike many of his contemporaries, he was politically uncommitted.

Macpherson James 1736–1796. Scottish writer and literary forger, author of *Fragments of Ancient Poetry collected in the Highlands of Scotland* 1760, followed by the epics *Fingal* 1761 and *Temora* 1763, which he claimed as the work of the 3rd-century bard *Ossian. After his death they were shown to be forgeries.

Macquarie Lachlan 1762–1824. Scottish administrator in Australia. He succeeded Admiral *Bligh as governor of New South Wales 1809, raised the demoralized settlement to prosperity, and did much to rehabilitate ex-convicts. In 1821 he returned to Britain in poor health, exhausted by struggles with his opponents. Lachlan River and Macquarie River and Island are named after him.

McQueen Steve (Terrence Steven) 1930–1980. US actor, a film star of the 1960s and 1970s, admired for his portrayals of the strong, silent loner, and noted for performing his own stunt work. After television success in the 1950s, he became a film star with *The Magnificent Seven* 1960. His films include *The Great Escape* 1963, *Bullitt* 1968, *Papillon* 1973, and *The Hunter* 1980.

macramé art of making decorative fringes and lacework with knotted threads. The name comes from the Arabic word for 'striped cloth', which is often decorated in this way.

macro in computer programming, a new com-

mand created by combining a number of existing ones. For example, if a programming language has separate commands for obtaining data from the keyboard and for displaying data on the screen, the programmer might create a macro that performs both these tasks with one command. A *macro key* on the keyboard combines the effects of pressing several individual keys.

macrobiotics dietary system of organically grown wholefoods. It originates in Zen Buddhism, and attempts to balance the principles of *yin and yang, which are thought to be present in foods in different proportions.

macroeconomics division of economics concerned with the study of whole (aggregate) economies or systems, including such aspects as government income and expenditure, the balance of payments, fiscal policy, investment, inflation, and unemployment. It seeks to understand the influence of all relevant economic factors on each other and thus to quantify and predict aggregate national income.

macromolecule in chemistry, a very large molecule, generally a *polymer.

macrophage type of *white blood cell, or leucocyte, found in all vertebrate animals. Macrophages specialize in the removal of bacteria and other microorganisms, or of cell debris after injury. Like phagocytes, they engulf foreign matter, but they are larger than phagocytes and have a longer life span. They are found throughout the body, but mainly in the lymph and connective tissues, and especially the lungs, where they ingest dust, fibres, and other inhaled particles.

Madagascar Democratic Republic of (*Repoblika Demokratika n'i Madagaskar*)

area 587,041 sq km/226,598 sq mi
capital Antananarivo
towns chief port Toamasina, Antseranana, Fianarantsoa, Toliary
physical temperate central highlands; humid valleys and tropical coastal plains; arid in S
environment according to 1990 UN figures, 93% of the forest area has been destroyed and about 100,000 species have been made extinct
head of state Albert Zafy from 1993

head of government Francisque Ravony from 1993

political system emergent democratic republic

exports coffee, cloves, vanilla, sugar, chromite, shrimps

currency Malagasy franc

population (1993 est) 13,000,000, mostly of Malayo-Indonesian origin; growth rate 3.2% p.a.

languages Malagasy (official), French, English

religion animist 50%, Christian 40%, Muslim 10%

GNP $254 per head (1992)

chronology

1885 Became a French protectorate.

1896 Became a French colony.

1960 Independence achieved from France, with Philibert Tsiranana as president.

1972 Army took control of the government.

1975 Martial law imposed under a national military directorate. New Marxist constitution proclaimed the Democratic Republic of Madagascar, with Didier Ratsiraka as president.

1976 Front-Line Revolutionary Organization (AREMA) formed.

1977 National Front for the Defence of the Malagasy Socialist Revolution (FNDR) became the sole legal political organization.

1980 Ratsiraka abandoned Marxist experiment.

1983 Ratsiraka re-elected, despite strong opposition from radical socialist National Movement for the Independence of Madagascar(MONIMA) under Monja Jaona.

1989 Ratsiraka re-elected for third term after restricting opposition parties.

1990 Political opposition legalized; 36 new parties created.

1991 Antigovernment demonstrations; opposition to Ratsiraka led to general strike. Nov: Ratsiraka formed new unity government.

1992 Constitutional reform approved.

1993 Albert Zafy, leader of coalition, elected president.

mad cow disease common name for *bovine spongiform encephalopathy, an incurable brain condition in cattle.

Madeira group of islands forming an autonomous region of Portugal off the NW coast of Africa, about 420 km/260 mi N of the Canary Islands. Madeira, the largest, and Porto Santo are the only inhabited islands. The Desertas and Selvagens are uninhabited islets. Their mild climate makes them a year-round resort

area 796 sq km/308 sq mi

capital Funchal, on Madeira

physical Pico Ruivo, on Madeira, is the highest mountain at 1,861 m/6,106 ft

products Madeira (a fortified wine), sugar cane, fruit, fish, handicrafts

population (1986) 269,500

history Portuguese from the 15th century; occupied by Britain 1801 and 1807–14. In 1980 Madeira gained partial autonomy but remains a Portuguese overseas territory.

Madeira River river of W Brazil; length 3,250 km/2,020 mi. It is formed by the rivers Beni and Mamoré, and flows NE to join the Amazon.

Madhya Pradesh state of central India; the largest of the Indian states

area 442,700 sq km/170,921 sq mi

capital Bhopal

towns Indore, Jabalpur, Gwalior, Durg-Bhilainagar, Raipur, Ujjain

products cotton, oilseed, sugar, textiles, engineering, paper, aluminium

population (1991) 66,135,400

language Hindi

history formed 1950 from the former British province of Central Provinces and Berar and the princely states of Makrai and Chattisgarh; lost some SW districts 1956, including *Nagpur, and absorbed Bhopal, Madhya Bharat, and Vindhya Pradesh. In 1984 some 2,600 people died in *Bhopal from an escape of poisonous gas.

Madison James 1751–1836. 4th president of the USA 1809–17. In 1787 he became a member of the Philadelphia Constitutional Convention and took a leading part in drawing up the US Constitution and the Bill of Rights. He allied himself firmly with Thomas *Jefferson against Alexander *Hamilton in the struggle between the more democratic views of Jefferson and the aristocratic, upper-class sentiments of Hamilton. As secretary of state in Jefferson's government 1801–09, Madison completed the *Louisiana Purchase negotiated by James Monroe. During his period of office the War of 1812 with Britain took place.

Madison Square Garden venue in New York, built as a boxing arena and also used for concerts. The current 'Garden' is the fourth to bear the name and staged its first boxing match 1968. It is situated over Pennsylvania Station on 7th Avenue, New York City and has a capacity of 20,000.

Madoc, Prince legendary prince of Gwynedd, Wales, supposed to have discovered the Americas and to have been an ancestor of a group of light-skinned, Welsh-speaking Indians in the American West.

Madonna Italian name for the Virgin *Mary, meaning 'my lady'.

Madonna Stage name of Madonna Louise Veronica Ciccone 1958– . US pop singer and actress who presents herself on stage and in videos with an exaggerated sexuality. Her first hit was 'Like a Virgin' 1984; others include 'Material Girl' 1985 and 'Like a Prayer' 1989. Her films include *Desperately Seeking Susan* 1985, *Dick Tracy* 1990, *In Bed with Madonna* 1991, and *A League of Their Own* 1992. Her book *Sex*, a collection of glossy, erotic photographs interspersed with explicit fantasies in the form of short stories, was published 1992, coinciding with the release of the dance album *Erotica*.

Madras industrial port (cotton, cement, chemicals, iron, and steel) and capital of Tamil Nadu, India, on the Bay of Bengal; population (1981) 4,277,000. Fort St George 1639 remains from the East India Company when Madras was the chief port on the east coast. Madras was occupied by the French 1746–48 and shelled by the German ship *Emden* 1914, the only place in India attacked in World War I.

Madrid industrial city (leather, chemicals, furniture, tobacco, paper) and capital of Spain and of Madrid province; population (1991) 2,984,600. Built on an elevated plateau in the centre of the country, at 655 m/2,183 ft it is the highest capital city in Europe and has excesses of heat and cold. Madrid province has an area of 8,000 sq km/

3,088 sq mi and a population of 4,855,000. Madrid began as a Moorish citadel captured from Castile 1083, became important in the times of Charles V and Philip II, and was designated capital 1561.

madrigal form of secular song in four or five parts, usually sung without instrumental accompaniment. It originated in 14th-century Italy. Madrigal composers include Giovanni Gabrieli (*c*. 1555–1612),Claudio *Monteverdi, Thomas *Morley, and Orlando Gibbons (1583–1625).

Maecenas Gaius Cilnius 69–8 BC. Roman patron of the arts who encouraged the work of *Horace and *Virgil.

maenad in Greek mythology, one of the women participants in the orgiastic rites of *Dionysus; maenads were also known as *Bacchae*.

Mafia (Italian 'swank') secret society reputed to control organized crime such as gambling, loan-sharking, drug traffic, prostitution, and protection; connected with the *Camorra of Naples. It originated in Sicily in the late Middle Ages and now operates chiefly there and in countries to which Italians have emigrated, such as the USA and Australia.

Magadha kingdom of ancient NE India, roughly corresponding to the middle and southern parts of modern *Bihar. It was the scene of many incidents in the life of Buddha and was the seat of the Maurya dynasty, founded in the 3rd century BC. Its capital Pataliputra was a great cultural and political centre.

magazine publication brought out periodically, typically containing articles, essays, short stories, reviews, and illustrations. The first magazine in the UK was the *Compleat Library* 1691. The US *Reader's Digest* 1922, with editions in many different countries and languages, was the world's best-selling magazine until overtaken by a Soviet journal in the mid-1980s.

Magdeburg industrial city (vehicles, paper, textiles, machinery) and capital of Saxony-Anhalt, Germany, on the river Elbe; population (1990) 290,000. A former capital of Saxony, Magdeburg became capital of Saxony-Anhalt on German reunification 1990. In 1938 the city was linked by canal with the Rhine and Ruhr rivers.

Magellan Ferdinand 1480–1521. Portuguese navigator. In 1519 he set sail in the *Victoria* from Seville with the intention of reaching the East Indies by a westerly route. He sailed through the *Magellan Strait* at the tip of South America, crossed an ocean he named the Pacific, and in 1521 reached the Philippines, where he was killed in a battle with the islanders. His companions returned to Seville 1522, completing the voyage under del *Cano.

Magellan NASA space probe to *Venus, launched May 1989; it went into orbit around Venus Aug 1990 to make a detailed map of the planet by radar. It revealed volcanoes, meteorite craters, and fold mountains on the planet's surface.

Magellanic Clouds in astronomy, the two galaxies nearest to our own galaxy. They are irregularly shaped, and appear as detached parts of the *Milky Way, in the southern constellations Dorado and Tucana.

maggot soft, plump, limbless larva of flies, a typical example being the larva of the blowfly which is deposited as an egg on flesh.

Maghreb name for NW Africa (Arabic 'far west', 'sunset'). The Maghreb powers – Algeria, Libya, Morocco, Tunisia, and Western Sahara – agreed on economic coordination 1964–65, with Mauritania cooperating from 1970. In 1989 these countries formed an economic union known as the Arab Maghreb Union. Chad and Mali are sometimes included. Compare *Mashraq, the Arab countries of the E Mediterranean.

magic art of controlling the forces of nature by supernatural means such as charms and ritual. The central ideas are that like produces like (*sympathetic magic*) and that influence carries by *contagion* or association; for example, by the former principle an enemy could be destroyed through an effigy, by the latter principle through personal items such as hair or nail clippings. See also *witchcraft.

magic bullet term sometimes used for a drug that is specifically targeted on certain cells or tissues in the body, such as a small collection of cancerous cells (see *cancer) or cells that have been invaded by a virus. Such drugs can be made in various ways, but *monoclonal antibodies are increasingly being used to direct the drug to a specific target.

magic realism in 20th-century literature, a fantastic situation realistically treated, as in the works of many Latin American writers such as Isabel Allende, Jorge Luis *Borges, and Gabriel *García Márquez.

magic square in mathematics, a square array of different numbers in which the rows, columns, and diagonals add up to the same total. A simple example employing the numbers 1 to 9, with a total of 15, is:

```
6 7 2
1 5 9
8 3 4
```

Maginot Line French fortification system along the German frontier from Switzerland to Luxembourg built 1929–36 under the direction of the war minister, André Maginot. It consisted of semi-underground forts joined by underground passages, and protected by antitank defences; lighter fortifications continued the line to the sea. In 1940 German forces pierced the Belgian frontier line and outflanked the Maginot Line.

magistrate in English law, a person who presides in a magistrates' court: either a justice of the peace (with no legal qualifications, and unpaid) or a stipendiary magistrate. Stipendiary magistrates are paid, qualified lawyers working mainly in London and major cities.

magistrates' court in England and Wales, a local law court that mainly deals with minor criminal cases. A magistrates' court consists of between two and seven lay justices of the peace (who are advised on the law by a clerk to the justices), or a single paid lawyer called a stipendiary magistrate.

maglev (acronym from *magnetic levitation*) high-speed surface transport using the repellent force of superconductive magnets (see *superconductivity) to propel and support, for

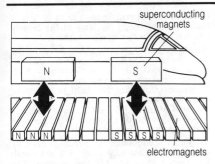

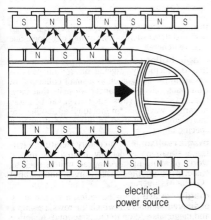

maglev The repulsion of superconducting magnets and electromagnets in the track keeps a maglev train suspended above the track.

example, a train above a track. Maglev trains have been developed in Japan, where a Tokyo–Osaka line was being planned 1990, and in Germany. A ship launched in Japan 1990 was to be fitted with superconducting thrusters instead of propellers for sea trials 1991.

magma molten rock material beneath the Earth's surface from which *igneous rocks are formed. *Lava is magma that has reached the surface and solidified, losing some of its components on the way.

magnesia common name for *magnesium oxide.

Magna Carta in English history, the charter granted by King John 1215, traditionally seen as guaranteeing human rights against the excessive use of royal power. As a reply to the king's demands for excessive feudal dues and attacks on the privileges of the church, Archbishop Langton proposed to the barons the drawing-up of a binding document 1213. John was forced to accept this at Runnymede (now in Surrey) 15 June 1215.

magnesium lightweight, very ductile and malleable, silver-white, metallic element, symbol Mg, atomic number 12, relative atomic mass 24.305. It is one of the *alkaline-earth metals, and the lightest of the commonly used metals. Magnesium silicate, carbonate, and chloride are widely distributed in nature. The metal is used in alloys and flash photography. It is a necessary trace element in the human diet, and green plants cannot grow without it since it is an essential constituent of chlorophyll ($C_{55}H_{72}MgN_4O_5$).

magnesium oxide or ***magnesia*** MgO white powder or colourless crystals, formed when magnesium is burned in air or oxygen; a typical basic oxide. It is used to treat acidity of the stomach, and in some industrial processes; for example, as a lining brick in furnaces, because it is very stable when heated (refractory oxide).

magnet any object that forms a magnetic field (displays *magnetism), either permanently or temporarily through induction, causing it to attract materials such as iron, cobalt, nickel, and alloys of these. It always has two *magnetic poles, called north and south.

magnetic field region around a permanent magnet, or around a conductor carrying an electric current, in which a force acts on a moving charge or on a magnet placed in the field. The field can be represented by lines of force, which by convention link north and south poles and are parallel to the directions of a small compass needle placed on them. A magnetic field's magnitude and direction are given by the *magnetic flux density, expressed in *teslas.

magnetic flux measurement of the strength of the magnetic field around electric currents and magnets. Its SI unit is the *weber; one weber per square metre is equal to one tesla.

magnetic pole region of a magnet in which its magnetic properties are strongest. Every magnet has two poles, called north and south. The north (or north-seeking) pole is so named because a freely suspended magnet will turn so that this pole points towards the Earth's magnetic north pole. The north pole of one magnet will be attracted to the south pole of another, but will be repelled by its north pole. Unlike poles may therefore be said to attract, like poles to repel.

magnetic resonance imaging (MRI) diagnostic scanning system based on the principles of nuclear magnetic resonance. MRI yields finely detailed three-dimensional images of structures within the body without exposing the patient to harmful radiation. The technique is invaluable for imaging the soft tissues of the body, such as the brain and the spinal cord.

magnetic storm in meteorology, a sudden disturbance affecting the Earth's magnetic field, causing anomalies in radio transmissions and magnetic compasses. It is probably caused by *sunspot activity.

magnetic tape narrow plastic ribbon coated with an easily magnetizable material on which data can be recorded. It is used in sound recording, audiovisual systems (videotape), and computing. For mass storage on commercial mainframe computers, large reel-to-reel tapes are still used, but for smaller mini- and microcomputers, tape cassettes and cartridges are more usual.

magnetism phenomena associated with *magnetic fields. Magnetic fields are produced by moving charged particles: in electromagnets, electrons flow through a coil of wire connected to a battery; in permanent magnets, spinning electrons within the atoms generate the field.

magnetite black iron ore, iron oxide (Fe_3O_4). Widely distributed, magnetite is found in nearly all igneous and metamorphic rocks. It is strongly magnetic and some deposits, called **lodestone**, are permanently magnetized. Lodestone has been used as a compass since the first millennium BC.

magnetosphere volume of space, surrounding a planet, controlled by the planet's magnetic field, and acting as a magnetic 'shell'. The Earth's magnetosphere extends 64,000 km/40,000 mi towards the Sun, but many times this distance on the side away from the Sun.

magnetron thermionic *valve (electron tube) for generating very high-frequency oscillations, used in radar and to produce microwaves in a microwave oven. The flow of electrons from the tube's cathode to one or more anodes is controlled by an applied magnetic field.

Magnificat in the New Testament, the song of praise sung by Mary, the mother of Jesus, on her visit to her cousin Elizabeth shortly after the Annunciation; it is used in the liturgy of some Christian churches.

magnification measure of the enlargement or reduction of an object in an imaging optical system. *Linear magnification* is the ratio of the size (height) of the image to that of the object. *Angular magnification* is the ratio of the angle subtended at the observer's eye by the image to the angle subtended by the object when viewed directly.

magnitude in astronomy, measure of the brightness of a star or other celestial object. The larger the number denoting the magnitude, the fainter the object. Zero or first magnitude indicates some of the brightest stars. Still brighter are those of negative magnitude, such as Sirius, whose magnitude is –1.46. *Apparent magnitude* is the brightness of an object as seen from Earth; *absolute magnitude* is the brightness at a standard distance of 10 parsecs (32.6 light years).

magnolia tree or shrub of the genus *Magnolia*, family Magnoliaceae, native to North America and E Asia. Magnolias vary in height from 60 cm/2 ft to 30 m/150 ft. The large, fragrant single flowers are white, rose, or purple. The southern magnolia *M. grandiflora* of the USA grows up to 24 m/80ft tall and has white flowers 23 cm/9 in across.

magnum opus (Latin) a great work of art or literature.

magpie any bird of a genus *Pica* in the crow family. It feeds on insects, snails, young birds, and carrion, and is found in Europe, Asia, N Africa, and W North America. The common magpie *p.pica* is about 45 cm 18 in long, and has black and white plumage, the long tail having a metallic gloss.

Magritte René 1898–1967. Belgian Surrealist painter whose paintings focus on visual paradoxes and everyday objects taken out of context. Recurring motifs include bowler hats, apples, and windows, for example *Golconda* 1953 where men in bowler hats are falling from the sky to a street below.

Maguire Seven seven Irish victims of a British

magnolia *In the magnolia's large flowers, the sepals are often indistinguishable from the petals and leaves.*

miscarriage of justice. In 1976 Annie Maguire, five members of her family, and a family friend were imprisoned in London for possessing explosives. All the convictions were overturned June 1991.

magus (plural *magi*) priest of the Zoroastrian religion of ancient Persia, noted for their knowledge of astrology. The term is used in the New Testament of the Latin Vulgate Bible where the Authorized Version gives 'wise men'. The magi who came to visit the infant Jesus with gifts of gold, frankincense, and myrrh (the *Adoration of the Magi*) were in later tradition described as 'the three kings' – Caspar, Melchior, and Balthazar.

Magyar member of the largest ethnic group in Hungary, comprising 92% of the population. Magyars are of mixed Ugric and Turkic origin, and they arrived in Hungary towards the end of the 9th century. The Magyar language (see *Hungarian language) belongs to the Uralic group.

Mahabad Kurdish town in Azerbaijan, W Iran, population (1983) 63,000. Occupied by Russian troops 1941, it formed the centre of a short-lived republic (1945–46) before being reoccupied by the Iranians. In the 1980s Mahabad was the focal point of resistance by Iranian Kurds against the Islamic republic.

Mahābhārata (Sanskrit 'great poem of the Bharatas') Sanskrit Hindu epic consisting of 18 books and 90,000 stanzas, probably composed in its present form about 300 BC. It forms with the *Rāmāyana* the two great epics of the Hindus. It contains the *Bhagavad-Gītā*, or *Song of the Blessed*, an episode in the sixth book.

Mahādeva (Sanskrit 'great god') title given to the Hindu god *Siva.

Mahādevī (Sanskrit 'great goddess') title given to Sakti, the consort of the Hindu god Siva. She is worshipped in many forms, including her more active manifestations as Kali or Durga and her peaceful form as Parvati.

Maharashtra state in W central India
area 307,800 sq km/118,811 sq mi
capital Bombay
towns Pune, Nagpur, Ulhasnagar, Sholapur, Nasik, Thana, Kolhapur, Aurangabad, Sangli, Amravati

products cotton, rice, groundnuts, sugar, minerals
population (1991) 78,706,700
language Marathi 50%
religions Hindu 80%, Parsee, Jain, and Sikh minorities
history formed 1960 from the southern part of the former Bombay state.

maharishi (Sanskrit *mahā* 'great', *rishi* 'sage') Hindu guru (teacher), or spiritual leader. The Maharishi Mahesh Yogi influenced the Beatles and other Westerners in the 1960s.

mahatma (Sanskrit 'great soul') title conferred on Mohandas K *Gandhi by his followers as the first great national Indian leader.

Mahāyāna (Sanskrit 'greater vehicle') one of the two major forms of *Buddhism, common in N Asia (China, Korea, Japan, and Tibet). Veneration of bodhisattvas (those who achieve enlightenment but remain on the human plane in order to help other living beings) is a fundamental belief in Mahāyāna, as is the idea that everyone has within them the seeds of Buddhahood.

Mahdi (Arabic 'he who is guided aright') in Islam, the title of a coming messiah who will establish a reign of justice on Earth. The title has been assumed by many Muslim leaders, notably the Sudanese sheik Muhammad Ahmed (1848–1885), who headed a revolt 1881 against Egypt and 1885 captured Khartoum.

Mahfouz Naguib 1911– . Egyptian novelist and playwright. His novels, which deal with the urban working class, include the semi-autobiographical *Khan al-Kasrain/The Cairo Trilogy* 1956–57. His *Children of Gebelawi* 1959 was banned in Egypt because of its treatment of religious themes. Nobel Prize for Literature 1988.

mah-jong or **mah-jongg** originally an ancient Chinese card game, dating from the Song dynasty 960–1279. It is now usually played by four people with 144 small ivory tiles, divided into six suits.

Mahler Gustav 1860–1911. Austrian composer and conductor whose work displays a synthesis of Romanticism and new uses of chromatic harmonies and musical forms. He composed 14 symphonies, including three unnumbered (as a student), nine massive repertoire symphonies, the titled *Das Lied von der Erde/Song of the Earth* 1909, and the incomplete *Symphony No. 10.* He also wrote song cycles.

Mahmud I 1696–1754. Ottoman sultan from 1730. After restoring order to the empire in Istanbul 1730, he suppressed the *Janissary rebellion 1731 and waged war against Persia 1731–46. He led successful wars against Austria and Russia, concluded by the Treaty of Belgrade 1739. He was a patron of the arts and also carried out reform of the army.

Mahmud II 1785–1839. Ottoman sultan from 1808 who attempted to westernize the declining empire, carrying out a series of far-reaching reforms in the civil service and army. The pressure for Greek independence after 1821 led to conflict with Britain, France, and Russia, and he was forced to recognize Greek independence 1830.

mahogany timber from any of several genera of trees found in the Americas and Africa. Mahogany is a tropical hardwood obtained chiefly by rainforest logging. It has a warm red colour and takes a high polish.

mahratta another name for *Maratha, a people of W India.

maidenhair any fern of the genus *Adiantum*, especially *A. capillus-veneris*, with hairlike fronds terminating in small kidney-shaped, spore-bearing pinnules. It is widely distributed in the Americas, and is sometimes found in the British Isles.

maidenhair tree another name for *ginkgo, a surviving member of an ancient group of gymnosperms.

Mailer Norman 1923– . US writer and journalist. He gained wide attention with his novel of World War II *The Naked and the Dead* 1948. A commentator on the US social, literary, and political scene, he has run for mayor of New York City.

Maimonides Moses (Moses Ben Maimon) 1135–1204. Jewish rabbi and philosopher, born in Córdoba, Spain. Known as one of the greatest Hebrew scholars, he attempted to reconcile faith and reason.

Maine northeasternmost state of the USA, largest of the New England states; nickname Pine Tree State
area 86,200 sq km/33,273 sq mi
capital Augusta
towns Portland, Lewiston, Bangor
physical Appalachian Mountains; 80% of the state is forested
products dairy and market garden produce, paper, pulp, timber, footwear, textiles, fish, lobster; tourism is important
population (1990) 1,228,000
famous people Henry Wadsworth Longfellow, Kate Douglas Wiggin, Edward Arlington Robinson, Edna St Vincent Millay
history permanently settled by the British from 1623; absorbed by Massachusetts 1691; became a state 1820.

mainframe large computer used for commercial data processing and other large-scale operations. Because of the general increase in computing power, the differences between the mainframe, *supercomputer, *minicomputer, and *microcomputer (personal computer) are becoming less marked.

maintenance in law, payments to support children or a spouse, under the terms of an agreement, or by a court order. In Britain, financial provision orders are made on divorce, but a court action can also be brought for maintenance without divorce proceedings. Applications for maintenance of illegitimate children are now treated in the same way as for legitimate children.

Maintenon Françoise d'Aubigné, Marquise de 1635–1719. Second wife of Louis XIV of France from 1684, and widow of the writer Paul Scarron (1610–1660). She was governess to the children of Mme de Montespan by Louis, and his mistress from 1667. She secretly married the king after the death of Queen Marie Thérèse 1683. Her political influence was considerable and, as a Catholic convert from Protestantism, her religious opinions were zealous.

Maitreya the Buddha to come, 'the kindly one', a principal figure in all forms of Buddhism; he is known as *Mi-lo-fo* in China and *Miroku* in Japan. Buddhists believe that a Buddha appears from time to time to maintain knowledge of the true path; Maitreya is the next future Buddha.

maize (North American *corn*) plant *Zea mays* of the grass family. Grown extensively in all subtropical and warm temperate regions, its range has been extended to colder zones by hardy varieties developed in the 1960s. It is widely used as animal feed.

majolica or *maiolica* tin-glazed *earthenware and the richly decorated enamel pottery produced in Italy in the 15th to 18th centuries. The name derives from the Italian form of Majorca, the island from where Moorish lustreware made in Spain was shipped to Italy. During the 19th century the word was used to describe moulded earthenware with relief patterns decorated in coloured glazes.

Major John 1943– . British Conservative politician, prime minister from Nov 1990. He was foreign secretary 1989 and chancellor of the Exchequer 1989–90. His earlier positive approach to European Community matters was hindered during 1991 by divisions within the Conservative Party. Despite continuing public dissatisfaction with the poll tax, the National Health Service, and the recession, Major was returned to power in the April 1992 general election. His subsequent handling of a series of political crises called into question his ability to govern the country effectively.

Majorca (Spanish *Mallorca*) largest of the *Balearic Islands, belonging to Spain, in the W Mediterranean
area 3,640 sq km/1,405 sq mi
capital Palma
products olives, figs, oranges, wine, brandy, timber, sheep; tourism is the mainstay of the economy
population (1981) 561,215
history captured 797 by the Moors, it became the kingdom of Majorca 1276, and was united with Aragon 1343.

Makarios III 1913–1977. Cypriot politician, Greek Orthodox archbishop 1950–77. A leader of the Resistance organization *EOKA, he was exiled by the British to the Seychelles 1956–57 for supporting armed action to achieve union with Greece (*enosis*). He was president of the republic of Cyprus 1960–77 (briefly deposed by a Greek military coup July–Dec 1974).

Makua member of a people living to the north of the Zambezi River in Mozambique. With the Lomwe people, they make up the country's largest ethnic group. The Makua are mainly farmers, living in villages ruled by chiefs. The Makua language belongs to the Niger-Congo family, and has about 5 million speakers.

Malabo port and capital of Equatorial Guinea, on the island of Bioko; population (1983) 15,253. It was founded in the 1820s by the British as *Port Clarence*. Under Spanish rule it was known as *Santa Isabel* (until 1973).

Malacca or *Melaka* state of W Peninsular Malaysia; capital Malacca; area 1,700 sq km/ 656 sq mi; products include rubber, tin, and wire; population (1980) 465,000 (about 70% Chinese). The town originated in the 13th century as a fishing village frequented by pirates, and later

developed into a trading port. Portuguese from 1511, then Dutch from 1641, it was ceded to Britain 1824, becoming part of the Straits Settlements.

malachite common *copper ore, basic copper carbonate, $Cu_2CO_3(OH)_2$. It is a source of green pigment and is polished for use in jewellery, ornaments, and art objects.

Málaga industrial seaport (sugar refining, distilling, brewing, olive-oil pressing, shipbuilding) and holiday resort in Andalusia, Spain; capital of Málaga province on the Mediterranean; population (1991) 524,800. Founded by the Phoenicians and taken by the Moors 711, Málaga was capital of the Moorish kingdom of Malaga from the 13th century until captured 1487 by the Catholic monarchs Ferdinand and Isabella.

Malagasy inhabitant of or native to Madagascar. The Malagasy language has about 9 million speakers; it belongs to the Austronesian family.

Malamud Bernard 1914–1986. US novelist and short-story writer. He first attracted attention with *The Natural* 1952, making a professional baseball player his hero. Later novels, often dealing with the Jewish immigrant tradition, include *The Assistant* 1957, *The Fixer* 1966, *Dubin's Lives* 1979, and *God's Grace* 1982.

malapropism amusing slip of the tongue, arising from the confusion of similar-sounding words. The term derives from the French *mal à propos* (inappropriate); historically, it is associated with Mrs Malaprop, a character in Sheridan's play *The Rivals* 1775, who was the pineapple (pinnacle) of perfection in such matters.

malaria infectious parasitic disease of the tropics transmitted by mosquitoes, marked by periodic fever and an enlarged spleen. When a female mosquito of the *Anopheles* genus bites a human who has malaria, it takes in with the human blood one of four malaria protozoa of the genus *Plasmodium*. This matures within the insect and is then transferred when the mosquito bites a new victim. Malaria affects some 200 million people a year on a recurring basis.

Malatya capital of a province of the same name in E central Turkey, lying west of the river Euphrates; population (1990) 281,800.

Malawi Republic of (*Malaŵi*)

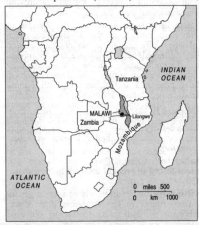

area 118,000 sq km/45,560 sq mi
capital Lilongwe
towns Blantyre (largest city and commercial centre), Mzuzu, Zomba
physical landlocked narrow plateau with rolling plains; mountainous W of Lake Malawi
head of state and government Bakili Muluzi from 1994
political system emergent democratic republic
exports tea, tobacco, cotton, peanuts, sugar
currency kwacha
population (1993 est) 9,700,000 (nearly 1 million refugees from Mozambique); growth rate 3.3% p.a.
languages English, Chichewa (both official)
religions Christian 75%, Muslim 20%
GNP $230 per head (1991)
chronology
1891 Became the British protectorate Nyasaland.
1964 Independence achieved from Britain, within the Commonwealth, as Malawi.
1966 Became a one-party republic, with Hastings Banda as president.
1971 Banda was made president for life.
1970s Reports of human-rights violations and murder of Banda's opponents.
1986–89 Influx of nearly a million refugees from Mozambique.
1992 Calls for multiparty politics. Countrywide industrial riots caused many fatalities. Western aid suspended over human-rights violations.
1993 Multiparty system introduced.
1994 Bakili Muluzi elected president in first free elections for 30 years.

Malawi, Lake or **Lake Nyasa** African lake, bordered by Malawi, Tanzania, and Mozambique, formed in a section of the Great *Rift Valley. It is about 500 m/1,650 ft above sea level and 560 km/350 mi long, with an area of 37,000 sq km/14,280 sq mi.

Malay member of a large group of peoples, comprising the majority population of the Malay Peninsula and Archipelago, and also found in S Thailand and coastal Sumatra and Borneo.

Malayalam southern Indian language, the official language of the state of Kerala. Malayalam is closely related to Tamil, also a member of the Dravidian language family; it is spoken by about 20 million people. Written records in Malayalam date from the 9th century AD.

Malay language member of the Western or Indonesian branch of the Malayo-Polynesian language family, used in the Malay peninsula and many of the islands of Malaysia and Indonesia. The Malay language can be written in either Arabic or Roman scripts. The dialect of the S Malay peninsula is the basis of both Bahasa Malaysia and Bahasa Indonesia, the official languages of Malaysia and Indonesia. Bazaar Malay is a pidgin variety used for trading and shopping.

Malayo-Polynesian family of languages spoken in Malaysia, better known as *Austronesian*.

Malaysia
area 329,759 sq km/127,287 sq mi
capital Kuala Lumpur
towns Johor Baharu, Ipoh, Georgetown (Penang), Kuching in Sarawak, Kota Kinabalu in Sabah

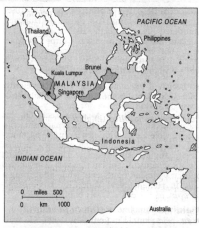

physical comprises Peninsular Malaysia (the nine Malay states – Johore, Kedah, Kelantan, Negri Sembilan, Pahang, Perak, Perlis, Selangor, Trengganu – plus Malacca and Penang); and E Malaysia (Sabah and Sarawak); 75% tropical jungle; central mountain range; swamps in E
head of state Jaafar bin Abd al-Rahman from 1994
head of government Mahathir bin Mohamad from 1981
political system liberal democracy
exports pineapples, palm oil, rubber, timber, petroleum (Sarawak), bauxite
currency ringgit
population (1993 est) 19,030,000 (Malaysian 47%, Chinese 32%, Indian 8%, others 13%); growth rate 2% p.a.
languages Malay (official), English, Chinese, Indian, and local languages
religions Muslim (official), Buddhist, Hindu, local beliefs
GNP $3,265 per head (1993)
chronology
1786 Britain established control.
1826 Became a British colony.
1963 Federation of Malaysia formed, including Malaya, Singapore, Sabah (N Borneo), and Sarawak (NW Borneo).
1965 Secession of Singapore from federation.
1969 Anti-Chinese riots in Kuala Lumpur.
1971 Launch of *bumiputra* ethnic-Malay-oriented economic policy.
1981 Election of Dr Mahathir bin Mohamad as prime minister.
1982 Mahathir bin Mohamad re-elected.
1986 Mahathir bin Mohamad re-elected.
1987 Arrest of over 100 opposition activists, including DAP leader, as Malay-Chinese relations deteriorated.
1988 Split in ruling UMNO party over Mahathir's leadership style; new UMNO formed.
1989 Semangat '46 set up by former members of UMNO including ex-premier Tunku Abdul Rahman.
1990 Mahathir bin Mohamad re-elected.
1991 New economic growth programme launched.

Malcolm four kings of Scotland, including:

Malcolm III called *Canmore* c. 1031–1093. King of Scotland from 1058, the son of Duncan I (murdered by *Macbeth 1040). He fled to England when the throne was usurped by Macbeth, but recovered S Scotland and killed Macbeth in battle 1057. He was killed at Alnwick while invading Northumberland, England.

Malcolm X assumed name of Malcolm Little 1926–1965. US black nationalist leader. While serving a prison sentence for burglary 1946–53, he joined the *Black Muslims sect. On his release he campaigned for black separatism, condoning violence in self-defence, but 1964 modified his views to found the Islamic, socialist Organization of Afro-American Unity, preaching racial solidarity. A year later he was assassinated by Black Muslim opponents while addressing a rally in Harlem, New York City. His *Autobiography of Malcolm X* was published 1964.

Maldives Republic of (*Divehi Jumhuriya*)
area 298 sq km/115 sq mi
capital Malé
towns Seenu
physical comprises 1,196 coral islands, grouped into 12 clusters of atolls, largely flat, none bigger than 13 sq km/5 sq mi, average elevation 1.8 m/6 ft; 203 are inhabited
environment the threat of rising sea level has been heightened by the frequency of flooding in recent years
head of state and government Maumoon Abdul Gayoom from 1978
political system authoritarian nationalism
exports coconuts, copra, bonito (fish related to tuna), garments
currency rufiya
population (1993 est) 238,400; growth rate 3.7% p.a.
languages Divehi (Sinhalese dialect), English
religion Sunni Muslim
GNP $460 per head (1991)
chronology
1887 Became a British protectorate.
1953 Long a sultanate, the Maldive Islands became a republic within the Commonwealth.
1954 Sultan restored.
1965 Achieved full independence outside the Commonwealth.
1968 Sultan deposed; republic reinstated with Ibrahim Nasir as president.
1978 Nasir retired; replaced by Maumoon Abdul Gayoom.
1982 Rejoined the Commonwealth.
1983 Gayoom re-elected.
1985 Became a founder member of South Asian Association for Regional Cooperation.
1988 Gayoom re-elected. Coup attempt by mercenaries thought to have the backing of former president Nasir was foiled by Indian paratroops.

Maldon English market town in Essex, at the mouth of the river Chelmer; population (1981) 14,750.

Malé capital of the Maldives in the Indian Ocean; population (1990) 55,100. It trades in copra, breadfruit, and palm products; it is also a tourist centre.

Malevich Kasimir 1878–1935. Russian abstract painter. In 1912 he visited Paris and became a Cubist, and 1913 he launched his own abstract movement, *Suprematism*. Later he returned to figurative themes treated in a semi-abstract style.

Mali Republic of (*République du Mali*)

area 1,240,142 sq km/478,695 sq mi
capital Bamako
towns Mopti, Kayes, Ségou, Timbuktu
physical landlocked state with river Niger and savanna in S; part of the Sahara in N; hills in NE; Senegal River and its branches irrigate the SW
environment a rising population coupled with recent droughts has affected marginal agriculture. Once in surplus, Mali has had to import grain every year since 1965
head of state and government Alpha Oumar Konare from 1992
political system emergent democratic republic
exports cotton, peanuts, livestock, fish
currency franc CFA
population (1993 est) 8,750,000; growth rate 2.9% p.a.
languages French (official), Bambara
religion Sunni Muslim 90%, animist 9%, Christian 1%
GNP $280 per head (1991)
chronology
1895 Came under French rule.
1959 With Senegal, formed the Federation of Mali.
1960 Became the independent Republic of Mali, with Modibo Keita as president.
1968 Keita replaced in an army coup by Moussa Traoré.
1974 New constitution made Mali a one-party state.
1976 New national party, the Malian People's Democratic Union, announced.
1983 Agreement between Mali and Guinea for eventual political and economic integration signed.
1985 Conflict with Burkina Faso lasted five days mediated by International Court of Justice.
1991 Demonstrations against one-party rule. Moussa Traoré ousted in a coup led by Lt-Col Amadou Toumani Toure. New constitution agreed, subject to referendum.
1992 Referendum endorsed new democratic constitution. Alliance for Democracy in Mali (ADEMA) won multiparty elections; Alpha Oumar Konare elected president.

malic acid $COOHCH_2CH(OH)COOH$ organic crystalline acid that can be extracted from apples plums, cherries, grapes, and other fruits, but occurs in all living cells in smaller amounts, being one of the intermediates of the *Krebs cycle.

Mali Empire Muslim state in NW Africa during the 7th–15th centuries. Thriving on its trade in gold, it reached its peak in the 14th century under Mansa Musa (reigned 1312–37), when it occupied an area covering present-day Senegal, Gambia, Mali, and S Mauritania. Mali's territory was similar to (though larger than) that of the Ghana Empire (see *Ghana, ancient), and gave way in turn to the *Songhai Empire.

Malinowski Bronislaw 1884–1942. Polish-born British anthropologist, one of the founders of the theory of functionalism in the social sciences. His classic study of the peoples of the Trobriand Islands led him to see customs and practices in terms of their function in creating and maintaining social order.

mallard common wild duck *Anas platyrhynchos*, found almost worldwide, from which domestic ducks were bred. The male, which can grow to a length of 60 cm/2 ft, usually has a green head and brown breast, while the female is mottled brown. Mallards are omnivorous, dabbling ducks.

Mallarmé Stéphane 1842–1898. French poet who founded the Symbolist school with Paul Verlaine. His belief that poetry should be evocative and suggestive was reflected in *L'Après-midi d'un faune/Afternoon of a Faun* 1876, which inspired the composer Debussy.

Malle Louis 1932– . French film director. After a period as assistant to director Robert Bresson, he directed *Les Amants/The Lovers* 1958, audacious for its time in its explicitness. His subsequent films, made in France and the USA, include *Zazie dans le métro* 1961, *Viva Maria* 1965, *Pretty Baby* 1978, *Atlantic City* 1980, *Au Revoir les enfants* 1988, and *Milou en mai* 1989.

Mallorca Spanish form of *Majorca, an island in the Mediterranean.

mallow any flowering plant of the family Malvaceae, especially of the genus *Malva*, including the European common mallow *M. sylvestris*; the tree mallow *Lavatera arborea*; and the marsh mallow *Althaea officinalis*. The *hollyhock is of the mallow family. Most mallows have pink or purple flowers.

Malmö industrial port (shipbuilding, engineering, textiles) in SW Sweden, situated across the Öresund from Copenhagen, Denmark; population (1990) 233,900. Founded in the 12th century, Malmö is Sweden's third largest city.

malnutrition condition resulting from a defective diet where certain important food nutrients (such as protein, vitamins, or carbohydrates) are absent. It can lead to deficiency diseases. A related problem is undernourishment, resulting from an insufficient diet; when this affects large numbers of people it is a *famine.

Malory Thomas 15th century. English author of the prose romance *Le Morte d'Arthur* about 1470. It is a translation from the French, modified by material from other sources, and it deals with the exploits of King Arthur's knights of the Round Table and the quest for the *Holy Grail.

Malpighi Marcello 1628–1694. Italian physiologist who made many anatomical discoveries

(still known by his name) in his microscope studies of animals and plants.

malpractice in law, *negligence by a professional person, usually a doctor, that may lead to an action for damages by the client. Such legal actions result in doctors having high insurance costs that are reflected in higher fees charged to their patients.

Malraux André 1901–1976. French writer. An active antifascist, he gained international renown for his novel *La Condition humaine/Man's Estate* 1933, set during the Nationalist/Communist Revolution in China in the 1920s. *L'Espoir/Days of Hope* 1937 is set in Civil War Spain, where he was a bomber pilot in the International Brigade. In World War II he supported the Gaullist resistance, and was minister of cultural affairs 1960–69.

malt in brewing, grain (barley, oats, or wheat) artificially germinated and then dried in a kiln. Malts are fermented to make beers or lagers, or fermented and then distilled to produce spirits such as whisky.

Malta Republic of (*Repubblika Ta'Malta*)

area 320 sq km/124 sq mi
capital and port Valletta
towns Rabat; port of Marsaxlokk
physical includes islands of Gozo 67 sq km/26 sq mi and Comino 2.5 sq km/1 sq mi
head of state Mifsud Bonnici from 1994
head of government Edward Fenech Adami from 1987
political system liberal democracy
currency Maltese lira
population (1993) 364,600; growth rate 0.7% p.a.
languages Maltese, English
religion Roman Catholic 98%
GNP $7,341 per head (1991)
chronology
1814 Annexed to Britain by the Treaty of Paris.
1947 Achieved self-government.
1955 Dom Mintoff of the Malta Labour Party (MLP) became prime minister.
1956 Referendum approved MLP's proposal for integration with the UK. Proposal opposed by the Nationalist Party.
1958 MLP rejected the British integration proposal.

1962 Nationalists elected, with Borg Olivier as prime minister.

1964 Independence achieved from Britain, within the Commonwealth.

1971 Mintoff re-elected. 1964 treaty declared invalid and negotiations began for leasing the NATO base in Malta.

1972 Seven-year NATO agreement signed.

1974 Became a republic.

1979 British military base closed.

1984 Mintoff retired and was replaced by Mifsud Bonnici as prime minister and MLP leader.

1987 Edward Fenech Adami (Nationalist) elected prime minister.

1989 Vincent Tabone elected president.

1990 Formal application made for European Community membership.

1992 Nationalist Party returned to power in general election.

1994 Mifsud Bonnici elected president.

Malta, Knights of another name for members of the military-religious order of the Hospital of *St John of Jerusalem.

Malthus Thomas Robert 1766–1834. English economist and cleric. His *Essay on the Principle of Population* 1798 (revised 1803) argued for population control, since populations increase in geometric ratio and food supply only in arithmetic ratio, and influenced Charles *Darwin's thinking on natural selection as the driving force of evolution.

Malthus theory projection of population growth made by Thomas Malthus. He based his theory on the *population explosion that was already becoming evident in the 18th century, and argued that the number of people would increase faster than the food supply. Population would eventually reach a resource limit (overpopulation). Any further increase would result in a population crash, caused by famine, disease, or war.

maltose $C_{12}H_{22}O_{11}$ a *disaccharide sugar in which both monosaccharide units are glucose.

Maluku or *Moluccas* group of Indonesian islands

area 74,500 sq km/28,764 sq mi

capital Ambon, on Amboina

population (1989 est) 1,814,000

history as the Spice Islands, they were formerly part of the Netherlands East Indies, and the S Moluccas attempted secession from the newly created Indonesian republic from 1949; exiles continue agitation in the Netherlands.

Malvinas Argentine name for the *Falkland Islands.

mamba one of two venomous snakes, genus *Dendroaspis*, of the cobra family Elapidae, found in Africa south of the Sahara. Unlike cobras, they are not hooded.

Mameluke member of a powerful political class that dominated Egypt from the 13th century until their massacre 1811 by Mehemet Ali.

Mamet David 1947– . US playwright. His plays, with their vivid, freewheeling language and sense of ordinary US life, include *American Buffalo* 1977, *Sexual Perversity in Chicago* 1978, *Glengarry Glen Ross* 1984, and *Oleanna* 1992.

mammal any vertebrate that suckles its young and has hair. Mammals maintain a constant body temperature in varied surroundings. Most mammals give birth to live young, but the platypus and echidna lay eggs. There are over 4,000 species, adapted to almost every way of life. The smallest shrew weighs only 2 g/0.07 oz, the largest whale up to 140 tonnes.

mammary gland in female mammals, a milk-producing gland derived from epithelial cells underlying the skin, active only after the production of young. In all but monotremes (egg-laying mammals), the mammary glands terminate in teats which aid infant suckling. The number of glands and their position vary between species. In humans there are two, in cows four, and in pigs between ten and fourteen.

mammography X-ray procedure used to screen for breast cancer. It can detect abnormal growths at an early stage, before they can be seen or felt.

Mammon evil personification of wealth and greed; originally a Syrian god of riches, cited in the New Testament as opposed to the Christian god.

mammoth extinct elephant of the genus *Mammuthus*, whose remains are found worldwide. Some were 50% taller than modern elephants.

Man, Isle of island in the Irish Sea, a dependency of the British crown, but not part of the UK

area 570 sq km/220 sq mi

capital Douglas

towns Ramsey, Peel, Castletown

features Snaefell 620 m/2,035 ft; annual TT (Tourist Trophy) motorcycle races, gambling casinos, Britain's first free port, tax haven; tailless Manx cat

products light engineering products; tourism, banking, and insurance are important

currency the island produces its own coins and notes in UK currency denominations

population (1986) 64,300

language English (Manx, nearer to Scottish than Irish Gaelic, has been almost extinct since the 1970s)

government crown-appointed lieutenant-governor, a legislative council, and the representative House of Keys, which together make up the Court of Tynwald, passing laws subject to the royal assent. Laws passed at Westminster only affect the island if specifically so provided

history Norwegian until 1266, when it was ceded to Scotland; it came under UK administration 1765.

Managua capital and chief industrial city of Nicaragua, on the lake of the same name; population (1985) 682,000. It has twice been destroyed by earthquake and rebuilt, 1931 and 1972; it was also badly damaged during the civil war in the late 1970s.

Manama (Arabic *Al Manamah*) capital and free trade port of Bahrain, on Bahrain Island; population (1988) 152,000. It handles oil and entrepôt trade.

manatee any plant-eating aquatic mammal of the genus *Trichechus* constituting the family Trichechidae in the order Sirenia (sea cows). Manatees occur in marine bays and sluggish rivers, usually in turbid water.

Manaus capital of Amazonas, Brazil, on the

Rio Negro, near its confluence with the Amazon; population (1991) 996,700. It can be reached by sea-going vessels, although it is 1,600 km/1,000 mi from the Atlantic. Formerly a centre of the rubber trade, it developed as a tourist centre in the 1970s.

Manchester city in NW England, on the river Irwell, 50 km/31 mi E of Liverpool. It is a manufacturing (textile machinery, chemicals, rubber, processed foods) and financial centre; population (1991) 397,400. It is linked by the Manchester Ship Canal, built 1894, to the river Mersey and the sea.

Manchester, Greater metropolitan county (1974–86) of NW England, replaced by a residuary body 1986 that covers some of its former functions

area 1,290 sq km/498 sq mi

towns Manchester, Bolton, Oldham, Rochdale, Salford, Stockport, and Wigan

features Manchester Ship Canal links it with the river Mersey and the sea; Old Trafford cricket ground at Stretford, and the football ground of Manchester United

products industrial

population (1991) 2,455,200

famous people John Dalton, James Joule, Emmeline Pankhurst, Gracie Fields, Anthony Burgess.

Manchu or *Qing* last ruling dynasty in China, from 1644 until its overthrow 1912; its last emperor was the infant *P'u-i. Originally a nomadic people from Manchuria, they established power through a series of successful invasions from the north, then granted trading rights to the USA and Europeans, which eventually brought strife and the *Boxer Rebellion.

Manchukuo former Japanese puppet state in Manchuria and Jehol 1932–45, ruled by the former Chinese emperor Henry *P'u-i.

Manchuria European name for the NE region of China, comprising the provinces of Heilongjiang, Jilin, and Liaoning. It was united with China by the Manchu dynasty 1644, but as the Chinese Empire declined, Japan and Russia were rivals for its control. The Russians were expelled after the *Russo-Japanese War 1904–05, and in 1932 Japan consolidated its position by creating a puppet state, *Manchukuo*, which disintegrated on the defeat of Japan in World War II.

Mandalay chief town of the Mandalay division of Myanmar (formerly Burma), on the river Irrawaddy, about 495 km/370 mi N of Yangon (Rangoon); population (1983) 533,000.

mandarin variety of the tangerine *orange *Citrus reticulata.*

Mandarin standard form of the *Chinese language. Historically it derives from the language spoken by *mandarins*, Chinese imperial officials, from the 7th century onwards. It is used by 70% of the population and taught in schools of the People's Republic of China.

mandate in history, a territory whose administration was entrusted to Allied states by the League of Nations under the Treaty of Versailles after World War I. Mandated territories were former German and Turkish possessions (including Iraq, Syria, Lebanon, and Palestine). When the United Nations replaced the League of Nations 1945, mandates that had not gained independence were dubbed *trust territories.

Mandela Nelson (Rolihlahla) 1918– . South African politician, president of South Africa from 1994. As organizer of the then banned *African National Congress (ANC), he was imprisoned 1964. In prison he became a symbol of unity for the worldwide anti-apartheid movement. After the lifting of the ANC ban he was released Feb 1990 and entered into negotiations with the government about a multiracial future for South Africa. The first free, nonracial elections were held April 1994, which the ANC and Mandela won, thus ending the era of apartheid. He was awarded the Nobel Prize for Peace (jointly with de Klerk) 1993.

Mandela Winnie (Nomzamo) 1934– . Civil-rights activist in South Africa and former wife of Nelson Mandela 1955–92. A leading spokesperson for the African National Congress during her husband's imprisonment 1964–90, she was jailed for a year and put under house arrest several times. In 1989 she was involved in the abduction of four youths, one of whom, Stompie Seipei, was later murdered. Winnie Mandela was convicted of kidnapping and assault, but her sentence was waived 1993. She was made deputy arts and science minister in the new government 1994. She was dismissed 1995 following allegations of dereliction of duty.

Mandelshtam Osip Emilevich 1891–1938. Russian poet. Son of a Jewish merchant, he was sent to a concentration camp by the communist authorities in the 1930s, and died there. His posthumously published work, with its classic brevity, established his reputation as one of the greatest 20th-century Russian poets.

mandolin musical instrument with four or five pairs of strings, tuned like a violin. It takes its name from its almond-shaped body (Italian *mandorla* 'almond').

mandragora or *mandrake* plant of the Old World genus *Mandragora* of almost stemless plants with narcotic properties, of the nightshade family Solanaceae. They have large leaves, pale blue or violet flowers, and globose berries known as devil's apples.

mandrake another name for the plant mandragora.

mandrill large W African forest-living baboon *Mandrillus sphinx*, most active on the ground. It has large canine teeth like the drill *M. leucophaeus*, to which it is closely related. The nose is bright red and the cheeks striped with blue. There are red callosities on the buttocks; the fur is brown, apart from a yellow beard.

Manet Edouard 1832–1883. French painter, active in Paris. Rebelling against the academic tradition, he developed a clear and unaffected Realist style. His subjects were mainly contemporary, such as *Un Bar aux Folies-Bergère/A Bar at the Folies-Bergère* 1882.

manganese hard, brittle, grey-white metallic element, symbol Mn, atomic number 25, relative atomic mass 54.9380. It resembles iron (and rusts), but it is not magnetic and is softer. It is used chiefly in making steel alloys, also alloys with aluminium and copper. It is used in fertilizers, paints, and industrial chemicals. It is a necessary trace element in human nutrition. The name is old, deriving from the French and Italian forms of Latin for *magnesia* (MgO), the white tasteless powder used as an antacid from ancient times.

manganese ore any mineral from which manganese is produced. The main ores are the oxides, such as *pyrolusite*, MnO_2; *hausmannite*, Mn_3O_4; and *manganite*, MnO(OH).

mangelwurzel or *mangold* variety of the common beet *Beta vulgaris* used chiefly as feed for cattle and sheep.

mango evergreen tree *Mangifera indica* of the cashew family Anacardiaceae, native to India but now widely cultivated for its oval fruits in other tropical and subtropical areas, such as the West Indies.

mangold another name for *mangelwurzel.

mangrove any of several shrubs and trees, especially of the mangrove family Rhizophoraceae, found in the muddy swamps of tropical coasts and estuaries. By sending down aerial roots from their branches, they rapidly form close-growing mangrove thickets. Their timber is impervious to water and resists marine worms. Mangrove swamps are rich breeding grounds for fish and shellfish. These habitats are being destroyed in many countries.

Manhattan island 20 km/12.5 mi long and 4 km/2.5 mi wide, lying between the Hudson and East rivers and forming a borough of the city of *New York, USA. It includes the Wall Street business centre and Broadway theatres.

Manhattan Project code name for the development of the *atom bomb in the USA in World War II, to which the physicists Enrico Fermi and J Robert Oppenheimer contributed.

manic depression mental disorder characterized by recurring periods of *depression which may or may not alternate with periods of inappropriate elation (mania) or overactivity. Sufferers may be genetically predisposed to the condition. Some cases have been improved by taking prescribed doses of *lithium.

Manila industrial port (textiles, tobacco, distilling, chemicals, shipbuilding) and capital of the Philippines, on the island of Luzon; population (1990) 1,598,900, metropolitan area (including *Quezon City) 5,926,000.

manioc another name for the plant *cassava.

Manipur state of NE India
area 22,400 sq km/8,646 sq mi
capital Imphal
products grain, fruit, vegetables, sugar, textiles, cement
population (1991) 1,826,700
language Hindi
religion Hindu 70%
history administered from the state of Assam until 1947 when it became a Union Territory. It became a state 1972.

Manitoba prairie province of Canada
area 650,000 sq km/250,900 sq mi
capital Winnipeg
exports grain, manufactured foods, beverages, machinery, furs, fish, nickel, zinc, copper, and the world's largest caesium deposits
population (1991) 1,092,600
history trading posts and forts were built here

by fur traders in the 18th century. What came to be known as the Red River settlement was first colonized 1811 by dispossessed Scottish Highlanders. The colony became the Canadian province of Manitoba 1870 after the Riel Rebellion 1869 ended. The area of the province was extended 1881 and 1912.

Manley Michael (Norman) 1924– . Jamaican politician, leader of the socialist People's National Party from 1969, and prime minister 1972–80 and 1989–92. He resigned the premiership because of ill health March 1992 and was succeeded by P J Patterson. Manley left parliament April 1992. His father, **Norman Manley** (1893–1969), was the founder of the People's National Party and prime minister 1959–62.

Mann Anthony. Stage name of Emil Anton Bundmann 1906–1967. US film director who made a series of violent but intelligent 1950s Westerns starring James Stewart, such as *Winchester '73* 1950. He also directed the epic *El Cid* 1961. His other films include *The Glenn Miller Story* 1954 and *A Dandy in Aspic* 1968.

Mann Thomas 1875–1955. German novelist and critic, concerned with the theme of the artist's relation to society. His first novel was *Buddenbrooks* 1901, which, followed by *Der Zauberberg/The Magic Mountain* 1924, led to a Nobel prize 1929. Notable among his works of short fiction is *Der Tod in Venedig/Death in Venice* 1913.

manna sweetish exudation obtained from many trees such as the ash and larch, and used in medicine. The manna of the Bible is thought to have been from the tamarisk tree, or a form of lichen.

Mannerism in painting and architecture, a style characterized by a subtle but conscious breaking of the 'rules' of classical composition – for example, displaying the human body in an off-centre, distorted pose, and using harsh, non-blending colours. The term was coined by Giorgio *Vasari and used to describe the 16th-century reaction to the peak of Renaissance classicism as achieved by Raphael, Leonardo da Vinci, and early Michelangelo.

Mannheim Karl 1893–1947. Hungarian sociologist who settled in the UK 1933. In *Ideology and Utopia* 1929 he argued that all knowledge, except in mathematics and physics, is ideological, a reflection of class interests and values; that there is therefore no such thing as objective knowledge or absolute truth.

manometer instrument for measuring the pressure of liquids (including human blood pressure) or gases. In its basic form, it is a U-tube partly filled with coloured liquid; pressure of a gas entering at one side is measured by the level to which the liquid rises at the other.

manor basic economic unit in *feudalism in Europe, established in England under the Norman conquest. It consisted of the lord's house and cultivated land, land rented by free tenants, land held by villagers, common land, woodland, and waste land.

Man Ray adopted name of Emmanuel Rudnitsky 1890–1977. US photographer, painter, and sculptor, active mainly in France; associated with the Dada movement. His pictures often showed

Surrealist images like the photograph *Le Violon d'Ingres* 1924.

Mansart Jules Hardouin. See *Hardouin-Mansart, Jules.

Mansell Nigel 1954– . English motor-racing driver. Runner-up in the world championship on two occasions, he became world champion 1992 and in the same year announced his retirement from Formula One racing, having won a British record 30 Grand Prix races. He returned to Grand Prix racing 1994.

Mansfield Katherine. Pen name of Kathleen Beauchamp 1888–1923. New Zealand writer who lived most of her life in England. Her delicate artistry emerges not only in her volumes of short stories – such as *In a German Pension* 1911, *Bliss* 1920, and *The Garden Party* 1923 – but also in her *Letters* and *Journal*.

manslaughter in English law, the unlawful killing of a human being in circumstances less culpable than *murder – for example, when the killer suffers extreme provocation, is in some way mentally ill (diminished responsibility), did not intend to kill but did so accidentally in the course of another crime or by behaving with criminal recklessness, or is the survivor of a genuine suicide pact that involved killing the other person.

manta another name for *devil ray, a large fish.

Mantegna Andrea *c.* 1431–1506. Italian Renaissance painter and engraver, active chiefly in Padua and Mantua, where some of his frescoes remain. Paintings such as *The Agony in the Garden c.* 1455 (National Gallery, London) reveal a dramatic linear style, mastery of perspective, and strongly Classical architectural detail.

mantis any insect of the family Mantidae, related to cockroaches. Some species can reach a length of 20 cm/8 in. There are about 2,000 species of mantis, mainly tropical.

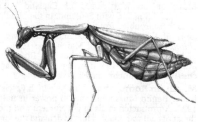

mantis *The praying mantis is a superbly designed predator.*

mantissa in mathematics, the decimal part of a *logarithm. For example, the logarithm of 347.6 is 2.5411; in this case, the 0.5411 is the mantissa, and the integral (whole number) part of the logarithm, the 2, is the characteristic.

mantle intermediate zone of the Earth between the crust and the core. It is thought to consist of silicate minerals such as olivine and spinel.

mantra in Hindu or Buddhist belief, a word repeatedly intoned to assist concentration and develop spiritual power; for example, *om*, which represents the names of Brahma, Vishnu, and Siva. Followers of a guru may receive their own individual mantra.

Manu in Hindu mythology, the founder of the human race, who was saved by *Brahma from a deluge.

manufacturing base share of the total output in a country's economy contributed by the manufacturing sector. This sector has greater potential for productivity growth than the service sector, which is labour-intensive; in manufacturing, productivity can be increased by replacing workers with technically advanced capital equipment. It is also significant because of its contribution to exports.

Manx Gaelic *Gaelic language of the Isle of Man.

Manzoni Alessandro, Count Manzoni 1785–1873. Italian poet and novelist, author of the historical romance *I promessi sposi/The Betrothed* 1825–27, set in Spanish-occupied Milan during the 17th century. Verdi's *Requiem* commemorates him.

Maoism form of communism based on the ideas and teachings of the Chinese communist leader *Mao Zedong. It involves an adaptation of *Marxism to suit conditions in China and apportions a much greater role to agriculture and the peasantry in the building of socialism, thus effectively bypassing the capitalist (industrial) stage envisaged by Marx.

Maori member of the indigenous Polynesian people of New Zealand, who numbered 294,200 in 1986, about 10% of the total population. Their language, Maori, belongs to the eastern branch of the Austronesian family.

Mao Zedong or *Mao Tse-tung* 1893–1976. Chinese political leader and Marxist theoretician. A founder of the Chinese Communist Party (CCP) 1921, Mao soon emerged as its leader. He organized the *Long March 1934–36 and the war of liberation 1937–49, following which he established a People's Republic and Communist rule in China; he headed the CCP and government until his death. His influence diminished with the failure of his 1958–60 *Great Leap Forward, but he emerged dominant again during the 1966–69 *Cultural Revolution. Mao adapted communism to Chinese conditions, as set out in the *Little Red Book*.

map diagrammatic representation of an area – for example, part of the Earth's surface or the distribution of the stars. Modern maps of the Earth are made using satellites in low orbit to take a series of overlapping stereoscopic photographs from which a three-dimensional image can be prepared. The earliest accurate large-scale maps appeared about 1580.

maple deciduous tree of the genus *Acer*, family Aceraceae, with lobed leaves and green flowers, followed by two-winged fruits, or samaras. There are over 200 species, chiefly in northern temperate regions.

Mapplethorpe Robert 1946–1989. US art photographer known for his use of racial and homoerotic imagery in chiefly fine platinum prints. He developed a style of polished elegance in his gallery art works, whose often culturally forbidden subject matter caused controversy.

map projection ways of depicting the spherical surface of the Earth on a flat piece of paper. Traditional projections include the *conic*, *azimuthal*, and *cylindrical*. The most famous cylindrical projection is the *Mercator projection, which dates from 1569. The weakness of these systems is that countries in different latitudes are disproportionately large, and lines of longitude and latitude appear distorted. In 1973 German historian Arno Peters devised the **Peters projection** in which the countries of the world retain their relative areas.

Maputo formerly (until 1975) **Lourenço Marques** capital of Mozambique, and Africa's second-largest port, on Delagoa Bay; population (1987) 1,006,800. Linked by rail with Zimbabwe and South Africa, it is a major outlet for minerals, steel, textiles, processed foods, and furniture.

maquis mostly evergreen vegetation common in many Mediterranean countries, consisting of scrub woodland with many low-growing tangled bushes and shrubs, typically including species of broom, gorse, and heather.

Maquis French *resistance movement that fought against the German occupation during World War II.

Mara (Sanskrit 'killing') in Buddhism, a supernatural being who attempted to distract the Buddha from the meditations that led to his enlightenment. In Hinduism, a goddess of death.

marabou stork *Leptoptilos crumeniferus* found in Africa. It is about 120 cm/4 ft tall, has a bald head, and eats snakes, lizards, insects, and carrion. It is largely dark grey and white and has an inflatable throat pouch.

Maracaibo oil-exporting port in Venezuela, on the channel connecting Lake Maracaibo with the Gulf of Venezuela; population (1989) 1,365,308. It is the second largest city in the country.

Maracaibo, Lake lake in NW Venezuela; area 14,000 sq km/5,400 sq mi. Oil was discovered here 1917.

Maracanã Stadium the world's largest football stadium, in Rio de Janeiro, Brazil, built 1950. It has a capacity of 175,000 but held a world record 199,854 spectators for the 1950 World Cup final between Brazil and Uruguay.

Maradona Diego 1960– . Argentine footballer who was voted the best player of the 1980s by the world's press. He has won 79 international caps, and has helped his country to two successive *World Cup finals. He was South American footballer of the year 1979 and 1980.

Marat Jean Paul 1743–1793. French Revolutionary leader and journalist. He was elected to the National Convention 1792, where he carried on a long struggle with the right-wing *Girondins, ending in their overthrow May 1793. In July he was murdered by Charlotte *Corday, a member of the Girondins.

Maratha or **Mahratta** member of a people living mainly in Maharashtra, W India. There are about 40 million speakers of Marathi, a language belonging to the Indo-European family. The Maratha are mostly farmers, and practise Hinduism.

marathon athletics endurance race over 42.195 km/26 mi 385 yd. It was first included in the Olympic Games in Athens 1896. The distance varied until it was standardized 1924. More recently, races have been opened to wider participation, including social runners as well as those competing at senior level.

Marathon, Battle of 490 BC. Fought between the Greeks, who were ultimately victorious, and invading Persians on the plain of Marathon, NE of Athens. Before the battle, news of the Persian destruction of the Greek city of Eretria was taken from Athens to Sparta by a courier, Pheidippides, who fell dead on arrival. His feat is commemorated by the **marathon race**.

Marbella port and tourist resort on the Costa del Sol between Málaga and Algeciras in Andalucia, S Spain; population (1991) 80,645. There are three bullrings, a Moorish castle, and the remains of a medieval defensive wall.

marble metamorphosed *limestone that takes and retains a good polish; it is used in building and sculpture. In its pure form it is white and consists almost entirely of calcite $CaCO_3$. Mineral impurities give it various colours and patterns. Carrara, Italy, is known for white marble.

Marble Arch triumphal arch in London designed by John *Nash to commemorate Nelson's victories. Intended as a ceremonial entry to Buckingham Palace, in 1851 it was moved to Hyde Park at the end of Oxford Street.

Marc Franz 1880–1916. German Expressionist painter, associated with Wassily Kandinsky in founding the *Blaue Reiter* movement. Animals played an essential part in his view of the world, and bold semi-abstracts of red and blue horses are characteristic of his work.

Marceau Marcel 1923– . French mime artist. He is the creator of the clown-harlequin Bip and mime sequences such as 'Youth, Maturity, Old Age, and Death'.

Marche, Le (English *the Marches*) region of E central Italy consisting of the provinces of Ancona, Ascoli Piceno, Macerata, and Pesaro e Urbino; capital Ancona; area 9,700 sq km/ 3,744 sq mi; population (1990) 1,435,600.

Marches boundary areas of England with Wales, and England with Scotland. In the Middle Ages these troubled frontier regions were held by lords of the Marches, sometimes called *marchiones* and later earls of March. The 1st Earl of March of the Welsh Marches was Roger de Mortimer (c. 1286–1330); of the Scottish Marches, Patrick Dunbar (died 1285).

March on Rome, the means by which Fascist leader Benito Mussolini came to power in Italy 1922. A protracted crisis in government and the threat of civil war enabled him to demand the formation of a Fascist government to restore order. On 29 Oct 1922, King Victor Emmanuel III invited Mussolini to come to Rome to take power. The 'march' was a propaganda myth: Mussolini travelled overnight by train from Milan to Rome, where he formed a government the following day, 30 Oct. Some 25,000 fascist Blackshirts were also transported to the city, where they marched in a ceremonial parade 31 Oct.

Marciano Rocky (Rocco Francis Marchegiano) 1923–1969. US boxer, world heavyweight champion 1952–56. He retired after 49 professional fights, the only heavyweight champion to retire undefeated.

Marconi Guglielmo 1874–1937. Italian electrical engineer and pioneer in the invention and development of radio. In 1895 he achieved radio communication over more than a mile, and in

England 1896 he conducted successful experiments that led to the formation of the company that became Marconi's Wireless Telegraph Company Ltd. He shared the Nobel Prize for Physics 1909.

Marco Polo see *Polo, Marco.

Marcos Ferdinand 1917–1989. Filipino right-wing politician, president from 1965 to 1986, when he was forced into exile in Hawaii. He was backed by the USA when in power, but in 1988 US authorities indicted him and his wife Imelda Marcos for racketeering, embezzlement, and defrauding US banks; Marcos was too ill to stand trial.

Marcos Imelda 1930– . Filipino politician and socialite, wife of Ferdinand Marcos, in exile 1986–91. She was acquitted 1990 of defrauding US banks. Under indictment for misuse of Philippine state funds, she returned to Manila Nov 1991 and was an unsuccessful candidate in the 1992 presidential elections.

Marcus Aurelius Antoninus AD 121–180. Roman emperor from 161 and Stoic philosopher. Although considered one of the best of the Roman emperors, he persecuted the Christians for political reasons. He wrote the philosophical *Meditations*.

Mardi Gras (French 'fat Tuesday' from the custom of using up all the fat in the household before the beginning of *Lent) Shrove Tuesday. A festival was traditionally held on this day in Paris, and there are carnivals in many parts of the world, including New Orleans, Louisiana; Italy; and Brazil.

mare (plural *maria*) dark lowland plain on the Moon. The name comes from Latin 'sea', because these areas were once wrongly thought to be water.

Marengo, Battle of defeat of the Austrians by the French emperor Napoleon on 14 June 1800, as part of his Italian campaign, near the village of Marengo in Piedmont, Italy.

Margaret (Rose) 1930– . Princess of the UK, younger daughter of George VI and sister of Elizabeth II. In 1960 she married Anthony Armstrong-Jones, later created Lord Snowdon, but they were divorced 1978. Their children are *David, Viscount Linley* (1961–) and *Lady Sarah Armstrong-Jones* (1964–).

Margaret of Anjou 1430–1482. Queen of England from 1445, wife of *Henry VI of England. After the outbreak of the Wars of the *Roses 1455, she acted as the leader of the Lancastrians, but was defeated and captured at the battle of Tewkesbury 1471 by Edward IV.

Margaret, St 1045–1093. Queen of Scotland, the granddaughter of King Edmund Ironside of England. She went to Scotland after the Norman Conquest, and soon after married Malcolm III. The marriage of her daughter Matilda to Henry I united the Norman and English royal houses.

margarine butter substitute made from animal fats and/or vegetable oils. The French chemist Hippolyte Mège-Mouriès invented margarine 1889. Today, margarines are usually made with vegetable oils, such as soy, corn, or sunflower oil, giving a product low in saturated fats (see *polyunsaturate) and fortified with vitamins A and D.

margay small cat *Felis wiedi* found from southern USA to South America in forested areas, where it hunts birds and small mammals. It is about 60 cm/2 ft long with a 40 cm/1.3 ft tail, has a rounded head, and has black spots and blotches on a yellowish-brown coat.

margin in finance, the difference between cost and selling price; also cash or collateral on deposit with a broker or lender to meet legal requirements against loss, as when stocks and other securities have been financed by funds supplied by the lender.

marginal cost pricing in economics, the setting of a price based on the additional cost to a firm of producing one more unit of output (the marginal cost), rather than the actual average cost per unit (total production costs divided by the total number of units produced). In this way, the price of an item is kept to a minimum, reflecting only the extra cost of labour and materials.

marginal utility in economics, the measure of additional satisfaction (utility) gained by a consumer who receives one additional unit of a product or service. The concept is used to explain why consumers buy more of a product when the price falls.

margrave German title (equivalent of marquess) for the 'counts of the march', who guarded the frontier regions of the Holy Roman Empire from Charlemagne's time. Later the title was used by other territorial princes. Chief among these were the margraves of Austria and of Brandenburg.

Margrethe II 1940– . Queen of Denmark from 1972, when she succeeded her father Frederick IX. In 1967, she married the French diplomat Count Henri de Laborde de Monpezat, who took the title Prince Hendrik. Her heir is Crown Prince Frederick (1968–).

marguerite European plant *Leucanthemum vulgare* of the daisy family Compositae. It is a shrubby perennial and bears white daisylike flowers. Marguerite is also the name of a cultivated variety of *chrysanthemum.

Marguerite of Navarre also known as *Margaret d'Angoulême* 1492–1549. Queen of Navarre from 1527, French poet, and author of the *Heptaméron* 1558, a collection of stories in imitation of Boccaccio's *Decameron*. The sister of Francis I of France, she was born in Angoulême. Her second husband 1527 was Henri d'Albret, king of Navarre.

Mariana Islands or *Marianas* archipelago in the NW Pacific E of the Philippines, divided politically into *Guam* (an unincorporated territory of the USA) and *Northern Marianas* (a commonwealth of the USA with its own internal government, of 16 mountainous islands, extending 560 km/350 mi N from Guam)
area 480 sq km/185 sq mi
capital Garapan on Saipan
government own constitutionally elected government
products sugar, coconuts, coffee
currency US dollar
population (1988) 21,000, mainly Micronesian
languages Chamorro 55%, English
religion mainly Roman Catholic
history sold to Germany by Spain 1899. The

islands were mandated by the League of Nations to Japan 1918, and taken by US Marines 1944–45 in World War II. The islands were part of the US Trust Territory of the Pacific 1947–78. Since 1978 they have been a commonwealth of the USA.

Mariana Trench lowest region on the Earth's surface; the deepest part of the sea floor. The trench is 2,400 km/1,500 mi long and is situated 300 km/200 mi E of the Mariana Islands, in the NW Pacific Ocean. Its deepest part is the gorge known as the Challenger Deep, which extends 11,034 m/36,210 ft below sea level.

Maria Theresa 1717–1780. Empress of Austria from 1740, when she succeeded her father, the Holy Roman emperor Charles VI; her claim to the throne was challenged and she became embroiled, first in the War of the *Austrian Succession 1740–48, then in the *Seven Years' War 1756–63; she remained in possession of Austria but lost Silesia. The rest of her reign was peaceful and, with her son Joseph II, she introduced social reforms.

Marie Antoinette 1755–1793. Queen of France from 1774. She was the daughter of Empress Maria Theresa of Austria, and married *Louis XVI of France 1770. Her reputation for extravagance helped provoke the *French Revolution of 1789. She was tried for treason Oct 1793 and guillotined.

Marie de' Medici 1573–1642. Queen of France, wife of Henry IV from 1600, and regent (after his murder) for their son Louis XIII. She left the government to her favourites, the Concinis, until Louis XIII seized power and executed them 1617. She was banished, but after she led a revolt 1619, *Richelieu effected her reconciliation with her son. When she attempted to oust him again 1630, she was exiled.

marigold any of several plants of the family Compositae, especially the genus *Tagetes*, including pot marigold *Calendula officinalis* and the tropical American *T. patula*, commonly known as French marigold.

marijuana dried leaves and flowers of the hemp plant *cannabis, used as a drug; it is illegal in most countries. Mexico is the world's largest producer.

marimba bass *xylophone with wooden rather than metal tubular resonators.

Mariner spacecraft series of US space probes that explored the planets Mercury, Venus, and Mars 1962–75.

marines fighting force that operates both on land and at sea. The *US Marine Corps* (1775) is constituted as an arm of the US Navy. It is made up of infantry and air support units trained and equipped for amphibious landings under fire.

Marinetti Filippo Tommaso 1876–1944. Italian author who in 1909 published the first manifesto of *Futurism, which called for a break with tradition in art, poetry, and the novel, and glorified the machine age.

marionette type of *puppet, a jointed figure controlled from above by wires or strings. Intricately crafted marionettes were used in Burma (now Myanmar) and Ceylon (now Sri Lanka) and later at the courts of Italian princes in the 16th–18th centuries.

maritime law that part of the law dealing with

the sea: in particular, fishing areas, ships, and navigation. Seas are divided into *internal waters* governed by a state's internal laws (such as harbours, inlets); **territorial waters* (the area of sea adjoining the coast over which a state claims rights); the *continental shelf* (the seabed and subsoil that the coastal state is entitled to exploit beyond the territorial waters); and the *high seas*, where international law applies.

Marivaux Pierre Carlet de Chamblain de 1688–1763. French novelist and dramatist. His sophisticated comedies include Le Jeu de l'amour et du hasard/The Game of Love and Chance 1730 and Les Fausses confidences/False Confidences 1737; his novel La Vie de Marianne/The Life of Marianne 1731–41 has autobiographical elements. Marivaux gave the word *marivaudage* (oversubtle lovers' conversation) to the French language.

marjoram aromatic herb of the mint family Labiatae. Wild marjoram *Origanum vulgare* is found both in Europe and Asia and has become naturalized in the Americas; the culinary sweet marjoram *O. majorana* is widely cultivated.

Mark Antony Antonius, Marcus 83–30 BC. Roman politician and soldier. He was tribune and later consul under Julius Caesar, serving under him in Gaul. In 44 BC he tried to secure for Caesar the title of king. After Caesar's assassination, he formed the Second Triumvirate with Octavian (*Augustus) and Lepidus. In 42 he defeated Brutus and Cassius at Philippi. He took Egypt as his share of the empire and formed a liaison with *Cleopatra. In 40 he returned to Rome to marry Octavia, the sister of Augustus. In 32 the Senate declared war on Cleopatra. Antony was defeated by Augustus at the battle of Actium 31 BC. He returned to Egypt and committed suicide.

market capitalization market value of a company, based on the market price of all its issued securities – a price that would be unlikely to apply, however, if a bid were actually made for control of them.

market forces in economics, the forces of demand (a want backed by the ability to pay) and supply (the willingness and ability to supply).

market gardening farming system that specializes in the commercial growing of vegetables, fruit, or flowers. It is an *intensive agriculture with crops often being grown inside greenhouses on small farms.

marketing promoting goods and services to consumers. In the 20th century, marketing has played an increasingly larger role in determining company policy, influencing product development, pricing, methods of distribution, advertising, and promotion techniques. Marketing skills are beginning to appear on the curriculum of some schools and colleges.

Markievicz Constance Georgina, Countess Markievicz (born Gore Booth) 1868–1927. Irish nationalist who married the Polish count Markievicz 1900. Her death sentence for taking part in the Easter Rising of 1916 was commuted, and after her release from prison 1917 she was elected to the Westminster Parliament as a Sinn Féin candidate 1918 (technically the first British woman member of Parliament), but did not take her seat.

Markova Alicia. Adopted name of Lilian Alicia Marks 1910– . British ballet dancer. Trained by *Pavlova, she was ballerina with *Diaghilev's company 1925–29, was the first resident ballerina of the Vic-Wells Ballet 1933–35, partnered Anton *Dolin in their own Markova-Dolin Company 1935–37, and danced with the Ballets Russes de Monte Carlo 1938–41 and Ballet Theatre, USA, 1941–46. She is associated with the great classical ballets, such as *Giselle*.

Marks Simon, 1st Baron of Broughton 1888–1964. English chain-store magnate. His father, Polish immigrant Michael Marks, had started a number of 'penny bazaars' with Yorkshireman Tom Spencer 1887; Simon Marks entered the business 1907 and built up a national chain of Marks and Spencer stores.

Mark, St 1st century AD. In the New Testament, Christian apostle and evangelist whose name is given to the second Gospel. It was probably written AD 65–70, and used by the authors of the first and third Gospels. He is the patron saint of Venice, and his emblem is a winged lion; feast day 25 April.

mark sensing in computing, a technique that enables pencil marks made in predetermined positions on specially prepared forms to be rapidly read and input to a computer. The technique makes use of the fact that pencil marks contain graphite and therefore conduct electricity. A **mark sense reader** scans the form by passing small metal brushes over the paper surface. Whenever a brush touches a pencil mark a circuit is completed and the mark is detected.

Marlborough John Churchill, 1st Duke of Marlborough 1650–1722. English soldier, created a duke 1702 by Queen Anne. He was granted the Blenheim mansion in Oxfordshire in recognition of his services, which included defeating the French army outside Vienna in the Battle of Blenheim 1704, during the War of the *Spanish Succession.

Marley Bob (Robert Nesta) 1945–1981. Jamaican reggae singer, a Rastafarian whose songs, many of which were topical and political, popularized reggae worldwide in the 1970s. One of his greatest hit songs is 'No Woman No Cry'; his albums include *Natty Dread* 1975 and *Exodus* 1977.

marlin or **spearfish** any of several genera of open-sea fishes known as billfishes, of the family Istiophoridae, order Perciformes. Some 2.5 m/7 ft long, they are found in warmer waters, have elongated snouts, and high-standing dorsal fins. Members of the family include the sailfish *Istiophorus platypterus*, the fastest of all fishes over short distances – reaching speeds of 100 kph/62 mph, and the blue marlin *Makaira nigricans*, highly prized as a 'game' fish.

Marlowe Christopher 1564–1593. English poet and dramatist. His work includes the blank-verse plays *Tamburlaine the Great* c. 1587, *The Jew of Malta* c. 1589, *Edward II* and *Dr Faustus*, both c. 1592, the poem *Hero and Leander* 1598, and a translation of Ovid's *Amores*.

Marmara, Sea of small inland sea separating Turkey in Europe from Turkey in Asia, connected through the Bosporus with the Black Sea, and through the Dardanelles with the Aegean; length 275 km/170 mi, breadth up to 80 km/50 mi.

marmoset small tree-dwelling monkey in the family Callithricidae, found in South and Central America. Most species have characteristic tufted ears, clawlike nails, and a handsome tail, and some only reach a body length of 18 cm/7 in. The tail is not prehensile. Some are known as tamarins.

marmot any of several large burrowing rodents of the genus *Marmota*, in the squirrel family Sciuridae. There are about 15 species. They eat plants and some insects. Marmots are found throughout Canada and the USA, and from the Alps to the Himalayas. Marmots live in colonies, make burrows (one to each family), and hibernate. In North America they are called **woodchucks** or **groundhogs**.

Marne, Battles of the in World War I, two unsuccessful German offensives. In the *First Battle* 6–9 Sept 1914, von Moltke's advance was halted by the British Expeditionary Force and the French under Foch; in the *Second Battle* 15 July–4 Aug 1918, Ludendorff's advance was defeated by British, French, and US troops under the French general Pétain, and German morale crumbled.

Maronite member of a Christian sect deriving from refugee Monothelites (Christian heretics) of the 7th century. They were subsequently united with the Roman Catholic Church and number about 400,000 in Lebanon and Syria, with an equal number scattered in southern Europe and the Americas.

maroon (Spanish *cimarrón* 'wild, untamed') in the West Indies and Surinam, a freed or escaped African slave. Maroons were organized and armed by the Spanish in Jamaica in the late 17th century and early 18th century. They harried the British with guerrilla tactics.

Marquesas Islands (French *Iles Marquises*) island group in *French Polynesia, lying north of the Tuamotu Archipelago; area 1,270 sq km/490 sq mi; population (1988) 7,500. The administrative headquarters is Atuona on Hiva Oa. The islands were annexed by France 1842.

marquess or **marquis** title and rank of a nobleman who in the British peerage ranks below a duke and above an earl. The wife of a marquess is a marchioness.

marquetry inlaying of various woods, bone, or ivory, usually on furniture, to create ornate patterns and pictures. *Parquetry* is the term used for geometrical inlaid patterns. The method is thought to have originated in Germany or Holland.

Márquez Gabriel García. See *García Márquez, Colombian novelist.

Marrakesh historic town in Morocco in the foothills of the Atlas Mountains, about 210 km/130 mi south of Casablanca; population (1982) 549,000. It is a tourist centre, and has textile, leather, and food processing industries. Founded 1062, it has a medieval palace and mosques, and was formerly the capital of Morocco.

marram grass coarse perennial grass *Ammophila arenaria*, flourishing on sandy areas.

Because of its tough, creeping rootstocks, it is widely used to hold coastal dunes in place.

Marrano (Spanish *marrano* 'pig') Spanish or Portuguese Jew who, during the 14th and 15th centuries, converted to Christianity to escape death or persecution at the hands of the *Inquisition. Many continued to adhere secretly to Judaism and carry out Jewish rites. During the Spanish Inquisition thousands were burned at the stake as 'heretics'.

marriage legally or culturally sanctioned union of one man and one woman (monogamy); one man and two or more women (polygamy); one woman and two or more men (polyandry). The basis of marriage varies considerably in different societies (romantic love in the West; arranged marriages in some other societies), but most marriage ceremonies, contracts, or customs involve a set of rights and duties, such as care and protection, and there is generally an expectation that children will be born of the union to continue the family line, and maintain the family property.

marrow trailing vine *Cucurbita pepo*, family Cucurbitaceae, producing large pulpy fruits, used as vegetables and in preserves; the young fruits of one variety are known as courgettes (US zucchini).

Mars in Roman mythology, the god of war, depicted as a fearless warrior. The month of March is named after him. He is equivalent to the Greek Ares.

Mars fourth planet from the Sun, average distance 227.9 million km/141.6 million mi. It revolves around the Sun in 687 Earth days, and has a rotation period of 24 hr 37 min. It is much smaller than Venus or Earth, with a diameter 6,780 km/4,210 mi, and mass 0.11 that of Earth. Mars is slightly pearshaped, with a low, level northern hemisphere, which is comparatively uncratered and geologically 'young', and a heavily cratered 'ancient' southern hemisphere.

Marsalis Wynton 1961– . US trumpet player. He has recorded both classical and jazz music. He was a member of Art Blakey's Jazz Messengers 1980–82 and also played with Miles Davis before forming his own quintet.

Marseillaise, La French national anthem; the words and music were composed 1792 as a revolutionary song by the army officer Claude Joseph Rouget de Lisle (1760–1836).

Marseille (English *Marseilles*) chief seaport of France, industrial centre (chemicals, oil refining, metallurgy, shipbuilding, food processing), and capital of the *département* Bouches-du-Rhône, on the Mediterranean Golfe du Lion; population (1990) 807,700.

marsh low-lying wetland. Freshwater marshes are common wherever groundwater, surface springs, streams, or run-off cause frequent flooding or more or less permanent shallow water. A marsh is alkaline whereas a *bog is acid. Marshes develop on inorganic silt or clay soils. Rushes are typical marsh plants. Large marshes dominated by papyrus, cattail, and reeds, with standing water throughout the year, are commonly called *swamps.

Marsh Ngaio 1899–1982. New Zealand detective fiction writer. Her first novel *A Man Lay Dead* 1934 introduced her hero Chief Inspector Roderick Alleyn.

Marshall Islands
area 180 sq km/69 sq mi
capital Dalap-Uliga-Darrit (on Majuro atoll)
physical comprises the Radak (13 islands) and Ralik (11 islands) chains in the W Pacific
head of state and government Amata Kabua from 1991
political system liberal democracy
products copra, phosphates, fish; tourism is important
currency US dollar
population (1990) 31,600
language English (official)
religions Christian, mainly Roman Catholic, and local faiths
GNP $16,516 per head (1990)
chronology
1855 Occupied by Germany.
1914 Occupied by Japan.
1920–45 Administered by Japan under United Nations mandate.
1946–63 Eniwetok and Bikini atolls used for US atom-bomb tests; islanders later demanded rehabilitation and compensation for the damage.
1947 Became part of the UN Pacific Islands Trust Territory, administered by the USA.
1986 Compact of free association with USA granted islands self-government, with USA retaining military control and taking tribute.
1990 UN trust status terminated.
1991 Independence agreed; UN membership granted.

Marshall Plan programme of US economic aid to Europe, set up at the end of World War II, totalling $13,000 billion 1948–52. Officially known as the European Recovery Programme, it was announced by Secretary of State George C Marshall in a speech at Harvard June 1947, but it was in fact the work of a State Department group led by Dean *Acheson. The perceived danger of communist takeover in postwar Europe was the main reason for the aid effort.

marsh gas gas consisting mostly of *methane. It is produced in swamps and marshes by the action of bacteria on dead vegetation.

marsh marigold plant *Caltha palustris* of the buttercup family Ranunculaceae, known as the kingcup in the UK and as the cowslip in the USA. It grows in moist sheltered spots and has five-sepalled flowers of a brilliant yellow.

Mars Observer NASA space probe launched 1992 to orbit Mars and survey the planet, its atmosphere, and the polar caps over two years. The probe was also scheduled to communicate information from the robot vehicles delivered by Russia's Mars 94 mission. The $1 billion project miscarried, however, when the probe unaccountably stopped transmitting Aug 1993, three days before it was due to drop into orbit.

Marston Moor, Battle of battle fought in the English Civil War 2 July 1644 on Marston Moor, 11 km/7 mi W of York. The Royalists were conclusively defeated by the Parliamentarians and Scots.

marsupial mammal in which the female has a pouch where she carries her young (born tiny and immature) for a considerable time after birth.

marten small bushy-tailed carnivorous mammal

of the genus *Martes* in the weasel family Mustelidae. Martens live in North America, Europe, and temperate regions of Asia, and are agile climbers of trees.

Martens Wilfried 1936– . Prime minister of Belgium 1979–92, member of the Social Christian Party. He was president of the Dutch-speaking CVP 1972–79 and, as prime minister, headed several coalition governments in the period 1979–92 when he was replaced by Jean-Luc Dehaene heading a new coalition.

Martial (Marcus Valerius Martialis) AD 41–104. Latin poet and epigrammatist. His poetry, often bawdy, reflects contemporary Roman life. He left over 15 books of miscellaneous verse, mostly elegiac couplets (a hexameter followed by a pentameter).

martial arts any of several styles of armed and unarmed combat developed in the East from ancient techniques and arts. Common martial arts include *aikido, *judo, *jujitsu, *karate, *kendo, and *kung fu.

martial law replacement of civilian by military authorities in the maintenance of order.

martin any of several species of birds in the swallow family, Hirundinidae.

Martin five popes, including:

Martin V 1368–1431. Pope from 1417. A member of the Roman family of Colonna, he was elected during the Council of Constance, and ended the Great Schism between the rival popes of Rome and Avignon.

Martinet Jean French inspector-general of infantry under Louis XIV whose constant drilling brought the army to a high degree of efficiency – hence the use of his name to mean a strict disciplinarian.

Martini Simone c. 1284–1344. Italian painter, a master of the Sienese school. He was a pupil of Duccio and continued the graceful linear patterns of Sienese art but introduced a fresh element of naturalism. His patrons included the city of Siena, the king of Naples, and the pope. Two of his frescoes are in the Town Hall in Siena: the *Maestà* about 1315 and the horseback warrior *Guidoriccio da Fogliano* (the attribution of the latter is disputed). From 1333 to 1339 Simone worked at Assisi where he decorated the chapel of St Martin with scenes depicting the life of the saint, regarded by many as his masterpiece.

Martinique French island in the West Indies (Lesser Antilles)
area 1,079 sq km/417 sq mi
capital Fort-de-France
products sugar, cocoa, rum, bananas, pineapples
population (1984) 327,000
history Martinique was reached by Spanish navigators 1493, and became a French colony 1635; since 1972 it has been a French overseas region.

Martinmas in the Christian calendar, the feast of St Martin, 11 Nov.

Martins Peter 1946– . Danish-born US dancer, choreographer, and ballet director, principal dancer with the New York City Ballet (NYCB) from 1965, its joint ballet master (with Anthony Tudor) from 1983, and its director from 1990. He

trained with August Bournonville and brought that teacher's influence to the NYCB.

martyr (Greek 'witness') one who voluntarily suffers death for refusing to renounce a religious faith. The first recorded Christian martyr was St Stephen, who was killed in Jerusalem shortly after Jesus' alleged ascension to heaven.

Marvell Andrew 1621–1678. English metaphysical poet and satirist. His poems include 'To His Coy Mistress' and 'Horatian Ode upon Cromwell's Return from Ireland'. He was committed to the parliamentary cause, and was member of Parliament for Hull from 1659. He devoted his last years mainly to verse satire and prose works attacking repressive aspects of government.

Marvin Lee 1924–1987. US film actor who began his career playing violent, often psychotic villains and progressed to playing violent, occasionally psychotic heroes. His work includes *The Big Heat* 1953, *The Killers* 1964, and *Cat Ballou* 1965.

Marx Karl (Heinrich) 1818–1883. German philosopher, economist, and social theorist whose account of change through conflict is known as historical, or dialectical, materialism (see *Marxism). His *Das Kapital/Capital* 1867–95 is the fundamental text of Marxist economics, and his systematic theses on class struggle, history, and the importance of economic factors in politics have exercised an enormous influence on later thinkers and political activists.

Marx Brothers team of US film comedians: Leonard *Chico* (from the 'chicks' – women – he chased) 1887–1961; Adolph, the silent *Harpo* (from the harp he played) 1888–1964; Julius *Groucho* (from his temper) 1890–1977; Milton *Gummo* (from his gumshoes, or galoshes) 1897–1977, who left the team before films; and Herbert *Zeppo* (born at the time of the first zeppelins) 1901–1979, part of the team until 1935. They made a total of 13 zany films 1929–49 including *Animal Crackers* 1930, *Duck Soup* 1933, *A Night at the Opera* 1935, and *Go West* 1940.

Marxism philosophical system, developed by the 19th-century German social theorists *Marx and *Engels, also known as *dialectical materialism*, under which matter gives rise to mind (materialism) and all is subject to change (from dialectic; see *Hegel). As applied to history, it supposes that the succession of feudalism, capitalism, socialism, and finally the classless society is inevitable. The stubborn resistance of any existing system to change necessitates its complete overthrow in the *class struggle* – in the case of capitalism, by the proletariat – rather than gradual modification.

Mary in the New Testament, the mother of Jesus through divine intervention (see *Annunciation), wife of *Joseph. The Roman Catholic Church maintains belief in her *Immaculate Conception and bodily assumption into heaven, and venerates her as a mediator. Feast day of the Assumption 15 Aug.

Mary Queen of Scots 1542–1587. Queen of Scotland 1542–67. Also known as *Mary Stuart*, she was the daughter of James V. Mary's connection with the English royal line from Henry VII made her a threat to Elizabeth I's hold on the

English throne, especially as she represented a champion of the Catholic cause. She was married three times. After her forced abdication she was imprisoned but escaped 1568 to England. Elizabeth I held her prisoner, while the Roman Catholics, who regarded Mary as rightful queen of England, formed many conspiracies to place her on the throne, and for complicity in one of these she was executed.

Mary Queen 1867–1953. Consort of George V of the UK. The daughter of the Duke and Duchess of Teck, the latter a grand-daughter of George II, in 1891 she became engaged to the Duke of Clarence, eldest son of the Prince of Wales (later Edward VII). After his death 1892, she married 1893 his brother George, Duke of York, who succeeded to the throne 1910.

Mary two queens of England:

Mary I *Bloody Mary* 1516–1558. Queen of England from 1553. She was the eldest daughter of Henry VIII by Catherine of Aragon. When Edward VI died, Mary easily secured the crown in spite of the conspiracy to substitute Lady Jane *Grey. In 1554 Mary married Philip II of Spain, and as a devout Roman Catholic obtained the restoration of papal supremacy and sanctioned the persecution of Protestants. She was succeeded by her half-sister Elizabeth I.

Mary II 1662–1694. Queen of England, Scotland, and Ireland from 1688. She was the Protestant elder daughter of the Catholic *James II, and in 1677 was married to her cousin *William III of Orange. After the 1688 revolution she accepted the crown jointly with William.

Maryland state of E USA; nickname Old Line State/Free State
area 31,600 sq km/12,198 sq mi
capital Annapolis
cities Baltimore, Silver Spring, Dundalk, Bethesda
products poultry, dairy products, machinery, steel, cars and parts, electric and electronic equipment, chemicals, fish and shellfish
population (1990) 4,781,500
famous people Stephen Decatur, Francis Scott Key, Edgar Allan Poe, Frederick Douglass, Harriet Tubman, Upton Sinclair, H L Mencken, Babe Ruth, Billie Holiday
history one of the original Thirteen Colonies, first settled 1634; it became a state 1788.

Mary Magdalene, St 1st century AD. In the New Testament, the woman whom Jesus cured of possession by evil spirits, was present at the Crucifixion and burial, and was the first to meet the risen Jesus. She is often identified with the woman of St Luke's gospel who anointed Jesus' feet, and her symbol is a jar of ointment; feast day 22 July.

Mary Rose greatest warship of Henry VIII of England, which sank off Southsea, Hampshire, 19 July 1545. The wreck was located 1971, and raised for preservation in dry dock in Portsmouth harbour 1982.

Masaccio (Tomaso di Giovanni di Simone Guidi) 1401–1428. Florentine painter, a leader of the early Italian Renaissance. His frescoes in Sta Maria del Carmine, Florence, 1425–28, which he painted with Masolino da Panicale (*c.* 1384–1447), show a decisive break with Gothic conventions. He was the first painter to apply

the scientific laws of perspective, newly discovered by the architect Brunelleschi.

Masai member of an E African people whose territory is divided between Tanzania and Kenya, and who number about 250,000. They were originally warriors and nomads, breeding humped zebu cattle, but some have adopted a more settled life. Their cooperation is being sought by the Kenyan authorities to help in wildlife conservation. They speak a Nilotic language belonging to the Nilo-Saharan family.

Masaryk Jan (Garrigue) 1886–1948. Czechoslovak politician, son of Tomáš Masaryk. He was foreign minister from 1940, when the Czechoslovak government was exiled in London in World War II. He returned 1945, retaining the post, but as a result of political pressure by the communists committed suicide.

Masaryk Tomáš (Garrigue) 1850–1937. Czechoslovak nationalist politician. He directed the revolutionary movement against the Austrian Empire, founding with Eduard Beneš and Stefanik the Czechoslovak National Council, and in 1918 was elected first president of the newly formed Czechoslovak Republic. Three times reelected, he resigned 1935 in favour of Beneš.

Masefield John 1878–1967. English poet and novelist. His early years in the navy inspired *Salt Water Ballads* 1902 and several adventure novels; he also wrote children's books, such as *The Box of Delights* 1935, and plays. He was poet laureate from 1930.

maser (acronym for *microwave amplification by stimulated emission of radiation*) in physics, a high-frequency microwave amplifier or oscillator in which the signal to be amplified is used to stimulate unstable atoms into emitting energy at the same frequency. Atoms or molecules are raised to a higher energy level and then allowed to lose this energy by radiation emitted at a precise frequency. The principle has been extended to other parts of the electromagnetic spectrum as, for example, in the *laser.

Maseru capital of Lesotho, southern Africa, on the Caledon River; population (1986) 289,000. Founded 1869, it is a centre for trade and diamond processing.

Mashraq (Arabic 'east') the Arab countries of the E Mediterranean: Egypt, Sudan, Jordan, Syria, and Lebanon. The term is contrasted with *Maghreb, comprising the Arab countries of NW Africa.

Masire Quett Ketumile Joni 1925– . President of Botswana from 1980. In 1962, with Seretse *Khama, he founded the Botswana Democratic Party (BDP) and in 1965 was made deputy prime minister. After independence 1966, he became vice president and, on Khama's death 1980, president, continuing a policy of nonalignment.

Maskelyne Nevil 1732–1811. English astronomer who accurately measured the distance from the Earth to the Sun by observing a transit of Venus across the Sun's face 1769. In 1774 he measured the mass of the Earth by noting the deflection of a plumb line near Mount Schiehallion in Scotland.

masochism desire to subject oneself to physical or mental pain, humiliation, or punishment, for erotic pleasure, to alleviate guilt, or out of destructive impulses turned inwards. The term is derived from Leopold von *Sacher-Masoch.

Mason James 1909–1984. English actor who portrayed romantic villains in British films of the 1940s. After *Odd Man Out* 1947 he worked in the USA, playing intelligent but troubled, vulnerable men, notably in *A Star Is Born* 1954. He returned to Europe 1960, where he made *Lolita* 1962, *Georgy Girl* 1966, and *Cross of Iron* 1977.

Mason–Dixon Line in the USA, the boundary line between Maryland and Pennsylvania (latitude 39° 43′ 26.3″ N), named after Charles Mason (1730–1787) and Jeremiah Dixon (died 1777), English astronomers and surveyors who surveyed it 1763–67. It was popularly seen as dividing the North from the South.

masque spectacular and essentially aristocratic entertainment with a fantastic or mythological theme in which music, dance, and extravagant costumes and scenic design figured larger than plot. Originating in Italy, it reached its height of popularity at the English court between 1600 and 1640, with the collaboration of Ben *Jonson as writer and Inigo *Jones as stage designer.

mass in physics, the quantity of matter in a body as measured by its inertia. Mass determines the acceleration produced in a body by a given force acting on it, the acceleration being inversely proportional to the mass of the body. The mass also determines the force exerted on a body by *gravity on Earth, although this attraction varies slightly from place to place. In the SI system, the base unit of mass is the kilogram.

Mass in Christianity, the celebration of the *Eucharist.

Mass in music, the setting of the invariable parts of the Christian Mass, that is *Kyrie, Gloria, Credo, Sanctus* with *Benedictus,* and *Agnus Dei.* A notable example is Bach's *Mass in B Minor.*

Massachusetts state of USA; nickname Bay State/Old Colony State
area 21,500 sq km/8,299 sq mi
capital Boston
cities Worcester, Springfield, New Bedford, Brockton, Cambridge
population (1990) 6,016,400
products electronic, communications, and optical equipment; precision instruments; non-electrical machinery; fish; cranberries; dairy products
famous people Samuel Adams, Louis Brandeis, Emily Dickinson, Ralph Waldo Emerson, Robert Goddard, Nathaniel Hawthorne, Oliver Wendell Holmes, Winslow Homer, William James, John F Kennedy, Robert Lowell, Paul Revere, Henry Thoreau, Daniel Webster
history one of the original Thirteen Colonies, it was first settled 1620 by the Pilgrims at Plymouth. After the *Boston Tea Party 1773, the American Revolution began at Lexington and Concord 19 April 1775, and the British evacuated Boston the following year. Massachusetts became a state 1788.

massage manipulation of the soft tissue of the body, the muscles, ligaments, and tendons, either to encourage the healing of specific injuries or to produce the general beneficial effects of relaxing muscular tension, stimulating blood circulation,

and improving the tone and strength of the skin and muscles.

mass–energy equation Albert *Einstein's equation $E = mc^2$, denoting the equivalence of mass and energy, where E is the energy in joules, m is the mass in kilograms, and c is the speed of light, in a vacuum, in metres per second.

Massenet Jules Emile Frédéric 1842–1912. French composer of opera, ballets, oratorios, and orchestral suites.

Massif Central mountainous plateau region of S central France; area 93,000 sq km/ 36,000 sq mi, highest peak Puy de Sancy 1,886 m/6,188 ft. It is a source of hydroelectricity.

Massine Léonide 1895–1979. Russian choreographer and dancer with the Ballets Russes. He was a creator of comedy in ballet and also symphonic ballet using concert music.

mass number or *nucleon number* sum (symbol A) of the numbers of protons and neutrons in the nucleus of an atom. It is used along with the *atomic number (the number of protons) in *nuclear notation: in symbols that represent nuclear isotopes, such as $^{14}_{6}C$, the lower number is the atomic number, and the upper number is the mass number.

Massorah collection of philological notes on the Hebrew text of the Old Testament. It was at first an oral tradition, but was committed to writing in the Aramaic language at Tiberias, Palestine, between the 6th and 9th centuries.

mass production manufacture of goods on a large scale, a technique that aims for low unit cost and high output. In factories mass production is achieved by a variety of means, such as division and specialization of labour and mechanization. These speed up production and allow the manufacture of near-identical, interchangeable parts. Such parts can then be assembled quickly into a finished product on an *assembly line.

mass spectrometer in physics, an apparatus for analysing chemical composition. Positive ions (charged particles) of a substance are separated by an electromagnetic system, which permits accurate measurement of the relative concentrations of the various ionic masses present, particularly isotopes.

mastiff breed of powerful dog, usually fawn in colour, that was originally bred in Britain for hunting purposes. It has a large head, wide-set eyes, and broad muzzle. It can grow up to 90 cm/ 3 ft at the shoulder, and weigh 100 kg/220 lb.

mastodon any of an extinct family (Mastodontidae) of mammals of the elephant order (Proboscidae). They differed from elephants and mammoths in the structure of their grinding teeth. There were numerous species, among which the American mastodon *Mastodon americanum,* about 3 m/10 ft high, of the Pleistocene era, is well known. They were hunted by humans for food.

Mastroianni Marcello 1924– . Italian film actor, most popular for his carefully understated roles as an unhappy romantic lover in such films as Antonioni's *La notte/The Night.* 1961. He starred in several films with Sophia Loren, including *Una giornata speciale/A Special Day* 1977, and worked with Fellini in *La dolce vita*

1960, $8^{1}/_{2}$ 1963, *Roma* 1971, and *Ginger and Fred* 1986.

Masur Kurt 1928– . German conductor, music director of the New York Philharmonic from 1990. He was conductor of the Dresden Philharmonic Orchestra 1955–58 and 1967–72, before making his London debut 1973 with the New Philharmonia. He was prominent in the political campaigning that took place prior to German unification.

Mata Hari Stage name of Gertrud Margarete Zelle 1876–1917. Dutch courtesan, dancer, and probable spy. In World War I she had affairs with highly placed military and government officials on both sides and told Allied secrets to the Germans. She may have been a double agent, in the pay of both France and Germany. She was shot by the French on espionage charges.

maté dried leaves of the Brazilian *holly Ilex paraguensis*, an evergreen shrub that grows in Paraguay and Brazil. The roasted, powdered leaves are made into a tea.

materialism philosophical theory that there is nothing in existence over and above matter and matter in motion. Such a theory excludes the possibility of deities. It also sees mind as an attribute of the physical, denying idealist theories that see mind as something independent of body; for example, Descartes' theory of 'thinking substance'.

mathematical induction formal method of proof in which the proposition $P(n + 1)$ is proved true on the hypothesis that the proposition $P(n)$ is true. The proposition is then shown to be true for a particular value of n, say k, and therefore by induction the proposition must be true for $n = k + 1, k + 2, k + 3,\ldots$. In many cases $k = 1$, so then the proposition is true for all positive integers.

mathematics science of spatial and numerical relationships. The main divisions of *pure mathematics* include geometry, arithmetic, algebra, calculus, and trigonometry. Mechanics, statistics, numerical analysis, computing, the mathematical theories of astronomy, electricity, optics, thermodynamics, and atomic studies come under the heading of *applied mathematics*.

Matilda 1102–1167. Claimant to the throne of England. On the death of her father, Henry I, 1135, the barons elected her cousin Stephen to be king. Matilda invaded England 1139, and was crowned by her supporters 1141. Civil war ensued until Stephen was finally recognized as king 1153, with Henry II (Matilda's son) as his successor.

Matisse Henri 1869–1954. French painter, sculptor, illustrator, and designer; one of the most original creative forces in early 20th-century art. His work concentrates on designs that emphasize curvaceous surface patterns, linear arabesques, and brilliant colour. Subjects include odalisques (women of the harem), bathers, and dancers; later works include pure abstracts, as in his collages of coloured paper shapes and the designs 1949–51 for the decoration of a chapel for the Dominican convent in Vence, near Nice.

Mato Grosso (Portuguese 'dense forest') area of SW Brazil, now forming two states, with their capitals at Cuiaba and Campo Grande. The for-ests, now depleted, supplied rubber and rare timbers; diamonds and silver are mined.

matriarchy form of social organization in which women head the family, and descent and relationship are reckoned through the female line. Matriarchy, often associated with polyandry (one wife with several husbands), occurs in certain parts of India, in the South Pacific, Central Africa, and among some North American Indian peoples. In *matrilineal* societies, powerful positions are usually held by men but acceded to through female kin.

matrix in mathematics, a square ($n \times n$) or rectangular ($m \times n$) array of elements (numbers or algebraic variables). They are a means of condensing information about mathematical systems and can be used for, among other things, solving *simultaneous linear equations and transform-ations.

matrix in biology, usually refers to the *extracellular matrix.

Matsuoka Yosuke 1880–1946. Japanese politician, foreign minister 1940–41. A fervent nationalist, Matsuoka led Japan out of the League of Nations when it condemned Japan for the seizure of Manchuria. As foreign minister, he allied Japan with Germany and Italy. At the end of World War II, he was arrested as a war criminal but died before his trial.

matter in physics, anything that has mass and can be detected and measured. All matter is made up of *atoms, which in turn are made up of *elementary particles; it exists ordinarily as a solid, liquid, or gas. The history of science and philosophy is largely taken up with accounts of theories of matter, ranging from the hard 'atoms' of Democritus to the 'waves' of modern quantum theory.

Matterhorn (French *le Cervin*, Italian *il Cervino*) mountain peak in the Alps on the Swiss-Italian border; 4,478 m/14,690 ft.

Matthau Walter. Stage name of Walter Matuschanskavasky 1922– . US character actor, impressive in both comedy and dramatic roles. He gained film stardom in the 1960s after his stage success in *The Odd Couple* 1965. His many films include *Kotch* 1971, *Charley Varrick* 1973, and *The Sunshine Boys* 1975.

Matthews Stanley 1915– . English footballer who played for Stoke City, Blackpool, and England. He played nearly 700 Football League games, and won 54 international caps. He was the first Footballer of the Year 1948 (again 1963), the first European Footballer of the Year 1956, and the first footballer to be knighted.

Matthew, St 1st century AD. Christian apostle and evangelist, the traditional author of the first Gospel. He is usually identified with Levi, who was a tax collector in the service of Herod Antipas, and was called by Jesus to be a disciple as he sat by the Lake of Galilee receiving customs dues. His emblem is a man with wings; feast day 21 Sept.

Matthias Corvinus 1440–1490. King of Hungary from 1458. His aim of uniting Hungary, Austria, and Bohemia involved him in long wars with Holy Roman emperor Frederick III and the kings of Bohemia and Poland, during which he cap-

mathematics signs

$a \rightarrow b$	*a* implies *b*
∞	infinity
lim	limiting value
$a \sim b$	numerical difference between *a* and *b*
$a \approx b$	*a* approximately equal to *b*
$a = b$	*a* equal to *b*
$a \equiv b$	*a* identical with *b* (for formulae only)
$a > b$	*a* greater than *b*
$a < b$	*a* smaller than *b*
$a \neq b$	*a* not equal to *b*
$b < a < c$	*a* greater than *b* and smaller than *c*, that is *a* lies between the values *b* & *c* but cannot equal either.
$a \geq b$	*a* equal to or greater than *b*, that is, *a* at least as great as *b*
$a \leq b$	*a* equal to or less than *b*, that is, *a* at most as great as *b*
$b \leq a \leq c$	*a* lies between the values *b* & *c* and could take the values *b* and *c*.
$|a|$	absolute value of *a*; this is always positive, for example $|-5|=5$
$+$	addition sign, positive
$-$	subtraction sign, negative
$\times$ or $\odot$	multiplication sign, times
$:$ or $\div$ or $/$	division sign, divided by
$a+b=c$	$a+b$, read as '*a* plus *b*', denotes the addition of *a* and *b*. The result of the addition, *c*, is also known as the sum.
$\int$	indefinite integral
$_a\int^b f(x)dx$	definite integral, or integral between $x=a$ and $x=b$
$a-b=c$	$a-b$, read as '*a* minus *b*', denotes subtraction of *b* from *a*.
	$a-b$, or *c*, is the difference. Subtraction is the opposite of addition.
$a \times b=c$ ⎫	$a \times b$, read as '*a* multiplied by *b*', denotes multiplication of *a* by *b*. $a \times b$, or *c*, is
$ab=c$ ⎬	the product, *a* and *b* are factors of *c*.
$a.b=c$ ⎭	
$a:b=c$	$a:c$, read as '*a* divided by *b*', denotes division. *a* is the dividend, *b* is the divisor; $a:b$, or *c*, is the quotient.
$a \div b=c$ ⎫	One aspect of division – repeated subtraction, is the opposite of multiplication – repeated addition.
$a/b=c$ ⎬	In fractions, or a/b, *a* is the numerator (= dividend), *b* the denominator (= divisor).
$a^b=c$	a^b, read as '*a* to the power *b*'; *a* is the base, *b* the exponent.
$^b\sqrt{a}=c$	$^b\sqrt{a}$, is the *b*th root of *a*, *b* being known as the root exponent. In the special case of $^2\sqrt{a}=c$, $^2\sqrt{a}$ or *c* is known as the square root of *a*, and the root exponent is usually omitted, that is, $^2\sqrt{a} = \sqrt{a}$.
e	exponential constant and is the base of natural (napierian) logarithms = 2.7182818284.......
π	ratio of the circumference of a circle to its diameter = 3.1415925535.......

tured Vienna (1485) and made it his capital. His father was János Hunyadi (1387–1456).

Maugham (William) Somerset 1874–1965. English writer. His work includes the novels *Of Human Bondage* 1915, *The Moon and Sixpence* 1919, and *Cakes and Ale* 1930; the short-story collections *The Trembling of a Leaf* 1921 and *Ashenden* 1928; and the plays *Lady Frederick* 1907 and *Our Betters* 1923.

Mau Mau Kenyan secret guerrilla movement 1952–60, an offshoot of the Kikuyu Central Association banned in World War II. Its aim was to end British colonial rule. This was achieved 1960 with the granting of Kenyan independence and the election of Jomo Kenyatta as Kenya's first prime minister.

Mauna Kea astronomical observatory in Hawaii, USA, built on a dormant volcano at

4,200 m/13,784 ft above sea level. Because of its elevation high above clouds, atmospheric moisture, and artificial lighting, Mauna Kea is ideal for infrared astronomy. The first telescope on the site was installed 1970.

Mauna Loa active volcano rising to a height of 4,169 m/13,678 ft on the Pacific island of Hawaii; it has numerous craters, including the second-largest active crater in the world.

Maundy Thursday in the Christian church, the Thursday before Easter. The ceremony of washing the feet of pilgrims on that day was instituted in commemoration of Jesus' washing of the apostles' feet and observed from the 4th century to 1754.

Maupassant Guy de 1850–1893. French author who established a reputation with the short story 'Boule de Suif/Ball of Fat' 1880 and wrote some 300 short stories in all. His novels include *Une Vie/A Woman's Life* 1883 and *Bel-Ami* 1885. He was encouraged as a writer by Gustave *Flaubert.

Mauriac François 1885–1970. French novelist. His novel *Le Baiser au lépreux/A Kiss for the Leper* 1922 describes the conflict of an unhappy marriage. The irreconcilability of Christian practice and human nature is examined in *Fleuve de feu/River of Fire* 1923, *Le Désert de l'amour/The Desert of Love* 1925, and *Thérèse Desqueyroux* 1927. Nobel Prize for Literature 1952.

Mauritania Islamic Republic of (*République Islamique de Mauritanie*)
area 1,030,700 sq km/397,850 sq mi
capital Nouakchott
towns port of Nouadhibou, Kaédi, Zouérate
physical valley of river Senegal in S; remainder arid and flat
head of state and government Maaouia Ould Sid Ahmed Taya from 1984
political system emergent democratic republic
exports iron ore, fish, gypsum
currency ouguiya
population (1993 est) 2,200,000 (30% Arab-Berber, 30% black Africans, 30% Haratine – descendants of black slaves, who remained slaves until 1980); growth rate 3% p.a.
languages French (official), Hasaniya Arabic, black African languages
religion Sunni Muslim 99%
GNP \$510 per head (1991)
chronology
1903 Became a French protectorate.
1960 Independence achieved from France, with Moktar Ould Daddah as president.
1975 Western Sahara ceded by Spain. Mauritania occupied the southern area and Morocco the north. Polisario Front formed in Sahara to resist the occupation by Mauritania and Morocco.
1978 Daddah deposed in bloodless coup; replaced by Mohamed Khouna Ould Haidalla. Peace agreed with Polisario Front.
1981 Diplomatic relations with Morocco broken.
1984 Haidalla overthrown by Maaouia Ould Sid Ahmed Taya. Polisario regime formally recognized.
1985 Relations with Morocco restored.
1989 Violent clashes between Mauritanians and Senegalese. Arab-dominated government expelled thousands of Africans into N Senegal; governments had earlier agreed to repatriate each other's citizens (about 250,000).
1991 Amnesty for political prisoners. Multiparty elections promised. Calls for resignation of President Taya.
1992 First multiparty elections won by ruling PRDS. Diplomacy with Senegal resumed.

Mauritius Republic of
area 1,865 sq km/720 sq mi; the island of Rodrigues is part of Mauritius; there are several small island dependencies
capital Port Louis
towns Beau Bassin-Rose Hill, Curepipe, Quatre Bornes
physical mountainous, volcanic island surrounded by coral reefs
head of state Cassam Uteem from 1992

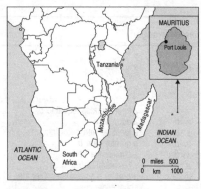

head of government Aneerood Jugnauth from 1982
political system liberal democratic republic
exports sugar, knitted goods, tea
currency Mauritius rupee
population (1993 est) 1,100,000, 68% of Indian origin; growth rate 1.5% p.a.
languages English (official), French, creole, Indian languages
religions Hindu 51%, Christian 30%, Muslim 17%
GNP \$3,000 per head (1992)
chronology
1814 Annexed to Britain by the Treaty of Paris.
1968 Independence achieved from Britain within the Commonwealth, with Seewoosagur Ramgoolam as prime minister.
1982 Aneerood Jugnauth became prime minister.
1983 Jugnauth formed a new party, the Mauritius Socialist Movement. Ramgoolam appointed governor general. Jugnauth formed a new coalition government.
1985 Ramgoolam died, succeeded by Veersamy Ringadoo.
1987 Jugnauth's coalition re-elected.
1990 Attempt to create a republic failed.
1991 Jugnauth's ruling MSM–MMM–OPR coalition won general election; pledge to secure republican status by 1992.
1992 Mauritius became a republic while remaining a member of the Commonwealth. Ringadoo became interim president.

Maurois André. Pen name of Emile Herzog 1885–1967. French novelist and writer whose works include the semi-autobiographical *Bernard Quesnay* 1926 and fictionalized biographies, such as *Ariel* 1923, a life of Shelley.

Maurya dynasty Indian dynasty c. 321–c. 185 BC, founded by **Chandragupta Maurya** (321–c. 279 BC). Under Emperor *Asoka most of India was united for the first time, but after his death in 232 the empire was riven by dynastic disputes.

Maxim Hiram Stevens 1840–1916. US-born British inventor of the first automatic machine gun, in 1884.

Maximilian 1832–1867. Emperor of Mexico 1864–67. He accepted that title when the French emperor Napoleon III's troops occupied the country, but encountered resistance from the deposed president Benito *Juárez. In 1866, after the French troops withdrew on the insistence of the USA, Maximilian was captured by Mexican republicans and shot.

Maximilian I 1459–1519. Holy Roman emperor from 1493, the son of Emperor Frederick III. He had acquired the Low Countries through his marriage to Mary of Burgundy 1477.

maximum and minimum in *coordinate geometry, points at which the slope of a curve representing a *function changes from positive to negative (maximum), or from negative to positive (minimum). A tangent to the curve at a maximum or minimum has zero gradient.

maxwell cgs unit (symbol Mx) of magnetic flux (the strength of a *magnetic field in an area multiplied by the area). It is now replaced by the SI unit, the *weber (one maxwell equals 10^{-8} weber).

Maxwell (Ian) Robert (born Jan Ludvik Hoch) 1923–1991. Czech-born British publishing and newspaper proprietor who owned several UK national newspapers, including the *Daily Mirror*, the Macmillan Publishing Company, and the New York *Daily News*. At the time of his death the Maxwell domain carried debts of some $3.9 billion.

Maxwell James Clerk 1831–1879. Scottish physicist. His main achievement was in the understanding of *electromagnetic waves: *Maxwell's equations* bring together electricity, magnetism, and light in one set of relations. He contributed to every branch of physical science – studying gases, optics, and the sensation of colour. His theoretical work in magnetism prepared the way for wireless telegraphy and telephony.

maya (Sanskrit 'illusion') in Hindu philosophy, mainly in the *Vedānta*, the cosmos which Isvara, the personal expression of Brahman, or the *atman, has called into being. This is real, yet also an illusion, since its reality is not everlasting.

Maya member of an American Indian civilization originating in the Yucatán Peninsula in Central America about 2600 BC, with later sites in Mexico, Guatemala, and Belize, and enjoying a classical period AD 325–925, after which it declined. Today they are Roman Catholic, and live in Yucatán, Guatemala, Belize, and W Honduras. Many still speak Maya, a member of the Totonac-Mayan (Penutian) language family, as well as Spanish.

Mayan art art of the Central American civilization of the Maya, between about AD 300 and 900. Mayan figures have distinctive squat proportions and squared-off composition. Large, steeply inclined pyramids were built, such as those at *Chichen Itzá, decorated with sculpture and inscription. Bonampak, Copan, Tikal, and Palenque were other sites of Mayan worship. In sculpture, human heads and giant reclining figures of Mayan deities are frequent motifs.

May Day first day of May. In many countries it is a national holiday in honour of labour; see also *Labour Day.

Mayer Julius Robert von 1814–1878. German physicist who in 1842 anticipated James *Joule in deriving the mechanical equivalent of heat, and Hermann von *Helmholtz in the principle of conservation of energy.

Mayer Louis B(urt). Adopted name of Eliezer Mayer 1885–1957. Russian-born US film producer, one of the founders of Metro-Goldwyn-Mayer (MGM) studios 1924. In charge of production, Mayer instituted the Hollywood 'star' system. He retired from MGM 1951.

Mayflower the ship in which the *Pilgrims sailed 1620 from Plymouth, England, to found Plymouth plantation and Plymouth colony in present-day Massachusetts.

mayfly any insect of the order Ephemerida (Greek *ephemeros* 'lasting for a day', an allusion to the very brief life of the adult). The larval stage, which can last a year or more, is passed in water, the adult form developing gradually from the nymph through successive moults. The adult has transparent, net-veined wings.

Mayhew Patrick (Barnabas Burke) 1929– . British lawyer and Conservative politician, Northern Ireland secretary from 1992. He was appointed Solicitor General 1983 and four years later Attorney General, becoming the government's chief legal adviser. His appointment as Northern Ireland secretary came at a propitious time and within two years he had witnessed the voluntary cessation of violence by both Republicans and Loyalists.

Mayo county in Connacht province, Republic of Ireland
area 5,400 sq km/2,084 sq mi
towns Castlebar (administrative town)
products sheep and cattle farming; salmon, potatoes, oats, and pigs
population (1991) 110,700.

mayor title of head of urban administration. In England, Wales, and Northern Ireland, the mayor is the principal officer of a district council that has been granted district-borough status under royal charter. In the USA a mayor is the elected head of a city or town.

mayweed any of several species of the daisy family Compositae native to Europe and Asia, and naturalized elsewhere, including the European dog fennel or stinking daisy *Anthemis cotula*, naturalized in North America, and Eurasian pineapple mayweed *Matricaria matricarioides*. All have finely divided leaves.

Mazarin Jules 1602–1661. French politician who succeeded Richelieu as chief minister of France 1642. His attack on the power of the nobility led to the *Fronde and his temporary exile, but his diplomacy achieved a successful conclusion to the Thirty Years' War, and, in alliance with Oliver Cromwell during the British protectorate, he gained victory over Spain.

Mazowiecki Tadeusz 1927– . Polish politician, founder member of *Solidarity, and Poland's first postwar noncommunist prime minister 1989–90.

mazurka lively national dance of Poland from the 16th century. In triple time, it is characterized by foot-stamping and heel-clicking, together with a turning movement.

Mazzini Giuseppe 1805–1872. Italian nationalist. He was a member of the revolutionary society, the *Carbonari, and founded in exile the nationalist movement Giovane Italia (Young Italy) 1832. Returning to Italy on the outbreak of the 1848 revolution, he headed a republican government established in Rome, but was forced into exile again on its overthrow 1849. He acted as a focus for the movement for Italian unity (see *Risorgimento).

Mbabane capital (since 1902) of Swaziland, 160 km/100 mi west of Maputo, in the Dalgeni Hills; population (1986) 38,000. Mining and tourism are important.

mbalax pop music of W Africa with polyrhythmic percussion and dramatic vocal harmonies. Evolving from the traditional rhythms of the Mandinka people, and absorbing a Cuban influence, it incorporated electric guitars and other Western instruments in the 1970s. The singer Youssou *N'Dour made *mbalax* known outside Africa.

mbaqanga or *township jive* South African pop music, an urban style that evolved in the 1960s, with high-pitched, choppy guitar and a powerful bass line; it draws on funk, reggae, and (vocally) on South African choral music. Mahlathini (1937–) and the Mahotella Queens are long-established exponents.

MDMA psychedelic drug (3,4-methylenedioxymethamphetamine), also known as *ecstasy.

ME abbreviation for *myalgic encephalitis*, a debilitating condition still not universally accepted as a genuine disease. The condition occurs after a flulike attack and has a diffuse range of symptoms. These strike and recur for years and include extreme fatigue, muscular pain, weakness, and depression.

mead alcoholic drink made from honey and water fermented with yeast, often with added spices. It was known in ancient times and was drunk by the Greeks, Britons, and Norse.

mean in mathematics, a measure of the average of a number of terms or quantities. The simple *arithmetic mean* is the average value of the quantities, that is, the sum of the quantities divided by their number. The *weighted mean* takes into account the frequency of the terms that are summed; it is calculated by multiplying each term by the number of times it occurs, summing the results and dividing this total by the total number of occurrences. The *geometric mean* of n quantities is the nth root of their product. In statistics, it is a measure of central tendency of a set of data.

meander loop-shaped curve in a river flowing across flat country. As a river flows, any curve in its course is accentuated by the current. The current is fastest on the outside of the curve where it cuts into the bank; on the curve's inside the current is slow and deposits any transported material. In this way the river changes its course across the flood plain.

mean free path in physics, the average distance travelled by a particle, atom, or molecule between successive collisions. It is of importance in the *kinetic theory of gases.

measles acute virus disease (rubeola), spread by airborne infection. Symptoms are fever, severe catarrh, small spots inside the mouth, and a raised, blotchy red rash appearing for about a week after two weeks' incubation. Prevention is by vaccination.

meat flesh of animals taken as food, in Western countries chiefly from domesticated herds of cattle, sheep, pigs, and poultry. Major exporters include Argentina, Australia, New Zealand, Canada, the USA, and Denmark (chiefly bacon). The practice of cooking meat is at least 600,000 years old. More than 40% of the world's grain is now fed to animals.

Meath county in the province of Leinster, Republic of Ireland
area 2,340 sq km/903 sq mi
county town Trim
products sheep, cattle
population (1991) 105,600.

Mecca (Arabic *Makkah*) city in Saudi Arabia and, as birthplace of Muhammad, the holiest city of the Islamic world; population (1974) 367,000. In the centre of Mecca is the Great Mosque, in the courtyard of which is the *Kaaba.

mechanical advantage the amount by which a machine can magnify a force. It is the load (the weight lifted or moved by the machine) divided by the effort (the force used by the operator).

mechanical equivalent of heat in physics, a constant factor relating the calorie (the c.g.s. unit of heat) to the joule (the unit of mechanical energy), equal to 4.1868 joules per calorie. It is redundant in the SI system of units, which measures heat and all forms of energy in joules (so that the mechanical equivalent of heat is 1).

mechanics branch of physics dealing with the motions of bodies and the forces causing these motions, and also with the forces acting on bodies in *equilibrium. It is usually divided into *dynamics and *statics.

mechanized infantry combat vehicle (MICV) tracked military vehicle designed to fight as part of an armoured battle group; that is, with tanks. It is armed with a quick-firing cannon and one or more machine guns. MICVs have replaced armoured personnel carriers.

Mechnikov Ilya 1845–1916. Russian scientist who discovered the function of white blood cells and *phagocytes. After leaving Russia and joining *Pasteur in Paris, he described how these 'scavenger cells' can attack the body itself (autoimmune disease). He shared the Nobel Prize for Medicine 1908 with Paul *Ehrlich.

Mecklenburg–West Pomerania (German *Mecklenburg-Vorpommern*) administrative *Land* (state) of Germany
area 22,887 sq km/8,840 sq mi
capital Schwerin
towns Rostock, Wismar, Stralsund, Neubrandenburg
products fish, ships, diesel engines, electronics, plastics, chalk
population (1990) 2,100,000
history the state was formerly the two grand duchies of Mecklenburg-Schwerin and Mecklenburg-Strelitz, which became free states of the Weimar Republic 1918–34, and were joined 1946 with part of Pomerania to form a region of East Germany. In 1952 it was split into the districts of Rostock, Schwerin, and Neubrandenburg. Following German reunification 1990, the districts were abolished and Mecklenburg–West Pomerania was reconstructed as one of the five new states of the Federal Republic.

Medan seaport and economic centre of the island of Sumatra, Indonesia; population (1980)

1,379,000. It trades in rubber, tobacco, and palm oil.

Medawar Peter (Brian) 1915–1987. Brazilian-born British immunologist who, with Australian physician Macfarlane Burnet (1899–1985), discovered that the body's resistance to grafted tissue is undeveloped in the newborn child, and studied the way it is acquired.

Mede member of a people of NW Iran who in the 9th century BC were tributaries to Assyria, with their capital at Ecbatana (now Hamadán), in the ancient SW Asian country of Media. Allying themselves with Babylon, they destroyed the Assyrian capital of *Nineveh 612 BC, and extended their conquests into central Anatolia. In 550 BC they were overthrown by the Persians, with whom they rapidly merged.

Medea in Greek mythology, the sorceress daughter of the king of Colchis. When *Jason reached the court, she fell in love with him, helped him acquire the Golden Fleece, and they fled together. When Jason married Creusa, Medea killed his bride with the gift of a poisoned garment, and then killed her own two children by Jason.

Medellín industrial town (textiles, chemicals, engineering, coffee) in the Central Cordillera, Colombia, 1,538 m/5,048 ft above sea level; population (1985) 2,069,000. It is the second city of Colombia, and its drug capital, with 7,000 violent deaths in 1990.

median in mathematics and statistics, the middle number of an ordered group of numbers. If there is no middle number (because there is an even number of terms), the median is the *mean (average) of the two middle numbers. For example, the median of the group 2, 3, 7, 11, 12 is 7; that of 3, 4, 7, 9, 11, 13 is 8 (the average of 7 and 9).

medical ethics moral guidelines for doctors. Traditionally these have been set out in the Hippocratic Oath (introduced by Greek physician *Hippocrates and including such injunctions as the command to preserve confidentiality, to help the sick to the best of one's ability, and to refuse fatal draughts), but in the late 20th century rapidly advancing technology has raised the question of how far medicine should intervene in natural processes.

Medici noble family of Florence, the city's rulers from 1434 until they died out 1737. Family members included *Catherine de' Medici, Pope *Leo X, Pope *Clement VII, *Marie de' Medici.

Medici Cosimo de' 1389–1464. Italian politician and banker. Regarded as the model for Machiavelli's *The Prince*, he dominated the government of Florence from 1434 and was a patron of the arts. He was succeeded by his inept son *Piero de' Medici* (1416–1469).

Medici Lorenzo de', *the Magnificent* 1449–1492. Italian politician, ruler of Florence from 1469. He was also a poet and a generous patron of the arts.

medicine science of preventing, diagnosing, alleviating, or curing disease, both physical and mental; also any substance used in the treatment of disease. The basis of medicine is anatomy (the structure and form of the body) and physiology (the study of the body's functions).

medicine, alternative forms of medical treatment that do not use synthetic drugs or surgery in response to the symptoms of a disease, but aim to treat the patient as a whole (*holism). The emphasis is on maintaining health (with diet and exercise) and on dealing with the underlying causes rather than just the symptoms of illness. It may involve the use of herbal remedies and techniques like *acupuncture, *homeopathy, and *chiropractic. Some alternative treatments are increasingly accepted by orthodox medicine, but the absence of enforceable standards in some fields has led to the proliferation of eccentric or untrained practitioners.

medieval art painting and sculpture of the Middle Ages in Europe and parts of the Middle East, dating roughly from the 4th century to the emergence of the Renaissance in Italy in the 1400s. This includes early Christian, Byzantine, Celtic, Anglo-Saxon, and Carolingian art. The Romanesque style was the first truly international style of medieval times, superseded by Gothic in the late 12th century.

Medina (Arabic *Madinah*) Saudi Arabian city, about 355 km/220 mi N of Mecca; population (1986 est) 500,000. It is the second-holiest city in the Islamic world, and is believed to contain the tomb of Muhammad. It produces grain and fruit.

meditation act of spiritual contemplation, practised by members of many religions or as a secular exercise. It is a central practice in Buddhism. The Sanskrit term is *dhyāna*. See also *transcendental meditation (TM).

Mediterranean Sea inland sea separating Europe from N Africa, with Asia to the east; extreme length 3,700 km/2,300 mi; area 2,966,000 sq km/1,145,000 sq mi. It is linked to the Atlantic (at the Strait of Gibraltar), Red Sea, and Indian Ocean (by the Suez Canal), Black Sea (at the Dardanelles and Sea of Marmara). The main subdivisions are the Adriatic, Aegean, Ionian, and Tyrrhenian seas. It is highly polluted.

medlar small shrub or tree *Mespilus germanica* of the rose family Rosaceae. Native to SE Europe, it is widely cultivated for its fruit, resembling a small brown-green pear or quince. These are palatable when decay has set in.

medulla central part of an organ. In the mammalian kidney, the medulla lies beneath the outer cortex and is responsible for the reabsorption of water from the filtrate. In plants, it is a region of packing tissue in the centre of the stem. In the vertebrate brain, the medulla is the posterior region responsible for the coordination of basic activities, such as breathing and temperature control.

Medusa in Greek mythology, a mortal woman who was transformed into a *Gorgon. Medusa was slain by Perseus; the winged horse *Pegasus was supposed to have sprung from her blood.

mefipristone (formerly *RU-486*) abortion pill first introduced in France 1989, and effective in 94% of patients up to 10 weeks pregnant when

WESTERN MEDICINE: CHRONOLOGY

c. 400 BC	Hippocrates recognized that disease had natural causes.
c. AD 200	Galen consolidated the work of the Alexandrian doctors.
1543	Andreas Vesalius gave the first accurate account of the human body.
1628	William Harvey discovered the circulation of the blood.
1768	John Hunter began the foundation of experimental and surgical pathology.
1785	Digitalis was used to treat heart disease; the active ingredient was isolated 1904.
1798	Edward Jenner published his work on vaccination.
1877	Patrick Manson studied animal carriers of infectious diseases.
1882	Robert Koch isolated the bacillus responsible for tuberculosis.
1884	Edwin Klebs isolated the diphtheria bacillus.
1885	Louis Pasteur produced a vaccine against rabies.
1890	Joseph Lister demonstrated antiseptic surgery.
1897	Martinus Beijerinck discovered viruses.
1899	Felix Hoffman developed aspirin; Sigmund Freud founded psychiatry.
1910	Paul Ehrlich developed the first specific antibacterial agent, Salvarsan, a cure for syphilis.
1922	Insulin was first used to treat diabetes.
1928	Alexander Fleming discovered penicillin.
1932	Gerhard Domagk discovered the first antibacterial sulphonamide drug, Prontosil.
1937	Electro-convulsive therapy (ECT) was developed.
1950s	Antidepressant drugs and beta-blockers for heart disease were developed. Manipulation of the molecules of synthetic chemicals became the main source of new drugs. Peter Medawar studied the body's tolerance of transplanted organs and skin grafts.
1953	Francis Crick and James Watson announced the structure of DNA. Jonas Salk developed a vaccine against polio.
1960s	A new generation of minor tranquillizers called benzodiazepines was developed.
1967	Christiaan Barnard performed the first human heart-transplant operation.
1972	The CAT scan, pioneered by Godfrey Hounsfield, was first used to image the human brain.
1975	César Milstein developed monoclonal antibodies.
1978	World's first 'test-tube baby' was born in the UK.
1980s	AIDS (acquired immune-deficiency syndrome) was first recognized in the USA.
1980	The World Health Organization reported the eradication of smallpox.
1983	The virus responsible for AIDS, now known as human immunodeficiency virus (HIV), was identified by Luc Montagnier at the Institut Pasteur, Paris; Robert Gallo at the National Cancer Institute, Maryland, USA discovered the virus independently 1984.
1984	The first vaccine against leprosy was developed.
1989	Grafts of fetal brain tissue were first used to treat Parkinson's disease.
1990	Gene for maleness discovered by UK researchers.
1991	First successful use of gene therapy (to treat severe combined immune deficiency) was reported in the USA.
1993	First trials of gene therapy against cystic fibrosis took place in the USA.

administered in conjunction with a prostaglandin. It was licensed in the UK in 1991.

mega- prefix denoting multiplication by a million. For example, a megawatt (MW) is equivalent to a million watts.

megabyte (Mb) in computing, a unit of memory equal to 1,024 *kilobytes. It is sometimes used, less precisely, to mean 1 million bytes.

megalith prehistoric stone monument of the late Neolithic or early Bronze Age. Most common in Europe, megaliths include single, large uprights (*menhirs*, for example, the Five Kings, Northumberland, England); *rows* (for example, Carnac, Brittany, France); *circles*, generally with a central 'altar stone' (for example, Stonehenge, Wiltshire, England); and the remains of burial chambers with the covering earth removed, looking like a hut (*dolmens*, for example Kits Coty, Kent, England).

megamouth deep-sea shark *Megachasma pelagios*, which feeds on plankton. It was first discovered 1976. It has a bulbous head with protruding jaws and blubbery lips, is 4.5 m/15 ft long, and weighs 750 kg/1,650 lb.

megapode large (up to 70 cm/2.3 ft long) chickenlike bird of the family Megapodiidae,

NOBEL PRIZE FOR PHYSIOLOGY OR MEDICINE

recent prizewinners

1989	Michael Bishop (USA) and Harold Varmus (USA): discovery of oncogenes, genes carried by viruses that can trigger cancerous growth in normal cells
1990	Joseph Murray (USA) and Donnall Thomas (USA): pioneering work in organ and cell transplants
1991	Erwin Neher (Germany) and Bert Sakmann (Germany): discovery of how gatelike structures (ion channels) regulate the flow of ions into and out of cells
1992	Edmond Fisher (USA) and Edwin Krebs (USA): isolating and describing the action of the enzyme responsible for reversible protein phosphorylation, a major biological control mechanism
1993	Phillip Sharp (USA) and Richard Roberts (UK): discovery of split genes (genes interrupted by nonsense segments of DNA)
1994	Alfred Gilman (USA) and Martin Rodbell (USA): discovery of a family of proteins (G proteins) that translate messages – in the form of hormones or other chemical signals – into action inside cells

found mainly in Australia, but also in SE Asia. Megapodes lay their eggs in a pile of rotting vegetation 4 m/13 ft across, and the warmth from this provides the heat for incubation. The male bird feels the mound with his tongue and adds or takes away vegetation to provide the correct temperature.

megaton one million (10^6) tons. Used with reference to the explosive power of a nuclear weapon, it is equivalent to the explosive force of one million tons of trinitrotoluene (TNT).

Meghalaya state of NE India
area 22,500 sq km/8,685 sq mi
capital Shillong
products potatoes, cotton, jute, fruit
minerals coal, limestone, white clay, corundum, sillimanite
population (1991) 1,760,600, mainly Khasi, Jaintia, and Garo
religion Hindu 70%
languages various.

Megiddo site of a fortress town in N Israel, where Thothmes III defeated the Canaanites about 1469 BC; the Old Testament figure Josiah was killed in battle about 609 BC; and in World War I the British field marshal Allenby broke the Turkish front 1918. It is identified with *Armageddon.

Mehemet Ali 1769–1849. Pasha (governor) of Egypt from 1805, and founder of the dynasty that ruled until 1953. An Albanian in the Ottoman service, he had originally been sent to Egypt to fight the French. As pasha, he established a European-style army and navy, fought his Turkish overlord 1831 and 1839, and conquered Sudan.

Mehta Zubin 1936– . Indian conductor who became music director of the New York Philharmonic 1978. He is known for his flamboyant style of conducting and his interpretations of the Romantic composers.

Meier Richard 1934– . US architect whose white designs spring from the poetic modernism of the *Le Corbusier villas of the 1920s. His abstract style is at its most mature in the Museum für Kunsthandwerk (Museum of Arts and Crafts), Frankfurt, Germany, which was completed 1984.

Meiji Mutsuhito 1852–1912. Emperor of Japan from 1867, when he took the title *meiji tennō* ('enlightened sovereign'). During his reign (known as the Meiji era) Japan became a world industrial and naval power. He abolished the feudal system and discrimination against the lowest caste, established state schools, and introduced conscription, the Western calendar, and other measures in an attempt to modernize Japan, including a constitution 1889.

Meinhof Ulrike 1934–1976. West German urban guerrilla, member of the *Baader–Meinhof gang* in the 1970s.

Mein Kampf (German 'my struggle') book dictated by Adolf *Hitler to Rudolf Hess 1923–24 during Hitler's jail sentence for his part in the abortive 1923 Munich beer-hall putsch. Part autobiography, part political philosophy, the book presents Hitler's ideas of German expansion, anticommunism, and anti-Semitism. It was published in two volumes, 1925 and 1927.

meiosis in biology, a process of cell division in which the number of *chromosomes in the cell is halved. It only occurs in *eukaryotic cells, and is part of a life cycle that involves sexual reproduction because it allows the genes of two parents to be combined without the total number of chromosomes increasing.

Meir Golda 1898–1978. Israeli Labour (*Mapai*) politician. Born in Russia, she emigrated to the USA 1906, and in 1921 went to Palestine. She was foreign minister 1956–66 and prime minister 1969–74. Criticism of the Israelis' lack of preparation for the 1973 Arab-Israeli War led to election losses for Labour, and unable to form a government, she resigned.

Meistersinger (German 'master singer') one of a group of German lyric poets, singers, and musicians of the 14th–16th centuries, who formed guilds for the revival of minstrelsy. Hans Sachs of Nuremberg (1494–1576) was a Meistersinger, and Richard Wagner's opera *Die Meistersinger von Nürnberg* 1868 depicts the tradition.

Mekong river rising as the Za Qu in Tibet and flowing to the South China Sea, through a vast delta (about 200,000 sq km/77,000 sq mi); length 4,425 km/2,750 mi. It is being developed for irrigation and hydroelectricity by Cambodia, Laos, Thailand, and Vietnam.

Melaka Malaysian form of *Malacca, state of Peninsular Malaysia.

melaleuca tree or *paperbark* tropical tree *Melaleuca leucadendron*, family Myrtaceae. The leaves produce *cajuput oil*, which has medicinal uses.

melamine $C_3N_6H_6$ thermosetting *polymer based on urea–formaldehyde. It is extremely resistant to heat and is also scratch-resistant. Its uses include synthetic resins.

Melanchthon Philip. Assumed name of Philip Schwarzerd 1497–1560. German theologian who helped Luther prepare a German translation of the New Testament. In 1521 he issued the first systematic formulation of Protestant theology, reiterated in the *Confession of *Augsburg* 1530.

Melanesia islands in the SW Pacific between Micronesia to the north and Polynesia to the east, embracing all the islands from the New Britain archipelago to Fiji.

melanoma mole or growth containing the dark pigment melanin. Malignant melanoma is a type of skin cancer developing in association with a pre-existing mole. Unlike other skin cancers, it is associated with brief but excessive exposure to sunlight.

Melbourne capital of Victoria, Australia, near the mouth of the river Yarra; population (1990) 3,080,000. Industries include engineering, shipbuilding, electronics, chemicals, food processing, clothing, and textiles.

Melchite or *Melkite* member of a Christian church in Syria, Egypt, Lebanon, and Israel. The Melchite Church was founded in Syria in the 6th–7th centuries and is now part of the Eastern Orthodox Church.

Méliès Georges 1861–1938. French film pioneer. From 1896 to 1912 he made over 1,000 films, mostly fantasies (*Le Voyage dans la Lune/A Trip to the Moon* 1902). He developed trick effects, slow motion, double exposure, and

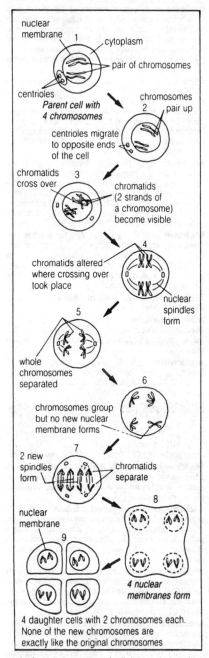

nuclear membrane 1

cytoplasm

pair of chromosomes

centrioles

Parent cell with 4 chromosomes

chromosomes 2 pair up

centrioles migrate to opposite ends of the cell

chromatids cross over 3

chromatids (2 strands of a chromosome) become visible

chromatids altered where crossing over took place 4

nuclear spindles form

5

whole chromosomes separated

6

chromosomes group but no new nuclear membrane forms

2 new spindles form 7

chromatids separate

8

nuclear membrane 9

4 nuclear membranes form

4 daughter cells with 2 chromosomes each. None of the new chromosomes are exactly like the original chromosomes

meiosis Meiosis is a type of cell division that produces gametes (sex cells, sperm and egg).

dissolves, and in 1897 built Europe's first film studio at Montreuil.

melodrama play or film with romantic and sensational plot elements, often unsubtly acted. Originally it meant a play accompanied by music. The early melodramas used extravagant theatrical effects to heighten violent emotions and actions artificially. By the end of the 19th century, melodrama had become a popular genre of stage play.

melon any of several large, juicy (95% water), thick-skinned fruits of trailing plants of the gourd family Cucurbitaceae. The muskmelon *Cucumis melo* and the large red watermelon *Citrullus vulgaris* are two of the many edible varieties.

meltdown the melting of the core of a nuclear reactor, due to overheating. To prevent such accidents all reactors have equipment intended to flood the core with water in an emergency. The reactor is housed in a strong containment vessel, designed to prevent radiation escaping into the atmosphere. The result of a meltdown is an area radioactively contaminated for 25,000 years or more.

melting point temperature at which a substance melts, or changes from a solid to liquid form. A pure substance under standard conditions of pressure (usually one atmosphere) has a definite melting point. If heat is supplied to a solid at its melting point, the temperature does not change until the melting process is complete. The melting point of ice is 0°C or 32°F.

Melville Herman 1819–1891. US writer whose novel *Moby-Dick* 1851 was inspired by his whaling experiences in the South Seas. These experiences were also the basis for earlier fiction, such as *Typee* 1846 and *Omoo* 1847. *Billy Budd* was completed just before his death and published 1924. Although most of his works were unappreciated during his lifetime, today he is one of the most highly regarded of US authors.

membrane in living things, a continuous layer, made up principally of fat molecules, that encloses a *cell or *organelles within a cell. Certain small molecules can pass through the cell membrane, but most must enter or leave the cell via channels in the membrane made up of special proteins. The *Golgi apparatus within the cell is thought to produce certain membranes.

Memling (or *Memlinc*) Hans *c.* 1430–1494. Flemish painter, born near Frankfurt-am-Main, Germany, but active in Bruges. He painted religious subjects and portraits. Some of his works are in the Hospital of St John, Bruges, including the *Adoration of the Magi* 1479.

memory in computing, the part of a system used to store data and programs either permanently or temporarily. There are two main types: immediate access memory and backing storage. Memory capacity is measured in *bytes or, more conveniently, in kilobytes (units of 1,024 bytes) or megabytes (units of 1,024 kilobytes).

memory ability to store and recall observations and sensations. Memory does not seem to be based in any particular part of the brain; it may depend on changes to the pathways followed by nerve impulses as they move through the brain. Memory can be improved by regular use as the connections between *nerve cells (neurons) become 'well-worn paths' in the brain. Events stored in ***short-term memory*** are forgotten quickly, whereas those in ***long-term memory*** can last for many years, enabling recall of information and recognition of people and places over long periods of time. Research is just beginning to uncover the biochemical and electrical bases of the human memory.

Memphis ruined city beside the Nile, 19 km/ 12 mi S of Cairo, Egypt. Once the centre of the worship of Ptah, it was the earliest capital of a united Egypt under King Menes about 3200 BC, but was superseded by Thebes under the new empire 1570 BC.

Memphis industrial port city (pharmaceuticals, food processing, cotton, timber, tobacco) on the Mississippi River, in Tennessee, USA; population (1990) 610,300. Its musical history includes Beale Street, home of the blues composer W C Handy, and Graceland, the home of Elvis Presley. The French built a fort here 1739, but Memphis was not founded until 1819.

Menander c. 342–291 BC. Greek comic dramatist, born in Athens. His work was virtually unknown until the discovery 1905 of substantial fragments of four of his plays in Eygptian papyri (many had been used as papier-mâché for Egyptian mummy cases). In 1957 the only complete Menander play, *Dyscholos/The Bad-Tempered Man*, was found.

Mencken H(enry) L(ouis) 1880–1956. US essayist and critic, known as 'the sage of Baltimore'. His unconventionally phrased, satiric contributions to the periodicals *The Smart Set* and *American Mercury* (both of which he edited) aroused controversy.

Mende member of a W African people living in the rainforests of central east Sierra Leone and W Liberia. They number approximately 1 million. The Mende are farmers as well as hunter-gatherers, and each of their villages is led by a chief and a group of elders. The Mende language belongs to the Niger-Congo family.

Mendel Gregor Johann 1822–1884. Austrian biologist, founder of *genetics. His experiments with successive generations of peas gave the basis for his theory of particulate inheritance rather than blending, involving dominant and recessive characters; see *Mendelism. His results, published 1865–69, remained unrecognized until the early 20th century.

mendelevium synthesized, radioactive metallic element of the *actinide series, symbol Md, atomic number 101, relative atomic mass 258. It was first produced by bombardment of Es-253 with helium nuclei. Its longest-lived isotope, Md-258, has a half-life of about two months. The element is chemically similar to thulium. It was named by the US physicists at the University of California at Berkeley who first synthesized it 1955 after the Russian chemist Mendeleyev, who in 1869 devised the basis for the periodic table of the elements.

Mendeleyev Dmitri Ivanovich 1834–1907. Russian chemist who framed the periodic law in chemistry 1869, which states that the chemical properties of the elements depend on their relative atomic masses. This law is the basis of the *periodic table of elements, in which the elements are arranged by atomic number and organized by their related groups.

Mendelism in genetics, the theory of inheritance originally outlined by Gregor Mendel. He

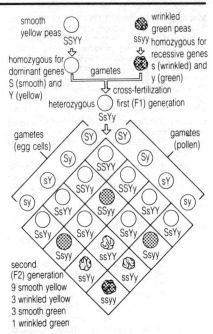

Mendelism Mendel's laws explain the proportion of offspring having various characteristics.

suggested that, in sexually reproducing species, all characteristics are inherited through indivisible 'factors' (now identified with *genes) contributed by each parent to its offspring.

Mendelssohn (-Bartholdy) (Jakob Ludwig) Felix 1809–1847. German composer, also a pianist and conductor. As a child he composed and performed with his own orchestra and as an adult was helpful to *Schumann's career. Among his best-known works are *A Midsummer Night's Dream* 1827; the *Fingal's Cave* overture 1832; and five symphonies, which include the Reformation 1830, the Italian 1833, and the Scottish 1842. He was instrumental in promoting the revival of interest in J S Bach's music.

Mendes Chico (Filho Francisco) 1944–1988. Brazilian environmentalist and labour leader. Opposed to the destruction of Brazil's rainforests, he organized itinerant rubber tappers into the Workers' Party (PT) and was assassinated by Darci Alves, a cattle rancher's son. Of 488 similar murders in land conflicts in Brazil 1985–89, his was the first to come to trial.

mendicant order religious order dependent on alms. In the Roman Catholic Church there are four orders of mendicant friars: Franciscans, Dominicans, Carmelites, and Augustinians. Hinduism has similar orders.

Mendoza Antonio de c. 1490–1552. First Spanish viceroy of New Spain (Mexico) 1535–51. He attempted to develop agriculture and mining and supported the church in its attempts to convert the Indians. The system he established lasted until the 19th century. He was subsequently viceroy of Peru 1551–52.

Menem Carlos (Saul) 1935– . Argentine politician, president from 1989; leader of the Peronist (Justicialist Party) movement. As president, he introduced sweeping privatization and public-spending cuts, released hundreds of political prisoners jailed under the Alfonsín regime, and sent two warships to the Persian Gulf to assist the USA against Iraq in the 1992 Gulf War (the only Latin American country to offer support to the USA). He also improved relations with the UK.

Menes c. 3200 BC. Traditionally, the first king of the first dynasty of ancient Egypt. He is said to have founded Memphis and organized worship of the gods.

Mengistu Haile Mariam 1937– . Ethiopian soldier and socialist politician, head of state 1977–91 (president 1987–91). He seized power in a coup and was confronted with severe problems of drought and secessionist uprisings, but survived with help from the USSR and the West until his violent overthrow.

menhir (Breton 'long stone') prehistoric standing stone; see *megalith.

meningitis inflammation of the meninges (membranes) surrounding the brain, caused by bacterial or viral infection. Bacterial meningitis, though treatable by antibiotics, is the more serious threat. Diagnosis is by *lumbar puncture.

meniscus in physics, the curved shape of the surface of a liquid in a thin tube, caused by the cohesive effects of *surface tension (capillary action). When the walls of the container are made wet by the liquid, the meniscus is concave, but with highly viscous liquids (such as mercury) the meniscus is convex. Meniscus is also the name of a concavo-convex or convexo-concave *lens.

Mennonite member of a Protestant Christian sect, originating as part of the *Anabaptist movement in Zürich, Switzerland, 1523. Members refuse to hold civil office or do military service, and reject infant baptism. They were named Mennonites after Menno Simons (1496–1559), leader of a group in Holland. Persecution drove other groups to Russia and North America.

menopause in women, the cessation of reproductive ability, characterized by menstruation (see *menstrual cycle) becoming irregular and eventually ceasing. The onset is at about the age of 50, but varies greatly. Menopause is usually uneventful, but some women suffer from complications such as flushing, excessive bleeding, and nervous disorders. Since the 1950s, *hormone replacement therapy (HRT), using *oestrogen alone or with *progesterone, has been developed to counteract such effects.

menorah seven-branched candlestick symbolizing Judaism and the state of Israel. Also, the candelabrum (having seven branches and a *shammes*, or extra candle with which to light the others) used on *Hanukkah.

Menshevik (Russian *menshinstvo* 'minority') member of the minority of the Russian Social Democratic Party, who split from the *Bolsheviks 1903. The Mensheviks believed in a large, loosely organized party and that, before socialist revolution could occur in Russia, capitalist society had to develop further. During the Russian Revolu-

tion they had limited power and set up a government in Georgia, but were suppressed 1922.

menstrual cycle cycle that occurs in female mammals of reproductive age, in which the body is prepared for pregnancy. At the beginning of the cycle, a Graafian (egg) follicle develops in the ovary, and the inner wall of the uterus forms a soft spongy lining. The egg is released from the ovary, and the lining of the uterus becomes vascularized (filled with blood vessels). If fertilization does not occur, the corpus luteum (remains of the Graafian follicle) degenerates, and the uterine lining breaks down, and is shed. This is what causes the loss of blood that marks menstruation. The cycle then begins again. Human menstruation takes place from puberty to menopause, occurring about every 28 days.

mental handicap impairment of intelligence. It can be very mild, but in more severe cases, it is associated with social problems and difficulties in living independently. A person may be born with a mental handicap (for example, *Down's syndrome) or may acquire it through brain damage. There are between 90 and 130 million people in the world suffering such disabilities.

mental illness abnormal working of the mind. Since normal working cannot easily be defined, the borderline between mild mental illness and normality is a matter of opinion. Mild forms are known as *neuroses*, affecting the emotions, whereas more severe forms, *psychoses*, distort conscious reasoning.

menthol pungent, waxy, crystalline alcohol $C_{10}H_{19}OH$, derived from oil of peppermint and used in medicines and cosmetics.

menu in computing, a list of options, displayed on screen, from which the user may make a choice – for example, the choice of services offered to the customer by a bank cash dispenser: withdrawal, deposit, balance, or statement. Menus are used extensively in *graphical user-interface (GUI) systems, where the menu options are often selected using a pointing device called a *mouse.

Menuhin Yehudi 1916– . US-born violinist and conductor. A child prodigy, he achieved great depth of interpretation, and was often accompanied on the piano by his sister *Hephzibah* (1921–1981). He conducted his own chamber orchestra and founded schools in Surrey, England, and Gstaad, Switzerland, for training young musicians.

Menzies Robert Gordon 1894–1978. Australian politician, leader of the United Australia (now Liberal) Party and prime minister 1939–41 and 1949–66.

Meo or *Miao* another name (sometimes considered derogatory) for the *Hmong, a SE Asian people.

MEP abbreviation for *Member of the *European Parliament*.

Mephistopheles or *Mephisto* another name for the *devil, or an agent of the devil, associated with the *Faust legend.

Mercalli scale scale used to measure the intensity of an *earthquake. It differs from the *Richter scale, which measures *magnitude*. It is named after the Italian seismologist Giuseppe Mercalli (1850–1914).

mercantilism economic theory, held in the 16th–18th centuries, that a nation's wealth (in the form of bullion or treasure) was the key to its prosperity. To this end, foreign trade should be regulated to create a surplus of exports over imports, and the state should intervene where necessary (for example, subsidizing exports and taxing imports). The bullion theory of wealth was demolished by Adam *Smith in Book IV of *The Wealth of Nations* 1776.

Mercator Gerardus 1512–1594. Latinized form of the name of the Flemish map-maker Gerhard Kremer. He devised the first modern atlas, showing *Mercator's projection* in which the parallels and meridians on maps are drawn uniformly at 90°. It is often used for navigational charts, because compass courses can be drawn as straight lines, but the true area of countries is increasingly distorted the further north or south they are from the equator. For other types, see *map projection.

Mercedes-Benz German car-manufacturing company created by a merger of the Daimler and Benz factories 1926. The first cars to carry the Mercedes name were those built by Gottlieb *Daimler 1901.

mercenary soldier hired by the army of another country or by a private army. Mercenary military service originated in the 14th century, when cash payment on a regular basis was the only means of guaranteeing soldiers' loyalty. In the 20th century mercenaries have been common in wars and guerrilla activity in Asia, Africa, and Latin America.

Merchant Ismail 1936– . Indian film producer, known for his stylish collaborations with James *Ivory on films including *Shakespeare Wallah* 1965, *The Europeans* 1979, *Heat and Dust* 1983, *A Room with a View* 1985, *Maurice* 1987, and *Howard's End* 1992.

merchant bank financial institution that specializes in the provision of corporate finance and financial and advisory services for business. Originally developed in the UK in the 19th century, merchant banks now offer many of the services provided by the commercial banks.

merchant navy the passenger and cargo ships of a country. Most are owned by private companies. To avoid strict regulations on safety, union rules on crew wages, and so on, many ships are today registered under 'flags of convenience', that is, flags of countries that do not have such rules.

Merchants Adventurers English trading company founded 1407, which controlled the export of cloth to continental Europe. It comprised guilds and traders in many N European ports. In direct opposition to the Hanseatic League, it came to control 75% of English overseas trade by 1550. In 1689 it lost its charter for furthering the traders' own interests at the expense of the English economy. The company was finally dissolved 1806.

Mercia Anglo-Saxon kingdom that emerged in the 6th century. By the late 8th century it dominated all England south of the Humber, but from about 825 came under the power of *Wessex. Mercia eventually came to denote an area

bounded by the Welsh border, the river Humber, East Anglia, and the river Thames.

Merckx Eddie 1945– . Belgian cyclist known as 'the Cannibal'. He won the Tour de France a joint record five times 1969–74.

mercury or *quicksilver* heavy, silver-grey, metallic element, symbol Hg (from Latin *hydrargyrum*), atomic number 80, relative atomic mass 200.59. It is a dense, mobile liquid with a low melting point (–38.87°C/–37.96°F). Its chief source is the mineral cinnabar, HgS, but it sometimes occurs in nature as a free metal.

Mercury in astronomy, the closest planet to the Sun, at an average distance of 58 million km/36 million mi. Its diameter is 4,880 km/3,030 mi, its mass 0.056 that of Earth. Mercury orbits the Sun every 88 days, and spins on its axis every 59 days. On its sunward side the surface temperature reaches over 400°C/752°F, but on the 'night' side it falls to –170°C/–274°F. Mercury has an atmosphere with minute traces of argon and helium. In 1974 the US space probe *Mariner 10* discovered that its surface is cratered by meteorite impacts. Mercury has no moons.

Mercury Roman god, identified with the Greek Hermes, and like him represented with winged sandals and a winged staff entwined with snakes. He was the messenger of the gods.

Mercury project US project to put a human in space in the one-seat Mercury spacecraft 1961–63.

merganser any of several diving ducks of the genus *Mergus* with long, serrated bills for catching fish, including the common merganser or goosander *M. merganser* and the red-breasted merganser *M. serrator*. Most have crested heads. They are widely distributed in the northern hemisphere.

Mergenthaler Ottmar 1854–1899. German-born American who invented a typesetting method. He went to the USA in 1872 and developed the first linotype machine (for casting hot-metal type in complete lines) 1876–86.

merger the linking of two or more companies, either by creating a new organization by consolidating the original companies or by absorption by one company of the others. Unlike a takeover, which is not always a voluntary fusion of the parties, a merger is the result of an agreement.

Mérida capital of Yucatán state, Mexico, a centre of the sisal industry; population (1986) 580,000. It was founded 1542, and has a cathedral 1598. Its port on the Gulf of Mexico is Progreso.

meridian half a *great circle drawn on the Earth's surface passing through both poles and thus through all places with the same longitude. Terrestrial longitudes are usually measured from the Greenwich Meridian.

Mérimée Prosper 1803–1870. French author. Among his works are the short novels *Colomba* 1841, *Carmen* 1846, and the *Lettres à une inconnue/Letters to an Unknown Girl* 1873.

merino breed of sheep. Its close-set, silky wool is highly valued. The merino, originally from Spain, is now found all over the world, and is the breed on which the Australian wool industry is built.

meristem region of plant tissue containing cells

that are actively dividing to produce new tissues (or have the potential to do so). Meristems found in the tip of roots and stems, the apical meristems, are responsible for the growth in length of these organs.

merlin small *falcon *Falco columbarius* of Eurasia and North America, where it is also called *pigeon hawk*. The male, 26 cm/10 in long, has a grey-blue back and reddish-brown barred front; the female, 32 cm/13 in long, is brown with streaks.

Merlin legendary magician and counsellor to King *Arthur. Welsh bardic literature has a cycle of poems attributed to him, and he may have been a real person.

mermaid mythical sea creature (the male is a *merman*), having a human head and torso and a fish's tail. The dugong and seal are among suggested origins for the idea.

Merovingian dynasty Frankish dynasty, named after its founder, *Merovech* (5th century AD). His descendants ruled France from the time of Clovis (481–511) to 751.

Mersey river in NW England; length 112 km/70 mi. Formed by the confluence of the Goyt and Etherow rivers, it flows west to join the Irish Sea at Liverpool Bay. It is linked to the Manchester Ship Canal. It is polluted by industrial waste, sewage, and chemicals.

Mersey beat pop music of the mid-1960s that originated in the northwest of England. It was also known as the Liverpool sound or *beat music in the UK. It was almost exclusively performed by all-male groups, of whom the most popular was the Beatles.

Merseyside former (1974–86) metropolitan county of NW England, replaced by a residuary body in 1986 which covers some of its former functions
area 650 sq km/251 sq mi
towns administrative headquarters Liverpool; Bootle, Birkenhead, St Helens, Wallasey, Southport
products chemicals, electrical goods, vehicles
population (1991) 1,376,800
famous people the Beatles, William Ewart Gladstone, George Stubbs.

Merv oasis in Turkmenistan, a centre of civilization from at least 1200 BC, and site of a town founded by Alexander the Great. Old Merv was destroyed by the emir of Bokhara 1787, and the modern town of Mary, founded by the Russians in 1885, lies 29 km/18 mi to its west.

mesa (Spanish 'table') flat-topped steep-sided plateau, consisting of horizontal weak layers of rock topped by a resistant formation; in particular, those found in the desert areas of the USA and Mexico. A small mesa is called a butte.

mescaline psychedelic drug derived from a small, spineless cactus *Lophophora williamsii* of N Mexico and the SW USA, known as *peyote. The tops (called mescal buttons), which scarcely appear above ground, are dried and chewed, or added to alcoholic drinks. Mescaline is a crystalline alkaloid $C_{11}H_{17}NO_3$. It is used by some North American Indians in religious rites.

Meskhetian member of a community of Turkish descent that formerly inhabited Meskhetia,

on the then Turkish-Soviet border. They were deported by Stalin 1944 to Kazakhstan and Uzbekistan, and have campaigned since then for a return to their homeland. In June 1989 at least 70 were killed in pogroms directed against their community in the Ferghana Valley of Uzbekistan by the ethnic Uzbeks.

Mesmer Friedrich Anton 1734–1815. Austrian physician, an early experimenter in *hypnosis, which was formerly (and popularly) called *mesmerism* after him.

Mesolithic the Middle Stone Age developmental stage of human technology and of *prehistory.

meson in physics, an unstable subatomic particle made up of two indivisible elementary particles called quarks. It has a mass intermediate between that of the electron and that of the proton, is found in cosmic radiation, and is emitted by nuclei under bombardment by very high-energy particles.

Mesopotamia the land between the Tigris and Euphrates rivers, now part of Iraq. Here the civilizations of Sumer and Babylon flourished. Sumer (3500 BC) may have been the earliest civilization.

mesosphere layer in the Earth's *atmosphere above the stratosphere and below the thermosphere. It lies between about 50 km/31 mi and 80 km/50 mi above the ground.

Mesozoic era of geological time 245–65 million years ago, consisting of the Triassic, Jurassic, and Cretaceous periods. At the beginning of the era, the continents were joined together as Pangaea; dinosaurs and other giant reptiles dominated the sea and air; and ferns, horsetails, and cycads thrived in a warm climate worldwide. By the end of the Mesozoic era, the continents had begun to assume their present positions, flowering plants were dominant, and many of the large reptiles and marine fauna were becoming extinct.

Messalina Valeria c. AD 22–48. Third wife of the Roman emperor *Claudius, whom she dominated. She was notorious for her immorality, forcing a noble to marry her AD 48, although still married to Claudius, who then had her executed.

Messerschmitt Willy 1898–1978. German aeroplane designer whose Me-109 was a standard Luftwaffe fighter in World War II, and whose Me-262 (1942) was the first mass-produced jet fighter.

Messiaen Olivier 1908–1992. French composer and organist. His music is mystical in character, vividly coloured, and incorporates transcriptions of birdsong. Among his works are the *Quartet for the End of Time* 1941, the large-scale *Turangalîla Symphony* 1949, and solo organ and piano pieces.

Messiah (from Hebrew *māshīach* 'anointed') in Judaism and Christianity, the saviour or deliverer. Jews from the time of the Old Testament exile in Babylon have looked forward to the coming of the Messiah. Christians believe that the Messiah came in the person of *Jesus, and hence called him the Christ.

Messier Charles 1730–1817. French astronomer who discovered 15 comets and in 1781 published a list of 103 star clusters and nebulae. Objects on this list are given M (for Messier) numbers, which astronomers still use today, such as M1 (the Crab nebula) and M31 (the Andromeda galaxy).

Messina, Strait of channel in the central Mediterranean separating Sicily from mainland Italy; in Greek legend a monster (Charybdis), who devoured ships, lived in the whirlpool on the Sicilian side, and another (Scylla), who devoured sailors, in the rock on the Italian side. The classical hero Odysseus passed safely between them.

metabolism the chemical processes of living organisms: a constant alternation of building up (**anabolism**) and breaking down (**catabolism**). For example, green plants build up complex organic substances from water, carbon dioxide, and mineral salts (photosynthesis); by digestion animals partially break down complex organic substances, ingested as food, and subsequently resynthesize them in their own bodies.

metal any of a class of chemical elements with certain chemical characteristics (*metallic character) and physical properties: they are good conductors of heat and electricity; opaque but reflect light well; malleable, which enables them to be cold-worked and rolled into sheets; and ductile, which permits them to be drawn into thin wires.

metal detector electronic device for detecting metal, usually below ground, developed from the wartime mine detector. In the head of the metal detector is a coil, which is part of an electronic circuit. The presence of metal causes the frequency of the signal in the circuit to change, setting up an audible note in the headphones worn by the user.

metallic bond the force of attraction operating in a metal that holds the atoms together. In the metal the *valency electrons are able to move within the crystal and these electrons are said to be delocalized. Their movement creates short-lived, positively charged ions. The electrostatic attraction between the delocalized electrons and the ceaselessly forming ions constitutes the metallic bond.

metallic character chemical properties associated with those elements classed as metals. These properties, which arise from the element's ability to lose electrons, are: the displacement of hydrogen from dilute acids; the formation of *basic oxides; the formation of ionic chlorides; and their reducing reaction, as in the *thermite process (see *reduction). In the periodic table of the elements, metallic character increases down any group and across a period from right to left.

metalloid or *semimetal* any chemical element having some of but not all the properties of metals; metalloids are thus usually electrically semiconducting. They comprise the elements germanium, arsenic, antimony, and tellurium.

metallurgy the science and technology of producing metals, which includes extraction, alloying, and hardening. Extractive, or **process, metallurgy** is concerned with the extraction of metals from their *ores and refining and adapting them for use. **Physical metallurgy** is concerned with their properties and application. **Metallography** establishes the microscopic structures that contribute to hardness, ductility, and strength.

metamorphic rock rock altered in structure and composition by pressure, heat, or chemically active fluids after original formation. (If heat is sufficient to melt the original rock, technically it becomes an igneous rock upon cooling.)

metamorphism geological term referring to the changes in rocks of the Earth's crust caused by increasing pressure and temperature. The resulting rocks are metamorphic rocks. All metamorphic changes take place in solid rocks. If the rocks melt and then harden, they become *igneous rocks.

metamorphosis period during the life cycle of many invertebrates, most amphibians, and some fish, during which the individual's body changes from one form to another through a major reconstitution of its tissues. For example, adult frogs are produced by metamorphosis from tadpoles, and butterflies are produced from caterpillars following metamorphosis within a pupa. In classical thought and literature, metamorphosis is the transformation of a living being into another shape, either living or inanimate. The Roman poet *Ovid wrote about this theme.

metaphor (Greek 'transfer') figure of speech using an analogy or close comparison between two things that are not normally treated as if they had anything in common. Metaphor is a common means of extending the uses and references of words. See also *simile.

metaphysical poet member of a group of 17th-century English poets whose work is characterized by conciseness; ingenious, often highly intricate wordplay; and striking imagery. Among the exponents of this genre are John *Donne and George *Herbert.

metaphysics branch of philosophy that deals with first principles, in particular 'being' (ontology) and 'knowing' (*epistemology), and that is concerned with the ultimate nature of reality. It has been maintained that no certain knowledge of metaphysical questions is possible.

metempsychosis another name for *reincarnation.

meteor flash of light in the sky, popularly known as a **shooting** or **falling star**, caused by a particle of dust, a **meteoroid**, entering the atmosphere at speeds up to 70 kps/45 mps and burning up by friction at a height of around 100 km/60 mi. On any clear night, several **sporadic meteors** can be seen each hour.

meteorite piece of rock or metal from space that reaches the surface of the Earth, Moon, or other body. Most meteorites are thought to be fragments from asteroids, although some may be pieces from the heads of comets. Most are stony, although some are made of iron and a few have a mixed rock-iron composition. Meteorites provide evidence for the nature of the solar system and may be similar to the Earth's core and mantle, neither of which can be observed directly.

meteorology scientific observation and study of the *atmosphere, so that weather can be accurately forecast. Data from meteorological stations and weather satellites are collated by computer at central agencies, and forecast and *weather maps based on current readings are issued at regular intervals. Modern analysis can give useful forecasts for up to six days ahead.

methanal (common name **formaldehyde**) HCHO gas at ordinary temperatures, condensing to a liquid at $-21°C/-5.8°F$. It has a powerful, penetrating smell. Dissolved in water, it is used as a biological preservative. It is used in the manufacture of plastics, dyes, foam (for example urea-formaldehyde foam, used in insulation), and in medicine.

methane CH_4 the simplest hydrocarbon of the paraffin series. Colourless, odourless, and lighter than air, it burns with a bluish flame and explodes when mixed with air or oxygen. It is the chief constituent of natural gas and also occurs in the explosive firedamp of coal mines. Methane emitted by rotting vegetation forms marsh gas, which may ignite by spontaneous combustion to produce the pale flame seen over marshland and known as *will-o'-the-wisp.

methanoic acid (common name **formic acid**) HCOOH, a colourless, slightly fuming liquid that freezes at $8°C/46.4°F$ and boils at $101°C/213.8°F$. It occurs in stinging ants, nettles, sweat, and pine needles, and is used in dyeing, tanning, and electroplating.

methanol (common name **methyl alcohol**) CH_3OH the simplest of the alcohols. It can be made by the dry distillation of wood (hence it is also known as wood alcohol), but is usually made from coal or natural gas. When pure, it is a colourless, flammable liquid with a pleasant odour, and is highly poisonous.

Method US adaptation of *Stanislavsky's teachings on acting and direction, in which importance is attached to the psychological building of a role rather than the technical side of its presentation. Emphasis is placed on improvisation, aiming for a spontaneous and realistic style of acting. One of the principal exponents of the Method was the US actor and director Lee Strasberg, who taught at the *Actors Studio in New York.

Methodism evangelical Protestant Christian movement that was founded by John *Wesley 1739 within the Church of England, but became a separate body 1795. The Methodist Episcopal Church was founded in the USA 1784. There are over 50 million Methodists worldwide.

Methuselah in the Old Testament, Hebrew patriarch who lived before the Flood; his lifespan of 969 years makes him a byword for longevity.

methyl alcohol common name for *methanol.

methylated spirit alcohol that has been rendered undrinkable, and is used for industrial purposes, as a fuel for spirit burners or a solvent.

metonymy (Greek 'transferred title') figure of speech that works by association, naming something closely connected with what is meant; for example, calling the theatrical profession 'the stage', horse racing 'the turf', or journalists 'the press'. See also *synecdoche.

metre SI unit (symbol m) of length, equivalent to 1.093 yards. It is defined by scientists as the length of the path travelled by light in a vacuum during a time interval of $1/299,792,458$ of a second.

metre in poetry, the rhythm determined by the number and type of feet (units of stressed and unstressed syllables) in a line. See also *verse.

metre in music, accentuation pattern characteristic of a musical line; the regularity underlying musical rhythm.

metric system system of weights and measures developed in France in the 18th century and recognized by other countries in the 19th century. In 1960 an international conference on weights and measures recommended the universal adoption of a revised International System (Système International d'Unités, or SI), with seven prescribed 'base units': the metre (m) for length, kilogram (kg) for mass, second (s) for time, ampere (A) for electric current, kelvin (K) for thermodynamic temperature, candela (cd) for luminous intensity, and mole (mol) for quantity of matter.

Metro-Goldwyn-Mayer (MGM) US film-production company 1924–1970s. MGM was formed by the amalgamation of the Metro Picture Corporation, the Goldwyn Picture Corporation, and Louis B Mayer Pictures. One of the most powerful Hollywood studios of the 1930s–1950s, it produced such prestige films as *David Copperfield* 1935 and *The Wizard of Oz* 1939. Among its stars were Greta Garbo, James Stewart, and Elizabeth Taylor.

metronome clockwork device, invented by Johann Maelzel 1814, using a sliding weight to regulate the speed of a pendulum to assist in keeping time, particularly in music.

metropolitan (Greek 'mother-state, capital') in the Christian church generally, a bishop who has rule over other bishops (termed **suffragans**). In the Eastern Orthodox Church, a metropolitan has a rank between an archbishop and a *patriarch.

metropolitan county in England, a group of six counties (1974–86) established under the Local Government Act 1972 in the largest urban areas outside London: Tyne and Wear, South Yorkshire, Merseyside, West Midlands, Greater Manchester, and West Yorkshire. Their elected assemblies were abolished 1986 when their areas of responsibility reverted to district councils.

Metternich Klemens (Wenzel Lothar), Prince von Metternich 1773–1859. Austrian politician, the leading figure in European diplomacy after the fall of Napoleon. As foreign minister 1809–48 (as well as chancellor from 1821), he tried to maintain the balance of power in Europe, supporting monarchy and repressing liberalism.

Mexican War war between the USA and Mexico 1846–48, begun in territory disputed between Texas (annexed by the USA 1845 but claimed by Mexico) and Mexico. It began when General Zachary Taylor invaded New Mexico after efforts to purchase what are now California and New Mexico failed. Mexico City was taken 1847, and under the Treaty of Guadaloupe Hidalgo that ended the war, the USA acquired New Mexico and California, as well as clear title to Texas in exchange for $15 million.

Mexico United States of (*Estados Unidos Mexicanos*)
area 1,958,201 sq km/756,198 sq mi
capital Mexico City
towns Guadalajara, Monterrey; port Veracruz

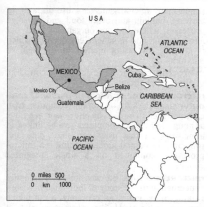

physical partly arid central highlands; Sierra Madre mountain ranges E and W; tropical coastal plains
head of state and government Ernesto Zedillo Ponce de Leon from 1994
political system federal democratic republic
exports silver, gold, lead, uranium, oil, natural gas, handicrafts, fish, shellfish, fruits and vegetables, cotton, machinery
currency peso
population (1993 est) 91,600,000 (mixed descent 60%, Indian 30%, Spanish descent 10%); 50% under 20 years of age; growth rate 2.6% p.a.
languages Spanish (official) 92%, Nahuatl, Maya, Zapoteco, Mixteco, Otomi
religion Roman Catholic 97%
GNP $2,870 per head (1991)
chronology
1821 Independence achieved from Spain.
1846–48 Mexico at war with USA; loss of territory.
1848 Maya Indian revolt suppressed.
1864–67 Maximilian of Austria was emperor of Mexico.
1917 New constitution introduced, designed to establish permanent democracy.
1983–84 Financial crisis.
1985 Institutional Revolutionary Party (PRI) returned to power. Earthquake in Mexico City.
1986 International Monetary Fund (IMF) loan agreement signed to keep the country solvent until at least 1988.
1988 PRI candidate Carlos Salinas de Gortari elected president. Debt reduction accords negotiated with USA.
1991 PRI won general election.
1992 Public outrage following Guadalajara gas-explosion disaster.
1993 Sept: electoral reforms passed. Donaldo Colosio Murrieta nominated PRI presidential candidate.
1994 Jan: attacks by rebel group, the Zapatista National Liberation Army (ZNLA), harshly put down by government troops. Government ceasefire announced; ZNLA awarded political recognition. March: peace accord signed. Colosio assassinated. Aug: Ernesto Zedillo Ponce de Leon (PRI) elected president.

Mexico City (Spanish **Ciudad de México**) capital, industrial (iron, steel, chemicals,

textiles), and cultural centre of Mexico, 2,255 m/ 7,400 ft above sea level on the S edge of the central plateau; population (1986) 18,748,000. It is thought to be one of the world's most polluted cities because of its position in a volcanic basin 2,000 m/7,400 ft above sea level. Pollutants gather in the basin causing a smog cloud.

Meyerbeer Giacomo. Adopted name of Jakob Liebmann Beer 1791–1864. German composer. His spectacular operas include *Robert le Diable* 1831 and *Les Huguenots* 1836. From 1826 he lived mainly in Paris, returning to Berlin after 1842 as musical director of the Royal Opera.

mezuza in Judaism, a small box containing a parchment scroll inscribed with a prayer, the Shema from Deuteronomy 6:4–9; 11:13–21, which is found on the doorpost of every home and every room in a Jewish house, except the bathroom.

mezzanine (Italian *mezzano* 'middle') architectural term for a storey with a lower ceiling placed between two main storeys, usually between the ground and first floors of a building.

mezzo-soprano female singing voice with a range between contralto and soprano. Janet Baker is a well-known mezzo-soprano.

mezzotint print produced by a method of etching in density of tone rather than line, popular in the 18th and 19th centuries. A copper or steel plate is worked with a tool that raises an even, overall burr (rough edge), which will hold ink. Areas of burr are then scraped and smoothed away to produce a range of lighter tones.

Mfecane in African history, a series of disturbances in the early 19th century among communities in what is today the eastern part of South Africa. They arose when chief *Shaka conquered the Nguni peoples between the Tugela and Pongola rivers, then created by conquest a centralized, militaristic Zulu kingdom from several communities, resulting in large-scale displacement of people.

mg symbol for **milligram**.

mi symbol for *mile*.

Miami industrial city (food processing, transportation and electronic equipment, clothing, and machinery) and port in Florida, USA; population (1990) 358,500. It is the hub of finance, trade, and air transport for the USA, Latin America, and the Caribbean. There has been an influx of immigrants from Cuba, Haiti, Mexico, and South America since 1959.

mica group of silicate minerals that split easily into thin flakes along lines of weakness in their crystal structure (perfect basal cleavage). They are glossy, have a pearly lustre, and are found in many igneous and metamorphic rocks. Their good thermal and electrical insulation qualities make them valuable in industry.

Michael in the Old Testament, an archangel, referred to as the guardian angel of Israel. In the New Testament Book of Revelation he leads the hosts of heaven to battle against Satan. In paintings, he is depicted with a flaming sword and sometimes a pair of scales. Feast day 29 Sept (Michaelmas).

Michael 1921– . King of Romania 1927–30 and 1940–47. The son of Carol II, he succeeded his grandfather as king 1927 but was displaced when his father returned from exile 1930. In 1940 he was proclaimed king again on his father's abdication, overthrew 1944 the fascist dictatorship of Ion Antonescu (1882–1946), and enabled Romania to share in the victory of the Allies at the end of World War II. He abdicated and left Romania 1947.

michaelmas daisy popular name for species of *aster, family Compositae, and also for the sea aster or starwort.

Michaelmas Day in Christian church tradition, the festival of St Michael and all angels, observed 29 Sept.

Michelangelo 1475–1564. Properly Michelangelo Buonarroti. Italian sculptor, painter, architect, and poet. He was active in his native Florence and in Rome. His giant talent dominated the High Renaissance. The marble *David* 1501–04 (Accademia, Florence) set a new standard in nude sculpture. His massive figure style was translated into fresco in the Sistine Chapel 1508–12 and 1536–41 (Vatican). Other works in Rome include the dome of St Peter's basilica.

Michelson Albert Abraham 1852–1931. German-born US physicist. In conjunction with Edward Morley, he performed in 1887 the **Michelson–Morley experiment** to detect the motion of the Earth through the postulated ether (a medium believed to be necessary for the propagation of light). The failure of the experiment indicated the nonexistence of the ether, and led *Einstein to his theory of *relativity. Michelson was the first American to be awarded a Nobel prize, in 1907.

Michigan state in N central USA; nickname Wolverine State/Great Lake State
area 151,600 sq km/58,518 sq mi
capital Lansing
cities Detroit, Grand Rapids, Flint
products motor vehicles and equipment; nonelectrical machinery; iron and steel; chemicals; pharmaceuticals; dairy products
population (1990) 9,295,300
famous people Edna Ferber, Gerald Ford, Henry Ford, Jimmy Hoffa, Iggy Pop, Diana Ross
history temporary posts established in early 17th century by French explorers Brulé, Marquette, Joliet, and La Salle; first settled 1668 at Sault Sainte Marie; present-day Detroit settled 1701; passed to the British 1763 and to the USA 1796; statehood achieved 1837.

Michigan, Lake lake in N central USA, one of the Great Lakes; area 58,000 sq km/22,390 sq mi. Chicago and Milwaukee are its main ports.

Mickey Mouse cartoon character created 1928 by US animator Walt Disney, characterized by black disc-shaped ears and white gloves. He made his film debut in *Plane Crazy* and starred in the first synchronized sound cartoon, *Steamboat Willie* 1928.

micro- prefix (symbol μ) denoting a one-millionth part (10^{-6}). For example, a micrometre, μm, is one-millionth of a metre.

microbe another name for *microorganism.

microbiology the study of microorganisms, mostly viruses and single-celled organisms such as bacteria, protozoa, and yeasts. The practical applications of microbiology are in medicine (since many microorganisms cause disease); in brewing, baking, and other food and beverage processes, where the microorganisms carry out fermentation; and in genetic engineering, which is creating increasing interest in the field of microbiology.

microchip popular name for the silicon chip, or *integrated circuit.

microcomputer or *micro* or **personal computer** small desktop or portable computer, typically designed to be used by one person at a time, although individual computers can be linked in a network so that users can share data and programs. Its central processing unit is a *microprocessor, contained on a single integrated circuit.

microeconomics the division of economics concerned with the study of individual decision-making units within an economy: a consumer, firm, or industry. Unlike macroeconomics, it looks at how individual markets work and how individual producers and consumers make their choices and with what consequences. This is done by analysing how relevant prices of goods are determined and the quantities that will be bought and sold.

micrometre one-millionth of a *metre (symbol μm).

Micronesia group of islands in the Pacific Ocean lying N of *Melanesia, including the Federated States of Micronesia, Belau, Kiribati, the Mariana and Marshall Islands, Nauru, and Tuvalu.

Micronesia Federated States of (FSM)
area 700 sq km/270 sq mi
capital Kolonia, in Pohnpei state
towns Moen, in Chuuk state; Lelu, in Kosrae state; Colonia, in Yap state
physical an archipelago in the W Pacific
head of state and government Bailey Olter from 1991
political system democratic federal state
products copra, fish products, tourism
currency US dollar
population (1990) 107,900
languages English (official) and local languages
religion Christianity
GNP $1,500 per head (1989)
chronology
16th century Colonized by Spain.
1885 Purchased from Spain by Germany.
1914 Occupied by Japan.
1920 Administered by Japan under League of Nations mandate.
1944 Occupied by USA.
1947 Became part of the UN Pacific Islands Trust Territory, administered by the USA.
1982 Compact of Free Association signed with USA.
1990 UN trust status terminated. Independent state established, with USA responsible for defence and foreign affairs.
1991 First independent president elected. Entered into UN membership.

microorganism or *microbe* living organism invisible to the naked eye but visible under a microscope. Microorganisms include viruses and single-celled organisms such as bacteria, protozoa, yeasts, and some algae. The term has no taxonomic significance in biology.

microphone primary component in a sound-reproducing system, whereby the mechanical energy of sound waves is converted into electrical signals by means of a *transducer. One of the simplest is the telephone receiver mouthpiece, invented by Alexander Graham Bell in 1876; other types of microphone are used with broadcasting and sound-film apparatus.

microprocessor complete computer *central processing unit contained on a single *integrated circuit, or chip. The appearance of the first microprocessors in 1971 heralded the introduction of the microcomputer. The microprocessor has led to a dramatic fall in the size and cost of computers, and *dedicated computers can now be found in washing machines, cars, and so on.

microscope instrument for magnification with high resolution for detail. Optical and electron microscopes are the ones chiefly in use; other types include acoustic and X-ray. In 1988 a scanning tunnelling microscope was used to photograph a single protein molecule for the first time. Laser microscopy is under development.

microsurgery surgical operation – rejoining a severed limb, for example – performed with the aid of a binocular microscope. Sewing of the nerves and blood vessels is done with a nylon thread so fine that it is only just visible to the naked eye. Restoration of movement and sensation in such cases may be comparatively limited.

microtubules tiny tubes found in almost all cells with a nucleus. They help to define the shape of a cell by forming scaffolding for cilia and form fibres of mitotic spindle.

microwave *electromagnetic wave with a wavelength in the range 0.3 to 30 cm/0.1 in to 12 in, or 300–300,000 megahertz (between radio waves and *infrared radiation). They are used in radar, as carrier waves in radio broadcasting, and in microwave heating and cooking.

microwave heating heating by means of microwaves. Microwave ovens use this form of heating for the rapid cooking or reheating of foods, where heat is generated throughout the food simultaneously. If food is not heated completely, there is a danger of bacterial growth that may lead to food poisoning. Industrially, microwave heating is used for destroying insects in grain and enzymes in processed food, pasteurizing and sterilizing liquids, and drying timber and paper.

MICV abbreviation for *mechanized infantry combat vehicle*.

Midas in Greek legend, a king of Phrygia who was granted the gift of converting all he touched to gold, and who, for preferring the music of Pan to that of Apollo, was given ass's ears by the latter.

MIDAS acronym for *Missile Defence Alarm System*.

Mid-Atlantic Ridge *ocean ridge, formed by the movement of plates described by *plate tectonics, that runs along the centre of the Atlantic Ocean, parallel to its edges, for some 14,000 km/8,800 mi – almost from the Arctic to the Antarctic.

Middle Ages period of European history between the fall of the Roman Empire in the 5th

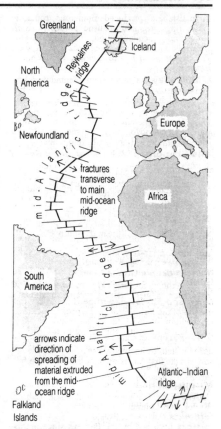

Mid-Atlantic Ridge The Mid-Atlantic Ridge is the boundary between the crustal plates that form America, and Europe and Africa.

century and the Renaissance in the 15th. Among the period's distinctive features were the unity of W Europe within the Roman Catholic Church, the feudal organization of political, social, and economic relations, and the use of art for largely religious purposes.

middle C white note at the centre of the piano keyboard, indicating the division between left- and right-hand regions and between the treble and bass staves of printed music.

Middle East indeterminate area now usually taken to include the Balkan States, Egypt, and SW Asia. Until the 1940s, this area was generally called the Near East, and the term Middle East referred to the area from Iran to Burma (now Myanmar).

Middle English the period of the *English language from about 1050 to 1550.

Middle Kingdom period of Egyptian history extending from the late 11th to the 13th dynasty (roughly 2040–1670 BC); Chinese term for China and its empire until 1912, describing its central position in the Far East.

Middleton Thomas c. 1570–1627. English

dramatist. He produced numerous romantic plays, tragedies, and realistic comedies, both alone and in collaboration, including *A Fair Quarrel* and *The Changeling* 1622 with Rowley; *The Roaring Girl* with Dekker; and *Women Beware Women* 1621.

Middle Way the path to enlightenment, taught by Buddha, which avoids the extremes of indulgence and asceticism.

midge common name for many insects resembling *gnats, generally divided into biting midges (family Ceratopogonidae) that suck blood, and non-biting midges (family Chironomidae).

Mid Glamorgan (Welsh *Morgannwg Ganol*) county in S Wales
area 1,020 sq km/394 sq mi
towns administrative headquarters Cardiff; resort Porthcawl; Aberdare, Merthyr Tydfil, Bridgend, Pontypridd
products the north was formerly a leading coal (Rhondda) and iron and steel area; Royal Mint at Llantrisant; agriculture in the south; Caerphilly mild cheese
population (1991) 536,500
languages 8% Welsh, English
famous people Geraint Evans.

MIDI acronym for *musical instrument digital interface*, a manufacturer's standard allowing different pieces of digital music equipment used in composing and recording to be freely connected.

Midi-Pyrénées region of SW France, comprising the *départements* of Ariège, Aveyron, Haute-Garonne, Gers, Lot, Haute-Pyrénées, Tarn, and Tarn-et-Garonne
area 45,300 sq km/17,486 sq mi
population (1986) 2,355,000
towns capital Toulouse; Montauban, Cahors, Rodez, and Lourdes
products fruit, wine, livestock
history occupied by the Basques since prehistoric times, this region once formed part of the prehistoric province of Gascony that was taken by the English 1154, recaptured by the French 1453, inherited by Henry of Navarre, and reunited with France 1607.

Midlands area of England corresponding roughly to the Anglo-Saxon kingdom of *Mercia. The *E Midlands* comprises Derbyshire, Leicestershire, Northamptonshire, and Nottinghamshire. The *W Midlands* covers the former metropolitan county of *West Midlands created from parts of Staffordshire, Warwickshire, and Worcestershire; and (often included) the *S Midlands* comprises Bedfordshire, Buckinghamshire, and Oxfordshire.

Midrash (Hebrew 'inquiry') medieval Hebrew commentaries on the Bible, in the form of sermons, in which allegory and legendary illustration are used. They were compiled mainly in Palestine between AD 400 and 1200.

midsummer the time of the summer *solstice, about 21 June. Midsummer Day, 24 June, is the Christian festival of St John the Baptist.

Midway Islands two islands in the Pacific, 1,800 km/1,120 mi NW of Honolulu; area 5 sq km/2 sq mi; population (1980) 500. They were annexed by the USA 1867, and are now administered by the US Navy. The naval *Battle of Midway* 3–6 June 1942, between the USA and Japan, was a turning point in the Pacific in World War II; the US victory marked the end of Japanese expansion in the Pacific.

Midwest or *Middle West* large area of the N central USA. It is loosely defined, but is generally taken to comprise the states of Illinois, Iowa, Wisconsin, Minnesota, Nebraska, Kansas, Missouri, North Dakota, and South Dakota and the portions of Montana, Wyoming, and Colorado that lie east of the Rocky Mountains. Ohio, Michigan, and Indiana are often variously included, as well. Traditionally its economy is divided between agriculture and heavy industry The main urban Midwest centre is Chicago.

Mies van der Rohe Ludwig 1886–1969 German architect who practised in the USA from 1937. He succeeded Walter *Gropius as director of the *Bauhaus 1929–33. He designed the bronze-and-glass Seagram building in New York City 1956–59 and numerous apartment buildings.

Mifune Toshiro 1920– . Japanese actor who appeared in many films directed by Akira *Kurosawa, including *Rashomon* 1950, *Shichinin no samurai/Seven Samurai* 1954, and *Throne of Blood* 1957. He has also appeared in European and American films: *Grand Prix* 1966, *Hell in the Pacific* 1969.

mignonette sweet-scented plant *Reseda odorata*, native to N Africa, bearing yellowish-green flowers in racemes (along the main stem), with abundant foliage; it is widely cultivated.

migraine acute, sometimes incapacitating headache (generally only on one side) accompanied by nausea, that recurs, often with advance symptoms such as flashing lights. No cure has been discovered, but *ergotamine normally relieves the symptoms. Some sufferers learn to avoid certain foods, such as chocolate, which suggests an allergic factor.

migrant labour people who leave their home lands to work elsewhere, usually because of economic or political pressures.

migration the movement, either seasonal or as part of a single life cycle, of certain animals chiefly birds and fish, to distant breeding or feeding grounds.

Mihailovič Draza 1893–1946. Yugoslav soldier, leader of the guerrilla *Chetniks of World War I against the German occupation. His feud with Tito's communists led to the withdrawal of Allied support and that of his own exiled government from 1943. He turned for help to the Italians and Germans, and was eventually shot for treason.

mikado (Japanese 'honourable palace gate') title until 1867 of the Japanese emperor, when it was replaced by the term *tennō* ('heavenly sovereign').

Milan (Italian *Milano*) industrial city (aircraft, cars, locomotives, textiles), financial and cultural centre, capital of Lombardy, Italy; population (1988) 1,479,000.

mildew any fungus that appears as a destructive growth on plants, paper, leather, or wood when exposed to damp; such fungi usually form a thin white coating.

mile imperial unit of linear measure. A statute mile is equal to 1,760 yards (1.60934 km), and an international nautical mile is equal to 2,026 yards (1,852 m).

Miles Bernard (Baron Miles) 1907– . English actor and producer. He appeared on stage as Briggs in *Thunder Rock* 1940 and Iago in *Othello* 1942, and his films include *Great Expectations* 1947. He founded a trust that in 1959 built the City of London's first new theatre for 300 years, the Mermaid.

Militant Tendency in British politics, left-wing faction originally within the Labour Party, aligned with the publication *Militant*. It became active in the 1970s, with radical socialist policies based on Trotskyism (see *Trotsky), and gained some success in local government, for example in the inner-city area of Liverpool. In the mid-1980s the Labour Party considered it to be a separate organization within the party and banned it.

militia body of civilian soldiers, usually with some military training, who are on call in emergencies, distinct from professional soldiers. In Switzerland, the militia is the national defence force, and every able-bodied man is liable for service in it. In the UK the **Territorial Army* and in the USA the **National Guard* have supplanted earlier voluntary militias.

milk secretion of the *mammary glands of female mammals, with which they suckle their young (during *lactation). Over 85% is water, the remainder comprising protein, fat, lactose (a sugar), calcium, phosphorus, iron, and vitamins. The milk of cows, goats, and sheep is often consumed by humans, but only Western societies drink milk after infancy; for people in most of the world, milk causes flatulence and diarrhoea.

Milky Way faint band of light crossing the night sky, consisting of stars in the plane of our Galaxy. The name Milky Way is often used for the Galaxy itself. It is a spiral *galaxy, about 100,000 light years in diameter, containing at least 100 billion stars. The Sun is in one of its spiral arms, about 25,000 light years from the centre.

Mill James 1773–1836. Scottish philosopher and political thinker who developed the theory of *utilitarianism. He is remembered for his political articles, and for the rigorous education he gave his son John Stuart Mill.

Mill John Stuart 1806–1873. English philosopher and economist who wrote *On Liberty* 1859, the classic philosophical defence of liberalism, and *Utilitarianism* 1863, a version of the 'greatest happiness for the greatest number' principle in ethics. His progressive views inspired *On the Subjection of Women* 1869.

Millais John Everett 1829–1896. British painter, a founder member of the **Pre-Raphaelite Brotherhood* (PRB) in 1848. By the late 1850s he had dropped out of the PRB, and his style became more fluent and less detailed.

millefiore (Italian 'a thousand flowers') ornamental glassmaking technique. Coloured glass rods are arranged in bundles so that the cross-section forms a pattern. When the bundle is heated and drawn out thinly, the design becomes reduced in scale. Slices of this are used in glass-bead manufacture and can be set side by side and fused into metalware.

Miller Arthur 1915– . US playwright. His plays deal with family relationships and contemporary American values, and include *Death of a Sales*man 1949 and *The Crucible* 1953, based on the Salem witch trials and reflecting the communist witch-hunts of Senator Joe *McCarthy. He was married 1956–61 to the film star Marilyn Monroe, for whom he wrote the film *The Misfits* 1960.

Miller Glenn 1904–1944. US trombonist and, as bandleader, exponent of the big-band swing sound from 1938. He composed his signature tune 'Moonlight Serenade' (a hit 1939). Miller became leader of the US Army Air Force Band in Europe 1942, made broadcasts to troops throughout the world during World War II, and disappeared without trace on a flight between England and France.

Miller Henry 1891–1980. US writer. From 1930 to 1940 he lived a bohemian life in Paris, where he wrote his novels *Tropic of Cancer* 1934 and *Tropic of Capricorn* 1938. They were so outspoken and sexually frank that they were banned in the USA and England until the 1960s.

millet any of several grasses, family Gramineae, of which the grains are used as a cereal food and the stems as fodder.

Millet Jean François 1814–1875. French artist, a leading member of the *Barbizon school, who painted scenes of peasant life and landscapes. *The Angelus* 1859 (Musée d'Orsay, Paris) was widely reproduced in his day.

Millett Kate 1934– . US radical feminist lecturer, writer, and sculptor whose book *Sexual Politics* 1970 was a landmark in feminist thinking. She was a founding member of the **National Organization of Women** (NOW). Later books include *Flying* 1974, *The Prostitution Papers* 1976, *Sita* 1977, and *The Loony Bin Trip* 1991, describing a period of manic depression and drug therapy.

milli- prefix (symbol m) denoting a one-thousandth part (10^{-3}). For example, a millimetre, mm, is one thousandth of a metre.

millibar unit of pressure, equal to one-thousandth of a *bar.

millilitre one-thousandth of a litre (ml), equivalent to one cubic centimetre (cc).

millimetre of mercury unit (symbol mmHg) of pressure, used in medicine for measuring blood pressure defined as the pressure exerted by a column of mercury one millimetre high, under the action of gravity.

milling metal machining method that uses a rotating toothed cutting wheel to shape a surface. The term also applies to grinding grain, cacao, coffee, pepper, and other spices.

millipede any arthropod of the class Diplopoda. It has a segmented body, each segment usually bearing two pairs of legs, and the distinct head bears a pair of short clubbed antennae. Most millipedes are no more than 2.5 cm/1 in long; a few in the tropics are 30 cm/12 in.

Mills John 1908– . English actor who appeared in films such as *In Which We Serve* 1942, *The Rocking Horse Winner* 1949, *The Wrong Box* 1966, and *Oh! What a Lovely War* 1969. He received an Academy Award for *Ryan's Daughter* 1971. He is the father of the actresses Hayley Mills and Juliet Mills.

Milne A(lan) A(lexander) 1882–1956. English writer. His books for children were based on the teddy bear and other toys of his son Christopher Robin (*Winnie-the-Pooh* 1926 and *The House at Pooh Corner* 1928). He also wrote children's verse (*When We Were Very Young* 1924 and *Now We Are Six* 1927) and plays, including an adaptation of Kenneth Grahame's *The Wind in the Willows* as *Toad of Toad Hall* 1929.

Milošević Slobodan 1941– . Serbian communist politician, party chief and president of Serbia from 1986; re-elected Dec 1990 in multi-party elections. Milosevic wielded considerable influence over the Serb-dominated Yugoslav federal army during the 1991–92 civil war and has continued to back Serbian militia in *Bosnia-Herzegovina 1992–93, although publicly disclaiming any intention to 'carve up' the newly independent republic. Widely believed to be the instigator of the conflict, Milošević changed tactics during 1993, adopting the public persona of peacemaker and putting pressure on his allies, the Bosnian Serbs, to accept UN-EC negotiated peace terms.

Milton John 1608–1674. English poet. His epic *Paradise Lost* 1667 is one of the landmarks of English literature. Early poems including *Comus* (a masque performed 1634) and *Lycidas* (an elegy 1638) showed Milton's superlative lyric gift. Latin secretary to Oliver Cromwell during the Commonwealth period, he also wrote many pamphlets and prose works, including *Areopagitica* 1644, which opposed press censorship.

Milwaukee industrial port (meatpacking, brewing, engineering, machinery, electronic and electrical equipment, chemicals) in Wisconsin, USA, on Lake Michigan; population (1990) 628,100. The site was settled 1818 and drew a large influx of German immigrants, beginning in the 1840s.

mime type of acting in which gestures, movements, and facial expressions replace speech. It has developed as a form of theatre, particularly in France, where Marcel *Marceau and Jean Louis *Barrault have continued the traditions established in the 19th century by Deburau and the practices of the *commedia dell'arte in Italy. In ancient Greece, mime was a crude, realistic comedy with dialogue and exaggerated gesture.

mimicry imitation of one species (or group of species) by another. The most common form is *Batesian mimicry* (named after English naturalist H W *Bates), where the mimic resembles a model that is poisonous or unpleasant to eat, and has aposematic, or warning, coloration; the mimic thus benefits from the fact that predators have learned to avoid the model. Hoverflies that resemble bees or wasps are an example. Appearance is usually the basis for mimicry, but calls, songs, scents, and other signals can also be mimicked.

Minamoto or *Genji* in Japanese history, an ancient Japanese clan, the members of which were the first ruling shoguns 1192–1219. Their government was based in Kamakura, near present-day Tokyo.

minaret slender turret or tower attached to a Muslim mosque or to buildings designed in that style. It has one or more balconies, from which the *muezzin* calls the people to prayer five times a day.

mind in philosophy, the presumed mental or physical being or faculty that enables a person to think, will, and feel; the seat of the intelligence and of memory; sometimes only the cognitive or intellectual powers, as distinguished from the will and the emotions.

Mindanao second-largest island of the Philippines
area 94,627 sq km/36,526 sq mi
towns Davao, Zamboanga
physical mountainous rainforest
products pineapples, coffee, rice, coconut, rubber, hemp, timber, nickel, gold, steel, chemicals, fertilizer
population (1980) 10,905,250.

mine explosive charge on land or sea, or in the atmosphere, designed to be detonated by contact, vibration (for example, from an enemy engine), magnetic influence, or a timing device. Countermeasures include metal detectors (useless for plastic types), specially equipped helicopters, and (at sea) *minesweepers.

mineral naturally formed inorganic substance with a particular chemical composition and a regularly repeating internal structure. Either in their perfect crystalline form or otherwise, minerals are the constituents of *rocks. In more general usage, a mineral is any substance economically valuable for mining (including coal and oil, despite their organic origins).

mineral extraction recovery of valuable ores from the Earth's crust. The processes used include open-cast mining, shaft mining, and quarrying, as well as more specialized processes such as those used for oil and sulphur (see, for example, *Frasch process).

mineralogy study of minerals. The classification of minerals is based chiefly on their chemical composition and the kind of chemical bonding that holds these atoms together. The mineralogist also studies their crystallographic and physical characters, occurrence, and mode of formation.

mineral salt in nutrition, a simple inorganic chemical that is required by living organisms. Plants usually obtain their mineral salts from the soil, while animals get theirs from their food. Important mineral salts include iron salts (needed by both plants and animals), magnesium salts (needed mainly by plants, to make chlorophyll), and calcium salts (needed by animals to make bone or shell). A *trace element is required only in tiny amounts.

Minerva in Roman mythology, the goddess of intelligence, and of handicrafts and the arts, equivalent to the Greek *Athena. From the earliest days of ancient Rome, there was a temple to her on the Capitoline Hill, near the Temple of Jupiter.

Ming dynasty Chinese dynasty 1368–1644, based in Nanjing. During the rule 1402–24 of Yongle (or Yung-lo), there was territorial expansion into Mongolia and Yunnan in the SW. The administrative system was improved, public works were carried out, and foreign trade was developed. Art and literature flourished and distinctive blue and white porcelain was produced.

Mingus Charles 1922–1979. US jazz bassist and composer. He played with Louis Armstrong, Duke Ellington, and Charlie Parker. His experimentation with *atonality and dissonant effects opened the way for the new style of free collective jazz improvisation of the 1960s.

miniature painting painting on a very small scale, notably early manuscript paintings, and later miniature portraits, sometimes set in jewelled cases. The art of manuscript painting was developed in Classical times in the West and revived in the Middle Ages. Several Islamic countries, for example Persia and India, developed strong traditions of manuscript art. Miniature portrait painting enjoyed a vogue in France and England in the 16th–19th centuries.

minicomputer multiuser computer with a size and processing power between those of a *mainframe and a *microcomputer. Nowadays almost all minicomputers are based on microprocessors.

Mini Disc digital audio disc that resembles a computer floppy disc in a 5 cm/2 in square case, with up to an hour's playing time. The system was developed by Sony for release 1993.

Minimalism movement beginning in the late 1960s in abstract art and music towards a severely simplified composition. In *painting*, it emphasized geometrical and elemental shapes. In *sculpture*, Carl André focused on industrial materials. In *music*, large-scale statements are based on layers of imperceptibly shifting repetitive patterns; its major exponents are Steve *Reich and Philip *Glass.

minimum lending rate (MLR) in the UK, the rate of interest at which the Bank of England lends to the money market; see also *bank rate.

mining extraction of minerals from under the land or sea for industrial or domestic uses. Exhaustion of traditionally accessible resources has led to development of new mining techniques; for example, extraction of oil from offshore deposits and from land shale reserves. Technology is also under development for the exploitation of minerals from entirely new sources such as mud deposits and mineral nodules from the sea bed.

mink two species of carnivores of the weasel family, genus *Mustela*, usually found in or near water. They have rich, brown fur, and are up to 50 cm/1.6 ft long with bushy tails 20 cm/8 in long. They live in Eurasia (*Mustela lutreola*) and North America (*M. vison*).

Minneapolis city in Minnesota, USA, forming with St Paul the Twin Cities area; population (1990) 368,400, metropolitan area 2,464,100. It is at the head of navigation of the Mississippi River. Industries include food processing and the manufacture of machinery, electrical and electronic equipment, precision instruments, transport machinery, and metal and paper products.

Minnelli Liza 1946– . US actress and singer, daughter of Judy *Garland and the director Vincente Minnelli. She achieved stardom in the Broadway musical *Flora, the Red Menace* 1965 and in the film *Cabaret* 1972. Her subsequent films include *New York, New York* 1977 and *Arthur* 1981.

Minnelli Vincente 1910–1986. US film director who specialized in musicals and occasional melodramas. His best films, such as *Meet Me in St Louis* 1944 and *The Band Wagon* 1953, display a powerful visual flair.

Minnesinger any of a group of German lyric poets of the 12th and 13th centuries who, in their songs, dealt mainly with the theme of courtly love without revealing the identity of the object of their affections. Minnesingers included Dietmar von Aist, Friedrich von Hausen, Heinrich von Morungen, Reinmar, and Walther von der Vogelweide.

Minnesota state in N midwest USA; nickname Gopher State/North Star State
area 218,700 sq km/84,418 sq mi
capital St Paul
cities Minneapolis, Duluth, Bloomington, Rochester
products cereals, soya beans, livestock, meat and dairy products, iron ore (about two-thirds of US output), nonelectrical machinery, electronic equipment
population (1990) 4,375,100
famous people F Scott Fitzgerald, Hubert H Humphrey, Sinclair Lewis, Charles and William Mayo
history first European exploration, by French fur traders, in the 17th century; region claimed for France by Daniel Greysolon, Sieur Duluth, 1679; part east of Mississippi River ceded to Britain 1763 and to the USA 1783; part west of Mississippi passed to the USA under the Louisiana Purchase 1803; became a territory 1849; statehood 1858.

minnow various small freshwater fishes of the carp family (Cyprinidae), found in streams and ponds worldwide. Most species are small and dully coloured, but some are brightly coloured. They feed on larvae and insects.

Minoan civilization Bronze Age civilization on the Aegean island of Crete. The name is derived from Minos, the legendary king of Crete, reputed to be the son of the god Zeus. The civilization is divided into three main periods: early Minoan, about 3000–2200 BC, middle Minoan, about 2200–1580 BC; and late Minoan, about 1580–1100 BC. Known from the Minoan civilization are the palaces of Knossos, Phaistos, and Mallia; sophisticated metalwork; and linear scripts. The Minoan language was deciphered by English archaeologist Michael Ventris (1922–1956). The civilization was suddenly destroyed by earthquake or war.

minor legal term for those under the age of majority, which varies from country to country but is usually between 18 and 21. In the USA (from 1971 for voting, and in some states for nearly all other purposes) and certain European countries (in Britain since 1970) the age of majority is 18.

Minorca (Spanish *Menorca*) second largest of the *Balearic Islands in the Mediterranean
area 689 sq km/266 sq mi
towns Mahon, Ciudadela
products copper, lead, iron; tourism is important
population (1985) 55,500.

Minotaur in Greek mythology, a monster, half man and half bull, offspring of Pasiphaë, wife of King Minos of Crete, and a bull. It lived in the Labyrinth at Knossos, and its victims were seven girls and seven youths, sent in annual tribute by Athens, until *Theseus killed it, with the aid of Ariadne, the daughter of Minos.

Minsk or **Mensk** industrial city (machinery, textiles, leather; a centre of the Russian computer industry) and capital of Belarus; population (1987) 1,543,000.

minster in the UK, a church formerly attached to a monastery: for example, York Minster. Originally the term meant a monastery, and in this sense it is often preserved in place names, such as Westminster.

mint in economics, a place where coins are made under government authority. In Britain, the official mint is the **Royal Mint**; the US equivalent is the **Bureau of the Mint**. The UK Royal Mint also manufactures coinages, official medals, and seals for Commonwealth and foreign countries.

mint in botany, any aromatic plant, genus *Mentha*, of the family Labiatae, widely distributed in temperate regions. The plants have square stems, creeping rootstocks, and flowers, usually pink or purplish, that grow in a terminal spike. Mints include garden mint *M. spicata* and peppermint *M. piperita*.

Mintoff Dom(inic) 1916– . Labour prime minister of Malta 1971–84. He negotiated the removal of British and other foreign military bases 1971–79 and made treaties with Libya.

Minton Thomas 1765–1836. English potter. He first worked under the potter Josiah Spode, but in 1789 established himself at Stoke-on-Trent as an engraver of designs (he originated the 'willow pattern') and in the 1790s founded a pottery there, producing high-quality bone china, including tableware.

minuet European courtly dance of the 17th century, later used with the trio as the third movement in a Classical symphony.

minute unit of time consisting of 60 seconds; also a unit of angle equal to one sixtieth of a degree.

Minuteman in weaponry, a US three-stage intercontinental ballistic missile (ICBM) with a range of about 8,000 km/5,000 mi. In US history the term was applied to members of the citizens' militia in the 1770s. These volunteer soldiers had pledged to be available for battle at a 'minute's notice' during the *American Revolution.

Miocene ('middle recent') fourth epoch of the Tertiary period of geological time, 25–5 million years ago. At this time grasslands spread over the interior of continents, and hoofed mammals rapidly evolved.

mips (acronym for **million instructions per second**) in computing, a measure of the speed of a processor. It does not equal the computer power in all cases.

mir (Russian 'peace' or 'world') in Russia before the 1917 Revolution, a self-governing village community in which the peasants distributed land and collected taxes.

Mir (Russian 'peace' or 'world') Russian space station, the core of which was launched 20 Feb 1986. *Mir* is intended to be a permanently occupied space station.

Mira or **Omicron Ceti** brightest long-period pulsating *variable star, located in the constellation *Cetus. Mira was the first star discovered to vary periodically in brightness.

Mirabeau Honoré Gabriel Riqueti, Comte de 1749–1791. French politician, leader of the National Assembly in the French Revolution. He wanted to establish a parliamentary monarchy on the English model. From May 1790 he secretly acted as political adviser to the king.

miracle play another name for *mystery play.

mirage illusion seen in hot climates of water on the horizon, or of distant objects being enlarged. The effect is caused by the *refraction, or bending, of light.

Miranda Carmen. Stage name of Maria de Carmo Miranda da Cunha 1909–1955. Portuguese dancer and singer who lived in Brazil from childhood. Her Hollywood musicals include *Down Argentine Way* 1940 and *The Gang's All Here* 1943. Her hallmarks were extravagant costumes and headgear adorned with tropical fruits, a staccato singing style, and fiery temperament.

Miró Joan 1893–1983. Spanish Surrealist painter, born in Barcelona. In the mid-1920s he developed a distinctive abstract style with amoeba shapes, some linear, some highly coloured, generally floating on a plain background.

Mirpur district in SW Kashmir, Pakistan, between the Jhelum River and the Indian state of Jammu and Kashmir; capital Mirpur. Its products include cotton and grain.

mirror any polished surface that reflects light; often made from 'silvered' glass (in practice, a mercury-alloy coating of glass). A plane (flat) mirror produces a same-size, erect 'virtual' image located behind the mirror at the same distance from it as the object is in front of it. A spherical concave mirror produces a reduced, inverted real image in front or an enlarged, erect virtual image behind it (as in a shaving mirror), depending on how close the object is to the mirror. A spherical convex mirror produces a reduced, erect virtual image behind it (as in a car's rear-view mirror).

MIRV abbreviation for **multiple independently targeted re-entry vehicle**, used in *nuclear warfare.

miscarriage spontaneous expulsion of a fetus from the womb before it is capable of independent survival. Often, miscarriages are due to an abnormality in the developing fetus.

misdemeanour in US law, an offence less serious than a *felony. A misdemeanour is an offence punishable by a relatively insevere penalty, such as a fine or short term in prison or a term of community service, while a felony carries more severe penalties, such as a term of imprisonment of a year or more up to the death penalty. In Britain the term is obsolete.

mise en scène (French 'stage setting') in cinema, the composition and content of the frame in terms of background scenery, actors, costumes, props, and lighting.

Mishima Yukio 1925–1970. Japanese novelist whose work often deals with sexual desire and perversion, as in *Confessions of a Mask* 1949 and *The Temple of the Golden Pavilion* 1956. He committed hara-kiri (ritual suicide) as a protest against what he saw as the corruption of the nation and the loss of the samurai warrior tradition.

Mishna or **Mishnah** collection of commentaries on written Hebrew law, consisting of discussions between rabbis, handed down orally from their inception in AD 70 until about 200, when, with the Gemara (the main body of rabbinical debate on interpretations of the Mishna) it was committed to writing to form the Talmud.

misrepresentation in law, an untrue statement of fact, made in the course of negotiating a contract, that induces one party to enter into the contract. The remedies available for misrepresentation depend on whether the representation is found to be fraudulent, negligent, or innocent.

missal in the Roman Catholic Church, a service book containing the complete office of Mass for the entire year. A simplified missal in the vernacular was introduced 1969 (obligatory from 1971): the first major reform since 1570.

missile rocket-propelled weapon, which may be nuclear-armed (see *nuclear warfare). Modern missiles are often classified as surface-to-surface missiles (SSM), air-to-air missiles (AAM), surface-to-air missiles (SAM), or air-to-surface missiles (ASM). A **cruise missile** is in effect a pilotless, computer-guided aircraft; it can be sea-launched from submarines or surface ships, or launched from the air or the ground.

mission organized attempt to spread a religion. Throughout its history Christianity has been the most assertive of missionary religions; Islam has also played a missionary role. Missionary activity in the Third World has frequently been criticized for its disruptive effects on indigenous peoples and their traditional social, political, and cultural systems.

Mississippi river in the USA, the main arm of the great river system draining the USA between the Appalachian and the Rocky mountains. The length of the Mississippi is 3,780 km/2,350 mi; with its tributary the Missouri 6,020 km/3,740 mi.

Mississippi state in SE USA; nickname Magnolia State/Bayou State
area 123,600 sq km/47,710 sq mi
capital Jackson
cities Biloxi, Meridian, Hattiesburg
products cotton, rice, soya beans, chickens, fish and shellfish, lumber and wood products, petroleum and natural gas, transportation equipment, chemicals
population (1990) 2,573,200
famous people Jefferson Davis, William Faulkner, Elvis Presley, Leontyne Price, Eudora Welty, Tennessee Williams, Richard Wright
history first explored by Hernando de Soto for Spain 1540; settled by the French 1699, the English 1763; ceded to the USA 1798; statehood achieved 1817.

Missouri state in central USA; nickname Show Me State/Bullion State
area 180,600 sq km/69,712 sq mi
capital Jefferson City
cities St Louis, Kansas City, Springfield, Independence
products meat and other processed food, aerospace and transport equipment, lead, zinc
population (1990) 5,117,100
famous people George Washington Carver, T S Eliot, Jesse James, Joseph Pulitzer, Harry S Truman, Mark Twain
history explored by de Soto 1541; acquired by

the USA under the Louisiana Purchase 1803; achieved statehood 1821, following the Missouri Compromise of 1820.

Missouri major river in the central USA, a tributary of the Mississippi, which it joins N of St Louis; length 4,320 km/2,683 mi.

Missouri Compromise in US history, the solution by Congress (1820–21) of a sectional crisis caused by the 1819 request from Missouri for admission to the union as a slave state, despite its proximity to existing nonslave states. The compromise was the simultaneous admission of Maine as a nonslave state to keep the same ratio.

mistletoe parasitic evergreen unisexual plant *Viscum album*, native to Europe. It grows on trees as a branched bush with translucent white berries. Used in many Western countries as a Christmas decoration, it also featured in *Druidism.

mistral cold, dry, northerly wind that occasionally blows during the winter on the Mediterranean coast of France. It has been known to reach a velocity of 145 kph/90 mph.

Mitchell Joni. Adopted name of Roberta Joan Anderson 1943– . Canadian singer, songwriter, and guitarist. She began in the 1960s folk style and subsequently incorporated elements of rock and jazz with confessional, sophisticated lyrics. Her albums include *Blue* 1971 and *Hejira* 1976.

Mitchell Margaret 1900–1949. US novelist, born in Atlanta, Georgia, which is the setting for her one book, the bestseller *Gone With the Wind* 1936, a story of the US Civil War. It was filmed starring Vivien Leigh and Clark Gable in 1939, becoming a cinematic classic worldwide.

Mitchell R(eginald) J(oseph) 1895–1937. British aircraft designer whose Spitfire fighter was a major factor in winning the Battle of Britain during World War II.

Mitchum Robert 1917– . US film actor, a star for more than 30 years as the big, strong, relaxed modern hero. His films include *Out of the Past* 1947, *The Night of the Hunter* 1955, and *The Friends of Eddie Coyle* 1973.

mite minute *arachnid of the subclass Acari.

Mitford sisters the six daughters of British aristocrat Lord Redesdale, including: **Nancy** (1904–1973), author of the semi-autobiographical *The Pursuit of Love* 1945 and *Love in a Cold Climate* 1949, and editor and part author of *Noblesse Oblige* 1956 elucidating 'U' (upper-class) and 'non-U' behaviour; **Diana** (1910–), who married Oswald *Mosley; **Unity** (1914–1948), who became an admirer of Hitler; **Jessica** (1917–), author of the autobiographical *Hons and Rebels* 1960 and *The American Way of Death* 1963.

Mithras in Persian mythology, the god of light. Mithras represented the power of goodness, and promised his followers compensation for present evil after death. He was said to have captured and killed the sacred bull, from whose blood all life sprang. Mithraism was introduced into the Roman Empire 68 BC. By about AD 250, it rivalled Christianity in strength.

Mithridates VI Eupator known as **the Great** 132–63 BC. King of Pontus (NE Asia Minor, on the Black Sea) from 120 BC. He massacred 80,000 Romans in overrunning the rest of Asia Minor and went on to invade Greece. He was defeated by *Sulla in the First Mithridatic War 88–84; by *Lucullus in the Second 83–81; and by *Pompey in the Third 74–64. He was killed by a soldier at his own order rather than surrender.

mitochondria (singular **mitochondrion**) membrane-enclosed organelles within *eukaryotic cells, containing enzymes responsible for energy production during *aerobic respiration. These rodlike or spherical bodies are thought to be derived from free-living bacteria that, at a very early stage in the history of life, invaded larger cells and took up a symbiotic way of life inside. Each still contains its own small loop of DNA, and new mitochondria arise by division of existing ones.

mitosis in biology, the process of cell division. The genetic material of *eukaryotic cells is carried on a number of *chromosomes. To control their movements during cell division so that both new cells get a full complement, a system of protein tubules, known as the spindle, organizes the chromosomes into position in the middle of the cell before they replicate. The spindle then controls the movement of chromosomes as the cell goes through the stages of division: *interphase*, *prophase*, *metaphase*, *anaphase*, and *telophase*. See also *meiosis.

mitre in the Christian church, the headdress worn by bishops, cardinals, and mitred abbots at solemn services. There are mitres of many different shapes, but in the Western church they usually take the form of a tall cleft cap. The mitre worn by the pope is called a tiara.

Mitre Bartólomé 1821–1906. Argentine president 1862–68. In 1852 he helped overthrow the dictatorial regime of Juan Manuel de Rosas, and in 1861 helped unify Argentina. Mitre encouraged immigration and favoured growing commercial links with Europe. He is seen as a symbol of national unity.

Mitsotakis Constantine 1918– . Greek politician, leader of the conservative New Democracy Party from 1984, prime minister 1990–93. He was minister for economic coordination 1965 and again 1978–80; foreign minister 1980–81. The military junta that seized power 1967 put him under house arrest, but he escaped and lived in exile until 1974. He was replaced as prime minister by Andreas *Papandreou.

Mitterrand François 1916– . French socialist politician, president from 1981. He held ministerial posts in 11 governments 1947–58, and founded the French Socialist Party (PS) 1971. In 1985 he introduced proportional representation, allegedly to weaken the growing opposition from left and right. Since 1982 his administrations have combined economic orthodoxy with social reform.

mixed economy type of economic structure that combines the private enterprise of capitalism with a degree of state monopoly. In mixed economies, governments seek to control the public services, the basic industries, and those industries that cannot raise sufficient capital investment from private sources. Thus a measure of economic planning can be combined with a measure of free enterprise. A notable example was US president F D Roosevelt's *New Deal in the 1930s.

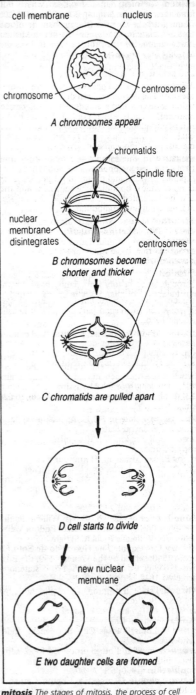

A chromosomes appear

B chromosomes become shorter and thicker

C chromatids are pulled apart

D cell starts to divide

new nuclear membrane

E two daughter cells are formed

mitosis *The stages of mitosis, the process of cell division that takes place when a plant or animal cell divides for growth or repair.*

mixed farming farming system where both arable and pastoral farming is carried out. Mixed farming is a lower-risk strategy than *monoculture. If climate, pests, or market prices are unfavourable for one crop or type of livestock, another may be more successful and the risk is shared. Animals provide manure for the fields and help to maintain soil fertility.

Mixtec ancient civilization of pre-colonial Mexico. The Mixtecs succeeded the *Zapotecs in the valley of Oaxaca. The Mixtecs produced historical records which contain biographies of rulers and noblemen and trace Mixtec history back to AD 692. They were skilled in the use of metals, including gold and silver.

mixture in chemistry, a substance containing two or more compounds that still retain their separate physical and chemical properties. There is no chemical bonding between them and they can be separated from each other by physical means (compare *compound).

Mizoram state of NE India
area 21,100 sq km/8,145 sq mi
capital Aizawl
products rice, hand-loom weaving
population (1991) 686,200
religion 84% Christian
history made a Union Territory 1972 from the Mizo Hills District of Assam. Rebels carried on a guerrilla war 1966–76, but 1976 acknowledged Mizoram as an integral part of India. It became a state 1986.

m.k.s. system system of units in which the base units metre, kilogram, and second replace the centimetre, gram, and second of the *c.g.s. system. From it developed the SI system (see *SI units).

ml symbol for *millilitre*.

MLR abbreviation for *minimum lending rate*.

mm symbol for *millimetre*.

Mmabatho or *Sun City* capital of Bophuthatswana South Africa; population (1985) 28,000. It is a casino resort frequented by many white South Africans.

moa extinct flightless kiwi-like bird, order Dinornithoformes, 19 species of which lived in New Zealand. They varied from 0.5 to 3.5 m/2 to 12 ft, with strong limbs, a long neck, and no wings. The last moa was killed in the 1800s.

Moab ancient country in Jordan east of the southern part of the river Jordan and the Dead Sea. The inhabitants were closely akin to the Hebrews in culture, language, and religion, but were often at war with them, as recorded in the Old Testament. Moab eventually fell to Arab invaders. The *Moabite Stone*, discovered 1868 at Dhiban, dates from the 9th century BC and records the rising of Mesha, king of Moab, against Israel.

moat ditch, often filled with water, surrounding a building or garden. Some 5,000 moats exist in England alone, many dating from the 12th–13th centuries; some were built for defence and others as a status symbol.

mobile ion in chemistry, ion that is free to move; mobile ions are only found in aqueous solutions or a melt of an *electrolyte. The mobility of the ions in an electrolyte is what allows it to conduct electricity.

Möbius strip structure made by giving a half twist to a flat strip of paper and joining the ends together. It has certain remarkable properties, arising from the fact that it has only one edge and one side. If cut down the centre of the strip, instead of two new strips of paper, only one long strip is produced. It was invented by the German mathematician August Möbius.

Mobutu Sese Seko Kuku Ngbeandu Wa Za Banga 1930– . Zairean president from 1965. He assumed the presidency in a coup, and created a unitary state under a centralized government. The harshness of some of his policies and charges of corruption have attracted widespread international criticism. In 1991 opposition leaders forced Mobutu to agree formally to give up some of his powers.

mockingbird North American songbird *Mimus polyglottos* of the mimic thrush family Mimidae, found in the USA and Mexico. About 25 cm/10 in long, it is brownish grey, with white markings on the black wings and tail. It is remarkable for its ability to mimic the songs of other species.

mock orange or *syringa* deciduous shrub of the genus *Philadelphus*, family Philadelphaceae, including *P. coronarius*, which has white, strongly scented flowers, resembling those of the orange.

mod British youth subculture that originated in London and Brighton in the early 1960s around the French view of the English; revived in the late 1970s. Mods were fashion-conscious, speedy, and upwardly mobile; they favoured scooters and soul music.

mode in mathematics, the element that appears most frequently in a given group. For example, the mode of the group 0, 0, 9, 9, 9, 12, 87, 87 is 9. (Not all groups have modes.)

model simplified version of some aspect of the real word. Models are produced to show the relationships between two or more factors, such as land use and the distance from the centre of a town (see *concentric-ring theory). Because models are idealized, they give only a general guide to what may happen.

Model Parliament English parliament set up 1295 by Edward I; it was the first to include representatives from outside the clergy and aristocracy, and was established because Edward needed the support of the whole country against his opponents: Wales, France, and Scotland. His sole aim was to raise money for military purposes, and the parliament did not pass any legislation.

modem (acronym for *modulator/demodulator*; also called an *acoustic coupler*) device for transmitting computer data over telephone lines. Such a device is necessary because the *digital signals produced by computers cannot, at present, be transmitted directly over the telephone network, which uses *analogue signals. The modem converts the digital signals to analogue, and back again. Modems are used for linking remote terminals to central computers and enable computers to communicate with each other anywhere in the world.

moderator in a nuclear reactor, a material such as graphite or heavy water used to reduce the speed of high-energy neutrons. Neutrons produced by nuclear fission are fast-moving and must be slowed to initiate further fission so that nuclear energy continues to be released at a controlled rate.

modern dance 20th-century dance idiom that evolved in opposition to traditional ballet by those seeking a freer and more immediate means of dance expression. Leading exponents include Martha *Graham and Merce *Cunningham in the USA, Isadora *Duncan and Loie Fuller in Europe.

Modernism in the arts, a general term used to describe the 20th century's conscious attempt to break with the artistic traditions of the 19th century; it is based on a concern with form and the exploration of technique as opposed to content and narrative.

Modigliani Amedeo 1884–1920. Italian artist, active in Paris from 1906. He painted and sculpted graceful nudes and portrait studies. His paintings – for example, the portrait of *Jeanne Hebuterne* 1919 (Guggenheim Museum, New York) – have a distinctive elongated, linear style.

modulation in radio transmission, the intermittent change of frequency, or amplitude, of a radio carrier wave, in accordance with the audio characteristics of the speaking voice, music, or other signal being transmitted. See *pulse-code modulation, *AM (amplitude modulation), and *FM (frequency modulation).

modulation in music, movement from one *key to another.

module in construction, a standard or unit that governs the form of the rest. For example, Japanese room sizes are traditionally governed by multiples of standard tatami floor mats; today prefabricated buildings are mass-produced in a similar way. The components of a spacecraft are designed in coordination; for example, for the Apollo Moon landings the craft comprised a command module (for working, eating, sleeping), service module (electricity generators, oxygen supplies, manoeuvring rocket), and lunar module (to land and return the astronauts).

modulus in mathematics, a number that divides exactly into the difference between two given numbers. Also, the multiplication factor used to convert a logarithm of one base to a logarithm of another base. Also, another name for *absolute value.

Mogadishu or **Mugdisho** capital and chief port of Somalia; population (1988) 1,000,000. It is a centre for oil refining, food processing, and uranium mining. During the struggle to overthrow President Barre and the ensuing civil war 1991–92, much of the city was devastated and many thousands killed. In April 1992 the UN Security Council voted to send military observers to monitor a cease-fire in the city.

Mogul dynasty N Indian dynasty 1526–1858, established by *Babur, Muslim descendant of Tamerlane, the 14th-century Mongol leader. The Mogul emperors ruled until the last one, *Bahadur Shah II, was dethroned and exiled by the British; they included *Akbar, *Aurangzeb, and *Shah Jahan.

Mohács, Battle of Austro-Hungarian defeat of the Turks 1687, which effectively marked the end of Turkish expansion into Europe. Named after the river port of that name on the Danube in Hungary, which is also the site of a Turkish victory 1526.

mohair (Arabic *mukhayyar* 'goat') yarn made from the long, lustrous hair of the *Angora goat or rabbit, loosely woven with cotton, silk, or wool to produce a fuzzy texture. It became popular for jackets, coats, and sweaters in the 1950s. Commercial mohair is now obtained from crossbred animals, pure-bred supplies being insufficient to satisfy demand.

Mohamad Mahathir bin 1925– . Prime minister of Malaysia from 1981 and leader of the United Malays' National Organization (UMNO). His 'look east' economic policy emulates Japanese industrialization.

Mohammed alternative form of *Muhammad, founder of Islam.

Moholy-Nagy Laszlo 1895–1946. US photographer. Born in Hungary, he lived in Germany 1923–29, where he was a member of the Bauhaus school, and fled from the Nazis 1935. Through the publication of his illuminating theories and practical experiments, he had great influence on 20th-century photography and design.

Mohorovičić discontinuity also **Moho** or **M-discontinuity** boundary that separates the Earth's crust and mantle, marked by a rapid increase in the speed of earthquake waves. It follows the variations in the thickness of the crust and is found approximately 32 km/20 mi below the continents and about 10 km/6 mi below the oceans. It is named after the Yugoslav geophysicist Andrija Mohorovičić (1857–1936), who suspected its presence after analysing seismic waves from the Kulpa Valley earthquake 1909.

Mohs' scale scale of hardness for minerals (in ascending order): 1 talc; 2 gypsum; 3 calcite; 4 fluorite; 5 apatite; 6 orthoclase; 7 quartz; 8 topaz; 9 corundum; 10 diamond.

Moi Daniel arap 1924– . Kenyan politician, president from 1978. Leader of Kenya African National Union (KANU), he became minister of home affairs 1964, vice president 1967, and succeeded Jomo Kenyatta as president. He enjoys the support of Western governments but has been widely criticized for Kenya's poor human-rights record. Since 1988 his rule has become increasingly authoritarian. In 1991, in the face of widespread criticism, he promised an eventual introduction of multiparty politics. In 1992 he was elected president in the first free elections amid widespread accusations of fraud.

Mojave Desert arid region in S California, USA, part of the Great Basin; area 38,500 sq km/15,000 sq mi.

molar one of the large teeth found towards the back of the mammalian mouth. The structure of the jaw, and the relation of the muscles, allows a massive force to be applied to molars. In herbivores the molars are flat with sharp ridges of enamel and are used for grinding, an adaptation to a diet of tough plant material. Carnivores have sharp powerful molars called carnassials, which are adapted for cutting meat.

molarity in chemistry, *concentration of a solution expressed as the number of *moles in grams of solute per cubic decimetre of solution.

molar volume volume occupied by one *mole (the molecular mass in grams) of any gas at standard temperature and pressure, equal to 2.24136×10^{-2} m^3.

Moldavia former principality in E Europe, on the river Danube, occupying an area divided today between Moldova (formerly a Soviet republic) and Romania. It was independent between the 14th and 16th centuries, when it became part of the Ottoman Empire. In 1861 Moldavia was united with its neighbouring principality Wallachia as Romania. In 1940 the eastern part, *Bessarabia, became part of the USSR, whereas the western part remained in Romania.

Moldova Republic of

area 33,700 sq km/13,012 sq mi
capital Chişinău (Kishinev)
towns Tiraspol, Beltsy, Bendery
physical hilly land lying largely between the rivers Prut and Dniester; N Moldova comprises the level plain of the Beltsy Steppe and uplands; the climate is warm and moderately continental
head of state Mircea Snegur from 1989
head of government Andrei Sangeli from 1994
political system emergent democracy
products wine, tobacco, canned goods
population (1992) 4,394,000 (Moldavian 64%, Ukrainian 14%, Russian 13%, Gagauzi 4%, Bulgarian 2%)
language Moldavian, allied to Romanian
religion Russian Orthodox
GNP $2,170 per head (1991)
chronology
1940 Bessarabia in the E became part of the Soviet Union whereas the W part remained in Romania.
1941 Bessarabia taken over by Romania–Germany.
1944 Red army reconquered Bessarabia.
1946–47 Widespread famine.
1988 A popular front, the Democratic Movement for Perestroika, campaigned for political reform.
1989 Jan–Feb: nationalist demonstrations in Chisinau. May: Moldavian Popular Front established. July: former Communist Party deputy leader Mircea Snegur became head of state. Aug: Moldavian language granted official status, triggering clashes between ethnic Russians and Moldavians. Nov: Gagauz-Khalky People's Movement formed to campaign for Gagauz autonomy.
1990 Feb: Popular Front polled strongly in supreme soviet elections. June: economic and political sovereignty declared; renamed Republic of Moldova. Oct: Gagauzi held unauthorized elections to independent parliament; state of emergency declared after interethnic clashes. Trans-Dniester region declared its sovereignty. Nov: state of emergency declared in Trans-Dniester region after interethnic killings.
1991 March: Moldova boycotted the USSR's constitutional referendum. Aug: independence declared after abortive anti-Gorbachev coup; Communist Party outlawed. Dec: Moldova joined new Commonwealth of Independent States.
1992 Admitted into United Nations and the Conference on Security and Cooperation in Europe; diplomatic recognition granted by USA. Possible union with Romania discussed. Trans-Dniester region fighting intensified; Russian peacekeeping force reportedly deployed after talks between Moldova and Russia. Andrei Sangheli became premier.
1993 Cease-fire in Gagauz and Trans-Dniester regions.
1994 Parliamentary elections won by Agrarian Democratic Party (ADP), led by former communist Petro Luchinsky. Plebiscite rejected nationalist demands for merger with Romania.

mole burrowing insectivore of the family Talpidae. Moles grow to 18 cm/7 in, and have acute senses of hearing, smell, and touch, but poor vision. They have shovel-like, clawed front feet for burrowing, and eat insects, grubs, and worms.

mole SI unit (symbol mol) of the amount of a substance. It is defined as the amount of a substance that contains as many elementary entities (atoms, molecules, and so on) as there are atoms in 12 g of the *isotope carbon-12.

mole person working subversively within an organization. The term has come to be used broadly for someone who gives out ('leaks') secret information in the public interest; it originally meant a person who spends several years working for a government department or a company with the intention of passing secrets to an enemy or a rival.

molecular biology study of the molecular basis of life, including the biochemistry of molecules such as DNA, RNA, and proteins, and the molecular structure and function of the various parts of living cells.

molecular clock use of rates of *mutation in genetic material to calculate the length of time elapsed since two related species diverged from each other during evolution. The method can be based on comparisons of the DNA or of widely occurring proteins, such as haemoglobin.

molecular formula in chemistry, formula indicating the actual number of atoms of each element present in a single molecule of a chemical compound. This is determined by two pieces of information: the *empirical formula and the *relative molecular mass, which is determined experimentally.

molecular mass (also known as *relative molecular mass) the mass of a molecule, calculated relative to one-twelfth the mass of an atom of carbon-12. It is found by adding the relative atomic masses of the atoms that make up the molecule.

molecular weight (also known as *relative molecular mass*) the mass of the molecule, calculated relative to one-twelfth the mass of an atom of carbon-12. It is found by adding the relative atomic masses of the atoms that make up the molecule.

molecule group of two or more *atoms bonded together. A molecule of an element consists of one or more like *atoms; a molecule of a compound consists of two or more different atoms bonded together. Molecules vary in size and complexity from the hydrogen molecule (H_2) to the large *macromolecules of proteins. They are held together by ionic bonds, in which the atoms gain or lose electrons to form *ions, or by covalent bonds, where electrons from each atom are shared in a new molecular orbital.

mole rat, naked small subterranean mammal *Heterocephalus glaber*, almost hairless, with a disproportionately large head. The mole rat is of importance to zoologists as one of the very few mammals that are eusocial, that is, living in colonies with sterile workers and one fertile female. This enables study of how under Darwinian evolution it is possible for sterile worker mole rats to be 'reproduced' from one generation to another.

Molière pen name of Jean-Baptiste Poquelin 1622–1673. French satirical dramatist and actor. Modern French comedy developed from his work. After the collapse of the Paris Illustre Théâtre (of which he was one ofthe founders), Molière performed in the provinces 1645–58. In 1655 he wrote his first play *L'Etourdi/The Blunderer*, followed by *Les Précieuses ridicules/The Affected Ladies* 1659. His satires include *L'Ecole des femmes/The School for Wives* 1662, *Le Misanthrope* 1666, *Le Bourgeois Gentilhomme/ The Would-Be Gentleman* 1670, and *Le Malade imaginaire/The Imaginary Invalid* 1673. Other satiric plays include *Tartuffe* 1664 (banned until 1697 for attacking the hypocrisy of the clergy), *Le Médecin malgré lui/Doctor in Spite of Himself* 1666, and *Les Femmes savantes/The Learned Ladies* 1672.

Molise mainly agricultural region of S central Italy, comprising the provinces of Campobasso and Isernia; area 4,400 sq km/1,698 sq mi; population (1990) 336,500. Its capital is Campobasso.

mollusc any invertebrate of the phylum Mollusca with a body divided into three parts, a head, a foot, and a visceral mass. The majority of molluscs are marine animals, but some inhabit fresh water, and a few are terrestrial. They include bivalves, mussels, octopuses, oysters, snails, slugs, and squids. The body is soft, limbless, and cold-blooded. There is no internal skeleton, but many species have a hard shell covering the body.

Molotov Vyacheslav Mikhailovich. Assumed name of V M Skriabin 1890–1986. Soviet communist politician. He was chair of the Council of People's Commissars (prime minister) 1930–41 and foreign minister 1939–49 and 1953–56. He negotiated the 1939 nonaggression treaty with Germany (the *Hitler–Stalin pact), and, after the German invasion 1941, the Soviet partnership with the Allies. His postwar stance prolonged the Cold War and in 1957 he was expelled from the government for Stalinist activities.

Molotov cocktail or *petrol bomb* homemade weapon consisting of a bottle filled with petrol, plugged with a rag as a wick, ignited, and thrown as a grenade. Resistance groups during World War II named them after the Soviet foreign minister Molotov.

Moluccas another name for *Maluku, Indonesia.

molybdenite molybdenum sulphide, MoS_2, the chief ore mineral of molybdenum. It possesses a hexagonal crystal structure similar to graphite, has a blue metallic lustre, and is very soft (1–1.5 on Mohs' scale).

molybdenum (Greek *malybdos* 'lead') heavy, hard, lustrous, silver-white, metallic element, symbol Mo, atomic number 42, relative atomic mass 95.94. The chief ore is the mineral molybdenite. The element is highly resistant to heat and conducts electricity easily. It is used in alloys, often to harden steels. It is a necessary trace element in human nutrition. It was named 1781 by Swedish chemist Karl Scheele, after its isolation by P J Hjelm (1746–1813), for its resemblance to lead ore.

Molyneaux Jim 1920– . Northern Ireland Unionist politician, leader of the Official Ulster Unionist Party (OUP) from 1979. A member of the House of Commons from 1970, he temporarily relinquished his seat, 1983–85, in protest at the *Anglo-Irish Agreement. Although a fervent supporter of the union between Britain and Northern Ireland, he is regarded as one of the more moderate loyalists.

Mombasa industrial port (oil refining, cement) in Kenya (serving also Uganda and Tanzania), built on Mombasa Island and adjacent mainland; population (1984) 481,000. It was founded by Arab traders in the 11th century and was an important centre for ivory and slave trading until the 16th century.

moment of a force in physics, measure of the turning effect, or torque, produced by a force acting on a body. It is equal to the product of the force and the perpendicular distance from its line of action to the point, or pivot, about which the body will turn. Its unit is the newton metre.

moment of inertia in physics, the sum of all the point masses of a rotating object multiplied by the squares of their respective distances from the axis of rotation. It is analogous to the *mass of a stationary object or one moving in a straight line.

momentum in physics, the product of the mass of a body and its linear velocity. The *angular momentum* of a body in rotational motion is the product of its moment of inertia and its angular velocity. The momentum of a body does not change unless it is acted on by an external force; angular momentum does not change unless it is acted upon by a turning force, or torque.

Momoyama in Japanese history, the period 1568–1616 or 1573–1603. During this time three great generals, Oda Nobunaga (1534–1582), Toyotomi Hideyoshi (1537–1598), and *Tokugawa Ieyasu, successively held power; Ieyasu established the Tokugawa shogunate. Portuguese missionaries and traders were an influence at this time, and *Japanese art, architecture (castles), and the tea ceremony flourished. The period is named after a castle built by Hideyoshi in Fushimi, central Honshu.

Monaco Principality of

area 1.95 sq km/0.75 sq mi
capital Monaco-Ville
towns Monte Carlo, La Condamine; heliport Fontvieille
physical steep and rugged; surrounded landwards by French territory; being expanded by filling in the sea
head of state Prince Rainier III from 1949
head of government Jacques Dupont from 1991
political system constitutional monarchy under French protectorate
exports some light industry; economy dependent on tourism and gambling
currency French franc
population (1990) 30,000; growth rate –0.5% p.a.
languages French (official), English, Italian
religion Roman Catholic 95%
chronology
1861 Became an independent state under French protection.
1918 France given a veto over succession to the throne.
1949 Prince Rainier III ascended the throne.
1956 Prince Rainier married US actress Grace Kelly.
1958 Birth of male heir, Prince Albert.
1959 Constitution of 1911 suspended.
1962 New constitution adopted.
1993 Joined the United Nations.

Monaghan (Irish **Mhuineachain**) county of the NE Republic of Ireland, province of Ulster; area 1,290 sq km/498 sq mi; products include cereals, linen, potatoes, and cattle; population (1991) 51,300. The county town is Monaghan. The county is low and rolling, and includes the rivers Finn and Blackwater.

monasticism devotion to religious life under vows of poverty, chastity, and obedience, known to Judaism (for example *Essenes), Buddhism, and other religions, before Christianity. In Islam, the Sufis formed monastic orders from the 12th century.

Monck or **Monk** George, 1st Duke of Albemarle

1608–1669. English soldier. During the Civil War he fought for King Charles I, but after being captured took command of the Parliamentary forces in Ireland. Under the Commonwealth he was commander in chief in Scotland, and in 1660 led his army into England and brought about the restoration of Charles II.

Mondrian Piet (Pieter Mondriaan) 1872–1944. Dutch painter, a pioneer of abstract art. He lived in Paris 1919–38, then in London, and from 1940 in New York. He was a founder member of the **de** *Stijl movement and chief exponent of Neo-Plasticism, a rigorous abstract style based on the use of simple geometric forms and pure colours. He typically painted parallel horizontal black lines which intersected vertical ones, creating square and rectangular blocks within the framework, some of which he filled with primary colours, mid-grey, or black, others being left white.

Monet Claude 1840–1926. French painter, a pioneer of Impressionism and a lifelong exponent of its ideals; his painting *Impression, Sunrise* 1872 gave the movement its name. In the 1870s he began painting the same subjects at different times of day to explore the effects of light on colour and form; the *Haystacks* and *Rouen Cathedral* series followed in the 1890s, and from 1899 he painted a series of *Water Lilies* in the garden of his house at Giverny, Normandy (now a museum).

monetarism economic policy, advocated by the economist Milton Friedman and the Chicago school of economists, that proposes control of a country's money supply to keep it in step with the country's ability to produce goods, with the aim of curbing inflation. Cutting government spending is advocated, and the long-term aim is to return as much of the economy as possible to the private sector, allegedly in the interests of efficiency.

monetary policy economic policy aimed at controlling the amount of money in circulation, usually through controlling the level of lending or credit. Increasing interest rates is an example of a contractionary monetary policy, which aims to reduce inflation by reducing the rate of growth of spending in the economy.

money any common medium of exchange acceptable in payment for goods or services or for the settlement of debts; legal tender. Money is usually coinage (invented by the Chinese in the second millennium BC) and paper notes (used by the Chinese from about AD 800). Developments such as the cheque and credit card fulfil many of the traditional functions of money.

money market institution that deals in gold and foreign exchange, and securities in the short term. Long-term transactions are dealt with on the capital market. There is no physical marketplace, and many deals are made by telephone or telex.

money supply quantity of money in circulation in an economy at any given time. It can include notes, coins, and clearing-bank and other deposits used for everyday payments. Changes in the quantity of lending are a major determinant of changes in the money supply. One of the main principles of *monetarism is that increases in the money supply in excess of the rate of economic growth are the chief cause of inflation.

Mongol member of any of the various Mongol (or Mongolian) ethnic groups of Central Asia. Mongols live in Mongolia, Russia, Inner Mongolia (China), Tibet, and Nepal. The Mongol language belongs to the Altaic family; some groups of Mongol descent speak languages in the Sino-Tibetan family, however.

Mongol Empire empire established by Genghis Khan, who extended his domains from Russia to N China and became khan of the Mongol tribes 1206. His grandson Kublai Khan conquered China and used foreigners such as Marco Polo as well as subjects to administer his empire. The Mongols lost China 1367 and suffered defeats in the West 1380; the empire broke up soon afterwards.

Mongolia State of
(*Outer Mongolia* until 1924; *People's Republic of Mongolia* until 1991)

area 1,565,000 sq km/604,480 sq mi
capital Ulaanbaatar
towns Darhan, Choybalsan
physical high plateau with desert and steppe (grasslands)
head of state Punsalmaagiyn Ochirbat from 1990
head of government Puntsagiyn Jasray from 1992
political system emergent democracy
exports meat and hides, minerals, wool, livestock, grain, cement, timber
currency tugrik
population (1993 est) 2,360,000; growth rate 2.8% p.a.
languages Khalkha Mongolian (official), Chinese, Russian, and Turkic languages
religion officially none (Tibetan Buddhist Lamaism suppressed 1930s)
GNP $112 per head (1990)
chronology
1911 Outer Mongolia gained autonomy from China.
1915 Chinese sovereignty reasserted.
1921 Chinese rule overthrown with Soviet help.
1924 People's Republic proclaimed.
1946 China recognized Mongolia's independence.

1966 20-year friendship, cooperation, and mutual-assistance pact signed with USSR. Relations with China deteriorated.
1984 Yumjaagiyn Tsedenbal, effective leader, deposed and replaced by Jambyn Batmonh.
1987 Soviet troops reduced; Mongolia's external contacts broadened.
1989 Further Soviet troop reductions.
1990 Democratization campaign launched by Mongolian Democratic Union. Ochirbat's Mongolian People's Revolutionary Party elected in free multiparty elections. Mongolian script readopted.
1991 Massive privatization programme launched as part of move towards a market economy. The word 'Republic' dropped from country's name.
1992 New constitution introduced. Worsening economic situation. Prime minister's resignation refused. Puntsagiyn Jasray appointed new prime minister.

Mongolia, Inner (Chinese *Nei Mongol*) autonomous region of NE China from 1947
area 450,000 sq km/173,700 sq mi
capital Hohhot
physical grassland and desert
products cereals under irrigation; coal; reserves of rare earth oxides europium, and yttrium at Bayan Obo
population (1990) 21,457,000.

mongolism former name (now considered offensive) for *Down's syndrome.

Mongoloid former racial classification, based on physical features, used to describe people of E Asian and North American origin; see *race.

mongoose any of various carnivorous mammals of the family Viverridae, especially the genus *Herpestes*. The Indian mongoose *H. mungo* is greyish in colour and about 50 cm/1.5 ft long, with a long tail. It may be tamed and is often kept for its ability to kill snakes. The white-tailed mongoose *Ichneumia albicauda* of central Africa has a distinctive grey or white bushy tail.

monism in philosophy, the theory that reality is made up of only one substance. This view is usually contrasted with *dualism, which divides reality into two substances, matter and mind. The Dutch philosopher Baruch Spinoza saw the one substance as God or Nature. Monism is also sometimes used as a description of a political system in which only one party is permitted to operate.

monitor any of various lizards of the family Varanidae, found in Africa, S Asia, and Australasia. Monitors are generally large and carnivorous, with well-developed legs and claws and a long powerful tail that can be swung in defence.

monk man belonging to a religious order under the vows of poverty, chastity, and obedience, and living under a particular rule; see *monasticism.

Monk Thelonious (Sphere) 1917–1982. US jazz pianist and composer who took part in the development of *bebop. He had a highly idiosyncratic style, but numbers such as 'Round Midnight' and 'Blue Monk' have become standards.

monkey any of the various smaller, mainly tree-dwelling anthropoid primates, excluding humans and the *apes. The 125 species live in Africa, Asia, and tropical Central and South America.

Monkeys eat mainly leaves and fruit, and also small animals. Several species are endangered due to loss of forest habitat, for example the woolly spider monkey and black saki of the Amazonian forest.

monkey puzzle or *Chilean pine* coniferous evergreen tree *Araucaria araucana* (see *araucaria), native to Chile; it has whorled branches covered in prickly leaves of a leathery texture.

Monmouth James Scott, Duke of Monmouth 1649–1685. Claimant to the English crown, the illegitimate son of Charles II and Lucy Walter. After James II's accession 1685, Monmouth landed in England at Lyme Regis, Dorset, claimed the crown, and raised a rebellion, which was crushed at *Sedgemoor in Somerset. He was executed with 320 of his accomplices.

monocarpic or *hapaxanthic* describing plants that flower and produce fruit only once during their lifecycle, after which they die. Most *annual plants and *biennial plants are monocarpic, but there are also a small number of monocarpic *perennial plants that flower just once, sometimes after as long as 90 years, dying shortly afterwards, for example, century plant *Agave* and some species of bamboo *Bambusa*. The general biological term related to organisms that reproduce only once during their lifetime is *semelparity.

monoclonal antibody (MAB) antibody produced by fusing an antibody-producing lymphocyte with a cancerous myeloma (bone-marrow) cell. The resulting fused cell, called a hybridoma, is immortal and can be used to produce large quantities of a single, specific antibody. By choosing antibodies that are directed against antigens found on cancer cells, and combining them with cytotoxic drugs, it is hoped to make so-called magic bullets that will be able to pick out and kill cancers.

monocotyledon angiosperm (flowering plant) having an embryo with a single cotyledon, or seed leaf (as opposed to *dicotyledons, which have two). Monocotyledons usually have narrow leaves with parallel veins and smooth edges, and hollow or soft stems. Their flower parts are arranged in threes. Most are small plants such as orchids, grasses, and lilies, but some are trees such as palms.

monoculture farming system where only one crop is grown. In Third World countries this is often a *cash crop, grown on *plantations. Cereal crops in the industrialized world are also frequently grown on a monoculture basis; for example, wheat in the Canadian prairies.

monody in music, declamation by accompanied solo voice, used at the turn of the 16th and 17th centuries.

monoecious having separate male and female flowers on the same plant. Maize (*Zea mays*), for example, has a tassel of male flowers at the top of the stalk and a group of female flowers (on the ear, or cob) lower down. Monoecism is a way of avoiding self-fertilization. *Dioecious plants have male and female flowers on separate plants.

monogamy practice of having only one husband or wife at a time in *marriage.

monomer chemical compound composed of simple molecules from which *polymers can be made. Under certain conditions the simple molecules (of the monomer) join together (polymerize) to form a very long chain molecule (macromolecule) called a polymer. For example, the polymerization of ethene (ethylene) monomers produces the polymer polyethene (polyethylene).

$$2nCH_2=CH_2$$
$$(CH_2-CH_2-CH_2-CH_2)_n$$

Monophysite (Greek 'one-nature') member of a group of Christian heretics of the 5th–7th centuries who taught that Jesus had one nature, in opposition to the orthodox doctrine (laid down at the Council of Chalcedon 451) that he had two natures, the human and the divine. Monophysitism developed as a reaction to *Nestorianism and led to the formal secession of the Coptic and Armenian churches from the rest of the Christian church. Monophysites survive today in Armenia, Syria, and Egypt.

Monopolies and Mergers Commission (MMC) UK government body re-established 1973 under the Fair Trading Act and, since 1980, embracing the Competition Act. Its role is to investigate and report when there is a risk of creating a monopoly by a company merger or takeover, or when a newspaper or newspaper assets are transferred. It also investigates companies, nationalized industries, or local authorities that are suspected of operating in a noncompetitive way. The US equivalent is the *Federal Trade Commission* (FTC).

monopoly in economics, the domination of a market for a particular product or service by a single company, which can therefore restrict competition and keep prices high. In practice, a company can be said to have a monopoly when it controls a significant proportion of the market (technically an *oligopoly).

Monopoly the world's biggest-selling copyrighted game, a board game of buying properties, building houses on them, and charging rent. It was devised in the USA 1934 by Charles B Darrow (1889–1967), with street names from Atlantic City, New Jersey, where he spent his holidays; he sold the game 1935 to Parker Brothers, US game manufacturers, for a royalty.

monorail railway that runs on a single rail; the cars can be balanced on it or suspended from it. It was invented 1882 to carry light loads, and when run by electricity was called a *telpher*.

monosaccharide or *simple sugar* *carbohydrate that cannot be hydrolysed (split) into smaller carbohydrate units. Examples are glucose and fructose, both of which have the molecular formula $C_6H_{12}O_6$.

monosodium glutamate (MSG) $NaC_5H_8NO_4$ a white, crystalline powder, the sodium salt of glutamic acid (an *amino acid found in proteins that plays a role in the metabolism of plants and animals). It is used to enhance the flavour of many packaged and 'fast foods', and in Chinese cooking. Ill effects may arise from its overconsumption, and some people are very sensitive to it, even in small amounts. It is commercially derived from vegetable protein.

monotheism belief or doctrine that there is only one God; the opposite of polytheism.

monotreme any member of the order Monotremata, the only living egg-laying mammals,
found in Australasia. They include the echidnas
and the platypus.

Monroe James 1758–1831. 5th president of the
USA 1817–25, a Democratic Republican. He
served in the American Revolution, was minister
to France 1794–96, and in 1803 negotiated the
*Louisiana Purchase. He was secretary of state
1811–17. His name is associated with the
*Monroe Doctrine.

Monroe Marilyn. Stage name of Norma Jean
Mortenson or Baker 1926–1962. US film actress,
the voluptuous blonde sex symbol of the 1950s,
who made adroit comedies such as *Gentlemen
Prefer Blondes* 1953, *How to Marry a Millionaire* 1953, *The Seven Year Itch* 1955, *Bus Stop*
1956, and *Some Like It Hot* 1959. Her second
husband was baseball star Joe di Maggio, and her
third was playwright Arthur *Miller, who wrote
The Misfits 1961 for her, a serious film that
became her last. She committed suicide, taking
an overdose of sleeping pills.

Monroe Doctrine declaration by US president
James Monroe 1823 that any further European
colonial ambitions in the western hemisphere
would be threats to US peace and security, made
in response to proposed European intervention
against newly independent former Spanish colonies in South America. In return the USA would
not interfere in European affairs. The doctrine,
subsequently broadened, has been a recurrent
theme in US foreign policy, although it has no
basis in US or international law.

Monrovia capital and port of Liberia; population (1985) 500,000. Industries include rubber,
cement, and petrol processing.

monsoon wind system that dominates the climate of a wide region, with seasonal reversals of
direction; in particular, the wind in S Asia that
blows towards the sea in winter and towards
the land in summer, bringing heavy rain. The
monsoon may cause destructive flooding all over
India and SE Asia from April to Sept. Thousands
of people are rendered homeless each year. The
Guinea monsoon is a southwesterly wind that
blows in W Africa from April to Sept, throughout
the rainy season.

monstera or *Swiss cheese plant* evergreen
climbing plant, genus *Monstera*, of the arum
family Araceae, native to tropical America. *M.
deliciosa* is cultivated as a house plant. Areas
between the veins of the leaves dry up, creating
deep marginal notches and ultimately holes.

montage in cinema, the juxtaposition of
several images or shots to produce an independent meaning. The term is also used more generally to describe the whole process of editing or a
rapidly edited series of shots. It was coined by
the Russian director S M *Eisenstein.

Montaigne Michel Eyquem de 1533–1592.
French writer, regarded as the creator of the essay
form. In 1580 he published the first two volumes
of his *Essais*, the third volume appeared in 1588.
Montaigne deals with all aspects of life from an
urbanely sceptical viewpoint. Through the translation by John Florio in 1603, he influenced
Shakespeare and other English writers.

Montana state of the W USA, on the Canadian
border; nickname Treasure State
area 318,100 sq km/147,143 sq mi
capital Helena
cities Billings, Great Falls, Butte
physical mountainous forests in the west, rolling
grasslands in the east
products wheat (under irrigation), cattle, coal,
copper, oil, natural gas, lumber, wood products
population (1990) 799,100
famous people Gary Cooper, Myrna Loy
history explored for France by Verendrye early
1740s; passed to the US 1803 in the Louisiana
Purchase; first settled 1809; W Montana obtained
from Britain in the Oregon Treaty 1846; influx of
gold-seeking immigrants mid-19th century; fierce
Indian wars 1867–77, which included 'Custer's
Last Stand' at the Little Bighorn with the Sioux;
achieved statehood 1889.

Montand Yves 1921–1991. French actor and
singer who achieved fame in the thriller *Le
Salaire de la peur/The Wages of Fear* 1953 and
continued to be popular in French and American
films, including *Let's Make Love* 1960 (with
Marilyn Monroe), *Le Sauvage/The Savage* 1976,
Jean de Florette 1986, and *Manon des sources*
1986.

Mont Blanc (Italian *Monte Bianco*) highest
mountain in the *Alps, between France and Italy;
height 4,807 m/15,772 ft. It was first climbed
1786.

Montcalm Louis-Joseph de Montcalm-Gozon,
Marquis de 1712–1759. French general, appointed military commander in Canada 1756. He
won a succession of victories over the British
during the French and Indian War, but was
defeated in 1759 by James *Wolfe at Québec,
where both he and Wolfe were killed; this battle
marked the end of French rule in Canada.

Monte Carlo town and luxury resort in
*Monaco, known for its casino (opened 1861)
and the Monte Carlo car rally and Monaco
Grand Prix; population (1982) 12,000.

Montenegro (Serbo-Croatian *Crna Gora*)
constituent republic of Yugoslavia
area 13,800 sq km/5,327 sq mi
capital Titograd
town Cetinje
physical mountainous
population (1986) 620,000, including 400,000
Montenegrins, 80,000 Muslims, and 40,000
Albanians
language Serbian variant of Serbo-Croat
religion Serbian Orthodox
famous people Milovan Djilas
history part of *Serbia from the late 12th
century, it became independent (under Venetian
protection) after Serbia was defeated by the Turks
1389. It was forced to accept Turkish suzerainty
in the late 15th century, but was never completely
subdued by Turkey. It was ruled by bishop
princes until 1851, when a monarchy was
founded, and became a sovereign principality
under the Treaty of Berlin 1878. The monarch
used the title of king from 1910 with Nicholas
I (1841–1921). Montenegro participated in the
Balkan Wars 1912 and 1913. It was overrun by
Austria in World War I, and in 1918 voted after
the deposition of King Nicholas to become part
of Serbia. In 1946 Montenegro became a repub-

lic of Yugoslavia. In a referendum March 1992 Montengrins voted to remain part of the Yugoslav federation; the referendum was boycotted by Montenegro's Muslim and Albanian communities.

Monterrey industrial city (iron, steel, textiles, chemicals, food processing) in NE Mexico; population (1986) 2,335,000. It was founded 1597.

Montessori Maria 1870–1952. Italian educationalist. From her experience with mentally handicapped children, she developed the *Montessori method*, an educational system for all children based on an informal approach, incorporating instructive play and allowing children to develop at their own pace.

Monteverdi Claudio (Giovanni Antonio) 1567–1643. Italian composer. He contributed to the development of the opera with *Orfeo* 1607 and *The Coronation of Poppea* 1642. He also wrote madrigals, *motets, and sacred music, notably the *Vespers* 1610.

Montevideo capital and chief port (grain, meat products, hides) of Uruguay, on the Río de la Plata; population (1985) 1,250,000. It was founded 1726.

Montezuma II 1466–1520. Aztec emperor 1502–20. When the Spanish conquistador Cortés invaded Mexico, Montezuma was imprisoned and killed during the Aztec attack on Cortés's force as it tried to leave Tenochtitlán, the Aztec capital city.

Montfort Simon de Montfort, Earl of Leicester c. 1208–1265. English politician and soldier. From 1258 he led the baronial opposition to Henry III's misrule during the second *Barons' War and in 1264 defeated and captured the king at Lewes, Sussex. In 1265, as head of government, he summoned the first parliament in which the towns were represented; he was killed at the Battle of Evesham during the last of the Barons' Wars.

Montgolfier Joseph Michel 1740–1810 and Étienne Jacques 1745–1799. French brothers whose hot-air balloon was used for the first successful human flight 21 Nov 1783.

Montgomery Bernard Law, 1st Viscount Montgomery of Alamein 1887–1976. British field marshal. In World War II he commanded the 8th Army in N Africa in the Second Battle of El *Alamein 1942. As commander of British troops in N Europe from 1944, he received the German surrender 1945.

month unit of time based on the motion of the Moon around the Earth. The time from one new or full Moon to the next (the *synodic* or *lunar month*) is 29.53 days. The time for the Moon to complete one orbit around the Earth relative to the stars (the *sidereal month*) is 27.32 days. The *solar month* equals 30.44 days, and is exactly one-twelfth of the solar or tropical year, the time taken for the Earth to orbit the Sun. The *calendar month* is a human invention, devised to fit the calendar year.

Montréal inland port, industrial city (aircraft, chemicals, oil and petrochemicals, flour, sugar, brewing, meat packing) of Québec, Canada, on Montreal island at the junction of the Ottawa and St Lawrence rivers; population (1986) 2,921,000.

Montréal Protocol international agreement, signed 1987, to reduce production of chemicals that are *ozone depleters by 35% by 1999. The protocol (under the Vienna Convention for the Protection of the Ozone Layer) was scheduled for review in 1992.

Montrose James Graham, 1st Marquess of Montrose 1612–1650. Scottish soldier, son of the 4th earl of Montrose. He supported the *Covenanters against Charles I, but after 1640 changed sides. Defeated in 1645 at Philiphaugh, he escaped to Norway. Returning in 1650 to raise a revolt, he survived shipwreck only to have his weakened forces defeated, and (having been betrayed to the Covenanters) was hanged in Edinburgh.

Montserrat volcanic island in the West Indies, one of the Leeward group, a British crown colony; capital Plymouth; area 110 sq km/ 42 sq mi; population (1985) 12,000. Practically all buildings were destroyed by hurricane Hugo Sept 1989.

moon in astronomy, any natural *satellite that orbits a planet. Mercury and Venus are the only planets in the Solar System that do not have moons.

Moon natural satellite of Earth, 3,476 km/ 2,160 mi in diameter, with a mass 0.012 (approximately one-eightieth) that of Earth. Its surface gravity is only 0.16 (one-sixth) that of Earth. Its average distance from Earth is 384,404 km/238,857 mi, and it orbits in a west-to-east direction every 27.32 days (the *sidereal month*). It spins on its axis with one side permanently turned towards Earth. The Moon has no atmosphere or water.

Moon Sun Myung 1920– . Korean industrialist and founder of the *Unification Church (*Moonies*) 1954. From 1973 he launched a major mission in the USA and elsewhere. The church has been criticized for its manipulative methods of recruiting and keeping members. He was convicted of tax fraud in the USA 1982.

Moonie popular name for a follower of the *Unification Church, a religious sect founded by Sun Myung Moon.

Moon probe crewless spacecraft used to investigate the Moon. Early probes flew past the Moon or crash-landed on it, but later ones achieved soft landings or went into orbit. Soviet probes included the Luna/Lunik series. US probes (Ranger, Surveyor, Lunar Orbiter) prepared the way for the Apollo crewed flights.

Moor any of the NW African Muslims, of mixed Arab and Berber origin, who conquered Spain and ruled its southern part from 711 to 1492. The name (English form of Latin *Maurus*) was originally applied to an inhabitant of the Roman province of Mauritania, in NW Africa.

Moorcock Michael 1939– . English writer, associated with the 1960s new wave in science fiction, editor of the magazine *New Worlds* 1964–69. He wrote the Jerry Cornelius novels, collected as *The Cornelius Chronicles* 1977, and *Gloriana* 1978.

Moore Dudley 1935– . English actor, comedian, and musician, formerly teamed with comedian Peter Cook. Moore became a Hollywood star after appearing in '*10*' 1979. His other films, mostly comedies, include *Bedazzled* 1968, *Arthur* 1981, and *Santa Claus* 1985.

Moore Henry 1898–1986. British sculptor. His subjects include the reclining nude, mother and child groups, the warrior, and interlocking abstract forms. Many of his post-1945 works are in bronze or marble, including monumental semi-abstracts such as *Reclining Figure* 1957–58 (outside the UNESCO building, Paris), and often designed to be placed in landscape settings.

Moore Roger 1928– . English actor who starred in the television series *The Saint* 1962–70, and assumed the film role of James Bond in 1973 in *Live and Let Die*.

moorhen marsh bird *Gallinula chloropus* of the rail family, common in water of swamps, lakes, and ponds in Eurasia, Africa, and North and South America. It is about 33 cm/13 in long, and mainly brown and grey, but with a red bill and forehead, and a vivid white underside to the tail. The big feet are not webbed or lobed, but the moorhen can swim well.

moose North American name for *elk.

moraine rocky debris or *till carried along and deposited by a *glacier. Material eroded from the side of a glaciated valley and carried along the glacier's edge is called lateral moraine; that worn from the valley floor and carried along the base of the glacier is called ground moraine. Rubble dropped at the foot of a melting glacier is called terminal moraine.

morality play didactic medieval European verse drama, in part a development of the *mystery play (or miracle play), in which human characters are replaced by personified virtues and vices, the limited humorous elements being provided by the Devil. Morality plays, such as *Everyman*, flourished in the 15th century. They exerted an influence on the development of Elizabethan drama and comedy.

Moral Rearmament (MRA) international movement calling for 'moral and spiritual renewal', founded by the Christian evangelist F N D Buchman in the 1920s as the **Oxford Group**. It based its teachings on the 'Four Absolutes' (honesty, purity, unselfishness, love).

Moravia (Czech **Morava**) district of central Europe, from 1960 two regions of Czechoslovakia:
South Moravia (Czech **Jihomoravský**)
area 15,030 sq km/5,802 sq mi
capital Brno
population (1991) 2,048,900.
North Moravia (Czech **Severomoravský**)
area 11,070 sq km/4,273 sq mi
capital Ostrava
population (1991) 1,961,500.
products maize, grapes, wine in the south; wheat, barley, rye, flax, sugar beet in the north; coal and iron
history part of the Avar territory since the 6th century; conquered by Charlemagne's Holy Roman Empire. In 874 the kingdom of Great Moravia was founded by the Slavic prince Sviatopluk, who ruled until 894. It was conquered by the Magyars 906, and became a fief of Bohemia 1029. It was passed to the Habsburgs 1526, and became an Austrian crown land 1849. It was incorporated in the new republic of Czechoslovakia 1918, forming a province until 1949.

Moravia Alberto. Pen name of Alberto Pincherle 1907–1991. Italian novelist. His first successful novel was *Gli indifferenti/The Time of Indifference* 1929, but its criticism of Mussolini's regime led to the government censoring his work until after World War II. Later books include *La romana/Woman of Rome* 1947, *La ciociara/Two Women* 1957, and *La noia/The Empty Canvas* 1961, a study of an artist's obsession with his model.

Moravian member of a Christian Protestant sect, the **Moravian Brethren**. An episcopal church that grew out of the earlier Bohemian Brethren, it was established by the Lutheran Count Zinzendorf in Saxony 1722.

Moray Earl of Moray another spelling of *Murray, regent of Scotland 1567–70.

Mordvin Finnish people inhabiting the middle Volga Valley in W Asia. They are known to have lived in the region since the 1st century AD. There are 1 million speakers of Mordvin scattered throughout W Russia, about one-third of whom live in the Mordvinian republic. Mordvin is a Finno-Ugric language belonging to the Uralic family.

More (St) Thomas 1478–1535. English politician and author. From 1509 he was favoured by *Henry VIII and employed on foreign embassies. He was a member of the privy council from 1518 and Lord Chancellor from 1529 but resigned over Henry's break with the pope. For refusing to accept the king as head of the church, he was executed. The title of his political book *Utopia* 1516 has come to mean any supposedly perfect society.

Moreau Jeanne 1928– . French actress who has appeared in international films, often in passionate, intelligent roles. Her work includes *Les Amants/The Lovers* 1958, *Jules et Jim/Jules and Jim* 1961, *Chimes at Midnight* 1966, and *Querelle* 1982.

morel any edible mushroom of the genus *Morchella*. The common morel *M. esculenta* grows in Europe and North America. The yellowish-brown cap is pitted like a sponge and about 2.5 cm/1 in long. It is used for seasoning gravies, soups, and sauces and is second only to the truffle as the world's most sought-after mushroom.

Morgagni Giovanni Battista 1682–1771. Italian anatomist. As professor of anatomy at Padua, Morgagni carried out more than 400 autopsies, and developed the view that disease was not an imbalance of the body's humours but a result of alterations in the organs. His work *On the Seats and Causes of Diseases as Investigated by Anatomy* 1761 formed the basis of *pathology.

Morgan Henry *c.* 1635–1688. Welsh buccaneer in the Caribbean. He made war against Spain, capturing and sacking Panama 1671. In 1674 he was knighted and appointed lieutenant governor of Jamaica.

Morgan J(ohn) P(ierpont) 1837–1913. US financier and investment banker whose company (sometimes criticized as 'the money trust') became the most influential private banking house after the Civil War, being instrumental in the formation of many trusts to stifle competition. He set up the US Steel Corporation 1901 and International Harvester 1902.

Morgan Thomas Hunt 1866–1945. US geneticist, awarded the 1933 Nobel Prize for Medicine for his pioneering studies in classical genetics. He was the first to work on the fruit fly *Drosophila*, which has since become a major subject of genetic studies. He helped establish that the genes were located on the chromosomes, discovered sex chromosomes, and invented the techniques of genetic mapping.

Morgan le Fay in the romance and legend of the English king *Arthur, an enchantress and healer, ruler of the island of Avalon and sister of the king, whom she tended after his final battle. In some versions of the legend she is responsible for the suspicions held by the king of his wife *Guinevere.

Morley Edward 1838–1923. US physicist who collaborated with Albert *Michelson on the *Michelson–Morley experiment* 1887. In 1895 he established precise and accurate measurements of the densities of oxygen and hydrogen.

Morley Robert 1908–1992. English actor and playwright, active in both Britain and the USA. His film work has been mainly character roles, in such movies as *Marie Antoinette* 1938, *The African Queen* 1952, and *Oscar Wilde* 1960.

Morley Thomas 1557–1602. English composer. A student of William *Byrd, he became organist at St Paul's Cathedral, London, and obtained a monopoly on music printing. A composer of the English madrigal school, he also wrote sacred music, songs for Shakespeare's plays, and a musical textbook.

Mormon or *Latter-day Saint* member of a Christian sect, the *Church of Jesus Christ of Latter-day Saints*, founded at Fayette, New York, in 1830 by Joseph *Smith. According to Smith, Mormon was an ancient prophet in North America whose *Book of Mormon*, of which Smith claimed divine revelation, is accepted by Mormons as part of the Christian scriptures. In the 19th century the faction led by Brigham *Young was polygamous. It is a missionary church with headquarters in Utah and a worldwide membership of about 6 million.

morning glory any twining or creeping plant of the genus *Ipomoea*, especially *I. purpurea*, family Convolvulaceae, native to tropical America, with dazzling blue flowers. Small quantities of substances similar to the hallucinogenic drug *LSD are found in the seeds of some species.

Moro Aldo 1916–1978. Italian Christian Democrat politician. Prime minister 1963–68 and 1974–76, he was expected to become Italy's president, but he was kidnapped and shot by Red Brigade urban guerrillas.

Moroccan Crises two periods of international tension 1905 and 1911 following German objections to French expansion in Morocco. Their wider purpose was to break up the Anglo-French entente 1904, but both crises served to reinforce the entente and isolate Germany.

Morocco Kingdom of (*al-Mamlaka al-Maghrebia*)
area 458,730 sq km/177,070 sq mi (excluding Western Sahara)
capital Rabat

towns Marrakesh, Fez, Meknès; ports Casablanca, Tangier, Agadir
physical mountain ranges NE–SW; fertile coastal plains in W
head of state Hassan II from 1961
head of government Abd al-Latif Filali from 1994
political system constitutional monarchy
exports dates, figs, cork, wood pulp, canned fish, phosphates
population (1993 est) 27,000,000; growth rate 2.5% p.a.
languages Arabic (official) 75%, Berber 25%, French, Spanish
religion Sunni Muslim 99%
GNP $1,030 per head (1991)
chronology
1912 Morocco divided into French and Spanish protectorates.
1956 Independence achieved as the Sultanate of Morocco.
1957 Sultan restyled king of Morocco.
1961 Hassan II came to the throne.
1972 Major revision of the constitution.
1975 Western Sahara ceded by Spain to Morocco and Mauritania.
1976 Guerrilla war in Western Sahara with the Polisario Front. Sahrawi Arab Democratic Republic (SADR) established in Algiers. Diplomatic relations between Morocco and Algeria broken.
1983 Peace formula for Western Sahara proposed by the Organization of African Unity (OAU), but soon collapsed.
1984 Hassan signed an agreement for cooperation and mutual defence with Libya.
1987 Cease-fire agreed with Polisario, but fighting continued.
1988 May: diplomatic relations with Algeria restored. Aug: United Nations peace plan accepted.
1989 Diplomatic relations with Syria restored.
1992 Muhammad Lamrani appointed prime minister; new constitution approved in referendum.
1993 Peace accord with Israel.
1994 Abd-al Latif Filali became prime minister.

Moroni capital of the Comoros Republic, on Njazídja (Grand Comore); population (1980) 20,000. It has a small natural harbour from which coffee, cacao, and vanilla are exported.

Morpheus in Greek and Roman mythology, the god of dreams, son of Hypnos or Somnus, the god of sleep.

morphine narcotic alkaloid $C_{17}H_{19}NO_3$ derived from *opium and prescribed only to alleviate severe pain. Its use produces serious side effects, including nausea, constipation, tolerance, and addiction, but its properties are highly valued for the relief of the terminally ill.

morphogen in medicine, one of a class of substances believed to be present in the growing embryo, controlling its growth pattern. It is thought that variations in the concentration of morphogens in different parts of the embryo cause these parts to grow at different rates.

morphology in biology, the study of the physical structure and form of organisms, in particular their soft tissues.

Morricone Ennio 1928– . Italian composer of film music. His atmospheric scores for 'spaghetti Westerns', notably the Clint *Eastwood movies *A Fistful of Dollars* 1964 and *The Good, the Bad and the Ugly* 1966, created a vogue for lyrical understatement. His highly ritualized, incantatory style pioneered the use of amplified instruments and solo voices, using studio special effects.

Morrigan in Celtic mythology, a goddess of war and death who could take the shape of a crow.

Morris William 1834–1896. English designer. A founder of the *Arts and Crafts movement, he was also a socialist and writer who shared the Pre-Raphaelite painters' fascination with medieval settings. In 1861 he cofounded a firm that designed and produced furniture, carpets, and a wide range of decorative wallpapers, many of which are still produced today. His Kelmscott Press, set up 1890 to print beautifully designed books, influenced printing and book design. The prose romances *A Dream of John Ball* 1888 and *News from Nowhere* 1891 reflect his socialist ideology. He also lectured on socialism.

morris dance English folk dance. In early times it was usually performed by six men, one of whom wore girl's clothing while another portrayed a horse. The others wore costumes decorated with bells. Morris dancing probably originated in pre-Christian ritual dances and is still popular in the UK and USA.

Morrison Herbert Stanley, Baron Morrison of Lambeth 1888–1965. British Labour politician. He was a founder member and later secretary of the London Labour Party 1915–45, and a member of the London County Council 1922–45. He entered Parliament in 1923, and organized the Labour Party's general election victory in 1945. He was twice defeated in the contest for leadership of the party, once to Clement Attlee in 1932, and then to Hugh Gaitskell 1955. A skilful organizer, he lacked the ability to unite the party.

Morrison Toni 1931– . US novelist. Her fiction records black life in the South, including *Song of Solomon* 1978, *Tar Baby* 1981, *Beloved* 1987, based on a true story about infanticide in Kentucky, which won the Pulitzer Prize 1988, and *Jazz* 1992. She won the Nobel Prize for Literature 1993.

Morrison Van (George Ivan) 1945– .

Northern Irish singer and songwriter. His jazz-inflected Celtic soul style was already in evidence on *Astral Weeks* 1968 and has been highly influential. Among other albums are *Tupelo Honey* 1971, *Veedon Fleece* 1974, and *Avalon Sunset* 1989.

Morrissey stage name of Steven Patrick Morrissey 1959– . English rock singer and lyricist. He was a founder member of the Smiths 1982–87 and subsequently a solo artist. His lyrics reflect on everyday miseries or glumly celebrate the England of his childhood. Solo albums include *Viva Hate* 1987 and *Your Arsenal* 1992.

Morse Samuel (Finley Breese) 1791–1872. US inventor. In 1835 he produced the first adequate electric telegraph (see *telegraphy), and in 1843 was granted $30,000 by Congress for an experimental line between Washington DC and Baltimore. With his assistant Alexander Bain (1810–1877) he invented the Morse code.

Morse code international code for transmitting messages by wire or radio using signals of short (dots) and long (dashes) duration, originated by US inventor Samuel Morse for use on his invention, the telegraph (see *telegraphy).

mortar method of projecting a bomb via a high trajectory at a target up to 6–7 km/3–4 mi away. A mortar bomb is stabilized in flight by means of tail fins. The high trajectory results in a high angle of attack and makes mortars more suitable than artillery for use in built-up areas or mountains; mortars are not as accurate, however. Artillery also differs in firing a projectile through a rifled barrel, thus creating greater muzzle velocity.

mortgage transfer of property, usually a house, as a security for repayment of a loan. The loan is normally repaid to a bank or building society over a period of years.

Mortimer John 1923– . English barrister and writer. His works include the plays *The Dock Brief* 1958 and *A Voyage Round My Father* 1970, the novel *Paradise Postponed* 1985, and the television series *Rumpole of the Bailey*, from 1978, centred on a fictional barrister.

Mortimer Roger de, 8th Baron of Wigmore and 1st Earl of March c. 1287–1330. English politician and adventurer. He opposed Edward II and with Edward's queen, Isabella, led a rebellion against him 1326, bringing about his abdication. From 1327 Mortimer ruled England as the queen's lover, until Edward III had him executed.

Morton Jelly Roll. Stage name of Ferdinand Joseph La Menthe 1885–1941. US New Orleans-style jazz pianist, singer, and composer. Influenced by Scott Joplin, he was a pioneer in the development of jazz from ragtime to swing by improvising and imposing his own personality on the music. His 1920s band was called the Red Hot Peppers.

mosaic design or picture, usually for a floor, wall or vault, produced by setting small pieces of marble, glass, or other materials in a cement ground. Mosaic was commonly used by the Romans for their baths and villas (for example Hadrian's Villa at Tivoli) and reached its highest development in the early Byzantine period (for example, San Vitale, Ravenna).

Moscow (Russian *Moskva*) industrial city, capital of Russia and of the Moskva region, and formerly (1922–91) of the USSR, on the Moskva River 640 km/400 mi SE of St Petersburg; population (1987) 8,815,000. Its industries include machinery, electrical equipment, textiles, chemicals, and many food products.

Moses c. 13th century BC. Hebrew lawgiver and judge who led the Israelites out of Egypt to the promised land of Canaan. On Mount Sinai he claimed to have received from Jehovah the oral and written Law, including the **Ten Commandments** engraved on tablets of stone. The first five books of the Old Testament – in Judaism, the *Torah* – are ascribed to him.

Moses 'Grandma' (born Anna Mary Robertson) 1860–1961. US painter. She was self-taught and began full-time painting about 1927 after many years as a farmer's wife. She painted naive and colourful scenes from rural American life.

Mosley Oswald (Ernald) 1896–1980. British politician, founder of the British Union of Fascists (BUF) 1932. He was a member of Parliament 1918–31, then led the BUF until his internment 1940–43 during World War II. In 1946 Mosley was denounced when it became known that Italy had funded his prewar efforts to establish *fascism in Britain, but in 1948 he resumed fascist propaganda with his Union Movement, the revived BUF.

mosque (Arabic *mesjid*) in Islam, a place of worship. Chief features are: the dome; the minaret, a balconied turret from which the faithful are called to prayer; the *mihrab*, or prayer niche, in one of the interior walls, showing the direction of the holy city of Mecca; and an open court surrounded by porticoes.

mosquito any fly of the family Culicidae. The female mosquito has needlelike mouthparts and sucks blood before laying eggs. Males feed on plant juices. Some mosquitoes carry diseases such as *malaria.

Mosquito Coast Caribbean coast of Honduras and Nicaragua, characterized by swamp, lagoons, and tropical rainforest. The territory is inhabited by Miskito Indians, Garifunas, and Zambos, many of whom speak English. Between 1823 and 1860 Britain maintained a protectorate over the Mosquito Coast which was ruled by a succession of 'Mosquito Kings'.

Moss Stirling 1929– . English racing-car driver. Despite being one of the best-known names in British motor racing, Moss never won the world championship. He was runner-up on four occasions, losing to Juan Manuel Fangio (1911–) in 1955, 1956, and 1957, and to fellow Briton Mike Hawthorn (1929–1959) in 1958.

moss small nonflowering plant of the class Musci (10,000 species), forming with the *liverworts and the *hornworts the order Bryophyta. The stem of each plant bears rhizoids (hairlike outgrowths) that anchor it; there are no true roots. Leaves spirally arranged on its lower portion have sexual organs at their tips. Most mosses flourish best in damp conditions where other vegetation is thin. The peat or bog moss *Sphagnum* was formerly used for surgical dressings.

Mössbauer Rudolf 1929– . German physicist who discovered in 1958 that in certain conditions a nucleus can be stimulated to emit very sharply defined beams of gamma rays. This became

known as the **Mössbauer effect**. Such a beam was used in 1960 to provide the first laboratory test of *Einstein's general theory of relativity. For his work on gamma rays Mössbauer shared the 1961 Nobel Prize for Physics with Robert *Hofstadter.

Mossi member of the majority ethnic group living in Burkina Faso. Their social structure, based on a monarchy and aristocracy, was established in the 11th century. The Mossi have been prominent traders, using cowrie shells as currency. There are about 4 million speakers of Mossi, a language belonging to the Gur branch of the Niger-Congo family.

Mostel Zero (Samuel Joel) 1915–1977. US comedian and actor, mainly in the theatre. His films include *Panic in the Streets* 1950, *A Funny Thing Happened on the Way to the Forum* 1966, *The Producers* 1967, and *The Front* 1976.

motet sacred, polyphonic music for unaccompanied voices in a form that originated in 13th-century Europe.

moth any of the various families of mainly night-flying insects of the order Lepidoptera, which also includes the butterflies. Their wings are covered with microscopic scales. The mouthparts are formed into a sucking proboscis, but certain moths have no functional mouthparts, and rely upon stores of fat and other reserves built up during the caterpillar stage. At least 100,000 different species of moth are known.

motherboard *printed circuit board that contains the main components of a microcomputer. The power, memory capacity, and capability of the microcomputer may be enhanced by adding expansion boards to the motherboard.

mother-of-pearl or *nacre* the smooth lustrous lining in the shells of certain molluscs – for example pearl oysters, abalones, and mussels. When this layer is especially heavy it is used commercially for jewellery and decorations. Mother-of-pearl consists of calcium carbonate. See *pearl.

Mother's Day day set apart in the USA, UK, and many European countries for honouring mothers. It is thought to have originated in Grafton, West Virginia, USA, in 1908 when Anna Jarvis observed the anniversary of her mother's death.

Motherwell Robert 1915–1991. US painter associated with the New York school of *action painting. Borrowing from Picasso, Matisse, and the Surrealists, Motherwell's style of Abstract Expressionism retained some suggestion of the figurative. His works include the 'Elegies to the Spanish Republic' 1949–76, a series of over 100 paintings devoted to the Spanish Revolution.

motor anything that produces or imparts motion; a machine that provides mechanical power – for example, an *electric motor. Machines that burn fuel (petrol, diesel) are usually called engines, but the internal-combustion engine that propels vehicles has long been called a motor, hence 'motoring' and 'motorcar'. Actually the motor is a part of the car engine.

motorboat small, waterborne craft for pleasure cruising or racing, powered by a petrol, diesel, or gas-turbine engine. A boat not equipped as a motorboat may be converted by a detachable outboard motor. For increased speed, such as in racing, motorboat hulls are designed to skim the water (aquaplane) and reduce frictional resistance. Plastics, steel, and light alloys are now used in construction as well as the traditional wood.

motorcar another term for *car.

motorcycle or **motorbike** two-wheeled vehicle propelled by a *petrol engine. The first successful motorized bicycle was built in France 1901, and British and US manufacturers first produced motorbikes 1903.

motorcycle racing speed contests on motorcycles. It has many different forms: *road racing* over open roads; *circuit racing* over purpose-built tracks; *speedway* over oval-shaped dirt tracks; *motocross* over natural terrain, incorporating hill climbs; and *trials*, also over natural terrain, but with the addition of artificial hazards.

motor effect tendency of a wire carrying an electric current in a magnetic field to move. The direction of the movement is given by the left-hand rule (see *Fleming's rules). This effect is used in the *electric motor. It also explains why streams of electrons produced, for instance, in a television tube can be directed by electromagnets.

motor nerve in anatomy, any nerve that transmits impulses from the central nervous system to muscles or body organs. Motor nerves cause voluntary and involuntary muscle contractions, and stimulate glands to secrete hormones.

motor neuron disease incurable wasting disease in which the nerve cells (neurons) controlling muscle action gradually die, causing progressive weakness and paralysis. It results from infection in childhood with the *polio virus; this is now largely eradicated, and it is thought that motor neuron disease will disappear by 2010.

motor racing competitive racing of motor vehicles. It has forms as diverse as hill-climbing, stock-car racing, rallying, sports-car racing, and Formula One Grand Prix racing. The first organized race was from Paris to Rouen 1894.

motorway main road for fast motor traffic, with two or more lanes in each direction, and with special access points (junctions) fed by slip roads. The first motorway (85 km/53 mi) ran from Milan to Varese, Italy, and was completed 1924; by 1939 some 500 km/300 mi of motorway (*autostrada*) had been built, although these did not attain the standards of later express highways. In Germany some 2,100 km/1,310 mi of *Autobahnen* had been completed by 1942. After World War II motorways were built in a growing number of countries, for example the USA, France, and the UK. The most ambitious building programme was in the USA, which by 1974 had 70,800 km/44,000 mi of 'expressway'.

Motown first black-owned US record company, founded in Detroit (Mo[tor] Town) 1959 by Berry Gordy, Jr (1929–). Its distinctive, upbeat sound (exemplified by the Four Tops and the *Supremes) was a major element in 1960s pop music.

Mott Nevill Francis 1905– . English physicist who researched the electronic properties of metals, semiconductors, and noncrystalline materials. He shared the Nobel Prize for Physics 1977 with US physicists Philip Anderson (1923–) and John Van Vleck (1899–1980).

mould mainly saprophytic fungi (see *fungus) living on foodstuffs and other organic matter, a few being parasitic on plants, animals, or each other. Many moulds are of medical or industrial importance; for example, penicillin.

moulding use of a pattern, hollow form, or matrix to give a specific shape to something in a plastic or molten state. It is commonly used for shaping plastics, clays, and glass. When metals are used, the process is called *casting.

moulting periodic shedding of the hair or fur of mammals, feathers of birds, or skin of reptiles. In mammals and birds, moulting is usually seasonal and is triggered by changes of day length.

Moundbuilder member of any of the various North American Indian peoples of the Midwest and the South who built earth mounds, from about 300 BC. The mounds were linear and pictographic in form for tombs, such as the Great Serpent Mound in Ohio, and truncated pyramids and cones for the platforms of chiefs' houses and temples. The *Hopewell and *Natchez were Moundbuilders.

mountain natural upward projection of the Earth's surface, higher and steeper than a hill. The process of mountain building (orogeny) consists of volcanism, folding, faulting, and thrusting, resulting from the collision and welding together of two tectonic plates.

mountain ash or **rowan** flowering tree *Sorbus aucuparia* of the family Rosaceae. It grows to 15 m/50 ft and has pinnate leaves and large clusters of whitish flowers, followed by scarlet berries.

mountain biking recreational sport that is enjoying increasing popularity in the 1990s. Mountain bikes first appeared on the mass market in the USA in 1981, in the UK in 1984, and have been used in all aspects of cycling. However, it is also a competition sport, and the first world championship was held in France in 1987. The second world championship was held 1990 in Mexico. National mountain-bike championships have been held in the USA since 1983 and in the UK since 1984. Mountain bikes have 10–15 gears, a toughened frame, and wider treads on the tyres than ordinary bicycles.

mountaineering art and practice of mountain climbing. For major peaks of the Himalayas it was formerly thought necessary to have elaborate support from Sherpas (local people), fixed ropes, and oxygen at high altitudes (*siege-style* climbing). In the 1980s the *Alpine style* was introduced. This dispenses with these aids, and relies on human ability to adapt, Sherpa-style, to high altitude.

mountain lion another name for *puma.

Mountbatten Louis, 1st Earl Mountbatten of Burma 1900–1979. British admiral and administrator. In World War II he became chief of combined operations 1942 and commander in chief in SE Asia 1943. As last viceroy of India 1947 and first governor general of India until 1948, he oversaw that country's transition to independence. He was killed by an Irish Republican

Army bomb aboard his yacht in the Republic of Ireland.

Mounties popular name for the *Royal Canadian Mounted Police*, known for their uniform of red jacket and broad-brimmed hat. Their Security Service, established 1950, was disbanded 1981 and replaced by the independent Canadian Security Intelligence Service.

mouse in computing, an input device used to control a pointer on a computer screen. It is a feature of *graphical user-interface (GUI) systems. The mouse is about the size of a pack of playing cards, is connected to the computer by a wire, and incorporates one or more buttons that can be pressed. Moving the mouse across a flat surface causes a corresponding movement of the pointer. In this way, the operator can manipulate objects on the screen and make menu selections.

mouse The mouse is one of the most adaptable and successful animals.

mouse in zoology, one of a number of small rodents with small ears and a long, thin tail, belonging largely to the Old World family Muridae. The house mouse *Mus musculus* is distributed worldwide. It is 75 mm/3 in long, with a naked tail of equal length, and has a grey-brown body.

mouth cavity forming the entrance to the digestive tract. In land vertebrates, air from the nostrils enters the mouth cavity to pass down the trachea. The mouth in mammals is enclosed by the jaws, cheeks, and palate.

mouth organ another name for *harmonica, a musical instrument.

movement in music, a section of a large work, such as a symphony, which is often complete in itself.

Mozambique People's Republic of (*República Popular de Moçambique*)
area 799,380 sq km/308,561 sq mi
capital and chief port Maputo
towns Beira, Nampula
physical mostly flat tropical lowland; mountains in W
head of state Joaquim Alberto Chissano from 1986
head of government Pascoal Mocumbi from 1994
political system emergent democratic republic
exports prawns, cashews, sugar, cotton, tea, petroleum products, copra
currency metical (replaced escudo 1980)
population (1993 est) 16,600,000 (mainly indigenous Bantu peoples; Portuguese 50,000); growth rate 2.8% p.a.; nearly 1 million refugees in Malawi

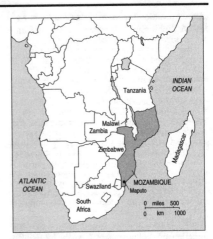

languages Portuguese (official), 16 African languages
religions animist 60%, Roman Catholic 18%, Muslim 16%
GNP $70 per head (1991)
chronology
1505 Mozambique became a Portuguese colony.
1962 Frelimo (liberation front) established.
1975 Independence achieved from Portugal as a socialist republic, with Samora Machel as president and Frelimo as the sole legal party.
1984 Nkomati accord of nonaggression signed with South Africa.
1986 Machel killed in air crash; succeeded by Joaquim Chissano.
1988 Tanzania announced withdrawal of its troops. South Africa provided training for Mozambican forces.
1989 Frelimo offered to abandon Marxism-Leninism; Chissano re-elected. Renamo continued attacks on government facilities and civilians.
1990 One-party rule officially ended. Partial cease-fire agreed.
1991 Peace talks resumed in Rome, delaying democratic process. Attempted antigovernment coup thwarted.
1992 Peace accord signed, but fighting continued.
1994 Demobilization of contending armies completed; hostilities ceased. Chissano re-elected in first multiparty elections.

Mozart Wolfgang Amadeus 1756–1791. Austrian composer and performer who showed astonishing precocity as a child and was an adult virtuoso. He was trained by his father, **Leopold Mozart** (1719–1787). From an early age he composed prolifically, his works including 27 piano concertos, 23 string quartets, 35 violin sonatas, and more than 50 symphonies including the E flat K543, G minor K550, and C major K551 ('Jupiter') symphonies, all composed 1788. His operas include *Idomeneo* 1781, *Le Nozze di Figaro/The Marriage of Figaro* 1786, *Don Giovanni* 1787, *Così fan tutte/Thus Do All Women* 1790, and *Die Zauberflöte/The Magic Flute* 1791. Strongly influenced by *Haydn, Mozart's music marks the height of the Classical age in its purity of melody and form.

MP abbreviation for *member of Parliament*.

MPLA (abbreviation for *Movimento Popular de Libertaçaõ de Angola*/Popular Movement for the Liberation of Angola) socialist organization founded in the early 1950s that sought to free Angola from Portuguese rule 1961–75 before being involved in the civil war against its former allies *UNITA and *FNLA 1975–76. The MPLA took control of the country, but UNITA guerrilla activity continues, supported by South Africa.

MS-DOS (abbreviation for *Microsoft Disc Operating System*) computer *operating system produced by Microsoft Corporation, widely used on *microcomputers with 16-bit microprocessors. A version called PC-DOS is sold by IBM specifically for their range of personal computers. MS-DOS and PC-DOS are usually referred to as DOS. MS-DOS first appeared in the early 1980s, and was based on an earlier system for computers with 8-bit microprocessors, CP/M.

MTBF abbreviation for *mean time between failures*, the statistically average time a component can be used before it goes wrong. The MTBF of a computer hard disc, for example, is around 150,000 hours.

Mubarak Hosni 1928– . Egyptian politician, president from 1981. Vice president to Anwar Sadat from 1975, Mubarak succeeded him on his assassination. He has continued to pursue Sadat's moderate policies, and has significantly increased the freedom of the press and of political association, while trying to repress the growing Islamic fundamentalist movement.

mucous membrane thin skin lining all animal body cavities and canals that come into contact with the air (for example, eyelids, breathing and digestive passages, genital tract). It secretes mucus, a moistening, lubricating, and protective fluid.

mucus lubricating and protective fluid, secreted by mucous membranes in many different parts of the body. In the gut, mucus smooths the passage of food and keeps potentially damaging digestive enzymes away from the gut lining. In the lungs, it traps airborne particles so that they can be expelled.

mudnester any of an Australian group of birds that make their nests from mud, including the apostle bird *Struthidea cinerea* (so called from its appearance in little flocks of about 12), the white-winged chough *Corcorax melanorhamphos*, and the magpie lark *Grallina cyanoleuca*.

mudpuppy brownish salamander of the genus *Necturus* in the family Proteidae. There are five species, living in fresh water in North America. They all breathe in water using external gills. *Necturus maculatus* is about 20 cm/8 in long.

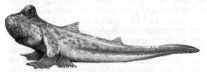

mudskipper Mudskippers use their fins as rudimentary legs.

mudskipper fish of the goby family, genus *Periophthalmus*, found in brackish water on shores in the tropics, except for the Americas. It can walk or climb over mudflats, using its strong pectoral fins as legs, and has eyes set close together on top of the head. It grows up to 30 cm/12 in long.

muezzin (Arabic) a person whose job is to perform the call to prayer five times a day from the minaret of a Muslim mosque.

mufti Muslim legal expert who guides the courts in their interpretation. In Turkey the *grand mufti* had supreme spiritual authority until the establishment of the republic in 1924.

Mugabe Robert (Gabriel) 1925– . Zimbabwean politician, prime minister from 1980 and president from 1987. He was in detention in Rhodesia for nationalist activities 1964–74, then carried on guerrilla warfare from Mozambique. As leader of *ZANU he was in an uneasy alliance with Joshua *Nkomo of ZAPU (Zimbabwe African People's Union) from 1976. The two parties merged 1987.

Muhammad or *Mohammed*, *Mahomet* c. 570–632. Founder of Islam, born in Mecca on the Arabian peninsula. In about 616 he claimed to be a prophet and that the *Koran* was revealed to him by God (it was later written down by his followers), through the angel Jibra'el. He fled from persecution to the town now known as Medina in 622: the flight, *Hegira*, marks the beginning of the Islamic era.

Mujaheddin (Arabic *mujahid* 'fighters', from *jihad* 'holy war') Islamic fundamentalist guerrillas of contemporary Afghanistan and Iran.

Mukalla seaport capital of the Hadhramaut coastal region of S Yemen; on the Gulf of Aden 480 km/300 mi E of Aden; population (1984) 158,000.

Mukden, Battle of taking of Mukden (now Shenyang), NE China, from Russian occupation by the Japanese 1905, during the *Russo-Japanese War. Mukden was later the scene of a surprise attack 18 Sept 1931 by the Japanese on the Chinese garrison, which marked the beginning of their invasion of China.

mulberry any tree of the genus *Morus*, family Moraceae, consisting of a dozen species, including the black mulberry *M. nigra*. It is native to W Asia and has heart-shaped, toothed leaves, and spikes of whitish flowers. It is widely cultivated for its fruit, which, made up of a cluster of small drupes, resembles a raspberry. The leaves of the Asiatic white mulberry *M. alba* are those used in feeding silkworms.

Muldoon Robert David 1921–1992. New Zealand National Party politician, prime minister 1975–84. He pursued austere economic policies such as a wage-and-price policy to control inflation.

mule hybrid animal, usually the offspring of a male ass and a female horse.

mullet two species of fish. The *red mullet* *Mullus surmuletus* is found in the Mediterranean and warm Atlantic as far north as the English Channel. It is about 40 cm/16 in long, red with yellow stripes, and has long barbels round the mouth. The *grey mullet* *Crenimugil labrosus* lives in ponds and estuaries. It is greyish above, with longitudinal dark stripes, and grows to 60 cm/24 in.

Mulliken Robert Sanderson 1896–1986. US chemist and physicist who received the 1966 Nobel Prize for Chemistry for his development of the molecular orbital theory.

Mulroney Brian 1939– . Canadian politician, Progressive Conservative Party leader 1983–93, prime minister from 1984–93. He achieved a landslide in the 1984 election, and won the 1988 election on a platform of free trade with the USA, but with a reduced majority. By 1991 his public-opinion standing had fallen to an unprecedented low level and in Feb 1993 he resigned the leadership of the Conservative Party.

multicultural education education aimed at preparing children to live in a multiracial society by giving them an understanding of the culture and history of different ethnic groups.

multilateralism trade among more than two countries without discrimination over origin or destination and regardless of whether a large trade gap is involved.

multimedia computer system that combines audio and video components to create an inter-active application that uses text, sound, and graphics (still, animated, and video sequences). For example, a multimedia database of musical instruments may allow a user not only to search and retrieve text about a particular instrument but also to see pictures of it and hear it play a piece of music.

multinational corporation or *trans-national corporation* company or enterprise operating in several countries, usually defined as one that has 25% or more of its output capacity located outside its country of origin.

multiple birth in humans, the production of more than two babies from one pregnancy. Multiple births can be caused by more than two eggs being produced and fertilized (often as the result of hormone therapy to assist pregnancy), or by a single fertilized egg dividing more than once before implantation.

multiple independently targeted re-entry vehicle (MIRV) nuclear-warhead-carry-ing part of a ballistic *missile that splits off in midair from the main body. Since each is individually steered and controlled, MIRVs can attack separate targets over a wide area.

multiple proportions, law of in chemistry, the principle that if two elements combine with each other to form more than one compound, then the ratio of the masses of one of them that combine with a particular mass of the other is a small whole number.

multiple sclerosis (MS) incurable chronic disease of the central nervous system, occurring in young or middle adulthood. It is characterized by degeneration of the myelin sheath that surrounds nerves in the brain and spinal cord. It is also known as disseminated sclerosis. Its cause is unknown.

multiplexer in telecommunications, a device that allows a transmission medium to carry a number of separate signals at the same time – enabling, for example, several telephone conversations to be carried by one telephone line, and radio signals to be transmitted in stereo.

multiplier in economics, the theoretical concept, formulated by John Maynard Keynes, of the effect on national income or employment by an adjustment in overall demand. For example, investment by a company in a new plant will stimulate new income and expenditure, which will in turn generate new investment, and so on, so that the actual increase in national income may be several times greater than the original investment.

multistage rocket rocket launch vehicle made up of several rocket stages (often three) joined end to end. The bottom stage fires first, boosting the vehicle to high speed, then it falls away. The next stage fires, thrusting the now lighter vehicle even faster. The remaining stages fire and fall away in turn, boosting the vehicle's payload (cargo) to an orbital speed that can reach 28,000 kph/17,500 mph.

multitasking or *multiprogramming* in computing, a system in which one processor appears to run several different programs (or different parts of the same program) at the same time. All the programs are held in memory together and each is allowed to run for a certain period.

multiuser system or *multiaccess system* in computing, an operating system that enables several users to access the same computer apparently at the same time. Each user has a terminal, which may be local (connected directly to the computer) or remote (connected to the computer via a modem and a telephone line). Multiaccess is usually achieved by *time-sharing*: the computer switches very rapidly between terminals and programs so that each user has sole use of the computer for only a fraction of a second but can work as if she or he had continuous access.

Muluzi Bakili 1943– . Malawi politician, president from 1994. Muluzi formed the United Democratic Front (UDF) 1992 when President *Banda agreed to end one-party rule, and went on to win almost half of the presidential votes. Since taking office, he has applied his business experience to the task of liberalizing trade and reviving the economy.

mummy any dead body, human or animal, that has been naturally or artificially preserved. Natural mummification can occur through freezing (for example, mammoths in glacial ice from 25,000 years ago), drying, or preservation in bogs or oil seeps. Artificial mummification may be achieved by embalming (for example, the mummies of ancient Egypt) or by freeze-drying (see *cryonics).

mumps virus infection marked by fever and swelling of the parotid salivary glands (such as those under the ears). It is usually minor in children, although meningitis is a possible complication. In adults the symptoms are severe and it may cause sterility in adult men.

Munch Edvard 1863–1944. Norwegian painter and printmaker. He studied in Paris and Berlin, and his major works date from the period 1892–1908, when he lived mainly in Germany. His paintings often focus on neurotic emotional states. The *Frieze of Life* 1890s, a sequence of highly charged, symbolic paintings, includes some of his most characteristic images, such as *Skriket/The Scream* 1893. He later reused these in etchings, lithographs, and woodcuts.

Münchhausen Karl Friedrich, Freiherr (Baron) von 1720–1797. German soldier, born in

Hanover. He served with the Russian army against the Turks, and after his retirement in 1760 told exaggerated stories of his adventures. This idiosyncrasy was utilized by the German writer Rudolph Erich Raspe (1737–1794) in his extravagantly fictitious *Adventures of Baron Munchausen* 1785, which he wrote in English while living in London.

Münchhausen's syndrome emotional disorder in which a patient feigns or invents symptoms to secure medical treatment. In some cases the patient will secretly ingest substances to produce real symptoms. It was named after the exaggerated tales of Baron Münchhausen.

Munda member of any one of several groups living in NE and central India, numbering about 5 million (1983). Their most widely spoken languages are Santali and Mundari, languages of the Munda group, an isolated branch of the Austro-Asiatic family. The Mundas were formerly nomadic hunter-gatherers, but now practise shifting cultivation. They are Hindus, but retain animist beliefs.

Munich (German *München*) industrial city (brewing, printing, precision instruments, machinery, electrical goods, textiles), capital of Bavaria, Germany, on the river Isar; population (1986) 1,269,400.

Munich Agreement pact signed on 29 Sept 1938 by the leaders of the UK (Neville *Chamberlain), France (Edouard *Daladier), Germany (Hitler), and Italy (Mussolini), under which Czechoslovakia was compelled to surrender its Sudeten-German districts (the *Sudetenland*) to Germany. Chamberlain claimed it would guarantee 'peace in our time', but it did not prevent Hitler from seizing the rest of Czechoslovakia in March 1939.

Munster southern province of the Republic of Ireland, comprising the counties of Clare, Cork, Kerry, Limerick, North and South Tipperary, and Waterford; area 24,140 sq km/9,318 sq mi; population (1991) 1,008,400.

muntjac small deer, genus *Muntiacus*, found in SE Asia. There are about six species. Males have short spiked antlers and two sharp canine teeth forming tusks. They are sometimes called 'barking deer' because of their voices.

Murakami Haruki 1949– . Japanese novelist and translator, one of Japan's best-selling writers, influenced by 20th-century US writers and popular culture. His dreamy, gently surrealist novels include *A Wild Sheep Chase* 1982 and *Norwegian Wood* 1987.

Murasaki Shikibu *c.* 978–*c.* 1015. Japanese writer, a lady at the court. Her masterpiece of fiction, *The Tale of Genji*, is one of the classic works of Japanese literature, and may be the world's first novel.

Murat Joachim 1767–1815. King of Naples 1808–1815. An officer in the French army, he was made king by Napoleon, but deserted him in 1813 in the vain hope that Austria and Great Britain would recognize him. In 1815 he attempted unsuccessfully to make himself king of all Italy, but when he landed in Calabria in an attempt to gain the throne he was captured and shot.

Murchison Roderick 1792–1871. Scottish geologist responsible for naming the *Silurian period (in his book *The Silurian System* 1839). He surveyed Russia 1840–45. In 1855 he became director-general of the UK Geological Survey.

Murcia autonomous region of SE Spain; area 11,300 sq km/4,362 sq mi; population (1986) 1,014,000. It includes the cities Murcia and Cartagena, and produces esparto grass, lead, zinc, iron, and fruit.

murder unlawful killing of one person by another. In the USA, first-degree murder requires proof of premeditation; second-degree murder falls between first-degree murder and *manslaughter.

Murdoch (Keith) Rupert 1931– . Australian-born US media magnate with worldwide interests. His UK newspapers, generally right-wing, include the *Sun*, the *News of the World*, and *The Times*; in the USA, he has a 50% share of 20th Century Fox, six Metromedia TV stations, and newspaper and magazine publishing companies. He purchased a 50% stake in a Hungarian tabloid, *Reform*, from 1989.

Murdoch Iris 1919– . English novelist, born in Dublin. Her novels combine philosophical speculation with often outrageous situations and tangled human relationships. They include *The Sandcastle* 1957, *The Sea, The Sea* 1978, and *The Message to the Planet* 1989.

Murillo Bartolomé Esteban *c.* 1617–1682. Spanish painter, active mainly in Seville. He painted sentimental pictures of the Immaculate Conception; he also specialized in studies of street urchins.

Murmansk seaport in NW Russia, on the Barents Sea; population (1987) 432,000. It is the largest city in the Arctic, Russia's most important fishing port, and the base of naval units and the icebreakers that keep the Northeast Passage open.

Murnau F W. Adopted name of Friedrich Wilhelm Plumpe 1889–1931. German silent-film director, known for his expressive images and 'subjective' use of a moving camera in *Der letzte Mamm/The Last Laugh* 1924. Other films include *Nosferatu* 1922 (a version of the Dracula story), *Sunrise* 1927, and *Tabu* 1931.

Muromachi in Japanese history, the period 1392–1568, comprising the greater part of the rule of the *Ashikaga shoguns; it is named after the area of Kyoto where their headquarters were sited.

Murphy Eddie 1961– . US film actor. His first film, *48 Hours* 1982 introduced the type of streetwise, comic character that has become his speciality. Its great success, and that of his next two films, *Trading Places* 1983 and *Beverly Hills Cop* 1984, made him one of the biggest box-office draws of the 1980s.

Murray principal river of Australia, 2,575 km/1,600 mi long. It rises in the Australian Alps near Mount Kosciusko and flows west, forming the boundary between New South Wales and Victoria, and reaches the sea at Encounter Bay, South Australia. With its main tributary, the Darling, it is 3,750 km/2,330 mi long.

Murray James Augustus Henry 1837–1915. Scottish philologist. He was the first editor of the *Oxford English Dictionary* (originally the *New*

English Dictionary) from 1878 until his death; the first volume was published 1884.

Murray James Stuart, Earl of Murray, or Moray 1531–1570. Regent of Scotland from 1567, an illegitimate son of James V. He was one of the leaders of the Scottish Reformation, and after the deposition of his half-sister *Mary Queen of Scots, he became regent. He was assassinated by one of her supporters.

Murray cod Australian freshwater fish *Maccullochella macquariensis* that grows to about 2 m/ 6 ft. It is named after the river in which it is found.

Muscat or *Masqat* capital of Oman, E Arabia, adjoining the port of Matrah, which has a deep-water harbour; combined population (1982) 80,000. It produces natural gas and chemicals.

muscle contractile animal tissue that produces locomotion and maintains the movement of body substances. Muscle is made of long cells that can contract to between one-half and one-third of their relaxed length.

muscovite white mica, $KAl_2(Al,Si_3O_{10}(OH,F)_2$, a common silicate mineral. It is colourless to silvery white with shiny surfaces, and like all micas it splits into thin flakes along its one perfect cleavage. Muscovite is a metamorphic mineral occurring mainly in schists; it is also found in some granites, and appears as shiny flakes on bedding planes of some sandstones.

muscular dystrophy any of a group of inherited chronic muscle disorders marked by weakening and wasting of muscle. Muscle fibres degenerate, to be replaced by fatty tissue, although the nerve supply remains unimpaired. Death occurs in early adult life.

Muses in Greek mythology, the nine daughters of Zeus and Mnemosyne (goddess of memory) and inspirers of creative arts: Calliope, epic poetry; Clio, history; Erato, love poetry; Euterpe, lyric poetry; Melpomene, tragedy; Polyhymnia, hymns; Terpsichore, dance; Thalia, comedy; and Urania, astronomy.

Museveni Yoweri Kaguta 1945– . Ugandan general and politician, president from 1986. He led the opposition to Idi Amin's regime 1971–78 and was minister of defence 1979–80 but, unhappy with Milton Obote's autocratic leadership, formed the National Resistance Army (NRA). When Obote was ousted in a coup in 1985, Museveni entered into a brief power-sharing agreement with his successor, Tito Okello, before taking over as president. Museveni leads a broad-based coalition government.

mushroom fruiting body of certain fungi, consisting of an upright stem and a spore-producing cap with radiating gills on the undersurface. There are many edible species belonging to the genus *Agaricus*. See also *fungus and *toadstool.

music art of combining sounds into a coherent perceptual experience, typically in accordance with fixed patterns and for an aesthetic purpose. Music is generally categorized as classical, *jazz, *pop music, *country and western, and so on.

musical 20th-century form of dramatic musical performance, combining elements of song, dance, and the spoken word, often characterized by lavish staging and large casts. It developed from the operettas and musical comedies of the 19th century.

musical instrument digital interface manufacturer's standard for digital music equipment; see *MIDI.

music hall British light theatrical entertainment, in which singers, dancers, comedians, and acrobats perform in 'turns'. The music hall's heyday was at the beginning of the 20th century, with such artistes as Marie Lloyd, Harry Lauder, and George Formby. The US equivalent is called vaudeville.

music therapy use of music as an adjunct to *relaxation therapy, or in *psychotherapy to elicit expressions of suppressed emotions by prompting patients to dance, shout, laugh, cry, or whatever, in response.

musk in botany, perennial plant *Mimulus moschatus* of the family Scrophulariaceae; its small oblong leaves exude the musky scent from which it takes its name; it is also called *monkey flower*. Also any of several plants with a musky odour, including the musk mallow *Malva moschata* and the musk rose *Rosa moschata*.

musk deer small deer *Moschus moschiferus* native to mountains of central Asia. A solitary animal, it is about 50 cm/20 in high, sure-footed, and has large ears and no antlers. Males have tusklike upper canine teeth. It is hunted and farmed for the musk secreted by an abdominal gland, which is used as medicine or perfume.

musk ox ruminant *Ovibos moschatus* of the family Bovidae, native to the Arctic regions of North America. It displays characteristics of sheep and oxen, is about the size of a small domestic cow, and has long brown hair. At certain seasons it exhales a musky odour.

muskrat rodent *Ondatra zibethicus* of the family Cricetidae, about 30 cm/12in long, living along streams, rivers, and lakes in North America. It has webbed hind feet, a side-to-side flattened tail, and shiny, light-brown fur. It builds up a store of food, plastering it over with mud, for winter consumption. It is hunted for its fur.

Muslim or *Moslem*, a follower of *Islam.

Muslim Brotherhood movement founded by members of the Sunni branch of Islam in Egypt in 1928. It aims at the establishment of a theocratic Islamic state and is headed by a 'supreme guide'. It is also active in Jordan, Sudan, and Syria.

mussel one of a number of bivalve molluscs, some of them edible, such as *Mytilus edulis*, found in clusters attached to rocks around the N Atlantic and American coasts. It has a blue-black shell.

Mussolini Benito 1883–1945. Italian dictator 1925–43. As founder of the Fascist Movement (see *fascism) 1919 and prime minister from 1922, he became known as *Il Duce* ('the leader'). He invaded Ethiopia 1935–36, intervened in the Spanish Civil War 1936–39 in support of Franco, and conquered Albania 1939. In June 1940 Italy entered World War II supporting Hitler. Forced by military and domestic setbacks to resign 1943, Mussolini established a breakaway government in N Italy 1944–45, but was killed trying to flee the country.

Mussorgsky Modest Petrovich 1839–1881. Russian composer who was largely self-taught.

His opera *Boris Godunov* was completed in 1869, although not produced in St Petersburg until 1874. Some of his works were 'revised' by *Rimsky-Korsakov, and only recently has their original beauty been recognized.

Mustafa Kemal Turkish leader who assumed the name of *Atatürk.

mustard any of several annual plants of the family Cruciferae, with sweet-smelling yellow flowers. Brown and white mustard are cultivated as a condiment in Europe and North America. The seeds of brown mustard *Brassica juncea* and white mustard *Sinapis alba* are used in the preparation of table mustard.

mutagen any substance that makes *mutation of genes more likely. A mutagen is likely to also act as a *carcinogen.

mutation in biology, a change in the genes produced by a change in the *DNA that makes up the hereditary material of all living organisms. Mutations, the raw material of evolution, result from mistakes during replication (copying) of DNA molecules. Only a few improve the organism's performance and are therefore favoured by *natural selection. Mutation rates are increased by certain chemicals and by radiation.

mute in music, any device used to dampen the vibration of an instrument and so affect the tone. Brass instruments use plugs of metal or cardboard inserted in the bell, while orchestral strings apply a form of clamp to the bridge.

mutiny organized act of disobedience or defiance by two or more members of the armed services. In naval and military law, mutiny has always been regarded as one of the most serious of crimes, punishable in wartime by death.

Mutsuhito personal name of the Japanese emperor *Meiji.

mutton bird any of various shearwaters and petrels that breed in burrows on Australasian islands. The young are very fat, and are killed for food and oil.

mutual fund another name for *unit trust, used in the USA.

mutual induction in physics, the production of an electromotive force (emf) or voltage in an electric circuit caused by a changing *magnetic flux in a neighbouring circuit. The two circuits are often coils of wire, as in a *transformer, and the size of the induced emf depends largely on the numbers of turns of wire in each of the coils.

mutualism or *symbiosis* an association between two organisms of different species whereby both profit from the relationship.

Muybridge Eadweard. Adopted name of Edward James Muggeridge 1830–1904. British photographer. He made a series of animal locomotion photographs in the USA in the 1870s and proved that, when a horse trots, there are times when all its feet are off the ground. He also explored motion in birds and humans.

Muzorewa Abel (Tendekayi) 1925– . Zimbabwean politician and Methodist bishop. He was president of the African National Council 1971–85 and prime minister of Rhodesia/Zimbabwe 1979–80. He was detained for a year in 1983–84. He was leader of the minority United Africa National Council, which merged with the Zimbabwe Unity Movement (ZUM) 1994.

MVD acronym for the Soviet Ministry of Internal Affairs, name (1946–53) of the Soviet secret police; later the *KGB.

Mwinyi Ali Hassan 1925– . Tanzanian socialist politician, president from 1985, when he succeeded Julius Nyerere. Mwinyi began a revival of private enterprise and control of state involvement and spending.

Myanmar Union of (*Thammada Myanmar Naingngandaw*) (formerly **Burma**, until 1989)

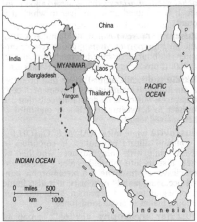

area 676,577 sq km/261,228 sq mi
capital and chief port Yangon (formerly Rangoon)
towns Mandalay, Moulmein, Pegu
physical over half is rainforest; rivers Irrawaddy and Chindwin in central lowlands ringed by mountains in N, W, and E
environment landslides and flooding during the rainy season (June–Sept) are becoming more frequent as a result of deforestation
head of state and government Than Shwe from 1992
political system military republic
exports rice, rubber, jute, teak, jade, rubies, sapphires
currency kyat
population (1993 est) 42,330,000; growth rate 1.9% p.a. (includes Shan, Karen, Raljome, Chinese, and Indian minorities)
language Burmese
religions Hinayana Buddhist 85%, animist, Christian
GNP $210 per head (1989)
chronology
1886 United as province of British India.
1937 Became crown colony in the British Commonwealth.
1942–45 Occupied by Japan.
1948 Independence achieved from Britain. Left the Commonwealth.
1962 General Ne Win assumed power in army coup.
1973–74 Adopted presidential-style 'civilian' constitution.
1975 Opposition National Democratic Front formed.
1986 Several thousand supporters of opposition leader Suu Kyi arrested.

1988 Government resigned after violent demonstrations. General Saw Maung seized power in military coup Sept; over 1,000 killed.
1989 Martial law declared; thousands arrested including advocates of democracy and human rights. Country renamed Myanmar and capital Yangon.
1990 Breakaway opposition group formed 'parallel government' on rebel-held territory.
1991 Martial law and human-rights abuses continued. Military offensives continued. Opposition leader, Aung San Suu Kyi, received Nobel Peace Prize.
1992 Jan-April: Pogrom against Muslim community in Arakan province, W Myanmar, carried out with army backing. April: Saw Maung replaced by Than Shwe. Several political prisoners liberated. Sept: martial law lifted.

myasthenia gravis in medicine, an uncommon condition characterized by loss of muscle power, especially in the face and neck. The muscles tire rapidly and fail to respond to repeated nervous stimulation. *Autoimmunity is the cause.

mycelium interwoven mass of threadlike filaments or *hyphae, forming the main body of most fungi. The reproductive structures, or 'fruiting bodies', grow from the mycelium.

Mycenae ancient Greek city in the E Peloponnese, which gave its name to the Mycenaean (Bronze Age) civilization. Its peak was 1400–1200 BC, when the Cyclopean walls (using close-fitting stones) were erected. The city ceased to be inhabited after about 1120 BC.

Mycenaean civilization Bronze Age civilization that flourished in Crete, Cyprus, Greece, the Aegean Islands, and W Anatolia about 4000–1000 BC. During this period, magnificent architecture and sophisticated artefacts were produced.

mycorrhiza mutually beneficial (mutualistic) association occurring between plant roots and a soil fungus. Mycorrhizal roots take up nutrients more efficiently than non-mycorrhizal roots, and the fungus benefits by obtaining carbohydrates from the tree.

myelin sheath insulating layer that surrounds nerve cells in vertebrate animals. It acts to speed up the passage of nerve impulses. Myelin is made up of fats and proteins and is formed from up to a hundred layers, laid down by special cells, the *Schwann cells*.

My Lai massacre killing of 109 civilians in My Lai, a village in South Vietnam, by US troops in March 1968. An investigation in 1969 was followed by the conviction of Lt William Calley, commander of the platoon.

mynah any of various tropical starlings, family Sturnidae, of SE Asia. The glossy blackhill mynah *Gracula religiosa* of India is a realistic mimic of sounds and human speech.

myoglobin globular protein, closely related to *haemoglobin and located in vertebrate muscle. Oxygen binds to myoglobin and is released only when the haemoglobin can no longer supply adequate oxygen to muscle cells.

myopia or *short-sightedness* defect of the eye in which a person can see clearly only those objects that are close up. It is caused either by the eyeball being too long or by the cornea and lens system of the eye being too powerful, both of which cause the images of distant objects to be formed in front of the retina instead of on it. Nearby objects are sharply perceived. Myopia can be corrected by suitable eyeglasses or contact lenses.

myopia, low-luminance poor night vision. About 20% of people have poor vision in twilight and nearly 50% in the dark. Low-luminance myopia does not show up in normal optical tests, but in 1989 a method was developed of measuring the degree of blurring by projecting images on a screen using a weak laser beam.

myrmecophyte plant that lives in association with a colony of ants and possesses specialized organs in which the ants live. For example, *Myrmecodia*, an epiphytic plant from Malaysia, develops root tubers containing a network of cavities inhabited by ants.

Myron c. 500–440 BC. Greek sculptor. His *Discobolus/Discus-Thrower* and *Athene and Marsyas*, much admired in his time, are known through Roman copies. They confirm his ancient reputation for brilliant composition and naturalism.

myrrh gum resin produced by small trees of the genus *Commiphora* of the bursera family, especially *C. myrrha*, found in Ethiopia and Arabia. In ancient times it was used for incense and perfume and in embalming.

myrtle evergreen shrub of the Old World genus *Myrtus*, family Myrtaceae. The commonly cultivated Mediterranean myrtle *M. communis* has oval opposite leaves and white flowers followed by purple berries, all of which are fragrant.

mystery play or *miracle play* medieval religious drama based on stories from the Bible. Mystery plays were performed around the time of church festivals, reaching their height in Europe during the 15th and 16th centuries. A whole cycle running from the Creation to the Last Judgement was performed in separate scenes on mobile wagons by various town guilds.

mystery religion any of various cults of the ancient world, open only to the initiated; for example, the cults of Demeter (see *Eleusinian Mysteries), Dionysus, Cybele, Isis, and Mithras. Underlying some of them is a fertility ritual, in which a deity undergoes death and resurrection and the initiates feed on the flesh and blood to attain communion with the divine and ensure their own life beyond the grave. The influence of mystery religions on early Christianity was considerable.

mystery reproductive syndrome (MRS) virus disease of pigs that causes sows to lose up to 10% of their litter. It was first seen in the USA 1987 and in Europe 1991. The symptoms are flulike.

mysticism religious belief or spiritual experience based on direct, intuitive communion with the divine. It does not always involve an orthodox deity, though it is found in all the major religions – for example, kabbalism in Judaism, Sufism in Islam, and the bhakti movement in Hinduism. The mystical experience is often rooted in ascetism and can involve visions, trances, and ecstasies; many religious traditions prescribe meditative and contemplative techniques for achieving mystical experience. Official churches fluctuate between acceptance of mysticism as a form of special grace, and suspicion of it as a dangerous deviation, verging on the heretical.

mythology study and interpretation of the stories symbolically underlying a given culture and of how they relate to similar stories told in other cultures. These stories describe gods and other supernatural beings, with whom humans may have relationships, and are intended to explain the workings of the universe and human history.

myxoedema thyroid-deficiency disease developing in adult life, most commonly in middle-aged women. The symptoms are loss of energy and appetite, inability to keep warm, mental dullness, and dry, puffy skin. It is completely reversed by giving the thyroid hormone known as thyroxine.

myxomatosis contagious, usually fatal, virus infection of rabbits which causes much suffering. It has been deliberately introduced in the UK and Australia since the 1950s to reduce the rabbit population.

16th century until 1859. An atom bomb was dropped on it by the USA 9 Aug 1945.

Nagorno-Karabakh autonomous region of *Azerbaijan

area 4,400 sq km/1,700 sq mi

capital Stepanakert

products cotton, grapes, wheat, silk

population (1987) 180,000 (76% Armenian, 23% Azeri), the Christian Armenians forming an enclave within the predominantly Shi'ite Muslim Azerbaijan

history an autonomous protectorate after the Russian Revolution 1917, Nagorno-Karabakh was annexed to Azerbaijan 1923 against the wishes of the largely Christian-Armenian population. Since 1989, when the local, ethnic Armenian council declared its intention to transfer control of the region to Armenia, the enclave has been racked by fighting between Armenian and Azeri troops, both attempting to assert control. By Feb 1992, the conflict had caused the loss of at least 1,000 lives (501 during 1991 alone) and the displacement of some 270,000 people, half of them Armenian and half Azeri.

Nagoya industrial seaport (cars, textiles, clocks) on Honshu Island, Japan; population (1990) 2,154,700. It has a shogun fortress 1610 and a notable Shinto shrine, Atsuta Jingu.

Nagpur industrial city (textiles, metals) in Maharashtra, India, on the river Pench; population (1981) 1,298,000. Pharmaceuticals, cotton goods, and hosiery are produced. Nagpur was founded in the 18th century, and was the former capital of Berar and Madhya Pradesh states.

Nagy Imre 1895–1958. Hungarian politician, prime minister 1953–55 and 1956. He led the Hungarian revolt against Soviet domination in 1956, for which he was executed.

Nahayan Sheik Sultan bin Zayed al- 1918– . Emir of Abu Dhabi from 1969, when he deposed his brother, Sheik Shakhbut. He was elected president of the supreme council of the United Arab Emirates 1971. In 1991 he was implicated, through his majority ownership, in the international financial scandals associated with the Bank of Commerce and Credit International.

Nahuatl member of any of a group of Mesoamerican Indian peoples (Mexico and Central America), of which the best-known group were the Aztecs. The Nahuatl are the largest ethnic group in Mexico, and their languages, which belong to the Uto-Aztecan (Aztec-Tanoan) family, are spoken by over a million people today.

naiad in classical mythology, a water nymph. Naiads lived in rivers and streams; nereids in the sea.

nail in biology, a hard, flat, flexible outgrowth of the digits of primates (humans, monkeys, and apes). Nails are composed of *keratin.

Naipaul V(idiadhar) S(urajprasad) 1932– . Trinidadian novelist living in Britain. His novels include *A House for Mr Biswas* 1961, *The Mimic Men* 1967, *A Bend in the River* 1979, and *Finding the Centre* 1984. His brother *Shiva(dhar) Naipaul* (1940–1985) was also a novelist (*Fireflies* 1970) and journalist.

Nairobi capital of Kenya, in the central highlands at 1,660 m/5,450 ft; population (1985) 1,100,000. It has light industry and food pro-

NAACP abbreviation for *National Association for the Advancement of Colored People*, a US civil rights organization.

Nabis, les group of French artists, active in the 1890s in Paris, united in their admiration of Paul Gauguin – the mystic content of his work, the surface pattern, and intense colour. In practice their work was decorative and influenced *Art Nouveau. Pierre *Bonnard and Edouard *Vuillard were leading members.

Nabokov Vladimir 1899–1977. US writer. He left his native Russia 1917 and began writing in English in the 1940s. His most widely known book is *Lolita* 1955, the story of the middle-aged Humbert Humbert's infatuation with a precocious girl of 12. His other books, remarkable for their word play and ingenious plots, include *Laughter in the Dark* 1938, *The Real Life of Sebastian Knight* 1945, *Pnin* 1957, and his memoirs *Speak, Memory* 1947.

nadir the point on the celestial sphere vertically below the observer and hence diametrically opposite the **zenith**. The term is used metaphorically to mean the low point of a person's fortunes.

naevus a mole, or patch of discoloration on the skin which has been present from birth. There are many different types of naevi, including those composed of a cluster of small blood vessels, such as the 'strawberry mark' (which usually disappears early in life), and the 'port-wine stain'.

NAFTA acronym for *North American Free Trade Agreement*.

Nagaland state of NE India, bordering Myanmar (Burma) on the E

area 16,721 sq km/6,456 sq mi

capital Kohima

products rice, tea, coffee, paper, sugar

population (1991) 1,215,600

history formerly part of Assam, the area was seized by Britain from Burma (now Myanmar) 1826. The British sent 18 expeditions against the Naga peoples in the N 1832–87. After India attained independence 1947, there was Naga guerrilla activity against the Indian government; the state of Nagaland was established 1963 in response to demands for self-government, but fighting continued sporadically.

Nagasaki industrial port (coal, iron, shipbuilding) on Kyushu Island, Japan; population (1990) 444,600. Nagasaki was the only Japanese port open to European trade from the cessing and is the headquarters of the United Nations Environment Programme.

Najibullah Ahmadzai 1947– . Afghan communist politician, state president 1986–92. A member of the Politburo from 1981, he was leader of the People's Democratic Party of Afghanistan (PDPA) from 1986. Although his government initially survived the withdrawal of Soviet troops Feb 1989, continuing pressure from the mujaheddin forces resulted in his eventual overthrow.

Nakasone Yasuhiro 1917– . Japanese conservative politician, leader of the Liberal Democratic Party (LDP) and prime minister 1982–87. He stepped up military spending and increased Japanese participation in international affairs, with closer ties to the USA. He was forced to resign his party post May 1989 as a result of having profited from insider trading in the *Recruit scandal. After serving a two-year period of atonement, he rejoined the LDP in April 1991.

Nakhichevan autonomous republic forming part of Azerbaijan, even though it is entirely outside the Azerbaijan boundary, being separated from it by Armenia; area 5,500 sq km/2,120 sq mi; population (1986) 272,000. Taken by Russia in 1828, it was annexed to Azerbaijan in 1924. 85% of the population are Muslim Azeris who maintain strong links with Iran to the south. Nakhichevan has been affected by the Armenia–Azerbaijan conflict; many Azeris have fled to Azerbaijan, and in Jan 1990 frontier posts and border fences with Iran were destroyed. In May 1992 Armenian forces made advances in the region, but Azerbaijan forces had regained control by Aug. The republic has sought independence from Azerbaijan.

Namib Desert coastal desert region in Namibia between the Kalahari Desert and the Atlantic Ocean. Its sand dunes are among the tallest in the world, reaching heights of 370 m/1,200 ft.

Namibia Republic of (formerly *South West Africa*)

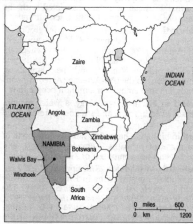

area 824,300 sq km/318,262 sq mi
capital Windhoek
towns Swakopmund, Rehoboth, Rundu
physical mainly desert

head of state and government Sam Nujoma from 1990
political system democratic republic
exports diamonds, uranium, copper, lead, zinc
currency Namibian dollar
population (1993 est) 1,550,000 (85% black African, 6% European)
languages Afrikaans (spoken by 60% of white population), German, English (all official), several indigenous languages
religion 51% Lutheran, 19% Roman Catholic, 6% Dutch Reformed Church, 6% Anglican
GNP $1,120 per head (1991)
chronology
1884 German and British colonies established.
1915 German colony seized by South Africa.
1920 Administered by South Africa, under League of Nations mandate, as British South Africa.
1946 Full incorporation in South Africa refused by United Nations (UN).
1958 South-West Africa People's Organization (SWAPO) set up to seek racial equality and full independence.
1966 South Africa's apartheid laws extended to the country.
1968 Redesignated Namibia by UN.
1978 UN Security Council Resolution 435 for the granting of full sovereignty accepted by South Africa and then rescinded.
1988 Peace talks between South Africa, Angola, and Cuba led to agreement on full independence for Namibia.
1989 Unexpected incursion by SWAPO guerrillas from Angola into Namibia threatened agreed independence. Transitional constitution created by elected representatives; SWAPO dominant party.
1990 Liberal multiparty 'independence' constitution adopted; independence achieved. Sam Nujoma elected president.
1991 Agreement on joint administration of Walvis Bay reached with South Africa, pending final settlement of dispute.
1992 Agreement on establishment of Walvis Bay Joint Administrative Body.

Nanak 1469–*c.* 1539. Indian guru and founder of Sikhism, a religion based on the unity of God and the equality of all human beings. He was strongly opposed to caste divisions.

Nancarrow Conlon 1912– . US composer who settled in Mexico 1940. Using a player-piano as a form of synthesizer, punching the rolls by hand, he experimented with complicated combinations of rhythm and tempo, producing a series of studies that anticipated minimalism and brought him recognition in the 1970s.

Nanchang industrial (textiles, glass, porcelain, soap) capital of Jiangxi province, China, about 260 km/160 mi SE of Wuhan; population (1989) 1,330,000.

Nanjing or *Nanking* capital of Jiangsu province, China, 270 km/165 mi NW of Shanghai; centre of industry (engineering, shipbuilding, oil refining), commerce, and communications; population (1989) 2,470,000. The bridge 1968 over the river Chang Jiang is the longest in China at 6,705 m/22,000 ft.

Nanning industrial river port, capital of Guangxi Zhuang autonomous region, China, on the river You Jiang; population (1989) 1,050,00. It was a supply town during the Vietnam War and the Sino-Vietnamese confrontation 1979.

nano- prefix used in *SI units of measurement, equivalent to a one-billionth part (10^{-9}). For example, a nanosecond is one-billionth of a second.

nanotechnology the building of devices on a molecular scale. Micromachines, such as gears smaller in diameter than a human hair, have been made at the AT & T Bell laboratories in New Jersey, USA. Building large molecules with useful shapes has been accomplished by research groups in the USA. A robot small enough to travel through the bloodstream and into organs of the body, inspecting or removing diseased tissue, was under development in Japan 1990.

Nansen Fridtjof 1861–1930. Norwegian explorer and scientist. In 1893, he sailed to the Arctic in the *Fram*, which was deliberately allowed to drift north with an iceflow. Nansen, accompanied by F Hjalmar Johansen (1867–1923), continued north on foot and reached 86° 14′ N, the highest latitude then attained. After World War I, Nansen became League of Nations high commissioner for refugees. Nobel Peace Prize 1923.

Nantes, Edict of decree by which Henry IV of France granted religious freedom to the *Huguenots 1598. It was revoked 1685 by Louis XIV.

napalm fuel used in flamethrowers and incendiary bombs. Produced from jellied petrol, it is a mixture of **na**phthenic and **palm**itic acids. Napalm causes extensive burns because it sticks to the skin even when aflame. It was widely used by the US Army during the Vietnam War.

naphtha the mixtures of hydrocarbons obtained by destructive distillation of petroleum, coal tar, and shale oil. It is raw material for the petrochemical and plastics industries. The term was originally applied to naturally occurring liquid hydrocarbons.

naphthalene $C_{10}H_8$ a solid, white, shiny, aromatic hydrocarbon obtained from coal tar. The smell of moth-balls is due to their napthalene content. It is used in making indigo and certain azo dyes, as a mild disinfectant, and as an insecticide.

Napier John 1550–1617. Scottish mathematician who invented *logarithms 1614 and 'Napier's bones', an early mechanical calculating device for multiplication and division.

Naples (Italian **Napoli**) industrial port (shipbuilding, cars, textiles, paper, food processing) and capital of Campania, Italy, on the Tyrrhenian Sea; population (1988) 1,201,000. To the south is the Isle of Capri, and behind the city is Mount Vesuvius, with the ruins of Pompeii at its foot.

Naples, Kingdom of the southern part of Italy, alternately independent and united with *Sicily in the Kingdom of the Two Sicilies.

Napoleon I Bonaparte 1769–1821. Emperor of the French 1804–14 and 1814–15. A general from 1796 in the *Revolutionary Wars, in 1799 he overthrew the ruling Directory (see *French Revolution) and made himself dictator. From 1803 he conquered most of Europe (the **Napoleonic Wars**) and installed his brothers as

puppet kings (see *Bonaparte). After the Peninsular War and retreat from Moscow 1812, he was forced to abdicate 1814 and was banished to the island of Elba. In March 1815 he reassumed power but was defeated by British forces at the Battle of *Waterloo and exiled to the island of St Helena. His internal administrative reforms and laws are still evident in France.

Napoleon II 1811–1832. Title given by the Bonapartists to the son of Napoleon I and *Marie Louise; until 1814 he was known as the king of Rome and after 1818 as the duke of Reichstadt. After his father's abdication 1814 he was taken to the Austrian court, where he spent the rest of his life.

Napoleon III 1808–1873. Emperor of the French 1852–70, known as **Louis-Napoleon**. After two attempted coups (1836 and 1840) he was jailed, then went into exile, returning for the revolution of 1848, when he became president of the Second Republic but soon turned authoritarian. In 1870 he was manoeuvred by the German chancellor Bismarck into war with Prussia (see *Franco-Prussian war); he was forced to surrender at Sedan, NE France, and the empire collapsed.

Napoleonic Wars 1803–15 a series of European wars conducted by Napoleon I following the *Revolutionary Wars, aiming for French conquest of Europe.

1803 Britain renewed the war against France, following an appeal from the Maltese against Napoleon's 1798 seizure of the island.

1805 Napoleon's planned invasion of Britain from Boulogne ended with Nelson's victory at *Trafalgar*. Coalition formed against France by Britain, Austria, Russia, and Sweden. Austria defeated at Ulm; Austria and Russia at *Austerlitz*.

1806 Prussia joined the coalition and was defeated at Jena; Napoleon instituted an attempted blockade, the **Continental System**, to isolate Britain from Europe.

1807 Russia defeated at Eylau and Friedland and, on making peace with Napoleon under the **Treaty of Tilsit**, changed sides, agreeing to attack Sweden, but was forced to retreat.

1808 Napoleon's invasion of Portugal and strategy of installing his relatives as puppet kings led to the *Peninsular War*.

1809 Revived Austrian opposition to Napoleon was ended by defeat at *Wagram*.

1812 The Continental System finally collapsed on its rejection by Russia, and Napoleon made the fatal decision to invade; he reached **Moscow** but was defeated by the Russian resistance and by the bitter winter as he retreated through a countryside laid waste by the retreating Russians (380,000 French soldiers died).

1813 Britain, Prussia, Russia, Austria, and Sweden formed a new coalition, which defeated Napoleon at the **Battle of the Nations**, Leipzig, Germany. He abdicated and was exiled to Elba.

1814 Louis XVIII became king of France, and the Congress of Vienna met to conclude peace.

1815 Napoleon returned to Paris. On 16 June the British commander Wellington defeated the French marshal Ney at Quatre Bras (in Belgium, SE of Brussels), and Napoleon was finally defeated at *Waterloo*, S of Brussels, 18 June.

Narasimha Rao P(amulaparti) V(enkata)

1921– . Indian politician, prime minister of India from 1991 and Congress (I) leader. He governed the state of Andhra Pradesh as chief minister 1971–73, and served in the Congress (I) cabinets of Indira and Rajiv Gandhi as minister of external affairs 1980–85 and 1988–90 and of human resources 1985–88. He took over the party leadership after the assassination of Rajiv Gandhi. Elected prime minister the following month, he instituted a reform of the economy.

narcissism in psychology, an exaggeration of normal self-respect and self-involvement which may amount to mental disorder when it precludes relationships with other people.

narcissus any bulbous plant of the genus *Narcissus*, family Amaryllidaceae. Species include the daffodil, jonquil, and narcissus. All have flowers with a cup projecting from the centre.

Narcissus in Greek mythology, a beautiful youth who rejected the love of the nymph Echo and was condemned to fall in love with his own reflection in a pool. He pined away and in the place where he died a flower sprang up that was named after him.

narcotic pain-relieving and sleep-inducing drug. The chief narcotics induce dependency, and include opium, its derivatives and synthetic modifications (such as morphine and heroin); alcohols (such as ethanol); and barbiturates.

Narmada River river that rises in the Maikala range in Madhya Pradesh state, central India, and flows 1,245 km/778 mi WSW to the Gulf of Khambat, an inlet of the Arabian Sea. Forming the traditional boundary between Hindustan and Deccan, the Narmada is a holy river of the Hindus. India's Narmada Valley Project is one of the largest and most controversial river development projects in the world. Between 1990 and 2040 it is planned to build 30 major dams, 135 medium-sized dams, and 3,000 smaller dams in a scheme that will involve moving 1 million of the valley's population of 20 million people.

narwhal *The male narwhal has a spiral tusk up to 2.7 m/9 ft long.*

narwhal toothed whale *Monodon monoceros*, found only in the Arctic Ocean. It grows to 5 m/16 ft long, has a grey and black body, a small head, and short flippers. The male has a single spirally fluted tusk that may be up to 2.7 m/9 ft long.

NASA (acronym for *National Aeronautics and Space Administration*) US government agency, founded 1958, for spaceflight and aeronautical research. Its headquarters are in Washington, DC and its main installation is at the *Kennedy Space Center in Florida. NASA's early

planetary and lunar programs included Pioneer spacecraft from 1958, which gathered data for the later crewed missions, the most famous of which took the first people to the Moon in *Apollo 11* on 16–24 July 1969.

Naseby, Battle of decisive battle of the English Civil War 14 June 1645, when the Royalists, led by Prince Rupert, were defeated by Oliver Cromwell and General Fairfax. It is named after the nearby village of Naseby, 32 km/20 mi S of Leicester.

Nash (Frederic) Ogden 1902–1971. US poet and wit. He published numerous volumes of humorous, quietly satirical light verse, characterized by unorthodox rhymes and puns. They include *I'm a Stranger Here Myself* 1938, *Versus* 1949, and *Bed Riddance* 1970. Most of his poems first appeared in the *New Yorker*, where he held an editorial post and did much to establish the magazine's tone.

Nash John 1752–1835. English architect. He laid out Regent's Park, London, and its approaches. Between 1813 and 1820 he planned Regent Street (later rebuilt), repaired and enlarged Buckingham Palace (for which he designed Marble Arch), and rebuilt Brighton Pavilion in flamboyant oriental style.

Nash Paul 1889–1946. English painter, an official war artist in world wars I and II. In the 1930s he was one of a group of artists promoting avant-garde styles in the UK. Two of his works are *Totes Meer/Dead Sea* (Tate Gallery, London) and *The Battle of Britain* (Imperial War Museum, London).

Nash (Richard) 'Beau' 1674–1762. British dandy. As master of ceremonies at Bath from 1705, he made the town a fashionable spa resort, and introduced a polished code of manners into polite society.

Nashe Thomas 1567–1601. English poet, satirist, and anti-Puritan pamphleteer. Born in Suffolk, he settled in London about 1588, where he was rapidly drawn into the Martin Marprelate controversy (a pamphleteering attack on the clergy of the Church of England by Puritans), and wrote at least three attacks on the Martinists. Among his later works are the satirical *Pierce Pennilesse* 1592 and the religious *Christes Teares over Jerusalem* 1593; his *The Unfortunate Traveller* 1594 is a picaresque narrative mingling literary parody and mock-historical fantasy.

Nashville port on the Cumberland River and capital of Tennessee, USA; population (1990) 488,300. It is a banking and commercial centre, and has large printing, music-publishing, and recording industries.

Nassau capital and port of the Bahamas, on New Providence Island; population (1980) 135,000.

Nassau agreement treaty signed 18 Dec 1962 whereby the USA provided Britain with Polaris missiles, marking a strengthening in Anglo-American relations.

Nasser Gamal Abdel 1918–1970. Egyptian politician, prime minister 1954–56 and from 1956 president of Egypt (the United Arab Republic 1958–71). In 1952 he was the driving power behind the Neguib coup, which ended the monarchy. His nationalization of the Suez Canal 1956 led to an Anglo-French invasion and the *Suez Crisis, and his ambitions for an Egyptian-led union of Arab states led to disquiet in the Middle East (and in the West). Nasser was also an early and influential leader of the nonaligned movement.

nastic movement plant movement that is caused by an external stimulus, such as light or temperature, but is directionally independent of its source, unlike *tropisms. Nastic movements occur as a result of changes in water pressure within specialized cells or differing rates of growth in parts of the plant. Examples include the opening and closing of crocus flowers following an increase or decrease in temperature (**thermonasty**), and the opening and closing of evening-primrose *Oenothera* flowers on exposure to dark and light (**photonasty**).

nasturtium any plant of the genus *Nasturtium*, family Cruciferae, including watercress *N. officinale*, a perennial aquatic plant of Europe and Asia, grown as a salad crop. It also includes plants of the South American family Tropaeolaceae, including the cultivated species *Tropaeolum majus*, with orange or scarlet flowers, and *T. minus*, which has smaller flowers.

Natal province of South Africa, NE of Cape Province, bounded on the east by the Indian Ocean
area 91,785 sq km/35,429 sq mi
capital Pietermaritzburg
towns Durban
physical slopes from the Drakensberg to a fertile subtropical coastal plain
products sugar cane, black wattle *Acacia mollissima*, maize, fruit, vegetables, tobacco, coal
population (1985) 2,145,000

Nataraja ('Lord of the Dance') in Hinduism, a title of *Siva.

Natchez member of a North American Indian people of the Mississippi area, one of the Mound-builder group of peoples. They had a highly developed caste system unusual in North America, headed by a ruler priest (the 'Great Sun'). Members of the highest caste always married members of the lowest caste. The system lasted until French settlers colonized the area 1731. Only a few Natchez now survive in Oklahoma. Their Muskogean language is extinct.

National Association for the Advancement of Colored People (NAACP) US civil-rights organization dedicated to ending inequality and segregation for African-Americans through nonviolent protest. Founded 1910, its first aim was to eradicate lynching. The NAACP campaigned to end segregation in state schools; it funded test cases that eventually led to the Supreme Court decision 1954 outlawing school segregation, although it was only through the *civil-rights movement of the 1960s that desegregation was achieved. In 1987 the NAACP had about 500,000 members, black and white.

national curriculum in the UK from 1988, a course of study in ten subjects common to all primary and secondary state schools. The national curriculum is divided into three core subjects – English, maths, and science – and seven foundation subjects: geography, history, technology, a foreign language (for secondary school pupils), art, music, and physical education. There are four stages, on completion of which the pupil's work is assessed. The stages are for ages 5–7, 7–11, 11–14, and 14–16.

national debt debt incurred by the central government of a country to its own people and institutions and also to overseas creditors. A government can borrow from the public by means of selling interest-bearing bonds, for example, or from abroad. Traditionally, a major cause of incurring national debt was the cost of war but in recent decades governments have borrowed heavily in order to finance development or nationalization, to support an ailing currency, or to avoid raising taxes.

National Economic Development Council (NEDC) known as '**Neddy**', the UK forum for economic consultation between government, management, and trade unions. It examines the country's economic and industrial performance, in both the public and private sectors, and seeks agreement on ways to improve efficiency. It was established 1962; its role diminished during the 1980s.

National Endowment for Democracy US political agency founded 1983 with government backing. It has funded a range of political organizations abroad, with over 95% of its $114 million annual income coming from the US government after 1984.

National Front in the UK, extreme right-wing political party founded 1967. In 1991, the party claimed 3,000 members. Some of its members had links with the National Socialist Movement of the 1960s (see *Nazism).

National Guard *militia force recruited by each state of the USA. The volunteer National Guard units are under federal orders in emergencies, and under the control of the governor in peacetime, and are now an integral part of the US Army. The National Guard has been used against demonstrators; in May 1970 at Kent State University, Ohio, they killed four students who were protesting against the bombing of Cambodia by the USA.

National Health Service (NHS) UK government medical scheme; see *health service.

national income the total income of a state in one year, comprising both the wages of individuals and the profits of companies. It is equal to the value of the output of all goods and services during the same period. National income is equal to gross national product (the value of a country's total output) minus an allowance for replacement of ageing capital stock.

national insurance in the UK, state social-security scheme that provides child allowances, maternity benefits, and payments to the unemployed, sick, and retired, and also covers medical treatment. It is paid for by weekly contributions from employees and employers.

National Insurance Act UK act of Parliament 1911, introduced by Lloyd George, Liberal chancellor, which first provided insurance for workers against ill health and unemployment.

nationalism in music, a 19th-century movement in which composers (such as Smetana and Grieg) included the folk material of their country in their works, projecting the national spirit and its expression.

nationalism in politics, a movement that consciously aims to unify a nation, create a state, or liberate it from foreign or imperialistic rule. Nationalist movements became a potent factor in European politics during the 19th century; since 1900 nationalism has become a strong force in Asia and Africa and in the late 1980s revived strongly in E Europe.

nationalization policy of bringing a country's essential services and industries under public ownership. It was pursued, for example, by the UK Labour government 1945–51. In recent years the trend towards nationalization has slowed and in many countries (the UK, France, and Japan) reversed (*privatization). Assets in the hands of foreign governments or companies may also be nationalized; for example, Iran's oil industry (see *Abadan), the *Suez Canal, and US-owned fruit plantations in Guatemala, all in the 1950s.

National Party, Australian Australian political party representing the interests of the farmers and people of the smaller towns. It developed from about 1860 as the *National Country Party*, and holds the power balance between Liberals and Labor. It gained strength following the introduction of proportional representation 1918, and has been in coalition with the Liberals since 1949.

National Rivers Authority UK environmental agency launched Sept 1989. It is responsible for managing water resources, investigating pollution controls, and taking over flood controls and land drainage from the former ten regional water authorities of England and Wales.

National Security Agency (NSA) largest and most secret of US intelligence agencies. Established 1952 to intercept foreign communications as well as to safeguard US transmissions, the NSA collects and analyses computer communications, telephone signals, and other electronic data, and gathers intelligence. Known as the Puzzle Palace, its headquarters are at Fort Meade, Maryland (with a major facility at Menwith Hill, England).

national security directive in the USA, secret decree issued by the president that can establish national policy and commit federal funds without the knowledge of Congress, under the National Security Act 1947. The National Security Council alone decides whether these directives may be made public; most are not. The directives have been criticized as unconstitutional, since they enable the executive branch of government to make laws.

national service *conscription into the armed services in peacetime.

National Socialism official name for the Nazi movement in Germany; see *Nazism and *fascism.

National Theatre, Royal British national theatre company established 1963, and the complex, opened 1976, that houses it on London's South Bank. The national theatre of France is the *Comédie Française, founded 1680.

National Trust British trust founded 1895 for the preservation of land and buildings of historic interest or beauty, incorporated by act of Parliament 1907. It is the largest private landowner in Britain. The National Trust for Scotland was established 1931.

national vocational qualification (NVQ) in the UK, a certificate of attainment of a standardized level of skill and competence. A national council for NVQs was set up 1986 in an effort by the government in cooperation with employers to rationalize the many unrelated vocational qualifications then on offer. The objective is to fit all qualifications to four levels of attainment, roughly equivalent to the GCSE, A level, and degree system of academic qualifications.

native element any nongaseous element that occurs naturally, uncombined with any other element(s). Examples of native nonmetals are carbon and sulphur.

native metal or *free metal* any of the metallic elements that occur in nature in the chemically uncombined or elemental form (in addition to any combined form). They include bismuth, cobalt, copper, gold, iridium, iron, lead, mercury, nickel, osmium, palladium, platinum, ruthenium, rhodium, tin, and silver. Some are commonly found in the free state, such as gold; others occur almost exclusively in the combined state, but under unusual conditions do occur as native metals, such as mercury.

nativity Christian festival celebrating a birth: *Christmas* is celebrated 25 Dec from AD 336 in memory of the birth of Jesus in Bethlehem; *Nativity of the Virgin Mary* is celebrated 8 Sept by the Catholic and Eastern Orthodox churches; *Nativity of John the Baptist* is celebrated 24 June by the Catholic, Eastern Orthodox, and Anglican churches.

NATO abbreviation for *North Atlantic Treaty Organization*.

Natron, Lake salt and soda lake in the Great Rift Valley, Tanzania; length 56 km/35 mi, width 24 km/15 mi.

natural in music, a sign cancelling a sharp or flat. A *natural trumpet* or *horn* is an instrument without valves, thus restricted to playing natural harmonics.

Natural Environment Research Council (NERC) UK organization established by royal charter 1965 to undertake and support research in the earth sciences, to give advice both on exploiting natural resources and on protecting the environment, and to support education and training of scientists in these fields of study. Research areas include geothermal energy, industrial pollution, waste disposal, satellite surveying, acid rain, biotechnology, atmospheric circulation, and climate. Research is carried out principally within the UK but also in Antarctica and in many Third World countries. It comprises 13 research bodies.

natural frequency the frequency at which a mechanical system will vibrate freely. A pendulum, for example, always oscillates at the same frequency when set in motion. More complicated systems, such as bridges, also vibrate with a fixed natural frequency. If a varying force with a frequency equal to the natural frequency is applied to such an object the vibrations can become violent, a phenomenon known as *resonance.

natural gas mixture of flammable gases found in the Earth's crust (often in association with petroleum), now one of the world's three main fossil fuels (with coal and oil). Natural gas is a mixture of *hydrocarbons, chiefly methane, with ethane, butane, and propane.

natural justice the concept that there is an inherent quality in law which compares favourably with arbitrary action by a government. It is largely associated with the idea of the rule of law. For natural justice to be present it is generally argued that no one should be a judge in his or her own case, and that each party in a dispute has an unalienable right to be heard and to prepare their case thoroughly (the rule of *audi alteram partem*).

natural logarithm in mathematics, the *exponent of a number expressed to base *e*, where *e* represents the *irrational number 2.71828... . Natural *logarithms are also called Napierian logarithms, after their inventor, the Scottish mathematician John Napier.

natural radioactivity radioactivity generated by those radioactive elements that exist in the Earth's crust. All the elements from polonium (atomic number 84) to uranium (atomic number 92) are radioactive. *Radioisotopes of some lighter elements are also found in nature (for example potassium-40).

natural selection the process whereby gene frequencies in a population change through certain individuals producing more descendants than others because they are better able to survive and reproduce in their environment. The accumulated effect of natural selection is to produce *adaptations such as the insulating coat of a polar bear or the spadelike forelimbs of a mole. The process is slow, relying firstly on random variation in the genes of an organism being produced by *mutation and secondly on the genetic *recombination of sexual reproduction. It was recognized by Charles Darwin and Alfred Russel Wallace as the main process driving *evolution.

Nature Conservancy Council (NCC) former name of UK government agency established by act of Parliament 1973 (Nature Conservancy created by royal charter 1949) with the aims of designating and managing national nature reserves and other conservation areas; advising government ministers on policies; providing advice and information; and commissioning or undertaking relevant scientific research. In 1991 the Nature Conservancy Council was dissolved and its three regional bodies became autonomous agencies. The English section became English Nature, and the Scottish and Welsh sections merged with their own countryside commissions to form Scottish Natural Heritage and the Countryside Council for Wales, respectively.

nature–nurture controversy or *environment–heredity controversy* long-standing dispute among philosophers and psychologists over the relative importance of environment, that is upbringing, experience and learning ('nurture'), and heredity, that is genetic inheritance ('nature'), in determining the make-up of an organism, as related to human personality and intelligence.

nature reserve area set aside to protect a habitat and the wildlife that lives within it, with only restricted admission for the public. A nature reserve often provides a sanctuary for rare species. The world's largest is Etosha Reserve, Namibia; area 99,520 sq km/38,415 sq mi.

naturopathy the facilitating of the natural self-healing processes of the body. Naturopaths are the GPs of alternative medicine and often refer clients to other specialists, particularly in manipulative therapies, to complement their own work of seeking, through diet, the prescription of natural medicines and supplements, and lifestyle counselling, to restore or augment the vitality of the body and thereby its optimum health.

Nauru Republic of (*Naoero*)
area 21 sq km/8 sq mi
capital (seat of government) Yaren District
physical tropical island country in SW Pacific; plateau encircled by coral cliffs and sandy beaches
head of state and government Bernard Dowiyogo from 1989
political system liberal democracy
political party Democratic Party of Nauru (DPN), opposition to government
exports phosphates
currency Australian dollar
population (1993 est) 10,000 (mainly Polynesian; Chinese 8%, European 8%); growth rate 1.7% p.a.
languages Nauruan (official), English
religion Protestant 66%, Roman Catholic 33%
GNP $9,091 per head (1985)
chronology
1888 Annexed by Germany.
1920 Administered by Australia, New Zealand, and UK until independence, except 1942–45, when it was occupied by Japan.
1968 Independence achieved from Australia, New Zealand, and UK with 'special member' Commonwealth status. Hammer DeRoburt elected president.
1976 Bernard Dowiyogo elected president.
1978 DeRoburt re-elected.
1986 DeRoburt briefly replaced as president by Kennan Adeang.
1987 DeRoburt re-elected; Adeang established the Democratic Party of Nauru.
1989 DeRoburt replaced by Kensas Aroi, who was later succeeded by Bernard Dowiyogo.
1992 DeRoburt died in Melbourne, Australia.

nautical mile unit of distance used in navigation, an internationally agreed-on standard (since 1959) equalling the average length of one minute of arc on a great circle of the Earth, or 1,852 m/6,076.12 ft. The term formerly applied to various units of distance used in navigation.

nautilus shelled *cephalopod, genus *Nautilus*, found in the Indian and Pacific oceans. The pearly nautilus *N. pompilius* has a chambered spiral shell about 20 cm/8 in in diameter. Its body occupies the outer chamber. The nautilus has a large number of short, grasping tentacles surrounding a sharp beak.

Navajo or *Navaho* (Tena *Navahu* 'large planted field') member of a North American Indian people related to the Apache, and numbering about 200,000, mostly in Arizona, and in New Mexico and Utah. They speak an Athabaskan language, belonging to the Na-Dené family. The Navajo were traditionally cultivators; many now herd sheep and earn an income from tourism, making and selling rugs, blankets, and silver and turquoise jewellery. The Navajo refer to themselves as *Dineh*, 'people'.

Navarino, Battle of decisive naval action 20 Oct 1827 off Pylos in the Greek war of liberation that was won by the combined fleets of the English, French, and Russians under Vice-Admiral Edward Codrington (1770–1851) over the Turkish and Egyptian fleets. Navarino is the Italian and historic name of Pylos Bay, Greece, on the SW coast of the Peloponnese.

Navarre (Spanish *Navarra*) autonomous mountain region of N Spain
area 10,400 sq km/4,014 sq mi
capital Pamplona
population (1986) 513,000

Navarre, Kingdom of former kingdom comprising the Spanish province of Navarre and part of what is now the French *département* of Basses-Pyrénées. It resisted the conquest of the *Moors and was independent until it became French 1284 on the marriage of Philip IV to the heiress of Navarre. In 1479 Ferdinand of Aragon annexed Spanish Navarre, with French Navarre going to Catherine of Foix (1483–1512), who kept the royal title. Her grandson became Henry IV of France, and Navarre was absorbed in the French crown lands 1620.

nave in architecture, the central part of a church, between the choir and the entrance.

navigation the science and technology of finding the position, course, and distance travelled by a ship, plane, or other craft. Traditional methods include the magnetic *compass and *sextant. Today the gyrocompass is usually used, together with highly sophisticated electronic methods, employing beacons of radio signals. Satellite navigation uses satellites that broadcast time and position signals.

Navigation Acts in British history, a series of acts of Parliament passed from 1381 to protect English shipping from foreign competition and to ensure monopoly trading between Britain and its colonies. The last was repealed 1849 (coastal trade exempt until 1853). The Navigation Acts helped to establish England as a major sea power, although they led to higher prices. They ruined the Dutch merchant fleet in the 17th century, and were one of the causes of the *American Revolution.

navigation, biological the ability of animals or insects to navigate. Although many animals navigate by following established routes or known landmarks, many animals can navigate without such aids; for example, birds can fly several thousand miles back to their nest site, over unknown terrain. Such feats may be based on compass information derived from the position of the Sun, Moon, or stars, or on the characteristic patterns of Earth's magnetic field.

Navratilova Martina 1956– . Czech tennis player who became a naturalized US citizen 1981. The most outstanding woman player of the 1980s, she had 55 Grand Slam victories by 1991, including 18 singles titles. She has won the Wimbledon singles title a record nine times, including six in succession 1982–87. She was defeated by Conchita Martinez in the final of her last Wimbledon 1994.

navy fleet of ships, usually a nation's *warships and the organization to maintain them. The USSR had one of the world's largest merchant fleets and the world's largest fishing, hydrographic, and oceanographic fleets. All ships had intelligence-gathering equipment.

Nazarbayev Nursultan 1940– . President of Kazakhstan from 1990. In the Soviet period he was prime minister of the republic 1984–89 and leader of the Kazakh Communist Party 1989–91, which established itself as the independent Socialist Party of Kazakhstan (SPK) Sept 1991. He advocates free-market policies, yet enjoys the support of the environmentalist lobby. He joined the Communist Party at 22 and left it after the failed Soviet coup 1991.

Nazareth town in Galilee, N Israel, SE of Haifa; population (1981) 64,000. According to the New Testament, it was the boyhood home of Jesus.

Nazism ideology based on racism, nationalism, and the supremacy of the state over the individual. The German Nazi party, the *National-sozialistiche Deutsche Arbeiterpartei* (National Socialist German Workers' Party), was formed from the German Workers' Party (founded 1919) and led by Adolf *Hitler 1921–45.

N'djamena capital of Chad, at the confluence of the Chari and Logone rivers, on the Cameroon border; population (1988) 594,000.

Ndola mining centre and chief city of the Copperbelt province of central Zambia; population (1988) 442,700.

N'Dour Youssou 1959– . Senegalese singer, songwriter, and musician whose fusion of traditional *mbalax* percussion music with bluesy Arab-style vocals, accompanied by African and electronic instruments, became popular in the West in the 1980s on albums such as *Immigrés* 1984 with the band Le Super Etoile de Dakar.

Neagh, Lough lake in Northern Ireland, 25 km/15 mi W of Belfast; area 396 sq km/153 sq mi. It is the largest lake in the British Isles.

Neanderthal hominid of the Mid-Late Palaeolithic, named after the Neander Thal (valley) near Düsseldorf, Germany, where a skeleton was found in 1856. *Homo sapiens neanderthalensis* lived from about 100,000 to 35,000 years ago and was similar in build to present-day people, but slightly smaller, stockier, and heavier-featured with a strong jaw and prominent brow ridges on a sloping forehead.

Neave Airey (Middleton Sheffield) 1916–1979. British intelligence officer and Conservative member of Parliament 1953–79, a close adviser to Prime Minister Thatcher. During World War II he escaped from Colditz, a German high-security prison camp. As shadow undersecretary of state for Northern Ireland from 1975, he became a target for extremist groups and was assassinated by an Irish terrorist bomb.

Nebraska state in central USA; nickname Cornhusker State/Blackwater State
area 200,400 sq km/77,354 sq mi
capital Lincoln
towns Omaha, Grand Island, North Platte
population (1990) 1,578,300
products cereals, livestock, processed foods, fertilizers, oil, natural gas

famous people Fred Astaire, William Jennings Bryan, Johnny Carson, Willa Cather, Henry Fonda, Harold Lloyd, Malcom X

history exploited by French fur traders in the early 1700s; ceded to Spain by France 1763; retroceded to France 1801; part of the Louisiana Purchase 1803; explored by Lewis and Clark 1804–06; first settlement at Bellevue 1823; became a territory 1854 and a state 1867 after the Union Pacific began its transcontinental railroad at Omaha 1865. Nebraska's farm economy was weakened in the 1930s by the Great Depression and dust storms, but World War II brought military airfields and war industries. Much of the industry developed since that time is related to agriculture.

Nebuchadnezzar or **Nebuchadrezzar II** king of Babylonia from 60 BC. Shortly before his accession he defeated the Egyptians at Carchemish and brought Palestine and Syria into his empire. Judah revolted, with Egyptian assistance, 596 and 587–586 BC; on both occasions he captured Jerusalem and took many Hebrews into captivity. He largely rebuilt Babylon and constructed the hanging gardens.

nebula cloud of gas and dust in space. Nebulae are the birthplaces of stars, but some nebulae are produced by gas thrown off from dying stars (see *planetary nebula; *supernova). Nebulae are classified depending on whether they emit, reflect, or absorb light.

Necker Jacques 1732–1804. French politician. As finance minister 1776–81, he attempted reforms, and was dismissed through Queen Marie Antoinette's influence. Recalled 1788, he persuaded Louis XVI to summon the States General (parliament), which earned him the hatred of the court, and in July 1789 he was banished. The outbreak of the French Revolution with the storming of the Bastille forced his reinstatement, but he resigned Sept 1790.

necrosis death or decay of tissue in a particular part of the body, usually due to bacterial poisoning or loss of local blood supply.

nectar sugary liquid secreted by some plants from a nectary, a specialized gland usually situated near the base of the flower. Nectar often accumulates in special pouches or spurs, not always in the same location as the nectary. Nectar attracts insects, birds, bats, and other animals to the flower for *pollination and is the raw material used by bees in the production of honey.

nectarine smooth, shiny-skinned variety of *peach, usually smaller than other peaches and with firmer flesh. It arose from a natural mutation.

Nefertiti or **Nofretete** queen of Egypt who ruled *c.* 1372–1350 BC; wife of the pharaoh *Ikhnaton.

Negev desert in S Israel that tapers to the port of Eilat. It is fertile under irrigation, and minerals include oil and copper.

negligence in law, doing some act that a 'prudent and reasonable' person would not do, or omitting to do some act that such a person would do. Negligence may arise in respect of a person's duty towards an individual or towards other people in general. Breach of the duty of care that results in reasonably foreseeable damage is a tort.

Negro term formerly used to refer to a member of the indigenous people of Africa south of the Sahara, today distributed around the world. The term generally preferred today is *black.

Nehru Jawaharlal 1889–1964. Indian nationalist politician, prime minister from 1947. Before the partition (the division of British India into India and Pakistan), he led the socialist wing of the nationalist *Congress Party, and was second in influence only to Mahatma Gandhi. He was imprisoned nine times by the British 1921–45 for political activities. As prime minister from the creation of the dominion (later republic) of India in Aug 1947, he originated the idea of nonalignment (neutrality towards major powers). His daughter was Prime Minister Indira Gandhi.

neighbourhood watch local crime-prevention scheme. Under the supervision of police, groups of residents agree to increase watchfulness in order to prevent crimes such as burglary and vandalism in their area.

Nelson Horatio, Viscount Nelson 1758–1805. English admiral. He joined the navy in 1770. In the Revolutionary Wars against France he lost the sight in his right eye 1794 and lost his right arm 1797. He became a national hero, and rear admiral, after the victory off Cape St Vincent, Portugal. In 1798 he tracked the French fleet to Aboukir Bay where he almost entirely destroyed it. In 1801 he won a decisive victory over Denmark at the Battle of *Copenhagen, and in 1805, after two years of blockading Toulon, another over the Franco-Spanish fleet at the Battle of *Trafalgar, near Gibraltar.

nematode unsegmented worm of the phylum Nematoda. Nematodes are pointed at both ends, with a tough, smooth outer skin. They include many free-living species found in soil and water, including the sea, and a large number are parasites, such as the roundworms and pinworms that live in humans, or the eelworms that attack plant roots. They differ from *flatworms in that they have two openings to the gut (a mouth and an anus).

Nemesis in Greek mythology, the goddess of retribution, who especially punished hubris (Greek *hybris*), violent acts carried out in defiance of the gods and human custom.

neo- (Greek *neos* 'new') prefix used to indicate a revival or development of an older form, often in a different spirit. Examples include **neo-Marxism** and **Neo-Classicism**.

Neo-Classicism movement in art, architecture, and design in Europe and North America about 1750–1850, characterized by a revival of classical Greek and Roman styles. It superseded the Rococo style and was partly inspired both by the excavation of Pompeii and Herculaneum. Leading figures of the movement were the architect Robert Adam; the painters David, Ingres, and Mengs; the sculptors Canova, Flaxman, and Thorvaldsen; and the designers Wedgwood, Hepplewhite, and Sheraton.

neocolonialism disguised form of *imperialism, by which a country may grant independence to another country but continue to dominate it by control of markets for goods or raw materials.

neo-Darwinism modern theory of *evolution, built up since the 1930s by integrating the 19th-century English scientist Charles *Darwin's theory of evolution through natural selection with the theory of genetic inheritance founded on the work of the Austrian biologist Gregor *Mendel.

neodymium yellowish metallic element of the *lanthanide series, symbol Nd, atomic number 60, relative atomic mass 144.24. Its rose-coloured salts are used in colouring glass, and neodymium is used in lasers.

Neo-Impressionism movement in French painting in the 1880s, an extension of Impressionist technique. It drew on contemporary theories on colour and perception, building up form and colour by painting dots side by side. Seurat was the chief exponent; his minute technique became known as *Pointillism*.

Neolithic last period of the *Stone Age, characterized by settled communities based on agriculture and domesticated animals, and identified by sophisticated, finely honed stone tools, and ceramic wares. The earliest Neolithic communities appeared about 9000 BC in the Middle East, followed by Egypt, India, and China. In Europe farming began in about 6500 BC in the Balkans and Aegean, spreading north and east by 1000 BC.

neon colourless, odourless, nonmetallic, gaseous element, symbol Ne, atomic number 10, relative atomic mass 20.183. It is grouped with the *inert gases, is non-reactive, and forms no compounds. It occurs in small quantities in the Earth's atmosphere.

neo-Nazism or **neo-Fascism** the upsurge in racial and political intolerance in western Europe of the early 1990s. In Austria, Belgium, France, Germany, and Italy, the growth of extreme right-wing political groupings, coupled with racial violence, particularly in Germany, was reminiscent of the Nazi period in Hitler's Germany. Ironically, the liberalization of politics in the post-Cold War world unleashed anti-liberal forces that had previously been held in check by authoritarian regimes.

neo-Platonism school of philosophy that flourished during the declining centuries of the Roman Empire (3rd–6th centuries AD). Neo-Platonists argued that the highest stage of philosophy is attained not through reason and experience, but through a mystical ecstasy. Many later philosophers, including Nicholas of Cusa, were influenced by neo-Platonism.

neoprene synthetic rubber, developed in the USA 1931 from the polymerization of chloroprene. It is much more resistant to heat, light, oxidation, and petroleum than is ordinary rubber.

Neo-Realism movement in Italian cinema that emerged in the 1940s. It is characterized by its naturalism, social themes, frequent use of non-professional actors, and the visual authenticity achieved through location filming. Exponents include the directors de Sica, Visconti, and Rossellini.

Nepal Kingdom of (*Nepal Adhirajya*)
area 147,181 sq km/56,850 sq mi
capital Katmandu
towns Pátan, Moráng, Bhádgáon
physical descends from the Himalayan mountain range in N through foothills to the river Ganges plain in S

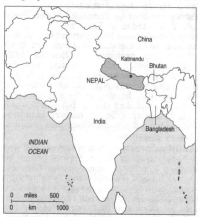

environment described as the world's highest rubbish dump, Nepal attracts 270,000 tourists, trekkers, and mountaineers each year. An estimated 1,100 lbs of rubbish is left by each expedition trekking or climbing in the Himalayas. Since 1952 the foothills of the Himalayas have been stripped of 40% of their forest cover
head of state King Birendra Bir Bikram Shah Dev from 1972
head of government Girija Prasad Koirala from 1991
political system constitutional monarchy Party (UNCP), Marxist-Leninist-Maoist; United Liberation Torchbearers; Democratic Front, radical republican
exports jute, rice, timber, oilseed
currency Nepalese rupee
population (1993 est) 20,400,000 (mainly known by name of predominant clan, the Gurkhas; the Sherpas are a Buddhist minority of NE Nepal); growth rate 2.3% p.a.
language Nepali (official); 20 dialects spoken
religions Hindu 90%; Buddhist, Muslim, Christian
GNP $180 per head (1991)
chronology
1768 Nepal emerged as unified kingdom.
1815–16 Anglo-Nepali 'Gurkha War'; Nepal became a British-dependent buffer state.
1846–1951 Ruled by the Rana family.
1923 Independence achieved from Britain.
1951 Monarchy restored.
1959 Constitution created elected legislature.
1960–61 Parliament dissolved by king; political parties banned.
1980 Constitutional referendum held following popular agitation.
1981 Direct elections held to national assembly.
1983 Overthrow of monarch-supported prime minister.
1986 New assembly elections returned a majority opposed to *panchayat* system of partyless government.
1988 Strict curbs placed on opposition activity; over 100 supporters of banned opposition party arrested; censorship imposed.
1989 Border blockade imposed by India in treaty dispute.

1990 *Panchayat* system collapsed after mass prodemocracy demonstrations; new constitution introduced; elections set for May 1991.
1991 Nepali Congress Party, led by Girija Prasad Koirala, won the general election.
1992 Communist-led demonstrations in Katmandu and Patan demanded government's resignation at time of economic austerity.

nephritis inflammation of the kidneys, caused by bacterial infection or, sometimes, by a body disorder that affects the kidneys, such as streptococcal infection of the throat. The degree of illness varies, and it may be acute or chronic, requiring a range of treatments from antibiotics to *dialysis. Acute nephritis is also known as *Bright's disease*.

nephron microscopic unit in vertebrate kidneys that forms *urine*. A human kidney is composed of over a million nephrons. Each nephron consists of a filter cup surrounding a knot of blood capillaries and a long narrow collecting tubule in close association with yet more capillaries. Waste materials and water pass from the bloodstream into the filter cup, and essential minerals and some water are reabsorbed from the tubule back into the blood. The urine that is left eventually passes out from the body.

Neptune in Roman mythology, god of the sea, the equivalent of the Greek *Poseidon.

Neptune in astronomy, the eighth planet in average distance from the Sun. Neptune orbits the Sun every 164.8 years at an average distance of 4.497 billion km/2.794 billion mi. It is a giant gas (hydrogen, helium, methane) planet, with a diameter of 48,600 km/30,200 mi and a mass 17.2 times that of Earth. Its rotation period is 16 hours 7 minutes. The methane in its atmosphere absorbs red light and gives the planet a blue colouring. It is believed to have a central rocky core covered by a layer of ice. Neptune has eight known moons.

neptunium silvery, radioactive metallic element of the *actinide series, symbol Np, atomic number 93, relative atomic mass 237.048. It occurs in nature in minute amounts in *pitchblende and other uranium ores, where it is produced from the decay of neutron-bombarded uranium in these ores. The longest-lived isotope, Np-237, has a half-life of 2.2 million years. The element can be produced by bombardment of U-238 with neutrons and is chemically highly reactive.

Nero AD 37–68. Roman emperor AD 54. He is said to have murdered his stepfather *Claudius' son Britannicus, his own mother, his wives Octavia and Poppaea, and many others. After the great fire of Rome 64, he persecuted the Christians, who were suspected of causing it. Military revolt followed 68; the Senate condemned Nero to death, and he committed suicide.

Neruda Pablo. Pen name of Neftalí Ricardo Reyes y Basualto 1904–1973. Chilean poet and diplomat. His work includes lyrics and the epic poem of the American continent *Canto General* 1950. He was awarded the Nobel Prize for Literature 1971. He served as consul and ambassador to many countries.

Nerva Marcus Cocceius Nerva AD c. 35–98. Roman emperor. He was proclaimed emperor on Domitian's death AD 96, and introduced state loans for farmers, family allowances, and allotments of land to poor citizens.

nerve strand of nerve cells enclosed in a sheath of connective tissue joining the *central and the *autonomic nervous systems with receptor and effector organs. A single nerve may contain both *motor and sensory nerve cells, but they act independently.

nerve cell or *neuron* elongated cell, part of the *nervous system, that transmits information between different parts of the body. A nerve impulse is a travelling wave of chemical and electrical changes that affects the surface membrane of the nerve fibre. Sequential changes in the permeability of the membrane to positive sodium (Na^+) ions and potassium (K^+) ions, produce electrical signals called action potentials. Impulses are received by the cell body and passed, as a pulse of electric charge, along the *axon. At the far end of the axon, the impulse triggers the release of chemical *neurotransmitters across a *synapse (junction), thereby stimulating another nerve cell or the action of an effector organ (for example, a muscle). Nerve impulses travel quickly, in humans as fast as 160 m/525 ft per second along a nerve cell.

Nervi Pier Luigi 1891–1979. Italian architect who used soft steel mesh within concrete to give it flowing form. For example, the Turin exhibition hall 1949, the UNESCO building in Paris 1952, and the cathedral at New Norcia, near Perth, Australia, 1960.

nervous breakdown popular term for a reaction to overwhelming psychological stress. It has no equivalent in medicine: patients said to be suffering from a nervous breakdown may in fact be going through an episode of depression, manic depression, anxiety, or even schizophrenia.

nervous system the system of interconnected *nerve cells of most invertebrates and all vertebrates. It is composed of the *central and *autonomic nervous systems. It may be as simple as the nerve net of coelenterates (for example, jellyfishes) or as complex as the mammalian nervous system, with a central nervous system comprising brain and spinal cord, and a peripheral nervous system connecting up with sensory organs, muscles, and glands.

Ness, Loch lake in Highland region, Scotland, forming part of the Caledonian Canal; 36 km/22.5 mi long, 229 m/754 ft deep. There have been unconfirmed reports of a *Loch Ness monster* since the 15th century.

Nestlé multinational corporation, the world's largest packaged-food company, best known for producing chocolate, coffee, and baby milk (the marketing of which in the Third World has been criticized as inappropriate). The company's market value 1991 was estimated at £.8 billion, and it employed 199,000 people.

Nestorianism Christian doctrine held by the Syrian ecclesiastic Nestorius (died c. 457), patriarch of Constantinople 428–431. He asserted that Jesus had two natures, human and divine. He was banished for maintaining that Mary was the mother of the man Jesus only, and therefore should not be called the Mother of God. His followers survived as the Assyrian church in Syria, Iraq, Iran, and as the Christians of St Thomas in S India.

net of a particular figure or price, calculated after the deduction of specific items such as commission, discounts, interest, and taxes. The opposite is *gross.

net assets either the total *assets of a company less its current liabilities (that is, the capital employed) or the total assets less current liabilities, debt capital, long-term loans and provisions, which would form the amount available to ordinary shareholders if the company were to be wound up.

netball game developed from basketball, played by two teams of seven players each on a hard court 30.5 m/100 ft long and 15.25 m/50 ft wide. At each end is a goal, consisting of a post 3.05 m/10 ft high, at the top of which is attached a circular hoop and net. The object of the game is to pass an inflated spherical ball through the opposing team's net. The ball is thrown from player to player; no contact is allowed between players, who must not run with the ball.

Netherlands Kingdom of the (*Koninkrijk der Nederlanden*), popularly referred to as *Holland*

area 41,863 sq km/16,169 sq mi
capital Amsterdam
towns The Hague (seat of government), Utrecht, Eindhoven, Maastricht; chief port Rotterdam
physical flat coastal lowland; rivers Rhine, Scheldt, Maas; Frisian Islands
territories Aruba, Netherlands Antilles (Caribbean)
environment the country lies at the mouths of three of Europe's most polluted rivers, the Maas, Rhine, and Scheldt. Dutch farmers contribute to this pollution by using the world's highest concentrations of nitrogen-based fertilizer per hectare/acre per year
head of state Queen Beatrix Wilhelmina Armgard from 1980
head of government Wim Kok from 1994
political system constitutional monarchy
exports dairy products, flower bulbs, vegetables, petrochemicals, electronics
currency guilder
population (1993) 15,240,000 (including 300,000 of Dutch-Indonesian origin absorbed 1949–64 from former colonial possessions); growth rate 0.4% p.a.
language Dutch

religions Roman Catholic 40%, Protestant 31%
GNP $21,030 per head (1992)
chronology
1940–45 Occupied by Germany during World War II.
1947 Joined Benelux customs union.
1948 Queen Juliana succeeded Queen Wilhelmina to the throne.
1949 Became a founding member of North Atlantic Treaty Organization (NATO).
1953 Dykes breached by storm; nearly 2,000 people and tens of thousands of cattle died in flood.
1958 Joined European Economic Community.
1980 Queen Juliana abdicated in favour of her daughter Beatrix.
1981 Opposition to cruise missiles averted their being sited on Dutch soil.
1989 Prime Minister Ruud Lubbers resigned; new Lubbers-led coalition elected.
1994 Government lost support in general election; new three-party coalition formed under Labour Party leader, Wim Kok.

Netherlands Antilles two groups of Caribbean islands, part of the Netherlands with full internal autonomy, comprising *Curaçao and Bonaire off the coast of Venezuela (*Aruba is considered separately), and St Eustatius, Saba, and the southern part of St Maarten in the Leeward Islands, 800 km/500 mi NE
area 797 sq km/308 sq mi
capital Willemstad on Curaçao
products oil from Venezuela refined here; tourism is important
language Dutch (official), Papiamento, English
population (1983) 193,000.

nettle any plant of the genus *Urtica*, family Urticaceae. Stinging hairs on the generally ovate leaves can penetrate the skin, causing inflammation. The common nettle *U. dioica* grows on waste ground in Europe and North America, where it was introduced.

network in computing, a method of connecting computers so that they can share data and *peripheral devices, such as printers. The main types are classified by the pattern of the connections – star or ring network, for example – or by the degree of geographical spread allowed; for example, local area networks (LANs) for communication within a room or building, and wide area networks (WANs) for more remote systems.

net worth the total *assets of a company less its total liabilities, equivalent to the interest of the ordinary shareholders in the company.

neuralgia sharp or burning pain originating in a nerve and spreading over its area of distribution. Trigeminal neuralgia, a common form, is a severe pain on one side of the face.

neural network artificial network of processors that attempts to mimic the structure of nerve cells (neurons) in the human brain. Neural networks may be electronic, optical, or simulated by computer software.

neurology the branch of medicine concerned with the study and treatment of the brain, spinal cord, and peripheral nerves.

neuron another name for a *nerve cell.

neurosis in psychology, a general term referring to emotional disorders, such as anxiety, depression, and obsessions. The main disturbance tends to be one of mood; contact with reality is relatively unaffected, in contrast to the effects of *psychosis.

neurotransmitter chemical that diffuses across a *synapse, and thus transmits impulses between *nerve cells, or between nerve cells and effector organs (for example, muscles). Common neurotransmitters are norepinephrine (which also acts as a hormone) and acetylcholine, the latter being most frequent at junctions between nerve and muscle. Nearly 50 different neurotransmitters have been identified.

neutrality the legal status of a country that decides not to choose sides in a war. Certain states, notably Switzerland and Austria, have opted for permanent neutrality. Neutrality always has a legal connotation. In peacetime, neutrality towards the big power alliances is called **nonalignment** (see *nonaligned movement).

neutralization in chemistry, a process occurring when the excess acid (or excess base) in a substance is reacted with added base (or added acid) so that the resulting substance is neither acidic nor basic.

neutrino in physics, any of three uncharged *elementary particles (and their antiparticles) of the *lepton class, having a mass too close to zero to be measured. The most familiar type, the antiparticle of the electron neutrino, is emitted in the beta decay of a nucleus. The other two are the muon and tau neutrinos.

neutron one of the three main subatomic particles, the others being the proton and the electron. The neutron is a composite particle, being made up of three quarks, and therefore belongs to the *baryon group of the *hadrons. Neutrons have about the same mass as protons but no electric charge, and occur in the nuclei of all atoms except hydrogen. They contribute to the mass of atoms but do not affect their chemistry.

neutron beam machine nuclear reactor or accelerator producing a stream of neutrons, which can 'see' through metals. It is used in industry to check molecular changes in metal under stress.

neutron bomb small hydrogen bomb for battlefield use that kills by radiation without destroying buildings and other structures. See *nuclear warfare.

neutron star very small, 'superdense' star composed mostly of *neutrons. They are thought to form when massive stars explode as *supernovae, during which the protons and electrons of the star's atoms merge, owing to intense gravitational collapse, to make neutrons. A neutron star may have the mass of up to three Suns, compressed into a globe only 20 km/12 mi in diameter.

Nevada state in W USA; nickname Silver State/Sagebrush State
area 286,400 sq km/110,550 sq mi
capital Carson City
towns Las Vegas, Reno
population (1990) 1,201,800
physical Mojave desert; lakes: Tahoe, Pyramid, Mead; mountains and plateaus alternating with valleys
products mercury, barite, gold
history explored by Kit Carson and John C Fre-

mont 1843–45; ceded to the USA after the Mexican War 1848; first permanent settlement a Mormon trading post 1848. Discovery of silver (the Comstock Lode) 1858 led to rapid population growth and statehood 1864. The building of the Hoover Dam in the 1930s provided the water and power needed for the growth of Las Vegas. In 1931 the state created two industries: divorce (Reno) and gambling (Las Vegas). Oil was discovered 1954, but gold exceeds all other mineral production. Tourism and gambling now generate more than half of the state's income.

new age movement of the late 1980s characterized by an emphasis on the holistic view of body and mind, alternative (or complementary) medicines, personal growth therapies, and a loose mix of theosophy, ecology, oriental mysticism, and a belief in the dawning of an astrological age of peace and harmony.

New Brunswick maritime province of E Canada
area 73,400 sq km/28,332 sq mi
capital Fredericton
towns St John, Moncton
products cereals, wood, paper, fish, lead, zinc, copper, oil, natural gas
population (1991) 725,600; 37% French-speaking
history first reached by Europeans (Cartier) 1534; explored by Champlain 1604; remained a French colony as part of Nova Scotia until ceded to England 1713. After the American Revolution many United Empire Loyalists settled there, and it became a province of the Dominion of Canada 1867.

New Caledonia island group in the S Pacific, a French overseas territory between Australia and the Fiji Islands
area 18,576 sq km/7,170 sq mi
capital Nouméa
physical fertile, surrounded by a barrier reef
products nickel (the world's third largest producer), chrome, iron
currency CFP franc
population (1983) 145,300, 43% Kanak (Melanesian), 37% European, 8% Wallisian, 5% Vietnamese and Indonesian, 4% Polynesian
language French (official)
religion Roman Catholic 60%, Protestant 30%
history New Caledonia was visited by Captain Cook 1774 and became French 1853. A general strike to gain local control of nickel mines 1974 was defeated. In 1981 the French socialist government promised moves towards independence. The 1985 elections resulted in control of most regions by Kanaks, but not the majority of seats. In 1986 the French conservative government reversed the reforms. The Kanaks boycotted a referendum Sept 1987 and a majority were in favour of remaining a French dependency. In 1989 the leader of the Socialist National Liberation front (the most prominent separatist group), Jean-Marie Tjibaou, was murdered.

Newcastle Thomas Pelham-Holles, Duke of Newcastle 1693–1768. British Whig politician, prime minster 1754–56 and 1757–62. He served as secretary of state for thirty years from 1724, then succeeded his younger brother Henry *Pelham as prime minister 1754. In 1756 he resigned as a result of setbacks in the Seven

Years' War, but returned to office 1757 with *Pitt the Elder (1st Earl of Chatham) taking responsibility for the conduct of the war.

Newcastle-upon-Tyne industrial port (coal, shipbuilding, marine and electrical engineering, chemicals, metals), commercial and cultural centre, in Tyne and Wear, NE England, administrative headquarters of Tyne and Wear and Northumberland; population (1991 est) 263,000.

New Deal in US history, programme introduced by President F D Roosevelt 1933 to counter the depression of 1929, including employment on public works, farm loans at low rates, and social reforms such as old-age and unemployment insurance, prevention of child labour, protection of employees against unfair practices by employers, and loans to local authorities for slum clearance.

New Delhi city in the Union Territory of Delhi, capital of India since 1912; population (1991) 294,100. The city was designed by British architect Edwin Lutyens.

New Democratic Party (NDP) Canadian political party, moderately socialist, formed 1961 by a merger of the Labour Congress and the Cooperative Commonwealth Federation.

New Economic Policy (NEP) economic policy of the USSR 1921–29 devised by the Soviet leader Lenin. Rather than requisitioning all agricultural produce above a stated subsistence allowance, the state requisitioned only a fixed proportion of the surplus; the rest could be traded freely by the peasant. The NEP thus reinstated a limited form of free-market trading, although the state retained complete control of major industries.

New England region of NE USA, comprising the states of Maine, New Hampshire, Vermont, Massachusetts, Rhode Island, and Connecticut. It is a geographic region rather than a political entity, with an area of 172,681 sq km/66,672 sq mi. Boston is the principal urban centre of the region, and Harvard and Yale its major universities.

Newfoundland breed of dog, said to have originated in Newfoundland. Males can grow to 70 cm/2.3 ft tall, and weigh 65 kg/145 lb; the females are slightly smaller. They have an oily, water-repellent undercoat and are excellent swimmers. Gentle in temperament, their fur is dense, flat, and usually dull black. Newfoundlands that are black and white or brown and white are called *Landseers*.

Newfoundland and Labrador Canadian province on the Atlantic Ocean
area 405,700 sq km/156,600 sq mi
capital St John's
towns Corner Brook, Gander
physical Newfoundland island and *Labrador on the mainland on the other side of the Straits of Belle Isle; rocky
products newsprint, fish products, hydroelectric power, iron, copper, zinc, uranium, offshore oil
population (1991) 571,600
history colonized by Vikings about AD 1000; Newfoundland reached by the English, under the Italian navigator Giovanni *Caboto, 1497. It was the first English colony, established 1583. French settlements made; British sovereignty was not recognized until 1713, although France retained

the offshore islands of St Pierre and Miquelon. Internal self-government was achieved 1855. In 1934, as Newfoundland had fallen into financial difficulties, administration was vested in a governor and a special commission. A 1948 referendum favoured federation with Canada and the province joined Canada 1949.

New Guinea island in the SW Pacific, N of Australia, comprising Papua New Guinea and the Indonesian province of West Irian (Irian Jaya area); total area about 885,780 sq km/342,000 sq mi. Part of the Dutch East Indies from 1828, West Irian was ceded by the United Nations to Indonesia 1963.

New Hampshire state in NE USA; nickname Granite State
area 24,000 sq km/9,264 sq mi
capital Concord
towns Manchester, Nashua
population (1990) 1,109,200 River forms boundary with Vermont; earliest presidential-election party primaries every four years; no state income tax or sales tax; ski and tourist resorts
products dairy, poultry, fruits and vegetables; electrical and other machinery; pulp and paper
famous people Mary Baker Eddy, Robert Frost
history settled as a fishing colony near Rye and Dover 1623; separated from Massachusetts colony 1679. As leaders in the Revolutionary cause, its leaders received the honour of being the first to declare independence of Britain on 4 July 1776. It became a state 1788, one of the original 13 states.

New Hebrides former name (until 1980) of *Vanuatu.

Ne Win adopted name of Maung Shu Maung 1911– . Myanmar (Burmese) politician, prime minister 1958–60, ruler from 1962 to 1974, president 1984–81, and chair until 1988 of the ruling Burma Socialist Programme Party (BSPP). His domestic 'Burmese Way to Socialism' policy programme brought the economy into serious decline.

New Jersey state in NE USA; nickname Garden State
area 20,200 sq km/7,797 sq mi
capital Trenton
towns Newark, Jersey City, Paterson, Elizabeth
population (1985) 7,562,000
products fruits and vegetables, fish and shellfish, chemicals, pharmaceuticals, soaps and cleansers, transport equipment, petroleum refining
famous people Stephen Crane, Thomas Edison, Thomas Paine, Paul Robeson, Frank Sinatra, Bruce Springsteen, Woodrow Wilson
history colonized in the 17th century by the Dutch (New Netherlands); ceded to England 1664; became a state 1787. It was one of the original 13 states.

Newlands John Alexander Reina 1838–1898. English chemist who worked as an industrial chemist; he prepared in 1863 the first *periodic table of the elements arranged in order of atomic weights (relative atomic masses), and pointed out the 'Law of Octaves' whereby every eighth element has similar properties. He was ridiculed at the time, but five years later Russian chemist Dmitri Mendeleyev published a more developed form of the table, also based on atomic masses, which forms the basis of the one used today (arranged by atomic number).

newly industrialized country (NIC) country that has in recent decades experienced a breakthrough into manufacturing and rapid export-led economic growth. The prime examples are Taiwan, Hong Kong, Singapore, and South Korea. Their economic development during the 1970s and 1980s was partly due to a rapid increase of manufactured goods in their exports.

Newman Barnett 1905–1970. US painter, sculptor, and theorist. His paintings are solid-coloured canvases with a few sparse vertical stripes. They represent a mystical pursuit of simple or elemental art. His sculptures, such as *Broken Obelisk* 1963–67, consist of geometric shapes on top of each other.

Newman John Henry 1801–1890. English Roman Catholic theologian. While still an Anglican, he wrote a series of *Tracts for the Times*, which gave their name to the Tractarian Movement (subsequently called the *Oxford Movement) for the revival of Catholicism. He became a Catholic 1845 and was made a cardinal 1879. In 1864 his autobiography, *Apologia pro vita sua*, was published.

Newman Paul 1925– . US actor and director, Hollywood's leading male star of the 1960s and 1970s. His films include *Somebody Up There Likes Me* 1956, *Cat on a Hot Tin Roof* 1958, *The Hustler* 1961, *Sweet Bird of Youth* 1962, *Hud* 1963, *Cool Hand Luke* 1967, *Butch Cassidy and the Sundance Kid* 1969, *The Sting* 1973, *The Verdict* 1983, *The Color of Money* 1986 (for which he won an Academy Award), *Mr and Mrs Bridge* 1991, and *The Hudsucker Proxy* 1994.

New Mexico state in SW USA; nickname Land of Enchantment
area 315,000 sq km/121,590 sq mi
capital Santa Fe
towns Albuquerque, Las Cruces, Roswell
population (1990) 1,515,000
physical more than 75% of the area lies over 3,900 ft/1,200 m above sea level; plains, mountains, caverns
products uranium, potash, copper, oil, natural gas, petroleum and coal products; sheep farming; cotton; pecans; vegetables
famous people Billy the Kid, Kit Carson, Georgia O'Keeffe
history explored by Francisco de Coronado for Spain 1540–42; Spanish settlement 1598 on the Rio Grande; Santa Fe founded 1610; most of New Mexico ceded to the USA by Mexico 1848; became a state 1912. The first atomic bomb, a test device, was exploded in the desert near Alamogordo 16 July 1945. Oil and gas development and tourism now contribute greatly to the state economy.

New Model Army army created 1645 by Oliver Cromwell to support the cause of Parliament during the English *Civil War. It was characterized by organization and discipline. Thomas Fairfax was its first commander.

New Orleans commercial and industrial city (banking, oil refining, rockets) and Mississippi river port in Louisiana, USA; population (1990) 496,900. It is the traditional birthplace of jazz.

news agency business handling news stories and photographs that are then sold to newspapers and magazines. International agencies include the Associated Press (AP, 1848), Agence France-Presse (AFP, 1944), United Press International (UPI, 1907), and *Reuters.

New Socialist Destour Party former name (1988–89) of Tunisian political party *Democratic Constitutional Rally (RCD).

New South Wales state of SE Australia
area 801,600 sq km/309,418 sq mi
capital Sydney
towns Newcastle, Wollongong, Broken Hill
physical Great Dividing Range (including Blue Mountains) and part of the Australian Alps (including Snowy Mountains and Mount Kosciusko); Riverina district, irrigated by the Murray-Darling-Murrumbidgee river system
products cereals, fruit, sugar, tobacco, wool, meat, hides and skins, gold, silver, copper, tin, zinc, coal; hydroelectric power from the Snowy River
population (1987) 5,570,000; 60% in Sydney
history called New Wales by James *Cook, who landed at Botany Bay 1770 and thought that the coastline resembled that of Wales. It was a convict settlement 1788–1850; opened to free settlement by 1819; achieved self-government 1856; became a state of the Commonwealth of Australia 1901. Since 1973 there has been decentralization to counteract the pull of Sydney, and the New England and Riverina districts have separatist movements.

newspaper daily or weekly publication in the form of folded sheets containing news and comment. News-sheets became commercial undertakings after the invention of printing and were introduced 1609 in Germany, 1616 in the Netherlands. In 1622 the first newspaper appeared in English, the *Weekly News*, edited by Nicholas Bourne and Thomas Archer. Improved *printing (steam printing 1814, the rotary press 1846 USA and 1857 UK), newsprint (paper made from woodpulp, used in the UK from the 1880s), and a higher literacy rate led to the growth of newspapers. In recent years, production costs have fallen with the introduction of new technology. The oldest national newspaper in the UK is *The Observer* 1791; the highest circulation UK newspaper is the Sunday *News of the World* (nearly 5 million copies weekly).

newt The crested newt, shown here, develops a crest of skin along the back in the spring mating season.

newt small salamander, of the family Salamandridae, found in Eurasia, NW Africa, and North America. The European newts, such as the smooth newt *Triturus vulgaris*, live on land for part of the year but enter a pond or lake to breed in the spring.

New Testament the second part of the **Bible*, recognized by the Christian church from the 4th century as sacred doctrine. The New Testament includes the Gospels, which tell of the life and teachings of Jesus, the history of the early church, the teachings of St Paul, and mystical writings. It was written in Greek during the 1st and 2nd centuries AD, and the individual sections have been ascribed to various authors by Biblical scholars.

newton SI unit (symbol N) of *force. One newton is the force needed to accelerate an object with mass of one kilogram by one metre per second per second. To accelerate a car weighing 1,000 kg/2,200 lb from 0 to 60 mph in 30 seconds would take about 2.5×10^5 N.

Newton Isaac 1642–1727. English physicist and mathematician who laid the foundations of physics as a modern discipline. He discovered the law of gravity, created calculus, discovered that white light is composed of many colours, and developed the three standard laws of motion still in use today. During 1665–66, he discovered the binomial theorem, and differential and integral calculus, and also began to investigate the phenomenon of gravitation. In 1685, he expounded his universal law of gravitation. His *Philosophiae naturalis principia mathematica*, usually referred to as *Principia*, was published in 1687, with the aid of Edmund *Halley.

Newton's laws of motion in physics, three laws that form the basis of Newtonian mechanics. (1) Unless acted upon by a net force, a body at rest stays at rest, and a moving body continues moving at the same speed in the same straight line. (2) A net force applied to a body gives it a rate of change of *momentum proportional to the force and in the direction of the force. (3) When a body A exerts a force on a body B, B exerts an equal and opposite force on A; that is, to every action there is an equal and opposite reaction.

Newton's rings in optics, an *interference phenomenon seen (using white light) as concentric rings of spectral colours where light passes through a thin film of transparent medium, such as the wedge of air between a large-radius convex lens and a flat glass plate. With monochromatic light (light of a single wavelength), the rings take the form of alternate light and dark bands. They are caused by interference (interaction) between light rays reflected from the plate and those reflected from the curved surface of the lens.

New Wave in pop music, a style that evolved parallel to punk in the second half of the 1970s. It shared the urban aggressive spirit of punk but was musically and lyrically more sophisticated; examples are the early work of Elvis Costello and Talking Heads.

New Wave (French *nouvelle vague*) French literary movement of the 1950s, a cross-fertilization of the novel, especially the **nouveau roman* (Marguerite Duras, Alain Robbe-Grillet, Nathalie Sarraute), and film (directors Jean-Luc Godard, Alain Resnais, and François Truffaut).

New World the Americas, so called by the first Europeans who reached them. The term also describes animals and plants of the western hemisphere.

New York largest city in the USA, industrial port (printing, publishing, clothing), cultural, financial, and commercial centre, in S New York State, at the junction of the Hudson and East rivers and including New York Bay. It comprises the boroughs of the Bronx, Brooklyn, Manhattan, Queens, and Staten Island; population (1990 census) 7,322,500, white 43.2%, black 25.2%, Hispanic 24.4%. New York is also known as the Big Apple.

New York state in NE USA; nickname Empire State/Excelsior State
area 127,200 sq km/49,099 sq mi
capital Albany
towns New York, Buffalo, Rochester, Yonkers, Syracuse
population (1990) 17,990,400
physical mountains: Adirondacks, Catskills; lakes: Champlain, Placid, Erie, Ontario; rivers: Mohawk, Hudson, St Lawrence (with Thousand Islands); Niagara Falls; Long Island; New York Bay.

New Zealand Dominion of

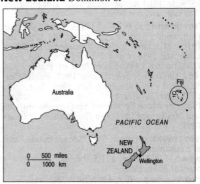

area 268,680 sq km/103,777 sq mi
capital and port Wellington
towns Hamilton, Palmerston North, Christchurch, Dunedin; port Auckland
physical comprises North Island, South Island, Stewart Island, Chatham Islands, and minor islands; mainly mountainous
overseas territories Tokelau (three atolls transferred 1926 from former Gilbert and Ellice Islands colony); Niue Island (one of the Cook Islands, separately administered from 1903: chief town Alafi); Cook Islands are internally self-governing but share common citizenship with New Zealand; Ross Dependency in Antarctica Waikato River; Kaingaroa state forest. On South Island are the Southern Alps and Canterbury Plains
head of state Elizabeth II from 1952 represented by governor general (Catherine Tizard from 1990)
head of government Jim Bolger from 1990
political system constitutional monarchy
exports lamb, beef, wool, leather, dairy products, processed foods, kiwi fruit; seeds and breeding stock; timber, paper, pulp, light aircraft
currency New Zealand dollar
population (1993 est) 3,490,000 (European

(mostly British) 87%; Polynesian (mostly Maori) 12%); growth rate 0.9% p.a.
languages English (official), Maori
religion Protestant 50%, Roman Catholic 15%
GNP $12,140 per head (1991)
chronology
1840 New Zealand became a British colony.
1907 Created a dominion of the British Empire.
1931 Granted independence from Britain.
1947 Independence within the Commonwealth confirmed by the New Zealand parliament.
1972 National Party government replaced by Labour Party, with Norman Kirk as prime minister.
1974 Kirk died; replaced by Wallace Rowling.
1975 National Party returned, with Robert Muldoon as prime minister.
1984 Labour Party returned under David Lange.
1985 Non-nuclear military policy created disagreements with France and the USA.
1987 National Party declared support for the Labour government's non-nuclear policy. Lange re-elected. New Zealand officially classified as a 'friendly' rather than 'allied' country by the USA because of its non-nuclear military policy.
1988 Free-trade agreement with Australia signed.
1989 Lange resigned over economic differences with finance minister (he cited health reasons); replaced by Geoffrey Palmer.
1990 Palmer replaced by Mike Moore. Labour Party defeated by National Party in general election; Jim Bolger became prime minister.
1991 Formation of amalgamated Alliance Party set to challenge two-party system.
1992 Ban on visits by US warships lifted. Constitutional voting change agreed.
1994 NP formed alliance with Labour.

Ney Michael, Duke of Elchingen, Prince of Ney 1769–1815. Marshal of France under *Napoleon I, who commanded the rearguard of the French army during the retreat from Moscow, and for his personal courage was called 'the bravest of the brave'. When Napoleon returned from Elba, Ney was sent to arrest him, but instead deserted to him and fought at Waterloo. He was subsequently shot for treason.

Ngorongoro Crater crater in the Tanzanian section of the African Great *Rift Valley notable for its large numbers of wildebeest, gazelle, and zebra.

Ngugi wa Thiong'o 1938– . Kenyan writer of essays, plays, short stories, and novels. He was imprisoned after the performance of the play *Ngaahika Ndeenda/I Will Marry When I Want* 1977 and lived in exile from 1982. His novels, written in English and Gikuyu, include *The River Between* 1965, *Petals of Blood* 1977, and *Caitaani Mutharaba-ini/Devil on the Cross* 1982, and deal with colonial and post-independence oppression.

NHS abbreviation for ***National Health Service***, the UK state-financed *health service.

niacin one of the 'B group' *vitamins, deficiency of which gives rise to pellagra, a disease that causes digestive disorders, skin eruptions, and mental disturbances.

Niagara Falls two waterfalls on the Niagara River, on the Canada–USA border, between lakes Erie and Ontario and separated by Goat Island.

The ***American Falls*** are 51 m/167 ft high, 330 m/1,080 ft wide; ***Horseshoe Falls***, in Canada, are 49 m/160 ft high, 790 m/2,600 ft across.

Niamey river port and capital of *Niger; population (1983) 399,000. It produces textiles, chemicals, pharmaceuticals, and foodstuffs.

Nibelungenlied *Song of the Nibelungs*, anonymous 12th-century German epic poem, derived from older sources. The composer Richard *Wagner made use of the legends in his *Ring* cycle.

Nicaea, Council of Christian church council held in Nicaea (now Iznik, Turkey) in 325, called by the Roman emperor Constantine. It condemned *Arianism as heretical and upheld the doctrine of the Trinity in the Nicene *Creed.

Nicaragua Republic of (*República de Nicaragua*)

area 127,849 sq km/49,363 sq mi
capital Managua
towns León, Granada; chief ports Corinto, Puerto Cabezas, El Bluff
physical narrow Pacific coastal plain separated from broad Atlantic coastal plain by volcanic mountains and lakes Managua and Nicaragua
head of state and government Violeta Barrios de Chamorro from 1990
political system emergent democracy
exports coffee, cotton, sugar, bananas, meat
currency cordoba
population (1993 est) 4,200,000 (mestizo 70%, Spanish descent 15%, Indian or black 10%); growth rate 3.3% p.a.
languages Spanish (official), Indian, English
religion Roman Catholic 95%
GNP $340 per head (1991)
chronology
1838 Independence achieved from Spain.
1926–1933 Occupied by US marines.
1936 General Anastasio Somoza elected president; start of near-dictatorial rule by Somoza family.
1962 Sandinista National Liberation Front (FSLN) formed to fight Somoza regime.
1979 Somoza government ousted by FSLN.
1982 Subversive activity against the government by right-wing Contra guerrillas promoted by the USA. State of emergency declared.
1984 The USA mined Nicaraguan harbours.

1985 Denunciation of Sandinista government by US president Ronald Reagan. FSLN won assembly elections.

1989 Demobilization of rebels and release of former Somoza supporters; cease-fire ended.

1990 FSLN defeated by UNO, a US-backed coalition; Violeta Barrios de Chamorro elected president. Antigovernment riots.

1991 First presidential state visit to USA for over fifty years.

1992 June: US aid suspended because of concern over role of Sandinistas in Nicaraguan government. 16,000 made homeless by earthquake.

1993 State of emergency declared in N Nicaragua following skirmishes between rival Contra and Sandinista rebel groups.

1994 Peace accord with remaining Contra rebels.

Nicaraguan Revolution the revolt 1978–79 in Nicaragua, led by the socialist *Sandinistas* against the US-supported right-wing dictatorship established by Anastasio *Somoza. His son, President Anastasio (Debayle) Somoza (1925–1980), was forced into exile 1979 and assassinated in Paraguay. The Sandinista National Liberation Front (FSLN) was named after Augusto César Sandino, a guerrilla leader killed by the US-trained National Guard 1934.

Nice city on the French Riviera; population (1982) 449,500. Founded in the 3rd century BC, it repeatedly changed hands between France and the Duchy of Savoy from the 14th to the 19th century. In 1860 it was finally transferred to France.

Nicene Creed a fundamental *creed of Christianity, promulgated by the Council of *Nicaea 325.

niche in ecology, the 'place' occupied by a species in its habitat, including all chemical, physical, and biological components, such as what it eats, the time of day at which the species feeds, temperature, moisture, the parts of the habitat that it uses (for example, trees or open grassland), the way it reproduces, etc.

Nichiren 1222–1282. Japanese Buddhist monk, founder of the sect that bears his name. The sect bases its beliefs on the *Lotus Sūtra*, which Nichiren held to be the only true revelation of the teachings of Buddha, and stresses the need for personal effort to attain enlightenment.

Nicholas two tsars of Russia:

Nicholas I 1796–1855. Tsar of Russia from 1825. His Balkan ambitions led to war with Turkey 1827–29 and the Crimean War 1853–56.

Nicholas II 1868–1918. Tsar of Russia 1894–1917. He was dominated by his wife, Tsarina *Alexandra, who was under the influence of the religious charlatan *Rasputin. His mismanagement of the Russo-Japanese War and of internal affairs led to the revolution of 1905, which he suppressed, although he was forced to grant limited constitutional reforms. He took Russia into World War I in 1914, was forced to abdicate in 1917 after the *Russian Revolution and was executed with his family.

Nicholas, St also known as *Santa Claus* 4th century AD. In the Christian church, patron saint of Russia, children, merchants, sailors, and pawnbrokers; bishop of Myra (now in Turkey). His legendary gifts of dowries to poor girls led to the custom of giving gifts to children on the eve of his feast day, 6 Dec, still retained in some countries, such as the Netherlands; elsewhere the custom has been transferred to Christmas Day. His emblem is three balls.

Nicholson Ben 1894–1982. English abstract artist. After early experiments influenced by Cubism and de Stijl (see *Mondrian), Nicholson developed a style of geometrical reliefs, notably a series of white reliefs (from 1933).

Nicholson Jack 1937– . US film actor who, in the late 1960s, captured the mood of nonconformist, uncertain young Americans in such films as *Easy Rider* 1969 and *Five Easy Pieces* 1970. He subsequently became a mainstream Hollywood star, appearing in *Chinatown* 1974, *One Flew over the Cuckoo's Nest* (Academy Award) 1975, *The Shining* 1979, *Terms of Endearment* (Academy Award) 1983, and *Batman* 1989.

nickel hard, malleable and ductile, silver-white metallic element, symbol Ni, atomic number 28, relative atomic mass 58.71. It occurs in igneous rocks and as a free metal (*native metal), occasionally occurring in fragments of iron-nickel meteorites. It is a component of the Earth's core, which is held to consist principally of iron with some nickel. It has a high melting point, low electrical and thermal conductivity, and can be magnetized. It does not tarnish and therefore is much used for alloys, electroplating, and for coinage.

Nicklaus Jack (William) 1940– . US golfer, nicknamed 'the Golden Bear'. He won a record 20 major titles, including 18 professional majors between 1962 and 1986.

Nicobar Islands group of Indian islands, part of the Union Territory of *Andaman and Nicobar Islands.

Nicolle Charles 1866–1936. French bacteriologist whose discovery in 1909 that typhus is transmitted by the body louse made the armies of World War I introduce delousing as a compulsory part of the military routine. Nobel Prize for Medicine 1928.

Nicosia capital of Cyprus, with leather, textile, and pottery industries; population (1987) 165,000. Nicosia was the residence of Lusignan kings of Cyprus 1192–1475. The Venetians, who took Cyprus 1489, surrounded Nicosia with a high wall, which still exists; the city fell to the Turks 1571. It was again partly taken by the Turks in the invasion 1974.

nicotine $C_{10}H_{14}N_2$ *alkaloid (nitrogenous compound) obtained from the dried leaves of the tobacco plant *Nicotiana tabacum* and used as an insecticide. A colourless oil, soluble in water, it turns brown on exposure to the air.

Nielsen Carl (August) 1865–1931. Danish composer. His works combine an outward formal strictness with an inner waywardness of tonality and structure. They include the Neo-Classical opera *Maskarade/Masquerade* 1906, a *Wind Quintet* 1922, six programmatic symphonies, numerous songs, and incidental music on Danish texts.

Niemeyer Oscar 1907– . Brazilian architect. He was joint designer of the United Nations headquarters in New York 1947 and from 1957 architect of many public buildings in the capital,

Brasília. His idiosyncratic interpretation of the Modernist idiom uses symbolic form to express the function of a building; for example, the Catholic Cathedral in Brasília.

Nietzsche Friedrich Wilhelm 1844–1900. German philosopher who rejected the accepted absolute moral values and the 'slave morality' of Christianity. He argued that 'God is dead' and therefore people were free to create their own values. His ideal was the *Übermensch*, or 'Superman', who would impose his will on the weak and worthless. Nietzsche claimed that knowledge is never objective but always serves some interest or unconscious purpose.

Niger third-longest river in Africa, 4,185 km/2,600 mi. It rises in the highlands bordering Sierra Leone and Guinea, flows NE through Mali, then SE through Niger and Nigeria to an inland delta on the Gulf of Guinea. Its flow has been badly affected by the expansion of the Sahara Desert. It is sluggish and frequently floods its banks. It was explored by the Scotsman Mungo Park 1795–96.

Niger Republic of (*République du Niger*)
area 1,186,408 sq km/457,953 sq mi
capital Niamey
towns Zinder, Maradi, Tahoua
physical desert plains between hills in N and savanna in S; river Niger in SW, Lake Chad in SE
head of state Mahamane Ousmane from 1993
head of government Mahamdou Issaufou from 1993
political system military republic
exports peanuts, livestock, gum arabic, uranium
currency franc CFA
population (1993) 8,500,000; growth rate 2.8% p.a.
languages French (official), Hausa, Djerma, and other minority languages
religions Sunni Muslim 85%, animist 15%
GNP $300 per head (1991)
chronology
1960 Achieved full independence from France; Hamani Diori elected president.
1974 Diori ousted in army coup led by Seyni Kountché.
1977 Cooperation agreement signed with France.
1987 Kountché died; replaced by Col Ali Saibu.
1989 Ali Saibu elected president without opposition.
1991 Saibu stripped of executive powers; transitional government formed.
1992 Transitional government collapsed. Referendum endorsed the adoption of multiparty politics.
1993 Mamahame Ousmane elected president in multiparty elections.

Niger-Congo languages the largest group of languages in Africa. It includes about 1,000 languages and covers a vast area south of the Sahara desert, from the W coast to the E, and down the E coast as far as South Africa. It is divided into groups and subgroups; the most widely spoken Niger-Congo languages are Swahili (spoken on the E coast), the members of the Bantu group (southern Africa), and Yoruba (Nigeria).

Nigeria Federal Republic of
area 923,773 sq km/356,576 sq mi
capital Abuja

towns Ibadan, Ogbomosho, Kano; ports Lagos, Port Harcourt, Warri, Calabar
physical arid savanna in N; tropical rainforest in S, with mangrove swamps along the coast; river Niger forms wide delta; mountains in SE
head of state and government General Sani Abacha from 1993
political system military republic
exports petroleum (largest oil resources in Africa), cocoa, peanuts, palm oil (Africa's largest producer), cotton, rubber, tin
currency naira
population (1993) 92,800 (Yoruba in W, Ibo in E, and Hausa-Fulani in N); growth rate 3.3% p.a.
languages English (official), Hausa, Ibo, Yoruba
religions Sunni Muslim 50% (in N), Christian 40% (in S), local religions 10%
GNP $290 per head (1991)
chronology
1914 N Nigeria and S Nigeria united to become Britain's largest African colony.
1954 Nigeria became a federation.
1960 Independence achieved from Britain within the Commonwealth.
1963 Became a republic, with Nnamdi Azikiwe as president.
1966 Military coup, followed by a counter-coup led by General Yakubu Gowon. Slaughter of many members of the Ibo tribe in north.
1967 Conflict over oil revenues led to declaration of an independent Ibo state of Biafra and outbreak of civil war.
1970 Surrender of Biafra and end of civil war.
1975 Gowon ousted in military coup; second coup put General Olusegun Obasanjo in power.
1979 Shehu Shagari became civilian president.
1983 Shagari's government overthrown in coup led by Maj-Gen Muhammadu Buhari.
1985 Buhari replaced in a bloodless coup led by Maj-General Ibrahim Babangida.
1989 Two new political parties approved. Babangida promised a return to pluralist politics; date set for 1992.
1991 Nine new states created. Babangida confirmed his commitment to democratic rule for 1992.
1992 Multiparty elections won by Babangida's Social Democratic Party.
1993 Results of presidential elections suspended by national commission, following complaints of ballot rigging. Aug: Babangida resigned, nominating Ernest Shonekan as interim prime minister.

General Sani Abacha took control, restoring military rule and dissolving political parties.

nightingale songbird of the thrush family with a song of great beauty, heard at night as well as by day. About 16.5 cm/6.5 in long, it is dull brown, lighter below, with a reddish-brown tail. It migrates to Europe and winters in Africa.

Nightingale Florence 1820–1910. English nurse, the founder of nursing as a profession. She took a team of nurses to Scutari (now Üsküdar, Turkey) in 1854 and reduced the *Crimean War hospital death rate from 42% to 2%. In 1856 she founded the Nightingale School and Home for Nurses in London.

nightjar any of about 65 species of night-hunting birds forming the family Caprimulgidae. They have wide, bristly mouths for catching flying insects. Their distinctive calls have earned them such names as whippoorwill and church-will's-widow. Some are called nighthawks.

Night Journey or **al-Miraj** (Arabic 'the ascent') in Islam, the journey of the prophet Muhammad, guided by the archangel Gabriel, from Mecca to Jerusalem, where he met the earlier prophets, including Adam, Moses, and Jesus; he then ascended to paradise, where he experienced the majesty of Allah, and was also shown hell.

nightshade any of several plants in the family Solanaceae, which includes the black nightshade *Solanum nigrum*, bittersweet or woody nightshade *S. dulcamara*, and deadly nightshade or *belladonna.

nihilism the rejection of all traditional values, authority, and institutions. The term was coined 1862 by Ivan Turgenev in his novel *Fathers and Sons*, and was adopted by the *Nihilists, the Russian radicals of the period. Despairing of reform, they saw change as possible only through the destruction of morality, justice, marriage, property, and the idea of God. Since then nihilism has come to mean a generally negative and destructive outlook.

Nijinsky Vaslav 1890–1950. Russian dancer and choreographer. Noted for his powerful but graceful technique, he was a legendary member of *Diaghilev's Ballets Russes, for whom he choreographed Debussy's *Prélude à l'après-midi d'un faune* 1912 and *Jeux* 1913, and Stravinsky's *Le Sacre du printemps/The Rite of Spring* 1913.

Nile river in Africa, the world's longest, 6,695 km/4,160 mi. The *Blue Nile* rises in Lake Tana, Ethiopia, the *White Nile* at Lake Victoria, and they join at Khartoum, Sudan. The river enters the Mediterranean Sea at a vast delta in N Egypt.

Nineteen Propositions demands presented by the English Parliament to Charles I 1642. They were designed to limit the powers of the crown, and their rejection represented the beginning of the Civil War.

Nineveh capital of the Assyrian Empire from the 8th century BC until its destruction by the Medes under King Cyaxares in 612 BC. It was situated on the river Tigris (opposite the present city of Mosul, Iraq) and was adorned with palaces.

Ningxia or **Ningxia Hui** autonomous region (formerly **Ninghsia-Hui**) of NW China

area 170,000 sq km/65,620 sq mi
capital Yinchuan
physical desert plateau
products cereals and rice under irrigation; coal
population (1990) 4,655,000

niobium soft, grey-white, somewhat ductile and malleable, metallic element, symbol Nb, atomic number 41, relative atomic mass 92.906. It occurs in nature with tantalum, which it resembles in chemical properties. It is used in making stainless steel and other alloys for jet engines and rockets and for making superconductor magnets.

nirvana in Buddhism, the attainment of perfect serenity by the eradication of all desires. To some Buddhists it means complete annihilation, to others it means the absorption of the self in the infinite.

Nirvana US rock group who popularized a hard-driving, dirty sound, a tuneful *grunge, exemplified by their second album, *Nevermind* 1991, and its hit single 'Smells Like Teen Spirit'. Vocalist and songwriter Kurt Cobain (1967–1994) committed suicide.

nitrate salt or ester of nitric acid, containing the NO_3^- ion. Nitrates are used in explosives, in the chemical and pharmaceutical industries, in curing meat (see *nitre), and as fertilizers. They are the most water-soluble salts known and play a major part in the nitrogen cycle. Nitrates in the soil, whether naturally occurring or from inorganic or organic fertilizers, can be used by plants to make proteins and nucleic acids.

nitre or **saltpetre** potassium nitrate, KNO_3, a mineral found on and just under the ground in desert regions; used in explosives. Nitre occurs in Bihar, India, Iran, and Cape Province, South Africa. The salt was formerly used for the manufacture of gunpowder, but the supply of nitre for explosives is today largely met by making the salt from nitratine (also called Chile saltpetre, $NaNO_3$). Saltpetre is a *preservative and is widely used for curing meats.

nitric acid or **aqua fortis** HNO_3 fuming acid obtained by the oxidation of ammonia or the action of sulphuric acid on potassium nitrate. It is a highly corrosive acid, dissolving most metals, and a strong oxidizing agent. It is used in the nitration and esterification of organic substances, and in the making of sulphuric acid, nitrates, explosives, plastics, and dyes.

nitrite salt or ester of nitrous acid, containing the nitrite ion (NO_2^-). Nitrites are used as preservatives (for example, to prevent the growth of botulism spores) and as colouring agents in cured meats such as bacon and sausages.

nitrogen colourless, odourless, tasteless, gaseous, nonmetallic element, symbol N, atomic number 7, relative atomic mass 14.0067. It forms almost 80% of the Earth's atmosphere by volume and is a constituent of all plant and animal tissues (in proteins and nucleic acids). Nitrogen is obtained for industrial use by the liquefaction and fractional distillation of air. Its compounds are used in the manufacture of foods, drugs, fertilizers, dyes, and explosives.

nitrogen cycle the process of nitrogen passing through the ecosystem. Nitrogen, in the form of inorganic compounds (such as nitrates) in the soil, is absorbed by plants and turned into organic compounds (such as proteins) in plant tissue. A proportion of this nitrogen is eaten by *herbivores, with some of this in turn being passed on to the carnivores, which feed on the herbivores. The nitrogen is ultimately returned to the soil as excrement and when organisms die and are converted back to inorganic form by *decomposers.

nitrogen fixation the process by which nitrogen in the atmosphere is converted into nitrogenous compounds by the action of microorganisms, such as cyanobacteria (see *blue-green algae) and bacteria, in conjunction with certain *legumes. Several chemical processes duplicate nitrogen fixation to produce fertilizers; see *nitrogen cycle.

nitrogen oxide any chemical compound that contains only nitrogen and oxygen. All nitrogen oxides are gases. Nitrogen monoxide and nitrogen dioxide contribute to air pollution. See also *nitrous oxide.

nitroglycerine $C_3H_5(ONO_2)_3$ flammable, explosive oil produced by the action of nitric and sulphuric acids on glycerol. Although poisonous, it is used in cardiac medicine. It explodes with great violence if heated in a confined space and is used in the preparation of dynamite, cordite, and other high explosives.

nitrous oxide or **dinitrogen oxide** N_2O colourless, nonflammable gas that, used in conjunction with oxygen, reduces sensitivity to pain. In higher doses it is an anaesthetic. Well tolerated, it is often combined with other anaesthetic gases to enble them to be used in lower doses. It may be self-administered; for example, in childbirth. It used to be known as 'laughing gas'.

Niven David 1909–1983. Scottish-born US film actor. In Hollywood from the 1930s, his films include *Wuthering Heights* 1939, *Around the World in 80 Days* 1956, *Separate Tables* 1958 (Academy Award), *The Guns of Navarone* 1961 and *The Pink Panther* 1964. He published two best-selling volumes of autobiography, *The Moon's a Balloon* 1972 and *Bring on the Empty Horses* 1975.

Nixon Richard (Milhous) 1913–1994. 37th president of the USA 1969–74, a Republican. He attracted attention as a member of the Un-American Activities Committee 1948, and was vice president to Eisenhower 1953–61. As president he was responsible for US withdrawal from Vietnam, and forged new links with China, but at home his culpability in the cover-up of the *Watergate scandal and the existence of a 'slush fund' for political machinations during his re-election campaign 1972 led to his resignation 1974 when threatened with *impeachment.

Nkomati Accord nonaggression treaty between South Africa and Mozambique concluded 1984, under which they agreed not to give material aid to opposition movements in each other's countries, which in effect meant that South Africa pledged itself not to support the Mozambique National Resistance (Renamo), while Mozambique was committed not to help the then outlawed African National Congress (ANC).

Nkomo Joshua 1917– . Zimbabwean politician, vice-president from 1988. As president of ZAPU (Zimbabwe African People's Union) from 1961, he was a leader of the black nationalist movement against the white Rhodesian regime. He was a member of Robert *Mugabe's cabinet 1980–82 and from 1987.

Nkrumah Kwame 1909–1972. Ghanaian nationalist politician, prime minister of the Gold Coast (Ghana's former name) 1952–57 and of newly independent Ghana 1957–60. He became Ghana's first president 1960 but was overthrown in a coup 1966. His 'African socialism' led to links with the communist bloc.

Nō or **Noh** classical, aristocratic Japanese drama which developed from the 14th to the 16th centuries and is still performed. There is a repertory of some 250 pieces, of which five, one from each of the several classes devoted to different subjects, may be put on in a performance lasting a whole day. Dance, mime, music, and chanting develop the mythical or historical themes. All the actors are men, some of whom wear masks and elaborate costumes; scenery is limited. Nō influenced *kabuki drama.

Noah in the Old Testament, the son of Lamech and father of Shem, Ham, and Japheth, who, according to God's instructions, built a ship, the ark, so that he and his family and specimens of all existing animals might survive the *Flood. There is also a Babylonian version of the tale, *The Epic of Gilgamesh*.

Nobel Alfred Bernhard 1833–1896. Swedish chemist and engineer. He invented *dynamite in 1867 and ballistite, a smokeless gunpowder, in 1889. He amassed a large fortune from the manufacture of explosives and the exploitation of the Baku oilfields in Azerbaijan, near the Caspian Sea. He left this fortune in trust for the endowment of five *Nobel prizes.

nobelium synthesized, radioactive, metallic element of the *actinide series, symbol No, atomic number 102, relative atomic mass 259. It is synthesized by bombarding curium with carbon nuclei.

Nobel prize annual international prize, first awarded 1901 under the will of Alfred Nobel, Swedish chemist, who invented dynamite. The interest on the Nobel endowment fund is divided annually among the persons who have made the greatest contributions in the fields of physics, chemistry, medicine, literature, and world peace.

noble gas alternative name for *inert gas.

nocturne in music, a lyrical, dreamy piece, often for piano, introduced by John Field (1782–1837) and adopted by Frédéric Chopin.

node in physics, a position in a *standing wave pattern at which there is no vibration. Points at which there is maximum vibration are called **antinodes**. Stretched strings, for example, can show nodes when they vibrate.

nodule in geology, a lump of mineral or other matter found within rocks or formed on the seabed surface; *mining technology is being developed to exploit them.

noise unwanted sound. Permanent, incurable loss of hearing can be caused by prolonged exposure to high noise levels (above 85 decibels). Over 55 decibels on a daily outdoor basis is regarded as an unacceptable level, to which an estimated 130 million people were exposed in 1991.

noise in pop music, a style that relies heavily on feedback, distortion, and dissonance. A loose term that came into use in the 1980s with the slogan 'noise annoys', it has been applied to *hardcore, industrial, and thrash metal bands, among others.

Nolan Sidney 1917–1992. Australian artist. He created atmospheric paintings of the outback, exploring themes from Australian history such as the life of the outlaw Ned Kelly and the folk heroine Mrs Fraser.

Noland Kenneth 1924– . US painter, associated with Abstract Expressionism. In the 1950s and early 1960s he painted targets, or concentric circles of colour, in a clean, hard-edged style on unprimed canvas. His work centred on geometry, colour, and symmetry. His later 1960s paintings experimented with the manipulation of colour vision and afterimages, pioneering the field of *Op art.

Nolde Emil. Adopted name of Emil Hansen 1867–1956. German Expressionist painter. Nolde studied in Paris and Dachau, joined the group of artists known as Die Brücke 1906–07, and visited Polynesia 1913; he then became almost a recluse in NE Germany. Many of his themes were religious.

nomadic pastoralism farming system where animals (cattle, goats, camels) are taken to different locations in order to find fresh pastures. It is practised in the developing world; for example, in central Asia and the Sahel region of W Africa. Increasing numbers of cattle may lead to overgrazing of the area and *desertification.

nominative in the grammar of some inflected languages – such as Latin, Russian, and Sanskrit – the form of a word used to indicate that a noun or pronoun is the subject of a finite verb.

Nomura Securities the world's largest financial institution, an investment house handling about 20% of all transactions on the Tokyo stock exchange. In 1991 Nomura admitted to paying Y16.5 billion in compensation to favoured clients (including companies in London and Hong Kong) for losses sustained on the stock market since the beginning of 1990, resulting in tax evasion of Y9 billion. It was also shown to have links with organized crime.

nonaligned movement countries adopting a strategic and political position of neutrality ('nonalignment') towards major powers, specifically the USA and former USSR. Although originally used by poorer states, the nonaligned position was later adopted by oil-producing nations. The 1989 summit in Belgrade was attended by 102 member states. With the ending of the Cold War, the movement's survival was in doubt.

Nonconformist in religion, originally a member of the Puritan section of the Church of England clergy who, in the Elizabethan age, refused to conform to certain practices, for example the wearing of the surplice and kneeling to receive Holy Communion.

Nonjuror any of the priests of the Church of England who, after the revolution of 1688, refused to take the oaths of allegiance to William and Mary. They continued to exist as a rival church for over a century, and consecrated their own bishops, the last of whom died 1805.

nonmetal one of a set of elements (around 20 in total) with certain physical and chemical properties opposite to those of metals. Nonmetals accept electrons (see *electronegativity) and are sometimes called electronegative elements.

Nono Luigi 1924–1990. Italian composer. His early vocal compositions have something of the spatial character of the works of Giovanni Gabrieli (*c.* 1555–1612), for example *Il Canto Sospeso* 1955–56. After the opera *Intolleranza* 1960 his style moved away from *serialism to become increasingly expressionistic. His music is frequently polemical in subject matter, and a number of works incorporate tape-recorded elements.

nonrenewable resource natural resource, such as coal or oil, that takes thousands or millions of years to form naturally and can therefore not be replaced once it is consumed. The main energy sources used by humans are nonrenewable; *renewable sources, such as solar, tidal, and geothermal power, have so far been less exploited.

non sequitur (Latin 'it does not follow') statement that has little or no relevance to the one that preceded it.

nonvolatile memory in computing, *memory that does not lose its contents when the power supply to the computer is disconnected.

noradrenaline in the body, a chemical that acts directly on specific receptors to stimulate the sympathetic nervous system. Released by nerve stimulation or by drugs, it causes an increase in blood pressure mainly by constricting arterioles (small, thin-walled divisions of arteries) and so raising total peripheral resistance. It is used therapeutically to treat septic shock.

Nordenskjöld Nils Adolf Erik 1832–1901. Swedish explorer. He made voyages to the Arctic with the geologist Torell and in 1878–79 discovered the Northeast Passage. He published the results of his voyages in a series of books, including *Voyage of the Vega round Asia and Europe* 1881.

Nordic ethnic designation for any of the various Germanic peoples, especially those of Scandinavia. The physical type of Caucasoid described under that term is tall, long-headed, blue-eyed, fair of skin and hair. The term is no longer in current scientific use.

Nord-Pas-de-Calais region of N France; area 12,400 sq km/4,786 sq mi; population (1986) 3,923,000. Its capital is Lille, and it consists of the *départements* of Nord and Pas-de-Calais.

Norfolk county on the east coast of England
area 5,360 sq km/2,069 sq mi
towns Norwich (administrative headquarters), King's Lynn; resorts: Great Yarmouth, Cromer, Hunstanton
physical low-lying with the Fens in the W and the *Norfolk Broads in the E; rivers: Ouse, Yare, Bure, Waveney
products cereals, turnips, sugar beets, turkeys, geese, offshore natural gas
population (1991) 736,700
famous people Fanny Burney, Thomas Paine, Horatio Nelson, John Crome ('old Crome'), John Sell Cotman, Rider Haggard.

Norfolk Broads area of some 12 interlinked freshwater lakes in E England, created about 600 years ago by the digging-out of peat deposits; the lakes are used for boating and fishing.

Noriega Manuel (Antonio Morena) 1940– . Panamanian soldier and politician, effective ruler of Panama from 1982, as head of the National Guard, until deposed by the USA 1989. An informer for the US Central Intelligence Agency, he was known to be involved in drug trafficking as early as 1972. He enjoyed US support until 1987. In the 1989 US invasion of Panama, he was forcibly taken to the USA, tried, and convicted of trafficking in 1992.

Norman any of the descendants of the Norsemen (to whose chief, Rollo, Normandy was granted by Charles III of France 911) who adopted French language and culture. During the 11th and 12th centuries they conquered England 1066 (under William the Conqueror), Scotland 1072, parts of Wales and Ireland, S Italy, Sicily, and Malta, and took a prominent part in the Crusades.

Norman architecture English term for *Romanesque, the style of architecture used in England 11th–12th centuries. Norman buildings are massive, with round arches (although trefoil arches are sometimes used for small openings). Buttresses are of slight projection, and vaults are barrel-roofed. Examples in England include the Keep of the Tower of London and parts of the cathedrals of Chichester, Gloucester, and Ely.

Normandy two regions of NW France: *Haute-Normandie and *Basse-Normandie. It was named after the Viking Norsemen (Normans), the people who conquered and settled in the area in the 9th century. As a French duchy it reached its peak under William the Conqueror and was renowned for its centres of learning established by Lanfranc and St Anselm. Normandy was united with England 1100–35. England and France fought over it during the Hundred Years' War, England finally losing it 1449 to Charles VII. In World War II the Normandy beaches were the site of the Allied invasion on D-day, 6 June 1944.

Normandy landings alternative name for *D-Day.

Norman French the form of French used by the Normans in Normandy from the 10th century, and by the Norman ruling class in England after the Conquest 1066. It remained the language of the English court until the 15th century, the official language of the law courts until the 17th century, and is still used in the Channel Islands.

Norris Frank 1870–1902. US novelist. A naturalist writer, he wrote *McTeague* 1899, about a brutish San Francisco dentist and the love of gold. He completed only two parts of his projected trilogy, the *Epic of Wheat: The Octopus* 1901, dealing with the struggles between wheat farmers, and *The Pit* 1903, describing the Chicago wheat exchange.

Norseman early inhabitant of Norway. The term Norsemen is also applied to Scandinavian *Vikings who during the 8th–11th centuries raided and settled in Britain, Ireland, France, Russia, Iceland, and Greenland.

North Frederick, 8th Lord North 1732–1792. British Tory politician. He entered Parliament in 1754, became chancellor of the Exchequer in 1767, and was prime minister in a government of Tories and 'king's friends' from 1770. His hard line against the American colonies was supported by George III, but in 1782 he was forced to resign by the failure of his policy. In 1783 he returned to office in a coalition with Charles *Fox, and after its defeat retired from politics.

North Oliver 1943– . US Marine lieutenant colonel. In 1981 he was inducted into the National Security Council (NSC), where he supervised the mining of Nicaraguan harbours 1983, an air-force bombing raid on Libya 1986, and an arms-for-hostages deal with Iran 1985 which, when uncovered 1986 (*Irangate), forced his dismissal and trial.

North Thomas 1535–1601. English translator, whose version of *Plutarch's *Lives* 1579 was the source for Shakespeare's Roman plays.

North America third largest of the continents (including Greenland and Central America), and over twice the size of Europe
area 24,000,000 sq km/9,400,000 sq mi
largest cities (population over 1 million) Mexico City, New York, Chicago, Toronto, Los Angeles, Montreal, Guadalajara, Monterrey, Philadelphia, Houston, Guatemala City, Vancouver, Detroit, San Diego, Dallas
physical occupying the northern part of the landmass of the western hemisphere between the Arctic Ocean and the tropical SE tip of the isthmus that joins Central America to South America; the northernmost point on the mainland is the tip of Boothia Peninsula in the Canadian Arctic; the northernmost point on adjacent islands is Cape Morris Jesup on Greenland; the most westerly point on the mainland is Cape Prince of Wales, Alaska; the most westerly point on adjacent islands is Attu Island in the Aleutians; the most easterly point on the mainland lies on the SE coast of Labrador; the highest point is Mount McKinley, Alaska, 6,194 m/20,320 ft; the lowest point is Badwater in Death Valley –86 m/

–282 ft. In Canada and the USA, the Great Plains of the interior separate mountain belts to the east (Appalachians, Laurentian Highlands) and west (Rocky Mountains, Coast Mountains, Cascade Range, Sierra Nevada). The western range extends south into Mexico as the Sierra Madre. The Mississippi river system drains from the central Great Plains into the Gulf of Mexico; low coastal plains on the Atlantic coast are indented by the Gulf of St Lawrence, Bay of Fundy, Delaware Bay, Chesapeake Bay; the St Lawrence and Great Lakes form a rough crescent (with Lake Winnipeg, Lake Athabasca, the Great Bear, and the Great Slave lakes) around the exposed rock of the great Canadian/Laurentian shield, into which Hudson Bay breaks from the north; Greenland (the largest island in the world next to Australia) is a high, ice-covered plateau with a deeply indented coastline of fjords

products with abundant resources and an ever-expanding home market, the USA's fast-growing industrial and technological strength has made it less dependent on exports and a dominant economic power throughout the continent. Canada is the world's leading producer of nickel, zinc, uranium, potash, and linseed, and the world's second largest producer of asbestos, silver, titanium, gypsum, sulphur, and molybdenum

population (1990 est) 395 million, rising to an estimated 450 million by 2000

languages English predominates in Canada, USA, and Belize; Spanish is the chief language of the countries of Latin America and a sizeable minority in the USA; French is spoken by about 25% of the population of Canada, and by people of the French *département* of St Pierre and Miquelon; indigenous non-European minorities, including the Inuit of Arctic Canada, the Aleuts of Alaska, North American Indians, and the Maya of Central America, have their own languages and dialects

religions Christian and Jewish religions predominate; 97% of Latin Americans, 47% of Canadians, and 21% of those living in the USA are Roman Catholic.

North American Free Trade Agreement

(NAFTA) trade agreement between the USA, Canada, and Mexico, signed Aug 1992; it was ratified by the Canadian parliament June 1993 and by the US Congress and Mexican Senate Nov 1993. The first trade pact of its kind to link two highly-industrialized countries to a developing one, it created a free market of 360 million people, with a total GDP of $6.45 trillion. Beginning Jan 1994, tariffs were to be progressively eliminated over a 10–15 year period and Canadian and US investment into low-wage Mexico progressively increased.

North American Indian

indigenous inhabitant of North America. Many describe themselves as 'Native Americans' rather than 'American Indians', the latter term having arisen because Columbus believed he had reached the East Indies. See also *American Indian.

Northamptonshire

county in central England

area 2,370 sq km/915 sq mi

towns Northampton (administrative headquarters), Kettering

products cereals, cattle

population (1991) 568,900

famous people John Dryden, Richard III, Robert Browne.

North Atlantic Drift

warm *ocean current in the N Atlantic Ocean; an extension of the *Gulf Stream. It flows east across the Atlantic and has a mellowing effect on the climate of NW Europe, particularly the British Isles and Scandinavia.

North Atlantic Treaty

agreement signed 4 April 1949 by Belgium, Canada, Denmark, France, Iceland, Italy, Luxembourg, the Netherlands, Norway, Portugal, the UK, the USA; Greece, Turkey 1952; West Germany 1955; and Spain 1982. They agreed that 'an armed attack against one or more of them in Europe or North America shall be considered an attack against them all'. The North Atlantic Treaty Organization (NATO) is based on this agreement.

North Atlantic Treaty Organization

(NATO) association set up 1949 to provide for the collective defence of the major Western European and North American states against the perceived threat from the USSR. Its chief body is the Council of Foreign Ministers (who have representatives in permanent session), and there is an international secretariat in Brussels, Belgium, and also the Military Committee consisting of the Chiefs of Staff. The military headquarters SHAPE (Supreme Headquarters Allied Powers, Europe) is in Chièvres, near Mons, Belgium. After the Eastern European *Warsaw Pact was disbanded 1991, an adjunct to NATO, the **North Atlantic Cooperation Council**, was established, including all the former Soviet republics, with the aim of building greater security in Europe.

North Brabant

(Dutch **Noord Brabant**) southern province of the Netherlands, lying between the Maas River (Meuse) and Belgium; area 4,940 sq km/1,907 sq mi; population (1991) 2,209,000. The capital is 's Hertogenbosch. Former heathland is now under mixed framing. Towns such as Breda, Tilburg, and Eindhoven are centres of brewing, engineering, microelectronics, and textile manufacture.

North Cape

(Norwegian **Nordkapp**) cape in the Norwegian county of Finnmark; the most northerly point of Europe.

North Carolina

state in E USA; nickname Tar Heel State/Old North State

area 136,400 sq km/52,650 sq mi

capital Raleigh

towns Charlotte, Greensboro, Winston-Salem

products tobacco, corn, soya beans, livestock, poultry, textiles, clothing, cigarettes, furniture, chemicals, machinery

population (1990) 6,628,600

famous people Billy Graham, O Henry, Jesse Jackson, Thomas Wolfe

history after England's Roanoke Island colony was unsuccessful 1585 and 1587, permanent settlement was made 1663; it was one of the original 13 states 1789.

Northcliffe

Alfred Charles William Harmsworth, 1st Viscount Northcliffe 1865–1922. British newspaper proprietor, born in Dublin. Founding the *Daily Mail* 1896, he revolutionized popular journalism, and with the *Daily Mirror* 1903 originated the picture paper. In 1908 he also obtained control of *The Times*. His brother **Harold Sidney Harmsworth, 1st Viscount**

Rothermere (1868–1940), was associated with him in many of his newspapers.

North Dakota state in N USA; nickname Flickertail State/Sioux State
area 183,100 sq km/70,677 sq mi
capital Bismarck
towns Fargo, Grand Forks, Minot
products cereals, meat products, farm equipment, oil, coal
population (1990) 638,800
famous people Maxwell Anderson, Louis L'Amour
history explored by La Verendrye's French Canadian expedition 1738–40; acquired by the USA partly in the Louisiana Purchase 1803 and partly by treaty with Britain 1813. The earliest settlement was Pembina 1812, by Scottish and Irish families, and North Dakota became a state 1889, attracting many German and Norwegian settlers.

North-East India area of India (Meghalaya, Assam, Mizoram, Tripura, Manipur, Nagaland, and Arunachal Pradesh) linked with the rest of India only by a narrow corridor. There is opposition to immigration from Bangladesh and the rest of India, and demand for secession.

Northeast Passage sea route from the N Atlantic, around Asia, to the N Pacific, pioneered by Swedish explorer Nils *Nordenskjöld 1878–79 and developed by the USSR in settling N Siberia from 1935. Russia owns offshore islands and claims it as an internal waterway; the USA claims that it is international.

Northern Areas districts north of Azad Kashmir, directly administered by Pakistan but not merged with it. India and Azad Kashmir each claim them as part of disputed Kashmir. They include Baltistan, Gilgit, Skardu, and Hunza (an independent principality for 900 years until 1974).

Northern Ireland see *Ireland, Northern.

northern lights common name for the *aurora borealis.

Northern Rhodesia former name (until 1964) of *Zambia.

Northern Territory territory of Australia
area 1,346,200 sq km/519,633 sq mi
capital Darwin (chief port)
towns Alice Springs
physical mainly within the tropics, although with wide range of temperature; very low rainfall
products beef cattle, prawns, bauxite (Gove), gold and copper (Tennant Creek), uranium (Ranger)
population (1987) 157,000
government there is an administrator and a legislative assembly, and the territory is also represented in the federal parliament
history originally part of New South Wales, it was annexed 1863 to South Australia but from 1911 until 1978 (when self-government was introduced) was under the control of the Commonwealth of Australia government. Mineral discoveries on land occupied by Aborigines led to a royalty agreement 1979.

North Holland (Dutch *Noord-Holland*) lowlying coastal province of the Netherlands occupying the peninsula jutting northwards between the North Sea and the IJsselmeer; area

2,670 sq km/1,031 sq mi; population (1991) 2,397,000. Most of it is below sea level, protected from the sea by a series of sand dunes and artificial dykes. The capital is Haarlem; other towns are Amsterdam, Hilversum, Den Helder, and the cheese centres Alkmaar and Edam. Famous for its bulbfields, the province also produces grain and vegetables.

North Korea see *Korea, North.

North Pole the northern point where an imaginary line penetrates the Earth's surface by the axis about which it revolves; see also *Poles and *Arctic.

North Rhine–Westphalia (German *Nordrhein-Westfalen*) administrative *Land* of Germany
area 34,100 sq km/13,163 sq mi
capital Düsseldorf
towns Cologne, Essen, Dortmund, Duisburg, Bochum, Wuppertal, Bielefeld, Bonn, Gelsenkirchen, Münster, Mönchengladbach
products iron, steel, coal, lignite, electrical goods, fertilizers, synthetic textiles
population (1988) 16,700,000
religion 53% Roman Catholic, 42% Protestant
history see *Westphalia.

North Sea sea to the east of Britain and bounded by the coasts of Belgium, the Netherlands, Germany, Denmark, and Norway; area 523,000 sq km/202,000 sq mi; average depth 55 m/180 ft, greatest depth 660 m/2,165 ft. In the northeast it joins the Norwegian Sea, and in the south it meets the Strait of Dover.

North–South divide geographical division of the world that theoretically demarcates the rich from the poor. The South includes all of Asia except Japan, Australia, and New Zealand; all of Africa, the Middle East, Central and South America. The North includes Europe, the USA, Canada, and all republics of the former Soviet Union. Newly industrialized countries such as South Korea and Taiwan could, however, be said to have more in common with the industrialized North than with *Third World countries.

Northumberland county in N England
area 5,030 sq km/1,942 sq mi
towns Newcastle-upon-Tyne (administrative headquarters), Berwick-upon-Tweed, Hexham
products sheep
population (1991) 300,600
famous people Thomas Bewick, Jack Charlton, Grace Darling.

Northumberland John Dudley, Duke of Northumberland *c.* 1502–1553. English politician, son of the privy councillor Edmund Dudley (beheaded 1510), and chief minister until Edward VI's death 1553. He tried to place his daughter-in-law Lady Jane *Grey on the throne, and was executed on Mary I's accession.

Northumbria Anglo-Saxon kingdom that covered NE England and SE Scotland, comprising the 6th-century kingdoms of Bernicia (Forth–Tees) and Deira (Tees–Humber), united in the 7th century. It accepted the supremacy of Wessex 827 and was conquered by the Danes in the late 9th century.

Northwest Passage Atlantic–Pacific sea route around the north of Canada. Canada, which owns offshore islands, claims it as an internal waterway; the USA insists that it is an international waterway and sent an icebreaker through without permission 1985.

Northwest Territories territory of Canada
area 3,426,300 sq km/1,322,552 sq mi
capital Yellowknife
physical extends to the North Pole, to Hudson's Bay in the east, and in the west to the edge of the Canadian Shield
products oil, natural gas, zinc, lead, gold, tungsten, silver
population (1991) 54,000; over 50% native peoples (Indian, Inuit)
history the area was the northern part of Rupert's Land, bought by the Canadian government from the Hudson's Bay Company 1869. An act of 1952 placed the Northwest Territories under a commissioner acting in Ottawa under the Ministry of Northern Affairs and Natural Resources. In 1990 territorial control of over 350,000 sq km/135,000 sq mi of the Northwest Territories was given to the *Inuit.

North Yorkshire county in NE England
area 8,320 sq km/3,212 sq mi
towns Northallerton (administrative headquarters), York, Harrogate; resorts: Scarborough, Whitby
products cereals, wool and meat from sheep, dairy products, coal, electrical goods
population (1991) 698,000
famous people Alcuin, W H Auden, Guy Fawkes.

Norway Kingdom of (*Kongeriket Norge*)

area 387,000 sq km/149,421 sq mi (includes Svalbard and Jan Mayen)
capital Oslo
towns Bergen, Trondheim, Stavanger
physical mountainous with fertile valleys and deeply indented coast; forests cover 25%; extends N of Arctic Circle
territories dependencies in the Arctic (Svalbard and Jan Mayen) and in Antarctica (Bouvet and Peter I Island, and Queen Maud Land)
environment an estimated 80% of the lakes and streams in the southern half of the country have been severely acidified by acid rain
head of state Harald V from 1991
head of government Gro Harlem Brundtland from 1990
political system constitutional monarchy
exports petrochemicals from North Sea oil and gas, paper, wood pulp, furniture, iron ore and

other minerals, high-tech goods, sports goods, fish
currency krone
population (1993 est) 4,300,000; growth rate 0.3% p.a.
languages Norwegian (official); there are Saami (Lapp) and Finnish-speaking minorities
religion Evangelical Lutheran (endowed by state) 94%
GNP $22,830 per head (1991)
chronology
1814 Became independent from Denmark; ceded to Sweden.
1905 Links with Sweden ended; full independence achieved.
1940–45 Occupied by Germany.
1949 Joined North Atlantic Treaty Organization (NATO).
1952 Joined Nordic Council.
1957 King Haakon VII succeeded by his son Olaf V.
1960 Joined European Free Trade Association (EFTA).
1972 Accepted into membership of European Economic Community; application withdrawn after a referendum.
1988 Gro Harlem Brundtland awarded Third World Prize.
1989 Jan P Syse became prime minister.
1990 Brundtland returned to power.
1991 King Olaf V died; succeeded by his son Harald V.
1992 Brundtland relinquished leadership of the Labour Party.

Norwegian person of Norwegian culture. There are 4–4.5 million speakers of Norwegian (including some in the USA), a Germanic language belonging to the Indo-European family. The seafaring culture of the Norwegians can be traced back to the Viking age, dating from about AD 800–1050, when people of Norwegian descent settled Iceland and Greenland, and voyaged to Vinland (coast of Newfoundland).

Norwich cathedral city in Norfolk, E England; population (1991) 121,000. Industries include shoes, clothing, chemicals, confectionery, engineering, and printing. It has Norman, medieval, Tudor, and Georgian architecture.

nose in humans, the upper entrance of the respiratory tract; the organ of the sense of smell. The external part is divided down the middle by a septum of *cartilage. The nostrils contain plates of cartilage that can be moved by muscles and have a growth of stiff hairs at the margin to prevent foreign objects from entering. The whole nasal cavity is lined with a *mucous membrane that warms and moistens the air and ejects dirt. In the upper parts of the cavity the membrane contains 50 million olfactory receptor cells (cells sensitive to smell).

Nostradamus Latinized name of Michel de Nôtredame 1503–1566. French physician and astrologer who was consulted by Catherine de' Medici and was physician to Charles IX. His book of prophecies in rhyme, *Centuries* 1555, has had a number of interpretations.

notary public legal practitioner who attests or certifies deeds and other documents. British diplomatic and consular officials may exercise notarial functions outside the UK.

notation in music, the use of symbols to represent individual sounds (such as the notes of the chromatic scale) so that they can be accurately interpreted and reproduced.

notation in dance, the recording of dances by symbols. There are several dance notation systems; prominent among them is *Labanotation.

note in music, the written symbol indicating pitch and duration, the sound of which is a tone.

notochord the stiff but flexible rod that lies between the gut and the nerve cord of all embryonic and larval chordates, including the vertebrates. It forms the supporting structure of the adult lancelet, but in vertebrates it is replaced by the vertebral column, or spine.

Nottingham industrial city (engineering, coal-mining, bicycles, textiles, knitwear, pharmaceuticals, tobacco, lace, electronics) and administrative headquarters of Nottinghamshire, England; population (1991) 261,500.

Nottinghamshire county in central England
area 2,160 sq km/834 sq mi
towns Nottingham (administrative headquarters), Mansfield, Worksop
features river Trent; remaining areas of Sherwood Forest in the 'Dukeries'; D H Lawrence commemorative walk from Eastwood (where he lived) to Old Brinsley Colliery
products cereals, cattle, sheep, light engineering, footwear, limestone, ironstone, oil
population (1991) 980,600
famous people William Booth, D H Lawrence, Alan Sillitoe

Nouakchott capital of Mauritania; population (1985) 500,000.

Nouméa port on the SW coast of New Caledonia; population (1989) 65,100.

noun grammatical *part of speech that names a person, animal, object, quality, idea, or time. Nouns can refer to objects such as *house*, *tree* (**concrete nouns**); specific persons and places such as *John Alden*, the *White House* (**proper nouns**); ideas such as *love*, *anger* (**abstract nouns**). In English many simple words are both noun and verb (*jump*, *reign*, *rain*). Adjectives are sometimes used as nouns ('a *local* man', 'one of the *locals*').

nouveau roman (French 'new novel') experimental literary form produced in the 1950s by French novelists of the *New Wave, including Alain Robbe-Grillet and Nathalie Sarraute. In various ways, these writers seek to eliminate character, plot, and authorial subjectivity in order to present the world as a pure, solid 'thing in itself'.

nouvelle cuisine (French 'new cooking') contemporary French cooking style that avoids traditional rich sauces, emphasizing fresh ingredients and attractive presentation. The phrase was coined in the British magazine *Harpers & Queen* in June 1975.

nova (plural *novae*) faint star that suddenly erupts in brightness by 10,000 times or more. Novae are believed to occur in close *double star systems, where gas from one star flows to a companion *white dwarf. The gas ignites and is thrown off in an explosion at speeds of 1,500 kps/930 mps or more. Unlike a *supernova, the star is not completely disrupted by the outburst.

After a few weeks or months it subsides to its previous state; it may erupt many more times.

Novalis Pen name of Friedrich Leopold von Hardenberg 1772–1801. Pioneer German Romantic poet who wrote *Hymnen an die Nacht/Hymns to the Night* 1800, prompted by the death of his fiancée Sophie von Kühn. He left two unfinished romances, *Die Lehrlinge zu Sais/The Novices of Sais* and *Heinrich von Ofterdingen*.

Nova Scotia province of E Canada
area 55,500 sq km/21,423 sq mi
capital Halifax (chief port)
towns Dartmouth, Sydney
products coal, gypsum, dairy products, poultry, fruit, forest products, fish products (including scallop and lobster)
population (1991) 897,500
history Nova Scotia was visited by the navigator Giovanni *Caboto 1497. A French settlement was established 1604, but expelled 1613 by English colonists from Virginia. The name of the colony was changed from *Acadia* to Nova Scotia 1621. England and France contended for possession of the territory until Nova Scotia (which then included present-day New Brunswick and Prince Edward Island) was ceded to Britain 1713; Cape Breton Island remained French until 1763. Nova Scotia was one of the four original provinces of the Dominion of Canada.

novel extended fictional prose narrative, often including some sense of the psychological development of the central characters and of their relationship with a broader world. The European novel is said to have originated in Greece in the 2nd century BC. Almost the only surviving Latin work that could be called a novel is the *Golden Ass* of Apuleius (late 2nd century), based on a Greek model. The modern novel took its name and inspiration from the Italian *novella*, the short tale of varied character which became popular in the late 13th century. As the main form of narrative fiction in the 20th century, the novel is frequently classified according to genres and subgenres such as the *historical novel, *detective fiction, fantasy, and *science fiction.

Novello Ivor. Stage name of Ivor Novello Davies 1893–1951. Welsh composer and actor-manager. He wrote popular songs, such as 'Keep the Home Fires Burning', in World War I, and musicals in which he often appeared as the romantic lead, including *Glamorous Night* 1925, *The Dancing Years* 1939, and *Gay's the Word* 1951.

Noverre Jean-Georges 1727–1810. French choreographer, writer, and ballet reformer. He promoted *ballet d'action* (with a plot) and simple, free movement, and is often considered the creator of modern classical ballet. *Les Petits Riens* 1778 was one of his works.

Novgorod industrial (chemicals, engineering, clothing, brewing) city on the Volkhov river, NW Russia; a major trading city in medieval times; population (1987) 228,000.

Novgorod school Russian school of icon and mural painters, active from the late 14th to the 16th century in Novgorod. They were inspired by the work of the 14th-century refugee Byzantine artist Theophanes the Greek. Russian artists imitated his linear style, but this became increasingly stilted and mannered.

Novi Sad industrial and commercial (pottery and cotton) city, capital of the autonomous province of Vojvodina in N Serbia, Yugoslavia, on the river Danube; population (1981) 257,700. Products include leather, textiles, and tobacco.

Novosibirsk industrial city (engineering, textiles, chemicals, food processing) in W Siberian Russia, on the river Ob; population (1987) 1,423,000. Winter lasts eight months here.

NSPCC abbreviation for *National Society for the Prevention of Cruelty to Children* (UK).

Nu U (Thakin) 1907– . Myanmar politician, prime minister of Burma (now Myanmar) for most of the period from 1948 to the military coup of 1962. Exiled from 1966, U Nu returned to the country 1980 and, in 1988, helped found the National League for Democracy opposition movement.

Nuba member of a minority ethnic group living in S Sudan, numbering about 1 million (1991). They speak related dialects of Nubian, which belongs to the Chari-Nile family. Forced Islamization threatens their cultural identity, and thousands were killed in the Sudan civil war.

nuclear arms verification the process of checking the number and types of nuclear weapons held by a country in accordance with negotiated limits. The chief means are: *reconnaissance satellites* that detect submarines or weapon silos, using angled cameras to give three-dimensional pictures of installations, penetrating camouflage by means of scanners, and partially seeing through cloud and darkness by infrared devices; *telemetry*, or radio transmission of instrument readings; *interception* to get information on performance of weapons under test; *on-site inspection* by experts visiting bases, launch sites, storage facilities, and test sites in another country; *radar tracking* of missiles in flight; *seismic monitoring* of underground tests, in the same way as with earthquakes. This is not accurate and on-site inspection is needed. Tests in the atmosphere, space, or the oceans are forbidden, and the ban is accepted because explosions are not only dangerous to all but immediately detectable.

nuclear energy energy from the inner core or *nucleus of the atom, as opposed to energy released in chemical processes, which is derived from the electrons surrounding the nucleus.

nuclear fusion process whereby two atomic nuclei are fused, with the release of a large amount of energy. Very high temperatures and pressures are thought to be required in order for the process to happen. Under these conditions the atoms involved are stripped of all their electrons so that the remaining particles, which together make up *plasma, can come close together at very high speeds and overcome the mutual repulsion of the positive charges on the atomic nuclei. At very close range another nuclear force will come into play, fusing the particles together to form a larger nucleus. As fusion is accompanied by the release of large amounts of energy, the process might one day be harnessed to form the basis of commercial energy production. Methods of achieving controlled

fusion are therefore the subject of research around the world.

nuclear physics the study of the properties of the nucleus of the *atom, including the structure of nuclei; nuclear forces; the interactions between particles and nuclei; and the study of radioactive decay. The study of elementary particles is *particle physics.

nuclear reactor device for producing *nuclear energy in a controlled manner. There are various types of reactor in use, all using nuclear fission. In a *gas-cooled reactor*, a circulating gas under pressure (such as carbon dioxide) removes heat from the core of the reactor, which usually contains natural uranium. The efficiency of the fission process is increased by slowing neutrons in the core by using a *moderator such as carbon. The reaction is controlled with neutron-absorbing rods made of boron. An *advanced gas-cooled reactor* (AGR) generally has enriched uranium as its fuel. A *water-cooled reactor*, such as the steam-generating heavy water (deuterium oxide) reactor, has water circulating through the hot core. The water is converted to steam, which drives turbo-alternators for generating electricity. The most widely used reactor is the *pressurized-water reactor*, which contains a sealed system of pressurized water that is heated to form steam in heat exchangers in an external circuit. The *fast reactor* has no moderator and uses fast neutrons to bring about fission. It uses a mixture of plutonium and uranium oxide as fuel. When operating, uranium is converted to plutonium, which can be extracted and used later as fuel. The fast breeder is so called because it produces more plutonium than it consumes. Heat is removed from the reactor by a coolant of liquid sodium. The world's largest fast breeder, the Superphénix, is at Creys-Malville in SW France; it began operation in 1986.

nuclear safety measures to avoid accidents in the operation of nuclear reactors and in the production and disposal of nuclear weapons and of *nuclear waste. There are no guarantees of the safety of any of the various methods of disposal.
nuclear accidents
Chernobyl, Ukraine. In April 1986 there was an explosive leak, caused by overheating, from a nonpressurized boiling-water reactor, one of the largest in Europe. The resulting clouds of radioactive material spread as far as Sweden; 31 people were killed in the explosion (many more are expected to die or become ill because of the long-term effects of radiation), and thousands of square kilometres of land were contaminated by fallout.
Three Mile Island, Harrisburg, Pennsylvania, USA. In 1979, a combination of mechanical and electrical failure, as well as operator error, caused a pressurized water reactor to leak radioactive matter.
Church Rock, New Mexico, USA. In July 1979, 380 million litres/100 million gallons of radioactive water containing uranium leaked from a pond into the Rio Purco, causing the water to become over 6,500 times as radioactive as safety standards allow for drinking water.
Ticonderoga, 130 km/80 mi off the coast of Japan. In 1965 a US Navy Skyhawk jet bomber fell off the deck of this ship, sinking in 4,900 m/16,000 ft of water. It carried a one-megaton

hydrogen bomb. The accident was only revealed in 1989.

Windscale (now Sellafield), Cumbria, England. In 1957, fire destroyed the core of a reactor, releasing large quantities of radioactive fumes into the atmosphere.

nuclear warfare war involving the use of nuclear weapons. The worldwide total of nuclear weapons in 1990 was about 50,000, and the number of countries possessing nuclear weapons stood officially at five – USA, USSR, UK, France, and China – although some other nations were thought either to have a usable stockpile of these weapons (Israel) or the ability to produce them quickly (Brazil, India, Pakistan, South Africa). Nuclear-weapons research began in Britain 1940, but was transferred to the USA after it entered World War II. The research programme, known as the Manhattan Project, was directed by J Robert Oppenheimer.

atom bomb The original weapon relied on use of a chemical explosion to trigger a chain reaction. The first test explosion was at Alamogordo, New Mexico, 16 July 1945; the first use in war was by the USA against Japan 6 Aug 1945 over Hiroshima and three days later at Nagasaki.

hydrogen bomb A much more powerful weapon than the atom bomb, it relies on the release of thermonuclear energy by the condensation of hydrogen nuclei to helium nuclei (as happens in the Sun). The first detonation was at Eniwetok Atoll, Pacific Ocean, 1952 by the USA.

neutron bomb or **enhanced radiation weapon** (ERW) A very small hydrogen bomb that has relatively high radiation but relatively low blast, designed to kill (in up to six days) by a brief neutron radiation that leaves buildings and weaponry intact.

nuclear methods of attack now include aircraft bombs, missiles (long-or short-range, surface to surface, air to surface, and surface to air), depth charges, and high-powered landmines ('atomic demolition munitions') to destroy bridges and roads.

nuclear waste the radioactive and toxic by-products of the nuclear-energy and nuclear-weapons industries. Nuclear waste may have an active life of several thousand years. Reactor waste is of three types: high-level spent fuel, or the residue when nuclear fuel has been removed from a reactor and reprocessed; intermediate, which may be long-or short-lived; and low-level, but bulky, waste from reactors, which has only short-lived radioactivity. Disposal, by burial on land or at sea, has raised problems of safety, environmental pollution, and security. In absolute terms, nuclear waste cannot be safely relocated or disposed of.

nuclear winter possible long-term effect of a widespread nuclear war. In the wake of the destruction caused by nuclear blasts and the subsequent radiation, it has been suggested that atmospheric pollution by dust, smoke, soot, and ash could prevent the Sun's rays from penetrating for a period of time sufficient to eradicate most plant life on which other life depends, and create a new Ice Age.

nucleic acid complex organic acid made up of a long chain of nucleotides. The two types, known as DNA (deoxyribonucleic acid) and RNA (ribonucleic acid), form the basis of heredity. The nucleotides are made up of a sugar (deoxyribose or ribose), a phosphate group, and one of four purine or pyrimidine bases. The order of the bases along the nucleic acid strand contains the genetic code.

nucleon in particle physics, either a *proton or a *neutron, both particles present in the atomic nucleus. **Nucleon number** is an alternative name for the *mass number of an atom.

nucleus in physics, the positively charged central part of an *atom, which constitutes almost all its mass. Except for hydrogen nuclei, which have only protons, nuclei are composed of both protons and neutrons. Surrounding the nuclei are electrons, which contain a negative charge equal to the protons, thus giving the atom a neutral charge.

nucleus in biology, the central, membrane-enclosed part of a eukaryotic cell (see *eukaryote), containing the chromosomes.

nuclide in physics, one of two or more atoms having the same atomic number (number of protons) and mass number (number of nucleons); compare *isotope.

Nuffield William Richard Morris, Viscount Nuffield 1877–1963. English manufacturer and philanthropist. Starting with a small cycle-repairing business, in 1910 he designed a car that could be produced cheaply, and built up Morris Motors Ltd at Cowley, Oxford.

nuisance in law, interference with enjoyment of, or rights over, land. There are two kinds of nuisance. **Private nuisance** affects a particular occupier of land, such as noise from a neighbour; the aggrieved occupier can apply for an *injunction and claim *damages. **Public nuisance** affects an indefinite number of members of the public, such as obstructing the highway; it is a criminal offence. In this case, individuals can claim damages only if they are affected more than the general public.

Nujoma Sam 1929– . Namibian left-wing politician, president from 1990, founder and leader of *SWAPO (the South-West Africa People's Organization) from 1959. He was exiled in 1960 and controlled guerrillas from Angolan bases until the first free elections were held 1989, taking office early the following year.

Nuku'alofa capital and port of Tonga on Tongatapu; population (1986) 29,000.

numbat or **banded anteater** Australian marsupial anteater *Myrmecobius fasciatus*. It is brown with white stripes on the back and has a long tubular tongue to gather termites and ants. The body is about 25 cm/10 in long, and the tongue can be extended 10 cm/4 in.

number symbol used in counting or measuring. In mathematics, there are various kinds of numbers. The everyday number system is the decimal ('proceeding by tens') system, using the base ten. *Real numbers include all rational numbers (integers, or whole numbers, and fractions) and irrational numbers (those not expressible as fractions). *Complex numbers include the real and unreal numbers (real-number multiples of the square root of –1). The *binary number system, used in computers, has two as its base. The ordinary numerals, 0, 1, 2, 3, 4, 5, 6, 7, 8, and 9, give a counting system that, in the decimal system, continues 10, 11, 12, 13, and so on. These are whole numbers (positive integers), with fractions represented as, for example, $\frac{1}{4}$, $\frac{1}{2}$, $\frac{3}{4}$, or as decimal fractions (0.25, 0.5, 0.75). They are also rational numbers. Irrational numbers cannot be represented in this way and require symbols, such as $\sqrt{2}$, π, and e. They can be expressed numerically only as the (inexact) approximations 1.414, 3.142 and 2.718 (to three places of decimals) respectively. The symbols π and e are also examples of transcendental numbers, because they (unlike $\sqrt{2}$) cannot be derived by solving a *polynomial equation (an equation with one *variable quantity) with rational *coefficients (multiplying factors). Complex numbers, which include the real numbers as well as unreal numbers, take the general form $a + bi$, where $i = \sqrt{-1}$ (that is, $i^2 = -1$), and a is the real part and bi the unreal part.

numismatics the study of *coins, and medals and decorations.

nun (Latin *nonna* 'elderly woman') woman belonging to a religious order under the vows of poverty, chastity, and obedience, and living under a particular rule. Christian convents are ruled by a superior (often elected), who is subject to the authority of the bishop of the diocese or sometimes directly to the pope. See *monasticism.

Nunn Trevor 1940– . British stage director, linked with the Royal Shakespeare Company from 1968. He received a Tony award (with John Caird 1948–) for his production of *Nicholas Nickleby* 1982 and for the musical *Les Misérables* 1987.

Nuremberg (German *Nürnberg*) industrial city (electrical and other machinery, precision instruments, textiles, toys) in Bavaria, Germany; population (1988) 467,000. From 1933 the Nuremberg rallies were held here, and in 1945 the Nuremberg trials of war criminals.

Nuremberg rallies annual meetings 1933–38 of the German Nazi Party. They were characterized by extensive torchlight parades, marches in party formations, and mass rallies addressed by Nazi leaders such as Hitler and Goebbels.

Nuremberg trials after World War II, the trials of the 24 chief *Nazi war criminals Nov 1945–Oct 1946 by an international military tribunal consisting of four judges and four prosecutors: one of each from the USA, UK, USSR, and France. An appendix accused the German cabinet, general staff, high command, Nazi leadership corps, *SS, *Sturmabteilung, and *Gestapo of criminal behaviour.

Nureyev Rudolf 1938–1993. Russian dancer and choreographer. A soloist with the Kirov Ballet, he defected to the West during a visit to Paris in 1961. Mainly associated with the Royal Ballet (London) and as Margot *Fonteyn's principal partner, he was one of the most brilliant dancers of the 1960s and 1970s. Nureyev danced in such roles as Prince Siegfried in *Swan Lake* and Armand in *Marguerite and Armand*, which was created specifically for Fonteyn and Nureyev. He also danced and acted in films and on television and choreographed several ballets.

nursery school or *kindergarten* semieducational establishment for children aged three to five. The first was established in Germany 1836 by Friedrich Froebel (1782–1852).

nursing care of the sick, the very young, the very old, and the disabled. Organized training originated 1836 in Germany, and was developed in Britain by the work of Florence *Nightingale, who, during the Crimean War, established standards of scientific, humanitarian care in military hospitals. Nurses give day-to-day care and carry out routine medical and surgical procedures under the supervision of a physician.

nut any dry, single-seeded fruit that does not split open to release the seed, such as the chestnut. A nut is formed from more than one carpel, but only one seed becomes fully formed, the remainder aborting. The wall of the fruit, the pericarp, becomes hard and woody, forming the outer shell.

nut and bolt common method of fastening pieces of metal or wood together. The nut consists of a small block (usually metal) with a threaded hole in the centre for screwing on to a threaded rod or pin (bolt or screw). The method came into use at the turn of the 19th century, following Henry Maudslay's invention of a precision screw-cutting *lathe.

nutation in botany, the spiral movement exhibited by the tips of certain stems during growth; it enables a climbing plant to find a suitable support. Nutation sometimes also occurs in tendrils and flower stalks.

nutation in astronomy, a slight 'nodding' of the Earth in space, caused by the varying gravitational pulls of the Sun and Moon. Nutation changes the angle of the Earth's axial tilt (average 23.5°) by about 9 seconds of arc to either side of its mean position, a complete cycle taking just over 18.5 years.

nuthatch small bird of the family Sittidae, with a short tail and pointed beak. Nuthatches climb head first up, down, and around tree trunks and branches, foraging for insects and their larvae.

nutmeg kernel of the seed of the evergreen tree *Myristica fragrans*, native to the Moluccas. Both the nutmeg and its secondary covering, known as *mace*, are used as spice in cookery.

nutrition the science of food, and its effect on human and animal life, health, and disease. Nutrition is the study of the basic nutrients required to sustain life, their bioavailability in foods and overall diet, and the effects upon them of cooking and storage.

Nuuk Greenlandic for *Godthaab, capital of Greenland.

Nyasa former name for Lake *Malawi.

Nyasaland former name (until 1964) for *Malawi.

Nyerere Julius (Kambarage) 1922– . Tanzanian socialist politician, president 1964–85. He devoted himself from 1954 to the formation of the Tanganyika African National Union and subsequent campaigning for independence. He became chief minister 1960, was prime minister of Tanganyika 1961–62, president of the newly formed Tanganyika Republic 1962–64, and first president of Tanzania 1964–85.

Nyers Rezso 1923– . Hungarian socialist leader. A member of the politburo from 1966 and the architect of Hungary's liberalizing economic reforms in 1968, he was ousted from power by hardliners 1974. In 1988 he was brought back into the politburo, and became head of the newly formed Hungarian Socialist Party in 1989.

nylon synthetic long-chain polymer similar in chemical structure to protein. Nylon was the first all-synthesized fibre, made from petroleum, natural gas, air, and water by the Du Pont firm in 1938. It is used in the manufacture of moulded articles, textiles, and medical sutures. Nylon fibres are stronger and more elastic than silk and are relatively insensitive to moisture and mildew. Nylon is used for hosiery and woven goods, simulating other materials such as silks and furs; it is also used for carpets.

Nyman Michael 1944– . British composer whose highly stylized music is characterized by processes of gradual modification by repetition of complex musical formulas. His compositions include scores for the British filmmaker Peter *Greenaway; a chamber opera, *The Man Who Mistook His Wife for a Hat* 1989; and three string quartets.

nymph in Greek mythology, a guardian spirit of nature. *Hamadryads* or *dryads* guarded trees; *naiads*, springs and pools; *oreads*, hills and rocks; and *nereids*, the sea.

nymph in entomology, the immature form of insects that do not have a pupal stage; for example, grasshoppers and dragonflies. Nymphs generally resemble the adult (unlike larvae), but do not have fully formed reproductive organs or wings.

oak any tree or shrub of the genus *Quercus* of the beech family Fagaceae, with over 300 known species widely distributed in temperate zones. Oaks are valuable for timber, the wood being durable and straight-grained. Their fruits are called acorns.

Oakley Annie (Phoebe Anne Oakley Mozee) 1860–1926. US sharpshooter, member of Buffalo Bill's Wild West Show (see William *Cody). Even though she was partially paralysed in a train crash 1901, she continued to astound audiences with her ability virtually until her death. Kaiser Wilhelm of Germany had such faith in her talent that he allowed her to shoot a cigarette from his mouth.

OAPEC abbreviation of *Organization of Arab Petroleum Exporting Countries*.

oarfish any of a family *Regalecidae* of deep-sea bony fishes, found in warm parts of the Atlantic, Pacific, and Indian oceans. Oarfish are large, up to 9 m/30 ft long, elongated, and compressed, with a fin along the back and a manelike crest behind the head. They have a small mouth, no teeth or scales, and large eyes. They are often reported as sea serpents.

OAS abbreviation for *Organization of American States*.

oasis area of land made fertile by the presence of water near the surface in an otherwise arid region. The occurrence of oases affects the distribution of plants, animals, and people in the desert regions of the world.

oat type of grass, genus *Avena*, a cereal food. The plant has long, narrow leaves and a stiff straw stem; the panicles of flowers, and later of grain, hang downwards. The cultivated oat *Avena sativa* is produced for human and animal food.

Oates Joyce Carol 1938– . US writer. Her novels, often containing surrealism and violence, include *A Garden of Earthly Delights* 1967, *Them* 1969, *Unholy Loves* 1979, *A Bloodsmoor Romance* 1982, and *Because It Is Bitter, and Because It Is My Heart* 1990.

Oates Laurence Edward Grace 1880–1912. British Antarctic explorer who accompanied Robert Falcon *Scott on his second expedition to the South Pole. On the return journey, suffering from frostbite, he went out alone into the blizzard to die rather than delay the others.

Oates Titus 1649–1705. English conspirator. A priest, he entered the Jesuit colleges at Valladolid,

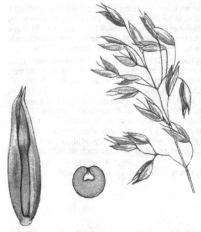

oat The oat plant has long, narrow leaves, with the grain hanging downwards.

Spain, and St Omer, France, as a spy 1677–78, and on his return to England announced he had discovered a 'Popish Plot' to murder Charles II and re-establish Catholicism. Although this story was almost entirely false, many innocent Roman Catholics were executed during 1678–80 on Oates's evidence.

oath solemn promise to tell the truth or perform some duty, combined with an appeal to a deity or something held sacred. In English courts witnesses normally swear to tell the truth holding a *New Testament in their right hand. In the USA witnesses raise their right hand in taking the oath. People who object to the taking of oaths, such as *Quakers and atheists, give a solemn promise (affirmation) to tell the truth. Jews swear holding the Torah (Pentateuch), with their heads covered. Muslims and Hindus swear by their respective sacred books.

OAU abbreviation for *Organization of African Unity*.

Ob river in Asian Russia, flowing 3,380 km/2,100 mi from the Altai Mountains through the W Siberian Plain to the Gulf of Ob in the Arctic Ocean. With its main tributary, the *Irtysh*, it is 5,600 km/3,480 mi.

ob. abbreviation for *obiit* (Latin 'he/she died').

OBE abbreviation for *Officer of the Order of the British Empire*, a British honour.

obelisk tall, tapering column of stone, much used in ancient Egyptian and Roman architecture. Examples are Cleopatra's Needles 1475 BC, one of which is in London, the other in New York.

Oberammergau village in Bavaria, Germany, 72 km/45 mi SW of Munich; population (1980) 5,000. A Christian *passion play has been performed here every ten years since 1634 (except during the world wars) to commemorate the ending of the Black Death plague.

Oberon in folklore, king of the elves or fairies and, according to the 13th-century French romance *Huon of Bordeaux*, an illegitimate son of Julius Caesar. Shakespeare used the character in *A Midsummer Night's Dream*.

obesity condition of being overweight (generally, 20% or more above the desirable weight for one's sex, build, and height). Obesity increases susceptibility to disease, strains the vital organs, and lessens life expectancy; it is remedied by healthy diet and exercise, unless caused by systemic (glandular) problems.

oboe musical instrument of the *woodwind family. Played vertically, it is a wooden tube with a bell, is double-reeded, and has a yearning, poignant tone. Its range is almost three octaves. Oboe concertos have been composed by Vivaldi, Albinoni, Richard Strauss, and others.

Obote (Apollo) Milton 1924– . Ugandan politician who led the independence movement from 1961. He became prime minister 1962 and was president 1966–71 and 1980–85, being overthrown by first Idi *Amin and then by Lt-Gen Tito Okello.

obscenity law law established by the Obscene Publications Act 1959 prohibiting the publishing of any material that tends to deprave or corrupt. In Britain, obscene material can be, for example, pornographic, violent, or can encourage drug taking. Publishing includes distribution, sale, and hiring of the material. There is a defence in support of the public good if the defendant can produce expert evidence to show that publication was in the interest of, for example, art, science, or literature.

observatory site or facility for observing astronomical or meteorological phenomena. The earliest recorded observatory was in Alexandria, N Africa, built by Ptolemy Soter in about 300 BC. The modern observatory dates from the invention of the telescope. Observatories may be ground-based, carried on aircraft, or sent into orbit as satellites, in space stations, and on the space shuttle.

obsession repetitive unwanted thought or compulsive action that is often recognized by the sufferer as being irrational, but which nevertheless causes distress. It can be associated with the irresistible urge of an individual to carry out a repetitive series of actions.

obsidian black or dark-coloured glassy volcanic rock, chemically similar to *granite, but formed by cooling rapidly on the Earth's surface at low pressure.

obstetrics medical speciality concerned with the management of pregnancy, childbirth, and the immediate postnatal period.

obtuse angle an angle greater than 90° but less than 180°.

O'Casey Sean. Adopted name of John Casey 1884–1964. Irish dramatist. His early plays are tragicomedies, blending realism with symbolism and poetic with vernacular speech: *The Shadow of a Gunman* 1922, *Juno and the Paycock* 1925, and *The Plough and the Stars* 1926. Later plays include *Red Roses for Me* 1946 and *The Drums of Father Ned* 1960.

occupation in law, the physical possession and control of land. In the UK, under the Land Registration Act 1925, the rights of a person in actual occupation may be an overriding interest binding a purchaser of registered land, unless the rights are disclosed on inquiry.

occupational psychology study of human behaviour at work. It includes dealing with problems in organizations, advising on management difficulties, and investigating the relationship between humans and machines (as in the design of aircraft controls; see also *ergonomics). Another area is *psychometrics and the use of assessment to assist in selection of personnel.

ocean great mass of salt water. Strictly speaking three oceans exist – the Atlantic, Indian, and Pacific – to which the Arctic is often added. They cover approximately 70% or 363,000,000 sq km/ 140,000,000 sq mi of the total surface area of the Earth. Water levels recorded in the world's oceans have shown an increase of 10–15 cm/4–6 in over the past 100 years.

oceanarium large display tank in which aquatic animals and plants live together much as they would in their natural environment. The first oceanarium was created by the explorer and naturalist W Douglas Burden 1938 in Florida, USA.

Oceania general term for the islands of the central and S Pacific, including Australia, New Zealand, and the eastern half of New Guinea; although situated in the world's largest ocean, Oceania is the smallest continent in the world in terms of land surface
area 8,500,000 sq km/3,300,000 sq mi (land area)
population 26 million, rising to 30 million by 2000; annual growth rate 1980 to 1985 1.5%; Australia accounts for 65% of the population.

oceanography study of the oceans, their origin, composition, structure, history, and wildlife (seabirds, fish, plankton, and other organisms). Much oceanography uses computer simulations to plot the possible movements of the waters, and many studies are carried out by remote sensing.

ocean ridge mountain range on the seabed indicating the presence of a constructive plate margin (where tectonic plates are moving apart and magma rises to the surface; see *plate tectonics). Ocean ridges, such as the *Mid-Atlantic Ridge, consist of many segments offset along *faults, and can rise thousands of metres above the surrounding seabed.

ocean trench deep trench in the seabed indicating the presence of a destructive margin (produced by the movements of *plate tectonics). The subduction or dragging downwards of one plate of the *lithosphere beneath another means that the ocean floor is pulled down. Ocean trenches are found around the edge of the Pacific Ocean and the NE Indian Ocean; minor ones occur in the Caribbean and near the Falkland Islands.

Oceanus in Greek mythology, one of the *Titans, the god of a river supposed to encircle the Earth. He was the ancestor of other river gods and the nymphs of the seas and rivers.

ocelot wild cat *Felis pardalis* of the southwestern USA, Mexico, and Central and South America, up to 1 m/3 ft long with a 45 cm/1.5 ft tail. It weighs about 18 kg/40 lbs and has a pale yellowish coat marked with longitudinal stripes and blotches. Hunted for its fur, it is close to extinction.

O'Connell Daniel 1775–1847. Irish politician, called 'the Liberator'. Although ineligible, as a Roman Catholic, to take his seat, he was elected member of Parliament for County Clare 1828 and so forced the government to grant Catholic emancipation. In Parliament he cooperated with the Whigs in the hope of obtaining concessions until 1841, when he launched his campaign for repeal of the union.

O'Connor Flannery 1925–1964. US novelist and short-story writer. Her works have a great sense of evil and sin, and often explore the religious sensibility of the Deep South. Her short stories include *A Good Man Is Hard to Find* 1955, *Everything That Rises Must Converge* 1965, *The Habit of Being* 1979, and *Flannery O'Connor: Collected Works* 1988.

OCR abbreviation for *optical character recognition*.

octal number system number system to the *base eight, used in computing, in which all numbers are made up of the digits 0 to 7. For example, decimal 8 is represented as octal 10, and decimal 17 as octal 21; see also *hexadecimal number system.

octane rating numerical classification of petroleum fuels indicating their combustion characteristics.

octave in music, a distance of eight notes as measured on the white notes of a piano keyboard. It corresponds to the consonance of first and second harmonics.

Octavian original name of *Augustus, the first Roman emperor.

October Revolution second stage of the *Russian Revolution 1917, when, on 24 Oct (6 Nov in the Western calendar), the Red Guards under Trotsky, and on orders from Lenin, seized the Winter Palace and arrested members of the Provisional Government. The following day the Second All-Russian Congress of Soviets handed over power to the Bolsheviks.

Octobrists group of Russian liberal constitutional politicians who accepted the reforming October Manifesto instituted by Tsar Nicholas II after the 1905 revolution and rejected more radical reforms.

octopus any of an order (Octopoda) of *cephalopods, genus *Octopus*, having a round or oval body and eight arms with rows of suckers on each. They occur in all temperate and tropical seas, where they feed on crabs and other small animals.

ODA abbreviation for *Overseas Development Administration*.

ode lyric poem of complex form, originally chanted to a musical accompaniment. Ancient Greek writers of odes include Sappho, Pindar, Horace, and Catullus; and, among English poets, Spenser, Milton, Dryden, and Keats.

Odessa seaport in Ukraine, on the Black Sea, capital of Odessa region; population (1989) 1,115,000. Products include chemicals, pharmaceuticals, and machinery.

Odin chief god of Scandinavian mythology, the **Woden** or **Wotan** of the Germanic peoples. A

octopus *The octopus can swim by using its legs or squirting water backwards to create a kind of jet propulsion.*

sky god, he lives in Asgard, at the top of the world-tree, and from the Valkyries (the divine maidens) receives the souls of heroic slain warriors, feasting with them in his great hall, Valhalla. The wife of Odin is Freya, or Frigga, and Thor is their son. Wednesday is named after Odin.

Odysseus chief character of Homer's *Odyssey*, and mentioned also in the *Iliad* as one of the leaders of the Greek forces at the siege of Troy, a man of courage and ingenuity. He is said to have been the ruler of the island of Ithaca.

OE abbreviation for *Old English*; see *English language.

OECD abbreviation for *Organization for Economic Cooperation and Development*.

oedema any abnormal accumulation of fluid in tissues or cavities of the body; waterlogging of the tissues due to excessive loss of *plasma through the capillary walls. It may be generalized (the condition once known as dropsy) or confined to one area, such as the ankles.

Oedipus in Greek legend, king of Thebes who unwittingly killed his father and married his mother, in fulfilment of a prophecy. When he learned what he had done, he put out his eyes.

Oedipus complex in psychology, term coined by Sigmund *Freud for the unconscious antagonism of a son to his father, whom he sees as a rival for his mother's affection. For a girl antagonistic to her mother, as a rival for her father's affection, the term is **Electra complex**. Contemporary theory places less importance on the Oedipus/Electra complex than did Freud.

oersted cgs unit (symbol Oe) of *magnetic field strength, now replaced by the SI unit ampere per metre. The Earth's magnetic field is about 0.5 oersted; the field near the poles of a small bar magnet is several hundred oersteds; and a powerful *electromagnet can have a field strength of 30,000 oersteds.

oesophagus passage by which food travels from mouth to stomach. The human oesophagus is about 23 cm/9 in long. Its upper end is at the bottom of the *pharynx, immediately behind the windpipe.

oestrogen group of hormones produced by the *ovaries of vertebrates; the term is also used for various synthetic hormones that mimic their effects. The principal oestrogen in mammals is oestradiol. Oestrogens promote the development of female secondary sexual characteristics; stimulate egg production; and, in mammals, prepare the lining of the uterus for pregnancy.

oestrus in mammals, the period during a female's reproductive cycle (also known as the oestrus cycle or *menstrual cycle) when mating is most likely to occur. It usually coincides with ovulation.

Offa died 796. King of Mercia, England, from 757. He conquered Essex, Kent, Sussex, and Surrey; defeated the Welsh and the West Saxons; and established Mercian supremacy over all England south of the river Humber.

Offaly county of the Republic of Ireland, in the province of Leinster, between Galway on the west and Kildare on the east; area 2,000 sq km/ 772 sq mi; population (1991) 58,500.

Offa's Dyke defensive earthwork along the Welsh border, of which there are remains from the mouth of the river Dee to that of the river Severn. It represents the boundary secured by *Offa's wars with Wales.

Offenbach Jacques 1819–1880. French composer. He wrote light opera, initially for presentation at the *Bouffes parisiens*. Among his works are *Orphée aux enfers/Orpheus in the Underworld* 1858, *La belle Hélène* 1864, and *Les contes d'Hoffmann/The Tales of Hoffmann* 1881.

Official Secrets Act UK act of Parliament 1989, prohibiting the disclosure of confidential material from government sources by employees; it remains an absolute offence for a member or former member of the security and intelligence services (or those working closely with them) to disclose information about their work. There is no public-interest defence, and disclosure of information already in the public domain is still a crime. Journalists who repeat disclosures may also be prosecuted.

offset printing the most common method of *printing, which uses smooth (often rubber) printing plates. It works on the principle of *lithography: that grease and water repel one another.

O'Flaherty Liam 1897–1984. Irish author, best known for his short stories published in volumes such as *Spring Sowing* 1924, *The Tent* 1926, and *Two Lovely Beasts* 1948. His novels, set in County Mayo, include *The Neighbour's Wife* 1923, *The Informer* 1925, and *Land* 1946.

Ogbomosho city and commercial centre in W Nigeria, 80 km/50 mi NE of Ibadan; population (1981) 590,600.

Ogden C(harles) K(ay) 1889–1957. English writer and scholar. With I A *Richards he developed the simplified form of English known as Basic English, built on a vocabulary of just 850 words. Together they wrote *Foundations of Aesthetics* 1921 and *The Meaning of Meaning* 1923.

O grade in Scottish education, Ordinary Grade, the equivalent of an English *GCSE taken by school students at the age of 16.

Ogun state of SW Nigeria; population (1988) 3,397,900; area 16,762 sq km/6,474 sq mi; capital Abeokuta.

O'Higgins Bernardo 1778–1842. Chilean revolutionary, known as 'the Liberator of Chile'. He was a leader of the struggle for independence from Spanish rule 1810–17 and head of the first permanent national government 1817–23.

Ohio state in N central USA; nickname Buckeye State
area 107,100 sq km/41,341 sq mi
capital Columbus
cities Cleveland, Cincinnati, Dayton, Akron, Toledo, Youngstown, Canton
population (1990) 10,847,100 long and about 5 m/18 ft across (built by *Hopewell Indians about 2nd–1st centuries BC)
products coal, cereals, livestock, dairy foods, machinery, chemicals, steel, motor vehicles, automotive and aircraft parts, rubber products, office equipment, refined petroleum.

ohm SI unit (symbol Ω) of electrical *resistance (the property of a substance that restricts the flow of electrons through it).

ohmic heating method of heating used in the food-processing industry, in which an electric current is passed through foodstuffs to sterilize them before packing. The heating effect is similar to that obtained by microwaves in that electrical energy is transformed into heat throughout the whole volume of the food, not just at the surface.

Ohm's law law that states that the current flowing in a metallic conductor maintained at constant temperature is directly proportional to the potential difference (voltage) between its ends. The law was discovered by Georg Ohm 1827.

oil flammable substance, usually insoluble in water, and composed chiefly of carbon and hydrogen. Oils may be solids (fats and waxes) or liquids. The three main types are: ***essential oils**, obtained from plants; **fixed oils**, obtained from animals and plants; and **mineral oils**, obtained chiefly from the refining of *petroleum.

oil crop plant from which vegetable oils are pressed from the seeds. Cool temperate areas grow rapeseed and linseed; warm temperate regions produce sunflowers, olives, and soya beans; tropical regions produce groundnuts (peanuts), palm oil, and coconuts.

oil palm African *palm tree *Elaeis guineensis*, the fruit of which yields valuable oils, used as food or processed into margarine, soaps, and livestock feeds.

okapi ruminant *Okapia johnstoni* of the giraffe family, although with much shorter legs and neck, found in the tropical rainforests of central Africa. Purplish brown with a creamy face and black and white stripes on the legs and hindquarters, it is excellently camouflaged. Okapis have remained virtually unchanged for millions of years.

Okavango Swamp marshy area in NW Botswana, fed by the **Okavango River**, which rises in Angola and flows SE about 1,600 km/1,000 mi.

O'Keeffe Georgia 1887–1986. US painter, based mainly in New York and New Mexico, known chiefly for her large, semi-abstract studies of flowers and bones, such as *Black Iris* 1926 (Metropolitan Museum of Art, New York) and the *Pelvis Series* of the 1940s.

Okhotsk, Sea of arm of the N Pacific between the Kamchatka Peninsula and Sakhalin and bordered southward by the Kuril Islands; area 937,000 sq km/361,700 sq mi. Free of ice only in summer, it is often fogbound.

Okinawa largest of the Japanese *Ryukyu Islands in the W Pacific
area 2,250 sq km/869 sq mi
capital Naha
population (1990) 3,145,500
history captured by the USA in the *Battle of Okinawa* 1 Apr–21 June 1945, with 47,000 US casualties (12,000 dead) and 60,000 Japanese (only a few hundred survived as prisoners). During the invasion over 150,000 Okinawans, mainly civilians, died; many massacred by Japanese forces. The island was returned to Japan 1972.

Oklahoma state in S central USA; nickname Sooner State
area 181,100 sq km/69,905 sq mi
capital Oklahoma City
towns Tulsa, Lawton, Norman, Enid
products cereals, peanuts, cotton, livestock, oil, natural gas, helium, machinery and other metal products
population (1990) 3,145,600
famous people John Berryman, Ralph Ellison, Woody Guthrie, Mickey Mantle, Will Rogers, Jim Thorpe
history explored for Spain by Francisco de Coronado 1541; most acquired by the USA from France with the *Louisiana Purchase 1803.

Oklahoma City industrial city (oil refining, machinery, aircraft, telephone equipment), capital of Oklahoma, USA, on the Canadian River; population (1990) 444,700. On 22 April, 1889, a tent city of nearly 10,000 inhabitants was set up overnight as the area was opened to settlement. In 1910 Oklahoma City had 64,000 people and became the state capital.

okra plant *Hibiscus esculentus* belonging to the Old World hibiscus family. Its red-and-yellow flowers are followed by long, sticky, green fruits known as *ladies' fingers* or *bhindi*. The fruits are cooked in soups and stews.

Okri Ben 1959– . Nigerian novelist, broadcaster, and journalist whose novel *The Famished Road* won the 1991 Booker Prize. He published his first book *Flowers and Shadows* 1980, and wrote his second, *The Landscapes Within* 1982, while still a student at university in Essex, England.

Olaf five kings of Norway, including:

Olaf I   Tryggvesson 969–1000. King of Norway from 995. He began the conversion of Norway to Christianity and was killed in a sea battle against the Danes and Swedes.

Olaf II Haraldsson 995–1030. King of Norway from 1015. He offended his subjects by his centralizing policy and zeal for Christianity, and was killed in battle by Norwegian rebel chiefs backed by *Canute of Denmark. He was declared the patron saint of Norway 1164.

Olaf V 1903–1991. King of Norway from 1957, when he succeeded his father, Haakon VII.

Olazabal Jose Maria 1966– . Spanish golfer, one of the leading players on the European circuit. After a distinguished amateur career he turned professional 1986. He was a member of

the European Ryder Cup teams 1987, 1989, and 1991.

Old Bailey popular name for the Central Criminal Court in London, situated in a street of that name in the City of London, off Ludgate Hill.

Old Catholic one of various breakaway groups from Roman Catholicism – including those in Holland (such as the *Church of Utrecht*, who separated from Rome 1724 after accusations of *Jansenism) and groups in Austria, Czechoslovakia, Germany, and Switzerland – who rejected the proclamation of *papal infallibility of 1870. Old Catholic clergy are not celibate.

Oldenburg Claes 1929– . US Pop artist, known for 'soft sculptures', gigantic replicas of everyday objects and foods, made of stuffed canvas or vinyl. One characteristic work is *Lipstick* 1969 (Yale University).

Old English general name for the range of dialects spoken by Germanic settlers in England between the 5th and 11th centuries AD, also known as *Anglo-Saxon. The literature of the period includes *Beowulf*, an epic in West Saxon dialect.

Old Pretender nickname of *James Edward Stuart, the son of James II of England.

Old Testament Christian term for the Hebrew *Bible*, which is the first part of the Christian Bible. It contains 39 (according to Christianity) or 24 (according to Judaism) books, which include the origins of the world, the history of the ancient Hebrews and their covenant with God, prophetical writings, and religious poetry. The first five books (*The five books of Moses*) are traditionally ascribed to Moses and known as the Pentateuch (by Christians) or the Torah (by Jews).

Olduvai Gorge deep cleft in the Serengeti steppe, Tanzania, where Louis and Mary *Leakey found prehistoric stone tools in the 1930s. They discovered Pleistocene remains of prehumans and gigantic animals 1958–59. The gorge has given its name to the *Olduvai culture*, a simple stone-tool culture of prehistoric hominids, dating from 2–0.5 million years ago.

Old Vic theatre in S London, England, former home of the National Theatre (1963–76). It was founded in 1818 as the Coburg. Taken over by Emma Cons 1880 (as the Royal Victoria Hall), it became a popular centre for opera and drama, and was affectionately dubbed the Old Vic.

Old World the continents of the eastern hemisphere, so called because they were familiar to Europeans before the Americas. The term is used as an adjective to describe animals and plants that live in the eastern hemisphere.

oleander or *rose bay* evergreen Mediterranean shrub *Nerium oleander* of the dogbane family Apocynaceae, with pink or white flowers and aromatic leaves that secrete the poison oleandrin.

olefin common name for *alkene.

O level, General Certificate of Education or *Ordinary level* formerly an examination taken by British school children at age 16. It was superseded by the *GCSE 1988.

oligarchy rule of the few, in their own interests. It was first identified as a form of government by the Greek philosopher, Aristotle. In modern times there have been a number of oligarchies, sometimes posing as democracies; the paramilitary rule of the *Duvalier family in Haiti, 1957–86, is an example.

Oligocene third epoch of the Tertiary period of geological time, 38–25 million years ago. The name, from Greek, means 'a little recent', referring to the presence of the remains of some modern types of animals existing at that time.

oligopoly in economics, a situation in which a few companies control the major part of a particular market and concert their actions to perpetuate such control. This may include an agreement to fix prices (a *cartel).

oligosaccharide *carbohydrate comprising a few *monosaccharide units linked together. It is a general term used to indicate that a carbohydrate is larger than a simple di-or trisaccharide but not as large as a polysaccharide.

olive evergreen tree *Olea europaea* of the family Oleaceae. Native to Asia but widely cultivated in Mediterranean and subtropical areas, it grows up to 15 m/50 ft high, with twisted branches and opposite, lance-shaped silvery leaves. The white flowers are followed by green oval fruits that ripen a bluish black. They are preserved in brine or oil, dried, or pressed to make olive oil.

olive branch ancient symbol of peace; in the Bible (Genesis 9), an olive branch is brought back by the dove to Noah to show that the flood has abated.

Olives, Mount of range of hills E of Jerusalem, associated with the Christian religion: a former chapel (now a mosque) marks the traditional site of Jesus' ascension to heaven, with the Garden of Gethsemane at its foot.

Olivier Laurence (Kerr), Baron Olivier 1907–1989. English actor and director. For many years associated with the Old Vic theatre, he was director of the National Theatre company 1962–73. His stage roles include Henry V, Hamlet, Richard III, and Archie Rice in John Osborne's *The Entertainer*. His acting and direction of filmed versions of Shakespeare's plays received critical acclaim for example, *Henry V* 1944 and *Hamlet* 1948.

olivine greenish mineral, magnesium iron silicate, $(Mg,Fe)_2SiO_4$. It is a rock-forming mineral, present in, for example, peridotite, gabbro, and basalt. Olivine is called *peridot* when pale green and transparent, and used in jewellery.

olm cave-dwelling aquatic salamander *Proteus anguinus*, the only European member of the family Proteidae, the other members being the North American mudpuppies. Olms are found in underground caves along the Adriatic seaboard in Italy, Croatia, and Yugoslavia. The adult is permanently larval in form, about 25 cm/10 in long, almost blind, with external gills and under-developed limbs. See *neoteny.

Olympia sanctuary in the W Peloponnese, ancient Greece, with a temple of Zeus, and the stadium (for foot races, boxing, and wrestling) and hippodrome (for chariot and horse races), where the original Olympic games were held.

Olympic Games sporting contests originally held in Olympia, ancient Greece, every four years during a sacred truce; records were kept from 776 BC. Women were forbidden to be present,

and the male contestants were naked. The ancient Games were abolished AD 394. The present-day games have been held every four years since 1896. Since 1924 there has been a separate winter Games programme. From 1994 the winter and summer Games will be held two years apart.

Olympus (Greek *Olimbos*) several mountains in Greece and elsewhere, one of which is **Mount Olympus** in N Thessaly, Greece, 2,918 m/ 9,577 ft high. In ancient Greece it was considered the home of the gods.

OM abbreviation for *Order of Merit*.

Om sacred word in Hinduism, used to begin prayers and placed at the beginning and end of books. It is composed of three syllables, symbolic of the Hindu Trimurti, or trinity of gods.

Oman Sultanate of (*Saltanat 'Uman*)
area 272,000 sq km/105,000 sq mi
capital Muscat
towns Salalah, Nizwa
physical mountains to N and S of a high arid plateau; fertile coastal strip
head of state and government Qaboos bin Said from 1970
political system absolute monarchy
exports oil, dates, silverware, copper
currency rial Omani
population (1993 est) 1,650,000; growth rate 3.0% p.a.
languages Arabic (official), English, Urdu, other Indian dialects
religion Ibadhi Muslim 75%, Sunni Muslim, Shi'ite Muslim, Hindu
GNP $4,660 per head (1992)
chronology
1951 The Sultanate of Muscat and Oman achieved full independence from Britain. Treaty of Friendship with Britain signed.
1970 After 38 years' rule, Sultan Said bin Taimur replaced in coup by his son Qaboos bin Said. Name changed to Sultanate of Oman.
1975 Left-wing rebels in south defeated.
1982 Memorandum of Understanding with UK signed, providing for regular consultation on international issues.
1985 Diplomatic ties established with USSR.

Omar 581–644. Adviser of the prophet Muhammad. In 634 he succeeded Abu Bakr as caliph (civic and religious leader of Islam), and conquered Syria, Palestine, Egypt, and Persia. He was assassinated by a slave. The Mosque of Omar in Jerusalem is attributed to him.

Omar Khayyám c. 1050–1123. Persian astronomer, mathematician, and poet. In the West, he is chiefly known as a poet through Edward *Fitzgerald's version of *The Rubaiyat of Omar Khayyám* 1859.

Omayyad dynasty Arabian dynasty of the Islamic empire who reigned as caliphs (civic and religious leaders of Islam) 661–750, when they were overthrown by Abbasids. A member of the family, Abd Al-Rahma1 m, escaped to Spain and in 756 assumed the title of emir of Córdoba. His dynasty, which took the title of caliph in 929, ruled in Córdoba until the early 11th century.

ombudsman (Swedish 'commissioner') official who acts on behalf of the private citizen in investigating complaints against the government. The post is of Scandinavian origin; it was introduced in Sweden 1809, Denmark 1954, and Norway

1962, and spread to other countries from the 1960s.

Omdurman city in Sudan, on the White Nile, a suburb of Khartoum; population (1983) 526,000. It was the residence of the Sudanese sheik known as the Mahdi 1884–98.

Omdurman, Battle of battle on 2 Sept 1898 in which the Sudanese, led by the Khalifa, were defeated by British and Egyptian troops under General Kitch ener.

omnivore animal that feeds on both plant and animal material. Omnivores have digestive adaptations intermediate between those of *herbivores and *carnivores, with relatively unspecialized digestive systems and gut microorganisms that can digest a variety of foodstuffs.

OMR abbreviation for *optical mark recognition*.

Omsk industrial city (agricultural and other machinery, food processing, sawmills, oil refining) in Russia, capital of Omsk region, W Siberia; population (1987) 1,134,000. Its oil refineries are linked with Tuimazy in the Bashkir republic by a 1,600-km/1,000-mi pipeline.

onager wild ass *Equus hemionus* found in W Asia. Onagers are sandy brown, lighter underneath, and about the size of a small horse.

Onassis Aristotle (Socrates) 1906–1975. Turkish-born Greek shipowner. In 1932 he started what became the largest independent shipping line and during the 1950s he was one of the first to construct supertankers. In 1968 he married Jacqueline Kennedy, widow of US president John F Kennedy.

oncogene gene carried by a virus that induces a cell to divide abnormally, forming a *tumour. Oncogenes arise from mutations in genes (protooncogenes) found in all normal cells. They are usually also found in viruses that are capable of transforming normal cells to tumour cells. Such viruses are able to insert their oncogenes into the host cell's DNA, causing it to divide uncontrollably. More than one oncogene may be necessary to transform a cell in this way.

oncology branch of medicine concerned with the diagnosis and treatment of neoplasms (lumps or tumours), especially cancer.

Onega, Lake second largest lake in Europe, NE of St Petersburg, partly in Karelia, Russia; area 9,600 sq km/3,710 sq mi. The *Onega canal*, along its south shore, is part of the Mariinsk system linking St Petersburg with the river Volga.

O'Neill Eugene (Gladstone) 1888–1953. US playwright, the leading dramatist between World Wars I and II. His plays include *Anna Christie* 1922, *Desire under the Elms* 1924, *The Iceman Cometh* 1946, and the posthumously produced autobiographical drama *Long Day's Journey into Night* 1956 (written 1940). He was awarded the Nobel prize for Literature 1936.

O'Neill Terence, Baron O'Neill of the Maine 1914–1990. Northern Irish Unionist politician. In the Ulster government he was minister of finance 1956–63, then prime minister 1963–69. He resigned when opposed by his party on measures to extend rights to Roman Catholics, including a universal franchise.

onion bulbous plant *Allium cepa* of the lily family Liliaceae. Cultivated from ancient times, it may have originated in Asia. The edible part is the bulb, containing an acrid volatile oil and having a strong flavour.

on-line system in computing, a system that allows the computer to work interactively with its users, responding to each instruction as it is given and prompting users for information when necessary. With the falling cost of computer operation, on-line operation has become increasingly attractive commercially.

onomatopoeia (Greek 'name-making') *figure of speech that copies natural sounds. Thus the word or name 'cuckoo' imitates the sound that the cuckoo makes.

Ontario province of central Canada
area 1,068,600 sq km/412,480 sq mi
capital Toronto
towns Hamilton, Ottawa (federal capital), London, Windsor, Kitchener, St Catharines, Oshawa, Thunder Bay, Sudbury
products nickel, iron, gold, forest products, motor vehicles, iron, steel, paper, chemicals, copper, uranium
population (1986) 9,114,000
history first explored by the French in the 17th century, it came under British control 1763 (Treaty of Paris). An attempt 1841 to form a merged province with French-speaking Québec failed, and Ontario became a separate province of Canada 1867. Under the protectionist policies of the new federal government, Ontario gradually became industrialized and urban. Since World War II, more than 2 million immigrants, chiefly from Europe, have settled in Ontario.

Ontario, Lake smallest and easternmost of the Great Lakes, on the US–Canadian border; area 19,200 sq km/7,400 sq mi. It is connected to Lake Erie by the Welland Canal and the Niagara River, and drains into the St Lawrence River. Its main port is Toronto.

ontogeny process of development of a living organism, including the part of development that takes place after hatching or birth. The idea that 'ontogeny recapitulates phylogeny' (the development of an organism goes through the same stages as its evolutionary history), proposed by the German scientist Ernst Heinrich Haeckel, is now discredited.

onyx semiprecious variety of chalcedonic *silica (SiO_2) in which the crystals are too fine to be detected under a microscope, a state known as cryptocrystalline. It has straight parallel bands of different colours: milk-white, black, and red.

oolite limestone made up of tiny spherical carbonate particles called *ooliths*. Ooliths have a concentric structure with a diameter up to 2 mm/0.08 in. They were formed by chemical precipitation and accumulation on ancient sea floors.

Oort Jan Hendrik 1900– . Dutch astronomer. In 1927, he calculated the mass and size of our Galaxy, the Milky Way, and the Sun's distance from its centre, from the observed movements of stars around the Galaxy's centre. In 1950 Oort proposed that comets exist in a vast swarm, now called the *Oort cloud*, at the edge of the solar system.

Oort cloud spherical cloud of comets beyond

Pluto, extending out to about 100,000 astronomical units (1.5 light years) from the Sun. The gravitational effect of passing stars and the rest of our Galaxy disturbs comets from the cloud so that they fall in towards the Sun on highly elongated orbits, becoming visible from Earth. As many as 10 trillion comets may reside in the Oort cloud, named after Jan Oort who postulated it 1950.

oosphere another name for the female gamete, or *ovum, of certain plants such as algae.

ooze sediment of fine texture consisting mainly of organic matter found on the ocean floor at depths greater than 2,000 m/6,600 ft. Several kinds of ooze exist, each named after its constituents.

opal form of *silica (SiO_2), often occurring as stalactites and found in many types of rock. The common opal is translucent, milk-white, yellow, red, blue, or green, and lustrous. Precious opal is opalescent, the characteristic play of colours being caused by close-packed silica spheres diffracting light rays within the stone.

Op art movement in modern art, popular in the 1960s. It uses scientifically based optical effects that confuse the spectator's eye. Precisely painted lines or dots are arranged in carefully regulated patterns that create an illusion of surface movement. Exponents include Victor Vasarely and Bridget Riley.

op. cit. abbreviation for *opere citato* (Latin 'in the work cited'), used in reference citation.

OPEC acronym for *Organization of Petroleum-Exporting Countries*.

opencast mining or *open-pit mining* or *strip mining* mining at the surface rather than underground. Coal, iron ore, and phosphates are often extracted by opencast mining. Often the mineral deposit is covered by soil, which must first be stripped off, usually by large machines such as walking draglines and bucket-wheel excavators. The ore deposit is then broken up by explosives.

Open College in the UK, a network launched by the Manpower Services Commission (now the Training Commission) 1987 to enable people to gain and update technical and vocational skills by means of distance teaching, such as correspondence, radio, and television.

open-hearth furnace method of steelmaking, now largely superseded by the *basic-oxygen process. It was developed in England by German-born William and Friedrich Siemens, and improved by Pierre and Emile Martin 1864. In the furnace, which has a wide, saucer-shaped hearth and a low roof, molten pig iron and scrap are packed into the shallow hearth and heated by overhead gas burners which use preheated air.

Open University institution established in the UK 1969 to enable mature students without qualifications to study to degree level without regular attendance. Open University teaching is based on a mixture of correspondence courses, TV and radio lectures and demonstrations, personal tuition organized on a regional basis, and summer schools.

opera dramatic musical work in which singing takes the place of speech. In opera the music accompanying the action has paramount import-ance, although dancing and spectacular staging may also play their parts. Opera originated in late 16th-century Florence when the musical declamation, lyrical monologues, and choruses of Classical Greek drama were reproduced in current forms.

operating system (OS) in computing, a program that controls the basic operation of a computer. A typical OS controls the *peripheral devices, organizes the filing system, provides a means of communicating with the operator, and runs other programs.

operational amplifier (op-amp) type of electronic circuit that is used to increase the size of an alternating voltage signal without distorting it.

operations research business discipline that uses logical analysis to find solutions to managerial and administrative problems, such as the allocation of resources, inventory control, competition, and the identification of information needed for decision-making.

operetta light form of opera, with music, dance, and spoken dialgoue. The story line is romantic and sentimental, often employing farce and parody. Its origins lie in the 19th-century *opéra comique* and it is intended to amuse. Examples of operetta are Jacques Offenbach's *Orphée aux enfers/Orpheus in the Underworld* 1858, Johann's Strauss's *Die Fledermaus/The Bat* 1874, and Gilbert and Sullivan's *Pirates of Penzance* 1879 and *The Mikado* 1885.

operon group of genes that are found next to each other on a chromosome, and are turned on and off as an integrated unit. They usually produce enzymes that control different steps in the same biochemical pathway. Operons were discovered 1961 (by the French biochemists F Jacob and J Monod) in bacteria.

ophthalmia inflammation of the eyeball or conjunctiva. *Sympathetic ophthalmia* is the diffuse inflammation of the sound eye that is apt to follow septic inflammation of the other.

ophthalmology medical speciality concerned with diseases of the eye and its surrounding tissues.

Ophuls Max. Adopted name of Max Oppenheimer 1902–1957. German film director, whose style is characterized by intricate camera movement. He worked in Europe and the USA, attracting much critical praise for such films as *Letter from an Unknown Woman* 1948 and *Lola Montès* 1955.

opiate, endogenous naturally produced chemical in the body that has effects similar to morphine and other opiate drugs; a type of neurotransmitter. Examples include *endorphins and encephalins (like endorphins, a variety of *peptides).

opinion poll attempt to measure public opinion by taking a survey of the views of a representative sample of the electorate; the science of opinion sampling is called *psephology*. Most standard polls take random samples of around a thousand voters which gives results that should be accurate to within three percentage points, 95% of the time. The first accurately sampled opinion poll was carried out by George *Gallup during the US presidential election 1936.

opium drug extracted from the unripe seeds of the opium poppy *Papaver somniferum* of SW Asia. An addictive narcotic, it contains several alkaloids, including **morphine**, one of the most powerful natural painkillers and addictive narcotics known, and **codeine**, a milder painkiller.

Opium Wars two wars, the *First Opium War* 1839–42 and the *Second Opium War* 1856–60, waged by Britain against China to enforce the opening of Chinese ports to trade in opium. Opium from British India paid for Britain's imports from China, such as porcelain, silk, and, above all, tea.

Oporto alternative form of *Porto in Portugal.

opossum any of a family (Didelphidae) of marsupials native to North and South America. Most opossums are tree-living, nocturnal animals, with prehensile tails, and hands and feet well adapted for grasping. They range from 10 cm/4 in to 50 cm/20 in in length and are insectivorous, carnivorous, or, more commonly, omnivorous.

Oppenheimer J(ulius) Robert 1904–1967. US physicist. As director of the Los Alamos Science Laboratory 1943–45, he was in charge of the development of the atom bomb (the Manhattan Project). When later he realized the dangers of radioactivity, he objected to the development of the hydrogen bomb, and was alleged to be a security risk 1953 by the US Atomic Energy Commission (AEC).

opposition in astronomy, the moment at which a body in the solar system lies opposite the Sun in the sky as seen from the Earth and crosses the *meridian at about midnight.

Opposition, Leader of His/Her Majesty's in UK politics, official title (from 1937) of the leader of the largest opposition party in the House of Commons. Since 1989 the post has received a government salary.

optical character recognition (OCR) in computing, a technique for inputting text to a computer by means of a document reader. First, a *scanner produces a digital image of the text; then character-recognition software makes use of stored knowledge about the shapes of individual characters to convert the digital image to a set of internal codes that can be stored and processed by computer.

optical disc in computing, a storage medium in which laser technology is used to record and read large volumes of digital data. Types include *CD-ROM, *WORM, and erasable optical disc.

optical fibre very fine, optically pure glass fibre through which light can be reflected to transmit an image or information from one end to the other. Optical fibres are increasingly being used to replace copper wire in telephone cables, the messages being coded as pulses of light rather than a fluctuating electric current.

optical illusion scene or picture that fools the eye. An example of a natural optical illusion is that the Moon appears bigger when it is on the horizon than when it is high in the sky, owing to the *refraction of light rays by the Earth's atmosphere.

optical mark recognition (OMR) in computing, a technique that enables marks made in predetermined positions on computer-input forms to be detected optically and input to a computer.

optical illusion

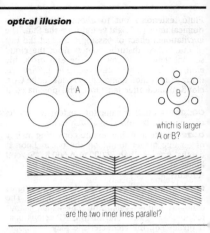

which is larger A or B?

are the two inner lines parallel?

An **optical mark reader** shines a light beam onto the input document and is able to detect the marks because less light is reflected back from them than from the paler, unmarked paper.

optic nerve large nerve passing from the eye to the brain, carrying visual information. In mammals, it may contain up to a million nerve fibres, connecting the sensory cells of the retina to the optical centres in the brain. Embryologically, the optic nerve develops as an outgrowth of the brain.

optics branch of physics that deals with the study of light and vision – for example, shadows and mirror images, lenses, microscopes, telescopes, and cameras. For all practical purposes light rays travel in straight lines, although *Einstein demonstrated that they may be 'bent' by a gravitational field. On striking a surface they are reflected or refracted with some absorption of energy, and the study of this is known as geometrical optics.

opting out in UK education, schools that choose to be funded directly from the Department of Education and Science are said to be opting out of local-authority control. The Education Act 1988 gave this option to all secondary schools and the larger primary schools, and in 1990 it was extended to all primary schools.

option in business, a contract giving the owner the right (as opposed to the obligation, as with futures contracts; see *futures trading) to buy or sell a specific quantity of a particular commodity or currency at a future date and at an agreed price, in return for a premium. The buyer or seller can decide not to exercise the option if it would prove disadvantageous.

optoelectronics branch of electronics concerned with the development of devices (based on the *semiconductor gallium arsenide) that respond not only to the *electrons of electronic data transmission, but also to *photons.

opus (Latin 'work') in music, a term, used with a figure, to indicate the numbering of a composer's works, usually in chronological order.

Opus Dei (Latin 'God's work') Roman Catholic institution aimed at the dissemination of the ideals of Christian perfection. Founded in Madrid 1928, and still powerful in Spain, it is now international. Its members may be of either sex, and lay or clerical.

oracle Greek sacred site where answers (also called oracles) were given by a deity to enquirers about future events; these were usually ambivalent, so that the deity was proven right whatever happened. The earliest was probably at Dodona (in *Epirus), but the most celebrated was that of Apollo at *Delphi.

Oracle *teletext system operated in the UK by Independent Television, introduced 1973. See also *Ceefax.

oral literature stories that are or have been transmitted in spoken form, such as public recitation, rather than through writing or printing. Most preliterate societies have had a tradition of oral literature, including short folk tales, legends, myths, proverbs, and riddles as well as longer narrative works; and most of the ancient epics – such as the Greek *Odyssey* and the Mesopotamian *Gilgamesh* – seem to have been composed and added to over many centuries before they were committed to writing.

Oran (Arabic **Wahran**) seaport in Algeria; population (1983) 663,500. Products include iron, textiles, footwear, and processed food; the port trades in grain, wool, vegetables, and native esparto grass.

orange any of several evergreen trees of the genus *Citrus*, family Rutaceae, which bear blossom and fruit at the same time. Thought to have originated in SE Asia, orange trees are commercially cultivated in Spain, Israel, the USA, Brazil, South Africa, and elsewhere. The sweet orange *C. sinensis* is the one commonly eaten fresh; the Jaffa, blood, and navel orange are varieties of this species.

Orange Free State province of the Republic of South Africa
area 127,993 sq km/49,405 sq mi
capital Bloemfontein
products grain, wool, cattle, gold, oil from coal, cement, pharmaceuticals
population (1987) 1,863,000; 82% ethnic Africans
history original settlements from 1810 were complemented by the *Great Trek, and the state was recognized by Britain as independent 1854. Following the South African, or Boer, War 1899–1902, it was annexed by Britain until it entered the union as a province 1910.

Orange, House of royal family of the Netherlands. The title is derived from the small principality of Orange in S France, held by the family from the 8th century to 1713. They held considerable possessions in the Netherlands, to which, after 1530, was added the German county of Nassau.

orang-utan ape *Pongo pygmaeus*, found solely in Borneo and Sumatra. Up to 1.65 m/5.5 ft in height, it is covered with long, red-brown hair and mainly lives a solitary, arboreal life, feeding chiefly on fruit. Now an endangered species, it is officially protected because its habitat is being systematically destroyed by *deforestation.

Oratorian member of the Roman Catholic order of secular priests, called in full *Congregation of the Oratory of St Philip Neri*, formally constituted by Philip Neri 1575 in Rome,

and characterized by the degree of freedom allowed to individual communities.

oratorio dramatic, non-scenic musical setting of religious texts, scored for orchestra, chorus, and solo voices. Its origins lie in the *Laudi spirituali* performed by St Philip Neri's Oratory in Rome in the 16th century, followed by the first definitive oratorio in the 17th century by Cavalieri. The form reached perfection in such works as J S Bach's *Christmas Oratorio*, and Handel's *Messiah*.

Orbison Roy 1936–1988. US pop singer and songwriter specializing in slow, dramatic ballads, such as 'Only the Lonely' 1960 and 'Running Scared' 1961. His biggest hit was the jaunty 'Oh, Pretty Woman' 1964.

orbit path of one body in space around another, such as the orbit of Earth around the Sun, or the Moon around Earth. When the two bodies are similar in mass, as in a *double star, both bodies move around their common centre of mass. The movement of objects in orbit follows Johann *Kepler's laws, which apply to artificial satellites as well as to natural bodies.

orbital, atomic region around the nucleus of an atom (or, in a molecule, around several nuclei) in which an *electron is most likely to be found. According to *quantum theory, the position of an electron is uncertain; it may be found at any point. However, it is more likely to be found in some places than in others, and it is these that make up the orbital.

orchestra group of musicians playing together on different instruments. In Western music, an orchestra typically contains various bowed string instruments and sections of wind, brass, and percussion. The size and format may vary according to the needs of composers.

orchid The orchid belongs to one of the largest flowering-plant families: there are possibly as many as 20,000 species.

orchid any plant of the family Orchidaceae, which contains at least 15,000 species and 700 genera, distributed throughout the world except in the coldest areas, and most numerous in damp equatorial regions. The flowers are the most evolved of the plant kingdom, have three sepals and three petals and are sometimes solitary, but more usually borne in spikes, racemes, or panicles, either erect or drooping.

ordeal, trial by in tribal societies and in Europe until the Renaissance, a method of testing guilt of an accused person based on the belief in heaven's protection of the innocent. Examples of such ordeals include walking barefoot over heated iron, and swallowing consecrated bread (causing the guilty to choke).

order in classical *architecture, the *column (including capital, shaft, and base) and the entablature, considered as an architectural whole. The five orders are Doric, Ionic, Corinthian, Tuscan, and Composite.

order in biological classification, a group of related *families. For example, the horse, rhinoceros, and tapir families are grouped in the order Perissodactyla, the odd-toed ungulates, because they all have either one or three toes on each foot. The names of orders are not shown in italic (unlike genus and species names) and by convention they have the ending '-formes' in birds and fish; '-a' in mammals, amphibians, reptiles, and other animals; and '-ales' in fungi and plants. Related orders are grouped together in a *class.

order in council in the UK, an order issued by the sovereign with the advice of the Privy Council; in practice it is issued only on the advice of the cabinet. Acts of Parliament often provide for the issue of orders in council to regulate the detailed administration of their provisions.

Order of Merit British order of chivalry founded 1902 by Edward VII and limited in number to 24 at any one time within the British Isles, plus additional honorary OMs for overseas peoples. It ranks below a knighthood. There are two types of OM, military and civil.

ordinate in *coordinate geometry, the y coordinate of a point; that is, the vertical distance of the point from the horizontal or x-axis. For example, a point with the coordinates (3,4) has an ordinate of 4. See *abscissa.

ordination religious ceremony by which a person is accepted into the priesthood or monastic life in various religions. Within the Christian church, ordination authorizes a person to administer the sacraments. The Anglican church in England and Australia voted in favour of the ordination of women priests Nov 1992. The Roman Catholic and Eastern Orthodox churches refuse to ordain women.

Ordnance Survey (OS) official body responsible for the mapping of Britain. It was established 1791 as the *Trigonometrical Survey* to continue work initiated 1784 by Scottish military surveyor General William Roy (1726–1790). Its first accurate maps appeared 1830, drawn to a scale of 1 in to the mile (1:63,000). In 1858 the OS settled on a scale of 1:2,500 for the mapping of Great Britain and Ireland (higher for urban areas, lower for uncultivated areas).

Ordovician period of geological time 510–439 million years ago; the second period of the *Palaeozoic era. Animal life was confined to the sea: reef-building algae and the first jawless fish are characteristic.

ore body of rock, a vein within it, or a deposit of sediment, worth mining for the economically valuable mineral it contains. The term is usually applied to sources of metals. Occasionally metals are found uncombined (native metals), but more often they occur as compounds such as carbon-ates, sulphides, or oxides. The ores often contain unwanted impurities that must be removed when the metal is extracted.

oregano any of several perennial herbs of the Labiatae family, especially the aromatic *Origanum vulgare*, also known as wild marjoram. It is native to the Mediterranean countries and W Asia and naturalized in the Americas. Oregano is extensively used to season Mediterranean cooking.

Oregon state in NW USA, on the Pacific; nickname Beaver State
area 251,500 sq km/97,079 sq mi
capital Salem
cities Portland, Eugene
population (1990) 2,842,300
products wheat, livestock, timber, electronics

Orestes in Greek legend, the son of *Agamemnon and *Clytemnestra, who killed his mother because she and her lover Aegisthus had murdered his father.

orfe fish *Leuciscus idus* of the carp family. It grows up to 50 cm/1.7 ft, and feeds on small aquatic animals. The species is generally greyish-black, but an ornamental variety is orange. It lives in rivers and lakes of Europe and NW Asia.

Orff Carl 1895–1982. German composer, an individual stylist whose work is characterized by sharp dissonances and percussion. Among his compositions are the cantata *Carmina Burana* 1937 and the opera *Antigone* 1949.

organ musical wind instrument of ancient origin. It produces sound from pipes of various sizes under applied pressure and has keyboard controls. Apart from its continued use in serious compositions and for church music, the organ has been adapted for light entertainment.

organ in biology, part of a living body, such as the liver or brain, that has a distinctive function or set of functions.

organelle discrete and specialized structure in a living cell; organelles include mitochondria, chloroplasts, lysosomes, ribosomes, and the nucleus.

organic chemistry branch of chemistry that deals with carbon compounds. Organic compounds form the chemical basis of life and are more abundant than inorganic compounds. In a typical organic compound, each carbon atom forms bonds covalently with each of its neighbouring carbon atoms in a chain or ring, and additionally with other atoms, commonly hydrogen, oxygen, nitrogen, or sulphur.

organic farming farming without the use of synthetic fertilizers (such as *nitrates and phosphates) or *pesticides (herbicides, insecticides, and fungicides) or other agrochemicals (such as hormones, growth stimulants, or fruit regulators).

Organization for Economic Cooperation and Development (OECD) international organization of 24 industrialized countries that provides a forum for discussion and coordination of member states' economic and social policies. Founded 1961, with its headquarters in Paris, the OECD superseded the Organization for European Economic Cooperation, which had been established 1948 to implement the *Marshall Plan.

Organization of African Unity (OAU) association established 1963 to eradicate colonialism and improve economic, cultural, and political cooperation in Africa. Its membership expanded to 51 countries when Namibia joined after independence 1990. The secretary general is Salim Ahmed Salim of Tanzania. Its headquarters are in Addis Ababa, Ethiopia.

Organization of American States (OAS) association founded 1948 by a charter signed by representatives of 30 North, Central, and South American states. It aims to maintain peace and solidarity within the hemisphere, and is also concerned with the social and economic development of Latin America.

Organization of Arab Petroleum Exporting Countries (OAPEC) body established 1968 to safeguard the interests of its members and encourage cooperation in economic activity within the petroleum industry. Its members are Algeria, Bahrain, Egypt, Iraq, Kuwait, Libya, Qatar, Saudi Arabia, Syria, and the United Arab Emirates; headquarters in Kuwait.

Organization of Central American States ODECA (*Organización de Estados Centroamericanos*) international association, first established 1951 and superseded 1962, promoting common economic, political, educational, and military aims in Central America. Its members are Costa Rica, El Salvador, Guatemala, Honduras, and Nicaragua, provision being made for Panama to join at a later date. The permanent headquarters are in Guatemala City.

Organization of Petroleum-Exporting Countries (OPEC) body established 1960 to coordinate price and supply policies of oil-producing states. Its concerted action in raising prices in the 1970s triggered worldwide recession but also lessened demand so that its influence was reduced by the mid-1980s. OPEC members in 1991 were: Algeria, Ecuador, Gabon, Indonesia, Iran, Iraq, Kuwait, Libya, Nigeria, Qatar, Saudi Arabia, the United Arab Emirates, and Venezuela.

organizer in embryology, a part of the embryo that causes changes to occur in another part, through *induction, thus 'organizing' development and *differentiation.

orienteering sport of cross-country running and route-finding. Competitors set off at one-minute intervals and have to find their way, using map and compass, to various checkpoints (approximately 0.8 km/0.5 mi apart), where their control cards are marked. World championships have been held since 1966.

original sin Christian doctrine that Adam's fall rendered humanity innately tainted and unable to achieve salvation except through divine grace.

Orinoco river in N South America, flowing for about 2,400 km/1,500 mi through Venezuela and forming for about 320 km/200 mi the boundary with Colombia; tributaries include the Guaviare, Meta, Apure, Ventuari, Caura, and Caroni. It is navigable by large steamers for 1,125 km/700 mi from its Atlantic delta; rapids obstruct the upper river.

oriole any of two families of brightly coloured songbirds. The Old World orioles of Africa and Eurasia belong to the family Oriolidae. New World orioles belong to the family Icteridae.

Orion in astronomy, a very prominent constellation in the equatorial region of the sky, identified with the hunter of Greek mythology. It contains the bright stars Betelgeuse and Rigel, as well as a distinctive row of three stars that make up Orion's belt. Beneath the belt, marking the sword of Orion, is the Orion nebula; nearby is one of the most distinctive dark nebulae, the Horsehead.

Orion in Greek mythology, a giant of *Boeotia, famed as a hunter.

Orion nebula luminous cloud of gas and dust 1,500 light years away, in the constellation Orion, from which stars are forming. It is about 15 light years in diameter, and contains enough gas to make a cluster of thousands of stars.

Orissa state of NE India
area 155,800 sq km/60,139 sq mi
capital Bhubaneswar
towns Cuttack, Rourkela
products rice, wheat, oilseed, sugar, timber, chromite, dolomite, graphite, iron
population (1991) 31,512,000
language Oriya (official)
religion 90% Hindu
history administered by the British 1803–1912 as a subdivision of Bengal, it joined with Bihar to become a province. In 1936 Orissa became a separate province, and in 1948–49 its area was almost doubled before its designation as a state 1950.

Orkney Islands island group off the NE coast of Scotland
area 970 sq km/375 sq mi
towns Kirkwall (administrative headquarters), on the island of Mainland (formerly known as Pomona)
products fishing and farming, wind power (Burgar Hill has the world's most productive wind-powered generator; a 300 kW wind turbine with blades 60 m/197 ft diameter, capable of producing 20% of the islands' energy needs)
population (1989) 19,400
famous people Edwin Muir, John Rae
history Harald I (Fairhair) of Norway conquered the islands 876; pledged to James III of Scotland 1468 for the dowry of Margaret of Denmark and annexed by Scotland (the dowry unpaid) 1472.

Ormuz alternative name for the Iranian island, *Hormuz.

Ormuzd another name for *Ahura Mazda*, the good god of *Zoroastrianism.

ornithology study of birds. It covers scientific aspects relating to their structure and classification, and their habits, song, flight, and value to agriculture as destroyers of insect pests. Worldwide scientific banding (or the fitting of coded rings to captured specimens) has resulted in accurate information on bird movements and distribution. There is an International Council for Bird Preservation with its headquarters at the Natural History Museum, London.

ornithophily *pollination of flowers by birds. Ornithophilous flowers are typically brightly coloured, often red or orange. They produce large quantities of thin, watery nectar, and are scentless because most birds do not respond well to smell. They are found mostly in tropical areas, with hummingbirds being important pollinators in North and South America, and the sunbirds in Africa and Asia.

Orpheus mythical Greek poet and musician. The son of Apollo and a muse, he married Eurydice, who died from the bite of a snake. Orpheus went down to Hades to bring her back and her return to life was granted on condition that he walk ahead of her without looking back. But he did look back and Eurydice was irretrievably lost. In his grief, he offended the Maenad women of Thrace, and was torn to pieces by them.

orrery mechanical device for demonstrating the motions of the heavenly bodies. Invented about 1710 by George Graham, it was named after his patron, the 4th Earl of Orrery. It is the forerunner of the planetarium.

orris root underground stem of a species of *iris grown in S Europe. Violet-scented, it is used in perfumery and herbal medicine.

Ortega Saavedra Daniel 1945– . Nicaraguan socialist politician, head of state 1981–90. He was a member of the Sandinista Liberation Front (FSLN), which overthrew the regime of Anastasio Somoza 1979. US-sponsored *Contra guerrillas opposed his government from 1982.

orthochromatic photographic film or paper of decreased sensitivity, which can be processed with a red safelight. Using it, blue objects appear lighter and red ones darker because of increased blue sensitivity.

orthodontics branch of *dentistry, mainly dealing with correction of malocclusion (faulty position of teeth).

Orthodox Church or *Eastern Orthodox Church* or *Greek Orthodox Church* federation of self-governing Christian churches mainly found in SE and E Europe and parts of Asia. The centre of worship is the Eucharist. There is a married clergy, except for bishops; the Immaculate Conception is not accepted. The highest rank in the church is that of Ecumenical Patriarch, or Bishop of Istanbul. There were approximately 130 million adherents in 1991.

ortolan songbird *Emberiza hortulana* of the bunting family, common in Europe and W Asia, migrating to Africa in the winter. Long considered a delicacy among gourmets, it has become rare and is now a protected species.

Orton Joe 1933–1967. English dramatist in whose black comedies surreal and violent action takes place in genteel and unlikely settings. Plays include *Entertaining Mr Sloane* 1964, *Loot* 1966, and *What the Butler Saw* 1968. His diaries deal frankly with his personal life. He was murdered by his lover Kenneth Halliwell.

Orwell George. Pen name of Eric Arthur Blair 1903–1950. English author. His books include the satire *Animal Farm* 1945, which included such sayings as 'All animals are equal, but some are more equal than others', and the prophetic *Nineteen Eighty-Four* 1949, portraying the dangers of excessive state control over the individual. Other works include *Down and Out in Paris and London* 1933.

oryx any of the genus *Oryx* of large antelopes native to Africa and Asia. The Arabian oryx *O.*

leucoryx, at one time extinct in the wild, has been successfully reintroduced into its natural habitat using stocks bred in captivity.

OS/2 single-user computer *operating system produced jointly by Microsoft Corporation and IBM for use on large microcomputers. Its main features are *multitasking and the ability to access large amounts of internal *memory.

Osaka industrial port (iron, steel, shipbuilding, chemicals, textiles) on Honshu island; population (1989) 2,535,000, metropolitan area 8,000,000. It is the oldest city of Japan and was at times the seat of government in the 4th–8th centuries.

Osborne John (James) 1929–1994. English dramatist. He became one of the first *Angry Young Men (anti-establishment writers of the 1950s) of British theatre with his debut play, *Look Back in Anger* 1956. Other plays include *The Entertainer* 1957, *Luther* 1960, and *Watch It Come Down* 1976.

oscillating universe in astronomy, a theory that states that the gravitational attraction of the mass within the universe will eventually slow down and stop the expansion of the universe. The outward motions of the galaxies will then be reversed, eventually resulting in a 'Big Crunch' where all the matter in the universe would be contracted into a small volume of high density. This could undergo a further *Big Bang, thereby creating another expansion phase. The theory suggests that the universe would alternately expand and collapse through alternate Big Bangs and Big Crunches.

oscillator any device producing a desired oscillation (vibration). There are many types of oscillator for different purposes, involving various arrangements of thermionic *valves or components such as *transistors, *inductors, *capacitors, and *resistors.

oscillograph instrument for displaying or recording the values of rapidly changing oscillations, electrical or mechanical.

oscilloscope or *cathode-ray oscilloscope* (CRO) instrument used to measure electrical voltages that vary over time and to display the waveforms of electrical oscillations or signals, by means of the deflection of a beam of *electrons. Readings are displayed graphically on the screen of a *cathode-ray tube.

Oshogbo city and trading centre on the river Niger, in W Nigeria, 200 km/125 mi NE of Lagos; population (1986) 405,000. Industries include cotton and brewing.

osier any of several trees and shrubs of the willow genus *Salix*, cultivated for basket making; in particular, *S. viminalis*.

Osiris ancient Egyptian god, the embodiment of goodness, who ruled the underworld after being killed by *Set. The sister-wife of Osiris was *Isis or Hathor, and their son *Horus captured his father's murderer.

Oslo capital and industrial port (textiles, engineering, timber) of Norway; population (1991) 461,600. The first recorded settlement was made in the 11th century by Harald III, but after a fire 1624, it was entirely replanned by Christian IV and renamed *Christiania* 1624–1924.

Osman I or *Othman I* 1259–1326. Turkish ruler

from 1299. He began his career in the service of the Seljuk Turks, but in 1299 he set up a kingdom of his own in Bithynia, NW Asia, and assumed the title of sultan. He conquered a great part of Anatolia, so founding a Turkish empire. His successors were known as 'sons of Osman', from which the term *Ottoman Empire is derived.

osmium (Greek *osme* 'odour') hard, heavy, bluish-white, metallic element, symbol Os, atomic number 76, relative atomic mass 190.2. It is the densest of the elements, and is resistant to tarnish and corrosion. It occurs in platinum ores and as a free metal (see *native metal) with iridium in a natural alloy called osmiridium, containing traces of platinum, ruthenium, and rhodium. Its uses include pen points and light-bulb filaments; like platinum, it is a useful catalyst.

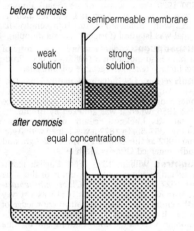

before osmosis

semipermeable membrane

weak solution

strong solution

after osmosis

equal concentrations

osmosis *Osmosis, the movement of liquid through a semipermeable membrane separating solutions of different concentrations, is essential for life.*

osmosis movement of solvent (liquid) through a semipermeable membrane separating solutions of different concentrations. The solvent passes from a less concentrated solution to a more concentrated solution until the two concentrations are equal. Applying external pressure to the solution on the more concentrated side arrests osmosis, and is a measure of the osmotic pressure of the solution.

osprey bird of prey *Pandion haliaetus*, the single member of the family Pandionidae; sometimes erroneously called 'fish hawk'. To catch fish, it plunges feet first into the water. Dark brown above and a striking white below, the osprey measures 60 cm/2 ft with a 2 m/6 ft wingspan. Once extinct in Britain, it is now breeding again in Scotland.

Ossa, Mount the highest peak on the island of Tasmania, Australia; height 1,617 m/5,250 ft.

Ossian (Celtic *Oisin*) legendary Irish hero, invented by the Scottish writer James *Macpherson. He is sometimes represented as the son of another hero, Finn Mac Cumhaill, about 250, and as having lived to tell the tales of Finn and the Ulster heroes to St Patrick, about 400. The publication 1760 of Macpherson's poems,

attributed to Ossian, made Ossian's name familiar throughout Europe.

ossification process whereby bone is formed in vertebrate animals by special cells (**osteoblasts**) that secrete layers of *extracellular matrix on the surface of the existing *cartilage. Conversion to bone occurs through the deposition of calcium phosphate crystals within the matrix.

osteomyelitis infection of bone, with spread of pus along the marrow cavity. Now quite rare, it may follow from a compound fracture (where broken bone protrudes through the skin), or from infectious disease elsewhere in the body.

osteopathy system of alternative medical practice that relies on physical manipulation to treat mechanical stress. It was developed over a century ago by US physician Andrew Taylor Still, who maintained that most ailments can be prevented or cured by techniques of spinal manipulation.

osteoporosis disease in which the bone substance becomes porous and brittle. It is common in older people, affecting more women than men. It may be treated with calcium supplements and etidronate.

Ostia ancient Roman town near the mouth of the Tiber. Founded about 330 BC, it was the port of Rome and had become a major commercial centre by the 2nd century AD. It was abandoned in the 9th century. The present-day seaside resort **Ostia Mare** is situated nearby.

ostinato (Italian 'obstinate') persistently repeated melodic or rhythmic figure.

Ostpolitik (German 'eastern policy') West German chancellor Willy *Brandt's policy of reconciliation with the communist bloc from 1971, pursued to a modified extent by his successors Schmidt and Kohl. The policy attained its goal with the reunification of Germany 1990.

ostracism deliberate exclusion of an individual, or group, from society. It was an ancient Athenian political device to preserve public order. Votes on pieces of broken pot (Greek *ostrakon*) were used to exile unpopular politicians for ten years.

Ostrava industrial city (iron works, furnaces, coal, chemicals) in Czechoslovakia, capital of Severomoravsky region, NE of Brno; population (1991) 327,600.

ostrich large flightless bird *Struthio camelus*, found in Africa. The male may be about 2.5 m/ 8 ft tall and weigh 135 kg/300 lb, and is the largest living bird. It has exceptionally strong legs and feet (two-toed) that enable it to run at high speed, and are also used in defence. It lives in family groups of one cock with several hens.

Ostrogoth member of a branch of the E Germanic people, the *Goths.

Oswald, St c. 605–642. King of Northumbria from 634, after killing the Welsh king Cadwallon. He became a Christian convert during exile on the Scottish island of Iona. With the help of St Aidan he furthered the spread of Christianity in N England.

Otago peninsula and coastal plain on South Island, New Zealand, constituting a district; area 64,230 sq km/ 25,220 sq mi; chief cities include Dunedin and Invercargill.

Othman c. 574–656. Third caliph (leader of the Islamic empire) from 644, a son-in-law of the prophet Muhammad. Under his rule the Arabs became a naval power and extended their rule to N Africa and Cyprus, but Othman's personal weaknesses led to his assassination. He was responsible for the compilation of the authoritative version of the Koran, the sacred book of Islam.

Othman I another name for the Turkish sultan *Osman I.

Otho I 1815–1867. King of Greece 1832–62. As the 17-year-old son of King Ludwig I of Bavaria, he was selected by the European powers as the first king of independent Greece. He was overthrown by a popular revolt.

Otis Elisha Graves 1811–1861. US engineer who developed a lift that incorporated a safety device, making it acceptable for passenger use in the first skyscrapers. The device, invented 1852, consisted of vertical ratchets on the sides of the lift shaft into which spring-loaded catches would engage and 'lock' the lift in position in the event of cable failure.

otitis inflammation of the ear. *Otitis externa*, occurring in the outer ear canal, is easily treated with antibiotics. Inflamed conditions of the middle ear (*otitis media*) or inner ear (*otitis interna*) are more serious, carrying the risk of deafness and infection of the brain.

O'Toole Peter 1932– . Irish-born English actor who made his name as *Lawrence of Arabia* 1962, and who then starred in such films as *Becket* 1964 and *The Lion in Winter* 1968. Subsequent appearances were few and poorly received by critics until *The Ruling Class* 1972, *The Stuntman* 1978, and *High Spirits* 1988.

otosclerosis overgrowth of bone in the middle ear causing progressive deafness. This inherited condition is gradual in onset, developing usually before middle age. It is twice as common in women as in men.

Ottawa capital of Canada, in E Ontario, on the hills overlooking the Ottawa river and divided by the Rideau Canal into the Upper (western) and Lower (eastern) towns; population (1986) 301,000, metropolitan area (with adjoining Hull, Québec) 819,000. Industries include timber, pulp and paper, engineering, food processing, and publishing. It was founded 1826–32 as Bytown, in honour of John By (1781–1836), whose army engineers were building the Rideau Canal. It was renamed 1854 after the Outaouac Indians.

otter any of various aquatic carnivores of the

otter *Eurasian otters are among the fastest aquatic mammals, swimming at speeds of up to 10 kph/ 6 mph.*

weasel family, found on all continents except Australia. Otters have thick, brown fur, short limbs, webbed toes, and long, compressed tails. They are social, playful, and agile.

Otto four Holy Roman emperors, including:

Otto I 912–973. Holy Roman emperor from 936. He restored the power of the empire, asserted his authority over the pope and the nobles, ended the Magyar menace by his victory at the Lechfeld 955, and refounded the East Mark, or Austria, as a barrier against them.

Otto IV c. 1182–1218. Holy Roman emperor, elected 1198. He engaged in controversy with Pope Innocent III, and was defeated by the pope's ally, Philip of France, at Bouvines 1214.

Ottoman Empire Muslim empire of the Turks 1300–1920, the successor of the *Seljuk Empire. It was founded by *Osman I and reached its height with *Suleiman in the 16th century. Its capital was Istanbul (formerly Constantinople).

Ouagadougou capital and industrial centre of Burkina Faso; population (1985) 442,000. Products include textiles, vegetable oil, and soap.

Oudh region of N India, now part of Uttar Pradesh. An independent kingdom before it fell under Mogul rule, Oudh regained independence 1732–1856, when it was annexed by Britain. Its capital was Lucknow, centre of the *Indian Mutiny 1857–58. In 1877 it was joined with Agra, from 1902 as the United Provinces of Agra and Oudh, renamed Uttar Pradesh 1950.

Oughtred William 1575–1660. English mathematician, credited as the inventor of the slide rule 1622. His major work *Clavis mathematicae/The Key to Mathematics* 1631 was a survey of the entire body of mathematical knowledge of his day. It introduced the '×' symbol for multiplication, as well as the abbreviations 'sin' for sine and 'cos' for cosine.

Oujda industrial and commercial city (lead and coalmining) in N Morocco, near the border with Algeria; population (1982) 471,000. It trades in wool, grain, and fruit.

ounce another name for the snow *leopard.

ounce unit of mass, one-sixteenth of a pound *avoirdupois, equal to 437.5 grains (28.35 g); also one-twelfth of a pound troy, equal to 480 grains.

outback the inland region of Australia. Its main inhabitants are Aborigines, miners (including opal miners), and cattle ranchers. Its harsh beauty has been recorded by such artists as Sidney Nolan.

output device in computing, any device for displaying, in a form intelligible to the user, the results of processing carried out by a computer.

ovary in female animals, the organ that generates the *ovum. In humans, the ovaries are two whitish rounded bodies about 25 mm/1 in by 35 mm/1.5 in, located in the abdomen near the ends of the *Fallopian tubes. Every month, from puberty to the onset of the menopause, an ovum is released from the ovary. This is called ovulation, and forms part of the *menstrual cycle. In botany, an ovary is the expanded basal portion of the *carpel of flowering plants, containing one or more *ovules. It is hollow with a thick wall to protect the ovules. Following fertilization of the ovum, it develops into the fruit wall or pericarp.

overdraft in banking, a loan facility on a current account. It allows the account holder to overdraw on his or her account up to a certain limit and for a specified time, and interest is payable on the amount borrowed. An overdraft is a cheaper form of borrowing than the credit options that major credit-card companies offer.

overfishing fishing at rates that exceed the *sustained-yield cropping of fish species, resulting in a net population decline. For example, in the North Atlantic, herring has been fished to the verge of extinction and the cod and haddock populations are severely depleted. In the Third World, use of huge factory ships, often by fisheries from industrialized countries, has depleted stocks for local people who cannot obtain protein in any other way. See also *fishing and fisheries.

overhead in economics, fixed costs in a business that do not vary in the short term. These might include property rental, heating and lighting, insurance, and administration costs.

Overijssel province of the E central Netherlands
area 3,340 sq km/1,289 sq mi
towns capital Zwolle; Enschede, Hengelo, Deventer
physical it is generally flat and contains the rivers Ijssel and Vecht
products livestock, dairy products, textiles
population (1991) 1,026,300
history ruled by the bishops of Utrecht during the Middle Ages, Overijssel was sold to Charles V of Spain 1527. Joining the revolt against Spanish authority, it became one of the United Provinces of the Netherlands 1579.

overlander one of the Australian drovers in the 19th century who opened up new territory by driving their cattle through remote areas to new stations, or to market, before the establishment of regular stock routes.

Overlord, Operation Allied invasion of Normandy 6 June 1944 (D-day) during World War II.

Overseas Development Administration (ODA) UK official body that deals with development assistance to overseas countries, including financial aid on concessionary terms and technical assistance, usually in the form of sending specialists to other countries and giving training in the UK.

overtone note that has a frequency or pitch that is a multiple of the fundamental frequency, the sounding body's *natural frequency. Each sound source produces a unique set of overtones, which gives the source its quality or timbre.

overture piece of instrumental music, usually preceding an opera. There are also overtures to suites and plays, ballets, and 'concert' overtures, such as Elgar's *Cockaigne* and John Ireland's descriptive *London Overture*.

Ovid (Publius Ovidius Naso) 43 BC–AD 17. Roman poet whose poetry deals mainly with the themes of love (*Amores* 20 BC, *Ars amatoria/ The Art of Love* 1 BC), mythology (*Metamorphoses* AD 2), and exile (*Tristia* AD 9–12).

ovipary method of animal reproduction in which eggs are laid by the female and develop outside her body, in contrast to ovovivipary and

vivipary. It is the most common form of reproduction.

ovovivipary method of animal reproduction in which fertilized eggs develop within the female (unlike ovipary), and the embryo gains no nutritional substances from the female (unlike vivipary). It occurs in some invertebrates, fishes, and reptiles.

ovulation in female animals, the process of releasing egg cells (ova) from the *ovary. In mammals it occurs as part of the *menstrual cycle.

ovule structure found in seed plants that develops into a seed after fertilization. It consists of an *embryo sac containing the female gamete (*ovum or egg cell), surrounded by nutritive tissue, the nucellus. Outside this there are one or two coverings that provide protection, developing into the testa, or seed coat, following fertilization.

ovum (plural *ova*) female gamete (sex cell) before fertilization. In animals it is called an egg, and is produced in the ovaries. In plants, where it is also known as an egg cell or oosphere, the ovum is produced in an ovule. The ovum is nonmotile. It must be fertilized by a male gamete before it can develop further, except in cases of *parthenogenesis.

Owen David 1938– . British politician, Labour foreign secretary 1977–79. In 1981 he was one of the founders of the *Social Democratic Party (SDP), and in 1983 became its leader. Opposed to the decision of the majority of the party to merge with the Liberals 1987, Owen stood down, but emerged 1988 as leader of a rump SDP, which was eventually disbanded 1990. In 1992 he became EC mediator in the peace talks on *Bosnia-Herzegovina with UN mediator Cyrus *Vance. He resigned from this post 1995.

Owen Robert 1771–1858. British socialist, born in Wales. In 1800 he became manager of a mill at New Lanark, Scotland, where by improving working and housing conditions and providing schools he created a model community. His ideas stimulated the *cooperative movement (the pooling of resources for joint economic benefit).

Owen Wilfred 1893–1918. English poet. His verse, owing much to the encouragement of Siegfried *Sassoon, expresses his hatred of war, for example *Anthem for Doomed Youth*, published 1921.

Owens Jesse (James Cleveland) 1913–1980. US track and field athlete who excelled in the sprints, hurdles, and the long jump. At the 1936 Berlin Olympics he won four gold medals.

owl any bird of the order Strigiformes, found worldwide. They are mainly nocturnal birds of prey, with mobile heads, soundless flight, acute hearing, and forward-facing immobile eyes, surrounded by 'facial discs' of rayed feathers. All species lay white eggs, and begin incubation as soon as the first is laid. They regurgitate indigestible remains of their prey in pellets (castings).

ox castrated male of domestic species of cattle, used in Third World countries for ploughing and other agricultural purposes. Also the extinct wild ox or *aurochs of Europe, and extant wild species such as buffaloes and yaks.

oxalic acid $(COOH)_2.2H_2O$ white, poisonous solid, soluble in water, alcohol, and ether. Oxalic acid is found in rhubarb, and its salts (oxalates) occur in wood sorrel (genus *Oxalis*, family Oxalidaceae) and other plants. It is used in the leather and textile industries, in dyeing and bleaching, ink manufacture, metal polishes, and for removing rust and ink stains.

oxbow lake curved lake found on the flood plain of a river. Oxbows are caused by the loops of *meanders being cut off at times of flood and the river subsequently adopting a shorter course. In the USA, the term *bayou* is often used.

Oxfam (acronym for *Oxford Committee for Famine Relief*) charity working to relieve poverty and famine worldwide. It was established in the UK 1942 by Canon Theodore Richard Milford (1896–1987), initially to assist the starving people of Greece.

Oxford university city and administrative centre of Oxfordshire in S central England, at the confluence of the rivers Thames and Cherwell; population (1991) 109,000. Features include Oxford University (1249), the Bodleian Library (1488), the Ashmolean Museum (1683), and Christopher Wren's Sheldonian Theatre (1664–68).

Oxford and Asquith, Earl of title of British Liberal politician Herbert Henry *Asquith.

Oxford Movement also known as *Tractarian Movement* or *Catholic Revival* movement that attempted to revive Catholic religion in the Church of England. Cardinal Newman dated the movement from a sermon in Oxford 1833 by John Keble (1792–1866). The Oxford Movement by the turn of the century had transformed the Anglican communion, and survives today as Anglo-Catholicism.

Oxfordshire county in S central England
area 2,610 sq km/1,007 sq mi
towns Oxford (administrative headquarters), Abingdon, Banbury, Henley-on-Thames, Witney
products cereals, cars, paper, bricks, cement
population (1991) 553,800
famous people William Davenant, Flora Thompson, Winston Churchill.

oxidation in chemistry, the loss of *electrons, gain of oxygen, or loss of hydrogen by an atom, ion, or molecule during a chemical reaction.

oxide compound of oxygen and another element, frequently produced by burning the element or a compound of it in air or oxygen.

oxlip plant closely related to the *cowslip.

Oxon. abbreviation for *Oxoniensis* (Latin 'of Oxford').

oxpecker African bird, of the genus *Buphagus*, of the starling family. It clambers about the bodies of large mammals, feeding on ticks and other parasites. It may help to warn the host of approaching dangers.

oxyacetylene torch gas torch that burns ethene (acetylene) in pure oxygen, producing a high-temperature (3,000°C/5,400°F) flame. It is widely used in welding to fuse metals. In the cutting torch, a jet of oxygen burns through metal already melted by the flame.

oxygen (Greek *oxys* 'acid' *genes* 'forming') colourless, odourless, tasteless, nonmetallic, gaseous element, symbol O, atomic number 8, relative atomic mass 15.9994. It is the most abundant element in the Earth's crust (almost 50% by mass), forms about 21% by volume of the atmosphere, and is present in combined form in water and many other substances. Life on Earth evolved using oxygen, which is a by-product of *photosynthesis and the basis for *respiration in plants and animals.

oxygen debt physiological state produced by vigorous exercise, in which the lungs cannot supply all the oxygen that the muscles need.

oxymoron (Greek 'sharply dull' or 'pointedly foolish') *figure of speech, the combination of two or more words that are normally opposites, in order to startle. *Bittersweet* is an oxymoron, as are *cruel to be kind* and *beloved enemy*.

oxytocin hormone that stimulates the uterus in late pregnancy to initiate and sustain labour. After birth, it stimulates the uterine muscles to contract, reducing bleeding at the site where the placenta was attached.

oyster bivalve *mollusc constituting the Ostreidae, or true oyster, family, having the upper valve flat, the lower concave, hinged by an elastic ligament. The mantle, lying against the shell, protects the inner body, which includes respiratory, digestive, and reproductive organs. Oysters commonly change their sex annually or more frequently; females may discharge up to a million eggs during a spawning period.

oyster catcher chunky shorebird of the family Haematopodidae, with a laterally flattened, heavy bill that can pry open mollusc shells.

oz abbreviation for *ounce*.

Ozal Turgut 1927–1993. Turkish Islamic right-wing politician, prime minister 1983–89, president from 1989. He has been responsible for improving his country's relations with Greece, but his prime objective has been to strengthen Turkey's alliance with the USA.

Ozalid process trademarked copying process used to produce positive prints from drawn or printed materials or film, such as printing proofs from film images. The film is placed on top of chemically treated paper and then exposed to ultraviolet light. The image is developed dry using ammonia vapour.

Ozark Mountains area in the USA (shared by Arkansas, Illinois, Kansas, Mississippi, Oklahoma) of ridges, valleys, and streams; highest point only 700 m/2,300 ft; area 130,000 sq km/50,000 sq mi. This heavily forested region between the Missouri and Arkansas rivers has agriculture and lead and zinc mines.

ozone O_3 highly reactive pale-blue gas with a penetrating odour. Ozone is an allotrope of oxygen (see *allotropy), made up of three atoms of oxygen. It is formed when the molecule of the stable form of oxygen (O_2) is split by ultraviolet radiation or electrical discharge. It forms a layer in the upper atmosphere, which protects life on Earth from ultraviolet rays, a cause of skin cancer. At lower atmospheric levels it is an air pollutant and contributes to the *greenhouse effect.

ozone depleter any chemical that destroys the ozone in the stratosphere. Most ozone depleters are chemically stable compounds containing chlorine or bromine, which remain unchanged for long enough to drift up to the upper atmosphere. The best known are *chlorofluorocarbons (CFCs), but many other ozone depleters are known, including halons, used in some fire extinguishers; methyl chloroform and carbon tetrachloride, both solvents; some CFC substitutes; and the pesticide methyl bromide.

p in music, abbreviation for *piano* (Italian 'softly').

p(p). abbreviation for *page(s)*.

p.a. abbreviation for *per annum* (Latin 'yearly').

paca large, tailless, nocturnal, burrowing *rodent of the genus *Cuniculus*, in the family Dasyproctidae, which also includes the agoutis. The paca, about 60 cm/2 ft long, is native to Central and South America.

pace (Latin) with deference to, followed by a name, used to acknowledge contradiction of the person named.

pacemaker medical device implanted in a patient whose heart beats irregularly. It delivers minute electric shocks to stimulate the heart muscles at regular intervals and restores normal heartbeat. The latest pacemakers are powered by radioactive isotopes for long life and weigh no more than 15 g/0.5 oz. They are implanted under the skin.

Pacific Islands former (1947–1990) UN Trust Territory in the W Pacific captured from Japan during World War II. The territory comprised over 2,000 islands and atolls and was assigned to the USA 1947. The islands were divided into four governmental units: the Northern Marianas (except Guam) which became a self-governing commonwealth in union with the USA 1975; the *Marshall Islands, the Federated States of *Micronesia, and the Republic of *Belau (formerly Palau) became self-governing 1979–80, signing agreements of free association with the USA 1982. In Dec 1990 the United Nations Security Council voted to dissolve its trusteeship over the islands with the exception of Belau.

Pacific Ocean world's largest ocean, extending from Antarctica to the Bering Strait; area 166,242,500 sq km/64,170,000 sq mi; average depth 4,188 m/13,749 ft; greatest depth of any ocean 11,034 m/36,210 ft in the *Mariana Trench.

Pacific Security Treaty military alliance agreement between Australia, New Zealand, and the USA, signed 1951 (acronym ANZUS). Military cooperation between the USA and New Zealand has been restricted by the latter's policy of banning ships that might be carrying nuclear weapons or nuclear power sources.

Pacific War war 1879–83 fought by an alliance of Bolivia and Peru against Chile. Chile seized Antofagasta and the coast between the mouths of the rivers Loa and Paposo, rendering Bolivia landlocked, and also annexed the southern Peruvian coastline from Arica to the mouth of the Loa, including the nitrate fields of the Atacama Desert.

pacifism belief that violence, even in self-defence, is unjustifiable under any conditions and that arbitration is preferable to war as a means of solving disputes. In the East, pacifism has roots in Buddhism, and nonviolent action was used by Mahatma *Gandhi in the struggle for Indian independence.

Pacino Al(berto) 1940– . US film actor who played powerful, introverted but violent roles in films such as *The Godfather* 1972, *Serpico* 1973, and *Scarface* 1983. *Dick Tracy* 1990 added comedy to his range of acting styles, and *The Godfather Part III* added subdued style to his virtuoso performances.

Packer Kerry (Francis Bullmore) 1937– . Australian media proprietor. He is chair of Consolidated Press Holdings, which he privatised in 1983, a conglomerate founded by his father. CPH also has interests in radio and television stations. In 1977 he created World Series Cricket, which introduced one-day matches and coloured kit to the game.

packet switching in computing, a method of transmitting data between computers connected in a *network. A complete packet consists of the data being transmitted and information about which computer is to receive the data. The packet travels around the network until it reaches the correct destination.

Padua (Italian *Padova*) city in N Italy, 45 km/28 mi W of Venice; population (1988) 224,000. The astronomer Galileo taught at the university, founded 1222.

paediatrics or *pediatrics* medical speciality concerned with the care of children.

paedomorphosis in biology, an alternative term for neoteny.

Pagan archaeological site in Myanmar with the ruins of the former capital (founded 847, taken by Kublai Khan 1287). These include Buddhist pagodas, shrines, and temples with wall paintings of the great period of Burmese art (11th–13th centuries).

Paganini Niccolò 1782–1840. Italian violinist and composer, a virtuoso soloist from the age of nine. He invented all the virtuoso techniques that have since been included in violin composition. His works for the violin ingeniously exploit the potential of the instrument. His raffish appearance, wild amours, and virtuosity (especially on a single string) fostered a rumour of his being in league with the devil.

page-description language in computing, a control language used to describe the contents and layout of a complete printed page. Page-description languages are frequently used to control the operation of *laser printers. The most popular page-description languages are Adobe Postscript and Hewlett-Packard Printer Control Language.

paging method of increasing a computer's apparent memory capacity. See *virtual memory.

Pagnol Marcel 1895–1974. French film director, producer, author, and playwright whose work includes *Fanny* 1932 and *Manon des sources* 1952. His autobiographical *La Gloire de mon père/My Father's Glory* 1957 was filmed 1991. He regarded the cinema as recorded theatre; thus his films, although strong on character and background, fail to exploit the medium fully as an independent art form.

Pahlavi dynasty Iranian dynasty founded by Reza Khan (1877–1944), an army officer who seized control of the government 1921 and was proclaimed shah 1925. During World War II, Britain and the USSR were nervous about his German sympathies and occupied Iran 1941–46. They compelled him to abdicate 1941 in favour of his son Muhammad Reza Shah Pahlavi, who took office in 1956, with US support, and was deposed in the Islamic revolution of 1979.

pain sense that gives an awareness of harmful effects on or in the body. It may be triggered by stimuli such as trauma, inflammation, and heat. Pain is transmitted by specialized nerves and also has psychological components controlled by higher centres in the brain. Drugs that control pain are also known as analgesics.

Paine Thomas 1737–1809. English left-wing political writer, active in the American and French revolutions. His pamphlet *Common Sense* 1776 ignited passions in the American Revolution; others include *The Rights of Man* 1791 and *The Age of Reason* 1793. He advocated republicanism, deism, the abolition of slavery, and the emancipation of women.

paint any of various materials used to give a protective and decorative finish to surfaces or for making pictures. A paint consists of a pigment suspended in a vehicle, or binder, usually with added solvents. It is the vehicle that dries and hardens to form an adhesive film of paint. Among the most common kinds are cellulose paints (or lacquers), oil-based paints, emulsion paints, and special types such as enamels and primers.

painting application of colour, pigment, or paint to a surface. The chief methods of painting are ***tempera*** emulsion painting, with a gelatinous (for example, egg yolk) rather than oil base; known in ancient Egypt; ***fresco*** watercolour painting on plaster walls; the palace of Knossos, Crete, contains examples from about 2,000 BC; ***ink*** developed in China from calligraphy in the Sung period and highly popular in Japan from the 15th century; ***oil*** ground pigments in linseed, walnut, or other oil; spread from N to S Europe in the 15th century; ***watercolour*** pigments combined with gum arabic and glycerol, which are diluted with water; the method was developed in the 15th–17th centuries from wash drawings; ***acrylic*** synthetic pigments developed after World War II; the colours are very hard and brilliant.

Pakistan Islamic Republic of
area 796,100 sq km/307,295 sq mi; one-third of Kashmir under Pakistani control
capital Islamabad
towns Karachi, Lahore, Rawalpindi, Peshawar
physical fertile Indus plain in E; Baluchistan plateau in W, mountains in N and NW
environment about 68% of irrigated land is waterlogged or suffering from salinization
head of state Farooq Leghari from 1993
head of government Benazir Bhutto from 1993

political system emergent democracy
exports cotton textiles, rice, leather, carpets
currency Pakistan rupee
population (1993 est) 122,400,000 (66% Punjabi, 13% Sindhi); growth rate 3.1% p.a.
languages Urdu and English (official); Punjabi, Sindhi, Pashto, Baluchi, other local dialects
religions Sunni Muslim 75%, Shi'ite Muslim 20%, Hindu 4%
GNP $400 per head (1991)
chronology
1947 Independence achieved from Britain, Pakistan formed following partition of British India.
1956 Proclaimed a republic.
1958 Military rule imposed by General Ayub Khan.
1969 Power transferred to General Yahya Khan.
1971 Secession of East Pakistan (Bangladesh). After civil war, power transferred to Zulfiqar Ali Bhutto.
1977 Bhutto overthrown in military coup by General Zia ul-Haq; martial law imposed.
1979 Bhutto executed.
1981 Opposition Movement for the Restoration of Democracy formed. Islamization process pushed forward.
1985 Nonparty elections held, amended constitution adopted, martial law and ban on political parties lifted.
1986 Agitation for free elections launched by Benazir Bhutto.
1988 Zia introduced Islamic legal code, the *Shari'a*. He was killed in a military plane crash in Aug. Benazir Bhutto elected prime minister in Nov.
1989 Pakistan rejoined the Commonwealth.
1990 Army mobilized in support of Muslim separatists in Indian Kashmir. Bhutto dismissed. Islamic Democratic Alliance (IDA), led by Nawaz Sharif, won Oct general election.
1991 *Sharia* (Islamic legal code) bill enacted; privatization and economic deregulation programme launched.
1992 Pakistan elected to UN Security Council 1993–95.
1993 Power struggle resulted in Khan ousting Sharif and dissolving the National Assembly. Balakh Sher Mazari appointed interim prime minister.

Palaeocene (Greek 'old' + 'recent') first epoch

of the Tertiary period of geological time, 65–55 million years ago. Many types of mammals spread rapidly after the disappearance of the great reptiles of the Mesozoic.

Palaeolithic earliest stage of human technology and development of the Stone Age; see *prehistory.

palaeomagnetism science of the reconstruction of the Earth's ancient magnetic field and the former positions of the continents from the evidence of **remanent magnetization** in ancient rocks; that is, traces left by the Earth's magnetic field in *igneous rocks before they cool. Palaeomagnetism shows that the Earth's magnetic field has reversed itself – the magnetic north pole becoming the magnetic south pole, and vice versa – at approximate half-million-year intervals, with shorter reversal periods in between the major spans.

palaeontology in geology, the study of ancient life that encompasses the structure of ancient organisms and their environment, evolution, and ecology, as revealed by their *fossils. The practical aspects of palaeontology are based on using the presence of different fossils to date particular rock strata and to identify rocks that were laid down under particular conditions, for instance giving rise to the formation of oil.

Palaeozoic era of geological time 570–245 million years ago. It comprises the Cambrian, Ordovician, Silurian, Devonian, Carboniferous, and Permian periods. The Cambrian, Ordovician, and Silurian constitute the Lower or Early Palaeozoic; the Devonian, Carboniferous, and Permian make up the Upper or Late Palaeozoic. The era includes the evolution of hard-shelled multicellular life forms in the sea; the invasion of land by plants and animals; and the evolution of fish, amphibians, and early reptiles. The earliest identifiable fossils date from this era.

Palatinate (called the **Pfalz** in Germany) historic division of Germany, dating from before the 8th century. It was ruled by a **count palatine** (a count with royal prerogatives) and varied in size.

Palau former name (until 1981) of the Republic of *Belau.

Palermo capital and seaport of Sicily; population (1988) 729,000. Industries include shipbuilding, steel, glass, and chemicals. It was founded by the Phoenicians in the 8th century BC.

Palestine (Arabic *Falastin* 'Philistine') geographical area at the E end of the Mediterranean sea, also known as the **Holy Land** because of its historic and symbolic importance for Jews, Christians and Muslims. In ancient times Palestine extended E of the river Jordan, though today it refers to the territory of the State of Israel and the two Israeli-occupied territories of the West Bank and the Gaza Strip. However, in Sept 1993 Israel agreed to withdraw from the Gaza Strip and the West Bank town of Jericho, giving the Palestinians partial self-rule in these areas. Early settlers included the Canaanites, Hebrews, and Philistines. Over the centuries it became part of the Egyptian, Assyrian, Babylonian, Macedonian, Ptolemaic, Seleucid, Roman, Byzantine, Arab, and Ottoman empires.

Palestine Liberation Organization (PLO) Arab organization founded 1964 to bring about an independent state in Palestine. It consists of several distinct groupings, the chief of which is al-*Fatah, led by Yassir *Arafat, the president of the PLO from 1969. The PLO's original main aim was the destruction of the Israeli state, but over time it has changed to establishing a Palestinian state alongside that of Israel. A historic peace accord was agreed Sept 1993 by the PLO and Israel allowing for partial Palestinian self-rule in Jericho and the Gaza Strip.

Palestine Wars another name for the *Arab-Israeli Wars.

Palestrina Giovanni Pierluigi da 1525–1594. Italian composer. He wrote secular and sacred choral music, and is regarded as the most perfect exponent of Renaissance *counterpoint. Apart from motets and madrigals, he also wrote 105 masses, including *Missa Papae Marcelli*.

Paley William 1743–1805. English Christian theologian and philosopher. He put forward the *argument from design theory, which reasons that the complexity of the universe necessitates a superhuman creator and that the existence of this being (God) can be deduced from a 'design' seen in all living creatures. His views were widely held until challenged by Charles *Darwin. His major treatises include *The Principles of Moral and Political Philosophy* 1785, *A View of the Evidences of Christianity* 1794, and *Natural Theology* 1802.

Pali ancient Indo-European language of N India, related to Sanskrit, and a classical language of Buddhism.

palisade cell cylindrical cell lying immediately beneath the upper epidermis of a leaf. Palisade cells normally exist as one closely packed row and contain many chloroplasts. During the hours of daylight palisade cells are photosynthetic, using the energy of the sun to create carbohydrates from water and carbon dioxide.

Palk Strait channel separating SE India from the island of Sri Lanka; it is 53 km/33 mi at the widest point.

Palladio Andrea 1518–1580. Italian Renaissance architect. He was noted for his harmonious and balanced classical structures. He designed numerous palaces and country houses in and around Vicenza, Italy, making use of Roman classical forms, symmetry, and proportion. The Villa Malcontenta and the Villa Rotonda are examples of houses designed from 1540 for patrician families of the Venetian Republic. He also designed churches in Venice and published his studies of classical form in several illustrated books.

palladium lightweight, ductile and malleable, silver-white, metallic element, symbol Pd, atomic number 46, relative atomic mass 106.4. It is one of the so-called platinum group of metals, and is resistant to tarnish and corrosion. It often occurs in nature as a free metal (see *native metal) in a natural alloy with platinum. Palladium is used as a catalyst, in alloys of gold (to make white gold) and silver, in electroplating, and in dentistry.

Pallas in Greek mythology, a title of the goddess *Athena.

Pallava dynasty hereditary Hindu rulers who dominated SE India between the 4th and 9th centuries. The dynasty's greatest kings were Simhavisnu (ruled *c.* 575–600) and Narasimhavarman I (ruled 630–668). Their capital was Kanchi, SW of Madras.

palm plant of the family Palmae, characterized by a single tall stem bearing a thick cluster of large palmate or pinnate leaves at the top. The majority of the numerous species are tropical or subtropical. Some, such as the coconut, date, sago, and oil palms, are important economically.

Palma (Spanish *Palma de Mallorca*) industrial port (textiles, cement, paper, pottery), resort, and capital of the Balearic Islands, Spain, on Majorca; population (1991) 308,600. Palma was founded 276 BC as a Roman colony. It has a Gothic cathedral, begun 1229.

Palmas, Las port in the Canary Islands; see *Las Palmas.

Palmer Arnold (Daniel) 1929– . US golfer who helped to popularize the professional sport in the USA in the 1950s and 1960s. He won the Masters 1958, 1960, 1962, and 1964; the US Open 1960; and the British Open 1961 and 1962.

Palmer Samuel 1805–1881. English landscape painter and etcher. He lived in Shoreham, Kent, 1826–35 with a group of artists who were all followers of William Blake and called themselves 'the Ancients'. Palmer's expressive landscape style during that period reflected a strongly spiritual inspiration.

Palmerston Henry John Temple, 3rd Viscount Palmerston 1784–1865. British politician. Initially a Tory, in Parliament from 1807, he was secretary-at-war 1809–28. He broke with the Tories 1830 and sat in the Whig cabinets of 1830–34, 1835–41, and 1846–51 as foreign secretary. He was prime minister 1855–58 (when he rectified Aberdeen's mismanagement of the Crimean War, suppressed the *Indian Mutiny, and carried through the Second Opium War) and 1859–65 (when he almost involved Britain in the American Civil War on the side of the South).

Palm Sunday in the Christian calendar, the Sunday before Easter and first day of Holy Week, commemorating Jesus' entry into Jerusalem, when the crowd strewed palm leaves in his path.

Palmyra ancient city and oasis in the desert of Syria, about 240 km/150 mi NE of Damascus. Palmyra, the biblical *Tadmor*, was flourishing by about 300 BC. It was destroyed AD 272 after Queen Zenobia had led a revolt against the Romans. Extensive temple ruins exist, and on the site is a village called Tadmor.

Palo Alto city in California, USA, situated SE of San Francisco at the centre of the high-tech region known as 'Silicon Valley'; population (1990) 55,900. It is the site of Stanford University.

Palomar, Mount astronomical observatory, 80 km/50 mi NE of San Diego, California, USA. It has a 5-m/200-in diameter reflector called the Hale. Completed 1948, it was the world's premier observatory during the 1950s.

Pamirs central Asian plateau mainly in Tajikistan, but extending into China and Afghanistan, traversed by mountain ranges. Its highest peak is Kommunizma Pik (Communism Peak 7,495 m/24,600 ft) in the Akademiya Nauk range.

Pampas flat, treeless, Argentine plains, lying between the Andes and the Atlantic and rising gradually from the coast to the lower slopes of the mountains. The E Pampas contain large cattle ranches and the flax-and grain-growing area of Argentina; the W Pampas are arid and unproductive.

pampas grass any grass of the genus *Cortaderia*, native to South America, especially *C. argentea*, which is grown in gardens and has tall leaves and large panicles of white flowers.

Pamyat (Russian 'memory') nationalist Russian popular movement. Founded 1979 as a cultural and historical group attached to the Soviet Ministry of Aviation Industry, it grew from the mid-1980s, propounding a violently conservative and anti-Semitic Russian nationalist message.

Pan in Greek mythology, the god (Roman *Sylvanus*) of flocks and herds, shown as a man with the horns, ears, and hoofed legs of a goat, and playing a shepherd's panpipe (or syrinx).

Pan-Africanist Congress (PAC) militant black South African nationalist group, which broke away from the African National Congress (ANC) 1959. More radical than the ANC, the Pan-Africanist Congress has a black-only policy for Africa. PAC was outlawed from 1960 to 1990. Its military wing is called Poqo ('we alone').

Panama Republic of (*República de Panamá*)

area 77,100 sq km/29,768 sq mi
capital Panamá (Panama City)
towns Cristóbal, Balboa, Colón, David
physical coastal plains and mountainous interior; tropical rainforest in E and NW; Pearl Islands in Gulf of Panama
head of state and government Ernesto Pérez Balladares from 1994
political system emergent democratic republic
exports bananas, petroleum products, copper, shrimps, sugar
currency balboa
population (1993 est) 2,510,000 (mestizo, or mixed race, 70%; West Indian 14%; European descent 10%; Indian (Cuna, Choco, Guayami) 6%); growth rate 2.2% p.a.
languages Spanish (official), English
religions Roman Catholic 93%, Protestant 6%
GNP $2,180 per head (1991)
chronology
1821 Achieved independence from Spain; joined confederacy of Gran Colombia.

1903 Full independence achieved on separation from Colombia.
1974 Agreement to negotiate full transfer of the Panama Canal from the USA to Panama.
1977 USA–Panama treaties transferred the canal to Panama, effective from 1990, with the USA guaranteeing its protection and an annual payment.
1984 Nicolás Ardito Barletta elected president.
1985 Barletta resigned; replaced by Eric Arturo del Valle.
1987 General Noriega (head of the National Guard and effective ruler) resisted calls for his removal, despite suspension of US military and economic aid.
1988 Del Valle replaced by Manuel Solis Palma. Noriega, charged with drug smuggling by the USA, declared a state of emergency.
1989 Opposition won election; Noriega declared results invalid; Francisco Rodríguez sworn in as president. Coup attempt against Noriega failed; Noriega declared head of government by assembly. 'State of war' with the USA announced. US invasion deposed Noriega; Guillermo Endara installed as president. Noriega sought asylum in Vatican embassy; later surrendered and taken to US for trial.
1991 Attempted antigovernment coup foiled. Constitutional reforms approved by assembly, including abolition of a standing army.
1992 Noriega found guilty of drug offences.
1994 Ernesto Pérez Balladares (PRD) elected president.

Panama Canal canal across the Panama isthmus in Central America, connecting the Pacific and Atlantic oceans; length 80 km/50 mi, with 12 locks. Built by the USA 1904–14 after an unsuccessful attempt by the French, it was formally opened 1920. The *Panama Canal Zone* was acquired 'in perpetuity' by the USA 1903, comprising land extending about 5 km/3 mi on either side of the canal. The zone passed to Panama 1979, and control of the canal itself was ceded to Panama by the USA in Jan 1990 under the terms of the Panama Canal Treaty 1977. The Canal Zone has several US military bases.

Panama City capital of the Republic of Panama, near the Pacific end of the Panama Canal; population (1990) 584,800. Products include chemicals, plastics, and clothing. An earlier Panama, to the NE, founded 1519, was destroyed 1671, and the city was founded on the present site 1673.

Pan-American Union former name (1910–48) of the *Organization of American States.

Panchen Lama 10th incarnation 1935–1989. Tibetan spiritual leader, second in importance to the *Dalai Lama. A protégé of the Chinese since childhood, the present Panchen Lama is not universally recognized. When the Dalai Lama left Tibet 1959, the Panchen Lama was deputed by the Chinese to take over, but was stripped of power 1964 for refusing to denounce the Dalai Lama.

panchromatic in photography, a term describing highly sensitive black-and-white film made to render all visible spectral colours in correct grey tones. Panchromatic film is always developed in total darkness.

pancreas in vertebrates, an accessory gland of the digestive system located close to the duodenum. When stimulated by the hormone secretin, it secretes enzymes into the duodenum that digest starches, proteins, and fats. In humans, it is about 18 cm/7 in long, and lies behind and below the stomach. It contains groups of cells called the *islets of Langerhans*, which secrete the hormones insulin and glucagon that regulate the blood sugar level.

panda *The lesser, or red, panda lives in the bamboo forests of Nepal, W Myanmar, and SW China.*

panda one of two carnivores of different families, native to NW China and Tibet. The *giant panda Ailuropoda melanoleuca* has black and white fur with black eye patches, and feeds mainly on bamboo shoots. It can grow up to 1.5 m/4.5 ft long, and weigh up to 140 kg/300 lb. It is an endangered species. The *lesser, or red, panda Ailurus fulgens*, of the raccoon family, is about 50 cm/1.5 ft long, and is black and chestnut, with a long tail.

Pandora in Greek mythology, the first mortal woman. Zeus sent her to Earth with a box of evils (to counteract the blessings brought to mortals by *Prometheus' gift of fire); she opened the box, and the evils all flew out. Only hope was left inside as a consolation.

Pangaea or *Pangea* world continent, named by Alfred *Wegener, that existed between 250 and 200 million years ago, made up of all the continental masses. It may be regarded as a combination of *Laurasia in the north and *Gondwanaland in the south, the rest of Earth being covered by the *Panthalassa ocean.

pangolin or *scaly anteater* any toothless mammal of the order Pholidota. There is only one genus (*Manis*), with seven species found in tropical Africa and SE Asia. They are long-tailed and covered with large, overlapping scales. The elongated skull contains a long, extensible tongue. Pangolins measure up to 1 m/3 ft in length; some are arboreal and others are terrestrial. All live on ants and termites.

Pankhurst Emmeline (born Goulden) 1858–1928. English suffragette. Founder of the Women's Social and Political Union 1903, she launched the militant suffragette campaign 1905. In 1926 she joined the Conservative Party and was a prospective Parliamentary candidate.

pansy cultivated violet derived from the European wild pansy *Viola tricolor*, and including many different varieties and strains. The flowers are usually purple, yellow, cream, or a mixture, and there are many highly developed varieties bred for size, colour, or special markings. Several of the 400 different species are scented.

Panthalassa ocean that covered the surface of the Earth not occupied by the world continent *Pangaea between 250 and 200 million years ago.

pantheism (Greek *pan* 'all'; *theos* 'God') doctrine that regards all of reality as divine, and God as present in all of nature and the universe. It is expressed in Egyptian religion and Brahmanism; stoicism, Neo-Platonism, Judaism, Christianity, and Islam can be interpreted in pantheistic terms. Pantheistic philosophers include Bruno, Spinoza, Fichte, Schelling, and Hegel.

pantheon originally a temple for worshipping all the gods, such as that in ancient Rome, rebuilt by the emperor Hadrian and still used as a church. In more recent times, the name has been used for a building where famous people are buried (as in the Panthéon, Paris).

panther another name for the *leopard.

pantomime in the British theatre, a traditional Christmas entertainment with its origins in the harlequin spectacle of the 18th century and burlesque of the 19th century, which gave rise to the tradition of the principal boy being played by an actress and the dame by an actor. The harlequin's role diminished altogether as themes developed on folktales such as *The Sleeping Beauty* and *Cinderella*, and with the introduction of additional material such as popular songs, topical comedy, and audience participation.

pantothenic acid water-soluble *vitamin ($C_9H_{17}NO_5$) of the B complex, found in a wide variety of foods. Its absence from the diet can lead to dermatitis, and it is known to be involved in the breakdown of fats and carbohydrates.

panzer German mechanized divisions and regiments in World War II, used in connection with armoured vehicles, mainly tanks.

Paolozzi Eduardo 1924– . English sculptor and graphic artist. He was a major force in the Pop art movement in London in the mid-1950s. In the 1940s he produced collages using images taken from popular magazines. From the 1950s he worked primarily as a sculptor, typically using bronze casts of pieces of machinery to create robotlike structures. *Cyclops* 1957 (Tate Gallery, London) is an example.

papal infallibility doctrine formulated by the Roman Catholic Vatican Council 1870, which stated that the pope, when speaking officially on certain doctrinal or moral matters, was protected from error by God, and therefore such rulings could not be challenged.

Papal States area of central Italy in which the pope was temporal ruler from 756 until the unification of Italy 1870.

Papandreou Andreas 1919– . Greek socialist politician, founder of the Pan-Hellenic Socialist Movement (PASOK), prime minister 1981–89, and from 1993. In 1989 he became implicated in the alleged embezzlement and diversion of funds to the Greek government of $200 million from the Bank of Crete, headed by George Koskotas, and as a result lost the election. In Jan 1992 a trial cleared Papandreou of all corruption charges, and he was re-elected prime minister 1993.

papaya tropical tree *Carica papaya* of the family Caricaceae, native from Florida to South America. Varieties are grown throughout the tropics. The edible fruits resemble a melon, with orange-coloured flesh and numerous blackish seeds in the central cavity; they may weigh up to 9 kg/20 lb.

Papeete capital and port of French Polynesia on the NW coast of Tahiti; population (1983) 79,000. Products include vanilla, copra, and mother-of-pearl.

paper thin, flexible material made in sheets from vegetable fibres (such as wood pulp) or rags and used for writing, drawing, printing, packaging, and various household needs. The name comes from papyrus, a form of writing material made from water reed, used in ancient Egypt. The invention of true paper, originally made of pulped fishing nets and rags, is credited to Tsai Lun, Chinese minister of agriculture, AD 105.

papier mâché craft technique that involves building up layer upon layer of pasted paper, which is then baked or left to harden. Used for trays, decorative objects, and even furniture, it is often painted, lacquered, or decorated with mother-of-pearl.

Papp Joseph 1921–1991. US theatre director. He was the founder of the New York Shakespeare Festival 1954 held in an open-air theatre in the city's Central Park. He also founded the New York Public Theater 1967, an off-Broadway forum for new talent, which staged the first productions of the musicals *Hair* 1967 and *A Chorus Line* 1975.

Pap test or *Pap smear* common name for *cervical smear.

Papuan native to or inhabitant of Papua New Guinea; a speaker of a Papuan language, used mainly on the island of New Guinea, although some 500 are used in New Britain, the Solomon Islands, and the islands of the SW Pacific. The Papuan languages belong to the Indo-Pacific family.

Papua New Guinea
area 462,840 sq km/178,656 sq mi
capital Port Moresby (on E New Guinea)
towns Lae, Rabaul, Madang
physical mountainous; includes tropical islands of New Ireland, New Britain, and Bougainville; Admiralty Islands, D'Entrecasteaux Islands, and Louisiade Archipelago
head of state Queen Elizabeth II of Britain, represented by governor general Wiwa Korowi from 1991
head of government Julius Chan from 1994
political system liberal democracy
exports copra, coconut oil, palm oil, tea, copper, gold, coffee
currency kina
population (1993 est) 3,900,000 (Papuans, Melanesians, Negritos, various minorities); growth rate 2.6% p.a.
languages English (official); pidgin English, 715 local languages
religions Protestant 63%, Roman Catholic 31%, local faiths
GNP $820 per head (1991)
chronology
1883 Annexed by Queensland; became the Australian Territory of Papua.

1884 NE New Guinea annexed by Germany; SE claimed by Britain.
1914 NE New Guinea occupied by Australia.
1921–42 Held as a League of Nations mandate.
1942–45 Occupied by Japan.
1975 Independence from Australia, within the Commonwealth, with Michael Somare as prime minister.
1980 Julius Chan became prime minister.
1982 Somare returned to power.
1985 Somare challenged by Paias Wingti, the deputy prime minister, who later formed a five-party coalition government.
1988 Wingti defeated on no-confidence vote and replaced by Rabbie Namaliu, who established a six-party coalition government.
1989 State of emergency imposed on Bougainville in response to separatist violence.
1990 Bougainville Revolutionary Army (BRA) issued unilateral declaration of independence.
1991 Economic boom as gold production doubled. Deputy Prime Minister Ted Diro found guilty of corruption. Wiwa Korowi replaced Vicent Serei Eri as governor general.
1992 Wingti elected premier.
1994 Julius Chan (PPP) elected premier. Peace agreement with BRA.

papyrus type of paper made by the ancient Egyptians from the stem of the papyrus or paper reed *Cyperus papyrus*, family Cyperaceae.

parabola in mathematics, a curve formed by cutting a right circular cone with a plane parallel to the sloping side of the cone. A parabola is one of the family of curves known as *conic sections. The graph of $y = x^2$ is a parabola.

Paracelsus Adopted name of Theophrastus Bombastus von Hohenheim 1493–1541. Swiss physician, alchemist, and scientist. He developed the idea that minerals and chemicals might have medical uses (iatrochemistry). He introduced the use of *laudanum (which he named) for pain-killing purposes. Considered by some to be something of a charlatan, his books were also criticised because of their mystical content. However, his rejection of the ancients and insistence on the value of experimentation make him a leading figure in early science.

paracetamol analgesic, particularly effective for musculoskeletal pain. It is as effective as aspirin in reducing fever, and less irritating to the stomach, but has little anti-inflammatory action (as for joint pain). An overdose can cause severe, often irreversible or even fatal, liver and kidney damage.

parachute any canopied fabric device strapped to a person or a package, used to slow down descent from a high altitude, or returning spent missiles or parts to a safe speed for landing, or sometimes to aid (through braking) the landing of a plane or missile. Modern designs enable the parachutist to exercise considerable control of direction, as in *skydiving.

paradigm all those factors, both scientific and sociological, that influence the research of the scientist. The term, first used by the US historian of science T S *Kuhn, has subsequently spread to social studies and politics.

paradise (Persian 'pleasure garden') in various religions, a place or state of happiness. Examples are the Garden of *Eden and the Messianic king-

dom; the Islamic paradise of the *Koran* is a place of sensual pleasure.

Paradise Lost epic poem in twelve books, by John Milton, first published 1667. The poem describes the Fall of Man and the battle between God and Satan, as enacted through the story of Adam and Eve in the Garden of Eden. A sequel, **Paradise Regained**, was published 1671 and relates the temptation of Christ in the wilderness.

paraffin common name for *alkane, any member of the series of hydrocarbons with the general formula C_nH_{2n+2}. The lower members are gases, such as methane (marsh or natural gas). The middle ones (mainly liquid) form the basis of petrol, kerosene, and lubricating oils, while the higher ones (paraffin waxes) are used in ointment and cosmetic bases. The fuel commonly sold as paraffin in Britain is more correctly called kerosene.

Paraguay Republic of (*República del Paraguay*)

area 406,752 sq km/157,006 sq mi
capital Asunción
towns Puerto Presidente Stroessner, Pedro Juan Caballero; port Concepción
physical low marshy plain and marshlands; divided by Paraguay River; Paraná River forms SE boundary
head of state and government General Juan Carlos Wasmosy from 1993
political system emergent democratic republic
exports cotton, soya beans, timber, vegetable oil, maté
currency guaraní
population (1993 est) 4,500,000 (95% mixed Guarani Indian–Spanish descent); growth rate 3.0% p.a.
languages Spanish 6% (official), Guarani 90%
religion Roman Catholic 97%
GNP $1,210 per head (1991)
chronology
1811 Independence achieved from Spain.
1865–70 War with Argentina, Brazil, and Uruguay; much territory lost.
1932–35 Territory won from Bolivia during the Chaco War.

1940–48 Presidency of General Higinio Morínigo.

1948–54 Political instability; six different presidents.

1954 General Alfredo Stroessner seized power.

1989 Stroessner ousted in coup led by General Andrés Rodríguez. Rodríguez elected president; Colorado Party won the congressional elections.

1991 Colorado Party successful in assembly elections.

parakeet any of various small *parrots.

parallax the change in the apparent position of an object against its background when viewed from two different positions. In astronomy, nearby stars show a shift owing to parallax when viewed from different positions on the Earth's orbit around the Sun. A star's parallax is used to deduce its distance.

parallel lines and parallel planes in mathematics, straight lines or planes that always remain a constant distance from one another no matter how far they are extended. This is a principle of Euclidean geometry. Some non-Euclidean geometries, such as elliptical and hyperbolic geometry, however, reject Euclid's parallel axiom.

parallelogram in mathematics, a quadrilateral (four-sided plane figure) with opposite pairs of sides equal in length and parallel, and opposite angles equal. The diagonals of a parallelogram bisect each other. Its area is the product of the length of one side and the perpendicular distance between this and the opposite side. In the special case when all four sides are equal in length, the parallelogram is known as a rhombus, and when the internal angles are right angles, it is a rectangle or square.

parallel processing emerging computer technology that allows more than one computation at the same time. Although in the 1980s this technology enabled only a small number of computer processor units to work in parallel, in theory thousands or millions of processors could be used at the same time.

paralysis loss of voluntary movement due to failure of nerve impulses to reach the muscles involved. It may result from almost any disorder of the nervous system, including brain or spinal-cord injury, poliomyelitis, stroke, and progressive conditions such as a tumour or multiple sclerosis. Paralysis may also involve loss of sensation due to sensory-nerve disturbance.

Paramaribo port and capital of Surinam, South America, 24 km/15 mi from the sea on the river Suriname; population (1980) 193,000. Products include coffee, fruit, timber, and bauxite. It was founded by the French on an Indian village 1540, made capital of British Surinam 1650, and placed under Dutch rule 1816–1975.

paramilitary uniformed, armed force found in many countries, occupying a position between the police and the military. In France such a force is called the Gendarmerie and in Germany the Federal Border Guard. In recent years the term has been extended to include also illegal organizations of a terrorist nature.

Paramount Studios US film production and distribution company, founded 1912 as the Famous Players Film Company by Adolph Zukor (1873–1976). In 1914 it merged with the distribution company Paramount Pictures. A major studio from the silent days of cinema, Paramount was adept at discovering new talent and Cecil B de Mille made many of his films for the studio. In 1966 the company was taken over by Gulf and Western Industries. In recent years it has produced such successful films as *Grease* 1978 and *Raiders of the Lost Ark* 1981.

Paraná river in South America, formed by the confluence of the Río Grande and Paranaiba; the Paraguay joins it at Corrientes, and it flows into the Río de la Plata with the Uruguay; length 4,500 km/2,800 mi. It is used for hydroelectric power by Argentina, Brazil, and Paraguay.

paranoia mental disorder marked by delusions of grandeur or persecution. In popular usage, paranoia means baseless or exaggerated fear and suspicion.

paraplegia paralysis of the lower limbs, involving loss of both movement and sensation; it is usually due to spinal injury.

parapsychology (Greek *para* 'beyond') study of phenomena that are not within range of, or explicable by established science, for example, extra-sensory perception. The faculty allegedly responsible for such phenomena, and common to humans and other animals, is known as *psi*.

paraquat $CH_3(C_5H_4N)_2CH_3.2CH_3SO_4$ (technical name 1,1-dimethyl-4,4-dipyridylium) non-selective herbicide (weedkiller). Although quickly degraded by soil microorganisms, it is deadly to human beings if ingested.

parasite organism that lives on or in another organism (called the 'host'), and depends on it for nutrition, often at the expense of the host's welfare. Parasites that live inside the host, such as liver flukes and tapeworms, are called *endoparasites*; those that live on the outside, such as fleas and lice, are called *ectoparasites*.

Paré Ambroise 1509–1590. French surgeon who introduced modern principles to the treatment of wounds. As a military surgeon, Paré developed new ways of treating wounds and amputations, which greatly reduced the death rate among the wounded. He abandoned the practice of cauterization (sealing with heat), using balms and soothing lotions instead, and used ligatures to tie off blood vessels.

parenchyma plant tissue composed of loosely packed, more or less spherical cells, with thin cellulose walls. Although parenchyma often has no specialized function, it is usually present in large amounts, forming a packing or ground tissue. It usually has many intercellular spaces.

parent governor elected parent representative on the governing body of a state school. The 1980 Education Act in the UK made it mandatory for all state schools to include parent governors, in line with the existing practice of some local education authorities. The 1986 Education Act increased parental representation.

parent–teacher association (PTA) group attached to a school consisting of parents and teachers who support the school by fund raising and other activities. In the UK, PTAs are organized into a national federation, the National Confederation of PTAs, which increasingly acts as a pressure group for state schools.

Pareto Vilfredo 1848–1923. Italian economist and political philosopher. A vigorous opponent of socialism and liberalism, he justified inequality of income on the grounds of his empirical observation (**Pareto's law**) that income distribution remained constant whatever efforts were made to change it.

Paris port and capital of France, on the river Seine; *département* in the Ile de France region; area 105 sq km/40.5 sq mi; population (1990) 2,175,200. Products include metal, leather, and luxury goods and chemicals, glass, and tobacco.

Paris in Greek legend, a prince of Troy whose abduction of Helen, wife of King Menelaus of Sparta, caused the Trojan War.

Paris Club international forum dating from the 1950s for the rescheduling of debts granted or guaranteed by official bilateral creditors; it has no fixed membership nor an institutional structure. In the 1980s it was closely involved in seeking solutions to the serious debt crises affecting many developing countries.

Paris Commune two periods of government in France: *The Paris municipal government 1789–94* was established after the storming of the *Bastille and remained powerful in the French Revolution until the fall of Robespierre 1794. *The provisional national government 18 March–May 1871* was formed while Paris was besieged by the Germans during the Franco-Prussian War. It consisted of socialists and left-wing republicans, and is often considered the first socialist government in history. Elected after the right-wing National Assembly at Versailles tried to disarm the National Guard, it fell when the Versailles troops captured Paris and massacred 20,000–30,000 people 21–28 May.

parish in Britain, a subdivision of a county often coinciding with an original territorial subdivision in Christian church administration, served by a parish church. In the US, the parish is an ecclesiastical unit committed to one minister or priest.

parish council unit of local government in England and Wales, based on church parishes. In Wales they are commonly called *community councils*.

Paris, Treaty of any of various peace treaties signed in Paris, including:
1763 ending the *Seven Years' War;
1783 recognizing American independence;
1814 and *1815* following the abdication and final defeat of *Napoleon I;
1856 ending the *Crimean War;
1898 ending the *Spanish-American War;
1919–20 the conference preparing the Treaty of *Versailles at the end of World War I was held in Paris;
1946 after World War II, the peace treaties between the *Allies and Italy, Romania, Hungary, Bulgaria, and Finland;
1951 treaty signed by France, West Germany, Italy, Belgium, Netherlands and Luxembourg, embodying the Schuman Plan to set up a single coal and steel authority;
1973 ending US participation in the *Vietnam War.

parity in economics, equality of price, rate of exchange, wages, and buying power. Parity ratios may be used in the setting of wages to establish similar status to different work groups. Parity in international exchange rates means that those on a par with each other share similar buying power. In the USA, agricultural output prices are regulated by a parity system.

parity of a number, the state of being either even or odd. In computing, the term refers to the number of 1s in the binary codes used to represent data. A binary representation has **even parity** if it contains an even number of 1s and **odd parity** if it contains an odd number of 1s.

Park Chung Hee 1917–1979. President of South Korea 1963–79. Under his rule South Korea had one of the world's fastest-growing economies, but recession and his increasing authoritarianism led to his assassination 1979.

Parker Charlie (Charles Christopher 'Bird', 'Yardbird') 1920–1955. US alto saxophonist and jazz composer, associated with the trumpeter Dizzy Gillespie in developing the *bebop style. His mastery of improvisation inspired performers on all jazz instruments.

Parker Dorothy (born Rothschild) 1893–1967. US writer and wit, a leading member of the Algonquin Round Table. She reviewed for the magazines *Vanity Fair* and *The New Yorker*, and wrote wittily ironic verses, collected in several volumes including *Not So Deep As a Well* 1940, and short stories.

Parkinson Norman. Adopted name of Ronald William Parkinson Smith 1913–1990. English fashion and portrait photographer who caught the essential glamour of each decade from the 1930s to the 1980s. Long associated with the magazines *Vogue* and *Queen*, he was best known for his colour work, and from the late 1960s took many official portraits of the royal family.

Parkinson's disease or *parkinsonism* or *paralysis agitans* degenerative disease of the brain characterized by a progressive loss of mobility, muscular rigidity, tremor, and speech difficulties. The condition is mainly seen in people over the age of 50.

parliament (French 'speaking') legislative body of a country. The world's oldest parliament is the Icelandic Althing which dates from about 930. The UK Parliament is usually dated from 1265. The legislature of the USA is called *Congress and comprises the *House of Representatives and the *Senate.

parliamentary paper in the UK, an official document, such as a White Paper or a report of a select committee, which is prepared for the information of members of Parliament.

Parliament, European governing body of the European Community; see *European Parliament.

Parliament, Houses of building where the UK legislative assembly meets. The present Houses of Parliament in London, designed in Gothic Revival style by the architects Charles Barry and A W Pugin, were built 1840–60, the previous building having burned down 1834. It incorporates portions of the medieval Palace of Westminster.

Parnassus mountain in central Greece, height 2,457 m/8,064 ft, revered by the ancient Greeks as the abode of Apollo and the Muses. The sacred site of Delphi lies on its southern flank.

Parnell Charles Stewart 1846–1891. Irish

nationalist politician. He supported a policy of obstruction and violence to attain *Home Rule, and became the president of the Nationalist Party 1877. In 1879 he approved the *Land League, and his attitude led to his imprisonment 1881. His career was ruined 1890 when he was cited as co-respondent in a divorce case.

parody in literature and the other arts, a work that imitates the style of another work, usually with mocking or comic intent; it is related to *satire.

parole conditional release of a prisoner from jail. The prisoner remains on licence until the date release would have been granted, and may be recalled if the authorities deem it necessary.

parquetry geometric version of *marquetry: a decorative veneer applied to furniture and floors, composed of shaped pieces of wood or other suitable materials, such as bone, horn, or ivory, to form a geometric pattern or mosaic.

Parr Catherine 1512–1548. Sixth wife of Henry VIII of England. She had already lost two husbands when in 1543 she married Henry VIII. She survived him, and in 1547 married Lord Seymour of Sudeley (1508–1549).

parrot any bird of the order Psittaciformes, abundant in the tropics, especially in Australia and South America. They are mainly vegetarian, and range in size from the 8.5 cm/3.5 in pygmy parrot to the 100 cm/40 in Amazon parrot. The smaller species are commonly referred to as parakeets. The plumage is often very colourful, and the call is usually a harsh screech. Several species are endangered.

Parry Charles Hubert Hastings 1848–1918. English composer. His works include songs, motets, and the setting of Milton's 'Blest Pair of Sirens' and Blake's 'Jerusalem'.

Parry William Edward 1790–1855. English admiral and Arctic explorer. He made detailed charts during explorations of the Northwest Passage (the sea route between the Atlantic and Pacific oceans) 1819–20, 1821–23, and 1824–25.

parsec in astronomy, a unit (symbol pc) used for distances to stars and galaxies. One parsec is equal to 3.2616 *light years, 2.063 x 10^5 *astronomical units, and 3.086×10^{13} km.

Parsee or *Parsi* follower of the religion *Zoroastrianism. The Parsees fled from Persia after its conquest by the Arabs, and settled in India in the 8th century AD. About 100,000 Parsees now live mainly in Bombay State.

Parsifal in Germanic legend, one of the knights who sought the Holy Grail; the father of Lohengrin.

parsley biennial herb *Petroselinum crispum* of the carrot family, Umbelliferae, cultivated for flavouring and its nutrient properties, being rich in vitamin C and minerals. Up to 45 cm/1.5 ft high, it has pinnate, aromatic leaves and yellow umbelliferous flowers.

parsnip temperate Eurasian biennial *Pastinaca sativa* of the carrot family Umbelliferae, with a fleshy edible root.

parthenocarpy in botany, the formation of fruits without seeds. This phenomenon, of no obvious benefit to the plant, occurs naturally in some plants, such as bananas. It can also be induced in some fruit crops, either by breeding or by applying certain plant hormones.

parthenogenesis development of an ovum (egg) without any genetic contribution from a male. Parthenogenesis is the normal means of reproduction in a few plants (for example, dandelions) and animals (for example, certain fish). Some sexually reproducing species, such as aphids, show parthenogenesis at some stage in their life cycle.

Parthenon temple of Athena Parthenos ('the Virgin') on the Acropolis at Athens; built 447–438 BC by Callicrates and Ictinus under the supervision of the sculptor Phidias, and the most perfect example of Doric architecture. In turn a Christian church and a Turkish mosque, it was then used as a gunpowder store, and reduced to ruins when the Venetians bombarded the Acropolis 1687. The *Elgin marbles were removed from the Parthenon in the early 19th century and are now in the British Museum, London.

Parthia ancient country in W Asia in what is now NE Iran, capital Ctesiphon. Originating about 248 BC, it reached the peak of its power under Mithridates I in the 2nd century BC, and was annexed to Persia under the Sassanids AD 226. Parthian horsemen feigned retreat and shot their arrows unexpectedly backwards, hence the use of 'Parthian shot', to mean a remark delivered in parting.

participle in grammar, a form of the verb, in English either a *present participle* ending in -ing (for example, 'working' in 'They were *working*', '*working* men', and 'a hard-*working* team') or a *past participle* ending in -ed in regular verbs (for example, 'trained' in 'They have been *trained* well', '*trained* soldiers', and 'a well-*trained* team').

particle in grammar, a category that includes such words as *up, down, in, out*, which may be used either as *prepositions (also called *prepositional particles*), as in *up the street* and *down the stairs*, or as *adverbs (identified as *adverbial particles*), as in *pick up the book/ pick the book up*. A verb with a particle (for example, *put up*) is a phrasal *verb.

particle physics study of the particles that make up all atoms, and of their interactions. More than 300 subatomic particles have now been identified by physicists, categorized into several classes according to their mass, electric charge, spin, magnetic moment, and interaction. Subatomic particles include the *elementary particles* (quarks, leptons, and gauge bosons), which are believed to be indivisible and so may be considered the fundamental units of matter; and the *hadrons* (baryons, such as the proton and neutron, and mesons), which are composite particles, made up of two or three quarks. The proton, electron, and neutrino are the only stable particles (the neutron being stable only when in the atomic nucleus). The unstable particles decay rapidly into other particles, and are known from experiments with particle accelerators and cosmic radiation. See *atomic structure.

particle, subatomic in physics, a particle that is smaller than an atom; see *particle physics.

partisan member of an armed group that operates behind enemy lines or in occupied territories during wars. The name 'partisans' was first given to armed bands of Russians who operated against Napoleon's army in Russia during 1812, but has since been used to describe Russian, Yugoslav, Italian, Greek, and Polish Resistance groups against the Germans during World War II.

part of speech grammatical function of a word, described in the grammatical tradition of the Western world, based on Greek and Latin. The four major parts of speech are the noun, verb, adjective, and adverb; the minor parts of speech vary according to schools of grammatical theory, but include the article, conjunction, preposition, and pronoun.

Parton Dolly 1946– . US country and western singer and songwriter whose combination of cartoonlike sex-symbol looks and intelligent, assertive lyrics made her popular beyond the genre, with hits like 'Jolene' 1974, but deliberate crossover attempts were less successful. She has also appeared in films, beginning with *9 to 5* 1980, and established a theme park Dollywood in Tennessee 1986.

partridge any of various medium-sized ground-dwelling fowl of the family Phasianidae, which also includes pheasants, quail, and chickens.

Parvati in Hindu mythology, the consort of Siva in one of her gentler manifestations, and the mother of Ganesa, the god of prophecy; she is said to be the daughter of the Himalayas.

PASCAL (French acronym for *program appliqué à la selection et la compilation automatique de la litterature*) a high-level computer-programming language. Designed by Niklaus Wirth (1934–) in the 1960s as an aid to teaching programming, it is still widely used as such in universities, but is also recognized as a good general-purpose programming language. It was named after 17th-century French mathematician Blaise Pascal.

pascal SI unit (symbol Pa) of pressure, equal to one newton per square metre. It replaces bars and millibars (10^5 Pa equals one bar). It is named after the French scientist Blaise Pascal.

Pascal Blaise 1623–1662. French philosopher and mathematician. He contributed to the development of hydraulics, the *calculus, and the mathematical theory of *probability.

pas de deux dance for two performers. A *grand pas de deux* is danced by the prima ballerina and the premier danseur.

Pashto language or *Pushto* or *Pushtu* Indo-European language, the official language of Afghanistan, also spoken in N Pakistan.

Pasolini Pier Paolo 1922–1975. Italian poet, novelist, and film director, an influential figure. His writings (making much use of first Friulan and later Roman dialect) include the novels *Ragazzi di vita/The Ragazzi* 1955 and *Una vita violenta/A Violent Life* 1959, filmed with success as *Accattone!* 1961.

Passchendaele village in W Flanders, Belgium, near Ypres. The Passchendaele ridge before Ypres was the object of a costly and unsuccessful British offensive in World War I, between July and Nov 1917; British casualties numbered nearly 400,000.

Passfield Baron Passfield. Title of the Fabian socialist Sidney *Webb.

passim (Latin 'in many places') indicates that a reference occurs repeatedly throughout the work.

passion flower climbing plant of the tropical American genus *Passiflora*, family Passifloraceae. It bears distinctive flower heads comprising a saucer-shaped petal base, a fringelike corona, and a central stalk bearing the stamens and ovary. Some species produce edible fruit.

passion play play representing the death and resurrection of a god, such as Osiris, Dionysus, or Jesus; it has its origins in medieval *mystery plays. Traditionally, a passion play takes place every ten years at *Oberammergau, Germany.

passive smoking inhalation of tobacco smoke from other people's cigarettes; see *smoking.

pass laws South African laws that required the black population to carry passbooks (identity documents) at all times and severely restricted freedom of movement. The laws, a major cause of discontent, formed a central part of the policies of *apartheid. They were repealed 1986.

Passover also called **Pesach** in Judaism, an eight-day spring festival which commemorates the exodus of the Israelites from Egypt and the passing over by the Angel of Death of the Jewish houses, so that only the Egyptian firstborn sons were killed.

passport document issued by a national government authorizing the bearer to go abroad and guaranteeing the bearer the state's protection. Some countries require an intending visitor to obtain a special endorsement or visa.

pasta food made from a dough of durum-wheat flour or semolina, water, and, sometimes egg, and cooked in boiling water. It is usually served with a sauce. Pasta is available either fresh or dried, and comes in a wide variety of shapes. It may be creamy yellow or coloured green with spinach or red with tomato. Pasta has been used in Italian cooking since the Middle Ages, but is now popular in many other countries.

Pasternak Boris Leonidovich 1890–1960. Russian poet and novelist. His novel *Dr Zhivago* 1957 was banned in the USSR as a 'hostile act', and was awarded a Nobel prize (which Pasternak declined). *Dr Zhivago* has since been unbanned and Pasternak has been posthumously rehabilitated.

Pasteur Louis 1822–1895. French chemist and microbiologist who discovered that fermentation is caused by microorganisms. He also developed a vaccine for *rabies, which led to the foundation of the Institut Pasteur in Paris 1888.

pasteurization treatment of food to reduce the number of microorganisms it contains and so protect consumers from disease. Harmful bacteria are killed and the development of others is delayed. For milk, the method involves heating it to 72°C/161°F for 15 seconds followed by rapid cooling to 10°C/50°F or lower. The process also kills beneficial bacteria and reduces the nutritive property of milk.

pastoral farming the rearing or keeping of animals in order to obtain meat or other products, such as milk, skins, and hair. Animals can be kept in one place or periodically moved (*nomadic pastoralism).

past participle form of the verb, see *participle.

Patagonia geographic area of South America, south of latitude 40° S, with sheep farming, and coal and oil resources. Sighted by Ferdinand Magellan 1520, it was claimed by both Argentina and Chile until divided between them 1881.

patchouli soft-wooded E Indian shrub *Pogostemon heyneanus* of the mint family Labiateae, source of the perfume patchouli.

patella or *knee cap* a flat bone embedded in the knee tendon of birds and mammals, which protects the joint from injury.

patent or *letters patent* documents conferring the exclusive right to make, use, and sell an invention for a limited period. Ideas are not eligible; neither is anything not new. The earliest known patent for an invention in England is dated 1449 (granted by Henry VI for making stained glass for Eton College).

Paternoster (Latin 'our father') in the Roman Catholic Church, the Lord's Prayer. The opening words of the Latin version are *Pater noster*.

Pathan member of a people of NW Pakistan and Afghanistan, numbering about 14 million (1984). The majority are Sunni Muslims. The Pathans speak Pashto, a member of the Indo-Iranian branch of the Indo-European family.

Pathé Charles 1863–1957. French film pioneer who began his career selling projectors in 1896 and with the profits formed Pathé Frères with his brothers. In 1901 he embarked on film production and by 1908 had become the world's biggest producer, with branches worldwide. He also developed an early colour process and established a weekly newsreel, *Pathé Journal*. World War I disrupted his enterprises and by 1918 he was gradually forced out of business by foreign competition.

pathogen (Greek 'disease producing') in medicine, a bacterium or virus that causes disease. Most pathogens are *parasites, and the diseases they cause are incidental to their search for food or shelter inside the host. Nonparasitic organisms, such as soil bacteria or those living in the human gut and feeding on waste foodstuffs, can also become pathogenic to a person whose immune system or liver is damaged. The larger parasites that can cause disease, such as nematode worms, are not usually described as pathogens.

pathology medical speciality concerned with the study of disease processes and how these provoke structural and functional changes in the body and its tissues.

patina effect produced on bronze by oxidation, which turns the surface green, and by extension any lacquering or finishing technique, other than gilding, applied to bronze objects. Patina can also mean the surface texture of old furniture, silver, and antique objects.

Paton Alan 1903–1988. South African writer. His novel *Cry, the Beloved Country* 1948 focused on racial inequality in South Africa. Later books include the study *Land and People of South Africa* 1956, *The Long View* 1968, and his autobiography *Towards the Mountain* 1980.

patriarch (Greek 'ruler of a family') in the Old Testament, one of the ancestors of the human race, and especially those of the ancient Hebrews, from Adam to Abraham, Isaac, Jacob, and his sons (who became patriarchs of the Hebrew tribes). In the Eastern Orthodox Church, the term refers to the leader of a national church.

patrician member of a privileged class in ancient Rome, descended from the original citizens. After the 4th century BC the rights formerly exercised by the patricians alone were made available to the ordinary people, the plebeians, and patrician descent became only a matter of prestige.

Patrick, St 389–c. 461. Patron saint of Ireland. Born in Britain, probably in S Wales, he was carried off by pirates to six years' slavery in Antrim, Ireland, before escaping either to Britain or Gaul – his poor Latin suggests the former – to train as a missionary. He is variously said to have landed again in Ireland 432 or 456, and his work was a vital factor in the spread of Christian influence there. His symbols are snakes and shamrocks; feast day 17 March.

Patriot missile ground-to-air medium-range missile system used in air defence. It has high-altitude coverage, electronic jamming capability, and excellent mobility. US Patriot missiles were tested in battle against *Scud missiles fired by the Iraqis in the 1991 Gulf War.

patronage power to give a favoured appointment to an office or position in politics, business, or the church; or sponsorship of the arts. Patronage was for centuries bestowed mainly by individuals (in Europe often royal or noble) or by the church. In the 20th century, patrons have tended to be political parties, the state, and – in the arts – private industry and foundations.

Patten Christopher Francis 'Chris' 1944– . British Conservative politician and governor of Hong Kong from 1992. A former director of the Conservative Party research department, he held junior ministerial posts under Margaret Thatcher and was later chairman of the party under John Major. He masterminded the successful 1992 Conservative election campaign but lost his own seat. He accepted the governorship of Hong Kong for the crucial five years prior to its transfer to China.

Patton George (Smith) 1885–1945. US general in World War II, known as 'Blood and Guts'. He was appointed to command the 2nd Armored Division 1940 and became commanding general of the First Armored Corps 1941. In 1942 he led the Western Task Force that landed at Casablanca, Morocco. After commanding the 7th Army, he led the 3rd Army across France and into Germany, and in 1945 took over the 15th Army.

Paul Les. Adopted name of Lester Polfuss 1915– . US inventor of the solid-body electric guitar in the early 1940s, and a pioneer of recording techniques including overdubbing and electronic echo. The Gibson Les Paul guitar was first marketed 1952 (the first commercial solid-body guitar was made by Leo Fender). As a guitarist in the late 1940s and 1950s he recorded with the singer Mary Ford (1928–1977).

Paul VI Giovanni Battista Montini 1897–1978. Pope from 1963. His encyclical *Humanae Vitae/Of Human Life* 1968 reaffirmed the church's traditional teaching on birth control, thus following the minority report of the commission originally appointed by Pope John rather than the majority view.

Pauli Wolfgang 1900–1958. Austrian physicist who originated the **exclusion principle**: in a given system no two fermions (electrons, protons, neutrons, or other elementary particles of half-integral spin) can be characterized by the same set of *quantum numbers. He also predicted the existence of neutrinos. He was awarded a Nobel prize 1945 for his work on atomic structure.

Pauling Linus Carl 1901–1994. US chemist, author of fundamental work on the nature of the chemical bond and on the discovery of the helical structure of many proteins. He also investigated the properties and uses of vitamin C as related to human health. He won the Nobel Prize for Chemistry 1954. An outspoken opponent of nuclear testing, he also received the Nobel Peace Prize in 1962.

Paul, St c. AD 3–c. AD 68. Christian missionary and martyr; in the New Testament, one of the apostles and author of 13 epistles. Originally opposed to Christianity, he took part in the stoning of St Stephen. He is said to have been converted by a vision on the road to Damascus. After his conversion he made great missionary journeys, for example to Philippi and Ephesus, becoming known as the Apostle of the Gentiles (non-Jews). His emblems are a sword and a book; feast day 29 June.

Pavarotti Luciano 1935– . Italian tenor whose operatic roles have included Rodolfo in *La Bohème*, Cavaradossi in *Tosca*, the Duke of Mantua in *Rigoletto*, and Nemorino in *L'Elisir d'amore*. He gave his first performance in the title role of *Otello* in Chicago, USA 1991.

Pavlov Ivan Petrovich 1849–1936. Russian physiologist who studied conditioned reflexes in animals. His work had a great impact on behavioural theory (see *behaviourism) and *learning theory. See also *conditioning. Nobel Prize for Medicine 1904.

Pavlova Anna 1881–1931. Russian dancer. Prima ballerina of the Imperial Ballet from 1906, she left Russia 1913, and went on to become one of the world's most celebrated exponents of classical ballet. With London as her home, she toured extensively with her own company, influencing dancers worldwide with roles such as Mikhail *Fokine's *The Dying Swan* solo 1905.

pawpaw or *papaw* small tree *Asimina triloba* of the custard-apple family Annonaceae, native to the eastern USA. It bears oblong fruits 13 cm/ 5 in long with yellowish, edible flesh. The name pawpaw is also used for the *papaya.

Paxton Joseph 1801–1865. English architect, garden superintendent to the Duke of Devonshire from 1826 and designer of the Great Exhibition building 1851 (the Crystal Palace), which was revolutionary in its structural use of glass and iron.

PAYE abbreviation for *Pay As You Earn*, system of tax collection in which a proportional amount of income tax is deducted on a regular basis by the employer before wages are paid. In the USA it is called withholding tax. PAYE tax deductions are calculated so that when added up they will approximately equal the total amount of tax likely to be due in that year.

Pays de la Loire agricultural region of W France, comprising the *départements* of Loire-Atlantique, Maine-et-Loire, Mayenne, Sarthe, and Vendée; capital Nantes; area 32,100 sq km/ 12,391 sq mi; population (1986) 3,018,000. Industries include shipbuilding and wine.

Paz (Estenssoro) Victor 1907– . President of Bolivia 1952–56, 1960–64, and 1985–89. He founded and led the Movimiento Nacionalista Revolucionario (MNR) which seized power 1952. His regime extended the vote to Indians, nationalized the country's largest tin mines, embarked on a programme of agrarian reform, and brought inflation under control.

Paz Octavio 1914– . Mexican poet and essayist. His works reflect many influences, including Marxism, surrealism, and Aztec mythology. His long poem *Piedra del sol/Sun Stone* 1957 uses contrasting images, centring upon the Aztec Calendar Stone (representing the Aztec universe), to symbolize the loneliness of individuals and their search for union with others. Nobel Prize for Literature 1990.

PCB abbreviation for *polychlorinated biphenyl*; *printed circuit board*.

PCM abbreviation for *pulse-code modulation*.

PCP abbreviation for *phencyclidine hydrochloride*, a drug popularly known as *angel dust.

pd abbreviation for *potential difference*.

pea climbing plant *Pisum sativum*, family Leguminosae, with pods of edible seeds, grown since prehistoric times for food. The pea is a popular vegetable and is eaten fresh, canned, dried, or frozen. The sweet pea *Lathyrus odoratus* of the same family is grown for its scented, butterfly-shaped flowers.

Peace Corps US organization of trained men and women, inspired by the British programme Voluntary Service Overseas (VSO) and established by President Kennedy 1961. The Peace Corps provides skilled volunteer workers for Third World countries, especially in the fields of teaching, agriculture, and health, for a period of two years.

peace movement collective opposition to war. The Western peace movements of the late 20th century can trace their origins to the pacifists of the 19th century and conscientious objectors during World War I. The campaigns after World War II have tended to concentrate on nuclear weapons, but there are numerous organizations devoted to peace, some wholly pacifist, some merely opposed to escalation.

peach tree *Prunus persica*, family Rosaceae. It has ovate leaves and small, usually pink flowers. The yellowish edible fruits have thick velvety skins; the nectarine is a smooth-skinned variety.

peacock technically, the male of any of various large pheasants. The name is most often used for the common peacock *Pavo cristatus*, a bird of the pheasant family, native to S Asia. It is rather larger than a pheasant. The male has a large fan-shaped tail, brightly coloured with blue, green, and purple 'eyes' on a chestnut background. The female (peahen) is brown with a small tail.

Peake Mervyn (Lawrence) 1911–1968. English writer and illustrator, born in China. His novels include the grotesque fantasy trilogy *Titus Groan* 1946, *Gormenghast* 1950, and *Titus Alone* 1959. Among his collections of verse are *The Glassblowers* 1950 and the posthumous *A Book of Nonsense* 1972.

peanut or **groundnut** or **monkey nut** South American vinelike annual plant *Arachis hypogaea*, family Leguminosae. After flowering, the flower stalks bend and force the pods into the earth to ripen underground. The nuts are a staple food in many tropical countries and are widely grown in the southern USA. They yield a valuable edible oil and are the basis for numerous processed foods.

pear tree *Pyrus communis*, family Rosaceae, native to temperate regions of Eurasia. It has a succulent edible fruit, less hardy than the apple.

pearl shiny, hard, rounded abnormal growth composed of nacre (or mother-of-pearl), a chalky substance. Nacre is secreted by many molluscs, and deposited in thin layers on the inside of the shell around a parasite, a grain of sand, or some other irritant body. After several years of the mantle (the layer of tissue between the shell and the body mass) secreting this nacre, a pearl is formed.

Pearl Harbor US Pacific naval base in Oahu, Hawaii, USA, the scene of a Japanese attack 7 Dec 1941, which brought the USA into World War II. The attack took place while Japanese envoys were holding so-called peace talks in Washington. More than 2,000 members of US armed forces were killed, and a large part of the US Pacific fleet was destroyed or damaged.

Pears Peter 1910–1986. English tenor. A co-founder with Benjamin *Britten of the Aldeburgh Festival, he was closely associated with the composer's work and sang the title role in *Peter Grimes*.

Pearse Patrick Henry 1879–1916. Irish poet prominent in the Gaelic revival, a leader of the *Easter Rising 1916. Proclaimed president of the provisional government, he was court-martialled and shot after its suppression.

Pearson Lester Bowles 1897–1972. Canadian politician, leader of the Liberal Party from 1958, prime minister 1963–68. As foreign minister 1948–57, he represented Canada at the United Nations, playing a key role in settling the *Suez Crisis 1956. Nobel Peace Prize 1957.

Peary Robert Edwin 1856–1920. US polar explorer who, after several unsuccessful attempts, became the first person to reach the North Pole on 6 April 1909. In 1988 an astronomer claimed Peary's measurements were incorrect.

Peasants' Revolt the rising of the English peasantry in June 1381, the culminative result of economic, social, and political disillusionment. It was sparked off by the imposition of a new poll tax, three times the rates of those imposed in 1377 and 1379. Led by Wat *Tyler and John *Ball, rebels from SE England marched to London and demanded reforms. The revolt was put down by deceit and force by the authorities.

peat fibrous organic substance found in bogs and formed by the incomplete decomposition of plants such as sphagnum moss. N Asia, Canada, Finland, Ireland, and other places have large deposits, which have been dried and used as fuel from ancient times. Peat can also be used as a soil additive.

pecan nut-producing *hickory tree *Carya illinoensis* or *C. pecan*, native to central USA and N Mexico and now widely cultivated. The tree grows to over 45 m/150 ft, and the edible nuts are smooth-shelled, the kernel resembling a smoothly ovate walnut.

peccary one of two species of the New World genus *Tayassu* of piglike hoofed mammals. A peccary has a gland in the middle of the back which secretes a strong-smelling substance. Peccaries are blackish in colour, covered with bristles, and have tusks that point downwards. Adults reach a height of 40 cm/16 in, and a weight of 25 kg/60 lb.

peck obsolete unit of dry measure, equalling eight quarts or a quarter bushel (9.002 litres).

Peck (Eldred) Gregory 1916– . US film actor specializing in strong, upright characters. His films include *Spellbound* 1945, *Duel in the Sun* 1946, *Gentleman's Agreement* 1947, *To Kill a Mockingbird* 1962, for which he won an Academy Award, and (cast against type as a Nazi doctor) *The Boys from Brazil* 1974.

Peckinpah Sam 1925–1985. US film director, often of Westerns, usually associated with slow-motion, blood-spurting violence. His best films, such as *The Wild Bunch* 1969, exhibit a thoughtful, if depressing, view of the world and human nature.

pectoral in vertebrates, the upper area of the thorax associated with the muscles and bones used in moving the arms or forelimbs. In birds, the *pectoralis major* is the very large muscle used to produce a powerful downbeat of the wing during flight.

pedicel the stalk of an individual flower, which attaches it to the main floral axis, often developing in the axil of a bract.

pediment in architecture, the triangular part crowning the fronts of buildings in Classical styles. The pediment was a distinctive feature of Greek temples.

Pedro two emperors of Brazil:

Pedro I 1798–1834. Emperor of Brazil 1822–31. The son of John VI of Portugal, he escaped to Brazil on Napoleon's invasion, and was appointed regent 1821. He proclaimed Brazil independent 1822 and was crowned emperor, but abdicated 1831 and returned to Portugal.

Pedro II 1825–1891. Emperor of Brazil 1831–89. He proved an enlightened ruler, but his anti-slavery measures alienated the landowners, who compelled him to abdicate.

Peel Robert 1788–1850. British Conservative politician. As home secretary 1822–27 and 1828–30, he founded the modern police force and in 1829 introduced Roman Catholic emancipation. He was prime minister 1834–35 and 1841–46, when his repeal of the *Corn Laws caused him and his followers to break with the party.

peepul another name for the *bo tree.

peerage in the UK, holders, in descending

order, of the titles of duke, marquess, earl, viscount, and baron. Some of these titles may be held by a woman in default of a male heir. In the late 19th century the peerage was augmented by the Lords of Appeal in Ordinary (the nonhereditary life peers) and, from 1958, by a number of specially created life peers of either sex (usually long-standing members of the House of Commons). Since 1963 peers have been able to disclaim their titles, usually to enable them to take a seat in the Commons (where peers are disqualified from membership).

peer group in the social sciences, people who have a common identity based on such characteristics as similar social status, interests, age, or ethnic group. The concept has proved useful in analysing the power and influence of co-workers, school friends, and ethnic and religious groups in socialization and social behaviour.

Pegasus in astronomy, a constellation of the northern hemisphere, near Cygnus, and represented as the winged horse of Greek mythology.

Pegasus in Greek mythology, the winged horse that sprang from the blood of the Gorgon Medusa. He was transformed into a constellation.

pegmatite extremely coarse-grained *igneous rock of any composition found in veins usually associated with large granite masses.

Pei Ieoh Ming 1917– . Chinese-born US Modernist/high-tech architect, noted for the use of glass walls. His buildings include the Bank of China Tower, Hong Kong, 1987, and the glass pyramid in front of the Louvre, Paris, 1989.

pekan or **fisher marten** North American marten (carnivorous mammal) *Martes penanti* about 1.2 m/4 ft long, with a doglike face, and brown fur with white patches on the chest. It eats porcupines.

Peking alternative transcription of *Beijing, capital of China.

pekingese breed of long-haired dog with a flat skull and flat face, typically less than 25 cm/10 in tall and weighing less than 5 kg/11 lb.

Peking man Chinese representative of an early species of human, found as fossils, 500,000–750,000 years old, in the cave of Choukoutien 1927 near Beijing (Peking). Peking man used chipped stone tools, hunted game, and used fire. Similar varieties of early human have been found in Java and E Africa. Their classification is disputed: some anthropologists classify them as *Homo erectus*, others as *Homo sapiens pithecanthropus*.

Pelagius 360–420. British theologian. He taught that each person possesses free will (and hence the possibility of salvation), denying Augustine's doctrines of predestination and original sin. Cleared of heresy by a synod in Jerusalem 415, he was later condemned by the pope and the emperor.

pelargonium flowering plant of the genus *Pelargonium* of the geranium family Geraniaceae, grown extensively in gardens, where it is familiarly known as the **geranium**. Ancestors of the garden hybrids came from S Africa.

Pelé Adopted name of Edson Arantes do Nascimento 1940– . Brazilian soccer player. A prolific goal scorer, he appeared in four World Cup competitions 1958–70 and led Brazil to three championships (1958, 1962, 1970).

Pelham Henry 1696–1754. British Whig politician. He held a succession of offices in Robert Walpole's cabinet 1721–42, and was prime minister 1743–54. His brother Thomas Pelham-Holles, 1st Duke of *Newcastle, succeeded him as prime minister.

pelican any of a family (Pelecanidae) of large, heavy water birds remarkable for the pouch beneath the bill which is used as a fishing net and temporary store for catches of fish. Some species grow up to 1.8 m/6 ft, and have wingspans of 3 m/10 ft.

Peloponnese (Greek **Peloponnesos**) peninsula forming the southern part of Greece; area 21,549 sq km/8,318 sq mi; population (1991) 1,077,000. It is joined to the mainland by the narrow isthmus of Corinth and is divided into the nomes (administrative areas) of Argolis, Arcadia, Achaea, Elis, Corinth, Lakonia, and Messenia, representing its seven ancient states.

Peloponnesian War conflict between Athens and Sparta and their allies, 431–404 BC, originating in suspicions about the 'empire-building' ambitions of the Athenian leader Pericles. It was ended by the Spartan general Lysander's capture of the Athenian fleet in 405, and his starving the Athenians into surrender in 404. Sparta's victory meant the destruction of the political power of Athens.

pelota or **jai alai** 'merry festival' very fast ball game of Basque derivation, popular in Latin American countries and in the USA where it is a betting sport. It is played by two, four, or six players, in a walled court, or *cancha*, and somewhat resembles squash, but each player uses a long, curved, wickerwork basket, or *cesta*, strapped to the hand, to hurl the ball, or pelota, against the walls.

Peltier effect in physics, a change in temperature at the junction of two different metals produced when an electric current flows through them. The extent of the change depends on what the conducting metals are, and the nature of change (rise or fall in temperature) depends on the direction of current flow. It is the reverse of the *Seebeck effect. It is named after the French physicist Jean Charles Peltier (1785–1845) who discovered it 1834.

pelvis in vertebrates, the lower area of the abdomen featuring the bones and muscles used to move the legs or hindlimbs. The **pelvic girdle** is a set of bones that allows movement of the legs in relation to the rest of the body and provides sites for the attachment of relevant muscles.

penance Roman Catholic sacrament, involving confession of sins and receiving absolution, and works performed (or punishment self-inflicted) in atonement for sin. Penance is worked out nowadays in terms of good deeds rather than routine repetition of prayers.

Penang (Malay **Pulau Pinang**) state in W Peninsular Malaysia, formed of Penang Island, Province Wellesley, and the Dindings on the mainland; area 1,030 sq km/398 sq mi; capital Penang (George Town); population (1990) 1,142,200. Penang Island was bought by Britain from the ruler of Kedah 1785; Province Wellesley was acquired 1800.

Penda *c.* 577–654. King of Mercia, an Anglo-Saxon kingdom in England, from about 632. He raised Mercia to a powerful kingdom, and defeated and killed two Northumbrian kings, Edwin 632 and Oswald 641. He was killed in battle by Oswy, king of Northumbria.

Penderecki Krzystof 1933– . Polish composer. His expressionist works, such as the *Threnody for the Victims of Hiroshima* 1961 for strings, employ cluster and percussion effects. He later turned to religious subjects and a more orthodox style, as in the *Magnificat* 1974 and the *Polish Requiem* 1980–83. His opera *The Black Mask* 1986 explored a new vein of surreal humour.

pendulum weight (called a 'bob') swinging at the end of a rod or cord. The regularity of a pendulum's swing was used in making the first really accurate clocks in the 17th century. Pendulums can be used for measuring the acceleration due to gravity (an important constant in physics), and in prospecting for oils and minerals.

Penelope in Greek legend, the wife of Odysseus, ruler of Ithaca and one of the leaders of the Greek forces in the Trojan War. During his absence after the siege of Troy she kept her many suitors at bay by asking them to wait until she had woven a shroud for her father-in-law, but unravelled her work each night. When Odysseus returned, after 20 years, he killed her suitors.

penetration technology the development of missiles that have low radar, infrared, and optical signatures and thus can penetrate an enemy's defences undetected. In 1980 the USA announced that it had developed such a piloted aircraft, known as Stealth. It comes in both fighter and bomber versions. In 1989 two out of three tests failed, and by 1990 the cost of the Stealth had risen to $815 million each.

penguin any of an order (Sphenisciformes) of marine flightless birds, mostly black and white, found in the southern hemisphere. They range in size from 40 cm/1.6 ft to 1.2 m/4 ft tall, and have thick feathers to protect them from the intense cold. They are awkward on land, but their wings have evolved into flippers, making them excellent swimmers. Penguins congregate to breed in 'rookeries', and often spend many months incubating their eggs while their mates are out at sea feeding.

penicillin any of a group of *antibiotic (bacteria killing) compounds obtained from filtrates of moulds of the genus *Penicillium* (especially *P. notatum*) or produced synthetically. Penicillin was the first antibiotic to be discovered (by Alexander *Fleming); it kills a broad spectrum of bacteria, many of which cause disease in humans.

peninsula land surrounded on three sides by water but still attached to a larger landmass. Florida, USA, is an example.

Peninsular War war 1808–14 caused by the French emperor Napoleon's invasion of Portugal and Spain. British expeditionary forces under Sir Arthur Wellesley (Duke of *Wellington), combined with Spanish and Portuguese resistance, succeeded in defeating the French at Vimeiro 1808, Talavera 1809, Salamanca 1812, and Vittoria 1813. The results were inconclusive, and the war was ended by Napoleon's abdication.

penis male reproductive organ, used for internal fertilization; it transfers sperm to the female reproductive tract. In mammals, the penis is made erect by vessels that fill with blood, and in most mammals (but not humans) is stiffened by a bone. It also contains the urethra, through which urine is passed. Snakes and lizards have a paired structure that serves as a penis, other reptiles have a single organ. A few birds, mainly ducks and geese, also have a type of penis, as do snails, barnacles, and some other invertebrates. Many insects have a rigid, nonerectile male organ, usually referred to as an intromittent organ.

Penn William 1644–1718. English member of the Society of Friends (Quakers), born in London. He joined the Society 1667, and in 1681 obtained a grant of land in America (in settlement of a debt owed by the king to his father) on which he established the colony of *Pennsylvania as a refuge for persecuted Quakers.

Pennines mountain system, 'the backbone of England', broken by a gap through which the river Aire flows to the east and the Ribble to the west; length (Scottish border to the Peaks in Derbyshire) 400 km/250 mi.

Pennsylvania state in NE USA: nickname Keystone State
area 117,400 sq km/45,316 sq mi
capital Harrisburg
cities Philadelphia, Pittsburgh, Erie, Allentown, Scranton
products hay, cereals, mushrooms, cattle, poultry, dairy products, cement, coal, steel, petroleum products, pharmaceuticals, motor vehicles and equipment, electronic components, textiles
population (1990) 11,881,600

Pennsylvanian US term for the upper *Carboniferous period of geological time, named after the US state.

pennyroyal European perennial plant *Mentha pulegium* of the mint family, with oblong leaves and whorls of purplish flowers. It is found growing in wet places on sandy soil.

pension organized form of saving for retirement. Pension schemes, which may be government-run or privately administered, involve regular payment for a qualifying period; when the person retires, a payment is made each week from the invested pension fund. Pension funds have today become influential investors in major industries.

pentadactyl limb typical limb of the mammals, birds, reptiles, and amphibians. These vertebrates (animals with backbone) are all descended from primitive amphibians whose immediate ancestors were fleshy-finned fish. The limb which evolved in those amphibians had three parts: a 'hand/foot' with five digits (fingers/toes), a lower limb containing two bones, and an upper limb containing one bone.

Pentagon the headquarters of the US Department of Defense, Arlington, Virginia. One of the world's largest office buildings (five-sided with a pentagonal central court), it houses the administrative and command headquarters for the US armed forces and has become synonymous with the military establishment bureaucracy.

pentanol $C_5H_{11}OH$ (common name *amyl alcohol*) clear, colourless, oily liquid, usually having a characteristic choking odour. It is obtained by the fermentation of starches and from the distillation of petroleum.

Pentateuch Greek (and Christian) name for the first five books of the *Bible*, ascribed to Moses, and called the *Torah* by Jews.

pentathlon five-sport competition. Pentathlon consists of former military training pursuits: swimming, fencing, running, horsemanship, and shooting. Formerly a five-event track and field competition for women, it was superseded by the seven-event heptathlon 1981.

Pentecost in Judaism, the festival of *Shavuot*, celebrated on the 50th day after *Passover in commemoration of the giving of the Ten Commandments to Moses on Mount Sinai, and the end of the grain harvest; in the Christian church, Pentecost is the day on which the apostles experienced inspiration of the Holy Spirit, commemorated on Whit Sunday.

Pentecostal movement Christian revivalist movement inspired by the baptism in the Holy Spirit with 'speaking in tongues' experienced by the apostles at the time of Pentecost. It represents a reaction against the rigid theology and formal worship of the traditional churches. Pentecostalists believe in the literal word of the Bible and disapprove of alcohol, tobacco, dancing, theatre, and so on. It is an intensely missionary faith, and recruitment has been rapid since the 1960s: worldwide membership is more than 10 million.

peony or *paeony* any perennial plant of the genus *Paeonia*, family Paeoniaceae, remarkable for their brilliant flowers. Most popular are the common peony *P. officinalis*, the white peony *P. lactiflora*, and the taller tree peony *P. suffruticosa*.

People's Charter the key document of *Chartism, a movement for reform of the British political system in the 1830s. It was used to mobilize working-class support following the restricted extension of the franchise specified by the 1832 Reform Act. It was drawn up in Feb 1837.

Pepin the Short *c.* 714–*c.* 768. King of the Franks from 751. The son of *Charles Martel, he acted as Mayor of the Palace to the last Merovingian king, Childeric III, deposed him and assumed the royal title himself, founding the *Carolingian dynasty. He was *Charlemagne's father.

pepper climbing plant *Piper nigrum* native to the E Indies, of the Old World pepper family Piperaceae. When gathered green, the berries are crushed to release the seeds for the spice called black pepper. When the berries are ripe, the seeds are removed and their outer skin is discarded, to produce white pepper. Chilli pepper, cayenne or red pepper and the sweet peppers used as a vegetable come from *capsicums native to the New World.

peppermint perennial herb *Mentha piperita* of the mint family, native to Europe, with ovate, aromatic leaves and purple flowers. Oil of peppermint is used in medicine and confectionery.

pepsin enzyme that breaks down proteins during digestion. It requires a strongly acidic environment and is found in the stomach.

peptide molecule comprising two or more *amino acid molecules (not necessarily different) joined by *peptide bonds*, whereby the acid group of one acid is linked to the amino group of the other (–CO.NH). The number of amino acid molecules in the peptide is indicated by referring to it as a di-, tri-, or polypeptide (two, three, or many amino acids).

Pepys Samuel 1633–1703. English diarist. His diary 1659–69 was a unique record of both the daily life of the period and the intimate feelings of the man. Written in shorthand, it was not deciphered until 1825. Pepys was imprisoned 1679 in the Tower of London on suspicion of being connected with the Popish Plot (see Titus *Oates).

Perak state of W Peninsular Malaysia; capital Ipoh; area 21,000 sq km/8,106 sq mi; population (1990) 2,222,200. It produces tin and rubber. The government is a sultanate. The other principal town is Taiping.

p/e ratio abbreviation for *price/earnings ratio*.

percentage way of representing a number as a *fraction of 100. Thus 45 percent (45%) equals 45100, and 45% of 20 is 45100 × 20 = 9.

perch any of the largest order of spiny-finned bony fishes, the Perciformes, with some 8,000 species. This order includes the sea basses, cichlids, damselfishes, mullets, barracudas, wrasses, and gobies. Perches of the freshwater genus *Perca* are found in Europe, Asia, and North America. They have varied shapes and are usually a greenish colour. They are very prolific, spawning when about three years old, and have voracious appetites.

percussion instrument musical instrument played by being struck with the hand or a beater. Percussion instruments can be divided into those that can be tuned to produce a sound of definite pitch, such as the kettledrum, tubular bells, glockenspiel, and xylophone and those without pitch including bass drum, tambourine, triangle, cymbals, and castanets.

Percy Henry 'Hotspur' 1364–1403. English soldier, son of the 1st Earl of Northumberland. In repelling a border raid, he defeated the Scots at Homildon Hill in Durham 1402. He was killed at the battle of Shrewsbury while in revolt against Henry IV.

perennating organ in plants, that part of a *biennial plant or herbaceous perennial that allows it to survive the winter; usually a root, tuber, rhizome, bulb, or corm.

perennial plant plant that lives for more than two years. Herbaceous perennials have aerial stems and leaves that die each autumn. They survive the winter by means of an underground storage (perennating) organ, such as a bulb or rhizome. Trees and shrubs or woody perennials have stems that persist above ground throughout the year, and may be either *deciduous or *evergreen. See also *annual plant, *biennial plant.

Peres Shimon 1923– . Israeli socialist politician, prime minister 1984–86. As foreign minister in Yitzhak Rabin's Labour government from 1992, he negotiated the 1993 peace agreement with the PLO. He was awarded the 1994 Nobel

Prize for Peace jointly with Israeli president, Rabin, and PLO leader, Yassir Arafat.

perestroika (Russian 'restructuring') in Soviet politics, the wide-ranging economic and political reforms initiated from 1985 by Mikhail Gorbachev, finally leading to the demise of the Soviet Union. Originally, in the economic sphere, *perestroika* was conceived as involving 'intensive development' concentrating on automation and improved labour efficiency. It evolved to attend increasingly to market indicators and incentives ('market socialism') and the gradual dismantling of the Stalinist central-planning system, with decision-taking being devolved to self-financing enterprises.

Perey Marguérite (Catherine) 1909–1975. French nuclear chemist who discovered the radioactive element francium in 1939. Her career, which began as an assistant to Marie Curie 1929, culminated with her appointment as professor of nuclear chemistry at the University of Strasbourg 1949 and director of its Centre for Nuclear Research 1958.

Pérez de Cuéllar Javier 1920– . Peruvian diplomat, secretary general of the United Nations 1982–91. He raised the standing of the UN by his successful diplomacy in ending the Iran–Iraq War 1988 and securing the independence of Namibia 1989.

perfect competition see *competition, perfect.

performing right permission to perform *copyright musical or dramatic works in public; this is subject to licence and the collection of fees. The first performing right society was established 1851 in France. In the UK the Copyright Act 1842 was the first to encompass musical compositions. The agent for live performances is the Performing Right Society, founded 1914; the rights for recorded and broadcast performance are administered by the Mechanical Copyright Protection Society, founded 1924.

perfume fragrant essence used to scent the body, cosmetics, and candles. More than 100 natural aromatic chemicals may be blended from a range of 60,000 flowers, leaves, fruits, seeds, woods, barks, resins, and roots, combined by natural animal fixatives and various synthetics. Favoured ingredients include *balsam, *civet (from the African civet cat) hyacinth, jasmine, lily of the valley, musk (from the *musk deer), orange blossom, rose, and tuberose.

Pergamum ancient Greek city in W Asia Minor, which became the capital of an independent kingdom 283 BC. As the ally of Rome it achieved great political importance in the 2nd century BC, and became a centre of art and culture. Close to its site is the modern Turkish town of Bergama.

Peri Jacopo 1561–1633. Italian composer who served the Medici family, the rulers of Florence. His experimental melodic opera *Euridice* 1600 established the opera form and influenced Monteverdi. His first opera, *Dafne* 1597, is now lost.

perianth in botany, a collective term for the outer whorls of the *flower, which protect the reproductive parts during development. In most *dicotyledons the perianth is composed of two distinct whorls, the calyx of *sepals and the co-rolla of *petals, whereas in many *monocotyledons the sepals and petals are indistinguishable and the segments of the perianth are then known individually as tepals.

pericarp wall of a *fruit. It encloses the seeds and is derived from the *ovary wall. In fruits such as the acorn, the pericarp becomes dry and hard, forming a shell around the seed. In fleshy fruits the pericarp is typically made up of three distinct layers. The **epicarp**, or **exocarp**, forms the tough outer skin of the fruit, while the **mesocarp** is often fleshy and forms the middle layers. The innermost layer or **endocarp**, which surrounds the seeds, may be membranous or thick and hard, as in the *drupe (stone) of cherries, plums, and apricots.

Pericles c. 490–429 BC. Athenian politician who dominated the city's affairs from 461 BC (as leader of the democratic party), and under whom Greek culture reached its height. He created a confederation of cities under the leadership of Athens, but the disasters of the *Peloponnesian War led to his overthrow 430 BC. Although quickly reinstated, he died soon after.

peridotite rock consisting largely of the mineral olivine; pyroxene and other minerals may also be present. Peridotite is an ultrabasic rock containing less than 45% silica by weight. It is believed to be one of the rock types making up the Earth's upper mantle, and is sometimes brought from the depths to the surface by major movements, or as inclusions in lavas.

perigee the point at which an object, travelling in an elliptical orbit around the Earth, is at its closest to the Earth. The point at which it is furthest from the Earth is the apogee.

perihelion the point at which an object, travelling in an elliptical orbit around the Sun, is at its closest to the Sun. The point at which it is furthest from the Sun is the aphelion.

period in physics, the time taken for one complete cycle of a repeated sequence of events. For example, the time taken for a pendulum to swing from side to side and back again is the period of the pendulum.

periodic table of the elements in chemistry, a table setting out the classification of the elements following the statement by Russian chemist Dmitri Mendeleyev 1869 that 'the properties of elements are in periodic dependence upon their atomic weight'. (Today elements are classified by their atomic number rather than by their relative atomic mass.)

periodontal disease formerly known as **pyorrhoea** disease of the gums and bone supporting the teeth, caused by the accumulation of plaque and microorganisms; the gums recede, and the teeth eventually become loose and may drop out unless treatment is sought.

peripheral device in computing, any item of equipment attached to and controlled by a computer. Peripherals are typically for input from and output to the user (for example, a keyboard or printer), storing data (for example, a disc drive), communications (such as a modem), or for performing physical tasks (such as a robot).

periscope optical instrument designed for observation from a concealed position such as from a submerged submarine. In its basic form it

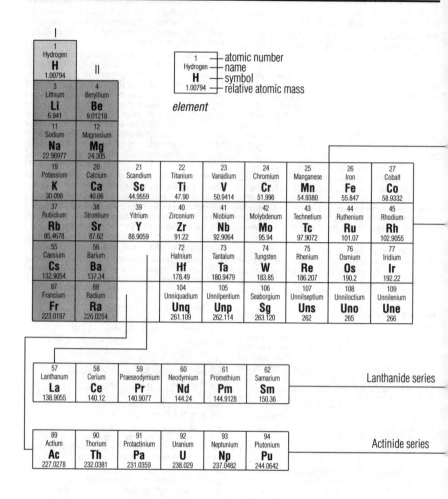

periodic table of the elements *The periodic table of the elements arranges the elements into horizontal rows (called periods) and vertical columns (called groups) according to their atomic numbers.*

consists of a tube with parallel mirrors at each end, inclined at 45° to its axis. The periscope attained prominence in naval and military operations of World War I.

peristalsis wavelike contractions, produced by the contraction of smooth muscle, that pass along tubular organs, such as the intestines. The same term describes the wavelike motion of earthworms and other invertebrates, in which part of the body contracts as another part elongates.

peritoneum tissue lining the abdominal cavity and digestive organs of vertebrates. *Peritonitis*, inflammation within the peritoneum, can occur due to infection or other irritation. It is sometimes seen following a burst appendix and quickly proves fatal if not treated.

periwinkle in botany, any of several trailing blue-flowered evergreen plants of the genus *Vinca* of the dogbane family Apocynaceae. They range in length from 20 cm/8 in to 1 m/3 ft.

periwinkle in zoology, any marine snail of the family Littorinidae, found on the shores of Europe and E North America. Periwinkles have a conical spiral shell, and feed on algae.

perjury the offence of deliberately making a false statement on *oath (or affirmation) when appearing as a witness in legal proceedings, on a point material to the question at issue. In Britain and the USA it is punishable by a fine, imprisonment, or both.

Perm industrial city (shipbuilding, oil refining, aircraft, chemicals, sawmills), and capital of Perm region, N Russia, on the Kama near the Ural mountains; population (1987) 1,075,000. It was called Molotov 1940–57.

						0
						2 Helium **He** 4002.60

	III	IV	V	VI	VII	
	5 Boron **B** 10.81	6 Carbon **C** 12.011	7 Nitrogen **N** 14.0067	8 Oxygen **O** 15.9994	9 Fluorine **F** 18.99840	10 Neon **Ne** 20.179
	13 Aluminium **Al** 26.98154	14 Silicon **Si** 28.066	15 Phosphorus **P** 30.9738	16 Sulphur **S** 32.06	17 Chlorine **Cl** 35.453	18 Argon **Ar** 39.948

28 Nickel **Ni** 58.70	29 Copper **Cu** 63.546	30 Zinc **Zn** 65.38	31 Gallium **Ga** 69.72	32 Germanium **Ge** 72.59	33 Arsenic **As** 74.9216	34 Selenium **Se** 78.96	35 Bromine **Br** 79.904	36 Krypton **Kr** 83.80
46 Palladium **Pd** 106.4	47 Silver **Ag** 107.868	48 Cadmium **Cd** 112.40	49 Indium **In** 114.82	50 Tin **Sn** 118.69	51 Antimony **Sb** 121.75	52 Tellurium **Te** 127.75	53 Iodine **I** 126.9045	54 Xenon **Xe** 131.30
78 Platinum **Pt** 195.09	79 Gold **Au** 196.9665	80 Mercury **Hg** 200.59	81 Thallium **Tl** 204.37	82 Lead **Pb** 207.37	83 Bismuth **Bi** 207.2	84 Polonium **Po** 210	85 Astatine **At** 211	86 Radon **Rn** 222.0176

63 Europium **Eu** 151.96	64 Gadolinium **Gd** 157.25	65 Terbium **Tb** 158.9254	66 Dysprosium **Dy** 162.50	67 Holmium **Ho** 164.9304	68 Erbium **Er** 167.26	69 Thulium **Tm** 168.9342	70 Ytterbium **Yb** 173.04	71 Lutetium **Lu** 174.97
95 Americium **Am** 243.0614	96 Curium **Cm** 247.0703	97 Berkelium **Bk** 247	98 Californium **Cf** 251.0786	99 Einsteinium **Es** 252.0828	100 Fermium **Fm** 257.0951	101 Mendelevium **Me** 258.0986	102 Nobelium **No** 259.1009	103 Lawrencium **Lr** 260.1054

permafrost condition in which a deep layer of soil does not thaw out during the summer but remains at below 0°C/32°F for at least two years, despite thawing of the soil above. It is claimed that 26% of the world's land surface is permafrost.

Permian period of geological time 290–245 million years ago, the last period of the Palaeozoic era. Its end was marked by a significant change in marine life, including the extinction of many corals and trilobites. Deserts were widespread, and terrestrial amphibians and mammal-like reptiles flourished. Cone-bearing plants (gymnosperms) came to prominence.

permutation in mathematics, a specified arrangement of a group of objects. It is the arrangement of a distinct objects taken b at a time in all possible orders. It is given by $a!/(a - b)!$, where '!' stands for *factorial. For example, the number of permutations of four letters taken from any group of six different letters is $6!/2! = (1 \times 2 \times 3 \times 4 \times 5 \times 6)/(1 \times 2) = 360$. The theoretical number of four-letter 'words' that can be made from an alphabet of 26 letters is $26!/22! = 358,800$.

Perón Evita (María Eva) (born Duarte) 1919–1952. Argentine populist leader. A successful radio actress, she married Juan *Perón in 1945. When he became president the following year, she became his chief adviser and virtually ran the health and labour ministries, devoting herself to helping the poor, improving education, and achieving women's suffrage. She was politically astute and sought the vice-presidency 1951, but was opposed by the army and withdrew.

Perón Juan (Domingo) 1895–1974. Argentine politician, dictator 1946–55 and from 1973 until his death. His populist appeal to the poor was enhanced by the charisma and political work of his second wife Eva (Evita) Perón. After her death in 1952 his popularity waned and he was deposed in a military coup 1955. He returned from exile to the presidency 1973, but died in office 1974, and was succeeded by his third wife Isabel Perón.

Perpendicular period of English Gothic architecture lasting from the end of the 14th century to the mid-16th century. It is characterized by window tracery consisting chiefly of vertical members, two or four arc arches, lavishly decorated vaults and use of traceried panels. Examples include the choir and cloister of Gloucester Cathedral, and King's College Chapel, Cambridge.

perpendicular in mathematics, at a right angle; also, a line at right angles to another or to a plane. For a pair of skew lines (lines in three dimensions that do not meet), there is just one common perpendicular, which is at right angles to both lines; the nearest points on the two lines are the feet of this perpendicular.

perpetual motion the idea that a machine can be designed and constructed in such a way that, once started, it will continue in motion indefinitely without requiring any further input of energy (motive power). Such a device contradicts the two laws of thermodynamics that state that (1) energy can neither be created nor destroyed (the law of conservation of energy) and (2) heat cannot by itself flow from a cooler to a hotter object. As a result, all practical (real) machines require a continuous supply of energy, and no heat engine is able to convert all the heat into useful work.

Perrault Charles 1628–1703. French author of the fairy tales *Contes de ma mère l'oye/Mother Goose's Fairy Tales* 1697, which include 'Sleeping Beauty', 'Little Red Riding Hood', 'Blue Beard', 'Puss in Boots', and 'Cinderella'.

Perrin Jean 1870–1942. French physicist who produced the crucial evidence that finally established the atomic nature of matter. Assuming the atomic hypothesis, Perrin demonstrated how the phenomenon of *Brownian movement could be used to derive precise values for *Avogadro's number. He was awarded the 1926 Nobel Prize for Physics.

Perry Matthew Calbraith 1794–1858. US naval officer, commander of the expedition of 1853 that reopened communication between Japan and the outside world after 250 years' isolation. Evident military superiority enabled him to negotiate the Treaty of Kanagawa 1854, giving the USA trading rights with Japan.

Persephone Greek goddess (Roman Proserpina), the daughter of Zeus and Demeter. She was carried off to the underworld as the bride of Pluto, who later agreed that she should spend six months of the year with her mother. The myth symbolizes the growth and decay of vegetation and the changing seasons.

Persepolis ancient capital of the Persian Empire, 65 km/40 mi NE of Shiraz. It was burned down after its capture in 331 BC by Alexander the Great.

Perseus in Greek mythology, son of Zeus and Danaë. He slew Medusa, the *Gorgon, and cut off her head, which he set in his shield, rescued *Andromeda, and became king of Tiryns.

Perseus in astronomy, a constellation of the northern hemisphere, near Cassiopeia, and represented as the mythological hero. The eye of the decapitated Gorgon, Medusa, is identified with the variable star Algol. Perseus lies in the Milky Way and contains the Double Cluster, a twin cluster of stars. Every August the Perseid meteor shower radiates from its northern part.

Persia, ancient kingdom in SW Asia. The early Persians were a nomadic Aryan people who migrated through the Caucasus to the Iranian plateau.

7th century BC The Persians were established in the present region of Fars, which then belonged to the Assyrians.

550 BC Cyrus the Great overthrew the empire of the Medes, to whom the Persians had been subject, and founded the Persian Empire.

539 BC Having conquered all Anatolia, Cyrus added Babylonia (including Syria and Palestine) to his empire.

529–485 BC Darius I organized an efficient centralized system of administration and extended Persian rule east into Afghanistan and NW India and as far north as the Danube, but the empire was weakened by internal dynastic struggles.

499–449 BC The Persian Wars with Greece ended Persian domination of the ancient world.

331 BC Alexander the Great drove the Persians under Darius III (died 330 BC) into retreat at Arbela on the Tigris, marking the end of the Persian Empire and the beginning of the Hellenistic period under the Seleucids.

AD 226 The Sassanian Empire was established in Persia and annexed Parthia.

637 Arabs took the capital, Ctesiphon, and introduced Islam in place of Zoroastrianism. For modern history see *Iran.

Persian Gulf or *Arabian Gulf* large shallow inlet of the Arabian Sea; area 233,000 sq km/90,000 sq mi. It divides the Arabian peninsula from Iran and is linked by the Strait of Hormuz and the Gulf of Oman to the Arabian Sea. Oilfields surround it in the Gulf States of Bahrain, Iran, Iraq, Kuwait, Oman, Qatar, Saudi Arabia, and the United Arab Emirates.

Persian language language belonging to the Indo-Iranian branch of the Indo-European family; see *Farsi.

Persian Wars series of conflicts between Greece and Persia 499–449 BC. The eventual victory of Greece marked the end of Persian domination of the ancient world and the beginning of Greek supremacy.

persimmon any tree of the genus *Diospyros* of the ebony family Ebenaceae, especially the common persimmon *D. virginiana* of the southeastern USA. Up to 19 m/60 ft high, the persimmon has alternate oval leaves and yellow-green unisexual flowers. The small, sweet, orange fruits are edible.

personal computer (PC) another name for *microcomputer. The term is also used, more specifically, to mean the IBM Personal Computer and computers based on it.

personal equity plan (PEP) investment scheme introduced in the UK 1987. Shares of public companies listed on the UK stock exchange are purchased by PEP managers on behalf of their clients. Up to certain limits, individuals may purchase such shares and, provided they hold them for at least a year, enjoy any capital gains and reinvested dividends tax-free.

personality individual's characteristic way of behaving across a wide range of situations. Two broad dimensions of personality are *extroversion and neuroticism. A number of more specific personal traits have also been described, including *psychopathy (antisocial behaviour).

personification figure of speech (poetic or imaginative expression) in which animals, plants, objects, and ideas are treated as if they were human or alive ('Clouds chased each other across the face of the Moon'; 'Nature smiled on their work and gave it her blessing'; 'The future beckoned eagerly to them').

Perspex trade name for a clear, lightweight, tough plastic first produced 1930. It is widely used for watch glasses, advertising signs, domestic baths, motorboat windshields, aircraft canopies, and protective shields. Its chemical name is polymethylmethacrylate (PMMA). It is manufactured under other names: Plexiglas (in the USA), Oroglas (in Europe) and Lucite.

perspiration excretion of water and dissolved substances from the *sweat glands of the skin of mammals. Perspiration has two main functions: body cooling by the evaporation of water from the skin surface, and excretion of waste products such as salts.

Perth capital of Western Australia, with its port at nearby Fremantle on the Swan River; population (1990) 1,190,100. Products include textiles, cement, furniture, and vehicles. It was founded 1829 and is the commercial and cultural centre of the state.

pertussis medical name for *whooping cough, an infectious disease mainly seen in children.

Peru Republic of (*República del Perú*)

area 1,285,200 sq km/496,216 sq mi
capital Lima, including port of Callao
towns Arequipa, Iquitos, Chiclayo, Trujillo
physical Andes mountains NW–SE cover 27% of Peru, separating Amazon river-basin jungle in NE from coastal plain in W; desert along coast N–S

environment an estimated 3,000 out of the 8,000 sq km/3,100 sq mi of coastal lands under irrigation are either waterlogged or suffering from saline water. Only half the population have access to clean drinking water
head of state and government Alberto Fujimori from 1990
political system democratic republic
exports coca, coffee, alpaca, llama and vicuña wool, fish meal, lead (largest producer in South America), copper, iron, oil
currency new sol
population (1993 est) 22,130,000 (46% Indian, mainly Quechua and Aymara; 43% mixed Spanish–Indian descent); growth rate 2.6% p.a.
languages Spanish 68%, Quechua 27% (both official), Aymara 3%
religion Roman Catholic 90%
GNP $1,020 per head (1991)
chronology
1824 Independence achieved from Spain.
1849–74 Some 80,000–100,000 Chinese labourers arrived in Peru to fill menial jobs such as collecting guano.
1902 Boundary dispute with Bolivia settled.
1927 Boundary dispute with Colombia settled.
1942 Boundary dispute with Ecuador settled.
1948 Army coup, led by General Manuel Odría, installed a military government.
1963 Return to civilian rule, with Fernando Belaúnde Terry as president.
1968 Return of military government in a bloodless coup by General Juan Velasco Alvarado.
1975 Velasco replaced, in a bloodless coup, by General Morales Bermúdez.
1980 Return to civilian rule, with Fernando Belaúnde as president.
1981 Boundary dispute with Ecuador renewed.
1985 Belaúnde succeeded by Social Democrat Alan García Pérez.
1987 President García delayed the nationalization of Peru's banks after a vigorous campaign against the proposal.
1988 García pressured to seek help from the International Monetary Fund.
1989 Mario Vargas Llosa entered presidential race; his Democratic Front won municipal elections Nov.
1990 Alberto Fujimori defeated Vargas Llosa in presidential elections. Assassination attempt on president failed.
1992 Fujimori sided with army to avert coup. Shining Path extremists continued campaign of violence. Their leader, Abimael Guzman Reynoso, arrested, tried, and given life sentence. Anti-government coup foiled; single-chamber legislature replaced two-chamber system.

Peru Current formerly known as **Humboldt Current** cold ocean *current flowing north from the Antarctic along the west coast of South America to S Ecuador, then west. It reduces the coastal temperature, making the west slopes of the Andes arid because winds are already chilled and dry when they meet the coast.

Perugino Pietro. Original name of Pietro Vannucci 1446–1523. Italian painter, active chiefly in Perugia. He taught Raphael who absorbed his soft and graceful figure style. Perugino produced paintings for the lower walls of the Sistine Chapel of the Vatican 1481 and in 1500 decorated the Sala del Cambio in Perugia.

perverting the course of justice in law, the criminal offence of acting in such a way as to prevent justice being done. Examples are tampering with evidence, misleading the police or a court, and threatening witnesses or jurors.

Pesach Jewish name for the *Passover festival.

Peshawar capital of North-West Frontier Province, Pakistan, 18 km/11 mi E of the Khyber Pass; population (1981) 555,000. Products include textiles, leather, and copper.

pest in biology, any insect, fungus, rodent, or other living organism that has a harmful effect on human beings, other than those that directly cause human diseases. Most pests damage crops or livestock, but the term also covers those that damage buildings, destroy food stores, and spread disease.

pesticide any chemical used in farming, gardening or indoors to combat pests. Pesticides are of three main types: *insecticides* (to kill insects), *fungicides* (to kill fungal diseases), and *herbicides* (to kill plants, mainly those considered weeds). The safest pesticides are those made from plants, such as the insecticides pyrethrum and derris. Pesticides cause a number of pollution problems through spray drift onto surrounding areas, direct contamination of users or the public, and as residues on food.

Pétain Henri Philippe 1856–1951. French general and right-wing politician. His defence of Verdun 1916 during World War I made him a national hero. In World War II he became prime minister June 1940 and signed an armistice with Germany. Removing the seat of government to Vichy, a health resort in central France, he established an authoritarian regime. He was imprisoned after the war.

petal part of a flower whose function is to attract pollinators such as insects or birds. Petals are frequently large and brightly coloured and may also be scented. Some have a nectary at the base and markings on the petal surface, known as honey guides, to direct pollinators to the source of the nectar. In wind-pollinated plants, however, the petals are usually small and insignificant, and sometimes absent altogether. Petals are derived from modified leaves, and are known collectively as a corolla.

Peter three tsars of Russia:

Peter I the Great 1672–1725. Tsar of Russia from 1682 on the death of his brother Tsar Feodor; he assumed control of the government 1689. He attempted to reorganize the country on Western lines; the army was modernized, a fleet was built, the administrative and legal systems were remodelled, education was encouraged, and the church was brought under state control. On the Baltic coast, where he had conquered territory from Sweden, Peter built his new capital, St Petersburg.

Peter II 1715–1730. Tsar of Russia from 1727. Son of Peter the Great, he had been passed over in favour of Catherine I 1725 but succeeded her 1727.

Peter III 1728–1762. Tsar of Russia 1762. Weak-minded son of Peter I's eldest daughter, Anne, he was adopted 1741 by his aunt *Elizabeth, Empress of Russia, and at her command married the future Catherine II 1745. He was deposed in favour of his wife, Alexius Orlov, and probably murdered by her lover, Alexius Orlov.

Peterloo massacre the events in St Peter's Fields, Manchester, England, 16 Aug 1819, when an open-air meeting in support of parliamentary reform was charged by yeomanry and hussars. Eleven people were killed and 500 wounded. The name was given in analogy with the Battle of Waterloo.

Peter, St Christian martyr, the author of two epistles in the New Testament and leader of the apostles. He is regarded as the first bishop of Rome, whose mantle the pope inherits. His real name was Simon, but he was nicknamed Kephas ('Peter', from the Greek for 'rock') by Jesus, as being the rock upon which he would build his church. His emblem is two keys; feast day 29 June.

petiole in botany, the stalk attaching the leaf blade, or *lamina, to the stem. Typically it is continuous with the midrib of the leaf and attached to the base of the lamina, but occasionally it is attached to the lower surface of the lamina, as in the nasturtium (a peltate leaf). Petioles that are flattened and leaflike are termed phyllodes. Leaves that lack a petiole are said to be sessile.

Petipa Marius 1818–1910. French choreographer who created some of the most important ballets in the classical repertory. For the Imperial Ballet in Russia he created masterpieces such as *The Sleeping Beauty* 1890 and *Swan Lake* 1895.

petition of right in British law, the procedure whereby, before the passing of the Crown Proceedings Act 1947, a subject petitioned for legal relief against the crown, for example for property of which the crown had taken possession.

Petra (Arabic *Wadi Musa*) ancient city carved out of the red rock at a site in Jordan, on the eastern slopes of the Wadi el Araba, 90 km/56 mi S of the Dead Sea. An Edomite stronghold and capital of the Nabataeans in the 2nd century, it was captured by the Roman emperor Trajan 106 and destroyed by the Arabs in the 7th century. It was forgotten in Europe until 1812 when the Swiss traveller Jacob Burckhardt (1818–1897) came across it.

Petrarch (Italian *Petrarca*) Francesco 1304–1374. Italian poet, born in Arezzo, a devotee of the Classical tradition. His *Il Canzoniere* is composed of sonnets in praise of his idealized love 'Laura', whom he first saw 1327 (she was a married woman and refused to become his mistress).

petrel any of various families of seabirds, including the worldwide *storm petrels* (family Procellariidae), which include the smallest seabirds (some only 13 cm/5 in long), and the *diving petrels* (family Pelecanoididae) of the southern hemisphere, which feed by diving underwater and are characterized by having nostril tubes. They include *fulmars and *shearwaters.

Petrie (William Matthew) Flinders 1853–1942. English archaeologist who excavated sites in Egypt (the pyramids at Gîza, the temple at Tanis, the Greek city of Naucratis in the Nile delta, Tell el Amarna, Naquada, Abydos, and Memphis) and Palestine from 1880.

petrochemical chemical derived from the processing of petroleum (crude oil). *Petrochemical industries* are those that obtain their raw materials from the processing of petroleum.

petrodollars in economics, dollar earnings of nations that make up the *Organization of Petroleum-Exporting Countries (OPEC).

Petrograd former name (1914–24) of St Petersburg, city in Russia.

petrol mixture of hydrocarbons derived from petroleum, mainly used as a fuel for internal combustion engines. It is colourless and highly volatile. *Leaded petrol* contains antiknock (a mixture of tetraethyl lead and dibromoethane), which improves the combustion of petrol and the performance of a car engine. The lead from the exhaust fumes enters the atmosphere, mostly as simple lead compounds. There is strong evidence that it can act as a nerve poison on young children and cause mental impairment. This has prompted a gradual switch to the use of *unleaded petrol* in the UK.

petrol engine the most commonly used source of power for motor vehicles, introduced by the German engineers Gottlieb Daimler and Karl Benz 1885. The petrol engine is a complex piece of machinery made up of about 150 moving parts. It is a reciprocating piston engine, in which a number of pistons move up and down in cylinders. The motion of the pistons rotate a crankshaft, at the end of which is a heavy flywheel. From the flywheel the power is transferred to the car's driving wheels via the transmission system of clutch, gearbox, and final drive.

petroleum or *crude oil* natural mineral oil, a thick greenish-brown flammable liquid found underground in permeable rocks. Petroleum consists of hydrocarbons mixed with oxygen, sulphur, nitrogen, and other elements in varying proportions. It is thought to be derived from ancient organic material that has been converted by, first, bacterial action, then heat and pressure (but its origin may be chemical also). From crude petroleum, various products are made by distillation and other processes; for example, fuel oil, petrol, kerosene, diesel, lubricating oil, paraffin wax, and petroleum jelly.

petrology branch of geology that deals with the study of rocks, their mineral compositions, and their origins.

Petronius Gaius, known as *Petronius Arbiter*, died *c.* AD 66. Roman author of the licentious romance *Satyricon*. He was a companion of the emperor Nero and supervisor of his pleasures.

pewter any of various alloys of mostly tin with varying amounts of lead, copper, or antimony. Pewter has been known for centuries and was once widely used for domestic utensils but is now used mainly for ornamental ware.

peyote spineless cactus *Lophophora williamsii* of N Mexico and the southwestern USA. It has white or pink flowers. Its buttonlike tops contain the hallucinogen *mescaline*, which is used by American Indians in religious ceremonies.

Pfalz German name of the historic division of Germany, the *Palatinate.

pH scale from 0 to 14 for measuring acidity or alkalinity. A pH of 7.0 indicates neutrality, below 7 is acid, while above 7 is alkaline. Strong acids, such as those used in car batteries, have a pH of

about 2; strong alkalis such as sodium hydroxide are pH 13.

Phaedra in Greek mythology, a Cretan, daughter of Minos and Pasiphae, married to Theseus of Athens. Her adulterous passion for her stepson Hippolytus led to her death. The story is told in plays by Euripides, Seneca, and Racine.

Phaethon in Greek mythology, the son of Helios, the Sun god, who was allowed for one day to drive the chariot of the Sun. Losing control of the horses, he almost set the Earth on fire and was killed by Zeus with a thunderbolt.

phage another name for a *bacteriophage, a virus that attacks bacteria.

phagocyte type of white blood cell, or *leucocyte, that can engulf a bacterium or other invading microorganism. Phagocytes are found in blood, lymph, and other body tissues, where they also ingest foreign matter and dead tissue. A *macrophage differs in size and life span.

Phalangist member of a Lebanese military organization (*Phalanges Libanaises*), since 1958 the political and military force of the *Maronite Church in Lebanon. The Phalangists' unbending right-wing policies and resistance to the introduction of democratic institutions helped contribute to the civil war in Lebanon.

phalarope any of a genus *Phalaropus* of small, elegant shorebirds in the sandpiper family (Scolopacidae). They have the habit of spinning in the water to stir up insect larvae. They are native to North America, the UK, and the polar regions of Europe.

Phanerozoic (Greek *phanero* 'visible') eon in Earth history, consisting of the most recent 570 million years. It comprises the Palaeozoic, Mesozoic, and Cenozoic eras. The vast majority of fossils come from this eon, owing to the evolution of hard shells and internal skeletons. The name means 'interval of well-displayed life'.

Pharaoh Hebrew form of the Egyptian royal title Per-'o. This term, meaning 'great house', was originally applied to the royal household, and after about 950 BC to the king.

Pharisee (Hebrew 'separatist') member of a conservative Jewish sect that arose in the 2nd century BC in protest against all movements favouring compromise with Hellenistic culture. The Pharisees were devout adherents of the law, both as found in the Torah and in the oral tradition known as the Mishnah.

pharmacology study of the origins, applications, and effects of chemical substances on living organisms. Products of the pharmaceutical industry range from aspirin to anticancer agents.

pharynx interior of the throat, the cavity at the back of the mouth. Its walls are made of muscle strengthened with a fibrous layer and lined with mucous membrane. The internal nostrils lead backwards into the pharynx, which continues downwards into the oesophagus and (through the epiglottis) into the windpipe. On each side, a Eustachian tube enters the pharynx from the middle ear cavity.

phase in astronomy, the apparent shape of the Moon or a planet when all or part of its illuminated hemisphere is facing the Earth. The Moon undergoes a full cycle of phases from new (when between the Earth and the Sun) through first quarter (when at 90° eastern elongation from the Sun), full (when opposite the Sun), and last quarter (when at 90° western elongation from the Sun).

phase in physics, a stage in an oscillatory motion, such as a wave motion: two waves are in phase when their peaks and their troughs coincide. Otherwise, there is a *phase difference*, which has consequences in *interference phenomena and *alternating current electricity.

PhD abbreviation for the degree of *Doctor of Philosophy*.

pheasant any of various large, colourful Asiatic fowls of the family Phasianidae, which also includes grouse, quail, and turkey. The plumage of the male Eurasian ring-necked or common pheasant *Phasianus colchicus* is richly tinted with brownish-green, yellow, and red markings, but the female is a camouflaged brownish colour. The nest is made on the ground. The male is polygamous.

phenol member of a group of aromatic chemical compounds with weakly acidic properties, which are characterized by a hydroxyl (OH) group attached directly to an aromatic ring. The simplest of the phenols, derived from benzene, is also known as phenol and has the formula C_6H_5OH. It is sometimes called *carbolic acid* and can be extracted from coal tar.

phenomenalism philosophical position that argues that statements about objects can be reduced to statements about what is perceived or perceivable. Thus English philosopher John Stuart Mill defined material objects as 'permanent possibilities of sensation'. Phenomenalism is closely connected with certain forms of *empiricism.

phenomenology the philosophical perspective, founded by the German philosopher Edmund *Husserl, that concentrates on phenomena as objects of perception (rather than as facts or occurrences that exist independently) in attempting to examine the ways people think about and interpret the world around them. It has been practised by the philosophers Martin Heidegger, Jean-Paul Sartre, and Maurice Merleau-Ponty.

phenotype in genetics, visible traits, those actually displayed by an organism. The phenotype is not a direct reflection of the *genotype because some alleles are masked by the presence of other, dominant alleles (see *dominance). The phenotype is further modified by the effects of the environment (for example, poor nutrition stunts growth).

pheromone chemical signal (such as an odour) that is emitted by one animal and affects the behaviour of others. Pheromones are used by many animal species to attract mates.

Phidias mid-5th century BC. Greek Classical sculptor. He supervised the sculptural programme for the Parthenon (most of it is preserved in the British Museum, London, and known as the *Elgin marbles*). He also executed the colossal statue of Zeus at Olympia, one of the Seven Wonders of the World.

Philadelphia ('the city of brotherly love') industrial city and port on the Delaware River in Pennsylvania, USA; population (1990) 1,585,600,

metropolitan area 5,899,300. Products include refined oil, chemicals, textiles, processed food, printing and publishing. Founded 1682, it was the first capital of the USA 1790–1800.

Philby Kim (Harold) 1912–1988. British intelligence officer from 1940 and Soviet agent from 1933. He was liaison officer in Washington 1949–51, when he was confirmed to be a double agent and asked to resign. Named in 1963 as having warned Guy Burgess and Donald Maclean (similarly double agents) that their activities were known, he fled to the USSR and became a Soviet citizen and general in the KGB. A fourth member of the ring was Anthony Blunt.

Philip Duke of Edinburgh 1921– . Prince of the UK, husband of Elizabeth II, a grandson of George I of Greece and a great-great-grandson of Queen Victoria. He was born in Corfu, Greece but brought up in England.

Philip six kings of France, including:

Philip II (Philip Augustus) 1165–1223. King of France from 1180. As part of his efforts to establish a strong monarchy and evict the English from their French possessions, he waged war in turn against the English kings Henry II, Richard I (with whom he also went on the Third Crusade), and John (against whom he won the decisive battle of Bouvines in Flanders 1214).

Philip IV *the Fair* 1268–1314. King of France from 1285. He engaged in a feud with Pope Boniface VIII and made him a prisoner 1303. Clement V (1264–1314), elected pope through Philip's influence 1305, moved the papal seat to Avignon 1309 and collaborated with Philip to suppress the *Templars, a powerful order of knights. Philip allied with the Scots against England and invaded Flanders.

Philip VI 1293–1350. King of France from 1328, first of the house of Valois, elected by the barons on the death of his cousin, Charles IV. His claim was challenged by Edward III of England, who defeated him at Crécy 1346.

Philip II of Macedon 382–336 BC. King of *Macedonia from 359 BC. He seized the throne from his nephew, for whom he was regent, conquered the Greek city states, and formed them into a league whose forces could be united against Persia. He was assassinated while he was planning this expedition, and was succeeded by his son *Alexander the Great.

Philip five kings of Spain, including:

Philip II 1527–1598. King of Spain from 1556. He was born at Valladolid, the son of the Habsburg emperor Charles V, and in 1554 married Queen Mary of England. On his father's abdication 1556 he inherited Spain, the Netherlands, and the Spanish possessions in Italy and the Americas, and in 1580 he annexed Portugal. His intolerance and lack of understanding of the Netherlanders drove them into revolt. Political and religious differences combined to involve him in war with England and, after 1589, with France. The defeat of the *Spanish Armada (the fleet sent to invade England in 1588) marked the beginning of the decline of Spanish power.

Philip V 1683–1746. King of Spain from 1700. A grandson of Louis XIV of France, he was the first Bourbon king of Spain. He was not recognized by the major European powers until 1713. See *Spanish Succession, War of the.

Philip Neri, St 1515–1595. Italian Roman Catholic priest who organized the Congregation of the Oratory (see *Oratorian).He built the oratory over the church of St Jerome, Rome, where prayer meetings were held and scenes from the Bible performed with music, originating the musical form *oratorio. Feast day 26 May.

Philippi ancient city of Macedonia founded by Philip of Macedon 358 BC.Near Philippi, Mark Antony and Augustus defeated Brutus and Cassius 42 BC.It was the first European town where St Paul preached, founding the congregation to which he addressed the Epistle to the Philippians (about AD 53).

Philippines Republic of the (*Republika ng Pilipinas*)

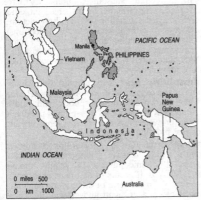

area 300,000 sq km/115,800 sq mi
capital Manila (on Luzon)
towns Quezon City (Luzon), Zamboanga (Mindanao); ports Cebu, Davao (on Mindanao), and Iloilo
physical comprises over 7,000 islands; volcanic mountain ranges traverse main chain N–S; 50% still forested. The largest islands are Luzon 108,172 sq km/41,754 sq mi and Mindanao 94,227 sq km/36,372 sq mi; others include Samar, Negros, Palawan, Panay, Mindoro, Leyte, Cebu, and the Sulu group
environment cleared for timber, tannin, and the creation of fish ponds, the mangrove forest was reduced from an area of 5,000 sq km/1,930 sq mi to 380 sq km/146 sq mi between 1920 and 1988
head of state and government Fidel Ramos from 1992
political system emergent democracy
exports sugar, copra (world's largest producer) and coconut oil, timber, copper concentrates, electronics, clothing
currency peso
population (1993 est) 65,660,000 (93% Malaysian); growth rate 2.4% p.a.
languages Tagalog (Filipino, official); English and Spanish
religions Roman Catholic 84%, Protestant 9%, Muslim 5%
GNP $850 per head (1992)

chronology
1542 Named the Philippines (Filipinas) by Spanish explorers.
1565 Conquered by Spain.
1898 Ceded to the USA after Spanish–American War.
1935 Granted internal self-government.
1942–45 Occupied by Japan.
1946 Independence achieved from USA.
1965 Ferdinand Marcos elected president.
1983 Opposition leader Benigno Aquino murdered by military guard.
1986 Marcos overthrown by Corazon Aquino's People's Power movement.
1987 'Freedom constitution' adopted, giving Aquino mandate to rule until June 1992; People's Power won majority in congressional elections. Attempted right-wing coup suppressed. Communist guerrillas active. Government in rightward swing.
1988 Land Reform Act gave favourable compensation to large estate-holders.
1989 Referendum on southern autonomy failed; Marcos died in exile; Aquino refused his burial in Philippines. Sixth coup attempt suppressed with US aid; Aquino declared state of emergency.
1990 Seventh coup attempt survived by President Aquino.
1991 June: eruption of Mount Pinatubo, hundreds killed. USA agreed to give up Clark Field airbase but keep Subic Bay naval base for ten more years. Sept: Philippines Senate voted to urge withdrawal of all US forces. US renewal of Subic Bay lease rejected. Nov: Imelda Marcos returned.
1992 Fidel Ramos elected to replace Aquino.

Philip, St 1st century AD. In the New Testament, one of the 12 apostles. He was an inhabitant of Bethsaida (N Israel), and is said to have worked as a missionary in Anatolia. Feast day 3 May.

Philistine member of a seafaring people of non-Semitic origin who founded city-states on the Palestinian coastal plain in the 12th century BC, adopting a Semitic language and religion. They were at war with the Israelites in the 11th–10th centuries BC (hence the pejorative use of their name in Hebrew records for anyone uncivilized in intellectual and artistic terms). They were largely absorbed into the kingdom of Israel under King David, about 1000 BC.

Philips Anton 1874–1951. Dutch industrialist and founder of an electronics firm. The Philips Bulb and Radio Works 1891 was founded with his brother Gerard, at Eindhoven. Anton served as chair of the company 1921–51, during which time the firm became the largest producer of electrical goods outside the USA.

philosophy (Greek 'love of wisdom') branch of learning that includes metaphysics (the nature of being), epistemology (theory of knowledge), logic (study of valid inference), ethics, and aesthetics. Philosophy is concerned with fundamental problems –including the nature of mind and matter, perception, self, free will, causation, time and space, and the existence of moral judgements – which cannot be resolved by a specific method.

Phiz pseudonym of Hablot Knight Browne 1815–1882. British artist who illustrated the greater part of the *Pickwick Papers* and other works by Charles Dickens.

phlebitis inflammation of a vein. It is sometimes associated with blockage by a blood clot (*thrombosis), in which case it is more accurately described as thrombophlebitis.

phloem tissue found in vascular plants whose main function is to conduct sugars and other food materials from the leaves, where they are produced, to all other parts of the plant.

phlox any plant of the genus *Phlox*, native to North America and Siberia. Phloxes are small with alternate leaves and showy white, pink, red, or purple flowers.

Phnom Penh capital of Cambodia, on the Mekong River, 210 km/130 mi NW of Saigon; population (1989) 800,000. Industries include textiles and food-processing.

phobia excessive irrational fear of an object or situation, for example, agoraphobia (fear of open spaces and crowded places), acrophobia (fear of heights), claustrophobia (fear of enclosed places). Behaviour therapy is one form of treatment.

Phobos one of the two moons of Mars, discovered 1877 by the US astronomer Asaph Hall (1829–1907). It is an irregularly shaped lump of rock, cratered by *meteorite impacts. Phobos is $27 \times 22 \times 19$ km/$17 \times 13 \times 12$ mi across, and orbits Mars every 0.32 days at a distance of 9,400 km/5,840 mi from the planet's centre. It is thought to be an asteroid captured by Mars' gravity.

Phoenicia ancient Greek name for N *Canaan on the E coast of the Mediterranean. The Phoenicians lived about 1200–332 BC. Seafaring traders and artisans, they are said to have circumnavigated Africa and established colonies in Cyprus, N Africa (for example Carthage), Malta, Sicily, and Spain. Their cities (Tyre, Sidon, and Byblos were the main ones) were independent states ruled by hereditary kings but dominated by merchant ruling classes. The fall of Tyre to Alexander the Great ended the separate history of Phoenicia.

phoenix mythical Egyptian bird that burned itself to death on a pyre every 500 years and rose rejuvenated from the ashes.

Phoenix capital of Arizona, USA; industrial city (steel, aluminium, electrical goods, food processing) and tourist centre on the Salt River; population (1990) 983,400.

phon unit of loudness, equal to the value in decibels of an equally loud tone with frequency 1,000 Hz. The higher the frequency, the louder a noise sounds for the same decibel value; thus an 80-decibel tone with a frequency of 20 Hz sounds as loud as 20 decibels at 1,000 Hz, and the phon value of both tones is 20. An aircraft engine has a loudness of around 140 phons.

phonetics identification, description, and classification of sounds used in articulate speech. These sounds are codified in the International Phonetic Alphabet (a highly modified version of the English/Roman alphabet).

phosphate salt or ester of *phosphoric acid. Incomplete neutralization of phosphoric acid gives rise to acid phosphates (see *acid salts and *buffer). Phosphates are used as fertilizers, and

are required for the development of healthy root systems. They are involved in many biochemical processes, often as part of complex molecules, such as *ATP.

phospholipid any *lipid consisting of a glycerol backbone, a phosphate group, and two long chains. Phospholipids are found everywhere in living systems as the basis for biological membranes.

phosphor any substance that is phosphorescent, that is, gives out visible light when it is illuminated by a beam of electrons or ultraviolet light. The television screen is coated on the inside with phosphors that glow when beams of electrons strike them. Fluorescent lamp tubes are also phosphor-coated. Phosphors are also used in Day-Glo paints, and as optical brighteners in detergents.

phosphorescence in physics, the emission of light by certain substances after they have absorbed energy, whether from visible light, other electromagnetic radiation such as ultraviolet rays or X-rays, or cathode rays (a beam of electrons). When the stimulating energy is removed phosphorescence ceases, although it may persist for a short time after (unlike *fluorescence, which stops immediately).

phosphoric acid acid derived from phosphorus and oxygen. Its commonest form (H_3PO_4) is also known as orthophosphoric acid, and is produced by the action of phosphorus pentoxide (P_2O_5) on water. It is used in rust removers and for rust-proofing iron and steel.

phosphorus (Greek *phosphoros* 'bearer of light') highly reactive, nonmetallic element, symbol P, atomic number 15, relative atomic mass 30.9738. It occurs in nature as phosphates (commonly in the form of the mineral *apatite), and is essential to plant and animal life. Compounds of phosphorus are used in fertilizers, various organic chemicals, for matches and fireworks, and in glass and steel.

photocell or *photoelectric cell* device for measuring or detecting light or other electromagnetic radiation, since its electrical state is altered by the effect of light. In a *photoemissive* cell, the radiation causes electrons to be emitted and a current to flow (*photoelectric effect); a *photovoltaic* cell causes an *electromotive force to be generated in the presence of light across the boundary of two substances. A *photoconductive* cell, which contains a semiconductor, increases its conductivity when exposed to electromagnetic radiation.

photochemical reaction any chemical reaction in which light is produced or light initiates the reaction. Light can initiate reactions by exciting atoms or molecules and making them more reactive: the light energy becomes converted to chemical energy. Many photochemical reactions set up a *chain reaction and produce *free radicals.

photocopier machine that uses some form of photographic process to reproduce copies of documents or illustrations. Most modern photocopiers, as pioneered by the Xerox Corporation, use electrostatic photocopying, or *xerography ('dry writing'). This employs a drum coated with a light-sensitive material such as selenium, which holds a pattern of static electricity charges corresponding to the dark areas of an image projected on to the drum by a lens. Finely divided pigment (toner) of opposite electric charge sticks to the charged areas of the drum and is transferred to a sheet of paper, which is heated briefly to melt the toner and stick it to the paper.

photoelectric effect in physics, the emission of *electrons from a substance (usually a metallic surface) when it is struck by *photons (quanta of electromagnetic radiation), usually those of visible light or ultraviolet radiation.

photography process for reproducing images on sensitized materials by various forms of radiant energy, including visible light, ultraviolet, infrared, X-rays, atomic radiations, and electron beams. Photography was developed in the 19th century; among the pioneers were L J M *Daguerre in France and Fox *Talbot in the UK. Colour photography dates from the early 20th century.

photogravure *printing process that uses a plate prepared photographically, covered with a pattern of recessed cells in which the ink is held. See *gravure.

photometer instrument that measures luminous intensity, usually by comparing relative intensities from different sources. Bunsen's grease-spot photometer 1844 compares the intensity of a light source with a known source by each illuminating one half of a translucent area. Modern photometers use *photocells, as in a photographer's exposure meter. A photomultiplier can also be used as a photometer.

photomultiplier instrument that detects low levels of electromagnetic radiation (usually visible light or *infrared radiation) and amplifies it to produce a detectable signal.

photon in physics, the *elementary particle or 'package' (quantum) of energy in which light and other forms of electromagnetic radiation are emitted. The photon has both particle and wave properties; it has no charge, is considered massless but possesses momentum and energy. It is one of the *gauge bosons, a particle that cannot be subdivided, and is the carrier of the *electromagnetic force, one of the fundamental forces of nature.

photoperiodism biological mechanism that determines the timing of certain activities by responding to changes in day length. The flowering of many plants is initiated in this way. Photoperiodism in plants is regulated by a light-sensitive pigment, *phytochrome*. The breeding seasons of many temperate-zone animals are also triggered by increasing or declining day length, as part of their *biorhythms.

photosphere visible surface of the Sun, which emits light and heat. About 300 km/200 mi deep, it consists of incandescent gas at a temperature of 5,800K (5,530°C/9,980°F).

photosynthesis process by which green plants trap light energy and use it to drive a series of chemical reactions, leading to the formation of carbohydrates. All animals ultimately depend on photosynthesis because it is the method by which the basic food (sugar) is created. For photosynthesis to occur, the plant must possess *chlorophyll and must have a supply of carbon dioxide and water. Actively photosynthesizing green plants store excess sugar as starch (this can be tested for in the laboratory using iodine).

phototropism movement of part of a plant toward or away from a source of light. Leaves are positively phototropic, detecting the source of light and orientating themselves to receive the maximum amount.

Phrygia former kingdom of W Asia covering the Anatolian plateau. It was inhabited in ancient times by an Indo-European people and achieved great prosperity in the 8th century BC under a line of kings bearing in turn the names Gordius and Midas, but then fell under Lydian rule. From Phrygia the cult of the Earth goddess Cybele was introduced into Greece and Rome.

phylacteries in Judaism, another name for *tefillin.

phylloxera any of a family (Phylloxeridae) of small plant-sucking insects (order Homoptera) that attack the leaves and roots of some plants.

phylogeny historical sequence of changes that occurs in a given species during the course of its evolution. It was once erroneously associated with ontogeny (the process of development of a living organism).

phylum (plural *phyla*) major grouping in biological classification. Mammals, birds, reptiles, amphibians, fishes, and tunicates belong to the phylum Chordata; the phylum Mollusca consists of snails, slugs, mussels, clams, squid, and octopuses; the phylum Porifera contains sponges; and the phylum Echinodermata includes starfish, sea urchins, and sea cucumbers. In classifying plants (where the term 'division' often takes the place of 'phylum'), there are between four and nine phyla depending on the criteria used; all flowering plants belong to a single phylum, Angiospermata, and all conifers to another, Gymnospermata. Related phyla are grouped together in a *kingdom; phyla are subdivided into *classes.

physical chemistry branch of chemistry concerned with examining the relationships between the chemical compositions of substances and the physical properties that they display. Most chemical reactions exhibit some physical phenomenon (change of state, temperature, pressure, or volume, or the use or production of electricity), and the measurement and study of such phenomena has led to many chemical theories and laws.

physics branch of science concerned with the laws that govern the structure of the universe, and the forms of matter and energy and their interactions. For convenience, physics is often divided into branches such as nuclear physics, particle physics, solid-and liquid-state physics, electricity, electronics, magnetism, optics, acoustics, heat, and thermodynamics. Before this century, physics was known as *natural philosophy*.

physiology branch of biology that deals with the functioning of living animals, as opposed to anatomy, which studies their structures.

physiotherapy treatment of injury and disease by physical means such as exercise, heat, manipulation, massage, and electrical stimulation.

Piaf Edith. Stage name of Edith Gassion 1915–1963. French singer and songwriter, a cab-

PHOTOGRAPHY: CHRONOLOGY

1515   Leonardo da Vinci described the camera obscura.

1750   The painter Canaletto used a camera obscura as an aid to his painting in Venice.

1790   Thomas Wedgwood in England made photograms – placing objects on leather, sensitized using silver nitrate.

1826   Nicephore Niépce (1765–1833), a French doctor, produced the world's first photograph from nature on pewter plates with a camera obscura and an eight-hour exposure.

1835   Niépce and L J M Daguerre produced the first Daguerreotype camera photograph.

1839   Daguerre was awarded an annuity by the French government and his process given to the world.

1841   Fox Talbot's calotype process was patented – the first multicopy method of photography using a negative/positive process, sensitized with silver iodide.

1845   Hill and Adamson began to use calotypes for portraits in Edinburgh.

1851   Fox Talbot used a one-thousandth of a second exposure to demonstrate high-speed photography.

1855   Roger Fenton made documentary photographs of the Crimean War from a specially constructed caravan with portable darkroom.

1859   Nadar in Paris made photographs underground using battery powered arc lights.

1860   Queen Victoria was photographed by Mayall. Abraham Lincoln was photographed by Matthew Brady for political campaigning.

1861   The single-lens reflex plate camera was patented by Thomas Sutton. The principles of three-colour photography were demonstrated by J C Maxwell.

1862   Nadar took aerial photographs over Paris.

1871   Gelatin-silver bromide was developed.

1878   In the USA Eadweard Muybridge analysed the movements of animals through sequential photographs, using a series of cameras.

1879   The photogravure process was invented.

1880   A silver bromide emulsion was fixed with hypo. Photographs were first reproduced in newspapers in New York using the half-tone engraving process. The first twin-lens reflex camera was produced in London.

1889   The Eastman Company in the USA produced the Kodak No 1 camera and roll film, facilitating universal, hand-held snapshots.

1902   In Germany, Deckel invented a prototype leaf shutter and Zeiss introduced the Tessar lens.

1904   The autochrome colour process was patented by the Lumière brothers.

1905   Alfred Stieglitz opened the gallery '291' in New York promoting photography. Lewis Hine used photography to expose the exploitation of children in American factories.

1907   The autochrome process began to be factory-produced.

1914   Oskar Barnack designed a prototype Leica camera for Leitz in Germany.

1924   Leitz launched the first 35mm camera, the Leica, delayed because of World War I. It became very popular with photojournalists.

1929   Rolleiflex produced a twin-lens reflex camera in Germany.

1935   In the USA, Mannes and Godowsky invented Kodachrome transparency film. Electronic flash was invented in the USA.

1936   *Life* magazine, significant for its photojournalism, was first published in the USA.

1938   *Picture Post* magazine was introduced in the UK.

1940   Multigrade enlarging paper by Ilford was made available in the UK.

1942   Kodacolour negative film was introduced.

1945   The zone system of exposure estimation was published in the book *Exposure Record* by Ansel Adams.

1947   Polaroid black and white instant process film was invented by Dr Edwin Land, who set up the Polaroid corporation in Boston, Massachusetts. The principles of holography were demonstrated in England by Dennis Gabor.

1955   Kodak introduced Tri-X, a black and white 200 ASA film.

1959   The zoom lens was invented by the Austrian firm of Voigtlander.

1960   The laser was invented in the USA, making holography possible. Polacolor, a self-processing colour film, was introduced by Polaroid.

1963   Cibachrome, paper and chemicals for printing directly from transparencies, was made available by Ciba-Geigy of Switzerland. One of the most permanent processes, it is marketed by Ilford in the UK.

1969   Photographs were taken on the Moon by US astronauts.

1972   The SX70 system, a single-lens reflex camera with instant prints, was produced by Polaroid.

1980   *Voyager 1* sent photographs of Saturn back to Earth across space.

1985   The Minolta Corporation in Japan introduced the Minolta 7000 – the world's first body-integral autofocus single-lens reflex camera.

1988   The electronic camera, which stores pictures on magnetic disc instead of on film, was introduced in Japan.

1990   Kodak introduced PhotoCD which converts 35mm camera pictures (on film) into digital form and stores them on compact disc (CD) for viewing on TV.

NOBEL PRIZE FOR PHYSICS

recent prizewinners

1984   Carlo Rubbia *(Italy)* and Simon van der Meer *(Netherlands)*: contributions to the discovery of the W and Z particles (weakons)

1985   Klaus von Klitzing *(West Germany)*: discovery of the quantized Hall effect

1986   Ernst Ruska *(West Germany)*: electron optics, and design of the first electron microscope. Gerd Binnig *(West Germany)*, and Heinrich Rohrer *(Switzerland)*: design of scanning tunnelling microscope

1987   Georg Bednorz *(West Germany)* and Alex Müller *(Switzerland)*: superconductivity in ceramic materials

1988   Leon Lederman, Melvin Schwartz, and Jack Steinberger *(USA)*: neutrino-beam method, and demonstration of the doublet structure of leptons through discovery of muon neutrino

1989   Norman Ramsey *(USA)*: measurement techniques leading to discovery of caesium atomic clock. Hans Dehmeit *(USA)* and Wolfgang Paul *(West Germany)*: ion-trap method for isolating single atoms

1990   Richard E Taylor *(Canada)*, Jerome I Friedman *(USA)*, and Henry W Kendall *(USA)*: experiments demonstrating that protons and neutrons are made up of quarks

1991   Pierre-Gilles de Gennes *(France)*: work on disordered systems including polymers and liquid crystals; development of mathematical methods for studying the behaviour of molecules in a liquid on the verge of solidifying

1992   Georges Charpak *(France)*: invention and development of detectors used in high-energy physics

1993   Joseph Taylor *(USA)* and Russell Hulse *(USA)*: discovery of first binary pulsar (confirming the existence of gravitational waves)

1994   Clifford G Shull *(USA)* and Berfram W Brockhouse *(Canada)*: development of technique known as 'neutron scattering' which led to advances in semiconductor technology.

---

aret singer in Paris from the late 1930s. She is remembered for the defiant song 'Je ne regrette rien/I Regret Nothing' and 'La Vie en rose' 1946.

piano or **pianoforte** stringed musical instrument, played by felt-covered hammers activated from a keyboard, and capable of soft (piano) or loud (forte) tones, hence its name. The first piano was constructed 1704 and introduced 1709 by Bartolommeo Cristofori, a harpsichord-maker of Padua. It uses a clever mechanism to make the keyboard touch-sensitive. Extensively developed during the 18th century, the piano attracted admiration among many composers, although it was not until 1768 that J C Bach gave one of the first public recitals on the instrument.

Picardy (French *Picardie*) region of N France, including Aisne, Oise, and Somme *départements*
area 19,400 sq km/7,488 sq mi
population (1986) 1,774,000
products chemicals and metals
history in the 13th century the name Picardy was used to describe the feudal smallholdings N of Paris added to the French crown by Philip II. During the Hundred Years' War the area was hotly contested by France and England, but it was eventually occupied by Louis XI 1477. Picardy once more became a major battlefield in World War I.

picaresque (Spanish *pícaro* 'rogue') genre of novel that takes a rogue or villain for its central character, telling his or her story in episodic form. The genre originated in Spain and was popular in the 18th century in Britain. Daniel Defoe's *Moll Flanders*, Tobias Smollett's *Roderick Random*, Henry Fielding's *Tom Jones*, and Mark Twain's *Huckleberry Finn* are typical picaresque novels.

Picasso Pablo Ruiz y 1881–1973. Spanish artist. Active chiefly in France, he was one of the most inventive and prolific talents in 20th-century art. His Blue Period 1901–04 and Rose Period 1905–06 preceded the revolutionary *Les Demoiselles d'Avignon* 1907 (Museum of Modern Art,

New York), which paved the way for Cubism. In the early 1920s he was considered a leader of the Surrealist movement. In the 1930s his work included metal sculpture, book illustration, and the mural *Guernica* 1937 (Prado, Madrid), a comment on the bombing of civilians in the Spanish Civil War. He continued to paint into his eighties.

Piccard Auguste 1884–1962. Swiss scientist. In 1931–32, he and his twin brother, **Jean Félix** (1884–1963), made ascents to 17,000 m/55,000 ft in a balloon of his own design, resulting in useful discoveries concerning stratospheric phenomena such as *cosmic radiation. He also built and used, with his son **Jacques Ernest** (1922–   ), bathyscaphs for research under the sea.

piccolo woodwind instrument, the smallest member of the flute family, for which Vivaldi composed three concertos.

Pict Roman term for a member of the peoples of N Scotland, possibly meaning 'painted' (tattooed). Of pre-Celtic origin, and speaking a Celtic language which died out in about the 10th century, the Picts are thought to have inhabited much of England before the arrival of the Celtic Britons. They were united with the Celtic Scots under the rule of Kenneth MacAlpin 844. Their greatest monument is a series of carved stones, whose symbols remain undeciphered.

pidgin language any of various trade jargons, contact languages, or *lingua francas arising in ports and markets where people of different linguistic backgrounds meet for commercial and other purposes. Usually a pidgin language is a rough blend of the vocabulary of one (often dominant) language with the syntax or grammar of one or more other (often dependent) groups. Pidgin English in various parts of the world, *français petit negre*, and Bazaar Hindi or Hindustani are examples of pidgins that have served long-term purposes to the extent of being acquired by children as one of their everyday languages. At this point they become *creole languages.

Piedmont (Italian *Piemonte*) region of N Italy,

PHYSICS: CHRONOLOGY

c. 400 BC	The first 'atomic' theory was put forward by Democritus.
c. 250	Archimedes' principle of buoyancy was established.
AD 1600	Magnetism was described by William Gilbert.
c. 1610	The principle of falling bodies descending to earth at the same speed was established by Galileo.
1642	The principles of hydraulics were put forward by Blaise Pascal.
c. 1665	Isaac Newton put forward the law of gravity, stating that the Earth exerts a constant force on falling bodies.
1677	The simple microscope was invented by Anton van Leeuwenhoek.
1690	The wave theory of light was propounded by Christiaan Huygens.
1704	The corpuscular theory of light was put forward by Isaac Newton.
1771	The link between nerve action and electricity was discovered by Luigi Galvani.
c. 1787	Charles's law relating the pressure, volume, and temperature of a gas was established by Jacques Charles.
1798	The link between heat and friction was discovered by Benjamin Rumford.
1800	Alessandro Volta invented the Voltaic cell.
1808	The 'modern' atomic theory was propounded by John Dalton.
1811	Avogadro's hypothesis relating volumes and numbers of molecules of gases was proposed by Amedeo Avogadro.
1815	Refraction of light was explained by Augustin Fresnel.
1819	The discovery of electromagnetism was made by Hans Oersted.
1821	The dynamo principle was described by Michael Faraday; the thermocouple was discovered by Thomas Seebeck.
1827	Ohm's law of electrical resistance was established by Georg Ohm; Brownian motion resulting from molecular vibrations was observed by Robert Brown.
1831	Electromagnetic induction was discovered by Faraday.
1842	The principle of conservation of energy was observed by Julius von Mayer.
c. 1847	The mechanical equivalent of heat was described by James Joule.
1849	A measurement of speed of light was put forward by French physicist Armand Fizeau (1819–1896).
1851	The rotation of the Earth was demonstrated by Jean Foucault.
1859	Spectrographic analysis was made by Robert Bunsen and Gustav Kirchhoff.
1873	Light was conceived as electromagnetic radiation by James Maxwell.
1887	The existence of radio waves was predicted by Heinrich Hertz.
1895	X-rays were discovered by Wilhelm Röntgen.
1896	The discovery of radioactivity was made by Antoine Becquerel.
1897	Joseph Thomson discovered the electron.
1899	Ernest Rutherford discovered alpha and beta rays.
1900	Quantum theory was propounded by Max Planck; the discovery of gamma rays was made by French physicist Paul-Ulrich Villard (1860–1934).
1904	The theory of radioactivity was put forward by Rutherford and Frederick Soddy.
1905	Albert Einstein propounded his special theory of relativity.
1911	The discovery of the atomic nucleus was made by Rutherford.
1916	Einstein put forward his general theory of relativity; mass spectrography was discovered by William Aston.
1926	Wave mechanics was introduced by Erwin Schrödinger.
1931	The cyclotron was developed by Ernest Lawrence.
1932	The discovery of the neutron was made by James Chadwick; the electron microscope was developed by Vladimir Zworykin.
1933	The positron, the antiparticle of the electron, was discovered by Carl Anderson.
1939	The discovery of nuclear fission was made by Otto Hahn and Fritz Strassmann.
1942	The first controlled nuclear chain reaction was achieved by Enrico Fermi.
1956	The neutrino, an elementary particle, was discovered by Clyde Cowan and Fred Reines.
1963	Maiman developed the first laser.
1964	Murray Gell-Mann and George Zweig discovered the quark.
1971	The theory of superconductivity was announced, where electrical resistance in some metals vanishes above absolute zero.
1973	The discovery of pulsars was made by Antony Hewish.
1979	The discovery of the asymmetry of elementary particles was made by US physicists James W Cronin and Val L Fitch.
1986	The discovery was made of high-temperature superconductors.
1983	Evidence of the existence of weakons (W and Z particles) was confirmed at CERN, validating the link between the weak nuclear force and the electromagnetic force.
1986	The first high-temperature superconductor was discovered, able to conduct electricity without resistance at a temperature of 35K.
1989	CERN's Large Electron–Positron Collider (LEP), a particle accelerator with a circumference of 27 km/16.8 mi, came into operation.
1991	LEP experiments demonstrated the existence of three generations of elementary particles, each with two quarks and two leptons.
1992	Japanese researchers developed a material that becomes superconducting at −103°C/−153°F (about 45°C/80°F warmer than the previous record).

bordering Switzerland to the N and France to the W, and surrounded, except to the E, by the Alps and the Apennines; area 25,400 sq km/9,804 sq mi; population (1990) 4,356,200. Its capital is Turin, and towns include Alessandria, Asti, Vercelli, and Novara. It also includes the fertile Po river valley. Products include fruit, grain, cattle, cars, and textiles. The movement for the unification of Italy started in the 19th century in Piedmont, under the house of Savoy.

Piero della Francesca c. 1420–1492. Italian painter. Active in Arezzo and Urbino, he was one of the major artists of the 15th century. His work has a solemn stillness and unusually solid figures, luminous colour, and compositional harmony. It includes a fresco series, *The Legend of the True Cross* (S Francesco, Arezzo), begun about 1452. Piero wrote two treatises, one on mathematics, one on the laws of perspective in painting.

Pietism religious movement within Lutheranism in the 17th century which emphasized spiritual and devotional faith rather than theology and dogma. It was founded by Philipp Jakob Spener (1635–1705), a minister in Frankfurt, Germany, who emphasized devotional meetings for 'groups of the Elect' rather than biblical learning; he wrote the *Pia Desideria* 1675. The movement was for many years associated with the University of Halle (founded 1694), Germany.

pietra dura (Italian 'hard stone') Italian technique of inlaying furniture with semiprecious stones, such as agate or quartz, in a variety of colours, to create pictures or patterns.

piezoelectric effect property of some crystals (for example, quartz) to develop an electromotive force or voltage across opposite faces when subjected to a mechanical strain, and, conversely, to expand or contract in size when subjected to an electromotive force. Piezoelectric crystal *oscillators are used as frequency standards (for example, replacing balance wheels in watches), and for producing *ultrasound.

pig any even-toed hoofed mammal of the family Suidae. They are omnivorous, and have simple, non-ruminating stomachs and thick hides. The Middle Eastern **wild boar** Sus scrofa is the ancestor of domesticated breeds; it is 1.5 m/4.5 ft long and 1 m/3 ft high, with formidable tusks, but not naturally aggressive.

pigeon any bird of the family Columbidae, sometimes also called doves, distinguished by their large crops, which, becoming glandular in the breeding season, secrete a milky fluid ('pigeon's milk') that aids digestion of food for the young. They are found worldwide.

pigeon hawk another name for the merlin, a small *falcon.

pigeon racing sport of racing pigeons against a clock. The birds are taken from their loft(s) and transported to a starting point, often hundreds of miles away. They have to return to their loft and a special clock times their arrival.

Piggott Lester 1935– . English jockey. He adopted a unique high riding style and is renowned as a brilliant tactician. A champion jockey 11 times between 1960 and 1982, he has ridden a record nine *Derby winners. Piggott retired from riding 1985 and took up training.

In 1987 he was imprisoned for tax evasion. He returned to racing in 1990.

pika or *mouse-hare* any small mammal of the family Ochotonidae, belonging to the order Lagomorpha (rabbits and hares). The single genus *Ochotona* contains about 15 species, most of which live in mountainous regions of Asia, although two species are native to North America.

pike any of a family Esocidae in the order Salmoniformes, of slender, freshwater bony fishes with narrow pointed heads and sharp, pointed teeth. The northern pike *Esox lucius*, of North America and Eurasia, may reach 2.2 m/7 ft and 9 kg/20 lb.

pikeperch any of various freshwater members of the perch family, resembling pikes, especially the walleye *Stizostedion vitreum*, common in Europe, W Asia, and North America. It reaches over 1 m/3 ft.

Pilate Pontius early 1st century AD. Roman procurator of Judea AD 26–36. The New Testament Gospels describe his reluctant ordering of Jesus' crucifixion, but there has been considerable debate about his actual role in it; many believe that pressure was put on him by Jewish conservative priests.

pilchard any of various small, oily members of the herring family, Clupeidae, especially the commercial sardine of Europe *Sardina pilchardus*, and the California sardine *Sardinops sagax*.

pilgrimage journey to sacred places inspired by religious devotion. For Hindus, the holy places include Varanasi and the purifying river Ganges; for Buddhists, the places connected with the crises of Buddha's career; for the ancient Greeks, the shrines at Delphi and Ephesus among others; for Jews, the sanctuary at Jerusalem; and for Muslims, Mecca.

Pilgrims the emigrants who sailed from Plymouth, Devon, England, in the *Mayflower* on 16 Sept 1620 to found the first colony in New England at New Plymouth, Massachusetts. Of the 102 passengers fewer than a quarter were Puritan refugees.

Pilgrim's Progress allegory by John Bunyan, published 1678–84, that describes the journey through life to the Celestial City of a man called Christian. On his way through the Slough of Despond, the House Beautiful, Vanity Fair, Doubting Castle, and other landmarks, he meets a number of allegorical figures.

Pill, the commonly used term for the contraceptive pill, based on female hormones. The combined pill, which contains oestrogen and progesterone, stops the production of eggs, and makes the mucus produced by the cervix hostile to sperm. It is the most effective form of contraception apart from sterilization, being more than 99% effective.

pilotfish small marine fish *Naucrates ductor* of the family Carangidae, which also includes pompanos. It hides below sharks, turtles, or boats, using the shade as a base from which to prey on smaller fish. It is found in all warm oceans and grows to about 36 cm/1.2 ft.

Pilsen German form of Czech town of *Plzeň.

pimento or *allspice* tree found in tropical parts of the New World. The dried fruits of the species

Pimenta dioica are used as a spice. Also, a sweet variety of *capsicum pepper (more correctly spelled *pimiento*).

pimpernel any plant of the genus *Anagallis* of the primrose family Primulaceae comprising about 30 species mostly native to W Europe. The European scarlet pimpernel *A. arvensis* grows in cornfields, the flowers opening only in full sunshine. It is naturalized in North America.

Pinatubo, Mount active volcano on Luzon Island, the Philippines, 88 km/55 mi N of Manila. Dormant for 600 years, it erupted June 1991, killing 343 people and leaving as many as 200,000 homeless. Surrounding rice fields were covered with 3 m/10 ft of volcanic ash.

Pindling Lynden (Oscar) 1930– . Bahamian prime minister 1967–92. After studying law in London, he returned to the island to join the newly formed Progressive Liberal Party and then became the first black prime minister of the Bahamas.

pindown punitive detention system used in some UK institutions for children and young people. Deprived of books, possessions, and most of their clothes, offenders are left in solitary confinement for up to several days. Strongly criticized when revealed in 1991, the method had been used in Staffordshire from 1985 and possibly elsewhere.

pine evergreen resinous tree of the genus *Pinus* with some 70–100 species, belonging to the Pinaceae, the largest family of conifers.

pineal body or *pineal gland* a cone-shaped outgrowth of the vertebrate brain. In some lower vertebrates, it develops a rudimentary lens and retina, which show it to be derived from an eye, or pair of eyes, situated on the top of the head in ancestral vertebrates. In fishes that can change colour to match the background, the pineal perceives the light level and controls the colour change. In birds, the pineal detects changes in daylight and stimulates breeding behaviour as spring approaches. Mammals also have a pineal gland, but it is located deeper within the brain. It secretes a hormonelike substance, melatonin, thought to influence rhythms of activity. In humans, it is a small piece of tissue attached to the posterior wall of the third ventricle of the brain.

pineapple plant *Ananas comosus* of the bromeliad family, native to South and Central America, but now cultivated in many other tropical areas, such as Hawaii and Queensland, Australia. The mauvish flowers are produced in the second year, and subsequently consolidate with their bracts into a fleshy fruit.

Pinero Arthur Wing 1855–1934. British dramatist. A leading exponent of 'well-made' play, he enjoyed great contemporary success with his farces, beginning with *The Magistrate* 1885. More substantial social drama followed with *The Second Mrs Tanqueray* 1893, and comedies including *Trelawny of the 'Wells'* 1898.

pink any annual or perennial plant of the genus *Dianthus* of the family Carophyllaceae. The stems have characteristically swollen nodes, and the flowers range in colour from white through pink to purple. Members of the pink family include carnations, sweet williams, and baby's breath *Gypsophila paniculata*.

Pinkerton Allan 1819–1884. US detective, born in Glasgow. In 1852 he founded *Pinkerton's National Detective Agency*, and built up the federal secret service from the espionage system he developed during the US Civil War.

Pink Floyd British psychedelic rock group, formed 1965. The original members were Syd Barrett (1946–), Roger Waters (1944–), Richard Wright (1945–), and Nick Mason (1945–). Their albums include *The Dark Side of the Moon* 1973 and *The Wall* 1979, with its spin-off film starring Bob Geldof.

pinnate leaf leaf that is divided up into many small leaflets, arranged in rows along either side of a midrib, as in ash trees (*Fraxinus*). It is a type of compound leaf. Each leaflet is known as a *pinna*, and where the pinnae are themselves divided, the secondary divisions are known as pinnules.

Pinochet (Ugarte) Augusto 1915– . Military ruler of Chile from 1973, when a coup backed by the US Central Intelligence Agency ousted and killed President Salvador Allende. Pinochet took over the presidency and governed ruthlessly, crushing all opposition. He was voted out of power when general elections were held in Dec 1989 but remains head of the armed forces until 1997.

pint imperial dry or liquid measure of capacity equal to 20 fluid ounces, half a quart, one-eighth of a gallon, or 0.568 litre. In the US, a liquid pint is equal to 0.473 litre, while a dry pint is equal to 0.550 litre.

Pinter Harold 1930– . English dramatist, originally an actor. He specializes in the tragicomedy of the breakdown of communication, broadly in the tradition of the Theatre of the *Absurd – for example, *The Birthday Party* 1958 and *The Caretaker* 1960. Later plays include *The Homecoming* 1965, *Old Times* 1971, *Betrayal* 1978, and *Mountain Language* 1988.

pinworm *nematode worm *Enterobius vermicularis*, an intestinal parasite of humans.

Pinyin Chinese phonetic alphabet approved 1956 by the People's Republic of China, and used since 1979 in transcribing all names of people and places from Chinese ideograms into other languages using the English/Roman alphabet. For example, the former transcription Chou Enlai becomes Zhou Enlai, Hua Kuo-feng became Hua Guofeng, Teng Hsiao-ping became Deng Xiaoping, Peking became Beijing.

pion or *pi meson* in physics, any of three *mesons (positive, negative, neutral) that play a role in binding together the neutrons and protons in the nucleus of an atom. They belong to the *hadron class of *elementary particles.

Pioneer probe any of a series of US solar-system space probes 1958–78. The probes *Pioneer 4–9* went into solar orbit to monitor the Sun's activity during the 1960s and early 1970s. *Pioneer 5*, launched 1960, was the first of a series to study the solar wind between the planets. *Pioneer 10*, launched March 1972, was the first probe to reach Jupiter (Dec 1973) and to leave the solar system 1983. *Pioneer 11*, launched April 1973, passed Jupiter Dec 1974, and was the first probe to reach Saturn (Sept 1979), before also leaving the solar system.

pipefish any of various long-snouted, thin, pipelike marine fishes in the same family (Syngnathidae) as seahorses. The great pipefish *S. acus* grows up to 50 cm/1.6 ft, and the male has a brood pouch for eggs and developing young.

Piper John 1903–1992. British painter, printmaker, and designer. His subjects include traditional Romantic views of landscape and architecture. As an official war artist in World War II he depicted damaged buildings. He also designed theatre sets and stained-glass windows for Coventry Cathedral and the Catholic Cathedral, Liverpool.

pipit any of various sparrow-sized ground-dwelling songbirds of the genus *Anthus* of the family Motacillidae, which also includes wagtails.

piracy the taking of a ship, aircraft, or any of its contents, from lawful ownership, punishable under international law by the court of any country where the pirate may be found or taken. When the craft is taken over to alter its destination, or its passengers held to ransom, the term is *hijacking. Piracy is also used to describe infringement of *copyright.

Pirandello Luigi 1867–1936. Italian writer. His plays include *La morsa/The Vice* 1912, *Sei personaggi in cerca d'autore/Six Characters in Search of an Author* 1921, and *Enrico IV/Henry IV* 1922. The themes and treatment of his plays anticipated the work of Brecht, O'Neill, Anouilh, and Genet. Nobel Prize 1934.

Piranesi Giambattista 1720–1778. Italian architect, most significant for his powerful etchings of Roman antiquities and as a theorist of architecture, advocating imaginative use of Roman models. Only one of his designs was built, Sta Maria del Priorato, Rome.

piranha any South American freshwater fish of the genus *Serrusalmus*, in the same order as cichlids. They can grow to 60 cm/2 ft long, and have razor-sharp teeth; some species may rapidly devour animals, especially if attracted by blood.

pirouette in dance, a movement comprising a complete turn of the body on one leg with the other raised.

Pisa city in Tuscany, Italy; population (1988) 104,000. It has an 11th–12th-century cathedral. Its famous campanile, the Leaning Tower of Pisa (repaired 1990) is 55 m/180 ft high and about 5 m/16.5 ft out of perpendicular. It has foundations only about 3 m/10 ft deep.

Pisanello nickname of Antonio Pisano *c.* 1395–1455. Italian artist active in Verona, Venice, Naples, Rome, and elsewhere. His panel paintings reveal a rich International Gothic style. He was also an outstanding portrait medallist. His frescoes are in the Palazzo Ducale in Mantua were rediscovered after World War II.

Pisces zodiac constellation, mainly in the northern hemisphere between Aries and Aquarius, near Pegasus. It is represented by two fish tied together by their tails. The Circlet, a delicate ring of stars, marks the head of the western fish in Pisces. The constellation contains the **vernal equinox**, the point at which the Sun's path

around the sky (the **ecliptic**) crosses the celestial equator. The Sun reaches this point around 21 March each year as it passes through Pisces from mid-March to late April. In astrology, the dates for Pisces are between about 19 Feb and 20 March (see *precession).

Piscis Austrinus or **Southern Fish** constellation of the southern hemisphere near Capricornus. Its brightest star is Fomalhaut.

Pisistratus *c.* 605–527 BC. Athenian politician. Although of noble family, he assumed the leadership of the peasant party, and seized power 561 BC. He was twice expelled, but recovered power from 541 BC until his death. Ruling as a dictator under constitutional forms, he was the first to have the Homeric poems written down, and founded Greek drama by introducing the Dionysiac peasant festivals into Athens.

Pissarro Camille 1831–1903. French Impressionist painter, born in the West Indies. He went to Paris in 1855, met Jean-Baptist-Camille Corot, then Claude Monet, and became a leading member of the Impressionists. He experimented with various styles, including *Pointillism, in the 1880s.

pistachio deciduous Eurasian tree *Pistacia vera* of the cashew family Anacardiaceae, with green nuts, which are eaten salted or used to enhance and flavour foods.

pistil general term for the female part of a flower, either referring to one single *carpel or a group of several fused carpels.

pistol any small *firearm designed to be fired with one hand. Pistols were in use from the early 15th century.

piston barrel-shaped device used in reciprocating engines (steam, petrol, diesel oil) to harness power. Pistons are driven up and down in cylinders by expanding steam or hot gases. They pass on their motion via a connecting rod and crank to a crankshaft, which turns the driving wheels. In a pump or compressor, the role of the piston is reversed, being used to move gases and liquids. See also *internal-combustion engine.

pit bull terrier or **American pit bull terrier** variety of dog that was developed in the USA solely as a fighting dog. It usually measures about 50 cm/20 in at the shoulder and weighs roughly 23 kg/50 lb, but there are no established criteria since it is not recognized as a breed by either the American or British Kennel Club.

Pitcairn Islands British colony in Polynesia, 5,300 km/3,300 mi NE of New Zealand
area 27 sq km/10 sq mi
capital Adamstown
products fruit and souvenirs to passing ships
population (1990) 52
language English
government the governor is the British high commissioner in New Zealand
history first settled 1790 by nine mutineers from the British ship the *Bounty* together with some Tahitians, their occupation remaining unknown until 1808.

pitch in chemistry, a black, sticky substance, hard when cold, but liquid when hot, used for waterproofing, roofing, and paving. It is made by the destructive distillation of wood or coal tar, and has been used since antiquity for caulking wooden ships.

pitch in music, the position of a note in the scale, dependent on the frequency of the predominant sound wave. In *standard pitch*, A above middle C has a frequency of 440 Hz. *Perfect pitch* is an ability to name or reproduce any note heard or asked for; it does not necessarily imply high musical ability.

pitchblende or *uraninite* brownish-black mineral, the major constituent of uranium ore, consisting mainly of uranium oxide (UO_2). It also contains some lead (the final, stable product of uranium decay) and variable amounts of most of the naturally occurring radioactive elements, which are products of either the decay or the fissioning of uranium isotopes. The uranium yield is 50–80%; it is also a source of radium, polonium, and actinium. Pitchblende was first studied by Pierre and Marie *Curie, who found radium and polonium in its residues in 1898.

pitcher plant any of various insectivorous plants of the family Sarraceniaceae, especially the genera *Nepenthes* and *Sarracenia*, the leaves of which are shaped like a pitcher and filled with a fluid that traps and digests insects.

Pitman Isaac 1813–1897. English teacher and inventor of Pitman's shorthand. He studied Samuel Taylor's scheme for shorthand writing, and in 1837 published his own system, *Stenographic Soundhand*, fast, accurate, and adapted for use in many languages.

Pitot tube instrument that measures fluid (gas and liquid) flow. It is used to measure the speed of aircraft, and works by sensing pressure differences in different directions in the airstream. It was invented in the 1730s by the French scientist Henri Pitot (1695–1771).

Pitt William, *the Elder*, 1st Earl of Chatham 1708–1778. British Whig politician, 'the Great Commoner'. As paymaster of the forces 1746–55, he broke with tradition by refusing to enrich himself; he was dismissed for attacking the duke of Newcastle, the prime minister. He served effectively as prime minister in coalition governments 1756–61 (successfully conducting the Seven Years' War) and 1766–68.

Pitt William, *the Younger* 1759–1806. British Tory prime minister 1783–1801 and 1804–06. He raised the importance of the House of Commons, clamped down on corruption, carried out fiscal reforms, and effected the union with Ireland. He attempted to keep Britain at peace but underestimated the importance of the French Revolution and became embroiled in wars with France from 1793; he died on hearing of Napoleon's victory at Austerlitz.

Pittsburgh industrial city (machinery, chemicals) in the USA and the nation's largest inland port, where the Allegheny and Monongahela rivers join to form the Ohio River in Pennsylvania; population (1990) 369,900, metropolitan area 2,242,800.

pituitary gland major *endocrine gland of vertebrates, situated in the centre of the brain. The anterior lobe secretes hormones, some of which control the activities of other glands (thyroid, gonads, and adrenal cortex); others are direct-acting hormones affecting milk secretion and controlling growth. Secretions of the posterior lobe control body water balance and contraction of the uterus. The posterior lobe is regulated by nerves from the *hypothalamus, and thus forms a link between the nervous and hormonal systems.

Pius 12 popes, including:

Pius IV 1499–1565. Pope from 1559, of the *Medici family. He reassembled the Council of Trent (see Counter-Reformation under *Reformation) and completed its work 1563.

Pius V 1504–1572. Pope from 1566. He excommunicated Elizabeth I of England, and organized the expedition against the Turks that won the victory of *Lepanto.

Pius VI (Giovanni Angelo Braschi) 1717–1799. Pope from 1775. He strongly opposed the French Revolution, and died a prisoner in French hands.

Pius VII 1742–1823. Pope from 1800. He concluded a concordat (papal agreement) with France 1801 and took part in Napoleon's coronation, but relations became strained. Napoleon annexed the papal states, and Pius was imprisoned 1809–14. After his return to Rome 1814, he revived the Jesuit order.

Pius IX 1792–1878. Pope from 1846. He never accepted the incorporation of the Papal States and of Rome in the kingdom of Italy. He proclaimed the dogmas of the Immaculate Conception of the Virgin 1854 and papal infallibility 1870; his pontificate was the longest in history.

Pius XII (Eugenio Pacelli) 1876–1958. Pope from 1939. He was conservative in doctrine and politics, and condemned *Modernism. He proclaimed the dogma of the bodily assumption of the Virgin Mary 1950 and in 1951 restated the doctrine (strongly criticized by many) that the life of an infant must not be sacrificed to save a mother in labour. He was criticized for failing to speak out against atrocities committed by the Germans during World War II and has been accused of collusion with the Nazis.

pixel (acronym for *picture element*) single dot on a computer screen. All screen images are made up of a collection of pixels, with each pixel being either off (dark) or on (illuminated, possibly in colour). The number of pixels available determines the screen's resolution. Typical resolutions of microcomputer screens vary from 320 × 200 pixels to 640 × 480 pixels, but screens with over 1,000 × 1,000 pixels are now quite common for high-quality graphic (pictorial) displays.

Pizarro Francisco *c.* 1475–1541. Spanish conquistador who took part in the expeditions of Vasco Núñez de Balboa and others. He explored the NW coast of South America in 1526–27, and conquered Peru 1531 with 180 followers. The Inca king Atahualpa was seized and murdered. In 1535 Pizarro founded the Peruvian city of Lima. Internal feuding led to Pizarro's assassination.

pizzicato (Italian 'pinched') in music, an instruction to pluck a bowed stringed instrument (such as the violin) with the fingers.

Plaatje Solomon Tshekiso 1876–1932. Pioneer South African black community leader who was the first secretary general and founder of the *African National Congress 1912.

placebo (Latin 'I will please') any harmless substance, often called a 'sugar pill', that has no chemotherapeutic value and yet produces physiological changes.

placenta organ that attaches the developing embryo or fetus to the *uterus in placental mammals (mammals other than marsupials, platypuses, and echidnas). Composed of maternal and embryonic tissue, it links the blood supply of the embryo to the blood supply of the mother, allowing the exchange of oxygen, nutrients, and waste products. The two blood systems are not in direct contact, but are separated by thin membranes, with materials diffusing across from one system to the other. The placenta also produces hormones that maintain and regulate pregnancy. It is shed as part of the afterbirth.

plague disease transmitted by fleas (carried by the black rat) which infect the sufferer with the bacillus *Pasteurella pestis*. An early symptom is swelling of lymph nodes, usually in the armpit and groin; such swellings are called 'buboes', hence **bubonic** plague. It causes virulent blood poisoning and the death rate is high.

plaice fish *Pleuronectes platessa* belonging to the flatfish group, abundant in the N Atlantic. It is white beneath and brownish with orange spots on the 'eyed' side. It can grow to 75 cm/2.5 ft long, and weigh about 2 kg/4.5 lb.

Plaid Cymru (Welsh 'Party of Wales') Welsh nationalist political party established 1925, dedicated to an independent Wales. In 1966 the first Plaid Cymru member of Parliament was elected.

plain or **grassland** land, usually flat, upon which grass predominates. The plains cover large areas of the Earth's surface, especially between the deserts of the tropics and the rainforests of the equator, and have rain in one season only. In such regions the climate belts move north and south during the year, bringing rainforest conditions at one time and desert conditions at another. Examples include the North European Plain, the High Plains of the USA and Canada, and the Russian Plain also known as the steppe.

Plains Indian member of any of the North American Indian peoples of the Great Plains, which extend over 3,000 km/2,000 mi from Alberta to Texas. The Plains Indians were drawn from diverse linguistic stocks fringing the Plains but shared many cultural traits, especially the nomadic hunting of bison herds once horses became available in the 18th century. The various groups include Blackfoot, Cheyenne, Comanche, Pawnee, and the Dakota or Sioux.

plainsong ancient chant of the Christian church first codified by Ambrose, bishop of Milan, and then by Pope Gregory in the 6th century. See *Gregorian chant.

Planck Max 1858–1947. German physicist who framed the quantum theory 1900. His research into the manner in which heated bodies radiate energy led him to report that energy is emitted only in indivisible amounts, called quanta, the magnitudes of which are proportional to the frequency of the radiation. His discovery ran counter to classical physics and is held to have marked the commencement of the modern science. Nobel Prize for Physics 1918.

Planck's constant in physics, a fundamental constant (symbol h) that is the energy of one quantum of electromagnetic radiation (the small-

est possible 'packet' of energy; see *quantum theory) divided by the frequency of its radiation. Its value is 6.626196×10^{-34} joule seconds.

plane in botany, any tree of the genus *Platanus*. Species include the oriental plane *P. orientalis*, a favourite plantation tree of the Greeks and Romans and the American plane or buttonwood *P. occidentalis*. A hybrid of these two is the London plane *P.* × *acerifolia*, with palmate, usually five-lobed leaves, which is widely planted in cities for its resistance to air pollution.

planet large celestial body in orbit around a star, composed of rock, metal, or gas. There are nine planets in the solar system: Mercury, Venus, Earth, Mars, Jupiter, Saturn, Neptune, Uranus, and Pluto. The inner four, called the **terrestrial planets**, are small and rocky, and include the planet Earth. The outer planets, with the exception of Pluto, are called the giant planets, large balls of rock, liquid, and gas; the largest is Jupiter, which contains more than twice as much mass as all the other planets combined. Planets do not produce light, but reflect the light of their parent star.

planetary nebula shell of gas thrown off by a star at the end of its life. Planetary nebulae have nothing to do with planets. They were named by William Herschel, who thought their rounded shape resembled the disc of a planet. After a star such as the Sun has expanded to become a *red giant, its outer layers are ejected into space to form a planetary nebula, leaving the core as a *white dwarf at the centre.

plankton small, often microscopic, forms of plant and animal life that live in the upper layers of fresh and salt water, and are an important source of food for larger animals. Marine plankton is concentrated in areas where rising currents bring mineral salts to the surface.

plant organism that carries out *photosynthesis, has cellulose cell walls and complex cells, and is immobile. A few parasitic plants have lost the ability to photosynthesize but are still considered to be plants. Plants are autotrophs, that is, they make carbohydrates from water and carbon dioxide, and are the primary producers in all food chains, so that all animal life is dependent on them. They play a vital part in the carbon cycle, removing carbon dioxide from the atmosphere and generating oxygen. The study of plants is known as botany.

Plantagenet English royal house, reigning 1154–1399, whose name comes from the nickname of Geoffrey, Count of Anjou (1113–1151), father of Henry II, who often wore in his hat a sprig of broom, *planta genista*. In the 1450s, Richard, Duke of York, took 'Plantagenet' as a surname to emphasize his superior claim to the throne over Henry VI's.

plantain any plant of the genus *Plantago*, family Plantaginaceae. The great plantain *P. major* has oval leaves, grooved stalks, and spikes of green flowers with purple anthers followed by seeds, which are used in bird food. The most common introduced species is *P. lanceolata* native to Europe and Asia and a widespread weed in Australia, Europe, and America. Many other species are troublesome weeds. A type of *banana is also known as plantain.

plantation large farm or estate where commer-

PLANETS

planet	main constituents	atmosphere	average distance from Sun in millions of km	time for one orbit in Earth years	diameter in thousands of km	average density if density of water is 1 unit
Mercury	rocky, ferrous	–	58	0.241	4.88	5.4
Venus	rocky, ferrous	carbon dioxide	108	0.615	12.10	5.2
Earth	rocky, ferrous	nitrogen, oxygen	150	1.00	12.76	5.5
Mars	rocky	carbon dioxide	228	1.88	6.78	3.9
Jupiter	liquid hydrogen, helium	–	778	11.86	142.80	1.3
Saturn	hydrogen, helium	–	1,427	29.46	120.00	0.7
Uranus	icy, hydrogen, helium	hydrogen, helium	2,870	84.00	50.80	1.3
Neptune	icy, hydrogen, helium	hydrogen, helium	4,497	164.80	48.60	1.8
Pluto	icy, rocky	methane	5,900	248.50	2.25	about 2

cial production of one crop – such as rubber (in Malaysia), palm oil (in Nigeria), or tea (in Sri Lanka) – is carried out. Plantations are usually owned by large companies, often *multinational corporations, and run by an estate manager. Many plantations were established in countries under colonial rule, using slave labour.

plant classification taxonomy or classification of plants. Originally the plant kingdom included bacteria, diatoms, dinoflagellates, fungi, and slime moulds, but these are not now thought of as plants. The groups that are always classified as plants are the bryophytes (mosses and liverworts), pteridophytes (ferns, horsetails, and club mosses), gymnosperms (conifers, yews, cycads, and ginkgos), and angiosperms (flowering plants). The angiosperms are split into monocotyledons (for example, orchids, grasses, lilies) and dicotyledons (for example, oak, buttercup, geranium, and daisy).

plant hormone substance produced by a plant that has a marked effect on its growth, flowering, leaf fall, fruit ripening, or some other process. Examples include *auxin, *gibberellin, *ethylene, and cytokinin.

plaque any abnormal deposit on a body surface, especially the thin, transparent film of sticky protein (called mucin) and bacteria on tooth surfaces. If not removed, this film forms tartar (calculus), promotes tooth decay, and leads to gum disease. Another form of plaque is a deposit of fatty or fibrous material in the walls of blood vessels that can block blood flow or break free to form blood clots.

plasma in biology, the liquid part of the *blood.

plasma in physics, an ionized gas produced at extremely high temperatures, as in the Sun and other stars, which contains positive and negative charges in approximately equal numbers. It is a good electrical conductor. In thermonuclear reactions the plasma produced is confined through the use of magnetic fields.

plasmapheresis removal from the body of large quantities of blood, which is then divided into its components (plasma and blood cells) by centrifugal force in a continuous-flow cell separator. Once separated, the elements of the blood are isolated and available for specific treatment. Restored blood is then returned to the venous system of the patient.

plasmid small, mobile piece of *DNA found in

bacteria and used in *genetic engineering. Plasmids are separate from the bacterial chromosome but still multiply during cell growth. Their size ranges from 3% to 20% of the size of the chromosome. There is usually only one copy of a single plasmid per cell, but occasionally several are found. Some plasmids carry 'fertility genes' that enable them to move from one bacterium to another and transfer genetic information between strains. Plasmid genes determine a wide variety of bacterial properties including resistance to antibiotics and the ability to produce toxins.

plastic any of the stable synthetic materials that are fluid at some stage in their manufacture, when they can be shaped, and that later set to rigid or semi-rigid solids. Plastics today are chiefly derived from petroleum. Most are polymers, made up of long chains of identical molecules.

plastic surgery branch of surgery concerned with the repair of congenital disfigurement and the reconstruction of tissues damaged by disease or injury; and **cosmetic surgery** undergone for reasons of vanity to conform to some aesthetic norm or counter the effects of ageing; for example, the removal of bags under the eyes or a double chin.

plastid general name for a cell *organelle of plants that is enclosed by a double membrane and contains a series of internal membranes and vesicles. Plastids contain *DNA and are produced by division of existing plastids. They can be classified into two main groups: the **chromoplasts**, which contain pigments such as carotenes and chlorophyll, and the **leucoplasts**, which are colourless; however, the distinction between the two is not always clear-cut.

Plata, Río de la or **River Plate** estuary in South America into which the rivers Paraná and Uruguay flow; length 320 km/200 mi and width up to 240 km/150 mi. The basin drains much of Argentina, Bolivia, Brazil, Uruguay, and Paraguay, which all cooperate in its development.

Plataea, Battle of battle 479 BC, in which the Greeks defeated the Persians during the *Persian Wars.

plateau elevated area of fairly flat land, or a mountainous region in which the peaks are at the same height. An **intermontane plateau** is one surrounded by mountains. A **piedmont**

plateau is one that lies between the mountains and low-lying land. A **continental plateau** rises abruptly from low-lying lands or the sea.

platelet tiny 'cell' found in the blood, which helps it to clot. Platelets are not true cells, but membrane-bound cell fragments that bud off from large cells in the bone marrow.

Plate, River English name of Río de *la Plata, an estuary in South America.

plate tectonics concept that attributes *continental drift and *seafloor spreading to the continual formation and destruction of the outermost layer of the Earth. This layer is seen as consisting of major and minor plates, curved to the planet's spherical shape and with a jigsaw fit to one another. Convection currents within the Earth's mantle produce upwellings of new material along joint lines at the surface, forming ridges (for example, the *Mid-Atlantic Ridge). The new material extends the plates, and these move away from the ridges. Where two plates collide, one overrides the other and the lower is absorbed back into the mantle. These subduction zones occur in the ocean trenches.

Plath Sylvia 1932–1963. US poet and novelist whose powerful, highly personal poems, often expressing a sense of desolation, are distinguished by their intensity and sharp imagery. Her *Collected Poems* 1981 was awarded a Pulitzer Prize. Her autobiographical novel *The Bell Jar* 1961 deals with the events surrounding a young woman's emotional breakdown.

platinum (Spanish *platina* 'little silver' (*plata* 'silver')) heavy, soft, silver-white, malleable and ductile, metallic element, symbol Pt, atomic number 78, relative atomic mass 195.09. It is the first of a group of six metallic elements (platinum, osmium, iridium, rhodium, ruthenium, and palladium) that possess similar traits, such as resistance to tarnish, corrosion, and attack by acid, and that often occur as free metals (*native metals). They often occur in natural alloys with each other, the commonest of which is osmiridium. Both pure and as an alloy, platinum is used in dentistry, jewellery, and as a catalyst.

Plato c. 428–347 BC. Greek philosopher, pupil of Socrates, teacher of Aristotle, and founder of the Academy school of philosophy. He was the author of philosophical dialogues on such topics as metaphysics, ethics, and politics. Central to his teachings is the notion of Forms, which are located outside the everyday world – timeless, motionless, and absolutely real.

platoon in the army, the smallest infantry subunit. It contains 30–40 soldiers and is commanded by a lieutenant or second lieutenant. There are three or four platoons in a company.

platypus monotreme, or egg-laying, mammal *Ornithorhynchus anatinus*, found in Tasmania and E Australia. Semiaquatic, it has small eyes and no external ears, and jaws resembling a duck's beak. It lives in long burrows along river banks, where it lays two eggs in a rough nest. It feeds on water worms and insects, and when full-grown is 60 cm/2 ft long.

Plautus c. 254–184 BC. Roman dramatist, born in Umbria, who settled in Rome and worked in a bakery before achieving success as a dramatist. He wrote at least 56 comedies, freely adapted

from Greek originals, of which 20 survive. Shakespeare based *The Comedy of Errors* on his *Menaechmi*.

plc abbreviation for *public limited company*.

pleadings in law, documents exchanged between the parties to court actions, which set out the facts that form the basis of the case they intend to present in court, and (where relevant) stating what damages or other remedy they are claiming.

plebeian member of the unprivileged class in ancient Rome, composed of aliens, freed slaves, and their descendants. During the 5th–4th centuries BC, plebeians waged a long struggle to win political and social equality with the patricians, eventually securing admission to the offices formerly reserved for patricians.

plebiscite referendum or direct vote by all the electors of a country or district on a specific question. Since the 18th century plebiscites have been employed on many occasions to decide to what country a particular area should belong; for example, in Upper Silesia and elsewhere after World War I, and in the Saar 1935.

Pléiade, La group of seven poets in 16th-century France, led by Pierre Ronsard, who were inspired by Classical models to improve French verse. Their name is derived from the seven stars of the Pleiades group.

Pleiades in astronomy, a star cluster about 400 light years away in the constellation Taurus, representing the Seven Sisters of Greek mythology. Its brightest stars (highly luminous, blue-white giants only a few million years old) are visible to the naked eye, but there are many fainter ones.

Pleiades in Greek mythology, the seven daughters of the giant Atlas who asked to be changed into a cluster of stars to escape the pursuit of the hunter Orion.

Pleistocene first epoch of the Quaternary period of geological time, beginning 1.8 million years ago and ending 10,000 years ago. Glaciers were abundant during the ice age of this period, and humans evolved into modern *Homo sapiens sapiens* about 100,000 years ago.

Plekhanov Georgi Valentinovich 1857–1918. Russian Marxist revolutionary and theorist, founder of the *Menshevik party. He led the first populist demonstration in St Petersburg, became a Marxist and, with Lenin, edited the newspaper *Iskra* (spark). In 1903 his opposition to Lenin led to the Bolshevik-Menshevik split.

plesiosaur prehistoric carnivorous marine reptile of the Jurassic and Cretaceous periods, which reached a length of 12 m/36 ft, and had a long neck and paddlelike limbs. The *pliosaurs evolved from the plesiosaurs.

pleurisy inflammation of the pleura, the thin, secretory membrane that covers the lungs and lines the space in which they rest. Pleurisy is nearly always due to bacterial or viral infection, which can be treated with antibiotics. It renders breathing painful.

Plimsoll Samuel 1824–1898. English social reformer, born in Bristol. He sat in Parliament as a Radical 1868–80, and through his efforts the Merchant Shipping Act was passed in 1876, providing for Board of Trade inspection of ships, and the compulsory painting of a **Plimsoll line** to indicate safe loading limits.

Plimsoll line loading mark painted on the hull of merchant ships, first suggested by Samuel Plimsoll. It shows the depth to which a vessel may be safely (and legally) loaded.

Pliny the Elder (Gaius Plinius Secundus) c. AD 23–79. Roman scientist and historian; only his works on astronomy, geography, and natural history survive. He was killed in an eruption of Vesuvius, the volcano near Naples.

Pliny the Younger (Gaius Plinius Caecilius Secundus) c. AD 61–113. Roman administrator, nephew of Pliny the Elder, whose correspondence is of great interest. Among his surviving letters are those describing the eruption of Vesuvius, his uncle's death, and his correspondence with the emperor *Trajan.

Pliocene ('almost recent') fifth and last epoch of the Tertiary period of geological time, 5–1.8 million years ago. The earliest hominid, the humanlike ape 'australopithecines', evolved in Africa.

pliosaur prehistoric carnivorous marine reptile, descended from the plesiosaurs, but with a shorter neck, and longer head and jaws. It was approximately 5 m/15 ft long. In 1989 the skeleton of one of a previously unknown species was discovered in northern Queensland, Australia. A hundred million years ago, it lived in the sea which once covered the Great Artesian Basin.

Plisetskaya Maya 1925– . Soviet ballerina and actress. She attended the Moscow Bolshoi Ballet School and succeeded Galina Ulanova as prima ballerina of the Bolshoi Ballet.

PLO abbreviation for *Palestine Liberation Organization*.

plotter or **graph plotter** device that draws pictures or diagrams under computer control. Plotters are often used for producing business charts, architectural plans, and engineering drawings. **Flatbed plotters** move a pen up and down across a flat drawing surface, whereas **roller plotters** roll the drawing paper past the pen as it moves from side to side.

Plough, the in astronomy, a popular name for the most prominent part of the constellation *Ursa Major.

plough agricultural implement used for tilling the soil. The plough dates from about 3500 BC, when oxen were used to pull a simple wooden blade, or ard. In about 500 BC the iron ploughshare came into use. By about AD 1000 horses as well as oxen were being used to pull wheeled ploughs, equipped with a ploughshare for cutting a furrow, a blade for forming the walls of the furrow (called a coulter), and a mouldboard to turn the furrow. In the 18th century an innovation introduced by Robert Ransome (1753–1830), led to a reduction in the number of animals used to draw a plough: from 8–12 oxen, or 6 horses, to a 2-or 4-horse plough.

plover any shore bird of the family Charadriidae, found worldwide. Plovers are usually black or brown above and white below, and have short bills. The European **golden plover** *Pluviatilis apricaria*, of heathland and sea coast, is about 28 cm/11 in long.

plum tree *Prunus domestica*, bearing edible fruits that are smooth-skinned with a flat kernel. There are many varieties, including the Victoria, czar, egg-plum, greengage, and damson; the sloe *P. spinosa* is closely related. Dried plums are known as prunes.

pluralism in political science, the view that decision-making in contemporary liberal democracies is the outcome of competition among several interest groups in a political system characterized by free elections, representative institutions, and open access to the organs of power. This concept is opposed by corporatism and other approaches that perceive power to be centralized in the state and its principal elites (the Establishment).

Plutarch c. AD 46–120. Greek biographer whose *Parallel Lives* has the life stories of pairs of Greek and Roman soldiers and politicians, followed by comparisons between the two. Thomas North's 1579 translation inspired Shakespeare's Roman plays.

Pluto in astronomy, the smallest and, usually, outermost planet of the solar system. The existence of Pluto was predicted by calculation by Percival Lowell and the planet was located by Clyde Tombaugh 1930. It orbits the Sun every 248.5 years at an average distance of 5.8 billion km/3.6 billion mi. Its highly elliptical orbit occasionally takes it within the orbit of Neptune, as in 1979–99. Pluto has a diameter of about 2,300 km/1,400 mi, and a mass about 0.002 of that of Earth. It is of low density, composed of rock and ice, with frozen methane on its surface and a thin atmosphere.

Pluto in Greek mythology, the lord of the underworld (Roman Dis). He was the brother of Zeus and Poseidon.

plutonic rock igneous rock derived from magma that has cooled and solidified deep in the crust of the Earth; granites and gabbros are examples of plutonic rocks.

plutonium silvery-white, radioactive, metallic element of the *actinide series, symbol Pu, atomic number 94, relative atomic mass 239.13. It occurs in nature in minute quantities in *pitchblende and other ores, but is produced in quantity only synthetically. It has six allotropic forms (see *allotropy) and is one of three fissile elements (elements capable of splitting into other elements – the others are thorium and uranium). The element has awkward physical properties and is the most toxic substance known.

Plymouth city and seaport in Devon, England, at the mouth of the river Plym, with dockyard, barracks, and a naval base at Devonport; population (1981) 244,000.

Plymouth Brethren fundamentalist Christian Protestant sect characterized by extreme simplicity of belief, founded in Dublin about 1827 by the Reverend John Nelson Darby (1800–1882). The Plymouth Brethren have no ordained priesthood, affirming the ministry of all believers, and maintain no church buildings. They hold prayer meetings and Bible study in members' houses. An assembly of Brethren was held in Plymouth 1831 to celebrate the sect's arrival in England, but by 1848 the movement had split into 'Open' and 'Closed' Brethren. The latter refuse communion with those not of their persuasion.

plywood manufactured panel of wood widely used in building. It consists of several thin sheets, or plies, of wood, glued together with the grain (direction of the wood fibres) of one sheet at right angles to the grain of the adjacent plies. This construction gives plywood equal strength in every direction.

Plzeň (German **Pilsen**) industrial city (heavy machinery, cars, beer) in W Czechoslovakia, at the confluence of the Radbuza and Mze rivers, capital of Západočeský (West Bohemia) region; 84 km/52 mi SW of Prague; population (1991) 173,100.

pneumatic drill drill operated by compressed air, used in mining and tunnelling, for drilling shot holes (for explosives), and in road repairs for breaking up pavements. It contains an air-operated piston that delivers hammer blows to the drill bit many times a second. The French engineer Germain Sommeiller (1815–1871) developed the pneumatic drill 1861 for tunnelling in the Alps.

pneumatophore erect root that rises up above the soil or water and promotes gas exchange. Pneumatophores, or breathing roots, are formed by certain swamp-dwelling trees, such as mangroves, since there is little oxygen available to the roots in waterlogged conditions. They have numerous pores or lenticels over their surface, allowing gas exchange.

pneumoconiosis disease of the lungs caused by dust, especially from coal, asbestos, or silica. Inhaled particles make the lungs gradually fibrous and the victim has difficulty breathing.

pneumonectomy surgical removal of all or part of a lung.

pneumonia inflammation of the lungs, generally due to bacterial or viral infection but also to particulate matter or gases. It is characterized by a build-up of fluid in the alveoli, the clustered air sacs (at the end of the air passages) where oxygen exchange takes place.

pneumothorax the presence of air in the pleural cavity, between a lung and the chest wall. It may be due to a penetrating injury of the lung or to lung disease, or it may arise without apparent cause. Prevented from expanding normally, the lung is liable to collapse.

Pnom Penh alternative form of *Phnom Penh, capital of Cambodia.

Po longest river in Italy, flowing from the Cottian Alps to the Adriatic; length 668 km/415 mi. Its valley is fertile and contains natural gas. The river is heavily polluted with nitrates, phosphates, and arsenic.

pochard any of various diving ducks found in Europe and North America, especially the genus *Aythya*.

Po Chu-i alternative transliteration of Bo Zhu Yi, Chinese poet.

pod in botany, a type of fruit that is characteristic of legumes (plants belonging to the Leguminosae family), such as peas and beans. It develops from a single *carpel and splits down both sides when ripe to release the seeds.

podzol or **podsol** type of light-coloured soil found predominantly under coniferous forests and on moorlands in cool regions where rainfall exceeds evaporation. The constant downward movement of water leaches nutrients from the upper layers, making podzols poor agricultural soils.

Poe Edgar Allan 1809–1849. US writer and poet. His short stories are renowned for their horrific atmosphere, as in 'The Fall of the House of Usher' 1839 and 'The Masque of the Red Death' 1842, and for their acute reasoning (ratiocination), as in 'The Gold Bug' 1843 and 'The Murders in the Rue Morgue' 1841 (in which the investigators Legrand and Dupin anticipate Conan Doyle's Sherlock Holmes). His poems include 'The Raven' 1845.

poet laureate poet of the British royal household, so called because of the laurel wreath awarded to eminent poets in the Graeco-Roman world. Early poets with unofficial status were Geoffrey Chaucer, John Skelton, Edmund Spenser, Samuel Daniel, and Ben Jonson. Ted Hughes was appointed poet laureate in 1984.

poetry the imaginative expression of emotion, thought, or narrative, frequently in metrical form and often using figurative language. Poetry has traditionally been distinguished from prose (ordinary written language) by rhyme or the rhythmical arrangement of words (metre), although the distinction is not always clear-cut. A distinction is made between lyrical, or songlike, poetry (sonnet, ode, elegy, pastoral), and narrative, or story-telling, poetry (ballad, lay, epic).

pogrom (Russian 'destruction') unprovoked violent attack on an ethnic group, particularly Jews, carried out with official sanction. The Russian pogroms against Jews began 1881, after the assassination of Tsar Alexander II, and again in 1903–06; persecution of the Jews remained constant until the Russian Revolution. Later there were pogroms in E Europe, especially in Poland after 1918, and in Germany under Hitler (see *Holocaust).

poikilothermy the condition in which an animal's body temperature is largely dependent on the temperature of the air or water in which it lives. It is characteristic of all animals except birds and mammals, which maintain their body temperatures by homeothermy (they are 'warm-blooded').

Poincaré Jules Henri 1854–1912. French mathematician who developed the theory of differential equations and was a pioneer in *relativity theory. He suggested that Isaac Newton's laws for the behaviour of the universe could be the exception rather than the rule. However, the calculation was so complex and time-consuming that he never managed to realize its full implication.

Poincaré Raymond Nicolas Landry 1860–1934. French politician, prime minister 1912–13, president 1913–20, and again prime minister 1922–24 (when he ordered the occupation of the Ruhr, Germany) and 1926–29.

Poindexter John Marlan 1936– . US rear admiral and Republican government official. In 1981 he joined the Reagan administration's National Security Council (NSC) and became national security adviser 1985. As a result of the

*Irangate scandal, Poindexter was forced to resign 1986, along with his assistant, Oliver North.

poinsettia or *Christmas flower* winter-flowering shrub *Euphorbia pulcherrima*, with large red leaves encircling small greenish-yellow flowers. It is native to Mexico and tropical America and is a popular houseplant in North America and Europe.

pointe (French 'toe of shoe') in dance, the tip of the toe. A dancer *sur les pointes* is dancing on her toes in blocked shoes, as popularized by the Italian dancer Marie *Taglioni 1832.

Pointe-Noire chief port of the Congo, formerly (1950–58) the capital; population (1984) 297,000. Industries include oil refining and shipbuilding.

pointer breed of dog, often white mixed with black, tan, or dark brown, about 60 cm/2 ft tall, and weighing 28 kg/62 lb.

Pointillism technique in oil painting developed in the 1880s by the Neo-Impressionist Georges Seurat. He used small dabs of pure colour laid side by side to create an impression of shimmering light when viewed from a distance.

poison or *toxin* any chemical substance that, when introduced into or applied to the body, is capable of injuring health or destroying life. The liver removes some poisons from the blood. The majority of poisons may be divided into *corrosives*, such as sulphuric, nitric, and hydrochloric acids; *irritants*, including arsenic and copper sulphate; *narcotics* such as opium, and carbon monoxide; and *narcotico-irritants* from any substances of plant origin including carbolic acid and tobacco.

poison pill in business, a tactic to avoid hostile takeover by making the target unattractive. For example, a company may give a certain class of shareholders the right to have their shares redeemed at a very good price in the event of the company being taken over, thus involving the potential predator in considerable extra cost.

Poitevin in English history, relating to the reigns of King John and King Henry III. The term is derived from the region of France south of the Loire (Poitou), which was controlled by the English for most of this period.

Poitier Sidney 1924– . US actor and film director, Hollywood's first black star. His films as an actor include *Something of Value* 1957, *Lilies of the Field* 1963, and *In the Heat of the Night* 1967, and as director *Stir Crazy* 1980.

Poitou-Charentes region of W central France, comprising the *départements* of Charente, Charente-Maritime, Deux-Sèvres, and Vienne
capital Poitiers
area 25,800 sq km/9,959 sq mi
population (1986) 1,584,000
products dairy products, wheat, chemicals, metal goods; brandy is made at Cognac
history once part of the Roman province of Aquitaine, this region was captured by the Visigoths in the 5th century and taken by the Franks AD 507. The area was contested by the English and French until the end of the Hundred Years' War in 1453, when it was incorporated into France by Charles II.

poker card game of US origin, in which two to eight people play (usually for stakes), and try to obtain a hand of five cards ranking higher than those of their opponents. The one with the highest scoring hand wins the central pool.

Poland Republic of (*Polska Rzeczpospolita*)

area 127,886 sq km/49,325 sq mi
capital Warsaw
towns Lódź, Kraków, Wrocław, Poznań, Katowice, Bydgoszcz, Lublin; ports Gdańsk, Szczecin, Gdynia
physical part of the great plain of Europe; Vistula, Oder, and Neisse rivers; Sudeten, Tatra, and Carpathian mountains on S frontier
environment atmospheric pollution derived from coal (producing 90% of the country's electricity), toxic waste from industry, and lack of sewage treatment have resulted in the designation of 27 ecologically endangered areas. Half the country's lakes have been seriously contaminated and three-quarters of its drinking water does not meet official health standards
head of state Lech Wałesa from 1990
head of government Waldemar Pawlak from 1993
political system emergent democratic republic
exports coal, softwood timber, chemicals, machinery, ships, vehicles, meat, copper (Europe's largest producer)
currency zloty
population (1993) 38,310,000; growth rate 0.6% p.a.
languages Polish (official), German
religion Roman Catholic 95%
GNP $1,830 per head (1991)
chronology
1918 Poland revived as independent republic.
1939 German invasion and occupation.
1944 Germans driven out by Soviet forces.
1945 Polish boundaries redrawn at Potsdam Conference.
1947 Communist people's republic proclaimed.
1956 Poznań riots. Władysław Gomułka installed as Polish United Workers' Party (PUWP) leader.
1970 Gomułka replaced by Edward Gierek after Gdańsk riots.
1980 Solidarity emerged as a free trade union following Gdańsk disturbances.

1981 Martial law imposed by General Wojciech Jaruzelski.
1983 Martial law ended.
1984 Amnesty for political prisoners.
1985 Zbigniew Messner became prime minister.
1987 Referendum on economic reform rejected.
1988 Solidarity-led strikes and demonstrations called off after pay increases. Messner resigned; replaced by the reformist Mieczysław F Rakowski.
1989 Solidarity relegalized. April: new 'socialist pluralist' constitution formed. June: widespread success for Solidarity in assembly elections, the first open elections in 40 years. July: Jaruzelski elected president. Sept: 'Grand coalition', first non-Communist government since World War II formed; economic restructuring undertaken on free-market lines; W Europe and US create $1 billion aid package.
1990 Jan: PUWP dissolved; replaced by Social Democratic Party and breakaway Union of Social Democrats. Lech Wałesa elected president.
1991 Oct: Multiparty general election produced inconclusive result. Five-party centre-right coalition formed under Jan Olszewski. Treaty signed agreeing to complete withdrawal of Soviet troops.
1992 June: Olszewski ousted on vote of no confidence; succeeded by Waldemar Pawlak. July: Hanna Suchocka replaced Pawlak.
1993 14% of workforce (2.6 million) unemployed. Suchocka lost vote of confidence. April: privatization bill passed. June: formal invitation to apply for European Community membership. Sept: inconclusive general election. Oct: Pawlak appointed prime minister.
1994 Joined NATO 'partnership for peace' programme.

Polanski Roman 1933– . Polish film director. His films include *Repulsion* 1965, *Cul de Sac* 1966, *Rosemary's Baby* 1968, *Chinatown* 1974, *Tess* 1979, *Frantic* 1988, and *Bitter Moon* 1992.

Polaris or *Pole Star* or *North Star* the bright star closest to the north celestial pole, and the brightest star in the constellation Ursa Minor. Its position is indicated by the 'pointers' in Ursa Major. Polaris is a yellow *supergiant about 500 light years away.

polarized light light in which the electromagnetic vibrations take place in one particular direction. In ordinary (unpolarized) light, the electric and magnetic fields vibrate in all directions perpendicular to the direction of propagation. After reflection from a polished surface or transmission through certain materials (such as Polaroid), the electric and magnetic fields are confined to one direction, and the light is said to be *plane polarized*. In *circularly polarized* and *elliptically polarized* light, the magnetic and electric fields are confined to one direction, but the direction rotates as the light propagates.

Polaroid camera instant-picture camera, invented by Edwin Land in the USA 1947. The original camera produced black-and-white prints in about one minute. Modern cameras can produce black-and-white prints in a few seconds, and colour prints in less than a minute. An advanced model has automatic focusing and exposure. It ejects a piece of film on paper immediately after the picture has been taken.

polder area of flat reclaimed land that used to be covered by a river, lake, or the sea. Polders have been artificially drained and protected from flooding by building dykes. They are common in the Netherlands, where the total land area has been increased by nearly one-fifth since AD 1200.

pole either of the geographic north and south points of the axis about which the Earth rotates. The geographic poles differ from the magnetic poles, which are the points towards which a freely suspended magnetic needle will point.

Pole person of Polish culture from Poland and the surrounding area. There are 37–40 million speakers of Polish (including some in the USA), a Slavic language belonging to the Indo-European family. The Poles are predominantly Roman Catholic, though there is an Orthodox Church minority. They are known for their distinctive cooking, folk festivals, and folk arts.

Pole Reginald 1500–1558. English cardinal from 1536 who returned from Rome as papal legate on the accession of Mary I in order to readmit England to the Catholic Church. He succeeded Cranmer as archbishop of Canterbury 1556.

polecat Old World weasel *Mustela putorius* with a brown back and dark belly and two yellow face patches. The body is about 50 cm/20 in long and it has a strong smell from anal gland secretions. It is native to Asia, Europe, and N Africa. In North America, *skunks are sometimes called polecats. A ferret is a domesticated polecat.

Pole Star *Polaris, the northern pole star. There is no bright star near the southern celestial pole.

police civil law-and-order force. In the UK it is responsible to the Home Office, with 56 autonomous police forces, generally organized on a county basis; mutual aid is given in circumstances such as mass picketing in the 1984–85 miners' strike, but there is no national police force or police riot unit (such as the French CRS riot squad). The predecessors of these forces were the ineffective medieval watch and London's Bow Street runners, introduced 1749 by Henry *Fielding which formed a model for the London police force established by Robert *Peel's government 1829 (hence 'peelers' or 'bobbies'); the system was introduced throughout the country from 1856.

Police Complaints Authority in the UK, an independent group of a dozen people set up under the Police and Criminal Evidence Act 1984 to supervise the investigation of complaints against the police by members of the public.

polio (*poliomyelitis*) viral infection of the central nervous system affecting nerves that activate muscles. The disease used to be known as infantile paralysis. Two kinds of vaccine are available, one injected (see *Salk) and one given by mouth. The World Health Organization expects that polio will be eradicated by 2000.

Polish Corridor strip of land designated under the Treaty of *Versailles 1919 to give Poland access to the Baltic. It cut off East Prussia from the rest of Germany. When Poland took over the southern part of East Prussia 1945, it was absorbed.

Polish language member of the Slavonic branch of the Indo-European language family, spoken mainly in Poland. Polish is written in the Roman and not the Cyrillic alphabet and its standard form is based on the dialect of Poznań in W Poland.

Politburo contraction of 'political bureau', the executive committee (known as the Presidium 1952–66) of the Supreme Soviet in the USSR, which laid down party policy. It consisted of about 12 voting and 6 candidate (nonvoting) members.

political action committee (PAC) in the USA, any organization that raises funds for political candidates and in return seeks to commit them to a particular policy. PACs also spend money on changing public opinion. In 1990, there were about 3,500 PACs, controlling some 25% of all funds spent in elections for *Congress. Donations to candidates amounted to $358.1 million, the largest PACs being the National Association of Realtors and the American Medical Association.

political correctness (PC) US shorthand term for a set of liberal attitudes about education and society, and the terminology associated with them. To be politically correct is to be sensitive to unconscious racism and sexism and to display environmental awareness. However, the real or alleged enforcement of PC speech codes ('people of colour' instead of 'coloured people', 'differently abled' instead of 'disabled', and so on) at more than 130 US universities by 1991 attracted derision and was criticized as a form of thought-policing.

political party association of like-minded people organized with the purpose of seeking and exercising political power. A party can be distinguished from an interest or *pressure group which seeks to influence governments rather than aspire to office, although some pressure groups, such as the Green movement, have over time transformed themselves into political parties.

politics ruling by the consent of the governed; an activity whereby solutions to social and economic problems are solved and different aspirations are met by the process of discussion and compromise rather than by the application of decree or force.

Polk James Knox 1795–1849. 11th president of the USA 1845–49, a Democrat, born in North Carolina. He allowed Texas admission to the Union, and forced the war on Mexico that resulted in the annexation of California and New Mexico.

polka folk dance in lively two-four time. The basic step is a hop followed by three short steps. The polka originated in Bohemia and spread with German immigrants to the USA, becoming a style of Texas country music.

pollack marine fish *Pollachius virens* of the cod family, growing to 75 cm/2.5 ft, and found close to the shore on both sides of the N Atlantic.

pollarding type of pruning whereby the young branches of a tree are severely cut back, about 2–4 m/6–12 ft above the ground, to produce a stumplike trunk with a rounded, bushy head of thin new branches.

pollen the grains of *seed plants that contain the male gametes. In *angiosperms (flowering plants) pollen is produced within *anthers; in most *gymnosperms (cone-bearing plants) it is produced in male cones. A pollen grain is typically yellow and, when mature, has a hard outer wall. Pollen of insect-pollinated plants (see *pollination) is often sticky and spiny and larger than the smooth, light grains produced by wind-pollinated species.

pollen tube outgrowth from a pollen grain that grows towards the *ovule, following germination of the grain on the *stigma. In *angiosperms (flowering plants) the pollen tube reaches the ovule by growing down through the *style, carrying the male gametes inside. These are discharged into the ovule and one fertilizes the egg cell.

pollination the process by which pollen is transferred from one plant to another. The male *gametes are contained in pollen grains, which must be transferred from the anther to the stigma in *angiosperms (flowering plants), and from the male cone to the female cone in *gymnosperms (cone-bearing plants). Fertilization (not the same as pollination) occurs after the growth of the pollen tube to the ovary.

Self-pollination occurs when pollen is transferred to a stigma of the same flower, or to another flower on the same plant; cross-pollination occurs when pollen is transferred to another plant. This involves external pollen-carrying agents, such as wind (see *anemophily), water, insects, birds (see *ornithophily), bats, and other small mammals.

Pollock Jackson 1912–1956. US painter, a pioneer of Abstract Expressionism and the foremost exponent of the technique of *action painting, a style he developed around 1946.

poll tax tax levied on every individual, without reference to income or property. Being simple to administer, it was among the earliest sorts of tax (introduced in England 1377), but because of its indiscriminate nature (it is a regressive tax, in that it falls proportionately more on poorer people) it has often proved unpopular. The **community charge**, a type of poll tax, was introduced in Scotland by the British government April 1989, and in England and Wales 1990, replacing the property-based local taxation (the *rates). Its unpopularity led to its replacement, 1993–94 by a *council tax, based both on property values and on the size of households.

polluter pays principle the idea that whoever causes pollution is responsible for the cost of repairing any damage. The principle is accepted in British law but has in practice often been ignored; for example, farmers causing the death of fish through slurry pollution have not been fined the full costs of restocking the river.

pollution the harmful effect on the environment of by-products of human activity, principally industrial and agricultural processes – for example, noise, smoke, car emissions, chemical and radioactive effluents in air, seas, and rivers, pesticides, radiation, sewage (see *sewage disposal), and household waste. Pollution contributes to the *greenhouse effect.

Pollux in Greek mythology, the twin brother of Castor (see *Castor and Pollux).

polo stick-and-ball game played between two teams of four on horseback. It originated in Iran, spread to India and was first played in England 1869. Polo is played on the largest pitch of any game, measuring up to 274 m/300 yd by 182 m/200 yd. A small solid ball is struck with the side of a long-handled mallet through goals at each end of the pitch. A typical match lasts about an hour, and is divided into 'chukkas' of 7½ minutes each. No pony is expected to play more than two chukkas in the course of a day.

Polo Marco 1254–1324. Venetian traveller and writer. He travelled overland to China 1271–75, and served the emperor Kublai Khan until he returned to Europe by sea 1292–95. He was captured while fighting for Venice against Genoa, and, while in prison 1296–98, dictated an account of his travels.

polonaise Polish dance in stately three-four time, that was common in 18th century Europe. The Polish composer Frédéric Chopin developed the polonaise as a pianistic form.

polonium radioactive, metallic element, symbol Po, atomic number 84, relative atomic mass 210. Polonium occurs in nature in small amounts and was isolated from *pitchblende. It is the element having the largest number of isotopes (27) and is 5,000 times as radioactive as radium, liberating considerable amounts of heat. It was the first element to have its radioactive properties recognized and investigated.

Pol Pot (also known as *Saloth Sar*, *Tol Saut*, and *Pol Porth*) 1925– . Cambodian politician and leader of the Khmer Rouge communist movement that overthrew the government 1975. After widespread atrocities against the civilian population, his regime was deposed by a Vietnamese invasion 1979. Pol Pot continued to help lead the Khmer Rouge until their withdrawal in 1989.

poltergeist (German 'noisy ghost') unexplained phenomenon that invisibly moves objects or hurls them about, starts fires, or causes other mischief.

polyandry system whereby a woman has more than one husband at the same time. It is found in many parts of the world, for example, in Madagascar, Malaysia, and certain Pacific isles, and among certain Inuit and South American Indian groups. In Tibet and parts of India, polyandry takes the form of the marriage of one woman to several brothers, as a means of keeping intact a family's heritage and property.

polyanthus cultivated variety of *primrose, with multiple flowers on one stalk, bred in a variety of colours.

Polybius c. 201–120 BC. Greek politician and historian. He was involved with the *Achaean League against the Romans and, following the defeat of the Macedonians at Pydna in 168 BC, he was taken as a political hostage to Rome. He returned to Greece in 151 and was present at the capture of Carthage by his friend Scipio in 146. His history of Rome in 40 books, covering the years 220–146, has largely disappeared.

polychlorinated biphenyl (PCB) any of a group of chlorinated isomers of biphenyl (C_6H_5)$_2$. They are dangerous industrial chemicals, valuable for their fire-resisting qualities. They constitute an environmental hazard because of their persistent toxicity. Since 1973 their use has been limited by international agreement.

polyester synthetic resin formed by the *condensation of polyhydric alcohols (alcohols containing more than one hydroxyl group) with dibasic acids (acids containing two replaceable hydrogen atoms). Polyesters are thermosetting *plastics, used in making synthetic fibres, such as Dacron and Terylene, and constructional plastics. With glass fibre added as reinforcement, polyesters are used in car bodies and boat hulls.

polyethylene or *polyethene* polymer of the gas ethylene (technically called ethene, C_2H_4). It is a tough, white, translucent, waxy thermoplastic (which means it can be repeatedly softened by heating). It is used for packaging, bottles, toys, electric cable, pipes and tubing.

polygamy the practice of having more than one spouse at the same time. It is found among many peoples. Normally it has been confined to the wealthy and to chiefs and nobles who can support several women and their offspring, as among ancient Egyptians, Teutons, Irish, and Slavs. Islam limits the number of legal wives a man may have to four. Certain Christian sects, for example, the Anabaptists of Münster, Germany, and the Mormons, have practised polygamy because it was the norm in the Old Testament.

polygon in geometry, a plane (two-dimensional) figure with three or more straight-line sides. Common polygons have names which define the number of sides (for example, triangle, quadrilateral, pentagon).

polyhedron in geometry, a solid figure with four or more plane faces. The more faces there are on a polyhedron, the more closely it approximates to a sphere. Knowledge of the properties of polyhedra is needed in crystallography and stereochemistry to determine the shapes of crystals and molecules. There are only five types of regular polyhedron (with all faces the same size and shape), as was deduced by early Greek mathematicians; they are the tetrahedron (four equilateral triangular faces), cube (six square faces), octahedron (eight equilateral triangles), dodecahedron (12 regular pentagons) and icosahedron (20 equilateral triangles).

Polykleitos 5th century BC. Greek sculptor whose *Spear Carrier* 450–440 BC (Roman copies survive) exemplifies the naturalism and harmonious proportions of his work. He created the legendary colossal statue of *Hera* in Argos, in ivory and gold.

polymer compound made up of a large long-chain or branching matrix composed of many repeated simple units (*monomers*). There are many polymers, both natural (cellulose, chitin, lignin) and synthetic (polyethylene and nylon, types of plastic). Synthetic polymers belong to two groups: thermosoftening and thermosetting (see *plastic).

polymerization chemical union of two or more (usually small) molecules of the same kind to form a new compound. *Addition polymerization* produces simple multiples of the same compound. *Condensation polymerization* joins molecules together with the elimination of water or another small molecule.

polymorphism in genetics, the coexistence of

several distinctly different types in a *population (groups of animals of one species). Examples include the different blood groups in humans and different colour forms in some butterflies.

polymorphism in minerology, the ability of a substance to adopt different internal structures and external forms, in response to different conditions of temperature and/or pressure. For example, diamond and graphite are both forms of the element carbon, but they have very different properties and appearance.

Polynesia islands of Oceania E of 170° E latitude, including Hawaii, Kiribati, Tuvalu, Fiji, Tonga, Tokelau, Samoa, Cook Islands, and French Polynesia.

Polynesian languages see *Malayo-Polynesian languages.

polynomial in mathematics, an algebraic expression that has one or more *variables (denoted by letters). A polynomial of degree one, that is, whose highest *power of x is 1, as in $2x + 1$, is called a linear polynomial; $3x^2 + 2x + 1$ is quadratic; $4x^3 + 3x^2 + 2x + 1$ is cubic.

polyp or *polypus* small 'stalked' benign tumour, most usually found on mucous membrane of the nose or bowels. Intestinal polyps are usually removed, since some have been found to be precursors of cancer.

polyphony music combining two or more 'voices' or parts, each with an individual melody.

polyploid in genetics, possessing three or more sets of chromosomes in cases where the normal complement is two sets (*diploid). Polyploidy arises spontaneously and is common in plants (mainly among flowering plants), but rare in animals. Many crop plants are natural polyploids, including wheat, which has four sets of chromosomes per cell (durum wheat) or six sets (common wheat). Plant breeders can induce the formation of polyploids by treatment with a chemical, colchicine.

polysaccharide long-chain *carbohydrate made up of hundreds or thousands of linked simple sugars (monosaccharides) such as glucose and closely related molecules.

polystyrene type of *plastic used in kitchen utensils or, in an expanded form in insulation and ceiling tiles.

polytechnic in the UK, an institution for higher education offering courses mainly at degree level and concentrating on full-time vocational courses, although many polytechnics provide a wide range of part-time courses at advanced levels. From April 1989 the 29 polytechnics in England became independent corporations.

polytetrafluoroethene (PTFE) polymer made from the monomer tetrafluoroethene (CF_2CF_2). It is a thermosetting plastic with a high melting point that is used to produce 'non-stick' surfaces on pans and to coat bearings. Its trade name is Teflon.

polytheism the worship of many gods, as opposed to monotheism (belief in one god). Examples are the religions of ancient Egypt, Babylon, Greece, Rome, Mexico, and modern Hinduism.

polyunsaturate type of *fat or oil containing a high proportion of triglyceride molecules whose *fatty-acid chains contain several double bonds. By contrast, the fatty-acid chains of the triglycerides in saturated fats (such as lard) contain only single bonds. Medical evidence suggests that polyunsaturated fats, used widely in margarines and cooking fats, are less likely to contribute to cardiovascular disease than saturated fats, but there is also some evidence that they may have adverse effects on health.

pome type of *pseudocarp, or false fruit, typical of certain plants belonging to the Rosaceae family. The outer skin and fleshy tissues are developed from the *receptacle (the enlarged end of the flower stalk) after fertilization, and the five *carpels (the true fruit) form the pome's core, which surrounds the seeds. Examples of pomes are apples, pears, and quinces.

pomegranate deciduous shrub or small tree *Punica granatum*, family Punicaceae, native to SW Asia but cultivated widely in tropical and subtropical areas. The round, leathery, reddish-yellow fruit contains numerous seeds that can be eaten fresh or made into wine.

pomeranian small breed of dog, about 15 cm/6 in high, weighing about 3 kg/6.5 lb. It has long straight hair with a neck frill, and the tail is carried over the back.

Pompadour Jeanne Antoinette Poisson, Marquise de Pompadour 1721–1764. Mistress of *Louis XV of France from 1744, born in Paris. She largely dictated the government's ill-fated policy of reversing France's anti-Austrian policy for an anti-Prussian one. She acted as the patron of the Enlightenment philosophers Voltaire and Diderot.

Pompeii ancient city in Italy, near the volcano *Vesuvius, 21 km/13 mi SE of Naples. In AD 63 an earthquake destroyed much of the city, which had been a Roman port and pleasure resort; it was completely buried beneath volcanic ash when Vesuvius erupted AD 79. Over 2,000 people were killed. Pompeii was rediscovered 1748 and the systematic excavation begun 1763 still continues.

Pompey the Great (Gnaeus Pompeius Magnus) 106–48 BC. Roman soldier and politician. From 60 BC to 53 BC, he was a member of the First Triumvirate with Julius *Caesar and Marcus Livius *Crassus.

Pompidou Georges 1911–1974. French conservative politician, president 1969–74. He negotiated a settlement with the Algerians 1961 and, as prime minister 1962–68, with the students in the revolt of May 1968.

Pondicherry union territory of SE India; area 480 sq km/185 sq mi; population (1991) 789,400. Its capital is Pondicherry, and products include rice, peanuts, cotton, and sugar. Pondicherry was founded by the French 1674 and changed hands several times among the French, Dutch, and British before being returned to France 1814 at the close of the Napoleonic Wars. In 1954 it was transferred to the government of India.

pony small horse under 1.47 m/4.5 ft (14.2 hands) shoulder height. Although of Celtic origin, all the pony breeds have been crossed with thoroughbred and Arab stock, except for the smallest – the hardy Shetland, which is less than 105 cm/42 in shoulder height.

poodle breed of gun dog, including standard (above 38 cm/15 in at shoulder), miniature (below 38 cm/15 in), and toy (below 28 cm/11 in) varieties. The dense curly coat is usually cut into an elaborate style.

poor law English system for poor relief, established by the Poor Relief Act 1601. Each parish was responsible for its own poor, paid for by a parish tax. The care of the poor was transferred to the Ministry of Health 1918, but the poor law remained in force until 1930.

Pop art movement of British and American artists in the mid-1950s and 1960s, reacting against the elitism of abstract art. Pop art imagery was drawn from advertising, comic strips, film, and television. Early exponents in the UK were Richard Hamilton, Peter Blake (1932–), and Eduardo Paolozzi, and in the USA Jasper Johns, Jim Dine, Andy Warhol, Roy Lichtenstein, and Claes Oldenburg.

pope the bishop of Rome, head of the Roman Catholic church, which claims he is the spiritual descendant of St Peter. Elected by the Sacred College of Cardinals, a pope dates his pontificate from his coronation with the tiara, or triple crown, at St Peter's Basilica, Rome. The pope had great political power in Europe from the early Middle Ages until the Reformation.

Pope Alexander 1688–1744. English poet and satirist. He established his reputation with the precocious *Pastorals* 1709 and *Essay on Criticism* 1711, which were followed by a parody of the heroic epic *The Rape of the Lock* 1712–14 and 'Eloisa to Abelard' 1717. Other works include a highly Neo-Classical translation of Homer's *Iliad* and *Odyssey* 1715–26.

pop music or ***popular music*** any contemporary music not categorizable as jazz or classical. Pop became distinct from folk music with the advent of sound-recording techniques, and has incorporated blues, country and western, and music-hall elements; electronic amplification and other technological innovations have played a large part in the creation of new styles. The traditional format is a song of roughly three minutes with verse, chorus, and middle eight bars.

Popper Karl (Raimund) 1902–1994. Austrian philosopher of science. He established 'falsifiability'; that although scientific assertions cannot be conclusively verified, they can be conclusively falsified by a counter-instance; therefore, science is not certain knowledge but a series of 'conjectures and refutations'.

poppy any plant of the genus *Papaver*, family Papaveraceae, that bears brightly coloured, often dark-centred, flowers and yields a milky sap. Species include the crimson European field poppy *P. rhoeas* and the Asian *opium poppies. Closely related are the California poppy *Eschscholtzia californica* and the yellow horned or sea poppy *Glaucium flavum*.

popular front political alliance of liberals, socialists, communists, and other centre and left-wing parties. This policy was proposed by the Communist International 1935 against fascism and was adopted in France and Spain, where popular-front governments were elected 1936; that in France was overthrown 1938 and the one in Spain fell in 1939.

POPES OF THE LAST 500 YEARS

1492–1503	Alexander VI
1503	Pius III
1503–13	Julius II
1513–21	Leo X
1522–3	Hadrian VI
1523–34	Clement VII
1534–49	Paul III
1550–5	Julius III
1555	Marcellus II
1555–9	Paul IV
1559–65	Pius IV
1566–72	Pius V
1572–85	Gregory XIII
1585–90	Sixtus V
1590	Urban VII
1590–1	Gregory XIV
1591	Innocent IX
1592–1605	Clement VIII
1605	Leo XI
1605–21	Paul V
1621–3	Gregory XV
1623–44	Urban VIII
1644–55	Innocent X
1655–67	Alexander VII
1667–9	Clement IX
1670–6	Clement X
1676–89	Innocent XI
1689–91	Alexander VIII
1691–1700	Innocent XII
1700–21	Clement XI
1721–4	Innocent XIII
1724–30	Benedict XIII
1730–40	Clement XII
1740 – 58	Benedict XIV
1758–69	Clement XIII
1769–74	Clement XIV
1775–99	Pius VI
1800–23	Pius VII
1823–9	Leo XII
1829–30	Pius VIII
1831–46	Gregory XVI
1846–78	Pius IX
1878–1903	Leo XIII
1903–14	Pius X
1914–22	Benedict XV
1922–39	Pius XI
1939–58	Pius XII
1958–63	John XXIII
1963–78	Paul VI
1978	John Paul I
1978–	John Paul II

population in biology and ecology, a group of animals of one species, living in a certain area and able to interbreed; the members of a given species in a *community of living things.

population the number of people inhabiting a country, region, area, or town. Population statistics are derived from many sources; for example, through the registration of births and deaths, and from censuses of the population. The first national censuses were taken in 1800 and 1801 and provided population statistics for Italy, Spain, the UK, Ireland, and the USA; and the cities of London, Paris, Vienna, Berlin, and New York.

population control measures taken by some governments to limit the growth of their countries' populations by trying to reduce *birth rates.

porcupine *Porcupines can release their quills at an attacker.*

Propaganda, freely available contraception, and tax disincentives for large families are some of the measures that have been tried.

population cycle in biology, regular fluctuations in the size of a population, as seen in lemmings, for example. Such cycles are often caused by density-dependent mortality: high mortality due to overcrowding causes a sudden decline in the population, which then gradually builds up again. Population cycles may also result from interaction between predator and prey.

population explosion the rapid and dramatic rise in world population that has occurred over the last few hundred years. Between 1959 and 1990, the world's population increased from 2.5 billion to over 5 billion people. It is estimated that it will be at least 6 billion by the end of the century. Most of this growth is now taking place in the developing world, where rates of natural increase are much higher than in developed countries.

Populism in US history, a late 19th-century political movement that developed out of farmers' protests against economic hardship. The Populist, or People's Party was founded 1892 and ran several presidential candidates. It failed, however, to reverse increasing industrialization and the relative decline of agriculture in the USA.

porcelain (hardpaste) translucent ceramic material with a shining finish, see *pottery and porcelain.

porcupine any *rodent with quills on its body, belonging to either of two families: Old World porcupines (family Hystricidae), terrestrial in habit and having long black-and-white quills; or New World porcupines (family Erethizontidae), tree-dwelling, with prehensile tails and much shorter quills.

pornography obscene literature, pictures, photos, or films considered to be of no artistic merit and intended only to arouse sexual desire. Standards of what is obscene and whether a particular work has artistic value are subjective, hence there is often difficulty in determining whether a work violates the *obscenity laws. Opponents of pornography claim that it is harmful and incites violence to women and children. Others oppose its censorship claiming that it is impossible to distinguish pornography from art.

porphyria group of genetic disorders caused by an enzyme defect. Porphyria affects the digestive tract, causing abdominal distress; the nervous system, causing psychotic disorder, epilepsy, and weakness; the circulatory system, causing high blood pressure; and the skin, causing extreme sensitivity to light. No specific treatments exist.

porphyry any *igneous rock containing large crystals in a finer matrix.

porpoise any small whale of the family Delphinidae that, unlike dolphins, have blunt snouts without beaks. Common porpoises of the genus *Phocaena* can grow to 1.8 m/6 ft long; they feed on fish and crustaceans.

Porsche Ferdinand 1875–1951. German car designer. Among his designs were the Volkswagen (German 'people's car', popularly known as the Beetle), first produced in the 1930s, which became an international success in the 1950s–1970s, and Porsche sports cars.

port sweet red, tawny, or white dessert wine, fortified with brandy, made from grapes grown in the Douro basin of Portugal and exported from Oporto, hence the name.

port in computing, a socket that enables a computer processor to communicate with an external device. It may be an *input port* (such as a joystick port), or an *output port* (such as a printer port), or both (an *i/o port*).

port point where goods are loaded or unloaded from a water-based to a land-based form of transport. Most ports are coastal, though inland ports on rivers also exist.

portable computer computer that can be carried from place to place. The term embraces a number of very different computers – from those that would be carried only with some reluctance to those, such as *laptop computers and notebook computers, that can be comfortably carried and used in transit.

Port Arthur former name (until 1905) of the port and naval base of Lüshun in NE China, now part of Lüdz.

Port-au-Prince capital and industrial port (sugar, rum, textiles) of Haiti; population (1982) 763,000.

Port Elizabeth industrial port (engineering, steel, food processing) in Cape Province, South Africa, about 710 km/440 mi E of Cape Town on Algoa Bay; population (1980) 492,140.

Porter Cole (Albert) 1892–1964. US composer and lyricist, mainly of musical comedies. His witty, sophisticated songs like 'Let's Do It' 1928, 'I Get a Kick Out of You' 1934, and 'Don't Fence Me In' 1944 have been widely recorded and admired. His shows, many of which were made into films, include *The Gay Divorcee* 1932 and *Kiss Me Kate* 1948.

Porter Edwin Stanton 1869–1941. US director, a pioneer of silent films. His 1903 film *The Great Train Robbery* lasted 12 minutes – then an unusually long time for a film – and contained an early use of the close-up.

Portillo Michael (Denzil Xavier) 1953– . British Conservative politician, employment secretary from 1994. His progress up the ministerial ladder was swift, leading some advisers to regard him as John Major's eventual successor. He is an avowed 'Thatcherite' convinced of the supremacy of the market and suspicious of the encroaching powers of the European Union (EU).

Portland William Henry Cavendish Bentinck, 3rd Duke of Portland 1738–1809. British politician, originally a Whig, who in 1783 became nominal prime minister in the Fox–North coalition government. During the French Revolution he joined the Tories, and was prime minister 1807–09.

Port Laoise or **Portlaoighise** (formerly **Maryborough**) county town of County Laois, Republic of Ireland, 80 km/50 mi WSW of Dublin; population (1981) 7,756. It has woollen and flour-milling industries, and is the site of a top-security prison.

Port Louis capital of Mauritius, on the island's NW coast; population (1987) 139,000. Exports include sugar, textiles, watches, and electronic goods.

Port Moresby capital and port of Papua New Guinea on the S coast of New Guinea; population (1987) 152,000.

Porto (English **Oporto**) industrial city (textiles, leather, pottery) in Portugal, on the river Douro, 5 km/3 mi from its mouth; population (1984) 327,000. It exports port.

Pôrto Alegre port and capital of Rio Grande do Sul state, S Brazil; population (1991) 1,254,600. It is a freshwater port for ocean-going vessels, and is Brazil's major commercial centre.

Port-of-Spain port and capital of Trinidad and Tobago, on Trinidad; population (1988) 58,000.

Porton Down site of the Chemical and Biological Defence Establishment (until 1991 Chemical Defence Establishment (CDE)) in Wiltshire, SW England. Its prime role is to conduct research into means of protection from chemical attack.

Porto Novo capital of Benin, W Africa; population (1982) 208,258. It was a former Portuguese centre for the slave and tobacco trade with Brazil and became a French protectorate 1863.

Port Rashid port serving Dubai in the United Arab Emirates.

Port Said port in Egypt, on reclaimed land at the northern end of the *Suez Canal; population (1983) 364,000. During the 1967 Arab-Israeli war the city was damaged and the canal blocked; Port Said was evacuated by 1969 but by 1975 had been largely reconstructed.

Portsmouth city and naval port in Hampshire, England, opposite the Isle of Wight; population (1991) 174,700. The naval dockyard was closed 1981 although some naval facilities remain.

Portugal Republic of (*República Portuguesa*)

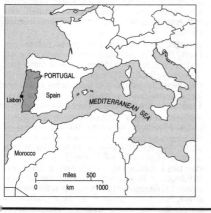

area 92,000 sq km/35,521 sq mi (including the Azores and Madeira)
capital Lisbon
towns Coimbra, ports Porto, Setúbal
physical mountainous in N, plains in S
head of state Mario Alberto Nobre Lopes Soares from 1986
head of government Aníbal Cavaco Silva from 1985
political system democratic republic
exports wine, olive oil, resin, cork, sardines, textiles, clothing, pottery, pulpwood
currency escudo
population (1993 est) 10,450,000; growth rate 0.5% p.a.
language Portuguese
religion Roman Catholic 97%
GNP $5,620 per head (1991)
chronology
1928–68 Military dictatorship under António de Oliveira Salazar.
1968 Salazar succeeded by Marcello Caetano.
1974 Caetano removed in military coup led by General Antonio Ribeiro de Spínola. Spínola replaced by General Francisco da Costa Gomes.
1975 African colonies became independent.
1976 New constitution, providing for return to civilian rule, adopted. Minority government appointed, led by Socialist Party leader Mario Soares.
1978 Soares resigned.
1980 Francisco Balsemão formed centre-party coalition after two years of political instability.
1982 Draft of new constitution approved, reducing powers of presidency.
1983 Centre-left coalition government formed.
1985 Aníbal Cavaco Silva became prime minister.
1986 Mario Soares elected first civilian president in 60 years. Portugal joined European Community.
1988 Portugal joined Western European Union.
1989 Constitution amended to allow major state enterprises to be denationalized.
1991 Mario Soares re-elected president; Social Democrats (PSD) majority slightly reduced in assembly elections.

Portuguese inhabitant of Portugal. The Portuguese have a mixed cultural heritage that can be traced back to the Lusitanian Celts who were defeated by the Romans about 140 BC. In the 5th century AD the Suebi, a Germanic group, overran the Iberian peninsula, and were later subdued by the Visigoths. In the 8th century AD S Portugal was invaded by the Moors. The Portuguese are predominantly Roman Catholic.

Portuguese East Africa former name of *Mozambique.

Portuguese Guinea former name of *Guinea-Bissau in W Africa.

Portuguese language member of the Romance branch of the Indo-European language family; spoken by 120–135 million people worldwide, it is the national language of Portugal, closely related to Spanish and strongly influenced by Arabic. Portuguese is also spoken in Brazil, Angola, Mozambique, and other former Portuguese colonies.

Portuguese man-of-war any of a genus *Physalia* of phylum *Coelenterata* (see *coelenterate). They live in the sea, in colonies, and have a large air-filled bladder (or 'float') on top and numerous hanging tentacles made up of feeding, stinging, and reproductive individuals. The float can be 30 cm/1 ft long.

Portuguese West Africa former name of *Angola.

Poseidon Greek god (Roman Neptune), the brother of Zeus and Pluto. The brothers dethroned their father, Kronos, and divided his realm, Poseidon taking the sea; he was also worshipped as god of earthquakes. His son was the merman sea god *Triton.

positivism theory that confines genuine knowledge within the bounds of science and observation. The theory is associated with the French philosopher Auguste Comte and *empiricism. *Logical positivism* developed in the 1920s. It rejected any metaphysical world beyond everyday science and common sense, and confined statements to those of formal logic or mathematics.

positron in physics, the antiparticle of the electron; an *elementary particle having the same magnitude of mass and charge as an electron but exhibiting a positive charge. The positron was discovered in 1932 by US physicist Carl Anderson at Caltech, USA, its existence having been predicted by the British physicist Paul Dirac 1928.

positron emission tomography (PET) a technique which enables doctors to observe the operation of the human body by following the progress of a radioactive chemical that has been inhaled or injected. PET scanners pinpoint the location of the chemical by bombarding the body with low energy *gamma radiation. The technique has been used to study a wide range of diseases including schizophrenia, Alzheimer's disease and Parkinson's disease.

possible world in philosophy, a consistent set of propositions describing a logically, if not physically, possible state of affairs. The term was invented by German philosopher *Leibniz who argued that God chose to make real one world from an infinite range of possible worlds. Since God could only choose the best, our world is 'the best of all possible worlds'.

possum another name for the *opossum, a marsupial animal with a prehensile tail found in North, Central and South America. The name is also used for many of the smaller marsupials found in Australia.

postcard card with space for a written message that can be sent through the mail without an envelope. The postcard's inventor was Emmanual Hermann, of Vienna, who in 1869 proposed a 'postal telegram', sent at a lower fee than a normal letter with an envelope. The first picture postcard was produced 1894.

poste restante (French) a system whereby mail is sent to a certain post office and kept there until collected by the person to whom it is addressed.

Post-Impressionism various styles of painting that followed *Impressionism in the 1880s and 1890s. The term was first used by the British critic Roger Fry in 1911 to describe the works of Paul Cézanne, Vincent van Gogh, and Paul Gauguin. These painters moved away from the spontaneity of Impressionism, attempting to give their work more serious meaning and permanence.

Post-Modernism late 20th-century movement in the arts and architecture that rejects the preoccupation of *Modernism and *Functionalism with pure form and technique rather than content. Post-Modern designers use an amalgam of style elements from the past, such as the Classical and the Baroque, and apply them to spare modern forms. Their slightly off-key familiarity creates a more immediate appeal than the austerities of Modernism.

postmortem or *autopsy* dissection of a dead body to determine the cause of death.

postnatal depression mood change occurring in many mothers a few days after the birth of a baby, also known as 'baby blues'. It is usually a short-lived condition but can sometimes persist; the most severe form of post-natal depressive illness, *puerperal psychosis*, requires hospital treatment. In mild cases, antidepressant drugs and hormone treatment may help.

Post Office (PO) government department or authority with responsibility for postal services. The Post Office has responsibility for paying out social security and collecting revenue for state insurance schemes. Post Office activities were divided in 1981 to separate telecommunications activities, and in 1984 these were privatized, forming a new company, British Telecom (later BT).

potash general name for any potassium-containing mineral, most often applied to potassium carbonate (K_2CO_3) or potassium hydroxide (KOH). Potassium carbonate, originally made by roasting plants to ashes in earthenware pots, is commercially produced from the mineral sylvite (potassium chloride, KCl) and is used mainly in making artificial fertilizers, glass, and soap.

potassium (Dutch *potassa* 'potash') soft, waxlike, silver-white, metallic element, symbol K (Latin *kalium*), atomic number 19, relative atomic mass 39.0983. It is one of the *alkali metals and has a very low density – it floats on water, and is the second lightest metal (after lithium). It oxidizes rapidly when exposed to air and reacts violently with water. Of great abundance in the Earth's crust, it is widely distributed with other elements and found in salt and mineral deposits in the form of potassium aluminium silicates.

potato perennial plant *Solanum tuberosum*, family Solanaceae, with edible tuberous roots that are rich in starch. Used by the Andean Indians for at least 2,000 years before the Spanish Conquest, the potato was introduced to Europe by the mid-16th century, and reputedly to England by the explorer Walter Raleigh.

Potemkin Grigory Aleksandrovich, Prince Potemkin 1739–1791. Russian politician. He entered the army and attracted the notice of Catherine II, whose friendship he kept throughout his life. An active administrator, he reformed the army, built the Black Sea Fleet, conquered the Crimea, developed S Russia, and founded the Kherson arsenal 1788 (the first Russian naval base on the Black Sea).

potential difference (pd) measure of the electrical potential energy converted to another form for every unit charge moving between two points in an electric circuit (see *potential, electric). The unit of potential difference is the volt.

potential, electric in physics, the relative electrical state of an object. A charged conductor, for example, has a higher potential than the Earth, whose potential is taken by convention to be zero. An electric *cell (battery) has a potential in relation to emf (*electromotive force), which can make current flow in an external circuit. The difference in potential between two points – the **potential difference** – is expressed in *volts; that is, a 12 V battery has a potential difference of 12 volts between its negative and positive terminals.

potential energy *energy possessed by an object by virtue of its relative position or state (for example, as in a compressed spring). It is contrasted with kinetic energy, the form of energy possessed by moving bodies.

potentiometer in physics, an electrical *resistor that can be divided so as to compare, measure, or control voltages. In radio circuits, any rotary variable resistance (such as volume control) is referred to as a potentiometer.

Potomac river in W Virginia, Virginia, and Maryland states, USA, rising in the Allegheny mountains, and flowing SE through Washington, DC, into Chesapeake Bay. It is formed by the junction of the N Potomac, about 153 km/95 mi long, and S Potomac, about 209 km/130 mi long; the Potomac itself 459 km/285 mi long.

Potsdam Conference conference held in Potsdam, Germany, 17 July–2 Aug 1945 between representatives of the USA, the UK, and the USSR. They established the political and economic principles governing the treatment of Germany in the initial period of Allied control at the end of World War II, and sent an ultimatum to Japan demanding unconditional surrender on pain of utter destruction.

Potter Beatrix 1866–1943. English writer and illustrator of children's books, beginning with *Peter Rabbit* 1900 and *The Tailor of Gloucester* 1902, based on her observation of family pets and wildlife around her home from 1905 in the English Lake District.

Potteries, the home of the china and earthenware industries, in central England. Wedgwood and Minton are factory names associated with the Potteries.

pottery and porcelain *ceramics in domestic and ornamental use including: **earthenware** made of porous clay and fired, whether unglazed (when it remains porous, for example, flowerpots, winecoolers) or glazed (most tableware); **stoneware** made of non-porous clay with a high silica content, fired at high temperature, which is very hard; **bone china** (softpaste) semi-porcelain made of 5% bone ash and *china clay; first made in the West in imitation of Chinese porcelain; **porcelain** (hardpaste) characterized by its hardness, ringing sound when struck, translucence, and shining finish, like that of a cowrie shell (Italian *porcellana*); made of kaolin and petuntse (fusible *feldspar consisting chiefly of silicates reduced to a fine, white powder); first developed

in China. Porcelain is high-fired at 1,400°C/ 2,552°F.

potto arboreal, nocturnal, African prosimian primate *Perodicticus potto* belonging to the *loris family. It has a thick body, strong limbs, and grasping feet and hands, and grows to 40 cm/ 16 in long, with horny spines along its backbone, which it uses in self-defence. It climbs slowly, and eats insects, snails, fruit, and leaves.

Poulenc Francis (Jean Marcel) 1899–1963. French composer and pianist. A self-taught composer of witty and irreverent music, he was a member of the group of French composers known as *Les Six*. Among his many works are the operas *Les Mamelles de Tirésias* 1947, and *Dialogues des Carmélites* 1957, and the ballet *Les Biches* 1923.

poultry domestic birds such as chickens, turkeys, ducks, and geese. They were domesticated for meat and eggs by early farmers in China, Europe, Egypt, and the Americas. Chickens were domesticated from the SE Asian jungle fowl *Gallus gallus* and then raised in the East as well as the West. Turkeys are New World birds, domesticated in ancient Mexico. Geese and ducks were domesticated in Egypt, China, and Europe.

pound imperial unit (abbreviation lb) of mass. The commonly used avoirdupois pound, also called the **imperial standard pound** (7,000 grains/0.45 kg), differs from the **pound troy** (5,760 grains/0.37 kg), which is used for weighing precious metals. It derives from the Roman weight called a *libra*, which weighed 0.327 kg.

pound British standard monetary unit, issued as a gold sovereign before 1914, as a note 1914–83, and as a circular yellow metal alloy coin from 1983. The pound is also the name given to the unit of currency in Egypt, Lebanon, Malta, Sudan, and Syria.

Pound Ezra 1885–1972. US poet who lived in London from 1908. His *Personae* and *Exultations* 1909 established the principles of *Imagism. His largest work was the series of *Cantos* 1925–1969 (intended to number 100), which attempted a massive reappraisal of history.

Poussin Nicolas 1594–1665. French painter, active chiefly in Rome; court painter to Louis XIII 1640–43. He was one of France's foremost landscape painters in the 17th century. He painted mythological and literary scenes in a strongly Classical style; for example, *Rape of the Sabine Women* about 1636–37 (Metropolitan Museum of Art, New York).

poverty condition that exists when the basic needs of human beings (shelter, food, and clothing) are not being met. Many different definitions of poverty exist, since there is little agreement on the standard of living considered to be the minimum adequate level (known as the **poverty level**) by the majority of people.

poverty cycle set of factors or events by which poverty, once started, is likely to continue unless there is outside intervention. Once an area or a person has become poor, this tends to lead to other disadvantages, which may in turn result in further poverty. The situation is often found in *inner-city areas and shanty towns. Applied to countries, the poverty cycle is often called the *development trap*. One way of breaking the cycle may be through *aid.

Powell (John) Enoch 1912– . British Conservative politician. He was minister of health 1960–63, and contested the party leadership 1965. In 1968 he made a speech against immigration that led to his dismissal from the shadow cabinet. He resigned from the party 1974, and was Official Unionist Party member for South Down, Northern Ireland 1974–87.

Powell Cecil Frank 1903–1969. English physicist. From the 1930s he and his team at Bristol University investigated the charged subatomic particles in cosmic radiation by using photographic emulsions carried in weather balloons. This led to his discovery of the pion (pi meson) 1946, a particle whose existence had been predicted by the Japanese physicist Hideki Yukawa 1935. Powell was awarded a Nobel prize in 1950.

Powell Colin (Luther) 1937– . US general, chair of the Joint Chiefs of Staff from 1989 and, as such, responsible for the overall administration of the Allied forces in Saudi Arabia during the *Gulf War 1991. A Vietnam War veteran, he first worked in government 1972 and was national security adviser 1987–89.

Powell Michael 1905–1990. English film director and producer. Some of his most memorable films were made in collaboration with Hungarian screenwriter Emeric Pressburger. Their richly imaginative films include *A Matter of Life and Death* 1946, *Black Narcissus* 1947, and *The Red Shoes* 1948.

Powell Mike 1963– . US long jumper who in 1991 broke US athlete Bob Beamon's world long-jump record of 8.90 m (which had stood since 1968) with a leap of 8.95 m. At the same time, he dealt Carl Lewis his first long-jump defeat since 1981. Powell also topped the world long-jump rankings in 1990.

power in mathematics, that which is represented by an *exponent or index, denoted by a superior small numeral. A number or symbol raised to the power of 2, that is, multiplied by itself, is said to be squared (for example, 3^2; x^2), and when raised to the power of 3, it is said to be cubed (for example, 2^3; y^3).

power in physics, the rate of doing work or consuming energy. It is measured in watts (joules per second) or other units of work per unit time.

power in optics, a measure of the amount by which a lens will deviate light rays. A powerful converging lens will converge parallel rays steeply, bringing them to a focus at a short distance from the lens. The unit of power is the *dioptre*, which is equal to the reciprocal of focal length in metres. By convention, the power of a converging (or convex) lens is positive and that of a diverging (or concave) lens negative.

power of attorney in law, legal authority to act on behalf of another, for a specific transaction, or for a particular period.

power station building where electrical power is generated (see *electricity; *nuclear reactor). The largest in Europe is the Drax power station near Selby, Yorkshire, which supplies 10% of Britain's electricity.

Powys county in central Wales
area 5,080 sq km/1,961 sq mi

towns Llandrindod Wells (administrative headquarters)
products agriculture, dairy cattle, sheep
population (1991) 116,500
languages 20% Welsh, English

Powys John Cowper 1872–1963. English novelist. His mystic and erotic books include *Wolf Solent* 1929 and *A Glastonbury Romance* 1933. He was one of three brothers (*Theodore Francis Powys* 1875–1953 and *Llewelyn Powys* 1884–1939), all writers.

Poznań (German *Posen*) industrial city (machinery, aircraft, beer) in W Poland; population (1985) 553,000. Founded 970, it was settled by German immigrants 1253 and passed to Prussia 1793; it was restored to Poland 1919.

pp abbreviation for *per procurationem* (Latin 'by proxy'); in music, *pianissimo* (Italian 'very softly').

PR abbreviation for *public relations*; *proportional representation*; *Puerto Rico*.

praetor in ancient Rome, a magistrate, elected annually, who assisted the *consuls (the chief magistrates) and presided over the civil courts. After a year in office, a praetor would act as a provincial governor for a further year. The number of praetors was finally increased to eight.

pragmatism philosophical tradition that interprets truth in terms of the practical effects of what is believed and, in particular, the usefulness of these effects. The US philosopher Charles Peirce is often accounted the founder of pragmatism; it was further advanced by William James.

Prague (Czech *Praha*) city and capital of Czechoslovakia on the river Vltava; population (1991) 1,212,000. Industries include cars, aircraft, chemicals, paper and printing, clothing, brewing, and food processing. It became the capital 1918.

Prague Spring the 1968 programme of liberalization, begun under a new Communist Party leader in Czechoslovakia. In Aug 1968 Soviet tanks invaded Czechoslovakia and entered the capital Prague to put down the liberalization movement initiated by the prime minister Alexander Dubček, who had earlier sought to assure the Soviets that his planned reforms would not threaten socialism. Dubček was arrested but released soon afterwards. Most of the Prague Spring reforms were reversed.

Praha Czech name for *Prague.

Praia port and capital of the Republic of Cape Verde, on the island of São Tiago (Santiago); population (1980) 37,500. Industries include fishing and shipping.

prairie the central North American plain, formerly grass-covered, extending over most of the region between the Rockies on the west and the Great Lakes and Ohio River on the east.

prairie dog any of the North American genus *Cynomys* of burrowing rodents in the squirrel family (Sciuridae). They grow to 30 cm/12 in, plus a short 8 cm/3 in tail. Their 'towns' can contain up to several thousand individuals. Their barking cry has given them their name. Persecution by ranchers has brought most of the five species close to extinction.

Prasad Rajendra 1884–1963. Indian politician.

He was national president of the Indian National Congress several times between 1934 and 1948 and India's first president after independence 1950–62.

praseodymium (Greek *praseo* 'leek-green' + *dymium*) silver-white, malleable, metallic element of the *lanthanide series, symbol Pr, atomic number 59, relative atomic mass 140.907. It occurs in nature in the minerals monzanite and bastnasite, and its green salts are used to colour glass and ceramics. It was named in 1885 by Austrian chemist Carl von Welsbach (1858–1929).

prawn any of various *shrimps of the suborder Natantia ('swimming'), of the crustacean order Decapoda, as contrasted with lobsters and crayfishes, which are able to 'walk'. Species called prawns are generally larger than species called shrimps.

Praxiteles mid-4th century BC. Greek sculptor, active in Athens. His *Aphrodite of Knidos* about 350 BC (known through Roman copies) is thought to have initiated the tradition of life-size freestanding female nudes in Greek sculpture.

prayer address to divine power, ranging from a magical formula to attain a desired end, to selfless communication in meditation. Within Christianity the Catholic and Orthodox churches sanction prayer to the Virgin Mary, angels, and saints as intercessors, whereas Protestantism limits prayer to God alone.

Precambrian in geology, time from the formation of Earth (4.6 billion years ago) up to 570 million years ago. Its boundary with the succeeding Cambrian period marks the time when animals first developed hard outer parts (exoskeletons) and so left abundant fossil remains. It comprises about 85% of geological time and is divided into two periods: the Archaean and the Proterozoic.

precedent the common law principle that, in deciding a particular case, judges are bound to follow any applicable principles of law laid down by superior courts in earlier reported cases.

precession slow wobble of the Earth on its axis, like that of a spinning top. The gravitational pulls of the Sun and Moon on the Earth's equatorial bulge cause the Earth's axis to trace out a circle in the sky every 25,800 years. The position of the celestial poles (see *celestial sphere) is constantly changing owing to precession, as are the positions of the equinoxes (the points at which the celestial equator intersects the Sun's path around the sky). The *precession of the equinoxes* means that there is a gradual westward drift in the ecliptic – the path that the Sun appears to follow – and in the coordinates of objects on the celestial sphere.

precipitation meteorological term for water that falls to the Earth from the atmosphere. It includes rain, snow, sleet, hail, dew, and frost.

precipitation in chemistry, the formation of a suspension of solid, insoluble particles in a liquid as a result of a reaction within the liquid between two or more soluble substances. If the particles settle, they form a *precipitate*; if the particles are very small and remain in suspension, they form a *colloidal precipitate* (see *colloid).

predestination in Christian theology, the doctrine asserting that God has determined all events beforehand, including the ultimate salvation or damnation of the individual human soul. Today Christianity in general accepts that humanity has free will, though some forms, such as Calvinism, believe that salvation can only be attained by the gift of God. The concept of predestination is also found in Islam.

pre-eclampsia or **toxaemia of pregnancy** potentially serious condition marked by high blood pressure, swelling, and sometimes convulsions. Arising from unknown causes, it disappears when pregnancy is over. It may progress to eclampsia if untreated.

preference share in finance, a share in a company with rights in various ways superior to those of ordinary shares; for example, priority to a fixed dividend and priority over ordinary shares in the event of the company being wound up.

Preferential Trade Area for Eastern and Southern African States (PTA) organization established 1981 with the object of increasing economic and commercial cooperation between member states, harmonizing tariffs, and reducing trade barriers, with the eventual aim of creating a common market. Members include (1992) Angola, Burundi, Comoros, Djibouti, Ethiopia, Kenya, Lesotho, Malawi, Mauritius, Mozambique, Rwanda, Somalia, Sudan, Swaziland, Tanzania, Uganda, Zaire, Zambia, and Zimbabwe. The headquarters of the PTA are in Lusaka, Zambia.

prefix letter or group of letters that can be added to the beginning of a word to make a new word. For example, *over*time, *out*rage, *non*sense.

pregnancy in humans, the period during which an embryo grows within the womb. It begins at conception and ends at birth, and the normal length is 40 weeks. Menstruation usually stops on conception. About one in five pregnancies fails, but most of these failures occur very early on, so the woman may notice only that her period is late. After the second month, the breasts become tense and tender, and the areas round the nipples become darker. Enlargement of the uterus can be felt at about the end of the third month, and thereafter the abdomen enlarges progressively. Pregnancy in animals is called *gestation.

prehistoric life the diverse organisms that inhabited Earth from the origin of life about 3.5 billion years ago to the time when humans began to keep written records, about 3500 BC. During the course of evolution, new forms of life developed and many other forms, such as the dinosaurs, became extinct. Prehistoric life evolved over this vast timespan from simple bacteria-like cells in the oceans to algae and protozoans and complex multicellar forms such as worms, molluscs, crustaceans, fishes, insects, land plants, amphibians, reptiles, birds, and mammals. On a geological timescale human beings evolved relatively recently, about 4 million years ago, although the exact dating is a matter of some debate.

prehistory human cultures before the use of writing. A classification system was devised 1816 by Danish archaeologist Christian Thomsen, based on the predominant materials used by early

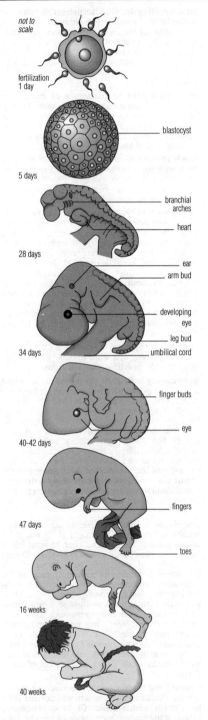

not to
scale

fertilization
1 day

blastocyst

5 days

branchial
arches

heart

28 days

ear

arm bud

developing
eye

leg bud

34 days

umbilical cord

finger buds

eye

40–42 days

fingers

47 days

toes

16 weeks

40 weeks

pregnancy *The development of a human embryo.*

humans for tools and weapons: *Stone Age, *Bronze Age, *Iron Age.

prelude in music, a composition intended as the preface to further music, to set a mood for a stage work, as in Wagner's *Lohengrin*; as used by Chopin, a short piano work.

Premadasa Ranasinghe 1924–1993. Sri Lankan politician, a United National Party member of Parliament from 1960, prime minister 1978–89, and president 1988–93, having gained popularity through overseeing a major house-building and poverty-alleviation programme. He sought peace talks with the Tamil Tiger guerrillas. He was assassinated.

prematurity the condition of an infant born before the full term. In obstetrics, an infant born after less than 37 weeks' gestation is described as premature.

premenstrual tension (PMT) or **premenstrual syndrome** medical condition caused by hormone changes and comprising a number of physical and emotional features that occur cyclically before menstruation and disappear with its onset. Symptoms include mood changes, breast tenderness, a feeling of bloatedness, and headache.

Preminger Otto (Ludwig) 1906–1986. Austrian-born US film producer, director, and actor. He directed *Margin for Error* 1942, *Laura* 1944, *The Moon Is Blue* 1953, *The Man with the Golden Arm* 1955, *Anatomy of a Murder* 1959, *Skidoo!* 1968, and *Rosebud* 1974. His films are characterized by an intricate technique of story-telling and a masterly use of the wide screen and the travelling camera.

premium price difference between the current market price of a security and its issue price (where the current price is the greater).

premolar in mammals, one of the large teeth toward the back of the mouth. In herbivores they are adapted for grinding. In carnivores they may be carnassials.

Premonstratensian Roman Catholic monastic order founded 1120 by St Norbert (*c.* 1080–1134), a German bishop, at Prémontré, N France. Members were known as White Canons. The rule was a stricter version of that of the St Augustine Canons.

preparatory school fee-paying independent school. In the UK, it is a junior school that prepares children for entry to a senior school at about age 13. In the USA, it is a school that prepares students for university entrance at about age 18.

preposition in grammar, a *part of speech coming before a noun or a pronoun to show a location (*in, on*), time (*during*), or some other relationship (for example, figurative relationships in phrases like '*by* heart' or '*on* time').

Pre-Raphaelite Brotherhood (PRB) group of British painters 1848–53; Dante Gabriel Rossetti, John Everett Millais, and Holman Hunt were founding members. They aimed to paint serious subjects, to study nature closely, and to shun the influence of the styles of painters after Raphael.

presbyopia vision defect, an increasing inability with advancing age to focus on near objects. It is caused by thickening and loss of elasticity in the lens, which is no longer able to relax to the near-spherical shape required for near vision.

Presbyterianism system of Christian Protestant church government, expounded during the Reformation by John Calvin, which gives its name to the established Church of Scotland, and is also practised in England, Wales, Ireland, Switzerland, North America, and elsewhere. There is no compulsory form of worship and each congregation is governed by presbyters or elders (clerical or lay), who are of equal rank. Congregations are grouped in presbyteries, synods, and general assemblies.

Prescott John Leslie 1938– . British Labour Party politician, deputy leader from 1994.

prescription in English law, the legal acquisition of title or right (for example, an *easement such as a right of way) by uninterrupted use or possession.

prescription in medicine, an order written in a recognized form by a practitioner of medicine, dentistry, or veterinary surgery to a pharmacist for a preparation of medications to be used in treatment.

present participle part of speech, see *participle.

preservative substance (*additive) added to a food in order to inhibit the growth of bacteria, yeasts, mould, and other microorganisms, and therefore extend its shelf-life. The term sometimes refers to *antioxidants (substances added to oils and fats to prevent their becoming rancid) as well. All preservatives are potentially damaging to health if eaten in sufficient quantity. Both the amount used, and the foods in which they can be used, are restricted by law.

president in government, the usual title of the head of state in a republic; the power of the office may range from the equivalent of a constitutional monarch to the actual head of the government. For presidents of the USA, see *United States of America.

presidential medal of freedom highest peacetime civilian award in the USA, instituted 1963, conferred annually on Independence Day by the president on those making significant contributions to the 'quality of American life'. It replaced the Medal of Freedom awarded from 1945 for acts and service aiding US security.

presidium name (1952–66) of the *Politburo, the executive committee of the Supreme Soviet in the USSR.

Presley Elvis (Aaron) 1935–1977. US singer and guitarist, the most influential performer of the rock-and-roll era. With his recordings for Sun Records in Memphis, Tennessee, 1954–55 and early hits such as 'Heartbreak Hotel', 'Hound Dog', and 'Love Me Tender', all 1956, he created an individual vocal style, influenced by Southern blues, gospel music, country music, and rhythm and blues. His records continued to sell in their millions into the 1990s.

press the news media, in particular *newspapers, journals, and periodical literature generally. The term is used also to describe journalists and reporters.

Pressburger Emeric 1902–1988. Hungarian director, producer, and screenwriter, known for his partnership with Michael *Powell.

Press Council in the UK, an organization (1953–91) founded to preserve the freedom of the press, maintain standards, consider complaints, and report on monopoly developments. The Press Council was replaced by the Press Complaints Commission, which began operations in Jan 1991.

press, freedom of absence of political *censorship in the press or other media, a concept regarded as basic to Western democracy. Access to and expression of views are, however, in practice restricted by the commercial interests of the owners and advertisers. In the UK the government imposed a ban 1988 on broadcast interviews with Provisional IRA members, which was upheld by the courts 1989.

press gang method used to recruit soldiers and sailors into the British armed forces in the 18th and early 19th centuries. In effect it was a form of kidnapping carried out by the services or their agents, often with the aid of armed men. This was similar to the practice of 'shanghaiing' sailors for duty in the merchant marine, especially in the Far East.

pressure in physics, the force acting normally (at right angles) to a body per unit surface area. The SI unit of pressure is the pascal (newton per square metre), equal to 0.01 millibars. In a fluid (liquid or gas), pressure increases with depth. At the edge of Earth's atmosphere, pressure is zero, whereas at sea level atmospheric pressure due to the weight of the air above is about 100 kilopascals (1,013 millibars or 1 atmosphere). Pressure is commonly measured by means of a barometer, manometer, or Bourdon gauge.

pressure cooker closed pot in which food is cooked in water under pressure, where water boils at a higher temperature than normal boiling point (100°C/212°F) and therefore cooks food quickly. The modern pressure cooker has a quick-sealing lid and a safety valve that can be adjusted to vary the steam pressure inside.

pressure group or *interest group* or *lobby* association that puts pressure on governments or parties to ensure laws and treatment favourable to its own interest. Pressure groups have played an increasingly prominent role in contemporary Western democracies. In general they fall into two types: groups concerned with a single issue, such as nuclear disarmament, and groups attempting to promote their own interest, such as oil producers.

pressurized water reactor (PWR) a nuclear reactor design used in nuclear power stations in many countries, and in nuclear-powered submarines. In the PWR, water under pressure is the coolant and *moderator. It circulates through a steam generator, where its heat boils water to provide steam to drive power *turbines.

Prestel the *viewdata service provided by British Telecom (BT), which provides information on the television screen via the telephone network. BT pioneered the service 1975.

Prester John legendary Christian prince. During the 12th and 13th centuries, Prester John was believed to be the ruler of a powerful empire in Asia. From the 14th to the 16th century, he was generally believed to be the king of Abyssinia (now Ethiopia) in N E Africa.

prestressed concrete reinforced concrete in which ducts enclose mechanically tensioned steel cables. This allows the most efficient use of the tensile strength of steel with the compressive strength of concrete.

pretender claimant to a throne. In British history, the term is widely used to describe the Old Pretender (*James Edward Stuart) and the Young Pretender (*Charles Edward Stuart).

Pretoria administrative capital of the Republic of South Africa from 1910 and capital of Transvaal province from 1860; population (1985) 741,300. Industries include engineering, chemicals, iron, and steel. Founded 1855, it was named after Boer leader Andries Pretorius (1799–1853).

Previn André (George) 1929– . US conductor and composer, born in Berlin. After a period working as a composer and arranger in the US film industry, he concentrated on conducting. He was principal conductor of the London Symphony Orchestra 1968–79. He was appointed music director of Britain's Royal Philharmonic Orchestra 1985 (a post he relinquished the following year, staying on as principal conductor), and of the Los Angeles Philharmonic in 1986.

Prévost d'Exiles Antoine François 1697–1763. French novelist, known as Abbé Prévost, who combined a military career with his life as a monk. His *Manon Lescaut* 1731 inspired operas by Massenet and Puccini.

Priam in Greek mythology, the last king of Troy. He was killed by Pyrrhus, son of Achilles, when the Greeks entered the city of Troy concealed in a huge wooden horse which the Trojans believed to be a gift to the city.

Priapus Greek god of fertility, son of Dionysus and Aphrodite, represented as grotesquely ugly, with an exaggerated phallus. He was also a god of gardens, where his image was frequently used as a scarecrow.

price/earnings ratio or *p/e ratio* company's share price divided by its earnings per share after tax.

prickly pear cactus of the genus *Opuntia*, native to Central and South America, mainly Mexico and Chile, but naturalized in S Europe, N Africa, and Australia, where it is a pest. The common prickly pear *Opuntia vulgaris* is low-growing, with flat, oval, stem joints, bright yellow flowers, and prickly, oval fruit; the flesh and seeds of the peeled fruit have a pleasant taste.

Pride's purge the removal of about 100 Royalists and Presbyterians from the English House of Commons from Parliament by a detachment of soldiers led by Col Thomas Pride (died 1658) in 1648. They were accused of negotiating with Charles I and were seen as unreliable by the army. The remaining members were termed the *Rump and voted in favour of the king's trial.

Priestley J(ohn) B(oynton) 1894–1984. English novelist and playwright. His first success was a novel about travelling theatre, *The Good Companions* 1929. He followed it with a realist novel about London life, *Angel Pavement* 1930. As a playwright he was often preoccupied with theories of time, as in *An Inspector Calls* 1945.

primary in presidential election campaigns in the USA, a statewide election to decide the candidates for the two main parties. Held in 35 states, primaries begin with New Hampshire in Feb and continue until June; they operate under varying complex rules.

primate in zoology, any member of the order of mammals that includes monkeys, apes, and humans (together called **anthropoids**, as well as lemurs, bushbabies, lorises, and tarsiers, together called **prosimians**). Generally, they have forward-directed eyes, gripping hands and feet, opposable thumbs, and big toes. They tend to have nails rather than claws, with gripping pads on the ends of the digits, all adaptations to the arboreal, climbing mode of life.

primate in the Christian church, the official title of an archbishop.

primate city city that is by far the largest within a country or area. Such a city holds a larger proportion of the population, economic activity and social functions than other settlements within that area. It is also likely to dominate politically together with the surrounding core area.

prime minister or **premier** head of a parliamentary government, usually the leader of the largest party. In countries with an executive president, the prime minister is of lesser standing, whereas in those with dual executives, such as France, power is shared with the president.

prime number a number that can be divided only by 1 or itself, that is, having no other factors. There is an infinite number of primes, the first ten of which are 2, 3, 5, 7, 11, 13, 17, 19, 23, and 29 (by definition, the number 1 is excluded from the set of prime numbers). The number 2 is the only even prime because all other even numbers have 2 as a factor.

prime rate the interest rate charged by commercial banks to their best customers. It is the lowest interest or base rate on which other rates are calculated according to the risk involved. Only borrowers who have the highest credit rating qualify for the prime rate.

Primitive Methodism Protestant Christian movement, an offshoot of Wesleyan *Methodism, that emerged in England 1811 when evangelical enthusiasts organized camp meetings at places such as Mow Cop 1807. Inspired by American example, open-air sermons were accompanied by prayers and hymn singing. In 1932 the Primitive Methodists became a constituent of a unified Methodist church.

Primo de Rivera Miguel 1870–1930. Spanish soldier and politician, dictator from 1923 as well as premier from 1925. He was captain-general of Catalonia when he led a coup against the ineffective monarchy and became virtual dictator of Spain with the support of Alfonso XIII. He resigned 1930.

Primorye territory of Russia, SE Siberia, on the Sea of Japan; area 165,900 sq km/64,079 sq mi; population (1985) 2,136,000; capital Vladivostok. Timber and coal are produced.

primrose any plant of the genus *Primula*, family Primulaceae, with showy five-lobed flowers. The common primrose *P. vulgaris* is a woodland plant, native to Europe, bearing pale

PRIME MINISTERS OF BRITAIN

Sir Robert Walpole	(Whig)	1721	Earl of Derby	(Conservative)	1866
Earl of Wilmington	(Whig)	1742	Benjamin Disraeli	(Conservative)	1868
Henry Pelham	(Whig)	1743	W E Gladstone	(Liberal)	1886
Duke of Newcastle	(Whig)	1754	Benjamin Disraeli	(Conservative)	1874
Duke of Devonshire	(Whig)	1756	W E Gladstone	(Liberal)	1880
Duke of Newcastle	(Whig)	1757	Marquess of Salisbury	(Conservative)	1885
Earl of Bute	(Tory)	1762	W E Gladstone	(Liberal)	1886
George Grenville	(Whig)	1763	Marquess of Salisbury	(Conservative)	1886
Marquess of Rockingham	(Whig)	1765	W E Gladstone	(Liberal)	1892
Duke of Grafton	(Whig)	1766	Earl of Rosebery	(Liberal)	1894
Lord North	(Tory)	1770	Marquess of Salisbury	(Conservative)	1895
Marquess of Rockingham	(Whig)	1782	Sir H Campbell-Bannerman	(Liberal)	1905
Earl of Shelbourne	(Whig)	1782	H H Asquith	(Liberal)	1908
William Pitt	(Tory)	1783	H H Asquith	(Coalition)	1915
Duke of Portland	(Coalition)	1783	D Lloyd George	(Coalition)	1916
Henry Addington	(Tory)	1801	A Bonar Law	(Conservative)	1922
William Pitt	(Tory)	1804	Stanley Baldwin	(Conservative)	1923
Lord Grenville	(Whig)	1806	Ramsay MacDonald	(Labour)	1924
Duke of Portland	(Tory)	1807	Stanley Baldwin	(Conservative)	1924
Spencer Percival	(Tory)	1809	Ramsay MacDonald	(Labour)	1929
Earl of Liverpool	(Tory)	1812	Ramsay MacDonald	(National)	1931
George Canning	(Tory)	1827	Stanley Baldwin	(National)	1935
Viscount Goderich	(Tory)	1827	N Chamberlain	(National)	1937
Duke of Wellington	(Tory)	1828	Sir Winston Churchill	(Coalition)	1940
Earl Grey	(Whig)	1830	Clement Attlee	(Labour)	1945
Viscount Melbourne	(Whig)	1834	Sir Winston Churchill	(Conservative)	1951
Sir Robert Peel	(Conservative)	1834	Sir Anthony Eden	(Conservative)	1955
Viscount Melbourne	(Whig)	1835	Harold Macmillan	(Conservative)	1957
Sir Robert Peel	(Conservative)	1841	Sir Alec Douglas-Home	(Conservative)	1963
Lord J Russell	(Liberal)	1846	Harold Wilson	(Labour)	1964
Earl of Derby	(Conservative)	1852	Edward Heath	(Conservative)	1970
Lord Aberdeen	(Peelite)	1852	Harold Wilson	(Labour)	1974
Viscount Palmerston	(Liberal)	1855	James Callaghan	(Labour)	1976
Earl of Derby	(Conservative)	1858	Margaret Thatcher	(Conservative)	1979
Viscount Palmerston	(Liberal)	1859	John Major	(Conservative)	1990
Lord J Russell	(Liberal)	1865			

yellow flowers in spring. Related to it is the *cowslip.

prince royal or noble title. In Rome and medieval Italy it was used as the title of certain officials, for example, *princeps senatus* (Latin 'leader of the Senate'). The title was granted to the king's sons in 15th-century France, and in England from Henry VII's time.

Prince Stage name of Prince Rogers Nelson 1960– . US pop musician who composes, arranges, and produces his own records and often plays all the instruments. His albums, including *1999* 1982 and *Purple Rain* 1984, contain elements of rock, funk, and jazz. His stage shows are energetic and extravagant.

Prince Edward Island province of E Canada
area 5,700 sq km/2,200 sq mi
capital Charlottetown
products potatoes, dairy products, lobsters, oysters, farm vehicles
population (1991) 129,900
history first recorded visit by Cartier 1534, who called it Isle St-Jean; settled by French; taken by British 1758; annexed to Nova Scotia 1763; separate colony 1769; settled by Scottish 1803; joined Confederation 1873.

Princess Royal title borne only by the eldest daughter of the British sovereign, granted by royal declaration. It was first borne by Mary, eldest daughter of Charles I, probably in imitation of the French court where the eldest daughter of the king was styled 'Madame Royale'. The title is currently held by Princess Anne.

Prince William Sound channel in the Gulf of Alaska, extending 200 km/125 mi NW from Kayak Island. In March 1989 the oil tanker *Exxon Valdez* ran aground here, spilling 12 million gallons of crude oil in what was then reckoned to be the world's greatest oil-pollution disaster.

printed circuit board (PCB) electrical circuit created by laying (printing) 'tracks' of a conductor such as copper on one or both sides of an insulating board. The PCB was invented in 1936 by Austrian scientist Paul Eisler, and was first used on a large scale in 1948.

printer in computing, an output device for producing printed copies of text or graphics. Types include the *daisywheel printer*, which produces good-quality text but no graphics; the *dot-matrix printer*, which produces text and graphics by printing a pattern of small dots; the *ink-jet printer*, which creates text and graphics by spraying a fine jet of quick-drying ink onto the paper; and the *laser printer*, which uses electrostatic technology very similar to that used by a photocopier to produce high-quality text and graphics.

printing reproduction of text or illustrative material on paper, as in books or newspapers, or on an increasing variety of materials; for example, on plastic containers. The first printing used woodblocks, followed by carved wood type or moulded metal type and hand-operated presses. Modern printing processes include *offset printing, and *gravure print.

printmaking creating a picture or design by printing from a plate (woodblock, stone, or metal sheet) that holds ink or colour. The oldest form of print is the woodcut, common in medieval Europe, followed by line *engraving (from the 15th century), and *etching (from the 17th century); coloured woodblock prints flourished in Japan from the 18th century. *Lithography was invented 1796.

prion exceptionally small microorganism, a hundred times smaller than a virus. Composed of protein, and without any detectable amount of nucleic acid (genetic material), it is thought to cause diseases such as scrapie in sheep, and certain degenerative diseases of the nervous system in humans. How it can operate without nucleic acid is not yet known.

Pripet (Russian *Pripyat*) river in E Europe, a tributary of the river Dnieper, which it joins 80 km/50 mi above Kiev, Ukraine, after a course of about 800 km/500 mi. The *Pripet marshes* near Pinsk were of strategic importance in both world wars.

prism in mathematics, a solid figure whose cross section is constant in planes drawn perpendicular to its axis. A cube, for example, is a rectangular prism with all faces (bases and sides) the same shape and size.

prism in optics, a triangular block of transparent material (plastic, glass, silica) commonly used to 'bend' a ray of light or split a beam into its spectral colours. Prisms are used as mirrors to define the optical path in binoculars, camera viewfinders, and periscopes. The dispersive property of prisms is used in the *spectroscope.

prison place of confinement for those convicted of contravening the laws of the state; most countries claim to aim also at rehabilitation. The average number of people in prison in the UK (1990) was 43,314 (about 97 people per 100,000 of the population) with almost 20% of these under the age of 21. About 22% were on *remand (awaiting trial or sentence). Because of overcrowding in prisons, almost 2,000 prisoners were held in police cells (1988). 55% of male prisoners and 34% of female prisoners were reconvicted within two years of being discharged from prison (1984). The US prison population (1988) was 800,000 (about 426 per 100,000 people). There were an estimated 10 million prisoners in Chinese prisons in 1991.

privacy the right of the individual to be free from secret surveillance (by scientific devices or other means) and from the disclosure to unauthorized persons of personal data, as accumulated in computer data banks. Always an issue complicated by considerations of state security, public welfare (in the case of criminal activity), and other factors, it has been rendered more complex by present-day technology.

privateer privately owned and armed ship commissioned by a state to attack enemy vessels. The crews of such ships were, in effect, legalized pirates; they were not paid but received a share of the spoils. Privateering existed from ancient times until the 19th century, when it was declared illegal by the Declaration of Paris 1856.

private limited company a registered company which has limited liability (the shareholders cannot lose more than their original shareholdings), and a minimum of two shareholders and a maximum of fifty. It cannot offer its shares or debentures to the public and their transfer is restricted.

privatization policy or process of selling or transferring state-owned or public assets and services (notably nationalized industries) to private investors. Privatization of services involves the government contracting private firms to supply services previously supplied by public authorities.

privet any evergreen shrub of the genus *Ligustrum* of the olive family Oleaceae, with dark green leaves, including the European common privet *L. vulgare*, with white flowers and black berries, naturalized in North America, and the native North American California privet *L. ovalifolium*, also known as hedge privet.

privilege in law, a special right or immunity in connection with legal proceedings. *Public-interest privilege* may be claimed by the government seeking to preserve the confidentiality of state documents. *Private privilege* can only attach to an individual by virtue of rank or office; for example, for members of Parliament in defence of defamation proceedings.

Privy Council council composed originally of the chief royal officials of the Norman kings in Britain; under the Tudors and early Stuarts it became the chief governing body. It was replaced from 1688 by the *cabinet, originally a committee of the council, and the council itself now retains only formal powers in issuing royal proclamations and orders-in-council. Cabinet ministers are automatically members, and it is presided over by the Lord President of the Council.

privy purse personal expenditure of the British sovereign, which derives from his/her own resources (as distinct from the *civil list, which now finances only expenses incurred in pursuance of official functions and duties). The office that deals with this expenditure is also known as the Privy Purse.

Privy Seal, Lord until 1884, the UK officer of state in charge of the royal seal to prevent its misuse. The honorary title is now held by a senior cabinet minister who has special nondepartmental duties.

Prix Goncourt French literary prize for fiction, given by the Académie Goncourt (founded by Edmond de *Goncourt 1903).

probability likelihood, or chance, that an event will occur, often expressed as odds, or in mathematics, numerically as a fraction or decimal. In general, the probability that n particular events will happen out of a total of m possible events is n/m. A certainty has a probability of 1; an impossibility has a probability of 0. Empirical probability is defined as the number of successful events divided by the total possible number of events.

probate formal proof of a will. In the UK, if a will's validity is unquestioned, it is proven in 'common form'; the executor, in the absence of other interested parties, obtains at a probate registry a grant upon his or her own oath. Otherwise, it must be proved in 'solemn form': its validity established at a probate court (in the Chancery Division of the High Court), with those concerned being made parties to the action.

probation in law, the placing of offenders under supervision of probation officers in the community, as an alternative to prison.

procedure in computing, a small part of a computer program that performs a specific task, such as clearing the screen or sorting a file. A *procedural language*, such as BASIC, is one in which the programmer describes a task in terms of how it is to be done, as opposed to a *declarative language*, such as PROLOG, in which it is described in terms of the required result. See *programming.

process control automatic computerized control of a manufacturing process, such as glassmaking. The computer receives *feedback information from sensors about the performance of the machines involved, and compares this with ideal performance data stored in its control program. It then outputs instructions to adjust automatically the machines' settings.

Proconsul prehistoric ape skull found on Rusinga Island in Lake Victoria (Nyanza), E Africa, by Mary *Leakey. It is believed to be 20 million years old.

procurator fiscal officer of a Scottish sheriff's court who (combining the role of public prosecutor and coroner) inquires into suspicious deaths and carries out the preliminary questioning of witnesses to crime.

productivity in economics, the output produced by a given quantity of labour, usually measured as output per person employed in the firm, industry, sector, or economy concerned. Productivity is determined by the quality and quantity of the fixed *capital used by labour, and the effort of the workers concerned. The level of productivity is a major determinant of cost-efficiency: higher productivity tends to reduce average costs of production.

profit-sharing scheme in a company, arrangements for some or all the employees to receive cash or shares on a basis generally related to the performance of the company.

Profumo John (Dennis) 1915– . British Conservative politician, secretary of state for war from 1960 to June 1963, when he resigned on the disclosure of his involvement with Christine Keeler, mistress also of a Soviet naval attaché. In 1982 Profumo became administrator of the social and educational settlement Toynbee Hall in London.

progesterone *steroid hormone that occurs in vertebrates. In mammals, it regulates the menstrual cycle and pregnancy. Progesterone is secreted by the corpus luteum (the ruptured Graafian follicle of a discharged ovum).

prognosis in medicine, prediction of the course or outcome of illness or injury, particularly the chance of recovery.

program in computing, a set of instructions that controls the operation of a computer. There are two main kinds: applications programs, which carry out tasks for the benefit of the user – for example, word processing; and *systems programs, which control the internal workings

of the computer. A *utility program is a systems program that carries out specific tasks for the user. Programs can be written in any of a number of *programming languages but are always translated into machine code before they can be executed by the computer.

program counter in computing, an alternative name for sequence control register.

program loop a part of a computer program that is repeated several times. The loop may be repeated a fixed number of times (*counter-controlled loop*) or until a certain condition is satisfied (*condition-controlled loop*). For example, a counter-controlled loop might be used to repeat an input routine until exactly ten numbers have been input; a condition-controlled loop might be used to repeat an input routine until the data terminator 'XXX' is entered.

programme music music that tells a story, depicts a scene or painting, or illustrates a literary or philosophical idea, such as Richard Strauss's *Don Juan*.

programming writing instructions in a programming language for the control of a computer. *Applications programming* is for end-user programs, such as accounts programs or word-processing packages. *Systems programming* is for operating systems and the like, which are concerned more with the internal workings of the computer.

programming language in computing, a special notation in which instructions for controlling a computer are written. Programming languages are designed to be easy for people to write and read, but must be capable of being mechanically translated (by a *compiler or an *interpreter) into the *machine code that the computer can execute.

progression sequence of numbers each formed by a specific relationship to its predecessor. An *arithmetic progression* has numbers that increase or decrease by a common sum or difference (for example, 2, 4, 6, 8); a *geometric progression* has numbers each bearing a fixed ratio to its predecessor (for example, 3, 6, 12, 24); and a *harmonic progression* has numbers whose *reciprocals are in arithmetical progression, for example 1, $\frac{1}{2}$, $\frac{1}{3}$, $\frac{1}{4}$.

progressive education teaching methods that take as their starting point children's own aptitudes and interests, and encourage them to follow their own investigations and lines of inquiry.

Progressivism in US history, the name of both a reform movement and a political party, active in the two decades before World War I. Mainly middle-class and urban-based, Progressives secured legislation at national, state, and local levels to improve the democratic system, working conditions, and welfare provision.

Prohibition in US history, the period 1920–33 when alcohol was illegal, representing the culmination of a long campaign by church and women's organizations, temperance societies, and the Anti-Saloon League. This led to bootlegging (the illegal distribution of liquor, often illicitly distilled), to the financial advantage of organized crime, and public opinion insisted on repeal 1933.

projection see *map projection.

project management technique for matching available resources (time, money, and people) against business project aims (early completion date, final cost, and so on). The technique originated in the shipbuilding industry during World War I, when Henry Laurence Gantt developed what is now known as the **Gantt chart**, a bar chart deploying use of resources over time.

projector any apparatus that projects a picture on to a screen. In a **slide projector**, a lamp shines a light through the photographic slide or transparency, and a projection *lens throws an enlarged image of the slide onto the screen. A **film projector** has similar optics, but incorporates a mechanism that holds the film still while light is transmitted through each frame (picture). A shutter covers the film when it moves between frames.

prokaryote in biology, an organism whose cells lack organelles (specialized segregated structures such as nuclei, mitochondria, and chloroplasts). Prokaryote DNA is not arranged in chromosomes but forms a coiled structure called a **nucleoid**. The prokaryotes comprise only the **bacteria** and **cyanobacteria** (see *blue-green algae); all other organisms are eukaryotes.

Prokhorov Aleksandr 1916– . Russian physicist whose fundamental work on microwaves in 1955 led to the construction of the first practical *maser (the microwave equivalent of the laser) by Charles Townes, for which they shared the 1964 Nobel Prize for Physics.

Prokofiev Sergey (Sergeyevich) 1891–1953. Soviet composer. His music includes operas such as *The Love for Three Oranges* 1921; ballets for Sergei *Diaghilev, including *Romeo and Juliet* 1935; seven symphonies including the *Classical Symphony* 1916–17; music for films; piano and violin concertos; songs and cantatas (for example, that composed for the 30th anniversary of the October Revolution); and *Peter and the Wolf* 1936.

prolapse displacement of an organ due to the effects of strain in weakening the supporting tissues. The term is most often used with regard to the rectum (due to chronic bowel problems) or the uterus (following several pregnancies).

proletariat in Marxist theory, those classes in society that possess no property, and therefore depend on the sale of their labour or expertise (as opposed to the capitalists or bourgeoisie, who own the means of production, and the petty bourgeoisie, or working small-property owners). They are usually divided into the industrial, agricultural, and intellectual proletariat.

PROM (acronym for **programmable read-only memory**) in computing, a memory device in the form of an integrated circuit (chip) that can be programmed after manufacture to hold information permanently. PROM chips are empty of information when manufactured, unlike ROM (read-only memory) chips, which have information built into them. Other memory devices are *EPROM (erasable programmable read-only memory) and *RAM (random-access memory).

promenade concert originally a concert in which the audience walked about, now in the UK the name of any one of an annual BBC series (the Proms) at the Royal Albert Hall, London, at which part of the audience stands. They were originated by English conductor Henry Wood 1895.

Prometheus in Greek mythology, a *Titan who stole fire from heaven for the human race. In revenge, Zeus had him chained to a rock where an eagle came each day to feast on his liver, which grew back each night, until he was rescued by the hero *Heracles.

promethium radioactive, metallic element of the *lanthanide series, symbol Pm, atomic number 61, relative atomic mass 145. It occurs in nature only in minute amounts, produced as a fission product/by-product of uranium in *pitchblende and other uranium ores; for a long time it was considered not to occur in nature. The longest-lived isotope has a half-life of slightly more than 20 years.

prominence bright cloud of gas projecting from the Sun into space 100,000 km/60,000 mi or more. **Quiescent prominences** last for months, and are held in place by magnetic fields in the Sun's corona. **Surge prominences** shoot gas into space at speeds of 1,000 kps/600 mps. **Loop prominences** are gases falling back to the Sun's surface after a *solar flare.

pronghorn ruminant mammal *Antilocapra americana* constituting the family Antilocapridae, native to the western USA. It is not a true antelope. It is light brown and about 1 m/3 ft high. It sheds its horns annually and can reach speeds of 100 kph/60 mph. The loss of prairies to agriculture, combined with excessive hunting, has brought this unique animal close to extinction.

pronoun in grammar, a part of speech that is used in place of a noun, usually to save repetition of the noun (for example 'The people arrived around nine o'clock. *They* behaved as though we were expecting *them*').

pronunciation the way in which words are rendered into human speech sounds; either a language as a whole ('French pronunciation') or a particular word or name ('what is the pronunciation of *allophony*?'). The pronunciation of languages forms the academic subject of *phonetics.

proof spirit numerical scale used to indicate the alcohol content of an alcoholic drink. Proof spirit (or 100% proof spirit) acquired its name from a solution of alcohol in water which, when used to moisten gunpowder, contained just enough alcohol to permit it to burn.

propaganda systematic spreading (propagation) of information or disinformation, usually to promote a religious or political doctrine with the intention of instilling particular attitudes or responses. Examples of the use of propaganda are the racial doctrines put forth by Nazism in World War II, and some of the ideas and strategies propagated by the USA and the USSR during the *Cold War (1945–90).

propane C_3H_8 gaseous hydrocarbon of the *alkane series, found in petroleum and used as fuel.

propanol or **propyl alcohol** third member of the homologous series of *alcohols. Propanol is usually a mixture of two isomeric compounds (see *isomer): propan-1-ol ($CH_3CH_2CH_2OH$) and propan-2-ol ($CH_3CHOHCH_3$). Both are colourless liquids that can be mixed with water and are used in perfumery.

propanone CH_3COCH_3 (common name **acetone**) colourless flammable liquid used extensively as a solvent, as in nail-varnish remover. It boils at 56.5°C/133.7°F, mixes with water in all proportions, and has a characteristic odour.

propellant substance burned in a rocket for propulsion. Two propellants are used: oxidizer and fuel are stored in separate tanks and pumped independently into the combustion chamber. Liquid oxygen (oxidizer) and liquid hydrogen (fuel) are common propellants, used, for example, in the space-shuttle main engines. The explosive charge that propels a projectile from a gun is also called a propellant.

propeller screwlike device used to propel some ships and aeroplanes. A propeller has a number of curved blades that describe a helical path as they rotate with the hub, and accelerate fluid (liquid or gas) backwards during rotation. Reaction to this backward movement of fluid sets up a propulsive thrust forwards. The marine screw propeller was developed by Francis Pettit Smith in the UK and Swedish-born John Ericson in the USA and was first used 1839.

proper motion gradual change in the position of a star that results from its motion in orbit around our galaxy, the Milky Way. Proper motions are slight and undetectable to the naked eye, but can be accurately measured on telescopic photographs taken many years apart. Barnard's Star is the star with the largest proper motion, 10.3 arc seconds per year.

Propertius Sextus c. 47–15 BC. Roman elegiac poet, a member of Maecenas' circle, who wrote of his love for his mistress 'Cynthia'.

property the right to control the use of a thing (such as land, a building, a work of art, or a computer program). In English law, a distinction is made between *real property*, which involves a degree of geographical fixity, and *personal property*, which does not. Property is never absolute, since any society places limits on an individual's property (such as the right to transfer that property to another). Different societies have held widely varying interpretations of the nature of property and the extent of the rights of the owner of that property.

prophet person thought to speak from divine inspiration or one who foretells the future. In the Bible, the chief prophets were Elijah, Amos, Hosea, and Isaiah. In Islam, *Muhammad is believed to be the last and greatest of a long line of prophets beginning with Adam and including Moses and Jesus.

prophylaxis any measure taken to prevent disease, including exercise and *vaccination. Prophylactic (preventive) medicine is an aspect of public-health provision that is receiving increasing attention.

proportion two variable quantities x and y are proportional if, for all values of x, $y = kx$, where k is a constant. This means that if x increases, y increases in a linear fashion.

proportional representation (PR) electoral system in which distribution of party seats corresponds to their proportion of the total votes cast, and minority votes are not wasted (as opposed to a simple majority, or 'first past the post', system). Forms include: *party list* (PLS) or additional member system (AMS). As recommended by the Hansard Society 1976 for introduction in the UK, three-quarters of the members would be elected in single-member constituencies on the traditional majority-vote system, and the remaining seats be allocated according to the overall number of votes cast for each party (a variant of this is used in Germany); *single transferable vote* (STV), in which candidates are numbered in order of preference by the voter, and any votes surplus to the minimum required for a candidate to win are transferred to second preferences, as are second-preference votes from the successive candidates at the bottom of the poll until the required number of elected candidates is achieved (this is in use in the Republic of Ireland).

propyl alcohol common name for *propanol.

propylene common name for propene.

prose spoken or written language without metrical regularity; in literature, prose corresponds more closely to the patterns of everyday speech than *poetry. In modern literature, the distinction between verse and prose is not always clear cut.

Prosecution Service, Crown body established by the Prosecution of Offences Act 1985, responsible for prosecuting all criminal offences in England and Wales. It is headed by the Director of Public Prosecutions (DPP), and brings England and Wales in line with Scotland (see *procurator fiscal) in having a prosecution service independent of the police.

Proserpina Roman equivalent of *Persephone, goddess of the underworld.

Prost Alain 1955– . French motor-racing driver who was world champion 1985, 1986, 1989, and 1993, and the first French world drivers' champion. To the end of the 1993 season he had won 51 Grands Prix from 199 starts. He retired 1993.

prostaglandin any of a group of complex fatty acids that act as messenger substances between cells. Effects include stimulating the contraction of smooth muscle (for example, of the womb during birth), regulating the production of stomach acid, and modifying hormonal activity. In excess, prostaglandins may produce inflammatory disorders such as arthritis. Synthetic prostaglandins are used to induce labour in humans and domestic animals.

prostate gland gland surrounding and opening into the *urethra at the base of the *bladder in male mammals.

prosthesis replacement of a body part with an artificial substitute. Prostheses include artificial limbs, hearing aids, false teeth and eyes, and for the heart, a *pacemaker and plastic heart valves and blood vessels.

prostitution receipt of money for sexual acts. Society's attitude towards prostitution varies according to place and period. In some countries, tolerance is combined with licensing of brothels and health checks on the prostitutes (both male and female). In the UK it is legal to be a prostitute, but soliciting for customers publicly, keeping a brothel, living on 'immoral earnings', and 'procuring' (arranging to make someone into a prostitute) and kerb crawling (driving slowly seeking to entice someone into the car for sexual purposes) are illegal. In the US, laws vary from state to state, with Nevada having legalized prostitution.

protactinium (Latin *proto* 'before' + actinium) silver-grey, radioactive, metallic element of the *actinide series, symbol Pa, atomic number 91, relative atomic mass 231.036. It occurs in nature in very small quantities, in *pitchblende and other uranium ores. It has 14 known isotopes; the longest-lived, Pa-231, has a half-life of 32,480 years.

protectionism in economics, the imposition of heavy duties or import quotas by a government as a means of discouraging the import of foreign goods likely to compete with domestic products. Price controls, quota systems, and the reduction of surpluses are among the measures taken for agricultural products in the European Community (see *agriculture). The opposite practice is *free trade.

protectorate formerly in international law, a small state under the direct or indirect control of a larger one. The 20th-century equivalent was a *trust territory. In English history the rule of Oliver and Richard *Cromwell 1653–59 is referred to as *the Protectorate*.

protein complex, biologically important substance composed of amino acids joined by *peptide bonds. Other types of bond, such as sulphur–sulphur bonds, hydrogen bonds, and cation bridges between acid sites, are responsible for creating the protein's characteristic three-dimensional structure, which may be fibrous, globular, or pleated.

Proterozoic period of geological time, 2.5 billion to 570 million years ago, the second division of the Precambrian era. It is defined as the time of simple life, since many rocks dating from this eon show traces of biological activity, and some contain the fossils of bacteria and algae.

Protestantism one of the main divisions of Christianity, which emerged from Roman Catholicism at the *Reformation. The chief denominations are the Anglican Communion (Episcopalian in the USA), Baptists, Lutherans, Methodists, Pentecostals, and Presbyterians, with a total membership of about 300 million.

Proteus in Greek mythology, an old man, the warden of the sea beasts of the sea god Poseidon, who possessed the gift of prophecy and could transform himself into any form he chose to evade questioning.

prothallus short-lived gametophyte of many ferns and other *pteridophytes (such as horsetails or clubmosses). It bears either the male or female sex organs, or both. Typically it is a small, green, flattened structure that is anchored in the soil by several *rhizoids (slender, hairlike structures, acting as roots) and needs damp conditions to survive. The reproductive organs are borne on the lower surface close to the soil. See also *alternation of generations.

protist in biology, a single-celled organism which has a eukaryotic cell, but which is not member of the plant, fungal, or animal kingdoms. The main protists are *protozoa.

protocol in computing, an agreed set of standards for the transfer of data between different devices. They cover transmission speed, format of data, and the signals required to synchronize the transfer. See also *interface.

proton (Greek 'first') in physics, a positively charged subatomic particle, a constituent of the nucleus of all atoms. It belongs to the baryon subclass of the *hadrons. A proton is extremely long-lived, with a lifespan of at least 10^{32} years. It carries a unit positive charge equal to the negative charge of an *electron. Its mass is about 1,836 times that of an electron, or 1.67×10^{-24} g. The number of protons in the atom of an element is equal to the atomic number of that element.

proton number alternative name for *atomic number.

protoplasm contents of a living cell. Strictly speaking it includes all the discrete structures (organelles) in a cell, but it is often used simply to mean the jellylike material in which these float. The contents of a cell outside the nucleus are called *cytoplasm.

prototype in technology, any of the first few machines of a new design. Prototypes are tested for performance, reliability, economy, and safety; then the main design can be modified before full-scale production begins.

protozoa group of single-celled organisms without rigid cell walls. Some, such as amoeba, ingest other cells, but most are *saprotrophs or parasites. The group is polyphyletic (containing organisms which have different evolutionary origins).

protractor instrument used to measure a flat *angle.

Proudhon Pierre Joseph 1809–1865. French anarchist, born in Besançon. He sat in the Constituent Assembly of 1848, was imprisoned for three years, and had to go into exile in Brussels. He published *Qu'est-ce que la propriété/What is Property?* 1840 and *Philosophie de la misère/Philosophy of Poverty* 1846; the former contains the dictum 'property is theft'.

Proust Marcel 1871–1922. French novelist and critic. His immense autobiographical work *A la Recherche du temps perdu/Remembrance of Things Past* 1913–27, consisting of a series of novels, is the expression of his childhood memories coaxed from his subconscious; it is also a precise reflection of life in France at the end of the 19th century.

Provençal language member of the Romance branch of the Indo-European language family, spoken in and around Provence in SE France. It is now regarded as a dialect or patois.

Provence-Alpes-Côte d'Azur region of SE France, comprising the *départements* of Alpes-de-Haute-Provence, Hautes-Alpes, Alpes-Maritimes, Bouches-du-Rhône, Var, and Vaucluse; area 31,400 sq km/12,120 sq mi; capital Marseille; population (1986) 4,059,000. The *Côte d'Azur*, on the Mediterranean, is a tourist centre. Provence was an independent kingdom in the 10th century, and the area still has its own language, Provençal.

proviso in law, a clause in a statute, deed, or

some other legal document introducing a qualification or condition to some other provision, frequently the one immediately preceding the proviso itself.

Proxima Centauri the closest star to the Sun, 4.2 light years away. It is a faint *red dwarf, visible only with a telescope, and is a member of the Alpha Centauri triple-star system.

proxy in law, a person authorized to stand in another's place; also the document conferring this right. The term usually refers to voting at meetings, but marriages by proxy are possible.

Prud'hon Pierre 1758–1823. French Romantic painter. He became drawing instructor and court painter to the emperor Napoleon's wives.

Prussia N German state 1618–1945 on the Baltic coast. It was an independent kingdom until 1867, when it became, under Otto von *Bismarck, the military power of the North German Confederation and part of the German Empire 1871 under the Prussian king Wilhelm I. West Prussia became part of Poland under the Treaty of *Versailles, and East Prussia was largely incorporated into the USSR after 1945.

prussic acid former name for *hydrocyanic acid.

Prut river that rises in the Carpathian Mountains of SW Ukraine, and flows 900 km/565 mi to meet the Danube at Reni. For part of its course it follows the eastern frontier of Romania.

psalm sacred poem or song of praise. The Book of Psalms in the Old Testament is divided into five books containing 150 psalms. They are traditionally ascribed to David, the second king of Israel.

PSBR abbreviation for ***public-sector borrowing requirement**.

pseudocarp fruitlike structure that incorporates tissue that is not derived from the ovary wall. The additional tissues may be derived from floral parts such as the *receptacle and *calyx. For example, the coloured, fleshy part of a strawberry develops from the receptacle and the true fruits are small *achenes – the 'pips' embedded in its outer surface. Rose hips are a type of pseudocarp that consists of a hollow, fleshy receptacle containing a number of achenes within. Different types of pseudocarp include pineapples, figs, apples, and pears.

pseudocopulation attempted copulation by a male insect with a flower. It results in *pollination of the flower and is common in the orchid family, where the flowers of many species resemble a particular species of female bee. When a male bee attempts to mate with a flower, the pollinia (groups of pollen grains) stick to its body. They are transferred to the stigma of another flower when the insect attempts copulation again.

pseudomorph mineral that has replaced another *in situ* and has retained the external crystal shape of the original mineral.

PSFD abbreviation for *public sector financial deficit*; see *public-sector borrowing requirement.

psi in parapsychology, a hypothetical faculty common to humans and other animals said to be responsible for extra-sensory perception (ESP) and telekinesis.

Psilocybe genus of mushroom with hallucinogenic properties, including the Mexican sacred mushroom *P. mexicana*, which contains compounds with effects similar to LSD (lysergic acid diethylamide, a hallucinogen). A related species *P. semilanceata* is found in N Europe.

psoriasis chronic, recurring skin disease characterized by raised, red, scaly patches, usually on the scalp, back, arms, and/or legs. Tar preparations, steroid creams, and ultraviolet light are used to treat it, and sometimes it disappears spontaneously. Psoriasis may be accompanied by a form of arthritis (inflammation of the joints).

Psyche late Greek personification of the soul as a winged girl or young woman. The goddess Aphrodite was so jealous of Psyche's beauty that she ordered her son Eros, the god of love, to make Psyche fall in love with the worst of men. Instead, he fell in love with her himself.

psychedelic rock or *acid rock* pop music that usually involves advanced electronic equipment for both light and sound. The free-form improvisations and light shows that appeared about 1966, attempting to suggest or improve on mind-altering drug experiences, had by the 1980s evolved into stadium performances with lasers and other special effects.

psychiatry branch of medicine dealing with the diagnosis and treatment of mental disorder, normally divided into the areas of *neurotic conditions* including anxiety, depression, and hysteria and *psychotic* disorders such as schizophrenia. Psychiatric treatment consists of analysis, drugs, or electroconvulsive therapy.

psychoanalysis theory and treatment method for neuroses, developed by Sigmund *Freud. The main treatment method involves the free association of ideas, and their interpretation by patient and analyst. It is typically prolonged and expensive and its effectiveness has been disputed.

psychology systematic study of human and animal behaviour. The first psychology laboratory was founded 1879 by Wilhelm *Wundt at Leipzig, Germany. The subject includes diverse areas of study and application, among them the roles of instinct, heredity, environment, and culture; the processes of sensation, perception, learning and memory; the bases of motivation and emotion; and the functioning of thought, intelligence, and language. Significant psychologists have included Gustav Fechner (1801–1887) founder of psychophysics; Wolfgang Köhler (1887–1967), one of the *gestalt or 'whole' psychologists; Sigmund Freud and his associates Carl Jung, Alfred Adler, and Hermann Rorschach (1884–1922); William James, Jean Piaget; Carl Rogers; Hans Eysenck; J B Watson, and B F Skinner.

psychometrics measurement of mental processes. This includes intelligence and aptitude testing to help in job selection and in the clinical assessment of cognitive deficiencies resulting from brain damage.

psychopathy personality disorder characterized by chronic antisocial behaviour (violating the rights of others, often violently) and an absence of feelings of guilt about the behaviour.

psychosis or *psychotic disorder* general term for a serious mental disorder where the indi-

PSYCHOLOGY: CHRONOLOGY

1890	William James published the first comprehensive psychology text, *Principles of Psychology*.
1895	Freud's first book on psychoanalysis was published.
1896	The first clinical psychology clinic was founded by Witner at the University of Pennsylvania.
1897	Wilhelm Wundt founded the first psychological laboratory in Leipzig.
1903	Ivan Pavlov reported his early study on conditioned reflexes in animals.
1905	Alfred Binet and Théodore Simon developed the first effective intelligence test.
1908	A first textbook of social psychology was published by William McDougall.
1913	John B Watson published *Behaviorism*, which laid the basis for the school and doctrine of that name.
1926	Jean Piaget presented his first book on child development.
1947	Hans Eysenck published *Dimensions of Personality*, a large-scale study of neuroticism and extra-version.
1953	B F Skinner's *Science of Human Behaviour*, a text of operant conditioning, was published.
1957	Noam Chomsky's *Syntactic Structures*, which stimulated the development of psycholinguistics, the study of language processes, was published.
1963	Milgram's studies of compliance with authority indicated conditions under which individuals behave cruelly to others when instructed to do so.
1967	Neisser's *Cognitive Psychology* marked renewed interest in the study of cognition after years in which behaviourism had been dominant.
1972	Newell and Simon simulated human problem-solving abilities by computer; an example of artificial intelligence.
1989	Jeffrey Masson attacked the fundamental principles of Freudian analytic psychotherapy in his book *Against Therapy*.

vidual commonly loses contact with reality and may experience hallucinations (seeing or hearing things that do not exist) or delusions (fixed false beliefs). For example, in a paranoid psychosis, an individual may believe that others are plotting against him or her. A major type of psychosis is *schizophrenia (which may be biochemically induced).

psychosomatic a physical symptom or disease, thought to arise from emotional or mental factors.

psychosurgery operation to achieve some mental effect. For example, *lobotomy* is the separation of the white fibres in the prefrontal lobe of the brain, as a means of relieving a deep state of anxiety.

psychotherapy treatment approaches for psychological problems involving talking rather than surgery or drugs. Examples include *cognitive therapy and *psychoanalysis.

psychotic disorder another name for *psychosis*.

ptarmigan any of a genus (Lagopus) of hardy, northern ground-dwelling birds (family Phasianidae, which also includes *grouse), with feathered legs and feet.

pteridophyte simple type of *vascular plant. The pteridophytes comprise four classes: the Psilosida, including the most primitive vascular plants, found mainly in the tropics; the Lycopsida, including the club mosses; the Sphenopsida, including the horsetails; and the Pteropsida, including the ferns. They do not produce seeds.

pterodactyl genus of *pterosaur.

pterosaur extinct flying reptile of the order Pterosauria, existing in the Mesozoic age. They ranged from starling size to a 12 m/40 ft wingspan. Some had horns on their heads that, when in flight, made a whistling to roaring sound.

PTFE abbreviation for *polytetrafluoroethene*.

Ptolemy (Claudius Ptolemaeus) *c.* AD 100–AD 170. Egyptian astronomer and geographer who worked in Alexandria. His *Almagest* developed the theory that Earth is the centre of the universe, with the Sun, Moon, and stars revolving around it. In 1543 the Polish astronomer *Copernicus proposed an alternative to the **Ptolemaic system**. Ptolemy's *Geography* was a standard source of information until the 16th century.

Ptolemy dynasty of kings of Macedonian origin who ruled Egypt over a period of 300 years; they included:

Ptolemy I *c.* 367–283 BC. Ruler of Egypt from 323 BC, king from 304. He was one of *Alexander the Great's generals, and possibly his half-brother (and married his lover, Thaïs). He established the library in Alexandria.

Ptolemy XIII 63–47 BC. Joint ruler of Egypt with his sister-wife Cleopatra; she put him to death.

puberty stage in human development when the individual becomes sexually mature. It may occur from the age of ten upwards. The sexual organs take on their adult form and pubic hair grows. In girls, menstruation begins, and the breasts develop; in boys, the voice breaks and becomes deeper, and facial hair develops.

pubes lowest part of the front of the human trunk, the region where the external generative organs are situated. The underlying bony structure, the pubic arch, is formed by the union in the midline of the two pubic bones, which are the front portions of the hip bones. In women this is more prominent than in men, to allow more room for the passage of the child's head at birth, and it carries a pad of fat and connective tissue, the *mons veneris* (mountain of Venus), for its protection.

Public Against Violence (Slovak *Verejnosť Proti Násil'u*) the Slovak half of the Czechoslovak democratic movement, counterpart of the Czech organization *Civic Forum.

public corporation company structure that is similar in organization to a public limited company but with no shareholder rights. Such corporations are established to carry out state-owned activities, but are financially independent of the state and are run by a board. The first public corporation to be formed in the UK was the Central Electricity Board in the 1920s.

public inquiry in English law, a legal invest-igation where witnesses are called and evidence is produced in a similar fashion to a court of law. Inquiries may be held as part of legal procedure, or into a matter of public concern.

public lending right (PLR) method of paying a royalty to authors when books are borrowed from libraries, similar to a royalty on perform-ance of a play or piece of music. Payment to the copyright holder for such borrowings was introduced in Australia 1974 and in the UK 1984.

public limited company (plc) a registered company in which shares and debentures may be offered to the public. It must have a minimum of seven shareholders and there is no upper limit. The company's financial records must be avail-able for any member of the public to scrutinize, and the company's name must carry the words 'public limited company' or initials 'plc'. A public company can raise enormous financial resources to fuel its development and expansion by inviting the public to buy shares.

Public Order Act UK act of Parliament 1986 that abolished the common-law offences of riot, rout, unlawful assembly, and affray and created a new expanded range of statutory offences: riot, violent disorder, affray, threatening behaviour, and disorderly conduct. These are all arrestable offences that may be committed in both private and public places. Prosecution for riot requires the consent of the Director of Public Prosecutions.

public school in England and Wales, a pres-tigious fee-paying independent school. In Scot-land, the USA, and many other English-speaking countries, a 'public' school is a state-maintained school, and independent schools are generally known as 'private' schools.

public-sector borrowing requirement (PSBR) amount of money needed by a govern-ment to cover any deficit in financing its own activities.

public spending expenditure by government, covering the military, health, education, infra-structure, development projects, and the cost of servicing overseas borrowing.

Puccini Giacomo (Antonio Domenico Michele Secondo Maria) 1858–1924. Italian opera com-poser whose music shows a strong gift for melody and dramatic effect and whose operas combine exotic plots with elements of *verismo* (realism). They include *Manon Lescaut* 1893, *La Bohème* 1896, *Tosca* 1900, *Madame Butterfly* 1904, and the unfinished *Turandot* 1926.

puddle clay clay, with sand or gravel, that has had water added and mixed thoroughly so that it becomes watertight. The term was coined 1762 by the canal builder James Brindley, although the use of such clay in dams goes back to Roman times.

Pudovkin Vsevolod Illationovich 1893–1953. Russian film director whose films include the silent *Mother* 1926, *The End of St Petersburg* 1927, and *Storm over Asia* 1928; and the sound films *Deserter* 1933 and *Suvorov* 1941.

Pueblo (Spanish 'village') generic name for the American Indians of SW North America known for their communal terraced villages of mud brick or stone. Surviving groups include the *Hopi.

Puerto Rico the Commonwealth of, Eastern-most island of the Greater Antilles, situated between the US Virgin Islands and the Domin-ican Republic
area 9,000 sq km/3,475 sq mi
capital San Juan
towns ports Mayagüez, Ponce
exports sugar, tobacco, rum, pineapples, tex-tiles, plastics, chemicals, processed foods
currency US dollar
population (1990) 3,522,000
language Spanish and English (official)
religion Roman Catholic
government under the constitution of 1952, similar to that of the USA, with a governor elected for four years, and a legislative assembly with a senate and house of representatives
history visited 1493 by Columbus; annexed by Spain 1509; ceded to the USA after the *Spanish-American War 1898; achieved commonwealth status with local self-government 1952.

Puerto Sandino major port on the Pacific W coast of Nicaragua, known as *Puerto Somoza* until 1979.

puff adder variety of *adder, a poisonous snake.

puffball globulous fruiting body of certain fungi (see *fungus) that cracks with maturity, releasing the enclosed spores in the form of a brown powder; for example, the common puffball *Lyco-perdon perlatum*.

puffer fish fish of the family Tetraodontidae. As a means of defence it inflates its body with air or water until it becomes spherical and the skin spines become erect. Puffer fish are mainly found in warm waters, where they feed on mol-luscs, crustaceans, and coral.

puffin any of various sea birds of the genus *Fratercula* of the *auk family, found in the N Atlantic and Pacific. The puffin is about 35 cm/ 14 in long, with a white face and front, red legs, and a large deep bill, very brightly coloured in summer. Having short wings and webbed feet, puffins are poor fliers but excellent swimmers. They nest in rock crevices, or make burrows, and lay a single egg.

pug breed of small dog with short wrinkled face, chunky body, and tail curled over the hip. It weighs 6–8 kg/13–18 lb.

Puget Sound inlet of the Pacific Ocean on the W coast of Washington State, USA.

Pugin Augustus Welby Northmore 1812–1852. English architect, collaborator with Charles *Barry in the detailed design of the Houses of Parliament. He did much to revive Gothic archi-tecture in England.

Puglia (English *Apulia*) region of Italy, the southeastern 'heel'; area 19,300 sq km/ 7,450 sq mi; capital Bari; population (1990) 4,081,500. Products include wheat, grapes, almonds, olives, and vegetables. The main indus-trial centre is Taranto.

P'u-i (or *Pu-Yi*) Henry 1906–1967. Last emperor of China (as Hsuan Tung) from 1908 until his deposition 1912; he was restored for a week

1917. After his deposition he chose to be called Henry. He was president 1932–34 and emperor 1934–45 of the Japanese puppet state of Manchukuo (see *Manchuria).

pūjā worship, in Hinduism, Buddhism, and Jainism.

Pulitzer Joseph 1847–1911. Hungarian-born US newspaper publisher. He acquired *The World* 1883 in New York City and, as a publisher, his format set the style for the modern newspaper. After his death, funds provided in his will established 1912 the school of journalism at Columbia University and the annual Pulitzer Prizes in journalism, literature, and music (from 1917).

pulley simple machine consisting of a fixed, grooved wheel, sometimes in a block, around which a rope or chain can be run. A simple pulley serves only to change the direction of the applied effort (as in a simple hoist for raising loads). The use of more than one pulley results in a mechanical advantage, so that a given effort can raise a heavier load.

Pullman George 1831–1901. US engineer who developed the Pullman railway car. In an attempt to improve the standard of comfort of rail travel, he built his first Pioneer Sleeping Car 1863. He formed the Pullman Palace Car Company 1867 and in 1881 the town of Pullman, Illinois, was built for his workers.

pulmonary pertaining to the *lungs.

pulsar celestial source that emits pulses of energy at regular intervals, ranging from a few seconds to a few thousandths of a second. Pulsars were discovered 1967, and are thought to be rapidly rotating *neutron stars, which flash at radio and other wavelengths as they spin. Over 400 radio pulsars are known in our Galaxy, although a million or so may exist.

pulse crop such as peas and beans. Pulses are grown primarily for their seeds, which provide a concentrated source of vegetable protein, and make a vital contribution to human diets in poor countries where meat is scarce, and among vegetarians. Soya beans are the major temperate protein crop in the West; most are used for oil production or for animal feed. In Asia, most are processed into soya milk and beancurd. Groundnuts dominate pulse production in the tropical world and are generally consumed as human food.

pulse impulse transmitted by the heartbeat throughout the arterial systems of vertebrates. When the heart muscle contracts, it forces blood into the *aorta (the chief artery). Because the arteries are elastic, the sudden rise of pressure causes a throb or sudden swelling through them. The actual flow of the blood is about 60 cm/2 ft a second in humans. The pulse rate is generally about 70 per minute. The pulse can be felt where an artery is near the surface, for example in the wrist or the neck.

pulse-code modulation (PCM) method of converting a continuous electrical signal (such as that produced by a microphone) into a series of pulses (a digital signal) for transmission along a telephone line.

puma also called *cougar* or *mountain lion* large wild cat *Felis concolor* found in North and South America. Tawny-coated, it is 1.5 m/4.5 ft long with a 1 m/3 ft tail. Cougars live alone, with each male occupying a distinct territory; they eat deer, rodents, and cattle. They have been hunted nearly to extinction.

pumice light volcanic rock produced by the frothing action of expanding gases during the solidification of lava. It has the texture of a hard sponge and is used as an abrasive.

pump any device for moving liquids and gases, or compressing gases. Some pumps, such as the traditional *lift pump* used to raise water from wells, work by a reciprocating (up-and-down) action. Movement of a piston in a cylinder with a one-way valve creates a partial vacuum in the cylinder, thereby sucking water into it.

pumped storage hydroelectric plant that uses surplus electricity to pump water back into a high-level reservoir. In normal working conditions the water flows from this reservoir through the *turbines to generate power for feeding into the grid. At times of low power demand electricity is taken from the grid to turn the turbines into pumps that then pump the water back again. This ensures that there is always a maximum 'head' of water in the reservoir to give the maximum output when required.

pumpkin gourd *Cucurbita pepo* of the family Cucurbitaceae. The large, spherical fruit has a thick, orange rind, pulpy flesh, and many seeds.

pun figure of speech, a play on words, or double meaning that is technically known as *paronomasia* (Greek 'adapted meaning'). Double meaning can be accidental, often resulting from homonymy, or the multiple meaning of words puns, however, are deliberate, intended as jokes or as clever and compact remarks.

punctuated equilibrium model evolutionary theory developed by Niles Eldridge and Stephen Jay Gould 1972 to explain discontinuities in the fossil record. It claims that periods of rapid change alternate with periods of relative stability (stasis), and that the appearance of new lineages is a separate process from the gradual evolution of adaptive changes within a species.

punctuation system of conventional signs (punctuation marks) and spaces by means of which written and printed language is organized in order to be as readable, clear, and logical as possible.

Pune formerly *Poona* city in Maharashtra, India; population (1985) 1,685,000. Products include chemicals, rice, sugar, cotton, paper, and jewellery.

Punic (Latin *Punicus* 'a Phoenician') relating to *Carthage, ancient city in N Africa founded by the Phoenicians.

Punic Wars three wars between *Rome and *Carthage:
First 264–241 BC, resulted in the defeat of the Carthaginians under *Hamilcar Barca and the cession of Sicily to Rome
Second 218–201 BC, Hannibal invaded Italy, defeated the Romans under *Fabius Maximus at Cannae, but was finally defeated by *Scipio Africanus Major at Zama (now in Algeria)
Third 149–146 BC, ended in the destruction of Carthage, and its possessions becoming the Roman province of Africa.

Punjab (Sanskrit 'five rivers': the Indus tributar

ies Jhelum, Chenab, Ravi, Beas, and Sutlej) former state of British India, now divided between India and Pakistan. Punjab was annexed by Britain 1849, after the Sikh Wars 1845–46 and 1848–49, and formed into a province with its capital at Lahore. Under the British, W Punjab was extensively irrigated, and land was granted to Indians who had served in the British army.

Punjab state of NW India
area 50,400 sq km/19,454 sq mi
capital Chandigarh
towns Amritsar
population (1991) 20,190,800
language Punjabi
religions 60% Sikh, 30% Hindu; there is friction between the two groups.

Punjab state of NE Pakistan
area 205,344 sq km/79,263 sq mi
capital Lahore
population (1981) 47,292,000
language Punjabi, Urdu
religion Muslim.

Punjabi member of the majority ethnic group living in the Punjab. Approximately 37 million live in the Pakistan half of Punjab, while another 14 million live on the Indian side of the border. In addition to Sikhs, there are Rajputs in Punjab, some of whom have adopted Islam. The Punjabi language belongs to the Indo-Iranian branch of the Indo-European family. It is considered by some to be a variety of Hindi, by others to be a distinct language.

punk movement of disaffected youth of the late 1970s, manifesting itself in fashions and music designed to shock or intimidate. *Punk rock* began in the UK and stressed aggressive performance within a three-chord, three-minute format, as exemplified by the Sex Pistols.

pupa nonfeeding, largely immobile stage of some insect life cycles, in which larval tissues are broken down, and adult tissues and structures are formed.

puppet figure manipulated on a small stage, usually by an unseen operator. The earliest known puppets are from 10th-century BC China. The types include *finger* or *glove puppets* (such as Punch); *string marionettes* (which reached a high artistic level in ancient Burma and Sri Lanka and in Italian princely courts from the 16th to 18th centuries, and for which the composer Franz Joseph Haydn wrote his operetta *Dido* 1778); *shadow silhouettes* (operated by rods and seen on a lit screen, as in Java); and *bunraku* (devised in Osaka, Japan), in which three or four black-clad operators on stage may combine to work each puppet about 1 m/3 ft high.

Purana one of a number of sacred Hindu writings dealing with ancient times and events, and dating from the 4th century AD onwards. The 18 main texts include the *Vishnu Purāna* and *Bhāgavata*, which encourage devotion to Vishnu, above all in his incarnation as Krishna.

Purcell Henry 1659–1695. English Baroque composer. His work can be highly expressive, for example, the opera *Dido and Aeneas* 1689 and music for Dryden's *King Arthur* 1691 and for *The Fairy Queen* 1692. He wrote more than 500 works, ranging from secular operas and incidental music for plays to cantatas and church music.

purchasing-power parity system for comparing standards of living between different countries. Comparing the gross domestic product of different countries involves first converting them to a common currency (usually US dollars or pounds sterling), a conversion which is subject to large fluctuations with variations in exchange rates. Purchasing-power parity aims to overcome this by measuring how much money in the currency of those countries is required to buy a comparable range of goods and services.

purdah (Persian and Hindu 'curtain') seclusion of women practised by some Islamic and Hindu peoples. It had begun to disappear with the adoption of Western culture, but the fundamentalism of the 1980s revived it; for example, the wearing of the chador (an all-enveloping black mantle) in Iran.

Pure Land Buddhism dominant form of Buddhism in China and Japan. It emphasizes faith in and love of Buddha, in particular Amitābha (Amida in Japan, Amituofo in China), the ideal 'Buddha of boundless light', who has vowed that all believers who call on his name will be reborn in his Pure Land, or Western Paradise. This also applies to women, who had been debarred from attaining salvation through monastic life. There are over 16 million Pure Land Buddhists in Japan.

purgatory in Roman Catholic belief, a purificatory state or place where the souls of those who have died in a state of grace can expiate their venial sins, with a limited amount of suffering.

purge removal (for example, from a political party) of suspected opponents or persons regarded as undesirable (often by violent means). In 1934 the Nazis carried out a purge of their party and a number of party leaders were executed for an alleged plot against Adolf Hitler. During the 1930s purges were conducted in the USSR under Joseph Stalin, carried out by the secret police against political opponents, Communist Party members, minorities, civil servants, and large sections of the armed forces' officer corps. Some 10 million people were executed or deported to labour camps from 1934 to 1938.

Purim Jewish festival celebrated in Feb or March (the 14th of Adar in the Jewish calendar), commemorating Esther, who saved the Jews from destruction in 473 BC during the Persian occupation.

Puritan from 1564, a member of the Church of England who wished to eliminate Roman Catholic survivals in church ritual, or substitute a presbyterian for an episcopal form of church government. The term also covers the separatists who withdrew from the church altogether. The Puritans were identified with the parliamentary opposition under James I and Charles I, and after the Restoration were driven from the church, and more usually known as *Dissenters or *Nonconformists.

purpura condition marked by purplish patches on the skin or mucous membranes due to localized spontaneous bleeding. It may be harmless, as sometimes with the elderly, or linked with disease, allergy, or drug reactions.

pus yellowish liquid that forms in the body as a result of bacterial attack; it includes white blood cells (leucocytes) 'killed in battle' with the bacteria, plasma, and broken-down tissue cells. An enclosed collection of pus is called an abscess.

Pusan or **Busan** chief industrial port (textiles, rubber, salt, fishing) of South Korea; population (1985) 3,797,600. It was invaded by the Japanese 1592 and opened to foreign trade 1883.

Pushkin Aleksandr 1799–1837. Russian poet and writer. His works include the novel in verse *Eugene Onegin* 1823–31 and the tragic drama *Boris Godunov* 1825. Pushkin's range was wide, and his willingness to experiment freed later Russian writers from many of the archaic conventions of the literature of his time.

Pushtu another name for the *Pashto language of Afghanistan and N Pakistan.

Pu-Yi alternative transliteration of the name of the last Chinese emperor, Henry *P'u-i.

PWR abbreviation for ***pressurized water reactor***, a type of nuclear reactor.

pyelitis inflammation of the renal pelvis, the central part of the kidney where urine accumulates before discharge. It is caused by bacterial infection and is more common in women than in men.

Pygmalion in Greek legend, a king of Cyprus who fell in love with an ivory statue he had carved. When Aphrodite brought it to life as a woman, Galatea, he married her.

Pygmy (sometimes ***Negrillo***) member of any of several groups of small-statured, dark-skinned peoples of the rainforests of equatorial Africa. They were probably the aboriginal inhabitants of the region, before the arrival of farming peoples from elsewhere. They live nomadically in small groups, as hunter-gatherers; they also trade with other, settled people in the area.

pylon steel lattice tower that supports high-tension electrical cables. In ancient Egyptian architecture, a pylon is one of a pair of inward-sloping towers that flank an entrance.

Pym John 1584–1643. English Parliamentarian, largely responsible for the *Petition of Right 1628. As leader of the Puritan opposition in the *Long Parliament from 1640, he moved the impeachment of Charles I's advisers the Earl of Strafford and William Laud, drew up the *Grand Remonstrance, and was the chief of five members of Parliament Charles I wanted arrested 1642. The five hid themselves and then emerged triumphant when the king left London.

Pynaker Adam 1622–1673. Dutch landscape painter. It is thought that Pynaker spent some three years in Italy. His landscape style reflects the Italianate influence in the way it combines cloudless skies with the effect of clear, golden light on a foreground of trees and foliage. *Barges on a River* (Hermitage, St Petersburg) is his masterpiece but *Landscape with Sportsmen and Game* (Dulwich Picture Gallery), is a more typical work.

Pynchon Thomas 1937– . US novelist who created a bizarre, labyrinthine world in his books, the first of which was *V* 1963. *Gravity's Rainbow* 1973 represents a major achievement in 20th-century literature, with its fantastic imagery and esoteric language, drawn from mathematics and science.

Pyongyang capital and industrial city (coal,

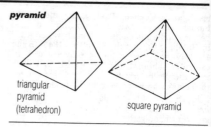

pyramid

triangular pyramid (tetrahedron)

square pyramid

iron, steel, textiles, chemicals) of North Korea; population (1984) 2,640,000.

pyramid in geometry, a solid figure with triangular side-faces meeting at a common vertex (point) and with a *polygon as its base. The volume V of a pyramid is given by $V = \frac{1}{3}Bh$, where B is the area of the base and h is the perpendicular height.

pyramid four-sided building with triangular sides. They were used in ancient Egypt as a royal tomb; for example, the Great Pyramid of Khufu/Cheops at Gîza, near Cairo, 230 m/755 ft square and 147 m/481 ft high. In Babylon and Assyria broadly stepped pyramids (ziggurats) were used as the base for a shrine to a god: the Tower of *Babel was probably one of these.

Pyrenees (French ***Pyrénées***; Spanish ***Pirineos***) mountain range in SW Europe between France and Spain; length about 435 km/270 mi; highest peak Aneto (French Néthon) 3,404 m/11,172 ft. *Andorra is entirely within the range. Hydroelectric power has encouraged industrial development in the foothills of the mountains.

pyrethrum popular name for some flowers of the genus *Chrysanthemum*, family Compositae. The ornamental species *C. coccineum*, and hybrids derived from it, are commonly grown in gardens. Pyrethrum powder, made from the dried flower heads of some species, is a powerful contact pesticide for aphids and mosquitoes.

pyridine C_5H_5N a heterocyclic compound (see *cyclic compounds). It is a liquid with a sickly smell that occurs in coal tar. It is soluble in water, acts as a strong *base, and is used as a solvent, mainly in the manufacture of plastics.

pyridoxine or ***vitamin B6*** $C_8H_{11}NO_3$ member of the *vitamin B complex. There is no clearly identifiable disease associated with deficiency but its absence from the diet can give rise to malfunction of the central nervous system and general skin disorders. Good sources are liver, meat, milk, and cereal grains. Related compounds may also show vitamin B6 activity.

pyrite common iron ore, iron sulphide FeS_2; also called ***fool's gold*** because of its yellow metallic lustre. Pyrite has a hardness of 6–6.5 on the Mohs' scale. It is used in the production of sulphuric acid.

pyrometer instrument used for measuring high temperatures.

pyroxene any one of a group of minerals, silicates of calcium, iron, and magnesium with a general formula X, YSi_2O_6, found in igneous and metamorphic rocks. The internal structure is based on single chains of silicon and oxygen.

Diopside (X = Ca, Y = Mg) and augite (X = Ca, Y = Mg,Fe,Al) are common pyroxenes.

Pyrrho c. 360–c. 270 BC. Greek philosopher, founder of *Scepticism, who maintained that since certainty was impossible, peace of mind lay in renouncing all claims to knowledge.

Pyrrhus c. 318–272 BC. King of *Epirus, Greece, from 307, who invaded Italy 280, as an ally of the Tarentines against Rome. He twice defeated the Romans but with such heavy losses that a **Pyrrhic victory** has come to mean a victory not worth winning. He returned to Greece 275 after his defeat at Beneventum, and was killed in a riot in Argos.

Pythagoras c. 580–500 BC. Greek mathematician and philosopher who formulated Pythagoras' theorem.

Pythagoras' theorem in geometry, a theorem stating that in a right-angled triangle, the area of the square on the hypotenuse (the longest side) is equal to the sum of the areas of the squares drawn on the other two sides. If the hypotenuse is h units long and the lengths of the other sides are a and b, then $h^2 = a^2 + b^2$.

python any constricting snake of the Old World subfamily Pythoninae of the family Boidae, which also includes *boas and the *anaconda. Pythons are found in the tropics of Africa, Asia, and Australia. Unlike boas, they lay eggs rather than produce living young. Some species are small, but the reticulated python *Python reticulatus* of SE Asia can grow to 10 m/33 ft.

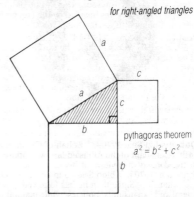

for right-angled triangles

pythagoras theorem
$$a^2 = b^2 + c^2$$

Pythagoras *Pythagoras' theorem for right-angled triangles is likely to have been known long before the time of Pythagoras.*

pyx (Latin *pyxis* 'small box') in the Roman Catholic Church, the container used for the wafers of the sacrament.

Qaboos bin Said 1940– . Sultan of Oman, the 14th descendant of the Albusaid family. Opposed to the conservative views of his father, he overthrew him 1970 in a bloodless coup and assumed the sultanship. Since then he has followed more liberal and expansionist policies, while maintaining his country's position of international nonalignment.

Qaddafi alternative form of *Khaddhafi, Libyan leader.

Qadisiya, Battle of battle fought in S Iraq 637. A Muslim Arab force defeated a larger Zoroastrian Persian army and ended the *Sassanian Empire. The defeat is still resented in Iran, where Muslim Arab nationalism threatens to break up the Iranian state.

qat shrub *Catha edulis* of the staff-tree family Celastraceae. The leaves are chewed as a mild narcotic in some Arab countries. Its use was banned in Somalia 1983.

Qatar State of (*Dawlat Qatar*)
area 11,400 sq km/4,402 sq mi
capital and chief port Doha
town Dukhan, centre of oil production
physical mostly flat desert with salt flats in S
head of state and government Sheik Khalifa bin Hamad al-Thani from 1972
political system absolute monarchy
exports oil, natural gas, petrochemicals, fertilizers, iron, steel
currency riyal
population (1993 est) 510,000 (half in Doha; Arab 40%, Indian 18%, Pakistani 18%); growth rate 3.7% p.a.
languages Arabic (official), English
religion Sunni Muslim 95%
GNP $15.870 per head (1990)
chronology
1916 Qatar became a British protectorate.
1970 Constitution adopted, confirming the emirate as an absolute monarchy.
1971 Independence achieved from Britain.
1972 Emir Sheik Ahmad replaced in bloodless coup by his cousin, Crown Prince Sheik Khalifa.

QC abbreviation for *Queen's Counsel*.

QED abbreviation for *quod erat demonstrandum* (Latin 'which was to be proved'), added at the end of a geometry proof.

Qin dynasty Chinese imperial dynasty 221–206 BC. *Shi Huangdi was its most renowned emperor. The Great Wall of China was built at this time.

Qinghai or *Tsinghai* province of NW China

area 721,000 sq km/278,306 sq mi
capital Xining
products oil, livestock, medical products
population (1990) 4,457,000; minorities include 900,000 Tibetans (mostly nomadic herders); Tibetan nationalists regard the province as being under colonial rule.

Qom or *Qum* holy city of Shi'ite Muslims, in central Iran, 145 km/90 mi S of Tehran; population (1986) 551,000. The Islamic academy of Madresseh Faizieh 1920 became the headquarters of Ayatollah *Khomeini.

quadrathon sports event in which the competitors must swim two miles, walk 30 miles, cycle 100 miles, and run 26.2 miles (a marathon) within 22 hours.

quadratic equation in mathematics, a polynomial equation of second degree (that is, an equation containing as its highest power the square of a variable, such as x^2). The general formula of such equations is $ax^2 + bx + c = 0$, in which a, b, and c are real numbers, and only the coefficient a cannot equal 0. In *coordinate geometry, a quadratic function represents a *parabola.

quadrilateral a *plane figure with four straight sides. The following are all quadrilaterals, each with distinguishing properties: *square* with four equal angles, four axes of symmetry; *rectangle* with four equal angles, two axes of symmetry; *rhombus* with four equal sides, two axes of symmetry; *parallelogram* with two pairs of parallel sides, rotational symmetry; and *trapezium* one pair of parallel sides.

Quadruple Alliance in European history, three military alliances of four nations:
the Quadruple Alliance 1718 Austria, Britain, France, and the United Provinces (Netherlands) joined forces to prevent Spain from annexing Sardinia and Sicily;
the Quadruple Alliance 1813 Austria, Britain, Prussia, and Russia allied to defeat the French emperor Napoleon; renewed 1815 and 1818. See Congress of *Vienna.
the Quadruple Alliance 1834 Britain, France, Portugal, and Spain guaranteed the constitutional monarchies of Spain and Portugal against rebels in the Carlist War.

quaestor Roman magistrate whose duties were mainly concerned with public finances. The quaestors originated as assistants to the consuls. Both urban and military quaestors existed, the latter being attached to the commanding generals in the provinces.

quail any of several genera of small grounddwelling birds of the family Phasianidae, which also includes grouse, pheasants, bobwhites, and prairie chickens.

Quaker popular name, originally derogatory, for a member of the Society of *Friends.

qualitative analysis in chemistry, a procedure for determining the identity of the component(s) of a single substance or mixture. A series of simple reactions and tests can be carried out on a compound to determine the elements present.

quango (acronym for *quasi-autonomous nongovernmental organization*) any administrative body that is nominally independent but relies on government funding; for example, the Equal Opportunities Commission (1975). Many quangos (such as the Location of Offices Bureau) were abolished by the Thatcher government 1979–90.

Quant Mary 1934– . British fashion designer who popularized the miniskirt in the UK. Her Chelsea boutique, Bazaar, revolutionized women's clothing and make-up in the 'swinging London' of the 1960s. In the 1970s she extended into cosmetics and textile design.

quantitative analysis in chemistry, a procedure for determining the precise amount of a known component present in a single substance or mixture. A known amount of the substance is subjected to particular procedures. *Gravimetric analysis* determines the mass of each constituent present; *volumetric analysis* determines the concentration of a solution by *titration against a solution of known concentration.

quant. suff. abbreviation for *quantum sufficit* (Latin 'as much as suffices').

quantum chromodynamics (QCD) in physics, a theory describing the interactions of quarks, the elementary particles that make up all hadrons (subatomic particles such as protons and neutrons). In quantum chromodynamics, quarks are considered to interact by exchanging particles called gluons, which carry the strong nuclear force, and whose role is to 'glue' quarks together. The mathematics involved in the theory is complex, and although a number of successful predictions have been made, as yet the theory does not compare in accuracy with *quantum electrodynamics, upon which it is modelled. See *elementary particles and *forces, fundamental.

quantum electrodynamics (QED) in physics, a theory describing the interaction of charged subatomic particles within electric and magnetic fields. It combines quantum theory and relativity, and considers charged particles to interact by the exchange of photons. QED is remarkable for the accuracy of its predictions – for example, it has been used to calculate the value of some physical quantities to an accuracy of ten decimal places, a feat equivalent to calculating the distance between New York and Los Angeles to within the thickness of a hair. The theory was developed by US physicists Richard Feynman and Julian Schwinger, and by Japanese physicist Sin-Itiro Tomonaga 1948.

quantum number in physics, one of a set of four numbers that uniquely characterize an *electron and its state in an *atom. The *principal quantum number* n defines the electron's main energy level. The *orbital quantum number* l relates to its angular momentum. The *magnetic quantum number* m describes the energies of electrons in a magnetic field. The *spin quantum number* m_s gives the spin direction of the electron.

quantum theory or *quantum mechanics* in physics, the theory that *energy does not have a continuous range of values, but is, instead, absorbed or radiated discontinuously, in multiples of definite, indivisible units called quanta. Just as earlier theory showed how light, generally seen as a wave motion, could also in some ways be seen as composed of discrete particles (*photons), quantum theory shows how atomic

particles such as electrons may also be seen as having wavelike properties. Quantum theory is the basis of particle physics, modern theoretical chemistry, and the solid-state physics that describes the behaviour of the silicon chips used in computers.

quarantine (from French *quarantaine* '40 days') any period for which people, animals, plants, or vessels may be detained in isolation when suspected of carrying contagious disease.

quark in physics, the *elementary particle that is the fundamental constituent of all hadrons (baryons, such as neutrons and protons, and mesons). There are six types, or 'flavours': up, down, top, bottom, strange, and charm, each of which has three varieties, or 'colours': red, yellow, and blue (visual colour is not meant, although the analogy is useful in many ways). To each quark there is an antiparticle, called an antiquark.

quart imperial liquid or dry measure, equal to two pints or 1.136 litres. In the USA, a liquid quart is equal to 0.946 litre, while a dry quart is equal to 1.101 litres.

quarter day in the financial year, any of the four dates on which such payments as ground rents become due: in England 25 March (Lady Day), 24 June (Midsummer Day), 29 Sept (Michaelmas), and 25 Dec (Christmas Day).

quartermaster in a military unit, usually a battalion, the officer in charge of its administration. In combat the quartermaster is responsible for supplying the unit with rations, fuel, and ammunition.

quartz crystalline form of *silica SiO_2, one of the most abundant minerals of the Earth's crust (12% by volume). Quartz occurs in many different kinds of rock, including sandstone and granite. It ranks 7 on the Mohs' scale of hardness and is resistant to chemical or mechanical breakdown. Quartzes vary according to the size and purity of their crystals. Crystals of pure quartz are coarse, colourless, and transparent, and this form is usually called rock crystal. Impure coloured varieties, often used as gemstones, include *agate, citrine quartz, and *amethyst. Quartz is used in ornamental work and industry, where its reaction to electricity makes it valuable in electronic instruments (see *piezoelectric effect). Quartz can also be made synthetically.

quartzite *metamorphic rock consisting of pure quartz sandstone that has recrystallized under increasing heat and pressure.

quasar (from *quasi*-stell*ar* object or QSO) one of the most distant extragalactic objects known, discovered 1964–65. Quasars appear starlike, but each emits more energy than 100 giant galaxies. They are thought to be at the centre of galaxies, their brilliance emanating from the stars and gas falling towards an immense *black hole at their nucleus.

quasi (Latin 'as if') apparently but not actually.

quassia any tropical American tree of the genus *Quassia*, family Simaroubaceae, with a bitter bark and wood. The heartwood of *Q. amara* is a source of quassiin, an infusion of which was formerly used as a tonic; it is now used in insecticides.

Quaternary period of geological time that

began about 1.64 million years ago and is still in process. It is divided into the *Pleistocene and *Holocene epochs.

Quatre Bras, Battle of battle fought 16 June 1815 during the Napoleonic Wars, in which the British commander Wellington defeated French forces under Marshal Ney. It is named after a hamlet in Brabant, Belgium, 32 km/20 mi SE of Brussels.

Quayle (J) Dan(forth) 1947– . US Republican politician, vice president from 1989–93. A congressman for Indiana 1977–81, he became a senator 1981. He is on the right of the party.

Quebec capital and industrial port (textiles, leather, timber, paper, printing, and publishing) of Québec province, on the St Lawrence River, Canada; population (1986) 165,000, metropolitan area 603,000.

Québec province of E Canada
area 1,540,700 sq km/594,710 sq mi
capital Quebec
towns Montreal, Laval, Sherbrooke, Verdun, Hull, Trois-Rivières
products iron, copper, gold, zinc, cereals, potatoes, paper, textiles, fish, maple syrup (70% of world's output)
population (1991) 6,811,800
language French (the only official language since 1974, although 17% speak English). Language laws 1989 prohibit the use of English on street signs
history known as New France 1534–1763; captured by the British and became province of Québec 1763–90, Lower Canada 1791–1846, Canada East 1846–67; one of the original provinces 1867. Nationalist feelings 1960s (despite existing safeguards for Québec's French-derived civil law, customs, religion, and language) were encouraged by French president de Gaulle's exclamation '*Vive le Québec libre/Long live free Québec*' on a visit to the province, and led to the foundation of the Parti Québecois by René Lévesque 1968. The Québec Liberation Front (FLQ) separatists had conducted a bombing campaign in the 1960s and fermented an uprising 1970; Parti Québecois won power 1976; a referendum on 'sovereignty-association' (separation) was defeated 1980. In 1982, when Canada severed its last legal ties with the UK, Québec opposed the new Constitution Act as denying the province's claim to an absolute veto over constitutional change. Robert Bourassa and Liberals returned to power 1985 and enacted restrictive English-language legislation. The right of veto was proposed for all provinces of Canada 1987, but the agreement failed to be ratified by its 1990 deadline and support for independence grew. The Parti Québecois was defeated by the Liberal Party 1989.

Quechua or *Quichua* or *Kechua* member of the largest group of South American Indians. The Quechua live in the Andean region. Their ancestors included the Inca, who established the Quechua language in the region. Quechua is the second official language of Peru and is widely spoken as a lingua franca in Ecuador, Bolivia, Columbia, Argentina, and Chile; it belongs to the Andean-Equatorial family.

Queen Anne style decorative art in England

1700–20, characterized by plain, simple lines mainly in silver and furniture.

Queen Maud Land region of Antarctica W of Enderby Land, claimed by Norway since 1939.

Queens mainly residential borough and county at the W end of Long Island, New York City USA; population (1980) 1,891,300.

Queensberry John Sholto Douglas, 8th Marquess of Queensberry 1844–1900. British patron of boxing. In 1867 he formulated the *Queensberry Rules*, which form the basis of today's boxing rules.

Queen's Counsel (QC) in England, a barrister appointed to senior rank by the Lord Chancellor. When the monarch is a king the term is *King's Counsel (KC)*. A QC wears a silk gown, and takes precedence over a junior member of the Bar.

Queensland state in NE Australia
area 1,727,200 sq km/666,699 sq mi
capital Brisbane
towns Townsville, Toowoomba, Cairns
products sugar, pineapples, beef, cotton, wool, tobacco, copper, gold, silver, lead, zinc, coal, nickel, bauxite, uranium, natural gas
population (1987) 2,650,000
history part of New South Wales until 1859 when it became self-governing. In 1989 the ruling National Party was defeated after 32 years in power and replaced by the Labor Party.

quenching *heat treatment used to harden metals. The metals are heated to a certain temperature and then quickly plunged into cold water or oil.

question mark punctuation mark (?) used to indicate enquiry or doubt. When indicating enquiry, it is placed at the end of a *direct question* ('Who is coming?') but never at the end of an *indirect question* ('He asked us who was coming'). When indicating doubt, it usually appears between brackets, to show that a writer or editor is puzzled or uncertain about quoted text.

quetzal long-tailed Central American bird *Pharomachus mocinno* of the *trogon family. The male is brightly coloured, with green, red, blue, and white feathers, and is about 1.3 m/4.3 ft long including tail. The female is smaller and lacks the tail and plumage.

Quetzalcoatl in pre-Columbian cultures of Central America, a feathered serpent god of air and water. In his human form, he was said to have been fair-skinned and bearded and to have reigned on Earth during a golden age. He disappeared across the eastern sea, with a promise to return; the Spanish conquistador Hernán *Cortés exploited the coincidence of description when he invaded. Ruins of Quetzalcoatl's temples survive in various ancient Mesoamerican ceremonial centres, including the one at Teotihuacán in Mexico. (See also *Aztec, *Mayan, and *Toltec civilizations).

Quezon City former capital of the Philippines 1948–76, NE part of metropolitan *Manila (the present capital), on Luzon Island; population (1990) 1,166,800. It was named after the Philippines' first president, Manuel Luis Quezon (1878–1944).

quicksilver former name for the element *mercury.

quid pro quo (Latin 'something for something') an exchange of one thing in return for another.

quietism a religious attitude, displayed periodically in the history of Christianity, consisting of passive contemplation and meditation to achieve union with God. The founder of modern quietism was the Spanish priest Molinos who published a *Guida Spirituale/Spiritual Guide* 1675.

quince small tree *Cydonia oblonga*, family Rosaceae, native to W Asia. The bitter, yellow, pear-shaped fruit is used in preserves. Flowering quinces, genus *Chaenomeles*, are cultivated for their flowers.

quinine antimalarial drug extracted from the bark of the cinchona tree. Peruvian Indians taught French missionaries how to use the bark in 1630, but quinine was not isolated until 1820. It is a bitter alkaloid $C_{20}H_{24}N_2O_2$.

Quinn Anthony 1915– . Mexican-born US actor, in films from 1935. Famous for the title role in *Zorba the Greek* 1964, he later played variations on this larger-than-life character. Other films include Fellini's *La Strada* 1954.

Quintilian (Marcus Fabius Quintilianus) *c.* AD 35–95. Roman rhetorician. He was born at Calgurris, Spain, taught rhetoric in Rome from AD 68, and composed the *Institutio Oratoria/ The Education of an Orator*, in which he advocated a simple and sincere style of public speaking.

Quirinal one of the seven hills on which ancient Rome was built. Its summit is occupied by a palace built 1574 as a summer residence for the pope and occupied 1870–1946 by the kings of Italy. The name Quirinal is derived from that of Quirinus, local god of the *Sabines.

Quisling Vidkun 1887–1945. Norwegian politician. Leader from 1933 of the Norwegian Fascist Party, he aided the Nazi invasion of Norway 1940 by delaying mobilization and urging non-resistance. He was made premier by Hitler 1942, and was arrested and shot as a traitor by the Norwegians 1945. His name became a generic term for a traitor who aids an occupying force.

Quito capital and industrial city (textiles, chemicals, leather, gold, silver) of Ecuador, about 3,000 m/9,850 ft above sea level; population (1986) 1,093,300. It was an ancient settlement, taken by the Incas about 1470 and by the Spanish 1534. It has a temperate climate all year round.

Qum alternative spelling of *Qom, city of Iran.

Qumran or *Khirbet Qumran* archaeological site in Jordan, excavated from 1951, in the foothills NW of the Dead Sea. Originally an Iron Age fort (6th century BC), it was occupied in the late 2nd century BC by a monastic community, the *Essenes, until the buildings were burned by Romans AD 68. The monastery library once contained the *Dead Sea Scrolls, which had been hidden in caves for safekeeping and were discovered 1947.

quorum minimum number of members required to be present for the proceedings of an assembly to be valid. The actual number of people required for a quorum may vary.

quota in international trade, a limitation on the quantities exported or imported. Restrictions may be imposed forcibly or voluntarily. The justification of quotas include protection of a home industry from an influx of cheap goods, prevention of a heavy outflow of goods (usually raw materials) because there are insufficient numbers to meet domestic demand, allowance for a new industry to develop before it is exposed to competition, or prevention of a decline in the world price of a particular commodity.

quo vadis? (Latin) where are you going?

qv abbreviation for *quod vide* (Latin 'which see'); indicates a cross-reference.

QwaQwa black homeland of South Africa that achieved self-governing status 1974; population (1985) 181,600.

raccoon *Raccoons are good climbers and spend much of their time in trees.*

RA abbreviation for **Royal Academy**, London, founded 1768.

Rabat capital of Morocco, industrial port (cotton textiles, carpets, leather goods) on the Atlantic coast, 177 km/110 mi W of Fez; population (1982) 519,000, Rabat-Salé 842,000. It is named after its original *ribat* or fortified monastery.

rabbi in Judaism, the chief religious leader of a synagogue or the spiritual leader (not a hereditary high priest) of a Jewish congregation; also, a scholar of Judaic law and ritual from the 1st century AD.

rabbit any of several genera of hopping mammals of the order Lagomorpha, which together with *hares constitute the family Leporidae. Rabbits differ from hares in bearing naked, helpless young and in occupying burrows.

Rabelais François 1495–1553. French satirist, monk, and physician. His name has become synonymous with bawdy humour. He was educated in the Renaissance humanist tradition and was the author of satirical allegories, including *La Vie inestimable de Gargantua/The Inestimable Life of Gargantua* 1535 and *Faits et dits héroïques du grand Pantagruel/Heroic Deeds and Sayings of the Great Pantagruel* 1533.

rabies or **hydrophobia** viral disease of the central nervous system that can afflict all warm-blooded creatures. It is almost invariably fatal once symptoms have developed. Its transmission to humans is generally by a bite from an infected animal.

Rabin Yitzhak 1922– . Israeli Labour politician, prime minister 1974–77 and from 1992. His policy of Palestinian self-government in the occupied territories contributed to the success of the centre-left party in the 1992 elections. In 1993 a historic peace agreement with the PLO led to a withdrawal of Israeli forces from Gaza and Jericho. He was awarded the 1994 Nobel Prize for Peace jointly with Shimon Peres and Yassir Arafat.

Rabuka Sitiveni 1948– . Fijian soldier and politician, head of state from 1992. When the 1987 elections in Fiji produced an Indian-dominated government, Rabuka staged two successive coups (the first short-lived). Within months of the second, he stepped down, allowing a civilian government to take over. In May 1992 he was nominated as the new Fijian premier.

raccoon any of several New World species of carnivorous mammals of the genus *Procyon*, in the family Procyonidae. The common raccoon *P. lotor* is about 60 cm/2 ft long, with a grey-brown body, a black-and-white ringed tail, and a black 'mask' around its eyes. The crab-eating raccoon *P. cancrivorus* of South America is slightly smaller and has shorter fur.

race in anthropology, term sometimes applied to a physically distinctive group of people, on the basis of their difference from other groups in skin colour, head shape, hair type, and physique. Formerly anthropologists divided the human race into three hypothetical racial groups: Caucasoid, Mongoloid, and Negroid. However, scientific studies have produced no proof of definite genetic racial divisions. Many anthropologists today, therefore, completely reject the concept of race, and social scientists tend to prefer the term ethnic group (see *ethnicity).

Rachmaninov Sergei (Vasilevich) 1873–1943. Russian composer, conductor, and pianist. After the 1917 Revolution he emigrated to the USA. His music is melodious and emotional and includes operas, such as *Francesca da Rimini* 1906, three symphonies, four piano concertos, piano pieces, and songs. Among his other works are the *Prelude in C-Sharp Minor* 1882 and *Rhapsody on a Theme of Paganini* 1934 for piano and orchestra.

Racine Jean 1639–1699. French dramatist. He was an exponent of the classical tragedy in French drama, taking his subjects from Greek mythology and observing the rules of classical Greek drama. Most of his tragedies have women in the title role, for example *Andromaque* 1667, *Iphigénie* 1674, and *Phèdre* 1677.

racism belief in, or set of implicit assumptions about, the superiority of one's own *race or ethnic group, often accompanied by prejudice against members of an ethnic group different from one's own. Racism may be used to justify *discrimination, verbal or physical abuse, or even genocide, as in Nazi Germany, or as practised by European settlers against American Indians in both North and South America.

rackets or **racquets** indoor game played on an enclosed court. Although first played in the Middle Ages, rackets developed in the 18th century and was played against the walls of London buildings.

rad unit of absorbed radiation dose, now replaced in the SI system by the *gray (one rad equals 0.01 gray), but still commonly used. It is defined as the dose when one kilogram of matter absorbs 0.01 joule of radiation energy (formerly, as the dose when one gram absorbs 100 ergs).

radar (acronym for *radio direction and ranging*) device for locating objects in space, direction finding, and navigation by means of transmitted and reflected high-frequency radio waves.

radar astronomy bouncing of radio waves off objects in the Solar System, with reception and analysis of the 'echoes'. Radar contact with the Moon was first made 1945 and with Venus 1961. The travel time for radio reflections allows the distances of objects to be determined accurately. Analysis of the reflected beam reveals the rotation period and allows the object's surface to be mapped. The rotation periods of Venus and Mercury were first determined by radar. Radar maps of Venus were obtained first by Earth-based radar and subsequently by orbiting space probes.

radian SI unit (symbol rad) of plane angles, an alternative unit to the *degree. It is the angle at the centre of a circle when the centre is joined to the two ends of an arc (part of the circumference) equal in length to the radius of the circle. There are 2π (approximately 6.284) radians in a full circle (360°).

radiation in physics, emission of radiant *energy as particles or waves – for example, heat, light, alpha particles, and beta particles (see *electromagnetic waves and *radioactivity). See also *atomic radiation.

radiation sickness sickness resulting from exposure to radiation, including X-rays, gamma rays, neutrons, and other nuclear radiation, as from weapons and fallout. Such radiation ionizes atoms in the body and causes nausea, vomiting, diarrhoea, and other symptoms. The body cells themselves may be damaged even by very small doses, causing *leukaemia; genetic changes may be induced in the germ plasm, causing infants to be born damaged or mutated.

radiation units units of measurement for radioactivity and radiation doses. Continued use of the units introduced earlier this century (the curie, rad, rem, and roentgen) has been approved while the derived SI units (becquerel, gray, sievert, and coulomb) become familiar. One curie equals 3.7×10^{-10} becquerels (activity); one rad equals 10^{-2} gray (absorbed dose); one rem equals 10^{-2} sievert (dose equivalent); one roentgen equals 2.58×10^{-4} coulomb/kg (exposure to ionizing radiation).

radical in chemistry, a group of atoms forming part of a molecule, which acts as a unit and takes part in chemical reactions without disintegration, yet often cannot exist alone; for example, the methyl radical – CH_3, or the carboxyl radical –COOH.

radical in politics, anyone with opinions more extreme than the main current of a country's major political party or parties. It is more often applied to those with left-wing opinions, although the radical right also exists.

Radical in Britain, supporter of parliamentary reform before the Reform Bill 1832. As a group the Radicals later became the progressive wing of the Liberal Party. During the 1860s (led by Cobden, Bright, and J S Mill) they campaigned for extension of the franchise, free trade, and *laissez faire, but after 1870, under the leadership of Joseph Chamberlain and Charles Dilke, they adopted a republican and semi-socialist pro-

gramme. With the growth of *socialism in the later 19th century, Radicalism ceased to exist as an organized movement.

radicle part of a plant embryo that develops into the primary root. Usually it emerges from the seed before the embryonic shoot, or plumule, its tip protected by a root cap, or calyptra, as it pushes through the soil. The radicle may form the basis of the entire root system, or it may be replaced by adventitious roots (positioned on the stem).

radio transmission and reception of radio waves. In radio transmission a microphone converts *sound waves (pressure variations in the air) into *electromagnetic waves that are then picked up by a receiving aerial and fed to a loudspeaker, which converts them back into sound waves.

radioactive decay process of continuous disintegration undergone by the nuclei of radioactive elements, such as radium and various isotopes of uranium and the transuranic elements. This changes the element's atomic number, thus transmuting one element into another, and is accompanied by the emission of radiation. Alpha and beta decay are the most common forms.

radioactive tracer any of various radioactive *isotopes used in labelled compounds; see *tracer.

radioactive waste any waste that emits radiation in excess of the background level. See *nuclear waste.

radioactivity spontaneous alteration of the nuclei of radioactive atoms, accompanied by the emission of radiation. It is the property exhibited by the radioactive *isotopes of stable elements and all isotopes of radioactive elements, and can be either natural or induced. See *radioactive decay.

radio astronomy study of radio waves emitted naturally by objects in space, by means of a *radio telescope. Radio emission comes from hot gases (**thermal radiation**); electrons spiralling in magnetic fields (**synchrotron radiation**); and specific wavelengths (**lines**) emitted by atoms and molecules in space, such as the 21-cm/8-in line emitted by hydrogen gas.

radio beacon radio transmitter in a fixed location, used in marine and aerial navigation. Ships and aircraft pinpoint their positions by reference to continuous signals given out by two or more beacons.

radiocarbon dating or **carbon dating** method of dating organic materials (for example, bone or wood), used in archaeology. Plants take up carbon dioxide gas from the atmosphere and incorporate it into their tissues, and some of that carbon dioxide contains the radioactive isotope of carbon, carbon-14. This decays at a known rate (half of it decays every 5,730 years); the time elapsed since the plant died can therefore be measured in a laboratory. Animals take carbon-14 into their bodies from eating plant tissues and their remains can be similarly dated. After 120,000 years so little carbon-14 is left that no measure is possible (see *half-life).

radio, cellular portable telephone system; see *cellular phone.

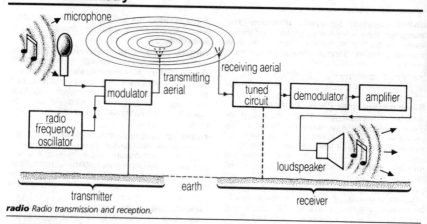

radio Radio transmission and reception.

radiochemistry chemical study of radioactive isotopes and their compounds (whether produced from naturally radioactive or irradiated materials) and their use in the study of other chemical processes.

radio frequencies and wavelengths classification of, see *electromagnetic waves.

radio galaxy galaxy that is a strong source of electromagnetic waves of radio wavelengths. All galaxies, including our own, emit some radio waves, but radio galaxies are up to a million times more powerful.

radiography branch of science concerned with the use of radiation (particularly *X-rays) to produce images on photographic film or fluorescent screens. X-rays penetrate matter according to its nature, density, and thickness. In doing so they can cast shadows on photographic film, producing a radiograph. Radiography is widely used in medicine for examining bones and tissues and in industry for examining solid materials; for example, to check welded seams in pipelines.

radioisotope (contraction of *radioactive *isotope*) in physics, a naturally occurring or synthetic radioactive form of an element. Most radioisotopes are made by bombarding a stable element with neutrons in the core of a nuclear reactor. The radiations given off by radioisotopes are easy to detect (hence their use as *tracers), can in some instances penetrate substantial thicknesses of materials, and have profound effects (such as genetic *mutation) on living matter. Although dangerous, radioisotopes are used in the fields of medicine, industry, agriculture, and research.

radioisotope scanning use of radioactive materials (radioisotopes or radionuclides) to pinpoint disease. It reveals the size and shape of the target organ and whether any part of it is failing to take up radioactive material, usually an indication of disease.

radiometric dating method of dating rock by assessing the amount of *radioactive decay of naturally occurring *isotopes. The dating of rocks may be based on the gradual decay of uranium into lead. The ratio of the amounts of 'parent' to 'daughter' isotopes in a sample gives a measure of the time it has been decaying, that is, of its age. Different elements and isotopes are used

depending on the isotopes present and the age of the rocks to be dated. Once-living matter can often be dated by *radiocarbon dating, employing the half-life of the isotope carbon-14, which is naturally present in organic tissue.

radio telescope instrument for detecting radio waves from the universe in *radio astronomy. Radio telescopes usually consist of a metal bowl that collects and focuses radio waves the way a concave mirror collects and focuses light waves. Radio telescopes are much larger than optical telescopes, because the wavelengths they are detecting are much longer than the wavelength of light. The largest single dish is 305 m/1,000 ft across, at Arecibo, Puerto Rico.

radiotherapy treatment of disease by *radiation from X-ray machines or radioactive sources. Radiation, which reduces the activity of dividing cells, is of special value for its effect on malignant tissues, certain nonmalignant tumours, and some diseases of the skin.

radio wave electromagnetic wave possessing a long wavelength (ranging from about 10^{-3} to 10^4 m) and a low frequency (from about 10^5 to 10^{11} Hz). Included in the radio-wave part of the spectrum are *microwaves, used for both communications and for cooking; ultra high and very high frequency waves, used for television and FM (*frequency modulation) radio communications; and short, medium, and long waves, used for AM (*amplitude modulation) radio communications. Radio waves that are used for communications have all been modulated (see *modulation) to carry information. Stars emit radio waves, which may be detected and studied using *radio telescopes.

radish annual herb *Raphanus sativus*, family Cruciferae. It is native to Europe and Asia, and cultivated for its fleshy, pungent, edible root, which is usually reddish but sometimes white or black.

radium (Latin *radius* 'ray') white, radioactive, metallic element, symbol Ra, atomic number 88, relative atomic mass 226.02. It is one of the *alkaline earth elements, found in nature in *pitchblende and other uranium ores. Of the 16 isotopes, the commonest, Ra-226, has a half-life of 1.622 years. The element was discovered and named in 1898 by Pierre and Marie *Curie.

radon colourless, odourless, gaseous, radioactive, nonmetallic element, symbol Rn, atomic number 86, relative atomic mass 222. It is grouped with the *inert gases and was formerly considered non-reactive, but is now known to form some compounds with fluorine. Of the 20 known isotopes, only three occur in nature; the longest half-life is 3.82 days.

RAF abbreviation for *Royal Air Force*.

Raffles Thomas Stamford 1781–1826. British colonial administrator, born in Jamaica. He served in the British East India Company, took part in the capture of Java from the Dutch in 1811, and while governor of Sumatra 1818–23 was responsible for the acquisition and founding of Singapore 1819.

rafflesia or *stinking corpse lily* any parasitic plant without stems of the genus *Rafflesia*, family Rafflesiaceae, native to Malaysia, Indonesia, and Thailand. There are 14 species, several of which are endangered by logging of the forests where they grow; the fruit is used locally for medicine. The largest flowers in the world are produced by *R. arnoldiana*. About 1 m/3 ft across, they exude a smell of rotting flesh, which attracts flies to pollinate them.

Rafsanjani Hojatoleslam Ali Akbar Hashemi 1934– . Iranian politician and cleric, president from 1989. When his former teacher Ayatollah *Khomeini returned after the revolution of 1979–80, Rafsanjani became the speaker of the Iranian parliament and, after Khomeini's death, state president and effective political leader.

raga in *Indian music, a scale of notes and style of ornament for music associated with a particular mood or time of day; the equivalent term in rhythm is *tala*. A choice of raga and tala forms the basis of improvised music; however, a written composition may also be based on (and called) a raga.

ragga type of *reggae music with a rhythmic, rapid-fire, semi-spoken vocal line. A macho swagger is a common element in the lyrics. Ragga developed around 1990 from 'toasting', itself an offshoot of reggae. Ragga performers include the Jamaicans Shabba Ranks, Anthony Red Rose, and Ninja Man. Performers and fans of ragga call themselves *ragamuffins*.

Raglan FitzRoy James Henry Somerset, 1st Baron Raglan 1788–1855. English general. He took part in the Peninsular War under Wellington, and lost his right arm at Waterloo. He commanded the British forces in the Crimean War from 1854. The *raglan sleeve*, cut right up to the neckline with no shoulder seam, is named after him.

Ragnarök in Norse mythology, the ultimate cataclysmic battle between gods and forces of evil, from which a new order will come. In Germanic mythology, this is known as *Götterdämmerung*.

ragtime syncopated music ('ragged time') in 2/4 rhythm, usually played on piano. It developed in the USA among black musicians in the late 19th century; it was influenced by folk tradition, minstrel shows, and marching bands, and was later incorporated into jazz. Scott *Joplin was a leading writer of ragtime pieces, called 'rags'.

ragwort any of several European perennial plants of the genus *Senecio*, family Compositae, usually with yellow-rayed flower heads; some are poisonous.

Rahman Tunku Abdul 1903–1990. Malaysian politician, first prime minister of independent Malaya 1957–63 and of Malaysia 1963–70.

rail any wading bird of the family Rallidae, including the rails proper (genus *Rallus*), coots, moorhens, and gallinules. Rails have dark plumage and wings, and long legs. They are 10–45 cm/4–18 in long.

Railtrack government-owned public limited company responsible for the commercial operation of the railway network in Britain. Ownership of the infrastructure was transferred from British Rail 1 April 1994 as a major step towards privatization of the railways.

railway method of transport in which trains convey passengers and goods along a twin rail track. Following the work of English steam pioneers such as Scottish engineer James *Watt, English engineer George *Stephenson built the first public steam railway, from Stockton to Darlington, England, in 1825. This heralded extensive railway building in Britain, continental Europe, and North America, providing a fast and economical means of transport and communication. After World War II, steam engines were replaced by electric and diesel engines. At the same time, the growth of road building, air services, and car ownership destroyed the supremacy of the railways.

rain form of *precipitation in which separate drops of water fall to the Earth's surface from clouds. The drops are formed by the accumulation of fine droplets that condense from water vapour in the air. The condensation is usually brought about by rising and subsequent cooling of air.

rainbow arch in the sky displaying the seven colours of the *spectrum in bands. It is formed by the refraction, reflection, and dispersion of the Sun's rays through rain or mist. Its cause was discovered by *Theodoric of Freiburg in the 14th century.

rainforest dense forest usually found on or near the *equator where the climate is hot and wet. Heavy rainfall results as the moist air brought by the converging tradewinds rises because of the heat. Over half the tropical rainforests are in Central and South America, the rest in SE Asia and Africa. They provide the bulk of the oxygen needed for plant and animal respiration. Tropical rainforest once covered 14% of the Earth's land surface, but are now being destroyed at an increasing rate as their valuable timber is harvested and the land cleared for agriculture, causing problems of *deforestation. Although by 1991 over 50% of the world's rainforest had been removed, they still comprise about 50% of all growing wood on the planet, and harbour at least 40% of the Earth's species (plants and animals).

Rainier III 1923– . Prince of Monaco from 1949. He was married to the US film actress Grace *Kelly.

Raj, the the period of British rule in India before independence in 1947.

Rajasthan state of NW India

area 342,200 sq km/132,089 sq mi
capital Jaipur
products oilseed, cotton, sugar, asbestos, copper, textiles, cement, glass
population (1991) 43,880,600
languages Rajasthani, Hindi
religions 90% Hindu, 3% Muslim
history formed 1948; enlarged 1956.

Rajneesh meditation meditation based on the teachings of the Indian Shree Rajneesh (born Chaadra Mohan Jain), established in the early 1970s. Until 1989 he called himself *Bhagwan* (Hindi 'God'). His followers, who number about half a million worldwide, regard themselves as Sannyas, or Hindu ascetics; they wear orange robes and carry a string of prayer beads. They are not expected to observe any specific prohibitions but to be guided by their instincts.

Raleigh or *Ralegh* Walter *c.* 1552–1618. English adventurer. He made colonizing and exploring voyages to North America 1584–87 and South America 1595, and naval attacks on Spanish ports. His aggressive actions against Spanish interests brought him into conflict with the pacific James I. He was imprisoned for treason 1603–16 and executed on his return from an unsuccessful final expedition to South America.

RAM (acronym for *random-access memory*) in computing, a memory device in the form of a collection of integrated circuits (chips), frequently used in microcomputers. Unlike *ROM (read-only memory) chips, RAM chips can be both read from and written to by the computer, but their contents are lost when the power is switched off. Microcomputers of the 1990s may have 10–20 megabytes of RAM.

Rama incarnation of *Vishnu, the supreme spirit of Hinduism. He is the hero of the epic poem the *Rāmāyana*, and he is regarded as an example of morality and virtue.

Ramadan in the Muslim *calendar, the ninth month of the year. Throughout Ramadan a strict fast is observed during the hours of daylight; Muslims are encouraged to read the whole Koran in commemoration of the Night of Power (which falls during the month) when, it is believed, Muhammad first received his revelations from the angel Gabriel.

Ramakrishna 1834–1886. Hindu sage, teacher, and mystic (one dedicated to achieving oneness with or a direct experience of God or some force beyond the normal world). Ramakrishna claimed that mystical experience was the ultimate aim of religions, and that all religions which led to this goal were equally valid.

Rāmāyana Sanskrit epic of *c.* 300 BC, in which Rama (an incarnation of the god Vishnu) and his friend Hanuman (the monkey chieftain) strive to recover Rama's wife, Sita, abducted by the demon king Ravana.

Rambert Marie. Adopted name of Cyvia Rambam 1888–1982. British ballet dancer and teacher born in Poland, who became a British citizen 1918. One of the major innovative and influential figures in modern ballet, she was with the Diaghilev ballet 1912–13, opened the Rambert School 1920, and in 1926 founded the *Ballet Rambert* which she directed. It became a modern dance company from 1966 with Norman Morrice as director, and was renamed the Rambert Dance Company 1987.

Rameau Jean-Philippe 1683–1764. French organist and composer. He wrote *Treatise on Harmony* 1722 and his varied works include keyboard and vocal music and many operas, such as *Castor and Pollux* 1737.

Rameses alternative spelling of *Ramses, name of kings of ancient Egypt.

ramjet simple jet engine (see under *jet propulsion) used in some guided missiles. It only comes into operation at high speeds. Air is then 'rammed' into the combustion chamber, into which fuel is sprayed and ignited.

Ramos Fidel (Eddie) 1928– . Philippine politician and president from 1992. He was Corazón *Aquino's staunchest ally as defence secretary, and was later nominated her successor.

Ramsay Allan 1713–1784. Scottish portrait painter. After studying in Edinburgh and Italy, he established himself as a portraitist in London and became painter to George III in 1760. His Portraits include *The Artist's Wife* about 1755 (National Gallery, Edinburgh).

Ramsay William 1852–1916. Scottish chemist who, with Lord Rayleigh, discovered argon 1894. In 1895 Ramsay produced helium and in 1898, in cooperation with Morris Travers, identified neon, krypton, and xenon. In 1903, with Frederick Soddy, he noted the transmutation of radium into helium, which led to the discovery of the density and relative atomic mass of radium. Nobel prize 1904.

Ramses or *Rameses* 11 kings of ancient Egypt, including:

Ramses II or *Rameses II* king of Egypt about 1304–1236 BC, the son of Seti I. He campaigned successfully against the Hittites, and built two rock temples at *Abu Simbel in Upper Egypt.

Ramses III or *Rameses III* king of Egypt about 1200–1168 BC. He won a naval victory over the Philistines and other Middle Eastern peoples, and asserted his control over Palestine.

random number one of a series of numbers having no detectable pattern. Random numbers are used in *computer simulation and *computer games. It is impossible for an ordinary computer to generate true random numbers, but various techniques are available for obtaining pseudo-random numbers – close enough to true randomness for most purposes.

rangefinder instrument for determining the range or distance of an object from the observer; used to focus a camera or to sight a gun accurately. A *rangefinder camera* has a rotating mirror or prism that alters the image seen through the viewfinder, and a secondary window. When the two images are brought together into one the lens is sharply focussed.

Rangoon former name (until 1989) of *Yangon, capital of Myanmar (Burma).

Ranjit Singh 1780–1839. Indian maharajah. He succeeded his father as a minor Sikh leader 1792, and created a Sikh army that conquered Kashmir and the Punjab. In alliance with the British he established himself as 'Lion of the Punjab', ruler of the strongest of the independent Indian states.

Rank J(oseph) Arthur 1888–1972. British film magnate. Having entered films in 1933 to promote the Methodist cause, by the mid-1940s he controlled, through the Rank Organization, half the British studios and more than 1,000 cinemas.

Ranke Leopold von 1795–1886. German historian whose quest for objectivity in history had great impact on the discipline. His attempts to explain 'how it really was' dominated both German and outside historical thought until 1914 and beyond. His *Weltgeschichte/World History* (nine volumes 1881–88) exemplified his ideas.

Ransome Arthur 1884–1967. English journalist (correspondent in Russia for the *Daily News* during World War I and the Revolution) and writer of adventure stories for children, such as *Swallows and Amazons* 1930 and *Peter Duck* 1932.

Rao P(amulaparti) V(enkata) Narasinha 1921– . Indian politician, see *Narasimah Rao.

Rapa Nui another name for *Easter Island, an island in the Pacific.

rape in botany, two plant species of the mustard family Cruciferae, *Brassica rapa* and *B. napus*, grown for their seeds, which yield a pungent edible oil. The common turnip is a variety of the former, and the swede turnip of the latter.

rape in law, sexual intercourse without the consent of the subject. Most cases of rape are of women by men. In Islamic law a rape accusation requires the support of four independent male witnesses.

Raphael Sanzio (Raffaello Sanzio) 1483–1520. Italian painter, one of the greatest of the High Renaissance, active in Perugia, Florence, and Rome (from 1508), where he painted frescoes in the Vatican and for secular patrons. His religious and mythological scenes are harmoniously composed; his portraits enhance the character of his sitters and express dignity. Many of his designs were engraved. Much of his later work was the product of his studio.

rap music rapid, rhythmic chant over a prerecorded repetitive backing track. Rap emerged in New York 1979 as part of the *hip-hop culture, although the macho, swaggering lyrics that initially predominated have roots in ritual boasts and insults. Different styles were flourishing by the 1990s, such as jazz rap, funk rap, and reggae rap.

rare-earth element alternative name for *lanthanide.

rare gas alternative name for *inert gas.

Rarotonga Treaty agreement that formally declares the South Pacific a nuclear-free zone. The treaty was signed 1987 by Australia, Fiji, Indonesia, New Zealand, and the USSR.

raspberry prickly cane plant of the genus *Rubus* of the Rosaceae family, native to Eurasia and North America, with white flowers followed by red fruits. These are eaten fresh and used for jam and wine.

Rasputin (Russian 'dissolute') Grigory Efimovich 1871–1916. Siberian Eastern Orthodox mystic who acquired influence over the tsarina *Alexandra, wife of *Nicholas II, and was able to make political and ecclesiastical appointments. His abuse of power and notorious debauchery (reputedly including the tsarina) led to his murder by a group of nobles.

Rastafarianism religion originating in the West Indies, based on the ideas of Marcus *Garvey, who called on black people to return to Africa and set up a black-governed country there. When Haile Selassie (**Ras Tafari**, 'Lion of Judah') was crowned emperor of Ethiopia 1930, this was seen as a fulfilment of prophecy and some Rastafarians acknowledged him as an incarnation of God (**Jah**), others as a prophet. The use of ganja (marijuana) is a sacrament. There are no churches. There were about one million Rastafarians by 1990.

raster graphics computer graphics that are stored in the computer memory by using a map to record data (such as colour and intensity) for every *pixel that makes up the image. When transformed (enlarged, rotated, stretched, and so on), raster graphics become ragged and suffer loss of picture resolution, unlike *vector graphics. Raster graphics are typically used for painting applications, which allow the user to create artwork on a computer screen much as if they were painting on paper or canvas.

rat any of numerous long-tailed *rodents (especially of the families Muridae and Cricetidae) larger than mice and usually with scaly, naked tails. The genus *Rattus* in the family Muridae includes the rats found in human housing.

rate of reaction the speed at which a chemical reaction proceeds. It is usually expressed in terms of the concentration (usually in *moles per litre) of a reactant consumed, or product formed, in unit time; so the units would be moles per litre per second (mol l^{-1} s^{-1}). The rate of a reaction may be affected by the concentration of the reactants, the temperature of the reactants, and the presence of a *catalyst. If the reaction is entirely in the gas state, the rate is affected by pressure, and, for solids, it is affected by the particle size.

rates in the UK, a *local government tax levied on industrial and commercial property, and until the introduction of the community charge (see *poll tax) 1989/90, also on residential property to pay for local amenities such as roads, footpaths, refuse collection and disposal, and community and welfare activities.

ratio measure of the relative size of two quantities or of two measurements (in similar units), expressed as a proportion. For example, the ratio of vowels to consonants in the alphabet is 5:21; the ratio of 500 m to 2 km is 500:2,000, or 1:4.

rationalism in theology, the belief that human reason rather than divine revelation is the correct means of ascertaining truth and regulating behaviour. In philosophy, rationalism takes the view that self-evident propositions deduced by reason are the sole basis of all knowledge (disregarding experience of the senses). It is usually contrasted with *empiricism, which argues that all knowledge must ultimately be derived from the senses.

rational number in mathematics, any number that can be expressed as an exact fraction (with a denominator not equal to 0), that is, as a/b where a and b are integers. For example, 2, $\frac{1}{4}$, $1\frac{5}{4}$, $-\frac{3}{4}$ are all rational numbers, whereas π

(which represents the constant 3.141592...) is not. Numbers such as π are called *irrational numbers.

ratite flightless bird with a breastbone without the keel to which flight muscles are attached. Examples are ostrich, rhea, emu, cassowary, and kiwi.

rat-tail or **grenadier** any fish of the family Macrouridae of deep-sea bony fishes. They have stout heads and bodies, and long tapering tails. They are common in deep waters on the continental slopes. Some species have a light-emitting organ in front of the anus.

rattlesnake any of various New World pit *vipers of the genera *Crotalus* and *Sistrurus* (the massasaugas and pygmy rattlers), distinguished by horny flat segments of the tail, which rattle when vibrated as a warning to attackers. They can grow to 2.5 m/8 ft long. The venom injected by some rattlesnakes can be fatal.

Rauschenberg Robert 1925– . US Pop artist, a creator of happenings (art in live performance) and incongruous multimedia works such as *Monogram* 1959 (Moderna Museet, Stockholm), a car tyre around the body of a stuffed goat daubed with paint. In the 1960s he returned to painting and used the silk-screen printing process to transfer images to canvas. He also made collages.

Ravel (Joseph) Maurice 1875–1937. French composer. His work is characterized by its sensuousness, unresolved dissonances, and 'tone colour'. Examples are the piano pieces *Pavane pour une infante défunte* 1899 and *Jeux d'eau* 1901, and the ballets *Daphnis et Chloë* 1912 and *Boléro* 1928.

raven any of several large *crows (genus *Corvus*). The common raven *C. corax* is about 60 cm/2 ft long, and has black, lustrous plumage. It is a scavenger, and is found only in the northern hemisphere.

Rawalpindi city in Punjab province, Pakistan, in the foothills of the Himalayas; population (1981) 928,400. Industries include oil refining, iron, chemicals, and furniture.

ray any of several orders (especially Ragiformes) of cartilaginous fishes with a flattened body, winglike pectoral fins, and a whiplike tail.

Ray John 1627–1705. English naturalist who devised a classification system accounting for nearly 18,000 plant species. It was the first system to divide flowering plants into *monocotyledons and *dicotyledons, with additional divisions made on the basis of leaf and flower characters and fruit types.

Ray Nicholas. Adopted name of Raymond Nicholas Kienzle 1911–1979. US film director, critically acclaimed for his socially aware dramas such as *Rebel Without a Cause* 1955. His films include *In a Lonely Place* 1950, *Johnny Guitar* 1954, and *55 Days at Peking* 1963.

Ray Satyajit 1921–1992. Indian film director, internationally known for his trilogy of life in his native Bengal: *Pather Panchali, Unvanquished,* and *The World of Apu* 1955–59. Later films include *The Music Room* 1963, *Charulata* 1964, *The Chess Players* 1977, and *The Home and the World* 1984.

rayon any of various shiny textile fibres and fabrics made from *cellulose. It is produced by pressing whatever cellulose solution is used through very small holes and solidifying the resulting filaments. A common type is *viscose, which consists of regenerated filaments of pure cellulose. Acetate and triacetate are kinds of rayon consisting of filaments of cellulose acetate and triacetate.

razorbill North Atlantic sea bird *Alca torda* of the auk family, which breeds on cliffs and migrates south in winter. It has a curved beak and is black above and white below. It uses its wings as paddles when diving. Razorbills are common off Newfoundland.

razor-shell or **razor-fish**; US name **razor clam** any bivalve mollusc in two genera *Ensis* and *Solen* with narrow, elongated shells, resembling an old-fashioned razor handle and delicately coloured. They can burrow rapidly into sand and are good swimmers.

re abbreviation for Latin 'with regard to'.

reaction in chemistry, the coming together of two or more atoms, ions, or molecules with the result that a *chemical change takes place. The nature of the reaction is portrayed by a chemical equation.

reaction principle principle stated by *Newton as his third law of motion: to every action, there is an equal and opposite reaction.

reactivity series chemical series produced by arranging the metals in order of their ease of reaction with reagents such as oxygen, water, and acids. This arrangement aids the understanding of the properties of metals, helps to explain differences between them, and enables predictions to be made about a metal's behaviour, based on a knowledge of its position or properties.

Reagan Ronald (Wilson) 1911– . 40th president of the USA 1981–89, a Republican. He was governor of California 1966–74, and a former Hollywood actor. Reagan was a hawkish and popular president. He adopted an aggressive policy in Central America, attempting to overthrow the government of Nicaragua, and invading *Grenada 1983. In 1987, *Irangate was investigated by the Tower Commission; Reagan admitted that USA–Iran negotiations had become an 'arms for hostages deal', but denied knowledge of resultant funds being illegally sent to the Contras in Nicaragua. He increased military spending (sending the national budget deficit to record levels), cut social programmes, introduced deregulation of domestic markets, and cut taxes. His *Strategic Defense Initiative, announced 1983, proved controversial owing to the cost and unfeasibility. He was succeeded by George *Bush.

realism in medieval philosophy, the theory that 'universals' have existence, not simply as names for entities but as entities in their own right. It is thus opposed to nominalism. In contemporary philosophy, the term stands for the doctrine that there is an intuitively appreciated reality apart from what is presented to the consciousness. It is opposed to *idealism.

real number in mathematics, any of the *rational numbers (which include the integers) or *irrational numbers. Real numbers exclude *imaginary numbers, found in *complex numbers of the general form $a + bi$ where $i = \sqrt{-1}$, although these do include a real component a.

realpolitik (German *Realpolitik* 'politics of realism') the pragmatic pursuit of self-interest and power, backed up by force when convenient. The term was coined 1853 to describe *Bismarck's policies in Prussia during the 1848 revolutions.

real tennis racket and ball game played in France, from about the 12th century, over a central net in an indoor court, but with a sloping roof let into each end and one side of the court, against which the ball may be hit. The term 'real' here means 'royal', not 'genuine'. Basic scoring is as for lawn *tennis, but with various modifications.

real-time system in computing, a program that responds to events in the world as they happen, as, for example, an automatic pilot program in an aircraft must respond instantly in order to correct deviations from its course. Process control, robotics, games, and many military applications are examples of real-time systems.

rearmament re-equipping a country with new weapons and other military hardware. The German dictator Adolf Hitler concentrated on rearmament in Germany after he achieved power in 1934. During the late 1930s Britain followed a policy of rearmament.

Réaumur René Antoine Ferchault de 1683–1757. French scientist. His work on metallurgy *L'Arte de convertir le fer forge en acier* 1722 described how to convert iron into steel and stimulated the development of the French steel industry. He produced a six-volume work 1734–42 on entomology, *L'Histoire des insectes/ History of Insects*, which threw much new light on the social insects. He also contributed to other areas of science.

receiver in law, a person appointed by a court to collect and manage the assets of an individual, company, or partnership in serious financial difficulties. In the case of bankruptcy, the assets may be sold and distributed by a receiver to creditors.

receptacle the enlarged end of a flower stalk to which the floral parts are attached. Normally the receptacle is rounded, but in some plants it is flattened or cup-shaped. The term is also used for the region on that part of some seaweeds which becomes swollen at certain times of the year and bears the reproductive organs.

recession in economics, a fall in business activity lasting more than a few months, causing stagnation in a country's output.

recessive gene in genetics, an *allele (alternative form of a gene) that will show in the *phenotype (observed characteristics of an organism) only if its partner allele on the paired chromosome is similarly recessive. Such an allele will not show if its partner is dominant, that is if the organism is *heterozygous for a particular characteristic. Alleles for blue eyes in humans, and for shortness in pea plants are recessive. Most mutant alleles are recessive and therefore are only rarely expressed (see *haemophilia and *sickle cell disease).

Recife industrial seaport (cotton textiles, sugar refining, fruit canning, flour milling) and naval base in Brazil; capital of Pernambuco state, at the mouth of the river Capibaribe; population (1991) 1,335,700. It was founded 1504.

reciprocal in mathematics, the result of dividing a given quantity into 1. Thus the reciprocal of 2 is $\frac{1}{2}$; of $\frac{2}{3}$ is $\frac{3}{2}$; of x^2 is $\frac{1}{x^2}$ or x^{-2}. Reciprocals are used to replace division by multiplication, since multiplying by the reciprocal of a number is the same as dividing by that number.

recitative in opera, on-pitch speechlike declamation used in narrative episodes.

recombination in genetics, any process that recombines, or 'shuffles', the genetic material, thus increasing genetic variation in the offspring. The two main processes of recombination both occur during meiosis (reduction division of cells). One is *crossing over*, in which chromosome pairs exchange segments; the other is the random reassortment of chromosomes that occurs when each gamete (sperm or egg) receives only one of each chromosome pair.

Reconquista (Spanish 'reconquest') the Christian defeat of the *Moors 9th–15th centuries, and their expulsion from Spain.

Reconstruction in US history, the period 1865–77 after the Civil War during which the nation was reunited under the federal government after the defeat of the Southern Confederacy.

recorder in the English legal system, a part-time judge who usually sits in the *crown courts in less serious cases but may also sit in the county courts or the High Court. Recorders are chosen from barristers of standing and also, since the Courts Act of 1971, from solicitors. They may eventually become circuit judges.

recorder in music, a pure-toned instrument of the *woodwind family, in which the single reed is integrated with the mouthpiece. Recorders are played in a consort (ensemble) of matching tone and comprise sopranino, descant, treble, tenor, and bass.

recording the process of storing information, or the information store itself. Sounds and pictures can be stored on discs or tape. The gramophone record or *compact disc stores music or speech as a spiral groove on a plastic disc and the sounds are reproduced by a record player. In *tape recording, sounds are stored as a magnetic pattern on plastic tape. The best-quality reproduction is achieved using digital audio tape.

Record Office, Public government office containing the English national records since the Norman Conquest, brought together from courts of law and government departments, including the Domesday Book, the Gunpowder Plot papers, and the log of HMS *Victory* at Trafalgar. It was established 1838 in Chancery Lane, London; records dating from the 18th century onwards have been housed at Kew, London, since 1976.

record player device for reproducing recorded sound stored as a spiral groove on a vinyl disc. A motor-driven turntable rotates the record at a constant speed, and a stylus or needle on the head of a pick-up is made to vibrate by the undulations in the record groove. These vibrations are then converted to electrical signals by a *transducer in the head (often a *piezoelectric crystal). After amplification, the signals pass to one or more loudspeakers, which convert them into sound. Alternative formats are *compact disc and *tape recording, magnetic.

Recruit scandal in Japanese politics, the revelation 1988 that a number of politicians and business leaders had profited from insider trading. It led to the resignation of several cabinet ministers, including Prime Minister Takeshita, whose closest aide committed suicide, and to the arrest of 20 people.

rectangle quadrilateral (four-sided plane figure) with opposite sides equal and parallel and with each interior angle a right angle (90°). Its area A is the product of the length l and width w; that is, $A = l \times w$. A rectangle with all four sides equal is a *square.

rectifier in electrical engineering, a device used for obtaining one-directional current (DC) from an alternating source of supply (AC). Types include plate rectifiers, thermionic *diodes, and *semiconductor diodes.

rector Anglican priest, formerly entitled to the whole of the *tithes levied in the parish, as opposed to a *vicar* (Latin 'deputy') who was only entitled to part.

rectum lowest part of the digestive tract of animals, which stores faeces prior to elimination (defecation).

recursion in computing and mathematics, a technique whereby a *function or *procedure calls itself into use in order to enable a complex problem to be broken down into simpler steps. For example, a function that finds the factorial of a number n (calculates the product of all the whole numbers between 1 and n) would obtain its result by multiplying n by the factorial of $n - 1$.

recycling processing of industrial and household waste (such as paper, glass, and some metals and plastics) so that it can be reused. This saves expenditure on scarce raw materials, slows down the depletion of *nonrenewable resources, and helps to reduce pollution.

Red Army name of the army of the USSR until 1946; later known as the **Soviet Army**. It developed from the Red Guards, volunteers who carried out the Bolshevik revolution, and received its name because it fought under the *red flag. The Chinese revolutionary army was also called the Red Army.

red blood cell or **erythrocyte** the most common type of blood cell, responsible for transporting oxygen around the body. It contains haemoglobin, which combines with oxygen from the lungs to form oxyhaemoglobin. When transported to the tissues, these cells are able to release the oxygen because the oxyhaemoglobin splits into its original constituents.

Red Cross international relief agency founded by the Geneva Convention 1864 at the instigation of the Swiss doctor Henri Dunant to assist the wounded and prisoners in war. Its symbol is a symmetrical red cross on a white ground. In addition to dealing with associated problems of war, such as refugees and the care of the disabled, the Red Cross is increasingly concerned with victims of natural disasters – floods, earthquakes, epidemics, and accidents.

red dwarf any star that is cool, faint, and small (about one-tenth the mass and diameter of the Sun). Red dwarfs burn slowly, and have estimated lifetimes of 100 billion years. They may be the most abundant type of star, but are difficult to see because they are so faint. Two of the closest stars to the Sun, *Proxima Centauri and *Barnard's Star, are red dwarfs.

Redford (Charles) Robert 1937– . US actor and film director. His first starring role was in *Barefoot In The Park* 1967, followed by *Butch Cassidy and the Sundance Kid* 1969, and *The Sting* (both with Paul *Newman).

red giant any large bright star with a cool surface. It is thought to represent a late stage in the evolution of a star like the Sun, as it runs out of hydrogen fuel at its centre. Red giants have diameters between 10 and 100 times that of the Sun. They are very bright because they are so large, although their surface temperature is lower than that of the Sun, about 2,000–3,000K (1,700–2,700°C).

Redgrave Michael 1908–1985. British actor. His stage roles included Hamlet and Lear (Shakespeare), Uncle Vanya (Chekhov), and the schoolmaster in Rattigan's *The Browning Version* (filmed 1951). On screen he appeared in *The Lady Vanishes* 1938, *The Importance of Being Earnest* 1952, and *Goodbye Mr Chips* 1959. He was the father of Vanessa and Lynn Redgrave, both actresses.

Redgrave Vanessa 1937– . British actress. She has played Shakespeare's Lady Macbeth and Cleopatra on the stage, and Olga in Chekhov's *Three Sisters* 1990. She won an Academy Award for the title role in the film *Julia* 1976; other films include *Howards End* 1992. She is active in left-wing politics.

Red Guard one of the school and college students, wearing red armbands, active in the *Cultural Revolution in China 1966–69. The armed workers who took part in the *Russian Revolution of 1917 were also called Red Guards.

red-hot poker any plant of the African genus *Kniphofia*, family Liliaceae, in particular *K uvaria*, with a flame-coloured spike of flowers.

Redmond John Edward 1856–1918. Irish politician, Parnell's successor as leader of the Nationalist Party 1890–1916. The 1910 elections saw him holding the balance of power in the House of Commons, and he secured the introduction of a *Home Rule bill, which was opposed by Protestant Ulster.

Redon Odilon 1840–1916. French Symbolist painter and graphic artist. He used fantastic symbols and images, sometimes mythological. From the 1890s he painted still lifes and landscapes. His work was much admired by the Surrealists.

Redoubt, Mount active volcanic peak rising to 3,140 m/10,197 ft, W of Cook inlet in Alaska, USA. There were eruptions in 1966 and 1989.

redox reaction chemical change where one reactant is reduced and the other reactant oxidized. The reaction can only occur if both reactants are present and each changes simultaneously. For example, hydrogen reduces copper(II) oxide to copper while it is itself oxidized to water. The corrosion of iron and the reactions taking place in electric and electrolytic cells are just a few instances of redox reactions.

Red Scare in US history, campaign against radicals and dissenters which took place in the aftermath of World War I and the Russian Revolution, during a period of labour disorders in the USA. A wave of strikes in 1919 was seen as a prelude to revolution and violently suppressed. Thousands of people were arrested on suspicion, and communists were banned from entry to the country.

Red Sea submerged section of the *Great Rift Valley (2,000 km/1,200 mi long and up to 320 km/200 mi wide). Egypt, Sudan, and Ethiopia (in Africa) and Saudi Arabia (Asia) are on its shores.

redshank wading bird *Tringa totanus* of N Europe and Asia, a type of sandpiper. It nests in swampy areas, rarely in Europe, since most redshanks winter in the south. It is greyish and speckled black, and has long red legs.

red shift in astronomy, the lengthening of the wavelengths of light from an object as a result of the object's motion away from us. It is an example of the *Doppler effect. The red shift in light from galaxies is evidence that the universe is expanding.

redstart any bird of the genus Phoenicurus. A member of the thrush family, it winters in Africa and spends the summer in Eurasia. The male has a dark grey head (with white mark on the forehead and black face) and dark grey back, brown wings with lighter underparts, and a red tail. The American redstart *Setophaga ruticulla* belongs to the family Parulidae.

reduction in chemistry, the gain of electrons, loss of oxygen, or gain of hydrogen by an atom, ion, or molecule during a chemical reaction.

redwing type of thrush *Turdus iliacus*, smaller than the song thrush, with reddish wing and body markings. It breeds in the north of Europe and Asia, flying south in winter.

redwood giant coniferous tree, one of the two types of *sequoia.

reed any of various perennial tall, slender grasses of wet or marshy environments; in particular, species of the genera *Phragmites* and *Arundo*; also the stalk of any of these plants. The common reed *P. australis* attains a height of 3 m/10 ft, having stiff, erect leaves and straight stems bearing a plume of purplish flowers.

Reed Lou 1942– . US rock singer, songwriter, and guitarist; former member (1965–70) of the New York avant-garde group **the Velvet Underground**, perhaps the most influential band of the period. His solo work deals largely with urban alienation and angst, and includes the albums *Berlin* 1973, *Street Hassle* 1978, and *New York* 1989.

reel in cinema, plastic or metal spool used for winding and storing film. As the size of reels became standardized it came to refer to the running time of the film: a standard 35-mm reel holds 313 m/900 ft of film, which runs for ten minutes when projected at 24 frames per second; hence a 'two-reeler' was a film lasting 20 minutes. Today's projectors, however, hold bigger reels.

referendum procedure whereby a decision on proposed legislation is referred to the electorate for settlement by direct vote of all the people. It is most frequently employed in Switzerland, the

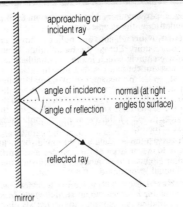

reflection *The law of reflection: the angle of incidence of a light beam equals the angle of reflection of the beam.*

first country to use it, but has become increasingly widespread. In 1992 several European countries (Ireland, Denmark, France) held referenda on whether or not to ratify the *Maastricht Treaty on closer European economic and political union.

refining any process that purifies or converts something into a more useful form. Metals usually need refining after they have been extracted from their ores by such processes as *smelting. Petroleum, or crude oil, needs refining before it can be used; the process involves fractional *distillation, the separation of the substance into separate components or 'fractions'.

reflection the throwing back or deflection of waves, such as *light or *sound waves, when they hit a surface. The *law of reflection* states that the angle of incidence (the angle between the ray and a perpendicular line drawn to the surface) is equal to the angle of reflection (the angle between the reflected ray and a perpendicular to the surface).

reflex in animals, a very rapid automatic response to a particular stimulus. It is controlled by the *nervous system. A reflex involves only a few nerve cells, unlike the slower but more complex responses produced by the many processing nerve cells of the brain.

reflex angle an angle greater than 180° but less than 360°.

reflex camera camera that uses a mirror and prisms to reflect light passing through the lens into the viewfinder, showing the photographer the exact scene that is being shot. When the shutter button is released the mirror springs out of the way, allowing light to reach the film. The most common type is the single-lens reflex (*SLR) camera. The twin-lens reflex (*TLR) camera has two lenses: one has a mirror for viewing, the other is used for exposing the film.

reflexology manipulation and massage of the feet to ascertain and treat disease or dysfunction elsewhere in the body.

Reform Acts UK acts of Parliament 1832, 1867, and 1884 that extended voting rights and redistributed parliamentary seats; also known as Representation of the People Acts.

Reformation religious and political movement in 16th-century Europe to reform the Roman Catholic church, which led to the establishment of Protestant churches. Anticipated from the 12th century by the Waldenses, Lollards, and Hussites, it was set off by German priest Martin *Luther 1517, and became effective when the absolute monarchies gave it support by challenging the political power of the papacy and confiscating church wealth.

refraction the bending of a wave of light, heat, or sound when it passes from one medium to another. Refraction occurs because waves travel at different velocities in different media.

refractory (of a material) able to resist high temperature, for example *ceramics made from clay, minerals, or other earthy materials. Furnaces are lined with refractory materials such as silica and dolomite.

refrigeration use of technology to transfer heat from cold to warm, against the normal temperature gradient, so that a body can remain substantially colder than its surroundings. Refrigeration equipment is used for the chilling and deep freezing of food in *food technology, and in air conditioners and industrial processes.

refugee person fleeing from oppressive or dangerous conditions (such as political, religious, or military persecution) and seeking refuge in a foreign country. In 1991 there were an estimated 17 million refugees worldwide, whose resettlement and welfare were the responsibility of the United Nations High Commission for Refugees (UNHCR). An estimated average of 3,000 people a day become refugees.

regelation phenomenon in which water refreezes to ice after it has been melted by pressure at a temperature below the freezing point of water. Pressure makes an ice skate, for example, form a film of water that freezes once again after the skater has passed.

Regency in Britain, the years 1811–20 during which *George IV (then Prince of Wales) acted as regent for his father *George III.

Regency style style of architecture and interior furnishings popular in England during the late 18th and early 19th centuries. The style is characterized by its restrained simplicity and its imitation of ancient classical elements, often Greek.

regeneration in biology, regrowth of a new organ or tissue after the loss or removal of the original. It is common in plants, where a new individual can often be produced from a 'cutting' of the original. In animals, regeneration of major structures is limited to lower organisms; certain lizards can regrow their tails if these are lost, and new flatworms can grow from a tiny fragment of an old one. In mammals, regeneration is limited to the repair of tissue in wound healing and the regrowth of peripheral nerves following damage.

regent person who carries out the duties of a sovereign during the sovereign's minority, incapacity, or lengthy absence from the country. In England since the time of Henry VIII, Parliament has always appointed a regent or council of regency when necessary.

reggae predominant form of West Indian popular music of the 1970s and 1980s, characterized by a heavily accented offbeat and a thick bass line. The lyrics often refer to *Rastafarianism. Musicians include Bob Marley, Lee 'Scratch' Perry (1940– , performer and producer), and the group Black Uhuru (1974–). Reggae is also played in the UK, South Africa, and elsewhere.

regiment military formation equivalent to a battalion in parts of the British army, and to a brigade in the armies of many other countries. In the British infantry, a regiment may include more than one battalion, and soldiers belong to the same regiment throughout their career.

Regina industrial city (oil refining, cement, steel, farm machinery, fertilizers), and capital of Saskatchewan, Canada; population (1986) 175,000. It was founded 1882 as *Pile of Bones* and renamed in honour of Queen Victoria of England.

Regional Crime Squad in the UK, local police force that deals with serious crime; see under *Scotland Yard, New.

register in computing, a memory location that can be accessed rapidly; it is often built into the computer's central processing unit. Some registers are reserved for special tasks – for example, an *instruction register* is used to hold the machine-code command that the computer is currently executing, while a *sequence-control register* keeps track of the next command to be executed. Other registers are used for holding frequently used data and for storing intermediate results.

Rehnquist William 1924– . Chief justice of the US *Supreme Court from 1986. Under his leadership, the court has established a reputation for conservative rulings on such issues as abortion and capital punishment.

Rehoboam king of Judah about 932–915 BC, son of Solomon. Under his rule the Jewish nation split into the two kingdoms of *Israel* and *Judah*. Ten of the tribes revolted against him and took Jeroboam as their ruler, leaving Rehoboam only the tribes of Judah and Benjamin.

Reich (German 'empire') three periods in European history. The First Reich was the Holy Roman Empire 962–1806, the Second Reich the German Empire 1871–1918, and the *Third Reich Nazi Germany 1933–45.

Reich Steve 1936– . US composer. His Minimalist music consists of simple patterns carefully superimposed and modified to highlight constantly changing melodies and rhythms; examples are *Phase Patterns* for four electronic organs 1970, *Music for Mallet Instruments, Voices, and Organ* 1973, and *Music for Percussion and Keyboards* 1984.

Reich Wilhelm 1897–1957. Austrian doctor, who emigrated to the USA 1939. He combined *Marxism and *psychoanalysis to advocate the positive effects of directed sexual energies and sexual freedom. His works include *Die Sexuelle Revolution/The Sexual Revolution* 1936–45 and *Di Funktion des Orgasmus/The Function of the Orgasm* 1948.

Reims (English *Rheims*) capital of Champagne-Ardenne region, France; population (1982) 199,000. It is the centre of the champagne industry and has textile industries as well. It was known in Roman times as *Durocorturum*. From 987 all but six French kings were crowned here. Ceded to England 1420 under the Treaty of Troyes, it was retaken by Joan of Arc, who had Charles VII consecrated in the 13th-century cathedral. In World War II, the German High Command formally surrendered here to US general Eisenhower 7 May 1945.

reincarnation belief that after death the human soul or the spirit of a plant or animal may live again in another human or animal. It is part of the teachings of many religions and philosophies, for example ancient Egyptian and Greek (the philosophies of Pythagoras and Plato), Buddhism, Hinduism, Jainism, certain Christian heresies (such as the Cathars), and theosophy. It is also referred to as *transmigration* or metempsychosis.

reindeer or *caribou* deer *Rangifer tarandus* of Arctic and subarctic regions, common to North America and Eurasia. About 120 cm/4 ft at the shoulder, it has a thick, brownish coat and broad hooves well adapted to travel over snow. It is the only deer in which both sexes have antlers; these can grow to 150 cm/5 ft long, and are shed in winter.

Reinhardt Django (Jean Baptiste) 1910–1953. Belgian jazz guitarist and composer, who was coleader, with Stephane Grappelli, of the Quintet de Hot Club de France 1934–39. He had a lyrical acoustic style and individual technique, and influenced many US musicians.

relative atomic mass the mass of an atom relative to one-twelfth the mass of an atom of carbon-12. It depends on the number of protons and neutrons in the atom, the electrons having negligible mass. If more than one *isotope of the element is present, the relative atomic mass is calculated by taking an average that takes account of the relative proportions of each isotope, resulting in values that are not whole numbers. The term *atomic weight*, although commonly used, is strictly speaking incorrect.

relative density or *specific gravity* the density (at 20°C/68°F) of a solid or liquid relative to (divided by) the maximum density of water (at 4°C/39.2°F). The relative density of a gas is its density divided by the density of hydrogen (or sometimes dry air) at the same temperature and pressure.

relative humidity the concentration of water vapour in the air. It is expressed as the percentage that its moisture content represents of the maximum amount that the air could contain at the same temperature and pressure. The higher the temperature the more water vapour the air can hold.

relative molecular mass the mass of a molecule, calculated relative to one-twelfth the mass of an atom of carbon-12. It is found by adding the relative atomic masses of the atoms that make up the molecule. The term *molecular weight* is often used, but strictly this is incorrect.

relativity in physics, the theory of the relative rather than absolute character of motion and mass, and the interdependence of matter, time, and space, as developed by Albert *Einstein in two phases:

special theory (1905) Starting with the premisses that (1) the laws of nature are the same for all observers in unaccelerated motion, and (2) the speed of light is independent of the motion of its source, Einstein postulated that the time interval between two events was longer for an observer in whose frame of reference the events occur in different places than for the observer for whom they occur at the same place.

general theory of relativity (1915) The geometrical properties of space-time were to be conceived as modified locally by the presence of a body with mass. A planet's orbit around the Sun (as observed in three-dimensional space) arises from its natural trajectory in modified space-time; there is no need to invoke, as Isaac Newton did, a force of *gravity coming from the Sun and acting on the planet. Einstein's theory predicted slight differences in the orbits of the planets from Newton's theory, which were observable in the case of Mercury. The new theory also said light rays should bend when they pass by a massive object, owing to the object's effect on local space-time. The predicted bending of starlight was observed during the eclipse of the Sun 1919, when light from distant stars passing close to the Sun was not masked by sunlight.

relaxation therapy development of regular and conscious control of physiological processes and their related emotional and mental states, and of muscular tensions in the body, as a way of relieving stress and its results. Meditation, *hypnotherapy, *autogenics, and *biofeedback are techniques commonly employed.

relay in electrical engineering, an electromagnetic switch. A small current passing through a coil of wire wound around an iron core attracts an *armature whose movement closes a pair of sprung contacts to complete a secondary circuit, which may carry a large current or activate other devices. The solid-state equivalent is a thyristor switching device.

relic part of some divine or saintly person, or something closely associated with them. Christian examples include the arm of St Teresa of Avila, the blood of St Januarius, and the *True Cross. Buddhist relics include the funeral ashes of the historic Buddha, placed in a number of stupas or burial mounds.

relief in architecture, carved figures and other forms that project from the background. The Italian terms *basso-rilievo* (low relief), *mezzo-rilievo* (middle relief), and *alto-rilievo* (high relief) are used according to the extent to which the sculpture projects. The French term *bas-relief* is commonly used to mean low relief.

religion (Latin *religare* 'to bind'; perhaps humans to God) code of belief or philosophy, which often involves the worship of a *God or gods. Belief in a supernatural power is not essential (absent in, for example, Buddhism and Confucianism), but faithful adherence is usually considered to be rewarded, for example by escape from human existence (Buddhism), by a future existence (Christianity, Islam), or by worldly benefit (Sōka Gakkai Buddhism). Among the chief religions are:
ancient and pantheist religions of Babylonia, Assyria, Egypt, Greece, and Rome;
oriental Hinduism, Buddhism, Jainism, Parseeism, Confucianism, Taoism, and Shinto;
'religions of a book' Judaism, Christianity (the

RELIGIOUS FESTIVALS

date	festival	religion	event commemorated
6 Jan	Epiphany	Western Christian	coming of the Magi
6–7 Jan	Christmas	Orthodox Christian	birth of Jesus
18–19 Jan	Epiphany	Orthodox Christian	coming of the Magi
Jan–Feb	New Year	Chinese	Return of Kitchen god to heaven
Feb–March	Shrove Tuesday	Christian	day before Lent
	Ash Wednesday	Christian	first day of Lent
	Purim	Jewish	story of Esther
	Mahashivaratri	Hindu	Siva
March–April	Palm Sunday	Western Christian	Jesus' entry into Jerusalem
	Good Friday	Western Christian	crucifixion of Jesus
	Easter Sunday	Western Christian	resurrection of Jesus
	Passover	Jewish	escape from slavery in Egypt
	Holi	Hindu	Krishna
	Holi Mohalla	Sikh	(coincides with Holi)
	Rama Naumi	Hindu	birth of Rama
	Ching Ming	Chinese	remembrance of the dead
13 April	Baisakhi	Sikh	founding of the Khalsa
April–May	Easter	Orthodox Christian	death and resurrection of Jesus
May–June	Shavuot	Jewish	giving of ten Commandments to Moses
	Pentecost (Whitsun)	Western Christian	Jesus' followers receiving the Holy Spirit
	Wesak	Buddhist	day of the Buddha's birth, enlightenment and death
	Martyrdom of Guru Arjan	Sikh	death of fifth guru of Sikhism
June	Dragon Boat Festival	Chinese	Chinese martyr
	Pentecost	Orthodox Christian	Jesus' followers receiving the Holy Spirit
July	Dhammacakka	Buddhist	preaching of Buddha's first sermon
Aug	Raksha Bandhan	Hindu	family
Aug–Sept	Janmashtami	Hindu	birthday of Krishna
Sept	Moon Festival	Chinese	Chinese hero
Sept–Oct	Rosh Hashana	Jewish	start of Jewish New Year
	Yom Kippur	Jewish	day of atonement
	Succot	Jewish	Israelites' time in the wilderness
Oct	Dusshera	Hindu	goddess Devi
Oct–Nov	Divali	Hindu	goddess Lakshmi
	Divali	Sikh	release of Guru Hargobind from prison
Nov	Guru Nanak's birthday	Sikh	founder of Sikhism
Nov–Dec	Bodhi Day	Buddhist (Mahayana)	Buddha's enlightenment
Dec	Hanukkah	Jewish	recapture of Temple of Jerusalem
	Winter Festival	Chinese	time of feasting
25 Dec	Christmas	Western Christian	birth of Christ
Dec–Jan	Birthday of Guru Gobind Sind	Sikh	last (tenth) human guru of Sikhism
	Martyrdom of Guru Tegh Bahadur	Sikh	ninth guru of Sikhism

principal divisions are Roman Catholic, Eastern Orthodox, and Protestant), and Islam (the principal divisions are Sunni and Shi'ite); **combined derivation** such as Baha'ism, the Unification Church, and Mormonism.

REM US four-piece rock group formed 1980 in Georgia. Their songs are characterized by melodic bass lines, driving guitar, and evocative lyrics partly buried in the mix. Albums include *Reckoning* 1984, *Green* 1988, and the mass-market breakthrough *Out of Time* 1991.

rem acronym of *roentgen equivalent man* SI unit of radiation dose equivalent.

remand in law, the committing of an accused but not convicted person into custody or to release on bail pending a court hearing.

Rembrandt Harmensz van Rijn 1606–1669. Dutch painter and etcher, one of the most prolific and significant artists in Europe of the 17th century. Between 1629 and 1669 he painted some 60 penetrating self-portraits. He also painted religious subjects, and produced about 300 etchings and over 1,000 drawings. His group portraits include *The Anatomy Lesson of Dr Tulp* 1632 (Mauritshuis, The Hague) and *The Night Watch* 1642 (Rijksmuseum, Amsterdam).

Remembrance Sunday (known until 1945 as **Armistice Day**) in the UK, national day of remembrance for those killed in both world wars and later conflicts, on the second Sunday of Nov. In Canada 11 Nov is **Remembrance Day**. The US equivalent is *Veterans Day.

Remington Philo 1816–1889. US inventor of the breech-loading rifle that bears his name. He began manufacturing typewriters 1873, using the patent of Christopher *Sholes (1819–1890), and made improvements that resulted five years later in the first machine with a shift key, thus providing lower-case letters as well as capital letters. The Remington rifle and carbine, which had a falling block breech and a tubular magazine, were developed in collaboration with his father *Eliphalet Remington* (1793–1861).

remix in pop music, the studio practice of reassembling a recording from all or some of its individual components, often with the addition of new elements. As a commercial concept, remixes accompanied the rise of the 12-in single in the 1980s.

remora any of a family of warm-water fishes that have an adhesive disc on the head, by which they attach themselves to whales, sharks, and turtles. These provide the remora with shelter and transport, as well as food in the form of parasites on the host's skin.

remote sensing gathering and recording information from a distance. Space probes have sent back photographs and data about planets as distant as Neptune. In archaeology, surface survey techniques provide information without disturbing subsurface deposits.

remote terminal in computing, a terminal that communicates with a computer via a modem (or acoustic coupler) and a telephone line.

REM sleep (acronym for **rapid-eye-movement sleep**) phase of sleep that recurs several times nightly in humans and is associated with dreaming. The eyes flicker quickly beneath closed lids.

Renaissance period and intellectual movement in European cultural history that is traditionally seen as ending the Middle Ages and beginning modern times. The Renaissance started in Italy in the 14th century and flourished in W Europe until about the 17th century. The broad aim of Renaissance education was to produce the 'complete human being' (**Renaissance man**), conversant in the humanities, mathematics and science (including their application in war), the arts and crafts, and athletics and sport; to enlarge the bounds of learning and geographical knowledge; to encourage the growth of scepticism and free thought, and the study and imitation of Greek and Latin literature and art. The revival of interest in classical Greek and Roman culture inspired artists such as Leonardo da Vinci, Michelangelo, and Dürer, architects such as Brunelleschi and Alberti, writers such as Petrarch and Boccaccio. Scientists and explorers proliferated as well.

Renaissance art movement in European art of the 15th and 16th centuries. It began in Florence, Italy, with the rise of a spirit of humanism and a new appreciation of the Classical past. In painting and sculpture this led to greater naturalism and interest in anatomy and perspective. Renaissance art peaked around 1500 with the careers of Leonardo da Vinci, Raphael, Michelangelo, and Titian in Italy and Dürer in Germany.

René France-Albert 1935– . Seychelles left-wing politician, the country's first prime minister after independence and president from 1977 after a coup. He has followed a non-nuclear policy of nonalignment.

renewable energy power from any source that replenishes itself. Most renewable systems rely on *solar energy directly or through the weather cycle as *wave power, *hydroelectric power, or wind power via *wind turbines, or solar energy collected by plants (alcohol fuels, for example). In addition, the gravitational force of the Moon can be harnessed through *tidal power stations, and the heat trapped in the centre of the Earth is used via *geothermal energy systems.

renewable resource natural resource that is replaced by natural processes in a reasonable amount of time. Soil, water, forests, plants, and animals are all renewable resources as long as they are properly conserved. Solar, wind, wave, and geothermal energies are based on renewable resources.

Reni Guido 1575–1642. Italian painter, active in Bologna and Rome (about 1600–14), whose work includes the fresco *Phoebus and the Hours Preceded by Aurora* 1613 (Casino Rospigliosi, Rome). His workshop in Bologna produced numerous religious images, including Madonnas.

Rennes industrial city (oil refining, chemicals, electronics, cars) and capital of Ille-et-Vilaine *département*, W France, at the confluence of the Ille and Vilaine, 56 km/35 mi SE of St Malo; population (1982) 234,000. It was the old capital of Brittany.

rennet extract, traditionally obtained from a calf's stomach, that contains the enzyme rennin, used to coagulate milk in the cheesemaking process. The enzyme can now be chemically produced.

Renoir Jean 1894–1979. French director whose films, characterized by their profound humanism, include *Boudu sauvé des eaux/Boudu Saved from Drowning* 1932, *La grande Illusion* 1937, and *La Règle du jeu/The Rules of the Game* 1939. In 1975 he received an honorary Academy Award for his life's work. He was the son of the painter Pierre-Auguste Renoir.

Renoir Pierre-Auguste 1841–1919. French Impressionist painter. He met Monet and Sisley in the early 1860s, and together they formed the nucleus of the Impressionist movement. He developed a lively, colourful painting style with feathery brushwork and painted many voluptuous female nudes, such as *The Bathers* about 1884–87 (Philadelphia Museum of Art, USA). In his later years he turned to sculpture.

repellent anything whose smell, taste, or other properties discourages nearby creatures. *Insect repellent* is usually a chemical substance that keeps, for example, mosquitoes at bay; natural substances include citronella, lavender oil, and eucalyptus oils. A device that emits ultrasound waves is also claimed to repel insects and small mammals. The bitter-tasting denatonium saccharide may be added to medicines to prevent consumption by children, and to plastic garbage bags to repel foraging animals.

repetitive strain injury (RSI) inflammation of tendon sheaths, mainly in the hands and wrists, which may be disabling. It is found predominantly in factory workers involved in constant repetitive movements, and in high-speed typists. Some victims have successfully sued their employers for damages.

replication in biology, production of copies of the genetic material, DNA; it occurs during cell division (*mitosis and *meiosis). Most mutations are caused by mistakes during replication.

repression in psychology, unconscious process said to protect a person from ideas, impulses, or memories that would threaten emotional stability were they to become conscious.

reprieve legal temporary suspension of the execution of a sentence of a criminal court. It is usually associated with the death penalty. It is distinct from a pardon (extinguishing the sentence) and commutation (alteration) of a sentence (for example, from death to life imprisonment).

reproduction in biology, process by which a living organism produces other organisms similar to itself. There are two kinds: *asexual reproduction and *sexual reproduction.

reptile any member of a class (Reptilia) of vertebrates. Unlike amphibians, reptiles have hard-shelled, yolk-filled eggs that are laid on land and from which fully formed young are born. Some snakes and lizards retain their eggs and give birth to live young. Reptiles are cold-blooded, produced from eggs, and the skin is usually covered with scales. The metabolism is slow, and in some cases (certain large snakes) intervals between meals may be months. Reptiles date back over 300 million years.

republic country where the head of state is not a monarch, either hereditary or elected, but usually a president whose role may or may not include political functions.

Republican Party one of the USA's two main political parties, formed 1854. It is a right-wing party, favouring capital and big business and opposing state subvention and federal controls. In the late 20th century most presidents have come from the Republican Party, but in Congress Republicans have been outnumbered.

requiem in the Roman Catholic church, a mass for the dead. Musical settings include those by Palestrina, Mozart, Berlioz, and Verdi.

research the primary activity in science, a combination of theory and experimentation directed towards finding scientific explanations of phenomena. It is commonly classified into two types: *pure research*, involving theories with little apparent relevance to human concerns; and *applied research*, concerned with finding solutions to problems of social importance – for instance in medicine and engineering. The two types are linked in that theories developed from pure research may eventually be found to be of great value to society.

reserve currency in economics, a country's holding of internationally acceptable means of payment (major foreign currencies or gold); central banks also hold the ultimate reserve of money for their domestic banking sector. On the asset side of company balance sheets, undistributed profits are listed as reserves.

residual current device or *earth leakage circuit breaker* device that protects users of electrical equipment from electric shock by interrupting the electricity supply if a short circuit or current leakage occurs.

residue in chemistry, a substance or mixture of substances remaining in the original container after the removal of one or more components by a separation process.

resin substance exuded from pines, firs, and other trees in gummy drops that harden in air. Varnishes are common products of the hard resins, and ointments come from the soft resins.

resistance in physics, that property of a substance that restricts the flow of electricity through it, associated with the conversion of electrical energy to heat; also the magnitude of this property. Resistance depends on many factors, such as the nture of the material, its temperature, dimensions, and thermal properties; degree of impurity; the nature and state of illumination of the surface; and the frequency and magnitude of the current. The SI unit of resistance is the ohm.

resistance movement opposition movement in a country occupied by an enemy or colonial power, especially in the 20th century; for example, the French resistance to Nazism in World War II.

resistivity in physics, a measure of the ability of a material to resist the flow of an electric current. It is numerically equal to the *resistance of a sample of unit length and unit cross-sectional area, and its unit is the ohm metre. A good conductor has a low resistivity ($1.7 - 10^{-8}$ ohm metres for copper); an insulator has a very high resistivity (10^{15} ohm metres for polyethane).

resistor in physics, any component in an electrical circuit used to introduce *resistance to a current. Resistors are often made from wire-wound coils or pieces of carbon. *Rheostats and *potentiometers are variable resistors.

resolution in computing, the number of dots per unit length in which an image can be reproduced on a screen or printer. A typical screen resolution for colour monitors is 75 dpi (dots per inch). A *laser printer will typically have a printing resolution of 300 dpi, and *dot-matrix printers typically have resolutions from 60 dpi to 180 dpi. Photographs in books and magazines have a resolution of 1,200 dpi or 2,400 dpi.

resonance rapid and uncontrolled increase in the size of a vibration when the vibrating object is subject to a force varying at its *natural frequency. In a trombone, for example, the length of the air column in the instrument is adjusted until it resonates with the note being sounded. Resonance effects are also produced by many electrical circuits. Tuning a radio, for example, is done by adjusting the natural frequency of the receiver circuit until it coincides with the frequency of the radio waves falling on the aerial.

resources materials that can be used to satisfy human needs. Because human needs are diverse and extend from basic physical requirements such as food and shelter, to ill-defined aesthetic needs, resources encompass a vast range of items. The intellectual resources of a society – its ideas and technologies – determine which aspects of the environment meet that society's needs, and therefore become resources. For example, in the 19th century, uranium was used only in the manufacture of coloured glass. Today, with the advent of nuclear technology, it is a military and energy resource. Resources are often categorized into *human resources*, such as labour, supplies and skills, and *natural resources*, such as climate, fossil fuels, and water. Natural resources are divided into *nonrenewable resources and *renewable resources.

respiration biochemical process whereby food molecules are progressively broken down (oxidized) to release energy in the form of *ATP. In most organisms this requires oxygen, but in some bacteria the oxidant is the nitrate or sulphate ion instead. In all higher organisms, respiration occurs in the *mitochondria

Respiration is also used to mean breathing, although this is more accurately described as a form of *gas exchange.

rest mass in physics, the mass of a body when its velocity is zero. For subatomic particles, it is their mass at rest or at velocities considerably below that of light. According to the theory of *relativity, at very high velocities, there is a relativistic effect that increases the mass of the particle.

Restoration in English history, the period when the monarchy, in the person of Charles II, was re-established after the English Civil War and the fall of the *Protectorate 1660.

Restoration comedy style of English theatre, dating from the Restoration. It witnessed the first appearance of women on the English stage, most notably in the 'breeches part', specially created in order to costume the actress in male attire, thus revealing her figure to its best advantage. The genre placed much emphasis on sexual antics. Examples include Wycherley's *The Country Wife* 1675, Congreve's *The Way of the World* 1700, and Farquhar's *The Beaux' Stratagem* 1707.

restrictive trade practices agreements between people in a particular trade or business that keep the cost of goods or services artificially high (for example, an agreement to restrict output) or provide barriers to outsiders entering the trade or business.

resurrection in Christian, Jewish, and Muslim belief, the rising from the dead that all souls will experience at the Last Judgement. The Resurrection also refers to Jesus rising from the dead on the third day after his crucifixion, a belief central to Christianity and celebrated at Easter.

resuscitation steps taken to revive anyone on the brink of death. The most successful technique for life-threatening emergencies, such as electrocution, near-drowning, or heart attack, is mouth-to-mouth resuscitation. Medical and paramedical staff are trained in cardiopulmonary resuscitation: the use of specialized equipment and techniques to attempt to restart the breathing and/or heartbeat and stabilize the patient long enough for more definitive treatment.

retail sale of goods and services to a consumer. The retailer is the last link in the distribution chain. A retailer's purchases are usually made from a wholesaler.

retail price index (RPI) indicator of variations in the *cost of living, superseded in the USA by the consumer price index.

retail-price maintenance (RPM) exceptions to the general rule that shops can charge whatever price they choose for goods. The main areas where RPM applies in the UK are books (where the Net Book Agreement prevents booksellers charging less than the publisher's price) and some pharmaceutical products.

retina light-sensitive area at the back of the *eye connected to the brain by the optic nerve. It has several layers and in humans contains over a million rods and cones, sensory cells capable of converting light into nervous messages that pass down the optic nerve to the brain.

retriever any of several breeds of hunting dogs, often used as guide dogs for the blind. The commonest breeds are the **Labrador retriever**, large, smooth-coated, and usually black or yellow; and the **golden retriever**, with either flat or wavy coat. They can grow to 60 cm/2 ft high and weigh 40 kg/90 lb.

retrovirus any of a family (*Retroviridae*) of *viruses containing the genetic material *RNA rather than the more usual *DNA.

Réunion French island of the Mascarenes group, in the Indian Ocean, 650 km/400 mi E of Madagascar and 180 km/110 mi SW of Mauritius
area 2,512 sq km/970 sq mi
capital St Denis
physical forested, rising in Piton de·Neiges to 3,069 m/10,072 ft
products sugar, maize, vanilla, tobacco, rum
population (1987) 565,000
history explored by Portuguese (the first European visitors) 1513; annexed by Louis XIII of France 1642; overseas *département* of France 1946; overseas region 1972.

reuse multiple use of a product (often a form of packaging), by returning it to the manufacturer or processor each time. Many such returnable items are sold with a deposit which is reimbursed if the item is returned. Reuse is usually more energy-and resource-efficient than *recycling unless there are large transport or cleaning costs.

Reuter Paul Julius, Baron de 1816–1899. German founder of the international news agency **Reuters**. He began a continental pigeon post 1849, and in 1851 set up a news agency in London. In 1858 he persuaded the press to use his news telegrams, and the service became worldwide. Reuters became a public company 1984.

Revelation last book of the New Testament, traditionally attributed to the author of the Gospel of St John but now generally held to be the work of another writer. It describes a vision of the end of the world, of the Last Judgement, and of a new heaven and earth ruled by God from Jerusalem.

Revere Paul 1735–1818. American revolutionary, a Boston silversmith, who carried the news of the approach of British troops to Lexington and Concord (see *American Revolution) on the night of 18 April 1775. On the next morning the first shots of the Revolution were fired at Lexington. Longfellow's poem 'The Midnight Ride of Paul Revere' commemorates the event.

reverse takeover in business, a *takeover where a company sells itself to another (a *white knight) to avoid being the target of a purchase by an unwelcome predator.

reversible reaction chemical reaction that proceeds in both directions at the same time, as the product decomposes back into reactants as it is being produced. Such reactions do not run to completion, provided that no substance leaves the system. Examples include the manufacture of ammonia from hydrogen and nitrogen, and the oxidation of sulphur dioxide to sulphur trioxide. The term is also applied to those reactions that can be made to go in the opposite direction by changing the conditions, but these run to completion because some of the substances escape from the reaction. Examples are the decomposition of calcium hydrogencarbonate on heating and the loss of water of crystallization by copper(II) sulphate pentahydrate.

revisionism political theory derived from Marxism that moderates one or more of the basic tenets of Marx, and is hence condemned by orthodox Marxists.

revolution any rapid, far-reaching, or violent change in the political, social, or economic structure of society. It is usually applied to political change: examples include the American Revolution, where colonists broke free from their colonial ties and established a sovereign, independent nation; the French Revolution, where an absolute monarchy was overthrown by opposition from inside the country and a popular uprising; and the Russian Revolution, where a repressive monarchy was overthrown by those seeking to institute widespread social and economic changes based on a socialist model. In the 1970s and 1980s a 'high-tech revolution' based on the silicon chip took place, facilitating the global use of computers.

Revolutionary Wars series of wars 1791–1802 between France and the combined armies of England, Austria, Prussia, and others, during the period of the *French Revolution.

revolutions of 1989 popular uprisings in many countries of Eastern Europe against communist rule, prompted by internal reforms in the USSR that permitted dissent within its sphere of influence. By 1990 nearly all the Warsaw Pact countries had moved from one-party to pluralist political systems, in most cases peacefully but with growing hostility between various nationalist and ethnic groups.

revolutions of 1848 series of revolts in various parts of Europe against monarchical rule. While some of the revolutionaries had republican ideas, many more were motivated by economic grievances. The revolution began in France with the overthrow of Louis Philippe and then spread to Italy, the Austrian Empire, and Germany, where the short-lived Frankfurt Parliament put forward ideas about political unity in Germany. None of the revolutions enjoyed any lasting success, and most were violently suppressed within a few months.

revue stage presentation involving short satirical and topical items in the form of songs, sketches, and monologues; it originated in the late 19th century.

Reykjavik capital (from 1918) and chief port of Iceland, on the SW coast; population (1988) 93,000. Fish processing is the main industry. Reykjavik is heated by underground mains fed by volcanic springs. It was a seat of Danish administration from 1801 to 1918.

Reynolds Albert 1933– . Irish politician, prime minister 1992–1994. He joined Fianna Faíl 1977, and held various government posts including minister of finance 1989–92. He became prime minister when Charles *Haughey was forced to resign Jan 1992, but his government was defeated on a vote of confidence Nov 1992. In subsequent elections, Reynolds succeeded in forming a Fianna Faíl-Labour coalition.

Reynolds Joshua 1723–1792. English portrait painter, active in London from 1752. He became the first president of the Royal Academy 1768. His portraits display a facility for striking and characterful compositions in a consciously grand manner. He often borrowed classical poses, for example *Mrs Siddons as the Tragic Muse* 1784 (San Marino, California, USA).

rhapsody in music, instrumental *fantasia, often based on folk melodies, such as Lizst's *Hungarian Rhapsodies* 1853–54.

rhea one of two flightless birds of the family Rheidae. The common rhea *Rhea americana* is 1.5 m/5 ft high and is distributed widely in South America. The smaller Darwin's rhea *Pterocnemia pennata* occurs only in the south of South America. They differ from the ostrich in their smaller size and in having a feathered neck and head, three-toed feet, and no plumelike tail feathers.

Rhee Syngman 1875–1965. Korean right-wing politician. A rebel under Chinese and Japanese rule, he became president of South Korea from 1948 until riots forced him to resign and leave the country 1960.

Rheims English version of *Reims, city in France.

Rheinland-Pfalz German name for the *Rhineland-Palatinate region of Germany.

rhenium (Latin *Rhenus* 'Rhine') heavy, silver-white, metallic element, symbol Re, atomic number 75, relative atomic mass 186.2. It has chemical properties similar to those of manganese and a very high melting point (3,180°C/5,756°F), which makes it valuable as an ingredient in alloys.

rheostat in physics, a variable *resistor, usually consisting of a high-resistance wire-wound coil with a sliding contact. It is used to vary electrical resistance without interrupting the current (for example, when dimming lights). The circular type in electronics (which can be used, for example, as the volume control of an amplifier) is also known as a *potentiometer.

rhesus factor *protein on the surface of red blood cells of humans, which is involved in the rhesus blood group system. Most individuals possess the main rhesus factor (Rh+), but those without this factor (Rh−) produce *antibodies if they come into contact with it. The name comes from rhesus monkeys, in whose blood rhesus factors were first found.

rhesus monkey macaque monkey *Macaca mulatta* found in N India and SE Asia. It has a pinkish face, red buttocks, and long, straight, brown-grey hair. It can grow up to 60 cm/2 ft long, with a 20 cm/8 in tail.

rhetoric (Greek *rhetor* 'orator') traditionally, the art of public speaking and debate. Rhetorical skills are valued in such occupations as politics, teaching, law, religion, and broadcasting.

rhetorical question question, often used by public speakers and debaters, that either does not require an answer or for which the speaker intends to provide his or her own answer ('Where else in the world can we find such brave young men as these?').

rheumatic fever or *acute rheumatism* acute or chronic illness characterized by fever and painful swelling of joints. Some victims also experience involuntary movements of the limbs and head, a form of *chorea.

rheumatism nontechnical term for a variety of ailments associated with inflammation and stiffness of the joints and muscles.

rheumatoid arthritis inflammation of the joints; a form of *arthritis.

Rhine (German **Rhein**, French **Rhin**) European river rising in Switzerland and reaching the North Sea via Germany and the Netherlands; length 1,320 km/820 mi. Tributaries include the Moselle and the Ruhr. The Rhine is linked with the Mediterranean by the Rhine–Rhône Waterway, and with the Black Sea by the Rhine–Main–Danube Waterway. It is the longest, and the dirtiest, river in Europe.

Rhineland former province of Prussia, ceded in 1815. Its unchallenged annexation by Nazi Germany 1936 was a harbinger of World War II.

Rhineland-Palatinate (German **Rheinland-Pfalz**) administrative region (German *Land*) of Germany
area 19,800 sq km/7,643 sq mi
capital Mainz
towns Ludwigshafen, Koblenz, Trier, Worms
physical wooded mountain country, river valleys of Rhine and Moselle
products wine (75% of German output), tobacco, chemicals, machinery, leather goods, pottery
population (1992) 3,702,000

rhinoceros odd-toed hoofed mammal of the family Rhinocerotidae. The one-horned Indian rhinoceros *Rhinoceros unicornis* is up to 2 m/6 ft high at the shoulder, with a tubercled skin, folded into shieldlike pieces; the African rhinoceroses are smooth-skinned and two-horned. All are endangered.

rhizome or *rootstock horizontal underground plant stem. It is a *perennating organ in some species, where it is generally thick and fleshy, while in other species it is mainly a means of *vegetative reproduction, and is therefore long and slender, with buds all along it that send up new plants. The potato is a rhizome that has two distinct parts, the tuber being the swollen end of a long, cordlike rhizome.

Rhode Island smallest state of the USA, in New England; nickname Little Rhody or the Ocean State
area 3,100 sq km/1,197 sq mi
capital Providence
towns Cranston, Newport, Woonsocket
products apples, potatoes, poultry (notably Rhode Island Reds), dairy products, jewellery (30% of the workforce), textiles, silverware, machinery, rubber, plastics, electronics
population (1990) 1,003,464
history founded 1636 by Roger Williams, exiled from Massachusetts Bay colony for religious dissent; one of the original Thirteen States.

Rhodes (Greek **Ródhos**) Greek island, largest of the Dodecanese, in the E Aegean Sea
area 1,412 sq km/545 sq mi
capital Rhodes
products grapes, olives
population (1981) 88,000
history settled by Greeks about 1000 BC; the *Colossus of Rhodes (fell 224 BC), was one of the *Seven Wonders of the World; held by the Knights Hospitallers of St John 1306–1522; taken from Turkish rule by the Italian occupation 1912; ceded to Greece 1947.

Rhodes Cecil (John) 1853–1902. South African politician, born in the UK, prime minister of Cape Colony 1890–96. Aiming at the formation of a South African federation and the creation of a block of British territory from the Cape to Cairo, he was responsible for the annexation of Bechuanaland (now Botswana) in 1885. He formed the British South Africa Company in 1889, which occupied Mashonaland and Matabeleland, thus forming **Rhodesia** (now Zambia and Zimbabwe).

Rhodesia former name of *Zambia (Northern Rhodesia) and *Zimbabwe (Southern Rhodesia).

rhodium (Greek *rhodon* 'rose') hard, silver-white, metallic element, symbol Rh, atomic number 45, relative atomic mass 102.905. It is one of the so-called platinum group of metals and is resistant to tarnish, corrosion, and acid. It occurs as a free metal in the natural alloy osmiridium and is used in jewellery, electroplating, and thermocouples.

rhododendron any of numerous shrubs of the genus *Rhododendron* of the heath family Ericaceae. Most species are evergreen. The leaves are usually dark and leathery, and the large racemes of flowers occur in all colours except blue. They thrive on acid soils. *Azaleas belong to the same genus.

Rhodope Mountains range of mountains on the frontier between Greece and Bulgaria, rising to 2,925 m/9,497 ft at Musala.

rhombus in geometry, an equilateral (all sides equal) *parallelogram. Its diagonals bisect each other at right angles, and its area is half the product of the lengths of the two diagonals. A rhombus whose internal angles are 90° is called a *square.

Rhône river of S Europe; length 810 km/500 mi. It rises in Switzerland and flows through Lake Geneva to Lyon in France, where at its confluence with the Saône the upper limit of navigation is reached. The river turns due south, passes Vienne and Avignon, and takes in the Isère and other tributaries. Near Arles it divides into the **Grand** and **Petit Rhône**, flowing respectively SE and SW into the Mediterranean W of Marseille.

Rhône-Alpes region of E France in the upper reaches of the Rhône; area 43,700 sq km/16,868 sq mi; population (1992) 5,344,000. It consists of the *départements* of Ain, Ardèche, Drôme, Isère, Loire, Rhône, Savoie, and Haute-Savoie. The chief town is Lyon. There are several notable wine-producing areas, including Chenas, Fleurie, and Beaujolais. Industrial products include chemicals, textiles, and motor vehicles.

rhubarb perennial plant *Rheum rhaponticum* of the buckwheat family Polygonaceae, grown for its pink, edible leaf stalks. The leaves contain oxalic acid, and are poisonous. There are also wild rhubarbs native to Europe and Asia.

rhyme identity of sound, usually in the endings of lines of verse, such as *wing* and *sing*. Avoided in Japanese, it is a common literary device in other Asian and European languages. Rhyme first appeared in Europe in late Latin poetry but was not used in Classical Latin or Greek.

rhythm and blues (R & B) US popular music of the 1940s–60s, which drew on swing and jump-jazz rhythms and blues vocals, and was a progenitor of rock and roll. It diversified into soul, funk, and other styles. R & B artists include

Bo Diddley (1928–), Jackie Wilson (1934–84), and Etta James (c. 1938–).

rhythm method method of natural contraception that works by avoiding intercourse when the woman is producing egg cells (ovulating). The time of ovulation can be worked out by the calendar (counting days from the last period), by temperature changes, or by inspection of the cervical mucus. All these methods are unreliable because it is possible for ovulation to occur at any stage of the menstrual cycle.

rib long, usually curved bone that extends laterally from the *spine in vertebrates. Most fishes and many reptiles have ribs along most of the spine, but in mammals they are found only in the chest area. In humans, there are 12 pairs of ribs. The ribs protect the lungs and heart, and allow the chest to expand and contract easily.

Ribbentrop Joachim von 1893–1946. German Nazi politician and diplomat, foreign minister 1938–45, during which time he negotiated the Non-Aggression Pact between Germany and the USSR. He was tried at Nuremberg as a war criminal 1946 and hanged.

Ribera José (Jusepe) de 1591–1652. Spanish painter, active in Italy from 1616 under the patronage of the viceroys of Naples. His early work shows the impact of Caravaggio, but his colours gradually lightened. He painted many full-length saints and mythological figures and genre scenes, which he produced without preliminary drawing.

riboflavin or *vitamin B₂* *vitamin of the B complex whose absence in the diet causes stunted growth.

ribonucleic acid full name of *RNA.

ribosome in biology, the protein-making machinery of the cell. Ribosomes are located on the endoplasmic reticulum (ER) of eukaryotic cells, and are made of proteins and a special type of *RNA, ribosomal RNA. They receive messenger RNA (copied from the *DNA) and *amino acids, and 'translate' the messenger RNA by using its chemically coded instructions to link amino acids in a specific order, to make a strand of a particular protein.

Ricardo David 1772–1823. English economist, author of *Principles of Political Economy* 1817. Among his discoveries were the principle of *comparative advantage (that countries can benefit by specializing in goods they produce efficiently and trading internationally to buy others), and the law of diminishing returns (that continued increments of capital and labour applied to a given quantity of land will eventually show a declining rate of increase in output).

rice principal cereal of the wet regions of the tropics; derived from grass of the species *Oryza sativa*, probably native to India and SE Asia. It is unique among cereal crops in that it is grown standing in water. The yield is very large, and rice is said to be the staple food of one-third of the world population.

Richard Cliff. Stage name of Harry Roger Webb 1940– . English pop singer. In the late 1950s he was influenced by Elvis Presley, but became a Christian family entertainer, continuing to have hits in the UK through the 1980s. His original

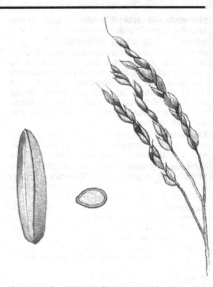

rice Rice takes 150–200 days to mature in warm, wet conditions.

backing group was the *Shadows* (1958–68 and later re-formed).

Richard three kings of England:

Richard I *the Lion-Heart* (French *Coeur-de-Lion*) 1157– . King of England from 1189, who spent all but six months of his reign abroad. He was the third son of Henry II, against whom he twice rebelled. In the third *Crusade 1191–92 he won victories at Cyprus, Acre, and Arsuf (against *Saladin), but failed to recover Jerusalem. While returning overland he was captured by the Duke of Austria, who handed him over to the emperor Henry VI, and he was held prisoner until a large ransom was raised. He then returned briefly to England, where his brother John I had been ruling in his stead. His later years were spent in warfare in France, where he was killed.

Richard II 1367–1400. King of England from 1377, effectively from 1389, son of Edward the Black Prince. He reigned in conflict with Parliament; they executed some of his associates 1388, and he executed some of the opposing barons 1397, whereupon he made himself absolute. Two years later, forced to abdicate in favour of *Henry IV, he was jailed and probably assassinated.

Richard III 1452–1485. King of England from 1483. The son of Richard, Duke of York, he was created duke of Gloucester by his brother Edward IV, and distinguished himself in the Wars of the *Roses. On Edward's death 1483 he became protector to his nephew Edward V, and soon secured the crown for himself on the plea that Edward IV's sons were illegitimate. He proved a capable ruler, but the suspicion that he had murdered Edward V and his brother undermined his popularity. In 1485 Henry, Earl of Richmond (later *Henry VII), raised a rebellion, and Richard III was defeated and killed at *Bosworth.

Richards Gordon 1905–1986. English jockey and trainer who was champion on the flat a record 26 times between 1925 and 1953.

Richards Viv (Isaac Vivian Alexander) 1952– . West Indian cricketer, captain of the West Indies team 1986–91. He played for the Leeward Islands and, in the UK, for Somerset and Glamorgan. A prolific run-scorer, he holds the record for the greatest number of runs made in test cricket in one calendar year (1,710 runs in 1976). He retired from international cricket in 1991.

Richardson Ralph (David) 1902–1983. English actor. He played many stage parts, including Falstaff (Shakespeare), Peer Gynt (Ibsen), and Cyrano de Bergerac (Rostand). He shared the management of the Old Vic theatre with Laurence Olivier 1944–50. In later years he revealed himself as an accomplished deadpan comic.

Richardson Samuel 1689–1761. English novelist, one of the founders of the modern novel. *Pamela* 1740–41, written in the form of a series of letters and containing much dramatic conversation, was sensationally popular all across Europe, and was followed by *Clarissa* 1747–48 and *Sir Charles Grandison* 1753–54.

Richardson Tony 1928–1991. English director and producer. With George Devine he established the English Stage Company 1955 at the Royal Court Theatre, with productions such as *Look Back in Anger* 1956. His films include *Saturday Night and Sunday Morning* 1960, and *Joseph Andrews* 1977.

Richelieu Armand Jean du Plessis de 1585–1642. French cardinal and politician, chief minister from 1624. He aimed to make the monarchy absolute; he ruthlessly crushed opposition by the nobility and destroyed the political power of the *Huguenots, while leaving them religious freedom. Abroad, he sought to establish French supremacy by breaking the power of the Habsburgs and in 1635 brought France into the Thirty Years' War.

Richter Burton 1931– . US particle physicist. In the 1960s he designed the Stanford Positron–Electron Accelerating Ring (SPEAR), a machine designed to collide positrons and electrons at high energies. In 1974 Richter and his team used SPEAR to produce a new subatomic particle, the ψ (psi) meson. This was the first example of a particle formed from a charmed quark, the quark whose existence had been postulated by Sheldon Glashow ten years earlier. Richter shared the 1976 Nobel Physics Prize with Samuel Ting, who had discovered the particle independently.

Richter Charles Francis 1900–1985. US seismologist, deviser of the *Richter scale used to measure the strength of the waves from earthquakes.

Richter scale scale based on measurement of seismic waves, used to determine the magnitude of an *earthquake at its epicentre. The magnitude of an earthquake differs from its intensity, measured by the *Mercalli scale, which is subjective and varies from place to place for the same earthquake. The scale is named after US seismologist Charles Richter.

Richthofen Manfred, Freiherr von (the 'Red Baron') 1892–1918. German aviator. In World War I he commanded the 11th Chasing Squadron, known as *Richthofen's Flying Circus*, and shot down 80 aircraft before being killed in action.

ricin extremely toxic extract from the seeds of the *castor-oil plant. When combined with *monoclonal antibodies, ricin can attack cancer cells, particularly in the treatment of lymphoma and leukaemia.

rickets defective growth of bone in children due to an insufficiency of calcium deposits. The bones, which do not harden adequately, are bent out of shape. It is usually caused by a lack of vitamin D and insufficient exposure to sunlight. Renal rickets, also a condition of malformed bone, is associated with kidney disease.

Ridley Nicholas *c.* 1500–1555. English Protestant bishop. He became chaplain to Henry VIII 1541, and bishop of London 1550. He took an active part in the Reformation and supported Lady Jane Grey's claim to the throne. After Mary's accession he was arrested and burned as a heretic.

Riefenstahl Leni 1902– . German filmmaker. Her film of the Nazi rallies at Nuremberg, *Triumph des Willens/Triumph of the Will* 1934, vividly illustrated Hitler's charismatic appeal but tainted her career. After World War II her work was blacklisted by the Allies until 1952.

Rienzi Cola di *c.* 1313–1354. Italian political reformer. In 1347, he tried to re-establish the forms of an ancient Roman republic. His second attempt seven years later ended with his assassination.

Rietvelt Gerrit Thomas 1888–1964. Dutch architect, an exponent of De *Stijl. He designed the Schroeder House at Utrecht 1924; he is also known for colourful, minimalist chair design.

Rifkind Malcolm Leslie 1946– . British lawyer and Conservative politician, defence secretary from 1992. His incisive intellect has enabled him to manage the 'peace dividend', with its inevitable rundown of parts of the armed forces, more successfully than some of his predecessors.

Riff member of a *Berber people of N Morocco, who under *Abd el-Krim long resisted the Spanish and French.

rifle *firearm that has spiral grooves (rifling) in its barrel. When a bullet is fired, the rifling makes it spin, thereby improving accuracy. Rifles were first introduced in the late 18th century.

rift valley valley formed by the subsidence of a block of the Earth's *crust between two or more parallel *faults. Rift valleys are steep-sided and form where the crust is being pulled apart, as at *ocean ridges, or in the Great Rift Valley of E Africa.

Rift Valley, Great volcanic valley formed 10–20 million years ago by a crack in the Earth's crust and running about 8,000 km/5,000 mi from the Jordan Valley through the Red Sea to central Mozambique in SE Africa. It is marked by a series of lakes, including Lake Turkana and volcanoes, such as Mount Kilimanjaro.

Riga capital and port of Latvia; population (1987) 900,000. A member of the *Hanseatic League from 1282, Riga has belonged in turn to Poland 1582, Sweden 1621, and Russia 1710. It was the capital of independent Latvia 1918–40 and was occupied by Germany 1941–44, before being annexed by the USSR. It again became independent Latvia's capital 1991.

Rigel or **Beta Orionis** brightest star in the constellation Orion. It is a blue-white supergiant, with an estimated diameter 50 times that of the Sun. It is 900 light years from Earth, and is about 100,000 times more luminous than our Sun. It is the seventh brightest star in the sky.

right-angled triangle triangle in which one of the angles is a right angle (90°). It is the basic form of triangle for defining trigonometrical ratios (for example, sine, cosine, and tangent) and for which *Pythagoras' theorem holds true. The longest side of a right-angled triangle is called the hypotenuse; its area is equal to half the product of the lengths of the two shorter sides.

rights an individual's automatic entitlement to certain freedoms and other benefits, usually, in liberal democracies such as the UK, in the context of the individual's relationship with the government of the country. The struggle to assert political and civil rights against arbitrary government has been a major theme of Western political history.

rights issue in finance, new shares offered to existing shareholders to raise new capital. Shareholders receive a discount on the market price while the company benefits from not having the costs of a relaunch of the new issue.

Rights of Man and the Citizen, Declaration of the historic French document. According to the statement of the French National Assembly 1789, these rights include representation in the legislature; equality before the law; equality of opportunity; freedom from arbitrary imprisonment; freedom of speech and religion; taxation in proportion to ability to pay; and security of property. In 1946 were added equal rights for women; right to work, join a union, and strike; leisure, social security, and support in old age; and free education.

right wing the more conservative or reactionary section of a political party or spectrum. It originated in the French national assembly 1789, where the nobles sat in the place of honour on the president's right, whereas the commons were on his left (hence *left wing).

rigor medical term for shivering or rigidity. *Rigor mortis* is the stiffness that ensues in a corpse soon after death, owing to the coagulation of muscle proteins.

Rig-Veda oldest of the *Vedas*, the chief sacred writings of Hinduism. It consists of hymns to the Aryan gods, such as Indra, and to nature gods.

Riley Bridget (Louise) 1931– . English Op art painter. In the early 1960s she invented her characteristic style, arranging hard-edged black and white dots or lines in regular patterns that created disturbing effects of scintillating light and movement; *Fission* 1963 (Museum of Modern Art, New York) is an example. She introduced colour in the late 1960s and experimented with silk-screen prints on Perspex.

Rilke Rainer Maria 1875–1926. Austrian writer. His prose works include the semi-autobiographical *Die Aufzeichnungen des Malte Laurids Brigge/Notebook of Malte Laurids Brigge* 1910.

His verse is characterized by a form of mystic pantheism that seeks to achieve a state of ecstasy in which existence can be apprehended as a whole.

Rimbaud (Jean Nicolas) Arthur 1854–1891. French Symbolist poet. His verse was chiefly written before the age of 20, notably *Les Illuminations* published 1886. From 1871 he lived with *Verlaine.

Rimsky-Korsakov Nikolay Andreyevich 1844–1908. Russian composer. He used Russian folk idiom and rhythms in his Romantic compositions and published a text on orchestration. His operas include *The Maid of Pskov* 1873, *The Snow Maiden* 1882, *Mozart and Salieri* 1898, and *The Golden Cockerel* 1907, a satirical attack on despotism that was banned until 1909.

ring circuit household electrical circuit in which appliances are connected in series to form a ring with each end of the ring connected to the power supply.

ringworm any of various contagious skin infections due to related kinds of fungus, usually resulting in circular, itchy, discoloured patches covered with scales or blisters. The scalp and feet (athlete's foot) are generally involved. Treatment is with *antifungal preparations.

Rio de Janeiro port and resort in E Brazil; population (1991) 5,487,300. The name (Portuguese 'river of January') commemorates the arrival of Portuguese explorers 1 Jan 1502, but there is in fact no river. Sugar Loaf Mountain stands at the entrance to the harbour. Rio was the capital of Brazil 1763–1960.

Rio Grande river rising in the Rocky Mountains in S Colorado, USA, and flowing S to the Gulf of Mexico, where it is reduced to a trickle by irrigation demands on its upper reaches; length 3,050 km/1,900 mi. Its last 2,400 km/1,500 mi form the US–Mexican border (Mexican name *Río Bravo del Norte*).

Rio Grande do Sul most southerly state of Brazil, on the frontier with Argentina and Uruguay; capital Pôrto Alegre; area 282,184 sq km/108,993 sq mi; population (1990) 9,348,300.

Río Muni the mainland portion of *Equatorial Guinea.

riot disturbance caused by a potentially violent mob. In the UK, riots formerly suppressed under the Riot Act are now governed by the Public Order Act 1986. Methods of riot control include plastic bullets, stun bags (soft canvas pouches filled with buckshot which spread out in flight), water cannon, and CS gas (tear gas).

RIP abbreviation for *requiescat in pace* (Latin 'may he/she rest in peace').

ripple tank in physics, shallow water-filled tray used to demonstrate various properties of waves, such as reflection, refraction, diffraction, and interference, by programming and manipulating their movement.

RISC (acronym for *reduced instruction-set computer*) in computing, a microprocessor (processor on a single chip) that carries out fewer instructions than other (*CISC) microprocessors in common use in the 1990s. Because of the low number of *machine-code instructions, the processor carries out those instructions very quickly.

risk capital or **venture capital** finance provided by venture capital companies, individuals, and merchant banks for medium-or long-term business ventures that are not their own and in which there is a strong element of risk.

Risorgimento movement for Italian national unity and independence from 1815. Leading figures in the movement included *Cavour, *Mazzini, and *Garibaldi. Uprisings 1848–49 failed, but with help from France in a war against Austria – to oust it from Italian provinces in the north – an Italian kingdom was founded 1861. Unification was finally completed with the addition of Venetia 1866 and the Papal States 1870.

ritualization in ethology, a stereotype that occurs in certain behaviour patterns when these are incorporated into displays. For example, the exaggerated and stylized head toss of the goldeneye drake during courtship is a ritualization of the bathing movement used to wet the feathers; its duration and form have become fixed. Ritualization may make displays clearly recognizable, so ensuring that individuals mate only with members of their own species.

river long water course that flows down a slope along a channel. It originates at a point called its **source**, and enters a sea or lake at its **mouth**. Along its length it may be joined by smaller rivers called **tributaries**. A river and its tributaries are contained within a *drainage basin.

Rivera Diego 1886–1957. Mexican painter, active in Europe until 1921. He received many public commissions for murals exalting the Mexican revolution. A vast cycle on historical themes (National Palace, Mexico City) was begun 1929. In the 1930s he visited the USA and with Ben Shan produced murals for the Rockefeller Center, New York (later overpainted because he included a portrait of Lenin).

Rivera Primo de. Spanish politician; see *Primo de Rivera.

riveting method of joining metal plates. A hot metal pin called a rivet, which has a head at one end, is inserted into matching holes in two overlapping plates, then the other end is struck and formed into another head, holding the plates tight. Riveting is used in building construction, boilermaking, and shipbuilding.

Riviera the Mediterranean coast of France and Italy from Marseille to La Spezia.

Riyadh (Arabic **Ar Riyād**) capital of Saudi Arabia and of the Central Province, formerly the sultanate of Nejd, in an oasis, connected by rail with Dammam on the Arabian Gulf; population (1986) 1,500,000.

Rizzio David 1533–1566. Italian adventurer at the court of Mary Queen of Scots. After her marriage to *Darnley, Rizzio's influence over her incited her husband's jealousy, and he was murdered by Darnley and his friends.

RKO (Radio Keith Orpheum) US film production and distribution company, formed 1928 through mergers and acquisitions. It was the most financially unstable of the major Hollywood studios, despite the success of many of its films, including *King Kong* 1933 and the series of musicals starring Fred Astaire and Ginger Rogers. In 1948, Howard *Hughes bought the studio and acceler-

MAJOR RIVERS

name and location	km	mi
Nile (NE Africa)	6,695	4,160
Amazon (South America)	6,570	4,080
Chang Jiang (China)	6,300	3,900
Mississippi–Missouri (USA)	6,020	3,740
Ob–Irtysh (China/Kazakhstan/Russia)	5,600	3,480
Huang He (China)	5,464	3,395
Paraná (Brazil)	4,500	2,800
Zaïre (Africa)	4,500	2,800
Mekong (Asia)	4,425	2,750
Amur (Asia)	4,416	2,744
Lena (Russia)	4,400	2,730
Mackenzie (Canada)	4,241	2,635
Niger (Africa)	4,185	2,600
Yenisei (Russia)	4,100	2,550
Mississippi (USA)	3,780	2,350
Murray–Darling (Australia)	3,750	2,330
Missouri (USA)	3,725	2,328
Volga (Russia)	3,685	2,290
Euphrates (Iraq)	3,600	2,240
Madeira (Brazil)	3,240	2,013
São Francisco (Brazil)	3,199	1,988
Yukon (USA/Canada)	3,185	1,979
Indus (Tibet/Pakistan)	3,180	1,975
Syrdar'ya (Kazakhstan)	3,078	1,913
Rio Grande (USA/Mexico)	3,050	1,900
Purus (Brazil)	2,993	1,860
Danube (Europe)	2,858	1,776
Brahmaputra (Asia)	2,850	1,770
Japurá (Brazil)	2,816	1,750
Salween (Myanmar/China)	2,800	1,740
Tocantins (Brazil)	2,699	1,677
Zambezi (Africa)	2,650	1,650
Paraguay (Paraguay)	2,591	1,610
Nelson–Saskatchewan (Canada)	2,570	1,600
Orinoco (Venezuela)	2,600	1,600
Amu Darya (Tajikistan/Turkmenistan/Uzbekistan)	2,540	1,578
Ural (Russia/Kazakhstan)	2,534	1,575
Kolyma (Russia)	2,513	1,562
Ganges (India/Bangladesh)	2,510	1,560
Orinoco (Venezuela)	2,400	1,490

ated its decline by poor management. The company ceased production 1953.

RN abbreviation for **Royal Navy**; see under *navy.

RNA **ribonucleic acid** nucleic acid involved in the process of translating the genetic material *DNA into proteins. It is usually single-stranded, unlike the double-stranded DNA, and consists of a large number of nucleotides strung together, each of which comprises the sugar ribose, a phosphate group, and one of four bases (uracil, cytosine, adenine, or guanine). RNA is copied from DNA by the formation of *base pairs, with uracil taking the place of thymine.

roach any freshwater fish of the Eurasian genus *Rutilus*, of the carp family, especially *R. rutilus* of N Europe. It is dark green above, whitish below, with reddish lower fins; it grows to 35 cm/1.2 ft.

Roach Hal 1892–1992. US film producer, usually of comedies, who was active from the 1910s to the 1940s. He worked with *Laurel and Hardy, and also produced films for Harold Lloyd and Charley Chase. His work includes *The*

roadrunner *The greater roadrunner feeds on ground-dwelling insects, which it kills by a sudden pounce on the prey.*

Music Box 1932, *Way Out West* 1936, and *Of Mice and Men* 1939.

road specially constructed route for wheeled vehicles to travel on. Reinforced tracks became necessary with the invention of wheeled vehicles in about 3000 BC and most ancient civilizations had some form of road network. The Romans developed engineering techniques that were not equalled for another 1,400 years.

roadrunner crested North American ground-dwelling bird *Geococcyx californianus* of the *cuckoo family, found in the SW USA and Mexico. It can run at a speed of 25 kph/15 mph.

Robbe-Grillet Alain 1922– . French writer, the leading theorist of *le nouveau roman* ('the new novel'), for example his own *Les Gommes/The Erasers* 1953, *La Jalousie/Jealousy* 1957, and *Dans le labyrinthe/In the Labyrinth* 1959, which concentrates on the detailed description of physical objects. He also wrote the script for the film *L'Année dernière à Marienbad/Last Year in Marienbad* 1961.

Robben Island prison island in Table Bay, Cape Town, South Africa.

robbery in law, a variety of *theft: stealing from a person, using force, or the threat of force, to intimidate the victim.

Robbia, della Italian family of sculptors and architects, active in Florence. *Luca della Robbia* (1400–1482) created a number of major works in Florence, notably the marble *cantoria* (singing gallery) in the cathedral 1431–38 (Museo del Duomo), with lively groups of choristers. Luca also developed a characteristic style of glazed terracotta work.

Robbins Jerome 1918– . US dancer and choreographer, codirector of the New York City Ballet 1969–83 (with George Balanchine). His ballets are internationally renowned and he is considered the greatest US-born ballet choreographer. He also choreographed the musicals *The King and I* 1951, *West Side Story* 1957, and *Fiddler on the Roof* 1964.

Robert two dukes of Normandy:

Robert I the Devil Duke of Normandy from 1028. He was the father of William the Conqueror, and is the hero of several romances; he was legendary for his cruelty.

Robert II *c.* 1054–1134. Eldest son of *William I (the Conqueror), succeeding him as duke of Normandy (but not on the English throne) 1087. His brother *William II ascended the English

throne, and they warred until 1096, after which Robert took part in the First Crusade. When his other brother *Henry I claimed the English throne 1100, Robert contested the claim and invaded England unsuccessfully 1101. Henry invaded Normandy 1106, and captured Robert, who remained a prisoner in England until his death.

Robert three kings of Scotland:

Robert I Robert the Bruce 1274–1329. King of Scotland from 1306, and grandson of Robert de *Bruce. He shared in the national uprising led by William *Wallace, and, after Wallace's execution 1305, rose once more against Edward I of England, and was crowned at Scone 1306. He defeated Edward II at *Bannockburn 1314. In 1328 the treaty of Northampton recognized Scotland's independence and Robert as king.

Robert II 1316–1390. King of Scotland from 1371. He was the son of Walter (1293–1326), steward of Scotland, who married Marjory, daughter of Robert I. He was the first king of the house of Stuart.

Robert III *c.* 1340–1406. King of Scotland from 1390, son of Robert II. He was unable to control the nobles, and the government fell largely into the hands of his brother, Robert, Duke of Albany (*c.* 1340–1420).

Robeson Paul 1898–1976. US bass singer and actor. He graduated from Columbia University as a lawyer, but limited opportunities for blacks led him instead to the stage. He appeared in *The Emperor Jones* 1924 and *Showboat* 1928, in which he sang 'Ol' Man River'. He played *Othello* in 1930, and his films include *Sanders of the River* 1935 and *King Solomon's Mines* 1937. An ardent advocate of black rights, he had his passport withdrawn 1950–58 because of his association with left-wing movements. He then left the USA to live in England.

Robespierre Maximilien François Marie Isidore de 1758–1794. French politician in the *French Revolution. As leader of the *Jacobins in the National Convention, he supported the execution of Louis XVI and the overthrow of the right-wing republican Girondins, and in July 1793 was elected to the Committee of Public Safety. A year later he was guillotined; many believe that he was a scapegoat for the Reign of *Terror since he ordered only 72 executions personally.

robin migratory songbird *Erithacus rubecula* of the thrush family, found in Europe, W Asia, Africa, and the Azores. About 13 cm/5 in long, both sexes are olive brown with a red breast. The nest is constructed in a sheltered place, and from five to seven white freckled eggs are laid.

Robin Hood legendary English outlaw and champion of the poor against the rich. He is said to have lived in Sherwood Forest, Nottinghamshire, during the reign of Richard I (1189–99). He feuded with the sheriff of Nottingham, accompanied by Maid Marian and a band of followers known as his 'merry men'. He appears in ballads from the 13th century, but his first datable appearance is in Langland's *Piers Plowman* about 1377.

Robinson Edward G. Stage name of Emanuel

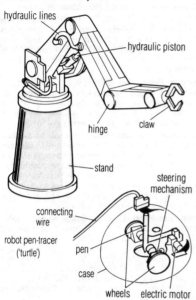

robot arm on assembly line

hydraulic lines

hydraulic piston

hinge

claw

stand

steering mechanism

connecting wire

robot pen-tracer ('turtle')

pen

case

wheels   electric motor

robot Two simple robots.

Goldenberg 1893–1973. US film actor, born in Romania, who emigrated with his family to the USA 1903. He was noted for his gangster roles, such as *Little Caesar* 1930.

Robinson Mary 1944– . Irish Labour politician, president from 1990. She became a professor of law at 25. A strong supporter of women's rights, she has campaigned for the liberalization of Ireland's laws prohibiting divorce and abortion.

Robinson Smokey (William) 1940– . US singer, songwriter, and record producer, associated with *Motown records from its conception. He was lead singer of the Miracles 1957–72 (hits include 'Shop Around' 1961, 'The Tears of a Clown' 1970) and his solo hits include 'Cruisin' 1979 and 'Being With You' 1981. His light tenor voice and wordplay characterize his work.

Robinson W(illiam) Heath 1872–1944. English cartoonist and illustrator who made humorous drawings of bizarre machinery for performing simple tasks, such as raising one's hat. A clumsily designed apparatus is often described as a 'Heath Robinson' contraption.

Robinson Sugar Ray. Adopted name of Walker Smith 1920–1989. US boxer, world welterweight champion 1945–51; he defended his title five times. Defeating Jake LaMotta 1951, he took the middleweight title. He lost the title six times and won it seven times. He retired at the age of 45.

robot any machine controlled by electronic chip or computer that can be programmed to do work (robotics, as opposed to mechanical work, called automation). The most common types are robotic 'arms'; when fixed to the floor or a workbench, they perform functions such as paint spraying or assembling parts in factories. Others include

radio-directed or computer-controlled vehicles for carrying materials, and a miscellany of devices from cruise missiles and deep-sea and space-exploration craft to robotic toys.

Rocard Michel 1930– . French socialist politician, prime minister 1988–91. A former radical, he joined the Socialist Party (PS) 1973, emerging as leader of its moderate social-democratic wing. He held ministerial office under President François Mitterrand 1981–85.

rock constituent of the Earth's crust, composed of mineral particles and/or materials of organic origin consolidated into a hard mass as *igneous, *sedimentary, or *metamorphic rocks.

rock and roll pop music born of a fusion of rhythm and blues and country and western and based on electric guitar and drums. In the mid-1950s, with the advent of Elvis Presley, it became the heartbeat of teenage rebellion in the West and also had considerable impact on other parts of the world. It found perhaps its purest form in late-1950s *rockabilly*, the style of white Southerners in the USA; the blanket term 'rock' later came to comprise a multitude of styles.

rock climbing sport originally an integral part of mountaineering. It began as a form of training for Alpine expeditions and is now divided into three categories: the *outcrop climb* for climbs of up to 30 m/100 ft; the *crag climb* on cliffs of 30–300 m/100–1,000 ft, and the *big wall climb*, which is the nearest thing to Alpine climbing, but without the hazards of snow and ice.

Rockefeller John D(avison) 1839–1937. US millionaire, founder of Standard Oil 1870 (which achieved control of 90% of US refineries by 1882). He founded the philanthropic *Rockefeller Foundation* 1913, to which his son *John D(avison) Rockefeller Jr* (1874–1960) devoted his life.

rocket projectile driven by the reaction of gases produced by a fast-burning fuel. Unlike jet engines, which are also reaction engines, modern rockets carry their own oxygen supply to burn their fuel and do not require any surrounding atmosphere. For warfare, rocket heads carry an explosive device.

Rocky Mountains or *Rockies* largest North American mountain system. They extend from the junction with the Mexican plateau, northwards through the west central states of the USA, through Canada to S Alaska. The highest mountain is Mount McKinley (6,194 m/20,320 ft).

Rococo movement in the arts and architecture in 18th-century Europe, tending towards lightness, elegance, delicacy, and decorative charm. The term 'Rococo' refers to *rocaille* (rock-or shell-work), a style of interior decoration based on S-curves and scroll-like forms. Watteau's paintings and Sèvres porcelain belong to the French Rococo vogue. In the 1730s the movement became widespread in Europe, notably in the churches and palaces of S Germany and Austria.

rodent any mammal of the worldwide order Rodentia, making up nearly half of all mammal species. Besides ordinary 'cheek teeth', they have a single front pair of incisor teeth in both upper and lower jaw, which continue to grow as they are worn down.

rodeo originally a practical means of rounding up cattle in North America. It is now a professional sport in the USA and Canada. Ranching skills such as bronco busting, bull riding, steer wrestling, and calf roping are all rodeo events. Because rodeo livestock is valuable, rules for its handling are laid out by the American Humane Association, yet criticism has been levelled at rodeos for cruel treatment of their animals.

Rodgers Richard (Charles) 1902–1979. US composer. He collaborated with librettist Lorenz Hart (1895–1943) on songs such as 'Blue Moon' 1934 and musicals such as *On Your Toes* 1936, and with Oscar *Hammerstein II (1895–1960) wrote musicals such as *Oklahoma!* 1943, *South Pacific* 1949, *The King and I* 1951, and *The Sound of Music* 1959.

Ródhos Greek name for the island of *Rhodes.

Rodin Auguste 1840–1917. French sculptor, often considered the greatest of his day. Through his work he freed sculpture from the idealizing conventions of the time by his realistic treatment of the human figure, introducing a new boldness of style and expression. Examples are *Le Penseur/The Thinker* 1880 (Musée Rodin, Paris), *Le Baiser/The Kiss* 1886 (marble version in the Louvre, Paris), and *The Burghers of Calais* 1884–86 (copy in Embankment Gardens, Westminster, London).

roebuck male of the Eurasian roe *deer.

Roeg Nicolas 1928– . English film director and writer. He was initially a camera operator. His striking visual style is often combined with fractured, disturbing plots, as in *Performance* 1970, *Don't Look Now* 1973, *The Man Who Fell to Earth* 1976, and *The Witches* 1989.

roentgen or **röntgen** unit (symbol R) of radiation exposure, used for X-rays and gamma rays. It is defined in terms of the number of ions produced in one cubic centimetre of air by the radiation. Exposure to 1,000 roentgens gives rise to an absorbed dose of about 870 rads (8.7 grays), which is a dose equivalent of 870 rems (8.7 sieverts).

Roe v Wade US Supreme Court decision 1973 dealing with the constitutionality of state anti-abortion laws. The case challenged a Texas statute prohibiting the abortion of pregnancies that did not threaten the mother's life. The Court struck down the Texas law, ruling that state prohibition of abortion is unconstitutional on two grounds: (1) women are guaranteed the right to privacy by the 14th Amendment, and (2) unborn fetuses are not persons with the right to equal protection of the law. The highly controversial ruling limited state regulation to the prohibition of third-trimester abortions.

Rogers Carl 1902–1987. US psychologist who developed the client-centred approach to counselling and psychotherapy. This stressed the importance of clients making their own decisions and developing their own potential (self-actualization).

Rogers Ginger. Stage name of Virginia Katherine McMath 1911–1995. US actress, dancer, and singer. She worked from the 1930s to the 1950s, often starring with Fred Astaire in such films as *Top Hat* 1935 and *Swing Time*

1936. Her later work includes *Bachelor Mother* 1939 and *Kitty Foyle* 1940 (Academy Award).

Rogers Richard 1933– . English High Tech architect. His works include the Pompidou Centre in Paris 1977 (jointly with Renzo Piano), the Lloyd's of London building in London 1986, and the Reuters building at Blackwall Yard, London, 1992.

Roget Peter Mark 1779–1869. English physician, one of the founders of the University of London, and author of a *Thesaurus of English Words and Phrases* 1852, a text constantly revised and still in print, offering synonyms.

Rohmer Eric. Adopted name of Jean-Marie Maurice Schérer 1920– . French film director and writer. Part of the French *New Wave, his films are often concerned with the psychology of self-deception. They include *Ma Nuit chez Maud/My Night at Maud's* 1969, *Le Genou de Claire/Claire's Knee* 1970, and *Die Marquise von O/The Marquise of O* 1976.

Roh Tae-woo 1932– . South Korean right-wing politician and general, president 1988–93. He held ministerial office from 1981 under President Chun, and became chair of the ruling Democratic Justice Party 1985. He was elected president 1988, amid allegations of fraud and despite being connected with the massacre of about 2,000 anti-government demonstrators 1980.

Roland French hero whose real and legendary deeds of valour and chivalry inspired many romances, including the 11th-century *Chanson de Roland* and Ariosto's *Orlando furioso*. A knight of *Charlemagne, Roland was killed in 778 with his friend Oliver and the 12 peers of France at Roncesvalles (in the Pyrenees) by Basques. He headed the rearguard during Charlemagne's retreat from his invasion of Spain.

role in the social sciences, the part(s) a person plays in society, either in helping the social system to work or in fulfilling social responsibilities towards others. *Role play* refers to the way in which children learn adult roles by acting them out in play (mothers and fathers, cops and robbers). Everyone has a number of roles to play in a society: for example, a woman may be an employee, mother, and wife at the same time.

roller any brightly coloured bird of the Old World family Coraciidae, resembling crows but in the same order as kingfishers and hornbills. Rollers grow up to 32 cm/13 in long. The name is derived from the habit of some species of rolling over in flight.

rolling common method of shaping metal. Rolling is carried out by giant mangles, consisting of several sets, or stands, of heavy rollers positioned one above the other. Red-hot metal slabs are rolled into sheet and also (using shaped rollers) girders and rails.

Rolling Stones, the British band formed 1962, once notorious as the 'bad boys' of rock. Original members were Mick Jagger (1943–), Keith Richards (1943–), Brian Jones (1942–1969), Bill Wyman (1936–), Charlie Watts (1941–), and the pianist Ian Stewart (1938–1985). A rock-and-roll institution, the Rolling Stones were still performing and recording in the 1990s.

Rollins Sonny (Theodore Walter) 1930– . US tenor saxophonist and jazz composer. A leader of the hard-bop school, he is known for the intensity and bravado of his music and for his skilful improvisation.

Rollo First duke of Normandy c. 860–932. Viking leader. He left Norway about 875 and marauded, sailing up the Seine to Rouen. He besieged Paris 886, and in 912 was baptized and granted the province of Normandy by Charles III of France. He was its duke until his retirement to a monastery 927. He was an ancestor of William the Conqueror.

Rolls Charles Stewart 1877–1910. British engineer who joined with Henry *Royce in 1905 to design and produce cars.

ROM (acronym for **read-only memory**) in computing, a memory device in the form of a collection of integrated circuits (chips), frequently used in microcomputers. ROM chips are loaded with data and programs during manufacture and, unlike *RAM (random-access memory) chips, can subsequently only be read, not written to, by computer. However, the contents of the chips are not lost when the power is switched off, as happens in RAM.

Romagna area of Italy on the Adriatic coast, under papal rule 1278–1860 and now part of the region of *Emilia-Romagna.

Roman art sculpture and painting of ancient Rome, from the 4th century BC to the fall of the Western Empire 5th century AD. Much Roman art was intended for public education, notably the sculpted triumphal arches and giant columns, such as Trajan's Column AD 106–113, and portrait sculptures of soldiers, politicians, and emperors. Surviving mural paintings (in Pompeii, Rome, and Ostia) and mosaic decorations show Greek influence. Roman art was to prove of lasting inspiration in the West.

Roman Britain period in British history from the mid-1st century BC to the mid-4th century AD. England was rapidly Romanized, but north of York fewer remains of Roman civilization have been found. Roman towns include London, York, Chester, St Albans, Colchester, Lincoln, Gloucester, and Bath. The most enduring mark of the occupation was the system of military roads radiating from London.

Roman Catholicism one of the main divisions of the Christian religion, separate from the Eastern Orthodox Church from 1054, and headed by the pope. For history and beliefs, see *Christianity. Membership is about 585 million worldwide, concentrated in S Europe, Latin America, and the Philippines.

romance in literature, tales of love and adventure, in verse or prose, that became popular in France about 1200 and spread throughout Europe. There were Arthurian romances about the legendary King Arthur and his knights, and romances based on the adventures of Charlemagne and on classical themes. In the 20th century the term 'romantic novel' is often used disparagingly, to imply a contrast with a realist novel.

Romance languages branch of Indo-European languages descended from the Latin of the Roman Empire ('popular' or 'vulgar' as opposed to 'classical' Latin). The present-day Romance languages with national status are French, Italian, Portuguese, Romanian, and Spanish.

Roman Empire from 27 BC to the 5th century AD; see *Rome, ancient.

Romanesque architecture style of W European *architecture of the 10th to 12th centuries, marked by rounded arches, solid volumes, and emphasis on perpendicular elements. In England the style is also known as *Norman architecture.

Romania

area 237,500 sq km/91,699 sq mi
capital Bucharest
towns Braşov, Timişoara, Cluj-Napoca, Iaşi; ports Galaţi, Constanta, Brăila
physical mountains surrounding a plateau, with river plains S and E
environment although sulphur-dioxide levels are low, only 20% of the country's rivers can provide drinkable water
head of state Ion Iliescu from 1989
head of government Nicolai Vacaroiu from 1992
political system emergent democratic republic
exports petroleum products and oilfield equipment, electrical goods, cars, cereals
currency leu
population (1993) 23,200,000 (Romanians 89%, Hungarians 7.9%, Germans 1.6%); growth rate 0.5% p.a.
languages Romanian (official), Hungarian, German
religions Romanian Orthodox 80%, Roman Catholic 6%
GNP $1,340 per head (1991)
chronology
1944 Pro-Nazi Antonescu government overthrown.
1945 Communist-dominated government appointed.
1947 Boundaries redrawn. King Michael abdicated and People's Republic proclaimed.
1949 New Soviet-style constitution adopted. Joined Comecon.
1952 Second new Soviet-style constitution.
1955 Romania joined Warsaw Pact.
1958 Soviet occupation forces removed.
1965 New constitution adopted.
1974 Ceauşescu created president.

1985–86 Winters of austerity and power cuts.
1987 Workers demonstrated against austerity programme.
1988–89 Relations with Hungary deteriorated over 'systematization programme'.
1989 Announcement that all foreign debt paid off. Razing of villages and building of monuments to Ceauşescu. Communist orthodoxy reaffirmed; demonstrations violently suppressed; massacre in Timisoara. Army joined uprising; heavy fighting; bloody overthrow of Ceauşescu regime in 'Christmas Revolution'; Ceauşescu and wife tried and executed; estimated 10,000 dead in civil warfare. Power assumed by new National Salvation Front, headed by Ion Iliescu.
1990 Securitate secret police replaced by new Romanian Intelligence Service; religious practices resumed; mounting strikes and protests against effects of market economy.
1991 Treaty on cooperation and good neighbourliness signed with USSR. Privatization law passed. Prime minister Petre Roman resigned following riots; succeeded by Theodor Stolojan heading a new cross-party coalition government. New constitution endorsed by referendum.
1992 Iliescu re-elected president; Nicolai Vacaroiu appointed prime minister.
1993 Formal invitation to apply for European Community membership.

Romanian language member of the Romance branch of the Indo-European language family, spoken in Romania, Macedonia, Albania, and parts of N Greece. It has been strongly influenced by the Slavonic languages and by Greek. The Cyrillic alphabet was used until the 19th century, when a variant of the Roman alphabet was adopted.

Roman law legal system of ancient Rome that is now the basis of *civil law, one of the main European legal systems.

Roman numerals ancient European number system using symbols different from Arabic numerals (the ordinary numbers 1, 2, 3, 4, 5, and so on). The seven key symbols in Roman numerals, as represented today, are I (1), V (5), X (10), L (50), C (100), D (500) and M (1,000). There is no zero, and therefore no place-value as is fundamental to the Arabic system. The first ten Roman numerals are I, II, III, IV (or IIII), V, VI, VII, VIII, IX, and X. When a Roman symbol is preceded by a symbol of equal or greater value, the values of the symbols are added (XVI = 16). When a symbol is preceded by a symbol of less value, the values are subtracted (XL = 40). A horizontal bar over a symbol indicates a multiple of 1,000 ($\bar{X}$ = 10,000). Although addition and subtraction are fairly straightforward using Roman numerals, the absence of a zero makes other arithmetic calculations (such as multiplication) clumsy and difficult.

Romano Giulio. See *Giulio Romano, Italian painter and architect.

Romanov dynasty rulers of Russia from 1613 to the *Russian Revolution 1917. Under the Romanovs, Russia developed into an absolutist empire.

Romanticism in literature, music, and art, a style that emphasizes the imagination, emotions, and creativity of the individual artist. The term is often used to characterize the culture of 19th-century Europe, as contrasted with 18th-century *Classicism.

Romanticism in music, term that generally refers to a preoccupation with the expression of emotion and with nature and folk history as a source of inspiration. Often linked with nationalistic feelings, the Romantic movement reached its height in the late 19th century, as in the works of Schumann and Wagner.

Romany member of a nomadic people, also called *Gypsy* (a corruption of 'Egyptian', since they were erroneously thought to come from Egypt). They are now believed to have originated in NW India, and live throughout the world. The Romany language, spoken in several different dialects, belongs to the Indic branch of the Indo-European family.

Rome (Italian *Roma*) capital of Italy and of Lazio region, on the river Tiber, 27 km/17 mi from the Tyrrhenian Sea; population (1987) 2,817,000. Rome has few industries but is an important cultural, road, and rail centre. A large section of the population finds employment in government offices. Remains of the ancient city include the Forum, Colosseum, and Pantheon.

Rome, ancient civilization based in Rome, which lasted for about 800 years. Traditionally founded 753 BC, Rome became a republic 510 BC. From then, its history is one of almost continual expansion until the murder of Julius *Caesar and foundation of the empire under *Augustus and his successors. At its peak under *Trajan, the Roman Empire stretched from Britain to Mesopotamia and the Caspian Sea. A long train of emperors ruling by virtue of military, rather than civil, power marked the beginning of Rome's long decline; under *Diocletian, the empire was divided into two parts – East and West – although temporarily reunited under *Constantine, the first emperor formally to adopt Christianity. The end of the Roman Empire is generally dated by the sack of Rome by the Goths AD 410, or by the deposition of the last emperor in the west AD 476. The Eastern Empire continued until 1453 at *Constantinople.

Rome–Berlin Axis another name for the *Axis.

Rome, Sack of AD 410. The invasion and capture of the city of Rome by the Goths, generally accepted as marking the effective end of the Roman Empire.

Rome, Treaties of two international agreements signed 25 March 1957 by Belgium, France, West Germany, Italy, Luxembourg, and the Netherlands, which established the European Economic Community (*European Community) and the European Atomic Energy Commission (EURATOM).

Rommel Erwin 1891–1944. German field marshal. He served in World War I, and in World War II he played an important part in the invasions of central Europe and France. He was commander of the N African offensive from 1941 (when he was nicknamed 'Desert Fox') until defeated in the Battles of El *Alamein.

Romney George 1734–1802. English portrait painter, active in London from 1762. He became, with Gainsborough and Reynolds, one of the most successful portrait painters of the late 18th century. He painted several portraits of Lady Hamilton, Admiral Nelson's mistress.

Romulus in Roman mythology, legendary founder and first king of Rome, the son of Mars and Rhea Silvia, daughter of Numitor, king of Alba Longa. Romulus and his twin brother Remus were thrown into the Tiber by their great-uncle Amulius, who had deposed Numitor, but were suckled by a she-wolf and rescued by a shepherd. On reaching adulthood they killed Amulius and founded Rome.

Romulus Augustulus born c. AD 461. Last Roman emperor in the West. He was made emperor by his father Orestes, a soldier, about 475 but was compelled to abdicate 476 by Odoacer, leader of the barbarian mercenaries, who nicknamed him Augustulus. Orestes was executed and Romulus Augustulus confined to a Neapolitan villa.

rondo form of instrumental music in which the principal section returns like a refrain. Rondo form is often used for the last movement of a sonata or concerto.

Rondônia state in NW Brazil; the centre of Amazonian tin and gold mining and of experiments in agricultural colonization; area 243,044 sq km/93,876 sq mi; population (1991) 1,373,700. Known as the Federal Territory of **Guaporé** until 1956, it became a state 1981.

Ronsard Pierre de 1524–1585. French poet, leader of the *Pléiade group of poets. Under the patronage of Charles IX, he published original verse in a lightly sensitive style, including odes and love sonnets, such as *Odes* 1550, *Les Amours/Lovers* 1552–53, and the 'Marie' cycle, *Continuation des amours/Lovers Continued* 1555–56.

röntgen alternative spelling for *roentgen, unit of X-and gamma-ray exposure.

Röntgen (or **Roentgen**) Wilhelm Konrad 1845–1923. German physicist who discovered X-rays 1895. While investigating the passage of electricity through gases, he noticed the *fluorescence of a barium platinocyanide screen. This radiation passed through some substances opaque to light, and affected photographic plates. Developments from this discovery have revolutionized medical diagnosis.

rook gregarious European *crow *Corvus frugilegus*. The plumage is black and lustrous and the face bare; a rook can grow to 45 cm/18 in long. Rooks nest in colonies at the tops of trees.

Rooney Mickey. Stage name of Joe Yule 1920– . US actor who began his career aged two in his parents' stage act. He played Andy Hardy in the Hardy family series of B-films (1936–46) and starred opposite Judy Garland in several musicals, including *Babes in Arms* 1939.

Roosevelt (Anna) Eleanor 1884–1962. US social worker, lecturer and First Lady; her newspaper column 'My Day' was widely syndicated. She was a delegate to the UN general assembly and chair of the UN commission on human rights 1946–51. She helped to draw up the Declaration of Human Rights at the UN 1945. Within the Democratic Party she formed the left-wing Americans for Democratic Action group 1947. She was married to President Franklin Roosevelt.

Roosevelt Franklin D(elano) 1882–1945. 32nd president of the USA 1933–45, a Democrat. He served as governor of New York 1929–33. Becoming president during the *Depression, he launched the *New Deal* economic and social reform programme, which made him popular with the people. After the outbreak of World War II he introduced *lend-lease for the supply of war materials and services to the Allies and drew up the *Atlantic Charter of solidarity. Once the USA had entered the war 1941, he spent much time in meetings with Allied leaders (see *Québec, *Tehran, and *Yalta conferences).

Roosevelt Theodore 1858–1919. 26th president of the USA 1901–09, a Republican. After serving as governor of New York 1898–1900 he became vice president to *McKinley, whom he succeeded as president on McKinley's assassination 1901. He campaigned against the great trusts (associations of enterprises that reduce competition), while carrying on a jingoist foreign policy designed to enforce US supremacy over Latin America.

root the part of a plant that is usually underground, and whose primary functions are anchorage and the absorption of water and dissolved mineral salts. Roots usually grow downwards and towards water (that is, they are positively geotropic and hydrotropic; see *tropism). Plants such as epiphytic orchids, which grow above ground, produce aerial roots that absorb moisture from the atmosphere. Others, such as ivy, have climbing roots arising from the stems, which serve to attach the plant to trees and walls.

root of an equation, a value that makes the equation true. For example, $x = 0$ and $x = 5$ are roots of the equation $x^2 - 5x = 0$.

root crop plant cultivated for its swollen edible root (which may or may not be a true root). Potatoes are the major temperate root crop; the major tropical root crops are cassava, yams, and sweet potatoes. Together they are second in importance only to cereals as human food. Roots have a high carbohydrate content, but their protein content rarely exceeds 2%. Consequently, communities relying almost exclusively upon roots may suffer from protein deficiency. Food production for a given area from roots is greater than from cereals.

root hair tubular outgrowth from a cell on the surface of a plant root. It is a delicate structure, which survives for a few days only and does not develop into a root. New root hairs are continually being formed near the root tip to replace the ones that are lost. The majority of land plants possess root hairs, which greatly increase the surface area available for the absorption of water and mineral salts from the soil. The layer of the root's epidermis that produces root hairs is known as the *piliferous layer*.

roots music term originally denoting *reggae, later encompassing any music indigenous to a particular culture; see *world music.

rootstock another name for *rhizome.

rope stout cordage with circumference over 2.5 cm/1 in. Rope is made similarly to thread or twine, by twisting yarns together to form strands, which are then in turn twisted around one another in the direction opposite to that of the yarns. Although *hemp is still used to make rope, nylon is increasingly used.

Rorschach test in psychology, method of diagnosis involving the use of inkblot patterns that subjects are asked to interpret, to help indicate personality type, degree of intelligence, and emotional stability. It was invented by the Swiss psychiatrist Hermann Rorschach (1884–1922).

rosary string of beads used in a number of religions, including Buddhism, Christianity, and Islam. The term also refers to a form of prayer used by Catholics, consisting of 150 *Ave Marias and 15 *Paternosters and Glorias, or to a string of 165 beads for keeping count of these prayers; it is linked with the adoration of the Virgin Mary.

Roscoff port N Brittany, France with a ferry link to Plymouth in England; population (1982) 4,000.

Roscommon (originally Ros-Comain, 'wood around a monastery') county of the Republic of Ireland in the province of Connacht
area 2,460 sq km/950 sq mi
towns Roscommon (county town)
physical bounded on the E by the river Shannon; lakes: Gara, Key, Allen; rich pastures
population (1991) 51,900.

rose *There are many species of rose, and many cultivated varieties.*

rose any shrub or climber of the genus *Rosa*, family Rosaceae, with prickly stems and fragrant flowers in many different colours. Numerous cultivated forms have been derived from the Eurasian sweetbrier or eglantine *R. rubiginosa* and dogrose *R. canina*. There are many climbing varieties, but the forms more commonly cultivated are bush roses and standards (cultivated roses grafted on to a briar stem).

Roseau formerly ***Charlotte Town*** capital of *Dominica, West Indies; population (1981) 20,000.

rosebay willowherb common perennial weed. See *willowherb.

Rosebery Archibald Philip Primrose, 5th Earl of Rosebery 1847–1929. British Liberal politician. He was foreign secretary 1886 and 1892–94, when he succeeded Gladstone as prime minister, but his government survived less than a year. After 1896 his imperialist views gradually placed him further from the mainstream of the Liberal Party.

Roseires, Er port at the head of navigation of the Blue Nile in Sudan. A hydroelectric scheme here provides the country with 70% of its electrical power.

rosemary evergreen shrub *Rosemarinus officinalis* of the mint family Labiatae, native to the Mediterranean and W Asia, with small, scented leaves. It is widely cultivated as a culinary herb and for the aromatic oil extracted from the clusters of pale blue or purple flowers.

Rosenberg Alfred 1893–1946. German politician, born in Tallinn, Estonia. He became the chief Nazi ideologist and was minister for eastern occupied territories 1941–44. He was tried at *Nuremberg 1946 as a war criminal and hanged.

Roses, Wars of the civil wars in England 1455–85 between the houses of *Lancaster (badge, red rose) and *York (badge, white rose), both of whom claimed the throne through descent from the sons of Edward III. As a result of *Henry VI's lapse into insanity, Richard, Duke of York, was installed as protector of the realm. Upon his recovery, Henry forced York to take up arms in self-defence.

Rosetta Stone slab of basalt with inscriptions from 197 BC, found near the town of Rosetta, Egypt, 1799. Giving the same text in three versions – Greek, hieroglyphic, and demotic script – it became the key to deciphering other Egyptian inscriptions.

Rosh Hashanah two-day holiday that marks the start of the Jewish New Year (first new moon after the autumn equinox), traditionally announced by blowing a ram's horn (a shofar).

Rosicrucians group of early 17th-century philosophers who claimed occult powers and employed the terminology of *alchemy to expound their mystical doctrines (said to derive from *Paracelsus). The name comes from books published in 1614 and 1615, attributed to Christian Rosenkreutz ('rosy cross'), most probably a pen name but allegedly a writer living around 1460. Several societies have been founded in Britain and the USA that claim to be their successors, such as the Rosicrucian Fraternity (1614 in Germany, 1861 in the USA).

Ross James Clark 1800–1862. English explorer who discovered the magnetic North Pole 1831. He also went to the Antarctic 1839; Ross Island, Ross Sea, and Ross Dependency are named after him.

Ross Ronald 1857–1932. British physician and bacteriologist, born in India. From 1881 to 1899 he served in the Indian medical service, and during 1895–98 identified mosquitoes of the genus *Anopheles* as being responsible for the spread of malaria. Nobel prize 1902.

Ross Dependency all the Antarctic islands and territories between 160° E and 150° W longitude and S of 60° S latitude; it includes Edward VII Land, Ross Sea and its islands, and parts of Victoria Land.

Rossellini Roberto 1906–1977. Italian film director. His World War II trilogy, *Roma città aperta/Rome, Open City* 1945, *Paisà/Paisan* 1946, and *Germania anno zero/Germany Year Zero* 1947, is considered a landmark of European cinema. He and actress Ingrid *Bergman were the parents of actress Isabella Rossellini (1952–).

Rossetti Christina (Georgina) 1830–1894. English poet, sister of Dante Gabriel Rossetti and a devout High Anglican (see *Oxford movement). Her verse includes *Goblin Market and Other Poems* 1862 and expresses unfulfilled spiritual yearning and frustrated love. She was a skilful technician and made use of irregular rhyme and line length.

Rossetti Dante Gabriel 1828–1882. British painter and poet, a founding member of the *Pre-Raphaelite Brotherhood (PRB) in 1848. As well as romantic medieval scenes, he produced many idealized portraits of women. His verse includes 'The Blessed Damozel' 1850. His sister was the poet Christina Rossetti.

Rossi Aldo 1931– . Italian architect and theorist. He is strongly influenced by rationalist thought and Neo-Classicism. His main works include the Gallaratese II apartment complex, Milan, 1970; the Modena cemetery, 1973; and the Teatro del Mondo/Floating Theatre, Venice, 1979.

Rossini Gioacchino (Antonio) 1792–1868. Italian composer. His first success was the opera *Tancredi* 1813. In 1816 his 'opera buffa' *Il barbiere di Siviglia/The Barber of Seville* was produced in Rome. During 1815–23 he produced 20 operas, and created (with *Donizetti and *Bellini) the 19th-century Italian operatic style.

Rostand Edmond 1869–1918. French dramatist, who wrote *Cyrano de Bergerac* 1897 and *L'Aiglon* 1900 (based on the life of Napoleon III), in which Sarah Bernhardt played the leading role.

rotational bush fallowing type of *shifting cultivation.

Roth Philip 1933– . US novelist whose portrayals of 20th-century Jewish-American life include *Goodbye Columbus* 1959 and *Portnoy's Complaint* 1969. Psychosexual themes are prominent in his work.

Rothermere Vere (Harold Esmond Harmsworth), 3rd Viscount 1925– . British newspaper proprietor. As chair of Associated Newspapers (1971–) he controls the right-wing *Daily Mail* (founded by his great-uncle Lord *Northcliffe) and *Mail on Sunday* (launched 1982), the London *Evening Standard*, and a string of regional newspapers.

Rothko Mark 1903–1970. Russian-born US painter, an Abstract Expressionist and a pioneer of *Colour Field* painting (abstract, dominated by areas of unmodulated, strong colour). Rothko produced several series of paintings in the 1950s and 1960s, including one at Harvard University; one in the Tate Gallery, London; and one for a chapel in Houston, Texas, 1967–69.

Rothschild European family active in the financial world for two centuries. *Mayer Anselm* (1744–1812) set up as a moneylender in Frankfurt-am-Main, Germany, and business houses were established throughout Europe by his ten children.

rotifer any of the tiny invertebrates, also called 'wheel animalcules', of the phylum Rotifera. Mainly freshwater, some marine, rotifers have a ring of *cilia that carries food to the mouth and also provides propulsion. They are the smallest of multicellular animals, few reach 0.05 cm/0.02 in.

rotten borough English parliamentary constituency, before the Great Reform Act 1832, that returned members to Parliament in spite of having small numbers of electors. Such a borough could easily be manipulated by those with sufficient money or influence.

Rotterdam industrial port (brewing, distilling, shipbuilding, sugar and petroleum refining, margarine, tobacco) in the Netherlands and one of the foremost ocean cargo ports in the world, in the Rhine-Maas delta, linked by canal 1866–90 with the North Sea; population (1991) 582,266.

Rottweiler breed of dog originally developed in Rottweil, Germany, as a herding and guard dog, and subsequently used as a police dog. Powerfully built, the dog is about 63–66 cm/25–27 in high at the shoulder, black with tan markings, a short coat and docked tail.

Rouault Georges 1871–1958. French painter, etcher, illustrator, and designer. Early in his career he was associated with the *Fauves but created his own style using heavy, dark colours and bold brushwork. His subjects included sad clowns, prostitutes, and evil lawyers; from about 1940 he painted mainly religious works.

Roubiliac or *Roubillac*, Louis François *c.* 1705–1762. French sculptor, a Huguenot who fled religious persecution to settle in England 1732. He became a leading sculptor of the day, creating a statue of Handel for Vauxhall Gardens 1737 (Victoria and Albert Museum, London).

roughage alternative term for dietary *fibre, material of plant origin that cannot be digested by enzymes normally present in the human *gut.

rounders bat-and-ball game similar to *baseball but played on a much smaller pitch. The first reference to rounders was in 1744.

Roundhead member of the Parliamentary party during the English Civil War 1640–60, opposing the royalist Cavaliers. The term referred to the short hair then worn only by men of the lower classes.

Rousseau Henri 'Le Douanier' 1844–1910. French painter, a self-taught naive artist. His subjects included scenes of the Parisian suburbs and exotic junglescapes, painted with painstaking detail; for example, *Surprised! Tropical Storm with a Tiger* 1891 (National Gallery, London).

Rousseau Jean-Jacques 1712–1778. French social philosopher and writer whose *Du Contrat social/Social Contract* 1762, emphasizing the rights of the people over those of the government, was a significant influence on the French Revolution. In the novel *Emile* 1762 he outlined a new theory of education.

rowan another name for the European *mountain ash tree.

rowing propulsion of a boat by oars, either by one rower with two oars (sculling) or by crews (two, four, or eight persons) with one oar each, often with a coxswain. Major events include the world championship, first held in 1962 for men and 1974 for women, and the Boat Race, first held in 1829.

Rowland Tiny (Roland W.) Adopted name of Roland Fuhrhop 1917– . British entrepreneur, chief executive and managing director of Lonrho, and owner from 1981 of the *Observer* Sunday newspaper.

Rowlandson Thomas 1756–1827. English painter and illustrator, a caricaturist of Georgian social life. He published the series of drawings *Tour of Dr Syntax in Search of the Picturesque* 1809 and its two sequels 1812–21.

Rowley William *c.* 1585–*c.* 1642. English actor and dramatist who collaborated with Thomas *Middleton on *The Changeling* 1621 and with Thomas Dekker and John *Ford on *The Witch of Edmon-ton* published 1658.

Rowling Wallace 'Bill' 1927– . New Zealand Labour politician, party leader 1969–75, prime minister 1974–75.

Rowntree Benjamin Seebohm 1871–1954. British entrepreneur and philanthropist. Much of the money he acquired as chair (1925–41) of the family firm of confectioners, H I Rowntree, he used to fund investigations into social conditions. His writings include *Poverty, A Study of Town Life* 1900. The three **Rowntree Trusts**, which were founded by his father **Joseph Rowntree** (1836–1925) in 1904, fund research into housing, social care, and social policy, support projects relating to social justice, and give grants to pressure groups working in these areas.

Rowse A(lfred) L(eslie) 1903– . English popular historian. He published a biography of Shakespeare 1963, and in 1973 controversially identified the 'Dark Lady' of Shakespeare's sonnets as Emilia Lanier, half-Italian daughter of a court musician, with whom the Bard is alleged to have had an affair 1593–95.

Royal Air Force (RAF) the *air force of Britain. The RAF was formed 1918 by the merger of the Royal Naval Air Service and the Royal Flying Corps.

royal assent in the UK, formal consent given by a British sovereign to the passage of a bill through Parliament, after which it becomes an *act of Parliament. The last instance of a royal refusal was the rejection of the Scottish Militia Bill of 1702 by Queen Anne.

Royal Ballet title under which the British Sadler's Wells Ballet (at Covent Garden), Sadler's Wells Theatre Ballet, and the Sadler's Wells Ballet School were incorporated 1956.

Royal Botanic Gardens, Kew botanic gardens in Richmond, Surrey, England, popularly known as *Kew Gardens.

royal commission in the UK and Canada, a group of people appointed by the government (nominally by the sovereign) to investigate a matter of public concern and make recommendations on any actions to be taken in connection with it, including changes in the law. In cases where agreement on recommendations cannot be reached, a minority report can be submitted by dissenters.

Royal Greenwich Observatory the national astronomical observatory of the UK, founded 1675 at Greenwich, E London, England, to provide navigational information for sailors. After World War II it was moved to Herstmonceux Castle, Sussex; in 1990 it was transferred to Cambridge. It also operates telescopes on La Palma in the Canary Islands, including the 4.2-m/165-

in William Herschel Telescope, commissioned 1987.

Royal Institution of Great Britain organization for the promotion, diffusion, and extension of science and knowledge, founded in London 1799 by the Anglo-American physicist Count Rumford (1753–1814). Michael *Faraday and Humphry *Davy were among its directors.

Royal Marines British military force trained for amphibious warfare. See *Marines.

Royal Opera House leading British opera house, Covent Garden, London; the original theatre opened 1732 and the present building dates from 1858.

royal prerogative powers, immunities, and privileges recognized in common law as belonging to the crown. Most prerogative acts in the UK are now performed by the government on behalf of the crown. The royal prerogative belongs to the Queen as a person as well as to the institution called the crown, and the award of some honours and dignities remain her personal choice. As by prerogative 'the king can do no wrong', the monarch is immune from prosecution.

Royal Shakespeare Company (RSC) British professional theatre company that performs Shakespearean and other plays. It was founded 1961 from the company at the Shakespeare Memorial Theatre 1932 (now the Royal Shakespeare Theatre) in Stratford-upon-Avon, Warwickshire, England.

Royal Society oldest and premier scientific society in Britain, originating 1645 and chartered 1660; Christopher *Wren and Isaac *Newton were prominent early members. Its Scottish equivalent is the Royal Society of Edinburgh 1783.

Royal Society for the Prevention of Cruelty to Animals (RSPCA) British organization formed 1824 to safeguard the welfare of animals; it promotes legislation, has an inspectorate to secure enforcement of existing laws, and runs clinics.

royalty in law, payment to the owner for rights to use or exploit literary or artistic copyrights and patent rights in new inventions of all kinds.

Royce (Frederick) Henry 1863–1933. British engineer, who so impressed Charles *Rolls by the car he built for his own personal use 1904 that Rolls-Royce Ltd was formed 1906 to produce automobiles and engines.

RPI abbreviation for **retail price index**; see *cost of living.

rpm abbreviation for **revolutions per minute**.

RSFSR abbreviation for **Russian Soviet Federal Socialist Republic**, the largest republic of the former Soviet Union; renamed the *Russian Federation 1991.

RSI abbreviation for *repetitive strain injury, a condition affecting workers, such as typists, who repeatedly perform certain movements with their hands and wrists.

RSPB abbreviation for **Royal Society for the Protection of Birds**.

RSPCA abbreviation for *Royal Society for the Prevention of Cruelty to Animals*.

RSVP abbreviation for *répondez s'il vous plaît* (French 'please reply').

Rt Hon. abbreviation for *Right Honourable*, the title of British members of Parliament.

RU-486 former name for *mefipristone, an abortion pill.

Ruanda part of the former Belgian territory of Ruanda-Urundi until it achieved independence as *Rwanda, country in central Africa.

rubato (from *tempo rubato*, Italian 'robbed time') in music, a pushing or dragging against the beat for extra expressive effect.

rubber coagulated latex of a variety of plants, mainly from the New World. Most important is Para rubber, which derives from the tree *Hevea brasiliensis* of the spurge family. It was introduced from Brazil to SE Asia, where most of the world supply is now produced, the chief exporters being Peninsular Malaysia, Indonesia, Sri Lanka, Cambodia, Thailand, Sarawak, and Brunei. At about seven years the tree, which may grow to 20 m/60 ft, is ready for 'tapping'. Small incisions are made in the trunk and the latex drips into collecting cups. In pure form, rubber is white and has the formula $(C_5H_8)_n$.

rubber another name for a *condom.

rubber plant Asiatic tree *Ficus elastica* of the mulberry family Moraceae, native to Asia and N Africa, producing latex in its stem. It has shiny, leathery, oval leaves, and young specimens are grown as house plants.

Rubbia Carlo 1934– . Italian physicist and, from 1989, director-general of *CERN, the European nuclear research organization. In 1983 he led the team that discovered the weakons (W and Z particles), the agents responsible for transferring the weak nuclear force. Rubbia shared the Nobel Prize for Physics with his colleague Simon van der Meer (1925–).

Rubbra Edmund 1901–1986. British composer. He studied under *Holst and was a master of contrapuntal writing, as exemplified in his study *Counterpoint* 1960. His compositions include 11 symphonies, chamber music, and songs.

rubella technical term for *German measles.

Rubens Peter Paul 1577–1640. Flemish painter, who brought the exuberance of Italian Baroque to N Europe, creating, with an army of assistants, innumerable religious and allegorical paintings for churches and palaces. These show mastery of drama in large compositions, and love of rich colour. He also painted portraits and, in his last years, landscapes.

Rubicon ancient name of the small river flowing into the Adriatic which, under the Roman Republic, marked the boundary between Italy proper and Cisalpine Gaul. When *Caesar led his army across it 49 BC he therefore declared war on the republic; hence to 'cross the Rubicon' means to take an irrevocable step.

rubidium (Latin *rubidus* 'red') soft, silver-white, metallic element, symbol Rb, atomic number 37, relative atomic mass 85.47. It is one of the *alkali metals, ignites spontaneously in air, and reacts violently with water. It is used in photoelectric cells and vacuum-tube filaments.

Rubik Erno 1944– . Hungarian architect who invented the *Rubik cube*, a multicoloured

puzzle that can be manipulated and rearranged in only one correct way, but about 43 trillion wrong ones. Intended to help his students understand three-dimensional design, it became a fad that swept around the world.

ruby the red transparent gem variety of the mineral *corundum Al_2O_3, aluminium oxide. Small amounts of chromium oxide, Cr_2O_3, substituting for aluminium oxide, give ruby its colour. Natural rubies are found mainly in Myanmar (Burma), but rubies can also be produced artificially and such synthetic stones are used in *lasers.

rudd freshwater fish *Scardinius erythrophthalmus*, a type of minnow, belonging to the carp family Cypridae, common in lakes and slow rivers of Europe; now introduced in the USA. Brownish green above and silvery below, with red fins and golden eyes, it can reach a length of 45 cm/1.5 ft and a weight of 1 kg/2.2 lb.

Rudolf, Lake former name of Lake *Turkana in E Africa.

Rudolph 1858–1889. Crown prince of Austria, the only son of Emperor Franz Joseph. From an early age he showed progressive views that brought him into conflict with his father. He conceived and helped to write a history of the Austro-Hungarian empire. In 1881, he married Princess Stephanie of Belgium, and they had one daughter, Elizabeth. In 1889 he and his mistress, Baroness Marie Vetsera, were found shot in his hunting lodge at Mayerling, near Vienna. The official verdict was suicide, although there were rumours that it was perpetrated by Jesuits, Hungarian nobles, or the baroness's husband.

Rudolph two Holy Roman emperors:

Rudolph I 1218–1291. Holy Roman emperor from 1273. Originally count of Habsburg, he was the first Habsburg emperor and expanded his dynasty by investing his sons with the duchies of Austria and Styria.

Rudolph II 1552–1612. Holy Roman emperor from 1576, when he succeeded his father Maximilian II. His policies led to unrest in Hungary and Bohemia, which led to the surrender of Hungary to his brother Matthias 1608 and religious freedom for Bohemia.

rue shrubby perennial herb *Ruta graveolens*, family Rutaceae, native to S Europe and temperate Asia. It bears clusters of yellow flowers. An oil extracted from the strongly scented, blue-green leaves is used in perfumery.

ruff bird *Philomachus pugnax* of the sandpiper family Scolopacidae. The name is taken from the frill of erectile feathers developed in the breeding season around the neck of the male. The ruff is found across N Europe and Asia, and migrates south in winter. It is a casual migrant throughout North America.

rug small *carpet.

rugby contact sport that originated at Rugby School, England, 1823 when a boy, William Webb Ellis, picked up the ball and ran with it while playing football (now soccer). Rugby is played with an oval ball. It is now played in two forms: *Rugby League* and *Rugby Union*.

Rugby League professional form of rugby football founded in England 1895 as the Northern Union when a dispute about pay caused northern clubs to break away from the Rugby Football

Union. The game is similar to *Rugby Union, but the number of players was reduced from 15 to 13 in 1906, and other rule changes have made the game more open and fast-moving.

Rugby Union amateur form of rugby football in which there are 15 players on each side. 'Tries' are scored by 'touching down' the ball beyond the goal line or by kicking goals from penalties. The Rugby Football Union was formed 1871 and has its headquarters in England (Twickenham, Middlesex).

Ruhr river in Germany; it rises in the Rothaargebirge and flows W to join the Rhine at Duisburg. The *Ruhr valley* (228 km/142 mi), a metropolitan industrial area (petrochemicals, cars; iron and steel at Duisburg and Dortmund) was formerly a coalmining centre.

Ruisdael or *Ruysdael* Jacob van c. 1628–1682. Dutch landscape painter, active in Amsterdam from about 1655. He painted rural scenes near his native town of Haarlem and in Germany, and excelled in depicting gnarled and weatherbeaten trees. The few figures in his pictures were painted by other artists.

rule of law doctrine that no individual, however powerful, is above the law. The principle had a significant influence on attempts to restrain the arbitrary use of power by rulers and on the growth of legally enforceable human rights in many Western countries. It is often used as a justification for separating legislative from judicial power.

rum spirit fermented and distilled from sugar cane. Scummings from the sugar pans produce the best rum, molasses the lowest grade. Puerto Rico and Jamaica are the main producing countries.

rumba Latin American ballroom dance; the music for this. Rumba originated in Cuba and its rhythms are the basis of much Afro-Cuban music.

ruminant any even-toed hoofed mammal with a rumen, the 'first stomach' of its complex digestive system. Plant food is stored and fermented before being brought back to the mouth for chewing (chewing the cud) and then is swallowed to the next stomach. Ruminants include cattle, antelopes, goats, deer, and giraffes, all with a four-chambered stomach. Camels are also ruminants, but they have a three-chambered stomach.

Rump, the English parliament formed between Dec 1648 and Nov 1653 after *Pride's purge of the *Long Parliament to ensure a majority in favour of trying Charles I. It was dismissed 1653 by Cromwell, who replaced it with the *Barebones Parliament.

Runcie Robert (Alexander Kennedy) 1921– . English cleric, archbishop of Canterbury 1980–91, the first to be appointed on the suggestion of the Church Crown Appointments Commission (formed 1977) rather than by political consultation. He favoured ecclesiastical remarriage for the divorced and the eventual introduction of the ordination of women.

Rundstedt Karl Rudolf Gerd von 1875–1953. German field marshal in World War II. Largely responsible for the German breakthrough in France 1940, he was defeated on the Ukrainian front 1941. As commander in chief in France from 1942, he resisted the Allied invasion 1944

and in Dec launched the temporarily successful Ardennes offensive.

rune character in the oldest Germanic script, chiefly adapted from the Latin alphabet, the earliest examples being from the 3rd century, and found in Denmark. Runes were scratched on wood, metal, stone, or bone.

runner in botany, aerial stem that produces new plants; also called a *stolon.

Runyon (Alfred) Damon 1884–1946. US journalist, primarily a sports reporter, whose short stories in *Guys and Dolls* 1932 deal wryly with the seamier side of New York City life in his own invented jargon.

Rupert Prince 1619–1682. English Royalist general and admiral, born in Prague, son of the Elector Palatine Frederick V (1596–1632) and James I's daughter Elizabeth. Defeated by Cromwell at *Marston Moor and *Naseby in the Civil War, he commanded a privateering fleet 1649–52, until routed by Admiral Robert Blake, and, returning after the Restoration, was a distinguished admiral in the Dutch Wars. He founded the *Hudson's Bay Company.

rupture in medicine, another name for *hernia.

rush any grasslike plant of the genus *Juncus*, family Juncaceae, found in wet places in cold and temperate regions. The round stems and flexible leaves of some species have been used for making mats and baskets since ancient times.

Rushdie (Ahmed) Salman 1947– . British writer, born in India of a Muslim family. His novel *The Satanic Verses* 1988 offended many Muslims with alleged blasphemy. In 1989 the Ayatollah Khomeini of Iran called for Rushdie and his publishers to be killed.

Rusk Dean 1909– . US Democrat politician. He was secretary of state to presidents J F Kennedy and L B Johnson 1961–69, and became unpopular through his involvement with the *Vietnam War.

Ruskin John 1819–1900. English art critic and social critic. He published five volumes of *Modern Painters* 1843–60 and *The Seven Lamps of Architecture* 1849, in which he stated his philosophy of art. His writings hastened the appreciation of painters considered unorthodox at the time, such as J M W *Turner and the *Pre-Raphaelite Brotherhood. His later writings were concerned with social and economic problems.

Russell Bertrand (Arthur William), 3rd Earl Russell 1872–1970. English philosopher and mathematician who contributed to the development of modern mathematical logic and wrote about social issues. His works include *Principia Mathematica* 1910–13 (with A N *Whitehead), in which he attempted to show that mathematics could be reduced to a branch of logic; *The Problems of Philosophy* 1912; and *A History of Western Philosophy* 1946. He was an outspoken liberal pacifist.

Russell Jane 1921– . US actress who was discovered by producer Howard Hughes. Her first film, *The Outlaw* 1943, was not properly released for several years because of censorship problems. Other films include *The Paleface* 1948, *Gentlemen Prefer Blondes* 1953, and *The Revolt of Mamie Stover* 1957.

Russell John, 1st Earl Russell 1792–1878. British Liberal politician, son of the 6th Duke of Bedford. He entered the House of Commons 1813 and supported Catholic emancipation and the Reform Bill. He held cabinet posts 1830–41, became prime minister 1846–52, and was again a cabinet minister until becoming prime minister again 1865–66. He retired after the defeat of his Reform Bill 1866.

Russell Ken 1927– . English film director whose work includes *Women in Love* 1969, *The Devils* 1971, and *Gothic* 1986. He has made television documentaries of the lives of the composers Elgar, Delius, and Richard Strauss.

Russell Lord William 1639–1683. British Whig politician. Son of the 1st Duke of Bedford, he was among the founders of the Whig Party, and actively supported attempts in Parliament to exclude the Roman Catholic James II from succeeding to the throne. In 1683 he was accused of complicity in the Rye House Plot to murder Charles II, and was executed.

Russia originally the name of the pre-revolutionary Russian Empire (until 1917), now accurately restricted to the *Russian Federation.

Russian member of the majority ethnic group living in Russia. Russians are also often the largest minority in neighbouring republics. The Russian language is a member of the East Slavonic branch of the Indo-European language family and was the official language of the USSR, with 130–150 million speakers. It is written in the Cyrillic alphabet. The ancestors of the Russians migrated from central Europe between the 6th and 8th centuries AD.

Russian Federation formerly (until 1991) *Russian Soviet Federal Socialist Republic*

area 17,075,500 sq km/6,591,100 sq mi
capital Moscow
towns St Petersburg (Leningrad), Nizhni-Novgorod (Gorky), Rostov-on-Don, Samara (Kuibyshev), Tver (Kalinin), Volgograd, Vyatka (Kirov), Ekaterinburg (Sverdlovsk)
physical fertile Black Earth district; extensive forests; the Ural Mountains with large mineral resources (Makhachkala); Kabardino-Balkar (Nalchik); Kalmyk (Elista); Karelia (Petrozavodsk); Komi (Syktyvkar); Mari (Yoshkar-Ola); Mordovia (Saransk); Vladikavkaz (formerly Ordzhonikidze); Tatarstan (Kazan); Tuva (Kizyl); Udmurt (Izhevsk); Yakut (Yakutsk)
head of state Boris Yeltsin from 1990/91

head of government Viktor Chernomyrdin from 1992
political system emergent democracy
products iron ore, coal, oil, gold, platinum, and other minerals, agricultural produce
currency rouble
population (1993) 150,000,000 (82% Russian, Tatar 4%, Ukrainian 3%, Chuvash 1%)
language Great Russian
religion traditionally Russian Orthodox
GNP $3,220 per head (1991)
chronology
1945 Became a founding member of United Nations.
1988 Aug: Democratic Union formed in Moscow as political party opposed to totalitarianism. Oct: Russian-language demonstrations in Leningrad, tsarist flag raised.
1989 March: Boris Yeltsin elected to USSR Congress of People's Deputies. Sept: conservative-nationalist Russian United Workers' Front established in Sverdlovsk.
1990 May: anticommunist May Day protests in Red Square, Moscow; Yeltsin narrowly elected RSFSR president by Russian parliament. June: economic and political sovereignty declared; Ivan Silaev became Russian prime minister. Aug: Tatarstan declared sovereignty. Dec: rationing introduced in some cities; private land ownership allowed.
1991 June: Yeltsin directly elected president under a liberal-radical banner. July: Yeltsin issued a decree to remove Communist Party cells from workplaces; sovereignty of the Baltic republics recognized by the republic. Aug: Yeltsin stood out against abortive anti-Gorbachev coup, emerging as key power-broker within Soviet Union; national guard established and pre-revolutionary flag restored. Sept: Silaev resigned as Russian premier. Nov: Yeltsin named prime minister; Soviet and Russian Communist Parties banned; Yeltsin's goverment gained control of Russia's economic assets and armed forces. Oct: Chechnya declared its independence. Dec: Yeltsin negotiated formation of new confederal Commonwealth of Independent States; Russia admitted into UN; independence recognized by USA and European Community.
1992 Jan: admitted into Conference on Security and Cooperation in Europe; assumed former USSR's permanent seat on UN Security Council; prices freed. Feb: demonstrations in Moscow and other cities as living standards fell. March: 18 out of 20 republics signed treaty agreeing to remain within loose Russian Federation; Tatarstan and Chechnya refused to sign. Dec: Victor Chernomyrdin elected prime minister; new constitution agreed in referendum. START II arms-reduction agreement signed with USA.
1993 March: power struggle between Yeltsin and Congress of People's Deputies. Referendum gave vote of confidence in Yeltsin's presidency but did not support constitutional change. Sept: Yeltsin dissolved parliament. Sept-Oct: attempted coup, led by conservative opponents, foiled by troops loyal to Yeltsin. Dec: new constitution approved in plebiscite. New parliament elected, with surprising successes for extremist Liberal Democratic Party.
1994 Jan: prominent reformers quit cabinet. Feb: Russian diplomatic intervention in Bosnia-Herzegovina conflict; 400 Russian peacekeeping

troops sent to region. Dec: Russian forces invaded breakaway republic of Chechnya.

1995 Conflict in Chechnya intensified; widespread criticism of Russia's conduct of the war as casualties mounted.

Russian Orthodox Church another name for the *Orthodox Church.

Russian Revolution two revolutions of Feb and Oct 1917 (Julian *calendar) that began with the overthrow of the Romanov dynasty and ended with the establishment of a communist soviet (council) state, the Union of Soviet Socialist Republics (USSR). In Oct Bolshevik workers and sailors under *Lenin seized government buildings and took over power.

Russo-Japanese War war between Russia and Japan 1904–05, which arose from conflicting ambitions in Korea and *Manchuria, specifically, the Russian occupation of Port Arthur (modern Dalian) 1896 and of the Amur province 1900. Japan successfully besieged Port Arthur May 1904–Jan 1905, took Mukden (modern Shenyang, see *Mukden, Battle of) on 29 Feb–10 March, and on 27 May defeated the Russian Baltic fleet, which had sailed halfway around the world to Tsushima Strait. A peace was signed 23 Aug 1905. Russia surrendered its lease on Port Arthur, ceded S Sakhalin to Japan, evacuated Manchuria, and recognized Japan's interests in Korea.

russula any fungus of the genus *Russula*, comprising many species. They are medium to large mushrooms with flattened caps, and many are brightly coloured.

rust reddish-brown oxide of iron formed by the action of moisture and oxygen on the metal. It consists mainly of hydrated iron(III) oxide ($Fe_2O_3.H_2O$ and iron(III) hydroxide ($Fe(OH)_3$).

rust in botany, common name for the minute parasitic fungi of the order Uredinales, which appear on the leaves of their hosts as orange-red spots, later becoming darker. The commonest is the wheat rust *Puccinia graminis*.

Ruth in the Old Testament, a Moabite (see *Moab) ancestor of David (king of Israel) by her second marriage to Boaz. When her first husband died, she preferred to stay with her mother-in-law, Naomi, than return to her own people.

ruthenium hard, brittle, silver-white, metallic element, symbol Ru, atomic number 44, relative atomic mass 101.07. It is one of the so-called platinum group of metals; it occurs in platinum ores as a free metal and in the natural alloy osmiridium. It is used as a hardener in alloys and as a catalyst; its compounds are used as colouring agents in glass and ceramics.

Rutherford Ernest 1871–1937. New Zealand physicist, a pioneer of modern atomic science. His main research was in the field of radioactivity, and he discovered alpha, beta, and gamma rays. He named the nucleus, and was the first to recognize the nuclear nature of the atom. Nobel prize 1908.

rutherfordium name proposed by US scientists for the element currently known as *unnilquadium (atomic number 104), to honour New Zealand physicist Ernest Rutherford.

rutile TiO_2, titanium oxide, a naturally occurring ore of titanium. It is usually reddish brown to black, with a very bright (adamantine) surface lustre. It crystallizes in the tetragonal system. Rutile is common in a wide range of igneous and metamorphic rocks and also occurs concentrated in sands; the coastal sands of E and W Australia are a major source. It is used as a pigment giving a brilliant white to paint, paper, and plastics.

Rutskoi Aleksander 1947– . Russian politician, founder of the reformist Communists for Democracy group, and vice president of the Russian Federation from 1991. During the abortive Aug 1991 coup he led the Russian delegation to rescue Soviet leader Mikhail Gorbachev from his forced confinement in the Crimea.

Ruwenzori mountain range on the frontier between Zaire and Uganda, rising to 5,119 m/16,794 ft at Mount Stanley.

Ruysdael Jacob van. See *Ruisdael, Dutch painter.

Ruyter Michael Adrianszoon de 1607–1676. Dutch admiral who led his country's fleet in the wars against England. On 1–4 June 1666 he forced the British fleet under Rupert and Albemarle to retire into the Thames, but on 25 July was heavily defeated off the North Foreland, Kent.

Rwanda Republic of (*Republika y'u Rwanda*)

area 26,338 sq km/10,173 sq mi
capital Kigali
towns Butare, Ruhengeri
physical high savanna and hills, with volcanic mountains in NW
head of state Pasteur Bizimungu from 1994
head of government Faustin Twagiramungu from 1994
political system transitional
exports coffee, tea, pyrethrum
currency franc
population (1993 est) 7,700,000 (Hutu 90%, Tutsi 9%, Twa 1%); growth rate 3.3% p.a. During the 1993–94 civil war, hundreds of thousands were killed and many thousands more fled to neighbouring countries
languages Kinyarwanda, French (official); Kiswahili
religions Roman Catholic 54%, animist 23%, Protestant 12%, Muslim 9%
GNP $260 per head (1991)
chronology
1916 Belgian troops occupied Rwanda; League of Nations mandated Rwanda and Burundi to Belgium as Territory of Ruanda-Urundi.

1959 Interethnic warfare between Hutu and Tutsi.
1962 Independence from Belgium achieved, with Grégoire Kayibanda as president.
1972 Renewal of interethnic fighting.
1973 Kayibanda ousted in a military coup led by Maj-Gen Juvenal Habyarimana.
1978 New constitution approved; Rwanda remained a military-controlled state.
1980 Civilian rule adopted.
1988 Refugees from Burundi massacres streamed into Rwanda.
1990 Government attacked by Rwandan Patriotic Front (FPR), a Tutsi military-political organization based in Uganda.
1992 Peace accord with FPR.
1993 Power-sharing agreement with government repudiated by FPR. Peace talks resumed. Aug: peace accord formally signed. United Nations mission sent to monitor peace agreement.
1994 President Habyarimana, with Burundian president Ntaryamira, killed in air crash, with fears that FPR responsible. Hundreds of thousands killed in ensuing civil war, with many Tutsis massacred by Hutu death squads; mass exodus of refugees to neighbouring countries. June: interim government fled capital as FPR forces closed in. French peacekeeping troops drafted in; 'safe zone' established in southwest. July: FPR installed transitional coalition government; moderate Hutu and FPR leader, Pasteur Bizimungu, appointed interim head of state.

Rydberg constant in physics, a constant that relates atomic spectra to the *spectrum of hydrogen. Its value is 1.0977×10^7 per metre.

Ryder Albert Pinkham 1847–1917. US painter. He developed one of the most original styles of his time. He painted with broad strokes that tended to simplify form and used yellowish colours that gave his works an eerie, haunted quality. His works are poetic, romantic, and filled with unreality; *Death on a Pale Horse* about 1910 (Cleveland Museum of Art) is typical.

Ryder Cup golf tournament for professional men's teams from the USA and Europe. It is played every two years, and the match is made up of a series of singles, foursomes, and fourballs played over three days.

rye cereal *Secale cereale* grown extensively in N Europe and other temperate regions. The flour is used to make dark-coloured ('black') breads. Rye is grown mainly as a forage crop, but the grain is also used to make whisky and breakfast cereals.

rye-grass any perennial, wiry grass of the genus *Lolium*, especially *L. perenne*, common in pastures and waste places. It grows up to 60 cm/24 in high, flowers in midsummer, and sends up abundant nutritious leaves, good for cattle. It is a Eurasian genus but has been introduced to Australia and North America.

Ryle Martin 1918–1984. English radioastronomer. At the Mullard Radio Astronomy Observatory, Cambridge, he developed the technique of sky-mapping using 'aperture synthesis', combining smaller dish aerials to give the characteristics of one large one. His work on the distribution of radio sources in the universe brought confirmation of the *Big Bang theory. He won, with Antony *Hewish, the Nobel Prize for Physics 1974.

Ryukyu Islands southernmost island group of Japan, stretching towards Taiwan and including Okinawa, Miyako, and Ishigaki
area 2,254 sq km/870 sq mi
capital Naha, on Okinawa
products sugar, pineapples, fish
population (1985) 1,179,000
history originally an independent kingdom; ruled by China from the late 14th century until seized by Japan 1609 and controlled by the Satsuma feudal lords until 1868, when the Japanese government took over. Chinese claims to the islands were relinquished 1895. In World War II the islands were taken by USA 1945 (see under *Okinawa); northernmost group, Oshima, restored to Japan 1953, the rest 1972.

Ryzhkov Nikolai Ivanovich 1929– . Soviet communist politician. He held governmental and party posts from 1975 before being brought into the Politburo and serving as prime minister 1985–90 under *Gorbachev. A low-profile technocrat, Ryzhkov was the author of unpopular economic reforms.

S

Saami (or *Lapp*) a member of a group of herding people living in N Scandinavia and the Kola Peninsula, and numbering about 46,000 (1983). Some are nomadic, others lead a more settled way of life. They live by herding reindeer, hunting, fishing, and producing handicrafts. Their language belongs to the Finno-Ugric family. Their religion is basically animist, but incorporates elements of Christianity.

SAARC abbreviation for *South Asian Association for Regional Cooperation*.

Saarinen Eero 1910–1961. Finnish-born US architect distinguished for a wide range of innovative modern designs using a variety of creative shapes for buildings. His works include the US embassy, London, the TWA terminal, New York, and Dulles Airport, Washington, DC. He collaborated on a number of projects with his father, Eliel Saarinen.

Saarinen Eliel 1873–1950. Finnish architect and town planner, founder of the Finnish Romantic school. In 1923 he emigrated to the USA, where he contributed to US skyscraper design by his work in Chicago, and later turned to functionalism.

Saarland (French *Sarre*) *Land* (state) of Germany
area 2,570 sq km/992 sq mi
capital Saarbrücken
products cereals and other crops; cattle, pigs, poultry. Former flourishing coal and steel industries survive only by government subsidy
population (1988) 1,034,000
history in 1919, the Saar district was administered by France under the auspices of the League of Nations; a plebiscite returned it to Germany 1935; Hitler gave it the name Saarbrücken. Part of the French zone of occupation 1945, it was included in the economic union with France 1947. It was returned to Germany 1957.

Sabah self-governing state of the federation of Malaysia, occupying NE Borneo, forming (with Sarawak) East Malaysia
area 73,613 sq km/28,415 sq mi
capital Kota Kinabalu (formerly Jesselton)
physical chiefly mountainous (highest peak Mount Kinabalu 4,098 m/13,450 ft) and forested
products hardwoods (25% of the world's supplies), rubber, fish, cocoa, palm oil, copper, copra, and hemp
population (1990) 1,470,200, of which the Kadazans form the largest ethnic group at 30%; also included are 250,000 immigrants from Indonesia and the Philippines
languages Malay (official) and English
religions Sunni Muslim and Christian (the Kadazans, among whom there is unrest about increasing Muslim dominance).
government consists of a constitutional head of state with a chief minister, cabinet, and legislative assembly
history in 1877–78 the Sultan of Sulu made concessions to the North Borneo Company, which was eventually consolidated with Labuan as a British colony 1946, and became the state of Sabah within Malaysia 1963. The Philippines advanced territorial claims on Sabah 1962 and 1968 on the grounds that the original cession by the Sultan was illegal, Spain having then been sovereign in the area.

Sabah Sheik Jabir al Ahmadal Jabir al-1928– . Emir of Kuwait from 1977. He suspended the national assembly 1986, after mounting parliamentary criticism, ruling in a feudal, paternalistic manner. On the invasion of Kuwait by Iraq 1990 he fled to Saudi Arabia, returning to Kuwait in March 1991.

Sabatini Gabriela 1970– . Argentine tennis player who in 1986 became the youngest Wimbledon semifinalist for 99 years. Her highest was ranking number three in the world behind Monica Seles and Steffi Graf in 1991.

Sabbatarianism belief held by some Protestant Christians in the strict observance of the Sabbath, Sunday, following the fourth commandment of the *Bible. It began in the 17th century.

Sabbath (Hebrew *shābath*, 'to rest') the seventh day of the week, commanded by God in the Old Testament as a sacred day of rest; in Judaism, from sunset Friday to sunset Saturday; in Christianity, Sunday (or, in some sects, Saturday).

Sabine member of an ancient people of central Italy, conquered by the Romans and amalgamated with them in the 3rd century BC. The so-called *rape of the Sabine women* – a mythical attempt by *Romulus in the early days of Rome to carry off the Sabine women to colonize the new city – is frequently depicted in art.

sable marten *Martes zibellina*, about 50 cm/20 in long and usually brown. It is native to N Eurasian forests, but now found mainly in E Siberia. The sable has diminished in numbers because of its valuable fur, which has long attracted hunters. Conservation measures and sable farming have been introduced to save it from extinction.

saccharide another name for a *sugar molecule.

saccharin or *ortho-sulpho benzimide* $C_7H_5NO_3S$ sweet, white, crystalline solid derived from coal tar and substituted for sugar. Since 1977 it has been regarded as potentially carcinogenic. Its use is not universally permitted and it has been largely replaced by other sweetening agents.

Sacco-Vanzetti case murder trial in Massachusetts, USA, 1920–21. Italian immigrants Nicola Sacco (1891–1927) and Bartolomeo Vanzetti (1888–1927) were convicted of murder during an alleged robbery. The conviction was upheld on appeal, with application for retrial denied. Prolonged controversy delayed execution until 1927. In 1977 the verdict was declared unjust (by Massachusetts governor Michael Dukakis) because of the judge's prejudice against the accuseds' anarchist views.

Sacher-Masoch Leopold von 1836–1895. Austrian novelist. His books dealt with the sexual pleasure of having pain inflicted on oneself, hence *masochism.

sacrament in Christian usage, observances forming the visible sign of inward grace. In the Roman Catholic Church there are seven sacraments: baptism, Holy Communion (Eucharist or mass), confirmation, rite of reconciliation (confession and penance), holy orders, matrimony, and the anointing of the sick.

sacred cow any person, institution, or custom that is considered above criticism. The term comes from the Hindu belief that cows are sacred and must not be killed.

Sacred Thread ceremony Hindu initiation ceremony which marks the passage to maturity for boys of the upper three castes; it usually takes place between the ages of five and twelve. It is regarded as a second birth and the castes whose males are entitled to undergo the ceremony are called 'twice born'.

Sadat Anwar 1918–1981. Egyptian politician. Succeeding *Nasser as president 1970, he restored morale by his handling of the Egyptian campaign in the 1973 war against Israel. In 1974 his plan for economic, social, and political reform to transform Egypt was unanimously adopted in a referendum. In 1977 he visited Israel to reconcile the two countries, and shared the Nobel Peace Prize with Israeli prime minister Menachem Begin 1978. He was assassinated by Islamic fundamentalists.

Sadducee (Hebrew 'righteous') member of the ancient Hebrew political party and sect of *Judaism that formed in pre-Roman Palestine in the first century BC. They were the group of priestly aristocrats in Jerusalem until the final destruction of the Temple AD 70.

Sade Donatien Alphonse François, Comte de, known as the *Marquis de Sade* 1740–1814. French author who was imprisoned for sexual offences and finally committed to an asylum. He wrote plays and novels dealing explicitly with a variety of sexual practices, including *sadism.

sadism tendency to derive pleasure (usually sexual) from inflicting physical or mental pain on others. The term is derived from the Marquis de *Sade.

Sadowa, Battle of or *Battle of Königgrätz* Prussian victory over the Austrian army 13 km/8 mi NW of Hradec Kralove (German Königgrätz) 3 July 1866, ending the 'Seven Weeks' War. It confirmed Prussian hegemony over the German states and led to the formation of the North German Confederation 1867. It is named after the nearby village of Sadowa (Czech Sadová) in Czechoslovakia.

safety glass glass that does not splinter into sharp pieces when smashed. *Toughened glass* is made by heating a glass sheet and then rapidly cooling it with a blast of cold air; it shatters into rounded pieces when smashed. *Laminated glass* is a 'sandwich' of a clear plastic film between two glass sheets; when this is struck, it simply cracks, the plastic holding the glass in place.

safety lamp portable lamp designed for use in places where flammable gases such as methane may be encountered; for example, in coal mines. The electric head lamp used as a miner's working light has the bulb and contacts in protected enclosures. The flame safety lamp, now used primarily for gas detection, has the wick enclosed within a strong glass cylinder surmounted by wire gauzes. Humphry *Davy 1815 and George *Stephenson each invented flame safety lamps.

safflower Asian plant *Carthamus tinctorius*, family Compositae. It is thistlelike, and widely grown for the oil from its seeds, which is used in cooking, margarine, and paints and varnishes; the seed residue is used as cattle feed.

saffron plant *Crocus sativus* of the iris family, probably native to SW Asia, and formerly widely cultivated in Europe; also the dried orange-yellow *stigmas of its purple flowers, used for colouring and flavouring.

saga prose narrative written down in the 11th–13th centuries in Norway and Iceland. The sagas range from family chronicles, such as the *Landnamabok* of Ari (1067–1148), to legendary and anonymous works such as the *Njala* saga.

sage perennial herb *Salvia officinalis* with grey-green aromatic leaves used for flavouring. It grows up to 50 cm/20 in high and has bluish-lilac or pink flowers.

Sagittarius zodiac constellation in the southern hemisphere, represented as a centaur aiming a bow and arrow at neighbouring Scorpius. The Sun passes through Sagittarius from mid-Dec to mid-Jan, including the winter solstice, when it is farthest south of the equator. The constellation contains many nebulae and *globular clusters, and open *star clusters. Kaus Australis and Nunki are its brightest stars. The centre of our Galaxy, the Milky Way, is marked by the radio source Sagittarius A. In astrology, the dates for Sagittarius are between about 22 Nov and 21 Dec (see *precession).

sago starchy material obtained from the pith of the sago palm *Metroxylon sagu*. It forms a nutritious food and is used for manufacturing glucose and sizing textiles.

Sahara largest desert in the world, occupying 5,500,000 sq km/2,123,000 sq mi of N Africa from the Atlantic to the Nile, covering: W Egypt; part of W Sudan; large parts of Mauritania, Mali, Niger, and Chad; and southern parts of Morocco, Algeria, Tunisia, and Libya. Small areas in Algeria and Tunisia are below sea level, but it is mainly a plateau with a central mountain system, including the Ahaggar Mountains in Algeria, the Aïr Massif in Niger, and the Tibesti Massif in Chad, of which the highest peak is Emi Koussi 3,415 m/11,208 ft. The area of the Sahara expanded by 650,000 sq km/251,000 sq mi 1940–90, but reafforestation is being attempted in certain areas.

Saigon former name (until 1976) of *Ho Chi Minh City, Vietnam.

Saigon, Battle of during the Vietnam War, battle 29 Jan–23 Feb 1968, when 5,000 Vietcong were expelled by South Vietnamese and US forces. The city was finally taken by North Vietnamese forces 30 April 1975, after South Vietnamese withdrawal from the central highlands.

saint holy man or woman respected for their wisdom, spirituality, and dedication to their faith. Within the Roman Catholic church a saint is officially recognized through *canonization by the pope. Many saints are associated with miracles and canonization usually occurs after a thorough investigation of the lives and miracles attributed to them. In the Orthodox church saints are recognized by the patriarch and Holy Synod after recommendation by local churches. The term is also used in Buddhism for individuals who have led a virtuous and holy life, such as Kūkai (775–835), founder of the Japanese Shingon sect of Buddhism. For individual saints, see under forename, for example *Paul, St.

St Andrews town at the eastern tip of Fife, Scotland, 19 km/12 mi SE of Dundee; population (1981) 11,400. Its university (1411) is the oldest in Scotland, and the Royal and Ancient Club (1754) is the ruling body of golf.

St Bartholomew, Massacre of slaughter of *Huguenots (Protestants) in Paris, 24 Aug–17 Sept 1572, and until 3 Oct in the provinces. About 25,000 people are believed to have been killed. When *Catherine de' Medici's plot to have Admiral Coligny assassinated failed, she resolved to have all the Huguenot leaders killed, persuading her son Charles IX it was in the interest of public safety.

St Bernard breed of large, heavily built dog 70 cm/30 in high at the shoulder, weight about 70 kg/150 lb. They have pendulous ears and lips, large feet, and drooping lower eyelids. They are usually orange and white.

St Christopher (St Kitts)–Nevis Federation of

area 269 sq km/104 sq mi (St Christopher 176 sq km/68 sq mi, Nevis 93 sq km/36 sq mi)
capital Basseterre (on St Christopher)
towns Charlestown (largest on Nevis)
physical both islands are volcanic
head of state Elizabeth II from 1983 represented by governor general
head of government Kennedy Simmonds from 1980
political system federal constitutional monarchy
exports sugar, molasses, electronics, clothing
currency E Caribbean dollar
population (1993 est) 44,800; growth rate 0.2% p.a.
language English
religions Anglican 36%, Methodist 32%, other Protestant 8%, Roman Catholic 10% (1985 est)
GNP $3,960 per head (1991)
chronology
1871–1956 Part of the Leeward Islands Federation.
1958–62 Part of the Federation of the West Indies.
1967 St Christopher, Nevis, and Anguilla achieved internal self-government, within the British Commonwealth, with Robert Bradshaw, Labour Party leader, as prime minister.
1971 Anguilla returned to being a British dependency.
1978 Bradshaw died; succeeded by Paul Southwell.

1979 Southwell died; succeeded by Lee L Moore.
1980 Coalition government led by Kennedy Simmonds.
1983 Full independence achieved within the Commonwealth.
1984 Coalition government re-elected.
1989 Prime Minister Simmonds won a third successive term.

St Elmo's fire bluish, flamelike electrical discharge that sometimes occurs above ships' masts and other pointed objects or about aircraft in stormy weather. Although high voltage, it is low current and therefore harmless. St Elmo (or St Erasmus) is the patron saint of sailors.

Saint-Exupéry Antoine de 1900–1944. French author who wrote the autobiographical *Vol de nuit/Night Flight* 1931 and *Terre des hommes/Wind, Sand, and Stars* 1939. His children's book *Le Petit Prince/The Little Prince* 1943 is also an adult allegory.

St George's port and capital of *Grenada; population (1986) 7,500, urban area 29,000.

St Helena British island in the S Atlantic, 1,900 km/1,200 mi W of Africa, area 122 sq km/47 sq mi; population (1987) 5,600. Its capital is Jamestown, and it exports fish and timber. Ascension and Tristan da Cunha are dependencies.

St Helens, Mount volcanic mountain in Washington State, USA. When it erupted 1980 after being quiescent since 1857, it devastated an area of 600 sq km/230 sq mi and its height was reduced from 2,950 m/9,682 ft to 2,560 m/8,402 ft.

St James's Palace palace in Pall Mall, London, a royal residence 1698–1837.

St John, Order of (full title *Knights Hospitallers of St John of Jerusalem*) oldest order of Christian chivalry, named from the hospital at Jerusalem founded about 1048 by merchants of Amalfi for pilgrims, whose travel routes the knights defended from the Muslims. Today there are about 8,000 knights (male and female), and the Grand Master is the world's highest ranking Roman Catholic lay person.

St John's capital and chief port of Newfoundland, Canada; population (1986) 96,000, urban area 162,000. The main industry is fish processing; other products include textiles, fishing equipment, furniture, and machinery.

St John's port and capital of Antigua and Barbuda, on Antigua; population (1982) 30,000.

Saint-Just Louis Antoine Léon Florelle de 1767–1794. French revolutionary. A close associate of *Robespierre, he became a member of the Committee of Public Safety 1793, and was guillotined with Robespierre.

St Kitts–Nevis contracted form of *St Christopher-Nevis.

Saint-Laurent Yves (Henri Donat Mathieu) 1936– . French fashion designer who has had an exceptional influence on fashion in the second half of the 20th century. He began working for Christian *Dior 1955 and succeeded him as designer on Dior's death 1957. He established his own label 1962 and went on to create the first 'power-dressing' looks for men and women: classical, stylish city clothes.

St Lawrence river in E North America. From

ports on the *Great Lakes it forms, with linking canals (which also give great hydroelectric capacity to the river), the St Lawrence Seaway for oceangoing ships, ending in the Gulf of St Lawrence. It is 1,200 km/745 mi long and is ice-bound annually for four months.

St Leger horse race held at Doncaster, England, every Sept. It is a flat race over 2.8 km/3,060 yd, and is the last of the season. First held 1776, it is the oldest of the English classic races. Because of damage to the course, the 1989 race was held at Ayr, the first time Scotland had staged a classic.

St Louis city in Missouri, USA, on the Mississippi River; population (1990) 396,700, metropolitan area 2,444,100. Its products include aerospace equipment, aircraft, vehicles, chemicals, electrical goods, steel, and beer.

St Lucia

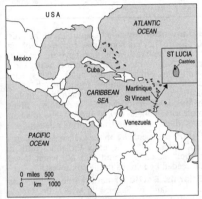

USA
ATLANTIC OCEAN
ST LUCIA
Castries
Mexico
Cuba
Martinique
CARIBBEAN SEA
St Vincent
Venezuela
PACIFIC OCEAN

0 miles 500
0 km 1000

area 617 sq km/238 sq mi
capital Castries
towns Vieux-Fort, Soufrière
physical mountainous island with fertile valleys; mainly tropical forest
head of state Elizabeth II from 1979 represented by governor general
head of government John Compton from 1982
political system constitutional monarchy
exports coconut oil, bananas, cocoa, copra
currency E Caribbean dollar
population (1993 est) 136,000; growth rate 2.8% p.a.
languages English; French patois
religion Roman Catholic 90%
GNP $2,872 per head (1991)
chronology
1814 Became a British crown colony following Treaty of Paris.
1967 Acquired internal self-government as a West Indies associated state.
1979 Independence achieved from Britain within the Commonwealth, with John Compton, leader of the United Workers' Party (UWP), as prime minister. Allan Louisy, leader of the St Lucia Labour Party (SLP), replaced Compton as prime minister.
1981 Louisy resigned; replaced by Winston Cenac.
1982 Compton returned to power at the head of a UWP government.
1987 Compton re-elected with reduced majority.

1991 Integration with Windward Islands proposed.
1992 UWP won general election.

St Moritz winter sports centre in SE Switzerland; it contains the Cresta Run (built 1885) for toboggans, bobsleighs, and luges. It was the site of the Winter Olympics 1928 and 1948.

St Petersburg capital of the St Petersburg region, Russia, at the head of the Gulf of Finland; population (1987) 4,948,000. Industries include shipbuilding, machinery, chemicals, and textiles. It was renamed **Petrograd** 1914 and was called **Leningrad** from 1924 until 1991, when its original name was restored.

St Peter's Cathedral, Rome Roman Catholic cathedral church of the Vatican City State, built 1506–1626, chiefly by the architects Bramante and Michelangelo, successively. The cathedral has an internal length of 180 m/600 ft and a width at the transepts of 135 m/450 ft. The dome has an internal diameter of 42 m/137 ft and rises externally 138 m/452 ft to the crowning cross of the lantern.

St Pierre and Miquelon territorial dependency of France, eight small islands off the S coast of Newfoundland, Canada
area St Pierre group 26 sq km/10 sq mi; Miquelon-Langlade group 216 sq km/83 sq mi
capital St Pierre
products fish
currency French franc
population (1987) 6,300
language French
religion Roman Catholic
government French-appointed commissioner and elected local council; one representative in the National Assembly in France
history settled 17th century by Breton and Basque fisherfolk; French territory 1816–1976; overseas *département* until 1985; violent protests 1989 when France tried to impose its claim to a 200-mi/320-km fishing zone around the islands; Canada maintains that there is only a 12-mi/19-km zone.

Saint-Saëns (Charles) Camille 1835–1921. French composer, pianist, and organist. Among his many lyrical Romantic pieces are concertos, the symphonic poem *Danse macabre* 1875, the opera *Samson et Dalila* 1877, and the orchestral *Carnaval des animaux/Carnival of the Animals* 1886.

Saint-Simon Claude Henri, Comte de 1760–1825. French socialist who fought in the American Revolution and was imprisoned during the French Revolution. He advocated an atheist society ruled by technicians and industrialists in *Du Système industrielle/The Industrial System* 1821.

Saint-Simon Louis de Rouvroy, Duc de 1675–1755. French soldier, courtier, and politician whose *Mémoires* 1691–1723 are unrivalled as a description of the French court.

St Valentine's Day Massacre the murder in Chicago, USA, of seven unarmed members of the 'Bugs' Moran gang on 14 Feb 1929 by members of Al Capone's gang disguised as policemen. The killings testified to the intensity of gangland warfare for the control of the trade in illicit liquor during *Prohibition.

St Vincent and the Grenadines
area 388 sq km/150 sq mi, including islets of the Northern Grenadines 43 sq km/17 sq mi
capital Kingstown
towns Georgetown, Chateaubelair
physical volcanic mountains, thickly forested
head of state Elizabeth II from 1979 represented by governor general
head of government James Mitchell from 1984
political system constitutional monarchy
exports bananas, taros, sweet potatoes, arrowroot, copra
currency E Caribbean dollar
population (1993 est) 115,000; growth rate – 4% p.a.
languages English; French patois
religion 47% Anglican, 28% Methodist, 13% Roman Catholic
GNP $1,730 per head (1991)
chronology
1783 Became a British crown colony.
1958-62 Part of the West Indies Federation.
1969 Achieved internal self-government.
1979 Achieved full independence from Britain within the Commonwealth, with Milton Cato as prime minister.
1984 James Mitchell became prime minister.
1989 Mitchell decisively re-elected.
1991 Integration with Windward Islands proposed.

St Vitus's dance former name for *chorea, a nervous disorder. St Vitus, martyred under the Roman emperor Diocletian, was the patron saint of dancers.

sake Japanese wine made from rice. It is usually served heated but may also be drunk at room temperature. There are both dry and sweet types. Sake contains 14–18% alcohol.

Sakhalin (Japanese *Karafuto*) island in the Pacific, N of Japan, that since 1947, with the Kurils, forms a region of Russia; capital Yuzhno-Sakhalinsk (Japanese *Toyohara*); area 74,000 sq km/28,564 sq mi; population (1981) 650,000, including aboriginal *Ainu and Gilyaks. There are two parallel mountain ranges, rising to over 1,525 m/5,000 ft, which extend throughout its length, 965 km/600 mi.

Sakharov Andrei Dmitrievich 1921–1989. Soviet physicist, known both as the 'father of the Soviet H-bomb' and as an outspoken human-rights campaigner. In 1948 he joined Igor Tamm in developing the hydrogen bomb; he later protested against Soviet nuclear tests and was a founder of the Soviet Human Rights Committee, winning the Nobel Peace Prize 1975. In 1980 he was sent to internal exile in Gorky (now Nizhni-Novgorod) for criticizing Soviet action in Afghanistan. At the end of 1986 he was allowed to return to Moscow and resume his place in the Soviet Academy of Sciences.

Sakti the female principle in *Hinduism.

Śākyamuni the historical *Buddha, called Shaka in Japan (because Gautama was of the Śakya clan).

Saladin or *Sala-ud-din* 1138–1193. Born a Kurd, sultan of Egypt from 1175, in succession to the Atabeg of Mosul, on whose behalf he conquered Egypt 1164–74. He subsequently conquered Syria 1174–87 and precipitated the third *Crusade by his recovery of Jerusalem from the Christians 1187. Renowned for knightly courtesy, Saladin made peace with Richard I of England 1192.

Salamanca, Battle of victory of the British commander Wellington over the French army in the *Peninsular War, 22 July 1812.

salamander The fire salamander is seldom far from water, preferring moist areas.

salamander any tailed amphibian of the order *Urodela*. They are sometimes confused with lizards, but unlike lizards they have no scales or claws. Salamanders have smooth or warty moist skin. The order includes some 300 species, arranged in nine families, found mainly in the northern hemisphere. Salamanders include hellbenders, mudpuppies, waterdogs, sirens, mole salamanders, newts, and lungless salamanders (dusky, woodland, and spring salamanders).

Salamis ancient city on the east coast of Cyprus, the capital under the early Ptolemies until its harbour silted up about 200 BC, when it was succeeded by Paphos in the southwest.

Salamis, Battle of naval battle off the coast of the island of Salamis in which the Greeks defeated the Persians 480 BC.

Salazar Antonio de Oliveira 1889–1970. Portuguese prime minister 1932–68 who exercised a virtual dictatorship. During World War II he maintained Portuguese neutrality but fought long colonial wars in Africa (Angola and Mozambique) that impeded his country's economic development as well as that of the colonies.

Salic law a law adopted in the Middle Ages by several European royal houses, excluding women from succession to the throne. The name derives mistakenly from the Salian or northern division of the Franks, who supposedly practised it.

salicylic acid HOC_6H_4COOH the active chemical constituent of aspirin, an analgesic drug. The acid and its salts (salicylates) occur naturally in many plants; concentrated sources include willow bark and oil of wintergreen.

Salieri Antonio 1750–1825. Italian composer. He taught Beethoven, Schubert, and Liszt, and was the musical rival of Mozart, whom it has been suggested, without proof, that he poisoned, at the emperor's court in Vienna, where he held the position of court composer.

Salinas de Gortiari Carlos 1948– . Mexican politician, president 1988–1994, a member of the dominant Institutional Revolutionary Party (PRI).

Salinger J(erome) D(avid) 1919– . US writer, author of the classic novel of mid-20th-century adolescence *The Catcher in the Rye* 1951. He also wrote short stories about a Jewish family named Glass, including *Franny and Zooey* 1961.

Salisbury city and market town in Wiltshire, England, 135 km/84 mi SW of London; population (1981) 35,355. Salisbury is an agricultural centre, and industries include brewing and carpet manufacture (in nearby Wilton). The cathedral of St Mary, built 1220–66, is an example of Early English architecture; its decorated spire 123 m/404 ft is the highest in England; its clock (1386) is one of the oldest still working. The cathedral library contains one of only four copies of the *Magna Carta*.

Salisbury former name (until 1980) of *Harare, capital of Zimbabwe.

saliva in vertebrates, a secretion from the salivary glands that aids the swallowing and digestion of food in the mouth. In mammals, it contains the enzyme amylase, which converts starch to sugar. The salivary glands of mosquitoes and other blood-sucking insects produce *anticoagulants.

Salk Jonas Edward 1914– . US physician and microbiologist. In 1954 he developed the original vaccine that led to virtual eradication of paralytic *polio in industrialized countries. He was director of the Salk Institute for Biological Studies, University of California, San Diego, 1963–75.

Sallust Gaius Sallustius Crispus 86–*c*. 34 BC. Roman historian, a supporter of Julius Caesar. He wrote accounts of Catiline's conspiracy and the Jugurthine War in an epigrammatic style.

salmon any of the various bony fishes of the family Salmonidae. More specifically the name is applied to several species of game fishes of the genera Salmo and Oncorhynchus of North America and Eurasia that mature in the ocean but, to spawn, return to the freshwater streams where they were born. Their normal colour is silvery with a few dark spots, but the colour changes at the spawning season.

Salmond Alexander Elliott Anderson (Alex) 1954– . Scottish politician, leader of Scottish National Party (SNP) from 1990. He joined the SNP and in 1987 was elected to the House of Commons, representing Banff and Buchan. He became SNP leader 1990 and, through his ability to project a moderate image, did much to improve his party's credibility.

salmonella very broad group of bacteria. They can be divided into three broad groups. One of these causes typhoid and paratyphoid fevers, while a second group causes salmonella *food poisoning, which is characterized by stomach pains, vomiting, diarrhoea, and headache. It can be fatal in elderly people, but others usually recover in a few days without antibiotics. Most cases are caused by contaminated animal products, especially poultry meat.

salsa Latin big-band dance music popularized by Puerto Ricans in New York City in the 1980s and by, among others, the Panamanian singer Rubén Blades (1948–).

salsify or *vegetable oyster* hardy biennial *Tragopogon porrifolius*, family Compositae. Its white fleshy roots and spring shoots are cooked and eaten.

salt in chemistry, any compound formed from an acid and a base through the replacement of all or part of the hydrogen in the acid by a metal or electropositive radical. **Common salt** is sodium chloride (see *salt, common).

SALT abbreviation for *Strategic Arms Limitation Talks*, a series of US–Soviet negotiations 1969–79.

salt, common or *sodium chloride* NaCl white crystalline solid, found dissolved in sea water and as rock salt (halite) in large deposits and salt domes. Common salt is used extensively in the food industry as a preservative and for flavouring, and in the chemical industry in the making of chlorine and sodium.

Salt Lake City capital of Utah, USA, on the river Jordan, 18 km/11 mi SE of the Great Salt Lake; population (1990) 159,900.

salt marsh wetland with halophytic vegetation (tolerant to sea water). Salt marshes develop around estuaries and on the sheltered side of sand and shingle spits. Salt marshes usually have a network of creeks and drainage channels by which tidal waters enter and leave the marsh.

saluki breed of dog resembling the greyhound. It is about 65 cm/26 in high and has a silky coat, which is usually fawn, cream, or white.

Salvador port and naval base in Bahia state, NE Brazil, on the inner side of a peninsula separating Todos Santos Bay from the Atlantic; population (1991) 2,075,400. Products include cocoa, tobacco, and sugar. Founded 1510, it was the capital of Brazil 1549–1763.

Salvador, El republic in Central America; see *El Salvador.

Salvation Army Christian evangelical, social-service, and social-reform organization, originating 1865 in London, England, with the work of William *Booth. Originally called the Christian Revival Association, it was renamed the East London Christian Mission in 1870 and from 1878 has been known as the Salvation Army, now a worldwide organization. It has military titles for its officials, is renowned for its brass bands, and its weekly journal is the *War Cry*.

sal volatile another name for *smelling salts.

Salyut (Russian 'salute') series of seven space stations launched by the USSR 1971–82. Salyut was cylindrical in shape, 15 m/50 ft long, and weighed 19 tonnes/21 tons. It housed two or three cosmonauts at a time, for missions lasting up to eight months.

Salzburg capital of the state of Salzburg, W Austria, on the river Salzach, in W Austria; population (1981) 139,400. The city is dominated by the Hohensalzburg fortress. It is the seat of an archbishopric founded by St Boniface about 700 and has a 17th-century cathedral. It is the birthplace of the composer Wolfgang Amadeus Mozart and an annual music festival has been held here since 1920. Industries include stock rearing, dairy farming, forestry, and tourism.

Salzburg federal province of Austria; area 7,200 sq km/2,779 sq mi; population (1987) 462,000. Its capital is Salzburg.

samara in botany, a winged fruit, a type of *achene.

Samara capital of Kuibyshev region, W central Russia, and port at the junction of the rivers

Samara and Volga, situated in the centre of the fertile middle Volga plain; industries include aircraft, locomotives, cables, synthetic rubber, textiles, fertilizers, petroleum refining, and quarrying; population (1987) 1,280,000. From 1935–91 it was called *Kuibyshev*, reverting to its former name Jan 1991.

Samaria region of ancient Israel. The town of Samaria (now Sebastiyeh) on the west bank of the river Jordan was the capital of Israel in the 10th–8th centuries BC. It was renamed Sebarte in the 1st century BC by the Roman administrator Herod the Great. Extensive remains have been excavated.

Samaritan member or descendant of the colonists forced to settle in Samaria (now N Israel) by the Assyrians after their occupation of the ancient kingdom of Israel 722 BC. Samaritans adopted a form of Judaism, but adopted only the Pentateuch, the five books of Moses of the Old Testament, and regarded their temple on Mount Gerizim as the true sanctuary.

Samaritans voluntary organization aiding those tempted to suicide or despair, established in 1953 in the UK. Groups of lay people, often consulting with psychiatrists, psychotherapists, and doctors, offer friendship and counselling to those using their emergency telephone numbers, day or night.

samarium hard, brittle, grey-white, metallic element of the *lanthanide series, symbol Sm, atomic number 62, relative atomic mass 150.4. It is widely distributed in nature and is obtained commercially from the minerals monzanite and bastnasite. It is used only occasionally in industry, mainly as a catalyst in organic reactions. Samarium was discovered by spectroscopic analysis of the mineral samarskite and named in 1879 by French chemist Paul Lecoq de Boisbaudran (1838–1912) after its source.

Samarkand city in E Uzbekistan, capital of Samarkand region, near the river Zerafshan, 217 km/135 mi E of Bukhara; population (1987) 388,000. Industries include cotton-ginning, silk manufacture, and engineering.

samba Latin American ballroom dance; the music for this. Samba originated in Brazil and became popular in the West in the 1940s. There are several different samba rhythms; the bossa nova is a samba-jazz fusion.

samizdat (Russian 'self-published') in the USSR and eastern Europe before the 1989 uprisings, written material circulated underground to evade state censorship; for example, reviews of Solzhenitzyn's banned novel *August 1914* 1972.

Samoa volcanic island chain in the SW Pacific. It is divided into the state of Western Samoa and American Samoa.

Samoa, American group of islands 4,200 km/ 2,610 mi S of Hawaii, administered by the USA
area 200 sq km/77 sq mi
capital Fagatogo on Tutuila
exports canned tuna, handicrafts
currency US dollar
population (1990) 46,800
language Samoan and English
religion Christian
government as a non-self-governing territory

of the USA, under Governor A P Lutali, it is constitutionally an unincorporated territory of the USA, administered by the Department of the Interior
history the islands were acquired by the USA in Dec 1899 by agreement with Britain and Germany under the Treaty of Berlin. A constitution was adopted 1960 and revised 1967.

Samoa, Western Independent State of (*Samoa i Sisifo*)

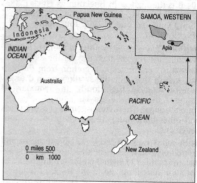

area 2,830 sq km/1,093 sq mi
capital Apia (on Upolu island)
physical comprises South Pacific islands of Savai'i and Upolu, with two smaller tropical islands and islets; mountain ranges on main islands
head of state King Malietoa Tanumafili II from 1962
head of government Tofilau Eti Alesana from 1988
political system liberal democracy
exports coconut oil, copra, cocoa, fruit juice, cigarettes, timber
currency talà
population (1993 est) 200,000; growth rate 1.1% p.a.
languages English, Samoan (official)
religions Protestant 70%, Roman Catholic 20%
GNP $930 per head (1991)
chronology
1899–1914 German protectorate.
1920–61 Administered by New Zealand.
1959 Local government elected.
1961 Referendum favoured independence.
1962 Independence achieved within the Commonwealth, with Fiame Mata Afa Mulinu'u as prime minister.
1975 Mata Afa died.
1976 Tupuola Taisi Efi became first nonroyal prime minister.
1982 Va'ai Kolone became prime minister; replaced by Tupuola Efi. Assembly failed to approve budget; Tupuola Efi resigned; replaced by Tofilau Eti Alesana.
1985 Tofilau Eti resigned; head of state invited Va'ai Kolone to lead the government.
1988 Elections produced a hung parliament, with first Tupuola Efi as prime minister and then Tofilau Eti Alesana.
1990 Universal adult suffrage introduced.
1991 Tofilau Eti Alesana re-elected. Fiame Naome became first woman in cabinet.

samoyed breed of dog, originating in Siberia. It weighs about 25 kg/60 lb and is 58 cm/23 in tall. It resembles a *chow chow, but has a more pointed face and a white or cream coat.

samphire or **glasswort** or **sea asparagus** perennial plant *Crithmum maritimum* found on sea cliffs in Europe. The aromatic leaves are fleshy and sharply pointed; the flowers grow in yellow-green umbels. It is used in salads, or pickled.

sampler (Latin *exemplar* 'pattern') embroidered panel, originally one on which various types of stitches or motifs had been worked to serve as models or samples. Since the 16th century the term has been used to mean a panel worked in various stitches to demonstrate the skill of the maker.

Sampras Pete(r) 1971– . US tennis player, winner of Wimbledon 1993 and 1994. At 19 years, he was the youngest winner of the US Open 1990. He also won the inaugural Grand Slam Cup in Munich 1990.

Samson 11th century BC. In the Old Testament, a hero of Israel. He was renowned for exploits of strength against the Philistines, which ended when his lover Delilah cut off his hair, the source of his strength, as told in the Book of Judges.

Samuel 11th–10 centuries BC. In the Old Testament, the last of the judges who ruled the ancient Hebrews before their adoption of a monarchy, and the first of the prophets; the two books bearing his name cover the story of Samuel and the reigns of kings Saul and David.

samurai member of the military caste in Japan from the mid-12th century until 1869, when the feudal system was abolished and all samurai pensioned off by the government. A samurai was an armed retainer of a *daimyō* (large landowner) with specific duties and privileges and a strict code of honour. A *rōnin* was a samurai without feudal allegiance.

San (formerly **Bushman**) member of a small group of hunter-gatherer peoples living in and around the Kalahari Desert. Their language belongs to the Khoisan family.

Sana'a capital of Yemen, SW Arabia, 320 km/200 mi N of Aden; population (1986) 427,000. A walled city, with fine mosques and traditional architecture, it is rapidly being modernized.

San Andreas fault geological fault line stretching for 1,125 km/700 mi in a NW–SE direction through the state of California, USA. The friction caused by tectonic movements along the fault gives rise to periodic earthquakes.

San Antonio city in S Texas, USA; population (1990) 936,000. It is a commercial and financial centre; industries include aircraft maintenance, oil refining, and meat packing.

sanction economic or military measure taken by a state or number of states to enforce international law. The first use of sanctions was the attempted economic boycott of Italy (1935–36) during the Abyssinian War by the League of Nations.

Sanctorius Sanctorius 1561–1636. Italian physiologist who pioneered the study of *metabolism and invented the clinical thermometer and a device for measuring pulse rate.

sanctuary (Latin *sanctuarium* 'sacred place')

the holiest area of a place of worship; also, a place of refuge from persecution or prosecution, usually in or near a place of worship. The custom of offering sanctuary in specific places goes back to ancient times and was widespread in Europe in the Middle Ages.

sand loose grains of rock, sized 0.02–2.00 mm/0.0008–0.0800 in in diameter, consisting chiefly of *quartz, but owing their varying colour to mixtures of other minerals. Sand is used in cement-making, as an abrasive, in glass-making, and for other purposes.

Sand George. Pen name of Amandine Aurore Lucie Dupin 1804–1876. French author whose prolific literary output was often autobiographical. In 1831 she left her husband after nine years of marriage and, while living in Paris as a writer, had love affairs with Alfred de Musset, *Chopin, and others. Her first novel *Indiana* 1832 was a plea for women's right to independence.

sandalwood fragrant heartwood of any of certain Asiatic and Australian trees of the genus *Santalum*, family Santalaceae, used for ornamental carving, in perfume, and burned as incense.

sandbar ridge of sand built up by the currents across the mouth of a river or bay. A sandbar may be entirely underwater or it may form an elongated island that breaks the surface. A sandbar stretching out from a headland is a *sand spit*.

Sandburg Carl August 1878–1967. US poet. He worked as a farm labourer and a bricklayer, and his poetry celebrates ordinary life in the USA, as in *Chicago Poems* 1916, *The People, Yes* 1936, and *Complete Poems* 1951 (Pulitzer prize). In free verse, it is reminiscent of Walt Whitman's poetry. Sandburg also wrote a monumental biography of Abraham Lincoln, *Abraham Lincoln: The Prairie Years* 1926 (two volumes) and *Abraham Lincoln: The War Years* 1939 (four volumes; Pulitzer Prize). *Always the Young Strangers* 1953 is his autobiography.

Sanders George 1906–1972. Russian-born British actor, usually cast as a smooth-talking cad. Most of his film career was spent in the USA where he starred in such films as *Rebecca* 1940, *The Moon and Sixpence* 1942, and *The Picture of Dorian Gray* 1944.

sandgrouse any bird of the family Pteroclidae. They look like long-tailed grouse, but are actually closely related to pigeons. They live in warm, dry areas of Europe, Asia, and Africa and have long wings, short legs, and thick skin.

sand hopper or **beachflea** any of various small crustaceans belonging to the order Amphipeda, with laterally compressed bodies, that live in beach sand and jump like fleas. The eastern sand hopper *Orchestia agilis* of North America is about 1.3 cm/0.5 in long.

San Diego city and military and naval base in California, USA; population (1990) 1,110,600, metropolitan area 2,498,000. It is an important Pacific Ocean fishing port. Manufacturing includes aerospace and electronic equipment, metal fabrication, printing and publishing, seafood canning, and shipbuilding.

Sandinista member of the socialist movement that carried out the *Nicaraguan Revolution.

Sandoz pharmaceutical company whose plant

in Basel, Switzerland, suffered an environmentally disastrous chemical fire in Nov 1986. Hundreds of tonnes of pesticides, including mercury-based fungicides, spilled into the river Rhine, rendering it lifeless for 100–200 km/60–120 mi and killing about half a million fish.

sandpiper any of various shorebirds belonging to the family Scolopacidae, which includes godwits, *curlews, and *snipes.

Sandringham House private residence of the British sovereign, built 1863 by the Prince of Wales (afterwards Edward VII) 1869–1971.

sandstone *sedimentary rocks formed from the consolidation of sand, with sand-sized grains (0.0625–2 mm/0.0025–0.08 in) in a matrix or cement. The principal component is quartz. Sandstones are classified according to the matrix or cement material (whether derived from clay or silt; for example, as calcareous sandstone, ferruginous sandstone, siliceous sandstone).

Sandwich John Montagu, 4th Earl of Sandwich 1718–1792. British politician. He was an inept First Lord of the Admiralty 1771–82 during the American Revolution, and his corrupt practices were blamed for the British navy's inadequacies.

Sandwich Islands former name of *Hawaii, a group of islands in the Pacific.

Sandys Duncan Edwin Sandys, Baron Duncan-Sandys 1908–1987. British Conservative politician. As minister for Commonwealth relations 1960–64, he negotiated the independence of Malaysia 1963. He was created a life peer in 1974.

San Francisco chief Pacific port of the USA, in California; population (1990) 724,000, metropolitan area of San Francisco and Oakland 3,686,600. The city stands on a peninsula, south of the Golden Gate 1937, the world's second longest single-span bridge, 1,280 m/4,200 ft. The strait gives access to San Francisco Bay. Manufactured goods include textiles, fabricated metal products, electrical equipment, petroleum products, chemicals, and pharmaceuticals.

San Francisco conference conference attended by representatives from 50 nations who had declared war on Germany before March 1945; held in San Francisco, California, USA. The conference drew up the United Nations Charter, which was signed 26 June 1945.

Sanger Frederick 1918– . English biochemist, the first person to win a Nobel Prize for Chemistry twice: the first in 1958 for determining the structure of insulin, and the second in 1980 for work on the chemical structure of genes.

sang-froid (French 'cold blood') coolness, composure.

Sangha in Buddhism, the monastic orders, one of the Three Treasures of Buddhism (the other two are Buddha and the law, or dharma). The term Sangha is sometimes used more generally by Mahāyāna Buddhists to include all believers.

San José capital of Costa Rica; population (1989) 284,600. Products include coffee, cocoa, and sugar cane. Founded 1737; capital since 1823.

San José city in Santa Clara Valley, California, USA; population (1990) 782,200. It is the centre of 'Silicon Valley', the site of many high-

technology electronic firms turning out semiconductors and other computer components. There are also electrical, aerospace, missile, rubber, metal, and machine industries, and it is a commercial and transportation centre for orchard crops and wines produced in the area.

San Juan capital of Puerto Rico; population (1990) 437,750. It is a port and industrial city. Products include chemicals, pharmaceuticals, machine tools, electronic equipment, textiles, plastics, and rum.

San Luis Potosí silver-mining city and capital of San Luis Potosí state, central Mexico; population (1986) 602,000. Founded 1586 as a Franciscan mission, it became the colonial administrative headquarters and has fine buildings of the period.

San Marino Republic of (*Repubblica di San Marino*)

area 61 sq km/24 sq mi
capital San Marino
towns Serravalle (industrial centre)
physical on the slope of Mount Titano
head of state and government two captains regent, elected for a six-month period
political system direct democracy
exports wine, ceramics, paint, chemicals, building stone
currency Italian lira
population (1993 est) 24,000; growth rate 0.1% p.a.
language Italian
religion Roman Catholic 95%
chronology
1862 Treaty with Italy signed; independence recognized under Italy's protection.
1947–86 Governed by a series of left-wing and centre-left coalitions.
1986 Formation of Communist and Christian Democrat 'grand coalition'.
1992 Joined the United Nations.

San Martín José de 1778–1850. South American revolutionary leader. He served in the Spanish army during the Peninsular War, but after 1812 he devoted himself to the South American struggle for independence, playing a large part in the liberation of Argentina, Chile, and Peru from Spanish rule.

sannyasin in Hinduism, a person who has renounced worldly goods to live a life of asceticism and seek *moksha*, or liberation from reincarnation, through meditation and prayer.

San Pedro Sula main industrial and commercial city in NW Honduras, the second-largest city in the country; population (1989) 300,900. It trades in bananas, coffee, sugar, and timber and manufactures textiles, plastics, furniture, and cement.

San Salvador capital of El Salvador 48 km/30 mi from the Pacific, at the foot of San Salvador volcano (2,548 m/8,360 ft); population (1984) 453,000. Industries include food processing and textiles. Since its foundation 1525, it has suffered from several earthquakes.

sans-culotte (French 'without knee breeches') in the French Revolution, a member of the working classes, who wore trousers, as opposed to the aristocracy and bourgeoisie, who wore knee breeches.

Sanskrit the dominant classical language of the Indian subcontinent, a member of the Indo-Iranian group of the Indo-European language family, and the sacred language of Hinduism. The oldest form of Sanskrit is **Vedic**, the variety used in the *Vedas* and *Upanishads* (about 1500–700 BC).

sans souci (French) without cares or worries.

Santa Ana periodic warm Californian *wind.

Santa Anna Antonio López de 1795–1876. Mexican revolutionary who became general and dictator of Mexico for most of the years between 1824 and 1855. He led the attack on the *Alamo fort in Texas 1836.

Santa Claus another name for Father Christmas; see St *Nicholas.

Santa Fe Trail US trade route 1821–80 from Independence, Missouri, to Santa Fe, New Mexico.

Santayana George 1863–1952. Spanish-born US philosopher and critic. He developed his philosophy based on naturalism and taught that everything has a natural basis.

Sant'Elia Antonio 1888–1916. Italian architect. His drawings convey a Futurist vision of a metropolis with skyscrapers, traffic lanes, and streamlined factories.

Santer Jacques 1937– . Luxembourg politician, prime minister 1984–94. In Jan 1995 he succeeded Jacques Delors as president of the European Commission.

Santiago capital of Chile; population (1990) 4,385,500. Industries include textiles, chemicals, and food processing. It was founded 1541 and is famous for its broad avenues.

Santo Domingo capital and chief sea port of the Dominican Republic; population (1982) 1,600,000. Founded 1496 by Bartolomeo, brother of Christopher Columbus, it is the oldest colonial city in the Americas. Its cathedral was built 1515–40.

San Yu 1919– . Myanmar (Burmese) politician. A member of the Revolutionary Council that came to power 1962, he became president 1981 and was re-elected 1985. He was forced to resign July 1988, along with Ne Win, after riots in Yangon (formerly Rangoon).

São Paulo city in Brazil, 72 km/45 mi NW of its port Santos; population (1991) 9,700,100,

metropolitan area 15,280,000. It is 900 m/3,000 ft above sea level, and 2°S of the Tropic of Capricorn. It is South America's leading industrial city, producing electronics, steel, and chemicals; it has meat-packing plants and is the centre of Brazil's coffee trade. It originated as a Jesuit mission in 1554.

São Tomé e Príncipe Democratic Republic of
area 1,000 sq km/386 sq mi
capital São Tomé
towns Santo Antonio, Santa Cruz
physical comprises two main islands and several smaller ones, all volcanic; thickly forested and fertile
head of state and government Miguel Trovoada from 1991
political system emergent democratic republic
exports cocoa, copra, coffee, palm oil, and kernels
currency dobra
population (1993 est) 130,000; growth rate 2.5% p.a.
languages Portuguese (official), Fang (Bantu)
religion Roman Catholic 80%, animist
GNP $350 per head (1991)
chronology
1471 Discovered by Portuguese.
1522–1973 A province of Portugal.
1973 Achieved internal self-government.
1975 Independence achieved from Portugal, with Manuel Pinto da Costa as president.
1984 Formally declared a nonaligned state.
1987 Constitution amended.
1988 Unsuccessful coup attempt against da Costa.
1990 New constitution approved.
1991 First multiparty elections held; Miguel Trovoada replaced Pinto da Costa.

sap the fluids that circulate through *vascular plants, especially woody ones. Sap carries water and food to plant tissues. Sap contains alkaloids, protein, and starch; it can be milky (as in rubber trees), resinous (as in pines), or syrupy (as in maples).

saponification in chemistry, the *hydrolysis (splitting) of an *ester by treatment with a strong alkali, resulting in the liberation of the alcohol from which the ester had been derived and a salt of the constituent fatty acid. The process is used in the manufacture of soap.

sapphire deep-blue, transparent gem variety of the mineral *corundum Al_2O_3, aluminium oxide. Small amounts of iron and titanium give it its colour. A corundum gem of any colour except red (which is a ruby) can be called a sapphire; for example, yellow sapphire.

Sappho c. 612–580 BC. Greek lyric poet, friend of the poet *Alcaeus and leader of a female literary coterie at Mytilene (now **Lesvos**, hence *lesbianism). Legend says she committed suicide when her love for the boatman Phaon was unrequited.

Sapporo capital of *Hokkaido, Japan; population (1989) 1,637,000. Industries include rubber and food processing. It is a winter sports centre and was the site of the 1972 Winter Olympics. Giant figures are sculpted in ice at the annual snow festival.

saprotroph (formerly **saprophyte**) organism that feeds on the excrement or the dead bodies or tissues of others. They include most fungi (the rest being parasites); many bacteria and protozoa; animals such as dung beetles and vultures; and a few unusual plants, including several orchids. Saprotrophs cannot make food for themselves, so they are a type of *heterotroph. They are useful scavengers, and in sewage farms and refuse dumps break down organic matter into nutrients easily assimilable by green plants.

Saracen ancient Greek and Roman term for an Arab, used in the Middle Ages by Europeans for all Muslims. The equivalent term used in Spain was *Moor.

Sarajevo capital of Bosnia-Herzegovina; population (1991) 526,000. Industries include engineering, brewing, chemicals, carpets, and ceramics. A Bosnian, Gavrilo Princip, assassinated Archduke *Franz Ferdinand here 1914, thereby precipitating World War I. From April 1992 the city was the target of a siege by Bosnian Serb forces in their fight to carve up the newly independent republic. A United Nations ultimatum and the threat of NATO bombing led to a cease-fire Feb 1994 and the effective end of the siege as Serbian heavy weaponry was withdrawn. Hostilities resumed later in the year.

Saratov industrial port (chemicals, oil refining) on the river Volga in W central Russia; population (1987) 918,000. It was established in the 1590s as a fortress to protect the Volga trade route.

Sarawak state of Malaysia, on the NW corner of the island of Borneo
area 124,400 sq km/48,018 sq mi
capital Kuching
products it has a tropical climate and produces timber, oil, rice, pepper, rubber, and coconuts
population (1991) 1,669,000; 24 ethnic groups make up almost half this number
physical mountainous; the rainforest, which may be 10 million years old, contains several thousand tree species. A third of all its plant species are endemic to Borneo. 30% of the forest was cut down 1963–89; timber expected to run out 1995–2001
history Sarawak was granted by the Sultan of Brunei to James Brooke 1841, who became 'Rajah of Sarawak'. It was a British protectorate from 1888 until captured by the Japanese in World War II. It was a crown colony from 1946 until 1963, when it became part of Malaysia.

sarcoidosis disease of unknown cause which may affect the lungs, eyes, and skin, and leads to blindness or death in a small minority. Many cases resolve spontaneously or may be successfully treated using *corticosteroids.

sarcoma malignant *tumour arising from the fat, muscles, bones, cartilage, or blood and lymph vessels and connective tissues. Sarcomas are much less common than *carcinomas.

sardine common name for various small fishes (*pilchards) in the herring family.

Sardinia (Italian *Sardegna*) mountainous island, special autonomous region of Italy; area 24,100 sq km/9,303 sq mi; population (1990) 1,664,400. Its capital is Cagliari, and it exports cork and petrochemicals. It is the second-largest Mediterranean island and includes Costa Smeralda (Emerald Coast) tourist area in the northeast and *nuraghi* (fortified Bronze Age dwellings).

After centuries of foreign rule, it became linked 1720 with Piedmont, and this dual kingdom became the basis of a united Italy 1861.

Sargasso Sea part of the N Atlantic (between 40° and 80°W and 25° and 30°N) left static by circling ocean currents, and covered with floating weed *Sargassum natans*.

Sargent John Singer 1856–1925. US portrait painter. Born in Florence of American parents, he studied there and in Paris, then settled in London around 1885. He was a fashionable and prolific painter.

Sargon two Mesopotamian kings:

Sargon I king of Akkad c. 2334–2279 BC, and founder of the first Babylonian empire. Like Moses, he was said to have been found floating in a cradle on the local river, in his case the Euphrates.

Sargon II died 705 BC. King of Assyria from 722 BC, who assumed the name of his predecessor. To keep conquered peoples from rising against him, he had whole populations moved from their homelands, including the Israelites from Samaria.

Sark one of the *Channel Islands, 10 km/6 mi E of Guernsey; area 5 sq km/2 sq mi; there is no town or village. It is divided into Great and Little Sark, linked by an isthmus, and is of great natural beauty. The Seigneurie of Sark was established by Elizabeth I, the ruler being known as Seigneur/Dame, and has its own parliament, the Chief Pleas. There is no income tax, and cars are forbidden; immigration is controlled.

Sarney (Costa) José 1930– . Brazilian politician, member of the centre-left Democratic Movement (PMDB), president 1985–90.

sarsaparilla drink prepared from the long twisted roots of several plants in the genus *Smilax* (family Liliaceae), native to Central and South America; it is used as a tonic.

Sartre Jean-Paul 1905–1980. French author and philosopher, a leading proponent of *existentialism. He published his first novel, *La Nausée/Nausea*, 1937, followed by the trilogy *Les Chemins de la Liberté/Roads to Freedom* 1944–4 and many plays, including *Huis Clos/In Camera* 1944. *L'Etre et le néant/Being and Nothingness* 1943, his first major philosophical work, sets out a radical doctrine of human freedom. In the later work *Critique de la raison dialectique/Critique of Dialectical Reason* 1960 he tried to produce a fusion of existentialism and Marxism.

SAS abbreviation for *Special Air Service*; also for *Scandinavian Airlines System*.

Saskatchewan (Cree *Kis-is-ska-tche-wan* 'swift flowing') province of W Canada
area 652,300 sq km/251,788 sq mi
capital Regina
towns Saskatoon, Moose Jaw, Prince Albert
physical prairies in the south; to the north, forests, lakes, and subarctic tundra; Prince Albert National Park
products more than 60% of Canada's wheat, oil, natural gas, uranium, zinc, potash (world's largest reserves), copper, helium (the only western reserves outside the USA)
population (1991) 995,300
history once inhabited by Indians speaking Athabaskan, Algonquin, and Sioux languages

Saudi Arabia 791

who depended on caribou and moose in the north and buffalo in the south. French trading posts established about 1750; owned by Hudson's Bay Company, first permanent settlement 1774; ceded to Canadian government 1870 as part of Northwest Territories; became a province 1905.

Sassanian Empire Persian empire founded AD 224 by Ardashir, a chieftain in the area of what is now Fars, in Iran, who had taken over *Parthia; it was named after his grandfather, Sasan. The capital was Ctesiphon, near modern *Baghdad, Iraq. After a rapid period of expansion, when it contested supremacy with Rome, it was destroyed in 637 by Muslim Arabs at the Battle of *Qadisiya.

Sassau-Nguesso Denis 1943– . Congolese socialist politician, president 1979–92. He progressively consolidated his position within the ruling left-wing Congolese Labour Party (PCT), at the same time as improving relations with France and the USA. In 1990, in response to public pressure, he agreed that the PCT should abandon Marxism-Leninism and that a multiparty system should be introduced.

Sassoon Siegfried 1886–1967. English writer, author of the autobiography *Memoirs of a Foxhunting Man* 1928. His *War Poems* 1919 express the disillusionment of his generation.

Satan a name for the *devil.

satellite any small body that orbits a larger one, either natural or artificial. Natural satellites that orbit planets are called moons. The first **artificial satellite**, Sputnik 1, was launched into orbit around the Earth by the USSR 1957. Artificial satellites are used for scientific purposes, communications, weather forecasting, and military applications. The largest artificial satellites can be seen by the naked eye.

satellite television transmission of broadcast signals through artificial communications satellites. Mainly positioned in *geostationary orbit, satellites have been used since the 1960s to relay television pictures around the world. Higher-power satellites have more recently been developed to broadcast signals to cable systems or directly to people's homes.

Satie Erik (Alfred Leslie) 1866–1925. French composer. His piano pieces, such as *Gymnopédies* 1888, often combine wit and melancholy. His orchestral works include *Parade* 1917, among whose sound effects is a typewriter. He was the mentor of the group of composers known as *Les Six*.

satire poem or piece of prose that uses wit, humour, or irony, often through *allegory or extended metaphor, to ridicule human pretensions or expose social evils. Satire is related to *parody* in its intention to mock, but satire tends to be more subtle and to mock an attitude or a belief, whereas parody tends to mock a particular work (such as a poem) by imitating its style, often with purely comic intent.

satrap title of a provincial governor in ancient Persia. Under Darius I, the Persian Empire was divided between some 20 satraps, each owing allegiance only to the king.

satsuma small, hardy, loose-skinned orange *Citrus reticulata* of the tangerine family, orig-

inally from Japan. It withstands cold conditions well.

saturated compound organic compound, such as propane, that contains only single covalent bonds. Saturated organic compounds can only undergo further reaction by *substitution reactions, as in the production of chloropropane from propane.

saturated fatty acid *fatty acid in which there are no double bonds in the hydrocarbon chain.

saturated solution in physics, a solution obtained when a solvent (liquid) can dissolve no more of a solute (usually a solid) at a particular temperature. Normally, a slight fall in temperature causes some of the solute to crystallize out of solution. If this does not happen the phenomenon is called supercooling, and the solution is said to be **supersaturated**.

Saturn in astronomy, the second-largest planet in the solar system, sixth from the Sun, and encircled by bright and easily visible equatorial rings. Viewed through a telescope it is ochre. Saturn orbits the Sun every 29.46 years at an average distance of 1,427,000,000 km/886,700,000 mi. Its equatorial diameter is 120,000 km/75,000 mi, but its polar diameter is 12,000 km/7,450 mi smaller, a result of its fast rotation and low density, the lowest of any planet.

Saturn in Roman mythology, the god of agriculture (Greek **Kronos**), whose period of rule was the ancient Golden Age. He was dethroned by his sons Jupiter, Neptune, and Pluto. At his festival, the Saturnalia in Dec, gifts were exchanged, and slaves were briefly treated as their masters' equals.

Saturn rocket family of large US rockets, developed by Wernher von Braun for the *Apollo project. The two-stage Saturn IB was used for launching Apollo spacecraft into orbit around the Earth. The three-stage Saturn V sent Apollo spacecraft to the Moon, and launched the *Skylab space station. The liftoff thrust of a Saturn V was 3,500 tonnes. After Apollo and Skylab, the Saturn rockets were retired in favour of the *space shuttle.

satyr in Greek mythology, a lustful, drunken woodland creature characterized by pointed ears, two horns on the forehead, and a tail. Satyrs attended the god of wine, *Dionysus. Roman writers confused satyrs with goat-footed fauns.

Saudi Arabia Kingdom of (al-Mamlaka al-'Arabiya as-Sa'udiya)
area 2,200,518 sq km/849,400 sq mi
capital Riyadh
towns Mecca, Medina, Taif; ports Jidda, Dammam
physical desert, sloping to the Persian Gulf from a height of 2,750 m/9,000 ft in the W
environment oil pollution caused by the Gulf War 1990–91 has affected 460 km/285 mi of the Saudi coastline, threatening desalination plants and damaging the wildlife of saltmarshes, mangrove forest, and mudflats
head of state and government King Fahd Ibn Abdul Aziz from 1982
political system absolute monarchy
exports oil, petroleum products
currency rial

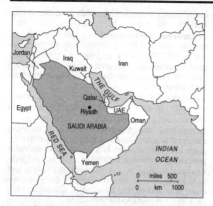

population (1993 est) 17,500,000 (16% nomadic); growth rate 3.1% p.a.
language Arabic
religion Sunni Muslim; there is a Shi'ite minority
GNP $7,070 per head (1990)
chronology
1926–32 Territories united and kingdom established.
1953 King Ibn Saud died and was succeeded by his eldest son, Saud.
1964 King Saud forced to abdicate; succeeded by his brother, Faisal.
1975 King Faisal assassinated; succeeded by his half-brother, Khalid.
1982 King Khalid died; succeeded by his brother, Crown Prince Fahd.
1987 Rioting by Iranian pilgrims caused 400 deaths in Mecca; diplomatic relations with Iran severed.
1990 Iraqi troops invaded and annexed Kuwait and massed on Saudi Arabian border. King Fahd called for help from US and UK forces.
1991 King Fahd provided military and financial assistance in Gulf War. Calls from religious leaders for 'consultative assembly' to assist in government of kingdom. Saudi Arabia attended Middle East peace conference.
1992 Formation of a 'consultative council' seen as possible move towards representative government.

Saul in the Old Testament, the first king of Israel. He was anointed by Samuel and warred successfully against the neighbouring Ammonites and Philistines, but fell from God's favour in his battle against the Amalekites. He became jealous and suspicious of David and turned against him and Samuel. After being wounded in battle with the Philistines, in which his three sons died, he committed suicide.

sauna bath causing perspiration by means of dry heat. It consists of a small room in which the temperature is raised to about 90°C/200°F. The bather typically stays in it for only a few minutes and then follows it with a cold shower or swim. Saunas are popular in health clubs and sports centres.

Saussure Ferdinand de 1857–1913. Swiss language scholar, a pioneer of modern linguistics and the originator of the concept of *structural-

ism as used in linguistics, anthropology, and literary theory.

savanna or **savannah** extensive open tropical grasslands, with scattered trees and shrubs. Savannas cover large areas of Africa, North and South America, and N Australia.

Save the Children Fund organization established 1919 to promote the rights of children to care, good health, material welfare, and moral, spiritual, and educational development. It operates in more than 50 Third World countries and the UK; projects include the provision of health care, education, community development, and emergency relief. Save the Children had an income 1989–90 of 52,196,368. Its headquarters are in London.

Savimbi Jonas 1934– . Angolan soldier and right-wing revolutionary, founder and leader of the National Union for the Total Independence of Angola (UNITA). From 1975 UNITA under Savimbi's leadership tried to overthrow the government. An agreement between the two parties was reached May 1991, but fighting broke out again following elections Sept 1992.

savings unspent income, after deduction of tax. In economics a distinction is made between *investment, involving the purchase of capital goods, such as buying a house, and saving (where capital goods are not directly purchased; for example, buying shares).

savings and loan association (S&L) in the USA, an institution that makes loans for home improvements, construction, and purchase. In the late 1980s a crisis developed, with S&Ls making huge losses on unsecured loans. A federal bailout pledging more than $100 billion in tax-payer funds was negotiated 1989.

Savonarola Girolamo 1452–1498. Italian reformer, a Dominican friar and an eloquent preacher. His crusade against political and religious corruption won him popular support, and in 1494 he led a revolt in Florence that expelled the ruling Medici family and established a democratic republic. His denunciations of Pope *Alexander VI led to his excommunication in 1497, and in 1498 he was arrested, tortured, hanged, and burned for heresy.

Savoy area of France between the Alps, Lake Geneva, and the river Rhône. A medieval duchy, it was made into the *départements* of Savoie and Haute-Savoie, in the Rhône-Alpes region.

sawfish any fish of an order *Pristiformes* of large, sharklike *rays, characterized by a flat, sawlike snout edged with teeth. The common sawfish *P. pectinatus*, also called the smalltooth, is more than 6 m/19 ft long. It has some 24 teeth along an elongated snout (2 m/6 ft) that can be used as a weapon.

sawfly any of several families of insects of the order Hymenoptera, related to bees, wasps, and ants, but lacking a 'waist' on the body. The egg-laying tube (ovipositor) of the female is surrounded by a pair of sawlike organs, which it uses to make a slit in a plant stem to lay its eggs. Horntails are closely related.

Saxe-Coburg-Gotha Saxon duchy. Albert, the Prince Consort of Britain's Queen Victoria, was a son of the 1st Duke, Ernest I (1784–1844), who was succeeded by Albert's elder brother, Ernest II

(1818–1893). It remained the name of the British royal house until 1917, when it was changed to Windsor.

saxhorn family of brass musical instruments played with valves, invented by the Belgian Adolphe Sax (1814–1894) in 1845.

saxifrage any plant of the genus *Saxifraga*, family Saxifragaceae, occurring in rocky, mountainous, and alpine situations in the northern hemisphere. They are low plants with groups of small white, pink, or yellow flowers.

Saxon member of a Teutonic people who invaded Britain in the early Middle Ages; see *Anglo-Saxon.

Saxony (German *Sachsen*) administrative *Land* (state) of Germany
area 17,036 sq km/6,580 sq mi
capital Dresden
towns Leipzig, Chemnitz, Zwickau
physical on the plain of the river Elbe north of the Erzgebirge mountain range
products electronics, textiles, vehicles, machinery, chemicals, coal
population (1990) 5,000,000
history conquered by Charlemagne 792, Saxony became a powerful medieval German duchy. The electors of Saxony were also kings of Poland 1697–1763. Saxony was part of East Germany 1946–90, forming a region with Anhalt.

Saxony-Anhalt administrative *Land* (state) of Germany
area 20,450 sq km/10,000 sq mi
capital Magdeburg
towns Halle, Dessau
products chemicals, electronics, rolling stock, footwear, cereals, vegetables
population (1990) 3,000,000
history Anhalt became a duchy 1863 and a member of the North German Confederation 1866. Between 1946 and 1990 it was joined to the former Prussian province of Saxony as a region of East Germany.

saxophone large family of wind instruments combining woodwind and brass features, the single reed of the clarinet and the wide bore of the bugle. Patented in 1846 by Adolphe Sax (1814–1894), a Belgian instrument maker, the saxophone is a lively and versatile instrument that has played a prominent part in the history of jazz. Four of the original eight sizes remain in common use: soprano, alto, tenor, and baritone. The soprano is usually straight, the others curved back at the mouthpiece end, and with an upturned bell.

Sayers Dorothy L(eigh) 1893–1957. English writer of crime novels featuring detective Lord Peter Wimsey and heroine Harriet Vane, including *Strong Poison* 1930, *The Nine Tailors* 1934, and *Gaudy Night* 1935. She also wrote religious plays for radio, and translations of Dante.

Say's law in economics, the 'law of markets' formulated by Jean-Baptiste Say (1767–1832) to the effect that supply creates its own demand and that resources can never be underused.

scabies contagious infection of the skin caused by the parasitic itch mite *Sarcoptes scaboi*, which burrows under the skin to deposit eggs. Treatment is by antiparasitic creams and lotions.

scabious any plant of the Eurasian genus *Scabiosa* of the teasel family Dipsacaceae, with many small, usually blue, flowers borne in a single head on a tall stalk. The small scabious *S. columbaria* and the Mediterranean sweet scabious *S. atropurpurea* are often cultivated.

scalar quantity in mathematics and science, a quantity that has magnitude but no direction, as distinct from a *vector quantity, which has a direction as well as a magnitude. Temperature, mass, and volume are scalar quantities.

scalawag or *scallywag* in US history, a derogatory term for white Southerners who, during and after the Civil War of 1861–65, supported the Republican Party, and black emancipation and enfranchisement.

scale in music, a sequence of pitches that establishes a key, and in some respects the character of a composition. A scale is defined by its starting note and may be *major* or *minor* depending on the order of intervals. A *chromatic* scale is the full range of 12 notes: it has no key because there is no fixed starting point.

scale in chemistry, *calcium carbonate deposits that form on the inside of a kettle or boiler as a result of boiling *hard water.

scallop any marine bivalve *mollusc of the family Pectinidae, with a fan-shaped shell. There are two 'ears' extending from the socketlike hinge. Scallops use water-jet propulsion to move through the water to escape predators such as starfish. The giant Pacific scallop found from Alaska to California can reach 20 cm/8 in width.

scaly anteater another name for the *pangolin.

scampi (Italian 'shrimps') any of several large *shrimps (prawns) prepared broiled or fried and served hot.

Scandinavia peninsula in NW Europe, comprising Norway and Sweden; politically and culturally it also includes Denmark, Iceland, the Faroe Islands and Finland.

scanner device, usually electronic, used to sense and reproduce an image. Magnetic resonance imaging was being used in 1990 to tell stale food from fresh: the image of a fresh vegetable is different from that of one frozen and thawed.

scanner in computing, a device that can produce a digital image of a document for input and storage in a computer. It uses technology similar to that of a photocopier. Small scanners can be passed over the document surface by hand; larger versions have a flat bed, like that of a photocopier, on which the input document is placed and scanned.

scanning in medicine, the noninvasive examination of body organs to detect abnormalities of structure or function. Detectable waves – for example, *ultrasound, magnetic, or *X-rays – are passed through the part to be scanned. Their absorption pattern is recorded, analysed by computer, and displayed pictorially on a screen.

scapula or *shoulder blade* large bone forming part of the pectoral girdle, assisting in the articulation of the arm with the chest region. Its flattened shape allows a large region for the attachment of muscles.

scarab any of a family Scarabaeidae of beetles, often brilliantly coloured, and including *cockchafers, June beetles, and dung beetles. The *Scarabeus sacer* was revered by the ancient Egyptians as the symbol of resurrection.

Scargill Arthur 1938– . British trade-union leader. Elected president of the National Union of Miners (NUM) 1981, he embarked on a collision course with the Conservative government of Margaret Thatcher. The damaging strike of 1984–85 split the miners' movement.

Scarlatti (Giuseppe) Domenico 1685–1757. Italian composer, eldest son of Alessandro *Scarlatti, who lived most of his life in Portugal and Spain in the service of the Queen of Spain. He wrote highly original harpsichord sonatas.

Scarlatti (Pietro) Alessandro (Gaspare) 1660–1725. Italian Baroque composer, Master of the Chapel at the court of Naples, who developed the opera form. He composed more than 100 operas, including *Tigrane* 1715, as well as church music and oratorios.

scarlet fever or *scarlatina* acute infectious disease, especially of children, caused by the bacterium *Streptococcus pyogenes*. It is marked by a sore throat and a bright red rash spreading from the upper to the lower part of the body. The rash is followed by the skin peeling in flakes. It is treated with antibiotics.

scarp and dip in geology, the two slopes formed when a sedimentary bed outcrops as a landscape feature. The scarp is the slope that cuts across the bedding plane; the dip is the opposite slope which follows the bedding plane. The scarp is usually steep, while the dip is a gentle slope.

scatter diagram or *scattergram* a diagram whose purpose is to establish whether or not a connection or *correlation exists between two variables, for example between life expectancy and GNP. Each observation is marked with a dot in a position that shows the value of both variables. The pattern of dots is then examined to see if they show any underlying trend by means of a *best-fit line* (a straight line drawn so that its distance from the various points is as short as possible).

scent gland gland that opens onto the outer surface of animals, producing odorous compounds that are used for communicating between members of the same species (*pheromones), or for discouraging predators.

scepticism ancient philosophical view that absolute knowledge of things is ultimately unobtainable, hence the only proper attitude is to suspend judgement. Its origins lay in the teachings of the Greek philosopher Pyrrho, who maintained that peace of mind lay in renouncing all claims to knowledge.

Scheele Karl Wilhelm 1742–1786. Swedish chemist and pharmacist. In the book *Experiments on Air and Fire* 1777, he argued that the atmosphere was composed of two gases. One, which supported combustion (oxygen), he called 'fire air', and the other, which inhibited combustion (nitrogen), he called 'vitiated air'. He thus anticipated Joseph *Priestley's discovery of oxygen by two years.

Scheherazade the storyteller in the *Arabian Nights*.

scherzo (Italian 'joke') in music, a lively piece, usually in rapid triple (3/4) time; often used for the third movement of a symphony, sonata, or quartet.

Schiaparelli Elsa 1896–1973. Italian couturier and knitwear designer. Her innovative fashion ideas included padded shoulders, sophisticated colours ('shocking pink'), and the pioneering use of zips and synthetic fabrics.

Schiele Egon 1890–1918. Austrian Expressionist artist. Originally a landscape painter, he was strongly influenced by Art Nouveau and developed a contorted linear style. His subject matter included portraits and nudes. In 1911 he was arrested for alleged obscenity.

Schiller Johann Christoph Friedrich von 1759–1805. German dramatist, poet, and historian. He wrote *Sturm und Drang* ('storm and stress') verse and plays, including the dramatic trilogy *Wallenstein* 1798–99. Much of his work concerns the aspirations for political freedom and the avoidance of mediocrity.

Schinkel Karl Friedrich 1781–1841. Prussian Neo-Classical architect. Major works include the Old Museum, Berlin, 1823–30, the Nikolaikirche in Potsdam 1830–37, and the Roman Bath 1833 in the park of Potsdam.

schism formal split over a doctrinal difference between religious believers, as in the *Great Schism in the Roman Catholic Church; over the doctrine of papal infallibility, as with the Old Catholics in 1879; and over the use of the Latin Tridentine mass 1988.

schist *metamorphic rock containing *mica or another platy or elongate mineral, whose crystals are aligned to give a foliation (planar texture) known as schistosity. Schist may contain additional minerals such as *garnet.

schizocarp dry *fruit that develops from two or more carpels and splits, when mature, to form separate one-seeded units known as mericarps.

schizophrenia mental disorder, a psychosis of unknown origin, which can lead to profound changes in personality and behaviour including paranoia and hallucinations. Contrary to popular belief, it does not involve a split personality. Modern treatment approaches include drugs, family therapy, stress reduction, and rehabilitation.

Schlesinger John 1926– . English film and television director who was responsible for such British films as *Billy Liar* 1963 and *Darling* 1965. His first US film, *Midnight Cowboy* 1969, was a big commercial success and was followed by *Sunday, Bloody Sunday* 1971, *Marathon Man* 1976, and *Yanks* 1979.

Schleswig-Holstein *Land* (state) of Germany
area 15,700 sq km/6,060 sq mi
capital Kiel
towns Lübeck, Flensburg, Schleswig
products shipbuilding, mechanical and electrical engineering, food processing
population (1988) 2,613,000
religions 87% Protestant; 6% Roman Catholic
history Schleswig (Danish *Slesvig*) and Holstein were two duchies held by the kings of Denmark from 1460, but were not part of the kingdom; a number of the inhabitants were German, and Holstein was a member of the Confederation of the Rhine formed 1815. Possession of the duchies had long been disputed by Prussia, and when

Frederick VII of Denmark died without an heir 1863, Prussia, supported by Austria, fought and defeated the Danes 1864, and in 1866 annexed the two duchies. A plebiscite held 1920 gave the northern part of Schleswig to Denmark, which made it the province of Haderslev and Aabenraa; the rest, with Holstein, remained part of Germany.

Schlieffen Plan military plan produced Dec 1905 by German chief of general staff, General Count Alfred von Schlieffen (1833–1913), that formed the basis of German military planning before World War I, and inspired Hitler's plans for the conquest of Europe in World War II. It involved a simultaneous attack on Russia and France, the object being to defeat France quickly and then deploy all available resources against the Russians.

Schliemann Heinrich 1822–1890. German archaeologist. He earned a fortune in business, retiring in 1863 to pursue his lifelong ambition to discover a historical basis for Homer's *Iliad*. In 1871 he began excavating at Hissarlik, Turkey, a site which yielded the ruins of nine consecutive cities and was indeed the site of Troy. His later excavations were at Mycenae 1874–76, where he discovered the ruins of the *Mycenaean civilization.

Schlüter Poul Holmskov 1929– . Danish right-wing politician, leader of the Conservative People's Party (KF) from 1974 and prime minister from 1982. Having joined the KF in his youth, he trained as a lawyer and then entered the Danish parliament (Folketing) in 1964. His centre-right coalition survived the 1990 election and was reconstituted, with Liberal support.

Schmidt Helmut 1918– . German socialist politician, member of the Social Democratic Party (SPD), chancellor of West Germany 1974–83. As chancellor, Schmidt introduced social reforms and continued Brandt's policy of *Ostpolitik. With the French president Giscard d'Estaing, he instigated annual world and European economic summits. He was a firm supporter of *NATO and of the deployment of US nuclear missiles in West Germany during the early 1980s.

Schoenberg Arnold (Franz Walter) 1874–1951. Austro-Hungarian composer, a US citizen from 1941. After Romantic early works such as *Verklärte Nacht/Transfigured Night* 1899 and the *Gurrelieder/Songs of Gurra* 1900–11, he experimented with *atonality (absence of key), producing works such as *Pierrot Lunaire* 1912 for chamber ensemble and voice, before developing the 12-tone system of musical composition. This was further developed by his pupils Alban *Berg and Anton *Webern.

scholasticism the theological and philosophical systems that were studied in both Christian and Judaic schools in Europe in the medieval period. Scholasticism sought to integrate biblical teaching with Platonic and Aristotelian philosophy.

Schopenhauer Arthur 1788–1860. German philosopher whose *The World as Will and Idea* 1818 expounded an atheistic and pessimistic world view: an irrational will is considered as the inner principle of the world, producing an ever-frustrated cycle of desire, of which the only

escape is aesthetic contemplation or absorption into nothingness.

Schrödinger Erwin 1887–1961. Austrian physicist who advanced the study of wave mechanics (see *quantum theory). Born in Vienna, he became senior professor at the Dublin Institute for Advanced Studies 1940. He shared (with Paul Dirac) a Nobel prize 1933.

Schubert Franz (Peter) 1797–1828. Austrian composer. His ten symphonies include the incomplete eighth in B minor (the 'Unfinished') and the 'Great' in C major. He wrote chamber and piano music, including the 'Trout Quintet', and over 600 lieder (songs) combining the Romantic expression of emotion with pure melody. They include the cycles *Die schöne Müllerin/The Beautiful Maid of the Mill* 1823 and *Die Winterreise/The Winter Journey* 1827.

Schulz Charles M(onroe) 1922– . US cartoonist who created the 'Peanuts' strip, syndicated from 1950. His characters Snoopy, Charlie Brown, Lucy, and Linus have been merchandised worldwide and featured in a 1967 musical, *You're a Good Man, Charlie Brown*.

Schumacher Fritz (Ernst Friedrich) 1911–1977. German economist who believed that the increasing size of institutions, coupled with unchecked economic growth, created a range of social and environmental problems. He argued his case in books like *Small is Beautiful* 1973, and tested it practically through establishing the Intermediate Technology Development Group.

Schuman Robert 1886–1963. French politician. He was prime minister 1947–48, and as foreign minister 1948–53 he proposed in May 1950 a common market for coal and steel (the **Schuman Plan**), which was established as the European Coal and Steel Community 1952, the basis of the European Community.

Schumann Robert Alexander 1810–1856. German Romantic composer. His songs and short piano pieces show simplicity combined with an ability to portray mood and emotion. Among his compositions are four symphonies, a violin concerto, a piano concerto, sonatas, and song cycles, such as *Dichterliebe/Poet's Love* 1840. Mendelssohn championed many of his works.

Schwarzenegger Arnold 1947– . Austrian-born US film actor, one of the biggest box-office attractions of the late 1980s and early 1990s. He starred in sword-and-sorcery films such as *Conan the Barbarian* 1982 and later graduated to large-scale budget action movies such as *Terminator* 1984, *Predator* 1987, and *Terminator II* 1991.

Schwarzkopf (H) Norman (nicknamed 'Stormin' Norman') 1934– . US general who was supreme commander of the Allied forces in the *Gulf War 1991. He planned and executed a blitzkrieg campaign, Desert Storm, sustaining remarkably few casualties in the liberation of Kuwait. He was a battalion commander in the Vietnam War and deputy commander of the 1983 US invasion of Grenada.

Schwinger Julian 1918– . US quantum physicist. His research concerned the behaviour of charged particles in electrical fields. This work, expressed entirely through mathematics, combines elements from quantum theory and relativity theory. Schwinger shared the Nobel Prize for Physics 1963 with Richard *Feynman and Sin-Itiro Tomonaga (1906–1979).

Schwitters Kurt 1887–1948. German artist, a member of the *Dada movement. He moved to Norway in 1937 and to England in 1940. From 1918 he developed a variation on collage, using discarded rubbish such as buttons and bus tickets to create pictures and structures.

sciatica persistent pain in the back and down the outside of one leg, along the sciatic nerve and its branches. Causes of sciatica include inflammation of the nerve or pressure of a displaced disc on a nerve root leading out of the lower spine.

science (Latin *scientia* 'knowledge') any systematic field of study or body of knowledge that aims, through experiment, observation, and deduction, to produce reliable explanation of phenomena, with reference to the material and physical world.

science fiction or **speculative fiction** (also known as **sci-fi** or **SF**) genre of fiction and film with an imaginary scientific, technological, or futuristic basis. It is sometimes held to have its roots in the works of Mary Shelley, notably *Frankenstein* 1818. Often taking its ideas and concerns from current ideas in science and the social sciences, science fiction aims to shake up standard perceptions of reality.

Scientology (Latin *scire* 'to know' and Greek *logos* 'branch of learning') 'applied religious philosophy' based on *dianetics, founded in California in 1954 by L Ron *Hubbard as the **Church of Scientology**. It claims to 'increase man's spiritual awareness', but its methods of recruiting and retaining converts have been criticized. Its headquarters from 1959 have been in Sussex, England.

Scilly, Isles of or **Scilly Isles/Islands**, or **Scillies** group of 140 islands and islets lying 40 km/25 mi SW of Land's End, England; administered by the Duchy of Cornwall; area 16 sq km/6.3 sq mi; population (1981) 1,850. The five inhabited islands are **St Mary's**, the largest, on which is Hugh Town, capital of the Scillies; **Tresco**, the second largest, with subtropical gardens; **St Martin's**, noted for beautiful shells; **St Agnes**; and **Bryher**.

scintillation counter instrument for measuring very low levels of radiation. The radiation strikes a scintillator (a device that emits a unit of light when a charged elementary particle collides with it), whose light output is 'amplified' by a *photomultiplier; the current pulses of its output are in turn counted or added by a scaler to give a numerical reading.

Scipio Africanus Major 237–*c*. 183 BC. Roman general. He defeated the Carthaginians in Spain 210–206 BC, invaded Africa 204 BC, and defeated Hannibal at Zama 202 BC.

Scipio Africanus Minor *c*. 185–129 BC (also **Scipio Aemilianus**). Roman general, the adopted grandson of Scipio Africanus Major. He destroyed Carthage 146, and subdued Spain 133. He was opposed to his brothers-in-law, the Gracchi (see *Gracchus).

sclerenchyma plant tissue whose function is to strengthen and support, composed of thick-walled cells that are heavily lignified (toughened). On maturity the inner cell dies, and only its walls remain.

sclerosis any abnormal hardening of body tissues, especially the nervous system or walls of the arteries. See *multiple sclerosis and *atherosclerosis.

Scofield Paul 1922– . English actor. His wide-ranging roles include the drunken priest in Graham Greene's *The Power and the Glory* 1956, Lear in *King Lear* 1962, and Salieri in Peter Shaffer's *Amadeus*. He appeared as Sir Thomas More in both stage and film versions of Robert Bolt's *A Man for All Seasons* (stage 1960–61, film 1966).

scorched earth in warfare, the policy of burning and destroying everything that might be of use to an invading army, especially the crops in the fields. It was used to great effect in Russia in 1812 against the invasion of Napoleon and again during World War II to slow the advance of German forces in 1941.

scorpion any arachnid of the order Scorpiones. Common in the tropics and subtropics, scorpions have large pincers and long tails ending in upcurved poisonous stings, though the venom is not usually fatal to a healthy adult human. Some species reach 25 cm/10 in. They produce live young, and hunt chiefly by night.

Scorpius zodiacal constellation in the southern hemisphere between Libra and Sagittarius, represented as a scorpion. The Sun passes briefly through Scorpius in the last week of Nov. The heart of the scorpion is marked by the red supergiant star Antares. Scorpius contains rich Milky Way star fields, plus the strongest *X-ray source in the sky, Scorpius X-1. In astrology, the dates for Scorpius are between about 24 Oct and 21 Nov (see *precession).

Scorsese Martin 1942– . US director, screenwriter, and producer. His films concentrate on complex characterization and the themes of alienation and guilt. Drawing from his Italian-American Catholic background, his work often deals with sin and redemption, as in his first major film *Boxcar Bertha* 1972. His passionate and forceful movies include *Mean Streets* 1973, *Taxi Driver* 1976, *Raging Bull* 1980, *The Last Temptation of Christ* 1988, *GoodFellas* 1990, *Cape Fear* 1991, and *The Age of Innocence* 1993.

Scotland the northernmost part of Britain, formerly an independent country, now part of the UK

area 78,470 sq km/30,297 sq mi

capital Edinburgh

towns Glasgow, Dundee, Aberdeen

industry electronics, marine and aircraft engines, oil, natural gas, chemicals, textiles, clothing, printing, paper, food processing, tourism

currency pound sterling

population (1988 est) 5,094,000

languages English; Scots, a lowland dialect (derived from Northumbrian Anglo-Saxon); Gaelic spoken by 1.3%, mainly in the Highlands

religions Presbyterian (Church of Scotland), Roman Catholic

famous people Robert Bruce, Walter Scott, Robert Burns, Robert Louis Stevenson, Adam Smith

government Scotland sends 72 members to the UK Parliament at Westminster. Local government is on similar lines to that of England, but there is a differing legal system (see *Scottish law). There is a movement for an independent or devolved Scottish assembly.

Scotland: history

1st millenium BC Picts reached Scotland from mainland Europe.

563 St Colomba founded the monastery on Iona and began conversion of Picts to Christianity.

c. 843 Unification of Picts, Scots, Britons, and Angles under Kenneth I MacAlpine.

1018 At Battle of Carham Malcolm II defeated Northumbrian army, bringing Lothian under Scottish rule.

1034 Duncan became king of United Scotland.

1263 Battle of Largs: defeat of Scots by Norwegian king Haakon.

1296 Edward I of England invaded and declared himself King of Scotland.

1297 William Wallace and Andrew Moray defeated English at Battle of Stirling Bridge.

1314 Robert Bruce defeated English under Edward II at Battle of Bannockburn.

1328 Scottish independence under Robert Bruce recognised by England.

1371 Robert II, first Stuart king, crowned.

1513 Scots defeated by English (and King James IV killed) at Battle of Flodden.

1559 John Knox returned permanently to Scotland, to participate in shift of Scottish Church to Protestantism.

1567 Mary Queen of Scots forced to abdicate and following year fled to England.

1603 Crowns of England and Scotland united under James VI who became James I of England.

1638 National Covenant condemned Charles I's changes in Church ritual; Scottish rebellion.

1643 Solemn League and Covenant: Scottish Covenanters ally with English Parliament against Charles I.

1651 Cromwell invaded Scotland and defeated Scots at Dunbar and Inverkeithing.

1689 At Killiecranke Jacobite forces under Graham of Claverhouse, Viscount Dundee, defeated William of Orange's army, but Dundee mortally wounded.

1692 Massacre of Glencoe: William of Orange ordered MacDonalds of Glencoe murdered in their sleep.

1707 Act of Union unites Scottish and English parliaments.

1715 The 'Fifteen': Jacobite rebellion in support of James Edward Stuart, 'James VII'.

1745 The 'Fortyfive': Charles Edward Stuart landed in Scotland and marched as far south as Derby before turning back.

1888 James Kier Hardie founded Scottish Labour Party.

1926 Secretary for Scotland became British Cabinet post.

1928 National Party of Scotland formed (became Scottish National Party 1934).

1979 Referendum rejected proposal for directly elected Scottish assembly.

Scotland Yard, New headquarters of the *Criminal Investigation Department (CID) of Britain's London Metropolitan Police, established in 1878.

Scots language the form of the English language as traditionally spoken and written in Scotland, regarded by some scholars as a distinct language. Scots derives from the Northumbrian dialect of Anglo-Saxon or Old English, and has been a literary language since the 14th century.

Scots law the legal system of Scotland. Owing to its separate development, Scotland has a system differing from the rest of the UK, being based on *civil law. Its continued separate existence was guaranteed by the Act of Union with England in 1707.

Scott (George) Gilbert 1811–1878. English architect. As the leading practical architect in the mid-19th-century Gothic revival in England, Scott was responsible for the building or restoration of many public buildings, including the Albert Memorial, the Foreign Office, and St Pancras Station, all in London.

Scott Giles Gilbert 1880–1960. English architect, grandson of George Gilbert Scott. He designed Liverpool Anglican Cathedral, Cambridge University Library, and Waterloo Bridge, London, 1945. He supervised the rebuilding of the House of Commons after World War II.

Scott Robert Falcon (known as **Scott of the Antarctic**) 1868–1912. English explorer who commanded two Antarctic expeditions, 1901–04 and 1910–12. On 18 Jan 1912 he reached the South Pole, shortly after Norwegian Roald *Amundsen, but on the return journey he and his companions died in a blizzard only a few miles from their base camp. His journal was recovered and published in 1913.

Scott Walter 1771–1832. Scottish novelist and poet. His first works were translations of German ballads, followed by poems such as 'The Lady of the Lake' 1810 and 'Lord of the Isles' 1815. He gained a European reputation for his historical novels such as *Heart of Midlothian* 1818, *Ivanhoe* 1819, and *The Fair Maid of Perth* 1828. His last years were marked by frantic writing to pay off his debts, after the bankruptcy of his publishing company in 1826.

Scottish Gaelic language see *Gaelic language.

Scout member of a worldwide youth organization that emphasizes character, citizenship, and outdoor life. It was founded (as the Boy Scouts) in England 1908 by Robert *Baden-Powell. His book *Scouting for Boys* 1908 led to the incorporation in the UK of the Boy Scout Association by royal charter in 1912.

scrapie fatal disease of sheep and goats that attacks the central nervous system, causing deterioration of the brain cells. It is believed to be caused by a submicroscopic organism known as a prion and may be related to *bovine spongiform encephalopathy, the disease of cattle known as 'mad cow disease'.

screamer any South American marsh-dwelling bird of the family Anhimidae; there are only three species, all in the genus *Anhima*. They are about 80 cm/30 in long, with short curved beaks, long toes, dark plumage, spurs on the fronts of the wings, and a crest or horn on the head.

scree pile of rubble and sediment that forms an ascending slope at the foot of a mountain or cliff.

screening or *health screening* the systematic search for evidence of a disease, or of conditions that may precede it, in people who are not suffering from any symptoms. The aim of screening is to try to limit ill health from diseases that are difficult to prevent and might otherwise go undetected. Examples are hypothyroidism and phenylketonuria, for which all newborn babies in Western countries are screened; breast cancer (*mammography) and cervical cancer; and stroke, for which high blood pressure is a known risk factor.

screw in construction, cylindrical or tapering piece of metal or plastic (or formerly wood) with a helical groove cut into it. Each turn of a screw moves it forward or backwards by a distance equal to the pitch (the spacing between neighbouring threads).

Scriabin alternative transcription of *Skryabin, Russian composer.

scrip issue or *subscription certificate* UK term for *bonus issue.

scrolling in computing, the action by which data displayed on a VDU screen are automatically moved upwards and out of sight as new lines of data are added at the bottom.

scuba acronym for *self-contained underwater breathing apparatus*, another name for *aqualung.

Scud Soviet-produced surface-to-surface *missile that can be armed with a nuclear, chemical, or conventional warhead. The *Scud-B*, deployed on a mobile launcher, was the version most commonly used by the Iraqi army in the Gulf War 1991. It is a relatively inaccurate weapon.

Scudamore Peter 1958– . British National Hunt jockey who was champion jockey 1982 (shared with John Francome) and from 1986 to 1991 inclusive. In 1988–89 he rode a record 221 winners, and after the 1990–91 season his total of winners stood at a world record 1,374.

sculpture the artistic shaping in relief or in the round of materials such as wood, stone, metal, and, more recently, plastic and other synthetics. The earliest sculptures are Palaeolithic stone, bone, and ivory carvings. All ancient civilizations, including the Assyrian, Egyptian, Indian, Chinese, and Mayan, have left examples of sculpture. Traditional European sculpture descends from that of Greece, Rome, and Renaissance Italy. The indigenous tradition of sculpture in Africa, South America, and the Caribbean has inspired much contemporary sculpture.

scurvy disease caused by deficiency of vitamin C (ascorbic acid), which is contained in fresh vegetables and fruit. The signs are weakness and aching joints and muscles, progressing to bleeding of the gums and then other organs, and drying-up of the skin and hair. Treatment is by giving the vitamin.

Scylla and Charybdis in classical mythology, a sea monster and a whirlpool, between which Odysseus had to sail. Later writers located them in the Straits of Messina, between Sicily and Italy.

scythe harvesting tool with long wooden handle and sharp, curving blade. It is similar to a *sickle. The scythe was in common use in the Middle East and Europe from the dawn of agriculture until the early 20th century, by which time it had generally been replaced by machinery.

Scythia region north of the Black Sea between the Carpathian mountains and the river Don, inhabited by the Scythians 7th–1st centuries BC. From the middle of the 4th century, they were slowly superseded by the Sarmatians. The Scythians produced ornaments and vases in gold and electrum with animal decoration. Although there is no surviving written work, there are spectacular archaeological remains, including vast royal burial mounds which often contain horse skeletons.

SDI abbreviation for *Strategic Defense Initiative*.

SDLP abbreviation for *Social Democratic Labour Party* (Northern Ireland).

SDP abbreviation for *Social Democratic Party*.

SDR abbreviation for *special drawing right*.

sea anemone invertebrate marine animal of the class Cnidaria with a tubelike body attached by the base to a rock or shell. The other end has an open 'mouth' surrounded by stinging tentacles, which capture crustaceans and other small organisms. Many sea anemones are beautifully coloured, especially those in tropical waters.

seaborgium synthesized radioactive element of the *transactinide series, symbol Sg, atomic number 106, relative atomic mass 263. It was first synthesized 1974 in the USA and given the temporary name unnilhexium. The discovery was not confirmed until 1993. It was officially named 1994 after US nuclear chemist Glenn Seaborg.

sea cucumber any echinoderm of the class Holothuroidea with a cylindrical body that is tough-skinned, knobbed, or spiny. The body may be several feet in length. Sea cucumbers are sometimes called 'cotton-spinners' from the sticky filaments they eject from the anus in self-defence.

seafloor spreading growth of the ocean *crust outwards (sideways) from ocean ridges. The concept of seafloor spreading has been combined with that of continental drift and incorporated into *plate tectonics.

sea horse any marine fish of several related genera, especially *Hippocampus*, of the family Syngnathidae, which includes the *pipefishes. The body is small and compressed and covered with bony plates raised into tubercles or spines. The tail is prehensile, and the tubular mouth sucks in small shellfish and larvae as food. The head and foreparts, usually carried upright, resemble those of a horse.

seakale perennial plant *Crambe maritima* of the family Cruciferae. In Europe the young shoots are cultivated as a vegetable.

seal aquatic carnivorous mammal of the families Otariidae and Phocidae (sometimes placed in a separate order, the Pinnipedia). The eared seals or sea lions (Otariidae) have small external ears, unlike the true seals (Phocidae). Seals have a streamlined body with thick blubber for insulation, and front and hind flippers. They feed on fish, squid, or crustaceans, and are commonly found in Arctic and Antarctic seas, but also in

sea horse *The dwarf sea horse swims in an upright position, propelled by gentle movements of its dorsal fin.*

Mediterranean, Caribbean, and Hawaiian waters.

seal mark or impression made in a block of wax to authenticate letters and documents. Seals were used in ancient China and are still used in China, Korea, and Japan.

sea lion any of several genera of *seals of the family Otariidae (eared seals), which also includes the fur seals. These streamlined animals have large fore flippers which they use to row themselves through the water. The hind flippers can be turned beneath the body to walk on land.

Sea Peoples unidentified seafaring warriors who may have been Achaeans, Etruscans, or *Philistines, who ravaged and settled the Mediterranean coasts in the 12th–13th centuries BC. They were defeated by Ramses III of Egypt 1191.

seaplane aeroplane capable of taking off from, and landing on, water. There are two major types, floatplanes and flying boats. The floatplane is similar to an ordinary aeroplane but has floats in place of wheels; the flying boat has a broad hull shaped like a boat and may also have floats attached to the wing tips.

searching in computing, extracting a specific item from a large body of data, such as a file or table. The method used depends on how the data are organized. For example, a binary search, which requires the data to be in sequence, involves first deciding which half of the data contains the required item, then which quarter, then which eighth, and so on until the item is found.

Searle Ronald 1920– . British cartoonist and illustrator, who created the schoolgirls of St Trinian's in 1941 and has made numerous cartoons of cats. His drawings, made as a Japanese prisoner of war during World War II, established him as a serious artist. His sketches of places and people include *Paris Sketch Book* 1950 and *Rake's Progress* 1955.

sea slug any of an order (Nudibranchia) of marine gastropod molluscs in which the shell is reduced or absent. The order includes some very colourful forms, especially in the tropics. They are largely carnivorous, feeding on hydroids and *sponges.

season period of the year having a characteristic climate. The change in seasons is mainly due to the change in attitude of the Earth's axis in relation to the Sun, and hence the position of the Sun in the sky at a particular place. In temperate latitudes four seasons are recognized: spring, summer, autumn (fall), and winter. Tropical regions have two seasons – the wet and the dry. Monsoon areas around the Indian Ocean have three seasons: the cold, the hot, and the rainy.

seasonal adjustment in statistics, an adjustment of figures designed to take into account influences that are purely seasonal, and relevant only for a short time. The resulting figures are then thought to reflect long-term trends more accurately.

seasonal affective disorder (SAD) recurrent depression characterized by an increased incidence at a particular time of year. One type of seasonal affective disorder increases in incidence in autumn and winter, and is associated with increased sleeping and appetite.

sea squirt or **tunicate** any solitary or colonial-dwelling saclike *chordate of the class Ascidiacea. A pouch-shaped animal attached to a rock or other base, it draws in food-carrying water through one siphon and expels it through another after straining it through numerous gill slits. The young are free-swimming tadpole-shaped organisms, which, unlike the adults, have a notochord.

SEATO abbreviation for *Southeast Asia Treaty Organization*.

Seattle port (grain, timber, fruit, fish) of the state of Washington, USA, situated between Puget Sound and Lake Washington; population (1990) 516,300, metropolitan area (with Everett) 2,559,200. It is a centre for the manufacture of jet aircraft (Boeing), and also has shipbuilding, food processing, and paper industries.

sea urchin any of various orders of the class Echinoidea among the *echinoderms. They all have a globular body enclosed with plates of lime and covered with spines. Sometimes the spines are anchoring organs, and they also assist in locomotion. Sea urchins feed on seaweed and the animals frequenting them, and some are edible.

seaweed any of a vast collection of marine and freshwater, simple, multicellular plant forms belonging to the *algae and found growing from about high-water mark to depths of 100–200 m/300–600 ft. Some have holdfasts, stalks, and fronds, sometimes with air bladders to keep them afloat, and are green, blue-green, red, or brown.

Sebastiano del Piombo c. 1485–1547. Italian painter, born in Venice, one of the great painters of the High Renaissance. Sebastiano was a pupil of *Giorgione and developed a similar style of painting. In 1511 he moved to Rome, where his friendship with Michelangelo (and rivalry with Raphael) inspired him to his greatest works, such as *The Raising of Lazarus* 1517–19 (National Gallery, London). He also painted powerful portraits.

Sebastian, St Roman soldier, traditionally a member of Emperor Diocletian's bodyguard until his Christian faith was discovered. He was martyred by being shot with arrows. Feast day 20 Jan.

seborrhoeic dermatitis common skin disease affecting any sebum (natural oil) producing area of the skin. It is thought to be caused by the yeast *Pityrosporum*, and is characterized by yellowish-red, scaly areas on the skin, and dandruff. Antidandruff shampoos are often helpful.

SEC abbreviation for *Securities and Exchange Commission*, US government body.

secant in trigonometry, the function of a given angle in a right-angled triangle, obtained by dividing the length of the hypotenuse (the longest side) by the length of the side adjacent to the angle. It is the *reciprocal of the *cosine (sec = 1/cos).

secession (Latin *secessio*) in politics, the withdrawal from a federation of states by one or more of its members, as in the secession of the Confederate states from the Union in the USA 1860.

second basic SI unit (symbol sec or s) of time, one-sixtieth of a minute. It is defined as the duration of 9,192,631,770 periods of the radiation corresponding to the transition between two hyperfine levels of the ground state of the caesium-133 isotope. In mathematics, the second is a unit (symbol ") of angular measurement, equalling one-sixtieth of a minute, which in turn is one-sixtieth of a degree.

secondary emission in physics, an emission of electrons from the surface of certain substances when they are struck by high-speed electrons or other particles from an external source. See also *photomultiplier.

secondary growth or *secondary thickening* increase in diameter of the roots and stems of certain plants (notably shrubs and trees) that results from the production of new cells by the *cambium. It provides the plant with additional mechanical support and new conducting cells, the secondary *xylem and *phloem. Secondary growth is generally confined to *gymnosperms and, among the *angiosperms, to the dicotyledons. With just a few exceptions, the monocotyledons (grasses, lilies) exhibit only primary growth, resulting from cell division at the apical meristems.

secondary sexual characteristic in biology, an external feature of an organism that is characteristic of its gender (male or female), but not the reproductive organs themselves. They include facial hair in men and breasts in women, combs in cockerels, brightly coloured plumage in many male birds, and manes in male lions. In many cases, they are involved in displays and contests for mates and have evolved by *sexual selection. Their development is stimulated by sex hormones.

Second World War alternative name for *World War II, 1939–45.

secretary bird ground-hunting, long-legged, mainly grey-plumaged bird of prey *Sagittarius serpentarius*, about 1.2 m/4 ft tall, with an erectile head crest. It is protected in southern Africa because it eats poisonous snakes.

secretary of state in the UK, a title held by a number of ministers; for example, the secretary of state for foreign and commonwealth affairs.

secretin *hormone produced by the small intestine of vertebrates that stimulates the production of digestive secretions by the pancreas and liver.

secretion in biology, any substance (normally a fluid) produced by a cell or specialized gland, for example, sweat, saliva, enzymes, and hormones. The process whereby the substance is discharged from the cell is also known as secretion.

secret police any state security force that operates internally, against political dissenters or subversives; for example, the US *Federal Bureau of Investigation and the UK *Special Branch.

secret service any government *intelligence organization. In the USA the Secret Service is a law-enforcement unit of the Treasury Department and provides the president's bodyguard.

secret society society with membership by invitation only, often involving initiation rites, secret rituals, and dire punishments for those who break the code. Often founded for religious reasons or mutual benefit, some have become the province of corrupt politicians or gangsters, like the *Mafia, *Ku Klux Klan, and the *Triad. See also *Freemasonry.

sect small ideological group, usually religious in nature, that may have moved away from a main group, often claiming a monopoly of access to truth or salvation. Sects are usually highly exclusive. They demand strict conformity, total commitment to their code of behaviour, and complete personal involvement, sometimes to the point of rejecting mainstream society altogether in terms of attachments, names, possessions, and family.

secularization the process through which religious thinking, practice, and institutions lose their religious and/or social significance. The concept is based on the theory, held by some sociologists, that as societies become industrialized their religious morals, values, and institutions give way to secular ones and some religious traits become common secular practices.

Securities and Exchange Commission (SEC) official US agency created 1934 to ensure full disclosure to the investing public and protection against malpractice in the securities (stocks and shares) and financial markets (such as insider trading).

Securities and Investment Board UK body with the overall responsibility for policing financial dealings in the City of London. Introduced in 1987 following the deregulation process of the so-called *Big Bang, it acts as an umbrella organization to such self-regulating bodies as the Stock Exchange.

sedan chair enclosed chair for one passenger carried on poles by two or more bearers. Introduced into England by Sir Sanders Dunscombe in 1634, by the 18th century it was the equivalent of a one-person taxi. The name derives from S Italy rather than from the French town of Sedan.

sedative any medication with the effect of lessening nervousness, excitement, or irritation. Sedatives will induce sleep in larger doses. Examples are *barbiturates, *narcotics, and benzodiazepines.

sedge any perennial grasslike plant of the family Cyperaceae, especially the genus *Carex*, usually with three-cornered solid stems, common in low water or on wet and marshy ground.

Sedgemoor, Battle of in English history, a battle 6 July 1685 in which *Monmouth's rebellion was crushed by the forces of James II, on a tract of marshy land 5 km/3 mi SE of Bridgwater, Somerset.

sediment any loose material that has 'settled' – deposited from suspension in water, ice, or air, generally as the water current or wind speed decreases. Typical sediments are, in order of increasing coarseness, clay, mud, silt, sand, gravel, pebbles, cobbles, and boulders.

sedimentary rock rock formed by the accumulation and cementation of deposits that have been laid down by water, wind, ice, or gravity. Sedimentary rocks cover more than two-thirds of the Earth's surface and comprise three major categories: *clastic*, *chemically precipitated*, and *organic*. Clastic sediments are the largest group and are composed of fragments of pre-existing rocks; they include clays, sands, and gravels. Chemical precipitates include limestones such as chalk, and evaporated deposits such as gypsum and halite (rock salt). Coal, oil shale, and limestone made of fossil material are examples of organic sedimentary rocks.

sedition in the UK, the offence of inciting unlawful opposition to the crown and government. Unlike treason, sedition does not carry the death penalty.

Seebeck effect in physics, the generation of a voltage in a circuit containing two different metals, or semiconductors, by keeping the junctions between them at different temperatures. Discovered by the German physicist Thomas Seebeck (1770–1831), it is also called the thermoelectric effect, and is the basis of the *thermocouple. It is the opposite of the *Peltier effect (in which current flow causes a temperature difference between the junctions of different metals).

seed the reproductive structure of higher plants (*angiosperms and *gymnosperms). It develops from a fertilized ovule and consists of an embryo and a food store, surrounded and protected by an outer seed coat, called the testa. The food store is contained either in a specialized nutritive tissue, the *endosperm, or in the *cotyledons of the embryo itself. In angiosperms the seed is enclosed within a *fruit, whereas in gymnosperms it is usually naked and unprotected, once shed from the female cone. Following *germination the seed develops into a new plant.

seed drill machine for sowing cereals and other seeds, developed by Jethro Tull in England 1701, although simple seeding devices were known in Babylon 2000 BC.

seed plant any seed-bearing plant; also known as a *spermatophyte*. The seed plants are subdivided into two classes, the *angiosperms, or flowering plants, and the *gymnosperms, principally the cycads and conifers. Together, they comprise the major types of vegetation found on land.

Seine French river rising on the Langres plateau NW of Dijon, and flowing 774 km/472 mi in a NW direction to join the English Channel near Le Havre, passing through Paris and Rouen.

seismology study of earthquakes and how their shock waves travel through the Earth. By examining the global pattern of waves produced by an earthquake, seismologists can deduce the nature of the materials through which they have

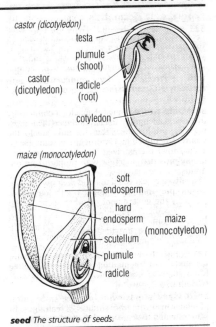

castor (dicotyledon)

- testa
- plumule (shoot)
- radicle (root)
- cotyledon

castor (dicotyledon)

maize (monocotyledon)

- soft endosperm
- hard endosperm
- scutellum
- plumule
- radicle

maize (monocotyledon)

seed The structure of seeds.

passed. This leads to an understanding of the Earth's internal structure.

select committee any of several long-standing committees of the UK House of Commons, such as the Environment Committee and the Treasury and Civil Service Committee. These were intended to restore parliamentary control of the executive, improve the quality of legislation, and scrutinize public spending and the work of government departments. Select committees represent the major parliamentary reform of the 20th century, and a possible means – through their all-party membership – of avoiding the automatic repeal of one government's measures by its successor.

Selene in Greek mythology, the goddess of the Moon. She was the daughter of Titan, and the sister of Helios and Eos. In later times she was identified with *Artemis.

selenium (Greek *Selene* 'Moon') grey, nonmetallic element, symbol Se, atomic number 34, relative atomic mass 78.96. It belongs to the sulphur group and occurs in several allotropic forms that differ in their physical and chemical properties. It is an essential trace element in human nutrition. Obtained from many sulphide ores and selenides, it is used as a red colouring for glass and enamel.

Seles Monica 1973– . Yugoslavian-born lawn-tennis player who won her first Grand Slam title, the French Open, at the age of 16. In 1991 she became the youngest woman player ever to achieve number-one ranking. In 1993 she was stabbed by a fan of her rival, Steffi Graf, during the Hamburg Open. She took an enforced break from the game and announced her return June 1995.

Seleucus I Nicator c. 358–280 BC. Macedonian general under Alexander the Great and founder of the *Seleucid Empire*. After Alexander's death 323 BC, Seleucus became governor and then (312 BC) ruler of Babylonia, founding the city of Seleucia on the river Tigris. He conquered Syria and had himself crowned king 306 BC, but his expansionist policies brought him into conflict with the Ptolemies of Egypt, and he was assassinated by Ptolemy Ceraunus. He was succeeded by his son Antiochus I.

self-help project any scheme for a community to help itself under official guidance. The most popular self-help projects in the developing world are aimed at improving conditions in shanty towns. Organized building lots are commonly provided, together with properly laid-out drains, water supplies, roads, and lighting. *Squatters are expected to build their own homes on the prepared sites, perhaps with loans provided by the government or other agencies. An example is the Arumbakkam scheme in Madras, India, begun 1977. Alternatively, 'basic shell' housing may be provided, as in parts of São Paulo, Brazil, and Salop in W Colombia.

self-induction or **self-inductance** in physics, the creation of a counter emf (*electromotive force) in a coil because of variations in the current flowing through it.

Selfridge Harry Gordon 1857–1947. US entrepreneur who in 1909 founded Selfridges in London, the first large department store in Britain.

Seljuk Empire empire of the Turkish people (converted to Islam during the 7th century) under the leadership of the invading Tatars or Seljuk Turks. The Seljuk Empire 1055–1243 included all Anatolia and most of Syria. It was succeeded by the *Ottoman Empire.

Sellafield site of a nuclear power station on the coast of Cumbria, NW England. It was known as **Windscale** until 1971, when the management of the site was transferred from the UK Atomic Energy Authority to British Nuclear Fuels Ltd. The plant is the world's greatest discharger of radioactive waste: between 1968 and 1979 180 kg of plutonium was discharged into the Irish Sea.

Sellers Peter 1925–1980. English comedian and film actor. He made his name in the madcap British radio programme *The Goon Show* 1949–60; his films include *The Ladykillers* 1955, *I'm All Right Jack* 1960, *Dr Strangelove* 1964, five *Pink Panther* films 1964–78 (as the bumbling Inspector Clouseau), and *Being There* 1979.

Selznick David O(liver) 1902–1965. US film producer whose early work includes *King Kong*, *Dinner at Eight*, and *Little Women* all 1933. His independent company, Selznick International (1935–40), made such lavish films as *Gone With the Wind* 1939, *Rebecca* 1940, and *Duel in the Sun* 1946.

semantics branch of *linguistics dealing with the meaning of words.

semaphore visual signalling code in which the relative positions of two moveable pointers or hand-held flags stand for different letters or numbers. The system is used by ships at sea and for railway signals.

Semarang port in N Java, Indonesia; population (1980) 1,027,000. There is a shipbuilding industry, and exports include coffee, teak, sugar, tobacco, kapok, and petroleum from nearby oilfields.

Semele in Greek mythology, mother of Dionysus by Zeus. At Hera's suggestion she demanded that Zeus should appear to her in all his glory, but when he did so she was consumed by lightning.

semelparity in biology, the occurrence of a single act of reproduction during an organism's lifetime. Most semelparous species produce very large numbers of offspring when they do reproduce, and normally die soon afterwards. Examples include the Pacific salmon and the pine loop moth. Many plants are semelparous, or *monocarpic. Repeated reproduction is called *iteroparity.

semicircular canal one of three looped tubes that form part of the labyrinth in the inner *ear. They are filled with fluid and detect changes in the position of the head, contributing to the sense of balance.

semicolon punctuation mark (;) with a function halfway between the separation of sentence from sentence by means of a period, or full stop, and the gentler separation provided by a comma. It also helps separate items in a complex list: 'pens, pencils, and paper; staples, such as rice and beans; tools, various; and rope'.

semiconductor crystalline material with an electrical conductivity between that of metals (good) and insulators (poor). The conductivity of semiconductors can usually be improved by minute additions of different substances or by other factors. Silicon, for example, has poor conductivity at low temperatures, but this is improved by the application of light, heat, or voltage; hence silicon is used in transistors, rectifiers, and integrated circuits (silicon chips).

semiology or **semiotics** the study of the function of signs and symbols in human communication, both in language and by various nonlinguistic means. Beginning with the notion of the Swiss linguist Ferdinand de *Saussure that no word or other sign (**signifier**) is intrinsically linked with its meaning (**signified**), it was developed as a scientific discipline, especially by Claude *Lévi-Strauss and Roland *Barthes.

Semiramis lived *c.* 800 BC. Assyrian queen, later identified with the chief Assyrian goddess *Ishtar.

Semite member of any of the peoples of the Middle East originally speaking a Semitic language, and traditionally said to be descended from Shem, a son of Noah in the Bible. Ancient Semitic peoples include the Hebrews, Ammonites, Moabites, Edomites, Babylonians, Assyrians, Chaldaeans, Phoenicians, and Canaanites. The Semitic peoples founded the monotheistic religions of Judaism, Christianity, and Islam.

Semitic languages branch of the *Hamito-Semitic language.

Semtex plastic explosive, manufactured in Czechoslovakia. It is safe to handle (it can only be ignited by a detonator) and difficult to trace, since it has no smell. It has been used by extremist groups in the Middle East and by the IRA in Northern Ireland.

senate in ancient Rome, the 'council of elders'. Originally consisting of the heads of patrician families, it was recruited from ex-magistrates and persons who had rendered notable public service, but was periodically purged by the censors. Although nominally advisory, it controlled finance and foreign policy.

Sendai city in Tōhoku region, NE Honshu, Japan; population (1989) 889,100. Industries include metal goods (a metal museum was established 1975), electronics, metal goods, textiles, pottery, and food processing. It was a feudal castle town from the 16th century.

Sendak Maurice 1928– . US writer and book illustrator, whose children's books with their deliberately arch illustrations include *Where the Wild Things Are* 1963, *In the Night Kitchen* 1970, and *Outside Over There* 1981.

Sendero Luminoso (Shining Path) Maoist guerrilla group active in Peru, formed 1980 to overthrow the government. Until 1988 its activity was confined to rural areas. By June 1988 an estimated 9,000 people had been killed in the insurgency, about half of them guerrillas.

Seneca Lucius Annaeus *c.* 4 BC–AD 65. Roman Stoic playwright, author of essays and nine tragedies. He was tutor to the future emperor Nero but lost favour after the latter's accession to the throne and was ordered to commit suicide. His tragedies were accepted as classical models by 16th-century dramatists.

Senefelder Alois 1771–1834. German engraver, born in Prague. He is thought to have invented *lithography.

Senegal Republic of (*République du Sénégal*)

area 196,200 sq km/75,753 sq mi
capital and chief port Dakar
towns Thiès, Kaolack
physical plains rising to hills in SE; swamp and tropical forest in SW
head of state and government Abdou Diouf from 1981
political system emergent socialist democratic republic
exports peanuts, cotton, fish, phosphates
currency franc CFA
population (1993 est) 7,970,000; growth rate 3.1% p.a.
languages French (official); African dialects are spoken
religions Muslim 80%, Roman Catholic 10%, animist
literacy men 37%, women 19% (1985 est)
GNP $720 per head (1991)

chronology
1659 Became a French colony.
1854–65 Interior occupied by French.
1902 Became a territory of French West Africa.
1959 Formed the Federation of Mali with French Sudan.
1960 Independence achieved from France, but withdrew from the federation. Léopold Sédar Senghor, leader of the Senegalese Progressive Union (UPS), became president.
1966 UPS declared the only legal party.
1974 Pluralist system re-established.
1976 UPS reconstituted as Senegalese Socialist Party (PS). Prime Minister Abdou Diouf nominated as Senghor's successor.
1980 Senghor resigned; succeeded by Diouf. Troops sent to defend Gambia.
1981 Military help again sent to Gambia.
1982 Confederation of Senegambia came into effect.
1983 Diouf re-elected. Post of prime minister abolished.
1988 Diouf decisively re-elected.
1989 Violent clashes between Senegalese and Mauritanians in Dakar and Nouakchott killed more than 450 people; over 50,000 people repatriated from both countries. Senegambia federation abandoned.
1991 Constitutional changes outlined.
1992 Diplomatic links with Mauritania re-established.
1993 Diouf re-elected.

Senghor Léopold (Sédar) 1906– . Senegalese politician and writer. He was the first president of independent Senegal 1960–80. Previously he was Senegalese deputy to the French National Assembly 1946–58, and founder of the Senegalese Progressive Union. He was also a well-known poet and a founder of *négritude*, a black literary and philosophical movement.

senile dementia *dementia associated with old age, often caused by *Alzheimer's disease.

Senna Ayrton 1960–1994. Brazilian motor-racing driver. He had his first Grand Prix win in the 1985 Portuguese Grand Prix, and progressed to the world driver's title in 1988, 1990, and 1991. By the end of the 1993 season he had 41 wins in 158 starts. He died in a crash during the San Marino Grand Prix.

Sennacherib died 681 BC. King of Assyria from 705 BC. Son of *Sargon II, he rebuilt the city of Nineveh on a grand scale, sacked Babylon 689, and defeated *Hezekiah, king of Judah, but failed to take Jerusalem. He was assassinated by his sons, and one of them, Esarhaddon, succeeded him.

Sennett Mack. Stage name of Michael Sinnott 1880–1960. Canadian-born US film producer. He was originally an actor. In 1911 he founded the Keystone production company, responsible for slapstick silent films featuring the Keystone Kops, Fatty Arbuckle, and Charlie Chaplin. He did not make the transition to sound with much enthusiasm and retired 1935. His films include *Tillie's Punctured Romance* 1914, *The Shriek of Araby* 1923, and *The Barber Shop* (sound) 1933.

sense organ any organ that an animal uses to gain information about its surroundings. All sense organs have specialized receptors (such as light receptors in the eye) and some means of translating their response into a nerve impulse that travels to the brain. The main human sense organs are the eye, which detects light and colour (different wavelengths of light); the ear, which detects sound (vibrations of the air) and gravity; the nose, which detects some of the chemical molecules in the air; and the tongue, which detects some of the chemicals in food, giving a sense of taste. There are also many small sense organs in the skin, including pain, temperature, and pressure sensors, contributing to our sense of touch.

sensor in computing, a device designed to detect a physical state or measure a physical quantity, and produce an input signal for a computer. For example, a sensor may detect the fact that a printer has run out of paper or may measure the temperature in a kiln.

sentence in law, the judgement of a court stating the punishment to be imposed following a plea of guilty or a finding of guilt by a jury. Before a sentence is imposed, the antecedents (criminal record) and any relevant reports on the defendant are made known to the judge and the defence may make a plea in mitigation of the sentence.

Seoul or **Sŏul** capital of South *Korea (Republic of Korea), near the Han River, and with its chief port at Inchon; population (1985) 10,627,800. Industries include engineering, textiles, food processing, electrical and electronic equipment, chemicals, and machinery.

sepal part of a flower, usually green, that surrounds and protects the flower in bud. The sepals are derived from modified leaves, and are collectively known as the *calyx.

separation of powers an approach to limiting the powers of government by separating governmental functions into the executive, legislative, and judiciary. The concept has its fullest practical expression in the the the US constitution (see *federalism).

Sephardi (plural **Sephardim**) Jew descended from those expelled from Spain and Portugal in the 15th century, or from those forcibly converted during the Inquisition to Christianity (Marranos). Many settled in N Africa and in the Mediterranean countries, as well as in the Netherlands, England, and Dutch colonies in the New World. Sephardim speak Ladino, a 15th-century Romance dialect, as well as the language of their nation.

sepia brown pigment produced from the black fluid of cuttlefish. After 1870 it replaced the use of bistre (made from charred wood) in wash drawings due to its warmer range of colours. Sepia fades rapidly in bright light.

Sepoy Rebellion alternative name for the *Indian Mutiny, a revolt of Indian soldiers against the British in India 1857–58.

sepsis general term for infectious change in the body caused by bacteria or their toxins.

septicaemia general term for any form of *blood poisoning.

septic shock life-threatening fall in blood pressure caused by blood poisoning (septicaemia). Toxins produced by bacteria infecting the blood induce a widespread dilation of the blood vessels throughout the body, and it is this that causes

the patient's collapse (see *shock). Septic shock can occur following bowel surgery, after a penetrating wound to the abdomen, or as a consequence of infection of the urinary tract. It is usually treated in an intensive care unit and has a high mortality rate.

Septuagint (Latin *septuagint* 'seventy') the oldest Greek version of the Old Testament or Hebrew Bible, traditionally made by 70 scholars.

sequencing in biochemistry, determining the sequence of chemical subunits within a large molecule. Techniques for sequencing amino acids in proteins were established in the 1950s, insulin being the first for which the sequence was completed. Efforts are now being made to determine the sequence of base pairs within *DNA.

sequestrator person or organization appointed by a court of law to control the assets of another person or organization within the jurisdiction of that court.

sequoia two species of conifer in the redwood family Taxodiaceae, native to W USA. The redwood *Sequoia sempervirens* is a long-lived timber tree, and one specimen, the Howard Libbey Redwood, is the world's tallest tree at 110 m/361 ft, with a circumference of 13.4 m/ 44 ft. The giant sequoia *Sequoiadendron giganteum* reaches up to 30 m/100 ft in circumference at the base, and grows almost as tall as the redwood. It is also (except for the bristlecone pine) the oldest living tree, some specimens being estimated at over 3,500 years of age.

Serapis ancient Graeco-Egyptian god, a combination of Apis and Osiris, invented by the Ptolemies; his finest temple was the Serapeum in Alexandria.

Serb member of Yugoslavia's largest ethnic group, found mainly in Serbia, but also in the neighbouring independent republics of Bosnia-Herzegovina and Croatia. Their language, generally recognized to be the same as Croat and hence known as Serbo-Croatian, belongs to the Slavic branch of the Indo-European family. It has more than 17 million speakers.

Serbia (Serbo-Croatian *Srbija*) constituent republic of Yugoslavia, which includes Kosovo and Vojvodina

area 88,400 sq km/34,122 sq mi

capital Belgrade

physical fertile Danube plains in the N, mountainous in the S

population (1986) 9,660,000

language the Serbian variant of Serbo-Croatian

religion Serbian Orthodox

history The Serbs settled in the Balkans in the 7th century and became Christians in the 9th century. They were united as one kingdom about 1169; the Serbian hero Stephan Dushan (1331–1355) founded an empire covering most of the Balkans. After their defeat at Kosovo 1389 they came under the domination of the Turks, who annexed Serbia 1459. Uprisings 1804–16, led by Kara George and Milosh Obrenovich, forced the Turks to recognize Serbia as an autonomous principality under Milosh. The assassination of Kara George on Obrenovich's orders gave rise to a long feud between the two houses. After a war with Turkey 1876–78, Serbia became an independent kingdom. On the assassination of the last Obrenovich 1903 the Karageorgevich dynasty came to the throne. The two Balkan Wars 1912–13 greatly enlarged Serbia's territory at the expense of Turkey and Bulgaria. Serbia's designs on Bosnia-Herzegovina, backed by Russia, led to friction with Austria, culminating in the outbreak of war 1914. Serbia was overrun 1915–16 and was occupied until 1918, when it became the nucleus of the new kingdom of the Serbs, Croats, and Slovenes, and subsequently *Yugoslavia. Rivalry between Croats and Serbs continued within the republic. During World War II Serbia was under a puppet government set up by the Germans; after the war it became a constituent republic of Yugoslavia. From 1986 Slobodan Milošević as Serbian party chief and president waged a populist campaign to end the autonomous status of the provinces of Kosovo and Vojvodina. Despite a violent Albanian backlash in Kosovo 1989–90 and growing pressure in Croatia and Slovenia to break away from the federation, Serbia formally annexed Kosovo Sept 1990. Milošević was re-elected by a landslide majority Dec 1990, but in March 1991 there were anticommunist and anti-Milošević riots in Belgrade. The 1991 civil war in Yugoslavia arose from the Milošević nationalist government attempting the forcible annexation of Serb-dominated regions in Croatia, making use of the largely Serbian federal army. In Oct 1991 Milošević renounced territorial claims on Croatia pressured by threats of European Community (EC) and United Nations (UN) sanctions, but the fighting continued until a cease-fire was agreed Jan 1992. EC recognition of Slovenia's and Croatia's independence in Jan 1992 and Bosnia-Herzegovina's in April left Serbia dominating a greatly reduced 'rump' Yugoslavia. A successor Yugoslavia, announced by Serbia and Montenegro April 1992, was rejected by the USA and EC because of concerns over serious human rights violations in Kosovo and Serbia's continued attempted partition of Bosnia-Herzegovina. In March 1992, and again in June, thousands of Serbs marched through Belgrade, demanding the ousting of President Milošević and an end to the war in Bosnia-Herzegovina. Milošević was re-elected Dec 1992.

Serbo-Croatian (or **Serbo-Croat**) the most widely spoken language in Yugoslavia. It is a member of the South Slavonic branch of the Indo-European family. Its different dialects tend to be written by the Greek Orthodox Serbs in the Cyrillic script, and by the Roman Catholic Croats in the Latin script.

serenade musical piece for chamber orchestra or wind instruments in several movements, originally for informal evening entertainment, such as Mozart's *Eine kleine Nachtmusik/A Little Night Music*.

serfdom the legal and economic status of peasants under *feudalism. Serfs could not be sold like slaves, but they were not free to leave their master's estate without his permission. They had to work the lord's land without pay for part of the week, more at busy seasons, and pay a percentage of their produce to the lord; in return they were allowed to cultivate a portion of the estate for their own benefit. They also served as soldiers.

Sergius, St of Radonezh 1314–1392. Patron saint of Russia, who founded the Eastern Orthodox monastery of the Blessed Trinity near Moscow 1334. Mediator among Russian feudal princes, he inspired the victory of Dmitri, Grand Duke of Moscow, over the Tatar khan Mamai at Kulikovo 1380.

serialism in music, a later form of the *twelve-tone system of composition.

series circuit electrical circuit in which the components are connected end to end, so that the current flows through them all one after the other.

serpentine group of minerals, hydrous magnesium silicate, $Mg_3Si_2O_5(OH)_4$, occurring in soft *metamorphic rocks and usually dark green. The fibrous form **chrysolite** is a source of *asbestos; other forms are **antigorite, talc, and meerschaum.** Serpentine minerals are formed by hydration of ultrabasic rocks during metamorphism. Rare snake-patterned forms are used in ornamental carving.

SERPS acronym for **State Earnings-Related Pension Schemes**, the UK state *pension scheme.

serum clear fluid that remains after blood clots. It is blood plasma with the anticoagulant proteins removed, and contains *antibodies and other proteins, as well as the fats and sugars of the blood. It can be produced synthetically, and is used to protect against disease.

Servetus Michael (Miguel Serveto) 1511–1553. Spanish Christian Anabaptist theologian and physician. He was a pioneer in the study of the circulation of the blood and found that it circulates to the lungs from the right chamber of the heart. He was burned alive by the church reformer Calvin in Geneva, Switzerland, for publishing attacks on the doctrine of the Trinity.

service industry commercial activity that provides and charges for various services to customers (as opposed to manufacturing or supplying goods), such as restaurants, the tourist industry, cleaning, hotels, and the retail trade (shops and supermarkets).

services, armed the air, sea, and land forces of a country; see *army, *navy; also called the armed forces.

service tree deciduous Eurasian tree *Sorbus domestica* of the rose family Rosaceae, with alternate pinnate leaves, white flowers, and small, edible, oval fruit. The European wild service tree *Sorbus torminalis* has oblong rather than pointed leaflets. It is related to the *mountain ash.

servomechanism automatic control system used in aircraft, motor cars, and other complex machines. A specific input, such as moving a lever or joystick, causes a specific output, such as feeding current to an electric motor that moves, for example, the rudder of the aircraft. At the same time, the position of the rudder is detected and fed back to the central control, so that small adjustments can continually be made to maintain the desired course.

sesame annual plant *Sesamum indicum* of the family Pedaliaceae, probably native to SE Asia. It produces oily seeds used for food and soap making.

sessile in botany, a leaf, flower, or fruit that

lacks a stalk and sits directly on the stem, as with the sessile acorns of certain *oaks. In zoology, it is an animal that normally stays in the same place, such as a barnacle or mussel. The term is also applied to the eyes of *crustaceans when these lack stalks and sit directly on the head.

Session, Court of one of the civil courts in Scotland; see *Court of Session.

set or **class** in mathematics, any collection of defined things (elements), provided the elements are distinct and that there is a rule to decide whether an element is a member of a set. It is usually denoted by a capital letter and indicated by curly brackets.

Set in Egyptian mythology, the god of night, the desert, and of all evils. He was the murderer of *Osiris, portrayed as a grotesque animal.

setter any of various breeds of gun dog, about 66 cm/2.2 ft high and weighing about 25 kg/55 lb. They have a long, smooth coat, feathered tails, and spaniel-like faces. They are called 'setters' because they were trained in crouching or 'setting' on the sight of game to be pursued.

Settlement, Act of in Britain, a law passed 1701 during the reign of King William III, designed to ensure a Protestant succession to the throne by excluding the Roman Catholic descendants of James II in favour of the Protestant House of Hanover. Elizabeth II still reigns under this act.

settlement out of court a compromise reached between the parties to a legal dispute. Most civil legal actions are settled out of court, reducing legal costs and avoiding the uncertainty of the outcome of a trial.

Seurat Georges 1859–1891. French artist. He originated, with Paul Signac, the Neo-Impressionist technique of *Pointillism (painting with small dabs rather than long brushstrokes). Examples of his work are *Bathers at Asnières* 1884 (National Gallery, London) and *Sunday on the Island of La Grande Jatte* 1886 (Art Institute of Chicago).

seven deadly sins in Christian theology, anger, avarice, envy, gluttony, lust, pride, and sloth.

Seventh-Day Adventist or *Adventist member of the Protestant religious sect of the same name. It originated in the USA in the fervent expectation of Christ's Second Coming, or advent, that swept across New York State following William Miller's prophecy that Christ would return on 22 Oct 1844. When this failed to come to pass, a number of Millerites, as his followers were called, reinterpreted his prophetic speculations and continued to maintain that the millennium was imminent. Adventists observe Saturday as the Sabbath and emphasize healing and diet; many are vegetarians. The sect has about 500,000 members in the USA.

Seven Weeks' War war 1866 between Austria and Prussia, engineered by the German chancellor *Bismarck. It was nominally over the possession of *Schleswig-Holstein, but it was actually to confirm Prussia's superseding Austria as the leading German state. The Battle of *Sadowa was the culmination of General von Moltke's victories.

Seven Wonders of the World in antiquity, the pyramids of Egypt, the hanging gardens of Babylon, the temple of Artemis at Ephesus, the statue of Zeus at Olympia, the mausoleum at Halicarnassus, the Colossus of Rhodes, and the Pharos (lighthouse) at Alexandria.

Seven Years' War (in North America known as the **French and Indian War**) war 1756–6. arising from the conflict between Austria and Prussia, and between France and Britain over colonial supremacy. Britain and Prussia defeated France, Austria, Spain, and Russia; Britain gained control of India and many of France's colonies, including Canada. Spain ceded Florida to Britain in exchange for Cuba. Fighting against great odds, Prussia was eventually successful in becoming established as one of the great European powers. The war ended with the Treaty of Paris 1763, signed by Britain, France, and Spain

Severn river of Wales and England, rising on the NE side of Plynlimmon, N Wales, and flowing 338 km/210 mi through Shrewsbury, Worcester and Gloucester to the Bristol Channel. The *Severn bore* is a tidal wave up to 2 m/6 ft high

Severus Lucius Septimus 146–211. Roman emperor. He held a command on the Danube when in 193 the emperor Pertinax was murdered. Proclaimed emperor by his troops, Severus proved an able administrator. He was born in N Africa, and was the only African to become emperor. He died at York while campaigning in Britain against the Caledonians.

Seville (Spanish *Sevilla*) city in Andalusia Spain, on the Guadalquivir River, 96 km/60 m N of Cadiz; population (1991) 683,500. Products include machinery, spirits, porcelain, pharmaceuticals, silk, and tobacco.

Sèvres fine porcelain produced at a factory in Sèvres, France, now a Paris suburb, since the early 18th century. It is characterized by the use of intensely coloured backgrounds (such as pink and royal blue), against which flowers are painted in elaborately embellished frames, often in gold.

Sèvres, Treaty of the last of the treaties that ended World War I. Negotiated between the Allied powers and the Ottoman Empire, it was finalized Aug 1920 but never ratified by the Turkish government.

sewage disposal the disposal of human excreta and other waterborne waste products from houses, streets, and factories. Conveyed through sewers to sewage works, sewage has to undergo a series of treatments to be acceptable for discharge into rivers or the sea, according to various local laws and ordinances. Raw sewage, or sewage that has not been treated adequately, is one serious source of water pollution and a cause of *eutrophication.

Sewell Anna 1820–1878. English author whose only published work, *Black Beauty* 1877, tells the life story of a horse. Although now read as a children's book, it was written to encourage sympathetic treatment of horses by adults.

sewing machine apparatus for the mechanical sewing of cloth, leather, and other materials by a needle, powered by hand, treadle, or belted electric motor. The popular lockstitch machine, using a double thread, was invented independently in the USA by both Walter Hunt 1834 and

Elias *Howe 1846. Howe's machine was the basis of the machine patented 1851 by Isaac *Singer.

sex determination process by which the sex of an organism is determined. In many species, the sex of an individual is dictated by the two sex chromosomes (X and Y) it receives from its parents. In mammals, some plants, and a few insects, males are XY, and females XX; in birds, reptiles, some amphibians, and butterflies the reverse is the case. In bees and wasps, males are produced from unfertilized eggs, females from fertilized eggs. Environmental factors can affect some fish and reptiles, such as turtles, where sex is influenced by the temperature at which the eggs develop.

sexism belief in (or set of implicit assumptions about) the superiority of one's own sex, often accompanied by a *stereotype or preconceived idea about the opposite sex. Sexism may also be accompanied by *discrimination on the basis of sex, generally as practised by men against women.

sex linkage in genetics, the tendency for certain characteristics to occur exclusively, or predominantly, in one sex only. Human examples include red-green colour blindness and haemophilia, both found predominantly in males. In both cases, these characteristics are *recessive and are determined by genes on the *X chromosome.

sextant navigational instrument for determining latitude by measuring the angle between some heavenly body and the horizon. It was invented by John Hadley (1682–1744) in 1730 and can be used only in clear weather.

sexually transmitted disease (STD) any disease transmitted by sexual contact, involving transfer of body fluids. STDs include not only traditional *venereal disease, but also a growing list of conditions, such as *AIDS and scabies, which are known to be spread primarily by sexual contact. Other diseases that are transmitted sexually include viral *hepatitis.

sexual reproduction reproductive process in organisms that requires the union, or *fertilization, of gametes (such as eggs and sperm). These are usually produced by two different individuals, although self-fertilization occurs in a few *hermaphrodites such as tapeworms. Most organisms other than bacteria and cyanobacteria (*blue-green algae) show some sort of sexual process. Except in some lower organisms, the gametes are of two distinct types called eggs and sperm. The organisms producing the eggs are called females, and those producing the sperm, males. The fusion of a male and female gamete produces a **zygote**, from which a new individual develops.

sexual selection process similar to *natural selection but relating exclusively to success in finding a mate for the purpose of sexual reproduction and producing offspring. Sexual selection occurs when one sex (usually but not always the female) invests more effort in producing young than the other. Members of the other sex compete for access to this limited resource (usually males competing for the chance to mate with females).

female reproductive system

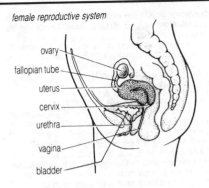

male reproductive system

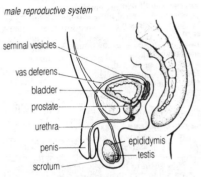

sexual reproduction The human reproductive organs.

Seychelles Republic of

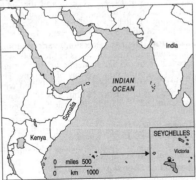

area 453 sq km/175 sq mi
capital Victoria (on Mahé island)
towns Cascade, Port Glaud, Misere
physical comprises two distinct island groups, one concentrated, the other widely scattered, totalling over 100 islands and islets
head of state and government France-Albert René from 1977
political system one-party socialist republic
political party Seychelles People's Progressive Front (SPPF), nationalist socialist
exports copra, cinnamon

currency Seychelles rupee
population (1993) 80,000; growth rate 2.2% p.a.
languages creole (Asian, African, European mixture) 95%, English, French (all official)
religion Roman Catholic 90%
GNP $5,430 per head (1991)
chronology
1744 Became a French colony.
1794 Captured by British.
1814 Ceded by France to Britain; incorporated as a dependency of Mauritius.
1903 Became a separate British colony.
1975 Internal self-government agreed.
1976 Independence achieved from Britain as a republic within the Commonwealth, with James Mancham as president.
1977 Albert René ousted Mancham in an armed coup and took over presidency.
1979 New constitution adopted; Seychelles People's Progressive Front (SPPF) sole legal party.
1981 Attempted coup by South African mercenaries thwarted.
1984 René re-elected.
1987 Coup attempt foiled.
1989 René re-elected.
1991 Multiparty politics promised.
1992 Mancham returned from exile. Constitutional commission elected.

Seyfert galaxy galaxy whose small, bright centre is caused by hot gas moving at high speed around a massive central object, possibly a *black hole. Almost all Seyferts are spiral galaxies. They seem to be closely related to *quasars, but are about 100 times fainter. They are named after their discoverer Carl Seyfert (1911–1960).

Seymour Jane c. 1509–1537. Third wife of Henry VIII, whom she married in 1536. She died soon after the birth of her son Edward VI.

Seymour Lynn 1939– . Canadian ballerina of rare dramatic talent. She was principal dancer of the Royal Ballet from 1959 and artistic director of the Munich State Opera Ballet 1978–80.

Sezession (German 'secession') various groups of German and Austrian artists in the 1890s who 'seceded' from official academic art institutions in order to found new schools of painting. The first was in Munich 1892; the next, linked with the paintings of Gustav *Klimt, was the Vienna Sezession 1897; the Berlin Sezession followed in 1899.

Sforza Italian family that ruled the duchy of Milan 1450–99, 1512–15, and 1522–35. Its court was a centre of Renaissance culture and its rulers prominent patrons of the arts.

Shaanxi or **Shensi** province of NW China
area 195,800 sq km/75,579 sq mi
capital Xian
physical mountains; Huang He valley, one of the earliest settled areas of China
products iron, steel, mining, textiles, fruit, tea, rice, wheat
population (1990) 32,882,000.

shackle unit of length, used at sea for measuring cable or chain. One shackle is 15 fathoms (90 ft/27 m).

Shackleton Ernest 1874–1922. Irish Antarctic explorer. In 1907–09, he commanded an expedition that reached 88° 23′ S latitude, located the magnetic South Pole, and climbed Mount *Erebus.

shad any of several marine fishes, especially the genus *Alosa*, the largest (60 cm/2 ft long and 2.7 kg/6 lb in weight) of the herring family (Clupeidae). They migrate in shoals to breed in rivers.

shadoof or **shaduf** machine for lifting water consisting typically of a long, pivoted wooden pole acting as a lever, with a weight at one end. The other end is positioned over a well, for example. The shadoof was in use in ancient Egypt and is still used in Arab countries today.

shadow area of darkness behind an opaque object that cannot be reached by some or all of the light coming from a light source in front. Its presence may be explained in terms of light rays travelling in straight lines and being unable to bend round obstacles. A point source of light produces an umbra, a completely black shadow with sharp edges. An extended source of light produces both a central umbra and a penumbra, a region of semidarkness with blurred edges where darkness gives way to light.

shadow cabinet the chief members of the British parliamentary opposition, each of whom is responsible for commenting on the policies and performance of a government ministry.

Shaftesbury market town and agricultural centre in Dorset, England, 30 km/19 mi SW of Salisbury; population (1985) 6,000. King Alfred is said to have founded an abbey on the site 880. Canute died at Shaftesbury 1035.

Shaftesbury Anthony Ashley Cooper, 1st Earl of Shaftesbury 1621–1683. English politician, a supporter of the Restoration of the monarchy. He became Lord Chancellor in 1672, but went into opposition in 1673 and began to organize the *Whig Party. He headed the Whigs' demand for the exclusion of the future James II from the succession, secured the passing of the Habeas Corpus Act 1679, then, when accused of treason 1681, fled to Holland.

Shaftesbury Anthony Ashley Cooper, 7th Earl of Shaftesbury 1801–1885. British Tory politician. He strongly supported the Ten Hours Act of 1847 and other factory legislation, including the 1842 act forbidding the employment of women and children underground in mines. He was also associated with the movement to provide free education for the poor.

shag common name for the double-crested *cormorant *Phalacrocorax auritis.*

shah (more formally, **shahanshah** 'king of kings') traditional title of ancient Persian rulers and also of those of the recent *Pahlavi dynasty in Iran.

Shah Jahan 1592–1666. Mogul emperor of India 1628–58. During his reign the *Taj Mahal and the Pearl Mosque at Agra were built. From 1658 he was a prisoner of his son Aurangzeb.

Shaka or **Chaka** c. 1787–1828. Zulu chief who formed a Zulu empire in SE Africa. He seized power from his half-brother 1816 and then embarked on a bloody military campaign to unite the Zulu clans. He was assassinated by his two half-brothers.

Shaker member of the Christian sect of the **United Society of Believers in Christ's**

SHAKESPEARE: THE PLAYS

title	performed

early plays

Henry VI Part I	1589–92
Henry VI Part II	1589–92
Henry VI Part III	1589–92
The Comedy of Errors	1592–93
The Taming of the Shrew	1593–94
Titus Andronicus	1593–94
The Two Gentlemen of Verona	1594–95
Love's Labours Lost	1594–95
Romeo and Juliet	1594–95

histories

Richard III	1592–93
Richard II	1593–96
King John	1596–97
Henry IV Part I	1597–98
Henry IV Part II	1597–98
Henry V	1599

Roman plays

Julius Caesar	1599–1600
Antony and Cleopatra	1607–08
Coriolanus	1607–08

the 'great' or 'middle' comedies

A Midsummer Night's Dream	1595–96
The Merchant of Venice	1596–97
Much Ado About Nothing	1598–99
As You Like It	1599–1600
The Merry Wives of Windsor	1600–01
Twelfth Night	1601–02

the great tragedies

Hamlet	1600–01
Othello	1604–05
King Lear	1605–06
Macbeth	1605–06
Timon of Athens	1607–08

the 'dark' comedies

Troilus and Cressida	1601–02
All's Well That Ends Well	1602–03
Measure for Measure	1604–05

Late plays

Pericles	1608–09
Cymbeline	1609–10
The Winter's Tale	1610–11
The Tempest	1611–12
Henry VIII	1612–13

Second Appearing, called Shakers because of their ecstatic shakings in worship. The movement was founded by James and Jane Wardley in England about 1747, and taken to North America 1774 by Ann Lee (1736–1784).

Shakespeare William 1564–1616. English dramatist and poet. Established in London by 1589 as an actor and a playwright, he was England's unrivalled dramatist until his death, and is considered the greatest English playwright. His plays, written in blank verse, can be broadly divided into lyric plays, including *Romeo and Juliet* and *A Midsummer Night's Dream*; comedies, including *The Comedy of Errors, As You Like It, Much Ado About Nothing*, and *Measure For Measure*; historical plays, such as *Henry VI* (in three parts), *Richard III*, and *Henry IV* (in two parts), which often showed cynical political wisdom; and tragedies, such as *Hamlet, Macbeth,* and *King Lear*. He also wrote numerous sonnets.

shale fine-grained and finely layered *sedimentary rock composed of silt and clay, usually formed in lowland areas. It is a weak rock, splitting easily along bedding planes to form thin, even slabs (by contrast, mudstone splits into irregular flakes). Oil shale contains kerogen, a solid bituminous material that yields *petroleum when heated.

shallot small onion *Allium ascalonicum* in which bulbs are clustered like garlic; used for cooking and in pickles.

shaman (Tungu *samân*) ritual leader who acts as intermediary between society and the supernatural world in many indigenous cultures of Asia, Africa, and the Americas. Also known as a **medicine man, seer,** or **sorcerer,** the shaman is expected to use special powers to cure illness and control good and evil spirits. The term is used for any tribal sorcerer or medicine man regardless of geography.

Shamir Yitzhak 1915– . Polish-born Israeli right-wing politician; prime minister 1983–84 and 1986–92; leader of the Likud (Consolidation Party) from 1983. He was foreign minister under Menachem Begin 1980–83, and again foreign minister in the *Peres unity government 1984–86.

shamrock several trifoliate plants of the family Leguminosae, including *clovers. St Patrick is said to have used one to illustrate the doctrine of the Holy Trinity, and it was made the national badge of Ireland.

Shandong or **Shantung** province of NE China
area 153,300 sq km/59,174 sq mi
capital Jinan
towns ports: Yantai, Weihai, Qingdao, Shigiusuo
products cereals, cotton, wild silk, varied minerals
population (1990) 84,393,000.

Shanghai port on the Huang-pu and Wusong rivers, Jiangsu province, China, 24 km/15 mi from the Chang Jiang estuary; population (1986) 6,980,000, the largest city in China. The municipality of Shanghai has an area of 5,800 sq km/ 2,239 sq mi and a population of 13,342,000. Industries include textiles, paper, chemicals, steel, agricultural machinery, precision instruments, shipbuilding, flour and vegetable-oil milling, and oil refining. It handles about 50% of China's imports and exports.

Shankar Ravi 1920– . Indian composer and musician. A virtuoso of the *sitar, he has composed film music and founded music schools in Bombay and Los Angeles.

Shannon longest river in Ireland, rising in County Cavan and flowing 386 km/240 mi through loughs Allen and Ree and past Athlone, to reach the Atlantic through a wide estuary below Limerick. It is the greatest source of electric power in the republic, with hydroelectric installations at and above Ardnacrusha, 5 km/ 3 mi N of Limerick.

Shanxi or **Shansi** province of NE China
area 157,100 sq km/60,641 sq mi
capital Taiyuan
products coal, iron, fruit
population (1990) 28,759,000

history saw the outbreak of the Boxer Rebellion 1900.

SHAPE acronym for *Supreme Headquarters Allied Powers Europe*, situated near Mons, Belgium, and the headquarters of NATO's Supreme Allied Commander Europe (SACEUR).

share in finance, that part of the capital of a company held by a member (shareholder). Shares may be numbered and are issued as units of definite face value; shareholders are not always called on to pay the full face value of their shares, though they bind themselves to do so.

sharecropping farming someone else's land, where the farmer gives the landowner a proportion of the crop instead of money. This system of rent payment was common in the USA, especially the South, until after World War II. It is still common in parts of the developing world; for example, in India. Often the farmer is left with such a small share of the crop that he or she is doomed to poverty.

share option in finance, see *option.

Shari'a the law of *Islam believed by Muslims to be based on divine revelation, and drawn from a number of sources, including the Koran, the Hadith, and the consensus of the Muslim community. Under this law, *qisās*, or retribution, allows a family to exact equal punishment on an accused; *diyat*, or blood money, is payable to a dead person's family as compensation. From the latter part of the 19th century, the role of the Shari'a courts in the majority of Muslim countries began to be taken over by secular courts, and the Shari'a to be largely restricted to family law. Modifications of Koranic maxims have resulted from the introduction of Western law; for example, compensation can now be claimed only after a conviction by a criminal court.

Sharjah or *Shariqah* third largest of the seven member states of the *United Arab Emirates, situated on the Arabian Gulf NE of Dubai; area 2,600 sq km/1,004 sq mi; population (1985) 269,000. Since 1952 it has included the small state of Kalba. In 1974 oil was discovered offshore. Industries include ship repair, cement, paint, and metal products.

shark any member of various orders of cartilaginous fishes (class Chondrichthyes), found throughout the oceans of the world. There are about 400 known species of shark. They have tough, usually grey, skin covered in denticles (small toothlike scales). A shark's streamlined body has side pectoral fins, a high dorsal fin, and a forked tail with a large upper lobe. Five open gill slits are visible on each side of the generally pointed head. Most sharks are fish-eaters, and a few will attack humans. They range from several feet in length to the great *white shark Carcharodon carcharias*, 9 m/30 ft long, and the harmless plankton-feeding *whale shark Rhincodon typus*, over 15 m/50 ft in length.

Sharman Helen 1963– . The first Briton to fly in space, chosen from 13,000 applicants for a 1991 joint UK-Soviet space flight. Sharman, a research chemist by profession, was launched on 18 May 1991 in *Soyuz TM-12* and spent six days with Soviet cosmonauts aboard the *Mir* space station.

sharp in music, sounding higher in pitch than the indicated note value, or than expected. A sharp sign in front of a written note indicates that the note is to be raised by a semitone. It is cancelled by a natural sign.

Sharpeville black township in South Africa, 65 km/40 mi S of Johannesburg and N of Vereeniging; 69 people were killed here when police fired on a crowd of anti-apartheid demonstrators 21 March 1960.

Shastri Lal Bahadur 1904–1966. Indian politician, prime minister 1964–66. He campaigned for national integration, and secured a declaration of peace with Pakistan at the Tashkent peace conference 1966.

Shatt-al-Arab (Persian *Arvand*) the waterway formed by the confluence of the rivers *Euphrates and *Tigris; length 190 km/120 mi to the Persian Gulf. Basra, Khorramshahr, and Abadan stand on it.

Shaw George Bernard 1856–1950. Irish dramatist. He was also a critic and novelist, and an early member of the socialist *Fabian Society. His plays combine comedy with political, philosophical, and polemic aspects, aiming to make an impact on his audience's social conscience as well as their emotions. They include *Arms and the Man* 1894, *Devil's Disciple* 1897, *Man and Superman* 1905, *Pygmalion* 1913, and *St Joan* 1924. Nobel prize 1925.

shearwater any sea bird of the genus *Puffinus*, in the same family (Procellariidae) as the diving *petrels.

sheath another name for a *condom.

Sheba ancient name for S *Yemen (Sha'abijah). It was once renowned for gold and spices. According to the Old Testament, its queen visited Solomon; until 1975 the Ethiopian royal house traced its descent from their union.

Shechem ancient town in Palestine, capital of Samaria. In the Old Testament, it is the traditional burial place of Joseph; nearby is Jacob's well. Shechem was destroyed about AD 67 by the Roman emperor Vespasian; on its site stands Nablus (a corruption of Neapolis) built by the Roman emperor *Hadrian.

sheep any of several ruminant, even-toed, hoofed mammals of the family Bovidae. Wild species survive in the uplands of central and eastern Asia, N Africa, southern Europe and North America. The domesticated breeds are all classified as *Ovis aries*. Various breeds of sheep are reared worldwide for meat, wool, milk, and cheese, and for rotation on arable land to maintain its fertility.

sheepdog any of several breeds of dog, bred originally for herding sheep. The Old English sheepdog is grey or blue-grey, with white markings, and is about 56 cm/22 in tall at the shoulder. The Shetland sheepdog is much smaller, 36 cm/14 in tall, and shaped more like a long-coated collie. The dog now most commonly used by shepherds and farmers to tend sheep is the border collie.

sheep scab highly contagious disease of sheep, caused by mites that penetrate the animal's skin. Painful irritation, infection, loss of fleece, and death may result. The disease is notifiable in the UK.

Sheffield industrial city on the river Don,

South Yorkshire, England; population (1991 est) 499,700. From the 12th century, iron smelting was the chief industry, and by the 14th century, Sheffield cutlery, silverware, and plate were made. During the Industrial Revolution the iron and steel industries developed rapidly. It now produces alloys and special steels, cutlery of all kinds, permanent magnets, drills, and precision tools.

sheik leader or chief of an Arab family or village.

shelduck duck *Tadorna tadorna* with a dark-green head and red bill, with the rest of the plumage strikingly marked in black, white, and chestnut. Widely distributed in Europe and Asia, it lays 10–12 white eggs in rabbit burrows on sandy coasts, and is usually seen on estuary mudflats.

shelf sea relatively shallow sea, usually no deeper than 200 m/650 ft, overlying the continental shelf around the coastlines. Most fishing and marine mineral exploitations are carried out in shelf seas.

shellac resin derived from secretions of the lac insect.

Shelley Mary Wollstonecraft 1797–1851. English writer, the daughter of Mary Wollstonecraft and William Godwin. In 1814 she eloped with the poet Percy Bysshe Shelley, whom she married in 1816. Her novels include *Frankenstein* 1818, *The Last Man* 1826, and *Valperga* 1823.

Shelley Percy Bysshe 1792–1822. English lyric poet, a leading figure in the Romantic movement. Expelled from Oxford University for atheism, he fought all his life against religion and for political freedom. This is reflected in his early poems such as *Queen Mab* 1813. He later wrote tragedies including *The Cenci* 1818, lyric dramas such as *Prometheus Unbound* 1820, and lyrical poems such as 'Ode to the West Wind'. He drowned while sailing in Italy.

shellfish popular name for molluscs and crustaceans, including the whelk and periwinkle, mussel, oyster, lobster, crab, and shrimp.

shell shock or *combat neurosis* or *battle fatigue* any of the various forms of mental disorder that affect soldiers exposed to heavy explosions or extreme *stress. Shell shock was first diagnosed during World War I.

Shenyang industrial city and capital of Liaoning province, China; population (1990) 4,500,000. It was the capital of the Manchu emperors 1644–1912; their tombs are nearby.

Shenzen special economic zone established in 1980 opposite Hong Kong on the coast of Guangdong province, S China. Its status provided much of the driving force of its spectacular development in the 1980s when its population rose from 20,000 in 1980 to 600,000 in 1989.

Shepard E(rnest) H(oward) 1879–1976. British illustrator of books by A A Milne (*Winnie-the-Pooh* 1926) and Kenneth Grahame (*The Wind in the Willows* 1908).

Shephard Gillian Patricia 1940– . British Conservative politician, education secretary from 1994. After holding cabinet posts in employment and agriculture, she took over education at a time when teachers' morale was low and relations between government and the profession particularly fraught. Although her open conciliatory approach did much initially to alleviate the situation, teachers' patience rapidly dissolved in the face of on-going cuts in eduction budgets.

Sheraton Thomas *c.* 1751–1806. English designer of elegant inlaid furniture. He was influenced by his predecessors *Hepplewhite and *Chippendale.

Sheridan Philip Henry 1831–1888. Union general in the American *Civil War. General Ulysses S *Grant gave him command of his cavalry in 1864, and soon after of the Army of the Shenandoah Valley, Virginia. Sheridan laid waste to the valley, cutting off grain supplies to the Confederate armies. In the final stage of the war, Sheridan forced General Robert E *Lee to surrender.

Sheridan Richard Brinsley 1751–1816. Irish dramatist and politician, born in Dublin. His social comedies include *The Rivals* 1775, celebrated for the character of Mrs Malaprop, *The School for Scandal* 1777, and *The Critic* 1779. In 1776 he became lessee of the Drury Lane Theatre. He became a member of Parliament in 1780.

sheriff (Old English *scīr* 'shire', *gerēfa* 'reeve') in England and Wales, the crown's chief executive officer in a county for ceremonial purposes; in Scotland, the equivalent of the English county-court judge, but also dealing with criminal cases; and in the USA the popularly elected head law-enforcement officer of a county, combining judicial authority with administrative duties.

Sherman William Tecumseh 1820–1891. Union general in the American *Civil War. In 1864 he captured and burned Atlanta; continued his march eastward, to the sea, laying Georgia waste; and then drove the Confederates northward. He was US Army chief of staff 1869–83.

Sherpa member of a people in NE Nepal related to the Tibetans and renowned for their mountaineering skill. A Sherpa, Tensing Norgay, was one of the first two people to climb to the summit of Everest.

Sherwood Forest hilly stretch of parkland in W Nottinghamshire, England, area about 520 sq km/200 sq mi. Formerly a royal forest, it is associated with the legendary outlaw *Robin Hood.

Shetland Islands islands off the north coast of Scotland, beyond the Orkneys
area 1,400 sq km/541 sq mi
towns Lerwick (administrative headquarters), on Mainland, largest of 19 inhabited islands
physical over 100 islands including Muckle Flugga (latitude 60° 51′ N) the northernmost of the British Isles
products processed fish, handknits from Fair Isle and Unst, miniature ponies. Europe's largest oil port is Sullom Voe, Mainland
population (1987) 22,000
language dialect derived from Norse, the islands having been a Norse dependency from the 8th century until 1472.

Shevardnadze Eduard 1928– . Georgian politician, Soviet foreign minister 1985–91, head of state of Georgia from 1992. A supporter of *Gorbachev, he was first secretary of the Georgian Communist Party from 1972 and an advocate of economic reform. In July 1991, he resigned from the Communist Party (CPSU) and, along with other reformers and leading democrats, established the Democratic Reform Movement. In March 1992 he was chosen as chair of Georgia's ruling military council, and in October elected speaker of parliament.

Shiah or **Shi'ite* member of one of the two main sects of *Islam.

shiatsu Japanese method of massage derived from *acupuncture and sometimes referred to as 'acupressure', which treats organic or physiological dysfunctions by applying finger or palm-of-the-hand pressure to parts of the body remote from the affected part.

shield in geology, alternative name for *craton, the ancient core of a continent.

shield in technology, any material used to reduce the amount of radiation (electrostatic, electromagnetic, heat, nuclear) reaching from one region of space to another, or any material used as a protection against falling debris, as in tunnelling. Electrical conductors are used for electrostatic shields, soft iron for electromagnetic shields, and poor conductors of heat for heat shields. Heavy materials such as lead and concrete are used for protection against *X-rays and nuclear radiation. See also *biological shield and heat shield.

shifting cultivation farming system where farmers move on from one place to another. The most common form is slash-and-burn agriculture: land is cleared by burning, so that crops can be grown. After a few years, soil fertility is reduced and the land is abandoned. A new area is cleared while the old land recovers its fertility.

Shi Huangdi or *Shih Huang Ti* 259–210 BC. Emperor of China who succeeded to the throne of the state of Qin in 246 BC and reunited China as an empire by 228 BC. He burned almost all existing books in 213 BC to destroy ties with the past; rebuilt the *Great Wall; and was buried at Xian in a tomb complex guarded by 10,000 life-size terracotta warriors (excavated by archaeologists in the 1980s).

Shi'ite or *Shiah* member of a sect of Islam who believe that *Ali was *Muhammad's first true successor. They are doctrinally opposed to the Sunni Muslims. They developed their own law differing only in minor directions, such as inheritance and the status of women. Holy men have greater authority in the Shi'ite sect than in the Sunni sect. They are prominent in Iran, the Lebanon, and Indo-Pakistan, and are also found in Iraq and Bahrain.

Shikoku smallest of the four main islands of Japan, S of Honshu, E of Kyushu; area 18,800 sq km/7,257 sq mi; population (1986) 4,226,000; chief town Matsuyama. Products include rice, wheat, soya beans, sugar cane, orchard fruits, salt, and copper.

Shilton Peter 1949– . English international footballer, an outstanding goalkeeper, who has set records for the highest number of Football League appearances (over 900) and England caps (125). First capped by England 1970 he retired from international football 1990, after the England–West Germany World Cup semifinal. In 1992 he became manager of Plymouth Argyle.

shingles common name for *herpes zoster, a disease characterized by infection of sensory nerves, with pain and eruption of blisters along the course of the affected nerves.

Shinkansen (Japanese 'new trunk line') fast railway network operated by Japanese Railways, on which the bullet trains run. The network, opened 1964, uses specially built straight and level track, on which average speeds of 160 kph/100 mph are attained.

Shinto (Chinese *shin tao* 'way of the gods') the indigenous religion of Japan. It combines an empathetic oneness with natural forces and loyalty to the reigning dynasty as descendants of the Sun goddess, Amaterasu-Omikami. Traditional Shinto followers stressed obedience and devotion to the emperor, and an aggressive nationalistic aspect was developed by the Meiji rulers. Today Shinto has discarded these aspects.

shinty (Gaelic *camanachd*) stick-and-ball game resembling hurling, popular in the Scottish Highlands. It is played between teams of 12 players each, on a field 132–183 m/144–200 yd long and 64–91 m/70–99 yd wide. A curved stick (*caman*) is used to propel a leather-covered cork and worsted ball into the opposing team's goal (*hail*). The premier tournament, the Camanachd Cup, was instituted 1896.

ship large seagoing vessel. The Greeks, Phoenicians, Romans, and Vikings used ships extensively for trade, exploration, and warfare. The 14th century was the era of European exploration by sailing ship, largely aided by the invention of the compass. In the 15th century Britain's Royal Navy was first formed, but in the 16th–19th centuries Spanish and Dutch fleets dominated the shipping lanes of both the Atlantic and Pacific. The ultimate sailing ships, the fast US and British tea clippers, were built in the 19th century. Also in the 19th century, iron was first used for some shipbuilding instead of wood. Steam-propelled ships of the late 19th century were followed by compound engine and turbine-propelled vessels from the early 20th century.

shire administrative area formed in Britain for the purpose of raising taxes in Anglo-Saxon times. By AD 1000 most of southern England had been divided into shires with fortified strongholds at their centres. The Midland counties of England are still known as *the Shires*; for example Derbyshire, Nottinghamshire, and Staffordshire.

Shiva alternative spelling of *Siva, Hindu god.

shock in medicine, circulatory failure marked by a sudden fall of blood pressure and resulting in pallor, sweating, fast (but weak) pulse, and sometimes complete collapse. Causes include disease, injury, and psychological trauma.

shock absorber in technology, any device for absorbing the shock of sudden jarring actions or movements. Shock absorbers are used in conjunction with coil springs in most motor-vehicle suspension systems and are usually of the telescopic type, consisting of a piston in an oil-filled cylinder. The resistance to movement of the piston through the oil creates the absorbing effect.

Shockley William 1910–1989. US physicist and amateur geneticist who worked with John Bardeen and Walter Brattain on the invention of the *transistor. They were jointly awarded a Nobel prize 1956. During the 1970s Shockley was criticized for his claim that blacks were genetically inferior to whites in terms of intelligence.

shoebill or **whale-headed stork** large, grey, long-legged, swamp-dwelling African bird *Balaeniceps rex*. Up to 1.5 m/5 ft tall, it has a large wide beak 20 cm/8 in long, with which it scoops fish, molluscs, reptiles, and carrion out of the mud.

Shoemaker Willie (William Lee) 1931– . US jockey 1949–90. He rode 8,833 winners from 40,351 mounts and his earnings exceeded $123 million. He retired Feb 1990 after finishing fourth on Patchy Groundfog at Santa Anita, California.

shogun in Japanese history, title of a series of military dictators 1192–1867 who relegated the emperor's role to that of figurehead. Technically an imperial appointment, the office was treated as hereditary and was held by the Minamoto clan 1192–1219, by the Ashikaga 1336–1573, and by the Tokugawa 1603–1867. The shogun held legislative, judicial, and executive power.

Sholes Christopher Latham 1819–1890. American printer and newspaper editor who, in 1867, invented the first practicable typewriter in association with Carlos Glidden and Samuel Soulé. In 1873, they sold their patents to *Remington & Sons, a firm of gunsmiths in New York, who developed and sold the machine commercially. In 1878 Sholes developed a shift-key mechanism that made it possible to touch-type.

Sholokhov Mikhail Aleksandrovich 1905–1984. Soviet novelist. His *And Quiet Flows the Don* 1926–40 depicts the Don Cossacks through World War I and the Russian Revolution. Nobel prize 1965.

Shona member of a Bantu-speaking people of southern Africa, comprising approximately 80% of the population of Zimbabwe. They also occupy the land between the Save and Pungure rivers in Mozambique, and smaller groups are found in South Africa, Botswana, and Zambia. The Shona are mainly farmers, living in scattered villages. The Shona language belongs to the Niger-Congo family.

shoot in botany, the parts of a *vascular plant growing above ground, comprising a stem bearing leaves, buds, and flowers. The shoot develops from the plumule of the embryo.

shooting star another name for a *meteor.

shop steward trade-union representative in a 'shop', or department of a factory, who recruits for the union, inspects contribution cards, and reports grievances to the district committee. This form of organization originated in the engineering industry and has spread to all large industrial undertakings.

short circuit direct connection between two points in an electrical circuit. Its relatively low resistance means that a large current flows through it, bypassing the rest of the circuit, and this may cause the circuit to overheat dangerously.

shorthand any system of rapid writing, such as the abbreviations practised by the Greeks and Romans. The first perfecter of an entirely phonetic system was Isaac *Pitman, by which system speeds of about 300 words a minute are said to be attainable.

Short Parliament the English Parliament that was summoned by Charles I on 13 April 1640 to raise funds for his war against the Scots. It was succeeded later in the year by the *Long Parliament.

short-sightedness nontechnical term for *myopia.

short story short work of prose fiction, which typically either sets up and resolves a single narrative point or depicts a mood or an atmosphere. Noted short-story writers include Anton Chekhov, Rudyard Kipling, Guy de Maupassant, Saki, Jorge Luis Borges, Edgar Allan Poe, and Ernest Hemingway.

short tennis a variation of lawn tennis. It is played on a smaller court, largely by children. It can be played indoors or outdoors.

Shostakovich Dmitry (Dmitriyevich) 1906–1975. Soviet composer. His music is tonal, expressive, and sometimes highly dramatic; it was not always to official Soviet taste. He wrote 15 symphonies, chamber music, ballets, and operas, the latter including *Lady Macbeth of Mtsensk* 1934, which was suppressed as 'too divorced from the proletariat', but revived as *Katerina Izmaylova* 1963.

shot put or **putting the shot** in athletics, the sport of throwing (or putting) overhand from the shoulder a metal ball (or shot). Standard shot weights are 7.26 kg/16 lb for men and 4 kg/8.8 lb for women.

shoveler fresh-water duck *Anas clypeata*, so named after its long and broad flattened beak. Spending the summer in N Europe or North America, it winters further south.

Shrapnel Henry 1761–1842. British army officer who invented shells containing bullets, to increase the spread of casualties, first used 1804; hence the word **shrapnel** to describe shell fragments.

shrew insectivorous mammal of the family Soricidae, found in Eurasia and the Americas. It is mouselike, but with a long nose and pointed teeth. Its high metabolic rate means that it must eat almost constantly. The common shrew *Sorex araneus* is about 7.5 cm/3 in long.

shrike 'butcher-bird' of the family Laniidae, of which there are over 70 species, living mostly in Africa, but also in Eurasia and North America. They often impale insects and small vertebrates on thorns. They can grow to 35 cm/14 in long, and have grey, black, or brown plumage.

shrimp crustacean related to the *prawn. It has a cylindrical, semi-transparent body, with ten jointed legs. Some shrimps grow as large as 25 cm/10 in long.

Shropshire county in W England. Sometimes abbreviated to *Salop*, it was officially known by this name from 1974 until local protest reversed the decision 1980
area 3,490 sq km/1,347 sq mi
towns Shrewsbury (administrative headquarters), Telford, Oswestry, Ludlow
physical bisected, on the Welsh border, NW to SE by the river Severn; Ellesmere, the largest of several lakes; the Clee Hills rise to about 610 m/1,800 ft in the SW
products chiefly agricultural: sheep and cattle
population (1991) 401,600

famous people Charles Darwin, Wilfred Owen, Gordon Richards.

shroud of Turin Christian relic; see *Turin shroud.

Shrove Tuesday in the Christian calendar, the day before the beginning of Lent. It is also known as *Mardi Gras*.

shrub perennial woody plant that typically produces several separate stems, at or near ground level, rather than the single trunk of most trees. A shrub is usually smaller than a tree, but there is no clear distinction between large shrubs and small trees.

Shultz George P 1920– . US Republican politician, economics adviser to President *Reagan 1980–82, and secretary of state 1982–89. Shultz taught as a labour economist at the University of Chicago before serving in the 1968–74 *Nixon administration, including secretary of labor 1969–70 and secretary of the Treasury 1972–74.

Shushkevich Stanislav 1934– . Belarus politician, president from 1991 after the attempted Soviet coup in Moscow. He was elected to parliament as a 'reform communist' 1990 and played a key role in the creation of the Commonwealth of Independent States.

shuttle diplomacy in international relations, the efforts of an independent mediator to achieve a compromise solution between belligerent parties, travelling back and forth from one to the other.

SI abbreviation for *Système International [d'Unités]* (French 'International System [of Metric Units]'); see *SI units.

sial in geochemistry and geophysics, the substance of the Earth's continental *crust, as distinct from the *sima of the ocean crust. The name is derived from *si*lica and *al*umina, its two main chemical constituents.

SIB abbreviation for *Securities and Investments Board*, UK regulating body.

Sibelius Jean (Christian) 1865–1957. Finnish composer. His works include nationalistic symphonic poems such as *En saga* 1893 and *Finlandia* 1900, a violin concerto 1904, and seven symphonies.

Siberia Asian region of Russia, extending from the Urals to the Pacific
area 12,050,000 sq km/4,650,000 sq mi
towns Novosibirsk, Omsk, Krasnoyarsk, Irkutsk
products hydroelectric power from rivers Lena, Ob, and Yenisei; forestry; mineral resources, including gold, diamonds, oil, natural gas, iron, copper, nickel, cobalt

Sibyl in Roman mythology, priestess of Apollo. She offered to sell *Tarquinius Superbus nine collections of prophecies, the *Sibylline Books*, but the price was too high. When she had destroyed all but three, he bought those for the identical price, and these were kept for consultation in emergency at Rome.

sic (Latin 'thus', 'so') sometimes found in brackets within a printed quotation to show that an apparent error is in the original.

Sichuan or *Szechwan* province of central China
area 569,000 sq km/219,634 sq mi
capital Chengdu

towns Chongqing
products rice, coal, oil, natural gas
population (1990) 107,218,000.

Sicily (Italian *Sicilia*) largest Mediterranean island, an autonomous region of Italy; area 25,700 sq km/9,920 sq mi; population (1990) 5,196,800. Its capital is Palermo, and towns include the ports of Catania, Messina, Syracuse, and Marsala. It exports Marsala wine, olives, citrus, refined oil and petrochemicals, pharmaceuticals, potash, asphalt, and marble. The autonomous region of Sicily also includes the islands of Lipari, Egadi, Ustica, and Pantelleria. Etna, 3,323 m/10,906 ft high, is the highest volcano in Europe; its last major eruption was in 1971.

sick building syndrome malaise diagnosed in the early 1980s among office workers and thought to be caused by such pollutants as formaldehyde (from furniture and insulating materials), benzene (from paint), and the solvent trichloroethene, concentrated in air-conditioned buildings. Symptoms include headache, sore throat, tiredness, colds, and flu. Studies have found that it can cause a 40% drop in productivity and a 30% rise in absenteeism.

Sickert Walter (Richard) 1860–1942. English artist. His Impressionist cityscapes of London and Venice, portraits, and domestic and music-hall interiors capture subtleties of tone and light, often with a melancholy atmosphere.

sickle harvesting tool of ancient origin characterized by a curving blade with serrated cutting edge and short wooden handle. It was widely used in the Middle East and Europe for cutting wheat, barley, and oats from about 10,000 BC to the 19th century.

sickle-cell disease hereditary chronic blood disorder common among people of black African descent; also found in the E Mediterranean, parts of the Persian Gulf, and in NE India. It is characterized by distortion and fragility of the red blood cells, which are lost too rapidly from the circulation. This often results in *anaemia.

Siddons Sarah 1755–1831. Welsh actress. Her majestic presence made her suited to tragic and heroic roles such as Lady Macbeth, Zara in Congreve's *The Mourning Bride*, and Constance in *King John*.

sidewinder rattlesnake *Crotalus cerastes* that lives in the deserts of the SW USA and Mexico, and moves by throwing its coils into a sideways 'jump' across the sand. It can grow up to 75 cm/ 30 in long.

Sidney Philip 1554–1586. English poet and soldier, author of the sonnet sequence *Astrophel and Stella* 1591, *Arcadia* 1590, a prose romance, and *Apologie for Poetrie* 1595, the earliest work of English literary criticism.

SIDS acronym for *sudden infant death syndrome*, the technical name for *cot death.

Siegfried or *Sigurd* legendary Germanic hero. It is uncertain whether his story has a historical basis, but it was current about AD 700. A version of the story is in the German *Nibelungenlied/ Song of the Nibelung*. In the poems of the Norse *Elder *Edda* and in the prose *Völsunga Saga*, Siegfried appears under the name of Sigurd.

Siegfried Line in World War I, a defensive line

established 1918 by the Germans in France; in World War II, the Allies' name for the West Wall, a German defensive line established along its western frontier, from the Netherlands to Switzerland.

siemens SI unit (symbol S) of electrical conductance, the reciprocal of the *impedance of an electrical circuit. One siemens equals one ampere per volt. It was formerly called the mho or reciprocal ohm.

Siemens German industrial empire created by four brothers. The eldest, *Ernst Werner von Siemens* (1812–1892), founded the original electrical firm of Siemens und Halske 1847 and made many advances in telegraphy. *William (Karl Wilhelm)* (1823–1883) moved to England; he perfected the open-hearth production of steel, pioneered the development of the electric locomotive and the laying of transoceanic cables, and improved the electric generator.

Sierra Leone Republic of

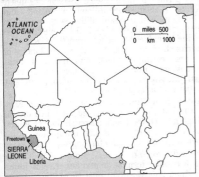

area 71,740 sq km/27,710 sq mi
capital Freetown
towns Koidu, Bo, Kenema, Makeni
physical mountains in E; hills and forest; coastal mangrove swamps
head of state and government military council headed by Capt Valentine Strasser from 1992
political system transitional
exports palm kernels, cocoa, coffee, ginger, diamonds, bauxite, rutile
currency leone
population (1993 est) 4,400,000; growth rate 2.5% p.a.
languages English (official), local languages
religions animist 52%, Muslim 39%, Protestant 6%, Roman Catholic 2% (1980 est)
GNP $210 per head (1991)
chronology
1808 Became a British colony.
1896 Hinterland declared a British protectorate.
1961 Independence achieved from Britain within the Commonwealth, with Milton Margai, leader of Sierra Leone People's Party (SLPP), as prime minister.
1964 Milton succeeded by his half-brother, Albert Margai.
1967 Election results disputed by army, who set up a National Reformation Council and forced the governor general to leave.
1968 Army revolt made Siaka Stevens, leader of the All People's Congress (APC), prime minister.

1971 New constitution adopted, making Sierra Leone a republic, with Stevens as president.
1978 APC declared only legal party. Stevens sworn in for another seven-year term.
1985 Stevens retired; succeeded by Maj-Gen Joseph Momoh.
1989 Attempted coup against President Momoh foiled.
1991 Referendum endorsed multiparty politics.
1992 Military take-over; President Momoh fled. National Provisional Ruling Council (NPRC) established under Capt Valentine Strasser.

Sierra Madre chief mountain system of Mexico, consisting of three ranges, enclosing the central plateau of the country; highest point Pico de Orizaba 5,700 m/18,700 ft. The Sierra Madre del Sur ('of the south') runs along the SW Pacific coast.

sievert SI unit (symbol Sv) of radiation dose equivalent. It replaces the rem (1 Sv equals 100 rem). Some types of radiation do more damage than others for the same absorbed dose – for example, the same absorbed dose of alpha radiation causes 20 times as much biological damage as the same dose of beta radiation. The equivalent dose in sieverts is equal to the absorbed dose of radiation in rays multiplied by the relative biological effectiveness. Humans can absorb up to 0.25 Sv without immediate ill effects; 1 Sv may produce radiation sickness; and more than 8 Sv causes death.

sight the detection of light by an *eye, which can form images of the outside world.

Sigismund 1368–1437. Holy Roman emperor from 1411. He convened and presided over the council of Constance 1414–18, where he promised protection to the religious reformer *Huss, but imprisoned him after his condemnation for heresy and acquiesced in his burning. King of Bohemia from 1419, he led the military campaign against the *Hussites.

Signac Paul 1863–1935. French artist. In 1884 he joined with Georges Seurat in founding the Salon des Artistes Indépendants and developing the technique of *Pointillism.

signal any sign, gesture, sound, or action that conveys information. Examples include the use of flags (*semaphore), light (traffic and railway signals), radio telephony, radio telegraphy (*Morse code), and electricity (telecommunications and computer networks).

significant figures the figures in a number that, by virtue of their place value, express the magnitude of that number to a specified degree of accuracy. The final significant figure is rounded up if the following digit is greater than 5. For example, 5,463,254 to three significant figures is 5,460,000; 3.462891 to four significant figures is 3.463; 0.00347 to two significant figures is 0.0035.

Sigurd in Norse mythology, a hero who appears in both the *Nibelungenlied/Song of the Nibelung* (under his German name of *Siegfried) and the *Edda.

Sihanouk Norodom 1922– . Cambodian politician, king 1941–55, prime minister 1955–70, when his government was overthrown by a military coup led by Lon Nol. With Pol Pot's resistance front, he overthrew Lon Nol 1975 and again became prime minister 1975–76, when he was forced to resign by the *Khmer Rouge. He returned from exile Nov 1991 under the auspices of a United Nations-brokered peace settlement to head the Supreme National Council, a new coalition comprising all Cambodia's warring factions, including the Khmer Rouge.

Sikhism religion professed by 14 million Indians, living mainly in the Punjab. Sikhism was founded by Nanak (1469–c. 1539). Sikhs believe in a single God who is the immortal creator of the universe and who has never been incarnate in any form, and in the equality of all human beings; Sikhism is strongly opposed to caste divisions. Their holy book is the *Guru Granth Sahib*. Guru Gobind Singh (1666–1708) instituted the *Khanda-di-Pahul*, the baptism of the sword, and established the Khalsa ('pure'), the company of the faithful. The Khalsa wear the five Ks: *kes*, long hair; *kangha*, a comb; *kirpan*, a sword; *kachh*, short trousers; and *kara*, a steel bracelet. Sikh men take the last name 'Singh' ('lion') and women 'Kaur' ('princess').

Sikh Wars two wars in India between the Sikhs and the British: The **First Sikh War 1845–46** followed an invasion of British India by Punjabi Sikhs. The Sikhs were defeated and part of their territory annexed. The **Second Sikh War 1848–49** arose from a Sikh revolt in Multan. They were defeated, and the British annexed the Punjab.

Sikkim or **Denjong** state of NE India; formerly a protected state, it was absorbed by India 1975, the monarchy being abolished. China does not recognize India's sovereignty
area 7,300 sq km/2,818 mi
capital Gangtok
products rice, grain, tea, fruit, soya beans, carpets, cigarettes, lead, zinc, copper
population (1991) 403,600
languages Bhutia, Lepecha, Khaskura (Nepali) – all official
religions Mahayana Buddhism, Hinduism
history ruled by the Namgyol dynasty from the 14th century to 1975, when the last chogyal, or king, was deposed. Allied to Britain in 1886, Sikkim became a protectorate of India 1950 and a state of India 1975.

Sikorski Wladyslaw 1881–1943. Polish general and politician; prime minister 1922–23, and 1939–43 of the Polish government in exile in London during World War II. He was killed in an aeroplane crash near Gibraltar in controversial circumstances.

Sikorsky Igor 1889–1972. Ukrainian-born US engineer who built the first successful helicopter. He emigrated to the USA 1918, where he first constructed multi-engined flying boats. His first helicopter (the VS300) flew 1939 and a commercial version (the R3) went into production 1943.

silage fodder preserved through controlled fermentation in a *silo, an airtight structure that presses green crops. It is used as a winter feed for livestock. The term also refers to stacked crops that may be preserved indefinitely.

Silayev Ivan Stepanovich 1930– . Prime minister of the USSR Aug–Dec 1991, a founder member of the Democratic Reform Movement (with former foreign minister *Shevardnadze). A member of the Communist Party 1959–91 and of

its Central Committee 1981–91, Silayev emerged as a reformer in 1990.

Silbury Hill steep, rounded artificial mound (40 m/130 ft high) of the Bronze Age 2660 BC, in Wiltshire, near *Avebury, England. Excavation has shown it not to be a barrow (grave), as was previously thought.

silencer (North American **muffler**) device in the exhaust system of cars and motorbikes. Gases leave the engine at supersonic speeds, and the exhaust system and silencer are designed to slow them down, thereby silencing them.

Silesia region of Europe that has long been disputed because of its geographical position, mineral resources, and industrial potential; now in Poland and Czechoslovakia. Dispute began in the 17th century with claims on the area by both Austria and Prussia. It was seized by Prussia's Frederick the Great, which started the War of the *Austrian Succession; this was finally recognized by Austria 1763, after the Seven Years' War. After World War I, it was divided in 1919 among newly formed Czechoslovakia, revived Poland, and Germany, which retained the largest part. In 1945, after World War II, all German Silesia east of the Oder-Neisse line was transferred to Polish administration; about 10 million inhabitants of German origin, both there and in Czechoslovak Silesia, were expelled.

silhouette profile or shadow portrait filled in with black or a dark colour. A common pictorial technique in Europe in the late 18th and early 19th centuries, it was named after Etienne de Silhouette (1709–1767), a French finance minister who made paper cut-outs as a hobby.

silica silicon dioxide, SiO_2, the composition of the most common mineral group, of which the most familiar form is quartz. Other silica forms are *chalcedony, chert, *opal, tridymite, and cristobalite.

silicon (Latin *silicium* 'silica') brittle, nonmetallic element, symbol Si, atomic number 14, relative atomic mass 28.086. It is the second most abundant element (after oxygen) in the Earth's crust and occurs in amorphous and crystalline forms. In nature it is found only in combination with other elements, chiefly with oxygen in silica (silicon dioxide, SiO_2) and the silicates. These form the mineral *quartz, which makes up most sands, gravels, and beaches.

silicon chip *integrated circuit with microscopically small electrical components on a piece of silicon crystal only a few millimetres square.

Silicon Valley nickname given to Santa Clara County, California, since the 1950s the site of many high-technology electronic firms, whose prosperity is based on the silicon chip.

silicosis chronic disease of miners and stone cutters who inhale *silica dust, which makes the lung tissues fibrous and less capable of aerating the blood. It is a form of *pneumoconiosis.

silk fine soft thread produced by the larva of the *silkworm moth when making its cocoon. It is soaked, carefully unwrapped, and used in the manufacture of textiles. The introduction of synthetics originally harmed the silk industry, but rising standards of living have produced an increased demand for real silk. It is manufactured in China, India, Japan, and Thailand.

silk in UK law, a *Queen's Counsel, a senior barrister entitled to wear a silk gown in court.

Silk Road ancient and medieval overland route of about 6,400 km/4,000 mi by which silk was brought from China to Europe in return for trade goods; it ran west via the Gobi Desert, Samarkand, and Antioch to Mediterranean ports in Greece, Italy, the Middle East, and Egypt.

silk-screen printing or **serigraphy** method of *printing based on stencils. It can be used to print on most surfaces, including paper, plastic, cloth, and wood. An impermeable stencil (either paper or photographic) is attached to a finely meshed silk screen that has been stretched on a wooden frame, so that the ink passes through to the area beneath only where the image is required. The design can also be painted directly on the screen with varnish. A series of screens can be used to add successive layers of colour to the design.

silkworm usually the larva of the **common silkworm moth** Bombyx mori. After hatching from the egg and maturing on the leaves of white mulberry trees (or a synthetic substitute), it spins a protective cocoon of fine silk thread 275 m/ 900 ft long. To keep the thread intact, the moth is killed before emerging from the cocoon, and several threads are combined to form the commercial silk thread woven into textiles.

Silurian period of geological time 439–409 million years ago, the third period of the Palaeozoic era. Silurian sediments are mostly marine and consist of shales and limestone. Luxuriant reefs were built by coral-like organisms. The first land plants began to evolve during this period, and there were many ostracoderms (armoured jawless fishes). The first jawed fishes (called acanthodians) also appeared.

silver white, lustrous, extremely malleable and ductile, metallic element, symbol Ag (from Latin *argentum*), atomic number 47, relative atomic mass 107.868. It occurs in nature in ores and as a free metal; the chief ores are sulphides, from which the metal is extracted by smelting with lead. It is one of the best metallic conductors of both heat and electricity; its most useful compounds are the chloride and bromide, which darken on exposure to light and are the basis of photographic emulsions.

silverfish wingless insect, a type of *bristletail.

silverpoint drawing material consisting of silver wire encased in a holder, used on paper prepared with opaque white. Lead, copper, and gold metalpoints were also used, but silver was most popular in the 15th and 16th centuries. Its limited application and the impossibility of erasure caused it to be superseded by the graphite pencil in the 18th century. A fine example of silverpoint is Dürer's Self-portrait 1484 (Albertina, Vienna).

sima in geochemistry and geophysics, the substance of the Earth's oceanic *crust, as distinct from the *sial of the continental crust. The name, now used rarely, is derived from **si**lica and **ma**gnesia, its two main chemical constituents.

Simenon Georges 1903–1989. Belgian crime writer. Initially a pulp fiction writer, in 1931 he created Inspector Maigret of the Paris Sûreté who appeared in a series of detective novels.

simile *figure of speech that in English uses the conjunctions *like* and *as* to express comparisons ('run like the devil'; 'as deaf as a post'). It is sometimes confused with *metaphor.

Simon (Marvin) Neil 1927– . US dramatist and screenwriter. His stage plays (which were made into films) include the wryly comic Barefoot in the Park 1963 (filmed 1967), The Odd Couple 1965 (filmed 1968), and The Sunshine Boys 1972 (filmed 1975), and the more serious, autobiographical trilogy Brighton Beach Memoirs 1983 (filmed 1986), Biloxi Blues 1985 (filmed 1988), and Broadway Bound 1986 (filmed 1991). He has also written screenplays and co-written musicals.

Simon Paul 1942– . US pop singer and songwriter. In a folk-rock duo with Art Garfunkel (1942–), he had such hits as 'Mrs Robinson' 1968 and 'Bridge Over Troubled Water' 1970. Simon's solo work includes the critically acclaimed album Graceland 1986, for which he drew on Cajun and African music, and The Rhythm of the Saints 1990.

simony in the Christian church, the buying and selling of church preferments, now usually regarded as a sin.

Simplon (Italian **Sempione**) Alpine pass Switzerland–Italy. The road was built by Napoleon 1800–05, and the Simplon Tunnel 1906, 19.8 km/ 12.3 mi, is one of Europe's longest.

Simpson Wallis Warfield, Duchess of Windsor 1896–1986. US socialite, twice divorced. She married *Edward VIII 1937, who abdicated in order to marry her. He was given the title Duke of Windsor by his brother, George VI, who succeeded him.

simultaneous equations in mathematics, one of two or more algebraic equations that contain two or more unknown quantities that may have a unique solution. For example, in the case of two linear equations with two unknown variables, such as (i) $x + 3y = 6$ and (ii) $3y - 2x = 4$, the solution will be those unique values of x and y that are valid for both equations. Linear simultaneous equations can be solved by using algebraic manipulation to eliminate one of the variables, *coordinate geometry, or matrices (see *matrix).

sin transgression of the will of God or the gods, as revealed in the moral code laid down by a particular religion. In Roman Catholic theology, a distinction is made between **mortal sins**, which, if unforgiven, result in damnation, and **venial sins**, which are less serious. In Islam, the one unforgivable sin is **shirk**, denial that Allah is the only god.

Sinai Egyptian peninsula, at the head of the Red Sea; area 65,000 sq km/25,000 sq mi. Resources include oil, natural gas, manganese, and coal; irrigation water from the river Nile is carried under the Suez Canal.

Sinai, Battle of battle 6–24 Oct 1973 during the Yom Kippur War between Israel and Egypt. It was one of the longest tank battles in history. Israeli troops crossed the Suez canal 16 Oct, cutting off the Egyptian 3rd Army.

Sinan 1489–1588. Ottoman architect. He was chief architect to Suleiman the Magnificent from 1538. Among the hundreds of buildings he designed are the Suleimaniye mosque complex in Istanbul 1551–58 and the Selimiye mosque in Adrinople (now Edirne) 1569–74.

Sinatra Frank (Francis Albert) 1915– . US singer and film actor. Celebrated for his phrasing and emotion, especially on love ballads, he is particularly associated with the song 'My Way'. His films from 1941 include *From Here to Eternity* 1953 (Academy Award) and *Guys and Dolls* 1955.

Sinclair Clive 1940– . British electronics engineer who produced the first widely available pocket calculator, pocket and wristwatch televisions, a series of home computers, and the innovative but commercially disastrous 'C5' personal transport (a low cyclelike three-wheeled vehicle powered by a washing-machine motor).

Sinclair Upton 1878–1968. US novelist. His concern for social reforms is reflected in *The Jungle* 1906, an important example of naturalistic writing, which exposed the horrors of the Chicago meat-packing industry and led to a change in food-processing laws; *Boston* 1928; and his Lanny Budd series 1940–53, including *Dragon's Teeth* 1942, which won a Pulitzer prize.

Sindhi member of the majority ethnic group living in the Pakistani province of Sind. The Sindhi language is spoken by about 15 million people. Since the partition of India and Pakistan 1947, large numbers of Urdu-speaking refugees have moved into the region from India, especially into the capital, Karachi.

sine in trigonometry, a function of an angle in a right-angled triangle which is defined as the ratio of the length of the side opposite the angle to the length of the hypotenuse (the longest side).

sine rule in trigonometry, a rule that relates the sides and angles of a triangle, stating that the ratio of the length of each side and the sine of the angle opposite is constant (twice the radius of the circumscribing circle). If the sides of a triangle are a, b, and c, and the angles opposite are A, B, and C, respectively, then the sine rule may be expressed as $a/\sin A = b/\sin B = c/\sin C$.

Singapore Republic of
area 622 sq km/240 sq mi
capital Singapore City
towns Jurong, Changi
physical comprises Singapore Island, low and flat, and 57 small islands
head of state Ong Teng Cheong from 1993
head of government Goh Chok Tong from 1990
political system liberal democracy with strict limits on dissent
exports electronics, petroleum products, rubber, machinery, vehicles
currency Singapore dollar
population (1993) 2,800,000 (Chinese 75%, Malay 14%, Tamil 7%); growth rate 1.2% p.a.
languages Malay (national tongue), Chinese, Tamil, English (all official)
religions Buddhist, Taoist, Muslim, Hindu, Christian
GNP $13,098 per head (1992)

chronology
1819 Singapore leased to British East India Company.
1858 Placed under crown rule.
1942 Invaded and occupied by Japan.
1945 Japanese removed by British forces.
1959 Independence achieved from Britain; Lee Kuan Yew became prime minister.
1963 Joined new Federation of Malaysia.
1965 Left federation to become an independent republic.
1988 Ruling conservative party elected to all but one of available assembly seats; increasingly authoritarian rule.
1990 Lee Kuan Yew resigned as prime minister; replaced by Goh Chok Tong.
1991 People's Action Party (PAP) and Goh Chok Tong re-elected.
1992 Lee Kuan Yew surrendered PAP leadership to Goh Chok Tong.
1993 Ong Teng Cheong elected president.

Singer Isaac Bashevis 1904–1991. Polish-born US novelist and short-story writer. He lived in the USA from 1935. His works, written in Yiddish, often portray traditional Jewish life in Poland and the USA, and the loneliness of old age. They include *The Family Moskat* 1950 and *Gimpel the Fool and Other Stories* 1957. Nobel prize 1978.

Singer Isaac Merit 1811–1875. US inventor of domestic and industrial sewing machines. Within a few years of opening his first factory 1851, he became the world's largest manufacturer (despite charges of patent infringement by Elias *Howe), and by the late 1860s more than 100,000 Singer sewing machines were in use in the USA alone.

Singh, Gobind see *Gobind Singh, Sikh guru.

Single European Market single market for all 12 member countries of the European Union (formerly the European Community), which came into operation 1 January 1993. Established under the Single European Act 1987, the market created 'an area without internal frontiers in which the free movement of goods, persons, services, and capital is ensured'. The single market has had the effect of removing all customs barriers (although check points such as those in airports still remain) and is one more step towards the creation of a genuine economic, monetary, and according to its most ardent advocates, political community.

singularity in astrophysics, the point in *space–time at which the known laws of physics break down. Singularity is predicted to exist at the centre of a black hole, where infinite gravitational forces compress the infalling mass of a collapsing star to infinite density. It is also thought, according to the Big Bang model of the origin of the universe, to be the point from which the expansion of the universe began.

Sinhalese member of the majority ethnic group of Sri Lanka (70% of the population). The Sinhalese are Buddhists. Since 1971 they have been involved in a violent struggle with the Tamil minority, who are seeking independence.

Sinn Féin Irish nationalist party founded by Arthur Griffith (1872–1922) in 1905; in 1917 Eamon *de Valera became its president. It is the political wing of the Irish Republican Army, and is similarly split between comparative moderates and extremists. In 1985 it gained representation in 17 out of 26 district councils in Northern Ireland. Its president from 1978 is Gerry *Adams. In 1994, following a ceasefire declaration by the IRA, Sinn Fein was poised to enter the political peace process.

Sino-Japanese Wars two wars waged by Japan against China 1894–95 and 1931–45 to expand to the mainland. Territory gained in the First Sino-Japanese War (Korea) and in the 1930s (Manchuria, Shanghai) was returned at the end of World War II.

Sino-Tibetan languages group of languages spoken in SE Asia. This group covers a large area, and includes Chinese and Burmese, both of which have numerous dialects. Some classifications include the Tai group of languages (including Thai and Lao) in the Sino-Tibetan family.

Sinuiju capital of North Pyongan province, near the mouth of the Yalu River, North Korea; population (1984) 754,000. It was founded 1910.

sinusitis painful inflammation of one of the sinuses, or air spaces, that surround the nasal passages. Most cases clear with antibiotics and nasal decongestants, but some require surgical drainage.

Sioux (or **Dakota**) a member of a group of North American *Plains Indians, now living on reservations in South Dakota and Nebraska, and among the general public. Their language belongs to the Macro-Siouan family.

siphon tube in the form of an inverted U with unequal arms. When it is filled with liquid and the shorter arm is placed in a tank or reservoir, liquid flows out of the longer arm provided that its exit is below the level of the surface of the liquid in the tank.

siren in Greek mythology, a sea nymph who lured sailors to their deaths along rocky coasts by her singing. *Odysseus, in order to hear the sirens safely, tied himself to the mast of his ship and stuffed his crew's ears with wax.

Sirius or **Dog Star** or **Alpha Canis Majoris** the brightest star in the sky, 8.6 light years from Earth in the constellation Canis Major. Sirius is a white star with a mass 2.3 times that of the Sun, a diameter 1.8 times that of the Sun, and a luminosity of 23 Suns. It is orbited every 50 years by a white dwarf, Sirius B, also known as the Pup.

sirocco hot, normally dry and dust-laden wind that blows from the deserts of N Africa across the Mediterranean into S Europe. It occurs mainly in the spring. The name 'sirocco' is also applied to any hot oppressive wind.

sisal strong fibre made from various species of *agave, such as *Agave sisalina*.

siskin greenish-yellow bird *Carduelis spinus* in the finch family Fringillidae, about 12 cm/5 in long, found in Eurasia.

Sistine Chapel chapel in the Vatican, Rome, begun under Pope Sixtus IV in 1473 by Giovanni del Dolci, and decorated by (among others) Michelangelo. It houses the conclave that meets to select a new pope.

Sisulu Walter 1912– . South African civil-rights activist, one of the first full-time secretary generals of the African National Congress (ANC), in 1964, with Nelson Mandela. He was imprisoned following the 1964 Rivonia Trial for opposition to the apartheid system and released, at the age of 77, as a gesture of reform by President F W *de Klerk 1989. In 1991, when Mandela became ANC president, Sisulu became his deputy.

Sisyphus in Greek mythology, king of Corinth who, after his evil life, was condemned in the underworld to roll a huge stone uphill, which always fell back before he could reach the top.

Sita in Hinduism, the wife of Rama, an avatar (manifestation) of the god Vishnu; a character in the *Rāmāyana* epic, characterized by chastity and kindness.

sitar Indian stringed instrument. It has a pear-shaped body, long neck, and an additional gourd resonator at the opposite end. A principal solo instrument, it has seven metal strings extending over movable frets and two concealed strings that provide a continuous singing drone.

site of special scientific interest (SSSI) in the UK, land that has been identified as having animals, plants, or geological features that need to be protected and conserved. From 1991 these sites were designated and administered by English Nature, Scottish Natural Heritage, and the Countryside Council for Wales.

Sitting Bull c. 1834–1893. North American Indian chief who agreed to *Sioux resettlement 1868. When the treaty was broken by the USA, he led the Sioux against Lieutenant Colonel *Custer at the Battle of the *Little Bighorn 1876.

situationism in ethics, the doctrine that any action may be good or bad depending on its context or situation. Situationists argue that no moral rule can apply in all situations and that what may be wrong in most cases may be right if the end is sufficiently good. In general, situationists believe moral attitudes are more important than moral rules.

SI units (French *Système International d'Unités*) standard system of scientific units used by scientists worldwide. Originally proposed in 1960, it replaces the *m.k.s., *c.g.s., and *f.p.s. systems. It is based on seven basic units: the metre (m) for length, kilogram (kg) for weight, second (s) for time, ampere (A) for electrical current, kelvin (K) for temperature, mole (mol) for amount of substance, and candela (cd) for luminosity.

Siva or **Shiva** in Hinduism, the third chief god (with Brahma and Vishnu). As Mahadeva (great lord), he is the creator, symbolized by the phallic *lingam*, who restores what as Mahakala he destroys. He is often sculpted as Nataraja, performing his fruitful cosmic dance. His consort or female principle (*sakti*) is Parvati, otherwise known as Durga or Kali.

Six, the the original six signatory countries to the Treaty of Rome, which created the *European Community.

Six Acts in British history, acts of Parliament passed 1819 by Lord Liverpool's Tory administration to curtail political radicalism in the aftermath of the *Peterloo massacre and during a period of agitation for reform when *habeas corpus was suspended and the powers of magistrates extended.

Six Articles act introduced by Henry VIII in England in 1539 to settle disputes over dogma in the English church.

Six Counties the six counties that form Northern Ireland: Antrim, Armagh, Down, Fermanagh, Londonderry, and Tyrone.

Six-Day War another name for the third *Arab-Israeli War.

Six, Les group of French 20th-century composers; see *Les Six.

sixth form in UK education, an inclusive term used for pupils who study for one or two years beyond school-leaving age in order to gain *A level or other post-16 qualifications.

ska or **bluebeat** Jamaican pop music, a precursor of reggae, mingling the local calypso, *mento*, with rhythm and blues. Ska emerged in the early 1960s (a slower style, **rock steady**, evolved 1966–68) and enjoyed a revival in the UK in the late 1970s. Prince Buster (1938–) was an influential ska singer. In the late 1980s, the term *skacid* was coined for a speeded-up ska with rap and electronic effects.

Skara Brae preserved Neolithic village on Mainland in the Orkney Islands, Scotland.

skate any of several species of flatfish of the ray group. The common skate *Raja batis* is up to 1.8 m/6 ft long and greyish, with black specks. Its egg cases ('mermaids' purses') are often washed ashore by the tide.

skateboard single flexible board mounted on wheels and steerable by weight positioning. As a land alternative to surfing, skateboards developed in California in the 1960s and became a worldwide craze in the 1970s. Skateboarding is practised in urban environments and has enjoyed a revival since the late 1980s.

skating self-propulsion on ice by means of bladed skates, or on other surfaces by skates with small rollers (wheels of wood, metal, or plastic). The chief competitive ice-skating events are figure skating, for singles or pairs, ice-dancing, and simple speed skating. The first world ice-skating championships were held in 1896.

skeleton the rigid or semirigid framework that supports an animal's body, protects its internal organs, and provides anchorage points for its muscles. The skeleton may be composed of bone and cartilage (vertebrates), chitin (arthropods) calcium carbonate (molluscs and other invertebrates), or silica (many protists).

skiffle British popular music style, introduced by singer and banjo player Lonnie Donegan (1931–) in 1956, using improvised percussion instruments such as tea chests and washboards.

skiing self-propulsion on snow by means of elongated runners (skis) for the feet, slightly bent upward at the tip. It is a popular recreational sport, as cross-country ski touring or as downhill runs on mountain trails; events include downhill; slalom, in which a series of turns between flags have to be negotiated; cross-country racing and ski jumping, when jumps of over 150 m/490 ft are achieved from ramps up to 90 m/295 ft high. Speed-skiing uses skis approximately one third longer and wider than normal with which speeds of up to 200 kph/125 mph have been recorded. Recently **monoboarding** or the use of a single, very broad ski, similar to a surf board, used with the feet facing the front and placed together, has become popular.

skin the covering of the body of a vertebrate. In mammals, the outer layer (epidermis) is dead and protective, and its cells are constantly being rubbed away and replaced from below. The lower layer (dermis) contains blood vessels, nerves, hair roots, and sweat and sebaceous glands, and i supported by a network of fibrous and elastic cells.

skink lizard of the family Scincidae, a large family of about 700 species found throughout the tropics and subtropics. The body is usually long and the legs are reduced. Some skinks are legless and rather snakelike. Many are good burrowers, or can 'swim' through sand, like the **sandfish** genus *Scincus* of N Africa. Some skinks lay eggs, others bear live young.

Skinner B(urrhus) F(rederic) 1903–1990. US psychologist, a radical behaviourist who rejected mental concepts, seeing the organism as a 'black box' where internal processes are not significant in predicting behaviour. He studied operant conditioning and maintained that behaviour is shaped and maintained by its consequences.

skittles or **ninepins** game in which nine wooden pins, arranged in a diamond-shape frame at the end of an alley, are knocked down in two rolls from the other end of the alley with a wooden ball. Two or more players can compete. Skittles resembles *tenpin bowling.

Skopje capital and industrial city of Macedonia, Yugoslavia; population (1981) 506,547. Industries include iron, steel, chromium mining, and food processing.

Skryabin or **Scriabin** Alexander (Nikolayevich) 1872–1915. Russian composer and pianist. His powerfully emotional tone poems such as *Prometheus* 1911, and symphonies such as *Divine Poem* 1903, employed unusual scales and harmonies.

skua dark-coloured gull-like seabird living in Arctic and Antarctic waters. Skuas can grow up to 60 cm/2 ft long and are good fliers. They are aggressive scavengers, and seldom fish for them selves but force gulls to disgorge their catch, and also eat chicks of other birds.

skull in vertebrates, the collection of flat and irregularly shaped bones (or cartilage) that enclose the brain and the organs of sight, hearing, and smell, and provide support for the jaws. In mammals, the skull consists of 22 bones joined by sutures. The floor of the skull is pierced by a large hole for the spinal cord and a number of smaller apertures through which other nerves and blood vessels pass.

skunk North American mammal of the weasel family. The common skunk *Mephitis mephitis* has a long, arched body, short legs, a bushy tail, and black fur with white streaks on the back. In self-defence, it discharges a foul-smelling fluid.

skydiving sport of freefalling from an aircraft at a height of up to 3,650 m/12,000 ft, performing aerobatics, and opening a parachute when 600 m/2,000 ft from the ground.

Skye largest island of the Inner Hebrides, Scotland; area 1,740 sq km/672 sq mi; population (1987) 8,100. It is separated from the mainland by the Sound of Sleat. The chief port is Portree. The economy is based on crofting, tourism, and livestock.

Skylab US space station, launched 14 May 1973, made from the adapted upper stage of a Saturn V rocket. At 75 tonnes/82.5 tons, it was the heaviest object ever put into space, and was 25.6 m/84 ft long. *Skylab* contained a workshop for carrying out experiments in weightlessness, an observatory for monitoring the Sun, and cameras for photographing the Earth's surface.

skylark a type of *lark.

skyscraper building so tall that it appears to 'scrape the sky', developed 1868 in New York, USA, where land prices were high and the geology allowed such methods of construction. Skyscrapers are now found in cities throughout the world. The world's tallest free-standing structure is the CN (Canadian National) Tower, Toronto, 555 m/1,821 ft.

slag in chemistry, the molten mass of impurities that is produced in the smelting or refining of metals.

slaked lime Ca(OH)$_2$ (technical name **calcium hydroxide**) substance produced by adding water to quicklime (calcium oxide, CaO). Much heat is given out and the solid crumbles as it absorbs water. A solution of slaked lime is called limewater.

slander spoken defamatory statement; if written, or broadcast on radio or television, it constitutes *libel.

slang extremely informal language usage that often serves to promote a feeling of group membership. It is not usually accepted in formal speech or writing and includes expressions that may be impolite or taboo in conventional terms.

slash and burn simple agricultural method whereby natural vegetation is cut and burned, and the clearing then farmed for a few years until the soil loses its fertility, whereupon farmers move on and leave the area to regrow. Although this is possible with a small, widely dispersed population, it becomes unsustainable with more people and is now a form of *deforestation.

slate fine-grained, usually grey metamorphic rock that splits readily into thin slabs along its *cleavage plane. It is the metamorphic equivalent of *shale.

Slav member of an Indo-European people in central and E Europe, the Balkans, and parts of N Asia, speaking closely related *Slavonic languages. The ancestors of the Slavs are believed to have included the Sarmatians and Scythians. Moving west from Central Asia, they settled in E and SE Europe during the 2nd and 3rd millennia BC.

slavery the enforced servitude of one person (a slave) to another or one group to another. A slave has no personal rights and is the property of another person through birth, purchase, or capture. Slavery goes back to prehistoric times but declined in Europe after the fall of the Roman Empire. During the imperialism of Spain, Portugal, and Britain in the 16th–18th centuries and in the American South in the 17th–19th centuries, slavery became a mainstay of an agricultural factory economy, with millions of Africans sold to work on plantations in North and South America. Millions more died in the process, but the profits from this trade were enormous. Slavery was abolished in the British Empire 1833 and in the USA at the end of the Civil War 1863–65, but continues illegally in some countries.

Slavonia region of E Croatia bounded by the Sava, Drava, and Danube rivers; Osijek is the largest town. Slavonia was the scene of fierce fighting between Croatian forces and Serb-dominated Yugoslav federal troops 1991–92. Following Croatia's declaration of independence from Yugoslavia 1991, Eastern and Western Slavonia declared themselves autonomous provinces of Serbia. The region experienced intense fighting during the 1991–92 civil war in Croatia and after the cease-fire 1992, 10,000 UN troops were deployed in E and W Slavonia and contested Krajina.

Slavonic languages or **Slavic languages** branch of the Indo-European language family spoken in central and E Europe, the Balkans, and parts of N Asia. The family comprises the **southern group** (Slovene, Serbo-Croatian, Macedonian, and Bulgarian); the **western group** (Czech and Slovak, Sorbian in Germany, and Polish and its related dialects); and the **eastern group** (Russian, Ukrainian, and Belarusian).

Slavophile intellectual and political group in 19th-century Russia that promoted the idea of an Eastern orientation for the empire in opposition to those who wanted the country to adopt Western methods and ideas of development.

sleep state of reduced awareness and activity that occurs at regular intervals in most mammals and birds, though there is considerable variation in the amount of time spent sleeping. Sleep differs from hibernation in that it occurs daily rather than seasonally, and involves less drastic reductions in metabolism. The function of sleep is unclear. People deprived of sleep become irritable, uncoordinated, forgetful, hallucinatory, and even psychotic.

Sleep Wayne 1948– . British dancer who was a principal dancer with the Royal Ballet 1973–83. He formed his own company, Dash, in 1980, and in 1983 adapted his TV *Hot Shoe Show* for the stage, fusing classical, modern, jazz, tap, and disco.

sleeping pill any pill or capsule that contains a drug (especially one of the *barbiturates) that induces sleep; in small doses, such drugs may relieve anxiety.

sleeping sickness or *trypanosomiasis* infectious disease of tropical Africa. Early symptoms include fever, headache, and chills, followed by *anaemia and joint pains. Later, the disease attacks the central nervous system, causing drowsiness, lethargy, and, if left untreated, death. Sleeping sickness is caused by either of two trypanosomes, *Trypanosoma gambiense* or *T. rhodiense*. Control is by eradication of the tsetse fly, which transmits the disease to humans.

sleet precipitation consisting of a mixture of water and ice.

slide rule mathematical instrument with pairs of logarithmic sliding scales, used for rapid calculations, including multiplication, division, and the extraction of square roots. It has been largely superseded by the electronic calculator.

Sligo county in the province of Connacht, Republic of Ireland, situated on the Atlantic coast of NW Ireland; area 1,800 sq km/695 sq mi; population (1991) 54,700. The county town is Sligo; there is livestock and dairy farming.

Slim William Joseph, 1st Viscount 1891–1970. British field marshal in World War II. He commanded the 1st Burma Corps 1942–45, stemming the Japanese invasion of India, and then forcing them out of Burma (now Myanmar). He was governor general of Australia 1953–60.

slime mould or *myxomycete* extraordinary organism that shows some features of *fungus and some of *protozoa. Slime moulds are not closely related to any other group, although they are often classed, for convenience, with the fungi. There are two kinds, cellular slime moulds and plasmodial slime moulds, differing in their complex life cycles.

slip decoration traditional decoration for earthenware with designs trailed in a thin, smooth mixture of clay and water (slip) or incised through a coating of slip. It is usually finished with a transparent lead glaze.

Sloane Hans 1660–1753. British physician, born in County Down, Ireland. He settled in London, and in 1721 founded the Chelsea Physic Garden. He was president of the Royal College of Physicians 1719–35, and in 1727 succeeded the physicist Isaac Newton as president of the Royal Society. His library, which he bequeathed to the nation, formed the nucleus of the British Museum.

sloe fruit of the *blackthorn.

sloth South American mammal, about 70 cm/2.5 ft long, of the order Edentata. Sloths are greyish brown and have small rounded heads, rudimentary tails, and prolonged forelimbs. Each foot has long curved claws adapted to clinging upside down from trees. They are vegetarian.

Slovak Republic (*Slovenská Republika*)
area 49,035 sq km/18,940 sq mi
capital Bratislava
towns Košice, Nitra, Prešov, Banská Bystrica

physical W range of the Carpathian Mountain including Tatra and Beskids in N; Danube plai in S; numerous lakes and mineral springs
features fine beech and oak forests with bear and wild boar
head of state Michal Kovak from 1993
head of government Vladimir Meciar fror 1994
political system emergent democracy
exports iron ore, copper, mercury, magnesite armaments, chemicals, textiles, machinery
currency koruna (based on Czechoslova koruna)
population (1992) 5,300,900 (with Hungaria and other minorities); growth rate 0.4% p.a.
language Slovak (official)
religions Roman Catholic (over 50% Lutheran, Reformist, Orthodox
GNP $1,887 per head (1990)
chronology
906–1918 Under Magyar domination.
1918 Independence achieved from Austro-Hur garian Empire; Slovaks joined Czechs in formir Czechoslovakia as independent nation.
1948 Communists assumed power in Czech slovakia.
1968 Slovak Socialist Republic created unde new federal constitution.
1989 Prodemocracy demonstrations in Bratis lava; new political parties formed, includir Slovak-based People Against Violence (PAV Communist Party stripped of powers. Dec: ne government formed, including former dissident political parties legalized; Václav Have appointed president of Czechoslovakia.
1991 Evidence of increasing Slovak separatism March: PAV splinter group, the Movement fe a Democratic Slovakia (MFDS), formed und Slovak premier Vladimir Meciar, pledged t greater autonomy for Slovakia. April: Meciar di missed, replaced by Jan Carnogursky; pro-Meci rallies held in Bratislava.
1992 March: PAV renamed Civic Democrat Union (CDU). June: MFDS emerged as domina political grouping in assembly elections; Meciar resigned, following Slovak gains in assembl elections. Aug: agreement on creation of separat Czech and Slovak states.
1993 Jan: Slovak Republic became sovereig

state, with Meciar, leader of the MFDS, as prime minister. Feb: Michal Kovak became president. June: gained membership of United Nations and Council of Europe; formal invitation to apply for EC membership.
1994 Jan: joined NATO 'partnership for peace' programme. March: Meciar ousted on a vote of no-confidence; replaced by Jozcef Moravcik, heading a non-MFDS coalition government. Oct: Meciar returned to power.

Slovenia Republic of (*Slovenija*)

area 20,251 sq km/7,817 sq mi
capital Ljubljana
towns Maribor, Kranj, Celji; chief port: Koper
physical mountainous; Sava and Drava rivers
head of state Milan Kučan from 1990
head of government Janez Drnovšek from 1992
political system emergent democracy
products grain, sugarbeet, livestock, timber, cotton and woollen textiles, steel, vehicles
currency tolar
population (1993) 2,000,000 (Slovene 91%, Croat 3%, Serb 2%)
languages Slovene, resembling Serbo-Croat, written in Roman characters
religion Roman Catholic
GNP $7,150 per head (1991)
chronology
1918 United with Serbia and Croatia.
1929 The kingdom of Serbs, Croats, and Slovenes took the name of Yugoslavia.
1945 Became a constituent republic of Yugoslav Socialist Federal Republic.
mid-1980s The Slovenian Communist Party liberalized itself and agreed to free elections. Yugoslav counterintelligence (KOV) began repression.
1989 Jan: Social Democratic Alliance of Slovenia launched as first political organization independent of Communist Party. Sept: constitution changed to allow secession from federation.
1990 April: nationalist DEMOS coalition secured victory in first multiparty parliamentary elections; Milan Kučan became president. July: sovereignty declared. Dec: independence approved in referendum.
1991 June: independence declared; 100 killed after federal army intervened; cease-fire brokered by European Community (EC). July: cease-fire

agreed between federal troops and nationalists. Oct: withdrawal of Yugoslav National Army (JNA) completed.
1992 Jan: European Community recognized Slovenia's independence. April: Janez Drnovsek appointed prime minister designate; independence recognized by USA. May: admitted into United Nations and Conference on Security and Cooperation in Europe.

slow-worm harmless species of lizard *Anguis fragilis*, once common in Europe, now a protected species in Britain. Superficially resembling a snake, it is distinguished by its small mouth and movable eyelids. It is about 30 cm/1 ft long, and eats worms and slugs.

SLR abbreviation for *single-lens reflex*, a type of *camera in which the image can be seen through the lens before a picture is taken.

slug air-breathing gastropod related to the snails, but with absent or much reduced shell.

Sluis, Battle of (or *Sluys*) 1340 naval victory for England over France which marked the beginning of the Hundred Years' War. England took control of the English Channel and seized 200 great ships from the French navy of Philip IV; there were 30,000 French casualties.

slum area of poor-quality housing. Slums are typically found in parts of the *inner city in rich countries and in older parts of cities in poor countries. Slum housing is usually densely populated, in a bad state of repair, and has inadequate services (poor sanitation, for example).

slurry form of manure composed mainly of liquids. Slurry is collected and stored on many farms, especially when large numbers of animals are kept in factory units (see *factory farming). When slurry tanks are accidentally or deliberately breached, large amounts can spill into rivers, killing fish and causing *eutrophication.

Sluter Claus *c.* 1380–1406. N European Gothic sculptor, probably of Dutch origin, active in Dijon, France. His work includes the *Well of Moses c.* 1395–1403 (now in the grounds of a hospital in Dijon) and the kneeling mourners, or *gisants*, for the tomb of his patron Philip the Bold, Duke of Burgundy (Dijon Museum and Cleveland Museum, Ohio).

smack slang term for *heroin, an addictive depressant drug.

small arms one of the two main divisions of firearms: guns that can be carried by hand. The first small arms were portable handguns in use in the late 14th century, supported on the ground and ignited by hand. Today's small arms range from breech-loading single-shot rifles and shotguns to sophisticated automatic and semiautomatic weapons. In 1980, there were 11,522 deaths in the USA caused by hand-held guns; in the UK, there were 8. From 1988 guns accounted for more deaths among teenage US males than all other causes put together.

small claims court in the USA, a court that deals with small civil claims, using a simple procedure, often without attorney intervention.

smallpox acute, highly contagious viral disease, marked by aches, fever, vomiting, and skin eruptions leaving pitted scars. Widespread vaccination programmes have almost eradicated this often fatal disease.

smart card plastic card with an embedded microprocessor and memory. It can store, for example, personal data, identification, and bank-account details, to enable it to be used as a credit or debit card. The card can be loaded with credits, which are then spent electronically, and reloaded as needed. Possible other uses range from hotel door 'keys' to passports.

smart drug any drug containing nutrients said to enhance the functioning of the brain, increase mental energy, lengthen the span of attention, and improve the memory; also described as a brain tonic. Smart drugs, developed in the USA, have been successfully used on Alzheimer's disease sufferers. As yet there is no scientific evidence to suggest that these drugs have any significant effect on healthy people. Smart drugs have not been approved by the British Department of Health and are not officially available in the UK.

smart weapon programmable bomb or missile that can be guided to its target by laser technology, TV homing technology, or terrain-contour matching (TERCOM). A smart weapon relies on its pinpoint accuracy to destroy a target rather than on the size of its warhead.

Smeaton John 1724–1792. British engineer, recognized as England's first civil engineer. He rebuilt the Eddystone lighthouse in the English Channel 1759, founded the Society of Engineers 1771, and rediscovered high-quality cement, unknown since Roman times.

smell sense that responds to chemical molecules in the air. It works by having receptors for particular chemical groups, into which the airborne chemicals must fit to trigger a message to the brain.

smelling salts or *sal volatile* a mixture of ammonium carbonate, bicarbonate, and carbamate together with other strong-smelling substances, formerly used as a restorative for dizziness or fainting.

smelt small fish, usually marine, although some species are freshwater. They occur in Europe and North America. The most common European smelt is the sparling *Osmerus eperlanus*.

smelting processing a metallic ore in a furnace to produce the metal. Oxide ores such as iron ore are smelted with coke (carbon), which reduces the ore into metal and also provides fuel for the process.

Smetana Bedřich 1824–1884. Czech composer whose music has a distinct national character, as in, for example, the operas *The Bartered Bride* 1866 and *Dalibor* 1868, and the symphonic suite *My Country* 1875–80. He conducted the National Theatre of Prague 1866–74.

Smiles Samuel 1812–1904. Scottish writer, author of the popular Victorian didactic work *Self Help* 1859.

Smirke Robert 1780–1867. English Classical architect, designer of the British Museum, London (1823–47).

Smith Adam 1723–1790. Scottish economist, often regarded as the founder of political economy. His *The Wealth of Nations* 1776 defined national wealth in terms of labour. The cause of wealth is explained by the division of labour – dividing a production process into several repetitive operations, each carried out by different workers. Smith advocated the free working of individual enterprise, and the necessity of 'free trade'.

Smith Bessie 1894–1937. US jazz and blues singer, born in Chattanooga, Tennessee. Known as the 'Empress of the Blues', she established herself in the 1920s after she was discovered by Columbia Records. She made over 150 recordings accompanied by such greats as Louis Armstrong and Benny Goodman.

Smith David 1906–1965. US sculptor and painter, whose work made a lasting impact on sculpture after World War II. He trained as a steel welder in a car factory. His pieces are large open-work metal abstracts.

Smith Ian (Douglas) 1919– . Rhodesian politician. He was a founder of the Rhodesian Front 1962 and prime minister 1964–79. In 1965 he made a unilateral declaration of Rhodesia's independence and, despite United Nations sanctions, maintained his regime with tenacity. In 1979 he was succeeded as prime minister by Bishop Abel Muzorewa, when the country was renamed Zimbabwe. He was suspended from the Zimbabwe parliament April 1987 and resigned in May as head of the white opposition party.

Smith John 1580–1631. English colonist. After an adventurous early life he took part in the colonization of Virginia, acting as president of the North American colony 1608–09. He explored New England in 1614, which he named, and published pamphlets on America and an autobiography. His trade with the Indians may have kept the colonists alive in the early years.

Smith John 1938–1994. British Labour politician, party leader 1992–94. He was Trade and Industry Secretary 1978–79 and from 1979 held various shadow cabinet posts, culminating in that of shadow chancellor 1987–92. As Leader of the Opposition, he won a reputation as a man of transparent honesty and a formidable parliamentarian. His sudden death from a heart attack shocked British politicians of all parties.

Smith Joseph 1805–1844. US founder of the *Mormon religious sect.

Smith Maggie (Margaret Natalie) 1934– . English actress, notable for her commanding presence. Her films include *The Prime of Miss Jean Brodie* 1969 (Academy Award), *California Suite* 1978, *A Private Function* 1984, and *A Room with a View* 1986.

Smith William 1769–1839. British geologist, the founder of stratigraphy. Working as a canal engineer, he observed while supervising excavations that different beds of rock could be identified by their fossils, and so established the basis of *stratigraphy. He also produced the first geological maps of England and Wales.

smog natural fog containing impurities (unburned carbon and sulphur dioxide) from domestic fires, industrial furnaces, certain power stations, and internal-combustion engines (petrol or diesel).

smokeless fuel fuel that does not give off any smoke when burned, because all the carbon is fully oxidized to carbon dioxide (CO_2). Natural gas, oil, and coke are smokeless fuels.

smoking inhaling the fumes from burning substances, generally *tobacco in the form of *cigarettes. The practice can be habit-forming and is dangerous to health, since carbon monoxide and other toxic materials result from the combustion process. A direct link between lung cancer and tobacco smoking was established 1950; the habit is also linked to respiratory and coronary heart diseases. In the West, smoking is now forbidden in many public places because even *passive smoking* – breathing in fumes from other people's cigarettes – can be harmful.

Smollett Tobias George 1721–1771. Scottish novelist who wrote the picaresque novels *Roderick Random* 1748, *Peregrine Pickle* 1751, *Ferdinand Count Fathom* 1753, *Sir Launcelot Greaves* 1760–62, and *Humphrey Clinker* 1771.

smuggling the illegal import or export of prohibited goods or the evasion of customs duties on dutiable goods. Smuggling has a long tradition in most border and coastal regions; goods smuggled include tobacco, spirits, diamonds, gold, and illegal drugs.

Smuts Jan Christian 1870–1950. South African politician and soldier; prime minister 1919–24 and 1939–48. He supported the Allies in both world wars and was a member of the British imperial war cabinet 1917–18.

Smythson Robert 1535–1614. English architect who built Elizabethan country houses, including Longleat 1568–75, Wollaton Hall 1580–88, and Hardwick Hall 1590–97. Their castlelike silhouettes, symmetry, and large gridded windows are a uniquely romantic, English version of Classicism.

snail air-breathing gastropod mollusc with a spiral shell. There are thousands of species, on land and in water. The typical snails of the genus *Helix* have two species in Europe. The common garden snail *H. aspersa* is very destructive to plants.

snake reptile of the suborder Serpentes of the order Squamata, which also includes lizards. Snakes are characterized by an elongated limbless body, possibly evolved because of subterranean ancestors. One of the striking internal modifications is the absence or greatly reduced size of the left lung. The skin is covered in scales, which are markedly wider underneath where they form. There are 3,000 species found in the tropical and temperate zones, but none in New Zealand, Ireland, Iceland, and near the poles. Only three species are found in Britain: the adder, smooth snake, and grass snake.

snapdragon perennial herbaceous plant of the genus *Antirrhinum*, family Scrophulariaceae, with spikes of brightly coloured two-lipped flowers.

Snell Willebrord 1581–1626. Dutch mathematician and physicist who devised the basic law of refraction, known as *Snell's law*, in 1621. This states that the ratio between the sine of the angle of incidence and the sine of the angle of refraction is constant.

snellen unit expressing the visual power of the eye.

snipe European marsh bird of the family Scolopacidae, order Charadriiformes; species include common snipe *Gallinago gallinago* and the rare great snipe *G. media*, of which the males hold spring gatherings to show their prowess. It is closely related to the *woodcock.

snooker indoor game derived from *billiards (via *pool). It is played with 22 balls: 15 red, one each of yellow, green, brown, blue, pink, and black, and one white cueball. Red balls are worth one point when sunk, while the coloured balls have ascending values from two points for the yellow to seven points for the black. The world professional championship was first held in 1927. The world amateur championship was first held 1963.

snoring loud noise during sleep made by vibration of the soft palate (the rear part of the roof of the mouth), caused by streams of air entering the nose and mouth at the same time. It is most common when the nose is partially blocked.

snow precipitation in the form of soft, white, crystalline flakes caused by the condensation in air of excess water vapour below freezing point. Light reflecting in the crystals, which have a basic hexagonal (six-sided) geometry, gives snow its white appearance.

Snow C(harles) P(ercy), Baron Snow 1905–1980. English novelist and physicist. He held government scientific posts in World War II and 1964–66. His sequence of novels *Strangers and Brothers* 1940–64 portrayed English life from 1920 onwards. His *Two Cultures* (Cambridge Rede lecture 1959) discussed the absence of communication between literary and scientific intellectuals in the West, and added the phrase 'the two cultures' to the language.

Snowdon (Welsh *Yr Wyddfa*) highest mountain in Wales, 1,085 m/3,560 ft above sea level. It consists of a cluster of five peaks. At the foot of Snowdon are the Llanberis, Aberglaslyn, and Rhyd-ddu passes. A rack railway ascends to the summit from Llanberis. *Snowdonia*, the surrounding mountain range, was made a national park 1951. It covers 2,188 sq km/845 sq mi of mountain, lakes, and forest land.

snowdrop bulbous plant *Galanthus nivalis*, family Amaryllidaceae, native to Europe, with white, bell-shaped flowers, tinged with green, in early spring.

snow leopard a type of *leopard.

snuff finely powdered *tobacco for sniffing up the nostrils (or sometimes chewed or rubbed on the gums) as a stimulant or sedative. Snuff taking was common in 17th-century England and the Netherlands, and spread in the 18th century to other parts of Europe, but was largely superseded by cigarette smoking.

Soane John 1753–1837. English architect. His refined Neo-Classical designs anticipated contemporary taste. He designed his own house in Lincoln's Inn Fields, London, 1812–13, now the *Soane Museum*. Little remains of his extensive work at the Bank of England, London.

soap mixture of the sodium salts of various *fatty acids: palmitic, stearic, and oleic acid. It is made by the action of sodium hydroxide (caustic soda) or potassium hydroxide (caustic potash) on fats of animal or vegetable origin. Soap makes grease and dirt disperse in water in a similar manner to a *detergent.

soap opera television or radio serial melodrama. It originated in the USA as a series of daytime programmes sponsored by soap-powder and detergent manufacturers.

soapstone compact, massive form of impure *talc.

Soares Mario 1924– . Portuguese socialist politician, president from 1986. Exiled 1970, he returned to Portugal 1974, and, as leader of the Portuguese Socialist Party, was prime minister 1976–78. He resigned as party leader 1980, but in 1986 he was elected Portugal's first socialist president.

Sobchak Anatoly 1937– . Soviet centrist politician, mayor of St Petersburg from 1990, cofounder of the Democratic Reform Movement (with former foreign minister *Shevardnadze), and member of the Soviet parliament 1989–91. He prominently resisted the abortive anti-Gorbachev coup of Aug 1991.

Sobers Gary (Garfield St Aubrun) 1936– . West Indian test cricketer. One of the game's great all-rounders, he scored more than 8,000 test runs, took over 200 wickets, and held more than 100 catches. He also held the record for the highest test innings (365 not out) until Brian Lara (1974–) broke it 1994 by 10 runs.

Sobieski John. Alternative name for *John III, king of Poland.

soca Latin Caribbean dance music, a mixture of **so**ul and **ca**lypso but closer to the latter. A soca band is likely to include conga drums, synthesizer, and a small horn section, as well as electric guitar, bass, and drums. Soca originated on Trinidad in the 1970s.

Social and Liberal Democrats official name for the British political party formed 1988 from the former Liberal Party and most of the Social Democratic Party. The common name for the party is the *Liberal Democrats*.

social behaviour in zoology, behaviour concerned with altering the behaviour of other individuals of the same species. Social behaviour allows animals to live harmoniously in groups by establishing hierarchies of dominance to discourage disabling fighting. It may be aggressive or submissive (for example, cowering and other signals of appeasement), or designed to establish bonds (such as social grooming or preening).

social contract the idea that government authority derives originally from an agreement between ruler and ruled in which the former agrees to provide order in return for obedience from the latter. It has been used to support both absolutism (*Hobbes) and democracy (*Locke, *Rousseau).

social costs and benefits in economics, the costs and benefits to society as a whole that result from economic decisions. These include private costs (the financial cost of production incurred by firms) and benefits (the profits made by firms and the value to people of consuming goods and services) and external costs and benefits (affecting those not directly involved in production or consumption); pollution is one of the external costs.

social democracy political ideology or belief in the gradual evolution of a democratic *socialism within existing political structures. The earliest was the German Sozialdemokratische Partei (SPD), today one of the two main German parties, created in 1875 from August Bebel's earlier German Social Democratic Workers' Party, founded 1869. Parties along the lines of the German model were founded in the last two decades of the 19th century in a number of countries, including Austria, Belgium, the Netherlands, Hungary, Poland, and Russia. The British Labour Party is in the social democratic tradition.

Social Democratic Federation (SDF) in British history, a socialist society, founded as the Democratic Federation in 1881 and renamed in 1884. It was led by H M Hyndman (1842–1921), a former conservative journalist and stockbroker who claimed Karl *Marx as his inspiration without obtaining recognition from his mentor. In 1911 it became the British Socialist Party.

Social Democratic Labour Party (SDLP) Northern Irish left-wing political party, formed in 1970. It aims ultimately at Irish unification, but distances itself from the violent tactics of the Irish Republican Army (IRA), adopting a constitutional, conciliatory role. The SDLP, led by John Hume (1937–), was responsible for setting up the New Ireland Forum in 1983.

Social Democratic Party (SDP) British centrist political party 1981–90, formed by members of Parliament who resigned from the Labour Party. The 1983 and 1987 general elections were fought in alliance with the Liberal Party as the *Liberal/SDP Alliance*. A merger of the two parties was voted for by the SDP 1987, and the new party became the *Social and Liberal Democrats, leaving a rump SDP that folded 1990.

social history branch of history that documents the living and working conditions of people rather than affairs of state. In recent years television programmes, books, and museums have helped to give social history a wide appeal.

socialism movement aiming to establish a classless society by substituting public for private ownership of the means of production, distribution, and exchange. The term has been used to describe positions as widely apart as anarchism and social democracy. Socialist ideas appeared in classical times; in early Christianity; among later Christian sects such as the *Anabaptists and *Diggers; and, in the 18th and early 19th centuries, were put forward as systematic political aims by Jean-Jacques Rousseau, Claude Saint-Simon, François Fourier, and Robert Owen, among others. See also Karl *Marx and Friedrich *Engels.

'socialism in one country' concept proposed by *Stalin in 1924. In contrast to *Trotsky's theory of the permanent revolution, Stalin suggested that the emphasis be changed away from promoting revolutions abroad to the idea of building socialism, economically and politically, in the USSR without help from other countries.

Socialist Realism artistic doctrine set up by the USSR during the 1930s setting out the optimistic, socialist terms in which society should be portrayed in works of art – in music and the visual arts as well as writing.

socialization process, beginning in childhood, by which a person becomes a member of a society, learning its norms, customs, laws, and ways of living. The main agents of socialization are the family, school, peer groups, work, religion, and the mass media. The main methods of socialization are direct instruction, rewards and punishment, imitation, experimentation, role play, and interaction.

Social Realism in painting, art that realistically depicts subjects of social concern, such as poverty and deprivation. The French artist Courbet provides a 19th-century example of the genre. Subsequently, in the USA, the Ashcan school and Ben Shahn are among those described as Social Realists.

social science the group of academic disciplines that investigate how and why people behave the way they do, as individuals and in groups. The term originated with the 19th-century French thinker Auguste *Comte. The academic social sciences are generally listed as sociology, economics, anthropology, political science, and psychology.

social security state provision of financial aid to alleviate poverty. The term 'social security' was first applied officially in the USA, in the Social Security Act 1935. In Britain it was first used officially 1944, and following the *Beveridge Report 1942 a series of acts was passed from 1945 to widen the scope of social security. Basic entitlements of those paying National Insurance contributions in Britain include an old-age pension, unemployment benefit, widow's pension, and payment during a period of sickness in one's working life. Other benefits include family credit, child benefit, and attendance allowance for those looking after sick or disabled people.

Society Islands (French *Archipel de la Société*) archipelago in *French Polynesia, divided into Windward Islands and Leeward Islands; area 1,685 sq km/650 sq mi; population (1983) 142,000. The administrative headquarters is Papeete on *Tahiti. The *Windward Islands* (French *Îles du Vent*) have an area of 1,200 sq km/460 sq mi and a population (1983) of 123,000. They comprise Tahiti, Moorea (area 132 sq km/51 sq mi; population 7,000), Maio (or Tubuai Manu; 9 sq km/3.5 sq mi; population 200), and the smaller Tetiaroa and Mehetia. The *Leeward Islands* (French *Îles sous le Vent*) have an area of 404 sq km/156 sq mi and a population of 19,000. They comprise the volcanic islands of Raiatea (including the main town of Uturoa), Huahine, Bora-Bora, Maupiti, Tahaa, and four small atolls. Claimed by France 1768, the group became a French protectorate 1843 and a colony 1880.

Socinianism 17th-century Christian belief that rejects such traditional doctrines as the Trinity and original sin, named after *Socinus*, the Latinized name of Lelio Francesco Maria Sozzini (1525–1562), Italian Protestant theologian. It is an early form of *Unitarianism.

sociobiology study of the biological basis of all social behaviour, including the application of population genetics to the evolution of behaviour. It builds on the concept of *inclusive fitness, contained in the notion of the 'selfish gene'. Contrary to some popular interpretations, it does not assume that all behaviour is genetically determined.

sociology systematic study of society, in particular of social order and social change, social conflict and social problems. It studies insti-tutions such as the family, law, and the church, as well as concepts such as norm, role, and culture. Sociology attempts to study people in their social environment according to certain underlying moral, philosophical, and political codes of behaviour.

Socrates c. 469–399 BC. Athenian philosopher. He wrote nothing but was immortalized in the dialogues of his pupil Plato. In his desire to combat the scepticism of the *sophists, Socrates asserted the possibility of genuine knowledge. In ethics, he put forward the view that the good person not knowingly does wrong. True knowledge emerges through dialogue and systematic questioning and an abandoning of uncritical claims to knowledge.

Socratic method method of teaching used by Socrates, in which he aimed to guide pupils to clear thinking on ethics and politics by asking questions and then exposing their inconsistencies in cross-examination. This method was effective against the *sophists.

soda lime powdery mixture of calcium hydroxide and sodium hydroxide or potassium hydroxide, used in medicine and as a drying agent.

Soddy Frederick 1877–1956. English physical chemist who pioneered research into atomic disintegration and coined the term *isotope. He was awarded a Nobel prize 1921 for investigating the origin and nature of isotopes.

sodium soft, waxlike, silver-white, metallic element, symbol Na (from Latin *natrium*), atomic number 11, relative atomic mass 22.898. It is one of the *alkali metals and has a very low density, being light enough to float on water. It is the sixth most abundant element (the fourth most abundant metal) in the Earth's crust. Sodium is highly reactive, oxidizing rapidly when exposed to air and reacting violently with water. Its most familiar compound is sodium chloride (common salt), which occurs naturally in the oceans and in salt deposits left by dried-up ancient seas.

sodium chloride or *common salt* or *table salt* NaCl white, crystalline compound found widely in nature. It is a a typical ionic solid with a high melting point (801°C/1,474°F); it is soluble in water, insoluble in organic solvents, and is a strong electrolyte when molten or in aqueous solution. Found in concentrated deposits, it is widely used in the food industry as a flavouring and preservative, and in the chemical industry in the manufacture of sodium, chlorine, and sodium carbonate.

sodium hydrogencarbonate chemical name for *bicarbonate of soda.

Sodom and Gomorrah two ancient cities in the Dead Sea area of the Middle East, recorded in the Old Testament (Genesis) as being destroyed by fire and brimstone for their wickedness.

sodomy another term for *buggery.

Sofia or *Sofiya* capital of Bulgaria since 1878; population (1990) 1,220,900. Industries include textiles, rubber, machinery, and electrical equipment. It lies at the foot of the Vitosha Mountains.

softball bat and ball game, a form of baseball played with similar equipment. The two main differences are the distances between the bases (18.29 m/60 ft) and that the ball is pitched underhand in softball. There are two forms of the game, **fast pitch** and **slow pitch**; in the latter the ball must be delivered to home plate in an arc that must be not less than 2.4 m/8 ft at its height. The fast-pitch world championship was instituted 1965 for women, 1966 for men; it is now contested every four years.

soft currency vulnerable currency that tends to fall in value on foreign-exchange markets because of political or economic uncertainty. Governments are unwilling to hold soft currencies in their foreign-exchange reserves, preferring strong or hard currencies, which are easily convertible.

software in computing, a collection of programs and procedures for making a computer perform a specific task, as opposed to *hardware, the physical components of a computer system. Software is created by programmers and is either distributed on a suitable medium, such as the *floppy disc, or built into the computer in the form of *firmware. Examples of software include *operating systems, *compilers, and application programs, such as payrolls. No computer can function without some form of software.

soft water water that contains very few dissolved metal ions such as calcium (Ca^{2+}) or magnesium (Mg^{2+}). It lathers easily with soap, and no *scale is formed inside kettles or boilers. It has been found that the incidence of heart disease is higher in soft-water areas.

softwood any coniferous tree, or the wood from it. In general this type of wood is softer and easier to work, but in some cases less durable, than wood from flowering (or angiosperm) trees.

soil loose covering of broken rocky material and decaying organic matter overlying the bedrock of the Earth's surface. Various types of soil develop under different conditions: deep soils form in warm wet climates and in valleys; shallow soils form in cool dry areas and on slopes. **Pedology**, the study of soil, is significant because of the relative importance of different soil types to agriculture.

soil creep gradual movement of soil down a slope. As each soil particle is dislodged by a raindrop it moves slightly further downhill. This eventually results in a mass downward movement of soil on the slope.

soil erosion the wearing away and redistribution of the Earth's soil layer. It is caused by the action of water, wind, and ice, and also by improper methods of *agriculture. If unchecked, soil erosion results in the formation of deserts (see *desertification). It has been estimated that 20% of the world's cultivated topsoil was lost between 1950 and 1990.

soil mechanics branch of engineering that studies the nature and properties of the soil. Soil is investigated during construction work to ensure that it has the mechanical properties necessary to support the foundations of dams, bridges, and roads.

sol *colloid of very small solid particles dispersed in a liquid that still retains the physical properties of a liquid.

solar energy energy derived from the Sun's

radiation. The amount of energy falling on just 1 sq km/0.3861 sq mi is about 4,000 megawatts, enough to heat and light a small town. In one second the Sun gives off 13 million times more energy than all the electricity used in the USA in one year. **Solar heaters** have industrial or domestic uses. They usually consist of a black (heat-absorbing) panel containing pipes through which air or water, heated by the Sun, is circulated, either by thermal *convection or by a pump. Solar energy may also be harnessed indirectly using **solar cells** (photovoltaic cells) made of panels of *semiconductor material (usually silicon), which generate electricity when illuminated by sunlight. Although it is difficult to generate a high output from solar energy compared to sources such as nuclear or fossil fuels, it is a major nonpolluting and renewable energy source used as far north as Scandinavia as well as in the SW USA and in Mediterranean countries.

solar pond natural or artificial 'pond', such as the Dead Sea, in which salt becomes more soluble in the Sun's heat. Water at the bottom becomes saltier and hotter, and is insulated by the less salty water layer at the top. Temperatures at the bottom reach about 100°C/212°F and can be used to generate electricity.

solar radiation radiation given off by the Sun, consisting mainly of visible light, *ultraviolet radiation, and *infrared radiation, although the whole spectrum of *electromagnetic waves is present, from radio waves to *X-rays. High-energy charged particles such as electrons are also emitted, especially from solar *flares. When these reach the Earth, they cause magnetic storms (disruptions of the Earth's magnetic field), which interfere with radio communications.

Solar System the Sun (a star) and all the bodies orbiting it: the nine planets (Mercury, Venus, Earth, Mars, Jupiter, Saturn, Uranus, Neptune, and Pluto), their moons, the asteroids, and the comets. It is thought to have formed from a cloud of gas and dust in space about 4.6 billion years ago. The Sun contains 99% of the mass of the Solar System. The edge of the Solar System is not clearly defined, marked only by the limit of the Sun's gravitational influence, which extends about 1.5 light years, almost halfway to the nearest star, Alpha Centauri, 4.3 light years away.

solar wind stream of atomic particles, mostly protons and electrons, from the Sun's corona, flowing outwards at speeds of between 300 kps/200 mps and 1,000 kps/600 mps.

solder any of various alloys used when melted for joining metals such as copper, its common alloys (brass and bronze), and tin-plated steel, as used for making food cans.

sole flatfish found in temperate and tropical waters. The **common sole** Solea solea, also called **Dover sole**, is found in the southern seas of NW Europe. Up to 50 cm/20 in long, it is a prized food fish, as is the **sand** or **French sole** Pegusa lascaris further south.

solenoid coil of wire, usually cylindrical, in which a magnetic field is created by passing an electric current through it (see *electromagnet). This field can be used to move an iron rod placed on its axis. Mechanical valves attached to the rod can be operated by switching the current on or off, so converting electrical energy into mechanical energy. Solenoids are used to relay energy from the battery of a car to the starter motor by means of the ignition switch.

sole trader or **sole proprietor** one person who runs a business, receiving all profits and responsible for all liabilities. Many small businesses are sole traders.

sol-fa short for **tonic sol-fa**, a method of teaching music, usually singing, systematized by John Curwen (1816–1880). The notes of a scale are named by syllables (doh, ray, me, fah, soh, lah, te, with the *key indicated) to simplify singing by sight.

Solferino, Battle of Napoleon III's victory over the Austrians 1859 at a village near Verona, N Italy, 8 km/5 mi S of Lake Garda.

solicitor in the UK, a member of one of the two branches of the English legal profession, the other being a *barrister. A solicitor is a lawyer who provides all-round legal services (making wills, winding up estates, conveyancing, divorce, and litigation). A solicitor cannot appear at High Court level, but must brief a barrister on behalf of his or her client. Solicitors may become circuit judges and recorders. In the USA the general term is lawyer or attorney.

Solicitor General in the UK, a law officer of the Crown, deputy to the *Attorney General, a political appointee with ministerial rank.

solid in physics, a state of matter that holds its own shape (as opposed to a liquid, which takes up the shape of its container, or a gas, which totally fills its container). According to *kinetic theory, the atoms or molecules in a solid are not free to move but merely vibrate about fixed positions, such as those in crystal lattices.

Solidarity (Polish *Solidarność*) national confederation of independent trade unions in Poland, formed under the leadership of Lech *Walesa Sept 1980. An illegal organization from 1981 to 1989, it was then elected to head the Polish government. Divisions soon emerged in the leadership. Solidarity had 2.8 million members in 1991.

solidification change of state of a substance from liquid or vapour to solid on cooling. It is the opposite of melting or sublimation.

solid-state circuit electronic circuit where all the components (resistors, capacitors, transistors, and diodes) and interconnections are made at the same time, and by the same processes, in or on one piece of single-crystal silicon. The small size of this construction accounts for its use in electronics for space vehicles and aircraft.

solipsism in philosophy, a view that maintains that the self is the only thing that can be known to exist. It is an extreme form of *scepticism. The solipsist sees himself or herself as the only individual in existence, assuming other people to be a reflection of his or her own consciousness.

soliton non-linear solitary wave that maintains its shape and velocity, and does not widen and disperse in the normal way. Such behaviour is characteristic of the waves of *energy that constitute the particles of atomic physics, and the mathematical equations that sum up the behaviour of solitons are being used to further research in nuclear fusion and superconductivity.

Solomon c. 974–c. 937 BC. In the Old Testament, third king of Israel, son of David by Bathsheba. During a peaceful reign, he was famed for his wisdom and his alliances with Egypt and Phoenicia. The much later biblical Proverbs, Ecclesiastes, and Song of Songs are attributed to him. He built the temple in Jerusalem with the aid of heavy taxation and forced labour, resulting in the revolt of N Israel.

Solomon Islands

area 27,600 sq km/10,656 sq mi
capital Honiara (on Guadalcanal)
towns Gizo, Yandina
physical comprises all but the northernmost islands (which belong to Papua New Guinea) of a Melanesian archipelago stretching nearly 1,500 km/900 mi. The largest is Guadalcanal (area 6,500 sq km/2,510 sq mi); others are Malaita, San Cristobal, New Georgia, Santa Isabel, Choiseul; mainly mountainous and forested
head of state Elizabeth II represented by governor general
head of government Francis Billy Hilly from 1993
political system constitutional monarchy
exports fish products, palm oil, copra, cocoa, timber
currency Solomon Island dollar
population (1993 est) 349,500 (Melanesian 95%, Polynesian 4%); growth rate 3.9% p.a.
languages English (official); there are some 120 Melanesian dialects
religions Anglican 34%, Roman Catholic 19%, South Sea Evangelical 17%
GNP $560 per head (1991)
chronology
1893 Solomon Islands placed under British protection.
1978 Independence achieved from Britain within the Commonwealth, with Peter Kenilorea as prime minister.
1981 Solomon Mamaloni replaced Kenilorea as prime minister.
1984 Kenilorea returned to power, heading a coalition government.
1986 Kenilorea resigned after allegations of corruption; replaced by his deputy, Ezekiel Alebua.
1988 Kenilorea elected deputy prime minister. Joined Vanuatu and Papua New Guinea to form the Spearhead Group, aiming to preserve Melanesian cultural traditions and secure independence for the French territory of New Caledonia.
1989 Solomon Mamaloni, now leader of the People's Action Party (PAP), elected prime minister.
1990 Mamaloni resigned as PAP party leader, but continued as head of a government of national unity.
1993 Francis Billy Hilly elected prime minister.

Solomon's seal any perennial plant of the genus *Polygonatum* of the lily family Liliaceae, native to Europe and found growing in moist, shady woodland areas. They have bell-like white or greenish-white flowers drooping from the leaf axils of arching stems, followed by blue or black berries.

Solon c. 638–558 BC. Athenian statesman. As one of the chief magistrates c. 594 BC, he carried out the cancellation of all debts from which land or liberty was the security and the revision of the constitution that laid the foundations of Athenian democracy.

solstice either of the days on which the Sun is farthest north or south of the celestial equator each year. The **summer solstice**, when the Sun is farthest north, occurs around June 21; the **winter solstice** around Dec 22.

Solti Georg 1912– . Hungarian-born British conductor. He was music director at the Royal Opera House, Covent Garden, London, 1961–71, and became director of the Chicago Symphony Orchestra 1969. He was also principal conductor of the London Philharmonic Orchestra 1979–83.

solubility in physics, a measure of the amount of solute (usually a solid or gas) that will dissolve in a given amount of solvent (usually a liquid) at a particular temperature. Solubility may be expressed as grams of solute per 100 grams of solvent or, for a gas, in parts per million (ppm) of solvent.

solute substance that is dissolved in another substance (see *solution).

solution two or more substances mixed to form a single, homogenous phase. One of the substances is the **solvent** and the others (**solutes**) are said to be dissolved in it.

solution in earth science, the dissolving in water of minerals within a rock. It may result in weathering (for example, when weakly acidic rainfall causes carbonation) and erosion (when flowing water passes over rocks).

Solvay process industrial process for the manufacture of sodium carbonate.

solvent substance, usually a liquid, that will dissolve another substance (see *solution). Although the commonest solvent is water, in popular use the term refers to low-boiling-point organic liquids, which are harmful if used in a confined space. They can give rise to respiratory problems, liver damage, and neurological complaints.

Solzhenitsyn Alexander (Isayevich) 1918– . Soviet novelist. He became a US citizen 1974. He was in prison and exile 1945–57 for anti-Stalinist comments. Much of his writing is semi-autobiographical and highly critical of the system, including *One Day in the Life of Ivan Denisovich* 1962, which deals with the labour camps under Stalin, and *The Gulag Archipelago* 1973, an exposé of the whole Soviet labour-camp network. This led to his expulsion from the USSR 1974. He was awarded a Nobel prize 1970.

soma intoxicating drink made from the fermented sap of the *Asclepias acida* plant, used in Indian religious ritual as a sacrifice to the gods. As *haoma*, its consumption also constituted the central rite in Zoroastrian ritual. Some have argued that the plant was in fact a hallucogenic mushroom.

Somalia Somali Democratic Republic (*Jamhuriyadda Dimugradiga Somaliya*)
area 637,700 sq km/246,220 sq mi
capital Mogadishu
towns Hargeisa, Kismayu, port Berbera
physical mainly flat, with hills in N
head of state and government Ali Mahdi Mohammed from 1991
political system transitional

exports livestock, skins, hides, bananas, fruit
currency Somali shilling
population (1993 est) 8,000,000 (including 350,000 refugees in Ethiopia and 50,000 in Djibouti); growth rate 3.1% p.a.
languages Somali, Arabic (both official) Italian, English
religion Sunni Muslim 99%
GNP $170 per head (1989)
chronology
1884–87 British protectorate of Somaliland established.
1889 Italian protectorate of Somalia established.
1960 Independence achieved from Italy and Britain.
1963 Border dispute with Kenya; diplomatic relations broken with Britain.
1968 Diplomatic relations with Britain restored.
1969 Army coup led by Maj-Gen Mohamed Siad Barre; constitution suspended, Supreme Revolutionary Council set up; name changed to Somali Democratic Republic.
1978 Defeated in eight-month war with Ethiopia. Armed insurrection began in north.
1979 New constitution for socialist one-party state adopted.
1982 Antigovernment Somali National Movement formed. Oppressive countermeasures by government.
1987 Barre re-elected president.
1989 Dissatisfaction with government and increased guerrilla activity in north.
1990 Civil war intensified. Constitutional reforms promised.
1991 Mogadishu captured by rebels; Barre fled. Ali Mahdi Mohammed named president; free elections promised. Secession of NE Somalia, as the Somaliland Republic, announced. Cease-fire signed, but later collapsed. Thousands of casualties as a result of heavy fighting in capital.
1992 Relief efforts to ward off impending famine severely hindered by unstable political situation; relief convoys hijacked by 'warlords'. Dec: UN peacekeeping troops, mainly US Marines, sent in to protect relief operations; dominant warlords agreed truce.
1993 March: leaders of armed factions agreed to federal system of government, based on 18 autonomous regions. May: UN took control of relief operations. June: US-led UN force destroyed headquarters of warlord General Muhammad Farah Aidid, after killing of Paki

tani peacekeeping troops. All-out search for Aidid launched. July-Sept: peacekeeping troops engaged in intermittent combat, with mounting UN and Somali casualties. Nov: search for Aidid halted.

1994 Clan-based fighting continued. March: Western peacekeeping troops withdrawn, including majority of US Marines.

Somaliland region of Somali-speaking peoples in E Africa including the former British Somaliland Protectorate (established 1887) and Italian Somaliland (made a colony 1927, conquered by Britain 1941 and administered by Britain until 1950) – which both became independent 1960 as the Somali Democratic Republic, the official name for *Somalia – and former French Somaliland, which was established 1892, became known as the Territory of the Afars and Issas 1967, and became independent as *Djibouti 1977.

Somerset county in SW England
area 3,460 sq km/1,336 sq mi
towns administrative headquarters Taunton; Wells, Bridgwater, Glastonbury, Yeovil
physical rivers Avon, Parret, and Exe; marshy coastline on the Bristol Channel; Mendip Hills (including Cheddar Gorge and Wookey Hole, a series of limestone caves where Stone Age flint implements and bones of extinct animals have been found); the Quantock Hills; Exmoor
products engineering, dairy products, cider
population (1991) 459,100
famous people Ernest Bevin, Henry Fielding, John Pym.

Somme, Battle of the Allied offensive in World War I July–Nov 1916 at Beaumont-Hamel-Chaulnes, on the river Somme in N France, during which severe losses were suffered by both sides. It was planned by the Marshal of France, Joseph Joffre, and UK commander in chief Douglas Haig; the Allies lost over 600,000 soldiers and advanced 32 km/20 mi. It was the first battle in which tanks were used. The German offensive around St Quentin March–April 1918 is sometimes called the Second Battle of the Somme.

Somoza García Anastasio 1896–1956. Nicaraguan soldier and politician, president 1937–47 and 1950–56. A protégé of the USA, who wanted a reliable ally to protect their interests in Central America, he was virtual dictator of Nicaragua from 1937 until his assassination in 1956. He exiled most of his political opponents and amassed a considerable fortune in land and businesses. Members of his family retained control of the country until 1979, when they were overthrown by popular forces.

sonar (acronym for ***sound navigation and ranging***) method of locating underwater objects by the reflection of ultrasonic waves. The time taken for an acoustic beam to travel to the object and back to the source enables the distance to be found since the velocity of sound in water is known. Sonar devices, or ***echo sounders***, were developed 1920.

sonata (Italian 'sounded') an essay in instrumental composition for a solo player or a small ensemble and consisting of a single movement or series of movements. The name signifies that the work is not beholden to a text or existing dance form, but is self-sufficient.

sonata form in music, rules determining the structure of a *sonata first movement, typically divided into exposition, development, and recapitulation sections. It introduced the new possibility of open and continuous development to an 18th-century music previously limited to closed dance routines. It provides the framework for first movements in general, including symphonies, concertos, and string quartets.

Sondheim Stephen (Joshua) 1930– . US composer and lyricist. He wrote the lyrics of Leonard Bernstein's *West Side Story* 1957 and composed witty and sophisticated musicals, including *A Little Night Music* 1973, *Pacific Overtures* 1976, *Sweeney Todd* 1979, *Into the Woods* 1987, and *Sunday in the Park with George* 1989.

son et lumière (French 'sound and light') outdoor night-time dramatization of the history of a notable building, monument, or town, using theatrical lighting effects, sound effects, music, and narration; it was invented by Paul Robert Houdin, curator of the Château de Chambord, France, and the first show was held here 1952.

song setting of words to music for one or more singers, with or without instrumental accompaniment. Song may be sacred, for example a psalm, motet, or cantata, or secular, for example a folk song or ballad. In verse song, the text changes in mood while the music remains the same; in *lied and other forms of art song, the music changes in response to the emotional development of the text.

Songhai Empire former kingdom of NW Africa, founded in the 8th century, which developed into a powerful Muslim empire under Sonni Ali (reigned 1464–92). It superseded the *Mali Empire and extended its territory, occupying an area that included parts of present-day Guinea, Burkina Faso, Senegal, Gambia, Mali, Mauritania, Niger, and Nigeria. In 1591 it was invaded and overthrown by Morocco.

sonic boom noise like a thunderclap that occurs when an aircraft passes through the *sound barrier, or begins to travel faster than the speed of sound. It happens when the cone-shaped shock wave caused by the plane touches the ground.

sonnet fourteen-line poem of Italian origin introduced to England by Thomas Wyatt in the form used by Petrarch (rhyming *abba abba cdcdcd* or *cdecde*) and followed by Milton and Wordsworth; Shakespear used the form *abab cdcd efef gg.*

sonoluminescence emission of light by a liquid that is subjected to high-frequency sound waves. The rapid changes of pressure induced by the sound cause minute bubbles to form in the liquid, which then collapse. Light is emitted at the final stage of the collapse, probably because it squeezes and heats gas inside the bubbles.

Sons of Liberty in American colonial history, the name adopted by those colonists opposing the *Stamp Act of 1765. Merchants, lawyers, farmers, artisans, and labourers joined what was an early instance of concerted resistance to British rule, causing the repeal of the act in March 1766.

Sony Japanese electronics hardware company

that produced the *Walkman, the first easily portable cassette player with headphones, 1980. It diversified into entertainment by the purchase of CBS Records 1988 and Columbia Pictures 1989.

Sophia Electress of Hanover 1630–1714. Twelfth child of Frederick V, elector palatine of the Rhine and king of Bohemia, and Elizabeth, daughter of James I of England. She married the elector of Hanover in 1658. Widowed in 1698, she was recognized in the succession to the English throne in 1701, and when Queen Anne died without issue in 1714, her son George I founded the Hanoverian dynasty.

sophist (Greek 'wise man') one of a group of 5th-century BC lecturers on culture, rhetoric, and politics. Sceptical about the possibility of achieving genuine knowledge, they applied bogus reasoning and were concerned with winning arguments rather than establishing the truth. *Plato regarded them as dishonest and **sophistry** came to mean fallacious reasoning.

Sophocles 495–406 BC. Greek dramatist who, with Aeschylus and Euripides, is one of the three great tragedians. He modified the form of tragedy by introducing a third actor and developing stage scenery. He wrote some 120 plays, of which seven tragedies survive. These are *Antigone* 441 BC, *Oedipus Tyrannus, Electra, Ajax, Trachiniae, Philoctetes* 409 BC, and *Oedipus at Colonus* 401 BC.

soprano in music, the highest range of the female voice about an octave higher than a contralto. Its range stretches from F above middle C to the C an octave and half above; however, some operatic roles require the extended upper range of a *coloratura* soprano such as Kiri *Te Kanawa.

Sopwith Thomas Octave Murdoch 1888–1989. English designer of the Sopwith Camel biplane, used in World War I, and joint developer of the Hawker Hurricane fighter plane used in World War II.

sorbic acid CH₃CH:CHCH:CHCOOH tasteless acid found in the fruit of the mountain ash (genus *Sorbus*) and prepared synthetically. It is widely used in the preservation of food – for example, cider, wine, soft drinks, animal feeds, bread, and cheese.

Sorbonne common name for the University of Paris, originally a theological institute founded 1253 by Robert de Sorbon, chaplain to Louis IX.

Sorel Georges 1847–1922. French philosopher who believed that socialism could only come about through a general strike; his theory of the need for a 'myth' to sway the body of the people was used by fascists.

Sørensen Søren 1868–1939. Danish chemist who in 1909 introduced the concept of using the *pH scale as a measure of the acidity of a solution. On Sørensen's scale, still used today, a pH of 7 is neutral; higher numbers represent alkalinity, and lower numbers acidity.

sorghum or ***great millet*** or ***Guinea corn*** any cereal grass of the genus *Sorghum*, native to Africa but cultivated widely in India, China, the USA, and S Europe. The seeds are used for making bread. Durra is a member of the genus.

sorrel (Old French *sur* 'sour') any of several plants of the genus *Rumex* of the buckwheat family Polygonaceae. *R. acetosa* is grown for its bitter salad leaves. *Dock plants are of the same genus.

sorting arranging data in sequence. When sorting a collection, or file, of data made up of several different *fields, one must be chosen as the *key field* used to establish the correct sequence. For example, the data in a company's mailing list might include fields for each customer's first names, surname, address, and telephone number. For most purposes the company would wish the records to be sorted alphabetically by surname; therefore, the surname field would be chosen as the key field.

sorus in ferns, a group of sporangia, the reproductive structures that produce *spores. These occur on the lower surface of fern fronds.

SOS internationally recognized distress signal using letters of the *Morse code (... – ...).

Sōseki Natsume, pen name of Natsume Kinnosuke 1867–1916. Japanese novelist whose works are deep psychological studies of urban intellectual lives. Strongly influenced by English literature, his later works are somewhat reminiscent of Henry James; for example, the unfinished *Meian/Light and Darkness* 1916. Sōseki is regarded as one of Japan's greatest writers.

Sosnowiec chief city of the Darowa coal region in the Upper Silesian province of Katowice, Poland; population (1990) 259,300.

Sotho member of a large ethnic group in southern Africa, numbering about 7 million (1987) and living mainly in Botswana, Lesotho, and South Africa. The Sotho are predominantly farmers living in small village groups. They speak a variety of closely related languages belonging to the Bantu branch of the Niger-Congo family. With English, Sotho is the official language of Lesotho.

soul according to many religions, the intangible and immortal part of a human being that survives the death of the physical body.

soul music emotionally intense style of *rhythm and blues sung by, among others, Sam Cooke (1931–1964), Aretha Franklin (1942–) and Al Green (1946–). A synthesis of blues, gospel music, and jazz, it emerged in the 1950s. Sometimes all popular music made by Afro-Americans is labelled soul music.

sound physiological sensation received by the ear, originating in a vibration (pressure variation in the air) that communicates itself to the air, and travels in every direction, spreading out as a expanding sphere. All sound waves in air travel with a speed dependent on the temperature; under ordinary conditions, this is about 330 m/1,070 ft per second. The pitch of the sound depends on the number of vibrations imposed on the air per second, but the speed is unaffected. The loudness of a sound is dependent primarily on the amplitude of the vibration of the air.

sound barrier concept that the speed of sound, or sonic speed (about 1,220 kph/760 mph at sea level), constitutes a speed limit to flight through the atmosphere, since a badly designed aircraft suffers severe buffeting at near sonic speed owing to the formation of shock waves. US test pilot Chuck Yeager first flew through the 'barrier' in 1947 in a Bell X-1 rocket plane. Now, by careful design, such aircraft as Concorde can fly at super sonic speed with ease, though they create in their wake a *sonic boom.

sound synthesis the generation of sound (usually music) by electronic *synthesizer.

soundtrack band at one side of a cine film on which the accompanying sound is recorded. Usually it takes the form of an optical track (a pattern of light and shade). The pattern is produced on the film when signals from the recording microphone are made to vary the intensity of a light beam. During playback, a light is shone through the track on to a photocell, which converts the pattern of light falling on it into appropriate electrical signals. These signals are then fed to loudspeakers to recreate the original sounds.

source language in computing, the language in which a program is written, as opposed to *machine code, which is the form in which the program's instructions are carried out by the computer. Source languages are classified as either *high-level languages or *low-level languages, according to whether each notation in the source language stands for many or only one instruction in machine code.

souring change that occurs to wine on prolonged exposure to air. The ethanol in the wine is oxidized by the air (oxygen) to ethanoic acid. It is the presence of the ethanoic (acetic) acid that produces the sour taste.
$$CH_3CH_2OH_{(aq)} + O_{2(g)} = CH_3COOH_{(aq)} + H_2O_{(l)}$$

Sousa John Philip 1854–1932. US bandmaster and composer of marches. He wrote 'The Stars and Stripes Forever!' 1897.

sousaphone large bass *tuba designed to wrap round the player in a circle and having a forward-facing bell. The form was suggested by US bandmaster John Sousa. Today sousaphones are largely fabricated in lightweight fibreglass.

South Africa Republic of (*Republiek van Suid-Afrika*)

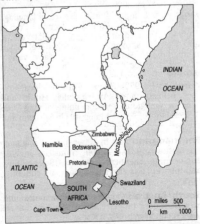

area 1,223,181 sq km/472,148 sq mi (includes independent black homelands)
capital and port Cape Town (legislative), Pretoria (administrative), Bloemfontein (judicial)
towns Johannesburg; ports Durban, Port Elizabeth, East London

physical southern end of large plateau, fringed by mountains and lowland coastal margin
territories Marion Island and Prince Edward Island in the Antarctic
head of state and government Nelson Mandela from 1994
political system emergent democracy
exports maize, sugar, fruit, wool, gold (world's largest producer), platinum, diamonds, uranium, iron and steel, copper; mining and minerals are largest export industry, followed by arms manufacturing
currency rand
population (1993) 32,590,000 (73% black: Zulu, Xhosa, Sotho, Tswana; 18% white: 3% mixed, 3% Asian); growth rate 2.5% p.a.
languages Afrikaans and English (both official), Bantu
religions Dutch Reformed Church 40%, Anglican 11%, Roman Catholic 8%, other Christian 25%, Hindu, Muslim
GNP $2,530 per head (1991)
chronology
1910 Union of South Africa formed from two British colonies and two Boer republics.
1912 African National Congress (ANC) formed.
1948 Apartheid system of racial discrimination initiated by Daniel Malan, leader of National Party (NP).
1955 Freedom Charter adopted by ANC.
1958 Malan succeeded as prime minister by Hendrik Verwoerd.
1960 ANC banned.
1961 South Africa withdrew from Commonwealth and became a republic.
1962 ANC leader Nelson Mandela jailed.
1964 Mandela, Walter Sisulu, Govan Mbeki, and five other ANC leaders sentenced to life imprisonment.
1966 Verwoerd assassinated; succeeded by B J Vorster.
1976 Soweto uprising.
1977 Death in custody of Pan African Congress activist Steve Biko.
1978 Vorster resigned and was replaced by Pieter W Botha.
1984 New constitution adopted, giving segregated representation to Coloureds and Asians and making Botha president. Nonaggression pact with Mozambique signed but not observed.
1985 Growth of violence in black townships.
1986 Commonwealth agreed on limited sanctions. US Congress voted to impose sanctions. Some major multinational companies closed down their South African operations.
1987 Government formally acknowledged the presence of its military forces in Angola.
1988 Botha announced 'limited constitutional reforms'. South Africa agreed to withdraw from Angola and recognize Namibia's independence as part of regional peace accord.
1989 Botha gave up NP leadership and state presidency. F W de Klerk became president. ANC activists released; beaches and public facilities desegregated. Elections held in Namibia to create independence government.
1990 ANC ban lifted; Nelson Mandela released from prison. NP membership opened to all races. ANC leader Oliver Tambo returned. Daily average of 35 murders and homicides recorded.
1991 Mandela and Zulu leader Mangosuthu Buthelezi urged end to fighting between ANC

and Inkatha. Mandela elected ANC president. Revelations of government support for Inkatha threatened ANC cooperation. De Klerk announced repeal of remaining apartheid laws. South Africa readmitted to international sport; USA lifted sanctions. PAC and Buthelezi withdrew from negotiations over new constitution. *1992* Constitution leading to all-races majority rule approved by whites-only referendum. Massacre of civilians at black township of Boipatong near Johannesburg by Inkatha, aided and abetted by police, threatened constitutional talks.
1993 Feb: de Klerk and Nelson Mandela agreed to formation of government of national unity after free elections. April: ANC leader Chris Hani assassinated by white extremist. July: township riots followed announcement of April 1994 date for nonracial elections, initiated by groups opposed to ANC-negotiated constitutional changes. Oct: on-going constitutional talks boycotted by new Freedom Alliance (coalition of Inkatha, right-wing groups, and black homelands of Ciskei and Bophuthatswana). Dec: new majority-rule constitution adopted.
1994 March: annexation of Bophuthatswana after popular uprising and attempted takeover by white right-wing extremists. Massacre of Inkatha supporters in Johannesburg; state of emergency declared in Natal/KwaZulu after dramatic escalation in Inkatha violence. April: Inkatha persuaded to enter elections and call off campaign of violence, by assurances that the status of Zulu king would be enshrined in constitution. Ultraright bombings in Johannesburg and Pretoria. ANC won landslide election victory. May: Mandela inaugurated as president.

South African Wars two wars between the Boers (settlers of Dutch origin) and the British; essentially fought for the gold and diamonds of the Transvaal. The *War of 1881* was triggered by the attempt of the Boers of the *Transvaal to reassert the independence surrendered 1877 in return for British aid against African peoples. The British were defeated at Majuba, and the Transvaal again became independent. The *War of 1899–1902*, also known as the *Boer War*, followed the armed Jameson Raid into the Boer Transvaal; a failed attempt, inspired by the Cape Colony prime minister Rhodes, to precipitate a revolt against Kruger, the Transvaal president. The *uitlanders* (non-Boer immigrants) were still not given the vote by the Boers, negotiations failed, and the Boers invaded British territory, besieging Ladysmith, Mafeking (now Mafikeng), and Kimberley. The war ended with the Peace of Vereeniging following the Boer defeat.

South America fourth largest of the continents, nearly twice as large as Europe (13% of the world's land surface), extending S from *Central America
area 17,864,000 sq km/6,900,000 sq mi
largest cities (population over 3.5 million) Buenos Aires, São Paulo, Rio de Janeiro, Bogotá, Santiago, Lima, Caracas
physical occupying the southern part of the landmass of the western hemisphere, the South American continent stretches from Point Gallinas on the Caribbean coast of Colombia to Cape Horn at the southern tip of Horn Island, which lies adjacent to Tierra del Fuego; the most southerly point on the mainland is Cape Froward on the Brunswick peninsula, S Chile; at its maximum width (5,120 km/3,200 mi) the continent stretches from Point Pariñas, Peru, in the extreme W to Point Coqueiros, just N of Recife, Brazil, in the E; five-sixths of the continent lies in the southern hemisphere and two-thirds within the tropics. South America can be divided into the following physical regions: 1) the Andes mountain system, which begins as three separate ranges in the N and stretches the whole length of W coast approximately 7,200 km/4,500 mi; a narrow coastal belt lies between the Andes and the Pacific Ocean; 2) the uplifted remains of the old continental mass, with interior plains at an elevation of 610–1,520 m/2,000–5,000 ft, are found in E and NE, in the Brazilian Highlands and Guiana Highlands; 3) the plain of the Orinoco river, which is an alluvial tropical lowland lying between the Venezuelan Andes and the Guiana Highlands; 4) the tropical Amazon Plain, which stretches 3,200 km/2,000 mi from the eastern foothills of the Andes to the Atlantic Ocean, separating the Brazilian and Guiana Highlands; 5) the Pampa-Chaco plain of Argentina, Paraguay, and Bolivia; 6) the Patagonian Plateau in the S consists of a series of terraces that rise from the Atlantic Ocean to the foothills of the Andes. Rivers include the Amazon (world's largest and second longest), Parana, Orinoco, Araguaia, Negro, Uruguay
products produces 44% of the world's coffee (Brazil, Colombia), 22% of its cocoa (Brazil), 35% of its citrus fruit, meat (Argentina, Brazil), soya beans (Argentina, Brazil), cotton (Brazil), linseed (Argentina); Argentina is the world's second largest producer of sunflower seed; Brazil is the world's largest producer of bananas, its second largest producer of tin, and its third largest producer of manganese, tobacco, and mangoes; Peru is the world's second largest producer of silver; Chile is the world's largest producer of copper
population (1988) 285 million, rising to 550 million (est) by 2000
languages Spanish, Portuguese (chief language in Brazil), Dutch (Surinam), French (French Guiana), Amerindian languages; Hindi, Javanese, and Chinese spoken by descendants of Asian immigrants to Surinam and Guyana; a variety of Creole dialects spoken by those of African descent
religions 90–95% Roman Catholic; local animist beliefs among Amerindians; Hindu and Muslim religions predominate among the descendants of Asian immigrants in Surinam and Guyana.

Southampton port in Hampshire, S England; population (1981) 204,600. Industries include engineering, chemicals, plastics, flour-milling, and tobacco; it is also a passenger and container port.

South Australia state of the Commonwealth of Australia
area 984,000 sq km/379,824 sq mi
capital Adelaide (chief port)
towns Whyalla, Mount Gambier
products meat and wool (80% of area cattle and sheep grazing), wines and spirits, dried and canned fruit, iron (Middleback Range), coal (Leigh Creek), copper, uranium (Roxby Downs),

oil and natural gas in the NE, lead, zinc, iron, opals, household and electrical goods, vehicles
population (1987) 1,388,000; 1% Aborigines
history possibly known to the Dutch in the 16th century; surveyed by Dutch navigator Abel Tasman 1644; first European settlement 1834; province 1836; became a state 1901. In 1963 British nuclear tests were made at Maralinga, in which Aborigines were said to have died.

South Carolina state in SE USA; nickname Palmetto State
area 80,600 sq km/31,112 sq mi
capital Columbia
cities Charleston, Greenville-Spartanburg
population (1990) 3,486,700
products tobacco, soya beans, lumber, textiles, clothing, paper, wood pulp, chemicals, nonelectrical machinery, primary and fabricated metals

South Dakota state of the USA; nickname Coyote or Sunshine State
area 199,800 sq km/77,123 sq mi
capital Pierre
cities Sioux Falls, Rapid City, Aberdeen
physical Great Plains; Black Hills (which include granite Mount Rushmore, on whose face giant relief portrait heads of former presidents Washington, Jefferson, Lincoln, and T Roosevelt are carved); Badlands
products cereals, hay, livestock, gold (second-largest US producer), meat products
population (1990) 696,000
famous people Crazy Horse, Sitting Bull, Ernest O Lawrence

Southeast Asia Treaty Organization (SEATO) collective military system 1954–77 established by Australia, France, New Zealand, Pakistan, the Philippines, Thailand, the UK, and the USA, with Vietnam, Cambodia, and Laos as protocol states. After the Vietnam War, SEATO was phased out.

Southern Cone Common Market free-trade zone between Brazil, Argentina, Uruguay, and Paraguay, agreed March 1991 for complete implementation by Jan 1995. It allows for a steady reduction of customs tariffs between members. Established by the Treaty of Asunción, it has headquarters in Montevideo.

Southern Cross popular name for the constellation Crux.

southern lights common name for the *aurora australis, coloured light in southern skies.

Southern Ocean corridor linking the Pacific, Atlantic, and Indian oceans, all of which receive cold polar water from the world's largest ocean surface current, the Antarctic Circumpolar current, which passes through the Southern Ocean.

Southern Uplands one of the three geographical divisions of Scotland, occupying most of the hilly Scottish Borderland to the south of a geological fault line that stretches from Dunbar on the North Sea to Girvan on the Firth of Clyde. The Southern Uplands, largely formed by rocks of the Silurian and Ordovician age, are intersected by the broad valleys of the Nith and Tweed rivers.

South Georgia island in the S Atlantic, a British crown colony administered with the South Sandwich Islands; area 3,757 sq km/1,450 sq mi.

South Georgia lies 1,300 km/800 mi SE of the Falkland Islands, of which it was a dependency until 1985. The British Antarctic Survey has a station on nearby Bird Island.

South Glamorgan (Welsh **De Morgannwg**) county in S Wales
area 420 sq km/162 sq mi
towns Cardiff (administrative headquarters), Barry, Penarth
products dairy farming, industry (steel, plastics, engineering) in the Cardiff area
population (1991) 383,300
language 6% Welsh; English
famous people Sarah Siddons, Shirley Bassey, R S Thomas.

South Holland (Dutch **Zuid-Holland**) low-lying coastal province of the Netherlands
area 2,910 sq km/1,123 sq mi
population (1991) 3,245,300
capital The Hague
towns Rotterdam, Dordrecht, Leiden, Delft, Gouda
products bulbs, horticulture, livestock, dairy products, chemicals, textiles
history once part of the former county of Holland, which was divided into two provinces 1840.

South Korea see *Korea, South.

South Sea Bubble financial crisis in Britain in 1720. The South Sea Company, founded 1711, which had a monopoly of trade with South America, offered in 1719 to take over more than half the national debt in return for further concessions. Its 100 shares rapidly rose to 1,000, and an orgy of speculation followed. When the 'bubble' burst, thousands were ruined. The discovery that cabinet ministers had been guilty of corruption led to a political crisis.

South West Africa former name (until 1968) of *Namibia.

South Yorkshire metropolitan county of England, created 1976, originally administered by an elected council; its powers reverted to district councils from 1986
area 1,560 sq km/602 sq mi
towns Barnsley, Sheffield, Doncaster
products metal work, coal, dairy, sheep, arable farming
population (1991) 1,269,300
famous people Ian Botham, Arthur Scargill.

Soutine Chaim 1894–1943. Lithuanian-born French Expressionist artist. He painted landscapes and portraits, including many of painters active in Paris in the 1920s and 1930s. He had a distorted style, using thick application of paint (impasto) and brilliant colours.

sovereign British gold coin, introduced by Henry VII, which became the standard monetary unit in 1817. Minting ceased for currency purposes in the UK in 1914, but the sovereign continued to be used as 'unofficial' currency in the Middle East. It was minted for the last time in 1987 and has now been replaced by the **Britannia**.

sovereignty absolute authority within a given territory. The possession of sovereignty is taken to be the distinguishing feature of the state, as against other forms of community. The term has an internal aspect, in that it refers to the ultimate source of authority within a state, such as a parliament or monarch, and an external aspect, where it denotes the independence of the state from any outside authority.

soviet (Russian 'council') originally a strike committee elected by Russian workers in the 1905 revolution; in 1917 these were set up by peasants, soldiers, and factory workers. The soviets sent delegates to the All-Russian Congress of Soviets to represent their opinions to a future government. They were later taken over by the *Bolsheviks.

Soviet Union alternative name for the former *Union of Soviet Socialist Republics (USSR).

Soweto (acronym for *South West Township*) racially segregated urban settlement in South Africa, SW of Johannesburg; population (1983) 915,872. It has experienced civil unrest because of the *apartheid regime.

soya bean leguminous plant *Glycine max*, native to E Asia, in particular Japan and China. Originally grown as a forage crop, it is increasingly used for human consumption in cooking oils and margarine, as a flour, soya milk, soy sauce, or processed into tofu, miso, or textured vegetable protein.

Soyinka Wole 1934– . Nigerian author who was a political prisoner in Nigeria 1967–69. His works include the play *The Lion and the Jewel* 1963; his prison memoirs *The Man Died* 1972; *Aké, The Years of Childhood* 1982, an autobiography, and *Isara*, a fictionalized memoir 1989. He was the first African to receive the Nobel Prize for Literature, in 1986.

Soyuz (Russian 'union') Soviet series of spacecraft, capable of carrying up to three cosmonauts. Soyuz spacecraft consist of three parts: a rear section containing engines; the central crew compartment; and a forward compartment that gives additional room for working and living space. They are now used for ferrying crews up to space stations, though they were originally used for independent space flight.

Spaak Paul-Henri 1899–1972. Belgian socialist politician. From 1936 to 1966 he held office almost continuously as foreign minister or prime minister. He was an ardent advocate of international peace.

space the void that exists beyond Earth's atmosphere. Above 120 km/75 mi, very little atmosphere remains, so objects can continue to move quickly without extra energy. The space between the planets is not entirely empty, but filled with the tenuous gas of the *solar wind as well as dust specks.

Spacelab small space station built by the European Space Agency, carried in the cargo bay of the US space shuttle, in which it remains throughout each flight, returning to Earth with the shuttle. Spacelab consists of a pressurized module in which astronauts can work, and a series of pallets, open to the vacuum of space, on which equipment is mounted.

space probe any instrumented object sent beyond Earth to collect data from other parts of the solar system and from deep space. The first probe was the Soviet *Lunik 1*, which flew past the Moon 1959. The first successful planetary probe was the US *Mariner 2*, which flew past Venus 1962, using *transfer orbit. The first space probe to leave the solar system was *Pioneer 10* 1983. Space probes include *Giotto*, the *Moon probes, and the Mariner, Pioneer, Viking, and Voyager series. Japan launched its first space probe 1990.

space shuttle reusable crewed spacecraft. The first was launched 12 April 1981 by the USA. It was developed by NASA to reduce the cost of using space for commercial, scientific, and military purposes. After leaving its payload in space, the space-shuttle orbiter can be flown back to Earth to land on a runway, and is then available for reuse.

space station any large structure designed for human occupation in space for extended periods of time. Space stations are used for carrying out astronomical observations and surveys of Earth, as well as for biological studies and the processing of materials in weightlessness. The first space station was *Salyut 1*, and the USA has launched *Skylab.

space-time in physics, combination of space and time used in the theory of *relativity. When developing relativity, Einstein showed that time was in many respects like an extra dimension (or direction) to space. Space and time can thus be considered as entwined into a single entity, rather than two separate things.

Spain (*España*)

area 504,750 sq km/194,960 sq mi
capital Madrid
towns Zaragoza, Seville, Murcia, Córdoba; ports Barcelona, Valencia, Cartagena, Málaga, Cádiz, Vigo, Santander, Bilbao
physical central plateau with mountain ranges; lowlands in S
territories Balearic and Canary Islands; in N Africa: Ceuta, Melilla, Alhucemas, Chafarinas Is, Peñón de Vélez
head of state King Juan Carlos I from 1975
head of government Felipe González Márquez from 1982
political system constitutional monarchy
exports citrus fruits, grapes, pomegranates, vegetables, wine, sherry, olive oil, canned fruit and fish, iron ore, cork, vehicles, textiles, petroleum products, leather goods, ceramics
currency peseta
population (1993 est) 39,200,000; growth rate 0.2% p.a.

languages Spanish (Castilian, official), Basque, Catalan, Galician, Valencian, Majorcan
religion Roman Catholic 99%
GNP $14,290 per head (1992)
chronology
1936–39 Civil war; General Francisco Franco became head of state and government; fascist party Falange declared only legal political organization.
1947 General Franco announced restoration of the monarchy after his death, with Prince Juan Carlos as his successor.
1975 Franco died; succeeded as head of state by King Juan Carlos I.
1978 New constitution adopted with Adolfo Suárez, leader of the Democratic Centre Party, as prime minister.
1981 Suárez resigned; succeeded by Leopoldo Calvo Sotelo. Attempted military coup thwarted.
1982 Socialist Workers' Party (PSOE), led by Felipe González, won a sweeping electoral victory. Basque separatist organization (ETA) stepped up its guerrilla campaign.
1985 ETA's campaign spread to holiday resorts.
1986 Referendum confirmed NATO membership. Spain joined the European Economic Community.
1988 Spain joined the Western European Union.
1989 PSOE lost seats to hold only parity after general election. Talks between government and ETA collapsed and truce ended.
1992 ETA's 'armed struggle' resumed.

spaniel any of several breeds of dog, characterized by large, drooping ears and a wavy, long, silky coat. The *Sussex spaniel* is believed to be the oldest variety, weighs 20 kg/45 lb, is 40 cm/15 in tall, and is a golden liver colour.

Spanish-American War brief war 1898 between Spain and the USA over Spanish rule in Cuba and the Philippines; the complete defeat of Spain made the USA a colonial power. The Treaty of Paris ceded the Philippines, Guam, and Puerto Rico to the USA; Cuba became independent. The USA paid $20 million to Spain. Thus ended Spain's colonial presence in the Americas.

Spanish Armada fleet sent by Philip II of Spain against England in 1588. Consisting of 130 ships, it sailed from Lisbon and carried on a running fight up the Channel with the English fleet of 197 small ships under Howard of Effingham and Francis *Drake. The Armada anchored off Calais but fireships forced it to put to sea, and a general action followed off Gravelines. What remained of the Armada escaped around the N of Scotland and W of Ireland, suffering many losses by storm and shipwreck on the way. Only about half the original fleet returned to Spain.

Spanish Civil War 1936–39. See *Civil War, Spanish.

Spanish Guinea former name of the Republic of *Equatorial Guinea.

Spanish language member of the Romance branch of the Indo-European language family, traditionally known as Castilian and originally spoken only in NE Spain. As the language of the court, it has been the standard and literary language of the Spanish state since the 13th century. It is now a world language, spoken in Mexico and all South and Central American countries (except Brazil, Guyana, Surinam, and French Guiana) as well as in the Philippines, Cuba, Puerto Rico, and much of the USA.

Spanish Main common name for the Caribbean in the 16th–17th centuries, but more properly the South American mainland between the river Orinoco and Panama.

Spanish Sahara former name for *Western Sahara.

Spanish Succession, War of the war 1701–14 of Britain, Austria, the Netherlands, Portugal, and Denmark (the Allies) against France, Spain, and Bavaria. It was caused by Louis XIV's acceptance of the Spanish throne on behalf of his grandson, Philip V of Spain, in defiance of the Partition Treaty of 1700, under which it would have passed to Archduke Charles of Austria (later Holy Roman emperor Charles VI).

spark chamber electronic device for recording tracks of charged subatomic *particles, decay products, and rays. In combination with a stack of photographic plates, a spark chamber enables the point where an interaction has taken place to be located, to within a cubic centimetre. At its simplest, it consists of two smooth threadlike *electrodes that are positioned 1–2 cm/0.5–1 in apart, the space between being filled by an inert gas such as neon. Sparks jump through the gas along the ionized path created by the radiation.

spark plug plug that produces an electric spark in the cylinder of a petrol engine to ignite the fuel mixture. It consists essentially of two electrodes insulated from one another. High-voltage (18,000 V) electricity is fed to a central electrode via the distributor. At the base of the electrode, inside the cylinder, the electricity jumps to another electrode earthed to the engine body, creating a spark. See also *ignition coil.

sparrow any of a family (Passeridae) of small Old World birds of the order Passeriformes with short, thick bills, including the now worldwide house or English sparrow *Passer domesticus*. Many numbers of the New World family Emberizidae, which includes warblers, orioles, and buntings are also called sparrows; for example, the North American song sparrow *Melospize melodia*.

sparrow hawk small woodland *hawk *Accipiter nisus* found in Eurasia and N Africa. It has a long tail and short wings. The male grows to 28 cm/11 in long, and the female to 38 cm/15 in. It hunts small birds.

Sparta ancient Greek city-state in the S Peloponnese (near Sparte), developed from Dorian settlements in the 10th century BC. The Spartans, known for their military discipline and austerity, took part in the Persian and Peloponnesian wars.

Spartacist member of a group of left-wing radicals in Germany at the end of World War I, founders of the *Spartacus League*, which became the German Communist Party in 1919. The league participated in the Berlin workers' revolt of Jan 1919, which was suppressed by the Freikorps on the orders of the socialist government. The agitation ended with the murder of Spartacist leaders Karl *Liebknecht and Rosa *Luxemburg.

Spartacus Thracian gladiator who in 73 BC led

a revolt of gladiators and slaves in Capua, near Naples. He was eventually caught by Roman general *Crassus and crucified.

spathe in flowers, the single large bract surrounding the type of inflorescence known as a spadix. It is sometimes brightly coloured and petal-like, as in the flamingo plant *Anthurium andreanum* from South America.

spa town town with a spring, the water of which, it is claimed, has the power to cure illness and restore health. Spa treatment involves drinking and bathing in the naturally mineralized spring water.

speakeasy bar that illegally sold alcoholic beverages during the *Prohibition period (1920–33) in the USA. The term is probably derived from the need to speak quickly or quietly to the doorkeeper in order to gain admission.

Speaker presiding officer charged with the preservation of order in the legislatures of various countries. In the UK the equivalent of the Speaker in the House of Lords is the Lord Chancellor; in the House of Commons the Speaker is elected for each parliament, usually on an agreed basis among the parties, but often holds the office for many years. The original appointment dates from 1377.

Special Air Service (SAS) specialist British regiment recruited from regiments throughout the army. It has served in Malaysia, Oman, Yemen, the Falklands, Northern Ireland, and during the 1991 Gulf War, as well as against international urban guerrillas, as in the siege of the Iranian embassy in London 1980.

Special Branch section of the British police originally established 1883 to deal with Irish Fenian activists. All 42 police forces in Britain now have their own Special Branches. They act as the executive arm of MI5 (British *intelligence) in its duty of preventing or investigating espionage, subversion, and sabotage; carry out duties at air and sea ports in respect of naturalization and immigration; and provide armed bodyguards for public figures.

special constable in the UK, a part-time volunteer who supplements local police forces as required. Special constables were established by the Special Constabulary Act 1831. They number some 16,000. They have no extra powers other than normal rights as citizens, although they wear a police-style uniform. They work alongside the police at football matches, demonstrations, and similar events.

special drawing right (SDR) the right of a member state of the *International Monetary Fund to apply for money to finance its balance of payments deficit. Originally, the SDR was linked to gold and the US dollar. After 1974 SDRs were defined in terms of a 'basket' of the 16 currencies of countries doing 1% or more of the world's trade. In 1981 the SDR was simplified to a weighted average of US dollars, French francs, German marks, Japanese yen, and UK pounds sterling.

special education education, often in separate 'special schools', for children with specific physical or mental problems or disabilities.

special relationship belief that ties of common language, culture, and shared aims of the defence of democratic principles should sustain a political relationship between the USA and the UK, and that the same would not apply to relationships between the USA and other European states.

speciation emergence of a new species during evolutionary history. One cause of speciation is the geographical separation of populations of the parent species, followed by reproductive isolation, so that they no longer produce viable offspring unless they interbreed. Other causes are *assortative mating and the establishment of a *polyploid population.

species in biology, a distinguishable group of organisms that resemble each other or consist of a few distinctive types (as in *polymorphism), and that can all interbreed to produce fertile offspring. Species are the lowest level in the system of biological classification.

specific gravity alternative term for *relative density.

specific heat capacity in physics, quantity of heat required to raise unit mass (1 kg) of a substance by one *kelvin (1°C). The unit of specific heat capacity in the SI system is the *joule per kilogram kelvin ($J kg^{-1} K^{-1}$).

spectacles pair of lenses fitted in a frame and worn in front of the eyes to correct or assist defective vision. Common defects of the eye corrected by spectacle lenses are short sight (myopia) by using concave (spherical) lenses, long sight (hypermetropia) by using convex (spherical) lenses, and astigmatism by using cylindrical lenses.

Spector Phil 1940– . US record producer, known for the 'wall of sound', created using a large orchestra, distinguishing his work in the early 1960s with vocal groups such as the Crystals and the Ronettes. He withdrew into semiretirement in 1966 but his influence can still be heard.

spectroscopy study of spectra (see *spectrum) associated with atoms or molecules in solid, liquid, or gaseous phase. Spectroscopy can be used to identify unknown compounds and is an invaluable tool in science, medicine, and industry (for example, in checking the purity of drugs).

spectrum (plural **spectra**) in physics, an arrangement of frequencies or wavelengths when electromagnetic radiations are separated into their constituent parts. Visible light is part of the *electromagnetic spectrum and most sources emit waves over a range of wavelengths that can be broken up or 'dispersed'; white light can be separated into red, orange, yellow, green, blue, indigo, and violet. The visible spectrum was first studied by Isaac *Newton, who showed in 1672 how white light could be broken up into different colours.

speculative action law case taken on a 'nowin, no-fee' basis, legal in the USA and Scotland, but not in England.

Spee Maximilian, Count von Spee 1861–1914. German admiral, born in Copenhagen. He went down with his flagship in the 1914 battle of the Falkland Islands, and the *Graf Spee* battleship was named after him.

speech recognition or *voice input* in computing, any technique by which a computer can understand ordinary speech. Spoken words are divided into 'frames', each lasting about one-thirtieth of a second, which are converted to a wave form. These are then compared with a series of stored frames to determine the most likely word. Research into speech recognition started in 1938, but the technology did not become sufficiently developed for commercial applications until the late 1980s.

speech synthesis or *voice output* computer-based technology for generating speech. A speech synthesizer is controlled by a computer, which supplies strings of codes representing basic speech sounds (phonemes); together these make up words. Speech-synthesis applications include children's toys, car and aircraft warning systems, and talking books for the blind.

speed common name for *amphetamine, a stimulant drug.

speed the rate at which an object moves. The constant speed v of an object may be calculated by dividing the distance s it has travelled by the time t taken to do so, and may be expressed as: $v = s/t$. The usual units of speed are metres per second or kilometres per hour.

speed of light speed at which light and other *electromagnetic waves travel through empty space. Its value is 299,792,458 m/186,281 mi per second. The speed of light is the highest speed possible, according to the theory of *relativity, and its value is independent of the motion of its source and of the observer. It is impossible to accelerate any material body to this speed because it would require an infinite amount of energy.

speed of sound speed at which sound travels through a medium, such as air or water. In air at a temperature of 0°C/32°F, the speed of sound is 331 m/1,087 ft per second. At higher temperatures, the speed of sound is greater; at 18°C/64°F it is 342 m/1,123 ft per second. It is greater in liquids and solids; for example, in water it is around 1,440 m/4,724 ft per second, depending on the temperature.

speedway sport of motorcycle racing on a dirt track. Four riders compete in each heat over four laps. A series of heats make up a match or competition. In Britain there are two leagues, the British League and the National League. World championships exist for individuals, pairs (first held 1970), four-rider teams (first held 1960), long-track racing, and ice speedway.

speedwell any flowering plant of the genus *Veronica* of the snapdragon family Scrophulariaceae. Of the many wild species, most are low-growing with small, bluish flowers.

Speer Albert 1905–1981. German architect and minister in the Nazi government during World War II. Commissioned by Hitler, Speer, like his counterparts in Fascist Italy, chose an overblown Classicism to glorify the state, as, for example, in his plan for the Berlin and Nuremberg Party Congress Grounds 1934.

speleology scientific study of caves, their origin, development, physical structure, flora, fauna, folklore, exploration, mapping, photography, cave-diving, and rescue work. *Potholing*, which involves following the course of underground rivers or streams, has become a popular sport.

Spence Basil 1907–1976. British architect. He was professor of architecture at the Royal Academy, London, 1961–68, and his works include Coventry Cathedral, Sussex University, and the British embassy in Rome.

Spencer Stanley 1891–1959. English painter who was born and lived in Cookham-on-Thames, Berkshire, and recreated the Christian story in a Cookham setting. His detailed, dreamlike compositions had little regard for perspective and used generalized human figures.

Spender Stephen (Harold) 1909– . English poet and critic. His earlier poetry has a left-wing political content, as in *Twenty Poems* 1930, *Vienna* 1934, *The Still Centre* 1939, and *Poems of Dedication* 1946. Other works include the verse drama *Trial of a Judge* 1938, the autobiography *World within World* 1951, and translations. His *Journals 1939–83* were published 1985.

Spenser Edmund c. 1552–1599. English poet, who has been called the 'poet's poet' because of his rich imagery and command of versification. His major work is the moral allegory *The Faerie Queene*, of which six books survive (three published 1590 and three 1596). Other books include *The Shepheard's Calendar* 1579, *Astrophel* 1586, the love sonnets *Amoretti* and the *Epithalamion* 1595.

sperm or *spermatozoon* in biology, the male *gamete of animals. Each sperm cell has a head capsule containing a nucleus, a middle portion containing *mitochondria (which provide energy), and a long tail (flagellum). See *sexual reproduction.

spermatophore small, nutrient-rich packet of *sperm produced in invertebrates, newts, and cephalopods.

spermatophyte in botany, another name for a *seed plant.

spermicide any cream, jelly, pessary, or other preparation that kills the *sperm cells in semen. Spermicides are used for contraceptive purposes, usually in combination with a *condom or *diaphragm. Sponges impregnated with spermicide have been developed but are not yet in widespread use. Spermicide used alone is only 75% effective in preventing pregnancy.

Sperry Elmer Ambrose 1860–1930. US engineer who developed various devices using *gyroscopes, such as gyrostabilizers (for ships and torpedoes) and gyro-controlled autopilots.

sphalerite the chief ore of zinc, composed of zinc sulphide with a small proportion of iron, formula $(Zn,Fe)S$. It is brown with a nonmetallic lustre unless an appreciable amount of iron is present (up to 26% by weight). Sphalerite usually occurs in ore veins in limestones, where it is often associated with galena. It crystallizes in the cubic system but does not normally form perfect cubes.

sphere in mathematics, a perfectly round solid with all points on its surface the same distance from the centre. This distance is the radius of the sphere. For a sphere of radius r, the volume $V = \frac{4}{3}\pi r^3$ and the surface area $A = 4\pi^2$.

sphincter ring of muscle found at various points in the alimentary canal, which contracts and relaxes to control the movement of food. The **pyloric sphincter**, at the base of the stomach, controls the release of the gastric contents into the duodenum. After release the sphincter contracts, closing off the stomach.

Sphinx mythological creature, represented in Egyptian, Assyrian, and Greek art as a lion with a human head. In Greek myth the Sphinx was female and killed travellers who failed to answer a riddle; she killed herself when *Oedipus gave the right answer.

sphygmomanometer instrument for measuring blood pressure. Consisting of an inflatable arm cuff joined by a rubber tube to a pressure-recording device (often a column-of-mercury scale), it is used, together with a stethoscope, to measure arterial blood pressure.

spice any aromatic vegetable substance used as a condiment and for flavouring food. Spices are mostly obtained from tropical plants, and include pepper, nutmeg, ginger, and cinnamon. They have little food value but increase the appetite and may facilitate digestion.

spider any arachnid (eight-legged animal) of the order Araneae. There are about 30,000 known species. Unlike insects, the head and breast are merged to form the cephalothorax, connected to the abdomen by a characteristic narrow waist. There are eight legs, and usually eight simple eyes. On the undersurface of the abdomen are spinnerets, usually six, which exude a viscid fluid. This hardens on exposure to the air to form silky threads, used to make silken egg cases, silk-lined tunnels, or various kinds of webs and snares for catching prey that is then wrapped. The fangs of spiders inject substances to subdue and digest prey, the juices of which are then sucked into the stomach by the spider.

spider plant African plant of the genus *Chlorophytum* of the lily family. Two species, *C. comosum* and *C. elatum*, are popular house plants. They have long narrow variegated leaves and produce flowering shoots from which the new plants grow. The flowers are small and white. Spider plants absorb toxins from the air and therefore have a purifying action on the local atmosphere.

Spielberg Steven 1947– . US film director, writer, and producer. His credits as director include such phenomenal box-office successes as *Jaws* 1975, *Close Encounters of the Third Kind* 1977, *Raiders of the Lost Ark* 1981, *ET* 1982, and *Jurassic Park* 1993. Immensely popular, his films usually combine cliff-hanging suspense with heartfelt sentimentality and a childlike sensibility. *Schindler's List* 1993, his powerful evocation of the Holocaust, won him his first Academy Award.

spikelet in botany, one of the units of a grass *inflorescence. It comprises a slender axis on which one or more flowers are borne.

spin in physics, the intrinsic *angular momentum of a subatomic particle, nucleus, atom, or molecule, which continues to exist even when the particle comes to rest. A particle in a specific energy state has a particular spin, just as it has a particular electric charge and mass. According to *quantum theory, this is restricted to discrete and indivisible values, specified by a spin *quantum number. Because of its spin, a charged particle acts as a small magnet and is affected by magnetic fields.

spina bifida congenital defect in which part of the spinal cord and its membranes are exposed, due to incomplete development of the spine (vertebral column). It is a neural tube defect.

spinach annual plant *Spinacia oleracea* of the goosefoot family Chenopodiaceae. It is native to Asia and widely cultivated for its leaves, which are eaten as a vegetable.

spinal tap another term for *lumbar puncture, a medical test.

Spinans Hill prehistoric site on a hill near Baltinglass, County Wicklow, in the Republic of Ireland, 48 km/30 miles SW of Dublin. Discovered 1992, it is the largest Bronze Age hillfort yet to be found in the British Isles, covering an area of 130 hectares/320 acres.

spine backbone of vertebrates. In most mammals, it contains 26 small bones called vertebrae, which enclose and protect the spinal cord (which links the peripheral nervous system to the brain). The spine articulates with the skull, ribs, and hip bones, and provides attachment for the back muscles.

spinet 17th-century laterally tapered domestic keyboard instrument of up to a three-and-a-half octave range, having a plucking action and single strings. It was the precursor of the *harpsichord.

spinning art of drawing out and twisting fibres (originally wool or flax) into a long thread, or yarn, by hand or machine. Synthetic fibres are extruded as a liquid through the holes of a spinneret. Spinning was originally done by hand, then with the spinning wheel, and in about 1767 in England James *Hargreaves built the **spinning jenny**, a machine that could spin 8, then 16, bobbins at once. Later, Samuel *Crompton's **spinning mule** 1779 had a moving carriage carrying the spindles and is still in use today.

Spinoza Benedict or Baruch 1632–1677. Dutch philosopher who believed in a rationalistic pantheism that owed much to Descartes' mathematical appreciation of the universe. Mind and matter are two modes of an infinite substance that he called God or Nature, good and evil being relative. He was a determinist, believing that human action was motivated by self-preservation.

spiny anteater alternative name for *echidna.

spiracle in insects, the opening of a *trachea, through which oxygen enters the body and carbon dioxide is expelled. In cartilaginous fishes (sharks and rays), the same name is given to a circular opening that marks the remains of the first gill slit.

spiraea any herbaceous plant or shrub of the genus *Spiraea*, family Rosaceae, which includes many cultivated species with ornamental panicles of flowers.

spiral a plane curve formed by a point winding round a fixed point from which it distances itself at regular intervals, for example the spiral traced by a flat coil of rope. Various kinds of spirals can be generated mathematically – for example, an equiangular or logarithmic spiral (in which a tangent at any point on the curve always makes the same angle with it) and an *involute. Spirals also occur in nature as a normal consequence of acce-

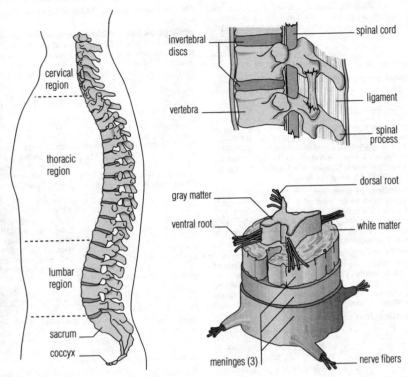

spine *The human spine extends every night during sleep.*

lerating growth, such as the spiral shape of the shells of snails and some other molluscs.

spiritualism belief in the survival of the human personality and in communication between the living and those who have 'passed on'. The spiritualist movement originated in the USA in 1848. Adherents to this religious denomination practise ***mediumship***, which claims to allow clairvoyant knowledge of distant events and spirit healing.

spit ridge of sand or shingle projecting from the land into a body of water. It is deposited by waves carrying material from one direction to another across the mouth of an inlet (*longshore drift). Deposition in the brackish water behind a spit may result in the formation of a *salt marsh.

Spitsbergen mountainous island with a deeply indented coastline in the Arctic Ocean, the main island in the Norwegian archipelago of *Svalbard, 657 km/408 mi N of Norway; area 39,043 sq km/15,075 sq mi. Fishing, hunting, and coal mining are the chief economic activities.

Spitz Mark 1950– . US swimmer. He won a record seven gold medals at the 1972 Olympic Games, all in world record times.

spleen organ in vertebrates, part of the lymphatic system, which helps to process *lymphocytes. It also regulates the number of red blood cells in circulation by destroying old cells, and stores iron. It is situated on the left side of the body, behind the stomach.

Split (Italian ***Spalato***) port in Croatia, on the Adriatic coast; population (1981) 236,000. Industries include engineering, cement, and textiles. Split was bombed during 1991 as part of Yugoslavia's blockade of the Croatian coast.

Spock Benjamin McLane 1903– . US paediatrician and writer on child care. His *Common Sense Book of Baby and Child Care* 1946 urged less rigidity in bringing up children than had been advised by previous generations of writers on the subject, but this was misunderstood as advocating permissiveness. He was also active in the peace movement, especially during the Vietnam War.

Spode Josiah 1754–1827. English potter. Around 1800, he developed bone porcelain (made from bone ash, china stone, and china clay), which was produced at all English factories in the 19th century. Spode became potter to King George III 1806.

spoils system in the USA, the granting of offices and favours among the supporters of a party in office. The spoils system, a type of *patronage, was used by President Jefferson and was enlarged in scope by the 1820 Tenure of Office Act, which gave the president and Senate the power to reappoint posts that were the gift of the government after each four-year election. The practice remained common in the 20th century in US local government.

sponge any saclike simple invertebrate of the

phylum Porifera, usually marine. A sponge has a hollow body, its cavity lined by cells bearing flagellae, whose whiplike movements keep water circulating, bringing in a stream of food particles. The body walls are strengthened with protein (as in the bath sponge) or small spikes of silica, or a framework of calcium carbonate.

spontaneous generation or *abiogenesis* erroneous belief that living organisms can arise spontaneously from non-living matter. This survived until the mid-19th century, when the French chemist Louis Pasteur demonstrated that a nutrient broth would not generate microorganisms if it was adequately sterilized. The theory of biogenesis holds that spontaneous generation cannot now occur; it is thought, however, to have played an essential role in the origin of *life on this planet 4 billion years ago.

spooling in computing, the process in which information to be printed is stored temporarily in a file, the printing being carried out later. It is used to prevent a relatively slow printer from holding up the system at critical times, and to enable several computers or programs to share one printer.

spoonbill any of several large wading birds of the Ibis family (Threskiornithidae), characterized by a long, flat bill, dilated at the tip in the shape of a spoon. Spoonbills are white or pink, and up to 90 cm/3 ft tall.

spoonerism exchange of elements in a flow of words. Usually a slip of the tongue, a spoonerism can also be contrived for comic effect (for example 'a troop of Boy Scouts' becoming 'a scoop of Boy Trouts'). William Spooner (1844–1930) gave his name to the phenomenon.

spore small reproductive or resting body, usually consisting of just one cell. Unlike a *gamete, it does not need to fuse with another cell in order to develop into a new organism. Spores are produced by the lower plants, most fungi, some bacteria, and certain protozoa. They are generally light and easily dispersed by wind movements. Plant spores are haploid and are produced by the sporophyte, following *meiosis; see *alternation of generations.

sporophyte diploid spore-producing generation in the life cycle of a plant that undergoes *alternation of generations.

spreadsheet in computing, a program that mimics a sheet of ruled paper, divided into columns and rows. The user enters values in the sheet, then instructs the program to perform some operation on them, such as totalling a column or finding the average of a series of numbers. Highly complex numerical analyses may be built up from these simple steps.

spring device, usually a metal coil, that returns to its original shape after being stretched or compressed. Springs are used in some machines (such as clocks) to store energy, which can be released at a controlled rate. In other machines (such as engines) they are used to close valves.

spring in geology, a natural flow of water from the ground, formed where the water table meets the ground's surface. The source of water is rain that has percolated through the overlying rocks. During its underground passage, the water may have dissolved mineral substances, which may then be precipitated at the spring (hence, a mineral spring).

springbok South African antelope *Antidorcas marsupialis* about 80 cm/30 in at the shoulder, with head and body 1.3 m/4 ft long. It may leap 3 m/10 ft or more in the air when startled or playing, and has a fold of skin along the middle of the back which is raised to a crest in alarm. Springboks once migrated in herds of over a million, but are now found only in small numbers where protected.

Springsteen Bruce 1949– . US rock singer, songwriter, and guitarist, born in New Jersey. His music combines melodies in traditional rock idiom and reflective lyrics about working-class life on albums such as *Born to Run* 1975 and *Born in the USA* 1984, maturing into the 1992 albums *Human Touch* and *Lucky Town*.

sprite in computing, a graphics object made up of a pattern of *pixels (picture elements) defined by a computer programmer. Some *high-level languages and applications programs contain routines that allow a user to define the shape, colours, and other characteristics of individual graphics objects. These objects can then be manipulated and combined to produce animated games or graphic screen displays.

spruce coniferous tree of the genus *Picea* of the pine family, found over much of the northern hemisphere. Pyramidal in shape, spruces have rigid, prickly needles and drooping, leathery cones. Some are important forestry trees, such as sitka spruce *P. sitchensis*, native to W North America, and the Norway spruce *P. abies*, now planted widely in North America.

Sputnik (Russian 'fellow traveller') series of ten Soviet Earth-orbiting satellites. *Sputnik 1* was the first artificial satellite, launched 4 Oct 1957. It weighed 84 kg/185 lb, with a 58 cm/23 in diameter, and carried only a simple radio transmitter which allowed scientists to track it as it orbited Earth. It burned up in the atmosphere 92 days later. Sputniks were superseded in the early 1960s by the Cosmos series.

SQL (abbreviation of *structured query language*) high-level computer language designed for use with relational databases. Although it can be used by programmers in the same way as other languages, it is often used as a means for programs to communicate with each other. Typically, one program (called the 'client') uses SQL to request data from a database 'server'.

square in geometry, a quadrilateral (four-sided) plane figure with all sides equal and each angle a right angle. Its diagonals bisect each other at right angles. The area A of a square is the length l of one side multiplied by itself ($A = l \times l$). Also, any quantity multiplied by itself is also termed a square, represented by an *exponent of power 2; for example, $4 \times 4 = 4^2 = 16$ and $6.8 \times 6.8 = 6.8^2 = 46.24$.

square root in mathematics, a number that when squared (multiplied by itself) equals a given number. For example, the square root of 25 (written $\sqrt{25}$) is $+5$, because $5 \times 5 = 25$, and $(-5) \times (-5) = 25$. As an *exponent, a square root is represented by $1/2$, for example, $16^{1/2} = 4$.

squash or *squash rackets* racket-and-ball game usually played by two people on an enclosed court, derived from *rackets. Squash became a popular sport in the 1970s and then a fitness craze as well as a competitive sport. There are two forms of squash: the American form, which is played in North and some South American countries, and the English, which is played mainly in Europe and Commonwealth countries such as Pakistan, Australia, and New Zealand.

squatter person illegally occupying someone else's property; for example, some of the urban homeless in contemporary Britain making use of vacant houses. Squatters commit a criminal offence if they take over property where there is a 'residential occupier'; for example, by moving in while the owner is on holiday.

squill bulb-forming perennial plant of the genus *Scilla*, family Liliaceae, found growing in dry places near the sea in W Europe. Cultivated species usually bear blue flowers either singly or in clusters at the top of the stem.

squint or *strabismus* common condition in which one eye deviates in any direction. A squint may be convergent (with the bad eye turned inward), divergent (outward), or, in rare cases, vertical. A convergent squint is also called *cross-eye*.

squirrel The northern flying squirrel stretches all four limbs when gliding from tree to tree.

squirrel rodent of the family Sciuridae. Squirrels are found worldwide except for Australia, Madagascar, and polar regions. Some are tree dwellers; these generally have bushy tails, and some, with membranes between their legs, are called *flying squirrels. Others are terrestrial, generally burrowing forms called ground squirrels; these include chipmunks, gophers, marmots, and prairie dogs.

SRAM (acronym for *static random-access memory*) computer memory device in the form of a silicon chip used to provide *immediate-access memory. SRAM is faster but more expensive than *DRAM (dynamic random-access memory).

Sri Lanka Democratic Socialist Republic of (*Prajathanrika Samajawadi Janarajaya Sri Lanka*) (until 1972 **Ceylon**)
area 65,600 sq km/25,328 sq mi
capital (and chief port) Colombo
towns Kandy; ports Jaffna, Galle, Negombo, Trincomalee
physical flat in N and around the coast; hills and mountains in S and central interior
head of state Dingiri Banda Wijetunge from 1993
head of government Chandrika Kumaratunga from 1994

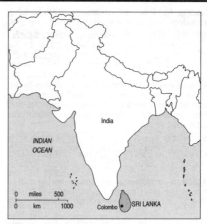

political system liberal democratic republic
exports tea, rubber, coconut products, graphite, sapphires, rubies, other gemstones
currency Sri Lanka rupee
population (1993 est) 17,800,000 (Sinhalese 74%, Tamils 17%, Moors 7%); growth rate 1.8% p.a.
languages Sinhala, Tamil, English
religions Buddhist 69%, Hindu 15%, Muslim 8%, Christian 7%
GNP $539 per head (1992)
chronology
1802 Ceylon became a British colony.
1948 Ceylon achieved independence from Britain within the Commonwealth.
1956 Sinhala established as the official language.
1959 Prime Minister Solomon Bandaranaike assassinated.
1972 Socialist Republic of Sri Lanka proclaimed.
1978 Presidential constitution adopted by new government headed by Junius Jayawardene of the UNP.
1983 Tamil guerrilla violence escalated; state of emergency imposed.
1987 President Jayawardene and Indian prime minister Rajiv Gandhi signed Colombo Accord. Violence continued despite cease-fire policed by Indian troops.
1988 Left-wing guerrillas campaigned against Indo-Sri Lankan peace pact. Prime Minister Ranasinghe Premadasa elected president.
1989 Premadasa became president; Dingiri Banda Wijetunga, prime minister. Leaders of the TULF and the banned Sinhala extremist People's Liberation Front (JVP) assassinated.
1991 March: defence minister Ranjan Wijeratne assassinated; Sri Lankan army killed 2,552 Tamil Tigers at Elephant Pass. Oct: impeachment motion against President Premadasa failed. Dec: new party, the Democratic United National Front (DUNF), formed by former members of the UNP.
1992 Several hundred Tamil Tiger rebels killed in army offensive, code-named 'Strike Force Two'.
1993 DUNF leader assassinated; government responsibility suspected. President Premadasa assassinated; succeeded by Dingiri Banda Wijetunge. Tamil hostility to government forces continued.
1994 UNP narrowly defeated in general election; Chandrika Kumaratunga became prime minister,

leading SLFP-led left-of-centre coalition. UNP presidential candidate assassinated.

SS Nazi elite corps (German **Schutz-Staffel** 'protective squadron') established 1925. Under *Himmler its 500,000 membership included the full-time **Waffen-SS** (armed SS), which fought in World War II, and spare-time members. The SS performed state police duties and was brutal in its treatment of the Jews and others in the concentration camps and occupied territories. It was condemned at the Nuremberg Trials of war criminals.

stabilizer one of a pair of fins fitted to the sides of a ship, especially one governed automatically by a *gyroscope mechanism, designed to reduce side-to-side rolling of the ship in rough weather.

stack in computing, a method of storing data in which the most recent item stored will be the first to be retrieved. The technique is commonly called 'last in, first out'.

stadholder or **stadtholder** leader of the United Provinces of the Netherlands from the 15th to the 18th century.

Staël Anne Louise Germaine Necker, Madame de 1766–1817. French author. She wrote semi-autobiographical novels such as *Delphine* 1802 and *Corinne* 1807, and the critical work *De l'Allemagne* 1810, on German literature. She was banished from Paris by Napoleon 1803 because of her advocacy of political freedom.

Staffordshire county in W central England
area 2,720 sq km/1,050 sq mi
towns Stafford (administrative headquarters), Stoke-on-Trent
products coal in the N; china and earthenware in the Potteries and the upper Trent basin
population (1991) 1,020,300
famous people Arnold Bennett, Peter de Wint, Robert Peel.

stag in finance, a subscriber for new *share issues who expects to profit from a rise in price on early trading in the shares.

stagflation economic condition (experienced in Europe in the 1970s) in which rapid inflation is accompanied by stagnating, even declining, output and by increasing unemployment. Its cause is often sharp increases in costs of raw materials and/or labour.

stain in chemistry, a coloured compound that will bind to other substances. Stains are used extensively in microbiology to colour microorganisms and in histochemistry to detect the presence and whereabouts in plant and animal tissue of substances such as fats, cellulose, and proteins.

stained glass coloured pieces of glass that are joined by lead strips to form a pictorial window design.

stainless steel widely used *alloy of iron, chromium, and nickel that resists rusting. Its chromium content also gives it a high tensile strength. It is used for cutlery and kitchen fittings. Stainless steel was first produced in the UK 1913 and in Germany 1914.

Stakhanov Aleksei 1906–1977. Soviet miner who exceeded production norms; he gave his name to the **Stakhanovite** movement of the 1930s, when workers were offered incentives to simplify and reorganize work processes in order to increase production.

stalactite and stalagmite cave structures formed by the deposition of calcite dissolved in ground water. **Stalactites** grow downwards from the roofs or walls and can be icicle-shaped, straw-shaped, curtain-shaped, or formed as terraces. **Stalagmites** grow upwards from the cave floor and can be conical, fir-cone-shaped, or resemble a stack of saucers. Growing stalactites and stalagmites may meet to form a continuous column from floor to ceiling.

Stalin Joseph. Adopted name (Russian 'steel') of Joseph Vissarionovich Djugashvili 1879–1953. Soviet politician. A member of the October Revolution Committee 1917, Stalin became general secretary of the Communist Party 1922. After *Lenin's death 1924, Stalin sought to create 'socialism in one country' and clashed with *Trotsky, who denied the possibility of socialism inside Russia until revolution had occurred in W Europe. Stalin won this ideological struggle by 1927, and a series of five-year plans was launched to collectivize industry and agriculture from 1928. All opposition was eliminated in the Great Purge 1936–38. During World War II, Stalin intervened in the military direction of the campaigns against Nazi Germany. His role was denounced after his death by Khrushchev and other members of the Soviet regime.

Stalingrad former name (1925–61) of the Russian city of *Volgograd.

Stallone Sylvester 1946– . US film actor, a bit player who rocketed to fame as the boxer in *Rocky* 1976. Other films include *First Blood* 1982 and the *Rambo* series from 1985.

Stamboul old part of the Turkish city of *Istanbul, the area formerly occupied by *Byzantium.

stamen male reproductive organ of a flower. The stamens are collectively referred to as the *androecium. A typical stamen consists of a stalk, or filament, with an anther, the pollen-bearing organ, at its apex, but in some primitive plants, such as *Magnolia*, the stamen may not be markedly differentiated.

Stamp Act UK act of Parliament in 1765 that sought to raise enough money from the American colonies to cover the cost of their defence. Refusal to use the required tax stamps and a blockade of British merchant shipping in the colonies forced repeal of the act the following year. It was a precursor of the *American Revolution.

standard atmosphere alternative term for *atmosphere, a unit of pressure.

standard deviation in statistics, a measure of the spread of data. The deviation (difference) of each of the data items from the mean is found, and their values squared. The mean value of these squares is then calculated. The standard deviation is the square root of this mean.

standard form method of writing numbers often used by scientists, particularly for very large or very small numbers. The numbers are written with one digit before the decimal point and multiplied by a power of 10. The number of digits given after the decimal point depends on the accuracy required. For example, the *speed of light is 2.9979×10^8 metres/1.8628×10^5 mi per second.

standard gravity acceleration due to gravity, generally taken as 9.81274 m/32.38204 ft per second per second.

standard illuminant any of three standard light intensities, A, B, and C, used for illumination when phenomena involving colour are measured. A is the light from a filament at 2,848 K (2,575°C/4,667°F), B is noon sunlight, and C is normal daylight. B and C are defined with respect to A. Standardization is necessary because colours appear different when viewed in different lights.

standard model in physics, the modern theory of *elementary particles and their interactions. According to the standard model, elementary particles are classified as leptons (light particles, such as electrons), hadrons (particles, such as neutrons and protons, that are formed from quarks), and gauge bosons. Leptons and hadrons interact by exchanging gauge bosons, each of which is responsible for a different fundamental force: photons mediate the electromagnetic force, which affects all charged particles; gluons mediate the strong nuclear force, which affects quarks; gravitons mediate the force of gravity; and the weakons (intermediate vector bosons) mediate the weak nuclear force. See also *quantum electrodynamics and *quantum chromodynamics.

standard of living in economics, the measure of consumption and welfare of a country, community, class, or person. Individual standard-of-living expectations are heavily influenced by the income and consumption of other people in similar jobs.

Standard Oil US company founded 1870 by John D *Rockefeller; it was divided 1911 under anti-monopoly laws into 34 independent companies, of which 14 remained in 1990 and three retain the Standard Oil name: the Standard Oil Company of California (Socal), Standard Oil Company (Indiana), and Standard Oil Company (Ohio). The former Standard Oil Company (New Jersey) became the *Exxon Corporation 1972.

standard temperature and pressure (STP) in chemistry, a standard set of conditions for experimental measurements, to enable comparisons to be made between sets of results. Standard temperature is 0°C and standard pressure 1 atmosphere (101,325 Pa).

standard volume in physics, the volume occupied by one kilogram molecule (the molecular mass in kilograms) of any gas at standard temperature and pressure. Its value is approx 22.414 cubic metres.

standing committee committee of the UK House of Commons that examines parliamentary bills (proposed acts of Parliament) for detailed correction and amendment. The committee comprises members of Parliament from the main political parties, with a majority usually held by the government. Several standing committees may be in existence at any time, each usually created for a particular bill.

standing order in banking, an instruction (banker's order) by a depositor with the bank to pay a certain sum of money at regular intervals. In some cases, the bank may be billed by a third party such as a supplier of gas or electricity, who is authorized by the depositor to invoice the bank directly, which in turn will pay out the sum demanded (known as **direct debit**).

standing wave in physics, a wave in which the positions of *nodes (positions of zero vibration) and antinodes (positions of maximum vibration) do not move. Standing waves result when two similar waves travel in opposite directions through the same space.

Stanislavsky Konstantin Sergeivich 1863–1938. Russian actor, director, and teacher of acting. He rejected the declamatory style of acting in favour of a more realistic approach, concentrating on the psychological basis for the development of character. The *Actors Studio is based on this approach.

Stanley town on E Falkland, capital of the *Falkland Islands; population (1986) 1,200. After changing its name only once between 1843 and 1982, it was renamed five times in the space of six weeks during the Falklands War April–June 1982.

Stanley Henry Morton. Adopted name of John Rowlands 1841–1904. Welsh-born US explorer and journalist who made four expeditions to Africa. He and David *Livingstone met at Ujiji 1871 and explored Lake Tanganyika. He traced the course of the river Zaïre (Congo) to the sea 1874–77, established the Congo Free State (Zaire) 1879–84, and charted much of the interior 1887–89.

Stanton Elizabeth Cady 1815–1902. US feminist who, with Susan B *Anthony, founded the National Woman Suffrage Association 1869, the first women's movement in the USA and was its first president. She and Anthony wrote and compiled the *History of Women's Suffrage* 1881–86. Stanton also worked for the abolition of slavery.

stanza (Italian 'resting or stopping place') group of lines in a poem. Each stanza has a set, repeatable pattern of metre and rhyme, and is normally divided from the following stanza by a blank line.

star luminous globe of gas, producing its own heat and light by nuclear reactions. Stars are born from *nebulae, and consist mostly of hydrogen and helium gases. Surface temperatures range from 2,000°C/3,600°F to above 30,000°C/54,000°F and the corresponding colours range from red to blue-white. The brightest stars have the highest masses, 100 times that of the Sun, and emit as much light as millions of suns; they live for less than a million years before exploding as *supernovae. The faintest stars are the *red dwarfs, less than one-thousandth the brightness of the Sun.

starch widely distributed, high-molecular-mass *carbohydrate, produced by plants as a food store; main dietary sources are cereals, legumes, and tubers, including potatoes. It consists of varying proportions of two *glucose polymers (*polysaccharides): straight-chain (amylose) and branched (amylopectin) molecules.

Star Chamber in English history, a civil and criminal court, named after the star-shaped ceiling decoration of the room in the Palace of Westminster, London, where its first meetings were held. Created in 1487 by Henry VII, the Star Chamber comprised some 20 or 30 judges. It was abolished 1641 by the *Long Parliament.

star cluster group of related stars, usually held together by gravity. Members of a star cluster are thought to form together from one large cloud of gas in space. **Open clusters** such as the Pleiades contain from a dozen to many hundreds of young stars, loosely scattered over several light years. *Globular clusters are larger and much more densely packed, containing perhaps 100,000 old stars.

starfish or **seastar** any *echinoderm of the subclass Asteroidea with arms radiating from a central body. Usually there are five arms, but some species have more. They are covered with spines and small pincerlike organs. There are also a number of small tubular processes on the skin surface that assist in locomotion and respiration. Starfish are predators, and vary in size from 1.2 cm/0.5 in to 90 cm/3 ft.

star fruit fruit of the *carambola tree.

Stark Johannes 1874–1957. German physicist. In 1902 he predicted, correctly, that high-velocity rays of positive ions (canal rays) would demonstrate the *Doppler effect, and in 1913 showed that a strong electric field can alter the wavelength of light emitted by atoms (the **Stark effect**). He was awarded the Nobel Prize for Physics 1919.

starling any member of a large widespread Old World family (Sturnidae) of chunky, dark, generally gregarious birds of the order Passeriformes. The European starling *Sturnus vulgaris* is common in N Eurasia and has been naturalized in North America from the late 19th century. The black, speckled plumage is glossed with green and purple. Its own call is a bright whistle, but it is a mimic of the songs of other birds. It is about 20 cm/8 in long.

Star of David or **Magen David** six-pointed star (made with two equilateral triangles), a symbol of Judaism since the 17th century. It is the central motif on the flag of Israel, and, since 1897, the emblem of Zionism.

START acronym for ***Strategic Arms Reduction Talks**.

Star Wars popular term for the *Strategic Defense Initiative announced by US president Reagan in 1983.

state territory that forms its own domestic and foreign policy, acting through laws that are typically decided by a government and carried out, by force if necessary, by agents of that government. It can be argued that growth of regional international bodies such as the European Community means that states no longer enjoy absolute sovereignty.

state change in science, a change in the physical state (solid, liquid, or gas) of a material. For instance, melting, boiling, and evaporation, and their opposites (solidification and condensation) are changes of state.

State Department (Department of State) US government department responsible for *foreign relations, headed by the *secretary of state, the senior cabinet officer of the executive branch.

statement in UK education, the results of an assessment of the special educational needs of a child with physical or mental disabilities. Under the Education Act 1981, less able children are entitled to such an assessment by various pro-

fessionals, to establish what their needs are an how they might be met. Approximately 2.4% children were in receipt of statements in 1990.

States General former French parliament tha consisted of three estates: nobility, clergy, an commons. First summoned 1302, it declined i importance as the power of the crown grew. I was not called at all 1614–1789 when the crow needed to institute fiscal reforms to avoid finar cial collapse. Once called, the demands made b the States General formed the first phase in th *French Revolution. States General is also th name of the Dutch parliament.

states of matter forms (solid, liquid, or ga: in which material can exist. Whether a materi: is solid, liquid, or gas depends on its temperatu and the pressure on it. The transition betwee states takes place at definite temperatures, calle melting point and boiling point.

static electricity *electric charge that : stationary, usually acquired by a body by mear of electrostatic induction or friction. Rubbing di ferent materials can produce static electricity, a seen in the sparks produced on combing one hair or removing a nylon shirt. In some processe static electricity is useful, as in paint sprayir where the parts to be sprayed are charged wit electricity of opposite polarity to that on the pai droplets, and in *xerography.

statics branch of mechanics concerned with th behaviour of bodies at rest and forces in equilil rium, and distinguished from *dynamics.

Stationery Office, His/Her Majesty' (HMSO) organization established 1786 to supp books and stationery to British governme departments, and to superintend the printing (government reports and other papers, and bool and pamphlets on subjects ranging from nation: works of art to industrial and agricultural pr cesses. The corresponding establishment in th USA is the Government Printing Office.

statistics branch of mathematics concerne with the collection and interpretation of dat For example, to determine the *mean age of t children in a school, a statistically acceptab answer might be obtained by calculating an ave age based on the ages of a representative sampl consisting, for example, of a random tenth of t pupils from each class. *Probability is the branc of statistics dealing with predictions of events.

status in the social sciences, an individual social position, or the esteem in which he (she is held by others in society. Both within ar between most occupations or social positio there is a status hierarchy. **Status symbols**, suc as insignia of office or an expensive car, ofte accompany high status.

Stauffenberg Claus von 1907–1944. Germa colonel in World War II who, in a conspiracy assassinate Hitler, planted a bomb in the di tator's headquarters conference room in th Wolf's Lair at Rastenburg, East Prussia, 20 Ju 1944. Hitler was merely injured, and Stauffe berg and 200 others were later executed by th Nazi regime.

Stavropol territory of the Russian Federatio lying N of the Caucasus Mountains; ar 80,600 sq km/31,128 sq mi; population (198 2,715,000. The capital is Stavropol. Irrigated la produces grain and sheep are also reared. There are natural gas deposits.

STD abbreviation for *sexually transmitted disease*.

steady-state theory theory that the universe appears the same wherever (and whenever) viewed. This seems to be refuted by the existence of *cosmic background radiation.

stealth technology methods used to make an aircraft as invisible as possible, primarily to radar detection but also to detection by visual means and heat sensors. This is achieved by a combination of aircraft-design elements: smoothing off all radar-reflecting sharp edges; covering the aircraft with radar-absorbent materials; fitting engine coverings that hide the exhaust and heat signatures of the aircraft; and other, secret technologies.

steam in chemistry, a dry, invisible gas formed by vaporizing water. The visible cloud that normally forms in the air when water is vaporized is due to minute suspended water particles. Steam is widely used in chemical and other industrial processes and for the generation of power.

steam engine engine that uses the power of steam to produce useful work. It was the principal power source during the British Industrial Revolution in the 18th century. The first successful steam engine was built 1712 by Thomas Newcomen, and it was developed further by James Watt from 1769 and by Richard Trevithick, whose high-pressure steam engine 1802 led to the development of the steam locomotive.

stearic acid $CH_3(CH_2)_{16}COOH$ saturated long-chain *fatty acid, soluble in alcohol and ether but not in water. It is found in many fats and oils, and is used to make soap and candles and as a lubricant. The salts of stearic acid are called stearates.

steel alloy or mixture of iron and up to 1.7% carbon, sometimes with other elements, such as manganese, phosphorus, sulphur, and silicon. The USA, Russia, Ukraine, and Japan are the main steel producers. Steel has innumerable uses, including ship and automobile manufacture, skyscraper frames, and machinery of all kinds.

steel band musical ensemble common in the West Indies, consisting mostly of percussion instruments made from oil drums that give a sweet, metallic ringing tone.

Steele Richard 1672–1729. Irish essayist who founded the journal *The Tatler* 1709–11, in which Joseph *Addison collaborated. They continued their joint work in *The Spectator*, also founded by Steele, 1711–12, and *The Guardian* 1713. He also wrote plays, such as *The Conscious Lovers* 1722.

Steen Jan 1626–1679. Dutch painter. Born in Leiden, he was also active in The Hague, Delft, and Haarlem. He painted humorous everyday scenes, mainly set in taverns or bourgeois households, as well as portraits and landscapes.

Stefan–Boltzmann law in physics, a law that relates the energy, E, radiated away from a perfect emitter (a *black body), to the temperature, T, of that body. It has the form $M = \sigma T^4$, where M is the energy radiated per unit area per second, T is the temperature, and σ is the **Stefan–Boltzmann constant**. Its value is 5.6697×10^{-8} W m^{-2}

K^{-4}. The law was derived by Austrian physicists Joseph Stefan and Ludwig Boltzmann.

Stein Gertrude 1874–1946. US writer who influenced authors Ernest *Hemingway, Sherwood *Anderson, and F Scott *Fitzgerald with her conversational tone, cinematic technique, use of repetition, and absence of punctuation: devices intended to convey immediacy and realism. Her work includes the self-portrait *The Autobiography of Alice B Toklas* 1933.

Steinbeck John (Ernst) 1902–1968. US novelist. His realist novels, such as *In Dubious Battle* 1936, *Of Mice and Men* 1937, and *The Grapes of Wrath* 1939 (Pulitzer prize 1940), portray agricultural life in his native California, where migrant farm labourers from the Oklahoma dust bowl struggled to survive. Nobel prize 1962.

Steinem Gloria 1934– . US journalist and liberal feminist who emerged as a leading figure in the US women's movement in the late 1960s. She was also involved in radical protest campaigns against racism and the Vietnam War. She cofounded the Women's Action Alliance 1970 and *Ms* magazine. In 1983 a collection of her articles was published as *Outrageous Acts and Everyday Rebellions*.

Steiner Rudolf 1861–1925. Austrian philosopher, originally a theosophist who developed his own mystic and spiritual teaching, anthroposophy, designed to develop the whole human being. A number of Steiner schools follow a curriculum laid down by him with a strong emphasis on the arts, although the schools also include the possibilities for pupils to take state exams.

Stella Frank 1936– . US painter, a pioneer of the hard-edged geometric trend in abstract art that followed Abstract Expressionism. From around 1960 he also experimented with the shape of his canvases.

stem main supporting axis of a plant that bears the leaves, buds, and reproductive structures; it may be simple or branched. The plant stem usually grows above ground, although some grow underground, including *rhizomes, *corms, *rootstocks, and *tubers. Stems contain a continuous vascular system that conducts water and food to and from all parts of the plant.

Stendhal pen name of Marie Henri Beyle 1783–1842. French novelist. His novels *Le Rouge et le noir/The Red and the Black* 1830 and *La Chartreuse de Parme/The Charterhouse of Parma* 1839 were pioneering works in their treatment of disguise and hypocrisy; a review of the latter by fellow novelist *Balzac in 1840 furthered Stendhal's reputation.

stenosis narrowing of a body vessel, duct, or opening, usually due to disease.

Stephen c. 1097–1154. King of England from 1135. A grandson of William I, he was elected king 1135, although he had previously recognized Henry I's daughter *Matilda as heiress to the throne. Matilda landed in England 1139, and civil war disrupted the country until 1153, when Stephen acknowledged Matilda's son, Henry II, as his own heir.

Stephen I, St 975–1038. King of Hungary from 997, when he succeeded his father. He completed the conversion of Hungary to Christianity and was canonized in 1803.

Stephen, St died c. AD 35. The first Christian martyr; he was stoned to death. Feast day 26 Dec.

Stephenson George 1781–1848. English engineer who built the first successful steam locomotive, and who also invented a safety lamp in 1815. He was appointed engineer of the Stockton and Darlington Railway, the world's first public railway, in 1821, and of the Liverpool and Manchester Railway in 1826. In 1829 he won a £500 prize with his locomotive *Rocket*.

Stephenson Robert 1803–1859. English civil engineer who constructed railway bridges such as the high-level bridge at Newcastle upon Tyne, England, and the Menai and Conway tubular bridges in Wales. He was the son of George Stephenson.

steppe the temperate grasslands of Europe and Asia. Sometimes the term refers to other temperate grasslands and semi-arid desert edges.

stepper motor electric motor that can be precisely controlled by signals from a computer. The motor turns through a precise angle each time it receives a signal pulse from the computer. By varying the rate at which signal pulses are produced, the motor can be run at different speeds or turned through an exact angle and then stopped. Switching circuits can be constructed to allow the computer to reverse the direction of the motor.

Steptoe Patrick Christopher 1913–1988. English obstetrician who pioneered *in vitro fertilization. Steptoe, together with biologist Robert Edwards, was the first to succeed in implanting in the womb an egg fertilized outside the body. The first 'test-tube baby' was Louise Brown, born by Caesarean section in 1978.

steradian SI unit (symbol sr) of measure of solid (three-dimensional) angles, the three-dimensional equivalent of the *radian. One steradian is the angle at the centre of a sphere when an area on the surface of the sphere equal to the square of the sphere's radius is joined to the centre.

stereophonic sound system of sound reproduction using two complementary channels leading to two loudspeakers, which gives a more natural depth to the sound. Stereo recording began with the introduction of two-track magnetic tape in the 1950s. See *hi-fi.

stereotype (Greek 'fixed impression') in sociology, a fixed, exaggerated, and preconceived description about a certain type of person, group, or society. It is based on prejudice rather than fact, but by repetition and with time, stereotypes become fixed in people's minds, resistant to change or factual evidence to the contrary.

sterilization any surgical operation to terminate the possibility of reproduction. In women, this is normally achieved by sealing or tying off the *Fallopian tubes (tubal ligation) so that fertilization can no longer take place. In men, the transmission of sperm is blocked by *vasectomy.

sterilization the killing or removal of living organisms such as bacteria and fungi. A sterile environment is necessary in medicine, food processing, and some scientific experiments. Methods include heat treatment (such as boiling), the use of chemicals (such as disinfect-ants), irradiation with gamma rays, and filtration. See also *asepsis.

sterling silver *alloy containing 925 parts o silver and 75 parts of copper. The copper harden the silver, making it more useful.

Sternberg Josef von 1894–1969. Austrian film director, in the USA from childhood. He is bes remembered for his seven films with Marlen Dietrich, including *The Blue Angel/Der blaue Engel* 1930, *Blonde Venus* 1932, and *The Devi Is a Woman* 1935, all of which are marked b his expressive use of light and shadow.

Sterne Laurence 1713–1768. Irish writer creator of the comic anti-hero Tristram Shandy *The Life and Opinions of Tristram Shandy Gent* 1759–67, an eccentrically whimsical an bawdy novel which foreshadowed many of the techniques and devices of 20th-century novelists including James Joyce. His other works include *A Sentimental Journey through France and Italy* 1768.

steroid in biology, any of a group of cyclic unsaturated alcohols (lipids without fatty acid components), which, like sterols, have a comple molecular structure consisting of four carbon rings. Steroids include the sex hormones, such as *testosterone, the corticosteroid hormones produced by the *adrenal gland, bile acids, and *cholesterol. The term is commonly used to refe to *anabolic steroid.

sterol any of a group of solid, cyclic, unsaturated alcohols, with a complex structure that includes four carbon rings; cholesterol is an example. Steroids are derived from sterols.

stethoscope instrument used to ascertain the condition of the heart and lungs by listening to their action. It consists of two earpieces connected by flexible tubes to a small plate that is placed against the body. It was invented in 1819 in France by René Théophile Hyacinthe *Laënnec.

Stevens Wallace 1879–1955. US poet. An insurance company executive, he was not recognized as a major poet until late in life. His volumes of poems include *Harmonium* 1923, *The Man with the Blue Guitar* 1937, and *Transport to Summer* 1947. *The Necessary Angel* 1951 is a collection of essays. An elegant and philosophical poet, he won the Pulitzer Prize 1954 for his *Collected Poems*.

Stevenson Adlai 1900–1965. US Democrat politician. As governor of Illinois 1949–53 he campaigned vigorously against corruption in public life, and as Democratic candidate for the presidency 1952 and 1956 was twice defeated by Eisenhower. In 1945 he was chief US delegate at the founding conference of the United Nations.

Stevenson Robert Louis 1850–1894. Scottish novelist and poet. He wrote the adventure novel *Treasure Island* 1883. Later works included the novels *Kidnapped* 1886, *The Master of Ballantrae* 1889, *The Strange Case of Dr Jekyll and Mr Hyde* 1886, and the anthology *A Child's Garden of Verses* 1885.

Stewart Jackie (John Young) 1939– . Scottish motor-racing driver. Until surpassed by Alain *Prost (France) 1987, Stewart held the record for the most Formula One Grand Prix wins (27).

Stewart James 1908–1993. US actor. He made his Broadway debut 1932 and soon after worked

1 Hollywood. Speaking with a soft, slow drawl, e specialized in the role of the stubbornly onest, ordinary American in such films as *Mr mith Goes to Washington* 1939, *The Philadel-hia Story* 1940 (Academy Award), *It's a Won-erful Life* 1946, *Harvey* 1950, *The Man from aramie* 1955, and *Anatomy of a Murder* 1959. His films with director Alfred Hitchcock include *Rope* 1948, *Rear Window* 1954, *The Man Who Knew Too Much* 1956, and *Vertigo* 1958.

tick insect insect of the order Phasmida, losely resembling a stick or twig. Many species re wingless. The longest reach a length of 30 cm/ ft.

stickleback any fish of the family Gasterostei-dae, found in marine and fresh waters of the northern hemisphere. It has a long body that can grow to 18 cm/7 in. The spines along a stickle-back's back take the place of the first dorsal fin, and can be raised to make the fish difficult to eat for predators. The male builds a nest for the female's eggs, which he then guards.

Stieglitz Alfred 1864–1946. US photographer. After forming the Photo Secession group in 1903, he started up the magazine *Camera Work*. Through exhibitions at his gallery '291' in New York he helped to establish photography as an art form. His works include *Winter, Fifth Avenue* 1893 and *Steerage* 1907. In 1924 he married the painter Georgia O'Keeffe, who was the model in many of his photographs.

stigma in a flower, the surface at the tip of a *carpel that receives the *pollen. It often has short outgrowths, flaps, or hairs to trap pollen and may produce a sticky secretion to which the grains adhere.

Stijl, De (Dutch 'the style') group of 20th-century Dutch artists and architects led by *Mondrian from 1917. The group promoted Mondrian's 'Neo-Plasticism', an abstract style that sought to establish universal principles of design based on horizontal and vertical lines, the three primary colours, and black, white, and grey. They had a strong influence on the *Bauhaus school.

Stilwell Joseph Warren ('Vinegar Joe') 1883–1946. US general in World War II. In 1942 he became US military representative in China, when he commanded the Chinese forces cooperating with the British (with whom he quarrelled) in Burma (now Myanmar); he later commanded all US forces in China, Burma, and India until recalled to the USA 1944 after differences over nationalist policy with the *Guomindang (nationalist) leader Chiang Kai-shek. Subsequently he commanded the US 10th Army on the Japanese island of Okinawa.

stimulant any substance that acts on the brain to increase alertness and activity; for example, *amphetamine. When given to children, stimulants may have a paradoxical, calming effect. Stimulants cause liver damage, are habit-forming, have limited therapeutic value, and are now prescribed only to treat *narcolepsy and severe obesity.

stinkwood any of various trees with unpleasant-smelling wood. The S African tree *Ocotea bullata*, family Lauraceae, has offensive-smelling wood when newly felled, but fine, durable timber used for furniture. Another stink-wood is *Gustavia augusta* from tropical America.

Stirling administrative headquarters of Central Region, Scotland, on the river Forth; population (1981) 39,000. Industries include the manufacture of agricultural machinery, textiles, and carpets. The castle, which guarded a key crossing of the river, pre-dates the 12th century and was long a Scottish royal residence. William Wallace won a victory at Stirling bridge 1297. Edward II of England (in raising a Scottish siege of the town) went into battle at Bannockburn 1314 and was defeated by Robert I (the Bruce).

Stirling James 1926–1992. Scottish architect. While in partnership with James Gowan (1924–), he designed the Leicester University Engineering Building 1959–63 in a Constructivist vein. He later adopted a more eclectic approach, exemplified in the Staatsgalerie, Stuttgart, 1977–82, a blend of Constructivism, Modernism, and several strands of Classicism. He also designed the Clore Gallery 1982–86 to house the Tate Collection of the Tate Gallery, London.

stoat carnivorous mammal *Mustela erminea* of the northern hemisphere, in the weasel family, about 37 cm/15 in long including the black-tipped tail. It has a long body and a flattened head. The upper parts and tail are red-brown, and the underparts are white. In the colder regions, the coat turns white (ermine) in winter.

stock in botany, any of several herbaceous plants of the genus *Matthiola* of the Crucifer family, commonly grown as garden ornamentals. Many cultivated varieties, including simple-stemmed, queen's, and ten-week, have been derived from the wild stock *M. incana*; *M. bicornis* becomes aromatic at night and is known as night-scented (or evening) stock.

stock in finance, the UK term for the fully paid-up capital of a company. It is bought and sold by subscribers not in units or shares, but in terms of its current cash value. In US usage the term stock generally means an ordinary share. See also *stocks and shares.

stock-car racing sport popular in the UK and USA, but in two different forms. In the UK, the cars are 'old bangers', which attempt to force the other cars off the track or to come to a standstill. This format is known in the USA as 'demolition derbies'. In the USA, stock cars are high-powered sports cars that race on purpose-built tracks at distances up to 640–800 km/400–500 mi.

stock exchange institution for the buying and selling of stocks and shares (securities). The world's largest stock exchanges are London, New York (Wall Street), and Tokyo. The oldest stock exchanges are Antwerp 1460, Hamburg 1558, Amsterdam 1602, New York 1790, and London 1801. The former division on the London Stock Exchange between brokers (who bought shares from jobbers to sell to the public) and jobbers (who sold them only to brokers on commission, the 'jobbers' turn') was abolished in 1986.

Stock Exchange Automation System (SEAQ) a computerized system of share price monitoring. From October 1987, SEAQ began displaying market makers' quotations for UK stocks, having only been operational previously for overseas equities.

Stockhausen Karlheinz 1928– . German composer of avant-garde music who has continued to explore new musical sounds and compositional techniques since the 1950s. His major works include *Gesang der Jünglinge* 1956 and *Kontakte* 1960 (electronic music); and *Sirius* 1977.

Stockholm capital and industrial port of Sweden; population (1990) 674,500. It is built on a number of islands. Industries include engineering, brewing, electrical goods, paper, textiles, and pottery.

stocks wooden frame with holes used in Europe and the USA until the 19th century to confine the legs and sometimes the arms of minor offenders, and expose them to public humiliation. The pillory had a similar purpose.

stocks and shares investment holdings (securities) in private or public undertakings. Although distinctions have become blurred, in the UK stock usually means fixed-interest securities – for example, those issued by central and local government – while *shares represent a stake in the ownership of a trading company which, if they are ordinary shares, yield to the owner dividends reflecting the success of the company. In the USA the term stock generally signifies what in the UK is an ordinary share.

stoicism (Greek *stoa* 'porch') Greek school of philosophy, founded about 300 BC by Zeno of Citium. The stoics were pantheistic materialists who believed that happiness lay in accepting the law of the universe. They emphasized human brotherhood, denounced slavery, and were internationalist. The name is derived from the porch on which Zeno taught.

Stoker Bram (Abraham) 1847–1912. Irish novelist, actor, theatre manager, and author. His novel *Dracula* 1897 crystallized most aspects of the traditional vampire legend and became the source for all subsequent fiction and films on the subject.

stokes cgs unit (symbol St) of kinematic viscosity (a liquid's resistance to flow).

Stokes George Gabriel 1819–1903. Irish physicist. During the late 1840s, he studied the *viscosity (resistance to relative motion) of fluids. This culminated in **Stokes' law**, $F = 6\pi\varepsilon rv$, which applies to a force acting on a sphere falling through a liquid, where ε is the liquid's viscosity and r and v are the radius and velocity of the sphere.

STOL (acronym for *short takeoff and landing*) aircraft fitted with special devices on the wings (such as sucking flaps) that increase aerodynamic lift at low speeds. Small passenger and freight STOL craft may become common with the demand for small airports, especially in difficult terrain.

stolon in botany, a type of *runner.

stolport (abbreviation for *short takeoff and landing port*) airport that can be used by planes adapted to a shorter than normal runway. Such planes tend to have a restricted flying range. Stolport sites are found in built-up areas (such as London Docklands) where ordinary planes would not be able to land safely.

stoma (plural *stomata*) in botany, a pore in the epidermis of a plant. Each stoma is surrounded

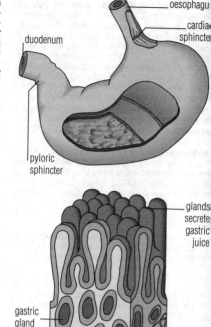

stomach *The human stomach can hold about 1.5 l/ 0.3 gal of liquid.*

by a pair of guard cells that are crescent-shaped when the stoma is open but can collapse to an oval shape, thus closing off the opening between them. Stomata allow the exchange of carbon dioxide and oxygen (needed for *photosynthesis and *respiration) between the internal tissues of the plant and the outside atmosphere. They are also the main route by which water is lost from the plant, and they can be closed to conserve water, the movements being controlled by changes in turgidity of the guard cells.

stomach the first cavity in the digestive system of animals. In mammals it is a bag of muscle situated just below the diaphragm. Food enters it from the oesophagus, is digested by the acid and *enzymes secreted by the stomach lining, and then passes into the duodenum. Some plant-eating mammals have multichambered stomachs that harbour bacteria in one of the chambers to assist in the digestion of *cellulose. The gizzard is part of the stomach in birds.

stone (plural *stone*) imperial unit (abbreviation st) of mass. One stone is 14 pounds (6.35 kg).

Stone Lucy 1818–1893. US feminist orator and editor. Married to the radical Henry Blackwell in 1855, she gained wide publicity when, after a mutual declaration rejecting the legal superiority of the man in marriage, she chose to retain her own surname despite her marriage. The term

Lucy Stoner' was coined to mean a woman who advocated doing the same.

Stone Age the developmental stage of humans in *prehistory before the use of metals, when tools and weapons were made chiefly of stone, especially flint. The Stone Age is subdivided into the Old or Palaeolithic, the Middle or Mesolithic, and the New or Neolithic. The people of the Old Stone Age were hunters and gatherers, whereas the Neolithic people took the first steps in agriculture, the domestication of animals, weaving, and pottery.

stonechat small insectivorous *thrush *Saxicola torquata* frequently found in Eurasia and Africa on open land with bushes. The male has a black head and throat, tawny breast, and dark back; the female is browner.

stonecrop any of several plants of the genus *Sedum* of the orpine family Crassulaceae, a succulent herb with fleshy leaves and clusters of starlike flowers. Stonecrops are characteristic of dry, rocky places and some grow on walls.

stonefish any of a family (Synanceiidae) of tropical marine bony fishes with venomous spines and bodies resembling encrusted rocks.

Stonehenge megalithic monument dating from about 2800 BC on Salisbury Plain, Wiltshire, England. It consisted originally of a circle of 30 upright stones, their tops linked by lintel stones to form a continuous circle about 30 m/100 ft across. Within the circle was a horseshoe arrangement of five trilithons (two uprights plus a lintel, set as five separate entities), and a so-called 'altar stone' – an upright pillar – on the axis of the horseshoe at the open, NE end, which faces in the direction of the rising sun. It has been suggested that it served as an observatory.

stoneware very hard opaque pottery made of nonporous clay with feldspar and a high silica content, fired at high temperature.

Stopes Marie (Carmichael) 1880–1958. Scottish birth-control campaigner. With her husband H V Roe (1878–1949), an aircraft manufacturer, she founded a London birth-control clinic 1921. The Well Woman Centre in Marie Stopes House, London, commemorates her work. She wrote plays and verse as well as the best-selling manual *Married Love* 1918.

Stoppard Tom 1937– . Czechoslovak-born British playwright whose works use wit and wordplay to explore logical and philosophical ideas. His play *Rosencrantz and Guildenstern are Dead* 1966 was followed by comedies including *The Real Inspector Hound* 1968, *Jumpers* 1972, *Travesties* 1974, *Dirty Linen* 1976, *The Real Thing* 1982, *Hapgood* 1988 and *Arcadia* 1993. He has also written for radio, television, and the cinema.

stork any of a family (Ciconiidea) of long-legged, long-necked wading birds with long, powerful wings, and long bills used for spearing prey. Some species grow up to 1.5 m/5 ft tall.

Stowe Harriet Beecher 1811–1896. US suffragist, abolitionist, and author of the antislavery novel *Uncle Tom's Cabin*, first published serially 1851–52. The inspiration came to her in a vision in 1848, and the book brought immediate success.

STP abbreviation for *standard temperature and pressure*.

strabismus technical term for a *squint.

Strachey (Giles) Lytton 1880–1932. English critic and biographer, a member of the *Bloomsbury Group of writers and artists. He wrote *Landmarks in French Literature* 1912. The mocking and witty treatment of Cardinal Manning, Florence Nightingale, Thomas Arnold, and General Gordon in *Eminent Victorians* 1918 won him recognition. His biography of *Queen Victoria* 1921 was more affectionate.

Stradivari Antonio (Latin form *Stradivarius*) 1644–1737. Italian stringed instrument maker, generally considered the greatest of all violin makers. He was born in Cremona and studied there with Niccolo *Amati. He produced more than 1,100 instruments from his family workshops, over 600 of which survive. The secret of his mastery is said to be in the varnish but is probably a combination of fine proportioning and ageing.

Strafford Thomas Wentworth, 1st Earl of Strafford 1593–1641. English politician, originally an opponent of Charles I, but from 1628 on the Royalist side. He ruled despotically as Lord Deputy of Ireland 1632–39, when he returned to England as Charles's chief adviser and received an earldom. He was impeached in 1640 by Parliament, abandoned by Charles as a scapegoat, and beheaded.

Straits Settlements former province of the *East India Company 1826–58, a British crown colony 1867–1946; it comprised Singapore, Malacca, Penang, Cocos Islands, Christmas Island, and Labuan.

strange attractor in physics, a point that moves irregularly within a given region at all times. Such movement describes, for example, the motion of turbulent fluids.

Strasberg Lee 1902–1982. US actor and artistic director of the *Actors Studio from 1948, who developed Method acting from *Stanislavsky's system; pupils have included Marlon Brando, Paul Newman, Julie Harris, Kim Hunter, Geraldine Page, Al Pacino, and Robert de Niro.

Strasbourg city on the river Ill, in Bas-Rhin *département*, capital of Alsace, France; population (1982) 373,000. Industries include car manufacture, tobacco, printing and publishing, and preserves. The *Council of Europe meets here, and sessions of the European Parliament alternate between Strasbourg and Luxembourg.

strata (singular **stratum**) layers or *beds of *sedimentary rock.

Strategic Air Command (SAC) the headquarters commanding all US land-based strategic missile and bomber forces. It is located in Colorado in an underground complex with an instant communications link to the president of the USA.

Strategic Arms Limitation Talks (SALT) series of US-Soviet discussions 1969–79 aimed at reducing the rate of nuclear-arms build-up (as opposed to *disarmament, which would reduce the number of weapons, as discussed in *Strategic Arms Reduction Talks (START).

Strategic Arms Reduction Talks (START) phase in US-Soviet peace discussions dealing with *disarmament. START began with talks in Geneva 1983, leading to the signing of the *Intermediate Nuclear Forces (INF) Treaty 1987. Reductions of about 30% in strategic nuclear weapons systems were agreed 1991 and more significant cuts Jan 1993.

Strategic Defense Initiative (SDI) also called *Star Wars*, attempt by the USA to develop a defence system against incoming nuclear missiles, based in part outside the Earth's atmosphere. It was announced by President Reagan in March 1983, and the research had by 1990 cost over $16.5 billion. In 1988, the joint Chiefs of Staff announced that they expected to be able to intercept no more than 30% of incoming missiles. Scientists maintain that the system is basically unworkable.

strategic islands islands (Azores, Canary Islands, Cyprus, Iceland, Madeira, and Malta) of great political and military significance likely to affect their stability; they held their first international conference in 1979.

strategy, military the planning of warfare. *Grand strategy* requires both political and military input and designs the overall war effort at national level. Planning for a campaign at army-group level or above is *strategy* proper. *Operational strategy* involves military planning at corps, divisional, and brigade level. *Tactics* is the art of warfare at unit level and below; that is, the disposition of relatively small numbers of soldiers over relatively small distances.

Stratford-upon-Avon market town on the river Avon, in Warwickshire, England; population (1981) 21,000. It is the birthplace of William *Shakespeare.

Strathclyde region of Scotland
area 13,900 sq km/5,367 sq mi
towns Glasgow (administrative headquarters), Paisley, Greenock, Kilmarnock, Clydebank, Hamilton, Coatbridge, Prestwick
products dairy, pig, and poultry products; shipbuilding; engineering; coal from Ayr and Lanark.
population (1991) 2,218,200, half the population of Scotland
famous people William Burrell, James Keir Hardie, David Livingstone.

stratigraphy branch of geology that deals with the sequence of formation of *sedimentary rock layers and the conditions under which they were formed. Its basis was developed by William *Smith, a British canal engineer.

stratosphere that part of the atmosphere 10–40 km/6–25 mi from Earth, where the temperature slowly rises from a low of –55°C/–67°F to around 0°C/32°F. The air is rarefied and at around 25 km/15 mi much *ozone is concentrated.

Strauss Johann (Baptist) 1825–1899. Austrian conductor and composer, the son of composer Johann Strauss (1804–1849). In 1872 he gave up conducting and wrote operettas, such as *Die Fledermaus* 1874, and numerous waltzes, such as *The Blue Danube* and *Tales from the Vienna Woods*, which gained him the title 'the Waltz King'.

Strauss Richard (Georg) 1864–1949. German composer and conductor. He followed the German Romantic tradition but had a strongly

personal style, characterized by his bold, colourful orchestration. He first wrote tone poems such as *Don Juan* 1889, *Till Eulenspiegel's Merry Pranks* 1895, and *Also sprach Zarathustra* 1896. He then moved on to opera with *Salome* 1905 and *Elektra* 1909, both of which have elements of polytonality. He reverted to a more traditional style with *Der Rosenkavalier* 1911.

Stravinsky Igor 1882–1971. Russian composer later of French (1934) and US (1945) nationality. He studied under *Rimsky-Korsakov and wrote the music for the Diaghilev ballets *The Firebird* 1910, *Petrushka* 1911, and *The Rite of Spring* 1913 (controversial at the time for their unorthodox rhythms and harmonies). His versatile work ranges from his Neo-Classical ballet *Pulcinella* 1920 to the choral-orchestral *Symphony of Psalms* 1930. He later made use of serial techniques in such works as the *Canticum Sacrum* 1955 and the ballet *Agon* 1953–57.

strawberry low-growing perennial plant of the genus *Fragaria*, family Rosaceae, widely cultivated for its red, fleshy fruits, which are rich in vitamin C. Commercial cultivated forms bear one crop of fruit in summer and multiply by runners.

streaming in education, the practice of dividing pupils for all classes according to an estimate of their overall ability, with arrangements for 'promotion' and 'demotion' at the end of each academic year.

streamlining shaping a body so that it offers the least resistance when travelling through a medium such as air or water. Aircraft, for example, must be carefully streamlined to reduce air resistance, or *drag.

stream of consciousness narrative technique in which a writer presents directly the uninterrupted flow of a character's thoughts, impressions, and feelings, without the conventional devices of dialogue and description. It first came to be widely used in the early 20th century. Leading exponents have included the novelists Virginia Woolf, James Joyce, and William Faulkner.

Streep Meryl 1949– . US actress known for her strong character roles. She became a leading star of the 1980s, winning numerous awards. Her films include *The Deer Hunter* 1978, *Kramer vs Kramer* 1979 (Academy Award), *The French Lieutenant's Woman* 1980, *Sophie's Choice* 1982 (Academy Award), *Out of Africa* 1985, *Ironweed* 1988, and *A Cry in the Dark* 1989.

street hockey form of hockey played on roller skates. At one time played mostly on streets in the USA, it is now played in indoor arenas.

Streisand Barbra (Barbara Joan) 1942– . US singer and actress who became a film star in *Funny Girl* 1968. Her subsequent films include *What's Up Doc?* 1972, *The Way We Were* 1973, and *A Star Is Born* 1979. *Yentl* 1983 was her masterwork, which she directed, scripted, composed, and starred in.

streptomycin antibiotic drug discovered in 1944, used to treat tuberculosis, influenzal meningitis, and other infections, some of which are unaffected by *penicillin.

stress in psychology, any event or situation that makes demands on a person's mental or emotional resources. Stress can be caused by overwork, anxiety about exams, money, or job security, unemployment, bereavement, poor relationships, marriage breakdown, sexual difficulties, poor living or working conditions, and constant exposure to loud noise.

stress and strain in the science of materials, measures of the deforming force applied to a body (stress) and of the resulting change in its shape (strain). For a perfectly elastic material, stress is proportional to strain (*Hooke's law).

stride piano jazz piano style alternating left-hand chords with single bass notes; it was popularized in the 1930s by such musicians as Fats *Waller.

stridulatory organs in insects, organs that produce sound when rubbed together. Crickets rub their wings together, but grasshoppers rub a hind leg against a wing. Stridulation is thought to be used for attracting mates, but may also serve to mark territory.

strike stoppage of work by employees, often as members of a trade union, to obtain or resist change in wages, hours, or conditions. A **lockout** is a weapon of an employer to thwart or enforce such change by preventing employees from working. Another measure is **work to rule**, when production is virtually brought to a halt by strict observance of union rules.

Strindberg August 1849–1912. Swedish playwright and novelist. His plays, influential in the development of dramatic technique, are in a variety of styles including historical plays, symbolic dramas (the two-part *Dödsdansen/The Dance of Death* 1901) and 'chamber plays' such as *Spöksonaten/The Ghost [Spook] Sonata* 1907. *Fadren/The Father* 1887 and *Fröken Julie/Miss Julie* 1888 are among his works.

string group of characters manipulated as a single object by the computer. In its simplest form a string may consist of a single letter or word – for example, the single word SMITH might be established as a string for processing by a computer. A string can also consist of a combination of words, spaces, and numbers – for example, 33 HIGH STREET ANYTOWN ALLSHIRE could be established as a single string.

stringed instrument musical instrument that produces a sound by making a stretched string vibrate. Today the strings are made of gut, metal, and Pearlon (a plastic). Types of stringed instruments include: **bowed** violin family, viol family; **plucked** guitar, ukelele, lute, sitar, harp, banjo, lyre; **plucked mechanically** harpsichord; **struck mechanically** piano, clavichord; **hammered** dulcimer.

string quartet *chamber music ensemble consisting of first and second violins, viola, and cello. The 18th-century successor to the domestic viol consort, the string quartet with its stronger and more rustic tone formed the basis of the symphony orchestra. Important composers for the string quartet include Haydn (more than 80 string quartets), Mozart (27), Schubert (20), Beethoven (17), Dvořák (8), and Bartók (6).

string theory mathematical theory developed in the 1980s; see *superstring theory.

stroboscope instrument for studying continuous periodic motion by using light flashing at the same frequency as that of the motion; for example, rotating machinery can be optically 'stopped' by illuminating it with a stroboscope flashing at the exact rate of rotation.

Stroessner Alfredo 1912– . Military leader and president of Paraguay 1954–89. As head of the armed forces from 1951, he seized power in a coup in 1954 sponsored by the right-wing ruling Colorado Party. Accused by his opponents of harsh repression, his regime spent heavily on the military to preserve his authority. Despite criticisms of his government's civil-rights record, he was re-elected seven times and remained in office until ousted in an army-led coup 1989.

Stroheim Erich von. Assumed name of Erich Oswald Stroheim 1885–1957. Austrian actor and director, in Hollywood from 1914. He was successful as an actor in villainous roles, but his career as a director was wrecked by his extravagance (*Greed* 1923) and he returned to acting in such international films as *La Grande Illusion* 1937 and *Sunset Boulevard* 1950.

stroke or **cerebrovascular accident** or **apoplexy** interruption of the blood supply to part of the brain due to a sudden bleed in the brain (cerebral haemhorrhage) or *embolism or *thrombosis. Strokes vary in severity from producing almost no symptoms to proving rapidly fatal. In between are those (often recurring) that leave a wide range of impaired function, depending on the size and location of the event.

strong nuclear force one of the four fundamental *forces of nature, the other three being the electromagnetic force, gravity, and the weak nuclear force. The strong nuclear force was first described by Japanese physicist Hideki Yukawa 1935. It is the strongest of all the forces, acts only over very small distances (within the nucleus of the atom), and is responsible for binding together *quarks to form *hadrons, and for binding together protons and neutrons in the atomic nucleus. The particle that is the carrier of the strong nuclear force is the *gluon, of which there are eight kinds, each with zero mass and zero charge.

strontium soft, ductile, pale-yellow, metallic element, symbol Sr, atomic number 38, relative atomic mass 87.62. It is one of the *alkaline-earth metals, widely distributed in small quantities only as a sulphate or carbonate. Strontium salts burn with a red flame and are used in fireworks and signal flares.

structuralism 20th-century philosophical movement that has influenced such areas as linguistics, anthropology, and literary criticism. Inspired by the work of the Swiss linguist Ferdinand de Saussure, structuralists believe that objects should be analysed as systems of relations, rather than as positive entities.

structured programming in computing, the process of writing a program in small, independent parts. This makes it easier to control a program's development and to design and test its individual component parts. Structured programs are built up from units called **modules**, which normally correspond to single *procedures or *functions. Some programming languages, such as PASCAL and Modula-2, are better suited to structured programming than others.

strychnine $C_{21}H_{22}O_2N_2$ bitter-tasting, poisonous alkaloid. It is a poison that causes violent muscular spasms, and is usually obtained by powdering the seeds of plants of the genus *Strychnos* (for example *S. nux vomica*). Curare is a related drug.

Stuart or **Stewart** royal family who inherited the Scottish throne in 1371 and the English throne in 1603.

Stubbs George 1724–1806. English artist, known for paintings of horses. After the publication of his book of engravings *The Anatomy of the Horse* 1766, he was widely commissioned as an animal painter.

student finance payment for higher education, whether by grants, loans, parents, or the student working part time. In the UK, students in higher education have their fees paid by their local education authority and are eligible for a maintenance grant, means-tested on their parents' income. In 1990 the government introduced a system of top-up loans intended gradually to replace 50% of the grant entitlement. At the same time students were debarred from previously available welfare benefits, and the National Union of Students argued that this left many worse off.

sturgeon any of a family (Acipenseridae) of large, primitive, bony fishes with five rows of bony plates, small sucking mouths, and chin barbels used for exploring the bottom of the water for prey.

Sturluson Snorri 1179–1241. Icelandic author of the Old Norse poems called *Eddas and the Heimskringla*, a saga chronicle of Norwegian kings until 1177.

Sturmabteilung (SA) German terrorist militia, also known as **Brownshirts**, of the Nazi Party, established 1921 under the leadership of Ernst *Röhm, in charge of physical training and political indoctrination.

Sturm und Drang (German 'storm and stress') German early Romantic movement in literature and music, from about 1775, concerned with the depiction of extravagant passions. Writers associated with the movement include Herder, Goethe, and Schiller. The name is taken from a play by Friedrich von Klinger 1776.

Stuttgart capital of Baden-Württemberg, Germany; population (1988) 565,000. Industries include publishing and the manufacture of vehicles and electrical goods.

style in flowers, the part of the *carpel bearing the *stigma at its tip. In some flowers it is very short or completely lacking, while in others it may be long and slender, positioning the stigma in the most effective place to receive the pollen.

Styx in Greek mythology, the river surrounding the underworld.

Suárez González Adolfo 1933– . Spanish politician, prime minister 1976–81. A friend of King Juan Carlos, he was appointed by the king to guide Spain into democracy after the death of the fascist dictator Franco.

subatomic particle in physics, a particle that is smaller than an atom. Such particles may be indivisible *elementary particles, such as the electron and quark, or they may be composites, such as the proton, neutron, and alpha particle. See also *particle physics.

sublimation in chemistry, the conversion of a solid to vapour without passing through the liquid phase.

submarine underwater warship. The first underwater boat was constructed for James I of England by the Dutch scientist Cornelius van Drebbel (1572–1633) in 1620. A naval submarine, or submersible torpedo boat, the *Gymnote*, was launched by France 1888. The conventional submarine of World War I was driven by diesel engine on the surface and by battery-powered electric motors underwater. The diesel engine also drove a generator that produced electricity to charge the batteries.

submersible vessel designed to operate under water, especially a small submarine used by engineers and research scientists as a ferry craft to support diving operations. The most advanced submersibles are the so-called lock-out type, which have two compartments: one for the pilot, the other to carry divers. The diving compartment is pressurized and provides access to the sea.

subpoena (Latin 'under penalty') in law, an order requiring someone who might not otherwise come forward of his or her own volition to give evidence before a court or judicial official at a specific time and place. A witness who fails to comply with a subpoena is in *contempt of court.

subroutine in computing, a small section of a program that is executed ('called') from another part of the program. Subroutines provide a method of performing the same task at more than one point in the program, and also of separating the details of a program from its main logic. In some computer languages, subroutines are similar to *functions or *procedures.

subsidiary in business, a company that is legally controlled by another company having 50% or more of its shares.

subsidy government payment or concession granted to a state or private company, or an individual. A subsidy may be provided to keep prices down, to stimulate the market for a particular product, or because it is perceived to be in the public interest.

substitution reaction in chemistry, the replacement of one atom or *functional group in an organic molecule by another.

substrate in biochemistry, a compound or mixture of compounds acted on by an enzyme. The term also refers to a substance such as *agar that provides the nutrients for the metabolism of microorganisms. Since the enzyme systems of microorganisms regulate their metabolism, the essential meaning is the same.

succession in ecology, a series of changes that occur in the structure and composition of the vegetation in a given area from the time it is first colonized by plants (**primary succession**), or after it has been disturbed by fire, flood, or clearing (**secondary succession**).

Succot or **Sukkoth** in Judaism, a harvest festival celebrated in Oct, also known as the **Feast of Booths**, which commemorates the time when the Israelites lived in the wilderness during the *Exodus from Egypt. As a reminder of the shelters used in the wilderness, huts are built and used for eating and sleeping during the seven days of the festival.

succubus a female spirit; see *incubus.

succulent plant thick, fleshy plant that stores water in its tissues; for example, cacti and stonecrops *Sedum*. Succulents live either in areas where water is very scarce, such as deserts, or in places where it is not easily obtainable because of the high concentrations of salts in the soil, as in salt marshes. Many desert plants are *xerophytes.

suckering in plants, reproduction by new shoots (suckers) arising from an existing root system rather than from seed. Plants that produce suckers include elm, dandelion, and members of the rose family.

Sucre legal capital and judicial seat of Bolivia; population (1988) 95,600. It stands on the central plateau at an altitude of 2,840 m/9,320 ft.

Sucre Antonio José de 1795–1830. South American revolutionary leader. As chief lieutenant of Simón *Bolívar, he won several battles in freeing the colonies of Ecuador and Bolivia from Spanish rule, and in 1826 became president of Bolivia. After a mutiny by the army and invasion by Peru, he resigned 1828 and was assassinated 1830.

sucrose or *cane sugar* or *beet sugar* $C_{12}H_{22}O_{10}$ a sugar found in the pith of sugar cane and in sugar beets. It is popularly known as *sugar.

Sudan Democratic Republic of (*Jamhuryat es-Sudan*)

area 2,505,800 sq km/967,489 sq mi
capital Khartoum
towns Omdurman, Juba, Wadi Medani, al-Obeid, Kassala, Atbara, al-Qadarif, Kosti; chief port Port Sudan
physical fertile valley of river Nile separates Libyan Desert in W from high rocky Nubian Desert in E
environment the building of the Jonglei Canal to supply water to N Sudan and Egypt threatens the grasslands of S Sudan
head of state General Omar Hassan Ahmed el-Bashir from 1989
head of government Sadiq al-Mahdi from 1993
political system military republic
exports cotton, gum arabic, sesame seed, peanuts, sorghum
currency Sudanese pound
population (1993) 30,830,000; growth rate 2.9% p.a.

languages Arabic 51% (official), local languages
religions Sunni Muslim 73%, animist 18%, Christian 9% (in south)
GNP $400 per head (1990)
chronology
1820 Sudan ruled by Egypt.
1885 Revolt led to capture of Khartoum by self-proclaimed Mahdi.
1896–98 Anglo-Egyptian offensive led by Lord Kitchener subdued revolt.
1899 Sudan administered as an Anglo-Egyptian condominium.
1955 Civil war between Muslim north and non-Muslim south broke out.
1956 Sudan achieved independence from Britain and Egypt as a republic.
1958 Military coup replaced civilian government with Supreme Council of the Armed Forces.
1964 Civilian rule reinstated.
1969 Coup led by Col Gaafar Mohammed Nimeri established Revolutionary Command Council (RCC); name changed to Democratic Republic of Sudan.
1970 Union with Egypt agreed in principle.
1971 New constitution adopted; Nimeri confirmed as president; Sudanese Socialist Union (SSU) declared only legal party.
1972 Proposed Federation of Arab Republics, comprising Sudan, Egypt, and Syria, abandoned. Addis Ababa conference proposed autonomy for southern provinces.
1974 National assembly established.
1983 Nimeri re-elected. Shari'a (Islamic law) introduced.
1985 Nimeri deposed in a bloodless coup led by General Swar al-Dahab; transitional military council set up. State of emergency declared.
1986 More than 40 political parties fought general election; coalition government formed.
1987 Virtual civil war with Sudan People's Liberation Army (SPLA).
1988 Sadiq al-Mahdi formed a new coalition. Another flare-up of civil war between north and south created tens of thousands of refugees. Floods made 1.5 million people homeless. Peace pact signed with SPLA.
1989 Sadiq al-Mahdi overthrown in coup led by General Omar Hassan Ahmed el-Bashir.
1990 Civil war continued with new SPLA offensive.
1991 Federal system introduced, with division of country into nine states.
1993 March: SPLA leaders announced unilateral cease-fire. April: peace talks began. Oct: civilian government, headed by Sadiq al-Mahdi, replaced military council; army retained ultimate control.
1994 Feb: government renewed attacks on SPLA strongholds in S.

sudden infant death syndrome (SIDS) in medicine, the technical term for *cot death.

Sudetenland mountainous region of N Czechoslovakia (now the Czech Republic), annexed by Germany under the *Munich Agreement 1938; it was returned to Czechoslovakia 1945.

Suetonius (Gaius Suetonius Tranquillus) *c.* AD 69–140. Roman historian. He was the author of *Lives of the Caesars* (Julius Caesar to Domitian).

Suez Canal artificial waterway, 160 km/100 mi

long, from Port Said to Suez, linking the Mediterranean and Red seas, separating Africa from Asia, and providing the shortest eastwards sea route from Europe. It was opened 1869, nationalized 1956, blocked by Egypt during the Arab-Israeli war 1967, and not re-opened until 1975.

Suez Crisis military confrontation Oct–Dec 1956 following the nationalization of the Suez Canal by President Nasser of Egypt. In an attempt to reassert international control of the canal, Israel launched an attack, after which British and French troops landed. Widespread international censure (Soviet protest, US non-support, and considerable domestic opposition) forced the withdrawal of British and French troops. The crisis resulted in the resignation of British prime minister Eden. British, French, and Australian relations with the USA were greatly strained during this period.

suffix letter or group of letters added to the end of a word in order to form a new word. For example, the suffix *-ist* can be added to *sex* to form the word *sexist*.

Suffolk county of E England
area 3,800 sq km/1,467 sq mi
towns Ipswich (administrative headquarters), Bury St Edmunds, Lowestoft, Felixstowe
physical low undulating surface and flat coastline; rivers: Waveney, Alde, Deben, Orwell, Stour; Little Ouse.
products cereals, sugar beet, working horses (Suffolk punches), fertilizers, agricultural machinery
population (1991) 629,900

suffragette or **suffragist** woman fighting for the right to vote. In the UK, women's suffrage bills were repeatedly introduced and defeated in Parliament between 1886 and 1911, and a militant campaign was launched 1906 by Emmeline *Pankhurst and her daughters. In 1918 women were granted limited franchise; in 1928 it was extended to all women over 21. In the USA the 19th amendment to the constitution 1920 gave women the vote in federal and state elections.

Sufism mystical movement of *Islam that originated in the 8th century. Sufis believe that deep intuition is the only real guide to knowledge. The movement has a strong strain of asceticism. The name derives from Arabic *suf*, a rough woollen robe worn as an indication of disregard for material things. There are a number of groups or brotherhoods within Sufism, each with its own method of meditative practice, one of which is the whirling dance of the *dervishes.

Sugar Alan 1947– . British entrepreneur, founder in 1968 of the Amstrad electronics company, which holds a strong position in the European consumer electronics and personal-computer market. In 1985 he introduced a complete word-processing system at the price of £399. Subsequent models consolidated his success internationally.

sugar or **sucrose** sweet, soluble crystalline carbohydrate found in the pith of sugar cane and in sugar beet. It is a *disaccharide* sugar, each of its molecules being made up of two simple-sugar (*monosaccharide*) units: glucose and fructose. Sugar is easily digested and forms a major source of energy in humans, being used in cooking and in the food industry as a sweetener and, in high concentrations, as a preservative. A high consumption is associated with obesity and tooth decay. In the UK, sucrose may not be used in baby foods.

sugar maple E North American *maple tree *Acer saccharum*.

Suharto Raden 1921– . Indonesian politician and general. He ousted Sukarno to become president 1967. He ended confrontation with Malaysia, invaded East Timor 1975, and reached a cooperation agreement with Papua New Guinea 1979. His authoritarian rule has met with domestic opposition from the left. He was re-elected 1973, 1978, 1983, and 1988.

suicide the act of killing oneself intentionally; a person who does this.

suite in music, formerly a grouping of old dance forms; later the term came to be used to describe a set of instrumental pieces, sometimes assembled from a stage work, such as Tchaikovsky's *Nutcracker Suite* 1891–92.

Sukarno Achmed 1901–1970. Indonesian nationalist, president 1945–67. During World War II he cooperated in the local administration set up by the Japanese, replacing Dutch rule. After the war he became the first president of the new Indonesian republic, becoming president-for-life in 1966; he was ousted by *Suharto.

Sulawesi formerly **Celebes** island in E Indonesia, one of the Sunda Islands; area (with dependent islands) 190,000 sq km/73,000 sq mi; population (1980) 10,410,000. It is mountainous and forested and produces copra and nickel.

Suleiman or **Solyman** 1494–1566. Ottoman sultan from 1520, known as **the Magnificent** and **the Lawgiver**. Under his rule, the Ottoman Empire flourished and reached its largest extent. He made conquests in the Balkans, the Mediterranean, Persia, and N Africa, but was defeated at Vienna in 1529 and Valletta (on Malta) in 1565. He was a patron of the arts, a poet, and an administrator.

Sulla Lucius Cornelius 138–78 BC. Roman general and politician, a leader of the senatorial party. Forcibly suppressing the democrats in 88 BC, he departed for a successful campaign against *Mithridates VI of Pontus. The democrats seized power in his absence, but on his return Sulla captured Rome and massacred all opponents. The reforms he introduced as dictator, which strengthened the power of the Senate, were backward-looking and short-lived. He retired 79 BC.

Sullivan Arthur (Seymour) 1842–1900. English composer who wrote operettas in collaboration with William Gilbert, including *HMS Pinafore* 1878, *The Pirates of Penzance* 1879, and *The Mikado* 1885. Their partnership broke down in 1896. Sullivan also composed serious instrumental, choral, and operatic works – for example, the opera *Ivanhoe* 1890 – which he valued more highly than the operettas.

sulphate SO_4^{2-} salt or ester derived from sulphuric acid. Most sulphates are water soluble (the exceptions are lead, calcium, strontium, and barium sulphates), and require a very high temperature to decompose them.

sulphide compound of sulphur and another element in which sulphur is the more electro negative element (see *electronegativity). Sulphides occur in a number of minerals. Some of the more volatile sulphides have extremely unpleasant odours (hydrogen sulphide smells of bad eggs).

sulphite SO_3^{2-} salt or ester derived from sulphurous acid.

sulphonamide any of a group of compounds containing the chemical group sulphonamide (SO_2NH_2) or its derivatives, which were, and still are in some cases, used to treat bacterial diseases. Sulphadiazine ($C_{10}H_{10}N_4O_2S$) is an example.

sulphur brittle, pale-yellow, nonmetallic element, symbol S, atomic number 16, relative atomic mass 32.064. It occurs in three allotropic forms: two crystalline (called rhombic and monoclinic, following the arrangements of the atoms within the crystals) and one amorphous. It burns in air with a blue flame and a stifling odour. Insoluble in water but soluble in carbon disulphide, it is a good electrical insulator. Sulphur is widely used in the manufacture of sulphuric acid (used to treat phosphate rock to make fertilizers) and in making paper, matches, gunpowder and fireworks, in vulcanizing rubber, and in medicines and insecticides.

sulphur dioxide SO_2 pungent gas produced by burning sulphur in air or oxygen. It is widely used for disinfecting food vessels and equipment, and as a preservative in some food products. It occurs in industrial flue gases and is a major cause of *acid rain.

sulphuric acid or *oil of vitriol* H_2SO_4 a dense, viscous, colourless liquid that is extremely corrosive. It gives out heat when added to water and can cause severe burns. Sulphuric acid is used extensively in the chemical industry, in the refining of petrol, and in the manufacture of fertilizers, detergents, explosives, and dyes. It forms the acid component of car batteries.

sulphurous acid H_2SO_3 solution of sulphur dioxide (SO_2) in water. It is a weak acid.

Sumatra or *Sumatera* second largest island of Indonesia, one of the Sunda Islands; area 473,600 sq km/182,800 sq mi; population (1989) 36,882,000. East of a longitudinal volcanic mountain range is a wide plain; both are heavily forested. Products include rubber, rice, tobacco, tea, timber, tin, and petroleum.

Sumerian civilization the world's earliest civilization, dated about 3500 BC, and located at the confluence of the Tigris and Euphrates rivers in lower Mesopotamia (present-day Iraq). It was a city-state with priests as secular rulers. After 2000 BC, Sumer was absorbed by the Babylonian empire.

summer time practice introduced in the UK 1916 whereby legal time from spring to autumn is an hour in advance of Greenwich mean time. Continental Europe 'puts the clock back' a month earlier than the UK in autumn. British summer time was permanently in force Feb 1940–Oct 1945 and Feb 1968–Oct 1971. Double summer time (2 hours in advance) was in force during the summers of 1941–45 and 1947. In North America the practice is known as *daylight saving time*.

summit or *summit conference* meeting of heads of government to discuss common interests, especially the US-Soviet summits 1959–90, of which there were 15. The term was first used during World War II, and the *Yalta Conference and *Potsdam Conference 1945 were summits that did much to determine the political structure of the postwar world. Later summits have been of varying importance, partly as public-relations exercises.

summons in law, a court order officially delivered, requiring someone to appear in court on a certain date.

Sumner James 1887–1955. US biochemist. In 1926 he succeeded in crystallizing the enzyme urease and demonstrating its protein nature. For this work Sumner shared the 1946 Nobel Prize for Chemistry with John Northrop and Wendell Stanley.

sumo wrestling national sport of Japan. Fighters of larger than average size (rarely less than 130 kg/21 st or 285 lb) try to push, pull, or throw each other out of a circular ring.

Sun the *star at the centre of the solar system. Its diameter is 1,392,000 km/865,000 mi; its temperature at the surface is about 5,800K (5,530°C/9,980°F), and at the centre 15,000,000K (15,000,000°C/27,000,000°F). It is composed of about 70% hydrogen and 30% helium, with other elements making up less than 1%. The Sun's energy is generated by nuclear fusion reactions that turn hydrogen into helium at its centre. The gas core is far denser than mercury or lead on Earth. The Sun is about 4.7 billion years old, with a predicted lifetime of 10 billion years.

Sun City alternative name for *Mmabatho, resort in Bophuthatswana, South Africa.

Sundanese member of the second largest ethnic group in the Republic of Indonesia. There are more than 20 million speakers of Sundanese, a member of the western branch of the Austronesian family. Like their neighbours, the Javanese, the Sundanese are predominantly Muslim. They are known for their performing arts, especially *jaipongan* dance traditions, and distinctive batik fabrics.

Sunday trading buying and selling on Sunday; this was banned in the UK by the Shops Act 1950, but the ban may be in breach of Article 30 of the Treaty of Rome as amounting to an unlawful restraint on the free movement of goods. A bill to enable widespread Sunday trading was defeated April 1986. Similar legislation in the USA has long been very laxly enforced, and in some cases repealed. The conflict is between the free market on the one hand and, on the other, the trade unions' fear of longer working hours, and the Christian lobby's traditional opposition to secular activity on the Sabbath.

sundew any insectivorous plant of the genus *Drosera*, family Droseraceae, with viscid hairs on the leaves for catching prey.

sundial instrument measuring time by means of a shadow cast by the Sun. Almost completely superseded by the proliferation of clocks, it survives ornamentally in gardens. The dial is marked with the hours at graduated distances, and a style or gnomon (parallel to Earth's axis and pointing to the north) casts the shadow.

sunfish marine fish *Mola mola* with disc-shaped body 3 m/10 ft long found in all temperate and tropical oceans. The term also applies to fish of the North American freshwater Centrarchidae family, which have compressed, almost circular bodies, up to 80 cm/30 in long, and are nestbuilders and avid predators.

sunflower tall plant of the genus *Helianthus*, family Compositae. The common sunflower *H. annuus*, probably native to Mexico, grows to 4.5 m/15 ft in favourable conditions. It is commercially cultivated in central Europe, the USA, Russia, Ukraine, and Australia for the oil-bearing seeds that follow the yellow-petalled flowers.

Sunni member of the larger of the two main sects of *Islam, with about 680 million adherents. Sunni Muslims believe that the first three caliphs were all legitimate successors of the prophet Muhammad, and that guidance on belief and life should come from the Koran and the Hadith, and from the Shari'a, not from a human authority or spiritual leader. Imams in Sunni Islam are educated lay teachers of the faith and prayer leaders. The name derives from the *Sunna*, Arabic 'code of behaviour', the body of traditional law evolved from the teaching and acts of Muhammad.

Sunningdale Agreement pact Dec 1973 between the UK and Irish governments, together with the Northern Ireland executive, drawn up in Sunningdale, England. The agreement included provisions for a power-sharing executive in Northern Ireland. However, the executive lasted only five weeks before the UK government was defeated in a general election, and a general strike May 1974 brought down the Northern Ireland government. The experiment has not been repeated.

Sunshine Coast chain of sandy beaches on the coast of Queensland, Australia, stretching for about 100 km/60 mi from Bribie Island, N of Brisbane, to Rainbow Beach. It includes the resorts of Noosa Heads and Caloundra.

sunshine recorder device for recording the hours of sunlight during a day. The *Campbell-Stokes sunshine recorder* consists of a glass sphere that focuses the sun's rays on a graduated paper strip. A track is burned along the strip corresponding to the time that the Sun is shining.

sunspot dark patch on the surface of the Sun, actually an area of cooler gas, thought to be caused by strong magnetic fields that block the outward flow of heat to the Sun's surface. Sunspots consist of a dark central *umbra*, about 4,000K (3,700°C/6,700°F), and a lighter surrounding *penumbra*, about 5,500K (5,200°C/9,400°F). They last from several days to over a month, ranging in size from 2,000 km/1,250 mi to groups stretching for over 100,000 km/62,000 mi. The number of sunspots visible at a given time varies from none to over 100 in a cycle averaging 11 years.

Sun Yat-sen or *Sun Zhong Shan* 1867–1925. Chinese revolutionary leader, founder of the *Guomindang (Nationalist party) 1894, and provisional president of the Republic of China 1912 after playing a vital part in deposing the emperor. He was president of a breakaway government from 1921.

superactinide any of a theoretical series of superheavy, radioactive elements, starting with atomic number 113, that extend beyond the *transactinide series in the periodic table. They

do not occur in nature and none has yet been synthesized.

supercomputer the fastest, most powerful type of computer, capable of performing its basic operations in picoseconds (thousand-billionths of a second), rather than nanoseconds (billionths of a second), like most other computers.

superconductivity in physics, increase in electrical conductivity at low temperatures. The resistance of some metals and metallic compounds decreases uniformly with decreasing temperature until at a critical temperature (the superconducting point), within a few degrees of absolute zero (0 K/–273.16°C/–459.67°F), the resistance suddenly falls to zero. The phenomenon was discovered by Dutch scientist Heike Kamerlingh-Onnes (1853–1926) in 1911.

supercooling in physics, the lowering in temperature of a *saturated solution without crystallization taking place, forming a supersaturated solution. Usually crystallization rapidly follows the introduction of a small (seed) crystal or agitation of the supercooled solution.

superego in Freudian psychology, the element of the human mind concerned with the ideal, responsible for ethics and self-imposed standards of behaviour. It is characterized as a form of conscience, restraining the *ego, and responsible for feelings of guilt when the moral code is broken.

supergiant the largest and most luminous type of star known, with a diameter of up to 1,000 times that of the Sun and absolute magnitudes of between –5 and –9.

superheterodyne receiver the most widely used type of radio receiver, in which the incoming signal is mixed with a signal of fixed frequency generated within the receiver circuits. The resulting signal, called the intermediate-frequency (i.f.) signal, has a frequency between that of the incoming signal and the internal signal. The intermediate frequency is near the optimum frequency of the amplifier to which the i.f. signal is passed. This arrangement ensures greater gain and selectivity. The superheterodyne system is also used in basic television receivers.

Superior, Lake largest and deepest of the *Great Lakes of North America, and the second largest lake in the world; area 83,300 sq km/32,200 sq mi.

supernova the explosive death of a star, which temporarily attains a brightness of 100 million Suns or more, so that it can shine as brilliantly as a small galaxy for a few days or weeks. Very approximately, it is thought that a supernova explodes in a large galaxy about once every 100 years. Many supernovae remain undetected because of obscuring by interstellar dust -astronomers estimate some 50%.

superpower term used to describe the USA and the USSR from the end of World War II 1945, when they emerged as significantly stronger than all other countries.

supersaturation in chemistry, the state of a solution that has a higher concentration of *solute than would normally be obtained in a *saturated solution.

supersonic speed speed greater than that at

which sound travels, measured in *Mach numbers. In dry air at 0°C/32°F, sound travels at about 1,170 kph/727 mph, but decreases with altitude until, at 12,000 m/39,000 ft, it is only 1,060 kph/658 mph.

superstring theory in physics, a mathematical theory developed in the 1980s to explain the properties of *elementary particles and the forces between them (in particular, gravity and the nuclear forces) in a way that combines *relativity and *quantum theory. In string theory, the fundamental objects in the universe are not pointlike particles but extremely small stringlike objects. These objects exist in a universe of ten dimensions, although, for reasons not yet understood, only three space dimensions and one dimension of time are discernible.

supersymmetry in physics, a theory that relates the two classes of elementary particle, the *fermions and the *bosons. According to supersymmetry, each fermion particle has a boson partner particle, and vice versa. It has not been possible to marry up all the known fermions with the known bosons, and so the theory postulates the existence of other, as yet undiscovered fermions, such as the photinos (partners of the photons), gluinos (partners of the gluons), and gravitinos (partners of the gravitons). Using these ideas, it has become possible to develop a theory of gravity – called supergravity – that extends Einstein's work and considers the gravitational, nuclear, and electromagnetic forces to be manifestations of an underlying superforce. Supersymmetry has been incorporated into the *superstring theory, and appears to be a crucial ingredient in the 'theory of everything' sought by scientists.

supplementary benefit in Britain, former name (1966–88) for *income support; weekly *social security payments by the state to those with low incomes.

supply and demand one of the fundamental approaches to economics, which examines and compares the supply of a good with its demand (usually in the form of a graph of supply and demand curves plotted against price). For a typical good, the supply curve is upward-sloping (the higher the price, the more the manufacturer is willing to sell), while the demand curve is downward-sloping (the cheaper the good, the more demand there is for it). The point where the curves intersect is the equilibrium price at which supply equals demand.

supply-side economics school of economic thought advocating government policies that allow market forces to operate freely, such as privatization, cuts in public spending and income tax, reductions in trade-union power, and cuts in the ratio of unemployment benefits to wages. Supply-side economics developed as part of the monetarist (see *monetarism) critique of *Keynesian economics.

Supremacy, Acts of two UK acts of Parliament 1534 and 1559, which established Henry VIII and Elizabeth I respectively as head of the English church in place of the pope.

Suprematism Russian abstract-art movement developed about 1913 by Kasimir *Malevich. The Suprematist paintings gradually became more severe, until in 1918 they reached a climax with the *White on White* series showing white geometrical shapes on a white ground.

Supreme Court highest US judicial tribunal, composed since 1869 of a chief justice (William Rehnquist from 1986) and eight associate justices. Appointments are made for life by the president, with the advice and consent of the Senate, and justices can be removed only by impeachment.

Supremes, the US vocal group, pioneers of the Motown sound, formed 1959 in Detroit. Beginning in 1962, the group was a trio comprising, initially, Diana Ross (1944–   ), Mary Wilson (1944–   ), and Florence Ballard (1943–1976). The most successful female group of the 1960s, they had a string of pop hits beginning with 'Where Did Our Love Go?' 1964 and 'Baby Love' 1964. Diana Ross left to pursue a solo career 1969.

Surabaya port on the island of Java, Indonesia; population (1980) 2,028,000. It has oil refineries and shipyards and is a naval base.

Suraj-ud-Dowlah 1728–1757. Nawab of Bengal, India. He captured Calcutta from the British 1756 and imprisoned some of the British in the Black Hole of Calcutta (a small room in which a number of them died), but was defeated in 1757 by Robert *Clive, and lost Bengal to the British at the Battle of Plassey. He was killed in his capital, Murshidabad.

surd an expression containing the root of an *irrational number that can never be exactly expressed – for example, $\sqrt{3} = 1.732050808...$.

surface-area-to-volume ratio the ratio of an animal's surface area (the area covered by its skin) to its total volume. This is high for small animals, but low for large animals such as elephants.

surface tension in physics, the property that causes the surface of a liquid to behave as if it were covered with a weak elastic skin; this is why a needle can float on water. It is caused by the exposed surface's tendency to contract to the smallest possible area because of unequal cohesive forces between *molecules at the surface. Allied phenomena include the formation of droplets, the concave profile of a meniscus, and the *capillary action by which water soaks into a sponge.

surfing sport of riding on the crest of large waves while standing on a narrow, keeled surfboard, usually of light synthetic material such as fibreglass, about 1.8 m/6 ft long (or about 2.4–7 m/8–9 ft known as the Malibu), as first developed in Hawaii and Australia. *Windsurfing is a recent development.

surge abnormally high tide brought about by a combination of a severe atmospheric depression over a shallow sea area, particularly high spring tides, and winds blowing from the appropriate direction. The low atmospheric pressure causes the water surface to rise, pushed up by greater pressures in the surrounding region, and the winds blow it towards the land, causing flooding.

surgeon fish any fish of the tropical marine family Acanthuridae. It has a flat body up to 50 cm/20 in long, is brightly coloured, and has a movable spine on each side of the tail that can be used as a weapon.

surgery in medicine, originally the removal of diseased parts or foreign substances from the body through cutting and other manual operations. It now includes such techniques as beamed high-energy ultrasonic waves, binocular magnifiers for microsurgery, and lasers. Circumstances permitting, surgery is carried out under sterile conditions, using *anaesthesia.

surgical spirit *ethanol to which has been added a small amount of methanol to render it unfit to drink. It is used to sterilize surfaces and to cleanse skin abrasions and sores.

Surinam Republic of (*Republiek Suriname*)
area 163,820 sq km/63,243 sq mi
capital Paramaribo
towns Nieuw Nickerie, Brokopondo, Nieuw Amsterdam
physical hilly and forested, with flat and narrow coastal plain
head of state and government Ronald Venetiaan from 1991
political system emergent democratic republic
exports alumina, aluminium, bauxite, rice, timber
currency Surinam guilder
population (1991) 404,300 (Hindu 37%, Creole 31%, Javanese 15%); growth rate 1.1% p.a.
languages Dutch (official), Sranan (creole), English, others

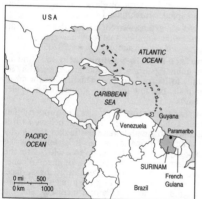

religions Christian 30%, Hindu 27%, Muslim 20%
GNP $3,610 per head (1991)
chronology
1667 Became a Dutch colony.
1954 Achieved internal self-government as Dutch Guiana.
1975 Independence achieved from the Netherlands, with Dr Johan Ferrier as president and Henck Arron as prime minister; 40% of the population emigrated to the Netherlands.
1980 Arron's government overthrown in army coup; Ferrier refused to recognize military regime; appointed Dr Henk Chin A Sen to lead civilian administration. Army replaced Ferrier with Dr Chin A Sen.
1982 Army, led by Lt Col Desi Bouterse, seized power, setting up a Revolutionary People's Front.
1985 Ban on political activities lifted.
1986 Antigovernment rebels brought economic chaos to Surinam.
1987 New constitution approved.

1988 Ramsewak Shankar elected president.
1989 Bouterse rejected peace accord reached by President Shankar with guerrilla insurgents, vowed to continue fighting.
1990 Shankar deposed in army coup.
1991 Johan Kraag became interim president. New Front for Democracy won assembly majority. Ronald Venetiaan elected president.
1992 Peace accord with guerrilla groups.

Surrealism movement in art, literature, and film that developed out of *Dada around 1922. Led by André *Breton, who produced the *Surrealist Manifesto* 1924, the Surrealists were inspired by the thoughts and visions of the subconscious mind. They explored varied styles and techniques, and the movement became the dominant force in Western art between World Wars I and II.

Surrey county in S England
area 1,660 sq km/641 sq mi
towns Kingston upon Thames (administrative headquarters), Guildford, Woking
products vegetables, agricultural products, service industries
population (1991) 997,000
famous people Eric Clapton, John Galsworthy, Aldous Huxley, Laurence Olivier.

Surrey Henry Howard, Earl of Surrey c. 1517–1547. English courtier and poet, executed on a poorly based charge of high treason. With Thomas Wyatt, he introduced the sonnet to England and was a pioneer of *blank verse.

surrogacy practice whereby a woman is sought, and usually paid, to bear a child for an infertile couple or a single parent.

surveying the accurate measuring of the Earth's crust, or of land features or buildings. It is used to establish boundaries, and to evaluate the topography for engineering work. The measurements used are both linear and angular, and geometry and trigonometry are applied in the calculations.

Sūrya in Hindu mythology, the sun god, son of the sky god Indra. His daughter, also named Sūrya, is a female personification of the Sun.

suspension mixture consisting of small solid particles dispersed in a liquid or gas, which will settle on standing. An example is milk of magnesia, which is a suspension of magnesium hydroxide in water.

Sussex former county of England, on the south coast, now divided into *East Sussex and *West Sussex.

sustainable capable of being continued indefinitely. For example, the sustainable yield of a forest is equivalent to the amount that grows back. Environmentalists made the term a catchword, in advocating the sustainable use of resources.

Sutherland Donald 1934– . Canadian-born US film actor who usually appears in offbeat roles. He starred in *M.A.S.H.* 1970, and his subsequent films include *Klute* 1971, *Don't Look Now* 1973, and *Revolution* 1986. He is the father of actor Kiefer Sutherland.

Sutherland Graham (Vivian) 1903–1980. English painter, graphic artist, and designer, active ainly in France from the late 1940s. He painted ortraits, landscapes, and religious subjects.

utherland Joan 1926– . Australian soprano. he went to England in 1951, where she made er debut the next year in *The Magic Flute*; later oles included *Lucia di Lammermoor*, Donna anna in *Don Giovanni*, and Desdemona in *Otello*. She retired from the stage in 1990.

uttee Hindu custom whereby a widow committed suicide by joining her husband's funeral yre, often under public and family pressure. anned in the 17th century by the Mogul mperors, the custom continued even after it was ade illegal under British rule 1829. There continue to be sporadic revivals.

utton Hoo archaeological site in Suffolk, ngland, where in 1939 a Saxon ship burial was xcavated. It is the funeral monument of Raedvald, King of the East Angles, who died about 24 or 625. The jewellery, armour, and weapons iscovered were placed in the British Museum, ondon.

uu Kyi Aung San 1945– . Myanmar Burmese) politician and human rights camaigner, leader of the National League for Democracy (NLD), the main opposition to the ilitary junta. When the NLD won the 1990 elecions, the junta refused to surrender power, and laced Suu Kyi under house arrest. She was warded the Nobel Peace Prize 1991 in recogition of her 'non-violent struggle for democracy nd human rights' in Myanmar. She is the daughr of former Burmese premier *Aung San.

uzhou or **Soochow**, formerly **Wuhsien** 912–49; city south of the Yangtze river delta and ast of the *Grand Canal, in Jiangsu province, China; population (1983) 670,000. It has mbroidery and jade-carving traditions and Shizin and Zhuozheng gardens. The city dates from bout 1000 BC, and the name Suzhou from the th century AD; it was reputedly visited by the enetian Marco *Polo.

uzuki Zenkō 1911– . Japanese politician. Originally a socialist member of the Diet in 1947, e became a conservative (Liberal Democrat) in 949, and was prime minister 1980–82.

valbard Norwegian archipelago in the Arctic Ocean. The main island is Spitsbergen; other lands include North East Land, Edge Island, arents Island, and Prince Charles Foreland.

vedberg Theodor 1884–1971. Swedish chemt. In 1924 he constructed the first ultracentrige, a machine that allowed the rapid separation f particles by mass. He was awarded the Nobel rize for Chemistry 1926.

vengali person who moulds another into a erformer and masterminds his or her career. The riginal Svengali was a character in the novel rilby 1894 by George *Du Maurier.

verdlovsk former name 1924–91 of *Ekater-*nburg*.

wabia (German *Schwaben*) historic region of W Germany, an independent duchy in the Middle Ages. It includes Augsburg and Ulm and rms part of the *Länder* (states) of Baden-Würtemberg, Bavaria, and Hessen.

wahili (Arabic *sawahil* 'coasts') language elonging to the Bantu branch of the Nigerongo family, widely used in east and central

Africa. Swahili originated on the E African coast as a *lingua franca* used among traders, and contains many Arabic loan words. It is an official language in Kenya and Tanzania.

swallow any bird of the family Hirundinidae of small, insect-eating birds in the order Passeriformes, with long, narrow wings and deeply forked tails. Swallows feed while flying.

swamp permanently or periodically waterlogged tract of wet, spongy land, often overgrown with plants.

swan any of several large, long-necked, aquatic, web-footed birds of the family Anatidae, which also includes ducks and geese.

Swan Joseph Wilson 1828–1914. English inventor of the incandescent-filament electric lamp and of bromide paper for use in developing photographs.

Swanson Gloria. Stage name of Gloria Josephine Mae Svenson 1897–1983. US actress, a star of silent films who influenced American tastes and fashion for more than 20 years. She retired in 1932 but made several major comebacks. Her work includes *Sadie Thompson* 1928, *Queen Kelly* 1928 (unfinished), and *Sunset Boulevard* 1950.

SWAPO (*South West Africa People's Organization*) organization formed 1959 in South West Africa (now *Namibia) to oppose South African rule. SWAPO guerrillas, led by Sam Nujoma, began attacking with support from Angola. In 1966 SWAPO was recognized by the United Nations as the legitimate government of Namibia, and won the first independent election 1989.

swastika (Sanskrit *svastika*) cross in which the bars are extended at right angles in the same clockwise or anticlockwise direction. An ancient good-luck symbol in both the New and the Old World and an Aryan and Buddhist mystic sign, it was adopted by Hitler as the emblem of the Nazi Party and incorporated into the German national flag 1935–45.

Swazi kingdom S African kingdom, established by Sobhuza I (died 1839), and named after his successor Mswati (ruled 1840–75).

Swaziland Kingdom of (*Umbuso weSwatini*)

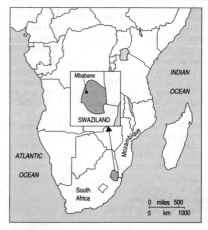

area 17,400 sq km/6,716 sq mi
capital Mbabane
towns Manzini, Big Bend
physical central valley; mountains in W (Highveld); plateau in E (Lowveld and Lubombo plateau)
head of state and government King Mswati III from 1986
political system near-absolute monarchy
political party Imbokodvo National Movement (INM), nationalist monarchist
exports sugar, canned fruit, wood pulp, asbestos
currency lilangeni
population (1993 est) 835,000; growth rate 3% p.a.
languages Swazi 90%, English (both official)
religions Christian 57%, animist
GNP $1,060 per head (1991)
chronology
1903 Swaziland became a special High Commission territory.
1967 Achieved internal self-government.
1968 Independence achieved from Britain, within the Commonwealth, as the Kingdom of Swaziland, with King Sobhuza II as head of state.
1973 The king suspended the constitution and assumed absolute powers.
1978 New constitution adopted.
1982 King Sobhuza died; his place was taken by one of his wives, Dzeliwe, until his son, Prince Makhosetive, reached the age of 21.
1983 Queen Dzeliwe ousted by another wife, Ntombi.
1984 After royal power struggle, it was announced that the crown prince would become king at 18.
1986 Crown prince formally invested as King Mswati III.
1987 Power struggle developed between advisory council Liqoqo and Queen Ntombi over accession of king. Mswati dissolved parliament; new government elected with Sotsha Dlamini as prime minister.
1991 Calls for democratic reform.
1992 Mswati dissolved parliament, assuming 'executive powers'.
1993 General election. Prince Jameson Mbilini Dlamini became prime minister.

sweat gland *gland within the skin of mammals that produces surface perspiration. In primates, sweat glands are distributed over the whole body, but in most other mammals they are more localized; for example, in cats and dogs, they are restricted to the feet and around the face.

sweatshop workshop or factory where employees work long hours under substandard conditions for low wages. Exploitation of labour in this way is associated with unscrupulous employers, who often employ illegal immigrants or children in their labour force.

swede annual or biennial plant *Brassica napus*, widely cultivated for its edible root, which is purple, white, or yellow. It is similar in taste to the turnip *B. rapa* but is of greater food value, firmer fleshed, and longer keeping.

Sweden Kingdom of (*Konungariket Sverige*)
area 450,000 sq km/173,745 sq mi
capital Stockholm
towns Göteborg, Malmö, Uppsala, Norrköping, Västerås

physical mountains in W; plains in S; thickly forested; more than 20,000 islands off the Stockholm coast
environment of the country's 90,000 lakes, 20,000 are affected by acid rain; 4,000 are so severely acidified that no fish are thought to survive in them
head of state King Carl XVI Gustaf from 1973
head of government Ingvar Carlsson from 1994
political system constitutional monarchy
exports aircraft, vehicles, ballbearings, drills, missiles, electronics, petrochemicals, textiles, furnishings, ornamental glass, paper, iron and steel
currency krona
population (1993 est) 8,700,000 (including 17,000 Saami [Lapps] and 1.2 million immigrants from Turkey, Yugoslavia, Greece, Iran, Finland and other Nordic countries); growth rate 0.1% p.a.
languages Swedish; there are Finnish- and Saami-speaking minorities
religion Lutheran (official) 95%
GNP $25,490 per head (1991)
chronology
12th century United as an independent nation.
1397–1520 Under Danish rule.
1914–45 Neutral in both world wars.
1951–76 Social Democratic Labour Party (SAP) in power.
1969 Olof Palme became SAP leader and prime minister.
1971 Constitution amended, creating a single-chamber Riksdag, the governing body.
1975 Monarch's last constitutional powers removed.
1976 Thorbjörn Fälldin, leader of the Centre Party, became prime minister, heading centre-right coalition.
1982 SAP, led by Palme, returned to power.
1985 SAP formed minority government, with communist support.
1986 Olof Palme murdered. Ingvar Carlsson became prime minister and SAP party leader.
1988 SAP re-elected with reduced majority; Green Party gained representation in Riksdag.
1990 SAP government resigned.
1991 Formal application for European Community (EC) membership. Election defeat for SAP; Carlsson resigned. Centre-right coalition formed; Carl Bildt became new prime minister.
1994 Carlsson formed minority government after SAP won most seats in general election. National

referendum narrowly supported application for European Union (formerly EC) membership.

Swedenborg Emanuel 1688–1772. Swedish theologian and philosopher. He trained as a scientist, but from 1747 concentrated on scriptural study, and in *Divine Love and Wisdom* 1763 concluded that the Last Judgement had taken place in 1757, and that the **New Church**, of which he was the prophet, had now been inaugurated. His writings are the scriptures of the sect popularly known as Swedenborgians, and his works are kept in circulation by the Swedenborg Society, London.

sweet pea plant of the *pea family.

sweet potato tropical American plant *Ipomoea batatas* of the morning-glory family Convolvulaceae; the white-orange tuberous root is used as a source of starch and alcohol and eaten as a vegetable.

sweet william biennial to perennial plant *Dianthus barbatus* of the pink family Caryophyllaceae, native to S Europe. It is grown for its fragrant red, white, and pink flowers.

swift any fast-flying, short-legged bird of the family Apodidae, of which there are about 75 species, found largely in the tropics. They are 9–23 cm/4–11 in long, with brown or grey plumage, long, pointed wings, and usually a forked tail. They are capable of flying 110 kph/70 mph.

Swift Jonathan 1667–1745. Irish satirist and Anglican cleric. He wrote *Gulliver's Travels* 1726, an allegory describing travel to lands inhabited by giants, miniature people, and intelligent horses. Other works include *The Tale of a Tub* 1704, attacking corruption in religion and learning; contributions to the Tory paper *The Examiner*, of which he was editor 1710–11; the satirical *A Modest Proposal* 1729, which suggested that children of the poor should be eaten; and many essays and pamphlets.

swimming self-propulsion of the body through water. There are four strokes in competitive swimming: freestyle, breaststroke, backstroke, and butterfly. Distances of races vary between 50 and 1,500 m. Olympic-size pools are 50 m/55 yd long and have eight lanes.

swimming, synchronized aquatic sport that demands artistry as opposed to speed. Competitors, either individual (solo) or in pairs, perform rhythmic routines to music. Points are awarded for interpretation and style. It was introduced into the Olympic swimming programme in 1984.

Swinburne Algernon Charles 1837–1909. English poet. He attracted attention with the choruses of his Greek-style tragedy *Atalanta in Calydon* 1865, but he and *Rossetti were attacked 1871 as leaders of 'the fleshly school of poetry', and the revolutionary politics of *Songs before Sunrise* 1871 alienated others.

swing music jazz style popular in the 1930s–40s, a big-band dance music with a simple harmonic base of varying tempo from the rhythm section (percussion, guitar, piano), harmonic brass and woodwind sections (sometimes strings), and superimposed solo melodic line from, for example, trumpet, clarinet, or saxophone. Exponents included Benny Goodman, Duke Ellington, and Glenn Miller, who introduced jazz to a mass white audience.

swing wing correctly *variable-geometry wing* aircraft wing that can be moved during flight to provide a suitable configuration for either low-speed or high-speed flight. The British engineer Barnes *Wallis developed the idea of the swing wing, first used on the US-built Northrop X-4, and since used in several aircraft, including the US F-111, F-114, and the B-1, the European Tornado, and several Soviet-built aircraft. These craft have their wings projecting nearly at right angles for takeoff and landing and low-speed flight, and swung back for high-speed flight.

Swiss cheese plant common name for *monstera, a plant of the arum family.

Swithun, St or *Swithin* English priest, chancellor of King Ethelwolf and bishop of Winchester from 852. According to legend, the weather on his feast day (15 July) is said to continue as either wet or fine for 40 days.

Switzerland Swiss Confederation (German *Schweiz*, French *Suisse*, Romansch *Svizzera*)

area 41,300 sq km/15,946 sq mi
capital Bern
towns Zürich, Geneva, Lausanne; river port Basel (on the Rhine)
physical most mountainous country in Europe (Alps and Jura mountains); highest peak Dufourspitze 4,634 m/15,203 ft in Apennines
environment an estimated 43% of coniferous trees, particularly in the central Alpine region, have been killed by acid rain, 90% of which comes from other countries. Over 50% of bird species are classified as threatened
head of state and government Otto Stich from 1994
government federal democratic republic
exports electrical goods, chemicals, pharmaceuticals, watches, precision instruments, confectionery
currency Swiss franc
population (1992) 6,911,000; growth rate 0.2% p.a.
languages German 65%, French 18%, Italian 12%, Romansch 1% (all official)
religions Roman Catholic 50%, Protestant 48%
GNP $32,250 per head (1992)

chronology
1648 Became independent of the Holy Roman Empire.
1798–1815 Helvetic Republic established by French revolutionary armies.
1847 Civil war resulted in greater centralization.
1874 Principle of the referendum introduced.
1971 Women given the vote in federal elections.
1984 First female cabinet minister appointed.
1986 Referendum rejected proposal for membership of United Nations.
1989 Referendum supported abolition of citizen army and military service requirements.
1991 18-year-olds allowed to vote for first time in national elections. Four-party coalition remained in power.
1992 René Felber elected president with Adolf Ogi as vice president. Closer ties with European Community rejected in national referendum.
1993 Ogi replaced Felber as head of state.
1994 Stich replaced Ogi as head of state.

swordfish marine bony fish *Xiphias gladius*, the only member of its family (Xiphiidae), characterized by a long swordlike beak protruding from the upper jaw. It may reach 4.5 m/15 ft in length and weigh 450 kg/1,000 lb.

SWOT analysis breakdown of an organization into its **s**trengths and **w**eaknesses (the internal analysis), with an assessment of the **o**pportunities open to it and the **t**hreats confronting it. SWOT analysis is commonly used in marketing and strategic studies.

sycamore tree *Acer pseudoplatanus* native to Europe. The leaves are five-lobed, and the hanging racemes of flowers are followed by winged fruits. The timber is used for furniture making.

Sydenham Thomas 1624–1689. English physician, the first person to describe measles and to recommend the use of quinine for relieving symptoms of malaria. His original reputation as 'the English Hippocrates' rested upon his belief that careful observation is more useful than speculation. His *Observationes medicae* was published in 1676.

Sydney capital and port of New South Wales, Australia; population (1990) 3,656,900. Industries include engineering, oil refining, electronics, scientific equipment, chemicals, clothing, and furniture. It is a financial centre, and has three universities. The 19th-century Museum of Applied Arts and Sciences is the most popular museum in Australia.

syenite grey, crystalline, plutonic (intrusive) *igneous rock, consisting of feldspar and hornblende; other minerals may also be present, including small amounts of quartz.

syllogism set of philosophical statements devised by Aristotle in his work on logic. It establishes the conditions under which a valid conclusion follows or does not follow by deduction from given premises. The following is an example of a valid syllogism: 'All men are mortal, Socrates is a man, therefore Socrates is mortal.'

Sylvanus in Roman mythology, another version of *Silvanus.

symbiosis any close relationship between two organisms of different species, and one where both partners benefit from the association. A well-known example is the pollination relationship between insects and flowers, where the insects feed on nectar and carry pollen from one flower to another. This is sometimes known as *mutualism. Symbiosis in a broader sense includes *commensalism and parasitism.

symbolic address in computing, a symbol used in *assembly-language programming to represent the binary *address of a memory location.

symbolic processor computer purpose-built to run so-called symbol-manipulation programs rather than programs involving a great deal of numerical computation. They exist principally for the *artificial intelligence language *LISP although some have also been built to run *PROLOG.

symbolism in the arts, the use of symbols as a device for concentrating or intensifying meaning. In particular, the term is used for a late 19th-century movement in French poetry, associated with Verlaine, Mallarmé, and Rimbaud, who used words for their symbolic rather than concrete meaning.

Symbolism movement in late 19th-century painting that emerged in France inspired by the trend in poetry. The subjects were often mythological, mystical, or fantastic. Gustave Moreau was a leading Symbolist painter.

Symington William 1763–1831. Scottish engineer who built the first successful steamboat. He invented the steam road locomotive in 1787 and a steamboat engine in 1788. His steamboat the *Charlotte Dundas* was completed in 1802.

symmetry exact likeness in shape about a given line (axis), point, or plane. A figure has symmetry if one half can be rotated or reflected onto the other. In a wider sense, symmetry exits if a change in the system leaves the essential features of the system unchanged; for example, reversing the sign of electric charges does not change the electrical behaviour of an arrangement of charges.

symphonic poem in music, a term originated by Franz Liszt for his 13 one-movement orchestral works that interpret a story from literature or history, also used by many other composers. Richard Strauss preferred the title 'tone poem'.

symphony musical composition for orchestra, traditionally in four separate but closely related movements. It developed from the smaller *sonata form, the Italian overture, and the dance suite of the 18th century.

symptom any change or manifestation in the body suggestive of disease as perceived by the sufferer. Symptoms are subjective phenomena. In strict usage, *symptoms* are events or changes reported by the patient; *signs* are noted by the doctor during the patient's examination.

synagogue in Judaism, a place of worship, also (in the USA) called a temple. As an institution it dates from the destruction of the Temple in Jerusalem AD 70, though it had been developing from the time of the Babylonian exile as a substitute for the Temple. In antiquity it was a public meeting hall where the Torah was also read, but today it is used primarily for prayer and service. A service requires a quorum (*minyan*) of ten adult Jewish men.

synapse junction between two *nerve cells, or between a nerve cell and a muscle (a neuromuscular junction), across which a nerve impulse is transmitted. The two cells are separated by a narrow gap called the **synaptic cleft**. The gap is bridged by a chemical *neurotransmitter, released by one nerve impulse.

synchrotron another name for a particle *accelerator.

syncline geological term for a fold in the rocks of the Earth's crust in which the layers or *beds dip inwards, thus forming a trough-like structure with a sag in the middle. The opposite structure, with the beds arching upwards, is an *anticline.

syncopation in music, the deliberate upsetting of rhythm by shifting the accent to a beat that is normally unaccented.

syndicalism (French *syndicat* 'trade union') political movement in 19th-century Europe that rejected parliamentary activity in favour of direct action, culminating in a revolutionary general strike to secure worker ownership and control of industry. After 1918 syndicalism was absorbed in communism, although it continued to have an independent existence in Spain until the late 1930s.

syndrome in medicine, a set of signs and symptoms that always occur together, thus characterizing a particular condition or disorder.

synecdoche (Greek 'accepted together') *figure of speech that uses either the part to represent the whole ('There were some *new faces* at the meeting', rather than *new people*), or the whole to stand for the part ('The West Indies beat England at cricket', rather than naming the national teams in question).

synergy (Greek 'combined action') in architecture, the augmented strength of systems, where the strength of a wall is greater than the added total of its individual units.

synergy in medicine, the 'cooperative' action of two or more drugs, muscles, or organs; applied especially to drugs whose combined action is more powerful than their simple effects added together.

Synge J(ohn) M(illington) 1871–1909. Irish playwright, a leading figure in the Irish dramatic revival of the early 20th century. His six plays reflect the speech patterns of the Aran Islands and W Ireland. They include *In the Shadow of the Glen* 1903, *Riders to the Sea* 1904, and *The Playboy of the Western World* 1907, which caused riots at the Abbey Theatre, Dublin, when first performed.

Synge Richard 1914–1994. British biochemist who investigated paper *chromatography (a means of separating mixtures). By 1940 techniques of chromatography for separating proteins had been devised. Still lacking were comparable techniques for distinguishing the amino acids that constituted the proteins. By 1944, Synge and his colleague Archer Martin had worked out a procedure, known as ascending chromatography, which filled this gap and won them the 1952 Nobel Prize for Chemistry.

synonymy near or identical meaning between or among words. There are very few strict synonyms in any language, although there may be many near-synonyms, depending upon the contexts in which the words are used. Thus *brotherly* and *fraternal* are synonyms in English, but a

brotherhood is not the same as a *fraternity*. People talk about the brotherhood of man but seldom if ever about the 'fraternity of man'. *Brotherhood* and *fraternity* are not therefore strictly synonymous.

synovial fluid viscous colourless fluid that bathes movable joints between the bones of vertebrates. It nourishes and lubricates the *cartilage at the end of each bone.

synthesis in chemistry, the formation of a substance or compound from more elementary compounds. The synthesis of a drug can involve several stages from the initial material to the final product; the complexity of these stages is a major factor in the cost of production.

synthesizer device that uses electrical components to produce sounds. In **preset synthesizers**, the sound of various instruments is produced by a built-in computer-type memory. In **programmable synthesizers** any number of new instrumental or other sounds may be produced at the will of the performer. **Speech synthesizers** can break down speech into 128 basic elements (allophones), which are then combined into words and sentences, as in the voices of electronic teaching aids.

synthetic fibre fibre made by chemical processes, unknown in nature. There are two kinds. One is made from natural materials that have been chemically processed in some way; *rayon, for example, is made by processing the cellulose in wood pulp. The other type is the true synthetic fibre, made entirely from chemicals. *Nylon was the original synthetic fibre, made from chemicals obtained from petroleum (crude oil).

syphilis sexually transmitted disease caused by the spiral-shaped bacterium (spirochete) *Treponema pallidum*. Untreated, it runs its course in three stages over many years, often starting with a painless hard sore, or chancre, developing within a month on the area of infection (usually the genitals). The second stage, months later, is a rash with arthritis, hepatitis, and/or meningitis. The third stage, years later, leads eventually to paralysis, blindness, insanity, and death. The Wassermann test is a diagnostic blood test for syphilis.

Syracuse (Italian *Siracusa*) industrial port (chemicals, salt) in E Sicily; population (1988) 124,000. It has a cathedral and remains of temples, aqueducts, catacombs, and an amphitheatre. Founded 734 BC by the Corinthians, it became a centre of Greek culture under the elder and younger *Dionysius. After a three-year siege it was taken by Rome 212 BC. In AD 878 it was destroyed by the Arabs, and the rebuilt town came under Norman rule in the 11th century.

Syria Syrian Arab Republic (*al-Jamhuriya al-Arabya as-Suriya*)
area 185,200 sq km/71,506 sq mi
capital Damascus
towns Aleppo, Homs, Hama; chief port Latakia
physical mountains alternate with fertile plains and desert areas; Euphrates River
head of state and government Hafez al-Assad from 1971
political system socialist republic
exports cotton, cereals, oil, phosphates, tobacco
currency Syrian pound
population (1993) 13,400,000; growth rate 3.5% p.a.

languages Arabic 89% (official), Kurdish 6%, Armenian 3%
religions Sunni Muslim 74%; ruling minority Alawite, and other Islamic sects 16%; Christian 10%
GNP $1,110 per head (1991)
chronology
1946 Achieved full independence from France.
1958 Merged with Egypt to form the United Arab Republic (UAR).
1961 UAR disintegrated.
1967 Six-Day War resulted in the loss of territory to Israel.
1970–71 Syria supported Palestinian guerrillas against Jordanian troops.
1971 Following a bloodless coup, Hafez al-Assad became president.
1973 Israel consolidated its control of the Golan Heights after the Yom Kippur War.
1976 Substantial numbers of troops committed to the civil war in Lebanon.
1978 Assad re-elected.
1981–82 Further military engagements in Lebanon.
1982 Islamic militant uprising suppressed; 5,000 dead.
1984 Presidents Assad and Gemayel approved plans for government of national unity in Lebanon.
1985 Assad secured the release of 39 US hostages held in an aircraft hijacked by extremist Shi'ite group, Hezbollah. Assad re-elected.
1987 Improved relations with USA and attempts to secure the release of Western hostages in Lebanon.
1989 Diplomatic relations with Morocco restored. Continued fighting in Lebanon; Syrian forces reinforced in Lebanon; diplomatic relations with Egypt restored.
1990 Diplomatic relations with Britain restored.
1991 Syria fought against Iraq in Gulf War. President Assad agreed to US Middle East peace plan. Assad re-elected president.
1993 Syria joined Iraq and other Arab countries in boycotting UN treaty outlawing production and use of chemical weapons.
1994 Israeli offer of partial withdrawal from Golan Heights.

Syriac language ancient Semitic language, originally the Aramaic dialect spoken in and around Edessa (now in Turkey) and widely used in W Asia from about 700 BC to AD 700. From the 3rd to 7th centuries it was a Christian liturgical and literary language.

syringa common, but incorrect, name for the *mock orange *Philadelphus*. The genus *Syringa* includes *lilac *Syringa vulgaris*, and is not related to mock orange.

Système International d'Unités official French name for *SI units.

systemic in medicine, relating to or affecting the body as a whole. A systemic disease is one where the effects are present throughout the body, as opposed to local disease, such as *conjunctivitis, which is confined to one part.

system implementation in computing, the process of installing a new computer system.

systems analysis in computing, the investigation of a business activity or clerical procedure with a view to deciding if and how it can be computerized. The analyst discusses the existing procedures with the people involved, observes the flow of data through the business, and draws up an outline specification of the required computer system (see also *systems design).

systems design in computing, the detailed design of an *applications package. The designer breaks the system down into component programs, and designs the required input forms, screen layouts, and printouts. Systems design forms a link between systems analysis and *programming.

systems program in computing, a program that performs a task related to the operation and performance of the computer system itself. For example, a systems program might control the operation of the display screen, or control and organize backing storage. In contrast, an *applications program is designed to carry out tasks for the benefit of the computer user.

System X in communications, a modular, computer-controlled, digital switching system used in telephone exchanges.

Szczecin (German **Stettin**) industrial (shipbuilding, fish processing, synthetic fibres, tools, iron) port on the river Oder, in NW Poland; population (1990) 413,400.

Székesfehérvár industrial city (metal products) in W central Hungary; population (1988) 113,000. It is a market centre for wine, tobacco, and fruit.

Szent-Györgyi Albert 1893–1986. Hungarian-born US biochemist who isolated vitamin C and studied the chemistry of muscular activity. He was awarded the Nobel Prize for Medicine 1937.

Szilard Leo 1898–1964. Hungarian-born US physicist who, in 1934, was one of the first scientists to realize that nuclear fission, or atom splitting, could lead to a chain reaction releasing enormous amounts of instantaneous energy. He emigrated to the USA in 1938 and there influenced *Einstein to advise President Roosevelt to begin the nuclear arms programme. After World War II he turned his attention to the newly emerging field of molecular biology.

1912 election. Taft served as chief justice of the Supreme Court 1921–30.

Tagalog member of the majority ethnic group living around Manila on the island of Luzon, in the Philippines, and numbering about 10 million (1988). The Tagalog live by fishing and trading. In its standardized form, known as Pilipino, Tagalog is the official language of the Philippines, and belongs to the Western branch of the Austronesian family. The Tagalogs' religion is a mixture of animism, Christianity, and Islam.

tagging, electronic long-distance monitoring of the movements of people charged with or convicted of a crime, thus enabling them to be detained in their homes rather than in prison. In the UK, legislation passed 1991 allowed for its use as an aid to bail and as a means of enforcing punishment, for example a curfew. The system is in use in the USA.

Taglioni Marie 1804–1884. Italian dancer. A ballerina of ethereal style and exceptional lightness, she was the first to use *pointe work, or dancing on the toes, as an expressive part of ballet rather than as sheer technique. She created many roles, including the title role in *La Sylphide* 1832, first performed at the Paris Opéra, and choreographed by her father *Filippo* (1771–1871).

Tagore Rabindranath 1861–1941. Bengali Indian writer, born in Calcutta, who translated into English his own verse *Gitanjali* ('song offerings') 1912 and his verse play *Chitra* 1896. Nobel Prize for Literature 1913.

Tahiti largest of the Society Islands, in *French Polynesia; area 1,042 sq km/402 sq mi; population (1983) 116,000. Its capital is Papeete. Tahiti was visited by Captain James *Cook 1769 and by Admiral *Bligh of the *Bounty* 1788. It came under French control 1843 and became a colony 1880.

T'ai Chi series of 108 complex, slow-motion movements, each named (for example, the White Crane Spreads its Wings) and designed to ensure effective circulation of the *chi*, or intrinsic energy of the universe, through the mind and body. It derives partly from the Shaolin *martial arts of China and partly from *Taoism.

taiga or **boreal forest** Russian name for the forest zone south of the *tundra, found across the northern hemisphere. Here, dense forests of conifers (spruces and hemlocks), birches, and poplars occupy glaciated regions punctuated with cold lakes, streams, bogs, and marshes. Winters are prolonged and very cold, but the summer is warm enough to promote dense growth.

taipan species of small-headed cobra *Oxyuranus scutellatus* found in NE Australia and New Guinea. It is about 3 m/10 ft long, and has a brown back and yellow belly. Its venom is fatal within minutes.

Taipei or **Taibei** capital and commercial centre of Taiwan; industries include electronics, plastics, textiles, and machinery; population (1990) 2,719,700. The National Palace Museum 1965 houses the world's greatest collection of Chinese art, taken there from the mainland 1948.

Taira or **Heike** in Japanese history, a military clan prominent in the 10th–12th centuries and

t symbol for *tonne*, *ton*.

table tennis or **ping pong** indoor game played on a rectangular table by two or four players. It was developed in Britain about 1880 and derived from lawn tennis. World championships were first held 1926.

taboo (Polynesian *tabu*, 'forbidden') prohibition applied to magical and religious objects. In psychology and the social sciences the term refers to practices that are generally prohibited because of religious or social pressures; for example, *incest is forbidden in most societies.

tacet (Latin 'it is silent') in music, score indication used when an instrument is to be silent for a complete movement or section of a movement.

tachograph combined speedometer and clock that records a vehicle's speed (on a small card disc, magnetic disc, or tape) and the length of time the vehicle is moving or stationary. It is used to monitor a lorry driver's working hours.

Tacitus Publius Cornelius *c.* AD 55–*c.* 120. Roman historian. A public orator in Rome, he was consul under Nerva 97–98 and proconsul of Asia 112–113. He wrote histories of the Roman Empire, *Annales* and *Historiae*, covering the years AD 14–68 and 69–97 respectively. He also wrote a *Life of Agricola* 97 (he married Agricola's daughter in 77) and a description of the German tribes, *Germania* 98.

Tadmur Arabic name for the ancient city of *Palmyra in Syria.

Taegu largest inland city of South Korea after Seoul; population (1990) 2,228,800.

Taejon (Korean 'large rice paddy') capital of South Chungchong province, central South Korea; population (1990) 1,062,100. Korea's tallest standing Buddha and oldest wooden building are found NE of the city at Popchusa in the Mount Songnisan National Park.

tae kwon do Korean *martial art similar to *karate, which includes punching and kicking. It was included in the 1988 Olympic Games as a demonstration sport.

taffeta (Persian 'spun') light, plain-weave fabric with a high lustre, originally silk but today also manufactured from artificial fibres.

Taft William Howard 1857–1930. 27th president of the USA 1909–13, a Republican. He was secretary of war 1904–08 in Theodore Roosevelt's administration, but as president his conservatism provoked Roosevelt to stand against him in the

dominant at court 1159–85. Their destruction by their rivals, the *Minamoto, 1185 is the subject of the 13th-century literary classic *Heike Monogatari/The Tale of the Heike.*

Taiwan Republic of China (*Chung Hua Min Kuo*)

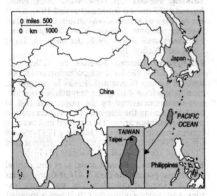

area 36,179 sq km/13,965 sq mi
capital Taipei
towns ports Kaohsiung, Keelung
physical island (formerly Formosa) off People's Republic of China; mountainous, with lowlands in W
head of state Lee Teng-hui from 1988
head of government Lien Chan from 1993
political system emergent democracy
exports textiles, steel, plastics, electronics, foodstuffs
currency New Taiwan dollar
population (1993) 21,000,000 (Taiwanese 84%, mainlanders 14%); growth rate 1.4% p.a.
languages Mandarin Chinese (official); Taiwan, Hakka dialects
religions officially atheist; Taoist, Confucian, Buddhist, Christian
GNP $8,815 per head (1991)
chronology
1683 Taiwan (Formosa) annexed by China.
1895 Ceded to Japan.
1945 Recovered by China.
1949 Flight of Nationalist government to Taiwan after Chinese communist revolution.
1954 US-Taiwanese mutual defence treaty.
1971 Expulsion from United Nations.
1972 Commencement of legislature elections.
1975 President Chiang Kai-shek died; replaced as Kuomintang leader by his son, Chiang Ching-kuo.
1979 USA severed diplomatic relations and annulled 1954 security pact.
1986 Democratic Progressive Party (DPP) formed as opposition to the nationalist Kuomintang.
1987 Martial law lifted; opposition parties legalized; press restrictions lifted.
1988 President Chiang Ching-kuo died; replaced by Taiwanese-born Lee Teng-hui.
1989 Kuomintang won assembly elections.
1990 Formal move towards normalization of relations with China. Hau Pei-tsun became prime minister.
1991 President Lee Teng-hui declared end to

state of civil war with China. Constitution amended. Kuomintang won landslide victory in assembly elections.
1992 Diplomatic relations with South Korea broken. Dec: Kuomintang lost support to DPP in first fully democratic elections but still secured majority of seats.
1993 Lien Chan appointed prime minister. Cooperation pact with China signed.

Taiyuan capital of Shanxi province, on the river Fen He, NE China; population (1989) 1,900,000; industries include iron, steel, agricultural machinery, and textiles; It is a walled city founded in the 5th century AD, and is the seat of Shanxi University.

Tajik or *Tadzhik* member of the majority ethnic group living in Tajikistan. Tajiks also live in Afghanistan and parts of Pakistan and W China. The Tajiki language belongs to the West Iranian subbranch of the Indo-European family, and is similar to Farsi; it is written in the Cyrillic script. The Tajiks have long been associated with neighbouring Turkic peoples and their language contains Altaic loan words.

Tajikistan Republic of

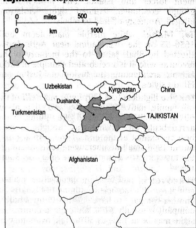

area 143,100 sq km/55,251 sq mi
capital Dushanbe
towns Khodzhent (formerly Leninabad) Kurgan-Tyube, Kulyab
physical mountainous, more than half of its territory lying above 3,000 m/10,000 ft; huge mountain glaciers, which are the source of many rapid rivers
head of state Imamali Rakhmanov from 1992
head of government Abduljalil Samadov from 1993
political system emergent democracy
products fruit, cereals, cotton, cattle, sheep, silks, carpets, coal, lead, zinc, chemicals, oil, gas
currency Russian rouble
population (1992) 5,568,000 (Tajik 63%, Uzbek 24%, Russian 8%, Tatar 1%, Kyrgyz 1%, Ukrainian 1%)
language Tajik, similar to Farsi (Persian)
religion Sunni Muslim
GNP $1,050 per head (1991)

chronology
1921 Part of Turkestan Soviet Socialist Autonomous Republic.

1929 Became a constituent republic of USSR.

1990 Ethnic Tajik-Armenian conflict in Dushanbe resulted in rioting against Communist Party of Tajikistan (CPT); state of emergency and curfew imposed.

1991 Jan: curfew lifted in Dushanbe. March: maintenance of Soviet Union endorsed in referendum; President Makhkamov forced to resign after failed anti-Gorbachev coup; CPT broke links with Moscow. Sept: declared independence; Rakhman Nabiyev elected president; CPT renamed Socialist Party of Tajikistan; state of emergency declared. Dec: joined new Commonwealth of Independent States.

1992 Jan: admitted into Conference for Security and Cooperation in Europe. Nabiyev temporarily ousted; state of emergency lifted. Feb: joined the Muslim Economic Cooperation Organization. March: admitted into United Nations; US diplomatic recognition achieved. May: coalition government formed. Sept: Nabiyev forced to resign; replaced by Imamali Rakhmanov.

1993 Civil war between ex-communist government forces and Islamic and prodemocracy groups continued. Human rights violations alleged. Amnesty offered to rebels.

Taj Mahal white marble mausoleum built 1630–53 on the river Jumna near Agra, India. Erected by Shah Jahan to the memory of his favourite wife, it is a celebrated example of Indo-Islamic architecture, the fusion of Muslim and Hindu styles.

takahe flightless bird *Porphyrio mantelli* of the rail family, native to New Zealand. It is about 60 cm/2 ft tall, with blue and green plumage and a red beak. The takahe was thought to have become extinct at the end of the 19th century, but in 1948 small numbers were rediscovered in the tussock grass of a mountain valley on South Island.

takeover in business, the acquisition by one company of a sufficient number of shares in another company to have effective control of that company – usually 51%, although a controlling stake may be as little as 30%. Takeovers may be agreed or contested; methods employed include the *dawn raid,* and methods of avoiding an unwelcome takeover include *reverse takeover, *poison pills,* or inviting a *white knight* to make a takeover bid.

Takeshita Noboru 1924– . Japanese rightwing politician. Elected to parliament as a Liberal Democratic Party (LDP) deputy 1958, he became president of the LDP and prime minister Oct 1987. He and members of his administration were shown in the *Recruit scandal to have been involved in insider-trading and he resigned in April 1989.

Talbot William Henry Fox 1800–1877. English pioneer of photography. He invented the paper-based *calotype process, the first negative/positive method. Talbot made *photograms several years before Louis Daguerre's invention was announced.

talc $Mg_3Si_4O_{10}(OH)_2$, mineral, hydrous magnesium silicate. It occurs in tabular crystals, but the massive impure form, known as **steatite** or

soapstone, is more common. It is formed by the alteration of magnesium compounds and usually found in metamorphic rocks. Talc is very soft, ranked 1 on the Mohs' scale of hardness. It is used in powdered form in cosmetics, lubricants, and as an additive in paper manufacture.

Talking Heads US New Wave rock group formed 1975 in New York; disbanded 1991. Their nervy minimalist music was inspired by African rhythms; albums include *More Songs About Buildings and Food* 1978, *Remain in Light* 1980, and *Naked* 1988.

Talleyrand Charles Maurice de Talleyrand-Périgord. 1754–1838. French politician and diplomat. As bishop of Autun 1789–91 he supported moderate reform during the *French Revolution, was excommunicated by the pope, and fled to the USA during the Reign of Terror (persecution of anti-revolutionaries). He returned and became foreign minister under the Directory 1797–99 and under Napoleon 1799–1807. He represented France at the Congress of *Vienna 1814–15.

Tallinn (German *Reval*) naval port and capital of Estonia; population (1987) 478,000. Industries include electrical and oil-drilling machinery, textiles, and paper. Founded 1219, it was a member of the *Hanseatic League; it passed to Sweden 1561 and to Russia 1750.

Tallis Thomas c. 1505–1585. English composer. He was a master of *counterpoint. His works include *Tallis's Canon* ('Glory to thee my God this night') 1567, the antiphonal *Spem in alium non habui* (about 1573) for 40 voices in various groupings, and a collection of 34 motets, *Cantiones sacrae,* 1575 (of which 16 are by Tallis and 18 by Byrd). In 1575 Elizabeth I granted Tallis and Byrd the monopoly for printing music and music paper in England.

Talmud the two most important works of post-Biblical Jewish literature. The Babylonian and the Palestinian (or Jerusalem) Talmud provide a compilation of ancient Jewish law and tradition. The Babylonian Talmud was edited at the end of the 5th century AD and is the more authoritative version for later Judaism; both Talmuds are written in a mix of Hebrew and Aramaic. They contain the commentary (*gemara*) on the *Mishna* (early rabbinical commentaries compiled about AD 200), and the material can be generally divided into *halakhah*, consisting of legal and ritual matters, and *haggadah*, concerned with ethical, theological, and folklorist matters.

tamarind evergreen tropical tree *Tamarindus indica*, family Leguminosae, native to the Old World, with pinnate leaves and reddish-yellow flowers, followed by pods. The pulp surrounding the seeds is used medicinally and as a flavouring.

tamarisk any small tree or shrub of the genus *Tamarix*, flourishing in warm, salty, desert regions of Europe and Asia where no other vegetation is found. The common tamarisk *T. gallica* has scalelike leaves and spikes of very small, pink flowers.

Tambo Oliver 1917–1993. South African nationalist politician, in exile 1960–90, president of the African National Congress (ANC) 1977–91. Because of poor health, he was given the honorary post of national chair July 1991, and Nelson *Mandela resumed the ANC presidency.

tambourine musical percussion instrument of ancient origin, almost unchanged since Roman times, consisting of a shallow drum with a single skin and loosely set jingles in the rim that accentuate the beat.

Tamerlane or *Tamburlaine* or *Timur i Leng* ('Timur the Lame') 1336–1405. Mongol ruler of Samarkand, in Uzbekistan, from 1369 who conquered Persia, Azerbaijan, Armenia, and Georgia. He defeated the *Golden Horde 1395, sacked Delhi 1398, invaded Syria and Anatolia, and captured the Ottoman sultan in Ankara 1402; he died invading China.

Tamil member of the majority ethnic group living in the Indian state of Tamil Nadu (formerly Madras). Tamils also live in S India, N Sri Lanka, Malaysia, Singapore, and South Africa, totalling 35–55 million worldwide. Tamil belongs to the Dravidian family of languages; written records in Tamil date from the 3rd century BC. The 3 million Tamils in Sri Lanka are predominantly Hindu, although some are Muslims, unlike the Sinhalese majority, who are mainly Buddhist. The *Tamil Tigers*, most prominent of the various Tamil groupings, are attempting to create a separate homeland in N Sri Lanka through both political and military means.

Tamil Nadu formerly (until 1968) *Madras State* state of SE India
area 130,100 sq km/50,219 sq mi
capital Madras
products mainly industrial: cotton, textiles, silk, electrical machinery, tractors, rubber, sugar refining
population (1991) 55,638,300
language Tamil
history the present state was formed 1956. Tamil Nadu comprises part of the former British Madras presidency (later province) formed from areas taken from France and Tipu Sahib, the sultan of Mysore, in the 18th century, which became a state of the Republic of India 1950. The northeast was detached to form Andhra Pradesh 1953; in 1956 other areas went to Kerala and Mysore (now Karnataka), and the Laccadive Islands (now Lakshadweep) became a separate Union Territory.

Tammany Hall Democratic Party organization in New York. It originated 1789 as the Society of St Tammany, named after an American Indian chief. It was dominant from 1800 until the 1930s and gained a reputation for corruption and rule by bosses; its domination was broken by Mayor *La Guardia in the 1930s and Mayor Koch in the 1970s.

Tampa port and resort on Tampa Bay in W Florida, USA; industries include fruit and vegetable canning, shipbuilding, and the manufacture of fertilizers, clothing, beer, and cigars; population (1990) 280,000.

Tampere (Swedish *Tammerfors*) city in SW Finland; industries include textiles, paper, footwear, and turbines; population (1990) 172,600, metropolitan area 258,000. It is the second largest city in Finland.

tanager any of various New World birds of the family Emberizidae. There are about 230 species in forests of Central and South America, all brilliantly coloured. They are 10–20 cm/4–8 in long, with plump bodies and conical beaks.

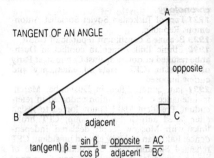

TANGENT OF AN ANGLE

opposite

adjacent

$$\tan(\text{gent})\ \beta = \frac{\sin \beta}{\cos \beta} = \frac{\text{opposite}}{\text{adjacent}} = \frac{AC}{BC}$$

tangent *The tangent of an angle is a mathematical function used in the study of right-angled triangles.*

Tananarive former name for *Antananarivo, capital of Madagascar.

Tanganyika former British colony in E Africa, which now forms the mainland of *Tanzania.

Tanganyika, Lake lake 772 m/2,534 ft above sea level in the Great Rift Valley, E Africa, with Zaire to the W, Zambia to the S, and Tanzania and Burundi to the E. It is about 645 km/400 mi long, with an area of about 31,000 sq km/12,000 sq mi, and is the deepest lake (1,435 m/4,710 ft) in Africa. The mountains around its shores rise to about 2,700 m/8,860 ft. The chief ports are Bujumbura (Burundi), Kigoma (Tanzania), and Kalémié (Zaire).

tangent in geometry, a straight line that touches a curve and has the same gradient as the curve at the point of contact. At a maximum or minimum, the tangent to a curve has zero gradient. Also, in trigonometry, a function of an acute angle in a right-angled triangle, defined as the ratio of the length of the side opposite the angle to the length of the side adjacent to it; a way of expressing the slope of a line.

Tangier or *Tangiers* or *Tanger* port in N Morocco, on the Strait of Gibraltar; population (1982) 436,227. It was a Phoenician trading centre in the 15th century BC. Captured by the Portuguese 1471, it passed to England 1662 as part of the dowry of Catherine of Braganza, but was abandoned 1684, and later became a lair of Barbary Coast pirates. From 1923 Tangier and a small surrounding enclave became an international zone, administered by Spain 1940–45. In 1956 it was transferred to independent Morocco and became a free port 1962.

tango couples dance of Latin-American origin or the music for it. The dance consists of two long sliding steps followed by three short steps and stylized body positions.

Tanizaki Jun-ichirō 1886–1965. Japanese novelist. His works include a version of *Murasaki's *The Tale of Genji* 1939–41, *The Makioka Sisters* in three volumes 1943–48, and *The Key* 1956.

tank armoured fighting vehicle that runs on tracks and is fitted with weapons systems capable of defeating other tanks and destroying life and property. The term was originally a code name for the first effective tracked and armoured fighting vehicle, invented by the British soldier and scholar Ernest Swinton, and used in the battle of the Somme 1916.

Tannenberg, Battle of two battles, named after a village now in N Poland:
1410 the Poles and Lithuanians defeated the Teutonic Knights, establishing Poland as a major power;
1914 during World War I, when Tannenberg was part of East Prussia, *Hindenburg defeated the Russians.

tannic acid or ***tannin*** $C_{14}H_{10}O_9$ yellow astringent substance, composed of several *phenol rings, occurring in the bark, wood, roots, fruits, and galls (growths) of certain trees, such as the oak. It precipitates gelatin to give an insoluble compound, used in the manufacture of leather from hides (tanning).

tanning treating animal skins to preserve them and make them into leather. In vegetable tanning, the prepared skins are soaked in tannic acid. Chrome tanning, which is much quicker, uses solutions of chromium salts.

tansy perennial herb *Tanacetum vulgare*, family Compositae, native to Europe. The yellow flower heads grow in clusters on stalks up to 120 cm/4 ft tall, and the aromatic leaves are used in cookery.

tantalum hard, ductile, lustrous, grey-white, metallic element, symbol Ta, atomic number 73, relative atomic mass 180.948. It occurs with niobium in tantalite and other minerals. It can be drawn into wire with a very high melting point and great tenacity, useful for lamp filaments subject to vibration. It is also used in alloys, for corrosion-resistant laboratory apparatus and chemical equipment, as a catalyst in manufacturing synthetic rubber, in tools and instruments, and in rectifiers and capacitors.

Tantrism forms of Hinduism and Buddhism that emphasize the division of the universe into male and female forces that maintain its unity by their interaction; this gives women equal status with men. Tantric Hinduism is associated with magical and sexual yoga practices that imitate the union of Siva and Sakti, as described in religious books known as the *Tantras*. In Buddhism, the *Tantras* are texts attributed to the Buddha, describing methods of attaining enlightenment.

Tanzania United Republic of (*Jamhuri ya Muungano wa Tanzania*)

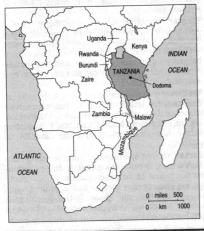

area 945,000 sq km/364,865 sq mi
capital Dodoma (since 1983)
towns Zanzibar Town, Mwanza; chief port and former capital Dar es Salaam
physical central plateau; lakes in N and W; coastal plains; lakes Victoria, Tanganyika, and Niasa
environment the black rhino faces extinction as a result of poaching
head of state and government Ali Hassan Mwinyi from 1985
political system one-party socialist republic
political party Revolutionary Party of Tanzania (CCM), African, socialist
exports coffee, cotton, sisal, cloves, tea, tobacco, cashew nuts, diamonds
currency Tanzanian shilling
population (1993 est) 28,200,000; growth rate 3.5% p.a.
languages Kiswahili, English (both official)
religions Muslim 35%, Christian 35%, traditional 30%
GNP $100 per head (1991)
chronology
16th–17th centuries Zanzibar under Portuguese control.
1890–1963 Zanzibar became a British protectorate.
1920–46 Tanganyika administered as a British League of Nations mandate.
1946–62 Tanganyika came under United Nations (UN) trusteeship.
1961 Tanganyika achieved independence from Britain, within the Commonwealth, with Julius Nyerere as prime minister.
1962 Tanganyika became a republic with Nyerere as president.
1964 Tanganyika and Zanzibar became the United Republic of Tanzania with Nyerere as president.
1967 East African Community (EAC) formed. Arusha Declaration.
1977 Revolutionary Party of Tanzania (CCM) proclaimed the only legal party. EAC dissolved.
1978 Ugandan forces repulsed after crossing into Tanzania.
1979 Tanzanian troops sent to Uganda to help overthrow the president, Idi Amin.
1985 Nyerere retired from presidency but stayed on as CCM leader; Ali Hassan Mwinyi became president.
1990 Nyerere surrendered CCM leadership; replaced by President Mwinyi.
1992 CCM agreed to abolish one-party rule. East African cooperation pact with Kenya and Uganda to be reestablished.

Taoiseach Gaelic name for the prime minister of the Irish Republic.

Taoism Chinese philosophical system, traditionally founded by the Chinese philosopher Lao Zi 6th century BC. He is also attributed authorship of the scriptures, *Tao Te Ching*, although these were apparently compiled 3rd century BC. The 'tao' or 'way' denotes the hidden principle of the universe, and less stress is laid on good deeds than on harmonious interaction with the environment, which automatically ensures right behaviour. The magical side of Taoism is illustrated by the *I Ching* or *Book of Changes*, a book of divination.

tap dancing rapid step dance, derived from clog dancing. Its main characteristic is the tapping of toes and heels accentuated by steel taps affixed to the shoes. It was popularized in vaudeville and in 1930s films by such dancers as Fred Astaire and Bill 'Bojangles' Robinson (1878–1949).

tape recording, magnetic method of recording electric signals on a layer of iron oxide, or other magnetic material, coating a thin plastic tape. The electrical signals from the microphone are fed to the electromagnetic recording head, which magnetizes the tape in accordance with the frequency and amplitude of the original signal. The impulses may be audio (for sound recording), video (for television), or data (for computer). For playback, the tape is passed over the same, or another, head to convert magnetic into electrical signals, which are then amplified for reproduction. Tapes are easily demagnetized (erased) for reuse, and come in cassette, cartridge, or reel form.

tapestry ornamental woven textile used for wall hangings, furniture, and curtains. The tapestry design is threaded into the warp with various shades of yarn. The great European centres of tapestry weaving were in Belgium, France, and England. The *Bayeux Tapestry is an embroidery rather than a true tapestry.

tapeworm any of various parasitic flatworms of the class Cestoda. They lack digestive and sense organs, can reach 15 m/50 ft in length, and attach themselves to the host's intestines by means of hooks and suckers. Tapeworms are made up of hundreds of individual segments, each of which develops into a functional hermaphroditic reproductive unit capable of producing numerous eggs. The larvae of tapeworms usually reach humans in imperfectly cooked meat or fish, causing anaemia and intestinal disorders.

tapioca granular starch used in cooking, produced from the *cassava root.

tapir any of the odd-toed hoofed mammals (perissodactyls) of the single genus *Tapirus*, now constituting the family Tapiridae. There are four species living in the American and Malaysian tropics. They reach 1 m/3 ft at the shoulder and weigh up to 350 kg/770 lb. Their survival is in danger because of destruction of the forests.

taproot in botany, a single, robust, main *root that is derived from the embryonic root, or *radicle, and grows vertically downwards, often to considerable depth. Taproots are often modified for food storage and are common in biennial plants such as the carrot *Daucus carota*, where they act as *perennating organs.

tar dark brown or black viscous liquid obtained by the destructive distillation of coal, shale, and wood. Tars consist of a mixture of hydrocarbons, acids, and bases. *Creosote and *paraffin are produced from wood tar. See also *coal tar.

tarantella peasant dance of southern Italy; also a piece of music composed for, or in the rhythm of, this dance, in fast six-eight time.

Taranto naval base and port in Puglia region, SE Italy; population (1988) 245,000. It is an important commercial centre, and its steelworks are part of the new industrial complex of S Italy. It was the site of the ancient Greek *Tarentum*, founded in the 8th century BC by *Sparta, and was captured by the Romans 272 BC.

tarantula wolf spider *Lycosa tarantula* with a 2.5 cm/1 in body. It spins no web, relying on its speed in hunting to catch its prey. The name 'tarantula' is also used for any of the numerous large, hairy spiders of the family Theraphosidae, with large poison fangs, native to the SW USA and tropical America.

tare alternative common name for *vetch.

tariff tax or duty placed on goods when they are imported into a country or trading bloc (such as the European Community) from outside. The aim of tariffs is to reduce imports by making them more expensive. Organizations such as the EC, the European Free Trade Association (EFTA), and the General Agreement on Tariffs and Trade (GATT) have worked towards mutual lowering of tariffs between countries.

Tarkovsky Andrei 1932–1986. Soviet film director whose work is characterized by an epic style combined with intense personal spirituality. His films include *Solaris* 1972, *Mirror* 1975, *Stalker* 1979, and *The Sacrifice* 1986.

taro or **eddo** plant *Colocasia esculenta* of the arum family Araceae, native to tropical Asia; the tubers are edible and are the source of Polynesian poi (a fermented food).

tarot cards fortune-telling aid consisting of 78 cards: the **minor arcana** in four suits (resembling playing cards) and the **major arcana**, 22 cards with densely symbolic illustrations that have links with astrology and the *Kabbala.

tarpon large silver-sided fish *Tarpon atlanticus* of the family Megalopidae. It reaches 2 m/6 ft and may weigh 135 kg/300 lb. It lives in warm W Atlantic waters.

Tarquinius Superbus lived 5th century BC. Last king of Rome 534–510 BC. He abolished certain rights of Romans, and made the city powerful. He was deposed when his son Sextus raped *Lucretia.

tarragon perennial bushy herb *Artemisia dracunculus* of the daisy family Compositae, native to the Old World, growing to 1.5 m/5 ft, with narrow leaves and small green-white flower heads arranged in groups. Tarragon contains an aromatic oil; its leaves are used to flavour salads, pickles, and tartar sauce. It is closely related to wormwood.

tarsier any of three species of the prosimian primates, genus *Tarsius*, of the East Indies and the Philippines. These survivors of early primates are about the size of a rat with thick, light-brown fur, very large eyes, and long feet and hands. They are nocturnal, arboreal, and eat insects and lizards.

tartan woollen cloth woven in specific chequered patterns individual to Scottish clans, with stripes of different widths and colours crisscrossing on a coloured background; used in making skirts, kilts, trousers, and other articles of clothing.

Tartar variant spelling of *Tatar, member of a Turkic people now living mainly in the autonomous region of Tatarstan, Russia.

tartrazine (E102) yellow food colouring produced synthetically from petroleum. Many people are allergic to foods containing it. Typical effects are skin disorders and respiratory problems. It has been shown to have an adverse effect on hyperactive children.

Tarzan fictitious hero inhabiting the African rainforest, created by US writer Edgar Rice *Burroughs in *Tarzan of the Apes* 1914, with numerous sequels. He and his partner Jane have featured in films, comic strips, and television series.

Tasaday member of an indigenous people of the rainforests of Mindanao in the *Philippines, contacted in the 1960s. Some anthropologists doubt their claim to leading a hunter-gatherer way of life.

Tashkent capital of Uzbekistan; population (1990) 2,100,000. Industries include the manufacture of mining machinery, chemicals, textiles, and leather goods. Founded in the 7th century, it was taken by the Turks in the 12th century and captured by Tamerlane 1361. In 1865 it was taken by the Russians. It was severely damaged by an earthquake 1966.

TASM (abbreviation for *tactical air-to-surface missile*) *missile with a range of under 500 km/ 300 mi and a nuclear warhead. TASMs are being developed independently by the USA and France to replace the surface-to-surface missiles being phased out by NATO from 1990.

Tasman Abel Janszoon 1603–1659. Dutch navigator. In 1642, he was the first European to see Tasmania. He also made the first European sightings of New Zealand, Tonga, and Fiji.

Tasmania former name (1642–1856) *Van Diemen's Land* island off the south coast of Australia; a state of the Commonwealth of Australia
area 67,800 sq km/26,171 sq mi
capital Hobart
towns Launceston (chief port)
products wool, dairy products, apples and other fruit, timber, iron, tin, coal, copper, silver
population (1987) 448,000
history the first European to visit here was Abel Tasman 1642; the last of the Tasmanian Aboriginals died 1876. Tasmania joined the Australian Commonwealth as a state 1901.

Tasmanian devil carnivorous marsupial *Sarcophilus harrisii*, in the same family (Dasyuridae) as native 'cats'. It is about 65 cm/ 2.1 ft long with a 25 cm/10 in bushy tail. It has a large head, strong teeth, and is blackish with white patches on the chest and hind parts. It is nocturnal, carnivorous, and can be ferocious when cornered. It has recently become extinct in Australia and survives only in remote parts of Tasmania.

Tasmanian wolf or *thylacine* carnivorous marsupial *Thylacinus cynocephalus*, in the family Dasyuridae. It is doglike in appearance and can be nearly 2 m/6 ft from nose to tail tip. It was hunted to probable extinction in the 1930s, but there are still occasional unconfirmed reports of sightings.

Tass acronym for *Telegrafnoye Agentstvo Sovyetskovo Soyuza*, the international news agency of the former Soviet Union. In Jan 1992 the creation of a replacement body, the Russian Information Telegraph Agency (RITA), was announced, although the name TASS was to be

retained for the domestic wire service within the Commonwealth of Independent States.

Tasso Torquato 1544–1595. Italian poet, author of the romantic epic poem of the First Crusade *Gerusalemme Liberata/Jerusalem Delivered* 1574, followed by the *Gerusalemme Conquistata/Jerusalem Conquered*, written during the period from 1576 when he was mentally unstable.

taste sense that detects some of the chemical constituents of food. The human *tongue can distinguish only four basic tastes (sweet, sour, bitter, and salty) but it is supplemented by the nose's sense of smell. What we refer to as taste is really a composite sense made up of both taste and smell.

Tatar or *Tartar* member of a Turkic people, the descendants of the mixed Mongol and Turkic followers of *Genghis Khan, called the Golden Horde because of the wealth they gained by plunder. The vast Tatar state was conquered by Russia 1552. The Tatars now live mainly in the Russian autonomous republic of Tatarstan, W Siberia, Turkmenistan, and Uzbekistan (where they were deported from the Crimea 1944). There are over 5 million speakers of the Tatar language, which belongs to the Turkic branch of the Altaic family. The Tatar people are mainly Muslim, although some have converted to the Orthodox Church.

Tatarstan formerly *Tatar Autonomous Republic* autonomous republic of E Russia
area 68,000 sq km/26,250 sq mi
capital Kazan
products oil, chemicals, textiles, timber
population (1986) 3,537,000 (48% Tatar, 43% Russian)
history a territory of Volga-Kama Bulgar state from the 10th century when Islam was introduced; conquered by the Mongols 1236; the capital of the powerful Khanate of Kazan until conquered by Russia 1552; an autonomous republic from 1920. In recent years the republic (mainly Muslim and an important industrial and oil-producing area) has seen moves towards increased autonomy. In Aug 1990 the republic's assembly upgraded Tatarstan to full republic status, proclaiming its economic and political 'sovereignty', and in April 1991 there were popular demonstrations in support of this action. In June 1991 it refused to participate in the Russian presidential election, and in March 1992 declined to be party to a federal treaty, signed in Moscow by 18 of Russia's other 20 main political subdivisions. A referendum 21 March 1992 favoured Tatarstan becoming a sovereign state within Russia.

Tati Jacques. Stage name of Jacques Tatischeff 1908–1982. French comic actor, director, and writer. He portrayed Monsieur Hulot, the embodiment of polite opposition to modern mechanization, in a series of films including *Les Vacances de M Hulot/Monsieur Hulot's Holiday* 1953.

Tatlin Vladimir 1885–1953. Russian artist, cofounder of *Constructivism*. After encountering Cubism in Paris 1913 he evolved his first Constructivist works, using raw materials such as tin, glass, plaster, and wood to create abstract sculptures that he suspended in the air.

Tatum Art(hur) 1910–1956. US jazz pianist

who, in the 1930s, worked mainly as a soloist. Tatum is considered among the most technically brilliant of jazz pianists and his technique and chromatic harmonies influenced many musicians, such as Oscar Peterson (1925–). He improvised with the guitarist Tiny Grimes (1916–) in a trio from 1943.

Tau Ceti one of the nearest stars visible to the naked eye, 11.9 light years from Earth in the constellation Cetus. It has a diameter slightly less than that of the Sun, and an actual luminosity of about 45% of the Sun's. Its similarity to the Sun is sufficient to suggest that Tau Ceti may possess a planetary system, although observations have yet to reveal evidence of this.

Taurus zodiacal constellation in the northern hemisphere near Orion, represented as a bull. The Sun passes through Taurus from mid-May to late June. Its brightest star is Aldebaran, seen as the bull's red eye. Taurus contains the Hyades and Pleiades open *star clusters, and the Crab nebula. In astrology, the dates for Taurus are between about 20 April and 20 May (see *precession).

tautology repetition of the same thing in different words, or the ungrammatical use of unnecessary words: for example, it is tautologous to say that something is *most unique*, since something unique cannot, by definition, be comparative.

Tavener John (Kenneth) 1944– . English composer whose individual and sometimes abrasive works include the dramatic cantata *The Whale* 1968 and the opera *Thérèse* 1979. He has also composed music for the Eastern Orthodox Church.

Taverner John 1495–1545. English organist and composer. He wrote masses and motets in polyphonic style, showing great contrapuntal skill, but as a Protestant renounced his art. He was imprisoned 1528 for heresy, and, as an agent of Thomas Cromwell, assisted in the dissolution of the monasteries.

taxation raising of money from individuals and organizations by the state in order to pay for the goods and services it provides. Taxation can be **direct** (a deduction from income) or **indirect** (added to the purchase price of goods or services, that is, a tax on consumption). The standard form of indirect taxation in Europe is **value-added tax (VAT)**. **Income tax** is the most common form of direct taxation.

taxis (plural **taxes**) or **tactic movement** in botany, the movement of a single cell, such as a bacterium, protozoan, single-celled alga, or gamete, in response to an external stimulus. A movement directed towards the stimulus is described as positive taxis, and away from it as negative taxis. The alga *Chlamydomonas*, for example, demonstrates positive **phototaxis** by swimming towards a light source to increase the rate of photosynthesis. **Chemotaxis** is a response to a chemical stimulus, as seen in many bacteria that move towards higher concentrations of nutrients.

taxonomy another name for the *classification of living organisms.

Tay longest river in Scotland; length 189 km/ 118 mi. Rising in NW Central region, it flows NE through Loch Tay, then E and SE past Perth to the Firth of Tay, crossed at Dundee by the Tay Bridge, before joining the North Sea. The Tay has numerous salmon fisheries; its main tributaries are the Tummel, Isla, and Earn.

Taylor A(lan) J(ohn) P(ercivale) 1906–1990. English historian and television lecturer. International history lecturer at Oxford University 1953–63, he established himself as an authority on modern British and European history and did much to popularize the subject, giving the first televised history lectures. His books include *The Struggle for Mastery in Europe 1848–1918* 1954, *The Origins of the Second World War* 1961, and *English History 1914–1945* 1965.

Taylor Elizabeth 1932– . English-born US actress whose films include *National Velvet* 1944, *Cat on a Hot Tin Roof* 1958, *Butterfield 8* 1960 (Academy Award), *Cleopatra* 1963, and *Who's Afraid of Virginia Woolf?* 1966 (Academy Award).

Taylor Frederick Winslow 1856–1915. US engineer and management consultant, the founder of scientific management. His ideas, published in *Principles of Scientific Management* 1911, were based on the breakdown of work to the simplest tasks, the separation of planning from execution of tasks, and the introduction of time-and-motion studies. His methods were clearly expressed in assembly-line factories, but have been criticized for degrading and alienating workers and producing managerial dictatorship.

Tay-Sachs disease inherited disorder, due to a defective gene, causing an enzyme deficiency that leads to blindness, retardation, and death in childhood. Because of their enforced isolation and inbreeding during hundreds of years, it is most common in people of E European Jewish descent.

Tayside region of Scotland
area 7,700 sq km/2,973 sq mi
towns Dundee (administrative headquarters), Perth, Arbroath, Forfar
products beef and dairy products, soft fruit from the fertile Carse of Gowrie (SW of Dundee)
population (1991) 385,300
famous people J M Barrie, John Buchan, Princess Margaret.

TB abbreviation for the infectious disease *tuberculosis*.

Tbilisi formerly *Tiflis* capital of the Republic of Georgia; industries include textiles, machinery, ceramics, and tobacco; population (1987) 1,194,000. Dating from the 5th century, it is a centre of Georgian culture, with fine medieval churches. Anti-Russian demonstrations were quashed here by troops 1981 and 1989; the latter clash followed rejected demands for autonomy from the Abkhazia enclave, and resulted in 19 or more deaths from poison gas (containing chloroacetophenone) and 100 injured. In Dec 1991 at least 50 people were killed as well-armed opposition forces attempted to overthrow President Gamsakhurdia, eventually forcing him to flee.

T cell or *T lymphocyte* immune cell (see *immunity and *lymphocyte) that plays several roles in the body's defences. T cells are so called because they mature in the *thymus.

Tchaikovsky Pyotr Il'yich 1840–1893. Russian composer. His strong sense of melody, personal expression, and brilliant orchestration are clear throughout his many Romantic works, which include six symphonies, three piano concertos, a violin concerto, operas (for example, *Eugene Onegin* 1879), ballets (for example, *The Nutcracker* 1892), orchestral fantasies (for example, *Romeo and Juliet* 1870), and chamber and vocal music.

TD abbreviation for *Teachta Dála* (Irish 'a member of the Irish parliament').

tea evergreen shrub *Camellia sinensis*, family Theaceae, of which the fermented, dried leaves are infused to make a beverage of the same name. Known in China as early as 2737 BC, tea was first brought to Europe AD 1610 and rapidly became a fashionable drink. In 1823 it was found growing wild in N India, and plantations were later established in Assam and Sri Lanka; producers today include Africa, South America, Georgia, Azerbaijan, Indonesia, and Iran.

teak tropical Asian timber tree *Tectona grandis*, family Verbenaceae, with yellowish wood used in furniture and shipbuilding.

teal any of various small, short-necked dabbling ducks of the genus *Anas*. The drakes generally have a bright head and wing markings. The green-winged teal *A. crecca* is about 35 cm/14 in long.

tear gas any of various volatile gases that produce irritation and tearing of the eyes, used by police against crowds and used in chemical warfare. The gas is delivered in pressurized, liquid-filled canisters or grenades, thrown by hand or launched from a specially adapted rifle. Gases (such as Mace) cause violent coughing and blinding tears, which pass when the victim breathes fresh air, and there are no lasting effects. Blister gases (such as mustard gas) and nerve gases are more harmful and may cause permanent injury or death.

teasel erect, prickly, biennial herb *Dipsacus fullonum*, family Dipsacaceae, native to Eurasia. The dry, spiny seed heads were once used industrially to tease, or raise the nap of, cloth.

tea tree shrub or small tree of the the genus *Leptospermum* of Australia and New Zealand. It is thought that some species of leptospermum were used by the explorer Captain Cook to brew tea; it was used in the first years of settlement for this purpose.

technetium (Greek *technetos* 'artificial') silver-grey, radioactive, metallic element, symbol Tc, atomic number 43, relative atomic mass 98.906. It occurs in nature only in extremely minute amounts, produced as a fission product from uranium in *pitchblende and other uranium ores. Its longest-lived isotope, Tc-99, has a half-life of 216,000 years. It is a superconductor and is used as a hardener in steel alloys and as a medical tracer.

Technicolor trade name for a film colour process using three separate negatives of blue, green, and red images. It was invented by Daniel F Comstock and Herbert T Kalmus in the USA 1922. Originally, Technicolor was a two-colour process in which superimposed red and green images were projected on to the screen by a special projector. This initial version proved expensive and imperfect, but when the three-colour process was introduced 1932, the system was widely adopted, culminating in its use in *The Wizard of Oz* and *Gone With the Wind*, both 1939. Technicolor remains the most commonly used colour process for cinematography.

technocracy society controlled by technical experts such as scientists and engineers. The term was invented by US engineer W H Smyth (1855–1940) 1919 to describe his proposed 'rule by technicians', and was popularized by James Burham (1905–1987) in *Managerial Revolution* 1941.

technology the use of tools, power, and materials, generally for the purposes of production. Almost every human process for getting food and shelter depends on complex technological systems, which have been developed over a 5-million-year period. Significant milestones include the advent of the *steam engine 1712, the introduction of *electricity and the *internal combustion engine in the mid-1800s, and recent developments in *communications, *electronics, and the nuclear and space industries. The *advanced technology* (highly automated and specialized) on which modern industrialized society depends is frequently contrasted with the *low technology* (labour-intensive and unspecialized) that characterizes some developing countries. *Intermediate technology* is an attempt to adapt scientifically advanced inventions to less developed areas by using local materials and methods of manufacture.

technology education training for the practical application of science in industry and commerce. Britain's Industrial Revolution preceded that of the rest of Europe by half a century and its prosperity stimulated other countries to encourage technological education. France established the Ecole Polytechnique, the first technological university 1794, and Germany founded the Technische Hochschulen in Berlin 1799. Britain founded the mechanics institutes for education in technology, notably the University of Manchester Institute of Science and Technology (UMIST) 1824.

tectonics in geology, the study of the movements of rocks on the Earth's surface. On a small scale tectonics involves the formation of *folds and *faults, but on a large scale *plate tectonics deals with the movement of the Earth's surface as a whole.

Tecumseh 1768–1813. North American Indian chief of the Shawnee. He attempted to unite the Indian peoples from Canada to Florida against the encroachment of white settlers, but the defeat of his brother *Tenskwatawa*, 'the Prophet', at the battle of Tippecanoe in Nov 1811 by W H Harrison, governor of the Indiana Territory, largely destroyed the confederacy built up by Tecumseh. He was commissioned a brigadier general in the British army during the War of 1812, and died in battle.

Teesside industrial area at the mouth of the river Tees, Cleveland, NE England; population (1981) 382,700. Industries include high technology, capital-intensive steelmaking, chemicals, an oil-fuel terminal, and the main North Sea natural-gas terminal. Middlesbrough is a large port.

tefillin or **phylacteries** in Judaism, two small leather boxes containing scrolls from the Torah, that are strapped to the left arm and the forehead by Jewish men for daily prayer.

Teflon trade name for polytetrafluoroethene (PTFE), a tough, waxlike, heat-resistant plastic used for coating nonstick cookware and in gaskets and bearings.

Tegucigalpa capital of Honduras; industries include textiles and food-processing; population (1989) 608,000. It was founded 1524 as a gold- and silver-mining centre.

Tehran capital of Iran; industries include textiles, chemicals, engineering, and tobacco; population (1986) 6,043,000. It was founded in the 12th century and made the capital 1788 by Muhammad Shah. Much of the city was rebuilt in the 1920s and 1930s. Tehran is the site of the Gulistan Palace (the former royal residence).

Tehran Conference conference held 1943 in Tehran, Iran, the first meeting of World War II Allied leaders Churchill, Roosevelt, and Stalin. The chief subject discussed was coordination of Allied strategy in W and E Europe.

Teilhard de Chardin Pierre 1881–1955. French Jesuit theologian, palaeontologist, and philosopher. He developed a creative synthesis of nature and religion, based on his fieldwork and fossil studies. Publication of his *Le Phénomène humain*/*The Phenomenon of Man*, written 1938–40, was delayed (due to his unorthodox views) until after his death by the embargo of his superiors. He saw humanity as being in a constant process of evolution, moving towards a perfect spiritual state.

Tej Bahadur 1621–1675. Indian religious leader, ninth guru (teacher) of Sikhism 1664–75, executed for refusing to renounce his faith.

Te Kanawa Kiri 1944– . New Zealand soprano. Te Kanawa's first major role was the Countess in Mozart's *The Marriage of Figaro* at Covent Garden, London, 1971. Her voice combines the purity and intensity of the upper range with an extended lower range of great richness and resonance. Apart from classical roles, she has also featured popular music in her repertoire, such as the 1984 recording of Leonard Bernstein's *West Side Story*.

tektite (from Greek *tektos* 'molten') small, rounded glassy stone, found in certain regions of the Earth, such as Australasia. Tektites are probably the scattered drops of molten rock thrown out by the impact of a large *meteorite.

Tel Aviv officially **Tel Aviv–Jaffa** city in Israel, on the Mediterranean Sea; industries include textiles, chemicals, sugar, printing, and publishing; population (1987) 320,000. Tel Aviv was founded 1909 as a Jewish residential area in the Arab town of Jaffa, with which it was combined 1949; their ports were superseded 1965 by Ashdod to the south.

telecommunications communications over a distance, generally by electronic means. Long-distance voice communication was pioneered 1876 by Alexander Graham Bell, when he invented the telephone as a result of Faraday's discovery of electromagnetism. Today it is possible to communicate with most countries by telephone cable, or by satellite or microwave link, with over 100,000 simultaneous conversations and several television channels being carried by the latest satellites. *Integrated-Services Digital Network (ISDN) makes videophones and high-quality fax possible; the world's first large-scale centre of ISDN began operating in Japan 1988. The chief method of relaying long-distance calls on land is microwave radio transmission.

telegraphy transmission of coded messages along wires by means of electrical signals. The first modern form of telecommunication, it now uses printers for the transmission and receipt of messages. Telex is an international telegraphy network.

Telemann Georg Philipp 1681–1767. German Baroque composer, organist, and conductor at the Johanneum, Hamburg, from 1721. He was exceedingly prolific, producing 25 operas, 1,800 church cantatas, hundreds of other vocal works, and 600 instrumental works.

telephone instrument for communicating by voice over long distances, invented by Alexander Graham *Bell 1876. The transmitter (mouthpiece) consists of a carbon microphone, with a diaphragm that vibrates when a person speaks into it. The diaphragm vibrations compress grains of carbon to a greater or lesser extent, altering their resistance to an electric current passing through them. This sets up variable electrical signals, which travel along the telephone lines to the receiver of the person being called. There they cause the magnetism of an electromagnet to vary, making a diaphragm above the electromagnet vibrate and give out sound waves, which mirror those that entered the mouthpiece originally.

telephoto lens photographic lens of longer focal length than normal that takes a very narrow view and gives a large image through a combination of telescopic and ordinary photographic lenses.

teleprinter or **teletypewriter** transmitting and receiving device used in telecommunications to handle coded messages. Teleprinters are automatic typewriters keyed telegraphically to convert typed words into electrical signals (using a 5-unit Baudot code, see *baud) at the transmitting end, and signals into typed words at the receiving end.

telescope optical instrument that magnifies images of faint and distant objects; any device for collecting and focusing light and other forms of electromagnetic radiation. It is a major research tool in astronomy, is used to sight over land and sea, and small telescopes can be attached to cameras and rifles. A telescope with a large aperture, or opening, can distinguish finer detail and fainter objects than one with a small aperture. The **refracting telescope** uses lenses, and the **reflecting telescope** uses mirrors. A third type, the **catadioptric telescope**, with a combination of lenses and mirrors, is used increasingly. See also *radio telescope.

teletext broadcast system of displaying information on a television screen. The information – typically about news items, entertainment, sport, and finance – is constantly updated. Teletext is a form of *videotext, pioneered in Britain by the

TELEVISION: CHRONOLOGY

1878	William Crookes in England invented the Crookes tube, which produced cathode rays.
1884	Paul Nipkow in Germany built a mechanical scanning device, the Nipkow disc, a rotating disc with a spiral pattern of holes in it.
1897	Karl Ferdinand Braun, also in Germany, modified the Crookes tube to produce the ancestor of the TV receiver picture tube.
1906	Boris Rosing in Russia began experimenting with the Nipkow disc and cathode-ray tube, eventually succeeding in transmitting some crude TV pictures.
1923	Vladimir Zworykin in the USA invented the first electronic camera tube, the iconoscope.
1926	John Logie Baird demonstrated a workable TV system, using mechanical scanning by Nipkow disc.
1928	Baird demonstrated colour TV.
1929	The BBC began broadcasting experimental TV programmes using Baird's system.
1936	The BBC began regular broadcasting using Baird's system from Alexandra Palace, London.
1940	Experimental colour TV transmission began in the USA, using the present-day system of colour reproduction.
1953	Successful colour TV transmissions began in the USA.
1956	The first videotape recorder was produced in California by the Ampex Corporation.
1962	TV signals were transmitted across the Atlantic via the Telstar satellite.
1970	The first videodisc system was announced by Decca in Britain and AEG-Telefunken in Germany, but it was not perfected until the 1980s, when laser scanning was used for playback.
1973	The BBC and Independent Television in the UK introduced the world's first teletext systems, Ceefax and Oracle, respectively.
1975	Sony introduced their videocassette tape-recorder system, Betamax, for domestic viewers, six years after their professional U-Matic system. The UK Post Office (now British Telecom) announced their Prestel viewdata system.
1979	Matsushita in Japan developed a pocket-sized, flat-screen TV set, using a liquid-crystal display.
1986	Data broadcasting using digital techniques was developed; an enhancement of teletext was produced.
1989	The Japanese began broadcasting high-definition television; satellite television was introduced in the UK.
1990	The BBC introduced a digital stereo sound system (NICAM); MAC, a European system allowing greater picture definition, more data, and sound tracks, was introduced.
1992	All-digital high-definition television (HDTV) demonstrated in the USA.

British Broadcasting Corporation (BBC) with Ceefax and by Independent Television with Oracle.

televangelist in North America, a fundamentalist Christian minister, often of a Pentecostal church, who hosts a television show and solicits donations from viewers. Well-known televangelists include Jim Bakker, convicted 1989 of fraudulent misuse of donations, and Jimmy Swaggart.

television (TV) reproduction at a distance by radio waves of visual images. For transmission, television camera converts the pattern of light it takes in into a pattern of electrical charges. This is scanned line by line by a beam of electrons from an electron gun, resulting in variable electrical signals that represent the picture. These signals are combined with a radio carrier wave and broadcast as magnetic waves. The TV aerial picks up the wave and feeds it to the receiver (TV set). This separates out the vision signals, which pass to a cathode-ray tube where a beam of electrons is made to scan across the screen line by line, mirroring the action of the electron gun in the TV camera. The result is a recreation of the pattern of light that entered the camera. Twenty-five pictures are built up each second with interlaced scanning in Europe (30 in North America), with a total of 625 lines in Europe (525 lines in North America and Japan).

telex (acronym for **teleprinter exchange**) international telecommunications network that handles telegraph messages in the form of coded signals. It uses *teleprinters for transmitting and receiving, and makes use of land lines (cables) and radio and satellite links to make connections between subscribers.

Telford Thomas 1757–1834. Scottish civil engineer who opened up N Scotland by building roads and waterways. He constructed many aqueducts and canals, including the Caledonian canal 1802–23, and erected the Menai road suspension bridge 1819–26, a type of structure scarcely tried previously in England. In Scotland he constructed over 1,600 km/1,000 mi of road and 1,200 bridges, churches, and harbours.

Tell Wilhelm (William) legendary 14th-century Swiss archer, said to have refused to salute the Habsburg badge at Altdorf on Lake Lucerne. Sentenced to shoot an apple from his son's head, he did so, then shot the tyrannical Austrian ruler Gessler, symbolizing his people's refusal to submit to external authority.

Tell el Amarna site of the ancient Egyptian capital *Akhetaton. The *Amarna tablets were found there.

Teller Edward 1908– . Hungarian-born US physicist known as the father of the *hydrogen bomb, which he worked upon, after taking part in the atom bomb project, at the Los Alamos research centre, New Mexico, 1946–52. He was a key witness against his colleague Robert *Oppenheimer at the security hearings 1954. He was widely believed to be the model for the leading character in Stanley Kubrick's 1964 film *Dr Strangelove*. More recently he has been one of the leading supporters of the Star Wars programme (*Strategic Defense Initiative).

tellurium (Latin *Tellus* 'Earth') silver-white, semi-metallic (*metalloid) element, symbol Te, atomic number 52, relative atomic mass 127.60. Chemically it is similar to sulphur and selenium, and it is considered as one of the sulphur group.

It occurs naturally in telluride minerals, and is used in colouring glass blue–brown, in the electrolytic refining of zinc, in electronics, and as a catalyst in refining petroleum.

Telstar US communications satellite, launched 10 July 1962, which relayed the first live television transmissions between the USA and Europe. *Telstar* orbited the Earth in 158 minutes, and so had to be tracked by ground stations, unlike the geostationary satellites of today.

Telugu language spoken in SE India. It is the official language of Andhra Pradesh, and is also spoken in Malaysia, giving a total number of speakers of around 50 million. Written records in Telugu date from the 7th century AD. Telugu belongs to the Dravidian family.

tempera painting medium in which powdered pigments are bound together, usually with egg yolk and water. A form of tempera was used in ancient Egypt, and egg tempera was the foremost medium for panel painting in late medieval and early Renaissance Europe. It was gradually superseded by oils from the late 15th century onwards.

temperament in music, a system of tuning the pitches of a mode or scale; in folk music to preserve its emotional or ritual meaning, in Western music to allow maximum flexibility for changing key. J S Bach wrote *The Well-Tempered Clavier* to demonstrate the superiority of this system of tuning.

temperature state of hotness or coldness of a body, and the condition that determines whether or not it will transfer heat to, or receive heat from, another body according to the laws of *thermodynamics. It is measured in degrees Celsius (before 1948 called centigrade), kelvin, or Fahrenheit.

tempering heat treatment for improving the properties of metals, often used for steel alloys. The metal is heated to a certain temperature and then cooled suddenly in a water or oil bath.

Templar member of a Christian military order, founded in Jerusalem 1119, the **Knights of the Temple of Solomon**. The knights took vows of poverty, chastity, and obedience and devoted themselves to the recovery of Palestine from the Muslims.

temple place of religious worship. In US usage, temple is another name for *synagogue.

Temple centre of Jewish national worship in Jerusalem in both ancient and modern days. The Western or **Wailing Wall** is the surviving part of the western wall of the enclosure of Herod's Temple. Since the destruction of the Temple AD 70, Jews have gone there to pray and to mourn their dispersion and the loss of their homeland.

Temple Shirley 1928– . US actress who became the most successful child star of the 1930s. Her films include *Bright Eyes* 1934 (Academy Award), in which she sang 'On the Good Ship Lollipop', *Curly Top* 1935, and *Rebecca of Sunnybrook Farm* 1938. Her film career virtually ended by the time she was 12. As Shirley Temple Black, she became active in the Republican Party and was US chief of protocol 1976–77. She was appointed US ambassador to Czechoslovakia 1989.

tempo (Italian 'time') in music, the speed at which a piece is played.

tench European freshwater bony fish *Tinca tinca*, a member of the carp family, now established in North America. It is about 45 cm/18 in long, weighing 2 kg/4.5 lb, coloured olive green above and grey beneath. The scales are small and there is a barbel at each side of the mouth.

Ten Commandments in the Old Testament, the laws given by God to the Hebrew leader Moses on Mt Sinai, engraved on two tablets of stone. They are: to have no other gods beside Jehovah; to make no idols; not to misuse the name of God; to keep the sabbath holy; to honour one's parents; not to commit murder, adultery, or theft; not to give false evidence; not to be covetous. They form the basis of Jewish and Christian moral codes; the 'tablets of the Law' given to Moses are also mentioned in the Koran. The giving of the Ten Commandments is celebrated in the Jewish festival of *Shavuot* (see *Pentecost).

tendon or **sinew** cord of tough, fibrous connective tissue that joins muscle to bone in vertebrates. Tendons are largely composed of the protein collagen, and because of their inelasticity are very efficient at transforming muscle power into movement.

tendril in botany, a slender, threadlike structure that supports a climbing plant by coiling around suitable supports, such as the stems and branches of other plants. It may be a modified stem, leaf, leaflet, flower, leaf stalk, or stipule (a small appendage on either side of the leaf stalk), and may be simple or branched. The tendrils of Virginia creeper *Parthenocissus quinquefolia* are modified flower heads with suckerlike pads at the end that stick to walls, while those of the grapevine *Vitis* grow away from the light and thus enter dark crevices where they expand to anchor the plant firmly.

Tenerife largest of the *Canary Islands, Spain; area 2,060 sq km/795 sq mi; population (1981) 557,000. *Santa Cruz* is the main town, and *Pico de Teide* is an active volcano.

Tennessee state in E central USA; nickname Volunteer State;
area 109,200 sq km/42,151 sq mi
capital Nashville
towns Memphis, Knoxville, Chattanooga, Clarksville
products cereals, cotton, tobacco, soya beans, livestock, timber, coal, zinc, copper, chemicals
population (1990) 4,877,200
famous people Davy Crockett, David Farragut, W C Handy, Cordell Hull, Andrew Jackson, Andrew Johnson, Dolly Parton, John Crowe Ransom, Bessie Smith
history first settled by Europeans 1757; became a state 1796. Tennessee was deeply divided in the Civil War and was a major war theatre, with the battles of Shiloh, Murfreesboro, Chattanooga, and Nashville among those fought in the state.

tennis or **lawn tennis** racket-and-ball game invented towards the end of the 19th century, derived from *real tennis. Although played on different surfaces (grass, wood, shale, clay, concrete), it is also called 'lawn tennis'. The aim of the two or four players is to strike the ball into the prescribed area of the court, with oval-headed rackets (strung with gut or nylon), in such a way that it cannot be returned. Major events include the *Davis Cup* and the annual All England Tennis Club championships, an open event for players of both sexes at *Wimbledon.

Tennyson Alfred, 1st Baron Tennyson 1809–1892. English poet, poet laureate 1850–92, whose verse has a majestic, musical quality. His works include 'The Lady of Shalott', 'The Lotus Eaters', 'Ulysses', 'Break, Break, Break', 'The Charge of the Light Brigade'; the longer narratives *Locksley Hall* 1832 and *Maud* 1855; the elegy *In Memoriam* 1850; and a long series of poems on the Arthurian legends *The Idylls of the King* 1857–85.

tenor in music, the highest range of adult male voice when not using *falsetto. It covers a two-octave range centred on middle C and is the preferred voice for operatic heroic roles. Exponents are Luciano *Pavarotti and Jose *Carreras.

Teotihuacán huge ancient city in central Mexico, a religious centre of Mesoamerican civilization that was inhabited by many cultures from 6000 BC on. It is one of the best-excavated archaeological sites in Mexico.

tequila Mexican alcoholic liquor distilled from the *agave plant. It is named after the place, near Guadalajara, where the conquistadors first developed it from Aztec *pulque*, which would keep for only a day.

terbium soft, silver-grey, metallic element of the *lanthanide series, symbol Tb, atomic number 81, relative atomic mass 158.925. It occurs in gadolinite and other ores, with yttrium and ytterbium, and is used in lasers, semiconductors, and television tubes. It was named in 1843 by Swedish chemist Carl Mosander (1797–1858) for the town of Ytterby, Sweden, where it was first found.

Teresa Mother. Born Agnes Bojaxhiu 1910– . Roman Catholic nun. She was born in Skopje, Albania, and at 18 entered a Calcutta convent and became a teacher. In 1948 she became an Indian citizen and founded the Missionaries of Charity, an order for men and women based in Calcutta that helps abandoned children and the dying. Nobel Peace Prize 1979.

terminal in computing, a device consisting of a keyboard and display screen (*VDU) – or, in older systems, a teleprinter – to enable the operator to communicate with the computer. The terminal may be physically attached to the computer or linked to it by a telephone line (remote terminal). A 'dumb' terminal has no processor of its own, whereas an 'intelligent' terminal has its own processor and takes some of the processing load away from the main computer.

termite any member of the insect order Isoptera. Termites are soft-bodied social insects living in large colonies which include one or more queens (of relatively enormous size and producing an egg every two seconds), much smaller kings, and still smaller soldiers, workers, and immature forms. Termites build galleried nests of soil particles that may be 6 m/20 ft high.

tern any of various lightly built seabirds placed in the same family (Laridae) as gulls and characterized by pointed wings and bill and usually a forked tail. Terns plunge-dive after aquatic prey. They are 20–50 cm/8–20 in long, and usually coloured in combinations of white and black.

terracotta (Italian 'baked earth') brownish-red baked clay, usually unglazed, used in building, sculpture, and pottery. The term is specifically applied to small figures or figurines, such as those found at Tanagra. Excavations at Xian, China, have revealed life-size terracotta figures of the army of the Emperor Shi Huangdi dating from the 3rd century BC.

terrapin member of some species of the order Chelonia (*turtles and *tortoises). Terrapins are small to medium-sized, aquatic or semi-aquatic, and are found widely in temperate zones. They are omnivorous, but generally eat aquatic animals. Some species are in danger of extinction owing to collection for the pet trade; most of the animals collected die in transit.

terrier any of various breeds of highly intelligent, active dogs. They are usually small. Types include the bull, cairn, fox, Irish, Scottish, Sealyham, Skye, and Yorkshire terriers. They were originally bred for hunting rabbits and following quarry such as foxes down into burrows.

territory in animal behaviour, a fixed area from which an animal or group of animals excludes other members of the same species. Animals may hold territories for many different reasons; for example, to provide a constant food supply, to monopolize potential mates, or to ensure access to refuges or nest sites. The size of a territory depends in part on its function: some nesting and mating territories may be only a few square metres, whereas feeding territories may be as large as hundreds of square kilometres.

terrorism systematic violence in the furtherance of political aims, often by small *guerrilla groups.

Tertiary period of geological time 65–1.64 million years ago, divided into five epochs: Palaeocene, Eocene, Oligocene, Miocene, and Pliocene. During the Tertiary, mammals took over all the ecological niches left vacant by the extinction of the dinosaurs, and became the prevalent land animals. The continents took on their present positions, and climatic and vegetation zones as we know them became established. Within the geological time column the Tertiary follows the Cretaceous period and is succeeded by the Quaternary period.

tesla SI unit (symbol T) of *magnetic flux density. One tesla represents a flux density of one *weber per square metre, or 10^4 *gauss. It is named after the Croatian engineer Nikola Tesla (1856–1943).

TESSA (acronym for *tax-exempt special savings account*) UK scheme, introduced 1991, to encourage longer-term savings by making interest tax-free on deposits of up to £9,000 over five years.

testis (plural *testes*) the organ that produces *sperm in male (and hermaphrodite) animals. In vertebrates it is one of a pair of oval structures that are usually internal, but in mammals (other than elephants and marine mammals), the paired testes (or testicles) descend from the body cavity during development, to hang outside the abdomen in a scrotal sac.

testosterone in vertebrates, hormone secreted chiefly by the testes, but also by the ovaries and the cortex of the adrenal glands. It promotes the development of secondary sexual characteristics in males. In animals with a breeding season, the onset of breeding behaviour is accompanied by a rise in the level of testosterone in the blood.

tetanus or **lockjaw** acute disease caused by the toxin of the bacillus *Clostridium tetani*, which usually enters the body through a wound. The bacterium is chiefly found in richly manured soil. Untreated, in seven to ten days tetanus produces muscular spasm and rigidity of the jaw spreading to the other muscles, convulsions, and death. There is a vaccine, and the disease may be treatable with tetanus antitoxin and antibiotics.

tetracycline one of a group of antibiotic substances having in common the four-ring structure of chlortetracycline, the first member of the group to be isolated. They are prepared synthetically or obtained from certain bacteria of the genus *Streptomyces*. They are broad-spectrum antibiotics, effective against a wide range of disease-causing bacteria.

Texas state in SW USA; nickname Lone Star State
area 691,200 sq km/266,803 sq mi
capital Austin
towns Houston, Dallas-Fort Worth, San Antonio, El Paso, Corpus Christi, Lubbock
products rice, cotton, sorghum, wheat, hay, livestock, shrimp, meat products, lumber, wood and paper products, petroleum (nearly one-third of US production), natural gas, sulphur, salt, uranium, chemicals, petrochemicals, nonelectrical machinery, fabricated metal products, transportation equipment, electric and electronic equipment
population (1990) 16,986,500
famous people James Bowie, George Bush, Buddy Holly, Sam Houston, Howard Hughes, Lyndon Johnson, Janis Joplin, Katherine Anne Porter, Tina Turner
history settled by the Spanish 1682; part of Mexico 1821–36; Santa Anna massacred the Alamo garrison 1836, but was defeated by Sam Houston at San Jacinto the same year; Texas became an independent republic 1836–45, with Houston as president; in 1845 it became a state of the USA. Texas is the only state in the USA to have previously been an independent republic.

Thackeray William Makepeace 1811–1863. English novelist and essayist, born in Calcutta, India. He was a regular contributor to *Fraser's Magazine* and *Punch*. *Vanity Fair* 1847–48 was his first novel, followed by *Pendennis* 1848, *Henry Esmond* 1852 (and its sequel *The Virginians* 1857–59), and *The Newcomes* 1853–55, in which Thackeray's tendency to sentimentality is most marked.

Thai member of the majority ethnic group living in Thailand and N Myanmar (Burma). Thai peoples also live in SW China, Laos, and N Vietnam. They speak Tai languages, all of which belong to the Sino-Tibetan language family. There are over 60 million speakers, the majority of whom live in Thailand. Most Thais are Buddhists, but the traditional belief in spirits, *phi*, remains.

Thailand Kingdom of (*Prathet Thai* or *Muang-Thai*)
area 513,115 sq km/198,108 sq mi
capital and chief port Bangkok
towns Chiangmai, Nakhon Sawan river port
physical mountainous, semi-arid plateau in NE, fertile central region, tropical isthmus in S
environment tropical rainforest was reduced to 18% of the land area 1988 (from 93% in 1961); logging was banned by the government 1988
head of state King Bhumibol Adulyadej from 1946
head of government Chuan Leekpai from 1992
political system military-controlled emergent democracy
currency baht
population (1993 est) 57,800,000 (Thai 75%, Chinese 14%); growth rate 2% p.a.
languages Thai and Chinese (both official); regional dialects
religions Buddhist 95%, Muslim 4%
GNP $1,580 per head (1991)
chronology
1896 Anglo-French agreement recognized Siam as independent buffer state.
1932 Constitutional monarchy established.
1939 Name of Thailand adopted.
1941–44 Japanese occupation.
1947 Military seized power in coup.
1972 Withdrawal of Thai troops from South Vietnam.
1973 Military government overthrown.
1976 Military reassumed control.
1980 General Prem Tinsulanonda assumed power.
1983 Civilian government formed; martial law maintained.
1988 Prime Minister Prem resigned; replaced by Chatichai Choonhavan.
1989 Thai pirates continued to murder, pillage, and kidnap Vietnamese 'boat people' at sea.
1991 Military seized power in coup. Interim civilian government formed under Anand Panyarachun. 50,000 demonstrated against new military-oriented constitution.
1992 General election produced five-party coalition. Appointment of General Suchinda Kraprayoon as premier provoked widespread riots. Krapayoon fled the country after army shooting of 100 demonstrators in May; Somboon Rahong nominated to succeed him. Nomination rejected by King Adulyadej; Panyarachun restored as prime minister. Antigovernment riots in Sept followed by general election; new coalition government led by Chuan Leekpai.

Thames river in S England; length 338 km/210 mi. It rises in the Cotswolds above Cirencester and is tidal as far as Teddington. Below London there is protection from flooding by means of the Thames barrier. The headstreams unite at Lechlade.

Thanksgiving (Day) national holiday in the US (fourth Thursday in Nov) and Canada (second Monday in Oct), first celebrated by the Pilgrim settlers in Massachusetts after their first harvest 1621.

Thant, U 1909–1974. Burmese diplomat, secretary general of the United Nations 1962–71. He helped to resolve the US–Soviet crisis over the Soviet installation of missiles in Cuba, and he made the controversial decision to withdraw the UN peacekeeping force from the Egypt–Israel border 1967.

Thatcher Margaret Hilda (born Roberts), Baroness Thatcher of Kesteven 1925– . British Conservative politician, prime minister 1979–90. She was education minister 1970–74 and Conservative Party leader from 1975. In 1982 she sent British troops to recapture the Falkland Islands from Argentina. She confronted trade-union power during the miners' strike 1984–85, sold off majority stakes in many public utilities to the private sector, and reduced the influence of local government through such measures as the abolition of metropolitan councils, the control of expenditure through 'rate-capping', and the introduction of the community charge, or *poll tax, from 1989. In 1990 splits in the cabinet over the issues of Europe and consensus government forced her resignation.

theatre performance by actors for an audience; it may include *drama, dancing, music, *mime, and *puppets. The term is also used for the place or building in which dramatic performances take place. Theatre history can be traced to Egyptian religious ritualistic drama as long ago as 3200 BC. The first known European theatres were in Greece from about 600 BC.

Thebes capital of Boeotia in ancient Greece. In the Peloponnesian War it was allied with Sparta against Athens. For a short time after 371 BC when Thebes defeated Sparta at Leuctra, it was the most powerful state in Greece. Alexander the Great destroyed it 336 BC and although it was restored, it never regained its former power.

Thebes Greek name of an ancient city (**Niut-Ammon**) in Upper Egypt, on the Nile. Probably founded under the first dynasty, it was the centre of the worship of Ammon, and the Egyptian capital under the New Kingdom about 1600 BC. Temple ruins survive near the villages of Karnak and Luxor, and in the nearby **Valley of the Kings** are buried the 18th–20th dynasty kings, including Tutankhamen and Amenhotep III.

Theodosius I 'the Great' c. AD 346–395. Roman emperor AD 388–95. A devout Christian and an adherent of the Nicene creed, he dealt harshly with heretics and in 391 crushed all forms of pagan religion in the empire. He thus founded the orthodox Christian state, acquiring his title. After his reign, the Roman empire was divided into eastern and western halves.

theology study of God or gods, either by reasoned deduction from the natural world or through revelation, as in the scriptures of Christianity, Islam, or other religions.

theosophy any religious or philosophical system based on intuitive insight into the nature of the divine, but especially that of the Theosophical Society, founded in New York 1875 by Madame Blavatsky and H S Olcott. It was based on Hindu ideas of *karma and *reincarnation, with *nirvana as the eventual aim.

Theravāda one of the two major forms of *Buddhism, common in S Asia (Sri Lanka, Thailand, Cambodia, and Myanmar); the other is the later *Mahāyāna.

thermodynamics branch of physics dealing with the transformation of heat into and from other forms of energy. It is the basis of the study of the efficient working of engines, such as the steam and internal-combustion engines. The three laws of thermodynamics are (1) energy can be neither created nor destroyed, heat and mechanical work being mutually convertible; (2) it is impossible for an unaided self-acting machine to convey heat from one body to another at a higher temperature; and (3) it is impossible by any procedure, no matter how idealized, to reduce any system to the *absolute zero of temperature (0K/−273°C) in a finite number of operations. Put into mathematical form, these laws have widespread applications in physics and chemistry.

thermoluminescence release in the form of light of stored energy from a substance heated by *irradiation. It occurs with most crystalline substances to some extent. It is used in archaeology to date pottery, and by geologists in studying terrestrial rocks and meteorites.

thermometer instrument for measuring temperature. There are many types, designed to measure different temperature ranges to varying degrees of accuracy. Each makes use of a different physical effect of temperature.

Theseus in Greek mythology, a hero of *Attica, supposed to have united the states of the area under a constitutional government in Athens. Ariadne, whom he later abandoned on Naxos, helped him find his way through the Labyrinth to kill the *Minotaur. He also fought the Amazons and was one of the *Argonauts.

Thessaloníki (English **Salonika**) port in Macedonia, NE Greece, at the head of the Gulf of Thessaloníki, the second largest city of Greece; population (1981) 706,200. Industries include textiles, shipbuilding, chemicals, brewing, and tanning. It was founded from Corinth by the Romans 315 BC as **Thessalonica** (to whose inhabitants St Paul addressed two epistles), captured by the Saracens AD 904 and by the Turks 1430, and restored to Greece 1912.

thiamine or **vitamin B₁** a water-soluble vitamin of the B complex. It is found in seeds and grain. Its absence from the diet causes the disease *beriberi.

Third Reich (Third Empire) term used by the Nazis to describe Germany during the years of Hitler's dictatorship after 1933. The idea of the Third Reich was based on the existence of two previous German empires, the medieval Holy Roman Empire and the second empire 1871–1918.

Third World or **developing world** those countries that are less developed than the industrialized free-market countries of the West (First World) and the industrialized former Communist countries (Second World). Third World countries are the poorest, as measured by their income per head of population, and are concentrated in Asia, Africa, and Latin America.

Thirteen Colonies 13 American colonies that signed the *Declaration of Independence from Britain 1776. Led by George Washington, the Continental Army defeated the British army in the *American Revolution 1776–81 to become the original 13 United States of America: Connecticut, Delaware, Georgia, Maryland, Massachusetts, New Hampshire, New Jersey, New York, North Carolina, Pennsylvania, Rhode

Island, South Carolina, and Virginia. They were united first under the Articles of *Confederation and from 1789, the US *constitution.

Thirty Years' War major war 1618–48 in central Europe. Beginning as a German conflict between Protestants and Catholics, it gradually became transformed into a struggle to determine whether the ruling Austrian Habsburg family would gain control of all Germany. The war caused serious economic and demographic problems in central Europe.

thistle prickly plant of several genera, such as *Carduus, Carlina, Onopordum*, and *Cirsium*, in the family Compositae. The stems are spiny, the flower heads purple, white, or yellow and cottony, and the leaves deeply indented with prickly margins. The thistle is the Scottish national emblem.

Thomas Dylan (Marlais) 1914–1953. Welsh poet. His poems, characterized by complex imagery and a strong musicality, include the evocation of his youth 'Fern Hill' 1946. His 'play for voices' *Under Milk Wood* 1954 describes with humour and compassion a day in the life of the residents of a small Welsh fishing village, Llareggub.

Thomas à Kempis 1380–1471. German Augustinian monk who lived at the monastery of Zwolle. He took his name from his birthplace Kempen; his real surname was Hammerken. His *De Imitatio Christi/Imitation of Christ* is probably the most widely known devotional work ever written.

Thomas, St in the New Testament, one of the 12 Apostles, said to have preached in S India, hence the ancient churches there were referred to as the 'Christians of St Thomas'. He is not the author of the Gospel of St Thomas, the Gnostic collection of Jesus' sayings.

Thompson Emma 1959– . English actress. She has worked in cinema, theatre, and television, ranging from song-and-dance to Shakespeare, often playing variations on the independent woman. In 1989 she married actor-director Kenneth *Branagh, and has appeared in all his films to date, including the role of Katharine in *Henry V* 1989, a dual role in *Dead Again* 1991, and as Beatrice in *Much Ado About Nothing* 1993. Her other films include *Howards End* 1992 (Academy Award) and *The Remains of the Day* 1993.

Thomson George Paget 1892–1975. English physicist whose work on *interference phenomena in the scattering of electrons by crystals helped to confirm the wavelike nature of particles. He shared a Nobel prize with C J Davisson 1937.

Thomson J(oseph) J(ohn) 1856–1940. English physicist who discovered the *electron. He was responsible for organizing the Cavendish atomic research laboratory at Cambridge University. His work inaugurated the electrical theory of the atom, and his elucidation of positive rays and their application to an analysis of neon led to Frederick *Aston's discovery of *isotopes. Nobel prize 1906.

Thor in Norse mythology, the god of thunder (his hammer), and represented as a man of enormous strength defending humanity against demons. He was the son of Odin and Freya, and Thursday is named after him.

thorax in tetrapod vertebrates, the part of the body containing the heart and lungs, and protected by the rib cage; in arthropods, the middle part of the body, between the head and abdomen.

Thoreau Henry David 1817–1862. US author. One of the most influential figures of 19th century US literature, he is best known for his vigorous defence of individualism and the simple life. His work *Walden, or Life in the Woods* 1854 stimulated the back-to-nature movement, and he completed some 30 volumes based on his daily nature walks. His essay *Civil Disobedience* 1849, prompted by his refusal to pay taxes, advocated peaceful resistance to unjust laws and had a wide impact, even in the 20th century.

thorium dark-grey, radioactive, metallic element of the *actinide series, symbol Th, atomic number 90, relative atomic mass 232.038. It occurs throughout the world in small quantities in minerals such as thorite and is widely distributed in monazite beach sands. It is one of three fissile elements (the others are uranium and plutonium), and its longest-lived isotope has a half- life of 1.39×10^{10} years. Thorium is used to strengthen alloys. It was discovered by Jöns Berzelius 1828 and was named by him after the Norse god Thor.

thorn apple or *jimson weed* annual plant *Datura stramonium* of the nightshade family, growing to 2 m/6 ft in northern temperate and subtropical areas; native to America and naturalized worldwide. It bears white or violet trumpet-shaped flowers and capsule like fruit that split to release black seeds. All parts of the plant are poisonous.

thoroughbred horse bred for racing purposes. All racehorses are thoroughbreds, and all male thoroughbreds are direct descendants of one of three stallions imported into Britain during the 17th and 18th centuries: the Darley Arabian, Byerley Turk, and Godolphin Barb.

Thoth in Egyptian mythology, god of wisdom and learning. He was represented as a scribe with the head of an *ibis, the bird sacred to him.

Thothmes four Egyptian kings of the 18th dynasty, including:

Thothmes I king of Egypt 1540–1501 BC. He founded the Egyptian empire in Syria.

Thothmes III king of Egypt c. 1500–1446 BC. He extended the empire to the river Euphrates and conquered Nubia. He was a grandson of Thothmes I.

Thrace (Greek *Thráki*) ancient empire (6000 BC–AD 300) in the Balkans, SE Europe, formed by parts of modern Greece and Bulgaria. It was held successively by the Greeks, Persians, Macedonians, and Romans.

Three Mile Island island in the Shenandoah River near Harrisburg, Pennsylvania, site of nuclear power station which was put out of action following a major accident March 1979. Opposition to nuclear power in the USA was reinforced after this accident and safety standards reassessed.

threshing agricultural process of separating cereal grains from the plant. Traditionally, the work was carried out by hand in winter months using the flail, a jointed beating stick. Today, threshing is done automatically inside the combine harvester at the time of cutting.

thrips any of a number of tiny insects of the order Thysanoptera, usually with feathery wings. Many of the 3,000 species live in flowers and suck their juices, causing damage and spreading disease. Others eat fungi, decaying matter, or smaller insects.

throat in human anatomy, the passage that leads from the back of the nose and mouth to the *trachea and *oesophagus. It includes the *pharynx and the *larynx, the latter being at the top of the trachea. The word 'throat' is also used to mean the front part of the neck, both in humans and other vertebrates; for example, in describing the plumage of birds. In engineering, it is any narrowing entry, such as the throat of a carburettor.

thrombosis condition in which a blood clot forms in a vein or artery, causing loss of circulation to the area served by the vessel. If it breaks away, it often travels to the lungs, causing pulmonary embolism.

throwing event field athletic contest. There are four at most major international track and field meetings: *discus, *hammer, *javelin, and *shot put.

thrush any bird of the large family Turdidae, order Passeriformes, found worldwide and known for their song. Thrushes are usually brown with speckles of other colours. They are 12–30 cm/5–12 in long.

thrush infection usually of the mouth (particularly in infants), but also sometimes of the vagina, caused by a yeastlike fungus (genus *Candida*). It is seen as white patches on the mucous membranes.

Thucydides c. 455–400 BC. Athenian historian who exercised command in the *Peloponnesian War with Sparta 424 with so little success that he was banished until 404. In his *History of the Peloponnesian War*, he attempted a scientific impartiality.

thug originally a member of a Hindu sect who strangled travellers as sacrifices to *Kali, the goddess of destruction. The sect was suppressed about 1830.

Thule Greek and Roman name for the northernmost land known. It was applied to the Shetlands, the Orkneys, and Iceland, and by later writers to Scandinavia.

thulium soft, silver-white, malleable and ductile, metallic element, of the *lanthanide series, symbol Tm, atomic number 69, relative atomic mass 168.94. It is the least abundant of the rare-earth metals, and was first found in gadolinite and various other minerals. It is used in arc lighting.

Thurber James (Grover) 1894–1961. US humorist. His short stories, written mainly for the *New Yorker* magazine, include 'The Secret Life of Walter Mitty' 1932, and his doodle drawings include fanciful impressions of dogs.

thylacine another name for the *Tasmanian wolf.

thyme herb, genus *Thymus*, of the mint family Labiatae. Garden thyme *T. vulgaris*, native to the Mediterranean, grows to 30 cm/1 ft high, and has pinkish flowers. Its aromatic leaves are used for seasoning.

thymus organ in vertebrates, situated in the upper chest cavity in humans. The thymus processes *lymphocyte cells to produce T-lymphocytes (T denotes 'thymus-derived'), which are responsible for binding to specific invading organisms and killing them or rendering them harmless.

thyristor type of *rectifier, an electronic device that conducts electricity in one direction only. The thyristor is composed of layers of *semiconductor material sandwiched between two electrodes called the anode and cathode. The current can be switched on by using a third electrode called the gate.

thyroid *endocrine gland of vertebrates, situated in the neck in front of the trachea. It secretes several hormones, principally thyroxine, an iodine-containing hormone that stimulates growth, metabolism, and other functions of the body. The thyroid gland may be thought of as the regulator gland of the body's metabolic rate. If it is overactive, as in thyrotoxicosis, the sufferer feels hot and sweaty, has an increased heart rate, diarrhoea, and weight loss. Conversely, an underactive thyroid leads to myxoedema, a condition characterized by sensitivity to the cold, constipation, and weight gain. In infants, an underactive thyroid leads to cretinism, a form of mental retardation.

Thyssen Fritz 1873–1951. German industrialist who based his business on the Ruhr iron and steel industry. Fearful of the communist threat, Thyssen became an early supporter of Hitler and contributed large amounts of money to his early political campaigns. By 1939 he had broken with the Nazis and fled first to Switzerland and later to Italy, where in 1941 he was sent to a concentration camp. Released 1945, he was ordered to surrender 15% of his property.

Tiahuanaco or **Tihuanaco** site of a Peruvian city, S of Lake Titicaca in the Andes, which gave its name to the 8th–14th-century civilization that preceded the Inca and built many of the roads the Inca are credited with building.

Tiananmen Square (Chinese 'Square of Heavenly Peace') paved open space in central Beijing (Peking), China, the largest public square in the world (area 0.4 sq km/0.14 sq mi). On 3–4 June 1989 more than 1,000 unarmed protesters were killed by government troops in a massacre that crushed China's emerging prodemocracy movement.

Tianjin or **Tientsin** port and industrial and commercial city in Hubei province, central China; population (1989) 5,620,000. The special municipality of Tianjin has an area of 4,000 sq km/1,544 sq mi and a population (1990) of 8,788,000. Its handmade silk and wool carpets are renowned. Dagan oilfield is nearby. Tianjin was opened to foreign trade 1860 and occupied by the Japanese 1937.

Tian Shan (Chinese *Tien Shan*) mountain system in central Asia. *Pik Pobedy* on the Xinjiang-Kyrgyz border is the highest peak at 7,440 m/24,415 ft.

tiara triple crown worn by the pope, or a semicircular headdress worn by women on formal occasions. The term was originally applied to a headdress worn by the ancient Persians.

Tiberius Claudius Nero 42 BC–AD 37. Roman emperor, the stepson, adopted son, and successor of Augustus from AD 14. A distinguished soldier, he was a conscientious ruler under whom the empire prospered.

Tibet autonomous region of SW China (Pinyin form *Xizang*)

area 1,221,600 sq km/471,538 sq mi
capital Lhasa

government Tibet is an autonomous region of China, with its own People's Government and People's Congress. The controlling force in Tibet is the Communist Party of China, represented locally by First Secretary Wu Jinghua from 1985. Tibetan nationalists regard the province as being under colonial rule

products wool, borax, salt, horn, musk, herbs, furs, gold, iron pyrites, lapis lazuli, mercury, textiles, chemicals, agricultural machinery

population (1987) 2,030,000; including 900,000 Tibetans (mostly nomadic herders, many Chinese have settled in Tibet. In 1988 the population of Tibet included 2 million Tibetans and 73,000 Han Chinese; there were 2 million Tibetans in China outside Tibet

religion traditionally Lamaist (a form of Mahāyāna Buddhism)

history Tibet was an independent kingdom from the 5th century AD. It came under nominal Chinese rule about 1700. Independence was regained after a revolt 1912. China regained control 1951 when the historic ruler and religious leader, the *Dalai Lama, was driven from the country and the monks (who formed 25% of the population) were forced out of the monasteries. Between 1951 and 1959 the Chinese People's Liberation Army (PLA) controlled Tibet, although the Dalai Lama returned as nominal spiritual and temporal head of state. In 1959 a Tibetan uprising spread from bordering regions to Lhasa and was supported by Tibet's local government. The rebellion was suppressed by the PLA, prompting the Dalai Lama and 9,000 Tibetans to flee to India. The Chinese proceeded to dissolve the Tibet local government, abolish serfdom, collectivize agriculture, and suppress *Lamaism. In 1965 Tibet became an autonomous region of China. Chinese rule continued to be resented, however, and the economy languished.

tick any of an arachnid group (Ixodoidea) of large bloodsucking mites. Many carry and transmit diseases to mammals (including humans) and birds.

tidal power station *hydroelectric power plant that uses the 'head' of water created by the rise and fall of the ocean tides to spin the water turbines. An example is located on the estuary of the river Rance in the Gulf of St Malo, Brittany, France, which has been in use since 1966.

tidal wave misleading name for a *tsunami.

tide rise and fall of sea level due to the gravitational forces of the Moon and Sun. High water occurs at an average interval of 12 hr 24 min 30 sec. The highest or *spring tides* are at or near new and full Moon; the lowest or *neap tides* when the Moon is in its first or third quarter.

Some seas, such as the Mediterranean, have very small tides.

Tientsin alternative form of *Tianjin, industrial city in NE China.

Tiepolo Giovanni Battista 1696–1770. Italian painter, born in Venice. He created monumental Rococo decorative schemes in palaces and churches in NE Italy, SW Germany, and Madrid (1762–70). The style is light-hearted, the palette light and warm, and he made great play with illusion.

Tierra del Fuego island group divided between Chile and Argentina. It is separated from the mainland of South America by the Strait of Magellan, and Cape Horn is at the southernmost point. The chief town, Ushuaia, Argentina, is the world's most southerly town. Industries include oil and sheep farming.

Tiffany Louis Comfort 1848–1933. US artist and glassmaker, son of Charles Louis Tiffany, who founded Tiffany and Company, the New York City jewellers. He produced stained-glass windows, iridescent Favrile (from Latin *faber* 'craftsman') glass, and lampshades in the Art Nouveau style. He used glass that contained oxides of iron and other elements to produce rich colours.

tiger largest of the great cats *Panthera tigris*, formerly found in much of central and S Asia but nearing extinction because of hunting and the destruction of its natural habitat. The tiger can grow to 3.6 m/12 ft long and weigh 300 kg/660 lbs; it has a yellow-orange coat with black stripes. It is solitary, and feeds on large ruminants. It is a good swimmer.

Tigré a people of N Ethiopia. The Tigré language is spoken by about 2.5 million people; it belongs to the SE Semitic branch of the Afro-Asiatic family. *Tigrinya* is a closely related language spoken slightly to the south.

Tigré or *Tigray* region in the northern highlands of Ethiopia; area 65,900 sq km/25,444 sq mi. The chief town is Mekele. The region had an estimated population of 2.4 million in 1984, at a time when drought and famine were driving large numbers of people to fertile land in the south or into neighbouring Sudan. Since 1978 a guerrilla group known as the Tigré People's Liberation Front (TPLF) has been fighting for regional autonomy. In 1989 government troops were forced from the province, and the TPLF advanced towards Addis Ababa, playing a key role in the fall of the Ethiopian government in May 1991.

Tigris (Arabic *Shatt Dijla*) river flowing through Turkey and Iraq (see also *Mesopotamia), joining the *Euphrates above Basra, where it forms the *Shatt-al-Arab; length 1,600 km/1,000 mi.

Tijuana city and resort in NW Mexico; population (1990) 742,700; known for horse races and casinos. *San Diego adjoins it across the US border.

till or *boulder clay* deposit of clay, mud, gravel, and boulders left by a *glacier. It is unsorted, with all sizes of fragments mixed up together, and shows no stratification; that is, it does not form clear layers or *beds.

Tilly Jan Tserklaes, Count von Tilly 1559–1632.

Flemish commander of the army of the Catholic League and imperial forces in the *Thirty Years' War. Notorious for his storming of Magdeburg, E Germany, 1631, he was defeated by the Swedish king Gustavus Adolphus at Breitenfeld and at the river Lech in SW Germany, where he was mortally wounded.

tilt-rotor aircraft type of vertical takeoff aircraft, also called a *convertiplane.

timber wood used in construction, furniture, and paper pulp. **Hardwoods** include tropical mahogany, teak, ebony, rosewood, temperate oak, elm, beech, and eucalyptus. All except eucalyptus are slow-growing, and world supplies are almost exhausted. **Softwoods** comprise the *conifers (pine, fir, spruce, and larch), which are quick to grow and easy to work but inferior in quality of grain. **White woods** include ash, birch, and sycamore; all have light-coloured timber, are fast-growing, and can be used as veneers on cheaper timber.

Timbuktu or **Tombouctou** town in Mali; population (1976) 20,500. A camel caravan centre from the 11th century on the fringe of the Sahara, since 1960 it has been surrounded by the southward movement of the desert, and the former canal link with the river Niger is dry. Products include salt.

time continuous passage of existence, recorded by division into hours, minutes, and seconds. Formerly the measurement of time was based on the Earth's rotation on its axis, but this was found to be irregular. Therefore the second, the standard *SI unit of time, was redefined 1956 in terms of the Earth's annual orbit of the Sun, and 1967 in terms of a radiation pattern of the element caesium.

time and motion study process of analysis applied to a job or number of jobs to check the efficiency of the work method, equipment used, and the worker. Its findings are used to improve performance. Time and motion studies were introduced in the USA by Frederick Taylor (1856–1915) at the beginning of the 20th century. Since then, the practice has spread throughout the industrialized world.

time-sharing in computing, a way of enabling several users to access the same computer at the same time. The computer rapidly switches between user *terminals and programs, allowing each user to work as if he or she had sole use of the system.

Timişoara capital of Timiş county, W Romania; population (1985) 319,000. The revolt against the Ceauşescu regime began here in Dec 1989 when demonstrators prevented the arrest and deportation of a popular Protestant minister who was promoting the rights of ethnic Hungarians. This soon led to large prodemocracy rallies.

Timor largest and most easterly of the Lesser Sunda Islands, part of Indonesia; area 33,610 sq km/12,973 sq mi. **West Timor** (capital Kupang) was formerly Dutch and was included in Indonesia on independence. **East Timor** (capital Dili), an enclave on the NW coast, and the islands of Atauro and Jaco formed an overseas province of Portugal until it was seized by Indonesia 1975. The annexation is not recognized by the United Nations, and guerrilla warfare by local people seeking independence continues. Since 1975 over 500,000 Timorese have been killed by Indonesian troops or have resettled in West Timor, according to Amnesty International. Products include coffee, maize, rice, and coconuts.

Timothy in the New Testament, companion to St *Paul, both on his missionary journeys and in prison. Two of the Pauline epistles are addressed to him.

tin soft, silver-white, malleable and somewhat ductile, metallic element, symbol Sn (from Latin *stannum*), atomic number 50, relative atomic mass 118.69. Tin exhibits *allotropy, having three forms: the familiar lustrous metallic form above 55.8°F/13.2°C; a brittle form above 321.8°F/161°C; and a grey powder form below 55.8°F/13.2°C (commonly called tin pest or tin disease). The metal is quite soft (slightly harder than lead) and can be rolled, pressed, or hammered into extremely thin sheets; it has a low melting point. In nature it occurs rarely as a free metal. It resists corrosion and is therefore used for coating and plating other metals.

Tinbergen Jan 1903–1988. Dutch economist. He shared a Nobel prize 1969 with Ragnar Frisch for his work on *econometrics (the mathematical-statistical expression of economic theory).

Tinbergen Niko(laas) 1907– . Dutch zoologist. He was one of the founders of *ethology, the scientific study of animal behaviour in natural surroundings. Specializing in the study of instinctive behaviour, he shared a Nobel prize with Konrad *Lorenz and Karl von *Frisch 1973. He is the brother of Jan Tinbergen.

tinnitus in medicine, constant internal sounds, inaudible to others. The phenomenon may originate from noisy conditions (drilling, machinery, or loud music) or from infection of the middle or inner ear. The victim may become overwhelmed by the relentless noise in the head.

tin ore mineral from which tin is extracted, principally cassiterite, SnO_2. The world's chief producers are Malaysia, Thailand, and Bolivia.

tinplate milled steel coated with tin, the metal used for most 'tin' cans. The steel provides the strength, and the tin provides the corrosion resistance, ensuring that the food inside is not contaminated. Tinplate may be made by *electroplating or by dipping in a bath of molten tin.

Tintoretto adopted name of Jacopo Robusti 1518–1594. Italian painter, active in Venice. His dramatic religious paintings are spectacularly lit and full of movement, such as his huge canvases of the lives of Christ and the Virgin in the Scuola di San Rocco, Venice, 1564–88.

Tipperary county in the Republic of Ireland, province of Munster, divided into north and south regions. **North Tipperary**: administrative headquarters Nenagh; area 2,000 sq km/772 sq mi; population (1991) 57,800. **South Tipperary**: administrative headquarters Clonmel; area 2,260 sq km/872 sq mi; population (1991) 74,800. It includes part of the Golden Vale, a dairy-farming region.

Tippett Michael (Kemp) 1905– . English composer whose works include the operas *The Midsummer Marriage* 1952, *The Knot Garden* 1970, and *New Year* 1989; four symphonies; *Songs for*

Ariel 1962; and choral music including *The Mask of Time* 1982.

Tirana or *Tiranë* capital (since 1920) of Albania; population (1990) 210,000. Industries include metallurgy, cotton textiles, soap, and cigarettes. It was founded in the early 17th century by Turks when part of the Ottoman Empire. Although the city is now largely composed of recent buildings, some older districts and mosques have been preserved.

Tiresias or *Teiresias* in Greek mythology, a man blinded by the gods and given the ability to predict the future.

Tîrgu Mureş city in Transylvania, Romania, on the river Mureş, 450 km/280 mi N of Bucharest; population (1985) 157,400. With a population comprising approximately equal numbers of ethnic Hungarians and Romanians, the city was the scene of rioting between the two groups following Hungarian demands for greater autonomy 1990.

Tirol federal province of Austria; area 12,600 sq km/4,864 sq mi; population (1989) 619,600. Its capital is Innsbruck, and it produces diesel engines, optical instruments, and hydroelectric power. Tirol was formerly a province (from 1363) of the Austrian Empire, divided 1919 between Austria and Italy (see *Trentino–Alto Adige*).

Tirpitz Alfred von 1849–1930. German admiral. As secretary for the navy 1897–1916, he created the German navy and planned the World War I U-boat campaign.

tissue in biology, any kind of cellular fabric that occurs in an organism's body. Several kinds of tissue can usually be distinguished, each consisting of cells of a particular kind bound together by cell walls (in plants) or extracellular matrix (in animals). Thus, nerve and muscle are different kinds of tissue in animals, as are *parenchyma and *sclerenchyma in plants.

tissue culture process by which cells from a plant or animal are removed from the organism and grown under controlled conditions in a sterile medium containing all the necessary nutrients. Tissue culture can provide information on cell growth and differentiation, and is also used in plant propagation and drug production. See also *meristem.

tit or *titmouse* any of 65 species of insectivorous, acrobatic bird of the family Paridae. Tits are 8–20 cm/3–8 in long and have grey or black plumage, often with blue or yellow markings. They are found in Eurasia and Africa, and also in North America, where they are called *chickadees*.

Titan in Greek mythology, any of the giant children of Uranus and Gaia, who included Kronos, Rhea, Themis (mother of Prometheus and personification of law and order), and Oceanus. Kronos and Rhea were in turn the parents of Zeus, who ousted Kronos as the ruler of the world.

Titanic British passenger liner, supposedly unsinkable, that struck an iceberg and sank off the Grand Banks of Newfoundland on its first voyage 14–15 April 1912; 1,513 lives were lost. In 1985 it was located by robot submarine 4 km/2.5 mi down in an ocean canyon, preserved by the cold environment. In 1987 salvage operations began.

titanium strong, lightweight, silver-grey, metallic element, symbol Ti, atomic number 22, relative atomic mass 47.90. The ninth most abundant element in the Earth's crust, its compounds occur in practically all igneous rocks and their sedimentary deposits. It is very strong and resistant to corrosion, so it is used in building high-speed aircraft and spacecraft; it is also widely used in making alloys, as it unites with almost every metal except copper and aluminium. Titanium oxide is used in high-grade white pigments.

titanium ore any mineral from which titanium is extracted, principally ilmenite (Fe,TiO$_3$) and rutile (TiO$_2$). Brazil, India, and Canada are major producers.

Titan rocket family of US space rockets developed from the Titan intercontinental missile. Two-stage Titan rockets launched the *Gemini crewed missions. More powerful Titans with additional stages and strap-on boosters were used to launch spy satellites and space probes, including *Viking and *Voyager.

tithe formerly, payment exacted from the inhabitants of a parish for the maintenance of the church and its incumbent; some religious groups continue the practice by giving 10% of members' incomes to charity.

Titian anglicized form of Tiziano Vecellio *c.* 1487–1576. Italian painter, active in Venice, one of the greatest artists of the High Renaissance. In 1533 he became court painter to Charles V, Holy Roman emperor, whose son Philip II of Spain later became his patron. Titian's work is richly coloured, with inventive composition. He produced a vast number of portraits, religious paintings, and mythological scenes including *Bacchus and Ariadne* 1520–23, *Venus and Adonis* 1554, and the *Entombment of Christ* 1559.

Titicaca lake in the Andes, 3,810 m/12,500 ft above sea level; area 8,300 sq km/3,200 sq mi, the largest lake in South America. It is divided between Bolivia (port at Guaqui) and Peru (ports at Puno and Huancane). It has enormous edible frogs.

Tito adopted name of Josip Broz 1892–1980. Yugoslav communist politician, in power from 1945. In World War II he organized the National Liberation Army to carry on guerrilla warfare against the German invasion 1941, and was created marshal 1943. As prime minister 1946–53 and president from 1953, he followed a foreign policy of 'positive neutralism'.

Titograd formerly (until 1948) *Podgorica* capital of Montenegro, Yugoslavia; population (1981) 132,300. Industries include metalworking, furniture-making, and tobacco. It was damaged in World War II and after rebuilding was renamed in honour of Marshal Tito. It was the birthplace of the Roman emperor Diocletian.

titration in analytical chemistry, a technique to find the concentration of one compound in a solution by determining how much of it will react with a known amount of another compound in solution.

Titus Flavius Sabinus Vespasianus AD 39–81. Roman emperor from AD 79. Eldest son of *Ves-asian, he stormed Jerusalem 70 to end the Jewish revolt in Roman Palestine. He completed the Colosseum, and enjoyed a peaceful reign, except for *Agricola's campaigns in Britain.

TLR camera twin-lens reflex camera that has a viewing lens of the same angle of view and focal length mounted above and parallel to the taking lens.

TM abbreviation for *transcendental meditation*.

TNT abbreviation for *trinitrotoluene*, $CH_3C_6H_2(NO_2)_3$, a powerful high explosive. It is a yellow solid, prepared in several isomeric forms from *toluene by using sulphuric and nitric acids.

toad any of the more terrestrial warty-skinned members of the tailless amphibians (order Anura). The name commonly refers to members of the genus *Bufo*, family Bufonidae, which are found worldwide, except for the Australian and polar regions.

toadstool inedible or poisonous type of *fungus with a fleshy, gilled fruiting body on a talk.

Toamasina formerly (until 1979) *Tamatave* port and resort town on the E coast of Madagascar; population (1985) 139,000. The principal port of Madagascar, it exports sugar, coffee, and tea.

tobacco any large-leaved plant of the genus *Nicotiana* of the nightshade family Solanaceae, native to tropical parts of the Americas. *N. tabacum* is widely cultivated in warm, dry climates for use in cigars and cigarettes, and in powdered form as snuff. The worldwide profits of the tobacco industry are estimated to be over $6 billion a year.

Tobago island in the West Indies; part of the republic of *Trinidad and Tobago.

Tobruk Libyan port; population (1984) 94,000. Occupied by Italy 1911, it was taken by Britain 1941 during World War II, and unsuccessfully besieged by Axis forces April–Dec 1941. It was captured by Germany June 1942 after the retreat of the main British force to Egypt, and this precipitated the replacement of Auchinleck by Montgomery as British commander.

Tocqueville Alexis de 1805–1859. French politician and political scientist, author of the first analytical study of the US constitution, *De la Démocratie en Amérique/Democracy in America* 1835, and of a penetrating description of France before the Revolution, *L'Ancien Régime et la Révolution/The Old Regime and he Revolution* 1856.

tofu or *dofu* or *doufu* pressed *soya bean curd derived from soya milk. It is a good source of protein and naturally low in fat.

tog unit of measure of thermal insulation used in the textile trade; a light summer suit provides .0 tog.

Togliatti Palmiro 1893–1964. Italian politician who was a founding member of the Italian Communist Party 1921 and effectively its leader for almost 40 years from 1926 until his death. In exile 1926–44, he returned after the fall of the fascist dictator Mussolini to become a member of Badoglio's government and held office until 1946.

Togo Republic of (*République Togolaise*)

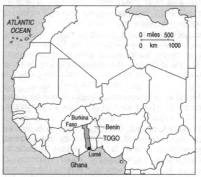

area 56,800 sq km/21,930 sq mi
capital Lomé
towns Sokodé, Kpalimé
physical two savanna plains, divided by range of hills NE–SW; coastal lagoons and marsh
environment the homes of thousands of people in Keto were destroyed by coastal erosion as a result of the building of the Volta dam
head of state Etienne Gnassingbé Eyadéma from 1967
head of government Edem Kodjo from 1994
political system emergent democracy
exports phosphates, cocoa, coffee, coconuts
currency franc CFA
population (1993 est) 4,100,000; growth rate 3% p.a.
languages French (official), Ewe, Kabre
religions animist 46%, Catholic 28%, Muslim 17%, Protestant 9%
GNP $1,530 million (1991). GNP per capita $410.
chronology
1885–1914 Togoland was a German protectorate until captured by Anglo-French forces.
1922 Divided between Britain and France under League of Nations mandate.
1946 Continued under United Nations trusteeship.
1956 British Togoland integrated with Ghana.
1960 French Togoland achieved independence from France as the Republic of Togo with Sylvanus Olympio as head of state.
1963 Olympio killed in a military coup. Nicolas Grunitzky became president.
1967 Grunitzky replaced by Lt-Gen Etienne Gnassingbé Eyadéma in bloodless coup.
1969 Assembly of the Togolese People (RPT) formed as sole legal political party.
1975 EEC Lomé convention signed in Lomé, establishing trade links with developing countries.
1979 Eyadéma returned in election. Further EEC Lomé convention signed.
1986 Attempted coup failed.
1991 Eyadéma legalized opposition parties. National conference elected Joseph Kokou Koffigoh head of interim government. Three anti-government coups foiled.
1992 Overwhelming referendum support for multiparty politics; new constitution adopted.
1993 President Eyadéma won first multiparty elections.

1994 Anti-government coup foiled. Opposition coalition won assembly elections. Eyadéma appointed Edem Kodjo prime minister, rejecting opposition nominee.

Tōgō Heihachirō 1846–1934. Japanese admiral who commanded the fleet at the battle of Tsushima 1905, when Japan defeated the Russians and effectively ended the Russo-Japanese War of 1904–05.

Tohoku mountainous region of N Honshu island, Japan; population (1988) 9,745,000; area 66,971 sq km/25,867 sq mi. Timber, fruit, fish, and livestock are produced. The chief city is Sendai. Aomori in the NE is linked to Hakodate on the island of Hokkaido by the **Seikan tunnel**, the world's longest underwater tunnel.

toilet place where waste products from the body are excreted. Simple latrines, with sewers to carry away waste, have been found in the Indus Valley and ancient Babylon; the medieval garderobe is essentially the same, even though flushing lavatories had been known to the Romans, for example at Housesteads Fort on Hadrian's Wall. The valve cistern, with a base that could be opened or closed, was invented by John Harington, godson of Queen Elizabeth I.

Tōjō Hideki 1884–1948. Japanese general and premier 1941–44 during World War II. Promoted to Chief of Staff of Japan's Guangdong army in Manchuria 1937, he served as minister for war 1940–41. He was held responsible for defeats in the Pacific 1944 and forced to resign. After Japan's defeat, he was hanged as a war criminal.

tokamak experimental machine designed by Soviet scientists to investigate controlled nuclear fusion. It consists of a doughnut-shaped chamber surrounded by electromagnets capable of exerting very powerful magnetic fields. The fields are generated to confine a very hot (millions of degrees) *plasma of ions and electrons, keeping it away from the chamber walls. See also *JET.

Tokugawa military family that controlled Japan as *shoguns 1603–1867. **Tokugawa Ieyasu** (1542–1616) was the Japanese general and politician who established the Tokugawa shogunate. The Tokugawa were feudal lords who ruled about one-quarter of Japan.

Tokyo capital of Japan, on Honshu Island; population (1989) 8,099,000, metropolitan area over 12 million. The Sumida River delta separates the city from its suburb of Honjo. It is Japan's main cultural and industrial centre (engineering, chemicals, textiles, electrical goods). Founded in the 16th century as **Yedo** (or **Edo**), it was renamed when the emperor moved his court there from Kyoto 1868. An earthquake 1923 killed 58,000 people and destroyed much of the city, which was again severely damaged by Allied bombing in World War II. The subsequent rebuilding has made it into one of the world's most modern cities.

Toledo city on the river Tagus, Castilla–La Mancha, central Spain; population (1982) 62,000. It was the capital of the Visigoth kingdom 534–711 (see *Goth), then became a Moorish city, and was the Castilian capital 1085–1560.

Tolkien J(ohn) R(onald) R(euel) 1892–1973. English writer who created the fictional world of Middle Earth in *The Hobbit* 1937 and the trilogy *The Lord of the Rings* 1954–55, fantasy novels peopled with hobbits, dwarves, and strange magical creatures. His work developed a cult following in the 1960s and had many imitators. A Oxford University he was professor of Anglo-Saxon 1925–45 and Merton professor of English 1945–59.

Tolpuddle Martyrs six farm labourers of Tolpuddle, a village in Dorset, SW England, who were transported to Australia in 1834 for forming a trade union. After nationwide agitation they were pardoned two years later. They returned to England and all but one migrated to Canada.

Tolstoy Leo Nikolaievich 1828–1910. Russian novelist who wrote *War and Peace* 1863–69 and *Anna Karenina* 1873–77. From 1880 Tolstoy underwent a profound spiritual crisis and took up various moral positions, including passive resistance to evil, rejection of authority (religious or civil) and private ownership, and a return to basic mystical Christianity. He was excommunicated by the Orthodox Church, and his late works were banned.

Toltec member of an ancient American Indian people who ruled much of Mexico in the 10th–12th centuries, with their capital and religious centre at Tula, NE of Mexico City. They also constructed a similar city at Chichén Itzá in Yucatán. After the Toltecs' fall in the 13th century, the Aztecs took over much of their former territory, except for the regions regained by the Maya.

toluene or **methyl benzene** $C_6H_5CH_3$ colourless, inflammable liquid, insoluble in water, derived from petroleum. It is used as a solvent in aircraft fuels, in preparing phenol (carbolic acid, used in making resins for adhesives, pharmaceuticals, and as a disinfectant), and the powerful high explosive *TNT.

Tomasi Giuseppe, Prince of Lampedusa. Italian writer; see *Lampedusa.

tomato annual plant *Lycopersicon esculentum* of the nightshade family Solanaceae, native to South America. It is widely cultivated for the many-seeded red fruit (technically a berry), used in salads and cooking.

ton imperial unit of mass. The **long ton**, used in the UK, is 1,016 kg/2,240 lb; the **short ton**, used in the USA, is 907 kg/2,000 lb. The **metric ton** or **tonne** is 1,000 kg/2,205 lb.

ton in shipping, unit of volume equal to 2.8 cubic metres/100 cubic feet. **Gross tonnage** is the total internal volume of a ship in tons; **net register tonnage** is the volume used for carrying cargo or passengers. **Displacement tonnage** is the weight of the vessel, in terms of the number of imperial tons of seawater displaced when the ship is loaded to its load line; it is used to describe warships.

tonality in music, the observance of a key structure; that is, the recognition of the importance of a tonic or key note and of the diatonic scale built upon it. See also *atonality and *polytonality.

Tone (Theobald) Wolfe 1763–1798. Irish nationalist, prominent in the revolutionary society of the United Irishmen. In 1798 he accompanied the French invasion of Ireland, was captured and condemned to death, but slit his own throat in prison.

tone poem in music, another name for *symphonic poem as used, for example, by Richard Strauss.

Tonga Kingdom of (*Pule'anga Fakatu'i 'o Tonga*) or *Friendly Islands*
area 750 sq km/290 sq mi
capital Nuku'alofa (on Tongatapu island)
towns Pangai, Neiafu
physical three groups of islands in SW Pacific, mostly coral formations, but actively volcanic in W
head of state King Taufa'ahau Tupou IV from 1965
head of government Baron Vaea from 1991
political system constitutional monarchy
currency Tongan dollar or pa'anga
population (1993 est) 105,000; growth rate 2.4% p.a.
languages Tongan (official), English
religions Wesleyan 47%, Roman Catholic 14%, Free Church of Tonga 14%, Mormon 9%, Church of Tonga 9%
GNP $1,100 per head (1991)
chronology
1831 Tongan dynasty founded by Prince Taufa'a-hau Tupou.
1900 Became a British protectorate.
1965 Queen Salote died; succeeded by her son, King Taufa'ahau Tupou IV.
1970 Independence achieved from Britain within the Commonwealth.
1990 Three prodemocracy candidates elected. Calls for reform of absolutist power.

tongue in tetrapod vertebrates, a muscular organ usually attached to the floor of the mouth. It has a thick root attached to a U-shaped bone (hyoid), and is covered with a *mucous membrane containing nerves and 'taste buds'. It directs food to the teeth and into the throat for chewing and swallowing. In humans, it is crucial for speech; in other animals, for lapping up water and for grooming, among other functions.

tonic in music, the first degree or key note of a scale (for example, the note C in the scale of C major).

tonne the metric ton of 1,000 kg/2,204.6 lb; equivalent to 0.9842 of an imperial *ton.

tonsillitis inflammation of the *tonsils.

tonsils in higher vertebrates, masses of lymphoid tissue situated at the back of the mouth and throat (palatine tonsils), and on the rear surface of the tongue (lingual tonsils). The tonsils contain many *lymphocytes and are part of the body's defence system against infection.

tonsure the full or partial shaving of the head as a symbol of entering clerical or monastic orders. Until 1973 in the Roman Catholic Church, the crown was shaved (leaving a surrounding fringe to resemble Jesus' crown of thorns); in the Eastern Orthodox Church the hair is merely shorn close. For Buddhist monks, the entire head is shaved except for a topknot.

Tonton Macoute member of a private army of death squads on Haiti. The Tontons Macoutes were initially organized by François *Duvalier, president of Haiti 1957–71, and continued to terrorize the population under his successor J C Duvalier. It is alleged that the organization continued to operate after Duvalier's exile to France.

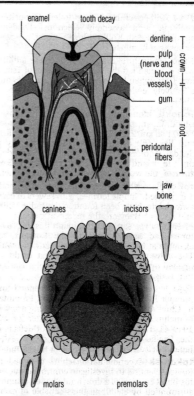

tooth Adults have 32 teeth: two incisors, one canine, two premolars, and three molars on each side of each jaw.

Tony award annual award by the League of New York Theaters to playwrights, performers, and technicians in *Broadway plays. It is named after the US actress and producer Antoinette Perry (1888–1946).

tool any implement that gives the user a *mechanical advantage, such as a hammer or a saw; a *machine tool* is a tool operated by power. Tools are the basis of industrial production; the chief machine tool is the lathe. The industrial potential of a country is often calculated by the number of machine tools available. Automatic control of machine tools, a milestone in industrial development, is known as *automation, and electronic control is called robotics (see *robot).

tooth in vertebrates, one of a set of hard, bone-like structures in the mouth, used for biting and chewing food, and in defence and aggression. In humans, the first set (20 milk teeth) appear from age six months to two and a half years. The permanent *dentition replaces these from the sixth year onwards, the wisdom teeth (third molars) sometimes not appearing until the age of 25 or 30. Adults have 32 teeth: two incisors, one canine (eye tooth), two premolars, and three molars on each side of each jaw. Each tooth consists of an enamel coat (hardened calcium deposits), dentine (a thick, bonelike layer), and an inner pulp cavity, housing nerves and blood vessels. Mammalian teeth have roots surrounded by cementum, which fuses them into their sockets in the jawbones. The neck of the tooth is covered by the *gum, while the enamel-covered crown protrudes above the gum line.

topaz mineral, aluminium fluosilicate, $Al_2SiO_4(F,OH)_2$. It is usually yellow, but pink if it has been heated, and is used as a gemstone when transparent. It ranks 8 on the Mohs' scale of hardness.

tope tumulus found in India and SE Asia; a Buddhist monument usually built over a relic of Buddha or his disciples. Topes date from 400–300 BC including ones at Sanchi, near Bhilsa, central India.

topi or **korrigum** antelope *Damaliscus korrigum* of equatorial Africa, head and body about 1.7 m/5.5 ft long, 1.1 m/3.5 ft high at the shoulder, with a chocolate-brown coat.

topiary clipping of trees and shrubs into ornamental shapes, originated by the Romans in the 1st century and revived in the 16th–17th centuries in formal European and American gardens.

topography the surface shape and aspect of the land, and its study. Topography deals with relief and contours, the distribution of mountains and valleys, the patterns of rivers, and all other features, natural and artificial, that produce the landscape.

topology branch of geometry that deals with those properties of a figure that remain unchanged even when the figure is transformed (bent, stretched) – for example, when a square painted on a rubber sheet is deformed by distorting the sheet. Topology has scientific applications, as in the study of turbulence in flowing fluids. The map of the London Underground

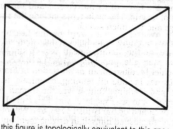

this figure is topologically equivalent to this one

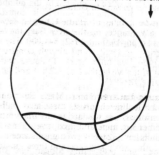

topology *Topology is often called 'rubber-sheet geometry'.*

system is an example of the topological representation of a network; connectivity (the way the lines join together) is preserved, but shape and size are not.

topsoil the upper, cultivated layer of soil, which may vary in depth from 8 to 45 cm/3 to 18 in. It contains organic matter – the decayed remains of vegetation, which plants need for active growth – along with a variety of soil organisms, including earthworms.

tor isolated mass of rock, usually granite, left upstanding on a hilltop after the surrounding rock has been broken down. Weathering takes place along the joints in the rock, reducing the outcrop into a mass of rounded blocks.

Torah in *Judaism, the first five books of the Hebrew Bible (Christian Old Testament). It contains a traditional history of the world from the Creation to the death of Moses; it also includes the Hebrew people's covenant with their one God, rules for religious observance, and guidelines for social conduct, including the Ten Commandments.

tornado extremely violent revolving storm with swirling, funnel-shaped clouds, caused by a rising column of warm air propelled by strong wind. A tornado can rise to a great height, but with a diameter of only a few hundred metres or yards or less. Tornadoes move with wind speeds of 160–480 kph/100–300 mph, destroying everything in their path. They are common in the central USA and Australia.

Toronto (North American Indian 'place of meeting') known until 1834 as *York*. Port and capital of Ontario, Canada, on Lake Ontario; metropolitan population (1985) 3,427,000. It is Canada's main industrial and commercial centre (banking, shipbuilding, cars, farm machinery, food processing, publishing) and also a cultural centre, with theatres and a film industry. The site became the provincial capital 1793.

torpedo self-propelled underwater missile, invented 1866 by British engineer Robert *Whitehead. Modern torpedoes are homing missiles; some resemble mines in that they lie on the seabed until activated by the acoustic signal of a passing ship. A television camera enables them to be remotely controlled, and in the final stage of attack they lock on to the radar or sonar signals of the target ship.

torpedo or **electric ray** any species of the order Torpediniformes of mainly tropical rays (cartilaginous fishes), whose electric organs between the pectoral fin and the head can give a powerful shock. They can grow to 180 cm/6 ft in length.

torque the turning effect of force on an object. A turbine produces a torque that turns an electricity generator in a power station. Torque is measured by multiplying the force by its perpendicular distance from the turning point.

torque converter device similar to a turbine, filled with oil, used in automatic transmission systems in motor vehicles and locomotives to transmit power (torque) from the engine to the gears.

torr unit of pressure equal to 1/760 of an *atmosphere, used mainly in high-vacuum technology.

Torreón industrial and agricultural city in Coahuila state, N Mexico, on the river Nazas at an altitude of 1,127 m/3,700 ft; population (1986) 730,000. Before the arrival of the railway 1907 Torreón was the largest of the three Laguna cotton-district cities (with Gómez Palacio and Ciudad Lerdo). Since then it has developed as a major thoroughfare and commercial centre.

Torricelli Evangelista 1608–1647. Italian physicist and pupil of *Galileo who devised the mercury *barometer.

tort in law, a wrongful act for which someone can be sued for damages in a civil court. It includes such acts as libel, trespass, injury done to someone (whether intentionally or by negligence), and inducement to break a contract (although breach of contract itself is not a tort).

tortoise reptile of the order Chelonia, family Testudinidae, with the body enclosed in a hard shell. Tortoises are related to the *terrapins and *turtles, and range in length from 10 cm/4 in to 150 cm/5 ft. The shell consists of a curved upper carapace and flattened lower plastron joined at the sides. The head and limbs may be withdrawn into it when the tortoise is in danger. Most land tortoises are herbivorous, feeding on plant material, and have no teeth. The mouth forms a sharp-edged beak. Tortoises have been known to live for 150 years.

torture infliction of bodily pain to extort evidence or confession. Legally abolished in England about 1640, torture was allowed in Scotland until 1708 and until 1789 in France. In the 20th century torture is widely (though, in most countries, unofficially) used. The human-rights organization *Amnesty International investigates and publicizes the use of torture on prisoners of conscience, and there is now a centre in Copenhagen, Denmark, where torture victims are rehabilitated and studies are carried out into the effects of torture.

Tory Party the forerunner of the British *Conservative Party about 1680–1830. It was the party of the squire and parson, as opposed to the Whigs (supported by the trading classes and Nonconformists). The name is still applied colloquially to the Conservative Party. In the USA a Tory was an opponent of the break with Britain in the War of American Independence 1775–83.

Toscana Italian name for the region of *Tuscany.

total internal reflection the complete reflection of a beam of light that occurs from the surface of an optically 'less dense' material. For example, a beam from an underwater light source can be reflected from the surface of the water, rather than escaping through the surface. Total internal reflection can only happen if a light beam hits a surface at an angle greater than the *critical angle for that particular pair of materials.

totalitarianism government control of all activities within a country, overtly political or otherwise, as in fascist or communist dictatorships. Examples of totalitarian regimes are Italy under Benito *Mussolini 1922–45; Germany under Adolph *Hitler 1933–45; the USSR under Joseph *Stalin from the 1930s until his death in 1953; more recently Romania under Nicolae *Ceauşescu 1974–89.

totemism (Algonquin Indian 'mark of my family') the belief in individual or clan kinship with an animal, plant, or object. This totem is sacred to those concerned, and they are forbidden to eat or desecrate it; marriage within the clan is usually forbidden. Totemism occurs among Pacific Islanders and Australian Aborigines, and was formerly prevalent throughout Europe, Africa, and Asia. Most North and South American Indian societies had totems as well.

toucan any South and Central American forest-dwelling bird of the family Ramphastidae. Toucans have very large, brilliantly coloured beaks and often handsome plumage. They live in small flocks and eat fruits, seeds, and insects. They nest in holes in trees, where the female lays 2–4 eggs; both parents care for the eggs and young. There are 37 species, ranging from 30 cm/1 ft to 60 cm/2 ft in size.

touch sensation produced by specialized nerve endings in the skin. Some respond to light pressure, others to heavy pressure. Temperature detection may also contribute to the overall sensation of touch. Many animals, such as nocturnal ones, rely on touch more than humans do. Some have specialized organs of touch that project from the body, such as whiskers or antennae.

touch screen in computing, an input device allowing the user to communicate with the computer by touching a display screen with a finger. In this way, the user can point to a required *menu option or item of data. Touch screens are used less widely than other pointing devices such as the *mouse or *joystick.

touch sensor in a computer-controlled *robot, a device used to give the robot a sense of touch, allowing it to manipulate delicate objects or move automatically about a room. Touch sensors provide the feedback necessary for the robot to adjust the force of its movements and the pressure of its grip. The main types include the strain gauge and the microswitch.

Toulon port and capital of Var *département*, SE France, on the Mediterranean Sea, 48 km/30 mi SE of Marseille; population (1983) 410,000. It is the chief Mediterranean naval station of France. Industries include oil refining, chemicals, furniture, and clothing. Toulon was the Roman *Telo Martius* and was made a port by Henry IV. It was occupied by the British 1793, and Napoleon first distinguished himself in driving them out. In World War II the French fleet was scuttled here to avoid its passing to German control.

Toulouse capital of Haute-Garonne *département*, SW France, on the river Garonne SE of Bordeaux; population (1982) 541,000. The chief industries are textiles and aircraft construction (Concorde was built here). Toulouse was the capital of the Visigoths (see *Goth) and later of Aquitaine 781–843.

Toulouse-Lautrec Henri Marie Raymond de 1864–1901. French artist, associated with the Impressionists. He was active in Paris, where he painted entertainers and prostitutes. From 1891 his lithograph posters were a great success.

touraco any fruit-eating African bird of the family Musophagidae. They have long tails, erectile crests, and short, rounded wings. The largest are 70 cm/28 in long.

tour de force (French 'feat of strength') a remarkable accomplishment.

Tour de France French road race for professional cyclists held annually over approximately 4,800 km/3,000 mi of primarily French roads. The race takes about three weeks to complete and the route varies each year, often taking in adjoining countries, but always ending in Paris. A separate stage is held every day, and the overall leader at the end of each stage wears the coveted 'yellow jersey' (French *maillot jaune*).

Toussaint L'Ouverture Pierre Dominique *c.* 1743–1803. Haitian revolutionary leader, born a slave. He joined the insurrection of 1791 against the French colonizers and was made governor by the revolutionary French government. He expelled the Spanish and British, but when the French emperor Napoleon reimposed slavery he revolted, was captured, and died in prison in France. In 1983 his remains were returned to Haiti.

Tower of London fortress on the Thames bank to the east of the City. The keep, or White Tower, was built about 1078 by Bishop Gundulf on the site of British and Roman fortifications. It is surrounded by two strong walls and a moat (now dry), and was for centuries a royal residence and the principal state prison.

toxaemia another term for *blood poisoning; **toxaemia of pregnancy** is another term for *pre-eclampsia.

toxic shock syndrome rare condition marked by rapid onset of fever, vomiting, and low blood pressure, sometimes leading to death. It is caused by a toxin of the bacterium *Staphylococcus aureus*, normally harmlessly present in the body, which may accumulate, for example, if a tampon used by a woman during a period remains unchanged beyond four to six hours.

toxic waste dumped *hazardous substance.

toxoplasmosis disease transmitted to humans by animals, often in pigeon or cat excrement. It causes flulike symptoms and damages the central nervous system, eyes, and visceral organs; it is caused by a protozoan, *Toxoplasma gondii*.

Toyota Japan's top industrial company, formed 1937, manufacturing motor vehicles. It was founded by Sakichi Toyoda (1894–1952), the inventor of an automatic loom.

trace element chemical element necessary in minute quantities for the health of a plant or animal. For example, magnesium, which occurs in chlorophyll, is essential to photosynthesis, and iodine is needed by the thyroid gland of mammals for making hormones that control growth and body chemistry.

tracer in science, a small quantity of a radioactive *isotope (form of an element) used to follow the path of a chemical reaction or a physical or biological process. The location (and possibly concentration) of the tracer is usually detected by using a Geiger–Muller counter.

trachea tube that forms an airway in air-breathing animals. In land-living *vertebrates, including humans, it is also known as the *windpipe* and runs from the larynx to the upper part of the chest. Its diameter is about 1.5 cm/0.6 in and its length 10 cm/4 in. It is strong and flexible, and

reinforced by rings of *cartilage. In the upper chest, the trachea branches into two tubes: the left and right bronchi, which enter the lungs. Insects have a branching network of tubes called tracheae, which conduct air from holes (*spiracles) in the body surface to all the body tissues. The finest branches of the tracheae are called tracheoles.

tracheostomy surgical opening in the windpipe (trachea), usually created for the insertion of a tube to enable the patient to breathe. It is done either to bypass the airway impaired by disease or injury, or to safeguard it during surgery or a prolonged period of mechanical ventilation.

trachoma chronic eye infection, resembling severe *conjunctivitis. The conjunctiva becomes inflamed, with scarring and formation of pus, and there may be damage to the cornea. It is caused by a viruslike organism (*chlamydia), and is a disease of dry tropical regions. Although it responds well to antibiotics, numerically it remains the biggest single cause of blindness worldwide.

Tractarianism another name for the *Oxford Movement, 19th-century movement for Catholic revival within the Church of England.

tractor in agriculture, a powerful motor vehicle, commonly having large rear wheels or caterpillar tracks, used for pulling farm machinery and loads. It is usually powered by a diesel engine and has a power-takeoff mechanism for driving machinery, and a hydraulic lift for raising and lowering implements.

Tracy Spencer 1900–1967. US actor distinguished for his understated, seemingly effortless, natural performances. His films include *Captains Courageous* 1937 and *Boys' Town* 1938 (for both of which he won Academy Awards), and he starred with Katharine Hepburn in nine films, including *Adam's Rib* 1949 and *Guess Who's Coming to Dinner* 1967, his final appearance.

trade cycle or *business cycle* period of time that includes a peak and trough of economic activity, as measured by a country's national income. In Keynesian economics, one of the main roles of the government is to smooth out the peaks and troughs of the trade cycle by intervening in the economy, thus minimizing 'overheating' and 'stagnation'. This is accomplished by regulating interest rates and government spending.

trade description description of the characteristics of goods, including their quality, quantity, and fitness for the purpose for which they are required. Under the Trade Descriptions Acts 1968 and 1972, making a false trade description is a criminal offence in English law.

trademark name or symbol that is distinctive of a marketed product. The owner may register the mark to prevent its unauthorized use. In the UK, the Trade Marks Act 1938 superseded the Trade Mark Registration Act 1875. Trademarks can be protected under common law or by registration, and cover a trader's goods or services. In 1988 the European Community adopted a directive to approximate the laws of member states relating to trademark laws.

Tradescant John 1570–1638. English gardener and botanist, who travelled widely in Europe and is thought to have introduced the cos lettuce to England from the Greek island bearing the same name. He was appointed gardener to Charles I and was succeeded by his son, **John Tradescant the Younger** (1608–1662), after his death. The younger Tradescant undertook three plant-collecting trips to Virginia, USA, and the Swedish botanist Carl Linnaeus named the genus *Tradescantia* in his honour.

tradescantia any plant of the genus *Tradescantia* of the family Commelinaceae, native to North and Central America. The spiderwort *T. virginiana* is a cultivated garden plant; the wandering jew *T. albiflora* is a common house plant, with green oval leaves tinged with pink or purple or silver-striped.

Trades Union Congress (TUC) voluntary organization of trade unions, founded in the UK 1868, in which delegates of affiliated unions meet annually to consider matters affecting their members. In 1991 there were 78 affiliated unions, with an aggregate membership of 10.4 million.

trade union organization of employed workers formed to undertake collective bargaining with employers and to try to achieve improved working conditions for its members. Attitudes of government to unions and of unions to management vary greatly from country to country. Probably the most effective trade-union system is that of Sweden, and the most internationally known is the Polish *Solidarity.

trade unionism, international worldwide cooperation between unions. In 1973 a European Trade Union Confederation was established, membership 29 million, and there is an International Labour Organization, established 1919 and affiliated to the United Nations from 1945, which formulates standards for labour and social conditions. Other organizations are the International Confederation of Free Trade Unions (1949) – which includes the American Federation of Labor and Congress of Industrial Organizations and the UK Trades Union Congress – and the World Federation of Trade Unions (1945).

trade wind prevailing wind that blows towards the equator from the northeast and southeast. Trade winds are caused by hot air rising at the equator and the consequent movement of air from north and south to take its place. The winds are deflected towards the west because of the Earth's west-to-east rotation. The unpredictable calms known as the *doldrums lie at their convergence.

Trafalgar, Battle of battle 21 Oct 1805 in the *Napoleonic Wars. The British fleet under Admiral Nelson defeated a Franco-Spanish fleet; Nelson was mortally wounded. The victory laid the foundation for British naval supremacy throughout the 19th century. It is named after Cape Trafalgar, a low headland in SW Spain, near the western entrance to the Straits of Gibraltar.

traffic vehicles using public roads. In 1970 there were 100 million cars and lorries in use worldwide; in 1990 there were 550 million. One-fifth of the space in European and North American cities is taken up by cars. In 1989 UK road-traffic forecasts predicted that traffic demand would rise between 83% and 142% by the year 2025.

tragedy in the theatre, a play dealing with a serious theme, traditionally one in which a character meets disaster either as a result of personal failings or circumstances beyond his or her control. Historically the Greek view of tragedy, as defined by Aristotle and expressed by the great tragedians Aeschylus, Euripides, and Sophocles, has been predominant in the western tradition. In the 20th century tragedies in the narrow Greek sense of dealing with exalted personages in an elevated manner have virtually died out. Tragedy has been replaced by dramas with 'tragic' implications or overtones, as in the work of Ibsen, O'Neill, Tennessee Williams, Pinter, and Osborne, for example, or by the hybrid tragicomedy.

tragicomedy drama that contains elements of tragedy and comedy; for example, Shakespeare's 'reconciliation' plays, such as *The Winter's Tale*, which reach a tragic climax but then lighten to a happy conclusion. A tragicomedy is the usual form for plays in the tradition of the Theatre of the *Absurd, such as Samuel *Beckett's *En attendant Godot/Waiting for Godot* 1953 and Tom *Stoppard's *Rosencrantz and Guildenstern are Dead* 1967.

trahison des clercs (French 'the treason of the intellectuals') the involvement of intellectuals in active politics.

Trajan Marcus Ulpius (Trajanus) AD 52–117. Roman emperor and soldier, born in Seville. He was adopted as heir by *Nerva, whom he succeeded AD 98.

trampolining gymnastics performed on a sprung canvas sheet which allows the performer to reach great heights before landing again. Marks are gained for carrying out difficult manoeuvres. Synchronized trampolining and tumbling are also popular forms of the sport.

tramway transport system for use in cities, where wheeled vehicles run along parallel rails. Trams are powered either by electric conductor rails below ground or by conductor arms connected to overhead wires. Greater manoeuvrability is achieved with the trolley bus, similarly powered by conductor arms overhead but without tracks.

trance mental state in which the subject loses the ordinary perceptions of time and space, and even of his or her own body.

tranquillizer common name for any drug for reducing anxiety or tension (*anxiolytic), such as *benzodiazepines, barbiturates, antidepressants, and beta-blockers. The use of drugs to control anxiety is becoming much less popular, because most of the drugs used are capable of inducing dependence.

transactinide element any of a series of nine radioactive, metallic elements with atomic numbers that extend beyond the *actinide series, those from 104 (rutherfordium) to 112 (unnamed). They are grouped because of their expected chemical similarities (all are bivalent), the properties differing only slightly with atomic number. All have half-lives of less than two minutes.

Trans-Alaskan Pipeline one of the world's greatest civil engineering projects, the construction of a pipeline to carry petroleum (crude oil) 1,285 km/800 mi from N Alaska to the ice-free port of Valdez. It was completed 1977 after three years' work and much criticism by ecologists.

Trans-Amazonian Highway or *Transamazonica* road in Brazil, linking Recife in the east with the provinces of Rondonia, Amazonas, and Acre in the west. Begun as part of the Brazilian National Integration Programme (PIN) in 1970, the Trans-Amazonian Highway was designed to enhance national security, aid the industrial development of the north of Brazil, and act as a safety valve for the overpopulated coastal regions.

transcendentalism philosophy inaugurated in the 18th century by Immanuel *Kant and developed in the USA in the mid-19th century into a mystical and social doctrine. As opposed to metaphysics in the traditional sense, transcendental philosophy is concerned with the conditions of possibility of experience, rather than the nature of being. It seeks to show the necessary structure of our 'point of view' on the world.

transcendental meditation (TM) technique of focusing the mind, based in part on Hindu meditation. Meditators are given a mantra (a special word or phrase) to repeat over and over to themselves; such meditation is believed to benefit the practitioner by relieving stress and inducing a feeling of wellbeing and relaxation. It was introduced to the West by Maharishi Mahesh Yogi and popularized by the Beatles in the late 1960s.

transcription in living cells, the process by which the information for the synthesis of a protein is transferred from the *DNA strand on which it is carried to the messenger *RNA strand involved in the actual synthesis.

transducer device that converts one form of energy into another. For example, a thermistor is a transducer that converts heat into an electrical voltage, and an electric motor is a transducer that converts an electrical voltage into mechanical energy. Transducers are important components in many types of *sensor, converting the physical quantity to be measured into a proportional voltage signal.

transfer orbit elliptical path followed by a spacecraft moving from one orbit to another, designed to save fuel although at the expense of a longer journey time.

transformational grammar theory of language structure initiated by Noam *Chomsky, which proposes that below the actual phrases and sentences of a language (its *surface structure*) there lies a more basic layer (its *deep structure*), which is processed by various transformational rules when we speak and write.

transformer device in which, by electromagnetic induction, an alternating current (AC) of one voltage is transformed to another voltage, without change of *frequency. Transformers are widely used in electrical apparatus of all kinds, and in particular in power transmission where high voltages and low currents are utilized.

transfusion intravenous delivery of blood or blood products (plasma, red cells) into a patient's circulation to make up for deficiencies due to disease, injury, or surgical intervention. Cross-matching is carried out to ensure the patient receives the right type of blood. Because of worries about blood-borne disease, self-trans-

fusion with units of blood 'donated' over the weeks before an operation is popular.

transgenic organism plant, animal, bacterium, or other living organism which has had a foreign gene added to it by means of *genetic engineering.

transhumance seasonal movement by pastoral farmers of their livestock between areas of different climate. There are three main forms: in *Alpine* regions, such as Switzerland, cattle are moved to high-level pastures in summer and returned to milder valley pastures in winter; in *Mediterranean* lands, summer heat and drought make it necessary to move cattle to cooler mountain slopes; in *W Africa*, the nomadic herders of the *Fulani peoples move cattle south in search of grass and water in the dry season and north in the wet season to avoid the *tsetse fly.

transistor solid-state electronic component, made of *semiconductor material, with three or more *electrodes, that can regulate a current passing through it. A transistor can act as an amplifier, *oscillator, *photocell, or switch, and (unlike earlier thermionic valves) usually operates on a very small amount of power. Transistors commonly consist of a tiny sandwich of germanium or silicon, alternate layers having different electrical properties.

transit in astronomy, the passage of a smaller object across the visible disc of a larger one. Transits of the inferior planets occur when they pass directly between the Earth and Sun, and are seen as tiny dark spots against the Sun's disc.

transition metal any of a group of metallic elements that have incomplete inner electron shells and exhibit variable valency – for example, cobalt, copper, iron, and molybdenum. They are excellent conductors of electricity, and generally form highly coloured compounds.

Transkei largest of South Africa's Bantustans, or homelands, extending northeast from the Great Kei River, on the coast of Cape Province, to the border of Natal; area 43,808 sq km/16,910 sq mi; population (1985) 3,000,000, including small white and Asian minorities. It became self-governing 1963, and achieved full 'independence' 1976. Its capital is Umtata, and it has a port at Mnganzana. It is one of the two homelands of the Xhosa people (the other is Ciskei), and products include livestock, coffee, tea, sugar, maize, and sorghum. It is governed by a military council since a 1987 coup (military leader Maj-Gen H B Holomisa from 1987).

translation in living cells, the process by which proteins are synthesized. During translation, the information coded as a sequence of nucleotides in messenger *RNA is transformed into a sequence of amino acids in a peptide chain. The process involves the 'translation' of the *genetic code. See also *transcription.

transmigration of souls another name for *reincarnation.

transparency in photography, a picture on slide film. This captures the original in a positive image (direct reversal) and can be used for projection or printing on positive-to-positive print material, for example by the Cibachrome or Kodak R-type process.

transpiration the loss of water from a plant by evaporation. Most water is lost from the leaves through pores known as *stomata, whose primary function is to allow *gas exchange between the plant's internal tissues and the atmosphere. Transpiration from the leaf surfaces causes a continuous upward flow of water from the roots via the *xylem, which is known as the transpiration stream.

transplant in medicine, the transfer of a tissue or organ from one human being to another or from one part of the body to another (skin grafting). In most organ transplants, the operation is for life-saving purposes, though the immune system tends to reject foreign tissue. Careful matching and immunosuppressive drugs must be used, but these are not always successful.

Transport and General Workers' Union (TGWU) UK trade union founded 1921 by the amalgamation of a number of dockers' and road-transport workers' unions, previously associated in the Transport Workers' Federation. It is the largest trade union in Britain.

transportation former punishment which involved sending convicted persons to overseas territories either for life or for shorter periods. It was introduced in England towards the end of the 17th century and was abolished 1857 after many thousands had been transported, mostly to Australia. It was also used for punishment of criminals by France until 1938.

transputer in computing, a member of a family of microprocessors designed for parallel processing, developed in the UK by Inmos. In the circuits of a standard computer the processing of data takes place in sequence; in a transputer's circuits processing takes place in parallel, greatly reducing computing time for those programs that have been specifically written for it.

transsexual person who identifies himself or herself completely with the opposite sex, believing that the wrong sex was assigned at birth. Unlike *transvestites*, who desire to dress in clothes traditionally worn by the opposite sex; transsexuals think and feel emotionally in a way typically considered appropriate to members of the opposite sex, and may undergo surgery to modify external sexual characteristics.

Trans-Siberian Railway railway line connecting the cities of European Russia with Omsk, Novosibirsk, Irkutsk, and Khabarovsk, and terminating at Vladivostok on the Pacific. It was built 1891–1905; from Leningrad to Vladivostok is about 8,700 km/5,400 mi. A 3,102 km/1,928 mi northern line was completed 1984 after ten years' work.

transubstantiation in Christian theology, the doctrine that the whole substance of the bread and wine changes into the substance of the body and blood of Jesus when consecrated in the *Eucharist.

transuranic element or **transuranium element** chemical element with an atomic number of 93 or more – that is, with a greater number of protons in the nucleus than has uranium. All transuranic elements are radioactive. Neptunium and plutonium are found in nature; the others are synthesized in nuclear reactions.

Transvaal province of NE South Africa, bordering Zimbabwe to the north; area 262,499 sq km/101,325 sq mi; population (1985) 7,532,000. Its capital is Pretoria, and towns include Johannesburg, Germiston, Brakpan, Springs, Benoni, Krugersdorp, and Roodepoort. Products include diamonds, coal, iron ore, copper, lead, tin, manganese, meat, maize, tobacco, and fruit. The main rivers are the Vaal and Limpopo with their tributaries. Swaziland forms an enclave on the Natal border. It was settled by *Voortrekkers*, Boers who left Cape Colony in the Great Trek from 1831. Independence was recognized by Britain 1852, until the settlers' difficulties with the conquered Zulus led to British annexation 1877. It was made a British colony after the South African War 1899–1902, and in 1910 became a province of the Union of South Africa.

Transylvania mountainous area of central and NW Romania, bounded to the south by the Transylvanian Alps (an extension of the *Carpathians), formerly a province, with its capital at Cluj. It was part of Hungary from about 1000 until its people voted to unite with Romania 1918. It is the home of the vampire legends.

trapezium (North American **trapezoid**) in geometry, a four-sided plane figure (quadrilateral) with two of its sides parallel. If the parallel sides have lengths a and b and the perpendicular distance between them is h (the height of the trapezium), its area $A=\frac{1}{2}h(a+b)$.

Trappist member of a Roman Catholic order of monks and nuns, renowned for the strictness of their rule, which includes the maintenance of silence, manual labour, and a vegetarian diet. The order was founded 1664 at La Trappe, in Normandy, France, by Armand de Rancé (1626–1700) as a reformed version of the *Cistercian order. In 1792 the monks were expelled (during the French Revolution) but the community remained together until it could return in 1817.

trauma in psychiatry, a painful emotional experience or shock with lasting psychic consequences; in medicine, any physical damage or injury.

traveller nomadic or itinerant wanderer; in Europe the term is frequently applied to *Romany and other travelling peoples.

Travers Morris William 1872–1961. English chemist who, with William Ramsay, between 1894 and 1908 first identified what were called the noble or *inert gases: krypton, xenon, and radon.

treason act of betrayal, in particular against the sovereign or the state to which the offender owes allegiance.

treasure trove in England, any gold or silver, plate or bullion, found concealed in a house or the ground, the owner being unknown. Normally, treasure originally hidden, and not abandoned, belongs to the crown, but if the treasure was casually lost or intentionally abandoned, the first finder is entitled to it against all but the true owner. Objects buried with no intention of recovering them, for example in a burial mound, do not rank as treasure trove, and belong to the owner of the ground.

treasury counsel in the UK, a group of barristers who receive briefs from the *Director of

Public Prosecutions to appear for the prosecution in criminal trials at the Central Criminal Court (*Old Bailey).

treaty written agreement between two or more states. Treaties take effect either immediately on signature or, more often, on ratification. Ratification involves a further exchange of documents and usually takes place after the internal governments have approved the terms of the treaty. Treaties are binding in international law, the rules being laid down in the Vienna Convention on the Law of Treaties 1969.

tree perennial plant with a woody stem, usually a single stem or 'trunk', made up of *wood and protected by an outer layer of *bark. It absorbs water through a *root system. There is no clear dividing line between *shrubs and trees, but sometimes a minimum height of 6 m/20 ft is used to define a tree.

trefoil any of several *clover plants of the genus *Trifolium* of the pea family Leguminosae, the leaves of which are divided into three leaflets. The name is also used for other plants with leaves divided into three lobes.

trematode parasitic flatworm with an oval non-segmented body, of the class Trematoda, including the *fluke.

Trent, Council of conference held 1545–63 by the Roman Catholic Church at Trento, N Italy initiating the *Counter-Reformation; see also *Reformation.

Trentino–Alto Adige autonomous region of N Italy, comprising the provinces of Bolzano and Trento; capital Trento; chief towns Trento in the Italian-speaking southern area, and Bolzano-Bozen in the northern German-speaking area of South Tirol (the region was Austrian until ceded to Italy 1919); area 13,600 sq km/5,250 sq mi; population (1990) 891,400.

trespass going on to the land of another without authority. In law, a landowner has the right to eject a trespasser by the use of reasonable force and can sue for any damage caused.

Trevithick Richard 1771–1833. British engineer, constructor of a steam road locomotive 1801 and the first steam engine to run on rails 1804.

Triad secret society, founded in China as a Buddhist cult AD 36. It became known as the Triad because the triangle played a significant part in the initiation ceremony. Today it is reputed to be involved in organized crime (drugs, gambling, prostitution) among overseas Chinese. Its headquarters are alleged to be in Hong Kong.

trial by ordeal in the Middle Ages, a test of guilt or innocence by which God's judgement of the case was supposedly revealed through the accused's exposure to fire, water, or blessed bread. The practice originated with the Franks in the 8th century, and survived until the 13th century. In the ordeal by cold water, the accused would be bound and thrown into the water. If he or she sank, it would prove innocence, but if they remained alive, it would show guilt.

triangle in geometry, a three-sided plane figure, the sum of whose interior angles is 180°. Triangles can be classified by the relative lengths of their sides. A **scalene triangle** has no sides of equal length; an **isosceles triangle** has at least two equal sides; an **equilateral triangle** has three equal sides (and three equal angles of 60°).

triangulation technique used in surveying and navigation to determine distances, using the properties of the triangle. To begin, surveyors measure a certain length exactly to provide a base line. From each end of this line they then measure the angle to a distant point, using a *theodolite. They now have a triangle in which they know the length of one side and the two adjacent angles. By simple trigonometry they can work out the lengths of the other two sides.

Triassic period of geological time 245–208 million years ago, the first period of the Mesozoic era. The continents were fused together to form the world continent *Pangaea. Triassic sediments contain remains of early dinosaurs and other reptiles now extinct. By late Triassic times, the first mammals had evolved.

triathlon test of stamina involving three sports: swimming 3.8 km/2.4 mi, cycling 180 km/112 mi, and running a marathon 42.195 km/26 mi 385 yd, each one immediately following the last.

tribal society way of life in which people govern their own affairs as independent local communities of families and clans without central government organizations or states. They are found in parts of SE Asia, New Guinea, South America, and Africa.

tribunal strictly, a court of justice, but used in English law for a body appointed by the government to arbitrate in disputes, or investigate certain matters. Tribunals usually consist of a lawyer as chair, sitting with two lay assessors.

tribune Roman magistrate of *plebeian family elected annually to defend the interests of the common people; only two were originally chosen in 494 BC, but there were later ten. They could veto the decisions of any other magistrate.

triceratops any of a genus *Triceratops* of massive, horned dinosaurs of the order Ornithischia. They had three horns and a neck frill and were up to 8 m/25 ft long; they lived in the Cretaceous period.

trichloromethane technical name for *chloroform.

tricolour (French *tricouleur*) the French national flag of three vertical bands of red, white, and blue. The red and blue were the colours of Paris and the white represented the royal house of Bourbon. The flag was first adopted on 17 July 1789, three days after the storming of the Bastille during the French Revolution.

Trident nuclear missile deployed on certain US nuclear-powered submarines and in the 1990s also being installed on four UK submarines. Each missile has eight warheads (*MIRVs) and each of the four submarines will have 16 Trident D-5 missiles. The Trident replaced the earlier Polaris and Poseidon missiles.

Trieste port on the Adriatic, opposite Venice in Friuli-Venezia-Giulia, Italy; population (1988) 237,000, including a large Slovene minority. It is the site of the International Centre for Theoretical Physics, established 1964.
history Trieste was under Austrian rule from 1382 (apart from Napoleonic occupation 1809–14) until transferred to Italy 1918. It wa

claimed after World War II by Yugoslavia, and the city and surrounding territory were divided 1954 between Italy and Yugoslavia.

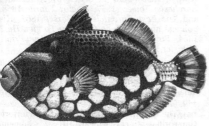

triggerfish The clown triggerfish of the rocky coasts and coral reefs of the Indian and Pacific oceans.

triggerfish any marine bony fish of the family Balistidae, with a laterally compressed body, up to 60 cm/2 ft long, and deep belly. They have small mouths but strong jaws and teeth. The first spine on the dorsal fin locks into an erect position, allowing them to fasten themselves securely in crevices for protection; it can only be moved by depressing the smaller third ('trigger') spine.

triglyceride chemical name for *fat.

trigonometry branch of mathematics that solves problems relating to plane and spherical triangles. Its principles are based on the fixed proportions of sides for a particular angle in a right-angled triangle, the simplest of which are known as the *sine, *cosine, and *tangent (so-called trigonometrical ratios). It is of practical importance in navigation, surveying, and simple harmonic motion in physics.

trilobite any of a large class (Trilobita) of extinct, marine, invertebrate arthropods of the Palaeozoic era, with a flattened, oval body, 1–65 cm/0.4–26 in long. The hard-shelled body was divided by two deep furrows into three lobes.

Trimurti the Hindu triad of gods, representing the Absolute Spirit in its three aspects: Brahma, personifying creation; Vishnu, preservation; and Siva, destruction.

Trinidad and Tobago Republic of

area Trinidad 4,828 sq km/1,864 sq mi and Tobago 300 sq km/116 sq mi

capital Port-of-Spain
towns San Fernando, Arima, Scarborough (Tobago)
physical comprises two main islands and some smaller ones; coastal swamps and hills E–W
head of state Noor Hassanali from 1987
head of government Patrick Manning from 1991
political system democratic republic
exports oil, petroleum products, chemicals, sugar, cocoa
currency Trinidad and Tobago dollar
population (1993 est) 1,300,000 (40% African descent, 40% Indian, 16% European, Chinese and others 2%), 1.2 million on Trinidad; growth rate 1.6% p.a.
languages English (official), Hindi, French, Spanish
religions Roman Catholic 32%, Protestant 29%, Hindu 25%, Muslim 6%
GNP $2,878 per head (1991)
chronology
1888 Trinidad and Tobago united as a British colony.
1956 People's National Movement (PNM) founded.
1959 Achieved internal self-government, with PNM leader Eric Williams as chief minister.
1962 Independence achieved from Britain, within the Commonwealth, with Williams as prime minister.
1976 Became a republic, with Ellis Clarke as president and Williams as prime minister.
1981 Williams died and was succeeded by George Chambers, with Arthur Robinson as opposition leader.
1986 National Alliance for Reconstruction (NAR), headed by Arthur Robinson, won general election.
1987 Noor Hassanali became president.
1990 Attempted antigovernment coup defeated.
1991 General election saw victory for PNM, with Patrick Manning as prime minister.

Trinity in Christianity, the union of three persons – Father, Son, and Holy Ghost/Spirit – in one godhead. The precise meaning of the doctrine has been the cause of unending dispute, and was the chief cause of the split between the Eastern Orthodox and Roman Catholic churches. **Trinity Sunday** occurs on the Sunday after Pentecost.

Triple Alliance pact from 1882 between Germany, Austria-Hungary, and Italy to offset the power of Russia and France. It was last renewed 1912, but during World War I Italy's initial neutrality gradually changed and it denounced the alliance 1915. The term also refers to other alliances: 1668 – England, Holland, and Sweden; 1717 – Britain, Holland, and France (joined 1718 by Austria); 1788 – Britain, Prussia, and Holland; 1795 – Britain, Russia, and Austria.

Triple Entente alliance of Britain, France, and Russia 1907–17. In 1911 this became a military alliance and formed the basis of the Allied powers in World War I against the Central Powers, Germany and Austria-Hungary.

triple jump field event in athletics comprising a hop, step and jump sequence from a take-off board into a sandpit landing area measuring 8 metres (minimum) in length. The takeoff board is usually 13 metres from the landing area. Each competitor has six trials and the winner is the one with the longest jump.

Tripoli (Arabic *Tarabolus al-Gharb*) capital and chief port of Libya, on the Mediterranean; population (1982) 980,000. Products include olive oil, fruit, fish, and textiles.

history Tripoli was founded about the 7th century BC by Phoenicians from Oea (now Tripoli in Lebanon). It was a base for Axis powers during World War II. In 1986 it was bombed by the US Air Force in retaliation for international guerrilla activity.

Tripura state of NE India since 1972, formerly a princely state, between Bangladesh and Assam;
area 10,500 sq km/4,053 sq mi
capital Agartala
products rice, cotton, tea, sugar cane; steel, jute
population (1991) 2,744,800
language Bengali
religion Hindu.

trireme ancient Greek warship with three banks of oars as well as sails, 38 m/115 ft long. They were used at the battle of *Salamis and by the Romans until the 4th century AD.

Tristan hero of Celtic legend who fell in love with Iseult, the bride he was sent to win for his uncle King Mark of Cornwall; the story became part of the Arthurian cycle and is the subject of Wagner's opera *Tristan und Isolde*.

tritium radioactive isotope of hydrogen, three times as heavy as ordinary hydrogen, consisting of one proton and two neutrons. It has a half-life of 12.5 years.

Triton in astronomy, the largest of Neptune's moons and one of the four largest in the solar system. It has a diameter of 2,700 km/1,680 mi, and orbits Neptune every 5.88 days in a retrograde (east to west) direction.

triumvir one of a group of three administrators sharing power in ancient Rome, as in the *First Triumvirate* 60 BC: Caesar, Pompey, Crassus; and *Second Triumvirate* 43 BC: Augustus, Antony, and Lepidus.

Trobriand Islands group of coral islands in the Solomon Sea, forming part of the province of Milne Bay, Papua New Guinea; chief town Losuia; area 440 sq km/170 sq mi.

troglodyte Greek term for a cave dweller, designating certain peoples in the ancient world. The troglodytes of S Egypt and Ethiopia were a pastoral people.

trogon any species of the order Trogoniformes of tropical birds, up to 50 cm/1.7 ft long, with resplendent plumage, living in the Americas and Afro-Asia. Most striking is the *quetzal.

Trojan horse in computing, a *virus program that appears to function normally but, while undetected by the normal user, causes damage to other files or circumvents security procedures. The earliest appeared in the UK in about 1988.

Trojan horse seemingly innocuous but treacherous gift from an enemy. In Greek legend, during the siege of Troy, the Greek army left an enormous wooden horse outside the gate of the city and retreated. When the Trojans had brought it in, Greek soldiers emerged from within the hollow horse and opened the city gates to enable it to be captured.

Trollope Anthony 1815–1882. English novelist who delineated provincial English middle-class society in a series of novels set in or around the imaginary cathedral city of Barchester. *The Warden* 1855 began the series, which includes *Barchester Towers* 1857, *Doctor Thorne* 1858 and *The Last Chronicle of Barset* 1867. His political novels include *Can You Forgive Her?* 1864, *Phineas Finn* 1867–69, and *The Prime Minister* 1875–76.

trombone *brass wind musical instrument developed from the sackbut. It consists of a tube bent double, varied notes being obtained by an inner sliding tube. Usual sizes of trombone are alto, tenor, bass, and contra-bass.

Tromp Maarten Harpertszoon 1597–1653 Dutch admiral. He twice defeated the occupying Spaniards 1639. He was defeated by English admiral Blake May 1652, but in Nov triumphed over Blake in the Strait of Dover. In Feb–June 1653 he was defeated by Blake and Monk, and was killed off the Dutch coast. His son, *Cornelius Tromp* (1629–1691), also an admiral, fought a battle against the English and French fleets in 1673.

trompe l'oeil (French 'deceives the eye') painting that gives a convincing illusion of three-dimensional reality. It has been common in most periods in the West, from Classical Greece through the Renaissance and later.

trophic level in ecology, the position occupied by a species (or group of species) in a *food chain. The main levels are *primary producers* (photosynthetic plants), *primary consumers* (herbivores), *secondary consumers* (carnivores), and *decomposers* (bacteria and fungi).

tropical disease any illness found mainly in hot climates. The most important tropical diseases worldwide are *malaria, schistosomiasis *leprosy, and *river blindness. Malaria kills about 1.5 million people each year, and produces chronic anaemia and tiredness in 100 times as many, while schistosomiasis is responsible for 1 million deaths a year. All the main tropical diseases are potentially curable, but the facilities for diagnosis and treatment are rarely adequate in the countries where they occur.

tropics the area between the tropics of Cancer and Capricorn, defined by the parallels of latitude approximately 23°30′ N and S of the equator. They are the limits of the area of Earth's surface in which the Sun can be directly overhead. The mean monthly temperature is over 20°C/68°F.

tropism or *tropic movement* the directional growth of a plant, or part of a plant, in response to an external stimulus such as gravity or light. If the movement is directed towards the stimulus, it is described as positive; if away from it, it is negative. *Geotropism* for example, the response of plants to gravity, causes the root (positively geotropic) to grow downwards, and the stem (negatively geotropic) to grow upwards.

troposphere lower part of the Earth's *atmosphere extending about 10.5 km/6.5 mi from the Earth's surface, where temperature decreases with height to about –60°C/–76°F except in local layers of temperature inversion. The *tropopause* is the upper boundary of the troposphere above which the temperature increases slowly with height within the atmosphere.

Trotsky Leon. Adopted name of Lev Davidovitch Bronstein 1879–1940. Russian revolutionary. He joined the Bolshevik party and took a leading part in the seizure of power 1917 and raising the Red Army that fought the Civil War 1918–20. In the struggle for power that followed *Lenin's death 1924, *Stalin defeated Trotsky, and this and other differences with the Communist Party led to his exile 1929. He settled in Mexico, where he was assassinated with an ice pick at Stalin's instigation. Trotsky believed in world revolution and in permanent revolution, and was an uncompromising, if liberal, idealist.

Trotskyism form of Marxism advocated by Leon Trotsky. Its central concept is that of **permanent revolution**. In his view a proletarian revolution, leading to a socialist society, could not be achieved in isolation, so it would be necessary to spark off further revolutions throughout Europe and ultimately worldwide. This was in direct opposition to the Stalinist view that socialism should be built and consolidated within individual countries.

troubadour one of a group of poet musicians in Provence and S France in the 12th–13th centuries, which included both nobles and wandering minstrels. The troubadours originated a type of lyric poetry devoted to themes of courtly love and the idealization of women and to glorifying the deeds of their patrons, reflecting the chivalric ideals of their period. Little is known of their music, which was passed down orally.

trout any of various bony fishes in the salmon family, popular for sport and food, usually speckled and found mainly in fresh water. They are native to the northern hemisphere. Trout have thick bodies and blunt heads, and vary in colour. The common trout *Salmo trutta* is widely distributed in Europe, occurring in British fresh and coastal waters. Sea trout are generally silvery and river trout olive-brown, both with spotted fins and sides.

Troy (Latin *Ilium*) ancient city of Asia Minor, besieged in the ten-year Trojan War (mid-13th century BC), which the poet Homer described in the *Iliad*. The city fell to the Greeks, who first used the stratagem of leaving behind, in a feigned retreat, a large wooden horse containing armed infiltrators to open the gates. Believing it to be a religious offering, the Trojans took it within the walls.

troy system system of units used for precious metals and gems. The pound troy (0.37 kg) consists of 12 ounces (each of 120 carats) or 5,760 grains (each equal to 65 mg).

Trudeau Pierre (Elliott) 1919– . Canadian Liberal politician. He was prime minister 1968–79 and 1980–84. In 1980, having won again by a landslide on a platform opposing Québec separatism, he helped to defeat the Québec independence movement in a referendum. He repatriated the constitution from Britain 1982, but by 1984 had so lost support that he resigned.

Truffaut François 1932–1984. French New Wave film director and actor, formerly a critic. A popular, romantic, and intensely humane filmmaker, he wrote and directed a series of semiautobiographical films starring Jean-Pierre Léaud, beginning with *Les Quatre Cent Coups/The 400 Blows* 1959. His other films include

Jules et Jim 1961, *Fahrenheit 451* 1966, *L'Enfant sauvage/The Wild Child* 1970, and *La Nuit américaine/Day for Night* 1973 (Academy Award).

truffle subterranean fungus of the order Tuberales. Certain species are valued as edible delicacies; in particular, *Tuber melanosporum*, generally found growing under oak trees. It is native to the Périgord region of France but cultivated in other areas as well. It is rounded, blackish brown, covered with warts externally, and with blackish flesh.

Trujillo city in NW Peru, with its port at Salaverry; population (1988) 491,000. Industries include engineering, copper, sugar milling, and vehicle assembly.

Truk group of about 55 volcanic islands surrounded by a coral reef in the E Caroline islands of the W Pacific, forming one of the four states of the Federated States of Micronesia. Fish and copra are the main products.

Truman Harry S 1884–1972. 33rd president of the USA 1945–53, a Democrat. In Jan 1945 he became vice president to F D Roosevelt, and president when Roosevelt died in April that year. He used the atom bomb against Japan, launched the *Marshall Plan to restore W Europe's economy, and nurtured the European Community and NATO (including the rearmament of West Germany).

Truman Doctrine US president Harry Truman's 1947 dictum that the USA would 'support free peoples who are resisting attempted subjugation by armed minorities or by outside pressures'. It was used to justify sending a counterinsurgency military mission to Greece after World War II and sending US troops abroad (for example, to Korea).

trumpet small high-register *brass wind instrument; a doubled tube with valves. Before the 19th century, the trumpet had no valves and was restricted to harmonies.

trumpeter any South American bird of the genus *Psophia*, family Psophiidae, up to 50 cm/20 in tall, related to the cranes. Trumpeters have long legs, a short bill, and dark plumage. The name is also applied to the trumpeter *swan.

trust arrangement whereby a person or group of people (the trustee(s)) holds property for others (the beneficiaries) entitled to the beneficial interest. A trust can be a legal arrangement under which A is empowered to administer property belonging to B for the benefit of C. A and B may be the same person; B and C may not.

Trust Territory country or area formerly held under the United Nations trusteeship system to be prepared for independence, either former *mandates, territories taken over by the Allies in World War II, or those voluntarily placed under the UN by the administering state.

trypanosomiasis any of several debilitating long-term diseases caused by a trypanosome (protozoan of the genus *Trypanosoma*). They include sleeping sickness (nagana) in Africa, transmitted by the bites of *tsetse flies, and Chagas' disease in the Americas, spread by assassin bugs.

tsar the Russian imperial title 1547–1721

(although it continued in popular use to 1917), derived from Latin *caesar*.

Tselinograd formerly (until 1961) *Akmolinsk*, a commercial and mining industrial city in N Kazakhstan, on the river Ishim; population (1983) 253,000. Situated at a railway junction, it produces agricultural machinery, textiles, and chemicals.

tsetse fly any of a number of blood-feeding African flies of the genus *Glossina*, some of which transmits the disease nagana to cattle and sleeping sickness to human beings. Tsetse flies may grow up to 1.5 cm/0.6 in long.

Tsumeb principal mining centre (diamonds, copper, lead, zinc) of N Namibia, NW of Grootfontein; population 13,500.

tsunami (Japanese 'harbour wave') giant wave generated by an undersea *earthquake or other disturbance. In the open ocean it may take the form of several successive waves, travelling at tens of kilometres/tens of miles per hour but with an amplitude (height) of approximately 1 m/3 ft. In the coastal shallows, tsunamis slow down and build up, producing towering waves that can sweep inland and cause great loss of life and property.

Tswana member of the majority ethnic group living in Botswana. The Tswana are divided into four subgroups: the Bakwena, the Bamangwato, the Bangwaketse, and the Batawana. Traditionally they are rural-dwelling farmers, though many now leave their homes to work as migrant labourers in South African industries. The Tswana language belongs to the Bantu branch of the Niger-Congo family.

Tuamotu Archipelago two parallel ranges of 78 atolls, part of *French Polynesia; area 690 sq km/266 sq mi; population (1983) 11,800, including the *Gambier Islands to the E. The atolls stretch 2,100 km/1,300 mi N and E of the Society Islands. The administrative headquarters is Apataki. The largest atoll is Rangiroa, the most significant is Hao; they produce pearl shell and copra. Mururoa and Fangataufa atolls to the SE have been a French nuclear test site since 1966. Spanish explorers landed 1606, and the islands were annexed by France 1881.

Tuareg Arabic name given to nomadic stockbreeders from west and central Sahara and Sahel (Algeria, Libya, Mali, Niger, and Burkina Faso). The eight Tuareg groups refer to themselves by their own names. Their language, Tamashek, belongs to the Berber branch of the Afro-Asiatic family and is spoken by 500,000–850,000 people. It is written in a noncursive script known as *tifinagh*, derived from ancient Numidian. Tuareg men wear dark-blue robes, turbans, and veils.

tuatara lizardlike reptile *Sphenodon punctatus*, found only on a few islands off New Zealand. It grows up to 70 cm/2.3 ft long, is greenish black, and has a spiny crest down its back. On the top of its head is the *pineal body, or so-called 'third eye', linked to the brain, which probably acts as a kind of light meter.

tuba large bass *brass wind musical instrument of the cornet family. The *Wagner tuba* combines features of the euphonium and french horn.

tuber swollen region of an underground stem or root, usually modified for storing food. The

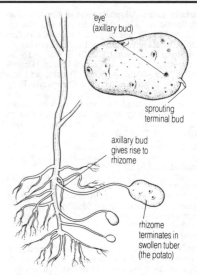

'eye'
(axillary bud)

sprouting
terminal bud

axillary bud
gives rise to
rhizome

rhizome
terminates in
swollen tuber
(the potato)

tuber *Tubers are produced underground from stems, as in the potato, or from roots, as in the dahlia.*

potato is a *stem tuber*, as shown by the presence of terminal and lateral buds, the 'eyes' of the potato. *Root tubers*, for example dahlias, developed from adventitious roots (growing from the stem, not from other roots) lack these. Both types of tuber can give rise to new individuals and so provide a means of *vegetative reproduction.

tuberculosis (TB) formerly known as *consumption* or *phthisis* infectious disease caused by the bacillus *Mycobacterium tuberculosis*. I takes several forms, of which pulmonary tuberculosis is by far the most common. A vaccine *BCG, was developed around 1920 and the first antituberculosis drug, streptomycin, in 1944.

Tubuai Islands or *Austral Islands* chain of volcanic islands and reefs 1,300 km/800 mi long in *French Polynesia, S of the Society Islands area 148 sq km/57 sq mi; population (1983 6,300. The main settlement is Mataura on Tubuai They were visited by Captain Cook 1777 and annexed by France 1880.

TUC abbreviation for *Trades Union Congress

Tudjman Franjo 1922– . Croatian nationalist leader and historian, president from 1990. As leader of the centre-right Croatian Democratic Union (HDZ), he led the fight for Croatian independence. During the 1991–92 civil war his troops were hampered by lack of arms and the military superiority of the Serb-dominated federal army, but recognition of Croatia's independence followed a successful UN-negotiated cease-fire Jan 1992, and Tudjman was re-elected president Aug 1992.

Tudor Anthony 1908–1987. English ballet dancer, choreographer, and teacher, who introduced psychological drama into ballet. His first works were for the *Rambert company (for example, *Lilac Garden* 1936); he cofounded the American Ballet Theater 1939 and created several works for it, including *Pillar of Fire* 1942

Romeo and Juliet 1943, and *The Tiller in the Fields* 1978.

Tudor dynasty English dynasty 1485–1603, descended from the Welsh Owen Tudor c. 1400–1461), second husband of Catherine of Valois (widow of Henry V of England). Their son Edmund married Margaret Beaufort 1443–1509), the great-granddaughter of *John of Gaunt, and was the father of Henry VII, who became king by overthrowing Richard III 1485. The dynasty ended with the death of Elizabeth I 1603.

Tufa or ***travertine*** soft, porous, *limestone rock, white in colour, deposited from solution from carbonate-saturated ground water around hot springs and in caves.

Tu Fu or ***Du Fu*** 712–770. Chinese poet of the Tang dynasty, with Li Po one of the two greatest Chinese poets. He wrote about the social injustices of his time, peasant suffering, and war, as in *The Army Carts* on conscription, and *The Beauties*, comparing the emperor's wealth with the lot of the poor.

Tukano member of an indigenous South American Indian people of the Vaupés region on the Colombian-Brazilian border, numbering approximately 2,000. An estimated 12,000 speak languages related to Tukano. The other main Tukanoan groups are Bara, Barasana, Cubeo, Desana, and Makuna.

Tulip plant of the genus *Tulipa*, family Liliaceae, usually with single goblet-shaped flowers on the end of an upright stem and leaves of a narrow oval shape with pointed ends. It is widely cultivated as a garden flower.

Tumour overproduction of cells in a specific area of the body, often leading to a swelling or lump. Tumours are classified as ***benign*** and ***malignant*** (see *cancer). Benign tumours grow more slowly, do not invade surrounding tissues, do not spread to other parts of the body, and do not usually recur after removal. However, benign tumours can be dangerous in areas such as the brain. The most familiar types of benign tumour are warts on the skin. In some cases, there is no sharp dividing line between benign and malignant tumours.

Tuna any of various large marine bony fishes of the mackerel family, especially the genus *Thunnus*, popular as food and game. Albacore *T. alalunga*, bluefin tuna *T. thynnus*, and yellowfin tuna *T. albacores* are commercially important.

Tundra region of high latitude almost devoid of trees, resulting from the presence of *permafrost. The vegetation consists mostly of grasses, sedges, heather, mosses, and lichens. Tundra stretches in a continuous belt across N North America and Eurasia.

Tungsten (Swedish *tung sten* 'heavy stone') hard, heavy, grey-white, metallic element, symbol W (from German *Wolfram*), atomic number 74, relative atomic mass 183.85. It occurs in the minerals wolframite, scheelite, and hubertite. It has the highest melting point of any metal (6,170°F/3,410°C) and is added to steel to make it harder, stronger, and more elastic; its other uses include high-speed cutting tools, electrical elements, and thermionic couplings. Its salts are used in the paint and tanning industries.

Tunguska Event explosion at Tunguska, central Siberia, Russia, in June 1908, which devastated around 6,500 sq km/2,500 sq mi of forest. It is thought to have been caused by either a cometary nucleus or a fragment of *Encke's comet. The magnitude of the explosion was equivalent to an atom bomb and produced a colossal shock wave; a bright falling object was seen 600 km/375 mi away and was heard up to 1,000 km/625 mi away.

Tunis capital and chief port of Tunisia; population (1984) 597,000. Industries include chemicals and textiles. Founded by the Arabs, it was captured by the Turks in 1533, then occupied by the French 1881 and by the Axis powers 1942–43. The ruins of ancient *Carthage are to the northeast.

Tunisia Tunisian Republic (*al-Jumhuriya at-Tunisiya*)

area 164,150 sq km/63,378 sq mi
capital and chief port Tunis
towns ports Sfax, Sousse, Bizerta
physical arable and forested land in N graduates towards desert in S
head of state Zine el-Abidine Ben Ali from 1987
head of government Hamed Karoui from 1989
political system emergent democratic republic
exports oil, phosphates, chemicals, textiles, food, olive oil
currency dinar
population (1993 est) 8,600,000; growth rate 2% p.a.
languages Arabic (official), French
religions Sunni Muslim 95%; Jewish, Christian
GNP $1,450 per head (1991)
chronology
1883 Became a French protectorate.
1955 Granted internal self-government.
1956 Independence achieved from France as a monarchy, with Habib Bourguiba as prime minister.
1957 Became a republic with Bourguiba as president.
1975 Bourguiba made president for life.
1987 Bourguiba appointed Zine el-Abidine Ben Ali as prime minister. Ben Ali seized power.
1988 Constitutional changes announced.
1989 Government party, RCD, won all assembly seats in general election.
1991 Crackdown on religious fundamentalists.

1992 Western criticism of human rights transgressions.
1994 Ben Ali and RCD re-elected.

Tunja capital city of Boyacá department, central Colombia, on the Pan-American Highway; population (1985) 93,800.

turbine engine in which steam, water, gas, or air (see *windmill) is made to spin a rotating shaft by pushing on angled blades, like a fan. Turbines are among the most powerful machines. Steam turbines are used to drive generators in power stations and ships' propellers; water turbines spin the generators in hydroelectric power plants; and gas turbines (as jet engines; see *jet propulsion) power most aircraft and drive machines in industry.

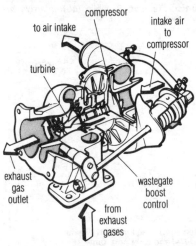

turbocharger *The turbocharger increases the power of a car engine by forcing compressed air into the engine cylinders.*

turbocharger turbine-driven device fitted to engines to force more air into the cylinders, producing extra power. The turbocharger consists of a 'blower', or compressor, driven by a turbine, which in most units is driven by the exhaust gases leaving the engine.

turbofan jet engine of the type used by most airliners, so called because of its huge front fan. The fan sends air not only into the engine for combustion but also around the engine for additional thrust. This results in a faster and more fuel-efficient propulsive jet (see *jet propulsion).

turbojet jet engine that derives its thrust from a jet of hot exhaust gases. Pure turbojets can be very powerful but use a lot of fuel.

turboprop jet engine that derives its thrust partly from a jet of exhaust gases, but mainly from a propeller powered by a turbine in the jet exhaust. Turboprops are more economical than turbojets but can be used only at relatively low speeds.

turbot any of various flatfishes of the flounder group prized as food, especially *Scophthalmus maximus* found in European waters. It grows up to 1 m/3 ft long and weighs up to 14 kg/30 lb. It is brownish above and whitish underneath.

Turgenev Ivan Sergeievich 1818–1883. Russia writer, notable for poetic realism, pessimism, an skill in characterization. His works include th play *A Month in the Country* 1849, and the novels *A Nest of Gentlefolk* 1858, *Fathers an Sons* 1862, and *Virgin Soil* 1877. His series *Sportsman's Sketches* 1852 criticized serfdom.

Turin (Italian **Torino**) capital of Piedmont, N Italy, on the river Po; population (198 1,025,000. Industries include iron, steel, cars, si and other textiles, fashion goods, chocolate, an wine. It was the first capital of united Ita 1861–64.

Turing Alan Mathison 1912–1954. Englis mathematician and logician. In 1936 h described a 'universal computing machine' th could theoretically be programmed to solve an problem capable of solution by a special designed machine. This concept, now called th **Turing machine**, foreshadowed the digit computer.

Turin shroud ancient piece of linen bearing th image of a body, claimed to be that of Jesu Independent tests carried out 1988 by scientis in Switzerland, the USA, and the UK showe that the cloth of the shroud dated from betwee 1260 and 1390. The shroud, property of the pop is kept in Turin Cathedral, Italy.

Turk member of any of the Turkic-speakir peoples of Asia and Europe, especially the princ pal ethnic group of Turkey. Turkic language belong to the Altaic family and include Uzbe Ottoman, Turkish, Azerbaijani, Turkoman, Tata Kirghiz, and Yakut.

Turkana, Lake formerly (to 1979) **Lake Rudo** lake in the Great Rift Valley, 375 m/1,230 above sea level, with its northernmost end Ethiopia and the rest in Kenya; area 9,000 sq km 3,475 sq mi. It is saline, and shrinking by evapo ation. Its shores were an early human huntir ground, and valuable remains have been foun that are accurately datable because of und turbed stratification.

Turkestan area of central Asia divided amor Kazakhstan, Kyrgyzstan, Tajikistan, Turkmeni tan, Uzbekistan, Afghanistan, and China (part Xinjiang Uygur).

turkey any of several large game birds of tl pheasant family, native to the Americas. The wi turkey *Meleagris galloparvo* reaches a length 1.3 m/4.3 ft, and is native to North and Centr American woodlands. The domesticated turk derives from the wild species. The ocellate turkey *Agriocharis ocellata* is found in Centr America; it has eyespots on the tail.

Turkey Republic of (*Türkiye Cumhuriyeti*)
area 779,500 sq km/300,965 sq mi
capital Ankara
towns ports Istanbul and Izmir
physical central plateau surrounded mountains
head of state Suleyman Demirel from 1993
head of government Tansu Ciller from 199?
political system democratic republic
exports cotton, yarn, hazelnuts, citrus, tobacc dried fruit, chromium ores
currency Turkish lira

population (1993) 58,870,000 (Turkish 85%, Kurdish 12%); growth rate 2.1% p.a.
languages Turkish (official), Kurdish, Arabic
religion Sunni Muslim 98%
GNP $1,820 per head (1991)
chronology
1919–22 Turkish War of Independence provoked by Greek occupation of Izmir. Mustafa Kemal (Atatürk), leader of nationalist congress, defeated Italian, French, and Greek forces.
1923 Treaty of Lausanne established Turkey as independent republic under Kemal. Westernization began.
1950 First free elections; Adnan Menderes became prime minister.
1960 Menderes executed after military coup by General Cemal Gürsel.
1965 Suleyman Demirel became prime minister.
1971 Army forced Demirel to resign.
1973 Civilian rule returned under Bulent Ecevit.
1974 Turkish troops sent to protect Turkish community in Cyprus.
1975 Demirel returned to head of a right-wing coalition.
1978 Ecevit returned, as head of coalition, in the face of economic difficulties and factional violence.
1979 Demeril returned. Violence grew.
1980 Army took over, and Bulent Ulusu became prime minister. Harsh repression of political activists attracted international criticism.
1982 New constitution adopted.
1983 Ban on political activity lifted. Turgut Özal became prime minister.
1987 Özal maintained majority in general election.
1988 Improved relations and talks with Greece.
1989 Turgut Özal elected president; Yildirim Akbulut became prime minister. Application to join European Community (EC) rejected.
1991 Mesut Yilmaz became prime minister. Turkey sided with UN coalition against Iraq in Gulf War. Conflict with Kurdish minority continued. Coalition government formed under Suleyman Demirel after inconclusive election result.
1992 Earthquake claimed thousands of lives.
1993 Özal died and was succeeded by Demirel. Tansu Ciller became prime minister. Kurdish separatist activity escalated, with attacks on Turkish premises in European cities.

turkish bath bathing that involves exposure to warm air and steam, followed by massage and cold-water immersion. Originating from Roman and East Indian traditions, the concept was introduced to Western Europe by the Crusaders but only became popular when hot water could be supplied in sufficient quantities.

Turkish language language of central and W Asia, the national language of Turkey. It belongs to the Altaic language family. Varieties of Turkish are spoken in NW Iran and several of the Central Asian Republics, and all have been influenced by Arabic and Persian. Originally written in Arabic script, it has been written within Turkey in a variant of the Roman alphabet since 1928.

Turkmenistan Republic of

area 488,100 sq km/188,406 sq mi
capital Ashgabat
towns Chardzhov, Mary (Merv), Nebit-Dag, Krasnovodsk
physical some 90% of land is desert including the Kara Kum 'Black Sands' desert (area 310,800 sq km/120,000 sq mi)
head of state Saparmurad Niyazov from 1991
head of government Sakhat Muradov from 1992
political system socialist pluralist
products silk, karakul, sheep, astrakhan fur, carpets, chemicals, rich deposits of petroleum, natural gas, sulphur, and other industrial raw materials
currency manat
population (1993) 4,000,000 (Turkmen 72%, Russian 10%, Uzbek 9%, Kazakh 3%, Ukrainian 1%)
language West Turkic, closely related to Turkish
religion Sunni Muslim
GNP $1,700 per head (1991)
chronology
1921 Part of Turkestan Soviet Socialist Autonomous Republic.
1925 Became a constituent republic of USSR.
1990 Economic and political sovereignty declared.
1991 Jan: After supreme soviet elections, Communist Party leader Niyazov became state president. March: endorsed maintenance of the Union in USSR referendum. Aug: President Niyazov

initially supported anti-Gorbachev attempted Moscow coup; democratic activists arrested. Oct: independence declared after overwhelming approval in referendum. Dec: joined new Commonwealth of Independent States; independence acknowledged by USA but diplomatic recognition withheld.

1992 March: admitted into United Nations; US diplomatic recognition achieved. Nov-Dec: parliament popularly elected with Sakhat Muradov as prime minister.

Turkoman or *Turkman* member of the majority ethnic group in Turkmenistan. They live to the E of the Caspian Sea, around the Kara Kum desert, and along the borders of Afghanistan and Iran. Traditionally the Turkomen were tent-dwelling pastoral nomads, though the majority are now sedentary farmers. Their language belongs to the Turkic branch of the Altaic family. They are predominantly Sunni Muslims.

Turks and Caicos Islands British crown colony in the West Indies, the SE archipelago of the Bahamas
area 430 sq km/166 sq mi
capital Cockburn Town on Grand Turk
features a group of some 30 islands, of which six are inhabited. Since 1982 the Turks and Caicos have developed as a tax haven
government governor, with executive and legislative councils (chief minister from 1987, Michael John Bradley, Progressive National Party)
exports crayfish and conch (flesh and shell)
currency US dollar
population (1980) 7,500, 90% of African descent
languages English, French Creole
religion Christian
history secured by Britain 1766 against French and Spanish claims, the islands were a Jamaican dependency 1873–1962, and in 1976 attained internal self-government.

Turku (Swedish *Aåbo*) port in SW Finland, near the mouth of the river Aura, on the Gulf of Bothnia; population (1990) 159,200. Industries include shipbuilding, engineering, textiles, and food processing. It was the capital of Finland until 1812.

turmeric perennial plant *Curcuma longa* of the ginger family, native to India and the East Indies; also the ground powder from its tuberous rhizomes, used in curries to give a yellow colour, and as a dyestuff.

Turner Joseph Mallord William 1775–1851. English landscape painter. He travelled widely in Europe, and his landscapes became increasingly Romantic, with the subject often transformed in scale and flooded with brilliant, hazy light. Many later works anticipate Impressionism; for example, *Rain, Steam and Speed* 1844 (National Gallery, London).

turnip biennial plant *Brassica rapa* cultivated in temperate regions for its edible white-or yellow-fleshed root and the young leaves, which are used as a green vegetable. Closely allied to it is the *swede Brassica napus*.

turnstone any of a genus *Arenaria* of small wading shorebirds, especially the ruddy turnstone *A. interpres*, which breeds in the Arctic and migrates to the southern hemisphere. It is

seen on rocky beaches, turning over stones for small crustaceans and insects.

turpentine solution of resins distilled from the sap of conifers, used in varnish and as a paint solvent but now largely replaced by *white spirit

Turpin Dick 1706–1739. English highwayman. The son of an innkeeper, he turned to highway robbery, cattle-thieving, and smuggling, and was hanged at York.

turquoise mineral, hydrous basic copper aluminium phosphate. Blue-green, blue, or green, i is a gemstone. Turquoise is found in Iran, Turkestan, Mexico, and southwestern USA.

turtle *The common musk turtle lives in the shallow, muddy streams of the USA.*

turtle freshwater or marine reptile whose body is protected by a shell. Turtles are related to tortoises, and some species can grow to a length of up to 2.5 m/8 ft. Turtles often travel long distances to lay their eggs on the beaches where they were born, and many species have suffered through destruction of their breeding sites as well as being hunted for food and their shell.

Tuscany (Italian *Toscana*) region of central Italy; area 23,000 sq km/8,878 sq mi; population (1990) 3,562,500. Its capital is Florence, and towns include Pisa, Livorno, and Siena. The area is mainly agricultural, with many vineyards, such as in the Chianti hills; it also has lignite and iron mines and marble quarries. The Tuscan dialect has been adopted as the standard form of Italian. Tuscany was formerly the Roman *Etruria*, and inhabited by Etruscans around 500 BC. In medieval times the area was divided into small states united under Florentine rule during the 15th–16th centuries. It became part of united Italy 1861.

Tussaud Madame (Anne Marie Grosholtz) 1761–1850. French wax-modeller. In 1802 she established an exhibition of wax models of celebrities in London. It was destroyed by fire 1925 but reopened 1928. Born in Strasbourg, she went to Paris 1766 to live with her wax-modeller uncle Philippe Curtius, whom she soon surpassed in technique. During the French Revolution they were forced to take death masks of many victims and leaders (some still exist in the Chamber of Horrors).

Tutankhamen king of Egypt of the 18th dynasty, about 1360–1350 BC. A son of Ikhnaton (also called Amenhotep IV), he was about 11 at his accession. In 1922 his tomb was discovered by the British archaeologists Lord Carnarvon and Howard Carter in the Valley of the Kings at Luxor, almost untouched by tomb robbers. The contents included many works of art and hi olid-gold coffin, which are now displayed in a Cairo museum.

Tutsi member of a minority ethnic group living n Rwanda and Burundi. Although fewer in number, they have traditionally been politically dominant over the Hutu majority and the Twa or Pygmies). The Tutsi are traditionally farmers; hey also hold virtually all positions of importance in Burundi's government and army. They have carried out massacres in response to Hutu rebellions, notably in 1972 and 1988. In Rwanda he balance of power is more even.

Tutu Desmond (Mpilo) 1931– . South African priest, Anglican archbishop of Cape Town and general secretary of the South African Council of Churches 1979–84. One of the leading figures in he struggle against apartheid in the Republic of South Africa, he was awarded the 1984 Nobel Prize for Peace.

Tuva (Russian **Tuvinskaya**) autonomous republic (administrative unit) of Russia, northwest of Mongolia
capital Kyzyl
area 170,500 sq km/65,813 sq mi
population (1986) 284,000
history part of Mongolia until 1911 and declared a Russian protectorate 1914; after the 1917 revolution it became the independent Tannu-Tuva republic 1920, until incorporated in he USSR as an autonomous region 1944. It was made the Tuva Autonomous Republic 1961.

Tuvalu South West Pacific State of (formerly **Ellice Islands**)
area 25 sq km/9.5 sq mi
capital Funafuti
physical nine low coral atolls forming a chain of 579 km/650 mi in the SW Pacific
head of state Elizabeth II from 1978 represented by governor general
head of government Kamuta Laafasi from 1993
political system liberal democracy
exports copra, handicrafts, stamps
currency Australian dollar
population (1993 est) 10,000 (Polynesian 96%); growth rate 3.4% p.a.
languages Tuvaluan, English
religion Christian (Protestant)
GDP (1983) $711 per head
chronology
1892 Became a British protectorate forming part of the Gilbert and Ellice Islands group.
1916 The islands acquired colonial status.
1975 The Ellice Islands were separated from the Gilbert Islands.
1978 Independence achieved from Britain within the Commonwealth with Toaripi Lauti as prime minister.
1981 Dr Tomasi Puapua replaced Lauti as premier.
1986 Islanders rejected proposal for republican status.
1989 Bikenibeu Paeniu elected new prime minister.

TVP (abbreviation for **texturized vegetable protein**) meat substitute usually made from soya beans. In manufacture, the soya-bean solids what remains after oil has been removed) are ground finely and mixed with a binder to form a sticky mixture. This is forced through a spinneret

and extruded into fibres, which are treated with salts and flavourings, wound into hanks, and then chopped up to resemble meat chunks.

Twain Mark. Pen name of Samuel Langhorne Clemens 1835–1910. US writer. He established his reputation with the comic masterpiece *The Innocents Abroad* 1869 and two classic American novels, in dialect, *The Adventures of Tom Sawyer* 1876 and *The Adventures of Huckleberry Finn* 1885. He also wrote satire, as in *A Connecticut Yankee at King Arthur's Court* 1889.

tweed cloth made of woollen yarn, usually of several shades, but in its original form without a regular pattern and woven on a hand loom in the more remote parts of Ireland, Wales, and Scotland.

Twelfth Day the 12th and final day of the Christmas celebrations, 6 Jan; the feast of the *Epiphany.

Twelver member of a Shi'ite Muslim sect who believes that the 12th imam (Islamic leader) did not die, but is waiting to return towards the end of the world as the Mahdi, the 'rightly guided one', to establish a reign of peace and justice on Earth.

twelve-tone system or **twelve-note system** system of musical composition in which the 12 notes of the chromatic scale are arranged in a particular order, called a 'series' or 'tone-row'. A work using the system consists of restatements of the series in any of its formations. Arnold *Schoenberg and Anton *Webern were exponents of this technique.

twin one of two young produced from a single pregnancy. Human twins may be genetically identical, having been formed from a single fertilized egg that split into two cells, both of which became implanted. Nonidentical twins are formed when two eggs are fertilized at the same time.

twitch alternative common name for *couch grass.

two-stroke cycle operating cycle for internal combustion piston engines. The engine cycle is completed after just two strokes (movement up or down) of the piston, which distinguishes it from the more common *four-stroke cycle. Power mowers and lightweight motorcycles use two-stroke petrol engines, which are cheaper and simpler than four-strokes.

Tyler Wat died 1381. English leader of the *Peasants' Revolt of 1381. He was probably born in Kent or Essex, and may have served in the French wars. After taking Canterbury he led the peasant army to Blackheath and occupied London. At Mile End King Richard II met the rebels and promised to redress their grievances, which included the imposition of a poll tax. At a further conference at Smithfield, Tyler was murdered.

Tyndale William 1492–1536. English translator of the Bible. The printing of his New Testament (the basis of the Authorized Version) was begun in Cologne 1525 and, after he had been forced to flee, completed in Worms. He was strangled and burned as a heretic at Vilvorde in Belgium.

Tyndall John 1820–1893. Irish physicist who 1869 studied the scattering of light by invisibly small suspended particles. Known as the **Tyndall**

effect, it was first observed with colloidal solutions, in which a beam of light is made visible when it is scattered by minute colloidal particles (whereas a pure solvent does not scatter light). Similar scattering of blue wavelengths of sunlight by particles in the atmosphere makes the sky look blue (beyond the atmosphere, the sky is black).

Tyne and Wear metropolitan county in NE England, created 1974, originally administered by an elected metropolitan council; its powers reverted to district councils 1986
area 540 sq km/208 sq mi
towns Newcastle-upon-Tyne (administrative headquarters), South Shields, Gateshead, Sunderland
products once a centre of heavy industry, it is now being redeveloped and diversified
population (1991) 1,087,000
famous people Thomas Bewick, Robert Stephenson, Harry Patterson ('Jack Higgins')

Tynwald parliament of the *Isle of Man.

typesetting means by which text, or copy, is prepared for *printing, now usually carried out by computer. Text is keyed on a typesetting machine in a similar way to typing. Laser or light impulses are projected on to light-sensitive film that, when developed, can be used to make plates for printing.

typewriter keyboard machine that produces characters on paper. The earliest known typewriter design was patented by Henry Mills in England 1714. However, the first practical typewriter was built 1867 in Milwaukee, Wisconsin, USA, by Christopher Sholes, Carlos Glidden, and Samuel Soulé. By 1873 *Remington and Sons, US gunmakers, produced under contract the first machines for sale and 1878 patented the first with lower-case as well as upper-case (capital) letters.

typhoid fever acute infectious disease of the digestive tract, caused by the bacterium *Salmonella typhi*, and usually contracted through a contaminated water supply. It is characterized by bowel haemorrhage and damage to the spleen. Treatment is with antibiotics.

typhoon violently revolving storm, a *hurricane in the W Pacific Ocean.

typhus acute infectious disease, often fatal, caused by bacteria transmitted by lice, fleas, mites, and ticks. Symptoms include fever, headache, and rash. Typhus is epidemic among people living in overcrowded conditions. Treatment is by antibiotics.

typography design and layout of the printed word. Typography began with the invention of

writing and developed as printing spread throughout Europe after the invention of metal moveable type by Johann *Gutenberg about 1440. Hundreds of variations have followed since, but the basic design of the Frenchman Nicholas Jensen (about 1420–80), with a few modifications, is still the ordinary ('roman') type used in printing.

Tyr in Norse mythology, the god of battles, whom the Anglo-Saxons called Týw, hence 'Tuesday'.

tyrannosaurus any of a genus *Tyrannosaurus* of gigantic flesh-eating *dinosaurs, order Saurischia, which lived in North America and Asia about 70 million years ago. They had two feet, were up to 15 m/50 ft long, 6.5 m/20 ft tall, weighed 10 tonnes, and had teeth 15 cm/6 in long.

Tyre (Arabic *Sur* or *Soûr*) town in SW Lebanon about 80 km/50 mi S of Beirut, formerly a port until its harbour silted up; population (1980 est) about 14,000. It stands on the site of the ancient city of the same name, a seaport of *Phoenicia.

tyre (North American **tire**) inflatable rubber hoop fitted round the rims of bicycle, car, and other road-vehicle wheels. The first pneumatic rubber tyre was patented in 1845 by the Scottish engineer Robert William Thomson (1822–73) but it was John Boyd Dunlop of Belfast who independently reinvented pneumatic tyres for use with bicycles 1888–89. The rubber for car tyres is hardened by *vulcanization.

Tyrone county of Northern Ireland
area 3,160 sq km/1,220 sq mi
towns Omagh (county town), Dungannon, Strabane, Cookstown
products mainly agricultural
population (1981) 144,000.

Tyrrhenian Sea arm of the Mediterranean sea, surrounded by mainland Italy, Sicily, Sardinia, Corsica, and the Ligurian Sea. It is connected to the Ionian Sea through the Straits of Messina. Islands include Elba, Ustica, Capri, Stromboli, and the Lipari Islands.

Tyson Mike (Michael Gerald) 1966– . US heavyweight boxer, undisputed world champion from Aug 1987 to Feb 1990. He won the World Boxing Council heavyweight title 1986 when he beat Trevor Berbick to become the youngest world heavyweight champion. He beat James 'Bonecrusher' Smith for the World Boxing Association title 1987 and later that year became the first undisputed champion since 1978 when he beat Tony Tucker for the International Boxing Federation title.

Tzu-Hsi alternative transliteration of *Zi Xi, dowager empress of China.

U

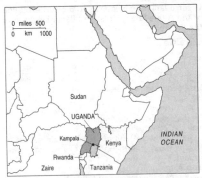

U-2 US military reconnaissance aeroplane, used in secret flights over the USSR from 1956 to photograph military installations. In 1960 a U-2 was shot down over the USSR and the pilot, Gary Powers, was captured and imprisoned. He was exchanged for a US-held Soviet agent two years later.

U2 Irish rock group formed 1977 by singer Bono Vox (born Paul Hewson, 1960–), guitarist Dave The Edge' Evans (1961–), bassist Adam Clayton (1960–), and drummer Larry Mullen (1961–). The band's albums include *The Unforgettable Fire* 1984, *The Joshua Tree* 1987, and *Zooropa* 1993.

Ubangi-Shari former name for the *Central African Republic.

Uccello Paolo. Adopted name of Paolo di Dono 1397–1475. Italian painter. Active in Florence, he was one of the first to experiment with perspective. His surviving paintings date from the 1430s onwards. Decorative colour and detail dominate his later pictures. His works include *St George and the Dragon* c.1460 (National Gallery, London).

Udmurt (Russian *Udmurtskaya*) autonomous republic in the W Ural foothills, central Russia
area 42,100 sq km/16,200 sq mi
capital Izhevsk
products timber, flax, potatoes, peat, quartz
population (1985) 1,559,000 (58% Russian, 33% Udmurt, 7% Tatar)
history conquered in the 15th–16th centuries; constituted the Votyak Autonomous Region 1920; name changed to Udmurt 1932; Autonomous Republic 1934; part of the independent republic of Russia from 1991.

Uganda Republic of
area 236,600 sq km/91,351 sq mi
capital Kampala
towns Jinja, M'Bale, Entebbe, Masaka
physical plateau with mountains in W; forest and grassland; arid in NE
head of state Kabuka Ronald Muwonda Mutebi from 1993
head of government Yoweri Museveni from 1986
political system emergent democratic republic
exports coffee, cotton, tea, copper
currency Uganda new shilling
population (1993) 19,000,000 (largely the Baganda, after whom the country is named; also Langi and Acholi, some surviving Pygmies); growth rate 3.3% p.a.

languages English (official), Kiswahili, Luganda, and other African languages
religions Roman Catholic 33%, Protestant 33%, Muslim 16%, animist
GNP $170 per head (1990)
chronology
1962 Independence achieved from Britain, within the Commonwealth, with Milton Obote as prime minister.
1963 Proclaimed a federal republic with King Mutesa II as president.
1966 King Mutesa ousted in coup led by Obote, who ended the federal status and became executive president.
1969 All opposition parties banned after assassination attempt on Obote.
1971 Obote overthrown in army coup led by Maj-Gen Idi Amin Dada; ruthlessly dictatorial regime established; nearly 49,000 Ugandan Asians expelled; over 300,000 opponents of regime killed.
1978 Amin forced to leave country by opponents backed by Tanzanian troops. Provisional government set up with Yusuf Lule as president. Lule replaced by Godfrey Binaisa.
1978–79 Fighting broke out against Tanzanian troops.
1980 Binaisa overthrown by army. Elections held and Milton Obote returned to power.
1985 After opposition by National Resistance Army (NRA), and indiscipline in army, Obote ousted by Brig Tito Okello; power-sharing agreement entered into with NRA leader Yoweri Museveni.
1986 Agreement ended; Museveni became president, heading broad-based coalition government.
1992 Announcement made that East African cooperation pact with Kenya and Tanzania would be revived.
1993 King of Baganda reinstated as formal monarch, in the person of Ronald Muwenda Mutebi II.
1994 Museveni won first general election in 14 years.

UHF (abbreviation for *ultra high frequency*) referring to radio waves of very short wavelength, used, for example, for television broadcasting.

UHT abbreviation for *ultra-heat treated* or *ultraheat treatment.

Uigur member of a Turkic people living in NW China and Kazakhstan; they form about 80% of the population of the Chinese province of Xinjiang Uygur. There are about 5 million speakers of

Uigur, a language belonging to the Turkic branch of the Altaic family; it is the official language of the province.

Ukraine

area 603,700 sq km/233,089 sq mi
capital Kiev
towns Kharkov, Donetsk, Odessa, Dneprope-trovsk, Lugansk (Voroshilovgrad), Lviv (Lvov), Mariupol (Zhdanov), Krivoi Rog, Zaporozhye
physical Russian plain; Carpathian and Crimean Mountains; rivers: Dnieper (with the Dnieper dam 1932), Donetz, Bug
head of state Leonid Kuchma from 1994
head of government Vitaly Masol from 1994
political system emergent democracy
products grain, coal, oil, various minerals
currency grivna
population (1993 est) 52,000,000 (Ukrainian 73%, Russian 22%, Byelorussian 1%, Russian-speaking Jews 1% – some 1.5 million have emigrated to the USA, 750,000 to Canada)
language Ukrainian (Slavonic)
religions traditionally Ukrainian Orthodox; also Ukrainian Catholic
GNP $2,340 per head (1991)
chronology
1918 Independent People's Republic proclaimed.
1920 Conquered by Soviet Red Army.
1921 Poland allotted charge of W Ukraine.
1932–33 Famine caused the deaths of more than 7.5 million people.
1941–44 Under Nazi control; Jews massacred at Babi Yar; more than 5 million Ukrainians and Ukrainian Jews deported and exterminated.
1944 Soviet control re-established.
1945 Became a founder member of the United Nations.
1946 Ukrainian Uniate Church proscribed and forcibly merged with Russian Orthodox Church.
1986 April: Chernobyl nuclear disaster.
1989 Rukh established as a political party.
1990 July: voted to proclaim sovereignty; former Communist Party (CP) leader Leonid Kravchuk indirectly elected president; sovereignty declared.
1991 Aug: demonstrations during the abortive anti-Gorbachev coup; independence declared, pending referendum; CP activities suspended. Oct: voted to create independent army. Dec: Kravchuk popularly elected president; independence endorsed in referendum; joined new Com-monwealth of Independent States; independenc acknowledged by USA and European Con munity.
1992 Jan: prices freed. Feb: prices 'temporaril' re-regulated. May: Crimean sovereignty declare then rescinded. Aug: joint control of Black Se fleet agreed with Russia.
1993 July: agreement to dismantle nuclea arsenal with US funding. Sept: President Krav chuk took direct rule, eliminating post of prim minister. Nov: START-1 nuclear arms reductio treaty ratified.
1994 April: election gains for radical nationalis in W and Russian unionists in E and Crime July: former premier Leonid Kuchma elect president. Oct: large-scale privatization an decentralization programme announced.

ukulele small four-stringed Hawaiian guitar, Portuguese origin; it is easy to play. Music f ukelele is written in a form of *tablature showin finger positions on a chart of the fingerboard.

Ulaanbaatar or **Ulan Bator**; formerly (un 1924) **Urga** capital of the Mongolian Republic; trading centre producing carpets, textiles, vodk population (1991) 575,000.

ulcer any persistent breach in a body surfac (skin or mucous membrane). It may be cause by infection, irritation, or tumour and is ofte inflamed. Common ulcers include aphtho (mouth), gastric (stomach), duodenal, an decubitus ulcers (pressure sores), and those cor plicating varicose veins.

ulna one of the two bones found in the low limb of the tetrapod (four-limbed) vertebrate. articulates with the shorter radius and humer (upper arm bone) at one end and with the radi and wrist bones at the other.

Ulster former kingdom in Northern Irelan annexed by England 1461, from Jacobean tim a centre of English, and later Scottish, settleme on land confiscated from its owners; divide 1921 into Northern Ireland (counties Antrii Armagh, Down, Fermanagh, Londonderry, an Tyrone) and the Republic of Ireland (counti Cavan, Donegal, and Monaghan).

Ulster Defence Association (UD, Northern Ireland Protestant paramilitary orga ization responsible for a number of sectarian kil ings. Fanatically loyalist, it established paramilitary (the Ulster Freedom Fighters) combat the *IRA on its own terms and by own methods. No political party has acknow edged any links with the UDA. In 1994, followin a cessation of military activities by the IRA, th UDA, along with other Protestant paramilita organizations, declared a cease-fire.

ultrasound pressure waves similar in nature sound waves but occurring at frequencies abo 20,000 Hz (cycles per second), the approxima upper limit of human hearing (15–16 Hz is t lower limit). Ultrasonics is concerned with th study and practical application of the phenomena.

ultrasound scanning or **ultrasonograph** in medicine, the use of ultrasonic pressure wav to create a diagnostic image. It is a safe, noni vasive technique that often eliminates the nee for exploratory surgery.

ultraviolet astronomy study of cosmic ultr

violet emissions using artificial satellites. The USA has launched a series of satellites for this purpose, receiving the first useful data 1968. Only a tiny percentage of solar ultraviolet radiation penetrates the atmosphere, this being the less dangerous longer-wavelength ultraviolet. The dangerous shorter-wavelength radiation is absorbed by gases in the ozone layer high in the Earth's upper atmosphere.

ultraviolet radiation electromagnetic radiation invisible to the human eye, of wavelengths from about 4×10^{-7} to 5×10^{-9} metres (where the *X-ray range begins). Physiologically, ultraviolet radiation is extremely powerful, producing sunburn and causing the formation of vitamin D in the skin.

Ulysses Roman name for *Odysseus, Greek mythological hero.

Ulysses space probe to study the Sun's poles, launched 1990 by a US space shuttle. It is a joint project by NASA and the European Space Agency. The gravity of Jupiter will swing *Ulysses* on to a path that loops it first under the Sun's south pole and then over the north pole to study the Sun and solar wind at latitudes not observable from the Earth.

Umar second caliph (head) of Islam, a strong disciplinarian. Under his rule Islam spread to Egypt and Persia. He was assassinated in Medina.

Umayyad alternative spelling of *Omayyad dynasty.

Umberto I 1844–1900. King of Italy from 1878, who joined the Triple Alliance 1882 with Germany and Austria-Hungary; his colonial ventures included the defeat at Aduwa, Abyssinia, 1896. He was assassinated by an anarchist.

Umberto II 1904–1983. Last king of Italy 1946. On the abdication of his father, Victor Emmanuel III, he ruled 9 May–13 June 1946, when he had to abdicate since a referendum established a republic. He retired to Portugal.

umbilical cord connection between the *embryo and the *placenta of placental mammals. It has one vein and two arteries, transporting oxygen and nutrients to the developing young, and removing waste products. At birth, the connection between the young and the placenta is no longer necessary. The umbilical cord drops off or is severed, leaving a scar called the navel.

umbrella bird bird of tropical South and Central America, family Contingidae. The Amazonian species *Cephalopterus ornatus* has an inflatable wattle at the neck to amplify its humming call, and in display elevates a long crest (12 cm/4 in) lying above the bill so that it rises umbrellalike above the head. These features are less noticeable in the female, which is brownish, whereas the male is blue-black.

Umm al Qaiwain one of the *United Arab Emirates.

Umtata capital of the South African Bantu homeland of Transkei; population (1976) 25,000.

UN abbreviation for the *_United Nations_.

uncertainty principle or *indeterminacy principle* in quantum mechanics, the principle that it is meaningless to speak of a particle's position, momentum, or other parameters, except as results of measurements; measuring, however, involves an interaction (such as a *photon of light bouncing off the particle under scrutiny), which must disturb the particle, though the disturbance is noticeable only at an atomic scale. The principle implies that one cannot, even in theory, predict the moment-to-moment behaviour of such a system.

Uncle Sam nickname for the US government. It was coined during the War of 1812 by opponents of US policy. It was probably derived from the initials 'US' placed on government property.

unconformity in geology, a break in the sequence of *sedimentary rocks. It is usually seen as an eroded surface, with the *beds above and below lying at different angles. An unconformity represents an ancient land surface, where exposed rocks were worn down by erosion and later covered in a renewed cycle of deposition.

unconscious in psychoanalysis, part of the personality of which the individual is unaware, and which contains impulses or urges that are held back, or repressed, from conscious awareness.

underground (North American **subway**) rail service that runs underground. The first underground line in the world was in London, opened 1863; it was essentially a roofed-in trench. The London Underground is still the longest, with over 400 km/250 mi of routes. Many large cities throughout the world have similar systems, and Moscow's underground, the Metro, handles up to 6.5 million passengers a day.

Underground Railroad in US history, a network established in the North before the *American Civil War to provide sanctuary and assistance for escaped black slaves. Safe houses, transport facilities, and 'conductors' existed to lead the slaves to safety in the North and Canada, although the number of fugitives who secured their freedom by these means may have been exaggerated.

Underwood Rory 1963– . English rugby union player who made his international debut 1984, and became the first English player to reach 50 international appearances. He helped England to win Grand Slams in 1991, 1992 and 1995.

unemployment lack of paid employment. The unemployed are usually defined as those out of work who are available for and actively seeking work. Unemployment is measured either as a total or as a percentage of those who are available for work, known as the working population or labour force. Periods of widespread unemployment in Europe and the USA in the 20th century include 1929–1930s, and the years since the mid-1970s.

UNESCO (acronym for *United Nations Educational, Scientific, and Cultural Organization*) agency of the UN, established 1946, with its headquarters in Paris. The USA, contributor of 25% of its budget, withdrew 1984 on grounds of its 'overpoliticization and mismanagement', and Britain followed 1985.

unfair dismissal sacking of an employee unfairly. Under the terms of the UK Employment Acts, this means the unreasonable dismissal of someone who has been in continuous employment for a period of two years; that is, dismissal on grounds not in accordance with the codes of disciplinary practice and procedures prepared by *ACAS. Dismissed employees may take their case to an industrial tribunal for adjudication.

Ungaretti Giuseppe 1888–1970. Italian poet who lived in France and Brazil. His lyrics show a cosmopolitan independence from Italian poetic tradition. His poems, such as the *Allegria di naufragi/Joy of Shipwrecks* 1919, are of great simplicity.

ungulate general name for any hoofed mammal. Included are the odd-toed ungulates (perissodactyls) and the even-toed ungulates (artiodactyls), along with subungulates such as elephants.

Uniate Church any of the *Orthodox churches that accept the Catholic faith and the supremacy of the pope, and are in full communion with the Roman Catholic Church, but retain their own liturgy and separate organization.

UNICEF acronym for *United Nations International Children's Emergency Fund*.

unicellular organism animal or plant consisting of a single cell. Most are invisible without a microscope but a few, such as the giant *amoeba, may be visible to the naked eye. The main groups of unicellular organisms are bacteria, protozoa, unicellular algae, and unicellular fungi or yeasts.

unicorn mythical animal referred to by Classical writers, said to live in India and resembling a horse, but with one spiralled horn growing from the forehead.

unidentified flying object or *UFO* any light or object seen in the sky whose immediate identity is not apparent. Despite unsubstantiated claims, there is no evidence that UFOs are alien spacecraft. On investigation, the vast majority of sightings turn out to have been of natural or identifiable objects, notably bright stars and planets, meteors, aircraft, and satellites, or to have been perpetrated by pranksters. The term *flying saucer* was coined in 1947 and has been in use since.

Unification Church or *Moonies* church founded in Korea 1954 by the Reverend Sun Myung *Moon. The number of members (often called 'moonies') is about 200,000 worldwide. The theology unites Christian and Taoist ideas and is based on Moon's book *Divine Principle*, which teaches that the original purpose of creation was to set up a perfect family, in a perfect relationship with God.

unified field theory in physics, the theory that attempts to explain the four fundamental forces (strong nuclear, weak nuclear, electromagnetic, and gravity) in terms of a single unified force (see *particle physics).

uniformitarianism in geology, the principle that processes that can be seen to occur on the Earth's surface today are the same as those that have occurred throughout geological time. For example, desert sandstones containing sand-dune structures must have been formed under conditions similar to those present in deserts today. The principle was formulated by James *Hutton and expounded by Charles *Lyell.

unilateralism in politics, support for *unilateral nuclear disarmament*: scrapping a country's nuclear weapons without waiting for other countries to agree to do so at the same time.

Unilateral Declaration of Independence (UDI) unnegotiated severing of relations with a colonial power; especially, the declaration made by Ian Smith's Rhodesian Front government 11 Nov 1965, announcing the independence of Rhodesia (now Zimbabwe) from Britain.

Union, Act of 1707 Act of Parliament that brought about the union of England and Scotland; that of 1801 united England and Ireland. The latter was revoked when the Irish Free State was constituted 1922.

Union Movement British political group. Founded as the *New Party* by Oswald *Mosley and a number of Labour members of Parliament 1931, it developed into the *British Union of Fascists* 1932. In 1940 the organization was declared illegal and its leaders interned, but it was revived as the Union Movement 1948, characterized by racist doctrines including anti-Semitism.

Union of Soviet Socialist Republics (USSR) former country in N Asia and E Europe that reverted to independent states following the resignation of Mikhail Gorbachev 1991; see *Armenia, *Azerbaijan, *Belarus, *Estonia, *Georgia, *Kazakhstan, *Kyrgyzstan, *Latvia, *Lithuania, *Moldova, *Russian Federation, *Tajikistan, *Turkmenistan, *Ukraine, and *Uzbekistan.

Soviet Union: history

1917 Revolution: provisional democratic government established by Mensheviks. Communist takeover by Bolsheviks under Lenin.
1922 Soviet Union established.
1924 Death of Lenin.
1928 Stalin emerged as absolute ruler after ousting Trotsky.
1930s Purges of Stalin's opponents took place.
1939 Nonaggression pact signed with Germany.
1941–45 'Great Patriotic War' against Germany.
1953 Stalin died; Beria removed; 'collective leadership' in power.
1955 Warsaw Pact created.
1956 Khrushchev made February 'secret speech'. Hungarian uprising.
1960 Sino-Soviet rift.
1962 Cuban missile crisis.
1964 Khrushchev ousted by new 'collective leadership'.
1968 Invasion of Czechoslovakia.
1969 Sino-Soviet border war.
1972 Salt I arms-limitation agreed with USA.
1977 Brezhnev elected president.
1979 Salt II. Soviet invasion of Afghanistan.
1980–81 Polish crisis.
1982 Deaths of Suslov and Brezhnev. Andropov became Communist Party leader.
1984 Chernenko succeeded Andropov.
1985 Gorbachev succeeded Chernenko and introduced wide-ranging reforms. Gromyko appointed president.
1986 Gorbachev's power consolidated at 27th Party Congress. Chernobyl nuclear disaster.

1987 USSR and USA agreed to scrap intermediate-range nuclear missiles. Boris Yeltsin, Moscow party chief, dismissed for criticizing slow pace of reform.

1988 Nationalists challenged in Kazakhstan, Baltic republics, Armenia, and Azerbaijan. Earthquake killed thousands in Armenia. Constitution radically overhauled; private sector encouraged at Special All-Union Party Conference. Gorbachev replaced Gromyko as head of state.

1989 Troops withdrew from Afghanistan. General election held. Nationalist riots in Georgia. Gorbachev elected state president. Communist regimes in Eastern Europe overthrown. Relations with Chinese normalized. Lithuania allowed multiparty elections. Gorbachev and US president Bush declared end of Cold War.

1990 Troops sent to Azerbaijan during civil war with Armenia. Gorbachev opposed independence of Baltic republics; sanctions imposed on Lithuania. Summit meeting with President Bush. Supreme soviet passed law allowing freedom of religious expression, ending official atheism.

1991 Plan to preserve USSR as federation of sovereign republics approved in unionwide referendum, though boycotted by six republics. April: cooperation pact signed by Gorbachev and presidents of nine republics. June: Boris Yeltsin elected president of Russian Republic in popular election and banned Communist Party cells in the RSFSR. New Union treaty approved by nine republics. July: START treaty signed with USA. Aug: coup by hardline communists removed Gorbachev from power; Gorbachev restored but position undermined by Yeltsin who began rapid dismantling of all existing communist structures. Sept: independence of Latvia, Lithuania, and Estonia internationally acknowledged; remaining republics seceded over following months. Nov: Efforts to form a new 'Union of Sovereign States' failed. Dec: Gorbachev resigned; new federated arrangement emerged, the Commonwealth of Independent States (CIS); Soviet parliament voted USSR out of existence.

unit standard quantity in relation to which other quantities are measured. There have been many systems of units. Some ancient units, such as the day, the foot, and the pound, are still in use. *SI units, the latest version of the metric system, are widely used in science.

UNITA (acronym for *União Nacional para a independência Total de Angola*/National Union for the Total Independence of Angola) Angolan nationalist movement founded by Jonas *Savimbi 1966. Backed by South Africa, UNITA continued to wage guerrilla warfare against the ruling MPLA regime after the latter gained control of the country in 1976. A peace agreement was signed May 1991, but fighting recommenced Sept 1992 after Savimbi disputed an election victory for the ruling party, and escalated into a bloody civil war 1993. A peace agreement was signed 1994.

Unitarianism Christian-derived sect that rejects the orthodox doctrine of the Trinity, asserts the fatherhood of God and the brotherhood of humanity, and gives a pre-eminent position to Jesus as a religious teacher, while denying his divinity.

United Arab Emirates (UAE) (*Ittihad al-Imarat al-Arabiyah*) federation of the emirates of Abu Dhabi, Ajman, Dubai, Fujairah, Ras al Khaimah, Sharjah, Umm al Qaiwain

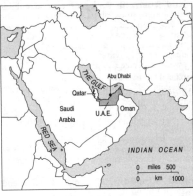

total area 83,657 sq km/32,292 sq mi
capital Abu Dhabi
towns (chief port) Dubai
physical desert and flat coastal plain; mountains in E
head of state and of government Sheik Sultan Zayed bin al-Nahayan of Abu Dhabi from 1971
political system absolutism
exports oil, natural gas, fish, dates
currency UAE dirham
population (1993 est) 2,100,000 (10% nomadic); growth rate 6.1% p.a.
languages Arabic (official), Farsi, Hindi, Urdu, English
religions Muslim 96%, Christian, Hindu
GNP $19,870 per head (1990)
chronology
1952 Trucial Council established.
1971 Federation of Arab Emirates formed; later dissolved. Six Trucial States formed United Arab Emirates, with ruler of Abu Dhabi, Sheik Zayed, as president.
1972 The seventh state joined.
1976 Sheik Zayed threatened to relinquish presidency unless progress towards centralization became more rapid.
1985 Diplomatic and economic links with USSR and China established.
1987 Diplomatic relations with Egypt restored.
1990–91 Iraqi invasion of Kuwait opposed; UAE fights with UN coalition.
1991 Bank of Commerce and Credit International (BCCI) controlled by Abu Dhabi's ruler collapses.

United Arab Republic union formed 1958, broken 1961, between *Egypt and *Syria. Egypt continued to use the name after the breach until 1971.

United Artists (UA) Hollywood film production, releasing, and distribution company formed 1919 by silent-screen stars Charles Chaplin, Mary Pickford, and Douglas Fairbanks, and director D W Griffith, in order to take control of their artistic and financial affairs. It concentrated on producing adaptations of literary works in the 1930s and 1940s, for example

Wuthering Heights 1939. The company nearly collapsed after the box-office disaster of Michael Cimino's *Heaven's Gate* 1980, and UA was subsequently bought by MGM.

United Australia Party Australian political party formed by Joseph *Lyons 1931 from the right-wing Nationalist Party. It was led by Robert Menzies after the death of Lyons. Considered to have become too dominated by financial interests, it lost heavily to the Labor Party 1943, and was reorganized as the *Liberal Party 1944.

United Democratic Front moderate multiracial political organization in South Africa, founded 1983. It was an important focus of anti-apartheid action in South Africa until 1989, when the African National Congress and Pan-Africanist Congress were unbanned.

United Irishmen society formed 1791 by Wolfe *Tone to campaign for parliamentary reform in Ireland. It later became a secret revolutionary group.

United Kingdom of Great Britain and Northern Ireland (UK)

area 244,100 sq km/94,247 sq mi
capital London
towns Birmingham, Glasgow, Leeds, Sheffield, Liverpool, Manchester, Edinburgh, Bradford, Bristol, Belfast, Newcastle-upon-Tyne, Cardiff
physical became separated from European continent about 6000 BC; rolling landscape, increasingly mountainous towards the N, with Grampian Mountains in Scotland, Pennines in N England, Cambrian Mountains in Wales; rivers include Thames, Severn, and Spey
territories Anguilla, Bermuda, British Antarctic Territory, British Indian Ocean Territory, British Virgin Islands, Cayman Islands, Falkland Islands, Gibraltar, Hong Kong (until 1997), Montserrat, Pitcairn Islands, St Helena and Dependencies (Ascension, Tristan da Cunha), Turks and Caicos Islands
environment an estimated 67% (the highest percentage in Europe) of forests have been damaged by acid rain
head of state Queen Elizabeth II from 1952
head of government John Major from 1990
political system liberal democracy
exports cereals, rape, sugar beet, potatoes, meat and meat products, poultry, dairy products, electronic and telecommunications equipment, engineering equipment and scientific instruments, oil and gas, petrochemicals, pharmaceuticals, fertilizers, film and television programmes, aircraft
currency pound sterling (£)
population (1993 est) 58,000,000 (81.5% English, 9.6% Scottish, 1.9% Welsh, 2.4% Irish, 1.8% Ulster); growth rate 0.1% p.a.
religions Christian (55% Protestant, 10% Roman Catholic); Muslim, Jewish, Hindu, Sikh
languages English, Welsh, Gaelic
GNP $16,080 per head (1991)
chronology
1707 Act of Union between England and Scotland under Queen Anne.
1721 Robert Walpole unofficially first prime minister, under George I.
1783 Loss of North American colonies that form USA; Canada retained.
1801 Act of Ireland united Britain and Ireland.
1819 Peterloo massacre: cavalry charged a meeting of supporters of parliamentary reform.
1832 Great Reform Bill became law, shifting political power from upper to middle class.
1838 Chartist working-class movement formed.
1846 Corn Laws repealed by Robert Peel.
1867 Second Reform Bill, extending the franchise, introduced by Disraeli and passed.
1906 Liberal victory; programme of social reform.
1914 Irish Home Rule Bill introduced.
1914–18 World War I.
1916 Lloyd George became prime minister.
1920 Home Rule Act incorporated NE of Ireland (Ulster) into the United Kingdom of Great Britain and Northern Ireland.
1921 Ireland, except for Ulster, became a dominion (Irish Free State, later Eire, 1937).
1924 First Labour government led by Ramsay MacDonald.
1926 General Strike.
1931 Coalition government; unemployment reached 3 million.
1939 World War II began.
1940 Winston Churchill became head of coalition government.
1945 Labour government under Clement Attlee; welfare state established.
1951 Conservatives under Winston Churchill defeated Labour.
1956 Suez Crisis.
1964 Labour victory under Harold Wilson.
1970 Conservatives under Edward Heath defeated Labour.
1972 Parliament prorogued in Northern Ireland; direct rule from Westminster began.
1973 UK joined European Economic Community.
1974 Three-day week, coal strike; Wilson replaced Heath.
1976 James Callaghan replaced Wilson as prime minister.
1979 Victory for Conservatives under Margaret Thatcher.
1981 Formation of Social Democratic Party (SDP). Riots occurred in inner cities.
1982 Unemployment over 3 million. Falklands War.
1983 Thatcher re-elected.
1984–85 Coal strike, the longest in British history.

County boundaries since 1974 (England and Wales) and since 1975 (Scotland)

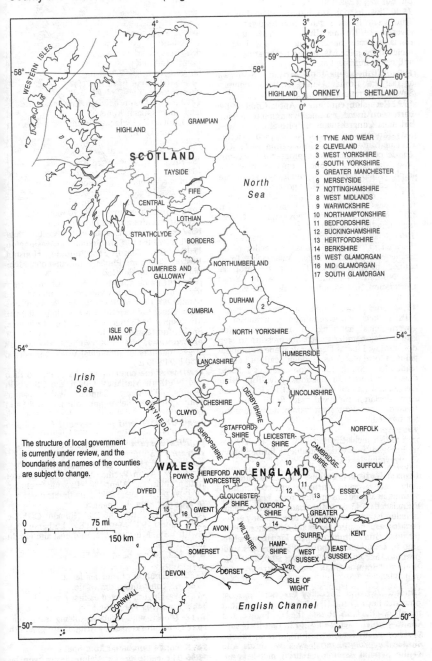

1 TYNE AND WEAR
2 CLEVELAND
3 WEST YORKSHIRE
4 SOUTH YORKSHIRE
5 GREATER MANCHESTER
6 MERSEYSIDE
7 NOTTINGHAMSHIRE
8 WEST MIDLANDS
9 WARWICKSHIRE
10 NORTHAMPTONSHIRE
11 BEDFORDSHIRE
12 BUCKINGHAMSHIRE
13 HERTFORDSHIRE
14 BERKSHIRE
15 WEST GLAMORGAN
16 MID GLAMORGAN
17 SOUTH GLAMORGAN

The structure of local government is currently under review, and the boundaries and names of the counties are subject to change.

0   75 mi
0   150 km

1988 Liberals and most of SDP merged into the Social and Liberal Democrats, leaving a splinter SDP. Inflation and interest rates rose.

1989 The Green Party polled 2 million votes in the European elections.

1990 Riots as poll tax introduced in England. Troops sent to the Persian Gulf following Iraq's invasion of Kuwait. Britain joined European exchange rate mechanism (ERM). Thatcher replaced by John Major as Conservative leader and prime minister.

1991 British troops took part in US-led war against Iraq under United Nations umbrella. Severe economic recession.

1992 Recession continued. April: Conservative Party won fourth consecutive general election, but with reduced majority. John Smith replaced Neil Kinnock as Labour leader. Sept: sterling devalued and UK withdrawn from ERM. Oct: drastic coal mine closure programme encountered massive public opposition; later implemented. Major's popularity at unprecedentedly low rating. Nov: government motion in favour of ratification of Maastricht Treaty narrowly passed. Revelations of past arms sales to Iraq implicated senior government figures, including the prime minister.

1993 Recession continued. Conservatives defeated in two by-elections; chancellor of the Exchequer replaced. July: Maastricht Treaty ratified by parliament. Dec: peace proposal for Northern Ireland, the Downing Street Declaration, issued jointly with Irish government.

1994 Series of scandals implicating Conservative MPs rocked public confidence. Criticism of government's handling of European Union issues. Major under increasing pressure to step down. May: Liberal Democrats made substantial gains in local elections. Sudden death of Labour leader, John Smith. June: Conservatives suffered defeats in European elections. July: Tony Blair elected new Labour leader. Aug: Irish Republican Army declared unilateral cease-fire in Northern Ireland. Oct: Protestant paramilitary cease-fire announced.

1995 April: devastating defeat for Conservatives in Scottish local elections. May: local elections in England and Wales produced further heavy Conservative losses.

United Nations (UN) association of states for international peace, security, and cooperation, with its headquarters in New York. The UN established 1945 as a successor to the *League of Nations, and has played a role in many areas, such as refugees, development assistance, disaster relief, and cultural cooperation. Its membership in early 1993 stood at 183 states. Its total proposed budget for 1992–93 was $2,006 million. Boutros *Boutros-Ghali became secretary general 1992.

United Nations Security Council the most powerful body of the UN. It has five permanent members – the USA, Russia, the UK, France, and China – which exercise a veto in that their support is requisite for all decisions, plus ten others, elected for two-year terms by a two-thirds vote of the General Assembly; retiring members are not eligible for re-election.

United States of America

area 9,368,900 sq km/3,618,770 sq mi

capital Washington DC

towns New York, Los Angeles, Chicago, Philadelphia, Detroit, San Francisco, Washington, Dallas, San Diego, San Antonio, Houston, Boston, Baltimore, Phoenix, Indianapolis, Memphis, Honolulu, San Jose

physical topography and vegetation from tropical (Hawaii) to arctic (Alaska); mountain range parallel with E and W coasts; the Rocky Mountains; Great Lakes in N; rivers include Hudson, Mississippi, Missouri, Colorado, Columbia, Snake, Rio Grande, Ohio

environment the USA produces the world's largest quantity of municipal waste per person (850 kg/1,900 lb)

territories the commonwealths of Puerto Rico and Northern Marianas; Guam, the US Virgin Islands, American Samoa, Wake Island, Midway Islands, Belau, and Johnston and San Islands

head of state and government Bill Clinton from 1993

political system liberal democracy

currency US dollar

population (1993) 257,000,000 (white 80%, black 12%, Asian/Pacific islander 3%, American Indian, Inuit, and Aleut 1%, Hispanic [included in above percentages] 9%); growth rate 0.9% p.a

languages English, Spanish

religions Christian 86.5% (Roman Catholic 26%, Baptist 19%, Methodist 8%, Lutheran 5%), Jewish 1.8%, Muslim 0.5%, Buddhist and Hindu under 0.5%

GNP $22,560 per head (1991)

chronology

1776 Declaration of Independence.

1787 US constitution drawn up.

1789 Washington elected as first president.

1803 Louisiana Purchase.

1812–14 War with England, arising from commercial disputes caused by Britain's struggle with Napoleon.

1819 Florida purchased from Spain.

1836 The battle of the Alamo, Texas, won by Mexico.

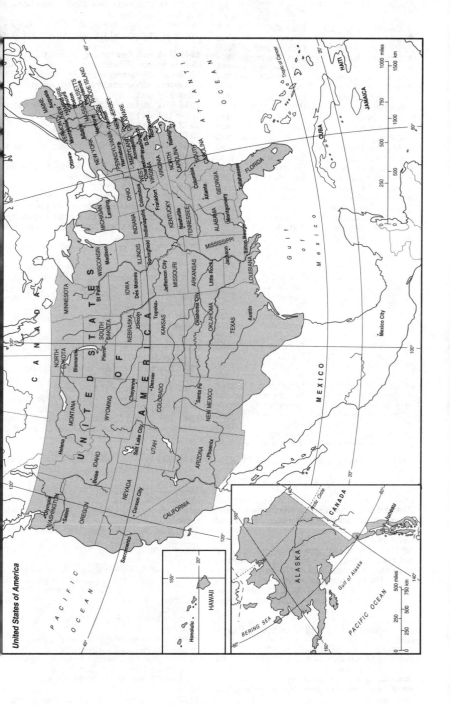

USA: PRESIDENTS AND ELECTIONS

name	party	took office
1. George Washington	Federalist	1789
2. John Adams	Federalist	1796
3. Thomas Jefferson	Dem. Republican	1800
4. James Madison	Dem. Republican	1808
5. James Monroe	Dem. Republican	1816
6. John Quincy Adams	Dem. Republican	1824
7. Andrew Jackson	Democrat	1828
8. Martin Van Buren	Democrat	1836
9. William Henry Harrison	Whig	1840
10. John Tyler	Whig	1841
11. James K Polk	Democrat	1844
12. Zachary Taylor	Whig	1848
13. Millard Fillmore	Whig	1850
14. Franklin Pierce	Democrat	1852
15. James Buchanan	Democrat	1856
16. Abraham Lincoln	Republican	1860
17. Andrew Johnson	Democrat	1865
18. Ulysses S Grant	Republican	1868
19. Rutherford B Hayes	Republican	1876
20. James A Garfield	Republican	1880
21. Chester A Arthur	Republican	1881
22. Grover Cleveland	Democrat	1884
23. Benjamin Harrison	Republican	1888
24. Grover Cleveland	Democrat	1892
25. William McKinley	Republican	1896
26. Theodore Roosevelt	Republican	1901
27. William H Taft	Republican	1908
28. Woodrow Wilson	Democrat	1912
29. Warren G Harding	Republican	1920
30. Calvin Coolidge	Republican	1923
31. Herbert Hoover	Republican	1928
32. Franklin D Roosevelt	Democrat	1932
33. Harry S Truman	Democrat	1945
34. Dwight D Eisenhower	Republican	1952
35. John F Kennedy	Democrat	1960
36. Lyndon B Johnson	Democrat	1963
37. Richard M Nixon	Republican	1968
38. Gerald R Ford	Republican	1974
39. Jimmy Carter	Democrat	1976
40. Ronald Reagan	Republican	1980
41. George Bush	Republican	1988
42. Bill Clinton	Democrat	1992

1841 First wagon train left Missouri for California.

1846 Mormons, under Brigham Young, founded Salt Lake City, Utah.

1846–48 Mexican War resulted in cession to USA of Arizona, California, part of Colorado and Wyoming, Nevada, New Mexico, Texas, and Utah.

1848–49 California gold rush.

1860 Lincoln elected president.

1861–65 Civil War between North and South.

1865 Slavery abolished. Lincoln assassinated.

1867 Alaska bought from Russia.

1890 Battle of Wounded Knee, the last major battle between American Indians and US troops.

1898 War with Spain ended with the Spanish cession of Philippines, Puerto Rico, and Guam; it was agreed that Cuba be independent. Hawaii annexed.

1917–18 USA entered World War I.

1919–1921 Wilson's 14 Points became base for League of Nations.

1920 Women achieved the vote.

1924 American Indians made citizens by Congress.

1929 Wall Street stock-market crash.

1933 F D Roosevelt's New Deal to alleviate the Depression put into force.

1941–45 The Japanese attack on Pearl Harbor Dec 1941 precipitated US entry into World War II.

1945 USA ended war in the Pacific by dropping atom bombs on Hiroshima and Nagasaki, Japan.

1950–53 US involvement in Korean War. McCarthy anticommunist investigations (HUAC) became a 'witch hunt'.

1954 Civil Rights legislation began with segregation ended in public schools.

1957 Civil Rights bill on voting.

1958 First US satellite in orbit.

1961 Abortive CIA-backed invasion of Cuba at the Bay of Pigs.

1963 President Kennedy assassinated; L B Johnson assumed the presidency.

1964–68 'Great Society' civil-rights and welfare measures in the Omnibus Civil Rights bill.

1964–75 US involvement in Vietnam War.

1965 US intervention in Dominican Republic.

1969 US astronaut Neil Armstrong was the first human on the Moon.

1973 OPEC oil embargo almost crippled US industry and consumers. Inflation began.

1973–74 Watergate scandal began in effort to re-elect Richard Nixon and ended just before impeachment; Nixon resigned as president replaced by Gerald Ford, who 'pardoned' Nixon

1975 Final US withdrawal from Vietnam.

1979 US–Chinese diplomatic relations normalized.

1979–80 Iranian hostage crisis; relieved by Reagan concessions and released on his inauguration day Jan 1981.

1981 Space shuttle mission was successful.

1983 US invasion of Grenada.

1986 'Irangate' scandal over secret US government arms sales to Iran, with proceeds to anti-government Contra guerrillas in Nicaragua.

1987 Reagan and Gorbachev (for USSR) signed intermediate-range nuclear forces treaty. Wall Street stock-market crash caused by programme trading.

1988 USA became world's largest debtor nation owing $532 billion. George Bush elected president.

1989 Bush met Gorbachev at Malta, end to Cold War declared; large cuts announced for US military; USA invaded Panama; Noriega taken into custody.

1990 Bush and Gorbachev met again. Nelson Mandela freed in South Africa, toured USA. US troops sent to Middle East following Iraq's invasion of Kuwait.

1991 Jan–Feb: US-led assault drove Iraq from Kuwait in Gulf War. US support was given to the USSR during the dissolution of communism and the recognition of independence of the Baltic republics. July: Strategic Arms Reduction Treaty (START) signed at US–Soviet summit in Moscow.

1992 Bush's popularity slumped as economic recession continued. Widespread riots in Los Angeles. Nov: Bill Clinton won presidential elections for the Democrats. Dec: dispatch of 28,000 US troops to Somalia to lead international relief effort.

1993 Jan: Clinton inaugurated. Feb: medium

UNITED STATES

State	capital	area in sq km/sq mi	date of joining the Union
Alabama	Montgomery	134,700/52,000	1819
Alaska	Juneau	1,531,100/591,200	1959
Arizona	Phoenix	294,100/113,600	1912
Arkansas	Little Rock	137,800/53,200	1836
California	Sacramento	411,100/158,700	1850
Colorado	Denver	269,700/104,100	1876
Connecticut	Hartford	13,000/5,000	1788
Delaware	Dover	5,300/2,000	1787
Florida	Tallahassee	152,000/58,700	1845
Georgia	Atlanta	152,600/58,900	1788
Hawaii	Honolulu	16,800/6,500	1959
Idaho	Boise	216,500/83,600	1890
Illinois	Springfield	146,100/56,400	1818
Indiana	Indianapolis	93,700/36,200	1816
Iowa	Des Moines	145,800/56,300	1846
Kansas	Topeka	213,200/82,300	1861
Kentucky	Frankfort	104,700/40,400	1792
Louisiana	Baton Rouge	135,900/52,500	1812
Maine	Augusta	86,200/33,300	1820
Maryland	Annapolis	31,600/12,200	1788
Massachusetts	Boston	21,500/8,300	1788
Michigan	Lansing	151,600/58,500	1837
Minnesota	St Paul	218,700/84,400	1858
Mississippi	Jackson	123,600/47,700	1817
Missouri	Jefferson City	180,600/69,700	1821
Montana	Helena	381,200/147,200	1889
Nebraska	Lincoln	200,400/77,400	1867
Nevada	Carson City	286,400/110,600	1864
New Hampshire	Concord	24,000/9,300	1788
New Jersey	Trenton	20,200/7,800	1787
New Mexico	Santa Fé	315,000/121,600	1912
New York	Albany	127,200/49,100	1788
North Carolina	Raleigh	136,400/52,700	1789
North Dakota	Bismarck	183,100/70,700	1889
Ohio	Columbus	107,100/41,400	1803
Oklahoma	Oklahoma City	181,100/69,900	1907
Oregon	Salem	251,500/97,100	1859
Pennsylvania	Harrisburg	117,400/45,300	1787
Rhode Island	Providence	3,100/1,200	1790
South Carolina	Columbia	80,600/31,100	1788
South Dakota	Pierre	199,800/77,100	1889
Tennessee	Nashville	109,200/42,200	1796
Texas	Austin	691,200/266,900	1845
Utah	Salt Lake City	219,900/84,900	1896
Vermont	Montpelier	24,900/9,600	1791
Virginia	Richmond	105,600/40,800	1788
Washington	Olympia	176,700/68,200	1889
West Virginia	Charleston	62,900/24,300	1863
Wisconsin	Madison	145,500/56,200	1848
Wyoming	Cheyenne	253,400/97,800	1890
District of Columbia	Washington	180/70	
Total		9,391,880/3,625,870	

term economic plan passed by Congress to cut federal budget deficit. July: air strike on Baghdad, Iraq. Oct: health-care reform package presented to Congress. Nov: North American Free Trade Agreement (NAFTA) between USA, Canada, and Mexico approved by Congress; wide-ranging anti-crime bill passed.
1994 Jan: Signs of economic recovery. Whitewater affair, alleging the Clintons' involvement in dubious financial dealings during the 1980s. Trade embargo against Vietnam lifted after 19 years. March: US backed NATO action against Serbs in Bosnia-Herzegovina. Most US troops withdrawn from Somalia.

1995 Republicans sought passage of 10-point populist manifesto, 'Contract with America'.

unit trust company that invests its clients' funds in other companies. The units represent holdings of shares, which means unit shareholders have a wider spread of capital than if they bought shares on the stock market.

universal indicator in chemistry, a mixture of *pH indicators, used to gauge the acidity or alkalinity of a solution. Each component changes colour at a different pH value, and so the indicator is capable of displaying a range of colours, according to the pH of the test solution, from red (at pH 1) to purple (at pH 13).

universal joint flexible coupling used to join rotating shafts; for example, the propeller shaft in a car. In a typical universal joint the ends of the shafts to be joined end in U-shaped yokes. They dovetail into each other and pivot flexibly about an X-shaped joint. This construction allows side-to-side and up-and-down movement, while still transmitting rotary motion.

universe all of space and its contents, the study of which is called cosmology. The universe is thought to be between 10 billion and 20 billion years old, and is mostly empty space, dotted with *galaxies for as far as telescopes can see. The most distant detected galaxies and *quasars lie 10 billion light years or more from Earth, and are moving farther apart as the universe expands. Several theories attempt to explain how the universe came into being and evolved, for example, the *Big Bang theory of an expanding universe originating in a single explosive event, and the contradictory *steady-state theory.

Unix multiuser *operating system designed for mini-computers but becoming increasingly popular on large microcomputers, workstations, mainframes, and supercomputers. It was developed by AT&T's Bell Laboratories in the USA during the late 1960s, using the programming language *C. It could therefore run on any machine with a C compiler, so ensuring its wide portability. Its wide range of functions and flexibility have made it widely used by universities and in commercial software.

unleaded petrol petrol manufactured without the addition of *antiknock. It has a slightly lower octane rating than leaded petrol, but has the advantage of not polluting the atmosphere with lead compounds. Many cars can be converted to running on unleaded petrol by altering the timing of the engine, and most new cars are designed to do so.

unnilennium synthesized radioactive element of the *transactinide series, symbol Une, atomic number 109, relative atomic mass 266. It was first produced in 1982 at the Laboratory for Heavy Ion Research in Darmstadt, Germany, by fusing bismuth and iron nuclei.

unnilhexium synthesized radioactive element of the *transactinide series, symbol Unh, atomic number 106, relative atomic mass 263. It was first synthesized in 1974 by two institutions, each of which claims priority. The University of California at Berkeley bombarded californium with oxygen nuclei to get isotope 263; the Joint Institute for Nuclear Research in Dubna, Russia, bombarded lead with chromium nuclei to obtain isotopes 259 and 260.

unniloctium synthesized, radioactive element of the *transactinide series, symbol Uno, atomic number 108, relative atomic mass 265. It was first synthesized in 1984 by the Laboratory for Heavy Ion Research in Darmstadt, Germany.

unnilpentium synthesized, radioactive, metallic element of the *transactinide series, symbol Unp, atomic number 105, relative atomic mass 262. Six isotopes have been synthesized, each with very short (fractions of a second) half-lives. Two institutions claim to have been the first to produce it: the Joint Institute for Nuclear

Research in Dubna, Russia, in 1967 (proposed name **nielsbohrium**); and the University of California at Berkeley, USA, who disputed the Soviet claim, in 1970 (proposed name **hahnium**).

unnilquadium synthesized, radioactive, metallic element, the first of the *transactinide series, symbol Unq, atomic number 104, relative atomic mass 262. It is produced by bombarding californium with carbon nuclei and has ten isotopes, the longest-lived of which, Unq-262, has a half-life of 70 seconds. Two institutions claim to be the first to have synthesized it: the Joint Institute for Nuclear Research in Dubna, Russia, in 1964 (proposed name **kurchatovium**); and the University of California at Berkeley, USA, in 1969 (proposed name **rutherfordium**).

unnilseptium synthesized, radioactive element of the *transactinide series, symbol Uns, atomic number 107, relative atomic mass 262. It was first synthesized by the Joint Institute for Nuclear Research in Dubna, Russia, in 1976; in 1981 the Laboratory for Heavy Ion Research in Darmstadt, Germany, confirmed its existence.

unsaturated compound chemical compound in which two adjacent atoms are bonded by a double or triple covalent bond.

unsaturated solution solution that is capable of dissolving more solute than it already contains at the same temperature.

untouchable or **harijan** member of the lowest Indian *caste, formerly forbidden to be touched by members of the other castes.

Unzen active volcano on the Shimbara peninsula, Kyushu Island, Japan, opposite the city of Kumamoto and 990 km/620 mi SW of Tokyo. Its eruption June 1991 led to the evacuation of 10,000 people.

Upanishad one of a collection of Hindu sacred treatises, written in Sanskrit, connected with the *Vedas but composed later, about 800–200 BC. Metaphysical and ethical, their doctrine equated the atman (self) with the Brahman (supreme spirit) – 'Tat tvam asi' ('Thou art that') – and developed the theory of the transmigration of souls.

Updike John (Hoyer) 1932– . US writer. Associated with the *New Yorker* magazine from 1955, he soon established a reputation for polished prose, poetry, and criticism. His novels include *The Poorhouse Fair* 1959, *The Centaur* 1963, *Couples* 1968, *The Witches of Eastwick* 1984, *Roger's Version* 1986, and *S.* 1988, and deal with the tensions and frustrations of contemporary US middle-class life and their effects on love and marriage.

Upper Volta former name (until 1984) of *Burkina Faso.

Ur ancient city of the *Sumerian civilization, in modern Iraq. Excavations by the British archaeologist Leonard Woolley show that it was inhabited 3500 BC. He discovered evidence of a flood that may have inspired the *Epic of *Gilgamesh* as well as the biblical account, and remains of ziggurats, or step pyramids, as well as social and cultural materials.

Ural Mountains (Russian **Ural'skiy Khrebet**) mountain system running from the Arctic to the Caspian Sea, traditionally separating Europe from Asia. The highest peak is Naradnaya 1,894 m/6,214 ft. It has vast mineral wealth.

uraninite uranium oxide, UO_2, an ore mineral of uranium, also known as *pitchblende* when occurring in massive form. It is black or brownish black, very dense, and radioactive. It occurs in veins and as massive crusts, usually associated with granite rocks.

uranium hard, lustrous, silver-white, malleable and ductile, radioactive, metallic element of the *actinide series, symbol U, atomic number 92, relative atomic mass 238.029. It is the most abundant radioactive element in the Earth's crust, its decay giving rise to essentially all radioactive elements in nature; its final decay product is the stable element lead. Uranium combines readily with most elements to form compounds that are extremely poisonous. The chief ore is *pitchblende, in which the element was discovered by German chemist Martin Klaproth 1789; he named it after the planet Uranus, which had been discovered 1781.

uranium ore material from which uranium is extracted, often a complex mixture of minerals. The main ore is uraninite (or pitchblende) UO_2, which is commonly found with sulphide minerals. The USA, Canada, and South Africa are the main producers in the West.

Uranus in Greek mythology, the primeval sky god. He was responsible for both the sunshine and the rain, and was the son and husband of *Gaia, the goddess of the Earth. Uranus and Gaia were the parents of *Kronos and the *Titans.

Uranus the seventh planet from the Sun, discovered by William *Herschel 1781. It is twice as far out as the sixth planet, Saturn. Uranus has a diameter of 50,800 km/31,600 mi and a mass 14.5 times that of Earth. It orbits the Sun in 84 years at an average distance of 2,870 million km/1,783 million mi. The spin axis of Uranus is tilted at 98°, so that one pole points towards the Sun, giving extreme seasons. It has 15 moons, and in 1977 was discovered to have thin rings around its equator.

Urban six popes, including:

Urban II *c.* 1042–1099. Pope 1088–99. He launched the First *Crusade at the Council of Clermont in France 1095.

urbanization process by which the proportion of a population living in or around towns and cities increases through migration as the agricultural population decreases. The growth of urban concentrations in the USA and Europe is a relatively recent phenomenon, dating back only about 150 years to the beginning of the Industrial Revolution (although the world's first cities were built more than 5,000 years ago).

urea $CO(NH_2)_2$ waste product formed in the mammalian liver when nitrogen compounds are broken down. It is excreted in urine. When purified, it is a white, crystalline solid. In industry it is used to make urea-formaldehyde plastics (or resins), pharmaceuticals, and fertilizers.

ureter tube connecting the kidney to the bladder. Its wall contains fibres of smooth muscle, whose contractions aid the movement of urine out of the kidney.

urethra in mammals, a tube connecting the

bladder to the exterior. It carries urine and, in males, semen.

Urey Harold Clayton 1893–1981. US chemist. In 1932 he isolated *heavy water and discovered *deuterium, for which he was awarded the 1934 Nobel Prize for Chemistry.

uric acid $C_5H_4N_4O_3$ nitrogen-containing waste substance, formed from the breakdown of food and body protein. It is only slightly soluble in water. Uric acid is the normal means by which most land animals that develop in a shell (birds, reptiles, insects, and land gastropods) deposit their waste products. The young are unable to get rid of their excretory products while in the shell and therefore store them in this insoluble form.

urinary system system of organs that removes nitrogenous waste products and excess water from the bodies of animals. In vertebrates, it consists of a pair of kidneys, which produce urine; ureters, which drain the kidneys; and (in bony fishes, amphibians, some reptiles, and mammals) a bladder, which stores the urine before its discharge. In mammals, the urine is expelled through the urethra; in other vertebrates, the urine drains into a common excretory chamber called a *cloaca, and the urine is not discharged separately.

urine amber-coloured fluid made by the kidneys from the blood. It contains excess water, salts, proteins, waste products in the form of urea, a pigment, and some acid.

Ursa Major (Latin 'Great Bear') third largest constellation in the sky, in the north polar region. Its seven brightest stars make up the familiar shape of the *Big Dipper* or *Plough*. The second star of the 'handle' of the dipper, called Mizar, has a companion star, Alcor. Two stars forming the far side of the 'bowl' act as pointers to the north pole star, Polaris.

Ursa Minor (Latin 'Little Bear') constellation in the northern sky. It is shaped like a dipper, with the north pole star Polaris at the end of the handle.

urticaria or *nettle rash* or *hives* irritant skin condition characterized by itching, burning, stinging, and the spontaneous appearance of raised patches of skin. Treatment is usually by antihistamines or steroids taken orally or applied as lotions. Its causes are varied and include allergy and stress.

Uruguay Oriental Republic of (*República Oriental del Uruguay*)
area 176,200 sq km/68,031 sq mi
capital Montevideo
towns Salto, Paysandú
physical grassy plains (pampas) and low hills
head of state and government Luis Lacalle Herrera from 1989
political system democratic republic
exports meat and meat products, leather, wool, textiles
currency nuevo peso
population (1993 est) 3,200,000 (Spanish, Italian; mestizo, mulatto, black); growth rate 0.7% p.a.
language Spanish
religion Roman Catholic 66%
GNP $2,860 per head (1991)

Brazil

PACIFIC
OCEAN

ATLANTIC
OCEAN

URUGUAY
Argentina Montevideo

0 miles 500
0 km 1000

chronology
1825 Independence declared from Brazil.
1836 Civil war.
1930 First constitution adopted.
1966 Blanco party in power, with Jorge Pacheco Areco as president.
1972 Colorado Party returned, with Juan Maria Bordaberry Arocena as president.
1976 Bordaberry deposed by army; Dr Méndez Manfredini became president.
1984 Violent antigovernment protests after ten years of repressive rule.
1985 Agreement reached between the army and political leaders for return to constitutional government; Colorado Party won general election; Dr Julio Maria Sanguinetti became president.
1986 Government of national accord established under President Sanguinetti's leadership.
1989 Luis Lacalle Herrera elected president.

Urumqi or **Urumchi** industrial city and capital of Xinjiang Uygur autonomous region, China, at the northern foot of the Tian Shan mountains; population (1989) 1,110,000. It produces cotton textiles, cement, chemicals, iron, and steel.

URUPABOL organization formed 1981 by Bolivia, Paraguay, and Uruguay to foster economic and commmercial cooperation.

USA abbreviation (official) for the ***United States of America***; US Army.

user interface in computing, the procedures and methods through which the user operates a program. These might include *menus, input forms, error messages, and keyboard procedures. A *graphical user interface (GUI or WIMP) is one that makes use of icons (small pictures) and allows the user to make menu selections with a mouse.

Ushuaia southernmost town in the world, at the tip of Tierra del Fuego, Argentina, less than 1,000 km/620 mi from Antarctica; population (1991) 29,700. It is a free port and naval base.

Ustashi Croatian militia that, during World War II, collaborated with the Nazis and killed thousands of Serbs, Romanies, and Jews.

Ustinov Peter 1921– . English stage and film actor, writer, and director. He won an Academy Award for *Spartacus* 1960. Other film appearances include *Topkapi* 1964, *Death on the Nile* 1978, and *Evil under the Sun* 1981. He published his autobiography *Dear Me* 1983.

usury former term for charging interest on a loan of money. In medieval times, usury was held to be a sin, and Christians were forbidden to lend (although not to borrow).

Utah state in W USA; nickname Beehive State/Mormon State
area 219,900 sq km/84,881 sq mi
capital Salt Lake City
towns Provo, Ogden
physical Colorado Plateau to the east, mountains in centre, Great Basin to the west, Great Salt Lake
products wool, gold, silver, copper, coal, salt, steel
population (1990) 1,722,900
famous people Brigham Young
history explored first by Franciscan friars for Spain 1776; Great Salt Lake discovered by US frontier scout Jim Bridger 1824; part of the area ceded by Mexico 1848; developed by Mormons, still by far the largest religious group in the state; territory 1850, but not admitted to statehood until 1896 because of Mormon reluctance to relinquish plural marriage.

Utamaro Kitagawa 1753–1806. Japanese artist of the *ukiyo-e* ('floating world') school, who created muted colour prints of beautiful women, including informal studies of prostitutes.

UTC abbreviation for *universal time coordinated*, the standard measurement of *time.

uterus hollow muscular organ of female mammals, located between the bladder and rectum, and connected to the Fallopian tubes above and the vagina below. The embryo develops within the uterus, and in placental mammals is attached to it after implantation via the *placenta and umbilical cord. The lining of the uterus changes during the *menstrual cycle. In humans and other higher primates, it is a single structure, but in other mammals it is paired.

U Thant Burmese diplomat; see *Thant, U.

Uthman alternative spelling of *Othman, third caliph of Islam.

utilitarianism philosophical theory of ethics outlined by the philosopher Jeremy *Bentham and developed by John Stuart Mill. According to utilitarianism, an action is morally right if it has consequences that lead to happiness, and wrong if it brings about the reverse. Thus society should aim for the greatest happiness of the greatest number.

utility program in computing, a systems program designed to perform a specific task related to the operation of the computer when requested to do so by the computer user. For example, a utility program might be used to complete a screen dump, format a disc, or convert the format of a data file so that it can be accessed by a different applications program.

Utopia (Greek 'no place') any ideal state in literature, named after philosopher Thomas More's ideal commonwealth in his book *Utopia* 1516. Other versions include Plato's *Republic*, Francis Bacon's *New Atlantis* 1626, and *City* *of the Sun* by the Italian Tommaso Campanella (1568–1639). Utopias are a common subject in *science fiction.

Utrecht province of the Netherlands lying SE of Amsterdam, on the Kromme Rijn (Crooked Rhine)
area 1,330 sq km/513 sq mi
population (1991) 1,026,800
capital Utrecht
towns Amersfoort, Zeist, Nieuwegeun, Veenendaal
products chemicals, livestock, textiles, electrical goods
history ruled by the bishops of Utrecht in the Middle Ages, the province was sold to the emperor Charles V of Spain 1527. It became a centre of Protestant resistance to Spanish rule and, with the signing of the Treaty of Utrecht, became one of the seven United Provinces of the Netherlands 1579.

Utrecht, Treaty of treaty signed 1713 that ended the War of the *Spanish Succession. Philip V was recognized as the legitimate king of Spain, thus founding the Spanish branch of the Bourbon dynasty and ending the French king Louis XIV's attempts at expansion; the Netherlands, Milan, and Naples were ceded to Austria; Britain gained Gibraltar; the duchy of Savoy was granted Sicily.

Utrecht, Union of in 1579, the union of seven provinces of the N Netherlands – Holland, Zeeland, Friesland, Groningen, Utrecht, Gelderland, and Overijssel – that became the basis of opposition to the Spanish crown and the foundation of the present-day Dutch state.

Utrillo Maurice 1883–1955. French artist. He painted townscapes of his native Paris, many depicting Montmartre, often from postcard photographs.

Uttar Pradesh state of N India
area 294,400 sq km/113,638 sq mi
capital Lucknow
towns Kanpur, Varanasi, Agra, Allahabad, Meerut
population (1991) 138,760,400
famous people Indira Gandhi, Ravi Shankar
language Hindi
religions 80% Hindu, 15% Muslim
history formerly the heart of the Mogul Empire and generating point of the *Indian Mutiny 1857 and subsequent opposition to British rule; see also the *United Provinces of *Agra and *Oudh.

Uzbek member of the majority ethnic group (almost 70%) living in Uzbekistan; minorities live in Turkmenistan, Tajikistan, Kazakhstan, and Afghanistan. There are 10–14 million speakers of the Uzbek language, which belongs to the Turkic branch of the Altaic family. Uzbeks are predominantly Sunni Muslims.

Uzbekistan Republic of
area 447,400 sq km/172,741 sq mi
capital Tashkent
towns Samarkand, Bukhara, Namangan
physical oases in the deserts; rivers: Amu Darya, Syr Darya; Fergana Valley; rich in mineral deposits
environment in 1993 around 75% of the popu-

lation living round the Aral Sea were suffering from illness, with alarming increases in typhoid and hepatitis A. Local fruit and vegetables contained dangerous levels of pesticides and nitrates, and infant mortality was three times the national average. In the former fishing town of Muynak 70% of the population of 2,000 had precancerous conditions
head of state Islam Karimov from 1990
head of government Abd al-Hashim Mutalov from 1991
political system socialist pluralist
products rice, dried fruit, vines (all grown by irrigation); cotton, silk
currency som
population (1993 est) 21,700,000 (Uzbek 71%, Russian 8%, Tajik 5%, Kazakh 4%)
language Uzbek, a Turkic language
religion Sunni Muslim
GNP $1,350 per head (1991)
chronology
1921 Part of Turkestan Soviet Socialist Autonomous Republic.
1925 Became constituent republic of the USSR.
1944 Some 160,000 Meskhetian Turks forcibly transported from their native Georgia to Uzbekistan by Stalin.
1989 Tashlak, Yaipan, and Ferghana were the scenes of riots in which Meskhetian Turks were attacked; 70 killed and 850 wounded.
1990 June: economic and political sovereignty declared; former Uzbek Communist Party (UCP) leader Islam Karimov became president.
1991 March: supported 'renewed federation' in USSR referendum. Aug: attempted anti-Gorbachev coup in Moscow initially supported by President Karimov, who later resigned from Soviet Communist Party (CPSU) Politburo; UCP broke with CPSU; independence declared. Dec: joined new Commonwealth of Independent States.
1992 Jan: violent food riots in Tashkent. March: joined the United Nations; US diplomatic recognition achieved. New constitution adopted.
1993 Crackdown on Islamic fundamentalists.
1994 Agreement to form single economic zone with Kazakhstan.

v in physics, symbol for *velocity*.

V1, V2 (German *Vergeltungswaffe* 'revenge weapons') German flying bombs of World War II, launched against Britain in 1944 and 1945. The V1, also called the doodlebug and buzz bomb, was an uncrewed monoplane carrying a bomb, powered by a simple kind of jet engine called a pulse jet. The V2, a rocket bomb with a preset guidance system, was the first long-range ballistic *missile. It was 14 m/47 ft long, carried a 1-tonne warhead, and hit its target at a speed of 5,000 kph/3,000 mph.

vaccination use of specially modified *pathogens (bacteria and viruses) to confer immunity to the diseases with which they are associated. When injected or taken by mouth, a vaccine stimulates the production of antibodies to protect against that particular disease. Vaccination is the oldest form of *immunization.

vaccine any preparation of modified viruses or bacteria that is introduced into the body, usually either orally or by a hypodermic syringe, to induce the specific *antibody reaction that produces *immunity against a particular disease.

vacuole in biology, a fluid-filled, membrane-bound cavity inside a cell. It may be a reservoir for fluids that the cell will secrete to the outside, or may be filled with excretory products or essential nutrients that the cell needs to store. In amoebae (single-cell animals), vacuoles are the sites of digestion of engulfed food particles. Plant cells usually have a large central vacuole for storage.

vacuum in general, a region completely empty of matter; in physics, any enclosure in which the gas pressure is considerably less than atmospheric pressure (101,325 *pascals).

vacuum cleaner cleaning device invented 1901 by the Scot Hubert Cecil Booth 1871–1955. Having seen an ineffective dust-blowing machine, he reversed the process so that his machine (originally on wheels, and operated from the street by means of tubes running into the house) operated by suction.

vacuum flask or *Dewar flask* or *Thermos flask* container for keeping things either hot or cold. It has two silvered glass walls with a vacuum between them, in a metal or plastic outer case. This design reduces the three forms of heat transfer: radiation (prevented by the silvering), conduction, and convection (both prevented by the vacuum). A vacuum flask is therefore equally efficient at keeping cold liquids cold, or hot liquids hot.

Vaduz capital of the European principality of Liechtenstein; industries include engineering and agricultural trade; population (1984) 5,000.

vagina the front passage in female mammals, linking the uterus to the exterior. It admits the penis during sexual intercourse, and is the birth canal down which the fetus passes during delivery.

vagrancy homelessness. English law classifies as vagrants tramps who do not make use of available shelter, but also prostitutes who behave indecently in public, pedlars who trade without a licence, those who collect for charity under false pretences, and those who are armed with offensive weapons.

Valdivia Pedro de *c.* 1497–1554. Spanish explorer who travelled to Venezuela about 1530 and accompanied Francisco *Pizarro on his second expedition to Peru. He then went south into Chile, where he founded the cities of Santiago 1541 and Valdivia 1544. In 1552 he crossed the Andes to explore the Negro River. He was killed by Araucanian Indians.

valence electron in chemistry, an electron in the outermost shell of an *atom. It is the valence electrons that are involved in the formation of ionic and covalent bonds (see *molecule). The number of electrons in this outermost shell represents the maximum possible valency for many elements and matches the number of the group that the element occupies in the *periodic table of the elements.

Valencia industrial city (wine, fruit, chemicals, textiles, ship repair) in Valencia region, E Spain; population (1991) 777,400. The Community of Valencia, consisting of Alicante, Castellón, and Valencia, has an area of 23,300 sq km/8,994 sq mi and a population of 3,772,000.

valency in chemistry, the measure of an element's ability to combine with other elements, expressed as the number of atoms of hydrogen (or any other standard univalent element) capable of uniting with (or replacing) its atoms. The number of electrons in the outermost shell of the atom dictates the combining ability of an element.

Valentine, St according to tradition a bishop of Terni martyred at Rome, now omitted from the calendar of saints' days as probably nonexistent. His festival was 14 Feb, but the custom of sending 'valentines' to a loved one on that day seems to have arisen because the day accidentally coincided with the Roman mid-February festival of *Lupercalia.

Valentino Rudolph. Adopted name of Rodolfo Alfonso Guglielmi di Valentina d'Antonguolla 1895–1926. Italian-born US film actor and dancer, the archetypal romantic lover of the Hollywood silent era. His screen debut was in 1919, but his first starring role was in *The Four Horsemen of the Apocalypse* 1921. His subsequent films include *The Sheik* 1921 and *Blood and Sand* 1922.

Valera Éamon de. Irish politician; see *de Valera.

valerian perennial plant of either of two genera, *Valeriana* and *Centranthus*, family Valerianaceae, native to the northern hemisphere, with clustered heads of fragrant tubular flowers in red, white, or pink. The root of the common valerian or garden heliotrope *Valeriana officinalis* is used medicinally to relieve flatulence and as a sedative.

Valéry Paul 1871–1945. French poet and mathematician. His poetry includes *La Jeune Parque/The Young Fate* 1917 and *Charmes/Enchantments* 1922.

Valhalla in Norse mythology, the hall in *Odin's palace where he feasts with the souls of heroes killed in battle.

validation in computing, the process of checking input data to ensure that it is complete, accurate, and reasonable. Although it would be impossible to guarantee that only valid data are entered into a computer, a suitable combination of validation checks should ensure that most errors are detected.

Valkyrie in Norse mythology, any of the female attendants of *Odin. They select the most valiant warriors to die in battle and escort them to Valhalla.

Valladolid industrial town (food processing, vehicles, textiles, engineering), and capital of Valladolid province, Spain; population (1991) 345,300.

Valle d'Aosta autonomous region of NW Italy; area 3,300 sq km/1,274 sq mi; population (1990) 116,000, many of whom are French-speaking. It produces wine and livestock. Its capital is Aosta.

Valletta capital and port of Malta; population (1987) 9,000; urban area 101,000.

Valley Forge site in Pennsylvania 32 km/20 mi NW of Philadelphia, USA, where George Washington's army spent the winter of 1777–78 in great hardship during the *American Revolution. Of the 10,000 men there, 2,500 died of disease and the rest suffered from lack of rations and other supplies; many deserted.

Valley of Ten Thousand Smokes valley in SW Alaska, on the Alaska Peninsula, where in 1912 Mount Katmai erupted in one of the largest volcanic explosions ever known, though without loss of human life since the area was uninhabited. It was dedicated as the Katmai National Monument 1918. Thousands of fissures in the valley floor continue to emit steam and gases.

Valley of the Kings burial place of ancient kings opposite *Thebes, Egypt, on the left bank of the Nile.

Valois branch of the Capetian dynasty, originally counts of Valois (see Hugh *Capet) in France, members of which occupied the French throne from Philip VI 1328 to Henry III 1589.

value added in business, see *added value.

value-added tax (VAT) tax on goods and services. VAT is imposed by the European Community on member states. The tax varies from state to state. An agreed proportion of the tax money is used to fund the EC.

valve device that controls the flow of a fluid. Inside a valve, a plug moves to widen or close the opening through which the fluid passes. The valve was invented by US radio engineer Lee de Forest (1873–1961).

valve in animals, a structure for controlling the direction of the blood flow. In humans and other vertebrates, the contractions of the beating heart cause the correct blood flow into the arteries because a series of valves prevent back flow. Diseased valves, detected as 'heart murmurs', have decreased efficiency. The tendency for low-pressure venous blood to collect at the base of limbs under the influence of gravity is counteracted by a series of small valves within the veins. It was the existence of these valves that prompted the 17th-century physician William Harvey to suggest that the blood circulated around the body.

valve or *electron tube* in electronics, a glass tube containing gas at low pressure, which is used to control the flow of electricity in a circuit. Three or more metal electrodes are inset into the tube. By varying the voltage on one of them, called the *grid electrode*, the current through the valve can be controlled, and the valve can act as an amplifier. Valves have been replaced for most applications by *transistors. However, they are still used in high-power transmitters and amplifiers, and in some hi-fi systems.

vampire (Magyar *vampir*) in Hungarian and Slavonic folklore, an 'undead' corpse that sleeps by day in its native earth, and by night, often in the form of a bat, sucks the blood of the living. *Dracula is a vampire in popular fiction.

vampire bat The vampire bat is the only mammal to live as a parasite.

vampire bat any South and Central American bat of the family Desmodontidae, of which there are three species. The *common vampire Desmodus rotundus* is found from N Mexico to central Argentina; its head and body grow to 9 cm/3.5 in. Vampires feed on the blood of birds and mammals; they slice a piece of skin from a sleeping animal with their sharp incisor teeth and lap up the flowing blood.

vanadium silver-white, malleable and ductile, metallic element, symbol V, atomic number 23, relative atomic mass 50.942. It occurs in certain iron, lead, and uranium ores and is widely distributed in small quantities in igneous and sedimentary rocks. It is used to make steel alloys, to which it adds tensile strength.

Van Allen radiation belts two zones of charged particles around the Earth's magnetosphere, discovered 1958 by US physicist James Van Allen. The atomic particles come from the Earth's upper atmosphere and the *solar wind, and are trapped by the Earth's magnetic field. The inner belt lies 1,000–5,000 km/620–3,100 mi above the equator, and contains *protons and *electrons. The outer belt lies 15,000–25,000 km/9,300–15,500 mi above the equator, but is lower around the magnetic poles. It contains mostly electrons from the solar wind.

Vanbrugh John 1664–1726. English Baroque architect and dramatist. He designed Blenheim Palace, Oxfordshire, and Castle Howard, Yorkshire, and wrote the comic dramas *The Relapse* 1696 and *The Provok'd Wife* 1697.

Van Buren Martin 1782–1862. Eighth president of the US 1837-41, a Democrat, who had helped establish the *Democratic Party. He was secretary of state 1829-31, minister to Britain 1831–33, vice president 1833-37, and president during the Panic of 1837, the worst US economic crisis until that time, caused by land speculation in the West. Refusing to intervene, he advocated the establishment of an independent treasury, one not linked to the federal government, worsening the depression and losing the 1840 election.

Vancouver industrial city (oil refining, engineering, shipbuilding, aircraft, timber, pulp and paper, textiles, fisheries) in Canada, its chief Pacific seaport, on the mainland of British Columbia; population (1986) 1,381,000.

Vancouver Island island off the west coast of Canada, part of British Columbia
area 32,136 sq km/12,404 sq mi
towns Victoria, Nanaimo, Esquimalt (naval base)
products coal, timber, fish.

Vandal member of a Germanic people related to the *Goths. In the 5th century AD the Vandals moved from N Germany to invade Roman *Gaul and Spain, many settling in Andalusia (formerly Vandalitia) and others reaching N Africa 429. They sacked Rome 455 but accepted Roman suzerainty in the 6th century.

van de Graaff Robert Jemison 1901–1967. US physicist who from 1929 developed a high-voltage generator, which in its modern form can produce more than a million volts. It consists of a continuous vertical conveyor belt that carries electrostatic charges (resulting from friction) up to a large hollow sphere supported on an insulated stand. The lower end of the belt is earthed, so that charge accumulates on the sphere. The size of the voltage built up in air depends on the radius of the sphere, but can be increased by enclosing the generator in an inert atmosphere, such as nitrogen.

Vanderbilt Cornelius 1794–1877. US industrialist who made a fortune of more than $100 million in steamships and (from the age of 70) by financing railways.

Van der Post Laurens (Jan) 1906– . South African writer whose books, many of them autobiographical, reflect his openness to diverse cultures and his belief in the importance of intuition, individualism, and myth in human experience. A formative influence was his time spent with the San Bushmen of the Kalahari while growing up, and whose disappearing culture he recorded in *The Lost World of the Kalahari* 1958, *The Heart of the Hunter* 1961, and *Testament to the Bushmen* 1984.

van der Waals Johannes Diderik 1837–1923. Dutch physicist who was awarded a Nobel prize 1910 for his theoretical study of gases. He emphasized the forces of attraction and repulsion between atoms and molecules in describing the behaviour of real gases, as opposed to the ideal gases dealt with in *Boyle's law and *Charles's law.

Van Diemen's Land former name (1642-1855) of *Tasmania, Australia. It was named by Dutch navigator Abel Tasman after the governor general of the Dutch East Indies, Anthony van Diemen. The name Tasmania was used from the 1840 and became official 1855.

van Dyck Anthony. Flemish painter, see *Dyck, Anthony van.

Vane Henry 1613–1662. English politician. In 1640 elected a member of the *Long Parliament he was prominent in the impeachment of Archbishop *Laud and in 1643–53 was in effect the civilian head of the Parliamentary government. At the Restoration of the monarchy he was executed.

Vane John 1927– . British pharmacologist who discovered the wide role of prostaglandins in the human body, produced in response to illness and stress. He shared the 1982 Nobel Prize for Medicine with Sune Bergström (1916-) and Bengt Samuelson (1934-) of Sweden.

van Eyck Jan. Flemish painter; see *Eyck, Jan van.

van Gogh Vincent. Dutch painter; see *Gogh, Vincent van.

vanilla any climbing orchid of the genus *Vanilla*, native to tropical America but cultivated elsewhere, with fragrant, large, white or yellow flowers. The dried and fermented fruit, or podlike capsules, of *Vanilla planifolia* are the source of the vanilla flavouring used in cookery and baking.

van Leyden Lucas. Dutch painter; see *Lucas van Leyden.

Vanuatu Republic of (*Ripablik Blong Vanuatu*)
area 14,800 sq km/5,714 sq mi
capital Vila (on Efate)
towns Luganville (on Espíritu Santo)
physical comprises around 70 islands, including Espíritu Santo, Malekula, and Efate; densely forested, mountainous
head of state Jean Marie Leye from 1994
head of government Maxime Carlot from 1991
political system democratic republic
exports copra, fish, coffee, cocoa
currency vatu
population (1993 est) 200,000 (90% Melanesian); growth rate 3.3% p.a.
languages Bislama 82%, English, French (all official)
religions Presbyterian 40%, Roman Catholic 16%, Anglican 14%, animist 15%
GNP $1,120 per head (1991)
chronology
1906 Islands jointly administered by France and Britain.
1975 Representative assembly established.
1978 Government of national unity formed, with Father Gerard Leymang as chief minister.
1980 Revolt on the island of Espíritu Santo delayed independence but it was achieved within the Commonwealth, with George Kalkoa (adopted name Sokomanu) as president and Father Walter Lini as prime minister.

1988 Dismissal of Lini by Sokomanu led to Sokomanu's arrest for treason. Lini reinstated.

1989 Sokomanu sentenced to six years' imprisonment; succeeded as president by Fred Timakata.

1991 Lini voted out by party members; replaced by Donald Kalpokas. General election produced UMP–NUP coalition under Maxime Carlot.

1994 Timakata succeeded as president by Jean Marie Leye.

vapour density density of a gas, expressed as the *mass of a given volume of the gas divided by the mass of an equal volume of a reference gas (such as hydrogen or air) at the same temperature and pressure. It is equal approximately to half the relative molecular weight (mass) of the gas.

vapour pressure pressure of a vapour given off by (evaporated from) a liquid or solid, caused by vibrating atoms or molecules continuously escaping from its surface. In an enclosed space, a maximum value is reached when the number of particles leaving the surface is in equilibrium with those returning to it; this is known as the *saturated vapour pressure*.

Varanasi or **Benares** holy city of the Hindus in Uttar Pradesh, India, on the river Ganges; population (1981) 794,000. There are 1,500 golden shrines, and a 5 km/3 mi frontage to the Ganges with sacred stairways (*ghats*) for purification by bathing.

Varèse Edgard 1885–1965. French composer who settled in New York 1916 where he founded the New Symphony Orchestra 1919 to advance the cause of modern music. His work is experimental and often dissonant, combining electronic sounds with orchestral instruments, and includes *Hyperprism* 1923, *Intégrales* 1931, and *Poème Electronique* 1958.

Vargas Getúlio 1883–1954. President of Brazil 1930–45 and 1951–54. He overthrew the republic 1930 and in 1937 set up a totalitarian, pro-fascist state known as the **Estado Novo**. Ousted by a military coup 1945, he returned as president 1951 but, amid mounting opposition and political scandal, committed suicide 1954.

Vargas Llosa Mario 1937– . Peruvian novelist, author of *La ciudad y los perros/The Time of the Hero* 1963 and *La guerra del fin del mundo/The War at the End of the World* 1982.

variable in mathematics, a changing quantity (one that can take various values), as opposed to a *constant. For example, in the algebraic expression $y = 4x^3 + 2$, the variables are x and y, whereas 4 and 2 are constants.

variable star in astronomy, a star whose brightness changes, either regularly or irregularly, over a period ranging from a few hours to months or even years. The *Cepheid variables regularly expand and contract in size every few days or weeks.

variation in biology, a difference between individuals of the same species, found in any sexually reproducing population. Variations may be almost unnoticeable in some cases, obvious in others, and can concern many aspects of the organism. Typically, variation in size, behaviour, biochemistry, or colouring may be found. The cause of the variation is genetic (that is,

inherited), environmental, or more usually a combination of the two. The origins of variation can be traced to the recombination of the genetic material during the formation of the gametes, and, more rarely, to mutation.

variations in music, a form based on constant repetition of a simple theme, each new version being elaborated or treated in a different manner. The theme is easily recognizable, either as a popular tune or – as a gesture of respect – as the work of a fellow composer; for example, Brahms honours Bach in the *Variations on the St Antony Chorale*.

varicose veins or **varicosis** condition where the veins become swollen and twisted. The veins of the legs are most often affected; other vulnerable sites include the rectum (*haemorrhoids) and testes.

variegation description of plant leaves or stems that exhibit patches of different colours. The term is usually applied to plants that show white, cream, or yellow on their leaves, caused by areas of tissue that lack the green pigment *chlorophyll. Variegated plants are bred for their decorative value, but they are often considerably weaker than the normal, uniformly green plant. Many will not breed true and require *vegetative reproduction.

Varna port in Bulgaria, on an inlet of the Black Sea; population (1990) 320,600. Industries include shipbuilding and the manufacture of chemicals.

Varuna in early Hindu mythology, the sky god and king of the universe.

Vasari Giorgio 1511–1574. Italian art historian, architect, and painter, author of *Lives of the Most Excellent Architects, Painters and Sculptors* 1550 (enlarged and revised 1568), in which he proposed the theory of a Renaissance of the arts beginning with Giotto and culminating with Michelangelo. He designed the Uffizi Palace, Florence.

vascular bundle strand of primary conducting tissue (a 'vein') in vascular plants, consisting mainly of water-conducting tissues, metaxylem and protoxylem, which together make up the primary *xylem, and nutrient-conducting tissue, *phloem. It extends from the roots to the stems and leaves. Typically the phloem is situated nearest to the epidermis and the xylem towards the centre of the bundle. In plants exhibiting *secondary growth, the xylem and phloem are separated by a thin layer of vascular *cambium, which gives rise to new conducting tissues.

vascular plant plant containing vascular bundles. *Pteridophytes (ferns, horsetails, and club mosses), *gymnosperms (conifers and cycads), and *angiosperms (flowering plants) are all vascular plants.

vas deferens in male vertebrates, a tube conducting sperm from the testis to the urethra. The sperms are carried in a fluid secreted by various glands, and can be transported very rapidly when the smooth muscle in the wall of the vas deferens undergoes rhythmic contraction, as in sexual intercourse.

vasectomy male sterilization; an operation to cut and tie the ducts (see *vas deferens) that carry sperm from the testes to the penis. Vasectomy does not affect sexual performance, but the semen produced at ejaculation no longer contains sperm.

vassal in medieval Europe, a person who paid feudal homage to a superior lord (see *feudalism), and who promised military service and advice in return for a grant of land. The term was used from the 9th century.

Vance Cyrus 1917– . US Democratic politician, secretary of state 1977–80. In 1992 he was chosen as UN negotiator in the peace talks on *Bosnia-Herzegovina. Together with EC negotiator Lord Owen, he devised the Vance–Owen peace plan for dividing the republic into 10 semi-autonomous provinces.

VAT abbreviation for *value-added tax*.

Vatican City State (*Stato della Città del Vaticano*)
area 0.4 sq km/109 acres
physical forms an enclave in the heart of Rome, Italy
head of state and government John Paul II from 1978
political system absolute Catholicism
currency Vatican City lira; Italian lira
population (1985) 1,000
languages Latin (official), Italian
religion Roman Catholic
chronology
1929 Lateran Treaty recognized sovereignty of the pope.
1947 New Italian constitution confirmed the sovereignty of the Vatican City State.
1978 John Paul II became the first non-Italian pope for more than 400 years.
1985 New concordat signed under which Roman Catholicism ceased to be Italy's state religion.

Vatican Council either of two Roman Catholic ecumenical councils called by Pope Pius IX 1869 (which met 1870) and by Pope John XXIII 1959 (which met 1962). These councils deliberated over elements of church policy.

Vaughan Sarah (Lois) 1924–1990. US jazz singer whose voice had a range of nearly three octaves. She began by singing bebop with such musicians as Dizzy Gillespie and later moved effortlessly between jazz and romantic ballads. She toured very widely and had several hit singles, including 'Make Yourself Comfortable' 1954, 'Mr Wonderful' 1956, and 'Broken-Hearted Melody' 1959.

Vaughan Williams Ralph 1872–1958. English composer. His style was tonal and often evocative of the English countryside through the use of folk themes. Among his works are the orchestral *Fantasia on a Theme by Thomas Tallis* 1910; the opera *Sir John in Love* 1929, featuring the Elizabethan song 'Greensleeves'; and nine symphonies 1909–57.

VDU abbreviation for *visual display unit*.

vector graphics computer graphics that are stored in the computer memory by using geometric formulas. Vector graphics can be transformed (enlarged, rotated, stretched, and so on) without loss of picture resolution. It is also possible to select and transform any of the components of a vector-graphics display because each is separately defined in the computer memory. In these respects vector graphics are superior to

raster graphics. Vector graphics are typically used for drawing applications, allowing the user to create and modify technical diagrams such as designs for houses or cars.

vector quantity any physical quantity that has both magnitude and direction (such as the velocity or acceleration of an object) as distinct from *scalar quantity (such as speed, density, or mass), which has magnitude but no direction. A vector is represented either geometrically by an arrow whose length corresponds to its magnitude and points in an appropriate direction, or by a pair of numbers written vertically and placed within brackets (x) (y) (z). Vectors can be added graphically by constructing a parallelogram of vectors (such as the parallelogram of forces commonly employed in physics and engineering).

Veda (Sanskrit 'divine knowledge') the most sacred of the Hindu scriptures, hymns written in an old form of Sanskrit; the oldest may date from 1500 or 2000 BC. The four main collections are: the *Rigveda* (hymns and praises); *Yajurveda* (prayers and sacrificial formulae); *Sâmaveda* (tunes and chants); and *Atharvaveda*, or Veda of the Atharvans, the officiating priests at the sacrifices.

Vedânta school of Hindu philosophy that developed the teachings of the *Upanishads*. One of its teachers was Śamkara, who lived in S India in the 8th century AD and is generally regarded as a manifestation of Siva. He taught that there is only one reality, Brahman, and that knowledge of Brahman leads finally to *moksha*, or liberation from reincarnation.

Vega or *Alpha Lyrae* brightest star in the constellation Lyra and the fifth brightest star in the sky. It is a blue-white star, 25 light years from Earth, with a luminosity 50 times that of the Sun.

Vega Lope Felix de (Carpio) 1562–1635. Spanish poet and dramatist, one of the founders of modern Spanish drama. He wrote epics, pastorals, odes, sonnets, novels, and, reputedly, over 1,500 plays (of which 426 are still in existence), mostly tragicomedies. He set out his views on drama in *Arte nuevo de hacer comedias/The New Art of Writing Plays* 1609, while reaffirming the classical form. *Fuenteovejuna* 1614 has been acclaimed as the first proletarian drama.

vegan vegetarian who eats no foods of animal origin whatever, including fish, eggs, and milk.

vegetarian person who eats only foods obtained without slaughter, for humanitarian, aesthetic, political, or health reasons. *Vegans abstain from all foods of animal origin.

vegetative reproduction type of *asexual reproduction in plants that relies not on spores, but on multicellular structures formed by the parent plant. Some of the main types are *stolons and runners, *gemma, bulbils, sucker shoots produced from roots (such as in the creeping thistle *Cirsium arvense*), *tubers, *bulbs, *corms, and *rhizomes. Vegetative reproduction has long been exploited in horticulture and agriculture, with various methods employed to multiply stocks of plants.

Veidt Conrad 1893–1943. German film actor, memorable as the sleepwalker in *Das Kabinett des Dr Caligari/The Cabinet of Dr Caligari*

1919 and as the evil caliph in *The Thief of Bagdad* 1940.

Veil Simone 1927– . French politician. A survivor of Hitler's concentration camps, she was minister of health 1974–79 and framed the French abortion bill. She was president of the European Parliament 1979–81.

vein in animals with a circulatory system, any vessel that carries blood from the body to the heart. Veins contain valves that prevent the blood from running back when moving against gravity. They always carry deoxygenated blood, with the exception of the veins leading from the lungs to the heart in birds and mammals, which carry newly oxygenated blood.

Velázquez Diego Rodríguez de Silva y 1599–1660. Spanish painter, born in Seville, the outstanding Spanish artist of the 17th century. In 1623 he became court painter to Philip IV in Madrid, where he produced many portraits of the royal family as well as occasional religious paintings, genre scenes, and other subjects. *Las Meninas/The Ladies-in-Waiting* 1655 (Prado, Madrid) is a complex group portrait that includes a self-portrait, but nevertheless focuses clearly on the doll-like figure of the Infanta Margareta Teresa.

Velcro (from 'velvet' and 'crochet') system of very small hooks and eyes for fastening clothing, developed by Swiss inventor Georges de Mestral (1902–1990) after studying why burrs stuck to his trousers and noting that they were made of thousands of tiny hooks.

Velde, van de family of Dutch artists. Both *Willem van de Velde* the Elder (1611–93) and his son *Willem van de Velde* the Younger (1633–1707) painted sea battles for Charles II and James II (having settled in London 1672). Another son *Adriaen van de Velde* (1636–1672) painted landscapes.

veldt subtropical grassland in South Africa, equivalent to the *Pampas of South America.

vellum type of parchment, often rolled in scrolls, made from the skin of a calf, kid, or lamb. It was used from the late Roman Empire and Middle Ages for exceptionally important documents and the finest manuscripts. For example, *Torahs* (the five books of Moses) are always written in Hebrew on parchment. The modern term now describes thick, high-quality paper that resembles fine parchment.

velocity speed of an object in a given direction. Velocity is a *vector quantity, since its direction is important as well as its magnitude (or speed).

velocity ratio (VR), or *distance ratio* in a machine, the ratio of the distance moved by an effort force to the distance moved by the machine's load in the same time. It follows that the velocities of the effort and the load are in the same ratio. Velocity ratio has no units.

velvet fabric of silk, cotton, nylon, or other textile, with a short, thick pile. Utrecht, Netherlands, and Genoa, Italy, are traditional centres of manufacture. It is woven on a double loom, then cut between the centre pile to form velvet nap.

vena cava one of the large, thin-walled veins found just above the *heart, formed from the junction of several smaller veins. The *posterior vena cava* receives oxygenated blood returning from the lungs, and empties into the left atrium. The *anterior vena cava* collects deoxygenated blood returning from the rest of the body and passes it into the right side of the heart, from where it will be pumped into the lungs.

Venda *Black National State from 1979, near the Zimbabwe border, in South Africa
area 6,500 sq km/2,510 sq mi
capital Thohoyandou
towns MaKearela
government military council since a coup 1990 (military leader Ramushwana from 1990)
products coal, copper, graphite, construction stone
population (1980) 343,500
language Luvenda, English.

Vendée, Wars of the in the French Revolution, a series of peasant uprisings against the revolutionary government that began in the Vendée *département*, W France 1793, and spread to other areas of France, lasting until 1795.

vendetta (Italian 'vengeance') any prolonged feud, in particular one in which the relatives of a dishonoured or murdered person seek revenge on the wrongdoer or members of the family. The tradition is Mediterranean, known in Europe and the USA as a way of settling wrongs in Corsica, Sardinia, and Sicily, as practised by the *Mafia.

veneer thin lamina of fine wood applied to the surface of furniture made with a coarser or cheaper wood. Veneer has been widely used from the second half of the 17th century.

venereal disease (VD) any disease mainly transmitted by sexual contact, although commonly the term is used specifically for gonorrhoea and syphilis, both occurring worldwide, and chancroid ('soft sore') and lymphogranuloma venerum, seen mostly in the tropics. The term *sexually transmitted diseases* (*STDs) is more often used to encompass a growing list of conditions passed on primarily, but not exclusively, in this way.

Veneto region of NE Italy, comprising the provinces of Belluno, Padova (Padua), Treviso, Rovigo, Venezia (Venice), and Vicenza; area 18,400 sq km/7,102 sq mi; population (1990) 4,398,100. Its capital is Venice, and towns include Padua, Verona, and Vicenza. The Veneto forms part of the N Italian plain, with the delta of the river Po; it includes part of the Alps and Dolomites, and Lake Garda. Products include cereals, fruit, vegetables, wine, chemicals, ships, and textiles.

Veneziano Domenico. Italian painter; see *Domenico Veneziano.

Venezuela Republic of (*República de Venezuela*)
area 912,100 sq km/352,162 sq mi
capital Caracas
towns Barquisimeto, Valencia; port Maracaibo
physical Andes Mountains and Lake Maracaibo in NW; central plains (llanos); delta of river Orinoco in E; Guiana Highlands in SE
head of state and of government Rafael Caldera from 1994
government federal democratic republic
exports coffee, timber, oil, aluminium, iron ore, petrochemicals

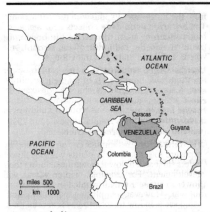

currency bolívar
population (1993) 20,410,000 (mestizos 70%, white (Spanish, Portuguese, Italian) 20%, black 9%, American Indian 2%); growth rate 2.8% p.a.
languages Spanish (official), Indian languages 2%
religions Roman Catholic 96%, Protestant 2%
GNP $2,610 per head (1991)
chronology
1961 New constitution adopted, with Rómulo Betancourt as president.
1964 Dr Raúl Leoni became president.
1969 Dr Rafael Caldera became president.
1974 Carlos Andrés Pérez became president.
1979 Dr Luis Herrera became president.
1984 Dr Jaime Lusinchi became president; social pact established between government, trade unions, and business; national debt rescheduled.
1987 Widespread social unrest triggered by inflation; student demonstrators shot by police.
1988 Carlos Andrés Pérez elected president. Payments suspended on foreign debts.
1989 Economic austerity programme enforced by $4.3 billion loan from International Monetary Fund. Price increases triggered riots; 300 people killed. Feb: martial law declared. May: General strike. Elections boycotted by opposition groups.
1992 Attempted anti-government coups failed.
1993 Pérez resigned, accused of corruption; Ramon José Velasquez succeeded him as interim head of state. Dec: former president Dr Rafael Caldera re-elected.
1994 Feb: Caldera sworn in as president. May: Pérez arrested.

Venice (Italian **Venezia**) city, port, and naval base, capital of Veneto, Italy, on the Adriatic; population (1990) 79,000. The old city is built on piles on low-lying islands. Apart from tourism (it draws 8 million tourists a year), industries include glass, jewellery, textiles, and lace. Venice was an independent trading republic from the 10th century, ruled by a doge, or chief magistrate, and was one of the centres of the Italian Renaissance.

veni, vidi, vici (Latin 'I came, I saw, I conquered') Julius *Caesar's description of his victory over King Pharnaces II (63–47 BC) at Zela in 47 BC.

Venn diagram in mathematics, a diagram representing a *set or sets and the logical relationships between them. The sets are drawn as circles. An area of overlap between two circles (sets) contains elements that are common to both sets, and thus represents a third set. Circles that do not overlap represent sets with no elements in common (disjoint sets). The method is named after the British logician John Venn (1834–1923).

venture capital or **risk capital** money put up by investors such as merchant banks to fund a new company or expansion of an established company. The organization providing the money receives a share of the company's equity and seeks to make a profit by rapid growth in the value of its stake, as a result of expansion by the start-up company or 'venture'.

Venturi Robert 1925– . US architect. He pioneered Post-Modernism through his books *Complexity and Contradiction in Architecture* 1967 (Pulitzer Prize 1991) and *Learning from Las Vegas* 1972. In 1986 he was commissioned to design the extension to the National Gallery London, opened 1991.

Venus in Roman mythology, the goddess of love and beauty (Greek *Aphrodite). The patrician Romans believed that they were descended from Aeneas, the son of the goddess and Anchises, a shepherd. She was venerated as the guardian of the Roman people.

Venus second planet from the Sun. It orbits the Sun every 225 days at an average distance of 108.2 million km/67.2 million mi and can approach the Earth to within 38 million km/24 million mi, closer than any other planet. Its diameter is 12,100 km/7,500 mi and its mass is 0.82 that of Earth. Venus rotates on its axis more slowly than any other planet, once every 243 days and from east to west, the opposite direction to the other planets (except Uranus and possibly Pluto). Venus is shrouded by clouds of sulphuric acid droplets that sweep across the planet from east to west every four days. The atmosphere is almost entirely carbon dioxide, which traps the Sun's heat by the *greenhouse effect and raises the planet's surface temperature to 480°C/900°F with an atmospheric pressure of 90 times that at the surface of the Earth.

Venus flytrap insectivorous plant *Dionaea muscipula* of the sundew family, native to the SE USA; its leaves have two hinged blades that close and entrap insects.

verb grammatical part of speech for what someone or something does (*to go*), experiences (*to live*), or is (*to be*). Verbs involve the grammatical categories known as number (singular or plural 'He *runs*; they *run*'), voice (active or passive: 'She *writes* books; it *is written*'), mood (statements, questions, orders, emphasis, necessity condition), aspect (completed or continuing action: 'She *danced*; she *was dancing*'), and tense (variation according to time: simple present tense, present progressive tense, simple past tense, and so on).

verbena any plant of the genus *Verbena*, family Verbenaceae, of about 100 species, mostly found in the American tropics. The leaves are fragrant and the tubular flowers arranged in close spikes in colours ranging from white to rose, violet, and purple. The garden verbena is a hybrid annual.

Vercingetorix Gallic chieftain. Leader of a revolt of all the tribes of Gaul against the Romans 52 BC; he lost, was captured, displayed in Julius

Caesar's triumph 46 BC, and later executed. This ended the Gallic resistance to Roman rule.

Verdi Giuseppe (Fortunino Francesco) 1813–1901. Italian opera composer of the Romantic period, who took his native operatic style to new heights of dramatic expression. In 1842 he wrote the opera *Nabucco*, followed by *Ernani* 1844 and *Rigoletto* 1851. Other works include *Il Trovatore* and *La Traviata* both 1853, *Aïda* 1871, and the masterpieces of his old age, *Otello* 1887 and *Falstaff* 1893. His *Requiem* 1874 commemorates Alessandro *Manzoni.

verdict in law, a jury's decision, usually a finding of 'guilty' or 'not guilty'.

verdigris green-blue coating of copper ethanoate that forms naturally on copper, bronze, and brass. It is an irritating, greenish, poisonous compound made by treating copper with ethanoic acid, and was formerly used in wood preservatives, antifouling compositions, and green paints.

Verdun fortress town in NE France on the Meuse. During World War I it became the symbol of French resistance, withstanding a German onslaught 1916.

Vergil alternative spelling for *Virgil, Roman poet.

verification in computing, the process of checking that data being input to a computer have been accurately copied from a source document. This may be done visually, by checking the original copy of the data against the copy shown on the VDU screen. A more thorough method is to enter the data twice, using two different keyboard operators, and then to check the two sets of input copies against each other. The checking is normally carried out by the computer itself, any differences between the two copies being reported for correction by one of the the keyboard operators.

Verlaine Paul 1844–1896. French lyric poet who was influenced by the poets Baudelaire and *Rimbaud. His volumes of verse include *Poèmes saturniens/Saturnine Poems* 1866, *Fêtes galantes/Amorous Entertainments* 1869, and *Romances sans paroles/Songs without Words* 1874. In 1873 he was imprisoned for attempting to shoot Rimbaud. His later works reflect his attempts to lead a reformed life. He was acknowledged as leader of the Symbolist poets.

Vermeer Jan 1632–1675. Dutch painter, active in Delft. Most of his pictures are *genre scenes, with a limpid clarity and distinct air of stillness, and a harmonious palette often focusing on yellow and blue. He frequently depicted solitary women in domestic settings, as in *The Lacemaker* (Louvre, Paris).

Vermont state in NE USA; nickname Green Mountain State
area 24,900 sq km/9,611 sq mi
capital Montpelier
towns Burlington, Rutland, Barre
products apples, maple syrup, dairy products, china clay, granite, marble, slate, business machines, paper and allied products; tourism is important
population (1990) 562,800
famous people Chester A Arthur, Calvin Coolidge, John Dewey

history explored by Champlain from 1609; settled 1724; state 1791.

vermouth sweet or dry white wine flavoured with bitter herbs and fortified with alcohol. It is made in France, Italy, and the USA.

vernacular architecture the domestic or peasant building tradition of different localities, not designed by trained architects; for example, thatched cottages in England, stone in Scotland, adobe huts in Mexico, and wooden buildings in the Nordic countries.

vernal equinox spring *equinox.

vernalization the stimulation of flowering by exposure to cold. Certain plants will not flower unless subjected to low temperatures during their development. For example, winter wheat will flower in summer only if planted in the previous autumn. However, by placing partially germinated seeds in low temperatures for several days, the cold requirement can be supplied artificially, allowing the wheat to be sown in the spring.

Verne Jules 1828–1905. French author of tales of adventure that anticipated future scientific developments: *Five Weeks in a Balloon* 1862, *Journey to the Centre of the Earth* 1864, *Twenty Thousand Leagues under the Sea* 1870, and *Around the World in Eighty Days* 1873.

Vernier Pierre 1580–1637. French mathematician who invented a means of making very precise measurements with what is now called the vernier scale. He was a French government official and in 1631 published *La construction, l'usage, et les propriétez du quadrant nouveau mathématique/The construction, uses and properties of a new mathematical quadrant*, in which he explained his method.

Verona industrial city (printing, paper, plastics, furniture, pasta) in Veneto, Italy, on the Adige; population (1988) 259,000. It also trades in fruit and vegetables.

Veronese Paolo c. 1528–1588. Italian painter, born in Verona, active mainly in Venice (from about 1553). He specialized in grand decorative schemes, such as his ceilings in the Doge's Palace in Venice, with *trompe l'oeil* effects and inventive detail. The subjects are religious, mythological, historical, and allegorical.

verruca growth on the skin; see *wart.

Versailles city in N France, capital of Les Yvelines *département*, on the outskirts of Paris; population (1982) 95,240. It grew up around the palace of Louis XV. Within the palace park are two small châteaux, Le Grand and Le Petit Trianon, built for Louis XIV (by Jules-Hardouin *Mansart) and Louis XV (by Jacques Gabriel 1698–1782) respectively.

Versailles, Treaty of peace treaty after World War I between the Allies and Germany, signed 28 June 1919. It established the League of Nations. Germany surrendered Alsace-Lorraine to France, and large areas in the east to Poland, and made smaller cessions to Czechoslovakia, Lithuania, Belgium, and Denmark. The Rhineland was demilitarized, German rearmament was restricted, and Germany agreed to pay reparations for war damage. The treaty was never ratified by the USA, which made a separate peace with Germany and Austria 1921.

verse arrangement of words in a rhythmic pattern, which may depend on the length of syllables (as in Greek or Latin verse), or on stress, as in English. Classical Greek verse depended upon quantity, a long syllable being regarded as occupying twice the time taken up by a short syllable.

vertebrate any animal with a backbone. The 41,000 species of vertebrates include mammals, birds, reptiles, amphibians, and fishes. They include most of the larger animals, but in terms of numbers of species are only a tiny proportion of the world's animals. The zoological taxonomic group Vertebrata is a subgroup of the *phylum *Chordata*.

vertex plural **vertices** in geometry, a point shared by three or more sides of a solid figure; the point farthest from a figure's base; or the point of intersection of two sides of a plane figure or the two rays of an angle.

vertigo dizziness; a whirling sensation accompanied by a loss of any feeling of contact with the ground. It may be due to temporary disturbance of the sense of balance (as in spinning for too long on one spot), psychological reasons, disease such as *labyrinthitis, or intoxication.

Verulamium Roman-British town whose remains have been excavated close to St Albans, Hertfordshire.

Verwoerd Hendrik (Frensch) 1901–1966. South African right-wing Nationalist Party politician, prime minister 1958–66. As minister of native affairs 1950–58, he was the chief promoter of apartheid legislation (segregation by race). He made the country a republic 1961. He was assassinated 1966.

Very Large Array (VLA) largest and most complex single-site radio telescope in the world. It is located on the Plains of San Augustine, 80 km/50 mi west of Socorro, New Mexico. It consists of 27 dish antennae, each 25 m/82 ft in diameter, arranged along three equally spaced arms forming a Y-shaped array. Two of the arms are 21 km/13 mi long, and the third, to the north, is 19 km/11.8 mi long. The dishes are mounted on railway tracks enabling the configuration and size of the array to be altered as required.

Vesalius Andreas 1514–1564. Belgian physician who revolutionized anatomy. His great innovations were to perform postmortem dissections and to make use of illustrations in teaching anatomy.

Vespasian (Titus Flavius Vespasianus) AD 9–79. Roman emperor from AD 69. He was the son of a moneylender, and had a distinguished military career. He was proclaimed emperor by his soldiers while he was campaigning in Palestine. He reorganized the eastern provinces, and was a capable administrator.

Vespucci Amerigo 1454–1512. Florentine merchant. The Americas were named after him as a result of the widespread circulation of his accounts of his explorations. His accounts of the voyage 1499–1501 indicate that he had been to places he could not possibly have reached (the Pacific Ocean, British Columbia, Antarctica).

Vesta in Roman mythology, the goddess of the hearth (Greek *Hestia*). In Rome, the sacred flame in her shrine in the Forum was kept constantly lit by the six **Vestal Virgins**.

vestigial organ in biology, an organ that remains in diminished form after it has ceased to have any significant function in the adult organism. In humans, the appendix is vestigial, having once had a digestive function in our ancestors.

Vesuvius (Italian **Vesuvio**) active volcano SE of Naples, Italy; height 1,277 m/4,190 ft. In 79 BC it destroyed the cities of Pompeii, Herculaneum, and Oplonti.

vetch trailing or climbing plant of any of several genera, family Leguminosae, usually having seed pods and purple, yellow, or white flowers, including the fodder crop alfalfa *Medicago sativa*.

Veterans Day in the USA, the name adopted 1954 for *Armistice Day and from 1971 observed by most states on the fourth Monday in Oct. The equivalent in the UK and Canada is *Remembrance Sunday.

veterinary science the study, prevention, and cure of disease in animals. More generally, it covers animal anatomy, breeding, and relations to humans.

veto (Latin 'I forbid') exercise by a sovereign, branch of legislature, or other political power, of the right to prevent the enactment or operation of a law, or the taking of some course of action.

VHF (abbreviation for **very high frequency**) referring to radio waves that have very short wavelengths (10 m-1 m). They are used for interference-free *FM (frequency-modulated) transmissions. VHF transmitters have a relatively short range because the waves cannot be reflected over the horizon like longer radio waves.

vibrato in music, a slight but rapid fluctuation of intensity or pitch in voice or instrument.

viburnum any small tree or shrub of the genus *Viburnum* of the honeysuckle family Caprifoliaceae, found in temperate and subtropical regions, including the *wayfaring tree, the laurustinus, and the guelder rose of Europe and Asia, and the North American blackhaws and arrowwoods.

vicar Church of England priest, originally one who acted as deputy to a *rector, but now also a parish priest.

viceroy chief official representing a sovereign in a colony, dominion or province, as in many Spanish and Portuguese American colonies and as in the British administration of India.

vice versa (Latin) the other way around.

Vichy health resort with thermal springs, known to the Romans, on the river Allier in Allier *département*, central France. During World War II it was the seat of the French general *Pétain's government 1940–44 (known also as the Vichy government), which collaborated with the Nazis.

Vichy government in World War II, the right-wing government of unoccupied France after the country's defeat by the Germans June 1940, named after the spa town of Vichy, France, where the national assembly was based under Prime Minister Pétain until the liberation 1944. **Vichy France** was that part of France not occupied by German troops until Nov 1942. Authoritarian and collaborationist, the Vichy regime cooperated with the Germans even after they had moved to the unoccupied zone Nov 1942. It imprisoned some 135,000 people, interned another 70,000, deported some 76,000 Jews, and sent 650,000 French workers to Germany.

Vico Giambattista 1668–1744. Italian philosopher, considered the founder of the modern philosophy of history. He argued that we can understand history more adequately than nature, since it is we who have made it. He believed that the study of language, ritual, and myth was a way of understanding earlier societies. His cyclical theory of history (the birth, development, and decline of human societies) was put forward in *New Science* 1725.

Victor Emmanuel three kings of Italy, including:

Victor Emmanuel II 1820–1878. First king of united Italy from 1861. He became king of Sardinia on the abdication of his father Charles Albert 1849. In 1855 he allied Sardinia with France and the UK in the Crimean War. In 1859 in alliance with the French he defeated the Austrians and annexed Lombardy. By 1860 most of Italy had come under his rule, and in 1861 he was proclaimed king of Italy. In 1870 he made Rome his capital.

Victor Emmanuel III 1869–1947. King of Italy from the assassination of his father, Umberto I, 1900. He acquiesced in the Fascist regime of Mussolini from 1922 and, after the dictator's fall 1943, relinquished power to his son Umberto II, who cooperated with the Allies. Victor Emmanuel formally abdicated 1946.

Victoria state of SE Australia
area 227,600 sq km/87,854 sq mi
capital Melbourne
towns Geelong, Ballarat, Bendigo
physical part of the Great Dividing Range, running E–W and including the larger part of the Australian Alps; Gippsland lakes; shallow lagoons on the coast; the mallee shrub region
products sheep, beef cattle, dairy products, tobacco, wheat, vines for wine and dried fruit, orchard fruits, vegetables, gold, brown coal (Latrobe Valley), oil and natural gas (Bass Strait)
population (1987) 4,184,000; 70% in the Melbourne area
history annexed for Britain by Captain Cook 1770; settled in the 1830s; after being part of New South Wales became a separate colony 1851, named after the queen; became a state 1901.

Victoria industrial port (shipbuilding, chemicals, clothing, furniture) on Vancouver Island, capital of British Columbia, Canada; population (1986) 66,303.

Victoria port and capital of the Seychelles, on Mahé island; population (1987) 24,300.

Victoria 1819–1901. Queen of the UK from 1837, when she succeeded her uncle William IV, and empress of India from 1876. In 1840 she married Prince *Albert of Saxe-Coburg and Gotha. Her relations with her prime ministers ranged from the affectionate (Melbourne and Disraeli) to the stormy (Peel, Palmerston, and Gladstone). Her golden jubilee 1887 and diamond jubilee 1897 marked a waning of republican sentiment, which had developed with her withdrawal from public life on Albert's death 1861.

Victoria and Albert Museum museum of decorative arts in South Kensington, London, founded 1852. It houses prints, paintings, and temporary exhibitions, as well as one of the largest collections of decorative arts in the world.

Victoria Cross British decoration for conspicuous bravery in wartime, instituted by Queen Victoria 1856.

Victoria Falls or *Mosi-oa-tunya* waterfall on the river Zambezi, on the Zambia–Zimbabwe border. The river is 1,700 m/5,580 ft wide and drops 120 m/400 ft to flow through a gorge, 30 m/100 ft wide.

Victoria, Lake or *Victoria Nyanza* largest lake in Africa; area over 69,400 sq km/26,800 sq mi; length 410 km/255 mi. It lies on the equator at an altitude of 1,136 m/3,728 ft, bounded by Uganda, Kenya, and Tanzania. It is a source of the Nile.

Victorian the mid- and late 19th century in England, covering the reign of Queen Victoria 1837–1901. Victorian style was often very ornate, markedly so in architecture, and Victorian Gothic drew on the original Gothic architecture of medieval times. It was also an era when increasing mass production by machines threatened the existence of crafts and craft skills.

vicuna *ruminant mammal *Lama vicugna* of the camel family that lives in herds on the Andean plateau. It can run at speeds of 50 kph/30 mph. It has good eyesight, fair hearing, and a poor sense of smell. It was hunted close to extinction for its meat and soft brown fur, which was used in textile manufacture, but the vicuna is now a protected species; populations are increasing thanks to strict conservation measures. It is related to the *alpaca, the *guanaco, and the *llama.

Vidal Gore 1925– . US writer and critic. Much of his fiction deals satirically with history and politics and includes the novels *Myra Breckinridge* 1968, *Burr* 1973, and *Empire* 1987, plays and screenplays, including *Suddenly Last Summer* 1958, and essays, such as *Armageddon?* 1987.

video camera portable television camera that takes moving pictures electronically on magnetic tape. It produces an electrical output signal corresponding to rapid line-by-line scanning of the field of view. The output is recorded on video cassette and is played back on a television screen via a videotape recorder.

video cassette recorder (VCR) device for recording and playing back video cassettes; see *videotape recorder.

video disc disc with pictures and sounds recorded on it, played back by laser. The video disc is a type of *compact disc.

video game electronic game played on a visual-display screen or, by means of special additional or built-in components, on the screen of a television set. The first commercially sold was a simple bat-and-ball game developed in the USA 1972, but complex variants are now available in colour and with special sound effects.

videotape recorder (VTR) device for recording pictures and sound on cassettes or spools of magnetic tape. The first commercial VTR was launched 1956 for the television broadcasting industry, but from the late 1970s cheaper models developed for home use, to record broadcast programmes for future viewing and to view rented or owned video cassettes of commercial films.

videotext system in which information (text and simple pictures) is displayed on a television (video) screen. There are two basic systems, known as *teletext and *viewdata. In the teletext system information is broadcast with the ordinary television signals, whereas in the viewdata system information is relayed to the screen from a central data bank via the telephone network. Both systems require the use of a television receiver with special decoder.

Vidor King 1894–1982. US film director who made such epics as *The Big Parade* 1925 and *Duel in the Sun* 1946. He has been praised as a cinematic innovator, and received an honorary Academy Award 1979. His other films include *The Crowd* 1928 and *Guerra e Pace/War and Peace* 1956.

Vienna (German *Wien*) capital of Austria, on the river Danube at the foot of the Wiener Wald (Vienna Woods); population (1986) 1,481,000. Industries include engineering and the production of electrical goods and precision instruments.

Vienna, Congress of international conference held 1814–15 that agreed the settlement of Europe after the Napoleonic Wars. National representatives included the Austrian foreign minister Metternich, Alexander I of Russia, the British foreign secretary Castlereagh and military commander Wellington, and the French politician Talleyrand.

Vientiane (Lao *Vieng Chan*) capital and chief port of Laos on the Mekong River; population (1985) 377,000.

Vietcong (Vietnamese 'Vietnamese communists') in the Vietnam War 1954–75, the members of the National Front for the Liberation of South Vietnam, founded 1960, who fought the South Vietnamese and US forces. The name was coined by the South Vietnamese government to differentiate these communist guerrillas from the *Vietminh.

Viète François 1540–1603. French mathematician who developed algebra and its notation. He was the first mathematician to use letters of the alphabet to denote both known and unknown quantities.

Vietminh the Vietnam Independence League, founded 1941 to oppose the Japanese occupation of Indochina and later directed against the French colonial power. The Vietminh were instrumental in achieving Vietnamese independence through military victory at Dien Bien Phu 1954.

Vietnam Socialist Republic of (*Công Hòa Xã Hội Chu Nghĩa Việt Nam*)
area 329,600 sq km/127,259 sq mi
capital Hanoi
towns ports Ho Chi Minh City (formerly Saigon), Da Nang, Haiphong
physical Red River and Mekong deltas, centre of cultivation and population; tropical rainforest; mountainous in N and NW
environment during the Vietnam War an estimated 2.2 million hectares of forest were destroyed. The country's National Conservation

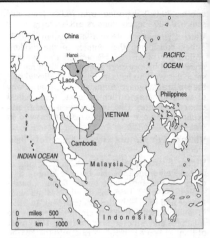

Strategy is trying to replant 500 million trees each year
head of state Le Duc Anh from 1992
head of government Vo Van Kiet from 1991
political system communism
exports rice, rubber, coal, iron, apatite
currency dong
population (1993 est) 70,400,000 (750,000 refugees, majority ethnic Chinese left 1975–79, some settled in SW China, others fled by sea – the 'boat people' – to Hong Kong and elsewhere); growth rate 2.4% p.a.
languages Vietnamese (official), French, English, Khmer, Chinese, local
religions Buddhist, Taoist, Confucian, Christian
GNP $200 per head (1990)
chronology
1945 Japanese removed from Vietnam at end of World War II.
1946 Commencement of Vietminh war against French.
1954 France defeated at Dien Bien Phu. Vietnam divided along 17th parallel.
1964 US troops entered Vietnam War.
1973 Paris cease-fire agreement.
1975 Saigon captured by North Vietnam.
1976 Socialist Republic of Vietnam proclaimed.
1978 Admission into Comecon. Vietnamese invasion of Cambodia.
1979 Sino-Vietnamese border war.
1986 Retirement of 'old guard' leaders.
1987–88 Over 10,000 political prisoners released.
1988–89 Troop withdrawals from Cambodia continued.
1989 'Boat people' leaving Vietnam murdered and robbed at sea by Thai pirates. Troop withdrawal from Cambodia completed. Hong Kong forcibly repatriated some Vietnamese refugees.
1991 Vo Van Kiet replaced Do Muoi as prime minister. Cambodia peace agreement signed. Relations with China normalized.
1992 Le Duc Anh elected president. Relations with South Korea normalized; USA eased 30-year-old trade embargo.

Vietnam War 1954–75. War between communist North Vietnam and US-backed South Vietnam. 200,000 South Vietnamese soldiers, million North Vietnamese soldiers, and 500,000 civilians were killed. 56,555 US soldiers were killed 1961–75, a fifth of them by their own troops. The war destroyed 50% of the country's forest cover and 20% of agricultural land. Cambodia, a neutral neighbour, was bombed by the US 1969–75, with 1 million killed or wounded.

viewdata system of displaying information on a television screen in which the information is extracted from a computer data bank and transmitted via the telephone lines. It is one form of *videotext. The British Post Office (now British Telecom) developed the first viewdata system, Prestel, 1975. Similar systems are now in widespread use in other countries. Users have access to a store of information, presented on the screen in the form of 'pages'.

vigilante in US history, originally a member of a 'vigilance committee', a self-appointed group to maintain public order in the absence of organized authority. The vigilante tradition continues with present-day urban groups patrolling streets and subways to deter muggers and rapists; for example, the Guardian Angels in New York.

Vigo Jean. Adopted name of Jean Almereida 1905–1934. French director of intensely lyrical experimental films. He made only two shorts, *A Propos de Nice* 1930 and *Taris Champion de Natation* 1934; and two feature films, *Zéro de conduite/Nothing for Conduct* 1933 and *L'Atalante* 1934.

Viking or **Norseman** medieval Scandinavian sea warrior. They traded with and raided Europe in the 8th–11th centuries, and often settled there. In France the Vikings were given *Normandy. Under Sweyn I they conquered England 1013, and his son Canute was king of England as well as Denmark and Norway. In the east they established the first Russian state and founded *Novgorod. They reached the Byzantine Empire in the south, and in the west sailed the seas to Ireland, Iceland, Greenland, and North America; see *Eric the Red, Leif *Ericsson, *Vinland.

Viking probes two US space probes to Mars, each one consisting of an orbiter and a lander. They were launched 20 Aug and 9 Sept 1975. They transmitted colour pictures, and analysed the soil.

vilayet administrative division of the Ottoman Empire under a law of 1864, with each vilayet, or province, controlled by a vali; some were subdivided into sanjaks. The vilayet system was an attempt by the Ottoman rulers to gain more power over the provinces, but many retained a large degree of autonomy.

Villa-Lobos Heitor 1887–1959. Brazilian composer. His style was based on folk tunes collected on travels in his country; for example, in the *Bachianas Brasileiras* 1930–44, he treats them in the manner of Bach. His works range from guitar solos to film scores to opera; he produced 2,000 works, including 12 symphonies.

Villehardouin Geoffroy de c. 1160–1213. French historian, the first to write in the French language. He was born near Troyes, and was a leader of the Fourth *Crusade, of which his *Conquest of Constantinople* (about 1209) is an account.

villeinage system of serfdom that prevailed in Europe in the Middle Ages. A villein was a peasant who gave dues and services to his lord in exchange for land. In France until the 13th century, 'villeins' could refer to rural or urban non-nobles, but after this, it came to mean exclusively rural non-noble freemen. In Norman England, it referred to free peasants of relatively high status.

Villon François 1431–c. 1465. French poet who used satiric humour, pathos, and lyric power in works written in the slang of the time. Among the little of his work that survives, *Petit Testament* 1456 and *Grand Testament* 1461 are prominent (the latter includes the 'Ballade des dames du temps jadis/Ballad of the Ladies of Former Times').

villus plural **villi** small fingerlike projection extending into the interior of the small intestine and increasing the absorptive area of the intestinal wall. Digested food, including sugars and amino acids, pass into the villi and are carried away by the circulating blood.

Vilnius capital of Lithuania; population (1987) 566,000. Industries include engineering and the manufacture of textiles, chemicals, and foodstuffs.

Vimy Ridge hill in N France, taken in World War I by Canadian troops during the battle of Arras, April 1917, at the cost of 11,285 lives. It is a spur of the ridge of Nôtre Dame de Lorette, 8 km/5 mi NE of Arras.

Vincent de Paul, St c. 1580–1660. French Roman Catholic priest and founder of the two charitable orders of Dazarists 1625 and Sisters of Charity 1634. After being ordained 1600, he was captured by Barbary pirates and held as a slave in Tunis until he escaped 1607. He was canonized 1737; feast day 19 July.

vincristine *alkaloid extracted from the blue periwinkle plant (*Vinca rosea*). Developed as an anticancer agent, it has revolutionized the treatment of childhood acute leukaemias; it is also included in *chemotherapy regimens for some lymphomas (cancers arising in the lymph tissues) and lung and breast cancers. Side effects, such as nerve damage and loss of hair, are severe but usually reversible.

vine or **grapevine** any of various climbing woody plants of the genus *Vitis*, family Vitaceae, especially *V. vinifera*, native to Asia Minor and cultivated from antiquity. Its fruit is eaten or made into wine or other fermented drinks; dried fruits of certain varieties are known as raisins and currants. Many other species of climbing plant are also termed vines.

vinegar sour liquid consisting of a 4% solution of acetic acid produced by the oxidation of alcohol, used to flavour food and as a preservative in pickling. **Malt vinegar** is brown and made from malted cereals; **white vinegar** is distilled from it. Other sources of vinegar include cider, wine, and honey. **Balsamic vinegar** is wine vinegar aged in wooden barrels.

Vinland Norse name for the area of North America, probably the coast of Nova Scotia or New England, which the Norse adventurer and explorer Leif *Ericsson visited about 1000. It was named after the wild grapes that grew there and is celebrated in an important Norse saga.

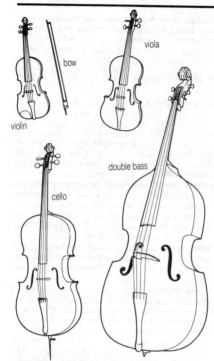

violin family *All the members of the violin family share a common design with minor variations, except the double bass.*

viol family of bowed stringed instruments prominent in the 16th–18th centuries, before their role was taken by the violins. Developed for close-harmony chamber music, they have a pure and restrained tone. Viols normally have six strings, a flat back, and narrow shoulders.

viola bowed, stringed musical instrument, alto member of the *violin family.

violet any plant of the genus *Viola*, family Violaceae, with toothed leaves and mauve, blue, or white flowers, such as the heath dog violet *V. canina* and sweet violet *V. odorata*. A *pansy is a kind of violet.

violin bowed, four-stringed musical instrument, the smallest and highest pitched of the violin family. The strings are tuned in fifths (G, D, A, and E), with G as the lowest, tuned below middle C.

violin family family of bowed stringed instruments developed in Italy during the 17th century, which eventually superseded the viols and formed the basis of the modern orchestra. There are four instruments: violin, viola, and cello (or violoncello); the double bass is descended from the double bass viol (or violone).

violoncello or *cello* bowed, stringed musical instrument, tenor member of the *violin family.

VIP abbreviation for *very important person*.

viper any front-fanged venomous snake of the family Viperidae. Vipers range in size from 30 cm/1 ft to 3 m/10 ft, and often have diamon or jagged markings. Most give birth to live young

Virchow Rudolf Ludwig Carl 1821–1902 German pathologist, the founder of cellula pathology. Virchow was the first to describe leu kaemia (cancer of the blood). In his book *Di Cellulare Pathologie/Cellular Pathology* 1858 he proposed that disease is not due to sudde invasions or changes, but to slow processes i which normal cells give rise to abnormal ones.

Viren Lasse 1949– . Finnish long-distance runner who won the 5,000 metres and 10,000 metres at the 1972 Munich and 1976 Montréa Olympics, becoming the first Olympic athlete successfully to defend both titles at these dis tances.

Virgil (Publius Vergilius Maro) 70–19 BC Roman poet who wrote the *Eclogues* 37 BC, a series of pastoral poems; the *Georgics* 30 BC, fou books on the art of farming; and his epic master-piece, the *Aeneid*.

virginal in music, a small type of *harpsichord.

Virginia state in E USA; nickname Old Dominion
area 105,600 sq km/40,762 sq mi
capital Richmond
towns Norfolk, Virginia Beach, Newport News, Hampton, Chesapeake, Portsmouth Hall (Robert E Lee's birthplace at Lexington); Williamsburg restoration; Jamestown and Yorktown historic sites
products sweet potatoes, maize, tobacco, apples, peanuts, coal, ships, lorries, paper, chemicals, processed food, textiles
population (1990) 6,187,40.

Virgin Islands group of about 100 small islands, northernmost of the Leeward Islands in the Antilles, West Indies. Tourism is the main industry. They comprise the *US Virgin Islands* St Thomas (with the capital, Charlotte Amalie), St Croix, St John, and about 50 small islets; area 350 sq km/135 sq mi; population (1990) 101,800; and the *British Virgin Islands* Tortola (with the capital, Road Town), Virgin Gorda, Anegada, and Jost van Dykes, and about 40 islets; area 150 sq km/58 sq mi; population (1987) 13,250.

Virgo zodiacal constellation, the second largest in the sky. It is represented as a maiden holding an ear of wheat. The Sun passes through Virgo from late Sept to the end of Oct. Virgo's brightest star is the first-magnitude Spica. Virgo contains the nearest large cluster of galaxies to us, 50 million light years away, consisting of about 3,000 galaxies centred on the giant elliptical galaxy M87. Also in Virgo is the nearest *quasar, 3C 273, an estimated 3 billion light years distant. In astrology, the dates for Virgo are between about 23 Aug and 22 Sept (see *precession).

virion a single mature *virus particle.

virtual memory in computing, a technique whereby a portion of the computer backing stor-age, or external, *memory is used as an extension of its immediate-access, or internal, memory. The contents of an area of the immediate-access memory are stored on, say, a hard disc while they are not needed, and brought back into main memory when required.

virtual reality advanced form of computer simulation, in which a participant has the illusion f being part of an artificial environment. The participant views the environment through two tiny 3-D television screens built into a visor. Sensors detect movements of the participant's head or body, causing the apparent viewing position to change. Gloves (datagloves) fitted with sensors may be worn, which allow the participant seemingly to pick up and move objects in the environment.

virus infectious particle consisting of a core of nucleic acid (DNA or RNA) enclosed in a protein shell. Viruses are acellular and able to function and reproduce only if they can invade a living cell to use the cell's system to replicate themselves. In the process they may disrupt or alter the host cell's own DNA. The healthy human body reacts by producing an antiviral protein, *interferon, which prevents the infection spreading to adjacent cells.

virus in computing, a piece of *software that can replicate itself and transfer itself from one computer to another, without the user being aware of it. Some viruses are relatively harmless, but others can damage or destroy data. They are written by anonymous programmers, often maliciously, and are spread along telephone lines or on *floppy discs. Antivirus software can be used to detect and destroy well-known viruses, but new viruses continually appear and these may bypass existing antivirus programs.

vis-à-vis (French 'face-to-face') with regard to.

Visby historic town and bishopric on the Swedish island of Gotland in the Baltic that became the centre of the German *Hanseatic League.

viscera general term for the organs contained in the chest and abdominal cavities.

Visconti dukes and rulers of Milan 1277–1447. They originated as north Italian feudal lords who attained dominance over the city as a result of alliance with the Holy Roman emperors. Despite papal opposition, by the mid-14th century they ruled 15 other major towns in northern Italy. The duchy was inherited by the *Sforzas 1447.

Visconti Luchino 1906–1976. Italian film, opera, and theatre director. The film *Ossessione* 1942 pioneered neorealist cinema despite being subject to censorship problems from the fascist government; later works include *Rocco and His Brothers* 1960, *The Leopard* 1963, *The Damned* 1969, and *Death in Venice* 1971. His powerful social commentary led to clashes with the Italian government and Roman Catholic Church.

viscose yellowish, syrupy solution made by treating cellulose with sodium hydroxide and carbon disulphide. The solution is then regenerated as continuous filament for the making of *rayon and as cellophane.

viscosity in physics, the resistance of a fluid to flow, caused by its internal friction, which makes it resist flowing past a solid surface or other layers of the fluid. It applies to the motion of an object moving through a fluid as well as the motion of a fluid passing by an object.

viscount in the UK peerage, the fourth degree of nobility, between earl and baron.

Vishnu in Hinduism, the second in the triad of gods (with Brahma and Siva) representing three aspects of the supreme spirit. He is the **Preserver**, and is believed to have assumed human appearance in nine *avatāras*, or incarnations, in such forms as Rama and Krishna. His worshippers are the Vaishnavas.

Visigoth member of the western branch of the *Goths, an E Germanic people.

vision defect any abnormality of the eye that causes less than perfect sight. In a **short-sighted** eye, the lens is fatter than normal, causing light from distant objects to be focused in front and not on the retina. A person with this complaint, called *myopia, cannot see clearly for distances over a few metres, and needs spectacles with diverging lenses. **Long sight**, also called hypermetropia, is caused by an eye lens thinner than normal that focuses light from distant objects behind the retina. The sufferer cannot see close objects clearly, and needs converging-lens spectacles. There are other vision defects, such as *colour blindness and *astigmatism.

visual display unit (VDU) computer terminal consisting of a keyboard for input data and a screen for displaying output. The oldest and the most popular type of VDU screen is the *cathode-ray tube (CRT), which uses essentially the same technology as a television screen. Other types use plasma display technology and *liquid-crystal displays.

vitamin any of various chemically unrelated organic compounds that are necessary in small quantities for the normal functioning of the body. Many act as coenzymes, small molecules that enable *enzymes to function effectively. They are normally present in adequate amounts in a balanced diet. Deficiency of a vitamin will normally lead to a metabolic disorder ('deficiency disease'), which can be remedied by sufficient intake of the vitamin. They are generally classified as **water-soluble** (B and C) or **fat-soluble** (A, D, E, and K).

vitamin C alternative name for *ascorbic acid.

vitreous humour transparent jellylike substance behind the lens of the vertebrate *eye. It gives rigidity to the spherical form of the eye and allows light to pass through to the retina.

vitriol any of a number of sulphate salts. Blue, green, and white vitriols are copper, ferrous, and zinc sulphate, respectively. **Oil of vitriol** is sulphuric acid.

Vitus, St Christian saint, perhaps Sicilian, who was martyred in Rome early in the 4th century. Feast day 15 June.

Vivaldi Antonio (Lucio) 1678–1741. Italian Baroque composer, violinist, and conductor. He wrote 23 symphonies, 75 sonatas, over 400 concertos, including the *Four Seasons* (about 1725) for violin and orchestra, over 40 operas, and much sacred music. His work was largely neglected until the 1930s.

vivipary in animals, a method of reproduction in which the embryo develops inside the body of the female from which it gains nourishment (in contrast to *ovipary and *ovovivipary). Vivipary is best developed in placental mammals, but also occurs in some arthropods, fishes, amphibians, and reptiles that have placentalike structures. In plants, it is the formation of young plantlets or bulbils instead of flowers. The term also describes seeds that germinate prematurely, before falling from the parent plant.

vivisection literally, cutting into a living animal. Used originally to mean experimental surgery or dissection practised on a live subject, the term is often used by *antivivisection campaigners to include any experiment on animals, surgical or otherwise.

viz abbreviation for **videlicet** (Latin 'that is to say', 'namely').

Vladimir I St 956–1015. Russian saint, prince of Novgorod, and grand duke of Kiev. Converted to Christianity 988, he married Anna, Christian sister of the Byzantine emperor *Basil II, and established the Byzantine rite of Orthodox Christianity as the Russian national faith.

Vladivostok port (naval and commercial) in E Siberian Russia, at the Amur Bay on the Pacific coast; population (1987) 615,000. It is kept open by icebreakers during winter. Industries include shipbuilding and the manufacture of precision instruments.

Vlaminck Maurice de 1876–1958. French painter who began using brilliant colour as an early member of the **Fauves** (see *Fauvism), mainly painting landscapes. He later abandoned Fauve colour. He also wrote poetry, novels, and essays.

VLSI (abbreviation for **very large-scale integration**) in electronics, the early-1990s level of advanced technology in the microminiaturization of *integrated circuits, and an order of magnitude smaller than *LSI (large-scale integration).

vocal cords folds of tissue within a mammal's larynx, and a bird's syrinx. Air passing over them makes them vibrate, producing sounds. Muscles in the larynx change the pitch of the sound by adjusting the tension of the vocal cords.

vocative in the grammar of certain inflected languages, for example Latin, the form of a word, especially a name, that is used to indicate that a person or thing is being addressed.

vodka strong colourless alcoholic liquor distilled from rye, potatoes, or barley.

Vogel Hans-Jochen 1926– . German socialist politician, chair of the Social Democratic Party (SPD) 1987–91. A former leader of the SPD in Bavaria and mayor of Munich, he served in the Brandt and Schmidt West German governments in the 1970s as housing and then justice minister and then, briefly, as mayor of West Berlin.

voice sound produced through the mouth and by the passage of air between the *vocal cords. In humans the sound is much amplified by the hollow sinuses of the face, and is modified by the movements of the lips, tongue, and cheeks.

Vojvodina autonomous area in N Serbia, Yugoslavia; area 21,500 sq km/8,299 sq mi; population (1986) 2,050,000, including 1,110,000 Serbs and 390,000 Hungarians. Its capital is Novi Sad. In Sept 1990 Serbia effectively stripped Vojvodina of its autonomous status, causing anti-government and anti-communist riots in early 1991.

vol abbreviation for **volume**.

volatile in chemistry, term describing a substance that readily passes from the liquid to the vapour phase. Volatile substances have a high *vapour pressure.

volatile memory in computing, *memory that loses its contents when the power supply to the computer is disconnected.

volcanic rock *igneous rock formed at the surface of the Earth. It is usually fine-grained, unlike the more coarse-grained intrusive (under the surface) types of igneous rocks. Volcanic rock can be either **lava** (solidified magma) or a **pyroclastic deposit** (fragmentary lava or ash), such as tuff (volcanic ash that has fused to form rock).

volcano vent in the Earth's *crust from which molten rock, lava, ashes, and gases are ejected. Usually it is cone-shaped with a pitlike opening at the top called the crater. Some volcanoes, for example, Stromboli and Vesuvius in Italy, eject the material with explosive violence; others, for example on Hawaii, are quiet and the lava simply rises into the crater and flows over the rim.

vole any of various rodents of the family Cricetidae, subfamily Microtinae, distributed over Europe, Asia, and North America, and related to hamsters and lemmings. They are characterized by stout bodies and short tails. They have brown or grey fur, and blunt noses, and some species reach a length of 30 cm/12 in. They feed on grasses, seeds, aquatic plants, and insects. Many show remarkable fluctuations in numbers over 3–4 year cycles.

Volga longest river in Europe; 3,685 km/2,290 mi, 3,540 km/2,200 mi of which are navigable. It drains most of the central and eastern parts of European Russia, rises in the Valdai plateau, and flows into the Caspian Sea 88 km/55 mi below Astrakhan.

Volgograd formerly (until 1925) *Tsaritsyn* and (1925–61) *Stalingrad* industrial city (metal goods, machinery, sawmills, oil refining) in SW Russia, on the river Volga; population (1987) 988,000.

Volkswagen (VW) German car manufacturer. The original VW, with its distinctive beetle shape, was produced in Germany 1938, a design by Ferdinand *Porsche. It was still in production in Latin America in the late 1980s, by which time it had exceeded 20 million sales.

volleyball indoor and outdoor team game played on a court between two teams of six players each. A net is placed across the centre of the court, and players hit the ball with their hands over it, the aim being to ground it in the opponents' court.

volt SI unit of electromotive force or electric potential, symbol V. A small battery has a potential of 1.5 volts; the domestic electricity supply in the UK is 240 volts (110 volts in the USA) and a high-tension transmission line may carry up to 765,000 volts.

Volta main river in Ghana, about 1,600 km/1,000 mi long, with two main upper branches, the Black and White Volta. It has been dammed to provide power.

Volta, Upper name until 1984 of *Burkina Faso.

Volta Alessandro 1745–1827. Italian physicist who invented the first electric cell (the voltaic pile), the electrophorus (an early electrostatic generator), and an *electroscope.

Voltaire Pen name of François-Marie Arouet 1694–1778. French writer who believed in deism and devoted himself to tolerance, justice, and humanity. He was threatened with arrest for *lettres philosophiques sur les Anglais/Philosophical Letters on the English* 1733 (essays in favour of English ways, thought, and political practice) and had to take refuge. Other writings include *Le Siècle de Louis XIV/The Age of Louis XIV* 1751; *Candide* 1759, a parody on Leibniz's 'best of all possible worlds'; and *Dictionnaire philosophique* 1764.

voltmeter instrument for measuring potential difference (voltage). It has a high internal resistance (so that it passes only a small current), and is connected in parallel with the component across which potential difference is to be measured. A common type is constructed from a sensitive current-detecting moving-coil *galvanometer placed in series with a high-value resistor (multiplier). To measure an AC (*alternating-current) voltage, the circuit must usually include a rectifier; however, a moving-iron instrument can be used to measure alternating voltages without the need for such a device.

volume in geometry, the space occupied by a three-dimensional solid object. A prism (such as a cube) or a cylinder has a volume equal to the area of the base multiplied by the height. For a pyramid or cone, the volume is equal to one-third of the area of the base multiplied by the perpendicular height. The volume of a sphere is equal to $4/3\pi r^3$, where r is the radius. Volumes of irregular solids may be calculated by the technique of *integration.

volumetric analysis procedure used for determining the concentration of a solution. A known volume of a solution of unknown concentration is reacted with a solution of known concentration (standard). The standard solution is delivered from a burette so the volume added is known. This technique is known as *titration. Often an indicator is used to show when the correct proportions have reacted. This procedure is used for acid–base, *redox, and certain other reactions involving solutions.

vomiting expulsion of the contents of the stomach through the mouth. It may have numerous causes, including direct irritation of the stomach, severe pain, dizziness, and emotion. Sustained or repeated vomiting may indicate serious disease, and dangerous loss of water, salt, and acid may result (as in *bulimia).

von Braun Wernher 1912–1977. German rocket engineer who developed German military rockets (*V1 and V2) during World War II and later worked for the space agency *NASA in the USA.

Vonnegut Kurt, Jr 1922– . US writer whose work generally has a science-fiction or fantasy element; his novels include *The Sirens of Titan* 1958, *Cat's Cradle* 1963, *Slaughterhouse-Five* 1969, which draws on his World War II experience of the fire-bombing of Dresden, Germany, *Galapagos* 1985, and *Hocus Pocus* 1990.

Von Neumann John 1903–1957. Hungarian-born US scientist and mathematician, known for his pioneering work on computer design. He invented his 'rings of operators' (called Von Neumann algebras) in the late 1930s, and also contributed to set theory, games theory, cybernetics (with his theory of self-reproducing automata, called **Von Neumann machines**), and the development of the atomic and hydrogen bombs.

voodoo set of magical beliefs and practices, followed in some parts of Africa, South America, and the West Indies, especially Haiti. It arose in the 17th century on slave plantations as a combination of Roman Catholicism and W African religious traditions; believers retain membership in the Roman Catholic church. Beliefs include the existence of *loa*, spirits who closely involve themselves in human affairs, and some of whose identities mesh with those of Christian saints. The loa are invoked by the priest (*houngan*) or priestess (*manbo*) at ceremonies, during which members of the congregation become possessed by the spirits and go into trance.

Vorticism short-lived movement in British painting, begun 1913 by Wyndham *Lewis. Influenced by Cubism and Futurism, he believed that painting should reflect the complexity and change of the modern world. He had a harsh, angular, semi-abstract style.

Voskhod (Russian 'ascent') Soviet spacecraft used in the mid-1960s; it was modified from the single-seat Vostok, and was the first spacecraft capable of carrying two or three cosmonauts. During *Voskhod* 2's flight 1965, Aleksi Leonov made the first space walk.

Vostok (Russian 'east') first Soviet spacecraft, used 1961–63. Vostok was a metal sphere 2.3 m/7.5 ft in diameter, capable of carrying one cosmonaut. It made flights lasting up to five days. *Vostok 1* carried the first person into space, Yuri *Gagarin.

vote expression of opinion by *ballot, show of hands, or other means. In systems that employ direct vote, the *plebiscite and *referendum are fundamental mechanisms. In parliamentary elections the results can be calculated in a number of ways. The main electoral systems are: **simple plurality** or **first past the post**, with single-member constituencies (USA, UK, India, Canada); **absolute majority**, achieved for example by the **alternative vote**, where the voter, in single-member constituencies, chooses a candidate by marking preferences (Australia), or by the **second ballot**, where, if a clear decision is not reached immediately, a second ballot is held (France, Egypt); **proportional representation**, achieved for example by the **party list** system (Israel, most countries of Western Europe, and several in South America), the **additional member** system (Germany), the **single transferable vote** (Ireland and Malta), and the **limited vote** (Japan).

Voyager probes two US space probes, originally *Mariners. *Voyager 1*, launched 5 Sept 1977, passed Jupiter March 1979, and reached Saturn Nov 1980. *Voyager 2* was launched earlier, 20 Aug 1977, on a slower trajectory that took it past Jupiter July 1979, Saturn Aug 1981, Uranus Jan 1986, and Neptune Aug 1989. Like the *Pioneer probes, the Voyagers are on their way out of the Solar System. Their tasks now include helping scientists to locate the position of the heliopause, the boundary at which the influence of the Sun gives way to the forces exerted by other stars.

Voysey Charles Francis Annesley 1857–1941.

English architect and designer. He designed country houses which were characteristically asymmetrical with massive buttresses, long sloping roofs, and rough-cast walls. He also designed textiles and wallpaper.

Vranitzky Franz 1937– . Austrian socialist politician, federal chancellor from 1986. A banker, he entered the political arena through the moderate, left-of-centre Socialist Party of Austria (SPÖ), and became minister of finance 1984. He succeeded Fred Sinowatz as federal chancellor 1986, heading an SPÖ-ÖVP (Austrian People's Party) coalition.

VSTOL (abbreviation for *vertical/short take-off and landing*) aircraft capable of taking off and landing either vertically or using a very short length of runway (see *STOL). Vertical takeoff requires a vector-control system that permits the thrust of the aircraft engine to be changed from horizontal to vertical for takeoff and back again to horizontal to permit forward flight. An alternative VSTOL technology developed in the USA involves tilting the wings of the aircraft from vertical to horizontal and along with them the aircraft propellers, thus changing from vertical lift to horizontal thrust.

Vuillard (Jean) Edouard 1886–1940. French painter and printmaker, a founding member of les *Nabis. His work is mainly decorative, with an emphasis on surface pattern reflecting the influence of Japanese prints. With *Bonnard he produced numerous lithographs and paintings of simple domestic interiors, works that are generally categorized as *intimiste*.

Vukovar river port in Croatia at the junction of rivers Vuka and Danube, 32 km/20 mi SE of Osijek; population (1981) 81,200. Industries include foodstuffs manufacture, fishing, and agricultural trade. In 1991 the town resisted three months of siege by the Serb-dominated Yugoslav army before capitulating. It suffered the severest damage inflicted to any European city since the bombing of Dresden during World War II.

Vulcan in Roman mythology, the god of fire and destruction, later identified with the Greek god *Hephaestus.

vulcanization technique for hardening rubber by heating and chemically combining it with sulphur. The process also makes the rubber stronger and more elastic. If the sulphur content is increased to as much as 30%, the product is the inelastic solid known as ebonite. More expensive alternatives to sulphur, such as selenium and tellurium, are used to vulcanize rubber for specialized products such as vehicle tyres. The process was discovered accidentally by US inventor Charles *Goodyear 1839 and patented 1844.

Vulgate (Latin 'common') the Latin translation of the Bible produced by St Jerome in the 4th century.

vulture *The vulture is a heavily built bird.*

vulture any of various carrion-eating birds of prey with naked heads and necks and with keen senses of sight and smell. Vultures are up to 1 m/3.3 ft long, with wingspans of up to 3.5 m/11.5 ft. The plumage is usually dark, and the head brightly coloured.

wadi in arid regions of the Middle East, a steep-sided valley containing an intermittent stream that flows in the wet season.

wafer in microelectronics, a 'superchip' some 8–10 cm/3–4 in diameter, for which wafer-scale integration (WSI) is used to link the equivalent of many individual *silicon chips, improving reliability, speed, and cooling.

Wagner Otto 1841–1918. Viennese architect. Initially designing in the Art Nouveau style, for example Vienna Stadtbahn 1894–97, he later rejected ornament for rationalism, as in the Post Office Savings Bank, Vienna, 1904–06. He influenced such Viennese architects as Josef Hoffmann, Adolf Loos, and Joseph Olbrich.

Wagner Richard 1813–1883. German opera composer. He revolutionized the 19th-century conception of opera, envisaging it as a wholly new art form in which musical, poetic, and scenic elements should be unified through such devices as the *leitmotif. His operas include *Tannhäuser* 1845, *Lohengrin* 1850, and *Tristan und Isolde* 1865. In 1872 he founded the Festival Theatre in Bayreuth; his masterpiece *Der Ring des Nibelungen/The Ring of the Nibelung*, a sequence of four operas, was first performed there in 1876. His last work, *Parsifal*, was produced in 1882.

wagtail any slim narrow-billed bird of the genus *Motacilla*, about 18 cm/7 in long, with a characteristic flicking movement of the tail. There are about 30 species, found mostly in Eurasia and Africa.

Wahabi puritanical Saudi Islamic sect founded by Muhammad ibn-Abd-al-Wahab (1703–1792), which regards all other sects as heretical. By the early 20th century it had spread throughout the Arabian peninsula; it still remains the official ideology of the Saudi Arabian kingdom.

Wailing Wall or (in Judaism) *Western Wall* the remaining part of the *Temple in Jerusalem, a sacred site of pilgrimage and prayer for Jews. There they offer prayers either aloud ('wailing') or on pieces of paper placed between the stones of the wall.

Waite Terry (Terence Hardy) 1939– . British religious adviser to the archbishop of Canterbury, then Dr Robert *Runcie 1980–87. As the archbishop's special envoy, Waite disappeared 20 Jan 1987 while engaged in secret negotiations to free European hostages in Beirut, Lebanon. He had been taken hostage by an Islamic group and was released 18 Nov 1991.

Wajda Andrzej 1926– . Polish film and theatre director, one of the major figures in postwar European cinema. His films are concerned with the predicament and disillusion of individuals caught up in political events. His works include *Ashes and Diamonds* 1958, *Man of Marble* 1977, *Man of Iron* 1981, *Danton* 1982, and *Korczak* 1990.

wake watch kept over the body of a dead person during the night before their funeral; it originated in Anglo-Saxon times as the eve before a festival.

Waksman Selman Abraham 1888–1973. US biochemist, born in Ukraine. He coined the word 'antibiotic' for bacteria-killing chemicals derived from microorganisms. Waksman was awarded a Nobel prize in 1952 for the discovery of streptomycin, an antibiotic used against tuberculosis.

Walachia alternative spelling of *Wallachia, part of Romania.

Walcott Derek 1930– . West Indian poet and playwright. His work fuses Caribbean and European, classical and contemporary elements, and deals with the divisions within colonial society and his own search for cultural identity. His works include the long poem 'Omeros' 1990, and his adaptation for the stage of Homer's *The Odyssey* 1992; his *Collected Poems* were published in 1986. Nobel Prize for literature 1992.

Waldenses also known as *Waldensians* or *Vaudois* Protestant religious sect, founded *c.* 1170 by Peter Waldo, a merchant of Lyons. They were allied to the *Albigenses. They lived in voluntary poverty, refused to take oaths or take part in war, and later rejected the doctrines of transubstantiation, purgatory, and the invocation of saints. Although subjected to persecution until the 17th century, they spread in France, Germany, and Italy, and still survive in Piedmont.

Waldheim Kurt 1918– . Austrian politician and diplomat, president from 1986. He was secretary general of the United Nations 1972–81, having been Austria's representative there 1964–68 and 1970–71. He was elected president of Austria despite revelations that during World War II he had been an intelligence officer in an army unit responsible for transporting Jews to death camps. His election therefore led to some diplomatic isolation of Austria, and in 1991 he announced that he would not run for re-election.

Waldsterben (German 'forest death') tree die-back related to air pollution, common throughout the industrialized world. It appears to be caused by a mixture of pollutants; the precise chemical mix varies between locations, but it includes acid rain, ozone, sulphur dioxide, and nitrogen oxides.

Wales (Welsh *Cymru*) Principality; constituent part of the UK, in the west between the British Channel and the Irish Sea
area 20,780 sq km/8,021 sq mi
capital Cardiff
towns Swansea, Wrexham, Newport, Carmarthen
exports traditional industries (coal and steel) have declined, but varied modern and high-technology ventures are being developed; Wales has the largest concentration of Japanese-owned plants in the UK. It also has the highest density of sheep in the world and a dairy industry; tourism is important
currency pound sterling
population (1987) 2,836,000

languages Welsh 19% (1981), English
religions Nonconformist Protestant denominations; Roman Catholic minority
government returns 38 members to the UK Parliament.

Wales: history for ancient history, see also *Britain, ancient.

c. 400 BC Wales occupied by Celts from central Europe.
AD 50–60 Wales became part of the Roman Empire.
c. 200 Christianity adopted.
c. 450–600 Wales became the chief Celtic stronghold in the west since the Saxons invaded and settled in S Britain. The Celtic tribes united against England.
8th century Frontier pushed back to *Offa's Dyke.
9th–11th centuries Vikings raided the coasts. At this time Wales was divided into small states organized on a clan basis, although princes such as Rhodri (844–878), Howel the Good (*c.* 904–949), and Griffith ap Llewelyn (1039–1063) temporarily united the country.
11th–12th centuries Continual pressure on Wales from the Normans across the English border was resisted, notably by *Llewelyn I and II.
1277 Edward I of England accepted as overlord by the Welsh.
1284 Edward I completed the conquest of Wales that had been begun by the Normans.
1294 Revolt against English rule put down by Edward I.
1350–1500 Welsh nationalist uprisings against the English; the most notable was that led by Owen Glendower.
1485 Henry Tudor, a Welshman, became Henry VII of England.
1536–43 Acts of Union united England and Wales after conquest under Henry VIII. Wales sent representatives to the English Parliament; English law was established in Wales; English became the official language.
18th century Evangelical revival made Nonconformism a powerful factor in Welsh life. A strong coal and iron industry developed in the south.
19th century The miners and ironworkers were militant supporters of Chartism, and Wales became a stronghold of trade unionism and socialism.
1893 University of Wales founded.
1920s–30s Wales suffered from industrial depression; unemployment reached 21% 1937, and a considerable exodus of population took place.
post-1945 Growing nationalist movement and a revival of the language, earlier suppressed or discouraged.
1966 *Plaid Cymru, the Welsh National Party, returned its first member to Westminster.
1979 Referendum rejected a proposal for limited home rule.
1988 Bombing campaign against estate agents selling Welsh properties to English buyers. For other history, see also *England, history; *United Kingdom.

Walesa Lech 1943– . Polish trade-union leader and president of Poland from 1990, founder of *Solidarity (Solidarność) in 1980, an organization, independent of the Communist

Party, which forced substantial political and economic concessions from the Polish government 1980–81 until being outlawed. He was awarded the Nobel Prize for Peace 1983.

Wales, Prince of title conferred on the eldest son of the UK's sovereign. Prince *Charles was invested as 21st prince of Wales at Caernarvon 1969 by his mother, Elizabeth II.

walkabout Australian Aboriginal English for a nomadic ritual excursion into the bush. The term was adopted in 1970, during tours of Australia and New Zealand by Elizabeth II, for informal public-relations walks by politicians and royalty.

Walker Alice 1944– . US poet, novelist, critic, and essay writer. She was active in the US civil rights movement in the 1960s and, as a black woman, wrote about the double burden of racist and sexist oppression that such women bear. Her novel *The Color Purple* 1983 (filmed 1985) won the Pulitzer Prize.

Walkman trade name of a personal stereo manufactured by the Sony corporation. Introduced 1980, it was the first easily portable cassette player with headphones, and the name Walkman is often used as a generic term.

wallaby any of various small and medium-sized members of the *kangaroo family.

Wallace Alfred Russel 1823–1913. English naturalist who collected animal and plant specimens in South America and SE Asia, and independently arrived at a theory of evolution by natural selection similar to that proposed by Charles *Darwin.

Wallace George Corley 1919– . US politician who was opposed to integration; he was governor of Alabama 1963–67, 1971–79, and 1983–87. He contested the presidency in 1968 as an independent (the American Independent Party) and in 1972 campaigned for the Democratic nomination but was shot at a rally and became partly paralysed.

Wallace line imaginary line running down the Lombok Strait in SE Asia, between the island of Bali and the islands of Lombok and Sulawesi. It was identified by naturalist Alfred Russel Wallace as separating the S Asian (Oriental) and Australian biogeographical regions, each of which has its own distinctive animals.

Wallachia independent medieval principality founded 1290, with allegiance to Hungary until 1330 and under Turkish rule 1387–1861, when it was united with the neighbouring principality of Moldavia to form Romania.

Wallenstein Albrecht Eusebius Wenzel von 1583–1634. German general who, until his defeat at Lützen 1632, led the Habsburg armies in the Thirty Years' War. He was assassinated.

Waller Fats (Thomas Wright) 1904–1943. US jazz pianist and composer with a forceful *stride piano style. His songs, many of which have become jazz standards, include 'Ain't Misbehavin'' 1929, 'Honeysuckle Rose' 1929, and 'Viper's Drag' 1934.

wallflower European perennial garden plant *Cheiranthus cheiri*, family Cruciferae, with fragrant red or yellow flowers in spring.

Wallis Barnes (Neville) 1887–1979. British aeronautical engineer who designed the airship R

00, and during World War II perfected the bouncing bombs' used by the Royal Air Force Dambusters Squadron to destroy the German Möhne and Eder dams in 1943. He also assisted n the development of the Concorde supersonic airliner and developed the *swing-wing aircraft.

Walloon member of a French-speaking people of SE Belgium and adjacent areas of France. The name 'Walloon' is etymologically linked to 'Welsh'.

Wall Street street in Manhattan, New York, on which the stock exchange is situated, and a synonym for stock dealing in the USA. It is so called from a stockade erected 1653.

Wall Street crash 1929 panic selling on the New York Stock Exchange following an artificial boom 1927–29 fed by speculation. On 24 Oct 1929, 13 million shares changed hands, with further heavy selling on 28 Oct and the disposal of 16 million shares on 29 Oct. Many shareholders were ruined, banks and businesses failed, and in the *Depression that followed, unemployment rose to approximately 17 million.

walnut tree *Juglans regia*, probably originating in SE Europe. It can reach 30 m/100 ft, and produces a full crop of edible nuts about a dozen years from planting; the timber is used in furniture and the oil is used in cooking.

Walpole Horace, 4th Earl of Orford 1717–1797. English novelist, letter writer and politician, the son of Robert Walpole. He was a Whig member of Parliament 1741–67. He converted his house at Strawberry Hill, Twickenham (then a separate town SW of London), into a Gothic castle; his *The Castle of Otranto* 1764 established the genre of the Gothic, or 'romance of terror', novel. More than 4,000 of his letters have been published.

Walpole Robert, 1st Earl of Orford 1676–1745. British Whig politician, the first 'prime minister' as First Lord of the Treasury and chancellor of the Exchequer 1715–17 and 1721–42. He encouraged trade and tried to avoid foreign disputes (until forced into the War of Jenkins's Ear with Spain 1739).

Walpurga, St English abbess who preached Christianity in Germany. *Walpurgis Night*, the night of 1 May (one of her feast days), became associated with witches' sabbaths and other superstitions. Her feast day is 25 Feb.

walrus Arctic marine carnivorous mammal

walrus *Like the sea lion, the walrus can bring its hind flippers forward under the body to help it move on land.*

Odobenus rosmarus of the same family (Otaridae) as the eared *seals. It can reach 4 m/13 ft in length, and weigh up to 1,400 kg/3,000 lb. It has webbed flippers, a bristly moustache, and large tusks. It is gregarious except at breeding time and feeds mainly on molluscs. It has been hunted close to extinction for its ivory tusks, hide, and blubber. The Alaskan walrus is close to extinction.

Walsh Raoul 1887–1981. US film director, originally an actor. He made a number of outstanding films, including *The Thief of Bagdad* 1924, *The Roaring Twenties* 1939, and *White Heat* 1949.

Walsingham Francis *c.* 1530–1590. English politician who, as secretary of state from 1573, both advocated a strong anti-Spanish policy and ran the efficient government spy system that made it work.

Walther von der Vogelweide *c.* 1170–1230. German poet, greatest of the *Minnesingers, whose songs dealt mainly with courtly love. Of noble birth, he lived in his youth at the Austrian ducal court in Vienna, adopting a wandering life after the death of his patron in 1198. His lyrics deal mostly with love, but also with religion and politics.

Walton Izaak 1593–1683. English author of the classic fishing text *Compleat Angler* 1653. He was born in Stafford, and settled in London as an ironmonger. He also wrote short biographies of the poets George Herbert and John Donne and the theologian Richard Hooker.

Walton William (Turner) 1902–1983. English composer. Among his works are *Façade* 1923, a series of instrumental pieces designed to be played in conjunction with the recitation of poems by Edith Sitwell; the oratorio *Belshazzar's Feast* 1931; and *Variations on a Theme by Hindemith* 1963.

waltz ballroom dance in three-four time evolved from the Austrian *Ländler* (traditional peasants' country dance) and later made popular by the *Strauss family in Vienna.

Wandering Jew in medieval legend, a Jew named Ahasuerus, said to have insulted Jesus on his way to Calvary and to have been condemned to wander the world until the Second Coming.

Wang An 1920–1990. Chinese-born US engineer, founder of Wang Laboratories 1951, one of the world's largest computer companies in the 1970s. He emigrated to the USA 1945 and three years later invented the computer memory core, the most common device used for storing computer data before the invention of the integrated circuit (chip).

Wankel engine rotary petrol engine developed by the German engineer Felix Wankel (1902–) in the 1950s. It operates according to the same stages as the *four-stroke petrol engine cycle, but these stages take place in different sectors of a figure-eight chamber in the space between the chamber walls and a triangular rotor. Power is produced once on every turn of the rotor. The Wankel engine is simpler in construction than the four-stroke piston petrol engine, and produces rotary power directly (instead of via a crankshaft). Problems with rotor seals have prevented its widespread use.

wapiti or *elk* species of deer *Cervus canaden-*

sis, native to North America, Europe, and Asia, including New Zealand. It is reddish brown in colour, about 1.5 m/5 ft at the shoulder, weighs up to 450 kg/1,000 lb, and has antlers up to 1.2 m/4 ft long. It is becoming increasingly rare.

Wapping district of the Greater London borough of Tower Hamlets; situated between the Thames and the former London Docks. Since the 1980s it has become a centre of the UK newspaper industry.

war act of force, usually on behalf of the state, intended to compel a declared enemy to obey the will of the other. The aim is to render the opponent incapable of further resistance by destroying its capability and will to bear arms in pursuit of its own aims. War is therefore a continuation of politics carried on with violent and destructive means, as an instrument of policy.

Warbeck Perkin *c.* 1474–1499. Flemish pretender to the English throne. Claiming to be Richard, brother of Edward V, he led a rising against Henry VII in 1497, and was hanged after attempting to escape from the Tower of London.

War between the States another (usually Southern) name for the American *Civil War.

warbler any of two families of songbirds, order Passeriformes.

Warburg Otto 1878–1976. German biochemist who in 1923 devised a manometer (pressure gauge) sensitive enough to measure oxygen uptake of respiring tissue. By measuring the rate at which cells absorb oxygen under differing conditions, he was able to show that enzymes called cytochromes enable cells to process oxygen. He was awarded the Nobel Prize for Medicine 1931. Warburg also demonstrated that cancerous cells absorb less oxygen than normal cells.

war crime offence (such as murder of a civilian or a prisoner of war) that contravenes the internationally accepted laws governing the conduct of wars, particularly The Hague Convention 1907 and the Geneva Convention 1949. A key principle of the law relating to such crimes is that obedience to the orders of a superior is no defence. In practice, prosecutions are generally brought by the victorious side.

ward of court in the UK, a child whose guardian is the High Court. Any person may, by issuing proceedings, make the High Court guardian of any child within its jurisdiction. No important step in the child's life can then be taken without the court's leave.

warfarin poison that induces fatal internal bleeding in rats; neutralized with sodium hydroxide, it is used in medicine as an anticoagulant: it prevents blood clotting by inhibiting the action of vitamin K. It can be taken orally and begins to act several days after the initial dose.

Warhol Andy. Adopted name of Andrew Warhola 1928–1987. US Pop artist and filmmaker. He made his name in 1962 with paintings of Campbell's soup cans, Coca-Cola bottles, and film stars. In his New York studio, the Factory, he produced series of garish silk-screen prints. His films include the semidocumentary *Chelsea Girls* 1966 and *Trash* 1970.

warlord in China, any of the provincial leaders who took advantage of central government weak-

ness, after the death of the first president o Republican China 1912, to organize their owr private armies and fiefdoms. They engaged ir civil wars until Chiang Kai-shek's Northern Expedition against them 1926, but they exerted power until the Communists came to powe under Mao Zedong 1949.

Warner Bros US film production company founded 1923 by Harry, Albert, Sam, and Jack Warner. It became one of the major Hollywood studios after releasing the first talking film, *The Jazz Singer* 1927. During the 1930s and 1950s company stars included Humphrey Bogart, Errol Flynn, and Bette Davis. It suffered in the 1960s through competition with television and was taken over by Seven Art Productions. In 1969 there was another takeover by Kinney National Service, and the whole company became known as *Warner Communications*.

warning coloration in biology, an alternative term for *aposematic coloration.

War of 1812 war between the USA and Britain caused by British interference with US trade as part of the economic warfare against Napoleonic France. Tensions within the British in Canada led to plans for a US invasion but these were never realized and success was limited to the capture of Detroit and a few notable naval victories. In 1814, British forces occupied Washington, DC and burned many public buildings. A treaty signed in Ghent, Belgium, Dec 1814 ended the conflict.

War Powers Act legislation passed 1973 enabling the US president to deploy US forces abroad for combat without prior Congressional approval. The president is nevertheless required to report to both Houses of Congress within 48 hours of having taken such action. Congress may restrict the continuation of troop deployment despite any presidential veto.

Warren Robert Penn 1905–1989. US poet and novelist, the only author to receive a Pulitzer prize for both prose and poetry. His novel *All the King's Men* 1946 was modelled on the career of Huey *Long, and he also won Pulitzer prizes for *Promises* 1968 and *Now and Then: Poems* 1976–78. He was the first official US poet laureate 1986–88.

Warsaw (Polish *Warszawa*) capital of Poland, on the river Vistula; population (1990) 1,655,700. Industries include engineering, food processing, printing, clothing, and pharmaceuticals.

Warsaw Pact or *Eastern European Mutual Assistance Pact* military alliance 1955–91 between the USSR and East European communist states, originally established as a response to the admission of West Germany into NATO. Its military structures and agreements were dismantled early in 1991; a political organization remained until the alliance was officially dissolved July 1991.

warship fighting ship armed and crewed for war. The supremacy of the battleship at the beginning of the 20th century was rivalled during World War I by the development of *submarine attack, and was rendered obsolescent in World War II with the advent of long-range air attack. Today the largest and most important surface warships are the *aircraft carriers.

wart protuberance composed of a local overgrowth of skin. The common wart (*verruca vulgaris*) is due to a virus infection. It usually disappears spontaneously within two years, but can be treated with peeling applications, burning away (cautery), or freezing (cryosurgery).

wart hog African wild *pig *Phacochoerus aethiopicus*, which has a large head with a bristly mane, fleshy pads beneath the eyes, and four large tusks. It has short legs and can grow to 80 cm/2.5 ft at the shoulder.

Warwick Richard Neville, Earl of Warwick 1428–1471. English politician, called **the Kingmaker**. During the Wars of the *Roses he fought at first on the Yorkist side against the Lancastrians, and was largely responsible for placing Edward IV on the throne. Having quarrelled with him, he restored Henry VI in 1470, but was defeated and killed by Edward at Barnet, Hertfordshire.

Warwickshire county in central England
area 1,980 sq km/764 sq mi
towns Warwick (administrative headquarters), Leamington, Nuneaton, Rugby, Stratford-upon-Avon
products mainly agricultural, engineering, textiles
population (1991) 477,000
famous people Rupert Brooke, George Eliot, William Shakespeare.

Wash, the bay of the North Sea between Norfolk and Lincolnshire, England.

washing soda $a_2CO_3.10H_2O$ (chemical name **sodium carbonate decahydrate**) substance added to washing water to 'soften' it (see water, hardness of).

Washington state in NW USA; nickname Evergreen State/Chinook State
area 176,700 sq km/68,206 sq mi
capital Olympia
towns Seattle, Spokane, Tacoma
products apples and other fruits, potatoes, livestock, fish, timber, processed food, wood products, paper and allied products, aircraft and aerospace equipment, aluminium
population (1990) 4,866,700; including 1.4% Indians, mainly of the Yakima people
famous people Bing Crosby, Jimi Hendrix, Mary McCarthy, Theodore Roethke
history explored by Spanish, British, and Americans in the 18th century; settled from 1811; became a territory 1853 and a state 1889.

Washington Booker T(aliaferro) 1856–1915. US educationist, pioneer in higher education for black people in the South. He was the founder and first principal of Tuskegee Institute, Alabama, in 1881, originally a training college for blacks, which has become a respected academic institution. He maintained that economic independence was the way to achieve social equality.

Washington George 1732–1799. First president of the USA 1789–97. As a strong opponent of the British government's policy, he sat in the *Continental Congresses of 1774 and 1775, and on the outbreak of the War of *American Independence was chosen commander in chief. After the war he retired to his Virginia estate, Mount Vernon, but in 1787 he re-entered politics as president of the Constitutional Convention.

Although he attempted to draw his ministers from all factions, his aristocratic outlook alienated his secretary of state, Thomas Jefferson, who resigned in 1793, thus creating the two-party system.

Washington Convention alternative name for *CITES*, the international agreement that regulates trade in endangered species.

Washington, DC (District of Columbia) national capital of the USA, on the Potomac River
area 180 sq km/69 sq mi
capital the District of Columbia covers only the area of the city of Washington
population (1983) 623,000 (metropolitan area, extending outside the District of Columbia, 3 million)
history the District of Columbia, initially land ceded from Maryland and Virginia, was established by Act of Congress 1790–91, and was first used as the seat of Congress 1800. The right to vote in national elections was not granted to residents until 1961. Local self-rule began 1975. In 1988 Washington had the highest murder rate of any large city in the USA.

wasp any of several families of winged stinging insects of the order Hymenoptera, characterized by a thin stalk between the thorax and the abdomen. Wasps can be social or solitary. Among social wasps, the queens devote themselves to egg laying, the fertilized eggs producing female workers; the males come from unfertilized eggs and have no sting. The larvae are fed on insects, but the mature wasps feed mainly on fruit and sugar. In winter, the fertilized queens hibernate, but the other wasps die.

WASP acronym for *white Anglo-Saxon Protestant*, common (frequently derogatory) term to describe the white elite in American society, specifically those educated at Ivy League universities and belonging to the Episcopalian Church.

waste materials that are no longer needed and are discarded. Examples are household waste, industrial waste (which often contains toxic chemicals), medical waste (which may contain organisms that cause disease), and *nuclear waste (which is radioactive). By *recycling, some materials in waste can be reclaimed for further use. In 1990 the industrialized nations generated 2 billion tonnes of waste. In the USA, 40 tonnes of solid waste is generated annually per person.

waste disposal depositing waste. Methods of waste disposal vary according to the materials in the waste and include incineration, burial at designated sites, and dumping at sea. Organic waste can be treated and reused as fertilizer (see *sewage disposal). *Nuclear waste and *toxic waste is usually buried or dumped at sea, although this does not negate the danger.

watch portable timepiece. In the early 20th century increasing miniaturization, mass production, and, in World War I, the advantages of the wristband led to the watch moving from the pocket to the wrist. Watches were also subsequently made waterproof, antimagnetic, selfwinding, and shock-resistant. In 1957 the electric watch was developed, and in the 1970s came the digital watch, which dispensed with all moving parts.

water H_2O liquid without colour, taste, or

odour. It is an oxide of hydrogen. Water begins to freeze at 0°C or 32°F, and to boil at 100°C or 212°F. When liquid, it is virtually incompressible; frozen, it expands by 111 of its volume. At 39.2°F/4°C, one cubic centimetre of water has a mass of one gram; this is its maximum density, forming the unit of specific gravity. It has the highest known specific heat, and acts as an efficient solvent, particularly when hot. Most of the world's water is in the sea; less than 0.01% is fresh water.

water boatman any water *bug of the family Corixidae that feeds on plant debris and algae. It has a flattened body 1.5 cm/0.6 in long, with oarlike legs.

water-borne disease disease associated with poor water supply. In the Third World four-fifths of all illness is caused by water-borne diseases, with diarrhoea being the leading cause of childhood death. Malaria, carried by mosquitoes dependent on stagnant water for breeding, affects 400 million people every year and kills 5 million. Polluted water is also a problem in industrialized nations, where industrial dumping of chemical, hazardous, and radioactive wastes causes a range of diseases from headache to cancer.

waterbuck any of several African *antelopes of the genus *Kobus* which usually inhabit swampy tracts and reedbeds. They vary in size from 1.4 m/6 ft to 2.1 m/7.25 ft long, are up to 1.4 m/4.5 ft tall at the shoulder, and have long brown fur. The large curved horns, normally carried only by the males, have corrugated surfaces. Some species have white patches on the buttocks. Lechwe, kor, and defassa are alternative names for some of the species.

water closet (WC) flushing lavatory that works by siphon action. The first widely used WC was produced in the 1770s by Alexander Cummings in London. The present type dates from Davis Bostel's invention of 1889, which featured a ball-cock valve system to refill the flushing cistern.

watercolour painting method of painting with pigments mixed with water, known in China as early as the 3rd century. The art as practised today began in England in the 18th century with the work of Paul Sandby and was developed by Thomas Girtin and J M W Turner. Other watercolourists were Raoul Dufy, Paul Cézanne, and John Marin. The technique of watercolour painting requires great skill since its transparency rules out overpainting.

watercress perennial aquatic plant *Nasturtium officinale* of the crucifer family, found in Europe and Asia, and cultivated as a salad crop.

water cycle in ecology, the natural circulation of water through the *biosphere. Water is lost from the Earth's surface to the atmosphere either by evaporation from the surface of lakes, rivers, and oceans or through the transpiration of plants. This atmospheric water forms clouds that condense to deposit moisture on the land and sea as rain or snow. The water that collects on land flows to the ocean in streams and rivers.

waterfall cascade of water in a river or stream. It occurs when a river flows over a bed of rock that resists erosion; weaker rocks downstream are worn away, creating a steep, vertical drop and a plunge pool into which the water falls. As the river ages, continuing erosion causes the water-fall to retreat upstream forming a deep valley, or gorge.

water flea any aquatic crustacean in the order Cladocera, of which there are over 400 species. The commonest species is *Daphnia pulex*, used in the pet trade to feed tropical fish.

Waterford county in Munster province, Republic of Ireland; area 1,840 sq km/710 sq mi; population (1991) 91,600. The county town is Waterford. The county includes the rivers Suir and Blackwater, and the Comeragh and Monavallagh mountain ranges in the north and centre. Products include cattle, beer, whiskey, and glassware.

waterfowl any water bird, but especially any member of the family Anatidae, which consists of ducks, geese, and swans.

Watergate US political scandal, named after the building in Washington, DC that housed the Democrats' campaign headquarters in the 1972 presidential election. Five men, hired by the Republican Committee to Re-elect the President (CREEP), were caught after breaking into the Watergate with complex electronic surveillance equipment. Investigations revealed that the White House was implicated in the break-in, and that there was a 'slush fund', used to finance unethical activities. In Aug 1974, President *Nixon was forced by the Supreme Court to surrender to Congress tape recordings of conversations he had held with administration officials, which indicated his complicity in a cover-up. Nixon resigned rather than face impeachment for obstruction of justice and other crimes.

water glass common name for sodium metasilicate (Na_2SiO_3). It is a colourless, jellylike substance that dissolves readily in water to give a solution used for preserving eggs and fireproofing porous materials such as cloth, paper, and wood. It is also used as an adhesive for paper and cardboard and in the manufacture of soap and silica gel, a substance that absorbs moisture.

water hyacinth tropical aquatic plant *Eichhornia crassipes* of the pickerelweed family Pontederiaceae. In one growing season 25 plants can produce 2 million new plants. It is liable to choke waterways, depleting the water of nutrients and blocking the sunlight, but can be used as a purifier of sewage-polluted water as well as in making methane gas, compost, concentrated protein, paper, and baskets. Originating in South America, it now grows in more than 50 countries.

water lily aquatic plant of the family Nymphaeaceae. The fleshy roots are embedded in mud and the large round leaves float on the water. The cup-shaped flowers may be white, pink, yellow, or blue.

Waterloo, Battle of battle on 18 June 1815 in which British forces commanded by Wellington defeated the French army of Emperor Napoleon near the village of Waterloo, 13 km/8 mi S of Brussels, Belgium. Napoleon found Wellington's army isolated from his allies and began a direct offensive to smash them, but the British held on until joined by the Prussians under General Blücher. Four days later Napoleon abdicated for the second and final time.

water meadow irrigated meadow. By flooding the land for part of each year, increased yields of nay are obtained. Water meadows were common in Italy, Switzerland, and England (from 1523) but have now largely disappeared.

watermelon large *melon Citrullus vulgaris of the gourd family, native to tropical Africa, with pink, white, or yellow flesh studded with black seeds and a green rind. It is widely cultivated in subtropical regions.

water mill machine that harnesses the energy n flowing water to produce mechanical power, typically for milling (grinding) grain. Water from a stream is directed against the paddles of a water wheel to make it turn. Simple gearing transfers his motion to the millstones. The modern equivalent of the water wheel is the water turbine, used in *hydroelectric power plants.

water pollution any addition to fresh or sea water that disrupts biological processes or causes a health hazard. Common pollutants include nitrate, pesticides, and sewage (see *sewage disposal), though a huge range of industrial contaminants, such as chemical byproducts and residues created in the manufacture of various goods, also enter water – legally, accidentally, and through illegal dumping.

water polo water sport developed in England 869, originally called 'soccer-in-water'. The aim s to score goals, as in soccer, at each end of a swimming pool. It is played by teams of seven a side (from squads of 13).

water skiing water sport in which a person is towed across water on a ski or skis, wider than those used for skiing on snow, by means of a rope (23 m/75 ft long) attached to a speedboat. Competitions are held for overall performances, slalom, tricks, and jumping.

water softener any substance or unit that removes the hardness from water. Hardness is caused by the presence of calcium and magnesium ions, which combine with soap to form an insoluble scum, prevent lathering, and cause deposits to build up in pipes and cookware (kettle fur). A water softener replaces these ions with sodium ions, which are fully soluble and cause no scum.

water supply distribution of water for domestic, municipal, or industrial consumption. Water supply in sparsely populated regions usually comes from underground water rising to the surface in natural springs, supplemented by pumps and wells. Urban sources are deep artesian wells, rivers, and reservoirs, usually formed from enlarged lakes or dammed and flooded valleys, from which water is conveyed by pipes, conduits, and aqueducts to filter beds. As water seeps through layers of shingle, gravel, and sand, harmful organisms are removed and the water is then distributed by pumping or gravitation through mains and pipes. Often other substances are added to the water, such as chlorine and fluorine; aluminium sulphate, a clarifying agent, is the most widely used chemical in water treatment. In towns, domestic and municipal (road washing, sewage) needs account for about 35 l/30 gal per head each day. In coastal desert areas, such as the Arabian peninsula, desalination plants remove salt from sea water. The earth's waters, both fresh and saline, have been polluted by industrial and domestic chemicals, some of which are toxic and others radioactive.

water table the upper level of ground water (water collected underground in porous rocks). Water that is above the water table will drain downwards; a spring forms where the water table cuts the surface of the ground. The water table rises and falls in response to rainfall and the rate at which water is extracted, for example, for irrigation.

Watling Street Roman road running from London to Wroxeter (*Viroconium*) near Chester, NW England.

Watson James Dewey 1928– . US biologist whose research on the molecular structure of DNA and the genetic code, in collaboration with Francis *Crick, earned him a shared Nobel prize in 1962. Based on earlier works, they were able to show that DNA formed a double helix of two spiral strands held together by base pairs.

Watson John Broadus 1878–1958. US psychologist, founder of behaviourism. He rejected introspection (observation by an individual of his or her own mental processes) and regarded psychology as the study of observable behaviour, within the scientific tradition.

Watson-Watt Robert Alexander 1892–1973. Scottish physicist who developed a forerunner of *radar. During a long career in government service (1915–1952) he proposed in 1935 a method of radiolocation of aircraft – a key factor in the Allied victory over German aircraft in World War II.

watt SI unit (symbol W) of power (the rate of expenditure or consumption of energy). A light bulb may use 40, 100, or 150 watts of power; an electric heater will use several kilowatts (thousands of watts). The watt is named after the Scottish engineer James Watt.

Watt James 1736–1819. Scottish engineer who developed the steam engine. He made Thomas *Newcomen's steam engine vastly more efficient by cooling the used steam in a condenser separate from the main cylinder.

Watteau Jean-Antoine 1684–1721. French Rococo painter. He developed a new category of genre painting known as the *fête galante*, scenes of a kind of aristocratic pastoral fantasy world. One of these pictures, *The Embarkation for Cythera* 1717 (Louvre, Paris), won him membership in the French Academy.

wattle certain species of *acacia in Australia, where their fluffy golden flowers are the national emblem. The leathery leaves, adapted to drought conditions, further avoid loss of water through transpiration by turning their edges to the direct rays of the sun. Wattles are used for tanning and in fencing.

wattle and daub method of constructing walls consisting of upright stakes bound together with withes (strong flexible shoots or twigs, usually of willow), and covered in mud or plaster. This was the usual way of building houses in medieval Europe; it was also the traditional method used in Australia, Africa, the Middle East, and the Far East.

Watts George Frederick 1817–1904. English painter and sculptor. He painted allegorical, biblical, and classical subjects, investing his work with a solemn morality, such as *Hope* 1886 (Tate Gallery, London). Many of his portraits are in the National Portrait Gallery, London. As a sculptor he executed *Physical Energy* 1904 for Cecil Rhodes's memorial in Cape Town, South Africa; a replica is in Kensington Gardens, London.

Waugh Evelyn (Arthur St John) 1903–1966. English novelist. His social satires include *Decline and Fall* 1928, *Vile Bodies* 1930, and *The Loved One* 1948. A Roman Catholic convert from 1930, he developed a serious concern with religious issues in *Brideshead Revisited* 1945. *The Ordeal of Gilbert Pinfold* 1957 is largely autobiographical.

wave in the oceans, a ridge or swell formed by wind or other causes. The power of a wave is determined by the strength of the wind and the distance of open water over which the wind blows (the fetch). Waves are the main agents of *coastal erosion and deposition: sweeping away or building up beaches, creating *spits and berms, and wearing down cliffs by their hydraulic action and by the corrosion of the sand and shingle that they carry. A *tsunami (misleadingly called a 'tidal wave') is a type of freak wave.

wave in physics, a disturbance consisting of a series of oscillations that propagate through a medium (or space). There are two types: in a *longitudinal wave* (such as a *sound wave) the disturbance is parallel to the wave's direction of travel; in a *transverse wave* (such as an *electromagnetic wave) it is perpendicular. The medium only vibrates as the wave passes; it does not travel outward from the source with the waves.

wavelength the distance between successive crests of a *wave. The wavelength of a light wave determines its colour; red light has a wavelength of about 700 nanometres, for example. The complete range of wavelengths of electromagnetic waves is called the electromagnetic *spectrum.

Wavell Archibald, 1st Earl 1883–1950. British field marshal in World War II. As commander in chief Middle East, he successfully defended Egypt against Italy July 1939. He was transferred as commander in chief India in July 1941, and was viceroy 1943–47.

wave power power obtained by harnessing the energy of water waves. Various schemes have been advanced since 1973, when oil prices rose dramatically and an energy shortage threatened. In 1974 the British engineer Stephen Salter developed the duck – a floating boom whose segments nod up and down with the waves. The nodding motion can be used to drive pumps and spin generators. Another device, developed in Japan, uses an oscillating water column to harness wave power.

wax solid fatty substance of animal, vegetable, or mineral origin. Waxes are composed variously of *esters, *fatty acids, free *alcohols, and solid hydrocarbons.

waxbill any of a group of small mainly African seed-eating birds in the family Estrildidae, order Passeriformes, which also includes the grass finches of Australia. Waxbills grow to 15 cm/6 in long, are brown and grey with yellow, red, or brown markings, and have waxy-looking red or pink beaks.

wayfaring tree European shrub *Viburnum*

lantana of the honeysuckle family, with clusters of fragrant white flowers, found on limy soils; naturalized in the NE USA.

Wayne John ('Duke'). Stage name of Marion Morrison 1907–1979. US actor, the archetypal Western hero: plain-speaking, brave, and solitary. His films include *Stagecoach* 1939, *Red River* 1948, *She Wore a Yellow Ribbon* 1949, *The Searchers* 1956, *Rio Bravo* 1959, *The Man Who Shot Liberty Valance* 1962, and *True Grit* 1969 (Academy Award). He was active in conservative politics.

w.c. abbreviation for *water closet*, another name for a *toilet.

weak nuclear force one of the four fundamental forces of nature, the other three being gravity, the electromagnetic force, and the strong nuclear force. It causes radioactive decay and other subatomic reactions. The particles that carry the weak force are called *weakons (or intermediate vector bosons) and comprise the positively and negatively charged W particles and the neutral Z particle.

weakon or *intermediate vector boson* in physics, a *gauge boson that carries the weak nuclear force, one of the fundamental forces of nature. There are three types of weakon, the positive and negative W particle and the neutral Z particle.

weapon any implement used for attack and defence, from simple clubs, spears, and bow and arrows in prehistoric times to machine guns and nuclear bombs in modern times. The first revolution in warfare came with the invention of *gunpowder and the development of cannons and shoulder-held guns. Many other weapons now exist, such as grenades, shells, torpedoes, rockets, and guided missiles. The ultimate in explosive weapons are the atomic (fission) and hydrogen (fusion) bombs. They release the enormous energy produced when atoms split or fuse together (see *nuclear warfare). There are also chemical and bacteriological weapons.

Wear river in NE England; length 107 km/67 mi. From its source in the Pennines it flows east, past Durham to meet the North Sea at Sunderland.

weasel any of various small, short-legged, lithe carnivorous mammals with bushy tails, especially the genus *Mustela*, found worldwide except Australia. They feed mainly on small rodents, although some, like the mink *M. vison*, hunt aquatic prey. Most are 12–25 cm/5–10 in long, excluding tail.

weather day-to-day variation of climatic and atmospheric conditions at any one place, or the state of these conditions at a place at any one time. Such conditions include humidity, precipitation, temperature, cloud cover, visibility, and wind. To a meteorologist the term 'weather' is limited to the state of the sky, precipitation, and visibility as affected by fog or mist. See *meteorology and *climate.

weather area any of the divisions of the sea around the British Isles for the purpose of weather forecasting for shipping. The areas are used to indicate where strong or gale-force winds are expected.

weathering process by which exposed rocks are broken down on the spot by the action of rain, frost, wind, and other elements of the weather. It differs from *erosion in that no movement or transportion of the broken-down material takes place. Two types of weathering are recognized: physical (or mechanical) and chemical. They usually occur together.

weaver any small bird of the family Ploceidae, order Passeriformes, mostly about 15 cm/6 in long, which includes the house *sparrow. The majority of weavers are African, a few Asian. The males use grasses to weave elaborate globular nests in bushes and trees. Males are often more brightly coloured than females.

weaving the production of textile fabric by means of a loom. The basic process is the interlacing at right angles of longitudinal threads (the warp) and horizontal threads (the weft), the latter being carried across from one side of the loom to the other by a type of bobbin called a shuttle.

Webb (Martha) Beatrice (born Potter) 1858–1943 and Sidney (James), Baron Passfield 1859–1947. English social reformers, writers, and founders of the London School of Economics (LSE) 1895. They were early members of the socialist *Fabian Society, and were married in 1892. They argued for social insurance in their minority report (1909) of the Poor Law Commission, and wrote many influential books, including *The History of Trade Unionism* 1894, *English Local Government* 1906–29, and *Soviet Communism* 1935.

Webb Philip (Speakman) 1831–1915. English architect. He mostly designed private houses, including the Red House, Bexley Heath, Sussex, for William *Morris, and was one of the leading figures, with Richard Norman *Shaw and C F A *Voysey, in the revival of domestic English architecture in the late 19th century.

Webber Andrew Lloyd. English composer of musicals; see *Lloyd Webber.

weber SI unit (symbol Wb) of *magnetic flux the magnetic field strength multiplied by the area through which the field passes). One weber equals 10^8 *maxwells.

Weber Carl Maria Friedrich Ernst von 1786–1826. German composer who established the Romantic school of opera with *Der Freischütz* 1821 and *Euryanthe* 1823. He was kapellmeister (chief conductor) at Breslau 1804–06, Prague 1813–16, and Dresden 1816. He died during a visit to London where he produced his opera *Oberon* 1826, written for the Covent Garden theatre.

Weber Max 1864–1920. German sociologist, one of the founders of modern sociology. He emphasized cultural and political factors as key influences on economic development and individual behaviour.

Weber Wilhelm Eduard 1804–1891. German physicist who studied magnetism and electricity, brother of Ernst Weber. Working with Karl Gauss, he made sensitive magnetometers to measure magnetic fields, and instruments to measure direct and alternating currents. He also built an electric telegraph. The SI unit of magnetic flux, the **weber**, is named after him.

Webern Anton (Friedrich Wilhelm von) 1883–1945. Austrian composer. He was a pupil of *Schoenberg, whose 12-tone technique he adopted. He wrote works of extreme brevity; for example, the oratorio *Das Augenlicht/The Light of Eyes* 1935, and songs to words by Stefan George and poems of Rilke.

Webster John c. 1580–1634. English dramatist who ranks after Shakespeare as the greatest tragedian of his time and is the Jacobean whose plays are most frequently performed today. His two great plays *The White Devil* 1608 and *The Duchess of Malfi* 1614 are dark, violent tragedies obsessed with death and decay and infused with poetic brilliance.

Webster Noah 1758–1843. US lexicographer whose books on grammar and spelling and *American Dictionary of the English Language* 1828 standardized US English.

Weddell Sea arm of the S Atlantic Ocean that cuts into the Antarctic continent SE of Cape Horn; area 8,000,000 sq km/3,000,000 sq mi. Much of it is covered with thick pack ice for most of the year.

Wedekind Frank 1864–1918. German dramatist. He was a forerunner of Expressionism with *Frühlings Erwachen/The Awakening of Spring* 1891, and *Der Erdgeist/The Earth Spirit* 1895 and its sequel *Der Marquis von Keith. Die Büchse der Pandora/Pandora's Box* 1904 was the source for Berg's opera *Lulu*.

wedge block of triangular cross-section that can be used as a simple machine. An axe is a wedge: it splits wood by redirecting the energy of the downward blow sideways, where it exerts the force needed to split the wood.

Wedgwood Josiah 1730–1795. English pottery manufacturer. He set up business in Staffordshire in the early 1760s to produce his agateware as well as unglazed blue or green stoneware decorated with white Neo-Classical designs, using pigments of his own invention.

weedkiller or **herbicide** chemical that kills some or all plants. Selective herbicides are effective with cereal crops because they kill all broad-leaved plants without affecting grasslike leaves. Those that kill all plants include sodium chlorate and *paraquat; see also *Agent Orange. The widespread use of weedkillers in agriculture has led to a dramatic increase in crop yield but also to pollution of soil and water supplies and killing of birds and small animals, as well as creating a health hazard for humans.

weever fish any of a family (Trachinidae) of marine bony fishes of the perch family, especially the genus *Trachinus*, with poison glands on dorsal fin and gill cover that can give a painful sting. It grows up to 5 cm/2 in long, has eyes near the top of the head, and lives on sandy seabeds.

weevil any of a superfamily (Curculionoidea) of *beetles, usually less than 6 mm/0.25 in long, and with a head prolonged into a downward beak, which is used for boring into plant stems and trees for feeding.

Wegener Alfred Lothar 1880–1930. German meteorologist and geophysicist, whose theory of *continental drift, expounded in *Origin of Continents and Oceans* 1915, was originally known as Wegener's hypothesis. His ideas can now be explained in terms of plate tectonics, the idea that the Earth's crust consists of a number of plates, all moving with respect to one another.

Wei Jingsheng 1951– . Chinese pro-democracy activist and essayist, imprisoned from 1979 for attacking the Chinese communist system. He is regarded as one of China's most important political prisoners.

weight the force exerted on an object by *gravity. The weight of an object depends on its mass – the amount of material in it – and the strength of the Earth's gravitational pull, which decreases with height. Consequently, an object weighs less at the top of a mountain than at sea level. On the Moon, an object has only one-sixth of its weight on Earth, because the pull of the Moon's gravity is one-sixth that of the Earth.

weightlessness condition in which there is no gravitational force acting on a body, either because gravitational force is cancelled out by equal and opposite acceleration, or because the body is so far outside a planet's gravitational field that it no force is exerted upon it.

weightlifting sport of lifting the heaviest possible weight above one's head to the satisfaction of judges. In international competitions there are two standard lifts: *snatch* and *jerk*.

weights and measures see under *c.g.s. system, *f.p.s. system, *m.k.s. system, *SI units.

Weil Simone 1909–1943. French writer who became a practising Catholic after a mystical experience in 1938. Apart from essays, her works (advocating political passivity) were posthumously published, including *Waiting for God* 1951, *The Need for Roots* 1952, and *Notebooks* 1956.

Weill Kurt (Julian) 1900–1950. German composer, US citizen from 1943. He wrote chamber and orchestral music and collaborated with Bertolt *Brecht on operas such as *Die Dreigroschenoper/The Threepenny Opera* 1928 and *Aufsteig und Fall der Stadt Mahagonny/The Rise and Fall of the City of Mahagonny* 1930, all attacking social corruption (*Mahagonny* caused a riot at its premiere in Leipzig). He tried to evolve a new form of music theatre, using subjects with a contemporary relevance and the simplest musical means. In 1935 he left Germany for the USA where he wrote a number of successful scores for Broadway, among them the antiwar musical *Johnny Johnson* 1936 (including the often covered 'September Song') and *Street Scene* 1947 based on an Elmer Rice play of the Depression.

Weil's disease or *leptospirosis* infectious disease of animals that is occasionally transmitted to human beings, usually by contact with water contaminated with rat urine. It is characterized by acute fever, and infection may spread to the liver, kidneys, and heart.

Weimar Republic the constitutional republic in Germany 1919–33, which was crippled by the election of antidemocratic parties to the Reichstag (parliament), and then subverted by the Nazi leader Hitler after his appointment as chancellor 1933. It took its name from the city where in Feb 1919 a constituent assembly met to draw up a democratic constitution.

Weinberger Caspar (Willard) 1917– . US

Republican politician. He served under presi dents Nixon and Ford, and was Reagan's defenc secretary 1981–87.

weir low wall built across a river to raise th water level. The oldest surviving weir in Englan is at Chester, across the river Dee, dating fro around 1100.

Weir Peter 1938– . Australian film director. H films have an atmospheric quality and often con tain a strong spiritual element. They includ *Picnic at Hanging Rock* 1975, *Witness* 198 and *The Mosquito Coast* 1986.

Weismann August 1834–1914. German biol gist. His failing eyesight forced him to turn fro microscopy to theoretical work. In 1892 he pr posed that changes to the body do not in tu cause an alteration of the genetic material.

Weizmann Chaim 1874–1952. Zionist leade the first president of Israel (1948–52), and chemist. He conducted the negotiations leadin up to the Balfour Declaration, by which Brita declared its support for an independent Jewis state.

Weizsäcker Richard, Baron von 1920– German Christian Democrat politician, preside from 1984. He began his career as a lawyer an was also active in the German Protestant churc and in Christian Democratic Union party po tics. He was elected to the West German Bunde tag (parliament) 1969 and served as mayor West Berlin from 1981, before being elected fe eral president 1984.

welding joining pieces of metal (or nonmeta at faces rendered plastic or liquid by heat or pre sure (or both). The principal processes today a gas and arc welding, in which the heat from a g flame or an electric arc melts the faces to b joined. Additional 'filler metal' is usually adde to the joint.

Welensky Roy 1907–1991. Rhodesian pol tician. He was instrumental in the creation a federation of North Rhodesia (now Zambia Southern Rhodesia (now Zimbabwe), and Nya aland (now Malawi) in 1953 and was prime mi ister 1956–63, when the federation w disbanded. His Southern Rhodesian Feder Party was defeated by Ian Smith's Rhodesi Front in 1964. In 1965, following Smith's un lateral declaration of Southern Rhodesian ind pendence from Britain, Welensky le politics.

welfare state political system under which th state (rather than the individual or the priva sector) has responsibility for the welfare of citizens. Services such as unemployment ar sickness benefits, family allowances and incom supplements, pensions, medical care, and ed cation may be provided and financed throu state insurance schemes and taxation.

Welles (George) Orson 1915–1985. US act and film and theatre director, whose first film w *Citizen Kane* 1941, which he produced, directe and starred in. Using innovative lighting, came angles and movements, he made it a landma in the history of cinema, yet he directed very fe films subsequently in Hollywood. His perfor ances as an actor include the character of Har Lime in *The Third Man* 1949.

Wellington capital and industrial po

woollen textiles, chemicals, soap, footwear, ~~b~~ricks) of New Zealand in North Island on Cook ~~S~~trait; population (1989) 324,600. The harbour ~~w~~as sighted by Captain Cook 1773.

Wellington Arthur Wellesley, 1st Duke of Wellington 1769–1852. British soldier and Tory poli~~t~~ician. As commander in the *Peninsular War, he ~~e~~xpelled the French from Spain 1814. He ~~d~~efeated Napoleon Bonaparte at Quatre-Bras ~~a~~nd Waterloo 1815, and was a member of the ~~C~~ongress of Vienna. As prime minister 1828–30, ~~h~~e was forced to concede Roman Catholic eman~~c~~ipation.

Wells H(erbert) G(eorge) 1866–1946. English ~~w~~riter of 'scientific romances' such as *The Time Machine* 1895 and *The War of the Worlds* 1898. His later novels had an anti-establishment, anti-conventional humour remarkable in its day, for example *Kipps* 1905 and *Tono-Bungay* 1909. His many other books include *Outline of History* 1920 and *The Shape of Things to Come* 1933, a ~~n~~umber of his prophecies from which have since been fulfilled. He also wrote many short stories.

Welsh corgi breed of dog with a foxlike head and pricked ears. The coat is dense, with several varieties of colouring. Corgis are about 30 cm/ 1 ft at the shoulder, and weigh up to 12 kg/27 lbs.

Welsh language in Welsh *Cymraeg* member of the Celtic branch of the Indo-European language family, spoken chiefly in the rural north and west of Wales; it is the strongest of the surviving Celtic languages, and in 1981 was spoken by 18.9% of the Welsh population.

Weltpolitik (German 'world politics') term applied to German foreign policy after about 1890, which represented Emperor Wilhelm II's attempt to make Germany into a world power through an aggressive foreign policy on colonies and naval building combined with an increase in nationalism at home.

Wembley Stadium sports ground in N London, England, completed 1923 for the British Empire Exhibition 1924–25. It has been the scene of the annual Football Association (FA) Cup final since 1923. The 1948 Olympic Games and many concerts, including the Live Aid concert 1985, were held here. Adjacent to the main stadium, which holds 78,000 people, are the Wembley indoor arena (which holds about 10,000, depending on the event) and conference centre.

Wenceslas, St 907–929. Duke of Bohemia who attempted to Christianize his people and was murdered by his brother. He is patron saint of Czechoslovakia and the 'good King Wenceslas' of a popular carol. Feast day 28 Sept.

Wends NW Slavonic peoples who settled east of the rivers Elbe and Saale in the 6th–8th centuries. By the 12th century most had been forcibly Christianized and absorbed by invading Germans; a few preserved their identity and survive as the Sorbs of Lusatia (E Germany/Poland).

werewolf in folk belief, a human being either turned by spell into a wolf or having the ability to assume a wolf form. The symptoms of *porphyria may have fostered the legends.

Wesker Arnold 1932– . English playwright. His socialist beliefs were reflected in the successful trilogy *Chicken Soup with Barley, Roots,* and *I'm Talking About Jerusalem* 1958–60. He established a catchphrase with *Chips with Everything* 1962.

Wesley Charles 1707–1788. English Methodist, brother of John *Wesley and one of the original Methodists at Oxford. He became a principal preacher and theologian of the Wesleyan Methodists, and wrote some 6,500 hymns.

Wesley John 1703–1791. English founder of *Methodism. When the pulpits of the Church of England were closed to him and his followers, he took the gospel to the people. For 50 years he rode about the country on horseback, preaching daily, largely in the open air. His sermons became the doctrinal standard of the Wesleyan Methodist Church.

Wessex the kingdom of the West Saxons in Britain, said to have been founded by Cerdic about AD 500, covering present-day Hampshire, Dorset, Wiltshire, Berkshire, Somerset, and Devon. In 829 Egbert established West Saxon supremacy over all England. Thomas *Hardy used the term Wessex in his novels for the SW counties of England.

West Benjamin 1738–1820. American Neo-Classical painter, active in London from 1763. He enjoyed the patronage of George III for many years and painted historical pictures.

West Mae 1892–1980. US vaudeville, stage, and film actress. She wrote her own dialogue, setting herself up as a provocative sex symbol and the mistress of verbal innuendo. She appeared on Broadway in *Sex* 1926, *Drag* 1927, and *Diamond Lil* 1928, which was the basis of the film (with Cary Grant) *She Done Him Wrong* 1933. Her other films include *I'm No Angel* 1933, *Going to Town* 1934, *My Little Chickadee* 1944 (with W C Fields), *Myra Breckinridge* 1969, and *Sextette* 1977. Both her plays and her films led to legal battles over censorship.

West Rebecca. Pen name of Cicely Isabel Fairfield 1892–1983. British journalist and novelist, an active feminist from 1911. *The Meaning of Treason* 1959 deals with the spies Burgess and Maclean. Her novels have political themes and include *The Fountain Overflows* 1956 and *The Birds Fall Down* 1966.

West African Economic Community international organization established 1975 to end barriers in trade and to achieve cooperation in development. Members include Burkina Faso, Ivory Coast, Mali, Mauritania, Niger, and Senegal; Benin and Togo have observer status.

West, American the Great Plains region of the USA to the east of the Rocky Mountains from Canada to Mexico.

West Bank area (5,879 sq km/2,270 sq mi) on the west bank of the river Jordan; population (1988) 866,000. The West Bank was taken by the Jordanian army 1948 at the end of the Arab-Israeli war that followed the creation of the state of Israel, and was captured by Israel during the Six-Day War 5–10 June 1967. The continuing Israeli occupation and settlement of the area has created tensions with the Arab population.

West Bengal state of NE India
area 87,900 sq km/33,929 sq mi
capital Calcutta
towns Asansol, Durgarpur
physical occupies the west part of the vast allu-

vial plain created by the rivers Ganges and Brahmaputra, with the Hooghly River; annual rainfall in excess of 250 cm/100 in
products rice, jute, tea, coal, iron, steel, cars, locomotives, aluminium, fertilizers
population (1991) 67,982,700

Westerlies prevailing winds from the west that occur in both hemispheres between latitudes of about 35° and 60°. Unlike the *trade winds, they are very variable and produce stormy weather.

western genre of popular fiction based on the landscape and settlement of the western USA. It developed in US dime novels and frontier literature. The western became established in written form with novels such as *The Virginian* 1902 by Owen Wister (1860–1938) and *Riders of the Purple Sage* 1912 by Zane Grey. See also *western film.

Western Australia state of Australia
area 2,525,500 sq km/974,843 sq mi
capital Perth
towns main port Fremantle, Bunbury, Geraldton, Kalgoorlie-Boulder, Albany
products wheat, fresh and dried fruit, meat and dairy products, natural gas (NW shelf) and oil (Canning Basin), iron (the Pilbara), copper, nickel, uranium, gold, diamonds
population (1987) 1,478,000
history a short-lived convict settlement at King George Sound 1826; the state founded at Perth 1829 by Captain James Stirling (1791–1865); self-government 1890; state 1901.

Western European Union (WEU) organization established 1955 as a consultative forum for military issues among the W European governments: Belgium, France, the Netherlands, Italy, Luxembourg, the UK, Germany, and (from 1988) Spain and Portugal.

Western film genre of films based loosely on the history of the American *West and evolved from the written Western. As a genre, the Western is virtually as old as the cinema. Italian 'spaghetti Westerns' and Japanese Westerns established it as an international form. The genre became less popular in the 1970s. There have been only four commercially successful films since: *Pale Rider* 1985 and *Unforgiven* 1992 (both starring Clint *Eastwood), *Young Guns* 1988 and Oscar award-winning *Dances with Wolves* 1990.

Western Isles island area of Scotland, comprising the Outer Hebrides (Lewis, Harris, North and South Uist, and Barra)
area 2,900 sq km/1,120 sq mi
towns Stornoway on Lewis (administrative headquarters)
products Harris tweed, sheep, fish, cattle
population (1991) 29,100
famous people Flora MacDonald.

Western Sahara formerly **Spanish Sahara** disputed territory in NW Africa bounded to the N by Morocco, to the W and S by Mauritania, and to the E by the Atlantic Ocean
area 266,800 sq km/103,011 sq mi
capital AD Dakhla
towns La'Youn, phosphate mining town of Bou Craa
exports phosphates
currency dirham
population (1988) 181,400; another estimated 165,000 live in refugee camps near Tindouf, SW

Algeria. Ethnic composition: Sawraw (traditionally nomadic herders)
language Arabic
religion Sunni Muslim
government administered by Morocco

West Germany see *Germany, West.

West Glamorgan (Welsh **Gorllewi Morgannwg**) county in SW Wales
area 820 sq km/317 sq mi
towns Swansea (administrative headquarters) Port Talbot, Neath
products tinplate, copper, steel, chemicals
population (1991) 357,800
languages 16% Welsh, English
famous people Richard Burton, Anthony Hopkins, Dylan Thomas.

West Indies archipelago of about 1,200 islands dividing the Atlantic from the Gulf of Mexico and the Caribbean. The islands are divided into **Bahamas**; **Greater Antilles** Cuba, Hispaniola (Haiti, Dominican Republic), Jamaica, and Puerto Rico **Lesser Antilles** Aruba, Netherlands Antilles, Trinidad and Tobago, the Windward Islands (Grenada, Barbados, St Vincent, St Lucia, Martinique, Dominica, Guadeloupe), the Leeward Islands (Montserrat, Antigua, St Christopher (St Kitts)–Nevis, Barbuda, Anguilla, St Martin, British and US Virgin Islands), and many smaller islands.

West Indies, Federation of the federal union 1958–62 comprising Antigua, Barbados, Dominica, Grenada, Jamaica, Montserrat, St Christopher (St Kitts)–Nevis and Anguilla, St Lucia, St Vincent, and Trinidad and Tobago. This federation came to an end when first Jamaica and then Trinidad and Tobago withdrew.

Westinghouse George 1846–1914. US inventor and founder of the Westinghouse Corporation 1886. He patented a powerful air brake for trains 1869, which allowed trains to run more safely with greater loads at higher speeds. In the 1880s he turned his attention to the generation of electricity. Unlike Thomas *Edison, Westinghouse introduced alternating current (AC) into his power stations.

West Irian former name of *Irian Jaya.

Westmeath inland county of Leinster province, Republic of Ireland
area 1,760 sq km/679 sq mi
town Mullingar (county town)
physical rivers: Shannon, Inny, Brosna; lakes: Ree, Sheelin, Ennell
products agricultural and dairy products, limestone, textiles
population (1991) 61,900

West Midlands metropolitan county in central England, created 1974, originally administered by an elected council; its powers reverted to district councils from 1986
area 900 sq km/347 sq mi
towns Birmingham (administrative headquarters)
products industrial goods
population (1991) 2,500,400

Westminster Abbey Gothic church in central London, officially the Collegiate Church of St Peter. It was built 1050–1745 and consecrated under Edward the Confessor 1065. The west towers are by Nicholas *Hawksmoor 1740. Since

William I nearly all English monarchs have been crowned in the abbey, and several are buried here; many poets are buried or commemorated here, at Poets' Corner.

West Pakistan a province of *Pakistan.

Westphalia independent medieval duchy, incorporated in Prussia by the Congress of Vienna 1815, and made a province 1816 with Münster as its capital. Since 1946 it has been part of the German *Land* (region) of *North Rhine–Westphalia.

Westphalia, Treaty of agreement 1648 ending the *Thirty Years' War. The peace marked the end of the supremacy of the Holy Roman Empire and the emergence of France as a dominant power. It recognized the sovereignty of the German states, Switzerland, and the Netherlands; Lutherans, Calvinists, and Roman Catholics were given equal rights.

West Point former fort in New York State, on the Hudson River, 80 km/50 mi N of New York City, site of the US Military Academy (commonly referred to as West Point), established 1802. Women were admitted 1976. West Point has been a military post since 1778.

West Sussex county on the south coast of England
area 2,020 sq km/780 sq mi
towns Chichester (administrative headquarters), Crawley, Horsham, Haywards Heath, Shoreham (port); resorts: Worthing, Littlehampton, Bognor Regis
physical the Weald, South Downs; rivers: Arun, West Rother, Adur
population (1991) 692,800
famous people William Collins, Richard Cobden, Percy Bysshe Shelley.

West Virginia state in E central USA; nickname Mountain State
area 62,900 sq km/24,279 sq mi
capital Charleston
towns Huntington, Wheeling
physical Allegheny Mountains; Ohio River
products apples, maize, poultry, dairy and meat products, coal, natural gas, oil, chemicals, synthetic fibres, plastics, steel, glass, pottery
population (1990) 1,793,500
famous people Pearl S. Buck, Thomas 'Stonewall' Jackson, Walter Reuther, Cyrus Vance

West Yorkshire metropolitan county in NE England, created 1976, originally administered by an elected metropolitan council; its powers reverted to district councils from 1986
area 2,040 sq km/787 sq mi
towns Wakefield, Leeds, Bradford, Halifax, Huddersfield
products coal, woollen textiles
population (1987) 2,052,000
famous people the Brontës, David Hockney, Henry Moore, J B Priestley.

wetland permanently wet land area or habitat. Wetlands include areas of *marsh, fen, *bog, flood plain, and shallow coastal areas. Wetlands are extremely fertile. They provide warm, sheltered waters for fisheries, lush vegetation for grazing livestock, and an abundance of wildlife. Estuaries and seaweed beds are more than 16 times as productive as the open ocean.

Wexford county in the Republic of Ireland, province of Leinster
area 2,350 sq km/907 sq mi
towns Wexford (county town), Rosslare
products fish, livestock, oats, barley, potatoes
population (1991) 102,000

Weyden Rogier van der *c.* 1399–1464. Netherlandish painter, official painter to the city of Brussels from 1436. He painted portraits and religious subjects, such as *The Last Judgment* about 1450 (Hôtel-Dieu, Beaune). His refined style had considerable impact on Netherlandish painting.

whale any marine mammal of the order Cetacea, with front limbs modified into flippers and with internal vestiges of hind limbs. The order is divided into the toothed whales (Odontoceti) and the baleen whales (Mysticeti). The toothed whales include *dolphins and *porpoises, along with large forms such as sperm whales. The baleen whales, with plates of modified mucous membrane called baleen in the mouth, are all large in size and include finback and right whales. There were hundreds of thousands of whales at the beginning of the 20th century, but they have been hunted close to extinction (see *whaling).

whaling the hunting of whales, largely discontinued 1986. Whales are killed for whale oil (made from the thick layer of fat under the skin called 'blubber'), used for food and cosmetics; for the large reserve of oil in the head of the sperm whale, used in the leather industry; and for *ambergris*, a waxlike substance from the intestines, used in making perfumes. There are synthetic substitutes for all these products. Whales are also killed for their meat, which is eaten by the Japanese and was used as pet food in the USA and Europe.

Wharton Edith (born Jones) 1862–1937. US novelist. Her work, known for its subtlety and form and influenced by her friend Henry James, was mostly set in New York society. It includes *The House of Mirth* 1905, which made her reputation; the grim, uncharacteristic novel of New England *Ethan Frome* 1911; *The Custom of the Country* 1913; and *The Age of Innocence* 1920.

wheat cereal plant derived from the wild *Triticum*, a grass native to the Middle East. It is the chief cereal used in breadmaking and is widely cultivated in temperate climates suited to its growth. Wheat is killed by frost, and damp renders the grain soft, so warm, dry regions produce the most valuable grain.

Wheatstone Charles 1802–1875. English physicist and inventor. With William Cooke he patented a railway telegraph in 1837, and, developing an idea of Samuel Christie, devised the *Wheatstone bridge*, an electrical network for measuring resistance. Originally a musical-instrument maker, he invented the harmonica and the concertina.

wheel and axle simple machine with a rope wound round an axle connected to a larger wheel with another rope attached to its rim. Pulling on the wheel rope (applying an effort) lifts a load attached to the axle rope. The velocity ratio of the machine (distance moved by load divided by distance moved by effort) is equal to the ratio of the wheel radius to the axle radius.

whelk any of various families of large marine snails with a thick spiral shell, especially the family Buccinidae. Whelks are scavengers, and also eat other shellfish. The largest grow to 40 cm/16 in long. Tropical species, such as the conches, can be very colourful.

whey watery by-product of the cheesemaking process, which is drained off after the milk has been heated and *rennet (a curdling agent) added to induce its coagulation.

Whig Party in the UK, predecessor of the Liberal Party. The name was first used of rebel *Covenanters and then of those who wished to exclude James II from the English succession (as a Roman Catholic). They were in power continuously 1714–60 and pressed for industrial and commercial development, a vigorous foreign policy, and religious toleration. During the French Revolution, the Whigs demanded parliamentary reform in Britain, and from the passing of the Reform Bill in 1832 became known as Liberals.

Whig Party in the USA, political party opposed to the autocratic presidency of Andrew Jackson from 1834. The Whig presidents were W H Harrison, Taylor, and Fillmore. The party diverged over the issue of slavery 1852: the Northern Whigs joined the Republican party; the Southern or 'Cotton' Whigs joined the Democrats. The title was taken from the British Whig Party which supported Parliament against the king. During the American Revolution, colonial patriots described themselves as Whigs, while those remaining loyal to Britain were known as Tories.

whip (the whipper-in of hounds at a foxhunt) in UK politics, the member of Parliament who ensures the presence of colleagues in the party when there is to be a vote in Parliament at the end of a debate. The written appeal sent by the whips to MPs is also called a whip; this letter is underlined once, twice, or three times to indicate its importance. A **three-line whip** is the most urgent, and every MP is expected to attend and vote with their party.

whiplash injury damage to the neck vertebrae and their attachments caused by a sudden backward jerk of the head and neck. It is most often seen in vehicle occupants as a result of the rapid deceleration experienced in a crash.

whippet breed of dog resembling a small greyhound. It grows to 56 cm/22 in at the shoulder, and 9 kg/20 lb in weight.

Whipple George 1878–1976. US physiologist whose research interest concerned the formation of haemoglobin in the blood. He showed that anaemic dogs, kept under restricted diets, responded well to a liver regime, and that their haemoglobin quickly regenerated. This work led to a cure for pernicious anaemia. He shared the 1934 Nobel Prize for Medicine with George Minot (1885–1950) and William Murphy (1892–1987).

whippoorwill North American *nightjar *Caprimulgus vociferus*, so called from its cry.

whip snake any of the various species of non-poisonous slender-bodied tree-dwelling snakes of the New World genus *Masticophis*, family Colubridae, also called **coachwhips**. They are closely allied to members of the genus *Coluber* of SW North America, Eurasia, Australasia, an N Africa, some of which are called whip snake in the Old World, but racers in North America.

whisky or **whiskey** distilled spirit made fror cereals: Scotch whisky from malted barley, Iris whiskey usually from barley, and North Ameri can whiskey and bourbon from maize and rye Scotch is usually blended; pure malt whisky i more expensive. Whisky is generally aged in wooden casks for 4–12 years.

whist card game for four, predecessor c *bridge, in which the partners try to win majority of the 13 tricks (the highest card playe being the winner of the trick).

Whistler James Abbott McNeill 1834–1903. U painter and etcher, active in London from 1859 His riverscapes and portraits show subtle compo sition and colour harmonies: for example *Arrangement in Grey and Black: Portrait of th Painter's Mother* 1871 (Louvre, Paris).

Whitby, Synod of council summoned by Kin Oswy of Northumbria 664, which decided t adopt the Roman rather than the Celtic form o Christianity for Britain.

White counter-revolutionary, especially durin the Russian civil wars 1917–21. Originally th term described the party opposing the Frenc Revolution, when the royalists used the white lil of the French monarchy as their badge.

White Gilbert 1720–1793. English cleric and naturalist, born at Selborne, Hampshire, and author of *Natural History and Antiquities of Selborne* 1789.

White Patrick (Victor Martindale) 1912–1990. Australian writer who did more than any other to put Australian literature on the international map. His partly allegorical novels explore the lives of early settlers in Australia and often deal with misfits or inarticulate people. They include *The Aunt's Story* 1948, *The Tree of Man* 1955, and *Voss* 1957 (based on the ill-fated 19th-century explorer Leichhardt). Nobel Prize for Literature 1973.

whitebait any of the fry (young) of various silvery fishes, especially *herring. It is also the name for a Pacific smelt *Osmerus mordax*.

whitebeam tree *Sorbus aria*, native to S Europe, usually found growing on chalk or limestone. It can reach 20 m/60 ft. It takes its name from the pinnately compound leaves, which have a dense coat of short white hairs on the underside.

white blood cell or **leucocyte** one of a number of different cells that play a part in the body's defences and give immunity against disease. Some (*phagocytes and *macrophages) engulf invading microorganisms, others kill infected cells, while *lymphocytes produce more specific immune responses. White blood cells are colourless, with clear or granulated cytoplasm, and are capable of independent amoeboid movement. They occur in the blood, *lymph and elsewhere in the body's tissues.

white-collar worker non-manual employee, such as an office worker or manager. With more mechanized production methods, the distinction between white-and blue-collar (manual) workers is becoming increasingly blurred.

white dwarf small, hot *star, the last stage in

he life of a star such as the Sun. White dwarfs have a mass similar to that of the Sun, but only 1% of the Sun's diameter, similar in size to the Earth. Most have surface temperatures of 8,000°C/14,400°F or more, hotter than the Sun. Yet, being so small, their overall luminosities may be less than 1% of that of the Sun. The Milky Way contains an estimated 50 billion white dwarfs.

white elephant any useless and cumbersome gift. In Thailand the monarch would formerly present a white elephant to a person out of favour: being the country's sacred animal, it could not be used for work, and its upkeep was ruinously expensive.

whitefish any of various freshwater fishes, genera *Coregonus* and *Prosopium* of the salmon family, found in lakes and rivers of North America and Eurasia. They include the whitefish *C. clupeaformis* and cisco *C. artedi*.

Whitehall street in central London, England, between Trafalgar Square and the Houses of Parliament, with many government offices and the Cenotaph war memorial.

Whitehead Robert 1823–1905. English engineer who invented the self-propelled torpedo 1866.

Whitehorse capital of Yukon Territory, Canada; population (1986) 15,199. Whitehorse is on the NW Highway. It replaced Dawson as capital in 1953.

White Horse any of several hill figures in England, including the one on Bratton Hill, Wiltshire, said to commemorate Alfred the Great's victory over the Danes at Ethandun 878; and the one at Uffington, Berkshire, 110 m/360 ft long, and probably a tribal totem of the early Iron Age, 1st century BC.

White House official residence of the president of the USA, in Washington, DC. It is a plain edifice of sandstone, built in the Italian Renaissance style 1792–99 to the designs of James Hoban, who also restored it after it was burned by the British 1814; it was then painted white to hide the scars.

Whitehouse Mary 1910– . British media activist. A founder of the National Viewers' and Listeners' Association, she has campaigned to censor radio and television for their treatment of sex and violence.

white knight in business, a company invited by the target of a takeover bid to make a rival bid. The company invited to bid is usually one that is already on good terms with the target company.

whiteout 'fog' of grains of dry snow caused by strong winds in temperatures of between –18°C/0°F and –1°C/30°F. The uniform whiteness of the ground and air causes disorientation in humans.

White Paper in the UK and some other countries, an official document that expresses government policy on an issue. It is usually preparatory to the introduction of a parliamentary bill (a proposed act of Parliament). Its name derives from its having fewer pages than a government 'blue book', and therefore needing no blue paper cover.

White Russia English translation of *Belarus.

white spirit colourless liquid derived from petrol; it is used as a solvent and in paints and varnishes.

White terror general term used by socialists and Marxists to describe a right-wing counterrevolution: for example, the attempts by the Chinese Guomindang to massacre the communists 1927–31; see *White.

whiting predatory fish *Merlangius merlangus* common in shallow sandy N European waters. It grows to 70 cm/2.3 ft.

Whitlam Gough (Edward) 1916– . Australian politician, leader of the Labor Party 1967–78 and prime minister 1972–75. He cultivated closer relations with Asia, attempted redistribution of wealth, and raised loans to increase national ownership of industry and resources.

Whitman Walt(er) 1819–1892. US poet who published *Leaves of Grass* 1855, which contains the symbolic 'Song of Myself'. It used unconventional free verse (with no rhyme or regular rhythm) and scandalized the public by its frank celebration of sexuality.

Whit Sunday Christian church festival held seven weeks after Easter, commemorating the descent of the Holy Spirit on the Apostles. The name is probably derived from the white garments worn by candidates for baptism at the festival. Whit Sunday corresponds to the Jewish festival of Shavuot (Pentecost).

Whittle Frank 1907– . British engineer who patented the basic design for the turbojet engine 1930. In the Royal Air Force he worked on jet propulsion 1937–46. In May 1941 the Gloster E 28/39 aircraft first flew with the Whittle jet engine. Both the German (first operational jet planes) and the US jet aircraft were built using his principles.

WHO acronym for *World Health Organization*.

Who, the English rock group, formed 1964, with a hard, aggressive sound, high harmonies, and a propensity for destroying their instruments on stage. Their albums include *Tommy* 1969, *Who's Next* 1971, and *Quadrophenia* 1973.

wholesale the business of selling merchandise to anyone other than the final customer. Most manufacturers or producers sell in bulk to a wholesale organization which distributes the smaller quantities required by retail outlets.

whooping cough or *pertussis* acute infectious disease, seen mainly in children, caused by colonization of the air passages by the bacterium *Bordetella pertussis*. There may be catarrh, mild fever, and loss of appetite, but the main symptom is violent coughing, associated with the sharp intake of breath that is the characteristic 'whoop', and often followed by vomiting and severe nose bleeds. The cough may persist for weeks.

whortleberry a form of *bilberry.

Whymper Edward 1840–1911. English mountaineer. He made the first ascent of many Alpine peaks, including the Matterhorn 1865, and in the Andes scaled Chimborazo and other mountains.

wickerwork furniture or other objects made from flexible rods or shoots, usually willow, as developed from stake-frame basketry. It is made by weaving strands in and out of a wicker frame.

Wicklow county in the Republic of Ireland, province of Leinster
area 2,030 sq km/784 sq mi
towns Wicklow (county town)
physical Wicklow Mountains; rivers: Slane, Liffey
population (1991) 97,300.

wide-angle lens photographic lens of shorter focal length than normal, taking in a wider angle of view.

Widmark Richard 1914– . US actor who made his film debut in *Kiss of Death* 1947 as a psychopath. He subsequently appeared in a great variety of *film noir* roles as well as in *The Alamo* 1960, *Madigan* 1968, and *Coma* 1978.

Wiener Norbert 1894–1964. US mathematician, credited with the establishment of the science of cybernetics in his book *Cybernetics* 1948. In mathematics, he laid the foundation of the study of stochastic processes (those dependent on random events), particularly *Brownian movement.

Wien's law in physics, a law of radiation stating that the wavelength carrying the maximum energy is inversely proportional to the body's absolute temperature: the hotter a body is, the shorter the wavelength. It has the form $\lambda_{max}T$ = constant, where λ_{max} is the wavelength of maximum intensity and T is the temperature. The law is named after German physicist Wilhelm Wien.

wig artificial head of hair, either real or synthetic, worn as an adornment, disguise, or to conceal baldness. Wigs were known in the ancient world and have been found on Egyptian mummies. Today they remain part of the uniform of judges, barristers, and some parliamentary officials in the UK and certain Commonwealth countries.

Wight, Isle of island and county in S England
area 380 sq km/147 sq mi
towns Newport (administrative headquarters), resorts: Ryde, Sandown, Shanklin, Ventnor
products chiefly agricultural; tourism
population (1991) 126,600
famous people Thomas Arnold, Robert Hooke.

Wightman Cup annual tennis competition between international women's teams from the USA and the UK. The trophy, first contested 1923, was donated by Hazel Hotchkiss Wightman (1886–1974), a former US tennis player who won singles, doubles, and mixed-doubles titles in the US Championships 1909–1911. Because of US domination of the contest it was abandoned 1990, but was reinstated 1991 with the UK side assisted by European players.

Wigner Eugene Paul 1902– . Hungarian-born US physicist who introduced the notion of parity into nuclear physics with the consequence that all nuclear processes should be indistinguishable from their mirror images. For this, and other work on nuclear structure, he shared the 1963 Nobel Prize for Physics with Maria Goeppert-Mayer and Hans Jensen (1906–1973).

Wilberforce William 1759–1833. English reformer who was instrumental in abolishing slavery in the British Empire. He entered Parliament 1780; in 1807 his bill for the abolition of the slave trade was passed, and in 1833, largely through his efforts, slavery was abolished throughout the empire.

Wilde Oscar (Fingal O'Flahertie Wills 1854–1900. Irish writer. With his flamboyant style and quotable conversation, he dazzled London society and, on his lecture tour 1882, the USA He published his only novel, *The Picture of Dorian Gray*, 1891, followed by witty plays including *A Woman of No Importance* 1893 and *The Importance of Being Earnest* 1895. In 1895 he was imprisoned for two years for homosexual offences; he died in exile.

wildebeest another name for *gnu.

Wilder Billy 1906– . Austrian-born accomplished US screenwriter and film director, in the USA from 1934. He directed and coscripted *Double Indemnity* 1944, *The Lost Weekend* (Academy Award for best director) 1945, *Sunset Boulevard* 1950, *Some Like It Hot* 1959, and the Academy Award-winning *The Apartment* 1960.

Wilder Thornton (Niven) 1897–1975. US playwright and novelist. He won Pulitzer prizes for the novel *The Bridge of San Luis Rey* 1927, and for the plays *Our Town* 1938 and *The Skin of Our Teeth* 1942. His farce *The Matchmaker* 1954 was filmed 1958. In 1964 it was adapted into the hit stage musical *Hello, Dolly!*, also made into a film.

wildlife trade international trade in live plants and animals, and in wildlife products such as skins, horns, shells, and feathers. The trade has made some species virtually extinct, and whole ecosystems (for example, coral reefs) are threatened. Wildlife trade is to some extent regulated by *CITES.

Wilhelm (English *William*) two emperors of Germany:

Wilhelm I 1797–1888. King of Prussia from 1861 and emperor of Germany from 1871; the son of Friedrich Wilhelm III. He served in the Napoleonic Wars 1814–15 and helped to crush the 1848 revolution. After he succeeded his brother Friedrich Wilhelm IV to the throne of Prussia, his policy was largely dictated by his chancellor *Bismarck, who secured his proclamation as emperor.

Wilhelm II 1859–1941. Emperor of Germany from 1888, the son of Frederick III and Victoria daughter of Queen Victoria of Britain. In 1890 he forced Chancellor Bismarck to resign and began to direct foreign policy himself, which proved disastrous. He encouraged warlike policies and built up the German navy. In 1914 he first approved Austria's ultimatum to Serbia and then, when he realized war was inevitable, tried in vain to prevent it. In 1918 he fled to Holland after Germany's defeat and his abdication.

Wilkes John 1727–1797. British Radical politician, imprisoned for his political views; member of Parliament 1757–64 and from 1774. He championed parliamentary reform, religious toleration, and US independence.

Wilkins Maurice Hugh Frederick 1916– . New Zealand-born British scientist. In 1962 he shared the Nobel Prize for Medicine with Francis *Crick and James *Watson for his work on the molecular structure of nucleic acids, particularly *DNA, using X-ray diffraction.

Wilkins William 1778–1839. English architect. He pioneered the Greek revival in England with his design for Downing College, Cambridge. Other works include the main block of University College London 1827–28, and the National Gallery, London, 1834–38.

will in law, declaration of how a person wishes his or her property to be disposed of after death. It also appoints administrators of the estate (*executors) and may contain wishes on other matters, such as place of burial or use of organs for transplant. Wills must comply with formal legal requirements of the local jurisdiction.

Willem Dutch form of *William.

William four kings of England:

William I *the Conqueror* c. 1027–1087. King of England from 1066. He was the illegitimate son of Duke Robert the Devil and succeeded his father as duke of Normandy 1035. Claiming that his relative King Edward the Confessor had bequeathed him the English throne, William invaded the country 1066, defeating *Harold II at Hastings, Sussex, and was crowned king of England.

William II *Rufus, the Red* c. 1056–1100. King of England from 1087, the third son of William I. He spent most of his reign attempting to capture Normandy from his brother *Robert II, duke of Normandy. His extortion of money led his barons to revolt and caused confrontation with Bishop Anselm. He was killed while hunting in the New Forest, Hampshire, and was succeeded by his brother Henry I.

William III *William of Orange* 1650–1702. King of Great Britain and Ireland from 1688, the son of William II of Orange and Mary, daughter of Charles I. He was offered the English crown by the parliamentary opposition to James II. He invaded England 1688 and in 1689 became joint sovereign with his wife, *Mary II. He spent much of his reign campaigning, first in Ireland, where he defeated James II at the battle of the Boyne 1690, and later against the French in Flanders. He was succeeded by Mary's sister, Anne.

William IV 1765–1837. King of Great Britain and Ireland from 1830, when he succeeded his brother George IV; third son of George III. He was created duke of Clarence 1789, and married Adelaide of Saxe-Meiningen (1792–1849) 1818. During the Reform Bill crisis he secured its passage by agreeing to create new peers to overcome the hostile majority in the House of Lords. He was succeeded by Victoria.

William three kings of the Netherlands, including:

William I 1772–1844. King of the Netherlands 1815–40. He lived in exile during the French occupation 1795–1813 and fought against the emperor Napoleon at Jena and Wagram. The Austrian Netherlands were added to his kingdom by the Allies 1815, but secured independence (recognized by he major European states 1839) by the revolution of 1830. William's unpopularity led to his abdication 1840.

William II 1792–1849. King of the Netherlands 1840–49, son of William I. He served with the British army in the Peninsular War and at Waterloo. In 1848 he averted revolution by conceding liberal constitution.

William *William the Lion* 1143–1214. King of Scotland from 1165. He was captured by Henry II while invading England 1174, and forced to do homage, but Richard I abandoned the English claim to suzerainty for a money payment 1189. In 1209 William was forced by King John to renounce his claim to Northumberland.

William *the Silent* 1533–1584. Prince of Orange from 1544. Leading a revolt against Spanish rule in the Netherlands from 1573, he briefly succeeded in uniting the Catholic south and Protestant northern provinces, but the former provinces submitted to Spain while the latter formed a federation 1579 which repudiated Spanish suzerainty 1581.

William (full name William Arthur Philip Louis) 1982– . Prince of the UK, first child of the Prince and Princess of Wales.

William of Malmesbury c. 1080–c. 1143. English historian and monk. He compiled the *Gesta regum/Deeds of the Kings* c. 1120–40 and *Historia novella*, which together formed a history of England to 1142.

Williams British racing-car manufacturing company started by Frank Williams in 1969 when he modified a Brabham BT26A. The first Williams Grand Prix car was designed by Patrick Head in 1978 and since then the team has been one of the most successful in Grand Prix racing.

Williams Tennessee (Thomas Lanier) 1911–1983. US playwright, born in Mississippi. His work is characterized by fluent dialogue and searching analysis of the psychological deficiencies of his characters. His plays, usually set in the Deep South against a background of decadence and degradation, include *The Glass Menagerie* 1945, *A Streetcar Named Desire* 1947, and *Cat on a Hot Tin Roof* 1955, the last two of which earned Pulitzer Prizes.

Williams William Carlos 1883–1963. US poet. His spare images and language reflect everyday speech. His epic poem *Paterson* 1946–58 celebrates his home town in New Jersey. *Pictures from Brueghel* 1963 won him, posthumously, a Pulitzer prize. His vast body of prose work includes novels, short stories, and the play *A Dream of Love* 1948. His work had a great impact on younger US poets.

Williamson Henry 1895–1977. English author whose stories of animal life include *Tarka the Otter* 1927. He described his experiences in restoring an old farm in *The Story of a Norfolk Farm* 1941 and wrote the fictional, 15-volume sequence *Chronicles of Ancient Sunlight*.

Willis Norman (David) 1933– . British trade-union leader. A trade-union official since leaving school, he succeeded Len Murray as the general secretary of the Trades Union Congress (TUC) 1984.

will-o'-the-wisp light sometimes seen over marshy ground, believed to be burning gas containing methane from decaying organic matter.

willow any tree or shrub of the genus *Salix*, family Salicaceae. There are over 350 species, mostly in the northern hemisphere, and they flourish in damp places. The leaves are often lance-shaped, and the male and female catkins are found on separate trees.

willowherb any plant of either of two genera

Epilobium and *Chamaenerion* of perennial weeds. The rosebay willowherb or fireweed *C. angustifolium* is common in woods and wasteland. It grows to 1.2 m/4 ft with long terminal racemes of red or purplish flowers.

willow warbler bird *Phylloscopus trochilus* that migrates from N Eurasia to Africa. It is about 11 cm/4 in long, similar in appearance to the chiffchaff, but with a distinctive song, and found in woods and shrubberies.

Wilson Edward O 1929– . US zoologist whose books have stimulated interest in biogeography, the study of the distribution of species, and sociobiology, the evolution of behaviour. His works include *Sociobiology: The New Synthesis* 1975 and *On Human Nature* 1978.

Wilson (James) Harold, Baron Wilson of Rievaulx 1916–1995. British Labour politician, party leader from 1963, prime minister 1964–70 and 1974–76. His premierships were dominated by the issue of UK admission to membership of the European Community, the social contract (unofficial agreement with the trade unions), and economic difficulties.

Wilson Richard 1714–1782. British painter whose English and Welsh landscapes are infused with an Italianate atmosphere and recomposed in a Classical manner. His work influenced the development of English landscape painting.

Wilson Teddy (Theodore) 1912–1986. US bandleader and jazz pianist. He toured with Benny Goodman 1935–39 and during that period recorded in small groups with many of the best musicians of the time; some of his 1930s recordings feature the singer Billie Holiday. Wilson led a big band 1939–40 and a sextet 1940–46.

Wilson (Thomas) Woodrow 1856–1924. 28th president of the USA 1913–21, a Democrat. He kept the USA out of World War I until 1917, and in Jan 1918 issued his 'Fourteen Points' as a basis for a just peace settlement. At the peace conference in Paris he secured the inclusion of the *League of Nations in individual peace treaties, but these were not ratified by Congress, so the USA did not join the League. Nobel Peace Prize 1919.

wilting the loss of rigidity (turgor) in plants, caused by a decreasing wall pressure within the cells making up the supportive tissues. Wilting is most obvious in plants which have little or no wood.

Wiltshire county in SW England
area 3,480 sq km/1,343 sq mi
towns Trowbridge (administrative headquarters), Salisbury, Swindon, Wilton
physical Marlborough Downs; Savernake Forest; rivers: Kennet, Wylye, Salisbury and Bristol Avons; Salisbury Plain
products wheat, cattle, pig and sheep farming, rubber, engineering
population (1990) 553,300
famous people Isaac Pitman, William Talbot, Christopher Wren.

Wimbledon English lawn-tennis centre used for international championship matches, situated in south London. There are currently 18 courts.

WIMP (acronym for *windows, icons, menus, pointing device*) in computing, another name for *graphical user interface (GUI).

Winchester drive in computing, a small hard disc drive commonly used with microcomputers *Winchester disc* has become synonymous with *hard disc.

wind lateral movement of the Earth's atmosphere from high-to low-pressure areas. Although modified by features such as land and water there is a basic worldwide system of *trade winds, *Westerlies, *monsoons, and others.

wind-chill factor or *wind-chill index* estimate of how much colder it feels when a wind is blowing. It is the sum of the temperature (in £°F below zero) and the wind speed (in miles per hour). So for a wind of 15 mph at an air temperature of –5°F, the wind-chill factor is 20.

Windermere largest lake in England, in Cumbria, 17 km/10.5 mi long and 1.6 km/1 mi wide

wind farm array of windmills or *wind turbines used for generating electrical power. A wind farm at Altamont Pass, California, USA, consists of 300 wind turbines, the smallest producing 60 kW and the largest 750 kW of electricity. To produce 1,200 megawatts of electricity (an output comparable with that of a nuclear power station), a wind farm would need to occupy around 370 sq km/140 sq mi.

Windhoek capital of Namibia; population (1988) 115,000. It is just north of the Tropic of Capricorn, 290 km/180 mi from the west coast.

wind instrument musical instrument that uses the performer's breath, sometimes activating a reed or reeds, to make a column of air vibrate. The pitch of the note is controlled by the length of the column. The main types are *woodwind instruments and *brass instruments.

windmill mill with sails or vanes that, by the action of wind upon them, drive machinery for grinding corn or pumping water, for example. Wind turbines, designed to use wind power on a large scale, usually have a propeller-type rotor mounted on a tall shell tower. The turbine drives a generator for producing electricity.

wind power the harnessing of wind energy to produce power. The wind has long been used as a source of energy: sailing ships and windmills are ancient inventions. After the energy crisis of the 1970s *wind turbines began to be used to produce electricity on a large scale. By the year 2000, 10% of Denmark's energy is expected to come from wind power.

Windscale former name of *Sellafield, nuclear power station in Cumbria, England.

Windsor, House of official name of the British royal family since 1917, adopted in place of Saxe-Coburg-Gotha. Since 1960 those descendants of Elizabeth II not entitled to the prefix HRH (His/Her Royal Highness) have borne the surname Mountbatten-Windsor.

Windsor Duchess of. Title of Wallis Warfield *Simpson.

Windsor Duke of. Title of *Edward VIII.

Windsor Castle British royal residence in Windsor, Berkshire, founded by William the Conqueror on the site of an earlier fortress. It includes the Perpendicular Gothic St George's Chapel and the Albert Memorial Chapel, beneath which George III, George IV, and William IV are buried. In the Home Park adjoining the castle is he Royal Mausoleum where Queen Victoria and Prince Albert are buried.

windsurfing or **boardsailing** or **sailboarding** water sport combining elements of surfing and sailing, first developed in the USA 1968. The windsurfer stands on a board which is propelled and steered by means of a sail attached to a mast that is articulated at the foot. Since 1984 the sport has been included in the Olympic Games as part of the yachting events. From 1992 men and women have to compete in separate categories. There are also annual boardsailing world championships.

wind tunnel test tunnel in which air is blown over, for example, a stationary model aircraft, motor vehicle, or locomotive to simulate the effects of movement. Lift, drag, and airflow patterns are observed by the use of special cameras and sensitive instruments. Wind-tunnel testing assesses aerodynamic design, preparatory to full-scale construction.

wind turbine windmill of advanced aerodynamic design connected to an electricity generator and used in *wind-power installations. Wind turbines can be either large propeller-type rotors mounted on a tall tower, or flexible metal strips fixed to a vertical axle at top and bottom. In 1990, over 20,000 wind turbines were in use throughout the world, generating 1,600 megawatts of power.

Windward Islands islands in the path of the prevailing wind, notably: **West Indies** see under *Antilles; *Cape Verde Islands; *French Polynesia (Tahiti, Moorea, Makatea).

wine alcoholic beverage, usually made from fermented grape pulp, although wines have also traditionally been made from many other fruits such as damsons and elderberries. **Red wine** is the product of the grape with the skin; **white wine** of the inner pulp of the grape. The sugar content is converted to ethyl alcohol by the yeast *Saccharomyces ellipsoideus*, which lives on the skin of the grape. The largest wine-producing countries are Italy, France, Russia, Georgia, Moldova, Armenia, and Spain; others include almost all European countries, Australia, South Africa, the USA, and Chile. For **dry wine** the fermentation is allowed to go on longer than for **sweet** or **medium**; *Champagne (sparkling wine from the Champagne region of France) is bottled while still fermenting, but other sparkling wines are artificially carbonated. Some wines are fortified with additional alcohol obtained from various sources, and with preservatives. Some of the latter may cause dangerous side effects (see *additive). For this reason, organic wines, containing no preservatives, have recently become popular.

wing in biology, the modified forelimb of birds and bats, or the membranous outgrowths of the *exoskeleton of insects, which give the power of flight. Birds and bats have two wings. Bird wings have feathers attached to the fused digits ('fingers') and forearm bones, while bat wings consist of skin stretched between the digits. Most insects have four wings, which are strengthened by wing veins.

Winnipeg capital and industrial city (processed foods, textiles, transportation, and transportation equipment) in Manitoba, Canada, on the Red

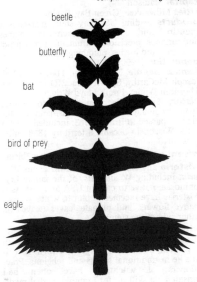

comparison of wing shapes

beetle

butterfly

bat

bird of prey

eagle

wing Birds can fly because of the specialized shape of their wings: a rounded leading edge, flattened underneath and round on top.

River, south of Lake Winnipeg; population (1986) 623,000. Established as Winnipeg 1870 on the site of earlier forts, the city expanded with the arrival of the Canadian Pacific Railroad 1881.

Winnipeg, Lake lake in S Manitoba, Canada, draining much of the Canadian prairies; area 24,500 sq km/9,460 sq mi.

winter of discontent the winter of 1978–79 in Britain, marked by a series of strikes that contributed to the defeat of the Labour government in the general election of spring 1979. The phrase is from Shakespeare's *Richard III*: 'Now is the winter of our discontent/Made glorious summer by this sun of York.'

Winterson Jeanette 1959– . English novelist. Her autobiographical first novel *Oranges Are Not the Only Fruit* 1985, humorously describes her upbringing as an Evangelical Pentecostalist in Lancashire, and her subsequent realisation of her homosexuality. The novel was successfully made into a television serial. Later novels include *The Passion* 1987, *Sexing the Cherry* 1989, and *Written On The Body* 1992.

wire thread of metal, made by drawing a rod through progressively smaller-diameter dies. Fine-gauge wire is used for electrical power transmission; heavier-gauge wire is used to make load-bearing cables.

wireless original name for a radio receiver. In early experiments with transmission by radio waves, notably by *Marconi in Britain, signals were sent in Morse code, as in telegraphy. Radio, unlike the telegraph, used no wires for transmission, and the means of communication was termed 'wireless telegraphy'.

Wisconsin state in N central USA; nickname Badger State

area 145,500 sq km/56,163 sq mi
capital Madison
cities Milwaukee, Green Bay, Racine
products leading US dairy state; maize, hay, industrial and agricultural machinery, engines and turbines, precision instruments, paper products, cars and lorries, plumbing equipment
population (1990) 4,891,800
famous people Edna Ferber, Harry Houdini, Joseph McCarthy, Spencer Tracy, Orson Welles, Thornton Wilder, Frank Lloyd Wright
history explored by Jean Nicolet for France 1634; originally settled near Ashland by the French; passed to Britain 1763; included in USA 1783. Wisconsin became a territory 1836 and a state 1848.

wisent another name for the European *bison.

wisteria any climbing shrub of the genus *Wisteria*, including *W. sinensis*, of the family Leguminosae, native to eastern USA and east Asia. Wisterias have racemes of bluish, white, or pale mauve flowers, and pinnate leaves (leaves on either side of the stem).

witchcraft the alleged possession and exercise of magical powers – *black magic* if used with evil intent, and *white magic* if benign. Its origins lie in traditional beliefs and religions. Practitioners of witchcraft have often had considerable skill in, for example, herbal medicine and traditional remedies; this prompted the World Health Organization in 1976 to recommend the integration of traditional healers into the health teams of African states.

witch hazel any flowering shrub or small tree of the genus *Hamamelis* of the witch-hazel family, native to North America and E Asia, especially *H. virginiana*. An astringent extract prepared from the bark or leaves is used in medicine as an eye lotion and a liniment.

witch-hunt persecution of minority political opponents or socially nonconformist groups without any regard for their guilt or innocence. Witch-hunts are often accompanied by a degree of public hysteria; for example, the *McCarthy anticommunist hearings during the 1950s in the USA.

withholding tax personal income tax on wages, salaries, dividends, or other income that is taxed at source to ensure that it reaches the tax authority. Those not liable to pay the tax can reclaim it by filing a tax return.

witness in law, a person who was present at some event (such as an accident, a crime, or the signing of a document) or has relevant special knowledge (such as a medical expert) and can be called on to give evidence in a court of law.

Witt Johann de 1625–1672. Dutch politician, grand pensionary of Holland and virtual prime minister from 1653. His skilful diplomacy ended the Dutch Wars of 1652–54 and 1665–67, and in 1668 he formed a triple alliance with England and Sweden against Louis XIV of France. He was murdered by a rioting mob.

Wittelsbach Bavarian dynasty, who ruled Bavaria as dukes from 1180, electors from 1623, and kings 1806–1918.

Wittgenstein Ludwig 1889–1951. Austrian philosopher. *Tractatus Logico-Philosophicus* 1922 postulated the 'picture theory' of language: that words represent things according to social agreement. He subsequently rejected this idea, and developed the idea that usage was more important than convention.

Witwatersrand or **the Rand** the economic heartland of S Transvaal, South Africa. Its reef, which stretches nearly 100 km/60 mi, produces over half the world's gold. Gold was first found there 1854. The chief city of the region is Johannesburg. Forming a watershed between the Vaal and the Olifant rivers, the Rand comprises a series of parallel ranges which extend 100 km/60 mi E–W and rise to 1,525–1,830 m/5,000–6,000 ft above sea level. Gold occurs in reefs that are mined at depths of up to 3,050 m/10,000 ft.

Wodehouse P(elham) G(renville) 1881–1975. English novelist, a US citizen from 1955, whose humorous novels portray the accident-prone world of such characters as the socialite Bertie Wooster and his invaluable and impeccable man-servant Jeeves, and Lord Emsworth of Blandings Castle with his prize pig, the Empress of Blandings.

Woden or **Wodan** the foremost Anglo-Saxon god, whose Norse counterpart is *Odin.

Wöhler Friedrich 1800–1882. German chemist, a student of Jöns *Berzelius, who in 1828 was the first person to synthesize an organic compound (*urea) from an inorganic compound (ammonium cyanate). He also devised a method 1827 that isolated the metals aluminum, beryllium, yttrium, and titanium. from their ores.

wolf any of two species of large wild dogs of the genus *Canis*. The grey or timber wolf *C. lupus*, of North America and Eurasia, is highly social, measures up to 90 cm/3 ft at the shoulder, and weighs up to 45 kg/100 lb. It has been greatly reduced in numbers except for isolated wilderness regions.

Wolfe James 1727–1759. British soldier who served in Canada and commanded a victorious expedition against the French general Montcalm in Québec on the Plains of Abraham, during which both commanders were killed. The British victory established their supremacy over Canada.

Wolfe Thomas 1900–1938. US novelist. He wrote four long and hauntingly powerful autobiographical novels, mostly of the South: *Look Homeward, Angel* 1929, *Of Time and the River* 1935, *The Web and the Rock* 1939, and *You Can't Go Home Again* 1940 (the last two published posthumously).

Wolfe Tom. Pen name of Thomas Kennerly, Jr 1931– . US journalist and novelist. In the 1960s he was a founder of the 'New Journalism', which brought fiction's methods to reportage. Wolfe recorded US mores and fashions in pop-style essays in, for example, *The Kandy-Kolored Tangerine-Flake Streamline Baby* 1965. His sharp social eye is applied to the New York of the 1980s in his novel *The Bonfire of the Vanities* 1988.

wolfram alternative name for *tungsten.

wolframite iron manganese tungstate, $(Fe,Mn)Wo_4$, an ore mineral of tungsten. It is dark grey with a submetallic surface lustre, and often occurs in hydrothermal veins in association with ores of tin.

Wollaston William 1766–1828. British chemist

and physicist. He amassed a large fortune through his discovery in 1804 of how to make malleable platinum. He went on to discover the new elements palladium 1804 and rhodium 1805. He also contributed to optics through the invention of a number of ingenious and still useful measuring instruments.

Wollongong industrial city (iron, steel) in New South Wales, Australia, 65 km/40 mi S of Sydney; population (1985, with Port Kembla) 238,000.

Wollstonecraft Mary 1759–1797. British feminist, member of a group of radical intellectuals called the English Jacobins, whose book *A Vindication of the Rights of Women* 1792 demanded equal educational opportunities for women. She married William Godwin and died giving birth to a daughter, Mary (later Mary *Shelley).

Wolof member of the majority ethnic group living in Senegal. There is also a Wolof minority in Gambia. There are about 2 million speakers of Wolof, a language belonging to the Niger-Congo family. The Wolof are Muslims.

Wolsey Thomas c. 1475–1530. English cleric and politician. In Henry VIII's service from 1509, he became archbishop of York 1514, cardinal and lord chancellor 1515, and began the dissolution of the monasteries. His reluctance to further Henry's divorce from Catherine of Aragon, partly because of his ambition to be pope, led to his downfall 1529. He was charged with high treason 1530 but died before being tried.

Wolverhampton industrial town (metalworking, chemicals, tyres, aircraft, commercial vehicles) in West Midlands, England, 20 km/12 mi NW of Birmingham; population (1991) 239,800.

wolverine largest land member *Gulo gulo* of the weasel family (Mustelidae), found in Europe, Asia, and North America. It is stocky in build, about 1 m/3.3 ft long. Its long, thick fur is dark brown on the back and belly and lighter on the sides. It covers food that it cannot eat with an unpleasant secretion. Destruction of habitat and trapping for its fur have greatly reduced its numbers.

wombat *The wombat is a powerfully built marsupial.*

wombat any of a family (Vombatidae) of burrowing, herbivorous marsupials, native to Tasmania and S Australia. They are about 1 m/3.3 ft long, heavy, with a big head, short legs and tail, and coarse fur.

Women's Institute (WI) local organization in country districts in the UK for the development of community welfare and the practice of rural crafts.

Women's Land Army organization founded 1916 for the recruitment of women to work on farms during World War I. At its peak Sept 1918 it had 16,000 members. It re-formed June 1939, before the outbreak of World War II. Many 'Land Girls' joined up to help the war effort and, by Aug 1943, 87,000 were employed in farm work.

women's movement the campaign for the rights of women, including social, political, and economic equality with men. Early European campaigners of the 17th–19th centuries fought for women's right to own property, to have access to higher education, and to vote (see *suffragette). Once women's suffrage was achieved in the 20th century, the emphasis of the movement shifted to the goals of equal social and economic opportunities for women, including employment. A continuing area of concern in industrialized countries is the contradiction between the now generally accepted principle of equality and the demonstrable inequalities that remain between the sexes in state policies and in everyday life. See page 907.

Women's Social and Political Union (WSPU) British political movement founded 1903 by Emmeline *Pankhurst to organize a militant crusade for female suffrage.

Wonder Stevie. Stage name of Steveland Judkins Morris 1950– . US pop musician, singer, and songwriter, associated with Motown Records. Blind from birth, he had his first hit, 'Fingertips', at the age of 12. Later hits, most of which he composed and sang, and on which he also played several instruments, include 'My Cherie Amour' 1973, 'Master Blaster (Jammin')' 1980, and the album *Innervisions* 1973.

wood the hard tissue beneath the bark of many perennial plants; it is composed of water-conducting cells, or secondary *xylem, and gains its hardness and strength from deposits of *lignin. **Hardwoods**, such as oak, and **softwoods**, such as pine, have commercial value as structural material and for furniture.

Wood Henry (Joseph) 1869–1944. English conductor, from 1895 until his death, of the London Promenade Concerts, now named after him. He promoted a national interest in music and encouraged many young composers.

woodcarving art form practised in many parts of the world since prehistoric times: for example, the NW Pacific coast of North America, in the form of totem poles, and W Africa, where there is a long tradition of woodcarving, notably in Nigeria. Woodcarvings survive less often than sculpture in stone or metal because of the comparative fragility of the material.

woodcock either of two species of wading birds, genus *Scolopax*, of the family Scolopacidae, which have barred plumage, long bills, and live in wet woodland areas.

woodcut print made by a woodblock in which a picture or design has been cut in relief. The woodcut is the oldest method of *printing, invented in China in the 5th century AD. In the Middle Ages woodcuts became popular in Europe, illustrating early printed books and broadsides.

WOMEN'S MOVEMENT: UK CHRONOLOGY

1562	The Statute of Artificers made it illegal to employ men or women in a trade before they had served seven years' apprenticeship. (It was never strictly enforced for women, as many guilds still allowed members to employ their wives and daughters in workshops.)
1753	Lord Hardwick's Marriage Act brought marriage under state control and created a firmer distinction between the married and unmarried.
1803	Abortion was made illegal.
1839	The Custody of Infants Act allowed mothers to have custody of their children under seven years old.
1840s	A series of factory acts limited the working day and occupations of women and children. A bastardy amendment put all the responsibility for the maintenance of an illegitimate child onto its mother.
1857–82	The Married Women's Property Acts allowed them to own possessions of various kinds for the first time.
1861	Abortion became a criminal offence even if performed as a life-saving act or done by the woman herself.
1862–70	The Contagious Diseases Acts introduced compulsory examination of prostitutes for venereal disease; the Acts were repealed in 1883.
1860s	Fathers could be named and required to pay maintenance for illegitimate children.
1864	Schools Enquiry Commission recommendations led to the establishment of high schools for girls.
1869	Women ratepayers were allowed to vote in municipal (local) elections.
1871	Newham College, Cambridge, was founded for women.
1872	The Elizabeth Garrett Anderson Hospital for women opened in London.
1874	The London School of Medicine for women was founded.
1878	Judicial separation of a married couple became possible. Maintenance orders could be enforced in court.
1880	The Trades Union Congress (TUC) adopted the principle of equal pay for women.
1882	The Married Women's Property Act gave wives legal control over their own earned income.
1885	The age of consent was raised to 16.
1887	The National Union of Women's Suffrage Societies became a nationwide group under Millicent Fawcett.
1903	The Women's Social and Political Union (WSPU) was founded by Emmeline and Christabel Pankhurst.
1905–10	Militant campaigns split the WSPU. Sylvia Pankhurst formed the East London Women's Federation.
1918	The Parliament (Qualification of Women) Act gave the vote to women householders over 30.
1923	Wives were given equal rights to sue for divorce on the grounds of adultery.
1925	The Guardianship of Infants Act gave women equal rights to the guardianship of their children.
1928	The 'Flapper' Vote: all women over 21 were given the vote.
1944	The Butler Education Act introduced free secondary education for all.
1946	A Royal Commission on equal pay was formed.
1948	Cambridge University allowed women candidates to be awarded degrees.
1960	Legal aid became available for divorce cases.
1967	The Abortion Law Reform Act made abortion legal under medical supervision and within certain criteria.
1969	Divorce reform was introduced that reduced the time a petitioner needed to wait before applying for a divorce.
1973	The Matrimonial Causes Act provided legislation to enable financial provision to be granted on divorce.
1975	The Sex Discrimination and Equal Pay Acts were passed. The National and Scottish Women's Aid Federations were formed.
1976	The Domestic Violence and Matrimonial Proceedings Act came into effect. The Sexual Offences (Amendment) Act attempted to limit a man's defence of consent in rape cases.
1977	The employed married women's option to stay partially out of the National Insurance system was phased out. Women qualified for their own pensions.
1980	The Social Security Act allowed a married woman to claim supplementary benefit and family income supplement if she was the main wage earner.
1983	The government was forced to amend the 1975 Equal Pay Act to conform to European Community directives.
1984	The Matrimonial and Family Proceedings Act made it less likely for a woman to be granted maintenance on divorce. It also reduced the number of years a petitioner must wait before applying for a divorce to one.
1986	The granting of invalid-care allowance was successfully challenged in the European Court of Justice. The Sex Discrimination Act (Amendment) allowed women to retire at the same age as men, and lifted legal restrictions preventing women from working night shifts in manufacturing industries. Firms with less than five employees were no longer exempt from the act.
1990	The legal limit for abortion was reduced to 24 weeks.
1991	Rape within marriage became a prosecutable offence in the UK.

woodland area in which trees grow more or less thickly; generally smaller than a forest. Temperate climates, with four distinct seasons a year, tend to support a mixed woodland habitat, with some conifers but mostly broad-leaved and deciduous trees, shedding their leaves in autumn and regrowing them in spring. In the Mediterranean region and parts of the southern hemisphere, the trees are mostly evergreen.

woodlouse crustacean of the order Isopoda. Woodlice have segmented bodies and flattened undersides. The eggs are carried by the female in a pouch beneath the thorax.

woodpecker bird of the family Picidae, which drills holes in trees to obtain insects. There are about 200 species worldwide. The largest of these, the imperial woodpecker *Campephilus imperialis* of Mexico, is very rare and may already be extinct.

wood pulp wood that has been processed into a pulpy mass of fibres. Its main use is for making paper, but it is also used in making *rayon and other cellulose fibres and plastics.

Woodstock the first free rock festival, held near Bethel, New York State, USA, over three days in Aug 1969. It was attended by 400,000 people, and performers included the Band, Country Joe and the Fish, the Grateful Dead, Jimi Hendrix, Jefferson Airplane, and the Who. The festival was a landmark in the youth culture of the 1960s (see *hippie) and was recorded in the film *Woodstock*.

Woodward Robert 1917–1979. US chemist who worked on synthesizing a large number of complex molecules. These included quinine 1944, cholesterol 1951, chlorophyll 1960, and vitamin B_{12} 1971. Nobel prize 1965.

woodwind musical instrument from which sound is produced by blowing into a tube, causing the air within to vibrate. Woodwind instruments include those, like the flute, originally made of wood but now more commonly of metal. The saxophone, made of metal, is an honorary woodwind because it is related to the clarinet. The oboe, bassoon, flute, and clarinet make up the normal woodwind section of an orchestra.

woodworm common name for the larval stage of certain wood-boring beetles. Dead or injured trees are their natural target, but they also attack structural timber and furniture.

Wookey Hole natural cave near Wells, Somerset, England, in which flint implements of Old Stone Age people and bones of extinct animals have been found.

wool the natural hair covering of the sheep, and also of the llama, angora goat, and some other *mammals. The domestic sheep *Ovis aries* provides the great bulk of the fibres used in (textile) commerce. Lanolin is a by-product.

Woolf Virginia (born Virginia Stephen) 1882–1941. English novelist and critic. Her first novel, *The Voyage Out* 1915, explored the tensions experienced by women who want marriage and a career. In *Mrs Dalloway* 1925 she perfected her 'stream of consciousness' technique. Among her later books are *To the Lighthouse* 1927, *Orlando* 1928, and *The Years* 1937, which considers the importance of economic independence for women.

Woolman John 1720–1772. American Quaker, born in Ancocas (now Rancocas), New Jersey. He was one of the first antislavery agitators and left an important *Journal*. He supported those who refused to pay a tax levied by Pennsylvania, to conduct the French and Indian War, on the grounds that it was inconsistent with pacifist principles.

Woolworth Frank Winfield 1852–1919. US entrepreneur. He opened his first successful 'five and ten cent' store in Lancaster, Pennsylvania, in 1879, and, together with his brother C S Woolworth (1856–1947), built up a chain of similar stores throughout the USA, Canada, the UK, and Europe.

Woosnam Ian 1958– . Welsh golfer who, in 1987, became the first UK player to win the World Match-Play Championship. He has since won many tournaments, including the World Cup 1987, World Match-Play 1990, and US Masters 1991. He was ranked Number One in the world for 50 weeks in 1991–92.

Worcestershire former Midland county of England, merged 1974 with Herefordshire in the new county of Hereford and Worcester, except for a small projection in the north, which went to West Midlands. Worcester was the county town.

word processor in computing, a program that allows the input, amendment, manipulation, storage, and retrieval of text; or a computer system that runs such software. Since word-processing programs became available to microcomputers, the method has been gradually replacing the typewriter for producing letters or other text.

Wordsworth William 1770–1850. English Romantic poet. In 1797 he moved with his sister Dorothy to Somerset to be near *Coleridge, collaborating with him on *Lyrical Ballads* 1798 (which included 'Tintern Abbey'). From 1799 he lived in the Lake District, and later works include *Poems* 1807 (including 'Intimations of Immortality') and *The Prelude* (written by 1805, published 1850). He was appointed poet laureate in 1843.

work in physics, a measure of the result of transferring energy from one system to another to cause an object to move. Work should not be confused with *energy (the capacity to do work, which is also measured in *joules) or with *power (the rate of doing work, measured in joules per second).

workhouse in the UK, a former institution to house and maintain people unable to earn their own living. Groups of parishes in England combined to build workhouses for the poor, the aged, the disabled, and orphaned children from about 1815 until about 1930.

Works Progress Administration (WPA, renamed *Works Projects Administration* 1939) in US history, a government initiative to reduce unemployment during the Depression (11 million in 1934). Formed 1935, it provided useful work for 8.5 million people during its eight-year existence, mainly in construction projects, at a total cost of $11 billion, and was discontinued only in 1943 when the change to a war economy eliminated unemployment. The WPA was an integral part of President Roosevelt's *New Deal.

work to rule industrial action whereby employees work strictly according to the legal terms of their contract of employment, usually resulting in a slowing-down of the work process.

World Bank popular name for the *International Bank for Reconstruction and Development* specialized agency of the United Nations that borrows in the commercial market and lends on commercial terms. It was established 1945 under the 1944 Bretton Woods agreement, which also created the International Monetary Fund. The *International Development Association* is an arm of the World Bank.

World Council of Churches (WCC) international organization aiming to bring together diverse movements within the Christian church. Established 1945, it has a membership of more than 100 countries and more than 300 churches; headquarters in Geneva, Switzerland.

World Cup the most prestigious competition in international soccer; World Cup events are also held in rugby union, cricket, and other sports.

World Health Organization (WHO) agency of the United Nations established 1946 to prevent the spread of diseases and to eradicate them. In 1990–91 it had 4,500 staff and a budget of £843 million. Its headquarters are in Geneva, Switzerland.

World Intellectual Property Organization (WIPO) specialist agency of the United Nations established 1974 to coordinate the international protection (initiated by the Paris convention 1883) of inventions, trademarks, and industrial designs, and also literary and artistic works (as initiated by the Berne convention 1886).

world music or *roots music* any music whose regional character has not been lost in the melting pot of the pop industry. Examples are W African *mbalax*, E African *soukous*, S African *mbaqanga*, French Antillean *zouk*, Javanese *gamelan*, Latin American *salsa* and *lambada*, Cajun music, European folk music, and rural blues.

World Trade Organization (WTO) world trade monitoring body established Jan 1995, following approval of the Final Act of the Uruguay Round of the General Agreement on Tariffs and Trade (GATT). Under the Final Act, the WTO, a permanent trading body with a status commensurate with that of the International Monetary Fund or the World Bank, effectively replaced GATT. The WTO monitors agreements to reduce barriers to trade, such as tariffs, subsidies, quotas, and regulations which discriminate against imported products.

World War I 1914–1918. War between the Central European Powers (Germany, Austria-Hungary, and allies) on one side and the Triple Entente (Britain and the British Empire, France, and Russia) and their allies, including the USA (which entered 1917), on the other side. An estimated 10 million lives were lost and twice that number were wounded. It was fought on the eastern and western fronts, in the Middle East, Africa, and at sea. Towards the end of the war Russia withdrew because of the Russian Revolution 1917. The peace treaty of Versailles 1919 was the formal end to the war.

World War II 1939–1945. War between Germany, Italy, and Japan (the Axis powers) on one side, and Britain, the Commonwealth, France, the USA, the USSR, and China (the Allied powers) on the other. An estimated 55 million lives were lost, 20 million of them citizens of the USSR. The war was fought in the Atlantic and Pacific theatres. In 1945, Germany surrendered (May) but Japan fought on until the USA dropped atomic bombs on Hiroshima and Nagasaki (Aug).

World Wide Fund for Nature (WWF, formerly the *World Wildlife Fund*) international organization established 1961 to raise funds for conservation by public appeal.

worm any of various elongated limbless invertebrates belonging to several phyla. Worms include the *flatworms, such as *flukes and *tapeworms; the roundworms or *nematodes, such as the eelworm and the hookworm; the marine ribbon worms or nemerteans; and the segmented worms or *annelids.

WORM (acronym for *write once read many times*) in computing, a storage device, similar to *CD-ROM. The computer can write to the disc directly, but cannot later erase or overwrite the same area. WORMs are mainly used for archiving and backup copies.

Worms industrial town in Rhineland-Palatinate, Germany, on the Rhine; population (1984) 73,000. Liebfraumilch wine is produced here. The Protestant reformer Luther appeared before the *Diet* (Assembly) *of Worms* 1521 and was declared an outlaw by the Roman Catholic church.

wormwood any plant of the genus *Artemisia*, family Compositae, especially the aromatic herb *A. absinthium*, the leaves of which are used in *absinthe. *Tarragon is a member of this genus.

Wounded Knee site on the Oglala Sioux Reservation, South Dakota, USA, of a confrontation between the US Army and American Indians.

W particle type of *elementary particle.

wrack any of the large brown *seaweeds characteristic of rocky shores. The bladder wrack *Fucus vesiculosus* has narrow, branched fronds up to 1 m/3.3 ft long, with oval air bladders, usually in pairs on either side of the midrib or central vein.

wren any of a family (Troglodytidae) of small birds of order Passeriformes, with slender, slightly curved bills, and uptilted tails.

Wren Christopher 1632–1723. English architect, designer of St Paul's Cathedral, London, built 1675–1710; many London churches including St Bride's, Fleet Street, and St Mary-le-Bow, Cheapside; the Royal Exchange; Marlborough House; and the Sheldonian Theatre, Oxford.

wrestling sport popular in ancient Egypt, Greece, and Rome, and included in the Olympics from 704 BC. The two main modern international styles are *Greco-Roman*, concentrating on above-waist holds, and *freestyle*, which allows the legs to be used to hold or trip; in both the aim is to throw the opponent to the ground.

Wright Frank Lloyd 1869–1959. US architect who rejected Neo-Classicist styles for 'organic architecture', in which buildings reflected their natural surroundings. Among his buildings are his Wisconsin home Taliesin East 1925; Falling

Water, near Pittsburgh, Pennsylvania, 1936, a house built straddling a waterfall; and the Guggenheim Museum, New York, 1959.

Wright Joseph 1734–1797. British painter, known as *Wright of Derby* from his birthplace. He painted portraits, landscapes, and scientific experiments. His work is often dramatically lit – by fire, candlelight, or even volcanic explosion.

Wright Orville 1871–1948 and Wilbur 1867–1912. US inventors; brothers who pioneered piloted, powered flight. Inspired by Otto *Lilienthal's gliding, they perfected their piloted glider 1902. In 1903 they built a powered machine, a 12-hp 341-kg/750-lb plane, and became the first to make a successful powered flight, near Kitty Hawk, North Carolina. Orville flew 36.6 m/120 ft in 12 sec; Wilbur, 260 m/852 ft in 59 sec.

Wright Peter 1917–1995. British intelligence agent. His book *Spycatcher* 1987, written after his retirement, caused an international stir when the British government tried unsuccessfully to block its publication anywhere in the world because of its damaging revelations about the secret service. Unsuccessful worldwide litigation to suppress *Spycatcher* cost the UK taxpayer over £1 million and gave rise to the phrase 'economical with the truth' (Robert Armstrong).

Wright Richard 1908–1960. US novelist. He was one of the first to depict the condition of black people in 20th-century US society with *Native Son* 1940 and the autobiography *Black Boy* 1945.

writ in law, a document issued by a court requiring performance of certain actions.

writing any written form of communication using a set of symbols: see *alphabet, *cuneiform, *hieroglyphic. The last two used ideographs (picture writing) and phonetic word symbols side by side, as does modern Chinese. Syllabic writing, as in Japanese, develops from the continued use of a symbol to represent the sound of a short word. Some 8,000-year-old inscriptions, thought to be pictographs, were found on animal bones and tortoise shells in Henan province, China, at a Neolithic site at Jiahu. They are thought to predate by 2,500 years the oldest known writing (Mesopotamian cuneiform of 3,500 BC).

Wrocław industrial river port in Poland, on the river Oder; population (1990) 643,200. Under the German name of *Breslau*, it was the capital of former German Silesia. Industries include shipbuilding, engineering, textiles, and electronics.

wrought iron fairly pure iron containing some beads of slag, widely used for construction work before the days of cheap steel. It is strong, tough, and easy to machine. It is made in a puddling furnace, invented by Henry Colt in England 1784. Pig iron is remelted and heated strongly in air with iron ore, burning out the carbon in the metal, leaving relatively pure iron and a slag containing impurities. The resulting pasty metal is then hammered to remove as much of the remaining slag as possible. It is still used in fences and grating.

Wuhan river port and capital of Hubei province, China, at the confluence of the Han and Chang Jiang rivers, formed 1950 as one of China's greatest industrial areas by the amalgamation of Hankou, Hanyang, and Wuchang; population (1989) 3,710,000. It produces iron, steel, machine tools, textiles, and fertilizer.

Wundt Wilhelm Max 1832–1920. German physiologist who regarded psychology as the study of internal experience or consciousness. His main psychological method was introspection; he also studied sensation, perception of space and time, and reaction times.

Wycliffe John c. 1320–1384. English religious reformer. Allying himself with the party of John of Gaunt, which was opposed to ecclesiastical influence at court, he attacked abuses in the church, maintaining that the Bible rather than the church was the supreme authority. He criticized such fundamental doctrines as priestly absolution, confession, and indulgences, and set disciples to work on translating the Bible into English.

Wye (Welsh *Gwy*) river in Wales and England; length 208 km/130 mi. It rises on Plynlimmon, NE Dyfed, flowing SE and E through Powys, and Hereford and Worcester, then follows the Gwent- Gloucestershire border before joining the river Severn south of Chepstow.

Wyeth Andrew (Newell) 1917– . US painter. His portraits and landscapes, usually in watercolour or tempera, are naturalistic, minutely detailed, and often have a strong sense of the isolation of the countryside: for example, *Christina's World* 1948 (Museum of Modern Art, New York).

Wyndham John. Pen name of John Wyndham Parkes Lucas Beynon Harris 1903–1969. English science-fiction writer who wrote *The Day of the Triffids* 1951, *The Chrysalids* 1955, and *The Midwich Cuckoos* 1957. A recurrent theme in his work is people's response to disaster, whether caused by nature, aliens, or human error.

Wyoming state in W USA: nickname Equality State
area 253,400 sq km/97,812 sq mi
capital Cheyenne
cities Casper, Laramie
products oil, natural gas, sodium salts, coal, uranium, sheep, beef
population (1990) 453,600
famous people Buffalo Bill Cody, Jackson Pollock
history acquired by USA from France as part of the *Louisiana Purchase 1803; Fort Laramie, a trading post, settled 1834; granted women the vote 1869; state 1890.

WYSIWYG (acronym for *what you see is what you get*) in computing, a program that attempts to display on the screen a faithful representation of the final printed output. For example, a WYSIWYG *word processor would show actual line widths, page breaks, and the sizes and styles of type.

Wyss Johann David 1743–1818. Swiss author of the children's classic *Swiss Family Robinson* 1812–13.

xanthophyll yellow pigment in plants that, like *chlorophyll, is responsible for the production of carbohydrates by photosynthesis.

Xavier, St Francis 1506–1552. Spanish Jesuit missionary. He went to the Portuguese colonies in the East Indies, arriving at Goa 1542. He was in Japan 1549–51, establishing a Christian mission that lasted for 100 years. He returned to Goa in 1552, and sailed for China, but died of fever there. He was canonized 1622.

X chromosome larger of the two sex chromosomes, the smaller being the *Y chromosome. These two chromosomes are involved in sex determination. Genes carried on the X chromosome produce the phenomenon of *sex linkage.

xenon (Greek *xenos* 'stranger') colourless, odourless, gaseous, non-metallic element, symbol Xe, atomic number 54, relative atomic mass 131.30. It is grouped with the *inert gases and was long believed not to enter into reactions, but is now known to form some compounds, mostly with fluorine. It is a heavy gas present in very small quantities in the air (about one part in 20 million).

Xenophon c. 430–354 BC. Greek historian, philosopher, and soldier. He was a disciple of *Socrates (described in Xenophon's *Symposium*). In 401 he joined a Greek mercenary army aiding the Persian prince Cyrus, and on the latter's death took command. His *Anabasis* describes how he led 10,000 Greeks on a 1,600-km/1,000-mile march home across enemy territory. His other works include *Memorabilia* and *Apology*.

xerography dry, electrostatic method of producing images, without the use of negatives or sensitized paper, invented in the USA by Chester Carlson 1938 and applied in the Xerox *photocopier. Toner powder is sprayed on paper in highly charged areas and fixed with heat.

xerophyte plant adapted to live in dry conditions. Common adaptations to reduce the rate of *transpiration include a reduction of leaf size, sometimes to spines or scales; a dense covering of hairs over the leaf to trap a layer of moist air (as in edelweiss); and permanently rolled leaves or leaves that roll up in dry weather (as in marram grass). Many desert cacti are xerophytes.

Xerxes c. 519–465 BC. King of Persia from 485 BC when he succeeded his father Darius and continued the Persian invasion of Greece. In 480, at the head of an army of some 400,000 men and supported by a fleet of 800 ships, he crossed the *Hellespont strait (now the Dardanelles) over a bridge of boats. He defeated the Greek fleet at Artemisium and captured and burned Athens, but Themistocles retaliated by annihilating the Persian fleet at Salamis and Xerxes was forced to retreat. He spent his later years working on a grandiose extension of the capital Persepolis and was eventually murdered in a court intrigue.

Xhosa member of a Bantu people of southern Africa, living mainly in the Black National State of *Transkei. Traditionally, the Xhosa were farmers and pastoralists, with a social structure based on a monarchy. Many are now town-dwellers, and provide much of the unskilled labour in South African mines and factories. Their Bantu language belongs to the Niger-Congo family.

Xian industrial city and capital of Shaanxi province, China; population (1989) 2,710,000. It produces chemicals, electrical equipment, and fertilizers.

Xi Jiang or *Si-Kiang* river in China, that rises in Yunnan and flows into the South China Sea; length 1,900 km/1,200 mi. Guangzhou lies on the N arm of its delta, and Hong Kong island at its mouth. The name means 'west river'.

Xingú region in Pará, Brazil, crossed by branches of the Xingu1 River which flows for 1,900 km/1,200 mi to the Amazon Delta. In 1989 Xingú Indians protested at the creation of a vast, intrusive lake for the Babaquara and Kararao dams of the Altamira complex.

Xining or *Sining* industrial city and capital of Qinghai province, China; population (1989) 640,000.

Xinjiang Uygur or *Sinkiang Uighur* autonomous region of NW China
area 1,646,800 sq km/635,665 sq mi
capital Urumqi
features largest of Chinese administrative areas
products cereals, cotton, fruit in valleys and oases; uranium, coal, iron, copper, tin, oil
population (1990) 15,156,000; the region has 13 recognized ethnic minorities, the largest being 6 million Uigurs (Muslim descendants of Turks)
religion 50% Muslim
history under Manchu rule from the 18th century. Large sections were ceded to Russia 1864 and 1881; China has raised the question of their return and regards the frontier between Xinjiang Uygur and Tajikistan, which runs for 480 km/300 mi, as undemarcated.

X-ray band of electromagnetic radiation in the wavelength range 10^{-11} to 10^{-9} m (between gamma rays and ultraviolet radiation; see *electromagnetic waves). Applications of X-rays make use of their short wavelength (as in X-ray crystallography) or their penetrating power (as in medical X-rays of internal body tissues). X-rays are dangerous and can cause cancer.

X-ray astronomy detection of X-rays from intensely hot gas in the universe. Such X-rays are prevented from reaching the Earth's surface by the atmosphere, so detectors must be placed in rockets and satellites. The first celestial X-ray source, Scorpius X-1, was discovered by a rocket flight 1962.

X-ray diffraction method of studying the

atomic and molecular structure of crystalline substances by using *X-rays. X-rays directed at such
substances spread out as they pass through the
crystals owing to *diffraction (the slight spreading of waves around the edge of an opaque
object) of the rays around the atoms. By using
measurements of the position and intensity of
the diffracted waves, it is possible to calculate the
shape and size of the atoms in the crystal. The
method has been used to study substances such
as *DNA that are found in living material.

xylem tissue found in *vascular plants, whose
main function is to conduct water and dissolved
mineral nutrients from the roots to other parts
of the plant. Xylem is composed of a number of
different types of cell, and may include long, thin,
usually dead cells known as tracheids; fibres
(schlerenchyma); thin-walled *parenchyma cells;
and conducting vessels.

xylophone musical *percussion instrument in
which wooden bars of varying lengths are
arranged according to graded pitch, or as a piano
keyboard, over resonators to produce sounds
when struck with hammers.

yachting pleasure cruising or racing a small and light vessel, whether sailing or power-driven. At the Olympic Games, seven sail-driven categories exist: Soling, Flying Dutchman, Star, Finn, Tornado, 470, and Windglider or *windsurfing (boardsailing). The Finn and Windglider are solo events; the Soling class is for three-person crews; all other classes are for crews of two.

Yahya Khan Agha Muhammad 1917–1980. Pakistani president 1969–71. His mishandling of the Bangladesh separatist issue led to civil war, and he was forced to resign.

yak species of cattle *Bos grunniens*, family Bovidae, which lives in wild herds at high altitudes in Tibet. It stands about 2 m/6 ft at the shoulder and has long shaggy hair on the underparts. It has large, upward-curving horns and humped shoulders. It is in danger of becoming extinct.

Yakut (Russian *Yakutskaya*) autonomous republic in Siberian Russia
area 3,103,000 sq km/1,197,760 sq mi
capital Yakutsk
products furs, gold, natural gas, some agriculture in the south
population (1986) 1,009,000; 50% Russians, 37% Yakuts
history the nomadic Yakuts were conquered by Russia 17th century; Yakut was a Soviet republic 1922–91. It remained an autonomous republic within the Russian Federation after the collapse of the Soviet Union 1991, since when it has agitated for greater independence.

yakuza (Japanese 'good for nothing') Japanese gangster. Organized crime in Japan is highly structured, and the various syndicates between them employed some 110,000 people 1989, with a turnover of an estimated 1.5 trillion yen. The *yakuza* are unofficially tolerated and very powerful.

Yalta Conference in 1945, a meeting at which the Allied leaders Churchill (UK), Roosevelt (USA), and Stalin (USSR) completed plans for the defeat of Germany in World War II and the foundation of the United Nations. It took place in Yalta, a Soviet holiday resort in the Crimea.

yam any climbing plant of the genus *Dioscorea*, family Dioscoreaceae, cultivated in tropical regions; its starchy tubers are eaten as a vegetable. The Mexican yam *D. composita* contains a chemical used in the manufacture of the contraceptive pill.

Yamoussoukro capital of *Ivory Coast; population (1986) 120,000. The economy is based on tourism and agricultural trade.

Yanamamo or *Yanomamo* (plural *Yanamami*) a member of a semi-nomadic South American Indian people, numbering approximately 15,000, who live in S Venezuela and N Brazil. The Yanamamo language belongs to the Macro-Chibcha family, and is divided into several dialects, although there is a common ritual language. Together with other Amazonian peoples, the Yanamami have been involved in trying to conserve the rainforest where they live. In Nov 1991 Brazil granted them possession of their original land, 58,395 km/36,293 sq mi on its northern border.

Yanayev Gennady 1937– . Soviet communist politician, leader of the failed Aug 1991 coup against *Gorbachev, after which he was arrested and charged with treason. He was vice president of the USSR 1990–91.

Yangon since 1989 the name for *Rangoon* capital and chief port of Myanmar (Burma) on the Yangon river, 32 km/20 mi from the Indian Ocean; population (1983) 2,459,000. Products include timber, oil, and rice. The city *Dagon* was founded on the site AD 746; it was given the name Rangoon (meaning 'end of conflict') by King Alaungpaya 1755.

Yang Shangkun 1907– . Chinese communist politician. He held a senior position in the party 1956–66 but was demoted during the Cultural Revolution. He was rehabilitated 1978, elected to the Politburo 1982, and to the position of state president 1988–93.

Yangtze-Kiang alternative transcription of *Chang Jiang, the longest river in China.

Yankee colloquial (often disparaging) term for an American. Outside the USA the term is applied to any American.

Yao member of a people living in S China, N Vietnam, N Laos, Thailand, and Myanmar (Burma), and numbering about 4 million (1984). The Yao language may belong to either the Sino-Tibetan or the Thai language family. The Yao incorporate elements of ancestor worship in their animist religion.

Yaoundé capital of Cameroon, 210 km/130 mi E of the port of Douala; population (1984) 552,000. Industry includes tourism, oil refining, and cigarette manufacturing.

yard imperial unit (symbol yd) of length, equivalent to three feet (0.9144 m).

yarmulke or *kippa* skullcap worn by Jewish men.

yarrow or *milfoil* perennial herb *Achillea millefolium* of the family Compositae, with feathery, scented leaves and flat-topped clusters of white or pink flowers.

Y chromosome smaller of the two sex chromosomes. In male mammals it occurs paired with the other type of sex chromosome (X), which carries far more genes. The Y chromosome is the smallest of all the mammalian chromosomes and is considered to be largely inert (that is, without direct effect on the physical body). See also *sex determination.

yd abbreviation for *yard*.

year unit of time measurement, based on the

rbital period of the Earth around the Sun. The *tropical year*, from one spring *equinox to the ext, lasts 365.2422 days. It governs the occurrence of the seasons, and is the period on which he calendar year is based. The *sidereal year* s the time taken for the Earth to complete one rbit relative to the fixed stars, and lasts 365.2564 ays (about 20 minutes longer than a tropical ear). The difference is due to the effect of *precession, which slowly moves the position of the quinoxes. The *calendar year* consists of 365 ays, with an extra day added at the end of Feb ach leap year. *Leap years* occur in every year nat is divisible by four, except that a century ear is not a leap year unless it is divisible by 00. Hence 1900 was not a leap year, but 2000 vill be.

east one of various single-celled fungi specially the genus *Saccharomyces*) that form nasses of minute circular or oval cells by buding. When placed in a sugar solution the cells nultiply and convert the sugar into alcohol and arbon dioxide. Yeasts are used as fermenting gents in baking, brewing, and the making of vine and spirits. Brewer's yeast *S. cerevisiae* is a ich source of vitamin B.

east artificial chromosome (YAC) fragnent of *DNA from the human genome inserted nto a yeast cell. The yeast replicates the fragment long with its own DNA. In this way the fragnents are copied to be preserved in a gene library. ACs are characteristically between 250,000 and million base pairs in length. A *cosmid works n the same way.

eats W(illiam) B(utler) 1865–1939. Irish poet. Ie was a leader of the Celtic revival and a ounder of the *Abbey Theatre in Dublin. His arly work was romantic and lyrical, as in the oem 'The Lake Isle of Innisfree' and the plays *he Countess Cathleen* 1892 and *The Land of Ieart's Desire* 1894. His later books of poetry nclude *The Wild Swans at Coole* 1917 and *The Vinding Stair* 1929. He was a senator of the rish Free State 1922–28. Nobel Prize for Literaure 1923.

edo or **Edo** former name of *Tokyo, Japan, ntil 1868.

ellow fever or **yellow jack** acute tropical iral disease, prevalent in the Caribbean area, 3razil, and on the west coast of Africa. Its sympoms include a high fever, headache, joint and auscle pains, vomiting and yellowish skin aundice, possibly leading to liver failure); the eart and kidneys may also be affected. Mortality high in serious cases.

ellowhammer Eurasian bird *Emberiza citnella* of the bunting family Emberizidae. About 6.5 cm/6.5 in long, the male has a yellow head nd underside, a chestnut rump, and a browntreaked back. The female is duller.

ellowknife capital of Northwest Territories, 'anada, on the northern shore of Great Slave ake; population (1986) 11,753. It was founded 935 when gold was discovered in the area and ecame the capital 1967.

ellow River English name for the *Huang He tiver, China.

ellow Sea gulf of the Pacific Ocean between 'hina and Korea; area 466,200 sq km/

180,000 sq mi. It receives the Huang He (Yellow River) and Chang Jiang.

Yellowstone National Park largest US nature reserve, established 1872, on a broad plateau in the Rocky Mountains, chiefly in NW Wyoming, but also in SW Montana and E Idaho; area 8,983 sq km/3,469 sq mi. The park contains more than 3,000 geysers and hot springs, including periodically erupting Old Faithful. It is one of the world's greatest wildlife refuges. Much of the park was ravaged by forest fires 1988.

Yeltsin Boris Nikolayevich 1931– . Russian politician, president of the Russian Soviet Federative Socialist Republic (RSFSR) 1990–91, and president of the newly independent Russian Federation from 1991. He directed the Federation's secession from the USSR and the formation of a new, decentralized confederation, the *Commonwealth of Independent States (CIS), with himself as the most powerful leader. A referendum April 1993 supported his policies of price deregulation and accelerated privatization, despite severe economic problems and civil unrest. He survived a coup attempt in Sept of the same year, but was subsequently forced to compromise on the pace and extent of his reforms after right-wing nationalists made unexpected gains in assembly elections.

Yemen Republic of (*al Jamhuriya al Yamaniya*)

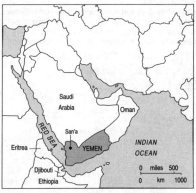

area 531,900 sq km/205,367 sq mi
capital San'ā
towns Ta'iz; and chief port Aden
physical hot moist coastal plain, rising to plateau and desert
head of state Ali Abdullah Saleh from 1990
head of government (interim) Muhammad Said al-Attar
political system emergent democratic republic
exports cotton, coffee, grapes, vegetables
currency rial in the north, dinar in the south
population (1993) 13,000,000; growth rate 2.7% p.a.
language Arabic
religions Sunni Muslim 63%, Shi'ite Muslim 37%
GNP $540 per head (1991)
chronology
1918 Yemen became independent.
1962 North Yemen declared the Yemen Arab Republic (YAR), with Abdullah al-Sallal as presi-

dent. Civil war broke out between royalists and republicans.

1967 Civil war ended with the republicans victorious. Sallal deposed and replaced by Republican Council. The People's Republic of South Yemen was formed.

1970 People's Republic of South Yemen renamed People's Democratic Republic of Yemen.

1971-72 War between South Yemen and the YAR; union agreement signed but not kept.

1974 Ibrahim al-Hamadi seized power in North Yemen and Military Command Council set up.

1977 Hamadi assassinated and replaced by Ahmed ibn Hussein al-Ghashmi.

1978 Constituent people's assembly appointed in North Yemen and Military Command Council dissolved. Ghashmi killed by envoy from South Yemen; succeeded by Ali Abdullah Saleh. War broke out again between the two Yemens. South Yemen president deposed and YSP formed.

1979 Cease-fire agreed with commitment to future union.

1983 Saleh elected president of North Yemen for a further five-year term.

1984 Joint committee on foreign policy for the two Yemens met in Aden.

1985 Ali Nasser re-elected secretary general of the YSP in South Yemen; removed his opponents. Three bureau members killed.

1986 Civil war in South Yemen; Ali Nasser dismissed. New administration under Haydar Abu Bakr al-Attas.

1988 President Saleh re-elected in North Yemen.

1989 Draft constitution for single Yemen state published.

1990 Border between two Yemens opened; countries formally united 22 May as Republic of Yemen.

1991 New constitution approved.

1992 Anti-government riots.

1993 General People's Congress won most seats in general elections but no overall majority; five-member presidential council elected, including Ali Abdullah Saleh as president and YSP leader, Ali Salim al-Baidh, as vice president.

1994 Fighting erupted between northern forces, led by President Saleh, and southern forces, led by Vice President al-Baidh. May: southern Yemen announced its secession. July: Saleh inflicted crushing defeat on al-Baidh, effectively ending civil war.

Yenisei river in Asian Russia, rising in the Tuva region and flowing across the Siberian plain into the Arctic Ocean; length 4,100 km/2,550 mi.

Yeomen of the Guard English military corps, popularly known as **Beefeaters**, the sovereign's bodyguard since the corps was founded by Henry VII 1485. Its duties are now purely ceremonial.

Yerevan industrial city (tractor parts, machine tools, chemicals, bricks, bicycles, wine, fruit canning) and capital of Armenia, a few miles N of the Turkish border; population (1987) 1,168,000. It was founded in the 7th century and was alternately Turkish and Persian from the 15th century until ceded to Russia 1828. Armenia became an independent republic 1991.

Yerkes Observatory astronomical centre in Wisconsin, USA, founded by George Hale 1897. It houses the world's largest refracting optical *telescope, with a lens of diameter 102 cm/40 in.

Yersin Alexandre Emile Jean 1863–1943. Swis: bacteriologist who discovered the buboni plague bacillus in Hong Kong 1894 and prepare a serum against it.

Yesenin Sergei alternative form of *Esenir Russian poet.

yeti Tibetan for the *abominable snowman.

Yevtushenko Yevgeny Aleksandrovich 1933- Soviet poet, born in Siberia. He aroused contro versy with his anti-Stalinist 'Stalin's Heirs' 195(published with Khrushchev's support, and 'Bab Yar' 1961. His autobiography was publishe 1963.

yew any evergreen coniferous tree of the genu *Taxus* of the family Taxaceae, native to th northern hemisphere. The leaves and bright re berrylike seeds are poisonous; the wood is har and close-grained.

Yi member of a people living in S China; ther are also Yi populations in Laos, Thailand, an Vietnam, totalling about 5.5 million (1987). Th Yi are farmers, producing both crops and liv stock. Their language belongs to the Sino-Tibeta family; their religion is animist.

Yiddish language member of the west Ge manic branch of the Indo-European languag family, deriving from 13th–14th-century Rhine land German and spoken by northern, centra and eastern European Jews, who have carried to Israel, the USA, and many other parts of th world. It is written in the Hebrew alphabet an has many dialects reflecting European areas (residence, as well as many borrowed words fro Polish, Russian, Lithuanian, and other language encountered.

yin and yang Chinese for 'dark' and 'brigh respectively, referring to the passiv (characterized as feminine, negative, intuitiv and active (characterized as masculine, positiv intellectual) principles of nature. Their inte action is believed to maintain equilibrium an harmony in the universe and to be present i all things. In Taoism and Confucianism they a represented by two interlocked curved shape within a circle, one white, one black, with a spc of the contrasting colour within the head of each

Yinchuan capital of Ningxia autonomou region, NW China; population (1989) 576,000.

yoga (Sanskrit 'union') Hindu philosophic system attributed to Patanjali, who lived abou 150 BC at Gonda, Uttar Pradesh, India. H preached mystical union with a personal dei through the practice of self-hypnosis and a risir above the senses by abstract meditation, ado(tion of special postures, and ascetic practices. A practised in the West, yoga is more a system (mental and physical exercise, and of induce relaxation as a means of relieving stress.

yoghurt or **yogurt** or **yoghourt** semisol curdlike dairy product made from milk fermente with bacteria. It was originally made by nomad tribes of Central Asia from mare's milk in leath(pouches attached to their saddles. It is drun plain throughout the Asian and Mediterranea region, to which it spread, but honey, sugar, an fruit were added in Europe and the USA, and th product made solid and creamy, to be eaten t spoon.

Yokohama Japanese port on Tokyo Bay; pop|

tion (1989) 3,176,000. Industries include shipbuilding, oil refining, engineering, textiles, glass,
and clothing.

olk store of food, mostly in the form of fats and
proteins, found in the *eggs of many animals. It
provides nourishment for the growing embryo.

olk sac sac containing the yolk in the egg of
most vertebrates. The term is also used for the
embranous sac formed below the developing
ammalian embryo and connected with the
umbilical cord.

om Kippur the Jewish Day of *Atonement.

om Kippur War the surprise attack on Israel
October 1973 by Egypt and Syria; see *Arab-
raeli Wars. It is named after the Jewish national
holiday on which it began, the holiest day of the
Jewish year.

ork cathedral and industrial city (railway rol-
ng stock, scientific instruments, sugar, choc-
ate, and glass) in North Yorkshire, N England;
population (1991) 100,600. The city is visited by
million tourists a year.

atures The Gothic York Minster contains
medieval stained glass; the south transept was
severely damaged by fire 1984, but has been
stored. Much of the 14th-century city wall sur-
ves, with four gates or 'bars', as well as the
medieval streets collectively known as the Sham-
es (after the slaughterhouse). The Jorvik Viking
entre, opened 1984 after excavation of a site at
oppergate, contains wooden remains of Viking
ouses. There are fine examples of 17th- to 18th-
ntury domestic architecture; the Theatre Royal,
e of a theatre since 1765; the Castle Museum;
e National Railway Museum; and the university
63.

story Traditionally the capital of the N of
gland, the city became from AD 71 the Roman
rtress of *Eboracum*. Recent excavations of the
man city have revealed the fortress, baths, and
mples to Serapis and Mithras. The first bishop
York (Paulinus) was consecrated 627 in the
oden church that preceded York Minster. Pau-
us baptized King Edwin there 627, and York
as created an archbishopric 732. In the 10th
ntury it was a Viking settlement. During the
ddle Ages its commercial prosperity depended
the wool trade. An active Quaker element in
e 18th and 19th centuries included the Rown-
e family that founded the chocolate factory.

ork English dynasty founded by Richard, Duke
York (1411–60). He claimed the throne
rough his descent from Lionel, Duke of Clar-
ce (1338–1368), third son of Edward III,
ereas the reigning monarch, Henry VI of the
al house of Lancaster, was descended from
e fourth son. The argument was fought out
the Wars of the *Roses. York was killed at the
ttle of Wakefield 1460, but next year his son
came King Edward IV, in turn succeeded by
son Edward V and then by his brother
chard III, with whose death at Bosworth the
e ended. The Lancastrian victor in that battle
s crowned Henry VII and consolidated his
im by marrying Edward IV's eldest daughter,
zabeth.

ork archbishop of. Metropolitan of the
rthern province of the Anglican Church in
gland, hence Primate of England.

orkshire former county in NE England on the

North Sea divided administratively into N, E,
and W ridings (thirds), but reorganized to form
a number of new counties 1974: the major part
of **Cleveland** and **Humberside**, **North Yorkshire**, **South Yorkshire**, and **West Yorkshire**.
Small outlying areas also went to Durham, Cumbria, Lancashire, and Greater Manchester.

Yoruba member of the majority ethnic group
living in SW Nigeria; there is a Yoruba minority
in E Benin. They number approximately 20
million in all, and their language belongs to the
Kwa branch of the Niger-Congo family. The
Yoruba established powerful city states in the
15th century, known for their advanced culture
which includes sculpture, art, and music.

Young Arthur 1741–1820. English writer and
publicizer of the new farm practices associated
with the *agricultural revolution. When the
Board of Agriculture was established 1792,
Young was appointed secretary, and was the
guiding force behind the production of a county-
by-county survey of British agriculture.

Young Brigham 1801–1877. US *Mormon
religious leader, born in Vermont. He joined the
Mormon Church, or Church of Jesus Christ of
Latter-day Saints, 1832, and three years later was
appointed an apostle. After a successful recruiting mission in Liverpool, England, he returned
to the USA and, as successor of Joseph Smith
(who had been murdered), led the Mormon
migration to the Great Salt Lake in Utah 1846,
founded Salt Lake City, and headed the colony
until his death.

Young Lester (Willis) 1909–1959. US tenor saxophonist and jazz composer. He was a major
figure in the development of his instrument for
jazz music from the 1930s and was an accompan-
ist for the singer Billie Holiday, who gave him the
nickname 'President', later shortened to 'Pres'.

Young Neil 1945– . Canadian rock guitarist,
singer, and songwriter, in the USA from 1966.
His high, plaintive voice and loud, abrasive guitar
make his work instantly recognizable, despite
abrupt changes of style throughout his career.
Rust Never Sleeps 1979 and *Arc Weld* 1991
(both with the group Crazy Horse) are among
his best work.

Young Thomas 1773–1829. British physicist
who revived the wave theory of light and identified the phenomenon of *interference in 1801.

Young Ireland Irish nationalist organization,
founded 1840 by William Smith O'Brien
(1803–1864), who attempted an abortive insurrection of the peasants against the British in Tipperary 1848. O'Brien was sentenced to death, but
later pardoned.

Young Italy Italian nationalist organization
founded 1831 by Giuseppe *Mazzini while in
exile in Marseille. The movement, which was
immediately popular, was followed the next year
by Young Germany, Young Poland, and similar
organizations. All the groups were linked by
Mazzini in his Young Europe movement, but
none achieved much practical success; attempted
uprisings by Young Italy 1834 and 1844 failed
miserably. It was superseded in Italy by the
*Risorgimento.

young offender institution in the UK,
establishment of detention for lawbreakers under

17 (juveniles) and 17–21 (young adults). The period of detention depends on the seriousness of the offence and on the age and sex of the offender. The institution was introduced by the Criminal Justice Act 1988.

Young Pretender nickname of *Charles Edward Stuart, claimant to the Scottish and English thrones.

Young Turk member of a reformist movement of young army officers in the Ottoman Empire founded 1889. The movement was instrumental in the constitutional changes of 1908 and the abdication of Sultan Abdul-Hamid II 1909. It gained prestige during the Balkan Wars 1912–13 and encouraged Turkish links with the German empire. Its influence diminished after 1918. The term is now used for a member of any radical or rebellious faction within a party or organization.

Yourcenar Marguerite. Pen name of Marguerite de Crayencour 1903–1987. French writer, born in Belgium. She first gained recognition as a novelist in France in the 1930s with books such as *La Nouvelle Euridyce/The New Euridyce* 1931. Her evocation of past eras and characters, exemplified in *Les Mémoires d'Hadrien/The Memoirs of Hadrian* 1951, brought her acclaim as a historical novelist. In 1939 she settled in the USA. In 1980 she became the first woman to be elected to the French Academy.

Youth Training Scheme (YTS) in the UK, a one- or two-year course of training and work experience for unemployed school leavers aged 16 and 17, from 1989 provided by employer-led Training and Enterprise Councils at local levels and renamed Youth Training.

Ypres (Flemish *Ieper*) Belgian town in W Flanders, 40 km/25 mi S of Ostend, a site of three major battles 1914–17 fought in World War I. The Menin Gate 1927 is a memorial to British soldiers lost in these battles.

ytterbium soft, lustrous, silvery, malleable, and ductile element of the *lanthanide series, symbol Yb, atomic number 70, relative atomic mass 173.04. It occurs with (and resembles) yttrium in gadolinite and other minerals, and is used in making steel and other alloys.

yttrium silver-grey, metallic element, symbol Y, atomic number 39, relative atomic mass 88.905. It is associated with and resembles the *rare-earth elements (*lanthanides), occurring in gadolinite, xenotime, and other minerals. It is used in colour-television tubes and to reduce steel corrosion.

Yucatán peninsula in Central America, divided among Mexico, Belize, and Guatemala; area 180,000 sq km/70,000 sq mi. Tropical crops are grown. It is inhabited by Maya Indians and contains the remains of their civilization.

yucca plant of the genus *Yucca*, family Liliaceae, with over 40 species found in Latin America and southwest USA. The leaves are stiff and sword-shaped and the flowers white and bell-shaped.

Yugoslavia

area 58,300 sq km/22,503 sq mi
capital Belgrade
towns Kraljevo, Leskovac, Pristina, Novi Sad, Titograd
head of state Zoran Lilic from 1993

head of government Radoje Kontic from 1993
political system socialist pluralist republic
exports machinery, electrical goods, chemicals, clothing, tobacco
currency dinar
population (1992) 10,460,000
languages Serbian variant of Serbo-Croatian, Slovenian
religion Eastern Orthodox 41% (Serbs), Roman Catholic 12% (Croats), Muslim 3%
GNP $6,540 per head (1988)
chronology
1918 Creation of Kingdom of the Serbs, Croats, and Slovenes.
1929 Name of Yugoslavia adopted.
1941 Invaded by Germany.
1945 Yugoslav Federal Republic formed under leadership of Tito; communist constitution introduced.
1948 Split with USSR.
1953 Self-management principle enshrined in constitution.
1961 Nonaligned movement formed under Yugoslavia's leadership.
1974 New constitution adopted.
1980 Tito died; collective leadership assumed power.
1987 Threatened use of army to curb unrest.
1988 Economic difficulties: 1,800 strikes, 250% inflation, 20% unemployment. Ethnic unrest in Montenegro and Vojvodina; party reshuffled and government resigned.
1989 Reformist Croatian Ante Marković became prime minister. Twenty-nine died in ethnic riots in Kosovo province, protesting against Serbian attempt to end autonomous status of Kosovo and Vojvodina; state of emergency imposed. May: inflation rose to 490%; tensions with ethnic Albanians rose.
1990 Multiparty systems established in Serbia and Croatia.
1991 June: Slovenia and Croatia declared independence, resulting in clashes between federal and republican armies; Slovenia accepted European Community (EC)-sponsored peace pact. Fighting continued in Croatia; repeated calls for cease-fires failed. Dec: President Stipe Mesic and Prime Minister Ante Marković resigned.

1992 Jan: EC-brokered cease-fire established in Croatia; EC and USA recognized Slovenia's and Croatia's independence. Bosnia-Herzegovina and Macedonia declared independence. April: Bosnia-Herzegovina recognized as independent by EC and USA amid increasing ethnic hostility. New Federal Republic of Yugoslavia (FRY) proclaimed by Serbia and Montenegro but not recognized externally. International sanctions imposed against Serbia and Montenegro. Hostilities continued. Sept: UN membership suspended.
1993 Anti-government rioting in Belgrade. Macedonia recognized as independent under name of Former Yugoslav Republic of Macedonia. Yugoslav economy severely damaged by international sanctions.

Yukon territory of NW Canada
area 483,500 sq km/186,631 sq mi
capital Whitehorse
towns Dawson, Mayo
products gold, silver, lead, zinc, oil, natural gas, coal

population (1991) 26,500
history settlement dates from the gold rush 1896–1910, when 30,000 people moved to the *Klondike river valley (silver is now worked there). It became separate from the Northwest Territories 1898, with Dawson as the capital 1898–1951. Construction of the Alcan Highway during World War II helped provide the basis for further development.

Yukon River river in North America, 3,185 km/ 1,979 mi long, flowing from Lake Tagish in Yukon Territory into Alaska, where it empties into the Bering Sea.

Yunnan province of SW China, adjoining Myanmar (Burma), Laos, and Vietnam
area 436,200 sq km/168,373 sq mi
capital Kunming
physical rivers: Chang Jiang, Salween, Mekong; crossed by the Burma Road; mountainous and well forested
products rice, tea, timber, wheat, cotton, rubber, tin, copper, lead, zinc, coal, salt
population (1990) 36,973,000.

Zagreb industrial city (leather, linen, carpets, paper, and electrical goods) and capital of Croatia, on the Sava river; population (1981) 1,174,512. Zagreb was a Roman city (*Aemona*) and has a Gothic cathedral. Its university was founded 1874. The city was damaged by bombing Oct 1991 during the Croatian civil war.

Zahir ud-din Muhammad 1483–1530. First Great Mogul of India from 1526, called Babur (Arabic 'lion'). He was the great-grandson of the Mongol conqueror Tamerlane and, at the age of 12, succeeded his father, Omar Sheik Mirza, as ruler of Ferghana (Turkestan).

Zahir Shah Mohammed 1914– . King of Afghanistan 1933–73. Zahir served in the government 1932–33 before being crowned king. He was overthrown 1973 by a republican coup and went into exile. He became a symbol of national unity for the *Mujaheddin Islamic fundamentalist resistance groups.

Zaire Republic of (*République du Zaïre*) (formerly **Congo**)

area 2,344,900 sq km/905,366 sq mi
capital Kinshasa
towns Lubumbashi, Kananga, Kisangani; ports Matadi, Boma
physical Zaïre River basin has tropical rainforest and savanna; mountains in E and W
head of state Mobutu Sese Seko Kuku Ngbendu wa Zabanga from 1965

head of government Leon Kengo Wa Dondo from 1994
political system transitional
exports coffee, copper, cobalt (80% of world output), industrial diamonds, palm oil
currency zaïre
population (1993 est) 40,256,000; growth rate 2.9% p.a.
languages French (official), Swahili, Lingala, other African languages; over 300 dialects
religions Christian 70%, Muslim 10%
GNP $220 per head (1990)
chronology
1908 Congo Free State annexed to Belgium.
1960 Independence achieved from Belgium as Republic of the Congo. Civil war broke out between central government and Katanga province.
1963 Katanga war ended.
1965 Col Mobutu seized power in coup.
1967 New constitution adopted.
1970 Mobutu elected president.
1971 Country became the Republic of Zaire.
1972 The Popular Movement of the Revolution (MPR) became the only legal political party. Katanga province renamed Shaba.
1974 Foreign-owned businesses and plantations seized by Mobutu and given in political patronage.
1977 Original owners of confiscated properties invited back. Mobutu re-elected; Zairians invaded Shaba province from Angola, repulsed by Belgian paratroopers.
1978 Second unsuccessful invasion from Angola.
1990 Mobutu announced end of ban on multiparty politics, following internal dissent.
1991 Sept: after antigovernment riots, Mobutu agreed to share power with opposition; Etienne Tshisekedi appointed premier. Oct: Tshisekedi dismissed; opposition government formed.
1992 Aug: Tshisekedi reinstated against Mobutu's wishes. Oct: renewed rioting. Dec: interim parliament, the High Council of the Republic (HCR), formed, with Tshisekedi as premier.
1993 Jan: army mutiny. March: Tshisekedi dismissed by Mobutu and replaced by Faustin Birindwa, but Tshisekedi disputed decision.
1994 Reconstituted interim parliament installed the Parliament of Transition, incorporating HCR. April: interim constitution adopted. Kengo Wa Dondo elected prime minister, with Mobutu's agreement.

Zaïre River formerly (until 1971) **Congo** second longest river in Africa, rising near the Zambia-Zaire border (and known as the **Lualaba River** in the upper reaches) and flowing 4,500 km/2,800 mi to the Atlantic, running in great curve that crosses the equator twice, and discharging a volume of water second only to the Amazon.

Zama, Battle of battle fought in 202 BC in Numidia (now Algeria), in which the Carthaginians under Hannibal were defeated by the Romans under Scipio, so ending the Second Punic War.

Zambezi river in central and SE Africa; length 2,650 km/1,650 mi from NW Zambia through Mozambique to the Indian Ocean, with a wide delta near Chinde. Major tributaries include the Kafue in Zambia. It is interrupted by rapids, and

...cludes on the Zimbabwe–Zambia border the ...ictoria Falls (Mosi-oa-tunya) and Kariba Dam, ...hich forms the reservoir of Lake Kariba with ...rge fisheries.

...ambia Republic of

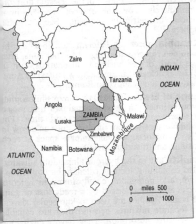

...area 752,600 sq km/290,579 sq mi
capital Lusaka
towns Kitwe, Ndola, Kabwe, Chipata, Livingstone
physical forested plateau cut through by rivers
head of state and government Frederick Chiluba from 1991
political system socialist pluralist republic
exports copper, cobalt, zinc, emeralds, tobacco
currency kwacha
population (1993) 9,000,000; growth rate 3.3% p.a.
languages English (official); Bantu dialects
religions Christian 66%, animist, Hindu, Muslim
GNP $420 per head (1990)
chronology
1899–1924 As Northern Rhodesia, under administration of the British South Africa Company.
1924 Became a British protectorate.
1964 Independence achieved from Britain, within the Commonwealth, as the Republic of Zambia with Kenneth Kaunda as president.
1972 United National Independence Party (UNIP) declared the only legal party.
1976 Support for the Patriotic Front in Rhodesia declared.
1980 Unsuccessful coup against President Kaunda.
1988 Kaunda re-elected unopposed for sixth term.
1990 Multiparty system announced for 1991.
1991 Movement for Multiparty Democracy won landslide election victory; Frederick Chiluba became president.
1992 Food and water shortages caused by severe drought.

ZANU (acronym for *Zimbabwe African National Union*) political organization founded in 1963 by the Reverend Ndabaningi Sithole and later led by Robert Mugabe. It was banned 1964 by the Rhodesian Front government, against

which it conducted a guerrilla war from Zambia until the free elections of 1980, when the ZANU Patriotic Front party, led by Mugabe, won 63% of the vote. In 1987 it merged with *ZAPU in preparation for making Zimbabwe a one-party state.

Zanzibar island region of Tanzania
area 1,658 sq km/640 sq mi (80 km/50 mi long)
towns Zanzibar
products cloves, copra
population (1985) 571,000
history settled by Arab traders in the 7th century; occupied by the Portuguese in the 16th century; became a sultanate in the 17th century; under British protection 1890–1963. Together with the island of Pemba, some nearby islets, and a strip of mainland territory, it became a republic 1963. It merged with Tanganyika as Tanzania 1964.

Zapata Emiliano 1879–1919. Mexican Indian revolutionary leader. He led a revolt against dictator Porfirio Díaz (1830–1915) from 1911 under the slogan 'Land and Liberty', to repossess for the indigenous Mexicans the land taken by the Spanish. By 1915 he was driven into retreat, and was assassinated.

Zapotec member of a North American Indian people of S Mexico, now numbering approximately 250,000, living mainly in Oaxaca. The Zapotec language, which belongs to the Oto-Mangean family, has nine dialects. The ancient Zapotec developed one of the classic Mesoamerican civilizations by AD 300, but declined under pressure from the Mixtecs from 900 until the Spanish Conquest 1530s.

Zappa Frank (Francis Vincent) 1940–1993. US rock musician, bandleader, and composer. His complex orchestral and electronic compositions (*Hot Rats* 1969) and crudely satirical songs made his work hard to categorize. He led the group the Mothers of Invention 1965–73.

ZAPU (acronym for *Zimbabwe African People's Union*) political organization founded by Joshua Nkomo 1961 and banned 1962 by the Rhodesian government. It engaged in a guerrilla war in alliance with *ZANU against the Rhodesian regime until late 1979. In the 1980 elections ZAPU was defeated and was then persecuted by the ruling ZANU Patriotic Front party. In 1987 the two parties merged.

zebra black and white striped member of the horse genus *Equus* found in Africa; the stripes serve as camouflage or dazzle and confuse predators. It is about 1.5 m/5 ft high at the shoulder, with a stout body and a short, thick mane. Zebras live in family groups and herds on mountains and plains, and can run at up to 60 kph/40 mph. Males are usually solitary.

zebu any of a species of *cattle *Bos indicus* found domesticated in E Asia, India, and Africa. It is usually light-coloured, with large horns and a large fatty hump near the shoulders. It is used for pulling loads, and is held by some Hindus to be sacred. There are about 30 breeds.

Zedekiah last king of Judah 597–586 BC. Placed on the throne by Nebuchadnezzar, he rebelled, was forced to witness his sons' execution, then was blinded and sent to Babylon. The witness to these events was the prophet Jeremiah, who describes them in the Old Testament.

zebra Burchell's zebras show great variation in stripe pattern, both between individuals and over the geographical range.

Zeebrugge small Belgian ferry port on the North Sea, linked to Bruges by a canal (built 1896–1907), 14 km/9 mi long. In March 1987 it was the scene of a disaster in which over 180 passengers lost their lives when the car ferry *Herald of Free Enterprise* put to sea from Zeebrugge with its car-loading doors open.

Zeeland province of the SW Netherlands
area 1,790 sq km/691 sq mi
capital Middelburg
towns Vlissingen, Terneuzen, Goes
population (1991) 357,500
products cereals, potatoes
history disputed by the counts of Flanders and Holland during the Middle Ages, Zeeland was annexed to Holland in 1323 by Count Willam III.

Zeeman Pieter 1865–1943. Dutch physicist who discovered 1896 that when light from certain elements, such as sodium or lithium (when heated), is passed through a spectroscope in the presence of a strong magnetic field, the spectrum splits into a number of distinct lines. His discovery, known as the **Zeeman effect**, won him a share of the 1902 Nobel Prize for Physics.

Zeffirelli Franco 1923– . Italian theatre, opera and film director, and stage designer, acclaimed for his stylish designs and lavish productions. His films include *La Traviata* 1983, *Otello* 1986, and *Hamlet* 1990.

Zeiss Carl 1816–1888. German optician. He opened his first workshop in Jena 1846, and in 1866 joined forces with Ernst Abbe (1840–1905) producing cameras, microscopes, and binoculars.

Zen (abbreviation of Japanese *zenna* 'quiet mind concentration') form of *Buddhism introduced from India to Japan via China in the 12th century. *Kōan* (paradoxical questions), tea-drinking, and sudden enlightenment are elements of Zen practice. Soto Zen was spread by the priest Dōgen (1200–1253), who emphasized work, practice, discipline, and philosophical questions to discover one's Buddha-nature in the 'realization of self'.

Zend-Avesta sacred scriptures of *Zoroastrianism, today practised by the Parsees. They comprise the *Avesta* (liturgical books for the priests), the *Gathas* (the discourses and revelations of Zoroaster); and the *Zend* (commentary upon them).

zenith uppermost point of the celestial horizon immediately above the observer; the *nadir is below, diametrically opposite. See *celestial sphere.

Zenobia queen of Palmyra AD 266–272. She assumed the crown as regent for her sons, after the death of her husband Odaenathus, and in 272 was defeated at Emesa (now Homs) by Aurelian and taken captive to Rome.

Zeno of Elea *c.* 490–430 BC. Greek philosopher who pointed out several paradoxes that raised 'modern' problems of space and time. For example, motion is an illusion, since an arrow in flight must occupy a determinate space at each instant, and therefore must be at rest.

zeolite any of the hydrous aluminium silicates, also containing sodium, calcium, barium, strontium, and potassium, chiefly found in igneous rocks and characterized by a ready loss or gain of water. Zeolites are used as 'molecular sieves' to separate mixtures because they are capable of selective absorption. They have a high ion-exchange capacity and can be used to make petrol, benzene, and toluene from low-grade raw materials, such as coal and methanol.

Zeppelin Ferdinand, Count von Zeppelin 1838–1917. German airship pioneer. On retiring from the army 1891, he devoted himself to the study of aeronautics, and his first airship was built and tested 1900. During World War I a number of Zeppelin airships bombed England. They were also used for luxury passenger transport but the construction of hydrogen-filled airships with rigid keels was abandoned after several disasters in the 1920s and 1930s. Zeppelin also helped to pioneer large multi-engine bomber planes.

Zernike Frits 1888–1966. Dutch physicist who developed the phase-contrast microscope 1935. Earlier microscopes allowed many specimens to be examined only after they had been transformed by heavy staining and other treatment. The phase-contrast microscope allowed living cells to be directly observed by making use of the difference in refractive indices between specimens and medium. He was awarded the Nobel Prize for Physics 1953.

Zeus in Greek mythology, chief of the gods (Roman Jupiter). He was the son of Kronos, whom he overthrew; his brothers included Hades and Poseidon, his sisters Demeter and Hera. As the supreme god he dispensed good and evil and was the father and ruler of all humankind. His emblems are the thunderbolt and aegis (shield), representing the thundercloud.

Zhangjiakou or **Changchiakow** historic town and trade centre in Hebei province, China, 160 km/100 mi NW of Beijing, on the Great Wall; population (1980) 1,100,000. Zhangjiakou is on the border of Inner Mongolia (its Mongolian name is **Kalgan**, 'gate') and on the road and railway to Ulaanbaatar in Mongolia. It developed under the Manchu dynasty, and was the centre of the tea trade from China to Russia.

Zhao Ziyang 1918–. Chinese politician, prime minister 1980–87 and secretary of the Chinese Communist Party 1987–89. His reforms included self-management and incentives for workers and factories. He lost his secretaryship and other posts after the Tiananmen Square massacre in Beijing June 1989.

Zhejiang or **Chekiang** province of SE China
area 101,800 sq km/39,295 sq mi
capital Hangzhou
products rice, cotton, sugar, jute, maize; timber on the uplands
population (1990) 41,446,000.

Zhelev Zhelyu 1935– . Bulgarian politician, president from 1990. In 1989 he became head of the opposition Democratic Forces coalition. He is a proponent of market-centred economic reform and social peace.

Zhengzhou or **Chengchow** industrial city (light engineering, cotton textiles, foods) and capital (from 1954) of Henan province, China, on the Huang Ho; population (1989) 1,660,000.

Zhivkov Todor 1911– . Bulgarian Communist Party leader 1954–89, prime minister 1962–71, president 1971–89. His period in office was one of caution and conservatism. In 1991 he was tried for gross embezzlement.

Zhou Enlai or **Chou En-lai** 1898–1976. Chinese politician. Zhou, a member of the Chinese Communist Party (CCP) from the 1920s, was prime minister 1949–76 and foreign minister 1949–58. He was a moderate Maoist and weathered the Cultural Revolution. He played a key role in foreign affairs.

Zhubov scale scale for measuring ice coverage, developed in the USSR. The unit is the **ball**; one ball is 10% coverage, two balls 20%, and so on.

Zhu De or **Chu Teh** 1886–1976. Chinese Red Army leader from 1931. He devised the tactic of mobile guerrilla warfare and organized the *Long March to Shaanxi 1934–36. He was made a marshal 1955.

Zhukov Georgi Konstantinovich 1896–1974. Marshal of the USSR in World War II and minister of defence 1955–57. As chief of staff from 1941, he defended Moscow 1941, counterattacked at Stalingrad (now Volgograd) 1942, organized the relief of Leningrad (now St Petersburg) 1943, and led the offensive from the Ukraine March 1944 which ended in the fall of Berlin.

Zia ul-Haq Mohammad 1924–1988. Pakistani general, in power from 1977 until his death, probably an assassination, in an aircraft explosion. He became army chief of staff 1976, led the military coup against Zulfiqar Ali *Bhutto 1977, and became president 1978. Zia introduced a fundamentalist Islamic regime and restricted political activity.

zidovudine (formerly **AZT**) antiviral drug used in the treatment of *AIDS. It is not a cure for AIDS but is effective in suppressing the causative virus (HIV) for as long as it is being administered.

ZIFT abbreviation for **zygote inter-Fallopian transfer** modified form of *in vitro fertilization in which the fertilized ovum is reintroduced into the mother's *Fallopian tube before the ovum has undergone its first cell division. This mimics the natural processes of fertilization (which normally occurs in the Fallopian tube) and implantation more effectively than older techniques.

ziggurat in ancient Babylonia and Assyria, a step pyramid of sun-baked brick faced with glazed bricks or tiles on which stood a shrine. The Tower of Babel as described in the Bible may have been a ziggurat.

Zimbabwe extensive stone architectural ruins near Victoria in Mashonaland, Zimbabwe. The structure was probably the work of the *Shona people who established their rule about AD 1000 and who mined minerals for trading. The word *zimbabwe* means 'house of stone' in Shona language. The new state of Zimbabwe took its name from these ruins.

Zimbabwe Republic of
area 390,300 sq km/150,695 sq mi
capital Harare
towns Bulawayo, Gweru, Kwekwe, Mutare, Hwange
physical high plateau with central high veld and mountains in E; rivers Zambezi, Limpopo
head of state and government Robert Mugabe from 1987

political system effectively one-party socialist republic
exports tobacco, asbestos, cotton, coffee, gold, silver, copper
currency Zimbabwe dollar
population (1993 est) 10,700,000 (Shona 80%, Ndbele 19%; about 100,000 whites); growth rate 3.5% p.a.
languages English (official), Shona, Sindebele
religions Christian, Muslim, Hindu, animist
GNP $620 per head (1991)
chronology
1889–1923 As Southern Rhodesia, under administration of British South Africa Company.
1923 Became a self-governing British colony.
1961 Zimbabwe African People's Union (ZAPU) formed, with Joshua Nkomo as leader.
1962 ZAPU declared illegal.
1963 Zimbabwe African National Union (ZANU) formed, with Robert Mugabe as secretary general.
1964 Ian Smith became prime minister. ZANU banned. Nkomo and Mugabe imprisoned.
1965 Smith declared unilateral independence.

1966–68 Abortive talks between Smith and UK prime minister Harold Wilson.
1974 Nkomo and Mugabe released.
1975 Geneva conference set date for constitutional independence.
1979 Smith produced new constitution and established a government with Bishop Abel Muzorewa as prime minister. New government denounced by Nkomo and Mugabe. Conference in London agreed independence arrangements (Lancaster House Agreement).
1980 Independence achieved from Britain, with Robert Mugabe as prime minister.
1981 Rift between Mugabe and Nkomo.
1982 Nkomo dismissed from the cabinet, leaving the country temporarily.
1984 ZANU–PF party congress agreed to create a one-party state in future.
1985 Relations between Mugabe and Nkomo improved. Troops sent to Matabeleland to suppress rumoured insurrection; 5,000 civilians killed.
1986 Joint ZANU–PF rally held amid plans for merger.
1987 White-roll seats in the assembly were abolished. President Banana retired; Mugabe combined posts of head of state and prime minister with the title executive president.
1988 Nkomo returned to the cabinet and was appointed vice president.
1989 Opposition party, the Zimbabwe Unity Movement, formed by Edgar Tekere; draft constitution drawn up, renouncing Marxism–Leninism; ZANU and ZAPU formally merged.
1990 ZANU–PF re-elected. State of emergency ended. Opposition to creation of one-party state.
1992 United Front formed to oppose ZANU–PF.

zinc (Germanic *zint* 'point') hard, brittle, bluish-white, metallic element, symbol Zn, atomic number 30, relative atomic mass 65.37. The principal ore is sphalerite or zinc blende (zinc sulphide, ZnS). Zinc is little affected by air or moisture at ordinary temperatures; its chief uses are in alloys such as brass and in coating metals (for example galvanized iron). Its compounds include zinc oxide, used in ointments (as an astringent) and cosmetics, paints, glass, and printing ink.

zinc ore mineral from which zinc is extracted, principally sphalerite $(Zn,Fe)S$, but also zincite, ZnO_2, and smithsonite, Zn,CO_3, all of which occur in mineralized veins. Ores of lead and zinc often occur together, and are common worldwide; Canada, the USA, and Australia are major producers.

Zinneman Fred(erick) 1907– . Austrian film director, in the USA from 1921, latterly in the UK. His films include *High Noon* 1952, *The Nun's Story* 1959, *The Day of the Jackal* 1973, and *Five Days One Summer* 1982.

zinnia any annual plant of the genus *Zinnia*, family Compositae, native to Mexico and South America, notably the cultivated hybrids of *Z. elegans*, with brightly coloured, daisylike flowers.

Zinoviev Grigory 1883–1936. Russian communist politician whose name was attached to a forgery, the *Zinoviev letter*, inciting Britain's communists to rise, which helped to topple the Labour government 1924.

Zion Jebusite (Amorites of Canaan) stronghold in Jerusalem captured by King David, and the hill on which he built the Temple, symbol of Jerusalem and of Jewish national life.

Zionism political movement advocating the re-establishment of a Jewish homeland in Palestine, the 'promised land' of the Bible, with its capital Jerusalem, the 'city of Zion'.

zip fastener fastening device used in clothing, invented in the USA by Whitcomb Judson 1891, originally for doing up shoes. It has two sets of interlocking teeth, meshed by means of a slide that moves up and down.

zircon zirconium silicate, $ZrSiO_4$, a mineral that occurs in small quantities in a wide range of igneous, sedimentary, and metamorphic rocks. It is very durable and is resistant to erosion and weathering. It is usually coloured brown, but can be other colours, and when transparent may be used as a gemstone.

zirconium (Germanic *zircon*, from Persian *zargun* 'golden') lustrous, greyish-white, strong, ductile, metallic element, symbol Zr, atomic number 40, relative atomic mass 91.22. It occurs in nature as the mineral zircon (zirconium silicate), from which it is obtained commercially. It is used in some ceramics, alloys for wire and filaments, steel manufacture, and nuclear reactors, where its low neutron absorption is advantageous.

zither Austrian Alpine folk instrument, consisting of up to 45 strings, stretched across a flat wooden soundbox about 60 cm/24 in long. Five strings are plucked with a plectrum for melody, and pass over frets, while the rest are plucked with the fingers for harmonic accompaniment.

Zi Xi or **Tz'u-hsi** 1836–1908. Dowager empress of China. She was presented as a concubine to the emperor Hsien-feng. On his death 1861 she became regent for her son T'ung Chih and, when he died 1875, for her nephew Guang Xu (1871–1908).

zodiac zone of the heavens containing the paths of the Sun, Moon, and planets. When this was devised by the ancient Greeks, only five planets were known, making the zodiac about 16° wide. The stars in it are grouped into 12 signs (constellations), each 30° in extent: Aries, Taurus, Gemini, Cancer, Leo, Virgo, Libra, Scorpius, Sagittarius, Capricornus, Aquarius, and Pisces. Because of the *precession of the equinoxes, the current constellations do not cover the same areas of sky as the zodiacal signs of the same name.

Zoë *c.* 978–1050. Byzantine empress who ruled from 1028 until 1050. She gained the title by marriage to the heir apparent Romanus III Argyrus, but was reputed to have poisoned him (1034) in order to marry her lover Michael. He died 1041 and Zoë and her sister Theodora were proclaimed joint empresses. Rivalry led to Zoë marrying Constantine IX Monomachus with whom she reigned until her death.

Zog Ahmed Beg Zogu 1895–1961. King of Albania 1928–39. He became prime minister of Albania 1922, president of the republic 1925, and proclaimed himself king 1928. He was driven out by the Italians 1939 and settled in England.

Zola Émile Edouard Charles Antoine 1840–1902. French novelist and social reformer.

With *La Fortune des Rougon/The Fortune of the Rougons* 1867 he began a series of some 20 naturalistic novels, portraying the fortunes of a French family under the Second Empire. They include *Le Ventre de Paris/The Underbelly of Paris* 1873, *Nana* 1880, and *La Débâcle/The Debacle* 1892. In 1898 he published *J'accuse/I Accuse*, a pamphlet indicting the persecutors of *Dreyfus, for which he was prosecuted for libel but later pardoned.

zoo abbreviation for **zoological gardens**, a place where animals are kept in captivity. Originally created purely for visitor entertainment and education, zoos have become major centres for the breeding of endangered species of animals; a 1984 report identified 2,000 vertebrate species in need of such maintenance. The Arabian oryx has already been preserved in this way; it was captured 1962, bred in captivity, and released again in the desert 1972, where it has flourished.

zoology branch of biology concerned with the study of animals. It includes description of present-day animals, the study of evolution of animal forms, anatomy, physiology, embryology, behaviour, and geographical distribution.

zoonosis any infectious disease that can be transmitted to humans by other vertebrate animals. Probably the most feared example is *rabies. The transmitted microorganism sometimes causes disease only in the human host, leaving the animal host unaffected.

Zoroaster or **Zarathustra** 6th century BC. Persian prophet and religious teacher, founder of Zoroastrianism. Zoroaster believed that he had seen God, Ahura Mazda, in a vision. His first vision came at the age of 30 and, after initial rejection and violent attack, he converted King Vishtaspa. Subsequently, his teachings spread rapidly, becoming the official religion of the kingdom. According to tradition, Zoroaster was murdered at the age of 70 while praying at the altar.

Zoroastrianism pre-Islamic Persian religion founded by the Persian prophet Zoroaster in the 6th century BC, and still practised by the *Parsees in India. The **Zendavesta** are the sacred scriptures of the faith. The theology is dualistic, **Ahura Mazda** or **Ormuzd** (the good God) being perpetually in conflict with **Ahriman** (the evil God), but the former is assured of eventual victory. There are approximately 100,000 (1991) Zoroastrians worldwide; membership is restricted to those with both parents belonging to the faith.

Z particle in physics, an *elementary particle, one of the weakons responsible for carrying the *weak nuclear force.

Zsigmondy Richard 1865–1929. Austrian chemist who devised and built an ultramicroscope in 1903. The microscope's illumination was placed at right angles to the axis. (In a conventional microscope the light source is placed parallel to the instrument's axis.) Zsigmondy's arrangement made it possible to observe gold particles with a diameter of 10-millionth of a millimetre. He received the Nobel Prize for Chemistry 1925.

zucchini alternative name for the courgette, a type of *marrow.

Zuider Zee former sea inlet in Holland, cut off from the North Sea by the closing of a dyke 1932, much of which has been reclaimed as land. The remaining lake is called the *IJsselmeer.

Zulu member of a group of southern African peoples mainly from Natal, South Africa. Their present homeland, KwaZulu, represents the nucleus of the once extensive and militaristic Zulu kingdom. Today many Zulus work in the industrial centres around Johannesburg and Durban. The Zulu language, closely related to Xhosa, belongs to the Bantu branch of the Niger-Congo family. Many Zulus, as supporters of the political organization *Inkatha, violently opposed the nonracial constitution adopted in South Africa 1993, threatening to boycott the 1994 elections unless their demands for greater autonomy were met.

Zululand region in Natal, South Africa, largely corresponding to the Black National State Kwa-Zulu. It was formerly a province, annexed to Natal 1897.

Zürich financial centre and industrial city (machinery, electrical goods, textiles) on Lake Zürich; capital of Zürich canton and the largest city in Switzerland; population (1990) 341,300.

Zweig Stefan 1881–1942. Austrian writer, author of plays, poems, and many biographies of writers (Balzac, Dickens) and historical figures (Marie Antoinette, Mary Stuart). He and his wife, exiles from the Nazis from 1934, despaired at what they saw as the end of civilization and culture and committed suicide in Brazil.

Zwingli Ulrich 1484–1531. Swiss Protestant, born in St Gallen. He was ordained a Roman Catholic priest 1506, but by 1519 was a Reformer and led the Reformation in Switzerland with his insistence on the sole authority of the Scriptures. He was killed in a skirmish at Kappel during a war against the cantons that had not accepted the Reformation.

zwitterion ion that has both a positive and a negative charge, such as an *amino acid in neutral solution. For example, glycine contains both a basic amino group (NH_2) and an acidic carboxyl group (-COOH); when both these are ionized in aqueous solution, the acid group loses a proton to the amino group, and the molecule is positively charged at one end and negatively charged at the other.

Zworykin Vladimir Kosma 1889–1982. Russian-born US electronics engineer, in the USA from 1919. He invented a television camera tube and the *electron microscope.

zygote *ovum (egg) after *fertilization but before it undergoes cleavage to begin embryonic development.

Conversion tables

To convert from imperial to metric	multiply by	to convert from metric to imperial	multiply by
length			
inches	25.4	millimetres	0.039,37
feet	0.3048	metres	3.2808
yards	0.9144	metres	1.0936
furlongs	0.201	kilometres	4.971
miles	1.6093	kilometres	0.6214
area			
square inches	6.4516	square centimetres	0.1550
square feet	0.0929	square metres	10.7639
square yards	0.8361	square metres	1.1960
square miles	2.5900	square kilometres	0.3861
acres	4046.86	square metres	0.000,247
acres	0.4047	hectares	2.47105
hectares	0.001	square kilometres	1,000
volume, capacity			
cubic inches	16.3871	cubic centimetres	0.0610
cubic feet	0.02832	cubic metres	35.3134
cubic yards	0.7646	cubic metres	1.3079
fluid ounces	28.4131	millilitres	0.0352
pints	0.5683	litres	1.760
quarts	1.1365	litres	0.88
imperial gallons	4.54609	litres	0.21997
US gallons	3.7854	litres	0.2642
mass/weight			
ounces	28.3495	grams	0.03527
pounds	0.4536	kilograms	2.2046
stone (14 lb)	6.3503	kilograms	0.1575
tons (imperial)	1016.05	kilograms	0.00098
tons (US)	907.2	kilograms	0.001
tons (imperial)	0.9842	tonnes	1.0161
tons (US)	0.9072	tonnes	1.102
speed			
miles per hour	1.6093	kilometres per hour	0.6214
feet per second	0.3048	metres per second	3.2808
force			
pound force	4.448	newton	0.2248
kilogram force	9.8096	newton	0.1019
pressure			
pounds per square inch	6.894,76	kilopascals	0.1450
tons per square inch	15.4443	megapascals	0.0647
atmospheres	101,325	newtons per square metre	0.000,009,86
atmospheres	14.69	pounds per square inch	0.068
energy			
calorie	4.186	joule	0.238
kilowatt hour	3,600,000	joule	0.000,000,277
power			
horsepower	0.7457	kilowatts	1.341
fuel consumption			
miles per gallon	0.3540	kilometres per litre	2.825
miles per US gallon	0.4251	kilometres per litre	2.3521
gallons per mile	2.8248	litres per kilometre	0.3540
US gallons per mile	2.3521	litres per kilometre	0.4251

Miscellaneous measures

acoustic ohm	c.g.s. unit of acoustic impedance (the ratio of sound pressure on a surface to sound flux through the surface)
acre	traditional English land measure equal to 4,480 square yards (4,047 sq m or 0.405 ha)
acre-foot	unit sometimes used to measure large volumes of water such as reservoirs; 1 acre-foot = 1,233.5 cu m/43,560 cu ft
astronomical unit	unit (symbol AU) equal to the mean distance of the Earth from the Sun: 149,597,870 km/92,955,800 mi
atmosphere	unit of pressure (abbreviation atm); 1 standard atmosphere = 101,325 pascals
barn	unit of area, especially the cross-sectional area of an atomic nucleus; 1 barn = 10^{-28} sq m
barrel	unit of liquid capacity; volume depends on liquid being measured. One barrel of oil = 159 litres/35 imperial gallons; one barrel of alcohol = 189 litres/41.5 imperial gallons
base box	imperial unit of area used in metal plating; 1 base box = 20.232 sq m/31,360 sq in
baud	unit of electrical signalling speed equal to one pulse per second; 300 baud = approximately 300 words per minute
brewster	unit (symbol B) for measuring reaction of optical materials to stress
British thermal unit	imperial unit of heat (symbol Btu); 1 Btu = approximately 1,055 joules
bushel	dry or liquid measure equal to 8 gallons or 4 pecks (36.37 litres/2,219.36 cu in) in the UK
cable	unit of length used on ships, taken as one-tenth of a nautical mile (185.3 m/608 ft)
calorie	c.g.s. unit of heat, now replaced by the joule; 1 calorie = approximately 4.2 joules
carat	unit for measuring mass of precious stones; 1 carat = 0.2 g/0.00705 oz
carat	unit of purity in gold; pure gold is 24-carat
carcel	obsolete unit of luminous intensity
cental	name for the short hundredweight; 1 cental = 45.4 kg/100 lb
chaldron	obsolete unit measuring capacity; 1 UK chaldron = 1.309 cubic metres or 288 gallons
clausius	in engineering, a unit of entropy; defined as the ratio of energy to temperature above absolute zero
cleanliness unit	unit for measuring air pollution, equal to the number of particles greater than 0.5 micrometres in diameter per cubic foot of air
clo	unit of thermal insulation of clothing; standard clothes have insulation of about 1 clo, the warmest is about 4 clo per 2.5 cm/1 in of thickness
clusec	unit for measuring the power of a vacuum pump
condensation number	in physics, the ratio of the number of molecules condensing on a surface to the number of molecules touching that surface
cord	unit for measuring the volume of wood cut for fuel; 1 cord = 3,456 cu m/128 cu ft, or a stack 2.4 m/8 ft long, 1.2 m/4 ft wide and 1.2 m/4 ft high
crith	unit of mass for weighing gases; 1 crith = the mass of 1 litre of hydrogen gas at standard temperature and pressure
cubit	earliest known unit of length; 1 cubit = approximately 50.5 cm/20.6 in, the length of the human forearm from tip of the middle finger to the elbow
curie	former unit of radioactivity (symbol Ci); 1 curie = 37 x 10^9 becquerels
cwt	symbol for hundredweight, unit of weight equal to 50.802 kg/112 pounds; 45.36 kg/100 lb in the USA
dalton	international atomic mass unit, equivalent to one-twelfth of the mass of a neutral carbon-12 atom
darcy	c.g.s. unit (symbol D) of permeability, used mainly in geology to describe the permeability of rock
darwin	unit of measurement of evolutionary rate of change
decontamination factor	unit measuring the effectiveness of radiological decontamination; ratio of original contamination to the radiation remaining
demal	unit measuring concentration; 1 demal = 1 gram-equivalent of solute in 1 cubic decimetre of solvent
denier	unit used to measure the fineness of yarns; 9,000 metres of 15 denier nylon weighs 15 g/0.5 oz
dioptre	optical unit measuring the power of a lens; the reciprocal of the focal length in metres
drachm	unit of apothecaries' measure; 1 drachm = 60 grains = 3.887 grams
dyne	c.g.s. unit of force; 10^5 dynes = 1 newton
einstein unit	unit for measuring photoenergy in atomic physics
eotvos unit	unit (symbol E) for measuring small changes in intensity of the Earth's gravity with horizontal distance
erg	c.g.s. unit of work, equal to the work done by a force of 1 dyne moving through 1 cm
erlang	unit for measuring telephone traffic intensity
fathom	unit of depth measurement in mining, seafaring and handling timber; 1 fathom = 1.83 m/6 ft
finsen unit	unit (symbol FU) for measuring intensity of ultraviolet light; UV light of 2 FU causes sunburn in 15 minutes
fluid ounce	measure of capacity, equivalent in the USA to $\frac{1}{16}$ of a pint; in the UK and Canada, equals $\frac{1}{20}$ of a pint
foot	imperial unit of length (symbol ft), equivalent to 0.3048 m
foot-candela	unit of illuminance, replaced by the lux; 1 foot-candela = 10.674 lux
foot-pound	imperial unit of energy (symbol ft-lb); 1 ft-lb = 1.356 joule

Miscellaneous measures (cont.)

frigorie	unit (symbol fg) used in refrigeration engineering to measure heat energy; 1 frigorie = 1,000 calories = 4,185 joules
furlong	unit of measurement, originating in Anglo-Saxon England, equivalent to 201.168 m/ 220 yd
galileo	unit (symbol Gal) of acceleration, used in geological surveying; 1 galileo = 10^{-2} metres per second per second
gallon	imperial liquid or dry measure, equal to 4.546 litres, and subdivided into 4 quarts or 8 pints; US gallon = 3.785 litres
gauss	c.g.s. unit (symbol) of magnetic flux density, replaced by the tesla
gill	imperial unit of volume for liquid measure, equal to one-quarter of a pint or 5 fluid ounces (0.142 litre)
grain	smallest unit of mass in the three English systems (avoirdupois, troy, apothecaries' weights) used in the UK and USA; 1 grain = 0.0648 g
hand	unit used in measuring the height of a horse from front hoof to shoulder (withers); 1 hand = 10.2 cm/4 in
hardness number	unit measuring hardness of materials. There are three different hardness scales: Brinell Rockwell and Vickers
hartree	atomic unit of energy, equivalent to atomic unit of charge divided by atomic unit of length; 1 hartree = 4.850×10^{-18} joule
haze factor	unit of visibility in mist or fog; the ratio of brightness of mist compared with that of the object
Hehner number	unit measuring concentration of fatty acids in oils; a Hehner number of 1 = 1 kg of fatty acid in 100 kg of oil or fat
hide	unit of measurement used in the 12th century to measure the extent of arable land; 1 hide = 256 acres (104 hectares)
horsepower	imperial unit (abbreviation hp) of power, now replaced by the watt
hundredweight	imperial unit (abbreviation cwt) of mass; 1 cwt = 50.8 kg/112 lb
inch	imperial unit (abbreviation in) of linear measure, a twelfth of a foot; 1 in = 2.54 cm
inferno	unit used in astrophysics for describing the temperature inside a star; 1 inferno = 1 billion K
iodine number	unit measuring percentage of iodine absorbed in a substance
jansky	unit used in radio astronomy to measure radiation received from space; 1 jansky = 10^{-} watts per square metre per hertz
kayser	unit used in spectroscopy to measure wave number (number of waves in a unit length a wavelength of 1.0 cm has a wave number of 10 kaysers
knot	unit used in navigation to measure a ship's speed; 1 knot = 1 nautical mile per hour, or about 1.15 miles per hour
league	obsolete imperial unit of length; 1 league = 3 miles = 4,828 metres
light year	unit used in astronomy to measure distance; the distance travelled by light in a year, approximately 9.46×10^{12} km/5.88×10^{12} miles
mache	obsolete unit of radioactive concentration; 1 mache is a concentration of 3.7×10^{-7} curies of radioactive material in one cubic metre of a medium
maxwell	c.g.s. unit (symbol Mx) of magnetic flux
megaton	measurement of the explosive power of a nuclear weapon; 1 megaton = one million tons of trinitrotoluene (TNT)
mil	(a) thousandth of a litre; contraction of the word millilitre. (b) imperial measure of length, equal to 10^{-3} inch; also known as the thou
mile	imperial unit of linear measure; a statute mile = 1.60934 km/1.760 yards, and an international nautical mile = 1,852/2,226 yards
millimetre of mercury	unit of pressure (symbol mmHg) used in medicine for measuring blood pressure
morgan	arbitrary unit used in genetics; 1 morgan is the distance along the chromosome in a gene that gives a recombination frequency of 1%
nautical mile	unit of distance used in navigation, equal to the average length of one minute of arc on a great circle of the earth, or 1,852 m/6,076.12 ft
neper	unit used in telecommunications; gives the attenuation of amplitudes of currents or powers as the natural logarithm of the ratio
oersted	c.g.s. unit (symbol Oe) of magnetic field strength, now replaced by amperes per metre
ounce	unit of mass, one-sixteenth of a pound avoirdupois, equal to 437.5 grains (28.35 g; also one-twelfth of a pound troy, equal to 480 grains
parsec	unit (symbol pc) used in astronomy for distances to stars and galaxies; 1 parsec = 3.2 light years, 2.063 x astronomical units and 3.086×10^{13} km
peck	obsolete unit of dry measure, equal to 8 quarts or a quarter bushel (9.002 litres)
pennyweight	imperial unit of mass; 1 dwt = 24 grains = 1.555×10^{-3} kg
perch	obsolete imperial unit of length; 1 perch = 5½ yards = 5.029 metres. Also called the rod or pole
pint	imperial unit of liquid or dry measure, equal to 20 fluid ounces, half a quart, one-eighth of a gallon, or 0.568 litre; in the USA, a liquid pint = 0.473 litre, while a dry pint = 0.550 litre
point	metric unit of mass used in relation to gemstones; 1 point = 0.01 metric carat = 2×10^{-6} kg
poise	c.g.s. unit of dynamic viscosity; 1 poise = 1 dyne-second per square centimetre

Miscellaneous measures (cont.)

pound	imperial unit (abbreviation lb) of mass; the avoirdupois pound or imperial standard pound = 0.45 kg/7,000 grains, while the pound troy (used for weighing precious metals) = 0.37 kg/5,760 grains
poundal	imperial unit (abbreviation pdl) of force; 1 poundal = 0.1383 newtons
quart	imperial liquid or dry measure, equal to 2 pints or 1.136 litres; in the USA a liquid quart = 0.946 litre, while a dry quart = 1.101 litres
rad	unit of absorbed radiation dose, replaced in the SI system by the gray; 1 rad = 0.01 joule of radiation absorbed by 1 kg of matter
relative biological effectiveness	relative damage caused to living tissue by different types of radiation
rood	imperial unit of area; 1 rood = ¼ acre = 1,011.7 square metres
roentgen	unit (symbol R) of radiation exposure, used for X- and gamma ray
rydberg	atomic unit of energy, equivalent to atomic unit of charge divided by twice atomic unit of length; 1 rydberg = 2.425 x 10^{-18} joule
sabin	unit of sound absorption, used in acoustical engineering; 1 sabin = absorption of 1 sq ft (0.093 sq m) of a perfectly absorbing surface
scruple	imperial unit of apothecaries measure; 1 scruple = 20 grains = 1.3 x 10^{-4} kg
shackle	unit of length used at sea for measuring cable or chain; 1 shackle = 15 fathoms (90 ft/ 27 m)
slug	obsolete imperial unit of mass, equal to 14.6 kg/32.17 lb
snellen	unit expressing the visual power of the eye
sone	unit of subjective loudness
standard volume	in physics, the volume occupied by 1 kilogram molecule (molecular mass in kilograms) of any gas at standard temperature and pressure; approximately 22.414 cu m
stokes	c.g.s. unit (symbol St) of kinematic viscosity
stone	imperial unit (abbreviation st) of mass; 1 stone = 6.35 kg/14 lb
strontium unit	measures concentration of strontium-90 in organic medium relative to concentration of calcium
tex	metric unit of line density; 1 tex is the line density of a thread with a mass of 1 gram and a length of 1 kilometre
tog	measure of thermal insulation, used in textile trade; a light summer suit = 1 tog
ton	imperial unit of mass. The long ton (UK) is 1,016 kg/2,240 lb; the short ton (USA) is 907 kg/2,000 lb
yard	imperial unit (symbol yd) of length, equivalent to 0.9144 m/3 ft

Decibels

Decibels (dB) measure the relative intensity or loudness of sound. A difference of 10 dB between two sounds means that the intensity of one sound is ten times louder than that of the other. Because of the way the ear responds to such differences in sound intensity, this tenfold difference results in one sound's being perceived to be twice as loud as the other. So, for example, a 20 dB sound is twice as loud as a 10 dB sound; 30 dB is four times louder; 40 dB is eight times louder; and so on. One decibel is the smallest difference that the ear can detect between sounds. Sounds of 120 dB and upwards cause physical pain.

Decibels	typical sound		
	threshold of hearing	60–65	restaurant; factory or warehouse office
10	rustle of leaves in gentle breeze	65	large office
10	quiet whisper	65–70	traffic on busy street
10	average whisper	65–90	train
10–50	quiet conversation	75–80	factory (light/medium work)
20	house in country (average situation)	95–100	riveter
25	house in city (average situation)	90	heavy traffic
40–45	hotel; theatre (between performances)	90–100	thunder
40–65	loud conversation	110–140	jet aircraft on take-off
50–55	small retail establishment	130	threshold of pain
55	commercial garage	140–190	space rocket at take-off
55–60	medium-size office; residential street		

Temperature scales

The freezing point and boiling point of water are 0°C and 100°C on the Celsius (centigrade) scale (100 degrees), and 32°F and 212°F on the Fahrenheit scale (180 degrees). So Celsius and Fahrenheit temperatures can be converted as follows:

$C = (F - 32) \times {}^{100}/_{180}$

$F = (C \times {}^{180}/_{100}) + 32$

Is there a temperature that is the same on both scales? The answer is yes: -40° (F and C).

Table of equivalent temperatures

°C	°F	°C	°F	°C	°F	°C	°F
100	212.0	70	158.0	40	104.0	10	50
99	210.2	69	156.2	39	102.2	9	48
98	208.4	68	154.4	38	100.4	8	46
97	206.6	67	152.6	37	98.6	7	44
96	204.8	66	150.8	36	96.8	6	42
95	203.0	65	149.0	35	95.0	5	41
94	201.2	64	147.2	34	93.2	4	39
93	199.4	63	145.4	33	91.4	3	37
92	197.6	62	143.6	32	89.6	2	35
91	195.8	61	141.8	31	87.8	1	33
90	194.0	60	140.0	30	86.0	0	32
89	192.2	59	138.2	29	84.2	-1	30
88	190.4	58	136.4	28	82.4	-2	28
87	188.6	57	134.6	27	80.6	-3	26
86	186.8	56	132.8	26	78.8	-4	24
85	185.0	55	131.0	25	77.0	-5	23
84	183.2	54	129.2	24	75.2	-6	21
83	181.4	53	127.4	23	73.4	-7	19
82	179.6	52	125.6	22	71.6	-8	17
81	177.8	51	123.8	21	69.8	-9	15
80	176.0	50	122.0	20	68.0	-10	14
79	174.2	49	120.2	19	66.2	-11	12
78	172.4	48	118.4	18	64.4	-12	10
77	170.6	47	116.6	17	62.6	-13	8
76	168.8	46	114.8	16	60.8	-14	6
75	167.0	45	113.0	15	59.0	-15	5
74	165.2	44	111.2	14	57.2	-16	3
73	163.4	43	109.4	13	55.4	-17	1
72	161.6	42	107.6	12	53.6	-18	-0
71	159.8	41	105.8	11	51.8	-19	-2

orld's 100 largest countries by area

untry	Area sq km	sq mi	Country	Area sq km	sq mi
ussian Federation	17,075,500	6,592,883	Turkmenistan	488,100	188,456
anada	9,970,610	3,849,671	Cameroon	475,440	183,568
ited States of America	9,638,900	3,721,597	Papua New Guinea	462,840	178,703
hina	9,596,960	3,705,404	Morocco	458,730	177,117
azil	8,511,965	3,286,486	Sweden	450,000	173,746
ustralia	7,682,300	2,966,150	Uzbekistan	447,400	172,742
dia	3,166,829	1,222,719	Iraq	434,924	167,925
gentina	2,780,092	1,073,399	Paraguay	406,752	157,048
zakhstan	2,717,300	1,049,155	Zimbabwe	390,300	150,696
dan	2,505,800	967,494	Norway	387,000	149,421
geria	2,381,741	919,595	Japan	377,535	145,767
ire	2,344,900	905,370	Germany	357,041	137,854
udi Arabia	2,200,518	849,624	Congo	342,000	132,047
exico	1,958,201	756,065	Finland	338,145	130,558
donesia	1,919,443	741,101	Malaysia	329,759	127,321
ya	1,759,540	679,362	Vietnam	329,600	127,259
n	1,648,000	636,296	Ivory Coast	322,463	124,504
ongolia	1,565,000	604,249	Italy	301,300	116,332
ru	1,285,200	496,218	Philippines	300,000	115,831
ad	1,284,000	495,755	Burkina Faso	274,122	105,839
gola	1,246,700	481,353	Oman	272,000	105,020
ali	1,240,142	478,821	Ecuador	270,670	104,506
uth Africa	1,223,181	472,272	New Zealand	268,680	103,738
hiopia	1,221,900	471,778	Gabon	267,667	103,347
ger	1,186,408	458,074	Guinea	245,857	94,926
lombia	1,141,748	440,831	United Kingdom	244,100	94,247
livia	1,098,581	424,164	Ghana	238,305	92,010
auritania	1,030,700	397,955	Romania	237,500	91,699
ypt	1,001,450	386,662	Laos	236,790	91,425
nzania	945,000	364,866	Uganda	236,600	91,352
geria	923,773	356,670	Guyana	214,969	83,000
nezuela	912,000	352,125	Belarus	207,600	80,155
mibia	824,300	318,264	Kyrgyzstan	198,500	76,641
ozambique	799,380	308,642	Senegal	196,200	75,753
kistan	796,100	307,376	Syria	185,200	71,506
rkey	779,500	300,966	Cambodia	181,035	69,898
ile	756,950	292,260	Uruguay	176,200	68,031
mbia	752,600	290,580	Tunisia	164,150	63,379
anmar	676,577	261,228	Surinam	163,820	63,251
ghanistan	652,090	251,773	Nepal	147,181	56,827
malia	637,700	246,217	Bangladesh	144,000	55,599
ntral African Republic	622,436	240,324	Tajikistan	143,100	55,251
raine	603,700	233,090	Greece	131,957	50,949
dagascar	587,041	226,658	Poland	127,886	49,377
nya	582,600	224,943	Nicaragua	127,849	49,363
tswana	582,000	224,711	Korea, North	120,538	46,540
nce	543,965	210,026	Malawi	118,000	45,560
men	531,900	205,368	Benin	112,622	43,484
ailand	513,115	198,115	Honduras	112,100	43,282
ain	504,750	194,885	Liberia	111,370	43,000

Worldwide population growth

Figures are for population growth rates as a percentage per annum.

Brunei	12.00	Lesotho	2.70	Trinidad and Tobago	1.
United Arab Emirates	6.10	Yemen	2.70	Argentina	1.
Kuwait	5.50	Congo	2.60	Australia	1.
Bahrain	4.40	Costa Rica	2.60	Mauritius	1.
Kenya	4.20	Mexico	2.60	Korea, South	1.
Solomon Islands	3.90	Papua New Guinea	2.60	Liechtenstein	1.
Maldives	3.70	Peru	2.60	Taiwan	1.
Qatar	3.70	Angola	2.50	Antigua and Barbuda	1.
Iraq	3.60	Belize	2.50	Dominica	1.
Jordan	3.60	Ethiopia	2.50	China	1.
Botswana	3.50	Korea, North	2.50	Cyprus	1.
Syria	3.50	Morocco	2.50	Singapore	1.
Tanzania	3.50	São Tomé Principe	2.50	Canada	1.
Zimbabwe	3.50	Sierra Leone	2.50	Samoa, Western	1.
Djibouti	3.40	South Africa	2.50	Surinam	1.
Tuvalu	3.40	Burkina Faso	2.40	New Zealand	0.
Ivory Coast	3.30	Guinea-Bissau	2.40	United States of America	0.
Malawi	3.30	Philippines	2.40	Iceland	0
Nicaragua	3.30	Tonga	2.40	Malta	0.
Nigeria	3.30	Vietnam	2.40	Uruguay	0.
Rwanda	3.30	Central African Republic	2.30	Afghanistan	0.
Uganda	3.30	Chad	2.30	Cuba	0
Vanuatu	3.30	Dominican Republic	2.30	Poland	0.
Zambia	3.30	Guinea	2.30	Barbados	0.
Ghana	3.20	Nepal	2.30	Finland	0.
Iran	3.20	Brazil	2.20	Japan	0.
Madagascar	3.20	Cambodia	2.20	Portugal	0.
Comoros	3.10	Colombia	2.20	Romania	0.
Honduras	3.10	Equatorial Guinea	2.20	Czech Republic	0.
Libya	3.10	Jamaica	2.20	Netherlands	0.
Pakistan	3.10	Laos	2.20	Slovakia	0.
Saudi Arabia	3.10	Panama	2.20	France	0.
Senegal	3.10	Seychelles	2.20	Greece	0.
Somalia	3.10	Bangladesh	2.17	Norway	0.
Algeria	3.00	Fiji	2.10	Hungary	0.
Benin	3.00	Turkey	2.10	Spain	0.
Liberia	3.00	Bhutan	2.00	St Christopher-Nevis	0.
Mauritania	3.00	Guyana	2.00	Switzerland	0.
Oman	3.00	India	2.00	Austria	0.
Paraguay	3.00	Indonesia	2.00	Belgium	0.
Swaziland	3.00	Malaysia	2.00	Bulgaria	0.
Togo	3.00	Thailand	2.00	Ireland	0.
Ecuador	2.90	Tunisia	2.00	Italy	0.
El Salvador	2.90	Albania	1.90	San Marino	0.
Mali	2.90	Cape Verde	1.90	Sweden	0.
Sudan	2.90	Gambia	1.90	United Kingdom	0
Zaire	2.90	Myanmar	1.90	Denmark	0
Burundi	2.80	Bahamas	1.80	Luxembourg	0
Guatemala	2.80	Israel	1.80	Lebanon	−0
Mongolia	2.80	Sri Lanka	1.80	Grenada	−0.
Mozambique	2.80	Haiti	1.70	Monaco	−0.
Niger	2.80	Kiribati	1.70	Germany	−0.
St Lucia	2.80	Nauru	1.70	St Vincent and the	−4
Venezuela	2.80	Chile	1.60	Grenadines	
Bolivia	2.70	Gabon	1.60		
Cameroon	2.70				

World literacy

Figures are percentages of the population of each country. Where separate figures are given for male and female literacy, the ranking is based on a simple average of the two.

	Men	Women	Average		Men	Women	Average
Andorra	100	100	100	Jamaica	82	82	82
Czech Republic	100	100	100	Dominica	80	80	80
Iceland	100	100	100	Malaysia	80	80	80
Luxembourg	100	100	100	Seychelles	80	80	80
Norway	100	100	100	Brazil	79	76	78
Slovakia	100	100	100	Dominican Republic	78	77	78
Australia	99	99	99	Albania	75	75	75
Canada	99	99	99	Lebanon	75	75	75
Cyprus	99	99	99	Bolivia	84	65	75
Denmark	99	99	99	China	82	66	74
Finland	99	99	99	Indonesia	83	65	74
France	99	99	99	Turkey	86	62	74
Germany	99	99	99	Zimbabwe	81	67	74
Hungary	99	99	99	Bahrain	79	64	72
Japan	99	99	99	Jordan	71	71	71
Korea, North	99	99	99	Kuwait	71	71	71
Monaco	99	99	99	Swaziland	70	66	68
Nauru	99	99	99	United Arab Emirates	68	68	68
Netherlands	99	99	99	Congo	79	55	67
New Zealand	99	99	99	Myanmar	66	66	66
Sweden	99	99	99	Nicaragua	66	66	66
Switzerland	99	99	99	Surinam	65	65	65
United Kingdom	99	99	99	Zaire	79	45	62
United States of America	99	99	99	Gabon	70	53	62
Austria	98	98	98	Honduras	61	58	60
Belgium	98	98	98	Qatar	60	60	60
Bulgaria	98	98	98	Solomon Islands	60	60	60
Poland	98	98	98	Syria	76	43	60
Romania	98	98	98	Cambodia	78	39	59
Italy	97	97	97	São Tomé Principe	73	42	58
San Marino	97	97	97	Uganda	70	45	58
Spain	97	97	97	Cameroon	68	45	57
Trinidad and Tobago	97	97	97	Equatorial Guinea	55	55	55
Argentina	96	95	96	Guatemala	63	47	55
Cuba	96	95	96	Tunisia	68	41	55
Uruguay	96	96	96	Ghana	64	43	54
Bahamas	95	95	95	Madagascar	53	53	53
Brunei	95	95	95	Vanuatu	53	53	53
Chile	94	94	94	Iran	62	39	51
Costa Rica	94	93	94	Algeria	63	37	50
Belize	93	93	93	Cape Verde	61	39	50
Greece	96	89	93	Iraq	68	32	50
Korea, South	92	92	92	Kenya	50	50	50
Antigua and Barbuda	90	90	90	Rwanda	50	50	50
Kiribati	90	90	90	Papua New Guinea	55	36	46
Malta	90	90	90	Egypt	59	30	45
Mexico	92	88	90	India	57	29	43
Samoa, Western	90	90	90	Nigeria	54	31	43
St Christopher-Nevis	90	90	90	Central African Republic	53	29	41
Taiwan	90	90	90	Togo	53	28	41
Yugoslavia (former)	90	90	90	Somalia	40	40	40
Mongolia	89	89	89	Mozambique	55	22	39
Thailand	89	89	89	Haiti	40	35	38
Colombia	89	87	88	Maldives	36	36	36
Paraguay	91	85	88	Burundi	43	26	35
Philippines	88	88	88	Ivory Coast	35	35	35
Venezuela	88	88	88	Liberia	47	23	35
Panama	87	87	87	Morocco	45	22	34
Peru	91	78	85	Bangladesh	43	22	33
Singapore	93	79	86	Guinea-Bissau	46	17	32
Grenada	85	85	85	Sudan	30	30	30
St Vincent and the Grenadines	85	85	85	Pakistan	40	19	30
				Sierra Leone	38	21	30
Portugal	89	80	85	Guinea	40	17	29
Botswana	84	84	84	Senegal	37	19	28
Ecuador	85	80	83	Benin	37	16	27
Fiji	88	77	83	Chad	40	11	26

World literacy rates (cont.)

Gambia	36	15	26	Oman	20	20	2
Nepal	39	12	26	Mauritania	17	17	1
Malawi	25	25	25	Comoros	15	15	1
Afghanistan	39	8	24	Burkina Faso	21	6	1
Saudi Arabia	34	12	23	Yemen	20	3	1
Angola	20	20	20	Mali	10	10	1
Djibouti	20	20	20	Bhutan	5	5	

World life expectancy

Figures are ages of the population of each country. Where separate figures are given for male and female life expectancy, the ranking is based on a simple average of the two.

Nation	men	women	average	Nation	men	women	average
Liechtenstein	78	83	81	Poland	66	74	70
Japan	76	82	79	Romania	67	73	70
Switzerland	74	82	78	Paraguay	67	72	70
Australia	75	80	78	Tunisia	68	71	70
Netherlands	74	81	78	Sri Lanka	67	72	70
Sweden	74	81	78	Argentina	66	73	70
Iceland	74	80	77	Korea, South	66	73	70
Spain	74	80	77	Bahrain	67	71	69
Italy	73	80	77	Jordan	67	71	69
Jamaica	75	78	77	Vanuatu	67	71	69
Norway	73	80	77	Fiji	67	71	69
Canada	72	79	76	Grenada	69	69	69
United States of America	72	79	76	Solomon Islands	66	71	69
Belgium	72	78	75	Guyana	66	71	69
Denmark	72	78	75	Chile	64	73	69
France	71	79	75	Surinam	66	71	69
New Zealand	72	78	75	Syria	67	69	68
United Kingdom	72	78	75	China	67	69	68
Israel	73	76	75	Malaysia	65	70	68
Luxembourg	71	78	75	Mauritius	64	71	68
Malta	72	77	75	Lebanon	65	70	68
Portugal	71	78	75	Libya	64	69	67
Brunei	74	74	74	Samoa, Western	64	69	67
Kuwait	72	76	74	Philippines	63	69	66
Singapore	71	77	74	Seychelles	66	66	66
Cyprus	72	76	74	Saudi Arabia	64	67	66
Finland	70	78	74	Mongolia	63	67	65
Greece	72	76	74	Thailand	62	68	65
Costa Rica	71	76	74	El Salvador	63	66	65
Cuba	72	75	74	Turkey	63	66	65
San Marino	70	77	74	Ecuador	62	66	64
Austria	70	77	74	Vietnam	62	66	64
Panama	71	75	73	Peru	61	66	64
Ireland	70	76	73	Morocco	62	65	64
Taiwan	70	75	73	Colombia	61	66	64
Barbados	70	75	73	Brazil	61	66	64
Yugoslavia (former)	69	75	72	Dominican Republic	61	65	63
Tonga	69	74	72	Iraq	62	63	63
Uruguay	68	75	72	Nicaragua	61	63	62
Czech Republic	68	75	72	São Tomé Principe	62	62	62
Slovakia	68	75	72	Maldives	60	63	62
Bulgaria	69	74	72	Tuvalu	60	63	62
St Vincent and the Grenadines	69	74	72	Kenya	59	63	61
Albania	69	73	71	Zimbabwe	59	63	61
Germany	68	74	71	Algeria	59	62	61
St Lucia	68	73	71	Lesotho	59	62	61
St Christopher-Nevis	69	72	71	Honduras	58	62	60
Hungary	67	74	71	Belize	60	60	60
United Arab Emirates	68	72	70	Botswana	59	59	59
Qatar	68	72	70	Guatemala	57	61	59
Venezuela	67	73	70	Cape Verde	57	61	59
Mexico	67	73	70	Egypt	57	60	59
Korea, North	67	73	70	Dominica	57	59	58
Trinidad and Tobago	68	72	70	Iran	57	57	57
Antigua and Barbuda	70	70	70	Oman	55	58	57
				Zambia	54	57	56

India	56	55	56	Laos	48	51	50
Togo	53	57	55	Niger	48	50	49
Pakistan	54	55	55	Gabon	47	51	49
Liberia	53	56	55	Yemen	47	50	49
Myanmar	53	56	55	Nigeria	47	49	48
Ivory Coast	52	55	54	Malawi	46	50	48
Papua New Guinea	53	54	54	Burundi	45	48	47
Indonesia	52	55	54	Mozambique	45	48	47
Somalia	53	53	53	Congo	45	48	47
Sudan	51	55	53	Equatorial Guinea	44	48	46
Senegal	51	54	53	Mauritania	43	48	46
Zaire	51	54	53	Mali	44	47	46
Bolivia	51	54	53	Burkina Faso	44	47	46
Haiti	51	54	53	Benin	42	46	44
Ghana	50	54	52	Sierra Leone	41	47	44
Tanzania	49	54	52	Chad	42	45	44
Madagascar	50	53	52	Cambodia	42	45	44
Rwanda	49	53	51	Bhutan	44	43	44
Cameroon	49	53	51	Central African Republic	41	45	43
Bangladesh	50	52	51	Angola	40	44	42
Swaziland	47	54	51	Guinea-Bissau	42	42	42
Djibouti	50	50	50	Gambia	42	42	42
Uganda	49	51	50	Afghanistan	43	41	42
Comoros	48	52	50	Guinea	39	42	41
Nepal	50	49	50	Ethiopia	38	38	38

Roman numerals

The basic Roman numerals are:

I	1
V	5
X	10
L	50
C	100
D	500
M	1,000

Other numbers are formed from these by adding or subtracting. The value of a symbol following another of the same or greater value is added: II = 2; III = 3; CC = 200. The value of a symbol preceding one of greater value is subtracted: IX = 9; CM = 900. The value of a symbol standing between two of greater value is subtracted from that of the second, the remainder being added to the first: XIX = 19.

The first twelve numbers are best known from the clock face:

I	1
II	2
III	3
IV	4
V	5
VI	6
VII	7
VIII	8
IX	9
X	10
XI	11
XII	12

Roman numerals are usually written in capital letters, but may be written in lower case, as in numbering subdivisions (Act I scene iv), or the preliminary pages of a book.

A bar over a symbol indicates multiplication by 1,000:

D̄   500,000

Time zones and relative times

The surface of the earth is divided into 24 time zones. Each zone represents 15° of longitude or 1 hour of time. Countries to the east of London and the Greenwich meridian are ahead of Greenwich Mean Time (GMT) and countries to the west are behind. The time indicated in the table below is fixed by law and is called standard time. Use of daylight saving time (such as British Summer Time) varies widely. At 12.00 noon, Greenwich Mean Time, the standard time elsewhere around the world is as follows:

Abu Dhabi	16.00	Dubai	16.00	Nicosia	14.00
Accra	12.00	Dublin	12.00	Oslo	13.00
Addis Ababa	15.00	Florence	13.00	Ottawa	07.00
Adelaide	21.30	Frankfurt	13.00	Panama City	07.00
Alexandria	14.00	Gdansk	13.00	Paris	13.00
Algiers	13.00	Geneva	13.00	Perth	20.00
Amman	14.00	Gibraltar	13.00	Port Said	14.00
Amsterdam	13.00	Hague, The	13.00	Prague	13.00
Anchorage	02.00	Harare	14.00	Quebec	07.00
Ankara	14.00	Havana	07.00	Rangoon	18.30
Athens	14.00	Helsinki	14.00	Rawalpindi	17.00
Auckland	24.00	Ho Chi Minh City	19.00	Reykjavik	12.00
Baghdad	15.00	Hobart	22.00	Rio de Janeiro	09.00
Bahrain	15.00	Hong Kong	20.00	Riyadh	15.00
Bangkok	19.00	Istanbul	14.00	Rome	13.00
Barcelona	13.00	Jakarta	19.00	San Francisco	04.00
Beijing	20.00	Jerusalem	14.00	Santiago	08.00
Beirut	14.00	Johannesburg	14.00	Seoul	21.00
Belgrade	13.00	Karachi	17.00	Shanghai	20.00
Belgrade	13.00	Kiev	15.00	Singapore	20.00
Berlin	13.00	Kuala Lumpur	20.00	Sofia	14.00
Berne	13.00	Kuwait	15.00	St Petersburg	15.00
Bogota	07.00	Kyoto	21.00	Stockholm	13.00
Bombay	17.30	Lagos	13.00	Sydney	22.00
Bonn	13.00	Le Havre	13.00	Taipei	20.00
Brazzaville	13.00	Lima	07.00	Tashkent	18.00
Brisbane	22.00	Lisbon	12.00	Tehran	15.30
Brussels	13.00	Los Angeles	04.00	Tel Aviv	14.00
Bucharest	14.00	Luanda	13.00	Tenerife	12.00
Budapest	13.00	Luxembourg	13.00	Tokyo	21.00
Buenos Aires	09.00	Lyon	13.00	Toronto	07.00
Cairo	14.00	Madras	17.30	Tripoli	13.00
Calcutta	17.30	Madrid	13.00	Tunis	13.00
Canberra	22.00	Manila	20.00	Valparaiso	08.00
Cape Town	14.00	Marseille	13.00	Vancouver	04.00
Caracas	08.00	Mecca	15.00	Vatican City	13.00
Casablanca	12.00	Melbourne	22.00	Venice	13.00
Chicago	06.00	Mexico City	06.00	Vienna	13.00
Cologne	13.00	Milan	13.00	Vladivostok	22.00
Colombo	17.30	Minsk	15.00	Volgograd	16.00
Copenhagen	13.00	Monrovia	11.00	Warsaw	13.00
Dacca	18.00	Montevideo	09.00	Washington	07.00
Damascus	14.00	Montreal	07.00	Wellington	24.00
Dar es Salaam	15.00	Moscow	15.00	Winnipeg	06.00
Darwin	21.30	Munich	13.00	Yokohama	21.00
Delhi	17.30	Nairobi	15.00	Zagreb	13.00
Denver	05.00	New Orleans	06.00	Zurich	13.00
Djakarta	20.00	New York	07.00		